HOLT TEACHER'S EDITION

WORLD HISTORY
HUMAN LEGACY

MODERN ERA

Authors
Susan Elizabeth Ramírez
Peter Stearns
Sam Wineburg

Senior Consulting Author
Steven A. Goldberg

HOLT, RINEHART AND WINSTON
A Harcourt Education Company
Orlando • Austin • New York • San Diego • London

Acknowledgments appear on page R147, which is an extension of the copyright page.

Printed in the United States of America

ISBN-13: 978-0-03-093890-0

ISBN 0-03-093890-2

1 2 3 4 5 6 7 8 9 048 12 11 10 09 08 07

Authors

Susan Ramírez

Susan Elizabeth Ramírez is the Penrose Chair of History and Latin American Studies at Texas Christian University. She received her Ph.D. in History from the University of Wisconsin, Madison, and taught for many years at DePaul University. A specialist in the history and culture of the Andean region, Professor Ramírez is the author of numerous articles and books, including *The World Upside Down: Cross-Cultural Contact and Conflict in Sixteenth Century Peru*. Her most recent book, *To Feed and Be Fed: The Cosmological Bases of Authority and Identity in the Andes*, offers a new interpretation of the rise and fall of the Inca Empire. She serves on the editorial boards of the *Hispanic American Historical Review* and *The Americas*.

Peter Stearns

Peter N. Stearns is Professor of History and Provost at George Mason University. Founder and longtime editor of the *Journal of Social History*, Stearns is also author and editor of numerous books, including the *Encyclopedia of World History* and the six-volume *Encyclopedia of European Social History from 1350 to 2000*. Professor Stearns received his Ph.D. from Harvard University and has taught for over 40 years. He is a member of the American Historical Society and the Social Science History Association, among other professional organizations. His current research topics include the history of gender, body image, and emotion. His most recent book is *Childhood in World History*.

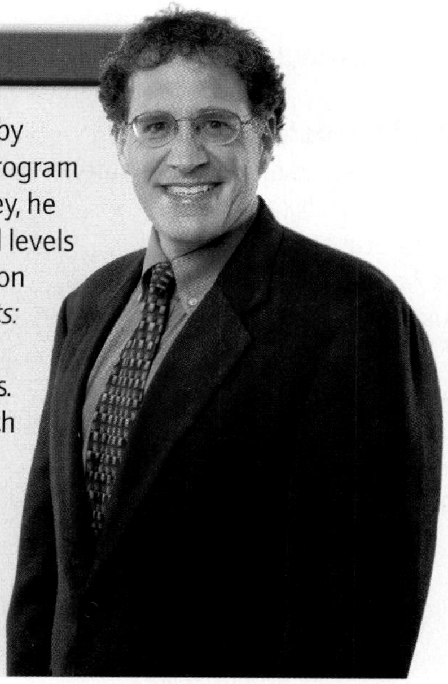

Sam Wineburg

Sam Wineburg is Professor of Education and Professor of History (by courtesy) at Stanford University, where he directs the only Ph.D. program in History Education in the nation. Educated at Brown and Berkeley, he spent several years teaching history at the middle and high school levels before completing a doctorate in Psychological Studies in Education at Stanford. His book *Historical Thinking and Other Unnatural Acts: Charting the Future of Teaching the Past* won the Frederic W. Ness Award from the Association of American Colleges and Universities. His work on teacher community won the 2002 Exemplary Research on Teaching and Teacher Education Award from the American Educational Research Association. He was a member of the blue-ribbon commission of the National Research Council that wrote the widely circulated report, *How People Learn: Brain, Mind, Experience, and School*. He is also the Senior Consulting Author on Holt's *American Anthem*.

Consultants

Program Consultant

Kylene Beers, Ed.D.
Senior Reading Researcher
School Development Program
Yale University
New Haven, Connecticut

Senior Consulting Author

Steve Goldberg
NCSS Board of Directors
Social Studies Department Chair
New Rochelle High School
New Rochelle, New York
Elizabeth Shanks

Academic Consultants

Alexander, Ph.D.
Professor of Rabbinic Judaism and Talmudic Literature
Department of Religious Studies
University of Virginia
Charlottesville, Virginia

Elizabeth A. Clark, Ph.D.
John Carlisle Kilgo Professor of Religion
Department of Religion
Duke University
Durham, North Carolina

Ahmet T. Karamustafa, Ph.D.
Professor of History and Religious Studies
Department of History
Washington University in St. Louis
St. Louis, Missouri

Christopher L. Salter, Ph.D.
Professor of Geography and Chair Emeritus
Department of Geography
University of Missouri-Columbia
Columbia, Missouri

Program Advisers

Academic Reviewers

Christian Appy, Ph.D.
Department of History
University of Massachusetts, Amherst
Amherst, Massachusetts

Jonathan Beecher, Ph.D.
Department of History
University of California, Santa Cruz
Santa Cruz, California

Stanley M. Burstein, Ph.D.
Professor Emeritus of Ancient History
Department of History
California State University, Los Angeles
Los Angeles, California

Prasenjit Duara, Ph.D.
Department of History
University of Chicago
Chicago, Illinois

Benjamin Ehlers, Ph.D.
Department of History
University of Georgia
Athens, Georgia

Lamont King, Ph.D.
Department of History
James Madison University
Harrisonburg, Virginia

Geoff Koziol, Ph.D.
Department of History
University of California
Berkeley, California

Robert J. Meier, Ph.D.
Department of Anthropology
Indiana University
Bloomington, Indiana

Vasudha Narayannan
Department of Religion
University of Florida
Gainesville, Florida

David L. Ransel, Ph.D.
Department of History
Indiana University
Bloomington, Indiana

Susan Schroeder, Ph.D.
Department of History
Tulane University
New Orleans, Louisiana

Helaine Silverman, Ph.D.
Department of Anthropology
University of Illinois
Urbana, Illinois

Paolo Squatriti, Ph.D.
Department of History
University of Michigan
Ann Arbor, Michigan

Marc Van De Mieroop, Ph.D.
Department of History
Columbia University
New York, New York

Educational Reviewers

Sally Adams
Garden Grove High School
Garden Grove, California

Chris Axtell
Sheldon High School
Sacramento, California

Tim Bayne
Lincoln East High School
Lincoln, Nebraska

Derrick Davis
Reagan High School
Austin, Texas

Terry Dawdy
Lake Travis High School
Austin, Texas

Nick Douglass
Anderson High School
Cincinnati, Ohio

Lynn M. Garcia
Hutchinson Central Technical High School
Buffalo, New York

Barbara Harper
Bryant High School
Bryant, Arkansas

Saundra J. Harris
Lane Technical College Prep High School
Chicago, Illinois

Marc Hechter
Palo Verde High School
Las Vegas, Nevada

Preya Krishna-Kennedy
Bethlehem Central High School
Delmar, New York

Brian Loney
Jefferson County Public School
Golden, Colorado

Jennifer Ludford
Princess Anne High School
Virginia Beach, Virginia

Patrick Teagarden
Homestead High School
Fort Wayne, Indiana

Reagan Williams
DH Conley High School
Greenville, North Carolina

Ernestine Woody
Freedom High School
Tampa, Florida

Field Test Teachers

Bruce P. Beichner
Allegheny-Clarion Valley High School
Foxburg, Pennsylvania

Earl Derkatch
Owasso High School
Owasso, Oklahoma

Steve Goldberg
New Rochelle High School
New Rochelle, New York

David Futransky
Cosby High School
Cosby, Tennessee

Anthony L. Marshall
Booker T. Washington High School
Tulsa, Oklahoma

Josh Mullis
Barr-Reeve Junior/Senior High School
Montgomery, Indiana

Michael B. Shuran
Tullahoma High School
Tullahoma, Tennessee

Nancy Webber
E. E. Waddell High School
Charlotte, North Carolina

Krissie Williams
Barnstable High School
Hyannis, Massachusetts

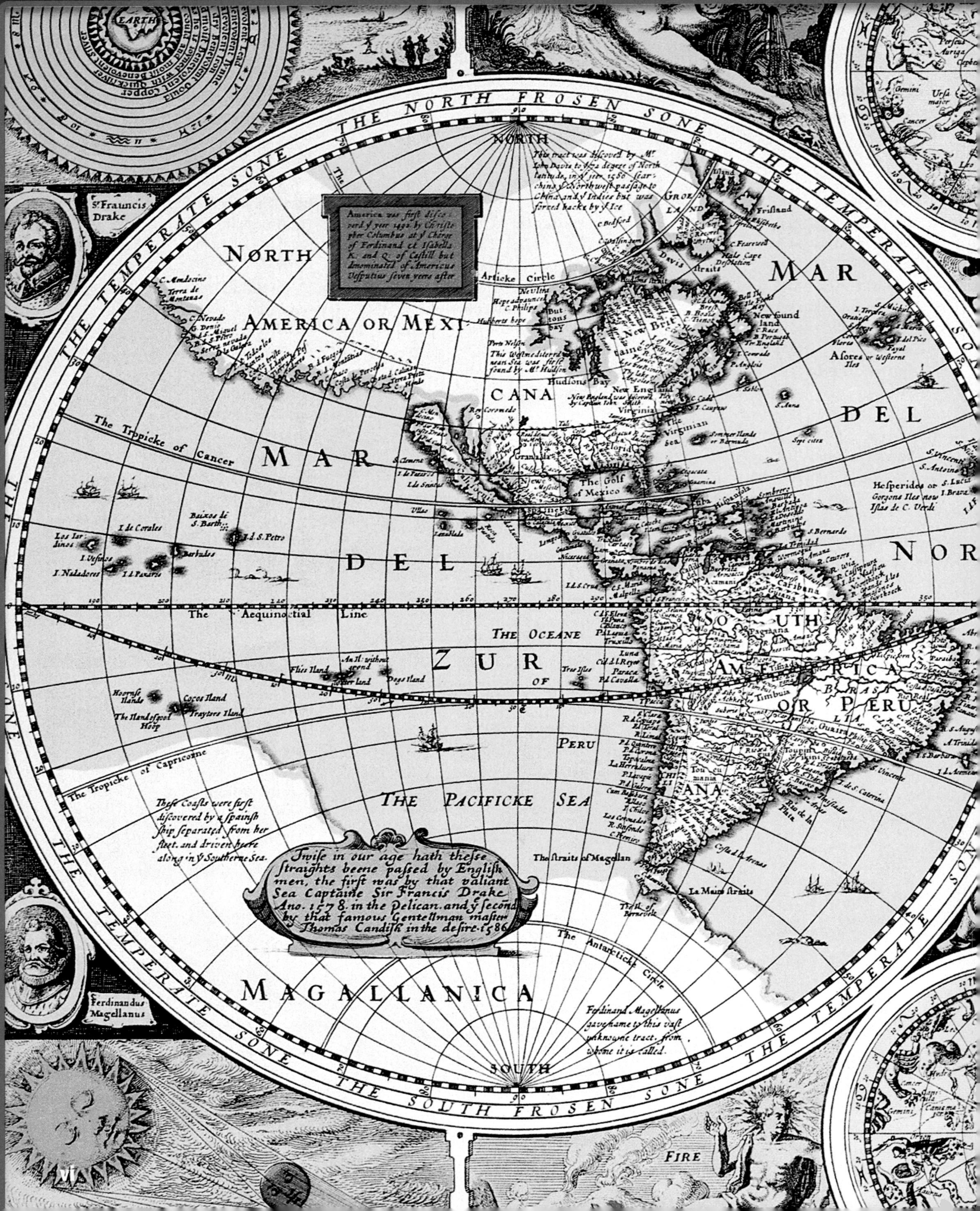
THE NORTH FROSEN SONE
NORTH
THE TEMPERATE SONE
S.r Frauncis Drake
EARTH
America was first discoverd y̆ yeare 1492. by Christopher Columbus at y̆ Charge of Ferdinand et Isabella K. and Q. of Castill but denominated of Americus Vespatius seven yeere after
NORTH
AMERICA OR MEXI
CANA
Artícke Circle
Hudsons Bay
New England
Virginia
The Golf of Mexico
The Tropicke of Cancer
MAR DEL ZUR
MAR DEL NOR
The Aequinoctial Line
THE OCEANE
SOUTH AMERICA OR PERU
PERU
The Tropicke of Capricorne
THE PACIFICKE SEA
These Coasts were first discovered by a spainsh ship separated from her fleet. and driven heere along in y̆ Southerne Sea.
Twise in our age hath these straights beene passed by English men, the first was by that valiant Sea Captaine Sir Francis Drake Ano. 1578. in the Pelican. and y̆ second by that famous Gentellman master Thomas Candish in the desire. 1586
The Straits of Magellan
La Maire Straits
The Antarcticke Circle
MAGALLANICA
Ferdinand Magellanus gave name to this vast unknowne tract. from whome it is called.
Ferdinandus Magellanus
SOUTH
THE SOUTH FROSEN SONE
FIRE

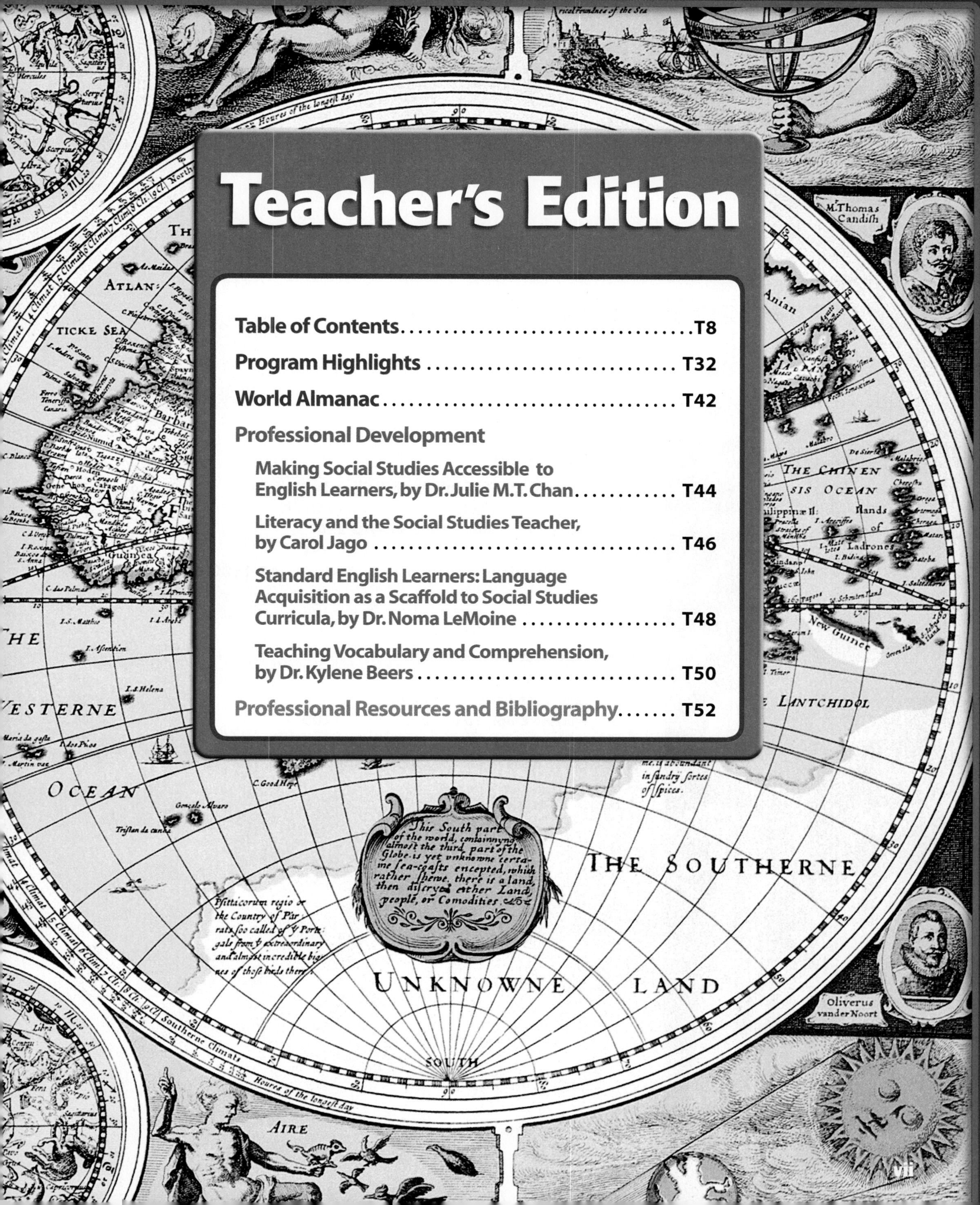

Teacher's Edition

Contents

UNIT 1

1200–1800

New Ideas, New Empires

UNIT 2

1500–1820

Changes in European Society

N°6
MUSÉE DES HORREURS
le Traître!

UNIT 4

1914–1945

The World at War 377

UNIT 5

1945–Present
The Contemporary World

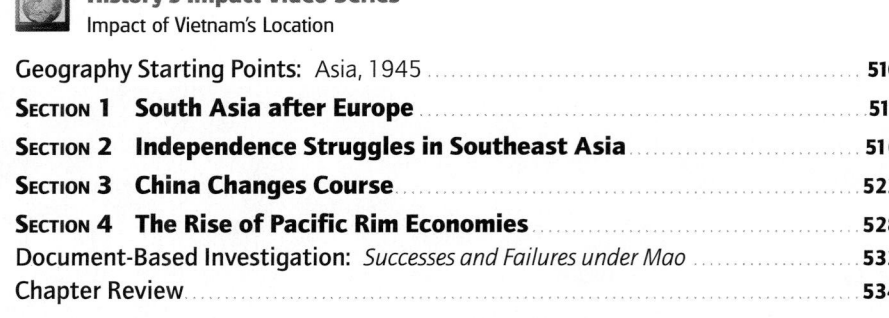

UNIT 6

Case Studies: Issues in the Contemporary World

Document-Based Investigation

Reference Section

Features

HISTORY & Geography

Explore the relationships between history and geography.

READING LIKE A HISTORIAN

Analyze and interpret primary and secondary source documents on world history.

World Religions

Learn about some of the major religions that have shaped world history.

Focus on Themes

Explore a world history theme in two contexts—the past and the present.

Themes Through Time

Study historical themes through key dates and moments in world history.

World Literature

Learn about the beliefs and experiences of people who lived in other times and places through excerpts from world literature.

Document-Based Investigation

Analyze topics in world history by using a variety of primary and secondary source documents.

History and Economics

Explore basic economic concepts in the context of world history.

Primary Sources

Examine key documents, speeches, political cartoons, and other primary sources that tell the story of world history.

Counterpoints

Examine some issues in world history through different viewpoints.

History Close-Up

Explore key developments and events in world history through in-depth and close-up illustrations and photo essays.

Forensics in History

Uncover a mystery in history using the tools of modern science.

The Arts Around the World

Take a closer look at a period in world history by examining the arts of that period.

FACES OF HISTORY

Meet the people who have made history and learn about their lives.

GEOGRAPHY Starting Points Maps

Interactive *Start with a map that establishes the geographical setting of the chapter.*

Linking TO Today

Link the people and events of world history to the world you live in today.

Maps

Interpret maps to see where important events happened and analyze how geography influenced world history.

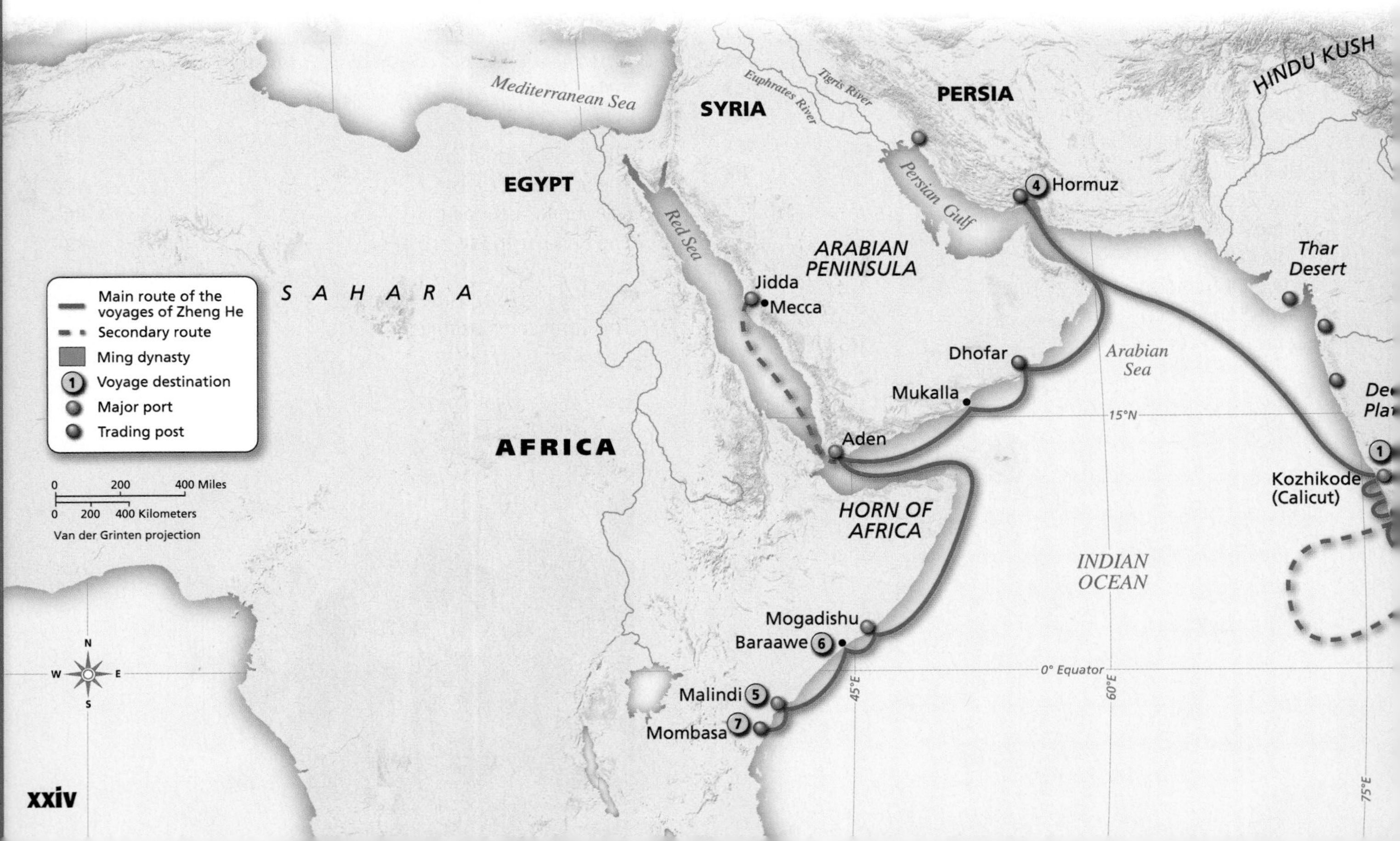

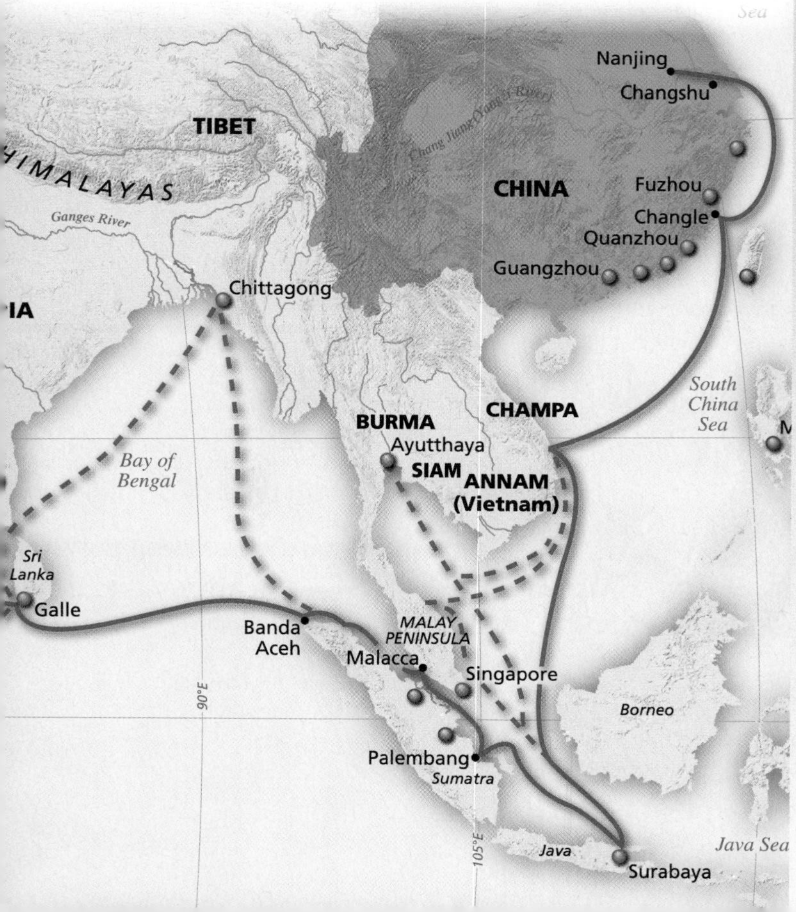
Nanjing
Changshu
TIBET
CHINA
Fuzhou
Changle
Quanzhou
Guangzhou
Ganges River
Chittagong
South China Sea
CHAMPA
BURMA
Ayutthaya
SIAM
ANNAM (Vietnam)
Bay of Bengal
Sri Lanka
Galle
Banda Aceh
MALAY PENINSULA
Malacca
Singapore
Borneo
90°E
Palembang
Sumatra
105°E
Java
Java Sea
Surabaya

Interactive

Charts and Graphs

Charts, Graphs, and Time Lines

Analyze information presented visually to learn more about history. To examine key facts and concepts, look for this special logo:

QUICK FACTS

CHARTS

GRAPHS

TIME LINE

Russia in Turmoil

August 1914 Russia enters World War I on the side of the Allied Powers.

March 1917 Russian citizens revolt and force Czar Nicholas II to give up power. A provisional government is established.

November 1917 In the Bolshevik Revolution, Communists led by Vladimir Lenin take over the Russian government.

TIME LINES

◀ A Bolshevik poster seeks to recruit soldiers during the Russian Civil War.

March 1918 The Bolshevik government signs the Treaty of Brest-Litovsk, which ends Russian involvement in World War I.

November 1920 After three years of fighting, the Russian Civil War ends with a Bolshevik victory.

December 1922 The Soviet Union is formed.

Primary Sources

Relive history through eyewitness accounts, literature, and documents.

THE MACMILLION.

HOLT brings history to life with an engaging narrative and instructional visuals

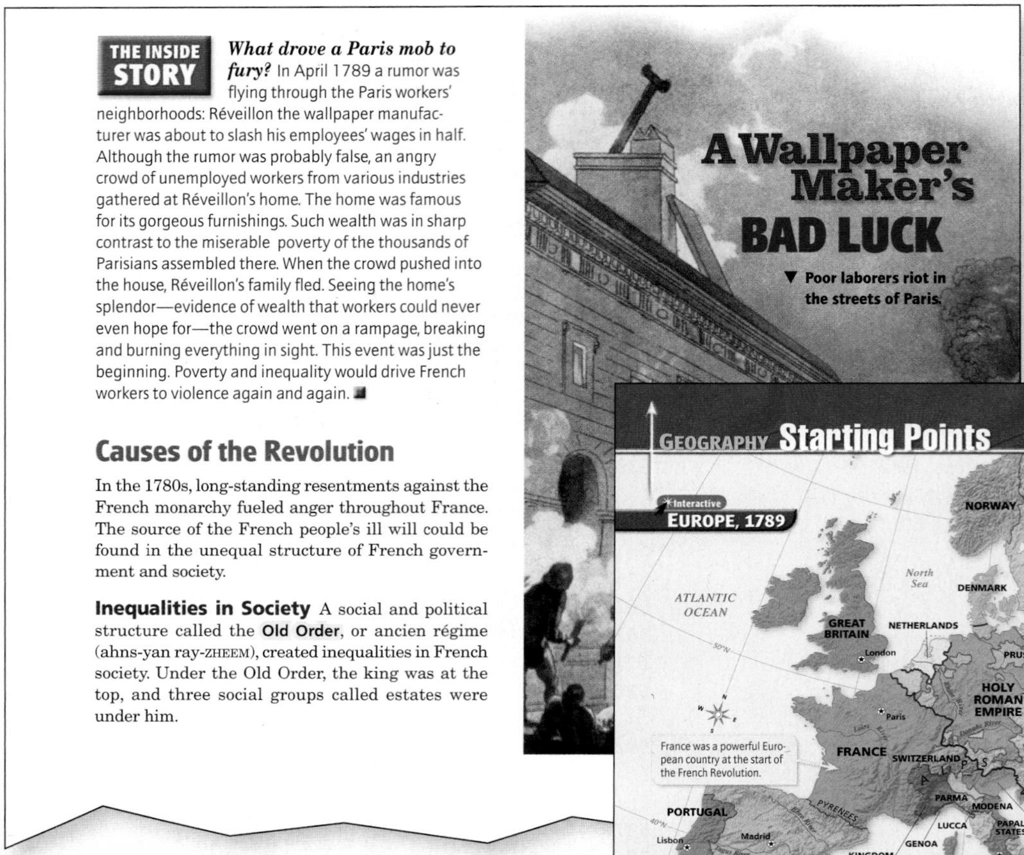

THE INSIDE STORY ***What drove a Paris mob to fury?*** In April 1789 a rumor was flying through the Paris workers' neighborhoods: Réveillon the wallpaper manufacturer was about to slash his employees' wages in half. Although the rumor was probably false, an angry crowd of unemployed workers from various industries gathered at Réveillon's home. The home was famous for its gorgeous furnishings. Such wealth was in sharp contrast to the miserable poverty of the thousands of Parisians assembled there. When the crowd pushed into the house, Réveillon's family fled. Seeing the home's splendor—evidence of wealth that workers could never even hope for—the crowd went on a rampage, breaking and burning everything in sight. This event was just the beginning. Poverty and inequality would drive French workers to violence again and again. ■

Causes of the Revolution

In the 1780s, long-standing resentments against the French monarchy fueled anger throughout France. The source of the French people's ill will could be found in the unequal structure of French government and society.

Inequalities in Society A social and political structure called the **Old Order**, or ancien régime (ahns-yan ray-ZHEEM), created inequalities in French society. Under the Old Order, the king was at the top, and three social groups called estates were under him.

▼ Poor laborers riot in the streets of Paris.

The Inside Story introduces each section with a "story behind the story" that looks at key events and crystallizes them in compelling human terms.

GEOGRAPHY Starting Points

Starting Points In the late 1700s France was one of Europe's large and powerful kingdoms. At that time, Europe was made up of a few large kingdoms and empires as well as many smaller states and territories. Then in 1789, the French Revolution set off a chain of events that reshaped Europe's political map.

1. **Analyze** Compare France on the large map to the French Empire on the inset map. What might have happened to allow France to become an empire?
2. **Predict** How do you think leaders of other European countries might have reacted as France expanded into other parts of Europe?

Listen to History

Go online to listen to an explanation of the starting points for this chapter.

go.hrw.com
Keyword: SHL NAP

592 CHAPTER 20

Geography Starting Points provides geographical orientation for what students are studying.

History's Impact Video Program
Watch the video to understand the impact of the French Revolution.

History's Impact Video Program helps students make connections between the impact of historical events and the world students live in today.

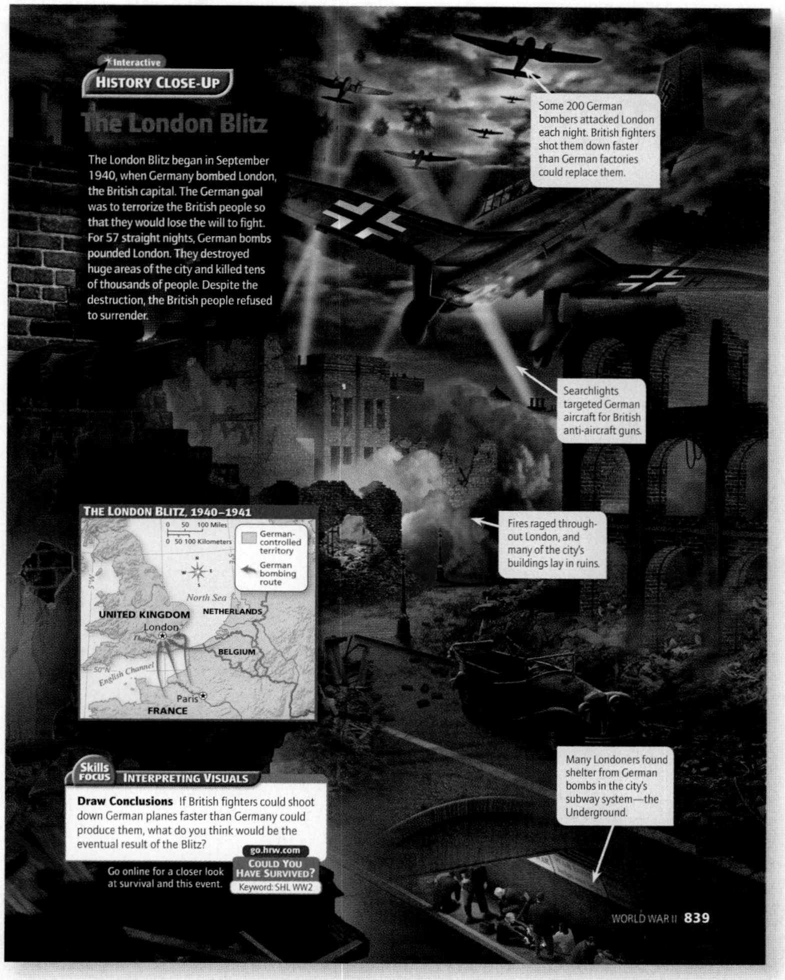

History Close-up features put students into the context of the time period, bringing to life the people, places, and concepts that they will learn.

Listening to History Audio CD Program includes musical and oratory selections that stimulate student interest and help them understand the sounds of an era.

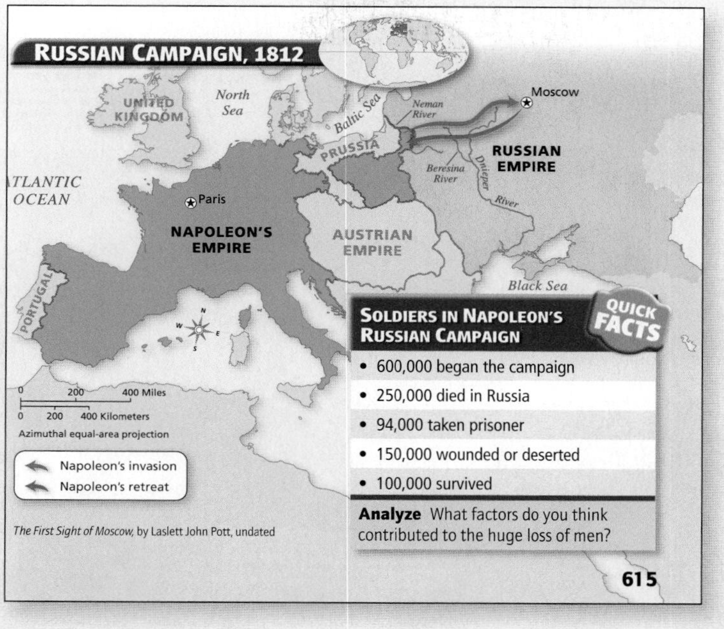

Dynamic Maps and Quick Facts Charts offer a way to engage students and help review key content.

HOLT integrates reading strategies and fosters **strong comprehensive skill development**

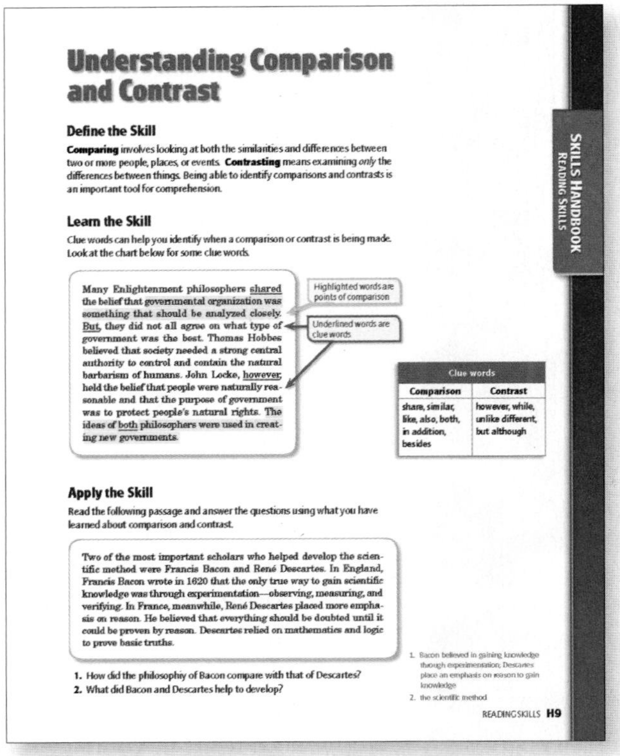

Understanding Comparison and Contrast

Define the Skill

Comparing involves looking at both the similarities and differences between two or more people, places, or events. **Contrasting** means examining *only* the differences between things. Being able to identify comparisons and contrasts is an important tool for comprehension.

Learn the Skill

Clue words can help you identify when a comparison or contrast is being made. Look at the chart below for some clue words.

Many Enlightenment philosophers shared the belief that governmental organization was something that should be analyzed closely. But, they did not all agree on what type of government was the best. Thomas Hobbes believed that society needed a strong central authority to control and contain the natural barbarism of humans. John Locke, however, held the belief that people were naturally reasonable and that the purpose of government was to protect people's natural rights. The ideas of both philosophers were used in creating new governments.

Highlighted words are points of comparison

Underlined words are clue words

Clue words	
Comparison	**Contrast**
share, similar, like, also, both, in addition, besides	however, while, unlike different, but although

Apply the Skill

Read the following passage and answer the questions using what you have learned about comparison and contrast.

Two of the most important scholars who helped develop the scientific method were Francis Bacon and René Descartes. In England, Francis Bacon wrote in 1620 that the only true way to gain scientific knowledge was through experimentation—observing, measuring, and verifying. In France, meanwhile, René Descartes placed more emphasis on reason. He believed that everything should be doubted until it could be proven by reason. Descartes relied on mathematics and logic to prove basic truths.

1. How did the philosophy of Bacon compare with that of Descartes?
2. What did Bacon and Descartes help to develop?

1. Bacon believed in gaining knowledge through experimentation; Descartes place an emphasis on reason to gain knowledge
2. the scientific method

SKILLS HANDBOOK READING SKILLS

READING SKILLS **H9**

Reading Skills lessons focus on reading skills to help students learn how to access information that they will learn.

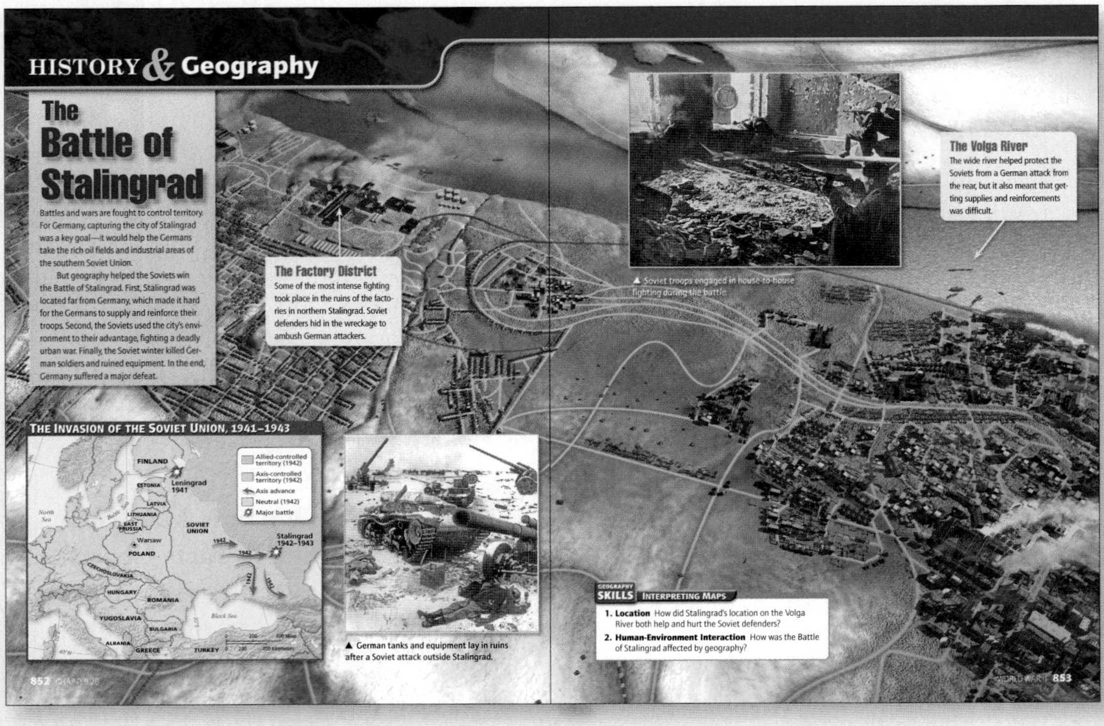

HISTORY & Geography

The Battle of Stalingrad

Battles and wars are fought to control territory. For Germany, capturing the city of Stalingrad was a key goal—it would help the Germans take the rich oil fields and industrial areas of the southern Soviet Union.

But geography helped the Soviets win the Battle of Stalingrad. First, Stalingrad was located far from Germany, which made it hard for the Germans to supply and reinforce their troops. Second, the Soviets used the city's environment to their advantage, fighting a deadly urban war. Finally, the Soviet winter killed German soldiers and ruined equipment. In the end, Germany suffered a major defeat.

The Factory District
Some of the most intense fighting took place in the ruins of the factories in northern Stalingrad. Soviet defenders hid in the wreckage to ambush German attackers.

The Volga River
The wide river helped protect the Soviets from a German attack from the rear, but it also meant that getting supplies and reinforcements was difficult.

▲ Soviet troops engaged in house-to-house fighting during the battle.

THE INVASION OF THE SOVIET UNION, 1941–1943

▲ German tanks and equipment lay in ruins after a Soviet attack outside Stalingrad.

GEOGRAPHY SKILLS INTERPRETING MAPS

1. **Location** How did Stalingrad's location on the Volga River both help and hurt the Soviet defenders?
2. **Human-Environment Interaction** How was the Battle of Stalingrad affected by geography?

852 CHAPTER 28

WORLD WAR II 853

History and Geography features incorporate visual images and special-purpose map activities that help students see the connection geography has to history.

Interactive Reader and Study Guide
HOLT
WORLD HISTORY
HUMAN LEGACY
• Learn main ideas through easy-to-read summaries
• Build skills
• Assess understanding of chapter content
• Extend lesson through Challenge Activities
HOLT, RINEHART AND WINSTON

The **Interactive Reader and Study Guide** helps **all** students understand and master the content using

- visual summary and critical thinking questions to organize chapter content
- section-by-section interactive note-taking to master main ideas
- challenge activities to extend concept learning

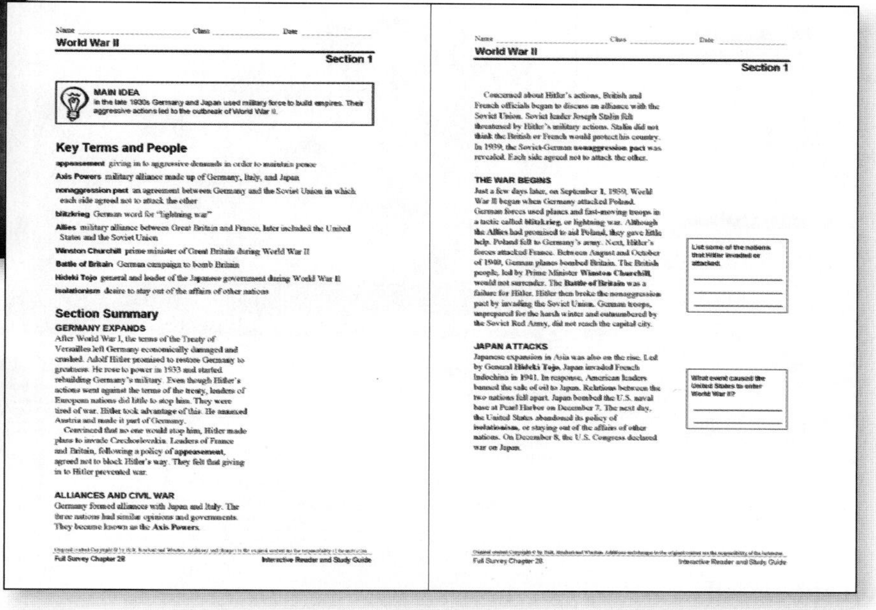

Name ______ Class ______ Date ______

World War II

Section 1

MAIN IDEA
In the late 1930s Germany and Japan used military force to build empires. Their aggressive actions led to the outbreak of World War II.

Key Terms and People

appeasement giving in to aggressive demands in order to maintain peace
Axis Powers military alliance made up of Germany, Italy, and Japan
nonaggression pact an agreement between Germany and the Soviet Union in which each side agreed not to attack the other
blitzkrieg German word for "lightning war"
Allies military alliance between Great Britain and France, later included the United States and the Soviet Union
Winston Churchill prime minister of Great Britain during World War II
Battle of Britain German campaign to bomb Britain
Hideki Tojo general and leader of the Japanese government during World War II
isolationism desire to stay out of the affairs of other nations

Section Summary

GERMANY EXPANDS
After World War I, the terms of the Treaty of Versailles left Germany economically damaged and crushed. Adolf Hitler promised to restore Germany to greatness. He rose to power in 1933 and started rebuilding Germany's military. Even though Hitler's actions went against the terms of the treaty, leaders of European nations did little to stop him. They were tired of war. Hitler took advantage of this. He annexed Austria and made it part of Germany.

Convinced that no one would stop him, Hitler made plans to invade Czechoslovakia. Leaders of France and Britain, following a policy of **appeasement**, agreed not to block Hitler's way. They felt that giving in to Hitler prevented war.

ALLIANCES AND CIVIL WAR
Germany formed alliances with Japan and Italy. The three nations had similar opinions and governments. They became known as the **Axis Powers**.

Full Survey Chapter 28 Interactive Reader and Study Guide

Name ______ Class ______ Date ______

World War II

Section 1

Concerned about Hitler's actions, British and French officials began to discuss an alliance with the Soviet Union. Soviet leader Joseph Stalin felt threatened by Hitler's military actions. Stalin did not think the British or French would protect his country. In 1939, the Soviet-German **nonaggression pact** was revealed. Each side agreed not to attack the other.

THE WAR BEGINS
Just a few days later, on September 1, 1939, World War II began when Germany attacked Poland. German forces used planes and fast-moving troops in a tactic called **blitzkrieg**, or lightning war. Although the **Allies** had promised to aid Poland, they gave little help. Poland fell to Germany's army. Next, Hitler's forces attacked France. Between August and October of 1940, German planes bombed Britain. The British people, led by Prime Minister **Winston Churchill**, would not surrender. The **Battle of Britain** was a failure for Hitler. Hitler then broke the nonaggression pact by invading the Soviet Union. German troops, unprepared for the harsh winter and outnumbered by the Soviet Red Army, did not reach the capital city.

List some of the nations that Hitler invaded or attacked.

JAPAN ATTACKS
Japanese expansion in Asia was also on the rise. Led by General **Hideki Tojo**, Japan invaded French Indochina in 1941. In response, American leaders banned the sale of oil to Japan. Relations between the two nations fell apart. Japan bombed the U.S. naval base at Pearl Harbor on December 7. The next day, the United States abandoned its policy of **isolationism**, or staying out of the affairs of other nations. On December 8, the U.S. Congress declared war on Japan.

What event caused the United States to enter World War II?

Full Survey Chapter 28 Interactive Reader and Study Guide

Also available
Spanish/English Interactive
Reader and Study Guide

Focus on Themes

Government and Citizenship

The 1789 Declaration of the Rights of Man and of the Citizen described how the French government would treat its citizens. The first article of the declaration states, "Men are born and remain free and equal in rights." The declaration uses the word *men*, but many asserted that the article applied to women, too. That women were equal to men was a truly revolutionary idea, and it frightened many people in France and the rest of Europe.

▲ **NOW Young workers in Rennes, France, protest unfair working conditions.**

EQUALITY THEN Equality was a key goal of the National Convention, which took control of France in 1792. Determined that everyone should be treated the same, the Convention went so far as to ban the titles *monsieur* and *madame*, the French equivalents of *Mr.* and *Mrs.* These titles, Convention leaders argued, had been derived from the words for *lord* and *lady*—noble titles—and should be abolished. Instead, people were required to address one another as "Citizen". For example, when King Louis XVI was overthrown, he became Citizen Capet, after his family's ancient name.

Despite the government's intentions, however, people were not treated equally. Women in particular had few rights. Although many women had taken part in the Revolution, they were not allowed to participate in the new government. Other people banned from the government included servants, men under 25, and people who did not pay taxes.

▶ **THEN Parisians marching on the Legislative Assembly.**

EQUALITY NOW Just as it was in France during the French Revolution, the idea that all people are equal is important in democracies around the world today. In most modern democracies, all citizens—men and women—are free to take part in the government. In addition, laws have made it illegal to discriminate against people based on their gender, race, occupation, or income.

In spite of the progress made by many democracies, equality for all is still a goal—not a reality—for many governments and their citizens. In many places, for example, women cannot vote, hold office, drive cars, or even appear in public alone. Consequently, groups of people all around the world are working hard to make equality a reality. The ideal of equality supported in the French Revolution, though not fully achieved, is alive in the world today.

Skills Focus UNDERSTANDING THEMES
1. **Summarize** What does the Declaration of the Rights of Man and of the Citizen say about equality?
2. **Analyze** How did the treatment of women during the French Revolution differ from the Declaration's goals?
3. **Predict** Do you think women around the world will gain rights or lose rights in the future? Why?

THE FRENCH REVOLUTION AND NAPOLEON 607

Focus on Themes and **Themes and Global Connections** encourage students to closely examine the content in context of a theme, developing their understanding of how historical events relate over time and to the present.

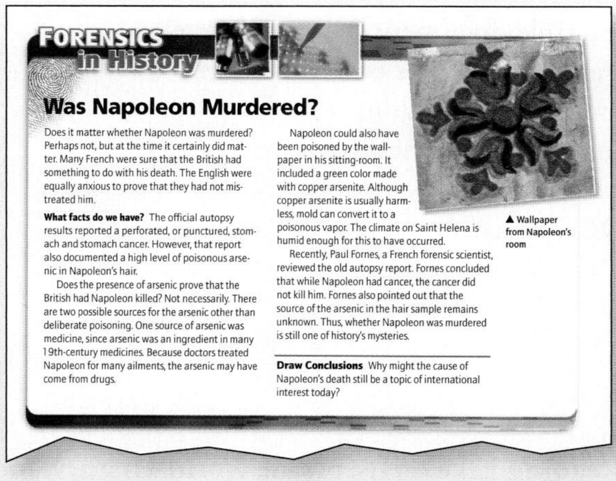

FORENSICS in History

Was Napoleon Murdered?

Does it matter whether Napoleon was murdered? Perhaps not, but at the time it certainly did matter. Many French were sure that the British had something to do with his death. The English were equally anxious to prove that they had not mistreated him.

What facts do we have? The official autopsy results reported a perforated, or punctured, stomach and stomach cancer. However, that report also documented a high level of poisonous arsenic in Napoleon's hair.

Does the presence of arsenic prove that the British had Napoleon killed? Not necessarily. There are two possible sources for the arsenic other than deliberate poisoning. One source of arsenic was medicine, since arsenic was an ingredient in many 19th-century medicines. Because doctors treated Napoleon for many ailments, the arsenic may have come from drugs.

Napoleon could also have been poisoned by the wallpaper in his sitting-room. It included a green color made with copper arsenite. Although copper arsenite is usually harmless, mold can convert it to a poisonous vapor. The climate on Saint Helena is humid enough for this to have occurred.

Recently, Paul Fornes, a French forensic scientist, reviewed the old autopsy report. Fornes concluded that while Napoleon had cancer, the cancer did not kill him. Fornes also pointed out that the source of the arsenic in the hair sample remains unknown. Thus, whether Napoleon was murdered is still one of history's mysteries.

▲ **Wallpaper from Napoleon's room**

Draw Conclusions Why might the cause of Napoleon's death still be a topic of international interest today?

Forensics in History features uncover a mystery in history using the tools of modern science.

HOLT encourages the investigation of history and prepares students to succeed on tests through **document-based instruction**

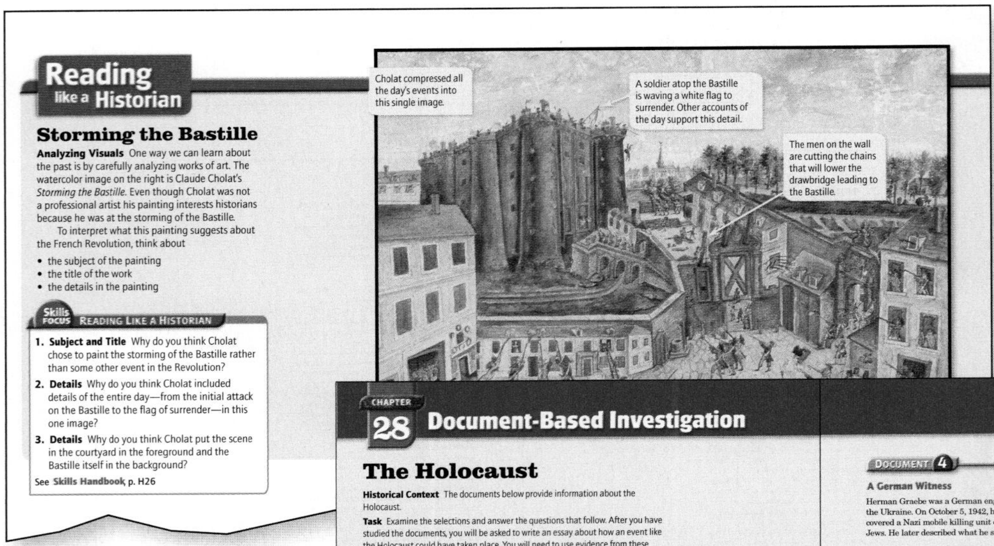

Reading like a Historian

Storming the Bastille

Analyzing Visuals One way we can learn about the past is by carefully analyzing works of art. The watercolor image on the right is Claude Cholat's *Storming the Bastille*. Even though Cholat was not a professional artist his painting interests historians because he was at the storming of the Bastille.

To interpret what this painting suggests about the French Revolution, think about

- the subject of the painting
- the title of the work
- the details in the painting

Cholat compressed all the day's events into this single image.

A soldier atop the Bastille is waving a white flag to surrender. Other accounts of the day support this detail.

The men on the wall are cutting the chains that will lower the drawbridge leading to the Bastille.

Skills Focus READING LIKE A HISTORIAN

1. **Subject and Title** Why do you think Cholat chose to paint the storming of the Bastille rather than some other event in the Revolution?
2. **Details** Why do you think Cholat included details of the entire day—from the initial attack on the Bastille to the flag of surrender—in this one image?
3. **Details** Why do you think Cholat put the scene in the courtyard in the foreground and the Bastille itself in the background?

See **Skills Handbook**, p. H26

Reading Like a Historian, integrated throughout the text, teaches students to analyze written and visual documents.

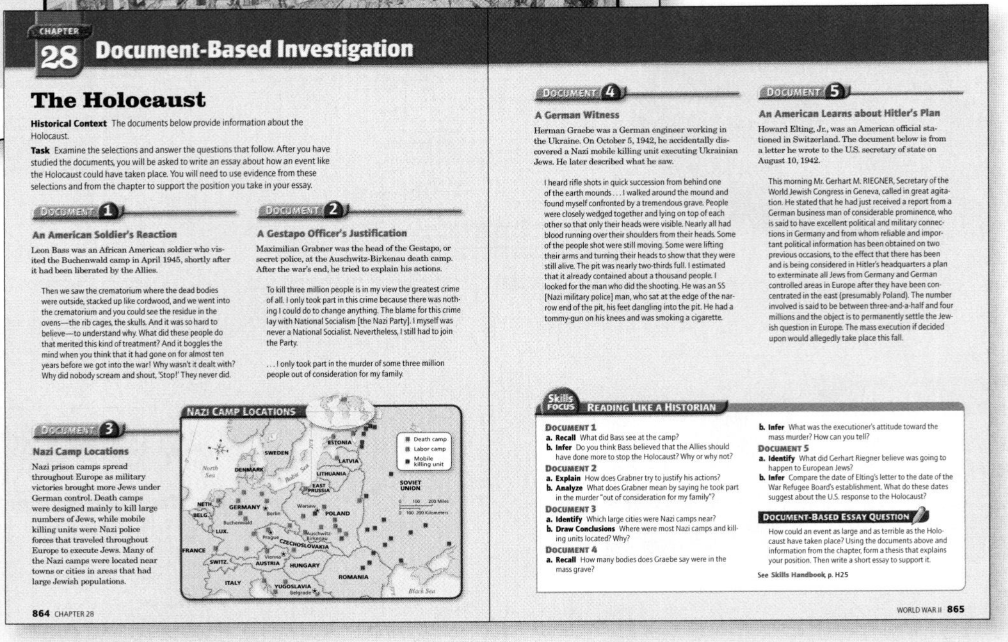

CHAPTER 28 **Document-Based Investigation**

The Holocaust

Historical Context The documents below provide information about the Holocaust.

Task Examine the selections and answer the questions that follow. After you have studied the documents, you will be asked to write an essay about how an event like the Holocaust could have taken place. You will need to use evidence from these selections and from the chapter to support the position you take in your essay.

DOCUMENT 1

An American Soldier's Reaction

Leon Bass was an African American soldier who visited the Buchenwald camp in April 1945, shortly after it had been liberated by the Allies.

> Then we saw the crematorium where the dead bodies were outside, stacked up like cordwood, and we went into the crematorium and you could see the residue in the ovens—the rib cages, the skulls. And it was so hard to believe—to understand why. What did these people do that merited this kind of treatment? And it boggles the mind when you think that it had gone on for almost ten years before we got into the war! Why wasn't it dealt with? Why did nobody scream and shout, 'Stop!' They never did.

DOCUMENT 2

A Gestapo Officer's Justification

Maximilian Grabner was the head of the Gestapo, or secret police, at the Auschwitz-Birkenau death camp. After the war's end, he tried to explain his actions.

> To kill three million people is in my view the greatest crime of all. I only took part in this crime because there was nothing I could do to change anything. The blame for this crime lay with National Socialism [the Nazi Party]. I myself was never a National Socialist. Nevertheless, I still had to join the Party.
>
> . . . I only took part in the murder of some three million people out of consideration for my family.

DOCUMENT 3

Nazi Camp Locations

Nazi prison camps spread throughout Europe as military victories brought more Jews under German control. Death camps were designed mainly to kill large numbers of Jews, while mobile killing units were Nazi police forces that traveled throughout Europe to execute Jews. Many of the Nazi camps were located near towns or cities in areas that had large Jewish populations.

DOCUMENT 4

A German Witness

Herman Graebe was a German engineer working in the Ukraine. On October 5, 1942, he accidentally discovered a Nazi mobile killing unit executing Ukrainian Jews. He later described what he saw.

> I heard rifle shots in quick succession from behind one of the earth mounds . . . I walked around the mound and found myself confronted by a tremendous grave. People were closely wedged together and lying on top of each other so that only their heads were visible. Nearly all had blood running over their shoulders from their heads. Some of the people shot were still moving. Some were lifting their arms and turning their heads to show that they were still alive. The pit was nearly two-thirds full. I estimated that it already contained about a thousand people. I looked for the man who did the shooting. He was an SS [Nazi military police] man, who sat at the edge of the narrow end of the pit, his feet dangling into the pit. He had a tommy-gun on his knees and was smoking a cigarette.

DOCUMENT 5

An American Learns about Hitler's Plan

Howard Elting, Jr., was an American official stationed in Switzerland. The document below is from a letter he wrote to the U.S. secretary of state on August 10, 1942.

> This morning Mr. Gerhart M. RIEGNER, Secretary of the World Jewish Congress in Geneva, called in great agitation. He stated that he had just received a report from a German business man of considerable prominence, who is said to have excellent political and military connections in Germany and from whom reliable and important political information has been obtained on two previous occasions, to the effect that there has been and is being considered in Hitler's headquarters a plan to exterminate all Jews from Germany and German controlled areas in Europe after they have been concentrated in the east (presumably Poland). The number involved is said to be between three-and-a-half and four millions and the object is to permanently settle the Jewish question in Europe. The mass execution if decided upon would allegedly take place this fall.

Skills Focus READING LIKE A HISTORIAN

DOCUMENT 1
a. **Recall** What did Bass see at the camp?
b. **Infer** Do you think Bass believed that the Allies should have done more to stop the Holocaust? Why or why not?

DOCUMENT 2
a. **Explain** How does Grabner try to justify his actions?
b. **Analyze** What does Grabner mean by saying he took part in the murder "out of consideration for my family"?

DOCUMENT 3
a. **Identify** Which large cities were Nazi camps near?
b. **Draw Conclusions** Where were most Nazi camps and killing units located? Why?

DOCUMENT 4
a. **Recall** How many bodies does Graebe say were in the mass grave?
b. **Infer** What was the executioner's attitude toward the mass murder? How can you tell?

DOCUMENT 5
a. **Identify** What did Gerhart Riegner believe was going to happen to European Jews?
b. **Infer** Compare the date of Elting's letter to the date of the War Refugee Board's establishment. What do these dates suggest about the U.S. response to the Holocaust?

DOCUMENT-BASED ESSAY QUESTION

How could an event as large and as terrible as the Holocaust have taken place? Using the documents above and information from the chapter, form a thesis that explains your position. Then write a short essay to support it.

See **Skills Handbook**, p. H25

864 CHAPTER 28

WORLD WAR II 865

Document-Based Investigation features have students analyze multiple documents, reach conclusions based on the investigation, answer critical thinking questions, and write DBQ essays.

HOLT
Reading Like A Historian: World History Toolkit
Encourage students to be history detectives
Analyze sources from a variety of perspectives
Investigate key historical topics
LUCHA por la HUMANIDAD
HOLT, RINEHART AND WINSTON

Reading Like a Historian: World History Toolkit
encourages students to be history detectives through analysis of sources from a variety of perspectives on key historical topics. Includes:

- Professional essays
- Teaching strategies
- Primary and secondary sources
- Transparencies
- A classroom poster
- Online presentation resources

PRIMARY SOURCES

Hiroshima

Father John A. Siemes, a German priest, was in Hiroshima when the atomic bomb was dropped on August 6, 1945. He later described the explosion:

> "Suddenly . . . the whole valley is filled by a garish light which resembles the magnesium light used in photography, and I am conscious of a wave of heat. I jump to the window to find out the cause of this remarkable phenomenon, but I see nothing more than that brilliant yellow light . . . I realize now that a bomb has burst . . .
>
> "The bright day now reveals the frightful picture ... Where the city stood everything, as far as the eye could reach, is a waste of ashes and ruin. Only several skeletons of buildings completely burned out in the interior remain. The banks of the river are covered with dead and wounded, and the rising waters have here and there covered some of the corpses . . .
>
> "As a result of the explosion of the bomb ... almost the entire city was destroyed at a single blow."

Skills FOCUS READING LIKE A HISTORIAN

1. **Make Generalizations** What does this source tell you about the power of the atomic bomb?
2. **Analyze Primary Sources** How would you expect the Japanese government to respond to the bombing of Hiroshima?

See **Skills Handbook**, p. H25

Primary Sources help students analyze written and visual sources.

World Literature

CHARLES DICKENS (1812–1870)

About the Reading The French Revolution is the setting for *A Tale of Two Cities*, but the book was written many years later, in 1859. In both cities—London and Paris—the reader meets people who show the best and worst of human qualities. The passage below introduces one of the book's villains, here called Monsieur the Marquis, as he rides through Paris in his carriage. The scene takes place before the Revolution has truly begun.

AS YOU READ **Think about why the poor people in the street react as they do.**

Excerpt from

A Tale of Two Cities

by Charles Dickens

Driving his Mail Coach in Nice, by Alphonse de Toulouse-Lautrec-Monfa, 1881

With a wild rattle and clatter, and an inhuman abandonment of consideration not easy to be understood in these days, the carriage dashed through streets and swept round corners, with women screaming before it, and men clutching each other and clutching children out of its way. At last, swooping at a street corner by a fountain, one of its wheels came to a sickening little jolt, and there was a loud cry from a number of voices, and the horses reared and plunged.

But for the latter inconvenience, the carriage probably would not have stopped; carriages were often known to drive on, and leave their wounded behind, and why not? But the frightened valet had got down in a hurry . . .

"What has gone wrong?" said Monsieur, calmly looking out.

A tall man in a nightcap had caught up a bundle from among the feet of the horses, and had laid it on the basement of the fountain, and was down in the mud and wet, howling over it like a wild animal.

"Pardon, Monsieur the Marquis!" said a ragged and submissive man, "it is a child."

"Why does he make that abominable noise? Is it his child?"

"Excuse me, Monsieur the Marquis—it is a pity—yes." . . .

The people closed round, and looked at Monsieur the Marquis. . . [He] ran his eyes over them all, as if they had been mere rats come out of their holes.

He took out his purse.

"It is extraordinary to me," said he, "that you people cannot take care of yourselves and your children. One or the other of you is for ever in the way. How do I know what injury you have done my horses?"

Skills FOCUS READING LIKE A HISTORIAN

go.hrw.com World Literature Keyword: SHL WRLIT

1. **Explain** What was the Monsieur's main concern?
2. **Interpret Literature as a Source** What bias may show in Dickens's novel? What sources do you think Dickens used for information on the Revolution?

See **Skills Handbook**, p. H28

600 CHAPTER 20

World Literature features present students with the opportunity to analyze significant literature excerpts of the time period.

A World History Teacher's Guide to Analyzing Movies provides full classroom support for critically viewing commercial movies with historical content and helps teachers use film as a source document.

HOLT ensures you can **differentiate instruction** for all students

live ink®
a new way to read
READING HELP

Live Ink Online Reading Help is an online tool that displays the text of the ***Holt Interactive Online Editions*** in a way that improves comprehension and increases test scores.

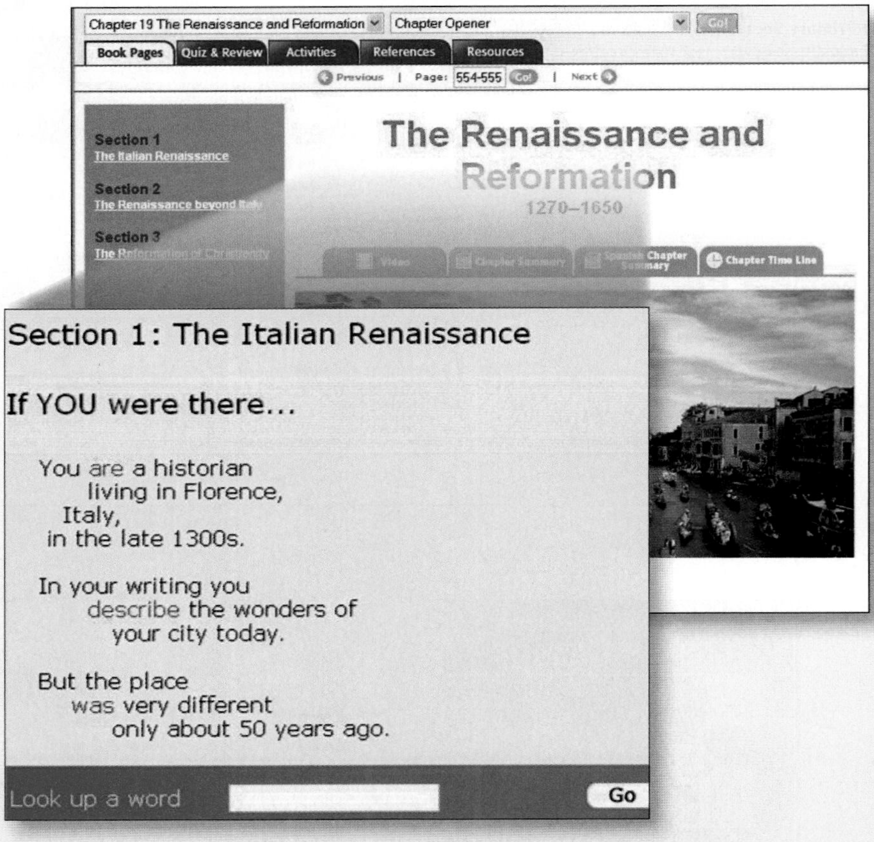

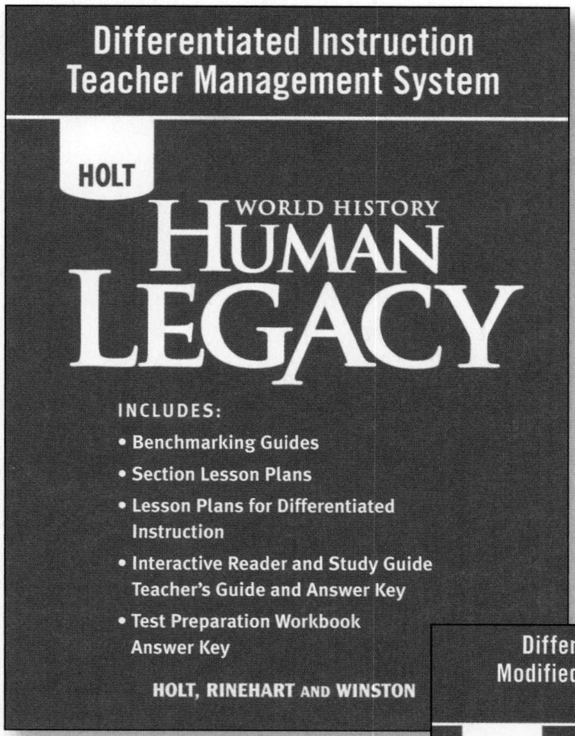

The **Differentiated Instruction Teacher Management System** provides Section Lesson Plans, Benchmarking guides, Lesson Plans for Differentiated Instruction, Teaching Guide, and Answer Keys.

The **Differentiated Instruction Modified Worksheets and Tests CD-ROM** provides all the key resources for the program modified to meet the specifications for students' Individualized Education Plans (IEPs.)

Interactive Skills Tutor CD-ROM helps students learn the Social Studies skills presented in the program. Each skill is introduced, practiced through interactive student activities, and then assessed for student mastery.

HOLT includes a range of **assessment options** to monitor students' progress effectively

The **Progress Assessment Support System (PASS)** includes all the assessment for every chapter and unit to help you monitor students' progress.

PASS includes:

- Test-Taking Tips
- Diagnostic Test
- Section Quizzes
- Chapter Tests
- Unit Tests
- End-of-the-Year Test
- Answer Keys

One-Stop Planner®
with Test Generator

The ExamView® Version 5 Assessment Suite, on the **Teacher's One-Stop Planner® CD-ROM**, makes it easy for you to reteach and offer more support to those students who need it.

Document-Based Activities for World History and the **Test Preparation Workbook** prepare students to succeed on high-stakes exams.

Quiz Game CD-ROM is an interactive multimedia game that assesses student understanding, makes learning fun, and tracks student performance.

A new technology, **Holt Online Assessment** helps you assess students' mastery of the content.

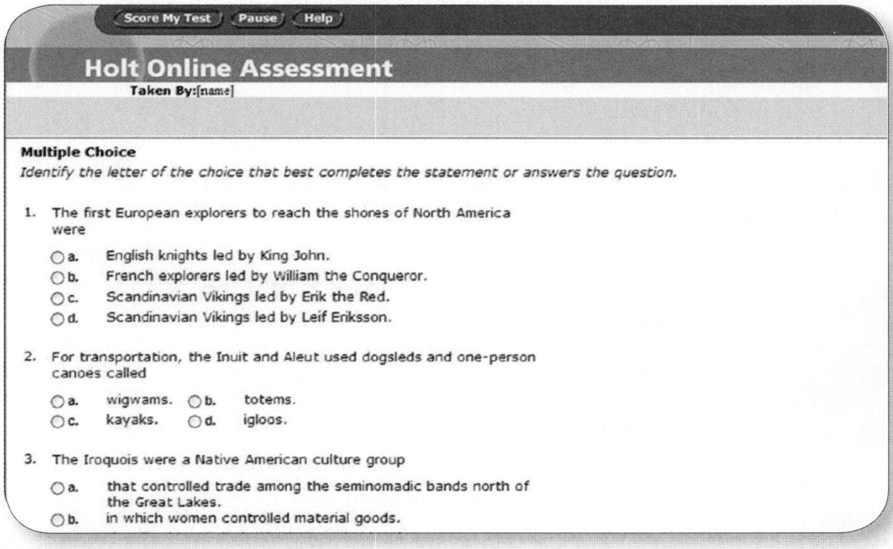

Step 1
Create a test

Step 2
Assign a test

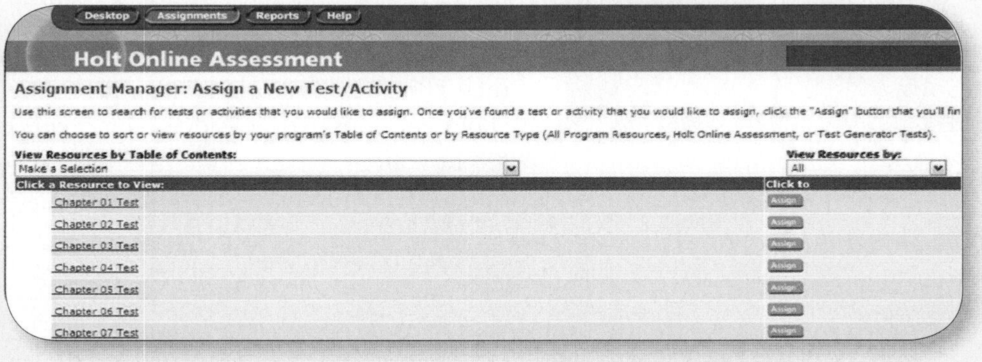

Step 3
View Reports

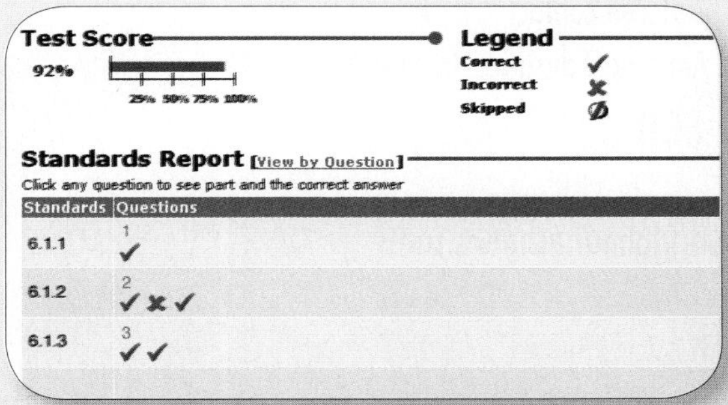

THE WORLD ALMANAC EDUCATION GROUP

Teaching Readers About Our World Since 1868

The World Almanac and Book of Facts has been delivering information about our world since the presidency of Johnson—Andrew Johnson! First published in 1868, *The World Almanac and Book of Facts* is America's all-time best-selling reference book, with more than 80 million copies sold.

Today, The World Almanac's experience and expertise at compiling, authenticating and distributing information extends throughout The World Almanac Education Group. We specialize in helping illuminate World History and the other social studies for students.

World Almanac **Key Events** in World History is a brief summary of important turning points in World History. It provides a capsule description of an event or movement, along with brief accounts of its significance. Use the section to review the content of Holt *World History Human Legacy.*

The World Almanac and Book of Facts itself devotes more than 200 pages to world history, providing quick answers about elections, world leaders, and events of the most recent year.

Social Studies Books, Kits and Databases for Your Classroom and Library

The World Almanac Education Group comprises ***World Almanac Books, Facts On File News Services, World Almanac Education Library Services,*** and ***Gareth Stevens Inc.*** These companies all offer valuable resources for world history and the other social studies. From engaging worksheet activities and supplemental classroom books that delve deeper into key curriculum areas to online database subscriptions, these materials can help you inspire your students to inquire about the world around them.

Social Studies Books

Gareth Stevens publishes acclaimed books series (with Teacher's Guides) in U.S. and World Geography, American and World History and American Government. Popular series include: ***Great Cities of the World, Places in History,*** and the ***Great Rivers of the World.***

Teaching Kits

World Almanac Education Library Services offers skills kits that combine class sets of authoritative reference works with worksheets, videos, and posters to teach students valuable map and research skills. With a set of almanacs or atlases at hand, students quickly learn how to find and use information, while discovering the world around the corner and around the globe.

On-line Databases

Facts On File News Services delivers award-winning on-line subscription databases at **FACTS.com.** These easy-to-use, accessible-from-anywhere databases teach kids about current events, topical issues, and science news. For a free trial visit: **www.facts.com/legacy.** Teachers also love the ***Issues & Controversies Yearbooks,*** which give students a quick understanding of more than sixty of the year's most talked-about topics.

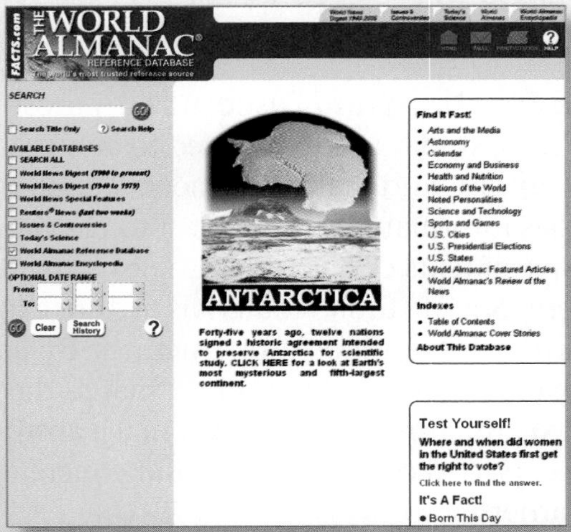

The World Almanac & World Almanac Book of Records

The World Almanac Education Group is founded on the reputation of ***The World Almanac and Book of Facts,*** the perennial number-one bestseller. Also look for the brand new ***World Almanac Book of Records,*** which includes fun and extensive coverage of World History.

Making Social Studies Accessible to English Learners

by Dr. Julie M.T. Chan

Dr. Julie M.T. Chan, Ed.D., is Director of Literacy Instruction in the Newport-Mesa Unified School District, located in Costa Mesa, California. She is a member of the California Reading and Literature Project, UCI/Orange County region, and serves on the state level CRLP Secondary Academic Language Tools development team. In addition, Dr. Chan teaches graduate courses on "The Sociocultural Contexts of Literacy and Learning" in the Masters of Reading program at California State University, Fullerton, and "Linguistics in Action in the Multicultural Classroom" at Concordia University in Irvine, California.

As increasing numbers of English-Language Learners (ELLs) enter the nation's secondary schools each year, it is incumbent upon all of us to help each student fully access the Social Studies curriculum.

Social Studies instruction relies heavily on language—oral language (listening/speaking) and written language (reading/writing). Because of their limited—but developing—proficiency in the English language, ELLs have a difficult time grasping the information presented orally by the teacher. In addition, they struggle when reading the printed text in Social Studies textbooks.

Chamot and O'Malley (1994) identified six areas where teachers can support ELLs: (1) Conceptual understanding, (2) Vocabulary, (3) Language functions and discourse, (4) Structures, (5) Academic language skills, and (6) Study skills and learning strategies. Here are some ways that teachers can make Social Studies accessible to English-Language Learners.

Conceptual Understanding While all students need to develop the concepts of time, chronology, distance, and differing ways of life, some ELLs may have never studied history or geography. Teachers could approach unfamiliar concepts and content by reading aloud trade books to build background knowledge and/or to provide a mental model at the beginning of a unit of study.

Vocabulary Students need to learn the content-specific, specialized terminology of Social Studies in order to discuss and report on the ideas studied. As students move up through the grades, the academic vocabulary of Social Studies becomes increasingly difficult because of the complexity of the concepts it represents. Thus, knowing which words to introduce and how and when to introduce them is critical.

Language Functions and Discourse In most school districts, students are expected to analyze, compare, contrast, and make judgments about Social Studies information. In contrast to the narrative discourse of texts designed for English language development, Social Studies materials feature expository patterns across various text structures. By using graphic organizers or mind maps that match the different text structures, teachers can make abstract ideas, concepts, and content visible and concrete for English Learners.

Differentiating Instruction

Below Level

English-Language Learners

1. Have students make a diagram of the power and social structure of feudal Japan. Students should write "Shogun" at the top edge of their papers. Have a volunteer name the next ruling class below the shogun. Have students add this to their papers.
2. Have students refer to the map and information in the section to make an approximate count of the daimyos. They can count the areas on the map and record an appropriate number next to the word (around 35).
3. Have volunteers name the working classes in descending order. Have students add the information to their own diagrams.
4. As a last step, have students work in mixed-ability pairs to add important details next to each class. LS **Verbal-Linguistic, Visual-Spatial**

Alternative Assessment Handbook, Rubric 1: Acquiring Information

Lessons designed to support instruction for English-Language Learners can be found throughout the Teacher's Edition.

Structures Oral and written language structures present special challenges to English-Language Learners. When teachers use research-based effective strategies to support oral and written language as well as published text structures, they can nudge their ELLs toward thinking, talking, reading, and writing like historians.

Academic Language Skills Students typically learn Social Studies through the receptive modes of listening and reading. In contrast, they "show what they know" through the productive modes of class discussions, oral presentations, and written products such as projects, reports, and expository/analytical essays. When the academic vocabulary of the content/concept to be studied is explicitly taught, ELLs can be more productive and therefore more successful at showing what they know.

Study Skills and Learning Strategies Chamot and O'Malley (1994) note that study skills, thinking skills, and social skills are also important components of the Social Studies curriculum. ELLs may not have, as yet, developed the learning strategies essential to these three skill areas. Thus teachers should help ELLs develop these skills so they can be better prepared to cope with the growing demands of new and abstract information found in grade-level Social Studies classrooms, textbooks, print materials, and primary source documents.

Teachers who are aware of the difficulties that ELLs encounter in their Social Studies classes will use this as an opportunity to explicitly teach those skills and strategies needed to be successful learners. Whether a teacher instructs regular Social Studies classes or a sheltered section, the result will be ELLs who have greater access to the Social Studies curriculum and who experience greater success as students moving toward the mainstream.

Billmeyer, Rachel (1996). *Teaching Reading in the Content Areas: If Not Me, Then Who?* Aurora, CO: McREL.

Buehl, Doug (2001). *Classroom Strategies for Interactive Learning*. Newark, DE: International Reading Association.

Chamot, Anna Uhl and J. Michael O'Malley (1994). *The CALLA Handbook: Implementing the Cognitive Academic Language Learning Approach.* Reading, MA: Addison-Wesley Publishing Company.

Roe, Betty, et al (1991). *Secondary School Reading Instruction: The Content Areas.* Boston, MA: Houghton Mifflin.

Tompkins, Gail E. (1997). *Literacy for the Twenty-First Century: A Balanced Approach.* Upper Saddle River, N.J.: Merrill.

ELL Instructional Support Services

- Use graphic organizers to teach abstract ideas.
- Teach specialized Social Studies vocabulary and usage.
- Promote development of study skills, thinking skills, and social skills.
- Read aloud content-related materials to help students build background knowledge.

Literacy and the Social Studies Teacher

by Carol Jago

Carol Jago teaches English at Santa Monica High School and directs the California Reading and Literature Project at UCLA. She is the author of *Cohesive Writing: Why Concept Is Not Enough* and *Papers, Papers, Papers: A Teacher's Survival Guide* (Heinemann 2005).

Q: Why should a Social Studies teacher have to teach reading and writing?

A: With a full curriculum of their own, many Social Studies teachers wonder why they should be expected to provide instruction in reading and writing? Isn't there enough to do just teaching history? There certainly is, but without strong literacy skills, students' ability to learn history is impaired. The idea is not that Social Studies teachers should become reading and writing teachers but rather that they should emphasize the classroom practices that are specific to learning history. For example, by helping students learn how to determine how to determine the gist of a textbook passage, Social Studies teachers reinforce what students need to know about distinguishing between important concepts and supporting details. By encouraging students to write like a historian, Social Studies teachers help students see how writing can be a powerful tool for thinking about controversial issues. By guiding students as they examine conflicting historical sources, Social Studies teachers help their students become critical readers with an eye for detail and point of view. The more students read and write, the more likely they are to retain what has been taught. Reading and writing help students learn history.

Q: What does research say about writing in Social Studies curriculum?

A: The National Commission on Writing in America's Schools and Colleges issued a report titled "The Neglected 'R'" calling for a writing revolution. NAEP research shows that only 50 percent of students meet "basic" levels of performance in writing and only one in five can be called "proficient." One student in five produces completely unsatisfactory prose. The 2003 report recommends that writing be incorporated into all state standards and that writing be required in every curriculum at all grade levels. "Very few things are more important to improving student achievement that restoring writing to its proper place in the classroom," said Commission Vice-Chair Arlene Ackerman, San Francisco superintendent of schools. "Writing is how we can teach students complex skills of synthesis, analysis, and problem solving." Given the controversial nature of so many topics in their curriculum, Social Studies teachers are uniquely positioned to help students develop these skills through persuasive writing.

Q: But how am I supposed to grade all those papers?

A: It isn't possible for teachers to work any harder. We need to work smarter. One method for assessing student writing effectively is to use rubrics. When the features of each numerical rubric score are laid out alongside a writing task, it is possible to assign a number to each student paper with confidence and, if not ease, efficiency.

Sample Scoring Rubric: Persuasive Essays

4 The Writing

- Clearly addresses all parts of the writing task
- Authoritatively defends a position with precise and relevant evidence
- Demonstrates a clear understanding of purpose and audience
- Maintains a consistent point of view, focus, and organizational structure, including the effective use of transitions
- Includes a clearly presented central idea with relevant facts, details, and/or explanations
- Includes a variety of sentence types
- Contains few, if any, errors in the conventions of the English language

3 The Writing

- Addresses all parts of the writing task
- Generally defends a position with relevant evidence and addresses the reader's concerns, biases, and expectations
- Demonstrates a general understanding of purpose and audience
- Maintains a mostly consistent point of view, focus, and organizational structure, including the effective use of some transitions
- Includes a central idea with relevant facts, details, and/or explanations
- Includes a variety of sentence types
- Contains some errors in the conventions of the English language

2 The Writing

- Addresses only parts of the writing task
- Defends a position with little, if any, evidence and may address the reader's concerns, biases, and expectations
- Demonstrates little understanding of purpose and audience
- Maintains an inconsistent point of view, focus, and organizational structure, which may include ineffective or awkward transitions that do not unify important ideas
- Suggests a central idea with relevant facts, details, and/or explanations
- Includes little variety of sentence types
- Contains several errors in the conventions of the English language

1 The Writing

- Addresses only one part of the writing task
- Fails to defend a position with any evidence and fails to address the reader's concerns, biases, and expectations
- Demonstrates no understanding of purpose and audience
- Lacks a point of view, focus, organizational structure, and transitions that unify important ideas
- Lacks a central idea but may contain marginally relevant facts, details, and/or explanations
- Includes no sentence variety
- Contains serious errors in the conventions of the English language

Scoring rubrics help Social Studies teachers assess student writing efficiently and effectively.

Social Studies teachers needn't feel that they must teach the mechanics of correctness. Language arts teachers recognize that this as their primary responsibility. By assigning writing, Social Studies teachers reinforce the lessons learned in English.

Q: With so much history to read, why are we asking students to read literature?

A: Literature helps bring history to life, animating historical events and allowing students to walk in the shoes of those who have lived long ago in places distant from their own experience. Good literature is also disturbing. It forces readers to examine the lives of others from the inside out, exposing young people to the complexity of the world they live in. Literature doesn't offer simple solutions. While reading fiction is not a vaccine for small-mindedness, it does make it difficult to think only of one's self. If one purpose of public education is to prepare students for the complex responsibilities of citizenship, I can think of no better preparation for these responsibilities than reading the work of Stephen Crane, Jack London, Frank Norris, Theodore Dreiser, and Upton Sinclair. Literature creates empathy and without empathy there can be little hope of a civilized society.

Standard English Learners

Language Acquisition as a Scaffold to Social Studies Curricula

by Dr. Noma LeMoine

Dr. Noma LeMoine, Ph.D., is a nationally recognized expert on issues of language variation and learning in African American and other students for whom Standard English is not native. She is Director of Academic English Mastery and Closing the Achievement Gap Branch for the Los Angeles Unified School District. She is a member of the National Citizen's Commission on African American Education, an arm of the Congressional Black Caucus Education Brain Trust. Dr. LeMoine is also the author of *English for Your Success: A Language Development Program for African American Students.*

Standard English Learners arrive at school in kindergarten as competent users of the language of their home but demonstrating limited proficiency in the language of school, that is, Standard American English. They are generally classified as English Only on school language surveys even though many of the rules that govern their home language are based in languages other than English. Because of their designation as English Only, these students' need for structured programs that support their acquisition of standard and academic English is often overlooked.

Who are Standard English Learners?

Standard English Learners (SELs) are students for whom standard English is not native or whose home language—the language acquired between infancy and five years of age—structurally does not match the language of school. Standard English Learners include African American, Hawaiian American, Mexican American, and Native American students who have in common a linguistic history grounded in languages other than English. Prior to coming in contact with English their ancestors spoke African languages, Hawaiian languages, Latin American Spanish, or Native American languages. In each case these "involuntary minorities"—people who were enslaved, colonized, conquered, or otherwise subordinated in the context of America—combined English vocabulary with their native language and fashioned new ways of communicating in their new environments. These language forms, African American Language (often referred to as Black English); Hawaiian American Language (referred

SEL Administrative Support Strategies

- Provide ongoing, comprehensive professional development for teachers and paraeducators including "literature circles" centered around the literature on the culturally and linguistically responsive instruction.
- Support the development of cooperative learning communities at the school site that engage teachers in review of the research, lesson study, peer coaching, and analysis of student work as a condition necessary for effectively educating SELs.
- Infuse information on the origin and historical development of standard and non-standard languages into the instructional curriculum.

to as Hawaiian Pidgin English); Mexican American Language (referred to as Chicano English); and Native American Language (sometimes referred to as Red English) incorporate English vocabulary, but differ in structure and form from standard American English.

Language Variation and Learning in SELs

In order for culturally and linguistically diverse Standard English Learners to succeed academically they must acquire the language, culture, and literacies of school. They must become literate in the forms of English that appear in newspapers, magazines, textbooks, voting materials, and consumer contracts. How best to facilitate this learning in Standard English Learners has proven elusive for most American public educational institutions and minimal emphasis has been placed on identifying instructional methodologies that scaffold SELs' access to core curricula. Learning is viewed as a social phenomenon and knowledge is recognized as a social construction that is influenced by the cultural and linguistic experiences, perspectives, and frames of references both students and teachers bring to the learning environment. For Standard English Learners this suggests that an instructional model, which validates and builds on prior knowledge experiences, language and culture while supporting the acquisition of school language through content learning is an appropriate pedagogy.

The Social Studies curriculum is perhaps the best vehicle for creating learning opportunities in both content and language acquisition areas. Opportunities to engage in critical thinking and participate in knowledge building abound in the Social Studies curriculum. As teachers help students develop skills as historians who re-create and share knowledge, students can also be provided opportunities to develop skills as speakers, readers, and writers.

SELs must be provided opportunities to add school language and literacy to their repertoire of skills using instructional approaches that build on the culture and language they bring to the classroom. In order for SELs to experience greater success in accessing core curricula, teachers will need to construct learning environments that are authentic, culturally responsive, support language acquisition, and build upon the experiences, learning styles, and strengths of SELs.

SEL Instructional Support Strategies

- Incorporate contrastive analysis strategies (linguistic, contextual, situational, and elicited) into the daily instruction of SELs to facilitate mastery of academic language.
- Incorporate applicable SDAIE (Specially Designed Academic Instruction in English) strategies into instruction including utilization of visuals, manipulatives, graphic organizers, media and other tools to explain concepts.
- Provide continuous and varied opportunities for students to use language to interact with each other and the content through instructional conversations.
- Provide 30 to 45 minutes per day of Mainstream English Language Development (MELD) instruction that promotes the development of listening, speaking, reading, and writing skills in standard and academic English.
- Establish classroom libraries that include culturally relevant books and provide opportunities for SELs to be read to and to engage in free voluntary reading (FVR) on a daily basis.
- Encourage student/classroom development of a personal thesaurus of conceptually coded words to support the acquisition of academic vocabulary.
- Convey knowledge on ancient Africa, Mexico, Hawaii, and North America; their cultures and history.
- Convey knowledge of the impact of diverse cultures on the modern world with an emphasis on historical and contemporary achievers.
- Make connections to students' prior knowledge, experiences, and cultural funds of knowledge to support learning and retention of learned concepts.

Teaching Vocabulary and Comprehension

by Dr. Kylene Beers

Dr. Kylene Beers, Ed.D., is a Senior Reading Researcher in the School Development Program of the Child Study Center at Yale University. A former middle school teacher, Dr. Beers is a respected authority on struggling readers. She is the current editor of *Voices from the Middle,* the journal of the National Council of Teachers of English; co-editor of *Into Focus: Understanding and Creating Middle School Readers;* and the author of *When Kids Can't Read—What Teachers Can Do.* Dr. Beers was the 2001 recipient of the Richard W. Halle Award given by NCTE for outstanding contributions to middle school education.

Effective Vocabulary Instruction

"Preteaching vocabulary . . . requires that the words to be taught must be key words . . . be taught in semantically and topically related sets, . . . and that only a few words be taught per lesson."

—Tierney and Cunningham

The Right Words and the Right Number

The more vocabulary words we give students to learn weekly, the less chance students have of learning a word to the level needed to move it from short-term to long-term memory. Keeping the number between 5 and 10 means students have a better chance of retaining that word beyond the end of the week (Beers, 2002).

Consequently, choose wisely the words to be taught. Avid readers benefit by studying rare words—those highly unusual ones—because these students already have a solid vocabulary of the more common words. Struggling readers, however, benefit by focusing on high-utility words—those more common words that they are likely to see in other contexts. So, in the sentence, "The boys banked the canoe to the lee side of the rock," the inclination might be to teach the word *lee,* a rare word. However, if students don't know what *banked* means in this context or don't know the word *canoe,* it matters little what *lee* means. For struggling readers, a focus on high-utility words is more beneficial than a focus on rare words.

The Right Instructional Approach

Tierney and Cunningham (1984) explain that offering students a list of vocabulary words with their definitions is not as effective as placing each word within a semantic context. Students learn how to use words as they read or hear them used correctly. This textbook lists the key terms and people for each section at the beginning of that section. Defining these terms and using them in a sentence provides students with the semantic placement that most helps them learn words. Choosing the right number of the right words and presenting words in a semantic context helps students build their vocabulary and, as a consequence, improve their comprehension.

Improving Comprehension

"Comprehension is both a product and a process, something that requires purposeful, strategic effort on the reader's part as he or she predicts, visualizes, clarifies, questions, connects, summarizes, and infers."

—Kylene Beers

When the Text is Tough

"Comprehension is only tough when you can't do it," explained the eleventh-grader. I almost dismissed his words until I realized what truth they offered. We aren't aware of all the thinking we do to comprehend a text until faced with a difficult text. Then all too clearly, we're aware of what words we don't understand, what syntax seems convoluted, and what ideas are beyond our immediate grasp. As skilled readers, we know what to do—we slow our pace, reread, ask questions, connect whatever we do understand to what we don't understand, summarize what we've read thus far, and make inferences about what the author is saying. In short, we make that invisible act of comprehension visible as we consciously push our way through the difficult text. At those times, we realize that, indeed, comprehension is tough.

Reading Strategies for Struggling Readers

It's even tougher if you lack strategies that would help you through the difficult text. Many struggling readers believe they aren't successful readers because that's just the way things are (Beers, 2002). They believe successful readers know some secret that they haven't been told (Duffy, 2002). While we don't mean to keep comprehension a secret, at times that is what we do. For example, though we tell students to "reread," we haven't shown them how to alter their reading. We tell them to "make inferences," or "make predictions," but we haven't taught them how to do such things. In other words, we tell them what to do, but don't show them how to do it, in spite of several decades of research showing the benefit of direct instruction in reading strategies to struggling readers (Baumann, 1984; Pearson, P. D., 1984; Dole, et al., 1996; Beers, 2002).

Direct Instruction Direct instruction means telling students what you are going to teach them, modeling it for them, providing assistance as they practice it, then letting them practice it on their own. It's not saying, "visualize while you read," but, instead, explaining, "today, I'm going to read this part aloud to you. I'm going to focus on seeing some of the action in my mind as I read. I'm going to stop occasionally and tell you what I'm seeing and what in the text helped me see that." When we directly teach comprehension strategies to students by means of modeling and repeated practice, we show students that good readers don't just get it. They work hard to get it. Direct instruction takes the secret out of comprehension as it provides teachers the support they need to reach struggling readers.

Baumann, J. 1984.
"Effectiveness of a Direct Instruction Paradigm for Teaching Main Idea Comprehension." *Reading Research Quarterly,* 20: 93–108.

Beers, K. 2002.
When Kids Can't Read—What Teachers Can Do. Portsmouth: Heinemann.

Dole, J., Brown, K., and Trathen, W. 1996.
"The Effects of Strategy Instruction on the Comprehension Performance of At-Risk Students." *Reading Research Quarterly,* 31: 62–89.

Duffy, G. 2002.
"The Case for Direct Explanation of Strategies." *Comprehension Instruction: Research-Based Best Practices.* Eds. C. Block and M. Pressley. New York: Guilford Press. 28–41.

Pearson, P. D. 1984.
"Direct Explicit Teaching of Reading Comprehension." *Comprehension Instruction: Perspectives and Suggestions.* Eds. G. Duffy, L. Roehler, and J. Mason. New York: Longman. 222–233.

Tierney, R. J., and Cunningham, J. W. 1984.
"Research on Teaching Reading Comprehension." *Handbook of Reading Research.* Eds. P. D. Pearson, R. Barr, M. Kamil, P. Mosenthal. New York: Longman. 609–656.

Professional Resources and Bibliography

Professional References

This section provides information about resources that can enrich your Social Studies class. Included is information about guest speakers, museum visits, electronic field trips, nonprofit organizations, and many others. Since addresses change frequently, you may want to verify them before you send your requests. You may also want to refer to the HRW Web site at http://www.hrw.com for current information.

GUEST SPEAKERS

National Council for History Education
26915 Westwood Rd., Suite B-2
Westlake, Ohio 44145
440-835-1776
www.nche.net

K-12 Outreach for International and Area Studies
University of California, Berkeley
2223 Fulton Street Room 338 #2324
Berkeley, CA 94720-2324
510-643-0868
orias@berkeley.edu

MUSEUM VISITS

American Association of Museums
1575 Eye Street NW, Suite 400
Washington, DC 20005
202-289-1818
www.aam-us.org

ELECTRONIC FIELD TRIPS

Library of Congress/Congressional Server
www.loc.gov

E3 Electronic Field Trips
Teachers College (TC 1008)
Ball State University
Muncie IN 47306
866-279-8716
www.bsu.edu/eft

eFieldTrips.org
2960 W. Player Dr.
Snowflake, Arizona 85937
928-536-4954

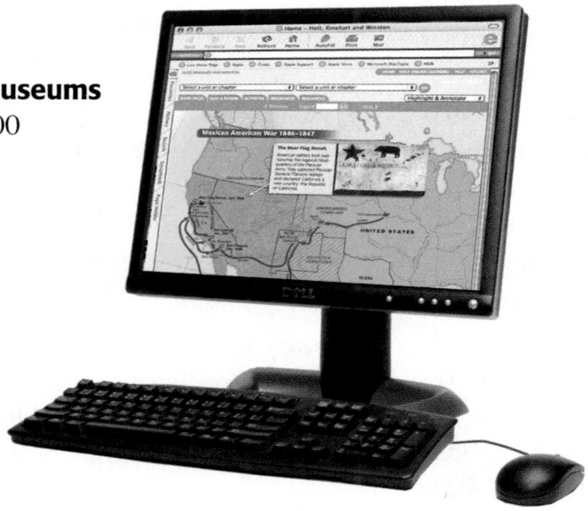

NONPROFIT ORGANIZATIONS

The World History Association
Sakamaki Hall
A203, 2530 Dole St.
University of Hawai'i at Manoa
Honolulu Hawai'i 96822-2383
808-956-7688
www.thewha.org

PBS
www.pbs.org/history/history_world html

National Council for the Social Studies
8555 Sixteenth Street, Suite 500
Silver Spring, MD 20910
301-588-1800
www.socialstudies.org

National Trust for Historic Preservation
1785 Massachusetts Ave. NW
Washington, DC 20036
202-588-6000
www.nationaltrust.org

National History Day
University of Maryland
at College Park
0119 Cecil Hall
College Park, MD 20742
301-314-9739
www.nationalhistoryday.org

GOVERNMENT RESOURCES

U.S. Department of Education
400 Maryland Ave., SW
Washington, D.C. 20202-0498
800-USA-LEARN
www.ed.gov

Smithsonian Institution
Smithsonian Information
P.O. Box 37012
SI Building, Room 153, MRC 010
Washington, DC 20013-7012
202-357-2700
www.si.edu

The Library of Congress
101 Independence Ave, SE
Washington, DC 20540
202-707-5000
www.loc.gov

National Register of Historic Places
National Park Service
1201 Eye Street, NW MS 2280
Washington, DC 20005
202-354-2213
www.cr.nps.gov/nr

SUBSCRIPTION SERVICES

Magazines.com Inc.
P.O. Box 682108
Franklin, TN 37068
800-929-2691
www.magazines.com

MISCELLANEOUS

Educational Resources Information Center (ERIC)
ERIC Project
c/o Computer Sciences Corporation
4483-A Forbes Blvd.
Lanham, MD 20705
800-538-3742
www.eric.ed.gov

The International Initiatives Program
American Council on Education
One Dupont Circle NW, Washington DC 20036

Busy Teachers' WebSite K-12
http://www.ceismc.gatech.edu/busyt

A Bibliography for the Social Studies Teacher

This bibliography is a select compilation of resources available for professional enrichment.

SELECTED AND ANNOTATED LIST OF READINGS

Social Studies and Language Arts

Burke, Jim. *Writing Reminders: Tools, Tips, and Techniques*
Portsmouth, NH: Heinemann, 2003
Burke offers a collection of strategies for teaching writing, complete with the instructional tools for implementing the strategies.

Jago, Carol. *Cohesive Writing: Why Concept Is Not Enough*
Portsmouth, NH: Heinemann, 2002
This book provides a coherent roadmap for teaching students how to write in each of the writing types required for the STAR assessment: summary, narrative, response to literature, and persuasion.

Social Studies and Standard English Mastery

LeMoine, N. and Los Angeles Unified School District. *English for Your Success: A Language Development Program for African American Students. Handbook of Successful Strategies for Educators.*
New Jersey: The Peoples Publishing Group, 1999
English for Your Success provides lessons using proven strategies for facilitating language acquisition and learning in African American Standard English Learners.

Ornstein-Galicia, J. *Form and Function in Chicano English*
Malabar, FL: Krieger Publishing Co., 1988
This text address issues of language and learning in Mexican American Standard English Learners (SELs) who speak mainly Chicano English.

Social Studies and English Learners

Billmeyer, Rachel and Mary Lee Barton. *Teaching Reading in the Content Areas: If Not Me, Then Who?* Second Edition
Aurora, CO: Mid-Continent Regional Educational Laboratory (McREL), 1998
These 40 strategies help students of all ages expand their vocabularies, understand different types of texts, and discuss what they have read.

Buehl, Doug. *Classroom Strategies for Interactive Learning,* Second Edition
Newark, DE: International Reading Assoc., 2001
More than 40 literacy strategies for middle school and high school educators outside the reading field.

Readance, John, Thomas W. Bean and R. Scott Baldwin. *Content Area Literacy: An Integrated Approach.* Eighth Edition
Dubuque, IA: Kendall/Hunt Publishing Company, 2000
The authors provide strategies for helping students read, understand, and enjoy nonfiction. A CD accompanies this widely used text.

Themes of History

No two historical events or periods are exactly alike, but there are common themes that can be traced through all of human history. As you read *Human Legacy,* look for the eight themes described below. They appear again and again, not just in this textbook, but throughout history. These themes help you see ways all peoples and societies are alike and ways they are different.

ARTS AND IDEAS

Some of the noblest human aspirations and achievements have been enshrined in artworks and in ideas. The arts can inspire us, and ideas can move us to action.

- What ideas unite and motivate a society?
- How does a culture express itself through its arts and ideas?
- How do the arts of different societies express enduring human needs and beliefs?

BELIEF SYSTEMS

Beliefs can be powerful forces for societies as well as individuals. Religious beliefs, for instance, have inspired great works of devotion, sacrifice, and art. They can also serve to define and divide people.

- What do people believe about the nature of the universe?
- What do people believe about how society should be ordered and governed?
- How do beliefs motivate people?

Economic Systems

ECONOMIC SYSTEMS

Because resources are scarce and people's needs and wants are many, every society needs an economic system by which to allocate available resources. Economic systems may change—from a simple barter system to today's complex global capitalism—but the need to order the exchange of goods, services, and resources remains a constant in human history.

- How are scarce resources allocated in a society?
- Why have some people or groups of people had more resources than others?
- How do economic systems affect political and social systems?
- How do different systems strive to ensure efficiency? fairness?

GEOGRAPHY AND ENVIRONMENT

Geography and environment influence the way societies develop. A desert society develops different economic and social practices than a sea faring one. People both modify their environment and adapt to it in order to best meet their needs.

- How do people change their environment and make changes to their environment?
- In what ways do geography and environment influence a society?

NORTH POLE
Since 1979 more than 20% of the Polar Ice Cap has melted away.
ARCTIC SEA ICE BOUNDARY IN 1979
Geography and Environment

Government and Citizenship

Today, most people believe that a government's power comes from the consent of the governed—that in government, citizens are the ultimate authority. But that belief is relatively new. Different societies—in the past and even today—adopt different forms of government.

- What is the proper form of government?
- Who should be a citizen? Why has that question had different answers at different times?
- What is the relationship between those who govern or rule and those who are governed or ruled?

Migration and Diffusion

From the days of the earliest humans in Africa, people have been on the move, hunting animals, looking for fresh fields to plant, and seeking new places for trade. The movement of peoples, goods, and ideas has the power to transform and even destroy empires and nations.

- What are the large patterns of movement that shape human history?
- How are new ideas, ways of doing things, and diseases spread?
- What motivates people to seek new lands?

Science and Technology

Humans use science to try to understand their environment, and they use technology to try to shape and control it. The urge to understand the world and to invent new tools to shape it is a fundamental aspect of human nature.

- What are the different concepts that people have had about the world? How have they changed over time?
- How have the tools people used changed over time, often radically reshaping the limits of human possibility?
- How have technological advances given one society advantages over another?

Society

The complex pattern of relationships—political, economic, cultural—that bind people together make a society. In any historical period, these patterns may be loosely defined or they may be embodied in institutions such as governments and churches.

- What are the social classes that make up a society?
- How is political and economic power distributed?
- What are the customs and norms that unite a society?

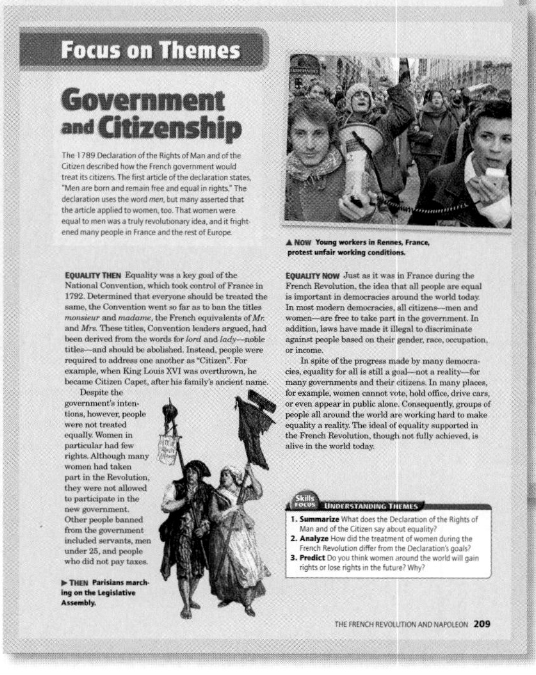

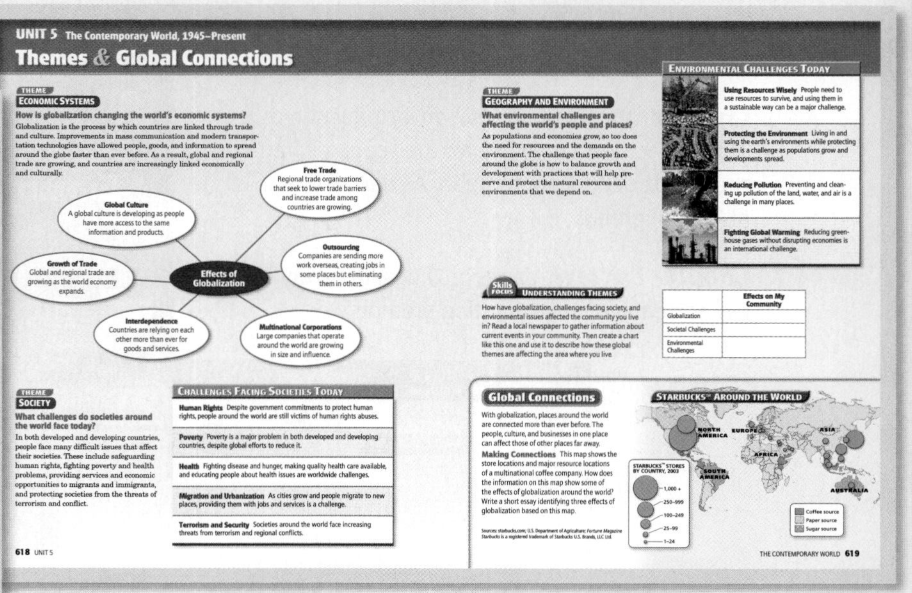

Human Legacy allows you to track important themes through history. Look for special themes of history features as you read.

How to Use Your Textbook

Holt World History: The Human Legacy, Modern Era was created to make your study of world history an enjoyable, meaningful experience. Take a few minutes to become familiar with the book's easy-to-use organization and special features.

Unit

Unit Openers list the chapter titles and the years the chapters cover. Each unit opener identifies the main themes covered in the unit. A historic photograph or painting illustrates the time period you are about to explore.

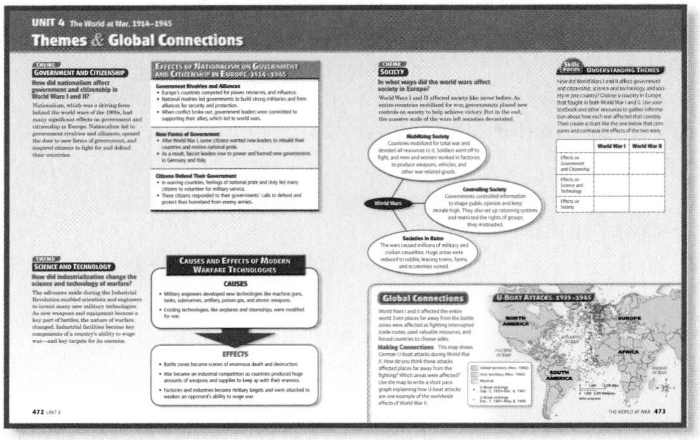

Themes and Global Connections features end each unit. Graphic organizers and tables show how each unit theme relates to the period of history covered in the unit. Global Connections helps you examine the global impact of key developments in history.

Chapter

Chapter Openers include an introduction called The Big Picture, a time line for the years covered in the chapter, and a photograph. A chapter theme is also highlighted.

Chapter Review pages provide a full array of assessments, including writing prompts.

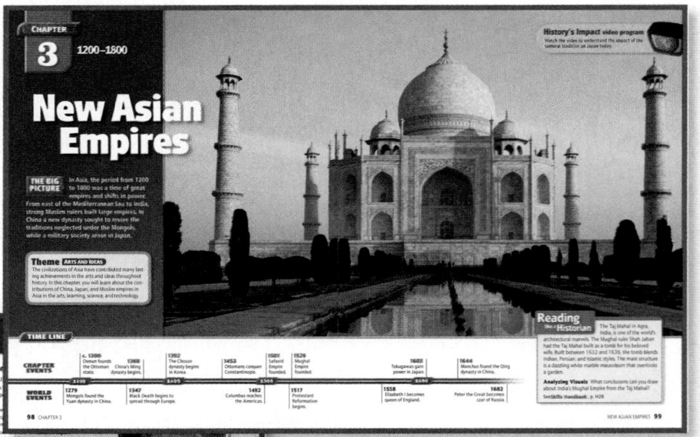

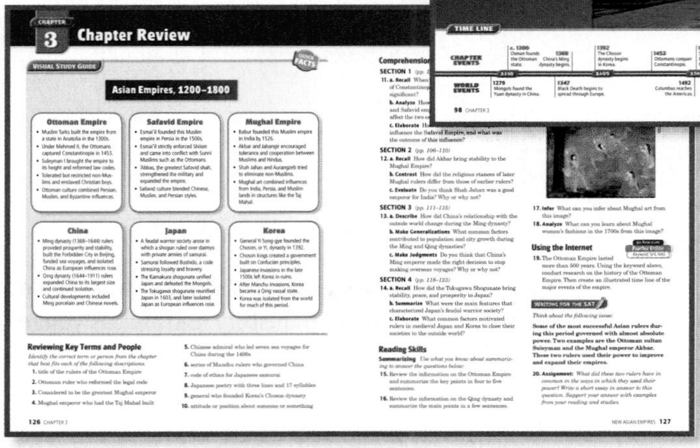

Section

Each section begins with a Main Idea statement, Focus Questions, and Key Terms and People. In addition, each section includes the following special features:

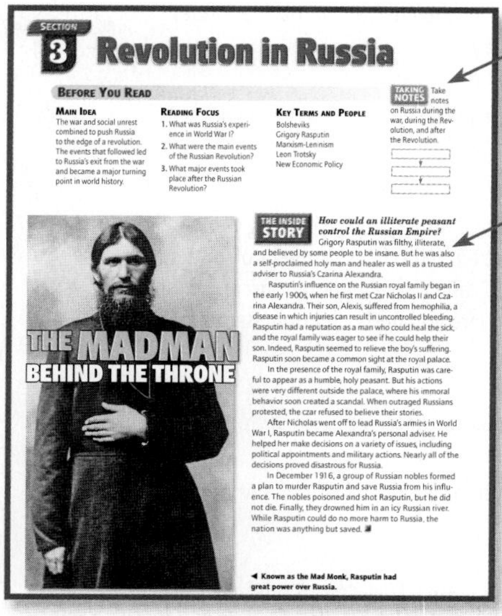
Section 3 Revolution in Russia

Before You Read

The Inside Story: How could an illiterate peasant control the Russian Empire?

THE MADMAN BEHIND THE THRONE

Taking Notes graphic organizers help you record key ideas as you read.

The Inside Story begins the section with an on-the-scene story from history.

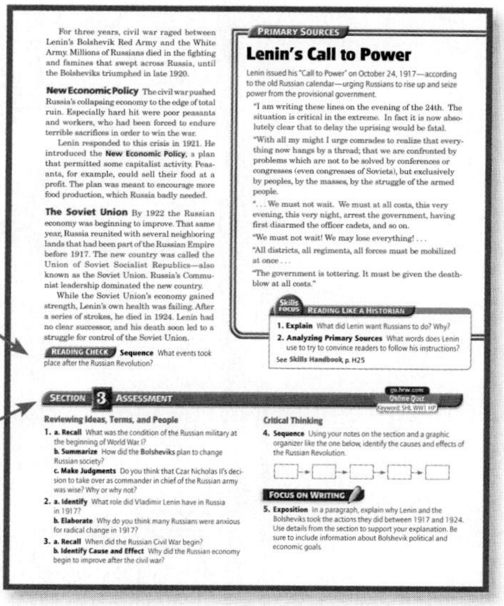
Primary Sources: Lenin's Call to Power

Section 3 Assessment

Reading Check questions provide frequent opportunities to review and assess your understanding.

Section Assessment questions help you check your understanding of a section's main ideas. There is also assessment practice online.

Test Prep and Practice

Holt World History: Human Legacy, Modern Era provides many opportunities to help you prepare for standardized tests.

Document-Based Investigation features appear at the end of every chapter. They allow you to analyze and write about historical documents.

Standardized Test Practice tests appear at the end of every unit. They follow a format like the kind used on many standardized tests.

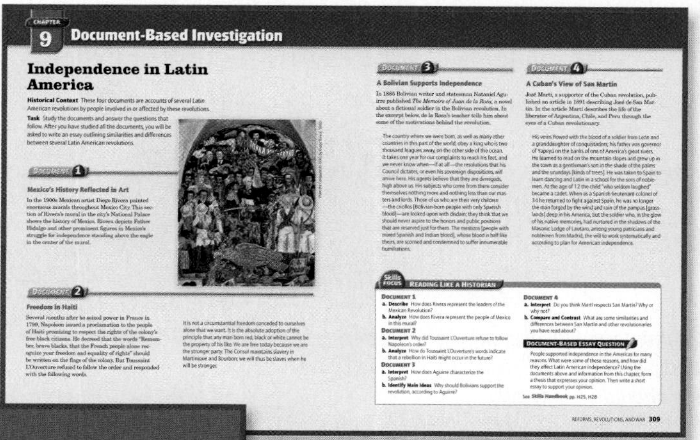
Chapter 9 Document-Based Investigation

Independence in Latin America

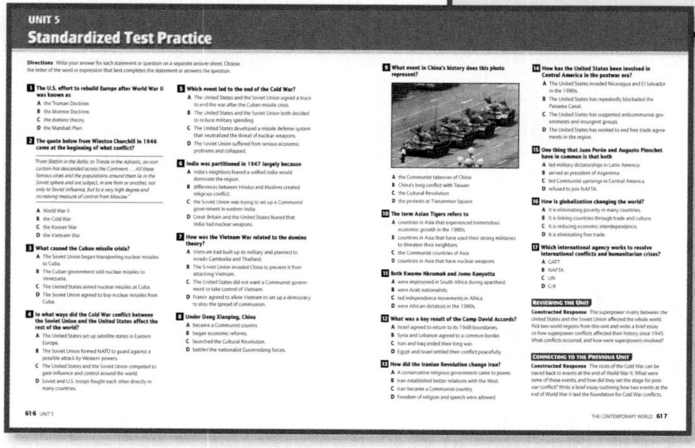
Unit 5 Standardized Test Practice

Scavenger Hunt

Holt World History: Human Legacy: The Modern Era opens a window on the past. Before you begin your journey into the past, take a minute to familiarize yourself with this book and its contents.

On a separate piece of paper, write the answers to the Scavenger Hunt questions below. Enjoy your journey.

1. How many units and chapters are in the book? How do you know?
2. Where in *Human Legacy* do you find the atlas?
3. The Reading Like a Historian section in the front of the book offers students instruction in various skills, such as analyzing primary sources. Name two other places in *Human Legacy* where you find additional Reading Like a Historian skills practice.
4. Where and how do you find key terms and people for Chapter 5, Section 2?
5. Where in *Human Legacy* do you find visuals to further your understanding of World War II?
6. Where do you find important academic vocabulary words defined?
7. Where do you find review questions to help you study?
8. If you want help with test-taking strategies, where do you look?
9. Where do you look to find a list of all of the primary sources used?
10. Where can you find a map that gives you an introduction to Chapter 12?

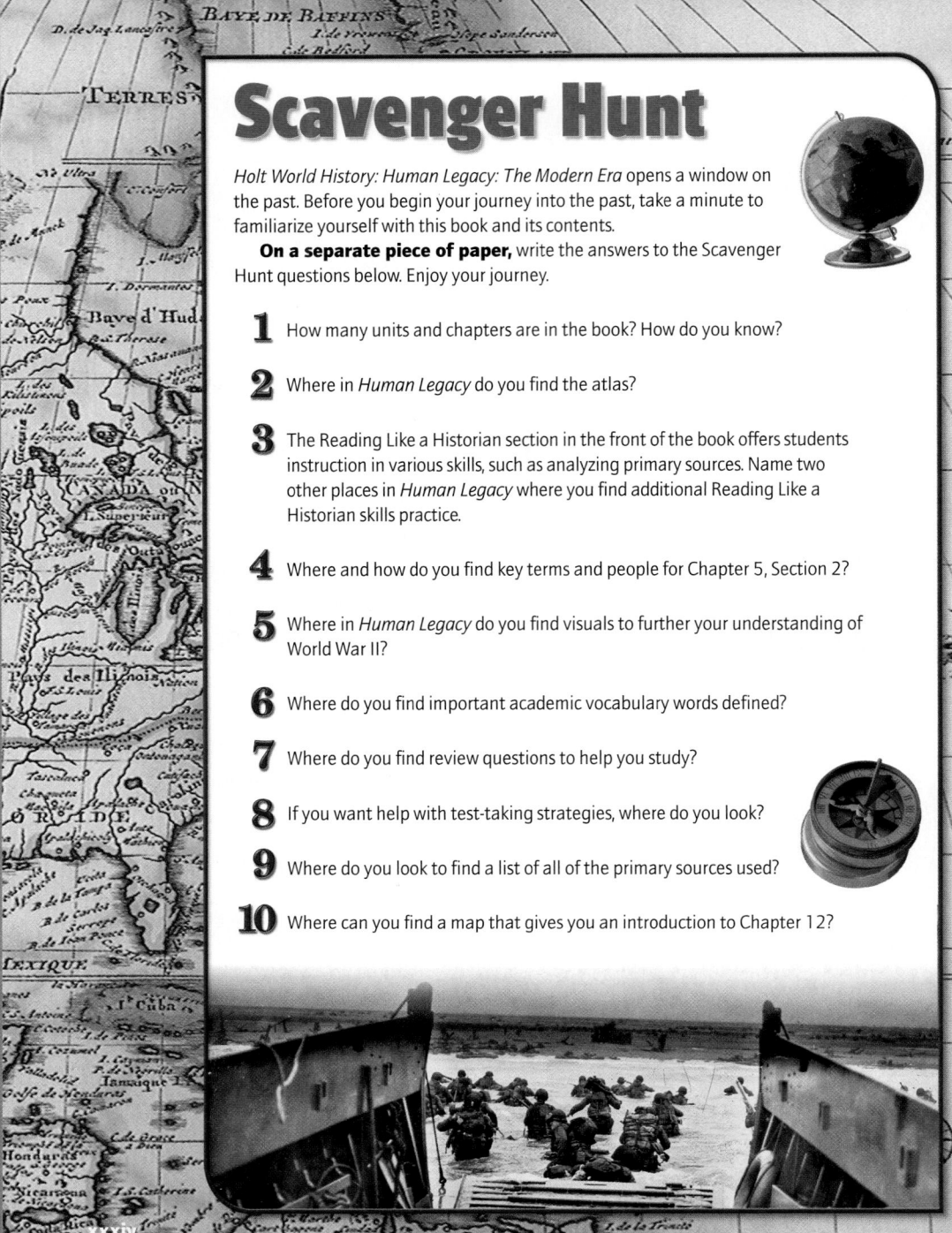

xxxiv

Answers

1. six units and 19 chapters; by checking the table of contents; 2. in the end matter; 3. Students should list any two of the following features: Reading Like a Historian, Primary Sources, World Literature, and Document-Based Investigation. 4. beneath the heading "Key Terms and People" at the top of page 176; 5. in Chapter 14; 6. in the side margins of each chapter; 7. the Reading Check questions throughout each section, the Section Assessment questions at the end of each section, and in the Chapter Reviews; 8. in the Test-Taking Strategies on page H40; 9. in the table of contents; 10. in the Geography Starting Points feature on page 380

Skills Handbook

with Test-Taking Strategies

Reading Skills

Social Studies Skills

Reading Like a Historian Skills

Writing and Speaking Skills

Test-Taking Strategies

Becoming an Active Reader

by Dr. Kylene Beers

Do you read a letter or email from a friend the same way you read a newspaper article? What about a poem and the instructions to an exam? Or a novel and a textbook? Chances are the answer is no: you read differently depending on your purpose for reading. When you are reading for information, such as when you are reading a textbook, you have a different purpose than when you are reading just for fun.

A different purpose calls for a different way of reading. In a textbook, especially a history book, there are a lot of facts, concepts, and unfamiliar words and names. You can't expect to absorb all that if you just let the words slide by. You have to be an active reader—questioning what you read, anticipating, making connections, stopping to review.

Human Legacy is structured to help you be an active reader. Sections, for example, are organized in outline format, with main heads and subheads to help you navigate the material. There are frequent review questions to help you assess whether or not you are absorbing the main points. Take a moment to familiarize yourself with some of the ways that this textbook facilitates reading comprehension.

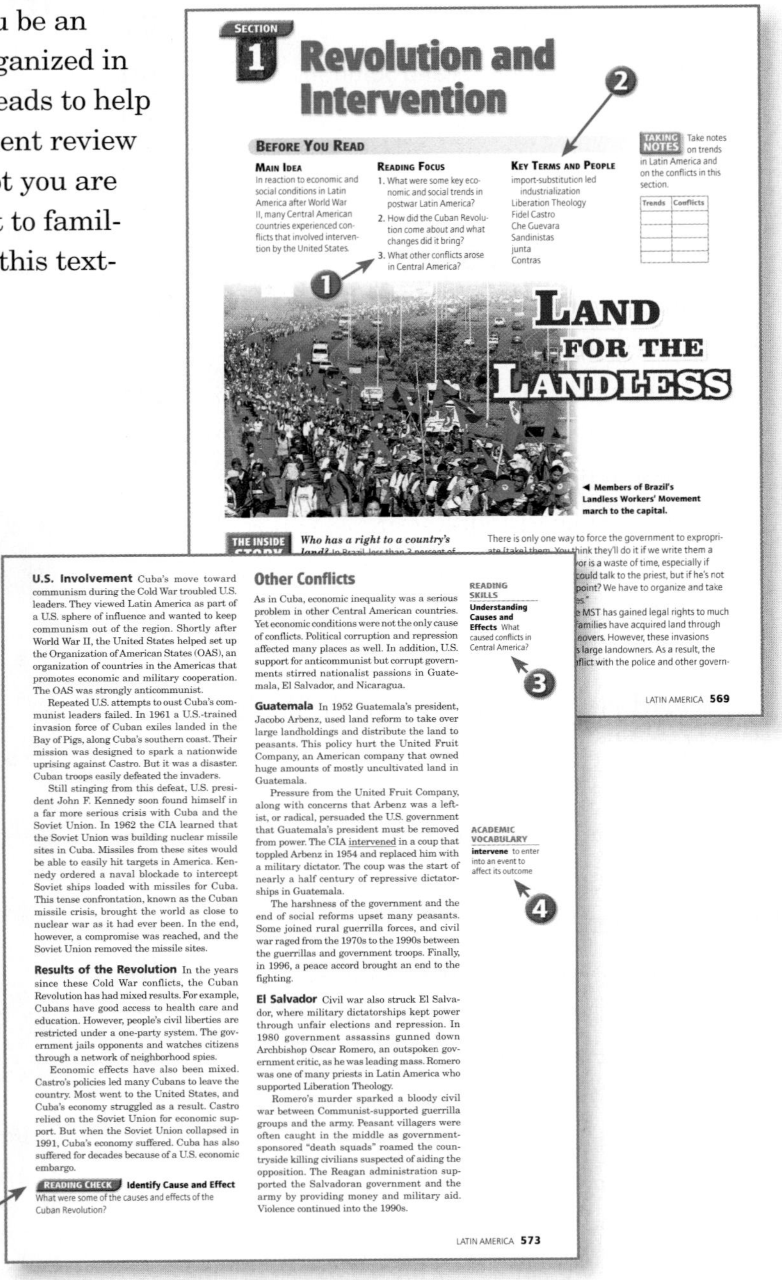

1. **Reading Focus and Reading Check** The Reading Focus questions act as a type of outline for each section. The Reading Check questions offer opportunities to assess what you have learned as you go.
2. **Key Terms and People** At the beginning of each section you will find a list of terms, people, places, and events that you will need to know. Watch for these words as you read.
3. **Reading Skills** Good readers use a number of reading skills and strategies to make sure they understand what they are reading. In the margins, look for questions that reinforce the reading skills you will be learning in this handbook.
4. **Academic Vocabulary** When we use a word that is important in all classes, not just in social studies, we define it in the margin under the heading Academic Vocabulary. You will see these words in other textbooks, so you should learn what they mean while reading this book.

Read Like a Skilled Reader

How can you become a more skilled reader? For starters, you first need to *think* about how to become a better reader. You also can use the following ideas and strategies.

Skilled readers . . .

- Preview what they are supposed to read before they begin reading. They look for titles of chapters and sections, listings of main ideas and focus questions, vocabulary words and key terms, information in the margin such as Academic Vocabulary, and visuals such as charts, graphs, maps, and photographs
- Construct tables or K-W-L charts into which they organize ideas from the reading. They write notes in the tables or charts as they read.
- Use clues from the text, such as the signal words shown below, to help determine or cement understanding.

  Sequencing words: *first, second, third, before, after, soon, later, next, then, following that, earlier, finally*

  Cause and effect words: *because, so, since, due to, as a result of, the reason for, therefore, brought about, led to, thus, consequently*

  Comparison and contrast words: *likewise, similarly, also, as well as, unlike, however, on the other hand*

Active Reading

Successful readers are ***active readers****. Active readers know that it is up to them to figure out what the text means. Here are some steps you can take to become an active and successful reader.*

Predict what will happen next on the basis of what already has happened in the text. When your predictions do not match what happens in the text, reread to clarify meaning.

Question what is happening as you read. Constantly ask yourself why events happen, what certain ideas mean, and what causes events to occur.

Summarize what you are reading frequently. Do not try to summarize an entire chapter! Instead, break a chapter into smaller parts. Read some of the text and summarize. Then move on.

Connect events in the text to what you already know or have read.

Clarify your understanding by pausing occasionally to ask questions and check for meaning. You may need to reread to clarify or read further to collect more information before you gain understanding.

Visualize people, places, and events in the text. Envision events or places by drawing maps, making charts, or taking notes about what you are reading.

Building Your Vocabulary

Holt Human Legacy helps you build your vocabulary by highlighting two types of vocabulary words. Key terms and people are listed at the beginning of every section. These are words you need to know to master the social studies content. You will encounter the definitions of the terms as you read the section. You can also turn to the Glossary for definitions. Academic vocabulary are words you need to know for other classes. They appear in the margins of sections. Below is a list of these academic vocabulary words, along with their definitions.

Academic Word/Definition	
amendment	a written change to a legal document
assessed	evaluated or determined
blockade	to isolate an enemy by using troops or warships
currency	money
deviate	to turn away from a course or topic
discrimination	the act of treating a person differently because of race, gender, or national origin
displace	to force to leave home or homeland
ethnic	common background or culture
export	item sent to other regions for trade
fundamental	basic
generation	group of people born and living about the same time
hypothesis	assumption or theory
ideology	a system of ideas, often political
immigrate	to move to another country to live
import	bring goods into a place or country
infrastructure	public works, such as buildings and roads, that are needed to support a population
initiate	to begin
institute	to originate and establish
integrate	to join together or blend
intervene	to enter into an event to affect its outcome
invest	to commit money in order to make a financial return
labor	work
legislation	laws or rules passed by a governing body
legitimacy	the right to rule

SKILLS HANDBOOK

Academic Word/Definition
liberal supporter of political and social reform
preclude to prevent something or someone from doing something
prejudiced biased against a racial, religious, or nation group
privileges special rights granted to certain people because of their position in society
proportion the size or amount of a thing in relation to another thing
prosperity wealth or success
rational having reason or understanding
regime a specific and often harsh government
region an area with one or more common features
regulation a law designed to control or govern conduct
sector a subdivision of society
security freedom from change or fear
stance an attitude, position, or view about someone or something
subsequent later; following in time
sufficient enough of what is needed
theories plausible general principles offered to explain what has been observed
utilize to make use of
valid correct or justified
violate break or ignore
welfare well-being

A Note about Chronological Terms

Historians like to fix exact dates on events, but that isn't as easy as it seems. Different cultures and different historical eras use different methods for dating events. Important political or religious events are often seen to mark the beginnings of new eras. The ancient Romans, for example, measured dates by the years in the reign of an emperor. Japan today officially does the same thing. From 1911 to 1949, China, by contrast, dated events from the overthrow of the last of its emperors, making 1929, for instance, "the 18th year of the Republic."

The system of dating used in the West began around AD 525, though it did not gain general acceptance in Europe until the 1200s. *Holt Human Legacy* follows this common usage. The table below shows some of the terms used in dating events and their meanings.

Chronological Terms	
BC short for "Before Christ", it refers to dates before the birth of Jesus	**BCE** short for "Before the Common Era," it refers to dates before the birth of Jesus
AD short for Anno Domini, Latin for "in the Year of the Lord," it refers to dates after the birth of Jesus	**CE** short for "Common Era," it refers to dates after the birth of Jesus

SKILLS HANDBOOK
READING SKILLS

Identifying Main Ideas and Details

Define the Skill

The **main idea** is the central thought in a passage. It is a general statement that conveys the key concept the author wants the reader to know. The main idea can come at the beginning, middle, or end of a passage, although it is most often found at the beginning. The main idea can be one or two sentences and can be implied or directly stated.

Details are statements that support or explain the main idea. Details are specific and provide additional information to the reader, such as the *who, what, when, where, why,* and *how* of the main idea. Details include statements, statistics, examples, explanations, and descriptions.

Learn the Skill

Read the passage below and note how the details support the main idea.

France continued to grow and change during the era of the Third Republic. Officials wrote a new constitution under which the government would have a two-house legislature and a president. Public education laws required free education for children between the ages of 6 and 13. Union membership became legal. All men now had the right to vote.

Main Idea
France continued to grow and change during the era of the Third Republic.

Details			
Detail 1	**Detail 2**	**Detail 3**	**Detail 4**
Officials wrote a new constitution that would have a two-house legislature and a president.	Public education laws required free education for children aged 6 to 13.	Union membership became legal.	All men had the right to vote.

Apply the Skill

Turn to Section 4 of the chapter titled Reforms, Revolutions, and War and locate the blue head titled "Effects on Native Americans." Use a graphic organizer like the one above to identify the main idea and details of the passage.

1. Identify the main idea in the passage. Restate it in your own words.
2. What details support the main idea?
3. Explain how the details add to the main idea.

1. By moving west, white settlers were often moving onto land that had been inhabited for thousands of years by Native Americans. Conflict between Native Americans and settlers was frequent.
2. Indian Removal Act, Trail of Tears
3. Answers will vary; possible answer: Supporting details give the results of the conflicts between settlers and Native Americans.

Sequencing

Define the Skill

Placing events in chronological order is called **sequencing**. By sequencing, you can gain a greater, more accurate understanding of the events that took place. Learning to sequence can also help you to understand relationships among events, including how a past event can influence present and future events.

Learn the Skill

Days, months, and years can help in determining sequence. Clue words, such as *before, after, then, by, first,* and *next,* can also help.

First Event World War I
Date 1914

By 1914 conditions in Russia were so bad that the arrival of World War I provided some relief for Nicholas and his top government officials. In late 1915 Czar Nicholas II decided to take personal command of the Russian forces. After the czar took command of the troops, things grew even worse for Russia. By the end of 1916, Russia was once again on the edge of a revolution. Change finally arrived in Russia on March 8, 1917 as unhappy citizens took to the streets of Petrograd, the Russian capital, to protest the lack of food.

Second Event Czar Nicholas II takes command of Russian forces.
Date 1915

Third Event Things grew worse for Russia.
Clue Word *after*

Last Event Citizens take to the streets.
Date March 8, 1917

Apply the Skill

Identify the three main events in the passage below and place them in correct chronological order. List the clue words or dates that signal the order of the events.

The year 1917 went badly for the Allies. A failed French offensive in the spring caused rebellion among some French troops. In July, the British launched an offensive near Ypres, in Belgium. Known as the Third Battle of Ypres, it was a disaster for the British. The Germans held the only bit of high ground in the very flat area, and they used it effectively to defend the region. In November, the British assault was finally called off.

1. In what year did the British launch the offensive near Ypres?
2. What happened in November 1917?
3. How long did the Battle of Ypres last?

1. 1917
2. the British assault was called off
3. 5 months

Identifying Causes and Effects

Define the Skill

By understanding **causes and effects** and seeing connections between them, you can determine why certain events occurred and whether events are related. A *cause* is something that makes something else happen. Often times a cause will be directly stated in the text. Occasionally, a cause will be implied—or stated indirectly. An *effect* is something that happens as the result of a cause. One cause may have more than one effect and, similarly, an effect may have several causes. Identifying causes and effects can help you better understand what you have read.

Learn the Skill

Identify the causes and effects in the passage. Start by identifying a cause and then look for one or more of the effects. Look for clue words such as *since, because, therefore,* and *however.*

First cause

The Treaty of Versailles, which ended World War I, had seriously damaged the German economy. The terms of the treaty left the Germans feeling humiliated. Adolf Hitler wanted the nation to have more "living room" in which the German people could grow and prosper. In other words, Hitler wanted more territory for Germany.

Last effect

Cause
The Treaty of Versailles

Effect
The German economy was damaged.

Effect
Germans felt humiliated.

Effect
Hitler wanted more territory for Germany.

Apply the Skill

Read the following sentences and answer the questions using what you have learned about identifying causes and effects.

At the end of the war, much of Europe and Asia lay in ruins. Tens of millions of people had died in the war, many of them civilians. In many areas the physical devastation was nearly complete. Entire cities, villages, and farms had been destroyed or damaged heavily, and national economies were near collapse.

1. What were the effects of the war on civilians?
2. What caused the collapse of national economies?
3. Identify one effect of the war on cities and villages.

1. millions of civilians died
2. the devastation of farms from the war
3. entire villages and cities were destroyed

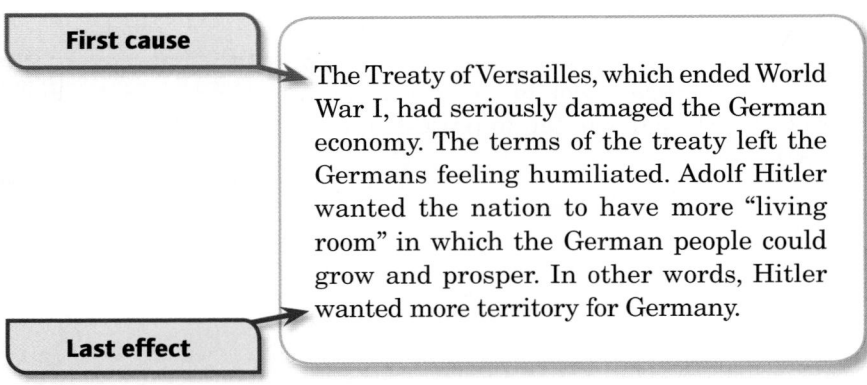

Understanding Comparison and Contrast

Define the Skill

Comparing involves looking at both the similarities and differences between two or more people, places, or events. **Contrasting** means examining *only* the differences between things. Being able to identify comparisons and contrasts is an important tool for comprehension.

Learn the Skill

Clue words can help you identify when a comparison or contrast is being made. Look at the chart below for some clue words.

Many Enlightenment philosophers shared the belief that governmental organization was something that should be analyzed closely. But, they did not all agree on what type of government was the best. Thomas Hobbes believed that society needed a strong central authority to control and contain the natural barbarism of humans. John Locke, however, held the belief that people were naturally reasonable and that the purpose of government was to protect people's natural rights. The ideas of both philosophers were used in creating new governments.

Highlighted words are points of comparison.

Underlined words are clue words.

Clue Words	
Comparison	**Contrast**
share, similar, like, also, both, in addition, besides	however, while, unlike, different, but, although

Apply the Skill

Read the following passage and answer the questions using what you have learned about comparison and contrast.

Two of the most important scholars who helped develop the scientific method were Francis Bacon and René Descartes. In England, Francis Bacon wrote in 1620 that the only true way to gain scientific knowledge was through experimentation—observing, measuring, and verifying. In France, meanwhile, René Descartes placed more emphasis on reason. He believed that everything should be doubted until it could be proven by reason. Descartes relied on mathematics and logic to prove basic truths.

1. How did the philosophy of Bacon compare with that of Descartes?
2. What did Bacon and Descartes help to develop?

1. Bacon believed in gaining knowledge through experimentation; Descartes place an emphasis on reason to gain knowledge.
2. the scientific method

Making Inferences

Define the Skill

Sometimes reading effectively means understanding both what the writer tells you directly and what the writer implies. By filling in the gaps, you are **making inferences**, or educated guesses. Making inferences involves using clues in the text to connect implied ideas with ideas that are stated. You also draw on your own prior knowledge and use common sense to make inferences.

Learn the Skill

To make an inference, study what the passage says. Think about what else you know about the subject, and then make an educated guess about the implied meaning.

> Though he became prime minister through democratic means, Mussolini quickly became a dictator. Not satisfied with simply having political control, he sought to influence the thoughts, feelings and behaviors of the Italian people. This attempt to control all aspects of life is called totalitarianism.

1. What the passage says Mussolini favored a totalitarian form of government.

2. What you know about the topic or can connect to your experience. In their drive for control, dictators violate the democratic rights of their citizens.

3. Make an inference. Totalitarianism threatened democracy in Italy.

Apply the Skill

Read the following passage and then use the three steps described above to make an inference about it.

> The worst day was October 29, known as Black Tuesday. On that single day, investors sold off 16 million shares. With few people wanting to buy the stocks that flooded the Market, stock prices collapsed completely. Many investors who had borrowed money to buy stocks were forced to sell at a loss to repay their loans.

1. On Black Tuesday, what economic crisis did the United States face?
2. Using the reading and your prior knowledge, explain the effects that a major economic crisis can have on a country's people.
3. What can you infer about the effects of the stock market crash?

1. the stock market collapse
2. possible answers: unemployment, loss of savings, homelessness
3. Answers will vary; possible answer: The collapse of the stock market led to such economic crises as unemployment and loss of life savings on a large scale.

Identifying Problems and Solutions

Define the Skill

Throughout history, people have faced problems and sought solutions to those problems. As a result, historians describing historical events often structure their writing by identifying a problem and then describing its actual or possible solutions. By **identifying problems and solutions**, you can better understand the challenges that people have faced over time and the means by which they have resolved such difficulties.

Learn the Skill

Look for problems that are identified in the reading and then determine what solutions were or are being pursued. Most problems have more than one solution.

In spite of international agreements, people around the world continue to suffer human rights abuses. Arbitrary arrest, torture, slavery, and even killing are daily occurrences in some countries. The United Nations works to protect human rights by monitoring areas of concern, investigating abuses, and working with national governments to improve conditions. Moreover, as globalization advances, stronger economic conditions can help foster adherence to human rights standards. Not only do opportunities increase, helping children to get an education and more women to find jobs, but businesses gain an incentive to follow practices that will help them avoid potentially ruinous publicity.

Problem
Human rights are being violated in the world.

Solution 1
The UN works to protect human rights.

Solution 2
Globalization improves economic situations in many countries.

Apply the Skill

Use a graphic organizer like the one above to identify the problems and solutions in the following passage.

During recent years, the number of worldwide terrorist attacks has increased, as has the violence of these attacks. After September 11, 2001, the United States government took many actions to prevent future terrorist attacks. It sought to strengthen its international and domestic intelligence services. It increased its focus on the security of the nation's borders and transportation networks. It sought to find and cut off the funding sources for terrorist networks.

1. What problem does the U.S. face from terrorism in recent years?
2. Identify two solutions that the U.S. used to address these problems after September 11.

1. the number of worldwide terrorist attacks have increased as well as the violence level of such attacks
2. strengthened its international and domestic intelligence service; increased its focus on the security of the nation's borders; found and cut off the funding sources for terrorist networks

Drawing Conclusions

Define the Skill

Historical writing provides you with facts and information. But often you have to determine the meaning of events on your own. You need to combine the facts and information, along with your prior knowledge, to draw conclusions about the reading. In **drawing conclusions**, you analyze the reading and form opinions about its meaning.

Learn the Skill

To draw conclusions, combine the information you find in the reading with what you already know. Look for a common link or theme. Then put it all together.

Drawing on the work of Faraday and Swan, Thomas Edison developed the first usable and practical lightbulb in 1879. The new invention caused a sensation. Having created a demand for lightbulbs, Edison then needed to supply the electricity that powered them. So he built the world's first central electric power plant in New York City. The plant illuminated several city blocks. As a result of Edison's work, life during the Industrial Age became easier and more convenient.

Information gathered from the passage you are reading		What you already know about the topic		What all the information adds up to—your conclusion
Thomas Edison invented the lightbulb in 1879 and built the world's first central electric plant.	+	Electricity is a huge part of people's lives today and is used in many capacities in everyday life.	=	The invention of the lightbulb was one of the first steps towards the modernized world we know today.

Apply the Skill

Read the following sentences. Think about what you know about telephone usage today. Use the process above to draw conclusions about the passage.

One day, Bell and his assistant Thomas Watson were working on a new device. Bell suddenly yelled, "Mr. Watson, come here, I need you!" Watson was pleased to hear Bell's voice not just from across the room, but through the device's receiver as well. The telephone was born.

During the 1880s, demand for telephones increased, and telephone companies quickly laid thousands of miles of phone lines in every region of the United States. By 1900 almost 1.5 million telephones were in American homes and offices. The telephone was on its way to becoming the ubiquitous instrument it is today.

1. When did telephone usage become commonplace in the United States?
2. What information can you conclude about the importance of the telephone in creating modern communications?

1. 1900
2. Answers will vary; possible answer: Modern communications rely heavily on the use of the telephone and related products that have been made after its advent, like the cell phone.

Making Generalizations

Define the Skill

A generalization is a statement that applies to different examples or situations not just to one. When **making generalizations**, you collect different examples, identify what they have in common, and then make a statement that applies equally to all examples.

Learn the Skill

In the passage, identify examples that have something in common. Then try to make a generalization that applies to all the examples.

For many years, right-wing military dictatorships ruled Argentina. They struggled with declining industry as well as rising unemployment, inflation, and foreign debt. Meanwhile, they cracked down on dissent by severely limiting personal freedoms.

In Brazil, as opposition to their military dictatorship grew, the economy crashed. Oil prices rose in the 1970s and the economy fell into debt and hyperinflation, a very high level of inflation that grows rapidly in a short period of time. The inflation rate exceeded 2,500 percent by 1993.

Example 1:		Example 2:		Generalization:
Argentina's military dictatorships struggled with declining industry, inflation, and foreign debt.	+	In Brazil, the military dictatorships led the economy into debt and hyperinflation.	=	Many Latin American countries under military dictatorships had struggling economies.

Apply the Skill

Using the process described above, make a generalization about the struggles in Latin America.

In El Salvador, a civil war broke out in which Communist-supported groups battled the army. Villagers were often caught in the middle as the government's army roamed the countryside killing civilians suspected of aiding the opposition.

In Nicaragua, control was in the hands of the Somoza family who had ruled for four decades. The Somozas' anticommunist views kept them in favor with the United States, but their corruption and violent repressive tactics alarmed many Nicaraguans. An anti-Somoza movement gained strength.

1. What conflict took place in El Salvador?
2. What was a problem of the Somoza family in Nicaragua?
3. Make a generalization about Latin American political struggles.

1. a civil war
2. They were corrupt and violent.
3. Answers will vary; possible answer: Many Latin American countries are plagued with violence and war as a result of their governments.

Interpreting Time Lines

Define the Skill

A **time line** organizes events that occurred during a specific period of time into chronological order. It has a beginning date and an ending date. The *time span* is the years between the beginning date and the ending date. *Time intervals* mark shorter increments of time within the time span. They appear at regular intervals, for example, every 5 or 10 years. Two time lines can be used to list events that happened within a certain time span but at different places. These are called *parallel time lines*. There are parallel time lines at the beginning of each chapter in this book.

By organizing events chronologically, time lines can help you see how events are related. Seeing how events are related can help you find cause-and-effect relationships between the events. Time lines also allow you to compare, contrast, and draw conclusions about historical events.

Learn the Skill

Use the following strategies to read the time line.

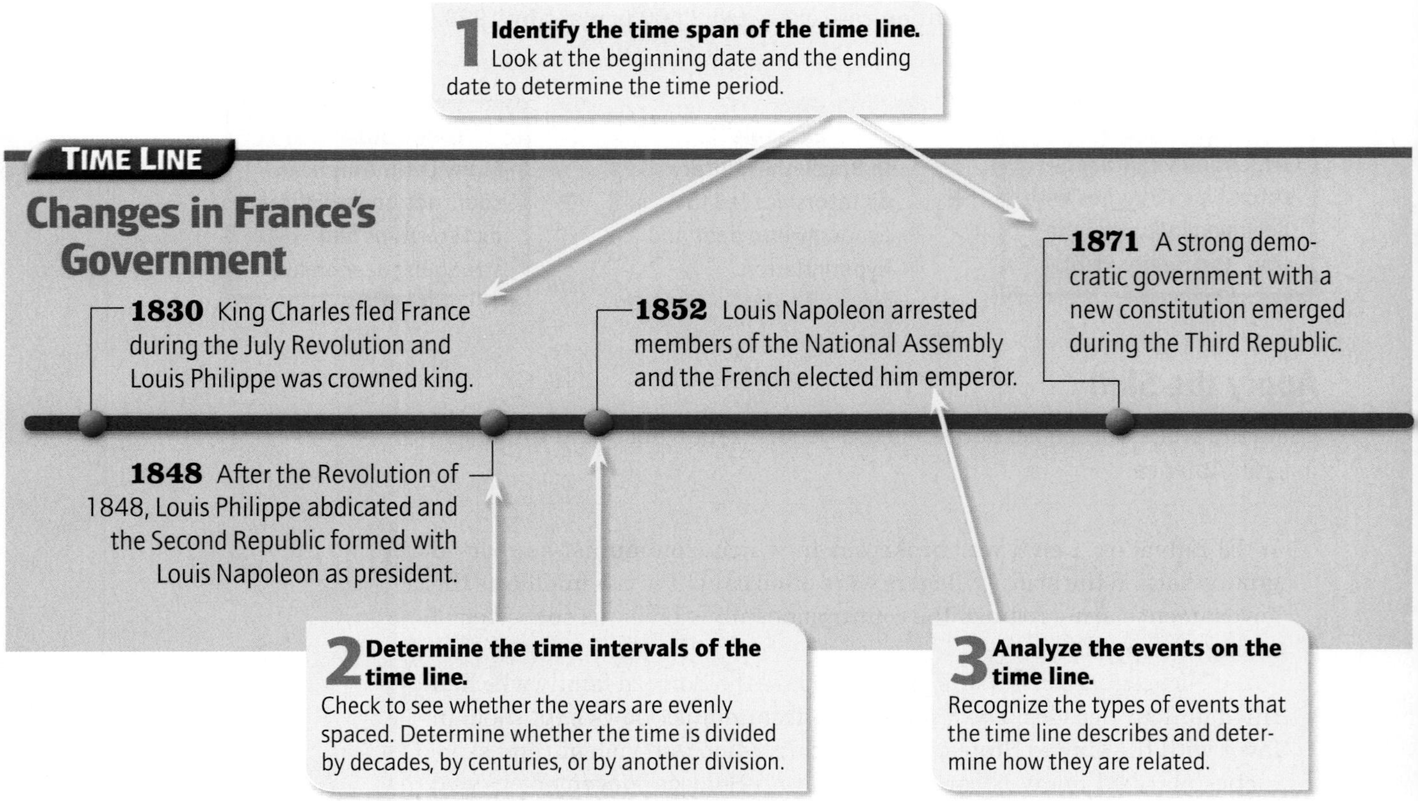

1 Identify the time span of the time line. Look at the beginning date and the ending date to determine the time period.
TIME LINE
Changes in France's Government
1830 King Charles fled France during the July Revolution and Louis Philippe was crowned king.
1848 After the Revolution of 1848, Louis Philippe abdicated and the Second Republic formed with Louis Napoleon as president.
1852 Louis Napoleon arrested members of the National Assembly and the French elected him emperor.
1871 A strong democratic government with a new constitution emerged during the Third Republic.
2 Determine the time intervals of the time line. Check to see whether the years are evenly spaced. Determine whether the time is divided by decades, by centuries, or by another division.
3 Analyze the events on the time line. Recognize the types of events that the time line describes and determine how they are related.

Apply the Skill

1. What is the time span of the time line?
2. What are the time intervals of the time line?
3. How are the events on the time line related?

1. 1830–1871
2. They vary: 18 years, 4 years, 19 years.
3. They all deal with changes in the French government in the mid-1800s.

Interpreting Line and Bar Graphs

Define the Skill

Graphs are diagrams that present statistical or numeric data. They can display amounts, trends, ratios, or changes over time. A **line graph** is a visual representation of data organized so that you can see a pattern of change over time. In most cases, the *vertical axis* of a line graph shows quantities while the *horizontal axis* shows time. A **bar graph** compares quantities. A single bar graph compares one set of data, while a double bar graph compares two sets of data. Knowing how to interpret line graphs and bar graphs can help you recognize historical trends.

Learn the Skill

Use the following strategies to interpret the line graph.

Use the following strategies to interpret the bar graph.

1 **Read the title of the graph.** The title tells you the subject or purpose of the graph.

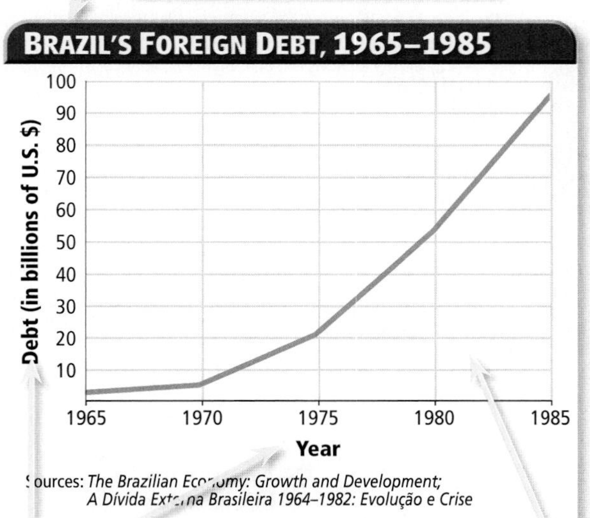

1 **Read the title of the graph.** Read the title and the legend to determine the subject of the graph.

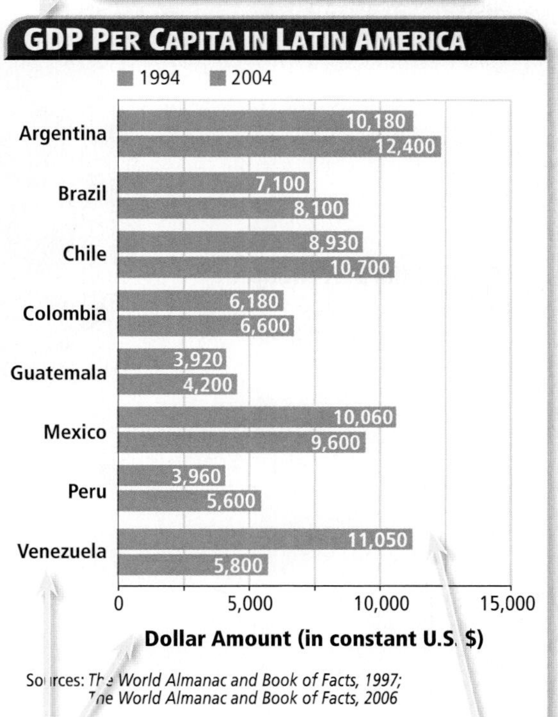

BRAZIL'S FOREIGN DEBT, 1965–1985

Debt (in billions of U.S. $) vs. Year

Sources: *The Brazilian Economy: Growth and Development;
A Dívida Externa Brasileira 1964–1982: Evolução e Crise*

GDP PER CAPITA IN LATIN AMERICA

■ 1994 ■ 2004

Country	1994	2004
Argentina	10,180	12,400
Brazil	7,100	8,100
Chile	8,930	10,700
Colombia	6,180	6,600
Guatemala	3,920	4,200
Mexico	10,060	9,600
Peru	3,960	5,600
Venezuela	11,050	5,800

Dollar Amount (in constant U.S. $)

Sources: *The World Almanac and Book of Facts, 1997;
The World Almanac and Book of Facts, 2006*

2 **Read the horizontal and vertical axis labels.** The labels explain what the graph measures and gives the units of measurement.

3 **Analyze the information on the graph.** Look at the slant of the line. The closer the line is to being parallel to the horizontal axis, the slower the change. The closer the line is to being perpendicular to the horizontal axis, the quicker the change.

2 **Read the horizontal and vertical axis labels.** The labels tell what the bar graph measures and gives the units of measurement.

3 **Analyze the information on the graph.** Compare the amounts shown on the bar graph.

Apply the Skill

1. What information does the line graph compare?
2. What information does the bar graph compare?
3. What conclusion can you draw from the data in the bar graph?

1. Brazil's foreign debt from the years 1965 to 1985
2. the GDP per capita for selected countries in Latin America in 1994 and 2004

3. possible answers: Venezuela had a greater GDP per capita in 1994 than in 2004; Argentina had a greater GDP per capita in 2004 than in 1994; Guatemala had the lowest GDP per capita in both years.

Interpreting Pie Graphs

Define the Skill

A **pie graph** is a circular chart that shows how individual parts relate to the whole. The circle of the pie symbolizes the whole amount. The slices of the pie represent the individual parts of the whole. Knowing how to interpret pie graphs will allow you to better understand and evaluate historical data as well as to recognize historical trends.

Learn the Skill

Use the following strategies to interpret the pie graph.

1 Read the title of the graph. The title tells you the subject or purpose of the graph.

2 Read the percentages. Compare the sizes of each piece within the graph.

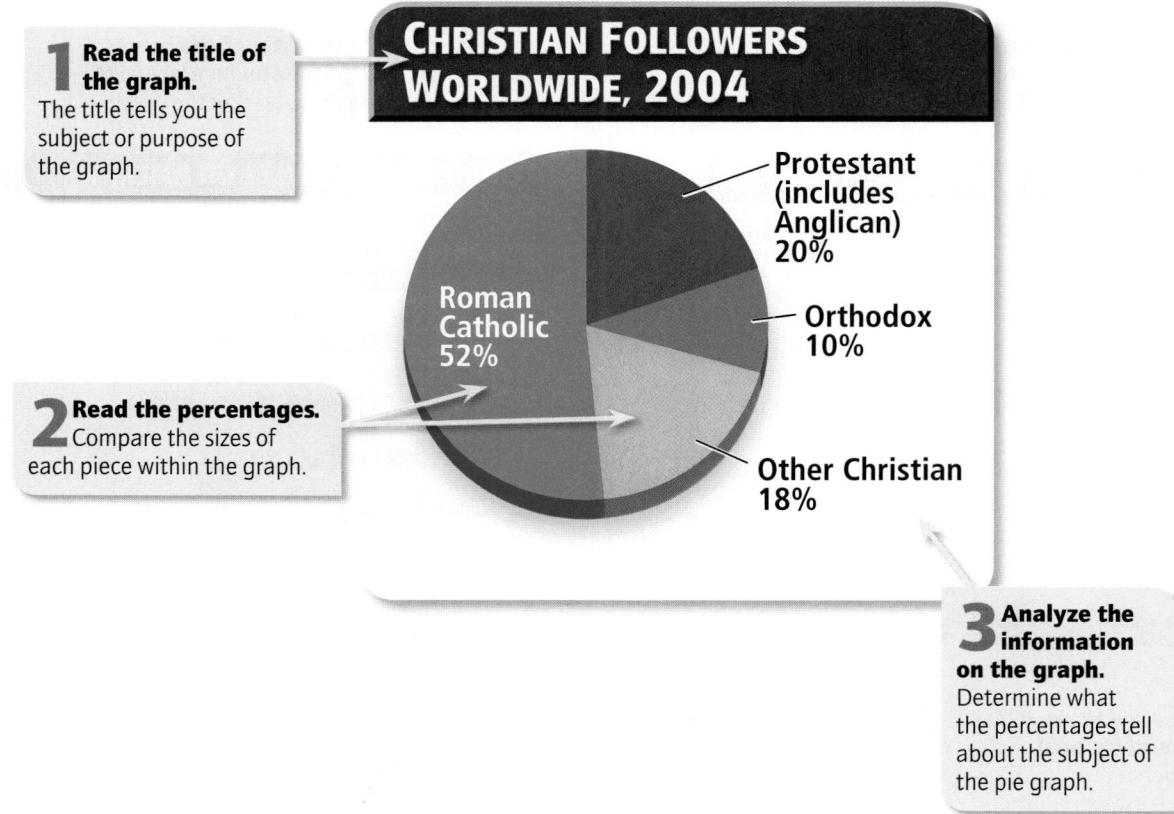

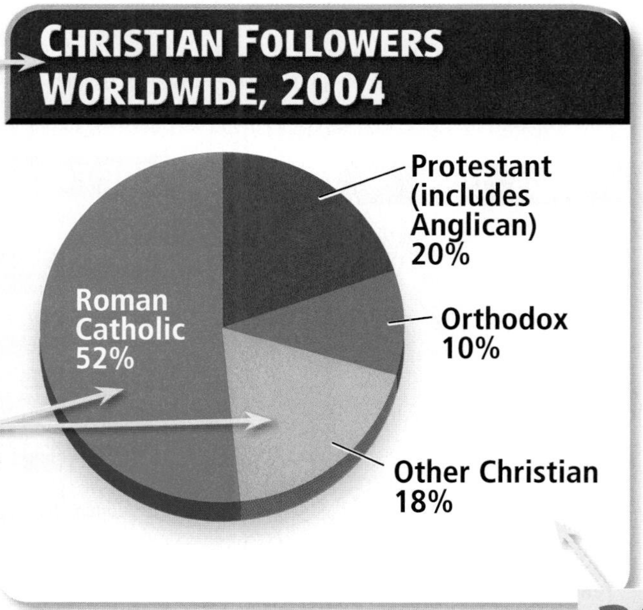

3 Analyze the information on the graph. Determine what the percentages tell about the subject of the pie graph.

Apply the Skill

1. What information does the pie graph compare?
2. Which religion has the fewest number of followers?
3. What percentage of the world follows other religions not listed in the graph?

1. the percentage of people who practice each religion
2. Orthodox
3. 55%

Interpreting Charts

Define the Skill

Charts are visual representations of information. Historians use charts to organize, condense, simplify, and summarize information in a convenient, easy-to-read format.

Simple charts combine or compare information. *Tables* classify information by groups. Numbers, percentages, dates, and other data can be classified in the columns and rows of a table for reference and comparison. *Diagrams* illustrate the steps involved in a process so that the information is easier to understand. Knowing how to read and use charts allows you to interpret, compare, analyze, and evaluate historical information.

Learn the Skill

Use the following strategies to interpret the chart.

1 Read the title of the chart. The title tells you the subject of the chart.

2 Look at the way the information is organized. Charts can be organized alphabetically, chronologically, or by topic.

3 Analyze the information found in the chart. Interpret, compare, and contrast the information in the chart to draw conclusions and make inferences or predictions.

QUICK FACTS

MAJOR JAPANESE EVENTS 1929 TO 1940

1929	The Great Depression hits Japan.
1931	Japan takes control of Manchuria, China.
1933	Japan withdraws from the League of Nations.
1934	Japan announces it will no longer submit to limits on its navy.
1936	Japan signs agreement with Germany.
1937	Japanese troops kill hundreds of thousands of civilians in Nanjing, China.
1940	Japan attempts to expand its power in Asia by proposing an economic alliance of Asian nations.

▼ Japanese troops in Shanghai, China

Apply the Skill

1. How is the information in the chart organized?
2. How many events are listed on the chart?
3. According to the chart, what major event occurred in Japan in 1931?

1. by date
2. 7
3. Japan took control of Manchuria, China.

Interpreting Movement Maps

Define the Skill

Different types of maps are used for different purposes. **Movement maps** show travel from one point to another. They can track sea voyages, explorations, or migrations. They can span a week, a few months, or thousands of years. Understanding how to read and interpret a movement map can help you learn more about historical events, their chronology, and the geographical locations they have affected.

Learn the Skill

Use the following strategies to interpret movement maps.

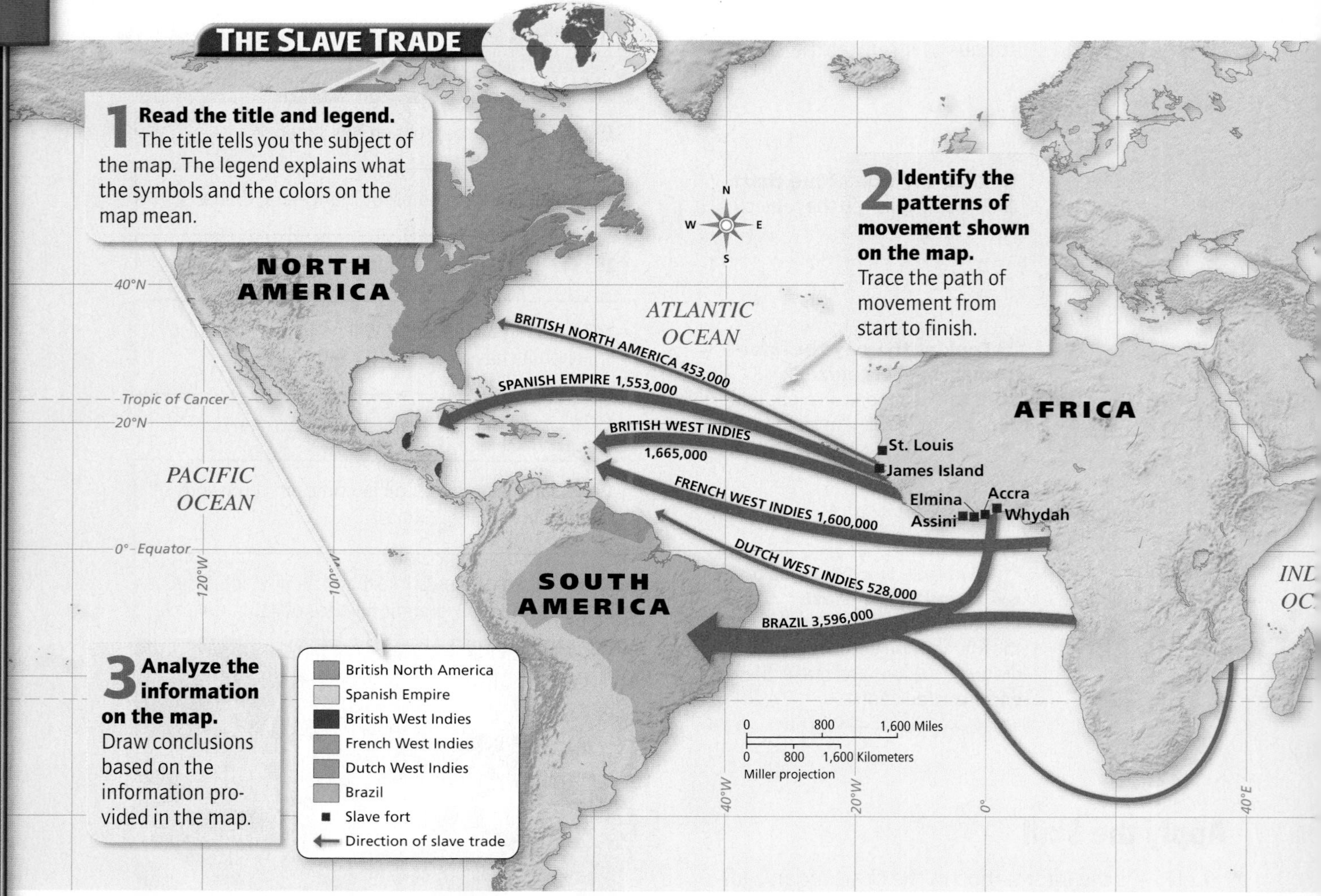

1 Read the title and legend. The title tells you the subject of the map. The legend explains what the symbols and the colors on the map mean.

2 Identify the patterns of movement shown on the map. Trace the path of movement from start to finish.

3 Analyze the information on the map. Draw conclusions based on the information provided in the map.

Apply the Skill

1. What was the path of the slave trade?
2. Which continents were directly involved in the slave trade?
3. To which continent were most enslaved people sent?

1. from Africa to South and North America
2. Africa, South America, and North America
3. North America

Interpreting Historical Maps

Define the Skill

Historical maps provide information about a place at a certain time in history. You can use historical maps to locate historical events, to learn how geography influences history, or to trace human interaction with the environment. Historical maps can show information such as population density, economic activity, political alliances, battles, and movement of people and goods. Historical maps can help you learn how places have changed over time.

Learn the Skill

Use the following strategies to interpret historical maps.

1 Read the title and legend. The title will help you identify the subject and the purpose of the map. The legend explains the meaning of the symbols and the colors on the map.

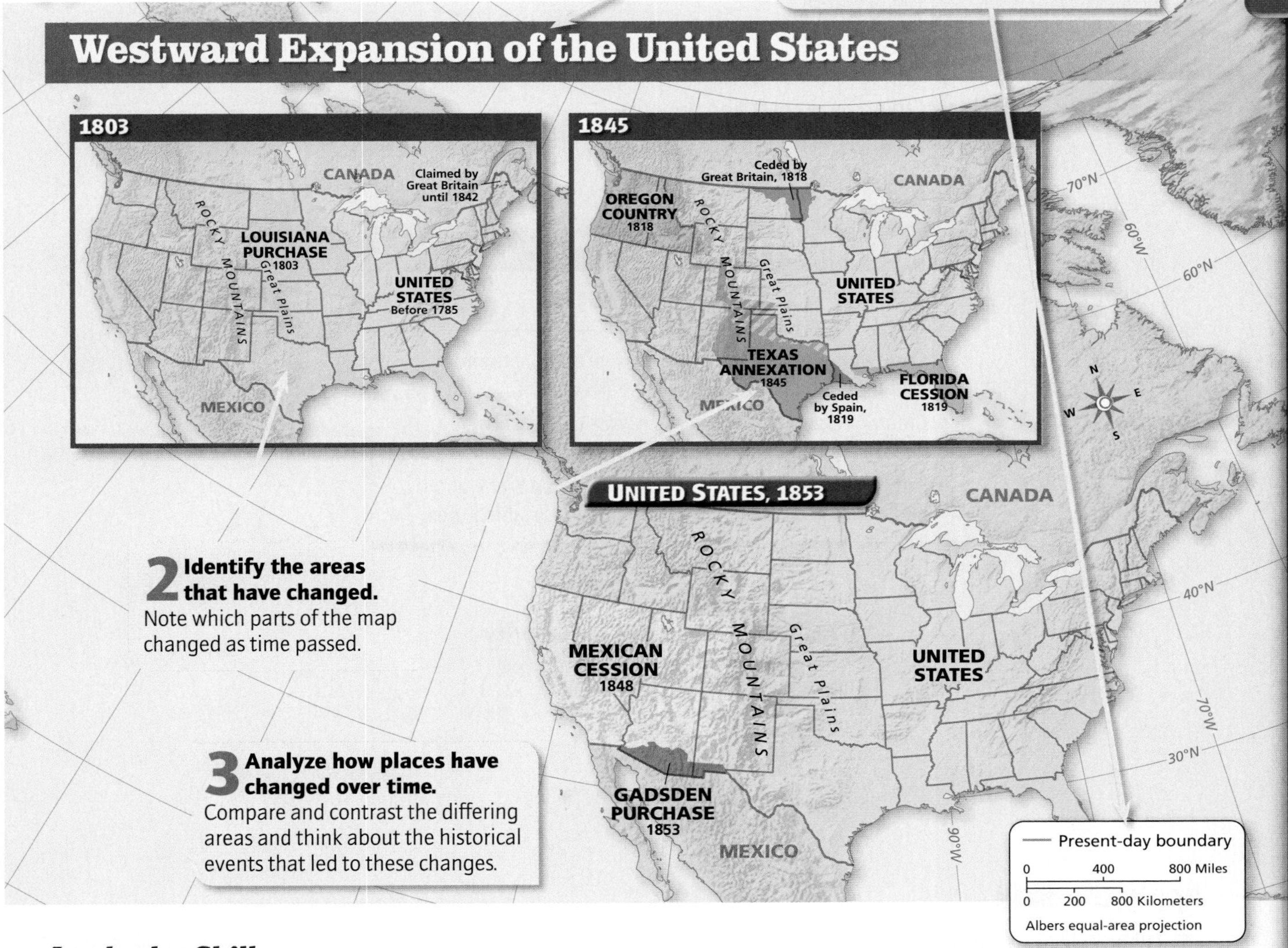

2 Identify the areas that have changed. Note which parts of the map changed as time passed.

3 Analyze how places have changed over time. Compare and contrast the differing areas and think about the historical events that led to these changes.

Apply the Skill

1. What is the purpose of these historical maps?
2. How did the United States change from 1803 to 1853?

1. to show how the United States gained more territory in the mid-1800s
2. The United States gained a third of the land that it already owned and stretched from the Atlantic Ocean to the Pacific.

Analyzing Costs and Benefits

Define the Skill

A **cost-benefit analysis** is a process that measures whether a project or a policy is worthwhile by calculating its benefits and comparing those benefits to its costs. Businesses large and small as well as government agencies all conduct cost-benefit analyses before deciding on a course of action.

Historians have the benefit of hindsight. They can look at events that have already happened and make cost-benefit analyses to determine whether a decision was the right one. The process is relatively straightforward when costs and benefits can be expressed in terms of money or basic economic indicators such as employment figures, gross domestic product, and inflation. Some costs and benefits, however, such as time or safety, are not easily measured by how much money is earned or lost. Also, people may disagree about the value of the costs and benefits.

Learn the Skill

Use the following strategies to analyze costs and benefits.

1 Identify the costs. Determine the costs of this project.

BUILDING VERSAILLES

COSTS	BENEFITS
• Cost five percent of the country's annual revenue • Created resentment among the people • Palace uncomfortable and crowded	• Kept court safer from Paris crowds • Was clear symbol of king's power • Palace had many grand and beautiful features.

2 Identify the benefits. Determine the benefits of the proposed project.

3 Analyze the costs and the benefits and draw conclusions. Compare the costs with the benefits.

Apply the Skill

1. What was one cost of building Versailles?
2. What was one benefit of this project?
3. Based on the cost-benefit chart, do you think it was a good investment to build the palace? Explain.

1. five percent of country's annual revenue, resentment among the people, crowded and uncomfortable
2. court safe from Paris crowds, symbol of king's power, grand and beautiful features
3. Answers will vary.

Evaluating Information on the Internet

Define the Skill

The **Internet** is an international computer network that connects schools, businesses, government agencies, and individuals. Every Web site on the Internet has its own address called an *URL*. Each URL has a domain. The *domain* tells you the type of Web site you are visiting. Common domains in the United States are .com, .net, .org, .edu, and .gov. A Web site with the domain .edu means that it is sponsored by an educational institution. A Web site with the domain .gov means that it is sponsored by a government institution. The collection of Web sites throughout the world is called the *World Wide Web*.

The Internet can be a valuable research tool. Evaluating the content found on the Internet will help you determine the accuracy and reliability of the information.

Learn the Skill

Use the following strategies to evaluate information on the Internet.

1 Identify the Web site's domain.
Determine who sponsors the Web site. Web sites sponsored by reputable organizations, educational institutions, and government agencies usually provide accurate and reliable information.

2 Understand the purpose of the site.
Find out whether the purpose of the site is to inform, to persuade, or to entertain.

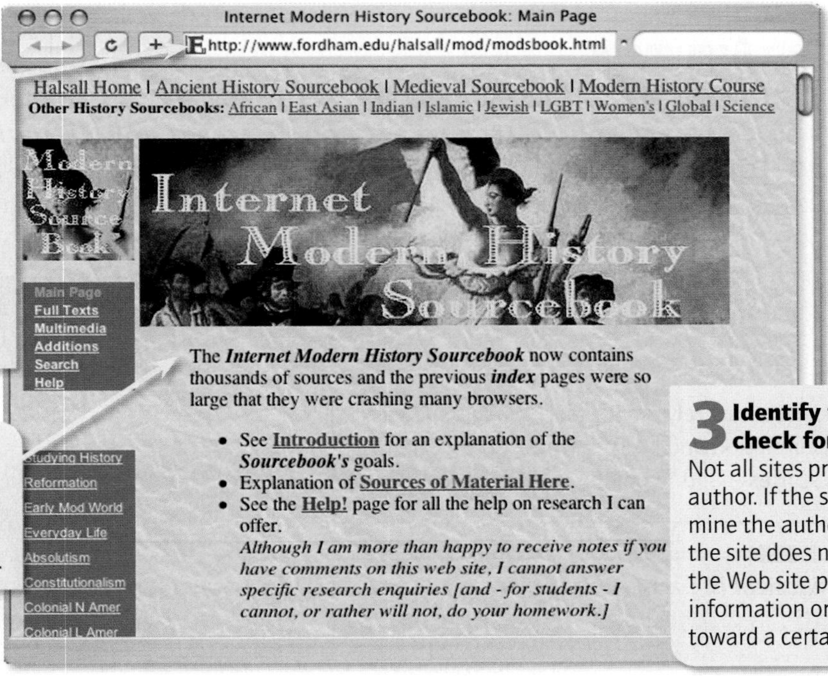

3 Identify the author and check for bias.
Not all sites provide you with an author. If the site does, try to determine the author's credentials. If the site does not, decide whether the Web site presents balanced information or is overly biased toward a certain point of view.

Apply the Skill

1. What is the domain of the Web site? Do you think the information on the Web site will be reliable? Why or why not?
2. What is the purpose of this Web site?
3. Do you think this Web site presents a balanced point of view or a biased point of view? Explain your response.

1. .edu. Yes, because it is sponsored by an educational institution.
2. to give information on modern history
3. Answers will vary.

Reading like a Historian

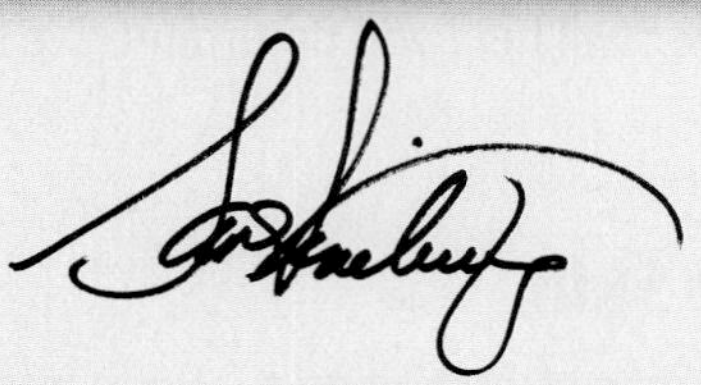

What does it mean to read like a historian? When I asked a group of 10th graders, they were stumped. "Maybe it's like having a mind that spins around like a computer, crammed with dates and facts and stuff," answered one. "Remembering everything you've ever read—you know, like a photographic memory," said another.

The truth is that historians are not computers and they have no better memories than the rest of us. While many historians know a lot about their areas of expertise, when you ask them questions about topics and eras they haven't studied, they seem pretty much like anyone else. So, if historians are not walking encyclopedias, what makes them distinctive?

How they read.

History as an Argument

When historians sit down to read a letter from a 16th century Spanish cleric, a novel from a 19th century Russian writer, or even a chapter from the textbook you are now holding, they approach it as an *argument*. Not in the sense of a brawl or street fight. But in the sense of someone making a claim, stating a position, trying to convince us that his or her description of events should be believed.

When we read like a historian we notice things we've never seen before. Look at the name of the book you're holding, ***Holt World History: Human Legacy***. Even the two little words "human legacy" form an argument—or the beginning of one.

Historians rely on primary sources, such as nonfiction and literary works, to tell their stories—and to bolster their arguments.

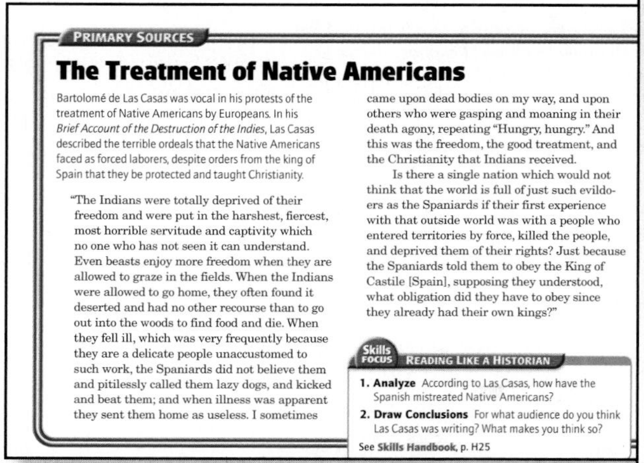

PRIMARY SOURCES

The Treatment of Native Americans

Bartolomé de Las Casas was vocal in his protests of the treatment of Native Americans by Europeans. In his *Brief Account of the Destruction of the Indies*, Las Casas described the terrible ordeals that the Native Americans faced as forced laborers, despite orders from the king of Spain that they be protected and taught Christianity.

"The Indians were totally deprived of their freedom and were put in the harshest, fiercest, most horrible servitude and captivity which no one who has not seen it can understand. Even beasts enjoy more freedom when they are allowed to graze in the fields. When the Indians were allowed to go home, they often found it deserted and had no other recourse than to go out into the woods to find food and die. When they fell ill, which was very frequently because they are a delicate people unaccustomed to such work, the Spaniards did not believe them and pitilessly called them lazy dogs, and kicked and beat them; and when illness was apparent they sent them home as useless. I sometimes came upon dead bodies on my way, and upon others who were gasping and moaning in their death agony, repeating "Hungry, hungry." And this was the freedom, the good treatment, and the Christianity that Indians received.

Is there a single nation which would not think that the world is full of just such evildoers as the Spaniards if their first experience with that outside world was with a people who entered territories by force, killed the people, and deprived them of their rights? Just because the Spaniards told them to obey the King of Castile [Spain], supposing they understood, what obligation did they have to obey since they already had their own kings?"

Skills FOCUS — READING LIKE A HISTORIAN

1. **Analyze** According to Las Casas, how have the Spanish mistreated Native Americans?
2. **Draw Conclusions** For what audience do you think Las Casas was writing? What makes you think so?

See **Skills Handbook**, p. H25

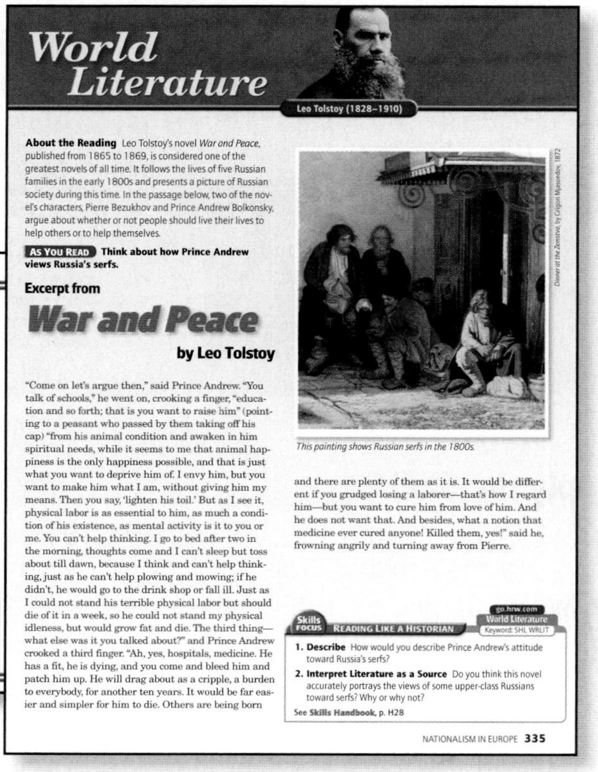

World Literature

Leo Tolstoy (1828–1910)

About the Reading Leo Tolstoy's novel *War and Peace*, published from 1865 to 1869, is considered one of the greatest novels of all time. It follows the lives of five Russian families in the early 1800s and presents a picture of Russian society during this time. In the passage below, two of the novel's characters, Pierre Bezukhov and Prince Andrew Bolkonsky, argue about whether or not people should live their lives to help others or to help themselves.

AS YOU READ **Think about how Prince Andrew views Russia's serfs.**

Excerpt from

War and Peace

by Leo Tolstoy

"Come on let's argue then," said Prince Andrew. "You talk of schools," he went on, crooking a finger, "education and so forth; that is you want to raise him" (pointing to a peasant who passed by them taking off his cap) "from his animal condition and awaken in him spiritual needs, while it seems to me that animal happiness is the only happiness possible, and that is just what you want to deprive him of. I envy him, but you want to make him what I am, without giving him my means. Then you say, 'lighten his toil.' But as I see it, physical labor is as essential to him, as much a condition of his existence, as mental activity is it to you or me. You can't help thinking. I go to bed after two in the morning, thoughts come and I can't sleep but toss about till dawn, because I think and can't help thinking, just as he can't help plowing and mowing; if he didn't, he would go to the drink shop or fall ill. Just as I could not stand his terrible physical labor but should die of it in a week, so he could not stand my physical idleness, but would grow fat and die. The third thing—what else was it you talked about?" and Prince Andrew crooked a third finger. "Ah, yes, hospitals, medicine. He has a fit, he is dying, and you come and bleed him and patch him up. He will drag about as a cripple, a burden to everybody, for another ten years. It would be far easier and simpler for him to die. Others are being born and there are plenty of them as it is. It would be different if you grudged losing a laborer—that's how I regard him—but you want to cure him from love of him. And he does not want that. And besides, what a notion that medicine ever cured anyone! Killed them, yes!" said he, frowning angrily and turning away from Pierre.

Dinner at the Zemstvo, by Grigori Mjasoedov, 1872

This painting shows Russian serfs in the 1800s.

Skills FOCUS — READING LIKE A HISTORIAN

go.hrw.com World Literature Keyword: SHL WRLIT

1. **Describe** How would you describe Prince Andrew's attitude toward Russia's serfs?
2. **Interpret Literature as a Source** Do you think this novel accurately portrays the views of some upper-class Russians toward serfs? Why or why not?

See **Skills Handbook**, p. H28

NATIONALISM IN EUROPE 335

Think about it. Compare your book with those written 30 or 40 years ago, which had titles like *Rise of Western Civilization* or the *Triumph of the West* or the *Tradition of Western Society*. These older books taught students that what mattered most was what happened in the West, particularly in Europe. They drew a straight line from the Greeks and Romans to Medieval Europe to the Renaissance and the "discovery" of the New World. Now and then the four-fifths of the world's population who are not heirs to the Western tradition would make an appearance. But the message was clear. The West and its peoples were at the center. Everyone else was in the margins.

Holt World History: Human Legacy makes a different argument: the whole of human history, not just the West, is our *legacy*, our inheritance. Accordingly, for us to truly understand the world we need to look beyond our narrow slice of it. Ancient China is as much a part of who we are, and who we will become, as ancient Greece.

Your Role in the Argument

Once you understand history as an argument you have a crucial role to play in it. History can no longer be served on a silver platter for you to swallow whole. Once you see history as an argument you realize that for every major historical interpretation, there are multiple ways of viewing things. You can't sit back and watch this happen; you have to make up your own mind. You see, calling something an argument means that it must be defended, must be backed by evidence rather than committed unquestioningly to memory.

Consider this: the Industrial Revolution occurred in England during the years 1780 to about 1830. While historians might dicker over the precise dates of the Industrial Revolution, few dispute that something big and important took place. But the moment we turn from this fact to the question of "why"—why did the Industrial Revolution occur in England and not, for example, in China or India we've landed ourselves in the middle of a raucous argument.

On one side are the historians who claim that the key factor in the birth of the Industrial Revolution was chance and something called "contingency." According to their argument, the British were lucky enough to have vast coal deposits in their soil, which fueled the ravenous industrial machine by providing a steady stream of cheap fuel. England also had a convenient source of cheap cotton and a ready market for finished textiles in her American colonies. These factors, so the argument goes, were not destined or preordained but were contingent: They happily came together at the right time and the right place to produce the Industrial Revolution. There's only one reason why China and India didn't industrialize before England, according to this reasoning. In the words of one historian: "They simply did not have colonies or coal."

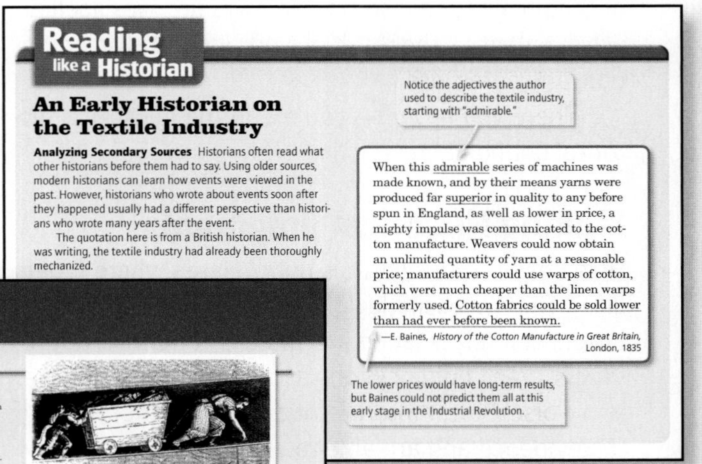

Reading like a Historian

An Early Historian on the Textile Industry

Analyzing Secondary Sources Historians often read what other historians before them had to say. Using older sources, modern historians can learn how events were viewed in the past. However, historians who wrote about events soon after they happened usually had a different perspective than historians who wrote many years after the event.

The quotation here is from a British historian. When he was writing, the textile industry had already been thoroughly mechanized.

Notice the adjectives the author used to describe the textile industry, starting with "admirable."

When this admirable series of machines was made known, and by their means yarns were produced far superior in quality to any before spun in England, as well as lower in price, a mighty impulse was communicated to the cotton manufacture. Weavers could now obtain an unlimited quantity of yarn at a reasonable price; manufacturers could use warps of cotton, which were much cheaper than the linen warps formerly used. Cotton fabrics could be sold lower than had ever before been known.

—E. Baines, *History of the Cotton Manufacture in Great Britain*, London, 1835

The lower prices would have long-term results, but Baines could not predict them all at this early stage in the Industrial Revolution.

Historians must read sources critically. That requires understanding a source's historical context—the knowledge and beliefs of the people at the time.

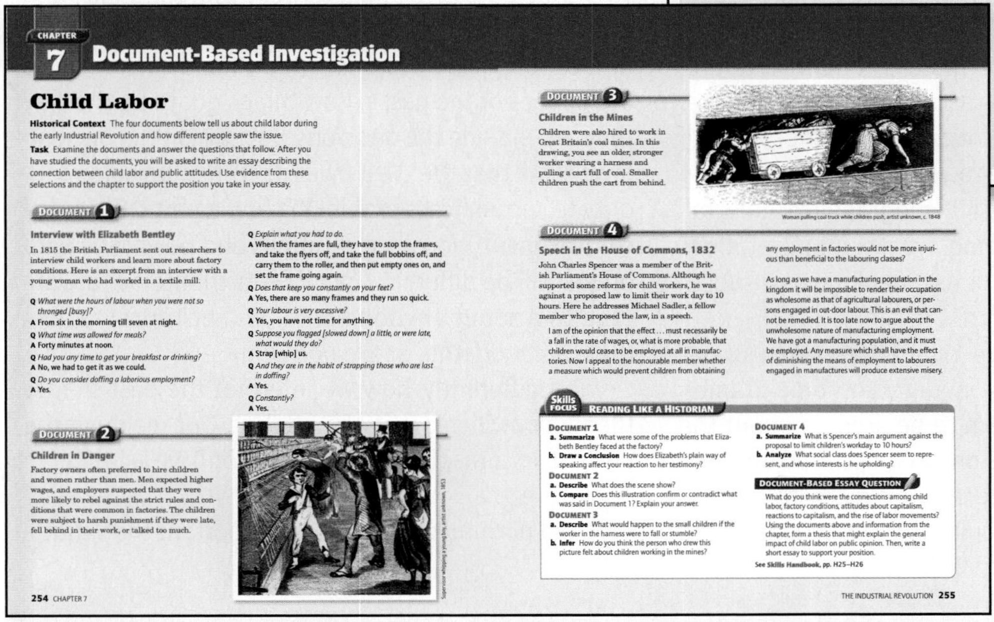

CHAPTER 7 **Document-Based Investigation**

Child Labor

Historical Context The four documents below tell us about child labor during the early Industrial Revolution and how different people saw the issue.

Task Examine the documents and answer the questions that follow. After you have studied the documents, you will be asked to write an essay describing the connection between child labor and public attitudes. Use evidence from these selections and the chapter to support the position you take in your essay.

DOCUMENT 1

Interview with Elizabeth Bentley

In 1815 the British Parliament sent out researchers to interview child workers and learn more about factory conditions. Here is an excerpt from an interview with a young woman who had worked in a textile mill.

Q *What were the hours of labour when you were not so thronged [busy]?*
A From six in the morning till seven at night.
Q *What time was allowed for meals?*
A Forty minutes at noon.
Q *Had you any time to get your breakfast or drinking?*
A No, we had to get it as we could.
Q *Do you consider doffing a laborious employment?*
A Yes.
Q *Explain what you had to do.*
A When the frames are full, they have to stop the frames, and take the flyers off, and take the full bobbins off, and carry them to the roller, and then put empty ones on, and set the frame going again.
Q *Does that keep you constantly on your feet?*
A Yes, there are so many frames and they run so quick.
Q *Your labour is very excessive?*
A Yes, you have not time for anything.
Q *Suppose you flagged [slowed down] a little, or were late, what would they do?*
A Strap [whip] us.
Q *And they are in the habit of strapping those who are last in doffing?*
A Yes.
Q *Constantly?*
A Yes.

DOCUMENT 2

Children in Danger

Factory owners often preferred to hire children and women rather than men. Men expected higher wages, and employers suspected that they were more likely to rebel against the strict rules and conditions that were common in factories. The children were subject to harsh punishment if they were late, fell behind in their work, or talked too much.

Supervisor whipping a young boy, artist unknown, 1853

254 CHAPTER 7

DOCUMENT 3

Children in the Mines

Children were also hired to work in Great Britain's coal mines. In this drawing, you see an older, stronger worker wearing a harness and pulling a cart full of coal. Smaller children push the cart from behind.

Woman pulling coal truck while children push, artist unknown, c. 1848

DOCUMENT 4

Speech in the House of Commons, 1832

John Charles Spencer was a member of the British Parliament's House of Commons. Although he supported some reforms for child workers, he was against a proposed law to limit their work day to 10 hours. Here he addresses Michael Sadler, a fellow member who proposed the law, in a speech.

I am of the opinion that the effect . . . must necessarily be a fall in the rate of wages, or, what is more probable, that children would cease to be employed at all in manufactories. Now I appeal to the honourable member whether a measure which would prevent children from obtaining any employment in factories would not be more injurious than beneficial to the labouring classes?

As long as we have a manufacturing population in the kingdom it will be impossible to render their occupation as wholesome as that of agricultural labourers, or persons engaged in out-door labour. This is an evil that cannot be remedied. It is too late now to argue about the unwholesome nature of manufacturing employment. We have got a manufacturing population, and it must be employed. Any measure which shall have the effect of diminishing the means of employment to labourers engaged in manufactures will produce extensive misery.

Skills FOCUS READING LIKE A HISTORIAN

DOCUMENT 1
a. Summarize What were some of the problems that Elizabeth Bentley faced at the factory?
b. Draw a Conclusion How does Elizabeth's plain way of speaking affect your reaction to her testimony?

DOCUMENT 2
a. Describe What does the scene show?
b. Compare Does this illustration confirm or contradict what was said in Document 1? Explain your answer.

DOCUMENT 3
a. Describe What would happen to the small children if the worker in the harness were to fall or stumble?
b. Infer How do you think the person who drew this picture felt about children working in the mines?

DOCUMENT 4
a. Summarize What is Spencer's main argument against the proposal to limit children's workday to 10 hours?
b. Analyze What social class does Spencer seem to represent, and whose interests is he upholding?

DOCUMENT-BASED ESSAY QUESTION

What do you think were the connections among child labor, factory conditions, attitudes about capitalism, reactions to capitalism, and the rise of labor movements? Using the documents above and information from the chapter, form a thesis that might explain the general impact of child labor on public opinion. Then, write a short essay to support your position.

See **Skills Handbook**, pp. H25–H26

THE INDUSTRIAL REVOLUTION 255

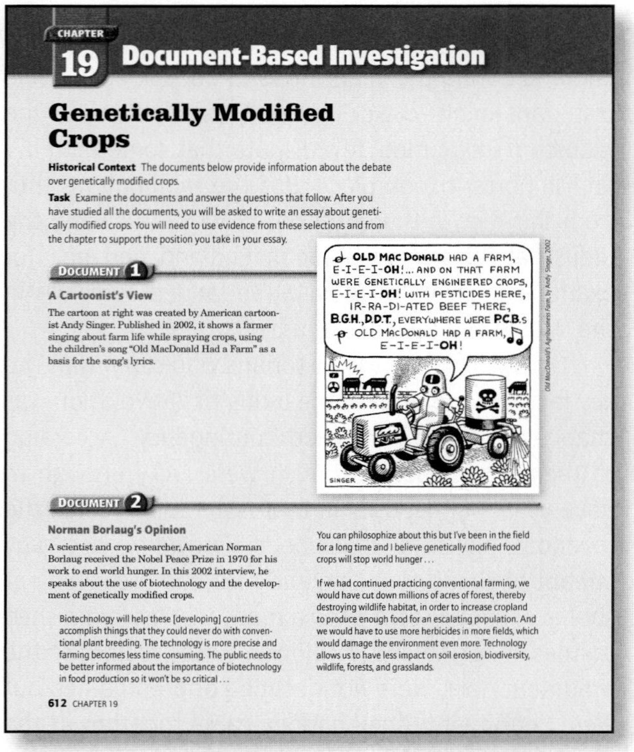
CHAPTER 19 Document-Based Investigation

Genetically Modified Crops

Historical Context The documents below provide information about the debate over genetically modified crops.

Task Examine the documents and answer the questions that follow. After you have studied all the documents, you will be asked to write an essay about genetically modified crops. You will need to use evidence from these selections and from the chapter to support the position you take in your essay.

DOCUMENT 1

A Cartoonist's View

The cartoon at right was created by American cartoonist Andy Singer. Published in 2002, it shows a farmer singing about farm life while spraying crops, using the children's song "Old MacDonald Had a Farm" as a basis for the song's lyrics.

DOCUMENT 2

Norman Borlaug's Opinion

A scientist and crop researcher, American Norman Borlaug received the Nobel Peace Prize in 1970 for his work to end world hunger. In this 2002 interview, he speaks about the use of biotechnology and the development of genetically modified crops.

Biotechnology will help these [developing] countries accomplish things that they could never do with conventional plant breeding. The technology is more precise and farming becomes less time consuming. The public needs to be better informed about the importance of biotechnology in food production so it won't be so critical . . .

You can philosophize about this but I've been in the field for a long time and I believe genetically modified food crops will stop world hunger . . .

If we had continued practicing conventional farming, we would have cut down millions of acres of forest, thereby destroying wildlife habitat, in order to increase cropland to produce enough food for an escalating population. And we would have to use more herbicides in more fields, which would damage the environment even more. Technology allows us to have less impact on soil erosion, biodiversity, wildlife, forests, and grasslands.

612 CHAPTER 19

Historians need to be able to understand *continuity* and *change*. For example, people have always needed food, but the technology of food production changes.

Hogwash, argue historians on the other side. The Industrial Revolution that swept England "was not a matter of chance, of 'things simply coming together.'" The scientific and technological superiority of Britain, writes a historian on this side, "was itself an achievement . . . the result of work, ingenuity, imagination, and enterprise."

There you have it—you are in the midst of a historical dogfight.

Making Historical Judgments

How do you know which is right? Here's where it gets dicey. There is no single right answer to big questions of historical interpretation like there is in math. Interpretations aren't right or wrong as much as they are better and worse. Better interpretations account for more of the evidence and are able to explain more of the big picture—incorporating social, geographical, cultural, and political factors in so doing. Weaker interpretations ignore pieces of evidence or use ideology as a substitute for hard thinking.

Sometimes interpretive differences come about because historians focus on different time frames. Even though they may seem to be arguing about the same thing, one may focus on what occurred during a decade or a century—while others may try to capture what happened over millennia. These time differences are what historians call differences in ***scale.*** Where historians come down on the issue of the technological progress represented by the Industrial Revolution will depend on whether their focus is a 50 year period or a 500 year one. Scale determines not only what historians see but what they choose to look at.

Even though historians argue over the meaning of the past, they often draw on the same concepts in doing so. At the heart of almost every historical interpretation is the notion of **continuity and change**: the idea that the world before us is both the same and different from the one inhabited by people in the past. We see the interplay of continuity and change when we compare the world today with the world around 1500. Then, as now, most of the world's population lived on just under seven percent of the earth's 60 million square miles of land. Over the past 500 or so years, that hasn't changed much: 70% of the world still lives on the same 4.25 million square miles. But consider this change: Since 1500, the world's population has mushroomed from 350 million to 6 billion, an increase of 1700%. Most of these people are crammed into the same inhabited territory that was known to the world in 1500!

Why History Matters

Why should we care about any of this—continuity and change, scale, contingency, the role of ideas, or even how to read like a historian? We should care because our images of the past—how things got to be the way they are—guide the decisions we make in the present. If we think that the West owes its technological superiority to certain ways of thinking and a particular set of cultural institutions, our positions and policies toward others will be different than if we attribute our advantage to a set of environmental and historical factors that came together at the right time.

Put differently, how we interpret the past shapes the reality we create in the present. Our reality in the present, in turn, gives birth to the world we'll inhabit in the future.

And nothing could be more important than that!

Analyzing Primary Sources

Define the Skill

Primary sources are documents or other artifacts created by people present at historical events either as witnesses or participants. Usually, you can identify a primary source by reading for first-person clues such as *I*, *we*, and *our*. These types of sources are valuable to historians because they give information about an event or a time period.

Primary sources can include:

- Letters
- Photographs
- Diaries
- Newspaper stories
- Pamphlets, books, or other writings
- Court opinions
- Autobiographies
- Pottery, weapons, and other artifacts
- Government data, laws, and statutes
- Speeches

Learn the Skill

Use the following strategies to analyze this primary source.

1 Identify the author or creator of the primary source and the date in which it was created.
The date gives you a historical context in which to place the primary-source document.

Vladimir Lenin issued his "Call to Power" speech on October 24, 1917, urging Russians to rise up and seize power from the provisional government. The Bolshevik Revolution began the next day.

"I am writing these lines on the evening of the 24th. The situation is critical in the extreme. In fact it is now absolutely clear that to delay the uprising would be fatal.

With all my might I urge comrades to realize that everything now hangs by a thread; that we are confronted by problems which are not to be solved by conferences or congresses (even congresses of Soviets), but exclusively by peoples, by the masses, by the struggle of the armed people.

... [W]e must not wait. We must at all costs, this very evening, this very night, arrest the government, having first disarmed the officer cadets, and so on.

We must not wait! We may lose everything! ..."

2 Compare details in the primary source to what you know about the historical event or time period.
The time frame of the primary source allows you to make connections between your previous knowledge and the information the document provides.

3 Determine what the author's intentions are in creating the primary source.
The document has a particular purpose and can be used by its author to inform, persuade, direct, or influence the audience.

Apply the Skill

1. What is Lenin's point of view?
2. How would this source help a historian write a historical interpretation of the Russian Revolution?

1. He wants to overthrow the current Russian government; he is a revolutionary.
2. Answers will vary; possible answer: The source was written a day before the revolution by one of the main players of the revolution and gives a first-hand account of the emotional tone of the time.

Analyzing Visuals

Define the Skill

Visuals, including paintings, drawings, photographs, and political cartoons, are another type of primary source. Like any primary source, they need to be analyzed critically. Sometimes visuals offer an accurate portrayal of the details of a historical figure or event. In other instances, they represent an exaggerated or biased point of view. Knowing and understanding an artist or photographer's point of view can sometimes reveal more to a historian than the actual image itself. By analyzing visuals, we are given an opportunity to see historical events through the eyes of the artist or photographer.

Learn the Skill

Use the following strategies to analyze visuals.

1 Identify the subject and determine the medium that is being used.
Visuals can be a photograph, a piece of fine art, an advertisement, or a cartoon. The type of visual being used can help you determine the audience.

3 Examine the details and the way in which the subject is depicted.
The details in the visual that surround the main subject can help you determine how the subject is depicted and what the artist wants you to know about the subject.

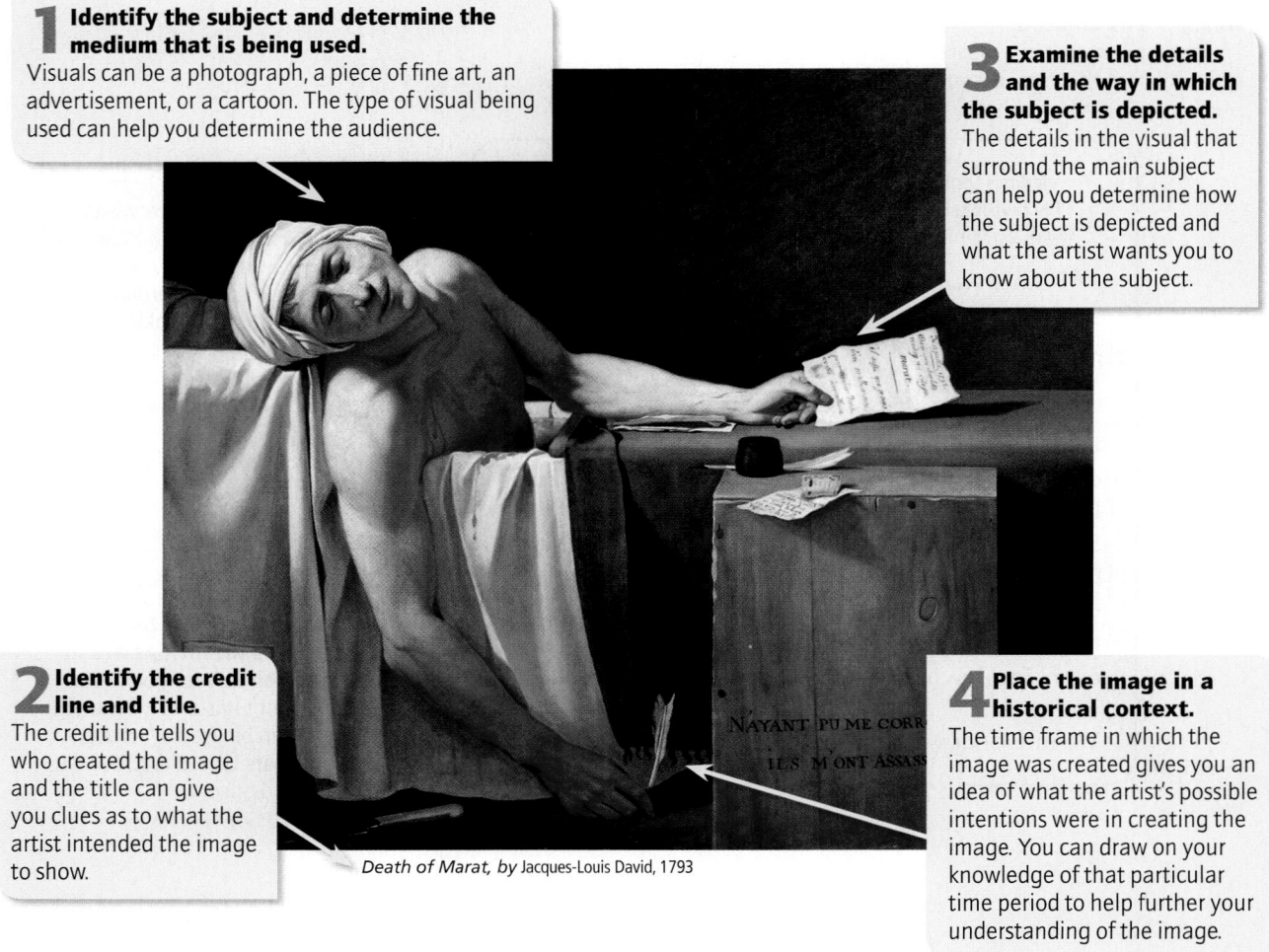

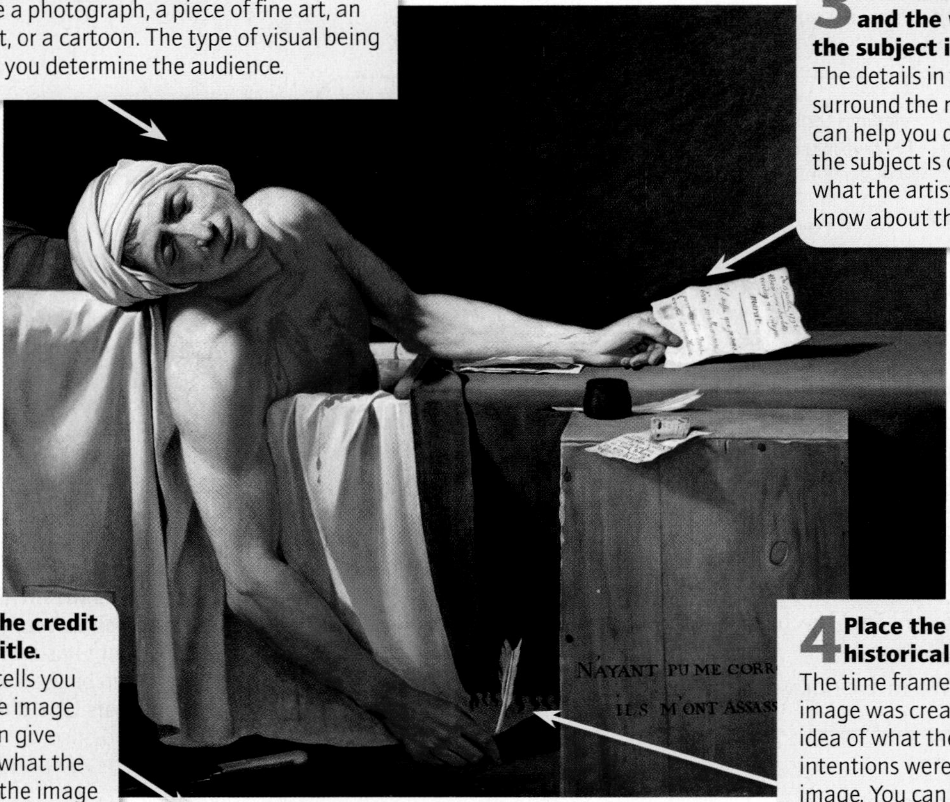

2 Identify the credit line and title.
The credit line tells you who created the image and the title can give you clues as to what the artist intended the image to show.

Death of Marat, by Jacques-Louis David, 1793

4 Place the image in a historical context.
The time frame in which the image was created gives you an idea of what the artist's possible intentions were in creating the image. You can draw on your knowledge of that particular time period to help further your understanding of the image.

Apply the Skill

1. What details of Marat's death are shown in this painting?
2. How does the artist portray Marat's death? What might his purpose be in portraying Marat in such a manner?

1. the knife, the tub, the letter
2. The artist portrays Marat as a victim, a martyr. Answers will vary; possible answer: to gain sympathy for the cause of the revolution

Interpreting Political Cartoons

Define the Skill

Political cartoons are another kind of visual used to help us understand a particular historical time period. These differ from visuals such as photographs and fine art because political cartoons express a point of view. They often exaggerate characteristics of subjects or events in order to convey a specific message, either about politics in particular or society in general. Historians use political cartoons to understand how a certain person or event was perceived at the time. To interpret political cartoons, examine all the elements while considering the social, political, and historical context of the time.

Learn the Skill

Use the acronym BASIC to interpret political cartoons.

B Background Knowledge
Place the political cartoon in its historical context. Use your prior knowledge of what is being depicted to analyze the cartoon's message about that particular event or person.

A Argument
Determine what the artist is trying to say in the political cartoon. Analyze the message that the artist is sending to the audience.

S Symbolism
Analyze any symbols in the cartoon. Symbols can be used to represent large groups that can't be depicted easily or to stand for a person or an event. Symbols can also be used to simplify the cartoon or make its message clearer to the audience.

I Irony
Examine the irony that is present in the cartoon. Irony is the use of words to express something different from their literal meaning. Sometimes in political cartoons, examples of irony are implied through the various symbols and pictures.

C Caricature (or exaggeration)
Often in political cartoons, facial features or people's bodies are exaggerated. Analyze any exaggerations present in the cartoon and consider what the meaning of such exaggerations might be.

Apply the Skill

1. Who are the parties being depicted in this cartoon?
2. What is the artist trying to say about the relationship between NAFTA and Mexican industries?

1. the United States and Mexico
2. Answers will vary; possible answer: While NAFTA is meant to help countries in the Americas, it can lead to losses for local industries as imported goods take over domestic goods.

Interpreting Literature as a Source

Define the Skill

Historians can sometimes use **literature** written during a particular time period to gain detailed insights into certain people, places, and events. For example, a poem set in the Middle Ages, such as Chaucer's *Canterbury Tales*, can provide historical details about the lifestyle of people in England in the 1300s. However, because most literature is fiction, it needs to be approached with special caution. Literature, even historical fiction, cannot be taken at face value or treated as a reliable source of information.

Learn the Skill

Use the following strategies to interpret literature.

1 Identify the author and time period of the piece. The time period allows you to place the literary work into a historical context. You can then draw on your knowledge of that time period to interpret the meaning of the piece.

2 Look for descriptive passages that help you determine the author's tone, or manner of expression. The author's tone helps us to understand how the author feels about the subject he or she is writing about. In historical literature the tone can be used to demonstrate a widely felt emotion of people during that particular time period.

Excerpt from *War and Peace*, by Leo Tolstoy, 1805

"Come on let's argue then," said Prince Andrew. "You talk of schools," he went on, crooking a finger, "education and so forth; that is you want to raise him (pointing to a peasant who passed by them taking off his cap) from his animal condition and awaken in him spiritual needs, while it seems to me that animal happiness is the only happiness possible, and that is just what you want to deprive him of. I envy him, but you want to make him what I am, without giving him my means. Then you say, 'lighten his toil.' But as I see it, physical labor is as essential to him, as much a condition of his existence, as mental activity is to you or me. You can't help thinking. I go to bed after two in the morning, thoughts come and I can't sleep but toss about till dawn, because I think and can't help thinking, just as he can't help plowing and mowing; if he didn't, he would go to the drink shop or fall ill. Just as I could not stand his terrible physical labor but should die of it in a week, so he could not stand my physical idleness, but would grow fat and die."

3 Determine whether the literature is meant to describe a certain historical event or to elicit an emotional response. Writers often try to elicit an emotional response from their audiences. Analyze the passage and decide whether or not the author is trying to make you feel one way or another about the subject matter.

Apply the Skill

1. What is the author's point of view?
2. What is the goal of the literature selection?
3. What can historians learn about social classes in Russia by reading this selection?

1. Answers will vary; possible answer: Tolstoy is writing from the perspective of the elite upper class in Europe.
2. Answers will vary; possible answer: to show class distinctions in Russia in the early 1800s
3. Answers will vary; possible answer: There was a great gap in social classes in Russia in the 1800s, which is one reason for the revolutions and uprisings of the time.

Recognizing Bias in Primary Sources

Define the Skill

To develop an effective analysis of primary sources, historians must learn to recognize bias and the source of **bias in primary sources**. A bias is a preference or inclination that inhibits a person from making an impartial judgment. A person's bias can be influenced by political, social, cultural, or personal beliefs. Most primary sources reflect some type of bias, either from the person who created the source or the person viewing the source. Bias can give clues about an author's intent or background. For example, the author may be trying to justify an action or sway an opinion.

Sometimes an author expresses a personal view without knowing that it is biased. Bias can help historians understand the different attitudes during a certain time in history. To avoid bias, a historian must look at many sources on the same incident or issue.

Learn the Skill

Use the following strategies to recognize bias.

1 Identify the speaker or author. The author's place in the context of a historical event or time period will give you an idea of what sort of bias he or she might have toward the subject.

Carelton Smith, visitor to the Lancashire mines, 1833

"The children, boys and girls, earned their wages by drawing the coals in tubs along the galleries by means of a belt and chain, which passed along their waists. Many girls were thus employed, and after a time became crooked and deformed."

2 Examine the author's point of view. Analyze what beliefs the author is trying to convey to his or her audience.

3 Compare the primary source with other sources and with historical evidence. Look to other sources available on this particular subject. Use a variety of sources to develop your own conclusions regarding the event or time period.

Apply the Skill

1. What is the author's goal in writing this passage?
2. Explain how a historian might use this document in preparing a historical account of child labor in coal mines.

1. to show the harsh conditions of children who were working in coal mines
2. Answers will vary; possible answer: This is an eyewitness account that a historian could use to prove that conditions in coal mines were unsuitable for children.

Analyzing Secondary Sources

Define the Skill

A **secondary source** is an account that is produced after a historical event by people who were not present at the actual event. These people rely on primary sources in order to write their secondary-source accounts. Secondary sources often contain summaries and analyses of events and time periods. Your textbook can be considered a secondary source.

Depending on the sorts of questions we ask, a document that we might have initially considered to be a secondary source can actually be a primary source. For example, a history textbook from the mid-1800s is normally considered to be a secondary source. But if we use that book to look at the ways in which history was written in the mid-1800s, the history text then becomes a primary source. It is important to pay attention to the ways in which a document is presented to us before determining whether it is a primary or secondary source.

Other kinds of secondary sources include
- Encyclopedia entries
- Web sites
- Articles and essays by historians
- Biographies

Learn the Skill

Use the following strategies to analyze secondary sources.

1 Identify the source. The author and the date give you a historical context for the source.

Einhard, the official biographer of Charlemagne,
The Life of Charlemagne, 830

"Charlemagne practised the Christian religion with great devotion and piety. . . As long as his health lasted he went to church morning and evening with great regularity, and also for early-morning Mass, and the late-night hours."

2 Analyze the summary of historical events provided by the source. The author of a secondary source usually offers a summary of events or a time period.

3 Primary-source possibilities. Determine whether or not this secondary source could also be considered a primary source. Use the date and your knowledge of the speaker to help you draw conclusions about how this source could be both primary and secondary.

Apply the Skill

1. What important information about Charlemagne can be found in this passage?
2. In what ways could this secondary source be viewed as a primary source?

1. He was very religious and went to church regularly.
2. Answers will vary; possible answer: This could be used as a primary source if someone wanted to look at the ways in which Charlemagne was viewed by historians over the centuries.

Recognizing Bias in Secondary Sources

Define the Skill

Most secondary sources, like most primary sources, contain some sort of bias based on the author's beliefs. Many secondary sources take a position on a historical event or time period and use that position to interpret the events that took place. Even secondary-source accounts that are meant to be neutral can reflect a bias of some sort. It is important to be able to notice when **bias exists in a secondary source** so that you can make your own assessment of the source's legitimacy.

Learn the Skill

Use the following strategies to recognize bias in secondary sources.

1 Identify the author and his or her purpose in writing the text. Secondary sources are written with a distinctive purpose toward the author's audience.

This excerpt is taken from a Chinese History textbook and is compiled by the Peoples' Education Company.

After the fight curtain was drawn back, the headquarters of the 29th troop of [the] Chinese defending army issued an order that they had to hold fast to Lugouqiao. Before this command was issued, the soldiers could not hold back their anger. So when the command reached them, the soldiers instantly ran out of the countryside, wishing they could wipe out the enemy immediately. The two lines of Chinese soldiers defended either side of the railroad bridge. Facing hundreds of Japanese attackers, they were not cowed in the least, and they engaged in intense hand-to-hand fights with [the] enemies. Nearly all of them died at the end of the battle of the bridge. Seeing their comrades fall in the battle, other soldiers, without showing much sorrow, clenched their teeth. They fought forward. Even the wounded who were ordered to retreat were still charging ahead.

2 Analyze the words the author uses to describe people, places, and events. The words or phrases that the author uses have a great deal to do with how he or she feels the subject. Identify and analyze these words in order to recognize what sort of bias the author has.

3 Determine the author's opinion about the subject being discussed. The author is looking at these events with particular feelings towards his or her subject. By analyzing where the author is coming from, you can recognize the bias in the writing.

Apply the Skill

1. What is the source?
2. Are there examples of emotional language in the excerpt? If so, what are they?
3. Is there bias in this passage? Explain your answer.

1. a Chinese history textbook
2. yes; "Japanese attackers;" "the soldiers could not hold back their anger;" "they were not cowed in the least;" "other soldiers, without showing much sorrow, clenched their teeth"
3. Yes; the author paints the Chinese in a very brave, positive light and the Japanese in a negative light, as the "attackers" and the "enemies."

Evaluating Historical Interpretation

Define the Skill

Historians and others **evaluate historical interpretations** to determine the credibility, level of bias, and relevance of the material. A historical interpretation is a way to explain the past. These interpretations can change over time as historians learn more about the people and events of the past.

Learn the Skill

Use the following strategies to evaluate historical interpretation.

1 Identify the author or publisher of the source to determine credibility.
The introduction tells you the author's name and his profession. You may have to do additional research to find out what the author's background is in order to determine credibility.

Excerpt from *The World of Rome*, by historians Peter Jones and Keith Sidwell, 1997

"Roman subjects have had a continuing appeal for cinema audiences. One thinks of *Ben-Hur* and *Spartacus*, for example, which established our view of galleys and chariot-races indelibly… There have been many novels devoted to Roman subjects. The best known in English, perhaps, are Robert Graves' *I, Claudius* and *Claudius the God*, adapted for TV in the 1960s…But it is not only the large-scale which shows the deep penetration of our consciousness by Roman images (even if these are merely images of images). All around, we can see trivial examples of this impact. There are Roman-style porticoes on fast-food stores and statue niches on minute houses on large estates. There are togas and gladiators in Bugs Bunny cartoons. There are Roman soldiers in Asterix books. There are Latin tags on British pound coins. There is a laurel wreath on the Whitehall cenotaph [a World War I monument in London].

For all this, the world of Rome is ultimately responsible."

2 Consider when the source was created.
The more current the publishing date is, the more recent the scholarship is and, therefore, the more credible the source.

3 Examine the level of bias in the interpretation.
The author or authors of historical interpretations take a position on the particular time period or event that they are discussing. Analyze the way in which their bias affects their interpretation of the event or time period.

Apply the Skill

1. Who are the authors of the interpretation?
2. When was the source created? How does this affect the scholarship?
3. How does bias affect the interpretation?

1. historians Peter Jones and Keith Sidwell
2. 1997; Answers will vary: possible answer: It's fairly recent scholarship, only about 10 years old; there may be more recent scholarship that could be take into consideration when assessing the validity of the source.
3. Answers will vary; possible answer: The bias of the authors is that Rome's legacy left only positive images on popular culture and life today. They don't discuss any of the possible lasting negative effects.

Analyzing Points of View

Define the Skill

Interpretations of past events often come from differing **points of view.** Two historians given the same primary-source documents may, and often do, look at the historical event or time period in two completely different ways. These differing interpretations may reflect an extreme bias for one view or another, or they may reflect two different schools of thought. Historians are often faced with alternative points of view of a time or an event in the past when conducting their research. Good historians do additional research to find the accuracies in each account.

Learn the Skill

Use the following strategies to analyze points of view.

1 Identify information given about the authors and the time during which their research was conducted. Knowing the authors' background and when they conducted their work gives you an insight into where their scholarship lies in the grand scheme of the subject material.

Archaeologists Dennis Stanford and Bruce Bradley's views on migration to the Americas, 1999

"We reason that generations of Solutrean hunters learned to cope with ice and weather conditions to follow resources such as Harp seals and Great Auks that migrated north and westward along with retreating ice in late spring. Through such activities they ended up (by accident and/or design) along the exposed continental shelf of North America discovering a New Land."

2 Define and analyze the main points in each argument. Determine what each author is saying about the topic.

Archaeologist Stuart J. Fiedel's view on migration to the Americas, 1987

"The striking similarity of fluted points and associated artifacts across the whole expanse of North America suggests that the continent was rapidly filled by Paleo-Indian hunting bands, each retaining for several centuries the tool-making traditions of an ancestral population that originally entered through the ice-free corridor around 10,000-9500 BC. But the only place from which this hypothetical group could have come is Alaska, where there is hardly any existing evidence of Clovis occupation."

3 Compare the points of view. Based on the time period of their study and their conclusions, analyze the author's alternative points of view in order to draw conclusions about the topic.

Apply the Skill

1. What is the main point of each selection?
2. Which source do you feel has more credibility? Why?

1. Selection 1: The first people were Solutrean hunters who came to North America along the continental shelf. Selection 2: The first people came to North America from Alaska.
2. Possible answer: the first one because it is more recent

CREATING WRITTEN PRESENTATIONS

Biographical Writing

A biography is the story of a person's life as told by someone else. Historical accounts usually include a great deal of biographical writing. Personalizing history in this way makes it more interesting and easier to understand for many people. Follow these steps when you write a biography.

1. Prewrite

Identifying the Subject Sometimes you will be assigned a subject; sometimes you will have a choice. When choosing, pick a person who interests you, one that you would like to know more about. Be sure to get your choice approved by your teacher.

Identifying a Thesis Decide on your point of view toward the person. Is he or she a leader, an artist, a scientist? Was he or she a hero, a failure; famous or infamous? Focus your thoughts in a single statement, which can serve as your *thesis statement.* A thesis statement tells what your paper will be about.

Gathering Information and Details You will be able to find information about your subject in encyclopedias and other reference books, in articles, on CD-ROMs and Web sites, and through other informational sources. You want to check with your teacher or librarian to make sure your sources are reliable and objective. Choose facts, examples, anecdotes, and other details that relate directly to your thesis. It's better to have a few paragraphs of carefully explained, related information than a running list of dates and other facts.

Organizing Information and Details Almost all biographical writing is organized in *chronological*, or time, order. Use an outline to gather specific details under a main idea for each paragraph in your paper. Be prepared to revise your thesis as you gather information and learn more about your subject. You will not be able to use all the information you find. Pick only what best supports and illustrates your thesis and main ideas.

2. Write

Use a Writer's Framework to create a draft.

Introduction

- Start with a quotation, anecdote or fascinating fact.
- Identify your subject, giving facts and details that reflect your point of view toward him or her.
- Clearly express the main focus, or thesis, of your paper in a single statement.

Body

- Choose three or four main events from the person's life to develop into paragraphs supporting your thesis.
- Give specific facts and examples that directly support the main idea in each paragraph.
- Use chronological order to organize your paper.

Conclusion

- Restate the main focus (thesis) of your paper.
- Give additional biographical information about the person to strengthen or expand your thesis.
- Relate the person to historical events at that time or to someone else in history.

3. Revise and Publish

Evaluating and Revising Look back at each paragraph. Revise wording or sentence structure to strengthen the links between your thesis and the supporting information.

Proofreading and Publishing Double-check the spelling of all names of people, places, and events. Also, check all dates.

Many historical societies, service clubs, and other groups sponsor essay contests. Check the guidelines for entering any such contests.

Expository Writing

Essay questions on tests, book reports, and other assignments that require you to explain or present information about a particular subject are types of expository writing—explaining or giving information about a topic. The specific information you give and what you say about it depends on not only your topic, but also the organization, or structure, of your writing. Follow these steps when you write an expository paper.

1. Prewrite

Identifying a Topic Most expository writing assignments include a topic or choice of topics. Often, the structure is assigned, too. Much of your expository writing will involve at least one of the following three common structures, shown here with example topics.

Comparison-contrast topic: *Explain three ways that the United Nations is like the League of Nations, and three ways they differ.*

Cause and effect topic: *How did industrialization change British social structure, and what results of those changes are seen in today's society?*

Sequence of events topic: *Trace the history of European exploration of the Americas.*

Writing a Thesis Statement Your response to your topic will guide the wording of your thesis statement. In a single sentence, state the main idea behind what you will write about the topic.

Comparison-contrast thesis: *Though similar in origin, aims and hopes, the United Nations and the League of Nations differed in organization, scope, and authority.*

Gathering and Organizing Information Some expository writing assignments involve research. Books, CD-ROMs, the Web, and other information sources can provide facts, examples, and other details about your topic. As a rule, you will want to organize your information in an outline according to the structure you chose or were assigned.

Organize by comparison-contrast: Sometimes you will want to give all your points of comparison first, then all the contrasting points. In other cases, you will give a point of comparison, then a contrast; then the next comparison, followed by the next contrast, etc.

Organize by cause and effect: Usually, you will give the cause(s) first, then the effect(s).

Organize by sequence of events: In most cases, you will use chronological, or time, order to organize a sequence of events.

2. Write

Use a Writer's Framework to create a draft.

Introduction

- Introduce your topic, providing any details or description readers will need to understand it.
- Briefly explain how you will develop your topic.
- Clearly state your thesis for your paper.

Body

- Follow your outline in presenting examples, facts, and other information in each paragraph.
- Use transitional words such as *then*, *as a result*, and *rather than* to relate ideas and information clearly.

Conclusion

- Briefly summarize (in a sentence or two) the key ideas and information in the body of your paper.
- Use information from the body of your paper to restate your thesis in more specific words.
- Expand on your thesis by explaining the importance, predicting future developments, or exploring some other aspect of your topic.

3. Revise and Publish

Evaluate and Revise Make sure that you have clearly introduced both your topic and the structure of your paper. Replace any weak transitional words with more precise words or phrases.

Proofread and Publish Proofread your paper to be sure that it is free of errors in punctuation, usage, and spelling. Transitional words often need to be set off by punctuation, so check them with special care.

CREATING WRITTEN PRESENTATIONS

Persuasive Writing

The purpose of persuasion is to convince others to believe something or do something. You'll most often find persuasive writing in advertisements, editorials written for newspapers and magazines, or in the speeches of political leaders. Persuasive writing turned into a speech is common in the great speeches of political leaders. Follow these steps when you write a persuasive paper.

1. Prewrite

Identifying an Issue One requirement for persuasion is a topic about which people disagree. If everyone agrees, there is no need to persuade. If you are asked to create a persuasive essay, an editorial, or a persuasive speech, start by identifying an issue with these characteristics:

1. You have an opinion about it.
2. There are clearly defined pro and con arguments about the issue.

Identifying a Thesis Once you have an issue, write a sentence that defines your opinion or position on it.

Example thesis: *Wealthier countries should help poorer countries develop their economies.*

Building an Argument The support provided for an opinion or thesis is called an argument. A persuasive argument must be based on logical proof and evidence. It may also include appeals to emotions or to a person's ethics.

Evidence: Facts, statistics, anecdotes, expert testimony, and precise examples

Emotional Appeals: Appeals to ideas people care about, such as love of country or human life and welfare

Ethical Appeals: Appeals to the readers' sense of right and wrong

Gathering and Organizing Support Unless you have already studied your topic, you will have to do some research for reasons and information to support your opinion. You can check online sources, textbooks, newspapers, etc.

Once you have gathered the support, you'll need to think about the order in which you should present it. Sometimes you will want to put the strongest and most compelling information or reason first, to capture your reader's attention. At other times you may want to save it for the end, to make a strong final impression.

2. Write

Use a Writer's Framework to create a draft:

Introduction

- Start with a question, quotation, or interesting fact.
- Clearly state your thesis.
- Give background information so readers understand the issue.

Body

- Include at least three reasons to support your thesis.
- Support each reason with evidence, emotional appeals, or ethical appeals.
- Organize the reasons by order of importance—most to least or least to most.

Conclusion

- Summarize your argument.
- Restate your thesis in different words.
- Include a call to action—a sentence that tells readers what you want them to do.

3. Revise and Publish

Evaluate and Revise Turn the statements in the Writer's Framework into questions and ask yourself what changes you need to make. For example, "Do I have a clear statement of my thesis in the introduction to my paper?"

Proofread and Publish Proofread your paper to be sure that it is free of errors in punctuation, usage, and spelling. If you have a computer with spell-check, be sure to use it. You also need someone to read what you have written. You could submit a persuasive paper to the editorial page of your school or local newspaper.

Research Writing

Unlike other expository writing, research writing requires you to present not only your own ideas and knowledge on a topic but those of others. Consequently, the success of your research papers will depend on how well you find, select, and use information sources. Follow these steps when you write a research paper.

1. Prewrite

Identifying a Topic and Research Question
In some cases, your teacher will assign the general subject, or topic, of your report. Other times, you will choose your own. Topics often include time periods, places, people, and events in history. To shape your topic, turn it into a research question. For example, if your topic were the Bolshevik Revolution, you might ask "What were the causes of the Bolshevik Revolution?"

Gathering and Recording Information To answer your research question, you will need to seek information about your topic in sources such as books, articles, and CD-ROMs. Information from all sources needs to be factual, up-to-date, logical, and objective.

Keep a numbered list of the sources you use. Record each note on a separate piece of paper or note card, including the source number and the page number(s) where the information appears.

Writing a Thesis Statement Gathering information will guide you in answering your research question. That answer can serve as a statement of the main idea, or thesis, you will develop in your report.

Example thesis: *The primary cause of the Bolshevik Revolution was long-term social unrest.*

Organizing Your Information Sort your notes into several major categories; then divide them further into subtopics. Organize all of these in an outline, according to how you want to present the information.

Depending on your thesis, you might organize by order of importance, chronological order, comparison and contrast, or cause and effect. With the example thesis on the Bolshevik Revolution, you might arrange causes in their order of importance or simply discuss causes before effects.

2. Write

Use a Writer's Framework to create a draft:

Introduction

- Grab readers' interest by opening with an interesting fact or anecdote.
- Give background information to acquaint readers with your topic and the research you've done.
- Clearly state your thesis.

Body

- Devote at least one paragraph to each main idea in your outline.
- Quote sources accurately and enclose all direct quotations in quotation marks.
- Insert a parenthetical source citation after each piece of research information that you use.

Conclusion

- Summarize your main points.
- Restate your thesis, relating it to your research.
- Create a Works Cited page listing your sources.

3. Revise and Publish

Evaluating and Revising Double check all quotations to make sure they're accurate. Where you have summarized or paraphrased information, make sure you have used your own words.

Proofreading and Publishing Proofread to be sure that you have enclosed each direct quotation in quotation marks. Check to be sure that you have given a parenthetical citation for the source for each piece of information used in your report.

Expository and Persuasive Speeches

Speeches are a common form of sharing information or persuading an audience. Preparing to give a speech usually involves the same steps as writing—planning, researching, organizing, drafting, and revising. Delivering a speech, however, requires an additional set of skills. Follow these steps when you prepare and deliver a speech about a historical event or issue.

1. Prepare the Speech

Identifying an Issue or Topic Sometimes you will be assigned a historical topic or issues for a speech. Other times you will be able to choose your own.

Identifying your Purpose

To Inform: Expository, or informative speeches, provide facts about and/or explain a historical event or situation.

To Persuade: Persuasive speeches attempt to change listeners' opinions about an issue on which there are clearly defined pro and con arguments. In addition to facts and examples, persuasive speeches rely on emotional appeals.

Identifying a Thesis A thesis statement is the statement of your main idea. You may be able to identify it as soon as you have a topic or an issue, but you may also wait until after you have done some research and gathered information. Here are examples of thesis statements.

Expository thesis: *Napoleon's Russian Campaign was troubled from the beginning, and it ended in failure.*

Persuasive thesis: *Napoleon's ego and pride were the cause of his failure in the Russian Campaign.*

Gathering Information Use reference books, history books, primary sources, and other sources to gather information. Persuasive speeches need *facts, statistics, anecdotes, expert testimony,* and *precise examples* just as much as expository speeches.

Organizing Your Notes Review the information you have gathered and identify the main points you want to make—the points that relate to and support your thesis. Then select a way to organize your presentation.

Typical ways to organize an *informative speech* include:

Organize by cause and effect: Discuss the cause(s) before the effect(s).

Organize by sequence: Discuss stages or actions in chronological order.

Organize by comparison-contrast: You might discuss one event or person and then discuss the other event and person. You can also organize by points of comparison. For example, you might compare two kings on political skills, military skills, and finally on their legacy to the world.

For a *persuasive speech*, you would typically:

Organize by order of importance: Save the most important and/or most dramatic point for last, to make a final impact on your audience.

Making Note Cards In most situations, you need to speak from a few note cards rather than a written paper. Make a separate card for:

- Each major point. Add reminder notes about facts, examples, or ideas you want to use to support that point.
- Direct quotations to be read word for word.
- When to show a map, chart, or other visual material to support your points.

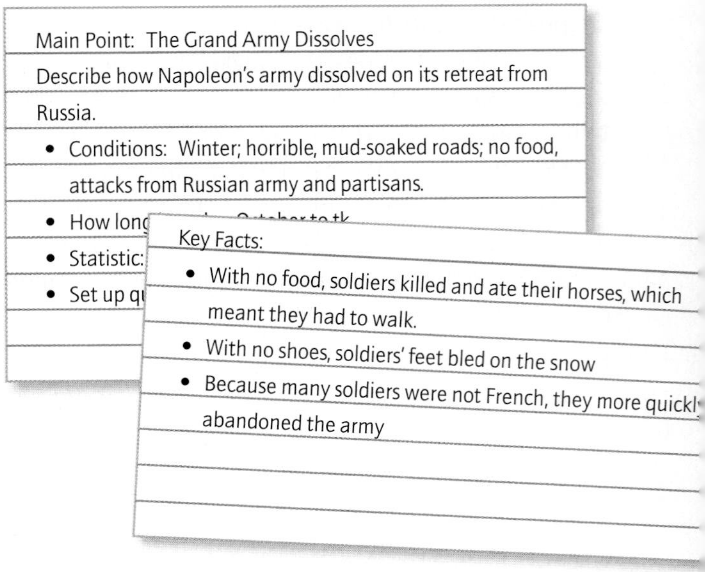
Main Point: The Grand Army Dissolves
Describe how Napoleon's army dissolved on its retreat from Russia.
• Conditions: Winter; horrible, mud-soaked roads; no food, attacks from Russian army and partisans.
• How long
• Statistic:
• Set up q
Key Facts:
• With no food, soldiers killed and ate their horses, which meant they had to walk.
• With no shoes, soldiers' feet bled on the snow
• Because many soldiers were not French, they more quickl abandoned the army

2. Practice the Speech

Practice will help build your self-confidence as well as help you spot and correct mistakes. You need to practice more than once, evaluating and changing your speech as you go.

Rehearse If possible, practice your speech in front of an audience—friends or family members. It is also helpful to practice in front of a mirror or make a video of your practice session. That way you can listen to the speech as well as observe the way you handled yourself while speaking.

Verbal Communication In a speech, it is not just the words that are important, it is also how the words are expressed. As you rehearse, adjust how well you do the following:

- Speak clearly and slowly
- Project your voice more loudly than in normal speech
- Stress words related to the main points
- Use small silences to suggest important points or give listeners time to think

Nonverbal Communication We use nonverbal signals whenever we speak, but when giving a speech, it is especially important to control and use these signals effectively. Practice controlling the following:

Facial Expressions: Frowning, smiling, etc. signal your feelings

Eye Contact: Maintaining eye contact with your audience makes them feel as though you are communicating directly to them

Gestures: Move your arms, hands, or head to emphasize your verbal message

Using Audiovisual Media Audiovisual media can make your speech more interesting and clarify your ideas. Audiovisual media include audio recordings, films, maps, charts, graphs, pictures, illustrations, power point presentations or anything else stored on a personal computer.

- Use visuals that are large enough for everyone in the audience to see and read.
- If you are going to use media as you present your speech, you need to include it when you rehearse.

3. Deliver the Speech

No matter how well you have planned and researched your topic—and you should know your topic inside and out—and how much you have practiced your presentation, actually standing in front of an audience and giving the speech is a challenge. Almost everyone is a little bit nervous when giving a speech, even people who have made a career as a speaker. Here are some things you can do to make speaking easier:

Check Your Audiovisual Media: Before the speech, make sure all electronic equipment is cued up and ready to go.

Read the Audience: Do they seem to be agreeing or disagreeing with the points you are making? Are they going to sleep or whispering to one another? You may need to adjust your verbal and nonverbal signals.

Slow Down: Force yourself to control the pace of your speech. Don't rush through it to get to the end.

Focus on What You Want to Say: Concentrate on your purpose for speaking. Don't be distracted or wander.

Finish with Finesse: Close your speech with emphasis on your main idea or point.

Multiple Choice

One of the most common questions you might see on a test is a **multiple-choice question.** These questions consist of a stem and several answer options. Use the strategies below to answer multiple-choice questions.

Learn

1. **Read the stem carefully and review each of the answer options.**
2. **Examine the question for key words and facts that indicate what the question is asking.**
3. **Pay careful attention to questions that are phrased in the negative.** Some questions contain words such as *not* and *except*. In these cases, look for the answer option that is not true.
4. **Eliminate answer options that you know are incorrect** This will help you narrow down your choices.
5. **Consider options such as *all of the above* and *none of the above* as you would any other possible response.**
6. **Watch for modifiers.** Answer options that include absolute words such as *always* or *never* are sometimes incorrect.
7. **Consider the options that remain and select the best.** If you are not sure of the answer, select the option that makes the most sense.

2 The word *best* indicates that you should look for the option that best explains why Henry broke from the church.

1

Stem

1. Which of the following best explains why Henry VIII broke away from the Catholic Church?

Answer Options

A The pope refused to grant him an annulment.
B He was a close friend and follower of Martin Luther.
C He wanted to be head of the church.
D He strongly opposed the sale of indulgences.

3

2. Which of the following was not a writer associated with the Renaissance?

A William Shakespeare
B Christine de Pisan
C Miguel de Cervantes
D Johannes Gutenberg

3. The Catholic Counter-Reformation led to

A improved relations between Catholics and Protestants.
B the formation of new religious orders.
~~**C** the creation of the Lutheran Church.~~
D all of the above.

4 You can eliminate option **C** if you recall that the Lutheran Church was a result of the *Protestant* Reformation.

4. Which of the following accurately describes Renaissance art?

A Renaissance art never focused on individuals.
B Renaissance art always had a religious theme.
C Renaissance artists rarely created sculptures.
D Renaissance paintings used a technique known as perspective.

5 Absolute words such as *always, never, all, none,* and *every* often signal an incorrect option.

Answers: 1 (A), 2 (D), 3 (B), 4 (D)

Historical Sources

Often, test questions will include historical sources in order to assess your ability to analyze documents or images. **Historical sources** are written or visual sources that tell us about important events or people in history. Historical sources can be primary-source documents created by people present at historical events or during a historical time period, or secondary sources created after an event by a person who was not present. Use the strategies below to answer questions using historical sources.

LEARN

1 Briefly examine the historical source and the questions that accompany it.
Look at the title and skim the source to identify the subject. Then read the questions to help you understand what information to focus on.

2 Examine the source carefully.
Take note of when the source was created and by whom. Look for key events, persons, or other details that provide information about the subject.

3 Study the source to determine its purpose and point of view.
Look for clues that might indicate why the source was created. Was it intended to create a reaction in the audience? Is it for informational purposes?

4 Re-read the questions that accompany the historical source and review the source to find the answers.

Answers: 1 (B), 2 (C)

1

Ferdinand Magellan

Magellan's greatness stands out, despite all attempts to disparage him. He not only had the gift of making the right decision at the right time; he was able to outwit enemies who were plotting to kill him, and to keep the loyalty of his men. And, as the Portuguese sailor who wrote the Leiden Narrative recorded, he was "an industrious man, and never rested," the kind of sea captain who slept little and woke at a moment's notice for anything like a change of wind. As a mariner and navigator he was unsurpassed; and although he did not live to complete the greatest voyage of discovery in the world's history, he planned it, and discovered the "Strait that shall forever bear his name," as well as the Marianas and the Philippines where no European had touched before.

—Samuel Eliot Morison, *The European Discovery of America: The Southern Voyages,* 1974, p. 320

2 These words indicate that the author thought highly of Magellan.

2

1. Which of the following correctly identifies an accomplishment of Ferdinand Magellan?

A He wrote the Leiden Narrative.

B He was the first European to reach the Marianas and the Philippines.

C He was the greatest explorer who ever lived.

D He discovered a sea route from Europe to Asia.

4

2. What is the author's point of view toward the subject?

A The author believes that Magellan's voyage was not very important in world history.

B He thinks that Europeans were wrong to colonize the Americas.

C The author thinks highly of Ferdinand Magellan.

D He believes that Magellan was a better sailor than Columbus

Political Cartoons

Another common type of test question asks you to analyze a political cartoon. **Political cartoons** are primary sources that use images and symbols to make a point about political figures or issues. Because cartoons often provide insight into the opinions and values of a historical period, exams use political cartoons to test your knowledge of a particular period. Use the strategies below to answer test questions that deal with political cartoons.

LEARN

1 Identify the cartoon's subject.
Read the cartoon's title and caption to help determine its subject. Information that indicates when the cartoon was created can also help you identify the subject matter.

2 Interpret symbols and images used in the cartoon.
Political cartoons often use symbols to express ideas. For example, an olive branch might represent the idea of peace. Exaggerated images or facial expressions often indicate emotions.

3 Determine the cartoonist's point of view.
Examine the cartoon to understand what point the artist is trying to make. Recognize whether the subject is portrayed positively or negatively. Does the cartoonist agree or disagree with the issue?

4 Read the questions carefully and study the political cartoon to find the answers.

Taille, Impots et Corvee (Tithes, Taxes, and Labor), France late 1700s

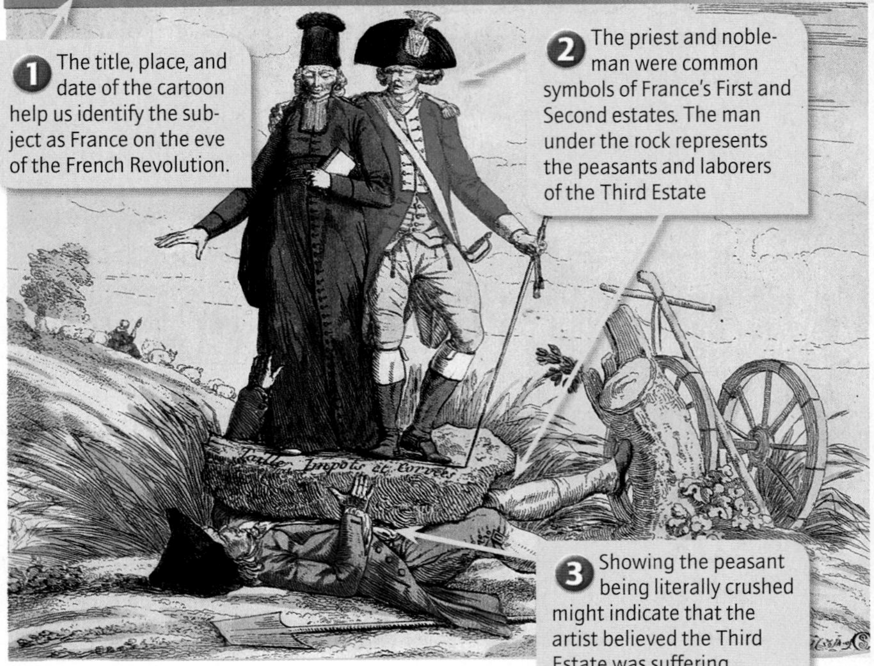

1 The title, place, and date of the cartoon help us identify the subject as France on the eve of the French Revolution.
2 The priest and nobleman were common symbols of France's First and Second estates. The man under the rock represents the peasants and laborers of the Third Estate
3 Showing the peasant being literally crushed might indicate that the artist believed the Third Estate was suffering.

4 **1.** The cartoon likely represents
- **A** France's economic difficulties under King Louis XVI.
- **B** religious disagreements that led to the French Revolution.
- **C** political reasons for Napoleon's rise to power.
- **D** social problems before the French Revolution.

2. What point is the artist most likely trying to make in this cartoon?
- **A** The First and Second estates oppress the Third Estate.
- **B** The First and Second estates share their wealth with the Third Estate.
- **C** Members of the Third Estate should not pay their taxes.
- **D** The three estates should work together to solve the country's economic problems.

Answers: 1 (D), 2 (A)

Line and Bar Graphs

Other test questions assess your ability to read graphs. Graphs are used to show statistical or numerical information in a visual way. **Line graphs** illustrate how quantities and trends change over time. **Bar graphs** compare groups of numbers within categories and sometimes show change over time. Use the strategies below to answer questions that cover line and bar graphs.

LEARN

1. **Read the title of the graph to determine its main idea**
2. **Read the questions that accompany the graph.**
   Reading the questions first will help you focus in on the most important part of the graph.
3. **Study the label on the vertical axis.**
   The vertical axis generally indicates what the graph measures.
4. **Examine the label on the horizontal axis.**
   The horizontal axis usually tells you the time period the graph covers.
5. **Read any legends or additional labels on the graph.**
   Legends and additional labels provide information about what the colors, patterns, or symbols on the graph mean.
6. **Identify any trends or patterns that the graph reveals.**
7. **Re-read the questions and review the graph to find the answers.**

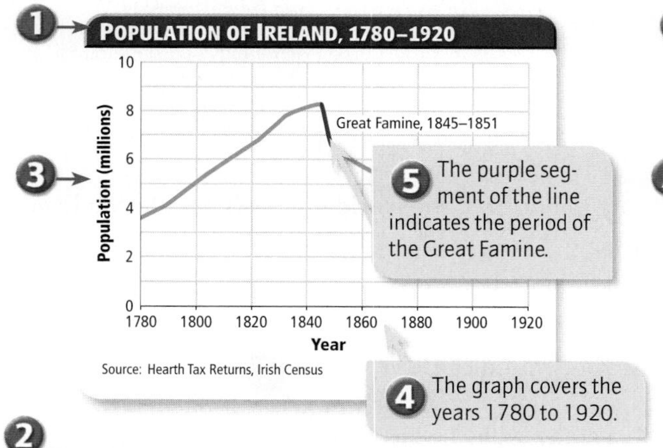

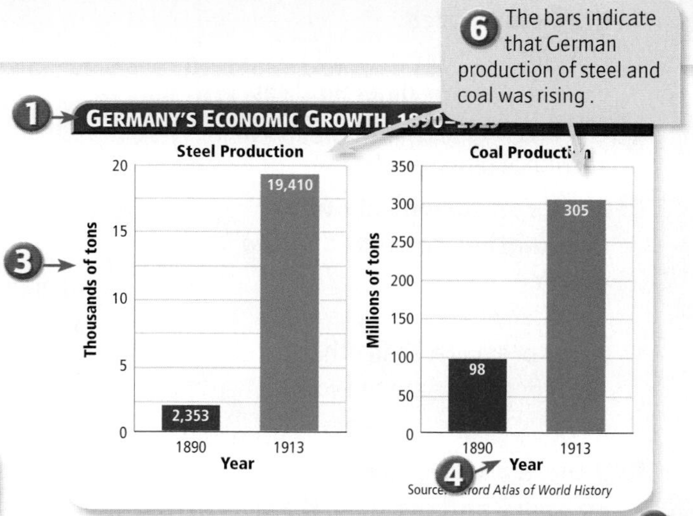

2

1. Which statement *best* summarizes the information in the line graph?

A The Irish population declined dramatically around 1900.

B The population of Ireland has always been smaller than that of Great Britain.

C Ireland's population increased dramatically as a result of the Industrial Revolution.

D After years of population growth, the Irish population declined rapidly around the time of the Great Famine.

2

2. According to the graphs, between 1890 and 1913, Germany's

A coal production declined as a result of the Great Depression.

B steel production and coal production both experienced dramatic increases.

C coal production declined, while steel production increased.

D. economy was relatively stable.

Answers: 1 (D), 2 (B)

Pie Graphs

Some tests include questions that require you to interpret information in pie graphs. A **pie graph** shows how parts are related to a whole. Slices of a pie graph should add up to 100% and are proportional to the percentage each represents. Sometimes exams will have two pie graphs side by side in order to show a comparison. Use the strategies below to answer questions about pie graphs.

LEARN

1. **Read the title of the graph to learn the topic and time period it covers.**
2. **Read the questions that accompany the pie graph.** Reading the questions first will help you focus in on the most important aspect of the graph.
3. **Identify the different "slices" into which the pie graph is divided.** Look for a legend or labels to explain what the different slices represent. What percentage does each slice represent?
4. **Draw conclusions about the information presented in the graph.** Consider why some slices are larger or smaller than others. What does the data tell you about the topic of the graph?
5. **If there are two graphs, compare and contrast them to identify and understand trends.**
6. **Re-read the questions and review the graph to find the answers.**

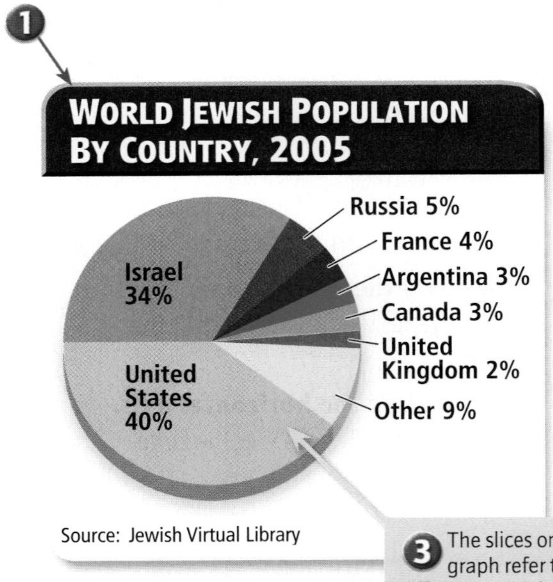

3 The slices on this graph refer to the different countries around the world where Jews lived in 2005.

2

1. In 2005 the majority of the world's Jewish population lived
- **A** in Europe.
- **B** in Israel.
- **C** outside Israel.
- **D** outside the United States.

4

2. Which of the following conclusions can accurately be drawn from the graph above?
- **A** In 2005 Jews lived in many different parts of the world.
- **B** Jews make up the largest religious group in Israel today.
- **C** A large number of Jews lived in Europe in 2005.
- **D** In 2005 Judaism was the third largest religion in the world.

Answers: 1 (C), 2 (A)

Political and Thematic Maps

Questions asking you to interpret maps frequently appear on tests. **Political maps** show countries and the political divisions within them. They may also highlight physical features such as mountains or bodies of water. **Thematic maps** focus on a specific topic and often show patterns of movement, distribution of resources, or location of events. Special symbols, such as icons or arrows, are often used on thematic maps. Use the strategies below to answer questions about political and thematic maps.

LEARN

1 Identify the map's subject and read the questions that accompany the map.
The map's title will often indicate the subject. Reading the questions will help you identify information you need to focus on.

2 Study the map legend.
The legend will help you identify what the different colors and symbols mean. These can give you details about the purpose of the map.

3 Examine the map's compass rose and scale.
The compass rose can help you determine direction, while the scale can help you estimate the distance between two places.

4 Study the information provided on the map.
Read all the labels and study the other information, such as colors, borders, or symbols.

5 Re-read the questions carefully and review the map to find the answers.

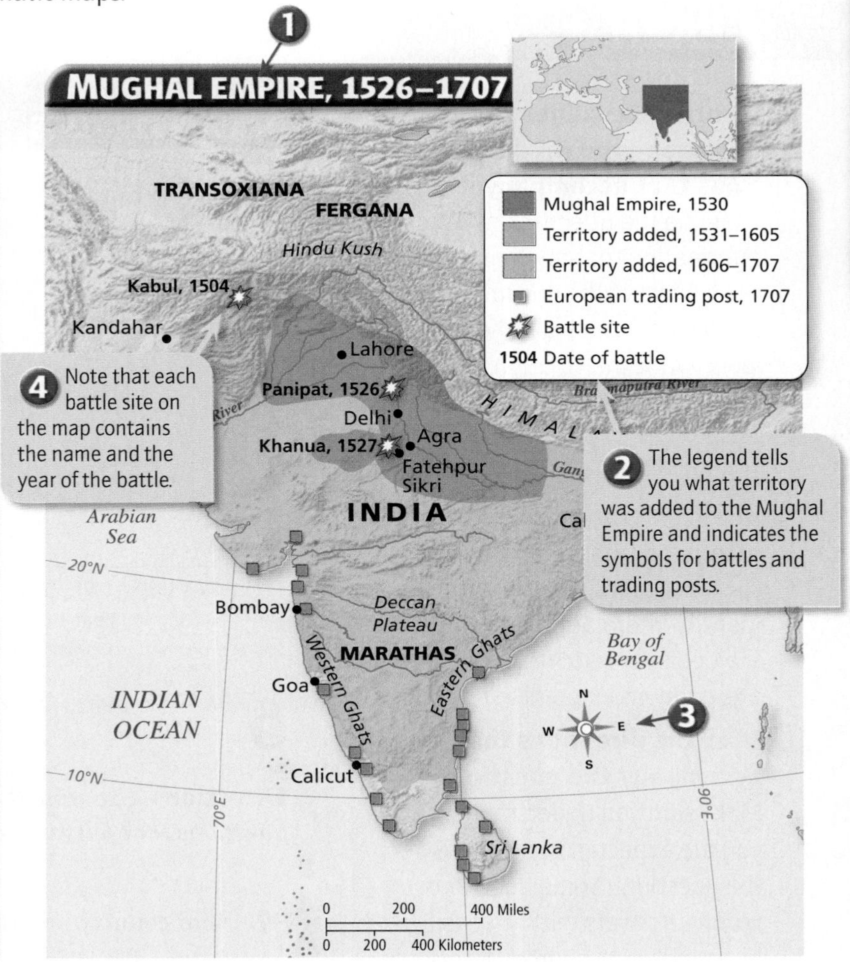

1. In 1530 the Mughal Empire was centered
   A around coastal cities.
   B in the Himalayas.
   C in northern India.
   D in southern India.

2. Why might European trading posts have been located along India's coasts?
   A to be close to valuable natural resources
   B to be near shipping routes
   C to be protected from invaders
   D to be nearby large cities

Answers: 1 (C), 2 (B)

Constructed Response

Some tests include constructed-response questions. **Constructed-response** questions ask you to interpret a source and answer open-ended, short-answer questions. Unlike multiple-choice questions, the answers are not given. You have to construct them. Use the strategies below to answer constructed-response questions.

LEARN

1 Identify the subject of the document and read the questions that accompany it. Examine the title and any other information that might indicate the subject of the document. Reading the questions help you identify the information you need to focus on.

2 Study the document carefully. Documents can include written excerpts, graphs, charts, political cartoons, maps, or other visuals. Identify information presented in the document such as facts, figure, opinions, or points of view.

3 Read the directions that accompany the questions. Make sure you understand what you are expected to do to answer the questions. Some questions require answers that can easily be found in the source. Others ask you to connect pieces of information from different parts of the source. Others may require you to make inferences using information not in the source.

4 Re-read the questions and then use the document and your knowledge of the subject to find the answers.

5 Write your answers. Use the space provided to write your answers to each question.

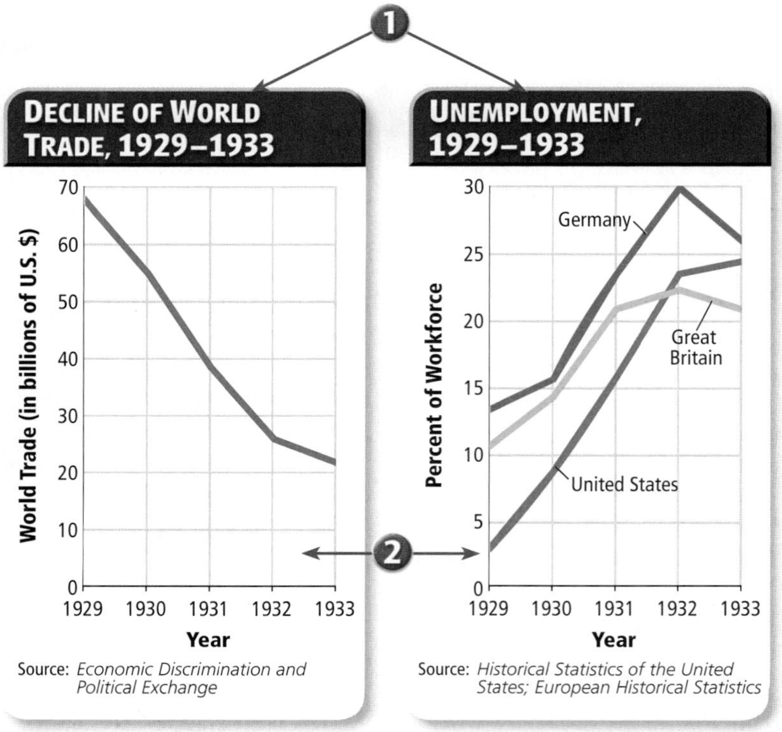

Source: *Economic Discrimination and Political Exchange*

Source: *Historical Statistics of the United States; European Historical Statistics*

3

Directions *Examine the line graphs carefully and answer the questions that follow in complete sentences.*

1. What country had the highest unemployment rate between 1929 and 1933?

Germany had the highest unemployment rate.

4 **2.** How might the decline in world trade have affected the unemployment rate?

The drop in world trade could have caused a decline in the number of available jobs. 5

3. What caused the decline of world trade and the rise of unemployment rates?

The Great Depression caused world trade to decline and unemployment rates to rise.

Extended Response

Extended-response questions are similar to constructed-response questions in that they ask you to analyze information presented in a document such as a chart, graph, or map and then to write a response. Extended-response answers, however, usually consist of a paragraph or essay. You will be assessed partly on your ability to write a coherent, grammatically correct response. In addition to your interpretation and analysis of the document, your answer should also include some prior knowledge of the topic.

To analyze and interpret the document, use the strategies you have already learned. To answer the question, use the strategies below.

LEARN

1. **Read the directions and question carefully to determine the purpose of your answer.** Be clear about what the question is asking you to do.
2. **Identify the subject and purpose of the document.** Examine the title, labels, and other details that can indicate a document's subject and purpose.
3. **Study the document carefully.** Read the text and note facts or details that might help you answer the question.
4. **Use the question and your notes to create a topic sentence.** Questions often point towards an effective topic sentence. However, avoid simply restating the question as a sentence.
5. **Develop an outline or graphic organizer to help organize your main points.**
6. **Write your answer in complete sentences.** Start with your topic sentence. Then refer to your outline as you write. Be sure to use correct grammar, spelling, and punctuation.

2

MAJOR TRADE ORGANIZATIONS AND AGREEMENTS

QUICK FACTS

ORGANIZATION [date formed]	Members (in 2006) and goals
General Agreement on Tariffs and Trade (GATT) [1948]	125 members (in 1995); worked to reduce tariffs and other international trade barriers; replaced by WTO
World Trade Organization (WTO) [1995]	Nearly 150 members; promotes lower trade barriers
Group of Eight (G-8) [1975, as G-6]	8 major industrial democracies; discuss international economic, environmental, and other issues
Organization of Petroleum Exporting Countries (OPEC) [1960]	11 major oil exporting countries, most in Middle East; coordinate oil policies of members
European Union (EU) [1993]	25 European nations; work for European economic and political integration

3

5 Use facts and examples from the document to help support your answer.

1

Directions *Use the table and your knowledge of world trade to write an essay that answers the question below.*

1. How have regional and international trade organizations affected world trade? What are the advantages and disadvantages of such organizations?

For the most part, international trade organizations have served to boost world trade. Some organizations, like the GATT were created to boost trade. Others, like OPEC, were created to strict oil sales of its members so that each will receive a high price for their products.

Document-Based Questions

Document-based questions ask you to analyze written and visual documents. Document-based questions usually consist of two parts. The first part asks short-answer questions about each document. The second part asks students to use their answers and information from the documents to produce an essay on a given topic. Use the strategies below to answer document-based questions.

LEARN

1. **Read the Historical Context information carefully.** This section will help you understand the background of the issue and documents that you will read.
2. **Review the Task information.** The task provides you with directions for answering the document-based question.
3. **Read the essay question carefully.** Be sure to pay attention to what the question is asking you to do.
4. **Skim each of the documents in Part A.** Briefly examine each document to get an idea of the issues it presents. Only two documents are shown here. Typically, document-based questions involve between four and eight documents.
5. **Carefully examine and study each document.** Look for points that might help you answer the essay question. If you are allowed to mark up the exam, underline or otherwise identify key points. You may also want to make notes in the margin.

1

Historical Context In 1917 the United States was debating whether or not to enter World War I, then raging in its third year in Europe. There was strong sentiment to maintain neutrality.

2

Task Using information from the documents and your knowledge of world history, answer the questions that follow each document in Part A. Your answers to the questions will help you write the Part B essay, in which you will be asked to:

Discuss the positions both pro and con for United States entry into World War I and describe the eventual course of events.

3 In this case, the question asks about United States neutrality in World War I.

Part A: Short-Answer Questions

Study each document carefully. Then answer the question or questions that follow each document in the space provided.

DOCUMENT 1

4

16 January 1917
"We intend to begin unrestricted submarine warfare on the first of February. We shall endeavor in spite of this to keep the United States neutral. In the event of this not succeeding, we make Mexico a proposal of an alliance on the following basis: Make war together, make peace together, generous financial support, and an understanding on our part that Mexico is to reconquer the lost territory in Texas, New Mexico, and Arizona...."

Zimmermann

5

1. What did the Zimmermann telegram propose to Mexico?
The Zimmermann telegram proposed that Mexico join in an alliance with Germany against the United States.

DOCUMENT 2

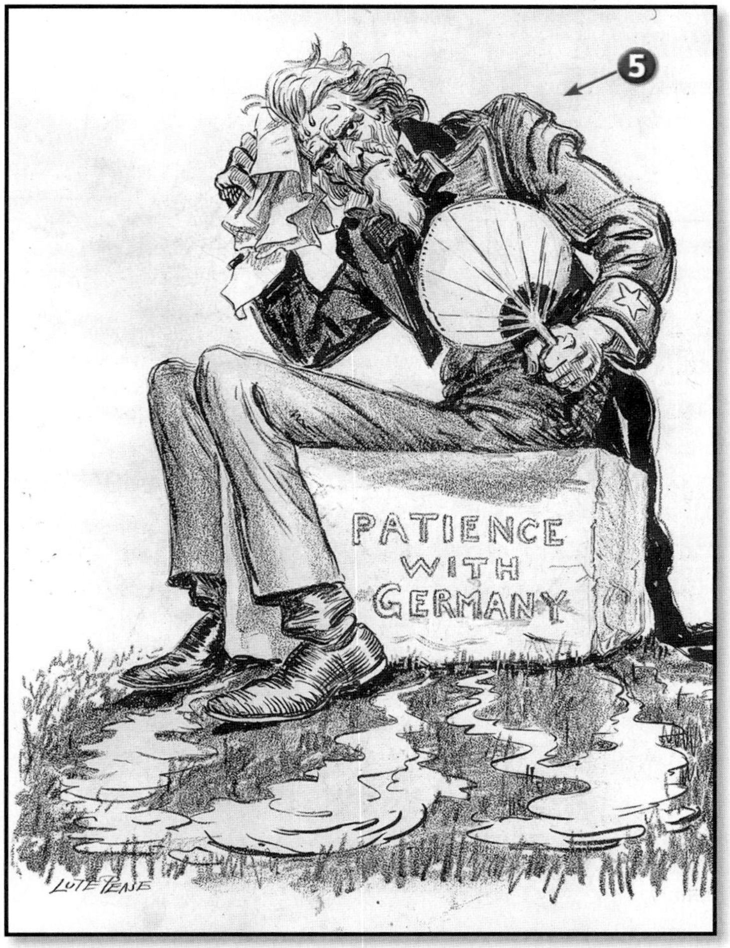

6

2. What point about United States neutrality in World War I is this political cartoon attempting to make?

It makes the point that American patience is wearing thin.

Part B: Essay

9

Using information from the documents and your knowledge of world history, write a well-organized essay recounting the debate over the United States's policy of neutrality in World War I and the events that altered that policy.

6 **Read and answer each of the document-specific questions.** As you answer the questions, think about how each connects to the essay topic.

7 **Return to the essay question to help you form a topic sentence or thesis.**

8 **Create an outline or graphic organizer to help organize your main points.** Review the document and any notes you made to find examples to support your points.

9 **Write your essay.** Include an introductory paragraph that frames your argument, a main body with details that explain it, and a closing paragraph that summarizes your position. Include specific details or documents to support your ideas.

Preparing for Standardized Tests

COUNTDOWN TO TESTING

Everyone wants to ace the big test, but doing well takes preparation and practice. *Holt World History: Human Legacy: The Modern Era* provides many opportunities for you to prepare for standardized tests.

Countdown to Testing

The Countdown to Testing section will help you study and prepare during the weeks before your test.

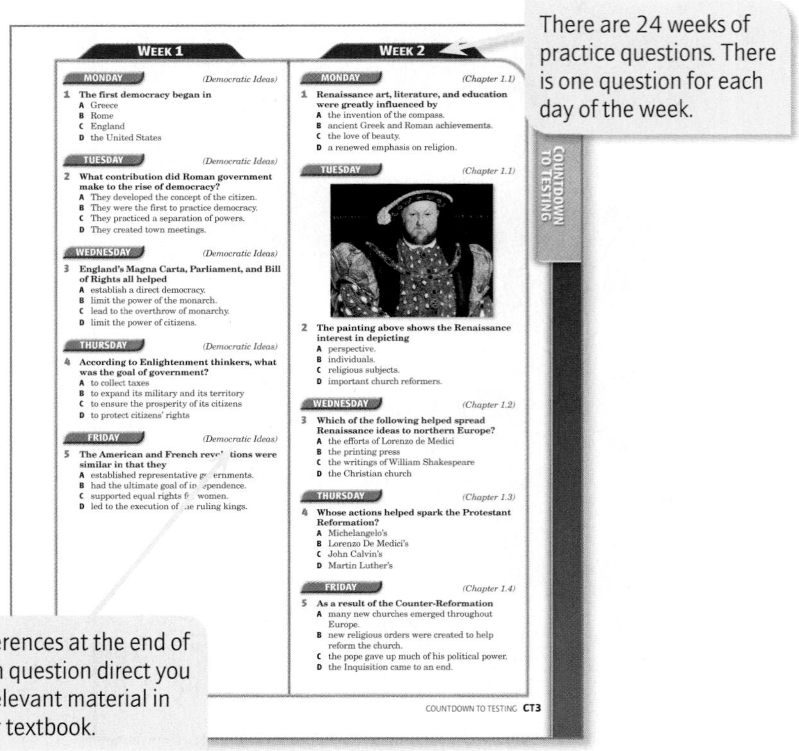

There are 24 weeks of practice questions. There is one question for each day of the week.
References at the end of each question direct you to relevant material in your textbook.

WEEK 1

MONDAY (Democratic Ideas)

1 The first democracy began in
A Greece
B Rome
C England
D the United States

TUESDAY (Democratic Ideas)

2 What contribution did Roman government make to the rise of democracy?
A They developed the concept of the citizen.
B They were the first to practice democracy.
C They practiced a separation of powers.
D They created town meetings.

WEDNESDAY (Democratic Ideas)

3 England's Magna Carta, Parliament, and Bill of Rights all helped
A establish a direct democracy.
B limit the power of the monarch.
C lead to the overthrow of monarchy.
D limit the power of citizens.

THURSDAY (Democratic Ideas)

4 According to Enlightenment thinkers, what was the goal of government?
A to collect taxes
B to expand its military and its territory
C to ensure the prosperity of its citizens
D to protect citizens' rights

FRIDAY (Democratic Ideas)

5 The American and French revolutions were similar in that they
A established representative governments.
B had the ultimate goal of independence.
C supported equal rights for women.
D led to the execution of the ruling kings.

WEEK 2

MONDAY (Chapter 1.1)

1 Renaissance art, literature, and education were greatly influenced by
A the invention of the compass.
B ancient Greek and Roman achievements.
C the love of beauty.
D a renewed emphasis on religion.

TUESDAY (Chapter 1.1)

2 The painting above shows the Renaissance interest in depicting
A perspective.
B individuals.
C religious subjects.
D important church reformers.

WEDNESDAY (Chapter 1.2)

3 Which of the following helped spread Renaissance ideas to northern Europe?
A the efforts of Lorenzo de Medici
B the printing press
C the writings of William Shakespeare
D the Christian church

THURSDAY (Chapter 1.3)

4 Whose actions helped spark the Protestant Reformation?
A Michelangelo's
B Lorenzo De Medici's
C John Calvin's
D Martin Luther's

FRIDAY (Chapter 1.4)

5 As a result of the Counter-Reformation
A many new churches emerged throughout Europe.
B new religious orders were created to help reform the church.
C the pope gave up much of his political power.
D the Inquisition came to an end.

COUNTDOWN TO TESTING CT3

Other Test Prep and Practice

Other opportunities to prepare and practice for the test include:

- Test-Taking Strategies Handbook in the Student Edition
- Unit-level Standardized Test Practice in the Student Edition
- *Test Preparation Workbook*

Test-Taking Tips

- **Use the Countdown to Testing questions to help you prepare.** Spend a few minutes every day answering that day's question.
- **Get plenty of sleep the night before the test.** A rested mind thinks more clearly and will help you focus during the test.
- **Arrive at the test prepared.** Remember your pencil and eraser and anything else you may need on test day.
- **Read each question carefully.** Be sure you know exactly what the question is asking.
- **Answer the easy questions first.** If you don't know the answer to a question, skip it and come back to it later.
- **Review your answers.** Before handing in your test, take a minute to look over your answers.

WEEK 1

MONDAY *(Democratic Ideas)*

1 The first democracy began in
- (A) Greece
- B Rome
- C England
- D the United States

TUESDAY *(Democratic Ideas)*

2 What contribution did Roman government make to the rise of democracy?
- A They developed the concept of the citizen.
- B They were the first to practice democracy.
- (C) They practiced a separation of powers.
- D They created town meetings.

WEDNESDAY *(Democratic Ideas)*

3 England's Magna Carta, Parliament, and Bill of Rights all helped
- A establish a direct democracy.
- (B) limit the power of the monarch.
- C lead to the overthrow of monarchy.
- D limit the power of citizens.

THURSDAY *(Democratic Ideas)*

4 According to Enlightenment thinkers, what was the goal of government?
- A to collect taxes
- B to expand its military and its territory
- C to ensure the prosperity of its citizens
- (D) to protect citizens' rights

FRIDAY *(Democratic Ideas)*

5 The American and French revolutions were similar in that they
- (A) established representative governments.
- B had the ultimate goal of independence.
- C supported equal rights for women.
- D led to the execution of the ruling kings.

WEEK 2

MONDAY *(Chapter 1.1)*

1 Renaissance art, literature, and education were greatly influenced by
- A the invention of the compass.
- (B) ancient Greek and Roman achievements.
- C the love of beauty.
- D a renewed emphasis on religion.

TUESDAY *(Chapter 1.1)*

2 The painting above shows the Renaissance interest in depicting
- A perspective.
- (B) individuals.
- C religious subjects.
- D important church reformers.

WEDNESDAY *(Chapter 1.2)*

3 Which of the following helped spread Renaissance ideas to northern Europe?
- A the efforts of Lorenzo de Medici
- (B) the printing press
- C the writings of William Shakespeare
- D the Christian church

THURSDAY *(Chapter 1.3)*

4 Whose actions helped spark the Protestant Reformation?
- A Michelangelo's
- B Lorenzo De Medici's
- C John Calvin's
- (D) Martin Luther's

FRIDAY *(Chapter 1.4)*

5 As a result of the Counter-Reformation
- A many new churches emerged throughout Europe.
- (B) new religious orders were created to help reform the church.
- C the pope gave up much of his political power.
- D the Inquisition came to an end.

WEEK 3

MONDAY (Chapter 2.1)

1 Which of the following was a cause of European overseas exploration?

- (A) the desire to spread Christianity
- B the need for more land for Europe's growing population
- C the lack of resources in Europe
- D the drive to compete with Chinese explorers

TUESDAY (Chapter 2.1)

2 Which of the following correctly identifies the European explorer with his key contribution?

- A Christopher Columbus—circumnavigated the world
- B Ferdinand Magellan—first European to reach Africa's Cape of Good Hope
- (C) Vasco da Gama—discovered a sea route to India
- D Bartolomeu Dias—first European to explore South America

WEDNESDAY (Chapter 2.3)

3 What impact did the Columbian Exchange have on life in the Americas?

- A Thousands of farmers in the Americas were left without lands to farm.
- B Population in the Americas boomed as a result of the introduction of new foods.
- (C) European diseases devastated the Native American population.
- D Native empires were overthrown in the search for gold.

THURSDAY (Chapter 2.4)

4 Which of the following explains the rise of slavery in the American colonies?

- (A) the need for a labor force to work plantations
- B the desire to convert Africans to Christianity
- C the lack of permanent settlers
- D the need for soldiers to defeat the Native Americans

FRIDAY (Chapter 2.3)

5 What role did mercantilism play in the establishment of colonial empires?

- A Mercantilism proposed that overcrowded countries seek new lands for colonies.
- B Mercantilism promoted the establishment of the slave trade.
- C Mercantilism supported the spread of Christianity to all parts of the world.
- (D) Mercantilism encouraged countries to seek out colonies for sources of wealth and new markets.

WEEK 4

MONDAY (Chapter 3.1)

1 In the 1300s what Muslim empire expanded into Europe?

- (A) the Ottoman Empire
- B the Safavid Empire
- C the Mughal Empire
- D the Ming Empire

TUESDAY (Chapter 3.2)

2 By the 1500s Muslim empires controlled all of the following regions except

- A the Byzantine Empire.
- B India.
- (C) Japan.
- D Persia.

WEDNESDAY (Chapter 3.3)

3 Under what dynasty did China expand to its largest size?

- A Ming
- (B) Qin
- C Tokugawa
- D Yuan

THURSDAY (Chapter 3.3)

> **"From the third year of Yongle till now we have seven times received the commission of ambassadors to countries of the western ocean . . . We have set eyes on barbarian regions far away."**
>
> —from a Chinese inscription dated to 1431

4 The quote above most likely describes the

- A establishment of the Ming dynasty.
- B Warring States period in Japan.
- C conquest of China by the Manchus.
- (D) voyages of Zheng He.

FRIDAY (Chapter 3.4)

5 Japanese feudalism was similar to European feudalism in that it featured

- A a code of ethics for samurai to follow.
- B a powerful central authority.
- C a class of professional warriors who governed.
- (D) an exchange of land between lords and vassals.

WEEK 5

MONDAY *(Chapter 4.1)*

1 Under the rule of Phillip II, Spain reached the peak of its wealth and power. What was the main source of Spain's wealth?
- **A** gold found by the Spanish Armada
- **B** taxes from citizens of its vast empire
- **(C)** riches from its American colonies
- **D** valuable trade with the Netherlands

TUESDAY *(Chapter 4.2)*

2 King Louis XIV's famous quote, "I am the state," best expresses
- **A** his dislike of Protestants.
- **B** the great wealth of Russia.
- **(C)** the idea of absolute monarchy.
- **D** his desire to expand his empire.

WEDNESDAY *(Chapter 4.2, 4.4)*

3 Which of the following is a similarity between Louis XIV and Peter the Great?
- **(A)** They both fought wars to expand their empires.
- **B** They both made efforts to westernize their empires.
- **C** They both believed the people should have a say in government.
- **D** They both ruled with the help of the pope.

THURSDAY *(Chapter 4.3)*

4 The English Bill of Rights is an important document because it
- **A** sparked the English Civil War.
- **(B)** limited the power of the monarch.
- **C** restored the English monarch to power.
- **D** created the first English Parliament.

FRIDAY *(Chapter 4.4)*

5 Which of the following is an example of the absolute rule of Peter the Great?
- **A** building an impressive castle at Versailles
- **B** granting the people the right to vote
- **C** traveling through Europe in disguise
- **(D)** gaining control of the Russian Orthodox Church

WEEK 6

MONDAY *(Chapter 5.1)*

1 Which of the following is *not* a part of the scientific method?
- **(A)** form a conclusion prior to testing
- **B** form a hypothesis that can be tested
- **C** perform experiments to test the hypothesis
- **D** analyze the results to form a conclusion that either proves or disproves the hypothesis

TUESDAY *(Chapter 5.1)*

2 What contribution did Nicolaus Copernicus make to the Scientific Revolution?
- **A** He concluded that the earth is the center of the universe.
- **B** He invented the microscope.
- **C** He developed the scientific method.
- **(D)** He theorized that the earth revolves around the sun.

WEDNESDAY *(Chapter 5.1)*

3 Which of the following was a characteristic of the Scientific Revolution?
- **A** the Inquisition
- **(B)** the belief in progress and the power of reason
- **C** the development of mass transportation systems
- **D** a growing desire to explore unknown parts of the world

THURSDAY *(Chapter 5.2)*

4 Which Enlightenment thinker argued that absolute monarchy was the best form of government?
- **A** Adam Smith
- **B** John Locke
- **(C)** Thomas Hobbes
- **D** Baron de Montesquieu

FRIDAY *(Chapter 5.3)*

5 How did the American Revolution express the ideals of the Enlightenment?
- **A** American Patriots supported absolute monarchy.
- **(B)** Colonists revolted against a government that failed to protect their rights.
- **C** The Patriots wanted to establish a direct democracy.
- **D** The new American government granted equal rights to women.

WEEK 7

MONDAY *(Chapter 6.1)*

1 **Which of the following was a key cause of the French Revolution?**
- A the desire for independence
- B dissatisfaction with the pope's power
- C the desire for equal rights for women
- (D) social inequalities

TUESDAY *(Chapter 6.1)*

2 **What type of government did the National Assembly establish at the beginning of the French Revolution?**
- (A) constitutional monarchy
- B absolute monarchy
- C representative government
- D dictatorship

WEDNESDAY *(Chapters 4.3, 6.2)*

3 **How did England's Glorious Revolution differ from the French Revolution?**
- A It established a British empire.
- B It created a representative government.
- C It led to the execution of the British monarch.
- (D) It was generally nonviolent.

THURSDAY *(Chapters 5.3, 6.2)*

4 **One similarity between the French and American revolutions was that they both**
- A led to a period of terror and violence.
- B resulted in the execution of the monarch.
- (C) asserted basic rights and freedoms of citizens.
- D led to the establishment of constitutional monarchies.

FRIDAY *(Chapter 6.2)*

5 **Following the Reign of Terror, the French government was controlled by**
- A Napoleon Bonaparte.
- (B) a weak and inefficient Directory.
- C the Jacobins.
- D a king.

WEEK 8

MONDAY *(Chapter 6.3)*

1 **Why might the French people have been willing to support the rule of Napoleon?**
- (A) They wanted a strong ruler who could restore order.
- B They hoped he would restore the king to power.
- C They believed Napoleon could build a powerful empire.
- D They wanted to revive the radical ideas of the Revolution.

TUESDAY *(Chapter 6.3)*

2 **As a result of Napoleon's rule,**
- A France industrialized.
- B Russia became a major world power.
- C British-French relations improved.
- (D) nationalism spread throughout Europe.

WEDNESDAY *(Chapter 6.3)*

3 **All of the following were reforms Napoleon enacted to strengthen France *except***
- A the creation of a national bank to regulate the economy.
- B the development of a uniform legal code.
- (C) the introduction of freedom of the press.
- D the establishment of a network of public schools.

THURSDAY *(Chapter 6.4)*

4 **What is the cartoon above *most likely* saying about Napoleon's grip on power?**
- A He controls everything with an iron fist.
- (B) He is on the verge of losing control.
- C He has no interest in gaining more power.
- D He chooses to give his power to other leaders.

FRIDAY *(Chapter 6.4)*

5 **Which of the following was a result of the Congress of Vienna?**
- A It established democratic governments throughout Europe.
- (B) It restored monarchies to power in Europe.
- C It led to the downfall of Napoleon.
- D It created a powerful European Army.

WEEK 9

MONDAY
(Chapter 7.1)

1 What factor explains Great Britain's industrialization?

- **A** improvements in social equality
- **(B)** growth of private investment
- **C** increasing political instability
- **D** expansion of cottage industries

TUESDAY
(Chapter 7.1)

2 The factors of production are

- **A** education, industrialization, and economics.
- **B** resources and industry.
- **(C)** land, labor, and capital.
- **D** transportation, communication, and investment.

WEDNESDAY
(Chapter 7.2)

3 Which of the following *most likely* explains the rise of labor unions?

- **A** Factory owners wanted better-trained workers.
- **B** Governments began regulating businesses.
- **C** The need for more workers was increasing.
- **(D)** Workers wanted their interests heard.

THURSDAY
(Chapter 7.2)

4 Which of the following was an effect of mass production?

- **(A)** More goods were available at lower prices.
- **B** Labor unions organized for the first time.
- **C** Fewer workers were available for factory jobs.
- **D** The demand for workers increased greatly.

FRIDAY
(Chapter 7.3)

5 Which statement describes a market economy?

- **A** Strict regulations govern businesses.
- **(B)** Businesses are free to compete for trade.
- **C** The government dictates what factories will produce.
- **D** Skilled workers are in high demand.

WEEK 10

MONDAY
(Chapter 7.3)

1 In contrast to capitalism, socialism proposed that

- **A** there should be no industry.
- **B** businesses and individuals should own and control industry.
- **(C)** society or the government should own and control industry.
- **D** the workers should own and control industry.

TUESDAY
(Chapter 8.1)

2 What contribution did Thomas Edison make to the Industrial Revolution?

- **A** He invented the telegraph.
- **B** He developed the Bessemer process.
- **(C)** He invented the first practical lightbulb.
- **D** He discovered electricity.

WEDNESDAY
(Chapter 8.2)

3 Who developed new techniques to help prevent diseases?

- **A** Albert Einstein
- **(B)** Louis Pasteur
- **C** Marie Curie
- **D** Eli Whitney

THURSDAY
(Chapter 8.3)

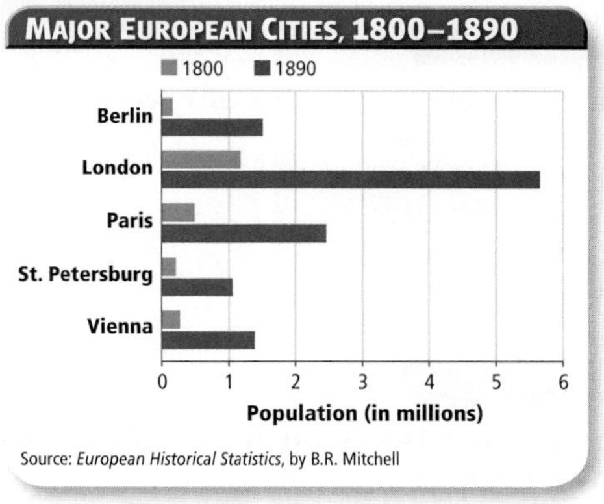

4 Between 1800 and 1890 the population of London grew by approximately

- **A** 1 million.
- **B** 2.5 million.
- **C** 3 million.
- **(D)** 4.5 million.

FRIDAY
(Chapter 8.3)

5 Romanticism emerged in response to the

- **(A)** abuses of the Industrial Revolution.
- **B** growth of cities.
- **C** development of powerful empires.
- **D** emergence of capitalism.

COUNTDOWN TO TESTING

WEEK 11

MONDAY (Chapter 9.1)

1 How did industrialization lead to reform movements?
- **A** Factory owners called for economic reforms.
- **B** The lack of industrialization in some industries led to a call for change.
- **(C)** The increased prosperity of factory workers and middle-class citizens led them to demand political change.
- **D** Industrialization did not affect the reform movement.

TUESDAY (Chapter 9.1, 9.2)

2 All of the following were reform movements in the mid-1800s *except*
- **A** organizing trade unions.
- **(B)** ending corruption among the clergy.
- **C** women's suffrage.
- **D** universal manhood suffrage.

WEDNESDAY (Chapter 9.3)

3 Unlike the French revolutions of the 1800s, the revolutions in Latin America sought
- **(A)** independence.
- **B** a return to absolute monarchy.
- **C** Communist government.
- **D** improvements in factory conditions.

THURSDAY (Chapter 9.3)

4 Who was the key leader of revolutions in South America?
- **A** Louis Napoleon
- **B** Miguel Hidalgo
- **(C)** Simón Bolivar
- **D** Toussaint L'Ouverture

FRIDAY (Chapter 9.4)

5 The Monroe Doctrine declared that the United States
- **A** would purchase the Louisiana Territory.
- **B** would create an alliance with France.
- **C** had the right to expand throughout North America.
- **(D)** would oppose further efforts to colonize the Americas.

WEEK 12

MONDAY (Chapter 10.1)

> *"A Country is not a mere territory . . .[it] is the idea which rises upon that foundation; it is the sentiment of love, the sense of fellowship which binds together all the sons of that territory."*
>
> —Giuseppe Mazzini, from *Duties of Man*

1 What concept does Mazzini's quote illustrate?
- **A** independence
- **(B)** nationalism
- **C** natural rights
- **D** universal suffrage

TUESDAY (Chapter 10.1, 10.2)

2 Unification efforts in Italy and Germany were similar in that they both
- **(A)** brought together smaller states into one nation.
- **B** resulted in economic growth and prosperity.
- **C** created powerful democratic governments.
- **D** relied on help from the United States.

WEDNESDAY (Chapter 10.3)

3 What effect did nationalism have on ethnic groups in Austria-Hungary?
- **A** It sparked warfare among the various ethnic groups.
- **B** It led to the unification of Austrian ethnic groups.
- **(C)** It encouraged some groups to rise up against Austrian control.
- **D** It had little or no effect on them.

THURSDAY (Chapter 10.3)

4 The Ottoman Empire lost much of its remaining territory in Europe as a result of
- **(A)** the Balkan War.
- **B** the Revolutions of 1848.
- **C** the rise of the Young Turks.
- **D** war with Italy.

FRIDAY (Chapter 10.4)

5 Which of the following was a reform of Czar Alexander II?
- **A** He funded the construction of the Trans-Siberian railroad.
- **(B)** He freed the Russian serfs.
- **C** He established a constitutional monarchy.
- **D** He granted women the right to vote.

WEEK 13

MONDAY
(Chapter 11.1)

1 Great Britain's most valuable colony was
- A China.
- B Egypt.
- (C) India.
- D Vietnam.

TUESDAY
(Chapter 11.2)

2 What effect did the opening of foreign trade have on Japan?
- A It led to war between Japan and Great Britain.
- B It led to the establishment of democracy.
- C It created tensions between Japan and China.
- (D) It encouraged Japan to modernize.

WEDNESDAY
(Chapter 11.3)

3 By the late 1800s European nations were eager to expand their empires into Africa in order to
- (A) gain valuable natural resources.
- B help lower the cost of transportation.
- C weaken the growing power of the United States.
- D experiment with new forms of government.

THURSDAY
(Chapter 11.4)

4 In what part of the world did the United States exert its influence?
- A Africa
- (B) Latin America
- C China
- D Russia

FRIDAY
(Chapter 11.1, 11.2, 11.3)

5 Which of the following accurately describes a response of colonized peoples toward their colonizers?
- A Japanese troops rebelled against British rulers.
- B West African merchants boycotted European trade goods.
- (C) Anti-western Chinese led the Boxer Rebellion against foreigners.
- D Indian students staged violent protests against imperialism.

WEEK 14

MONDAY
(Chapter 12.1)

1 Which of the following explains why the great powers of Europe were drawn into war in 1914?
- A Many countries wanted to spread democracy.
- B Most countries wished to gain more territory.
- C Most countries wanted to prevent the spread of communism.
- (D) Many countries were fulfilling promises made to their allies.

TUESDAY
(Chapter 12.2)

2 All of the following were theaters of battle during World War I *except*
- A the Eastern Front.
- (B) the Baltic Campaign.
- C the Western Front.
- D the Gallipoli Campaign.

WEDNESDAY
(Chapter 12.2)

3 What event during the war raised concerns about human rights violations?
- A the use of machine guns
- (B) the Armenian Massacre
- C the Treaty of Versailles
- D the Battle of Verdun

THURSDAY
(Chapter 12.2)

4 The men in the photo have equipment to protect them from what new weapon?
- A airplanes
- B machine guns
- (C) poison gas
- D tanks

FRIDAY
(Chapter 12.2)

5 Which of the following is a characteristic of total war?
- (A) Governments tell factories what to produce.
- B Governments encourage full and uncensored coverage of the war in the news media.
- C Governments cut military spending.
- D Neutral nations sell weapons to countries on both sides of the war.

COUNTDOWN TO TESTING

COUNTDOWN TO TESTING

WEEK 15

MONDAY
(Chapter 12.3)

1 What effect did the Russian Revolution have on World War I?

- (A) It forced Russia to withdraw from the war.
- B It left Germany with no more allies.
- C It led to the defeat of Austria-Hungary.
- D It encouraged the United States to enter the war.

TUESDAY
(Chapter 12.3)

2 Why is Vladimir Lenin a significant figure in Russian history?

- A He created Russia's first legislative body.
- (B) He instituted a Communist regime in Russia.
- C He curbed the government's control of the Russian economy.
- D He was the commander of Russian forces in World War I.

WEDNESDAY
(Chapter 12.4)

3 How did the U.S. entry into World War I affect the course of the war?

- A It aided the Central Powers.
- B It led Germany to adopt unrestricted submarine warfare.
- C It helped President Wilson win reelection.
- (D) It tipped the balance in favor of the Allied Powers.

THURSDAY
(Chapter 12.4)

4 What was the main purpose of the Treaty of Versailles?

- A to ensure that another world war could not take place
- (B) to punish Germany for its role in the war
- C to punish Russia for withdrawing from the war
- D to reward the Unites States for entering the war

FRIDAY
(Chapter 12.4)

5 How did the end of World War I affect territories in the Middle East?

- (A) Former Ottoman lands were placed under European control.
- B The Ottoman Empire gained new lands.
- C Several new Jewish nations were created.
- D Europeans lost control of their Middle Eastern colonies.

WEEK 16

MONDAY
(Chapter 13.1)

1 After World War I nationalist movements in European colonies increased as a result of

- A the fear that colonists might be pulled into another costly war.
- B the lack of financial support from Europe.
- C the fear that European nations would demand more resources to rebuild after the war.
- (D) the colonists' belief that they had earned their freedom by fighting in the war.

TUESDAY
(Chapter 13.2)

2 Which of the following was a cause of the U.S. stock market crash in 1929?

- (A) increasing speculation in the stock market
- B economic troubles brought on by the high cost of maintaining colonies
- C government regulation of the economy
- D lack of confidence in the government

WEDNESDAY
(Chapter 13.4)

3 Which of the following tactics did Joseph Stalin use to further his plan for economic modernization?

- A He worked to improve political rights for women.
- B He loosened government control of industry.
- (C) He instituted a policy of collectivization of small farms.
- D He encouraged capitalist ideas and beliefs.

THURSDAY
(Chapter 13.3, 13.4)

4 During the 1930s how were Germany and Japan similar?

- A Both joined an alliance with the Soviet Union.
- B Both established colonies in the Pacific.
- C Both had Communist governments.
- (D) Both built up their military forces.

FRIDAY
(Chapter 13.4)

5 What factor played a key role in widespread disillusionment with Germany's post-World War I government?

- A lack of industrial growth
- B the spread of communism
- C lack of democratic reforms
- (D) economic crisis

WEEK 17

MONDAY

(Chapter 14.1)

1 Which of the following is an example of German aggression prior to World War II?

A Germany remained neutral.
B Germany reclaimed and militarized the Rhineland.
C Germany gave up control of Austria.
D Germany signed a treaty with Russia.

TUESDAY

(Chapter 14.1)

2 What was the goal of the policy of appeasement?

A to demand payment of reparations
B to set up democratic government in Italy
C to prevent war with Germany
D to ensure the neutrality of Britain

WEDNESDAY

(Chapter 14.1)

3 What event triggered World War II?

A Germany invaded Poland.
B Italy attacked North Africa.
C Japan bombed Pearl Harbor.
D Germany and the Soviet Union signed a nonaggression pact.

THURSDAY

(Chapter 14.1)

THE LONDON BLITZ, 1940–1941

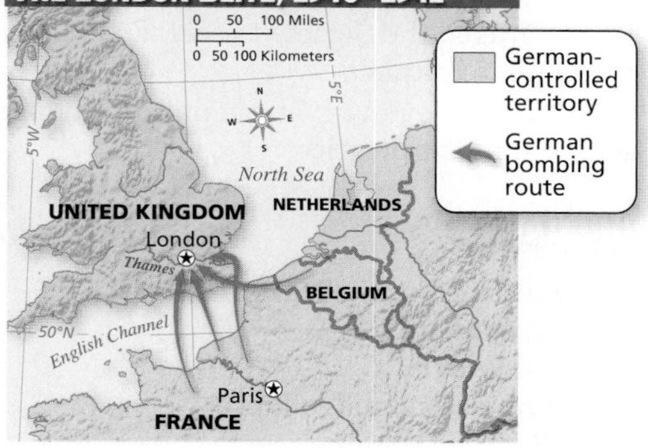

4 Based on the map, from which country did most German bombing raids originate?

A United Kingdom
B France
C Belgium
D Netherlands

FRIDAY

(Chapter 14.1)

5 What British leader encouraged the British to keep fighting during the Battle of Britain?

A George Marshall
B Franklin Roosevelt
C Winston Churchill
D Neville Chamberlain

WEEK 18

MONDAY

(Chapter 14.2)

1 Which battle was a turning point in the war in the Pacific?

A Battle of El Alamein
B Battle of the Bulge
C Battle of Midway
D Battle of Stalingrad

TUESDAY

(Chapter 14.3)

2 The Nazis implemented the Final Solution in order to

A leave the British with no allies.
B conquer all of Europe.
C defeat the Soviets.
D kill Europe's Jews.

WEDNESDAY

(Chapter 14.4)

3 What country suffered the greatest number of casualties in World War II?

A Soviet Union
B Japan
C United States
D Great Britain

THURSDAY

(Chapter 14.4)

4 What two countries emerged from the war as the world's most powerful nations?

A the United States and Japan
B Great Britain and the United States
C the Soviet Union and Germany
D the United States and the Soviet Union

FRIDAY

(Chapter 14.4)

5 In order to prevent the outbreak of future wars, the Allies created the

A Final Solution.
B policy of appeasement.
C Potsdam Conference.
D United Nations.

Week 19

MONDAY
(Chapter 15.1)

1 **Which of the following was a cause of the Cold War?**
(A) The Soviet Union set up Communist governments in Eastern Europe.
B The United States refused to force Germany to pay reparations.
C Soviet officials were charged with war crimes during the Nuremberg Trials.
D The United States refused to loan money to the Soviet Union after the war.

TUESDAY
(Chapter 15.1)

2 **The goal of the Truman Doctrine was to**
A permanently divide Europe between East and West.
B rebuild the war-torn nations of Eastern Europe.
(C) prevent the spread of communism.
D remove Stalin from power in the Soviet Union.

WEDNESDAY
(Chapter 15.1)

3 **What effect did the Cold War have on the nations of Europe?**
A To protect themselves from future attacks, European nations developed the most powerful armies in the world.
B The high cost of the Cold War forced European nations to seek more colonies.
C Europe was slow to rebuild after the war as a result of Cold War tensions.
(D) It divided Europe into two competing alliances—NATO and the Warsaw Pact.

THURSDAY
(Chapter 15.2)

4 **U.S. efforts to prevent the spread of communism led it to become involved in conflicts in all of the following places *except***
A Southeast Asia.
(B) Australia.
C Central America.
D Africa.

FRIDAY
(Chapter 15.2)

5 **All of the following are results of the U.S.-Soviet rivalry during the Cold War *except***
A the Cuban missile crisis.
B the development of a nuclear arms race.
(C) the creation of Israel.
D the Red Scare.

Week 20

MONDAY
(Chapter 15.3)

1 **Command economies differ from market economies in that**
A command economies rely heavily on barter.
B market forces determine economic decisions.
(C) governments make most economic decisions in command economies.
D command economies produce more goods.

TUESDAY
(Chapter 15.3)

2 **What was the result of uprisings in Eastern Europe in the 1950s and 1960s?**
A They led to democratic reforms in Eastern Europe and the Soviet Union.
(B) They resulted in a Soviet crackdown on political protest in Eastern Europe.
C They encouraged the United States to support rebellions in Eastern Europe.
D They led the Soviet government to grant equal rights to women.

WEDNESDAY
(Chapter 15.3)

3 **In what way did an economic crisis in the 1980s affect Soviet policies?**
A It increased Cold War tensions with the United States.
B It forced a Soviet crackdown on Eastern European nations.
C It encouraged the Soviets to seek an alliance with Great Britain.
(D) It forced the Soviet government to introduce some capitalist practices.

THURSDAY
(Chapter 15.4)

4 **The fall of the Berlin Wall in 1989 has become a symbol of**
A the Cold War.
B Germany's economic collapse.
(C) the collapse of communism.
D ethnic tensions in Eastern Europe.

FRIDAY
(Chapter 15.4)

5 **Since the end of the Cold War, the United States has been chiefly involved in conflicts in**
(A) the Middle East.
B Southeast Asia.
C Eastern Europe.
D Africa.

WEEK 21

MONDAY
(Chapter 16.1)

1 Who was a key figure in the independence movement in India?

A Benazir Bhutto
(B) Mohandas Gandhi
C Mao Zedong
D Indira Gandhi

TUESDAY
(Chapter 16.2)

2 What was the cause of fighting in Vietnam in the 1940s and early 1950s?

A The Vietnamese opposed the division of the country into North and South.
B The United States had tried to colonize Vietnam.
C Communist China had invaded Vietnam.
(D) The Vietnamese wanted their independence from France.

WEDNESDAY
(Chapter 16.3)

3 What was the main result of the Chinese Civil War?

A Japan invaded China.
(B) Communists took over the Chinese government.
C China was divided into two countries.
D The United States sent troops to China to prevent the spread of communism.

THURSDAY
(Chapter 16.3)

> *"If we combine a planned economy with a market economy, we shall be in a better position to liberate the productive forces and speed up economic growth."*
> —Deng Xiaoping, interview, 1985

4 According to the quote above, what did China hope to gain from its economic reforms?

(A) economic growth
B the end of communism
C reunification with Taiwan
D the creation of a planned economy

FRIDAY
(Chapter 16.4)

5 How did Japan change in the years following World War II?

A The power of the emperor was strengthened.
(B) Its economy experienced unprecedented growth.
C Its population declined dramatically.
D It lost markets for its goods.

WEEK 22

MONDAY
(Chapter 17.1)

1 What impact did World War II have on independence movements in Africa?

A African natives gained political strength by ruling the colonies during the war.
B The cost of the war made European nations more determined to hang on to their colonies' wealth.
(C) Independence movements gained strength as European countries lost power after the war.
D The atrocities of the war led many Africans to oppose foreign control.

TUESDAY
(Chapter 17.1)

2 Why might African colonies with large European populations have faced more difficulty in gaining independence?

A The United States often sent aid to support European settlers.
B European governments did not want to force their people to pay taxes.
C European settlers often supported independence movements.
(D) European settlers did not want to give up their land.

WEDNESDAY
(Chapter 17.2)

3 What African country was torn apart by ethnic conflict and genocide in 1994?

A Ghana
B Kenya
(C) Rwanda
D South Africa

THURSDAY
(Chapter 17.3)

4 The Zionist movement, immigration into Palestine, and the Holocaust led to

(A) the creation of a Jewish state in Palestine.
B the Persian Gulf War.
C the Iranian Revolution.
D the OPEC oil embargo.

FRIDAY
(Chapter 17.4)

5 All of the following have been major factors in conflicts in North Africa and the Middle East since 1945 *except*

A the Arab-Israeli dispute over Palestine.
B the region's large oil reserves.
C the growth of Islamism.
(D) the building of the Suez Canal.

COUNTDOWN TO TESTING

WEEK 23

MONDAY (Chapter 18.1)

1 Which of the following was a cause of the Cuban Revolution?
- **A** U.S. business interests supported Castro.
- **B** Military leaders wanted more power.
- **(C)** Cuba's poor were unhappy with their political and economic situation.
- **D** Cubans wanted independence from Spain.

TUESDAY (Chapter 18.1)

2 During the Cold War, the United States became involved in Latin America in order to
- **A** support the rights of the poor.
- **B** gain valuable natural resources.
- **(C)** stop the spread of communism.
- **D** end the rule of brutal dictators.

WEDNESDAY (Chapter 18.2)

3 What led to the rise of military dictatorships in South America?
- **(A)** economic problems
- **B** the desire to limit the power of the rich
- **C** growing distrust of the United States
- **D** democratic reforms

THURSDAY (Chapter 18.3)

4 What political reform has helped bring change to many Latin American nations?
- **A** the introduction of one-party rule
- **B** improvements in trade and production
- **(C)** the return of democratic governments
- **D** the rise of military dictatorships

FRIDAY (Chapter 18.3)

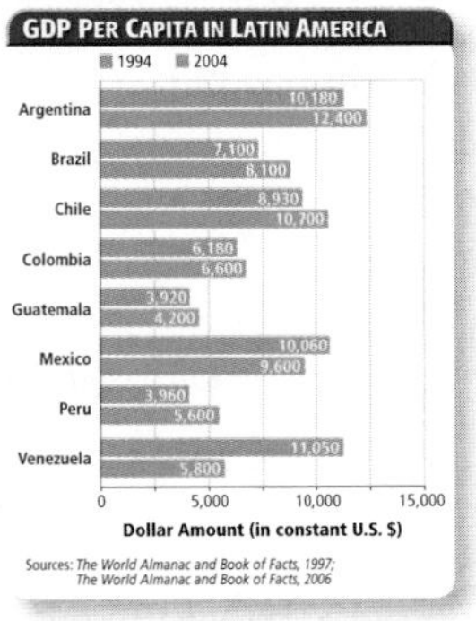

5 What overall trend does this graph illustrate?
- **A** per capita GDPs skyrocketed
- **(B)** per capita GDPs increased slightly
- **C** per capita GDPs declined dramatically
- **D** per capita GDPs remained constant

WEEK 24

MONDAY (Chapter 19.1)

1 The process by which countries are linked through trade and culture is known as
- **A** urbanization.
- **(B)** globalization.
- **C** international cooperation.
- **D** free trade.

TUESDAY (Chapter 19.1)

2 Which of the following is a result of global trade?
- **A** Developed countries support the spread of democracy.
- **(B)** Developing countries can participate in trade.
- **C** The global economy has declined.
- **D** Trade restrictions have increased.

WEDNESDAY (Chapter 19.2)

3 Countries around the world pledged to respect human rights in the
- **(A)** Universal Declaration of Human Rights.
- **B** North American Free Trade Agreement.
- **C** General Agreement on Tariffs and Trade.
- **D** Camp David Accords.

THURSDAY (Chapter 19.3)

4 Since 2001 governments have responded to terrorist attacks in all of the following ways *except*
- **A** strengthening transportation security.
- **B** improving intelligence services.
- **C** increasing border security.
- **(D)** creating new systems of alliances.

FRIDAY (Chapter 19.4)

5 How have the improvements in information technology affected the world?
- **A** They have led to increased global warming.
- **(B)** They have allowed almost instant communication between countries.
- **C** They have increased the trade gap between developed and developing countries.
- **D** They have led to increased urbanization.

Connecting with Past Learnings

Prehistory–1500

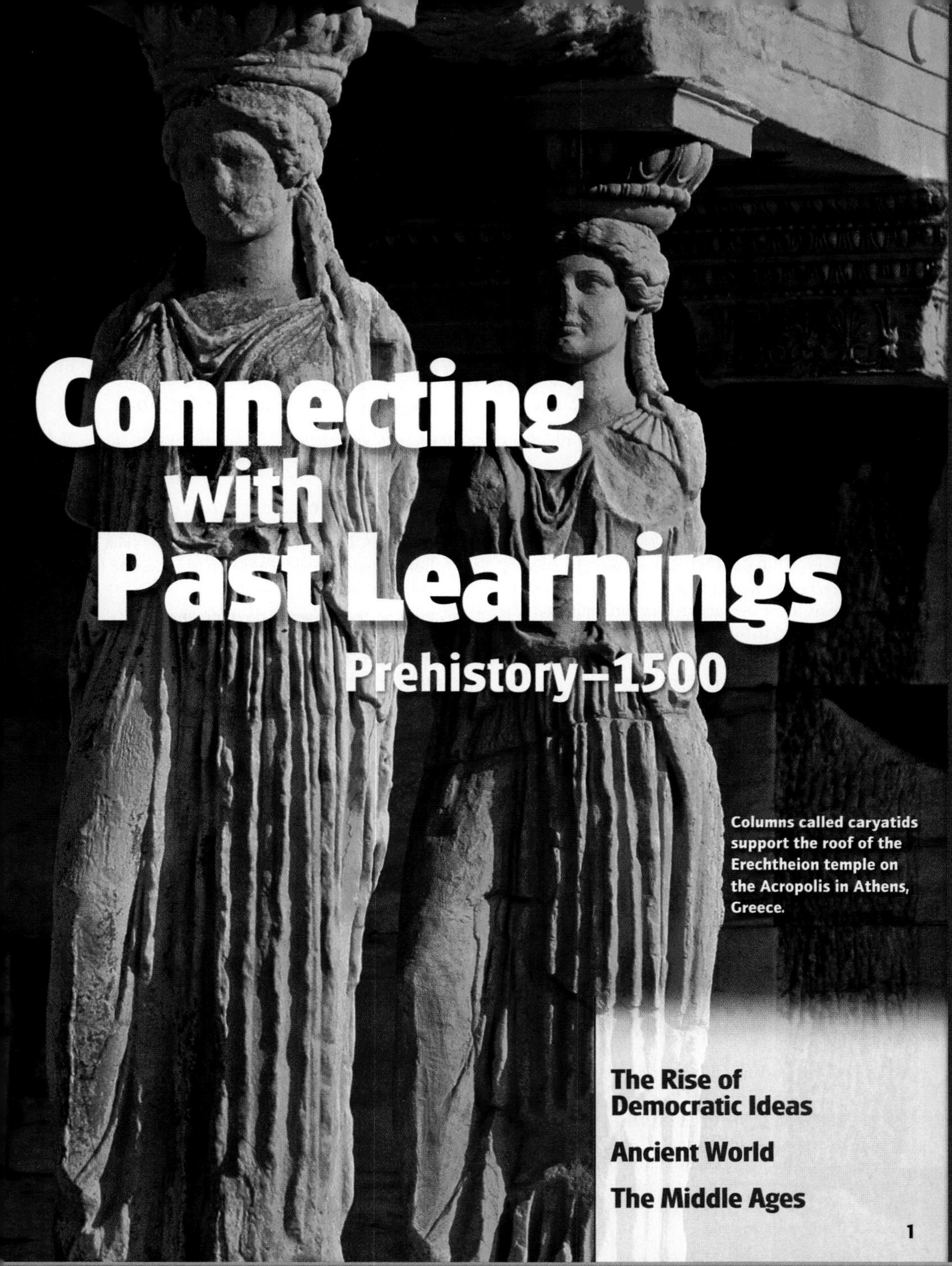

Columns called caryatids support the roof of the Erechtheion temple on the Acropolis in Athens, Greece.

The Rise of Democratic Ideas

Ancient World

The Middle Ages

1

Connections Preview

Connecting with Past Learnings

What Is Democracy? Have students define the word democracy. Then have students list examples of institutions that would be best run as a democracy. National governments, social clubs, and civic organizations are possible examples students might list. Next, have students list examples of entities that would not function well as a democracy (e.g. classrooms, football teams, the military). Have students share their lists and discuss with the class.

Teaching Tip

The CIA World Factbook Web site is a useful tool in learning how the practice of democracy around the world varies. The site includes updated information about the governments of the world's nations, including their branches, legal systems, and extension of suffrage.

Preteach

The Rise of Democratic Ideas

Motivate

Although they are too young to vote, have students think about how they can participate in their country's democratic government. Have students describe ways they may have already done so (e.g. wrote a letter to a senator, volunteered for a political campaign, etc.). Guide a class discussion about the importance of citizen participation in a democracy.

Reading Like a Historian

Interpreting Visuals Have students look at the statues pictured on the opposite page. Point out examples of current structures in the United States that reflect classical styles, such as the Supreme Court Building and the U.S. Capitol building in Washington, D.C. There may be similar examples in your state's capital city. Discuss with students why so many government buildings in the United States were built in the styles of ancient Greece and Rome.

The Rise of Democratic Ideas

Introduction

In the United States we tend to take democracy for granted. But the truth is democratic societies are very rare throughout history. Monarchies, tyrannies, dictatorships, oligarchies—the rule by a powerful few—all have been more common than democracies. So common, in fact, that for most of human history democracy seemed not just rare but unimaginable, unnatural, and even dangerous.

Where did the idea of democracy come from? If it was so rare and considered dangerous, how did it become the dominant form or government, in aspiration if not always in reality, that it is today? This short account traces the progress of democratic ideas.

Just what do we mean by democracy? The ancient Greeks invented the term. *Demos* meant "the people," and *kratos* or *cracy* meant "the rule of." But what the Greeks meant by democracy is very different from the modern meaning of the term. Today, a definition of democracy includes certain basic ideas:

- **Sovereignty and consent of the governed**
  Simply put, this means that those who are governed—the people—agree to be governed. The ultimate authority in political matters rests with the people and is only "on loan" to government. Two ideas follow from this. The first is that consent can be withheld or, in the case of the American Revolution, withdrawn. If government behaves tyrannically, the people have the right to rebel. The second idea is that there must be a way, short of rebellion, for the people to give or withhold their consent. That mechanism is *elections*.
- **All people possess natural and inherent rights**
  These are rights that all human beings possess and that no just government can take away arbitrarily. *The Bill of Rights* enumerated some of these rights: *freedom of the press, freedom of speech, freedom of assembly, freedom of association*, and *freedom of religion*.
- **Rule of law**
  John Adams famously described the United States constitution as "a government of laws and not of men." What he meant was that those in government and government itself had *powers limited by written laws*. To make the rule of law a reality, there needs to be a common respect for the law and a means to enforce it.
- **Limits on the power of government**
  This follows from the rule of law. If the people's rights are to be protected, government's power must be limited. The American Founders worked to devise practical means to limit government's power. Their solution was to disperse it—among separate branches and between the central or federal government and the governments of the states. This is the idea behind the *separation of powers, checks and balances, federalism,* and an *independent judiciary.*
- **Majority rule and minority rights**
  Decisions are made by a majority of citizens. Those on the losing end of political questions agree to abide by the decision of the majority. The majority, in turn, agrees not to use its power unfairly against the minority. These agreements form part of the *social contract* without which society cannot function.
- **Duties of citizenship**
  Citizenship carries responsibilities as well as rights. For democracy to function, citizens must be involved and, ideally, informed. They must uphold the law; participate in the political process either directly, as a representative, or indirectly, by voting in elections; and exercise reasoned judgment when considering public issues.

Skills Focus: Identifying Main Idea and Details

At Level

Research Required

Reading Skill

Types of Democracy

1. Copy the chart for students to see. Omit the italicized words. Have students identify three different types of government, in addition to democracy, and write them on the class chart.
2. Have students conduct research on the governments they identified to fill in the chart. **LS Visual-Spatial**

Alternative Assessment Handbook, Rubric 7: Charts

	Democracy	*Monarchy*	*Dictatorship*	*Oligarchy*
Power	*citizens who vote*	*king or queen*	*dictator*	*a small group of leaders*
Examples	*U.S., Great Britain*	*Saudi Arabia, pre-revolution France*	*Germany under Hitler; Iraq under Hussein*	*pre-democracy Greek city-states*

Representative Government in Greece and Rome

The ancient Greeks and Romans were the first people to experiment with democracy and representative government. For centuries afterward, their examples served by turns to frighten and to inspire people.

Greeks—Founders of Democracy Ancient Greece was divided into a number of city-states. The Greek word for city-state was *polis*, which gives us our word "politics." Each city-state was ruled by a king, or *tyrannos*. Not every *tyrannos* was a tyrant, but enough were that during the 150 years after about 650 BC, many Greek city-states overthrew their rulers. But what form of government should replace kingship? In many places, wealthy aristocrats took power. Slowly, however, the idea that people should rule themselves took root, nowhere more firmly than in Athens.

In 594 BC the Athenians turned to a leader named Solon to reorganize their government. He divided all Athenian citizens into four groups based on wealth. Only members of the three richest groups, or classes, could hold public office. All citizens, however, could sit in the **assembly**.

Solon's reforms did not solve Athens's problems. The wealthy continued to dominate government. In about 507 BC, a new leader, Cleisthenes, divided the citizens of Athens into 10 groups based on where people lived rather than their wealth or family. Each tribe chose 50 men who together made up the Council of Five Hundred. The Council proposed laws to the assembly, which had final authority. All free adult males were members of the assembly. The decisions of the assembly became law.

Unlike modern democracy, which depends on elected representatives to express the will of the citizens, Athens had a **direct democracy**. That meant that all citizens participated in the government. Athenians liked to boast that in their government, everyone was equal before the law. Athenian democracy, however, was an extremely limited one. Neither women nor slaves, who formed the majority of the population, could participate as citizens.

The ancient Greeks made another fundamental contribution to the rise of democratic ideas. Their philosophers were the first people to think and write about government in a systematic way. Greek philosophers believed that the world was based on certain natural laws, or truths, that could be discovered through the use of reason.

The Greek philosophers Plato and Aristotle studied the types of government. Plato distrusted democracy. In *The Republic* he described his perfect society. It was an aristocracy ruled by philosopher-kings chosen for their wisdom and high ideals. Aristotle, Plato's pupil, believed that monarchy, aristocracy, and democracy all had strengths and weaknesses. He wanted to combine the best elements from all three.

A Republic in Rome The early history of Rome was similar to that of Athens—a city-state ruled by a tyrant. In 509 BC Romans drove out their king and established a new form of government. They called it a *res publica*. We call it a **republic**. In a republic, power rests with citizens who elect officials to represent them

The Classical Heritage

Athenian Democracy
- Rights for all citizens
- Direct citizen participation in government
- Systematic inquiry into the nature of government

Roman Republic
- Citizens elect representatives to government
- Separation of powers among branches of government
- Checks and balances on branches of government

Greek philosopher Plato

Cicero addresses the Roman Senate.

Direct Teach

Reading Focus

Representative Government in Greece and Rome

Explain What concepts pioneered by the Roman Republic have been adopted by modern democracies? *voters elect representatives to run the government; checks and balances; separation of powers*

Compare and Contrast Why do you think direct democracy thrived in Athens, while Rome developed as a republic? *possible answers—As a city-state, Athens had a small voter base and could function as a direct democracy. Rome governed a large empire, creating a necessity for elected officials.*

Biography

Marcus Porcius Cato (Cato the Censor) (234 BC–149 BC) Cato was one of the best known statesmen and writers of the Roman Republic. After serving as a soldier in the Roman army for several years, Cato entered politics. He quickly rose through the ranks of Roman government and was elected as a consul, Rome's highest office, before the age of 40. A skilled orator, Cato used his political power to zealously promote morality, tax reform, and public building projects. After retiring from politics Cato wrote several important Latin works, including an encyclopedia.

Differentiating Instruction

Below Level

Learners Having Difficulty

1. Review with students the Greek leaders and philosophers discussed in this section: Solon, Cleisthenes, Pericles, Plato, and Aristotle. Have students list the names or write them in a chart. Have students work in mixed-ability pairs to write down examples of how each Greek leader or philosopher contributed to the rise of democracy.
2. Guide students in a discussion about what is required for a democracy to succeed. You might wish to discuss the importance of education and the active participation of citizens in the political process. Have students take notes during the discussion.
3. Have pairs organize their notes and review their leader/philosopher lists. Then have students refer to their notes and write a paragraph describing how the Greeks advanced the concept of democracy.

LS Visual-Spatial, Interpersonal

Alternative Assessment Handbook, Rubrics 11: Discussions; and 40: Writing to Describe

Direct Teach

Reading Focus

The Judeo-Christian Legacy

Explain How did the Hebrew religion influence Christianity? *Christianity arose in a Jewish culture; Jesus of Nazareth was a Jewish teacher; Jesus's teachings were grounded in Jewish tradition.*

Summarize Which principles of Judaism and Christianity are evident in Western democratic thought? *possible answers—kindness and respect for all people, appropriate punishments for crimes, acceptance of all people, a moral and just community*

Info to Know

The Apostle Paul The oldest documented Christian writings are the letters of the apostle Paul. These epistles are included in the New Testament and form the basis of much of Christianity's core doctrine. The earliest surviving letters of Paul were written in the AD 50s, about a quarter of a century after the crucifixion of Jesus.

in governing the state. The Romans introduced the idea of **representative government.**

The Romans divided government power among different bodies, what we would call branches. The Senate controlled public funds and decided foreign policy. Magistrates were the elected officials who carried out the laws. A variety of assemblies voted on laws and elected two senior magistrates, called consuls, to run the government. Judges called praetors were elected by an assembly to rule on the law. In theory, no branch could act independently of the other: There was a system of **checks and balances**. The principle of dispersing government's power became known as the **separation of powers.**

The Romans contributed to the **rule of law** by having a written law code. The Twelve Tables of the Law were posted in the Roman marketplace for all to see. No longer could the law be whatever the powerful said it was. Moreover, the law applied to all citizens equally. The Roman statesman Cicero (106–43 BC) put that idea this way: "We are born for Justice, and that right is based, not upon men's opinions, but upon Nature." In other words, justice is one of the **natural rights** that all people have. Cicero believed that laws had to be based on "right reason in agreement with nature." No law that was contrary to either reason or nature could be considered a just law.

The Romans were proud of their government and their laws. From this pride grew a strong sense of patriotism and a belief that citizenship carried with it a duty to serve the state. Ironically, it was partly this sense of duty to the state that impelled Rome on the path to empire, ultimately dooming its republican ideals.

Roman ideas about law, along with the separation of powers and checks and balances, laid the foundation for many future governments, including that of the United States. In practice, however, the Roman Republic was deeply flawed. As in Athens, citizenship in Rome excluded the majority of people, including women and slaves. The Senate, drawn from the upper classes, retained most of the governmental power. Worse, as the republic gave way to empire, it also became clear that the rulers placed themselves above the law. There was no force to stop them.

The Judeo-Christian Legacy

The moral and ethical principles of Judaism and Christianity profoundly influenced Western democratic thought. Over time, these principles contributed to the belief that all people, not just a limited group of citizens, deserve kindness and respect.

Morality and Sacred Law The ancestors of modern Jews were the Hebrews. According to the Bible, the forefather of the Hebrew people was Abraham. Abraham is a revered figure in Judaism, Christianity, and Islam. All three faiths trace their heritage to him through the line of prophets descended from his sons. According to the Bible, God made a covenant, or solemn promise, to Abraham. In return for Abraham's obedience, God would lead him and his descendants to a new land and make them a mighty people.

In the Jewish tradition, morality and the laws that govern human action derive ultimately from God. The most famous of these laws are the Ten Commandments, which in the biblical account were given to the Hebrew leader Moses by God. The Jewish tradition values justice and righteousness. People have a duty to show others respect and kindness and to strive to do what is right.

Christianity Much of Judaism's system of ethics carried over into the founding of Christianity. The first Christians were the followers of the Jewish teacher Jesus of Nazareth. According to Jesus, there is only one true God, who cares for all people. Jesus taught that people must love God and must love others as they love themselves.

Christianity teaches that all people are equal in the eyes of God. This belief in **human equality** was a powerful reason for the spread of Christianity. As life in the Roman Empire became more difficult, this message

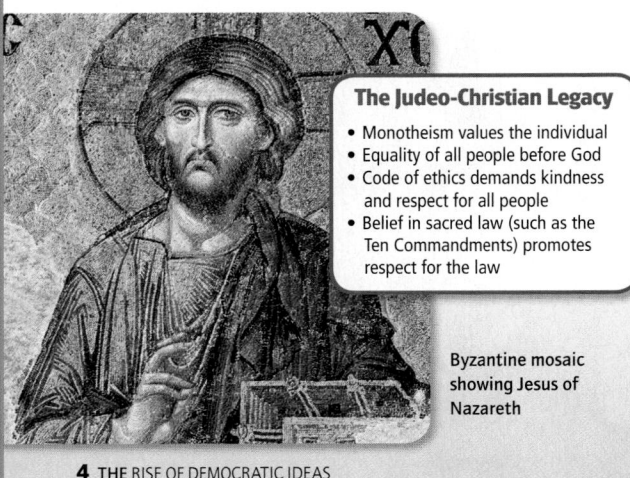

The Judeo-Christian Legacy

- Monotheism values the individual
- Equality of all people before God
- Code of ethics demands kindness and respect for all people
- Belief in sacred law (such as the Ten Commandments) promotes respect for the law

Byzantine mosaic showing Jesus of Nazareth

Skills Focus: Analyzing Primary Sources

At Level

Research Required

Reading Like a Historian Skill

The Ten Commandments

1. Organize students into groups of three and have each group conduct research about the Ten Commandments.
2. For each commandment, have students make a list of current United States laws that were likely inspired by the commandment.
3. Have groups share their lists with the class.
4. Guide the class in a discussion about how the Ten Commandments have influenced United States law. LS **Verbal-Linguistic**

Alternative Assessment Handbook, Rubrics 11: Discussions; and 14: Group Activity

offered people hope. Like Judaism, Christian morality valued righteousness and justice. It called on people to work for a morally just community that respected the value of each person.

The Judeo-Christian belief in human equality also had implications for democracy. If people were equal in the eyes of God, how could some be excluded from citizenship, be held as slaves, or be treated in a way that violated their human dignity? It took nearly 2,000 years, however, for these implications to alter political behavior. Western societies continued to practice slavery until the 1800s and to limit voting rights until the 1900s.

The Rise of Democracy in England

The long history of the struggle for democracy in England goes back nearly to the kingdom's founding. As royal subjects disputed the idea of absolute rule by a monarch, their actions helped to lay the foundation for revolutions that brought sweeping changes to England and, eventually, the United States.

Asserting Rights Around 1215, an English ruler named King John demanded that nobles pay more taxes to support his war in France. The nobles opposed the tax. A powerful group joined together, rebelled, and eventually forced the king to accept a document known as **Magna Carta**. Magna Carta restricted the king's power to tax—he had to get the agreement of his council—and ended his power to arrest people without cause. While it mainly protected the liberties of the nobles, later generations saw in Magna Carta an expanded significance. For them, it became an assertion of the rule of law and of **limits on executive power**. By accepting Magna Carta, the king admitted that even he had to obey the law—or face being overthrown.

By the end of the 1200s, the king's council had grown into a representative assembly known as **Parliament**. At first, membership in Parliament was restricted to nobles, important religious leaders, and the wealthier members of the middle class who represented the major towns. The body mainly served to advise the king. However, it also had the right to refuse new taxes sought by the king. Over time Parliament was divided into two parts, called houses—the House of Lords and the House of Commons. Parliament, much modified over the years, still operates today as Britain's lawmaking body.

The English Bill of Rights As England's central government grew, Parliament's power to accept or reject new taxes became more important. By the early 1600s, English monarchs began to claim absolute power over Parliament. A civil war broke out between those who supported the king and those who supported Parliament. After years of struggle, Parliament's supporters emerged victorious toward the end of the 1600s.

Signing of the Magna Carta

Democracy in England

- **Magna Carta** Limits power of executive (king); lists individuals' rights
- **Parliament** Representative assembly develops into legislative (lawmaking) body
- **English Bill of Rights** Asserts Parliamentary sovereignty and lists rights of individuals

John Locke

Direct Teach

Reading Focus

The Rise of English Democracy

Recall What were three events in English history that led to the growth of democracy? *signing of the Magna Carta; English Civil War; formalization of the English Bill of Rights*

Draw Conclusions How did English monarchs unintentionally promote democracy? *King John moved his nobles to action by demanding higher taxes from them; English kings in the 1600s provoked a civil war by claiming absolute power over Parliament and common law.*

Primary Source

"To understand political power right, and derive it from its original, we must consider, what state all men are naturally in, and that is, a state of perfect freedom to order their actions, and dispose of their possessions and persons, as they think fit, within the bounds of the law of nature, without asking leave, or depending upon the will of any other man."
—John Locke, from *Two Treaties of Government,* 1690

Collaborative Learning

At Level

Magna Carta Debate

1. Organize the students into small groups, and have each group prepare arguments supporting and opposing the Magna Carta. Students should consider the viewpoints of King John, the nobles, and the common people in England.
2. Serving as moderator, stage a class debate about whether or not the Magna Carta was a fair document.
3. Discuss the arguments presented in the debate as a class. Ask students which side of the argument they found most convincing and why.
4. Have students write a short essay explaining if and why the Magna Carta was revolutionary for its time. LS **Kinesthetic, Verbal-Linguistic**

Alternative Assessment Handbook, Rubrics 10: Debates; and 43: Writing to Persuade

Direct Teach

Reading Focus

Democratic Revolutions

Identify Cause and Effect What led to the American Revolution? *ideas about government and natural rights from Enlightenment thinkers; British tax policies sparking resistance from American colonists*

Compare How were the results of the American Revolution and the French Revolution similar? *possible answer—Both resulted in a federal system of government with separation of powers.*

Info to Know

Jean-Jacques Rousseau The turning point in Rousseau's life came in 1750, when, at the age of 38, he entered an essay contest. The theme of the contest, which was presented by the Dijon Academy of Letters, was whether the advancement of arts and science has resulted in an improvement in morals. Though he was certain the other entrants would praise the arts and sciences, Rousseau answered "no" to the question, arguing instead for the superiority of nature. Rousseau won the contest and instantly rose to prominence.

The Rise of Democratic Ideas

The battle between the king and Parliament produced a number of thinkers whose work influenced the rise of modern democracy. None was more important than John Locke (1632–1704). Like Cicero, Locke believed that people possessed natural rights—"life, liberty, and estate [property]"—and that just laws were based on reason. The purpose of a government was to protect these rights, and if it failed, rebellion was a lawful course of action. In that sense, government was a **social contract** that the people entered into with the king. If the king broke the contract by acting tyrannically, the people were no longer bound to obey. Finally, Locke believed that the best way to safeguard people's rights was to limit the power of government.

In 1689 Parliament passed the **English Bill of Rights**. It declared that Parliament would choose who ruled the country. The ruler would be subject to Parliamentary laws, could not impose taxes without Parliament's consent, and could not interfere with the election of its members. The Bill of Rights also protected private citizens from government injustice.

While England was not yet a democracy—that would have to wait until the 20th century—the English Bill of Rights did mark a turning point. It helped define the rights of individuals and placed limits on government power. Later, it served as a model for the Bill of Rights in the United States Constitution.

Democratic Revolutions

From the late 1700s until the early 1800s, a series of revolutions in Europe and the Americas helped spread the idea of democracy. The new republics experimented with different institutions of government.

Influence of the Enlightenment John Locke's faith in reason was characteristic of the **Enlightenment**, a time of philosophical inquiry that roughly spanned the 1700s. The ideas of Locke and other Enlightenment thinkers exerted a strong influence on the revolutionaries in Europe and the Americas. In *The Spirit of the Laws* Baron de Montesquieu (1689–1755) laid out in a freshly compelling way the idea of a separation of powers operating through a system of checks and balances. He emphasized the need for an **independent judiciary** to safeguard people's rights. "There is no liberty," he wrote, "if the judiciary

Presenting the Declaration of Independence

The "George Washington of South America," Simón Bolívar liberated several South American colonies from Spain.

Democratic Revolutions

American Revolution
- Inspired by the classical and Enlightenment thinkers
- **Declaration of Independence**
- **United States Constitution** Established a separation of powers between branches of government and federal system
- **Bill of Rights** Guarantees people's rights

French Revolution
- "Liberty, equality, and fraternity"
- Resulted in the end of monarchy; separation of powers between branches of government; federal system
- **Declaration of the Rights of Man and Citizen**

Latin American Revolutions
- Influenced by American and French revolutions
- Achieved independence for nations in Central and South America

Skills Focus: Identifying Cause and Effect

At Level

Research Required

Reading Skill

Causes of the Revolution

1. Organize students into small groups. Assign each group one of the three democratic revolutions: American, French, or Latin American.
2. Have students use reliable online or print resources to conduct research about conditions in their assigned country (or countries), prior to the outbreak of revolution.
3. Have each group present its findings to the class. Guide the class in a discussion about the causes of the democratic revolutions.

LS Interpersonal, Verbal-Linguistic

Alternative Assessment Handbook, Rubrics 24: Oral Presentations; and 30: Research

power be not separated from the legislative and the executive." In *The Social Contract* another Enlightenment thinker, Jean-Jacques Rousseau (1712–1778), argued for **popular sovereignty**—the idea that the ultimate authority in the state rests with the people. A true social contract, for Rousseau, involved all people surrendering certain rights in order to form a just community that expressed the "general will." Unlike Locke, Rousseau believed property to be a source of corruption and inequity.

The American Revolution The American Revolution began as an assertion by the colonists of their rights as British subjects. The colonists had no representation in the British Parliament. They considered it tyranny to be taxed without representation. The **Declaration of Independence,** written by Thomas Jefferson and other delegates to the Second Continental Congress in 1776, declared the United States to be an independent nation. It stated that all powers must come from the people and a government that fails to protect people's rights can be justly overthrown.

The **United States Constitution**, which was largely the work of James Madison and ratified in 1788, recognized that government exists to serve the people. It embraced the separation of governmental power into three branches—legislative, executive, and judicial—and a system of checks and balances between these branches. The Constitution also established a **federal system**, with powers distributed between the federal and the state and local governments. In 1791 ten amendments outlining basic individual freedoms were added. These are known as the **Bill of Rights**.

The French Revolution The success of the American Revolution inspired a similar effort in France. Disputes between a powerful monarch, King Louis XVI, the high nobles and clergy and the ordinary people led to the French Revolution, which changed the government dramatically. France's monarchy ended, and the new government adopted the **Declaration of the Rights of Man and of the Citizen**, which listed basic human rights and political powers of the people. The French constitution of 1791 limited the powers of the king and divided the government into three branches. By 1793, however, radicals pushed Rousseau's ideas of popular sovereignty and the general will to extremes, unleashing a terror campaign against anyone they considered an enemy of the revolution.

Independence in Latin America During the late 1700s and early 1800s, a series of independence movements swept Central and South America, from Haiti to Argentina. Rebellions broke out against France and Spain, which controlled most of the colonies. By 1822, almost all of Latin American colonies won their independence. The leaders of the fight for independence were familiar with the ideas of the Enlightenment and the French Revolution. In addition, many of the constitutions of the new republics owed substantial debts to the United States Constitution.

Conclusion

Democratic ideas lie implicit in the traditions and history of many cultures. The desire for justice and belief in the rule of law, for instance, can be traced in documents as disparate as the Code of Hammurabi of ancient Babylon and the Shari'ah, or law code, of Islam. Checks on executive power were known in the city-states of India and the kingdoms of Africa.

Democracy can be fragile. Its history is one of failure more than it is of success. But those very failures can be instructive and give people hope that once won, democratic government will be cherished.

Section Assessment

Define and Explain the Significance

1. natural rights
2. republic
3. Magna Carta
4. Parliament
5. Declaration of Independence

Reading Comprehension

6. How did Aristotle's view of government differ from Plato's?
7. In what way was the government of the Roman Republic an example of checks and balances?
8. What Judeo-Christian values supported the development democratic ideas?
9. How did the ideas of the Enlightenment influence the American Revolution?
10. What were the central features of the government created by the U.S. Constitution?

Critical Thinking

11. Although the United States was created with the Declaration of Independence, how could it be argued that the country was really launched in 1789?

Direct Teach

Reading Focus

Democratic Revolutions

Identify Who was the primary author of the Declaration of Independence? *Thomas Jefferson*

Summarize What ideas were reflected in all three major documents of American Revolution? *All three documents reflected ideas of natural rights and popular sovereignty.*

Contrast How were the Latin American revolutions different from the French Revolution? *The Latin American revolutions were anti-colonial movements that produced independent nations. The French Revolution resulted in a change of government within a single independent nation.*

Activity Revolution Posters Have students create a poster reflecting the ideas of one or more of the revolutions described on this page.
LS Visual-Spatial

Alternative Assessment Handbook, Rubric 28: Posters

Review & Assess

Close

Have students identify the historical period they believe was most important to advancing modern democratic ideas.

Review

Have students list four features of modern democratic government. Have students explain why the features they identified are important democratic ideas.

Section Assessment Answers

1. natural rights, page 4
2. republic, page 3
3. Magna Carta, page 5
4. Parliament, page 5
5. Declaration of Independence, page 7
6. Plato—aristocracy should rule by philosopher-kings; Aristotle—combine best elements of monarchy, aristocracy, and democracy
7. senate, magistrates, assemblies and consuls, judges; no branch of government could act independently of each other
8. belief in human equality; no one should be excluded from citizenship
9. checks and balances; idea that ultimate authority in the state rests with the people; power comes from the people
10. government divided into three branches, checks and balances among three branches, federal system, Bill of Rights
11. possible answer—The Constitution was adopted in 1789; the new nation with its democratic government was launched upon its signing.

•Prologue Preview•

Exploring the Time Line

The Ancient World Several civilizations arose in the ancient world. These advanced societies developed in different regions of the world at different time periods. Have students list the ancient civilizations with which they are familiar. Discuss how societies in the ancient world could have influenced each other's development.

Info to Know

Abu Hureyra Abu Hureyra is one of the earliest known urban centers in human history. Located in the Middle Euphrates Valley, the settlement was a base camp for hunter-gatherers between 10,500 and 9,000 BC. Around 8,500 BC, gazelle hunters built a permanent village of mud-brick houses at the site. A few centuries later, the people at Abu Hureyra started raising livestock and growing crops.

The Ancient World

The earliest humans appeared in Africa about 200,000 years ago and then slowly populated the planet. By about 3,000 years ago, the first civilizations began to arise in river valleys in Africa, the Near East, India, and China. Over time city-states grew and then gave way to empires. Great systems of philosophy and religion, some which still exist today, first began.

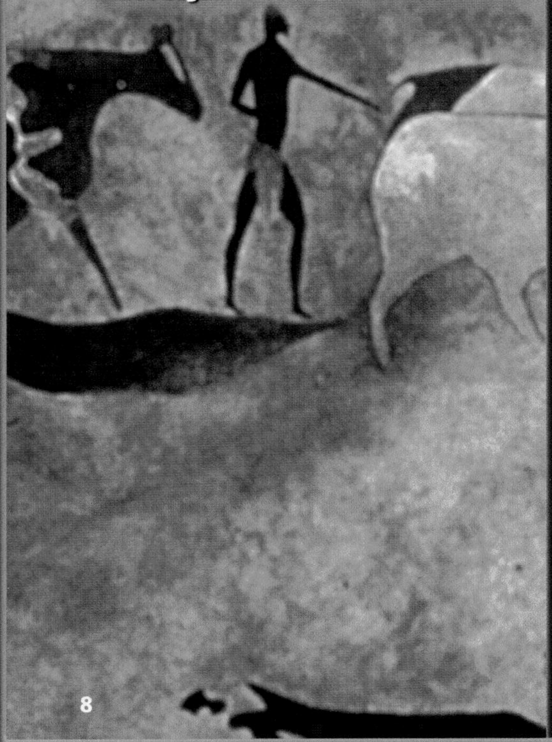

8

5000 BC

AFRICA

▶ The pyramids of Egypt, built during the Old Kingdom, served as tombs for pharaohs.

THE AMERICAS

▶ The Olmec, an influential early Mesoamerican people, carved colossal stone heads.

5000 BC

ASIA

c. 4000 BC
Large cities begin to appear in Sumer.

▶ Babylon was one of the greatest cities of the ancient world. Archaeologists have found the ruins of the Ishtar Gate (right).

EUROPE

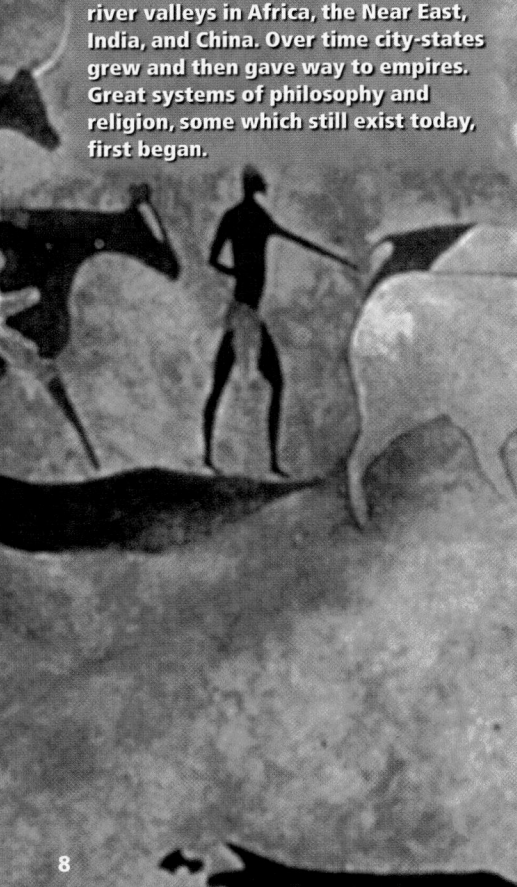

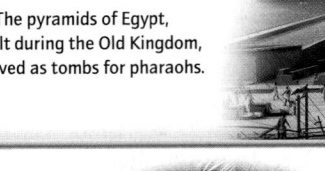

2500 BC

c. 3100 BC Menes unifies Upper and Lower Egypt.

The Old Kingdom c. 2650–2150 BC

The New Kingdom c. 1550–1070 BC

c. 730 BC Kush conquers Egypt.

c. 300 BC King Ezana of Aksum converts to Christianity

AD 1

1000 BC Maya civilization begins to develop

Olmecs 1200–300 BC

c. 300 BC First Hohokam communities begin in Arizona.

c. 400 BC The Moche culture develops in Peru's coastal desert.

2500 BC

c. 2500 BC The Indus Valley civilization develops.

1792 BC Hammurabi becomes king of Babylon.

c. 1250 BC Hinduism begins to develop.

Shang Dynasty c. 1766–1150 BC

c. 1200s BC Moses leads the Hebrews from Egypt to Canaan.

c. 500 BC The Buddha seeks enlightenment.

256 BC The Zhou dynasty ends.

AD 1

c 29 AD Jesus of Nazareth spreads his message in Judea.

c. 2100 BC Minoan culture appears in Crete.

1200s BC According to legend, the Trojan War is fought.

753 BC Romulus establishes the city of Rome.

509 BC The Roman Republic begins.

c. 500 BC Democracy begins in Athens.

323 BC Alexander the Great dies.

Pax Romana 27 BC–AD 180

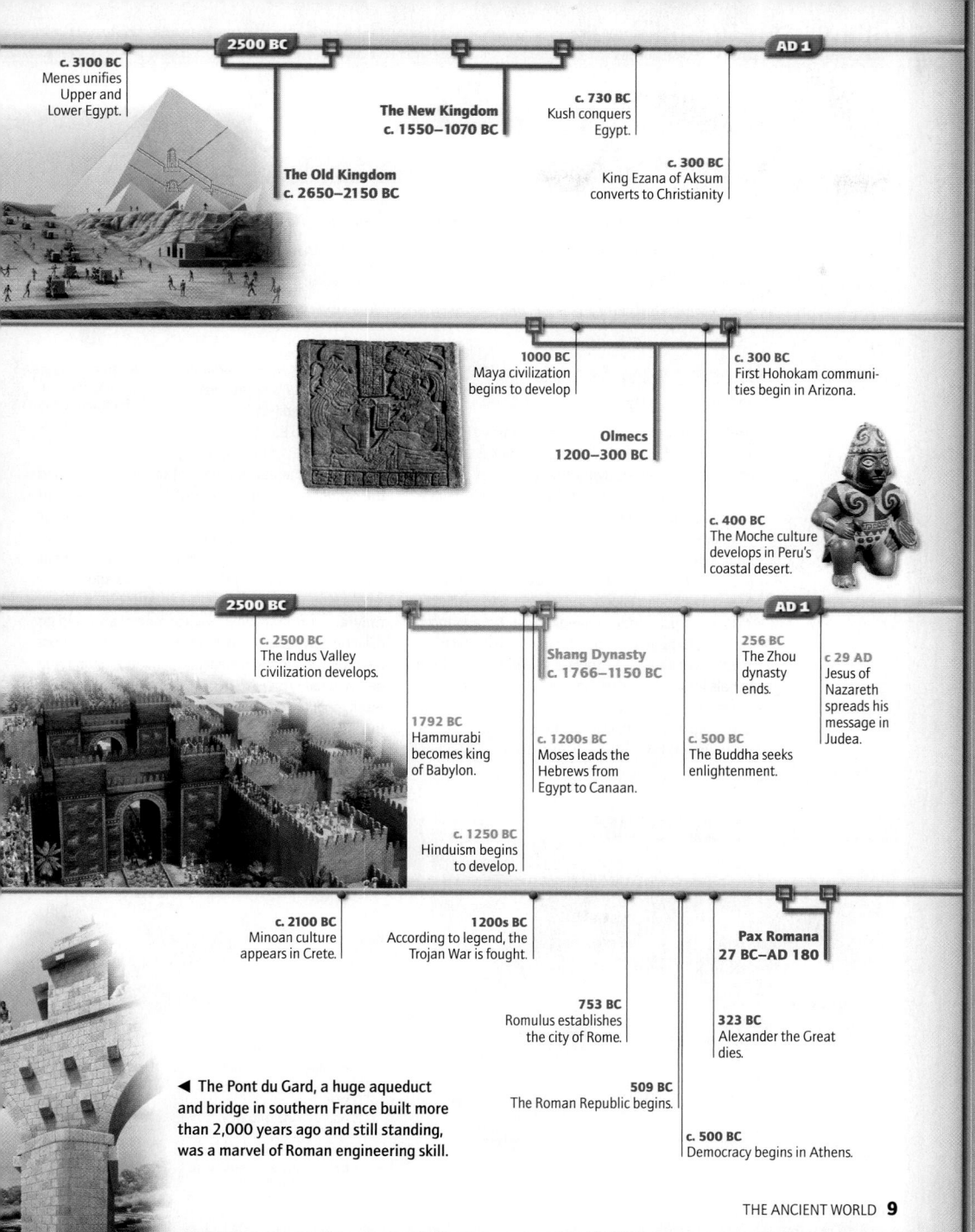

◀ The Pont du Gard, a huge aqueduct and bridge in southern France built more than 2,000 years ago and still standing, was a marvel of Roman engineering skill.

•Prologue Preview•

Primary Source

"Hail to thee, O Nile! Who manifests thyself over this land, and comes to give life to Egypt! Mysterious is thy issuing forth from the darkness, on this day whereon it is celebrated! Watering the orchards created by Re, to cause all the cattle to live, you give the earth to drink, inexhaustible one!"
—Ancient Egyptian Hymn to the Nile, c. 2100 BC

Reading Like a Historian

Analyzing Visuals The four time lines on this page show the chronological development of the world's ancient civilizations. The pyramids of ancient Egypt shown in the top image are just one of many engineering marvels of the ancient world. Around the same time the Egyptians were building the pyramids, the people of Mesopotamia built immense temples called ziggurats and people in the Indus Valley built the great cities of Harappa and Mohenjo Daro.

Preteach

Exploring the Topic

Have students write a definition of the word *civilization*. Next have students list what they believe were the characteristics of the world's earliest civilizations. Have students to describe the geographic features they think would have benefitted early civilizations.

Key Terms

Preteach the following terms:

artifacts objects used by hominids such as tools, clothing, and weapons (p. 10)

nomads people who wander from place to place in search of food (p. 11)

surplus extra food (p. 11)

division of labor people specializing in different kinds of work (p. 11)

civilizations complex and organized societies (p. 11)

artisans skilled workers of tools, pottery, and other goods (p. 11)

cultural diffusion the spread of ideas and other aspects of culture (p. 11)

Info to Know

Early Hominid Scientists working in Ethiopia recently discovered a 3.3 million-year-old skeleton of a young hominid. The female is believed to have been three years old at death, making this skeleton the oldest ever found of a hominid so young. Scientists described the fossil as belonging to a species in transition from ape to human. Researchers are hopeful that the skeleton will reveal more information about the evolution of the early ancestors of humans.

Teaching Tip

Using a large map of the ancient world, point out the locations of the four early civilizations identified in this section. Ask students why they think the earliest civilizations developed in those locations. *fertile soil in the river valleys supported agriculture; rivers could be used for transporting goods*

TERMS

artifact
nomads
surplus
division of labor
civilization
artisans
cultural diffusion

Prehistory and the Beginnings of Civilization

The earliest human ancestors appeared millions of years ago. By about 11,000 years ago, modern humans had spread from Africa to all continents except Antarctica. They developed stone tools and agriculture, setting the stage for the formation of civilizations. This time before recorded history is called prehistory.

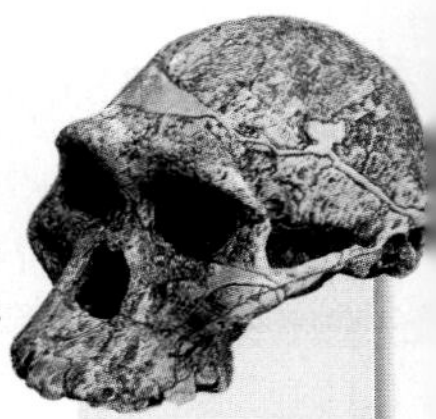

Australopithecine first appeared in Africa about 4–5 million years ago.

Unlocking the Secrets of Prehistory

Early humans are known as hominids. Hominids include humans as well as earlier humanlike creatures. By studying the remains of hominid skeletons, scientists can determine what hominids looked like and how long they lived.

Scientists called anthropologists study fossilized remains of early humans, while other scientists called archaeologists study objects used by hominids such as tools and weapons. These objects are called **artifacts**. Anthropologists and archaeologists use advanced technologies to date human remains and artifacts.

Early humans used tools and weapons to hunt animals for food. As they became successful hunters, they migrated, or moved over great distances, following the moving herds. Over many generations, hominids migrated from Africa to Asia. Eventually, a new human species called *Homo sapiens* appeared. *Homo sapiens* may have developed first in Africa and later spread to Europe and Asia.

The period of prehistory that begins with the development of stone tools is called the Stone Age. Almost all artifacts that have been found from this time were made of stone. The oldest part of the Stone Age is called the Paleolithic Era, or Old Stone Age. The Old Stone Age lasted from about 2.5 million years until about 10,000 years ago.

As later Stone Age people migrated out of Africa, they encountered new environments and had to develop new tools and skills to adapt to these environments. For example, in colder regions, later Stone Age people needed more than fire to keep them warm. As a result, people learned to make needles from bone and then used the needles to sew together animal skins for clothing.

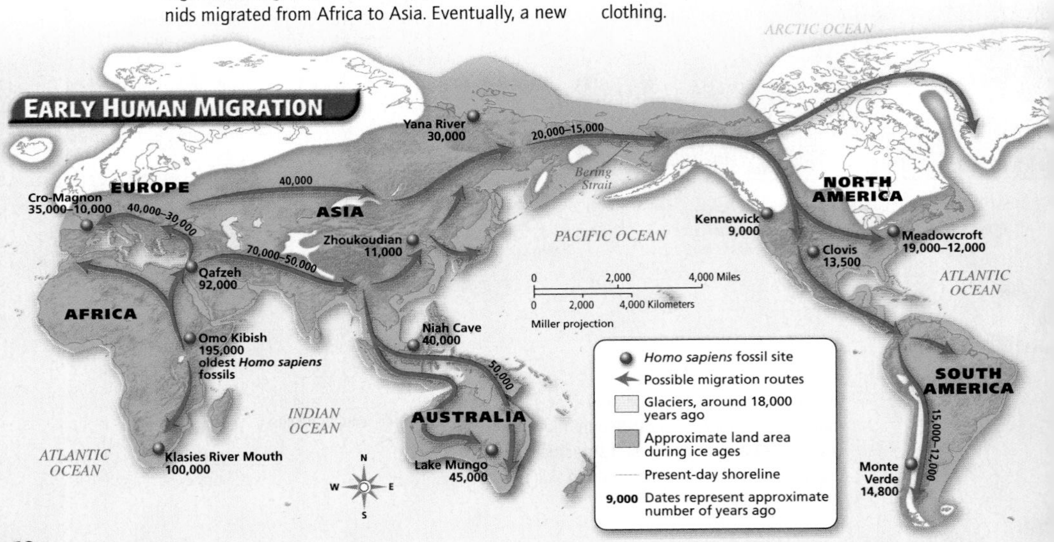

10

Differentiating Instruction

Below Level

Learners Having Difficulty

Background: Tell students that a major part of trying to understand the lives of prehistoric people is understanding the environment in which they lived.

1. Write the following headings for students to see:
   - Tools and Technology
   - Clothing and Shelter
   - Stone Age Societies
2. Have students work in pairs to list all the facts they can find in this section and place them under the appropriate heading. When possible, they should indicate whether a development took place during the Old Stone Age, the Middle Stone Age, or the New Stone Age.
3. Have volunteers read the items from their lists to the class.
4. Guide the class in a discussion of life in the Stone Age. **LS Interpersonal, Verbal-Linguistic**

Alternative Assessment Handbook, Rubric 14: Group Activity

100,000 BC — 10,000 BC — 5,000 BC

100,000 BC
Homo sapiens begin to migrate out of Africa.

8000 BC
The Paleolithic Era ends and the Neolithic Era begins as people start to develop agriculture.

6500 BC
More than 5,000 people live in Çatal Hüyük.

From Nomadism to Settled Communities

An advance in toolmaking ability marks the New Stone Age, or Neolithic Era. Polishing or grinding replaced chipping as the means to fashion stone tools.

Other important changes began to occur during the New Stone Age. In some places, humans ceased to be **nomads**, wandering from place to place in search for food. Over time, people learned that seeds from the plants and fruits that they gathered could be planted and grown. This knowledge was a major breakthrough in human progress.

The development of agriculture, or the raising of crops for food, allowed some Neolithic peoples to settle in permanent villages along rivers or in river valleys. They planted seeds for crops such as wheat, barley, and rice, most likely using sharpened sticks to make furrows in the earth. They also began to domesticate, or tame, animals such as cattle, goats, sheep, and pigs. This shift occurred between about 8000 BC and about 3000 BC and is known as the Neolithic agricultural revolution.

Some Neolithic farming settlements grew into villages of considerable size, with walls and mud-brick houses. One such village was Çatal Hüyük, in present-day Turkey. By 6500 BC, Çatal Hüyük was home to around 5,000 people.

Characteristics of Civilization

As societies became more settled, and villages grew in size and complexity, the first cities began to appear. Cities differed from villages in being larger, more densely populated, more formally organized, and more complex economically. Cities relied on people being able to produce an agricultural **surplus**, or extra food. This surplus allowed for a **division of labor**, with people specializing in different types of work and a method developing for the exchange of goods and services. For example, toolmakers could spend their time on their work and then trade their products for food.

Agricultural surplus, a division of labor, and large cities all needed to be in place in order for the first **civilizations**, or complex and organized societies, to appear. The first civilizations arose in four river valleys. These were (1) the Nile River valley in Africa, (2) the valley of the Tigris and Euphrates rivers in southwestern Asia, (3) the Indus River valley in southern Asia, and (4) the Huang River valley in eastern Asia.

In these four valleys, the rivers rise and flood during heavy rains. Except for rainy periods, however, little rain falls. The regular flooding and a warm climate helped farmers grow crops. Advances in farming enabled the populations of early civilizations to increase.

Different forms of leadership emerged to help run early civilizations. These were the first governments. Governments made rules to guide people's behavior and help them plan and regulate their work. Government leaders also enforced the rules.

This model from ancient Egypt depicts division of labor—pounding grain into flour, rolling dough, and baking bread.

A number of different social classes also developed. A class of skilled workers called **artisans** made tools, pottery, and other goods. Other people became merchants and traders, buying goods from farmers or artisans and then reselling them. Traders not only transported goods to be sold, they also passed along ideas. The spread of beliefs, customs, and technologies from one culture to another is called **cultural diffusion**.

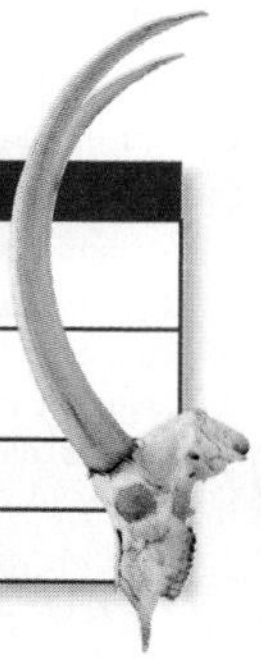

KEY FACTS

- *Homo sapiens* first emerged in Africa between 400,000 and 100,000 years ago.
- Animals such as dogs, cattle, goats, sheep, and pigs were first domesticated between 12,000 and 4,000 years ago.
- Agriculture developed in Africa and Asia about 10,000 years ago.
- The first civilizations emerged in the river valleys of Africa and Asia.

REVIEW

1. **Identify** (a) artifacts, (b) Neolithic Age, (c) civilization
2. **Define** (a) prehistory, (b) surplus, (c) division of labor, (d) cultural diffusion
3. How did the development of towns and cities affect early humans?

Direct Teach

Reading Focus

From Nomadism to Settled Communities

Name What is another name for the New Stone Age? *Neolithic Age*

Identifying Cause and Effect What key breakthroughs led to the development of settled communities? *planting seeds for crops; domesticating animals*

Reading Focus

Characteristics of Civilization

Recall What was about to occur at the end of the New Stone Age? *the development of civilizations*

Explain How do you think division of labor impacted work in early civilizations? *possible answer—It increased efficiency because workers could become proficient at their one task, rather than trying to learn many different tasks.*

Skill Focus: Interpreting Time Lines

At Level

Social Studies Skill
The Development of Humanity

1. Have students create a time line that includes the dates listed in this section.
2. Have students create their time lines to scale. Two inches, for example, could represent 100,000 years. The earliest date on their time lines (i.e. the date at the left end of the line) should be 400,000 years ago, to represent the first emergence of *Homo sapiens* in Africa.
3. Have a volunteer recreate his or her time line on the board. A new scale will be needed so the entire class can see it (e.g. two feet could represent 100,000 years).
4. Discuss as a class how the pace of change has accelerated over the course of human history.

LS Visual-Spatial

Alternative Assessment Handbook, Rubric 36: Time Line

Answers

1. **(a.)** *objects used by hominids such as tools, clothing, and weapons;* **(b.)** *the New Stone Age, beginning in 8000 BC;* **(c.)** *a complex, organized society;* **2. (a.)** *the period of time before writing was developed;* **(b.)** *extra food;* **(c.)** *people specializing in different kinds of work;* **(d.)** *the spread of ideas and other aspects of culture;* **3.** *possible answer—People settled in one location, produced their own food through agriculture, and eventually developed civilizations.*

Preteach

Exploring the Topic

Have students list five things that come to mind when they think of ancient Egypt. Then ask students why they think Egypt has been called the "Gift of the Nile." Have them explain what Mesopotamia could be considered the "gift of."

Key Terms

Preteach the following terms:

Menes king of Upper Egypt who united Egypt under one dynasty (p. 12)

pharaoh title of Egyptian rulers; means "great house" (p. 12)

polytheism belief in many gods (p. 12)

monotheism belief in only one god (p. 12)

Ahkenaten pharaoh who tried to change Egypt's religious beliefs from polytheism to monotheism (p. 12)

Ramses II pharaoh after Akhenaten; known as Ramses the Great (p. 12)

cuneiform Sumerian sign-based system of writing (p. 13)

ziggurats Sumerian temples (p. 13)

Solomon Hebrew king who ruled during the height of Israel's wealth and power (p. 13)

Diaspora scattering (p. 13)

Biography

Hatshepsut (1503 B.C.–1468 B.C.?)

Hatshepsut was the daughter of pharaoh Tuthmosis I and Ahmose, his Great Royal Wife. Hatshepsut married her half-brother Tuthmosis II, strengthening his claim to the Egyptian throne. After he died, their young son Tuthmosis III inherited the kingship. Hatshepsut, however, seized power. As Egypt's leader, she initiated a large-scale building program and sent trading expeditions to foreign lands. After Thuthmosis III reached adulthood, he overthrew his mother's government. After taking power, the new pharaoh ordered Hatshepsut's monuments destroyed. Her fate is unknown.

Answers

Old Kingdom Pyramids *possible answer—Believing their rulers to be divine, Egyptians wanted to properly honor the pharaohs and prepare them for the afterlife.*

TERMS
Menes
pharaoh
polytheism
monotheism
Akhenaten
Ramses II
cuneiform
ziggurats
Solomon
diaspora

Ancient Egypt and the Near East 5000–350 BC

About 5,000 years ago, two great centers of civilization developed in Africa and the Near East. Along the banks of the Nile River, the kingdom of Egypt built monuments to its rulers. In Mesopotamia, the "land between two rivers," a series of kingdoms rose and fell and the religion that became Judaism was born.

The Nile River offered Egyptians water for farming and abundant plant and wildlife.

Egypt—"Gift of the Nile"

Each year the Nile floods its banks, spreading soil rich for farming. Although early Egyptian farmers could not explain the floods, they learned to use the floods to their advantage. They also dug short canals to carry water to their fields. This system of irrigation helped farmers grow several crops a year.

Over time, a stable political and cultural system established itself in Egypt. Two distinct cultures developed along the Nile: Lower Egypt and Upper Egypt. Sometime after 3100 BC, **Menes,** a king of Upper Egypt, united Egypt under a dynasty, or family of rulers. Later, rulers took the title **pharaoh**, which means "great house." From the time of Menes until almost 300 BC, some 30 dynasties ruled Egypt. Historians have divided this time period into the Old Kingdom, the Middle Kingdom, and the New Kingdom.

During the Old Kingdom (about 2650 to 2150 BC), Egyptians built temples and pyramids to serve as tombs for their leaders. The Middle Kingdom (about 2055 to 1650 BC) was a golden age marked by stability and prosperity. During the New Kingdom (about 1550 to 1070 BC), strong pharaohs established rule over many peoples and territories.

Ancient Egyptians practiced **polytheism**, or the belief in many gods. They also believed in a life after death. To make this possible, however, the body had to be preserved. They developed a process called mummification and built elaborate tombs to protect the pharaoh's body.

Despite most Egyptians' polytheism, pharaoh Amenhotep IV (1380 to 1362 BC) believed in only one god. This belief is known as **monotheism**. Amenhotep's god was the sun, symbolized by a disk called Aten. To honor Aten, the pharaoh changed his name to **Akhenaten**, meaning "he who is pleasing Aten." Akhenaten attempted to change Egypt's religion. On his death, the old gods were restored.

Following the death of Akhenaten, Egypt returned to polytheism. In 1279 BC **Ramses II** became the new ruler. His reign lasted more than 60 years. Sometimes called Ramses the Great, he kept the Egyptian empire together and built many monuments and temples.

Old Kingdom Pyramids

The famous pyramids of Egypt were built during the Old Kingdom. Mostly located along the lower Nile, the pyramids were built as tombs for kings.

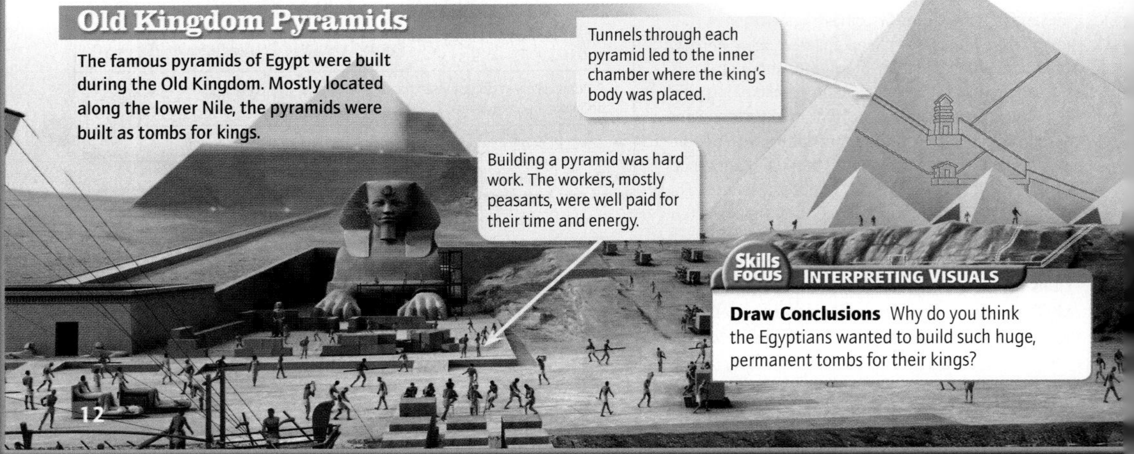

Tunnels through each pyramid led to the inner chamber where the king's body was placed.
Building a pyramid was hard work. The workers, mostly peasants, were well paid for their time and energy.

Skills FOCUS INTERPRETING VISUALS

Draw Conclusions Why do you think the Egyptians wanted to build such huge, permanent tombs for their kings?

12

Differentiating Instruction

Below Level

English-Language Learners

1. Organize the class into mixed-ability pairs. Have each pair review the information on this page about ancient Egypt.
2. Next, have each pair create a poster that illustrates life in ancient Egypt. Encourage students to include pictures, maps, their own drawings, and quotes in their posters.
3. Display student posters in the classroom. Guide a discussion about the aspects of ancient Egypt depicted in the posters.

LS Visual-Spatial, Interpersonal

Alternative Assessment Handbook, Rubric 28: Posters

5000 BC — 3000 BC — 1000 BC

c. 4000 BC Large cities begin to appear in Sumer.

c. 3100 BC Menes unifies Upper and Lower Egypt.

Old Kingdom Egypt c. 2650–2150 BC

c. 2330 BC Akkadian king Sargon I creates the world's first empire.

1792 BC Hammurabi becomes king of Babylon.

New Kingdom Egypt c. 1550–1070 BC

965 BC Solomon becomes king of Israel.

586 BC Chaldeans conquer Judah. Diaspora begins.

Mesopotamia

In southwestern Asia, another civilization was forming. In Neolithic times, people began to settle in the wide valley between the Tigris and Euphrates rivers. Called Mesopotamia, or the "land between two rivers," it was known for its fertile soil. In fact, historians call this crescent-shaped area the Fertile Crescent. A series of kingdoms rose and fell in the Fertile Crescent. Look at the chart below to learn more about them.

Around 4000 BC, the Sumerians created the first civilization to take root in the Fertile Crescent. The Sumerians were responsible for several important cultural developments. They created a unique form of writing. Sumerians wrote by pressing marks into wet clay tablets with a wedge-shaped tool. Sumerian writing is known today as **cuneiform**. Sumerians had about 600 cuneiform signs. They also developed a system of numbers. In addition, Sumerians built impressive temples known as **ziggurats.** Made of baked brick stacked in layers, ziggurats could be up to 150 feet high and look to us something like a wedding cake. The top of the ziggurat served as a shrine to a Sumerian god.

Judaism

About 1200 BC, as empires rose and fell in the Fertile Crescent, another people, the Hebrews, came from Egypt to occupy a strip of land known as Canaan. The Hebrews traced their roots to Mesopotamia, where they lived from around 2000 to 1500 BC. These early Hebrews were monotheists. Their religion became Judaism. The Hebrews also believed in prophets, messengers sent to reveal the will of God. These messages often formed the basis for Jewish moral standards.

Around 1000 BC, the Hebrews established a kingdom in Canaan called Israel, uniting their 12 tribes under a single ruler. Under its third king, **Solomon**, Israel reached the height of its wealth and power. In the late 900s BC, however, the 10 northern tribes revolted, splitting the kingdom in two. By about 722 BC, the Assyrians had conquered the northern kingdom, still called Israel. In 586 BC, the Chaldeans captured the southern kingdom, called Judah, and sent the Jews, as its people were known, into exile. This was the beginning of the **Diaspora**, or scattering, of Jews.

Key Facts

- About 5,000 years ago, advanced civilizations relying on irrigated agriculture developed in rivers valleys in Egypt and Mesopotamia.
- Old Kingdom pharaohs built pyramids.
- A series of city-states and kingdoms, including Sumer, Babylon, and Persia, dominated the Fertile Crescent from 4000 BC to 500 BC.
- In 1792, Babylonian king Hammurabi created the first major code of laws.
- Chaldeans conquered Judah in 586 BC; Jewish Diaspora began.

REVIEW

1. **Identify** (a) Nile River, (b) Mesopotamia, (c) Israel
2. **Define** (a) pharaoh, (b) polytheism, (c) monotheism, (d) diaspora
3. Name two peoples who established empires in the Fertile Crescent.

Mesopotamian Empires

AKKADIANS (c. 2330 BC)
People from northern Mesopotamia who conquered the Sumerians. Their empire lasted 150 years.

BABYLONIANS (c. 1750 BC)
Powerful group that united Mesopotamia and established their capital in the city of Babylon. Their ruler, Hammurabi, established the first code of laws, called the Code of Hammurabi.

HITTITES (c. 1250 BC)
Warlike people who invaded the Tigris-Euphrates Valley; they were among the first people to smelt iron.

ASSYRIANS (c. 650 BC)
Warlike people who used chariots in battle; they captured and destroyed Babylon around 700 BC. At its height, their empire stretched from Mesopotamia to the Nile Valley.

CHALDEANS (c. 600 BC)
Chaldeans conquered most of the Assyrian Empire. Their leader attempted to restore Babylon to its former glory.

PERSIANS (c. 500 BC)
Persians conquered Babylon in 539 BC; they expanded government and built many roads to connect cities.

Collaborative Learning — At Level

Empires of Mesopotamia

1. Organize students into six small groups. Assign one of the six Mesopotamian empires listed at the bottom of this page (Akkadian, Babylonian, Hittite, Assyrian, Chaldean, Persian) to each of the groups.
2. Have each group prepare a presentation on their assigned empire. Group members should share responsibilities in the researching, planning, and preparing of the presentation. Encourage students to include multimedia elements in their presentations.
3. Have each group synthesize the information its members found and present it to the class. Have groups explain why the empire they researched is important in world history.

LS **Verbal-Linguistic, Interpersonal**

Alternative Assessment Handbook, Rubrics 14: Group Activity; and 29: Presentations

Direct Teach

Reading Focus

Mesopotamia

Identify A fertile valley lay between which two rivers in Mesopotamia? *Tigris and Euphrates*

Speculate Why do you think the Sumerians developed a system of writing? *possible answers—to help them manage trade and other aspects of their expanding economy; to communicate; for religious rituals*

Reading Focus

Judaism

Name What was the name of Israel's first king? *Saul*

Analyze Why do you think the Hebrews were vulnerable to foreign conquest? *possible answers—division within their kingdom; smaller population than their conquerors*

MISCONCEPTION ALERT

Who was the world's first known author? An Egyptian? An Old Testament scribe? The title instead belongs to a woman named Enheduanna, daughter of Sargon the Great. After the Akkadian king Sargon conquered Sumer in the 2340s B.C., he installed Enheduanna as high priestess at the city of Ur. In this position, she wrote hymns to the goddess Inanna. Several of these hymns have survived, making them the earliest writings that can be attributed to a named author.

Answers

1. **(a.)** *river in Lower and Upper Egypt that flooded annually to create fertile land for farming;* **(b.)** *wide fertile valley in Southwest Asia between the Tigris and Euphrates Rivers;* **(c.)** *Hebrew kingdom in Canaan;* **2. (a.)** *title of Egyptian rulers meaning "great house;"* **(b.)** *belief in many gods;* **(c.)** *belief in one god;* **(d.)** *scattering;* **3.** *possible answer—Babylonians and Assyrians*

Preteach

Exploring the Topic

Have students list what they know about ancient India and ancient China. Ask them to explain how those civilizations still impact the world today. Then have them try to identify ways that they personally are affected by the ideas and achievements of ancient India and ancient China.

Key Terms

Preteach the following terms:

Aryans warrior civilization that entered India after the decline of the Harappans (p. 14)

Vedas great works of Aryan religious literature (p. 14)

Hinduism religion founded in India that teaches that souls are reborn over and over again (p. 14)

Chandragupta Maurya established the Mauryan Empire in India (p. 14)

Ashoka Chandragupta's grandson; increased size of his kingdom (p. 14)

Buddhism religion founded by Siddhartha Gautama (p. 14)

Mandate of Heaven right granted by the god of Heaven to rule China (p. 15)

Confucius a leading philosopher of ancient China (p. 15)

Daoism Chinese philosophy (p. 15)

Legalism people who believed harsh laws should be enforced to counter people's selfish, untrustworthy natures (p.15)

Recent Scholarship

Gregory Possehl's book *The Indus Civilization: A Contemporary Perspective*, presents an overview of the most current knowledge on the ancient society, exploring technology, subsistence, political organization, religion, and other aspects.

The Indus Civilization: A Contemporary Perspective by Gregory Possehl. AltaMira Press, 2003.

TERMS

Aryans
Vedas
Hinduism
Chandragupta Maurya
Ashoka
Buddhism
Mandate of Heaven
Confucius
Daoism
Legalism

Ancient India and China

2500 BC–AD 250

About 4,500 years ago, other great civilizations arose in the river valleys of India and China. The societies shared many key characteristics, but also developed distinctive cultures and patterns of life.

This statue was among the ruins of Mohenjo Daro in the Indus Valley.

Early Civilizations on the Indian Subcontinent

The first Indian civilization developed in the Indus River Valley on the Indian subcontinent, which extends south from central Asia to the Indian Ocean. About 2500 BC, two large cities, Harappa and Mohenjo Daro, arose. The civilization centered on these cities is known as the Harappan, after the first city.

After the decline of the Indus Valley civilization, a warrior civilization, the **Aryans**, came to dominate the region. Aryans had superior military technology, using armies of chariots, and undertook many cultural and religious changes.

Most of what is known about the Aryans comes from the **Vedas**, their great works of religious literature. The Vedas describe a complicated social structure divided into four classes, or *varnas*. Brahmins were the highest varna. The Brahmins were often priests who explained and interpreted the Vedas.

Over time, the Vedas formed one of the bases of the religion known as **Hinduism**, which spread throughout India. Among the most basic tenets of Hinduism is the belief in Brahman, the eternal being that created and preserves the world. Hinduism also teaches that souls are reborn over and over again. This belief is called reincarnation, or *samsara*. Another principle of Hinduism is *dharma*. *Dharma* involves a person's responsibility to live morally so that the soul can escape the cycle of rebirth.

Empires in India In 320 BC, an adventurer named **Chandragupta Maurya** appeared in India. He established the Mauryan Empire, which ruled for almost 150 years. Chandragupta's grandson, Ashoka, came to power in about 270 BC. **Ashoka** fought bloody wars to increase the size of his kingdom and proved to be an even greater ruler than his grandfather.

Before the time of the Mauryan Empire, the religion of **Buddhism** began. Its founder, Siddhartha Gautama, became known as the Buddha, or "Enlightened One." The Buddha accepted some Hindu ideas but also believed that desire had to be eliminated

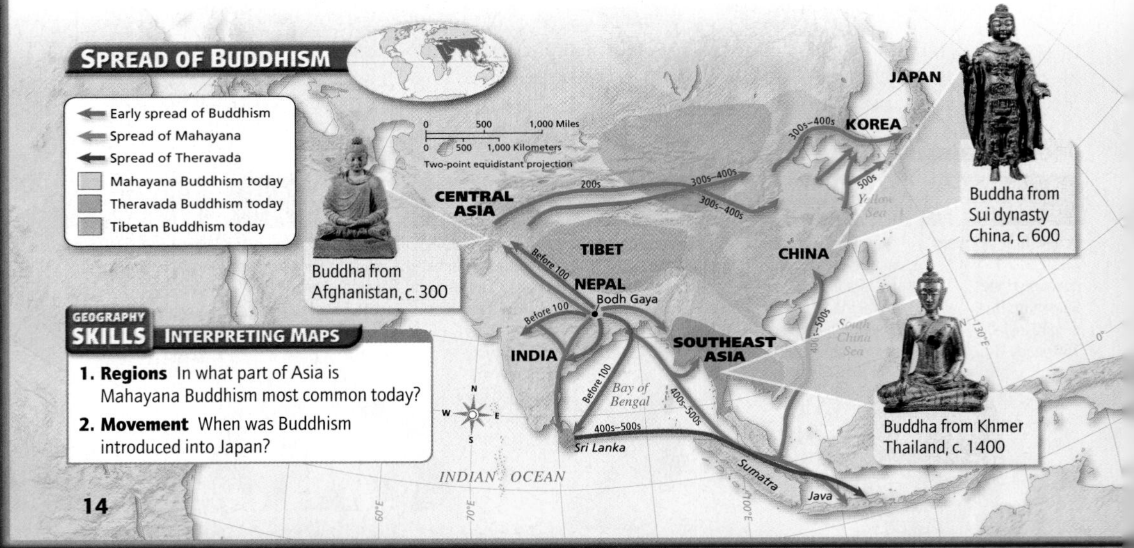

GEOGRAPHY SKILLS INTERPRETING MAPS

1. **Regions** In what part of Asia is Mahayana Buddhism most common today?
2. **Movement** When was Buddhism introduced into Japan?

14

Skills Focus: Identifying Cause and Effect

At Level

Research Required

Reading Skill

Harappan Civilization

1. Review with students the information in the text about the Harappan civilization.
2. Have students conduct research about the Harappan civilization to learn more about its characteristics.
3. Have students write an essay or prepare a multimedia presentation on the rise and decline of the Harappan civilization.
4. Have students present their work to the class. Guide a class discussion about the vulnerabilities of ancient civilizations.

LS Verbal-Linguistic

Alternative Assessment Handbook, Rubrics 29: Presentations; and 30: Research

Answers

Interpreting Maps 1. *China;* 2. *refer to map*

2500 BC — 1500 BC — 500 BC

c. 2500 BC The Indus Valley civilization develops.

Shang Dynasty c. 1766 BC–1150 BC

c. 1500 BC The Aryans gain power in India.

c. 1250 BC Hinduism begins to develop.

c. 500 BC The Buddha seeks enlightenment.

256 BC The Zhou dynasty ends.

from people's lives. He taught that salvation comes from knowing "Four Noble Truths."

Ashoka became a Buddhist and attempted to spread the Buddhist faith in India and to other countries. For nearly 500 years Buddhism flourished. However, around AD 320, a new dynasty called the Gupta arose. The Guptas favored Hinduism over Buddhism. Hinduism became the dominant religion of India and remains so today.

Civilization in China

A land of enormous size, China has great geographic diversity. Rugged mountains and harsh deserts isolated China from the civilizations of India and the west. As a result, China developed its own independent culture.

Early Kingdoms The first dynasty to unite most of China was the Shang, around 1766 BC. The Shang established a complex bureaucracy—a government organized into different levels. This system served as a model for future governments of China.

About 1150 BC, a people called the Zhou overthrew the Shang. Zhou rulers believed that the gods determined who should rule China, an idea known as the **Mandate of Heaven**. Throughout Chinese history, rulers of new dynasties claimed that the old dynasty had lost this mandate.

Zhou rulers instituted many changes. A leading philosopher who helped explain these changes was **Confucius.** Confucius's followers collected his ideas and teachings, and in time this body of teachings became known as Confucianism.

In 221 BC a dynasty called the Qin took power. The Qin emperor ruled harshly, and his dynasty lasted only 15 years. Still, it produced lasting changes in China. It built a series of defensive walls along China's northern border stretching about 1,500 miles. The wall became known as the Great Wall of China. The Qin also reunified China, building a strong central government.

In 206 BC the Han dynasty seized power from the Qin. Han rulers followed Confucianism and appointed Confucian scholars to high posts. China lived in relative peace during the Han dynasty. Trade in luxury goods flourished along the Silk Roads, which stretched from China to the Mediterranean Sea and linked China and the Greco-Roman world. One such good was paper, a Chinese invention that spread to the Western world.

Belief Systems Chinese philosophers and teachers sought to understand the human condition. Confucianism taught about the importance of family and respect for a person's ancestors. Confucius encouraged strong, positive behavior on the part of China's leaders, hoping they could solve the social and political problems of the time.

Laozi (top) and Confucius (right) brought the philosophies of Daoism and Confucianism to Chinese society, helping to shape many of the early dynasties.

At about the same time, another important Chinese philosophy, **Daoism**, appeared. Daoism taught that people should not strive for power or wealth. Instead, they should bring themselves into harmony with the Dao, a force governing the universe and nature. Over time, Daoism became second only to Confucianism in importance in Chinese life and appealed to many different people.

Another popular belief system was **Legalism**, which dealt with politics and rose to prominence during the Qin dynasty. Legalists believed in enforcing harsh laws because people were selfish and untrustworthy. The Han dynasty attempted to balance Legalist principles with the teachings of Confucianism.

Buddhism spread to China during the Han dynasty. When the Han dynasty fell in AD 220, Buddhism grew in popularity. Amid the unrest, many peasants found comfort in the teachings of the Buddha.

Key Facts
• India's first civilization developed along the Indus River at Mohenjo Daro and Harappa.
• Hinduism and Buddhism are religions first developed in India.
• A series of ruling dynasties made China a united and strong kingdom.

Review

1. **Identify** (a) Aryan, (b) Vedas, (c) Confucius
2. **Define** (a) Hinduism, (b) Buddhism, (c) Daoism, (d) Legalism
3. How did the idea of the Mandate of Heaven influence Chinese government?

Direct Teach

Reading Focus

Civilizations in China

Recall What was the first dynasty to rule China? *Shang*

Explain What were the major principles of Confucianism? *family is important, respect ancestors, leaders should exhibit strong, positive behavior*

Make Connections How was ancient China affected by cultural diffusion? *possible answer—Buddhism, a religion founded in India, spread to China and became popular.*

Primary Source

"Lead the people by laws and regulate them by penalties and the people will try to keep out of jail, but will have no sense of shame. Lead the people by virtue and restrain them by the rules of decorum, and the people will have a sense of shame, and moreover will become good."

—Confucius, *The Analects*

Skills Focus: Interpreting Literature as Historical Evidence

Belief Systems of Ancient India and China

Research Required **Above Level**

1. Organize students into five groups. Assign each group one of the following topics: Hinduism, Confucianism, Daoism, Buddhism, and Legalism.
2. Have students conduct research to find a passage of ancient literature written by a founder or follower of their assigned belief system. Passages should be at least 100 words.
3. Have each group prepare a report interpreting its selected passage. Reports should address the following questions: Why was this passage written? How might this passage have promoted its author's belief system among the people of ancient India or ancient China?
4. Have groups share their reports with the class. Discuss with students why the belief systems they studied gained popularity in ancient India or ancient China. **LS Verbal-Linguistic, Interpersonal**

Alternative Assessment Handbook, Rubrics 14: Group Activity; and 16: Judging Information

Answers

1. **(a.)** *warrior civilization that entered India after the decline of the Harappans;* **(b.)** *great works of Aryan religious literature;* **(c.)** *a leading philosopher of ancient China;* **2. (a.)** *religion founded in India that teaches that souls are reborn over and over again;* **(b.)** *religion founded by Siddhartha Gautama that teaches that people can attain salvation by knowing the "Four Noble Truths";* **(c.)** *Chinese philosophy that teaches that people should bring themselves into harmony with the Dao;* **(d.)** *Chinese belief system that promoted enforcing harsh laws because people were selfish and untrustworthy;* **3.** *possible answer—After overthrowing the government a new dynasty in China would claim to have the Mandate of Heaven to give it legitimacy.*

Preteach

Exploring the Topic

The influences of ancient Greece and Rome are still prevalent today. Have students identify examples of such influences in their community and nation. Possible ideas include classical architecture, system of government, currency, literature, and movies. Have students explain why they think the influences of ancient Greece and Rome have been so enduring.

Key Terms

Preteach the following terms:

polis Greek word for city-state (p. 16)

democracy system of government in which all citizens participate in making decisions (p. 16)

Peloponnesian War war between Athens and Sparta that ended the Greek Classical Age (p. 16)

Alexander the Great Greek conqueror of Egypt, Mesopotamia, and Persia; his conquests spread Greek culture and language (p. 16)

Hellenistic Greek-like culture (p. 16)

republic system of government in which voters elect officials to run the state (p. 17)

Julius Caesar a popular Roman general (p. 17)

Augustus title given to Octavian, the first emperor of Rome (p. 17)

Pax Romana "Roman Peace" (p. 17)

Jesus of Nazareth Jewish spiritual leader; Christianity is based on his teachings (p. 17)

Constantine Roman emperor who converted the empire to Christianity (p. 17)

MISCONCEPTION ALERT

For centuries, the *Iliad* and the *Odyssey* have been attributed to Homer. However, many scholars who have studied the texts doubt that both works were written by the same individual. They instead believe that the *Iliad* was written about a century earlier than the *Odyssey*.

TERMS
polis
democracy
Peloponnesian War
Alexander the Great
Hellenistic
republic
Julius Caesar
Augustus
Pax Romana
Jesus of Nazareth
Constantine

Ancient Greece and Rome

2000 BC–AD 400

The achievements of the civilizations of Greece and Rome had a lasting influence, especially on the cultures of Europe. Greek art, architecture, and political philosophy remained models for centuries. Rome's power and grand civic monuments inspired later generations with awe.

Artifacts like this Greek plate and this Roman coin give insight into Greek and Roman culture.

Greece in the Bronze Age

The first civilization to appear in Greece was that of the Minoans, which developed on the island of Crete as early as 3000 BC. In about 1400 BC, Mycenaeans from the Greek mainland conquered Crete. The Mycenaeans, a warlike people with strong kings, adopted many elements of Minoan culture.

In the 700s BC, long after the Mycenaean civilization had been destroyed, a blind poet named Homer wrote two long epic poems recalling the glory days of Mycenaean warfare. The poems, the *Iliad* and the *Odyssey,* tell the story of the Trojan War and its aftermath. The Greeks were polytheists, so numerous gods and goddesses appear in the poems.

Greek City-States

In the 800s and 700s BC the Greeks formed a number of independent city-states. The Greek word for city-state is **polis**. A polis usually developed around an existing fort and gave local Greeks a sense of identity. While Greeks shared a common language and culture, each polis was politically independent. This led to political disunity and rivalry. The Greeks based their governments on tribes and chiefs. Many tribes developed into small kingdoms that often went to war with one another.

The two most important city-states, Athens and Sparta, showed great differences. Athens was a direct **democracy**. All citizens participated in making decisions. Sparta, by contrast, was ruled by two kings. Sparta was known for its military strength and the discipline of its people.

In about 490 BC a series of conflicts between Greece and Persia known as the Persian Wars began. The various Greek city-states set aside their rivalries to defeat the common enemy. Following the victory over Persia, however, tension grew between Athens and Sparta. In 431 BC, the **Peloponnesian War** broke out between the two leading Greek powers. The war, which Sparta won, effectively ended what had been a classical age in Greece.

Alexander and the Spread of Hellenistic Culture

In 359 BC Philip II of Macedon conquered Greece. His 20-year-old son, Alexander, succeeded him in 336 BC, after Philip was assassinated. Philip's son would become known as **Alexander the Great.**

Alexander crushed the rebellions that broke out in Greece after his father's death. Then he set out to conquer the world. By 331 BC, Alexander ruled a huge territory that included Egypt, Mesopotamia, and Persia. He spread the Greek language and Greek ideas wherever his armies marched, influencing local cultures from the Nile River to lands bordering India. This blended culture became known as **Hellenistic**, or Greek-like. Trade routes to China, India, and Egypt also helped spread Hellenistic culture.

GREEK ACHIEVEMENTS — QUICK FACTS

- **Architecture:** built the Acropolis, a temple complex on a hill in the center of Athens; considered the finest example of Greek architecture.
- **Drama:** invented drama—plays with dialogue, conflict, and emotion.
- **Philosophy & Science:** used philosophy to understand the world; philosophers such as Aristotle laid foundations for anatomy, botany, and zoology.
- **Sports:** held athletic contests called the Olympic Games every four years to honor the Greek god Zeus.

16

Differentiating Instruction

Below Level

Special Education Students

1. Organize students into mixed-ability small groups.
2. Have students prepare a scrapbook about ancient Greece. Each group's scrapbook should include images and information about Greek literature, architecture, government, and wars.
3. Members of each group should work together to compile the scrapbook: brainstorming ideas, conducting research, note taking, placing pictures in the book, etc. Allow students enough time to compile their scrapbooks.
4. Display the completed scrapbooks on a table in the classroom. Allow students time to examine the books created by other groups.
LS Visual-Spatial, Kinesthetic

Alternative Assessment Handbook, Rubrics 14: Group Activity; and 32: Scrapbooks

2000 BC — 1000 BC — AD 1

- **c. 2100 BC** Minoan culture appears in Crete.
- **1200s BC** According to legend, the Trojan War is fought.
- **753 BC** Romulus establishes the city of Rome.
- **509 BC** The Roman Republic begins.
- **c. 500 BC** Democracy begins in Athens.
- **323 BC** Alexander the Great dies.
- **Pax Romana 27 BC–AD 180**
- **c. AD 312** Constantine becomes Christian.

The Rise of Rome

In about 750 BC some villages joined to form the city-state of Rome. At first ruled by a king, by 509 BC Rome had become a **republic.** Voters elected some of the officials who ran the state, though most people were not represented. Roman culture leaned heavily on Greek models. Romans adapted Greek gods, philosophy, architecture and literature to their own ends.

As Roman power grew, it came into conflict with Carthage, a powerful city-state on the north coast of Africa. The Punic Wars between the two city-states resulted in the destruction of Carthage. Rome also expanded to the west, conquering Macedon and Greece. By about 129 BC, Rome controlled much of the land around the Mediterranean Sea.

Internal political rivalries, class divisions, and civil war weakened the Roman Republic. A popular general named **Julius Caesar** sought power but was killed by conspirators. His grandnephew, Octavian, defeated the conspirators and, in 27 BC, made himself emperor. This was the beginning of the Roman Empire. The Roman Senate gave Octavian the title of **Augustus**, or "revered one." His reign began a period called the **Pax Romana**, or "Roman Peace," which lasted 200 years.

Rome's Fall and the Rise of Christianity

Eventually the empire grew corrupt and began to fail. Rival generals fought to become emperor. In the late AD 200s the empire was divided between East and West. During the 300s and 400s a series of invasions by Germanic tribes overwhelmed the empire's frontiers and left many people longing for new beliefs.

In this atmosphere, the Christian religion gave people hope. Based on the teachings of a Jewish spiritual leader, **Jesus of Nazareth**, Christianity at first spread slowly in the face of Roman persecution. However, by the 300s, many Romans had adopted Christianity. The Emperor **Constantine** converted to Christianity in 312 and ended the persecution of Christians the next year. Emperor Theodosius went further. In 391 he made Christianity the official religion of the empire. The last Roman emperor in the West was overthrown in 476.

ROMAN ACHIEVEMENTS — QUICK FACTS

- **Law:** Roman civil law became the basis for many of the world's law codes.
- **Engineering:** Romans built a network of roads, bridges, and aqueducts, as well as massive public works such as courthouses, theaters, and stadiums.

Engineers used human-powered cranes to lift heavy blocks of stone into place.
Arches made the overall structure incredibly strong.

KEY FACTS

- Democracy was first established in the Greek city-state of Athens.
- The conquests of Alexander the Great spread Hellenistic culture throughout the eastern Mediterranean and the Near East.
- Rome became the dominant power in the Mediterranean but lost its republican form of government in the process.
- Emperor Constantine converted to Christianity in 312. Emperor Theodosius made Christianity the official religion of the empire in 391.

REVIEW

1. **Identify** (a) Homer, (b) Alexander, (c) Jesus of Nazareth, (d) Constantine
2. **Define** (a) polis, (b) democracy, (c) republic, (d) Pax Romana
3. How did Greece influence Roman culture?

Direct Teach

Reading Focus

The Rise of Rome

Identify Which two powers fought each other in the Punic Wars? *Rome and Carthage*

Make Inferences What do you think led to the Pax Romana? *possible answer—With its great military strength, Rome defeated its rivals and was able to dominate the Mediterranean without any serious threats from other powers.*

Reading Focus

Rome's Fall and the Rise of Christianity

Identify Cause and Effect What caused the decline of the Roman Empire? *corruption, failing economy, unstable government, invasions from Germanic tribes*

Explain What role did Constantine play in the rise of Christianity? *possible answer—As emperor, he converted to Christianity, giving the religion legitimacy in the empire.*

Collaborative Learning

At Level

Research Required

Eyewitness News in Rome

1. Organize students into small groups. Have each group conduct research about an event that occurred in the Roman Republic or Roman Empire (e.g. assassination of Caesar, start of Second Punic War, Constantine's conversion).
2. Have groups prepare a television newscast reporting on the event they have selected. Students should cover the event during, or immediately following, its occurrence. Group members should play different roles in the newscast (e.g. reporters, participants in the events, eyewitnesses, etc.).
3. Have groups present their "newscasts" to the class. Discuss how the spread of news today differs from the spread of news in Roman times. **LS Interpersonal, Kinesthetic**

Alternative Assessment Handbook, Rubrics 14: Group Activity; and 33: Skit's and Reader's Theater

Answers

1. (a.) *blind Greek poet who wrote the Iliad and the* Odyssey; **(b.)** *Macedonian king who conquered a vast empire, including Persia, Egypt, and Mesopotamia;* **(c.)** *Jewish spiritual leader whose teachings underlie Christianity;* **(d.)** *Roman emperor who converted to Christianity and built the city of Constantinople;* **2. (a.)** *Greek word for city-state;* **(b.)** *system of government in which all citizens participate in making decisions;* **(c.)** *system of government in which voters elect officials to run the state;* **(d.)** *"Roman Peace;"* **3.** *possible answer—Alexander's conquests spread Greek ideas to many different lands; when the Romans later conquered many of these territories, they adopted the Hellenistic culture that had spread to those places.*

Preteach

Exploring the Topic

Have students make a list of what they know about the ancient civilizations in the Americas. Write some of their responses on the board. Discuss how the characteristics of the ancient American civilizations were similar to the characteristics of the other ancient civilizations they have previously studied.

Key Terms

Preteach the following terms:

maize corn (p. 18)

kiva underground chamber used by the Anasazi for religious ceremonies (p. 19)

Info to Know

Maya Calendar Among their many notable achievements, the Maya developed a calendar based on astronomical observation. They used this calendar to create a cycle of worship and to record the chronology of their dynasties. Many scholars believe that the Maya understood the concept of time better than any other ancient civilization.

TERMS
maize
kiva

Ancient Civilizations in the Americas 1000 BC–1500 AD

As in Africa, Asia and the Mediterranean, great civilizations also grew in the Americas. In Mexico and along the west coast of South America, mighty empires united vast territories. In North America diverse cultures thrived by adapting to an array of environments.

An Olmec sculpture of a giant head may represent a ruler, a lord, or a god.

Civilizations in Central America

Many historians think that early peoples migrated from Asia to the Americas between 35,000 or more years ago and about 8,000 years ago. Some people moved into eastern and central areas of North America. Others migrated farther south through Mexico and Central America, an area called Mesoamerica.

The Olmec civilization was the earliest culture in Mexico, starting about 1200 BC. Olmec society seems to have been mostly based on farming **maize**, or corn. The growing of maize became the foundation of all the civilizations in Mesoamerica.

Olmec civilization collapsed about 300 BC. Another, more advanced people were the Maya, who occupied rainforests on the Yucatan Peninsula and in present-day Guatemala and El Salvador starting about 1000 BC. The Maya were skilled architects and engineers. They created a series of 40 city-states in their region but did not have a unified empire. They built many steep, pyramid-shaped temples that were several stories tall, and they developed the only complete writing system in the Americas. Maya writing was based on pictographic characters called hieroglyphs. The Maya thrived from AD 300 to 900.

In about 800, a people called the Toltecs invaded the central valley of Mexico from the north. Their empire spread as far south as the Yucatán Peninsula, where their religion and designs influenced Maya pyramids and cities. In about 1200, a number of northern invaders fought one another in central Mexico. The strong group to emerge from these struggles was a people called the Aztecs.

The Aztecs were a warlike people who gradually came to rule central Mexico. Their empire grew quickly. Conquered peoples paid taxes to Aztec rulers. The Aztecs built a large capital city, Tenochtitlán,

EARLY MESOAMERICAN CIVILIZATIONS

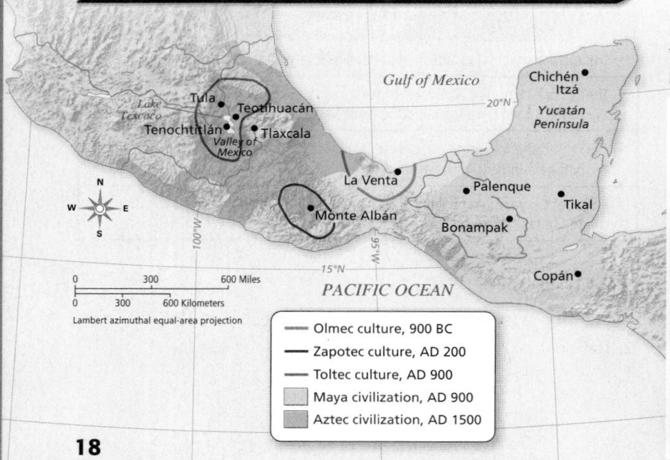

18

▼ This Maya pyramid at Tikal was the tallest structure in the Americas before the Europeans' arrival. Maya pyramids were often topped with temples.

Differentiating Instruction

Above Level

Advanced Learners/Gifted and Talented

1. Have students conduct further research into the decline of Maya civilization.
2. Have students form a thesis explaining why Maya civilization declined and build a case to support it.
3. Have students prepare short presentations in which they state their theses and give evidence to support them. Have students use presentation software to support their theses. Encourage students to ask the presenters questions. **LS Verbal-Linguistic**

Alternative Assessment Handbook, Rubrics 24: Oral Presentations; and 22: Multimedia Presentations

1000 BC — AD 1 — AD 1000

c. 1000 BC
Maya civilization begins to develop.

c. 400 BC
The Moche culture develops in Peru's coastal desert.

c. 750
The Anasazi develop pueblo architecture.

1325
The Aztecs establish their capital at Tenochtitlán.

c. 1440
Pachacuti begins to expand the Inca Empire.

Classic Age of Maya Civilization
250–900

which had pyramid temples, markets, and palaces for wealthy families. The Aztecs believed that the sun god was in a constant struggle with the forces of darkness. They "fed" the sun god with human sacrifices. The Aztecs's frequent wars gave the them a ready supply of prisoners to sacrifice. For their deeds, Aztec warriors earned prestige, wealth, and power.

Incas of South America

During the height of Aztec power in Mexico, the Inca civilization was emerging in the Andes Mountains of South America. The Incas worshiped the sun and moon. Their name meant "children of the sun." By the end of the 1400s, the Inca Empire stretched along most of the west coast of South America, including present-day Peru, Ecuador, Bolivia, and Chile. The Inca emperor had absolute power but used it to improve the empire. The Incas built fortresses and irrigation systems. They also laid roads, many of which were paved, and built bridges. Inca government was efficient, establishing an educational system that taught the imperial language and laws as well as Inca religion and history. The excellent system of roads, education, and communication helped to unify the vast empire.

North America

The greatest diversity of early American peoples was found in what is now the United States and Canada. Regional cultures developed, as people in different areas adapted to different environments. Peoples in what is now the southwestern United States, for example, lived in desert areas and learned to farm in the harsh, dry climate.

The Hohokam were one such people. Their major communities, in present-day southern Arizona, have been dated from about 300 BC to AD 500. Another ancient civilization, the Anasazi, also flourished in this area. The Anasazi built large villages on steep cliffs. The buildings were made of stone and adobe brick. The villages were later called pueblos by the Spanish. Each village had a large underground chamber called a **kiva** that was used for religious ceremonies.

Some of North America's most sophisticated cultures developed in the eastern woodlands region. This area stretches from what is now Canada to the Gulf of Mexico and from the Atlantic Ocean to the Mississippi River. A group called the Hopewell settled in the Ohio Valley region sometime around 300 to 200 BC. The Hopewell left behind many earthen mounds, which were perhaps used for burial. Some of the mounds are in the shapes of animals.

Another group that lived in the eastern woodlands was the Mississippians. They lived from about 700 to 1550 along the Mississippi River and as far east as present-day South Carolina. Like the Hopewell, the Mississippians were great mound builders. Many of their settlements centered on a ceremonial mound in a plaza on which stood a temple. The city of Cahokia, near the present-day city of East St. Louis, Illinois, was the largest such ceremonial center in North America. It had over 20,000 people and 100 mounds.

Eastern Woodlands

- Peoples included the Adena, Hopewell, Mississippian, Iroquois, Mohawk, and Seminole
- Warm and temperate forests
- Relied on hunting and gathering, as well as farming some native crops
- Longhouses built from forest materials

Adena Serpent Mound in Ohio.

Key Facts

- Early peoples migrated from Asia to North America and South America.
- Maya farmers grew maize, which became the foundation of Mesoamerican civilization.
- The Maya, Incas, and Aztecs developed sophisticated civilizations in Central and South America.
- Many different peoples, including the Anasazi and the Mississippians, lived in North America.

Review

1. **Identify** (a) Olmec, (b) Inca, (c) Hopewell
2. **Define** (a) maize, (b) kiva
3. Why did the Aztecs sacrifice human beings?

Direct Teach

Reading Focus

Inca of South America

Recall What does the name "Inca" mean? *children of the sun*

Explain How were the Inca able maintain a large unified empire? *educational system, excellent roads, strong communication system*

Reading Focus

North America

Identify What challenges did the ancient peoples of western North America face? *possible answers—lack of water, difficulty growing food*

Speculate Why do you think the Hopewell built earthen mounds? *possible answer—burial of important people; to honor gods many different tasks*

Info to Know

Cahokia Native Americans built a large city on the Illinois side of the Mississippi River across from what is now St. Louis, Missouri. Called Cahokia, this urban center thrived between A.D. 700 and A.D. 1250. The city served as the center of a trading network that stretched across North America. Cahokia's trade links extended to the Pacific Northwest, the Great Lakes, the Gulf Coast, and Florida. Surrounded by a wooden palisade that contained more than 20,000 logs, Cahokia was the largest Native American urban center north of Mexico.

Skills Focus: Evaluating Information on the Internet

At Level

Research Required

Social Studies Skill

Examining Artifacts

1. Organize the class into several small groups. Assign each of the small groups a different civilization discussed in this section.
2. Have groups use reliable online sources to conduct online research on structures or artifacts from these civilizations. Have groups choose three structures or artifacts they found and determine what information has been learned from them. Have students evaluate conclusions that have been drawn from what has been learned about the artifacts or structures.
3. Have each of the groups write a short essay describing the results of their research.

LS Verbal-Linguistic

Alternative Assessment Handbook, Rubrics 12: Drawing Conclusions; and 30: Research

Answers

1. (a.) *early Mesoamerican civilization that thrived in Mexico after 1200 BC;* **(b.)** *civilization that ruled a large empire in the Andes Mountains of South America;* **(c.)** *Native American group that built earthen mounds in the Ohio Valley region;* **2. (a.)** *corn;* **(b.)** *underground chamber used for religious ceremonies;* **3.** *to feed the sun god they worshipped*

Prologue Preview

Exploring the Time line

The Middle Ages The Middle Ages period was a time of continued growth and development among many of the world's civilizations. The period, however, was also a time of conquest and warfare. Have students consider the term "Middle Ages." Discuss with the class the reasons why this period in history is called the Middle Ages.

MISCONCEPTION ALERT

Europeans were not the first sailors to master overseas exploration. Starting in 1405, nearly a century before Columbus crossed the Atlantic, Zheng He led a series of Chinese naval expeditions to the Indian Ocean. Zheng's fleets promoted Chinese commercial interests throughout the Indian Ocean region, sailing as far as the coast of East Africa. In 1433, however, the Ming emperor brought an abrupt halt to China's overseas expeditions.

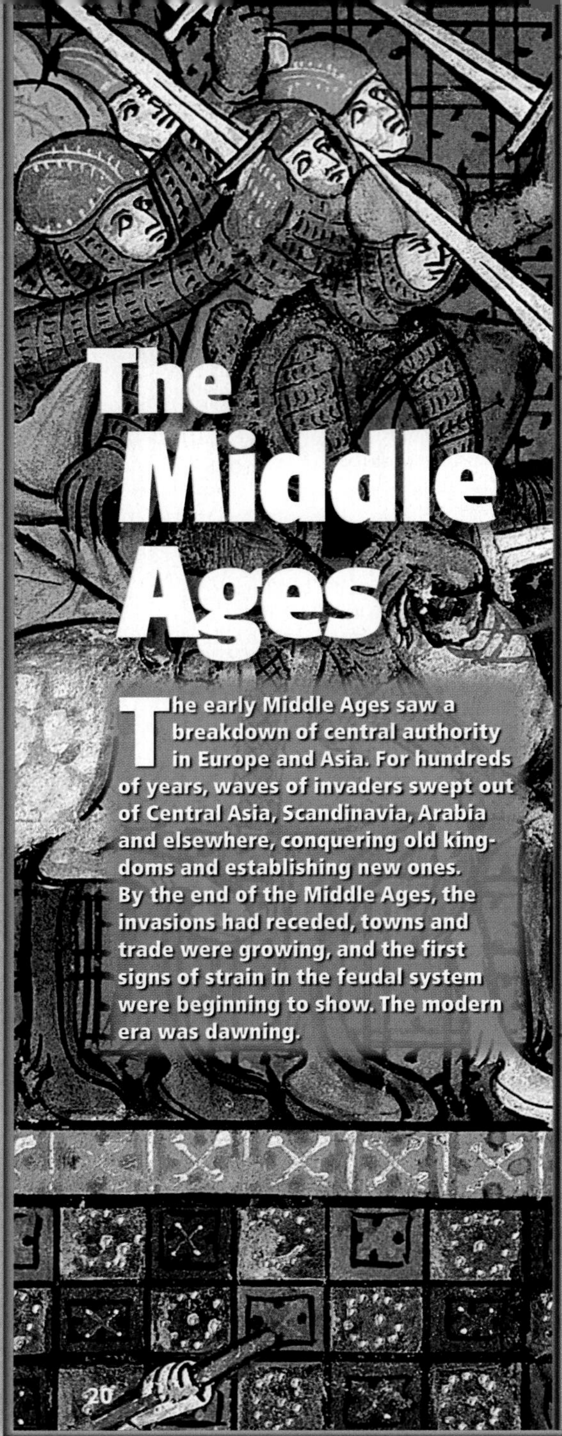

The Middle Ages

The early Middle Ages saw a breakdown of central authority in Europe and Asia. For hundreds of years, waves of invaders swept out of Central Asia, Scandinavia, Arabia and elsewhere, conquering old kingdoms and establishing new ones. By the end of the Middle Ages, the invasions had receded, towns and trade were growing, and the first signs of strain in the feudal system were beginning to show. The modern era was dawning.

500 AD

AFRICA

Ghana c. 750–1203

800 Ghana begins to emerge as a major trading empire in West Africa.

THE AMERICAS

c. 750 The Anasazi develop pueblo architecture.

800 Toltec dominate central Mexico.

▶ The Aztec capital of Tenochtitlán covered five square miles and was home to 400,000 people in 1519.

500 AD

ASIA

c. 550 Buddhism spreads from China to Japan.

618 Tang dynasty begins a classical age in China.

622 Muhammad travels to Medina—the hegira.

786 Harun al-Rashid leads the Abbasid caliphate to its height.

794 Heian period begins a golden age in Japan.

EUROPE

732 Muslim advance in Europe stopped in the Battle of Tours, in France.

800 The pope crowns Charlemagne Emperor of the Romans.

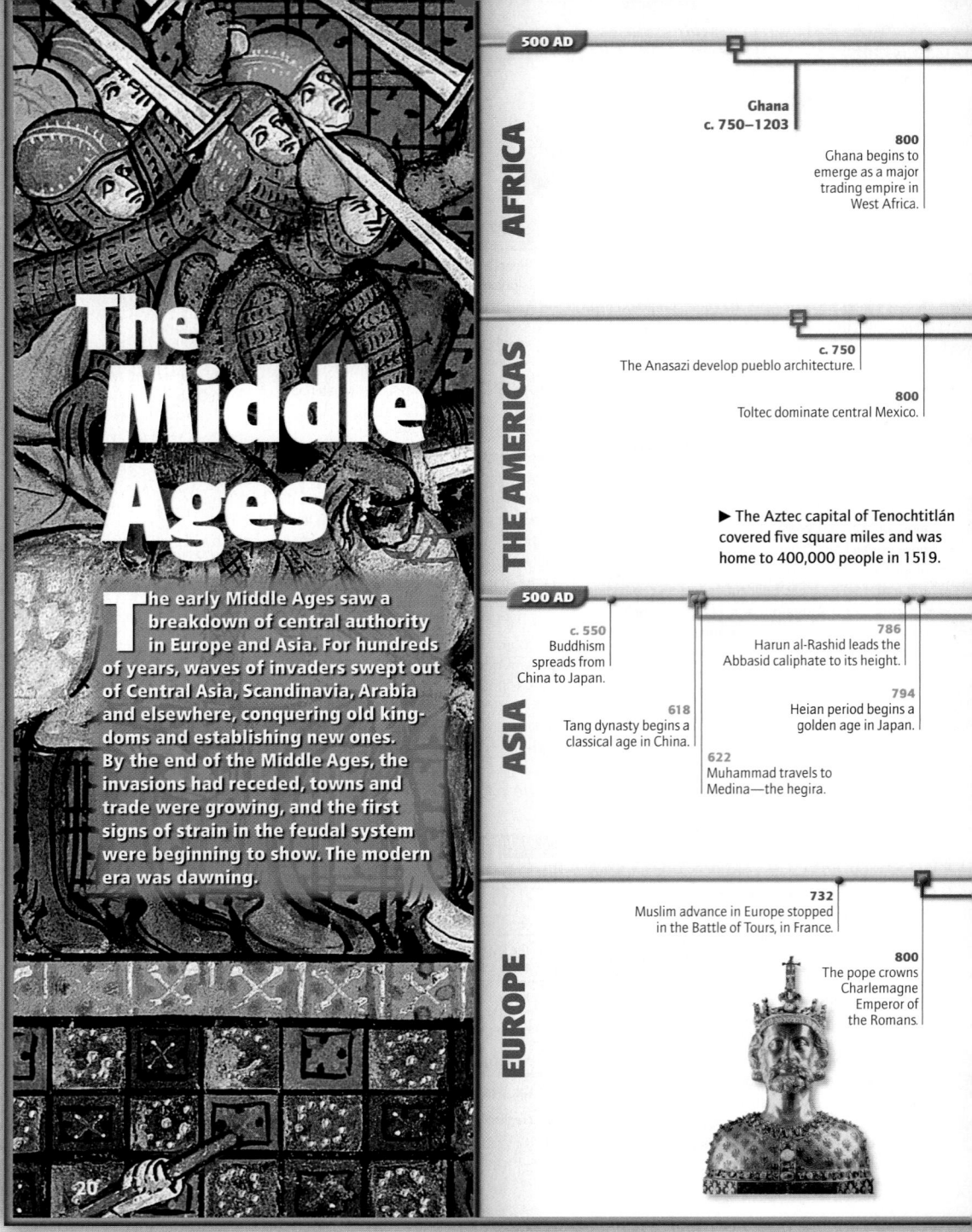

1000 AD

1500 AD

c. 1100
East African city-state Kilwa is a leading port and trade center.

c. 1235
Muslim rulers establish the empire of Mali.

1324
Mansa Musa of Mali begins a hajj to Mecca.

▶ Mansa Musa's impressive caravan included more than 60,000 people.

Mississippian Mound Builders 700–1550

1325
The Aztecs establish their capital at Tenochtitlán.

c. 1440
Pachacuti begins to expand the Inca Empire.

1492
Columbus lands in the Americas

1000 AD

1500 AD

939
Kingdom of Dai Viet gains independence from China.

969
The Fatimid dynasty is established.

1055
The Seljuk Turks take Baghdad.

1258
The Mongols capture Baghdad.

1279
Mongols take over China and found the Yuan dynasty.

1392
Choson dynasty begins in Korea.

Tang Dynasty 618–907

▶ The Mongols were one of history's most efficient military forces, conquering large parts of Asia and Europe.

Viking raids in Europe 800–1150

962
Otto the Great becomes emperor of the Holy Roman Empire.

1066
William the Conqueror wins the Battle of Hastings.

1096
The first Crusaders leave Europe to battle for the Holy Land.

1163
The building of Notre Dame cathedral begins.

1291
The Crusades end.

The Hundred Years' War 1337–1453

1347
The Black Death begins to spread through Europe.

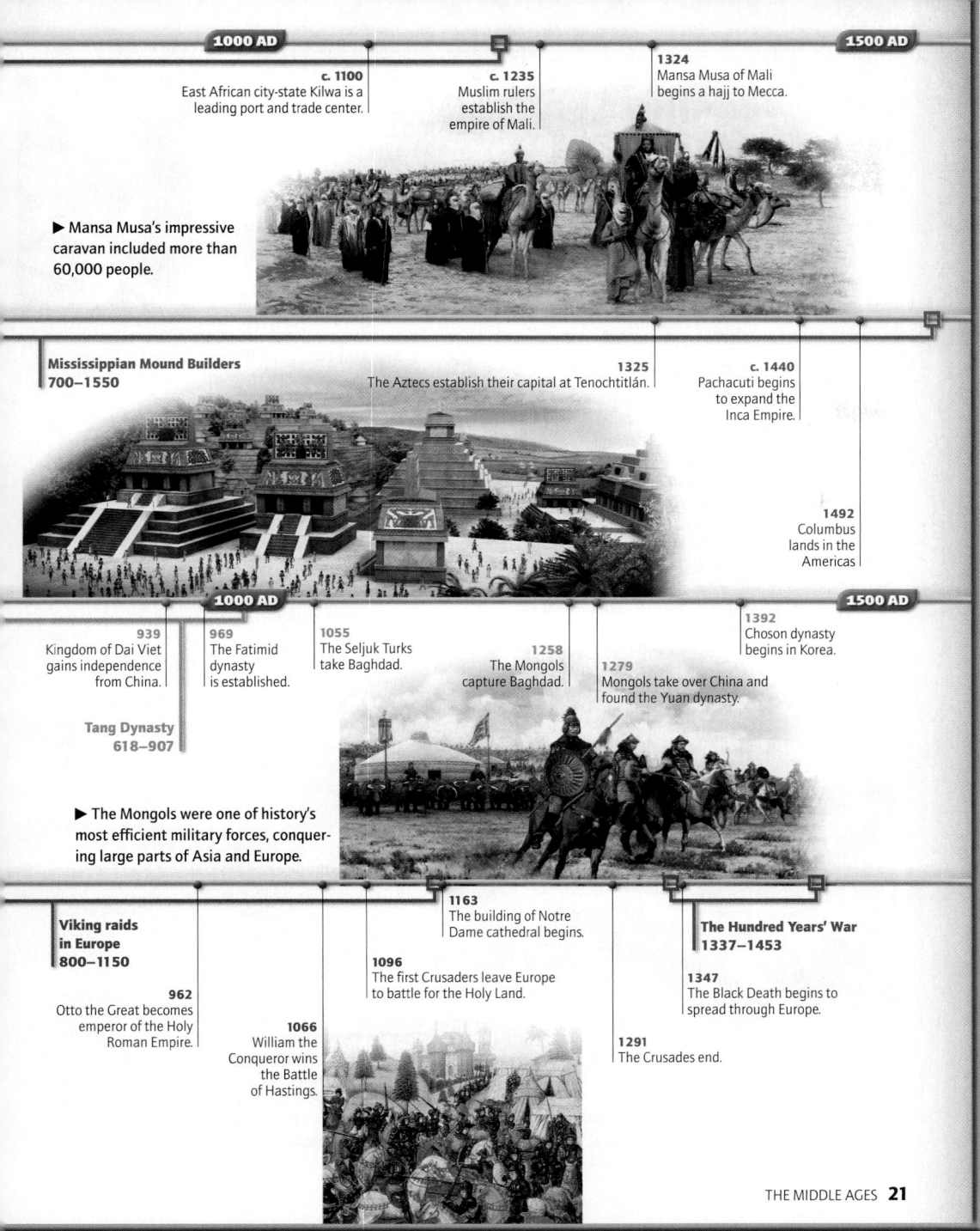

•Prologue Preview•

Teaching Tip

Students sometimes learn about historical events in a given location without considering what is happening at the same time in other parts of the world. Choose a date between 500 and 1500 and write it on the board. Using a large world map, point to several locations on different continents. Discuss with students what was occurring in those locations during the year you selected.

Reading Like a Historian

Interpreting Time Lines The four time lines on this page list events that happened in different parts of the world during the Middle Ages. As the world became more interconnected during this period, some of the events on the different timelines were related to each other. Discuss with students possible examples of these connections. *possible answers—The rise of Abbasid caliphate in 786 spreads Islam to new lands, eventually leading to the establishment of the Muslim empire of Mali in 1235; Mongol conquest of Asia in the late 1200s likely promoted the spread of the Black Death to Europe in 1347.*

Preteach

Exploring the Topic

Have students make a list of factors that contribute to the battlefield success of an army. Randomly select a few students to share an idea from their lists. Write their responses on the board. Have students consider how religion could affect soldiers in an army. Discuss the specific ways that religion could motivate a military force in battle.

Key Terms

Preteach the following terms:

Muhammad man born in AD 570 in Mecca who spread the religion of Islam across Arabia (p. 22)

Islam religion based on the belief that there is only one God and that each believer must obey God's will (p. 22)

Muslims followers of Islam (p. 22)

Qur'an holy book of Islam (p. 22)

caliph title meaning "successor to the Prophet" that was given to Muslim leaders (p. 22)

Umayyads clan that ruled the Muslim empire in the early 700s (p. 22)

Abbasids dynasty that ruled the Muslim empire from the 740s until 1258 (p. 22)

Recent Scholarship

When Baghdad Ruled the Muslim World: The Rise and Fall of Islam's Greatest Dynasty is a fascinating look at Baghdad and the Islamic Empire during the eighth and ninth centuries. Author Hugh Kennedy focuses on the human dimension of the time, and he provides a thorough discussion of the flourishing culture of the empire.

When Baghdad Ruled the Muslim World: The Rise and Fall of Islam's Greatest Dynasty by Hugh Kennedy. Da Capo Press, 2005.

TERMS
Muhammad
Islam
Qur'an
Muslim
caliph
Umayyad
Abbasid

Muslim Civilization
550–1260

A new civilization inspired by the teachings of a religious leader named Muhammad arose in the early 600s. Soon a mighty empire carried those teachings over a vast area stretching from India to Spain. Though the empire eventually splintered, Muslim civilization continued to thrive.

This illustration is an artistic depiction of Muhammad's name.

Muhammad and the Rise of Islam

In about AD 570 a man named **Muhammad** was born in Mecca, a city on a major trading route in the Arabian desert. Muhammad made his living as a trader and came into contact with both monotheists, such as Christians and Jews, and polytheists. When he was about 40 years old, Muhammad reported that the angel Jibreel (Gabriel) told him he had been called to be a prophet of Allah (Arabic for God). He reported that the angel instructed him to teach others. By 632, when he died, Muhammad had converted many Arab tribes to the religion known as **Islam**.

Islam is based on two central beliefs: that there is only one God and that each believer must obey God's will. Followers of Islam are called **Muslims**. The holy book of Islam is the **Qur'an**, which Muslims believe is the word of God as revealed to Muhammad.

Islam has five basic rules called the Five Pillars of Islam. Following these rules is required of all Muslims. Muslims recite their prayers in mosques. Mosques have no furnishings except for mats or rugs on which to kneel for prayer.

FIVE PILLARS OF ISLAM

1st pillar:	Professing the faith—Allah is the only God and Muhammad is his prophet
2nd pillar:	Praying five times daily
3rd pillar:	Giving charity to the poor
4th pillar:	Fasting during the holy month of Ramadan
5th pillar:	Making a hajj, or pilgrimage, to Mecca at least once

The Spread of Islam

By 642, the growing armies of Islam, drawn mainly from the Arabian Peninsula, had defeated the Persian Empire and taken control of what today is Iraq. Within 25 years of Muhammad's death, the expanding empire included Syria, Persia, and parts of North Africa.

In 711 a powerful Muslim force from North Africa invaded Spain and brought Islam to Europe. These Muslims were called Moors. They would continue to rule parts of Spain for more than 700 years.

By the late 900s, large numbers of Turks had converted to Islam. The Turks were located on the fringes of the Muslim world in Central Asia. Their warlike culture encouraged expansion and conquest. During the 1000s, Turkish Muslims seized control of Muslim Persia, Mesopotamia, and Syria. They also began raiding northern India on horseback. Along with Mongol converts, Turkish Muslims spread Islam across much of Asia.

During the period of Arab rule, the Muslim empire was organized into provinces. Muslim leaders were given the title of **caliph**, meaning "successor to the Prophet." Struggles over succession led to a split in Islam. The Shias believed Muhammad's son-in-law, Ali, should be caliph. The Sunnis believed that a just ruler recognized by the Muslim community could be caliph. Eventually, most Sunnis accepted leaders from a clan called the **Umayyads** as caliphs. In the late 740s the Umayyads were overthrown by a new dynasty known as the **Abbasids**. The Abbasids, who ruled until the 1258, created a new capital, Baghdad, which grew into a great city. It was under the Abbasids that Muslim civilization reached its height.

Differentiating Instruction

Above Level

Advanced Learners/Gifted and Talented

1. Organize students into small groups.
2. Instruct students to use reliable online or print sources to research the rise of Islam during the 600s and 700s. Students should focus their research on the government and spread of the Islamic empire.
3. Have students prepare a multimedia presentation based on their research.
4. After students have had enough time to prepare their presentations, have each group give its presentation to the class. **LS Verbal-Linguistic, Interpersonal**

Alternative Assessment Handbook, Rubrics 22: Multimedia Presentations; and 30: Research

500 — 900 — 1300

c. 570 Muhammad is born in Arabia.

610 Muhammad reports the first revelations from Allah.

622 Muhammad travels to Medina—the hegira.

732 Muslim advance in Europe is stopped at the Battle of Tours in France.

786 Harun al-Rashid leads the Abbasid caliphate to its height.

969 The Fatimid dynasty is established.

1055 The Seljuk Turks take Baghdad.

1258 The Mongols capture Baghdad.

Muslim Culture

Islam became more than just a religion. It was also a great cultural movement that affected most aspects of life in the lands ruled by Muslims. The Arabic language, the language in which the Qur'an was written, unified peoples across the region. Muslims learned from the people they conquered and the merchants with whom they traded. They preserved classical learning by translating the scientific and philosophical works of the Greeks into Arabic. In Persia a distinctive Muslim culture developed that drew on ancient Persian culture.

Muslims throughout the empire, or caliphate, lived according to the Qur'an and other religious writings. These guided both their religious and daily life. In their treatment of other religions, Muslim rulers allowed considerable religious freedom. For example, they did not demand that all conquered peoples convert to Islam. Non-Muslims had to pay an extra tax instead. Christians and Jews, referred to as "People of the Book" because Muhammad had accepted some of the Christian Bible's and the Torah's teachings, had a special, though still inferior, status.

The unity of the caliphate eventually broke down. A Umayyad dynasty continued to rule in Spain. A new dynasty, the Fatimids, conquered Egypt. Turkish Muslims, largely settled around the caliphate of Baghdad, served the Abbasid caliph as troops. Their growing power gradually shifted political authority away from the caliph. A different kind of Turkish ruler called a sultan emerged, leaving the caliph to play an important but symbolic role. By the 1000s, the Turks had seized control of Baghdad. Christians from the West captured Muslim cities during a series of wars. In 1258, a force from Central Asia, the Mongols, sacked Baghdad.

Key Facts
• Muhammad preached Islam, which spread from the Arabia in the 600s.
• Islam and the Arabic language eventually united peoples on three continents.
• Turks became the rulers of the caliphate.
• Muslim culture blended ideas from Arabia, Greece, and Persia.

REVIEW

1. **Identify** (a) Muhammad, (b) Abbasid, (c) sultan
2. **Define** (a) Islam, (b) Qur'an, (c) Muslim, (d) caliph
3. **Compare** How was Islam similar to other Judaism and Christianity?

EXPANSION OF ISLAM, 632–760

Muslim armies quickly triumphed from India to Spain. ***In what directions did Islam spread?***

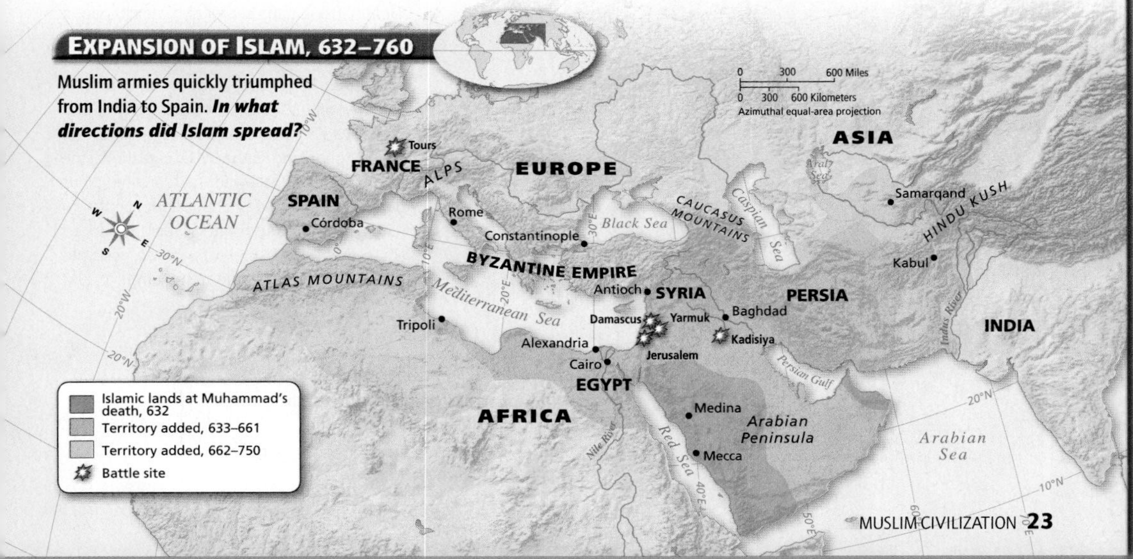

Skill Focus: Summarizing

At Level

Reading Skill

Muslim Rule

1. Review the material in the text about how Muslims impacted the lands they conquered with their government and culture.
2. Organize students into small groups. Have each group create a skit about life in a land recently conquered by Islamic armies. The people in the conquered land should be non-Muslims, such as Christians and/or Jews.
3. Allow enough time for students to write and rehearse their skits. Have students perform their skits for the class.
4. Discuss each of the skits as a class. Have students describe how dramatic depictions can further illustrate material included in a textbook. **LS Kinesthetic, Visual-Spatial**

Alternative Assessment Handbook, Rubric 33: Skits and Reader's Theater

Direct Teach

Reading Focus

Muslim Culture

Recall How did Muslims refer to Christians and Jews? *"People of the Book"*

Explain How did Islam become more than a religion? *by becoming a great cultural movement that affected all aspects of life in Muslim lands*

Identify Cause and Effect What led to the decline of the caliphate's power in the Middle Ages? *internal divisions; attacks from external enemies such as the Christians and Mongols*

Biography

Abu Ali al-Husayn Ibn Sina (980–1037)

Known as Avicenna in Europe, Abu Ali al-Husayn Ibn Sina gained international fame as a physician, scientist, and philosopher. The son of a Persian official, Ibn Sina studied science and medicine as a young man. He later wrote several academic books that advanced existing knowledge of the natural sciences. Ibn Sina's most famous work is the *Canon of Medicine*, which became a standard medical reference work in the Islamic world and Europe. Ibn Sina was also well-known for his writings on philosophy, which combined elements of Greek tradition with the teachings of Islamic scripture.

Answers

Expansion of Islam *east, north, south, and west*

1. (a.) *man born in AD 570 in Mecca who spread the religion of Islam across Arabia;* **(b.)** *dynasty that ruled the Muslim empire from the 740s through 1258;* **(c.)** *a Turkish ruler;* **2. (a.)** *religion based on the belief that there is only one God and that each believer must obey God's will;* **(b.)** *holy book of Islam;* **(c.)** *follower of Islam;* **(d.)** *title meaning "successor to the Prophet" that was given to Muslim leaders;* **3.** *possible answer—All three religions were monotheistic; all three religions recognized prophets and had a holy book of scripture.*

Preteach

Exploring the Topic

Have students list what they believe were the three most important factors that contributed to the wealth of past kingdoms. Have volunteers share their ideas with the class. If not mentioned by anyone, have students consider the importance of trade. Lead a discussion about how trade could have contributed to the wealth of kingdoms in past centuries.

Key Terms

Preteach the following terms:

Mansa Musa Mali leader who made Timbuktu a leading center of Islamic thought (p. 24)

Sunni 'Ali Songhai king who followed traditional religious beliefs and expanded his kingdom into an empire (p. 24)

Askia Muhammad Songhai king who restored Islam and expanded the territory and prosperity of his empire (p. 24)

Ezana Aksum king who conquered Kush (p. 25)

Biography

Abu-Ishaq Ibrahim-es-Saheli (mid-1300s AD) An architect from Andalusia, Spain named Abu-Ishaq Ibrahim-es-Saheli, met Mansa Musa during his famous hajj. The architect befriended Mansa Musa along the Nile River. Es-Saheli was well versed in techniques of mud and burnt-brick construction. The king offered him the equivalent of over $3 million to convince him to travel to Mali and build a vast palace and mosque. Es-Saheli agreed to come and build Mansa Musa's palace. He also constructed the great Djingareyber Mosque and at Timbuktu, another one at Djenné, and a third in Gao. Es-Saheli is credited with the introduction of burnt bricks, flat roofs, and the pyramid-shaped minaret to the area's architecture. His tomb is located in Timbuktu.

TERMS

Mansa Musa
Sunni 'Ali
Askia Mohammed
Ezana

African Kingdoms

100–1600

For centuries a series of kingdoms flourished in Africa. Traders from West African kingdoms crossed the vast Sahara bringing gold and salt in caravans of camels. In East Africa, traders traveled by sea, along the Nile River, the Red Sea, and the Indian Ocean.

Traditional African drum from Guinea.

West African Trading Kingdoms

Trade kept parts of Africa well-connected with the rest of the world. In West Africa, several important trading kingdoms emerged. The wealth and strength of these kingdoms depended on their control of trade routes across the Sahara.

The southern edge of the Sahara is a region known as the Sahel. Commerce developed in the Sahel, with gold mined in the south traded for salt mined in the desert. Where this gold-for-salt exchange took place, cities grew and flourished, making areas of West Africa major trading centers. Camel caravans, the main form of transportation, crossed the desert. The caravans operated for centuries and linked West Africa with the Muslim states in North Africa and the Middle East.

The earliest of the West African kingdoms was Ghana. Ghana was established sometime after the AD 300s. By the 800s, Ghana was dominating the gold-for-salt exchange. Their long-range trade networks encouraged high levels of political organization.

Ghana's hold on the trans-Sahara trade gradually weakened. By about 1235, control of the trade was in the hands of the kingdom of Mali. Mali's power reached its peak in the early 1300s under the rule of **Mansa Musa**. A devout Muslim, Mansa Musa made the city of Timbuktu a leading center of Islamic thought, attracting scholars from Egypt and Arabia.

Disputes over Mansa Musa's successor weakened Mali. The kingdom of Songhai, centered on the important trading city of Gao on the Niger River, took advantage. In 1464 the Songhai king, **Sunni 'Ali,** captured Timbuktu. Sunni 'Ali followed traditional religious beliefs. He expanded the kingdom into an empire and divided it into several provinces. His successor, **Askia Mohammed**, restored Islam, further extended the empire, and

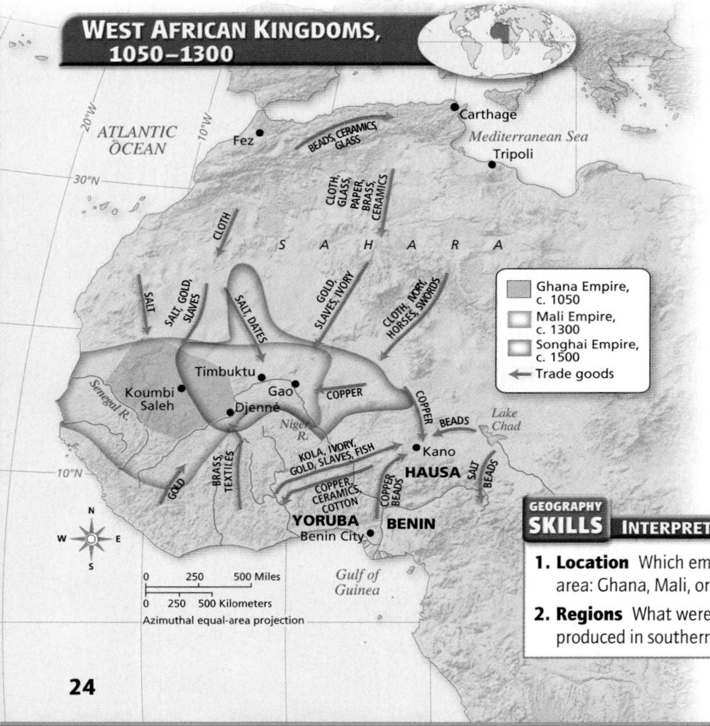

GEOGRAPHY SKILLS INTERPRETING MAPS

1. **Location** Which empire controlled the greatest area: Ghana, Mali, or Songhai?
2. **Regions** What were the main trade goods being produced in southern West Africa?

Differentiating Instruction

Below Level

Struggling Readers

1. Organize students into mixed-ability pairs. Have each pair conduct research using reliable print and online sources to learn about the trade caravans that crossed the Sahara to reach Ghana, Mali, and Songhai.
2. Have each pair create a diorama depicting a caravan on its way to or from one of the three West African kingdoms.
3. Have students display their dioramas throughout the classroom.
4. Have pairs describe their diorama to the class. Have the class discuss the risks of leading a trade caravan across the Sahara and the reasons why merchants were willing to take those risks. **LS Visual-Spatial**

Alternative Assessment Handbook, Rubric 23: Artwork

Answers

Interpreting Maps 1. *Songhai;* 2. *Refer to map.*

100						1500
c. 350 The kingdom of Aksum defeats Kush.	**800** Ghana begins to emerge as a major trading empire in West Africa.	**c. 1100** East African city-state Kilwa is a leading port and trade center.	**c. 1235** Muslim rulers establish the empire of Mali.	**1324** Mansa Musa of Mali begins a hajj to Mecca.	**1464** Sunni Ali founds the Songhai empire.	

developed Timbuktu into a great commercial center. Arab, Jewish, and Italian merchants brought goods from as faraway as Europe, India, and China. Despite its prosperity, however, the Songhai Empire steadily declined after the reign of Askia Mohammed. The empire was defeated by a Moroccan army in 1591.

Kush and Aksum

One of the earliest recorded kingdoms in East Africa was the kingdom of Kush. Kush arose along the upper Nile River in a region known as Nubia. Because of its close connection with Egypt, Kush's culture resembled Egyptian culture in many ways. In about 1500 BC, Egypt's rulers brought Nubia and Kush under their control. By about 1100 BC, Kush gained its independence, and in 730 BC, Kush conquered Egypt.

In the mid-600s BC, the Assyrians invaded Kush. Their attack greatly weakened the kingdom. The kingdom reorganized, however, and a new period of growth and cultural achievement began about 80 years later, centered on the new capital city of Meroë. Historians believe that Kush's civilization reached its height between about 250 BC and about AD 150. The people of Meroë built impressive pyramids and temples, crafted beautiful pottery, and developed a written form of their language.

By about the AD 100s, a rival kingdom to Kush called Aksum straddled the trade routes that stretched from Egypt to the interior of Africa. As Kush declined, Aksum increasingly competed with it for control of trade. By about AD 320, Aksum was a military power led by **King Ezana**. Ezana conquered Kush and set up a thriving kingdom that became a major center of long-distance trade. During his reign, Ezana converted to Christianity and made it the kingdom's official religion. Christianity became a powerful influence throughout the region, laying the foundations for the development of the Ethiopian church that continues today.

Coastal City-States

Several city-states dominated trade on the East African coast. Important trade routes were established in the Indian Ocean. East Africans exported gold, ivory, tortoise shells, and enslaved people. They imported porcelain and weapons. Among the earliest of the trading city-states along the Indian Ocean coast were Mogadishu, Pate, and Mombasa. By the late AD 1100s, Kilwa had also become a leading port where gold that had been mined in south-central Africa was brought for trade. Many kingdoms competed for control over the mining and shipping of gold.

Trade led to a blending of African, Arab, and Asian cultural influences along East Africa's coast. Local Africans, who spoke a Bantu language, adopted many Arab words. As the two languages blended, a new language called Swahili developed. Because many foreign traders were Muslim, Islam gained a hold along the East African coast as well.

The growing wealth of Africa's overseas trade also stimulated developments in Africa's interior. There, the Shona people established kingdom called Great Zimbabwe by the 1300s. This kingdom was located in southeastern Africa, along a trade route linking Africa's interior gold mines to the city-states on the coast. Supplying the coastal city-states made Great Zimbabwe wealthy. At its height, Great Zimbabwe was home to over 18,000 people.

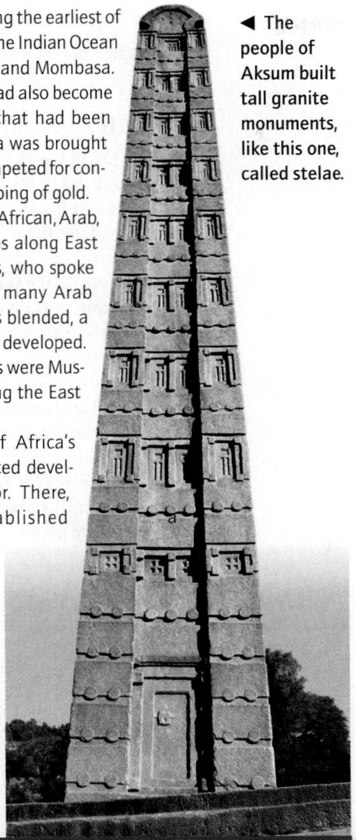

◄ The people of Aksum built tall granite monuments, like this one, called stelae.

KEY FACTS

- Trade routes across the Sahara strongly influenced civilizations in West Africa.
- Around AD 350, Aksum succeeded Kush as the strongest East African kingdom.
- Trade routes in the Indian Ocean strongly influenced civilizations in East Africa.

REVIEW

1. **Identify** (a) Mansa Musa, (b) Askia Mohammed, (c) King Ezana
2. **Define** (a) Nubia, (b) Ghana, (c) Timbuktu, (d) Great Zimbabwe
3. How did trade affect the development of both Kush and Aksum?

Direct Teach

Reading Focus

Kush and Aksum

Locate Where was the kingdom of Kush located? *along the upper Nile River in Nubia*

Explain How did Aksum eventually gain enough strength to conquer Kush? *possible answer—Aksum gained control of African trade routes to increase its own wealth while weakening that of Kush.*

Reading Focus

Coastal City-States

Name Who established the kingdom of Great Zimbabwe? *the Shona*

Analyze Why do you think so many city-states developed along the coast of East Africa? *possible answer—Their location on the East African coast allowed these city-states to serve as prosperous commercial centers that linked the Indian Ocean trade routes with the trade routes of the African interior.*

Collaborative Learning

At Level

Kingdoms of Africa

Research Required

1. Organize students into four groups. Assign one of the African kingdoms described on this page (Kush, Aksum, East African city-states, Great Zimbabwe) to each of the groups.
2. Have each group conduct research to prepare a large poster on its assigned kingdom. Encourage students to include photographs, paintings, maps, quotes, graphs, their own original drawings, and time lines on their posters.
3. Have each group assign responsibilities to its members. Duties include researching, locating and creating items, and placing the items on the poster.
4. Display the completed posters in the classroom. Have groups explain why the kingdom they researched is important to African and world history. **LS Visual-Spatial, Interpersonal**

Alternative Assessment Handbook, Rubrics 14: Group Activity; and 28: Posters

Answers

1. (a.) *Mali leader who made Timbuktu a leading center of Islamic thought;* **(b.)** *Songhai king who restored Islam and expanded the territory and prosperity of his empire;* **(c.)** *Aksum king who conquered Kush;* **2. (a.)** *region along the upper Nile River;* **(b.)** *the earliest of the West African trading kingdoms;* **(c.)** *West African city that was a leading center of commerce and Islamic thought;* **(d.)** *kingdom in southeastern Africa established by the Shona people;* **3.** *possible answer—Trade allowed Kush to build up great wealth and power; when Aksum became a major trading power, it gained enough strength to conquer Kush.*

Preteach

Exploring the Topic

Have students consider how governments ruled large empires in premodern times. Point out that, even 1,000 years ago, China had a vast territory and a large population. Have students identify what would have helped the past dynastic governments of China to effectively rule the country. *roads, bureaucratic structure, common cultural links among the population, strong military*

Key Terms

Preteach the following terms:

Genghis Khan Mongol leader who captured the Chinese capital in the early 1200s (p. 27)

Kublai Khan grandson of Genghis Khan who established a dynasty in China in the late 1200s (p. 27)

shogun top general who controlled the military, finances, and law in feudal Japan (p. 27)

daimyo lords who were responsible for running most of Japanese society at the local level (p. 27)

samurai powerful warriors who protected the daimyo (p. 27)

Info to Know

Chinese Population Growth China's population reached 60 million while under the rule of the Tang dynasty. During the Song/Sung period, Chinese farmers used new seeds from Southeast Asia and technological advances to increase their crop output. This growth in agricultural productivity sparked further population increases. By the year 1100 there were nearly 100 million people living in China.

TERMS

Genghis Khan
Kublai Khan
shogun
daimyo
samurai

Cultures of East Asia

550–1400

Beginning in the late 500s a series of strong dynasties emerged to rule China. The influence of China's advanced civilization spread across East Asia. Korea and Japan borrowed from China, producing vibrant cultures of their own.

Tang artists made lively figurines, such as this female polo player.

Golden Ages in China

The fall of the Han dynasty in the 200s led to a long era of instability and decline in China. Hordes of invaders destroyed Han cities and set up new kingdoms. In the late 500s, one of these groups succeeded in reuniting China under its rule. The new dynasty, known as the Sui, came into power in 589. Sui rulers reestablished Chinese bureaucracy, increased the size of the state education system, and reformed the civil service system. Sui emperors also built the Grand Canal, the world's oldest and longest canal system. The canal became a convenient way to travel and transport goods between northern and southern China. However, the Sui dynasty proved unpopular. Forced labor on the Grand Canal produced discontent. An uprising in 618 ended Sui rule and brought the Tang dynasty to power.

China's first "Golden Age" occurred under the Tang dynasty. Buddhism reached its peak, becoming for a time the state religion. Wealthy Buddhists donated land for monasteries. Chinese inventions spread to the outside world through China's increased contact with other peoples. Later Tang emperors, seeking to counter Buddhist influence, restored Confucianism, building temples to Confucius.

The Tang dynasty ended in 907. In 960 the Sung dynasty was established and a second "Golden Age" began. The Sung required government officials to study the works of Confucius. The movement was called "neo-Confucianism." Foreign trade expanded, key port cities were established, and caravans brought in goods from Central Asia and India.

TANG AND SONG DYNASTIES, 618–1279

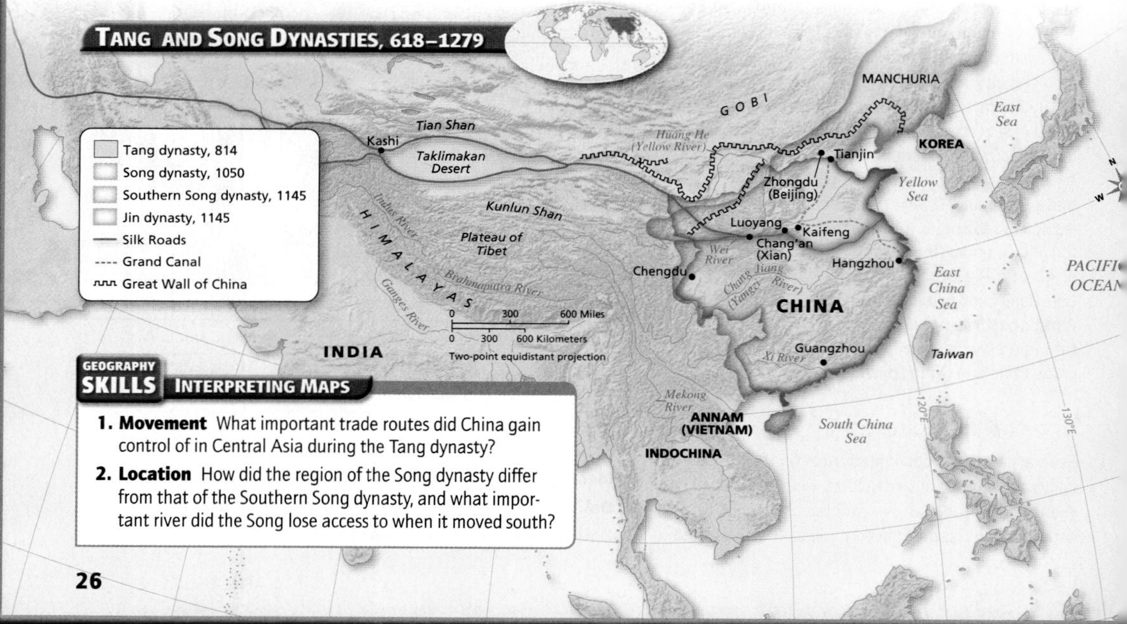

GEOGRAPHY SKILLS INTERPRETING MAPS

1. **Movement** What important trade routes did China gain control of in Central Asia during the Tang dynasty?
2. **Location** How did the region of the Song dynasty differ from that of the Southern Song dynasty, and what important river did the Song lose access to when it moved south?

Skills Focus: Comparing and Contrasting

At Level

Reading Skill

Tang Dynasty and Song/Sung Dynasty

1. Have students draw a Venn diagram like the one shown and complete it showing the differences and similarities between China under the Tang dynasty and China under the Song/Sung dynasty.
2. Have volunteers share their answers and complete the graphic organizer with the class. Have students use the information in their diagrams to write a paragraph describing how the Tang and Song/Sung dynasties were similar and different. **LS Verbal-Linguistic, Visual-Spatial**

Alternative Assessment Handbook, Rubrics 9: Comparing and Contrasting; and 13: Graphic Organizers

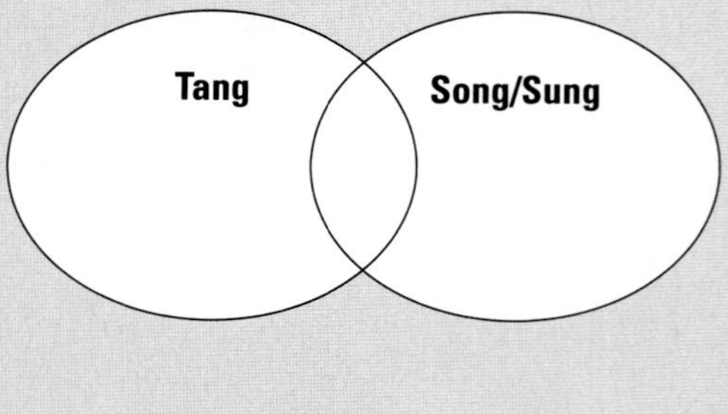

Answers

Interpreting Maps 1. *Silk Roads;* 2. *Song/Sung dynasty controlled a larger region that included the river valleys of northern China; Huang He River*

500 — 800 — 1100 — 1400

c. 550 Buddhism spreads from China to Japan

618 Tang dynasty begins a classical age in China.

794 Heian period begins a golden age in Japan.

939 Kingdoms of Vietnam gain independence from China.

c. 1094 World's first paper money printed in China

1279 Mongols take over China and found the Yuan dynasty.

1392 Choson dynasty begins in Korea.

Under Sung government policies, China also underwent a period of major economic change. International trade with Japan and Southeast Asia grew. The overall increase in trade created new opportunities for rural peasants, many of whom engaged in timber-growing, papermaking, and other new occupations. A cash economy also emerged, replacing a barter system. The world's first paper money was printed in 1024.

The Mongol Invasions

The Mongols, a fierce warrior people, lived north of China. In the early 1200s a Mongol force led by **Genghis Khan** captured the Chinese capital, which today is called Beijing. The Mongols went on to capture the rest of China, along with large parts of Europe.

In 1271 **Kublai Khan**, a grandson of Genghis Khan, announced the beginning of his own dynasty in China. Under Mongol rule, China prospered in many ways. Kublai Khan extended the length of the Grand Canal by hundreds of miles, and also linked China with India and Persia. Improved trade and communication with other parts of the world encouraged China's economic growth.

Following Kublai Khan's death in 1294, China experienced many problems, including rebellions. Chinese rebels pushed the Mongols back beyond the Great Wall in 1368, ending their dynasty.

Korea

Korea's political and cultural development was strongly shaped by China. A rugged, mountainous peninsula that juts south into the sea between China and Japan, Korea has long served as a bridge allowing the passage of people and ideas from eastern Asia to neighboring island chains. As early as 300 BC, immigrants from China began to arrive in Korea, bringing with them knowledge of metalworking and agriculture.

These immigrants helped to found the first true kingdom in Korea. Korean rulers adopted Chinese as their written language and embraced Confucian traditions and ideas along with the Chinese model of government. Despite the strength of China's influence, Koreans worked to maintain their own culture and traditions. Korean society developed a distinctive form of Buddhism. During the Koryo period, Korean artisans developed celadon pottery. Koreans also advanced the Chinese technology of movable type by casting the type blocks in metal.

During the Koryo period, Korean artists became famous for their celadon pottery.

Japan

The islands of Japan, off the east coast of Asia, were also influenced by China. The Japanese adopted Chinese writing in the early 700s and Buddhism in the mid-500s. Chinese art, science, government, and fashion also influenced Japanese society. In 702 the Japanese emperor issued a new law code modeled on Tang dynasty laws. This code centralized the government and gave the emperor more power over the lives of his people.

After the 800s, however, the political system adapted from China began to decline. A new system called the feudal system took its place by the 1100s. Under the feudal system in Japan, the emperor still reigned, but he was now considered a figurehead. The **shogun**, or top general, had more power, including control over the military, finances, and law. The shogun, in turn, granted power to the **daimyo**, lords who were responsible for running most of Japanese society at the local level. The daimyo, who were protected by warriors called the **samurai**, became the most powerful people in Japan.

Key Facts
• China experienced "golden ages" during the Tang and Song dynasties.
• Mongol invasions of China in the 1200s led to Mongol rule in much of Eurasia.
• Korea and Japan adopted many cultural practices from China.
• Japan developed into a feudal society during the 1100s.

REVIEW

1. **Identify** (a) Tang dynasty, (b) Genghis Khan, (c) shogun
2. **Define** (a) Mongols, (b) daimyo, (c) samurai
3. How did the culture of Korea differ from earlier Chinese culture?

Direct Teach

Reading Focus

The Mongol Invasions, Korea, and Japan

Recall When did the Mongol dynasty in China end? *1368*

Explain How did Japanese shoguns rule the country? *shoguns ruled by controlling the military, finances, and law; they governed at the local level through daimyo who employed samurai for protection*

Compare In what ways were Korea and Japan similar? *possible answer—Both were influenced by China; Korea adopted elements from China's government, Confucian traditions, movable type technology, and Buddhism; Japan was influenced by writing, art, science, government, fashion, and the Buddhist religion from China.*

MISCONCEPTION ALERT

Many of the soldiers who rode with Genghis Khan and his successors were not Mongols; they were Turkic peoples who were also nomads from Central Asia. Early in his campaigns, Genghis began adding loyal Turkish tribesmen to his forces until the Turks outnumbered the Mongols. As a result, the Turkish language spread in the wake of the conquest.

Differentiating Instruction

Below Level

English-Language Learners

Research Required

1. Organize the class into small, mixed-ability groups.
2. Have each group create a poster that depicts a large time line of East Asian history between 550 and 1400. Have students conduct outside research to locate additional important dates and events beyond what is included in the textbook pages. Each time line should include at least 10 events. Encourage students to use pictures to illustrate some of the events on their time lines.
3. Have groups share their time lines with the class and explain the events they selected.
4. Synthesizing the information from the time lines, review the major events in East Asian history between 550 and 1400. **LS Visual-Spatial, Interpersonal**

Alternative Assessment Handbook, Rubrics 14: Group Activity; and 36: Time Lines

Answers

1. (a.) *government that ruled China from 618 to 907;* **(b.)** *Mongol leader who captured the Chinese capital in the early 1200s;* **(c.)** *top general who controlled the military, finances, and law in feudal Japan;* **2. (a.)** *fierce warrior people who lived north of China;* **(b.)** *lords who were responsible for running most of Japanese society at the local level;* **(c.)** *powerful warriors who protected the daimyo;* **3.** *distinctive form of Buddhism; celadon pottery; use of metal movable type blocks*

Preteach

Exploring the Topic

Have students make a list of what they know about the Byzantine Empire and a list of what they know about the Roman Empire. Have volunteers share their lists with the class. Write some of their responses on the board. Lead a discussion about why people today are generally less familiar with the Byzantine Empire than ancient Rome.

Key Terms

Preteach the following terms:

Justinian Byzantine emperor who added new lands to his empire (p. 28)

icon holy image of Jesus, the Virgin Mary, or the saints (p. 29)

Orthodox Church Christian Church in the East that split from the Roman Catholic Church (p. 29)

Vladimir Grand Prince of Kiev who made Orthodox Christianity the state religion (p. 29)

Yaroslav the Wise Kievan king who made many cultural and administrative improvements during his reign between 1019 and 1054 (p. 29)

Teaching Tip

Provide students with pictures of famous Byzantine paintings, sculptures, and artwork to give them a better idea of the richness and variety of art at this time.

Biography

Vladimir Monomakh (1053–1125) Vladimir Monomakh assumed the Kievan throne in 1113, at a time when division threatened his state. Known as Vladimir II, the new leader brought unity to his people with his firm and wise rule. Well educated, Vladimir II gained fame for both his skill as a military leader and a writer. His work *Testament* displays the love he felt for his citizens, as well as his sense of responsibility. After his death in 1125, Vladimir II's eldest son Mstislav succeeded him as king.

TERMS
Justinian I
icon
Orthodox Church
Vladimir
Yaroslav the Wise

The Byzantine Empire and Russia 350–1200

While the Western Roman Empire fell to invaders in AD 476, the Eastern Roman Empire, also called the Byzantine Empire, survived. It included Greece, Syria, Egypt, and other areas. The success of the Byzantine Empire also influenced the development of another major kingdom, Russia.

Justinian and Theodora ruled the Byzantine Empire from 527 to 565.

Byzantium

In AD 330, the Roman emperor Constantine ordered a new city built on the grounds of the town of Byzantium. Originally founded in 667 BC by a band of ancient Greeks, Byzantium had stood for more than 1,000 years. However, Constantine wanted the new Christian city to become a "New Rome," a new capital for the Roman Empire. The city was called the City of Constantine, or Constantinople.

Since its ancient days as Byzantium, Constantinople had been a gateway between Asia and Europe. Constantinople was an important city for trade and commerce because of its harbor and location. It also was a melting pot of cultures and ideas about art, science, mathematics, and religion. However, it was a constant target of foreign emperors and invaders.

Following Constantine's death in 337, the Roman Empire became divided between east and west. After a series of battles with "barbarians," the name that Romans gave to the Germanic peoples living outside the empire, the Western Roman Empire was finally conquered in AD 476. Constantinople remained the capital of the Eastern Empire. Known as the Byzantine Empire, this state lasted until 1453.

Justinian's Code

Many leaders of the Byzantine Empire hoped to revive the glory and power of the Roman Empire. One of the most successful was the emperor **Justinian I**. During his reign from 527 to 565, the Byzantines recaptured much of North Africa, Italy, and southern Spain. Justinian's conquests left the empire exhausted, and many of the newly won lands were lost shortly after his death.

Justinian's reform of the laws of the empire proved a more lasting achievement. In 528, he ordered his scholars to collect the laws of the Roman Empire and to preserve them. This collection, known as Justinian's Code, was organized into four parts, including:

- useful Roman Laws
- Roman legal options
- guide for law students
- laws passed after AD 534

City at a Crossroads

Constantinople stands on the edge of Europe looking out towards Asia. Its location made it an important trading and political center.

Differentiating Instruction

Below Level

Struggling Readers

1. Organize students into small, mixed-ability groups.
2. Have students prepare a set of three maps of the Byzantine Empire. The maps should show Byzantine territory before, during, and after the reign of Justinian. Beyond that requirement, students are free to choose any date for their maps.
3. The members of each group should work together to complete the various tasks of compiling the maps: researching dates, taking notes, creating the maps, etc. Allow students enough time to complete their maps.
4. Have groups present their maps to the class, explaining their reasoning for the dates they selected. Discuss as a class how Byzantine power varied over time. **LS Visual-Spatial, Interpersonal**

Alternative Assessment Handbook, Rubrics 14: Group Activity; and 20: Map Creation

300	600		900		1200
330 Constantinople is founded as the new capital of the Roman Empire.	**527** Justinian I rules the Eastern Roman Empire.	**726** Leo III calls for the destruction of icons.	**1019** Yaroslav the Wise becomes Grand Prince of Kiev.	**1054** The Great Schism divides the Christian Church.	**1453** Constantinople falls, ending the Byzantine Empire.

The Code of Justinian formed the basis of Byzantine law. It preserved the Roman idea that people should be ruled by laws rather than by the whims of leaders. By the 1100s, the Code was being used in western Europe.

After the loss of Justinian's conquests in the west, Greek cultural influences in the empire grew stronger. During the reign of Emperor Heraclius (610–641), Greek replaced Latin as the empire's official language, and old Roman imperial titles gave way to Greek ones.

Schism in the Christian Church

Christianity was an important part of life in the Byzantine Empire. However, church leaders in the west and east had different ideas about church doctrine and practice. Over time, these differences led to schism, or division, in the Christian Church.

A controversy over **icons,** or holy images of Jesus, the Virgin Mary, or the saints, hastened the split. Many Byzantines kept icons in their homes and churches and honored them. Other Byzantines believed that this was wrong. They were called iconoclasts.

In 726 Emperor Leo III, an iconoclast, ordered the destruction of icons. However, many people refused to give them up. This became known as the Iconoclastic Controversy. In 731 Pope Gregory III decided that it was heresy not to allow the honoring of icons. He excommunicated, or expelled from the church, people who destroyed icons. This caused friction between the pope in Rome and the emperor in Constantinople.

While the controversy over iconoclasm eventually receded—later emperors accepted icons—the breach between the church in the west and that in the east widened. The Byzantines looked to a church leader known as a patriarch, appointed by the emperor. They did not recognize the authority of the pope in Rome. These and other differences led to the Great Schism in the Christian Church in 1054. The church in the West became the Roman Catholic Church, with the pope as its leader. The church in the East became the **Orthodox Church**. (*Orthodox* means "right opinion" in Greek.) Despite efforts at reconciliation over the centuries, the two churches remain separate today.

Russia

From its beginnings, Russia has had an important influence on European and Asian history because of its geography, origins, and people. Its first inhabitants, the Slavs, moved into the region after about the AD 400s. During the 800s, Vikings from Scandinavia traveled to the area and took control of Slavic cities such as Novgorod and Kiev, which became the capital of the first Russian state. In 860, a Viking ruler led his Rus warriors in a surprise attack against Constantinople. Although the early Russians were defeated, the two kingdoms became trading partners. Greek missionaries visited Kievan Russia in the late 800s, spreading Byzantine Christianity. In the 980s, the Grand Prince of Kiev, **Vladimir I,** converted to Orthodox Christianity. He also made it the state religion.

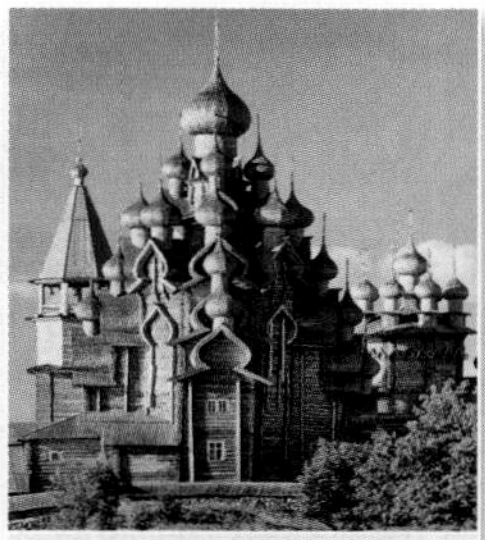
A Russian church that was built entirely of wood

The Kievan state's greatest king was **Yaroslav the Wise,** who ruled from 1019 to 1054. Yaroslav made many cultural and administrative improvements. He built many churches and introduced Russia's first law code, known as *Russkaya Pravda*. After his rule ended, Kiev declined in power. Internal conflicts allowed a new group of invaders, the Mongols, to conquer or destroy almost every city in Kievan Russia.

Key Facts
• The Byzantine Empire grew out of the Eastern Roman Empire, preserving the Greco-Roman heritage for over 1,000 years.
• The Great Schism in the Christian Church led to the Roman Catholic and the Eastern Orthodox churches.
• The early development of Russia, including its religion, was greatly influenced by the Byzantine Empire.

Review

1. **Identify** (a) Justinian I, (b) Leo III, (c) Vladimir I, (d) Yaroslav the Wise
2. **Define** (a) Justinian's Code, (b) icons, (c) Orthodox Church
3. Why was Justinian's Code important?
4. What was the result of the Iconoclastic Controversy?

Direct Teach

Reading Focus

Schism in the Christian Church

Identify After the Great Schism, which church dominated in the West? *Roman Catholic Church*

Speculate Why do you think the split between the church in the West and the church in the East has remained permanent? *possible answers—The split became a power struggle, in which neither side wanted to submit to the authority of the other; because the split was rooted in religious issues, each side believed its position reflected the will of God.*

Reading Focus

Russia

Identify Russia has influenced the history of which two continents? *Europe and Asia*

Describe How did Russia become a Christian state? *Greek missionaries spread Byzantine Christianity in Kievan Russia in the late 800s; Vladimir I converted to Orthodox Christianity in the 980s, making it the state religion.*

Skills Focus: Analyzing Alternative Points of View

At Level

Research Required

Reading Like a Historian Skill

Reporting the Great Schism

1. Tell students they are newspaper reporters covering the Great Schism in 1054.
2. Have each student write a newspaper article about the Great Schism. Students should conduct research to familiarize themselves with the positions of both sides. Articles should be balanced and should include "interview" excerpts with at least one person from each side.
3. Have volunteers read their articles to the class.
4. Discuss how modern journalism might have influenced the outcome of the Great Schism in 1054. **LS Interpersonal, Kinesthetic**

Alternative Assessment Handbook, Rubrics 30: Research; and 40: Writing to Describe

Answers

*1. **(a.)** Byzantine emperor who added new lands to his empire; **(b.)** Byzantine emperor who ordered the destruction of icons; **(c.)** Grand Prince of Kiev who made Orthodox Christianity the state religion; **(d.)** Kievan king who made many cultural and administrative improvements during his reign between 1019 and 1054; **2. (a.)** four-part collection of Roman laws the formed the basis of Byzantine Law; **(b.)** holy images of Jesus, the Virgin Mary, or the saints; **(c.)** Christian church in the East that split from the Roman Catholic Church; **3.** later adopted by the West, the Code preserved the Roman idea that people should by ruled by laws rather than the whims of leaders; **4.** It created a split between the church in the East and the church in the West. It later expanded into the Great Schism.*

Preteach

Exploring the Topic

Ask students to think about the current political, social, and religious settings in which they live. Next have them consider the political, social, and religious systems of the Middle Ages. Lead a discussion about how their lives would be different if they lived in feudal Europe.

Key Terms

Preteach the following terms:

Charlemagne great Frankish king who ruled from 768 to 814 (p. 30)

feudal system political organization in which lower nobles pledged loyalty and service to higher nobles in exchange for grants of land (p. 31)

fief grant of land from a powerful noble to a lesser noble (p. 31)

vassal person who received a fief (p. 31)

manorial system economic structure in which a lord allowed peasants to farm part of his land in exchange for some of their crops (p. 31)

canon law the code of law of the Christian church (p. 31)

MISCONCEPTION ALERT

Christopher Columbus and his men were not the first Europeans to reach the Americas. In 1000 a Viking named Lief Ericsson was driven off course as he tried to sail from Greenland to Norway. He instead landed on the North American coast at present-day Newfoundland. Evidence of Viking settlements has been found on the northern tip of that island. Three years later, another Viking expedition reached the North American coast. Viking contacts with Newfoundland continued until 1189.

TERMS

Charlemagne
feudal system
fief
vassal
manorial system
canon law

Early Middle Ages in Europe

800–1100

The barbarian peoples who overran much of the Western Roman Empire brought with them behaviors and traditions that gradually developed into a new and distinct European civilization. This period between the 400s and about 1500 is generally known as the Middle Ages.

Charlemagne, ruler of the Franks.

Germanic Invasions

For hundreds of years following the breakup of the Roman Empire, many Germanic tribes plundered Europe and established small kingdoms. The tribe that had the most impact on European history was known as the Franks.

The greatest of all Frankish kings, **Charlemagne**, ruled from 768 until 814. During his reign, he worked to build a "New Rome" centered in present-day France and Germany. Much of Europe regarded Charlemagne as a successor to Roman emperors. He was crowned by the pope as Emperor of the Romans. His empire was divided into regions, each governed on his behalf by an official known as a count.

Charlemagne helped spread church teachings and Christian beliefs, and did much to bring civilization, order, and learning to barbarian Europe during the 800s. He also placed great value on education. He started schools at his palace and appointed one of Europe's most respected thinkers to develop a curriculum based on the Roman model. However, his empire quickly crumbled following his death in 814.

Viking Raids

Charlemagne's empire was undermined by internal divisions and by invasions of peoples from beyond its frontiers. The most feared invaders during the 800s and 900s were the Vikings from Scandinavia. Vikings were Germanic peoples from what are now the countries of Norway, Sweden, and Denmark. Their customs and myths centered on pagan gods. During spring and summer, the Vikings traveled south and west along the coasts of mainland Europe and the British Isles. They would raid and loot settlements and bring captives back to work as slaves on their farms in Scandinavia. Over time they settled in England, Ireland, and other parts of Europe. A large Viking settlement in northwestern France gave the region its name, Normandy, from the French word for "Northman."

EUROPE, 815

Charlemagne's empire briefly reunited parts of the Western Roman Empire. ***What was the other great Christian empire in Europe at this time?***

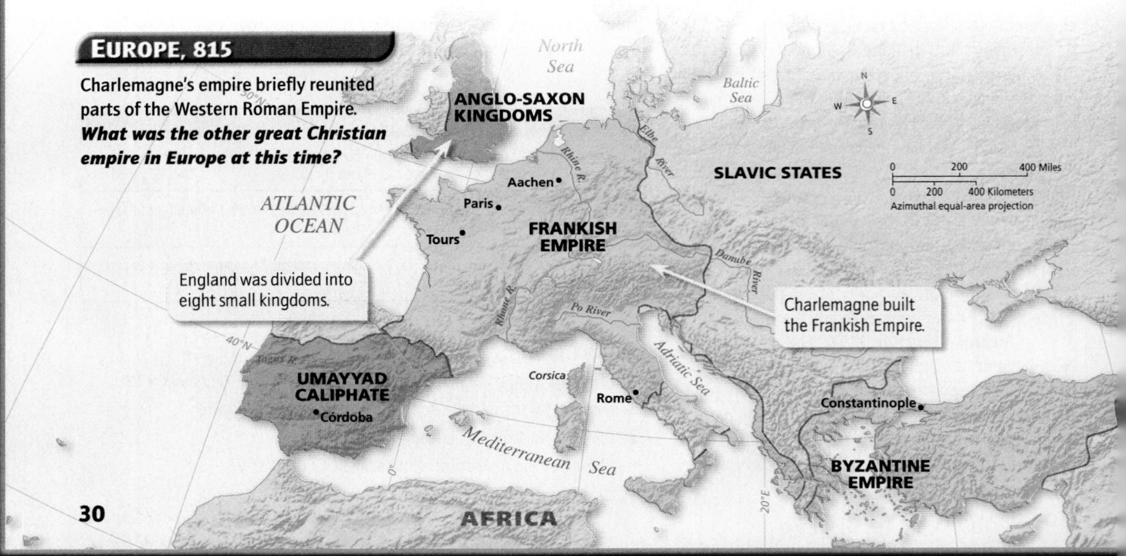

Collaborative Learning

At Level

Charlemagne and Rome

1. Remind students that Charlemagne sought to build his Frankish empire into a "New Rome."
2. Organize students into an even number of groups. Have students in each group prepare for a debate on this statement: The Frankish empire under Charlemagne was a true successor to the Roman Empire. Assign each group a pro or con side. Give students time to prepare their arguments. Students should write as many arguments to support their position as they can, and consider points the other side might make.
3. Call pairs of groups to debate before the class.
4. Have students write a paragraph summarizing the results of their group's debate. **LS Verbal-Linguistic, Auditory-Musical**

Alternative Assessment Handbook, Rubric 10: Debates

Answers

Europe, 815 *Byzantine Empire*

800 | 1000 | 1200

800
The pope crowns Charlemagne Emperor of the Romans.

962
Otto the Great becomes emperor of the Holy Roman Empire.

1066
William the Conqueror wins the Battle of Hastings.

Viking raids in Europe 800–1150

Feudal System

With kings unable to defend their realms from the waves of invaders, new arrangements for self-defense arose. Lower nobles pledged loyalty and military service to higher nobles. By the 900s, most Europeans were governed by local independent leaders who were often lords. The new political organization was known as the **feudal system**, or feudalism.

Within feudalism, a powerful noble granted land to a lesser noble. The noble who received the land could use it and its products, but could not own it. In return for maintaining the land, the lesser noble promised loyalty, military service, and other assistance to the lord who granted him the land. The grant of land was called a **fief,** and the person who received the fief was a **vassal**. Fiefs eventually became hereditary, with legal possession passing from a vassal to his eldest son.

Feudalism provided social and political structure to the culture of the middle ages. Another system, the **manorial system,** shaped the economic structure of Europe during these years. A lord and several peasant families shared the land of a manor, or large farming estate. The lord kept about one third of the manor's lands, called the domain, for himself. Peasants farmed the remaining two thirds of the land. In return for being allowed to work the land, the peasants gave the lord some of their crops and helped to farm his land. Most peasants, called serfs, could not leave the land without the lord's permission.

The Christian Church

Throughout the Middle Ages, the Christian church was one of the few sources of leadership and stability that people could rely upon. The medieval church had broad political powers and performed many of the functions of modern governments. By the 1100s, the church was one of Europe's leading landowners, and many of its leaders were powerful feudal overlords.

The pope held supreme authority in the church. His most important and powerful advisers were cardinals. From the late 1100s on, only cardinals could elect the pope. The church also had its own code of law, called **canon law,** and its own courts. The court could issue a ruling against an entire region, closing all churches in that region and limiting the powers of the clergy. The church did not allow anyone to question the basic principles of Christianity. People who denied the church's principles or preached other beliefs were considered heretics, unbelievers who deserved eternal damnation.

The medieval church also had the power to tax. Priests collected a tithe, or one tenth of a Christian's income. By the early 1200s, the church was perhaps the wealthiest single institution in Europe.

The church's wealth and influence led to many problems. Nobles began to appoint friends or relatives to high church positions. High positions within the church hierarchy were often sold to people hoping to gain wealth either from church income or by charging high fees for religious services. As time went on, these practices came under criticism from inside and outside the church, leading to many calls for reform.

Feudal Obligations — Quick Facts

Feudalism was built upon relationships of obligation and service.

A Knight's Duties to His Lord
- Provide military service
- Remain loyal and faithful
- Give money on special occasions

A Lord's Duties to His Knights
- Give land
- Protect from attack
- Resolve disputes between knights

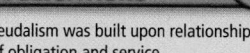

Key Facts

- Frankish king Charlemagne reunited much of western Europe, triggering a cultural rebirth during the 800s.
- The feudal and manorial systems shaped the social, political, and economic structures of Europe during the Middle Ages.
- The Christian Church became a political, social, and economic force during the 1000s and the 1100s.

Review

1. **Identify** (a) Franks, (b) Charlemagne, (c) fief, (d) vassal
2. **Define** (a) feudal system (b) manorial system (c) canon law
3. How was the church's organization similar to that of a modern government?

Direct Teach

Reading Focus

Feudal System

Explain Why did the feudal system emerge in Europe? *kings needed new self-defense arrangements*

Compare How were the feudal system and the manorial system similar? *Both systems were hierarchical.*

Reading Focus

The Christian Church

Identify Who was the head of the Christian Church in the Middle Ages? *the pope*

Summarize What were the church's sources of wealth in the Middle Ages? *land, tithes, and fees for religious services*

Recent Scholarship

In *Those Terrible Middle Ages: Debunking the Myths*, the author discusses many of the myths associated with the Middle Ages, including the idea that the Middle Ages were not dark, but instead produced a number of scholars of both genders.

Those Terrible Middle Ages: Debunking the Myths by Regine Pernoud. Ignatius Press, 2000.

Differentiating Instruction

Above Level

Advanced Learners/Gifted and Talented

Research Required

1. Review with students the information in the text about the manorial system.
2. Have students conduct outside research about daily life on a medieval manor.
3. Have students write a short story that takes place on a European manor during the Middle Ages. Students should include lords and serfs in their stories. Encourage students to write about additional characters who are nobles, priests, and monarchs.
4. Have volunteers read their stories to the class.
5. As an extension, students might want to present their stories as a short skit for the class. **LS Verbal-Linguistic**

Alternative Assessment Handbook, Rubric 39: Writing to Create

Answers

1. (a.) *Germanic tribe that built a large empire in Europe;* **(b.)** *great Frankish king who ruled from 768 to 814;* **(c.)** *grant of land from a powerful noble to a lesser noble;* **(d.)** *person granted a fief;* **2. (a.)** *political system; lower nobles pledged loyalty, service to higher nobles in exchange for land;* **(b.)** *economic structure in which peasants farmed part of a lord's land in exchange for some crops;* **(c.)** *law code of the Christian church;* **3.** *hierarchy; political power; law code; power to tax; corruption*

Preteach

Exploring the Topic

Have students make a list of the rights that are guaranteed to them as citizens of their nation. Have them discuss as a class how their lives would be different if these rights were not guaranteed—if their leaders could rule however they pleased. Continue by discussing the medieval influences on their current political system.

Key Terms

Preteach the following terms:

William the Conqueror ruler of England from 1066 to 1087 who brought feudalism from France and laid the foundation for a strong monarchy in England (p. 32)

Magna Carta document signed by King John that protected the liberties of the nobles and provided a basic outline of rights (p. 32)

Crusades military missions to take the Holy Land from the Muslims (p. 33)

Gothic style of church architecture named after the barbarian Goths (p. 33)

scholasticism efforts of European philosophers to reconcile Christian faith nd reason (p. 33)

Thomas Aquinas monk of the Dominican order whose principal work summarized medieval Christian thought (p. 33)

Black Death plague that killed one-third of Europe's population between 1347 and 1351 (p. 33)

Info to Know

Domesday Book In 1086 William sent officers out across England to conduct a vast survey. The king's men collected volumes of information about the size, ownership, and resources of every parcel of land in England. The results of this huge survey were compiled in the *Domesday Book,* which the government used as a basis for taxation and administration.

Answers

Interpreting Maps 1. *Paris; Antioch;* **2.** *possible answer—Muslim forces were based much closer to the Crusader states than the European kingdoms that tried to hold on to them.*

TERMS
William the Conqueror
Magna Carta
Crusades
Gothic
Thomas Aquinas
Black Death

High Middle Ages in Europe

1000–1500

Kings, nobles, and church leaders struggled with one another for power during the early Middle Ages. As the period progressed, however, royal power gained supremacy over the power of nobles in England and France.

In 1215 English nobles forced King John to sign Magna Carta.

The Magna Carta

The continual struggle for power between kings and local lords resulted in the emergence of two new kingdoms, England and France. The people of England were known as Anglo Saxons, after the two Germanic tribes from which they originated. In 1065 the Anglo-Saxon king died, and a French duke laid claim to the thrown. **William the Conqueror** invaded. He ruled England from 1066 to 1087. He brought feudalism from France and laid the foundation for a strong monarchy in England.

By 1215, King John, the son of one of William's successors, demanded that nobles pay more taxes to support his war in France. A powerful group of high nobles joined together against the king and forced him to sign a document known as the **Magna Carta.**

The Magna Carta protected the liberties of the nobles. It also provided a basic outline of rights. King John agreed not to collect any new taxes without the consent of important nobles and church leaders who advised him. He also agreed to let any accused person be judged by a jury of his or her peers. The acceptance of the Magna Carta meant that the king had to obey the law or face being overthrown. Over time, the Magna Carta became the basis for key democratic ideas such as limits on executive power.

THE CRUSADES, 1095–1204

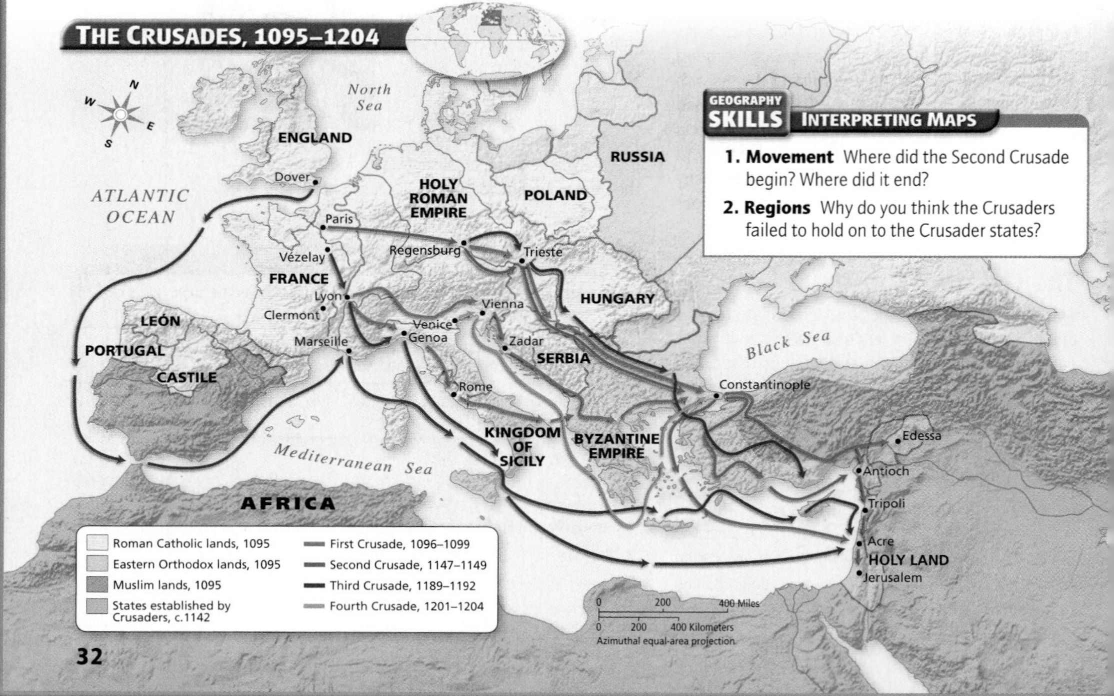

GEOGRAPHY SKILLS INTERPRETING MAPS

1. **Movement** Where did the Second Crusade begin? Where did it end?
2. **Regions** Why do you think the Crusaders failed to hold on to the Crusader states?

Skills Focus: Identifying Cause and Effect

At Level

Research Required

Reading Skill

King John and the Magna Carta

1. Have students conduct research using reliable sources to learn more about the events leading up to King John's signing of the Magna Carta.
2. Tell students they are nobles in England in 1215. Have students write a letter to King John to persuade him to sign the Magna Carta. Student letters may emphasize the positive benefits the document will bring or the negative consequences the king will face if he refuses to sign it. Students may wish to include elements of both arguments in their letters.
3. Have volunteers read their letters to the class.

LS Verbal-Linguistic

Alternative Assessment Handbook, Rubric 43: Writing to Persuade

1000 — 1250 — 1500

1096 The first Crusaders leave Europe to battle for the Holy Land.

1163 The building of Notre Dame cathedral begins.

1291 The Crusades end.

1347 The Black Death begins to spread through Europe.

The Hundred Years' War 1337–1453

The Crusades

During the late 1000s, the Seljuk Turks, a Muslim people from Central Asia, gained control of Jerusalem and the area around it—known to Christians as the Holy Land. The Turks went on to attack the Byzantine Empire, leading the Byzantine emperor to call on the pope in Rome for help. In 1095 the pope called a meeting of church leaders and feudal lords. It was the beginning of the **Crusades.**

At least 10,000 Europeans joined the military mission to take the Holy Land from the Muslims who controlled it. The First Crusade lasted from 1096 to 1099. French and Italian lords led several armies from Europe to Constantinople. From there, the Crusaders marched down the coast toward the Holy Land and eventually recaptured Jerusalem after a series of violent battles.

Other Crusades during the 1100s and 1200s were less successful, however. By 1291, when the Crusades ended, Muslims had regained control of the Holy Land. Still, the Crusades brought many change to Europe. These included the use of crossbows in warfare, advances in trade between Italian cities and the Holy Land, and an increase in the power of European kings due to the number of nobles who died in the fighting.

Life and Culture

Throughout the Middle Ages, European culture underwent many changes. During the early period, for example, few people received an education. Those who did were mainly nobles and the clergy, with schooling carried out at monasteries and in churches. As towns grew larger, however, other schools opened.

Between the late 1000s and the late 1200s, four great universities opened, including ones in Paris and at Oxford in England. By the end of the 1400s, many more universities had opened. Subjects of study included law, medicine, and theology.

Another change involved architecture. In the mid-1100s, builders developed a different style of church architecture called **Gothic**, after the barbarian Goths. The highest artistic skills of the medieval world went into the building of the new churches, which were considered monuments to God. Gothic cathedrals had high walls, tall spires, and rows of supports called flying buttresses on the outside walls. Every element of Gothic churches reached toward heaven. Cathedrals were constructed in many parts of Europe. Their tall buildings towered over the growing towns around them.

The recovery of Greek texts in Europe was also a key change. Muslim scholars had kept the works of Greek and Roman philosophers such as Aristotle alive. During the later period, European philosophers tried to reconcile Aristotle's ideas with those of early church writers. This attempt to bring together faith and reason was called **scholasticism**. One of the greatest philosophers of the Middle Ages was **Thomas Aquinas**, a monk of the Dominican order whose principal work summarized medieval Christian thought.

The cathedral of Notre Dame was built in Paris as a symbol of God's greatness.

The Black Death

A plague called the **Black Death** swept through Europe beginning in 1347. The plague, which began in Asia, spread to different ports via trading ships. Rats on the ships carried the disease. The plague was spread to people by bites from fleas on the rats.

Entire towns and villages were wiped out between 1347 and 1351. Roughly one third of Europe's population died. People's faith in God was shaken, and the church lost some of its power and importance. Available workers became harder to find, leading them to demand higher wages. Relations between the upper and lower classes changed, with peasants staging uprisings in several European countries.

Key Facts
• The Magna Carta, signed in 1215, limited the power of the English king.
• During the Crusades, Christians tried to end Muslim rule of the Holy Land.
• Universities and Gothic cathedrals became important parts of growing European towns.
• The Black Death killed millions of people during the late Middle Ages.

Review

1. **Identify** (a) King John, (b) Thomas Aquinas (c) Black Death
2. **Define** (a) Magna Carta (b) Crusades (c) Gothic
3. How did education change during the Middle Ages?

Direct Teach

Reading Focus

The Crusades

Recall Which force gained control of Jerusalem prior to the first Crusade? *Seljuk Turks*

Speculate Why do you think so many Europeans took part in the Crusades? *possible answers—belief that they were doing God's will; desire for wealth; seeking adventure*

Reading Focus

Life and Culture

Identify Who preserved the works of Greek and Roman philosophers? *Muslim scholars*

Describe What were the elements of Gothic architecture? *high walls, tall spires, rows of supports called flying buttresses on outside walls, towering churches that seemed to reach toward heaven*

Primary Source

"Three things are necessary for the salvation of man; to know what he ought to believe; to know what he ought to desire; and to know what he ought to do."
—Thomas Aquinas, *Two Precepts of Charity*

Differentiating Instruction

Below Level

English-Language Learners

Research Required

1. Have students work in pairs to make a list of at least five names of major participants in the Crusades.
2. Have pairs of students select one person from their list who interests them. Then have students conduct research about that person using reliable print or online sources. Students should consult at least two sources for their research.
3. Have each pair of students work together to write a one page biography of its chosen person. Biographies should include an illustration of the person and a bibliography citing all sources used.
4. Have volunteers read their biographies to the class. **LS Verbal-Linguistic, Interpersonal**

Alternative Assessment Handbook, Rubrics 4: Biographies; and 40: Writing to Describe

Answers

1. (a.) *English king who signed the Magna Carta in 1215;* **(b.)** *monk of the Dominican order whose principal work summarized medieval Christian thought;* **(c.)** *plague that killed one-third of Europe's population between 1347 and 1351;* **2. (a.)** *document signed by King John that protected the liberties of the nobles and provided a basic outline of rights;* **(b.)** *military missions to take the Holy Land from the Muslims;* **(c.)** *style of church architecture named after the barbarian Goths;* **3.** *Education became more accessible as more schools and universities opened.*

Answers

Review Key Terms and People

1. e
2. b
3. j
4. g
5. l
6. d
7. c
8. a
9. k
10. i
11. f
12. h

Comprehension and Critical Thinking

13. **a.** Nile River valley in Africa, Tigris and Euphrates Rivers valley in southwestern Asia, Indus River valley in southern Asia, Huang River valley in eastern Asia
    b. possible answer—Akkadians: conquered the Sumerians; Babylonians: ruler Hammurabi established first code of laws; Hittites: warlike invaders of Tigris-Euphrates Valley; among first people to smelt iron
    c. taught reincarnation and dharma
14. **a.** possible answer—Athens was a direct democracy; Sparta was led by two kings.
    b. It became the foundation of the civilizations.
    c. It unified people across the region.
15. **a.** Trade caravans linked West Africa with the Muslim states in North Africa and the Middle East; in East Africa, the powerful trading kingdoms of Kush and Aksum controlled trade from Egypt to the interior of Africa.
    b. Korea is located on the mainland, Japan is a chain of islands; Korea has long served as a bridge between eastern Asia and the neighboring islands; Japan developed a feudal system.
    c. possible answer—yes, the Code collected all Roman laws and organized them so that they could be accessed and preserved
16. **a.** manorial system
    b. it killed one-third of the European population, shook people's faith in God, caused the church to lose power and influence, allowed workers to demand higher wages since so few were left, and encouraged peasants to revolt against upper classes

Critical Reading

17. B
18. B

Prologue Assessment

Review Key Terms and People

Match each numbered description with the correct lettered item below.

1. Series of wars during which Christians tried to recapture holy lands from Muslims
2. Scientists who study objects used by early man
3. Prophet of Islam
4. Greek word for city-state
5. Mali ruler who made Timbuktu a center of Islamic thought
6. Greatest all Frankish kings
7. Period of Roman Peace
8. Sumerian form of writing
9. Underground chamber used for Anasazi religious ceremonies
10. Leading philosopher during China's Zhou dynasty
11. Religious images considered holy by Byzantines
12. Top general who was the real power in medieval Japan

a. cuneiform
b. archeologists
c. Pax Romana
d. Charlemagne
e. Crusades
f. icons
g. polis
h. shogun
i. Confucius
j. Muhammad
k. kiva
l. Mansa Musa

Comprehension and Critical Thinking

SECTIONS 1–3 *(pp. 10–15)*

13. **a. Identify** What four river valleys became important during the rise of civilization?
    b. Summarize Describe three states that dominated Mesopotamia.
    c. Elaborate How did the rise of Hinduism affect ancient India?

SECTIONS 4–6 *(pp. 16–19, 22–23)*

14. **a. Recall** What was one difference between the governments of Athens and Sparta?
    b. Analyze In what ways did maize change civilizations in Central America?
    c. Evaluate Why was the Arabic language important for the Muslim caliphate?

SECTIONS 7–9 *(pp. 24–29)*

15. **a. Describe** How were trade routes influential in West Africa? in East Africa?
    b. Contrast What differences developed between Korea and Japan?
    c. Evaluate Do you think Justinian's Code was a logical way to organize Roman law? Why or why not?

SECTIONS 10–11 *(pp. 30–33)*

16. **a. Recall** In addition to the feudal system, what system shaped the economic structure of Europe during the Middle Ages?
    b. Elaborate How did the Black Death affect life in Europe during the High Middle Ages?

Critical Reading

Read the passage on page 29 that begins with the heading "Schism in the Christian Church." Then answer the questions that follow.

17. You can infer from the passage that the Great Schism
    A. led to attacks on Muslims.
    B. had many causes that built up over time.
    C. helped in Russia becoming Christian.
    D. was all about icons.
18. In the third last sentence of the passage's third paragraph, "In 731 Pope Gregory III decided that it was heresy not to allow the honoring of icons," the word *heresy* means
    A. correct.
    B. contrary to church teaching.
    C. economical.
    D. reasonable.

34

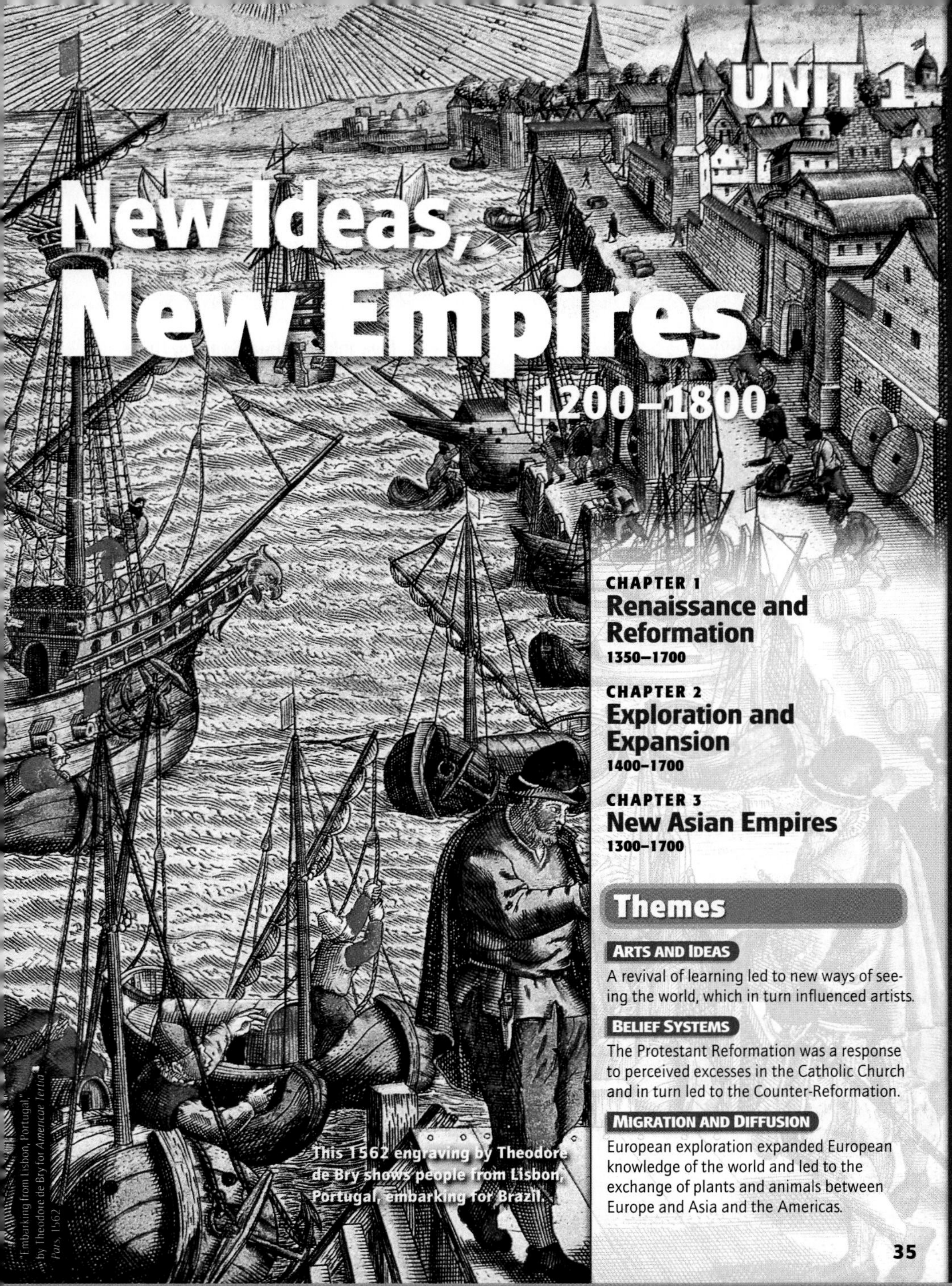

UNIT 1

New Ideas, New Empires

1200–1800

This 1562 engraving by Theodore de Bry shows people from Lisbon, Portugal, embarking for Brazil.

"Embarking from Lisbon, Portugal," by Theodore de Bry for *Americae Tertia Pars*, 1562

CHAPTER 1
Renaissance and Reformation
1350–1700

CHAPTER 2
Exploration and Expansion
1400–1700

CHAPTER 3
New Asian Empires
1300–1700

Themes

ARTS AND IDEAS
A revival of learning led to new ways of seeing the world, which in turn influenced artists.

BELIEF SYSTEMS
The Protestant Reformation was a response to perceived excesses in the Catholic Church and in turn led to the Counter-Reformation.

MIGRATION AND DIFFUSION
European exploration expanded European knowledge of the world and led to the exchange of plants and animals between Europe and Asia and the Americas.

Unit Preview

Introducing the Unit

Ask students to consider what it would be like to discover another planet that was suitable for human habitation. Have students make a list of the ways in which humans could use a new world. Write each item for the class to see. Then guide the class in a discussion of the items. Tell students that Europeans viewed the discovery of the Americas in much the same way—hence the nickname "New World."

Connecting to Themes

Activity Renaissance to Reformation Ask students how the Renaissance paved the way for the Protestant Reformation. Guide students in a discussion of the ways that a new focus on the secular and the individual led some people to question the Catholic Church.
LS Verbal-Linguistic

Reading Like a Historian

Interpreting Visuals

Voyages to Brazil The engraving shown on this page is part of a series illustrating voyages of discovery and exploration around the world. This engraving shows Portuguese caravels leaving Lisbon for Brazil. It comes from Part 3 of De Bry's *Grand Voyages*, which covered voyages to Brazil.

Unit Resources

Planning

- **Differentiated Instruction Teacher Management System:** Unit Pacing Guide
- OSP **One-Stop Planner CD-ROM:** Teacher Management System
- **Power Presentations with Video CD-ROM**

Differentiating Instruction

- **Differentiated Instruction Teacher Management System:** Lesson Plans for Differentiated Instruction
- **Differentiated Instruction Modified Worksheets and Tests CD-ROM**

Enrichment

- **A World History Teacher's Guide to Analyzing Movies**
- **Document-Based Activities for World History**
- **World History Outline Maps**
- **Reading Like a Historian: World History Toolkit**
- **World History Primary Source Library CD-ROM**

Assessment

- **PASS:** Unit Test, Forms A and B
- **Alternative Assessment Handbook**
- OSP **ExamView Test Generator**
- HOAP **Holt Online Assessment Program** (in the Premier Online Edition)

Chapter 1 Planning Guide

Renaissance and Reformation

Chapter Overview	Reproducible Resources	Technology Resources
CHAPTER 1 **pp. 36–67** **Overview: In this chapter, students will learn how the rediscovery of classical knowledge led to a period of creativity and learning known as the Renaissance. As emphasis was placed on the individual, new ideas about religion emerged, which led to the Reformation.**	**Differentiated Instruction Teacher Management System:*** • Pacing Guide • Lesson Plans for Differentiated Instruction **Interactive Reader and Study Guide:** Chapter Summary* **Chapter Resource File*** • Writing for the SAT • Social Studies Skill • Chapter Review **World History Outline Maps**	**Live Ink© Online Reading Help** **Student Edition on Audio CD Program** **Differentiated Instruction Modified Worksheets and Tests CD-ROM** **World History Primary Source Library CD-ROM** **Power Presentations with Video CD-ROM** **History's Impact: World History Video Program (VHS/DVD):** Renaissance and Reformation
Section 1: **The Italian Renaissance** **The Main Idea:** In Italy the growth of wealthy trading cities and new ways of thinking helped lead to a rebirth of the arts and learning. This era became known as the Renaissance.	**Differentiated Instruction Teacher Management System:** Section 1 Lesson Plan* **Interactive Reader and Study Guide:** Section 1 Summary* **Chapter Resource File*** • Vocabulary Builder: Section 1 • Biography: Sofonisba Anguissola • Primary Source: The School of Athens	**Daily Test Practice Transparency:** Section 1* **Map Transparency:** Europe, c. 1300* **Quick Facts Transparency:** Causes of the Renaissance*
Section 2: **The Northern Renaissance** **The Main Idea:** Renaissance ideas soon spread beyond Italy to northern Europe by means of trade, travel, and printed material, influencing the art and ideas of the north.	**Differentiated Instruction Teacher Management System:** Section 2 Lesson Plan* **Interactive Reader and Study Guide:** Section 2 Summary* **Chapter Resource File*** • Vocabulary Builder: Section 2 • Biography: Jan van Eyck • History and Geography: Trade Fuels City Growth • Literature: *The Canterbury Tales*	**Daily Test Practice Transparency:** Section 2* **Internet Activity:** The Printing Press
Section 3: **The Protestant Reformation** **The Main Idea:** Criticism of the Roman Catholic Church led to a religious movement called the Protestant Reformation and brought changes in religion and politics across Europe.	**Differentiated Instruction Teacher Management System:** Section 3 Lesson Plan* **Interactive Reader and Study Guide:** Section 3 Summary* **Chapter Resource File*** • Vocabulary Builder: Section 3 • Biography: Jan Hus	**Daily Test Practice Transparency:** Section 3* **Map Transparency:** Spread of Protestantism* **Internet Activity:** Reformation Leaders
Section 4: **The Counter-Reformation** **The Main Idea:** Catholics at all levels recognized the need for reform in the church. Their work turned back the tide of Protestantism in some areas and renewed the zeal of Catholics everywhere.	**Differentiated Instruction Teacher Management System:** Section 4 Lesson Plan* **Interactive Reader and Study Guide:** Section 4 Summary* **Chapter Resource File*** • Vocabulary Builder: Section 4 • Biography: Teresa of Avila	**Daily Test Practice Transparency:** Section 4* **Map Transparency:** Religions in Europe, 1600* **Quick Facts Transparency:** The Reformation*

go.hrw.com | Print Resource | Transparency
Learning Styles | Audio CD | CD-ROM
Video | SE Student Edition | TE Teacher's Edition
OSP One-Stop Planner CD-ROM
*also on One-Stop Planner CD-ROM

HOLT
History's Impact
World History Video Program (VHS/DVD)
Renaissance and Reformation

Review, Assessment, Intervention

- **Quick Facts Transparency:** Renaissance and Reformation*
- **Progress Assessment Support System (PASS):** Chapter Test*
- **Differentiated Instruction Modified Worksheets and Tests CD-ROM:** Modified Chapter Test
- OSP **One-Stop Planner CD-ROM:** ExamView Test Generator (English/Spanish)
- HOAP **Holt Online Assessment Program (HOAP),** in the Holt Premier Online Student Edition

- **PASS:** Section 1 Quiz*
- **Online Quiz:** Section 1
- **Alternative Assessment Handbook**

- **PASS:** Section 2 Quiz*
- **Online Quiz:** Section 2
- **Alternative Assessment Handbook**

- **PASS:** Section 3 Quiz*
- **Online Quiz:** Section 3
- **Alternative Assessment Handbook**

- **PASS:** Section 4 Quiz*
- **Online Quiz:** Section 4
- **Alternative Assessment Handbook**

Power Presentation with Video CD-ROM

Power Presentations with Video are visual presentations of each chapter's main ideas. Presentations can be customized by including Quick Facts charts, images and maps from the textbook, and video clips.

Holt Online Learning

go.hrw.com
Teacher Resources
KEYWORD: SHL TEACHER

go.hrw.com
Student Resources
KEYWORD: SHL REN

- Document-Based Questions
- Interactive Multimedia Activities
- Current Events
- Chapter-Based Internet Activities
- and more!

Holt Premier
Online Student Edition

Complete online support for interactivity, assessment, and reporting

- Interactive Maps and Notebook
- Homework Practice and Research Activities Online

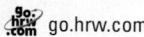

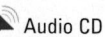

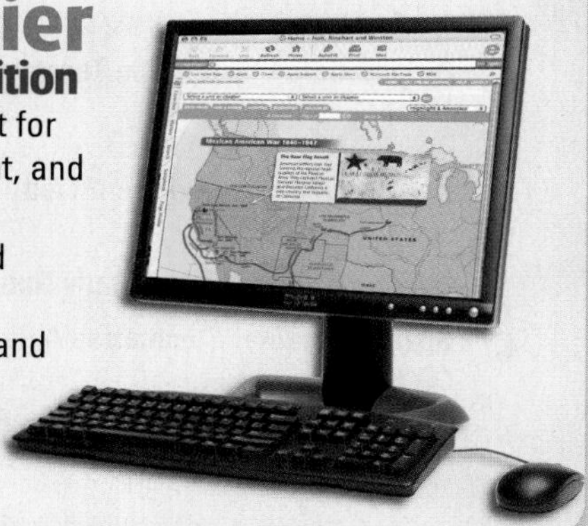

CHAPTER 1 PLANNING GUIDE

The Big Picture

Peter N. Stearns

The Big Changes Western Europe between 1350 and 1600 began to participate in two or three really big changes, all in a context in which Europe's world role began gradually to expand. First, the European economy began to become more commercial. Second, stronger governments began to emerge, and feudal controls weakened. Third, culture began to shift away from a primary emphasis on traditional religious values. The Renaissance, Reformation, and Counterreformation can be seen in terms of these big changes, though they had their own flavors and complexities. The Renaissance built on and encouraged growing trade and urbanism. The Reformation did ultimately contribute to more focus on economic life as a means of demonstrating God's favor. The Renaissance encouraged new political functions and values, initially in the Italian city-states; the Reformation, by cutting the power of the papacy, gave new leeway to secular rulers. The Renaissance encouraged a more secular culture; and while the Reformation sought exactly the opposite, its weakening of Christian unity encouraged some cultural change as well.

The Renaissance The Renaissance began in the particular context of late-medieval Italy, with unusual ties to the classical past and fewer feudal controls. The Renaissance achievements showed particularly in dramatically new cultural and artistic forms, and the more general sentiments described in humanism. How much the movement affected politics and, particularly, daily life must be debated. The Renaissance spread northward after about 1450. It was encouraged by the printing press and rising literacy. Encouragement to some of the great vernacular writers of all time showed the power of cultural change in Britain and France as well as Spain.

The Reformation and Counterreformation Concern about church corruption, national sentiment, and new readings of the Bible prompted Luther's defiance of the Catholic Church. Reformation leaders did not intend to destroy Christian unity but rather redefine it. Lutheranism, Calvinism, and Anglicanism produced a dramatically new religious map. Catholic revival, and new tools such as the powerful Jesuit order, preserved much territory for Catholicism, but it could not stem division. The result was a period of confusion and considerable conflict, including concern about witchcraft.

Recent Scholarship

Daily Life in Renaissance Italy (2001) by Elizabeth S. Cohen and Thomas V. Cohen shows the dramatic improvements in historians' ability not only to find out about patterns of daily life, but also to show why they deserve serious attention and not just antiquarian interest. Urban conditions produced new aspirations and some strikingly modern-seeming protest, though economic life was not fully transformed. Gender, family life, and sexuality showed a similar combination of change and continuity. The book takes its analysis up to about 1500, as the peak Renaissance impulses began to decline in Italy.

Differentiating Instruction

Differentiated Instruction Teacher Management System
- Pacing Guide
- Lesson Plans for Differentiated Instruction

Interactive Reader and Study Guide

Spanish Chapter Summaries Audio CD Program

Student Edition on Audio CD Program

Differentiated Instruction Modified Worksheets and Tests CD-ROM
- Vocabulary Flash Cards
- Modified Vocabulary Builder Activities
- Modified Chapter Review Activity
- Modified Chapter Test

OSP **One-Stop Planner CD-ROM**
- ExamView Test Generator (English/Spanish)
- PuzzlePro
- Quiz Show for ExamView
- Transparencies and Videos

TE **Differentiated Activities in the Teacher's Edition**
- Machiavelli's Theories, p. 44
- Political Cartoons: The Protestants, p. 53
- The Council of Trent, p. 59

BEFORE YOU TEACH

Reading Like a Historian

Sam Wineburg

The Prince Few political theorists in history are immortalized with their own adjective. But Nicolo Machiavelli has bequeathed to us "Machiavellian" —unscrupulous, lacking morals, bereft of conscience, an out-and-out rogue. There's even an online Machiavellian personality quiz: "Are you a cutthroat or a pussycat?" Agree or disagree: "Never tell anyone the real reason you did something unless it is useful to do so." Agree and you earn the right to be in the Machiavellian Club.

But there was more than one side to this Italian author and statesman. How do we reconcile the autocratic Machiavelli of *The Prince* with the life-long republican and author of *The Discourses*, an extended panegyric on the virtues of liberty and the advantages of representative government? This is the puzzle of reading Machiavelli.

One way to solve it is to cast *The Prince* as satire, so over the top that we have no choice but to conclude that it means the opposite of what it says —a view held by Garrett Mattingly, longtime professor of European history at Columbia University. Mattingly drew inspiration from Spinoza, who read *The Prince* as a cautionary tale that warns us what happens when rulers forswear morality to ensure the survival of the state. Others, like the German philosopher Fichte, read *The Prince* as an anti-religious tract, a frontal assault on Christianity. Benedetto Croce, the 20th century Italian philosopher, saw in Machiavelli the humanist. For him, *The Prince* embodied the author's view of the nobility of man and contained its own moral code.

But overwhelmingly, the most common reading of Machiavelli and his famous book is the one we already know: the chilling statement of statecraft by a philosophizing sociopath. In this vein, the British philosopher and public intellectual Bertrand Russell coined the most unforgettable epithet. Russell damned *The Prince* as a "handbook for gangsters."

Misreading Machiavelli? How is it that a book that has been widely acknowledged as lucid and transparent, a "model of clear Renaissance prose," one whose own author proclaimed that he had "not ornamented this work, nor filled it with fulsome phrases" is given to so many divergent readings? What other philosopher could we imagine being defended with the words—the title of a piece appearing on the webpage of New York's Italian American society—"Machiavelli was not Machiavellian"?

In a magisterial review that appeared in the New York Review of Books, Sir Isaiah Berlin claimed that Machiavelli challenged a core assumption of the Western tradition—and it is this challenge, never explicitly stated in *The Prince*—that has given rise to so many misreadings of the text. According to Berlin, at the heart of the Western tradition is the "idea of the world and of human society as a single intelligible structure," an organic whole whose pieces with much human toil can ultimately be aligned. "It is this rock, upon which Western beliefs and lives had been founded, that Machiavelli seems, in effect, to have split open."

In Berlin's reading, Machiavelli is not saying, as many would have him, that there is a conflict between the private realm of morality and the public realm of statecraft. Rather—and this is *The Prince's* most radical point—Machiavelli claimed that the two spheres are incommensurate. They can never be reconciled. "If Machiavelli is right, this entire tradition—the central current of Western thought—is fallacious. For if his position is valid then it is impossible to construct even the notion of a perfect society, for there exists at least two sets of virtues—let us call them the Christian and the pagan—which are not merely in practice, but in principle, incompatible."

If Berlin is right, we have misread Machiavelli because we have yet to read him correctly. *The Prince* called the bluff of the Western tradition, and it is easier to misread this book than to wrestle with the implications of its claim.

• Chapter Preview •

Chapter Main Ideas

Section 1 In Italy the growth of wealthy trading cities and new ways of thinking helped lead to a rebirth of the arts and learning. This era became known as the Renaissance.

Section 2 Renaissance ideas soon spread beyond Italy to northern Europe by means of trade, travel, and printed material, influencing the art and ideas of the north.

Section 3 Criticism of the Roman Catholic Church led to a religious movement called the Protestant Reformation and brought changes in religion and politics across Europe.

Section 4 Catholics at all levels recognized the need for reform in the church. Their work turned back the tide of Protestantism in some areas and renewed the zeal of Catholics everywhere.

CHAPTER 1 1300–1650

Renaissance and Reformation

THE BIG PICTURE Major changes in Europe caused the medieval period to give way to a new period. As trade with the East increased, Europeans rediscovered the classical knowledge of ancient Greece and Rome. This knowledge led to a period of creativity and learning called the Renaissance. A new focus on the individual emerged, contributing to new ideas about religion. These ideas caused a struggle in Christianity known as the Reformation.

Theme MIGRATION AND DIFFUSION

The migration of people and the diffusion of ideas have encouraged the development of a more global culture. In this chapter you will read about the diffusions of ideas that changed the cultural and religious lives of Europeans after the Middle Ages.

Battista Sforza and Federico da Montefeltro by Piero della Francesca, c. 1420–1492, Courtesy of Alinari/Art Resource, NY

TIME LINE

CHAPTER EVENTS

- **1300s** The Renaissance begins in Italy's city-states.
- **1434** The Medici family controls the city-state of Florence.
- **c. 1455** Gutenberg develops a printing press with moveable type.
- **1492** More than 100,000 Jews are expelled from Spain.

1300 — 1400

WORLD EVENTS

- **1368** The Ming dynasty begins in China.
- **1453** The Ottomans conquer Constantinople.
- **1464** Sunni Ali founds the Songhai Empire in West Africa.
- **1492** Christopher Columbus reaches the Americas.

Key to Differentiating Instruction

Below Level

Basic-level activities designed for all students encountering new material

At Level

Intermediate-level activities designed for average students

Above Level

Challenging activities designed for honors and gifted and talented students

Standard English Mastery

Activities designed to improve standard English usage

Introduce the Chapter

At Level

Prep Required

Renaissance and Reformation

1. Have students skim the chapter and list all the artwork depicted, noting the artists who created the pieces.
2. Guide students in a discussion of the similarities and differences of the pieces in terms of visual effects such as shadow and perspective, realism, and subject matter.
3. Tell students that in this chapter they will learn about a period of stunning advances in the arts and other fields. Around the same time, people began challenging some basic elements of Catholic doctrine.
4. Have students write a paragraph describing the different and similar styles used by artists mentioned in this chapter. LS **Visual-Spatial, Verbal-Linguistic**

Alternative Assessment Handbook, Rubrics 11: Discussions; and 40: Writing to Describe

History's Impact video program
Watch the video to understand the impact of the Renaissance and Reformation.

Reading like a Historian The Renaissance saw a rebirth in artistic creativity. New themes and techniques, such as perspective, made Renaissance art more realistic and three-dimensional than medieval art. During the 1400s Renaissance artist Piero della Francesca painted the portraits above of the Duke of Urbino and his wife.

Analyzing Visuals What aspects of the portraits show realism and a three-dimensional perspective?

See **Skills Handbook**, p. H26

1508
Michelangelo starts painting the Sistine Chapel.

1500

1537
Spanish conquistadors conquer the Inca Empire in South America.

• Chapter Preview •

HOLT
History's Impact
► **Video Program: Renaissance and Reformation**
See the Video Teacher's Guide for strategies for using the video segment.

Reading Like a Historian

Analyzing Visuals This Italian couple ruled in Urbino, Italy, during the 1400s. What about these two portraits might indicate that these people were rulers? *possible answers—The woman's clothing is formal and she wears jewels, indicating her wealth and status; the man wears a hat that may signify power.*

Explore the Time Line

1. What city-state was controlled by the Medici family? *Florence*
2. What important device was developed around the same time that the Ottomans conquered Constantinople? *printing press with movable type*
3. How many years after Michelangelo began painting the Sistine Chapel was the Inca Empire conquered? *about 29 years*
4. In what century did the Renaissance begin in Italy? *1300s*

Info to Know

Condotierri: The Mercenaries As the Italian city-states grew wealthy from trade, wars became nearly constant. City-states fought to maintain control over their holdings. Italian leaders turned to condotierri, who were mercenary generals. The Duke of Urbino, pictured above, was one of the most successful condotierri. As a young fighter, he lost his right eye and the bridge of his nose. Therefore, all portraits of him are profiles, presenting his left side.

Draw Conclusions What qualities would make an effective condotierre? *good military leader; no firm loyalty*

go.hrw.com
Online Resources
Chapter Resources:
KEYWORD: SHL REN
Teacher Resources:
KEYWORD: SHL TEACHER

Answers

Reading Like a Historian *realistic details and shadows in faces, clothing, and jewelry; scale of natural features diminishes in background, showing distance*

Preteach

Geography Starting Points

Mediterranean Trade In the late Middle Ages, wealth and urban development were concentrated in cities around the Mediterranean Sea, especially in Italy. With the exception of Paris, the only European cities with more than 10,000 people were Naples, Venice, Milan, and Constantinople. Venice financed trading ventures and organized fleets of ships that traded around the Mediterranean. Meanwhile, Arab caravans arrived in the Near East with silks, spices, and cotton. North African traders brought gold and ivory across the Sahara and within reach of the Mediterranean.

- **Map Transparency:** Europe, c. 1300
- **World History Outline Maps**
- **Interactive Map:** Europe, c. 1300

Answers

Geography Starting Points

1. *Naples, Venice;* 2. *possible answer—Asian traders might bring new ideas about religion, society, and government.*

Geography Starting Points

Interactive

Europe, c. 1300

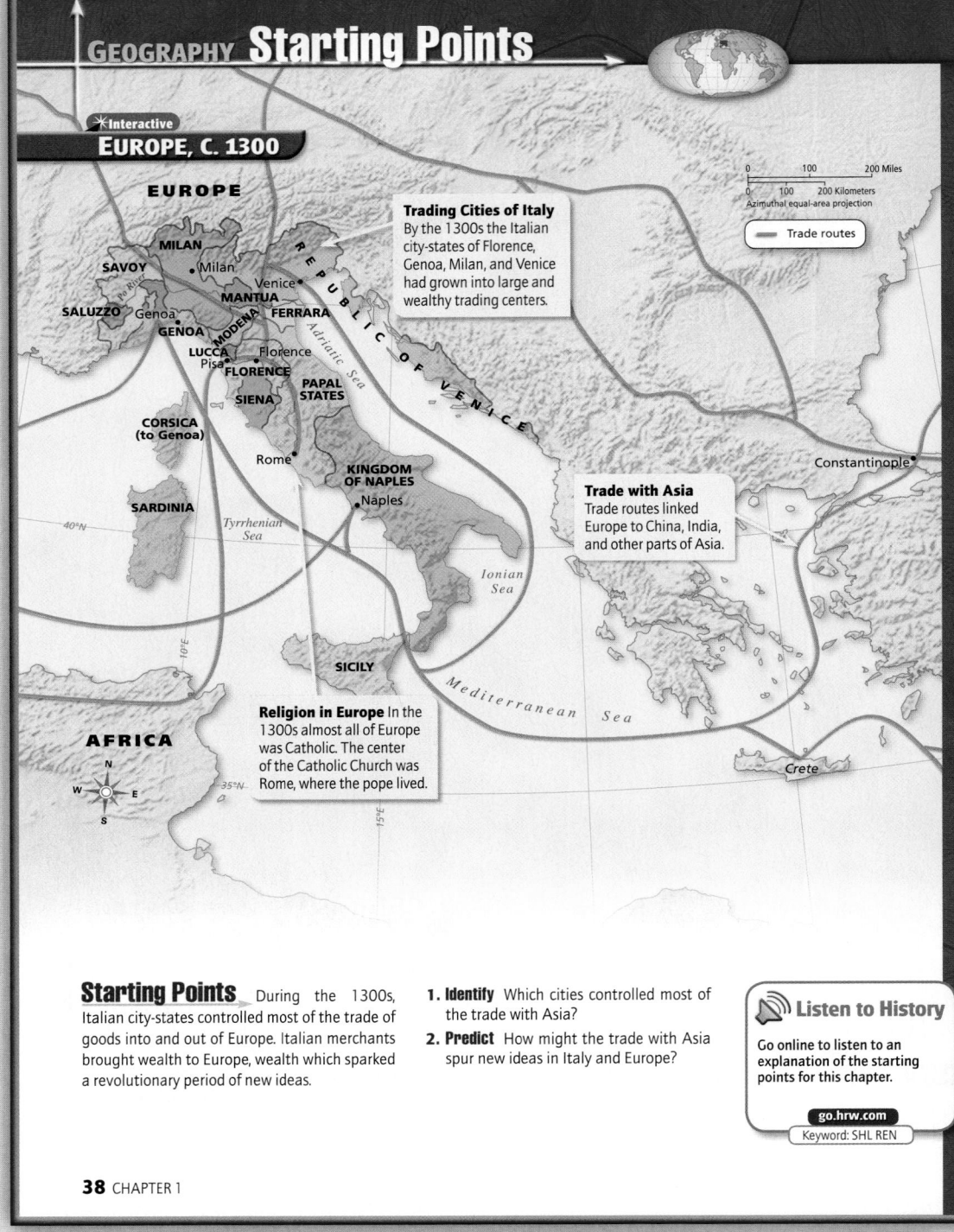

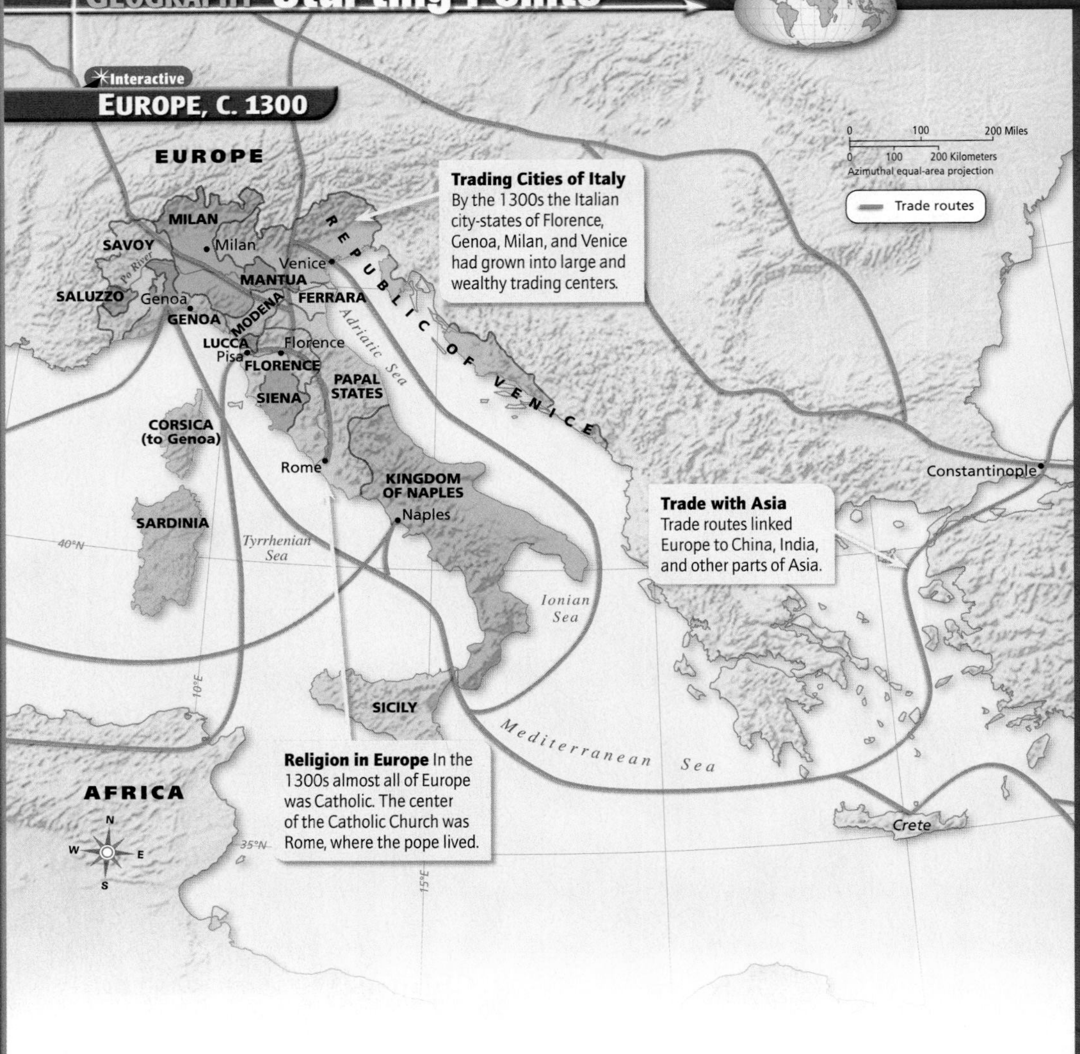

Starting Points During the 1300s, Italian city-states controlled most of the trade of goods into and out of Europe. Italian merchants brought wealth to Europe, wealth which sparked a revolutionary period of new ideas.

1. **Identify** Which cities controlled most of the trade with Asia?
2. **Predict** How might the trade with Asia spur new ideas in Italy and Europe?

Listen to History

Go online to listen to an explanation of the starting points for this chapter.

go.hrw.com

Keyword: SHL REN

Skills Focus: Analyzing Maps

At Level

Research Required

Social Studies Skill

Trader's Log

1. Have students conduct research to find what products were produced and traded in the 1300s in the locations listed on the map. For instance, Florence was well known for its woolen cloth.
2. Have students create a trader's log that describes a journey among some of the locations listed on the map. Tell students to list the transactions that occurred at each location. A log might begin "Jan. 26, 1307: Left Florence, via horse-drawn cart, headed north to Venice with a cargo of fine cloth."
3. Have volunteers present their logs to the class. **LS Verbal-Linguistic**

Alternative Assessment Handbook, Rubric 37: Writing Assignments

SECTION 1

The Italian Renaissance

Before You Read

Main Idea

In Italy the growth of wealthy trading cities and new ways of thinking helped lead to a rebirth of the arts and learning. This era became known as the Renaissance.

Reading Focus

1. What changes in society and in cities stimulated the beginning of the Renaissance?
2. What ideas formed the foundation of the Italian Renaissance?
3. What contributions did artists make to the Renaissance?

Key Terms and People

Renaissance
humanism
secular
Baldassare Castiglione
Niccolò Machiavelli
Lorenzo de Medici
Leonardo da Vinci
Michelangelo Buonarroti
Raphael

TAKING NOTES In a graphic organizer like this one, take notes on the beginnings of the Renaissance, its ideas, and its art.

Beginnings	Ideas and Art

Michelangelo, *Creation of the Stars and Planets*. Detail of God.

A VISION OF GOD

◀ **This painting by Michelangelo shows a Christian-inspired view of God creating the stars and planets. The painting decorates part of the ceiling of the Sistine Chapel in Rome.**

THE INSIDE STORY ***How did one man's vision turn a ceiling into a masterpiece?*** Weak light filtered through the arched windows of the Sistine Chapel in Rome. High above the ground, the artist Michelangelo stood on a platform. He looked up, raised his brush to the ceiling, and carefully applied paint to the wet plaster. For almost four years, this ceiling had been his canvas. Across it, he had painted vivid scenes of events and people from the Bible. The expressive, detailed figures were monumental, so they could be seen from far below.

Each day, Michelangelo and his assistants climbed a 40-foot ladder to a scaffolding. From there, steps rose another 20 feet to a platform 7 feet beneath the chapel's immense, vaulted ceiling. All day Michelangelo stood, his head craned back, his arm raised high to the ceiling.

Yet when the agony of the work was finally done, Michelangelo had created one of the world's great masterpieces. One observer wrote that the Sistine Chapel was so beautiful "as to make everyone astonished." ■

The Beginning of the Renaissance

Michelangelo's painting was not only beautiful but also very different from the art of the Middle Ages. A new direction in art was only one of the ways in which European society began changing after the 1300s.

Changes in Society The Black Death, starvation, and warfare had overtaken Europe about 1300. These catastrophic events and the enormous loss of life may have led to some of the changes of the 1300s.

Preteach

Getting Started

Use the **Interactive Reader and Study Guide** to familiarize students with the section content.

Interactive Reader and Study Guide, Section 1

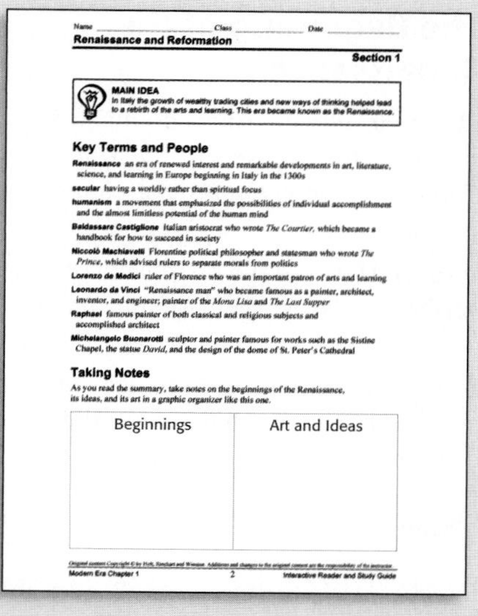

Name ______ Class ______ Date ______

Renaissance and Reformation

Section 1

MAIN IDEA
In Italy the growth of wealthy trading cities and new ways of thinking helped lead to a rebirth of the arts and learning. This era became known as the Renaissance.

Key Terms and People

Renaissance an era of renewed interest and remarkable developments in art, literature, science, and learning in Europe beginning in Italy in the 1300s

secular having a worldly rather than spiritual focus

humanism a movement that emphasized the possibilities of individual accomplishment and the almost limitless potential of the human mind

Baldassare Castiglione Italian aristocrat who wrote *The Courtier*, which became a handbook for how to succeed in society

Niccolò Machiavelli Florentine political philosopher and statesman who wrote *The Prince*, which advised rulers to separate morals from politics

Lorenzo de Medici ruler of Florence who was an important patron of arts and learning

Leonardo da Vinci "Renaissance man" who became famous as a painter, architect, inventor, and engineer; painter of the *Mona Lisa* and *The Last Supper*

Raphael famous painter of both classical and religious subjects and accomplished architect

Michelangelo Buonarroti sculptor and painter famous for works such as the Sistine Chapel, the statue *David*, and the design of the dome of St. Peter's Cathedral

Taking Notes

As you read the summary, take notes on the beginnings of the Renaissance, its ideas, and its art in a graphic organizer like this one.

Beginnings	Art and Ideas

Modern Era Chapter 1 2 Interactive Reader and Study Guide

Academic Vocabulary

Review with students the high-use academic term(s) in this section.

deviate to turn away from a course or topic (p. 43)

CRF: Vocabulary Builder: Section 1

Taking Notes

Beginnings:—thriving cities, increased trade, wealthy merchant class, renewed interest in art, literature, science, and learning, desire to beautify cities; Ideas and Art:— rebirth in art, literature, and science, secular focus, humanism, individualism, vernacular literature, interest in ancients

Teach the Main Idea

At Level

The Italian Renaissance

1. **Teach** Ask students the Reading Focus questions to teach this section.
2. **Apply** Have students scan the section, examine the pictures and charts, and read the captions. Tell students to make a list of these elements, leaving space for notes. Ask students what these elements reveal about the section.
3. **Review** As you review the section, have students take notes about each picture or chart, describing its significance to the broader themes of the Renaissance.
4. **Practice/Homework** Have students create a resumé for one of the artists or writers of the Italian Renaissance.
   LS Visual-Spatial, Verbal-Linguistic

Alternative Assessment Handbook, Rubric 31: Resumés

• Direct Teach •

Reading Focus

1 What changes in society and in cities stimulated the beginning of the Renaissance? *growth of important city-states; increased trade; new wealth*

The Beginning of the Renaissance

Identify Which groups dominated society in the city-states? *the Roman Catholic Church, nobles, merchants, artisans*

Recall How did the merchants of northern Italy use their wealth? *built up their cities, made them magnificent*

Draw Conclusions What advantage might banking have over other industries? *possible answer—easy access to money, money can be used for investment*

Info to Know

Communication Speed Although Venice established connections with ports around the Mediterranean Sea, the rate of travel and communication remained quite slow by today's standards. It took 9 days for news from Venice to reach Naples, 22 days to reach Sicily, and 37 days for it to reach Constantinople. Even by the year 1500, journeys were typically measured by weeks, not days.

The decrease in population allowed farmers to produce more food than they needed. Food prices declined, allowing people more money to spend on other things. The demand for agricultural goods increased, allowing various areas of Europe to begin to specialize in the products that were best suited to their environment. For example, England began to produce more wool and areas of Germany, more grain. As specialization increased, regions had to trade for the products they did not produce.

READING SKILLS
Predicting How might the change in economic structure change other parts of society?

The Rise of City-States Urban areas also began to specialize, particularly in Italy. The territory that today makes up Italy was divided into several large city-states in the north and various kingdoms and the Papal States in the south. The northern city-states of Venice, Milan, and Florence became bustling centers of commerce. In these city-states, the Roman Catholic Church, nobles, merchants, and artisans dominated society. Merchants were usually either bankers or traders. Artisans practiced such crafts as goldsmithing. Knowledge of arts such as painting, sculpture, and architecture increased as nobles and merchants sought to display their new wealth.

Venice, a city with access to the sea, built its economy and reputation on trade. Its people had a long history of trading with other ports along the Mediterranean Sea. Shipbuilding prospered, and sailors traveled to the Near East. As a result, Venetian merchants became some of the wealthiest in the world. They used this wealth to build a unique city that has been described as "a work of art."

Milan, to the west of Venice, based its economy on agriculture, silk, and weapons. Florence, to the south, was famous for its banking and cloth. Monarchs appealed to Florentine bankers for money to fund wars or other endeavors. Merchants refined raw wool into fine cloth and sold it abroad. The leading merchants and bankers poured their wealth into creating a city that rivaled any other in Europe. A citizen of Florence expressed his admiration:

HISTORY'S VOICES

> **"What wealth of buildings, what distinguished architecture there is in Florence! Indeed, how the great genius of the builders is reflected in these buildings, and what a pleasure there is for those who live in them."**
>
> —Leonardo Bruni, *Panegyric to the City of Florence*, 1403

READING CHECK **Find the Main Idea** How did society and cities change in the 1300s?

Florence and the Medici Family

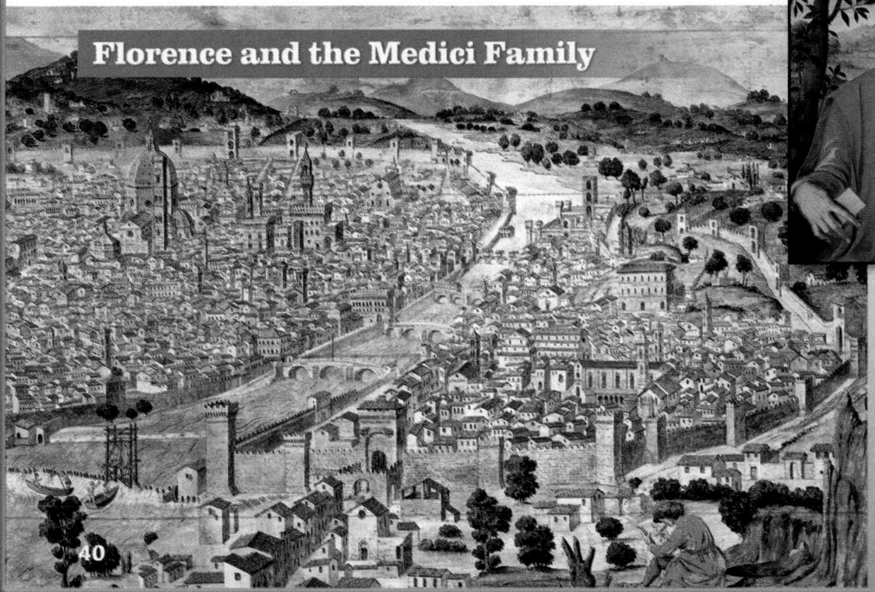

Detail from "Catena Map"

Lorenzo the Magnificent, Anonymous

The Medici family helped finance many new buildings in Florence. This portrait depicts the influential Lorenzo de Medici. ***How does Lorenzo's portrait show his importance?***

Answers

Reading Skills *possible answer—The wealthy classes might sponsor art and science.*

Florence and the Medici Family *possible answers—His appearance suggests that he is wealthy, he sits perched on a chair with Florence behind him.*

Reading Check *Specialization in agriculture increased, resulting in more trade; urban areas became centers of commerce; merchants and artisans became important; some cities became displays of wealth.*

Skills Focus: Summarizing

At Level

Research Required

Reading Skill
City-State Newspapers

1. Review with students the information in the text about Italy in the 1300s. Tell students that bitter rivalry existed between the Italian city-states.
2. Organize students into small groups. Assign each group an Italian city-state.
3. Have each group prepare a newspaper from its city-state in the 1300s. Have students write articles on politics, current events, and daily life of the period. Have them include at least one editorial about how society has changed after the Black Death. Remind students to include some references to appreciation of ancient Greece and Rome.
4. Have groups present their newspapers to the class. **LS Verbal-Linguistic, Visual-Spatial**

Alternative Assessment Handbook, Rubrics 14: Group Activity; and 23: Newspapers

Renaissance Ideas

As the economy and social structure changed, new ideas began to appear. The ideas led to a sustained period of renewed interest and remarkable developments in art, literature, science, and learning. This era became known as the **Renaissance**. (The word *renaissance* is French for "rebirth.") The Renaissance arose in Italy, in part because of its thriving cities, increased trade, and wealthy merchant class.

Inspiration from the Ancients Along with goods for trade, the ships of Venice carried Greek scholars seeking refuge in Italy from the Ottomans. These scholars brought works by ancient writers that the Italians had thought to be lost.

Suddenly the doors to a new world of ideas opened to Italians who could read. They began looking for more information, reading Arabic translations of original texts and searching the libraries and finding lost texts. As they read, they began to think about art, philosophy, and science in different ways. Along the way they began to think more like the classical thinkers who had believed in the human capacity to create and achieve.

Humanism The interest in ancient Greek and Roman culture drove scholars to think about the characteristics of a good education. Under their influence, the church's scholastic education began to give way to the classics: rhetoric, grammar, poetry, history, and Latin and Greek. These subjects came to be known as humanities, and the movement they inspired is known as **humanism**.

In contrast with Church teachings that individuality and achievement were relatively unimportant, humanists emphasized individual accomplishment. They believed that the potential of the human mind was almost limitless. A humanist from Florence, Giovanni Pico della Mirandola (mee-RAN-oh-lah) wrote about the importance of the human mind:

HISTORY'S VOICES

"On Man . . . the father conferred the seeds of . . . every way of life . . . If [a man is] rationale, he will grow into a heavenly being. If [a man is] intellectual, he will be an angel and the son of God."

—Giovanni Pico della Mirandola, *On the Dignity of Man*, 1486

QUICK FACTS: Causes of the Renaissance

- Increased trade with Asia and other regions as a result of the Crusades
- Growth of large, wealthy city-states in Italy
- Renewed interest in the classical learning of ancient Greece and Rome
- Rise of rich and powerful merchants, who became patrons of the arts
- Increased desire for scientific and technical knowledge
- Desire to beautify cities

The roots of humanism are sometimes traced back to the work of Dante Alighieri, a Florentine poet of the late middle ages. His work contains glimpses of what would become the humanist focus on human nature. Many historians believe the Renaissance itself began with two humanists who lived a generation after Dante. Giovanni Boccaccio (bo-KAH-chee-oh) and Francesco Petrarch (PEHT-rahrk) both wrote literature in the vernacular, or everyday language of the people. In the past, most writing had been done in formal Latin.

Humanists rediscovered ancient texts on anatomy, geography, and astronomy. Advances were made in medicine—notable among them were Leonardo da Vinci's studies of human anatomy. Progress was also made in astronomy. Philosophers and writers produced works that would influence Europeans for centuries.

Secular Writers After a period of war in the early 1500s, life in Italy seemed insecure and precarious. The church no longer served as a source of stability and peace. Looking for comfort and guidance in the midst of this instability, some people turned to a form of humanism developed from Petrarch's ideas. Their focus was also **secular**; that is, they had a worldly rather than a spiritual focus.

These humanists argued that individual achievement and education could be fully expressed only if people used their talents and abilities in the service of their cities. Under their influence, the ideal Renaissance man came to be the "universal man," accomplished in the classics, but also a man of action. Such a man could respond to all situations.

Direct Teach

Reading Focus

2 What ideas formed the foundation of the Italian Renaissance? *inspiration from the ancient Greeks and Romans; humanism; secular focus*

Renaissance Ideas

Recall When did the Renaissance take place? *from 1300s to 1550*

Contrast How were Renaissance viewpoints different from previous ideas? *Renaissance viewpoints stressed the importance of individuals, and individual accomplishments; previously group and society were considered more important.*

Make Inferences How do you think the use of vernacular languages might bring Renaissance ideas to a new audience? *possible answer—They could be read by the common people who did not read Latin.*

Quick Facts Transparency: Causes of the Renaissance

Biography

El Greco (1541–1614) Domenikos Theotokopoulos, better known as El Greco, meaning "The Greek," was born on the island of Crete. Little is known of his early life as a young artist, but he was inspired by Italian artists Titian and Michelangelo. In 1576 El Greco departed for Spain and soon received a commission to paint *The Assumption of the Virgin* in a church in Toledo. This painting distinguished El Greco's style from that of his Italian teachers. After several church commissions, El Greco painted *The Burial of Count Orgaz*, which is considered a masterpiece. El Greco became successful and often entertained friends in his fine home in Toledo. He died in 1614, leaving a rich legacy in his paintings.

Skills Focus: Identifying Problem and Solution — At Level

Reading Skill
Justifying the Arts

1. Review with students the information in the text about the role of the Medici family, particularly Lorenzo, in financing Renaissance art.
2. Have students write two letters. The first letter should be to Lorenzo from one of his relatives, criticizing his extravagant spending on the arts. The second should be a reply from Lorenzo, in which he justifies his spending and explains the importance of the arts to the city of Florence. Encourage students to form their own arguments to justify spending on the arts.
3. Have volunteers read their letters to the class.
4. As an extension, have some students play the roles of Lorenzo and his relative, and informally debate this issue. **LS Verbal-Linguistic**

Alternative Assessment Handbook, Rubrics 10: Debates; and 25: Personal Letters

Direct Teach

Reading Focus

Renaissance Ideas

Identify Cause and Effect How did *The Courtier* influence society? *It was used as a handbook for how to succeed in society.*

Analyze How were Machiavelli's views shaped by his experiences? *possible answer—saw political violence; came to believe that morals should play no part in politics*

Make Judgments Do you think Machiavelli was right when he said that a ruler must do whatever is necessary to maintain power? Why or why not? *possible answers—Yes, if not, the state would cease to exist. No, a ruler must always be fair and just, even if it means losing power.*

Primary Source

"[A gentleman should] speak not always of serious subjects, but also of amusing things such as games and jests and jokes, according to the occasion. He should always of course, speak out fully and frankly and avoid talking nonsense … [A gentlewoman should] know how to choose topics suitable for the kind of person she is addressing … She should not introduce jests and jokes into a discussion about serious things. She should not … [pretend] to know what she does not know, but she should seek modestly to win credit for knowing what she does."

—Baldassare Castiglione, *The Courtier*

One of these humanists, the Italian diplomat **Baldassare Castiglione** (cas-steel-YOH-nay) wrote a book called *The Courtier*. Published in 1528, it describes how the perfect Renaissance gentleman—and gentlewoman—should act. In the book Castiglione creates a fictional conversation between a duke and his guests. They discuss how courtiers and court ladies should behave, suggesting that they should

- Speak of serious subjects as well as amusing ones,
- Have a knowledge of Latin and Greek,
- Be well-acquainted with poetry and history,
- Be able to write prose as well as poetry.

Merchants also used Castiglione's book as a guide to behavior. They hoped that if they acted like courtiers, they would raise their status.

At about the same time that Castiglione was finishing *The Courtier*, a fellow Italian, **Niccolò Machiavelli** (mahk-ee-uh-VEL-ee) of Florence, was writing another influential book. Machiavelli was a political philosopher and statesman whose experiences with violent politics of the time influenced his opinions about how governments should rule. He set down his ideas in a book called *The Prince*.

Much of Machiavelli's advice seemed to encourage harsh treatment of citizens and rival states. He describes men as "ungrateful, fickle, liars, and deceivers" and advises rulers to separate morals from politics. Power and ruthlessness, Machiavelli says, are more useful than idealism to a ruler. He insists that a ruler must do whatever is necessary to maintain political power, even if it is viewed as cruel, for without it the state will cease to exist.

THE ARTS AROUND THE WORLD

Art and Architecture

The Italian Renaissance

What is it? Art and architecture of the Italian Renaissance did not follow a single style or method. Instead, works from the period of about 1350 to 1550 display a change in attitudes. Renaissance attitudes about the value of people affected artists and architects. These talented individuals competed with one another for paid assignments and for fame. Subject matter went beyond religious scenes to real people and their places in the natural world. Moreover, the works produced were for people to enjoy, not solely for the glory of God.

What are the key characteristics?

- Realistic portrayals of people and other subjects
- Use of perspective
- Influence of classical Greece and Rome
- Beauty, balance, and harmony
- Value of the individual

Why is it important?
With the Italian Renaissance, art and architecture entered the modern era. Not only are the paintings, sculptures, and buildings beautiful and inspiring, but they also reflect modern people's interest in competition, achievement, and the world we see around us.

▶ The Individual Leonardo da Vinci painted this portrait of an upper-class woman with her pet ermine in about 1490. The emotion shown on the woman's face, her clothing and jewelry, and the way she holds her pet express her unique personality.

Cecilia Gallerani, Leonardo da Vinci, c. 1490

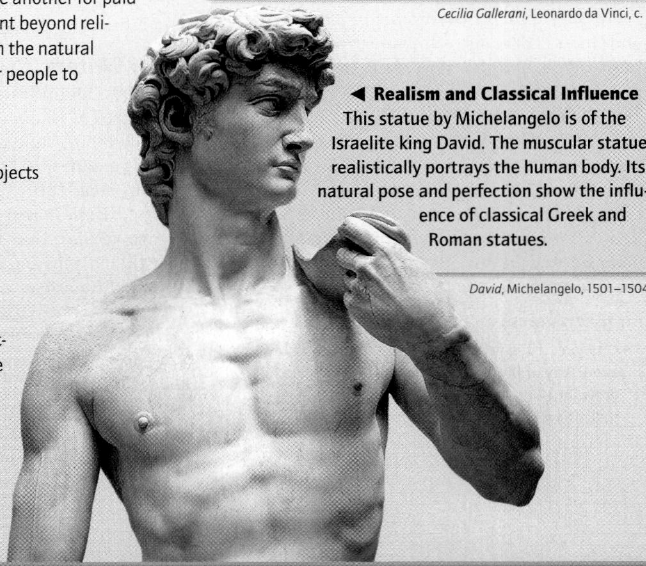

◀ Realism and Classical Influence This statue by Michelangelo is of the Israelite king David. The muscular statue realistically portrays the human body. Its natural pose and perfection show the influence of classical Greek and Roman statues.

David, Michelangelo, 1501–1504

Collaborative Learning

At Level

Design Competition

Materials: drawing paper

1. Organize students into groups of four to six students. Each group should designate a sculptor, a painter, at least one architect, and a detail person to work out design elements.
2. Tell students that they will compete with other groups to design a city hall for an Italian town during the Renaissance. Have students sketch concepts for each element of the building. Students may need to create several sketches before they arrive at their final design. The design proposal should include doors, an entry hall, a conference room, and a sample of the exterior façade.
3. Have groups present their design proposals to the class. You may wish to show students' proposals to another class and have them vote on the best design. **LS Visual-Spatial, Interpersonal**

Alternative Assessment Handbook, Rubrics 3: Artwork; and 14: Group Activity

HISTORY'S VOICES

"A prudent ruler cannot, and must not, honor his word when it places him at a disadvantage and when the reasons for which he made his promise no longer exist."

—Niccolò Machiavelli, *The Prince*, 1513

Machiavelli's theory that "the end justifies the means" deviated from accepted views of correct behavior. However, its idea that the state was an entity in itself, separate from its ruler, became the foundation for much later political philosophy.

Science of the Renaissance As humanists searched archives and Arab translations for classical texts, they discovered a wealth of scientific information. Although the majority of humanist scholars and writers during the Renaissance focused on human sciences such as history, geography, and politics, new ideas about the natural world were beginning to be explored. Science would soon become an important avenue of inquiry, challenging the church's teachings about the world.

Among other scientists who challenged the church's ideas about nature, viewers of the night sky began to claim that Earth was not the center of the universe as the church taught. Nicholas Copernicus, a Polish astronomer, suggested that the Sun sat at the center of the universe, orbited by the planets and stars. Galileo Galilei, an Italian astronomer who wrote that Earth orbited the Sun, was placed under house arrest by church officials for expressing his views.

ACADEMIC VOCABULARY
deviate to turn away from a course or topic

READING CHECK **Draw Conclusions** What were some important new ideas of the Renaissance?

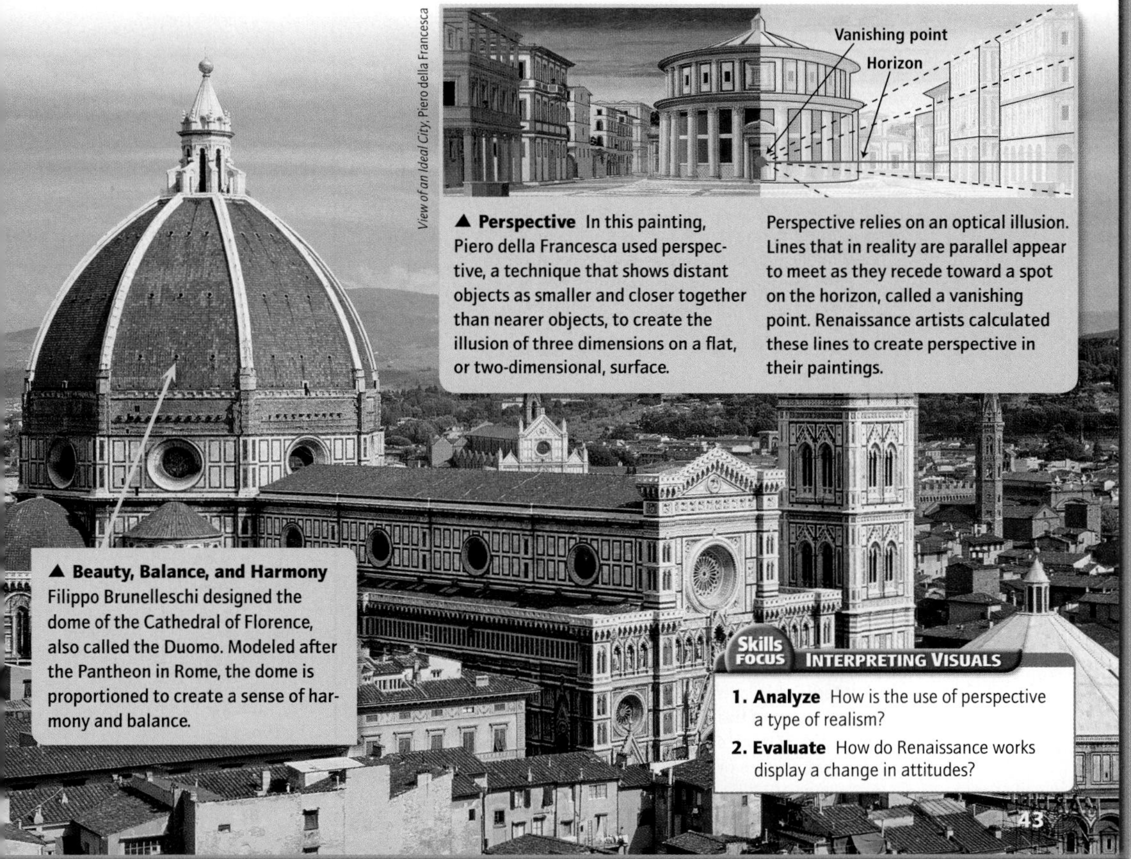

View of an Ideal City, Piero della Francesca

▲ **Perspective** In this painting, Piero della Francesca used perspective, a technique that shows distant objects as smaller and closer together than nearer objects, to create the illusion of three dimensions on a flat, or two-dimensional, surface.

Perspective relies on an optical illusion. Lines that in reality are parallel appear to meet as they recede toward a spot on the horizon, called a vanishing point. Renaissance artists calculated these lines to create perspective in their paintings.

▲ **Beauty, Balance, and Harmony** Filippo Brunelleschi designed the dome of the Cathedral of Florence, also called the Duomo. Modeled after the Pantheon in Rome, the dome is proportioned to create a sense of harmony and balance.

Skills FOCUS **INTERPRETING VISUALS**

1. **Analyze** How is the use of perspective a type of realism?
2. **Evaluate** How do Renaissance works display a change in attitudes?

43

Direct Teach

Reading Focus

Renaissance Ideas

Compare How were the theories of Copernicus and Galileo similar? *Both theories said that the sun was at the center of the universe.*

Make Inferences Based on the reaction to Galileo's universe theory, how do you think the Roman Catholic Church viewed Renaissance science? *did not agree with the new scientific theories; tried to silence scientists who challenged church teachings*

Teaching Tip

Coordinate with the art department of your school to create some interdisciplinary lessons on the Renaissance that include art, architecture, and history content.

Differentiating Instruction

Above Level

Prep Required

Materials: excerpts from Machiavelli's *The Prince*

1. Hand out excerpts from *The Prince* to each student. Allow enough time for students to read the excerpts.
2. Guide students in a discussion of the ideas Machiavelli presents in *The Prince*.
3. Ask students whether they agree with Machiavelli that morals should be separated from politics. What would be the results of this type of rule?
4. Have students write a short essay in which they defend Machiavelli's theories, or disagree with them. Essays should include a clear thesis and several supporting statements.

LS Verbal-Linguistic

Alternative Assessment Handbook, Rubrics 11: Discussions; and 37: Writing Assignments

Answers

Interpreting Visuals 1. *uses optical illusions to portray objects as they are seen in real life;* **2.** *show realistic portrayals, not idealistic portrayals of religious subjects; value beauty, balance, harmony, and the individual*

Reading Check *inspiration from the ancient Greeks and Romans; humanism; secular focus; new theories in science*

Direct Teach

Reading Focus

3 What contributions did artists make to the Renaissance? *new styles and techniques; focus on human personality; works inspired by Greek and Roman art*

Renaissance Art

Identify How did wealthy patrons support Renaissance art? *purchased artwork; gave money to artists, intellectuals, and musicians*

Contrast How did the subject matter of Renaissance art differ from the subject matter of medieval art? *included scenes from Greek and Roman myths; focused as much on human personality as on religious significance*

Info to Know

Renaissance Rivalry According to several sources, there was a bitter rivalry between Leonardo da Vinci and Michelangelo. When the two artists met in Florence, the young Michelangelo jokingly referred to one of da Vinci's failed projects, a bronze statue of a horse and rider. The comment apparently offended the old master. The two great artists' mutual dislike for one other only increased when they were commissioned to paint battle scenes on opposite walls of the city hall in Florence.

FACES OF HISTORY **Two Renaissance Masters**

LEONARDO
Da Vinci
1452–1519

MICHELANGELO
Buonarroti
1475–1564

Leonardo was born in Vinci and moved to Florence when he was 15. He was apprenticed to an artist, but Leonardo's skill soon surpassed his master's. He left for Milan, where he served the duke. While continuing as a painter, he advised the duke on architecture and weaponry.

Leonardo spent time in Milan, Florence, and Rome as power struggles gripped Italy. Today he is remembered for his masterful painting and for his wide-ranging knowledge of many topics, including anatomy, physics, and engineering.

Analyze How did Leonardo achieve fame?

Michelangelo considered himself a "son of Florence," although he was born in Caprese. His father was an official who relied on the Medici family for support. As a young artist, Michelangelo studied in the Medici garden school.

When Lorenzo de Medici died in 1492, Florence was torn into political factions. Michelangelo's art career became tied up with power struggles there and in Rome. The artist continued to receive important commissions, however, and to create what many consider to be the finest art in the world.

Infer Why was Michelangelo a successful artist?

Compare and Contrast How were the careers of these two artists alike and different?

Renaissance Art

Even more than politics, the arts reflected the new humanist spirit. Whereas medieval artists had used idealized and symbolic representations of religious themes, Renaissance artists depicted the things they observed in nature.

THE IMPACT TODAY

Today the U.S. government helps support artists and art education through grants and special programs. The National Endowment for the Arts oversees many of these programs.

Patrons of the Arts In medieval times, artwork was created by anonymous artists who worked for the church. During the Renaissance, artists worked for whoever offered them the highest price. The buyers of art, or patrons, might be wealthy individuals, city governments, or the church. Wealthy individuals competed against one another, displaying their wealth and modernity through the purchase of artworks.

In Florence, the Medici—a wealthy and powerful family who ruled the city—supported the arts. They gave huge sums of money to artists, intellectuals, and musicians. **Lorenzo de Medici**, himself a well-educated poet, supported some of the most talented artists of the day. The Sforza family, rulers of Milan, were also benefactors of artists and others.

Styles and Techniques Renaissance artists wanted to paint the natural world as realistically as possible, which was a change from the style of the Middle Ages. To help with this goal, they studied perspective. Using perspective, artists could represent three-dimensional objects on flat surfaces. Painters also experimented with new ways of using color to portray shapes and textures accurately.

Renaissance art also differed from that of the Middle Ages in its subject matter. Although many artists continued to choose religious subjects, artists began to paint and sculpt scenes from Greek and Roman myths. In addition, religious paintings focused as much on the human personality of the figures as their religious significance. This shift in themes displayed the humanist interest in classical learning and human nature.

During the Renaissance, the design of buildings also reflected humanist reverence of Greek and Roman culture. Churches, palaces, and public buildings incorporated columns and domes inspired by those of classical Greek and Roman architecture.

Skills Focus: Identifying Main Idea and Details — At Level

Reading Skill

Artists and their Works

1. Draw the chart for students to see. Omit the italicized answers.
2. Have students copy and complete the chart. Have volunteers fill in the class chart. **LS Visual-Spatial**

Alternative Assessment Handbook, Rubric 7: Charts

Artist	Field(s)	Achievement
Raphael	*painter, architect*	*"The School of Athens"*
Leonardo da Vinci	*painter, architect, engineer, mathematician, musician, etc.*	*"The Last Supper"; "The Mona Lisa"; observations and designs*
Bramante	*architecture*	*designed St. Peter's Basilica*
Michelangelo Buonarroti	*painter, sculptor, architect, poet*	*Sistine Chapel; "Pieta"; "David"*

Answers

Faces of History *alike—served as artists to important figures, lived in Florence, careers affected by power struggles in Italy; different—Leonardo da Vinci also known for accomplishments in physics, engineering, anatomy*

Leonardo da Vinci The genius **Leonardo da Vinci** was a highly talented painter; but he was also a writer, an inventor, an architect, an engineer, a mathematician, a musician, and a philosopher. Two of his paintings, *The Last Supper* and the *Mona Lisa*, continue to be studied and admired today. *The Last Supper* shows a gathering of the disciples of Jesus the night before his crucifixion. The *Mona Lisa* tries to capture the complexity of the human spirit with its mysterious smile.

Leonardo filled some 20,000 pages with notes recording his ideas for building an armored tank and a flying machine, sketches of human anatomy, and countless other things. He designed and built canals, developed a machine to cut threads in screws, and designed the first machine gun. His interests and enthusiasms were boundless.

Michelangelo The sculptors of the Renaissance studied anatomy to make their statues more lifelike. One of the most accomplished of these was Michelangelo.

In Rome at the age of 24, **Michelangelo Buonarroti** won fame with his *Pietà*, a sculpture of Mary, the mother of Jesus, holding her son after his death. Michelangelo's *Pietà* communicates themes of grief, love, acceptance, and immortality. Michelangelo soon amazed Rome again with his 13-foot marble statue of *David*. The statue's representation of the human form, suppressed energy, and depth of expression are unsurpassed.

In painting, Michelangelo is most famous for his artwork on the ceiling of the Sistine Chapel in Rome. The ceiling shows sweeping scenes from the Old Testament of the Bible. Many art historians consider it one of the greatest achievements in the history of painting because of the personalized characterizations of Biblical figures.

Raphael Raffaello Sanzio, who became known as **Raphael**, was a renowned painter and an accomplished architect. His most famous work, *The School of Athens*, is a fresco, a painting made on fresh, moist plaster. The fresco shows Plato and Aristotle surrounded by philosophers from the past and present who were admired by the humanists. He is also well known for his many paintings of the Madonna, or mother of Jesus.

Bramante Renaissance architecture reached its height with the work of Donato Bramante. He had already achieved fame with his designs when he was chosen architect of Rome. His design for St. Peter's Basilica influenced the appearance of many smaller churches.

READING CHECK **Find the Main Idea** What was the ideal of Renaissance art?

SECTION 1 ASSESSMENT

go.hrw.com Online Quiz Keyword: SHL REN HP

Reviewing Ideas, Terms, and People

1. **a. Recall** Which groups came to dominate Italian city-states in the 1300s and 1400s?
   b. Identify Cause and Effect How did the Black Death influence the economic system of Europe?
2. **a. Define** What is **humanism**?
   b. Draw Conclusions How did **Machiavelli's** *The Prince* reflect humanist and Renaissance ways of thinking?
   c. Evaluate How did Castiglione's book reveal a new idea about the role of achievement?
3. **a. Describe** How were Renaissance artists funded?
   b. Explain For what reason(s) is **Leonardo da Vinci** considered a Renaissance man?
   c. Predict How might the new ideas of the Renaissance affect society?

Critical Thinking

4. **Identify Cause and Effect** Using your notes on the section and the graphic organizer below, show what effect humanism had on arts and ideas during the Renaissance.

Painting	Sculpture	Architecture	Thinkers

FOCUS ON WRITING

5. **Exposition** Choose a person from the chapter and write a short paragraph explaining why he was important in the Renaissance. You should include a list of his achievements.

Section 1 Assessment Answers

1. **a.** church, nobles, merchants, artisans
   b. transformed it from farm-based system to commerce-based system
2. **a.** a school emphasizing the potential of the human mind
   b. possible answer—emphasized individual accomplishment, lacked idealism
   c. described new rules for social behavior
3. **a.** wealthy individuals, city governments, the church
   b. He pursued knowledge and achieved success in many subjects.
   c. possible answer—might encourage people to question accepted teachings
4. Painting—captured the human spirit; Sculpture—more lifelike, showed depth of expression; Architecture—reflected humanist love of Greek and Roman culture; Thinkers—human mind is almost limitless, focus on individualism
5. Student paragraphs should provide details about one of the artists, thinkers, or political figures in this section.

Direct Teach

Reading Focus

Renaissance Art

Identify What important sculpture did Michelangelo create when he was twenty-four? Pietà, *sculpture of Jesus and Mary*

Explain Why is Michelangelo's work on the Sistine Chapel considered so amazing? *showed personalized characterizations of Biblical figures*

Predict What do you think it would be like to meet Michelangelo? *possible answer—he would offer fascinating information about the process he used to create his masterpieces.*

CRF: Biography: Sofonisba Anguissola

CRF: Primary Source: The School of Athens by Raphael

Review & Assess

Close

Have students explain how the Italian Renaissance represented a major shift from the period before it.

Review

Online Quiz, Section 1

Assess

SE Section 1 Assessment

Progress Assessment: Section 1 Quiz

Alternative Assessment Handbook

Reteach/Intervene

Interactive Reader and Study Guide, Section 1

Interactive Skills Tutor CD-ROM

Answers

Reading Check *capturing the human personality, realism, human form*

Preteach

Getting Started

Use the **Interactive Reader and Study Guide** to familiarize students with the section content.

Interactive Reader and Study Guide, Section 2

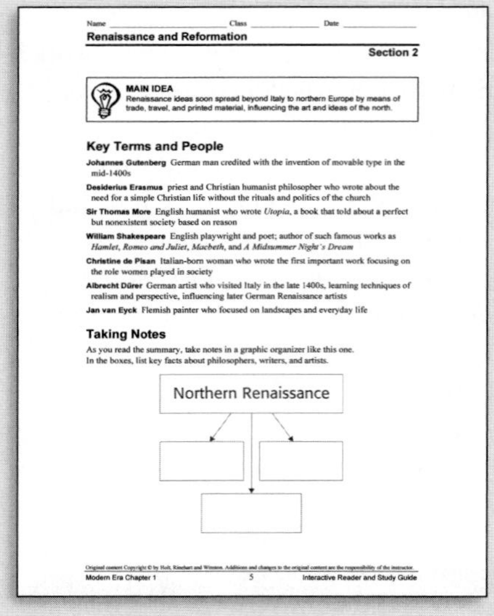

Name ______ Class ______ Date ______

Renaissance and Reformation

Section 2

MAIN IDEA
Renaissance ideas soon spread beyond Italy to northern Europe by means of trade, travel, and printed material, influencing the art and ideas of the north.

Key Terms and People

Johannes Gutenberg German man credited with the invention of movable type in the mid-1400s

Desiderius Erasmus priest and Christian humanist philosopher who wrote about the need for a simple Christian life without the rituals and politics of the church

Sir Thomas More English humanist who wrote *Utopia*, a book that told about a perfect but nonexistent society based on reason

William Shakespeare English playwright and poet; author of such famous works as *Hamlet*, *Romeo and Juliet*, *Macbeth*, and *A Midsummer Night's Dream*

Christine de Pisan Italian-born woman who wrote the first important work focusing on the role women played in society

Albrecht Dürer German artist who visited Italy in the late 1400s, learning techniques of realism and perspective, influencing later German Renaissance artists

Jan van Eyck Flemish painter who focused on landscapes and everyday life

Taking Notes

As you read the summary, take notes in a graphic organizer like this one. In the boxes, list key facts about philosophers, writers, and artists.

Northern Renaissance

Original content Copyright © by Holt, Rinehart and Winston. Additions and changes to the original content are the responsibility of the instructor.

Modern Era Chapter 1 5 Interactive Reader and Study Guide

CRF: Vocabulary Builder: Section 2

Taking Notes

Northern European cities and trade grow, trade spreads ideas to northern Europe, printing press speeds spread of ideas; Dürer brings Renaissance techniques to Germany, van Eyck and Brueghel use techniques for everyday subjects; Christian humanism, Erasmus writes about simple Christian life, More's history and philosophy; Shakespeare's plays and sonnets

go.hrw.com
Online Resources
KEYWORD: SHL REN
ACTIVITY: The Printing Press

SECTION 2 The Northern Renaissance

BEFORE YOU READ

MAIN IDEA

Renaissance ideas soon spread beyond Italy to northern Europe by means of trade, travel, and printed material, influencing the art and ideas of the north.

READING FOCUS

1. How did the Renaissance spread to northern Europe?
2. What contributions did writers and philosophers make to the northern Renaissance?
3. How did the works of northern artists differ from those of the Italian Renaissance?

KEY TERMS AND PEOPLE

Johannes Gutenberg
Desiderius Erasmus
Sir Thomas More
William Shakespeare
Christine de Pisan
Albrecht Dürer
Jan van Eyck

TAKING NOTES Using a graphic organizer like this one list key facts about philosophers, writers, and artists.

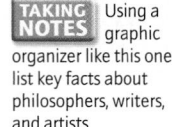

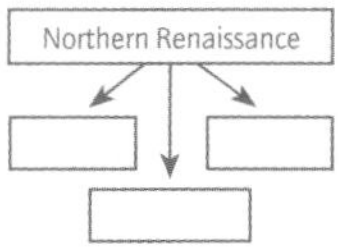

▲ **Albrecht Dürer, son of a Nuremberg goldsmith, is well known for his woodcuts.**

Self Portrait at the Age of Twenty-Eight, by Albrecht Dürer, 1500

THE INSIDE STORY ***How did a German artist find hope in Italy?*** In 1506, the German artist Albrecht Dürer was soon to end a visit to Italy. He wrote to a friend, "I want to ride to Bologna to learn the secrets of the art of perspective, which a man is willing to teach me. I will stay there about eight or ten days and then return to Venice . . . Here I am a gentleman; at home only a parasite." Dürer's letter provides evidence of the spread of Renaissance techniques and ideas to other parts of Europe. It also comments on the low position of artists in most parts of Europe during the 1400s and 1500s. That would soon change, as the Renaissance passion for art and culture raised the status of artists everywhere. Dürer's 1500 self-portrait shows his view of the importance of artists by portraying himself as the subject of a painting. ■

The Renaissance Spreads North

In the 1200s and 1300s, most cities in Europe were in Italy. By the 1500s, however, large cities had also sprouted in northern Europe. Soon the ideas of the Renaissance reached the growing cities of London, Paris, Amsterdam, and others. Trade, the movement of artists and scholars, and the development of printing helped spread Renaissance ideas northward.

Trading Goods and Ideas As cities grew, a vast trading network spread across northern Europe. This network was dominated by the Hanseatic League, a merchant organization that controlled trade throughout northern Europe. The league operated from the 1200s to the 1400s, working to protect its members from

Teach the Main Idea

At Level

The Northern Renaissance

1. **Teach** Ask students the Reading Focus questions to teach this section.
2. **Apply** Have students create flashcards to learn the names of the important writers and artists in this section. Have students write the name on one side of the card and a description of the person's achievements or famous work on the other side.
3. **Review** As you review the section, have students use their flashcards to quiz each other on the different writers and artists.
4. **Practice/Homework** Have students write a short compare-contrast paper on the Italian Renaissance and the Northern Renaissance.
LS Visual-Spatial, Verbal-Linguistic

Alternative Assessment Handbook, Rubric 9: Comparing and Contrasting pirates and other hazards. It also made shipping safer by building lighthouses and training ship captains. Along with goods, northern Europeans exchanged ideas with people from other places. Thus, trade helped the ideas of the Italian Renaissance spread to the north.

Renaissance ideas were also spread by Italian artists who fled to northern Europe to escape violent clashes between the armies of northern monarchs and the wealthy Italian cities. The artists brought their humanist ideas and new painting techniques with them.

In addition, some northern scholars traveled to Italy for an education. When these scholars returned home, they brought the humanist ideas they had learned with them. As newly wealthy northern Europeans became able to afford higher education, universities were established in France, the Netherlands, and Germany.

A Book Revolution In the mid-1400s, the German **Johannes Gutenberg** cast the letters of the alphabet onto metal plates and locked those plates into a wooden press. This movable type, which had its roots in China and Korea, resulted in one of the most dramatic upheavals the world has ever known. Other people had made steps toward this invention, but Gutenberg is traditionally given the credit.

With movable type, text could be quickly printed on both sides of a sheet of paper. Until this time, the only way to reproduce writing was by hand, which was a long, painstaking process. Movable type made producing books and other printed material faster and cheaper, making them available to more people.

Gutenberg's first publication was a 1,282-page Bible. Soon printers in other cities, such as Rome and Venice, appeared. Within 35 years, a Gutenberg press appeared as far away as Constantinople. Books could now be made quickly and inexpensively. A scholar wrote that "thirty buyers rise up for each volume . . . tearing one another's eyes out to get hold of them." Printed books provided more rapid access to new ideas. With easier access to books, more people learned to read and more books were printed. The explosion of printed material quickly spread Renaissance ideas.

READING CHECK **Find the Main Idea** How did Renaissance ideas spread to northern Europe?

Philosophers and Writers

As Renaissance ideas spread beyond Italy, northern humanists expressed their own ideas in works that combined the interests of theology, fiction, and history. They created philosophical works, novels, dramas, and poems.

Erasmus Some northern philosophers combined Christian ideas with humanism to create Christian humanism. The leading Christian humanist was **Desiderius Erasmus**. Working as a priest in what is now the Netherlands, Erasmus wrote extensively about the need for a pure and simple Christian life, stripped of the rituals and politics of the church on earth. He also advised readers on educating children.

Erasmus's writings fanned the flames of a growing discontent with the Roman Catholic Church. He himself was dismayed by this effect, but his works were later censored in Paris and condemned by the Church.

Advances in Printing

The illustration above shows Johannes Gutenberg in his printing shop, inspecting a page that has just been printed. The book to the right is one of the Bibles printed by Gutenberg in the 1400s. *Why was Gutenberg's printing press such an important invention?*

Direct Teach

Reading Focus

1. How did the Renaissance spread to northern Europe? *ideas exchanged with trade; artists and scholars traveled between Italy and north; printing press allowed easier bookmaking, ideas spread with printed material*

The Renaissance Spreads North

Recall Why did artists flee to northern Europe? *to escape violent clashes between northern monarchs and the wealthy Italian cities*

Identify Cause and Effect What was the effect of the printing press on books and bookmaking? *Text could be quickly printed on both sides of a page; books could be made quickly and cheaply.*

Activity **Journal Entries** Have students write a journal entry from the point of view of a young German artist traveling through Italy during the Renaissance. **LS Verbal-Linguistic**

Alternative Assessment Handbook, Rubric 15: Journals

CRF: History and Geography: Trade Fuels City Growth

Skills Focus: Identifying Cause and Effect

At Level

Reading Skill
The Printing Press

1. Draw the graphic organizer for students to see. Omit the italicized answers.
2. Have students copy and complete the graphic organizer, showing the effects triggered by the invention of the printing press. Have volunteers fill in the class chart. **LS Visual-Spatial**

Alternative Assessment Handbook, Rubric 13: Graphic Organizers

Effects of the Printing Press

printing press invented in Germany → *press technology spreads* → *easier and cheaper to make books* → *more books available* → *ideas spread quickly* → *people want to learn to read*

Answers

Advances in Printing *new ideas spread; more people learned to read*

Reading Check *Ideas were exchanged through trade; artists and scholars traveled between Italy and the north; printing press allowed easier bookmaking; ideas spread with printed material.*

Direct Teach

Reading Focus

2 What contributions did writers and philosophers make to the northern Renaissance? *created Christian humanism; fanned flames of discontent with Church; introduced humanism to England, spread Renaissance ideas to a mass audience*

Philosophers and Writers

Recall Explain the effects of Erasmus' writings. *fanned flames of discontent with Catholic Church*

Summarize What is *Utopia* about? *criticizes English government; describes perfect society based on reason*

Analyze In what ways is Shakespeare's work a good example of Renaissance ideals? *drew inspiration from ancient works; explored topics of humans and nature; included realistic characters*

CRF: Literature: *The Canterbury Tales*

Info to Know

The Praise of Folly Erasmus was an educated man and was also a great satirist. He took a light-hearted approach in writing a book called *The Praise of Folly*. In the book, Folly is personified as a woman, who explains why people of various rank and status choose her over common sense. Erasmus used this clever device to critique the church as well as society at large.

Northern Renaissance Art

Return of the Hunters, by Pieter Brueghel the Elder, 1565

Sir Thomas More Humanism was introduced to England by Italians living there and by English people who had studied in Italy. Erasmus also lived in England for a time. During his stay, he became friends with an important fellow humanist and English statesman, **Sir Thomas More**.

More's best-known humanist work is the novel *Utopia*. The book was meant for a humanist audience, and it was widely read across Europe. More's book contains both a criticism of English government and society and a vision of a perfect, but nonexistent, society based on reason. The title of his work has become a common word for any ideal society.

William Shakespeare In an age of great writers, many scholars believe the greatest was English playwright **William Shakespeare**. As one contemporary writer noted, Shakespeare "was not of an age, but for all time."

Shakespeare drew inspiration from ancient and contemporary works of literature. A wide knowledge of natural science and humanist topics, as well as a deep understanding of human nature, were expressed in his plays. His use of language and choice of themes, however, made his plays appeal even to uneducated people.

Through his plays, Shakespeare helped spread the ideas of the Renaissance to a mass audience. His dramatic plays were a shift from the religious morality plays that had become popular during the Middle Ages. Unlike morality plays, which focused on teaching ideal behavior, Shakespeare focused on the lives of realistic characters. The first public theaters were not built in London until the end of the 1500s, but by Shakespeare's death in 1616, London was the scene of a thriving theater district, with some theaters able to hold up to 2,000 spectators. Shakespeare's plays were a popular pastime for people from every class.

Christine de Pisan Italian-born writer **Christine de Pisan** wrote important works focusing on the role women played in society. Pisan grew up in the French court of Charles V. After she was widowed, she turned to writing as a way of supporting herself and her three children. Her writings included poetry, a biography of Charles V, and works that guided women on proper morality.

Pisan was recognized as a great writer during her lifetime. In her book *The City of Women*, she discusses different views of women and their roles in society. She was one of the few to champion equality and education for women.

READING CHECK **Summarize** What were some characteristics of Renaissance writers' work?

Skills Focus: Making Generalizations

At Level

Research Required

Reading Skill
Becoming a Docent

1. Tell students that docents are people who give tours of art and historical museums, so they need to be experts in art and history.
2. Have students choose a work of art from the Renaissance to research. Research should focus on the artist's approach to the subject matter, techniques and visual effects, and when the piece was created. Encourage students to locate unusual or anecdotal information about the artist or the work that a crowd of museum visitors would find interesting.
3. Have students present the artwork as a docent would in an art museum. Encourage students to use a pointer to refer to specific elements in the piece. **LS Verbal-Linguistic, Kinesthetic**

Alternative Assessment Handbook, Rubric 24: Oral Presentations

Answers

Reading Check *expressed humanist ideas, scientific knowledge, realistic experiences, and social conditions*

The Merchant Georg Gisze, by Hans Holbein the Younger, 1532

Northern Renaissance art contains more realistic scenes than Italian Renaissance art does. The hunting scene on the left portrays daily life, while the woodcut and portrait display intricate details and textures of clothing and objects. ***How did northern artists adapt Italian techniques to their own subject matter?***

Artists

Like their literary counterparts, the artists of northern Europe were influenced by the Italian Renaissance. They adopted Italian techniques, but their works reflected a more realistic view of humanity. Whereas Italian artists tried to capture the beauty of Greek and Roman gods in their paintings, northern artists often tried to depict people as they really were.

German artist **Albrecht Dürer** (DOOR-uhr) visited Italy in the late 1400s. On his return to Germany, he used the Italian techniques of realism and perspective in his own works.

Dürer's paintings also exhibit features that were unique to the northern Renaissance. For example, Dürer painted in oils, a medium that characterized the art of northern Europe. Oil paints also suited the northern artists' love of detail. They reproduced the texture of fabric, wood, and other material; the reflection of objects in a room in a mirror; scenes outside a window; and other tiny details.

Northern artists in the area of the Netherlands known as Flanders developed their own distinct style. Known as the Flemish School, they used a technique of oil painting that had been perfected in the 1400s by the Flemish painter **Jan van Eyck**. Van Eyck's work often focused on landscapes and domestic life. Northern artists fused the everyday with the religious through the use of symbolism in their paintings. A single lit candle or the light streaming through a window are representations of God's presence. German painter Hans Holbein used objects as symbols to characterize the subjects of his portraits.

In the 1500s Flemish artist Pieter Brueghel (BROY-guhl) the Elder used Italian techniques. In subject matter, however, Brueghel's art followed that of earlier northern artists. His paintings showed scenes from everyday peasant life, very different from the mythological scenes of Italian paintings.

READING CHECK **Contrast** How did northern Renaissance artwork differ from that of Italian artists?

SECTION 2 ASSESSMENT

go.hrw.com
Online Quiz
Keyword: SHL REN HP

Reviewing Ideas, Terms, and People

1. **a. Identify** Name four ways in which Renaissance ideas spread to northern Europe.
   b. Make Judgments Was the printing press or trade networks more important in spreading Renaissance ideas? Explain your answer.
2. **a. Define** What is Christian humanism?
   b. Interpret Explain the meaning of the description of **William Shakespeare** as "not of an age, but for all time."
3. **a. Identify** Who was **Albrecht Dürer**, and how did he influence German painting?
   b. Explain What was new in the subject matter of Northern Renaissance painting?

Critical Thinking

4. **Sequence** Using your notes and the graphic organizer below, describe some of the differences between Italian and northern Renaissance painting.

Italian Renaissance	Northern Renaissance

FOCUS ON SPEAKING

5. **Persuasion** Write a short speech that an Italian might make to a northern European to convince him or her that the Renaissance would bring beneficial changes to the culture. Give at least three reasons.

Direct Teach

Reading Focus

3 How did the works of northern artists differ from those of the Italian Renaissance? *Northern artists tried to depict things as they actually were*

Artists

Identify What Renaissance techniques did Dürer learn in Italy? *realism, perspective*

Evaluate What do you think Italian Renaissance artists would think about the Northern Renaissance artists' works? *possible answer—They probably would be impressed by the northern artists' techniques, but would find the subject matter strange.*

CRF: Biography: Jan van Eyck

Review & Assess

Close

Have students explain how Christian humanism was connected to the ideas of the Renaissance.

Review

Online Quiz, Section 2

Assess

SE Section 2 Assessment

Progress Assessment: Section 2 Quiz

Alternative Assessment Handbook

Reteach/Intervene

Interactive Reader and Study Guide, Section 2

Interactive Skills Tutor CD-ROM

Section 2 Assessment Answers

1. **a.** Trade spread new ideas; Italian artists went north; northern scholars went to Italy; printing press quickened the spread of ideas.
   b. possible answers—Printing press made books accessible; trade spread ideas faster.
2. **a.** school of thought seeking to simplify Christian life, separating it from rituals and politics of the church on earth
   b. possible answer—Works can always be appreciated; themes are timeless.
3. **a.** German painter; incorporated techniques of Italian Renaissance
   b. focused on people as they actually were
4. **a.** Italian Renaissance: try to capture beauty of Greek and Roman gods, used realism and perspective, mythological scenes
   b. Northern Renaissance: more realistic, showed people as they were, love of details, used oils, showed scnes of everyday life
5. possible answers—will encourage new ways of thinking about the world; will inspire great writers; will inspire artists to try new techniques

Answers

Northern Renaissance Art *showed a more realistic view of humanity*

Reading Check *depicted everyday objects, people as they actually were*

World Literature

Petrarch and Shakespeare

Meet the Writers

Petrarch (1304–1374) Francesco Petrarca, better known as Petrarch, grew up in the Italian province of Tuscany, and later in Avignon, France. He studied law and entered the service of the church around 1330. Petrarch spent much of his life traveling through Italy, France, Germany, and the Low Countries as a diplomat; his duties involved writing formal speeches. He wrote in Latin and Italian and produced poems, historical pieces, and artful personal letters.

William Shakespeare (1564–1616) Known for his many sonnets and plays, Shakespeare displays an impressive knowledge of human motivation and behavior through his characters. Born in the English town of Stratford-upon-Avon, he was married at the age of eighteen to Anne Hathaway. Shakespeare arrived in London around 1588 and acted in a theater troupe. He began writing plays to be staged by the troupe; he also produced sonnets. The company became successful, opened the Globe Theater in 1599, and frequently performed at the courts of Queen Elizabeth I and King James I.

Activity **Poetic Letters** Have students write a letter to one of their friends. Tell students to use poetic language in the style of Petrarch or Shakespeare. **LS Verbal-Linguistic**

Alternative Assessment Handbook, Rubric 25: Personal Letters

World Literature

About the Reading A form of poem called a sonnet became popular during the Renaissance, when poets began writing about more worldly matters, such as love or politics. A sonnet is a 14-line lyric poem that follows a strict pattern of rhyme and rhythm. Italian poet Francesco Petrarch perfected the Italian sonnet, which consists of two sections. English poets created their own version of the sonnet, perfected by English poet and playwright William Shakespeare. The English sonnet consists of three sections followed by two lines, called a couplet. A major theme in Renaissance sonnets is how the best things in life, such as youth and beauty, are fleeting and should be enjoyed before they fade away.

AS YOU READ **Think about how each poet expresses his personal feelings about love.**

Sonnet 61 (1329)
Petrarch

1304–1374

Blest be the day, and blest the month and year,
Season and hour and very moment blest,
The lovely land and place where first possessed
By two pure eyes I found me prisoner;
And blest the first sweet pain, the first most dear,
Which burned by heart when Love [Cupid, the god
of love] came in as guest;
And blest the bow, the shafts which shook my breast,
And even the wounds which Love delivered there.
Blest be the words and voices which filled grove
And glen [valley] with echoes of my lady's name;
The sighs, the tears, the fierce despair of love;
And blest the sonnet-sources of my fame;
And blest that thought of thoughts which is her own,
Of her, her only, of herself alone.

—translated by Joseph Auslander

Sonnet 116 (1609)
Shakespeare

1564–1616

Let me not to the marriage of true minds
Admit impediments [barriers]. Love is not love
Which alters when it alteration finds,
Or bends with the remover to remove:

O no! It is an ever-fixed mark [navigational beacon]
That looks on tempests [storms] and is never shaken;
It is the star [North Star] to every wandering bark [ship],
Whose worth's unknown, although his height be taken.

Love's not Time's fool, though rosy lips and cheeks
Within his bending sickle's compass come:
Love alters not with his brief hours and weeks,
But bears it out even to the edge of doom.

If this be error and upon me proved,
I never writ, nor no man ever loved.

go.hrw.com World Literature Keyword: SHL WRLIT

Skills FOCUS **READING LIKE A HISTORIAN**

1. **Find the Main Idea** How would you summarize the main idea of Petrarch's sonnet?
2. **Analyze** In what ways does Shakespeare's sonnet explore the theme of the nature of love?
3. **Interpret Literature as a Source** Both sonnets focus on worldly romantic love. How might the focus of these sonnets have been different if they had been written during the Middle Ages? Explain your answer.

See **Skills Handbook**, p. H28

Skills Focus: Analyzing Primary Sources

At Level

Standard English Mastery

Reading Like a Historian Skill
Analyzing Sonnets

Background: Tell students that sonnets follow strict guidelines. The two main forms of sonnets are represented here: the Italian or Petrarchan sonnet, and the English or Shakespearian sonnet.

1. Have students analyze the rhyme scheme of each sonnet.
2. Tell students that Shakespeare wrote in iambic pentameter, a line of verse with five metrical "feet," in which unstressed and stressed syllables alternate. You may want to demonstrate the meter to students by tapping on your desk.
3. Have students copy some lines of Shakespeare's sonnet onto their own papers. Then, have them divide the feet with vertical lines, placing an accent mark above accented syllables. Then have students use iambic pentameter to write their own sonnets. **LS Verbal-Linguistic**

Alternative Assessment Handbook, Rubric 26: Poems and Songs

Answers

Reading Like a Historian

1. *possible answer—Love is a blessed thing.* **2.** *explains that love does not change with the passage of time* **3.** *possible answer—might have focused on love for God instead of love for another human*

SECTION 3

The Protestant Reformation

BEFORE YOU READ

MAIN IDEA

Criticism of the Roman Catholic Church led to a religious movement called the Protestant Reformation and brought changes in religion and politics across Europe.

READING FOCUS

1. What was the state of Catholicism in the 1400s?
2. How did Martin Luther challenge the Catholic Church?
3. How did Protestantism spread to other areas?
4. What were the effects of the Reformation in England?

KEY TERMS AND PEOPLE

Protestant Reformation
indulgences
Martin Luther
theocracy
John Calvin
predestination
Henry VIII
annulled
Elizabeth I

TAKING NOTES Use a graphic organizer like this one. Take notes about the causes of the Protestant Reformation.

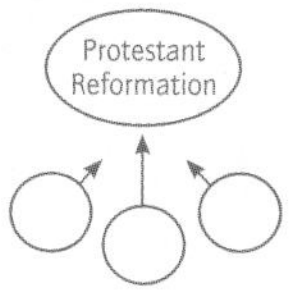

THE INSIDE STORY ***Why did a humble monk defy the Holy Roman Emperor?*** In the fall of 1517 a monk nailed a list of items to the door of Castle Church in Wittenberg. He listed certain financial and religious practices he wanted to debate with Catholic leaders and bring to an end. His list of complaints, posted where many people could see them, shocked the people who read it. In the early 1500s no one criticized the church publicly, certainly not a monk.

As people read the list, word spread around Germany. The complaints, called the Ninety-Five Theses, were soon printed and distributed around Europe. The pope, upset by the monk's defiance, banned the work, telling Roman Catholics not to read it.

Eventually the Holy Roman Emperor and German parliament got involved, demanding that the monk take back his words. The monk refused, saying that he must obey his conscience and stand by his work. The actions of that monk, named Martin Luther, are considered the beginning of the movement called the Protestant Reformation.

A MONK Defies THE EMPEROR

▼ In 1517 a Catholic monk named Martin Luther posted Ninety-five Theses criticizing the Roman Catholic Church.

Martin Luther, by Hugo Vogel, 1890

Catholicism in the 1400s

Over the centuries since its beginning, the Roman Catholic Church had gained power and wealth in Europe. As the influence, extravagance, and worldliness of the church grew, some people thought it had strayed too far from its spiritual roots. By the early 1500s, the concerns crystallized into a reform movement that eventually came to be called the **Protestant Reformation**.

Preteach

Getting Started

Use the **Interactive Reader and Study Guide** to familiarize students with the section content.

Interactive Reader and Study Guide, Section 3

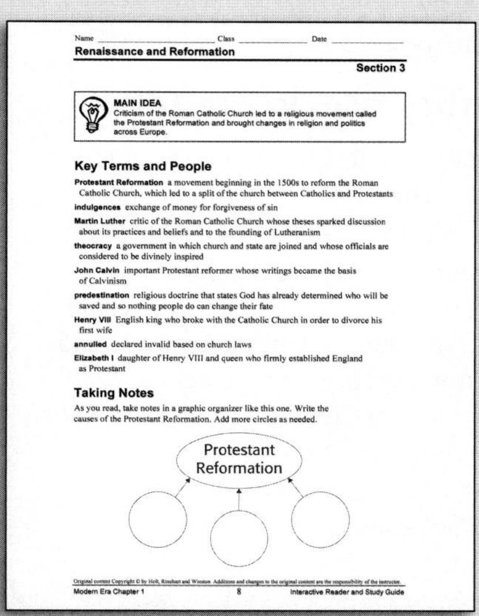

Name ________ Class ________ Date ________

Renaissance and Reformation

Section 3

MAIN IDEA
Criticism of the Roman Catholic Church led to a religious movement called the Protestant Reformation and brought changes in religion and politics across Europe.

Key Terms and People

Protestant Reformation a movement beginning in the 1500s to reform the Roman Catholic Church, which led to a split of the church between Catholics and Protestants

indulgences exchange of money for forgiveness of sin

Martin Luther critic of the Roman Catholic Church whose theses sparked discussion about its practices and beliefs and to the founding of Lutheranism

theocracy a government in which church and state are joined and whose officials are considered to be divinely inspired

John Calvin important Protestant reformer whose writings became the basis of Calvinism

predestination religious doctrine that states God has already determined who will be saved and so nothing people do can change their fate

Henry VIII English king who broke with the Catholic Church in order to divorce his first wife

annulled declared invalid based on church laws

Elizabeth I daughter of Henry VIII and queen who firmly established England as Protestant

Taking Notes

As you read, take notes in a graphic organizer like this one. Write the causes of the Protestant Reformation. Add more circles as needed.

Protestant Reformation

Original content Copyright © by Holt, Rinehart and Winston. Additions and changes to the original content are the responsibility of the instructor.

Modern Era Chapter 1 8 Interactive Reader and Study Guide

CRF: Vocabulary Builder: Section 3

Taking Notes

Causes—financial corruption, abuses of power, immorality, unfair taxes, rise of nationalism

go.hrw.com
Online Resources

KEYWORD: SHL REN
ACTIVITY: Reformation Leaders

Teach the Main Idea

At Level

The Protestant Reformation

1. **Teach** Ask students the Reading Focus questions to teach this section.
2. **Apply** Draw four ladders for students to see. Label the tops of the ladders with the names of the topics in this section: Catholicism in the 1400s, Martin Luther, The Spread of Protestantism, and Protestantism Spreads to England. Have students copy the ladders onto their own paper and fill in the rungs of the ladders with the main ideas of each topic.
3. **Review** As you review the section, have students explain how the actions of Protestant reformers challenged traditional Catholic doctrine.
4. **Practice/Homework** Have students write a letter to the editor about church problems during the 1400s. **LS Visual-Spatial, Verbal-Linguistic**

Alternative Assessment Handbook, Rubrics 13: Graphic Organizers; and 17: Letters to Editors

Direct Teach

Reading Focus

1 What was the state of Catholicism in the 1400s? *Church was wealthy and powerful, involved in politics, had moved away from spiritual roots, often financially corrupt, immorality of some clergy*

Catholicism in the 1400s

Recall What were common criticisms of the Church? *financially corrupt, abusive of power, immoral, taxed unfairly*

Develop If you had been a Church official during this period, what would you have done to fend off criticism and controversy? *possible answers—would try to reform Church from inside; would try to suppress criticism by focusing on positive aspects of the Church*

CRF: Biography: Jan Hus

Info to Know

Example of Corruption Most Germans who bought indulgences believed that the money would go to the construction of St. Peter's Basilica. The public didn't realize, however, that some of the money was going to Albert of Brandenburg. Albert had purchased the position of arch bishop of Mainz, but was too young to occupy it according to church law. Pope Leo decided that Albert could take the office provided that he pay the church a large sum of money, which he did by borrowing. Half the money raised by indulgences went to Albert to pay off his debt.

Dissatisfaction with the Church As the wealth and worldliness of the Church grew, so did instances of financial corruption, abuse of power, and immorality. In return, people's respect for priests, monks, and even popes weakened. Heavy taxation also caused discontent. The church financed Renaissance artists in elaborate projects, but it was the middle class and peasants who were taxed to pay for those projects.

In the early 1500s Pope Leo X needed money for the construction of Saint Peter's Basilica in Rome. To help raise money, he approved the sale of **indulgences**. Indulgences were pardons issued by the pope that people could buy to reduce a soul's time in purgatory. For almost a thousand years, Catholics had believed that after dying people went to purgatory, where their souls worked off the sins they had committed. The sale of indulgences, however, was one of the church's most criticized practices.

As unhappiness with taxation, the sale of indulgences, and other church practices grew, another major shift was occurring in Europe. Nationalism, or the devotion to a particular state or nation rather than to the church, began to grow. People began to consider themselves citizens of a government separate from the church.

READING SKILLS
Predicting How might reformers change the Catholic Church?

Early Reformers Earlier, two men had stepped forward to challenge the church. The first, John Wycliffe, was born in England about 1330. He believed that the church should give up its earthly possessions. His views proved unpopular with church officials, who removed him from his teaching position.

Another reformer, Jan Hus (yahn HOOS), was born in southern Bohemia about 1370. He became a priest and was soon preaching against the immorality and worldliness of the Catholic Church. In 1412 Hus was excommunicated by Pope Gregory XII. Hus was later arrested, tried for heresy, and burned at the stake.

These two men were some of the first and most influential theologians to openly criticize the church. Their views, though condemned by the church and not widely accepted by ordinary people, began a discussion that would eventually lead to reform.

READING CHECK **Summarize** What conditions led to the Protestant Reformation?

Reading like a Historian

Reformation Woodcuts

Analyzing Visuals Historians can learn about how events or people were viewed by analyzing visuals that convey a point of view. Some German Protestant reformers used woodcuts to spread their ideas. Woodcuts were cheap to produce and easy to print, and people did not have to be able to read to understand them. The two woodcuts here, made in 1521, attack Pope Leo X by comparing him unfavorably to Jesus.

To interpret these woodcuts, think about
- the subject of each illustration
- the details and symbols in each illustration
- the overall message of the pair of illustrations

Skills FOCUS **READING LIKE A HISTORIAN**

1. **Subject** How are the subjects of the two woodcut illustrations related?
2. **Details** What details in each of the woodcut illustrations show how Jesus and Pope Leo X view themselves and live their lives?
3. **Message** What is the overall message of the pair of woodcut illustrations?

See **Skills Handbook**, p. H26

Martin Luther

Although scholars, priests, and laypeople had criticized the church before 1517, this year symbolically marks the beginning of the Protestant Reformation. It was in this year that **Martin Luther** made public his complaints about the church.

The Ninety-five Theses To Martin Luther, selling indulgences was sinful. In his theses, Luther flatly denied that indulgences had any power to remit sin. He also criticized the power of the pope and the wealth of the church.

Luther's theses were not intended for the common people of his parish but for church leaders. They were written in academic Latin, which most people did not understand. In nailing them to the church door, Luther was following a common practice of the time. Church doors then served much as community bulletin boards do today.

Differentiating Instruction

Below Level

English-Language Learners

1. Review with students the information in the text about church abuses, Protestant criticisms of the Church, and various Protestant groups.
2. Organize students into mixed-ability pairs.
3. Have students create two political cartoons, one that portrays Protestants as crusaders against the evils of the Church, and the other that minimizes the Church problems and shows Protestants as fanatics.
4. Have volunteers present their political cartoons to the class. **LS Visual-Spatial**

Alternative Assessment Handbook, Rubric 27: Political Cartoons

Answers

Reading Like a Historian **1.** *Both involve leaders; but the leaders' attitudes toward their followers differ.* **2.** *Jesus is on his knees washing a disciple's feet; pope is sitting high above his visitors in a throne; they are kissing his feet.* **3.** *possible answer—The pope has departed from the original teachings of Jesus.*

Reading Check *Church's financial corruption; immorality; abuse of power*

Jesus is washing the feet of his disciples. He taught that people should serve others and not put themselves above others.

The pope has visiting world leaders kiss his feet. He raises himself above others and has them serve him.

The Pope as the Antichrist, by Lucas Cranach the Elder, 1521

Luther's theses, as he had intended, stimulated a discussion among university intellectuals. Soon, thanks to the newly invented printing press, the theses were published. The work spread across Europe and was widely read by intellectuals, clergy, and laypeople. The ideas expressed in the theses made sense to many people, and the desire for reform grew.

Luther's Message Following the publication of the theses, Luther continued to study and debate. He contradicted basic Catholic beliefs when he insisted that God's grace cannot be won by good works. Faith alone, he said, was needed. In Leipzig in 1519, he shocked many when he declared that the only head of the Christian Church is Jesus himself, not the pope. He also insisted that individual Christians should be their own interpreters of scripture and that Christian practices should come only from the Bible. To further this aim, Luther translated the Bible into German. The translation enabled many more people to read the Bible without the aid of the clergy.

Reactions to Luther In 1520 Pope Leo X excommunicated Luther, or expelled him from the Church. In 1521 Martin Luther was summoned to appear before the newly crowned Holy Roman emperor, Charles V, and the German Diet, or assembly, at the city of Worms. Luther refused to change his opinions.

The Holy Roman emperor handed down the Edict of Worms. This decree declared Luther to be an outlaw and condemned his writings. The edict did not prevent Luther's ideas from spreading, however. Although Martin Luther himself had not intended to begin a new religion, by 1530, Lutheranism was a formally recognized branch of Christianity.

In 1529, Charles V moved to suppress Lutherans in Germany. Lutheran princes in the German assembly issued a *protestatio*, or protest, against these measures. This is how the term *Protestant* came into being.

READING CHECK **Identify Supporting Details** Describe the ideas of Martin Luther and how they contradicted the church's teachings of his day.

Direct Teach

Reading Focus

2 How did Martin Luther challenge the Catholic Church? *wrote Ninety Five Theses; claimed Christ was the only head of the Church, salvation by faith alone, questioned basic beliefs of Catholicism*

Martin Luther

Identify Cause and Effect What was Luther's intention when he posted his theses? *to spark a discussion among intellectuals*

Make Inferences Do you think that Luther's writings put him in physical danger? *Definitely, he was challenging the most powerful institution of his time.*

Info to Know

"The Daughter of Printing" The invention of the printing press greatly affected change during the Renaissance and Reformation. Martin Luther's religious ideas spread quickly by print. Some historians have called the Reformation, "the daughter of printing." During Luther's lifetime, about 4,000 editions (books printed from one set of type) of his writings were published. In fact, one third of the books in Germany were written by him. Luther's Address to the Christian Nobility, which appeared in the 1520s, sold 4,000 copies in one week.

Skills Focus: Summarizing

At Level

Reading Skill

Press Conference with Martin Luther

1. Organize students into three groups: a small group of speechwriters, a medium-sized group of colleagues, and a large group of the press.
2. Have speechwriters write a speech for Martin Luther to be given a few months after he posted his theses. Have colleagues learn as much as they can about Luther's ideas and prepare to answer questions on his behalf.
3. Guide the press in narrowing down their questions to no more than one question per reporter. Give a copy of the questions to the advisors. Have colleagues discuss how they will answer any tricky questions.
4. Begin the press conference. Choose one of the speech writers to present the speech. Have members of the press stand up, ask their questions, and have colleagues answer them.

LS Kinesthetic, Verbal-Linguistic

Alternative Assessment Handbook, Rubric 14: Group Activity

Answers

Reading Check *God's grace cannot be won by good works but by faith; leader of church is Jesus, not pope; people can interpret scripture; practices come from Bible; challenged Catholic practices and the authority of the pope*

Direct Teach

Reading Focus

3 How did Protestantism spread to other areas? *Luther's stand against the Church opened the door for others to make differing ideas known*

The Spread of Protestantism

Describe What was the basis of Zwingli's church in Switzerland? *theocracy; government in which church and state are joined*

Compare What did John Calvin's church have in common with Zwingli's? *Protestant, in Switzerland, based on theocracy*

Evaluate Why do you think Calvin's church was successful when Zwingli's was not? *possible answer—Luther opposed Zwingli, Zwingli open to attack from Church because they lacked Lutheran support; Calvin had larger power base from citizens who embraced strictness*

Info to Know

Religion in Switzerland Today the population of Switzerland is approximately half Catholic and half Protestant. The country also has a small Jewish community.

FACES OF HISTORY

John CALVIN
1509–1564

Born into the French middle class, John Calvin studied law and the humanities. Calvin, unlike Martin Luther, was never a monk or priest in the Catholic Church. Calvin and Luther disagreed on several points of theology, but both rejected Catholicism.

Calvin arrived in Geneva in 1536 and became an influential leader of the reform movement there. Under his influence, his followers created a system of worship they called "the religion." He and his supporters instituted a religious government in Switzerland that controlled almost every aspect of people's lives. Calvin's ideas soon spread. People still follow his ideas today through religious denominations called "Reformed."

Infer How did Calvin approach to reform differ from Luther's?

The Spread of Protestantism

Martin Luther's stand against the Roman Catholic Church opened the door for others to put forth their differing ideas on religious matters. As Lutheranism arose in Germany, new religious movements began in Switzerland and other places in Europe.

Ulrich Zwingli Another Reformation priest, Ulrich Zwingli, was born in Switzerland within months of Luther. Zwingli entered the priesthood at the age of 22 and soon began preaching similar ideas to those of Martin Luther. His proposed reforms, however, went even farther than those of Luther.

Many of Zwingli's ideas about religion were viewed as radical. The church he established in Switzerland had the notion of theocracy at its base. A **theocracy** is a government in which church and state are joined and in which officials are considered to be divinely inspired.

Although Zwingli's movement gained support throughout Switzerland, some areas of the country opposed him and his supporters. His opponents included Martin Luther, who accused Zwingli of tampering with the word of God. Since the Swiss Protestants could not win the Lutherans' support, they were vulnerable to attack by the Catholics. When the disagreement between Swiss Protestants and Catholic officials erupted in war, Zwingli was one of the casualties. He died in battle in 1531.

John Calvin Next to Luther, **John Calvin** was the most important Protestant reformer. Born in 1509 and educated in France, Calvin was influenced by Erasmus and other Renaissance humanists. He also supported the reforms of Martin Luther in Germany.

Inspired by the ideas of Augustine, Calvin preached the doctrine of **predestination**. Predestination holds that God knows who will be saved, even before people are born, and therefore guides the lives of those destined for salvation. Thus, nothing humans can do, either good or bad, will change their predestined end.

Calvinism took root in Geneva, Switzerland, and the city became a theocracy under Calvin's leadership. Calvinists viewed people as sinful by nature, and strict laws were enacted that regulated people's behavior. In Geneva, church attendance was mandatory, and even matters such as the number of courses in each meal and the color of clothing were the subject of laws. Amusements such as feasting, dancing, singing, and wearing jewelry were forbidden.

This strictness was actually the heart of Calvinism's appeal. It gave its followers a sense of mission and discipline. Calvinists felt they were setting an example and making the world fit for the "elect," those who had been chosen for salvation.

Other Reformers Other reformers took the ideas of Martin Luther, Ulrich Zwingli, and John Calvin and adapted them to their own beliefs. John Knox became the spokesman for the Reformation in Scotland after spending time in John Calvin's Geneva. After years of religious turmoil in Scotland, Knox's Reformed Church replaced the Roman Catholic Church. His church structure laid the ground for the Presbyterian denomination that arose later.

Another group separated itself from the Lutherans, Calvinists, and other Protestant Reformers by its beliefs about baptism. The Anabaptists insisted on rebaptizing adults, which was a crime punishable by death at that time. The Anabaptist Church later evolved into several religious factions, including the Hutterites (named for their founder, Jakob Hutter), the Mennonites, and the Amish Mennonites.

READING CHECK **Make Generalizations** How did the ideas of reformers who came after Luther differ from those of Luther?

Skills Focus: Comparing and Contrasting

At Level

Reading Skill

Protestant Movements

1. Draw the Venn diagram for students to see. Omit the italicized answers.
2. Have students copy and complete the diagram. Have volunteers complete the class Venn diagram. **LS Visual-Spatial**

Alternative Assessment Handbook, Rubric 13: Graphic Organizers

Protestant Movements

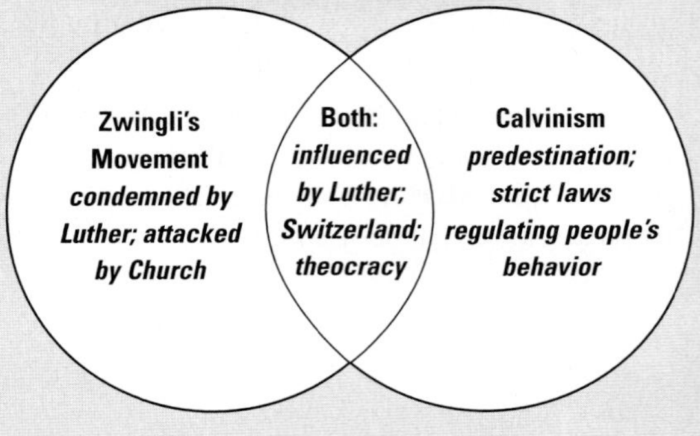

Answers

Faces of History *Calvin created religious government; strict laws, and controlled people's lives.*

Reading Check *some were more radical; included ideas of theoracy, predestination*

Protestantism Spreads to England

The Protestant Reformation began with criticism of the Catholic Church by priests and other religious thinkers. In England, the Reformation began with the king.

A King's Protest **Henry VIII** became king of England in 1509 at the age of 17. As a young king, he was a devout Catholic who wrote angry protests against the "venomous" ideas of Luther. Henry's actions won him the title "Defender of the Faith."

By 1525, Henry's wife, Catherine of Aragon, had borne only one child, a girl named Mary. This presented a problem for Henry, who wanted a male heir. It was thought that a female monarch could weaken England politically, and he believed Catherine would produce no male heir. Henry decided to have the marriage **annulled**, or declared invalid based on church laws, so that he could marry again.

The pope offered Henry several solutions to his problem but would not agree to the annulment because Catherine and her nephew, Holy Roman Emperor Charles V, opposed it. The dilemma became known as "the king's great matter." While Henry argued with the pope over his annulment, he fell in love with Anne Boleyn. Henry soon took matters into his own hands.

The Reformation Parliament Henry summoned Parliament. Known as the Reformation Parliament, the gathering led to a declaration that England no longer considered itself under the authority of the pope. Instead, Henry himself became the head of the Church of England. He changed the rituals of the church very little, but Henry closed Catholic monasteries and convents and distributed much of the land to nobles. This helped build more public support for the split from the Church.

In 1533, Anne Boleyn and Henry VIII were secretly married. Later that year, after Parliament had declared Henry's marriage to Catherine null and void, Anne gave birth to a girl, Elizabeth. The next year Parliament passed the Act of Supremacy, which required subjects to take an oath declaring Henry VIII to be "Supreme Head of the Church of England." The break with Rome was complete.

Religious Conflicts in England

The desire of King Henry VIII to end his marriage led to religious conflict in England. ***Why is King Henry VIII a key figure of the Reformation?***

▶ **1527** King Henry VIII asks the pope to annul his marriage, but the pope refuses.

▶ **1534** Henry VIII breaks from the Catholic Church. He founds the Church of England and serves as its head.

Portrait of Henry VIII, by Hans Holbein the Younger, 1540

▲ **1553** Queen Mary I restores the Catholic Church in England and executes many Protestants.

Execution of Protestants at Smithfield, 1557, Unknown, c. 1720

◀ **1558** Queen Elizabeth I restores the Church of England and support for Protestantism.

Elizabeth I, by Nicholas Hilliard

Direct Teach

Reading Focus

4 What were the effects of Protestantism in England? *Henry VIII broke from Catholic Church; Church of England formed*

Recall What was the "king's great matter"? *that the pope would not agree to annul his marriage to Catherine of Aragon*

Contrast How did Henry VIII's break with the church contrast with his actions as a young man? *As a young man he had supported the Catholic Church against Luther; was called "Defender of the Faith"*

Info to Know

Religious Conflicts in England When he organized the Church of England, Henry VIII changed little in the way of doctrine or ritual. The main difference was that the monarch, not the pope, was the head of the church. A generation later, Archbishop Thomas Cranmer wrote the first version of the Book of Common Prayer, which replaced the Latin liturgical books with prayers in English.

Skills Focus: Drawing Conclusions

At Level

Reading Skill

The King's Great Matter

1. Review with students the information in the text about "the king's great matter."
2. Organize students into two groups. Pose the following question to students: Was King Henry VIII justified in doing what he did to resolve this dilemma?
3. Have students in each group brainstorm ideas in support of their argument. Students in one group should list reasons they feel the king was justified in his actions; students in the other group should list reasons opposing the king's actions. One student in each group should take notes and compile a group list.
4. Serving as moderator, conduct a class debate, instructing students in each group to provide at least two reasons why they either support or oppose King Henry VIII's actions.

LS Verbal-Linguistic

Alternative Assessment Handbook, Rubrics 10: Debates; and 14: Group Activity

Answers

Religious Conflicts in England *broke from Catholic Church; founded Church of England*

Direct Teach

Interpreting Maps

Spread of Protestantism

Summarize What does this map show about the spread of Protestantism? *possible answer—Protestantism changed as it spread to different areas.*

Predict What might happen between Protestant nations and Catholic nations? *possible answers—might try to convert each other; might go to war*

Map Transparency: Spread of Protestantism

Review & Assess

Close

Have students compare and contrast official church doctrines and Luther's viewpoints.

Review

Online Quiz, Section 3

Assess

SE Section 3 Assessment

Progress Assessment: Section 3 Quiz

Alternative Assessment Handbook

Reteach/Intervene

Interactive Reader and Study Guide, Section 3

Interactive Skills Tutor CD-ROM

Spread of Protestantism

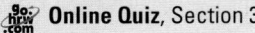

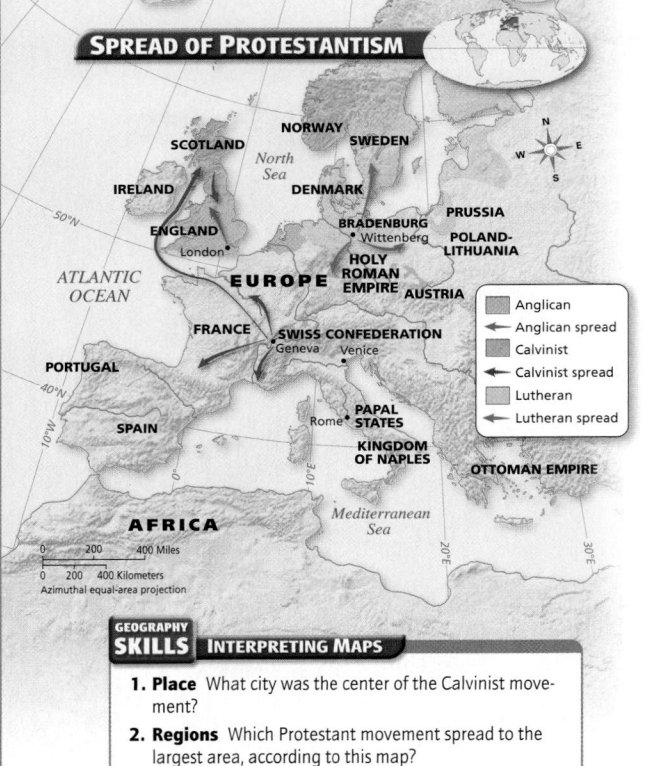

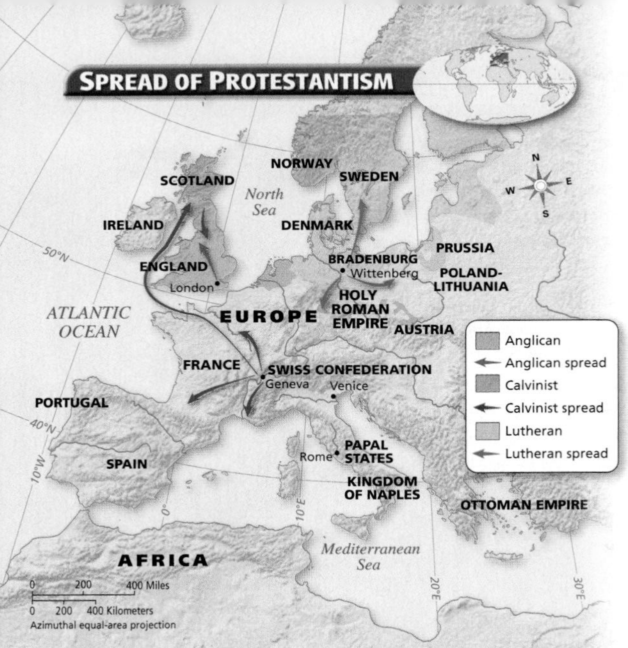

GEOGRAPHY SKILLS INTERPRETING MAPS

1. **Place** What city was the center of the Calvinist movement?
2. **Regions** Which Protestant movement spread to the largest area, according to this map?

Henry's Heirs In the end, Henry VIII had six wives. Henry's third wife, Jane Seymour, gave England its male heir, Edward VI. None of Henry's later three marriages produced any children.

When Edward VI took the throne in 1547 at age nine, Protestantism gained more ground under the guidance of his guardians. Edward died before his 16 birthday, and Henry's daughter Mary became queen of England.

Mary returned England to the authority of the pope. Hundreds of people were burned at the stake for their Protestant beliefs, earning the queen the title Bloody Mary. The news of Mary's death caused little sorrow among Protestants. Her 25-year-old half-sister Elizabeth, the daughter of Anne Boleyn, became queen.

Elizabeth's Reign **Elizabeth I** was a Protestant at heart. One of her first acts as queen was to draft a new Supremacy Act in 1559, splitting England once again from Rome.

Throughout her reign, Elizabeth was threatened by Catholics who plotted to place Mary, Queen of Scots, on the throne. In turn, Elizabeth persecuted any who dared to worship as Catholics. A strong queen, Elizabeth survived these struggles, firmly establishing the Church of England.

READING CHECK **Summarize** What caused the Reformation to spread to England?

Section 3 Assessment

go.hrw.com Online Quiz Keyword: SHL REN HP

Reviewing Ideas, Terms, and People

1. **a. Identify** Name three criticisms that were made of the Catholic Church in the 1500s.
   b. Summarize What other factors contributed to a weakening of the power of the Church in the 1500s?
2. **a. Recall** What were the **Ninety-five Theses**?
   b. Analyze What criticisms did **Martin Luther** have of the Catholic Church?
3. **a. Recall** Which Protestant reformer preached the doctrine of **predestination**?
   b. Draw Conclusions Why did Zwingli's followers wish to form an alliance with the Lutherans?
4. **a. Describe** What led to **Henry VIII**'s break with the Catholic Church?
   b. Make Judgments Based on the response to Henry VIII's break with Rome, what was likely to be the future relationship between the church and England? Explain your answer.

Critical Thinking

5. **Identify Cause and Effect** Using your notes and a graphic organizer like the one below, record the major reforms brought about by each reformer.

Reformers	Reforms

Focus on Writing

6. **Narration** Write a short paragraph that tells how England became a Protestant nation. Include important people, dates, and events.

Section 3 Assessment Answers

1. **a.** financially corrupt, abused power, immoral
   b. high taxes for middle class and peasants; rise of nationalism
2. **a.** Luther's propositions regarding the Church
   b. criticized power of the pope and church's wealth, the selling of indulgences
3. **a.** Calvin
   b. possible answer—to form a unified front against the Catholic Church
4. **a.** his desire to annul his marriage
   b. possible answer—There might be a power struggle between the king and the pope
5. Luther—began Protestant Reformation with the Ninety-five Theses; Zwingli—theocracy; Calvin—predestination, strict laws; Knox—his church replaced Catholic Church in Scotland; Anabaptist—rebaptism of adults
6. Student answers should include and explain the following events: Henry tries to get marriage annulled; pope won't agree to annulment; Henry forms Church of England.

Answers

Interpreting Maps **1.** *Geneva;* **2.** *Lutheran*

Reading Check *the desire of Henry VIII to annul his marriage*

SECTION 4

The Counter-Reformation

Before You Read

Main Idea

Catholics at all levels recognized the need for reform in the church. Their work turned back the tide of Protestantism in some areas and renewed the zeal of Catholics everywhere.

Reading Focus

1. What reforms were made in the Catholic Church?
2. What were the religious and social effects of the Counter-Reformation?
3. What wars occurred because of the Counter-Reformation?

Key Terms and People

Counter-Reformation
Jesuits
Ignatius of Loyola
Council of Trent
Charles Borromeo
Francis of Sales
Teresa of Avila

TAKING NOTES Use a graphic organizer to take notes on the reforms, effects, and wars related to the Counter-Reformation.

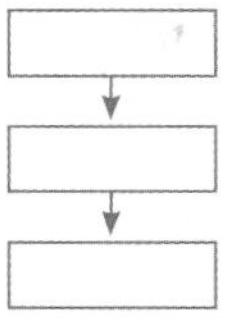

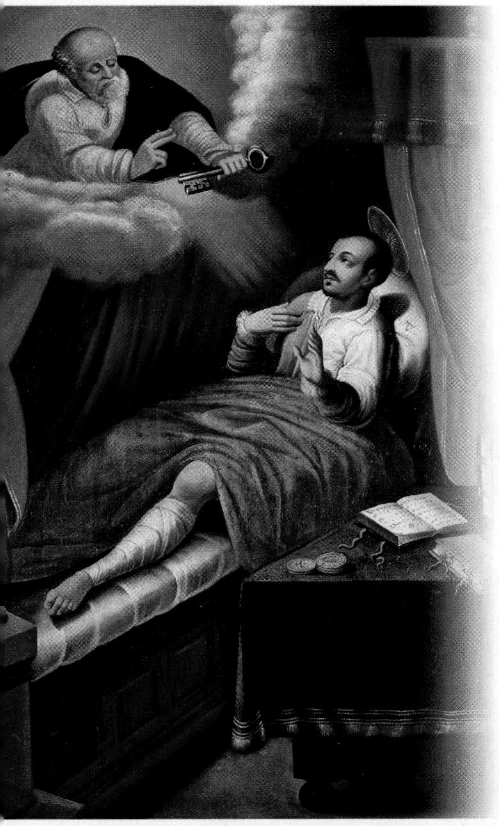

Saint Ignatius Loyola, anonymous

From SOLDIER to Saint

THE INSIDE STORY ***How does a soldier change his life to become a saint?*** A Spanish soldier, whose legs had been shattered by a cannonball, was taken by litter to a castle. His right leg had to be rebroken in order to be set correctly, and, eventually, part of the bone had to be sawed off. During the long months of recovery, the soldier's life changed.

The soldier needed something to occupy his time until he could walk again, so he read the only material available to him in the castle—biographies of saints. At first the soldier and former courtier in the Spanish royal court was bored by the stories of penance. But the ideas in the books soon filled his mind with the desire to find a religious purpose, and he began to see religious visions.

The books and visions inspired the soldier, whose name was Ignatius, to change his life—to become a "soldier of God" rather than a "soldier of man." Ignatius later founded a religious teaching order still active today—the Jesuits.

◄ This painting by an unknown artist shows Saint Peter offering a key to Ignatius of Loyola. The key allows one to enter Heaven.

Preteach

Getting Started

Use the **Interactive Reader and Study Guide** to familiarize students with the section content.

Interactive Reader and Study Guide, Section 4

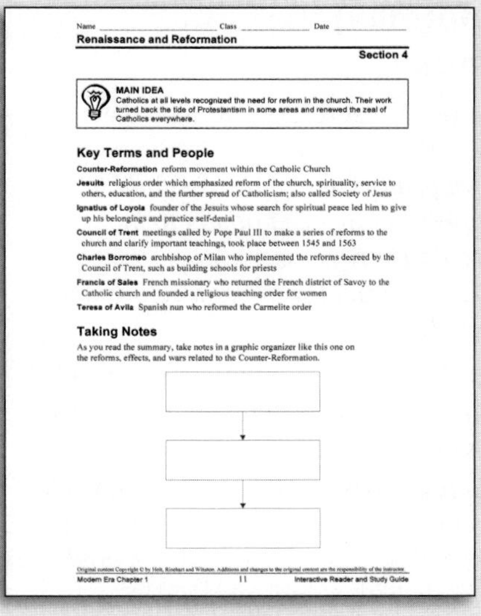

Name ______ Class ______ Date ______

Renaissance and Reformation

Section 4

MAIN IDEA
Catholics at all levels recognized the need for reform in the church. Their work turned back the tide of Protestantism in some areas and renewed the zeal of Catholics everywhere.

Key Terms and People

Counter-Reformation reform movement within the Catholic Church

Jesuits religious order which emphasized reform of the church, spirituality, service to others, education, and the further spread of Catholicism; also called Society of Jesus

Ignatius of Loyola founder of the Jesuits whose search for spiritual peace led him to give up his belongings and practice self-denial

Council of Trent meetings called by Pope Paul III to make a series of reforms to the church and clarify important teachings, took place between 1545 and 1563

Charles Borromeo archbishop of Milan who implemented the reforms decreed by the Council of Trent, such as building schools for priests

Francis of Sales French missionary who returned the French district of Savoy to the Catholic church and founded a religious teaching order for women

Teresa of Avila Spanish nun who reformed the Carmelite order

Taking Notes

As you read the summary, take notes in a graphic organizer like this one on the reforms, effects, and wars related to the Counter-Reformation.

Modern Era Chapter 1 11 Interactive Reader and Study Guide

Academic Vocabulary

Review with students the high-use academic term in this section.

proportion the size or amount of a thing in relation to another thing (p. 608)

CRF: Vocabulary Builder: Section 4

Taking Notes

reformed corruption and financial abuses, addressed Protestant challenges and reaffirmed some Catholic teachings; gave Catholicism a boost, Jesuits opened universities and sent out missionaries; increased influence on politics and worldwide

Teach the Main Idea

At Level

The Counter-Reformation

1. **Teach** Ask students the Reading Focus questions to teach this section.
2. **Apply** Draw three rectangles for students to see. Label them with the names of the topics in this section: Reforming the Catholic Church, Religious and Social Effects, Religious Wars of Unrest. Have students copy the rectangles onto their own papers. Have them write the main ideas of each topic in the appropriate rectangle.
3. **Review** As you review the section, have students describe how the Catholic Church dealt with the challenges of the Protestant Reformation.
4. **Practice/Homework** Have students write a letter from a priest who is attending the Council of Trent to his home parish, describing what is taking place at the council. **LS Visual-Spatial, Verbal-Linguistic**

Alternative Assessment Handbook, Rubric 25: Personal Letters

Direct Teach

Reading Focus

1 What reforms were made in the Catholic Church? *Savonarola's preaching against abuses in the Church; new religious orders such as the Jesuits*

Reforming the Catholic Church

Recall What reforms did Savonarola call for? *called for churches to melt down ornaments to provide food for the poor; convinced others to burn jewelry, mirrors, and trinkets, new religious orders worked to reform the Church*

Identify How did the Jesuits spread Catholicism? *by establishing missions, schools, and universities*

Analyze Why do you think Savonarola was first encouraged, then condemned? *possible answers—The Church feared he might become too powerful.*

Info to Know

Spiritual Exercises Ignatius of Loyola wrote a guide for meditation and discipline called "Spiritual Exercises." This book asked the reader to picture a thought or prayer, then to think of Jesus's actions, and sometimes to visualize oneself doing those actions. Loyola wanted the members of his order to be spiritual, but also to take an active role in the world.

Reforming the Catholic Church

Protestant reformers were not the only ones who were dissatisfied with the state of the Catholic Church. Even before Martin Luther posted his theses, some Catholics had been working toward reform of the church itself. Later, in response to the spread of Protestantism, the church began a series of reforms known as the **Counter-Reformation.**

Early Reformers A monk named Girolamo Savonarola (sahv-oh-nuh-ROH-luh) was one of the first reformers to try to change the church from within. During the late 1400s, he preached fiery sermons against the abuses of the church. He called for churches to melt down their gold and silver ornaments to buy bread for the hungry and poor members of the church.

Savonarola convinced people to gather and burn jewelry and trinkets. This enormous fire was known as "the bonfire of the vanities." Pope Alexander at first allowed Savonarola's work but eventually excommunicated him for spreading ideas the pope thought dangerous. In 1498, Savonarola was executed at Florence.

THE IMPACT TODAY
Several Jesuit colleges are today ranked among the best in the United States, including Fordham, Georgetown, and Loyola.

Jesuits Other leaders formed new religious orders whose members worked to reform the church. Their work renewed the church's emphasis on spirituality and service. The most influential of these groups was the Society of Jesus, or the **Jesuits.**

The Jesuit order was founded in 1534 by **Ignatius of Loyola**, a Basque nobleman and former soldier. The order was approved by the pope in 1539. Loyola, the Father General, ran the Jesuits like a military organization, emphasizing obedience to the church above all. The Jesuits concentrated on education as a means of combating the Protestant Reformation. They established missions, schools, and universities. With such effective organizations, the Catholic Church began to regain ground against Protestantism.

The Council of Trent Recognizing the need to redefine the doctrines of the Catholic faith, Pope Paul III convened the **Council of Trent** in 1545. It met on and off until 1563. Its delegates examined the criticisms made by Protestants about Catholic practices. In doing so, they clarified Catholic teaching on important points.

The delegates addressed the abuses that had weakened the church over the past century. A series of reforms addressed the corruption of the clergy. The training of priests was regulated and financial abuse was curbed. The sale of indulgences was abolished.

Above all, the Council of Trent rejected the Protestants' emphasis on self-discipline and individual faith. The council argued that the

The Council of Trent
Members of the Catholic clergy met in the Italian city of Trent to decide how to react to the rise of Protestantism. Members of the council signed decrees that outlined specific rules that Catholics were to follow.

The First Chapter of the 25th Council of Trent, anonymous, 1630

Skills Focus: Identifying Main Idea and Details

At Level

Reading Skill
The Jesuits

1. Draw the graphic organizer below for students to see. Omit the italicized answers.
2. Have students copy and complete the chart. Have volunteers fill in the class chart.
   LS Visual-Spatial

Alternative Assessment Handbook, Rubric 7: Charts

The Jesuits

started by	*Ignatius of Loyola*
goals	*obedience to Church and, above all, renewal of Church's spirituality and science, concentrated on education*
achievements	*starting schools and universities, missionary activity, knowledge of other cultures*

GEOGRAPHY SKILLS INTERPRETING MAPS

1. **Place** Which Protestant denomination was dominant in England in 1600?
2. **Regions** Which countries had a mix of Catholics and Protestants in 1600?

church could help believers achieve salvation by using mystery and magnificent ceremonies to inspire faith. This was consistent with the beliefs of millions of people, indeed the majority of Europeans, who remained Catholic.

The pronouncements of the Council of Trent meant that would be no compromise between Catholicism and Protestantism. The council's bold action was a great boost to Catholicism. Austria, Poland, and other parts of Europe returned to the Catholic Church. In addition, Catholics everywhere felt renewed energy and confidence.

The Jesuits used this renewed spirit to expand the scope of the church. By 1700, they operated 669 colleges in Italy, Germany, and other places. Many future leaders were educated at Jesuit schools. In this way, the order had some influence over political affairs. As they worked in India, Japan, China, and other places, the Jesuits also gained and passed along information about the cultures of other lands.

Reforming Catholics Several important figures in the Catholic Church helped to carry out the reforms decreed by the Council of Trent. **Charles Borromeo** (bohr-roh-MAY-oh) was the archbishop of Milan from 1560 to 1584. He took decisive steps to implement the reforms ordered by the council, such as building a new school for the education of priests.

In France, **Francis of Sales** worked to regain the district of Savoy, which had largely turned to Calvinism. As a result of his missionary work, most of the people of Savoy returned to the Catholic Church. He later founded a religious teaching order for women.

Women and the Church During the Renaissance, women in religious orders began to take on more active roles in the Church. Before the Renaissance, they lived in secluded convents. By the late Middle Ages, it was acceptable for nuns to help the poor, orphaned, or sick.

Direct Teach

Reading Focus

Reforming the Catholic Church

Identify What reforms were passed by the Council of Trent? *addressed clergy's corruption, regulated priests' training, curbed financial abuses, condemned sale of indulgences*

Predict How do you think Protestants would view the decisions of the council? *possible answer—good decisions, but didn't go far enough*

Map Transparency: Religions in Europe, 1600

Recent Scholarship

Girolamo Savonarola raged against church abuses such as profiting from the poor and charged the Medicis as accomplices. In *Fire in the City: Savonarola and the Struggle for the Soul of Renaissance Florence*, Lauro Martines has written about this pivotal moment in the Renaissance.

Fire in the City: Savonarola and the Struggle for the Soul of Renaissance Florence by Lauro Martines. Oxford University Press, 2006.

Differentiating Instruction

Below Level

English-Language Learners

1. Review with students the information in the text about the Council of Trent.
2. Organize students into mixed-ability pairs.
3. Have students create a poster that summarizes the decisions made at the Council of Trent. You may wish to have students write the first letter of each line in Renaissance-era calligraphy.
4. Have volunteers present their posters to the class. Display the posters in a classroom exhibit for all to see. **LS Verbal-Linguistic, Visual-Spatial**

Alternative Assessment Handbook, Rubric 28: Posters

Answers

Interpreting Maps **1.** *Anglican;* **2.** *France, Poland, Hungary, Russia, Holy Roman Empire*

Direct Teach

Reading Focus

Reforming the Catholic Church

Identify Name some women who began religious orders during this period. *Angela Merici, Jane of Chantal, Teresa of Avila*

Evaluate Why was the Inquisition considered an abuse of power? *people put on trial; torture and executions*

CRF: Biography: Teresa of Avila

Reading Focus

2 What were the religious and social effects of the Counter-Reformation? *changes in both Catholicism and Protestantism; persecution of non-Catholics, Jews, and Muslims; formation of independent states and nations*

Religious and Social Effects

Recall What groups were most often executed for alleged witchcraft? *women and the poor*

Describe Name three ways in which the Reformation and Counter-Reformation affected politics and government. *softened harsh rule of colonial governments; encouraged independent states; political power separated from churches*

READING SKILLS

Predicting Look at the head in the second column. What might be the effects of the Counter-Reformation?

Many women had a profound and important influence on others through their work with the church. In 1535 Italian nun Angela Merici began the Company of Saint Ursula, an order of women dedicated to teaching girls. Jane of Chantal and Francis of Sales cofounded the Visitation of Holy Mary order, which trained women to be teachers. Mary Ward of England began a network of schools for girls throughout Europe. At first her work was denounced by anti-Jesuits and the church because Ward's ideas about women were considered dangerously new. Later, however, her missionary influence was formally recognized by the church.

Perhaps the most famous female spiritual leader was **Teresa of Avila**. Born in Spain in 1515, Teresa decided to become a nun about the age of 20. Her father opposed her plan, but Teresa ran away to a convent about 1536. At the convent, after deciding that the practices were too lax, she followed her own strict rules regarding fasting, prayer, and sleep. Eventually the church gave her permission to reform the Carmelite order. Teresa's deep spirituality, reported visions of Christ, and fervor for the Catholic faith inspired many would-be Protestants to remain in the church.

ACADEMIC VOCABULARY

proportion the size or amount of a thing in relation to another thing

The Inquisition To counter the Reformation, the church established a church court, called the Roman Inquisition, in 1542 to fight Protestantism. Later popes increased the Inquisition's power. They tried people who were accused of being Protestants, of practicing witchcraft, or of breaking church law.

The Spanish monarchs set up and controlled the much harsher Spanish Inquisition in 1478. They used the Inquisition to impose religious uniformity, especially on converted Jews and Muslims, and later, on Protestants.

The church also tried to stamp out rebellion through its *Index of Forbidden Books*. The church warned the people not to read books on the lists or they would lose their souls. Accounts of torture and executions by the courts damaged the church's image. The Inquisition's actions during the Counter-Reformation are still seen as an abuse of the church's power.

READING CHECK **Summarize** What methods did the Catholic Church use to stop the spread of Protestantism?

Religious and Social Effects

The Counter-Reformation affected the whole world. Although the Roman Catholic Church was no longer the only religious authority in Europe, its policies influenced governments and societies wherever the church existed.

Changes in Religion A renewed zeal for the Catholic faith spread the religion to other continents, largely through the work of the Jesuits. In North America and elsewhere, their influence at times softened the harsh colonial rule of the governments under which they worked. Protestants broke away from the Catholic Church and then split into many factions. Religious turmoil increased as Catholics persecuted non-Catholics and non-Catholics persecuted Catholics and one another.

Adding to the religious discord, rifts soon opened between the various Protestant churches. Martin Luther and his followers denounced the radical ideas of the Anabaptists and Zwingli's followers. Those whose thinking coincided with John Calvin disapproved of some of the ideas on which Lutheranism was based. Martin Luther's theses had opened the door to religious freedom. That freedom brought an equal proportion of conflict and turmoil.

Persecution and Hysteria Both Catholics and Protestants, including Luther, viewed Jews and Muslims as heretics. In 1492, Jews and, in 1500, Muslims were forced to convert to Catholic Christianity or leave Spain. Many Jews resettled in eastern and southern Europe. The majority of the Jews who had earlier converted to Christianity and who were members of the educated elite, stayed in Spain.

In many of the areas in Europe where Jews were allowed to stay, they were not as restricted as they had been during the Middle Ages. However, in some places they were forced to live in a particular part of the city, called a ghetto. The ghettos were walled and their gates closed at a certain time each evening.

Across Europe, many people feared that witches roamed the land, killing children and cattle and working with the devil. Their fears increased in times of poor harvests or other hardships. The fears inspired hysteria in which accused witches were rounded up and tried for their alleged wrongdoing.

Skills Focus: Making Oral Presentations

At Level

Research Required

Reading Like a Historian Skill

Women and the Church

1. Tell students that women have always been involved in the Catholic Church, although their roles have changed over the years. Certain types of involvement by women have been and continue to be controversial.
2. Assign each student a famous Catholic woman, such as Mother Teresa or Catherine of Sienna.
3. Have students conduct research on their assigned person. Research should focus on the person's actions, her faith, and her relationship to the Catholic leadership.
4. Have students make a short presentation about their assigned person. **LS Verbal-Linguistic**

Alternative Assessment Handbook, Rubrics 24: Oral Presentations; and 30: Research

Answers

Reading Skills *possible answer—that the church might gain a broader following due to reforms*

Reading Check *spreading Catholicism through mission work and education reforms of the Council of Trent; Inquisition put people on trial, punished them*

World Religions

Christianity

The Reformation divided Christians in western Europe into Catholic and Protestant. Today Catholics, Protestants, and Orthodox Christians form the three main branches of Christianity.

Origins of Christianity The Christian faith is rooted in the beliefs of Judaism. Christians believe that a man named Jesus of Nazareth who lived in the first century AD was the promised Jewish Messiah and the Son of God. Jesus taught that all people who believe that he is the Son of God and follow his teachings will receive salvation—the forgiveness of sins and the promise of everlasting life.

The life and teachings of Jesus are described in the Gospels, the first four books of the New Testament. The New Testament along with the Hebrew Bible make up the Christian Bible, the sacred text of Christianity.

Christianity Today Christianity is now the religion with the most followers worldwide, with 2.1 billion followers. The nations with the highest percentages of Christians are in the Americas and Europe. In the United States, 85 percent of the population identifies themselves as Christian.

The chart breaks down Christianity into its major branches. Within these branches are many smaller groups called denominations. In all, Christianity has some 1,000 denominations in North America alone. Protestants account for most of these.

Some Christian denominations, including Catholics, perform the Eucharist, or Communion, which reenacts Jesus' Last Supper. An important holy day is Easter. On this day, Christians remember the Resurrection, when they believe Jesus rose from the dead.

Find the Main Idea What are the three main branches of Christianity?

Guell Colony Chapel, Antoni Gaudi

MAJOR CHRISTIAN DENOMINATIONS, 2004

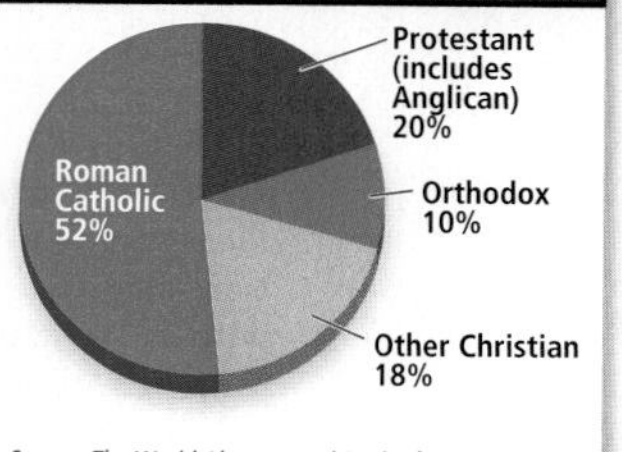

Source: *The World Almanac and Book of Facts, 2006*

The penalty for practicing witchcraft at this time was often death, and many innocent victims were executed for alleged witchcraft. The majority of executions for witchcraft occurred between 1580 and 1660. Thousands of people, most of them women or poor, were killed.

Political Effects A rising sense of national identity was interwoven with a decline in the power of the Catholic Church. The Protestant Reformation indirectly encouraged the formation of independent states and nations. Rulers and merchants both wanted the church to be less involved in state and business affairs, which they sought to control on their own. Political power became separated from churches, although nations and churches often aligned themselves with one another to increase their own influence in a region.

READING CHECK **Generalize** How did religious turmoil affect society during the 1500s?

Religious Wars and Unrest

In 1494, shortly before Michelangelo sculpted his *Pietà* and Savonarola was executed, King Charles VIII of France invaded Italy. This began a series of wars in which France and Spain vied for control of the Italian peninsula.

The Italian Wars During the Italian Wars, control of Italy bounced between these two powers. England also eventually became involved, as did several popes. The fighting finally culminated in the sack of Rome by the Spaniard and Holy Roman Emperor Charles V in 1527.

The Italian Wars officially ended in 1559. The real significance of the Italian Wars was that they were credited with expanding the Italian Renaissance throughout Europe. Troops returned home carrying ideas they had been exposed to in Italy. In addition, artists from Italy fled to the north, bringing new techniques and styles with them.

Skills Focus: Interpreting Pie and Bar Graphs

At Level

Research Required

Social Studies Skill

Religious Denominations

1. Have students review the pie graph on this page.
2. Have students conduct Internet research using reliable Web sites to find the percentages of religious followers in the United States in these categories: Protestants, Roman Catholics, Nonreligious or Atheists, Orthodox, Independent Christian, and Other Religions. Then, have them research these percentages in your home state.
3. Have students create basic pie graphs of their findings.
4. Have students write a paragraph describing how the percentages of religious followers worldwide compares to percentages in the United States and in your home state.
LS Verbal-Linguistic, Visual-Spatial

Alternative Assessment Handbook, Rubrics 7: Charts, and 30: Research

Direct Teach

Reading Focus

3 What wars occurred because of the Counter-Reformation? *Italian Wars; Peasants' War; fighting in France between Protestants and Catholics*

Religious Wars and Unrest

Recall What were the Italian Wars? *war between France and Spain over Italian peninsula, also involved England*

Identify How did the Italian Wars end? *sack of Rome*

Identify Cause and Effect What was one unintended effect of the Italian Wars? *spread Renaissance ideas*

Info to Know

Winning Followers During the Counter-Reformation Catholic efforts to regain followers often took the form of restoring splendid churches or commissioning new works of art. On the other hand, Protestants produced works of literature and writings on doctrine.

Answers

World Religions *Catholics, Orthodox Christians, Protestant*

Reading Check *caused changes in religion, fear and persecution of different religious groups, the creation of independent states*

Direct Teach

Quick Facts Transparency: The Reformation

Review & Assess

Close

Have students describe Catholic actions in response to the Protestant Reformation.

Review

Online Quiz, Section 4

Assess

SE Section 4 Assessment

Progress Assessment: Section 4 Quiz

Alternative Assessment Handbook

Reteach/Intervene

Interactive Reader and Study Guide, Section 4

Interactive Skills Tutor CD-ROM

Answers

Reading Check *peasants' high taxes, lack of power; Reformation ideas of freedom*

The Reformation (Quick Facts)

Causes

- Humanist values led people to question church authority.
- Some clergy were corrupt, worldly, or poorly educated.
- Martin Luther posted his Ninety-five Theses.
- The printing press helped spread Reformation ideas.

Effects

- Many Protestant sects developed.
- Church leaders reformed the Catholic Church.
- Religious intolerance and anti-Semitism increased.
- Religious conflicts spread across Europe.

Conflicts among Germans With new ideas circulating amongst a growing population, peasants were becoming more unhappy with high taxes and a lack of power. At the same time, Reformation preachers were giving backing to the idea of freedom. Stirred by these factors, in 1524 tens of thousands of German peasants stormed castles and monasteries, a rebellion known as the Peasants' War. The nobles harshly suppressed the uprising.

Martin Luther, accused of beginning the unrest, denounced it. The peasants, he wrote, "rob and rage and act like mad dogs." Luther's refusal to side with the peasants prevented the Reformation from spilling over into a social revolution that encouraged social equality.

Holy Roman Emperor Charles V, a devout Catholic, was determined to turn back the tide of Protestantism. In 1546 he began a war against the Lutheran princes of Germany. After years of battles, enthusiasm for the war waned, and the Peace of Augsburg was signed in 1555. Charles, who scorned religious compromise, would not attend the meeting.

The agreement reached in Augsburg allowed each prince to choose the religion that his subjects would practice. The only choices were Catholicism or Lutheranism, and the subjects had no say in the choice. Still, the seeds of religious freedom had been planted.

Conflicts between Religions In France the Huguenots, the Protestant minority, fought for years against the Catholics. The fighting ended when their leader, Henry of Navarre, became Catholic. His conversion led to political stability by encouraging Catholics to accept him as king. In 1598 Henry's Edict of Nantes granted religious freedom to Protestants.

READING CHECK **Identify Cause and Effect** What factors led to the Peasants' War?

Section 4 Assessment

go.hrw.com
Online Quiz
Keyword: SHL REN HP

Reviewing Ideas, Terms, and People

1. **a. Recall** On what issues did the reformer **Ignatius of Loyola** focus?
   b. Explain How did the Catholic Church try to keep people from becoming Protestant?
   c. Evaluate In your opinion, what was the main importance of the **Counter-Reformation** in European history?
2. **a. Describe** What were some of the effects of the Counter-Reformation on European society?
   b. Summarize What led to the persecution of witches across Europe during the 1500s?
3. **a. Identify** Who were the Huguenots?
   b. Interpret How did the Peace of Augsburg encourage religious toleration?
   c. Elaborate How did Luther's reaction to the Peasants' War affect the Counter-Reformation?

Critical Thinking

4. **Compare** Using your notes from the section and a graphic organizer like the one below, analyze causes, characteristics, and effects of the Counter-Reformation.

Counter-Reformation	
Causes	
Characteristics	
Effects	

Focus on Writing

5. **Exposition** Which Counter-Reformation reform do you think was most important? Write a paragraph identifying the reform and exploring why it was so important.

Section 4 Assessment Answers

1. a. obedience to the church above all, renewed emphasis on spirituality and service
   b. Counter-Reformation, redefined doctrine at Council of Trent
   c. possible answer—reformed the Church; brought people back to the faith; new converts
2. a. the Church's influence was restored, spirituality and service emphasized
   b. fear of different religious practices
3. a. French Protestants
   b. allowed each prince to choose the religion his subjects would practice; allowed different religions to coexist
   c. prevented Reformation from becoming a social revolution as well
4. Causes: response to spread of Protestantism, some Catholics left reform was overdue; Characteristics: Council of Trent redefined doctrines, Jesuits taught spirituality and service, worked to bring about reform, women took on more active roles; Effects: church regains supports of Catholics in many European countries, majority of Europeans remained Catholic
5. Student paragraphs should include one of the reforms and support their choice with logic and details from the section.

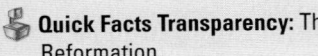

Focus on Themes

Migration and Diffusion

Before Gutenberg's press, books were rare and expensive. New ideas usually spread by word of mouth as people traveled from place to place. Although clergy and nobles might have been able to read the few books that existed, the majority of books were philosophical and religious works with little practical knowledge in them. Political ideas, technical knowledge about agriculture or medicine, and even laws, were usually learned directly from others.

▲ **NOW A Sotho woman in South Africa uses a laptop to access information on the Internet.**

DIFFUSION OF IDEAS THEN The movable type that Gutenberg developed changed the way people shared information. New forms of literature began to appear in Europe for new kinds of audiences. Novels were published for pleasure reading. Manuals on agriculture were published to help farmers learn techniques that produced more and better crops. Political tracts began appearing and changed the way people thought about their place in society. Printed sheets of news, the first European newspapers, appeared in German cities in the late 1400s. Italian news sheets were purchased for a small coin called a *gazeta*.

As printing presses spread throughout Europe and literacy rates grew, anyone who could read had access to ideas previously known only to the elite. For the first time, religious and political authorities had little control over the spread of information between people and places, although many tried to institute a measure of censorship.

◀ **THEN A woodcut shows printers working on a printing press, a revolutionary technology at the time.**

The Printer's Workshop, by Jost Ammann, 1568

DIFFUSION OF IDEAS NOW Today a similar revolution is occurring with the spread of computers and access to the Internet. An immense amount of information is available to people in areas that have no libraries or universities.

In addition, new forms of communication are being created that take advantage of the new technology. Music and graphics can accompany text in a way books do not allow and can make certain ideas more easily understood. Hyperlinked text allows readers instant access to more information on certain topics.

As with the technology of printing, Internet technology raises issues for modern authorities, who struggle to maintain a flow of information that respects the legal rights of all concerned. The illegal downloading of copyrighted material is one such issue.

Skills FOCUS — UNDERSTANDING THEMES

1. **Summarize** Why was the printing press such a revolutionary technology?
2. **Compare and Contrast** What are some similarities and differences between the printing revolution and the Internet revolution?
3. **Predict** Do you think the problems created by the technology of the Internet will be solved?

Focus on Themes

Info to Know

Copyrights and the Internet Copyright law seeks to protect the rights of creators of music, books, and many other original works, so that the creators may profit from their own work. With the Internet revolution, new challenges for copyright law arose. For example, in the 1990s, Internet music-sharing services arose, allowing people to share music files, sometimes without paying for them. Courts in the United States ruled that these services violated copyright laws, while courts in Canada ruled that the use of these services does not violate copyright. Distributors of electronic books and other electronic content have faced similar challenges.

Skills Focus: Comparing and Contrasting

At Level

Reading Skill

Diffusion of Ideas, Then and Now

1. Copy the graphic organizer for all to see, omitting the italicized answers.
2. Have students fill in the boxes of the flow chart. Then use the flow charts to compare the Internet revolution and the printing revolution. **LS Visual-Spatial**

Alternative Assessment Handbook, Rubric 7: Charts

Idea in era of printing revolution → printed on: *paper in book form* → idea accessible by: *anyone who could read*

Idea in era of Internet revolution → printed on: *Web site* → idea accessible by: *anyone with computer*

Answers

Understanding Themes 1. *allowed all readers access to new ideas; made spread of ideas faster;* **2.** *similarities—both increased speed of communication; differences—Internet revolution does not involve physical printing;* **3.** *possible answer—Yes, the problem is still quite new, and will probably take more time to solve.*

Document-Based Investigation

The Renaissance and Individualism

Info to Know

Anamorphosis The painting "The Ambassadors" contains one particularly unusual element—the object protruding from under the table. To create this object, artist Hans Holbein used a technique called anamorphosis. Looking at the object from straight ahead reveals nothing, but looking at it from a sharp angle, in this case from the right, reveals a human skull. It is possible that the painting was meant to be hung above and to the left of a doorway so that the viewer would see the skull upon entering the room. Although many have debated the symbolic meaning of the skull in this painting, no one is certain of Holbein's intent.

CHAPTER 1

Document-Based Investigation

The Renaissance and Individualism

Historical Context The documents below illustrate the changing view of individuals that occurred during the Renaissance.

Task Study the documents and answer the questions that follow. After you have studied all of the documents, you will be asked to write an essay explaining changes that occurred during the Renaissance.

DOCUMENT 1

A Medieval View

In 1195 Pope Innocent III published a work entitled *On the Misery of the Human Condition.* In it, he described all of humanity as sinful people who should focus all their energy on receiving God's forgiveness.

> [Man] does depraved [evil] things by which he offends God, offends his neighbors, offends himself. He does vain and shameful things by which he pollutes his fame, pollutes his person, pollutes his conscience. He does vain things by which he neglects serious things, neglects profitable things, neglects necessary things.

DOCUMENT 2

Individuals and Accomplishment

Wealthy people with access to education began learning not just religious or practical things, but things that interested them. Geography, music, art, and mathematics were learned because they interested the student, not in order to obtain employment or gain salvation. This painting of two French ambassadors by Hans Holbein shows items associated with subjects that the two men have studied.

The Ambassadors, Hans Holbein the Younger, 1533

Skills Focus: Analyzing Alternative Points of View

Below Level

Reading Like a Historian Skill

Pre- and Post-Renaissance Viewpoints

1. Explain to students that the introduction to each document is designed to help them gain a frame of reference. Write the following words and phrases for all to see: "1195," "focus all their energy on receiving God's forgiveness," "not in order to obtain employment or gain salvation."
2. Tell students that these words and phrases provide clues about the point of view conveyed in each document. Ask students to identify other clues, and write them for all to see.
3. Have students use these clues and their reading to determine which document represents a pre-Renaissance view, and which represents a post-Renaissance view. Have volunteers identify the documents, and explain how they arrived at their answer.

LS Visual-Spatial, Interpersonal

Alternative Assessment Handbook, Rubrics 12: Drawing Conclusions; and 16: Judging Information

Document 3

The Dignified Man

In 1487 an Italian nobleman and scholar, Giovanni Pico della Mirandola, prepared a speech called "Oration on the Dignity of Man." The work assumes the point of view of God speaking to Adam after his creation.

> The nature of all other beings is limited and constrained within the bounds of laws prescribed by Us. Thou [you], constrained by no limits, in accordance with thine own free will, in whose hand We have placed thee, shalt ordain for thyself the limits of thy nature. We have set thee at the world's center that thou mayest from thence more easily observe whatever is in the world. We have made thee neither of heaven nor of earth, neither mortal nor immortal, so that with freedom of choice and with honor, as though the maker and molder of thyself, thou mayest fashion [make] thyself in whatever shape thou shalt prefer.

Document 4

Christian Humanism

The writings of Desiderius Erasmus brought together the ideas of Christianity and the ideas of humanism. In a preface to his Latin version of the New Testament, he discusses why it is important for humanists to study Christianity.

> And in the first place, it's not pleasant to raise the complaint, not altogether new but all too just and never more timely than in these days when men are applying themselves singlemindedly each to his own studies, that the philosophy of Christ is singled out for derision [mockery] even by some Christians—is ignored by most and cultivated [studied] (coldly at that—I won't say insincerely) by only a few. In all other disciplines where human energy is invested, there's nothing so obscure and elusive that lawless curiosity has not explored it. Yet how does it happen that even those of us who lay claim to the Christian name fail to embrace this philosophy in full sincerity, as we should? Platonists, Pythagoreans, Academics, Stoics, Cynics, Peripatetics, and Epicureans all know the doctrines of their particular sects, they learn them by heart, and fight fiercely for them, ready to die rather than abandon the cause of their particular patron. Why then don't we stand up even more spiritedly on behalf of our maker and our leader, Christ?

Skills Focus: Reading Like a Historian

Document 1

a. Interpret How does Pope Innocent III's description of humanity view the individual?

b. Infer Why was secular learning discouraged before the Renaissance?

Document 2

a. Describe What subjects are the ambassadors interested in learning?

b. Interpret How might this painting be different from earlier paintings of important officials?

Document 3

a. Identify Why does humanity have a special place in the universe, according to Mirandola?

b. Compare How has the view of the relationship between God and humanity changed in Mirandola's eyes?

Document 4

a. Analyze Why does Erasmus say humanists should study Christianity?

b. Interpret How does Erasmus equate spiritual and secular learning?

Document-Based Essay Question

The change in the view of humanity during the Renaissance was a subtle and gradual shift that would have a profound effect. What changes occurred in the view of the individual? Using the documents above and information from the chapter, note some changes. Then write an essay about how they may have affected the way people lived.

See **Skills Handbook**, p. H22

Document-Based Investigation

Primary Source

"... we do not intend to tear up the old and commonly accepted edition, but to amend it in some places where it is corrupt, and to make it clear where it is obscure; and this not by the dreams of my own mind, nor, as they say, with unwashed hands, but partly by the evidence of the earliest manuscripts, and partly by the opinion of those whose learning and sanctity have been confirmed by the authority of the Church..."
—Erasmus, letter to Pope Leo X about his version of the New Testament

Skills Focus: Analyzing Primary Sources

At Level

Reading Like a Historian Skill
The Life of Erasmus

1. Explain to students that in order to understand Erasmus's introduction to the New Testament, they must understand some facts about his life.
2. Have students review the information about Erasmus in the chapter. Individually or in groups, have them conduct additional research to answer the following questions: Why did Erasmus create a Latin version of the New Testament? What was his relationship with the Church? How did Erasmus react to the teachings of Luther? What were some of Erasmus's other writings and what topics did they address?
3. Have students write several paragraphs to inform what they have learned about Erasmus. Have volunteers share their paragraphs with the rest of the class, in order to help them better understand Document 4. **LS Verbal-Linguistic**

Alternative Assessment Handbook, Rubric 42: Writing to Inform

Answers

Document 1 a. *sinful;* **b.** *because it was believed people should only focus on receiving God's forgiveness for sins;* **Document 2 a.** *geography, music, art, mathematics; b. possible answers—earlier officials were probably painted as being close to God, chosen by God;* **Document 3 a.** *because of free will;* **b.** *possible answer—God gave Adam free will, but in Mirandola's time, the Church controlled people's actions.* **Document 4 a.** *because secular groups are studying their areas with passion and singlemindedness, and Christianity is no less important;* **b.** *Christianity should be stood up for more spiritedly.* **Essay** *Student essays should use the documents and the chapter to identify that the role of the individual before the Renaissance was to cultivate a relationship with God, and that the individual had more freedoms and activities after the Renaissance. Essays should go on to explain the effect this shift would have on the way people lived.*

Visual Summary

Review and Inquiry Have students choose one of the lists in the Visual Study Guide on this page. Have students write a one-sentence summary of each person's accomplishments or each event's significance.

🖐 **Quick Facts Transparency**: Visual Study Guide: Renaissance and Reformation

Review Key Terms and People

1. The Renaissance was a period of renewed interest in art and science.
2. Humanism emphasized individual accomplishment.
3. Leonardo da Vinci was a Renaissance artist and inventor.
4. Johannes Gutenberg invented movable type.
5. Albrecht Dürer was a German painter who used techniques of the Italian Renaissance.
6. William Shakespeare's plays helped spread ideas of the Renaissance.
7. The Protestant Reformation reformed the Catholic Church.
8. The Reformation symbolically began in 1517 when Martin Luther posted the Ninety-five Theses.
9. Indulgences were pardons issued by the pope in exchange for money.
10. Henry VIII began the Church of England.
11. The Catholic Reformation followed the Protestant Reformation.
12. The Council of Trent reformed church practices.

Comprehension and Critical Thinking

13. **a.** a school of thought emphasizing the individual and the human mind
 b. religious subjects; idealized
 c. Wealthy patrons supported artists.

14. **a.** controlled trade throughout northern Europe; protected merchants; built lighthouses
 b. trade, travel, printing
 c. possible answer—works were censored, condemned by Church

QUICK FACTS

VISUAL STUDY GUIDE

People of the Renaissance

Lorenzo de Medici	▪ Ruler of Florence and patron of many artists
Leonardo da Vinci	▪ Italian artist, engineer, and scientist
Michelangelo	▪ Italian painter and sculptor
Baldassare Castiglione	▪ Italian writer and courtier
Niccolo Machiavelli	▪ Italian political writer and statesman
Albrecht Dürer	▪ German painter
Johannes Gutenberg	▪ German creator of movable type
Desiderius Erasmus	▪ Christian humanist philosopher and writer
William Shakespeare	▪ English playwright and poet
Martin Luther	▪ German religious reformer
John Calvin	▪ Swiss religious reformer
Henry VIII	▪ King of England
Elizabeth I	▪ Queen of England and daughter of Henry VIII
Ignatius of Loyola	▪ Spanish monk and founder of the Jesuits
Teresa of Avila	▪ Spanish nun and reformer of the Carmelite order

Events of the Renaissance

mid-1300s	▪ Italy experiences a rise of city-states.
1435	▪ Alberti writes an explanation of perspective for other artists.
1455	▪ Gutenberg develops a printing press with moveable type.
1506	▪ Dürer returns to Germany from a trip to Italy.
1508	▪ Michelangelo starts painting the Sistine Chapel.
1517	▪ Luther posts his Ninety-Five Theses at Wittenberg.
1518	▪ Castiglione completes *The Courtier*.
1533	▪ Henry VIII marries Anne Boleyn.
1537	▪ Teresa of Avila runs away from home to join a convent.
1540	▪ Ignatius of Loyola founds the Jesuits.
1542	▪ The Inquisition is established.
1545	▪ Pope Paul III convenes the Council of Trent.
1558	▪ Elizabeth I comes to the throne of England.
1593	▪ Shakespeare appears in London records.

Review Key Terms and People

For each term or name below, write a sentence explaining its significance to the Renaissance or Reformation.

1. Renaissance
2. humanism
3. Leonardo da Vinci
4. Johannes Gutenberg
5. Albrecht Dürer
6. William Shakespeare
7. Protestant Reformation
8. Martin Luther
9. indulgences
10. Henry VIII
11. Catholic Reformation
12. Council of Trent

15. **a.** the list of complaints that Martin Luther publicized in 1517
 b. the wife of Henry VIII did not produce a male heir; Henry VIII wanted an annulment; pope refused to grant annulment; Henry VIII founded Church of England
 c. possible sentence—Yes, earlier writers had also begun to criticize the Church.

16. **a.** to redefine Catholic doctrines; to examine criticisms made by Protestants
 b. possible answer—the Jesuits, because they used positive methods, such as education

c. possible answer—The two religions would continue to disagree with each other, leading to wars and further differences.

Reading Skills

17. possible answer—The Catholic Church might decline in power as a result of the Protestant Reformation.

18. possible answer—more wars between Catholic and Protestants

History's Impact video program
Review the video to answer the closing question: How have the Renaissance and Reformation influenced art and religion?

Comprehension and Critical Thinking

SECTION 1 *(pp. 39–45)*

13. a. Recall What was humanism?

b. Explain How did medieval artwork differ from the artwork created during the Renaissance?

c. Evaluate How did the success of Italian city-states help make the Renaissance possible?

SECTION 2 *(pp. 46–48)*

14. a. Identify Name the functions of the Hanseatic League.

b. Summarize What were the various ways that Renaissance ideas were spread?

c. Elaborate Why did it become dangerous to own a book by Erasmus?

SECTION 3 *(pp. 51–55)*

15. a. Define What were the Ninety-Five Theses?

b. Sequence Describe the sequence of events that led to England's break with the Roman Catholic Church.

c. Support a Position If Martin Luther had not posted his theses back in 1517, would the Reformation ever have happened? Take a position on this question and write a few sentences in support of that position.

SECTION 4 *(pp. 57–62)*

16. a. Identify Main Ideas What was the purpose of the Council of Trent?

b. Compare The Catholic Church used many methods to stop the spread of Protestantism. Compare the methods of the Jesuits to those of the Inquisition. Which had more far-reaching effects?

c. Predict "The pronouncements of the Council of Trent meant that no middle ground between Catholicism and Protestantism existed." Predict the future of both religions based on this statement and the other information in this chapter.

Reading Skills

Predicting *Use what you know about predicting to answer the following questions.*

17. If you know that the Catholic Church played an important role in society before the Renaissance and Reformation, what might you predict would happen after these movements?

18. After studying the religious wars in Europe during this time what do you think might happen next on this continent?

Analyzing Visuals

Reading Like a Historian *The painting below shows wealthy Italians at a daily meal during the Renaissance.*

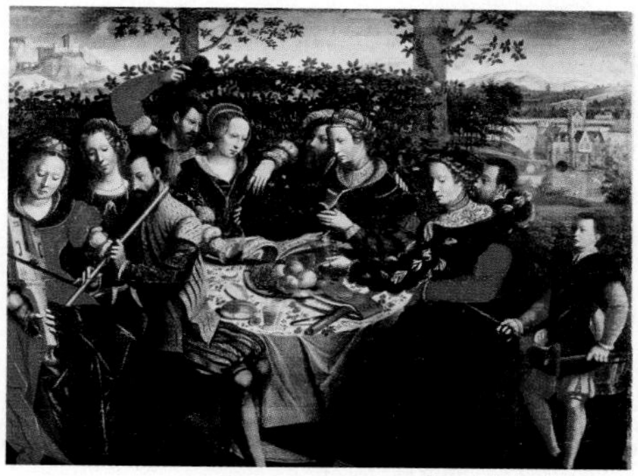

Concert, Ambrosius Benson

19. Draw Conclusions The musicians on the left side of the painting are performing a concert for the diners. What does this painting tell you about what wealthy Italians valued during the Renaissance?

Using the Internet

go.hrw.com
Practice Online
Keyword: SHL REN

20. Certain religious practices caused a number of people to call for change. Using the keyword above, do research to learn about leaders of the Reformation. Then use the information you learned to create a pamphlet on the topic.

WRITING FOR THE SAT

Think about the following issue:

Although drastic changes occurred during the Renaissance, most people's lives changed very little. The elite and nobles benefitted the most from the changes of the Renaissance.

21. Assignment: Why would the poor not benefit as much as nobles from changes of the Renaissance? Write a short essay discussing this issue. Support your point of view with examples.

Answers

Analyzing Visuals

19. possible answer—shows wealthy Italians valued art and music

Using the Internet

20. Go to the HRW Web site and enter the keyword shown to access a rubric for this activity.

KEYWORD: SHL REN

Writing for the SAT

21. Student essays should demonstrate an understanding of the Renaissance and its effects on people's lives. Essays should also point out that the lives of the wealthy were improving and that wealthy patrons financed art and music.
A rubric for this activity is provided in **CRF:** Writing for the SAT.

HOLT
History's Impact
▶ **Video Program: Renaissance and Reformation**
Refer to the Video Program Teacher's Guide for a discussion of the closing question.

Review and Assessment Resources

Review and Reinforce

- **CRF:** Chapter Review
- **Quick Facts Transparency**: Visual Study Guide: Renaissance and Reformation
- **Spanish Chapter Summaries Audio CD Program**
- HOAP **Online Chapter Summaries in Six Languages**
- OSP **Holt PuzzlePro**: Quiz Show for ExamView
- **Quiz Game CD-ROM**

Assess

- **PASS**: Chapter Test, Forms A and B
- **Alternative Assessment Handbook**
- OSP **ExamView Test Generator**, Chapter Test
- **Differentiated Instruction Modified Worksheets and Tests CD-ROM**: Chapter Test
- HOAP **Holt Online Assessment Program** (in the Premier Online Edition)

Reteach/Intervene

- **Interactive Reader and Study Guide**
- **Differentiated Instruction Teacher Management System**: Lesson Plans for Differentiated Instruction
- **Differentiated Instruction Modified Worksheets and Tests CD-ROM**: Chapter Test
- **Interactive Skills Tutor CD-ROM**

go.hrw.com
Online Resources
KEYWORD: SHL TEACHER

Chapter 2 Planning Guide

Exploration and Expansion

Chapter Overview	Reproducible Resources	Technology Resources
CHAPTER 16 **pp. 466–495** **Overview:** **In this chapter, students will learn about the explorations, conquests, and expansion that occurred between 1400 and 1700.**	**Differentiated Instruction Teacher Management System:*** • Pacing Guide • Lesson Plans for Differentiated Instruction **Interactive Reader and Study Guide:** Chapter Summary* **Chapter Resource File*** • Writing About History • Social Studies Skill • Chapter Review	**Live Ink© Online Reading Help** **Student Edition on Audio CD Program** **Differentiated Instruction Modified Worksheets and Tests CD-ROM** **World History Primary Source Library CD-ROM** **History's Impact: World History Video Program (VHS/DVD):** Exploration and Expansion
Section 1: **Voyages of Discovery** **The Main Idea:** During the 1400s and1500s European explorers—inspired by greed, curiosity, and the desire for glory and aided by new technologies—sailed to many previously unknown lands in the 1400s and 1500s.	**Differentiated Instruction Teacher Management System:** Section 1 Lesson Plan* **Interactive Reader and Study Guide:** Section 1 Summary* **Chapter Resource File*** • Vocabulary Builder: Section 1 • Biography: Vasco da Gama • History and Geography: Portuguese Explorers in Africa	**Daily Test Practice Transparency:** Section 1* **Map Transparency:** European Discovery, 1400–1700* **Map Transparency:** Explorers and Their Routes* **Internet Activity:** Navigation Tools
Section 2: **Conquest and Colonies** **The Main Idea:** The countries of Europe established colonies in the lands they had discovered but, in some cases, only after violently conquering the native people who lived there.	**Differentiated Instruction Teacher Management System:** Section 2 Lesson Plan* **Interactive Reader and Study Guide:** Section 2 Summary* **Chapter Resource File*** • Vocabulary Builder: Section 2 • Biography: Isabella I • Primary Source: An Aztec Account of the Spanish Arrival of Tenochtitlán	**Daily Test Practice Transparency:** Section 2* **Map Transparency:** Colonies in the Americas* **Quick Facts Transparency:** Causes and Effects of the French and Indian War* **Internet Activity:** Exploration and Expansion
Section 3: **New Patterns of Trade** **The Main Idea:** The creation of colonies in the Americas and elsewhere led to the exchange of new types of goods, the establishment of new patterns of trade, and new economic systems in Europe.	**Differentiated Instruction Teacher Management System:** Section 3 Lesson Plan* **Interactive Reader and Study Guide:** Section 3 Summary* **Chapter Resource File*** • Vocabulary Builder: Section 3 • Biography: Pocahontas	**Daily Test Practice Transparency:** Section 3* **Quick Facts Transparency:** The Columbian Exchange* **Quick Facts Transparency:** Basic Principles of Mercantilism*
Section 4: **The Atlantic Slave Trade** **The Main Idea:** Between the 1500s and the 1800s millions of Africans were captured, shipped across the Atlantic Ocean, and sold as slaves in the Americas.	**Differentiated Instruction Teacher Management System:** Section 4 Lesson Plan **Interactive Reader and Study Guide:** Section 4 Summary* **Chapter Resource File*** • Vocabulary Builder: Section 4 • Biography: Olaudah Equiano • Literature: *The Interesting Narrative and Other Writings*	**Daily Test Practice Transparency:** Section 4* **Map Transparency:** The Atlantic Slave Trade*

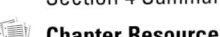

go.hrw.com | Print Resource | Transparency
LS Learning Styles | Audio CD | CD-ROM
Video | SE Student Edition | TE Teacher's Edition
OSP One-Stop Planner CD-ROM
*also on One-Stop Planner CD-ROM

Review, Assessment, Intervention

- **Quick Facts Transparency:** Exploration and Expansion*
- **Progress Assessment Support System (PASS):** Chapter Test*
- **Differentiated Instruction Modified Worksheets and Tests CD-ROM:** Modified Chapter Test
- OSP **One-Stop Planner CD-ROM:** ExamView Test Generator (English/Spanish)
- HOAP **Holt Online Assessment Program (HOAP),** in the Holt Premier Online Student Edition

---

- **PASS:** Section 1 Quiz*
- **Online Quiz:** Section 1
- **Alternative Assessment Handbook**

- **PASS:** Section 2 Quiz*
- **Online Quiz:** Section 2
- **Alternative Assessment Handbook**

- **PASS:** Section 3 Quiz*
- **Online Quiz:** Section 3
- **Alternative Assessment Handbook**

- **PASS:** Section 4 Quiz*
- **Online Quiz:** Section 4
- **Alternative Assessment Handbook**

HOLT
History's Impact
World History Video Program (VHS/DVD)
Exploration and Expansion

Power Presentation with Video CD-ROM

Power Presentations with Video are visual presentations of each chapter's main ideas. Presentations can be customized by including Quick Facts charts, images and maps from the textbook, and video clips.

Holt Online Learning

go.hrw.com
Teacher Resources
KEYWORD: SHL TEACHER

go.hrw.com
Student Resources
KEYWORD: SHL EXP

- Document-Based Questions
- Interactive Multimedia Activities
- Current Events
- Chapter-Based Internet Activities
- and more!

Holt Premier
Online Student Edition

Complete online support for interactivity, assessment, and reporting

- Interactive Maps and Notebook
- Homework Practice and Research Activities Online

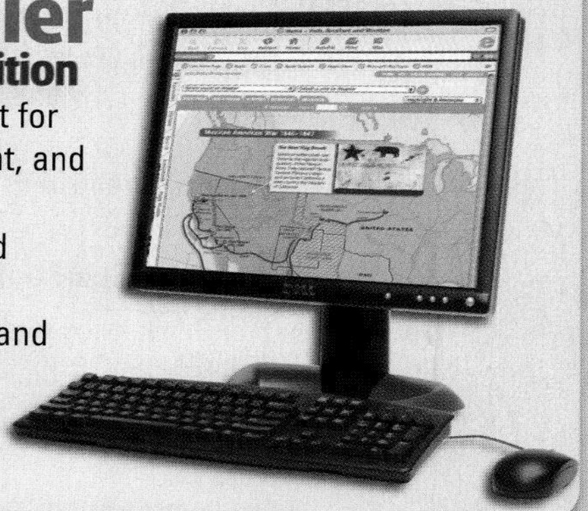

Before You Teach

The Big Picture

Peter N. Stearns

The European Surge Beginning as early as the 13th century Europeans began to undertake a widening series of sea voyages. There was great desire to gain direct access to the products of Asia without having to use Islamic traders as middlemen. Europeans had trouble paying for the Asian goods they wished, and direct trade and a desire to find new sources of gold were key responses. But political motives added in: explorations soon became part of interstate rivalry within Europe, particularly as France, Holland, and England joined the parade.

The Columbian Exchange European exploration of the Americas had a host of consequences. New food products were available to other parts of the world. To the Americas the same exchange brought new animals and grains, as well as new tools and weapons, with results that greatly changed the nature of life. Most important however were new diseases, like measles and chicken pox, which gradually killed off about 80 percent of the Native American population. The resultant labor shortage helped encourage the final component of the exchange, the importation of African slaves by the millions.

Colonies Spain formed colonial centers in Central America and the Andes, overtaking Aztec and Inca governments. Spanish control also loomed large in the Caribbean. Portugal's American empire focused on Brazil. Later, Britain, France and Holland gained colonial holdings in North America and the Caribbean. Colonial holdings also formed in several parts of Asia and Africa, where Europe's advantage in naval weaponry was particularly relevant.

A World Economy Europe's growing dominance over key ocean trade routes and its role in brokering American products, like silver, gained new profits for trading companies and governments alike. Capitalism spread, as did government involvement, later enshrined in the politically competitive doctrine of mercantilism. American economies were increasingly geared to produce crops and raw materials for world trade. European profits grew, and manufacturing opportunities expanded as well. Asian economies prospered through their strong manufacturing output.

Recent Scholarship

Several recent books have captured key elements of the new world economy that resulted from European ventures and the inclusion of the Americas. *White and Deadly: Sugar and Colonialism* (1999) does an excellent job in showing vital new connections. Sugar was a product that had already caught European fancy; it now became a mass consumer item dependent on global production and trade. Essays show the efforts to spread production of sugar not only in the Americas but in Africa and Indonesia. Labor systems receive appropriate attention, as does the rise of corporate involvement in sugar colonies.

Differentiating Instruction

Differentiated Instruction Teacher Management System
- Pacing Guide
- Lesson Plans for Differentiated Instruction

Interactive Reader and Study Guide

Spanish Chapter Summaries Audio CD Program

Student Edition on Audio CD Program

Differentiated Instruction Modified Worksheets and Tests CD-ROM
- Vocabulary Flash Cards
- Modified Vocabulary Builder Activities
- Modified Chapter Review Activity
- Modified Chapter Test

OSP **One-Stop Planner CD-ROM**
- ExamView Test Generator (English/Spanish)
- PuzzlePro
- Quiz Show for ExamView
- Transparencies and Videos

TE **Differentiated Activities in the Teacher's Edition**
- Explorers throughout History, p. 72
- Europeans Encounter the Aztecs and Incas, p. 79
- Markets and Manufactured Goods, p. 87
- Columbus and the Native Americans, p. 94

Reading Like a Historian

Sam Wineburg

Understatement can sometimes distance us from the grit of historical understanding, shaving off the very details that provide a toehold to insight. This may be the case with our chapter's description of the Aztecs and their neighbors. "Though the Aztec were very powerful," we are told, "they were very unpopular with the people they had conquered."Perhaps because they ate them?

The Scale of Aztec Sacrifice That the Aztecs practiced human sacrifice is widely known, but its dimensions—unless you've studied this culture—will be beyond you or your students' wildest calculations. The priestly blood cult was anything but a "remote, top of the pyramid" affair in the words of Inga Clendinnen, author of *Aztecs: An Interpretation*. Rather, the blood of sacred killing leached into all levels of Aztec society.

On the inauguration of the temple to Huitzilopochtli, Aztec god of war and sun, the air around Lake Texcoco was especially thick with the smell of fresh blood (could it be otherwise, when as many 20,000 humans were given over to the killing stone in a single day?). Such massive killings were special events. But smaller sacrifices—to lesser gods—stained the 18 months of the Aztec calendar. These killings were conducted locally in neighborhood temples, each staffed with its own team of priests. The priests themselves would pin down the victim's limbs as a flint knife punctured the chest below the rib cage to extract a still-pulsating heart. In the maintenance of this cult, all of the work leading up to and following the sacrifice, members of the Aztec laity were involved at every stage.

Prior to their sacrifice, victims had to be tended to and cared for, groomed in special cages that the Spanish, when they entered the capital Tenochtitlán, a thriving metropolis of about 200,000 people, mistakenly took for fattening cages. Commoners in the city's different wards were responsible for tending to the victims-to-be before their appointed date, dressing them up in the special sacrifice regalia, even plying them with wine on the night before "in order that they would not dread death."

It is afterwards, after victims' hearts were extracted and their skin flailed (so that warriors, draping the blood-drenched flesh over their backs, could parade through the streets), that we see how the cult of sacrifice infused all levels of Aztec society. As victims' bodies cascaded down the steps of the temple, old men collected the corpses and deposited them at the cultic butcher shops. Carvers severed the limbs—hands, feet and arms—and messengers would deliver the flesh to the waiting hearths of the commoners. For all, elite and commoner alike, the devouring and digesting of neighbors was a providential sign of their gods' favor. When these morsels of flesh came from close neighbors, the gods were especially pleased.

Bad Neighbors Sometimes war was waged for no other reason than to gain captives to feed this flesh industry and, as one might imagine, Tenochtitlán's unslakable blood-thirst made for bad neighbor policy. So, when Cortés laid siege to Tenochtitlán for four months in 1520, he had a lot already going for him as a recruiter. "The Indian empire," wrote Walter Prescott Webb some 150 years ago, "was in a manner conquered by Indians." According to Ross Hassig, author of three books on the Spanish conquest, the final defeat of Tenochtitlán was carried out by a small band of 350-400 Spaniards backed by an estimated 200,000 allies—Tlaxcalans, Huejotzincans, and other neighboring peoples—"even though they went virtually unacknowledged and certainly unrewarded."

The Aztec were "very unpopular" indeed. Eating your neighbors has never been a recipe for winning friends.

• Chapter Preview •

Chapter Main Ideas

Section 1 During the 1400s and 1500s European explorers—inspired by greed, curiosity, and the desire for glory and aided by new technologies—sailed to many previously unknown lands in the 1400s and 1500s.

Section 2 The countries of Europe established colonies in the lands they had discovered but, in some cases, only after violently conquering the native people who lived there.

Section 3 The creation of colonies in the Americas and elsewhere led to the exchange of new types of goods, the establishment of new patterns of trade, and new economic systems in Europe.

Section 4 Between the 1500s and 1800s millions of Africans were captured, shipped across the Atlantic Ocean, and sold as slaves in the Americas.

CHAPTER 2

1400–1700

Exploration and Expansion

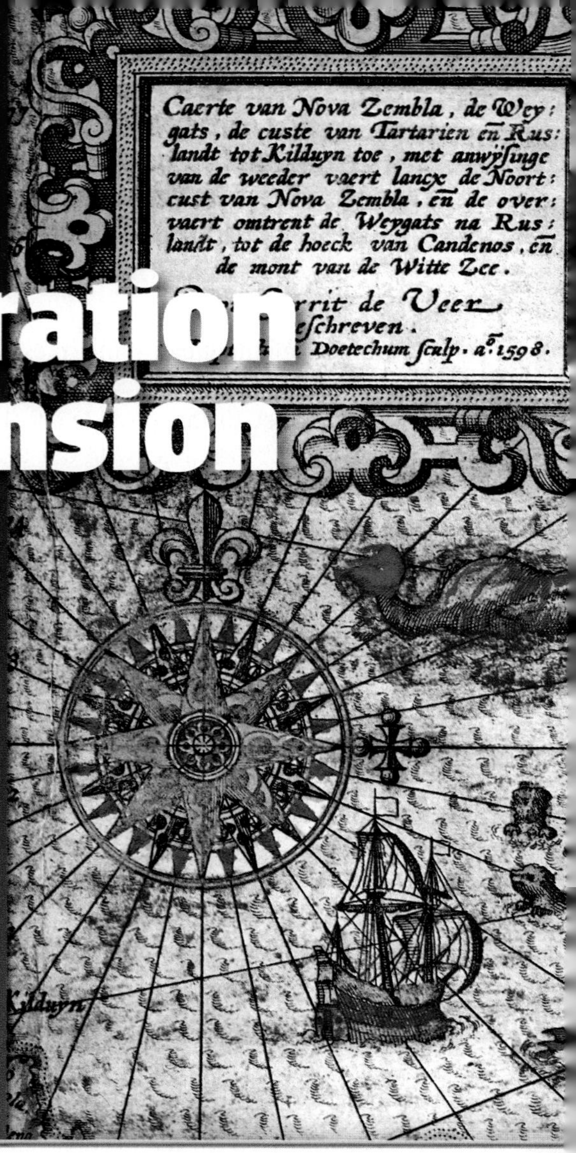

Caerte van Nova Zembla, de Wey: gats, de custe van Tartarien en Rus: landt tot Kilduyn toe, met anwysinge van de weeder vaert langx de Noort: cust van Nova Zembla, en de over: vaert omtrent de Weygats na Rus: landt, tot de hoeck van Candenos, en de mont van de Witte Zee.
Doetechum sculp. a°. 1598.
Kilduyn

Map showing the last voyage of Willem Barents, by Gerrit de Veer, 1596–97

THE BIG PICTURE Between 1400 and 1700, a new world opened up for Europe. Sailors set out on great voyages of discovery to lands that the people of Europe had not previously known existed. As news of the discoveries spread, countries scrambled to claim new lands, setting up colonies in hopes of gaining wealth and power. Once colonies were established, ships crossed the Atlantic in both directions laden with goods of all kinds.

Theme MIGRATION AND DIFFUSION

The arrival of Christopher Columbus in the Americas in 1492 was a turning point in world history. In the years that followed Columbus's voyage, European migration to the Americas took off, and the diffusion of goods and ideas changed societies worldwide.

TIME LINE

CHAPTER EVENTS

- **1419** Prince Henry the Navigator begins to support Portuguese exploration.
- **1488** Bartholomeu Dias rounds the tip of Africa.
- **1492** Christopher Columbus reaches the Americas.
- **1520** Magellan's ships sail around the southern tip of South America.

1400 — 1450 — 1500

WORLD EVENTS

- **1453** The Hundred Years' War ends.
- **1453** Constantinople falls to the Ottoman Turks.
- **1517** The Protestant Reformation begins.

Key to Differentiating Instruction

Below Level

Basic-level activities designed for all students encountering new material

At Level

Intermediate-level activities designed for average students

Above Level

Challenging activities designed for honors and gifted and talented students

Standard English Mastery

Activities designed to improve standard English usage

Introduce the Chapter

At Level

Exploration and Expansion

1. Tell students that during the period covered by this chapter, the nations of western Europe entered an Age of Exploration that resulted in the European discovery and colonization of the Americas.
2. Have each student prepare a list of reasons why one country would want to conquer another and colonize it. Then have volunteers share their lists with the class.
3. Guide students in a discussion of the reasons presented using the following questions: What advantages did the home country obtain from having colonies? What challenges might the home country face in ruling its colonies? What advantages, if any, would the colony get from foreign rule? What challenges would the colony face?
4. Tell students that in this chapter they will learn about how European nations established colonies in the New World. **LS Verbal-Linguistic**

Alternative Assessment Handbook, Rubrics 6: Cause and Effect; and 11: Discussions

History's Impact video program

Watch the video to understand the impact of the Columbian Exchange on Europe and the Americas.

Reading like a Historian

This map, drawn in the late 1500s, shows the region called Nova Zembla, a cluster of islands in the Arctic Ocean off the northern coast of Russia. This region was one of the many explored and mapped by Europeans in the Age of Discovery.

Analyzing Visuals What evidence on this map suggests the European drive to find and explore new lands and regions?

See **Skills Handbook**, p. H26

1600

1602 Dutch capitalists form the East India Company.

1644 The Ming dynasty ends in China.

1649 King Charles I is beheaded during the English Civil War.

• Chapter Preview •

HOLT

History's Impact

► **Video Program: Exploration and Expansion**

See the Video Teacher's Guide for strategies for using the video segment.

Reading Like a Historian

Analyzing Visuals Novaya Zemlya, or "new land," is the Russian name for Nova Zembla. In the 1950s, the Soviet Union used these islands as a nuclear test site.

Explore the Time Line

1. When did Prince Henry begin to support navigation? *1419*
2. How long after Columbus reached America did the Protestant Reformation begin? *25 years*
3. What event happened in 1520? *Magellan's ships sailed around the southern tip of South America.*

Info to Know

Nova Zembla Not all nautical expeditions looking for a shorter northern route to China sailed west to find a Northwest Passage. The English and Dutch also searched for a Northeast Passage, but never got any farther than Nova Zembla. The island, off the north coast of Russia, was first sighted by an English ship in 1553. Nova Zembla is shown on the right side of the map above.

Make Inferences Why did the English and Dutch hope to find a Northeast Passage to China? *They thought it would be shorter than the usual route.*

go.hrw.com

Online Resources

Chapter Resources:
KEYWORD: SHL EXP
Teacher Resources:
KEYWORD: SHL TEACHER

Answers

Reading Like a Historian *ships, navigation instruments, sea animals appear happy*

Preteach

Geography Starting Points

Ptolemy's *Geography* The Greek astronomer Ptolemy was also famous for his treatise on cartography, or map-making. In it, he drew a map of the world as it was known to the Greeks and Romans of his time, around AD 100–150. The known world stretched from the Atlantic Ocean to China and southeast Asia, and from the Baltic Sea to central Africa. Ptolemy's *Geography* also included instructions for reconstructing his map based on the longitudes and latitudes of some 8,000 localities. Early manuscripts and printings of the *Geography* often included beautifully detailed maps based on his instructions. His book was an early best seller. A Latin translation with maps was published in the 15th century. It inspired Columbus's fateful decision to try to reach Asia by sailing west.

Map Transparency: European Discovery, 1400–1700

World History Outline Maps

Interactive Map: European Discovery, 1400–1700

GEOGRAPHY Starting Points

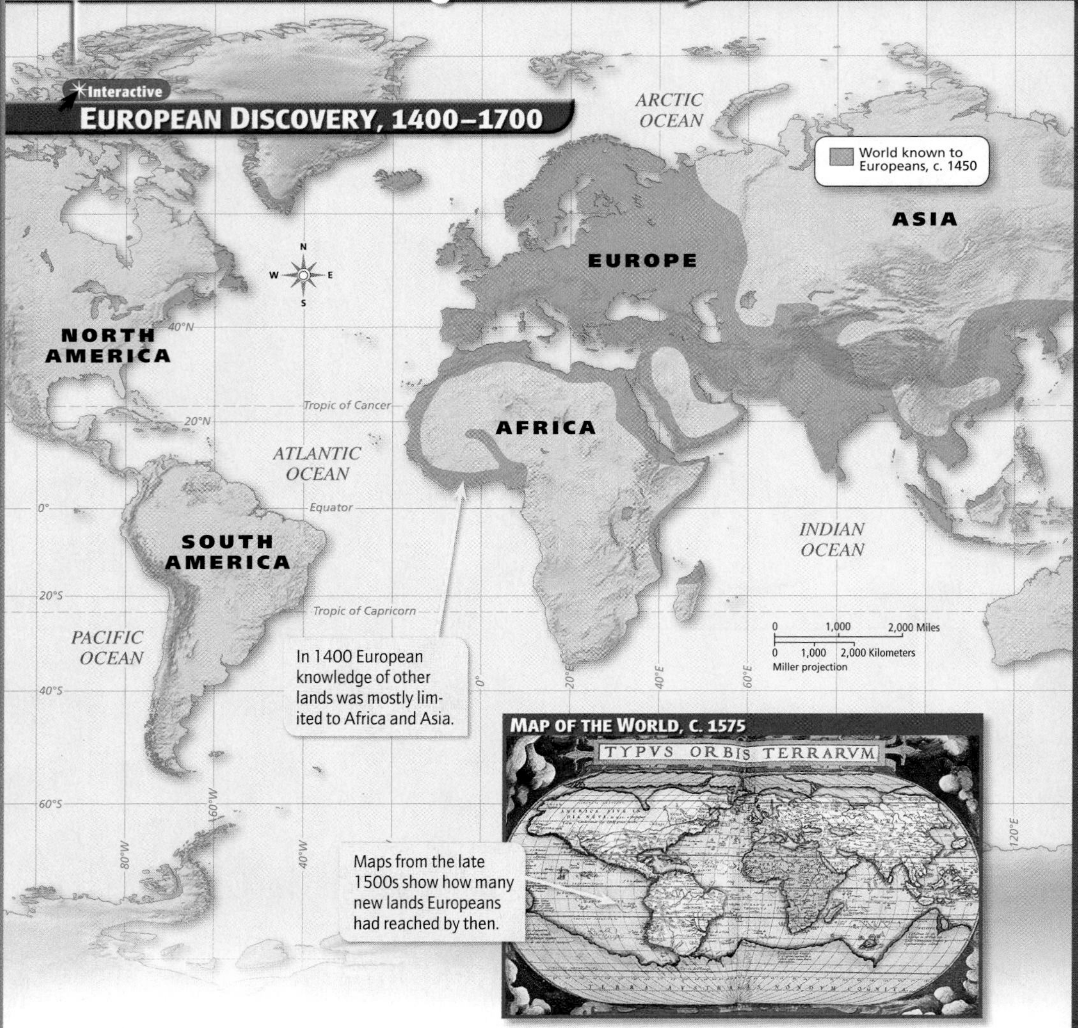

Starting Points By the early 1400s the people of Europe had fairly extensive contact with people as far away as China. However, there were still huge parts of the world that people did not even know existed. Within a few centuries, the situation had changed. European explorers had sailed all around the globe, and many countries had created global empires.

1. **Analyze** Compare the large map on this page with the historic map inset. Based on these two maps, what regions did Europeans learn of between 1400 and 1600?
2. **Predict** What do you think happened that enabled Europeans to learn about and explore distant lands?

Listen to History

Go online to listen to an explanation of the starting points for this chapter.

go.hrw.com
Keyword: SHL EXP

Skills Focus: Making Inferences

At Level

Reading Skill

A Different World

1. Have students consider what the world would be like if Europeans had never sailed west and discovered the Americas. Have students write a short essay describing what their lives might be like today if the Old World and New World had never come into contact. Where might they live? How might they live?
2. Have volunteers read their essays to the rest of the class.
3. Guide students in a discussion of the profound changes that were brought about as a result of the European voyages of discovery between 1400 and 1700. LS **Verbal-Linguistic**

Alternative Assessment Handbook, Rubrics 11: Discussions; and 40: Writing to Describe

Answers

Geography Starting Points

1. *southern Africa and North and South America;* **2.** *possible answer—better ships and navigational skills*

Section 1

Voyages of Discovery

Before You Read

Main Idea

During the 1400s and 1500s European explorers—Inspired by greed, curiosity, and the desire for glory and aided by new technologies—sailed to many previously unknown lands.

Reading Focus

1. What were the foundations upon which the Age of Exploration was built?
2. What discoveries were made by explorers from Portugal and Spain?
3. What drove explorers from the rest of Europe?

Key Terms and People

caravel
Henry the Navigator
Vasco da Gama
Christopher Columbus
Ferdinand Magellan
circumnavigate
Sir Francis Drake
Henry Hudson

Taking Notes Use a graphic organizer like this one to take notes on the reasons Europeans explored and where their explorations took place.

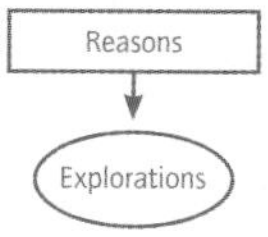

The Inside Story

How wide was the sea? When Christopher Columbus set out to reach Asia by sailing across the Atlantic in 1492, he did not expect the voyage to be long. Like many Europeans, Columbus was aware that the earth was round, but he did not realize how large it was. Nor did he realize that two continents—the Americas—lay between him and his goal.

For nearly a month, Columbus and his crew sailed with no land in sight. After weeks without even a glimpse of land, many of Columbus's sailors were getting restless. They feared that the small fleet would run out of food or water, and they wanted to return home to Spain.

Columbus convinced the crew to sail on for a few more days. Before long, watchful sailors began to spot signs of land, such as birds flying overhead. Finally, on October 12, the shout that the crew had been waiting for rang out: land had been spotted. That land was the Caribbean island now called San Salvador. Columbus was in a land previously unknown to Europeans, but he did not realize it. He firmly believed he had achieved his goal of reaching Asia by sailing west, a belief he held for the rest of his life. ■

LAND AHOY!

A statue of Christopher Columbus in the Dominican Republic commemorates his arrival in the Caribbean in 1492.

Foundations of Exploration

During the Renaissance, a spirit of discovery and innovation had been awakened in Europe. In the later part of the 1400s and 1500s, that spirit led Europeans to set sail on voyages of discovery to find new lands or new routes to places already known. Such voyages were so frequent and influential that the period is sometimes called the Age of Exploration.

Teach the Main Idea

At Level

Voyages of Discovery

1. **Teach** Ask students the Reading Focus questions to teach this section.
2. **Apply** Have students create charts of the explorers mentioned in this section. Student charts should include the explorers' names, dates, country for which they explored, and achievements or discoveries.
3. **Review** Review student charts as a class, and create a master chart for students to see. Guide students in a discussion of the accomplishments of the early explorers.
4. **Practice/Homework** Have each student choose one of the explorers and write a resumé of his accomplishments. (If necessary, review standard resumé formats with students or provide sample resumés for them to imitate.) **LS Visual-Spatial, Verbal-Linguistic**

Alternative Assessment Handbook, Rubrics 7: Charts; and 31: Resumés

Preteach

Getting Started

Use the **Interactive Reader and Study Guide** to familiarize students with the section content.

Interactive Reader and Study Guide, Section 1

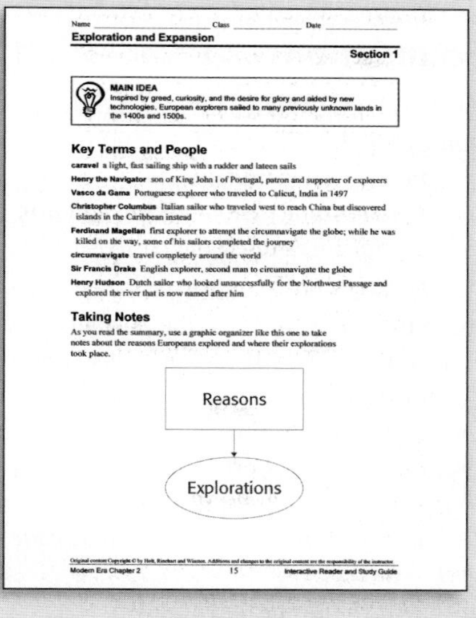

Name ______ Class ______ Date ______

Exploration and Expansion

Section 1

MAIN IDEA
Inspired by greed, curiosity, and the desire for glory and aided by new technologies, European explorers sailed to many previously unknown lands in the 1400s and 1500s.

Key Terms and People

caravel a light, fast sailing ship with a rudder and lateen sails
Henry the Navigator son of King John I of Portugal, patron and supporter of explorers
Vasco da Gama Portuguese explorer who traveled to Calicut, India in 1497
Christopher Columbus Italian sailor who traveled west to reach China but discovered islands in the Caribbean instead
Ferdinand Magellan first explorer to attempt the circumnavigate the globe; while he was killed on the way, some of his sailors completed the journey
circumnavigate travel completely around the world
Sir Francis Drake English explorer, second man to circumnavigate the globe
Henry Hudson Dutch sailor who looked unsuccessfully for the Northwest Passage and explored the river that is now named after him

Taking Notes

As you read the summary, use a graphic organizer like this one to take notes about the reasons Europeans explored and where their explorations took place.

Reasons
Explorations

Modern Era Chapter 2 15 Interactive Reader and Study Guide

CRF: Vocabulary Builder: Section 1

Taking Notes

Reasons—spirit of discovery and innovation during the Renaissance; search for wealth; desire for fame and glory; religious zeal; curiosity; advances in technology; Explorations—west coast of Africa; India; Brazil; Indonesia; Caribbean; South America; North America

go.hrw.com
Online Resources
KEYWORD: SHL EXP
ACTIVITY: Navigation Tools

Direct Teach

Reading Focus

1 What were the foundations upon which the Age of Exploration was built? *a spirit of discovery and innovation during the Renaissance, technology borrowed from other cultures*

Foundations of Exploration

Summarize What changes in technology helped improve navigation? *compass to determine direction, astrolabe to determine distance from equator, new type of ship called the caravel*

Rank What do you think was the main motive that drove the Age of Exploration? Why? *possible answer—Money was probably the motive; merchants outside Italy wanted to get expensive luxury goods without having to pay the high prices demanded by Italian merchants who controlled trade with Asia.*

CRF: Interdisciplinary Project: Geometry, Math, and Navigation

The Drive to Explore Like many other events in history, the Age of Exploration was driven in large part by the search for wealth. For years, Europeans had desired expensive luxury goods such as spices, silk, perfume, and jade from China and India. The flow of these goods to Europe was controlled by Italian merchants, who charged high prices for the rare goods. Many of the explorers who set out from Europe in the 1400s and 1500s hoped to find new, faster routes to Asia that they could use to gain a foothold in this trade.

Wealth was not the only goal that drove people to explore, though. Some people set out on voyages to find fame and glory. They hoped that making a great discovery would bring honor to their names.

Other explorers hoped to spread their faith into new lands. The Reformation and Counter-Reformation had brought a new religious zeal to Europe, and some Europeans saw the search for new lands as a chance to introduce new populations to Christian teachings.

One final motive for braving uncharted ocean waters was simple curiosity. Writings by medieval travelers such as Marco Polo, who had lived in the Mongol court of China for many years, were very popular in Europe. These writings intrigued many explorers with their tales of exotic lands and peoples.

Advances in Technology Whatever their reasons for exploring, Europeans could not have made their voyages of discovery without certain key advances in technology. Some of these advances were made in Europe during the Renaissance, and others were borrowed from people with whom the Europeans had contact, especially the Chinese and Muslims.

To make long voyages, sailors needed precise means to calculate their location. This means was provided by the introduction of the compass and the astrolabe to Europe. Brought to Europe from China, the compass let sailors know at any time which direction was north. The astrolabe, which Europeans first learned how to use from Muslims, allowed navigators to calculate their location based on the position of the sun and stars in relation to the horizon. Together, the compass and the astrolabe allowed sailors to plot courses even when they were out of sight of land.

Just as important as these advances in navigation were the advances Europeans made in shipbuilding. First, Europeans learned to build ships that rode lower in the water than earlier ships. These deep-draft ships, as they were called, were capable of withstanding heavier waves than earlier ships could. These ships also typically had larger cargo holds and thus could carry more supplies.

Themes Through Time

Exploration

MIGRATION AND DIFFUSION Though the spirit of exploration that struck Europe in the 1400s was new, exploration itself was not a new idea. People have been exploring the world around them since ancient times, and the drive to explore affects people even today.

c. 600 BC Phoenician sailors explore the west coast of Africa.

c. 1325–1350 Muslim writer Ibn Battutah travels through Southwest Asia, Africa, India, and China.

1200

1271–1292 European merchant Marco Polo travels through China and southeast Asia.

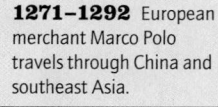

Marco Polo arriving at Hormuz, by the Boucicaut Master, c. 1400s

72

Differentiating Instruction

Below Level

Learners Having Difficulty

1. Have students name as many explorers from this time period as they can. Write the explorers' names for all students to see.
2. Group students together in mixed-ability pairs and have each pair choose one name from the list. Then have pairs write answers to the following questions: What discoveries did the explorer make? What country did he represent? When did he make his explorations? What were the immediate and long-term results of the explorer's discoveries?
3. Have pairs use the answers to write a paragraph about their chosen explorers.
4. Guide students in a discussion of exploration. What characteristics did all the explorers have in common? Where do today's explorers travel? How does exploration today differ from exploration in previous centuries?
LS Verbal-Linguistic

Alternative Assessment Handbook, Rubric 42: Writing to Inform

Another new ship that aided in exploration was the **caravel**, a light, fast sailing ship. The caravel had two features that made it highly maneuverable. First, it was steered with a rudder at the stern, or rear, of the ship rather than the side oars used on earlier ships. In addition, it was equipped with lateen sails, triangular sails that could be turned to catch wind from any direction. Lateen sails could even be used to sail directly into a headwind.

Another advantage of the caravel was that it could be equipped with weapons, including cannons. Armed with cannons, the ship's crew could face off against hostile ships at sea. Based on its maneuverability and defensive ability, the caravel quickly became the most popular ship for exploratory voyages.

READING CHECK **Summarize** How did advances in technology spur exploration?

Explorers from Portugal and Spain

Portugal and Spain share the Iberian Peninsula, the westernmost extent of continental Europe. As a result of their location facing the Atlantic Ocean, these two countries were well suited to kicking off the Age of Exploration.

The Portuguese Portugal was the first country to launch large-scale voyages of exploration. These voyages were begun largely due to the efforts of one man, Prince Henry, the son of King John I of Portugal. Though he is often called **Henry the Navigator**, the prince was not himself an explorer. Instead, he was a patron and supporter of those who wished to explore.

In the early 1400s Henry established a small court to which he brought sailors, mapmakers, astronomers, and others who were interested in navigation. From this court, Henry sent expeditions west to islands in the Atlantic and south to explore the western coast of Africa. As a result of these voyages, the Portuguese began to settle the Azores and Madeira Islands in the Atlantic. Portuguese sailors also learned a great deal about Africa's coast, including the fact that both gold and slaves were available in the area.

Prince Henry's ultimate goal was to find a water route around Africa to India. He died before that goal could be accomplished, but. Portuguese explorers did not abandon their attempts to find such a route. In 1488 Bartolomeu Dias became the first European to attempt to sail around the southern tip of Africa, a point today known as the Cape of Good Hope. Dias and his crew might have sailed farther, but violent storms forced to turn back.

READING SKILLS

Questioning As you read, ask yourself how Prince Henry supported exploration.

1405–1433 Chinese admiral Zheng He explores lands all around the Indian Ocean.

1492 Christopher Columbus sails to the Americas.

1600

1768–1779 Captain James Cook explores the South Pacific.

Mid-1800s Large-scale exploration of the polar regions begins.

Mid-1900s New technology allows the exploration of space to begin.

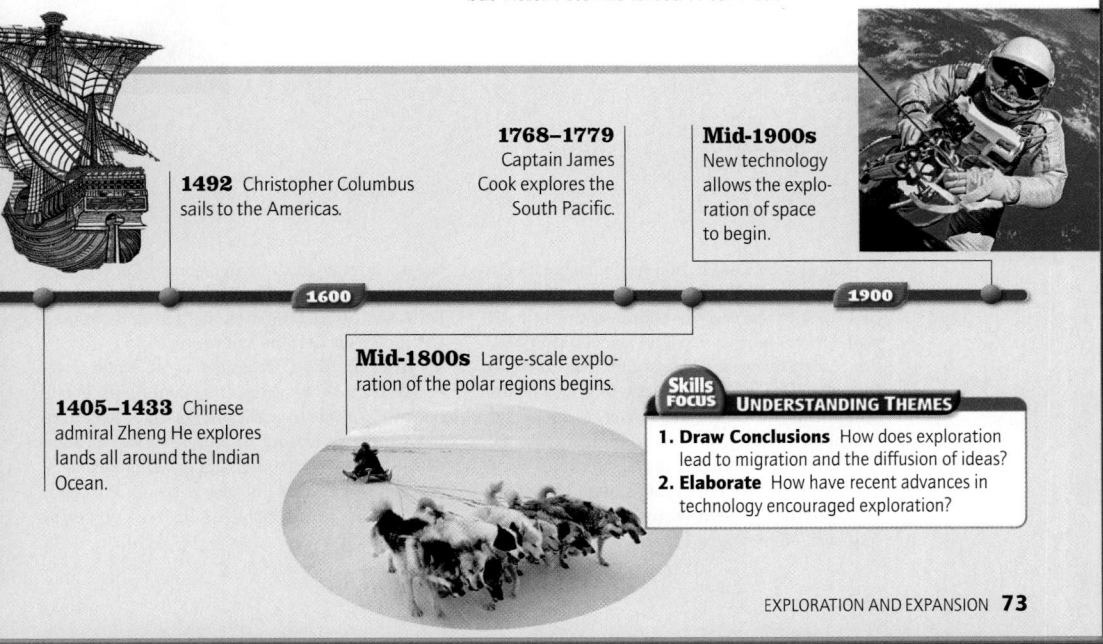

1900

Skills FOCUS **UNDERSTANDING THEMES**

1. **Draw Conclusions** How does exploration lead to migration and the diffusion of ideas?
2. **Elaborate** How have recent advances in technology encouraged exploration?

Direct Teach

Reading Focus

2 What discoveries were made by explorers from Portugal and Spain? *learned about Africa; found sea route to India; landed in the Americas; circumnavigated the world*

Explorers from Portugal and Spain

Explain Why did Portugal turn toward the Atlantic Ocean rather than the Mediterranean Sea for exploration? *possible answer—because Portugal borders the Atlantic instead of the Mediterranean*

Identify Cause and Effect What was Prince Henry's reason for bringing together people interested in navigation? *to raise his sailors' chances of success in exploring the African coast*

CRF: Biography: Vasco da Gama

CRF: History and Geography: Portuguese Explorers in Africa

Skills Focus: Summarizing

At Level

Reading Skill
The Technology of Exploration

1. Have students create a four-column chart about technology that aided overseas exploration in the 1400s. The first column should identify the technological advances. The second column should describe each advance and the third column should explain how it aided exploration. In the fourth column, students should number the advances to rank their importance, with 1 being most important.
2. Review student charts as a class, creating a master chart for all to see. How did students rank the advances? Was there a consensus, or did student opinions vary widely?
3. Guide students in a discussion of the ways in which technological advances combined with the drive to explore. **LS Visual-Spatial, Logical-Mathematical**

Alternative Assessment Handbook, Rubric 7: Charts

Answers

Reading Skills *possible response—He brought together people interested in exploration and navigation; financed expeditions*

Themes Through Time 1. *causes new lands to become available for settlement, causes different cultures to come into contact and share ideas;* **2.** *New technology has made the exploration of space possible.*

Reading Check *new ships faster and more maneuverable, could better handle sea voyages; navigational instruments allowed for voyages of exploration*

Direct Teach

Info to Know

The Astrolabe Sailors of the 1500s had only a few simple tools—such as the astrolabe—to guide them. Using the position of the sun and stars, these explorers sailed the oceans of the world. They could plot and hold a course and measure their progress. Astrolabes helped them estimate where they were with respect to land. These devices, which take their name from the Greek word for "star," were usually made of brass or iron. To use the astrolabe, a sailor would sight a star along the attached bar. By lining up the bar with markings on a disk, he could figure out the latitude of his ship's position. Astrolabes were used until the 18th century, when they were replaced by the more accurate sextant.

Pedro Cabral On his visit to Calicut, Pedro Cabral encountered problems with the Arab merchants controlling the port. The Arabs attacked the Portuguese trading booths, killing some of the sailors. Cabral bombarded the city and then sailed south to the rival city of Cochin to trade.

Ferdinand Magellan Ferdinand Magellan was convinced that he could reach the Spice Islands in East Asia by sailing west. The circumnavigation of the globe by his fleet was not only a great achievement of navigation and courage, it was also the first proof that the world was round.

Map Transparency: Explorers and Their Routes

Interactive Map: Explorers and Their Routes

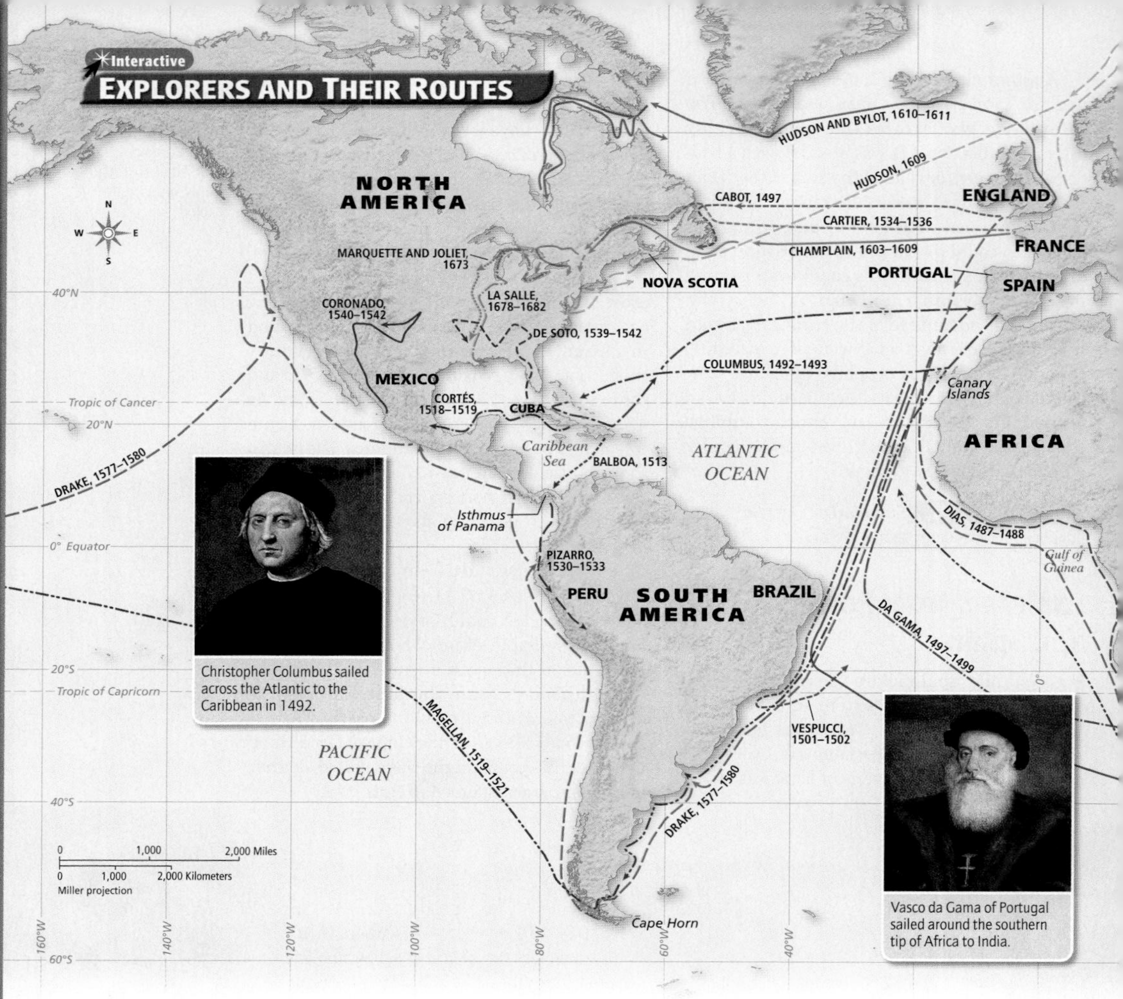

Christopher Columbus sailed across the Atlantic to the Caribbean in 1492.

Vasco da Gama of Portugal sailed around the southern tip of Africa to India.

Excited by Dias's success, another Portuguese explorer, **Vasco da Gama**, set out for India in 1497. On the way da Gama stopped at several African ports, where he learned that Muslim merchants were already actively involved in trade. Though the journey took more than 10 months, da Gama and his crew eventually reached the city of Calicut in India.

The return of da Gama caused great excitement among the Portuguese, who hurried to send another expedition to India. This second trip was led by Pedro Cabral, who sailed far to the west to avoid the windless Gulf of Guinea. Not only did Cabral keep the wind behind his sails, but he and his men sighted and claimed the land that became known as Brazil.

In India, the Portuguese established trading centers from which they could ship goods back to Europe. In addition, Portuguese sailors from India sailed out to find other lands, such as Indonesia, that could supply valuable goods. As a result of this lucrative trade, Portugal became one of the richest and most powerful nations in Europe.

74 CHAPTER 2

Collaborative Learning

At Level

School for Navigators

Materials: poster paper, colored pencils or markers

1. Organize students into small groups. Tell students they work for the admissions department of a navigation school in the late 1400s. Have each group create a set of posters, brochures, advertisements, and other materials to recruit students for the school. Recruitment materials should provide information about the school's programs and explain how they will prepare students for a maritime career.
2. Have volunteers from each group share their recruitment materials with the rest of the class. **LS Visual-Spatial, Interpersonal**

Alternative Assessment Handbook, Rubrics 28: Posters; and 43: Writing to Persuade

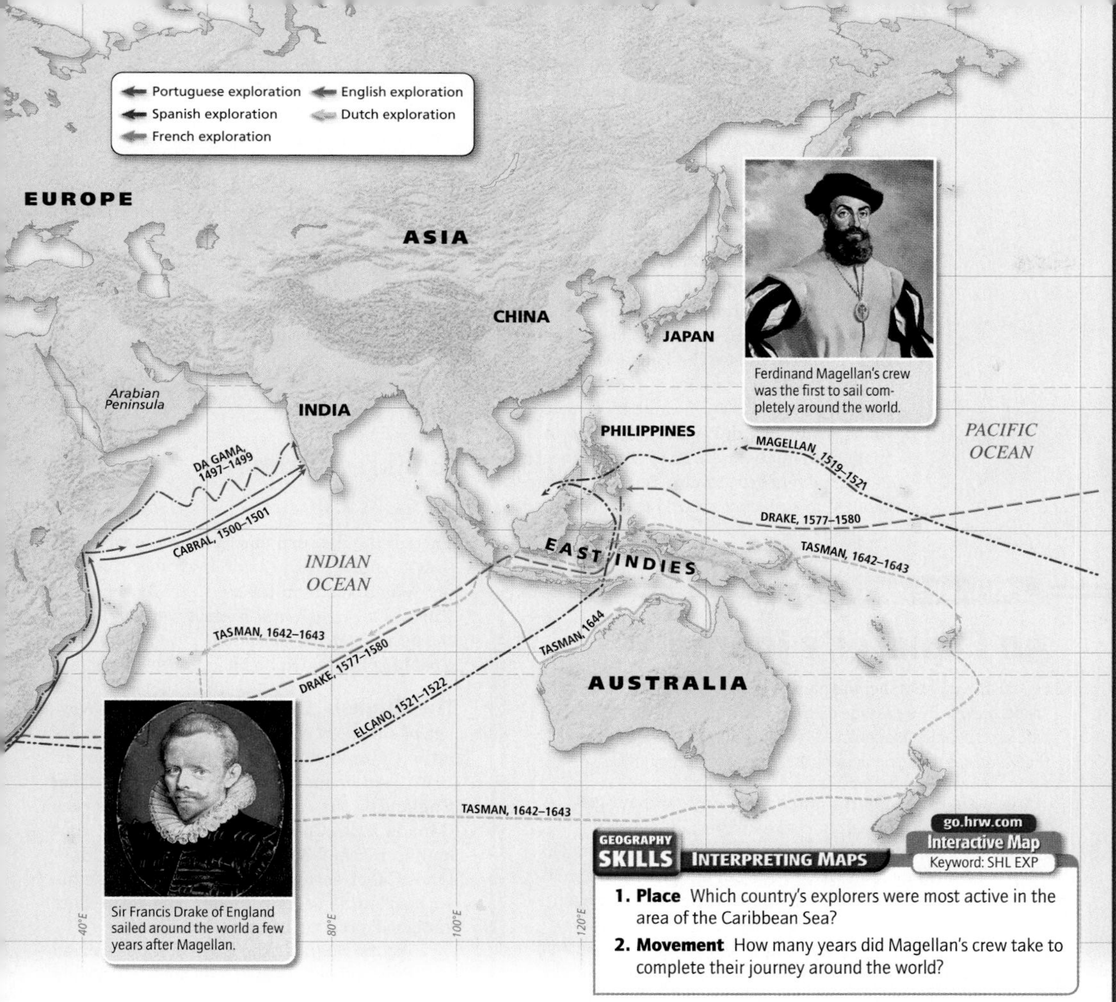

Ferdinand Magellan's crew was the first to sail completely around the world.

Sir Francis Drake of England sailed around the world a few years after Magellan.

GEOGRAPHY SKILLS INTERPRETING MAPS

go.hrw.com Interactive Map Keyword: SHL EXP

1. **Place** Which country's explorers were most active in the area of the Caribbean Sea?
2. **Movement** How many years did Magellan's crew take to complete their journey around the world?

The Spanish Like Portugal, Spain was eager to seek out new routes to the riches of the East. In 1492 the Spanish rulers, King Ferdinand and Queen Isabella, agreed to pay for a voyage by Italian sailor **Christopher Columbus**. Columbus believed that he could sail west around the world from Spain to reach China.

Although Columbus was correct in theory, the figures he presented to the king and queen about the earth's size were wrong. He also had no idea that the Americas lay across the Atlantic. As a result, when Columbus reached an island in the Caribbean after about two months at sea, he thought he had reached the Asian islands known as the Indies. As a result, he called the people living there Indians.

Columbus returned to Spain in March 1493 with many exotic items from the lands he had explored, including parrots, jewels, gold, and plants unknown in Europe. In addition, he brought several Native Americans back to Spain, where they were baptized as Christians. Believing that he had found a new route to Asia, the Spanish hailed Columbus as a hero.

Direct Teach

Biography

Fernando de Rojas (1465?–1541)
Although little is known about Spanish author Fernando de Rojas's life, it is believed that he was born into a Jewish family and that he received a degree in law from the University of Salamanca. His novel *Comedia de Celisto y Malibea* is considered the first Spanish prose masterpiece and the greatest literary work of the early Renaissance in Spain. The novel, which is popularly known as *La Celestina* after its main character, was originally published in 1499. It tells the story of two young lovers, the nobleman Calisto and Melibea, a lady of high birth. Celestina is the go-between who helps bring the two lovers together. Because it depicts romance in everyday life, *La Celestina* is often considered the first European novel. It was reprinted in Spanish over 100 times by the mid-17th century and had a major influence on the work of Miguel de Cervantes, author of *Don Quixote*. It was also translated into many languages; the first English version was published in 1631.

Info to Know

Maritime Trade Even before the Europeans, the Chinese sought to establish maritime trade routes. Between 1405 and 1433 the Chinese Muslim navigator Zheng He led seven naval expeditions in Chinese ships that visited Southeast Asia, India, East Africa, and Arabia to secure trade with these regions. A change in the Chinese government's foreign policies, however, prohibited additional expeditions. China returned to using other nations' commercial fleets to carry its goods.

Skills Focus: Evaluating Historical Interpretation — Above Level

Reading Like a Historian Skill

Trade and Exploration

1. Guide students in a discussion of the economic motivation of early exploration using the following questions: Before the voyages of discovery, how did Europeans get goods from Asia and what groups controlled trade with countries in Asia?
2. Have students use the map Explorers and Their Routes to answer the following questions: What factor(s) allowed Portugal to take the lead in finding a sea route to Asia? How did Dias and da Gama enable Portugal to trade directly with Asia? How did these explorations give Portugal a trade advantage over other European nations?
3. Have each student write a paragraph predicting how other European nations will react to Portugal's new dominance of trade with Asia.
4. Have volunteers read their predictions aloud.
LS Verbal-Linguistic

Alternative Assessment Handbook, Rubrics 11: Discussions; and 40: Writing to Describe

Answers

Interpreting Maps 1. *Spain's explorers;* **2.** *3 years*

Direct Teach

Reading Focus

Explorers from Portugal and Spain

Recall Which nation financed Columbus's voyages? *Spain*

Analyze Why did Columbus believe he had reached Asia? *His figures about the size of the earth were wrong; he did not know the Americas lay across the Atlantic.*

Interpret Why did mapmakers name America after Amerigo Vespucci and not Christopher Columbus? *Vespucci was the first to conclude the Americas were a new land and not part of Asia.*

Activity Slogans Have students create a slogan for Prince Henry's school for navigators. **LS Verbal-Linguistic**

Alternative Assessment Handbook, Rubric 24: Slogans and Banners

Reading Focus

3 What drove explorers from the rest of Europe? *desire for shorter route to Asia, new trading partners, search for Northwest Passage*

Explorers from the Rest of Europe

Identify What other European nations undertook voyages of exploration? *England, France, the Netherlands*

Explain What common goals did explorers from these nations share? *quicker passage to Asia via a Northeast Passage, and through the Americas via a Northwest Passage*

Answers

Primary Sources *no fresh food or water; rats, worms; sickness and death*

Reading Check *da Gama—reached India via sea; Columbus—landed in the Americas; Magellan—circumnavigated the earth*

Columbus made three more voyages to the Americas, still believing that he had reached Asia. His error was not realized until about 1502, when explorer Amerigo Vespucci sailed along the coast of South America and concluded that it was not Asia but a new land. Later mapmakers named the land America in his honor.

Now knowing that they had found a new land, the Spanish set out to explore it. In 1513 Vasco Núñez de Balboa led an expedition across the Isthmus of Panama. After more than three weeks of difficult travel, Balboa became the first European to see the Pacific Ocean.

After Balboa's discovery, the Spanish realized they needed to cross another ocean to reach Asia. What they did not know was how large that ocean might be. To answer that question, a daring adventurer named **Ferdinand Magellan** decided to sail west around the world.

Born in Portugal but sailing for Spain, Magellan set out in 1519 with five ships and about 250 men. His journey was long and difficult, and some of his men mutinied, or rebelled. After months at sea, Magellan's fleet reached the Philippines, where Magellan was killed in a fight against the native people. His men sailed on, however, led by Juan Sebastián de Elcano. In early September 8, 1522, 18 survivors of the original fleet arrived in Spain. They were the first people ever to **circumnavigate**, or sail completely around, the world.

READING CHECK **Analyze** What did da Gama, Columbus, and Magellan accomplish?

PRIMARY SOURCES

An Explorer's Journal

Life on an explorer's ship was harsh. Supplies were scarce, and many sailors grew ill. The passage below was written by an Italian writer who accompanied Magellan on his trip around the world. It describes the hardships the crew faced as they crossed the Pacific Ocean.

> "We were three months and twenty days without getting any kind of fresh food. We ate biscuit, which was no longer biscuit, but powder of biscuits swarming with worms, for they had eaten the good. It stank strongly of the urine of rats. We drank yellow water that had been putrid for many days. We also ate some ox hides that covered the top of the mainyard to prevent the yard from chafing the shrouds, and which had become exceedingly hard because of the sun, rain, and wind. We left them in the sea for four or five days, and then placed them for a few moments on top of the embers, and so ate them; and often we ate sawdust from boards. Rats were sold for one-half ducado [gold coin] apiece, and even we could not get them. But above all the other misfortunes the following was the worst. The gums of both the lower and upper teeth of some of our men swelled, so they could not eat under any circumstances and therefore died."

Skills Focus READING LIKE A HISTORIAN

Interpret What made the trip across the Pacific so difficult for Magellan's sailors?

See **Skills Handbook**, p. H25

Explorers from the Rest of Europe

Though the Spanish and Portuguese were the first to launch voyages of discovery, they did not remain alone in their efforts. By the early 1500s the English and French were exploring the northern parts of the Americas, and within a century the Dutch had joined the efforts.

The English The first major English voyage of discovery was launched just a few years after Columbus reached the Caribbean. In 1497 a sailor named John Cabot sailed from England to the Atlantic coast of what is now Canada. Like Columbus, Cabot thought that he had reached Asia. After returning to England, Cabot set out once more to repeat his voyage, but he never returned. His entire fleet vanished, presumably sunk.

Like the Spanish, the English soon realized that they had not reached Asia but a previously unknown land. In response, the English queen sent **Sir Francis Drake** to round the tip of South America and explore its west coast. After a stop in what is now California, Drake sailed north to seek a route around North America back to the Atlantic. However, the weather proved too cold, and he ended up heading west around the world to get back to England. He became the second man to circumnavigate the globe.

Eager for success, England's rulers wanted to find a shorter route to Asia than Magellan had found. In search of this route, they sent a Dutch-born sailor named **Henry Hudson**. In 1607 Hudson set out to the north, hoping to

Collaborative Learning

At Level

Explorers Wanted

1. Organize students into small groups. Tell students it is 1481 and King John II of Portugal has asked them to help him recruit explorers. Have each group think of characteristics that would make a good explorer—personality, education, background, etc.—and write a job description for the position. Job descriptions should mention risks involved in the profession, as well as compensation (salary, bonuses, and other benefits such as insurance and pension plans).
2. Next, have each group create a newspaper display advertisement to attract applicants. Student display ads might include artwork, and should list main points from the job description.
3. Have volunteers from each group share their job descriptions and newspaper ads with the rest of the class. **LS Interpersonal, Visual-Spatial**

Alternative Assessment Handbook, Rubrics 2: Advertisements; and 14: Group Activity find a Northeast Passage around Europe. Finding nothing but ice, he returned to England. Later, Hudson set out on two more voyages for the English and one for the Dutch.

The French Like the English, the French wanted to find a passage to Asia. They sent explorers to look for a Northwest Passage that would take them around the northern reaches of North America. One of the French explorers who sought this passage was Jacques Cartier, who left France in 1534. Cartier sailed past the island of Newfoundland into the St. Lawrence River. He claimed all the land along the river as the province of New France, or as it came to be called later, Canada. Later French explorers added to Cartier's claims, but none ever found a Northwest Passage.

The Dutch By the early years of the 1600s, the Netherlands—once a Spanish possession—had become a powerful trading nation. Already heavily involved in trade with Asia but hoping to find new products and new trading partners, the Dutch soon became involved in the exploration of the Americas as well.

One of these Dutch explorers was Henry Hudson, the same man who had sailed for the English before. In 1609, he once again set out to find a Northeast Passage around Asia. Once again unsuccessful, he instead headed west to seek a Northwest Passage through the Americas. Though he did not find the passage he sought, he did explore the river that now bears his name. Though the river is named for Hudson, it had actually been discovered years earlier by Giovanni da Verazzano, an Italian explorer sailing for France. Hudson also reached and explored Hudson Bay.

Henry Hudson greeted by Native Americans, The Granger Collection, New York

Henry Hudson

Henry Hudson, who sailed for both England and the Netherlands, explored the area we now call New York.

READING CHECK **Find the Main Idea** What did English, French, and Dutch explorers hope to find?

SECTION 1 ASSESSMENT

go.hrw.com
Online Quiz
Keyword: SHL EXP HP

Reviewing Ideas, Terms, and People

1. **a. Identify** What were four reasons that drove people to explore new lands?
   b. Explain How did devices like the astrolabe, compass, and **caravel** help promote exploration?
   c. Support a Position Do you agree or disagree with this statement: "The Age of Exploration could not have occurred without the Renaissance"? Support your answer.
2. **a. Describe** For what is **Vasco da Gama** best known? For what is **Ferdinand Magellan** known?
   b. Summarize Why was **Christopher Columbus** mistaken about the land he had found?
   c. Elaborate What role did **Henry the Navigator** play in launching the Age of Exploration?
3. **a. Recall** What goal did English, French, and Dutch explorers share with the Spanish and Portuguese? How was their approach to the Americas different?
   b. Explain Why did **Sir Francis Drake** end up sailing completely around the world?

Critical Thinking

4. **Categorize** Draw a chart like the one below. Using your notes, identify the major explorers that sailed for each country and the areas that they explored.

European Explorers				
Portugal	Spain	England	France	Netherlands

FOCUS ON WRITING

5. **Persuasion** Write a letter as though you were a European explorer trying to convince a monarch to fund your expedition. Your letter should point out why you want to explore.

• Review & Assess •

Close

Have students explain the impact of technology on exploration in the 1400s.

Review

go.hrw.com **Online Quiz,** Section 1

Assess

SE Section 1 Assessment

Progress Assessment: Section 1 Quiz

Alternative Assessment Handbook

Reteach/Intervene

Interactive Reader and Study Guide, Section 1

Interactive Skills Tutor CD-ROM

Answers

Reading Check *a shorter route to Asia*

Section 1 Assessment Answers

1. a. search for wealth, fame and glory, desire to spread faith, curiosity
   b. made longer sea voyages possible, improved navigation
   c. possible answer—agree: The Renaissance awakened a spirit of discovery and innovation in Europe.
2. a. da Gama—sea route to India; Magellan—circumnavigation of the world
   b. He believed he was in Asia.
   c. brought together people interested in exploration and navigation, financed expeditions
3. a. trade with Asia; sought a shorter route
   b. The weather was too cold to return the way he came, and he continued sailing west.
4. Portugal—Dias: southern Africa; da Gama: India; Cabral: India, Brazil; Spain—Columbus: Caribbean; Vespucci: South America; Balboa: Panama, Pacific Ocean; Magellan: circumnavigation of world; England—Drake: southern tip of South America, circumnavigation of world; Hudson: North America; France—Cartier: Newfoundland, Canada; Netherlands—Hudson: Hudson Bay
5. Student letters should include the major reasons for exploration during this period, including religious zeal, curiosity, and the search for wealth, fame, and glory.

Preteach

Getting Started

Use the **Interactive Reader and Study Guide** to familiarize students with the section content.

Interactive Reader and Study Guide, Section 2

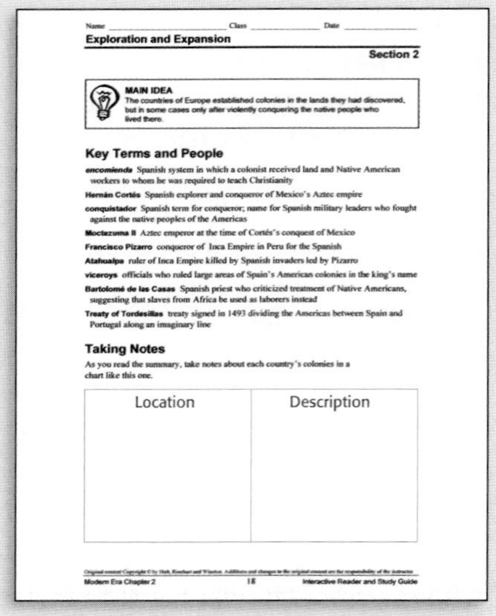
Name ______ Class ______ Date ______

Exploration and Expansion

Section 2

MAIN IDEA
The countries of Europe established colonies in the lands they had discovered, but in some cases only after violently conquering the native people who lived there.

Key Terms and People

encomienda Spanish system in which a colonist received land and Native American workers to whom he was required to teach Christianity

Hernán Cortés Spanish explorer and conqueror of Mexico's Aztec empire

conquistador Spanish term for conqueror; name for Spanish military leaders who fought against the native peoples of the Americas

Moctezuma II Aztec emperor at the time of Cortés's conquest of Mexico

Francisco Pizarro conqueror of Inca Empire in Peru for the Spanish

Atahualpa ruler of Inca Empire killed by Spanish invaders led by Pizarro

viceroys officials who ruled large areas of Spain's American colonies in the king's name

Bartolomé de las Casas Spanish priest who criticized treatment of Native Americans, suggesting that slaves from Africa be used as laborers instead

Treaty of Tordesillas treaty signed in 1493 dividing the Americas between Spain and Portugal along an imaginary line

Taking Notes

As you read the summary, take notes about each country's colonies in a chart like this one.

Location	Description

Modern Era Chapter 2 18 Interactive Reader and Study Guide

CRF: Vocabulary Builder: Section 2

Taking Notes

Spain—Location: Caribbean, Mexico, South America; Description: Aztec Empire, Inca Empire, gold, silver, farming; Portugal—Location: Brazil; Description: heavy jungles made mining and farming difficult; France—Location: New France, or Canada, south into North America; Description: rich in fish, furs, fewer colonists sent there; Netherlands—Location: Hudson River valley; Description: small settlement; England—Location: Virginia, Massachusetts; Description: marshy ground, impure water

go.hrw.com
Online Resources
KEYWORD: SHL EXP
ACTIVITY: Exploration and Expansion

SECTION 2

Conquest and Colonies

Before You Read

Main Idea
The countries of Europe established colonies in the lands they had discovered but, in some cases, only after violently conquering the native people who lived there.

Reading Focus
1. How did Spain build an empire in the Americas?
2. What kind of colony did the Portuguese establish in Brazil?
3. What was life like in the French, Dutch, and English colonies in the Americas?

Key Terms and People
encomienda
Hernán Cortés
conquistador
Moctezuma II
Francisco Pizarro
Atahualpa
viceroys
Bartolomé de Las Casas
Treaty of Tordesillas

TAKING NOTES For each country you read about, take notes about its colonies in a chart like this one.

Location	Description

A FATEFUL MEETING

◀ **The meeting between Cortés and Moctezuma was marked by the exchange of gifts.**

Miniature of the meeting of Cortés and Moctezuma, from *History of the Indians*, by Diego Duran, 1579

THE INSIDE STORY ***What happened when the Aztec king met Europeans for the first time?*** In 1519 Spaniard Hernán Cortés led a small force of soldiers into the interior of Mexico. His intention was to establish a Spanish colony there. Once in Mexico, he heard many tales of the powerful Aztec Empire and its mighty leader, Emperor Moctezuma II. Cortés and his troops set out to meet the emperor for themselves.

Just as Cortés had heard tales of Moctezuma, so the Aztec emperor had heard of the Spaniard. As Cortés neared the Aztec capital of Tenochtitlán, Moctezuma and his advisers headed out to meet him. According to one account, the two men met for the first time on one of the bridges that linked the island city to the mainland. Moctezuma, carried on a litter by four servants, was a magnificent sight. Draped in gold and precious stones, he was shaded by a canopy of green feathers decorated with more gold and stones.

As he approached Moctezuma, Cortés dismounted from his horse and bowed deeply. Moctezuma returned the bow, and the two leaders exchanged gifts. Cortés presented Moctezuma with an elaborate necklace of perfumed glass beads, receiving in return wreaths and garlands of flowers, gold collars, and other items. Through interpreters, the men exchanged greetings and respectful comments.

The meeting of the Aztecs and the Europeans changed society in the region forever. Before long, Moctezuma was dead, and the Spanish and Aztecs were at war. Aztec dominance was ending, and a new society was forming. ■

Teach the Main Idea

At Level

Conquest and Colonies

1. **Teach** Ask students the Reading Focus questions to teach this section.
2. **Apply** Have students create a time line of the major events in this section. Student time lines should begin with Cortés's expedition in 1519 and end with war between the British and French in 1754.
3. **Review** Review student time lines as a class. Have students identify the kinds of conflicts that might be expected to arise among the European nations colonizing the Americas.
4. **Practice/Homework** Each of the European nations that established colonies in the Americas had its own distinct system of governing its colonies. Have each student decide which nation's colony he or she would have preferred to live in and write a brief essay explaining why. **LS Visual-Spatial, Verbal-Linguistic**

Alternative Assessment Handbook, Rubrics 36: Time Lines; and 40: Writing to Describe

Spain Builds an Empire

After European explorers reached the Americas, countries began to scramble to establish colonies and empires in the lands they had found. Among the first countries to successfully settle in the Americas was Spain, which eventually conquered the two greatest native empires of the Americas, the Aztecs and Incas.

Spain in the Caribbean The first areas settled by the Spanish were Caribbean islands such as Hispaniola and Cuba. When Columbus first arrived in the area, he had hoped to find huge quantities of gold. In this, he was disappointed. However, the Spanish still hoped to make his discovery profitable by introducing the ***encomienda*** system to the Caribbean.

In the *encomienda* system, a colonist was given a certain amount of land and a number of Native Americans to work the land for him. In exchange, the colonist was required to teach the native workers about Christianity. This system became the basis for nearly all Spanish settlements on the mainland as well.

The *encomienda* system was disastrous for Native Americans. Overwork and mistreatment took a horrendous toll on the native population. Even worse, however, were the diseases spread by Europeans. Smallpox, tuberculosis, measles, and other deadly diseases had previously been unknown in the Americas. For this reason, Native Americans had no resistance to these illnesses, and millions died.

The Conquest of Mexico From the Caribbean some Spaniards moved to the mainland to set up colonies. One such person was **Hernán Cortés**, who led an expedition to Mexico that ended with the conquest of the Aztec Empire. Cortés was a **conquistador**, or conqueror, a term applied to Spanish military leaders who fought against the native peoples of the Americas.

At the time of the Spanish arrival in Mexico, the Aztec emperor was **Moctezuma II**. Though the Aztecs were very powerful and ruled much of Mexico, they were unpopular with those they had conquered. Cortés was able to use this lack of popularity to his advantage. By the time he reached the Aztec capital, Tenochtitlán, Cortés's small band of Spanish soldiers had been joined by thousands of Native Americans who wanted to defeat the Aztecs.

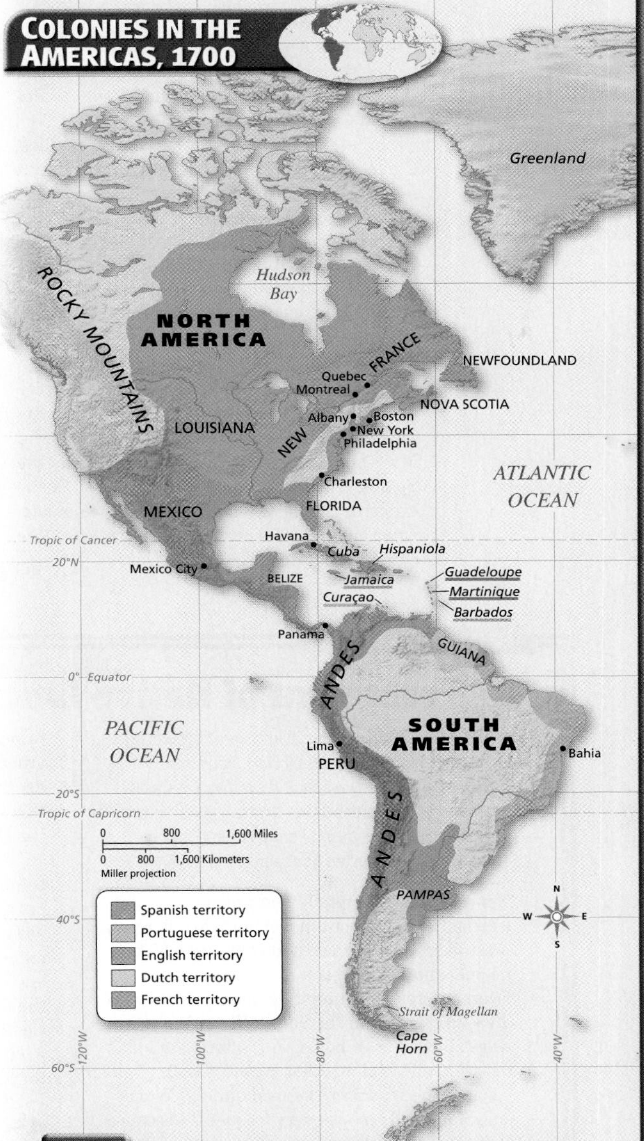

GEOGRAPHY SKILLS INTERPRETING MAPS

1. **Regions** Which countries established colonies in North America? Which had colonies on Caribbean islands?
2. **Place** Which European country controlled the most territory in the Americas?

Direct Teach

Reading Focus

❶ How did Spain build an empire in the Americas? *introduced* encomienda *system, conquered Aztec and Inca empires, viceroys governed land*

Spain Builds an Empire

Identify What was the *encomienda* system? *system in which a colonist was given land and Native Americans to work the land for him*

Make Inferences Why did Cortés find Malinche useful? *because she could serve as a translator between the Spanish and the Aztecs*

Predict What will be the outcome of Cortés's conquest of Tenochtitlán? *Mexico will become a major Spanish colony.*

Map Transparency: Colonies in the Americas

CRF: Biography: Isabella I

CRF: Primary Source: An Aztec Account of the Spanish Arrival in Tenochtitlán

Info to Know

Tenochtitlán In his letters, Hernán Cortés described Tenochtitlán: "This city has many squares where trading is done and markets are held continuously. There is also one square … where every kind of merchandise produced in these lands is found…. There are shops like apothecaries', where they sell ready-made medicines as well as liquid ointments and plasters. There are shops like barbers' where they have their hair washed and shaved, and shops where they sell food and drink."

Differentiating Instruction

Above Level

Advanced Learners/Gifted and Talented

Research Required

1. Have students research at least one aspect of either the Aztec or Inca civilization at the time the conquistadors first arrived, such as religion, architecture, or agriculture.
2. Tell students that they are members of either Cortés's expedition in Mexico or Pizarro's expedition in Peru, depending on the civilization they researched. Have students write a series of journal entries describing the civilization they discovered from the point of view of a 16th-century European encountering it for the first time.
3. Have volunteers read their journal entries to the class.
4. Guide students in a discussion of the Aztec and Inca cultures based on their research. How were these cultures different than the culture of the Europeans who conquered them? **LS Verbal-Linguistic**

Alternative Assessment Handbook, Rubrics 30: Research; and 42: Writing to Inform

Answers

Interpreting Maps 1. *North America—France, Spain, England; Caribbean—France, Spain, England, the Netherlands;* **2.** *Spain*

Direct Teach

Reading Focus

Spain Builds an Empire

Recall What two major empires did the conquistadors encounter in the Americas? *Aztec and Inca*

Evaluate What do you think was the motive of the Spanish in seeking to convert the Indians to Christianity? *possible answer—They probably believed that they were saving the Indians' souls and "civilizing" them.*

Info to Know

Aztec and Inca Unrest in the Aztec and Inca Empires contributed to their defeat by the Spanish. Both groups had built their empires in the 1400s, often through the conquest of their neighbors, and both had to put down frequent rebellions in the decades that followed. The Inca were in the midst of a civil war when the Spanish arrived in 1530. Cortés and Pizarro exploited such tensions among native peoples to gain control of both empires.

Among the Native Americans who joined Cortés was a woman named Malintzin, also called Malinche. Because she was able to speak the Aztec language, Malintzin became invaluable to Cortés as a translator.

In addition to his Native American allies, Cortés had several other advantages that helped him defeat the Aztecs. He had metal weapons and heavy armor, neither of which was known to the Aztecs, as well as guns. Also, Cortés and a few of his soldiers rode horses, animals never before seen in the Americas. Some Aztecs were so scared at their first sight of the horses that they fled in terror. As it had in the Caribbean, disease also swept through the Aztec Empire, killing thousands of people.

On November 8, 1519, Cortés and his army entered Tenochtitlán. Though Cortés and Moctezuma greeted each other respectfully, the Spanish soon took the emperor prisoner. Battle erupted, during which Moctezuma was killed. After months of heavy fighting, Cortés took the city and the entire Aztec Empire.

The Conquest of Peru About 10 years after the conquest of the Aztecs, a conquistador named **Francisco Pizarro** led an expedition to Peru. Pizarro had heard of the fabulous wealth of Peru's Inca Empire, and he hoped to win some of that wealth for himself.

The Inca Empire that Pizarro found was already weakened significantly. Smallpox had recently swept through, killing many people, including the emperor. In the wake of the emperor's death, civil war had broken out. A new ruler, **Atahualpa**, had only just taken control of the empire when the Spanish arrived.

Atahualpa heard of the Spaniards' arrival and agreed to meet with them in 1532. At that meeting, Pizarro demanded that Atahualpa accept Christianity and hand over his empire to Spain. Atahualpa refused, and the Spanish took him prisoner. Though Atahualpa gave Pizarro a huge fortune in gold and silver, the Spanish killed him and headed south to Cuzco, the Inca capital. There they destroyed the Inca army and took over the empire.

PRIMARY SOURCES

The Treatment of Native Americans

Bartolomé de Las Casas was vocal in his protests of the treatment of Native Americans by Europeans. In his *Brief Account of the Destruction of the Indies*, Las Casas described the terrible ordeals that the Native Americans faced as forced laborers, despite orders from the king of Spain that they be protected and taught Christianity.

"The Indians were totally deprived of their freedom and were put in the harshest, fiercest, most horrible servitude and captivity which no one who has not seen it can understand. Even beasts enjoy more freedom when they are allowed to graze in the fields. When the Indians were allowed to go home, they often found it deserted and had no other recourse than to go out into the woods to find food and die. When they fell ill, which was very frequently because they are a delicate people unaccustomed to such work, the Spaniards did not believe them and pitilessly called them lazy dogs, and kicked and beat them; and when illness was apparent they sent them home as useless. I sometimes came upon dead bodies on my way, and upon others who were gasping and moaning in their death agony, repeating "Hungry, hungry." And this was the freedom, the good treatment, and the Christianity that Indians received.

Is there a single nation which would not think that the world is full of just such evildoers as the Spaniards if their first experience with that outside world was with a people who entered territories by force, killed the people, and deprived them of their rights? Just because the Spaniards told them to obey the King of Castile [Spain], supposing they understood, what obligation did they have to obey since they already had their own kings?"

Skills Focus READING LIKE A HISTORIAN

1. **Analyze** According to Las Casas, how have the Spanish mistreated Native Americans?
2. **Draw Conclusions** For what audience do you think Las Casas was writing? What makes you think so?

See **Skills Handbook**, p. H25

Skills Focus: Identifying Problem and Solution

At Level

Reading Skill

Governing the Spanish Colonies in America

1. Guide students in a discussion of the *encomienda* system. How did the intentions of the *encomienda* system compare with the reality of it?
2. Organize students into small groups. Tell students they are advisers to the Spanish monarchs charged with developing a new system to replace the *encomienda* system. Have each group write a plan that will treat Native Americans well and still allow development of the colonies. Each system should have a means of enforcing the requirement to treat natives well.
3. Have volunteers from each group share their plans with the rest of the class.

LS Interpersonal, Verbal-Linguistic

Alternative Assessment Handbook, Rubrics 14: Group Activity; and 35: Solving Problems

Answers

Primary Sources **1.** *deprived them of freedom and made them slaves; mistreated them when they were ill and dying;* **2.** *possible answer—future Spanish colonists, because he implies that the Indians may fight back if they continue to suffer mistreatment*

Life in the Spanish Empire With the conquests of Mexico and Peru, Spain gained control of a huge empire in the Americas. To govern his American holdings, the Spanish king chose officials called **viceroys**, each of whom ruled a large area in the king's name.

The Spanish colonial economy was based largely on the mining of gold and silver, though farming was also common. For labor in both mines and on farms, the Spanish drafted Native Americans. However, disease and mistreatment took a toll on the native population, which dropped by more than 90 percent from an estimated 50 million to only 4 million.

Some Spaniards were appalled at the treatment of Native Americans and called on others to protect those who remained. The most vocal of these reformers was a priest named **Bartolomé de Las Casas**. In seeking to protect the Native Americans, however, Las Casas recommended replacing them as laborers with imported African slaves. Slave labor soon became a common practice in the Americas.

READING CHECK **Summarize** How did the Spanish create an empire in the Americas?

The Portuguese in Brazil

Like the Spanish, the Portuguese built an empire in the Americas. However, because of a treaty signed early in the Age of Exploration, their empire was not nearly as large as the Spanish one. The **Treaty of Tordesillas**, signed in 1494, drew an imaginary line through the Atlantic. Everything to the west of this line, including most of the then-undiscovered Americas, would belong to Spain. Everything to the east would be Portuguese. Of the Americas, only Brazil remained as a Portuguese colony.

Brazil's heavy jungles made both mining and farming difficult, so the Portuguese were in no hurry to settle there. Only in the 1530s did colonists slowly begin to move in, mostly along the Atlantic coast. When colonists did finally arrive, they established huge farming estates similar to those in the Spanish lands. Like the Spanish, the Portuguese first used Native American labor and then African slaves to work on their farms.

READING CHECK **Explain** Why did few colonists originally move to Brazil?

Shooting the Rapids, by Frances Anne Hopkins, c. 1879

French Traders

Most people who moved to French colonies in North America were traders, not settlers. ***What does this image suggest about life in French colonies?***

French, Dutch, and English Colonies in the Americas

As silver and gold from Spain's and Portugal's American colonies began to circulate throughout Europe, other European countries paid close attention. Leaders in France, England, and the Netherlands decided that they, too, needed to establish colonies in the Americas.

New France French explorers had established several colonies in an area known as New France, or Canada. The French hoped that this colony would be as rich a source of gold and silver as the Spanish lands to the south.

Although the French were disappointed in their hope of finding gold, silver, and other riches, they found other potentially valuable trade goods. For example, the waters of the North Atlantic were swarming with fish, a staple of the European diet. In addition, the forests yielded valuable furs. Fox, lynx, otter, and other furs, especially beaver, sold for high prices in Europe.

Unlike the Spanish and Portuguese, the French did not send large numbers of colonists to the Americas. Only small groups of traders moved across the sea. As a result, the French population in North America remained small.

THE IMPACT TODAY

Portuguese is still the official language of Brazil today.

Direct Teach

Reading Focus

2 What kind of colony did the Portuguese establish in Brazil? *a farming colony*

The Portuguese in Brazil

Identify What land did the Treaty of Tordesillas give to Portugal? *everything to the east of an imaginary line in the Atlantic; this ended up being Brazil*

Identify Cause and Effect What made farming and mining difficult in Brazil? *heavy jungles*

Reading Focus

3 What was life like in the French, Dutch, and English colonies in the Americas? *based on trade, fishing, furs*

French, Dutch, and English Colonies in the Americas

Contrast How did French explorations to the Americas differ from those of the Spanish and Porteugese? *The French sent small groups of traders, not large groups of colonists.*

Draw Conclusions Why did leaders in France, England, and the Netherlands decide they could no longer ignore the potential of the land to the west? *They saw the riches Spain was getting from its American colonies; they also still hoped to find a western route to Asia.*

Skills Focus: Analyzing Maps

At Level

Social Studies Skill

Europeans in the Americas

Materials: outline maps of the Americas

1. Organize students into small groups. Distribute outline maps to each group. Have students use the map Colonies in the Americas and information in this chapter to place the following on their maps: the names of the Europeans who first explored each region, their nationality, and the dates of their explorations.
2. Review student maps as a class.
3. Guide students in a discussion of each European nation's reasons for wanting to explore the Americas. **LS Interpersonal, Visual-Spatial**

Alternative Assessment Handbook, Rubrics 14: Group Activity; and 20: Map Creation

Answers

French Traders *possible answers—fishing was important; mostly male settlers*

Reading Check (top) *conquered Aztec and Inca empires; appointed viceroys to govern;* **(bottom)** *Heavy jungles made farming and mining difficult.*

Direct Teach

Reading Focus

French, Dutch, and English Colonies in the Americas

Identify What were the major French possessions in North America, and where were they located? *New France included possessions along the St. Lawrence River, Newfoundland, and Nova Scotia. Louisiana was the region of the Mississippi River and its tributaries.*

Draw Conclusions Why do you think the French did not enslave the Native Americans? *possible answer—Native Americans were important allies, helping the French to hunt animals.*

Activity **Attracting Settlers** Have students design their own recruiting slogan or flyer to attract settlers to Virginia. **LS Visual-Spatial**

Alternative Assessment Handbook, Rubric 34: Slogans and Banners

Also unlike the Spanish and Portuguese, the French did not enslave Native Americans. In fact, Native American hunters were the French traders' main source of furs, and they often became allies. Many French traders even married Native American women, intermingling the two cultures.

From New France, a few French explorers headed south to seek out more lands they could claim. Samuel de Champlain, for example, founded the city of Quebec in 1608. The French also explored the Mississippi River, which they believed flowed to the Pacific and thus would provide them with a route to Asia. Eventually, they realized their error. In 1682 René-Robert La Salle canoed down the entire Mississippi River to the Gulf of Mexico. La Salle claimed the enormous Mississippi region and its tributaries for France. He named this huge, fertile area Louisiana, after the king, Louis XIV.

The Dutch of New Netherland Like the French, the Dutch colonists who came to North America were mostly interested in trade. The only large Dutch colony in North America was New Netherland, located in the Hudson River valley. In 1626 the governor of New Netherland bought the island of Manhattan from the Wappinger people and founded the city of New Amsterdam, which later became New York City. The settlement remained small for some time, with fewer than 4,000 people in all of New Netherland in the 1650s.

One reason that New Netherland did not grow was that the Dutch were more focused on developing their colonies in other parts of the world. Those colonies were more profitable for the Dutch because they produced goods that could not be obtained in Europe or the Americas. For example, Dutch colonies in the Caribbean produced sugar. Even more valuable were the spices that the Dutch imported from their colonies in southeast Asia.

Reading like a Historian

Recruiting Colonists

Analyzing Primary Sources Posters and pamphlets can be important sources of information about the past. Such documents can tell us about what people considered important and how they tried to persuade others to agree with them.

To examine the meaning of a poster or a pamphlet, think about

- the creator of the document
- the purpose of the document
- the facts and evidence used to support the creator's ideas

Skills Focus READING LIKE A HISTORIAN

1. **Creator** Who was the creator of the pamphlet shown here? Who was the pamphlet's intended audience?
2. **Purpose** For what purpose was this pamphlet created?
3. **Facts and Evidence** What facts did the creators of the pamphlet use to try to convince people to listen to them?

See **Skills Handbook**, p. H25

Nova Britannia, or New England, was a name given to the English colonies in North America.

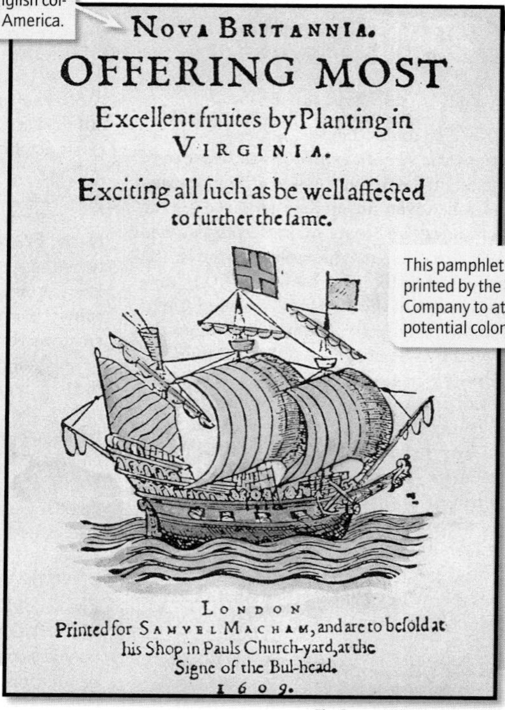
NOVA BRITANNIA.
OFFERING MOST
Excellent fruites by Planting in
VIRGINIA.
Exciting all ſuch as be well affected
to further the ſame.
LONDON
Printed for SAMVEL MACHAM, and are to be ſold at
his Shop in Pauls Church-yard, at the
Signe of the Bul-head.
1609.

This pamphlet was printed by the Virginia Company to attract potential colonists.

The Granger Collection, New York

Collaborative Learning

At Level

Colonial Life

Research Required

1. Organize students into small groups. Have each group research life in the early Spanish, Portuguese, French, Dutch, or English colonies in the Americas. Then have students write skits portraying scenes from everyday life in one of the colonies, including typical interactions between native people and the colonists. To ensure variety, you might wish to assign a nation to each group.
2. Have each group present its skit to the class.
3. Guide students in a discussion of life in the various early European colonies in the Americas. **LS Interpersonal, Kinesthetic**

Alternative Assessment Handbook, Rubrics 30: Research; and 33: Skits and Reader's Theater

Answers

Reading Like a Historian **1.** *the Virginia Company; potential colonists;* **2.** *to attract potential colonists;* **3.** *that farming was good, that the colonial life was exciting*

The English Colonies The English, too, set out to establish colonies in America. The first English colony was established at Jamestown, Virginia, in 1607. The settlers of Jamestown hoped to find gold and silver and possibly a river route to the Pacific. Instead, they found marshy ground and impure water. Some 80 percent of the settlers of Jamestown died during their first winter in America. Nevertheless, the colony endured.

In 1620 another group of settlers called the Pilgrims sailed from England. The Pilgrims, who had been persecuted in England for their religious beliefs, established a colony at Plymouth, Massachusetts. Despite initial difficulties, the Pilgrims persevered, and the settlement was self-sufficient within five years.

The English settlers did not share the same relationship with Native Americans as the French and Dutch. Although both the Jamestown and Plymouth colonies had received aid from local peoples during their early years, most English colonists viewed the Native Americans with distrust or even anger.

British-French Conflict The English also ran into conflict with French settlers in the Americas. In the mid-1700s English colonists began attempting to settle in French territory in the upper Ohio River valley. Tension between English and French settlers in the region grew, until war broke out in 1754. On one side were the English, and on the other were the French, though each side also had Native American allies. For that reason, the English named the conflict the French and Indian War.

At first, the war went badly for the British. The French had many more soldiers in America than they did. Before long, however, the British had turned the tide, taking the city of Quebec. Eventually, the French surrendered, yielding to England not only Canada but all French territory east of the Mississippi River.

Although the British now controlled much more of North America than they had before, the war had been very costly. The English king tried to place the costs of the war on his American colonists, which led to resentment on their part. Eventually, this resentment helped bring about the American Revolution.

READING CHECK **Sequence** What series of events led to the French and Indian War?

Causes and Effects of the French and Indian War

QUICK FACTS

CAUSES

- The English tried to settle on land in the Americas that had been claimed by the French.
- Native American groups allied with each side to fight their opponents.

EFFECTS

- The French lost nearly all of their territory in North America, including Canada.
- Great Britain amassed huge debts, which the British tried to recoup from the colonies.

Section 2 Assessment

go.hrw.com
Online Quiz
Keyword: SHL EXP HP

Reviewing Ideas, Terms, and People

1. **a. Identify** Who were **Hernán Cortés** and **Francisco Pizarro**? How did their actions shape Spain's empire in the Americas?
   b. Explain Why was the ***encomienda*** system originally created? What effect did it ultimately have on American society?
   c. Elaborate How might the history of Mexico and South America have been different if the Spanish had not discovered gold and silver there?
2. **a. Describe** What economic activities took place in Portuguese Brazil?
   b. Compare and Contrast What was one way in which Portuguese and Spanish colonies were similar? What was one way in which they differed?
3. **a. Describe** What was the main resource in France's colonies?
   b. Make Generalizations How did French and Dutch colonists relate to Native Americans? How did the English relate to Native Americans?
   c. Extend How did the French and Indian War shape American history?

Critical Thinking

4. **Analyze** Draw a chart like the one below. Using your notes, fill in the chart with details about each country's colonies: their locations, the activities that took place, and the colonists' relations with Native Americans.

	Location	Activities	Relations
Spain			
Portugal			
France			
Netherlands			
England			

FOCUS ON WRITING

5. **Exposition** The opinions of Bartolomé de Las Casas were influential in alerting Europeans to the treatment of Native Americans. Write a short paragraph explaining what his opinions were and how they affected attitudes in Europe.

Direct Teach

Causes and Effects of the French and Indian War

QUICK FACTS

Elaborate Why do you think the French and Indian War was so costly to the British? *possible answer—The French had more soldiers in America, so the British probably had to send reinforcements to defeat them.*

Quick Facts Transparency: Causes and Effects of the French and Indian War

Review & Assess

Close

Have students summarize the characteristics of each European nation's drive for conquest and colonies in the New World.

Review

Online Quiz, Section 2

Assess

SE Section 2 Assessment

Progress Assessment: Section 2 Quiz

Alternative Assessment Handbook

Reteach/Intervene

Interactive Reader and Study Guide, Section 2

Interactive Skills Tutor CD-ROM

Answers

Reading Check *English attempted to settle in Ohio River valley, tension grew between English and French, Native Americans allied with each side*

Section 2 Assessment Answers

1. **a.** Spanish conquistadors; conquered Aztec and Inca empires, claimed their land
   b. as a way to make the colonies profitable; resulted in the deaths of many Native Americans
   c. possible answer—Aztec and Inca empires might have continued.
2. **a.** farming
   b. similar—used Native Americans as laborers; different—no mining in Portuguese colonies
3. **a.** furs
   b. French—became allies with them; Dutch—purchased land from them; English—received help from Native Americans but still distrusted them
   c. made the territory mostly belong to England
4. Spain—Mexico, South America; conquest; harmful; Portugal—Brazil; farming; used laborers; France—North America; fishing and farming; allied with them; Netherlands—North America; trade; purchased land from them; England—North America; farming, search for gold and silver; received aid from them but distrusted them
5. believed Native Americans were mistreated; wanted future settlers to treat them better

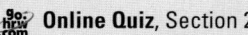

Preteach

Getting Started

Use the **Interactive Reader and Study Guide** to familiarize students with the section content.

Interactive Reader and Study Guide, Section 3

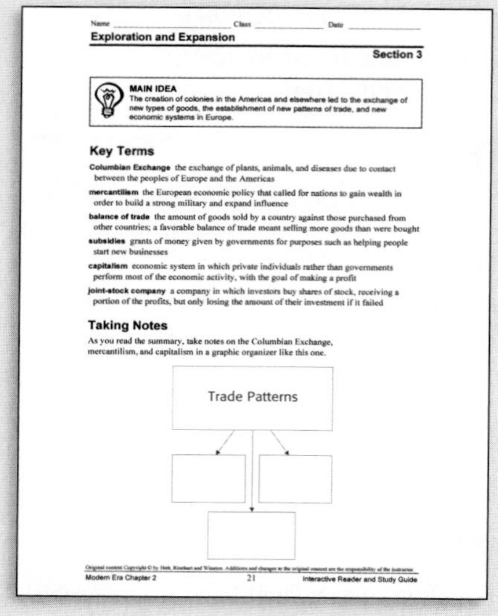

Name ____________ Class ____________ Date ____________

Exploration and Expansion

Section 3

MAIN IDEA
The creation of colonies in the Americas and elsewhere led to the exchange of new types of goods, the establishment of new patterns of trade, and new economic systems in Europe.

Key Terms

Columbian Exchange the exchange of plants, animals, and diseases due to contact between the peoples of Europe and the Americas

mercantilism the European economic policy that called for nations to gain wealth in order to build a strong military and expand influence

balance of trade the amount of goods sold by a country against those purchased from other countries; a favorable balance of trade meant selling more goods than were bought

subsidies grants of money given by governments for purposes such as helping people start new businesses

capitalism economic system in which private individuals rather than governments perform most of the economic activity, with the goal of making a profit

joint-stock company a company in which investors buy shares of stock, receiving a portion of the profits, but only losing the amount of their investment if it failed

Taking Notes

As you read the summary, take notes on the Columbian Exchange, mercantilism, and capitalism in a graphic organizer like this one.

Trade Patterns

Academic Vocabulary

Review with students the high-use academic term in this section.

intermittent happening from time to time, not constant (p. 484)

CRF: Vocabulary Builder: Section 3

Taking Notes

Columbian Exchange—widespread exchange of plants, animals and disease between the societies of Europe and the Americas; effects also felt in Africa and Asia; Mercantilism—system based on the idea that a nation's strength depended upon its wealth; needed favorable balance of trade; colonies helped provide raw materials, new markets; Capitalism—system in which most economic activity is carried on by private individuals or organizations seeking profit; joint-stock companies were one example of capitalism in the colonies

SECTION 3

New Patterns of Trade

Before You Read

Main Idea

The creation of colonies in the Americas and elsewhere led to the exchange of new types of goods, the establishment of new patterns of trade, and new economic systems in Europe.

Reading Focus

1. How did exploration result in a new exchange of plants and animals?
2. What was mercantilism, and how did it push the drive to establish colonies?
3. How did global trade lead to the rise of capitalism in Europe?

Key Terms

Columbian Exchange
mercantilism
balance of trade
subsidies
capitalism
joint-stock companies

TAKING NOTES Take notes on the Columbian Exchange, mercantilism, and capitalism in a graphic organizer like this one.

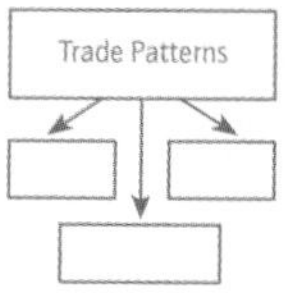

Europe's FIRST TASTE of CHOCOLATE

Painted tile showing chocolate drinkers, from Barcelona, Spain, 1790

▲ **Chocolate was first introduced in Europe as a drink, not as a candy or dessert.**

THE INSIDE STORY ***Why didn't many Europeans like chocolate?*** Before the 1500s the people of Europe had never tasted chocolate. Cacao, the bean from which chocolate is made, is native to the Americas. Until the Europeans arrived in South America during the Age of Exploration, they had never had a chance to sample the sweet treat.

Chocolate did not make much of an impression on Europeans at first. Christopher Columbus actually brought a few cacao beans back to Europe after his first voyage, but because the beans looked unimpressive—few people even noticed them. In the Americas, however, cacao was not only used in a popular beverage but also as a form of currency.

The use of cacao beans as money brought them to the attention of Hernán Cortés during his conquest of the Aztecs. Cortés actually sampled chocolate but did not like it; the chocolate drink made by the Aztecs included neither sugar nor milk and was considered bitter by the Europeans.

Chocolate did not come to the attention of many people in Europe until a few years later. Later, Europeans thought to mix the bitter drink with milk and sugar to produce something similar to modern hot chocolate. When a group of Dominican friars brought this new, sweeter chocolate drink to the court of Prince Philip of Spain, it became an instant hit. Chocolate became one of the favored drinks of the Spanish nobility. Because cacao was grown only in the Americas, the drink was very expensive, which added to its prestige. Chocolate remained a treat that only the very rich could afford, and drinking it was a sign of high status. ■

Teach the Main Idea

At Level

New Patterns of Trade

1. **Teach** Ask students the Reading Focus questions to teach this section.
2. **Apply** Have students create an outline of the section using the heads as main points. Have students identify at least two main ideas under each of the red subheadings.
3. **Review** Review student outlines as a class. Have students identify the points in their outlines they feel are most important or most interesting. Guide students in a discussion of the ways in which new business practices affected European nations' desire for colonial empires.
4. **Practice/Homework** Have students answer the following question in a brief essay: Which side gained the most as a result of the Columbian Exchange, or did both sides benefit equally? **LS Visual-Spatial, Verbal-Linguistic**

Alternative Assessment Handbook, Rubrics 11: Discussions; and 43: Writing to Express

The Columbian Exchange

QUICK FACTS

From the Americas

Animals
- guinea pigs
- llamas
- turkeys

Plants
- avocados
- beans
- cashews
- chili peppers
- chocolate
- corn
- papayas
- peanuts
- pecans
- pineapples
- potatoes
- rubber
- squash
- strawberries
- sweet potatoes
- tobacco
- tomatoes
- vanilla

From Europe, Africa, and Asia

Animals
- cattle
- chickens
- donkeys
- goats
- horses
- housecats
- mice and rats
- pigs
- rabbits
- sheep

Plants
- bananas
- black pepper
- citrus fruits
- coffee
- garlic and onions
- lettuce
- peaches and pears
- sugar
- wheat, rye, and oats

Diseases
- cholera
- influenza
- malaria
- measles
- smallpox

The Columbian Exchange

The voyages of Christopher Columbus and those that followed launched a period of large-scale contact between the societies of Europe and of the Americas. The arrival of colonists and their interaction with Native Americans led to sweeping cultural changes in both societies. Over time, contact between the two groups led to the widespread exchange of plants, animals, and disease. Historians call this global transfer the **Columbian Exchange**.

The Exchange of Goods Because of the physical isolation between the Eastern and Western Hemispheres, plants and animals had developed in very different ways. As a result, before contact with the Americas Europeans had never known foods like potatoes, corn, sweet potatoes, or turkeys. Peoples in the Americas had not known coffee, oranges, rice, wheat, sheep, or cattle.

The arrival of Europeans in the Americas changed that. Previously unknown foods were brought from the Americas—what Europeans of the time called the New World—back to Europe, as colonists were eager to share new discoveries. At the same time, colonists brought familiar foods from the so-called Old World to the Americas with them, which resulted in items previously unknown in the Americas being introduced there.

New foods were not the only benefit that resulted from the Columbian Exchange. The introduction of beasts of burden, especially horses, to the Americas was a significant development. Before European contact, almost the only domesticated beast of burden in the Americas was the llama, which lived only in the Andes. The introduction of the horse provided people in the rest of the Americas with a new source of labor and transportation.

Effects of the Columbian Exchange

The exchange of foods and animals had a dramatic impact on later societies. Over time, crops native to the Americas, such as corn and potatoes, became staples in the diets of people in Europe and other parts of the world. These foods provided substantial nutrition and helped people live longer. Also, later economic activities such as Texas cattle ranching or Brazilian coffee growing would not have been possible without the Columbian Exchange, since both cows and coffee were native to the Old World.

Even traditional cuisines changed because of the Columbian Exchange. Who today could imagine Italian food without tomatoes? Until contact with the Americas, however, Europeans had never tried tomatoes. In fact, most Europeans viewed tomatoes with suspicion when they first arrived from America, thinking them poisonous. By the late 1600s, however, tomatoes had begun to be included in Italian cookbooks.

Direct Teach

Reading Focus

1 How did exploration result in a new exchange of plants and animals? *As contact increased between Europe and the Americas, plants, animals, and disease traveled from one part of the world to another.*

The Columbian Exchange

Explain How did the Columbian Exchange work? *Europeans transported plants, animals, people, and diseases between the Eastern and Western hemispheres.*

Identify Cause and Effect What were the results of the Columbian Exchange? *New economic activities grew up and national cuisines changed. However, diseases brought to the Americas by Europeans wiped out much of the native population.*

Make Judgments If the Columbian Exchange had not taken place, would you rather have lived in the Old World or the New World? Why? *possible answer—the New World; the fruits, nuts, and vegetables found there tasted better than those found in the Old World*

Quick Facts Transparency: The Columbian Exchange

CRF: Biography: Pocahontas

Teaching Tip

Some students may not know what the items are on the Columbian Exchange chart. Review each term on the chart or have students use an illustrated dictionary to look up each new term.

Skills Focus: Comparing and Contrasting

Below Level

Reading Skill
The Columbian Exchange

Materials: blank note cards, tacks, or tape

1. Organize students into small groups. Give each group a list of plants and/or animals from the two lists in the Quick Facts chart on this page along with a stack of note cards. Each member of the group should have one item and one card.
2. Have groups find pictures of the plants and animals on their lists. Have each student draw and label one of the plants or animals on a card.
3. Create two display areas for all to see and label them "New World" and "Old World."
4. Collect all the cards, shuffle them, and hand them back so that each student gets one card. Have students tack or tape their cards in the appropriate area. **LS Interpersonal, Visual-Spatial**

Alternative Assessment Handbook, Rubrics 3: Artwork; and 14: Group Activity

Direct Teach

Reading Focus

2 What was mercantilism, and how did it push the drive to establish colonies? *system based on the idea that a nation's strength was based on its wealth; colonies helped provide wealth*

Mercantilism

Summarize How did the desire to create a favorable balance of trade help lead to the establishment of colonies? *European powers wanted to establish colonies so that they could control sources of raw materials and to provide new markets for manufactured goods.*

Elaborate How did the establishment of colonies in the New World lead to inflation? *Shiploads of gold and silver flowed to Europe from the Americas. They were made into new coins, increasing the amount of money in circulation. The increase of money pushed the prices of goods higher.*

Quick Facts Transparency: Basic Principles of Mercantilism

Effects of the Columbian Exchange were felt not only in Europe and the Americas. Africa and Asia, too, changed as a result of the exchange. For example, the arrival of corn, an easy-to-grow, nutritious crop, in China helped that country's population grow tremendously. China was also one of the main consumers of the silver mined in the Americas. In Africa, two crops native to the Americas, corn and peanuts, are still among the continent's most widely grown products. In fact, scholars estimate that a full one-third of all food crops grown around the world today are of American origin.

ACADEMIC VOCABULARY
intermittent happening from time to time, not constant

The Introduction of New Diseases Even more disastrous than overdependence on new foods were the diseases brought to the Americas by Europeans. As you read in the previous section, the Native Americans had no natural resistance to European diseases such as smallpox, measles, influenza, and malaria. Those diseases killed millions of Native Americans. A few new diseases were introduced in Europe as well, but they were much less deadly.

Often, the first epidemics following the arrival of Europeans were the most severe. By 1518 or 1519, for example, smallpox had killed perhaps one-half of the population of Santo Domingo. Historians have estimated that the population of central Mexico decreased by more than 30 per cent in the 10 years following the first contact with Europeans.

Epidemics returned again and again, with even more devastating effects. The Native American population continued to decline in subsequent centuries. Some historians estimate that the Inca Empire decreased from about 13 million people in 1492 to 2 million in 1600. The North American population fell from around 2 million in 1492 to 500,000 by 1900. Disease was not the only factor that led to such a dramatic decrease. Intermittent warfare and other violence contributed. But without question, diseases from Europe had a devastating impact on Native American populations.

READING CHECK **Find the Main Idea** What were two lasting effects of the Columbian Exchange?

Mercantilism

The founding of colonies in the Americas and the introduction of new goods to Europe led to significant changes in the European economy. During the 1500s, for example, Europeans developed a new type of economic policy called **mercantilism**. The basic principle of mercantilism was that a nation's strength depended on its wealth. A wealthy nation had the power to build a strong military to protect itself and expand its influence.

During the mercantilist era, wealth was measured by the amount of gold and silver that a nation possessed. Mercantilists believed that there was a fixed amount of wealth in the world. For one nation to become wealthier—and therefore more powerful—it had to take wealth and power away from another nation. As a result, mercantilism led to intense competition between nations for wealth during the 1500s and 1600s.

Balance of Trade Mercantilists believed that a nation could build wealth in two ways. It could extract gold and silver from mines at home or in its colonies, or it could sell more goods than it bought from foreign countries, thus creating a favorable **balance of trade**. With a favorable balance of trade, a country received more gold and silver from other nations than it paid to them. In the mercantilists' view, this situation increased the nation's power and weakened its foreign competitors. Therefore, a favorable balance of trade became a central goal for many mercantilist countries.

Basic Principles of Mercantilism (Quick Facts)
A nation's strength depends on its wealth as measured in gold and silver.
Only a fixed amount of wealth exists in the world, and nations have to compete for their share of that wealth.
A favorable balance of trade is an important step in gaining wealth.
Countries should seek to limit imports and maximize exports.
A country should have its own source for raw materials and precious metals to avoid dependence on others.
Colonies exist only as a way for the mother country to make profit.
A country's colonies should not trade with any other countries.

Skills Focus: Analyzing Primary Sources

Below Level

Reading Like a Historian Skill
The Columbian Exchange and Cuisine

1. Have students obtain or make copies of menus from local Chinese, Italian, or Mexican restaurants.
2. Have each student choose a meal to "order." Then have students find recipes for each item on his or her "order" and make a list of the ingredients. (Tell students they can ignore the amounts needed for each recipe.)
3. Next, have students identify which ingredients came from the New World and which originated in the Old World.
4. Have volunteers share their lists with the class.
5. Guide students in a discussion of ways in which these recipes illustrate how cuisines were affected by the Columbian Exchange.
LS Verbal-Linguistic

Alternative Assessment Handbook, Rubrics 11: Discussions; and 30: Research

Answers

Reading Check *possible answers—changes in cuisine, changes in crops grown around the world, epidemics*

COUNTERPOINTS

Two Sources on Colonies

European economists believed that the sole purpose of colonies was the make their mother countries rich. If a colony was unprofitable, then it should be abandoned.

“If it should be found impracticable for Great Britain to draw any considerable augmentation of revenue from any of the resources above mentioned; the only resource which can remain to her is a diminution of her expense . . . The expense of the peace establishment of the colonies was, before the commencement of the present disturbances, very considerable, and is an expense which may, and if no revenue can be drawn from them ought certainly to be saved altogether.”

Adam Smith
—*The Wealth of Nations*, 1776

Colonists, on the other hand, felt that they were risking their lives for king and country and should be cared for regardless of the colony's overall profitability.

“Look here, King of Spain! Do not be cruel and ungrateful to your vassals, because while your father and you stayed in Spain without the slightest bother, your vassals, at the price of their blood and fortune, have given you all the kingdoms and holding you have in these parts. Beware, King and lord, that you cannot take, under the title of legitimate king, any benefit from this land where you risked nothing, without first giving due gratification to those who have labored and sweated in it.”

Lope de Aguirre
—Letter to King Philip II of Spain, 1561

Skills FOCUS INVESTIGATING HISTORY

Analyze What was the driving force behind Smith's view of colonies? What force drove Aguirre's views?

A country could do several things to achieve a favorable balance of trade. One approach was to reduce the amount of goods imported from other countries by placing tariffs, or import taxes, on those goods. The importer of a particular good paid the tariff and added that cost to the price of the good. Imported goods were thus often more expensive than similar goods produced within the nation. The higher price, therefore, discouraged people from buying imported goods.

Another approach was to encourage exports that could sell for high prices. For example, manufactured goods sold to other nations fat highers prices than raw materials did. So woolen cloth could be sold at a higher profit than raw wool could. Countries therefore encouraged manufacturing and the export of manufactured goods. Governments provided **subsidies**, or grants of money, to help businesspeople start new industries.

A third approach to achieving a favorable balance of trade was to control overseas sources of raw materials and precious metals. A nation that controlled its own sources of these goods would not need to import them from competing nations. Why was this important? There were two main reasons. First, a country did not need to spend any of its own money on obtaining raw materials. Second, foreign countries were always considered rivals. At any time, a rival might become an active enemy and cut off supplies of raw materials. To minimize that risk, European nations worked to become more self-sufficient. For example, they began to establish colonies in the lands they controlled.

Colonies The building of colonial empires was essential to the mercantilist system. European powers wanted to establish colonies in order to control sources of raw materials and provide new markets for manufactured goods.

READING SKILLS
Questioning As you read, ask yourself how each mercantilist approach could lead to a favorable balance of trade.

Direct Teach

Reading Focus

Mercantilism

Recall Under mercantilism, why did wealthy nations build strong militaries? *to protect themselves and expand their influence*

Summarize How did nations create a favorable balance of trade? *They reduced the amount of import goods by placing tariffs on them. They also encouraged exports, and controlled overseas sources of raw materials and precious metals.*

Info to Know

The Legacy of Mercantilism The world's nations in 1948 launched a major effort to reduce international tensions in patterns of trade and commerce that emerged during mercantilism. A multinational treaty called the General Agreement on Tariffs and Trade (GATT) created a mechanism to reduce tariffs and other economic barriers between nations. Average tariffs on manufactured goods fell from about 40 percent to less than 5 percent by the 1980s, and regions adopted duty-free trade arrangements like the European Union and the North American Free Trade Agreement (NAFTA). However, some nations have introduced new subsidies or import quotas for certain industries or products, in a movement called neomercantilism.

Differentiating Instruction

Below Level

Learners Having Difficulty

1. Copy the diagram for students to see. Omit the italicized answers. Have students copy and complete the diagram.
2. Review student diagrams as a class, filling in the class diagram. Have students correct their own work. Guide students in a discussion of how raw materials and manufactured goods are related, and why markets are needed for manufactured goods. LS **Visual-Spatial**

Alternative Assessment Handbook, Rubrics 11: Discussions; and 13: Graphic Organizers

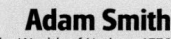

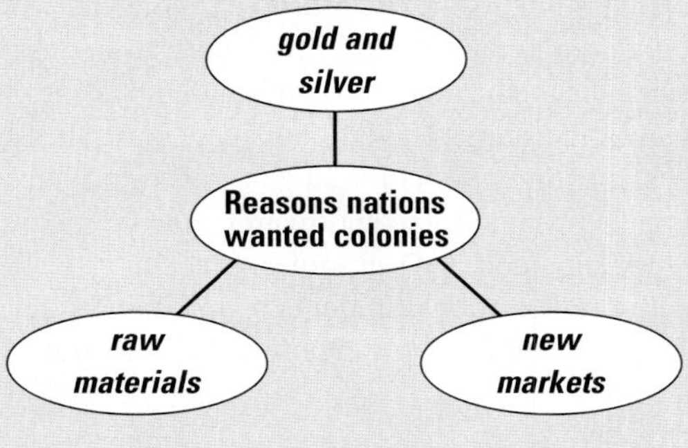

Answers

Counterpoints *Smith—the idea that colonies should make the mother country rich; Aguirre—that colonists should be cared for*

Reading Skills *tariffs—reduced imports; subsidies—increased exports; colonies—brought new markets and new sources of raw materials*

Direct Teach

Reading Focus

Mercantilism

Explain How did European monarchs restrict economic activities in their colonies to make sure that the colonies benefited only the home country? *by forbidding them to sell raw materials to any nation other than the home country; by forcing colonies to buy manufactured goods only from their home countries and forbidding them from manufacturing goods themselves*

Identifying Cause and Effect What was the impact of colonization on European societies? *growth of cities and towns; new class of wealthier merchants who wielded more power*

Info to Know

The New Commercial Economy World exploration led to a new kind of economy in Europe. Goods brought from Africa, Asia, and the New World made many countries in Europe rich. Spices, silks, gold, silver, and precious stones were some of the most sought-after items. The Portuguese, Spanish, and Dutch were the first European powers to build trading empires. Trade and commerce eventually replaced farming as the leading economic activity in Europe. Over time, the new commercial economy generally helped to spread wealth and improve living standards.

Saving and Investing In recent years the U.S. household savings rate has been declining. The household savings rate in Japan is double that of the United States, and Europe's savings rate is four times greater than the United States.

In the mercantilist view, colonies existed only to benefit the home country. In 1697 the English economist Charles D'Avenant explained how colonies benefited England.

HISTORY'S VOICES

> **"Our plantations . . . consume more of our home manufactures . . . they produce commodities indispensably necessary to this part of the world, and not to be produced elsewhere, and, with industry and conduct, may be made an inexhaustible mine of treasure to their mother kingdom."**
>
> —Charles D'Avenant, "An Essay on the East-India Trade"

To make sure that colonies benefited only the home country, European monarchs restricted economic activities in the colonies. People living in the colonies could not sell raw materials to any nation other than the home country or buy manufactured goods from other nations. Governments passed strict laws that forbade colonies from manufacturing goods. So colonies were forced to buy manufactured goods only from their home country. Mercantilists argued that such laws were justified because colonies existed to benefit the home country.

Impact on Society The changes taking place because of colonization also had an impact on European societies. Towns and cities grew as business activity increased. A new class of wealthier merchants emerged who began to wield more power in their towns.

HISTORY and Economics

Saving and Investing

What should you do with any money you have left over after paying for necessities? Consider making your money work for you by saving or investing it.

Saving and Investing in History Before the late 1500s opportunities for saving and investing were limited. Then banks began offering other services to customers, including a secure place for keeping money. Opportunities for investment also became available at that time. For example, many joint-stock companies were established to engage in the lucrative trade in Asian spices and textiles. These companies, in turn, played a significant role in financing exploration and trading voyages. The companies were frequently able to return large profits to investors when their ships came back from the East Indies laden with valuable merchandise.

Saving and Investing in Your Life One of the most important financial responsibilities you will have to learn is how to use your money wisely. Begin by opening a savings account. This is a risk-free way to finance your goals, because deposits are insured by the government. Saving is also profitable, since banks pay interest.

ENGLISH JOINT-STOCK COMPANIES, 1688

Company	Date of Creation	Value of Each Share	Number of Investors
East India	1600	£100	511
Royal African	1672	£100	203
Hudson's Bay	1670	£100	32
White Paper	1686	£50	unknown
Royal Lustring	1688	£25	134

Another option is investing in stocks or bonds. Investing money is riskier but can provide richer rewards. However, because you risk losing all your money if an investment fails, you should invest money only if you have adequate savings.

Analyze How can investing in a company be profitable? How can it be risky?

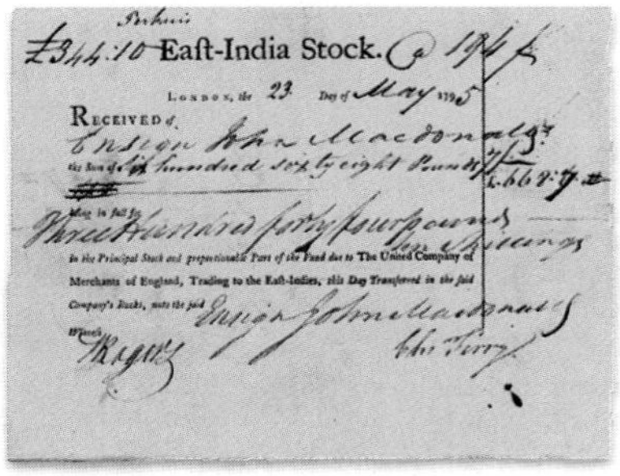

◀ Stock certificate from the East India Company, an early joint-stock company

Skills Focus: Identifying Cause and Effect

At Level

Reading Skill

The Effects of Mercantilism

1. Have students draw editorial cartoons that illustrate one of the effects of mercantilism, such as the accumulation of gold and silver, creating a favorable balance of trade, establishment of colonial empires, or policies that restricted trade and manufacturing in the home country's colonies. Since these are editorial cartoons, students should take a clear stand for or against the policy they illustrate.
2. Display student cartoons for the class to see.
3. Guide students in a discussion of the effects of mercantilism on society and the world. **LS Visual-Spatial**

Alternative Assessment Handbook, Rubrics 11: Discussions; and 27: Political Cartoons

Answers

History and Economics *profitable—might earn a lot of money; risky—might lose a lot of money*

The impact of colonization was not felt throughout society, though. Rural life continued much as it had for centuries. Generations would pass before many began to grow new foods from the Americas. In towns and cities, wealthy merchants enjoyed some social mobility, but most people remained poor.

READING CHECK **Summarize** What were the main principles of mercantilism?

The Rise of Capitalism

Increasing trade between European nations and their colonies resulted in the creation of new business practices during the 1500s and 1600s. These practices would have a profound impact on the economies of European nations.

Capitalism Emerges During this period, an economic system known as **capitalism** expanded. In capitalism, most economic activity is carried on by private individuals or organizations in order to seek a profit. Individuals, not just the government, began to amass great fortunes through overseas trade.

Merchants began to supply colonists with goods from Europe and, in return, brought back products and raw materials from the Americas. This overseas trade made many merchants rich, and this wealth enabled them to invest in still more business ventures. Business activity in Europe increased markedly.

Rising Prices Investors willingly took the risks of investing in overseas trade because of inflation, or a steady increase in prices. Demand for goods increased because of a growing population and a relative scarcity of goods. The rising demand drove prices higher.

Another factor leading to higher prices was the increase of the money supply in Europe. Shiploads of gold and silver flowed into Europe from the Americas to be made into new coins. Over time, the increase of money in circulation pushed prices for goods still higher.

A New Business Organization Overseas business ventures were very costly, often too expensive for individual investors. Soon, investors began to pool their money into **joint-stock companies** to fund ever-larger businesses. In a joint-stock company, investors bought shares of stock in the company. If the company achieved a profit, each shareholder would receive a portion of that profit, based on the number of shares owned. If the company failed, investors would lose only the amount of money they had invested in the business.

One of the first joint-stock companies was the British East India Company, founded in 1600 to import spices from Asia. Other joint-stock companies formed to bear the enormous cost of establishing new colonies. In 1607, for example, the Virginia Company of London established the first successful English colony in the Americas at Jamestown, Virginia.

THE IMPACT TODAY
The notion of investors sharing profits and risk is the norm in the business world today.

READING CHECK **Identify Cause and Effect** Why did new business practices develop in Europe?

SECTION 3 ASSESSMENT

go.hrw.com
Online Quiz
Keyword: SHL EXP HP

Reviewing Ideas, Terms, and People

1. **a. Define** What was the **Columbian Exchange**? What were some of the products exchanged?
   b. Explain How did the exchange of plants and animals change life in both Europe and the Americas?
   c. Elaborate What effect did the introduction of new diseases into the Americas have on Native American populations?
2. **a. Describe** What was the most important principle of **mercantilism**?
   b. Make Generalizations Why were colonies important under the principles of mercantilism?
   c. Extend How did the quest for a favorable **balance of trade** push the drive to establish colonies?
3. **a. Recall** Why did people form **joint-stock companies**?
   b. Elaborate How did the drive to establish colonies lead to the growth of **capitalism**?

Critical Thinking

4. **Compare and Contrast** Draw a Venn diagram like the one below. Using your notes, write three facts about mercantilism in the left oval. Then write three facts about capitalism in the right oval. Where the ovals overlap, identify one feature that the two systems have in common.

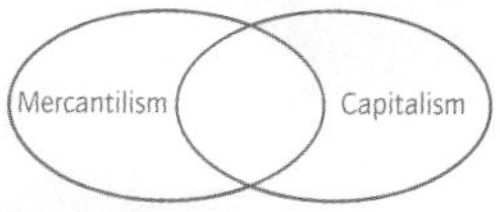

FOCUS ON WRITING

5. **Persuasion** Write a short letter as though you were one of the founders of a joint-stock company trying to convince a friend to invest his or her money in your venture. In your letter, explain what you hope your company will accomplish and why you feel it would be beneficial to your friend to take part.

Direct Teach

Reading Focus

3 How did global trade lead to the rise of capitalism in Europe? *It provided opportunities for individuals to invest money and build wealth.*

The Rise of Capitalism

Define What is capitalism? *system in which most economic activity is carried on by private individuals or organizations in order to seek a profit*

Make Generalizations How was the Virginia Company of London an example of capitalism? *Investors pooled their money in order to make a profit by establishing American colonies.*

Review & Assess

Close

Guide students in a discussion of the ways in which mercantilism encouraged European nations to establish colonial empires.

Review

Online Quiz, Section 3

Assess

SE Section 3 Assessment

Progress Assessment: Section 3 Quiz

Alternative Assessment Handbook

Reteach/Intervene

Interactive Reader and Study Guide, Section 3

Interactive Skills Tutor CD-ROM

Section 3 Assessment Answers

1. **a.** exchange of plants and animals between Europe and Americas; possible answers—tomatoes, cows, coffee, corn, peanuts
   b. changed cuisines, crops
   c. Millions died from the diseases.
2. **a.** that a nation's strength depended on its wealth
   b. Colonies could provide raw materials and new markets.
   c. allowed nations to control overseas sources of raw materials and precious metals
3. **a.** to pool their money in an attempt to make a profit
   b. Colonies provided opportunities for individuals to build wealth.
4. Mercantilism—nation's strength depended on wealth; favorable balance of trade; Capitalism—most economic activity carried on by private individuals or organizations seeking profit; Both—benefited from establishment of colonies
5. Student letters should explain how investors can make a profit in the venture.

Answers

Reading Skills (left) *nation's strength depended upon its wealth; needed a favorable balance of trade;* **(right)** *because of increasing trade between Europe and its colonies*

Preteach

Getting Started

Use the **Interactive Reader and Study Guide** to familiarize students with the section content.

Interactive Reader and Study Guide, Section 4

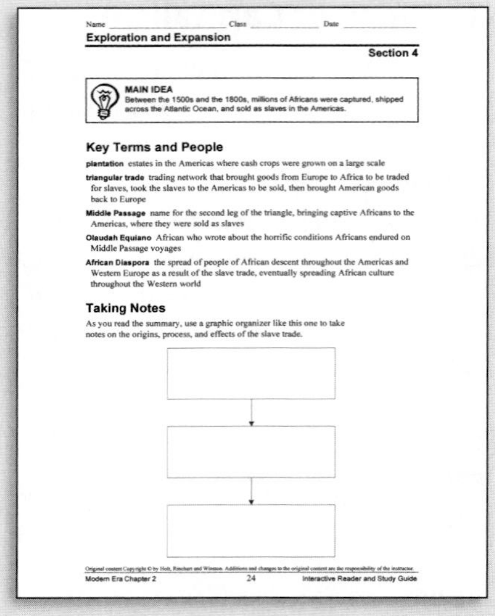

Name ______________ Class ______________ Date ______________

Exploration and Expansion

Section 4

MAIN IDEA
Between the 1500s and the 1800s, millions of Africans were captured, shipped across the Atlantic Ocean, and sold as slaves in the Americas.

Key Terms and People

plantation estates in the Americas where cash crops were grown on a large scale

triangular trade trading network that brought goods from Europe to Africa to be traded for slaves, took the slaves to the Americas to be sold, then brought American goods back to Europe

Middle Passage name for the second leg of the triangle, bringing captive Africans to the Americas, where they were sold as slaves

Olaudah Equiano African who wrote about the horrific conditions Africans endured on Middle Passage voyages

African Diaspora the spread of people of African descent throughout the Americas and Western Europe as a result of the slave trade, eventually spreading African culture throughout the Western world

Taking Notes

As you read the summary, use a graphic organizer like this one to take notes on the origins, process, and effects of the slave trade.

Original content Copyright © by Holt, Rinehart and Winston. Additions and changes to the original content are the responsibility of the instructor.

Modern Era Chapter 2 — 24 — Interactive Reader and Study Guide

CRF: Vocabulary Builder: Section 4

Taking Notes

Origins—need for workers on plantations in the Americas; Process—triangular trade began; Middle Passage brought Africans to Americas under inhumane conditions; Effects—an estimated 15 to 20 million Africans were shipped to the Americas; millions of people deprived of their freedom; resulted in countless deaths; harmed Africa; divided Africans from one another; enriched other parts of the world; led to African Diaspora and spread of African culture

SECTION 4

The Atlantic Slave Trade

Before You Read

Main Idea

Between the 1500s and the 1800s millions of Africans were captured, shipped across the Atlantic Ocean, and sold as slaves in the Americas.

Reading Focus

1. Where did the Atlantic slave trade originate?
2. How did slavery evolve in the American colonies?
3. What were the consequences of the slave trade?

Key Terms and People

plantations
triangular trade
Middle Passage
Olaudah Equiano
African Diaspora

TAKING NOTES Use a graphic organizer to take notes on the origins, process, and effects of the slave trade.

Origins → Process → Effects

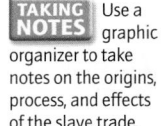

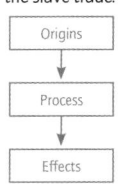

The view through the door of the House of Slaves on Gorée Island is a profound symbol of the slave trade.

THE INSIDE STORY ***How did the door of a Senegalese house become a powerful symbol for millions of people worldwide?*** On rocky Gorée Island off the coast of Senegal stands the House of Slaves. Millions of African captives spent their last days in Africa in this house or houses like it. Crowded into dark, dungeonlike rooms, they awaited the ships that would carry them into slavery in the Americas. Their last steps in Africa were through the Door of No Return, a narrow doorway facing the Atlantic Ocean. Once through it, they would leave behind everything they knew—to face an uncertain and terrifying future.

Though historians today are not sure how prominent a role Gorée Island played in the slave trade, the history of the House of Slaves draws about 200,000 people to visit each year. However many slaves actually departed through the Door of No Return, it remains a powerful symbol of the tragedy of slavery. ■

Origins of the Slave Trade

Throughout history, slavery has existed in many parts of the world, including Africa. The people who were forced into slavery came from various walks of life. Many were farmers, merchants, priests, soldiers, or musicians. They were fathers and mothers, sons and daughters.

The Atlantic Slave Trade A shortage of labor in the Americas led to the beginning of the Atlantic slave trade. European planters in the Americas needed large numbers of workers on their **plantations**, estates where

Teach the Main Idea

At Level

The Atlantic Slave Trade

1. **Teach** Ask students the Reading Focus questions to teach this section.
2. **Apply** Have students make a cause-and-effect chart about slavery in the Americas. Tell students that the reasons the slave trade was started are the causes, while the results, or consequences, of the slave trade are the effects.
3. **Review** Review student charts as a class. Guide students in a discussion of how the development of the American colonies would have been different if slavery had never been introduced in the New World.
4. **Practice/Homework** Have students write about the causes and effects of the African slave trade. **LS Visual-Spatial, Verbal-Linguistic**

Alternative Assessment Handbook, Rubrics 7: Charts; and 41: Writing to Express cash crops such as sugar or tobacco were grown on a large scale. Planters had first used Native Americans as workers, but European diseases had killed millions of them. In the 1600s planters used indentured servants—people who worked for a set period in exchange for passage to the Americas—from Europe, but such workers were expensive to support.

As a result, millions of Africans were forcibly taken to the Americas before the slave trade ended in the 1800s. Most came from the coast of West Africa, between Senegal and Angola. Some slaves were supplied by African rulers in exchange for European firearms or other goods. Others were kidnapped on slave raids organized by European traders.

Captured Africans were marched to slave ships where they became part of a network called the **triangular trade**. The first leg of the triangle consisted of ships carrying European goods to Africa to be exchanged for slaves. The second leg, or **Middle Passage**, brought Africans to the Americas to be sold as slaves. The third leg carried American products such as sugar, tobacco, and rice to Europe. Some slave traders from the Americas sailed directly to Africa, however, not following the triangular route.

The Middle Passage The Middle Passage was a terrifying ordeal. Captive Africans were chained together and forced into dark, cramped quarters below the ship's decks. In many cases, the Africans were packed into such a small space that they could neither sit nor stand. One African, **Olaudah Equiano**, later wrote about these horrific conditions.

HISTORY'S VOICES

"The stench of the hold . . . was so intolerably loathsome, that it was dangerous to remain there for any time . . . The closeness of the place, and the heat of the climate . . . almost suffocated us . . . The shrieks of the women, and the groans of the dying, rendered the whole scene of horror almost inconceivable."

—Olaudah Equiano, *The Interesting Narrative of the Life of Olaudah Equiano*, 1789

THE ATLANTIC SLAVE TRADE

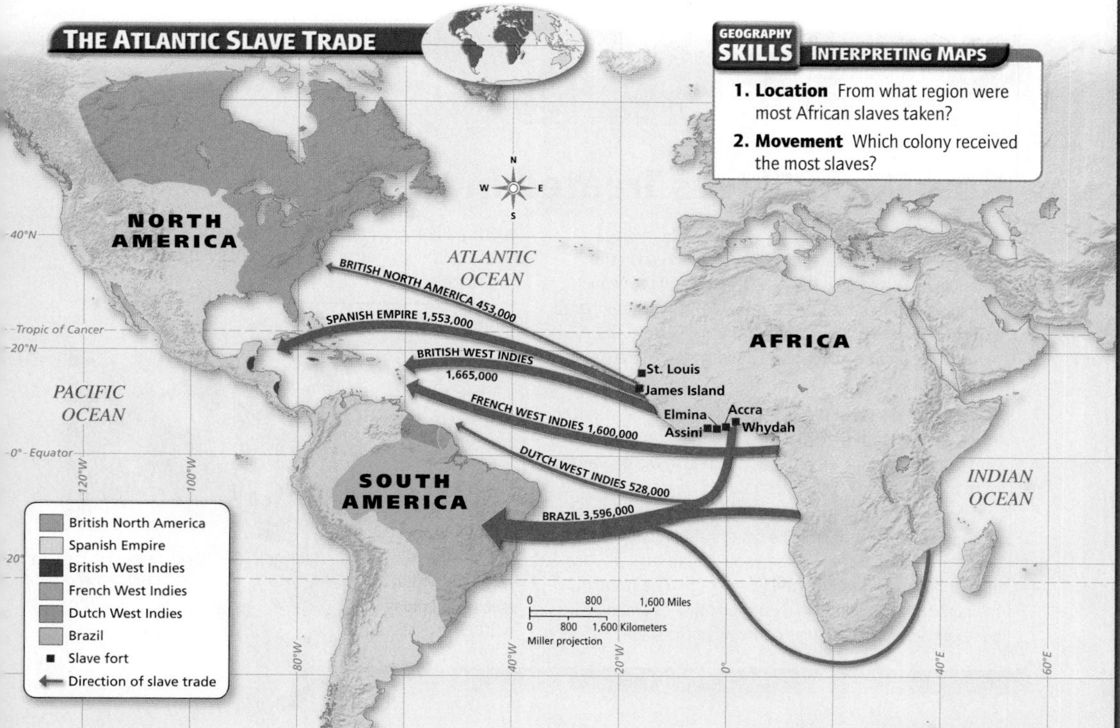

GEOGRAPHY SKILLS INTERPRETING MAPS

1. **Location** From what region were most African slaves taken?
2. **Movement** Which colony received the most slaves?

Direct Teach

Reading Focus

1 Where did the Atlantic slave trade originate? *along a triangular route connecting traders in Europe, Africa, and the Americas*

Origins of the Slave Trade

Recall What was the Middle Passage? *the second leg of the triangular trade route, bringing Africans to the Americas to be sold as slaves*

Identify Who was Olaudah Equiano? *an African who wrote about the conditions on a slave ship*

Explain What is a cash crop? *a crop such as sugar or tobacco that was raised for sale*

CRF: Biography: Olaudah Equiano

CRF: Economics and History: Prices in the Atlantic Slave Trade

Interpreting Maps

The Atlantic Slave Trade

Movement Where did most slaves come from and where did they end up? *from the west coast of Africa; to South America, Caribbean, and east coast of North America*

Map Transparency: The Atlantic Slave Trade

Info to Know

The Persistence of Slavery Freed African American slaves from the United States founded the African country of Liberia. There, some of them named settlements after slave states such as Mississippi and Louisiana, cleared land for huge plantations with Southern-style mansions, and modeled their government after that of the United States—complete with slavery. Slavery still exists in Liberia.

Skills Focus: Comparing and Contrasting

At Level

Reading Skill

Slavery in Africa and the Americas

1. Organize students into small groups. Have each group make a chart showing the similarities and differences between slavery as it existed in Africa and slavery in the New World.
2. Review student charts as a class.
3. Have each student write a brief essay answering the following question: Does the fact that Africans enslaved other Africans make the Europeans who engaged in the slave trade any less guilty of their offenses? Why or why not? **LS Visual-Spatial, Verbal-Linguistic**

Alternative Assessment Handbook, Rubrics 7: Charts; and 14: Group Activity

Answers

Interpreting Maps 1. *West Africa;* **2.** *Brazil*

Direct Teach

Reading Focus

2 How did slavery evolve in the American colonies? *By the end of the 1600s, England dominated the slave trade; living conditions for slaves were harsh; some enslaved people rebelled.*

Slavery in the Colonies

Describe Describe the living conditions for enslaved people. *They were harsh. Many owners and overseers inflicted degrading physical punishment for minor offenses. Enslaved people frequently had to endure brutal treatment and abuse.*

Summarize How did Africans resist slavery? *by slowing work, destroying equipment, committing acts of sabotage, revolting, or running away*

The journey to the Americas usually lasted three to six weeks. Between 10 and 20 percent of all captive Africans did not survive the voyage. When those who survived arrived in the Americas, they faced still more terrors—the auction block and an uncertain future.

READING CHECK **Describe** What was the Middle Passage of the slave trade like?

Slavery in the Colonies

Slave traders carried captive Africans to many parts of the Americas. Spanish traders took slaves to their Caribbean sugar plantations. Portuguese traders brought millions to Brazil. The English took most of their captives to the West Indies but also brought large numbers to colonies in North America. By the end of the 1600s England dominated the slave trade.

Living Conditions Most enslaved Africans worked on plantations, but others worked in mines, in towns, and in the countryside. Those who had been skilled craft workers—such as carpenters, metalworkers, or coopers—often continued their crafts in the Americas. Women were sometimes given domestic duties as servants and cooks.

Slaves had to meet their own basic needs in the short hours at the end of the workday. Daily tasks such as cooking, mending clothing, and tending the sick had to be fit in around the work they performed for the slaveholder.

Living conditions for many enslaved people were harsh. Owners and overseers inflicted physical and degrading punishment for minor offenses. As a result, many slaveholders lived in constant fear of rebellion by angry slaves who could not take the harsh treatment they faced on plantations anymore.

Resistance Laws in the Americas considered enslaved Africans to be property. Slaves had no rights and no freedoms, and slaveholders controlled most of the conditions under which they lived. In many cases, enslaved people endured brutal treatment and abuse.

FORENSICS in History

How Were Slaves Treated in the North?

In the United States, most people think of slavery as a southern phenomenon. Many more slaves lived in the American South than in the North, and, for many years, people assumed that those slaves who did live in the North were better treated than their southern counterparts. A recent discovery, however, has led many people to change their minds.

What facts do we have? In 1991 workers in Manhattan laying the foundation for a new skyscraper found a graveyard that dated back to the 1700s. Buried in the graveyard were the remains of 427 African slaves.

The remains were sent to Howard University in Washington, D.C., to be studied. The results of that study showed that many of the slaves had been pushed to their physical limit or beyond—literally worked to death. The strain of their labors had resulted in deformed muscles and broken bones. In addition, the fact that many of the slaves buried in the graveyard were children—several less than six months old—suggests that the slaves lived under terrible conditions.

Infer How could this study challenge the idea that northern slaves were well treated?

▶ The slaves found in the New York City graveyard were reburied in a special ceremony in 2003.

Skills Focus: Analyzing Alternative Points of View — At Level

Reading Like a Historian Skill

The Slave Trade

Materials: poster paper, colored markers or pencils

1. Organize students into small groups. Have each group discuss the advantages and disadvantages of the slave trade for one of the following individuals: a plantation owner in the Americas, an enslaved person, the owner of a slave ship, or the ruler of an African kingdom.
2. Have each student write an essay analyzing the different points of view involved in the slave trade.
3. Guide students in a discussion of the slave trade from the points of view that have been presented. **LS Interpersonal, Visual-Spatial**

Alternative Assessment Handbook, Rubric 37: Writing Assignments

Answers

Forensics in History *It shows that the slaves in New York had been worked to their physical limits and probably lived under terrible conditions.*

Reading Check *a terrifying ordeal; people were cramped, chained together; as many as one in four people did not survive the voyage*

Enslaved Africans and their descendants coped with these inhumane conditions in many different ways. Some resisted by trying to keep their cultural traditions alive. Others turned to religion for strength and hope for a better life.

Some slaves also fought back by slowing down their work or destroying equipment. Occasionally they revolted, attacking slaveholders and their families. Some slaves were able to flee plantations and establish communities of runaways in remote areas.

READING CHECK **Summarize** Why did many slaves fight back against their owners?

Effects of the Slave Trade

The Atlantic slave trade continued for 400 years and devastated societies in West Africa. Historians have estimated that about 15 to 20 million Africans were shipped to the Americas against their will. Millions more were sent to Europe, Asia, and the Middle East.

The human cost of the slave trade was enormous. Countless people died marching from the interior to the coast or crammed aboard slave ships. Slavery deprived millions of people of their freedom and doomed their descendants to lives of forced servitude.

In Africa, the effects of the slave trade were profound. Slave raiders captured many of the strongest young people—the future leaders of their societies. The slave trade also divided Africans from one another. For example, some African rulers waged wars against their own people and their neighbors to gain captives.

The forced labor of millions of Africans did not enrich Africa, but it did enrich other parts of the world. The labor of African slaves helped build the economies of many American colonies. Their knowledge of agriculture contributed to the growth of the rice industry in the southern English colonies.

As a result of the slave trade, people of African descent spread throughout the Americas and Western Europe. This dispersal is called the **African Diaspora**. The African Diaspora eventually led to the diffusion of African culture—including music, art, religion, and food—throughout the Western world.

READING CHECK **Explain** What effects did the Atlantic slave trade have in Africa?

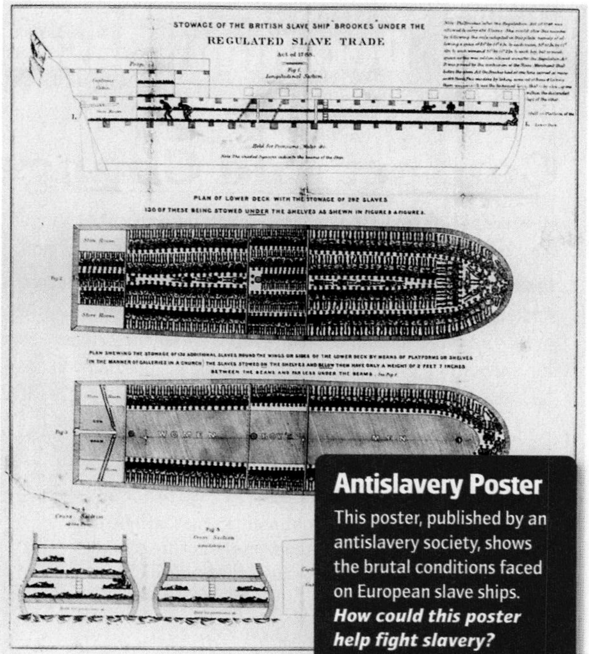

Antislavery Poster

This poster, published by an antislavery society, shows the brutal conditions faced on European slave ships.

How could this poster help fight slavery?

SECTION 4 ASSESSMENT

go.hrw.com
Online Quiz
Keyword: SHL EXP HP

Reviewing Ideas, Terms, and People

1. **a. Identify** From where did most of the slaves involved in the Atlantic slave trade come? Where were the slaves taken?
   b. Explain Why was the **triangular trade** developed?
   c. Elaborate How did the **plantation** system lead to the slave trade?
2. **a. Describe** What were living conditions like for most African slaves?
   b. Analyze What were three reactions of slaves to their loss of freedom?
3. **a. Define** What is the **African Diaspora**? How did it affect the world?
   b. Make Judgements What do you think was the most tragic result of the African slave trade? Why?

Critical Thinking

4. **Identify Cause and Effect** Draw a graphic organizer like the one below. Using your notes, identify the social, economic, and cultural effects of the Atlantic slave trade.

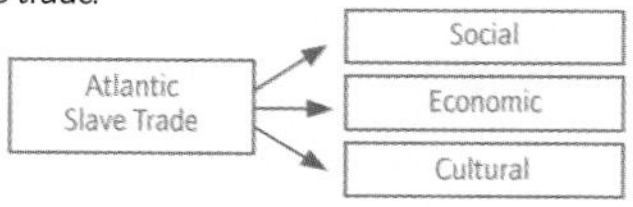

FOCUS ON WRITING

5. **Description** Write a short description of the Middle Passage experienced by enslaved Africans. Include in your description the conditions slaves had to endure and the effects of the passage on those slaves.

Direct Teach

Reading Focus

3 What were the consequences of the slave trade? *death or loss of freedom for millions, devastation of African societies*

Effects of the Slave Trade

Recall According to historians' estimates, how many Africans were shipped to the Americas against their will? *about 15 to 20 million*

Identify Cause and Effect What was one effect of the African Diaspora? *the spread of African culture throughout the Western world*

CRF: Literature: *The Interesting Narrative and Other Writings*

Review & Assess

Close

Review the origins, process, and effects of the Atlantic slave trade.

Review

Online Quiz, Section 4

Assess

SE Section 4 Assessment

Progress Assessment: Section 4 Quiz

Alternative Assessment Handbook

Reteach/Intervene

Interactive Reader and Study Guide, Section 4

Interactive Skills Tutor CD-ROM

Section 4 Assessment Answers

1. **a.** West Africa; the Americas
   b. to form a trade network between Europe, Africa, and Asia
   c. It required large numbers of workers.
2. **a.** harsh conditions, lack of freedom
   b. keeping cultural traditions alive, religion, rebellion
3. **a.** the spread of people of African descent throughout the Americas and Western Europe; spread African culture
   b. possible answer—the fact that millions of people were deprived of freedom; because freedom is a basic right
4. Social—led to lack of freedom for certain people in the Americas, separated Africans from one another, caused wars; Economic—enriched other parts of the world, but did not enrich Africa; Cultural—led to spread of African culture, the African Diaspora
5. Student descriptions should include details about inhumane treatment and point out that many people died on the voyage.

Answers

Antislavery Poster *might make people realize how brutal the conditions were and thus begin to oppose slavery*

Reading Check (top) *to cope with inhumane conditions;* **(bottom)** *took away future leaders; divided Africans from one another*

Document-Based Investigation

Contact and Change

Info to Know

The Dark Side of the Columbian Exchange Although few European explorers had active diseases, they still carried many germs that were highly contagious to Native Americans. Passing these germs to just a few people could rapidly infect large areas. Large, prosperous towns discovered by Spanish explorers in the early 1540s in what is now the southeastern United States no longer existed in 1560. During this time, Spanish colonists in Florida tried to find these towns to acquire food but diseases brought by the explorers had destroyed them. It is estimated that by the early 1600s, the Mesoamerican Indian population was 90 to 95 percent smaller than it had been a hundred years before.

Recent Scholarship

In his book *1491: New Revelations of the Americas Before Columbus*, Charles C. Mann makes many revelations. One of the chief of these is his assertion that the Americas were much more urban, more populated, and more technologically advanced than has generally been assumed. Far from living in harmony with nature, Native Americans engineered the landscape to meet their needs. The empty landscape that greeted later settlers was a result of the diseases carried by the first Europeans.

1491: New Revelations of the Americas Before Columbus by Charles C. Mann. Knopf, 2005.

CHAPTER 2

Document-Based Investigation

Contact and Change

Historical Context The four documents here describe changes that occurred in the Americas as a result of the arrival of Europeans in the region.

Task Study the selections and answer the questions that follow. After you have studied all the documents, you will be asked to write an essay describing how the year 1492 was a turning point in history. You will need to use evidence from these documents and from the chapter to support the position you take in your essay.

Document 1

The Arrival of Europeans

The arrival of Christopher Columbus in the Caribbean in 1492 had a tremendous impact on the future of that region. The passage below describes that arrival. It is taken from an abridgment of Columbus's personal journal made by Bartholomé de las Casas.

> The Admiral . . . called them as witnesses to certify that he in the presence of them all, was taking, as he in fact took possession of said island for the King and Queen his masters, making the declarations that were required as they will be found more fully in the attestations then taken down in writing. Soon after a large crowd of natives congregated there. What follows are the Admiral's own words in his book on the first voyage and discovery of these Indies. "In order to win the friendship and affection of that people, and because I was convinced that their conversion to our Holy Faith would be better promoted through love than through force, I presented some of them with red caps and some strings of glass beads which they placed around their necks, and with other trifles of insignificant worth that delighted them and by which we have got wonderful hold on their affections."

Document 2

The Impact of Disease

Among the most disastrous effects of the arrival of Europeans in the Americas was the rapid spread of disease. Historians estimate that about 90 percent of the Native American population was killed by diseases like smallpox, influenza, and malaria. The image shown here was drawn in the mid- to late 1500s by a Spanish friar named Bernardino de Sahagún, who had befriended many Aztecs. In his *General History of the Things of New Spain*, from which this image is taken, Sahagún describes the effects of these diseases on Aztec populations. The image shows Aztecs suffering through various stages of smallpox.

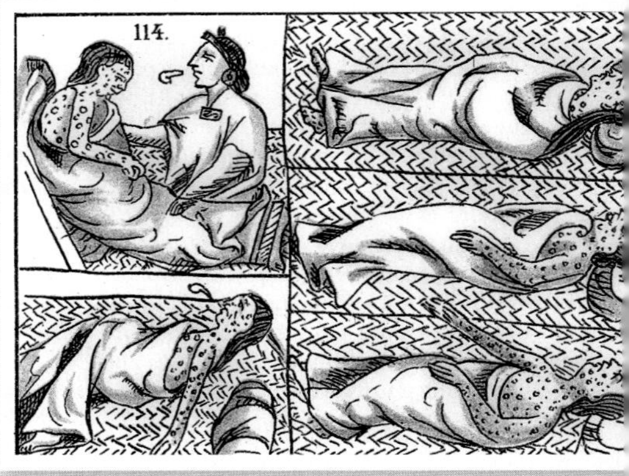

American Museum of Natural History

Differentiating Instruction

Below Level

Learners Having Difficulty

Materials: white paper, colored pencils or markers

1. Have students draw the scene that takes place in Document 1. Tell students that in order to create a detailed drawing, they will need to pay careful attention to the Admiral's quote.
2. Review student drawings as a class. Ask students: Do the people in their drawings appear to be getting along with one another? Why or why not?
3. Guide students in a discussion of the relationship of Columbus's men with Native Americans, and how it changed over time.
LS Visual-Spatial

Alternative Assessment Handbook, Rubric 3: Artwork

DOCUMENT 3

A New Economic System

When they established colonies in the Americas, the Spanish created a new economic system, the *encomienda* system, in which Native Americans worked on Spanish-owned estates. The basis for that system was laid out in a letter from King Ferdinand and Queen Isabella to the governor of Hispaniola in 1503.

> Our desire is that the Christians not lack people to work their holdings and to take out what gold there is. It also is our desire that the Indians be converted. All this can be better done by having the Indians live in community with the Christians, because they then will help each other cultivate and settle the island, take out the gold, and bring profit to Spain. Therefore, we command you, our governor, to compel the Indians to associate with the Christians. The Indians should work on the Christians' buildings, mine the gold, till the fields, and produce food for the Christians. This the Indians shall perform as free people, which they are, and not as slaves. Also, see to it that the Indians are well treated, with those who become Christians better treated than the others. Do not consent or allow any person to do them any harm or oppress them.

DOCUMENT 4

Changes in Society

The detail below comes from a map drawn by explorer Sebastian Cabot in 1544. The illustrations on the map depict many changes that had occurred in American society over the previous 50 years.

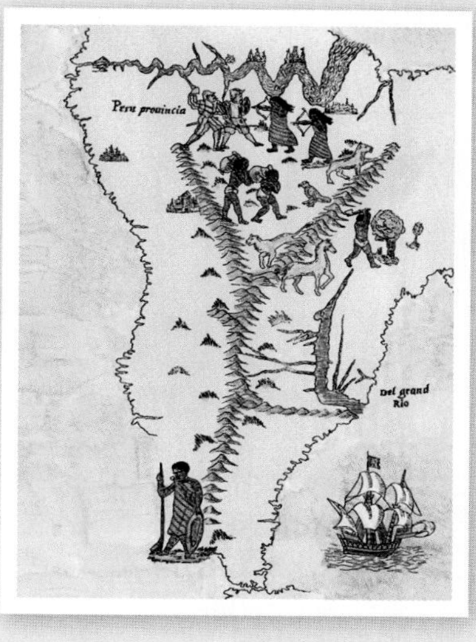

Map of Peru and South America, by Sebastian Cabot, 1544

Skills FOCUS — READING LIKE A HISTORIAN

DOCUMENT 1

a. Describe What was Columbus's first act upon arriving on the Caribbean island he had discovered?

b. Explain Why does Columbus say he gave gifts to the Native Americans he encountered?

DOCUMENT 2

a. Analyze What symptoms appear in this image?

b. Make Judgments Do you think Sahagún sympathized more with the Spanish or with the Aztecs? Why?

DOCUMENT 3

a. Interpret Why did Ferdinand and Isabella want Native Americans and Christians to live together?

b. Infer Do you think the governor of Hispaniola followed the monarchs' instructions fully? Why or why not?

DOCUMENT 4

a. Describe In what activities are the people shown on this map engaged? How do these activities reflect changes in American society?

b. Summarize What other changes are shown?

DOCUMENT-BASED ESSAY QUESTION

The year 1492 has been described as a turning point in world history. What does this phrase mean? Using the documents above and information from the chapter, form a thesis that might explain its meaning. Then write a short essay to support your position.

See **Skills Handbook**, pp. H25–H26

Document-Based Investigation

Info to Know

Stamina and Nutrition Levels of nutrition in the New World were probably much lower than in Europe, which would account for the smaller stature and lower energy levels in Native Americans. When Europeans tried to force Native Americans to do Old World levels of work, many were literally worked to death.

Skills Focus: Sequencing

At Level

Reading Skill

After 1492

1. Have students create a time line of events in the Americas in the years immediately following Columbus's arrival.
2. Tell students that their time lines should include the conquest of the Aztec and Inca Empires, as well as important explorations that took place during this time. Students should also indicate on the time line when Documents 1, 2, 3, and 4 were created.
3. Guide a class discussion about what happened in the Americas between 1492 and 1550. What effects did these events have on Native Americans and Europeans? **LS Visual-Spatial, Intrapersonal**

Alternative Assessment Handbook, Rubrics 11: Discussions; and 37: Time Lines

Answers

Reading Like a Historian

Document 1. a. *gave gifts to the Native Americans;* **b.** *because he could more easily convert them to Christianity through love than by force;* **Document 2. a.** *vomiting, spots on skin;* **b.** *with the Aztecs; the depiction of the disease makes it look painful;* **Document 3. a.** *because the Native Americans could help the Spanish Christians and might convert to Christianity themselves;* **b.** *no, because we know Native Americans were treated harshly under the* encomienda *system;* **Document 4. a.** *fighting and working; shows the natives fighting Europeans, and making use of horses;* **b.** *Native Americans are also shown laboring under heavy loads, possibly as slaves.* **Essay** *Student essays should use details from the documents and the chapter in order to show the changes in Europe and the Americas after 1492. Essays should discuss the effects of the Columbian Exchange, exploration, conquest, and colonization.*

Answers

Visual Study Guide

Review and Inquiry Organize students into three groups. One group will cover the Columbian Exchange, the second group will cover New Economic Systems, and the third group will cover the Atlantic Slave Trade. Have each group review the chart in the visual summary and write a brief explanation of how exploration and colonization led to its assigned topic.

Quick Facts Transparency: Visual Study Guide: Exploration and Expansion

Review Key Terms and People

1. Columbian Exchange
2. Vasco da Gama
3. caravel
4. African Diaspora
5. Ferdinand Magellan
6. subsidy

Comprehension and Critical Thinking

7. **a.** the Caribbean; Asia
b. for fame and glory, in search of wealth, to spread Christianity, because they were curious about the world
c. possible answer—Yes, because there was the appeal of wealth, fame, and glory.

8. **a.** building colonial empires
b. based on different trade goods (fish and furs); fewer colonists; allied with Native Americans
c. possible answer—Spain, because millions of Native Americans died in Spain's colonial empire.

9. **a.** the relationship between a nation's imports and exports; because having more exports than imports brought wealth
b. exchanged plants, animals, and disease between Europe and the Americas
c. possible answer—They probably disliked mercantilism because it focused on building the wealth of the mother country, not building the wealth of the colonies.

CHAPTER 2

Chapter Review

QUICK FACTS

VISUAL STUDY GUIDE

Exploration

- Explorers from countries throughout Europe set out in search of new routes to Asia.
- Instead of Asia, many explorers ended up in the Americas.

Colonization

- Europeans established colonies in the lands they had discovered.
- The Spanish conquered Native American tribes to build an empire.
- The Portuguese settled Brazil.
- The French, Dutch, and English established colonies in North America and the Caribbean.

Columbian Exchange

- New plants and animals were introduced to both Europe and the Americas.
- Diseases from Europe killed millions of Native Americans.
- The exchange of goods had effects worldwide.

New Economic Systems

- Mercantilism was based on the idea that a nation's power was determined by its wealth.
- Capitalism was based on businesses owned by individuals or groups of investors rather than the government.

Atlantic Slave Trade

- Millions of Africans were captured and shipped to the Americas as slaves.
- Slaves worked on plantations in various European colonies.
- Slaves endured horrific conditions once they arrived.

Review Key Terms and People

Finn each blank with the name or term that correctly completes each sentence.

1. The exchange of new plants, animals, and diseases between Europe and the Americas was called the __________.
2. A Portuguese explorer named _________ was the first person to sail around Africa to reach India.
3. A fast new type of ship, the __________, helped begin the Age of Exploration.
4. The spread of people of African descent through the Western world is called the __________.
5. The first voyage completely around the world was originally led by __________.
6. A __________ is a government grant of money intended to promote a business.

96 CHAPTER 2

10. **a.** the trading of goods and people between Europe, Africa, and the Americas
b. They were denied freedom and basic rights and lived under very poor conditions.
c. in Africa—led to loss of future leaders; wars; divisions between Africans; outside Africa—led to the loss of freedom for millions of enslaved people; enriched countries other than Africa

Using the Internet

11. Go to the HRW Web site and enter the keyword shown to access a rubric for this activity.

KEYWORD: SHL EXP

History's Impact video program

Review the video to answer the closing question: What were the positive and negative effects of the Columbian Exchange?

Comprehension and Critical Thinking

SECTION 1 *(pp. 71–77)*

7. a. Recall Where did Christopher Columbus travel on his first voyage? At what place did he think he had arrived?

b. Explain Why did Europeans of the 1400s and 1500s want to explore the world?

c. Develop Would you have wanted to leave Europe to explore? Why or why not?

SECTION 2 *(pp. 78-83)*

8. a. Identify Main Ideas What was main goal of Spanish and Portuguese colonists?

b. Contrast How did French colonies in the Americas differ from Spanish colonies?

c. Elaborate Which country's colonization efforts do you think had the greatest impact on Native American cultures? Why?

SECTION 3 *(pp. 84-89)*

9. a. Define What is a balance of trade? Why did countries want a favorable balance of trade?

b. Make Generalizations How did the Columbian Exchange change both Europe and the Americas?

c. Extend How do you think most colonists felt about mercantilism? Why do you think so?

SECTION 4 *(pp. 90-93)*

10. a. Describe What was involved in the triangular trade?

b. Summarize How were slaves treated in the American colonies?

c. Elaborate How did the slave trade affect people in Africa? How did it affect people outside of Africa?

Using the Internet

go.hrw.com
Practice Online
Keyword: SHL EXP

11. In order to attract settlers, many colonists in the Americas created posters and pamphlets that advertised the benefits of living in their colonies. Some posters, for example, pointed out pleasant climates or readily available land. Using the keyword above, do research to learn more about one of the colonies discussed in this chapter. Then create a poster that could have been used to attract new settlers.

Analyzing Primary Sources

Reading Like a Historian *The poster below was printed in Charleston, South Carolina, in 1769. Examine the poster and then answer the questions that follow.*

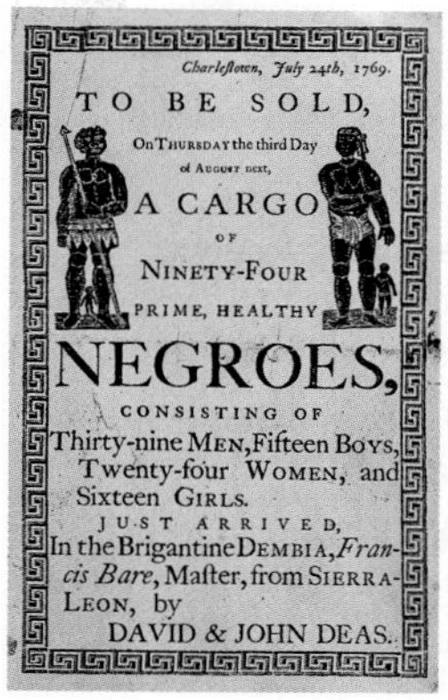

The Granger Collection, New York

12. Analyze What was the purpose of this poster?

13. Interpret Why did the creator of this poster include the details that he did?

Reading Skills

Questioning *Re-read the Inside Story feature that opens Section 3 of this chapter. As you read, ask yourself questions about what is happening in the story. Then answer the questions below.*

14. Where was chocolate originally made?

15. Who brought chocolate to Europe?

16. How was chocolate first received in Europe?

Writing About History

Narration: Writing a Biographical Essay *Many of the explorers who set out in search of new lands during the Age of Exploration did so to seek fame and fortune. As you have read, a number of explorers found the fame they sought and are still known today.*

17. Assignment: In an essay, write a biographical sketch of an explorer from the Age of Exploration. You can choose one of the explorers discussed in this chapter or another about whom you wish to learn more. Use information from this chapter and from other research in your sketch.

Answers

Analyzing Primary Sources

12. to sell the slaves listed on the poster

13. It states that the slaves are healthy in order to show that they will be strong workers.

Reading Skills

14. in the Americas

15. Christopher Columbus

16. People did not like chocolate at first; they considered it bitter.

Writing About History

17. Student biographical sketches should focus on one explorer of the Age of Exploration and provide details about that explorer's life and motivations for exploration, the area he explored, and the effects of his voyage.

A rubric for this activity is provided in **CRF:** Writing for the SAT.

HOLT

History's Impact

► **Video Program: Exploration and Expansion**

Refer to the Video Program Teacher's Guide for the answer to the closing question.

Review and Assessment Resources

Review and Reinforce

- **CRF:** Chapter Review
- **Quick Facts Transparency**: Visual Study Guide: Exploration and Expansion
- **Spanish Chapter Summaries Audio CD Program**
- OSP **Holt PuzzlePro**: Quiz Show for ExamView
- **Quiz Game CD-ROM**

Assess

- **PASS**: Chapter Test, Forms A and B
- **Alternative Assessment Handbook**
- OSP **ExamView Test Generator**, Chapter Test
- **Differentiated Instruction Modified Worksheets and Tests CD-ROM**: Chapter Test
- HOAP **Holt Online Assessment Program** (in the Premier Online Edition)

Reteach/Intervene

- **Interactive Reader and Study Guide**
- **Differentiated Instruction Teacher Management System**: Lesson Plans for Differentiated Instruction
- **Differentiated Instruction Modified Worksheets and Tests CD-ROM**: Chapter Test
- **Interactive Skills Tutor CD-ROM**

go.hrw.com
Online Resources
KEYWORD: SHL TEACHER

Chapter 3 Planning Guide

New Asian Empires

Chapter Overview	Reproducible Resources	Technology Resources
CHAPTER 3 **pp. 98–127** **Overview: In this chapter, students will learn about the great empires and shifts in power that occurred in Asia from 1200 to 1800.**	**Differentiated Instruction Teacher Management System:** * • Pacing Guide • Lesson Plans for Differentiated Instruction **Interactive Reader and Study Guide:** Chapter Summary* **Chapter Resource File*** • Writing for the SAT • Social Studies Skill • Chapter Review **World History Outline Maps**	**Live Ink© Online Reading Help** **Student Edition on Audio CD Program** **Differentiated Instruction Modified Worksheets and Tests CD-ROM** **World History Primary Source Library CD-ROM** **Power Presentations with Video CD-ROM** **History's Impact: World History Video Program (VHS/DVD):** New Asian Empires
Section 1: **The Ottoman and Safavid Empires** **The Main Idea:** The Ottoman and Safavid empires flourished under powerful rulers who expanded the territory and cultural influence of their empires.	**Differentiated Instruction Teacher Management System:** Section 1 Lesson Plan* **Interactive Reader and Study Guide:** Section 1 Summary* **Chapter Resource File*** • Vocabulary Builder: Section 1 • Biography: `Abbas • History and Geography: Muslim Rule in India Gains Foothold • Primary Source: Soldiers of the Ottoman Empire	**Daily Test Practice Transparency:** Section 1* **Map Transparency:** Asian Empires, c. 1600's* **Map Transparency:** The Ottoman Empire, 1300–1683* **Map Transparency:** The Safavid Empire, 1500–1639*
Section 2: **The Mughal Empire** **The Main Idea:** Mughal rulers created a powerful empire in which military might and artistic culture flourished.	**Differentiated Instruction Teacher Management System:** Section 2 Lesson Plan* **Interactive Reader and Study Guide:** Section 2 Summary* **Chapter Resource File*** • Vocabulary Builder: Section 2 • Biography: Nur Jahan	**Daily Test Practice Transparency:** Section 2* **Map Transparency:** Mughal Empire, 1526–1707* **Quick Facts Transparency:** Achievements of the Mughal Emperors*
Section 3: **The Ming and Qing Dynasties** **The Main Idea:** During the Ming and Qing dynasties China prospered, but the empire entered a period of isolation in response to increasing European contact.	**Differentiated Instruction Teacher Management System:** Section 3 Lesson Plan* **Interactive Reader and Study Guide:** Section 3 Summary* **Chapter Resource File*** • Vocabulary Builder: Section 3 • Biography: Zhang Juzheng	**Daily Test Practice Transparency:** Section 3* **Map Transparency:** Ming and Qing Dynasties, 1368–1911* **Map Transparency:** The Voyages of Zheng He* **Internet Activity:** Ming and Qing Art
Section 4: **Medieval Japan and Korea** **The Main Idea:** During the medieval period, a feudal warrior society developed in Japan, while Korea's rulers endured invasion and turned to isolation.	**Differentiated Instruction Teacher Management System:** Section 4 Lesson Plan* **Interactive Reader and Study Guide:** Section 4 Summary* **Chapter Resource File*** • Vocabulary Builder: Section 4 • Biography: Tomoe Gozen • Literature: Hokku Poems	**Daily Test Practice Transparency:** Section 4* **Map Transparency:** Japan and Korea, 1592–1597* **Internet Activity:** Japanese Theatre

go.hrw.com | Print Resource | Transparency
Learning Styles | Audio CD | CD-ROM
Video | **SE** Student Edition | **TE** Teacher's Edition
OSP One-Stop Planner CD-ROM
*also on One-Stop Planner CD-ROM

Review, Assessment, Intervention

- **Quick Facts Transparency:** New Asian Empires*
- **Progress Assessment Support System (PASS):** Chapter Test*
- **Differentiated Instruction Modified Worksheets and Tests CD-ROM:** Modified Chapter Test
- OSP **One-Stop Planner CD-ROM:** ExamView Test Generator (English/Spanish)
- HOAP **Holt Online Assessment Program (HOAP),** in the Holt Premier Online Student Edition

- **PASS:** Section 1 Quiz*
- **Online Quiz:** Section 1
- **Alternative Assessment Handbook**

- **PASS:** Section 2 Quiz*
- **Online Quiz:** Section 2
- **Alternative Assessment Handbook**

- **PASS:** Section 3 Quiz*
- **Online Quiz:** Section 3
- **Alternative Assessment Handbook**

- **PASS:** Section 4 Quiz*
- **Online Quiz:** Section 4
- **Alternative Assessment Handbook**

HOLT
History's Impact
World History Video Program (VHS/DVD)
New Asian Empires

Power Presentation with Video CD-ROM

Power Presentations with Video are visual presentations of each chapter's main ideas. Presentations can be customized by including Quick Facts charts, images and maps from the textbook, and video clips.

Holt Online Learning

go.hrw.com
Teacher Resources
KEYWORD: SHL TEACHER

go.hrw.com
Student Resources
KEYWORD: SHL NAS

- Document-Based Questions
- Interactive Multimedia Activities
- Current Events
- Chapter-Based Internet Activities
- and more!

Holt Premier
Online Student Edition

Complete online support for interactivity, assessment, and reporting

- Interactive Maps and Notebook
- Homework Practice and Research Activities Online

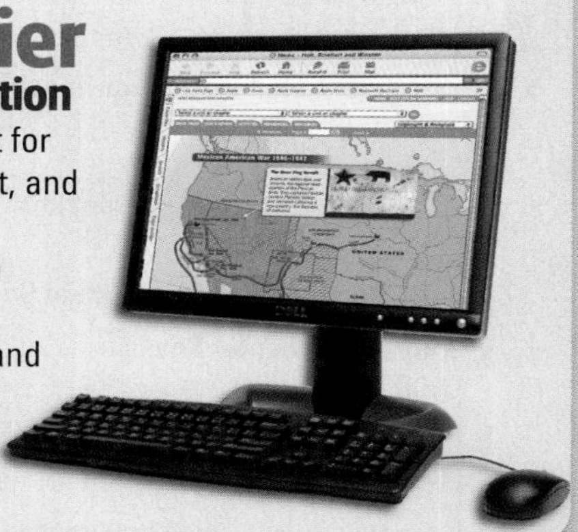

The Big Picture

Peter N. Stearns

Gunpowder Empires The emergence of large new empires in Asia, embracing many different cultures and language groups, was a crucial development during the early modern period. Based in part on the use of land-based guns, particularly siege cannons, new groups of invaders seized power in the Middle East/southeastern Europe, Persia, and India. Empire also revived in China. Japan did not form an empire, but did develop more centralized rule within the feudal system. For several centuries, the Asian empires maintained substantial political power, opulent cities, and a variety of new contributions in the arts. They also played a vigorous economic role.

The Ottoman, Safavid and Mughal Empires Three empires were Muslim-ruled, giving some renewed political coherence to Islam. During their initial phases, the empires were also tolerant, which contributed to their success. The empires made significant contributions to bureaucratic development, as well as to military strength. They also had a major cultural impact, through new artistic and architectural combinations and even linguistic innovation.

East Asia Generalizations about China in this period often miss the mark. Two major dynasties flourished during the early modern centuries. The second, the Qing, was imposed from the outside and had characteristics of the gunpowder empires of southern and western Asia. A brief flurry of international trade was followed by greater internal focus. Still China remained a center for global production and profited from European-mediated exchanges with the Americas. Japan adopted a more systematic policy of isolation, but even here trade with the Dutch persisted. The Tokugawa shogunate maintained the feudal social system and Confucianism gained ground, leading to educational expansion.

Decline Several of the gunpowder empires faltered by around 1700. The Mughal Empire fell into serious trouble because of military overextension and growing intolerance. The Ottoman Empire reached peak expansion in the 17th century. China displayed some new problems by the 18th century.

Recent Scholarship

India before Europe (2006) is a sympathetic and readable study of the varieties of Indian development in the early modern period, from the establishment of the Mughal Empire to important regional kingdoms. Catherine B. Asher and Cynthia Talbot deal well with Muslim-Hindu relationships, including the vitality of Indian Islam, as well as with urban, artistic, economic patterns. Also vital for the period and hugely influential in recent world history, is Kenneth Pomeranz's *The Great Divergence: China, Europe, and the Making of the Modern World Economy* (2000), which shows the vitality of Chinese world trade and challenges conventional interpretations of Europe's economic gains.

Differentiating Instruction

Differentiated Instruction Teacher Management System
- Pacing Guide
- Lesson Plans for Differentiated Instruction

Interactive Reader and Study Guide

Spanish Chapter Summaries Audio CD Program

Student Edition on Audio CD Program

Differentiated Instruction Modified Worksheets and Tests CD-ROM
- Vocabulary Flash Cards
- Modified Vocabulary Builder Activities
- Modified Chapter Review Activity
- Modified Chapter Test

OSP **One-Stop Planner CD-ROM**
- ExamView Test Generator (English/Spanish)
- PuzzlePro
- Quiz Show for ExamView
- Transparencies and Videos

TE **Differentiated Activities in the Teacher's Edition**
- Map of Constantinople, p. 103
- The Death of Akbar, p. 107
- The Mongols, p. 112
- Social Structure of Feudal Japan, p. 122

Reading Like a Historian

Sam Wineburg

Historical Imaginings Some seventy years before Columbus reached the New World, the fleet of Admiral Zheng He, the eunuch mariner and emissary of the Ming Emperor Yongle, set out on a remarkable voyage. From China, Zheng He's captains sailed their massive 500-feet long junks to the western coast of Africa, then crossed the Atlantic to modern day Mexico, Brazil, Patagonia, and California. Along the way they brought horses to the Americas, smelted copper in Greenland, and mined for lead and saltpeter in Australia.

Fantastic? Not according to former British submarine commander and amateur historian, Gavin Menzies, whose *1421: The Year China Discovered the World*, published in 2002 climbed to the top of best-seller lists and became a media sensation. It's not everyday that a thick book packed with multiple-page explanations of celestial navigation makes front-page news ("Did the Chinese beat out Columbus?" asked the *International Herald Tribune*, June 25, 2005.) Even if a fraction of Menzies' claims are true, then the textbook you are holding will have to undergo substantial revision.

On his website (http://www.1421.tv) Menzies has amassed over 100,000 notes from supporters, the preponderance of which are from like-minded enthusiasts eager to debunk accepted history. One scans the list in vain for endorsements by serious historians—Western, Chinese, or otherwise. They have not been forthcoming.

"Alternative History" Why have historians been slow to warm to what *1421*'s publisher calls "the incredible true story of the discovery of America before Columbus was even born"? The response can be summed up in one word: evidence.

Consider just a few of the hundreds of claims *1421* puts forth: that Ming voyagers reached South and North America, Antarctica and Australia, even though no Ming artifacts have been located and documented in those regions; that, while visiting the tip of Patagonia, sailors captured giant ground sloths, even though by *1421* such beasts had been extinct for about a thousand years; that animals aboard these ships were nourished by foods mixed with desalinated sea water, even though there's no evidence the Chinese had mastered this technology; or that during long stretches at sea, Ming mariners replenished their own food supply by impressing "trained otters working in pairs to heard shoal into nets" even though no evidence is provided of such miraculous creatures. And this is just the tip of a Patagonian iceberg.

Reviewing the book in the *Journal of World History*, University of Arkansas historian Robert Finlay called Menzies a man "gripped by a mania to bend everything to his purposes," someone who "flouts the basic rules of both historical study and elementary logic." University of London's T. H. Barrett goes one step further. He claims that Menzies' imagination casts him "upon the desolate shores of Alternative History. There spacemen, Altanteans, and Templars jostle endlessly … in a picture of the past that never was."

Not all historians see *1421* without use. Writing in *World History Connected*, John E. Wills suggests that the book's greatest value may lay as a tool to "teach students about the use and misuse of historical evidence."

Zheng He was a remarkable mariner whose bold expeditions to the Indian Ocean are well documented by historical sources. Unfortunately, the eunuch admiral died at sea and was thus denied the custom of being reunited with his missing parts, long sealed in a jar, so that he would not remain impotent in the next life.

A historical interpretation unbound by evidence remains impotent in this life.

Chapter Preview

Chapter Main Ideas

Section 1 The Ottoman and Safavid empires flourished under powerful rulers who expanded the territory and cultural influence of their empires.

Section 2 Mughal rulers created a powerful empire in which military might and artistic culture flourished.

Section 3 During the Ming and Qing dynasties, China prospered, but the empire entered a period of isolation in response to increasing European contact.

Section 4 During the medieval period, a feudal warrior society developed in Japan, while Korea's rulers endured invasion and turned to isolation.

CHAPTER 3

1200–1800

New Asian Empires

THE BIG PICTURE In Asia, the period from 1200 to 1800 was a time of great empires and shifts in power. From east of the Mediterranean Sea to India, strong Muslim rulers built large empires. In China a new dynasty sought to revive the traditions neglected under the Mongols, while a military society arose in Japan.

Theme ARTS AND IDEAS

The civilizations of Asia have contributed many lasting achievements in the arts and ideas throughout history. In this chapter, you will learn about the contributions of China, Japan, and Muslim empires in Asia in the arts, learning, science, and technology.

TIME LINE

CHAPTER EVENTS

- **c. 1300** Osman founds the Ottoman state.
- **1368** China's Ming dynasty begins.
- **1392** The Choson dynasty begins in Korea.
- **1453** Ottomans conquer Constantinople.
- **1501** Safavid Empire founded.
- **1526** Mughal Empire founded.

1300 — 1400 — 1500

WORLD EVENTS

- **1279** Mongols found the Yuan dynasty in China.
- **1347** Black Death begins to spread through Europe.
- **1492** Columbus reaches the Americas.
- **1517** Protestant Reformation begins.

Key to Differentiating Instruction

Below Level

Basic-level activities designed for all students encountering new material

At Level

Intermediate-level activities designed for average students

Above Level

Challenging activities designed for honors and gifted and talented students

Standard English Mastery

Activities designed to improve standard English usage

Introduce the Chapter

At Level

New Asian Empires

Materials: 4 large sheets of paper, colored markers

1. Tell students that through fierce competition for power, rulers gained control over different parts of Asia. Organize the class into four groups, and assign each group a section of this chapter.
2. Have each group look for major power struggles that are described within their assigned section.
3. Distribute one sheet of paper and one marker to each group. Have students record their assigned section number at the top, and record their findings on the paper.
4. When groups have finished their work, have them share their findings. Have students take notes during the presentations and ask them to retain their notes as a study tool.

LS Interpersonal, Verbal-Linguistic

Alternative Assessment Handbook, Rubrics 1: Acquiring Information; and 14: Group Activity

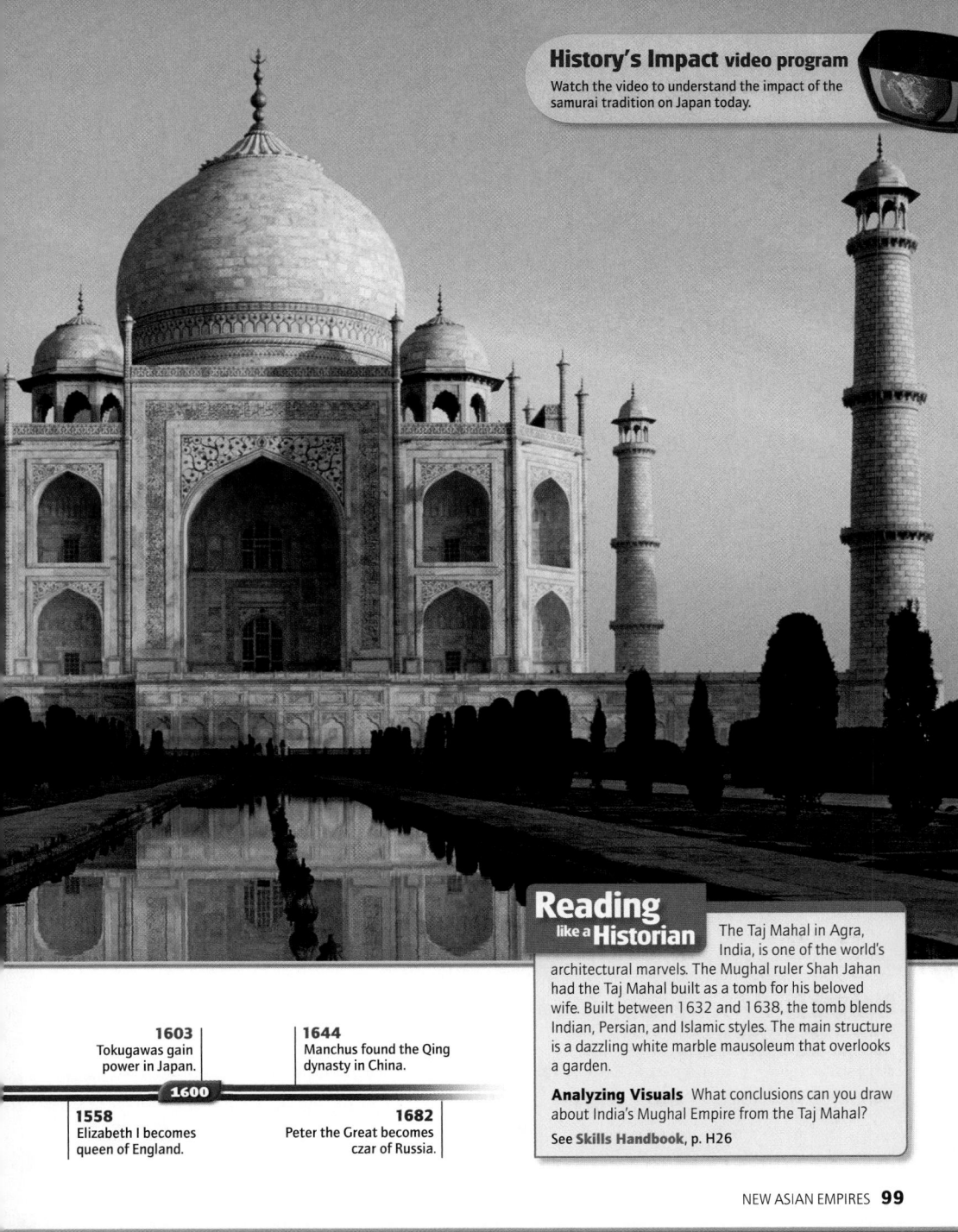

History's Impact video program
Watch the video to understand the impact of the samurai tradition on Japan today.

Reading like a Historian The Taj Mahal in Agra, India, is one of the world's architectural marvels. The Mughal ruler Shah Jahan had the Taj Mahal built as a tomb for his beloved wife. Built between 1632 and 1638, the tomb blends Indian, Persian, and Islamic styles. The main structure is a dazzling white marble mausoleum that overlooks a garden.

Analyzing Visuals What conclusions can you draw about India's Mughal Empire from the Taj Mahal?

See **Skills Handbook**, p. H26

1558 Elizabeth I becomes queen of England.

1600

1603 Tokugawas gain power in Japan.

1644 Manchus found the Qing dynasty in China.

1682 Peter the Great becomes czar of Russia.

Chapter Preview

HOLT
History's Impact
► **Video Program: New Asian Empires**
See the Video Teacher's Guide for strategies for using the video segment.

Reading Like a Historian
Analyzing Visuals This memorial mausoleum expresses not only love for the departed, but reminds the faithful to pray. Point out to students that the minarets are part of the overall plan, and that the spires atop the buildings guide one's eyes upward. Have students describe the effect of the reflecting pond and explain how the desert location of the Taj Mahal adds to the pond's importance.

Explore the Time Line
1. Which dynasty was founded in 1279? *the Yuan dynasty in China*
2. How much time elapsed between the founding of the Safavid Empire and the Mughal Empire? *25 years*
3. What event began in Europe in 1517? *the Protestant Reformation*
4. Who gained power in 1603 in Japan? *the Tokugawas*

Info to Know
The Taj Mahal The Taj Mahal was built during the reign of Shah Jahan, who brought workers from all over India and central Asia to work on the building. It took more than 20,000 workers and over 20 years to finish the job.

Make Inferences What statement does this building make about the reign of Shah Jahan? *possible answer—that he was a powerful ruler with unlimited financial resources, and that his reign lasted a long time*

go.hrw.com
Online Resources
Chapter Resources: KEYWORD: SHL NAS
Teacher Resources: KEYWORD: SHL TEACHER

Answers
Reading Like a Historian *possible answer—that the Mughals were wealthy and Muslim*

Preteach

Geography Starting Points

The Caucasus Mountains The name of these mountains is at the root of the term that is used to identify people with fair skin (Caucasian). In 1795, Johann Blumenbach, a German anthropologist, introduced the term, because he erroneously assumed that the ancestors of such people had originated somewhere in the Caucasus range. Though it is not a scientific term, it is still in use for want of a better one. The mountains themselves received their name from the Greek word *kaukhasis*, which came from the Scythian *kroy-khasis*, which literally means "(the mountain) ice-shining."

- **Map Transparency:** Asian Empires, c. 1600's
- **World History Outline Maps**
- **Interactive Map:** Asian Empires, c. 1600's

GEOGRAPHY Starting Points

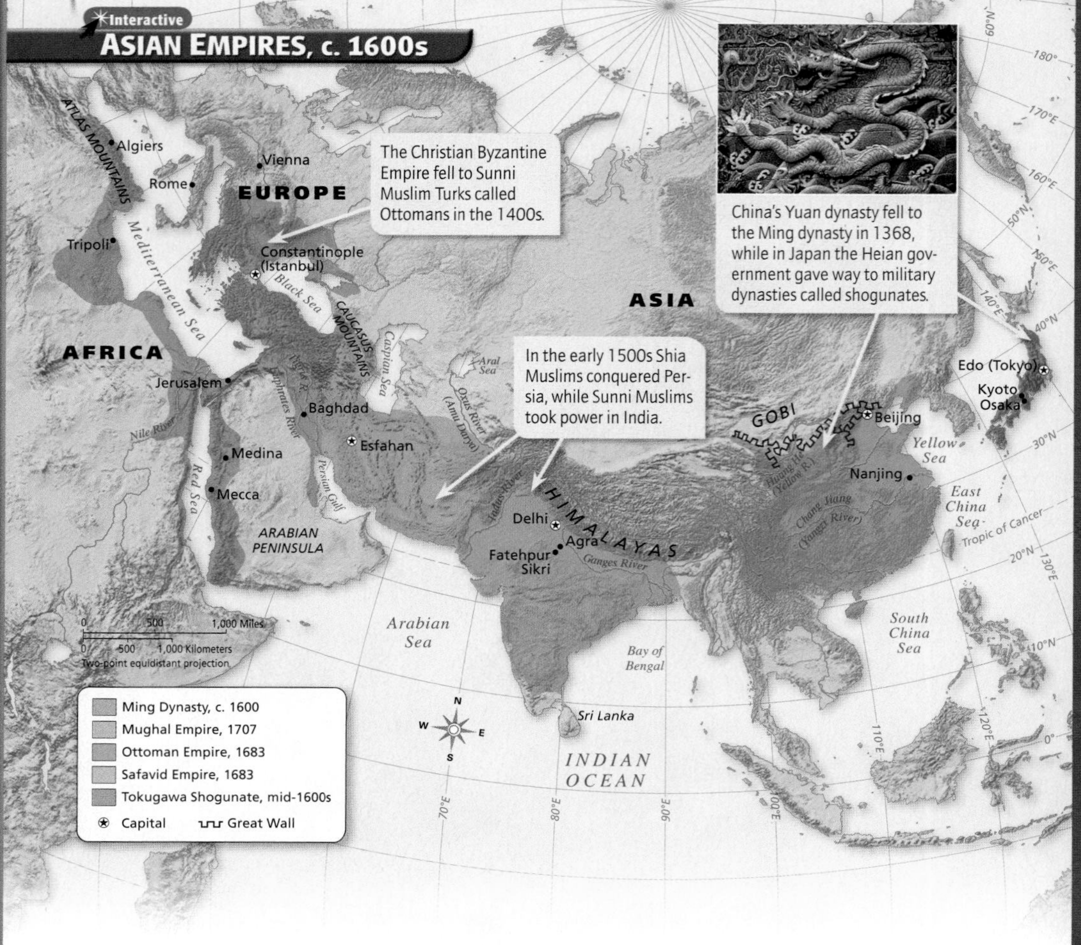

Starting Points Between 1300 and 1500 several powerful new empires arose in Asia. The rise of these empires represented major shifts in power in Asian society. In Turkey and India, for example, power shifted from the Christians and Hindus who had previously ruled to new Muslim rulers. In Japan, power shifted from a strong monarchy to rule by local rulers.

1. **Analyze** According to the map, what new dynasties took power in China and Japan during this period?
2. **Predict** What effects do you think the changes in government of the 1300s and 1400s had on Asian societies? Why do you think these changes took place?

Listen to History

Go online to listen to an explanation of the starting points for this chapter.

go.hrw.com
Keyword: SHL NAS

Answers

Geography Starting Points

1. *The Ming Dynasty and the Tokugawa Shogunate;* **2.** *New leaders would bring new styles of leadership, laws would change, and reforms would be introduced*

Skills Focus: Analyzing Maps

At Level

Social Studies Skill
Borders of Asian Empires

1. Tell students that they will identify the natural borders of each of the five Asian Empires.
2. Draw the chart for students to see. Omit the italicized answers. Organize students into small groups, and have groups focus on one map area at a time as they fill in the chart. **LS Interpersonal, Visual-Spatial**

Alternative Assessment Handbook, Rubrics 13: Graphic Organizers; and 21: Map Reading

Asian Empires	Natural Borders
Mughal	*Arabian Sea, Bay of Bengal, Indian Ocean, Himalaya's*
Ottoman	*Black Sea, Mediterranean Sea, Red Sea, Persian Gulf, Atlas Mountains, Caucasus Mountains*
Safavid	*Persian Gulf, Caspian Sea, Caucasus Mountains*
Ming	*Yellow, East China and South China Seas, Gobi Desert*
Tokugawa	*Yellow or East China Seas*

SECTION 1

The Ottoman and Safavid Empires

BEFORE YOU READ

MAIN IDEA

The Ottoman and Safavid empires flourished under powerful rulers who expanded the territory and cultural influence of their empires.

READING FOCUS

1. How did the Ottomans build a powerful empire, and what were their cultural accomplishments?
2. How was the Safavid Empire founded and enlarged, and what cultural elements did it combine?

KEY TERMS AND PEOPLE

ghazis
Ottomans
sultan
Janissaries
Mehmed II
Suleyman I
shah
'Abbas

TAKING NOTES Take notes in a graphic organizer like this one to record key facts about the Ottoman and Safavid empires.

Ottoman	Safavid

▲ Ottoman forces use massive cannons in their siege of Constantinople in 1453.

THE INSIDE STORY ***How might a black powder alter history?*** For more than 1,000 years, Constantinople had been the capital—the New Rome—of the Byzantine Empire, the eastern half of the old Roman Empire. By 1453, though, the once-great empire was crumbling, falling to invaders called Ottomans.

The 21-year-old Ottoman ruler, Mehmed II, burned with desire to take Constantinople. But how to break through its massive walls? The answer was an explosive black powder called gunpowder. Invented by the Chinese, gunpowder had slowly spread west. There, the Ottomans were among the first to use gunpowder weapons, such as cannons—weapons that changed warfare and the course of history.

Mehmed II surrounded Constantinople and aimed massive cannons at its walls. After some two months of battering, the city fell. Waves of Ottoman soldiers flooded in, killing and enslaving thousands. One witness said the "blood flowed through the streets like rainwater after a sudden storm." With Constantinople's conquest, the Ottoman Empire had become one of the great world powers. ■

The Ottoman Empire

The Mongol conquests of the 1200s had ripped apart the Seljuk Turk empire in Anatolia, a region also known as Asia Minor. A number of small, independent Turkish states then formed in the region. In the late 1200s a great chieftain, who was from one of these states, arose and went on to found the powerful Ottoman Empire.

Preteach

Getting Started

Use the **Interactive Reader and Study Guide** to familiarize students with the section content.

Interactive Reader and Study Guide, Section 1

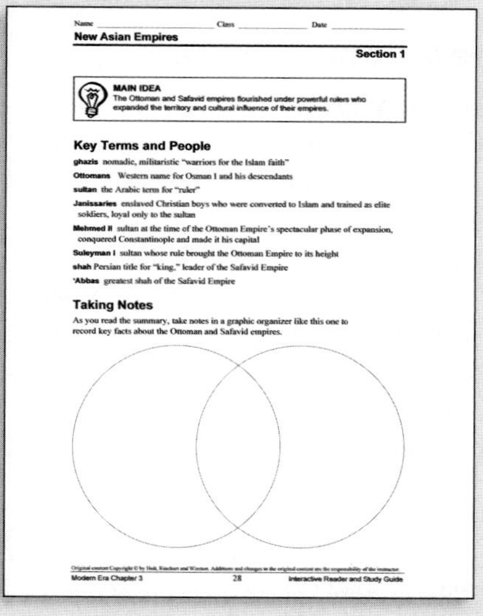
Name ______ Class ______ Date ______

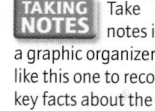

New Asian Empires

Section 1

MAIN IDEA
The Ottoman and Safavid empires flourished under powerful rulers who expanded the territory and cultural influence of their empires.

Key Terms and People

ghazis nomadic, militaristic "warriors for the Islam faith"
Ottomans Western name for Osman I and his descendants
sultan the Arabic term for "ruler"
Janissaries enslaved Christian boys who were converted to Islam and trained as elite soldiers, loyal only to the sultan
Mehmed II sultan at the time of the Ottoman Empire's spectacular phase of expansion, conquered Constantinople and made it his capital
Suleyman I sultan whose rule brought the Ottoman Empire to its height
shah Persian title for "king," leader of the Safavid Empire
'Abbas greatest shah of the Safavid Empire

Taking Notes

As you read the summary, take notes in a graphic organizer like this one to record key facts about the Ottoman and Safavid empires.

Modern Era Chapter 3 28 Interactive Reader and Study Guide

CRF: Vocabulary Builder: Section 1

Taking Notes

Ottoman Empire—Muslim Turks of Anatolia; took over the declining Christian Byzantine Empire; Constantinople fell to the Ottomans, became known as Istanbul; vast, diverse empire; sultan made all laws; magnificent mosques and palaces; began to decline in 1600s, lasted until 1900s; Safavid Empire—Persian Muslims began building an empire in the 1500s; Shia; laid foundation for the culture of present-day Iran; Both—Muslim empires who flourished under strong leaders

Teach the Main Idea

At Level

The Ottoman and Safavid Empires

Materials: 4 sheets of construction paper

1. **Teach** Ask students the Reading Focus questions to teach this section.
2. **Apply** Organize students into four groups. Assign one of the main topics of the section to each group. Have each group create a poster that shows the main ideas presented under their assigned heading.
3. **Review** Have groups display their posters and share the main ideas behind their illustrations.
4. **Practice/Homework** Have each student write a one-paragraph summary of the major ideas presented in this section. **LS Verbal-Linguistic, Visual-Spatial**

Alternative Assessment Handbook, Rubrics 24: Oral Presentations; and 28: Posters

Reading Focus

1 How did the Ottomans build a powerful empire, and what were their cultural accomplishments? *rich, diverse culture, many religious practices, built magnificent mosques and palaces*

The Ottoman Empire

Identify What were two advantages of the Ottoman military? *elite soldiers loyal to sultan, had superior new weapons*

Explain What was special about the location of Anatolia? *It lay at the strategic intersection of Asia and Europe.*

Develop What are some possible reasons the Ottomans might have shown cultural and religious tolerance? *possible answer—They would have faced less opposition from the conquered and benefited from their knowledge.*

CRF: Primary Source: Soldiers of the Ottoman Empire

Interpreting Maps

The Ottoman Empire, 1300–1683

Human/Environment Interaction Why do you think the Ottomans never expanded their territory west of the Nile? *It is a desert area without water or other resources needed to support human life.*

Movement In the expansion of 1451 to 1520, in which direction did the Ottomans travel to add territory that was not contiguous to their own? *north, to Crimea*

Map Transparency: The Ottoman Empire, 1300–1683

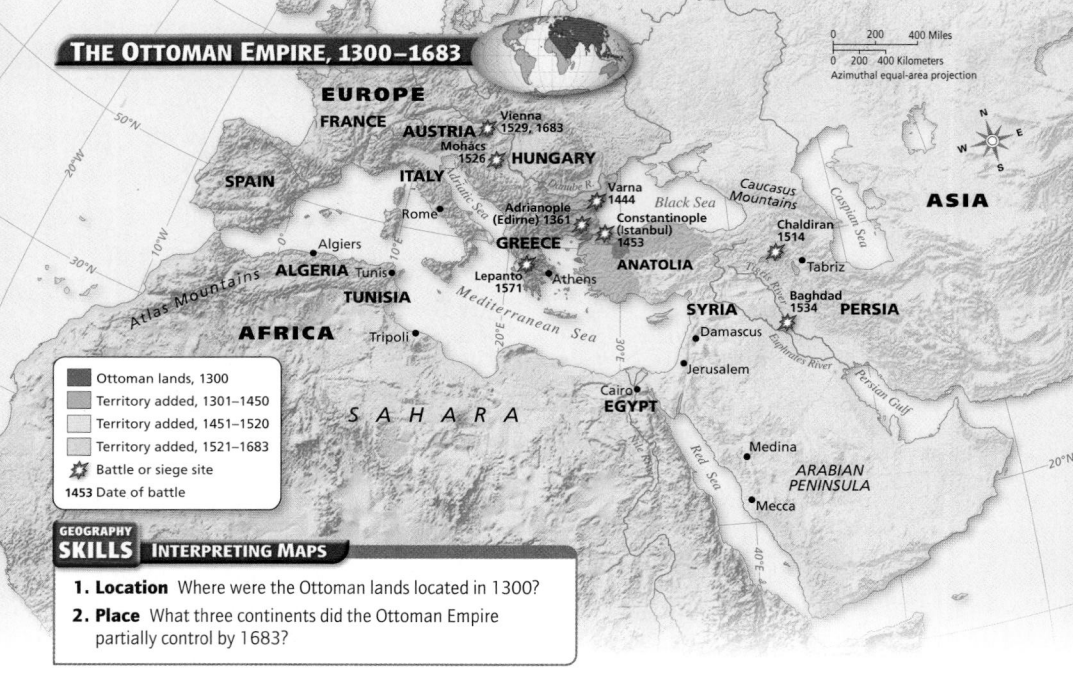

GEOGRAPHY SKILLS INTERPRETING MAPS

1. **Location** Where were the Ottoman lands located in 1300?
2. **Place** What three continents did the Ottoman Empire partially control by 1683?

Growth of the Empire Anatolia lies at the strategic intersection of Asia and Europe. In the early 1300s, the region was bordered by the declining Christian Byzantine Empire to the west and by Muslim empires to the east. To the north, beyond the Black Sea, lay Russia.

The Turks of Anatolia were mainly Muslim. A nomadic people with a militaristic society, they saw themselves as ***ghazis,*** or "warriors for the Islam faith." One of the ablest *ghazi* leaders was Osman I. By 1300 he had built a strong state in Anatolia. Westerners came to refer to Osman and his descendants as the **Ottomans**. Their power grew quickly, and by the mid-1300s the Ottomans controlled much of Anatolia.

Orhan I, Osman's son, became the second Ottoman ruler and declared himself **sultan**, Arabic for "ruler." Under Orhan and later sultans, Ottoman forces swept into the Balkans in southeastern Europe to attack the Byzantine Empire. In 1361 the Ottomans took Adrianople, the second-most important Byzantine city, renamed it Edirne, and made it their capital. By the early 1400s the Ottomans controlled much of the Balkan Peninsula. Within about 100 years, the Ottoman state had grown into a true empire and become a European power.

The key to the Ottomans' success was their military. As their empire grew, the Ottomans enslaved Christian boys from conquered areas. The boys were converted to Islam and trained as elite soldiers called **Janissaries**, who were loyal only to the sultan. Many Christians called this practice a blood tax. In addition, the Ottomans adopted gunpowder weapons such as cannons. The force of these weapons made it possible to take cities defended by heavy walls.

Invasion and Decline Despite their strong military, the Ottomans experienced a setback when the great Central Asian conqueror Timur (TEEM-uhr) attacked. Because of an old leg injury, Timur was known as Timur the Lame and in Europe as Tamerlane. At the Battle of Ankara in 1402, his army crushed the Ottoman forces. Timur soon withdrew, but the Ottoman Empire was left in shambles, its ruler dead. A bloody power struggle followed, which weakened the empire.

Skills Focus: Identifying Main Idea and Details

At Level

Research Required

Reading Skill

The Ottomans

1. Remind students that the Ottomans were remarkably tolerant of other cultures and religions. Review the information in the text about the treatment of conquered people.
2. Have students design an illustrated, public relations brochure explaining the changes that will be coming to a people that cannot withstand the Ottoman army. Have students first sketch their ideas and plan the layout for their brochures. Remind students that the illustrations are crucial, as not everyone spoke the same language.
3. Have volunteers present their work to the class.
4. As an extension, have students write a generalization statement about the Ottoman treatment of conquered peoples.

LS Interpersonal, Visual-Spatial

Alternative Assessment Handbook, Rubric 3: Artwork

Answers

Interpreting Maps 1. *Balkans, Greece, Anatolia;* **2.** *Africa, Asia, Europe*

Fall of Constantinople Following a period of decline, a spectacular phase of expansion began with the reign of **Mehmed II** in the mid-1400s. A strong military leader, Mehmed was determined to take Constantinople, the Byzantine capital. The Ottomans had failed to capture this city despite conquering the lands around it. Constantinople controlled the Bosporus Strait, a major trade route between Asia and Europe. Control of this vital waterway not only provided the Byzantines with great wealth but also divided the Ottoman Empire.

In 1453 the Ottomans led a major land and sea assault against Constantinople. Using massive cannons, Ottoman forces battered the city's walls. After a siege of almost two months, Constantinople fell. The Byzantine Empire no longer existed. Mehmed became known as "the Conqueror," and, in triumph, claimed the center of eastern Christianity for Islam.

Mehmed made Constantinople his capital, which became known as Istanbul. In keeping with tradition, he allowed his soldiers to pillage the city for three days, during which many residents were killed or enslaved. Mehmed then rebuilt Constantinople into a Muslim city. He had palaces and mosques built and even had Hagia Sophia, the great Orthodox Christian cathedral, turned into a mosque. To repopulate the city, he had people moved there from across the empire. Soon, the city was again a major trade center with people of many cultures.

Height of the Empire Under the next three sultans, expansion continued. The Ottomans expanded their empire east through the rest of Anatolia. They also addressed a new threat in Persia—the Safavid Empire. In 1514 Ottoman forces crushed the Safavids at the Battle of Chaldiran. The Ottomans then swept through Syria and into Egypt in North Africa. Soon afterward, the Ottoman army captured Mecca and Medina, the holy cities of Islam.

The Ottoman Empire reached its height under **Suleyman I** (soo-lay-MAHN), known in the West as Suleyman "the Magnificent." During his reign, from 1520 to 1566, Ottoman forces pushed through Hungary up to Vienna. Meanwhile, the navy gained control of the eastern Mediterranean and the North African coast.

Suleyman's domestic achievements were equally impressive. He reformed the tax system and overhauled the government bureaucracy. In addition, he improved the court system and legal code and had new laws issued to reduce corruption. For these actions, he earned the title Suleyman "the Lawgiver."

Society and Culture The Ottoman sultan ruled over a vast and diverse empire. As head of this empire, the sultan had immense power and issued all laws and made all major decisions. Numerous officials advised the sultan, however. These officials were considered his slaves—that is, they had to be completely loyal to the sultan and the empire, and they had to practice Islam and follow Ottoman customs.

This privileged ruling class formed one of two classes in Ottoman society. The second class consisted of everyone else in the empire. This group included people of many cultures who spoke many different languages and practiced many different religions.

In general, the Ottomans governed their diverse subjects with tolerance. At the same time, Non-Muslims had to pay heavy taxes and endure restrictions, although they did not have to serve in the military. Muslims did have to join the military but they were not taxed. Following Islamic law, the Ottomans allowed religious freedom. They required some religious groups, such as Christians and Jews—People of the Book to Muslims—to form millets, or religious communities. Each millet could follow its own religious laws and choose its own leaders, who were responsible to the sultan.

FACES OF HISTORY

SULEYMAN
c. 1494–1566

Suleyman was named for the Hebrew king Soloman, whom the Qur'an considers to be the wisest ruler of antiquity. Energetic, calm, and intelligent, Suleyman studied subjects from architecture to geography to poetry. He used his vast knowledge to improve the Ottoman Empire in many ways. His military campaigns extended the empire to the east and west. He had many bridges and mosques built and reformed the empire's administration and laws, for which his subjects gave him the title *Kanuni*, or "Lawgiver." In addition, some historians consider Suleyman's rule to have been the height of Ottoman cultural achievements.

Summarize How did Suleyman improve the Ottoman Empire?

Direct Teach

Reading Focus

The Ottoman Empire

Describe How were Janissaries created? *In the Balkans, some Christian boys were taken from their families and converted to Islam and trained soldiers.*

Evaluate What is your opinion of Mehmed II's conquest of Constantinople? *possible answer—It was cruel to kill so many and it was not necessary to destroy a great city.*

Recent Scholarship

Osman's Dream: The History of the Ottoman Empire by Caroline Finkel is an overview of an empire that lasted over six centuries. Finkel describes the richness and the complexity of the Ottoman Empire. She looks at the Ottomans as they saw themselves and their empire, not as a Westerner looking at the empire from the outside. Osman's Dream is a careful, well-researched history, complete with descriptions of the richness, complexity, and change that occurred in the empire over the centuries.

Osman's Dream: The History of the Ottoman Empire by Caroline Finkel. Basic Books, 2006.

Differentiating Instruction

Below Level

Learners Having Difficulty; English-Language Learners

1. Remind students that Constantinople was a well-defended city and only fell because Sultan Mehmed II carried out an effective siege plan.
2. Have students use the maps in this chapter or in the atlas of their textbook to create a map showing the location Byzantium, the Black Sea, and the Bosporus Straits.
3. Have students show the path that Mehmed II took when he laid siege to the city. Students should show the probable positions of forts, armed forces, and the armada which felled the city. Student maps should include a key and a means for measuring distance. **LS Visual-Spatial**

Alternative Assessment Handbook, Rubrics 1: Acquiring Information; and 20: Map Creation

Answers

Faces of History *expanded the empire; built mosques and bridges; reformed the empire's administration and laws*

Direct Teach

Reading Focus

2 How was the Safavid Empire founded and enlarged, and what cultural elements did it combine? *through conquest; blended the Shía religion with Persian tradition, built magnificent cities, palaces, and mosques and produced a golden age*

The Safavid Empire

Identify Who was the founder of the Safavid Empire? *a 14-year old boy named Esma'il*

Explain How did religion bring the Safavid Empire into conflict with the Ottoman Empire? *The Safavids were Shia Muslims, while most other Muslims were Sunnis.*

Map Transparency: The Safavid Empire, 1500–1639

Primary Source

"I gave my orders—make a dress for my beloved.
Use the sun to make the top,
Use the moon to make the lining, Use the white clouds for the trimmings,
Use the blue of the sea to make the threads.
Use the stars for buttons, And make the fastenings out of me."

—excerpt of a letter from Suleyman to his wife, former Ukrainian slave, Roxolana

Interactive Map: The Safavid Empire, 1500–1639

The mixing of many peoples created a rich Ottoman culture, which reached its peak under Suleyman. Architects built magnificent mosques and palaces. Many buildings showed a Byzantine influence, such as in the use of domes. One master designer was Sinan. His Mosque of Suleyman in Istanbul shows a graceful solution to the problem of combining a round dome with a rectangular building.

The Empire's Decline After Suleyman's reign, the Ottoman Empire gradually declined. One cause was the practice of dealing with heirs. Until the 1600s, new sultans had their brothers killed to eliminate rivals. Later, princes and heirs were locked up in the royal palace. When a prince or heir was released to become sultan, he had no experience with governing. Though there were periodic efforts to reform the system, a series of weak sultans resulted. Even so, the empire lasted until the early 1900s.

READING SKILLS
Summarizing After you read the information on the Safavid Empire, summarize the key points in three to five sentences.

READING CHECK **Analyze** Why is Suleyman's reign considered the height of the Ottoman Empire?

The Safavid Empire

East of the Ottomans, Persian Muslims called the Safavids (sah-FAH-vuhds) began building an empire around 1500. The Safavids soon came into conflict with the Ottomans and other Muslims. The conflict related to Islam's split into the rival Sunni and Shia sects. The Safavids were Shia; most other Muslims were Sunnis.

Growth of the Empire The founder of the Safavid Empire was a 14-year-old boy named Esma'il (is-mah-EEL). His father had died fighting Sunni Muslims, and in 1501 Esma'il took up the sword. Joined by his father's supporters, Esma'il led his army on a sweep of conquest in Persia. In a series of victories, he gained control of what is now Iran as well as part of Iraq. Esma'il then took the Persian title of **shah,** or "king," of the Safavid Empire.

As shah, Esma'il made Shiism the official Safavid religion. This act worried his advisers because most people in the empire were Sunnis. Unconcerned, Esma'il said the following:

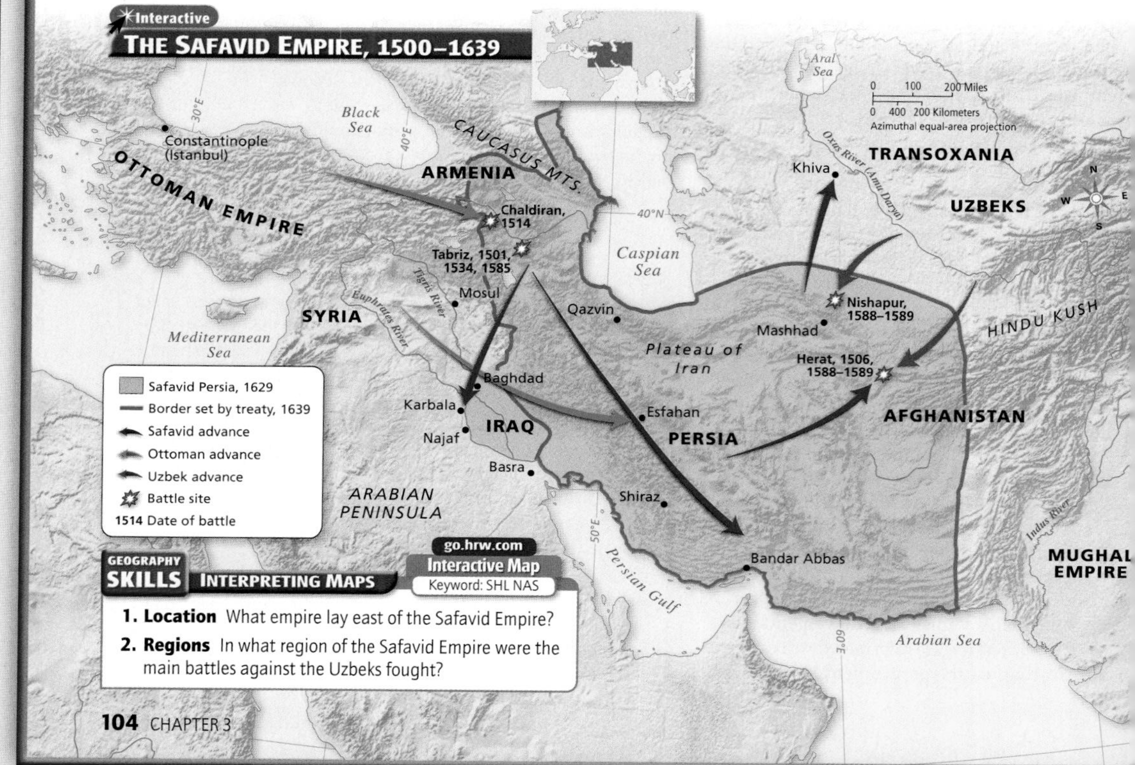

GEOGRAPHY SKILLS INTERPRETING MAPS

1. **Location** What empire lay east of the Safavid Empire?
2. **Regions** In what region of the Safavid Empire were the main battles against the Uzbeks fought?

Skills Focus: Comparing and Contrasting

At Level

Reading Skill

Expansion by Conquest

1. Review the rapid expansion of the Ottoman Empire with students. Use both the text and the maps in this section to help students understand the immensity of the Safavid Empire.
2. Organize students into an even number of groups, and have groups prepare for a debate on the topic "A civilization that expands by conquest will maintain power and spread their beliefs." Assign half of the groups to prepare statements to represent those who support this position. Assign the other groups to prepare statements to represent those who disagree.
3. When groups have prepared their statements, call upon pairs of groups to debate the issue.
4. When the debates are finished, have students write a short essay explaining their position on this topic. **LS Interpersonal, Verbal-Linguistic**

Alternative Assessment Handbook, Rubrics 10: Debates; and 14: Group Activity

Answers

Reading Skills *Student summaries should show an understanding of the Safavid Empire.*

Interpreting Maps **1.** *The Mughal Empire;* **2.** *in the northeast*

Reading Check *because Suleyman expanded the empire, built bridges and mosques, and reformed the administration and laws of the empire*

HISTORY'S VOICES

> "I am committed to this action; God and the Immaculate Imams [pure religious leaders] are with me, and I fear no one; by God's help, if the people utter one word of protest, I will draw the sword and leave not one of them alive."
>
> —Esma'il, quoted in *A Literary History of Persia, Volume 4,* by Edward G. Browne

The blending of Shia religion and Persian tradition gave the Safavid state a unique identity and laid the foundation for the national culture of present-day Iran. At the same time, Shiism sharply distinguished the Safavid state from its Sunni neighbors, notably the Ottomans to the west and the Uzbeks to the northeast.

Esma'il dreamed of converting all Sunnis to Shiism. He battled the Uzbeks with some success but suffered a crushing defeat by the Ottomans in 1514 at the Battle of Chaldiran. The Safavid army was no match for the Ottomans' superior gunpowder weapons. Esma'il died in 1524, and later Safavid shahs struggled to keep the empire together.

Then in 1588 the greatest Safavid leader, **'Abbas**, became shah. 'Abbas reformed the government, strengthened the military, and acquired modern gunpowder weapons. Copying the Ottoman model, 'Abbas had slave youths captured in Russia trained to be soldiers. Under 'Abbas's rule, the Safavids defeated the Uzbeks and gained back land lost to the Ottomans.

Culture and Economy 'Abbas's achievements produced a golden age in Safavid culture. Abbas brought in Chinese potters to improve the quality of glazed tiles and ceramics. The Safavids created public spaces with graceful arches and lush gardens. Colorful tiles and domes decorated mosques. During the 1600s the capital, Esfahan (es-fah-HAHN), was one of the world's most magnificent cities.

Safavid culture played a role in the empire's economy because 'Abbas encouraged the manufacturing of traditional products. Hand-woven Persian carpets became an important industry and export. Such trade goods brought wealth to the Safavid Empire and helped establish it as a major Muslim civilization. The empire lasted until 1722.

READING CHECK **Compare and Contrast** How were the achievements of Esma'il and 'Abbas similar, and how were they different?

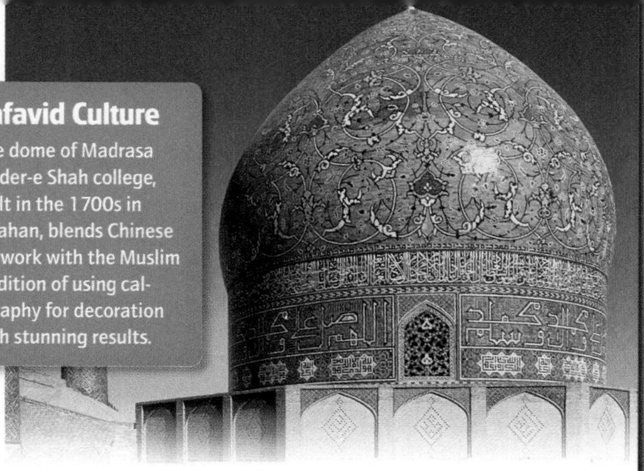

Safavid Culture
The dome of Madrasa Mader-e Shah college, built in the 1700s in Esfahan, blends Chinese tilework with the Muslim tradition of using calligraphy for decoration with stunning results.

SECTION 1 ASSESSMENT

go.hrw.com
Online Quiz
Keyword: SHL NAS HP

Reviewing Ideas, Terms, and People

1. **a. Identify** Who were the **Janissaries**, and what was their role in the success of the **Ottomans**?
   b. Draw Conclusions Why do you think Westerners referred to **Suleyman I** as "the Magnificent"?
   c. Elaborate What impact did the Ottoman Empire and its expansion have on European history? Support your explanation with examples from the reading.
2. **a. Recall** Why did the Safavid Empire come into conflict with other Muslim empires around it?
   b. Explain How did events of the Safavid period shape culture in the present-day country of Iran?
   c. Evaluate Who do you think was the better Safavid ruler—Esma'il or **'Abbas**? Provide reasons to support your opinion.

Critical Thinking

3. **Categorize** Using your notes and a graphic organizer like the one below, categorize and organize the information that you recorded about the Ottoman and Safavid empires.

	Ottoman	Safavid
Location		
Key People		
Key Events		
Society		
Culture		

FOCUS ON WRITING

4. **Persuasion** Write a short letter from the Ottoman sultan Mehmed II to his military advisors stating that he wants to attack the Byzantine capital of Constantinople. The letter should explain why capturing the city is so important to the Ottoman Empire and persuade the military advisors to support the campaign.

Direct Teach

Reading Focus

The Safavid Empire

Recall What were some achievements of 'Abbas? *He reformed the government, strengthened the military, and acquired gunpowder weapons.*

Interpret How did the Ottoman Empire defeat the Safavids in 1514? *by using superior gunpowder weapons*

CRF: Biography: `Abbas

Review & Assess

Close

Review the development of the Ottoman and Safavid dynasties, the means with which they expanded their territories, and the cultural influence of their empires.

Review

Online Quiz, Section 1

Assess

SE Section 1 Assessment

Progress Assessment: Section 1 Quiz

Alternative Assessment Handbook

Reteach/Intervene

Interactive Reader and Study Guide, Section 1

Interactive Skills Tutor CD-ROM

Section 1 Assessment Answers

1. **a.** Christian boys taken by the sultan, converted to Islam, trained to fight; became an elite fighting corps
   b. developed a code of laws, was responsible for empire's immense expansion
   c. led to the fall of Byzantine Empire
2. **a.**The Safavids were Shia Muslims, while most other Muslims were Sunnis.
   b. blended the Persian culture with Shia religion, laying the foundation for Iran's culture
   c. possible answer—`Abbas, because he gained back land that had been lost.
3. Ottoman—Anatolia, spreading into Africa, Asia, Europe; Mehmed II, Suleyman; fall of Constantinople; diverse society, two classes, religious tolerance; blended cultures; Safavid—east of the Ottomans, in Persia; Esma'il, 'Abbas; defeat by the Ottomans in 1514; 'Abbas's achievements brought a golden age in culture; magnificent city of Esfahan
4. Student letters should emphasize that Constantinople divided the Ottoman Empire. Acquiring it would provide great wealth and a trade route between Asia and Europe.

Answers

Reading Check *Both leaders focused on military. 'Abbas had more success in battle because he acquired gunpowder weapons.*

Preteach

Getting Started

Use the **Interactive Reader and Study Guide** to familiarize students with the section content.

Interactive Reader and Study Guide, Section 2

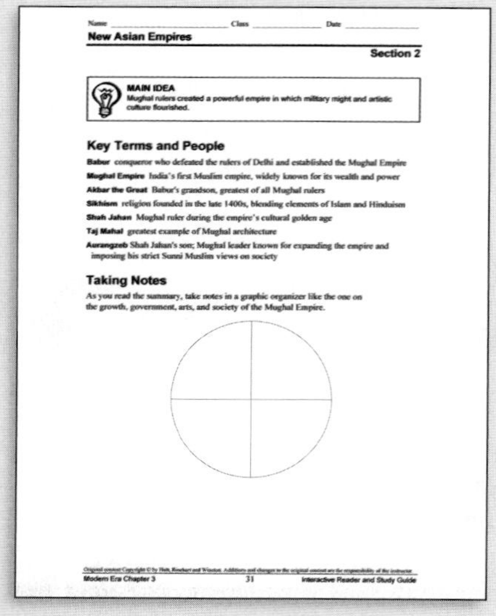

Name ______________ Class ________ Date ________

New Asian Empires

Section 2

MAIN IDEA
Mughal rulers created a powerful empire in which military might and artistic culture flourished.

Key Terms and People

Babur conqueror who defeated the rulers of Delhi and established the Mughal Empire
Mughal Empire India's first Muslim empire, widely known for its wealth and power
Akbar the Great Babur's grandson, greatest of all Mughal rulers
Sikhism religion founded in the late 1400s, blending elements of Islam and Hinduism
Shah Jahan Mughal ruler during the empire's cultural golden age
Taj Mahal greatest example of Mughal architecture
Aurangzeb Shah Jahan's son; Mughal leader known for expanding the empire and imposing his strict Sunni Muslim views on society

Taking Notes

As you read the summary, take notes in a graphic organizer like the one on the growth, government, arts, and society of the Mughal Empire.

Modern Era Chapter 3 — 31 — Interactive Reader and Study Guide

Academic Vocabulary

Review with students the high-use academic terms in this section.

stance attitude, position, or view about someone or something (p. 108)

regime a specific and often harsh government (p. 110)

CRF: Vocabulary Builder: Section 2

Taking Notes

Growth— defeated rulers of Delhi by 1526, established Mughal Empire, Akbar organized the empire, empire reached greatest size under Aurangzeb; Government—Akbar: won people's loyalty, fought to prevent rebellion, had firm grasp of government and finances; Shah Jahan imposed heavy taxes; Arts-cultural golden age during the reign of Shah Jahan, Taj Mahal built, along with other monuments of Mughal majesty such as the Peacock Throne; Society—religious tolerance, Jahangir came into conflict with Sikhs.

SECTION

2 The Mughal Empire

Before You Read

Main Idea

Mughal rulers created a powerful empire in which military might and artistic culture flourished.

Reading Focus

1. How was Muslim rule first established in India?
2. What was the new empire created by Babur and Akbar like?
3. What achievements were made by the rulers who held power at the height of the Mughal Empire?

Key Terms and People

Babur
Mughal Empire
Akbar the Great
Sikhism
Shah Jahan
Taj Mahal
Aurangzeb

TAKING NOTES Take notes in a graphic organizer like this one on the growth, government, arts, and society of the Mughal Empire.

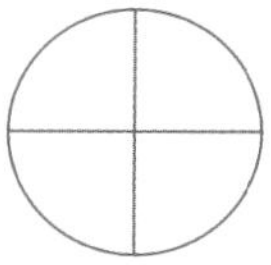

THE INSIDE STORY ***How did a young prince and his outnumbered army create an empire?*** From birth, Prince Babur seemed destined to be a conqueror. Babur, whose name means "tiger," was a descendant of both Timur, the great general from Central Asia, and Genghis Khan, perhaps the greatest conqueror in Asian history. At 11 Babur became king of Fergana, a small territory in Central Asia. By 14 he had led a victorious army to take the city of Samarqand.

Babur's ambition was to build a huge empire that rivaled that of his ancestor Timur. As part of his empire building, Babur set out to conquer India in 1525. He and his army marched deep into India, heading for the capital, Delhi. In response, the Indian army came out to meet them. The two armies faced off near the small village of Panipat.

Babur's army was vastly outnumbered by the Indians. He had only about 12,000 troops with which to fight an estimated 100,000 foes. In addition, the Indian army included some 1,000 elephants, while Babur's had none. At first glance, the battle appeared to be hopeless.

However, Babur's army was better trained and better disciplined than the Indians. In addition, Babur had a secret weapon—cannons—never before used in India. The first cannon shots astounded the Indians and terrified the elephants, who turned and stampeded through the Indian army. Within a few hours, Babur had won. Historians mark this victory as the beginning of a new empire in India. ■

◀ **Babur's cannons helped him overcome overwhelming odds to win the Battle of Panipat and create a new empire.**

Battle of Panipat illustration from the *Baburnama*, c. 1598

106

Teach the Main Idea

At Level

The Mughal Empire

1. **Teach** Ask students the Reading Focus questions to teach this section.
2. **Apply** Organize students into three groups. Assign each group one of the three topics in the section: Muslim Rule in India, A New Empire, Height of the Mughal Empire. Have each group plan a set of drawings to illustrate the main points of its assigned topic. Each member of the group should have one main point to illustrate. When students have finished their drawings, have them record the main point at the bottom of their papers.
3. **Review** Have each group present its work in the same order the topics are presented in the text. Create a class display of the drawings.
4. **Practice/Homework** Have students write a short summary of what they learned about the Mughal Empire. **LS Interpersonal, Visual-Spatial**

Alternative Assessment Handbook, Rubrics 3: Artwork; and 24: Oral Presentations

Muslim Rule in India

After the fall of the Gupta Empire in the 500s, India broke apart into a number of small kingdoms. For several centuries, no single ruler emerged to take charge of all India.

The Arrival of Islam During this period of small kingdoms, Arab Muslim traders arrived in India for the first time. These traders sailed to ports along India's west coast in search of goods such as spices. Over time, some Muslim traders settled in Indian towns, where they peacefully lived beside Hindus and Buddhists.

The next Muslims to arrive in India, however, were not so peaceful. In the early 700s Muslim raiders invaded and conquered the region of Sind in what is now Pakistan. About 300 years later, Muslims poured into north India from Afghanistan. By the 1200s, most of northern India was under Muslim control.

The Delhi Sultanate Once the Muslims had taken control of north India, they established a new government for the region. Because this new government was based in the city of Delhi, it became known as the Delhi sultanate.

The rulers of the Delhi sultanate were tolerant and allowed the Indian people to practice their traditional customs and religions. At the same time, though, they worked to spread Muslim culture through India by inviting artists and scholars from other parts of the Islamic world to Delhi. As a result, a new culture formed that blended Muslim and Indian elements. For example, a new language, Urdu, formed from a combination of Arabic and Sanskrit.

READING CHECK **Sequence** How did Muslims come to rule India?

A New Empire

The Delhi sultanate remained strong for about 300 years. By the early 1500s, however, its power was weakening. This weakening left India open to invasion.

Babur The man who took advantage of India's weakness was a young Central Asian conqueror named Zahir ud-Din, but better known as **Babur**, or "the tiger." After trying and failing to create an empire in Central Asia, Babur turned to India. By 1526 he had defeated the rulers of Delhi and founded the **Mughal Empire**. The Mughals—whose name comes from the Persian word *Mogul* for "Mongol"—reigned as India's first Muslim empire and were one of the great civilizations of history. The Mughal Empire was known for its wealth and power.

Akbar the Great Babur died shortly after his conquest of India, and the task of organizing what he had conquered fell to his descendants. Most of this organization was done by Babur's grandson **Akbar the Great**. Despite being only 13 when he took the throne in 1556, Akbar became the greatest of all Mughal rulers.

FACES OF HISTORY

AKBAR
1542–1605

A Mughal emperor of India, Akbar united Indian territory north of the Vindhya Range under one empire. His rule is noted for many reforms, including the abolition of slavery and the development of trade. He was a patron of the arts and encouraged the development of science. Although himself a Muslim, his tolerance for non-Muslims in his empire was remarkable. His enlightened leadership became a model for later Mughal rulers.

Analyze Why was Akbar considered a great ruler?

Akbar built a new capital called Fatehpur Sikri, or the "City of Victory," to commemorate his achievements as emperor.

107

Differentiating Instruction

Above Level

Research Required

Advanced Learners/Gifted and Talented

1. Remind students that historians sometimes differ in their opinions because they do not have access to an accurate, definitive accounts of an event, the references that are available contradict each other, or accounts of events show bias.
2. Organize students into small groups and have students in each group to locate and read three or more primary and secondary articles about the death of Akbar. Have students find what they can about the writer or sponsor of the Internet site and record any indication of possible bias.
3. When students have finished their research, have them review the documents and formulate their own answers to this question: Did Akbar poison his father or not? Have volunteers from each group present their positions and reasoning, supported by research findings, to the class. **LS Verbal-Linguistic**

Alternative Assessment Handbook, Rubrics 11: Discussions; and 30: Research

Direct Teach

Reading Focus

1 How was Muslim rule first established in India? *After the fall of the Gupta Empire, there were many small kingdoms; Muslim traders arrived and lived peacefully; Muslim raiders conquered the region in the early 700s; in the 1200s Delhi sultanate was established*

Muslim Rule in India

Recall What was the Delhi sultanate? *series of Muslim dynasties that arose in 1200s, expanded Muslim influence into southern India*

Judge How do you think Babur's failure to build an empire in Central Asia affected him? *possible answers—decided to become fierce warrior, determined not to lose battles again*

Reading Focus

2 What was the new empire created by Babur and Akbar like? *The rulers expanded the empire, believed in religious tolerance, developed strong, centralized government*

A New Empire

Explain How were Akbar and Jahangir related to Babur? *Akbar was Babur's grandson; Jahangir was Babur's great-grandson.*

Summarize Why was Jahangir a popular ruler? *continued religious tolerence, supported artists and writers, appointed Hindus and Muslims to office, adopted Persian influences*

CRF: History and Geography: Muslim Rule in India Gains a Foothold

Answers

Faces of History *He encouraged religious tolerance and instituted many beneficial reforms.*

Reading Check *Muslim raiders conquered the region in the early 700s; in the 1200s the Delhi sultanate was established*

Direct Teach

Reading Focus

3 What achievements were made by the rulers who held power at the height of the Mughal Empire? *supported literature and arts; built Taj Mahal and other monuments to Mughal greatness; expanded empire's borders*

Height of the Mughal Empire

Describe What was the architectural style of the Taj Mahal? *greatest example of Mughal architecture, included elements of Indian, Persian, Muslim architectural styles*

Evaluate In what ways, if any, did the golden age of architecture play a role in the decline of the Mughal Empire? *possible answer—The building projects were very costly, probably led to the taxation, resentment, and loss of prosperity within the empire.*

CRF: Biography: Nur Jahan

Interpreting Maps

Mughal Empire 1526–1707

Movement Of the three groups living in the northern section of the map, which one's descendants have a nation named after them today, and what is it called? *Uzbecks, Uzbekistan*

Place What are some possible reasons that trading centers were grouped close together in some areas? *possible answers—safe ports, concentration of available goods, political stability in the area*

Map Transparency: Mughal Empire, 1526–1707

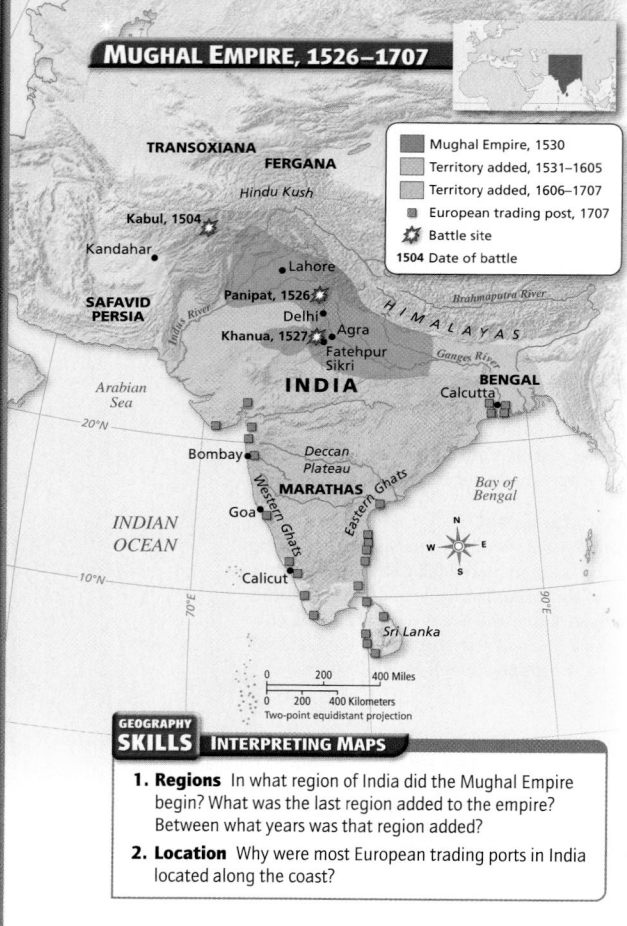

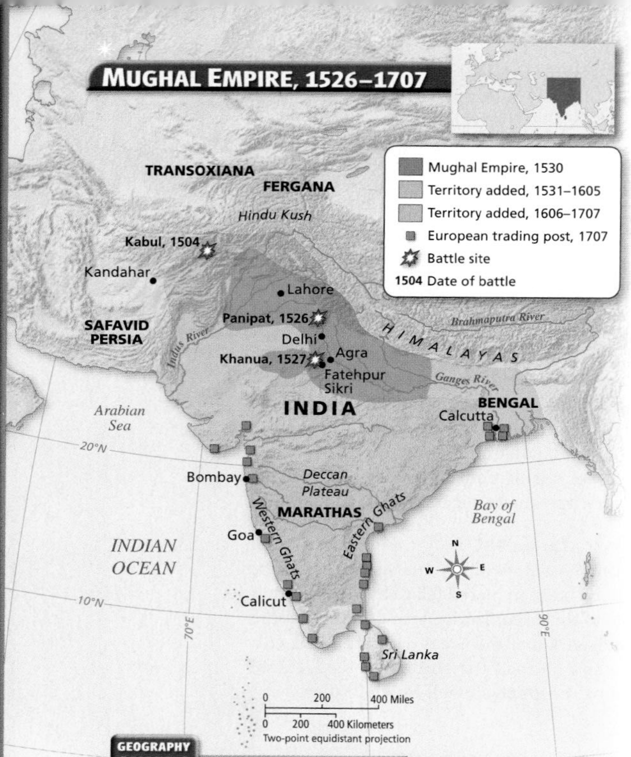

GEOGRAPHY SKILLS INTERPRETING MAPS

1. **Regions** In what region of India did the Mughal Empire begin? What was the last region added to the empire? Between what years was that region added?
2. **Location** Why were most European trading ports in India located along the coast?

Akbar realized that India had a diverse population, which he feared could lead to the breakdown of his empire. As a result, he did everything he could think of to win the people's loyalty. For example, he married the daughter of a local noble to win the noble's support and brought the sons of other nobles to live at his court. At the same time, Akbar was not hesitant to fight to prevent rebellion. By the time Akbar died in 1605, the Mughals ruled most of north India and much of the interior.

ACADEMIC VOCABULARY
stance an attitude, position, or view about someone or something

Akbar also worked to unify his diverse empire by promoting religious tolerance. His personal stance was that no single religion—including Islam, which he had been raised to practice—could provide all the answers to life's problems. As a result, he did not want to discourage people from practicing any religion or to discriminate against anyone for their beliefs. He abolished taxes that earlier rulers had placed on non-Muslims and appointed Hindus to several influential positions in his government. He also encouraged discussions and debates among Muslims, Hindus, Christians, and members of other religions.

Although flexible and generous in his support of different religions, Akbar kept a firm grasp on his government and its finances. He established a centralized government framework that gave him supreme civil and military authority over his empire. To keep better track of the empire's finances, Akbar reformed the tax system and appointed officials to oversee it. To try to prevent officials with regional loyalties, only about one-third of these officials were from India. The majority were from outside of the Mughal Empire.

READING CHECK **Explain** How did Babur and Akbar the Great help create a new empire in India?

Height of the Mughal Empire

Babur and Akbar laid the foundation for a powerful empire. The rulers who followed them built upon that foundation and raised Mughal India to new heights of power and wealth.

Jahangir Intelligent and impatient to rule, Akbar's son Jahangir rebelled against his father. The two later reconciled, and Jahangir became emperor after Akbar's death in 1605. Despite his ruthless start, Jahangir was known as a good ruler. He continued Akbar's practice of religious tolerance, appointing both Muslim and Hindu officials. He supported the arts and adopted many Persian influences into Indian society. Jahangir's acceptance of Persian customs was inspired by his wife, Nur Jahan, who had been born in Persia. A powerful woman, Nur Jahan actually ruled for several years while her husband was ill.

During his reign, Jahangir came into conflict with a religious group known as the Sikhs (SEEKS), some of whom had supported a rebellion against him. **Sikhism**, which had been founded by Guru Nanak (1469–c. 1539), blended elements of both Islam and Hinduism.

Skills Focus: Making Inferences

At Level

Reading Skill

The Mughal Shahs

1. Tell students that political cartoonists use their talent to express their opinions and beliefs, both positive and negative, about the actions of national rulers.
2. Have students select one of the shahs discussed in this section and create a political cartoon that makes a clear, visual political statement about his actions.
3. When students have had time to complete their work, have volunteers share their political cartoons to the class. Students should explain the reasoning for the viewpoint shown. **LS Visual-Spatial**

Alternative Assessment Handbook, Rubric 27: Political Cartoons

Answers

Interpreting Maps 1. *the northern region; the southern region; 1606–1707;* 2. *possible answer—to connect to Indian Ocean trade routes*

Reading Check *by commitment to justice, religious tolerance, and the expansion of the empire.*

Like Muslims, Sikhs believe that there is only one God, that God created the world, and that he has no physical form. But unlike Muslims, who believe in an afterlife, Sikhs believe in the Hindu concept of reincarnation. They believe that the goal of existence is to be freed from the cycle of rebirth and to attain unity with God. Sikhs do not practice rituals such as pilgrimage and yoga that came from the earlier religions.

Shah Jahan Jahangir's son and successor, **Shah Jahan** shared his father's love of literature and art. During his reign the Mughal Empire experienced a cultural golden age. The greatest example of Mughal architecture, the **Taj Mahal** in Agra, was built during his reign. Designed by Persian architects and displaying elements of Indian, Persian, and Muslim architectural styles, the Taj Mahal was built as a tomb for Shah Jahan's beloved wife.

In addition to the Taj Mahal, Shah Jahan built a new capital for India at Delhi. At the heart of the capital was a chamber that held the magnificent Peacock Throne. Flanked by two sculpted peacocks and encrusted with gold, diamonds, emeralds, and other gems, the throne became a symbol of Mughal majesty.

The cost of building monuments such as the Taj Mahal and the palaces of Delhi was enormous. To pay for the monuments, Shah Jahan imposed heavy taxes on the people of India. He demanded half of all crops grown in the country, which led to hardship and famine for many people. Adding to Shah Jahan's need for money was a series of wars he launched against India's neighbors. Many of these wars were fought in the name of Islam against Christians and Hindus because, unlike his father and grandfather, Shah Jahan was a Muslim who did not practice religious tolerance.

Aurangzeb In 1657 Shah Jahan grew terribly ill. His sons, thinking their father near death, began to maneuver to take the throne. Before long, war broke out between them. When Shah Jahan unexpectedly recovered, his son **Aurangzeb** captured him and locked him in a prison in Agra. Aurangzeb then killed his rivals, and brought the head of one brother in a box to show his father. With the way clear, Aurangzeb then declared himself emperor.

Early in his reign, Aurangzeb was chiefly concerned with expanding India's borders. The empire reached its greatest size at this time.

READING SKILLS

Summarizing After you read the information on the Height of the Mughal Empire, summarize the key points of the reigns of Jahangir, Shah Jahan, and Aurangzeb in four to six sentences.

Linking TO Today

The Sikhs

Today more than 20 million people identify themselves as Sikhs, making Sikhism the world's fifth-largest religion. The majority of Sikhs live in the Punjab region of India, where about 500 years ago a young spiritual teacher named Guru Nanak founded the faith. Nanak wrote his teachings as poems. These poems, along with the teachings of nine other gurus, or prophets, now form part of the holy book of Sikhism.

Sikhs strive to live according to these teachings, which they believe to be the living word of a single, all-powerful God. Serving others, living a truthful life, and the belief that all people are equal, regardless of gender or social class, are core to Sikh spirituality.

As an expression of their faith, Sikhs wear special clothing. The turban, for example, symbolizes the Sikhs' strong belief in social equality. In the early years of Sikhism, before India was under Mughal rule, only kings and noblemen could wear turbans. In response, a Sikh guru commanded all Sikhs, both men and women, to wear the turban as a symbol of their social equality. Today this tradition continues. Wearing the turban is required for all Sikh men but is optional for Sikh women.

Why do Sikhs continue to wear turbans today?

▲ Like the turban, uncut hair is a symbol of Sikh identity and faith. To honor the human form as created by God, Sikhs do not cut their hair or beards.

Direct Teach

Reading Focus

Height of the Mughal Empire

Recall What foundation did Babur and Akbar build for rulers who suceeded them? *legacy of wealth and power*

Explain In what ways did Sikhism blend elements of Islam and Hinduism? *Like Muslims, Sikhs believe in only one God, that God created the world, and that he has no physical form. Like Hindus, they believe in reincarnation.*

Make Inferences Why were there so many influences in Mughal cultural development? *possible answer—geographic location, trade, acceptance of foreign cultures and faiths, invasion and assimilation of neighboring people*

Activity **Shah Facts** Have students make a list of the shahs they have studied so far and record facts they have learned about each of them.

LS Verbal-Linguistic

Teaching Tip

Help students develop a connection to the Mughal Empire by holding an "East India Traders' Day." Students may bring examples or drawings of cotton fabrics, teas, and spiced goods to class. Suggest saris, teas, and food made with spices from India and Sri Lanka.

Skills Focus: Analyzing Costs and Benefits — At Level

Research Required

Social Studies Skill

Weighing the Value of Patronage

1. Have students name a few of the artistic achievements of the Mughals they read about in this section. Make a class list for students to see.
2. Have students select one shah they have studied in this section and identify one particular arts project he supported. Have students record these two pieces of information on a piece of paper that has been divided into a three-part chart.
3. On the bottom third of the paper, have students list the costs of the patronage on the left and the benefits on the right.
4. When students have finished, display the charts and guide the class in a discussion of the costs and benefits of art patronage.

LS Verbal-Linguistic, Visual-Spatial

Alternative Assessment Handbook, Rubrics 6: Cause and Effect; and 13: Graphic Organizers

Answers

Reading Skills *Student summaries will vary, but should show a clear understanding of each ruler's reign.*

Linking to Today *as an expression of their faith and a symbol of their belief in social equality*

Direct Teach

Info to Know

Women of Influence Women's patronage of the arts became significant under the rule of Shahs Jahangir and Jahan. During the reign of Shah Jahangir, his wife, Queen Nur Jahan, gained more influence in politics and the arts. She made many political decisions, introduced new styles of dress, and commissioned many buildings and gardens. She also arranged her son's marriage. When her son's wife died, his unmarried daughter, Jahanara assumed royal duties and commissioned many artistic works.

Quick Facts Transparency: Achievements of the Mughal Emperors

Review & Assess

Close

Have students describe the Mughal rulers, their achievements, and the characteristics of their reigns.

Review

Online Quiz, Section 2

Assess

SE Section 2 Assessment

Progress Assessment: Section 2 Quiz

Alternative Assessment Handbook

Reteach/Intervene

Interactive Reader and Study Guide, Section 2

Interactive Skills Tutor CD-ROM

Answers

Reading Check *His harsh regime led to rebellions.*

Later, however, Aurangzeb turned more to domestic affairs. A strict Sunni Muslim, he worked to impose his religious views on society. He issued strict decrees about morality and personal behavior and appointed officials to enforce them. He also persecuted Hindus and Sikhs, taxing them, forbidding them high positions in government, and destroying their temples. When crowds of Shia and Sufi Muslims gathered to protest his actions, Aurangzeb ordered soldiers mounted on elephants to crush them.

THE IMPACT **TODAY**

Persecution would later lead many Sikhs to move to California.

Aurangzeb's restrictions and his persecution of his subjects led many peasants to rebel. One rebellious subject wrote to the emperor:

HISTORY'S VOICES

> **"Your subjects are trampled underfoot; every province of your Empire is impoverished . . . If Your Majesty places any faith in those books by distinction called divine, you will be there instructed that God is the God of all mankind, not the God of Mussalmans [Muslims] alone."**
>
> —Anonymous Mughal citizen, quoted in *History of Aurangzeb* by Jadunath Sarkar

QUICK FACTS

ACHIEVEMENTS OF THE MUGHAL EMPERORS

Mughal rulers unified vast lands and peoples, and left a spectacular cultural legacy.

Babur (1526–1530)
- Conquered India
- Founded the Mughal Empire

Akbar (1556–1605)
- Expanded the size of the Mughal Empire
- Built a strong central government
- Promoted religious tolerance

Jahangir (1605–1627)
- Encouraged Persian culture in India
- Supported art and literature

Shah Jahan (1628–1658)
- Promoted literature and arts
- Built the Taj Majal and a capital at Delhi

Aurangzeb (1658–1707)
- Supported the growth of Sunni Islam
- Increased the empire to its largest size

Decline of the Mughals Although Aurangzeb had enlarged the Mughal Empire, his actions marked the beginning of its end. Due to the harsh measures of Aurangzeb's regime, frequent rebellions broke out in the later 1600s. When Aurangzeb died, rival claims to the throne led to civil war. Soon, invaders poured into India from the north.

ACADEMIC VOCABULARY
regime a specific and often harsh government

Although the Mughals continued to rule for about 150 more years, they held little power and controlled far less territory. In time, India fell under the sway of the British, who made it a colony and part of their global empire.

READING CHECK **Summarize** How did Aurangzeb contribute to the Mughals' decline?

SECTION 2 ASSESSMENT

go.hrw.com **Online Quiz** Keyword: SHL NAS HP

Reviewing Ideas, Terms, and People

1. **a. Identify** What was the first Muslim government established in India? Where did its name come from?
   b. Explain How did relationships between Muslims and members of other religions change in India?
   c. Elaborate How did the arrival of Islam in India lead to later changes in society?
2. **a. Describe** How did **Babur** establish the **Mughal Empire**?
   b. Make Generalizations What qualities helped Babur and **Akbar the Great** create a successful and prosperous empire in India?
   c. Rate Which of Akbar's accomplishments as emperor do you think was most impressive? Why?
3. **a. Identify** What were two artistic achievements made in India under **Shah Jahan**?
   b. Compare and Contrast How were Shah Jahan and **Aurangzeb** similar? How were they different?
   c. Extend How did the policies of Shah Jahan and Aurangzeb lead to the decline of Mughal civilization?

Critical Thinking

4. **Identify Cause and Effect** Using your notes and a graphic organizer like the one here, explain the reasons for the growth and decline of the Mughal Empire. List reasons for growth in the left arrow and reasons for decline in the right arrow.

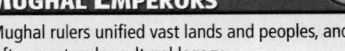

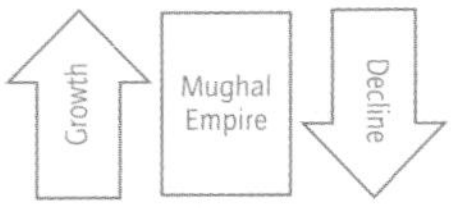

FOCUS ON WRITING

5. **Narration** Write a short paragraph about the founding of the Mughal Empire. In your paragraph, trace the key events in the empire's early history.

Section 2 Assessment Answers

1. **a.** Delhi sultanate; because the new government was based in Delhi
   b. possible answer—In the beginning of the empire, there was religious tolerance, but later, different religions clashed.
   c. A new culture formed, blending Muslim and Indian elements.
2. **a.** defeated the rulers of Delhi
   b. ambition, capable leaders
   c. possible answer—keeping peace among many different religions, because later emperors were unable to do this
3. **a.** Taj Mahal; Peacock Throne
   b. similar—did not believe in tolerance; different—Aurangzeb more interested in expansion
   c. possible answer—Policies led to rebellions.
4. Growth: religious tolerance, strong government, expansion of borders, wealth; building of great monuments; Decline: use of wealth for building projects, violence, heavy taxation, religious persecution, lack of religious tolerance
5. Student paragraphs should be supported by the text.

SECTION 3

The Ming and Qing Dynasties

BEFORE YOU READ

MAIN IDEA

During the Ming and Qing dynasties China prospered, but the empire entered a period of isolation in response to increasing European contact.

READING FOCUS

1. How did the Ming dynasty bring stability, prosperity, and isolation to China?
2. How did the Manchus of the Qing dynasty rule China?
3. What cultural developments occurred during the Ming and Qing periods?

KEY PEOPLE

Hongwu
Yonglo
Zheng He
Matteo Ricci
Kangxi
Qianlong
Lord George Macartney

TAKING NOTES As you read, use a graphic organizer like the one below to take notes on the Ming and Qing dynasties and their culture.

Ming	Qing

THE INSIDE STORY ***Why might a ruler build a city within a city?*** The Gate of Divine Might, the Hall of Supreme Harmony, the Palace of Heavenly Purity—these structures are part of China's Forbidden City. Set in the heart of Beijing, China's capital, the Forbidden City was built in the early 1400s for China's Ming emperor and his family, court, and servants. The vast complex is surrounded by a moat and a 35-foot-high wall, and includes dozens of imperial palaces, halls, temples, residences, and other buildings. This amazing city within a city earned its name because China's common people were not allowed to enter it.

For centuries, the golden-colored rooftops of this hidden city—all that China's people could see of it—symbolized China's imperial glory. ■

The Ming Dynasty

In 1279 the Mongol leader Kublai Khan conquered China and founded the Yuan dynasty. After Kublai Khan's death in 1294, however, the Yuan dynasty weakened. This weakness, combined with Chinese resentment of Mongol rule, made China ripe for rebellion—and the rise of a new dynasty.

A FORBIDDEN City

◄ The Hall of Supreme Harmony in China's Forbidden City

Teach the Main Idea

At Level

The Ming and Qing Dynasties

1. **Teach** Ask students the Reading Focus questions to teach this section.
2. **Apply** Organize students into small groups. Assign groups one of the two dynasties, Ming or Qing. Have groups record the main facts about their dynasty. For each red heading, have students write a one-sentence generalization and three supporting details.
3. **Review** Have volunteers share their generalizations and supporting details. Tell students to keep these notes and add to them as they study the section.
4. **Practice/Homework** When students have finished studying the section, have them write a short summary about what they learned about Chinese culture and history.
LS Interpersonal, Verbal-Linguistic

Alternative Assessment Handbook, Rubrics 1: Acquiring Information; and 14: Group Activity

Preteach

Getting Started

Use the **Interactive Reader and Study Guide** to familiarize students with the section content.

Interactive Reader and Study Guide, Section 3

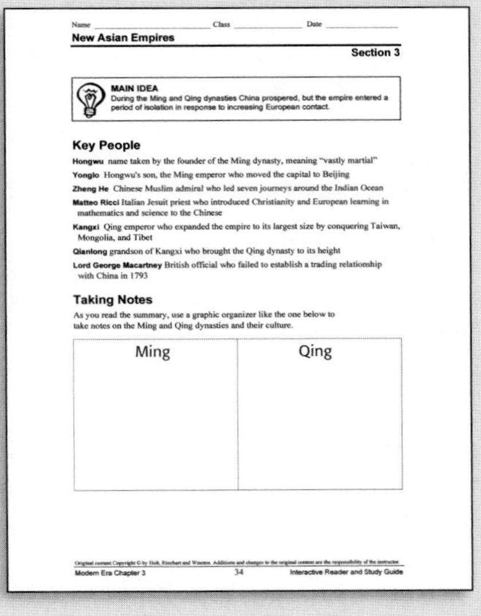

Name ______ Class ______ Date ______

New Asian Empires

Section 3

MAIN IDEA
During the Ming and Qing dynasties China prospered, but the empire entered a period of isolation in response to increasing European contact.

Key People

Hongwu name taken by the founder of the Ming dynasty, meaning "vastly martial"
Yonglo Hongwu's son, the Ming emperor who moved the capital to Beijing
Zheng He Chinese Muslim admiral who led seven journeys around the Indian Ocean
Matteo Ricci Italian Jesuit priest who introduced Christianity and European learning in mathematics and science to the Chinese
Kangxi Qing emperor who expanded the empire to its largest size by conquering Taiwan, Mongolia, and Tibet
Qianlong grandson of Kangxi who brought the Qing dynasty to its height
Lord George Macartney British official who failed to establish a trading relationship with China in 1793

Taking Notes

As you read the summary, use a graphic organizer like the one below to take notes on the Ming and Qing dynasties and their culture.

Ming	Qing

Original content Copyright © by Holt, Rinehart and Winston. Additions and changes to the original content are the responsibility of the instructor.
Modern Era Chapter 3 34 Interactive Reader and Study Guide

CRF: Vocabulary Builder: Section 3

Taking Notes

Ming—1368: Zhu Yuanzhang overthrew Mongol emperor and founded Ming dynasty, which lasted nearly 300 years; built Forbidden City; Zheng He led sea voyages; later Ming became isolated; built Great Wall of China; prosperity, population growth; overthrown in 1644 by Manchu, who formed Qing dynasty; Qing—last dynasty in 3,500 years of imperial rule in China; showed respect for Confucian traditions; largest empire in China's history; continued policies of isolation

go.hrw.com
Online Resources
KEYWORD: SHL NAS
ACTIVITY: Ming and Qing Art

Direct Teach

Reading Focus

1 How did the Ming dynasty bring stability, prosperity, and isolation to China? *gained independence from Mongol rule, rebuilt China, passed beneficial reforms, government officials were educated, corruption reduced; protected China from Mongol invasions, built the Great Wall, developed agriculture, industry, and the arts, set up trade with foreign nations; developed China's sea power; became a stable, prosperous time in history of China*

The Ming Dynasty

Recall Who led seven sea voyages for China during the early 1400s? *Zheng He*

Summarize Why was Hongwu considered a great emperor? *passed reforms; increased stability and prosperity; worked to eliminate Mongol influence and restore traditional Chinese values*

Analyze Why do you think the Ming emperors limited sea voyages and European trade? *possible answer—After years of Mongol rule, it was important to the Ming emperors to preserve China's traditions and keep away foreign influences.*

Activity The Forbidden City Tell students that a new capital on the site of the Mongol Yuan dynasty's capital city, now called Beijing, was built between 1406 and 1420. During most of the Ming and Qing dynasties, commoners were forbidden to enter the building. For this reason it became known as the Forbidden City. Ask students how the isolation of the Ming emperors inside the walls of the Forbidden City might have affected the way in which they governed. *Students should recognize the potential problems that arise when rulers are out of touch with the people they govern.*

CRF: Biography: Zhang Juzheng

China under Ming Rule In 1368 a peasant named Zhu Yuanzhang (JOO YOO-AHN-jahng) and his rebel army overthrew the last Mongol emperor. Zhu took the name **Hongwu**, meaning "vastly martial," and founded the Ming dynasty. *Ming* means "brilliant," and Ming China lasted nearly 300 years until 1644. During this period, China's rulers gained control of Korea, Mongolia, and parts of Central and Southeast Asia.

Having expelled the Mongols, Hongwu worked to rebuild China. He reduced taxes and passed reforms to improve agriculture and trade, increasing stability and prosperity in China. In addition, Hongwu worked to eliminate Mongol influences and to revive traditional Chinese values and practices, such as Confucian principles. For example, to obtain government officials educated in Confucian ideas, he restored and improved the civil service examination system. To root out corruption, he increased the influence of censors, officials who monitored government.

At the same time, Hongwu greatly expanded his power as emperor. He did away with the positions of some high-level officials and took over more control of the government. As a result, the Ming emperors were much more powerful than emperors of previous dynasties. In addition, Hongwu eliminated anyone whom he saw as challenging his authority, and over time he had thousands of his rivals killed.

Hongwu died in 1398. Following a power struggle, his son **Yonglo** (YOOHNG-LOH) became emperor, ruling from 1402 until 1424. Yonglo moved the Ming capital to Beijing, a city in the northeast of China. At the center of Beijing, he built a vast imperial city, which was surrounded by high walls. This city complex became known as the Forbidden City because most people were forbidden from entering it.

Ming Sea Voyages To extend China's influence, Yonglo sponsored overseas voyages. Between 1405 and 1433 **Zheng He** (juhng HUH), a Chinese Muslim admiral, led seven voyages around the Indian Ocean as far as Africa. To show China's power, Zheng He sailed with huge fleets of as many as 300 ships. These fleets included trading ships called junks as well as immense treasure ships, each about 400 feet long. Wherever he went, Zheng He presented gifts from China, and in return several foreign leaders sent tribute to China's emperor.

The Great Wall of China

Zheng He's voyages demonstrated Ming China's growing sea power. After 1433, however, a new emperor stopped the overseas voyages. They had been highly expensive, and some officials complained that China's resources would be better used to defend the frontiers.

Ming Foreign Relations The policy to end the voyages was part of a move in Ming China toward isolation from the outside world. This move toward isolation gained full force in the 1500s, when the Ming heavily restricted foreign trade and travel to limit outside contacts. Foreign merchants were allowed to trade only at a few Chinese ports, such as Canton, and only during certain times. Such policies were impossible to enforce, however. All along China's coast, ambitious Chinese smugglers carried out a brisk trade with foreign merchants.

One reason for the Ming emperors' decision to isolate China was the arrival of European traders and Christian missionaries in the 1500s. The Europeans introduced many new goods and ideas—including new products from the Americas. In fact, Europeans often paid with silver from the Americas. The Ming disliked the influence of the Europeans, though, and sought to preserve China's traditions.

Differentiating Instruction

Below Level

Learners Having Difficulty

1. Remind students that the Mongols were powerful, skilled warriors who had much success in battle, and they viewed Europeans as suspicious barbarians.
2. Remind students that the primary reason the Chinese had contact with Europeans was to acquire gold and silver, not to learn more about Europe or European culture. Review the information in the text about foreign merchants being allowed in China only during specific times.
3. Have students write a banner headline telling foreign merchants that they have to leave China because trading season is over.

LS Verbal-Linguistic

Alternative Assessment Handbook, Rubric 34: Slogans and Banners

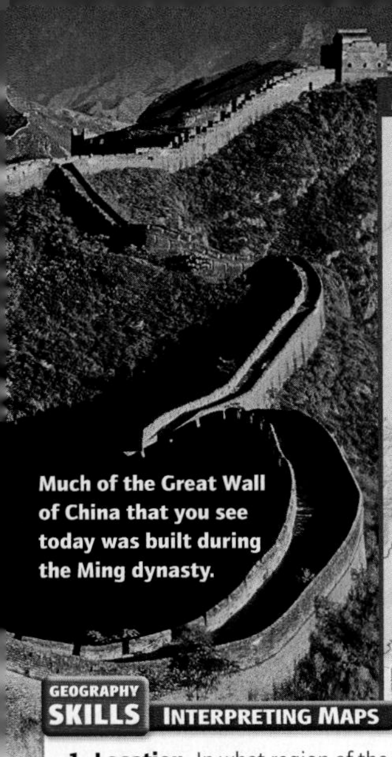

Much of the Great Wall of China that you see today was built during the Ming dynasty.

MING AND QING DYNASTIES, 1368–1911

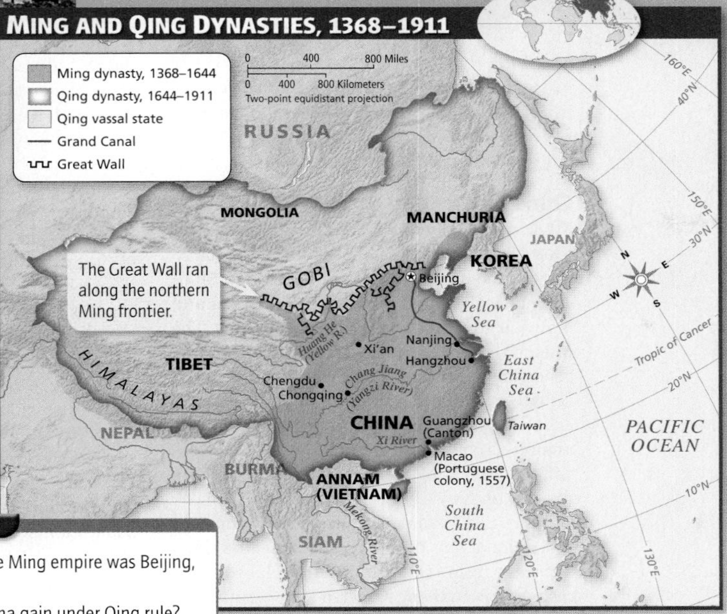

GEOGRAPHY SKILLS INTERPRETING MAPS

1. **Location** In what region of the Ming empire was Beijing, the capital, located?
2. **Regions** What regions did China gain under Qing rule?

Even so, some Europeans gained influence in China. One such European was **Matteo Ricci** (mah-TAY-oh REE-chee), an Italian Jesuit priest, who arrived in 1583. To gain acceptance, Ricci learned the Chinese language and adopted many Chinese customs. His efforts gained him entry to the Ming court, where he became highly respected. There, Ricci introduced European learning in mathematics and science.

In addition to dealing with the Europeans, the Ming faced a renewed Mongol threat to the north. To improve defense, the Ming restored China's Great Wall. Parts of earlier walls were repaired but most of the construction was new. In fact, much of the Great Wall that is seen today was built during the Ming period.

Ming Economy and Society Ming rule brought prosperity to China. Improved methods of irrigation increased farm production, and peasants produced huge crops of rice in the southern river valleys. In addition, new crops from the Americas, such as corn and sweet potatoes, reached China in the 1500s. These crops further increased farm output.

Stability and plentiful food led to substantial population growth. As the population grew, so did China's cities. In these cities, industries such as the manufacture of porcelain and silk expanded in response to a growing European demand for Chinese goods. At the same time, China remained a mainly agricultural society.

Ming Decline In the late 1500s, the Ming dynasty began to decline. Several weak rulers took the throne, and under their rule corruption increased. As defense efforts drained the treasury, Ming rulers raised taxes. High taxes combined with crop failures in the 1600s led to famine and hardship. Rebellions broke out.

As Ming China weakened, the Manchu—a people to the northwest in Manchuria—saw their chance. In 1644 the Manchu swept into Beijing and took the capital. The last Ming emperor killed himself to avoid capture. The Manchu then formed their own dynasty and gave it a Chinese name—Qing (CHING).

READING CHECK **Analyze** What were some of the strengths and weaknesses of the Ming dynasty?

READING SKILLS

Summarizing
After you read the information on the Ming Dynasty, summarize the key points in five to seven sentences.

Direct Teach

Reading Focus

The Ming Dynasty

Recall What did Matteo Ricci introduce to China? *Christianity, European learning in mathematics and science*

Summarize What were the reasons for the decline of the Ming dynasty? *Weak rulers became corrupt, draining resources and raising taxes, and rebellions broke out.*

Map Transparency: Ming and Qing Dynasties, 1368–1911

Info to Know

The Gobi Desert The great Gobi Desert of Central Asia, is known as Yintai shamo in Mandarin. It is sandy in the western part, but in the east, it is very rocky. Fierce winds from the northwest whip sand into dangerous dry storms. The very edge of the desert supports grasses and a small number of nomadic tribes who raise sheep and goats. It is about 1,000 miles wide.

Skill Focus: Comparing and Contrasting

At Level

Reading Skill

China Today and Yesterday

Materials: wall map of modern China, colored pencils

1. Guide students in a discussion of the ways that rulers of China struggled to defend its borders.
2. Have students use maps in this chapter and in the atlas of their texts draw a large outline map of modern-day China and the surrounding countries. Then have students draw the border of early China in a different color. Next, have students draw the border of modern China in a different color and Mongolia in another color.
3. Have students use a physical map to identify the geography and natural features of the land controlled by the Chinese and Mongols in the 1400s, and the land they control today.

LS Intrapersonal, Visual-Spatial

Alternative Assessment Handbook, Rubrics 9: Comparing and Contrasting; and 20: Map Creation

Answers

Reading Skills *Student summaries should demonstrate an understanding of the importance of the Ming Dynasty.*

Interpreting Maps 1. *the northern region;* **2.** *Manchuria, Mongolia, Tibet*

Reading Check *strengths—increased stability and prosperity; weaknesses—isolation from foreign influence, weak rulers in the late 1500s*

Direct Teach

Reading Focus

2 How did the Manchus of the Qing dynasty rule China? *with respect for Chinese traditions; keeping Manchu separate from Chinese; with isolation from foreign influence*

The Qing Dynasty

Recall What territory did Qianlong add to the empire? *Taiwan, Mongolia, Tibet*

Analyze Why do you think the Qing empire was stable? *possible answer—The Qing rulers showed respect for the Manchus traditions and gave them government positions.*

Reading Focus

3 What cultural developments occurred during the Ming and Qing periods? *developments in art, literature*

Ming and Qing Culture

Identify Cause and Effect What development led to a growth in popular fiction? *rising literacy rates*

Explain What made Ming porcelain so valuable in Europe? *its beauty and superb quality*

Counterpoints

Two Sources on China and Trade

Activity Trade Discussions To ensure that students understand the quotes, have them work individually or in pairs to write paraphrases of each quote. Have volunteers share their paraphrases with the class.

Answers

Counterpoints *possible answer—Macartney does not understand why the Chinese do not wish to trade and think that view is a mistake. Qianlong explains that the Chinese have everything they need and do not want his trade goods.*

The Qing Dynasty

The Qing dynasty, which ruled from 1644 to 1911, became the last dynasty in 3,500 years of imperial rule in China. Under the Qing dynasty's Manchu rulers, China again grew prosperous and expanded to its largest size in history.

China under Qing Rule As foreigners, the Manchu initially faced heavy resistance from their Chinese subjects, especially in the south. To win the support of the Chinese, the Manchu showed respect for Chinese customs and maintained China's Confucian traditions. The Manchu rulers carried over much of the Ming government structure and continued the civil service examination system. In addition, government positions were distributed equally among Chinese and Manchu officials. These actions eventually earned the Manchu the respect and loyalty of many of their Chinese subjects and restored stability to the empire.

At the same time, the Manchu remained separate from the Chinese and placed some restrictions on them. Manchu were not allowed to marry Chinese, and Manchu women were forbidden to bind their feet as Chinese women did. In addition, Chinese males had to wear their hair in the Manchu style—shaved in the front with a queue, or braid, in the back.

Qing China flourished under two outstanding emperors: **Kangxi** (KAHNG-SHEE) and his grandson **Qianlong** (chee-UHN-LOOHNG). Kangxi, who ruled from 1661 to 1772, reduced taxes for peasants and expanded the empire into parts of Central Asia. An intellectual, he supported the arts and entertained Jesuit priests at court. The Jesuits were highly educated, and Kangxi enjoyed learning from them about European advances in science and other areas.

Kangxi's grandson Qianlong brought the Qing dynasty to its height. Ruling from 1736 to 1796, Qianlong expanded the empire of China to its largest size by conquering Taiwan, Mongolia, and Tibet. During his reign, agricultural production continued to rise; and China's population boomed, surging to more than 300 million by 1750. The economy thrived as well, benefiting from improved transportation and from growing domestic and foreign markets.

COUNTERPOINTS

Two Sources on China and Trade

In a letter to King George III of England, Qing emperor Qianlong explains his refusal of the king's gifts and request for trade.

"Swaying the wide world, I have but one aim in view, to maintain a perfect governance and to fulfill the duties of the State: strange and costly objects do not interest me... Our dynasty's majestic virtue has penetrated unto every country under Heaven, and Kings of all nations have offered their costly tribute by land and sea. As your Ambassador can see for himself, we possess all things. I set no value on objects strange or ingenious [clever], and have no use for your country's manufactures [products]."

QIANLONG
—from a letter to King George III

Lord George Macartney led Great Britain's first attempt to expand trade relations with China. The Macartney Mission of 1792–1794 ended in failure.

"They receive us . . . with the highest distinction [and] show us every external mark of favour . . . Yet, in less than a couple months, they plainly discover that they wish us gone, refuse our requests without reserve . . ., and dismiss us dissatisfied . . . I must endeavour [try] to unravel this mystery if I can. Perhaps they have given way to impressions which they could not resist, but are ashamed to confess; perhaps they begin to find their mistake, and wish to make amends."

LORD MACARTNEY
—from an entry in Macartney's diary

Skills Focus INVESTIGATING HISTORY

Analyze How does Lord Macartney's view of the trade discussions compare with Emperor Qianlong's view?

Skills Focus: Identifying Problem and Solution — At Level

Reading Skill

Strengthening China

1. Explain to students that under the Mongols, China grew weak. Tell students that they will act as advisers to Hongwu.
2. Organize students into small, mixed-ability groups. Have students use information from the text to list things that needed to be improved in China during the late 1300s. Have students use their ideas to create a plan to improve the Chinese government and economy. When students have prepared their plans, have them create a petition that they could present to the Chinese emperor.
3. Have volunteers share their petitions with the class. You might wish to provide students with parchment paper and have them write their petitions in black ink. **LS Verbal-Linguistic**

Alternative Assessment Handbook, Rubrics 24: Oral Presentations; and 35: Solving Problems

Qing Foreign Relations Qianlong continued the Ming policy of isolation and restricting foreign trade. The Manchu, like the Chinese, saw Chinese civilization—and products—as superior and expected foreigners to trade on China's terms. Accepting these terms, the Dutch began a thriving trade in Chinese goods. Dutch traders obtained Chinese porcelain and silk along with a new good, tea. In fact, tea soon became the main Chinese export to Europe.

Other Europeans continued to try to change China's trade restrictions. In 1793 a British official, **Lord George Macartney**, came to China to discuss expanding trade. The Chinese found the British goods that he brought inferior to their own products. In addition, the Chinese demanded that Macartney show respect to Emperor Qianlong by kowtowing—kneeling in front of the emperor and touching the forehead to the ground nine times. Macartney refused, and the Chinese sent him away.

At the time, China was one of the most advanced civilizations in the world. Isolation, however, would help prevent the Chinese from keeping up with European advances. In the 1800s European efforts to open China's closed society would eventually topple the Qing dynasty—and imperial rule.

READING CHECK **Draw Conclusions** How did cultural differences hamper trade relations between the British and the Chinese during the Qing period?

Ming and Qing Culture

Under Ming and Qing rule, the Chinese made many developments in the arts and literature. Ming artisans produced exquisite blue-and-white porcelain. The beauty and superb quality of Ming porcelain made it a valuable trade item, especially in Europe.

During the Ming period, rising literacy rates contributed to the growth of popular fiction, or fiction written in everyday language for the common people. Short stories became more popular, and the first Chinese novels were published. In the 1700s the Qing writer Cao Zhan wrote the novel *Dream of the Red Chamber*. Considered China's greatest novel, it examines the decline of an upper-class Chinese family.

READING CHECK **Analyze** How did literature change during the Ming period?

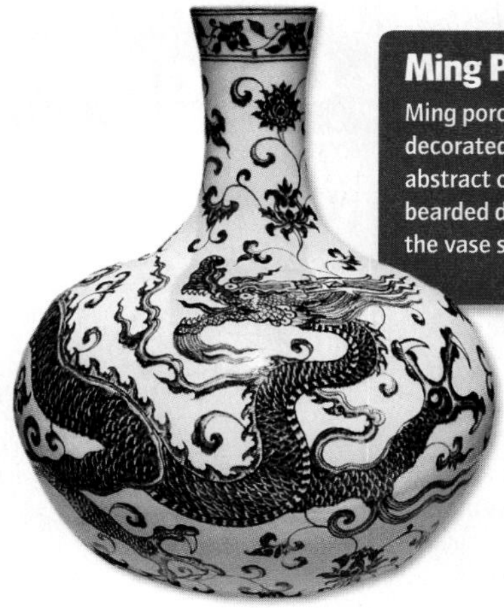

Ming Porcelain

Ming porcelain was often richly decorated with blue-and-white abstract or floral designs. A bearded dragon wraps around the vase shown here.

SECTION 3 ASSESSMENT

go.hrw.com
Online Quiz
Keyword: SHL NAS HP

Reviewing Ideas, Terms, and People

1. a. **Identify** Who were **Hongwu** and **Yonglo**, and what were their main achievements?
   b. **Draw Conclusions** How did **Zheng He**'s voyages demonstrate Ming China's sea power and increase China's influence?
   c. **Evaluate** How did interaction with foreigners affect China during the Ming period?
2. a. **Recall** How did the Manchu rulers of the Qing dynasty earn the support and loyalty of many of the Chinese people?
   b. **Explain** Why did the British fail in their efforts in the 1790s to expand trade relations with Qing China?
   c. **Rank** Based on what you have learned about the major Ming and Qing emperors, how would you rank them? Explain your reasoning.
3. a. **Identify** Which book is considered to be China's greatest novel, and when was it written?
   b. **Analyze** How did Ming porcelain contribute to China's economy?

Critical Thinking

4. **Compare and Contrast** Using your notes and a graphic organizer like the one here, compare and contrast the main accomplishments and challenges of the Ming and Qing dynasties.

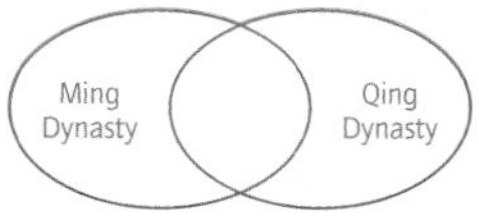

FOCUS ON WRITING

5. **Exposition** You are a Dutch merchant who conducts trade with China in the 1700s. Write a short letter to another European merchant giving the merchant advice on how to gain the right to trade with China.

Review & Assess

Close

Have students identify the changes that occurred in China during the Ming and Qing dynasties.

Review

Online Quiz, Section 3

Assess

SE Section 3 Assessment

Progress Assessment: Section 3 Quiz

Alternative Assessment Handbook

Reteach/Intervene

Interactive Reader and Study Guide, Section 3

Interactive Skills Tutor CD-ROM

Answers

Reading Check (top) *The British official who came to trade did not perform a traditional gesture of respect to the emperor, and was sent away.* **(bottom)** *Popular fiction was written in everyday language; short stories became popular.*

Section 3 Assessment Answers

1. **a.** Ming emporor; Hongwu—extended China's influence, stabilized China, began building the Great Wall; Yonglo—moved the capital to Beijing, large-scale diplomatic and economic contact with the Europeans, developed the world's largest commercial navy, launched historic trade expeditions under Zheng He
   b. He traveled with huge fleets of ships loaded with treasures, made contact with leaders who sent tribute to the emperor.
   c. It introduced European learning in mathematics and science.
2. **a.** showed respect for Chinese customs and traditions
   b. Chinese thought the British goods were inferior; British official refused to kowtow to the emperor.
   c. possible answer—Kangxi and Qianlong would rank highest because they reduced taxes, expanded the empire, and brought the Qing dynasty to its height.
3. **a.** Dream of the Red Chamber was written in the 1700s.
   b. It was a valuable trade item, especially in Europe.
4. Ming—built Forbidden City; Zheng He led sea voyages; built Great Wall of China; prosperity, population growth; Qing—China grew prosperous; showed respect for Confucian traditions; largest empire in China's history; Both—emphasized Chinese culture; isolated from foreign influence
5. Student letters should explain the importance of showing respect to the emperor and bringing quality items for trade.

History and Geography

The Voyages of Zheng He

Teaching Tip

The travels of Zheng He are recounted in a film titled *Ghost Fleet: The Epic Voyage of Zheng He*. Photojournalist Michael Yamashita, director Jonathan Finnigan, and a film crew covered over 10,000 miles to retrace these epic voyages. They began in Yunan, China and traveled all the way to the Swahili coast of Africa. Director Finnigan made a two-hour documentary from the lengthy shoot, which made its debut Asia in December 2005. It debuted in New York City in May 2006.

Activity Understanding Climate Have students compare the latitude of their hometown with that of the areas Zheng He traveled. Discuss the similarities and differences in the climate of various locations based on your own and students' experiences. Travel Web sites frequently offer a weather report for various destinations. Have volunteers locate several of Zheng He's stops on a weather Web site and report on current weather in those locations. **LS Visual-Spatial**

Activity Zheng He's Travels Have students compare the distance traveled by Zheng He with the distance across the continental United States (approximately 2,500 miles) or the distance from their town to the nearest large city. Have students estimate the number of times they would have to travel back and forth to equal the length of Zheng He's voyage. **LS Logical-Mathematical**

HISTORY & Geography

Interactive

The Voyages of Zheng He

Between 1405 and 1433 the Chinese admiral Zheng He led seven grand voyages throughout the Indian Ocean. During the seven voyages, Zheng He visited ports in Southeast Asia, India, Persia, the Arabian Peninsula, and Africa. The voyages consisted of huge fleets, some with hundred of ships. These ships were like traveling cities; and their crews included not only sailors but also astrologers, blacksmiths, cooks, doctors, officials, royal guards, and translators.

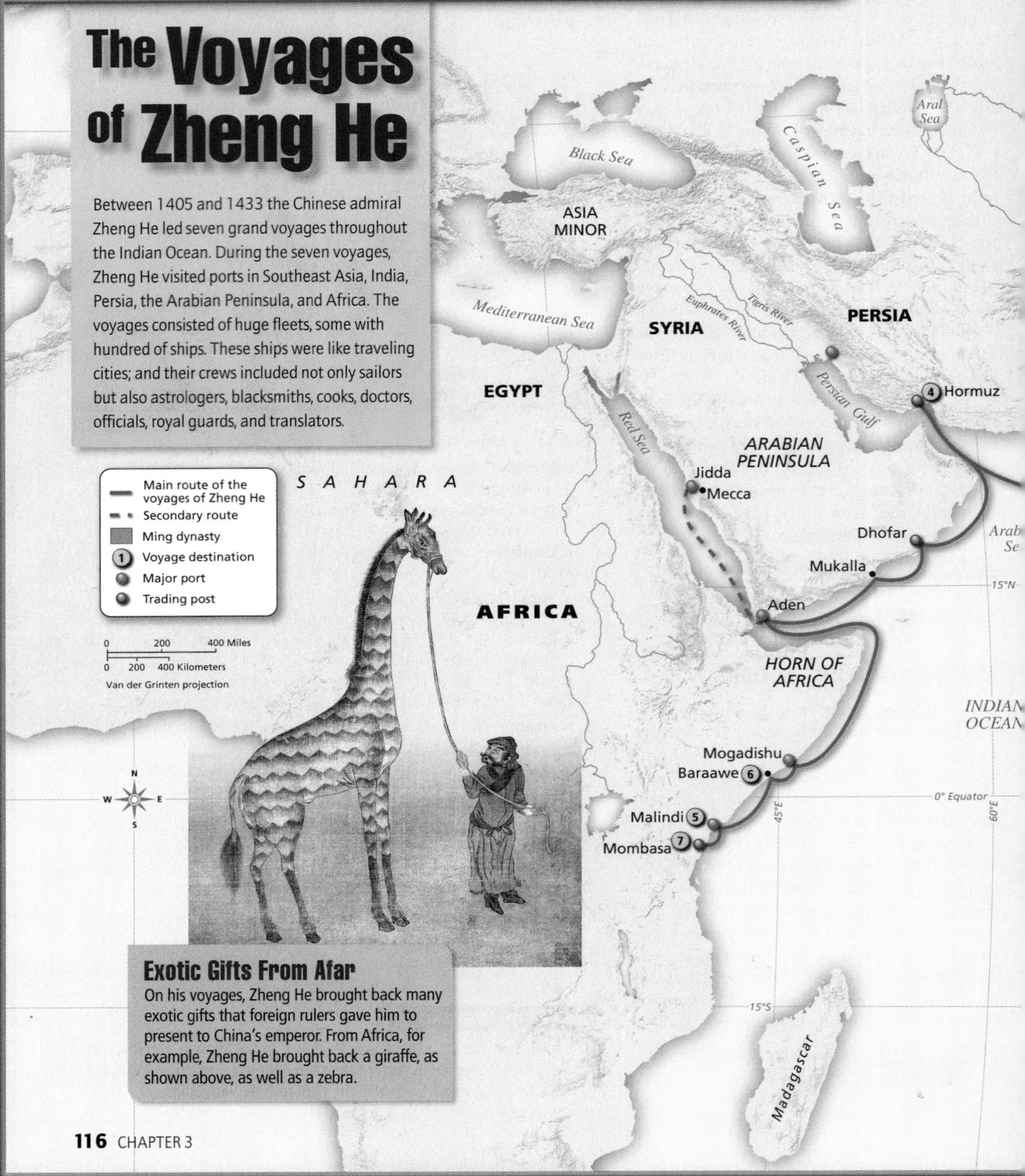

Exotic Gifts From Afar

On his voyages, Zheng He brought back many exotic gifts that foreign rulers gave him to present to China's emperor. From Africa, for example, Zheng He brought back a giraffe, as shown above, as well as a zebra.

116 CHAPTER 3

Skills Focus: Analyzing Secondary Sources

At Level

Research Required

Reading Like a Historian
Comparing Ships

1. Remind students that many explorers sailed in search of land and wealth. They sailed different ships and traveled to different areas. Have students compare the voyages of Zheng He with those of Christopher Columbus.
2. Organize students into small groups. Have students collect data about the ships of each explorer on the list. Students should document the sources of their data, especially when it conflicts with another source.
3. Next, have students record their information in bar graph form. Display completed work.
4. Discuss the difference in the estimated ship sizes. Finally, have students write a paragraph discussing whether size matters when comparing ships of Columbus and Zheng He. **LS Logical-Mathematical, Visual-Spatial**

Alternative Assessment Handbook, Rubrics 13: Graphic Organizers; and 30: Research

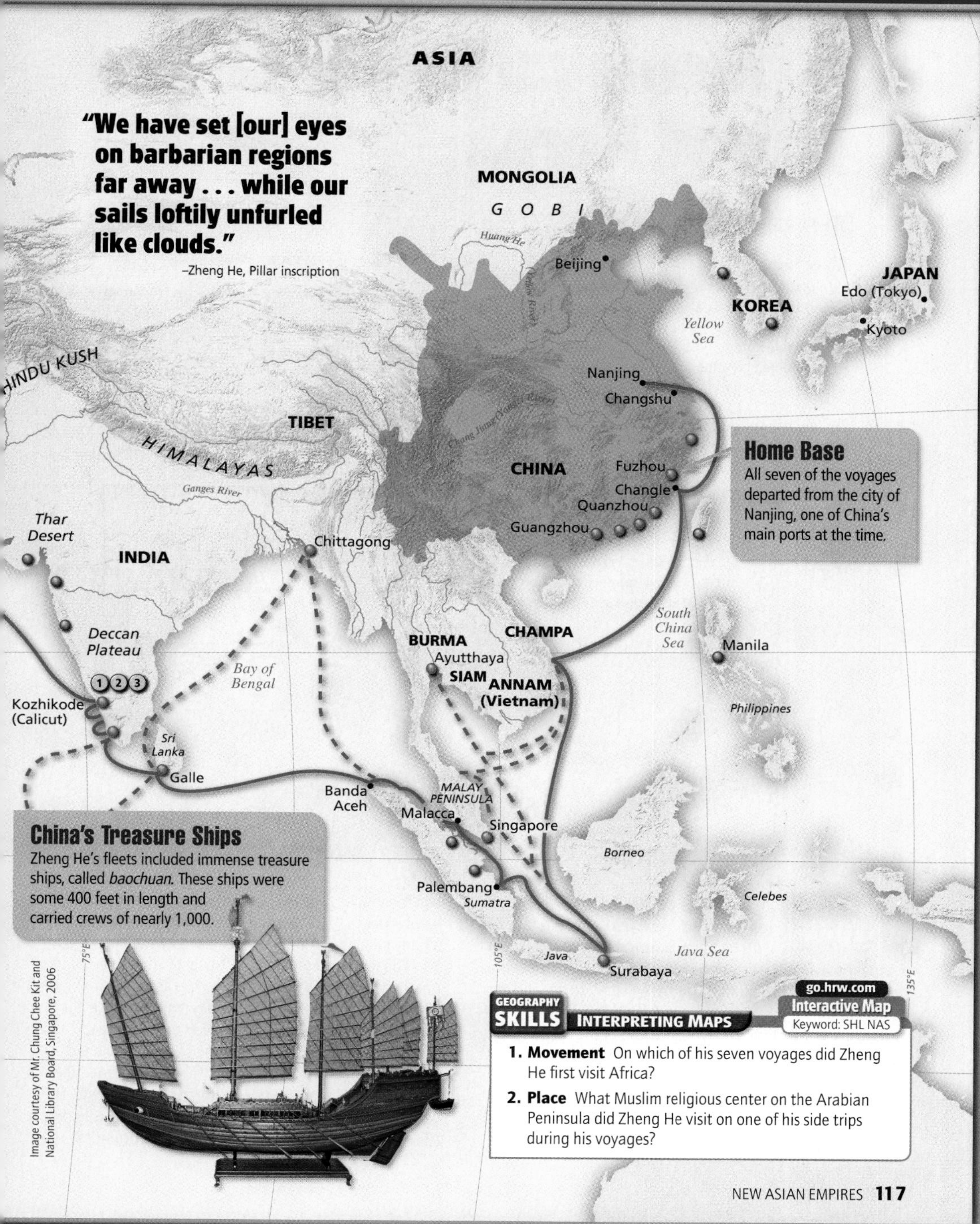

Home Base
All seven of the voyages departed from the city of Nanjing, one of China's main ports at the time.

China's Treasure Ships
Zheng He's fleets included immense treasure ships, called *baochuan*. These ships were some 400 feet in length and carried crews of nearly 1,000.

GEOGRAPHY SKILLS INTERPRETING MAPS

go.hrw.com
Interactive Map
Keyword: SHL NAS

1. **Movement** On which of his seven voyages did Zheng He first visit Africa?
2. **Place** What Muslim religious center on the Arabian Peninsula did Zheng He visit on one of his side trips during his voyages?

History and Geography

Info to Know

A Special Place of Honor The amazing voyages of Zheng He were nearly lost to history, at least to western historians. However, in China, he was famous enough to inspire a special honor on the 580th anniversary of his voyage. In 1985, in recognition of the importance of his accomplishment, a new tomb was crafted. The memorial hall at the Ming-style entrance includes paintings of the navigator and his maps. The steps to the tomb are divided in four sections of seven each, likely representing the four cardinal directions and the number of his voyages.

The Spice Islands The fabled Spice Islands attracted many sailors and explorers from afar. Zheng He was no exception. The Moluccas are located in eastern part of Indonesia and are now called the Maluku Province. Cloves, nutmeg, and mace are all grown on the small volcanic islands. Archaeologists have discovered evidence that cloves were traded in Persia over 3,000 years ago. In medieval Europe, spices were prized for their medicinal use, as well as to add interesting flavors to edibles. Spices were very expensive because of the great distance they had to be shipped. Many voyages of exploration were inspired by the desire to find an easier route to the Spice Islands.

Skills Focus: Interpreting Movement Maps

At Level

Research Required

Social Studies Skill
Zheng He and Spices

Materials: sticky notes, large world map

1. Tell students that several common spices come from India. It is likely that Zheng He's travels along the Malabar Coast led to the spread of spices.
2. Have students make a list of at least five of their favorite spices. Then have students conduct outside research to discover the origins of the spices. Students should record the sources of their information.
3. Have students share their lists and the results of their research with the class. As volunteers provide the information, place a label on the map for the origins of each spice discussed.
4. Have students write a paragraph about the spices, explaining why they think explorers were interested in finding them.

LS Intrapersonal, Verbal-Linguistic

Alternative Assessment Handbook, Rubrics 12: Drawing Conclusions; and 30: Research

Answers

Interpreting Maps 1. *on his fifth voyage* **2.** *Mecca*

Preteach

Getting Started

Use the **Interactive Reader and Study Guide** to familiarize students with the section content.

Interactive Reader and Study Guide, Section 4

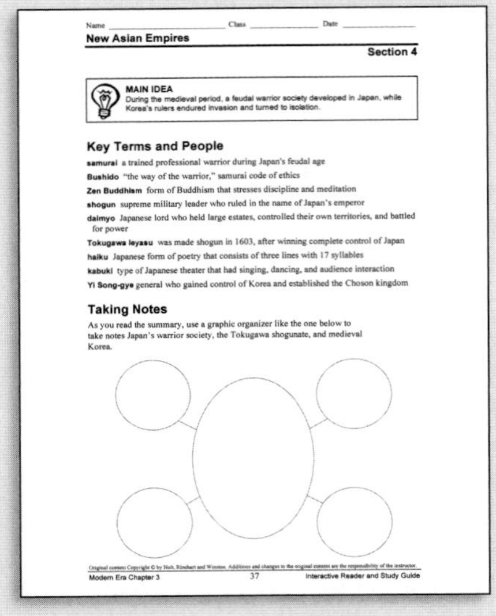

Name ______________ Class ________ Date ________

New Asian Empires

Section 4

MAIN IDEA
During the medieval period, a feudal warrior society developed in Japan, while Korea's rulers endured invasion and turned to isolation.

Key Terms and People

samurai a trained professional warrior during Japan's feudal age
Bushido "the way of the warrior," samurai code of ethics
Zen Buddhism form of Buddhism that stresses discipline and meditation
shogun supreme military leader who ruled in the name of Japan's emperor
daimyo Japanese lord who held large estates, controlled their own territories, and battled for power
Tokugawa Ieyasu was made shogun in 1603, after winning complete control of Japan
haiku Japanese form of poetry that consists of three lines with 17 syllables
kabuki type of Japanese theater that had singing, dancing, and audience interaction
Yi Song-gye general who gained control of Korea and established the Choson kingdom

Taking Notes

As you read the summary, use a graphic organizer like the one below to take notes Japan's warrior society, the Tokugawa shogunate, and medieval Korea.

Original content Copyright © by Holt, Rinehart and Winston. Additions and changes to the original content are the responsibility of the instructor.
Modern Era Chapter 3 37 Interactive Reader and Study Guide

Academic Vocabulary

Review with students the high-use academic term in this section.

preclude to prevent somthing or someone from acting (p. 121)

CRF: Vocabulary Builder: Section 4

Taking Notes

Japan—in feudal system, large landowners hired samurai, trained professional warriors; samurai were highly respected, followed code of ethics known as Bushido, adopted Zen Buddhism; shoguns: generals who ruled in emperor's name; daimyo: powerful warlords; Tokugawa shogunate ruled with strong central government, brought about period of peace and stability, increased contact with Europeans; haiku and kabuki were popular; Korea—Choson kings formed a government based on Confucianism; Korea became isolated

go.hrw.com
Online Resources

KEYWORD: SHL NAS
ACTIVITY: Japanese Theater

SECTION 4

Medieval Japan and Korea

Before You Read

MAIN IDEA

During the medieval period, a feudal warrior society developed in Japan, while Korea's rulers endured invasion and turned to isolation.

READING FOCUS

1. What were the key characteristics of the feudal warrior society in Japan?
2. How did the Tokugawa Shogunate rule Japan, and in what ways did culture flourish during the period?
3. How did the Choson dynasty shape events in medieval Korea?

KEY TERMS AND PEOPLE

samurai
Bushido
Zen Buddhism
shogun
daimyo
Tokugawa Ieyasu
haiku
kabuki
Yi Song-gye

TAKING NOTES Use a graphic organizer like this one to take notes on Japan's warrior society, the Tokugawa Shogunate, and medieval Korea.

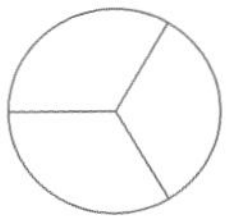

This image shows a portion of a famous Japanese folding screen of the summer siege of Osaka.

Japanese Folding Screen of Summer War of Osaka

THE INSIDE STORY

Would the castle be strong enough to withstand the attack? In 1614 a human wall of some 200,000 Japanese warriors stormed toward Osaka Castle. The castle, one of the greatest in Japan, had a five-story tower and was surrounded by double walls more than 100 feet high. Inside this fortress, Toyotomi Hideyori, the lord of the castle, grew desperate. He was surrounded and knew that Tokugawa Ieyasu, Japan's new military leader, was determined to defeat him to wipe out any possible rivals.

As some 300 cannons battered the castle's double walls, Hideyori sent his army out to meet the enemy. The two forces met in bloody engagement on the battlefield. Arrows flew, swords slashed with deadly force, and guns—a fairly new arrival in Japan—blasted away.

The winter siege of Osaka castle terrified the Toyotomi clan trapped within the two-mile-wide compound. Unable to endure any more, Hideyori finally signed a truce. But Ieyasu broke the truce and laid siege to Osaka Castle again in the summer of 1615. In June the castle's weakened walls finally fell. Ieyasu's forces overran the gates, burned the castle to the ground, and slaughtered the occupants. The victors took the head of Hideyori's son as a trophy. In defeat, Hideyori took his own life rather than be captured. ■

Teach the Main Idea

At Level

Medieval Japan and Korea

1. **Teach** Ask students the Reading Focus questions to teach this section.
2. **Apply** Have students make a list of the visuals in the section. Make a class list for all to see. Then have students work in pairs to scan the section and write a caption or information box about each of the visuals and how it relates to the section.
3. **Review** Have volunteers share their captions and information boxes with the class. Add the information to the class list.
4. **Practice/Homework** Have students select one of the visuals and write a paragraph about it and its relationship to the history of Japan and Korea. **LS Verbal-Linguistic, Visual-Spatial**

Alternative Assessment Handbook, Rubric 37: Writing Assignments

Japan's Warrior Society

By the 1100s Japan's central government had begun to lose control of the empire. Local clans began to fight each other for power and land. Law and order gave way to conflict and chaos, and bandits roamed the countryside. For protection, large landowners hired armies of **samurai** (SA-muh-ry), or trained professional warriors. Gradually, a feudal warrior society developed in Japan that was similar to that of medieval Europe—yet, uniquely Japanese.

Feudalism and the Samurai In Japan, as in medieval Europe, a feudal system gradually developed. In exchange for allegiance and military service, noble landowners gave property or payment to samurai warriors. Unlike in Europe, where knights were usually paid with land grants, only the most powerful samurai received land. Most of them were paid with food, generally rice. Those samurai who did receive land did not work or live on that land, but they did profit from it. The samurai's lands were worked by peasants, who gave the samurai money or food as payment each year.

The main role of the samurai was that of a warrior, and so they were highly skilled in that role. Like the medieval knights of Europe, samurai wore armor, were skilled with many weapons, and often fought on horseback. At all times, samurai were expected to be in fighting form, ready to do battle should the need arise. As time passed, samurai rose in status in Japanese society and enjoyed many privileges. When samurai strutted along Japan's streets, crowds parted to let them pass. People dropped their eyes out of respect—and fear—because a samurai had the right to kill anyone who showed him disrespect.

In addition to training as warriors, samurai had to follow a strict code of ethics known as **Bushido** (BOOH-shi-doh), which means "the way of the warrior." Bushido required samurai to be courageous, honorable, obedient, and most of all loyal. The Japanese word *samurai* means "those who serve," and each samurai had to serve and obey his lord without hesitation, even if the samurai or his family suffered as a result. Samurai who failed to obey or protect their lord were expected to commit seppuku—suicide by ritual disembowelment—rather than live with their shame.

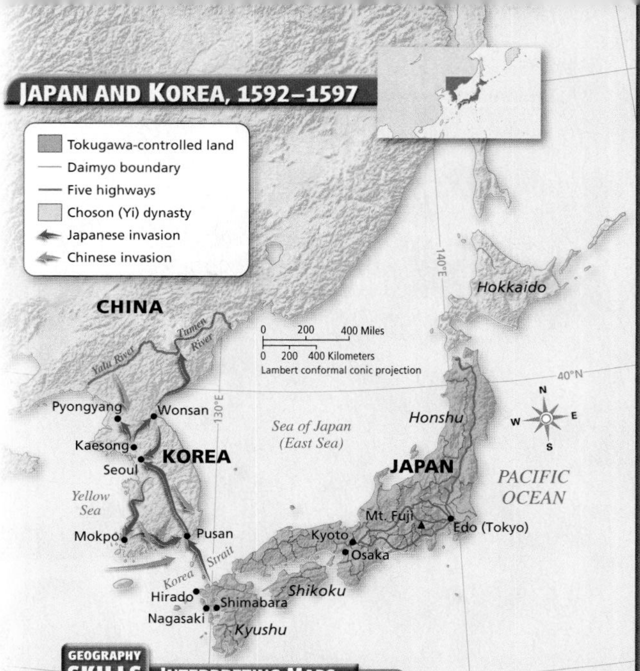

GEOGRAPHY SKILLS INTERPRETING MAPS

Movement What two major Japanese cities did the Five Highways connect?

Samurai strove to live disciplined lives, which they thought made them better warriors. To improve their self-discipline, many samurai pursued activities that required great focus, such as writing poetry, arranging flowers, and performing tea ceremonies. In addition, many samurai adopted **Zen Buddhism**, a form of Buddhism that spread from China to Japan in the 1100s. Zen stressed discipline and meditation as ways to focus the mind and gain wisdom.

Both men and women of samurai families learned to fight, though only men usually went to war. Like male samurai, female samurai had to follow Bushido and were prepared to die to protect their home and family honor. Honored in Japanese society, samurai women could inherit property and participate in business.

Rise of the Shoguns For most of the 1100s, Japan had no strong central government. The emperor was nominally in charge, but he had little control over the country. Local nobles, the heads of powerful clans, fought for power.

Direct Teach

Reading Focus

1 What were the key characteristics of the feudal warrior society in Japan? *It was a military government, led by the warrior class and a central governing figure, the shogun.*

Japan's Warrior Society

Identify Who were the samurai? *trained professional warriors, hired by landowners; highly respected in Japanese society*

Evaluate What advantages might there have been to the dominance of the military class? *possible answer—The samurai would enjoy the respect he received and would work hard to protect those whose safety depended on them.*

Interpreting Maps

Japan and Korea, 1592–1597

Movement Why do you think Japan decided to invade Korea? *possible answer—Korea would give Japan a land bridge to the rest of Asia.*

Place What sort of climate would you expect to find on Hokkaido Island, and why do you think there are no daimyo lands pictured there? *It would have been colder in the winter than the lower islands, and may have experienced storms from the north.*

Map Transparency: Japan and Korea, 1592–1597

Skills Focus: Identifying Main Idea and Details

At Level

Reading Skill

Comparing Feudal Systems

1. Remind students that the feudal system in Japan was similar to European feudalism, yet unique. Copy the Venn diagram and omit the italicized words.
2. Have students use the information in their text and conduct additional research to complete the diagram. When students have finished, complete the class diagram and have students correct their work. **LS Visual-Spatial**

Alternative Assessment Handbook, Rubrics 9: Comparing and Contrasting; and 13: Graphic Organizers

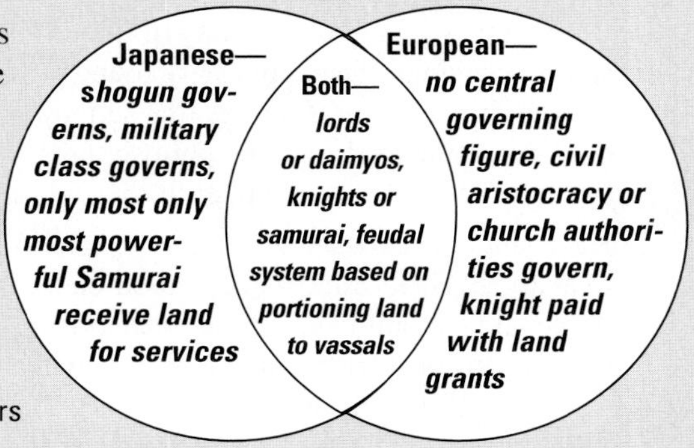

Answers

Interpreting Maps *Kyoto and Edo (Tokyo)*

Direct Teach

History Close-Up
The Way of the Warrior

Make Inferences Why was it important for samurai to follow Bushido? *It was expected that these men would be self-disciplined.*

Develop What are some possible reasons the samurai's protective clothes were not made of metal like those of knights? *possible answer—Japan may not have had sufficient metal resources; bamboo and leather may have provided adequate defense.*

CRF: Biography: Tomoe Gozen

About the Illustration

This illustration is an artist's conception based on available sources. Historians, however, are uncertain exactly what this scene looked like.

Info to Know

Japanese Swordmaking When Fujiyasu Masahira makes a sword, he follows the exacting traditional method of master craftsmen from hundreds of years ago. He makes his own charcoal, which he uses to smelt iron oxide sand into steel. When he has made a sufficient amount of steel with the right carbon content, he stacks pieces to form the blade. He wraps the stack in rice paper and dips it in clay before heating it in the forge. Some silicon from the rice straw ash becomes part of the steel. The metal is heated, folded and pounded flat repeatedly. It is then filed into a rough shape and tempered by repeated heating and quenching in water. After careful shaping and polishing, a custom sword guard and scabbard are made. Masahira is one of only fourteen Mukansa smiths. Mukansa smiths have won so many first prizes in their craft that they can no longer take part in competition.

Interactive
HISTORY CLOSE-UP

The Way of the Warrior

The elite, highly trained samurai followed a strict code of ethics called Bushido, or "the way of the warrior." Samurai were expected to serve with honor and loyalty in battle and to value duty and death over defeat. Terrifying and bloodthirsty in war, a samurai also found time to meditate, write poetry, and arrange flowers to focus his mind and body.

All samurai were skilled in the use of the longbow.

The samurai below are writing poetry. Writing poetry helped train the samurai to concentrate.

Samurai wore colorful armor and fierce-looking helmets. Most samurai carried and sometimes fought with two swords.

Skills Focus INTERPRETING VISUALS

go.hrw.com Interactive Keyword: SHL NAS

1. **Find the Main Idea** What equipment did the samurai use to protect themselves in battle?
2. **Draw Conclusions** Why do you think that samurai wore fierce-looking helmets with horns or other terrifying features?

120

Skill Focus: Analyzing Primary Sources

At Level

Prep Required

Reading Like a Historian Skill
Samurai Sayings

1. Before class, print out a variety of quotes or samurai sayings. They are easily found on the Internet. Remind students that samurai considered themselves to be philosophers, and have left behind a number of their ideas.
2. Have students choose one samurai quotation to analyze. Have students copy their chosen quote and explain its meaning. Remind students to consider the time it was written and if it might still be meaningful to people today.
3. Have volunteers share the quotations they selected and their analyses.
4. As an extension, have students illustrate their quotation. **LS Intrapersonal, Verbal-Linguistic**

Alternative Assessment Handbook, Rubrics 12: Drawing Conclusions; and 37: Writing Assignments

Answers

Interpreting Visuals 1. *armor, helmets;* **2.** *possible answer—to make themselves more intimidating*

After decades of warfare between clans, the Minamoto family defeated a rival to become Japan's most powerful clan. In 1192 the clan leader, Minamoto Yoritomo, forced the emperor to name him **shogun**, or "general." Japan's supreme military leader, the shogun ruled in the emperor's name. Although the emperor remained at the top of Japanese society, he became a mere figurehead. For nearly 700 years following, shoguns would rule Japan.

Yoritomo allowed the emperor to continue to hold court at Heian, which in time became known as Kyoto. The new shogun then formed a military government at Kamakura. The Kamakura Shogunate (SHOH-guhn-uht), or military dynasty, ruled Japan until 1333.

In the 1200s the Kamakura Shogunate faced a major threat—the Mongols. In 1274 and again in 1281, large Mongol fleets attacked Japan. Each time, the Japanese defeated the Mongols with the help of a powerful storm that wiped out the enemy fleet. The Japanese referred to these storms as the *kamikaze,* or "divine wind," and believed they showed that the gods favored Japan.

The Mongol invasions weakened the Kamukura Shogunate, however. Many lords did not think the shogun had rewarded them well enough for their part in the fighting and grew to resent the shogun's power over them. Loyalties began to break down, and in 1338 the Kamakura Shogunate was overthrown.

Rebellion and Order A new shogunate took power but was too weak to gain control of Japan. With the loss of centralized rule, Japan splintered into many competing factions. Numerous local **daimyo** (DY-mee-oh), powerful warlords who held large estates, gained control of their own territories and battled for power.

To defend their lands, the daimyo built large fortified castles. As in medieval Europe, these castles were often on hills, protected by walls, and surrounded by water. People came to the castles for protection, and towns often grew up around them. In time, the daimyo began to use peasants as foot soldiers in their armies in addition to samurai on horseback. After 1543 Portuguese traders introduced firearms to Japan. The daimyo gradually began to arm their soldiers with these weapons. Some samurai refused to use guns and later died wielding swords against superior firepower.

During the 1500s, three strong daimyo worked to take control of Japan. The first of these ambitious daimyo was Oda Nobunaga (ohd-ah noh-booh-nah-gah), who was the first daimyo to arm his soldiers with guns. With these weapons, Oda easily defeated his opponents' traditional samurai cavalry. By Oda's death in 1582 he controlled half of Japan.

Toyotomi Hideyoshi, Oda's greatest general, continued his leader's efforts and by 1590 controlled most of Japan. A few years later in 1600, **Tokugawa Ieyasu** (toh-koohg-ah-wuh ee-e-yahs-ooh) won a decisive battle to gain complete control of Japan. In 1603 the emperor made Tokugawa shogun. This event began the Tokugawa shogunate, which ruled until 1867.

READING CHECK **Find the Main Idea** What features defined Japan's feudal warrior society?

The Tokugawa Shogunate

Tokugawa Ieyasu established his capital at a quiet fishing village named Edo (AY-doh), which is now the city of Tokyo. By establishing a strong, central government, he and the later Tokugawa shoguns brought about a period of relative unity, peace, and stability in Japan.

Tokugawa Rule The Tokugawa shoguns closely controlled the daimyo, who still held power at the local level. To keep the daimyo loyal, the shoguns required them to live in Edo periodically and to leave their families there year-round as "hostages." These requirements forced the daimyo to maintain two residences, which was expensive, and were an attempt to preclude the daimyo from rebelling.

The stability and peace of Tokugawa rule brought prosperity to Japan. Agricultural production rose, the population and cities grew, and economic activity increased. New roads called the Five Highways linked the main cities and castle towns, further improving trade.

Under Tokugawa rule, Japan's strict feudal social structure became even more rigid. At the top of society was the emperor, in truth a figurehead. Next was the shogun, who held the real power as the top military ruler. Below the shogun were daimyo, who owed him their loyalty, and then samurai, who served the daimyo. Together, the emperor, shogun, daimyo, and samurai made up the ruling warrior class.

ACADEMIC VOCABULARY
preclude to prevent something or someone from acting

Direct Teach

Reading Focus

Japan's Warrior Society

Identify Who were the daimyo? *warlords who held large estates and battled one another for power*

Identify Cause and Effect How did the Mongol invasions affect the Kamukura Shogunate? *weakened the power of the shogunate, led to rebellions*

Reading Focus

2 How did the Tokugawa Shogunate rule Japan, and in what ways did culture flourish during this period? *required daimyos live in Edo periodically, requiring them to establish two residences, some family members were kept hostage in Edo, a strict social structure was maintained, cities became centers of culture in art, literature, and theater*

The Tokugawa Shogunate

Recall What were the Five Highways? *new roads linking the main cities and castle towns, increasing trade*

Make Inferences Why do you think the Tokugawa rulers found it necessary to impose such strict rules? *possible answer—The previous shogunate had lost power when it lost centralized rule; Tokugawa rulers wanted to keep this from happening again.*

Skills Focus: Identifying Cause and Effect

At Level

Reading Skill

Changes in Political Stability

1. Tell students that the rise and fall of power were the result of chains of events. Tell students they will create two such chains in class.
2. Write the following title for all to see: The Collapse of Central Government. Have volunteers share an event or situation that led to the collapse of centralized government in Japan during the feudal period, and add each event to the chain. When finished, arrange the events in order of occurrence and have students copy the information.
3. Next, repeat this process with the following title: The Establishment of Peaceful Rule.
4. Have students write a paragraph about the causes and effects involved in changes in political stability. **LS Verbal-Linguistic**

Alternative Assessment Handbook, Rubric 9: Comparing and Contrasting

Answers

Reading Check *Samurai gave military service in exchange for property or payment; shoguns ruled in the name of the emperor; daimyo were powerful warlords.*

Direct Teach

Reading Focus

The Tokugawa Shogunate

Identify What three classes were below the warrior class during the time of the Tokugawa Shogunate? *peasants, artisans, merchants*

Contrast What was the role of women during the Tokugawa period? *led restricted lives, obedient to male head of household, lost many rights and freedoms*

Describe How did relations with the West change during the Tokugawa Shogunate? *Initially European traders were welcomed, but the shoguns grew concerned with the spread of Christianity in Japan and began to restrict trade and travel. By 1650 Japan was again mostly closed to European trade.*

CRF: Literature: Hokku Poems

Info to Know

Korean Alphabet Hangul (Korean for "Great Script") is the name of the 24-letter Korean alphabet. Developed during the reign of Sejong in the mid-1440's, Hangul became the official writing system of the Korean language. However, Chinese influence and Japanese rule kept the language from being used by scholars or the upper class until the end of Japanese rule of Korea in 1945.

Answers

Reading Like a Historian 1. *possible answer—The servant's costume is very simple, while the woman's costume is elaborate and expensive-looking.*
2. *possible answer—that kabuki continues to be performed today*

Below the warrior class were three classes—peasants, artisans, and merchants. Members of these lower classes could not rise in social status, serve in the military or government, or hold government positions that might challenge the power of the warrior class.

Peasants made up the vast majority—about 80 percent—of Japan's population. Forbidden from doing anything but farming, they supported themselves by growing rice and other crops on daimyo and samurai estates. In Japan, farming was considered an honorable trade, and peasants enjoyed a relatively high status, just below samurai. At the same time, peasants paid most of the taxes and led hard lives.

Below the peasants were artisans, who often lived in castle towns and made goods such as armor and swords. At the bottom of society were the merchants, not honored because they did not produce anything. Yet merchants often grew wealthy and could use their wealth to improve their social position.

During the Tokugawa period, women's status gradually declined. Many women led restricted lives and had to obey the male head of the household absolutely. Even women in the samurai class lost many rights and freedoms, such as the right to inherit property.

While male samurai continued to command respect, their role changed. Peace put many samurai out of work. Because samurai were not allowed to engage in trade, many ronin—masterless samurai—fell on desperate times. Some became farmers, others warriors-for-hire, and still others roaming bandits.

Relations with the West The prosperity of the Tokugawa Period went hand in hand with Japan's increasing contact with Europeans. The Portuguese had arrived in Japan in 1543, and other Europeans soon followed. Initially, the Japanese welcomed European traders and missionaries and the new ideas, products, and technologies that they brought.

Reading like a Historian

Kabuki Theater

Analyzing Visuals Kabuki plays combine dance, song, music, dialogue, and pantomime with elaborate costumes and make-up to tell stories about historical events as well as everyday life. The photograph at right is a still from a 2001 London performance of Tsuri Onna, or "Fishing for a Wife," a kabuki comedy about a servant tricked into marrying an unattractive woman. To interpret this image think about

- the subject of the image
- the details of the image
- the creation of the image

Actors in female roles cover their face, hands, and feet with a thick white make-up that symbolizes delicate skin.

Some kabuki costumes can weigh up to 40 pounds. The servant's simple costume is an indicator of his social status.

Skills Focus READING LIKE A HISTORIAN

1. **Details** What details from the costumes of the two characters suggest a difference in social class?
2. **Creation** What does the date and information about the photograph's creation suggest about kabuki as an artform?

See **Skills Handbook**, p. H26

Differentiating Instruction

Below Level

English-Language Learners

1. Organize students into mixed-ability pairs. Tell students that the feudal social structure under the Tokugawa Shogunate was quite rigid.
2. Copy the chart for students to see, omitting the italicized items. Have students copy and complete the chart.
LS Verbal-Linguistic, Visual-Spatial

Alternative Assessment Handbook, Rubric 1: Acquiring Information

Feudal Social Structure (Most important ↑ … Least important ↓)

Title	Role
Emperor	*Figurehead ruler*
Shogun	*True ruling power*
Daimyo	*Warlord landowners, owed loyalty to shogun*
Samurai	*Warriors, served the daimyo*
Peasants	*Farmers*
Artisans	*Made goods like armor and swords*
Merchants	*Sold goods, not honored*

While trade with Europe boosted Japan's economy, Christian missionaries changed Japanese society. Many Japanese became Christian, and soon samurai could be heard chanting Christian prayers in battle. Over time, though, the Tokugawa shoguns grew concerned with the spread of Christianity in Japan. Shoguns began to persecute Christians and kill missionaries or force them to leave. At the same time, the shoguns began to restrict foreign trade and travel. For example, they banned the building of all large ships. By 1650 Japan had shut its doors to all Europeans except the Dutch. Japan continued this policy for more than 200 years.

Feudal Culture Japan's growing cities became centers of culture during the feudal period. In art, colorful woodblock prints called Ukiyo-e, or "pictures of the floating world," became popular. Many of these prints showed vibrant scenes of city life.

In literature, realistic stories became popular as well as a form of poetry called **haiku**. A haiku consists of three lines with 17 syllables. Many haiku, including the one below, deal with themes of nature and harmony.

HISTORY'S VOICES

"An old silent pond . . .
A frog jumps into the pond,
splash! Silence again."

—Matsuo Basho, translated by Harry Behn

In theater, Noh drama developed in the 1300s. Slow-moving, Noh plays told stories through the use of masks, stylized dance, and music. For more action, plot, and humor, Japanese audiences turned to a new type of theater in the 1600s—**kabuki**. A kabuki play could last all day as actors sang and danced, pausing to interact with the audience. Although women initially performed kabuki, they were later banned from performing and replaced by men.

READING CHECK **Summarize** What changes did Tokugawa rulers impose on Japanese society?

Medieval Korea

In 1392 a powerful general named **Yi Song-gye** gained control of Korea and established the Choson kingdom. The Choson, or Yi, dynasty that ruled the kingdom became one of Korea's longest ruling dynasties, lasting until 1910.

The Choson kings formed a government based on Confucianism. During this period, Korea prospered and produced many cultural achievements, including the creation of a Korean alphabet. Then in the late 1500s the Japanese invaded Korea twice. The Koreans held off the Japanese by using advanced Turtle ships—ironclad warships with cannons—and receiving help from Ming China. The fighting left Korea in ruins, though. In the early 1600s Korea faced another threat when the Chinese invaded. By the 1640s Korea had become a vassal state to the Qing dynasty in China.

As a result of these events, the Choson kings increasingly isolated Korea from the world except for trade with China. In the West, Korea became known as "the Hermit Kingdom" because of its isolation.

READING CHECK **Analyze** How did foreign influences both help and hurt Korea?

READING SKILLS

Summarizing
After you read the information on Medieval Korea, summarize the key points in two to four sentences.

SECTION 4 ASSESSMENT

go.hrw.com
Online Quiz
Keyword: SHL NAS HP

Reviewing Ideas, Terms, and People

1. **a. Identify** Who were Minamoto Yoritomo and **Tokugawa Ieyasu**, and why were they each significant in Japanese history?
   b. Compare How were the **samurai** of medieval Japan similar to the knights of medieval Europe?
   c. Elaborate How did the rise of the **daimyo** alter Japanese society?
2. **a. Describe** What was life like for Japanese peasants, merchants, women, and ronin during the Tokugawa Period?
   b. Summarize What actions did Tokugawa Ieyasu and later Tokugawa **shoguns** take to secure Japanese unity?
   c. Evaluate How did **kabuki** and **haiku** contribute to Japanese culture?
3. **a. Recall** Who founded the Choson dynasty in Korea, and when?
   b. Analyze How do you think isolation might have benefited Korea's development, and how might it have hurt it?

Critical Thinking

4. **Sequence** Using your notes and a graphic organizer like the one below, explain the sequence of events from the development of a feudal warrior society in Japan to the rise of the Tokugawa Shogunate. You may need to add circles to your graphic organizer.

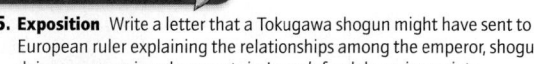

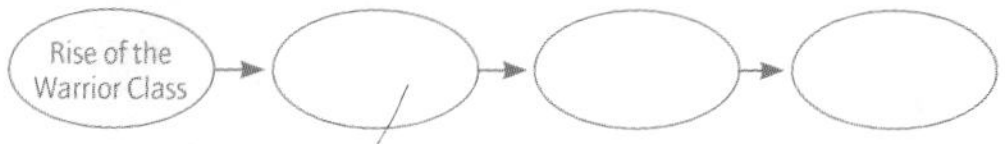

FOCUS ON WRITING

5. **Exposition** Write a letter that a Tokugawa shogun might have sent to a European ruler explaining the relationships among the emperor, shogun, daimyo, samurai, and peasants in Japan's feudal warrior society.

Direct Teach

Reading Focus

3 How did the Choson dynasty shape events in medieval Korea? *formed government based on Confucianism; isolated Korea from the world*

Medieval Korea

Recall What was one important cultural achievement in medieval Korea? *the creation of a Korean alphabet*

Analyze Why did the Choson kings isolate Korea from the rest of the world? *Foreign invasions left Korea in ruins.*

Review & Assess

Close

Review the Japanese feudal system and discuss the achievements made under the Tokugawa shogunate.

Review

Online Quiz, Section 4

Assess

SE Section 4 Assessment

Progress Assessment: Section 4 Quiz

Alternative Assessment Handbook

Reteach/Intervene

Interactive Reader and Study Guide, Section 4

Interactive Skills Tutor CD-ROM

Section 4 Assessment Answers

1. **a.** shoguns; Yorimoto was first shogun; Tokugawa began Tokugawa shogunate
   b. ethics based on religion, were skilled warriors
   c. decentralized power in Japan
2. **a.** required to obey rigid class structure; farmers considered honorable, but taxed highly. merchants lowest class, tended to prosper; women obedient, lost many rights and freedoms; during peacetime, ronin became farmers or bandits
   b. They placed restrictions on daimyo.
   c. They are distinct Japanese art forms.
3. **a.** Yi Song-gye, 1392
   b. possible answer—allowed Korean culture to flourish; limited positive foreign influences
4. Shogun established as ruler, land distributed to daimyos, then to samurai, factions compete, Tokugawa Ieyasu gains control and restricts daimyo, strict social structure
5. Student letters should define the different roles and explain the relationships among them.

Answers

Reading Check (left) *They required daimyos to live in Edo periodically and make expensive processions, some family members were kept hostage in Edo, a strict social structure was maintained, and they isolated Japan from outsiders* **(right)** *helped—Korea's government was formed on Confucianism, which was a foreign influence; harmed—Chinese and Japanese invaded Korea.*

Document-Based Investigation

Feudalism in Japan and Europe

Word Help

fealty the loyalty of a vassal or feudal tenant to his lord

fluid likely to change; variable

practicable possible to practice or perform

Activity Analyzing Primary Sources Ask students to volunteer what they know about European knights' code of chivalry. Tell students that *bushido* is roughly the samurai equivalent to chivalry. Write the following ten virtues of bushido for all to see: loyalty, self sacrifice, justice, sense of shame, refined manners, purity, modesty, frugality, martial spirit, honor, and affection. Ask students which of these Hojo Shigetoki discussed in Document 1. *loyalty and self sacrifice*

Info to Know

Matsumoto Castle Now a National Treasure of Japan, Matsumoto Castle was originally designed to withstand attack from *teppo*, the firearms used at that time. Construction of the castle began in the 1580s. It has three moats and small openings in the walls allowed the use of weapons. The castle also has a secret third floor, which invaders were unaware of until they were captured in the dark, windowless room. The fourth floor was the lord's chamber where he attended to castle business. The fifth floor provides excellent visibility on all sides, as does the tiny room on the top floor.

CHAPTER 3

Document-Based Investigation

Feudalism in Japan and Europe

Historical Context The documents in this investigation describe different aspects of feudalism in medieval Japan and in medieval Europe.

Task Study the documents and answer the questions that follow. Then, using evidence from these documents and from the chapter, write an essay comparing and contrasting feudalism in Japan and in Europe.

DOCUMENT 1

The Ideal Samurai in Medieval Japan

In about 1256, Hojo Shigetoki, a Buddhist monk and former deputy to the Kyoto Shogunate, wrote a series of essays outlining the ideal behavior and moral character of Japan's warrior class, the samurai.

> When one is serving officially or in the master's court, he should not think of a hundred or a thousand people, but should consider only the importance of the master. Nor should he draw the line at his own life or anything else he considers valuable. Even if the master is being phlegmatic [slow to rise to action] and one goes unrecognized, he should know that he will surely have the divine protection of the gods and Buddhas. While in the midst of duties, one should keep this principle in mind concerning service at the master's court, too. To think of receiving the blessings of the master without fulfilling the duties of court service is no different from trying to cross a rough sea without a boat.

DOCUMENT 2

Fortresses of Feudalism

Medieval fortresses such as Matsumoto Castle (left) in Japan and Bodiam Castle (right) in England were often built on hills and surrounded by water for defensive purposes. As in medieval Europe, the need for castles in Japan arose in a time marked by the absence of a strong central government and intense competition between local rulers. During this period of disorder and division in Japan, dozens of warlords fought each other and built castles to defend their lands.

Collaborative Learning

At Level

Research Required

Fortresses of Feudalism

1. Review with students the characteristics shared by Matsumoto and Bodiam castles. Tell students they will compare and contrast the physical characteristics of European and Japanese medieval fortresses.
2. Organize students into small groups. Have each group conduct research to locate information about the two castles pictured in Document 2. Have each group create a list of facts about the defensive structural advantages of each castle, and a bibliography of references for the facts it recorded.
3. Next, have each group mark list entries that have strong similarities.
4. Have groups post their lists for display and allow students time to circulate the room to view each group's results. **LS Interpersonal, Visual-Spatial**

Alternative Assessment Handbook, Rubrics 9: Comparing and Contrasting; and 14: Group Activity

DOCUMENT 3

Duties of a Knight in Medieval Europe

In about 1023 Duke William of Aquitaine, in present-day France, asked Bishop Fulbert of Chartres to advise on the duties of vassals and lords. The following excerpt is from the bishop's reply.

> To William most glorious duke of the Aquitanians . . . Asked to write something concerning the form of fealty, I have noted briefly for you on the authority of the books of the things we follow. He who swears fealty to his lord ought always to have these six things in memory; what is harmless, safe, honorable, useful, easy, practicable. Harmless, that is to say that he should not be injurious to his lord in his body; safe, that he should not be injurious to him in his secrets or in the defences through which he is able to be secure; honorable, that he should not be injurious to him in his justice or in other matters that pertain to his honor; useful, that he should not be injurious to him in his possessions; easy or practicable , that that good which his lord is able to do easily, he make not difficult, nor that which is practicable he make impossible to him.

DOCUMENT 4

A Historian's View

In the 1960s Peter Duus was one of many historians who debated whether or not "feudalism" was a valid concept for understanding Japanese history. In the following passage from his book *Feudalism in Japan,* published in 1969, Duus examines feudalism in Japan and Europe.

> Of course, we should not expect feudal Japan to be a mirror image of feudal Europe, either in its pattern of development or in its institutional structure. The history of Japan was conditioned by a geographic, economic, social, and intellectual environment vastly different from that of Europe. What we should expect to find is a family resemblance, not an exact likeness. Equally important we should not think of European feudalism as being more "normal" than Japanese feudalism. Building a model on the basis of the European experience is simple a convenience; a close study of both Japan and Europe may mean that we will have to modify the model. It may be that some things we assume to be indispensable aspects of feudalism were not present in both cultures and that certain things we had not assumed to be so were in fact common to both. In short, we are still at the beginning of the comparative study of feudalism, and our definition of it will have to remain a fluid one.

Skills FOCUS — READING LIKE A HISTORIAN

DOCUMENT 1

a. Identify According to Hojo Shigetok, what should be the foremost concern of a samurai?

b. Explain What does Hojo Shigetok mean when he says that expecting a master's blessing without fulfilling one's duties is like trying to cross a rough sea without a boat?

DOCUMENT 2

a. Describe What architectural features suggest that both castles were defensive structures?

b. Elaborate Why were castles important to the development and maintenance of feudalism in Europe and Japan?

DOCUMENT 3

a. Identify Main Ideas According to Bishop Fulbert, how should a knight in service to a lord act?

b. Compare Based on this document and Document 1, how did a knight's duties compare to those of a samurai?

DOCUMENT 4

a. Describe According to Duus what might account for the differences in feudalism in Japan and Europe?

b. Interpret How would a fluid definition of feudalism help historians study feudalism in Japan and Europe?

DOCUMENT-BASED ESSAY QUESTION

Using details from the documents and information from this chapter and other resources, write a short essay comparing and contrasting feudalism in Japan and Europe.

See **Skills Handbook**, p. H48

Document-Based Investigation

Biography

Bishop Fulbert, (c. 950s–1028) Bishop Fulbert of Chartres overcame a humble background by excelling as a student and then establishing a school at Chartres Cathedral. The school attracted students from across Europe, who held such respect for him that they referred to Fulbert as "the venerable Socrates." When Chartres burned down in 1020, Fulbert received help from various European kings to rebuild it. His writings are valued by the Catholic Church because they describe the liturgy and discipline of the church at the time.

Skills Focus: Making Inferences

At Level

Reading Skill
A Samurai Journal

1. Remind students that the life of a samurai was quite different from that of his European counterpart.
2. Have students write a journal entry for a samurai living at Matsumoto Castle in the 1600s. Students should review each document to help them infer what a samurai's life may have been like. Suggest that students include specific duties that would have been performed by the samurai or his servant, and describe specific places he would go.
3. When students have had time to write, have several volunteers share their work.
4. As homework, have students write a short essay about their new understanding of feudalism in Japan. **LS Verbal-Linguistic**

Alternative Assessment Handbook, Rubric 15: Journals

Answers

Reading Like a Historian

Document 1. a. *the importance of the master;* **b.** *possible answer—The fulfillment of one's duties to his master is a source of protection in bad times, just like a boat protects one during harsh seas;* **Document 2. a.** *moats, protective walls with narrow openings for defense;* **b.** *Castles protected people who lived and worked together, cooperating with each other under a behavioral code and the law of a single ruler. This protection allowed people to survive invasions.* **Document 3. a.** *A knight must remember what is harmless, safe, honorable, useful, easy, and practicable.* **b.** *A knight must concern himself with what is harmless, safe, and easy, but a samurai's focus is on the importance of his master, even disregarding his own safety.* **Document 4. a.** *The history of Japan was conditioned by a geographic, economic, social, and intellectual environment vastly different from that of Europe.* **b.** *possible answer—We should allow the definition of feudalism to change as we learn more.* **Essay** *Student essays should include several similarities and differences in feudalism in Japan and Europe.*

Answers

Visual Summary

Review and Inquiry Organize students into six groups. Assign one region from the Visual Study Guide to each group. Have groups create an oral presentation about their assigned region.

Quick Facts Transparency: Visual Study Guide: New Asian Empires

Review Key Terms and People

1. sultan
2. Suleyman
3. Akbar the Great
4. Shah Jahan
5. Zheng He
6. Qing dynasty
7. Bushido
8. haiku
9. Yi Song-gye
10. stance

Comprehension and Critical Thinking

11. **a.** 1453; provided Ottoman Empire with a trade route between Asia and Europe; marked the fall of the Byzantine Empire
b. Safavids were Shia Muslims, Ottomans were Sunni. Safavid emperors went to war with the Ottoman Empire to convert it.
c. Ottoman Empire defeated the Safavids at the Battle of Chaldiran, spread of Safavid Empire.

12. **a.** won loyalty of diverse population, promoted religious tolerance.
b. Later Mughal rulers did not practice religious tolerance.
c. possible answer—Yes, during his reign the empire experienced a golden age.

13. **a.** After European traders arrived, Ming rulers isolated China from the outside world to preserve China's traditions.
b. possible answer—stability, prosperity
c. possible answer—Yes, it helped preserve China's traditions.

CHAPTER 3

Chapter Review

VISUAL STUDY GUIDE

QUICK FACTS

Asian Empires, 1200–1800

Ottoman Empire

- Muslim Turks built the empire from a state in Anatolia in the 1300s.
- Under Mehmed II, the Ottomans captured Constantinople in 1453.
- Suleyman I brought the empire to its height and reformed law codes.
- Tolerated but restricted non-Muslims and enslaved Christian boys.
- Ottoman culture combined Persian, Muslim, and Byzantine influences.

Safavid Empire

- Esmai'il founded this Muslim empire in Persia in the 1500s.
- Esmai'il strictly enforced Shiism and came into conflict with Sunni Muslims such as the Ottomans.
- 'Abbas, the greatest Safavid shah, strengthened the military and expanded the empire.
- Safavid culture blended Chinese, Muslim, and Persian styles.

Mughal Empire

- Babur founded this Muslim empire in India by 1526.
- Akbar and Jahangir encouraged tolerance and cooperation between Muslims and Hindus.
- Shah Jahan and Aurangzeb tried to eliminate non-Muslims.
- Mughal art combined influences from India, Persia, and Muslim lands in structures like the Taj Mahal.

China

- Ming dynasty (1368–1644) rulers provided prosperity and stability, built the Forbidden City in Beijing, funded sea voyages, and isolated China as European influences rose.
- Qing dynasty (1644–1911) rulers expanded China to its largest size and continued isolation.
- Cultural developments included Ming porcelain and Chinese novels.

Japan

- A feudal warrior society arose in which a shogun ruled over daimyo with private armies of samurai.
- Samurai followed Bushido, a code stressing loyalty and bravery.
- The Kamakura shogunate unified Japan and defeated the Mongols.
- The Tokugawa shogunate reunified Japan in 1603, and later isolated Japan as European influences rose.

Korea

- General Yi Song-gye founded the Choson, or Yi, dynasty in 1392.
- Choson kings created a government built on Confucian principles.
- Japanese invasions in the late 1500s left Korea in ruins.
- After Manchu invasions, Korea became a Qing vassal state.
- Korea was isolated from the world for much of this period.

Reviewing Key Terms and People

Identify the correct term or person from the chapter that best fits each of the following descriptions.

1. title of the rulers of the Ottoman Empire
2. Ottoman ruler who reformed the legal code
3. Considered to be the greatest Mughal emperor
4. Mughal emperor who had the Taj Mahal built
5. Chinese admiral who led seven sea voyages for China during the 1400s
6. series of Manchu rulers who governed China
7. code of ethics for Japanese samurai
8. Japanese poetry with three lines and 17 syllables
9. general who founded Korea's Choson dynasty
10. attitude or position about someone or something

14. **a.** by re-establishing a strong central government in Japan
b. Samurai gave military service in exchange for property or payment; shoguns ruled in the name of the emperor; daimyo were powerful warlords.
c. Rulers in both Japan and Korea were concerned about how foreign influence would affect their cultures.

Reading Skills

15. key points—Ottomans built vast empire in Europe, Asia, and Africa; had strong military ruled by sultan; conquered Constantinople; diverse cultures created rich Ottoman culture
16. key points—Qing dynasty were Manchus who overthrew the Ming dynasty; last dynasty in China's history and the largest empire; respected Chinese customs and traditions; maintained Ming policy of isolation

History's Impact video program
Review the video to answer the closing question: Describe some influences of the samurai on the traditions of contemporary Japan.

Comprehension and Critical Thinking

SECTION 1 *(pp. 101–105)*

11. a. Recall When did the Ottomans capture the city of Constantinople, and why was the city's conquest significant?

b. Analyze How did religion divide the Ottoman and Safavid empires, and how did this division affect the two empires' relationship?

c. Elaborate How did the Ottoman Empire influence the Safavid Empire, and what was the outcome of this influence?

SECTION 2 *(pp. 106–110)*

12. a. Recall How did Akbar bring stability to the Mughal Empire?

b. Contrast How did the religious stances of later Mughal rulers differ from those of earlier rulers?

c. Evaluate Do you think Shah Jahan was a good emperor for India? Why or why not?

SECTION 3 *(pp. 111–115)*

13. a. Describe How did China's relationship with the outside world change during the Ming dynasty?

b. Make Generalizations What common factors contributed to population and city growth during the Ming and Qing dynasties?

c. Make Judgments Do you think that China's Ming emperor made the right decision to stop making overseas voyages? Why or why not?

SECTION 4 *(pp. 118–123)*

14. a. Recall How did the Tokugawa Shogunate bring stability, peace, and prosperity to Japan?

b. Summarize What were the main features that characterized Japan's feudal warrior society?

c. Elaborate What common factors motivated rulers in medieval Japan and Korea to close their societies to the outside world?

Reading Skills

Summarizing *Use what you know about summarizing to answer the questions below:*

15. Review the information on the Ottoman Empire and summarize the key points in four to five sentences.

16. Review the information on the Qing dynasty and summarize the main points in a few sentences.

Analyzing Visuals

Reading Like a Historian *The painting below, made during the 1700s shows young women relaxing and playing on swings during the Mughal Empire.*

Mughal miniature, c. 1700s

17. Infer What can you infer about Mughal art from this image?

18. Analyze What can you learn about Mughal women's fashions in the 1700s from this image?

Using the Internet

go.hrw.com
Practice Online
Keyword: SHL NAS

19. The Ottoman Empire lasted more than 500 years. Using the keyword above, conduct research on the history of the Ottoman Empire. Then create an illustrated time line of the major events of the empire.

WRITING FOR THE SAT

Think about the following issue:

Some of the most successful Asian rulers during this period governed with almost absolute power. Two examples are the Ottoman sultan Suleyman and the Mughal emperor Akbar. These two rulers used their power to improve and expand their empires.

20. Assignment: *What did these two rulers have in common in the ways in which they used their power? Write a short essay in answer to this question. Support your answer with examples from your reading and studies.*

Answers

Analyzing Visuals

17. possible answer—that Mughal art depicted daily life

18. Mughal women wore long, colorful skirts, blouses, and dresses.

Using the Internet

19. Go to the HRW Web site and enter the keyword shown to access a rubric for this activity.

KEYWORD: SHL NAS

Writing for the SAT

20. Student essays should include details from the chapter about the reigns of the Ottoman sultan Suleyman and the Mughal emperor Akbar. Essays should point out what the two rulers had in common. A rubric for this activity is provided in **CRF:** Writing for the SAT.

HOLT
History's Impact

► **Video Program: New Asian Empires**
See the Video Program Teacher's Guide for the answer to the closing question.

Review and Assessment Resources

Review and Reinforce

- **CRF**: Chapter Review
- **Quick Facts Transparency**: Visual Study Guide: New Asian Empires
- **Spanish Chapter Summaries Audio CD Program**
- OSP **Holt PuzzlePro**: Quiz Show for ExamView
- **Quiz Game CD-ROM**

Assess

- **PASS**: Chapter Test, Forms A and B
- **Alternative Assessment Handbook**
- OSP **ExamView Test Generator**, Chapter Test
- **Differentiated Instruction Modified Worksheets and Tests CD-ROM**: Chapter Test
- HOAP **Holt Online Assessment Program** (in the Premier Online Edition)

Reteach/Intervene

- **Interactive Reader and Study Guide**
- **Differentiated Instruction Teacher Management System**: Lesson Plans for Differentiated Instruction
- **Differentiated Instruction Modified Worksheets and Tests CD-ROM**: Chapter Test
- **Interactive Skills Tutor CD-ROM**

go.hrw.com
Online Resources
KEYWORD: TEACHER

Unit Review

You can use these pages to have students simultaneously review the unit and practice taking standardized tests.

Answers

1. D
   Exploration and Expansion, Section 3
2. B
   Renaissance and Reformation, Section 3
3. D
   Renaissance and Reformation, Section 4
4. A
   Renaissance and Reformation, Section 1
5. C
   Renaissance and Reformation, Section 1
6. A
   Renaissance and Reformation, Section 3
7. C
   Exploration and Expansion, Section 1
8. B
   Exploration and Expansion, Section 1
9. D
   Exploration and Expansion, Section 3

UNIT 1

Standardized Test Practice

Directions Write your answer for each statement or question on a separate answer sheet. Choose the letter of the word or expression that best completes the statement or answers the question.

1 The illustration shows an effect on Aztecs of the

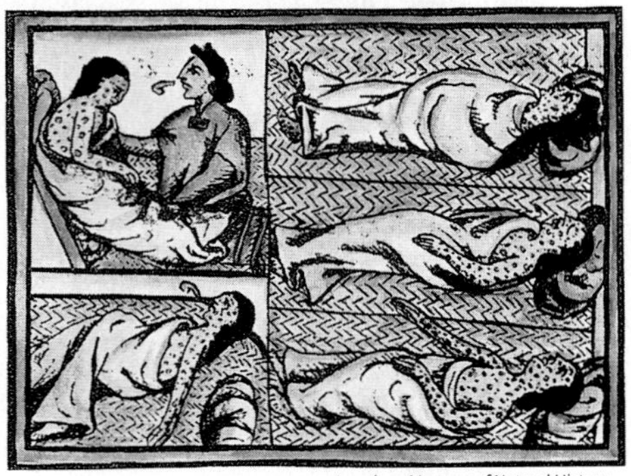

American Museum of Natural History

A Mayan attacks.
B famine.
C Spanish weapons.
D Columbian exchange.

2 Why were many people in the 1500s unhappy with the Roman Catholic Church?

A People wanted the Catholic Church to sell indulgences so they could have their sins forgiven.
B People thought that the Catholic Church had become too worldly, too wealthy, and had strayed from its spiritual roots.
C The newly invented printing press enabled heresy to spread quickly.
D They opposed the Diet of Worms.

3 One response of Catholics to the Reformation was

A the sack of Rome by the soldiers of the Holy Roman Emperor Charles V.
B Ignatius of Loyola calling the Council of Trent.
C encouraging people to read and criticize Luther's work.
D the formation of new religious orders, such as the Jesuits, who worked to reform the church.

4 Some of the factors that helped bring about the Renaissance are

A increased trade, the growth of wealthy city-states, and an interest in classical ideas and styles.
B decreased trade as a result of the Crusades.
C decreased interest in secular themes in literature.
D increased focus on finding ways to glorify God.

5 One of the characteristics of the Renaissance was

A a focus on religious art.
B a lack of trade among towns and cities.
C an emphasis on the individual.
D a return to traditional religious ideas.

6 Martin Luther taught that

A faith alone can lead to salvation.
B faith and good works lead to salvation.
C God has already chosen those who will be saved.
D the Bible and church tradition are both sources of truth.

7 During the 1300s and 1400s, Europeans set out on voyages of exploration to find

A a cure for the plague and other serious illnesses.
B the North and South poles.
C wealth and fame.
D the American continents.

8 The monarch who established a school for navigators was

A King John II of Portugal.
B Prince Henry of Portugal.
C Queen Isabella of Spain.
D King Henry VII of England.

9 The global transfer of plants, animals, people, and diseases between the Eastern and Western hemispheres became known as the

A mercantile exchange.
B European-Western Exchange.
C balance of trade.
D Columbian Exchange.

10 The Spanish conquistador Hernán Cortés
A captured and destroyed the Aztec capital, Tenochtitlan.
B conquered the Incas, who were weakened by disease.
C respected and admired the Aztec emperor Montezuma II.
D established the first Spanish colony in Hispaniola.

11 The voyage of enslaved Africans across the Atlantic Ocean was known as the
A African-American Passage.
B Middle Passage.
C Long Voyage.
D Passage of the Enslaved.

12 When the Ottomans conquered Constantinople they renamed it
A Byzantium.
B Adrianople.
C Anatolia.
D Istanbul.

13 Suleyman I (the Great) is best known for
A expanding the Ottoman Empire to its height of power.
B leading the Ottomans into Europe.
C defeating a crusade at the Battle of Nicopolis.
D conquering Constantinople.

14 During his reign as shah of the Mughal Empire, Akbar
A gained a foothold in India.
B established a religion that blended Muslim, Christian, and other beliefs.
C pursued artistic interests and allowed his wife and her family to govern.
D destroyed Hindu temples and kept Hindus out of high positions in government.

15 One of the achievements of the Ming dynasty under Hongwu was
A diplomatic and economic contact with Europeans.
B a dramatic increase in taxes.
C the complete defeat of the Mongols.
D shared government control between the emperor and the chief minister.

16 Japanese feudalism was similar to European feudalism in that it
A had a central governing figure.
B was governed by church and civil authorities.
C gave land to vassals who swore allegiance to a lord.
D had a code of ethics called the bushido.

17 One characteristic of Japanese life during the Tokugawa period was the
A respect and high social rank given to merchants.
B continued need for samurai.
C strictness of the social structure.
D power of the daimyo over the shogun.

18 Read this excerpt from Leonardo da Vinci's writings. What is his opinion about the art of painting?

"The painter will produce pictures of small merit if he takes for his standard the pictures of others, but if he will study from natural objects he will bear good fruit. As was seen in the painters after the Romans who always imitated each other and so their art constantly declined from age to age... Those who take for their standard any one but nature... weary themselves in vain."

A He recommends studying other painters' works.
B He supports copying Roman works.
C He thinks that an artist must study nature.
D He thinks that painting required little talent.

REVIEWING THE UNIT

Constructed Response From the 1300s through the 1600s, some empires expanded, some fell, and others closed their borders. Recall what you have learned about European, Asian, and American empires during this period. Choose one empire and write a brief essay identifying the causes and effects of its expansion, its fall, or its retreat from the outside world.

CONNECTING TO THE PREVIOUS UNIT

Constructed Response During the Renaissance and Reformation, Europeans began to change how they looked at the world. Recall what you learned about Europe during the Middle Ages. Then write a brief essay about medieval events that set the stage for the Renaissance, Reformation, and exploration.

Unit Review

Answers

10. A
Exploration and Expansion, Section 2

11. B
Exploration and Expansion, Section 4

12. D
New Asian Empires, Section 1

13. A
New Asian Empires, Section 1

14. B
New Asian Empires, Section 2

15. C
New Asian Empires, Section 3

16. C
New Asian Empires, Section 4

17. C
New Asian Empires, Section 4

18. C
Renaissance and Reformation, Section 1

Reviewing the Unit

Students essays will vary depending on the empire they chose to write about.

Connecting to the Previous Unit

Student essays should discuss the influence that medieval events had on the Renaissance, the Reformation, and exploration.

Unit Review

Migration and Diffusion

The Columbian Exchange One area in which the New World came out ahead in the Columbian Exchange was in terms of the exchange of animals. In the New World there were 25 species of large mammals, but none of them except the llama and alpaca were suitable for domestication. On the other hand, Europe and Asia had 72 large animal species, of which 13 were suitable for domestication, including horses, cattle, sheep, goats, and pigs.

Arts and Ideas

The Development of Printing Perhaps the most important development of the Renaissance took place in Northern Europe rather than in Italy: the printing press. In the first 50 years after the invention of movable type, more than 6,000 separate works were printed. The first books printed in Northern Europe were Bibles and other religious texts. In Italy, on the other hand, printers published Greek and Roman classics, as well as new literary and scientific works by Renaissance scholars. The religious and political controversies of the 16th and 17th centuries were spread largely by printed pamphlets.

Activity The Importance of Printing Tell students to envision what the world would be like without printing. How would it affect their lives? Have students write a paragraph about what life would be like without books, magazines, or newspapers.

LS Verbal-Linguistic

UNIT 1 New Ideas, New Empires, 1200–1800

Themes & Global Connections

THEME

MIGRATION AND DIFFUSION

Why can 1492 be considered a turning point in world history?

The encounters among the Americas, Africa, and Europe had profound affects on the populations, food sources, and diseases all over the world. For example, American foodstuffs introduced into Asia resulted in an increase in the population of China.

RESULTS OF EUROPEAN EXPLORATION

Europe	• New food sources enriched diets and led to a population boom. • Spain was enriched with American gold and silver, leading to global dominance and inflation. • Europeans raced to establish colonies. • European-American trade led to increased European business activity. • Mercantilist and capitalist ideas took hold.
Americas	• European diseases devastated Native American populations, which lacked immunity. • Millions of Africans were forcibly enslaved and brought to the Americas. • Europeans emigrated in great numbers to the Americas. • The wheel, iron tools, and guns were introduced. • New domesticated plants and animals were introduced.
Africa	• The Atlantic slave trade forcibly removed millions of Africans from the continent. • New food crops were introduced. • Guns were introduced into West Africa.
China	• New food sources enriched diets and led to a population boom. • China received American silver in payment for Chinese luxury goods.

THEME

ARTS AND IDEAS

How did the Renaissance influence Europeans' world view?

The Renaissance brought a shift in most Europeans' focus from spiritual concerns characteristic of the Middle Ages to a more secular and individualistic focus. Religion still played an important role in people's lives, but people increasingly focused their attention on their own interests and achievements.

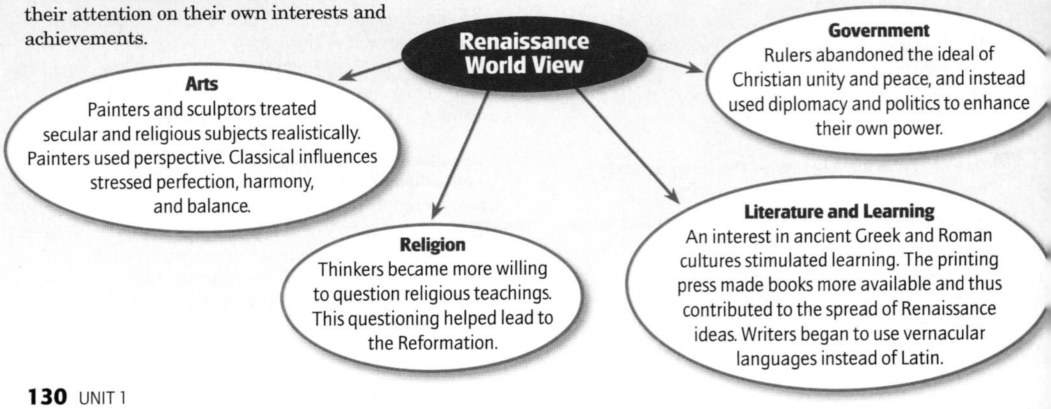

Renaissance World View
Arts
Painters and sculptors treated secular and religious subjects realistically. Painters used perspective. Classical influences stressed perfection, harmony, and balance.
Government
Rulers abandoned the ideal of Christian unity and peace, and instead used diplomacy and politics to enhance their own power.
Religion
Thinkers became more willing to question religious teachings. This questioning helped lead to the Reformation.
Literature and Learning
An interest in ancient Greek and Roman cultures stimulated learning. The printing press made books more available and thus contributed to the spread of Renaissance ideas. Writers began to use vernacular languages instead of Latin.

Differentiating Instruction

Below Level

English-Language Learners

1. Organize students into four groups. Assign each group one of the four areas affected by the Renaissance world view, as shown in the graphic organizer on this page. Have groups find or draw pictures that illustrate the area assigned to them and create a collage showing how that area affected the way people looked at the world.
2. Have volunteers from each group present their collages to the class. Place each collage on display for the class to see.
3. Guide the class in a discussion of the ways in which the Renaissance changed the way people looked at the world around them.
   LS Interpersonal, Visual-Spatial

Alternative Assessment Handbook, Rubrics 8: Collages; 11: Discussions; and 14: Group Activity

THEME
BELIEF SYSTEMS

How did conquest affect people's belief systems?

During this period conquest resulted in a change in the dominant religion in several areas of the world.

CONQUEST AND BELIEF SYSTEMS

Ottomans conquered Constantinople.	Orthodox Christian Constantinople became Muslim Istanbul.
Safavids expanded their empire.	Shia Islam became the state religion in what is today Iran, replacing a number of existing traditions.
Mughals conquered northern India.	Islam was promoted, but Hinduism remained dominant and Buddhism nearly disappeared.
Europeans conquered the Americas.	Christianity replaced Native American religions.

Skills FOCUS **UNDERSTANDING THEMES**

Conquest by Ottoman Turkish armies was a major factor in the diffusion of Ottoman culture. The Ottoman military kept Italian traders out of the eastern Mediterranean, took over much of Hungary, and laid siege to Vienna. Following the conquest of Constantinople, the Ottomans forced people of other cultures to migrate to the city. Use your textbook and other resources to gather information about how Europeans responded to the Ottoman expansion. Then create a chart like the one below to explain how Europeans responded. Add as many rows as you need.

Ottoman Empire	European Response
Control of the eastern Mediterranean ports through which Asian trade passed	
Conquest of Hungary	
Siege of Vienna	

Global Connections

Japan's feudal period bears some similarities to European feudalism. The samurai were the at the center of the warrior class much as knights had been. They served their daimyo, or lord, and received land for their services. The shogun was at the top of the hierarchy and the real ruler of Japan.

In the last unit you learned about European feudalism. There are similarities between the systems, but they are not identical. What in European and Japanese society might account for the differences and similarities? Use your textbook and other sources to create a chart that compares and contrasts Japanese and European feudal systems.

Making Connections Analyze your chart to determine whether or not you think the two systems were similar. Then state your conclusions in a short essay of two to three paragraphs explaining your position.

▼ **Matsumoto Castle is located in Japan.**

▼ **Bodiam Castle is located in England.**

131

Skill Focus: Identifying Problem and Solution

At Level

Reading Skill

The New World: An Alternate Version

1. Tell students that it is 1492, and Columbus has just discovered the Americas, but in this version of history, he realizes that he has not reached Asia but instead a new, previously unknown land. Instead of landing, he goes back to Spain and tells of his discovery.
2. Organize students into small groups. Tell them they are advisers to the Spanish monarchs who want to make sure that the people of the Americas are treated fairly and that their safety is guaranteed. Have each group develop a set of guidelines designed to protect the Native Americans from possible contamination and exploitation.
3. Have volunteers from each group present their guidelines to the rest of the class.

LS Interpersonal

Alternative Assessment Handbook, Rubrics 14: Group Activity; 35: Solving Problems

Unit Review

Belief Systems

The Catholic Monarchs Ferdinand of Aragon and Isabella of Castille ruled over the most diverse country in western Europe, which had large Muslim and Jewish populations. Spanish civilization owed much to this fact. The Jews had made their mark in business and government, while Muslims had dominated in the visual arts and architecture. The leader of the Spanish Inquisition, Tomás de Torquemada, began a campaign against the Jews. In 1492—the year Columbus discovered the Americas—the Catholic Monarchs conquered the Muslim kingdom of Granada in southern Spain, finally uniting Spain. After Muslims rebelled in 1499–1500, they were given the choice of converting to Catholicism or leaving the country. The expulsion of the Jews and Muslims deprived Spain of much of its educated middle class, which would have serious repercussions in the future.

Understanding Themes

Ottoman Empire	European Response
Control of eastern Mediterranean ports through which Asian trade passed	*One last crusade ended in a European defeat at Nicopolis, on the Danube.*
Conquest of Hungary	*For the next 200 years there was near-constant warfare in Hungary between the Hapsburg and Ottoman empires.*
Siege of Vienna	*Europe reacted with fear and resolved to fight to the death to turn back the Ottomans.*

Global Connections

Student charts and essays should indicate the following similarities: both were systems in which lords gave lands to vassals in exchange for service. Differences include the fact that there was a single central authority, the shogun, in Japan. Also, in Japan military leaders governed, rather than civil or religious authorities.

Unit Review

Summarizing the Unit

During the period covered in this unit, the world experienced great changes. Guide the class in a discussion of those changes. Have students identify the ways in which the Renaissance, Protestant Reformation, Counter-Reformation, European voyages of discovery, and the formation of Asian empires and dynasties were related to each other.

Answers

Thinking Like a Historian

Student charts or graphic organizers will vary, depending on which area students selected, but should summarize developments in all three areas—government, trade and the economy, and the arts.

UNIT 1 IN BRIEF

Below is a chapter-by-chapter summary of the main ideas in this unit, followed by a summary activity for the unit.

CHAPTER 1 Renaissance and Reformation
1300–1650

MAIN IDEA **As trade with the East increased, Europeans rediscovered the classical knowledge of ancient Greece and Rome. This knowledge led to a period of creativity and learning known as the Renaissance. A new focus on the individual emerged, leading to new ideas about religion, and ultimately the Reformation.**

SECTION 1 In Italy the growth of wealthy trading cities and new ways of thinking led to a rebirth of the arts and learning known as the Renaissance.

SECTION 2 Trade and printing helped spread the Renaissance beyond Italy to Northern Europe, where it affected artists and writers in many ways.

SECTION 3 The Protestant Reformation was a response to criticisms of the Roman Catholic Church. The Reformation led to changes in politics as well as religion.

SECTION 4 Many Catholics recognized the need for reform of the church, and their work renewed the faith of Catholics.

CHAPTER 2 Exploration and Expansion
1400–1700

MAIN IDEA **Between 1400 and 1700 explorers set out on great voyages of discovery, and as the news of new lands spread, countries scrambled to set up colonies in hopes of gaining wealth.**

SECTION 1 Aided by new technologies and inspired by greed, curiosity, and the desire for glory, European explorers sailed to previously unknown lands.

SECTION 2 The countries of Europe established colonies in the lands they had discovered but in some cases only after conquering the people who lived there.

SECTION 3 The creation of colonies in the Americas and elsewhere led to the establishment of new patterns of trade and new economic systems in Europe.

SECTION 4 Millions of Africans were captured, transported across the Atlantic Ocean, and sold as slaves in the Americas between the 1500s and the 1800s.

CHAPTER 3 New Asian Empires
1200–1800

MAIN IDEA **Several new Muslim empires arose in Asia. In China, Mongol rule came to an end with the rise of the Ming dynasty. In Japan, the Tokugawa Shogunate created a strong central government.**

SECTION 1 The Ottomans conquered Constantinople and developed a rich culture. The Safavid dynasties expanded their territories.

SECTION 2 Mughal rulers in India created a powerful empire and saw an artistic flowering.

SECTION 3 China's power and size reached new heights during the Ming and Qing dynasties, and trade and culture flourished.

SECTION 4 Japan's feudal system unified under a shogunate that also produced a cultural blossoming.

Thinking like a Historian — Summary and Extension Activity

The Renaissance and Reformation set the stage for European expansion into previously unknown lands. In Asia, new empires formed and expanded, and the arts flourished. Choose one of these areas and create a chart or graphic organizer that shows the developments in:

A. Government

B. Trade and the economy

C. The arts

Unit Resources

Review and Reinforce
- **CRF:** Chapter Review
- **Spanish Chapter Summaries Audio CD Program**
- OSP **Holt PuzzlePro**: Quiz Show for ExamView
- **Quiz Game CD-ROM**

Assess
- **PASS**: Unit Test, Forms A and B
- **Alternative Assessment Handbook**
- OSP **ExamView Test Generator**
- **Differentiated Instruction Modified Worksheets and Tests CD-ROM**: Chapter Test
- HOAP **Holt Online Assessment Program** (in the Premier Online Edition)

Reteach/Intervene
- **Interactive Reader and Study Guide**
- **Differentiated Instruction Teacher Management System**: Lesson Plans for Differentiated Instruction
- **Differentiated Instruction Modified Worksheets and Tests CD-ROM**: Chapter Test
- **Interactive Skills Tutor CD-ROM**

go.hrw.com
Online Resources
KEYWORDS: SHL REN, SHL EXP, SHL NAS

UNIT 2

Changes in European Society

1500–1820

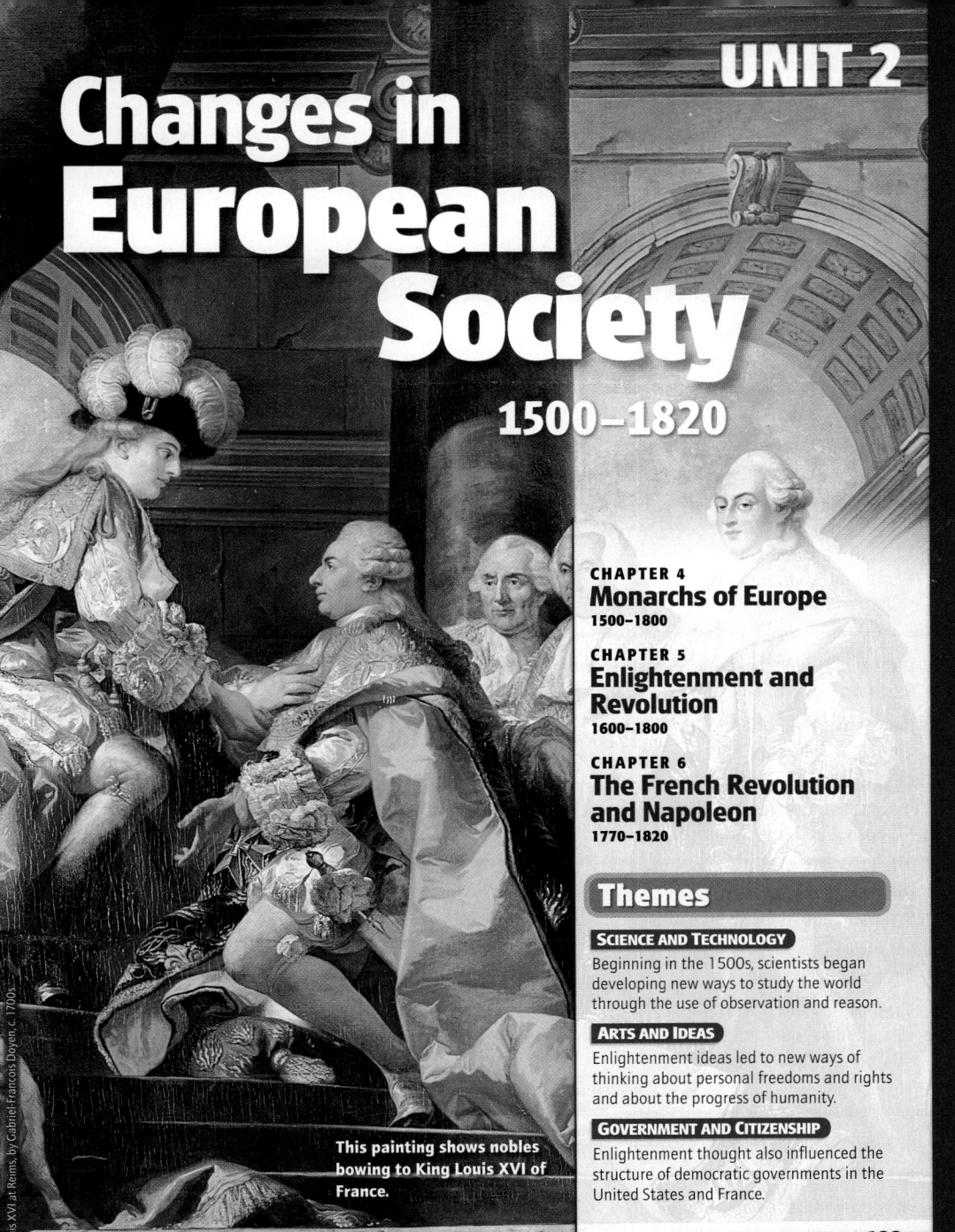

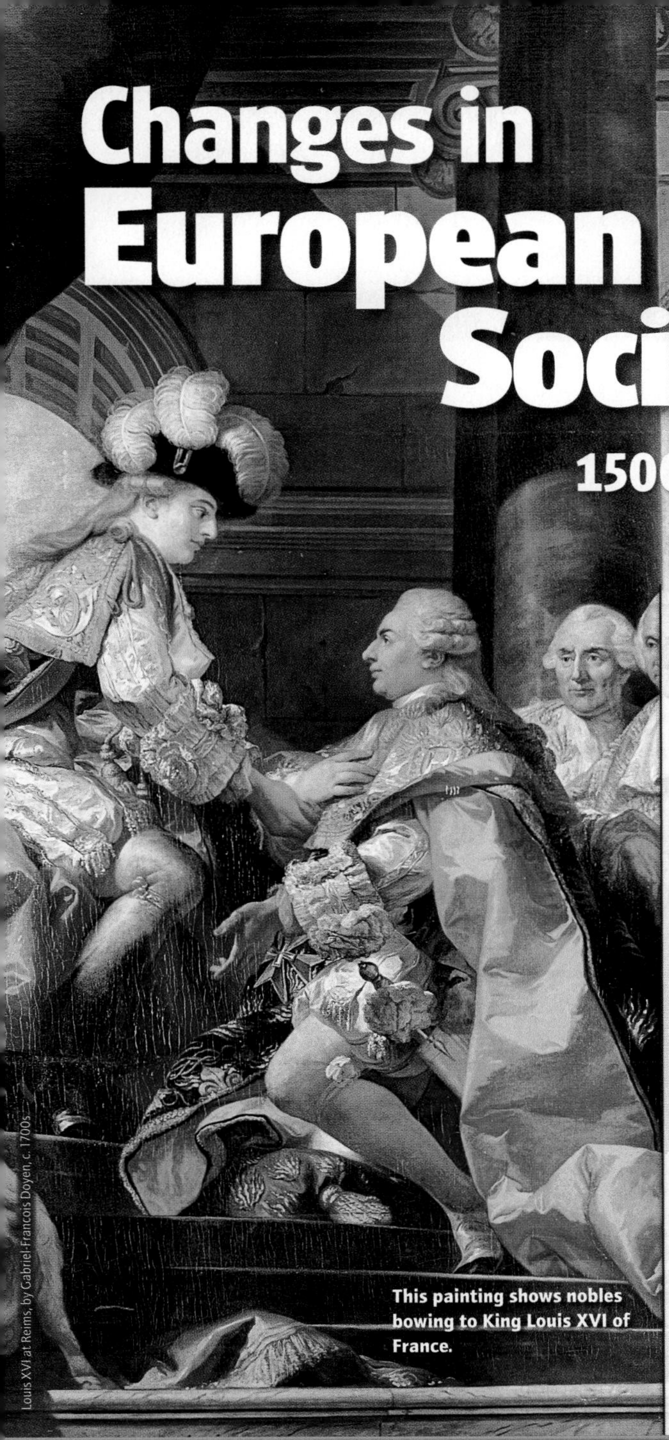

This painting shows nobles bowing to King Louis XVI of France.

Louis XVI at Reims, by Gabriel-François Doyen, c. 1700s

Themes

SCIENCE AND TECHNOLOGY
Beginning in the 1500s, scientists began developing new ways to study the world through the use of observation and reason.

ARTS AND IDEAS
Enlightenment ideas led to new ways of thinking about personal freedoms and rights and about the progress of humanity.

GOVERNMENT AND CITIZENSHIP
Enlightenment thought also influenced the structure of democratic governments in the United States and France.

Unit Preview

Introducing the Unit

Ask students to name a societal, economic, or political issue they feel strongly about, such as homelessness, hunger, war, or terrorism. Then have students list factors that might cause people involved in the issue to rebel against authority. Have students list what might have caused revolts against monarchs during the 1500s to 1800s.

Connecting to Themes

Activity New Ideas Bring Change
Ask students how changes in personal beliefs and in economic systems led to individualism and to changes in European society. Guide students in a discussion about the ways in which belief systems and economic systems changed during the Enlightenment.

Reading Like a Historian

Interpreting Visuals

Louis XVI When he came to the throne, Louis XVI was an awkward, timid twenty-year old, who was ill equipped to rule a country. Throughout his reign, he often expressed his desire to have been born a common man, free of his great responsibility. Louis' propensity to listen to self-interested advisors and give in to the extravagant demands of Queen Marie-Antoinette eventually cost him his life.

Unit Resources

Planning

- **Differentiated Instruction Teacher Management System:** Unit Pacing Guide
- OSP **One-Stop Planner CD-ROM:** Teacher Management System
- **Power Presentations with Video CD-ROM**

Differentiating Instruction

- **Differentiated Instruction Teacher Management System:** Lesson Plans for Differentiated Instruction
- **Differentiated Instruction Modified Worksheets and Tests CD-ROM**

Enrichment

- **A World History Teacher's Guide to Analyzing Movies**
- **Document-Based Activities for World History**
- **World History Outline Maps**
- **Reading Like a Historian: World History Toolkit**
- **World History Primary Source Library CD-ROM**

Assessment

- **PASS:** Unit Test, Forms A and B
- **Alternative Assessment Handbook**
- OSP **ExamView Test Generator**
- HOAP **Holt Online Assessment Program** (in the Premier Online Edition)

Chapter 4 Planning Guide

The Monarchs of Europe

Chapter Overview	Reproducible Resources	Technology Resources
CHAPTER 4 **pp. 134–165** **Overview: In this chapter, students will learn about the power of European monarchs and the various challenges they faced.**	**Differentiated Instruction Teacher Management System:*** • Pacing Guide • Lesson Plans for Differentiated Instruction **Interactive Reader and Study Guide:** Chapter Summary* **Chapter Resource File*** • Writing for the SAT • Social Studies Skill • Economics and History • Chapter Review	**Live Ink© Online Reading Help** **Student Edition on Audio CD Program** **Differentiated Instruction Modified Worksheets and Tests CD-ROM** **World History Primary Source Library CD-ROM** **History's Impact: World History Video Program (VHS/DVD):** The Monarchs of Europe
Section 1: **The Power of Spain** **The Main Idea:** Spain experienced a golden age during the 1500s, but economic problems and military struggles decreased Spanish power by the 1600s.	**Differentiated Instruction Teacher Management System:** Section 1 Lesson Plan* **Interactive Reader and Study Guide:** Section 1 Summary* **Chapter Resource File*** • Vocabulary Builder: Section 1 • Biography: Diego Velázquez	**Daily Test Practice Transparency:** Section 1* **Map Transparency:** Monarchs of Europe*
Section 2: **Absolute Monarchy and France** **The Main Idea:** Henry IV, Louis XIII, and Louis XIV strengthened the French monarchy, with Louis XIV setting the example of an absolute monarch for the rest of Europe.	**Differentiated Instruction Teacher Management System:** Section 2 Lesson Plan* **Interactive Reader and Study Guide:** Section 2 Summary* **Chapter Resource File*** • Vocabulary Builder: Section 2 • Biography: Louis de Rouvroy • Primary Source: The Edict of Nantes	**Daily Test Practice Transparency:** Section 2* **Internet Activity:** Louis XIV
Section 3: **Monarchy in England** **The Main Idea:** In contrast to the absolute monarchies of Spain and France, the English monarchy was limited by Parliament; following a civil war, Parliament became even more powerful.	**Differentiated Instruction Teacher Management System:** Section 3 Lesson Plan* **Interactive Reader and Study Guide:** Section 3 Summary* **Chapter Resource File*** • Vocabulary Builder: Section 3 • Biography: William and Mary • History and Geography: A King at War with Parliament • Literature: *The Life of King Henry V*	**Daily Test Practice Transparency:** Section 3*
Section 4: **Rulers of Russia and Central Europe** **The Main Idea:** The czars of Russia struggled with the westernization of their empire, while powerful families battled for control of Central Europe.	**Differentiated Instruction Teacher Management System:** Section 4 Lesson Plan* **Interactive Reader and Study Guide:** Section 4 Summary* **Chapter Resource File*** • Vocabulary Builder: Section 4 • Biography: Maria Theresa	**Daily Test Practice Transparency:** Section 4* **Map Transparency:** The Expansion of Russia* **Map Transparency:** Central Europe, 1763* **Internet Activity:** Peter the Great and Catherine the Great

go.hrw.com | Print Resource | Transparency
LS Learning Styles | Audio CD | CD-ROM
Video | SE Student Edition | TE Teacher's Edition
OSP One-Stop Planner CD-ROM
*also on One-Stop Planner CD-ROM

HOLT
History's Impact
World History Video Program (VHS/DVD)
The Monarchs of Europe

Review, Assessment, Intervention

- **Quick Facts Transparency:** The Monarchs of Europe
- **Progress Assessment Support System (PASS):** Chapter Test*
- **Differentiated Instruction Modified Worksheets and Tests CD-ROM:** Modified Chapter Test
- OSP **One-Stop Planner CD-ROM:** ExamView Test Generator (English/Spanish)
- HOAP **Holt Online Assessment Program (HOAP),** in the Premier Online Student Edition

- **PASS:** Section 1 Quiz*
- **Online Quiz:** Section 1
- **Alternative Assessment Handbook**

- **PASS:** Section 2 Quiz*
- **Online Quiz:** Section 2
- **Alternative Assessment Handbook**

- **PASS:** Section 3 Quiz*
- **Online Quiz:** Section 3
- **Alternative Assessment Handbook**

- **PASS:** Section 4 Quiz*
- **Online Quiz:** Section 4
- **Alternative Assessment Handbook**

Power Presentation with Video CD-ROM

Power Presentations with Video are visual presentations of each chapter's main ideas. Presentations can be customized by including Quick Facts charts, images and maps from the textbook, and video clips.

Holt Online Learning

go.hrw.com
Teacher Resources
KEYWORD: SHL TEACHER

go.hrw.com
Student Resources
KEYWORD: SHL MON

- Document-Based Questions
- Interactive Multimedia Activities
- Current Events
- Chapter-Based Internet Activities
- and more!

Holt Premier Online Student Edition

Complete online support for interactivity, assessment, and reporting

- Interactive Maps and Notebook
- Homework Practice and Research Activities Online

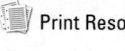

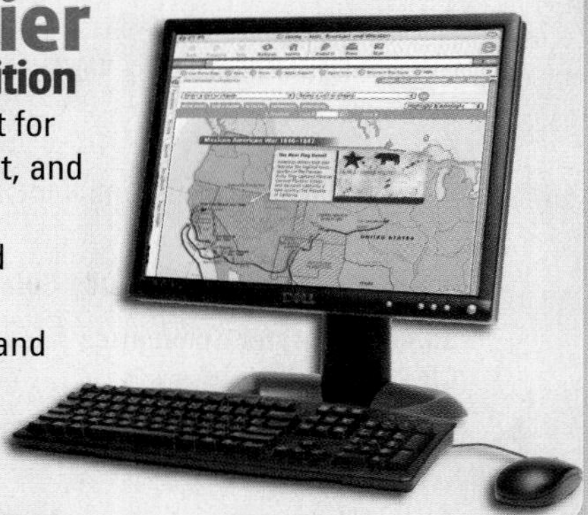

Before You Teach

The Big Picture

Peter N. Stearns

Politics and Diplomacy Three features predominate in the early modern period. First, major shifts occurred in the balance of power among nations. Second, important innovations occurred in the institutions of monarchy. In the 17th century, however, monarchical strength increased, notably in the rise of absolute monarchs. Absolutism also influenced Prussia and Russia, and to a degree the Hapsburgs. After Tudor gains, the English monarchy encountered new opposition. Through the English civil wars and the Glorious Revolution, a quite different parliamentary monarchy model emerged. Finally, European states gained new powers that outlasted the era of absolutism. Bureaucracies grew and became more specialized, and governments more actively intervened in the economy.

The Spanish Era Fueled by the Hapsburg dynastic link and the resources from the Americas, Spain served as Europe's major power during the 16th century. But naval defeat at British hands, economic lag, and overextension in other parts of Europe reduced Spain's power.

French Absolutism After the weaknesses of the later 16th century, the French monarchy rebounded and developed the clearest model of absolutism, with claims of untrammeled royal authority and divine right. Centralization increased, though in fact there were many limitations from the aristocracy and provincial institutions. Louis XIV's reign featured cultural and ritual splendor that reduced aristocratic interference. Mercantilist policies justified state economic intervention, new taxes, and colonialism.

Russia and Central Europe Absolutist policies and pomp spread to the Hapsburg monarchy and successful expansion against the Ottoman Empire was a distinctive theme. Prussian power increased, again with some territorial expansion as the result of careful wars and diplomacy. The Russian state shook off Tartar overlords and began a systematic policy of territorial expansion, making it a major player in central and east Asia as well as in Europe. Under Peter the Great, a very selective pattern of westernization emerged, designed to create a new elite culture, enhance the power of the czar, and create a more powerful and effective military.

Recent Scholarship

Absolutism in Central Europe (2000) provides a well-informed definition of absolutism in practice and its operation in central Europe. Author Peter H. Wilson reviews the major aspects of the historiography, in a subject that has gone through several interpretations. The focus on central Europe allows comparisons of different forms and attention to a region that can be somewhat slighted in general coverage, in favor of the showier developments in France. The book also allows discussion of the consequences of absolutism in the later political experience of the region, a subject on which the author is well versed.

Differentiating Instruction

Differentiated Instruction Teacher Management System
- Pacing Guide
- Lesson Plans for Differentiated Instruction

Interactive Reader and Study Guide

Spanish Chapter Summaries Audio CD Program

Student Edition on Audio CD Program

Differentiated Instruction Modified Worksheets and Tests CD-ROM
- Vocabulary Flash Cards
- Modified Vocabulary Builder Activities
- Modified Chapter Review Activity
- Modified Chapter Test

OSP **One-Stop Planner CD-ROM**
- ExamView Test Generator (English/Spanish)
- PuzzlePro
- Quiz Show for ExamView
- Transparencies and Videos

TE **Differentiated Activities in the Teacher's Edition**
- Monarch Family Trees, p. 1364
- Designing a Royal Compound, p. 545
- The English Civil War: Board Game, p. 550
- Imperial St. Petersburg Charts, p. 569
- Absolute Power Debate, p. 563

BEFORE YOU TEACH

Reading Like a Historian
Sam Wineburg

Tyndale's Translation Biblical translation is a contact sport and sometimes—as William Tyndale learned the hard way—the results can be fatal.

Inspired by Erasmus, whose ideas he encountered at Cambridge at the beginning of the 16th century, Tyndale believed that the way to God was through study of His word. A master of Greek and Hebrew, Tyndale was determined to produce a Biblical translation so accessible that even "a boy that driveth the plough" could understand it.

Tyndale's freethinking ways ran afoul of Henry VIII, and he took flight to Germany and then to Holland, where he was betrayed by an English spy. As he awaited death at the stake for heresy on October 6, 1536, he is reputed to have uttered the words, "Lord, open the King of England's eyes."

King Henry's eyes remained shut. A new translation would have to wait until 1604, when King James I, in an attempt to make peace between warring factions of Anglicans and Puritans, convened translators representing a wide swath of religious views and interests. Their charge was to produce a translation all sides of this religiously divided kingdom could approve.

At the end of the day, however, the resulting "King James Version" looked surprisingly like the text produced by that heretic William Tyndale. About 83 percent of the King James Bible was identical to Tyndale's, including such unforgettable phases as "Let there be light" (Genesis 1:3) and "In the beginning God created the Word" (John 1:1). Acknowledging this contribution, Biblical scholars today refer to the King James Bible as the "Tyndale-King James Version."

Comparing Translations There have been too many translations of the Bible to count, starting as early as the 7th century when the poet Caedmon rendered Biblical stories into Old English verse. One of the most widely used modern translations is the much-heralded 1952 Revised Standard Version (RSV) of the National Council of Churches, produced by America's most eminent Biblical scholars. Yet the RSV's reception, at least in its early days, showed that Biblical controversies die a hard death—an impression impossible to miss by scanning the titles of various reviews: "The Devil's Masterpiece," "Modernism's Unholy Bible," "A Sad Travesty," and—reflecting 1950s Cold War passions—"The New Communist Bible."

To almost all of these commentators, the touchstone remained the King James Version. Writing in *The New Yorker*, critic Dwight Macdonald noted that, "Literature, . . . and especially religious literature is not primarily concerned with being clear and reasonable; it is connotative rather than direct, suggestive rather than explicit. . . . To make the Bible readable in the modern sense means to flatten out, tone down and convert into tepid expository prose what in the King James Version is wild, full of awe, and passionate."

Four hundred years after its first appearance, the King James Bible is the metric for any attempt to render this Bible into English. Its hold is due, in part, to Tyndale's unique touch, seen unmistakably in his rendering of Psalm 23, which begins, "The Lord is my Shepard, I shall not want." Compare the elegance of Tyndale-King James to the Living Bible's clunky "Because the Lord is my Shepard, I have everything I need" or the New International Version's strained "The Lord is my Shepard, I shall not be in want."

The King James Bible is the most widely read book in the English language. Without it, King James, and his otherwise uneventful reign, would have been long forgotten.

Chapter Preview

Chapter Main Ideas

Section 1 Spain experienced a golden age during the 1500s, but economic problems and military struggles decreased Spanish power by the 1600s.

Section 2 Henry IV, Louis XIII, and Louis XIV strengthened the French monarchy, with Louis XIV setting the example of an absolute monarch for the rest of Europe.

Section 3 In contrast to the absolute monarchies of Spain and France, the English monarchy was limited by Parliament; following a civil war, Parliament became even more powerful.

Section 4 The czars of Russia struggled with the westernization of their empire, while powerful families battled for control of Central Europe.

CHAPTER 4

1500–1800

The Monarchs of Europe

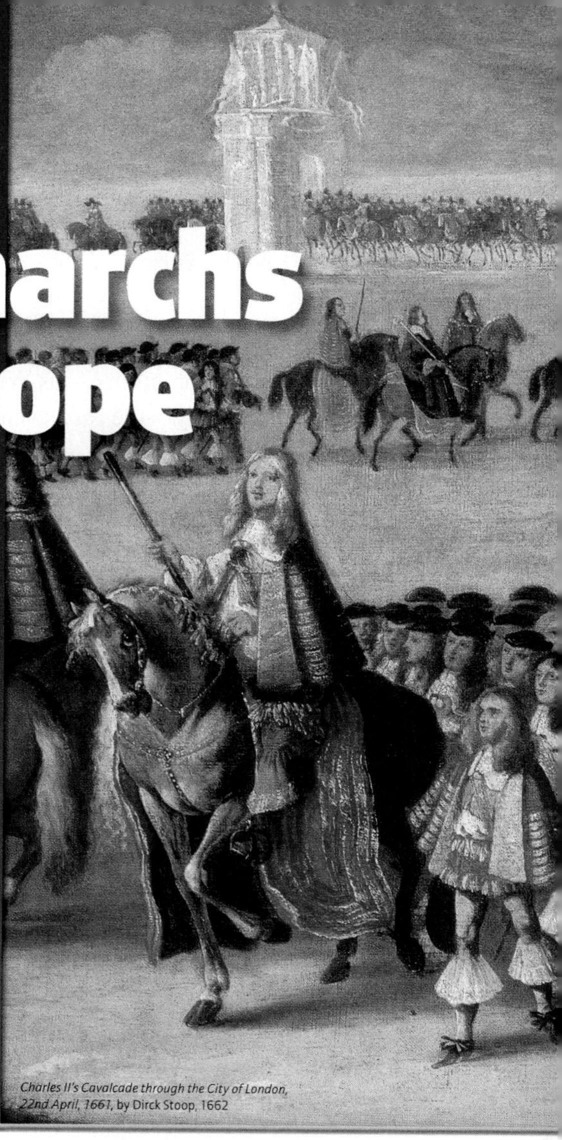

Charles II's Cavalcade through the City of London, 22nd April, 1661, by Dirck Stoop, 1662

THE BIG PICTURE Throughout the 1500s, global discoveries and exploration brought new wealth and prestige to Europe's monarchs. Kings, queens, and emperors ruled with few limits on their power. Over the next three centuries, their power was challenged by internal problems, rebellions, and wars.

Theme ARTS AND IDEAS

How should monarchs rule? How much power should they have? These were questions that Europeans tried to answer during the age of absolute monarchs. Although conflicts were common throughout these centuries, the arts and literature flourished.

TIME LINE

CHAPTER EVENTS

- **1519** Charles V begins rule of the Holy Roman Empire.
- **1547** Ivan IV becomes czar of Russia.
- **1572** Huguenots die in the Saint Bartholomew's Day Massacre.
- **1588** England defeats the Spanish Armada.
- **The Thirty Years' War 1618–1648**
- **1653** Oliver Cromwell is named Lord Protector in England.

1500 — 1600 — 1700

WORLD EVENTS

- **1501** Amerigo Vespucci explores the coast of Brazil.
- **1526** Babur founds the Mughal Empire in India.
- **1603** Tokugawa Ieyasu becomes shogun of Japan.
- **1620** The Pilgrims land on the Massachusetts coast.

Key to Differentiating Instruction

Below Level

Basic-level activities designed for all students encountering new material

At Level

Intermediate-level activities designed for average students

Above Level

Challenging activities designed for honors and gifted and talented students

Standard English Mastery

Activities designed to improve standard English usage

Introduce the Chapter

At Level

The Monarchs of Europe

1. Tell students that during the period covered by this chapter, the map of Europe continued to change as strong monarchs consolidated their control over their kingdoms and extended their territories through marriage or through conquest. At the same time, the spread of Protestantism created new conflicts, both within and between nations.
2. Organize students into small groups. Have each group prepare a list of the advantages and disadvantages of having a strong monarch in the historical context of the time. Have volunteers from each group share their lists with the class.
3. Guide the class in a discussion of the ideas presented. Did the advantages of having a strong monarch outweigh the disadvantages? Why or why not? In what ways could strong monarchs abuse their power? How could such abuses be remedied? **LS Interpersonal, Verbal-Linguistic**

Alternative Assessment Handbook, Rubric 11: Discussions

History's Impact video program
Watch the video to understand the impact of Spain's Golden Century.

Reading like a Historian Throughout the centuries from 1500 to 1800, monarchs liked to display their grandeur. In this painting, Charles II of England parades through London the day before he is crowned.

Analyzing Visuals What do you think historians can learn from this painting?

See **Skills Handbook**, p. H26

1714 The War of the Spanish Succession ends.

1762 Catherine the Great becomes czarina of Russia.

1800

1707 The Mughal Empire of India begins to disintegrate.

1776 The British colonies of North America declare their independence.

• Chapter Preview •

HOLT
History's Impact
► **Video Program:**
The Monarchs of Europe
See the Video Teacher's Guide for strategies for using the video segment.

Reading Like a Historian

Analyzing Visuals When Charles II returned to England to become king, he did so in grand style. His cavalcade, or large procession consisted of many men and horses. They passed through many arches along their route.

Explore the Time Line

1. When did Ivan IV become czar of Russia? *1547*
2. When did the Thirty Years' War take place? *1618–1648*
3. Who was Oliver Cromwell? *Lord Protector in England*
4. How long after the defeat of the Spanish Armada did the Pilgrims land on the Massachusetts coast? *about 32 years*

Info to Know

An Exiled King Charles II lived in exile for about a decade after his father, Charles I, was executed. Then, in 1660 Charles II was named King of England. The years that followed are known as the Restoration because monarchy was restored in England.

Make Inferences How do you think the people in the painting above felt about Charles's return? Why? *possible answer—happy; believed the restored monarchy would mean a return to stability*

go.hrw.com
Online Resources
Chapter Resources:
KEYWORD: SHL MON
Teacher Resources:
KEYWORD: SHL TEACHER

Answers

Reading Like a Historian *possible answers—the conditions under which Charles II returned to England as king; information about regal ceremonies, clothing, and weapons*

Preteach

Geography Starting Points

Primary Source

"It appears from all this that the person of the king is sacred, and that to attack him in any way is sacrilege. . . . Kings should be guarded as holy things, and whosoever neglects to protect them is worthy of death. . . ."
—Jacques Benigne Bossuet, on the divine right of kings

Teaching Tip

Remind students that the Protestant Reformation began in 1517 when Martin Luther publicized his complaints against the Roman Catholic Church. Have students predict how the Protestant Reformation might have affected the monarchs shown on the map.

Map Transparency: Monarchs of Europe
World History Outline Maps
Interactive Map: Monarchs of Europe

GEOGRAPHY Starting Points

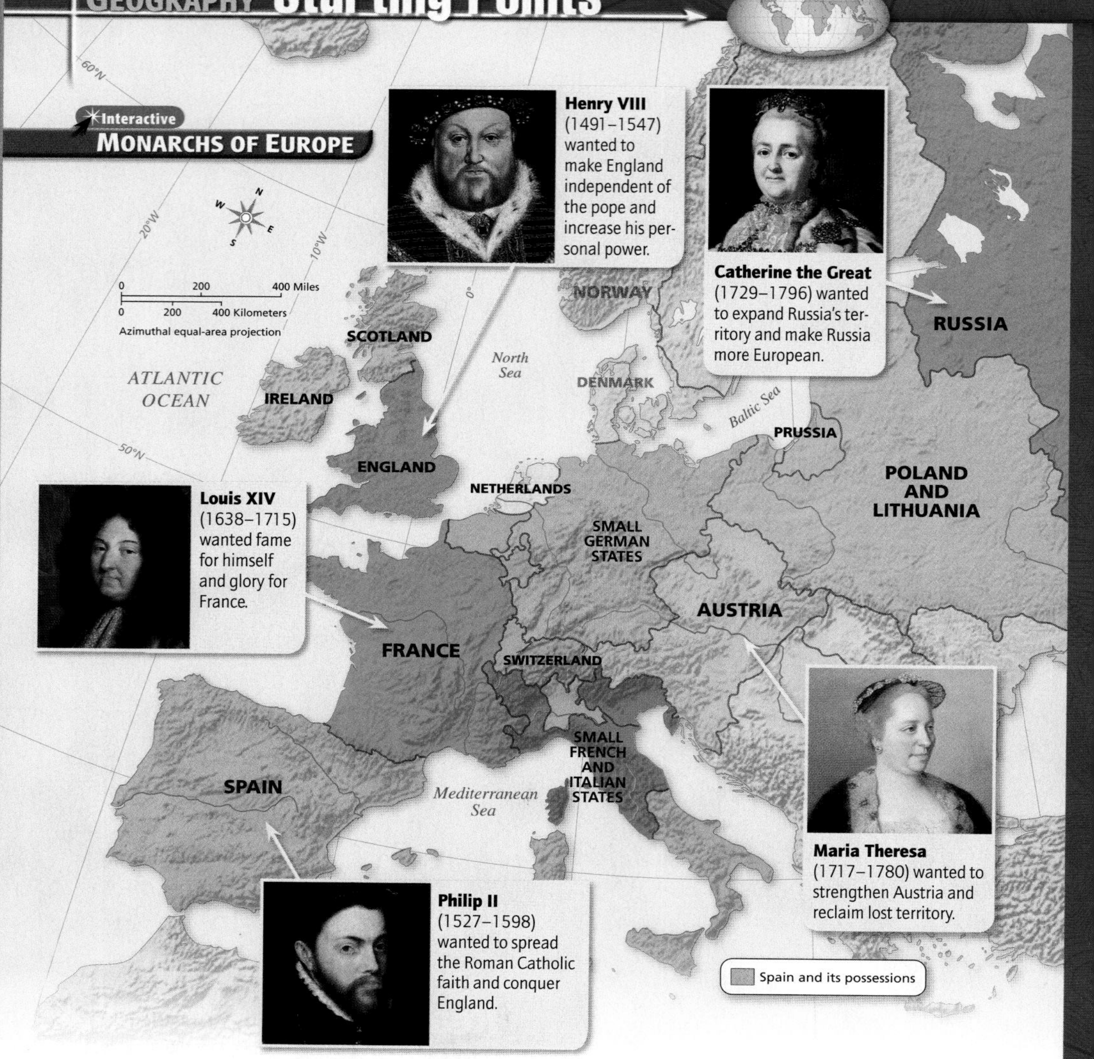

Interactive
MONARCHS OF EUROPE
Henry VIII (1491–1547) wanted to make England independent of the pope and increase his personal power.
Catherine the Great (1729–1796) wanted to expand Russia's territory and make Russia more European.
Louis XIV (1638–1715) wanted fame for himself and glory for France.
Maria Theresa (1717–1780) wanted to strengthen Austria and reclaim lost territory.
Philip II (1527–1598) wanted to spread the Roman Catholic faith and conquer England.
0 200 400 Miles
0 200 400 Kilometers
Azimuthal equal-area projection
60°N
50°N
20°W
10°W
0°
ATLANTIC OCEAN
North Sea
Baltic Sea
Mediterranean Sea
SCOTLAND
IRELAND
ENGLAND
NORWAY
DENMARK
RUSSIA
PRUSSIA
POLAND AND LITHUANIA
NETHERLANDS
SMALL GERMAN STATES
AUSTRIA
FRANCE
SWITZERLAND
SMALL FRENCH AND ITALIAN STATES
SPAIN
Spain and its possessions

Starting Points European monarchs, some of whom are pictured above, began to increase their power in about 1500. The kings, queens, emperors, and empresses had conflicting goals, though. As a result, wars were common. This map of Europe in 1650 gives clues to some of the issues these monarchs faced.

1. **Analyze** How might the location of Spain's possessions have been both an advantage and a disadvantage for Spain?
2. **Predict** Based on the map and the monarchs' goals described in the captions, what conflicts do you think developed? Where do you think wars broke out?

Listen to History
Go online to listen to an explanation of the starting points for this chapter.
go.hrw.com
Keyword: SHL MON

Differentiating Instruction

Above Level

Advanced Learners/Gifted and Talented

Research Required

1. Explain to students that many of the monarchs of Europe were related to one another by blood or marriage. Tell them that marriages between royal families were often used to strengthen alliances or prevent wars.
2. Have students conduct independent research to find out which of the monarchs shown on this page had family relationships, whether by blood or marriage. Remind students that these monarchs ruled at different times, so some of them will be generations apart.
3. Have students draw a simple family tree to illustrate one of the family connections they discovered. Have students write an essay analyzing the relationship they chose. Have students predict the effect the monarchs' connection might have upon their nations.

LS Visual-Spatial, Verbal-Linguistic

Alternative Assessment Handbook, Rubrics 30: Research; and 37: Writing Assignments

Answers

Geography Starting Point

1. *possible answer—advantage: gave Spain a foothold in Central Europe; disadvantage: hard to govern and protect the small, separate territories;* **2.** *possible conflicts and wars—Roman Catholic monarchs might struggle against Protestant monarchs; Spain might try to conquer England; Austria and Russia might try to expand; France might try to claim territory to add to its glory*

SECTION 1

The Power of Spain

BEFORE YOU READ

MAIN IDEA

Spain experienced a golden age during the 1500s, but economic problems and military struggles decreased Spanish power by the 1600s.

READING FOCUS

1. What challenges did King Charles I face when he became Emperor Charles V?
2. What were some artistic achievements of Spain's golden age?
3. How did Spain rise and then decline under Philip II?

KEY TERMS AND PEOPLE

absolute monarch
divine right
Charles V
Peace of Augsburg
Philip II
El Greco
Diego Velázquez
Miguel de Cervantes
Sister Juana Ines de la Cruz
Spanish Armada

TAKING NOTES Take notes to record examples of Spain's strengths and weaknesses during the 1500s and 1600s.

Strengths	
Weaknesses	

The KING of SPAIN SPEAKS NO SPANISH

Fasti Farnesiani, by Taddeo Zuccari, c. 1560s

THE INSIDE STORY ***Why did the king of Spain speak no Spanish?*** In 1516, a thin and sickly 16-year-old boy named Charles became king of Spain. In some ways, Charles would not seem to be a likely candidate for the Spanish throne. After all, he was born in Belgium, raised by Austrian relatives, and grew up speaking French. When Charles became king, his ignorance of the Spanish language made him a foreigner in the eyes of the Spanish. Charles proved to everyone that he could learn quickly, though. He mastered Spanish along with other languages. In fact, Charles is said to have spoken "Spanish to God, Italian to women, French to men, and German to his horse." He needed all those languages, because Charles became not only king of Spain but also Holy Roman Emperor. In that role, he ruled an empire that stretched across much of Europe. ■

The King Becomes Emperor

In 1516 the teenaged Charles became King Charles I of Spain. Although he was inexperienced, Charles had at least one kingly trait. As a member of the ancient and powerful Hapsburg family, he was prepared to rule as an **absolute monarch**—a ruler whose power was not limited by having to consult with the nobles, common people, or their representatives. Moreover, absolute monarchs generally believed that they ruled by **divine right**. This concept held that the monarchs received their power from God and therefore must not be challenged. From about 1500 through the 1700s, absolute monarchs tried to impose their will across much of Europe and even to lands far beyond. In Spain, Charles struggled to keep the territories within his empire under control.

Teach the Main Idea

At Level

The Power of Spain

1. **Teach** Ask students the Reading Focus questions to teach this section.
2. **Apply** Have students create charts comparing and contrasting the reign of Charles V with that of his son, Philip II.
3. **Review** Review student charts as a class. What similarities did they find between the reigns of the two monarchs? What differences were there? Guide students in a discussion of the two leaders' reigns. Which was a better ruler?
4. **Practice/Homework** Have students write an essay explaining why they think Charles V divided his empire between his brother and his son rather than passing it on intact.
LS Visual-Spatial, Verbal-Linguistic

Alternative Assessment Handbook, Rubrics 7: Charts; and 9: Comparing and Contrasting

Preteach

Getting Started

Use the **Interactive Reader and Study Guide** to familiarize students with the section content.

Interactive Reader and Study Guide, Section 1

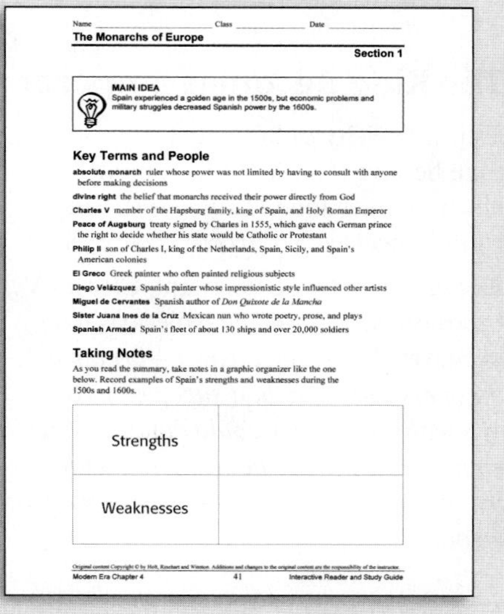

Name ______ Class ______ Date ______

The Monarchs of Europe

Section 1

MAIN IDEA
Spain experienced a golden age in the 1500s, but economic problems and military struggles decreased Spanish power by the 1600s.

Key Terms and People

absolute monarch ruler whose power was not limited by having to consult with anyone before making decisions
divine right the belief that monarchs received their power directly from God
Charles V member of the Hapsburg family, king of Spain, and Holy Roman Emperor
Peace of Augsburg treaty signed by Charles in 1555, which gave each German prince the right to decide whether his state would be Catholic or Protestant
Philip II son of Charles I, king of the Netherlands, Spain, Sicily, and Spain's American colonies
El Greco Greek painter who often painted religious subjects
Diego Velázquez Spanish painter whose impressionistic style influenced other artists
Miguel de Cervantes Spanish author of *Don Quixote de la Mancha*
Sister Juana Ines de la Cruz Mexican nun who wrote poetry, prose, and plays
Spanish Armada Spain's fleet of about 130 ships and over 20,000 soldiers

Taking Notes

As you read the summary, take notes in a graphic organizer like the one below. Record examples of Spain's strengths and weaknesses during the 1500s and 1600s.

Strengths	
Weaknesses	

Original content Copyright © by Holt, Rinehart and Winston. Additions and changes to the original content are the responsibility of the instructor.

Modern Era Chapter 4 41 Interactive Reader and Study Guide

Academic Vocabulary

Review with students the high-use academic term in this section.

region an area with one or more common features (p. 138)

CRF: Vocabulary Builder: Section 1

Taking Notes

Strengths—American possessions brought great wealth; strong military; Golden Age of Spanish art; Weaknesses—unrest and revolts; constant fighting; economic problems

Direct Teach

Reading Focus

1 What challenges did King Charles I face when he became Emperor Charles V? *ruling all the separate states, with enemies on all sides; the Protestant Reformation led to rebellions against Catholic rule*

The King Becomes Emperor

Explain Why did monarchs of this time believe their authority should never be questioned? *ruled by divine right, power came directly from God*

Evaluate Why do you think Charles V had more success in the Americas than in Europe? *possible answer—because there his explorers had superior weapons with which they could conquer huge empires; in Europe he was surrounded by enemies who had access to the same weapons*

Info to Know

The Peace of Augsburg The Peace of Augsburg was a temporary settlement that allowed each German prince to determine a state religion, either Catholicism or Lutheranism. Anyone who adhered to the other religion could move to a territory where that religion was recognized. Other Protestant sects, such as Calvinism, were not recognized by the agreement.

Achievements in Art and Literature

Spain's prominence in European affairs in the 1500s and 1600s is reflected in the important role it had in art and literature. ***How might wealth from the Americas have affected Spain's artistic achievements?***

Plate made of gold acquired in the Americas ▶

▲ Stormy skies over Toledo in an El Greco painting

View of Toledo, by El Greco, c. 1597

Charles V and the Empire When Charles became king of Spain, his territory also included the Low Countries of Belgium and the Netherlands, along with colonies in the Americas. He had inherited all these lands. Then in 1519 the throne of the Holy Roman Empire became vacant. The position was elective, so Charles borrowed money to buy the votes. He became Holy Roman Emperor as **Charles V**. As a result, his holdings expanded to parts of Italy, Austria, and various German states. The resulting empire was so vast that Charles liked to say the "sun never set" over it.

ACADEMIC VOCABULARY
region an area with one or more common features

Ruling all the separate states was not an easy task. Charles faced enemies on all sides. Ottoman Turks, the French, and rebellious German princes all fought him.

At the same time, Charles was fighting for religious control over Europe. As Holy Roman Emperor, Charles wanted Europe to be Roman Catholic. His power was closely connected to the power of the Catholic Church, so the growing Protestant movement threatened his influence. In 1521 Charles confronted Protestant leader Martin Luther directly, declaring him an outlaw. In spite of Charles's efforts, Protestants gained influence, and rebellions against Catholic rulers spread.

After years of devastating wars between Catholics and Protestants, Charles V had to sign the **Peace of Augsburg**. The agreement, signed in 1555, gave each German prince the right to decide whether his state would be Catholic or Protestant. Thus, Charles's vision of a Catholic Europe never became reality. Moreover, constant warfare had brought him to the brink of bankruptcy.

Charles V achieved more success in the Americas than he did in Europe. During his reign, Spanish explorers claimed much of the Americas for Spain. Among the explorers he supported were Hernán Cortés, who conquered the Aztec Empire, and Francisco de Coronado, who explored the American Southwest region. Within 20 years of those early explorations, silver and gold began to flow from the American colonies—especially those in Bolivia, Peru, and Mexico—bringing Spain fabulous wealth.

Dividing the Empire Charles V gave up his thrones in 1556, frustrated by his failures in Europe. He decided to divide his large empire between his brother and his son. His brother took over the old Hapsburg holdings in Austria. His son, who became **Philip II**, ruled the Netherlands, Spain, Sicily, and Spain's colonies in the Americas. Charles V lived the rest of his life in a Spanish monastery, his dream of a unified empire unfulfilled.

READING CHECK **Draw Conclusions** In what ways was Charles V successful as an emperor? In what ways was he unsuccessful?

Skills Focus: Interpreting Historical Maps

At Level

Research Required

Social Studies Skill

The Empire of Charles V

Materials: outline maps of Europe and the Americas, colored markers

1. Organize students into small groups. Give each group a copy of each of the two outline maps and colored markers.
2. Have each group use descriptions and historical maps to create detailed maps of Charles V's empire. Write the following instructions for students to see: Use pink to show lands Charles V inherited. Use orange to show lands he acquired during his rule. Use green to show countries with which Charles V formed alliances through marriages. Use red to outline the Holy Roman Empire as it existed in his lifetime.
3. Review student maps as a class.

LS Interpersonal, Visual-Spatial

Alternative Assessment Handbook, Rubrics 20: Map Creation; and 30: Research

Answers

Achievements in Art and Literature *possible answer—provided money to pay for court painters*

Reading Check *successful—exploration of the Americas, which brought fabulous wealth to Spain; unsuccessful—did not maintain religious control over Europe; constant wars brought financial problems*

Las Meninas, or *The Maids in Waiting*, by Diego Velázquez, c. 1656

◀ The painter can be seen before his easel in this scene of court life.

Sister Juana Ines de la Cruz with the small picture that was part of her nun's habit, or clothing

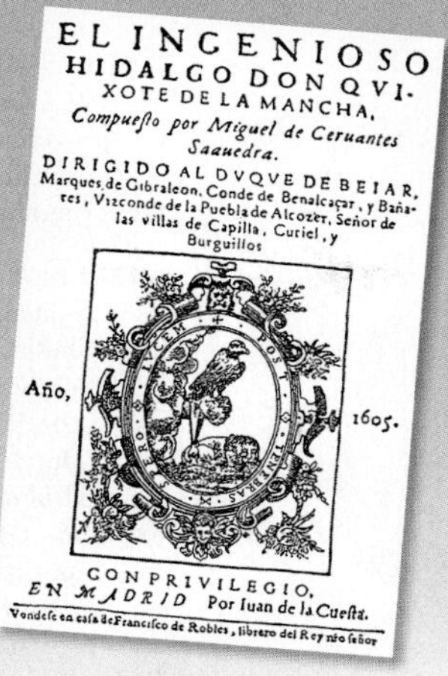

EL INGENIOSO HIDALGO DON QVI-XOTE DE LA MANCHA,
Compuesto por Miguel de Ceruantes Saauedra.
DIRIGIDO AL DVQVE DE BEIAR, Marques de Gibraleon, Conde de Benalcaçar, y Bañares, Vizconde de la Puebla de Alcozer, Señor de las villas de Capilla, Curiel, y Burguillos.
Año, 1605.
CON PRIVILEGIO, EN MADRID Por Iuan de la Cuesta.
Vendese en casa de Francisco de Robles, librero del Rey nro señor

▲ The title page of the first edition of *Don Quixote*

Artistic Achievements

Just as Spain exerted political power, it also influenced European culture. From about 1550 to 1650 Spain had a golden age, known as the Golden Century, of artistic achievement.

Art One of the most prominent painters was a Greek, Domenicos Theotocopoulos, who became known as **El Greco**. Much of his work was religious and reflected Spain's central role in the Counter-Reformation. El Greco's style is famous for elongated human figures.

Another Spanish painter, **Diego Velázquez**, created masterpieces that portray people of all social classes with great dignity. Velazquez had the privilege of being the court painter.

Literature The Spanish golden age also produced fine writers, the greatest being **Miguel de Cervantes**. His most famous work, *Don Quixote de la Mancha*, is about a man who is caught between the medieval and modern worlds.

Writers in Spain's colonies also produced works of merit. A Mexican nun named **Sister Juana Ines de la Cruz** wrote poetry, prose, and plays. Church officials criticized Sister Juana for some of her ideas, for example, her belief that women had a right to education.

READING CHECK **Summarize** What were some achievements of Spain's Golden Century?

Spain under Philip II

Spain reached the peak of its grandeur during the reign of Philip II. One reason for this prosperity was the steady stream of gold and silver that flowed from its American colonies. With this immense wealth, Spain's power grew considerably. Eventually, though, American gold could not solve Spain's problems.

Religion and Revolt Like his father, King Philip II was a devout Catholic and saw himself as a leader of the Counter-Reformation. A chance to spread Catholicism came when Philip married Queen Mary I of England, who was also Catholic. She died, though, before she could give birth to an heir who could have returned England to the Catholic faith.

Philip also wanted to secure the position of Catholicism in his European territories. But his faith clashed with the Calvinist Protestantism that was spreading through the northern provinces of the Low Countries (the Netherlands, Belgium, and Luxembourg). A bloody revolt began in the 1560s when the Dutch refused to declare allegiance to Philip. To punish them, he sent an army under the command of the Duke of Alba. Alba set up a court, known locally as the Court of Blood, that tortured and executed thousands of people suspected of being rebels. Such cruelties only made the situation worse, and rebellion broke out anew.

Direct Teach

Reading Focus

2 What were some artistic achievements of Spain's golden age? *paintings of El Greco and Diego Velázquez, writings of Miguel de Cervantes and Sister Juana Inez de la Cruz*

Artistic Achievements

Summarize What is *Don Quixote de la Mancha* about? *a man caught between the modern and medieval worlds*

Analyze Why is 1550 to 1650 known as Spain's Golden Century? *Spanish artists produced great works that influenced European culture.*

CRF: Biography: Diego Velázquez

Reading Focus

3 How did Spain rise and then decline under Philip II? *rose—colonies in America sent a steady stream of gold and silver to Spain; declined—wars, the defeat of the Spanish Armada, economic problems*

Spain under Philip II

Identify What was the source of Spain's immense wealth? *gold and silver from the American colonies*

Define What was the Council of Blood? *a Spanish court that executed and tortured thousands of people suspected of being rebels*

Skills Focus: Identifying Problem and Solution

At Level

Reading Skill
Spain's Troubles

1. Organize students into small groups. Tell groups they are advisers to Philip II of Spain. Have each group choose one of the following topics for discussion: the revolt in the Netherlands, the attempt to invade England with the Spanish Armada, or Spain's economic problems.
2. Have each group write a memorandum to Philip discussing the situation of their choice and examining the advantages and disadvantages of possible actions. Students should then make recommendations to Philip based on their analysis of the situation.
3. Have volunteers from each group read their memorandums to the class. **LS Interpersonal, Verbal-Linguistic**

Alternative Assessment Handbook, Rubrics 35: Solving Problems; and 37: Writing Assignments

Answers

Reading Check *paintings by El Greco and Velázquez, writings by Miguel de Cervantes and Juana Ines de la Cruz*

Direct Teach

Reading Focus

Spain under Philip II

Judge Why do you think the Spanish did not want the Netherlands to break away from the empire? *possible answer—They may have feared that other parts of the empire would follow the example of the Dutch and seek independence.*

Make Inferences What do you think Philip II could have done differently to prevent the decline of his empire? *possible answer—use some of the wealth from the American colonies for economic development in Spain*

Review & Assess

Close

Guide students in a discussion of the successes and failures of Charles V and Philip II.

Review

Online Quiz, Section 1

Assess

SE Section 1 Assessment

Progress Assessment: Section 1 Quiz

Alternative Assessment Handbook

Reteach/Intervene

Interactive Reader and Study Guide, Section 1

Interactive Skills Tutor CD-ROM

The revolt dragged on for decades. Finally, in 1609, a truce was reached. The seven northern provinces formed the independent nation of the Netherlands, while the southern provinces remained in Spanish hands.

Spain and England Long before the Dutch revolt ended, it had deepened another rivalry. That conflict was between Spain and England. As fellow Protestants, the English had sent aid to the Dutch rebels. England's assistance to the Dutch infuriated Philip, but he was also worried about English attacks on his ships. England's Queen Elizabeth I was allowing her ship captains to attack Spanish treasure ships coming from America. These ship captains, known as the sea dogs, stole the gold and silver for England. Sir Francis Drake was one of the most infamous sea dogs. Drake even destroyed 30 ships in a Spanish harbor.

King Philip II wanted to stop England from raiding his ships and to return England to the Catholic Church, from which it had broken in 1534. He decided to invade England.

Philip ordered his navy to assemble a great fleet, the **Spanish Armada**. It totaled about 130 ships and 20,000 soldiers and sailors. The fleet, which was called invincible, or unbeatable, sailed into the English Channel in 1588. Queen Elizabeth I rallied her troops, and the English prepared for attack.

The Spanish had packed the ships with soldiers for a land invasion. They had also planned to be joined by Spanish forces in the Netherlands. Instead, they faced a series of fierce naval battles that severely damaged their fleet. Then, the English set eight ships on fire and aimed them at the remaining ships of the Armada. In panic and disarray, the Spanish ships fled before the English fireships. As the damaged ships made their way home the long way around, several were wrecked. King Philip's Armada was not invincible.

An Empire in Decline The defeat of the Armada was not the end for Spain, which recovered from the loss. But England remained Protestant, defiant, and undefeated.

Spain's real problems were internal. Philip's government was so centralized that he insisted on approving every decision himself. In addition, because Philip trusted no one, the court was riddled by factions and suspicion. As a result, government action practically came to a standstill. Moreover, Philip spent the wealth from the Americas on constant warfare. It was never enough, though—he borrowed money often and went bankrupt four times. The flood of American gold and silver also drove up prices, leading to inflation. Nor did Spain develop industries, relying instead on its traditional agricultural economy. Therefore, the economy lagged behind that of other countries. Spain gradually declined as a major power.

READING CHECK **Recall** What were two events that caused problems for Spain?

SECTION 1 ASSESSMENT

go.hrw.com
Online Quiz
Keyword: SHL MON HP

Reviewing Ideas, Terms, and People

1. **a. Define** Write a brief definition of the following terms: absolute monarch, divine right.
   b. Explain How did Charles I become Holy Roman Emperor Charles V?
   c. Analyze How did the size of his empire affect the rule of Charles V?
2. **a. Identify** Who were El Greco and Diego Velázquez?
   b. Infer Why might church officials have been particularly critical of some works by Sister Juana Ines de la Cruz?
3. **a. Recall** What region of Spain's European territories rebelled, starting in the 1560s?
   b. Explain Why did Philip II want to invade England?
   c. Evaluate A Spanish official in the Americas is said to have commented, "If Death had to come from Spain, I would live forever." What was the official implying?

Critical Thinking

4. **Identify Cause and Effect** Use your notes and a graphic organizer like the one below to describe the rise and decline of the Spanish empire, paying particular attention to the role that strengths and weaknesses played.

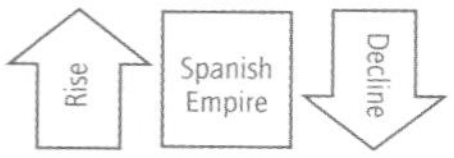

FOCUS ON SPEAKING

5. **Narration** Imagine that you are a Spanish or English sailor who survived the Spanish Armada's attempted invasion of England. Prepare and deliver the tale you tell other sailors when you return home.

Section 1 Assessment Answers

1. **a.** absolute monarch: ruler whose power was not limited; divine right: idea that monarchs received their power from God
   b. He bought the necessary votes.
   c. faced enemies on all sides; could not maintain religious control
2. **a.** painters during Spain's Golden Century
   b. Some of her beliefs were controversial, including women's right to education.
3. **a.** the Low Countries (the Netherlands, Belgium, and Luxembourg)
   b. to stop England from raiding his ships; to return England to Catholicism
   c. possible answer—that the transport of people and goods from Spain to the New World was very slow
4. Rise: Colonies in America sent a steady stream of gold and silver to Spain; Decline: caused by a series of wars, the defeat of the Spanish Armada, and economic problems
5. Student tales should show an understanding of the Spanish Armada's attempted invasion of England.

Answers

Reading Check *revolt in the Netherlands; defeat of the Spanish Armada*

Interactive
HISTORY CLOSE-UP

The Wreck of the Spanish Armada

A series of battles in the English Channel had weakened the Armada. Then, when the English launched fireships at the enemy, some of the Spanish sailors cut their anchor lines so they could escape. It was a fateful decision, because the Spanish ships were then at the mercy of storms in the North Atlantic, and many ships were wrecked. This illustration combines several events into one scene.

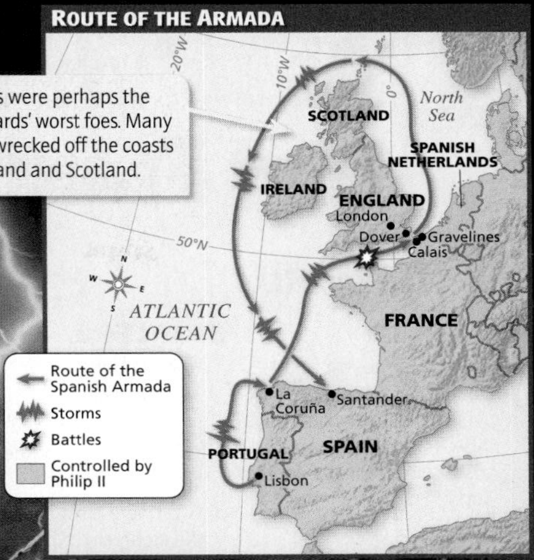

Rebels closed the Dutch harbor where Spanish ships were waiting to launch a second force against England.
The English set fire to ships rigged so that their cannons would fire automatically.
The Spanish sailors were already suffering from overcrowding, hunger, and disease by the time they encountered the English.

Skills Focus INTERPRETING VISUALS

Analyze What tactics did the English use against the Armada? How did those tactics, combined with poor weather, defeat the Armada?

go.hrw.com
COULD YOU HAVE SURVIVED?
Go online for a closer look at survival and this event.
Keyword: SHL MON

Direct Teach

History Close-Up

The Wreck of the Spanish Armada

"I have the heart and stomach of a king, and of a king of England, too; and think foul scorn that Parma or Spain or any prince of Europe should dare to invade the borders of my realm; to which rather than any dishonour should grow by me, I myself will take up arms, I myself will be your general, judge, and rewarder of every one of your virtues in the field."

—Speech by Queen Elizabeth I, 1588

Activity Analyzing Primary Sources Write the Queen Elizabeth quote above for all to see. Tell students that the queen gave this speech to the English army as it prepared for the Spanish invasion. Have a strong reader read the quote aloud. Then ask students the following questions: Why does Elizabeth call herself a king of England? How might this speech have motivated the army? **LS Verbal-Linguistic**

About the Illustration

This illustration is an artist's conception based on available sources. Historians, however, are uncertain exactly what this scene looked like.

Skills Focus: Identifying Cause and Effect

At Level

Reading Skill

What Caused the Armada's Defeat?

1. Draw the graphic organizer for all to see. Omit the italicized answers.
2. Have students copy and complete the graphic organizer. Guide a class discussion about what caused the wreck of the Spanish Armada. **LS Visual-Spatial**

Alternative Assessment Handbook, Rubrics 6: Cause and Effect; and 13: Graphic Organizers

Causes	Effects
1. *overcrowding, hunger, and disease on Spanish ships*	*Wreck of the Spanish Armada*
2. *storms*	
3. *English set fires on ships.*	
4. *Rebels closed Dutch harbor.*	

Answers

Interpreting Visuals *The storms wrecked many of Spain's ships, helping England, which was a Protestant nation; the Spanish were trying to escape by heading into the North Sea.*

Preteach

Getting Started

Use the **Interactive Reader and Study Guide** to familiarize students with the section content.

Interactive Reader and Study Guide, Section 2

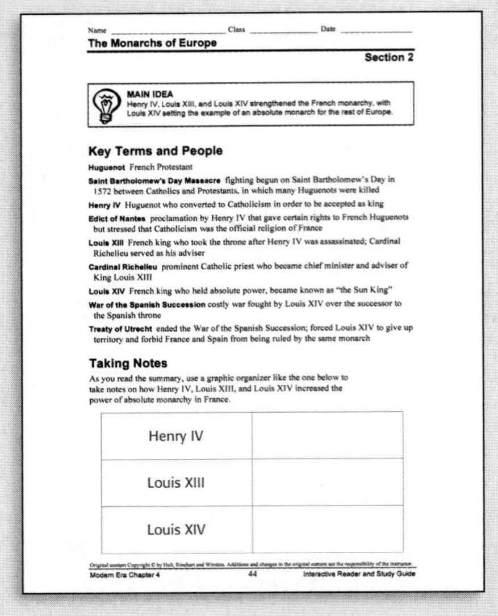

Name ______________ Class __________ Date __________

The Monarchs of Europe

Section 2

MAIN IDEA
Henry IV, Louis XIII, and Louis XIV strengthened the French monarchy, with Louis XIV setting the example of an absolute monarch for the rest of Europe.

Key Terms and People

Huguenot French Protestant

Saint Bartholomew's Day Massacre fighting begun on Saint Bartholomew's Day in 1572 between Catholics and Protestants, in which many Huguenots were killed

Henry IV Huguenot who converted to Catholicism in order to be accepted as king

Edict of Nantes proclamation by Henry IV that gave certain rights to French Huguenots but stressed that Catholicism was the official religion of France

Louis XIII French king who took the throne after Henry IV was assassinated; Cardinal Richelieu served as his adviser

Cardinal Richelieu prominent Catholic priest who became chief minister and adviser of King Louis XIII

Louis XIV French king who held absolute power, became known as "the Sun King"

War of the Spanish Succession costly war fought by Louis XIV over the successor to the Spanish throne

Treaty of Utrecht ended the War of the Spanish Succession; forced Louis XIV to give up territory and forbid France and Spain from being ruled by the same monarch

Taking Notes

As you read the summary, use a graphic organizer like the one below to take notes on how Henry IV, Louis XIII, and Louis XIV increased the power of absolute monarchy in France.

Henry IV	
Louis XIII	
Louis XIV	

Modern Era Chapter 4 44 Interactive Reader and Study Guide

CRF: Vocabulary Builder: Section 2

Taking Notes

Henry IV—went to war and accepted Catholicism as official religion to gain power; Louis XIII—chose a strong chief minister who worked with him to reduce the power of the Huguenots and the French nobles; became involved in Thirty Years' War; Louis XIV—after Mazarin's death, ruled by himself; created rituals and an extravagant lifestyle to build his image as a great ruler; fought wars to increase France's power abroad

go.hrw.com
Online Resources
KEYWORD: SHL MON
ACTIVITY: Louis XIV

SECTION 2

Absolute Monarchy and France

Before You Read

Main Idea

Henry IV, Louis XIII, and Louis XIV strengthened the French monarchy, with Louis XIV setting the example of an absolute monarch for the rest of Europe.

Reading Focus

1. How did Henry IV end France's wars of religion?
2. How did Louis XIII and Cardinal Richelieu strengthen the French monarchy?
3. What were the main events in the monarchy of Louis XIV?

Key Terms and People

Huguenot
Saint Bartholomew's Day Massacre
Henry IV
Edict of Nantes
Louis XIII
Cardinal Richelieu
Louis XIV
War of the Spanish Succession
Treaty of Utrecht

TAKING NOTES Take notes on how Henry IV, Louis XIII, and Louis XIV increased the power of absolute monarchy in France.

Henry IV	
Louis XIII	
Louis XIV	

THE INSIDE STORY ***Why did the streets of Paris run with blood?*** It was August 24, 1572, the Catholic feast day of Saint Bartholomew. Many Protestant nobles were in Paris for the wedding of Henry of Navarre, a Protestant nobleman, to Marguerite de Valois, a Catholic princess. The marriage was supposed to calm the hostilities between Catholics and Protestants that had been tearing France apart. But just two days before, Catherine de' Medici, the queen of France and the bride's mother, had ordered the murder of a prominent Protestant leader. The attempt failed, but then Catherine had another idea. While so many Protestants were in the city, she ordered their massacre. Just before dawn on August 24, the killing began, with a bloodbath as the result. ■

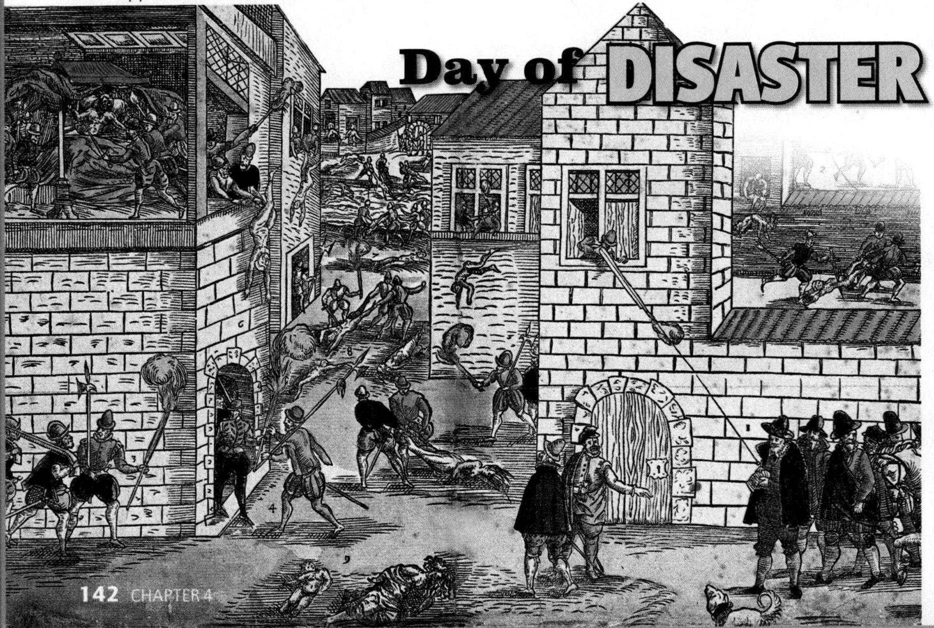

◀ **In Paris alone, some 3,000 Protestants were killed in the Saint Bartholomew's Day Massacre.**

St. Bartholomew's Day Massacre in Paris, artist unknown, c. 1572

Teach the Main Idea

At Level

Absolute Monarchy and France

1. **Teach** Ask students the Reading Focus questions to teach this section.
2. **Apply** Organize students into small groups. Have each group discuss the meaning of the term absolute monarch. Then have each group make lists of the traits it would expect in an absolute monarch.
3. **Review** Review group lists as a class, writing the traits each group mentioned for the class to see.
4. **Practice/Homework** Tell students that they are newspaper editors commenting on the War of the Spanish Succession. Have students write an editorial expressing their views on the war. Was it worth going to war when Spain lost most of its empire, France gave up much of the territory it hoped to claim, and England emerged as the big winner? **LS Interpersonal, Verbal-Linguistic**

Alternative Assessment Handbook, Rubrics 14: Group Activity; and 41: Writing to Express

Religious War and Henry IV

Soon after the Protestant Reformation began in Germany, it spread to France. By the 1560s, about one in ten French men and women was a **Huguenot** (HYOO-guh-NAHT), or French Calvinist Protestant. Many noble families were Huguenots. Such a large number of Protestants, especially among the nobles, threatened the Catholic French monarchy. The monarchy adhered to the idea that all loyal citizens of France should share *un roi, une loi, une foi*—"one king, one law, one religion." The religious conflict was a challenge to absolute monarchy.

Conflict and a New King Just as wars between Catholics and Protestants shook Germany, in France fighting broke out between Catholics and Huguenots in 1562 and raged for years. Hostilities took a particularly horrible turn in 1572, when the Catholic queen of France ordered the killing of Huguenots in Paris. Her assassins started with the Huguenot nobles who were in the city for the wedding of Henry of Navarre, a French nobleman. The event became known as the **Saint Bartholomew's Day Massacre**. From Paris, the violence spread to other parts of France. Estimates of the final death toll range from 10,000 to 70,000.

Henry of Navarre escaped death by denying his religion. Years later, he was in line to become king, but as a Huguenot in a heavily Catholic country, he had to fight Catholic troops to claim the throne. Finally, in 1593 Henry won acceptance by converting to Catholicism and was crowned **Henry IV**. According to some accounts, he explained his conversion by saying, "Paris is well worth a mass."

Compromise and Progress Henry knew that a compromise was needed to restore peace. In 1598 he granted some rights to Huguenots by issuing the **Edict of Nantes** (NAHNT). It gave Huguenots limited freedom of worship. Among other freedoms granted was the right of Huguenots to hold office and to rule 200 towns where they were already in the majority.

At the time, the Edict of Nantes was a remarkable document in that it represented a clear break with the conformity of the past. No longer were all the people forced to follow the monarch's religion. The concept of "one king, one law, one religion" was no longer in effect.

French Catholics accepted the edict because it ended the religious wars but still declared Catholicism the official religion of France. In addition, the edict required that Huguenots support the Catholic Church financially.

Following the edict's success, King Henry IV focused on repairing his war-torn country. A major achievement was improving France's financial situation. Henry eliminated France's debt and even built up a surplus. He also created new industries, drained swamps, built canals and roads, stimulated trade, and encouraged agriculture. Over time he became one of France's most respected monarchs.

READING CHECK **Summarize** What were some high points and low points in the life of Henry IV?

Louis XIII and Richelieu

Henry had only about 10 years to enjoy being king of France. In 1610 a fanatic Catholic stabbed him while his carriage was stopped in traffic. The next king, **Louis XIII**, was very young when he was crowned. For several years he depended upon his mother to serve as regent, that is, to govern in his place.

Once Louis XIII was old enough to rule, a Catholic churchman named **Cardinal Richelieu** (REESH-uhl-oo) became his chief minister and most trusted adviser. Louis XIII was a relatively weak ruler, but Cardinal Richelieu was determined to strengthen the monarchy. Doing so required that its opponents be crushed.

FACES OF HISTORY

Cardinal RICHELIEU
1585–1642

Armand-Jean du Plessis, duc de Richelieu, was determined to strengthen the monarchy and France. He used ruthless methods to fulfill his goal. To weaken the nobility's military power, Cardinal Richelieu demanded that all fortified castles not necessary for the defense of France be torn down. The nobles protested, but their precious castles were demolished anyway. In addition, Richelieu attacked the nobles' political power by appointing only local officials who supported the king. For some positions, he even appointed middle-class common people who disliked the nobles. These officials knew they served at his pleasure and behaved accordingly.

Analyze Why would the demolition of the nobles' castles diminish their military power?

Direct Teach

Reading Focus

1 How did Henry IV end France's wars of religion? *by converting to Catholicism and granting certain rights to the Huguenots*

Religious War and Henry IV

Explain Why did Catholics accept the Edict of Nantes? *because it ended the religious wars, but stilldeclared Catholicism as France's official religion*

Evaluate Why would the French royal family want to kill all the Huguenots? *France had been embroiled in religious strife between Huguenots and Catholics. Killing all the Huguenots would put an end to the fighting.*

CRF: Primary Source: The Edict of Nantes

Reading Focus

2 How did Louis XIII and Cardinal Richelieu strengthen the French monarchy? *reduced power of Huguenots; uncovered nobles' revolt; entered the Thirty Years' War*

Louis XIII and Richelieu

Recall What happened at La Rochelle? *Richelieu's forces besieged the city to deal with Huguenot rebels.*

Make Inferences How did Richelieu plan to strengthen the monarchy? *by crushing its opponents*

Skills Focus: Comparing and Contrasting

At Level

Reading Skill
Henry IV and Richelieu

1. The ongoing religious conflict in France between Huguenots and Catholics played a large part in the policies of both Henry IV and Cardinal Richelieu. Have students make a chart comparing and contrasting the policies of both men.
2. Review student charts as a class.
3. Guide students in a discussion of France's religious conflicts. Have students name modern nations that have experienced similar religious strife. **LS Visual-Spatial**

Alternative Assessment Handbook, Rubrics 7: Charts; and 11: Discussions

Answers

Faces of History *It meant nobles could not escape Richelieu's forces.*

Reading Check *possible answer—high points: being crowned king, Edict of Nantes, reforms; low points: Saint Bartholomew's Day Massacre, having to fight to claim throne*

Direct Teach

Reading Focus

Louis XIII and Richelieu

Recall Why did Richelieu become involved in the Thirty Years' War? *He wanted to bring down the Hapsburg family.*

Identify Cause and Effect What was one effect of Richelieu's victory at La Rochelle? *It gave the message to the Huguenots not to resist the monarchy.*

Recent Scholarship

Cardinal Richelieu: And the Making of France is a detailed biography of Richelieu. Author Anthony Levi gives a detailed look at the ways Richelieu made France into a great power, perhaps the most powerful nation in continental Europe. Levi discusses Richelieu's accomplishments within France and examines his determination to unify the nation.

Cardinal Richelieu: And the Making of France by Anthony Levi. Constable and Robinson, 2001.

Both Louis XIII and Richelieu wanted to reduce the recently won power of the Huguenots. To teach the Huguenots a lesson, in 1627 Richelieu used a situation at La Rochelle, a Huguenot port city. The people of La Rochelle had sided with English forces that had taken a nearby island. Richelieu's troops laid siege to the walled city, cutting off its supplies. After 14 months, the starving citizens surrendered. Richelieu ordered the city walls to be torn down and all the city's churches to become Catholic. His victory was a signal to all Huguenots that resistance to the monarchy carried risks.

Richelieu and the king also saw the nobles as a threat, so Richelieu turned to suppressing them. His spies uncovered a series of planned revolts by some nobles. Punishments were severe. For example, Richelieu had three prominent nobles publicly executed for treason.

As the king's chief minister, Richelieu also directed foreign policy. The Thirty Years' War, about which you will read more later, pitted Catholics against Protestants in Central Europe. Because he wanted to bring down the Hapsburg family, which led the Catholic side of the conflict, Richelieu involved France on the side of the Protestants.

READING CHECK **Identify** Who did Louis XIII and Cardinal Richelieu see as their enemies?

The Monarchy of Louis XIV

Richelieu died in 1642, and Louis XIII died one year later. In 1643 the son of Louis XIII was crowned **Louis XIV**. History's best example of an absolute monarch, Louis led France during a time of great power, prosperity, and glory. His reign had a lasting impact on France—both positive and negative.

Rise of the Sun King Like his father, Louis XIV became king, with his mother as regent, at a very young age. A churchman named Cardinal Mazarin, who became chief minister after Cardinal Richelieu, provided advice.

Louis was raised to be king. From childhood, he was taught all the skills that a king would eventually need—from interviewing foreign ambassadors and interpreting state papers to hunting and dancing.

The young king was quite different from his father. For example, he was supremely confident in his ability to rule. When Cardinal Mazarin died, Louis XIV, who was only 18 years old, declared that he would run the government himself. He declared, "L'état, c'est moi," meaning "I am the state." Louis chose the sun as his personal symbol, implying that the world revolved around him. He thus became known as the Sun King.

The Palace at Versailles

The royal family and some 10,000 officials, servants, and nobles lived at Versailles—making the place more a city than a palace.

View of Versailles, artist unknown, 1668

The king pointing to plans for Versailles

Louis XIV, artist unknown, 1600s

Skills Focus: Identifying Main Idea and Details

At Level

Reading Skill

The Monarchy of Louis XIV

1. Have each student write a series of newspaper headlines that report the course of Louis XIV's policies and actions as king. Student headlines may either be supportive or critical, but each student should express a consistent point of view.
2. Have volunteers read their headlines to the class.
3. Guide students in a discussion of their headlines. What do the events of Louis XIV's reign reveal about his attitude toward power? **LS Verbal-Linguistic**

Alternative Assessment Handbook, Rubric 23: Newspapers

Answers

Reading Check *Huguenots, nobles, the Hapsburg family*

HISTORY & Economics

Making Economic Decisions

Making economic decisions requires balancing benefits and costs. Often a decision has costs that one does not see at first. When you spend money on one thing, you cannot spend that money on something else. Those things that one cannot have as a result of an economic decision are called opportunity costs.

BUILDING VERSAILLES	
COSTS	**BENEFITS**
• Cost five percent of the country's annual revenue • Created resentment among the people • Helped cause revolution years later	• Kept court safer from Paris crowds • Was clear symbol of king's power • Allowed the king to keep the nobles in check

Economic Decisions in History Louis XIV faced opportunity costs when he decided to spend so much money on building the palace at Versailles. A major cost was in lost goodwill. The French people felt resentment when they saw their money going to build a huge, grand palace while they paid high taxes and sometimes went hungry. This resentment would help cause a revolution years later.

Economic Decisions and Your Life Your economic decisions have opportunity costs, too. Consider the decision of whether or not to buy the latest electronic gadget when it first comes on the market. Should you rush out to buy it, or should you wait for the price to come down? Either decision carries opportunity costs. Buying now means spending money that you could use for a long-term goal, such as building your college fund. Buying later means giving up the pleasure you might get from joining the newest fad.

▲ The decision to build Versailles had both costs and benefits.

Explain Why should you consider opportunity costs when making economic decisions?

Absolutism at Versailles For the rest of his long reign, Louis XIV retained absolute power. He began a tradition of absolute monarchy in France that would last for more than a century. Louis demanded that he be in charge of all military, political, and economic initiatives. The religion of his subjects was also to be under his direct control.

By drawing so much power to himself and the central government, Louis deprived the nobles of influence. They declined further in status when Louis built an enormous palace at Versailles (ver-SY), a few miles outside of Paris, and required that his nobles visit him there regularly. Nobles gained prestige by becoming servants in the king's Versailles court instead of by fighting or building local influence far from Paris. In addition, Louis urged the nobles to develop expensive new habits of dressing, dining, and gambling. As the nobles thus grew poorer, they had to depend on the king's generosity just to survive.

An immense complex of buildings and gardens, Versailles was a grand spectacle of kingly power. Louis XIV's style and ceremony emphasized his political strength. Practically every moment of the king's day required rituals performed by bowing courtiers. Eating, dressing, walking in the garden—all required a ritual. And Louis always knew who had given what he considered proper attention, as described in one courtier's memoir.

HISTORY'S VOICES

"If anyone habitually living at Court absented himself he insisted on knowing the reason; those who came there only for flying visits had also to give a satisfactory explanation; any one who seldom or never appeared there was certain to incur his displeasure."

—Duc de Saint-Simon, *The Court of Louis XIV*, 1746

Differentiating Instruction — Below Level

English-Language Learners

Materials: construction paper

1. Organize students into small groups. Tell students they have been chosen by the king to design a royal compound in the country with a royal palace, palaces to house members of the court, theaters, stables, and other buildings, as well as formal gardens, lawns, woods, and recreational spaces. Have each group draw up a plan and make illustrated displays of court life, including art, dance, dress, and social etiquette. Have students decide where the money should come from to build their royal compounds.
2. Display student designs for the class to see.
3. Guide students in a discussion of the finished designs. How do they think their royal compounds compare to Louis XIV's Versailles? **LS Interpersonal, Visual-Spatial**

Alternative Assessment Handbook, Rubrics 3: Artwork; and 14: Group Activity

Direct Teach

Reading Focus

3 What were the main events in the monarchy of Louis XIV? *building of Versailles, cancellation of Edict of Nantes, War of the Spanish Succession, Treaty of Utrecht*

The Monarchy of Louis XIV

Identify Who was Cardinal Mazarin? *the adviser who became chief minister after Cardinal Richelieu's death*

Analyze How did Louis XIV work at building his image? *created elaborate rituals to emphasize his power, built a grand palace at Versailles*

Evaluate Do you think that Louis XIV's extravagant lifestyle was worth the cost? Why or why not? *possible answer—Yes, it probably helped keep France politically stable by symbolizing his power.*

CRF: Biography: Louis de Rouvroy

Info to Know

The Boy King Louis XIV became king of France at the age of four. Although he was surrounded by the luxury of the French court, the first years of his reign were not easy. When he was just nine, Louis had to flee Paris when rebellions broke out between the French nobility and the monarch. From 1648 to 1652, Louis kept moving through France, suffering from hunger, cold, and fear. The memory of that hardship stayed with Louis forever. He never again trusted the people of Paris or the nobility.

The Arts in France Catherine de Medici introduced ballet into France in 1581, but under Louis XIV, ballet became a serious art form. He founded the first school for ballet in 1661. In 1681 female dancers first performed at the Paris Opera.

Answers

History & Economics *possible answer—While they are not immediately apparent, they help you make a more informed decision.*

Direct Teach

Reading Focus

The Monarchy of Louis XIV

Recall What country benefited most from the War of Spanish Succession? *England*

Identify Cause and Effect What were the causes and effects of the War of the Spanish Succession? *caused when other European powers did not want to see Louis XIV's son become king of Spain; resulted in giving Louis's grandson the Spanish throne, but keeping France and Spain from being ruled by the same monarch, and making France give up territory. England ended up benefiting at the expense of France and Spain.*

Review & Assess

Close

Guide students in a discussion of the reasons for the increasing power of the monarchy from Henry IV to Louis XIV.

Review

Online Quiz, Section 2

Assess

SE Section 2 Assessment

Progress Assessment: Section 2 Quiz

Alternative Assessment Handbook

Reteach/Intervene

Interactive Reader and Study Guide, Section 2

Interactive Skills Tutor CD-ROM

Louis and Protestantism Another way that Louis established absolute monarchy was by smashing the power of the Huguenots once and for all. Since the reign of Henry IV, the Edict of Nantes had protected the Huguenots. For all Richelieu's efforts, even he had not been able to eliminate that protection.

In 1685 Louis made his move. He revoked, or canceled, the edict and outlawed Protestantism in his realm. Over 200,000 Huguenots fled France, including many prosperous merchants and artisans. The loss of their skills and wealth helped cause a financial crisis.

READING SKILLS

Connecting How does the War of the Spanish Succession connect to other problems related to succession about which you have already read?

Money and the Military Louis's finances were always a matter of concern because the grand lifestyle he demanded required a great deal of money. The treasury was saved primarily by the efficient policies of the minister of finance, Jean-Baptiste Colbert (kawl-BER). Colbert limited imports and increased exports. In addition, he simplified the tax system. Colbert even reduced the government's debt. Still, Louis always wanted more money.

Louis needed cash to fulfill his greatest ambition—to build up the military and expand French territory. He succeeded in this goal, certainly, by enlarging the army from some 70,000 men to more than 200,000 disciplined soldiers. Louis also spent money on good equipment for his new army. With this mighty force, Louis became the most powerful ruler in Europe, taking France into war four times.

War over a Throne Louis XIV wanted to increase his power beyond the borders of France. He went to war to reclaim territory that France had lost, but his wars cost France dearly. In fact, they cost so much that Louis had to melt down royal silver to pay for army supplies. The most costly of his wars was the **War of the Spanish Succession**. It began when the Spanish king died without an heir. Three rulers claimed that they should name the successor. Louis was one of the three, because he wanted the Spanish throne for his oldest son.

The other European monarchs did not want France and Spain to be so closely connected. Such an alliance could cause economic and political problems for several countries. Therefore, in 1701 England, the Netherlands, and the Holy Roman Empire went to war against France. Fighting was not limited to Europe. In North America, the conflict was connected to a phase of the French and Indian Wars.

After many defeats, in 1713 Louis accepted the **Treaty of Utrecht**. Although the treaty said that Louis's grandson got the Spanish throne, it also said that France and Spain would never be ruled by the same monarch. Louis also had to give up most of the territory he had taken. The war benefited England at the expense of France and Spain. Despite the setback, Louis XIV remained in power until his death in 1715—still an absolute monarch.

READING CHECK **Find the Main Idea** What were some main events during Louis XIV's reign?

Section 2 Assessment

go.hrw.com
Online Quiz
Keyword: SHL MON HP

Reviewing Ideas, Terms, and People

1. **a. Define** Write a brief definition of the following terms: **Huguenot, Saint Bartholomew's Day Massacre, Edict of Nantes.**
   b. Sequence List in order the major events in the conflict between French Huguenots and Catholics.
   c. Elaborate Attributed to **Henry IV** is the quotation, "Paris is well worth a mass." What does this statement mean?
2. **a. Identify** Who was **Cardinal Richelieu**, and why was he significant?
   b. Interpret What were the effects of the siege of La Rochelle?
3. **a. Identify** What was Versailles? Why was it important?
   b. Explain What did **Louis XIV** mean by "L'état, c'est moi"?
   c. Evaluate How could Louis XIV have improved his legacy?

Critical Thinking

4. **Sequence** Copy the graphic organizer below and use it to describe how the power of the French monarchy increased under Henry IV, Louis XIII, and Louis XIV.

Henry IV → Louis XIII → Louis XIV

Focus on Writing

5. **Description** Study the illustrations in this section. Then write a brief description of either the St. Bartholomew's Day Massacre or the palace that Louis XIV built at Versailles. Use details that will help your reader visualize the scene.

Section 2 Assessment Answers

1. **a.** Huguenot: French Protestant; St. Bart's Day Massacre: killing of 10,000 to 70,000 Huguenots; Edict of Nantes: document giving certain rights to Huguenots
   b. St. Bartholomew's Day Massacre, Henry IV converted to Catholicism, Edict of Nantes, Thirty Years' War
   c. France was worth converting to Catholicism
2. **a.** chief minister, trusted adviser of Louis XIII
   b. all churches became Catholic; gave signal to Huguenots that resistance was unwise
3. **a.** Louis XIV's palace; symbol of king's power
   b. "I am the state"; could rule by himself
   c. possible answer—by placing less emphasis on appearance, and more on strategy
4. Henry IV: issued Edict of Nantes, made reforms; Louis XIII: took power from Huguenots, nobles; Louis XIV: absolute monarch, built Versailles
5. Student descriptions should include details about the illustration of a chosen event.

Answers

Reading Skills *possible answer—Another problem of succession was Henry IV becoming King of France.*

Reading Check *building of Versailles, cancellation of Edict of Nantes, War of the Spanish Succession, Treaty of Utrecht*

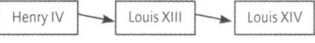

SECTION 3
Monarchy in England

BEFORE YOU READ

MAIN IDEA

In contrast to the absolute monarchies of Spain and France, the English monarchy was limited by Parliament; following a civil war, Parliament became even more powerful.

READING FOCUS

1. How did the Tudors work with Parliament?
2. What led the first two Stuart kings to clash with Parliament?
3. What were the causes and results of the English Civil War?
4. What happened when monarchy returned to England?

KEY TERMS AND PEOPLE

Puritans
Charles I
Royalists
Oliver Cromwell
commonwealth
Restoration
Charles II
William and Mary
Glorious Revolution
constitutional monarchy

TAKING NOTES As you read, take notes to record details about the decreasing power of the monarchy and increasing power of Parliament.

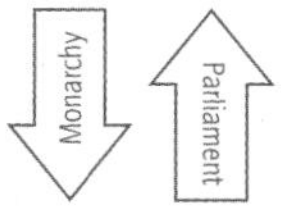

A BOLD QUEEN

Portrait of Elizabeth I, by unknown artist, 1500s

THE INSIDE STORY ***How did a queen get her way?*** Queen Elizabeth I had a very strong personality—and it showed in her relationship with England's Parliament. Early in her reign, the members of Parliament asked Elizabeth I when she planned to marry. In response, she told them that she planned to die without a husband, and that it was none of Parliament's business anyway. She was not interested in sharing power with a king. Elizabeth's close relationship with Parliament was assisted by her fierce and obvious love for England. In her last speech to Parliament she said, "Though you have had, and may have, many princes more mighty and wise sitting in this seat, yet you never had, nor shall have, any that will be more careful and loving." Later monarchs would not be as close to Parliament, or so skillful in dealing with it. ■

The Tudors and Parliament

Two prominent members of the Tudor dynasty, Henry VIII and his daughter Elizabeth I, ruled during the time when absolutism was common on the European continent. In England, though, Parliament placed curbs on absolute monarchy. Both father and daughter had to learn how to work with Parliament to fulfill their goals for England.

◀ **Queen Elizabeth at the height of her glory, as shown by the richness of her clothing and jewels**

Preteach

Getting Started

Use the **Interactive Reader and Study Guide** to familiarize students with the section content.

Interactive Reader and Study Guide, Section 3

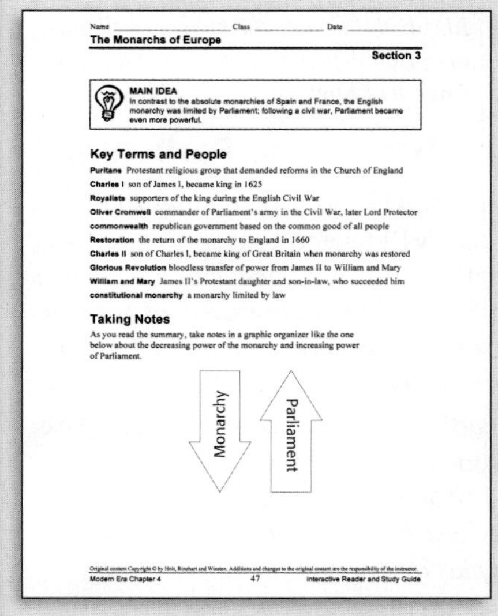

Name ______ Class ______ Date ______

The Monarchs of Europe

Section 3

MAIN IDEA
In contrast to the absolute monarchies of Spain and France, the English monarchy was limited by Parliament; following a civil war, Parliament became even more powerful.

Key Terms and People

Puritans Protestant religious group that demanded reforms in the Church of England
Charles I son of James I, became king in 1625
Royalists supporters of the king during the English Civil War
Oliver Cromwell commander of Parliament's army in the Civil War, later Lord Protector
commonwealth republican government based on the common good of all people
Restoration the return of the monarchy to England in 1660
Charles II son of Charles I, became king of Great Britain when monarchy was restored
Glorious Revolution bloodless transfer of power from James II to William and Mary
William and Mary James II's Protestant daughter and son-in-law, who succeeded him
constitutional monarchy a monarchy limited by law

Taking Notes

As you read the summary, take notes in a graphic organizer like the one below about the decreasing power of the monarchy and increasing power of Parliament.

Monarchy
Parliament

Original content Copyright © by Holt, Rinehart and Winston. Additions and changes to the original content are the responsibility of the instructor.
Modern Era Chapter 4 47 Interactive Reader and Study Guide

CRF: Vocabulary Builder: Section 3

Taking Notes

Tudors worked with Parliament to get what they wanted; Parliament forced Charles I to sign the Petition of Right; English Civil War resulted in Parliament defeating and executing Charles I; Parliament restored monarchy but continued to develop its role; Parliament invited William and Mary to replace James II; Parliament passed the Bill of Rights, further limiting royal power.

Teach the Main Idea

At Level

Monarchy in England

1. **Teach** Ask students the Reading Focus questions to teach this section.
2. **Apply** Have students create a time line of the major events in this section. Student time lines should begin with the passage of the Act of Supremacy in 1534 and end with the passage of the English Bill of Rights in 1689.
3. **Review** Guide students in a discussion of the events on their time lines. What events could be considered milestones in England's road to democracy? What events were setbacks?
4. **Practice/Homework** Tell students that it is the time of the English Civil War. Have each student decide whether he or she would have been on the side of the Cavaliers or the Roundheads and write an essay explaining why. Have students take into consideration the leadership of Charles I and Oliver Cromwell and the issues at stake.
LS Visual-Spatial, Verbal-Linguistic

Alternative Assessment Handbook, Rubrics 36: Time Lines; and 40: Writing to Describe

Direct Teach

Reading Focus

1. How did the Tudors work with Parliament? *Henry VIII teamed with Parliament to pass a series of laws to convert England to Protestantism and name him head of the Church of England. Elizabeth I needed the help of Parliament to re-establish herself as the head of the Church of England.*

The Tudors and Parliament

Summarize What measures did Henry VIII take to convert England to Protestantism? *teamed with Parliament to pass a series of laws, Act of Supremacy made the king head of the Church of England*

Predict What do you think would have happened if Elizabeth I had married? *possible answer—might have lost power because her husband would have wanted to play a part in governing England.*

CRF: Literature: *The Life of King Henry V*

Henry VIII created the Protestant Church of England so he could divorce his first wife. To effect the split with the Roman Catholic Church, Henry had Parliament pass laws ending the power of the pope in England. In 1534 the Act of Supremacy named the king as the head of the Church of England.

After Henry's death and the short reign of his son Edward, Henry's daughter Mary I became queen. Often called Bloody Mary, she briefly made England Catholic again. When Mary died in 1558, Elizabeth was crowned queen and returned England to the Anglican, or English Protestant, Church. Parliament helped her do so by passing laws that favored Protestantism.

Tension developed between Parliament and the queen when Parliament pressured her to marry so that she would have an heir to the throne. She refused, knowing that marriage to either an Englishman or a foreigner could limit her freedom. Still, she managed to talk Parliament into approving the funds she needed.

A major reason for Elizabeth's good relationship with Parliament was her willingness to let the members speak their minds without fear of punishment. Her close ties to Parliament show in the fact that she called it into session 10 times during her 45-year reign.

While Elizabeth was clearly in charge, she had some difficulty keeping her subjects from questioning her actions. For example, in 1601 one of her favorite courtiers, the Earl of Essex, rebelled against the queen's authority. He asked publicly, "Cannot princes err? Cannot subjects receive wrong? Is an earthly power or authority infinite?" Essex was tried and executed, but he was not the last to question the English monarch's authority.

READING CHECK **Recall** What did Henry VIII and Elizabeth I work with Parliament to do?

The Stuarts and Parliament

The Tudors' success with Parliament was not repeated by their successors. When Elizabeth I died in 1603, a relative of the Tudors from Scotland became king. James I was the first member of the Stuart dynasty to rule in England. His view of absolute monarchy caused conflict with Parliament.

James I Clashes with Parliament James faced problems from the start. He believed firmly in the divine right of kings and wanted to rule as an absolute monarch. But wars waged

Linking TO Today

The British Monarchy

Should the United Kingdom still have a king or queen? Ever since the conflict between king and Parliament in the 1600s, the monarch has had a restricted role in the government.

Critics of the monarchy sometimes claim that the royal family is an expensive luxury. Monarchy's defenders reply that Queen Elizabeth II's wealth—perhaps about $500 million—allows her to pay her own way. Her accountants agree. In 2006 a report from the office of Royal Public Finances stated that Queen Elizabeth II and her family cost each citizen of the United Kingdom only about $1.13 per year. In addition, the monarchy's supporters point out that the tourist industry, which is worth more than $300 billion per year, would suffer if the romance of royalty were eliminated. Elizabeth II can also sometimes defuse a touchy situation with other heads of state, since she does not represent a particular political viewpoint.

Perhaps the best argument for the monarchy is its power as a symbol. It represents continuity—the ability of the kingdom's people to survive centuries of global turmoil and still live in relative peace with each other.

Draw Conclusions Should the monarchy continue? Why or why not?

Queen Elizabeth II greets crowds celebrating her eightieth birthday. ▶

Collaborative Learning

At Level

The Reign of Queen Elizabeth I

1. Organize students into two groups for a classroom debate on the reign of Queen Elizabeth I. Have one side support her policies and the other side argue against them. Have students consider the historical context in evaluating the policies. Why did Elizabeth refuse to marry, re-establish herself as the head of the Church of England, and allow English captains to attack Spanish ships coming from America laden with treasure? Give each side time to prepare arguments.
2. Conduct a classroom debate on Elizabeth's policies. Which side presented the most convincing arguments? **LS Interpersonal**

Alternative Assessment Handbook, Rubric 10: Debates

Answers

Linking to Today *possible answers—Yes, it is a symbol of continuity, it encourages tourism; No, the royal family is expensive to maintain.*

Reading Check *to pass laws to help the monarch achieve desired results* by his predecessors, combined with his own spending, left him low on funds. In addition, because he was from Scotland, he was considered an outsider. For all of these reasons, he had difficulty getting along with Parliament. Although James called Parliament repeatedly during his reign, he was rarely able to get Parliament to approve all the money he wanted.

As Parliament increased its influence, another group was starting to make itself known. The **Puritans**, a group of strict Calvinists, demanded that the Church of England be further reformed. They wanted to "purify" the English church of practices they thought were still too Catholic. For example, priests still dressed in elaborate robes, and worshippers knelt during services.

Another of the Puritans' goals was to take power away from church officials. James saw this stance as a threat to his power because the church leadership supported him. As a result, he refused to pass most of the Puritans' requests for reform. One reform James agreed to was the publication of an English version of the Bible that became known as the King James Bible.

Charles I Defies Parliament When James I died in 1625, his younger son was crowned king as **Charles I**. He was popular at first, but married a Catholic princess and involved England in military adventures overseas.

In 1628 Charles summoned Parliament to request money. Parliament refused to grant it until Charles signed a document, called the Petition of Right, that placed limits on the king's power. Among the document's provisions was a statement that the king could not levy taxes without Parliament's approval. Nor could he imprison anyone without legal justification, force citizens to house soldiers, or declare martial law in peacetime. The Petition of Right was a direct challenge to absolute monarchy.

When Parliament refused to give him money again later, Charles taxed the English people on his own and forced bankers to loan him money. The members of Parliament were furious. In response, Charles dismissed Parliament and in 1629 decided to rule without consulting Parliament ever again.

READING CHECK **Find the Main Idea** Why did the Stuarts have trouble with Parliament?

The English Civil War

Conflict continued between a king who believed in absolute monarchy and a Parliament that saw itself as independent of the king. The conflict became so severe that it led to war and even the king's death.

Parliament Reconvened In 1640 Charles I was badly in debt, thanks to a religious rebellion in Scotland. He finally had to reconvene Parliament so he could ask for more money.

This session became known as the Long Parliament because it did not disband for many years. After being ignored for 11 years, the members of Parliament were in no mood to bow to the king's wishes, and they took the opportunity to further limit the king's powers. They demanded that Parliament must be called at least every three years, and the king could no longer dismiss Parliament. Charles I accepted these new rules, but he awaited the right moment to overturn them.

War with Parliament That moment came when a radical Puritan group within Parliament moved to abolish the appointment of bishops in the Anglican Church. The king, whose power was connected to the power of the church, was outraged.

For this insult, Charles decided to arrest the Puritan leaders for treason. He led troops into the House of Commons to make the arrest, but the men had already escaped. Now Charles had given away his intentions to take back power. Some members of Parliament decided to rise up against the king. Charles I called for the support of the English people. Within months, in 1642, the English Civil War began.

Without funding from Parliament, the king had to rely on contributions to pay for an army. His supporters, mainly wealthy nobles, were called **Royalists** for their allegiance to his royal person. On the other side, Parliament could back its army by voting for funding. Supporters of Parliament were called Roundheads, from their short, bowl-shaped haircuts, which contrasted with the Royalists' long wigs. The Roundheads included Puritans, merchants, and some members of the upper classes.

Leading the Roundhead forces was a member of Parliament named **Oliver Cromwell**. He had risen to leadership as an army general.

READING SKILLS

Connecting How does this information about the Puritans connect to what you already know about Puritans in America?

THE IMPACT TODAY

Today, England's monarch is allowed to enter the Houses of Parliament only once a year, to open a session of Parliament.

Direct Teach

Reading Focus

2 What led the first two Stuart kings to clash with Parliament? *went to Parliament to raise money, rarely able to get the money they wanted*

The Stuarts and Parliament

Recall What did Charles I do when Parliament refused to give him money after he signed the Petition of Right? *He taxed the English people and dismissed Parliament.*

Evaluate Do you think the English would have accepted James I as an absolute monarch if he had not been an "outsider"? Explain your answer. *possible answer—no; because they were used to having monarchs work with Parliament*

Reading Focus

3 What were the causes and results of the English Civil War? *causes—Long Parliament limited Charles I's powers and refused to give him money; results—Charles I executed; monarchy and House of Lords abolished; England became a commonwealth*

The English Civil War

Recall Why did Charles I call Parliament into session in 1640? *He needed money following a religious rebellion in Scotland*

Summarize How did Oliver Cromwell's role in government change over time? *started as member of Parliament; became army general and commander-in-chief; seized power as Lord Protector*

CRF: History and Geography: A King at War with Parliament

Skills Focus: Summarizing

Below Level

Reading Skill

The Role of Religion in English Politics

1. Have students work in mixed-ability pairs to make a chart summarizing the relations between religion and government during the reigns of Henry VIII, Mary, Elizabeth I, and James I.
2. Review student charts as a class, and make a class chart for all to see. Have students correct their own work as needed.
3. Guide students in a discussion of religious conflicts in England using the following questions: How did religious conflicts in England compare with conflicts elsewhere in Europe? What factors might account for differences in England? How did the fact that the English monarch was also the head of the Church of England affect English religious conflicts? **LS Visual-Spatial**

Alternative Assessment Handbook, Rubrics 7: Charts; and 11: Discussions

Answers

Reading Skills *Many Puritans left England and settled in America.*

Reading Check *Both wanted to rule as absolute monarchs.*

Direct Teach

Reading Focus

The English Civil War

Sequence List, in order, the events leading to the establishment of the commonwealth. *Cromwell led Roundheads in battle against Royalists; king surrendered; Cromwell dismissed members of Parliament who disagreed with him; king tried and executed; monarchy and House of Lords outlawed*

Make Judgments Do you think that England was better off under the commonwealth or under the monarchy? Explain. *possible answer—under the monarchy: in the end Cromwell proved to be as much of a tyrant as the king he had deposed by passing many restrictive laws*

Info to Know

Charles I Charles I originally attempted to marry the daughter of the Spanish king in order to form an alliance between Spain and England. When he failed to negotiate the marriage, he married the French princess Henrietta Maria instead, forming an alliance with France against Spain. His marriage to Henrietta, a Catholic, angered his Protestant subjects.

Reading like a Historian

A View of Oliver Cromwell

Interpreting Political Cartoons England faced problems both at home and abroad during the mid-1600s. Under Charles I, fighting had broken out in Ireland and Scotland. Oliver Cromwell inherited those tensions—and expenses. In addition, he had Parliament pass a law that damaged Dutch trade. A war with the Dutch was the result. Cromwell was also in conflict with the Royalists, of course.

Cromwell's foreign exploits made him very unpopular in the other countries. In England, though, Cromwell was popular enough that in 1657 Parliament offered him the crown, which he declined. As you study this Dutch cartoon about Cromwell titled "The Horrible Tail Man," consider:

- the identities of the characters in the cartoon
- what the various characters are doing
- where Cromwell's attention is focused
- the country where it was published

Cromwell is portrayed in a negative way. His face is ugly, and he has a long, fat tail filled with coins.

A Royalist, a Dutchman, an Irishman, and a Scot are cutting off sections of Cromwell's money-filled tail.

Skills Focus READING LIKE A HISTORIAN

1. **Details** Is Cromwell aware of what is going on behind him? How does this affect the meaning?
2. **Message** What was the cartoonist saying about the impact of Cromwell's foreign involvements?

See **Skills Handbook**, p. H27

In 1644, at the first truly decisive battle of the war, he led a victory in which 4,000 of the king's soldiers died. Cromwell continued to rise in power until he became commander-in-chief of Parliament's army.

The Royalist army was outmatched by Cromwell's disciplined troops. In 1646 the king surrendered. Now in full control, Cromwell dismissed all members of Parliament who disagreed with him. Those who were left made up what was called the Rump Parliament.

Trial and Execution Eventually the Rump Parliament charged the king with treason and put him on trial. During his trial, Charles defended himself with great eloquence but refused to even recognize Parliament's authority to try him. "I do stand more for the liberty of my people than any here that come to be my pretended judges," he declared. In the end, the king was sentenced to death for treason. On January 30, 1649, Charles I was publicly beheaded in front of his own palace—the first European monarch to be formally tried and sentenced to death by a court of law. To some people he was a martyr, to others a tyrant who got what he deserved.

England under Cromwell For the next 11 years, England's government changed completely. The House of Commons abolished the House of Lords and outlawed the monarchy.

England became a **commonwealth**, which is a republican government based on the common good of all the people. In 1653 Cromwell was given the title Lord Protector of England,

Differentiating Instruction

Above Level

Advanced Learners/Gifted and Talented

Research Required

Materials: poster board; colored markers

1. Organize students into small groups. Have each group create a board game for the English Civil War. The playing board should be a map of Great Britain and Ireland with major cities and sites of major battles marked on it. Game pieces should represent the Royalist forces (Cavaliers) and Parliamentary forces (Roundheads), with special pieces representing King Charles I and Oliver Cromwell.
2. Have each group conduct research about the progress of the English Civil War to mark the major battle sites on the map and to write rules for playing the game. Game rules should allow either two people or two teams to play.
3. Have each group demonstrate its board game for the rest of the class. Guide students in a discussion about the English Civil War.

LS Visual-Spatial, Kinesthetic

Alternative Assessment Handbook, Rubrics 20: Map Creation; and 30: Research

Answers

Reading Like a Historian 1. *no; shows he is not an effective leader;* **2.** *They were expensive and harmful to England.*

Scotland, and Ireland. Although Cromwell was a skilled leader, he demanded complete obedience. He clamped down on English social life by closing the theaters and limiting other forms of popular entertainment.

Cromwell had to deal with foreign issues, too. He led military expeditions to Scotland and Ireland. His economic policies led to a war with the Dutch over trade. To limit Spanish activity in the Americas, he also warred on Spain.

A Defender of Absolutism Cromwell, the king's death, and the war troubled many of the English people. One of them was Thomas Hobbes, a Royalist who fled to France during Cromwell's rule. Hobbes wrote what is now a classic work of political science, *Leviathan*. In it, Hobbes described humans as being naturally selfish and fearful. Life in nature, he wrote, was "solitary, poor, nasty, brutish, and short." Hobbes argued that people needed an all-powerful monarch to tell them how to live. His views sparked controversy during a time when England was trying to find a balance between government by the people's representatives and the monarchy.

READING CHECK **Identify Cause and Effect** What were some effects of the English Civil War?

The Monarchy Returns

Hobbes's ideas reflected the fact that many people were unhappy under Cromwell, especially when he dismissed Parliament to rule. Attitudes were changing so much that a return to monarchy became possible.

The Restoration When Cromwell died in 1658, his son took his place. Richard Cromwell lacked his father's leadership abilities, though, and his government collapsed. Eventually Parliament reconvened and voted to bring back the monarchy—an event known as the **Restoration**.

In the spring of 1660, Parliament invited the son of the dead Charles I, also named Charles, to be the new king. Parliament laid out certain conditions, which Charles accepted, along with the invitation. He would be crowned King **Charles II**. As he rode into London upon his return, the people shouted their good wishes. The writer Samuel Pepys recorded his impressions of the day in his diary:

HISTORY'S VOICES

> "Great joy all yesterday at London, and at night more bonfires than ever, and ringing of bells, and drinking of the King's health upon their knees in the streets, which methinks is a little too much. But every body seems to be very joyfull in the business . . ."
>
> —*The Diary of Samuel Pepys*, May 2, 1660

The Reign of Charles II Charles knew that as king he had to watch his step. When his policies were opposed, he usually gave in. Still, he had to address many issues. Conflict with the Dutch continued. Religious tensions remained. And the role of Parliament was still being developed. Charles supported religious toleration for Catholics, for example, but Parliament insisted upon laws to strengthen the Church of England.

The Restoration years were a mixture of positive and negative events. On one hand, Charles reopened the theaters, with a flowering of English drama as the result. Another positive event was passage of the Habeas Corpus Act of 1679. This act guaranteed that someone accused of a crime had the right to appear in court to determine if the accused should be held or released. The act is one of the most important in English history.

England also suffered setbacks during the reign of Charles II. In 1665 the bubonic plague returned, killing perhaps 100,000 people in London alone. The next year, the Great Fire of London destroyed large parts of the city—but also killed the rats that had spread the deadly plague. After the fire, though, Charles supported public construction projects.

James II Later in Charles's reign the question of who would succeed him remained. His brother, James, was next in line, but he was Catholic. In addition, James had married a Catholic princess whose Catholic son would outrank James's Protestant daughters from his first marriage. When Charles died in 1685, James II was crowned king. Many people wondered if another destructive war would follow.

James was not popular. Besides being a Catholic, he believed wholeheartedly in his right to rule as an absolute monarch. The English people, however, would no longer tolerate such a belief.

Direct Teach

Reading Focus

4 What happened when monarchy returned to England? *Charles II took the throne, followed by his brother, James II, a Catholic. Then, Protestants William and Mary became king and queen in the Glorious Revolution.*

The Monarchy Returns

Identify Cause and Effect Why did Parliament vote to bring back the monarchy? *People were unhappy with new Puritan laws, and Cromwell's son was an uninspiring leader.*

Evaluate What were the positive and negative aspects of the Restoration years? *positive—the theaters reopened, Habeas Corpus Act passed; negative—conflict with Dutch, religious tension, bubonic plague, Great Fire of London*

Analyze Why are the events of 1688 known as the Glorious Revolution? *A new king and queen took power without bloodshed.*

CRF: Biography: William and Mary

CRF: Economics and History: British Deficit Financing, 1688–1815

Info to Know

Hobbes and *Leviathan* When the struggle between Charles I and Parliament broke out, Thomas Hobbes began work on a defense of the powers of the monarch, using ideas that he later developed in *Leviathan*. Fearing arrest by Parliament, he fled to Paris. From 1646 to 1648 he taught mathematics to Charles I's son, the future King Charles II, who was living in exile in Paris. *Leviathan* was viewed by Prince Charles's advisers as justifying the Commonwealth, and by French authorities as attacking the papacy. Fearing arrest again, he returned to England. When Charles II came to the throne in 1660, he welcomed his former teacher back to his court.

Skills Focus: Identifying Main Idea and Details — At Level

Reading Skill

The Puritan Commonwealth

1. Guide students in a discussion of the effectiveness of Cromwell's Commonwealth using the following questions: Why was the monarchy abolished? How does the idea of a commonwealth fit in with Cromwell's dismissal of Parliament and seizure of power? How did Cromwell's behavior compare with that of King Charles? Did the English just replace one tyrant with another?
2. Have each student write a "job evaluation" assessing Oliver Cromwell's performance as the leader of England. First have students create an evaluation form with questions about different aspects of job performance, then have students fill in the answers.
3. Have volunteers read their job evaluations to the class. **LS Verbal-Linguistic**

Alternative Assessment Handbook, Rubrics 11: Discussions; and 40: Writing to Describe

Answers

Reading Check *temporarily ended monarchy and House of Lords, restricted English social life in certain ways*

Direct Teach

Analyzing Primary Sources

The English Bill of Rights

Activity **Comparing Documents**
Provide students with copies of the Bill of Rights from the United States Constitution. Have them search for similarities between the American Bill of Rights and the English Bill of Rights. **LS Verbal-Linguistic**

Review & Assess

Close

Have students summarize the important events in English history from the time of the Tudors to the Glorious Revolution.

Review

go.hrw.com Online Quiz, Section 3

Assess

SE Section 3 Assessment

Progress Assessment: Section 3 Quiz

Alternative Assessment Handbook

Reteach/Intervene

Interactive Reader and Study Guide, Section 3

Interactive Skills Tutor CD-ROM

PRIMARY SOURCES

The English Bill of Rights

These excerpts from The Bill of Rights illustrate the limits placed on the monarchy by Parliament. In the document, the members of Parliament made several declarations, including:

1. That the pretended power of suspending laws, or the execution of laws, by regal authority, without consent of parliament is illegal. . .
5. That it is the right of the subjects to petition the king, and all commitments and prosecutions for such petitioning are illegal. . .
8. That election of members of parliament ought to be free.
9. That the freedom of speech, and debates or proceedings in parliament, ought not to be impeached or questioned in any court or place out of parliament.
10. That excessive bail ought not to be required, nor excessive fines imposed, nor cruel and unusual punishments inflicted.

Skills Focus READING LIKE A HISTORIAN

1. **Analyze** In the fifth declaration, what does "petition the king" mean?
2. **Draw Conclusions** Which of these rights do we enjoy today?

See **Skills Handbook**, p. H25

The Glorious Revolution In 1688 a group of nobles invited James's daughter Mary and her husband William to become king and queen of England. **William and Mary** were both Protestants, living in the Netherlands. James, knowing that it was pointless to fight, fled to France. Parliament gave the throne to William III and Mary II as joint rulers. This transfer of power became known as the **Glorious Revolution**.

Changes in Government With the Glorious Revolution, Parliament had essentially crowned the new king and queen. More important was a document that William and Mary had to sign before taking the throne—the English Bill of Rights. This document prevented the monarch from levying taxes without the consent of Parliament, among many other provisions. Decades later, the Bill of Rights was reflected in the U.S. Constitution.

The Bill of Rights was central to England's growth as a **constitutional monarchy**, the term for a monarchy limited by law. The document's approval came after decades of dramatic changes in English government. England had rejected the concept of an absolute monarch who supposedly ruled by divine right for a monarchy ruled by law.

READING CHECK **Describe** What happened during the Glorious Revolution?

SECTION 3 ASSESSMENT

go.hrw.com
Online Quiz
Keyword: SHL MON HP

Reviewing Ideas, Terms, and People

1. **a. Identify** Which monarch separated England from the Roman Catholic Church?
   b. Explain Why did Elizabeth I need to get along with the English Parliament?
2. **a. Recall** How did the **Puritans** get their name?
   b. Summarize What was the basic conflict between James I and Parliament?
3. **a. Identify** When did the **English Civil War** begin?
   b. Explain Why did **Charles I** have a hard time raising money for an army, while Parliament did not?
   c. Develop Why did the English people differ in their views on the execution of Charles I?
4. **a. Recall** What is a **constitutional monarchy**?
   b. Compare and Contrast How were the **Restoration** and the **Glorious Revolution** similar and different?
   c. Make Judgments Why is the English Bill of Rights important to both the English and American people?

Critical Thinking

5. **Identify Cause and Effect** Using your notes and a graphic organizer like the one below, identify the causes of the decreasing power of the monarchy. Add more boxes as needed.

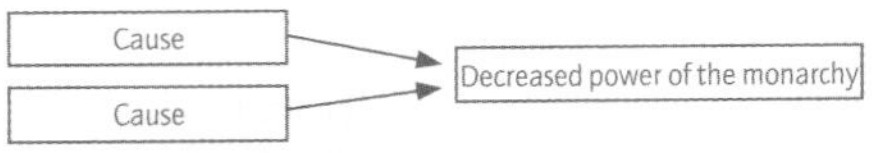

FOCUS ON WRITING

6. **Exposition** Imagine that you are a guide in a museum that has a copy of the English Bill of Rights. As a handout for museum visitors, write a brief explanation of the importance of this document.

Section 3 Assessment Answers

1. **a.** Henry VIII
   b. to pass laws supporting her policies
2. **a.** wanted to "purify" the Church of England
   b. James I could not get money from Parliament.
3. **a.** 1642
   b. Parliament was able to levy taxes.
   c. People who supported the monarchy believed Parliament did not have the authority to execute the king.
4. **a.** monarchy limited by law
   b. similar—both did not involve violence; different—in Glorious Revolution, the king and queen had to accept limits on their power
   c. provided rights that are important to this day; some rights later included in U.S. Bill of Rights
5. Kings believed in absolute monarchy while Parliament wanted to remain independent of King, Charles I overthrown by Parliament, English Bill of Rights passed
6. Student handouts should point out that Parliament's role was still being developed

Answers

Primary Sources **1.** *speak freely when asking for political change;* **2.** *free speech; free elections; no cruel and unusual punishment*

Reading Check *William and Mary were given the English throne by Parliament.*

THE ARTS AROUND THE WORLD

Music

Classical Music

What is it? The term "classical music" means different things to different people. It can describe a certain era of European music that began in the mid-1700s. Most people, though, probably think of classical music as beautiful concert music of any time period played by an orchestra—a large group of musicians.

Key characteristics:

- Includes many different forms—symphonies, operas, string quartets, art songs sung by individuals, and more
- Involves many different instruments—violins, violas, cellos, clarinets, horns, drums, pianos, drums, and many more
- Usually performed by highly trained musicians and singers

Maestro Seiji Ozawa conducts the Boston Symphony.

Why is it important?

- Classical music expresses the entire range of human emotions, from deep religious reverence to wild passion.
- It is an always-evolving form of musical expression that incorporates new instruments and modern topics.
- Although the performers are trained, one does not need to be trained to enjoy classical music.

This is an original score from one of classical music's greatest masters—Wolfgang Amadeus Mozart.

Franz Joseph Haydn Conducting a String Quartet by Schmid, artist unknown, no date

Composer Franz Josef Haydn was Austrian but visited London often. His many musical works inspired later composers.

Skills Focus INTERPRETING VISUALS

1. **Compare and Contrast** What do the performances pictured have in common? How are they different?
2. **Rank** What modern issues do you think would be good topics for symphonies or operas?

The Arts Around the World

Biography

Franz Joseph Haydn (1732–1809)

Joseph Haydn was one of the creators of the Classical style in music. During most of his career, he was the musical director at the court of the Esterhazys, one of the wealthiest families in the Austrian empire. During his regular visits to Vienna, Haydn developed a close friendship with Wolfgang Amadeus Mozart.

In 1791 he visited England. After he returned to Vienna, Ludwig van Beethoven went there to study with him. Haydn recognized his student's greatness, saying: "I shall be proud to be called his teacher." He visited England a second time in 1794. His 12 London symphonies won over British audiences and led King George III to invite him to stay, but he decided to return to Austria instead.

In 1797 Haydn wrote the national anthem of the Austrian monarchy, which was also used as the national anthem of Germany. "Papa" Haydn died in 1809, a famous and wealthy man.

Teaching Tip

Collaborate with the school music department or a local orchestra to present examples of classical music to students. Explain the history behind each piece of music presented.

Skills Focus: Comparing and Contrasting

At Level

Prep Required

Reading Skill
Classical Music

Materials: CDs featuring works of a classical composer such as Beethoven, and a modern orchestral composer such as Bela Bartok; CD player

1. Explain that the word "classical" can refer generally to orchestral music, or specifically to the Classical period.
2. Play a short selection from both CDs. Ask students which music came from the Classical period, and which is modern. Have volunteers give their guesses and explain their reasoning. Reveal who composed each selection.
3. Organize students into small groups. Play the CDs again. Have each group create a list of details about each piece, and compare the lists with the class. LS **Auditory-Musical, Interpersonal**

Alternative Assessment Handbook, Rubric 9: Comparing and Contrasting

Answers

Interpreting Visuals 1. *possible answer—both include conductors; one is a painted scene, the other is a photograph; one seems to be a large group; the other is a smaller group;* **2.** *Student answers will vary.*

Preteach

Getting Started

Use the **Interactive Reader and Study Guide** to familiarize students with the section content.

Interactive Reader and Study Guide, Section 4

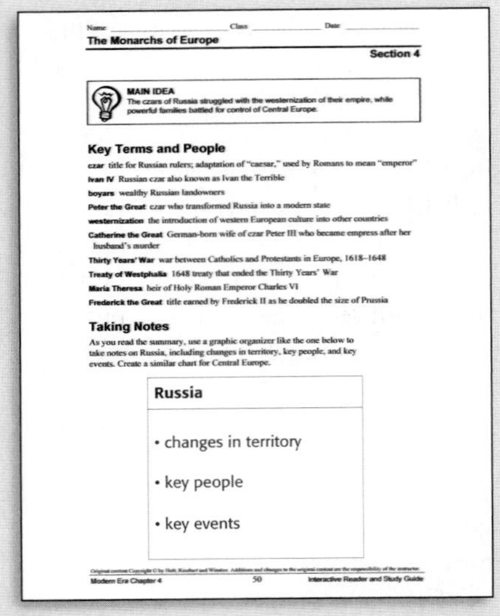

Name ______ Class ______ Date ______

The Monarchs of Europe

Section 4

MAIN IDEA
The czars of Russia struggled with the westernization of their empire, while powerful families battled for control of Central Europe.

Key Terms and People

czar title for Russian rulers; adaptation of "caesar," used by Romans to mean "emperor"
Ivan IV Russian czar also known as Ivan the Terrible
boyars wealthy Russian landowners
Peter the Great czar who transformed Russia into a modern state
westernization the introduction of western European culture into other countries
Catherine the Great German-born wife of czar Peter III who became empress after her husband's murder
Thirty Years' War war between Catholics and Protestants in Europe, 1618–1648
Treaty of Westphalia 1648 treaty that ended the Thirty Years' War
Maria Theresa heir of Holy Roman Emperor Charles VI
Frederick the Great title earned by Frederick II as he doubled the size of Prussia

Taking Notes

As you read the summary, use a graphic organizer like the one below to take notes on Russia, including changes in territory, key people, and key events. Create a similar chart for Central Europe.

Russia
• changes in territory • key people • key events

Modern Era Chapter 4   50   Interactive Reader and Study Guide

Academic Vocabulary

Review with students the high-use academic term in this section.

legitimacy definition the right to rule (p. 157)

CRF: Vocabulary Builder: Section 4

Taking Notes

Russia—Territory: expansion into Siberia, warm-water port at St. Petersburg; Key People—Ivan IV; Peter the Great; Catherine the Great; Events: Time of Troubles; Great Northern War, building of St. Petersburg; Central Europe—Territory: possessions of Hapsburgs and Hohenzollerns; Key People: Frederick I; Maria Theresa, Frederick the Great; Events: Thirty Years' War; Treaty of Westphalia; Seven Years' War

go.hrw.com
Online Resources
KEYWORD: SHL MON
ACTIVITY: Peter the Great and Catherine the Great

SECTION 4

Rulers of Russia and Central Europe

Before You Read

Main Idea

The czars of Russia struggled with the westernization of their empire, while powerful families battled for control of Central Europe.

Reading Focus

1. How did Ivan IV strengthen the Russian monarchy?
2. What reforms did Peter the Great make in Russia?
3. How did the rule of Catherine the Great affect Russia?
4. What states formed in Central Europe in the 1600s and 1700s?

Key Terms and People

boyars
czar
Ivan IV
Peter the Great
westernization
Catherine the Great
Thirty Years' War
Treaty of Westphalia
Maria Theresa
Frederick the Great

TAKING NOTES Take notes on Russia in a chart like this one, including changes in territory, key people, and key events. Create a similar chart for Central Europe.

Russia
• changes in territory • key people • key events

Tsar Ivan IV Vasilyevich 'the Terrible' (1530–84), by Victor Mikhailovich Vasnetsov, 1897

THE INSIDE STORY ***How did a ruler earn such a bad reputation?*** The young Russian emperor, Ivan IV, seemed reasonable at first and made several positive reforms. He also went to war to expand Russia's territory. When he seized the city of Kazan, the Russian people gave him the nickname *groznyi*, which means "fearsome" or "stern." However, the word has also been translated as "terrible." Ivan's actions did indeed become terrible, as he slipped into periods of uncontrollable rage, suspicion, and violence. Whole towns were burned and their people sent away. Ivan killed some enemies while they were in church. He had leading citizens publicly executed in grisly ways designed to horrify the many witnesses. Ivan even mortally wounded his own son in an argument. This incident probably sealed his reputation for all time as "Ivan the Terrible." ■

The Monarchy of Ivan IV

In the 1500s Russia was far behind western Europe in technological advancement and centralized government. At the time, Russia was run, in effect, by church officials and **boyars**, or landowners, usually with conservative viewpoints. Then, in 1546 a young prince claimed the title of **czar** (ZAHR) and put Russia on a different course. The title was a version of the Latin word *caesar*, or emperor, the title used by the Romans. The new czar, whose name was Ivan, intended to rule without limits on his power. But his own madness created chaos.

Teach the Main Idea

At Level

Rulers of Russia and Central Europe

1. **Teach** Ask students the Reading Focus questions to teach this section.
2. **Apply** Have students create an outline of the section using the heads as main points. Have students identify at least two main ideas under each of the red subheadings.
3. **Review** Review student outlines as a class. Guide students in a discussion of the relationship between Austria and Prussia during this period.
4. **Practice/Homework** Tell students that it is 1618 and they are mediators trying to prevent war after Protestants threw the Holy Roman Emperor's representatives out of the palace windows. Have students use the terms of the Peace of Augsburg and any other arguments they can think of to try to convince the emperor to negotiate rather than go to war.
LS Visual-Spatial, Verbal-Linguistic

Alternative Assessment Handbook, Rubrics 11: Discussions; and 43: Writing to Persuade

Reforms of Ivan IV During the early years of his rule, **Ivan IV** made many reforms. He created a general council that included merchants and lower-level nobles. He also began to promote military officers on merit rather than status and drew up a new legal code. These and similar reforms reduced the boyars' power.

Ivan also expanded Russia's borders and trade. He defeated the Tatars, who had succeeded the Mongols, and expanded Russian territory east to the Volga River. Controlling the length of the Volga to the Caspian Sea increased trade. As a result of such achievements, the years from 1547 to 1563 are known as Ivan's "good period."

Ivan the Terrible During the 1560s, Ivan changed. It was during this time that his strict policies and violent actions sealed his reputation as Ivan the Terrible. First, he became suspicious of his closest advisers and sent them away, killing many of their supporters. When his wife Anastasia died, he became convinced that she was murdered and that people were conspiring against him.

To investigate and punish the opposition, Ivan created a private police force of some 6,000 men. These men dressed in black and rode black horses. They controlled almost half of Russia's territory in Ivan's name and brutally punished anyone who spoke out against the czar's policies.

Ivan's harshness continued when in 1565 he seized land from 12,000 boyars. Soon after, he ordered the killing of thousands of people in the city of Novgorod because he suspected that they wanted to separate from Russia. Ivan's descent into mental illness seemed complete when in 1581 he killed his own son, who was next in line to be czar.

Although it may have been an accident, the death of Ivan's son left Russia without an heir to the throne. As a result, power changed hands many times. Uncertainty about the succession, economic problems, and foreign invasions added up to a chaotic period known as the Time of Troubles. It lasted until 1613, when Michael, a relative of Ivan's first wife, was crowned czar. Michael was the first of the Romanov dynasty, which ruled Russia until 1917.

READING CHECK **Contrast** How did the early rule of Ivan IV differ from his later years?

Peter the Great

About 70 years later, Peter I was crowned czar. Known later as **Peter the Great** for his efforts to transform Russia into a modern state, Peter had the strength to regain absolute power for the Russian monarchy.

Early Rule Peter became czar in 1682 while he was still a child, so his sister insisted on ruling in his place. At the age of 17, Peter removed his sister from the throne and took power for himself.

Peter was an impressive man. He was about six and a half feet tall, and it was said that he was so strong he could roll up a heavy silver platter as if it were foil. Peter also had a strong personality and boundless energy.

One of Czar Peter's first acts was to storm Azov, a Black Sea port held by Turks. The attack was a disaster, but it inspired Peter to build a navy. Peter labored side-by-side with thousands of carpenters to build hundreds of ships. When Peter's new navy took up the campaign against Azov, the Turks surrendered.

Modernization and Reform As Russia's ruler, Peter realized that his country needed to modernize to catch up with the rest of Europe. He was determined to bring elements of Western culture to Russia. This process is known as **westernization**.

In 1697 Peter began a journey to western Europe to see for himself what Russia needed to modernize. He traveled in disguise but was sometimes recognized anyway. Wherever Peter went, he learned hands-on skills, especially shipbuilding. He also recruited European experts to bring their skills to Russia.

This historic trip was cut short, though, by a rebellion among the *streltsy*, a military corps that also had political influence. Certain that the *streltsy* wanted to put his sister back on the throne, Peter had many members tortured and then executed. Finally, he disbanded the *streltsy* and organized a more modern army.

In addition to modernizing the army, Peter made many other reforms. He brought the church under state control, built up Russian industry, started the first newspaper in Russia, and sponsored new schools. Peter modernized the calendar and promoted officials based on service instead of their social status.

Direct Teach

Reading Focus

1 How did Ivan IV strengthen the Russian monarchy? *reduced opposition; expanded Russia; increased trade*

The Monarchy of Ivan IV

Recall What kinds of reforms did Ivan IV enact? *worked to create a general council, tried to make army and local governments more fair*

Predict How would Russia's history have been different if Ivan IV had not killed his son? *possible answer—probably would have avoided the "Time of Troubles" and might have developed more rapidly*

Reading Focus

2 What reforms did Peter the Great make in Russia? *strengthened the Russian navy, encouraged modernization and westernization, brought the church under state control, modernized army, built up industry, sponsored new schools, continued to decrease power of boyars*

Peter the Great

Make Inferences Why do you think Peter the Great wanted to westernize Russia? *possible answer—He was favorably impressed with what he saw on his travels in Europe.*

Predict How do you think Peter's emphasis on modernization and westernization will affect Russia's relations with the rest of Europe? *possible answer—draw it into more and more contact, including more wars*

Skills Focus: Comparing and Contrasting

At Level

Reading Skill

Westernization of Russia

Background: Russia westernization was initiated by its ruler, Peter the Great. In other times and places it has been imposed on nations by other nations—a process sometimes referred to as cultural imperialism.

1. Have each student make lists of the advantages and disadvantages of westernization in the Russia of Peter the Great.
2. Review student lists as a class. As you do so, create a class list of the advantages and disadvantages for all to see.
3. Guide students in a discussion of westernization. Have students identify other places westernization has occurred, and where—and in what ways—it has been resisted. **LS Visual-Spatial**

Alternative Assessment Handbook, Rubric 9: Comparing and Contrasting

Answers

Reading Check *early years marked by many reforms that strengthened the government; later years marked by suspicion, creation of royal police, terror*

Direct Teach

Reading Focus

Peter the Great

Recall What were some ways in which Peter the Great attempted to westernize Russia? *encouraged Russians to adopt European styles of clothing and grooming, gained a warm-water port to keep Russia open to western trade year-round*

Analyze In what ways was St. Petersburg significant? *provided warm-water port for Russia, symbolized westernization of Russia*

Teaching Tip

The word *czar* is sometimes spelled *tsar*. In American usage, *czar* is the more common spelling. However, most scholars of Slavic studies prefer the *tsar* spelling, which more closely follows the Russian spelling.

THE IMPACT TODAY

St. Petersburg is Russia's second-largest city and is still a cultural and educational center.

Peter also supported education, believing that Russians needed to learn more about science and other critical fields from the West.

Some reforms were less important but did affect people's daily lives. For example, Peter wanted Russians to adopt European styles of clothing and grooming. Peter even personally cut off the boyars' traditional long coats and beards so they would look more European. The boyars resented and resisted such actions.

Through these and other reforms, Peter tried to impose his will on the Russian people and make Russia a more modern country. Although he was not always successful, Peter the Great is often considered the founder of modern Russia for his efforts.

Founding of St. Petersburg In addition to his many reforms, Peter also founded a new city. In the early 1700s, Peter fought Sweden to acquire a warm-water port. Russia's other ports were choked by ice much of the year. A port farther south on the Baltic Sea would keep Russia open to western trade all year long and help connect Russia to the west.

On land he won from Sweden, Peter built a new capital, St. Petersburg, and Russia's government was moved to the new city. St. Petersburg featured Western-style architecture, rather than traditional Russian styles.

READING CHECK **Recall** Name three ways in which Peter the Great attempted to westernize Russia.

FACES OF HISTORY Peter the Great, 1672–1725

Notice the regal posture, shining armor, and rich fabrics in this official portrait.

Portrait of Peter I the Great, by Jean Marc Nattier, 1717

This Dutch painting shows Peter in a casual pose, with unkempt hair, beard stubble, and the clothing of a laborer.

Portrait of Peter the Great, Dutch school, no date

Do these two portraits really show the same person—the powerful Peter the Great? They do indeed! The portrait on the left shows him as Peter I, Czar of Russia. On the right, he is shown as a common Dutch shipbuilder, a disguise he adopted on a trip to Europe to learn firsthand the secrets of Western technology. Under an assumed name, Peter even earned a certificate as a qualified shipwright. Also in Europe, Peter learned new printing methods and participated in surgical operations. He even learned basic dentistry and enjoyed pulling his servants' teeth. To learn additional skills from the West, Peter persuaded hundreds of craft workers, doctors, engineers, naval officers, and other experts to come to Russia.

Skills Focus READING LIKE A HISTORIAN

1. **Analyze** If Peter had seen the portrait on the right, do you think he would have liked it? Why or why not?
2. **Evaluate** How do these portraits affect your evaluation of Peter the Great?

Skills Focus: Identifying Main Idea and Details

At Level

Reading Skill

The Greats

1. Tell students they are newspaper reporters in czarist Russia preparing to interview either Peter the Great or Catherine the Great. Have each student choose one of the two "great" Russian rulers and write that ruler's name at the top of a sheet of paper. Have students write a series of questions that they would like to ask that ruler.
2. Have students exchange questions. Now tell students they are the ruler whose name is at the top of the list of questions. Have students answer the questions as they think that ruler would have.
3. Have volunteers share the questions they answered, along with their answers, with the rest of the class.
4. Guide students in a discussion of the two rulers based on their interviews. **LS Verbal-Linguistic**

Alternative Assessment Handbook, Rubric 23: Newspapers

Answers

Faces of History **1.** *possible answer—yes, because he looks regal, wealthy, and strong;* **2.** *possible answer—They illustrate that Peter the Great was willing to go to great lengths to westernize Russia.*

Reading Check *by encouraging men to shave off their beards, encouraging people to adopt European styles of dress, building a new capital with Western-style architecture*

GEOGRAPHY SKILLS INTERPRETING MAPS

1. **Regions** During what time period was most of Siberia added to Russia?
2. **Movement** What was the general direction of Russian expansion?

Catherine the Great

Russia's next important ruler was actually a German princess who came to Russia to marry a grandson of Peter the Great. She became known as **Catherine the Great**.

Catherine Takes Power After her husband became Czar Peter III in 1761, Catherine and many Russian nobles grew angry at his weak and incompetent rule. With the help of her allies, Catherine seized power from the new czar, who was murdered. Catherine II was declared czarina of Russia. The word *czarina* is the female form of "czar."

Early Reforms Catherine saw herself as the true successor of Peter the Great and worked to build on his westernization efforts. To emphasize the legitimacy of her claim, she built a bronze statue in St. Petersburg honoring Peter. It was inscribed "To Peter the First, from Catherine the Second."

Catherine began an ambitious plan of reforms. She was influenced by major European thinkers of the time who believed that a strong and wise ruler could improve life for his or her subjects. Catherine reformed Russia's legal and education systems and removed some restrictions on trade. She also promoted science and the arts.

Challenges to Catherine's Rule As Catherine tried to reform Russia, she was soon distracted by conflict. A few years after taking power, she faced war in Poland, where people wanted freedom from Russian influence. In 1768 the Ottoman Empire joined the Polish cause. Eventually, Russia won the war and took over half of Poland and territory on the Black Sea, a valuable outlet for sea trade.

While the war was still raging, Catherine faced a popular rebellion inside Russia. A man named Yemelyan Pugachev was traveling the countryside claiming that he was Peter III and had not been murdered after all. Pugachev gained support among Russia's peasants and led a ragtag army that took over many areas before the rebellion was put down. In the end, Pugachev was captured and beheaded.

The revolt convinced Catherine that she needed to strengthen the authority of the monarchy in rural areas. She completely reorganized local governments and put their administration in the hands of area landowners and nobles. In return for their service as government officials, Catherine reduced their taxes and gave them absolute control over their lands and peasants.

ACADEMIC VOCABULARY
legitimacy the right to rule

READING CHECK **Analyze** What was one way that Catherine showed she was an absolute monarch?

Direct Teach

Reading Focus

3 How did the rule of Catherine the Great affect Russia? *Russia won a war with Poland and Turkey, splitting Poland with Austria and gaining key territory on the Black Sea.*

Catherine the Great

Recall Who was Catherine the Great? *a German princess who became czarina of Russia*

Explain Why did Catherine change her name and convert to the Russian Orthodox faith? *wanted Russians to accept her as their leader*

Rank Which ruler—Peter or Catherine—do you think was greater? Why? *possible answer—Peter, because he had the greater effect on Russia, westernizing and modernizing Russia and strengthening the monarchy; Catherine merely sought to assume some of his glory*

Map Transparency: The Expansion of Russia

Skills Focus: Drawing Conclusions

At Level

Research Required

Reading Skill

Enlightened Despot or Absolute Monarch?

1. Have students reread the information about Catherine the Great in the Enlightenment chapter.
2. Have students create a two-column chart. In one column, have students list the actions of Catherine the Great that would classify her as an enlightened despot. In the other column, have students list the actions of Catherine the Great that would classify her as an absolute monarch.
3. Organize students into two groups. One group will argue that Catherine was an enlightened despot, and the other will argue that Catherine was an absolute monarch.
4. Guide a class debate on whether Catherine the Great is best classified as an enlightened despot or an absolute monarch. **LS Visual-Spatial, Interpersonal**

Alternative Assessment Handbook, Rubrics 10: Debates; and 13: Graphic Organizers

Answers

Interpreting Maps 1. *by 1689;* **2.** *southward and westward*

Reading Check *possible answers—she strengthened the monarchy's authority in rural areas.*

Direct Teach

Reading Focus

4 What states formed in Central Europe in the 1600s and 1700s? *Estonia, Latvia, Lithuania, Belarus, Moldova, Ukraine, Georgia*

Monarchy and Conflict in Central Europe

Identify What was the Thirty Years' War? *a religious clash between Catholics and Protestants that began in 1618, involved the powerful empires of Central Europe*

Identify Cause and Effect What was one major effect of the Thirty Years' War? *The map of Europe changed.*

CRF: Biography: Maria Theresa

Info to Know

Balance of Power The emergence of Prussia as a major military power after the War of the Austrian Succession affected the balance of power in Europe. When England allied itself with Prussia, an alarmed France allied itself with Austria, and rivalries intensified.

Monarchy and Conflict in Central Europe

Unlike the monarchs of Russia and Western Europe, rulers in Central Europe in the 1500s and 1600s never became absolute monarchs. The Holy Roman Empire, which included most of Central Europe at that time, was headed by a single emperor, but he did not have total authority. His empire included dozens of small states, each with its own ruler, who fought vigorously against increased imperial power.

Since the 1450s, all of the Holy Roman Emperors had come from a single family, the Hapsburgs. In the early 1600s, an attempt by one of the Hapsburg emperors to exert his authority launched a terrible conflict known as the **Thirty Years' War.** Alliances between the Hapsburgs and other European monarchs helped make the war a continent-wide affair.

A Deadly Assault

The Holy Roman Emperor's forces stormed Magdeburg, Germany, in 1631 and butchered two-thirds of the townspeople. Outrage over the slaughter inspired the Swedes under Gustavus Adolphus to fight harder. ***Why could it be said that the battle of Magdeburg was both a victory and defeat for its conquerors?***

The Thirty Years' War The Thirty Years' War began as a religious dispute. In 1618 in Prague (now in the Czech Republic) an official representing Holy Roman Emperor Ferdinand II, who was Roman Catholic, ordered that two Protestant churches be shut down. Local Protestants were furious. They responded by throwing the emperor's representatives out of the palace windows. Although the men landed on a rubbish heap and were unhurt, their dignity was damaged.

The emperor's attempt to control people's religion sparked revolt throughout the region. Nobles in the German states of Bavaria and Austria rebelled against the emperor, and nobles from other states soon joined them. The rulers of other countries became involved in the war as well. The monarchs of Spain, who were also members of the Hapsburg family, joined the war on Ferdinand's side. In response, the king of France, Spain's rival, joined the Protestant opposition. The kings of Denmark and Sweden also joined on the Protestant side.

The Thirty Years' War dragged on until 1648, with devastating effects on Germany. Several million Germans died—in battle, from disease, or starvation because their fields were ruined. In the end, the two sides agreed to the **Treaty of Westphalia**, which ended the war. In addition to extending religious toleration to both Catholics and Protestants, the treaty further reduced the power of the Holy Roman emperor and strengthened the rulers of the states within it.

Austria and Prussia Among the rulers who gained from the treaty were the leaders of Austria and Prussia. Austria was governed by the Hapsburg family, while Prussia's rulers came from a rival family, the Hohenzollerns.

In 1740 the Hapsburg Holy Roman Emperor Charles VI died without a male heir. But before he died he had approved a document called the Pragmatic Sanction, which stated that the empire could be passed to a female heir. It seemed his daughter, **Maria Theresa**, would take the throne.

Skills Focus: Comparing and Contrasting

At Level

Reading Skill

The Hapsburgs and the Hohenzollerns

1. Maria Theresa and Frederick II came to power at the same time. Have students make charts comparing and contrasting the two rulers, including comparisons of their families and the history and geography of the nations they led.
2. Review student charts as a class.
3. Guide students in a discussion of the Hapsburgs and the Hohenzollerns based on their charts. Use the following questions: What effect did the histories of Austria and Prussia have on their rulers' behavior? How did their family backgrounds influence them? How did the fact that Maria Theresa was a woman affect relations between Austria and Prussia? Do you think her gender was really a factor, or just an excuse? Which ruler do you think was more effective? Why? Under which ruler would you rather have lived? Why? **LS Visual-Spatial**

Alternative Assessment Handbook, Rubrics 7: Charts; and 11: Discussions

Answers

A Deadly Assault *because many people died, but the loss inspired the Swedes to fight even harder*

The Hohenzollerns had a different plan. Frederick II of Prussia, also called **Frederick the Great**, seized the Austrian province of Silesia, which had minerals and industries. To avoid a long war, Frederick offered Maria Theresa an alliance. He also promised to help her husband become Holy Roman Emperor. Maria Theresa turned him down, and the War of the Austrian Succession broke out in 1740. Soon Spain, France, and two German states entered the war on Prussia's side, each hoping to gain territory. With so much against her, Maria Theresa asked for peace in 1748. Prussia kept Silesia, launching Prussia to a position of real power.

Continued Rivalry Prussia's victory only intensified the rivalry between Austria and Hungary, and it was not long before war broke out again. In 1756 the Seven Years' War began. On one side were Prussia—still ruled by Frederick the Great—and Great Britain. On the other were Austria, France, and Russia. Fighting occurred not just in Europe, but also in the enemies' colonies in North America and India.

During the first part of the war, Prussia was on the verge of defeat. At one point, Austrian and Russian forces even occupied the capital, Berlin. But then Russia pulled out of the war, allowing Prussia to regain strength. Eventually, Prussia emerged as the strongest military power in Europe. With his newfound might, Frederick pushed his opponents out of Prussia. As a result, the war ended in 1763 with both sides exhausted. However, the rivalry between Austria and Prussia was far from over. Hapsburgs and Hohenzollerns struggled for control of Central Europe for many more years.

CENTRAL EUROPE, 1763

GEOGRAPHY SKILLS INTERPRETING MAPS

Location Why might the locations of Hapsburg and Hohenzollern holdings have caused conflict with other powers?

READING CHECK **Recall** What were three wars that affected Central Europe?

SECTION 4 ASSESSMENT

go.hrw.com
Online Quiz
Keyword: SHL MON HP

Reviewing Ideas, Terms, and People

1. **a. Define** Write a brief definition for the following terms: czar, boyars.
   b. Explain Why was Ivan IV known as Ivan the Terrible?
   c. Develop Why would uncertainty about who would be czar contribute to a Time of Troubles?
2. **a. Identify** What was the significance of Russia's new capital at St. Petersburg?
   b. Draw Conclusions Do you think Peter I earned the name Peter the Great? Why or why not?
3. **a. Recall** How did Catherine the Great become czarina?
   b. Explain How did Pugachev's revolt affect her reign?
4. **a. Describe** How did the Thirty Years' War begin?
   b. Identify Cause and Effect How did the rivalry between the Hapsburgs and Hohenzollerns affect Central Europe?

Critical Thinking

5. **Compare and Contrast** Use your notes and a chart like the one below to identify major figures in Russia and Central Europe, key events, and the roles they played in those events.

Person	Event	Role

FOCUS ON WRITING

6. **Persuasion** Imagine that you are a German engineer who has moved to Russia to help Peter the Great build St. Petersburg. Write a letter in which you try to persuade another professional back home to come work with you in Russia.

Direct Teach

Info to Know

The Art of Governing Frederick William I worried about the worthiness of his son to rule because of Frederick II's interest in the arts and philosophy rather than in the military or government.

Map Transparency: Central Europe, 1763

Review & Assess

Close

Have students create a time line to place important events in Russia and Central Europe in chronological sequence.

Review

Online Quiz, Section 4

Assess

SE Section 4 Assessment

Progress Assessment: Section 4 Quiz

Alternative Assessment Handbook

Reteach/Intervene

Interactive Reader and Study Guide, Section 4

Interactive Skills Tutor CD-ROM

Answers

Interpreting Maps *possible answer—The Hapsburg and Hohenzollern lands bordered strong powers on all sides, and many of those powers hoped to expand.*

Section 4 Assessment Answers

1. **a.** czar: the title chosen by Ivan IV for himself, adapted from the word *caesar*, which the Romans used to mean "emperor"; boyars: wealthy Russian landowners
   b. latter part of his rule marked by terror
   c. possible answer—There was no strong leadership to keep order.
2. **a.** symbolized Peter the Great's efforts to modernize and westernize Russia, featured western-style architecture
   b. possible answers—yes, he expanded Russia's borders and increased trade, brought Russia into closer contact with western Europe, modernized Russia; no, cruel actions undermined achievements
3. **a.** married a grandson of Peter the Great
   b. showed Catherine she needed to strengthen her authority in rural areas
4. **a.** Most of Europe became involved for either religious or political reasons.
   b. intensified other European rivalries; led to War of Austrian Succession and Seven Years' War
5. Peter the Great—Events: Great Northern War; building of St. Petersburg; Role: westernizer and modernizer of Russia; Catherine the Great—Event: Pugachev's rebellion; Role: absolute ruler; Maria Theresa—Events: War of Austrian Succession; Seven Years' War; Roles: heir to Austrian throne; ally of France, Russia; Frederick the Great—Event: Seven Years' War; Role: ally of Great Britain, emerged as strongest power in Europe
6. Student letters should focus on the importance of St. Petersburg, both as a warm-water port and a symbol of westernization.

History and Geography

Imperial Saint Petersburg

Info to Know

A Changing City Peter designated St. Petersburg his capital in 1712, but Russia's capital returned to Moscow after the Bolsheviks seized power in 1917. After Lenin's death in 1924, the Communists renamed the city Leningrad. With the collapse of communism and the breakup of the Soviet Union, Leningrad became St. Petersburg again in 1991. Today St. Petersburg remains an important cultural center in Russia. The city is home to the Hermitage, a museum housed in the Winter Palace of Catherine the Great.

HISTORY & Geography

Imperial St. Petersburg

Cities reflect the history of the rulers who built and ruled them. St. Petersburg certainly reflects the determination of Peter the Great to create a grand new capital with a warm-water port. Peter started construction on the city in 1703—even before he had truly won the land from Sweden. The site he chose was actually a dank swamp—a place so hazardous that some 40,000 Swedish prisoners of war died while building the city. Their bones went into the city's foundations. After Peter's rule, his successors added more features that were heavily influenced by Western European styles.

▼ This 1712 map shows Peter's original plan for the city.

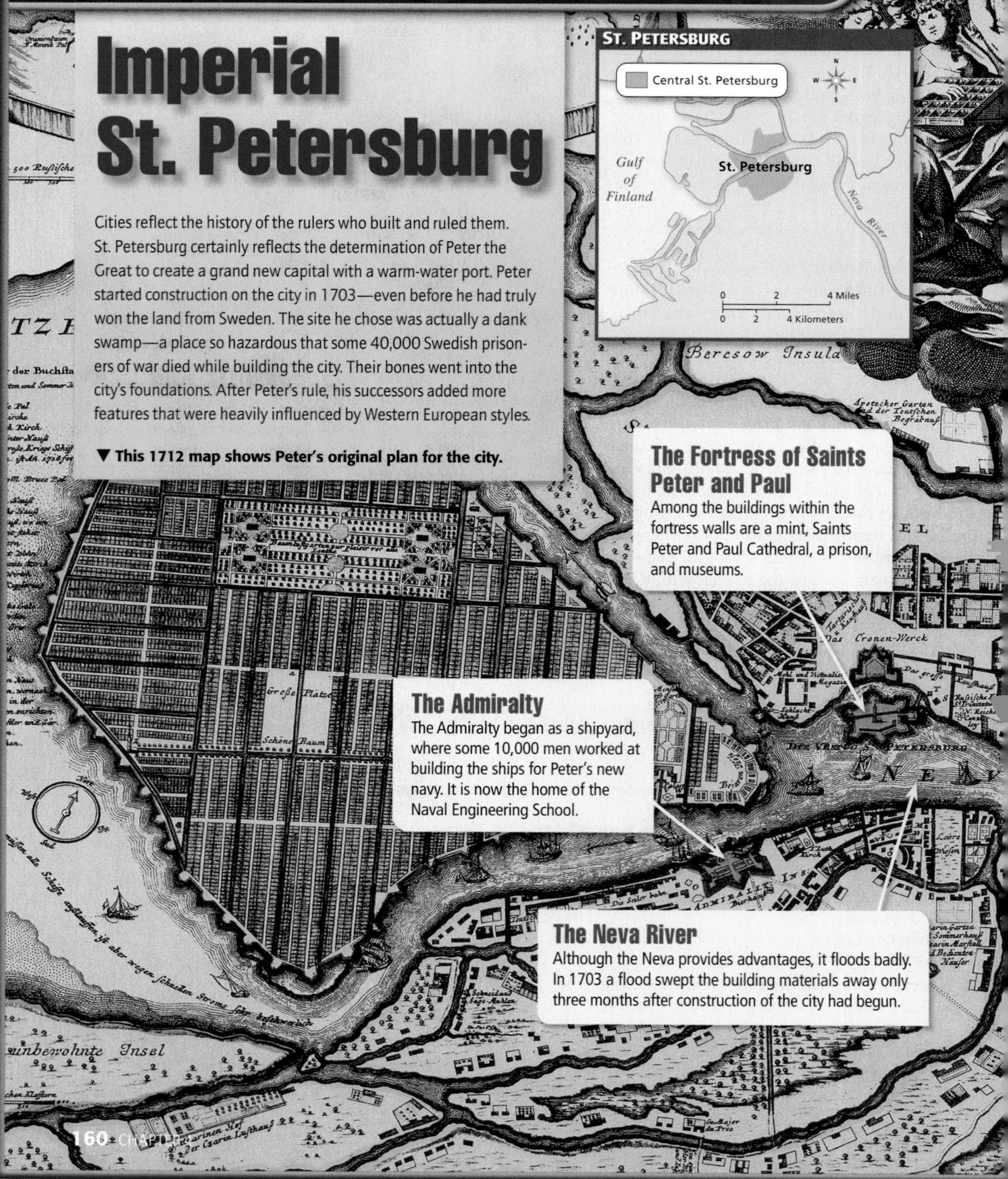

Beresow Insula
unbewohnte Insel
The Fortress of Saints Peter and Paul
Among the buildings within the fortress walls are a mint, Saints Peter and Paul Cathedral, a prison, and museums.
The Admiralty
The Admiralty began as a shipyard, where some 10,000 men worked at building the ships for Peter's new navy. It is now the home of the Naval Engineering School.
The Neva River
Although the Neva provides advantages, it floods badly. In 1703 a flood swept the building materials away only three months after construction of the city had begun.
ST. PETERSBURG
Central St. Petersburg
Gulf of Finland
St. Petersburg
Neva River
0 2 4 Miles
0 2 4 Kilometers

Skills Focus: Interpreting Historical Maps

At Level

Social Studies Skill

St. Petersburg in 1712

1. Explain to students that the map on this page is an actual historical map showing Peter the Great's plan for his capital city. Direct students' attention to the inset map. Ask students to identify why this location was chosen for St. Petersburg. What challenges might it have presented to city builders?
2. Organize students into groups of four to six. Tell them they are city planners for Peter the Great and will be presenting their plans for St. Petersburg to the czar, using this map as a visual source.
3. Have groups prepare oral presentations, which should answer the following questions: What advantages does the new capital provide to Russia? How have city planners overcome challenges, such as flooding? What buildings in the new city represent the glory and strength of Russia? Tell students they must convince the czar that these plans fulfill his dreams for a capital city.
4. Have groups give their presentations to the rest of the class. **LS Visual-Spatial, Interpersonal**

Alternative Assessment Handbook, Rubric 24: Oral Presentations

GEOGRAPHY SKILLS **INTERPRETING MAPS**

1. **Location** Peter's original plan was for Vasilevskiy Island, at the far left, to be the city's center. That plan was abandoned, and the city grew up around the Admiralty. What may have accounted for the change in plans?
2. **Place** How do you think early visitors to St. Petersburg reacted to the buildings pictured here?

▼ This view of a bridge over the Neva River shows the grandeur of St. Petersburg.

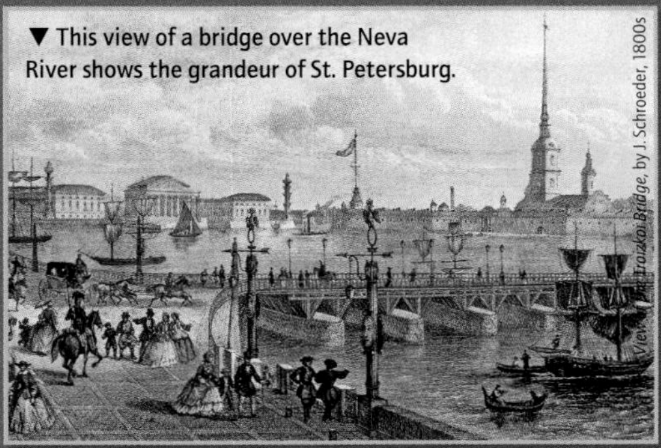

View of Troitsky Bridge, by J. Schroeder, 1800s

▲ Several palaces make up the Hermitage. The original palace was built for Peter's daughter Elizabeth, who took the Russian throne in 1741. Today, the Hermitage is one of the world's finest art museums.

▲ Peterhof, Peter the Great's own palace, is outside the city, linked directly to the Gulf of Finland by a canal. Pictured above is the Grand Cascade.

History and Geography

Teaching Tip

Remind students that the Renaissance writer Niccolò Machiavelli argued that it is safer for a monarch to be feared than to be loved. Have students interpret this argument and ask them if they think Peter the Great was more loved or feared. Explain that Peter's great accomplishments, such as the building of St. Petersburg, contrast with his disregard for the profound human suffering he caused. Discuss whether glorious ends justify brutal means.

Differentiating Instruction

Below Level

Learners Having Difficulty

1. Draw the chart for all to see. Omit the italicized answers.
2. Have students copy and complete the chart individually or in small groups, using the visuals on this spread. When charts are completed, review them as a class. Have students use their charts to make general observations about St. Petersburg. **LS Visual-Spatial**

Alternative Assessment Handbook, Rubrics 7: Charts; and 21: Map Reading

Imperial St. Petersburg

Buildings	Geography	Building Challenges
• *The Admiralty* • *Saints Peter and Paul Cathedral* • *Mint* • *Prison* • *Museums* • *Hermitage* • *Peterhof*	• *swampland* • *warm-water port* • *Neva River*	• *flooding* • *death of workers*

Answers

Interpreting Maps 1. *possible answers—island might have flooded, might have wanted city center closer to the Fortress of Saints Peter and Paul;* **2.** *possible answer—Visitors were probably awed by the grandeur of the buildings.*

Document-Based Investigation

Views of Absolutism

Activity Political Cartoons Review Document 1 with students, and have them answer the related questions. Then, have students draw the same political cartoon from the opposite point of view. Tell students they can do this simply by changing or removing certain elements of the original cartoon.
LS Visual-Spatial

Teaching Tip

Remind students that Louis XIV is famous for saying "L'état, c'est moi." In English this translates to "I am the state." Discuss with students how this short phrase captures the idea of absolutism.

CHAPTER 4 **Document-Based Investigation**

Views of Absolutism

Historical Context These documents reveal different reactions to absolutism, a dominant political theory in the 1500s through 1700s in parts of Europe.

Task Study the selections and answer the questions that follow. After you have studied all the documents, you will be asked to write an essay supporting or criticizing absolutism. You will need to use evidence from these selections and from the chapter to support the position you take in your essay.

DOCUMENT 1

Queen Catherine's Dream

This English cartoon shows Catherine the Great being offered the cities of Warsaw and Constantinople by the devil. The title is "Queen Catherine's Dream." Catherine claimed to be fighting the Turks to free Constantinople and the Ottoman Empire from Muslim rule. The English had a different view. They accused her of simply wanting more territory.

Queen Catherine's Dream, by Richard Newton, 1791

DOCUMENT 2

The Sun King's Emblem

Louis XIV chose the sun as his emblem because of the "unique quality of the radiance . . . the good it does in every place." He believed that "the profession of king is great, noble, a fount of delight" and that "God who made you king will give you the necessary guidance." The golden emblem shown here is from Versailles, the elaborate palace that Louis built outside the city of Paris.

Réunion des Musées Nationaux / Art Resource, NY

Skills Focus: Analyzing Visuals

Above Level

Reading Like a Historian Skill
The Treasure of Versailles

Materials: blank paper or posterboard

1. Explain to students that the gold emblem shown in Document 2 is just one of the many luxurious objects found in the palace of Louis XIV. Have students conduct independent research about the treasures of Versailles.
2. Have students create posters illustrating some of the treasures they found. Posters should include accompanying text that describes the objects and how they symbolize the power of the French monarchy.
3. Display student posters for all to see.
LS Visual-Spatial, Intrapersonal

Alternative Assessment Handbook, Rubrics 28: Posters; and 30: Research

Document 3

On the Divine Right of Kings

Jacques Benigne Bossuet, Bishop of Meaux, served as tutor to the French heir to the throne. Bossuet strongly supported absolutism in this excerpt from his treatise titled *Politics Derived from Holy Writ.*

> We have already seen that all power is of God . . . Rulers then act as the ministers of God and as his lieutenants on earth. It is through them that God exercises his empire . . . The royal throne is not the throne of a man, but the throne of God himself . . .
>
> Note what is said in Ecclesiasticus: "God has given to every people its ruler." . . . He therefore governs all peoples and gives them their kings . . .
>
> But kings, although their power comes from on high, . . . must employ it with fear and self-restraint, as a thing coming from God and of which God will demand an account . . .
>
> God is infinite, God is all. The prince, as prince, is not regarded as a private person: he is a public personage, all the state is in him; the will of all the people is included in his. As all perfection and all strength are united in God, so all the power of individuals is united in the person of the prince.

Document 4

Why Did Charles I Fight the Civil War?

Here British historian Conrad Russell expresses his views on the limitations that monarchs faced.

> The belief that it was the duty of a ruler to enforce uniformity in the true religion was one which caused difficulties . . . Philip II in the Netherlands failed in this task for reasons not altogether different from those of Charles I. Both felt themselves obliged to fight rather than give up the struggle . . .
>
> For him, [Charles I] then, the problem of religious unity was one of unity between kingdoms . . . On this point, Charles's Scottish opponents agreed with him. They too thought that unless there was unity of religion and church government between England and Scotland, there would be permanent instability . . . Charles, moreover, did not only have a King of England's resistance to Scottish notions of Presbyterianising England: he also had to view such a proposal through the eyes of the King of Ireland. A religious settlement in which it would have been a key point that no papists were to be tolerated would hardly have led to stability in Ireland . . . Of all the participants in the crisis of 1640–42, Charles was the only one whose position forced him to a genuinely British perspective.

Skills Focus: Reading Like a Historian

Document 1

a. Describe What elements of the cartoon suggest that the cartoonist is suspicious of Catherine's motives?

b. Infer How does the cartoon reflect the history of absolutism in England, in contrast to its history in Russia?

Document 2

a. Analyze Why do you think Louis chose this emblem? Is it an appropriate emblem for Louis XIV?

b. Infer What do you think the effect of this emblem might have been on the people who saw it at Versailles?

Document 3

a. Identify On what basis does Bossuet justify absolutism?

b. Analyze Does Bossuet think there are any limitations on the king's power? Why or why not?

Document 4

a. Describe What limited Charles I's choices?

b. Infer How does the writer view Charles I's decisions?

Document-Based Essay Question

People held different views on the proper role of the monarch and the limits of royal authority. Using the documents above and information from the chapter, form a thesis that supports a role for absolute monarchy or argues for limits on royal power. Consider if there were both benefits and hazards of absolutism. Then write a short essay to support your position.

See **Skills Handbook**, pp. H25, H26

Document-Based Investigation

Word Help

personage person of distinction

papist disparaging, or degrading term for a Roman Catholic

Info to Know

The Divine Right In England, the execution of Charles I symbolizes the end of divine right. Although the monarchy would eventually return to England, future monarchs were forced to accept limits on their power. Elsewhere in Europe, however, absolutism and the idea of divine right continued for many years. As late as the 1900s, Czar Nicholas II of Russia and Emperor Wilhelm II of Prussia claimed to receive their power from God.

Answers

Document 1. a. *She is being given territory by the devil.* **b.** *possible answer—By the time Catherine the Great ruled Russia, monarchs in England had been forced to accept limits on their power.* **Document 2. a.** *possible answer—Yes, the sun is present everywhere and affects almost everything.* **b.** *possible answer—might have inspired them to believe in the power of their king;* **Document 3. a.** *that God gave rulers their absolute power;* **b.** *Yes, God will punish rulers if they misuse their power.* **Document 4. a.** *the political and religious views of Scotland and Ireland;* **b.** *as genuinely British;* **Essay** *Student essays should either argue for limits on royal power, using examples from England and their reading in the chapter, or for absolute monarchy, using examples from Document 2, Document 3, and the chapter. Essays should be supported by detail and logic.*

Differentiating Instruction — Below Level

Learners Having Difficulty

1. Review each document with students. Have students summarize the message or significance of each document in their own words.
2. Tell students that the four documents represent different perspectives on absolute rule. Have students classify each document as either supporting absolute rule or supporting limits on royal power.
3. Organize a class debate on whether monarchs should rule with absolute power, or whether they should have limits on their power. Have students base their arguments on each document and the text in this chapter. **LS Interpersonal**

Alternative Assessment Handbook, Rubrics 10: Debates; and 38: Writing to Classify

Answers

Visual Summary

Review and Inquiry Organize students into five groups. Assign each group one of the areas shown in the Visual Study Guide. Have groups prepare an oral presentation to give to the rest of the class, reviewing key rulers and events of their area.

Quick Facts Transparency: Visual Study Guide: The Monarchs of Europe

Review Key Terms and People

1. Thirty Years' War
2. Glorious Revolution
3. Peace of Augsburg
4. Cardinal Richelieu
5. Huguenots
6. legitimacy
7. Spanish Armada
8. divine right
9. Royalists

Comprehension and Critical Thinking

10. a. its large size; conflict between Protestants and Catholics
b. naval battles, English fireships, and storms
c. possible answer—Despite great wealth, Spain faced economic failure and decline.

11. a. The Saint Bartholomew's Day Massacre began.
b. These groups threatened the absolute power of the monarch.
c. Over 200,000 Huguenots fled France after the edict was revoked, causing an economic crisis.

12. a. He placed restrictions on English social life.
b. because many people were unhappy during Cromwell's reign and the reign of his son
c. English monarchs accepted limits on their power.

13. a. Ivan the Terrible
b. high points—reforms, winning Great Northern War, building St. Petersburg; low points—storming of Azov, rebellion of *strelsky*
c. because most fighting took place in Germany, and several million Germans died in the war

Reading Skills

14. possible answer—that the Reformation began in Germany in 1517 and spread throughout Europe; key terms such as "Protestant Reformation" and "Calvinist"

CHAPTER 4

Chapter Review

QUICK FACTS

VISUAL STUDY GUIDE

Monarchs of Europe: 1500–1800

Spain

Ruler	Major Events	Results of Reign
Charles V	Many enemies, Reformation, Peace of Augsburg	Spain powerful; empire divided between heirs
Philip II	Dutch revolt, Armada defeat	Spain weakened

France

Ruler	Major Events	Results of Reign
Henry IV	Survived massacre, issued Edict of Nantes	Calmed religious conflict, repaired war-torn country
Louis XIII	La Rochelle, clash with nobles, Thirty Years' War	Huguenots and nobles weakened
Louis XIV	Versailles built, revocation of the Edict of Nantes, military buildup	Absolutism firmly established, economic growth, expensive wars

Central Europe

Ruler	Major Events	Results of Reign
Maria Theresa (Austria)	War of Austrian Succession, Seven Years War	Continued competition with Hohenzollerns
Frederick II (the Great) (Prussia)	War of Austrian Succession, Seven Years War	Prussia as major European power

England

Ruler	Major Events	Results of Reign
Henry VIII	Split with pope	Parliament strengthened
Elizabeth I	War with Spain	England undefeated
Charles I	Led troops into Parliament	Executed amid English Civil War
Cromwell	Civil War, conflicts abroad	Ruled alone, created resentment
Charles II	Restoration	Habeas Corpus Act
William and Mary	Glorious Revolution, English Bill of Rights	Parliament's power greatly increased

Russia

Ruler	Major Events	Results of Reign
Ivan IV	Reforms, expanded territory, terror	Time of Troubles
Peter I (the Great)	Reforms, *streltsy* rebellion, St. Petersburg built	Beginning of westernization
Catherine II (the Great)	Rebellion, rural government reform	More power for nobles over serfs

Review Key Terms and People

Identify the correct term or person from the chapter that best fits each of the following descriptions.

1. war that lasted from 1618 to 1648 and devastated Germany
2. transfer of power to William III and Mary II
3. treaty that gave the rulers of German states the right to decide the religion of their states
4. the most trusted adviser of King Louis XIII
5. French Protestants
6. the right to rule
7. fleet that tried to invade England in 1588
8. belief that God grants absolute power to monarchs
9. supporters of Charles I

History's Impact video program
Review the video to answer the closing question:
When was Spain's Golden Century, and how was it financed?

Comprehension and Critical Thinking

SECTION 1 *(pp. 137–140)*

10. a. Recall What were two reasons why Charles V had a difficult time ruling his empire?

b. Sequence What events foiled the Spanish Armada's invasion of England?

c. Elaborate Why might a historian title a book about Spain from 1550 to 1650 *A Glorious Failure*?

SECTION 2 *(pp. 142–146)*

11. a. Identify What happened in Paris early in the morning on August 24, 1572?

b. Explain Why did Cardinal Richelieu want to crush the power of the nobles and the Huguenots?

c. Elaborate Why was the revocation of the Edict of Nantes a problem for more people than just the Huguenots?

SECTION 3 *(pp. 147–152)*

12. a. Describe How did Cromwell change English society?

b. Infer Why did the people of London cheer Charles II when he returned from exile?

c. Develop The English monarchy developed in a very different direction than did the monarchies of Spain and France. How did it differ?

SECTION 4 *(pp. 154–159)*

13. a. Identify By what name is Ivan IV often remembered?

b. Compare and Contrast What were some high points and low points of Peter the Great's rule?

c. Draw Conclusions Why was the Thirty Years' War one of the worst disasters in German history?

Reading Skills

Connecting *Read the passage below from this chapter. Then answer the question that follows.*

"Soon after the Protestant Reformation began in Germany, it spread to France. By the 1560s, about one in ten French men and women was a Huguenot, or French Calvinist Protestant."

14. How does this passage connect with what you learned in a previous chapter about the Reformation? Which words help you remember what you have learned?

Interpreting Political Cartoons

Reading Like a Historian *Peter the Great wanted to westernize Russia. He even ordered Russian men to cut their beards so they would look more European.*

Woodcut showing Russian official cutting off a beard, artist unknown

15. Analyze Do you think the artist approved of Peter's rule? Why or why not?

Using the Internet

go.hrw.com
Practice Online
Keyword: SHL MON

16. The era of absolute monarchs was also a key period for the extension of government functions. Rulers set up more effective administrations and got involved in new activities, such as building hospitals. Using the keyword above, research expansion of the government's role in one country and write a report on your findings.

WRITING FOR THE SAT

Think about the following issue:

The concept of absolutism influenced monarchs to varying degrees, and the monarchs' reigns affected their countries long after their deaths.

17. Assignment: Some monarchs left their countries in better condition than when they began their rule, while others left lasting damage. Choose three of the monarchs from the chapter and, in a brief essay, compare and contrast how absolutism affected those rulers' impact on their countries.

Answers

Interpreting Political Cartoons

15. possible answer—The artist probably approved of Peter's rule because the tone of the cartoon is light, and he makes fun of the nobleman being forced to change his formal appearance.

Using the Internet

16. Go to the HRW Web site and enter the keyword shown to access a rubric for this activity.

KEYWORD: SHL MON

Writing for the SAT

17. Student essays should discuss three of the monarchs covered in the chapter. Essays should use supporting details and examples to make a logical argument about the rulers' impact on their countries. A rubric for this activity is provided in **CRF:** Writing for the SAT.

HOLT

History's Impact

► **Video Program: The Monarchs of Europe**
Refer to the Video Program Teacher's Guide for a discussion of the closing question.

Review and Assessment Resources

Review and Reinforce

- **CRF:** Chapter Review
- **Quick Facts Transparency**: Visual Study Guide: The Monarchs of Europe
- **Spanish Chapter Summaries Audio CD Program**
- OSP **Holt PuzzlePro**: Quiz Show for ExamView
- **Quiz Game CD-ROM**

Assess

- **PASS**: Chapter Test, Forms A and B
- **Alternative Assessment Handbook**
- OSP **ExamView Test Generator**, Chapter Test
- **Differentiated Instruction Modified Worksheets and Tests CD-ROM**: Chapter Test
- HOAP **Holt Online Assessment Program** (in the Premier Online Edition)

Reteach/Intervene

- **Interactive Reader and Study Guide**
- **Differentiated Instruction Teacher Management System**: Lesson Plans for Differentiated Instruction
- **Differentiated Instruction Modified Worksheets and Tests CD-ROM**: Chapter Test
- **Interactive Skills Tutor CD-ROM**

go.hrw.com
Online Resources
KEYWORD: SHL TEACHER

Chapter 5 Planning Guide

Enlightenment and Revolution

Chapter Overview	Reproducible Resources	Technology Resources
CHAPTER 5 **pp. 166–191** **Overview: In this chapter, students will study the effect of new discoveries and ideas about government and society during the Enlightenment. They will also learn how the influence of Enlightenment ideas led to the establishment of the United States.**	**Differentiated Instruction Teacher Management System:** * • Pacing Guide • Lesson Plans for Differentiated Instruction **Interactive Reader and Study Guide:** Chapter Summary* **Chapter Resource File*** • Writing About History • Social Studies Skill • Chapter Review **World History Outline Maps**	**Live Ink© Online Reading Help** **Student Edition on Audio CD Program** **Differentiated Instruction Modified Worksheets and Tests CD-ROM** **Interactive Skills Tutor CD-ROM** **World History Primary Source Library CD-ROM** **Power Presentations with Video CD-ROM** **History's Impact: World History Video Program (VHS/DVD):** Enlightenment and Revolution
Section 1: **The Scientific Revolution** **The Main Idea:** New ways of thinking led to remarkable discoveries during the Scientific Revolution.	**Differentiated Instruction Teacher Management System:** Section 1 Lesson Plan* **Interactive Reader and Study Guide:** Section 1 Summary* **Chapter Resource File*** • Vocabulary Builder: Section 1 • Biography: Carl Linnaeus • Primary Source: The Compatibility of Science and Religion	**Daily Test Practice Transarency:** Section 1* **Map Transparency:** European Centers of Learning, c. 1750* **Quick Facts Transparency:** The Scientific Method* **Quick Facts Transparency:** Causes and Effects of the Scientific Revolution*
Section 2: **The Enlightenment** **The Main Idea:** European thinkers developed new ideas about government and society during the Enlightenment.	**Differentiated Instruction Teacher Management System:** Section 2 Lesson Plan* **Interactive Reader and Study Guide:** Section 2 Summary* **Chapter Resource File*** • Vocabulary Builder: Section 2 • Biography: Madame Geoffrin	**Daily Test Practice Transparency:** Section 2* **Quick Facts Transparency:** Key Enlightenment Ideas* **Internet Activity:** John Locke
Section 3: **The American Revolution** **The Main Idea:** Enlightenment ideas led to revolution, independence, and a new government for the United States.	**Differentiated Instruction Teacher Management System:** Section 3 Lesson Plan* **Interactive Reader and Study Guide:** Section 3 Summary* **Chapter Resource File*** • Vocabulary Builder: Section 3 • Biography: Benjamin Franklin • Literature: *Rip Van Winkle* • History and Geography: Battles in the War for Independence	**Daily Test Practice Transparency:** Section 3* **Map Transparency:** The Revolutionary War* **Internet Activity:** The Enlightenment

go.hrw.com | Print Resource | Transparency
LS Learning Styles | Audio CD | CD-ROM
Video | SE Student Edition | TE Teachers Edition
OSP One-Stop Planner CD-ROM
*also on One-Stop Planner CD-ROM

HOLT
History's Impact
World History Video Program (VHS/DVD)
Enlightenment and Revolution

Review, Assessment, Intervention

- **Quick Facts Transparency:** Enlightenment and Revolution*
- **Spanish Chapter Summaries Audio CD Program**
- **Progress Assessment Support System (PASS):** Chapter Test*
- **Differentiated Instruction Modified Worksheets and Tests CD-ROM:** Modified Chapter Test
- OSP **One-Stop Planner CD-ROM:** ExamView Test Generator (English/Spanish)
- HOAP **Holt Online Assessment Program (HOAP),** in the Holt Premier Online Student Edition

---

- **PASS:** Section 1 Quiz*
- **Online Quiz:** Section 1
- **Alternative Assessment Handbook**

- **PASS:** Section 2 Quiz*
- **Online Quiz:** Section 2
- **Alternative Assessment Handbook**

- **PASS:** Section 3 Quiz*
- **Online Quiz:** Section 3
- **Alternative Assessment Handbook**

Power Presentation with Video CD-ROM

Power Presentations with Video are visual presentations of each chapter's main ideas. Presentations can be customized by including Quick Facts charts, images and maps from the textbook, and video clips.

Holt Online Learning

go.hrw.com
Teacher Resources
KEYWORD: SHL TEACHER

go.hrw.com
Student Resources
KEYWORD: SHL ENL

- Document-Based Questions
- Interactive Multimedia Activities
- Current Events
- Chapter-Based Internet Activities
- and more!

Holt Premier
Online Student Edition

Complete online support for interactivity, assessment, and reporting

- Interactive Maps and Notebook
- Homework Practice and Research Activities Online

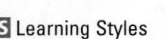

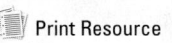

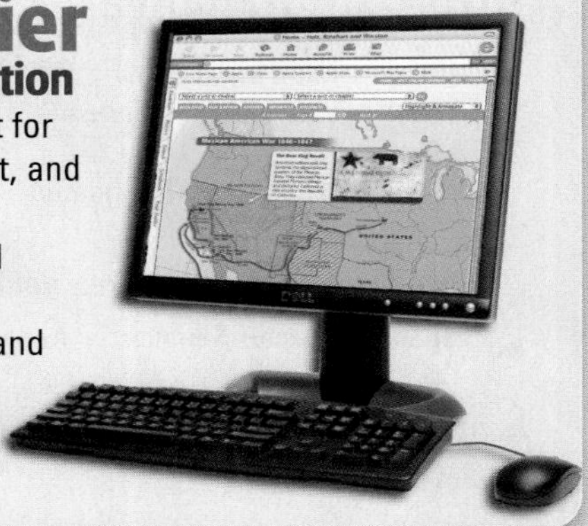

The Big Picture

Peter N. Stearns

Scientific Revolution The Scientific Revolution was a big development in world history, and certainly in European history. European science had not been very advanced, but now it surged forward. New discoveries overturned traditions and provided unprecedented knowledge about the physical universe and the workings of the human body. Clear definitions of scientific methods emerged. The result was not only great innovation, but also the establishment of science as the basis for human knowledge—the first time science had held this position in any culture. Of course there were struggles with established religions, some of which continue, but the basic trend was clear.

Implications of the Scientific Revolution: The Enlightenment Growing literacy and weariness with earlier religious quarrels set a context for wide popular interest in the new science. Various intellectuals also began to apply new thinking to political and social topics. John Locke held a central role in setting up the Enlightenment, both in his praise of popular sovereignty and religious tolerance and in his belief in the educability of children. Enlightenment thinkers, centered in France, applied new methods to the study of government, praising constitutions, legal equality, and, in some cases, democracy. Criticism of older institutions like the church and the aristocracy ran strong. Enlightenment figures also praised technological progress, urged a reform of criminal justice, and established new social sciences, including economics. A few maverick voices claimed even more, staking out feminist and socialist arguments. The Enlightenment set an intellectual basis for a wide variety of reform and protest movements.

The American Revolution New ideas, the examples of the earlier English civil wars, and new, widely resented colonial measures by the British government set the context for the American Revolution and the ultimate establishment of national independence. Enlightenment ideas figured strongly in the new United States Constitution, including its protection of personal freedoms in the Bill of Rights. In turn, the American Revolution helped spur political change in other regions, including France.

Recent Scholarship

In *The Household and the Making of History: A Subversive View of the Western Past* (2004), Mary S. Hartman offers a challenging interpretation of gender relations in European society. She argues that distinctive family patterns set up unusual collaborations and tensions between men and women that paralleled more familiar developments in the early modern centuries, including science, in establishing distinctive Western institutions and ideas.

Differentiating Instruction

Differentiated Instruction Teacher Management System
- Pacing Guide
- Lesson Plans for Differentiated Instruction

Interactive Reader and Study Guide

Spanish Chapter Summaries Audio CD Program

Student Edition on Audio CD Program

Differentiated Instruction Modified Worksheets and Tests CD-ROM
- Vocabulary Flash Cards
- Modified Vocabulary Builder Activities
- Modified Chapter Review Activity
- Modified Chapter Test

OSP **One-Stop Planner CD-ROM**
- ExamView Test Generator (English/Spanish)
- PuzzlePro
- Quiz Show for ExamView
- Transparencies and Videos

TE **Differentiated Activities in the Teacher's Edition**
- Foundations of Modern Science, p. 170
- Scientific Method Experiments, p. 171
- Odes to Reason, p. 177
- Discussing the Declaration of Independence, p. 186

Reading Like a Historian

Sam Wineburg

Our chapter quotes the Declaration of Independence and words familiar to many: "We hold these truths to be self-evident, that all men are created equal." However, as some of our students will point out, this documents' author, Thomas Jefferson, was himself a slaveholder. How could Jefferson write about equality while holding African Americans in bondage? Students will often see only one logical conclusion: Jefferson was a hypocrite.

Confronted with documents from the Mayan empire, we have little trouble recognizing the differences between that world and our own. But the Declaration of Independence presents a different kind of problem. Its language is so familiar that we presume it speaks directly to us. If there is a discrepancy between the words of this document and the behavior of its author, we conclude that the problem is not our understanding—but Jefferson's own moral failings.

The challenge in reading history is to understand what documents meant to the people who actually wrote them. This means trying to set aside our present-day conceptions long enough to ask what an author two hundred years ago might have meant. Is it possible that Jefferson intended something different by "all men are created equal" than how we understand the same words today?

The historian and journalist Garry Wills asks this question in his exhaustive study, *Inventing America: Jefferson's Declaration of Independence.* To understand Jefferson, Wills immersed himself in the same works of philosophy that Jefferson read.

Understanding Jefferson We should begin by recognizing that Jefferson shared in many of the taken-for-granted prejudices of his day—particularly in the way that European societies assumed intellectual superiority to those in Africa and Asia. However, Jefferson wrote this statement: "Whether further observation will or will not verify the conjecture that nature has been less bountiful to [Blacks] in the endowments of the head, I believe that in those of the heart she will be found to have done them justice."

Here Jefferson assumes a skeptical stance regarding differences in intellect between Blacks and Whites. But he concludes by stating that "nature" has done Africans "justice" —has put them on an equal footing—in issues of the heart. What are we to make of this curious statement? Is it a throw away line—a patronizing consolation prize in a world that valued head over heart?

Wills points out that this distinction was crucial to Jefferson. To him and the philosophers he drew on, it was the human heart that united humanity far more than the head. Blacks, for Jefferson, were equal to Whites in moral qualities that resided in the heart, in "benevolence, gratitude, and unshaken fidelity," and it is these qualities that represented the highest of human achievements. To the moral philosopher Thomas Hutcheson, whose thought influenced Jefferson's, all men are created equal in their moral capacity, "these natural rights equally belong to all. . . . Nature makes none masters, none slaves."

To us, the separation of head from heart seems like a cynical apology that permitted Jefferson to proclaim equality while enforcing bondage. But in Jefferson's world, this was a real distinction. To Jefferson, according to Wills, "accidental differences of body and mind were dwarfed by an all-important equality in the governing faculty of man. There is no inconsistency in his theory, whatever one may think of its validity. For him it was valid, and everything he wrote about Blacks . . . is derived from its principles."

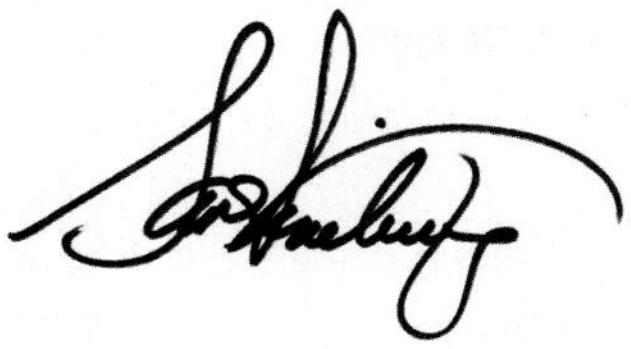

Chapter Preview

Chapter Main Ideas

Section 1 New ways of thinking led to remarkable discoveries during the Scientific Revolution.

Section 2 European thinkers developed new ideas about government and society during the Enlightenment.

Section 3 Enlightenment ideas led to independence and a new government for the United States.

CHAPTER 5

1550–1800

Enlightenment and Revolution

A Philosopher Giving a Lecture at the Orrery, by Joseph Wright of Derby, 1776

THE BIG PICTURE Beginning in the late 1500s, new discoveries and the use of reason in Europe during the Scientific Revolution and the Enlightenment led to changing ideas about government and society. Influenced by Enlightenment ideas, British colonists in North America established a new nation—the United States.

Theme SCIENCE AND TECHNOLOGY
Between about 1550 and 1800 scientists in Europe made advances in science through observation and experimentation. In this chapter you will study these discoveries in science and learn how they affected the world.

TIME LINE

CHAPTER EVENTS

- **1609** In Italy, Galileo develops the first telescope used for astronomy.
- **1690** John Locke publishes *Two Treatises on Civil Government*, arguing that government should protect people's natural rights.
- **1759** Voltaire publishes *Candide*, a novel attacking the church and other institutions of his time.

1600 — 1700 — 1750

WORLD EVENTS

- **1652** Dutch colonists arrive at the Cape of Good Hope.
- **1707** The Mughal Empire ends in India.
- **1769** Spanish missionaries begin founding missions in California.

Key to Differentiating Instruction

Below Level
Basic-level activities designed for all students encountering new material

At Level
Intermediate-level activities designed for average students

Above Level
Challenging activities designed for honors and gifted and talented students

Standard English Mastery
Activities designed to improve standard English usage

Introduce the Chapter

At Level

Enlightenment and Revolution

1. Write this John Locke quote for students to see: "New opinions are always suspected, and usually opposed, without any other reason but because they are not already common."
2. Guide students in a discussion of the meaning of the quote. When students understand the quote, ask them if they agree. Have them brainstorm examples, real or hypothetical, in which new ideas and opinions have been summarily rejected. As volunteers give responses, write them for students to see.
3. Tell students that in this chapter they will learn about a shift in ideas and opinions about nature and society.
4. Have students write a newspaper op-ed column in which they argue that new ideas should be given a fair chance and not rejected outright. Have students use examples from the class list to prove their point. **LS Verbal-Linguistic**

Alternative Assessment Handbook, Rubrics 23: Newspapers; and 43: Writing to Persuade

History's Impact video program
Watch the video to understand the impact of the Declaration of Independence.

Reading like a Historian In this painting, a scientist gives a demonstration of an orrery, a device that shows the movement of the planets around the sun. The spectators respond to their new understanding of the universe with wonder and awe.

Analyzing Visuals What do you think the darkened room and the illuminated faces of the spectators symbolize?

See **Skills Handbook**, p. H26

1775 The American Revolutionary War begins.

1780 Tupac Amaru leads a peasant revolt in Peru.

1783 The Treaty of Paris recognizes the United States as a nation.

1787 American leaders write the U.S. Constitution.

1789 The French Revolution begins.

Chapter Preview

HOLT
History's Impact
► **Video Program: Enlightenment and Revolution**
See the Video Teacher's Guide for strategies for using the video segment.

Reading Like a Historian
Analyzing Visuals Why do you think astronomers build models such as the one in the painting? *possible answers—to work out problems in three dimensions; to aid understanding; to educate others*

go.hrw.com
Online Resources
Chapter Resources:
KEYWORD: SHL ENL
Teacher Resources:
KEYWORD: SHL TEACHER

Explore the Time Line
1. Who published an important work first, Voltaire or Locke? *Locke*
2. What was the argument of *Two Treatises on Civil Government*? *Government should protect people's natural rights.*
3. What happened in 1775? *The American Revolution began.*
4. About how many years after the Treaty of Paris recognized the United States as a nationwas the U.S. Constitution written? *four years*

Info to Know
The Music of the Spheres During medieval times, people believed that Earth and the heavens were a series of huge spheres, one within the next. They also believed that Earth was at the center, the planets and stars were in the two closest spheres, and the outer spheres were inhabited by angels and other spirits. They thought that as these spheres revolved one inside another, they made heavenly music.

Make Inferences Where do you think these ideas about the solar system might have originated? *possible answers—based on descriptions in the Bible; opinions of scholars*

Answers
Reading Like a Historian *possible answer—The darkened room probably symbolizes lack of knowledge; the illuminated faces symbolize the enlightenment and knowledge that scientists experienced.*

Preteach

Geography Starting Points

The Scientific Community For the thinkers during the Enlightenment, a remarkable amount of communication occurred through letters. Scientists wrote to each other and to friends who were scientifically inclined. Science and math scholar Father Marin Mersenne, a close friend of Descartes, would compile many of the letters and ideas for scientists during the Enlightenment.

Make Inferences Look at the map on this page. Why do you think these scientists did not simply meet each other face to face? *possible answers—lived far away from one another; travel was difficult; may have had local commitments*

Map Transparency: European Centers of Learning c. 1750

World History Outline Maps

Interactive Map: European Center of Learning, c. 1750

GEOGRAPHY Starting Points

Interactive

EUROPEAN CENTERS OF LEARNING, c. 1750

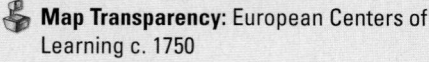

Starting Points In Europe, beginning about 1550, a period of revolutionary scientific discovery began that would change the world forever. Later, in an era known as the Enlightenment, philosophers introduced new ways of thinking about government and society. By 1750, academic centers and observatories thrived throughout Europe.

1. **Analyze** Which nation had a concentration of leading academic centers in 1750?
2. **Predict** How do you think centers of learning influenced how Europeans viewed the world in the 1700s?

Listen to History

Go online to listen to an explanation of the starting points for this chapter.

go.hrw.com
Keyword: SHL ENL

Skills Focus: Analyzing Maps

At Level

Research Required

Social Studies Skill
Tour of the Enlightenment

1. Review with students the various activities and events that occurred during the Enlightenment and Scientific Revolution.
2. Organize students into small groups. Tell them that they are members of the Royal Society of London, philosophers and scientists. Have students plan a trip that begins in London and travels to four other centers of the Enlightenment.
3. To make plans accurate, have students conduct research on cities, everyday life, and modes of travel in the 1600s and 1700s. Itineraries should include destinations, modes of travel, people to meet, and activities to undertake.
4. Have volunteers present their itineraries to the class. **LS Interpersonal**

Alternative Assessment Handbook, Rubric 40: Writing to Describe

Answers

Geography Starting Points **1.** *Great Britain;* **2.** *possible answer—probably changed their views dramatically and made them more open to new ideas*

SECTION 1

The Scientific Revolution

BEFORE YOU READ

MAIN IDEA

New ways of thinking led to remarkable discoveries during the Scientific Revolution.

READING FOCUS

1. What changes led to the dawn of modern science?
2. What discoveries occurred in astronomy, physics, and math during the Scientific Revolution?
3. How did early scientists advance knowledge in biology and chemistry?
4. How did scientific ideas move beyond the realm of science and affect society?

KEY TERMS AND PEOPLE

geocentric theory
Scientific Revolution
scientific method
René Descartes
Nicolaus Copernicus
heliocentric theory
Galileo Galilei
Isaac Newton

TAKING NOTES Take notes on new discoveries during the Scientific Revolution.

New Discoveries
astronomy
telescope
physics
math

THE INSIDE STORY *How was a college student inspired to change the future of science?*

Nicolaus Copernicus seemed destined to become an astronomer. He began his studies in Poland, where he studied many subjects, including astronomy. At that time, astronomy courses taught little more than methods of calculating the dates of holy days. But for Copernicus, the course ignited a passion for astronomy.

However, his uncle Lucas, a bishop, wanted Copernicus to have a church career. He soon sent Copernicus to the university in Bologna, Italy, to study church law. Copernicus rented a room from an astronomy professor and assisted with his research. In 1497 Copernicus observed the moon eclipse the sun. As a result, his excitement for astronomy continued to grow.

Copernicus eventually made a living as a doctor, but his first love was always astronomy. Throughout his life Copernicus carefully observed the heavens, made calculations, and developed a mathematical formula that proved the earth rotated around the sun. The world of science would never be the same. ■

DESTINED TO STUDY THE STARS

In the late 1400s astronomer Nicholas Copernicus proved the earth rotated around the sun. ▶

The Astronomer Copernicus: Conversation With God, by Jan Matejko, 1800s

Preteach

Getting Started

Use the **Interactive Reader and Study Guide** to familiarize students with the section content.

Interactive Reader and Study Guide, Section 1

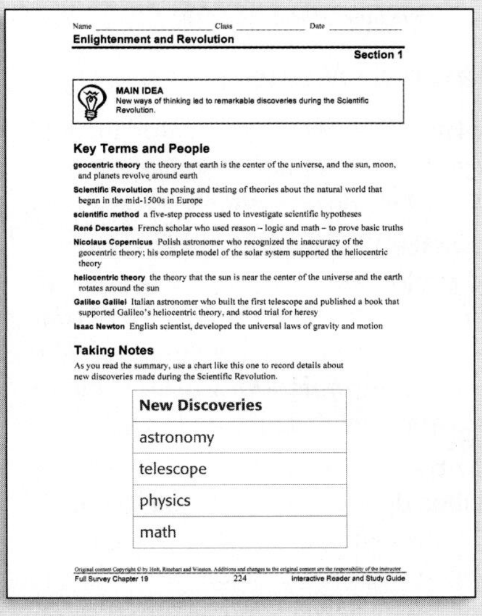

Name ______________ Class ________ Date ________

Enlightenment and Revolution

Section 1

MAIN IDEA
New ways of thinking led to remarkable discoveries during the Scientific Revolution.

Key Terms and People

geocentric theory the theory that earth is the center of the universe, and the sun, moon, and planets revolve around earth

Scientific Revolution the posing and testing of theories about the natural world that began in the mid-1500s in Europe

scientific method a five-step process used to investigate scientific hypotheses

René Descartes French scholar who used reason – logic and math – to prove basic truths

Nicolaus Copernicus Polish astronomer who recognized the inaccuracy of the geocentric theory; his complete model of the solar system supported the heliocentric theory

heliocentric theory the theory that the sun is near the center of the universe and the earth rotates around the sun

Galileo Galilei Italian astronomer who built the first telescope and published a book that supported Galileo's heliocentric theory, and stood trial for heresy

Isaac Newton English scientist, developed the universal laws of gravity and motion

Taking Notes

As you read the summary, use a chart like this one to record details about new discoveries made during the Scientific Revolution.

New Discoveries
astronomy
telescope
physics
math

Full Survey Chapter 19 224 Interactive Reader and Study Guide

CRF: Vocabulary Builder: Section 1

Taking Notes

Astronomy—heliocentric theory, elliptical orbits; Telescope—Galileo confirms that planets orbit the sun with first telescope used for astronomy in 1609; Physics and Math—calculus, universal laws of gravity and motion

Teach the Main Idea

At Level

The Scientific Revolution

1. **Teach** Ask students the Reading Focus questions to teach this section.
2. **Apply** Draw four rectangles for students to see. Label them with the names of the four topics in this section: Dawn of Modern Science; Discoveries in Astronomy, Physics, and Math; Discoveries in Biology and Chemistry, and Science and Society. Have students copy the rectangles onto their papers and fill them in with discoveries, names of key scientists, and other important details.
3. **Review** As you review the section, have students describe how scientific discoveries changed the way people viewed the world.
4. **Practice/Homework** Have students write a research proposal from the point of view of Galileo, Newton, or Vesalius. **LS Visual-Spatial, Verbal-Linguistic**

Alternative Assessment Handbook, Rubric 1: Acquiring Information

Direct Teach

Reading Focus

1 What changes led to the dawn of modern science? *traditional authorities challenged; new theories posed and tested; exploration led to closer study of natural world; development of scientific method*

Dawn of Modern Science

Define What is the geocentric theory? *earth is center of universe; sun, moon, and planets revolve around earth*

Identify Cause and Effect How did exploration affect the development of modern science? *discoveries outside the realm of ancient scholars; led to closer study of natural world; need for accurate knowledge*

Contrast How was the scientific method different from previous methods of understanding? *reliance on testing ideas by experimentation, rather than accepting the view of traditional authorities*

Info to Know

Scientists or Philosophers? During the 1600s, those who investigated nature were not referred to as scientists. Instead, they were called "natural philosophers." Their tools were referred to as "philosophical instruments." Mathematicians were usually called "geometers" after the most advanced branch of math at the time.

Primary Source

"The truth is the science of Nature has been already too long made only a work of the brain and the fancy: It is now high time that it should return to the plainness and soundness of observations on material and obvious things."
—Robert Hooke, *Micrographia*, 1665

Answers

Linking to Today *It allowed biologists to see whole cells for the first time.*

Dawn of Modern Science

When some scholars in the Middle Ages had questions about the natural world, they sought answers from traditional authorities—the church and ancient scholars. In the mid-1500s, however, scholars began to challenge tradition as they began to think in new ways.

The Old View One example of how scholars relied on traditional authorities was in their beliefs about the structure of the universe. People believed that the earth was the center of the universe and that the sun, moon, and planets revolved around the earth. This viewpoint was called the **geocentric theory**.

The Greek philosopher Aristotle proposed the geocentric theory in the 300s BC. The Greek astronomer Ptolemy expanded upon Aristotle's ideas in the AD 200s. These ideas were upheld by the church, which taught that God put the earth at the center of the universe. For centuries, scholars and the church were the accepted authorities for European intellectuals.

New Viewpoints In the Middle Ages, scholars in Europe learned about scientific advances in the Arab world. By the mid-1500s, they began to challenge traditional authorities. They posed theories about the natural world and developed procedures to test those ideas. Historians have called this new way of thinking the **Scientific Revolution**.

Why were Europeans open to new ideas at this time? One reason was exploration. When explorers journeyed to Africa, Asia, and the Americas, they found people and animals they had never seen before. The ancient scholars could provide no information about these new lands. Perhaps there were other things to be discovered that the ancients had not known.

The Age of Exploration also led scientists to study the natural world more closely. Navigators, for example, needed more accurate instruments and geographic knowledge to help find their way across vast oceans. The more that scientists examined the natural world, however, the more they found that it did not match ancient beliefs.

The Scientific Method Scientists eventually developed a new approach to investigation and discovery called the **scientific method**. The scientific method consists of five basic steps. First, scientists identify a problem. Next, they form a hypothesis that can be tested. They then perform experiments to test the hypothesis.

Linking to Today

The Science of Cells

Since the Scientific Revolution, scientists have continued to use the scientific method to make remarkable discoveries. Mary Osborn, a cell biologist in Göttingen, Germany, researches cytoskeletons, or the structures that form the skeleton of cells. In the 1970s she focused her research on microtubules, tiny tubes that move important substances throughout cells. She developed a new microscopic technique that allowed her to see that microtubules form continuous lines that snake through cells.

One of her colleagues in the scientific community, however, dismissed her findings as false. At that time, biologists used electron microscopes to study cells. Electron microscopes required scientists to slice cells very thinly to view them. For this reason, biologists had never before seen microtubules intact.

Mary Osborn's microscopic technique allowed biologists to see whole cells for the first time. Scientists now use her technique widely, most notably for improved cancer diagnoses. More reliable diagnoses allow doctors to treat cancer patients more effectively than ever before.

Analyze How did Osborn's technique allow scientists to see cells in an entirely new way?

Mary Osborn in her laboratory in Göttingen, Germany ▶

Differentiating Instruction

Below Level

Special Education Students

Materials: poster paper, current science and technology magazines, scissors, glue

1. Review with students the idea that the foundations of modern science were built during the Scientific Revolution.
2. Organize students into mixed-ability pairs.
3. Have students search current magazines for images of things made possible by modern science, particularly in the realm of astronomy, math, physics, biology, and chemistry. Possible images could include machines and people engaged in scientific study.
4. Have students create a collage with images they find. Display collages for students to see.
LS Visual-Spatial

Alternative Assessment Handbook, Rubric 8: Collages

They record the results of the experiments. Finally, they analyze the results of the experiments to form a conclusion that either proves or disproves the hypothesis.

Two of the most important scholars who helped develop the scientific method were Francis Bacon and **René Descartes** (day-KAHRT). In England, Francis Bacon wrote in 1620 that the only true way to gain scientific knowledge was through experimentation—observing, measuring, explaining, and verifying. In France, meanwhile, René Descartes placed more emphasis on reason. He believed that everything should be doubted until it could be proven by reason. Descartes relied on mathematics and logic to prove basic truths.

The ideas of Bacon and Descartes continue to influence modern scientific methods. Scientists today use observation and experimentation along with mathematical logic to achieve a deeper understanding of the natural world.

READING CHECK **Find the Main Idea** What was the Scientific Revolution?

THE SCIENTIFIC METHOD (QUICK FACTS)

The Scientific Method is a set of techniques for acquiring new knowledge about the natural world based on observable, measurable evidence.

Step 1 Identify a problem or a research question to be answered.

Step 2 Form a hypothesis that can be tested. A hypothesis is a proposed answer to the research question and is based on previous knowledge.

Step 3 Perform experiments to test the hypothesis.

Step 4 Record the results of the experiments.

Step 5 Analyze the results of the experiments to form a conclusion that either proves or disproves the hypothesis.

Discoveries in Astronomy, Physics, and Math

Early scientists made significant contributions in astronomy, physics, and math. Their work began to explain the complexities of the solar system and the limits of the physical world.

Copernicus In the early 1500s Polish astronomer **Nicolaus Copernicus** recognized that the geocentric theory did not explain the movements of the sun, moon, and planets accurately. After years of careful observation, he came to the conclusion that the sun, not the earth, was near the center of the solar system. Copernicus's discovery that the earth revolves around the sun is called the **heliocentric theory.**

The idea that the earth orbits the sun was not completely new. But Copernicus developed a detailed mathematical explanation of how the process worked. In addition, Copernicus was the first scientist to create a complete model of the solar system that combined physics, astronomy, and mathematics.

Copernicus did not publish his conclusions in his most famous book, *On the Revolutions of the Heavenly Spheres*, until the last year of his life. He knew the church would oppose his work because his work contradicted the teachings of the church. He was also concerned about the weaknesses of his theory. His mathematical formulas did not predict the positions of the planets very well, and Copernicus did not want to face ridicule for these weaknesses.

Copernicus died in 1543, shortly after his revolutionary work was published. Other scientists would further develop and expand upon Copernicus's ideas.

Brahe and Kepler One of those scientists was Tycho Brahe (brah), a Danish astronomer. When a bright object appeared in the sky over Denmark in 1572, Brahe wrote a book proving that the object was a newly visible star that was far away. He called it a supernova, the name still used for distant exploding stars that suddenly become visible on earth.

Brahe's book impressed King Frederick II of Denmark, who gave Brahe money to build two observatories. There, Brahe developed his own system to explain planetary movement. He believed that the sun revolved around the earth, but that the other five known planets in the solar system revolved around the sun.

Brahe later moved to Prague and hired a German mathematician named Johannes Kepler as his assistant. Brahe needed help to form a mathematical theory from the detailed measurements he had made of the planets.

READING SKILLS
Visualizing
To help you understand the heliocentric theory, draw a circle in the center of a piece of paper to represent the sun. Then draw circles around the "sun" to represent the earth and the planets.

Direct Teach

Reading Focus

2 What discoveries occurred in astronomy, physics, and math during the Scientific Revolution? *heliocentric theory; planets orbited sun; predictable laws of movement; law of universal gravitation; calculus*

Discoveries in Astronomy, Physics, and Math

Recall Why did Copernicus not publish his work until the last year of his life? *he knew the Church would oppose it; uncertain about weaknesses of theory*

Contrast What set Copernicus's work apart from that of previous scientists? *created a complex model of solar system that combined physics, astronomy, and mathematics*

Make Generalizations Based on Frederick II's actions, what role do you think rulers and patrons played in the Scientific Revolution? *financed projects and experiments*

CRF: Primary Source: The Compatibility of Science and Religion

The Scientific Method (QUICK FACTS)

Evaluate Why must scientists analyze results instead of skipping the final step and going on to the next experiment? *They must determine the meaning of results before deciding what the next experiment should be.*

Quick Facts Transparency: The Scientific Method

Differentiating Instruction — Above Level

Advanced Learners/Gifted and Talented

1. Review with students the steps in the scientific method. Briefly discuss the concept of a controlled experiment.
2. Give students some examples of simple experiments they could do at home. Have students generate short lists of experiments they would like to try.
3. Check student lists to make sure they are appropriate. Experiments should be controlled, relatively simple, safe, and ethical.
4. Have students choose an experiment, document their question, and form a hypothesis. Then, have them document their experiment and results. Remind students not to falsify data if the experiment did not go how they expected.
5. Have students create visuals to show the steps of their experiment. Have volunteers present their experiments to the class. **LS Logical-Mathematical, Visual-Spatial**

Alternative Assessment Handbook, Rubric 1: Acquiring Information

Answers

Reading Check *a new way of thinking about the natural world that challenged traditional views and instead relied upon experimentation*

Direct Teach

Reading Focus

Discoveries in Astronomy, Physics, and Math

Identify What valuable contribution did Kepler make? *proved that planets had elliptical orbits around the sun*

Make Inferences Why were Galileo's books so controversial? *They contradicted the official Church viewpoint that the sun orbited Earth.*

Evaluate What do you think was Newton's most important discovery? Why? *possible answers—idea that planets and stars move according to predictable laws, expressed mathematically; new view of the universe*

MISCONCEPTION ALERT

Though it is often perceived that scientists rely purely on facts and data, early scientists had a good measure of what might be perceived as superstition. Girolamo Cardano, a doctor, natural philosopher, and mathematician, supposedly had the gift of prophesy and predicted the date of his own death. Isaac Newton studied alchemy and spent his time searching the Bible for clues about the end of the world.

After Brahe's death, Johannes Kepler published the result of Brahe's measurements of the orbit of Mars. These measurements led Kepler to solve the main problem of Copernican theory. Copernicus had assumed that the planets orbited the sun in a circle. Kepler found through the Mars measurements that this assumption was not true. He was the first astronomer to prove that the planets orbited the sun in an oval pattern, or ellipse.

Brahe had wanted to prove Copernicus wrong. Instead, his measurements led Kepler to prove that the heliocentric theory was right. Kepler's mathematical model of the solar system was also correct.

Galileo Copernican theory was supported and by **Galileo Galilei**, an Italian scientist. After learning about a sailor's spyglass that allowed one to see distant objects, Galileo built the first telescope used for astronomy in 1609, which he used to scan the heavens.

Galileo was the first scientist to observe Saturn, the craters on the moon, sunspots, and the moons of Jupiter. He also discovered that the Milky Way was made up of stars. He described these amazing discoveries in 1610 in a book called *Starry Messenger*.

Sir Isaac Newton The English scientist **Isaac Newton** changed the world of science by bringing together astronomy, physics, and mathematics. As a young man, Newton wondered if gravity affected the universe the way that it affected objects on earth. Years later, his assistant wrote about Newton's questioning.

HISTORY'S VOICES

> "Whilst he was musing in a garden it came into his thought that the same power of gravity (which made an apple fall from the tree to the ground) was not limited to a certain distance from the earth, but must extend much farther than was usually thought—Why not as high as the Moon[?]"
>
> —John Conduitt, *Conduitt's Account of Newton's Life at Cambridge*, 1727

In 1687 Newton published his greatest work, *The Mathematical Principles of Natural Philosophy*, also known as the *Principia*. In this book, he explained his law of universal gravitation. This law states that gravity affects objects in the universe as well as on earth. Just as gravity causes an apple to fall from a tree, gravity keeps the planets in their orbits.

From these findings, Newton developed a new kind of mathematics called calculus, which he used to predict the effects of gravity. Controversy soon erupted, however. The German philosopher Gottfried von Leibniz independently developed calculus at the same time. Leibniz and Newton accused each other of plagiarism and feuded for many years. Historians now believe that it was simply a case of independent discovery by two very talented men.

READING CHECK **Contrast** How did Copernicus and Brahe differ in their views of the universe?

Themes Through Time

ASTRONOMY

SCIENCE AND TECHNOLOGY Early astronomers studied the sun, moon, and planets to help create calendars or assist with navigation. After the Scientific Revolution, the science of astronomy expanded to include the study of the solar system, the stars in the Milky Way galaxy, and other more distant galaxies and stellar formations.

c. 150 Ptolemy writes that the earth is the center of the universe. He remains the authority on astronomy until the 1600s.

499 During the Gupta Empire in India, the astronomer Aryabhata writes that the spherical earth rotates on its axis.

500

c. 600 Mayan astronomers compile detailed observations of the heavens and acquire the knowledge to predict solar eclipses.

Skills Focus: Identifying Main Idea and Details

At Level

Reading Skill

Astronomers and Their Achievements

1. Draw the graphic organizer for students to see. Omit the italicized answers.
2. Have students copy and complete the graphic organizer. Then, have volunteers fill in the class graphic organizer. **LS Visual-Spatial**

Alternative Assessment Handbook, Rubric 13: Graphic Organizers

Astronomers and Their Achievements

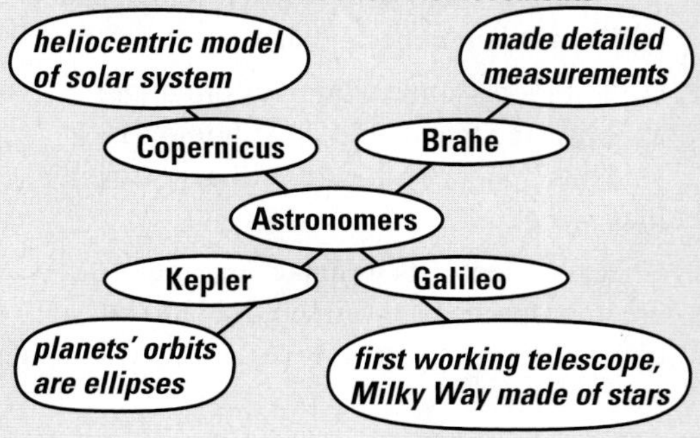

Answers

Reading Check *Copernicus—all planets orbit the sun; Brahe—sun orbits Earth, other planets orbit sun*

Discoveries in Biology and Chemistry

Just as astronomers moved away the works of ancient Greeks, other scientists used the scientific method to acquire new knowledge. As a result, during the Scientific Revolution, scientists made great discoveries in the fields of biology and chemistry.

Biology In the Middle Ages, European doctors relied on the works of the ancient Greek physician Galen. But Galen's works were inaccurate. He had assumed that human anatomy was similar to that of animals, because he had never dissected a human body.

Andreas Vesalius, a Flemish doctor, became known for his work in anatomy at the University of Padua in Italy. In 1539 a judge learned of his work and made the bodies of executed criminals available to Vesalius for dissection. Vesalius hired artists to produce accurate drawings. He published his greatest work, *On the Workings of the Human Body*, in 1543.

Vesalius laid the groundwork for English physician William Harvey to observe and explain the workings of the human heart in the early 1600s. Harvey described how blood and the circulatory system functioned.

Later in the 1600s Dutch scientist Antony van Leeuwenhoek used his interest in developing a magnifying lens to invent the microscope. He was the first person to describe the appearance of bacteria, red blood cells, yeast, and other microorganisms.

English physicist and inventor Robert Hooke used an early microscope to describe the appearance of plants at a microscopic level. In addition to his many achievements in physics and mathematics, Hooke is credited with creating the term *cell*.

Chemistry Robert Boyle is often called the father of modern chemistry. Boyle was the first chemist to define an element. His 1661 work, *The Sceptical Chemist*, described matter as a cluster of tiny particles (now called atoms or molecules). Boyle stated that changes in matter happened when these clusters were rearranged. His most significant contribution to chemistry was Boyle's law, which describes how temperature, volume, and pressure affect gases.

French chemist Antoine-Laurent Lavoisier (lah-VWAH-zee-ay) developed methods for precise measurements in the 1700s. He discovered the law of Conservation of Mass, which proved that matter could not be created or destroyed. Lavoisier recognized and named oxygen, introduced the metric system of measurements, and invented the first periodic table, which included 33 elements.

THE IMPACT TODAY

To pass a scuba diving certification test, divers must answer questions about how Boyle's law relates to safely ascending and descending underwater.

READING CHECK **Summarize** What were the major contributions made in biology and chemistry?

1610 Using a telescope, Galileo confirms that the planets orbit the sun and observes that the moon's surface is not smooth but rough and jagged.

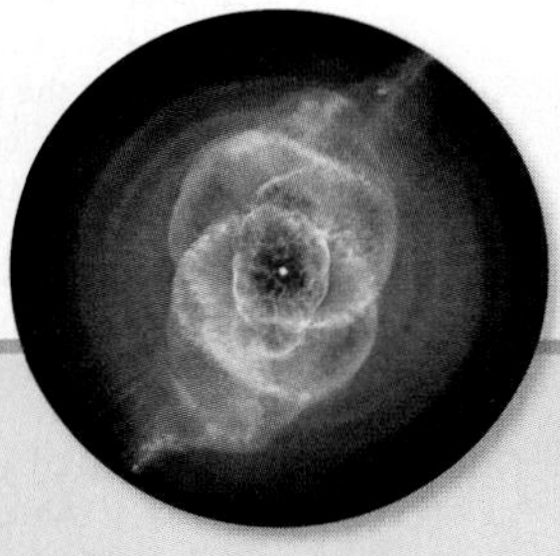

1990 The Hubble Telescope is launched and starts recording spectacular images of the universe like this one of a dying star.

1500 — 2000

1453 Nicolaus Copernicus publishes a book proposing that the sun is the center of the universe.

1905 Albert Einstein's theory of relativity changes the world's views on time and space.

Skills Focus UNDERSTANDING THEMES

Infer What impact did the invention and refinement of the telescope have on the field of astronomy?

Direct Teach

Reading Focus

3 How did early scientists advance knowledge in biology and chemistry? *anatomy studies, function of circulatory system, spontaneous generation disproved, microscopic observations; elements defined, animals need oxygen, Law of Conservation of Mass*

Discoveries in Biology and Chemistry

Analyze How did Vesalius record information learned from his dissections? *hired artists to produce accurate drawings of his procedures*

Predict What impact do you think Vesalius's work had on the medical community? *possible answers—expanded knowledge of anatomy; made them realize anatomy's importance*

Summarize What were Lavoisier's achievements? *developed precise measuring techniques, first to prove Law of Conservation of Mass, described the role of oxygen in chemistry*

CRF: Biography: Carl Linnaeus

Primary Source

"The Newtonian principle of gravitation is now more firmly established, on the basis of reason, than it would be were the government to step in, and to make it an article of necessary faith. Reason and experiment have been indulged, and error has fled before them."
—Thomas Jefferson, *Notes on the State of Virginia*, 1781-1785

Skills Focus: Making Oral Presentations

At Level

Research Required

Reading Like a Historian Skill
Scientific Conference

1. Assign each student to a scientist of the Scientific Revolution.
2. Have students conduct research to gain additional information about their scientists. Have them prepare a brief presentation for a scientific conference. Presentations should include biographical information, but should mainly focus on the scientist's work. Students should include visuals in their presentations.
3. When students are ready to give their presentations, organize the class into three or four groups. Have students in the first group set up at different stations in the room and give their presentations as the other groups rotate through the stations.
4. Have the next group of students set up at the stations and repeat the process. **LS Kinesthetic**

Alternative Assessment Handbook, Rubrics 24: Oral Presentations; and 30: Research

Answers

Themes Through Time *It allowed scientists to observe the universe and test hypotheses rather than accepting traditional views.*

Reading Check *importance of anatomy and dissection; function of blood and circulatory system; invention of microscope; discovery of certain laws of matter*

Direct Teach

Reading Focus

4 How did scientific ideas move beyond the realm of science and affect society? *Science and religion combined to produce artistic achievements of the Renaissance; scientists also challenged some of the traditional ideas of the Church.*

Science and Society

Contrast How did the basis of Christianity differ from the basis of science? *Christianity was based on faith; science was based on the pursuit of knowledge.*

Analyze How did Renaissance artists combine science and religion? *studied anatomy, experimented with chemistry of paints and nature of light, used math to create balance; works dedicated to God*

Info to Know

Other Discoveries During the Scientific Revolution, the barometer was developed and used to prove that air pressure varies with altitude. Newton and Descartes found that light occurs in waves and that colors result from varying frequencies of light. Boyle discovered that chemicals interact mechanically, and not through some spirit or principle within them. Finally, advances in medicine showed that wounds should be treated with a dressing rather than a red-hot iron, and that instruments should be used to aid difficult births.

Primary Source

"Cogito ergo sum." (Latin)
("I think, therefore I am.")
—René Descartes

▼ Standing before Church officials, Galileo defended his belief that the planets orbit the sun.

Galileo Galilei Before the Inquisition, 1633, by Joseph-Nicolas Robert-Fleury, 1847

FACES OF HISTORY

Galileo GALILEI

1564–1642

Many people considered the sentencing of Galileo in 1633 to life imprisonment a great tragedy. Efforts to clear his name continued for centuries after his death. But as late as 1822, the Vatican still banned Galileo's *Dialogue concerning Two Chief World Systems.*

The church gradually changed its views toward Galileo. A church commission reopened his case in 1983. In 1992 Pope John Paul II declared that the church had wrongfully condemned Galileo.

Infer Why do you think the Catholic Church decided to reexamine Galileo's case in the 1980s?

Science and Society

As science began to assume greater significance in society, the question of the role of the Roman Catholic Church in a changing culture became important. At this time the church opposed the views of many scientists, such as Galileo. However, the church benefitted from the new scientific discoveries that made Renaissance art and architecture possible.

Science and the Church As the most powerful institution in Europe during the Middle Ages, the church had also been the primary resource for knowledge and learning. The church had established cathedral schools, many of which became universities, to train people to run the church. How did scientists and their innovative views fit into the church's established structure?

Most European scientists were Christian and did not want to challenge the role of Christianity in society. However, conflicts between the church and science developed. The church explained the world through inspiration and revealed truth. Early science sought to explain the world through the accumulation of facts and logical reasoning.

The early church rejected some of the beliefs of ancient Greek scholars because they were not Christians. Some leaders in the church also feared reason as an enemy of faith. But, the church leaders eventually became convinced that reason could be used to serve the needs of the church instead of undermining them. To a limited extent, the church began to embrace some of the achievements of the Scientific Revolution.

Galileo's theories, however, brought him into direct conflict with the church. Church leaders pressured Galileo not to support the ideas of Copernicus. Still, Galileo continued his studies. In 1632 he published *Dialogue concerning Two Chief World Systems.* Although this book included the views of both Ptolemy and Copernicus, it clearly showed Galileo's support of Copernican theory. Pope Urban VII angrily ordered Galileo to Rome to stand trial before the Inquisition—the church institution to stamp out heresy, or dissenting views.

In April 1633 Galileo stood trial before the Inquisition. Galileo reluctantly stated that he would not use Copernican theory in his work so that he would receive a lenient sentence. The pope ordered Galileo placed under house arrest in his villa near Florence, where he spent the remainder of his life.

Science and Art During the Renaissance, the study of art and architecture were not separate from the study of science. Artists learned human anatomy so they could paint the body.

Skills Focus: Summarizing

At Level

Reading Skill

The Trial of Galileo

1. Review the information in the text about the trial of Galileo. You may wish to give students more information about the Inquisition.
2. Organize students into small groups. Have each group write a skit about Galileo's trial. Characters could include Galileo, a few inquisitors, and few spectators.
3. Allow enough time for students to prepare and rehearse their skits. Then, have students perform their skits for the class.

LS Kinesthetic, Interpersonal

Alternative Assessment Handbook, Rubric 33: Skits and Reader's Theater

Answers

Faces of History *possible answer—because his discoveries advanced science*

Artists experimented with the chemistry of paints and the nature of light. Painters used mathematics to create compositions of perfect balance. The use of mathematics and physics were crucial to the great architecture and engineering achievements of the time.

Science and religion thus combined to produce the great artistic achievements of the Renaissance. Much of the great art and architecture of the Renaissance was dedicated to the glory of God and would have been impossible without reason and science. But the artists and architects had not challenged a basic belief of the church. Rather, astronomers such as Galileo did.

Science and Community The Scientific Revolution had firmly established a new way of thinking about the physical world. Great advances had been made in the disciplines of astronomy, physics, biology, and chemistry. In turn, those advances had influenced developments in the arts and architecture. As the Scientific Revolution spread, its impact would reach far beyond the laboratories and observatories of scientists.

Soon, philosophers and scholars would seek new understandings about society. They would reexamine old ideas government, religion, education, and economics. They would also wonder if reason could solve the age-old problems of poverty, war, and ignorance. The new ways of thinking that emerged from the Scientific Revolution would lead to even more dramatic changes, as you will read about in the next section.

READING CHECK **Draw Conclusions** How did the Scientific Revolution have an impact beyond the realm of science?

Causes and Effects of the Scientific Revolution (QUICK FACTS)

CAUSES

- Exploration and expansion of trade
- Continuing study of ancient authorities
- Development of the scientific method

EFFECTS

- Beginnings of modern science
- Belief in progress and the power of reason
- New view of the universe as a well-ordered system

Section 1 Assessment

go.hrw.com
Online Quiz
Keyword: SHL ENL HP

Reviewing Ideas, Terms, and People

1. **a. Define** What was the **geocentric theory** of the universe?
   b. Analyze How did the **scientific method** change the way people learned about the natural world?
   c. Evaluate What effect would the scientific method have on the acceptance of the geocentric theory?
2. **a. Identify** What was the **heliocentric theory**?
   b. Contrast In what way did Galileo's view of the universe differ from Aristotle's view?
   c. Elaborate Why do you think the Catholic Church objected to the Galileo's theories so strongly?
3. **a. Recall** Who was the traditional authority on human anatomy before the Scientific Revolution?
   b. Explain How did Vesalius acquire more accurate knowledge about human anatomy?
4. **a. Describe** What effects did the Scientific Revolution have on art and architecture?
   b. Draw Conclusions Why do you think artists and architects were eager to embrace the ideas of the Scientific Revolution?

Critical Thinking

5. **Identify Cause and Effect** Copy the graphic organizer below and use it to list the causes and the effects of new discoveries made during the Scientific Revolution.

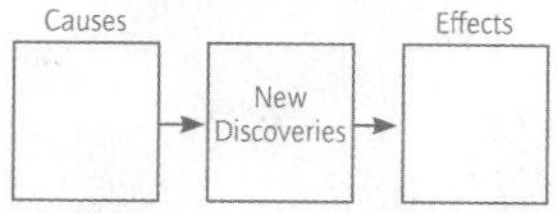

FOCUS ON WRITING

6. **Persuasion** Suppose that you are an astronomer during the mid-1500s. Write a short speech explaining why the scientific method would reveal truth more accurately than reliance upon traditional authorities.

Direct Teach

Reading Focus

Science and Society

Identity What were some of the long-term effects of the Scientific Revolution? *development of modern science; belief in progress and the power of reason*

Predict How might other parts of society be affected by the ideas of the Scientific Revolution? *possible answers—Government might be affected because people would become less willing to accept authority without reason; religion might become affected because people would be more likely to look for experimental proof.*

Quick Facts Transparency: Causes and Effects of the Scientific Revolution

Review & Assess

Close

Have students describe the changes in ideas brought about by the Scientific Revolution.

Review

Online Quiz, Section 1

Assess

SE Section 1 Assessment

Progress Assessment: Section 1 Quiz

Alternative Assessment Handbook

Reteach/Intervene

Interactive Reader and Study Guide, Section 1

Interactive Skills Tutor CD-ROM

Section 1 Assessment Answers

1. **a.** The earth was at the center of the universe.
   b. gave them step-by-step process to test their hypotheses
   c. possible answer—would disprove the geocentric theory
2. **a.** The sun was the center of universe.
   b. Aristotle—geocentric theory; Galileo—heliocentric theory
   c. possible answer—because his ideas challenged Church teachings
3. **a.** Galen
   b. by dissecting human bodies
4. **a.** New knowledge led to artistic achievement
   b. provided new way of depicting physical world
5. Causes—traditional theories challenged, age of exploration, examination of natural world, accurate instruments; Effects—scientific method, new models of solar system, advances in math, anatomy, and chemistry; conflicts with Church
6. Student speeches should explain the process of the scientific method.

Answers

Reading Check *led people to question the Church, inspired great artistic achievements, led to new ideas about government, religion, education, and economics*

Preteach

Getting Started

Use the **Interactive Reader and Study Guide** to familiarize students with the section content.

Interactive Reader and Study Guide, Section 2

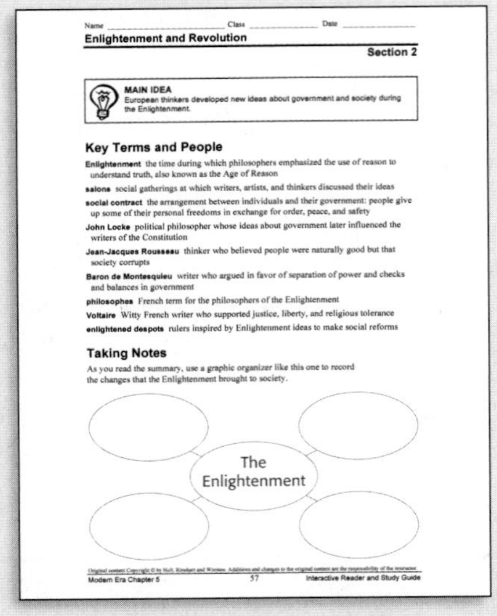

Name ______ Class ______ Date ______

Enlightenment and Revolution

Section 2

MAIN IDEA
European thinkers developed new ideas about government and society during the Enlightenment.

Key Terms and People

Enlightenment the time during which philosophers emphasized the use of reason to understand truth, also known as the Age of Reason

salons social gatherings at which writers, artists, and thinkers discussed their ideas

social contract the arrangement between individuals and their government: people give up some of their personal freedoms in exchange for order, peace, and safety

John Locke political philosopher whose ideas about government later influenced the writers of the Constitution

Jean-Jacques Rousseau thinker who believed people were naturally good but that society corrupts

Baron de Montesquieu writer who argued in favor of separation of power and checks and balances in government

philosophes French term for the philosophers of the Enlightenment

Voltaire Witty French writer who supported justice, liberty, and religious tolerance

enlightened despots rulers inspired by Enlightenment ideas to make social reforms

Taking Notes

As you read the summary, use a graphic organizer like this one to record the changes that the Enlightenment brought to society.

The Enlightenment

Modern Era Chapter 5 57 Interactive Reader and Study Guide

Academic Vocabulary

Review with students the high-use academic term in this section.

rational having reason or understanding (p. 178)

CRF: Vocabulary Builder: Section 2

Taking Notes

belief in reason as the key to all; new views on government—social contract, government's purpose to protect rights, otherwise it is in breach of contract, checks on power of king; new views on society

go.hrw.com
Online Resources
KEYWORD: SHL ENL
ACTIVITY: John Locke

SECTION 2

The Enlightenment

Before You Read

Main Idea

European thinkers developed new ideas about government and society during the Enlightenment.

Reading Focus

1. How was the Enlightenment influenced by reason?
2. What new views did philosophers have about government?
3. What new views did philosophers have about society?
4. How did Enlightenment ideas spread?

Key Terms and People

Enlightenment
salons
social contract
John Locke
Jean-Jacques Rousseau
Baron de Montesquieu
philosophes
Voltaire
enlightened despots

TAKING NOTES Take notes on the changes that the Enlightenment brought to society.

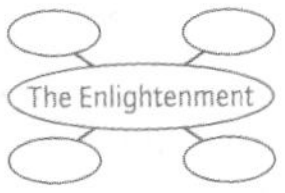

▲ Voltaire began writing an epic poem in prison.

Engraving of Voltaire imprisoned in the Bastille, by François Bouchot, 1800s.

THE INSIDE STORY ***Why was a French philosopher jailed for his writings?*** In the early 1700s François-Marie Arouet was the toast of Paris. His witty, satirical verses delighted Parisian aristocrats. But in 1717 he may have mocked the wrong man. The Duke of Orleans, who ruled France as regent until the young king Louis XV came of age, believed Arouet made fun of him. Outraged, the Duke of Orleans imprisoned Arouet in the Bastille prison for 11 months.

While in prison, Arouet began writing more serious works. He wrote his first play, called *Oedipe*, which would secure his reputation as the greatest French playwright of his time. He also completed an epic poem about Henry IV called *La Henriade*. But Arouet would be best known for his philosophical works, which he would write under the pen name Voltaire. ■

The Age of Reason

The Scientific Revolution convinced many European thinkers about the power of reason. With the scientific method and reason, scientists had made countless discoveries about the physical world. Could reason be used to study human nature and society as well?

In the 1600s a new generation of philosophers began to view reason as the best way to understand truth. They came to the remarkable conclusion that reason could be used to solve all human problems. This exciting time of optimism and possibility is now called the **Enlightenment**, or the Age of Reason.

Ideas of the Enlightenment inspired educated people throughout Europe and beyond. People gathered in cof-

Teach the Main Idea

At Level

The Enlightenment

1. **Teach** Ask students the Reading Focus questions to teach this section.
2. **Apply** Have students create flashcards to learn the ideas of the philosophers in this section. Have them write the idea on one side of the card and the philosopher's name on the other side. Some ideas are similar, so students should write them as they appear in the text.
3. **Review** As you review the section, have students use their flashcards to quiz each other on the philosophers and their ideas.
4. **Practice/Homework** Have students create a resume for one of the philosophers in this section. **LS Visual-Spatial, Verbal-Linguistic**

Alternative Assessment Handbook, Rubric 31: Resumés

feehouses and public spaces to debate the new ideas. Many writers published their ideas in books, magazines, and inexpensive pamphlets to help spread their ideas among educated readers. They were all inspired by the exciting notion that the problems of the world could be solved by educated people.

By the time the Enlightenment reached its peak in the 1700s, Paris was a center of intellectual activity. Eager to promote the new ideas, many wealthy Parisian women began hosting social gatherings called **salons**. These women brought together philosophers, artists, scientists, and writers regularly to discuss their ideas.

READING CHECK **Find the Main Idea** What exciting conclusion did philosophers reach during the Enlightenment?

New Views on Government

As the Enlightenment began, European thinkers began looking for ways to apply reason in order to improve the human condition. Some of these thinkers began to examine the organization of government.

Thomas Hobbes The English thinker Thomas Hobbes wrote about his views on government in his 1651 book, *Leviathan*. His experience of the violence and upheaval of the English civil war persuaded him that people were selfish and greedy. In the natural state, he wrote, people would lead lives that were "solitary, poor, nasty, brutish, and short."

Hobbes believed that people needed governments to impose order. He argued that people in a society should agree to give up some freedoms to a strong leader in exchange for the peace, safety, and order that government could provide. Hobbes called this exchange between society and government the **social contract**. He believed that absolute monarchy was the best form of government because an absolute monarchy had the power of a leviathan, a massive sea monster. That strong, centralized power could be used to impose law and order.

John Locke Another English philosopher, **John Locke**, believed that people were naturally happy, tolerant, and reasonable. He argued that all people were born equal with the natural rights of life, liberty, and property.

Locke stated that the purpose of government was to protect people's natural rights. He believed that monarchs were not chosen by God. Instead, the people consented to the government, whose power was limited by laws. In *Two Treatises on Government*, Locke described the importance of the fairness of law.

HISTORY'S VOICES

> "Those who are united into one body, and have a common established law and judicature [court system] to appeal to, with authority to decide controversies between them, and punish offenders, are in civil society one with another . . ."
>
> —John Locke, *Two Treatises on Government*, 1690

Locke believed that if a government failed to protect its citizens' natural rights, they had the right to overthrow it. Locke's belief in government by consent became a foundation for modern democracy. His ideas inspired later revolutionaries in Europe and the Americas.

Jean-Jacques Rousseau The French philosopher **Jean-Jacques Rousseau** (roo-SOH) believed that people were basically born good.

PRIMARY SOURCES

Rousseau's Social Contract

Jean-Jacques Rousseau believed that the social contract was not just between the governors and the governed but between all members of society.

> "What then is government? It is an intermediary body established between the subjects and the sovereign [king] to keep them in touch with each other. . . The government's power is only the public power vested in it. . . . when the [government] has a particular will of its own stronger than that of the sovereign. . . at that moment the social union will disappear and the body politic will be dissolved."
>
> —Jean-Jacques Rousseau, *The Social Contract*, 1763

Skills Focus READING LIKE A HISTORIAN

1. **Define** What did Rousseau mean by "an intermediary body" in the first line of this excerpt?
2. **Analyzing Primary Sources** What would happen if government carried out its own wishes in opposition to those of the people?

See **Skills Handbook**, p. H25

Direct Teach

Reading Focus

1 How was the Enlightenment influenced by reason? *like scientists, philosophers emphasized use of reason to understand truth; used reason to study human condition*

The Age of Reason

Recall What was the Enlightenment? *a time of optimism and possibility when people used reason to attempt to solve the problems of the world*

Describe What role did salons play in the Enlightenment? *brought together philosophers, artists, scientists, and writers to discuss new ideas*

Reading Focus

2 What new views did philosophers have about government? *Hobbes—social contract, limits to freedom, monarchy is best; Locke—people of equal value, government protects rights, people can rebel against government; Rousseau—government is for common good; Montesquieu—separation of powers*

New Views on Government

Analyze How did the views of Hobbes and Locke about humans in their natural state affect their political ideas? *Hobbes—people naturally bad, need all-powerful monarch to protect them; Locke—people naturally good, need government to protect rights*

Elaborate If applied, how would Locke's economic theory affect taxes? *possible answer—state has no natural right to property or money*

Differentiating Instruction

Below Level

Learners Having Difficulty

1. Review with students the importance of reason for the philosophes.
2. Have students write a poem or song called "Ode to Reason" that could have been written by a philosophe. Encourage students to find creative ways to praise reason and all of the things that could be accomplished through it.
3. Have volunteers recite their poems for the class. **LS Verbal-Linguistic, Auditory-Musical**

Alternative Assessment Handbook, Rubric 26: Poems and Songs

Answers

Primary Sources 1. *a group created to keep the subjects and the kings in touch with each other;* **2.** *The social contract would cease to exist.*

Reading Check *Reason could be used to solve all human problems.*

Direct Teach

Reading Focus

New Views on Government

Describe What is separation of powers? *power divided among several branches of government*

Explain According to Montesquieu, how was Great Britain's government an example of separation of powers? *divided into branches: parliament made laws, king carried out laws, court interpreted laws*

Reading Focus

3 What new views did philosophers have about society? *religious toleration, women's right's; an economic system without government regulation*

New Views on Society

Recall Why was Voltaire imprisoned? *criticisms of nobility, government, and the Church*

Explain How did Voltaire express his ideas? *by writing with sharp wit*

Info to Know

The Encyclopedia The word encyclopedia means "circle of teachings." Although a slim three-volume set was produced in English, French philosopher Denis Diderot edited perhaps the first work that is truly worthy of that name. *Encyclopedia or Systematic Dictionary of the Arts, Sciences, and Crafts* filled 35 volumes by the time it was completed in 1777. Contributors included many leading thinkers of the Enlightenment.

Answers

Counterpoints *Hobbes—human nature is violent; Locke—human nature is governed by natural laws*

Reading Check *Each philosopher had strong opinions about the power and purpose of government.*

COUNTERPOINTS

Two Views on Society

After living through the English civil war, Thomas Hobbes became convinced that society needed a strong central authority to control and contain the natural barbarism of humans.

"In [a state of nature], there is . . . no Knowledge of the face of the Earth; no account of Time; no Arts; no Letters; no Society; and which is worst of all, continuall feare, and danger of violent death; And the life of man, solitary, poor, nasty, brutish, and short."

Thomas Hobbes
—Leviathan, 1651

John Locke believed that under ideal conditions, people lived according to a law of nature. Because people could interpret the law differently, they needed an authority to enforce it.

"The state of nature has a law of nature to govern it. . . no one ought to harm another in his life, health, liberty, or possessions: . . . Every one . . . may not . . . take away, or impair . . . the life, the liberty, health, limb, or goods of another."

John Locke
—Two Treatises on Government, 1690

Skills Focus READING LIKE A HISTORIAN

Contrast How do Hobbes's and Locke's views of human nature differ?

ACADEMIC VOCABULARY
rational having reason or understanding

Rousseau also believed that society corrupted people. In *The Social Contract*, he wrote, "Man is born free but everywhere is in chains."

Rousseau believed that government should work for the benefit of the common good, not for the wealthy few. He argued that individuals should give up some of their freedoms for the benefit of the community as a whole.

Rousseau despised inequality in society. He believed that all people were equal and should be recognized as equal in society. His view would inspire revolutionaries in years to come.

Baron de Montesquieu Another French thinker, **Baron de Montesquieu** (MOHN-tes-kyoo), argued that the best form of government included a separation of powers. Dividing power among branches of government, he believed, would prevent any individual or group from abusing its power.

In 1748 Montesquieu published *The Spirit of the Laws.* In this book he wrote about his admiration for Great Britain's government, because its powers were divided into branches. Parliament (the legislative branch) made the laws. The king and his advisers (the executive branch) carried out the laws. The court system (the judicial branch) interpreted the laws.

In truth, Montesquieu had misunderstood the structures of the British government. His misunderstanding, however, led him to a rational conclusion. The separation of powers allowed each branch of government to serve as a check against the power of the others—a concept known as the system of checks and balances. This concept would become an important part of the structure of later democratic governments, especially that of the United States.

READING CHECK **Make Inferences** Why was the subject of government so important to Hobbes, Locke, Rousseau, and Montesquieu?

New Views on Society

While some Enlightenment philosophers focused their attention on government, others chose to deal with issues in society, such as religious toleration, women's rights, and economic systems.

Voltaire One of the most outspoken French philosophers, or **philosophes**, was François-Marie Arouet, who wrote under the name **Voltaire** (vohl-TAYR). With biting wit, Voltaire attacked injustice wherever he saw it—among

Skills Focus: Identifying Main Idea and Details

At Level

Reading Skill

Philosophers of the Enlightenment

1. Draw the chart for students to see. Omit the italicized answers.
2. Have students copy and complete the chart. Then, have volunteers fill in the class chart. Guide students in a discussion about the differences of each philosopher's beliefs.
   LS **Visual-Spatial**

Alternative Assessment Handbook, Rubrics 7: Charts; and 11: Discussions

Philosophers of the Enlightenment

Philosopher	Hobbes	Locke	Rousseau	Montesquieu
Main Work	*Leviathan*	*Two Treatises of Civil Government*	*Social Contract*	*The Spirit of Laws*
Idea of Government	*imposes order, prevents violence*	*protects rights, political equality*	*sovereignty comes from the people*	*democracy must be carefully maintained*
Preferred Government	*Monarchy*	*Democracy*	*Democracy*	*Republican (Democracy)*

the nobility, in the government, and in the church. His sharp wit created enemies, however, and Voltaire was imprisoned twice. He was later exiled to England for two years.

Voltaire used his pen to defend every principle that he held dear and to fight superstition and ignorance. Despite making enemies, Voltaire continued the struggle for justice, religious toleration, and liberty during his entire life.

Diderot and the *Encyclopedia* By the mid-1700s the great expansion of human knowledge convinced French philosophe Denis Diderot (DEE-de-roh) to compile it all into a single work, the *Encyclopedia*. This extensive 35-volume work explained new ideas about art, science, government, and religion. Its purpose was the promotion of knowledge.

Diderot worked on the *Encyclopedia* for 27 years, publishing the last volume in 1772. French leaders attacked the *Encyclopedia* because it criticized the church, the government, and the legal system. The government tried to stop publication in 1759, and Diderot completed the remaining volumes in secret. The *Encyclopedia* was an immediate success, and it helped spread Enlightenment ideas across Europe and to North America.

Mary Wollstonecraft Although Enlightenment thinkers questioned many established beliefs, they usually held traditional views about women. Many believed that women's proper roles were as wives and mothers, and that women should receive only enough education to prepare them for those roles.

The English writer Mary Wollstonecraft rejected that view. Wollstonecraft demanded equal rights for women, especially in education—a radical view at the time. In her 1792 book, *A Vindication of the Rights of Woman*, she argued that if men and women had equal education, they would be equal in society.

Adam Smith Some thinkers such as Scottish economist Adam Smith, used reason to analyze economic systems. In his 1776 book, *The Wealth of Nations*, Smith argued that business activities should take place in a free market. Smith was a strong believer in laissez-faire (les-ay FAYR) economics, an economic system that worked without government regulation. In French, laissez-faire means "leave alone". Smith believed that the economy would be stronger if the market forces of supply and demand were allowed to work freely.

READING CHECK **Summarize** How did philosophers apply reason to issues in society?

Reading like a Historian

Voltaire's *Candide*

Interpreting Literature as a Source Works of fiction can be very revealing about the times in which they were written. Through the actions and words of the characters, the writer may include information about how people lived, worked, and interacted with each other.

The main character in *Candide* is a young man named Candide who is on a journey around the world in search of enlightenment and wisdom. In the excerpt below, Voltaire describes Candide's view of the aftermath of an earthquake in Lisbon, Portugal. When analyzing a work of fiction, think about

- the details in the literature and known facts
- the author's point of view

An auto-da-fe was a ritual of penance for condemned heretics, who were usually executed afterward.

> After the earthquake, which had destroyed three-fourths of the city of Lisbon, the sages [wise men] of that country could think of no means more effectual to preserve the kingdom from utter ruin than to entertain the people with an auto-da-fe, it having been decided by the University of Coimbra, that the burning of a few people alive by a slow fire, and with great ceremony, is an infallible preventive of earthquakes.
>
> —Voltaire, *Candide*, 1759

Universities were controlled by the church and existed primarily to prepare students for church careers.

Skills Focus **READING LIKE A HISTORIAN**

1. **Details** What action did Portuguese leaders believe would save the country from further devastation?
2. **Author's Point of View** How does the phrase "entertain the people with an auto-da-fe" reveal Voltaire's disdain for Portuguese leaders?

See **Skills Handbook**, p. H28

Direct Teach

Reading Focus

New Views on Society

Explain What did Mary Wollstonecraft believe about women's education? *women should receive equal education; would hold equal place in society if they were equally educated*

Describe What was laissez-faire economics? *an economic system that works without government regulation*

CRF: Literature: *Rip Van Winkle*

Biography

Mary Wollstonecraft (1759–1797)
English author Mary Wollstonecraft left home in her early twenties to run a school with her sisters. When her first novel met with moderate success, she moved to London, where she found a job as a translator and joined an intellectual circle that included Thomas Paine and William Blake. Wollstonecraft briefly lived in Paris during the French Revolution.

Recent Scholarship

In *Jean-Jacques Rousseau: Restless Genius*, Leo Damrosch presents an insightful view of Rousseau's tumultuous life. Damrosch successfully explains the significance of *Emile, The Social Contract*, and the *Confessions*, and relates those works to Rousseau's conflicted psyche.

Jean-Jacques Rousseau: Restless Genius by Leo Damrosch. Houghton Mifflin, 2005.

Skills Focus: Summarizing

At Level

Reading Skill
Enlightenment Salon

1. Review the information in the text about Enlightenment salons.
2. Organize students into small groups.
3. Have each group write a short skit about a scene that would likely take place at a salon. Characters should discuss and debate ideas about man in his natural state, the purpose of government, the ideal government, and rights.
4. Have students rehearse and perform their skits for the class. **LS Kinesthetic, Interpersonal**

Alternative Assessment Handbook, Rubrics 14: Group Activity; and 33: Skits and Reader's Theater

Answers

Reading Like a Historian 1. *burning a few people alive;* **2.** *It reveals that the leaders did not think highly of the people they ruled.*

Reading Check *They used reason to challenge existing societal views and government policies.*

Direct Teach

Reading Focus

4 How did Enlightenment ideas spread? *Monarchs across Europe began to adopt Enlightenment ideas in their social policies.*

Enlightenment Ideas Spread

Recall Who were the enlightened despots? *monarchs who made reforms based on Enlightenment ideas*

Explain Why did Catherine the Great shift her focus from reform to building a Russian empire? *because she realized that if her reforms were too liberal she would lose the support of the wealthy landowners*

CRF: Biography: Madame Geoffrin

Teaching Tip

Arrange the classroom like a salon for a discussion. Place chairs or desks in a circle and sit in the circle with students. Keep pressure low, and ask thought-provoking questions that will encourage students to get involved. This will work well if you treat the activity as an incentive and make guidelines ahead of time. Afterwards, ask students how the reorganization of desks and chairs affected the discussion.

Enlightenment Society

In the late 1700s, Madame Geoffrin hosted some of the most popular salons and frequently invited Voltaire, Diderot, and Montesquieu.

An actor entertains the salon's guests by reading Voltaire's play *The Orphan of China.*

Salons were intellectually stimulating social gatherings held in the homes of wealthy Parisian women. Philosophers, writers, artists, and scientists gathered there to share their ideas. ***How do you think salons helped women gain more rights in Enlightenment society?***

Enlightenment Ideas Spread

The spirit of optimism and change was not confined to the salons and the coffeehouses of Europe. Enlightenment ideas quickly spread throughout Europe to Prussia, Russia, Austria, and beyond. Many philosophes appealed directly to European monarchs for change. As a result, a few monarchs developed a system of government in which they ruled according to Enlightenment ideas. These monarchs became known as **enlightened despots**.

Prussia Frederick II, the king of Prussia from 1740 to 1786, believed that his duty was to rule with absolute power in order to build Prussia's strength. But he was also strongly influenced by the ideas of Voltaire. While Frederick was building Prussia a military power in Europe, he also introduced a number of reforms.

Frederick ambitiously tried to establish a system of elementary education for all Prussian children. He abolished torture and supported most forms of religious tolerance. Frederick also reduced censorship.

Frederick's reforms were limited, however. For example, he did not extend religious tolerance to Jews; he tried to limit the number of Jews that could live in Prussia. Frederick also opposed serfdom, but he did not abolish it because he needed the support of the aristocracy. Like other enlightened despots, Frederick did not make reforms simply to achieve justice. He did so to build Prussia's strength and make his own rule more powerful.

Russia When Catherine II became the ruler of Russia in 1762, she dreamed of establishing order and justice in Russia while supporting education and culture. Catherine not only read the works of the philosophes also corresponded with both Voltaire and Diderot.

Inspired by the philosophes, Catherine set about reforming Russia. She drafted a Russian constitution and a code of laws, but they were considered far too liberal and were never put

Skills Focus: Make Inferences

At Level

Reading Skill

Recommendations for a Despot

1. Review with students the basic ideas of the Enlightenment philosophers.
2. Organize students into mixed-ability pairs.
3. Have each pair make a list of five recommendations for rulers who wanted to implement Enlightenment ideas. For example, rulers should not confiscate a person's property unless that person owes a large amount of money in taxes.
4. Have volunteers read their recommendations to the class. LS **Verbal-Linguistic**

Alternative Assessment Handbook, Rubric 35: Solving Problems

Answers

Enlightenment Society *possible answer—Intellectual gatherings probably inspired them to push for more rights.*

into practice. Before Catherine came to power, she intended to free the serfs but quickly realized that she would lose the support of wealthy landowners if she did. Catherine had no intentions of giving up power and she became a tyrant. During her reign she actually imposed serfdom on more Russians than ever before.

Austria The most radical enlightened despot was Joseph II, the son of Maria Theresa of Austria. When he became emperor in 1780, Joseph embarked upon an ambitious reform program. He eliminated torture and the death penalty and provided free food and medicine for poor citizens. As a Catholic emperor, he granted religious tolerance to Protestants and Jews. His most significant reform was abolishing serfdom and requiring that laborers be paid for their work.

These dramatic changes were resisted by the nobility and the church. They forced Joseph to revoke some of his reforms shortly before his death in 1790.

Later Times and Places During the Enlightenment, writers and philosophers questioned ideas that had been long held as absolute truths. They challenged beliefs in absolute monarchy, questioned the relationship between the church and state, and debated the roles and rights of people in society. Enlightenment philosophers promoted ideas that reformers and revolutionaries would later use to change society.

The Enlightenment belief in progress would spur many generations to enact reforms. People began to believe that human reason could solve any problem. Instead of accepting poverty, ignorance, and inequality as part of the human condition, people debated new ways of making society more just.

Enlightenment ideas about power and authority would inspire not only reforms but revolutions. For example, leaders in Great Britain's American colonies would use those ideas as inspiration to break free from the British monarchy. Strongly influenced by the political views of Locke and Rousseau, the colonists began to experience a new sense of national identity.

READING CHECK **Draw Conclusions** How successful were the reforms of the enlightened despots?

Key Enlightenment Ideas

QUICK FACTS

- The ability to reason is what makes humans unique.
- Reason can be used to solve problems and improve people's lives.
- Reason can free people from ignorance, superstition, and unfair government.
- The natural world is governed by laws that can be discovered through reason.
- Like the natural world, human behavior is governed by natural laws.
- Governments should reflect natural laws and encourage education and debate.

Section 2 Assessment

go.hrw.com
Online Quiz
Keyword: SHP ENL HP

1. **a. Define** What was the **Enlightenment**?
   b. Explain Why did philosophers believe reason was important?
   c. Elaborate Why would **salons** be an effective way to spread Enlightenment ideas?
2. **a. Identify** Who wrote *Leviathan*?
   b. Analyze How did Hobbes and Locke differ in their ideas about government?
3. **a. Recall** Who were the **philosophes**?
   b. Explain What radical idea did Mary Wollstonecraft support?
   c. Predict Why might Adam Smith's economic ideas appeal to business owners?
4. **a. Identify** What was an **enlightened despot**?
   b. Draw Conclusions How were Frederick II's reforms limited?
   c. Evaluate What do you think is the most significant legacy of the Enlightenment?

Critical Thinking

5. **Analyze** Use a concept map like this one below and your notes from this section to describe how Enlightenment ideas affected government.

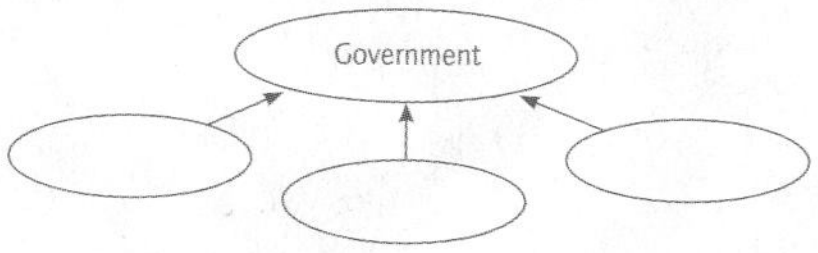

Focus on Speaking

6. **Persuasion** Suppose you are a philosophe who would like your monarch to make reforms based on Enlightenment ideas. Prepare a speech in which you try to convince Frederick the Great, Catherine the Great, or Joseph II to support your ideas. Be sure to include reasons why you believe it would be in the monarch's best interests to make your reforms.

Direct Teach

Reading Focus

Enlightenment Ideas Spread

Analyze Were the enlightened despots truly enlightened? *possible answers—yes, passed reforms; no, abandoned reforms when politically necessary*

Predict How might Enlightenment ideas inspire revolutions? *possible answer—People might rise up against governments who did not adhere to the social contract.*

Quick Facts Transparency: Key Enlightenment Ideas

Review & Assess

Close

Have students compare and contrast the ideas of the Enlightenment philosophers.

Review

Online Quiz, Section 2

Assess

SE Section 2 Assessment

Progress Assessment: Section 2 Quiz

Alternative Assessment Handbook

Reteach/Intervene

Interactive Reader and Study Guide, Section 2

Interactive Skills Tutor CD-ROM

Section 2 Assessment Answers

1. **a.** a time of optimism in which people used reason to solve human problems
   b. because it helped people to abandon traditional beliefs
   c. possible answer—Salons brought together many different groups of people to share ideas.
2. **a.** Thomas Hobbes
   b. Hobbes—government imposes order, monarch should be obeyed; Locke—government protects rights, should be limited
3. **a.** French philosophers of the Age of Reason
   b. equal rights for women
   c. did not want government regulations
4. **a.** a ruler who made reforms based upon Enlightenment ideas
   b. only helped certain people; made some reforms to increase his own power
   c. possible answer—American and French revolutions would not have occurred.
5. Notes should mention that people began to question traditional authorities.
6. Speeches should show an unerstanding of Enlightment ideas.

Answers

Reading Check *They were successful but limited by political opposition.*

Preteach

Getting Started

Use the **Interactive Reader and Study Guide** to familiarize students with the section content.

Interactive Reader and Study Guide, Section 3

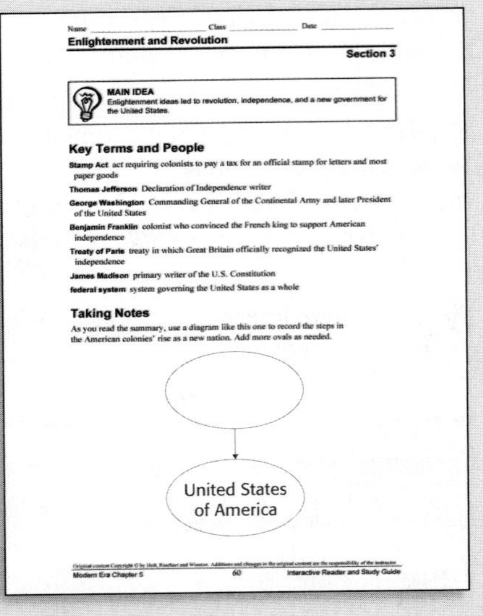

Name ______________ Class ______________ Date ______________

Enlightenment and Revolution

Section 3

MAIN IDEA
Enlightenment ideas led to revolution, independence, and a new government for the United States.

Key Terms and People

Stamp Act act requiring colonists to pay a tax for an official stamp for letters and most paper goods

Thomas Jefferson Declaration of Independence writer

George Washington Commanding General of the Continental Army and later President of the United States

Benjamin Franklin colonist who convinced the French king to support American independence

Treaty of Paris treaty in which Great Britain officially recognized the United States' independence

James Madison primary writer of the U.S. Constitution

federal system system governing the United States as a whole

Taking Notes

As you read the summary, use a diagram like this one to record the steps in the American colonies' rise as a new nation. Add more ovals as needed.

United States of America

Original content Copyright © by Holt, Rinehart and Winston. Additions and changes to the original content are the responsibility of the instructor.

Modern Era Chapter 5 60 Interactive Reader and Study Guide

Academic Vocabulary

Review with students the high-use academic term in this section.

regulation a law designed to control or govern conduct (p. 183)

CRF: Vocabulary Builder: Section 3

Taking Notes

first successful English colonies; Seven Years' War and new tax policies; opposition and increase in tensions; fighting breaks out; Common Sense; Declaration of Independence; America wins war

go.hrw.com
Online Resources
KEYWORD: SHL ENL
ACTIVITY: The Enlightenment

SECTION 3

The American Revolution

Before You Read

Main Idea

Enlightenment ideas led to revolution, independence, and a new government for the United States.

Reading Focus

1. What were some of the causes of change and crisis in the American colonies?
2. How was the struggle for independence affected by Enlightenment concepts?
3. How did American colonists form a new government?

Key Terms and People

Stamp Act
Thomas Jefferson
Benjamin Franklin
George Washington
Treaty of Paris
James Madison
federal system

TAKING NOTES Take notes on the steps in the American colonies' rise as a new nation. Add more ovals as needed.

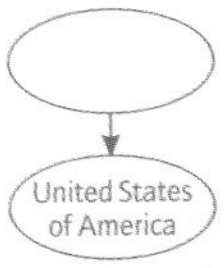

The Power of Ideas

◀ **French engraving of three titans of the Enlightenment: Voltaire, Jean-Jacques Rousseau, and Benjamin Franklin**

THE INSIDE STORY ***How did Enlightenment ideas influence an American leader?*** Benjamin Franklin was one of the great Enlightenment philosophers in America. Like Voltaire, Rousseau, and other Enlightenment philosophers, Franklin believed that reason and intelligence could be used to improve the lives of everyone.

Franklin was not just a philosopher; he was a scientist as well. His methodical observations and experiments led him to invent a number of useful items, such as the lightning rod, bifocals, and the Franklin stove. Through his inventions, Franklin showed that practical applications of scientific knowledge could be used to improve people's lives.

Although Franklin may be best remembered today for his inventions and experiments, his commitment to Enlightenment ideals would have an even longer-lasting impact. In the 1770s Franklin came together with other American Enlightenment thinkers, such as Thomas Jefferson, to put Enlightenment ideals into practice to create a new government and nation—the United States. ■

Teach the Main Idea

At Level

The American Revolution

1. **Teach** Ask students the Reading Focus questions to teach this section.
2. **Apply** Draw three ladders for students to see. Label the tops of the ladders with the names of the topics in this section: Change and Crisis, Struggle for Independence, and Forming a New Government. Have students copy the ladders and fill in the rungs of the ladders with the main ideas of each topic.
3. **Review** As you review the section, have students explain the various ideas that made an impact during the American Revolution.
4. **Practice/Homework** Have students write an open letter from an Enlightenment philosopher to the American colonists, encouraging them in their struggle against England. **LS Visual-Spatial, Verbal-Linguistic**

Alternative Assessment Handbook, Rubric 25: Personal Letters

Change and Crisis

By the mid-1700s dramatic new Enlightenment ideas had spread as far as North America. These ideas inspired Great Britain's colonists to seek independence and forge a new nation founded on the ideals of the Enlightenment.

Forming a New Identity Since the establishment of the first English settlement in North America in the early 1600s, the British colonies had expanded rapidly along the east coast. By 1770 the colonies had a population of more than 2.1 million people.

The colonies offered many opportunities that simply were not available in Great Britain. Land was plentiful and cheap. The English class system was largely absent, and individuals could more easily advance themselves through intelligence and hard work.

By the mid-1770s the colonies had been established for nearly 150 years. Although the colonists were British subjects, they were allowed a large measure of independence. Each colony had its own government and made most of its own laws. Over time, the colonists began to identify more closely with the colonies and less with Britain itself.

Opposing British Policies Trouble erupted when Britain began to assert its right to impose laws on the colonies. In the 1760s conflict between some colonists and Britain escalated rapidly.

Britain defeated France in the French and Indian War in 1763, and France had to give up its North American colonies. The war had been very expensive for Britain. Because removing the French benefited the colonists, Britain decided to make the colonies pay part of the cost in the form of new taxes.

In 1765 Parliament passed the **Stamp Act**, which required colonists to pay a tax for an official stamp on all newspapers, legal documents, and other public papers. Colonial leaders were outraged that Parliament taxed them without representatives there to plead their case. They called for a boycott of English goods, which caused Parliament to repeal the act in 1766.

The British, in 1767, imposed a new series of taxes on glass, paper, paints, and tea. Furious merchants in Boston, Massachusetts, one of the largest colonial cities and a major port, called for another boycott of English goods. The British sent in troops to keep order in the city. As a result, Bostonians harassed the troops constantly on the city's streets.

Finally, in 1770 British discipline snapped. Troops shot and killed five men in an incident known as the Boston Massacre. Most of the Townshend Acts were partially repealed after another colonial boycott. However, the tax on tea remained.

In 1773 a group of rebellious Bostonians called the Sons of Liberty boarded three ships in Boston Harbor. Led by Samuel Adams and Paul Revere, the Sons of Liberty dumped hundreds of crates of tea into the harbor to protest the tax, an act known as the Boston Tea Party. The British closed the port of Boston and passed the so-called Intolerable Acts, regulations that limited the freedoms of the colonists.

The colonists called the First Continental Congress in Philadelphia in 1774 to list their grievances against the British government. A plan to reconcile their differences with the British was presented, but it was voted down.

Revolution Begins The Sons of Liberty in Massachusetts expected a war. As a consequence, they hid weapons in the countryside and towns west of Boston. In April 1775 hundreds of British troops marched out of Boston toward the towns of Lexington and Concord, intending to find these weapons. At dawn on April 19, British troops confronted about 75 colonial militiamen in Lexington. Shots rang out, and the American Revolution began.

ACADEMIC VOCABULARY
regulation a law designed to control or govern conduct

FACES OF HISTORY

George WASHINGTON
1732–1799

George Washington's leadership was crucial to an American victory in the Revolutionary War. When he took command of the American forces in 1775, he faced the daunting task of leading an army of untrained militia men against one of the world's strongest military forces.

But Washington's leadership skills won him the loyalty of his troops. He enforced strict discipline, but he also demanded better food, clothing, and pay for them from the Continental Congress. Washington knew that if he looked after his soldiers' needs, they would be better prepared to defeat the British army.

Identify Supporting Details What were some of the ways in which Washington created an effective army against the British?

Direct Teach

Reading Focus

❶ What were some of the causes of change and crisis in the American colonies? *taxes to pay for war, Navigation Acts, Stamp Act, Townshend Acts, Boston Massacre, Boston Tea Party, Intolerable Acts, start of American Revolution, Common Sense published*

Change and Crisis

Recall What did the Stamp Act do? *required colonists to pay a tax for an official stamp on newspapers, legal documents, and other public papers*

Identify Cause and Effect What reactions did British tax policies prompt in the colonies? *boycotts of British goods, tension with British troops, Boston Massacre, Boston Tea Party*

Develop If you had been the ruler of Great Britain during the unrest in the colonies, what would you have done? *possible answer—appease the colonists by keeping taxes at a minimum; establish martial law*

Info to Know

British Revenues and Expenses In the year 1755, the Seven Years' War cost England about 3.5 million pounds sterling, approximately 700 million dollars today. Tax revenues were about 7 million pounds. By 1760, annual war expenditures had reached nearly 14 million pounds, although tax revenues had only been increased to about 9 million.

Primary Source

"You know that these two nations [France and England] have been at war over a few acres of snow near Canada, and they are spending on this fine struggle more than Canada itself is worth."
—Voltaire, *Candide*, Chapter 23

Collaborative Learning

At Level

Come to America!

Materials: poster paper, art supplies

Background: Tell students that the early colonies were run by companies that had a large interest in the colonies' lasting success. When England took over the colonies, it had a large strategic and economic interest in the colonies' success.

1. Review with students the various attractions of America during the colonial period.
2. Organize students into small groups. Each group should designate a designer, artist, letterer, and fact checker. The fact checker's job is to verify the historical accuracy of the images.
3. Have each group create a print advertisement to convince people to settle in America. Advertisements should showcase the attractions of America and feature a large slogan.
4. Have volunteers present their advertisements to the class. LS **Visual-Spatial**

Alternative Assessment Handbook, Rubric 2: Advertisements

Answers

Faces of History *enforced strict discipline; won loyalty of troops; demanded better pay, food, and clothing for his troops*

Direct Teach

Reading Focus

2 How was the struggle for independence affected by Enlightenment concepts? *The concept of the social contract led colonists to believe Great Britain could not rule the colonies without their consent; Enlightenment ideas were used in the Declaration of Independence.*

Struggle for Independence

Identify Who was on the committee to write the Declaration of Independence? *Thomas Jefferson, John Adams, Benjamin Franklin, and others*

Analyze Did the Declaration of Independence present new or old ideas? Explain your answer. *possible answer—was influenced by Magna Carta, English Bill of Rights, and Enlightenment ideas, but Declaration presented those ideas in a new way*

Predict How do you think the English government reacted to the Declaration? *possible answer—views unchanged; still needed to keep colonies under control for economic reasons*

CRF: Biography: Benjamin Franklin

About the Illustration

This illustration is an artist's conception based on available sources. Historians, however, are uncertain exactly what this scene looked like.

Info to Know

Indentured Servants Approximately half of the new settlers in the North American colonies were indentured servants. These people signed a contract called an indenture in order to gain passage to the colonies. Indentured servants were fairly expensive to obtain, but they worked on their employer's land from four to seven years. After they finished their term, they were given food, clothing, tools, and some money, and could stake their own claim to land.

Answers

Reading Check *Both imposed taxes on the colonies.*

Not all colonists were Patriots, or those who wanted independence from Britain. Many colonists remained loyal to the British. Others thought that such a war was too risky.

In his January 1776 pamphlet, *Common Sense,* writer Thomas Paine argued that the colonies had matured to the point that they no longer needed British rule. Instead, he argued, they deserved independence. Widely read, Thomas Paine's *Common Sense* helped the Patriots gain popular support for the cause of independence.

READING CHECK **Compare** What did the Stamp Act and the Townshend Acts have in common?

Struggle for Independence

The American Revolution was the first war in which old ideas about government were challenged by the ideas of the Enlightenment. The Patriots created a nation based on these ideas.

Declaring Independence During the meeting of the Second Continental Congress in 1776, a committee formed to write a document declaring the colonies' independence from Britain. Members of the committee were well-educated leaders, such as John Adams, **Thomas Jefferson**, and **Benjamin Franklin**, who were familiar with Enlightenment concepts. Jefferson wrote a draft of the Declaration, incorporating ideas from Locke and Rousseau. On July 4, 1776, the Continental Congress adopted the Declaration of Independence.

The Declaration of Independence was an elegant expression of Enlightenment political philosophy. Many of these ideas were presented in the Preamble.

HISTORY'S VOICES

> **"That to secure these rights, Governments are instituted among Men, deriving their just powers from the consent of the governed,—That whenever any Form of Government becomes destructive of these ends, it is the Right of the People to alter or to abolish it, and to institute new Government . . ."**
>
> —The Declaration of Independence, 1776

Interactive

HISTORY CLOSE-UP **Valley Forge**

From December 1777 to June 1778 the Continental Army camped at Valley Forge, a hilltop near Philadelphia. Here soldiers endured a harsh winter, very little food, and disease. Despite these hardships, the soldiers who left Valley Forge were a more unified and disciplined army.

Women at the camp cooked and took care of sick soldiers.
As many as 12 men shared a tiny hut like this one.

Skills Focus: Comparing and Contrasting

At Level

Reading Skill

British Policies and Taxes

1. Review with students the information in the text about British policies and taxes leading up to the American Revolution.
2. Have students create two political cartoons—one that opposes British policies, implying they are unjust, and the other that supports them, implying that the colonists are complaining unnecessarily.
3. Have volunteers present their political cartoons to the class.
4. Guide a class discussion about the differing viewpoints expressed in students' cartoons. **LS Visual-Spatial**

Alternative Assessment Handbook, Rubric 27: Political Cartoons

The Declaration of Independence drew ideas from the English Bill of Rights of 1689, which protected citizens' right to a trial, the right to elect members of Parliament, and the right to an independent judicial system.

The Revolutionary War Before independence had been declared, the Second Continental Congress assigned **George Washington** as the commanding general of the army in June 1775. The Americans had little money. However, they had a courageous and resourceful leader in General Washington, as well as the advantage of fighting in their own land.

The American Revolution began poorly for the British, who evacuated Boston in June 1775 after the Americans positioned cannons overlooking the city. British troops later defeated Washington in the Battle of Long Island, and the Continental Army was driven into New Jersey. Beaten and bruised, Washington engineered a surprising and daring victory by crossing the icy Delaware River and defeating British forces at Trenton.

In 1777 the British defeated Washington's forces in New Jersey, and Washington moved into Pennsylvania. Philadelphia fell to the British, and Washington's army spent a bitter and deadly winter at Valley Forge.

In upstate New York, the British were also winning battles in the summer of 1777. In October, however, the Americans trapped British general Burgoyne's army at the Battle of Saratoga. The British surrendered and the victory was a crucial win for the Americans. At the same time, Benjamin Franklin was in Paris seeking aid from the French. The victory at Saratoga was exactly the news he needed. Franklin was able to convince the French to contribute heavily to the American cause. This alliance became a turning point in the war.

Over the next two years, the Americans strengthened their forces. The British adopted a strategy to divide the colonies in two. They captured Savannah, Georgia in 1778 and Charleston, South Carolina in 1780. In South Carolina, the Americans made numerous attacks on the British.

In September 1781 the French and American armies surrounded the British army under Lord Cornwallis in Yorktown, Virginia. After a siege of several weeks, Cornwallis grew tired of waiting for the British reinforcements. Lord Cornwallis and his troops surrendered to General Washington on October 19, 1781. The American colonists had won their independence from Great Britain.

General George Washington led the Continental Army.

With marching drills and weapons training, General Steuben from Prussia helped transform the American soldiers into a professional army.

Skills Focus INTERPRETING VISUALS

Draw Conclusions How do you think surviving a harsh winter with few clothes and little food helped unite the soldiers in the Continental Army?

go.hrw.com
COULD YOU HAVE SURVIVED?
Keyword: SHL ENL

Go online for a closer look at survival and this event.

Skills Focus: Summarizing

At Level

Reading Skill
Rebel Soldier

1. Review with students the basic information about the campaigns of the American Revolution.
2. Have students write five brief letters home from the point of view of an American soldier serving under the command of George Washington. Have students date the letters so that they cover several events of the American Revolution.
3. Have volunteers read their letters to the class.
4. Discuss the letters as a class. Did the letters convey an accurate portrayal of George Washington's leadership? LS **Intrapersonal, Verbal-Linguistic**

Alternative Assessment Handbook, Rubric 25: Personal Letters

Direct Teach

Reading Focus

Struggle for Independence

Explain Why was the Battle of Saratoga a turning point in the war? *Americans captured large army; Franklin able to get aid from France*

Draw Conclusions How did American forces use their advantages to win the war? *relied on Washington's great leadership; used knowledge of land to launch guerilla attacks; surrounded British forces on peninsula*

CRF: History and Geography: Battles in the War for Independence

Info to Know

Wealth and the Revolution Many historians have pointed out that the American Revolution was primarily a power struggle among members of the upper class. The men who engineered the revolt generally belonged to the wealthy ruling class; George Washington, for instance, was the richest man in the colonies. The majority of soldiers, however, were poor men. Rich men could avoid being drafted by paying for substitutes to fight for them. The military also offered incentives to the poor such as money and a change in social status.

Primary Source

"These are the times that try men's souls. The summer soldier and the sunshine patriot will, in this crisis, shrink from the service of their country; but he that stands it *now*, deserves the love and thanks of man and woman."
—Thomas Paine, *The American Crisis,* no. 1, Dec. 23, 1776

Answers

History Close-Up *possible answer—improved their morale and proved that they were a strong, united force*

Direct Teach

Reading Focus

3 How did American colonists form a new government? *replaced Articles of Confederation with a new Constitution and Bill of Rights*

Forming a New Government

Identify What powers did the government lack under the Articles of Confederation? *had no power to tax or negotiate with foreign powers*

Contrast How did the Constitution differ from the Articles of Confederation? *created a federal system of government, divided power among three branches of government*

Explain How did the Bill of Rights become part of the Constitution? *A group of opponents wanted protection for individual rights to be added to the Constitution.*

Map Transparency: The Revolutionary War

Info to Know

Young Patriots Patriots of all ages fought in the Revolutionary War. Many boys between the ages of 14 and 16 enlisted in the American army. Other boys, some who were as young as 6, served as drummers for the troops. The job of drummer boys was to signal commands from generals to troops, which sometimes put them in the midst of battle. The American navy had its share of young sailors as well; these boys served as deckhands or "powder monkeys" who carried ammunition to the gunners during battle.

THE REVOLUTIONARY WAR

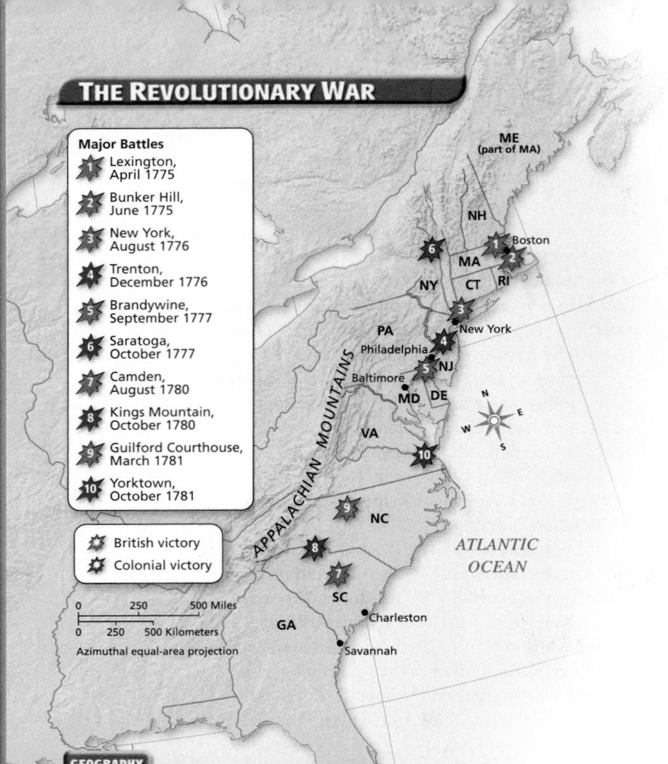

GEOGRAPHY SKILLS INTERPRETING MAPS

1. **Location** In which state were the first two major battles of the Revolutionary War fought in 1775?
2. **Regions** What physical feature served as a natural boundary for the thirteen colonies?

In September 1783 the British government formally recognized the independence of the United States by signing the **Treaty of Paris**. Benjamin Franklin and other American leaders signed the document in Paris. This treaty set the geographic boundaries for the new United States. The treaty gave the Americans not only independence but also much greater territory than the original 13 colonies. The Americans gained all land east of the Mississippi River and north of the 31st parallel.

The end of the war was just the beginning, however. The Americans now faced the daunting and difficult task of building a new nation.

READING CHECK **Sequence** What events led to the signing of the Declaration of Independence?

Forming a New Government

The American Revolution was over. Now the colonists had to figure out how to band together to form a new government and nation. Meanwhile, in France, revolutionaries inspired by the success of the American Revolution began to oppose the French monarchy.

The Articles of Confederation The first government of the new United States was established by the Articles of Confederation, approved in 1781. The framers of the Articles deliberately made the national government weak to avoid abuses of power. For example, the government had no power to tax. It also could not negotiate with foreign nations. The Articles of Confederation produced a government that proved too weak to govern effectively.

The Constitution In 1787, delegates met at a Constitutional Convention in Philadelphia to revise the Articles. Instead, they wrote a new constitution. The U.S. Constitution remains the oldest written constitution still in use today.

George Washington presided over the convention, but **James Madison** played a leading role in negotiating the main points. Delegates met for nearly four months, and the Constitution that emerged was a product of skillful compromise. The delegates signed the Constitution in 1787, which then went to the states to be ratified. The Constitution went into effect in 1789.

The Constitution created a **federal system** of government. In a federal system, certain powers are held by the federal government, and other powers are reserved for the state governments. The Constitution divides the national government's powers among three branches of government. The executive branch includes the president, who has the power to carry out laws. The judicial branch interprets the laws. Congress, the legislative branch, makes the laws. Congress consists of a lower house, called the House of Representatives, and an upper house, called the Senate. A system of checks and balances ensures that no branch of government becomes too powerful.

The influence of Enlightenment thought on the Constitution was very powerful. The founding principle of the Constitution is that government exists for the people. This principle

Differentiating Instruction

Above Level

Advanced Learners/Gifted and Talented

Prep Required

Materials: copies of the Declaration of Independence, the Constitution and Bill of Rights, various Enlightenment writings, the English Bill of Rights, and Magna Carta

1. Organize students into small groups. Give each group copies of the Declaration of Independence, the preamble to the Constitution, the Bill of Rights, and one other document. You may wish to find annotated versions.
2. Tell students that the early leaders of the United States were influenced by many earlier documents. Have students search for similarities in the documents. Suggest that students first read the American documents and then split up the other selection and search for similar language and ideas. Have students compile the similarities into an annotated list.
3. Have groups present their lists to the class.
LS Verbal-Linguistic

Alternative Assessment Handbook, Rubrics 9: Comparing and Contrasting; and 30: Research

Answers

Interpreting Maps **1.** *Massachusetts;* **2.** *The Atlantic Ocean*

Reading Check *Second Continental Congress declares colonies' independence from Britain; Washington assigned commander of army; American forces strengthened; French and American armies defeat British army; colonists win independence*

reflects Locke's and Rousseau's idea of government by consent of the people. The division of government into three branches reflects Montesquieu's idea of the separation of powers.

The Bill of Rights A group of opponents to the Constitution argued that it failed to protect the rights of citizens. They wanted protection for individuals' rights to be added to the Constitution. Congress responded with the Bill of Rights, the first 10 amendments to the Constitution. The Bill of Rights protected the natural rights advocated by Voltaire, Locke, and Rousseau, such as the freedoms of speech and religion. The Bill of Rights protected a number of other rights, but most important, it guaranteed people equality, or due process, of law.

Impact of American Government News of the American colonies' successful revolution had a tremendous impact on other governments, especially in France. The French king Louis XVI had supported the American Revolution. However, his form of government could not have been further from the ideals of the colonists. He was an absolute monarch who taxed his people without mercy and cared nothing for their suffering. The loss of the Seven Years' War had also added to France's troubles. Additionally, the king's support of the American war effort had been expensive and contributed to France's economic problems.

France would experience the upheaval of revolution beginning in 1789. One of the many reasons for that revolution was the inspiration of the American example. A group of distant British colonies had adopted the ideals of the Enlightenment and shown that it was possible to oppose tyranny. This new government was created based on the principles of liberty and equality. The courage and determination of the soldiers who fought in the Revolution, and the wisdom of the framers of the Constitution, have stood as shining examples to movements against oppression ever since.

Signing the Constitution
George Washington presided over the Constitutional Convention, held in Philadelphia from May to September 1787.

Scene at the Signing of the Constitution, by Howard Chandler Christy, 1940

READING CHECK **Find the Main Idea** How did the Constitution and the Bill of Rights change the government and society of the United States?

SECTION 3 ASSESSMENT

go.hrw.com
Online Quiz
Keyword: SHL ENL HP

Reviewing Ideas, Terms, and People

1. **a. Identify** Who was Thomas Paine, and what did he write?
   b. Analyze How did opposition to British tax policies affect the American colonies?
   c. Evaluate Do you think you would have joined the colonial rebellion in 1770? Why or why not?
2. **a. Recall** What was the **Treaty of Paris**?
   b. Draw Conclusions How did Enlightenment ideas influence the Continental Congress in 1776?
3. **a. Recall** When were the Articles of Confederation approved?
   b. Explain Why was a Constitutional Convention called in 1787?
   c. Make Judgments Do you think it was a wise decision to add the Bill of Rights to the Constitution? Why or why not?

Critical Thinking

4. **Categorize** Use the graphic organizer below to show four key events that led to the formation of the United States. Be sure to explain why you chose those four events.

FOCUS ON WRITING

5. **Persuasion** You are a young American colonist in the early 1770s. Write a short letter to your newspaper's editor stating why you support independence from Great Britain. Explain your reasons.

Direct Teach

Reading Focus

Forming a New Government

Compare In what ways were the American and French revolutions similar? *people rebelled against absolute monarchs and unfair taxation; replaced governments with Enlightenment principles of liberty, equality, democracy*

Analyze Why do you think the French king supported the American Revolution even though his own government was similar to Great Britain's? *possible answer—wanted to gain an advantage over Great Britain*

Review & Assess

Close

Have students explain the connections between Enlightenment ideas and the American colonial struggle.

Review

Online Quiz, Section 3

Assess

SE Section 3 Assessment

Progress Assessment: Section 3 Quiz

Alternative Assessment Handbook

Reteach/Intervene

Interactive Reader and Study Guide, Section 3

Interactive Skills Tutor CD-ROM

Section 3 Assessment Answers

1. **a.** writer and political theorist; *Common Sense*
   b. led to high tension with Britain, boycotts of British goods, Boston Tea Party
   c. possible answers—yes, struggle for basic rights; no, taxes are not this important
2. **a.** a document signed in Paris by American leaders in which the British government formally recognized U.S. independence
   b. They helped inspire the committee to draft the Declaration of Independence.
3. **a.** 1781
   b. to revise the Articles of Confederation
   c. possible answer—yes; guarantees that the nation will protect people's rights
4. Events should include some of the following—Stamp Act; Revolutionary War; Treaty of Paris signed; Constitution signed; Articles of Confederation, and Bill of Rights.
5. Letters should include details from the section, such as: no taxation without representation; colonies no longer needed British rule; people had right to form new government based on Enlightenment principles.

Answers

Reading Check *caused anger about taxation without representation; colonial leaders supported creation of new nation; committee formed at Continental Congress; Jefferson wrote draft; adopted by the Congress*

Document-Based Investigation

Word Help

allay reduce, relieve
redress compensation, payment
assail fight against
arbitrary unrestrained in the exercise of power

Info to Know

The Magna Carta and Democracy The Magna Carta is often cited as the first document in the development of modern democracy. While it is true that the Magna Carta did establish a foundation for later democratic documents, the document King John signed in 1215 was not so much democratic as it was a limitation of the powers of the king by the nobles. Nowhere in its pages did the Magna Carta provide for fully representative government, nor did it grant many rights to ordinary English people. Nevertheless, the Magna Carta did establish an important point: that even a king had to obey the law. Some of the rights granted to the nobles within the Magna Carta were later used to support modern political ideas such as due process of law, no taxation without representation, and the right to trial by jury.

CHAPTER 5 Document-Based Investigation

Documents of Democracy

Historical Context The four famous and significant documents below provide different views on the relationship between government and the people.

Task Examine the selections and answer the questions that follow. After you have studied the documents, you will be asked to write an essay about the ideal of democratic government. You will need to use evidence from these selections and from the chapter to support the position you take in your essay.

DOCUMENT 1

The Magna Carta, 1215

In 1215 a group of English noblemen demanded that King John sign the Magna Carta to protect their rights. This document established that the power of the king could be limited by a written document.

> Since we have granted all these things for God, for the better ordering of our kingdom, and to allay the discord that has arisen between us and our barons, . . . we give and grant to the barons the following security:
>
> The barons shall elect twenty-five of their number to keep . . . the peace and liberties granted and confirmed to them by this charter.
>
> If we . . . offend in any respect against any man . . . , and the offence is made known to four of the said twenty-five barons, they shall come to us . . . to declare it and claim immediate redress. If we . . . make no redress within forty days, . . . the twenty-five barons . . . may distrain upon and assail us in every way possible . . . by seizing our castles, lands, possessions, or anything else . . . until they have secured such redress as they have determined upon. Having secured the redress, they may then resume their normal obedience to us.

DOCUMENT 2

The Spirit of the Laws, 1748

In his 1748 work, *The Spirit of the Laws*, Baron de Montesquieu explained his views on the separation of powers.

> Again, there is no liberty, if the power of judging be not separated from the legislative and executive powers. Were it joined with the legislative, the life and liberty of the subject would be exposed to arbitrary control, for the judge would then be the legislator. Were it joined to the executive power, the judge might behave with all the violence of an oppressor.
>
> There would be an end of every thing were the same man, or the same body, whether of the nobles or of the people to exercise those three powers that of enacting laws, that of executing the public resolutions, and that of judging the crimes or differences of individuals.

Collaborative Learning

At Level

Research Required

Debating the King's Power

1. Organize students into two groups. Assign the first group to represent the point of view of a king. The second group will represent the point of view of the king's subjects.
2. Have students in the first group make a list of reasons why a king should have absolute power. Have students in the second group make a list of reasons why subjects should limit a king's power. Students should develop their lists by using their textbooks, other reference books, and their own ideas. Both groups should examine the four Documents as they develop their lists.
3. Have each group choose one or two representatives to serve as debaters. Then, lead a class debate on the following topic: Do people have the right to limit the power of a ruler? **LS Interpersonal, Verbal-Linguistic**

Alternative Assessment Handbook, Rubrics 1: Acquiring Information, and 10: Debates

DOCUMENT 3

Common Sense, 1776

Thomas Paine argued for independence in his 1776 pamphlet, *Common Sense*.

> Were a manifesto to be published, and despatched to foreign courts, setting forth the miseries we have endured, and the peaceable methods we have ineffectually used for redress; declaring, at the same time, that not being able, any longer, to live happily or safely under the cruel disposition of the British court, we had been driven to the necessity of breaking off all connections with her; at the same time, assuring all such courts of our peaceable disposition towards them, and of our desire of entering into trade with them: Such a memorial would produce more good effects to this Continent, than if a ship were freighted with petitions to Britain.
>
> Under our present denomination of British subjects, we can neither be received nor heard abroad: The custom of all courts is against us, and will be so, until, by an independence, we take rank with other nations.

DOCUMENT 4

Declaration of Independence, 1776

Thomas Jefferson wrote the Declaration of Independence in June 1776. The Declaration proclaimed the political philosophy of the American people—a philosophy drawn from Enlightenment ideals—and listed a set of grievances against the British king George III. The document was intended to justify the breaking of ties with Great Britain and the establishment of a newly independent United States.

> We hold these truths to be self-evident, that all men are created equal, that they are endowed by their creator with certain unalienable rights, that among these are life, liberty, and the pursuit of happiness. That to secure these rights, governments are instituted among men, deriving their just powers from the consent of the governed, that whenever any form of government becomes destructive of these ends, it is the right of the people to alter or to abolish it, and to institute new government, laying its foundation on such principles, and organizing its powers in such form, as to them shall seem most likely to effect their safety and happiness.

Skills Focus — READING LIKE A HISTORIAN

DOCUMENT 1

a. Recall What was the role of the 25 barons in relation to the Magna Carta?

b. Analyze How did the Magna Carta limit the power of the monarch?

DOCUMENT 2

a. Identify Which three powers did Montesquieu believe should be separated among branches of government?

b. Draw Conclusions What would be the consequences of not separating the three powers?

DOCUMENT 3

a. Describe What complaints of the colonists does Paine want foreign nations to know about?

b. Interpret Why does Paine want foreign nations to know about the colonies' unhappiness of living under British rule?

DOCUMENT 4

a. Define What did "unalienable rights" mean?

b. Explain What options are available to citizens whose government no longer protects their rights?

DOCUMENT-BASED ESSAY QUESTION

What were some key elements of the Enlightenment ideal of democratic government? Using the documents above and information from the chapter, form a thesis that explains your position. Then write a short essay to support your position.

See **Skills Handbook**, p. H25

Skills Focus: Interpreting Time Lines

At Level

Research Required

Social Studies Skill

Key Documents of Democracy

1. Draw a time line for students to see. The time line should begin at 1200 and continue in hundred-year increments to 1800. Have students copy the time line onto their own papers.
2. Have students add the Declaration of Independence (1776), *The Spirit of the Laws* (1748), Magna Carta (1215) and *Common Sense* (1776) to their time lines.
3. Write the following additional examples for students to see: Mayflower Compact (1620); English Bill of Rights (1689); *Two Treatises on Government* (1690); Virginia Declaration of Rights (1776); United States Constitution (1789). Have students add the new examples to their time lines.
4. Have students conduct research about each document and then write a one-sentence summary of each one. **LS Visual-Spatial**

Alternative Assessment Handbook, Rubric 36: Time Lines

Document-Based Investigation

Word Help

endowed provided naturally

just fair

Info to Know

John Locke English philosopher John Locke was one of the first people to coin many of the phrases in America's Declaration of Independence. Thomas Jefferson, who wrote the Declaration, was well schooled in Enlightenment philosophy, including Locke's natural rights theory. Many of his most memorable lines were inspired by Locke. For example, in 1690, Locke wrote in *Two Treatises on Government* that humans have a natural right to "life, liberty, and property." In the Declaration, Jefferson adapted this phrase to "life, liberty, and the pursuit of happiness." The ideas of Locke also lay behind the bold opening words of the Declaration: "We hold these truths to be self-evident: that all men are created equal..." Moreover, Jefferson gleaned from Locke the most central idea of independence: that the governed have the right to alter or abolish a government that does not protect the natural rights of the people.

Answers

Reading Like a Historian

Document 1. a. *elected officials responsible for bringing the barons' complaints to the king and securing payment for any wrongdoing; could seize property from the king if necessary;* **b.** *showed that the king could be punished for his actions;* **Document 2. a.** *the judicial, legislative, and executive;* **b.** *If power were not separated, it could become arbitrary and oppressive.* **Document 3. a.** *that the colonists cannot live happily or safely under British rule;* **b.** *in order to justify the call for independence;* **Document 4. a.** *rights that have been given to people by God and cannot be taken away;* **b.** *They may change their government, or get rid of it and start a new government.* **Essay** *possible answer—governments should rule with the consent of the governed; power of government should be limited*

Answers

Visual Summary

Review and Inquiry Organize students into three groups, and assign each group one of the topics in the Spread of Ideas flow chart: Scientific Revolution, Enlightenment, and American Revolution. Have each group write a short summary of its assigned topic.

Quick Facts Transparency: Visual Study Guide: Enlightenment and Revolution

Review Key Terms and People

1. Declaration of Independence
2. Catherine the Great
3. Nicolaus Copernicus
4. Stamp Act
5. John Locke
6. rational
7. heliocentric theory
8. Baron de Montesquieu
9. George Washington
10. scientific method

Comprehension and Critical Thinking

11. **a.** that the earth rotated around the sun
b. He supported Copernican theory, even though the Church pressured him not to support it.
c. possible answer—It inspired people to question old views; ideas also spread to government, society, and art.

12. **a.** period when philosophers believed in using reason to understand truth
b. believed in social contract; Hobbes believed human nature was violent, while Locke believed human nature followed natural laws
c. possible answer—Yes, they instituted some Enlightenment reforms, though often for their own reasons.

13. **a.** the first ten amendments to the Constitution; protected individual liberties
b. incorporated Enlightenment philosophers' ideas of the social contract, natural rights, equality, toleration
c. possible answer—John Locke, because his phrases were used in the Declaration of Independence; idea of social contract lay behind the entire Revolution

Reading Skills

14. had lived apart from Great Britain; had been allowed to rule themselves somewhat
15. caused tension
16. Causes—new identity for colonists, opposition to British policies; Enlightenment philosophy; Effects—independence for United States; other revolutions began

CHAPTER 5

Chapter Review

VISUAL STUDY GUIDE

QUICK FACTS

The Spread of Ideas

Scientific Revolution

- Francis Bacon and René Descartes develop the scientific method.
- Scientists learn more about the solar system and the limits of the physical world.
- Biologists learn more about the human body, and chemists define matter.
- Advances in science influence developments in art and architecture.

Enlightenment

- Enlightenment thinkers apply reason to the study of human nature.
- Thinkers develop new ways of organizing government.
- Philosophers use reason to deal with religious toleration, women's rights, and economic systems.

American Revolution

- Enlightenment ideas inspire American colonists to declare independence from Great Britain.
- The success of the American Revolution inspires people in France to revolt against their monarchy.

Major Scientists and Thinkers

Nicolaus Copernicus
- Developed the heliocentric theory of the solar system

Galileo Galilei
- Built first working telescope for astronomy

Sir Isaac Newton
- Developed calculus to explain all movement in the universe

Thomas Hobbes
- Believed people needed governments to impose order

John Locke
- Believed the purpose of government was to protect people's natural rights

Jean-Jacques Rousseau
- Believed all people should be equal in society

Voltaire
- Believed in justice and religious toleration in society

Denis Diderot
- Compiled the *Encyclopedia*, 28 volumes on art, science, government, and religion

Mary Wollstonecraft
- Believed women should have the same educational opportunities and rights as men

Review Key Terms and People

Identify the term or person from the chapter that best fits each of the following descriptions.

1. Document proclaiming that the United States was a free and independent nation
2. Enlightened despot from Russia
3. Polish astronomer who developed the heliocentric theory of the solar system
4. British policy that taxed newspapers and other public documents
5. English philosopher who believed in government by consent
6. Having reason or understanding
7. Theory that the sun was the center of the universe
8. French philosopher who believed in the separation of powers
9. Commander of colonial army during the American Revolution
10. Five-step process for testing theories in order to acquire new knowledge

History's Impact video program
Review the video to answer the closing question: How does the Declaration of Independence affect American life today?

Comprehension and Critical Thinking

SECTION 1 *(pp. 168–175)*

11. a. Recall What did Nicolaus Copernicus discover about the universe?

b. Explain How did Galileo's beliefs about Copernican theory bring him into conflict with the church?

c. Elaborate Did the Scientific Revolution bring about a modern way of thinking? Explain your answer.

SECTION 2 *(pp. 176–181)*

12. a. Define What was the Enlightenment?

b. Compare and Contrast Both Thomas Hobbes and John Locke believed in a social contract. How were their views similar? In what ways were they different?

c. Support a Position Were enlightened despots an improvement over traditional monarchs? Why or why not?

SECTION 3 *(pp. 182–187)*

13. a. Identify What was the Bill of Rights?

b. Analyze How did the Constitution and the Bill of Rights incorporate some of the ideas of Enlightenment thinkers Montesquieu, Voltaire, Locke, and Rousseau?

c. Rate Which Enlightenment thinker had the greatest influence on the framers of the U.S. Constitution? Explain your answer.

Reading Skills

Understanding Causes and Effects *Use what you know about understanding causes and effects to answer the questions below.*

14. Why did the colonists in the British colonies begin to develop a new identity?

15. What effects did the Stamp Act, Townshend Acts, and other British taxes have on the relationship between Great Britain and its colonies in North America?

16. List the causes and effects of the American Revolution.

Interpreting Literature as a Source

Reading Like a Historian *Voltaire wrote the short story "Micromégas" in 1752. In this early work of science fiction, visitors from outer space observe and comment on the frequency with which Europeans go to war.*

> "I assure you, at the end of 10 years, not a hundredth part of those wretches will be left; even if they had never drawn the sword, famine, fatigue, or intemperance will sweep them almost all away. Besides, it is not they who deserve punishment, but rather those armchair barbarians, who from the privacy of their cabinets, and during the process of digestion, command the massacre of a million men, and afterward ordain a solemn thanksgiving to God."
>
> —Voltaire, "Micromégas"

17. Explain Who does Voltaire blame for the evils of warfare?

18. Analyze What does Voltaire reveal about his view of European leaders?

Using the Internet

go.hrw.com
Practice Online
Keyword: SHL ENL

19. The U.S. Constitution was a result of skillful negotiation and compromise. Using the Internet, research the major issues that arose during the weeks of the Constitutional Convention. Then write a report about the issues and the compromises achieved, using eyewitness accounts and other documents to support your work.

WRITING ABOUT HISTORY

Exposition: Writing an Explanation *The Scientific Revolution resulted in a dramatic change in the way in which scientists viewed the natural world and the way in which they acquired knowledge about it. Most people, however, were not scientists. Nevertheless, the Scientific Revolution led to changes far beyond the realm of science.*

20. Assignment: In an essay, explain how the new ways of thinking that arose out of the Scientific Revolution led to the Enlightenment. To provide support for your explanation, use information from this chapter and from other research as needed. Be sure to use facts and examples to clearly illustrate the points you are making about the ways in which ideas led to concrete changes in the world.

Answers

Interpreting Literature as a Source

17. government leaders

18. He believes they are heartless and deserve punishment for their actions.

Using the Internet

19. Go to the HRW Web site and enter the keyword shown to access a rubric for this activity.

KEYWORD: SHL ENL

Writing About History

20. Student essays should include examples of concrete changes that occurred after the Age of Reason, including the women's rights movement, Adam Smith's laissez-faire economic system, new governments based on democracy and equality, and developments in art and architecture.
A rubric for the activity is provided in **CRF**: Writing about History.

HOLT

History's Impact

► **Video Program: Enlightenment and Revolution**
See the Video Program Teacher's Guide for the answer to the closing question.

Review and Assessment Resources

Review and Reinforce

- **CRF:** Chapter Review
- **Quick Facts Transparency**: Visual Study Guide: Enlightenment and Revolution
- **Spanish Chapter Summaries Audio CD Program**
- OSP **Holt PuzzlePro**: Quiz Show for ExamView
- **Quiz Game CD-ROM**

Assess

- **PASS**: Chapter Test, Forms A and B
- **Alternative Assessment Handbook**
- OSP **ExamView Test Generator**, Chapter Test
- **Differentiated Instruction Modified Worksheets and Tests CD-ROM**: Chapter Test
- HOAP **Holt Online Assessment Program** (in the Premier Online Edition)

Reteach/Intervene

- **Interactive Reader and Study Guide**
- **Differentiated Instruction Teacher Management System**: Lesson Plans for Differentiated Instruction
- **Differentiated Instruction Modified Worksheets and Tests CD-ROM**: Chapter Test
- **Interactive Skills Tutor CD-ROM**

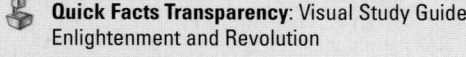

go.hrw.com
Online Resources
KEYWORD: SHL TEACHER

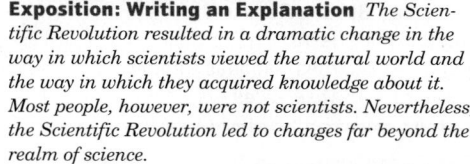

Chapter 6 Planning Guide

The French Revolution and Napoleon

Chapter Overview	Reproducible Resources	Technology Resources
CHAPTER 6 **pp. 192-225** **Overview:** **In this chapter, students will learn about events in France that led to a revolution, a period of chaos, and the emergence of a dictator.**	**Differentiated Instruction Teacher Management System:** • Pacing Guide • Lesson Plans for Differentiated Instruction **Interactive Reader and Study Guide:** Chapter Summary* **Chapter Resource File*** • Writing for the SAT • Social Studies Skill • Chapter Review **World History Outline Maps**	**Live Ink© Online Reading Help** **Student Edition on Audio CD Program** **Differentiated Instruction Modified Worksheets and Tests CD-ROM** **World History Primary Source Library CD-ROM** **Power Presentations with Video CD-ROM** **History's Impact: World History Video Program (VHS/DVD):** The French Revolution and Napoleon
Section 1: **The Revolution Begins** **The Main Idea:** Problems in French society led to a revolution, the formation of a new government, and the end of the monarchy.	**Differentiated Instruction Teacher Management System:** Section 1 Lesson Plan* **Interactive Reader and Study Guide:** Section 1 Summary* **Chapter Resource File*** • Vocabulary Builder: Section 1 • Biography: Marie-Antoinette • Biography: Georges-Jacques Danton • Literature: *Les Misérables*	**Quick Facts Transparency:** Causes of the Revolution* **Daily Test Practice Transparency:** Section 1* **Internet Activity:** Revolutions
Section 2: **The Republic** **The Main Idea:** An extreme government changed French society and tried through harsh means to eliminate its critics within France.	**Differentiated Instruction Teacher Management System:** Section 2 Lesson Plan* **Interactive Reader and Study Guide:** Section 2 Summary* **Chapter Resource File*** • Vocabulary Builder: Section 2	**Quick Facts Transparency:** Governments of Revolutionary France* **Daily Test Practice Transparency:** Section 2*
Section 3: **Napoleon's Europe** **The Main Idea:** Napoleon Bonaparte rose through military ranks to become emperor over France and much of Europe.	**Differentiated Instruction Teacher Management System:** Section 3 Lesson Plan* **Interactive Reader and Study Guide:** Section 3 Summary* **Chapter Resource File*** • Vocabulary Builder: Section 3 • Biography: Pope Pius VII • Primary Source: *The Plumb-pudding in Danger*	**Map Transparency:** Napoleon's Empire, 1812* **Daily Test Practice Transparency:** Section 3* **Internet Activity:** Napoleon Bonaparte
Section 4: **Napoleon's Fall and Europe's Reaction** **The Main Idea:** After defeating Napoleon, the European allies sent him into exile and held a meeting in Vienna to restore order and stability to Europe.	**Differentiated Instruction Teacher Management System:** Section 4 Lesson Plan* **Interactive Reader and Study Guide:** Section 4 Summary* **Chapter Resource File*** • Vocabulary Builder: Section 4 • Biography: Czar Alexander I • History and Geography: Napoleon Invades Russia	**Quick Facts Transparency:** Soldiers in Napoleon's Russian Campaign* **Map Transparency:** Russian Campaign, 1812* **Map Transparency:** Europe After the Congress of Vienna, 1815* **Daily Test Practice Transparency:** Section 4*

go.hrw.com | Print Resource | Transparency
Learning Styles | Audio CD | CD-ROM
Video | **SE** Student Edition | **TE** Teachers Edition
OSP One-Stop Planner CD-ROM
*also on One-Stop Planner CD-ROM

HOLT
History's Impact
World History Video Program (VHS/DVD)
The French Revolution and Napoleon

Review, Assessment, Intervention

- **Quick Facts Transparency:** The French Revolution and Napoleon*
- **Spanish Chapter Summaries Audio CD Program**
- **Program Assessment Support System (PASS):** Chapter Test*
- **Differentiated Instruction Modified Worksheets and Tests CD-ROM:** Modified Chapter Test
- **OSP One-Stop Planner CD-ROM:** ExamView Test Generator (English/Spanish)
- **HOAP Holt Online Assessment Program (HOAP),** in the Holt Premier Online Student Edition

- **PASS:** Section 1 Quiz*
- **Online Quiz:** Section 1
- **Alternative Assessment Handbook**

- **PASS:** Section 2 Quiz*
- **Online Quiz:** Section 2
- **Alternative Assessment Handbook**

- **PASS:** Section 3 Quiz*
- **Online Quiz:** Section 3
- **Alternative Assessment Handbook**

- **PASS:** Section 4 Quiz*
- **Online Quiz:** Section 4
- **Alternative Assessment Handbook**

Power Presentation with Video CD-ROM

Power Presentations with Video are visual presentations of each chapter's main ideas. Presentations can be customized by including Quick Facts charts, images and maps from the textbook, and video clips.

Holt Online Learning

go.hrw.com
Teacher Resources
KEYWORD: SHL TEACHER

go.hrw.com
Student Resources
KEYWORD: SHL NAP

- Document-Based Questions
- Interactive Multimedia Activities
- Current Events
- Chapter-Based Internet Activities
- and more!

Holt Premier
Online Student Edition

Complete online support for interactivity, assessment, and reporting

- Interactive Maps and Notebook
- Homework Practice and Research Activities Online

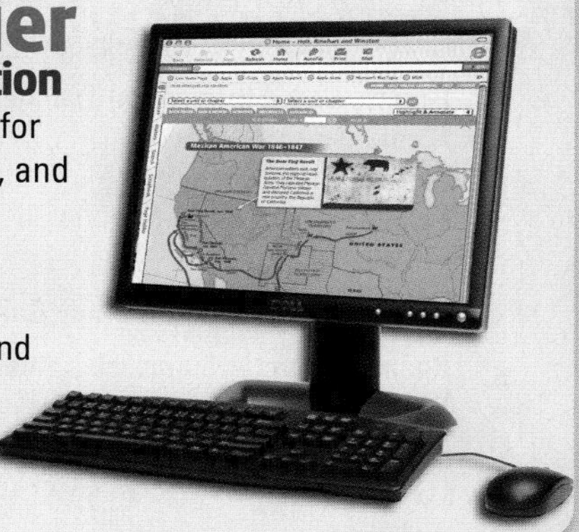

The Big Picture

Peter N. Stearns

Causes and Outcomes of the French Revolution Explaining the factors that prompted people to revolt against a longstanding political and social regime involves crucial historical issues. Political policy, ideas, social tensions and short-term economic problems feed the equation. Once launched, the Revolution went through several crucial stages, becoming for a time particularly bloodthirsty (though at levels tame by more recent standards). A key challenge is to understand the durable changes introduced by the Revolution, from the initial liberal phase through the more democratic Terror, without getting lost in the sequence of events or totally distracted by the Revolution's drawbacks and limitations. Changes in the position of the aristocracy and other legally privileged groups; recasting the relation between religion and state; and developing new bases for nationalism and for national military conscription are among the key results, though new constitutional freedoms, key voting systems, the attack on monarchy and even the introduction of the metric system deserve attention as well. The French Revolution also displayed classic patterns of revolution more generally, which can be teased out for comparison with similar events including the American Revolution.

Napoleon Napoleon's stormy rule invites another balancing act, between short-term conquests and ultimate failures, and the longer term role in spreading revolutionary achievements, including nationalism. Napoleon permanently installed some features of the Revolution in France—but not all of them. He spread key principles more widely, particularly in adjacent territories but also in more distant parts of Europe. The Vienna settlement that followed Napoleon's final defeat must be interpreted as a recognition of change along with a clear effort to install a more conservative diplomatic and political order. The settlement created issues for the future, but it has also been hailed as far more constructive than many more modern peace treaties. In the wake of Napoleon, it's important, finally, to think about how elements of the French Revolution spread across the Atlantic, but not, until much later, to Asia and Africa.

Recent Scholarship

Explaining the Revolution *Making Democracy in the French Revolution* (2001) by James Livesey is a much discussed recent effort to explain major features of the revolutionary achievement. Livesey puts some emphasis on new ideas, but also looks to the social base—the kinds of groups that supported dramatic political change—with particular reference to commercial practices. Not surprisingly, scholars have been trying to pinpoint causes of the French Revolution for a long time, and until recently, focus seemed to have shifted from social issues to ideologies. Livesey represents a new start on a more comprehensive approach. Acknowledging other interpretations while working beyond them, Livesey contributes to one of the great causation questions in modern history.

Differentiating Instruction

Differentiated Instruction Teacher Management System
- Pacing Guide
- Lesson Plans for Differentiated Instruction

Interactive Reader and Study Guide

Spanish Chapter Summaries Audio CD Program

Student Edition on Audio CD Program

Differentiated Instruction Modified Worksheets and Tests CD-ROM
- Vocabulary Flash Cards
- Modified Vocabulary Builder Activities
- Modified Chapter Review Activity
- Modified Chapter Test

OSP **One-Stop Planner CD-ROM**
- ExamView Test Generator (English /Spanish)
- PuzzlePro
- Quiz Show for ExamView
- Transparencies and Videos

TE **Differentiated Activities in the Teacher's Edition**
- France in the 1780s, p. 196
- National Assembly, p. 199
- Bastille Day, p. 199
- Concept of Irony, p. 202
- French Government and Society, p. 205
- Characteristics of Napoleon, p. 212
- Napoleon's Last Campaigns, p. 218
- Execution Debate, p. 223

Reading Like a Historian

Sam Wineburg

A Fairy Tale Ending? Few students will come to your class already knowing about the storming of the Bastille. But you can be fairly certain that they'll know a story about a little girl dressed in red, whose visit to grandma goes terribly awry. "What big teeth you have Grandma," says an unsuspecting Little Red Riding Hood to the beast disguised as grandma. "Better to eat you with," replies the wolf. As the wolf lunges toward his prey, the girl's screams alert a woodsman who, on entering the house, forces the wolf to spit out grandma (miraculously intact). The woodsman kills the beast and then goes on his way. In the words of one modern version: "Little Red Riding Hood and her grandma had a nice lunch and a long chat."

What in the world does Little Red Riding Hood have to do with the French Revolution? This is precisely the question asked by Princeton historian Robert Darnton, whose research draws on early versions of common folktales to reconstruct the worldviews of the people in the past. Darnton contrasts the happy ending of our familiar story with the same tale as recounted by peasants in pre-Revolutionary France. Accosting grandma, our French wolf does not swallow her whole, but kills her, then pours "her blood into a bottle" and slices "her flesh onto a platter." When little granddaughter arrives, the wolf-as-grandma invites her to a feast: "There is meat and wine in the pantry." The unsuspecting little cannibal dines on meat and wine and, sated, crawls into bed with grandma-wolf. In the French version no woodsman appears handily to save the little girl. Indeed, "What big teeth you have," are Little Red Riding Hood's parting words before she, too, becomes dinner. Hardly a happy ending.

Folktales as Historical Sources Darnton shows that it is not just this story that casts a dark shadow, but the antecedents to other familiar tales as well: Hansel and Gretel, Puss n' Boots, Cinderella. "Storytellers of 18th century France," he writes, "portrayed a world of raw and naked brutality."

And why should we expect otherwise? Peasants of the Third Estate eked out a hardscrabble existence. Our chapter describes the particularly harsh winter of 1788. But the truth is that this winter only made a bad situation worse. Hunger for the peasants of the Third Estate was a way of life and, for many, a way of death. A watery porridge seasoned by a wilted vegetable served as the daily staple. Meat was virtually unheard of, reserved for the few occasions when a holiday or marriage brightened the calendar. An oppressive tax system, ground rents, and forced tithes added to the peasant's burden. Life was dominated by basic needs, a fact which brings us back to Little Red Riding Hood.

Food—especially the height of extravagance, a meat meal—was an obsession for French peasants and major theme in their tales. Rather than offering an escape from their grim reality, the peasants' stories mirrored their bleak existence. As Darnton writes, such tales "erect warning signs around the seeking of fortune: 'Danger!' 'Road Out,' 'Go Slow!' 'Stop!'" The sin of our ill-fated French heroine was that she blithely avoided these warning signs and let her guard down. Instead of becoming suspicious by the offer of a meat and wine during an otherwise uneventful visit to grandma, she let her stomach triumph over her good sense—a mistake for which she paid dearly.

Viewing these early folktales as historical sources aquaints us with a world vastly different from our own. Often their precise meaning escapes us because of our inability to span the abyss separating our two worlds. But when we listen closely to an early version of a common folktale we can discern clues about the life of the voiceless masses of the Third Estate. In the process, we gain insight into the despair and misery that ultimately fueled the forces of the French Revolution.

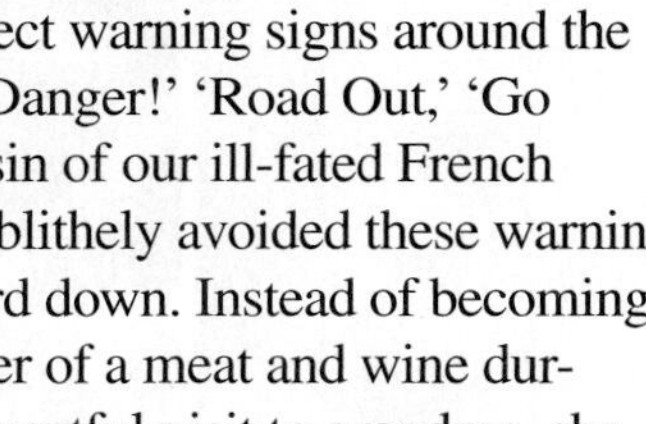

• Chapter Preview •

Chapter Main Ideas

Section 1 Problems in French society led to a revolution, the formation of a new government, and the end of the monarchy.

Section 2 An extreme government changed French society and tried through harsh means to eliminate its critics within France.

Section 3 Napoleon Bonaparte rose through military ranks to become emperor over France and much of Europe.

Section 4 After defeating Napoleon, the European allies sent him into exile and held a meeting in Vienna to restore order and stability to Europe.

CHAPTER 6 1789–1815

The French Revolution and Napoleon

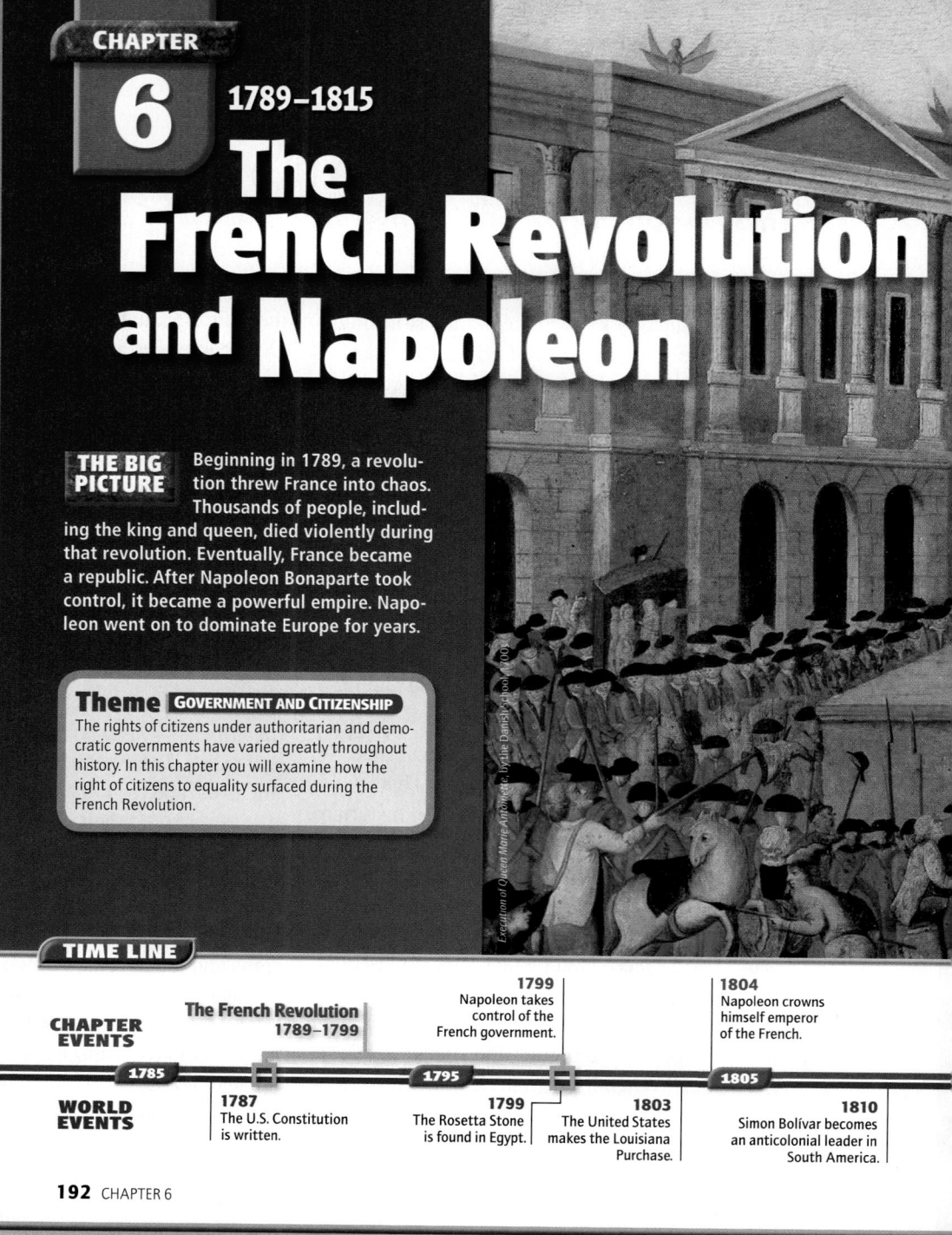

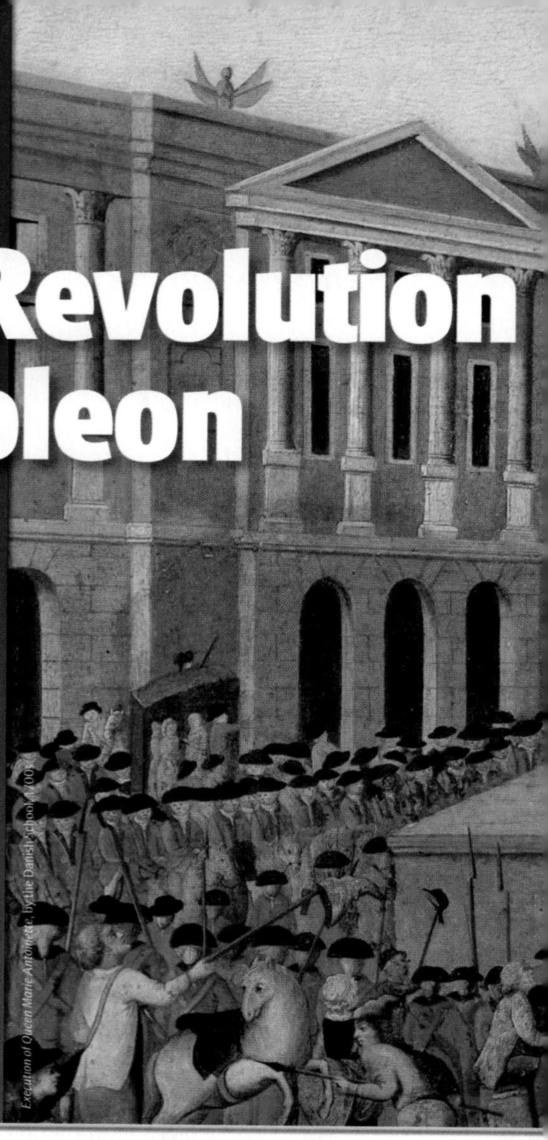

Execution of Queen Marie Antoinette, by the Danish School, 1700s

THE BIG PICTURE Beginning in 1789, a revolution threw France into chaos. Thousands of people, including the king and queen, died violently during that revolution. Eventually, France became a republic. After Napoleon Bonaparte took control, it became a powerful empire. Napoleon went on to dominate Europe for years.

Theme GOVERNMENT AND CITIZENSHIP
The rights of citizens under authoritarian and democratic governments have varied greatly throughout history. In this chapter you will examine how the right of citizens to equality surfaced during the French Revolution.

TIME LINE

CHAPTER EVENTS

- **The French Revolution** 1789–1799
- **1799** Napoleon takes control of the French government.
- **1804** Napoleon crowns himself emperor of the French.

1785 — 1795 — 1805

WORLD EVENTS

- **1787** The U.S. Constitution is written.
- **1799** The Rosetta Stone is found in Egypt.
- **1803** The United States makes the Louisiana Purchase.
- **1810** Simon Bolívar becomes an anticolonial leader in South America.

Key to Differentiating Instruction

Below Level
Basic-level activities designed for all students encountering new material

At Level
Intermediate-level activities designed for average students

Above Level
Challenging activities designed for honors and gifted and talented students

Standard English Mastery
Activities designed to improve standard English usage

Introduce the Chapter

At Level

The French Revolution and Napoleon

1. Tell students that in this chapter they will learn about events in France that led to a revolution, a period of chaos, and the emergence of a dictator.
2. Write these terms for students to see: liberty, equality, brotherhood/sisterhood. Then have students write a few sentences about what each of the words means to them. Have volunteers read their sentences to the class.
3. Guide students in a discussion about why some people might be willing to sacrifice everything for these principles, especially in an unjust society.
4. Have students scan the chapter and develop a list of the main topics and a list of the charts and maps that appear in the chapter.
5. Guide students in a review of the maps and charts. Have students explain what the maps and charts reveal about this time period.
LS Verbal-Linguistic

Alternative Assessment Handbook, Rubrics 1: Acquiring Information; and 11: Discussions

History's Impact video program
Watch the video to understand the impact of the French Revolution.

Reading like a Historian This painting shows the execution by guillotine of Queen Marie-Antoinette in 1793. The queen was killed during the French Revolution's Reign of Terror, an especially bloody time.

Analyzing Visuals How do you think the painter who created this picture felt about the queen's execution? Explain your answer.

See **Skills Handbook**, p. H27

1813 Mexico declares its independence from Spain.

1815

1815 Allied forces defeat Napoleon at the Battle of Waterloo.

1821 Napoleon dies in exile.

Chapter Preview

HOLT
History's Impact
► **Video Program: The French Revolution and Napoleon**
See the Video Teacher's Guide for strategies for using the video segment.

Reading Like a Historian
Analyzing Visuals Have students take a moment to examine the image on these pages. Ask students to look at the crowd. What kinds of people are represented? *soldiers, poor people* What are their reactions to the execution? *Some are excited and celebrating, others stand silently.*

go.hrw.com
Online Resources
Chapter Resources:
KEYWORD: SHL NAP
Teacher Resources:
KEYWORD: SHL TEACHER

Explore the Time Line
1. How many years did the French Revolution last? *ten*
2. What event happened the same year that the Rosetta Stone was found in Egypt? *Napoleon took control of the French government.*
3. What did Napoleon do in 1804? *crowned himself emperor of the French*
4. In which battle was Napoleon defeated? *Battle of Waterloo*

Info to Know
The Diamond Necklace Affair Before the revolution, a young adventuress named Madame Lamotte hatched a plot to advance her own place in society and gain wealth. Her plot involved the queen, Marie-Antoinette, a prominent clergyman, a jeweler, and a diamond necklace worth about $100 million today. Although Marie-Antoinette was innocent of involvement in the scheme, her reputation among the French was severely damaged.

Draw Conclusions Why was Marie-Antoinette's reputation damaged? *because she was implicated in a crime though she was innocent*

Answers
Reading Like a Historian *possible answer—felt that the execution was barbaric; executioner parades head, shows blood*

Preteach

Geography Starting Points

Where are Italy and Germany? By 1789, the outlines of the modern nations of Spain, France, and Portugal were clearly recognizable. At this time in history, Germany and Italy were divided into dozens of small states, although the German states were still organized into the Holy Roman Empire. During the Napoleonic Wars, France conquered or subjugated these small states, but could not hold them for long. Italy and Germany did not achieve complete unification until the 1870s.

Map Transparency: Europe, 1789

World History Outline Maps

GEOGRAPHY Starting Points

Interactive
EUROPE, 1789

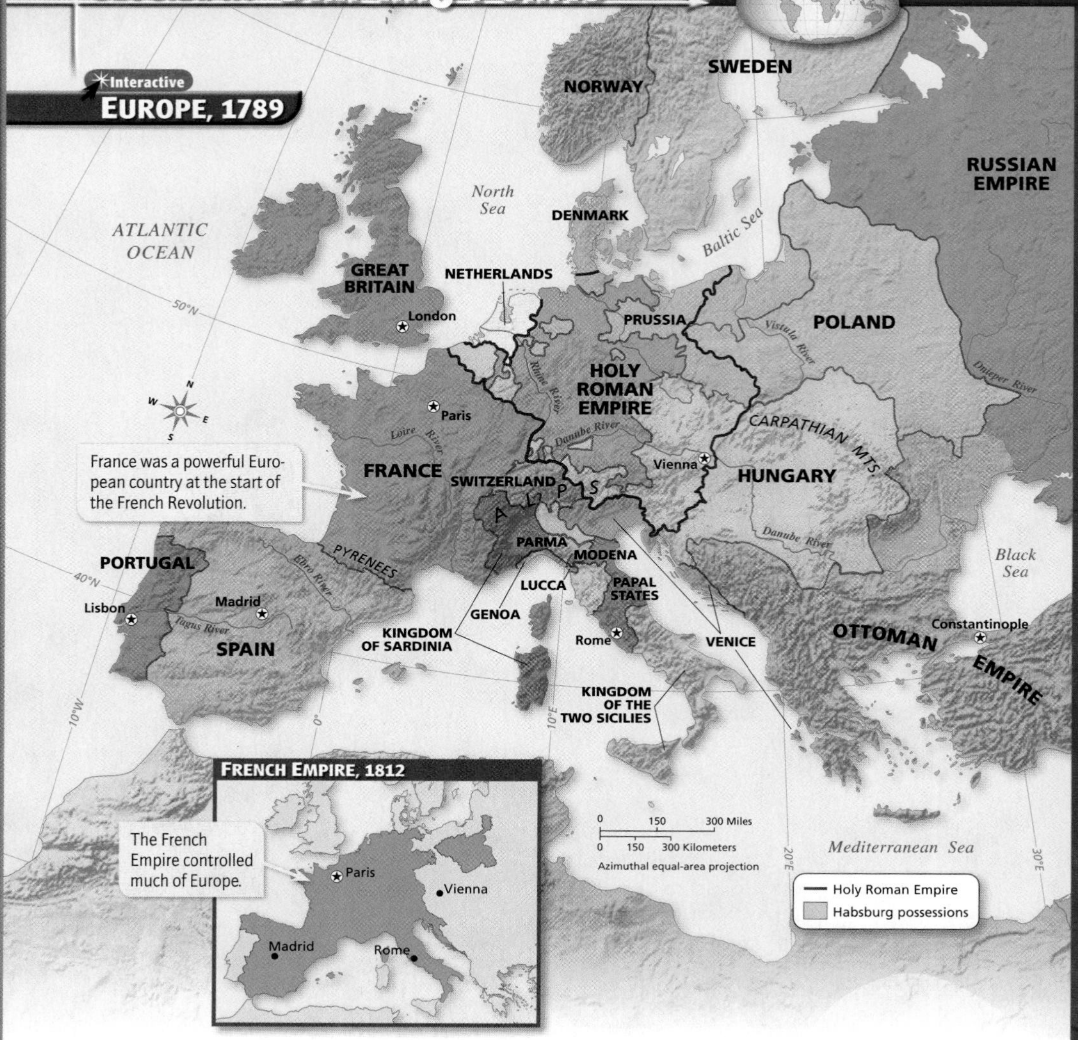

Starting Points In the late 1700s France was one of Europe's large and powerful kingdoms. At that time, Europe was made up of a few large kingdoms and empires as well as many smaller states and territories. Then in 1789, the French Revolution set off a chain of events that reshaped Europe's political map.

1. **Analyze** Compare France on the large map to the French Empire on the inset map. What might have happened to allow France to become an empire?
2. **Predict** How do you think leaders of other European countries might have reacted as France expanded into other parts of Europe?

Listen to History

Go online to listen to an explanation of the starting points for this chapter.

go.hrw.com
Keyword: SHL NAP

Skills Focus: Analyzing Maps

At Level

Social Studies Skill

French Expansion

Materials: outline maps, colored pencils

1. Give each student an outline map of Europe.
2. Have students use the information from the map on this page to create a new map that shows French expansion. Students should start by carefully outlining the 1789 French border and coloring in France.
3. Have students draw arrows that show the various directions of the French conquest. Then, have students outline the 1812 borders and color in the new territories with a different color. Tell students that most of this territory did not become part of France, but was controlled by France.
4. Have students locate major battles that occurred during the French conquest and add this information to the map. **LS Visual-Spatial**

Alternative Assessment Handbook, Rubric 20: Map Creation

Answers

Geography Starting Points

1. *possible answers—a strong military leader took control; values of country shifted to building an empire; weaker neighbors;* **2.** *possible answers—felt threatened; challenged French conquest*

Section 1
The Revolution Begins

Before You Read

Main Idea

Problems in French society led to a revolution, the formation of a new government, and the end of the monarchy.

Reading Focus

1. What caused the French Revolution?
2. What happened during the first events of the Revolution?
3. How did the French create a new nation?

Key Terms and People

Old Order
King Louis XVI
Marie-Antoinette
First Estate
Second Estate
Third Estate
bourgeoisie
sans culottes
Declaration of the Rights of Man and of the Citizen
radical

Taking Notes As you read, take notes in a graphic organizer like this one. Record details of the events that led up to the Revolution and the events that occurred immediately after it.

Events Before the Revolution
↓
Events After the Revolution

The Inside Story

What drove a Paris mob to fury? In April 1789 a rumor was flying through the Paris workers' neighborhoods: Réveillon the wallpaper manufacturer was about to slash his employees' wages in half. Although the rumor was probably false, an angry crowd of unemployed workers from various industries gathered at Réveillon's home. The home was famous for its gorgeous furnishings. Such wealth was in sharp contrast to the miserable poverty of the thousands of Parisians assembled there. When the crowd pushed into the house, Réveillon's family fled. Seeing the home's splendor—evidence of wealth that workers could never even hope for—the crowd went on a rampage, breaking and burning everything in sight. This event was just the beginning. Poverty and inequality would drive French workers to violence again and again. ■

▼ Poor laborers riot in the streets of Paris.

Causes of the Revolution

In the 1780s, long-standing resentments against the French monarchy fueled anger throughout France. The source of the French people's ill will could be found in the unequal structure of French government and society.

Inequalities in Society A social and political structure called the **Old Order**, or ancien régime (ahns-yan ray-ZHEEM), created inequalities in French society. Under the Old Order, the king was at the top, and three social groups called estates were under him.

Preteach

Getting Started

Use the **Interactive Reader and Study Guide** to familiarize students with the section content.

Interactive Reader and Study Guide, Section 1

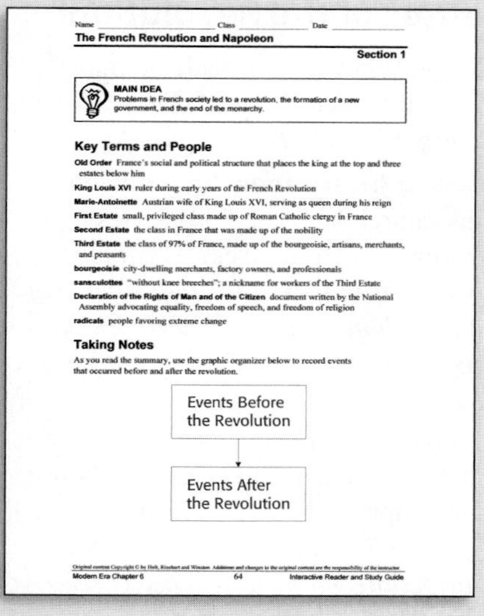
Name ______ Class ______ Date ______

The French Revolution and Napoleon

Section 1

MAIN IDEA
Problems in French society led to a revolution, the formation of a new government, and the end of the monarchy.

Key Terms and People

Old Order France's social and political structure that places the king at the top and three estates below him

King Louis XVI ruler during early years of the French Revolution

Marie-Antoinette Austrian wife of King Louis XVI, serving as queen during his reign

First Estate small, privileged class made up of Roman Catholic clergy in France

Second Estate the class in France that was made up of the nobility

Third Estate the class of 97% of France, made up of the bourgeoisie, artisans, merchants, and peasants

bourgeoisie city-dwelling merchants, factory owners, and professionals

sansculottes "without knee breeches"; a nickname for workers of the Third Estate

Declaration of the Rights of Man and of the Citizen document written by the National Assembly advocating equality, freedom of speech, and freedom of religion

radicals people favoring extreme change

Taking Notes

As you read the summary, use the graphic organizer below to record events that occurred before and after the revolution.

Events Before the Revolution
↓
Events After the Revolution

Original content Copyright © by Holt, Rinehart and Winston. Additions and changes to the original content are the responsibility of the instructor.

Modern Era Chapter 6 64 Interactive Reader and Study Guide

Academic Vocabulary

Review with students the high-use academic term in this section.

privileges special rights granted to certain people because of their position in society (p. 594)

CRF: Vocabulary Builder: Section 1

Taking Notes

Before Revolution— inequalities in society, Enlightenment ideas, poor leadership, financial crisis, hunger; After Revolution— National Assembly completed constitution, restricted king's power, gave citizens broad rights, formed Legislative Assembly, disbanded and formed National Convention, ended monarchy, declared France a republic

Teach the Main Idea

The Revolution Begins

1. **Teach** Ask students the Reading Focus questions to teach this section.
2. **Apply** Write the following question for students to see: How do you know when a system is unfair? Have students work in pairs to brainstorm answers to this question. Have each pair volunteer its best answer, and write all the answers for students to see. Have students provide brief examples of unfair systems they have encountered.
3. **Review** As you review the section, have students explain how the conditions in France led to the revolution.
4. **Practice/Homework** Have students write a one-page petition to the king of France in which they suggest reforms that might help France avoid revolution. **LS Verbal-Linguistic**

Alternative Assessment Handbook, Rubric 43: Writing to Persuade

Direct Teach

Reading Focus

1 What caused the French Revolution? *inequalities in society, Enlightenment ideas, poor leadership, financial crisis, hunger and cold*

Causes of the Revolution

Recall What groups made up the First and Second Estates? *First Estate—clergy; Second Estate—nobility*

Making Inferences Why do you think church lands and properties were exempt from taxes? *possible answer—tradition of the importance of the church in society; immoral to tax religious property*

Evaluate What are some possible reasons for the reluctance of the First and Second Estates to eliminate their tax exemptions? *possible answers—pride, tradition, lack of empathy for Third Estate*

- **CRF**: Biography: Marie-Antoinette
- **CRF**: Literature: *Les Misérables* by Victor Hugo
- **CRF**: Social Studies Skills: Interpreting Charts

Info to Know

Population Growth In 1700, France's population hovered around 20 million. As diseases and food shortages diminished, the population increased by 8 to 10 million over the next hundred years. This rapid growth contributed to social stress that in turn led to revolution.

The king at the time of the Revolution was **King Louis XVI**. He lived at the extravagant palace of Versailles, 10 miles outside of Paris. King Louis XVI was shy and indecisive but not cruel. His queen, **Marie-Antoinette**, was from Austria—a country that was a traditional enemy of France. Marie-Antoinette's nationality made her unpopular with the French, but she was also frivolous and self-indulgent. She enjoyed lavish parties and fancy clothes while many of the common people wore rags.

The rest of French society was divided into three classes, called estates. These groups varied widely in what they contributed to France, in terms of both work and taxes.

ACADEMIC VOCABULARY
privileges special rights granted to certain people because of their position in society

The **First Estate** was made up of the Roman Catholic clergy, about 1 percent of the population. The clergy had held several privileges since the Middle Ages. For example, only church courts could try priests and bishops for crimes, so the clergy did not have to answer to the same laws as everyone else. Furthermore, neither the clergy nor the Roman Catholic Church had to pay taxes. Land belonging to the Roman Catholic Church was also exempt from taxes. In addition, the church owned about 10 percent of France's land, which produced vast sums of money in rents and fees. Bishops and some other higher clergy controlled this wealth and became very rich. Although many of the priests who ministered to the common people were poor, many people resented the wealth and privileges of the clergy.

The **Second Estate** was made up of the nobility, less than 2 percent of the population. Although the nobility controlled much of the country's wealth, they paid few taxes. Members of the Second Estate held key positions in the government and military. Many lived on country estates where peasants did all the work and were forced to pay high fees and rents to the landowner. Some nobles lived in luxury at the king's court, where their only real jobs were ceremonial.

PRIMARY SOURCES

The Three Estates

This cartoon shows a member of the Third Estate crushed beneath a stone that represents taxes, land rent and fees, and labor the peasants had to perform without pay. Nobles paid some fees, but no taxes. The clergy did not pay taxes either. The graph below shows that the Third Estate contributed much more money to the country's treasury than the other estates.

REVENUE PAID BY ESTATES

Source: Simon Schama, Citizens

The First and Second Estates, represented by a priest and nobleman, stand on the stone and add to the peasant's misery.
The man under the rock represents the peasants and laborers of the Third Estate.

Taille, Impots et Corvee, anonymous, 1700s

Skills Focus READING LIKE A HISTORIAN

1. **Analyze** In the cartoon, which two estates appear to be allies?
2. **Analyze Primary Sources** How do you think members of the three estates might have reacted to this cartoon? Explain your answer.

See **Skills Handbook**, p. H25

Differentiating Instruction

Below Level

Special Education Students

Guide students in a discussion about the various types of people who lived in France during the 1780s. Copy the three-column chart at right for students to see. Omit the italicized words. Have students copy and complete the chart. **LS Visual-Spatial**

Alternative Assessment Handbook, Rubrics 7: Charts; and 11: Discussions

Estate	Title	Roles
First	*Clergy*	*control of 1/10th of the land; minister to common people*
Second	*Nobility*	*controlled much of country's wealth; ran government; served in military*
Third	*Bourgeoisie, sansculottes, peasants*	*merchants, factory owners, professionals, artisans, workers, farmers, laborers*

Answers

Reading Like a Historian 1. *the First and Second Estates;* **2.** *possible answer—First and Second: anger at this portrayal; Third: agreement and motivation to take action*

The **Third Estate**, by far the largest group of people, included about 97 percent of the population. The Third Estate was itself made up of several groups. At the top of the Third Estate was the **bourgeoisie** (boorhzh-wah-ZEE)—city-dwelling merchants, factory owners, and professionals such as lawyers and doctors. Although they had no role in the government, some of the bourgeoisie were highly educated and quite rich. Their wealth, however, did not buy them any influence in the government.

Below the bourgeoisie were the artisans and workers of the cities. These were the shoemakers, carpenters, bricklayers, dressmakers, and laborers. If these people had no work, they went hungry. The workers of the Third Estate were known as **sans culottes** (sanz-kooh-laht), or those "without knee breeches." They wore long pants—in contrast to the tight knee-length breeches, or pants, worn by the nobility. Sans culottes became a nickname of pride for the workers.

At the bottom of the Third Estate were the peasants who farmed the nobles' fields. Not only did they pay rents and fees to the landowners, but they also paid a tenth of their income to the church. In addition, they had to perform labor, such as working on roads, without pay. Many peasants were miserably poor and had no hope for a better life.

Enlightenment Ideas While social inequalities were driving poor people toward revolt, new ideas from the Enlightenment were also inspiring the French Revolution. Many educated members of the bourgeoisie knew about the writings of the great Enlightenment philosophers John Locke, Baron de Montesquieu, and Jean-Jacques Rousseau. Members of the bourgeoisie also knew that Great Britain's government limited the king's power. More recently, they had learned that American colonists, inspired by Enlightenment ideas, had successfully rebelled against Britain's king. Seeing how these ideas were transforming government and society in other countries, some of the bourgeoisie began to consider how these ideas might be used in France.

A Financial Crisis A third cause of the Revolution was a financial crisis, severe economic problems that affected much of the country.

CAUSES OF THE REVOLUTION — QUICK FACTS

- Inequalities in society
- Ideas of Enlightenment writers
- Poor leadership from Louis XVI
- Financial crisis
- Widespread hunger and record cold

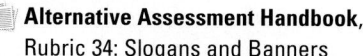

The Bread Famine and the Pawnbroker by Le Sueur brothers, 1700s

First, France was deeply in debt. Over the previous centuries, France had borrowed huge sums of money to spend on wars, including the American Revolution. But the king and his court continued to spend lavishly, leading to even more borrowing and debt. By the 1780s, this pattern of spending and borrowing had taken the country deeply into debt.

By 1787 King Louis XVI was desperate for money. He tried to tax the Second Estate, but the nobles refused to pay. The king, incapable of the strong leadership the situation required, backed down. A year later the country faced bankruptcy. Half the taxes collected were needed just to pay the country's debt.

At the same time, nature was creating other economic problems. First, a hailstorm and a drought ruined the harvest. Then the winter of 1788 was the worst in 80 years. Frozen rivers prevented waterwheels from powering the mills that ground wheat into flour. Food and firewood were scarce and expensive. As hunger and cold made life wretched for thousands of French citizens, misery grew into anger.

The country was broke, and people were hungry and angry. Eliminating the tax exemptions for the First and Second Estates could have helped the situation, but the clergy and the nobility resisted all such efforts.

READING CHECK **Summarize** What were the causes of the French Revolution?

Direct Teach

Reading Focus

Causes of the Revolution

Recall Who were the sansculottes? *workers of the Third Estate who wore long pants instead of fashionable knee breeches; became a nickname of pride for workers*

Summarize What spending patterns put France into deep debt by the 1780s? *borrowing huge sums of money to spend on wars; lavish spending by king and his court*

Predict What actions could King Louis have taken to avoid an economic crisis? *possible answer— eliminated tax exemptions for the First and Second Estates*

Activity **Reform Slogans** Have students create three slogans that members of the Third Estate might use to encourage reform in France. List slogans for the class to see. **LS Verbal-Linguistic**

Alternative Assessment Handbook, Rubric 34: Slogans and Banners

Quick Facts Transparency: Causes of the Revolution

go.hrw.com
Online Resources
KEYWORD: SHL NAP
ACTIVITY: Revolutions

Skills Focus: Identifying Problem and Solution — At Level

Reading Skill
Problems in France

Materials: butcher or poster paper, colored markers

1. Guide students in a discussion of the problems that France faced in the 1780s. Develop a class list of these problems and write them for students to see.
2. Organize students into six groups and assign each group a role: monarch, clergy, nobility, bourgeoisie, artisans, and peasants.
3. Have each group develop a plan to address three of France's problems. Remind students to suggest plans in accordance with their roles. Have groups write their plans on the poster paper.
4. Have volunteers share their plans with the class, and display their posters for the class to see. Have students discuss which plans seem most feasible. **LS Visual-Spatial, Interpersonal**

Alternative Assessment Handbook, Rubrics 11: Discussions; and 35: Solving Problems

Answers

Reading Check *inequalities in society, Enlightenment ideas, poor leadership, financial crisis, hunger and cold*

Direct Teach

Reading Focus

2 What happened during the first events of the Revolution? *Members of the Third Estate demanded more representation and rights; a mob stormed the Bastille; rumors of retaliation spread.*

First Events of the Revolution

Recall Why did a mob storm the Bastille? *to look for weapons to defend themselves; the Bastille was a symbol of oppression*

Contrast How was the 1789 meeting of the Estates General different from previous meetings? *Members of the Third Estate had a new sense of their importance; they demanded, and eventually received, increased voting rights.*

Make Judgments Did the National Assembly created by the Third Estate have the right to make laws for all of France? *possible answer—Yes, they represented 97 percent of the people in France.*

CRF: Biography: Georges-Jacques Danton

Primary Source

Louis XVI: "Is it a revolt?"
François Alexandre Frederic, Duc de La Rochefoucauld-Liancourt: "No, Sire, it is a revolution."
–Upon learning at Versailles of the fall of the Bastille, 1789

Answers

Reading Like a Historian **1.** *possible answer—Cholat participated in the storming and thought it was important.* **2.** *possible answer—He wanted to tell the story in one painting.* **3.** *possible answer—to show the perspective of the people moving toward the Bastille*

First Events of the Revolution

By the spring of 1789, no group was happy. The First and Second Estates—the upper clergy and the nobility—resented that they had lost power to the monarchy. The wealthy bourgeoisie resented government regulations that hampered the growth of businesses as well as being barred from government and military positions. The poorer members of the Third Estate resented the hunger and unemployment that plagued them now more then ever.

Meeting of the Estates-General One of the first events of the Revolution was a meeting that the nobility pressed Louis to call. The nobles wanted a meeting of the Estates-General, an assembly made up of the three estates, to approve new taxes on the Third Estate. In August 1788 Louis agreed that the Estates General should meet the following spring.

In the tense atmosphere that existed in the spring of 1789, representatives of the Estates-General came to Paris. Because the Estates-General had not met for 175 years, this was the first such meeting for all of the representatives. In preparation for the event, the representatives wrote "notebooks," called cahiers (kah-YAYZ), to document their grievances. As the notebooks arrived in Paris, excitement grew. It became clear that people wanted the Estates-General to pass sweeping reforms. However, the voting process threatened the possibility of reforms.

Each of the three estates had always had only one vote in the Estates-General. Usually the First and Second Estates voted together, outvoting the Third Estate. This time, though, the ideas of the Enlightenment philosophers had given members of the Third Estate a new sense of importance. The Third Estate wanted to change the voting process.

At the start of the first meeting, King Louis instructed the assembly to follow the old rules of voting by estate. But the Third Estate, which had more representatives than the First or Second, refused the king's order. When Louis did nothing to have the order enforced, the Third Estate acted. On June 17, 1789, they proclaimed themselves a legislature, the National Assembly, with the right to make laws for France.

Reading like a Historian

Storming the Bastille

Analyzing Visuals One way we can learn about the past is by carefully analyzing works of art. The watercolor image on the right is Claude Cholat's *Storming the Bastille.* Even though Cholat was not a professional artist his painting interests historians because he was at the storming of the Bastille.

To interpret what this painting suggests about the French Revolution, think about

- the subject of the painting
- the title of the work
- the details in the painting

Skills Focus READING LIKE A HISTORIAN

1. **Subject and Title** Why do you think Cholat chose to paint the storming of the Bastille rather than some other event in the Revolution?
2. **Details** Why do you think Cholat included details of the entire day—from the initial attack on the Bastille to the flag of surrender—in this one image?
3. **Details** Why do you think Cholat put the scene in the courtyard in the foreground and the Bastille itself in the background?

See **Skills Handbook**, p. H26

Only then did the king take action, by locking the Third Estate out of their meeting place. Not to be defeated, the representatives of the Third Estate met in an indoor tennis court. There they swore what became known as the Tennis Court Oath—that they would not leave the court until they had written a constitution for France. In the face of this event, Louis relented and allowed each representative to have a vote.

The Storming of the Bastille The next major event of the Revolution occurred because Louis made a serious mistake. He started ordering troops to Paris and Versailles in case he needed to preserve the monarchy by force. Seeing this, members of the National Assembly feared that the king would use violence to end their meetings. The people of Paris, in sympathy with the National Assembly, sought to arm themselves against any action the king might take.

Differentiating Instruction

Below Level

Learners Having Difficulty

1. Review the information in the text about the storming of the Bastille. Have students closely examine the painting by Claude Cholat.
2. Organize students into mixed-ability pairs. Have each pair write a poem or song lyrics that tell the story of the storming of the Bastille from the point of view of a member of the mob, the commander, the prison guard, or one of the prisoners.
3. Have volunteers recite their poem or song lyrics to the class. **LS Auditory-Musical**

Alternative Assessment Handbook, Rubric 26: Poems and Songs

Cholat compressed all the day's events into this single image.
A soldier atop the Bastille is waving a white flag to surrender. Other accounts of the day support this detail.
The men on the wall are cutting the chains that will lower the drawbridge leading to the Bastille.

Storming the Bastille, by Claude Cholat, 1789

On July 14, 1789, a mob of Parisians went to the Bastille, an ancient prison, looking for weapons. In the past, the French government imprisoned people at the Bastille who spoke out against the monarchy. However, at the time, the prison held only seven prisoners, but the people viewed the huge medieval building as a powerful sign of the people's oppression. At first, the mob tried to negotiate with the Bastille's commander for weapons. When negotiations broke down, the angry mob and the prison guard exchanged fire and the mob swarmed into the prison. The mob killed the commander, stuck his head on a long stick, and paraded it through the streets. The action of the storming of the Bastille became a powerful symbol of the French Revolution.

The Spread of Fear After the fall of the Bastille, many people were shocked by what they had done. They feared that the king would punish them and end the Revolution.

Some people spread rumors that the king had hired foreign soldiers to punish the Third Estate. As a result, a panic later called the Great Fear swept through France. This panic was based on both fiction and fact. For example, rumors of massacres spread from village to village, and many people believed all kinds of wild stories. In the region of Champagne, for example, 3,000 men tried to find a gang of thugs reportedly seen in their neighborhood. However, the gang turned out to just be a herd of cattle.

As a result of the years of abuse by landowners, some peasants took revenge. The peasants destroyed records listing feudal dues and rents and burned nobles' houses. There was violence in the countryside, but the violence did not come from foreign soldiers.

READING CHECK **Identify Cause and Effect** What was the connection between the fall of the Bastille and the Great Fear?

THE IMPACT TODAY

July 14, called Bastille Day, is now France's national holiday.

Direct Teach

Reading Focus

First Events of the Revolution

Recall What did people fear after the fall of the Bastille? *that the king would punish them and end the revolution*

Explain How were rumors of massacres misleading? *Some stories were untrue, such as a reported gang of thugs in Champagne that was really a herd of cattle.*

Reading Like a Historian

Storming the Bastille

Activity Guide students in a discussion about how this painting celebrates the storming of the Bastille. Have students create an illustration that portrays the same events in a negative light. **LS Visual-Spatial**

Alternative Assessment Handbook, Rubrics 3: Artwork; and 11: Discussions

Differentiating Instruction

Advanced Learners/ Gifted and Talented

Research Required **Above Level**

Have students conduct research on the National Assembly, including its decisions and individual members. Each student should write a short essay in which they evaluate decisions of the National Assembly on an item-by-item basis. Have volunteers read selections from their essays to the class. **LS Verbal-Linguistic**

Alternative Assessment Handbook, Rubric 37: Writing Assignments

English-Language Learners

Below Level

Materials: poster paper, colored markers

Have students review the material about the storming of the Bastille. Guide students in a discussion about the significance of Bastille Day and why it was made a national holiday in France. Have students create a poster in honor of Bastille Day. Display posters in a classroom exhibit. **LS Visual-Spatial**

Alternative Assessment Handbook, Rubric 28: Posters

Answers

Reading Check *possible answer— After the fall of the Bastille, people were terrified that the king would punish them.*

Direct Teach

Reading Focus

3 How did the French create a new nation? *National Assembly completed constitution; restricted king's power; created Legislative Assembly; gave citizens broad rights; ended monarchy*

Creating a New Nation

Recall What was the outcome of the women's march on Versailles? *Louis made peace with the crowd by promising to return to Paris.*

Make Inferences Why did the National Assembly turn the clergy into public employees? *possible answer—They wanted the clergy to be accountable to the public, not part of a separate institution.*

Teaching Tip

Highlight the lasting importance of the Declaration of the Rights of Man and of the Citizen by having students compare it with the Universal Declaration of Human Rights, passed by the United Nations after World War II. The similarities will be striking.

PRIMARY SOURCES

Declaration of the Rights of Man and of the Citizen

This excerpt from the Declaration states the principles of the French Revolution and shows the strong influence of Enlightenment ideals.

"The representatives of the French people, . . . believing that the ignorance, neglect, or contempt of the rights of man are the sole cause of public calamities and of the corruption of governments, have determined to set forth in a solemn declaration the natural, unalienable, and sacred rights of man. . .

1. Men are born and remain free and equal in rights. . .
2. The aim of all political association is the preservation of the . . . rights of man. These rights are liberty, property, security and resistance to oppression. . .
5. Law can only prohibit such actions as are hurtful to society. . .
6. Law is the expression of the general will. Every citizen has a right to participate personally, or through his representative, in its formation. It must be the same for all. . .
7. No person shall be accused, arrested, or imprisoned except in the cases and according to the forms prescribed by law. . .
9. As all persons are held innocent until they shall have been declared guilty. . .
11. The free communication of ideas and opinions is one of the most precious of the rights of man. . . .
12. A common contribution [tax] is essential. . . . This should be equitably distributed among all the citizens in proportion to their means."

Skills Focus — READING LIKE A HISTORIAN

1. **Explain** According to the Declaration, what are the natural rights of man?
2. **Analyze** What ideas do the Declaration and the American Declaration of Independence and U.S. Bill of Rights share?

See **Skills Handbook**, p. H25

Creating a New Nation

The violence that marked the beginning of the Revolutions eventually lessened.. At this stage, in the Revolution the National Assembly began transforming centuries of French tradition. The Assembly formed a new government and France's monarchy eventually crumbled.

Legislating New Rights By early August 1789, the National Assembly had eliminated all the feudal dues and services that the peasants owed the landowners. The Assembly also eliminated the First Estate's legal privileges.

In late August the National Assembly adopted the **Declaration of the Rights of Man and of the Citizen**. The Declaration laid out the basic principles of the French Revolution—"liberty, equality, fraternity [brotherhood]." Writers of the Declaration took their inspiration from the English Bill of Rights, the American Declaration of Independence, and the writings of Enlightenment philosophers.

READING SKILLS

Understanding Word Parts If you know that *philo* means "love" and *sophia* means "wisdom," how would you define *philosophers?*

The document stated that all men are born equal and remain equal before the law. Like the U.S. Bill of Rights, the Declaration guaranteed freedom of speech, the press, and religion.

However, these rights did not extend to women. A famous Paris playwright, Olympe de Gouges (duh-goozh), wrote a declaration of rights for women, but the National Assembly turned it down.

Restrictions on Power Alarmed by the National Assembly's actions, Louis made the same mistake he had made earlier in the summer. He called troops to Versailles to protect his throne. This angered the common people of Paris, who feared that the king would crush the Revolution. In October a crowd of perhaps 7,000 women marched through the rain from Paris to Versailles. Demanding bread, the mob broke into the palace. To make peace with the crowd, Louis agreed to return to Paris and live in the Tuileries Palace with his family.

Skills Focus: Analyzing Primary Sources

At Level

Reading Like a Historian Skill
French Revolution Principles

1. Guide students in a discussion about the main points of the Declaration of the Rights of Man and of the Citizen.
2. Organize students into eight groups. Assign each group one of the principles listed in the Declaration.
3. Have students in each group work together to paraphrase the principle in their own words. Remind students that assembly members felt strongly about the ideas they discussed.
4. Have a volunteer from each group read its paraphrased principle and discuss as a class.

LS Interpersonal, Verbal-Linguistic

Alternative Assessment Handbook, Rubrics 11: Discussions; and 14: Group Activity

Answers

Reading Like a Historian 1. *liberty, property, security, resistance to oppression;* **2.** *equality of man; listing basic human rights; free speech, innocent until proven guilty*

Reading Skills *possible answer—those who have a love of wisdom*

The seizure of the royal family encouraged the Revolution's leaders to take bolder steps, and they passed several anticlerical measures. In November, the National Assembly seized church lands and sold them to pay off France's huge debt. All religious orders were disbanded. The Assembly also passed an act that turned the clergy into public employees. This action outraged most members of the clergy and also horrified many peasants.

Formation of a New Government In 1791 the National Assembly finally completed its constitution. It created a new legislative body called the Legislative Assembly. Citizens gained broad voting rights, but only taxpaying men at least 25 years old had the right to vote. The constitution kept the monarchy but severely restricted the king's power. In June 1791 the king and queen suspected that they were not safe, so they put on disguises and fled Paris. However, they were recognized and brought back to the Tuileries Palace.

The Intervention of Foreign Powers In July 1792 Austria and Prussia issued a declaration warning against harming the French monarchs and hinting that any such action would provoke war. Although the declaration was not meant to be read as a serious threat, Austria sent 50,000 troops to the French border. In response, the Legislative Assembly declared war. France's army was in disarray, however, and was defeated.

In Paris the financial strain of war, food shortages and high prices, and foreign troops marching toward the city led to unrest. Many people blamed the army's defeats on the king. Parisians feared that the achievements of the Revolution would be overturned, and they decided they had nothing to lose from extreme action.

The End of the Monarchy Extreme action came on August 10, 1792, when a mob marched on the Tuileries Palace and slaughtered the guards. Louis, Marie-Antoinette, and the children—now demoted to commoners—were thrown in prison.

Faced with mob violence and foreign invasion, the Legislative Assembly felt powerless. It voted itself out of existence and called for the election of a new legislature, the National Convention. The violence in August helped put the **radical** faction, or those who favored extreme change, in control. Among the National Convention's first acts were abolishing the monarchy and declaring France a republic.

The same day the new National Convention met, the French won a battle against the foreign invaders. This victory inspired hope in the revolutionary troops. The French Republic had held its ground against Europe's Old Order.

READING CHECK **Sequence** What steps did National and Legislative Assemblies take to create a new nation?

SECTION 1 ASSESSMENT

go.hrw.com
Online Quiz
Keyword: SHL NAP HP

Reviewing Ideas, Terms, and People

1. **a. Recall** What was the **Old Order**, and who was at its top?
   b. Explain Why did members of the **Third Estate** feel they were treated unfairly by the **First** and **Second Estates**?
   c. Predict What do you think might have happened if, in the fall of 1789, harvests had been larger than usual?
2. **a. Explain** What happened on July 14, 1789?
   b. Analyze Why did **Third Estate** members of the Estates-General feel that the Tennis Court Oath was necessary?
   c. Evaluate Do you think the Great Fear was a logical reaction to the fall of the Bastille? Why or why not?
3. **a. Describe** What rights did the **Declaration of the Rights of Man and of the Citizen** grant?
   b. Sequence List the events that directly affected the royal family.

Critical Thinking

4. **Identify Cause and Effect** Copy the graphic organizer below and use it to list causes of the French Revolution and the immediate effects. Add rows as needed.

Causes	Effects

FOCUS ON WRITING

5. **Persuasion** You are a member of one of the French estates. Write a short letter to the editor of the newspaper, arguing for or against each representative to the Estates-General having one vote.

Direct Teach

Reading Focus

Creating a New Nation

Make Inferences Why do you think that Austria and Prussia warned against harming the French monarchs? *possible answer—to avoid provoking war against France*

Summarize What challenges were faced by the people of France in August 1792? *mob violence, foreign invasion, unstable government*

Review & Assess

Close

Have students describe the ways in which members of the Third Estate tried to address France's problems.

Review

Online Quiz, Section 1

Assess

SE Section 1 Assessment

Progress Assessment: Section 1 Quiz

Alternative Assessment Handbook

Reteach/Intervene

Interactive Reader and Study Guide, Section 1

Interactive Skills Tutor CD-ROM

Section 1 Assessment Answers

1. **a.** structure of French society in 1780s; King Louis XVI
   b. First and Second Estate—small tax burden, powerful positions and privileges; Third Estate—large tax burden, few rights
   c. possible answer—tensions would have eased, conflict would have been postponed
2. **a.** The Bastille was stormed.
   b. believed France needed a constitution soon
   c. possible answer—Yes, French peasants could expect punishment.
3. **a.** freedom of speech, press, and religion, right to participate in government, receive fair trial
   b. women's march to Versailles, 1791 constitution, march on Tuileries palace
4. Causes—huge inequalities, Enlightenment ideas, economic problems, poor harvest; Effects—resentment of upper class, gave people hope, country desperate for money, hunger and anger, end of monarchy
5. possible answers—letters for: balances interests of France; letters against: unfair because 97 percent of people are in Third Estate

Answers

Reading Check *National Assembly—completed constitution and created Legislative Assembly; Legislative Assembly—created a new legislature, the National Convention, which abolished the monarchy and declared France a republic*

World Literature

Excerpt from *A Tale of Two Cities*

Word Help

latter the second of two, last
basement lower part
Monsieur mister or sir
Marquis title of nobility
submissive obedient, compliant

Meet the Writer

Charles Dickens (1812-1870) One of the most celebrated English authors, Charles Dickens wrote such classic novels as *Oliver Twist* and *A Christmas Carol*. To highlight the injustices of the 19th century, Dickens depicted the harsh treatment of the poor in a society divided along lines of wealth. Rather than stating his critique directly, Dickens skillfully used his characters to bring out social issues. Dickens pioneered the serial method of publication, which was later widely copied. Magazines printed monthly installments of his novels, making the stories available to those who could not afford books.

World Literature

CHARLES DICKENS (1812–1870)

About the Reading The French Revolution is the setting for *A Tale of Two Cities*, but the book was written many years later, in 1859. In both cities—London and Paris—the reader meets people who show the best and worst of human qualities. The passage below introduces one of the book's villains, here called Monsieur the Marquis, as he rides through Paris in his carriage. The scene takes place before the Revolution has truly begun.

AS YOU READ **Think about why the poor people in the street react as they do.**

Driving his Mail Coach in Nice, by Alphonse de Toulouse-Lautrec-Monfa, 1881

Excerpt from

A Tale of Two Cities

by Charles Dickens

With a wild rattle and clatter, and an inhuman abandonment of consideration not easy to be understood in these days, the carriage dashed through streets and swept round corners, with women screaming before it, and men clutching each other and clutching children out of its way. At last, swooping at a street corner by a fountain, one of its wheels came to a sickening little jolt, and there was a loud cry from a number of voices, and the horses reared and plunged.

But for the latter inconvenience, the carriage probably would not have stopped; carriages were often known to drive on, and leave their wounded behind, and why not? But the frightened valet had got down in a hurry . . .

"What has gone wrong?" said Monsieur, calmly looking out.

A tall man in a nightcap had caught up a bundle from among the feet of the horses, and had laid it on the basement of the fountain, and was down in the mud and wet, howling over it like a wild animal.

"Pardon, Monsieur the Marquis!" said a ragged and submissive man, "it is a child."

"Why does he make that abominable noise? Is it his child?"

"Excuse me, Monsieur the Marquis—it is a pity—yes." . . .

The people closed round, and looked at Monsieur the Marquis. . . [He] ran his eyes over them all, as if they had been mere rats come out of their holes.

He took out his purse.

"It is extraordinary to me," said he, "that you people cannot take care of yourselves and your children. One or the other of you is for ever in the way. How do I know what injury you have done my horses?"

Skills FOCUS **READING LIKE A HISTORIAN**

go.hrw.com
World Literature
Keyword: SHL WRLIT

1. **Explain** What was the Monsieur's main concern?
2. **Interpret Literature as a Source** What bias may show in Dickens's novel? What sources do you think Dickens used for information on the Revolution?

See **Skills Handbook**, p. H28

Differentiating Instruction

Above Level

Advanced Learners/Gifted and Talented

1. Guide the class in a discussion about the concept of irony using the following example: Later in A Tale of Two Cities, the Marquis is killed to avenge the death of the young child. The killer leaves this note on the body: "Drive him fast to his tomb. This, from JACQUES."
2. Have students brainstorm ways in which a person unapologetically commits a crime or does something wrong and meets an ironic fate. For example, a thief leaves stolen goods in the trunk of his car and, ironically, his car is stolen.
3. Have students write down their ideas and have volunteers share their ideas with the class. Discuss how well the students captured the concept of irony. **LS Verbal-Linguistic**

Alternative Assessment Handbook, Rubric 11: Discussions

Answers

Reading Like a Historian 1. *his horses;* **2.** *bias against French nobility; sources sympathetic to the Third Estate*

SECTION 2

The Republic

Before You Read

Main Idea

An extreme government changed French society and tried through harsh means to eliminate its critics within France.

Reading Focus

1. What changes did the radical government make in French society and politics?
2. What was the Reign of Terror, and how did it end?

Key Terms and People

Maximilien Robespierre
guillotine
counterrevolution
Reign of Terror

TAKING NOTES As you read, take notes on the changes made in French government and society and on the Reign of Terror.

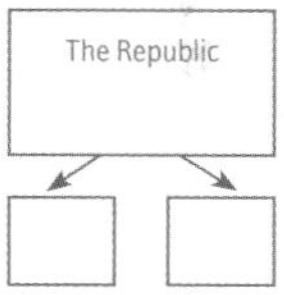

◀ Jacques-Louis David painted the *Death of Marat* in 1793. The painting provides a narrative of Marat's murder, showing Corday's letter and knife and Marat's wound and blood.

Death of Marat, by Jacques-Louis David, 1793

THE INSIDE STORY ***How did a skin disease help destroy a radical leader?*** On July 13, 1793, Charlotte Corday, who hated the radicals, set out on what she saw as a patriotic mission. Believing that only Jean-Paul Marat's death would save France's republic, the young woman made her way to Marat's home in Paris. A member of the National Convention, Marat was a leader of the radicals who had taken over the French government. Because he was suffering from a severe skin disease, he had taken to working at home while soaking in the tub. At Marat's home, Corday said that she had information about traitors. She was taken to Marat, who sat partially covered by a table across his tub. As the two talked, Corday slowly reached into a fold of her dress. Suddenly, she pulled out a large kitchen knife, leaned over, and plunged the blade into Marat's chest. Blood gushed from the wound, and Marat sank slowly into the water. The radical leader's skin disease gave an enemy the chance to destroy him. With his murder, Marat became a martyr to his followers. ■

Preteach

Getting Started

Use the **Interactive Reader and Study Guide** to familiarize students with the section content.

Interactive Reader and Study Guide, Section 2

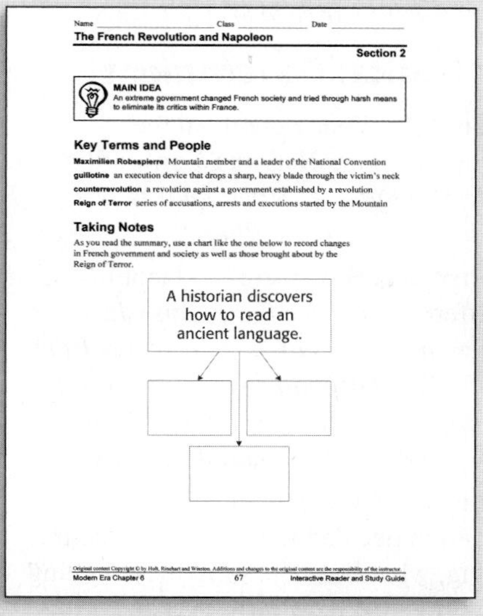
Name ______ Class ______ Date ______

The French Revolution and Napoleon

Section 2

MAIN IDEA
An extreme government changed French society and tried through harsh means to eliminate its critics within France.

Key Terms and People

Maximilien Robespierre Mountain member and a leader of the National Convention
guillotine an execution device that drops a sharp, heavy blade through the victim's neck
counterrevolution a revolution against a government established by a revolution
Reign of Terror series of accusations, arrests and executions started by the Mountain

Taking Notes

As you read the summary, use a chart like the one below to record changes in French government and society as well as those brought about by the Reign of Terror.

Modern Era Chapter 6 67 Interactive Reader and Study Guide

CRF: Vocabulary Builder: Section 2

Taking Notes

A radical government—three factions in government: Mountain, Girondins, and Plain; king executed, control tightened society transformed; The Reign of Terror—opposition to Revolution, civil war, trials and executions, Directory formed

Teach the Main Idea

At Level

The Republic

1. **Teach** Ask students the Reading Focus questions to teach this section.
2. **Apply** Draw two large circles for students to see. Label each circle with one of the topics of the section: A Radical Government and The Reign of Terror. Have students copy the circles. Then have students work in pairs and write the main ideas of each topic in the appropriate circle.
3. **Review** As you review the section, use the circles as a graphic organizer, and have students identify the main ideas they have written in their circles. Have students identify the links between the two circles.
4. **Practice/Homework** Have students write an editorial for a Paris newspaper, cautioning the people about excessive violence in the revolution. **LS Visual-Spatial, Verbal-Linguistic**

Alternative Assessment Handbook, Rubrics 13: Graphic Organizers; and 37: Writing Assignments

Direct Teach

Reading Focus

1 What changes did the radical government make in French society and politics? *tried and executed king; set up Committee of Public Safety and the Revolutionary Tribunal; closed churches; tried to undo old ways*

A Radical Government

Identify What were the three factions in the National Convention? *the Mountain or Montagnards, the Girondins, and the Plain*

Contrast How were the Jacobins different from the Girondins? *Jacobins were most radical, support came from the poor; Girondins were moderate; support came from provinces, supported a constitutional monarchy*

Interpret When the National Convention decided to try and execute the king, what message were they sending to France? *possible answer—The monarchy is over and cannot return.*

Info to Know

Slavery and the Haitian Revolution

Revolutionary leaders had proclaimed liberty as their highest ideal, which raised the issue of colonial slavery. France had several colonies in the Caribbean that followed a plantation system with a labor force of black slaves. After the Revolution began, free blacks and people of mixed race began calling for full rights and an end to the slave trade. Their cause was promoted in France by some National Assembly members and radical journalists. The white planters fought back, however, and a 1790 decree did nothing to change things. In 1791, tensions reached a breaking point; a huge slave revolt began and eventually led to the independence of Haiti.

A Radical Government

When the National Convention convened on September 20, 1792, the radical representatives were in control. Under their direction the Revolution took an extreme turn. France would no longer be a constitutional monarchy. It would be a republic.

Factions in the New Government All of the members of the National Convention supported the Revolution. They grouped themselves into three political factions, however. The Mountain, whose members were called Montagnards, were the most radical. Many Montagnards also belonged to the radical Jacobin (JAK-uh-bihn) Club, or Jacobins. The Montagnards support came from lower middle class and poor people. This support pushed the Montagnards to adopt more radical policies.

A second political faction, the Girondins, were moderates. They came mainly from the provinces and resented what they considered the excessive influence of the Paris mob on the Revolution. The Girondins generally supported a constitutional monarchy and resisted extremes on either side.

The third political faction, the Plain, was made up of the swing voters. In general, the members of the Plain originally supported the Girondins but later switched their support to the Mountain.

These groupings had no formal organization. They did not put forth programs or promote plans of action. Each member acted as an individual and was often strongly influenced by personal rivalries.

Radical Leaders Three members of radical groups played particularly important roles in the new government.

1. Jean-Paul Marat, an advocate of violence and a leader of the Paris sans culottes, was one of the National Convention's most radical leaders.
2. Georges-Jacques Danton, a violent agitator in the early days of the Revolution, was very popular with the public. A compromiser, he came to oppose what he considered the Revolution's excesses.
3. **Maximilien Robespierre** was known for his intense dedication to the Revolution. He became increasingly radical and led the National Convention during its most bloodthirsty time.

The Execution of the King Shortly after the National Convention convened, the king was placed on trial. The Girondins had hoped to avoid a trial, but they were in the minority. The more powerful Montagnards were eager to try and execute the king in order to prevent a return of the monarchy and to defend the Revolution from its enemies.

Quickly condemned, the king was scheduled to die the next day, January 21, 1793. That morning, the Paris streets were quiet. Soldiers lined the way to the place of execution, in case any supporters of the monarchy caused trouble. At the scaffold, Louis began to deliver a speech proclaiming his innocence, but a drumroll drowned out his voice. He was pushed into place on the **guillotine**, a device that dropped a sharp, heavy blade through the victim's neck.

Death of a King

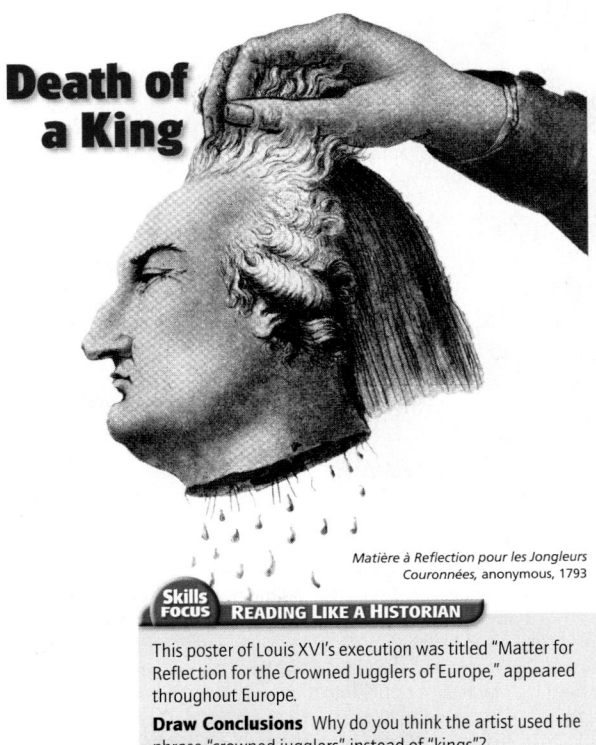

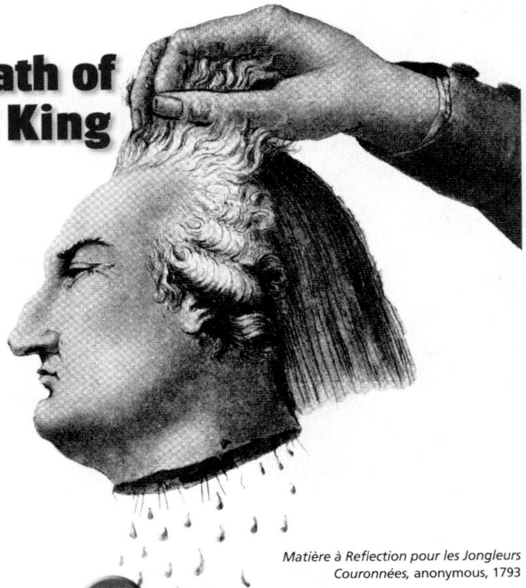

Matière à Reflection pour les Jongleurs Couronnées, anonymous, 1793

Skills Focus READING LIKE A HISTORIAN

This poster of Louis XVI's execution was titled "Matter for Reflection for the Crowned Jugglers of Europe," appeared throughout Europe.

Draw Conclusions Why do you think the artist used the phrase "crowned jugglers" instead of "kings"?

See **Skills Handbook**, p. H27

Collaborative Learning

At Level

The King on Trial?

1. Guide students in a discussion of the trial of the king, including the possible effects on France if the king were executed.
2. Organize students into mixed-ability pairs. Have half of the pairs write a letter to the National Convention explaining why the king should be put on trial. Have the other half write letters arguing against a trial.
3. Have volunteers read their letters to the class. As they read, make a list of arguments for and against a trial for students to see.
4. Tell students that they are the members of the National Convention and will vote on whether or not to put the king on trial. Remind students that they are not voting on the outcome of the trial.
5. Maintain a secret ballot and tally the votes for students to see. **LS Verbal-Linguistic, Interpersonal**

Alternative Assessment Handbook, Rubric 43: Writing to Persuade

Answers

Reading Like a Historian *possible answer—wanted to ridicule all monarchs as nothing more than entertainers*

When the deed was done, a young guard held up the dripping head for all to see.

Reports of the king's execution quickly spread across Europe. Outside of France, Europeans reacted with horror to the news of the French Revolution. The London *Times* newspaper condemned the Revolution and the execution of the king as savagery.

HISTORY'S VOICES

"Every [heart] burns with indignation in this kingdom, against the ferocious savages of Paris . . . A Republic founded on the blood of an innocent victim must have but a short duration."

—*London Times*, January 25, 1793

Tightening Control After the king's execution, the National Convention began to tighten its hold on France. First, it set up the Committee of Public Safety to manage the country's military defense against the foreign forces on France's borders. The committee promptly created an unprecedented draft of all able-bodied, unmarried men between 18 and 45 for military service. In addition, the National Convention established a court called the Revolutionary Tribunal. This court was supposed to root out and eliminate people who threatened the Revolution from within.

Transforming Society The Revolution not only transformed the French government but also attempted to completely transform French society. The leaders of the new government wanted to erase all connections to old ways of life, including religion. Many clergy members lost their positions. In Paris the local government closed the churches. To replace Roman Catholicism, Robespierre created the cult of the Supreme Being, in which enthusiasm for the Revolution was the object of worship.

Anticlerical feeling took many forms. Even statues of people holding Bibles were not safe. Workers changed the titles on the Bibles to read "Declaration of the Rights of Man."

A metric system replaced the old system of weights and measures. A new calendar also cut ties to the past. The months were renamed, and every month had 3 weeks of 10 days. The revolutionary calendar fell out of use, but the metric system was one change that was kept.

READING CHECK **Explain** Why did the National Convention want to change French government and society?

Daily Life and the French Revolution

Ideals of the Revolution influenced the design of many kinds of everyday objects. ***Why might objects such as playing cards have helped spread revolutionary ideas?***

▶ To erase connections with royalty, makers of playing cards replaced the traditional images of kings and queens with revolutionary ideals. For example, in place of the queens were the freedoms of worship, marriage, the press, and the professions.

French School, 1700s

◀ Instead of stiff fussy dresses, women began to wear light, loose ones that recalled the styles of ancient Greece—much admired for its democracy.

Incroyable and Merveilleuse in Paris, by Louis Leopold Boilly, 1801

▶ Household items also showed revolutionary themes. Here, a wallpaper panel displays revolutionary slogans and a red Phrygian (FRI-jee-uhn) cap. The Phrygian cap became a popular symbol of the Revolution because freed slaves of ancient Rome wore such caps.

French School, 1700s

Direct Teach

Reading Focus

A Radical Government

Recall What departments did the National Convention set up? *the Committee of Public Safety, the Revolutionary Tribunal*

Summarize How did the Revolution affect the church and the clergy? *some clergy lost positions, Parisian churches closed, Robespierre created new cult, statues altered*

Make Inferences Why do you think the Revolutionary government changed the calendar and the system of weights and measures? *It wanted to completely transform society, not just the government.*

Info to Know

French Republican Calendar Revolutionaries saw the old Gregorian calendar and its religious holidays as another symbol of the Church and the Old Order. The new calendar began on September 22, the anniversary of the proclamation of the French Republic. The names of the months translate as Vintage, Mist, Frost, Snow, Rain, Wind, Seedtime, Blossom, Meadow, Harvest, Heat, and Fruits. Five extra days were placed at the end of each year to make a total of 365.

Primary Source

"The tree of liberty only grows when watered by the blood of tyrants."
—Bertrand Barère de Vieuzac, speech to the National Convention, 1793

Differentiating Instruction

Below Level

English-Language Learners

1. Draw a two-column chart as shown for students to see. Omit the italicized answers.

French Government and Society	
Before Revolution	**After Revolution**
three estates	***National Convention***
monarchy	***Rights of Man***
heavy taxes	***taxes distributed***
privileges for church	***clergy public employees***
peace	***war***

2. Organize students into mixed-ability pairs. Have students copy the chart as shown onto their own paper. Have students work together to fill in their charts, but they should turn in their own individual charts. **LS Interpersonal, Visual-Spatial**

Alternative Assessment Handbook, Rubrics 7: Charts; and 14: Group Activity

Answers

Daily Life and the French Revolution *possible answer—Because many people played cards, pictures depicting new ideals became very accessible.*

Reading Check *It saw the old government and systems as oppressive and it wanted to create a better society.*

Direct Teach

Reading Focus

2 What was the Reign of Terror, and how did it end? *a period of accusations, trials, and executions that created a wave of fear; when those who began the terror were killed*

The Reign of Terror

Recall Where did the main opposition to the Revolution come from? *the countryside*

Explain Why did peasants generally oppose the Revolutionary government? *peasants were devoutly Catholic, some supported monarchy, opposed anticlerical moves*

Summarize What dramatic events occurred in the Vendée? *civil war; violence between counterrevolutionary and government forces*

Primary Source

"Anarchy within, invasion from without. A country cracking from outside pressure, disintegrating from internal strain. Revolution is at its height. War. Inflation. Hunger. Fear. Hate. Sabotage. Fanaticism. Hopes. Boundless idealism . . . and the dread that all the gains of the Revolution would be lost. And the faith that if they won, they would bring Liberty, Equality, Fraternity to the world."—R. R. Palmer, *Twelve Who Ruled*

The Reign of Terror

By the middle of 1793, many people were concerned about the course of the Revolution. Many of the French themselves were criticizing it. Outside France, the countries of Great Britain, Holland, Spain, Austria, and Prussia were worried enough about the Revolution to form a coalition and make war against France.

As a result, some of the revolutionary leaders feared that they would lose control. They decided to take drastic actions to avoid a possible **counterrevolution**, a revolution against a government that was established by a revolution. The Mountain began a series of accusations, trials, and executions that became known as the **Reign of Terror**, creating a wave of fear throughout the country.

An Outbreak of Civil War In France, real resistance to the Revolution lay in the countryside. Shortly after the peasants won their main goal—the end of feudal dues—they returned to their essentially conservative views. In general, they remained devoutly Catholic and opposed the Revolution's anticlerical moves.

When the National Convention instituted a draft, the peasants' hatred for the government erupted. Village rebels declared, "They have killed our king; chased away our priests; sold the goods of our church; eaten everything we have and now they want to take our bodies . . . no, they shall not have them."

In a region of western France called the Vendée (vahn-day), resistance to the government was so strong that it led to civil war. A counterrevolutionary force called the Catholic and Royal army, a name showing support for the Roman Catholic Church and the monarchy, fought government forces. Savage fighting spread across the region. The government eventually regained control of the Vendée, destroying everyone and everything it could.

Accusations and Trials Back in Paris, the Mountain, the leaders of the campaign to eliminate any resistance to the Revolution, used the Revolutionary Tribunal to rid the country of dissent. Robespierre declared the need to use terror to defend the republic from its many enemies.

The Reign of Terror

The Committee of Public Safety unleashed the Reign of Terror in the summer of 1793. The committee used its broad powers to eliminate all the Revolution's enemies—real and imagined. One member went so far as to accuse losing generals of treason and answered critics with the cry, "heads! heads! and more heads!" ***According to the map, where did most counterrevolutionary activity take place?***

Maximilien Robespierre
He dominated the Committee of Public Safety.

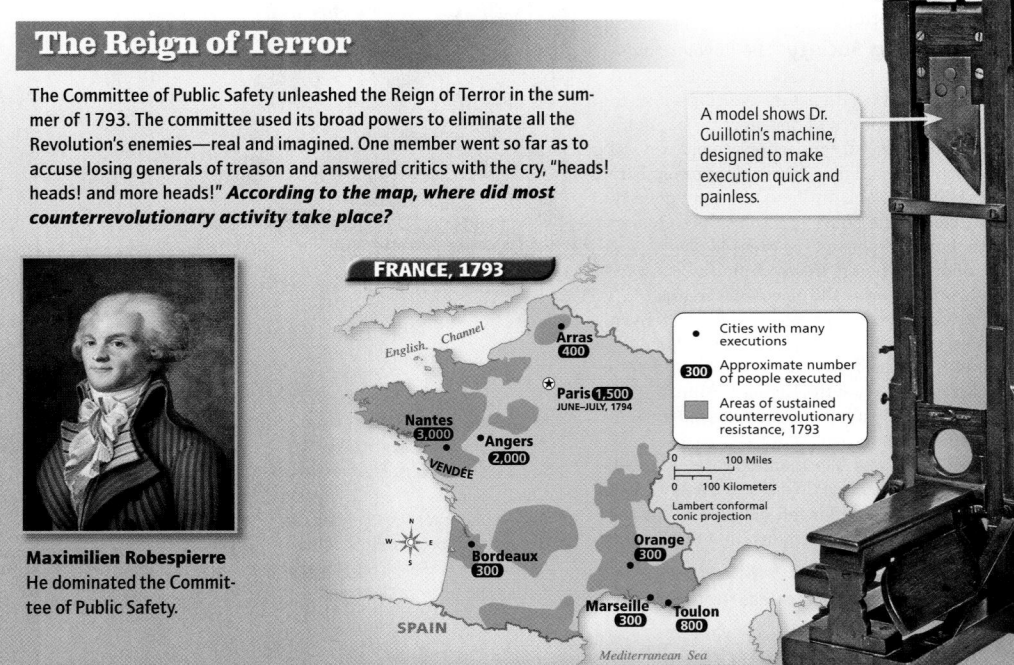

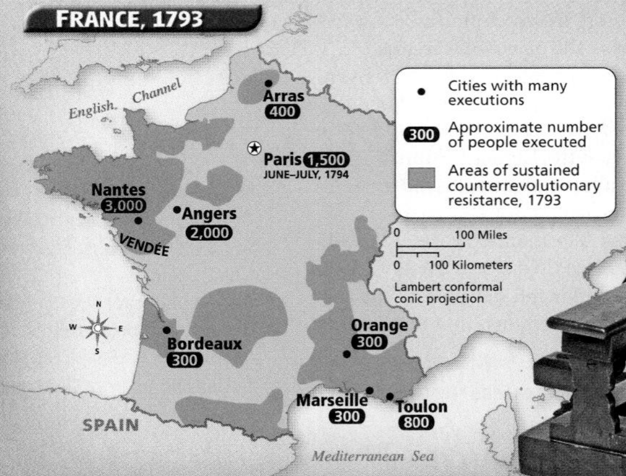

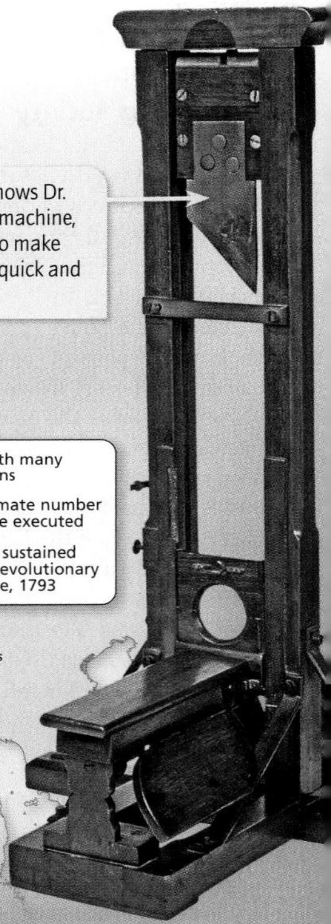

A model shows Dr. Guillotin's machine, designed to make execution quick and painless.

Skills Focus: Identifying Problem and Solution

At Level

Reading Skill

City Folk and Country Folk

Materials: three sheets of butcher paper, markers

1. Organize the class into three groups. The first group will represent revolutionaries in Paris, the second will represent people of the Vendée, and the third will represent a group of mediators.
2. Have the first two groups make a list of complaints about each other on the butcher paper. The third group will "float" between the first two, observe, and draft a list of proposals for compromise.
3. Have representatives from the first two groups read their lists to the class.
4. Have the third group read its proposals for compromise. Then allow the first and second groups to make suggestions to improve the compromise. Arrive at a consensus and write the final compromise on the third piece of butcher paper. **LS Visual-Spatial, Interpersonal**

Alternative Assessment Handbook, Rubric 14: Group Activity

Answers

The Reign of Terror *northwestern and southeastern corners of France, areas far from Paris*

HISTORY'S VOICES

"Now, what is the fundamental principle of the democratic or popular government? . . . It is virtue . . . which is nothing other than the love of country and of its laws. . . If the spring of popular government in time of peace is virtue, the springs of popular government in revolution are at once virtue and terror: virtue, without which terror is fatal; terror, without which virtue is powerless. Terror is nothing other than justice, prompt, severe, inflexible; it is therefore an emanation of virtue."

—Robespierre, *Justification of the Use of Terror,* speech February 5, 1794

The Revolutionary Tribunal started its campaign with the Girondists, who were seen as a threat to the Revolution because they had once favored a constitutional monarchy. Soon, anyone who had ever criticized the Revolution or who had had any connection to the Old Order was in danger of being hauled in for a trial. Some people were tried merely because they were suspected of counterrevolutionary activity. The accused had few rights and some were even forbidden to defend themselves.

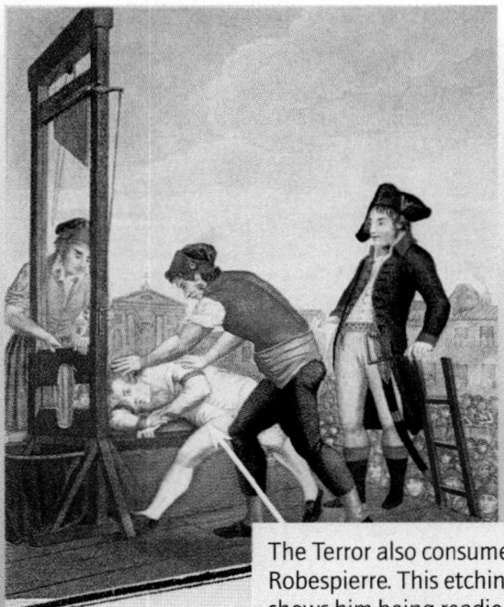

Le Morte de Robespierre, anonymous, c. 1794

The Terror also consumed Robespierre. This etching shows him being readied for the guillotine.

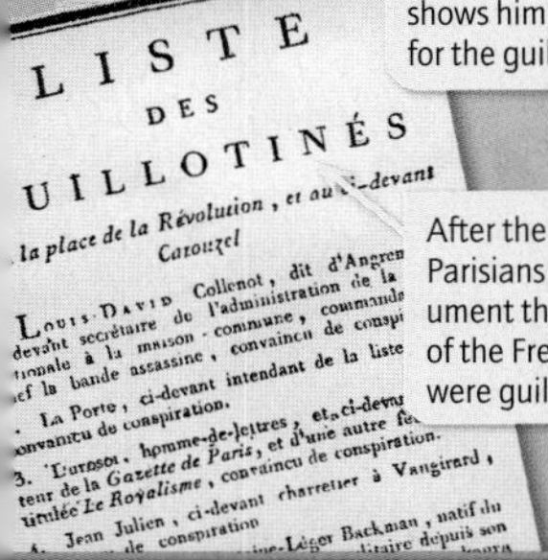

LISTE DES GUILLOTINÉS

la place de la Révolution, et au ci-devant Carouzel

After the Terror, curious Parisians bought this document that listed many of the French citizens who were guillotined.

Death by Guillotine The most common sentence was death by guillotine. Such a death was quick, in contrast to the agonizing methods of execution in use for centuries. To get to the scaffold where the guillotine waited, the condemned rode in an open cart that paraded through the streets of Paris. Crowds gathered along the cart's route to jeer at or sometimes cheer for the passengers. At the scaffold, mobs watched the gruesome executions. Women with radical sympathies sometimes sat near the scaffold and quietly knitted while the victims went to their deaths.

The guillotine was so efficient that the executioner could execute more than one person per minute. Executions became so common in Paris that residents complained about the blood overflowing the city's drainage ditches.

The Terror's Victims The Reign of Terror did not spare any particular class, occupation, or gender. Though many more common people than nobles were killed, the nobility was not entirely spared. The peasants and laborers—the same people the Revolution was supposed to aid—formed the largest group of victims. Nor did the Terror spare women. Marie-Antoinette, was one of the early victims, as were many women of the lower classes. Olympe de Gouges, who wrote the Declaration of the Rights of Woman and the Female Citizen, also went to the guillotine. Even the nuns who refused to close their convents were also sent to the guillotine.

Those who launched the Reign of Terror eventually fell victim themselves. Robespierre sent Danton and his followers to the guillotine for suggesting that the rule of terror might be relaxed. Then Robespierre himself became a victim. On July 27, 1794, Robespierre and his supporters were surrounded by National Convention soldiers and taken into custody. Soon after their arrest, the heads of Robespierre and about 100 of his supporters fell into the guillotine's basket where so many heads had fallen before.

How many victims had the Terror claimed? During the 10 months of the Terror, some 300,000 people were arrested, and about 17,000 were executed. Even though the dead were a small percentage of France's population, the widespread violence shocked the French and increased foreign opposition to the Revolution.

Direct Teach

Reading Focus

The Reign of Terror

Recall Who was in danger of being tried by the Revolutionary Tribunal? *Girondist critics of the Revolution, people with connections to the Old Order, anyone suspected of counterrevolutionary activity*

Elaborate How did the guillotine contribute to the Reign of Terror? *It was a quicker, more efficient method of execution.*

Make Judgments Why wasn't the Reign of Terror ended sooner? *If people challenged the policy, they would also be tried and executed.*

Info to Know

The Guillotine The Paris executioner complained that decapitation by sword dulled the blade. Sharpening a sword took time, and there were so many people to be executed. But hacking away at a victim's neck with a dull sword was cruel. To solve this dilemma, Dr. Joseph Guillotin, a member of the National Assembly, proposed the introduction of the decapitation machine already in use in other countries. Dr. Guillotin felt that painless executions were more in keeping with Enlightenment ideals. The machine was tested on corpses from a hospital and went into official use in 1792. Although the guillotine was designed to be a machine of mercy, it became of symbol of terror.

Primary Source

"Show my head to the people, it is worth seeing."

—Georges-Jacques Danton, last words, addressed to the executioner

Collaborative Learning

At Level

Monument for Victims of the Terror

Materials: poster board, colored pencils, markers

1. Organize students into small groups. Have each group design a monument to commemorate the Reign of Terror victims.
2. Have students write a short speech to be delivered during a ceremony in which their monument will be unveiled. Encourage students to be creative, but also to be respectful of the dead. You might want to show examples of other monuments such as the Vietnam Veterans Memorial and the Hiroshima Peace Memorial Park.
3. Have students present their monuments and speeches to the class. **LS Interpersonal, Visual-Spatial**

Alternative Assessment Handbook, Rubrics 3: Artwork; and 24: Oral Presentations

Direct Teach

Reading Focus

The Reign of Terror

Identify What was the new governing board called? *the Directory*

Explain Why was the new government ineffective? *directors were weak and corrupt, argued amongst themselves, fell into patterns of Old Order*

Quick Facts Transparency: Governments of Revolutionary France

Review & Assess

Close

Have students explain how the radical government disintegrated into the Reign of Terror.

Review

Online Quiz, Section 2

Assess

SE Section 2 Assessment

Progress Assessment: Section 2 Quiz

Alternative Assessment Handbook

Reteach/Intervene

Interactive Reader and Study Guide, Section 2

Interactive Skills Tutor CD-ROM

Governments of Revolutionary France

QUICK FACTS

Throughout the Revolution, legislative bodies dissolved to create new governments. Methods of electing the legislatures differed.

National Assembly, created June 17, 1789
- Ended feudalism and privileges of the First and Second Estates
- Approved the Declaration of the Rights of Man and of the Citizen
- Seized church lands and made clergy paid employees
- Wrote constitution that reduced the king's power

Legislative Assembly, first met September 1791
- Inexperienced representatives, often deadlocked on domestic issues
- Declared war on Austria in April 1792

National Convention, first met September 1792
- Ended monarchy, proclaimed France a republic
- Tried and executed Louis XVI for treason
- Instituted draft to increase size of army
- In power during Reign of Terror
- Began codifying laws and creating public education system
- Abolished slavery in French colonies
- Wrote a new constitution, and created the Directory

Directory, first met in 1795
- Run by an executive branch of five directors
- Weak, corrupt, and inefficient
- Ended in 1799 when Napoleon seized power

The actions of the Reign of Terror were intended to protect the Revolution but had in fact weakened it. As one woman shouted as she went to her death, "Oh Liberty, what crimes are committed in your name!"

After the Terror When the Terror ended, France had to start over with a new government. In 1795 the National Convention wrote yet another constitution. It restricted voting rights given in the previous constitution. Now, only men who owned property could vote.

After the new constitution was adopted, voters elected a governing board. Called the Directory, this governing board was made up of five men called directors. The directors did pass some financial reforms that helped farmers and improved trade, but the Directory was not an effective government.

Partly because the directors were weak and corrupt, France's troubles continued. The directors argued among themselves, failing to lead the exhausted country forward. Eventually, their rule shared many characteristics of the Old Order's—high prices, bankruptcy, citizen unrest. The result was a power vacuum. With no one really in control, something in France had to change.

READING CHECK **Summarize** Why was the period of mass executions called the Reign of Terror?

Section 2 Assessment

go.hrw.com
Online Quiz
Keyword: SHL NAP HP

Reviewing Ideas, Terms, and People

1. **a. Identify** Who was **Maximilien Robespierre**, and why is he important?
   b. Analyze How did anticlerical sentiment affect France's church and society?
   c. Support a Position What is your opinion about Louis XVI not having the opportunity to speak to the crowd before his execution? Explain your answer.
2. **a. Recall** What was the most common sentence given by the Revolutionary Tribunal?
   b. Identify Cause and Effect What are two reasons that many peasants opposed the Revolution?
   c. Make Judgments If you had been the king of Great Britain in 1793, would you have been nervous? Why or why not?

Critical Thinking

3. **Categorize** Copy the chart below and fill it in with ways in which the French Revolution affected the daily lives of the French people.

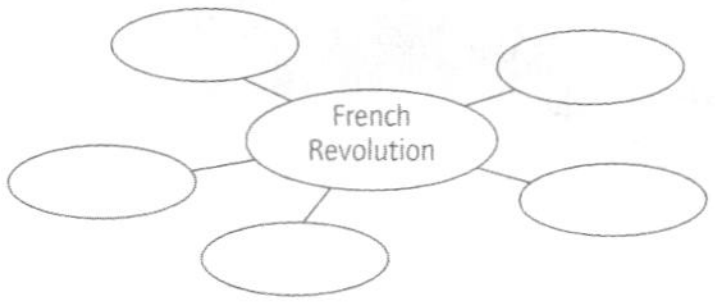

FOCUS ON SPEAKING

4. **Description** You are a peasant in the French countryside. Write and present a short speech describing the ways you think the Reign of Terror has changed your life.

Section 2 Assessment Answers

1. **a.** radical leader dedicated to the Revolution, led France during Reign of Terror
   b. clergy lost positions, Parisian churches closed, new cult created, statues altered
   c. possible answer—Louis might have given a passionate speech, captured public sympathy, and have been spared.
2. **a.** death by guillotine
   b. peasants were devoutly Catholic and supported the monarchy; opposed the draft
   c. possible answer—Yes, what happened in France could also happen in Britain.
3. military draft; anticlerical activity; metric system; new clock and calendar; Reign of Terror
4. possible ways life changed—live in environment of fear and despair, widespread violence, loss of life by guillotine

Answers

Reading Check *It was a period of accusations, trials, and executions that led to a wave of fear.*

Focus on Themes

Government and Citizenship

The 1789 Declaration of the Rights of Man and of the Citizen described how the French government would treat its citizens. The first article of the declaration states, "Men are born and remain free and equal in rights." The declaration uses the word *men*, but many asserted that the article applied to women, too. That women were equal to men was a truly revolutionary idea, and it frightened many people in France and the rest of Europe.

▲ **NOW Young workers in Rennes, France, protest unfair working conditions.**

EQUALITY THEN Equality was a key goal of the National Convention, which took control of France in 1792. Determined that everyone should be treated the same, the Convention went so far as to ban the titles *monsieur* and *madame*, the French equivalents of *Mr.* and *Mrs.* These titles, Convention leaders argued, had been derived from the words for *lord* and *lady*—noble titles—and should be abolished. Instead, people were required to address one another as "Citizen". For example, when King Louis XVI was overthrown, he became Citizen Capet, after his family's ancient name.

Despite the government's intentions, however, people were not treated equally. Women in particular had few rights. Although many women had taken part in the Revolution, they were not allowed to participate in the new government. Other people banned from the government included servants, men under 25, and people who did not pay taxes.

▶ **THEN Parisians marching on the Legislative Assembly.**

EQUALITY NOW Just as it was in France during the French Revolution, the idea that all people are equal is important in democracies around the world today. In most modern democracies, all citizens—men and women—are free to take part in the government. In addition, laws have made it illegal to discriminate against people based on their gender, race, occupation, or income.

In spite of the progress made by many democracies, equality for all is still a goal—not a reality—for many governments and their citizens. In many places, for example, women cannot vote, hold office, drive cars, or even appear in public alone. Consequently, groups of people all around the world are working hard to make equality a reality. The ideal of equality supported in the French Revolution, though not fully achieved, is alive in the world today.

Skills Focus UNDERSTANDING THEMES

1. **Summarize** What does the Declaration of the Rights of Man and of the Citizen say about equality?
2. **Analyze** How did the treatment of women during the French Revolution differ from the Declaration's goals?
3. **Predict** Do you think women around the world will gain rights or lose rights in the future? Why?

Focus on Themes

Government and Citizenship

Biography

Olympe de Gouges (1748?-1793) Marie Gouze was born in southern France into a humble family. When she became a widow at a young age, she moved to Paris and taught herself to write, taking the name Olympe de Gouges. After publishing her memoirs in 1784, she began writing political pamphlets and plays. One of her early plays was a protest against slavery. De Gouges believed that the philosophy of natural freedom should apply to all people. She was an outspoken advocate of equality of the sexes, especially with regards to marriage and children. During the Reign of Terror, she proposed government reforms by popular vote; for this, she was sent to the guillotine in 1793.

Primary Source

"Averse to all intrigue, beyond all parties whose passionate fight has divided France, I forged a new path for myself; trusting my own eyes alone, and listening to my own inner voice, I have confronted the foolish, have attacked the mean and have sacrificed all my assets to the revolution." –Olympe de Gouges

Differentiating Instruction

At Level

English-Language Learners

Research Required

1. Organize students into pairs. Have each pair conduct research on women's participation in government in various countries around the world, including the United States.
2. Students should investigate local, regional, and national offices held, as well as voting statistics. Statistics for women should be compared with those for men.
3. Have students compile their findings in a one-page report that includes a brief summary of their findings.
4. Have pairs present the results of their research to the class. **LS Logical-Mathematical, Verbal-Linguistic**

Alternative Assessment Handbook, Rubrics 1: Acquiring Information; and 30: Research

Answers

Understanding Themes 1. *"Men are born and remain free and equal in rights."* **2.** *Despite the government's promise of equality, women had few rights and could not participate in government.* **3.** *Possible answers should include that women will gain rights in the future, but it will depend on levels of activism and societal values.*

Preteach

Getting Started

Use the **Interactive Reader and Study Guide** to familiarize students with the section content.

Interactive Reader and Study Guide, Section 3

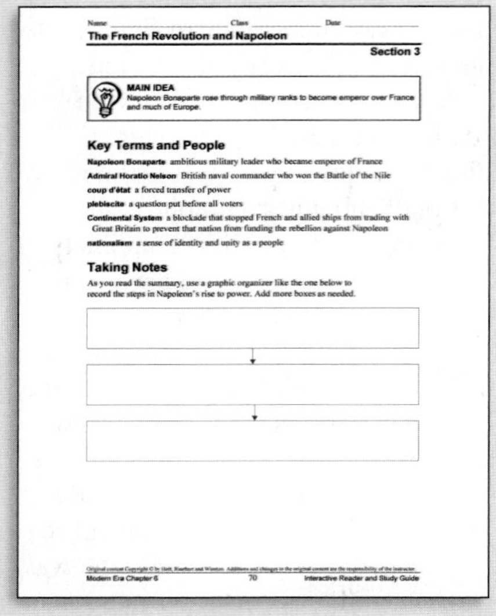

Name ______________ Class ______________ Date ______________

The French Revolution and Napoleon

Section 3

MAIN IDEA
Napoleon Bonaparte rose through military ranks to become emperor over France and much of Europe.

Key Terms and People

Napoleon Bonaparte ambitious military leader who became emperor of France
Admiral Horatio Nelson British naval commander who won the Battle of the Nile
coup d'état a forced transfer of power
plebiscite a question put before all voters
Continental System a blockade that stopped French and allied ships from trading with Great Britain to prevent that nation from funding the rebellion against Napoleon
nationalism a sense of identity and unity as a people

Taking Notes

As you read the summary, use a graphic organizer like the one below to record the steps in Napoleon's rise to power. Add more boxes as needed.

Modern Era Chapter 6 — 70 — Interactive Reader and Study Guide

Academic Vocabulary

Review with students the high-use academic term in this section.

blockade to isolate an enemy by using troops or warships (p. 610)

CRF: Vocabulary Builder: Section 3

Taking Notes

forced British out of Toulon; defeated Austrians in Italy; dispersed mob of royalists; assigned to defend French interior; defeated Austrians and Italians; won control of Egypt; lost battle with British, but covered it up; staged coup d'état in France; crowned himself emperor; began a series of wars to conquer Europe

go.hrw.com
Online Resources
KEYWORD: SHL NAP
ACTIVITY: Napoleon Bonaparte

Section 3 Napoleon's Europe

Before You Read

Main Idea

Napoleon Bonaparte rose through military ranks to become emperor over France and much of Europe.

Reading Focus

1. How did Napoleon rise to power?
2. How did Emperor Napoleon come to dominate Europe?
3. What were Napoleon's most important policies?

Key Terms and People

Napoleon Bonaparte
Admiral Horatio Nelson
coup d'état
plebiscite
Continental System
nationalism

TAKING NOTES As you read, take notes in a diagram like this one to record the steps in Napoleon's rise to power. Add more boxes as needed.

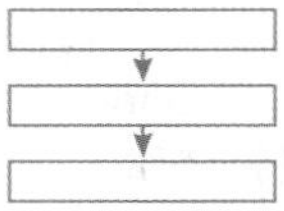

THE INSIDE STORY ***How did a young officer's chance to prove himself change Europe's future?*** Sometimes achieving greatness requires a little luck. For a young soldier named Napoleon Bonaparte, the lucky break came in the summer of 1793. British troops held the vital French port of Toulon. The French artillery battled courageously to retake the port but made little headway. During the fighting the French captain was wounded, and young Napoleon Bonaparte was chosen to take the wounded captain's place.

Napoleon made the most of his chance. He came up with a daring plan to retake the port by surrounding the harbor with 80 cannons. Napoleon convinced the officers above him that his plan would succeed. Within 48 hours, the port was his. The victory showed Napoleon's genius for military strategy and brought him both notice and promotion. There now appeared to be no stopping him. Within 20 years, he would rule most of Europe. ■

WITH A LITTLE LUCK...

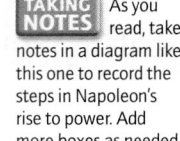

▼ Napoleon led French forces in a fierce battle for Toulon, a port on the Mediterranean Sea.

Teach the Main Idea

At Level

Napoleon's Europe

1. **Teach** Ask students the Reading Focus questions to teach this section.
2. **Apply** Have students draw a ladder that shows Napoleon's rise to power. Have students list Napoleon's policies at the top of their ladders.
3. **Review** As you review the section, have students discuss what steps Napoleon took to gain power and the policies he pursued when he was in power.
4. **Practice/Homework** Have students prepare a short illustrated biography of Napoleon. **LS Visual-Spatial, Verbal-Linguistic**

Alternative Assessment Handbook, Rubrics 13: Graphic Organizers; and 37: Writing Assignments

Napoleon's Rise to Power

Napoleon Bonaparte was a ruthlessly ambitious young man. The turmoil of the French Revolution gave him a prime opportunity to rise quickly to power. Within a few short years, he would rise from a mere army captain to become the ruler of France.

Opportunities for Glory Napoleon was a brilliant military leader who achieved many early successes. In 1793 he forced British troops out of the port of Toulon. The following year he won a dazzling victory over Austrian troops in Italy.

In 1795 Napoleon faced off against a mob of royalists trying to regain power in Paris. Using artillery to shoot into the crowd, Napoleon forced the royalists to flee. As a reward for stopping the uprising, Napoleon was put in charge of defending the French interior. He was only 26 years old.

The following year, the Directory placed Napoleon in command of French forces invading Italy. Poorly supplied, his troops had to take their food from the countryside. But Napoleon turned this hardship to his advantage. Because his troops were not slowed down by a supply train, they could strike quickly. In Italy, Napoleon won battles against the Austrians and Italians. His victories not only kept France's borders secure but also won territory for France. Napoleon's future looked very bright.

Next, Napoleon turned his attention to Egypt, where he wanted to disrupt the valuable trade between Great Britain and India. He took the French fleet and a large army across the Mediterranean Sea in 1798. Napoleon's forces quickly defeated Egypt's Ottoman defenders and won control of much of Egypt. But the British navy, under the command of **Admiral Horatio Nelson**, was on Napoleon's trail. Nelson trapped the French ships. In the long Battle of the Nile, the British destroyed most of the French fleet.

After his loss in the Battle of the Nile, Napoleon wanted to cover up his disastrous defeat. He left his army in Egypt under the command of another officer and sailed back to France. He kept his defeat out of the press and exaggerated the successes of the French army, becoming a national hero in the process.

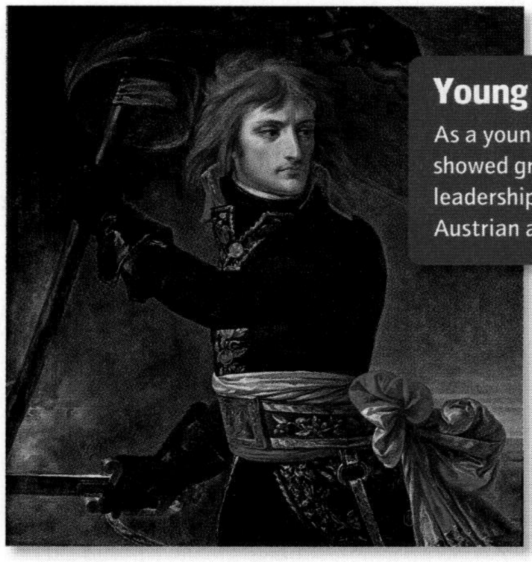

Le General Bonaparte a Arcole, by Antoine Jean Gros, 1797

Young Napoleon

As a young general, Napoleon showed great courage and leadership in battles against Austrian and Italian armies.

Napoleon Seizes Power Napoleon's ambitions continued to grow. Capitalizing on his status as a national hero, he decided to seize political power.

By this time, the Directory had grown weak and ineffective. As a result, some French leaders feared that royalists might conspire to place a monarchy in power. Others feared the growing opposition of European nations, such as Great Britain and Austria, against France. As a result, a group of conspirators began to plot to seize more power for Napoleon.

Armed supporters of Napoleon surrounded the Directory legislature and forced members to turn the government over to Napoleon in November 1799. This event was a **coup d'état** (koo day-TAH), a forced transfer of power.

A group of three consuls, called the Consulate, would replace the Directory as the government of France. Members voted Napoleon in charge as first Consul. The structure of a republic was still in place, but Napoleon had become a dictator.

Why would a nation that had overthrown its king now welcome a new dictator? Exhausted by the chaos of the Revolution and constant warfare, the French craved the order and stability Napoleon promised. Napoleon also pledged to uphold some key revolutionary reforms. The people would willingly give up some freedoms if Napoleon could bring peace, prosperity, and glory to France.

READING CHECK **Summarize** What events led to Napoleon's rise to power?

Direct Teach

Reading Focus

1 How did Napoleon rise to power? *achieved military successes, showed courage and leadership, covered up his defeat, his supporters staged coup d'état*

Napoleon's Rise to Power

Recall What was the outcome of Napoleon's campaigns in Italy? *He was victorious, kept France's borders secure and won territory for France.*

Explain How did Napoleon become the dictator of France? *His supporters staged a coup d'état; Napoleon was set up as first Consul, clearly in charge.*

Evaluate Did Napoleon achieve more by his victories or by covering up his defeats? *possible answer—Covering up his defeats made him seem invincible.*

MISCONCEPTION ALERT

Though Napoleon is often described by historians as a short man, he would not have been considered short during the time in which he lived. He stood about 5'6", which was an average height in early 19th century France.

Skills Focus: Sequencing

At Level

Research Required

Reading Skill

Life of Napoleon

Materials: butcher paper, art supplies

1. Organize students into small groups. Have each group use information in the text to create an illustrated time line of Napoleon's life.
2. Have students conduct additional research to find events and dates that are not in the text, and have them add this information to their time lines. Each time line should include at least four illustrations.
3. Display students time lines in the classroom. Ask students which events in Napoleon's life made a large impact on the course of history.

LS Interpersonal, Visual-Spatial

Alternative Assessment Handbook, Rubric 36: Time Lines

Answers

Reading Check *stopped royalists from regaining power, defended French interior, won battles in Italy, kept borders secure, won territory for France, covered up Battle of Nile, coup d'état*

Direct Teach

Reading Focus

2 How did Emperor Napoleon come to dominate Europe? *strengthened control over France; began a series of wars to conquer Europe*

Emperor Napoleon

Recall What question was submitted in the plebiscite? *whether France should be declared an empire*

Explain Why was Napoleon unable to conquer Great Britain? *Admiral Nelson and the British Navy defeated a combined French and Spanish force in the Battle of Trafalgar.*

Make Judgments Was a blockade of Great Britain a good strategy? *possible answers—Yes, because British economy depended on overseas trade; no—because it was hard to enforce trade restrictions.*

CRF: Biography: Pope Pius VII

CRF: Primary Source: *The Plumb-pudding in Danger*

Info to Know

Napoleon and Josephine As Napoleon entered the political realm, he began searching for a wife. He was introduced to Marie-Josephe-Rose de Beauharnais at a party and soon fell in love with her, calling her "Josephine." Although she had reservations at the beginning, she eventually agreed to marry him. During Napoleon's long absences for military campaigns, Josephe entertained other men and the rumors eventually reached him. Initially heartbroken, he began taking mistresses. The two remained married for many years, but the issue of an heir eventually arose; Josephine was barren. Napoleon divorced her and married Maria-Louisa of Austria.

Emperor Napoleon

As first consul, Napoleon moved quickly to strengthen his power over France. Once France was firmly under his control, he set about conquering Europe.

Napoleon Crowns Himself Napoleon wanted to make his own power permanent and hereditary. He submitted a **plebiscite**, a question put before all the voters, in 1804: Did they want to declare France an empire? French voters supported him and voted yes. Thus, Napoleon became Emperor Napoleon I.

Pope Pius VII came from Rome to crown Napoleon emperor in Paris. As the pope was about to place the crown on the new emperor's head, Napoleon grabbed the crown and placed it on his own head. This action told the world that no one gave Napoleon his authority—he took it for himself.

Desire for Empire Once Napoleon became emperor of France, he moved to build an empire. He wanted to rule Europe and to extend French power in the Americas. France controlled a number of territories in the Americas, including Louisiana, Florida, and the sugar-producing colony of Saint Domingue (now called Haiti). When civil war erupted in Saint Domingue, Napoleon sent an expedition to take back the colony and restore its profitable sugar industry. But the French expedition failed miserably.

ACADEMIC VOCABULARY
blockade to isolate an enemy by using troops or warships

This failure led Napoleon to abandon his dream of empire in the Americas. He sold the Louisiana Territory to the United States and turned his focus to Europe.

The Napoleonic Wars Begin In his quest to conquer Europe, Napoleon began a series of wars that became known as the Napoleonic Wars. These wars were an extension of the ones fought between France and other European nations during the French Revolution. During this period of warfare, France became the dominant European power. Although it grew rapidly under Napoleon's leadership, the French empire would fall apart even more quickly. The Napoleonic Wars lasted until 1815, keeping France in a state of near-continuous warfare for more than a decade.

Throughout the Napoleonic Wars, Great Britain remained France's greatest enemy. Britain helped organize a series of coalitions of European nations against France, and British funds helped strengthen resistance to Napoleon across Europe. Napoleon knew that until he could defeat Great Britain, he would have no peace in Europe.

Napoleon hoped to invade Britain and defeat it. However, Admiral Nelson and the British navy, the commander and fleet that had earlier defeated Napoleon in Egypt, stood in his way. The British navy proved its worth in October 1805 when it defeated a combined French and Spanish navy off the coast of Spain in the Battle of Trafalgar.

On land, Napoleon was more successful. Two months after his defeat at the Battle of Trafalgar, he won a devastating victory over Russian and Austrian troops at the Battle of Austerlitz, near Vienna, Austria.

The Continental System Great Britain continued to defy Napoleon. But this "nation of shopkeepers," as Napoleon disdainfully called the country, was vulnerable. Britain's economy depended on overseas trade. If Napoleon could disrupt that trade, he would weaken Britain's ability to fund rebellion in Europe against him.

In an effort to disrupt Great Britain's trade with other nations, he planned a blockade. This plan, called the **Continental System**, prohibited French or allied ships from trading with Britain. The British responded by requiring all ships from neutral countries to stop in British ports for permission to trade with the French.

While trying to enforce these trade restrictions, Britain and France were drawn into other conflicts. One conflict was the Peninsular War, which drew Portugal and Spain into the conflict between France and Great Britain.

The Peninsular War Portugal, which shares the Iberian Peninsula with Spain, was neutral during the Napoleonic Wars. The Portuguese refused to comply with the Continental System because they depended on trade with Britain. To enforce his power, Napoleon sent French troops into Portugal to take control and drive out the king. Napoleon then quickly conquered Spain and placed his brother Joseph on the Spanish throne. But the Spanish resented having a foreign ruler and revolted in 1808.

To support the Spanish revolt of French rule, Great Britain sent its military forces to Spain.

Differentiating Instruction

Below Level

Special Education Students

Prep Required

Materials: magazines, poster paper, paste, scissors, small photocopied images of Napoleon

1. Review the text about Napoleon's rise to power. Have students brainstorm adjectives, both positive and negative, that could be used to describe Napoleon. Create a class list for students to see.
2. Give each student a piece of poster paper and a photocopied image of Napoleon. The image should be pasted in the center or at the top of the poster paper. The title of the poster should be: Words that Describe Napoleon.
3. Have students search the magazines for images that could be used to illustrate the adjectives on the class list. Students should write the term on their poster paper and paste the image above it.
4. Display posters for students to see. **LS Visual-Spatial**

Alternative Assessment Handbook, Rubrics 3: Artwork; and 28: Posters

Now battling two military forces, Napoleon faced a serious threat. He responded by sending troops from central Europe, and they quickly won several victories over the British and Spanish troops.

Yet a more deadly enemy still threatened—the Spanish people. They began a guerrilla war in which bands of peasants ambushed French troops and raided French camps. To punish the Spanish guerrilla fighters, the French slaughtered many innocent Spanish civilians. Nevertheless, the war kept the French army pinned down, and eventually Napoleon had to pull his troops out of Spain.

Napoleon Dominates Europe In spite of this setback in Spain, Napoleon managed to take control of most of Europe through treaties, alliances, and victories in battle. The only nations free of his control were Great Britain, Sweden, Portugal, and the Ottoman Empire.

In many of the European nations Napoleon conquered, he put his relatives in power. He gave his brothers the thrones of Holland, the Italian states of Naples and Sicily, and the German state of Westphalia. His sisters, and even his stepson, also held powerful positions.

READING CHECK **Summarizing** What regions of Europe did Napoleon dominate?

FACES OF HISTORY Napoleon Bonaparte, 1769–1821

Napoleon actually rode a mule across the Alps instead of a fine horse like the one in this painting.
Napoleon looks like a big, impressive man in this portrait. In fact, he was 5'6" or shorter.

Napoleon on Horseback at the St. Bernard Pass, by Jacques-Louis David, 1801

Contrast Napoleon's slumped posture in this painting with his pose in the other one.
Notice the scuffed, dusty boots and rumpled coat.

Napoleon at Fontainebleau, by Paul Delaroche, 1814

The people who knew or met Napoleon held different opinions about him. He inspired fierce loyalty in his troops. His wife Josephine adored him. Some other observers, though, saw Napoleon as cold and unfeeling.

As is the case with famous people, historians and artists have also portrayed Napoleon in different ways, depending on their points of view. Compare the two portraits of Napoleon above and how the artists' viewpoints differed.

Skills Focus READING LIKE A HISTORIAN

1. **Draw Conclusions** Which of the portraits do you think is a more realistic painting?
2. **Analyze Visuals** How does each painting reflect different aspects of Napoleon's personality and the rise and fall of his fortunes?

See **Skills Handbook**, p. H26

Direct Teach

Reading Focus

Emperor Napoleon

Explain How did the Spanish people threaten French forces? *by waging a guerrilla war, ambushing French troops, and raiding French camps*

Summarize How did Napoleon establish dominance in Europe? *through treaties, alliances, and victories in battle; by putting his relatives in power*

Info to Know

The Napoleonic Code The Napoleonic Code, a system of laws organized by Napoleon, has had a widespread impact throughout history. The code went into effect in the lands that Napoleon controlled and influenced other areas as well. Laws of most western European countries still show some influence of the code. In addition, because Quebec and Louisiana were settled by the French, the present-day laws of those places are also based on the Napoleonic Code.

Skills Focus: Recognizing Bias in Primary Sources — At Level

Reading Like a Historian Skill

Bias in Paintings

1. Have students examine the two paintings of Napoleon on this page.
2. Discuss with students how these paintings reveal the bias of the artists. Highlight the idea that some of Napoleon's actions were controversial.
3. Organize students into mixed-ability pairs. Have each pair make two political cartoons of Napoleon, one that portrays his actions in a positive light and the other that portrays them in a negative light. **LS Interpersonal, Visual-Spatial**

Alternative Assessment Handbook, Rubrics 11: Discussions; and 27: Political Cartoons

Answers

Reading Like a Historian 1. *possible answer—the portrait on the right, because it shows him as an ordinary person, not a dramatic hero;* **2.** *left—reflects his courage and leadership; right—reflects his restlessness and disappointment*

Reading Check *all nations except Great Britain, Sweden, and the Ottoman Empire*

Direct Teach

Reading Focus

Emperor Napoleon

Identify In what countries did Napoleon place his relatives? *Spain, Holland, Italy, and Germany*

Make Judgments Do you think placing one's relatives in power is an effective way to lead a nation or territory? *possible answers—Yes, they can be manipulated and will do what the leader tells them; no, because they might be inexperienced or ineffective.*

Map Transparency: Napoleon's Empire, 1812

Info to Know

Napoleon's Empire, 1812 In all of the "satellite kingdoms" of France, efforts were made to introduce elements of French government. This meant trying to remove the old feudal privileges of the nobility and diminish the importance of the Church in society. Conscription, or a military draft, also occurred in regions throughout the empire.

Interactive Map: Napoleon's Empire, 1812

Interactive

NAPOLEON'S EMPIRE, 1812

Napoleon put his relatives into positions of power throughout Europe, and they helped him control the empire. Though some of these relatives were popular with the people they governed, the fact that each had the same last name served as a constant reminder that Napoleon ruled over them.

Louis-Napoleon, a younger brother, was king of Holland.

Jerome-Napoleon, the youngest brother, was king of Westphalia.

Joseph-Napoleon, the oldest brother, was king of Spain.

Joachim-Napoleon, a brother-in-law, ruled the Kingdom of Naples.

Eugene-Napoleon, a stepson, ruled the Kingdom of Italy.

Elisa-Napoleon, a sister, was grand duchess of Tuscany.

GEOGRAPHY **SKILLS** INTERPRETING MAPS

go.hrw.com Interactive Map Keyword: SHL NAP

1. **Location** How did the strategic placement of Napoleon's relatives affect his control of Europe?
2. **Movement** Was Napoleon's empire protected on all sides? If not, from where might enemies have attacked?

Collaborative Learning

At Level

Nepotism Debate

1. Discuss with students Napoleon's policy of placing relatives in control of conquered territories.
2. Organize students into two groups. Pose the following question to students: Is nepotism an effective leadership tool?
3. Have students in each group brainstorm ideas in support of their argument. One group should list reasons in favor of nepotism and the other group should list reasons against it. One student in each group should take notes and compile a group list.
4. Conduct a class debate, instructing students in each group to provide at least three reasons why they either support or oppose nepotism.

LS Interpersonal, Verbal-Linguistic

Alternative Assessment Handbook, Rubrics 10: Debates; and 14: Group Activity

Answers

Interpreting Maps 1. *enabled Napoleon to control the entire empire, and relatives had same last name, a constant reminder of who was in power;* 2. *No, it was vulnerable to attack on the east-central border; the Mediterranean Sea*

Napoleon's Policies

As Napoleon ruled his empire, he also strengthened the power of France's central government. He developed a plan to establish order and efficiency throughout France, which involved reforms in many areas of French society.

Reform of Church-State Relations Many French citizens had despised the antireligious nature of the French Revolution. Napoleon soothed these feelings by making an agreement with the pope. Called the Concordat, this agreement acknowledged that most French citizens were Roman Catholics. The agreement did not require that they be Catholics, because religious toleration was still the law. The Concordat recognized the influence of the Roman Catholic Church in France but did not return any control over national affairs to the church.

Economic Reforms Because Napoleon knew that a good financial system was essential for the stability of France, he established the Bank of France to regulate the economy. He also set up a more efficient tax collection system. These measures ensured that the government would not face the kinds of financial crises that occurred before the Revolution.

Legal and Educational Reforms Under Napoleon's leadership, scholars revised and organized French law and created the Napoleonic Code. This code made laws uniform across the nation and eliminated many injustices. However, it also promoted order and authority over individual rights. Freedom of the press, for example, was restricted by censors who banned books and newspapers for certain political content. In addition, the code was limited in that it only applied to male citizens. The code denied rights for women and allowed for husbands to have authority over their wives.

Napoleon also believed that a strong state depended on having strong leaders in government and military positions. He established a network of high schools, universities, and technical schools to educate young men in preparation for those jobs.

Napoleon's Legacy Napoleon left a legacy in France as well as throughout Europe. In France, Napoleon ensured that some basic ideas of the revolution would remain part of the French government. Historians speak of this period of Napoleon's domination of Europe as the Age of Napoleon.

Napoleon made some basic revolutionary ideas part of the French government. These democratic ideas included equality before the law and a representative system of government. In fact, these revolutionary principles were those that Napoleon had approved and supported.

Throughout Europe, Napoleon's actions helped fuel the spread of **nationalism**—a sense of identity and unity as a people. During the Revolution, the French people developed a new loyalty to France as a whole. In addition, similar feelings of nationalism spread to peoples that Napoleon had conquered.

READING CHECK **Identify Cause and Effect** How did Napoleon's reforms affect French society?

SECTION 3 ASSESSMENT

go.hrw.com
Online Quiz
Keyword: SHL NAP HP

Reviewing Ideas, Terms, and People

1. **a. Identify** What happened in November 1799?
   b. Analyze How did Napoleon use French citizens to gain power?
   c. Evaluate Do you think you would have welcomed Napoleon as a dictator? Why or why not?
2. **a. Recall** Who fought the battles at Trafalgar and Austerlitz? Which side won each battle?
   b. Analyze How did the **Continental System** affect countries beyond Europe?
   c. Make Judgments How do you think you would have reacted if you had been present at Napoleon's crowning?
3. **a. Define** What is **nationalism**, and how did it spread?
   b. Contrast In what way did Napoleon's support of revolutionary ideals contrast with other actions that he took?
   c. Elaborate Why do you think historians may hold different views of Napoleon?

Critical Thinking

4. **Sequence** Use the graphic organizer below to show the sequence of events that led to Napoleon's rise to power.

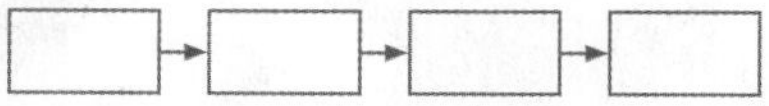

FOCUS ON WRITING

5. **Exposition** Write a one-paragraph letter to Napoleon from the viewpoint of a French officer stationed in Spain during the Peninsular War. In your letter, make suggestions about how to win the war.

Direct Teach

Reading Focus

3 What were Napoleon's most important policies? *recognized influence of the Church; established Bank of France; set up efficient tax system; Napoleonic Code revised and organized laws; promoted order and authority over individual rights; established schools*

Napoleon's Policies

Describe Describe the Napoleonic Code. *made laws uniform nationwide, eliminated injustices, promoted order and authority over individual rights*

Evaluate How well did Napoleon implement the principles of the French Revolution? *success—equality before the law, representative system of government; failure—individual rights and freedoms*

Review & Assess

Close

Guide students in a discussion about the effects of Napoleon's conquests and policies on France and other European countries.

Review

Online Quiz, Section 3

Assess

SE Section 3 Assessment

Progress Assessment: Section 3 Quiz

Alternative Assessment Handbook

Reteach/Intervene

Interactive Reader and Study Guide, Section 3

Interactive Skills Tutor CD-ROM

Section 3 Assessment Answers

1. a. Supporters of Napoleon staged a coup d'état.
   b. submitted a plebiscite asking whether France should be an empire
   c. possible answers—Yes, he established order; no—dictators take power from the people.
2. a. Trafalgar—British defeated French and Spanish; Austerlitz—French defeated Russians and Austrians.
   b. prohibited trade with Britain; created other conflicts
   c. possible answer—shocked that Napoleon crowned himself
3. a. sense of patriotism, identity, and unity as a people; through Napoleon's conquests
   b. Napoleon often suppressed individual freedoms.
   c. possible answer—Napoleon was a complex figure who took many diverse actions.
4. stopped royalists from regaining power, won battles and territory, secured borders, staged a coup d'état
5. Students' letters might mention attacks from peasants and propose reasonable ways to deal with guerrillas.

Answers

Reading Check *Napoleon made some basic revolutionary ideas part of the French government.*

Preteach

Getting Started

Use the **Interactive Reader and Study Guide** to familiarize students with the section content.

Interactive Reader and Study Guide, Section 4

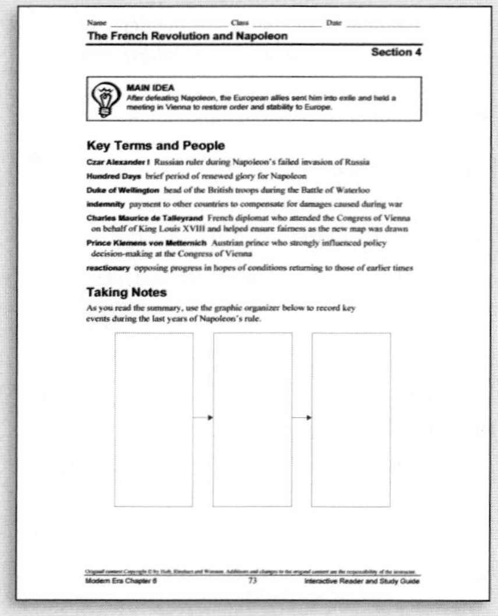

Name ________ Class ________ Date ________

The French Revolution and Napoleon

Section 4

MAIN IDEA
After defeating Napoleon, the European allies sent him into exile and held a meeting in Vienna to restore order and stability to Europe.

Key Terms and People

Czar Alexander I Russian ruler during Napoleon's failed invasion of Russia
Hundred Days brief period of renewed glory for Napoleon
Duke of Wellington head of the British troops during the Battle of Waterloo
indemnity payment to other countries to compensate for damages caused during war
Charles Maurice de Talleyrand French diplomat who attended the Congress of Vienna on behalf of King Louis XVIII and helped ensure fairness as the new map was drawn
Prince Klemens von Metternich Austrian prince who strongly influenced policy decision-making at the Congress of Vienna
reactionary opposing progress in hopes of conditions returning to those of earlier times

Taking Notes

As you read the summary, use the graphic organizer below to record key events during the last years of Napoleon's rule.

Original content Copyright © by Holt, Rinehart and Winston. Additions and changes to the original content are the responsibility of the instructor.
Modern Era Chapter 6 73 Interactive Reader and Study Guide

CRF: Vocabulary Builder: Section 4

Taking Notes

disastrous Russian campaign; defeat at Battle of Nations; exile to Elba; the Hundred Days; Battle of Waterloo; France returned to original size; map of Europe redrawn; monarchies restored; people's rights restricted

SECTION 4

Napoleon's Fall and Europe's Reaction

Before You Read

Main Idea

After defeating Napoleon, the European allies sent him into exile and held a meeting in Vienna to restore order and stability to Europe.

Reading Focus

1. What events caused disaster and defeat for Napoleon?
2. What were Napoleon's last campaigns?
3. What did the Congress of Vienna achieve?
4. What is the legacy of the French Revolution?

Key Terms and People

Czar Alexander I
Hundred Days
Duke of Wellington
Prince Klemens von Metternich
Charles Maurice de Talleyrand
indemnity
reactionary

TAKING NOTES As you read, record key events during the last years of Napoleon's rule in boxes like the ones below. Then summarize the changes after his fall.

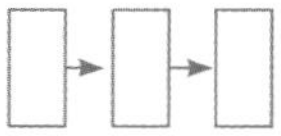

Catastrophe!

THE INSIDE STORY ***Did a bad omen doom an invasion from the start?*** On a moonlit June evening in 1812, Napoleon camped with his army near the Neman River in an area now known as Lithuania and Belarus. The army was ready to cross the river and invade the powerful empire of Russia.

With a few officers as company, Napoleon was riding his horse through a field. Suddenly, a rabbit sprang out between the legs of the emperor's horse. The horse swerved, and Napoleon lost his hold, tumbling to the ground. Only slightly bruised, Napoleon quickly stood and remounted his horse—all without speaking a word. The event worried the officers, who could not shake off their leader's tumble as a harmless accident. One officer said to another: "We should do better not to cross the Neman. That fall is a bad sign." ■

Teach the Main Idea

At Level

Napoleon's Fall and Europe's Reaction

1. **Teach** Ask students the Reading Focus questions to teach this section.
2. **Apply** Draw a four-column chart for students to see. Label the columns with the topics of this section—Disaster and Defeat, The Last Campaigns, The Congress of Vienna, and The Revolution's Legacy. Have students copy the chart and have them write the main points of each topic in the corresponding column.
3. **Review** As you review the section, have students explain the effects of the French Revolution and Napoleon over the short term and the long term.
4. **Practice/Homework** Have students write a one-page essay on the continuing importance of the French Revolution. **LS Visual-Spatial, Verbal-Linguistic**

Alternative Assessment Handbook, Rubrics 7: Charts; and 37: Writing Assignments

Disaster and Defeat

While some of Napoleon's officers believed they had seen a "bad sign" before they invaded Russia, Napoleon himself apparently did not see the sign. He decided to invade Russia.

The Russian Campaign When Napoleon stationed troops near the western border of Russia, **Czar Alexander I**, the Russian ruler, became very nervous. The czar, who was also concerned about the effects of the Continental System on his country's need to import goods, began to gather his own troops. Napoleon noticed those troop movements. To teach the czar a lesson, he decided to turn his troops east and move into Russia.

In June, Napoleon and an army of some 600,000 men marched across the Russian border. However, this invasion was troubled from the beginning. First, many of the soldiers were new recruits from conquered territories who felt no loyalty to Napoleon. Also, many of the army's supplies were lost or spoiled along the rough roads. In addition to those problems, the July heat made men and horses miserable. As a result, many men suffered from disease, desertion, and hunger, which thinned the army's ranks.

Napoleon wanted a quick victory over Russia, but there was no one for Napoleon to fight. The Russian troops withdrew as he advanced. Russian peasants, too, moved east after setting fire to their fields in order to leave nothing behind that the French troops could use. To Napoleon and his troops, all of western Russia seemed deserted.

In August, the French army was still moving east toward Moscow. Napoleon's troops finally clashed with the Russians. The French won the battle, but their casualties were very high. The Russian army, still 90,000 men strong, retreated.

What remained of the French army pushed on to Moscow in September. The troops found the city nearly deserted and in flames. No one knows whether the Russians or French looters lit the fires. Regardless of the cause, Napoleon could not support his troops in the ruined city through the winter. In October he had no choice: He left Moscow.

Napoleon's weary troops began the long retreat homeward. The Russians forced the French army to return the way it had come—across the same scorched fields Napoleon had crossed earlier in the summer. To make the journey even worse, Russian peasants attacked isolated French soldiers.

This painting shows Napoleon leading French troops to Moscow.

RUSSIAN CAMPAIGN, 1812

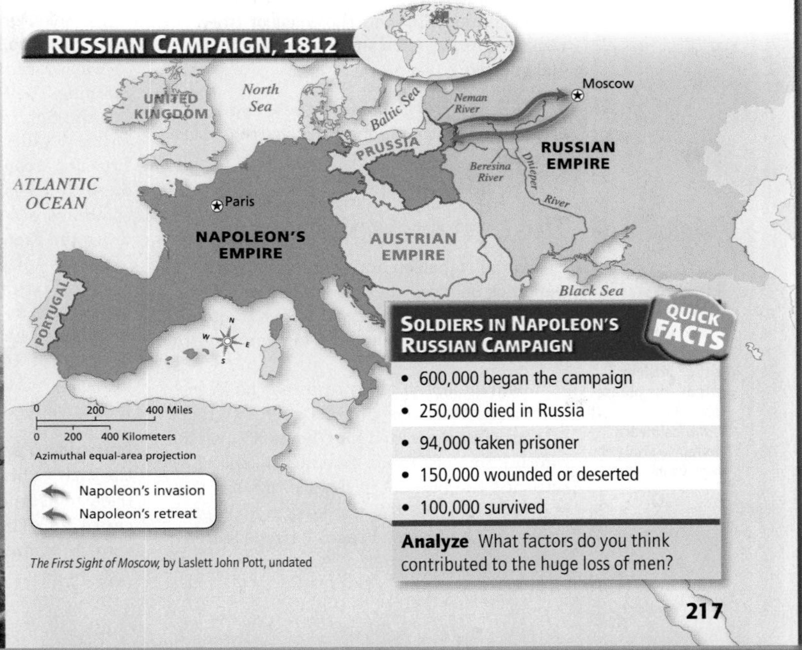

The First Sight of Moscow, by Laslett John Pott, undated

QUICK FACTS — Soldiers in Napoleon's Russian Campaign

- 600,000 began the campaign
- 250,000 died in Russia
- 94,000 taken prisoner
- 150,000 wounded or deserted
- 100,000 survived

Analyze What factors do you think contributed to the huge loss of men?

Direct Teach

Reading Focus

1 What events caused disaster and defeat for Napoleon? *miserable failure of Russian campaign; enemies allied themselves and attacked Napoleon's forces near Leipzig*

Disaster and Defeat

Explain Why did Napoleon attack Russia? *wanted to punish Russia for gathering troops near the border*

Analyze What strategic moves did Russian forces make? *not meeting French forces head-on; burning fields and cities to destroy supplies; retreating, forcing the French to follow*

Activity Have students write a letter home from a German soldier serving in Napoleon's army for the Russian campaign. **LS Verbal-Linguistic**

CRF: Biography: Czar Alexander I

CRF: History and Geography: Napoleon Invades Russia

Map Transparency: Russian Campaign, 1812

QUICK FACTS Soldiers in Napoleon's Russian Campaign

Predict How do you think Napoleon's Russian campaign affected surviving soldiers' morale? *soldiers probably tired, angry, upset at loss of fellow soldiers*

Quick Facts Transparency: Soldiers in Napoleon's Russian Campaign

Skills Focus: Identifying Problem and Solution

At Level

Reading Skill

Planning the Russian Campaign

Materials: outline maps

1. Review with students the information in the text about the disastrous Russian campaign and discuss the challenges faced by the invading French force.
2. Organize students into mixed-ability pairs. Have each pair plan a Russian campaign designed to avoid the military mistakes that Napoleon made.
3. Plans should include a written element and a map. Students should consider factors such as supply lines, what to do in harsh weather, and how to locate and engage the Russian forces. Remind students that they will not be able to use modern transportation or technology.
4. Have volunteers share their plans with the class. **LS Logical-Mathematical, Visual-Spatial**

Alternative Assessment Handbook, Rubrics 14: Group Activity; and 20: Map Creation

Answers

Russian Campaign, 1812 *harsh Russian winter, desertions due to low morale*

Direct Teach

Reading Focus

2 What were Napoleon's last campaigns? *The Hundred Days, Battle of Waterloo*

The Last Campaigns

Identify After Napoleon's exile, who became leader of France? *Louis XVIII, brother of Louis XVI*

Make Inferences Why do you think Napoleon was exiled rather than placed in prison? *possible answer—so that he would be far away, unable to bribe his way out or influence politics in any way*

Make Judgments If you lived in France at the time, would you have supported Napoleon's return? *possible answers—Yes, he made reforms and won glory for France; no—he dragged France through years of bitter warfare.*

Info to Know

War and Peace Leo Tolstoy's *War and Peace* is one of the greatest—and longest—novels ever written. Tolstoy relates a dramatic story of fictional characters against the backdrop of the Napoleonic Wars. The main characters are members of Russian nobility and the military who get caught up in the wars. Much of the book takes place during Napoleon's Russian campaign.

READING SKILLS

Understanding Word Origins If the root word *contra* means "against," what do you think the word *encounter* means?

Then true horror set in. The harsh Russian winter was the most terrifying enemy that the French army had encountered. As the exhausted men marched west, starvation and freezing temperatures killed thousands. The brutal Russian winter did what no military power had been able to do before. It decimated Napoleon's army.

What was left of French army staggered back to French territory without a leader. Napoleon had rushed back to Paris by sleigh, leaving his troops to face much of the awful trip without him. In the end, only about 94,000 out of the original 600,000 French troops made the journey back.

Defeat and Exile to Elba Napoleon's disaster in Russia gave his enemies new hope. Russia, Prussia, Austria, and Great Britain allied themselves against France. Meanwhile, Napoleon raised another army, but his troops were inexperienced. In October 1813 the allies met Napoleon's new troops near the German city of Leipzig. This battle was a clear defeat for Napoleon. In March 1814, the allies entered Paris in triumph.

As one of the terms of surrender, Napoleon had to give up his throne. The victors allowed him to keep the title of emperor, but his new empire was tiny—a small Mediterranean island named Elba, off the coast of Italy. He went into exile with a small pension and about 400 guards.

READING CHECK **Identify Cause and Effect** What factors contributed to Napoleon's failure in Russia?

The Last Campaigns

THE IMPACT TODAY

Waterloo has come to mean any sort of crushing defeat. The phrase *to meet one's Waterloo* means "to face a final and decisive moment."

By exiling Napoleon and sending him to Elba, the allies believed they had ended any threat from him. But Napoleon would not go quietly. He waited for an opportunity to regain control of France.

Meanwhile, the allies restored the French monarchy. They recognized Louis XVIII, the brother of the executed king Louis XVI, as the rightful king of France. In addition, the allies returned the borders of France to what they had been in 1792. But the king quickly grew unpopular, and many French citizens feared a return to the Old Order.

The Hundred Days After about a year in exile on Elba, Napoleon managed to hire a ship that took him and many supporters back to France. He landed on the north coast and headed for Paris.

As rumors of Napoleon's return spread, people began to react. Louis XVIII panicked and fled to Belgium, and the allies declared Napoleon an outlaw. The French people who despised Napoleon for dragging France through years of bitter warfare were not happy. Thousands of other French citizens, however, were excited to hear that Napoleon was back. They still adored their emperor for the reforms he had made and the glory he had won for France. In fact, the troops sent to arrest Napoleon pledged their loyalty to him instead. On March 20 Napoleon arrived in Paris to cheering crowds. This was the beginning of the **Hundred Days**, a brief period of renewed glory for Napoleon and of problems for his enemies.

The Battle of Waterloo Across Europe, Napoleon's enemies were gathering their troops for another showdown with Napoleon. After some indecisive battles, the final confrontation pitted Napoleon's troops against British troops led by the **Duke of Wellington**. Belgian, Dutch, and German troops increased Wellington's ranks. On June 18, 1815, the armies met near Waterloo, a Belgian village.

Heavy rain delayed the battle until late morning. The British forces stood their ground, but the fighting was ferocious all day. One of Britain's allies, Prussia, came to their aid. As Prussian troops arrived to help the British soldiers, Napoleon's army was no match for the combined strength of the two armies. They drove the French army off the field by the end of the day.

The French and the British both suffered huge losses at the Battle of Waterloo. Casualties totaled about 50,000 men. But for Napoleon, the Battle of Waterloo was a crushing defeat. It was the end of his military career and the end of the Napoleonic Wars.

Napoleon's Final Days Napoleon evaded the victors briefly. Having fled to a port, he tried to escape to America, but he was soon captured. This time, Napoleon's captors sent him much farther away than Elba.

Differentiating Instruction

Below Level

English-Language Learners

1. Review the information in the text about Napoleon's final campaigns. Remind students that Napoleon had been a popular figure in France for many years before his downfall.
2. Organize students into mixed-ability pairs. Have each pair work together to write a summary of Napoleon's last campaigns. Summaries should include campaigns from the end of the Russian campaign up until Napoleon's death.
3. Have volunteers present their summaries to the class. **LS Verbal-Linguistic**

Alternative Assessment Handbook, Rubric 37: Writing Assignments

Answers

Reading Skills *face, meet*

Reading Check (left) *soldiers lacked loyalty to Napoleon, extreme heat, supplies lost or spoiled, disease, desertion, hunger, Russian troops withdrew, harsh Russian winter* **(right)** *hired a ship to return him to France and won the support of people and the army*

FORENSICS in History

Was Napoleon Murdered?

Does it matter whether Napoleon was murdered? Perhaps not, but at the time it certainly did matter. Many French were sure that the British had something to do with his death. The English were equally anxious to prove that they had not mistreated him.

What facts do we have? The official autopsy results reported a perforated, or punctured, stomach and stomach cancer. However, that report also documented a high level of poisonous arsenic in Napoleon's hair.

Does the presence of arsenic prove that the British had Napoleon killed? Not necessarily. There are two possible sources for the arsenic other than deliberate poisoning. One source of arsenic was medicine, since arsenic was an ingredient in many 19th-century medicines. Because doctors treated Napoleon for many ailments, the arsenic may have come from drugs.

Napoleon could also have been poisoned by the wallpaper in his sitting-room. It included a green color made with copper arsenite. Although copper arsenite is usually harmless, mold can convert it to a poisonous vapor. The climate on Saint Helena is humid enough for this to have occurred.

Recently, Paul Fornes, a French forensic scientist, reviewed the old autopsy report. Fornes concluded that while Napoleon had cancer, the cancer did not kill him. Fornes also pointed out that the source of the arsenic in the hair sample remains unknown. Thus, whether Napoleon was murdered is still one of history's mysteries.

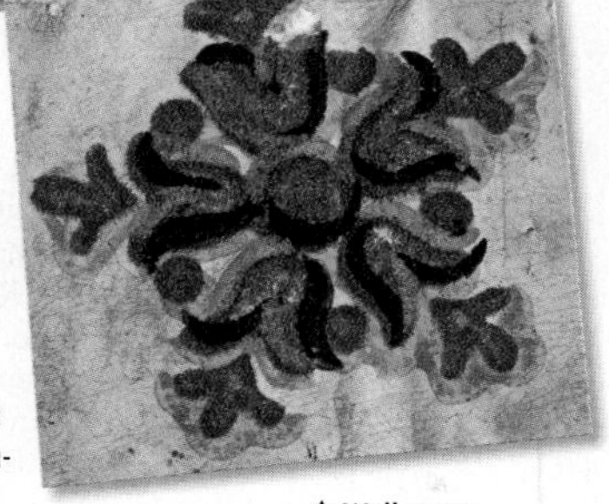

▲ Wallpaper from Napoleon's room

Draw Conclusions Why might the cause of Napoleon's death still be a topic of international interest today?

They exiled him to Saint Helena, a bleak volcanic island in the South Atlantic, some 1,200 miles from the nearest mainland.

Napoleon never escaped from his remote prison on Saint Helena. Nor did Napoleon serve a long sentence; he died six years later at the age of just 51. The cause of his death has never been determined definitively.

READING CHECK **Draw Conclusions** How was Napoleon able to escape exile in Elba and return to command the French army?

The Congress of Vienna

Just before Napoleon's escape from Elba, hundreds of diplomats had gathered in the city of Vienna. The purpose of this grand meeting, called the Congress of Vienna, was to create a plan to restore order and stability to Europe after the turmoil of the Napoleonic Wars. The diplomats' plan redrew the map of Europe.

The Negotiators Although about 700 diplomats attended the Congress, only a few played crucial roles in the negotiations: Lord Castlereagh (KAS-uhl-ray) of Great Britain, Czar Alexander I of Russia, King Frederick William III of Prussia, and **Prince Klemens von Metternich** (MET-ern-ik) of Austria. **Charles Maurice de Talleyrand** attended on behalf of King Louis XVIII, who had retaken the French throne.

Metternich, who had a strong distrust of democracy and political change, dominated the Congress of Vienna. He wanted to restore a balance of power, make Europe peaceful again, restore old monarchies, and compensate the Allies for their losses. Like Metternich, the other decision makers wanted to make sure that France could never again rise to such power. Perhaps more than anything, worried members of the Congress wanted to put down revolution wherever it might appear.

Direct Teach

Reading Focus

3 What did the Congress of Vienna achieve? *redrew map of Europe; formed the German Confederation; took and distributed France's conquered territories; restored some monarchies*

The Congress of Vienna

Identify Who was the most important figure at the Congress of Vienna? *Prince Klemens von Metternich*

Draw Conclusions Why did the Congress of Vienna want to suppress all revolutions? *saw revolutions as destabilizing force; wanted to stabilize Europe*

Forensics in History

Copper Arsenite Copper arsenite is a known carcinogen. It affects the central nervous system, the gastrointestinal tract, and the kidneys. Symptoms include coughs and headaches, as well as cardiac disorders and shock. When the chemical is heated, toxic fumes are released, and exposure to the chemical can lead to death.

Skills Focus: Summarizing

At Level

Reading Skill

The Congress of Vienna

1. Copy the graphic organizer as shown for students to see. Omit the italicized words. Have students copy the graphic organizer onto their papers and list the correct information for each heading.
2. Have volunteers take turns completing the class graphic organizer. LS **Visual-Spatial**

Alternative Assessment Handbook, Rubric 13: Graphic Organizers

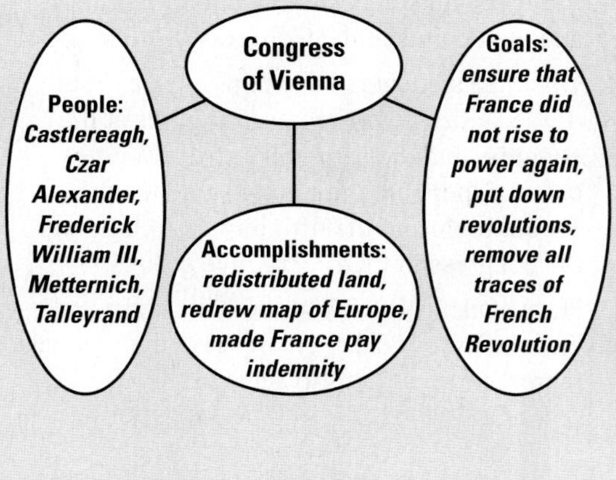

Answers

Forensics in History *possible answer—could lead to a different understanding of political or social events in history*

Direct Teach

Reading Focus

The Congress of Vienna

Explain How was it decided which nations gained territory and which nations lost it? *Those which aided France lost territory; those which opposed France won territory.*

Make Judgments Do you think France was treated fairly by the Congress of Vienna? *possible answers—Yes, France caused much suffering in Europe; no—other countries plundered French holdings.*

Map Transparency: Europe After the Congress of Vienna, 1815

Interpreting Maps

Europe After the Congress of Vienna, 1815

Movement Which countries were never controlled by France? *Great Britain, Russia*

Recent Scholarship

The Reign of Napoleon Bonaparte is the second book of a two-volume biography by Robert B. Asprey. Asprey, a former U.S. Marine captain, draws on his advanced knowledge of warfare to present a detailed and dramatic picture of Napoleon's life and campaigns. The book focuses on command strategy as well as the suffering endured by individual foot soldiers.

The Reign of Napoleon Bonaparte by Robert Asprey. Basic Books, 2002.

Answers

Interpreting Maps 1. *Netherlands, Prussia, Spain, Lesser German States, Switzerland, Kingdom of Sardinia;* 2. *Italy, Germany*

Reading Check *restore order, stability, and balance of power; ensure France could not rise again; suppress revolution*

They wanted to remove all traces of the French Revolution and Napoleon's rule. To do so, they changed boundaries across Europe.

Redrawing the Map The Congress of Vienna changed many national borders in order to strengthen the nations near France. Strengthening the states surrounding France was supposed to lessen the chance that France would invade its neighbors again.

The Dutch Republic and the Austrian Netherlands were united as the Kingdom of the Netherlands. Austria joined with 38 German states to form a loose organization of states called the German Confederation. Great Britain received overseas territories, rather than land in Europe.

The process of redrawing the map required complicated trades. Countries that had aided France lost territory. Those that had fought France gained territory. If one country seemed to be getting too much, it had to give up something else. Talleyrand was instrumental in arranging these trades.

In the end, France lost all its conquered territory. Its boundaries were pulled back to where they had been in 1792. France also had to pay a large **indemnity**—a payment to other countries to compensate them for damages.

Restoring Monarchies In addition to redrawing the map, the Congress of Vienna restored some of the monarchies that Napoleon had eliminated. Members of the old Bourbon royal family were returned to the thrones of Spain and Sicily. Monarchies were also restored in Portugal and the island nation of Sardinia.

Metternich's Influence After Napoleon's fall, reactionary attitudes deeply influenced politics and society. People with **reactionary** ideals not only oppose progress but also want conditions to return to those of an earlier time.

Metternich was a reactionary who wanted to return Europe to the years before 1789. He believed in absolute monarchy. Constitutions, voting rights, freedom of religion and the press—Metternich despised them all. In the areas where Metternich's influence was strong—Austria, the German states, and northern Italy—all such liberal ideas were suppressed. Secret police spied on people who disagreed with Metternich's ideas, and his opponents were often imprisoned or fined.

Interactive

EUROPE AFTER THE CONGRESS OF VIENNA, 1815

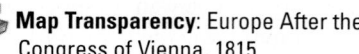

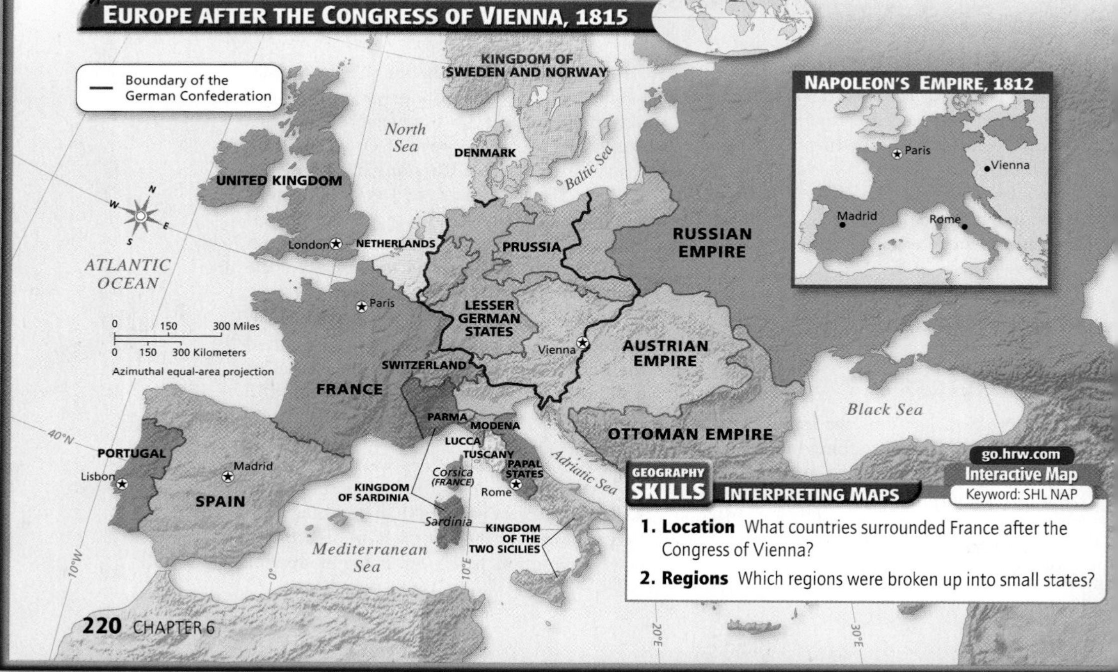

go.hrw.com
Interactive Map
Keyword: SHL NAP

GEOGRAPHY SKILLS INTERPRETING MAPS

1. **Location** What countries surrounded France after the Congress of Vienna?
2. **Regions** Which regions were broken up into small states?

Collaborative Learning

At Level

Delegates in Vienna

1. Review with students the main representatives and viewpoints at the Congress of Vienna.
2. Organize students into groups of five. Four of the students will represent figures at the congress and the fifth will serve as a note-taker. If there are remaining students, they should represent the fifth important figure at the congress in their respective groups.
3. Have students in each group brainstorm and create a list of goals each of the congressional representatives wants to achieve.
4. Have the note-taker in each group summarize the goals of the congress for the class.

LS **Interpersonal**

Alternative Assessment Handbook, Rubric 14: Group Activity

In addition, newspapers were not allowed to publish opposing views. For about 30 years, Metternich's conservative influence helped silence the liberal ideals of the Revolution.

READING CHECK **Summarize** What were the main goals of the Congress of Vienna?

The Revolution's Legacy

Given the results of the Congress of Vienna, was the French Revolution a failure? At first glance, you might think so. After the Congress of Vienna, monarchs ruled much of Europe once again. Citizens' rights were again restricted, and nobles enjoyed the privileges of a glittering lifestyle. Had so many revolutionaries died in vain? Had the principles of the Enlightenment died with them?

In fact, the French Revolution had changed many things. Never again would Europe's monarchs and nobles be secure in their privileged positions. They knew that Enlightenment ideas about human dignity, personal liberty, and the equality of all people would not go away.

The common people also remembered something important—that they could change the world. In the Revolution, French workers and peasants had taken control of their own destinies. No longer did people have to assume that nothing would ever change to make their lives better.

Though the Revolution was over within 10 years, the ideals that inspired it influenced people around the world for the next 200 years. Those ideals were so powerful that they could survive the worst horrors that the French Revolution and the Napoleonic Wars could create. Only a few years after Napoleon's empire ended, massive revolutions began from France to Romania. Enlightenment ideals crossed the Atlantic and inspired people in Latin America to throw off colonial rule. Eventually, the same ideals would inspire political movements in Asia and Africa.

READING CHECK **Draw Conclusions** Why could it be said that the French Revolution is still being fought today?

FACES OF HISTORY

Prince Klemens von METTERNICH
1773–1859

Metternich hated the republican form of government. This hatred most likely stemmed from an event during the French Revolution. The Metternich estate, which his family had held for 800 years, was seized by the French in 1794.

Metternich believed only monarchies working together could keep the peace: "Union between the monarchs... must... save society from total ruin." His repressive policies, however, helped bring on revolutions in 1848. During the revolution in Austria, Metternich fled Vienna in a laundry cart, but he eventually retired in peace.

Draw Conclusions Why do you think Metternich's policies sparked revolutions in 1848?

SECTION 4 ASSESSMENT

go.hrw.com
Online Quiz
Keyword: SHL NAP HP

Reviewing Ideas, Terms, and People

1. **a. Explain** What challenges did the French army face in the Russian campaign?
   b. Infer How did Russia's physical geography affect Napoleon's invasion?
2. **a. Recall** What was the **Hundred Days**?
   b. Draw Conclusions How do you think the results of the Battle of Waterloo affected morale on both sides?
3. **a. Identify** Who was Metternich, and why was he important?
   b. Make Generalizations Use the maps in this section to make a general statement about how Europe's boundaries changed between 1812 and 1815.
4. **a. Describe** What did Europe after the Congress of Vienna have in common with Europe before 1789?
   b. Make Judgments Do you think the French Revolution was effective? Why or why not?

Critical Thinking

5. **Analyze** Use the concept map below to describe possible long-term results of the French Revolution.

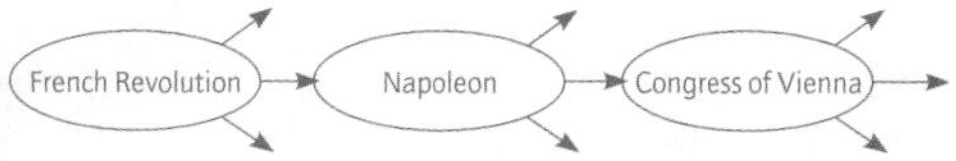

FOCUS ON WRITING

6. **Persuasion** Write a brief conversation between two leaders of the Congress of Vienna—Metternich and Talleyrand. In your conversation, have the speakers debate what the Congress should do to maintain peace in Europe.

Direct Teach

Reading Focus

4 What is the legacy of the French Revolution? *monarchs no longer secure in their positions, people realized they could change their governments and destinies*

The Revolution's Legacy

Recall In what way was the French Revolution unsuccessful? *Monarchs again ruled Europe; citizens' rights were restricted; nobles enjoyed a privileged lifestyle.*

Elaborate Why is the French Revolution considered so important? *ideals of revolution inspired people worldwide; gave knowledge that people could change their own destinies*

Review & Assess

Close

Have students discuss the lasting impact of the French Revolution.

Review

Online Quiz, Section 4

Assess

SE Section 4 Assessment
Progress Assessment: Section 4 Quiz
Alternative Assessment Handbook

Reteach/Intervene

Interactive Reader and Study Guide, Section 4
Interactive Skills Tutor CD-ROM

Section 4 Assessment Answers

1. a. supplies lost or spoiled, difficult to find Russian army, harsh Russian winter
   b. size of country meant long marches; harsh winter killed thousands
2. a. period when Napoleon returned from exile
   b. possible answer—French: heartbroken; British and Prussian: joyful
3. a. Austrian prince; guided decisions at the Congress of Vienna
   b. France shrank to original size; empires splintered into smaller countries; confederations formed
4. a. monarchs ruled much of Europe; citizens' rights restricted; nobles enjoyed privileges
   b. possible answer—Yes, high ideals inspired others worldwide.
5. Enlightenment ideals and nationalism spread, uniform government efficient, monarchy returns, people's rights restricted, territories redistributed
6. Students' conversations might include the following debate points: Metternich—absolute monarchy to ensure peace; Talleyrand—redistribution of land; balance of power.

Answers

Faces of History *His policies were undemocratic and repressive; people wanted more control.*

Reading Check *People still fight for the basic ideals of liberty and equality.*

Document-Based Investigation

Reactions to Revolution

Word Help

conspiracies plots to do harm
treason betraying one's country
fancy imagine, perceive
torpid powerless to move

Info to Know

Chappe's Mechanism During the French Revolution, inventor Claude Chappe devised a way to communicate quickly across long distances. Chappe's system was made up of tall towers, up to 10 miles apart, topped by moveable mechanical arms that could be arranged in dozens of different positions. Each arrangement signified a different message. Once a message had been posted, an operator on the nearest tower "read" it through a telescope. He then set his own mechanism with the same message, to be read farther down the line. In this way, a message could travel at more than 100 miles an hour. Unfortunately for Chappe, angry crowds twice attacked his equipment, thinking that he was communicating with enemies of the Revolution.

Activity **Analyzing Visuals** Have students closely examine Delaroche's painting. Have them write a list of adjectives that describe the people depicted in the painting. *possible answers—determined, angry, desperate, tired* **LS Verbal-Linguistic**

CHAPTER 6

Document-Based Investigation

Reactions to Revolution

Historical Context The four documents here reveal the reactions of people from various parts of the world to the events of the French Revolution.

Task Study the selections and answer the questions that follow. After you have studied all the documents, you will be asked to write an essay explaining why people's reactions to the revolution differed. You will need to use evidence from these selections and from the chapter to support the position you take in your essay.

DOCUMENT 1

A French Writer's Recollections

François-Auguste-René de Chateaubriand is one of the most famous authors in French history. A member of the nobility, he fled France when the Revolution began. Writing in England, he described how the upheaval in France, including changes to the names of days and months, affected the people still living there.

> The people, now hearing of nothing but conspiracies, invasion, and treason, were afraid of their own friends, and fancying themselves upon a mine which was ready to burst beneath them, sunk into a state of torpid terror. The unfortunate confounded [confused] people no longer knew where they were, nor whether they existed. They sought in vain for their ancient customs—these had vanished. They saw a foreign nation in strange attire, wandering through the public streets. As if condemned for ever to this new order of misery, the unknown months seemed to tell them that the revolution would extend to eternity; and in this land of prodigies, they had fears of losing themselves even in the midst of the streets, the names of which they no longer knew.

DOCUMENT 2

An Artist's View

The painting at right was created by French artist Paul Delaroche. Painted in the 1830s, it shows the artist's idea of what the mob that stormed the Bastille in 1789 may have looked like. The figure in white with the sword holds the keys to the Bastille. Other members of the crowd are carrying or dragging objects that they have taken from the prison.

The Conquerors of the Bastille before the Hotel de Ville in 1789, Paul Delaroche, 1839

Skills Focus: Recognizing Bias in Primary Sources — At Level

Reading Like a Historian Skill
Chateaubriand the Nobleman

1. Guide students in a discussion about Chateaubriand's writing. Ask students how Chateaubriand's position as a nobleman might have made him biased as an observer.
2. Have students write a one-page response to Chateaubriand's writing from a member of the National Convention or from a French worker. The response should acknowledge that things are not perfect under the Republic, but they are better than they were under the Old Order.
3. Have volunteers read their responses to the class. **LS Verbal-Linguistic**

Alternative Assessment Handbook, Rubric 37: Writing Assignments

DOCUMENT 3

A British Newspaper's Response

The trial and execution of King Louis XVI of France in 1793 shocked people around Europe. Descriptions of the execution were printed by newspapers around the world, many of them clearly expressing their opinions of the revolutionaries who had overthrown Louis. The following passage was printed in *The Times,* a London newspaper, on January 25, 1793.

> The Republican tyrants of France have now carried their bloody purposes to the uttermost diabolical stretch of savage cruelty. They have murdered their King without even the shadow of justice, and of course they cannot expect friendship nor [dealings] with any civilized part of the world. The vengeance of Europe will now rapidly fall on them; and, in process of time, make them the veriest wretches on the face of the earth. The name of Frenchman will be considered as the appellation [name] of savage, and their presence will be shunned as a poison, deadly destructive to the peace and happiness of Mankind.

DOCUMENT 4

An American Reaction to British Critics

Thomas Paine, one of the heroes of the American Revolution, was living in Europe when the French Revolution broke out. There, he read British writings (like Document 3) on events in France. Paine, in response to these writings, published his own thoughts on the French Revolution. The excerpt below is one of his published reactions.

> It was not against Louis XVI. but against the despotic principles of the Government, that the nation revolted. These principles had not their origin in him, but in the original establishment, many centuries back: and they were become too deeply rooted to be removed, and the … parasites and plunderers too abominably filthy to be cleansed by anything short of a complete and universal Revolution. When it becomes necessary to do anything, the whole heart and soul should go into the measure, or not attempt it. That crisis was then arrived, and there remained no choice but to act with determined vigor, or not to act at all…

Skills FOCUS READING LIKE A HISTORIAN

DOCUMENT 1

a. Describe How does Chateaubriand describe the lives of French people during the French Revolution?

b. Infer Do you think Chateaubriand supported the Revolution? Why or why not?

DOCUMENT 2

a. Identify Which elements of the image suggest that the people are not happy with the revolutionary government?

b. Compare Do you think the artist who created this image would agree with Chateaubriand's opinions? Why or why not?

DOCUMENT 3

a. Recall What does the author predict will happen to France?

b. Analyze What words or phrases in this selection reveal the author's bias? What impact do these words have?

DOCUMENT 4

a. Interpret Why does Paine say that a revolution was needed? Support your answer.

b. Interpret Does Paine agree with the writer of Document 3 about the execution of King Louis XVI? What words or phrases support your answer?

DOCUMENT-BASED ESSAY QUESTION

Responses to the French Revolution varied from country to country, and from person to person. Why do you think people had such different reactions to the idea of revolution? Using the documents above and information from the chapter, form a thesis that might explain these differences. Then write a short essay to support your position.

See **Skills Handbook**, pp. H25, H26, H30, H34

Document-Based Investigation

Word Help

veriest wretches most awful people

despotic having absolute power

parasite a person who receives help from another without giving anything in return

Info to Know

Thomas Paine Thomas Paine praised the French for setting up a constitutional government. Britain, he argued, did not have a true constitution, only a set of monarchical and aristocratic claims backed up by force. The French were so impressed with Paine's ideas that he was elected to the National Congress, even though he didn't speak French.

Teaching Tip

Have students conduct research about Chappe's mechanism and discuss their findings as a class. As an extension activity, have students build scale models to demonstrate how the mechanism worked.

Differentiating Instruction

Above Level

Advanced Learners /Gifted and Talented

1. Organize students into two groups. One will support the opinion expressed in the British newspaper. The other will support the opinion expressed by Thomas Paine. Give students time to go over the documents and organize their arguments.
2. Pair students from one group with members of the other group. If there is a remaining student, make one grouping of three.
3. Have students debate the following question: Was the execution of the king a necessary part of the Revolution?
4. Guide students in a discussion about strong points that were made on both sides.
LS Verbal-Linguistic

Alternative Assessment Handbook, Rubrics 10: Debates; and 14: Group Activity

Answers

Reading Like a Historian

Document 1. a. *afraid of friends, terrified, confused, felt they were in a foreign country;* **b.** *possible answer—no, because he was a displaced nobleman, saw only chaos and fear;* **Document 2. a.** *People hold swords and have sad, angry expressions.* **b.** *possible answer—yes, because the people depicted may be confused and were reacting to the Revolution;* **Document 3. a**. *Other countries will take vengeance, all French will be considered savages.* **b.** *tyrants, bloody purposes, murdered; get an emotional response from reader;* **Document 4. a.** *Revolution was the only way to destroy despotic principles of government.* **b.** *no; cleansed, complete and universal Revolution, act with determined vigor;* **Essay**

Answers

Visual Summary

Review and Inquiry Organize students into six groups, and assign each group one of these parts of the visual summary: short-term causes, long-term causes, short-term effects, long-term effects, 1789-1795, 1799-1815. Have each group prepare a two-minute oral summary of its assigned topic.

Quick Facts Transparency: Visual Study Guide: The French Revolution and Napoleon

Review Key Terms and People

1. coup d'état
2. Continental System
3. plebiscite
4. guillotine
5. indemnity
6. estates
7. nationalism
8. reactionary

Comprehension and Critical Thinking

9. a. bourgeoisie, artisans and workers, peasants
   b. stormed by mob, commander killed
   c. declaration by Austria and Prussia provoked war with France; war led to shortages and financial strain
10. a. shocked and horrified
    b. clergy became elected public employees or lost positions, Parisian churches closed, new cult
    c. No, directors were weak and corrupt.
11. a. made a compromise agreement with the pope, the Concordat
    b. efficient tax collecting system, revised and organized law, established schools
    c. possible answers—intense hatred of invaders, carefully planned ambushes, inability of French army to fight guerrilla war

CHAPTER 6

Chapter Review

QUICK FACTS

VISUAL STUDY GUIDE

Causes and Effects of the Revolution

CAUSES

Short-Term Causes
- Poor harvests, food shortage
- Massive government debt
- Louis XVI's refusal to accept financial reforms
- Fall of the Bastille

Long-Term Causes
- Great inequalities in society
- Spread of Enlightenment ideas
- Weak leadership from King Louis XVI

French Revolution

EFFECTS

Short-Term Effects
- A written constitution for France
- End of the monarchy and execution of the king and queen
- European alliance against France
- Reign of Terror

Long-Term Effects
- Napoleon's seizure of power
- Growth of nationalism in Europe
- Congress of Vienna
- Spread of revolutionary ideas to Latin America, Asia, and Africa

Major Events of the Revolution and Napoleonic Era

1789	▪ National Assembly forms ▪ Fall of the Bastille ▪ Declaration of the Rights of Man and of the Citizen
1791	▪ Legislative Assembly forms ▪ France declares war against Austria and Prussia
1792	▪ National Convention forms ▪ Monarchy ends
1793	▪ Louis XVI executed ▪ First coalition forms against France ▪ Reign of Terror begins
1795	▪ The Directory forms
1799	▪ Napoleon seizes power
1805	▪ French defeat at Trafalgar, victory at Austerlitz
1812	▪ Disastrous Russian campaign
1813	▪ Napoleon exiled to Elba
1815	▪ Napoleon's Hundred Days ▪ French defeat at Waterloo ▪ Napoleon exiled to Saint Helena ▪ Congress of Vienna

Review Key Terms and People

Identify the term or person from the chapter that best fits each of the following descriptions.

1. a forced transfer of power
2. Napoleon's plan for cutting off trade to enemy countries
3. a question put before all voters
4. execution device that dropped a heavy blade through the victim's neck
5. a payment to other countries to compensate them for damages
6. classes of French society
7. a sense of patriotism and unity as a people
8. opposing progress; wanting conditions to return to those of an earlier time

224 CHAPTER 6

12. a. so soldiers could not get any of the food, adding to challenges of invasion
    b. France reduced to original size, territories redistributed, German Confederation formed
    c. possible answers—yes, revolution had caused disorder; no—suppressing rights does not create order for long.

Reading Skills

13. Noblilty are those who are in a state or condition of being noble.
14. against the clergy
15. possible answer—concord; means agreement or harmony

History's Impact video program
Review the video to answer the closing question: How did the French Revolution impact the world?

Comprehension and Critical Thinking

SECTION 1 *(pp. 195–201)*

9. a. Identify What were the groups within the Third Estate?

b. Summarize What happened at the Bastille on July 14, 1789?

c. Elaborate How did events in other countries affect the development of the French government?

SECTION 2 *(pp. 203–207)*

10. a. Recall How did other European countries react to the execution of Louis XVI?

b. Analyze In what ways did the Revolution change religion in France?

c. Make Judgments Was the Directory an improvement on the National Convention? Why or why not?

SECTION 3 *(pp. 210–215)*

11. a. Explain How did Napoleon make peace with the Roman Catholic Church?

b. Draw Conclusion How did Napoleon's policies affect common people?

c. Predict What are some possible reasons for the success of the Spanish peasants' guerrilla war against Napoleon's troops?

SECTION 4 *(pp. 216–221)*

12. a. Explain Why did the Russian people burn their fields as they retreated eastward?

b. Contrast How did the Congress of Vienna change the map of Europe?

c. Rate Do you think Metternich's reaction to the French Revolution and Napoleon's rule was a logical one? Why or why not?

Reading Skills

Understanding Word Origins *Use what you know about prefixes, suffixes, and root words to answer the questions below.*

13. If you know that the suffix *–ity* means "state or condition," how do you explain the relationship between the word *nobles* and the word *nobility*?

14. What does the prefix *anti–* tell you about the meaning of the word *anticlerical*?

15. What do you think is the root of the word *concordat*? What does this root word suggest about the meaning of *concordat*?

Analyzing Visuals

Reading Like a Historian *The cartoon below shows Napoleon in front of his home, the palace at Fontainebleau.*

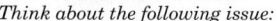

From High to Low... or the Causes and the Effects, artist unknown, c. 1814

16. Explain Does this cartoon show a period early in Napoleon's career or late in his career? Explain.

17. Draw Conclusions The buildings in the left corner are symbols for Spain. Those in the right corner stand for Russia. What do you think the cartoonist was trying to say by using these symbols?

Using the Internet

go.hrw.com
Practice Online
Keyword: SHL NAP

18. During the French Revolution, many political parties competed for power. Using the keyword above, do research to learn about the beliefs, leaders, and activities of some of these political parties. Then create a chart to clarify what the parties had in common and how they differed.

WRITING FOR THE SAT

Think about the following issue:

The Revolution threw France into chaos and cost thousands of lives. Still, millions of French people were fiercely loyal to the Revolution and believed that it offered a better life than they had known under King Louis XVI.

19. Assignment: Why were so many French willing to risk everything for revolutionary ideals? Write a short essay in which you develop your position on this issue. Support your point of view with reasoning and examples from your reading.

Answers

Analyzing Visuals

16. late; he is struggling to maintain his reach over the empire and has dropped his crown and scepter

17. that Napoleon has lost control over his empire

Using the Internet

18. Go to the HRW Web site and enter the keyword shown to access a rubric for this activity.

KEYWORD: SHL NAP

Writing for the SAT

19. possible reasoning—The French were willing to risk everything because the Old Order took their labor and tax money and gave them nothing in return. possible example—wanted the right to participate in government

A rubric for the activity is provided in **CRF:** Writing for the SAT.

HOLT
History's Impact
► **Video Program**
Refer to the Video Program Teacher's Guide for a discussion of the closing question.

Review and Assessment Resources

Review and Reinforce

- **CRF:** Chapter Review
- **Quick Facts Transparency:** Visual Study Guide: The French Revolution and Napoleon
- **Spanish Chapter Summaries Audio CD Program**
- OSP **Holt PuzzlePro**; Quiz Show for ExamView
- **Quiz Game CD-ROM**

Assess

- **PASS:** Chapter Test, Forms A and B
- **Alternative Assessment Handbook**
- OSP **ExamView Test Generator,** Chapter Test
- **Differentiated Instruction Modified Worksheets and Tests CD-ROM:** Chapter Test
- HOAP **Holt Online Assessment Program** (in the Premier Online Edition)

Reteach/Intervene

- **Interactive Reader and Study Guide**
- **Differentiated Instruction Teacher Management System:** Lesson Plans for Differentiated Instruction
- **Differentiated Instruction Modified Worksheets and Tests CD-ROM:** Chapter Test
- **Interactive Skills Tutor CD-ROM**

go.hrw.com
Online Resources
KEYWORD: SHL TEACHER

Unit Review

You can use these pages to have students simultaneously review the unit and practice taking standardized tests.

Answers

1. D
Monarchs of Europe, Section 1
2. C
Monarchs of Europe, Section 1
3. A
Monarchs of Europe, Section 1
4. A
Monarchs of Europe, Section 2
5. B
Monarchs of Europe, Section 4
6. A
Monarchs of Europe, Section 3
7. D
Enlightenment and Revolution, Section 1
8. A
Enlightenment and Revolution, Section 1
9. A
Enlightenment and Revolution, Section 1
10. A
Enlightenment and Revolution, Section 2

UNIT 2

Standardized Test Practice

Directions Write your answer for each statement or question on a separate answer sheet. Choose the letter of the word or expression that best completes the statement or answers the question.

1 Throughout the 1500s and 1600s, many European monarchs worked to

A create large trade associations throughout Europe.
B spread democracy in Europe.
C allow religious freedom in their kingdoms.
D centralize their political power.

2 King Philip II of Spain saw himself as a leader of the

A Protestant Reformation.
B Renaissance.
C Catholic Reformation.
D Spanish Succession.

3 In 1588 the Spanish Armada was defeated by

A England.
B France.
C Italy.
D Germany.

4 Absolute monarchy in France is most associated with which king?

A Cardinal Richelieu
B Philip II
C Louis XIV
D Henry IV

5 A key goal of Peter the Great was to

A isolate Russia.
B modernize Russia.
C democratize Russia.
D divide Russia.

6 With the Glorious Revolution in England in 1688,

A Parliament gained more power.
B England became less democratic.
C Parliament revoked the English Bill of Rights.
D William and Mary left England.

7 The work of which Scientific Revolution thinker produced this understanding of the solar system?

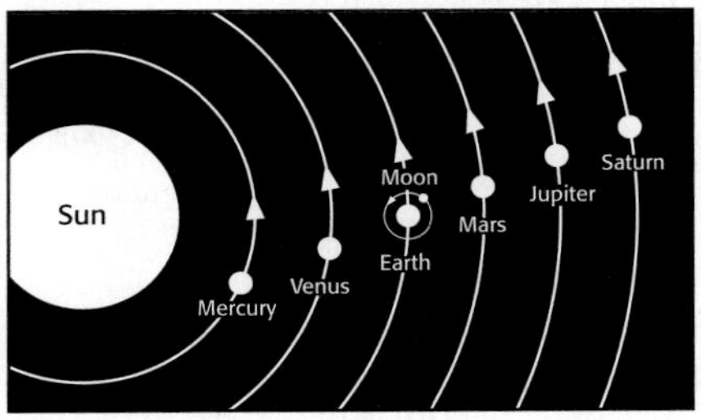

A Voltaire
B Thomas Aquinas
C Descartes
D Copernicus

8 Francis Bacon and René Descartes are credited with developing

A the scientific method.
B the law of motion.
C the theory of relativity.
D the geocentric model.

9 Which famous physicist studied the laws of motion and gravity?

A Isaac Newton
B William Harvey
C Ptolemy
D Robert Boyle

10 John Locke is best known for advancing which idea?

A People have a natural right to life, liberty, and property.
B Government power should not be limited.
C Governments should be separated into different branches.
D Monarchy is the best form of government.

11 **The Enlightenment idea that government should be created and controlled by the people is called**
- **A** divine right of kings.
- **B** enlightened despotism.
- **C** absolutism.
- **D** popular sovereignty.

12 **The passage below from *The Social Contract*, published in 1762, was written by which Enlightenment thinker?**

"Man is born free; and everywhere he is in chains. One thinks himself the master of others, and still remains a greater slave than they. How did this change come about? I do not know. What can make it legitimate? That question I think I can answer."

- **A** Voltaire
- **B** Locke
- **C** Montesquieu
- **D** Rousseau

13 **The Declaration of Independence put forth the idea that**
- **A** monarchs had more rights than their subjects.
- **B** monarchy should be abolished everywhere.
- **C** people had a right to overthrow unjust governments.
- **D** people should have no say in the independence of nations.

14 **The U.S. Constitution established a system of**
- **A** separation of powers into different branches of government.
- **B** constitutional monarchy in the colonies.
- **C** equal voting rights for men and women.
- **D** strategic military and trade alliances.

15 **Both the American and French revolutions**
- **A** resulted in a lasting constitution.
- **B** failed to overthrow their governments.
- **C** happened before the Enlightenment.
- **D** inspired others seeking democracy.

16 **One cause of the French Revolution was**
- **A** the strong leadership of Louis XVI.
- **B** nearby revolutions in Germany and Austria.
- **C** record government surpluses.
- **D** inequalities in society.

17 **Which person was a leader of France's Reign of Terror?**
- **A** Napoleon
- **B** Louis XVI
- **C** Robespierre
- **D** Prince Klemens von Metternich

18 **In his rise to power, Napoleon**
- **A** defeated British troops at the French port of Toulon.
- **B** defeated the British navy at the Battle of the Nile.
- **C** decided not to replace the Directory with a Consulate.
- **D** chose not to lead French forces invading Italy.

REVIEWING THE UNIT

Constructed Response Enlightenment ideas influenced key government documents that were created in the 1600s and 1700s. Recall what you have learned about the English Bill of Rights, the U.S. Declaration of Independence, the U.S. Constitution, and the French Declaration of the Rights of Man and of the Citizen. Then write a brief essay in which you summarize how each document reflected Enlightenment ideas.

CONNECTING TO THE PREVIOUS UNIT

Constructed Response The Protestant and Catholic Reformations affected many European monarchs, their governments, and their relations with other countries. Choose one country from this unit that was deeply affected by religious changes and divisions in Europe. Then write a brief essay explaining how the Protestant or Catholic Reformation affected the country's history, government, and society.

Unit Review

11. D
Enlightenment and Revolution, Section 2

12. D
Enlightenment and Revolution, Section 2

13. C
Enlightenment and Revolution, Section 3

14. A
Enlightenment and Revolution, Section 2

15. D
The French Revolution and Napoleon, Section 4

16. D
The French Revolution and Napoleon, Section 1

17. C
The French Revolution and Napoleon, Section 2

18. A
The French Revolution and Napoleon, Section 3

Reviewing the Unit

Student essays should mention that the English Bill of Rights gave citizens important civil rights, which reflected Enlightenment ideals about liberty, rights, equality, the social contract, and the limits of government. The Declaration of Independence reflected Enlightenment ideals such as the demand for certain unalienable rights. The U.S. Constitution reflected Enlightenment ideas about checks and balances. The Declaration of the Rights of Man and of the Citizen stated that all men are born equal and remain equal before the law, and it guaranteed freedom of speech and religion.

Connecting to the Previous Unit

Student essays will vary depending on choice of country, but essays should discuss one country from this unit that was affected by religious changes and divisions in Europe. Essays should explain how the Protestant or Catholic Reformation affected the country's history, government, and society.

Unit Review

Science and Technology

Deductive Reasoning René Descartes' life-long obsession with *how* we know what we know may have begun when he studied under the Jesuits. The Jesuits used reason to interpret and comprehend Christian teachings. This method of gaining knowledge may have inspired Descartes to ask questions like "How do you know what is true?" and "How can you tell what is true from what is false?" These are the fundamental questions that Descartes spent most of his career investigating to outline his methods of deductive reasoning.

Arts and Ideas

Tolerance Another important and influential idea to come out of the Enlightenment was the idea of tolerance. Tolerance was especially important to the *philosophes,* a group of French thinkers most active in the 18th century. As far as the *philosophes* were concerned, the worst crimes against humanity were instigated and carried out in the name of religion. They believed that without religious tolerance, a just and fair society was impossible.

Analyzing Primary Sources

Activity **Rousseau** Write the following quote by Rousseau for students to see: "Man is born free but everywhere is in chains." Explain that though Rousseau was describing the state of Europe, his statement still rings true today. Have students write a paragraph in which they explain how Rousseau's statement can be applied to recent global events.

UNIT 2 Changes in European Society, 1500–1820

Themes & Global Connections

THEME
SCIENCE AND TECHNOLOGY

How did advances in science lead to new ways of thinking?

For more than a thousand years, scientific thought in Europe had been dominated by the ideas of the ancient Greeks. But beginning in the 1500s, people began using reason to study the world in new ways. As a result, scientists made major advances that led to new ways of thinking about the world.

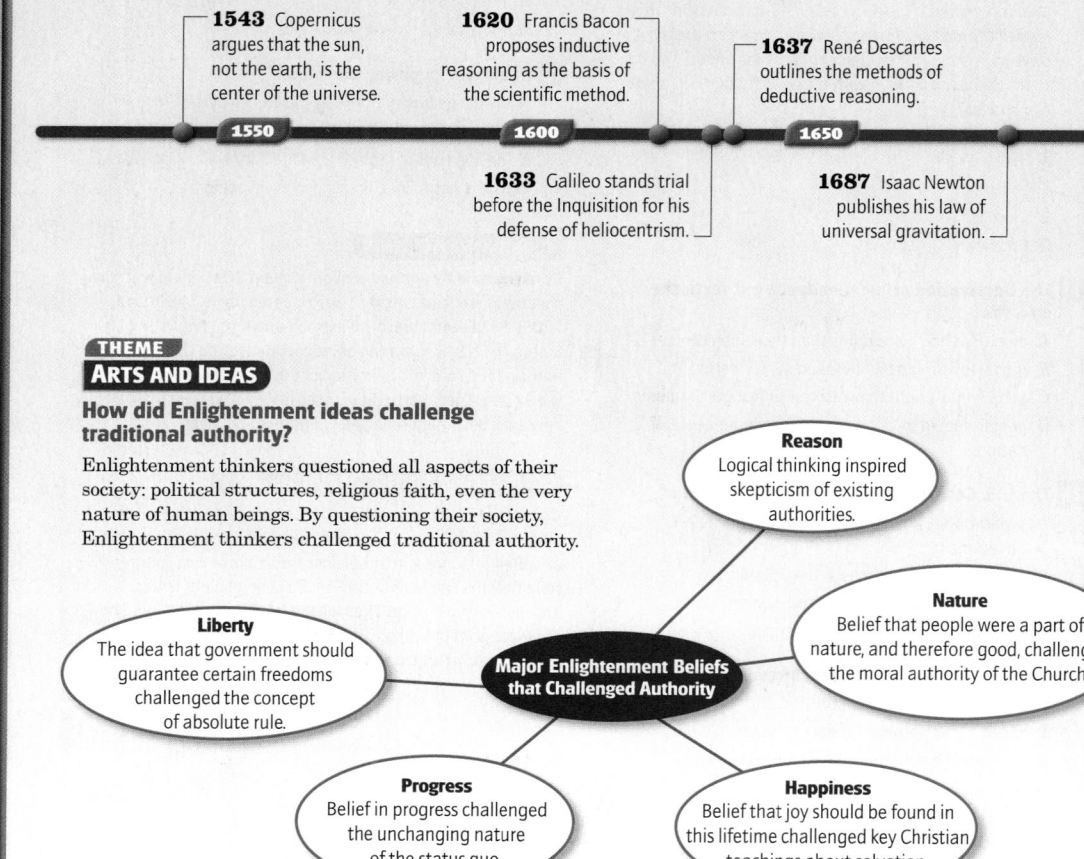

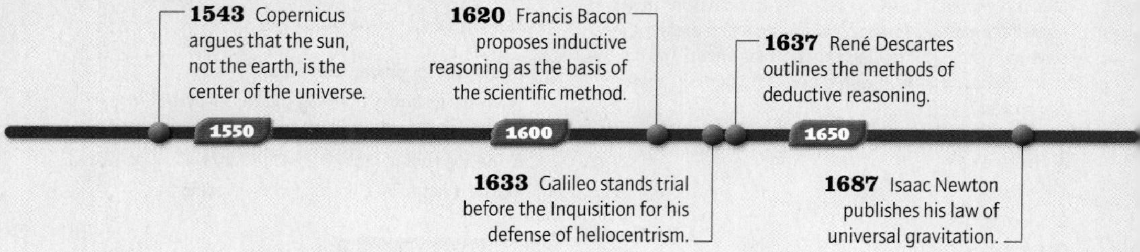

1543 Copernicus argues that the sun, not the earth, is the center of the universe.
1620 Francis Bacon proposes inductive reasoning as the basis of the scientific method.
1637 René Descartes outlines the methods of deductive reasoning.
1550
1600
1650
1633 Galileo stands trial before the Inquisition for his defense of heliocentrism.
1687 Isaac Newton publishes his law of universal gravitation.

THEME
ARTS AND IDEAS

How did Enlightenment ideas challenge traditional authority?

Enlightenment thinkers questioned all aspects of their society: political structures, religious faith, even the very nature of human beings. By questioning their society, Enlightenment thinkers challenged traditional authority.

Major Enlightenment Beliefs that Challenged Authority

Reason
Logical thinking inspired skepticism of existing authorities.

Liberty
The idea that government should guarantee certain freedoms challenged the concept of absolute rule.

Nature
Belief that people were a part of nature, and therefore good, challenged the moral authority of the Church.

Progress
Belief in progress challenged the unchanging nature of the status quo.

Happiness
Belief that joy should be found in this lifetime challenged key Christian teachings about salvation.

228 UNIT 2

Differentiating Instruction

Above Level

Advanced Learners/Gifted and Talented

Standard English Mastery

1. Organize students into five groups. Assign each group one of the five items listed on the time line.
2. Have each group conduct additional research on the event using reliable online or traditional print sources. Students should take notes about the significance and impact of the event as it related to society at the time.
3. Have students use information from their research to write a newspaper article announcing the event to the public. The article should explain the event's significance and its likely impact on society. Remind students to use the pyramid structure of journalism (information should be presented from most to least significant), and to use the five Ws and one H (who, what, where, when, why, and how).
4. Have a student from each group read the article to the class. **LS Interpersonal, Verbal-Linguistic**

Alternative Assessment Handbook, Rubric 23: Newspapers

THEME
GOVERNMENT AND CITIZENSHIP

How did the ideas of the Enlightenment influence the emergence of democratic government?

The ideas of the Enlightenment had a huge influence on the leaders of the American and French revolutions. When these leaders began to form new democratic governments in France and the United States, they built the ideas of thinkers like Locke, Montesquieu, Rousseau, and Voltaire into the very structures of their governments.

IMPACT OF ENLIGHTENMENT THOUGHT ON GOVERNMENT IN FRANCE AND THE UNITED STATES

John Locke	Wrote that government and the people were bound by a social contract	The U.S. Declaration of Independence upheld the social contract by stating that "governments are instituted among men, deriving their just powers from the consent of the governed."
John Locke	Argued that government should protect citizens' natural rights, which included life, liberty, and property	The French National Assembly protected citizens' rights in the Declaration of the Rights of Man and of the Citizen. The U.S. Declaration of Independence defined natural rights as "life, liberty, and the pursuit of happiness."
Montesquieu	Wrote that power in a republican democracy should be divided to avoid tyranny	Both the U.S. Constitution and the French Declaration of the Rights of Man and of the Citizen called for the separation of powers in government.
Rousseau	Argued that true democracy would require many people to share political power	Citizens in France and the United States voted for their representatives in government. Many participated directly as elected government officials.
Voltaire	Argued in favor of free speech and religious toleration	Both the United States and French governments protected the freedoms of speech and religion.

Skills FOCUS
UNDERSTANDING THEMES

How did the Scientific Revolution and the Enlightenment result in a new view of human beings and their world? Use your textbook and other resources to gather information about how people's views changed after the Scientific Revolution and Enlightenment. Then create a chart like the one below to contrast these changing views.

Changing Views		
	Old Ways and Ideas	**New Ways and Ideas**
Methods used to explain the world		
Relationship between the ruler and the people		
Importance of the individual		

Global Connections

Political revolutions have one common characteristic—they result in the overthrow of one government or ruler and the substitution of another. But each revolution has its own specific causes that arise because of particular conditions in that nation.

In this unit, you learned about three significant revolutions: the Glorious Revolution in England, the American Revolution, and the French Revolution. Create a chart that compares and contrasts their political, economic, and social causes.

Making Connections Analyze your chart to determine what the most common causes of revolution were. Then write a short essay of two to three paragraphs explaining your understanding of why those causes so frequently led to revolution.

CHANGES IN EUROPEAN SOCIETY **229**

Skills Focus: Making Oral Presentations

At Level

Reading Like a Historian Skill
Philosophers' Conference

1. Have students reread the chart on this page outlining the impact of Enlightenment and then tell them to choose one of the four philosophers.
2. Using the information in the chart, have students create a speech from the point of view of their chosen philosopher, asserting that philosopher's Enlightenment idea. Tell students they will present their speech at a philosophers' conference, which will be attended by French and American citizens and government officials.
3. Have volunteers present their speeches to the class, which will represent conference participants. Encourage students to use clear and loud voices, and to speak persuasively and passionately when presenting their speeches. LS **Verbal-Linguistic**

Alternative Assessment Handbook, Rubric 24: Oral Presentations

Unit Review

Government and Citizenship

The Social Contract Locke's idea of the social contract formed the foundation of his thoughts about government and those who are governed. Locke put forth that, in the social contract, government exists to protect those it governs. When government does not protect, it breaks the contract, leaving the governed free to choose new rulers or a new government. The idea of the social contract was the driving influence behind the Declaration of Independence.

Understanding Themes

Student charts should include the following information:
Method used to explain the world—old ways and ideas dominated by ideas of ancient Greek new ways and ideas: relied on systematic observation, precise instruments, and reasoning
Relationship between the ruler and the people—old ways and ideas: divine right of kings, absolutism; the governed supported their rulers, rulers did not support their subjects; new ways and ideas: social contract, government exists to protect the governed
Importance of the individual—old ways and ideas: community, authority, and tradition were foundation of society; new ways and ideas: individuals are in control of their own destiny; individual has ability to change the world

Global Connections

Student charts should compare and contrast the political, economic, and social causes of the Glorious Revolution, the American Revolution, and the French Revolution. Student essays will vary, but should demonstrate an understanding of the causes that led to each revolution.

Unit Review

Summarizing the Unit

Remind students that although many of America's customs and traditions come from British roots, other countries have also shaped American culture. Have students create a class chart of contributions from the other people discussed in this unit. To begin list ways that French philosophers of the Enlightenment influenced American social thought.

Answers

Thinking Like a Historian *Student charts or graphic organizers should show an understanding of causes and effects of Enlightenment ideas and how they influenced modern government structures, citizens' rights, and the use of reason to solve problems.*
possible responses—
A. *Modern governments reflect checks and separation of powers advocated by Enlightenment thinkers. Democratic governments are structured to ensure popular sovereignty.*
B. *Governments are expected to protect citizens' rights, such as the right to their own property. Many believe that governments should reflect peoples' right to popular sovereignty.* **C.** Philosophes *emphasized education and used reason to study the human condition, which continues today in the social sciences.*

UNIT 2 IN BRIEF

Below is a chapter-by-chapter summary of the main ideas in this unit, followed by a summary activity for the unit.

CHAPTER 4 Monarchs of Europe
1500–1800

MAIN IDEA Between 1500 and 1800, Europe's rulers in Spain, France, Russia, and other kingdoms held absolute power over their subjects.

SECTION 1 During the 1500s Spain grew powerful under the rule of absolute monarchs like Philip II and entered a Golden Age of art and literature. But beginning in the late 1500s, wars, revolts, and economic problems began to weaken Spain's empire.

SECTION 2 After a period of religious violence, Henry IV reunified France in the late 1500s. During the 1600s, French kings such as Louis XIV consolidated their political power as absolute rulers.

SECTION 3 In England, monarchs clashed with Parliament in the English Civil War. After the war, England became a constitutional monarchy, and Parliament limited the power of monarchs with the peaceful Glorious Revolution.

SECTION 4 Russia became a world power under Peter the Great and Catherine the Great, as they reformed and modernized the county. In Central Europe, powerful families ruled new states.

CHAPTER 5 Enlightenment and Revolution
1550–1800

MAIN IDEA New ideas and discoveries in Europe during the Scientific Revolution and the Enlightenment led to significant changes in government and society. Enlightenment ideas inspired a revolution, independence, and democracy in the United States.

SECTION 1 The beginnings of modern science can be traced back to the discoveries and methods of the Scientific Revolution.

SECTION 2 During the Enlightenment, philosophers began to argue that people have basic natural rights and governments are responsible for protecting them.

SECTION 3 Inspired by Enlightenment ideas, colonists in America rebelled against England, gaining independence and becoming the world's first modern democracy.

CHAPTER 6 The French Revolution and Napoleon
1770–1820

MAIN IDEA The French Revolution of 1789 overthrew the French monarchy and established a democracy based on Enlightenment ideas. But instability after the revolution allowed Napoleon Bonaparte to take power and create a large European empire until he was finally defeated.

SECTION 1 Inequalities in society and other problems led to the French Revolution and a democratic government in France. The new government worked to protect people's rights and to put an end to the monarchy.

SECTION 2 The French government soon became radical and began a Reign of Terror. Political opponents were put on trial and executed as the government tried to maintain power.

SECTION 3 As France's new government struggled, the young general Napoleon Bonaparte rose to power and seized control. Napoleon waged wars across Europe to build an empire and increase French power and influence.

SECTION 4 Napoleon was eventually defeated in Russia and at the Battle of Waterloo by an alliance of European powers. After his defeat, European leaders met at the Congress of Vienna to restore the balance of power in Europe, redraw Europe's borders, and restore European monarchies.

Thinking like a Historian — Summary and Extension Activity

Enlightenment ideas of the 1600s and 1700s caused changes in government and society that still influence the world today. Choose one of the following topics and create a chart or graphic organizer to show how Enlightenment ideas have influenced the modern world.

A. Structures of modern governments
B. Rights of citizens
C. Use of reason to solve problems

Unit Resources

Review and Reinforce

CRF: Chapter Review
Spanish Chapter Summaries Audio CD Program
OSP **Holt PuzzlePro**: Quiz Show for ExamView
Quiz Game CD-ROM

Assess

PASS: Unit Test, Forms A and B
Alternative Assessment Handbook
OSP **ExamView Test Generator**
Differentiated Instruction Modified Worksheets and Tests CD-ROM: Chapter Tests
HOAP **Holt Online Assessment Program** (in the Premier Online Edition)

Reteach/Intervene

Interactive Reader and Study Guide
Differentiated Instruction Teacher Management System: Lesson Plans for Differentiated Instruction
Differentiated Instruction Modified Worksheets and Tests CD-ROM: Chapter Tests
Interactive Skills Tutor CD-ROM

go.hrw.com
Online Resources
KEYWORDS: SHL MON, SHL ENL, SHL NAP

UNIT 3 Industrialization and Nationalism 1700–1920

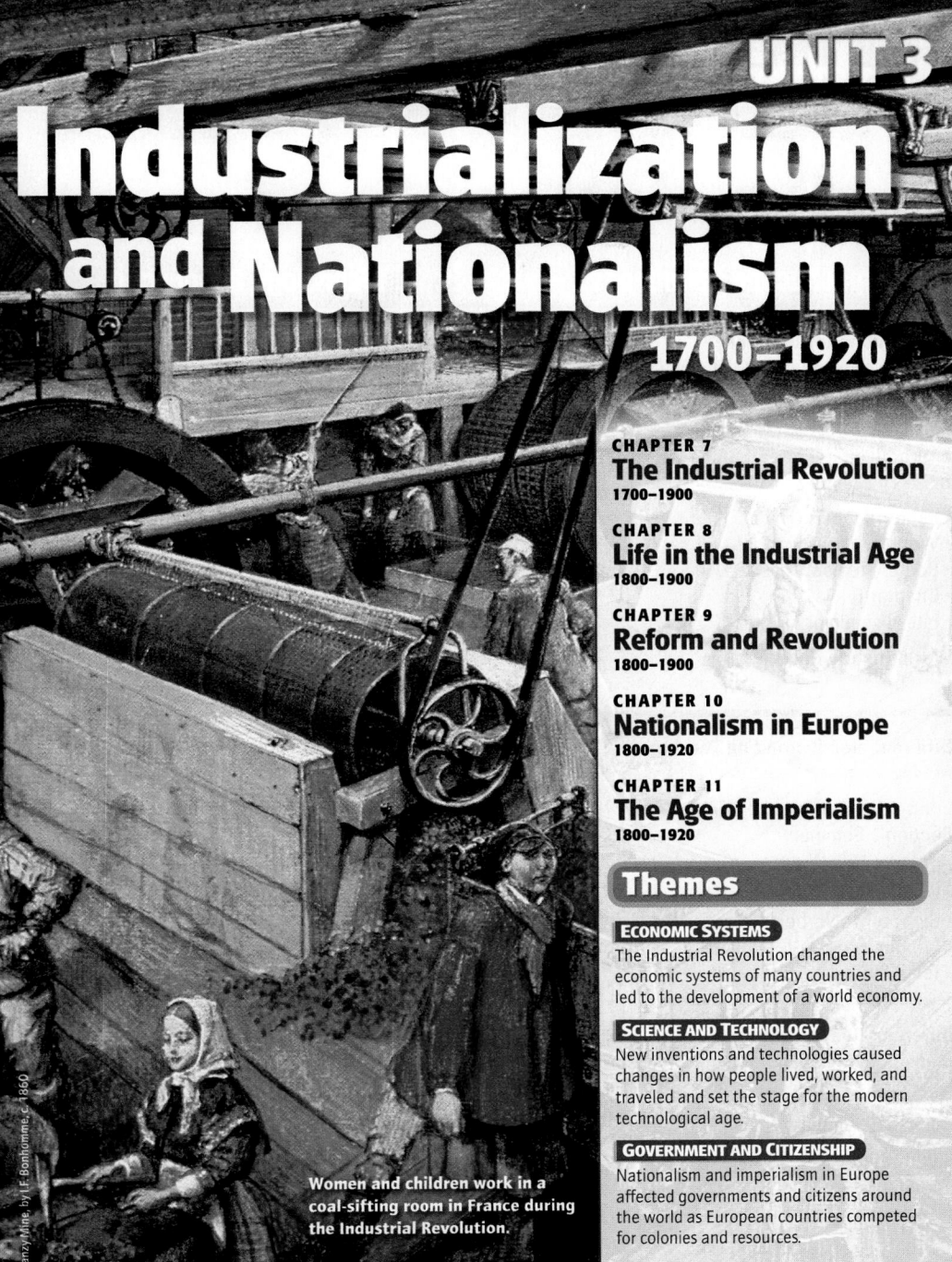

Women and children work in a coal-sifting room in France during the Industrial Revolution.

The Blanzy Mine, by I.F. Bonhomme, c. 1860

Themes

ECONOMIC SYSTEMS
The Industrial Revolution changed the economic systems of many countries and led to the development of a world economy.

SCIENCE AND TECHNOLOGY
New inventions and technologies caused changes in how people lived, worked, and traveled and set the stage for the modern technological age.

GOVERNMENT AND CITIZENSHIP
Nationalism and imperialism in Europe affected governments and citizens around the world as European countries competed for colonies and resources.

Unit Preview

Introducing the Unit

Have students list the factors that characterize modern society. As they do so, write them for the class to see. As a class, go through the list to determine which of those factors first evolved during the period covered by this unit. For example, globalization can be viewed as an outgrowth of the imperialism that led European nations to colonize much of Africa and Asia.

Connecting to Themes

Activity **The Effects of Industrialization** Have students identify the effects of the Industrial Revolution. Guide the class in a discussion of the ways in which industrialization led to urbanization, improvements in education, a rise in democracy at home, and imperialist policies abroad. LS **Verbal-Linguistic**

Reading Like a Historian

Interpreting Visuals

The French Industrial Revolution
Industrial development took place later in France than in Great Britain. At the time when Britain was rapidly industrializing, France was embroiled in a revolution. France had become an industrial power by 1848, but even after great growth during the Second Empire, it lagged behind Britain.

Unit Resources

Planning

- **Differentiated Instruction Teacher Management System:** Unit Pacing Guide
- OSP **One-Stop Planner CD-ROM:** Teacher Management System
- **Power Presentations with Video CD-ROM**

Differentiating Instruction

- **Differentiated Instruction Teacher Management System:** Lesson Plans for Differentiated Instruction
- **Differentiated Instruction Modified Worksheets and Tests CD-ROM**

Enrichment

- **A World History Teacher's Guide to Analyzing Movies**
- **Document-Based Activities for World History**
- **World History Outline Maps**
- **Reading Like a Historian: World History Toolkit**
- **World History Primary Source Library CD-ROM**

Assessment

- **PASS:** Unit Test, Forms A and B
- **Alternative Assessment Handbook**
- OSP **ExamView Test Generator**
- HOAP **Holt Online Assessment Program** (in the Premier Online Edition)

Chapter 7 Planning Guide

The Industrial Revolution

Chapter Overview	Reproducible Resources	Technology Resources
CHAPTER 7 **pp. 232–257** **Overview: In this chapter, students will learn how new processes and machines led to dramatic changes in industry–a period in history known as the Industrial Revolution.**	**Differentiated Instruction Teacher Management System:*** • Pacing Guide • Lesson Plans for Differentiated Instruction **Interactive Reader and Study Guide:** Chapter Summary* **Chapter Resource File*** • Writing About History • Social Studies Skill • Chapter Review • Interdisciplinary Project **World History Outline Maps**	**Live Ink© Online Reading Help** **Student Edition on Audio CD Program** **Differentiated Instruction Modified Worksheets and Tests CD-ROM** **Interactive Skills Tutor CD-ROM** **World History Primary Source Library CD-ROM** **Power Presentations with Video CD-ROM** **History's Impact: World History Video Program (VHS/DVD):** The Industrial Revolution
Section 1: **A New Kind of Revolution** **The Main Idea:** In the 1700s, conditions in Great Britain led to the rapid growth of the textile industry, which in turn led to huge changes in many other industries.	**Differentiated Instruction Teacher Management System:** Section 1 Lesson Plan* **Interactive Reader and Study Guide:** Section 1 Summary* **Chapter Resource File*** • Vocabulary Builder: Section 1 • Biography: Norbert Rillieux • Primary Source: Machines Transform the English Textile Industry	**Daily Test Practice Transparency:** Section 1* **Map Transparency:** Resources of Great Britain, 1800* **Quick Facts Transparency:** New Machines for an Old Industry*
Section 2: **Factories and Workers** **The Main Idea:** The transition from cottage industries changed how people worked in factories, what life was like in factory towns, labor conditions, and, eventually, processes within factories.	**Differentiated Instruction Teacher Management System:** Section 2 Lesson Plan* **Interactive Reader and Study Guide:** Section 2 Summary* **Chapter Resource File*** • Vocabulary Builder: Section 2 • Biography: Nelly Bly • Literature: *Hard Times*	**Daily Test Practice Transparency:** Section 2* **Map Transparency:** Effects of the Factory System* **Internet Activity:** Labor Unions
Section 3: **New Ideas in a New Society** **The Main Idea:** The Industrial Revolution inspired new ideas about economics and affected society in many ways.	**Differentiated Instruction Teacher Management System:** Section 3 Lesson Plan* **Interactive Reader and Study Guide:** Section 3 Summary* **Chapter Resource File*** • Vocabulary Builder: Section 3 • Biography: Louis Pasteur • History and Geography: The First Modern Railroad	**Daily Test Practice Transparency:** Section 3* **Quick Facts Transparency:** Effects of Industrialization on Women* **Map Transparency:** Industrialized Europe, 1900* **Internet Activity:** Historic Origins of Socialism and Capitalism

go.hrw.com | Print Resource | Transparency
Learning Styles | Audio CD | CD-ROM
Video | SE Student Edition | TE Teachers Edition
OSP One-Stop Planner CD-ROM
*also on One-Stop Planner CD-ROM

Review, Assessment, Intervention

- **Quick Facts Transparency:** The Industrial Revolution*
- **Spanish Chapter Summaries Audio CD Program**
- **Progress Assessment Support System (PASS):** Chapter Test*
- **Differentiated Instruction Modified Worksheets and Tests CD-ROM:** Modified Chapter Test
- OSP **One-Stop Planner CD-ROM:** ExamView Test Generator (English/Spanish)
- HOAP **Holt Online Assessment Program (HOAP),** in the Holt Premier Online Student Edition

- **PASS:** Section 1 Quiz*
- **Online Quiz:** Section 1
- **Alternative Assessment Handbook**

- **PASS:** Section 2 Quiz*
- **Online Quiz:** Section 2
- **Alternative Assessment Handbook**

- **PASS:** Section 3 Quiz*
- **Online Quiz:** Section 3
- **Alternative Assessment Handbook**

HOLT
History's Impact
World History Video Program (VHS/DVD)
The Industrial Revolution

Power Presentation with Video CD-ROM
Power Presentations with Video are visual presentations of each chapter's main ideas. Presentations can be customized by including Quick Facts charts, images and maps from the textbook, and video clips.

Holt Online Learning

go.hrw.com
Teacher Resources
KEYWORD: SHL TEACHER

go.hrw.com
Student Resources
KEYWORD: SHL IND

- Document-Based Questions
- Interactive Multimedia Activities
- Current Events
- Chapter-Based Internet Activities
- and more!

Holt Premier
Online Student Edition
Complete online support for interactivity, assessment, and reporting
- Interactive Maps and Notebook
- Homework Practice and Research Activities Online

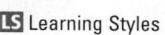

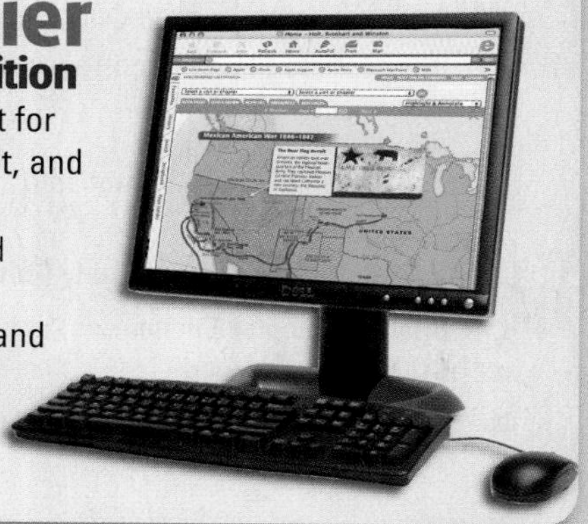

The Big Picture

Peter N. Stearns

The Industrial Revolution The Industrial Revolution is one of the big changes in human history, deservedly compared with the Neolithic Revolution much earlier in the course. Both the Industrial and the Neolithic revolutions fundamentally altered the ways people worked, where they lived, even what kinds of families they had. At the same time the Industrial Revolution is not quite like the set of events that make up a development such as the French Revolution. There are specific developments, like the key inventions, but the main focus is on broader processes that unfold over several decades. A good start involves basic definitions of early industrial technology including transportation, organizational forms beginning with the factory, and changes in levels of material goods. Discussion must also deal with the question of causes, including what distinctive factors existed in Great Britain.

Extensions and Impacts of Industrialization Britain led the world's industrial pack until the later 19th century. At the same time, it's vital to highlight broader participation in the process by 1850, with much of Western Europe and key parts of the United States joining in. How this expansion occurred, why these areas and not others, and what implications expanding industrialization had for the rest of the world are all important questions. Industrialization was a force that forever changed the human experience and gave rise to new forms of social organization and new social divisions, such as, the emergence of modern working class and middle class. A focus on how work and work values changed can help students understand human impact and the extent of change, while also raising questions about why people protested and also how many could accommodate to new experience. Western industrialization also had gender implications, rather different from what might be expected by more contemporary standards, which can help organize discussion of the broader consequences for family life. Finally, the Industrial Revolution occurred in an ideological framework, with the rise of liberal economics but also the emergence of Marxist critique. The two ideological systems need to be discussed through comparison but also through understanding of the political and social results of ideological competition during the industrialization process.

Recent Scholarship

My latest book, *The Industrial Revolution in World History* (2006), looks at industrialization from a global perspective. The book defines industrialization technologically and organizationally; it looks at social consequences, with particular reference to work, family and leisure; it deals with environmental impact. Discussions about causation issues, and particularly the balance between global and internal British or Western factors, are phrased in terms of active debates. The book looks at the Industrial Revolution in three phases, from Britain's launch to current globalization: early, with emphasis of course on Britain, Western Europe and the United States; late 19th to early 20th centuries, with attention to Russia and Japan along with further Western and global developments; and recent decades, when an additional 40 percent of the world's population are becoming more actively involved in the industrialization process. In all stages, global consequences and new inequalities play a crucial role.

Differentiating Instruction

Differentiated Instruction Teacher Management System
- Pacing Guide
- Lesson Plans for Differentiated Instruction

Interactive Reader and Study Guide

Spanish Chapter Summaries Audio CD Program

Student Edition on Audio CD Program

Differentiated Instruction Modified Worksheets and Tests CD-ROM
- Vocabulary Flash Cards
- Modified Vocabulary Builder Activities
- Modified Chapter Review Activity
- Modified Chapter Test

OSP **One-Stop Planner CD-ROM**
- ExamView Test Generator (English/Spanish)
- PuzzlePro
- Quiz Show for ExamView
- Transparencies and Videos

TE **Differentiated Activities in the Teacher's Edition**
- Britain's Industrial Success, p. 236
- Cottage Industries vs. Factory Work, p. 243
- Conditions in Manchester, p. 244
- Discontented Workers, p. 246
- New Industrialists, p. 249
- Rebuttal to Spencer, p. 255

Reading Like a Historian

Sam Wineburg

Accident or Achievement? Why did the Industrial Revolution take place in England? This seemingly inoffensive question hurls us into the epicenter of historical argument.

Consider how Robert B. Marks, author of *The Origins of the Modern World*, answers it. England did not achieve industrial eminence because of some inherent quality or essence of thought. "The West certainly did not 'rise' over other parts of the world because of cultural (or racial) superiority." For Marks, the engine in the machine is historical accident and a set of contingent circumstances. England was blessed with huge coal deposits, providing her with a steady supply of cheap fuel. That and the fact that Britain used slave labor to grow cheap cotton in her American colonies (which it then sold back at a handsome profit as finished textiles) kept the whole thing going. There was only one reason why the Chinese or the Indians didn't industrialize first: "They simply did not have colonies or coal."

David S. Landes, professor of history and economics at Harvard and author of *The Wealth and Poverty of Nations*, argues that there was nothing accidental about England's ascendance. The Industrial Revolution that swept this island nation "was not a matter of chance, of 'things simply coming together.'" The superiority of Britain "was itself an achievement . . . the result of work, ingenuity, imagination, and enterprise." For Landes, Britain possessed cultural and institutional features that created unique opportunities for industrial development. These included an ethos of inquiry, the development of a shared scientific language, and the building of a scholarly community that "routinized discovery" and in so doing elevated scientists and inventors to the status of rock stars. It was this cultural environment that gave birth to a technological hothouse that world had never before seen.

Marks focuses on the accident of cheap coal and pooh-poohs the role of scientific innovation. Landes places scientific and rational thinking at the center.

Who's RIght? Historical arguments that address "big" questions resist pat answers. Such arguments are never-ending, embracing earlier arguments as well as adopting new data and explanations that come in and out of fashion. Understanding all sides brings us closer to complexity, and helps us understand multi-faceted phenomena.

There's another reason why such arguments cannot be settled once and for all. They are as much about the present as the past. What stings Marks is the hubris of "Eurocentrism," the notion that "the West has some unique historical advantage . . . which gave this human community a permanent superiority." For him, Eurocentrism blinds us to unequal distribution of resources that have often come about by exploitation (slavery), greed (capitalism), and, in this case, the fickleness of historical accident (living atop huge coal deposits).

Landes views such thinking as a politically correct mist that obscures one enduring fact: "culture makes all the difference." And the culture that lead to technological innovation and prosperity? One that rewarded individual achievement, honesty in government, the protection of private property; that "afforded opportunity to individual or collective enterprise" and "encouraged initiative, competition, and emulation." England.

If you hear echoes of contemporary debates—clashing views about free markets, globalization, the policies of the G-8 and the World Bank, the inherent goodness or evil of capitalism—you should. To better understand why historians argue over the past, we must also ask why they, and we, argue over the present. Debates about what happened in the past will be settled only when we sign on to a collective vision for the future.

Don't hold your breath.

• Chapter Preview •

Chapter Main Ideas

Section 1 In the 1700s, conditions in Great Britain led to the rapid growth of the textile industry, which in turn led to huge changes in many other industries.

Section 2 The transition from cottage industries changed how people worked in factories, what life was like in factory towns, labor conditions, and eventually, processes within factories.

Section 3 The Industrial Revolution inspired new ideas about economics and affected society in many ways.

CHAPTER 7

1700–1900

The Industrial Revolution

THE BIG PICTURE The Scientific Revolution and Enlightenment led people to develop new ways of doing things. Among these new ways were processes and machines for raising crops, making cloth, and other jobs. These developments led to dramatic changes in industry and the world of work. Because so much changed, this era is called the Industrial Revolution. It began in Great Britain and then spread to other parts of the world.

Theme SCIENCE AND TECHNOLOGY
Industrialization made a dramatic impact on the world. In this chapter you will learn the remarkable ways in which technology altered how people worked and lived between 1700 and 1900.

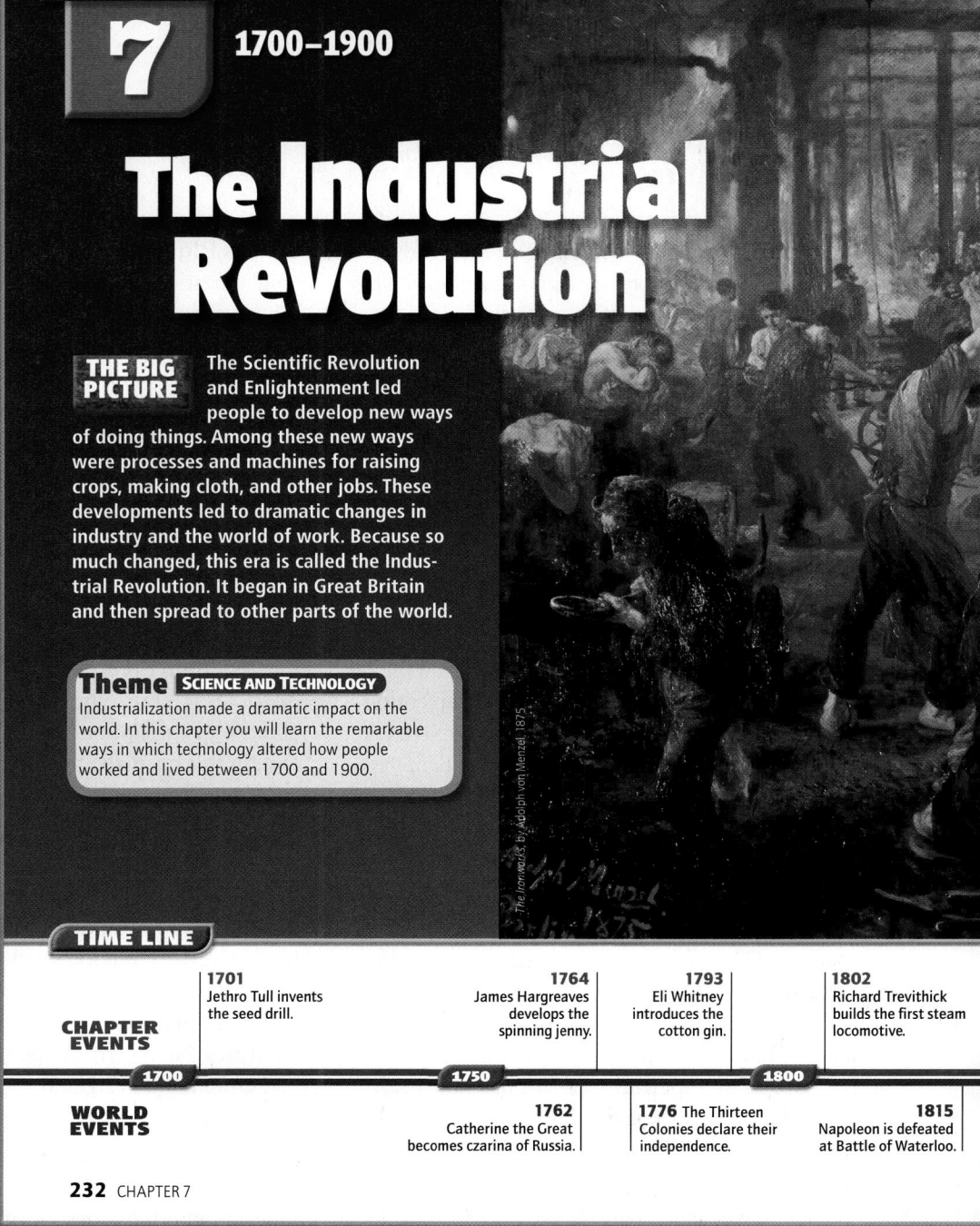

The Ironworks, by Adolph von Menzel, 1875

TIME LINE

CHAPTER EVENTS

- **1701** Jethro Tull invents the seed drill.
- **1764** James Hargreaves develops the spinning jenny.
- **1793** Eli Whitney introduces the cotton gin.
- **1802** Richard Trevithick builds the first steam locomotive.

1700 — 1750 — 1800

WORLD EVENTS

- **1762** Catherine the Great becomes czarina of Russia.
- **1776** The Thirteen Colonies declare their independence.
- **1815** Napoleon is defeated at Battle of Waterloo.

232 CHAPTER 7

Key to Differentiating Instruction

Below Level
Basic-level activities designed for all students encountering new material

At Level
Intermediate-level activities designed for average students

Above Level
Challenging activities designed for honors and gifted and talented students

Standard English Mastery
Activities designed to improve standard English usage

Introduce the Chapter

At Level

The Industrial Revolution

1. Have students write their own definitions of the word *revolution*. Have volunteers share their definitions, and write the responses for students to see. If student definitions focus on political revolts, ask leading questions that will guide students toward other types of major economic, social, or technological changes.
2. Have students create a single class definition for the term *revolution* using elements of various responses. Display the class definition in the classroom.
3. Tell students that in this chapter they will learn about a revolution in the ways that goods were produced. Industrialization is called a revolution because of the sweeping changes it brought.
4. Have students give examples of items they use in their daily lives that are produced by machines and items produced without solely relying on machines. **LS Verbal-Linguistic**

Alternative Assessment Handbook, Rubric 11: Discussions

History's Impact video program
Watch the video to understand the impact of the Industrial Revolution.

Reading like a Historian The painting shown here is of workers in a German factory flattening a sheet of hot iron. The artist, Adoph von Menzel, visited factories like this one so he could reproduce the details correctly.

Analyzing Visuals How many different tasks or activities can you see in the painting? How do you think the artist felt about the industry pictured? Explain your answer.

See **Skills Handbook**, p. H26

1848 Marx and Engels publish *The Communist Manifesto.*

1871 Trade unions are legalized in Britain.

1850

1848 Revolutions occur throughout Europe.

• Chapter Preview •

HOLT
History's Impact

► **Video Program: The Industrial Revolution**
See the Video Teacher's Guide for strategies for using the video segment.

Reading Like aw Historian

Analyzing Visuals Many of Adoph von Menzel's paintings are historical in theme, and he created a series of paintings about the accomplishments of Frederick the Great. In this painting, von Menzel captures a sense of the grim colors and harsh conditions of workers in an iron factory.

go.hrw.com
Online Resources
Chapter Resources:
KEYWORD: SHL IND
Teacher Resources:
KEYWORD: SHL TEACHER

Explore the Time Line

1. Who invented the seed drill? *Jethro Tull*
2. What did Richard Trevithick accomplish in 1802? *built the first steam locomotive*
3. What occurred the same year that *The Communist Manifesto* was published? *Revolutions occurred throughout Europe.*
4. How many years after *The Communist Manifesto* were trade unions legalized in Britain? *twenty-three years*

Info to Know

British Cloth Cloth production was the most important business activity in 18th century Britain. Families did much of the work in their homes, and they farmed as well. Woven cloth was sold to merchants who then took the cloth to the nearest market town. Many merchants also exported cloth to America, Russia, Sweden, Holland, and Germany.

Draw Conclusions Why do you think cloth makers sold their finished cloth to merchants, rather than taking cloth to market towns by themselves? *possible answers—could not leave farms, towns were far away, lack of transportation*

Answers

Reading Like a Historian *possible answers—three; felt that industry was a noble activity because workers are in heroic poses, but the work is very hard*

Preteach

Geography Starting Points

The Canal Builder One of the great canal-builders in Britain was Thomas Telford. He built the Ellesmere Canal in Wales, which included two giant aqueducts. Telford also built the Caledonian Canal, a waterway that connects the east coast of Scotland to the west coast.

- **Map Transparency:** Resources of Great Britain, 1800
- **Interactive Map:** Resources of Great Britain, 1800
- **World History Outline Maps**

★Interactive
RESOURCES OF GREAT BRITAIN, 1800

North Sea

Glasgow

Newcastle upon Tyne

Irish Sea

IRELAND

Bradford · Leeds
Manchester
Liverpool
Sheffield
Nottingham

Kingston upon Hull

Birmingham

GREAT BRITAIN

London ★

Bristol

:::: Major canal
▇ Coal field
⬥ Iron ore

English Channel

0 50 100 Miles
0 50 100 Kilometers
Lambert conformal conic projection

FRANCE

Interior of a mine in South Staffordshire

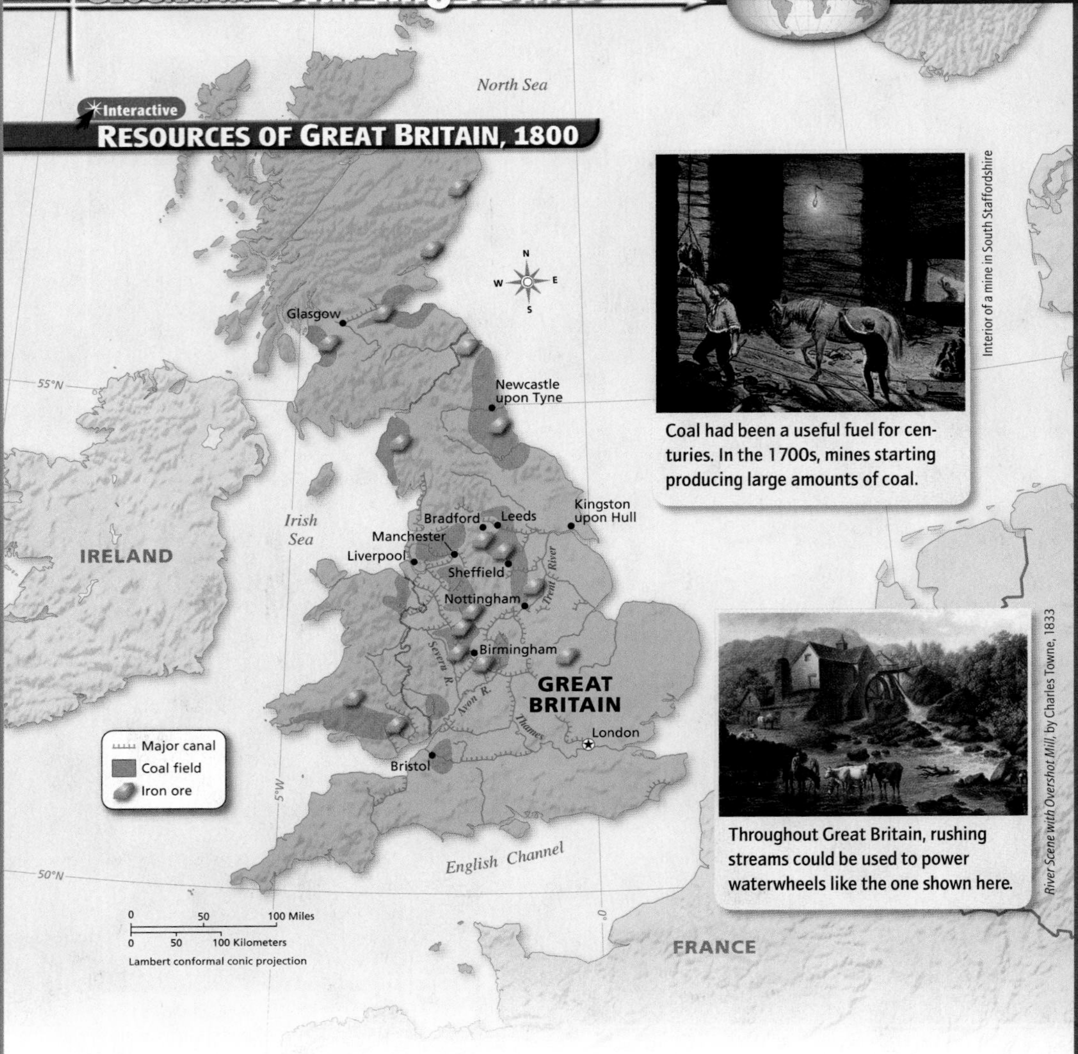

Coal had been a useful fuel for centuries. In the 1700s, mines starting producing large amounts of coal.

River Scene with Overshot Mill, by Charles Towne, 1833

Throughout Great Britain, rushing streams could be used to power waterwheels like the one shown here.

Starting Points In 1800, much of Europe's economy was still based on farming. Times were changing, though, particularly in Great Britain. There, fewer people were working on farms, and more were working in manufacturing. Great Britain's natural resources, such as coal and iron, were major factors in the growth of British industry.

1. **Analyze** What do you think is the connection between canals and rivers and industry?

2. **Predict** Based on the map, where do you think Great Britain's first industries grew?

Listen to History

Go online to listen to an explanation of the starting points for this chapter.

go.hrw.com
Keyword: SHL IND

234 CHAPTER 7

Skills Focus: Analyzing Maps

At Level

Social Studies Skill
Resource Development

Materials: drawing paper, colored pencils

1. Have students draw a map of a large island nation. Islands should not resemble England. Have students include one river, two cities, mountains and other natural features. Have students divide their islands into a grid system of 16 zones and label them A1, A2, B1, B2, etc.

2. Label six scraps of paper with zone names and place the papers in a hat. Draw three out and read the zone names. These will be the locations of coal deposits. The last three will be the locations of iron ore deposits. Have students create a map legend for the coal and iron deposits.

3. Based on the location of the iron and coal deposits, have students place two new towns, three canals, and two railroads on their maps.
LS Visual-Spatial

Alternative Assessment Handbook, Rubric 20: Map Creation

Answers

Geography Starting Points

1. *canals and rivers used to bring natural resources to industrial sites, transport goods;* **2.** *in the south central region, some coastal areas*

Section 1

A New Kind of Revolution

Before You Read

Main Idea
In the 1700s, conditions in Great Britain led to the rapid growth of the textile industry, which in turn led to huge changes in many other industries.

Reading Focus
1. Why did the Industrial Revolution begin in Great Britain?
2. How did industrialization cause a revolution in the production of textiles?
3. How did steam power the Industrial Revolution?
4. Where did industrialization spread beyond Great Britain?

Key Terms and People
Industrial Revolution
enclosure movement
factors of production
cottage industry
factory
industrialization
Jethro Tull
Richard Arkwright
James Watt
Robert Fulton

Taking Notes As you read, take notes on the early years of the Industrial Revolution.

A. In Britain
B. In Textiles
C. Steam Power
D. Spread

The Inside Story

How did one farmer's frustration help start a revolution? Jethro Tull had never planned to be a farmer. He had trained to be a lawyer but inherited the family farm. While running the farm, Tull was often annoyed by the workers' sloppy habits. For example, when planting, they wasted seeds by throwing big handfuls onto the ground. Sure that the job could be done more efficiently, Tull invented a horse-drawn machine that planted seeds one by one. He called it a seed drill. Without knowing it, Tull was helping to start a revolution—an agricultural revolution that would bring changes to nearly all aspects of life. ■

For centuries, workers had used muscle power to farm the land.

The Mowers, by Sir George Clausen, 1891

A Revolution in Great Britain

During the 1700s changes in technology began that would transform the world. These changes were based on a shift in how people worked. For centuries people had used human and animal power as their main energy sources. Then they began to develop water and steam power to drive new machines and perform countless tasks. This era, when the use of power-driven machinery was developed, is called the **Industrial Revolution**. For several reasons, it started in Great Britain.

Factors for Success By the 1700s several factors had come together to set the scene for the development of industry in Great Britain. Those factors included a range of political and economic events.

Teach the Main Idea

At Level

A New Kind of Revolution

1. **Teach** Ask students the Reading Focus questions to teach this section.
2. **Apply** Draw four circles for students to see. Label them with the main topics in this section: A Revolution in Great Britain, A Revolution in Textiles, Steam Powers the Revolution, and Industrialization Spreads. Have students copy the circles onto their papers and fill them in with the main ideas of each topic.
3. **Review** As you review the section, have students describe the conditions that led to the Industrial Revolution in Britain.
4. **Practice/Homework** Have students write an 18th century magazine article in which they explain specifically how new devices will change the textile industry. **LS Visual-Spatial, Verbal-Linguistic**

Alternative Assessment Handbook, Rubric 19: Magazines

Preteach

Getting Started

Use the **Interactive Reader and Study Guide** to familiarize students with the section content.

Interactive Reader and Study Guide, Section 1

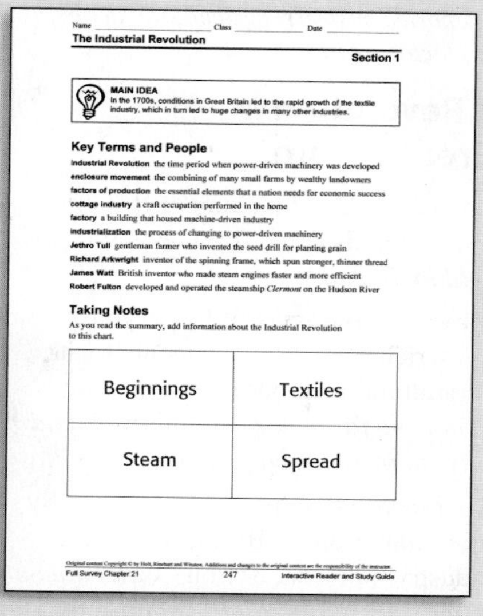
Name ________ Class ________ Date ________

The Industrial Revolution

Section 1

MAIN IDEA
In the 1700s, conditions in Great Britain led to the rapid growth of the textile industry, which in turn led to huge changes in many other industries.

Key Terms and People
Industrial Revolution the time period when power-driven machinery was developed
enclosure movement the combining of many small farms by wealthy landowners
factors of production the essential elements that a nation needs for economic success
cottage industry a craft occupation performed in the home
factory a building that housed machine-driven industry
industrialization the process of changing to power-driven machinery
Jethro Tull gentleman farmer who invented the seed drill for planting grain
Richard Arkwright inventor of the spinning frame, which spun stronger, thinner thread
James Watt British inventor who made steam engines faster and more efficient
Robert Fulton developed and operated the steamship *Clermont* on the Hudson River

Taking Notes
As you read the summary, add information about the Industrial Revolution to this chart.

Beginnings	Textiles
Steam	Spread

Original content Copyright © by Holt, Rinehart and Winston. Additions and changes to the original content are the responsibility of the instructor.
Full Survey Chapter 21 247 Interactive Reader and Study Guide

Academic Vocabulary

Review with students the high-use academic term in this section.

labor work, or people who do the work (p. 237)

CRF: Vocabulary Builder: Section 1

Taking Notes

Beginnings—expansion of colonialism, political stability, government support of business, growth of private investment led to industrialism, factors of production; Textiles—invention of cotton gin, spinning jenny, and water frame revolutionized textile industry; Steam—development of steam engine made several industries more efficient; Spread—industrialization spread quickly to societies with a degree of individual freedom and economic stability, spread to other countries as well

Direct Teach

Reading Focus

1 Why did the Industrial Revolution begin in Great Britain? *colonies provided raw materials, political stability encouraged commerce, powerful navy defended shipping, government supported business, agricultural factors, factors of production*

A Revolution in Great Britain

Recall Where did many of Britain's raw materials come from? *colonies held by Britain*

Make Inferences Why do you think rich farmers experimented with agricultural methods? *possible answers—to farm more efficiently, to find ways to increase crop yields*

Summarize Why was water initially more important to Britain's growing industry than coal or iron? *Water was readily available; it did not have to be mined or transported; waterways provided transportation among mines, factories, and markets.*

Info to Know

Enclosure Movement The enclosure movement greatly changed rural England as communal use and care of the land changed to private ownership. As individual landowners and tenants took control of defined areas of land, communities lost their land use rights. Open, unfenced fields and meadows were turned into privately owned hedged, fenced, or walled fields. Acts of Parliament, as well as private agreements between lords and their tenants, helped speed the change.

Answers

History and Economics **1.** *fossil fuels not found in Britain, skilled labor supply from China and India, investors from Asia and Middle East;* **2.** *possible answer—renewable power sources, more emphasis on technically skilled workforce*

- **Exploration and colonialism** Great Britain claimed colonies around the world that provided vast amounts of raw materials, such as cotton fiber. In addition, the colonies became new markets for British goods. (However, India's own textile industry was severely damaged by British competition.)
- **Seapower** Britain could bring in raw materials and send finished goods around the world because it had the largest, most powerful navy and merchant fleet in the world.
- **Political stability** Although Great Britain fought wars in Canada and North America during the 1700s, at home the country was at peace, and commerce thrived.
- **Government support** Parliament passed laws that favored business, helping the country compete successfully against other nations.
- **Growth of private investment** Private businesses funded experiments for creating better products—what we would call "research and development" today.

Agricultural Factors Much of the research and development took place on farms as some of Britain's so-called gentlemen farmers began to experiment with agricultural methods.

Jethro Tull was among these wealthier farmers. In about 1701 Tull invented the seed drill, a machine that made planting grain much more efficient.

Farmers experimented with other aspects of agriculture also. For example, they improved livestock breeding methods to raise healthier animals. Better varieties of food crops, such as potatoes, were developed. These improvements increased Britain's food supply. Since more food can support more people, Britain's population grew rapidly.

Another agricultural development had mixed results. Wealthy landowners could buy up fields that had previously been shared by rich and poor farmers alike. The new landowners combined the small fields to create large farms and fenced them, a transformation

HISTORY and Economics

Factors of Production

The basic factors of production are the essential elements that a nation needs to achieve economic success. They are land (natural resources), labor, and capital. The places where these factors can be found change over time.

Factors of Production in History In the 1700s the factors of production that sparked the Industrial Revolution were all in place in Great Britain. From these factors—coal, iron ore, waterways, unemployed farmers, cash, and human talent—the British built an industrial empire.

Factors of Production Today Much has changed since the 1700s. The land, labor, and capital that made Great Britain an industrial leader no longer have the same value. For example, running water is not as important a power source as it once was. Today, the industrial world depends more on fossil fuels, especially oil. Countries other than Great Britain provide most of the world's supply of the precious fuel. Labor resources can also be found elsewhere. Today, China and India have huge numbers of skilled workers. Capital resources have shifted, too. Investors from Asia and the Middle East now fund many factories in Western countries.

All these shifts in where the factors of production are located affect wealth and, therefore, political power. As you study different countries, keep track of how the factors of production have affected their economies—and their histories.

▲ A worker in Malaysia assembles TVs for a Japanese company.

1. Summarize How has the location of the factors of production changed in current times?
2. Predict How might the factors of production continue to change?

Differentiating Instruction

Below Level

Special Education Students; Learners Having Difficulty

Materials: construction paper, markers

1. Review what the term *industrialization* means and then guide students in a discussion of Britain's factors for success in industrialization. Make a list of Britain's five factors for industrial success for students to see.
2. Organize students into mixed-ability pairs.
3. Have each pair design a series of Web pages that explain the five factors of Britain's industrial success. There should be a home page and a separate page for each factor. Pages should include text and a picture or icon that illustrates the factor.
4. Have volunteers share their pages with the class. **LS Visual-Spatial**

Alternative Assessment Handbook, Rubric 3: Artwork

called the **enclosure movement**. The movement allowed for more efficient farming methods and, therefore, further increased the food supply. However, enclosure also threw countless farmers off the land. Unable to make a living in the countryside, these poor farmers went to the cities for jobs. There they would form the workforce for growing industries.

Britain's Big Advantage These conditions all point to the basic reason why the Industrial Revolution began in Great Britain. The country had the essential elements that a nation needs to achieve economic success—what economists call the **factors of production**. There are three factors: land, labor, and capital.

Land, in this context, means all of a place's natural resources. Great Britain had all the resources it needed for industry. It had coal to burn as fuel and iron to make into steel and machinery. But to get industry started, no resource was more important than water. People used Britain's streams and rivers to turn waterwheels and generate power, and many of those same waterways provided transportation between mines, factories, and markets. A network of canals connected major rivers. In the mid-1700s England already had about 1,000 miles of canals, which grew to about 4,000 miles by 1800. Also, for long-distance shipping, Great Britain had good deepwater harbors.

For labor, Britain had the growing population made possible by a greater food supply. Within this growing population were the thousands of people who had lost their farmland because of the enclosure movement. These were often entire families, and entire families would go to work in industry.

Britain's last factor of production was capital, which refers to funds for investment in business. The country was generally prosperous, and people had money to spend. Britain also had "human capital"—people with abilities and skills that are needed in industry. For example, Jethro Tull and later inventors were among this group of capable people. With all these factors of production in place, Great Britain was ready for a boom in business.

READING CHECK **Find the Main Idea** Why was Great Britain in the 1700s ideally suited to be the birthplace of the Industrial Revolution?

New Machines for an Old Industry

The inventors who revolutionized the textile industry improved on each other's ideas. The spinning frame shown here, invented by Richard Arkwright, twisted fibers together. As a result, it made thread that was much stronger than thread made by an earlier machine.

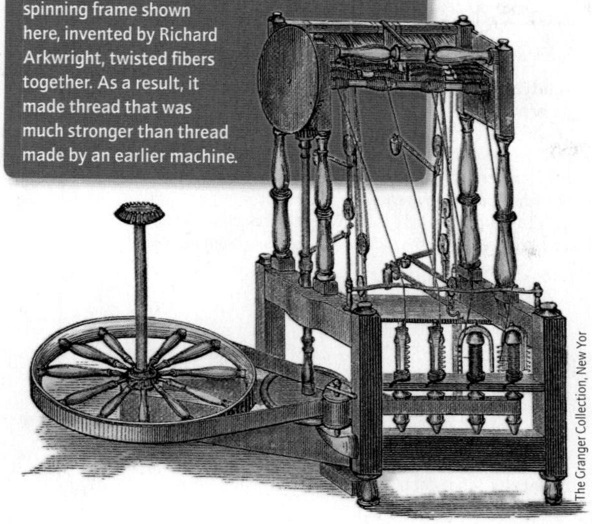
The Granger Collection, New Yor

A Revolution in Textiles

The Industrial Revolution began with the British cloth-making, or textile, industry. British workers had been handweaving woolen cloth for centuries. Weaving was a **cottage industry**—a craft occupation performed in the home. But the old ways of making cloth were completely transformed by **industrialization**, or the process of changing to power-driven machinery.

ACADEMIC VOCABULARY
labor work, or people who do the work

A New Way of Making Cloth In Great Britain most fabric was made of wool or cotton. During the 1700s the supply of both fibers increased. The wool supply increased because the enclosure movement converted so many farms to pastures for raising more sheep. Shipments of cotton fiber came from the British colonies, particularly in India and North America. In the southern American colonies the trade in cotton had a tragic result. Slave labor helped make cotton farming more profitable. Therefore, as Great Britain bought more and more American cotton, slavery became more entrenched throughout the South. A new invention also helped keep the American cotton industry—and slavery—profitable.

Direct Teach

Reading Focus

2 How did industrialization cause a revolution in the production of textiles? *new devices allowed faster and less labor-intensive production of cloth*

A Revolution in Textiles

Explain Why did the supply of wool and cotton increase in the 1700s? *enclosure movement converted farms to pastures for more sheep, cotton came from British colonies, including those in America*

Identify Cause and Effect How did Britain's demand for cotton affect the United States? *made growing cotton very profitable; increased the spread of slavery in the American South*

Quick Facts Transparency: New Machines for an Old Industry

CRF: Primary Source: Machines Transform the English Textile Industry

Skills Focus: Identifying Main Idea and Details — At Level

Reading Skill

Land, Labor, Capital

1. Draw the chart below for students to see. Omit the italicized answers.
2. Have students copy and complete the chart. **LS Visual-Spatial**

Alternative Assessment Handbook, Rubric 7: Charts

Factors of Production in Britain

Factor of Production	Land	Labor	Capital
what it means	*all natural resources*	*people available to work*	*funds for investment*
how it was an advantage	*had coal for fuel, iron for steel*	*growing population, people who had lost farmland*	*country prosperous, money to spend, people with abilities*

Answers

Reading Check *Colonies around the world supplied raw materials, powerful navy and merchant fleet facilitated trade, waterways provided power and transportation, enclosure movement led to large labor supply, private investors provided funds for investment, coal and iron deposits provided needed resources.*

Direct Teach

Reading Focus

A Revolution in Textiles

Recall What problem did Eli Whitney solve? *the slow, tedious process of pulling seeds from raw cotton; invented the cotton gin*

Identify What machines were developed to spin fiber into thread or yarn? *spinning jenny, spinning frame*

Evaluate Did inventors like Kay and Arkwright deserve to be honored or scorned? *possible answers—honored: their inventions changed the world; scorned: many people lost their jobs*

Activity Weavers Wanted Have students design a "Jobs Wanted" flyer inviting workers to leave their farms and come to work at a weaving factory. Remind students that many farm workers might not have been able to read or write at this time in history.
LS Visual-Spatial

CRF: Biography: Nobert Rillieux

Reading Like a Historian

Analyze Ask students how they think Baines might have described preindustrial methods of production. *primitive, backward*

Teaching Tip

If students have trouble grasping the changes brought by the Industrial Revolution, ask them to name products that have revolutionized their lives, such as cell phones and other technological devices that they consider necessities.

Answers

Reading Like a Historian **1.** *possible answer—No, Baines could not have understood the long-term effects during his own lifetime.* **2.** *positive adjectives, general tone*

Reading Check *spinning jenny and spinning frame spun thread into yarn, "flying shuttle" and power loom made weaving faster*

Reading like a Historian

An Early Historian on the Textile Industry

Analyzing Secondary Sources Historians often read what other historians before them had to say. Using older sources, modern historians can learn how events were viewed in the past. However, historians who wrote about events soon after they happened usually had a different perspective than historians who wrote many years after the event.

The quotation here is from a British historian. When he was writing, the textile industry had already been thoroughly mechanized.

Notice the adjectives the author used to describe the textile industry, starting with "admirable."

When this admirable series of machines was made known, and by their means yarns were produced far superior in quality to any before spun in England, as well as lower in price, a mighty impulse was communicated to the cotton manufacture. Weavers could now obtain an unlimited quantity of yarn at a reasonable price; manufacturers could use warps of cotton, which were much cheaper than the linen warps formerly used. Cotton fabrics could be sold lower than had ever before been known.

—E. Baines, *History of the Cotton Manufacture in Great Britain*, London, 1835

The lower prices would have long-term results, but Baines could not predict them all at this early stage in the Industrial Revolution.

Skills Focus READING LIKE A HISTORIAN

1. **Credibility** Would Baines be an authority on the long-term effects of industrialization? Why or why not?
2. **Details** What details show the author's attitude about the textile industry?

See **Skills Handbook**, p. H30

Pulling seeds from raw cotton blossoms was time-consuming when done by hand. An American named Eli Whitney solved the problem. He built a machine, called the cotton gin, that removed the seeds efficiently.

The fiber was then spun into thread or yarn. James Hargreaves, a weaver, revolutionized the spinning process with a machine he called the spinning jenny, which spun several threads at once. Hargreaves' machine was not perfect. The thread it produced was still thick and prone to break when woven into cloth. **Richard Arkwright**, another inventor, solved this problem with the spinning frame, which spun stronger, thinner thread.

Finally, the thread was woven into fabric. The traditional in-home weaving loom was about six feet wide—the width a man could reach from side to side to push the thread back and forth on a shuttle. The "flying shuttle," patented by John Kay, doubled the speed at which a weaver could do the job. Because many workers lost their jobs as a result, Kay was attacked and fled to France. He died in poverty.

Nevertheless, the ever-faster spinning machines soon created a demand for better weaving machines. To meet that demand, in 1785 Edmund Cartwright patented the power loom, a larger, faster weaving system.

Cloth-Making in Factories The new machines were too big for the weaver's cottage. They had to be housed in large buildings constructed specially for that purpose. A building that housed industrial machines became known as a **factory**, from the old word *manufactory*. Factories needed ready supplies of power. Arkwright built early factories to house a spinning system driven by water power. His system was known as the water frame.

From this flurry of invention and innovation, an industry was born. In 1770 England produced about 50,000 bolts of cloth. By 1800 the textile output had increased to 400,000 bolts.

READING CHECK **Identify Problem and Solution** How did machines solve problems that weavers faced?

Skills Focus: Making Oral Presentations

At Level

Research Required

Reading Like a Historian Skill

Inventors Showcase

1. Assign each student the role of an inventor mentioned in the section, such as Jethro Tull, James Hargreaves, or Robert Fulton.
2. Have each student conduct outside research on the assigned person and his most famous invention.
3. Have students prepare and present short, first-person accounts of their assigned inventor's most famous invention. Students should give some background on why they created the device and demonstrate how it works with drawings or models.
4. Hold an Inventors Showcase in which students present their inventions.
LS Intrapersonal, Kinesthetic

Alternative Assessment Handbook, Rubrics 24: Oral Presentations; and 30: Research

Steam Powers the Revolution

A simple fact of physics powered the Industrial Revolution: when water is heated and changes into steam, it expands. British inventors learned how to harness the force of steam to drive machines that transformed the world.

Development of the Steam Engine The first commercially successful steam engine was built in England in 1712, but it was very slow. Then an inventor named **James Watt** came up with crucial innovations. His engine was faster and more efficient at driving machinery. By 1800 about 500 of Watt's steam engines were chugging and hissing in mines and factories throughout Britain.

The widespread use of steam engines began when inventors put them to use in the textile mills. Using steam power instead of water power meant that factories no longer had to be built near ready supplies of water. Instead, they could be located where fuel was readily available and where workers already lived. Also, factories could be built closer to roads and ports from which raw materials and finished products could be shipped.

Steam was soon applied to other uses, eventually producing a revolution in transportation. In about 1802 Richard Trevithick used a steam engine to power the first locomotive. Steam-powered trains soon became essential to the Industrial Revolution. They made possible the fast shipment of finished goods even to faraway markets.

Steam also provided a power source for ships. An Irish-born American, **Robert Fulton**, became famous for developing a steamship called the *Clermont*. In 1807 the *Clermont* began operating on the Hudson River between New York City and Albany. Fulton's business was the first profitable use of steam navigation. Steamships would replace sailing ships on the open sea and the horse-drawn barges that hauled goods along canals.

Coal for British Steam Engines Steam engines required immense amounts of fuel to heat water. Wood was scarce, though, because most of England's forests had been cut down for farming. But the country had a big supply of another valuable fuel—coal. Consequently, as more factories were built to run on steam, the coal mining industry in northern and western England grew. By 1800, Great Britain produced 80 percent of Europe's coal.

Naturally, many factories were built near Britain's northern coal mines. Quiet agricultural landscapes changed into busy, noisy boom towns dotted with factories and surrounded by endless rows of workers' and miners' homes.

The miners' families often experienced tragedy. Working in the mines was a dangerous job. Mine explosions, coal dust, collapsing shafts, and the sheer hard labor took a heavy toll. Children were often hired to slip down the narrow shafts and pick and haul coal. Their lives were hard, as one account describes:

HISTORY'S VOICES

> **"The children, boys and girls, earned their wages by drawing the coals in tubs along the galleries by means of a belt and chain, which passed around their waists. Many girls were thus employed, and after a time became crooked and deformed."**
>
> —Carelton Smith, visitor to the Lancashire mines, 1833

Such reports caught the public's attention. Industrialization continued for some time, though, before the situation changed.

READING CHECK **Make Generalizations** What impact did the steam engine have on the growth of British industry?

THE IMPACT TODAY

Coal is still a major resource for the United Kingdom, which is the fifth-greatest coal producer in the European Union.

FACES OF HISTORY

James WATT

1736–1819

As a young man, Watt was an instrument maker at Scotland's Glasgow University. There he was given an early steam engine to repair. It was a slow contraption that wasted fuel. One day in 1765, as Watt strolled across the campus, he got an idea for how to improve the old engine. Watt built his new engine in secrecy, patented his design, and began manufacturing it. The engine was very popular and set off a revolution in the production of textiles, paper, and flour, in mining, and in transportation. Thanks to his steam engine and other inventions, Watt became rich and famous. Today in Glasgow, a stone marks the place where young Watt had his "Aha!" moment—the spark of inspiration that helped launch the Industrial Revolution.

A tribute to James Watt can be found on every light bulb in your home. The inventor played such a central role in the development of power generation that today we measure electric power in watts.

Identify Problem and Solution How did James Watt make sure that he would profit from his valuable design?

Direct Teach

Reading Focus

3 How did steam power the Industrial Revolution? *British inventors harnessed the force of steam to drive steam engines, first in textile mills, then in trains and steamships.*

Steam Powers the Revolution

Recall What was James Watt's main achievement? *built a more efficient steam engine*

Summarize How did the steam engine lead to a revolution in transportation? *Steam-powered trains made it possible to ship goods quickly; steam-powered ships replaced sailing ships and slow horse-drawn barges.*

Evaluate Could coal mining have been made more humane? *possible answers—Yes, children should not have been used for mine work; no, mine work is very dangerous and difficult, even today.*

Info to Know

Watt's Designs James Watt's improved steam engine relied on a condensing chamber that would prevent the loss of steam from the system. It was typically used to work pumps. In 1781 he invented the rotary engine, which drove machinery by turning a shaft in the machine. While these designs were under patent, the firm of Boulton and Watt built about 200 steam pumps and over 300 rotary engines. During his career, Watt also invented the double-acting engine and a pressure gauge.

Skills Focus: Identifying Cause and Effect

At Level

Reading Skill

Effects of Steam Power

1. Review the information in the text about the development of steam power and its effects.
2. Make a two-column chart titled Effects of Steam Power for students to see. Label one column Positive and the other column Negative.
3. Have volunteers fill in the chart with positive and negative effects of both the development and use of steam power.
4. Guide students in a discussion about the positive effects for workers, factory owners, and merchants. Would it have been possible to lessen the negative effects and still get all the positive ones? **LS Visual-Spatial**

Alternative Assessment Handbook, Rubric 7: Charts

Answers

Faces of History *built engine in secrecy, patented his design*

Reading Check *major impact; used in textile mills, factories could be located away from rivers, powered locomotives and ships, led to development of coal as a resource, more factories built near northern coal mines*

Direct Teach

Reading Focus

4 Where did industrialization spread beyond Great Britain? *America, continental Europe, Asia*

Industrialization Spreads

Explain How did Britain try to keep its discoveries secret? *outlawed export of certain machines, forbade skilled craftsmen from leaving the country*

Make Inferences What do Samuel Slater's accomplishments reveal about him? *possible answer—that the was technically skilled, highly motivated, and had a good memory*

Info to Know

Spread of Industry Britain remained a manufacturing powerhouse in the 19th century, but other nations began developing their own industrial bases, as well. In 1809 a visitor to the Ruhr and Wupper valleys in present-day Germany described them as a "miniature England." Large coalfields in France, Belgium, and present-day Germany became important centers of industrial growth.

Biography

William Blake (1757–1827) William Blake was a British artist and poet who defied convention. Apprenticed to an engraver, he drew copies of monuments in London's churches. After trying unsuccessfully to establish a print shop, Blake made a modest living as an engraver and illustrator. He developed a method of "illuminated printing," which combined art and text on a single plate of etching. Blake was also a poet, and he illustrated and printed his own poems with assistance from his wife. Inspired by nature and mystical vision, Blake rejected industrialization and political themes. In one poem, he writes of Britain's "dark Satanic mills." The greatness of Blake's works was not generally recognized during his lifetime, but he is now regarded as one of England's most original and lyric writers.

Industrialization Spreads

With steam driving British factories, industrialization increased rapidly and soon spread to western Europe and the United States. Other regions, including Asia and Africa, did not industrialize in the 1800s. Why did industry not take hold in some areas? What was it about Western countries that encouraged them to embrace industry?

Industry and the West Today's scholars have many ideas about why industrialization did not spread quickly to all parts of the world. Among those ideas is the impact of individual freedom on economic activity.

In Western countries, individual freedom was becoming a significant force in society. Although during the 1800s even Western countries were not truly democratic, the individual citizens enjoyed more political liberty than people elsewhere. People with a degree of freedom can compete against each other. Western societies saw competition as good. Wealth and fame rewarded those who competed well. For example, explorers raced to find new lands where merchants could do business. Fierce competition even led some Westerners to exploit other countries in their search for raw materials and markets. Then, during the Industrial Revolution, Western industrialists competed to improve on inventions and processes.

Industry Comes to America Although industrialization spread far beyond Great Britain, it was not because the British wanted to share the wealth. In fact, Britain outlawed the export of certain machines and even forbade some skilled craftsmen from leaving the country. As a result of these restrictions, from about 1760 to 1830, the Industrial Revolution took place mainly in Great Britain, giving the country a head start in economic development. But it was just a matter of time before knowledge of the machines and how to run them leaked out. The United States was one of the first places to benefit from that knowledge.

In his 1791 *Report on Manufactures*, U.S. Treasury Secretary Alexander Hamilton argued that industrialization would help the young United States gain economic independence from Great Britain. He even wanted the U.S. government to bribe British citizens into bringing their knowledge to this country.

Fortunately for the United States, Samuel Slater, a highly skilled young millworker, had already arrived from Britain. To avoid arrest, Slater had disguised himself as a farmworker and boarded a ship to America in 1789.

Slater had a dream—of making a fortune in America. He had detailed knowledge of the

Steamships and the Spread of Industrialization

Steamships helped spread industrialization. They carried raw materials to industrialized countries, finished products to markets, and immigrants to countries where they could get factory jobs. The ship in this print is the *Great Eastern* under construction in the 1850s. It was built to carry passengers and cargo from Europe to Australia.

Collaborative Learning

Prep Required | At Level

Interviewing Slater and Lowell

1. Find and provide students with supplementary information on Samuel Slater and Francis Cabot Lowell.
2. Organize students into small groups. Provide each group with the information about Slater and Lowell.
3. Have groups brainstorm interview questions that could be asked of Slater and Lowell. Questions should focus on the most important details of their lives.
4. Have groups develop their questions into a script for a radio round-table interview featuring Slater and Lowell and two interviewers. Encourage students to include dialogue and discussion between Slater and Lowell. Have groups rehearse and then present the interviews to the class.

LS Auditory-Musical, Kinesthetic

Alternative Assessment Handbook, Rubric 33: Skits and Reader's Theater machinery created by water frame inventor Richard Arkwright for combing and spinning cotton in a single, efficient process. But Slater did not have a copy of the English machines to use as a model. In a remarkable feat of memory, Slater built the complex Arkwright machinery from scratch at a Rhode Island mill.

Slater's bold move resulted in a big success. In 1793 he built what is known today as Slater's Mill in Pawtucket, Rhode Island. For his contribution, Slater became known as the Father of American Industry.

Textile mill technology spread rapidly throughout the northeast United States. The mill city of Lowell, Massachusetts, became the jewel of American industry. The mill's principle founder, Francis Cabot Lowell, used the power of a nearby waterfall to run his machinery. Lowell's mills, situated in 40 multi-story brick buildings on a network of six miles of canals, were models for modern industry.

Lowell had the world's first all-in-one mill that took raw cotton through the various processes from fiber to finished cloth. He hired young, single girls from nearby farms to work in the mills, providing good wages and clean, safe housing for them. Some 10,000 workers were employed there by 1850.

Industry Spreads to Europe A British engineer named William Cockerill brought industry to continental Europe. In 1807 he founded a textile factory in Belgium, which became the second industrialized European country after Great Britain.

Political unrest delayed the industrialization of France. In 1789 revolution erupted in France. The Napoleonic Wars further delayed the process. After Napoleon was defeated in 1815 the French government gave financial support for building industry. By 1848 France had become an industrial power.

In Germany, there was no central government to support industry. Railroads were being built, however, among the many small German states. The railroads paved the way for industrialization after about 1850. Treaties that dropped trade barriers among the states also helped industry grow.

Industry in Asia Eventually, industry spread to Asia. Although today Japan is one of the world's industrial leaders, the Industrial Revolution spread to Japan fairly late. Industrialization took hold there after 1868, when the Meiji government came to power and modernized Japan's economy. Within just a few decades, Japan had thriving industries.

Japan was far ahead of its Asian neighbors. The industrialization of other major world powers—including China, India, and Russia—would not occur until the 1900s.

READING SKILLS

Drawing Conclusions If you know the Meiji modernized Japan's economy, what can you conclude about the previous government's role in the country's economy?

READING CHECK **Compare and Contrast** How did industrialization in Britain compare to the process in America and Europe?

SECTION 1 ASSESSMENT

go.hrw.com
Online Quiz
Keyword: SHL IND HP

Reviewing Ideas, Terms, and People

1. **a. Describe** What were the **factors of production** that helped produce an **Industrial Revolution** in Great Britain?
   b. Identify Cause and Effect What effect did changes in agriculture have on the Industrial Revolution?
   c. Rate Which condition in mid-1700s England do you think was most crucial to the birth of the Industrial Revolution? Explain your answer.
2. **a. Identify** What did **Richard Arkwright** invent?
   b. Infer Why did some people not like the arrival of machines?
   c. Predict What effect might the shift from cottages to factories have on the lives of textile workers and on towns and cities?
3. **a. Recall** What industry stimulated the widespread use of steam engines?
   b. Evaluate How do you think people justified the use of children doing hard labor in coal mines?
4. **a. Identify** Why is Samuel Slater known as the Father of American Industry?
   b. Draw Conclusions How do you think visitors reacted when they saw the Lowell mills?

Critical Thinking

5. **Categorize** Use your notes and a graphic organizer like the one below to show how various factors helped start the Industrial Revolution.

Factors in the Start of the Industrial Revolution				
Government	Agriculture	Land	Labor	Capital

FOCUS ON WRITING

6. **Persuasion** Imagine that you are a highly skilled millworker living in Great Britain in about 1800. Write an outline for the main points you would make to government officials to persuade them that you should be allowed to go to the United States to start a textile business.

Direct Teach

Reading Focus

Industrialization Spreads

Explain What delayed industrialization in France and Germany? *French Revolution, Napoleonic wars; Germany had no central government*

Identify Cause and Effect How did the Meiji bring industry to Japan? *passed reforms to modernize political and economic systems*

Review & Assess

Close

Have students list the factors that brought about the Industrial Revolution and the inventions that pushed the revolution forward.

Review

Online Quiz, Section 1

Assess

SE Section 1 Assessment

Progress Assessment: Section 1 Quiz

Alternative Assessment Handbook

Reteach/Intervene

Interactive Reader and Study Guide, Section 1

Interactive Skills Tutor CD-ROM

Section 1 Assessment Answers

1. **a.** land, labor, and capital
   b. seed drill improvements in breeding increased food supply, population grew; evicted farmers joined industrial workforce
   c. possible answers—powerful navy protected shipping; enclosure movement
2. **a.** the spinning frame
   b. caused job loss, changed work pattern
   c. work under close supervision, unsafe conditions; rapid growth of towns and cities
3. **a.** textile industry
   b. possible answers—Families needed the money; children could fit into mine shafts.
4. **a.** brought industrial knowledge to America
   b. possible answer—amazed by the size of the operation and the advanced technology
5. Government—laws favored businesses; Agriculture—experimental farming methods; enclosure movement; Land—Britain had coal, iron, and water; Labor—growing population supplied a large workforce; Capital—Britain prospered, had skilled workers and inventors
6. Outlines should show an understanding of the textile industry during the Industrial Revolution.

Answers

Reading Skills *possible answer—The previous government took little interest in Japan's economy.*

Reading Check *Britain industrialized first, America and Europe benefited from earlier inventions; Lowell factory in Massachusetts was first all-in-one mill; political issues delayed industrial development in continental Europe*

Preteach

Getting Started

Use the **Interactive Reader and Study Guide** to familiarize students with the section content.

Interactive Reader and Study Guide, Section 2

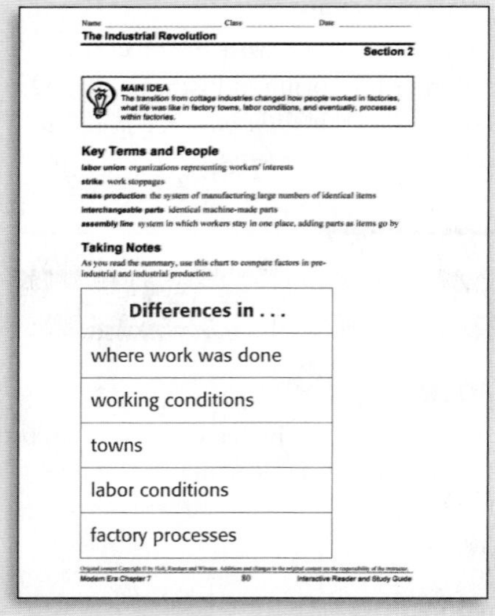

Name ________ Class ________ Date ________

The Industrial Revolution

Section 2

MAIN IDEA
The transition from cottage industries changed how people worked in factories, what life was like in factory towns, labor conditions, and eventually, processes within factories.

Key Terms and People

labor union organizations representing workers' interests
strike work stoppages
mass production the system of manufacturing large numbers of identical items
interchangeable parts identical machine-made parts
assembly line system in which workers stay in one place, adding parts as items go by

Taking Notes

As you read the summary, use this chart to compare factors in pre-industrial and industrial production.

Differences in . . .
where work was done
working conditions
towns
labor conditions
factory processes

Academic Vocabulary

Review with students the high-use academic term in this section.

invest to commit money in order to make a financial return (p. 245)

CRF: Vocabulary Builder: Section 2

Taking Notes

where work was done—homes vs. factories; working conditions—comfortable vs. unsanitary and noisy; towns—small towns and villages vs. large cities; labor conditions—direct contact with merchants vs. contact with managers and factory owners; factory processes—required wide range of skills vs. mass production, repetitive tasks

go.hrw.com
Online Resources

KEYWORD: SHL IND
ACTIVITY: Labor Unions

Section 2 Factories and Workers

Before You Read

Main Idea

The transition from cottage industries changed how people worked in factories, what life was like in factory towns, labor conditions, and, eventually, processes within factories.

Reading Focus

1. How was production organized before factories?
2. What were factories and factory towns like?
3. How did the factory system affect workers?
4. What was mass production, and what were its effects?

Key Terms

labor union
strike
mass production
interchangeable parts
assembly line

Taking Notes Create a table to compare the differences in pre-industrial and industrial production in terms of the factors listed.

Differences in . . .
where work was done
working conditions
towns
labor conditions
factory processes

The Inside Story ***How did the early Industrial Revolution affect families?*** In 1795 writer Hannah More told a story about a large family in Lancashire, in northern England. The father worked in the coal mine, and the wife and children worked at home spinning fiber into thread and running a small dairy farm. There was not enough work at home to keep all the children busy, though, so three of them, including nine-year-old Mary, went to work with their father in the coal mine. Gradually the family's income increased, thanks to the children's hard work. But tragedy soon struck. The father died in a mine accident, the mother lost her mind from so much grief, and Mary struggled to keep her sisters and brothers fed. Although we do not know if this story of Mary's family was true, the problems it describes were true for many real families. The early years of the Industrial Revolution brought hardships to many British families, whether they worked in the mines or the factories. ■

This scene of textile workers making cloth at home was a common one until the late 1700s.

Teach the Main Idea

At Level

Factories and Workers

1. **Teach** Ask students the Reading Focus questions to teach this section.
2. **Apply** Organize students into pairs. Have each pair create a two-column chart and write short descriptions of production, labor, and family life before and after industrialization.
3. **Review** As you review the section, have students describe the changes that industrialization brought to individuals, families, workplaces, and towns.
4. **Practice/Homework** Have students write a series of journal entries from the point of view of a worker who has been forced to switch from a cottage industry to factory work. **LS Verbal-Linguistic**

Alternative Assessment Handbook, Rubric 15: Journals

Production before Factories

Production of goods for others did not begin with the Industrial Revolution. Instead, it began many years earlier with cottage industries, when workers produced goods at home.

Work in the Home In cottage industries, workers who produced finished goods dealt directly with merchants. Like other such industries, the manufacturing of textiles followed several steps.

In the first step, a merchant delivered raw materials to the weaver's cottage. In the early textile industry, the raw material was usually wool. Next, the weavers and their families processed the wool in several stages, from raw material to finished product. They hand-spun the fiber into thread and wove the thread into cloth. When the cloth was finished, the merchant picked it up and took it to market.

Work at home had some clear benefits. The weavers controlled their work schedules and product quality. They could work faster when they needed to earn more money. Or, they could work more slowly to make cloth of the highest quality. Also, family life revolved around the business. Weavers made their own decisions on when to work and rest, depending on the family's needs. They could make adjustments for illness, holidays, and the seasons.

Problems for Cottage Industries Even though working in the home had benefits for workers such as weavers, it also had disadvantages. A fire or flood that destroyed the home's equipment could ruin a family in an instant. Also, cloth-making demanded a range of technical skills for the various steps—skills that took a long time to learn. Moreover, only adults had the physical strength that some jobs, such as weaving on a loom, required. The typical home loom was at least six feet wide and required strength to operate. So, if the parents fell ill or died, the children could not take their places. As textile production and then other occupations moved from the cottage to the factory, business owners were able to take advantage of the problems these drawbacks caused for workers.

READING CHECK **Find the Main Idea** What were some benefits of the cottage system of production?

Factories and Factory Towns

A major change from the cottage industry system to the factory system was where employees worked. A factory laborer had to leave his or her home and work in a place built especially for industry. For some workers, a job in a factory was a welcome way to support the family. For many workers, however, the factory system caused real hardship.

Working in a Factory Factory work was divided into several separate, easily learned tasks, and each worker was assigned to one task. As a result, children could learn jobs as well as adults could. Many families fleeing poverty in the countryside would send their boys and girls—some as young as six years old—to work in the factories. In fact, some factory owners preferred hiring children because they could pay them lower wages. Still, the majority of factory workers were adult men.

Factory work was dangerous for all workers, but children faced special hazards. For example, one problem with early weaving looms was that the threads often snapped. Children, with their small hands, could reach into the still-running machines to retrieve the broken threads more easily than adults. Some children lost fingers in the process. Because there was no safety protection from the massive machines, such severe injuries were common.

The workday was long—more than twelve hours for even very young children. Noise, lack of ventilation, poor sanitation, and inadequate food added to the hardship.

Poor factory conditions were common throughout the late 1700s and into the 1800s. In the 1830s, however, the public began to take notice and ask for improvements. Some of the requests came from the child workers:

HISTORY'S VOICES

> **"We respect our masters, and are willing to work for our support, and that of our parents, but we want time for more rest, a little play, and to learn to read and write. We do not think it right that we should know nothing but work and suffering, from Monday morning to Saturday night, to make others rich. Do, good gentlemen, inquire carefully into our concern."**
>
> —submission from the Manchester's Factory Children Committee to the House of Commons, 1836

Direct Teach

Reading Focus

1 How was production organized before factories? *in small cottage industries; a family worked together to produce goods such as cloth or barrels*

Production before Factories

Describe What happened after a merchant dropped off wool at a weaver's cottage? *family hand-spun the fiber into thread, wove threads into cloth; merchant picked up cloth, took it to market*

Evaluate Would you choose to work in a cottage industry or in a factory? Explain. *possible answers—cottage industry: time with family, freedom of work schedule; factory: easier to learn single task, some security in employment*

Reading Focus

2 What were factories and factory towns like? *factories—often dangerous; work divided into separate, easily-learned tasks; low wages; long hours; factory towns—comprised of shoddy, close-packed company dwellings; polluted; poor sanitation*

Factories and Factory Towns

Summarize What hardships were part of factory work? *dangerous conditions, long work days, noise, lack of ventilation, poor sanitation, inadequate food*

Draw Conclusions Why were children sent to work in factories? Explain. *Families desperately needed money; some factory owners preferred hiring children.*

Differentiating Instruction

Below Level

English-Language Learners

Materials: construction paper, colored markers

1. Review with students the information in the text about cottage industries and factory work.
2. Have each student create a two-panel drawing. The first panel should feature a family at work in a cottage industry. The second panel should show the same family members after they have begun working in a factory. Encourage students to highlight the differences between the two systems in their drawings. Have students present their drawings to the class.
3. As an extension, have students write a paragraph explaining why the family was forced to switch to factory work. **LS Visual-Spatial**

Alternative Assessment Handbook, Rubric 3: Artwork

Answers

Reading Check *workers made decisions about when to work, rest, and eat, how much to produce; family could adjust work schedule, all family members could be involved*

Factories and Factory Towns

Explain Why did companies provide housing to employees? *Families from the countryside needed housing.*

Identify What were the hazards of coal as a power source? *thick, dark soot; poisonous chemicals in the air*

Make Generalizations Why do you think conditions in Manchester became so terrible? *possible answer— city unable to cope with overcrowding; factory owners didn't care about conditions or the environment*

Activity **Manchester Poem** Have students write a poem lamenting the conditions in Manchester. **LS** **Auditory-Musical**

📖 **Alternative Assessment Handbook,** Rubric 26: Poems and Songs

Primary Source

"How little can the rich man know
Of what the poor man feels,
When Want like some dark demon foe,
Nearer and nearer steals!...

He never saw his darlings lie
Shivering, the grass their bed;
He never heard that maddening cry,
'Daddy, a bit of bread!'"
 —"Manchester Song", quoted by
 Elizabeth Gaskell in
 *Mary Barton: A Tale of
 Manchester Life*

Find several images that illustrate life before and after industrialization. Display them for students to see.

Answers

Reading Check *injuries, long workdays, noise, lack of ventilation, poor sanitation, inadequate food*

Life in Factory Towns Factories changed not just the lives of their workers, but also the towns where the factories were located. Along rivers, large mill operations sprang up quickly. Whole towns grew up around the factories. Some companies provided housing to their employees, many of whom arrived from the countryside with few belongings and nowhere to stay. Families crowded into shoddy, close-packed company dwellings.

When water power changed to steam power, manufacturing towns rose near the coal mines also. The hazards of burning coal for producing steam quickly became apparent. Thick soot from the burning coal blanketed towns, turning day into night. The smoke sent sulfur and other poisonous chemicals into the air.

Factories for smelting, or refining, iron were often built near coal mines. They sent more dark, smoky pollution into the air. The iron smelting factories in one region of northwestern England emitted so much pollution that the region was nicknamed "black country." Because the iron-smelting required fires, one American visitor to the region called it "black by day and red by night."

North of this region lay the textile city of Manchester—the British city that came to symbolize the problems of industrialization. Sanitation statistics provide detail. According to one account, some neighborhoods of Manchester had only two toilets for every 250 residents. Under such conditions, disease spread easily. As a result, about six children in ten died before the age of five.

READING CHECK **Identify Supporting Details** What are some facts that illustrate the difficulties of factory work?

★ Interactive
HISTORY CLOSE-UP

Factory Work

With industrialization, more and more people went to work in factories to produce goods such as textiles. Although factory jobs were difficult and dangerous, they provided a living.

In the large image you see what it was like to work in a textile factory in about 1835. The smaller drawing shows a cutaway view of a similar factory of a few years earlier.

Ventilation was poor. Dust and fibers drfiting in the air caused tuberculosis and other illnesses.

Workers who arrived at the factory late were punished. Keeping track of the time was hard for families who could not afford a clock.

Foremen sometimes beat children who talked too much or worked too slowly.

Children often had to scramble under the still-running machines, and accidents were common. One hospital reported that each year it treated 1,000 injuries caused by factory machines.

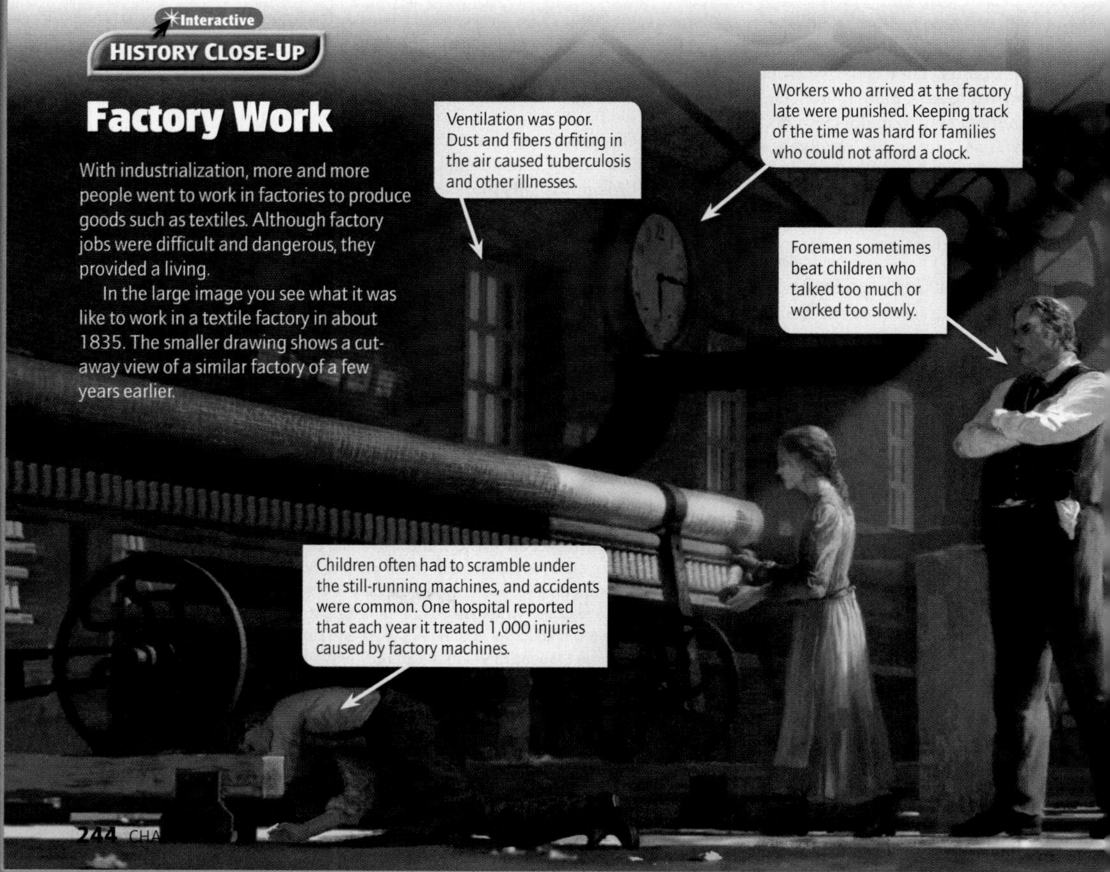

Differentiating Instruction

Above Level

Advanced Learners/Gifted and Talented

Materials: butcher paper, art supplies

1. Review the effects that industrialization had on towns such as Manchester.

2. Organize students into small groups. Have each group write an official petition to city officials in Manchester and a petition to Parliament asking for improved conditions within the city. Student petitions should focus on the need for improved sanitation, working conditions, child labor laws, and environmental conditions.

3. Have students share their petitions with the class.

4. Guide students in a discussion of the petitions. Did the petitions address all the needs of Manchester residents and workers? **LS** **Intrapersonal, Verbal-Linguistic**

📖 **Alternative Assessment Handbook,** Rubric 43: Writing to Persuade

The Factory System and Workers

Factories changed more than just families and towns. They also transformed the very nature of labor, as industry moved from the home to the factory.

Workers in a New Economy The factory system required large amounts of capital, or money, to pay for building the factories and installing the machinery. This produced three main levels of participants within the system:

- wealthy business people to <u>invest</u> in and own the factories
- mid-level employees to run the factories and supervise the day-to-day operations
- low-level employees to run the machines.

Employers who invested their money expected to make a profit. They shared little of their profits with their employees, who were paid only for the hours they worked. At the same time, no one worker was responsible for the product's quality, and factory workers had little incentive to improve their job performance. Quality could decline.

Also, workers were plentiful. British factories had no trouble finding former farm workers displaced by the enclosure movement. In the United States, immigrants were glad to find any work they could.

Employers often preferred hiring women and children because men expected higher wages. Men were also seen as not taking orders as readily. In addition, many people saw unskilled factory jobs as inappropriate for men. Factory work was seen as "women's work."

ACADEMIC VOCABULARY
invest to commit money in order to make a financial return

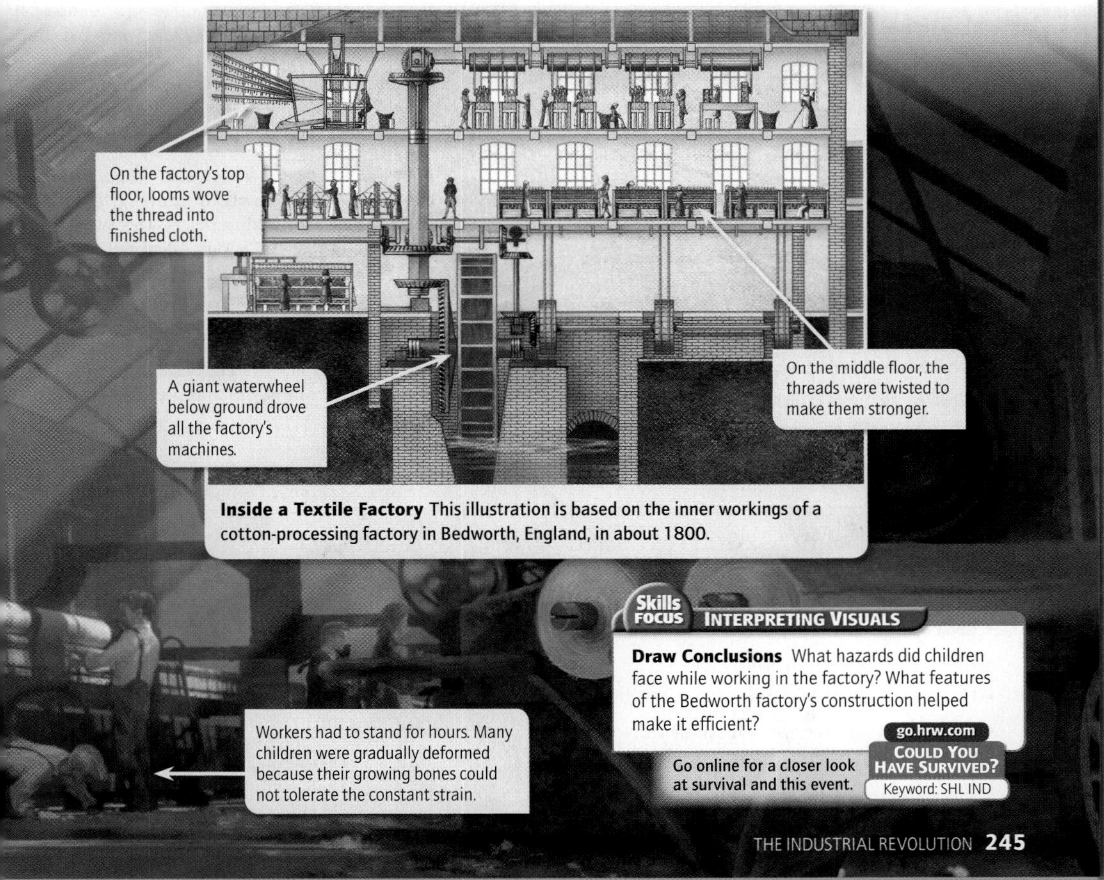

On the factory's top floor, looms wove the thread into finished cloth.
On the middle floor, the threads were twisted to make them stronger.
A giant waterwheel below ground drove all the factory's machines.
Workers had to stand for hours. Many children were gradually deformed because their growing bones could not tolerate the constant strain.

Inside a Textile Factory This illustration is based on the inner workings of a cotton-processing factory in Bedworth, England, in about 1800.

Skills Focus INTERPRETING VISUALS

Draw Conclusions What hazards did children face while working in the factory? What features of the Bedworth factory's construction helped make it efficient?

go.hrw.com
Go online for a closer look at survival and this event.
COULD YOU HAVE SURVIVED?
Keyword: SHL IND

Direct Teach

Reading Focus

3 How did the factory system affect workers? *workers paid only for hours worked; little incentive to improve job performance; large supply of unskilled workers; employers preferred women and children*

The Factory System and Workers

Compare What did mid-level and regular employees have in common? *Both worked for factory owners.*

Analyze How did the large labor supply hurt individual workers? *Discontented workers had few options; other workers were willing to replace them.*

CRF: Literature: *Hard Times*

History Close-Up

Factory Work

Development of Management
Originally, factory owners managed their factories personally. As factories grew and employed more people, one person could no longer supervise so many workers. Management positions were created and many administrative responsibilities fell to managers, who took instructions from owners. The role of managers has grown steadily and now they are an integral part of most industries. People in management positions are often well-paid, highly respected professionals.

About the Illustration
This illustration is an artist's conception based on available sources. Historians, however, are uncertain exactly what this scene looked like.

Skills Focus: Identifying Problem and Solution

Below Level

Reading Skill
Company Meeting

Materials: butcher paper, markers

1. Review with students the different levels of employees within the factory system and the working conditions within the factories.
2. Organize students into three groups: business owners, mid-level employees, and lower-level employees. Have each group work together to make a list of complaints to present at the company meeting. Have students write the complaints on butcher paper.
3. Hold a company meeting during class. Have volunteers from each group read its list of complaints to the class.
4. Post the lists for students to see, and guide students in a discussion about whether compromises could be reached on any common issues among the three groups.

LS Interpersonal, Verbal-Linguistic

Alternative Assessment Handbook, Rubrics 14: Group Activity; and 35: Solving Problems

Answers

History Close-Up *poor ventilation, machine-related injuries, punishment from foremen, bone deformation; tasks separated by floor*

Direct Teach

Reading Focus

The Factory System and Workers

Explain How did British workers react to the government's unwillingness to change labor conditions? *organized, formed labor unions, went on strike*

Draw Conclusions Why did the British government ignore the problems of workers and the unemployed? *did not believe these were government problems; thought people would lose incentive to work harder*

CRF: Biography: Nellie Bly

Effects of the Factory System

QUICK FACTS

Evaluate What effects do you think the factory system had on families? *possible answer—unable to spend much time together, informal education interrupted for children*

Quick Facts Transparency: Effects of the Factory System

Info to Know

Chartism The Reform Act of 1832 widened voting rights in Britain but included property requirements that excluded people of the lower classes. In 1836 organizers formed the London Working Men's Association and drew up a charter of political demands. The so-called Chartists used public meetings, petitions, and strikes to draw attention to their cause. Some Chartists even threatened physical force if their demands were not met. Although the movement eventually died out, its goals were taken on by others and many reforms were passed in the second half of the 19th century.

Cottage Workers' Unrest One group of people faced a particular challenge caused by the factory system. These were the weavers and other cottage industry workers still trying to earn their living by making goods at home. Their handmade goods were more expensive than factory-made items, so they had a hard time selling them. Facing ruin, some of these workers turned to violence.

One night in 1811, masked workers attacked a textile factory in Nottingham, England. The incident marked the beginning of the Luddite movement. The Luddites, named after a General Ned Ludd who probably did not exist, opposed machines that were "hurtful to the commonality"—in other words, that put them out of work. Luddites burned factories and smashed machines but tried to avoid injuring people. During 1812 the movement quickly spread to other cities. Several Luddites were caught and hanged, though, and the Luddite movement ended quickly.

THE IMPACT TODAY
People who resist using today's new technologies are sometimes called Luddites.

Changing Labor Conditions The severe treatment of the Luddites illustrates that the British government did not want to get involved in factory problems. Government leaders did not see regulating business as their job. Many citizens thought that if the government helped poor people too much, they would lose their incentive to work harder. As a result, the government did not pass laws relating to work hours, safety, or child labor.

Because the government took no action, in the early 1800s British workers started to organize. They formed the first **labor unions**, which are organizations representing workers' interests. To urge employers to raise wages and improve conditions, unions in Britain organized **strikes**, or work stoppages. At first, Parliament banned unions and strikes, fearing social and economic trouble.

Slowly, pressure from the public and unions brought change. Hearings in Parliament in 1832 produced the Sadler Report, which described abuses in the factories. Eventually Britain passed laws that limited work hours for adults and children. Another law required child workers to be at least nine years old. In 1871 Parliament legalized labor unions.

American workers also organized. In the United States, the first nationwide labor unions developed in the mid-1800s.

A New Class of Workers While factory conditions were slowly improving, another process was also taking place—the growth of the middle class. The middle class included the various groups, or types, of workers that were in the middle income range, between the rich factory owners and the poor factory workers.

Several groups of workers who were essential to the factory system became part of the middle class. Managers and accountants kept

EFFECTS OF THE FACTORY SYSTEM (QUICK FACTS)

Before the Factory System

- Goods were produced in the home.
- Work required a wide range of skills.
- Children did chores at home with the family.
- Families worked directly with merchants.
- Few people were members of the middle class.

After the Factory System

- Good were produced in factories.
- Work required a few easily learned skills.
- Children were employed in large numbers in factories.
- Workers dealt with managers and, sometimes, factory owners.
- More people joined the middle class.

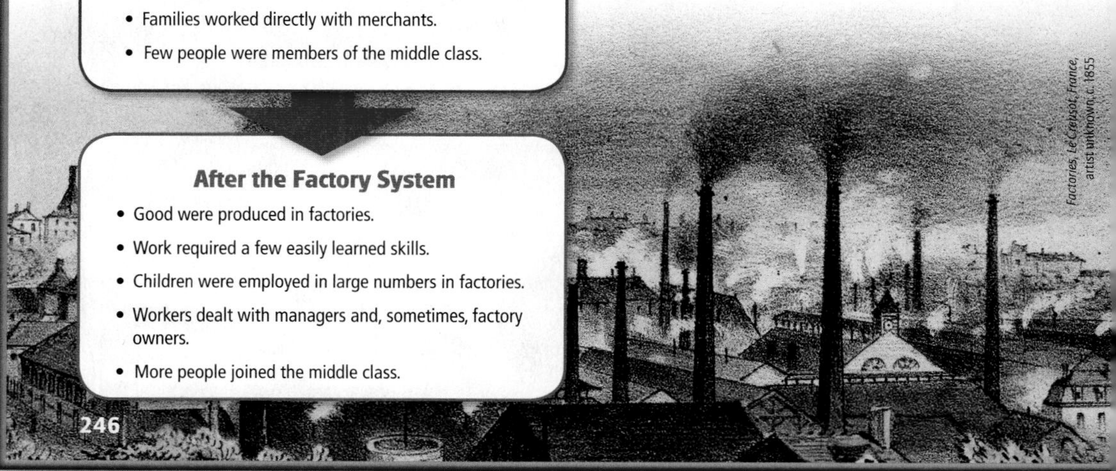

Factories, Le Creusot, France, artist unknown, c. 1855

246

Differentiating Instruction

Above Level

Advanced Learners/Gifted and Talented

1. Have students consider these questions: If you were a discontented worker in industrial Britain, what options would you have? What actions would you take to change your situation? Have students write a half-page response to these two questions.
2. Organize students into small groups. Have groups discuss their responses and select the one that they believe might be most effective and achievable.
3. Guide students in a discussion about the various options that discontented workers had. Also discuss the probable outcome of various actions.
4. As an extension, have students watch the classic silent film *Metropolis* and then discuss its imagery and symbolism. **LS Intrapersonal, Verbal-Linguistic**

Alternative Assessment Handbook, Rubrics 11: Discussions; and 41: Writing to Express

Answers

Reading Check *Different groups that were part of the factory system became part of the middle class.*

the factories running and their books balanced. Engineers designed the machines, and mechanics kept them in good repair. Other workers transported the goods to market while still others were engaged in sales of those goods. As the income from increased manufacturing, buying, and selling spread throughout the economy, more people entered the middle class.

READING CHECK **Identify Cause and Effect** How the factory system affected different groups?

Factories and Mass Production

The factory system certainly changed the world of work. In addition, new processes further changed how people worked in factories and what they could produce.

The Process of Mass Production Many changes in industry evolved fully in the United States. One of these changes was the development of **mass production**—the system of manufacturing large numbers of identical items. Elements of mass production, including interchangeable parts and the assembly line, came to be known as the American system.

Interchangeable parts are identical machine-made parts. They made production and repair of factory-made goods more efficient. Before industrialization, one skilled worker might have made an entire gun, clock, or other product by himself. He would make or gather all the parts and assemble them. The process could be slow, and because the parts were all handmade, the finished products were a little different from each other. With interchangeable parts, though, one worker could put together many identical products in a short time. Making repairs was easier, too, because replacement parts did not have to be custom-made to fit.

The other element of mass production related to movement within factories. In early workshops, the product stayed in one place and workers moved around it, adding parts and making refinements. An innovation was the **assembly line**. In an assembly line, the product moves from worker to worker, as each one performs a step in the manufacturing process. With this division of labor, workers can make many items quickly.

Effects of Mass Production Mass production had advantages and disadvantages. A big advantage was a dramatic increase in production. Businesses that made many items quickly could charge less per item. As a result, more people could afford to buy these mass-produced goods.

For employees, however, mass production could lead to more repetitious jobs. At first, some workers protested, refusing to work quickly. But the changes could not be stopped, and mass production became the norm in factories.

READING CHECK **Summarize** What was mass production?

SECTION 2 ASSESSMENT

go.hrw.com
Online Quiz
Keyword: SHL IND HP

Reviewing Ideas, Terms, and People

1. **a. Describe** How did the textile business work when it was a cottage industry?
   b. Compare List some advantages and disadvantages of cottage industry.
2. **a. Recall** Why were early factory towns unhealthy?
   b. Explain Why was factory work especially dangerous for children?
   c. Infer If working in factories and living in the cities was so terrible, why did people stay?
3. **a. Identify** What was the structure of authority within the new factories?
   b. Infer What factors combined to keep workers' wages low?
   c. Evaluate Why might workers have been reluctant to hold a **strike** in the early years of the factory system?
4. **a. Define** What were the two main components of the **American system** of mass production?
   b. Develop Why would the American system help many industries grow larger and richer?

Critical Thinking

5. **Analyze** Use your notes to fill in a chart like the one below by analyzing the effects of the factory system. Who do you think benefited the most and least from the changes?

Industrial Production	
Advantages	Disadvantages

FOCUS ON WRITING

6. **Narration** Write a paragraph or two in which you describe the changes that a typical English town and its residents might have experienced in the 1800s as industries developed in the town.

Direct Teach

Reading Focus

4 What was mass production, and what were its effects? *system of manufacturing large numbers of identical items; large increase in production, decrease in prices, standardization of measurements, repetitive jobs*

Factories and Mass Production

Describe How was a product made before the development of interchangeable parts? *One skilled worker made the entire product; as a result, each finished product was slightly different.*

Make Inferences Why do you think some workers resisted mass production? *possible answer—Working in factories might have been boring and repetitive.*

Review & Assess

Close

Have students explain how the factory system led to changes in all aspects of people's lives.

Review

Online Quiz, Section 2

Assess

SE Section 2 Assessment

Progress Assessment: Section 2 Quiz

Alternative Assessment Handbook

Reteach/Intervene

Interactive Reader and Study Guide, Section 2

Interactive Skills Tutor CD-ROM

Section 2 Assessment Answers

1. **a.** merchant brought wool to cottage, weaver made cloth, merchant took cloth to market
   b. advantage—worker could adjust schedule; disadvantage—fire or floods
2. **a.** chemicals, pollution, poor sanitation
   b. could be injured while using machines
   c. had no other way to make a living
3. **a.** business owner at top, mid-level employees, regular employees at bottom
   b. business owners who cared only about making a profit, willing workers were plentiful
   c. Unions and strikes were illegal.
4. **a.** interchangeable parts, assembly line
   b. allowed for increased production, lower prices, increased sales
5. advantages—increased production, lower prices, availability of products; disadvantages—harsh working conditions, pollution, child mortality, ended cottage industries; factory owners: most; employees: least
6. Student paragraphs or essays should convey the effect of industry on English towns.

Answers

Reading Check *a system of manufacturing large numbers of identical items*

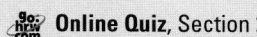

Preteach

Getting Started

Use the **Interactive Reader and Study Guide** to familiarize students with the section content.

Interactive Reader and Study Guide, Section 3

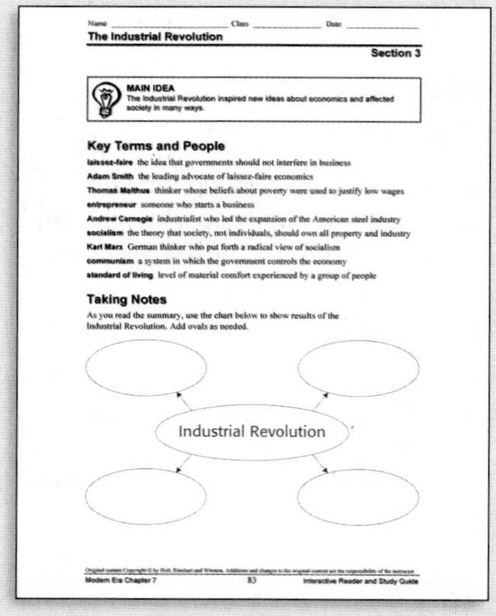

Name ______ Class ______ Date ______

The Industrial Revolution

Section 3

MAIN IDEA
The Industrial Revolution inspired new ideas about economics and affected society in many ways.

Key Terms and People

laissez-faire the idea that governments should not interfere in business
Adam Smith the leading advocate of laissez-faire economics
Thomas Malthus thinker whose beliefs about poverty were used to justify low wages
entrepreneur someone who starts a business
Andrew Carnegie industrialist who led the expansion of the American steel industry
socialism the theory that society, not individuals, should own all property and industry
Karl Marx German thinker who put forth a radical view of socialism
communism a system in which the government controls the economy
standard of living level of material comfort experienced by a group of people

Taking Notes

As you read the summary, use the chart below to show results of the Industrial Revolution. Add ovals as needed.

Industrial Revolution

Academic Vocabulary

Review with students the high-use academic term in this section.

stance attitude or position (p. 250)

CRF: Vocabulary Builder: Section 3

Taking Notes

new ideas about economics; entrepreneurs built fortunes; new industries developed; lives of women changed; migration of job seekers from countryside to city; cities became crowded and dangerous; pollution of air and water; population grew rapidly; standard of living in industrialized countries improved; Great Britain, France, and Germany emerged as global leaders; United States benefited from industrialization

go.hrw.com
Online Resources

KEYWORD: SHL IND
ACTIVITY: Historic Origins of Socialism and Capitalism

SECTION 3

New Ideas in a New Society

Before You Read

Main Idea

The Industrial Revolution inspired new ideas about economics and affected society in many ways.

Reading Focus

1. What new ideas about economics developed during the Industrial Revolution?
2. What competing economic ideas arose as a result?
3. How did the Industrial Revolution affect society?

Key Terms and People

laissez-faire
Adam Smith
Thomas Malthus
entrepreneur
Andrew Carnegie
socialism
Karl Marx
communism
standard of living

TAKING NOTES Take notes on the new ideas of the Industrial Revolution.

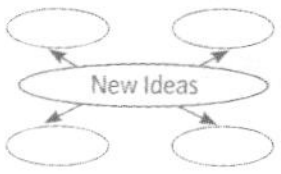

THE INSIDE STORY ***What marvels of industry were displayed in a glass palace?*** In 1851 the Great Exhibition in London drew residents and visitors to a huge glass and iron building called the Crystal Palace. Inside the marvelous structure were nearly 14,000 exhibits, many of which displayed industrial products and processes. English writer Charlotte Brontë was dazzled by the exhibition: "It is a wonderful place—vast, strange, new, and impossible to describe. Its grandeur does not consist in *one* thing, but in the unique assemblage of *all* things." Brontë was impressed by the wide range of exhibits, including "great compartments filled with railway engines and boilers, with mill machinery in full work . . ." All these remarkable exhibits showed the accomplishments of the Industrial Revolution. People came from far away to gawk at those achievements. In fact, some 6 million visitors from across Europe and elsewhere attended the exhibition. ■

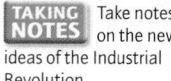

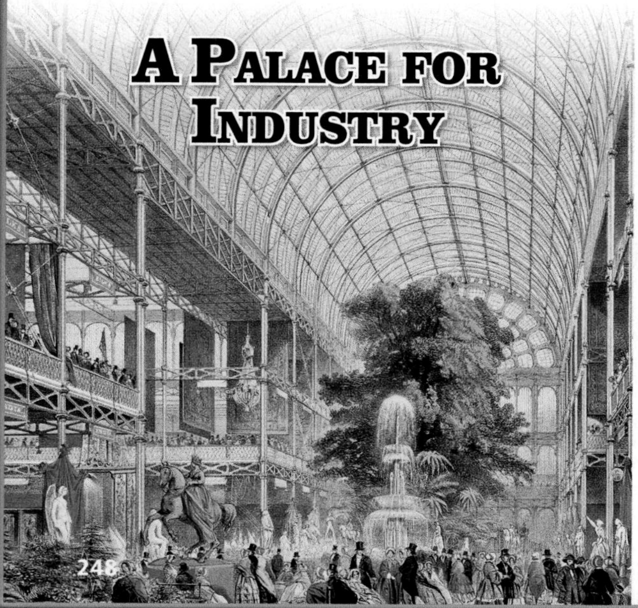

◀ Visitors crowded into the Crystal Palace to view the displays.

Dickinsons' Pictures of Great Exhibition, 1851

New Ideas about Economics

During the late 1700s and early 1800s industrialization was changing not just products and work, but also how people thought about economics. One change was that mercantilism was giving way to capitalism and competition.

Capitalism and Competition Under the old mercantile system, governments restricted trade to protect their own industries from foreign competition. Then, starting in the late 1700s, some people said that governments should not interfere in business. This idea is called **laissez-faire** (lehz-ay-FEHR) economics, from a French phrase meaning "free to do."

248

Teach the Main Idea

At Level

Results of the Industrial Revolution

1. **Teach** Ask students the Reading Focus questions to teach this section.
2. **Apply** Have students create two Web diagrams for the section, one that shows the key people and their ideas and the other that shows the costs and benefits of industrialization.
3. **Review** As you review the section, have students explain the different political and economic ideas that came out of the Industrial Revolution.
4. **Practice/Homework** Have students write a one-page essay on the positive and negative results of the Industrial Revolution.
LS Visual-Spatial, Verbal-Linguistic

Alternative Assessment Handbook, Rubric 37: Writing Assignments

Adam Smith became the leading advocate of laissez-faire economics. In 1776 he published *The Wealth of Nations*, in which he analyzed the definition and creation of wealth. Smith wrote that markets free from government interference benefited all. Such an economic system free from regulation is called a market economy. Also in a market economy, businesses can compete freely against each other for trade. The British government agreed with Smith's ideas and ended most regulations by the 1840s.

Smith influenced **Thomas Malthus**, who was concerned about population growth caused by the development of industry. Malthus wrote that the population would always grow faster than food production. Therefore, he concluded, poverty and misery would never go away. Population growth, Malthus said, was slowed only by war, disease, famine, and decreased reproduction. Because many people agreed that these problems were unavoidable, Malthus' ideas were used to justify low wages and laws that limited charity to the poor.

In time, Malthus was proved wrong. The disasters he predicted did not happen, but the population did grow. Still, the ideas of Smith and Malthus affected attitudes. As Smith predicted, industrialization succeeded and spread. Industrial capitalism emerged as the main economic pattern in the Western world.

New Roles for Business Leaders Industrialization also changed the roles that business leaders played in public life. Before the Industrial Revolution, people who owned land controlled the wealth and power. But by the mid-1800s, the leaders of industry began taking away the landowners' influence. Some industrialists became extremely wealthy, and their new wealth bought them political power.

The Industrial Revolution also highlighted the role of the **entrepreneur**, someone who starts a new business. Among the entrepreneurs were financiers, bankers, and investors who pooled their money to create large corporations. As demand increased for capital to build factories, banking and finance became more important occupations. Some industrialists made fortunes simply by buying and selling companies for a profit.

A few industrialists, mainly in the United States, built some of the largest corporate empires ever seen—and acquired wealth that few people could imagine. In the late 1800s, their stories helped make them famous.

Andrew Carnegie, who was born in Scotland, was an example of "rags to riches" success. His father, a weaver, was driven out of work by the textile mills. The family moved to America, and Carnegie started working in a mill at age 12. With hard work, creativity, intelligence, and tough business practices, he led the expansion of the American steel industry.

PRIMARY SOURCES

A View of Andrew Carnegie

Andrew Carnegie, who took the steel industry to new heights, gave away some $350 million to fund various charities. This cartoon from *Punch,* a satirical British magazine, shows Carnegie giving $2 million to Scottish universities. The original title is "The MacMillion."

Punch, May 29, 1901

Carnegie's clothing is a combination of the traditional Scottish kilt and the American flag.

The mortarboards, which are the headgear for college graduates, are labeled with the names of Scottish universities.

Skills Focus READING LIKE A HISTORIAN

1. **Analyze** What might Carnegie's clothing have meant to people at the time?
2. **Evaluate** How do you think the artist felt about Carnegie's donation? Explain your answer.

See **Skills Handbook**, p. H25

Direct Teach

Reading Focus

1 *What new ideas about economics developed during the Industrial Revolution? laissez-faire economics,* The Wealth of Nations, *increased role of entrepreneur*

New Ideas about Economics

Describe What is *The Wealth of Nations* about? *analyzes wealth and how it is created; states that markets free from regulation would benefit all*

Make Inferences How were Malthus's ideas used to justify low wages? *Poverty would never go away, so there was no reason to combat it with higher wages.*

Make Generalizations How did industrialists and entrepreneurs become extremely powerful? *took away influence of landowners, pooled money to create corporations, used tough business practices, acquired enormous wealth*

Primary Source

"Upon the sacredness of property civilization itself depends—the right of the laborer to his hundred dollars in the savings bank, and equally the legal right of the millionaire to his millions."

—Andrew Carnegie, "Wealth" from the *North American Review*, June 1889

Primary Source

"In a sense, the theory of the Communists may be summed up in a single sentence: Abolition of private property."

—Karl Marx and Friedrich Engels, *The Communist Manifesto*, 1848

Differentiating Instruction

Below Level

Learners Having Difficulty

1. Draw the graphic organizer for students to see. Omit the italicized answers.

New Industrialists

Who were they?	What did they do (positive)?	What did they do (negative)?
Carnegie, Rockefeller, Vanderbilt	*built large businesses, gave to charity*	*drove competitors out of business, did not allow unions*

2. Organize students into mixed-ability pairs. Have pairs copy and complete the graphic organizer. **LS Visual-Spatial**

Alternative Assessment Handbook, Rubric 13: Graphic Organizers

Answers

Reading Like a Historian 1. *His traditional Scottish clothing indicates he was pro Scottish.* **2.** *possible answer—thought Carnegie was too generous because artist shows him throwing money*

Direct Teach

Reading Focus

2 What competing economic ideas arose as a result? *socialism, communism*

Competing Economic Views

Contrast How is socialism different from capitalism? *Under capitalism, individuals own property and control industry, whereas under socialism, the government or society does.*

Interpret How were Robert Owen's ideas applied in New Lanark? *emphasis on good of all, good working conditions, nonprofit stores, free schooling, strict rules*

Predict What factors might have led to the failure of New Harmony? *possible answer—economic failure, conflicts within community*

Info to Know

Robert Owen Robert Owen began his career as an entrepreneur in the textile industry. When he purchased New Lanark, one of his first actions was to set up a school nearby. He stopped employing children under the age of ten, and sent them to school instead. Fearing a loss of money, Owen's partners protested. In response, Owen borrowed money to buy out his partners' shares of the business.

PRIMARY SOURCES

The Iron Law of Wages

The ideas of Adam Smith and Thomas Malthus had many admirers. Among them was David Ricardo (1772–1823), an English banker. In an 1817 work, Ricardo argued that natural economic forces would keep wages low—so low that workers barely had enough to survive. Ricardo's theory came to be called The Iron Law of Wages, indicating that the "law" was real and unchangeable. The theory was popular with factory owners, since it justified their paying low wages to their employees.

"It is when the market price of labour exceeds its natural price that the condition of the labourer is flourishing and happy, that he has it in his power to command a greater proportion of the necessaries and enjoyments of life, and therefore to rear a healthy and numerous family. When, however, by the encouragement which high wages give to the increase of population, the number of labourers is increased, wages again fall to their natural price, and indeed from a reaction sometimes fall below it."

—David Ricardo, *On Wages,* 1817

Like Malthus, Ricardo predicted a rise in population. According to Ricardo, what encourages population growth?

Skills Focus READING LIKE A HISTORIAN

1. **Sequence** According to Ricardo, what is the sequence of the rise and fall of wages?
2. **Draw Conclusions** Do you think Ricardo felt some sympathy with workers? Why or why not?

See **Skills Handbook**, p. H25

Other industrialists achieved similar feats. Examples include Cornelius Vanderbilt in railroads and John D. Rockefeller in oil. These men built giant corporations that drove out their competitors. They were both admired for their contributions to human progress and criticized for their treatment of workers. For example, they were generally against their employees' joining labor unions. Although some, like Andrew Carnegie, gave generously to charity, people who disapproved of their methods sometimes called them "robber barons."

READING CHECK **Summarize** What were some of the new ideas about economics?

Competing Economic Views

Not everyone agreed that laissez-faire capitalism was a good thing. Some thinkers blamed capitalism for bad working conditions and big gaps between the rich and poor. They took a different stance on economic sytems. Two of these men were Robert Owen and Karl Marx.

ACADEMIC VOCABULARY
stance attitude or position

Robert Owen In contrast to the gloomy views of Thomas Malthus, Robert Owen had a more hopeful view of how industry might affect people. He thought that for the good of all, society or the government, instead of individuals, should own property and control industry—a theory called **socialism**. The theory was a clear contrast to capitalism.

To demonstrate his ideas, Owen built a mill complex at New Lanark, Scotland, that gained widespread praise as a model industrial town. The workers there enjoyed good working conditions, shopped at nonprofit stores, lived in decent houses, and could earn sick pay. Because he felt that education improved character, Owen even provided free schooling for the workers' children. He also imposed strict rules on workers' personal lives, including curfews and bathing requirements.

Owen brought his ideas to the United States in 1825, when he founded a community called New Harmony in Indiana. New Harmony was to be a utopia, an ideal community where poverty and other evils of society did not exist. The belief that such communities can solve society's problems is called utopianism.

The efforts of Owens and other people who believed in socialism led to a movement called social democracy. Those who advocated social democracy wanted to move from capitalism to socialism by democratic means.

Skills Focus: Drawing Conclusions

Above Level

Reading Skill
Economic Issues of the Industrial Revolution

Background: Explain to students that for countries to determine whether their economics will be based on free enterprise or on socialism, they must decide what goods will be produced, how goods will be produced, and for whom. Other economic factors arose during the Industrial Revolution, such as monetary systems, and measures of wealth and value determination, which today include such indicators as CPI and GNP.

1. Organize students into small groups.
2. Have groups discuss why these various economic issues arose during the Industrial Revolution, and why different methods of value determination emerged.
3. Guide students in a class discussion about each group's conclusions. **LS Interpersonal, Verbal-Linguistic**

Alternative Assessment Handbook, Rubrics 11: Discussions; and 14: Group Activity

Answers

Primary Sources **1.** *high wages cause population to increase, laborers increase, wages fall;* **2.** *possible answer—Yes, he writes about the workers' happiness, health, and "enjoyments of life."*

Reading Check *mercantilism gave way to capitalism and competition, laissez-faire economics and The* Wealth of Nations *allowed for increased role of entrepeneur*

Karl Marx A more radical view of socialism was put forth by two Germans, Friedrich Engels and **Karl Marx**. They declared that as capitalism grew, more and more workers would sink into poverty. In time they would rebel, seize control of the "means of production"—such as factories and farms—and govern themselves. Capitalism would collapse. Workers would establish a society based on cooperation and equal distribution of wealth. Such a revolution was inevitable, the authors claimed.

In time, Marx would be better known than Engels. In 1867 Marx produced the first volume of *Das Kapital*. In this three-part work, he put forth his arguments against capitalism. One of its evils, Marx said, was how capitalism disrupts the relationship between labor and profit. He thought there should be a direct connection between one's work and one's pay. For example, he thought it was not fair that one worker could toil all day at back-breaking labor and make very little money while another person got rich doing nothing more than sitting in an office speculating on future markets.

Marx thought that socialism could help rid the world of these injustices. However, he believed that the transition to socialism would not happen quickly because many people, especially the wealthier classes, would not see any benefit for themselves. For that reason, he thought the workers would have to control the government. Because the government would then control the economy, a command economy would result. The system in which the government owns almost all the means of production and controls economic planning is called **communism**. Years later, some governments would adopt communism and use it to violate basic human rights and freedom of choice.

READING CHECK **Infer** Why did capitalism provoke strong response from the socialists?

Effects on Society

The rise of new economic ideas was among the countless effects of the Industrial Revolution. Other effects were felt in small and large ways, from how families lived to how countries dealt with each other. For example, the shift away from cottage industries affected home life and the roles of women in society.

Effects on Home Life When work was done in the home, women often worked alongside their husbands. Then when industry drew workers away from home, women were usually the ones who stayed home to care for children. The worlds of work and home began to separate. Women and men were seen as occupying "separate spheres"—the woman in the home and the man in the workplace to support the home and family.

Effects of Industrialization on Women

QUICK FACTS

Women Who Went from Cottage Industries to Factory Work
- Earned low wages in low-skill jobs
- Separated from their families
- No real improvement in their status

Other Working-Class Women
- Found jobs as cooks, maids, and child-care workers because more families could afford to hire them
- Found some new educational and cultural opportunities in cities
- Overall improvement for many women

Middle-Class Women
- Freed from chores because many could afford to hire domestic help
- Began to attend college and get jobs as teachers and nurses
- Those who did work often criticized by people who said that they should not work outside the home
- Most affected by idea of separate spheres

Time for Tea, by Valentine Prinsep, 1800s

The Terrace, by Silvestro Legato, 1868

Direct Teach

Reading Focus

Competing Economic Views

Summarize What did Marx and Engels think would happen to the capitalist system? *More workers would sink into poverty; workers would rebel, take over means of production, and then govern themselves.*

Elaborate Why did Marx support the idea of a command economy? *possible answer—thought government should control economy*

Reading Focus

3 How did the Industrial Revolution affect society? *growth of new industries, working class women in factories and other jobs, migration of job-seekers to cities, pollution, some countries became powerful, increased standard of living*

Effects on Society

Explain How did industrialization affect home life? *separate spheres—women stayed home, men worked in factories; women expected to teach morals at home*

Make Inferences Why do you think women who went from cottage industries to factory work had no improvement in their status? *possible answer—were still performing low-skilled work*

Quick Facts Transparency: Effects of Industrialization on Women

Skills Focus: Making Oral Presentations

At Level

Reading Like a Historian Skill

Women of Different Social Classes

1. Organize a talk show about the social differences among women during the Industrial Revolution. Have a number of volunteers represent women from different social classes in a talk-show format. Select one student to serve as the show host and moderator. Have students prepare their roles beforehand. The rest of the class will serve as the show audience.
2. Begin the talk show. Have the host ask each guest to explain how industrialization has changed her life. As the guests respond, have audience members jot down one or two questions to ask a specific guest.
3. Encourage the guests to engage with each other and then encourage the host to interject occasionally.
4. Allow the audience members to ask their questions. **LS Kinesthetic, Verbal-Linguistic**

Alternative Assessment Handbook, Rubric 14: Group Activity

Answers

Reading Check *Socialists blamed capitalism for harsh working conditions, polluted cities, and the big gaps between rich and poor.*

Direct Teach

Reading Focus

Effects on Society

Recall How did industrailization positively affect Great Britain, France, and Germany? *became leaders in global economy; mass produced ships and weapons*

Elaborate How might industrialization lead to cultural clashes and discrimination? *possible answer—limited number of jobs, housing, waves of immigrants looking for work*

Map Transparency: Industrialized Europe, 1900

CRF: History and Geography: The First Modern Railroad

Interactive Map: Industrialized Europe, 1900

Recent Scholarship

Many male writers who lived through the Industrial Revolution expressed a longing for an idealized past. According to Susan Zlotnick, professor of English at Vassar College, British women writers had a very different perspective. In her book *Women, Writing, and the Industrial Revolution,* Zlotnick argues that writers like Elizabeth Gaskell and Charlotte Brontë were more willing to accept industrialism and foresaw the possibility of improvement in the changes that it brought.

Women, Writing and the Industrial Revolution, by Susan Zlotnick, The Johns Hopkins University Press, 2001.

Answers

Interpreting Maps 1. *Britain, Belgium, parts of Germany and eastern Europe, northern Italy;* **2.** *industrial area grew up around a mine or power source*

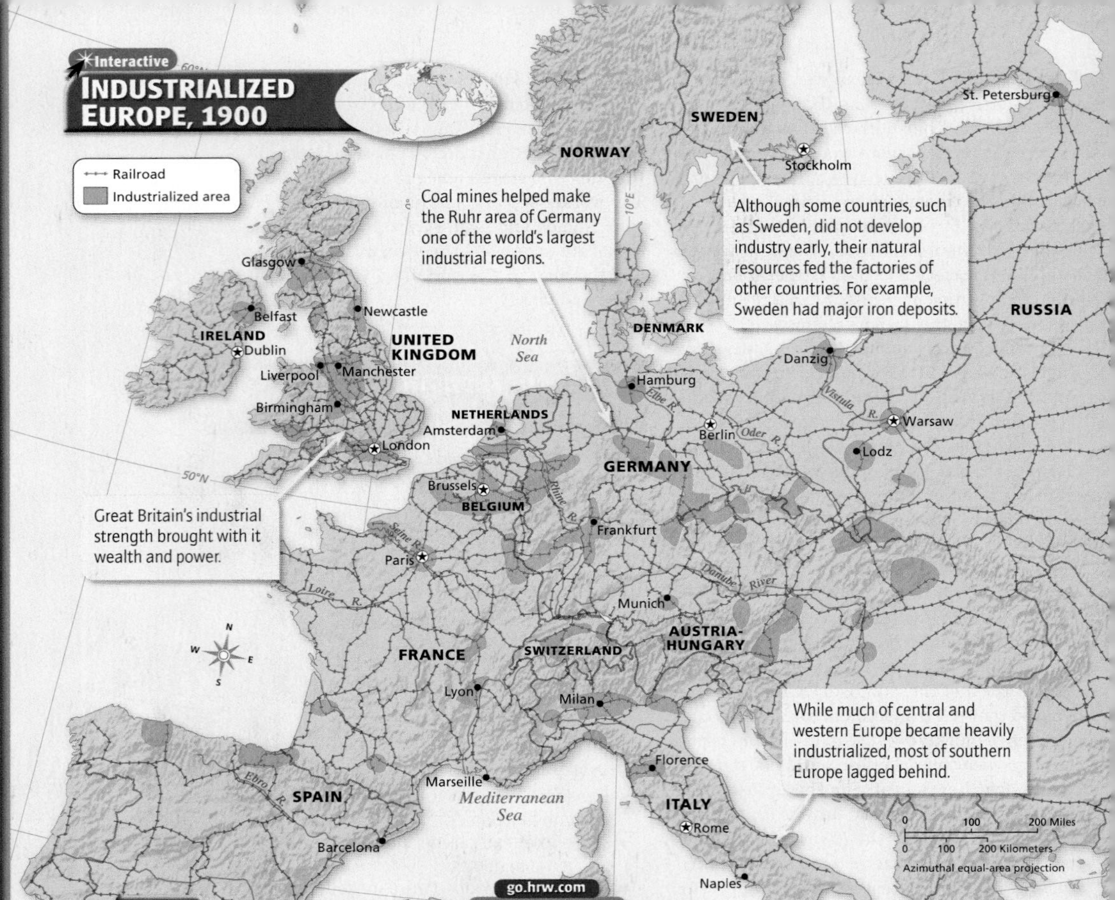

GEOGRAPHY SKILLS INTERPRETING MAPS

go.hrw.com Interactive Map Keyword: SHL IND

1. **Regions** What areas were heavily industrialized by 1900?
2. **Human-Environment Interaction** Some areas were heavily industrialized but did not have major cities. What do you think explains that situation?

The idea of separate spheres had another effect. Although so many people enjoyed what the new industrialized economy provided, in general they saw the business world as without moral controls. Women were expected to provide moral guidance in the home.

Middle-class families were more affected by this division between home and work than were lower-class families. Poorer families that depended on two incomes to survive could not afford for the wife to say home. However, belief in the home as society's moral center was equally powerful among lower-class families.

Effects on Countries On a scale much larger than the family home, industrialization also affected entire countries. For some nations, industry brought with it great power. For example, Great Britain, France, and Germany became leaders in the global economy.

Skills Focus: Analyzing Costs and Benefits

Above Level

Social Studies Skill
Analysis of Industrialization

1. Organize students into small groups.
2. Have groups discuss the following questions: How has the Industrial Revolution changed everyday life? How has it changed the way you view the world? Who has it benefited most and who has it benefited least? How might the negative impact of industrialization be diminished? For example, what could be done to reduce pollution that continues to occur? How might industry be refocused in the future to achieve the maximum benefits with minimum costs?
3. Guide students in a large group discussion of these questions. **LS Intrapersonal**

Alternative Assessment Handbook, Rubric 11: Discussions

Mass production increased their ability to build ships and make weapons. With increased military strength, some countries were able to conquer and control sources of raw materials around the world.

The powerful industrial giants could even control the economy of a place thousands of miles away. For example, India had made and exported cotton cloth for centuries already when Britain took control of the region. Indian textile workshops were not mechanized, however, so cotton cloth imported from Britain was cheaper. The Indian textile industry could not compete and was practically destroyed.

Back on this side of the world, the effect of industrialization on the United States was very dramatic. With its huge size, wealth of natural resources, and spirit of independence, the United States industrialized rapidly. Like the major industrial powers of Europe, the United States gained global political power based on its industrial strength. In addition, industry helped the country's population grow quickly. A large number of the new Americans had moved from other lands around the world, drawn by jobs in American factories. The immigrants, both skilled and unskilled, contributed to the nation's economic success and its cultural variety.

Long-Term Effects on Societies Overall, industrialized societies saw an increase in wealth. It is true that much of the wealth flowed into the pockets of a few rich industrialists. But manufacturing also created a new middle class of clerks, merchants, and managers. In general, the **standard of living**, or level of material comfort, for people in industrialized countries improved. Even many of the poorest people gradually benefited from labor-saving devices and cheap, machine-made goods.

The Industrial Revolution introduced something new to the middle class: leisure. People had more time on their hands and more money in their pockets. They could enjoy public sports events, a concert in the park, a day at the beach, or even a vacation. With increased leisure time, they could become more educated or participate more deeply in politics.

You will soon read how industrialization brought big changes to almost all aspects of daily life—from art to transportation. We are still experiencing those changes in our lives today. The full story of the Industrial Revolution has yet to be written.

READING CHECK **Identify Cause and Effect** What were some of the major effects industrialization had on families and countries?

SECTION 3 ASSESSMENT

go.hrw.com
Online Quiz
Keyword: SHL IND HP

Reviewing Ideas, Terms, and People

1. **a. Identify** What is the connection between **Adam Smith** and **laissez-faire** economics?
   b. Draw Conclusions Why do you think some economists believed that unrestricted capitalism would help all of society?
   c. Predict What are some of the groups of people who might have called the big industrialists "robber barons"? Who might have called them "captains of industry"?
2. **a. Describe** What was the role of **Karl Marx** and Friedrich Engels in the development of socialism?
   b. Analyze How would someone who advocated social democracy have responded to Marx's prediction?
3. **a. Recall** How did the Industrial Revolution affect the **standard of living** for people in industrialized countries?
   b. Interpret Why do you think Americans' spirit of independence encouraged the growth of capitalism?
   c. Predict How do you think the idea of separate spheres affected the children of middle-class families?

Critical Thinking

4. **Compare and Contrast** How did each of the major economic theories propose to change or benefit society? Fill in a table like the one below with as many changes as you can.

Theory	Proposed Social Change
Capitalism	
Utopianism	
Socialism	
Communism	

FOCUS ON WRITING

5. **Description** Imagine that you belong to a middle-class family in the late 1800s. Write a conversation that you have with your great-grandfather about the changes that your family has experienced over the years.

Direct Teach

Reading Focus

Effects on Society

Identify What benefits did industrialization bring to some nations? *great power, military strength, increase in overall wealth and standard of living, leisure time*

Evaluate Which do you think were greater, the costs or benefits of industrialization? *possible answers—costs; destroyed an older way of life and the environment; benefits; brought prosperity, wealth, and leisure time*

CRF: Biography: Louis Pasteur

CRF: Interdisciplinary Project

Review & Assess

Close

Guide students in a discussion about the positive and negative effects of industrialization.

Review

Online Quiz, Section 3

Assess

SE Section 3 Assessment

Progress Assessment: Section 3 Quiz

Alternative Assessment Handbook

Reteach/Intervene

Interactive Reader and Study Guide, Section 3

Interactive Skills Tutor CD-ROM

Section 3 Assessment Answers

1. **a.** Smith supported laissez-faire economics in his book, *The Wealth of Nations.*
   b. saw restrictions as obstacles that prevented the growth of companies
   c. factory workers; business owners, capitalists
2. **a.** developed communism, a more radical approach to socialist ideas
   b. possible answer—might agree with Marx because of his socialist views
3. **a.** increased standard of living
   b. possible answer—Americans wanted individual rights and fewer economic restrictions.
   c. possible answers—children's morals improved; probably missed their fathers
4. Capitalism—increased wealth, fewer government restrictions; Utopianism—poverty and social evils eliminated; Socialism—societal control of property and industry; Communism—workers control government and economy
5. Student conversations might include that the middle class can afford new products, enjoy leisure time, and live in cities.

Answers

Reading Check *families—wealth, leisure time, better educated; countries—increased power, wealth, and living standards; overcrowding of cities, pollution, rapid population growth*

Document-Based Investigation

Child Labor

Word Help

doffing removing completed spools from machinery

bobbins spools of thread

Teaching Tip

Review with students the difference between primary and secondary sources. Remind students that a primary source is from a firsthand source; it might be a poem, diary, interview, etc. A secondary source is an interpretation or analysis of a primary source. Tell students that their textbook is a secondary source.

MISCONCEPTION ALERT

Although students may think that child labor is a thing of the past, it continues to this day. As of 2006, 211 million children aged 5-14 could be found working. Founded in 1992, the International Programme on the Elimination of Child Labour (IPEC) is a organization that works with governments to abolish child labor and protect children.

CHAPTER 7 **Document-Based Investigation**

Child Labor

Historical Context The four documents below tell us about child labor during the early Industrial Revolution and how different people saw the issue.

Task Examine the documents and answer the questions that follow. After you have studied the documents, you will be asked to write an essay describing the connection between child labor and public attitudes. Use evidence from these selections and the chapter to support the position you take in your essay.

DOCUMENT 1

Interview with Elizabeth Bentley

In 1815 the British Parliament sent out researchers to interview child workers and learn more about factory conditions. Here is an excerpt from an interview with a young woman who had worked in a textile mill.

Q *What were the hours of labour when you were not so thronged [busy]?*
A From six in the morning till seven at night.

Q *What time was allowed for meals?*
A Forty minutes at noon.

Q *Had you any time to get your breakfast or drinking?*
A No, we had to get it as we could.

Q *Do you consider doffing a laborious employment?*
A Yes.

Q *Explain what you had to do.*
A When the frames are full, they have to stop the frames, and take the flyers off, and take the full bobbins off, and carry them to the roller, and then put empty ones on, and set the frame going again.

Q *Does that keep you constantly on your feet?*
A Yes, there are so many frames and they run so quick.

Q *Your labour is very excessive?*
A Yes, you have not time for anything.

Q *Suppose you flagged [slowed down] a little, or were late, what would they do?*
A Strap [whip] us.

Q *And they are in the habit of strapping those who are last in doffing?*
A Yes.

Q *Constantly?*
A Yes.

DOCUMENT 2

Children in Danger

Factory owners often preferred to hire children and women rather than men. Men expected higher wages, and employers suspected that they were more likely to rebel against the strict rules and conditions that were common in factories. The children were subject to harsh punishment if they were late, fell behind in their work, or talked too much.

Supervisor whipping a young boy, artist unknown, 1853

Skills Focus: Analyzing Secondary Sources

At Level

Research Required

Reading Like a Historian Skill

Child Labor

1. Tell students that child labor is still very common in the world.
2. Have students conduct research about an aspect of child labor and prepare a short research paper on their findings. Tell students to use secondary sources about their chosen topic, and to analyze each source for accuracy and potential bias. Possible topics include industries and corporations that employ children, hours and working conditions, children's access to education, connections to economic and political factors, and how child labor is justified by employers and families.
3. Have volunteers present their findings to the class.
4. Guide students in a discussion about things that can be done to abolish child labor.

LS Verbal-Linguistic

Alternative Assessment Handbook, Rubrics 29: Presentations; and 30: Research

DOCUMENT 3

Children in the Mines

Children were also hired to work in Great Britain's coal mines. In this drawing, you see an older, stronger worker wearing a harness and pulling a cart full of coal. Smaller children push the cart from behind.

Woman pulling coal truck while children push, artist unknown, c. 1848

DOCUMENT 4

Speech in the House of Commons, 1832

John Charles Spencer was a member of the British Parliament's House of Commons. Although he supported some reforms for child workers, he was against a proposed law to limit their work day to 10 hours. Here he addresses Michael Sadler, a fellow member who proposed the law, in a speech.

> I am of the opinion that the effect . . . must necessarily be a fall in the rate of wages, or, what is more probable, that children would cease to be employed at all in manufactories. Now I appeal to the honourable member whether a measure which would prevent children from obtaining any employment in factories would not be more injurious than beneficial to the labouring classes?
>
> As long as we have a manufacturing population in the kingdom it will be impossible to render their occupation as wholesome as that of agricultural labourers, or persons engaged in out-door labour. This is an evil that cannot be remedied. It is too late now to argue about the unwholesome nature of manufacturing employment. We have got a manufacturing population, and it must be employed. Any measure which shall have the effect of diminishing the means of employment to labourers engaged in manufactures will produce extensive misery.

Skills FOCUS — READING LIKE A HISTORIAN

DOCUMENT 1

a. Summarize What were some of the problems that Elizabeth Bentley faced at the factory?

b. Draw a Conclusion How does Elizabeth's plain way of speaking affect your reaction to her testimony?

DOCUMENT 2

a. Describe What does the scene show?

b. Compare Does this illustration confirm or contradict what was said in Document 1? Explain your answer.

DOCUMENT 3

a. Describe What would happen to the small children if the worker in the harness were to fall or stumble?

b. Infer How do you think the person who drew this picture felt about children working in the mines?

DOCUMENT 4

a. Summarize What is Spencer's main argument against the proposal to limit children's workday to 10 hours?

b. Analyze What social class does Spencer seem to represent, and whose interests is he upholding?

DOCUMENT-BASED ESSAY QUESTION

What do you think were the connections among child labor, factory conditions, attitudes about capitalism, reactions to capitalism, and the rise of labor movements? Using the documents above and information from the chapter, form a thesis that might explain the general impact of child labor on public opinion. Then, write a short essay to support your position.

See **Skills Handbook**, pp. H25–H26

Differentiating Instruction

Above Level

Advanced Learners/Gifted and Talented

1. Have students write a one-page rebuttal to Spencer's speech. Rebuttals should address Spencer's assumptions and flawed reasoning. They should also make original points in support of Sadler's proposal.
2. Have volunteers read their rebuttals aloud to the class. Encourage students to make their points dramatically.
3. As an extension, have pairs of students play the roles of Spencer and Sadler and participate in an extemporaneous debate on the subject of Sadler's proposal. **LS Verbal-Linguistic, Kinesthetic**

Alternative Assessment Handbook, Rubric 10: Debates

Document-Based Investigation

Info to Know

The Chadwick Report A report written by Edwin Chadwick, the secretary of the royal commission on reform of the poor laws and commissioner on the Board of Health, and published in 1842, stated that in his research of the living conditions in poor neighborhoods, he found that 43,000 women had become widows. His research also found that 112,000 children had become orphans as a result of poor sanitary conditions.

Answers

Reading Like a Historian

Document 1. a. *long hours, only one break time, continuous, fast-paced work, possibility of whipping;* ***b.*** *possible answer—She appears to be matter of fact, which makes her testimony shocking because it shows that she had gotten used to working in such deplorable conditions.* **Document 2. a.** *a child being punished;* **b.** *confirms; boys are being whipped for stopping work;* **Document 3. a.** *They would be injured* **b.** *sympathetic to their suffering by calling attention to the horrendous conditions;* **Document 4. a.** *Preventing children from working would hurt working classes by denying them jobs and money.* **b.** *seems to represent wealthy class because he states that the law might cause injury to "laboring classes"; upholds interests of business and factory owners;* **Essay** *Students essays should explain the differences in public opinion in reaction to child labor, such as the views of John Spencer in Document 4.*

Answers

Visual Summary

Review and Inquiry Organize students into small groups. Randomly choose bulleted phrases or items from the time line in the visual summary, and have groups take turns explaining the phrase's significance to the Industrial Revolution.

Quick Facts Transparency: Visual Study Guide: The Industrial Revolution

Review Key Terms and People

1. standard of living
2. factors of production
3. Jethro Tull
4. invest
5. entrepreneur
6. cottage industry
7. laissez-faire
8. industrialization

Comprehension and Critical Thinking

9. a. coal, iron, streams, rivers
b. made cotton production and slavery profitable
c. possible answers— Steam engine allowed factories to spread, and also created a transportation revolution; other machinery might have been used.
10. a. a group of workers who violently protested new machines
b. dangerous machines, pollution, long hours, abuse
c. possible answers— cottage industry, because loss of family business means loss of income for all family members; factory, because of the terrible working conditions
11. a. Andrew Carnegie, Cornelius Vanderbilt, John D. Rockefeller
b. Communism is a more radical view of socialism.
c. increased their ability to build ships and weapons, and thereby conquer and control new sources of raw materials

CHAPTER 7

Chapter Review

QUICK FACTS

VISUAL STUDY GUIDE

Causes and Effects of the Industrial Revolution

CAUSES

- Availability of raw materials and markets in colonies
- Great Britain's seapower and political stability
- Parliament's support of free enterprise
- Agricultural improvements in Great Britain
- Enclosure movement in Great Britain
- Great Britain's factors of production
- Invention of new machines in the textile industry
- Development of the steam engine
- Increased individual freedom in the West
- Western attitudes toward competition

Industrial Revolution

EFFECTS

- Development of labor-saving, time-saving machines
- The factory system
- Poor working conditions in factories
- Overcrowding, pollution, disease in cities
- Competing ideas about economics
- Rise in standard of living, growth of middle class
- Rise of new industries and powerful industrialists
- New emphasis on middle-class home life
- Increased power of industrialized countries

Key Events of the Industrial Revolution

1701	Jethro Tull invents the seed drill.
1765	James Watt develops idea for practical steam engine.
1776	Adam Smith publishes *The Wealth of Nations*.
1785	Edmund Cartwright patents the power loom.
1789	Samuel Slater arrives in the United States.
1793	Slater's Mill is established in Rhode Island.
1802	Richard Trevithick uses a steam engine to drive the first locomotive.
1807	William Cockerill builds a factory in Belgium.
1811	The Luddites stage their first attack on textile factories.
1832	The Sadler Report details the conditions in British factories.
1851	The Great Exhibition displays the marvels of industry to the world.
1867	Karl Marx publishes the first volume of *Das Kapital*.
1871	The British Parliament legalizes labor unions.

Reviewing Key Terms and People

Identify the correct term or person from the chapter that best fits each of the following descriptions.

1. level of material comfort
2. the essential elements that a nation needs to achieve economic success
3. invented a seed drill that made planting more efficient
4. to commit money in order to make a financial return
5. person who starts a business
6. a craft occupation performed in the home
7. economic system in which government does not regulate business and commerce
8. the process of changing to power-driven machinery

256 CHAPTER 7

Reading Skills

12. Children were hired as mine workers because of their small size.
13. Cotton production likely increased.

Analyzing Secondary Sources

14. possible answer—Yes, because livestock and farming changed dramatically.
15. He describes the appearance of the sheep with a lot of visual detail.

History's Impact video program

Review the video to answer the closing question: How did industrialization affect the United States?

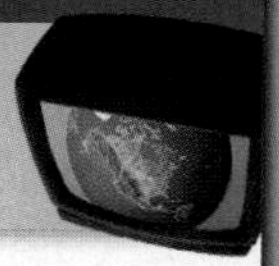

Comprehension and Critical Thinking

SECTION 1 *(pp. 235–241)*

9. a. Recall What natural resources enabled the Industrial Revolution to begin in Great Britain?

b. Sequence How did the cotton gin affect slavery in the United States?

c. Support a Position Defend or refute this statement: "Without the steam engine, the Industrial Revolution would not have amounted to more than a pile of rickety machines."

SECTION 2 *(pp. 242–247)*

10. a. Identify Who were the Luddites, and what did they do?

b. Explain What were some of the hazards of working in the early factories?

c. Rank Which family do you think faced more potential problems—a cottage industry family, or one whose members worked in a factory? Explain.

SECTION 3 *(pp. 248–253)*

11. a. Identify Who were some of the industrialists who gained wealth and power in the United States?

b. Compare How do socialism and communism differ?

c. Evaluate In what ways did industrialization give countries such as Great Britain and Germany an advantage over some of their neighbors?

Reading Skills

Drawing Conclusions *Use what you know about drawing conclusions to answer the questions below.*

12. If you know that coal mines had narrow passageways and low ceilings, what can you conclude about why many children were hired to work in the mines?

13. If you know that Eli Whitney's cotton gin speeded up the process of pulling seeds from raw cotton blossoms, what can you conclude about a change in the rate of cotton production during the 1800s?

Analyzing Secondary Sources

Reading Like a Historian

"Early breeders of better animals succeeded not because of a knowledge of chemistry, which was in its infancy, or of genetics, which did not exist, but because they backed hunches. Even so, the results were remarkable. The appearance of the livestock inhabiting the landscape changed; the scraggy medieval sheep whose backs resembled, in section, the Gothic arches of the monasteries which bred them, gave way to the fat, square, contented-looking animal familiar today."

—J. M. Roberts, *History of the World*, 1993

14. Explain Do you think Roberts would agreed that the changes in agriculture could be called an agricultural revolution? Why or why not?

15. Analyze How does Roberts's description of the sheep help the reader understand the change in their appearance over time?

Using the Internet

go.hrw.com
Practice Online
Keyword: SHL IND

16. The cities of Manchester and Birmingham, England, suffered some of the worst effects of the Industrial Revolution. The two cities also contributed much to Great Britain's rise to power and wealth. Choose one of these cities and use the Internet to research the role it played in industrialization. Then, create a chart showing the city's contributions and problems.

WRITING ABOUT HISTORY

Exposition: Writing an Explanation *The Industrial Revolution changed life in every society it touched. It affected individuals as well as groups, the rich as well as the poor, the cities as well as the rural areas.*

17. Assignment: In an essay, explain how this revolution affected people in three ways: how they worked, how they conducted business, and how they lived at home. To provide support for your explanation, use information from this chapter and from other research sources as needed. Be sure to use facts and examples to clearly illustrate the points you are making about the ways in which life changed.

Answers

Using the Internet

16. Go to the HRW Web site and enter the keyword shown to access a rubric for this activity.

KEYWORD: SHL IND

Writing for the SAT

17. Student essays should discuss how the Industrial Revolution affected the way people worked, conducted business, and lived at home. They should compare pre-industrial conditions to those observed during the process of industrialization. Possible answers may include that before industrialization, work was based in the home; after industrialization, work was based in factories.

A rubric for the activity is provided in **CRF:** Writing for the SAT.

HOLT

History's Impact

► **Video Program: The Industrial Revolution**
See the Video Program Teacher's Guide for the answer to the closing question.

Review and Assessment Resources

Review and Reinforce

- **CRF:** Chapter Review
- **Quick Facts Transparency**: Visual Study Guide: The Industrial Revolution
- **Spanish Chapter Summaries Audio CD Program**
- OSP **Holt PuzzlePro**: Quiz Show for ExamView
- **Quiz Game CD-ROM**

Assess

- **PASS**: Chapter Test, Forms A and B
- **Alternative Assessment Handbook**
- OSP **ExamView Test Generator**, Chapter Test
- **Differentiated Instruction Modified Worksheets and Tests CD-ROM**: Chapter Test
- HOAP **Holt Online Assessment Program** (in the Premier Online Edition)

Reteach/Intervene

- **Interactive Reader and Study Guide**
- **Differentiated Instruction Teacher Management System**: Lesson Plans for Differentiated Instruction
- **Differentiated Instruction Modified Worksheets and Tests CD-ROM**: Chapter Test
- **Interactive Skills Tutor CD-ROM**

go.hrw.com
Online Resources
KEYWORD: SHL TEACHER

Chapter 8 Planning Guide

Life in the Industrial Age

Chapter Overview	Reproducible Resources	Technology Resources
CHAPTER 8 **pp. 258–283** **Overview:** **In this chapter, students will learn about the far-reaching effects of the Industrial Revolution and its effects on many aspects of daily life.**	**Differentiated Instruction Teacher Management System:*** • Pacing Guide • Lesson Plans for Differentiated Instruction **Interactive Reader and Study Guide:** Chapter Summary* **Chapter Resource File*** • Writing for the SAT • Social Studies Skill • Chapter Review **World History Outline Maps**	**Live Ink© Online Reading Help** **Student Edition on Audio CD Program** **Differentiated Instruction Modified Worksheets and Tests CD-ROM** **Interactive Skills Tutor CD-ROM** **World History Primary Source Library CD-ROM** **Power Presentations with Video CD-ROM** **History's Impact: World History Video Program (VHS/DVD):** Life in the Industrial Age
Section 1 **Advances in Technology** **The Main Idea:** The technological breakthroughs of the Industrial Age included advances in electric power, transportation, and communication.	**Differentiated Instruction Teacher Management System:** Section 1 Lesson Plan* **Interactive Reader and Study Guide:** Section 1 Summary* **Chapter Resource File*** • Vocabulary Builder: Section 1 • Biography: Granville Woods	**Daily Test Practice Transparency:** Section 1* **Map Transparency:** Growth in the Industrial Age* **Map Transparency:** U.S. Railroads, 1870* **Internet Activity:** The Inventions of Thomas Edison
Section 2: **Science and Medical Achievements** **The Main Idea:** Advances in science, medicine, and the social sciences led to new theories about the natural world and human mind, an improved quality of life, and longer life spans.	**Differentiated Instruction Teacher Management System:** Section 2 Lesson Plan* **Interactive Reader and Study Guide:** Section 2 Summary* **Chapter Resource File*** • Vocabulary Builder: Section 2 • Biography: Elizabeth Blackwell • Literature: *Frankenstein*	**Daily Test Practice Transparency:** Section 2* **Quick Facts Transparency:** New Ideas in the Sciences* **Internet Activity:** Introduction of Anesthesia to Surgery
Section 3: **Daily Life in the Late 1800s** **The Main Idea:** During the late 1800s, cities grew and changed, while education, leisure time activities, and the arts reflected those changing times.	**Differentiated Instruction Teacher Management System:** vSection 3 Lesson Plan* **Interactive Reader and Study Guide:** Section 3 Summary* **Chapter Resource File*** • Vocabulary Builder: Section 3 • History and Geography: The Growth of Cities • Biography: Sarah Winnemucca	**Daily Test Practice Transparency:** Section 3* **Quick Facts Transparency:** Increase in Leisure Activities*

go.hrw.com | Print Resource | Transparency
LS Learning Styles | Audio CD | CD-ROM
Video | **SE** Student Edition | **TE** Teachers Edition
OSP One-Stop Planner CD-ROM
*also on One-Stop Planner CD-ROM

Review, Assessment, Intervention

- **Quick Facts Transparency:** Life in the Industrial Age*
- **Spanish Chapter Summaries Audio CD Program**
- **Progress Assessment Support System (PASS):** Chapter Test*
- **Differentiated Instruction Modified Worksheets and Tests CD-ROM:** Modified Chapter Test
- OSP **One-Stop Planner CD-ROM:** ExamView Test Generator (English/Spanish)
- HOAP **Holt Online Assessment Program (HOAP),** in the Holt Premier Online Student Edition

- **PASS:** Section 1 Quiz*
- **Online Quiz:** Section 1
- **Alternative Assessment Handbook**

- **PASS:** Section 2 Quiz*
- **Online Quiz:** Section 2
- **Alternative Assessment Handbook**

- **PASS:** Section 3 Quiz*
- **Online Quiz:** Section 3
- **Alternative Assessment Handbook**

HOLT
History's Impact
World History Video Program (VHS/DVD)
Life in the Industrial Age

Power Presentation with Video CD-ROM

Power Presentations with Video are visual presentations of each chapter's main ideas. Presentations can be customized by including Quick Facts charts, images and maps from the textbook, and video clips.

Holt Online Learning

go.hrw.com
Teacher Resources
KEYWORD: SHL TEACHER

go.hrw.com
Student Resources
KEYWORD: SHL LIF

- Document-Based Questions
- Interactive Multimedia Activities
- Current Events
- Chapter-Based Internet Activities
- and more!

Holt Premier
Online Student Edition

Complete online support for interactivity, assessment, and reporting

- Interactive Maps and Notebook
- Homework Practice and Research Activities Online

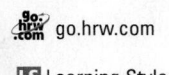

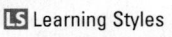

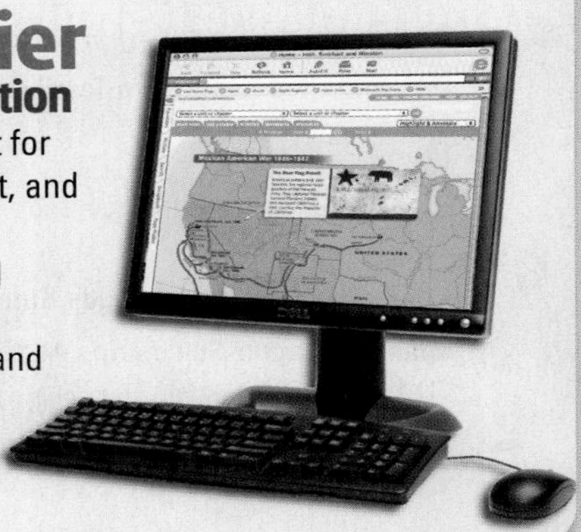

The Big Picture

Peter N. Stearns

Industrial Society From the 1830s onward, new social forms that constituted the essence of industrial society developed in Western Europe and the United States. Urbanism was a vital feature of the new industrial society and new technologies changed life outside as well as within the workplace. New forms of transportation and communication and electric lighting are key examples. Public health measures reduced urban disease and infant mortality rates.

Industrial Culture Scientific discoveries dominated the intellectual scene. The theory of evolution helped redefine biology. For many people, a general sense of scientific explanations of the natural world and a belief in the link between science and technological progress shaped basic outlooks in powerful new ways. Scientific thought spilled over into the social sciences and psychology. Artistic developments, such as impressionism, were somewhat separate. In literature, realism captured the scientific spirit, in seeking an objective examination of the human condition. Major artistic and scientific developments, though not easily compatible, created a common cultural framework from Russia to the United States.

Popular Culture Crucial changes occurred in ordinary life, too. Despite major social divisions, consumerism increased. Education spread more widely, and the majority of people in Western society were literate by the 1890s. Educational opportunities for women expanded as part of this general development. New leisure forms emerged, often emphasizing pleasure-seeking and spectatorship, or the enjoyment of professional sports and entertainments.

Assessment Obviously, many of these developments created a recognizably modern world—technology, suburbs, commercialized leisure, improved health. The developments correspondingly challenge assessment. They represented progress in many ways, as contemporaries often insisted, but they did not resolve all older problems—poverty remained, for example—and they created some new ones, such as more regimented leisure.

Recent Scholarship

In *Marianne in the Market: Envisioning Consumer Society in Fin-de-Siècle France* (2001), Lisa Tiersten deals with some of the leading developments of the later 19th century, obviously in a single national context. She discusses the new consumer role of women and how it related to living conditions and to the new criticisms levied both against women and consumerism. Aesthetic issues also figure in, as new products challenged older ideas of taste and artistry. Consumerism is portrayed as a major change in living standards and personal beliefs, but also as an unsettling process for many groups.

Differentiating Instruction

Differentiated Instruction Teacher Management System
- Pacing Guide
- Lesson Plans for Differentiated Instruction

Interactive Reader and Study Guide

Spanish Chapter Summaries Audio CD Program

Student Edition on Audio CD Program

Differentiated Instruction Modified Worksheets and Tests CD-ROM
- Vocabulary Flash Cards
- Modified Vocabulary Builder Activities
- Modified Chapter Review Activity
- Modified Chapter Test

OSP **One-Stop Planner CD-ROM**
- ExamView Test Generator (English/Spanish)
- PuzzlePro
- Quiz Show for ExamView
- Transparencies and Videos

TE **Differentiated Activities in the Teacher's Edition**
- Comparing Theories of Evolution, p. 269
- Leisure Activities in the 1800s, p. 276
- Examining Art of the 1800s, p. 281

Reading Like a Historian

Sam Wineburg

Reading Without Words How do historians read something without words—for example, Claude Monet's 1874 painting *Sunrise*, which inspired the term "impressionism"? They can use words to describe this seascape's most distinguishing features—its radiant sun or its contrast of serenity and movement. But in so doing historians are typically no better than anyone else. What they can do, however, is build a context for a work by asking about the circumstances of its creation. How and when did a painting come into being and for what purpose? What cultural forces did it draw on or react against?

The school of painting known as impressionism arose in Paris in the second half of the 19th century, a time of dizzying social change and unprecedented urbanization. It was in this environment that Monet quit the studio and took his canvas outside—a bold act that spurned artistic convention. His scenes of everyday life contrasted with the ornate designs of traditional painting, the castles, mythological figures, church scenes, and formal portraits that defined the French Academy of Fine Arts.

The word impressionism was first used as a term of disparagement, something unfinished, superficial, or half-baked. It appeared in a biting review of Monet's work by Louis Leroy, who ridiculed *Sunrise* by quipping that "wallpaper in its embryonic state is more finished than that seascape!" Monet and others adopted the term as the name of their new movement, pointing out that impression also carried the sense of leaving an indelible mark—of appealing directly and unrepentantly to the senses.

Impressionists became famous for their use of color—raw, bold, and thick stroked—applied directly to the canvas. Hamlin Garland, one of the first American critics to offer a defense of impressionism, noted that the "impressionist does not believe that nature needs toning. . . . He paints with nature's colors—red, blue, and yellow; and he places them fearlessly on the canvas side by side, leaving the eye to mix them as in nature." In a society becoming increasingly mechanized, impressionists created images no machine could imitate. If urbanization had separated Europeans from nature by breaking agricultural rhythms, painting a canvas *en plein air* restored the relationship between the artist and nature.

Technology and Change That the impressionists rebelled against the changes brought about by industrialization is true—but only to a point. No artist is an island. This is illustrated most vividly in their response to the new technology of photography.

The impressionists' renunciation of "copying" nature in all its detail can be interpreted as a response to photographic realism. Impressionism did not need to compete with the camera because its goal was to teach the eye to see in a way no photo could. Like many other Parisians of his day, Monet himself was a camera enthusiast who noticed that pictures taken at slow shutter speeds resulted in blurred images. These insights led him to experiment with their equivalents on the canvas: smudged images that resembled photographic blurs and afterimages. Photography opened up the eyes of the artist and taught him a new way of seeing.

Artists both react to and are subsumed by the forces of their age. Reading a painting does not mean reducing Monet or others to the material conditions of industrialization. Rather, placing art in time and space reminds us that creative forms arise in settings with their own particular stories. Reading a work of art historically means reuniting that work with its rightful story.

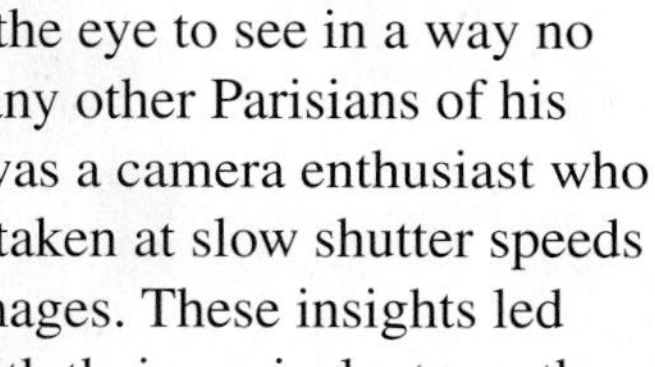

• Chapter Preview •

Chapter Main Ideas

Section 1 The technological breakthroughs of the Industrial Age included advances in electric power, transportation, and communication.

Section 2 Advances in science, medicine, and the social sciences led to new theories about the natural world and human mind, an improved quality of life, and longer life spans.

Section 3 During the late 1800s, cities grew and changed, while education, leisure time activities, and the arts reflected those changing times.

CHAPTER 8

1800–1900

Life in the Industrial Age

THE BIG PICTURE During the 1700s and 1800s, the Industrial Revolution changed practically everything about the world of work. Many of the changes were technological advances. As the rate of advances increased, many other aspects of daily life besides work were also transformed.

Theme SCIENCE AND TECHNOLOGY

Changes in science and technology accelerated rapidly during the 1800s. One discovery or invention led to another. The process repeated over and over, until practically every aspect of human experience was affected.

TIME LINE

CHAPTER EVENTS

- **1803** John Dalton develops modern atomic theory.
- **1817** Beethoven begins composing his Ninth Symphony.
- **1837** Samuel Morse invents the telegraph.
- **1849** Steamship service around South America begins.

1800 — 1820 — 1840

WORLD EVENTS

- **1813** Mexico declares its independence from Spain.
- **1816** Shaka Zulu founds the Zulu Empire in southern Africa.
- **1850** The Taiping Rebellion, which claims 20 million lives, begins in China.
- **1851** India's first railroad is built.

Key to Differentiating Instruction

Below Level

Basic-level activities designed for all students encountering new material

At Level

Intermediate-level activities designed for average students

Above Level

Challenging activities designed for honors and gifted and talented students

Standard English Mastery

Activities designed to improve standard English usage

Introduce the Chapter

At Level

Life in the Industrial Age

1. Write the following words for students to see: electricity, telephone, radio, automobile, airplane, vaccines, anesthesia, antiseptics. Remind students that all of these developments had their origins in the Industrial Age.
2. Organize students into small groups. Have each group choose from the list of developments the one that they think is most important. Then have students in each group make a list of the ways in which the development changed life.
3. Have volunteers from each group share their lists with the class. Guide students in a discussion of the ideas presented. Which development was chosen by the most groups? Why?
4. Tell students that in this chapter they will learn about the technological advances of the Industrial Age and how they changed everyday life in the 19th century. **LS Interpersonal**

Alternative Assessment Handbook, Rubrics 11: Discussions; and 14: Group Activity

History's Impact video program
Watch the video to understand the impact of the Industrial Age.

Reading like a Historian During the 1800s, a revolution in transportation occurred as railroads made travel faster and easier. At the same time, the middle class grew, and more people could take advantage of railroad service.

Analyzing Visuals This painting shows a crowded railroad platform in England in about 1860. What evidence of prosperity do you see in the painting?

See **Skills Handbook**, p. H26

1860

1861 The Civil War begins in the United States.

1879 Thomas Edison invents the lightbulb.

1880

1884 The Berlin Conference begins the partition of Africa.

1885 Louis Pasteur develops a vaccine against rabies.

Chapter Preview

HOLT
History's Impact
► **Video Program: Life in the Industrial Age**
See the Video Teacher's Guide for strategies for using the video segment.

Reading Like a Historian

Steam Power In 1802, British engineer Richard Trevithick designed a steam-powered coach. However, because they were so heavy, steam vehicles were soon banned from public roads, and their owners were forced to run them on tracks. Eventually, they were replaced by locomotives running on iron rails.

Explore the Time Line

1. How many years after the invention of the telegraph did the Civil War begin in the United States? *24 years*
2. When was the lightbulb invented, and by whom? *1879, by Thomas Edison*
3. How many years passed between the invention of the telegraph and the invention of the light-bulb? *42 years*

Info to Know

Industrial Revolution The Industrial Revolution is a term originally used to describe the transformation of England from a largely rural population to an urban manufacturing power. Other nations began to go through the same process soon afterward. Some nations, such as Japan and Russia, did not become industrialized until the first half of the 20th century. Today there are still nations that have not yet begun the process of industrialization.
Identify Where did the Industrial Revolution begin? *in England*

go.hrw.com
Online Resources
Chapter Resources:
KEYWORD: SHL LIF
Teacher Resources:
KEYWORD: SHL TEACHER

Answers

Reading Like a Historian 1. *fine clothing; travelers have many pieces of luggage filled with belongings; people appear content*

Preteach

Geography Starting Points

Activity **Analyzing Maps** Have students use a large map of the United States to locate the U.S. cities shown on the map in the text. Have students identify the waterways that are adjacent to each city. Then have students explain why early industrial cities developed along rivers, lakes, and oceans.
LS Visual-Spatial

- **Alternative Assessment Handbook,** Rubric 21: Map Reading
- **Map Transparency**: Growth in the Industrial Age
- **World History Outline Maps**
- **Interactive Map:** Urban Growth in the Industrial Age

GEOGRAPHY Starting Points

Interactive
URBAN GROWTH IN THE INDUSTRIAL AGE

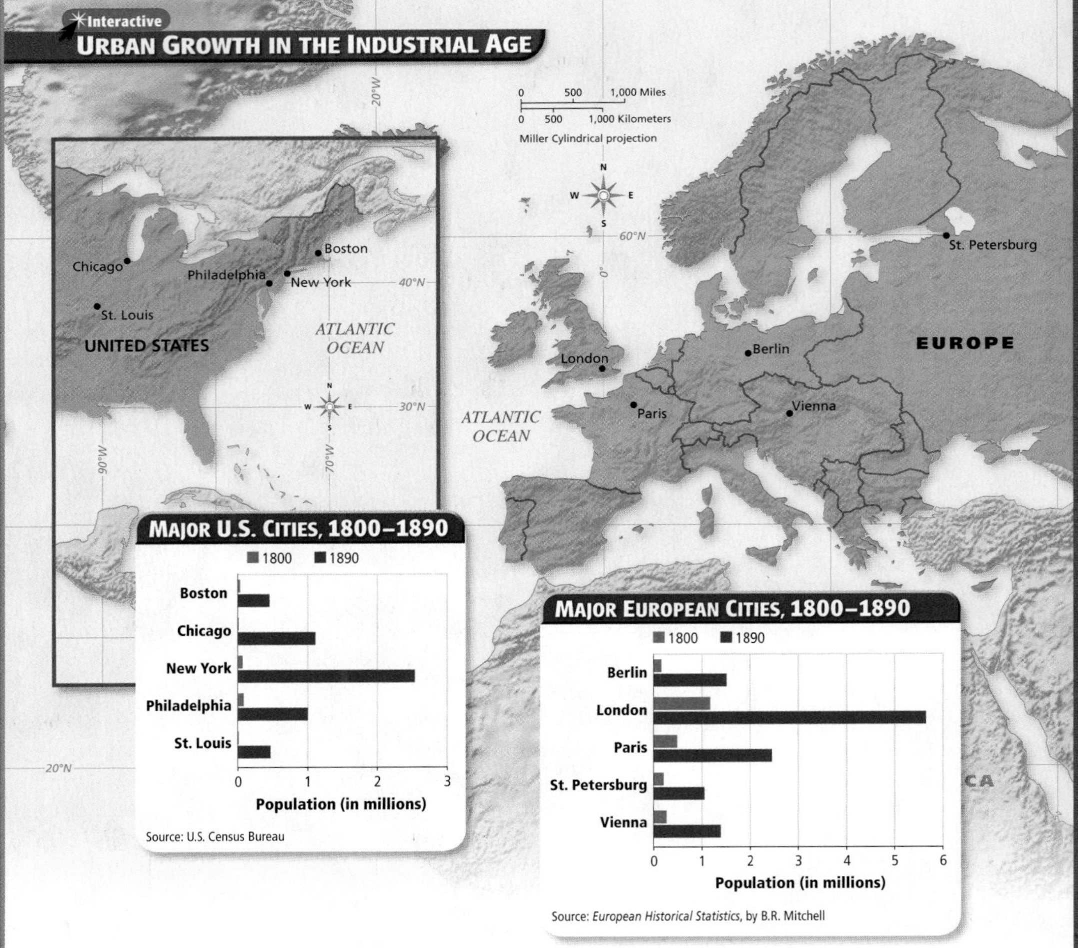

Starting Points

By the 1800s industrialization was causing cities in Europe and the United States to grow at a tremendous rate. In addition, society was changing rapidly in the cities. However, advances in technology, science, medicine, and other fields soon changed daily life far beyond the cities.

1. **Analyze** By about how many people did London grow from 1800 to 1890? What factors may have caused the population increase?
2. **Predict** How do you think the growth of cities affected the people who lived in them?

Listen to History

Go online to listen to an explanation of the starting points for this chapter.

go.hrw.com
Keyword: SHL LIF

Skills Focus: Analyzing Maps

At Level

Research Required

Social Studies Skill
The Industrial Age

1. Have students conduct outside research and compare the population of the cities shown on the map in three time periods, 1820, 1880, and 1920.
2. Have students calculate the percentages of growth or decline and show their results in tabular format, using the graphs above as a model.
3. Have students find photographs from one of these cities in the 1800s. Have students create multimedia presentations combining their graphs and photographs. Presentations should illustrate how population growth affected life in industrial cities during the 1800s.
LS Visual-Spatial, Logical-Mathematical

- **Alternative Assessment Handbook**, Rubrics 7: Charts, and 22: Multimedia Presentations

Answers

Geography Starting Points

1. *about 4 million people; people may have moved to cities to work in industrial jobs;* **2.** *possible answer—crowded living conditions, unhealthy environment*

SECTION 1

Advances in Technology

Before You Read

Main Idea

The technological breakthroughs of the Industrial Age included advances in electric power, transportation, and communication.

Reading Focus

1. How did electric power affect industry and daily life?
2. What advances in transportation occurred during the Industrial Age?
3. What were the advances in communication, and how were they achieved?

Key Terms and People

Michael Faraday
Thomas Edison
Bessemer process
Henry Ford
Wilbur and Orville Wright
telegraph
Samuel Morse
Alexander Graham Bell
Guglielmo Marconi

TAKING NOTES Use a graphic organizer like the one below to take notes on key technological advances of the Industrial Age.

THE INSIDE STORY ***What new technology wowed the world in 1900?*** As visitors approached the gates to the Paris Exhibition of 1900, they wondered what was lighting up the night sky so brilliantly. Many had heard about a new technology that was a great improvement over the oil and gas lighting they currently used in their homes. But what they saw was amazing—a spectacular display of electricity as 5,000 multicolored lights lit up an enormous steel and glass building. None of the 50 million people who visited the exhibition had ever before seen such a spectacle of electric power. Few could imagine how electricity would transform their lives. ■

In 1900, lights of the Palace of Electricity turned part of Paris into a fantasy land.
Palais de Electricité, artist unknown, c. 1900

261

Teach the Main Idea

At Level

Advances in Technology

1. **Teach** Ask students the Reading Focus questions to teach this section.
2. **Apply** Have students make a chart with the following headings: Electric Power, Transportation, Communication. Under each heading, have students list the important 19th-century developments in that area.
3. **Review** Review student charts as a class. Then have students identify the one change under each heading that they believe was the most important.
4. **Practice/Homework** Have students write editorials from the point of view of a 19th century editor. They should try to convince the public that the federal government should help fund a transcontinental railroad system. Student editorials should describe the benefits of such a system and explain why it will be worth the money to build it. **LS Visual-Spatial, Verbal-Linguistic**

Alternative Assessment Handbook, Rubrics 7: Charts; and 43: Writing to Persuade

Preteach

Getting Started

Use the **Interactive Reader and Study Guide** to familiarize students with the section content.

Interactive Reader and Study Guide, Section 1

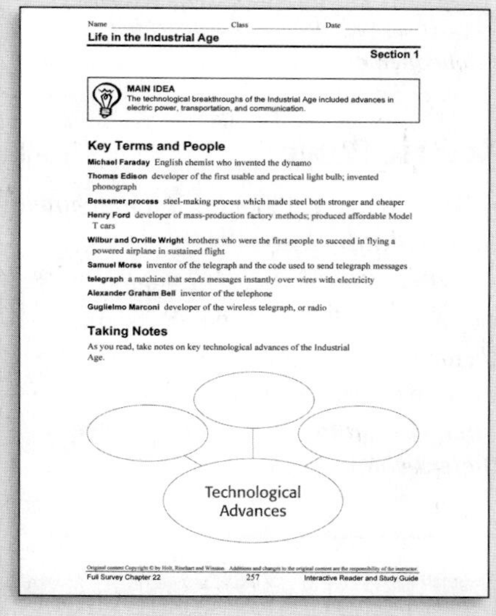

Name ________ Class ________ Date ________

Life in the Industrial Age

Section 1

MAIN IDEA
The technological breakthroughs of the Industrial Age included advances in electric power, transportation, and communication.

Key Terms and People

Michael Faraday English chemist who invented the dynamo
Thomas Edison developer of the first usable and practical light bulb; invented phonograph
Bessemer process steel-making process which made steel both stronger and cheaper
Henry Ford developer of mass-production factory methods; produced affordable Model T cars
Wilbur and Orville Wright brothers who were the first people to succeed in flying a powered airplane in sustained flight
Samuel Morse inventor of the telegraph and the code used to send telegraph messages
telegraph a machine that sends messages instantly over wires with electricity
Alexander Graham Bell inventor of the telephone
Guglielmo Marconi developer of the wireless telegraph, or radio

Taking Notes

As you read, take notes on key technological advances of the Industrial Age.

Technological Advances

Full Survey Chapter 22 257 Interactive Reader and Study Guide

CRF: Vocabulary Builder: Section 1

Taking Notes

Technological Advances—lightbulb; steam-powered trains; Bessemer process; steamships; automobile; airplane; telegraph; telephone; radio and phonograph

go.hrw.com
Online Resources
KEYWORD: SHL LIF
ACTIVITY: The Inventions of Thomas Edison

Direct Teach

Reading Focus

1. How did electric power affect industry and daily life? *drastically changed them; industry—factories no longer relied on steam engines powered by waterways, work day could extend past sunset; daily life—provided cheaper, convenient light source, led to other inventions*

Electric Power

Define What is a dynamo? *a machine that generates electricity by moving a magnet through a coil of copper wire*

Make Generalizations Why did inventors and scientists want to develop new power sources in the 1800s? *Water, coal, and steam were not very efficient sources of power.*

Recent Scholarship

Light! The Industrial Age 1750–1900, Art & Science, Technology & Science examines how the electric light bulb changed the way people live, work, and shop. It also describes how light influenced other inventions, including microscopes and cameras. The book identifies how the use of light led to dramatic changes in painting, with emphasis on the Romantics and the Impressionists.

Light! The Industrial Age 1750–1900, Art & Science, Technology & Science by Andreas Bluhm and Louise Lippincott. Thames & Hudson, 2001.

Electric Power

Before the late 1880s water, coal, and steam had powered industry. As the Industrial Age progressed, though, inventors and scientists were inspired to develop new technologies. One technology drastically changed industry and daily life more than any other—electricity.

Early Attempts at Electric Power For many centuries, scientists had known of and been interested in electricity. During the 1700s Benjamin Franklin and other scientists had performed important experiments. Still, no one had developed a way to harness electricity and put it to use. In 1831, however, English chemist **Michael Faraday** discovered the connection between magnetism and electricity. His discovery led to the dynamo, a machine that generated electricity by moving a magnet through a coil of copper wire. Faraday used the electricity to power an electric motor, and his discoveries led to the development of electrical generators.

During the 1800s other scientists also created devices that used electric power. For instance, in 1860 British chemist Joseph Swan developed a primitive electric lightbulb that gave off light by passing heat through a small strip of paper. However, Swan's lightbulb did not shine for very long, and its light was too dim. Swan's work was a beginning, but it was nearly 40 more years before the invention of a usable lightbulb.

Edison's Lightbulb Based on the work of Faraday and Swan, **Thomas Edison** developed the first usable and practical lightbulb in 1879. The new invention caused a sensation.

HISTORY'S VOICES

> **"Edison's electric light, incredible as it may appear, is produced from a tiny strip of paper that a breath would blow away. Through this little strip of paper is passed an electric current, and the result is a bright, beautiful light . . . and this light, the inventor claims, can be produced cheaper than that from the cheapest oil."**
>
> —Marshall Fox, *New York Herald*, 1879

This invention did not come easily, even to Edison. Instead, it came through trial and error and many hours of work in his laboratory in Menlo Park, New Jersey. As Edison's research became known, young people who shared his passion for inventing flocked to his lab to work for him. In addition to the lightbulb, Edison and his team made generators, motors, light sockets, and other electrical devices.

Edison also played a major role in the development of city electrical utility systems. He built the world's first central electric power plant in New York City. The plant produced enough power to light several city blocks. As a result of Edison's work, many aspects of life became easier.

Effects on Industry and Daily Life The wide availability of electric power transformed industry in both the United States and Europe. Electric power improved industry in three significant ways. First, by using electric power, factories no longer had to rely on large steam engines to power machines. Second, factories did not have to depend on waterways to power the steam engines. Third, factory production increased as factories became less dependent on sunlight. With electric lighting in factories, workers could stay on the job late into the night.

In addition to changing industry, electricity transformed daily life. Before people had electricity, they lit their homes with candles, gaslights, or oil lamps. Electricity provided a cheaper, more convenient light source. Inventors soon created other electrical devices that made daily life more convenient.

READING CHECK **Analyze** How did electricity change industry and daily life?

FACES OF HISTORY

Thomas EDISON
1847–1931

Thomas Edison, one of the world's most brilliant inventors, came from a humble background. He had only a few months of formal schooling. After working as a newsboy, Edison became a telegraph operator, where he got involved in electronic communication. In fact, improvements in the telegraph system were among his first inventions. Eventually, Edison held more than 1,090 patents for new inventions. His goal was to make things that could succeed on the market and, by doing so, prove their usefulness. He also believed in hard work, as he explained in this famous quote. "Genius is one percent inspiration and ninety-nine percent perspiration."

Draw Conclusions Do you think Edison saw himself as a genius? Why or why not?

Skills Focus: Identifying Problem and Solution

Level Tag

Reading Skill
Edison's Invention Factory

1. Organize students into small groups. Tell students that it is the 1890s and each group is a research team at Thomas Edison's "invention factory." Have each group decide on a new invention they want to work on. Students should get approval before proceeding with their invention.
2. Have groups write a proposal that explores the market for their product and the feasibility of producing it affordably. Then have groups develop sketches and diagrams of their product and write an explanation of how the invention will work.
3. Ask volunteers from each group to present their invention to the rest of the class. The rest of the class will represent potential investors. Which inventions would they invest in?

LS Kinesthetic, Visual-Spatial

Alternative Assessment Handbook, Rubrics 3: Artwork; and 14: Group Activity

Answers

Faces of History *possible answer—No, he credited hard work more than inspiration for his discoveries.*

Reading Check *Factories no longer needed steam engines or water sources to power them; production increased; people could light their homes and businesses more safely and effectively with electric lighting.*

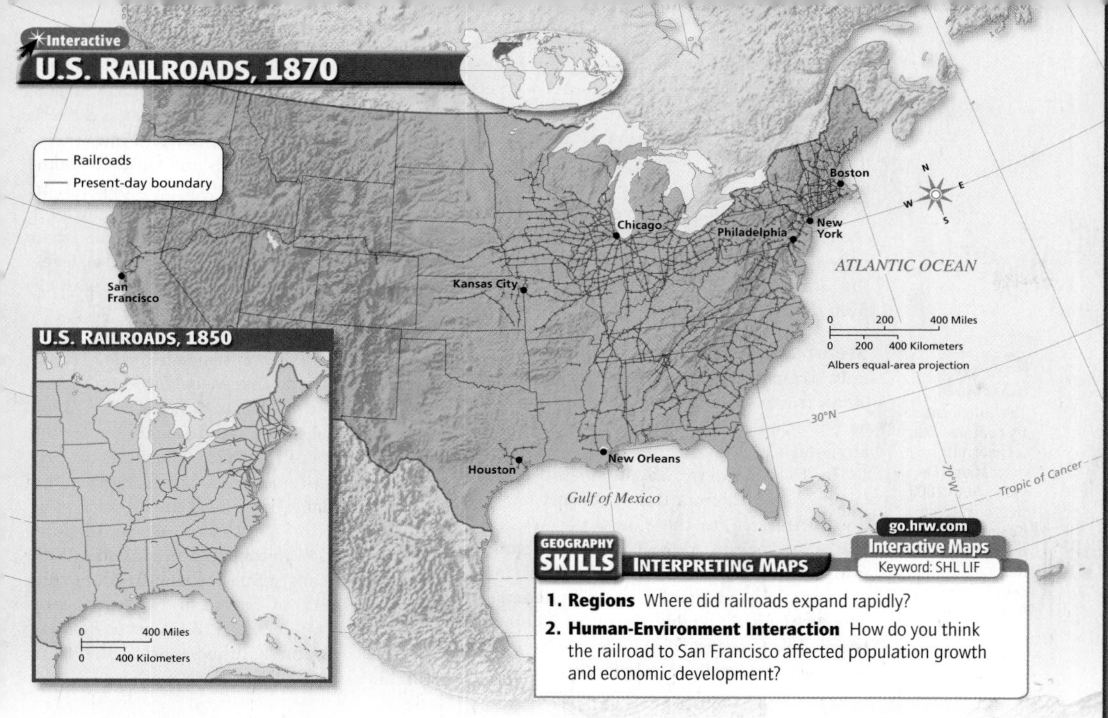

GEOGRAPHY SKILLS **INTERPRETING MAPS**

go.hrw.com
Interactive Maps
Keyword: SHL LIF

1. **Regions** Where did railroads expand rapidly?
2. **Human-Environment Interaction** How do you think the railroad to San Francisco affected population growth and economic development?

Advances in Transportation

In addition to power technology, the late 1800s brought improvements in transportation. The development of efficient steam engines led to trains and steamships, while the internal combustion engine led to cars and airplanes.

Steam-Powered Trains Throughout the early 1800s boats on canals and rivers provided the best means for long-distance travel. Then, with the development of efficient steam engines, trains began to replace boats. Trains could carry heavy loads, did not require waterways, and traveled faster than watercraft. By 1830 the world's first rail line linked two major British cities, Manchester and Liverpool. By 1840 about 3,000 miles of railroad tracks crisscrossed the eastern United States.

Improvements in steel production contributed to the expansion of the railroad system. A new process made steel stronger and was also cheaper and more efficient. Working separately, Englishman Henry Bessemer and American William Kelly developed the new process in the late 1850s. The **Bessemer process** involved forcing air through molten metal to burn out carbon and other impurities that make metal brittle. The process came to be named for Bessemer because he made it a financial success.

Using the Bessemer process, factories increased their production of locomotives and railroad tracks. In addition, engineers used the stronger steel to build bridges that allowed the trains to cross any type of terrain.

As the new steel-making process made building railroads easier, they expanded rapidly. By 1860 a 30,000-mile network of tracks linked the major American cities. West of the Mississippi River, new railroads brought people to unsettled or thinly settled areas of the country. As a result, cities in the American West grew and prospered along the tracks.

Engineers also took railroad technology around the world. India's first train ran in 1851. Just one year later, the first African railroad was built in Egypt. Construction on the world's longest railroad, the Trans-Siberian in Russia, began in 1891.

Direct Teach

Reading Focus

2 What advances in transportation occurred during the Industrial Age? *First, trains began to replace canal and river traffic. Later, automobiles began to replace carriages. In 1903, humans succeeded in flying a powered airplane.*

Advances in Transportation

Explain What advantages did the Bessemer process have over earlier steel-making processes? *made steel stronger by burning out impurities; cheaper and more efficient*

Identify Cause and Effect How did improvements in the production of steel lead to the expansion of the railroad system? *Factories were able to increase their production of locomotives and steel tracks, and engineers could build strong steel bridges.*

Evaluate What was the biggest advantage that railroads had over canals as a means of transportation? *possible answer—Railroads could easily be built anywhere.*

Map Transparency: U.S., 1870

Info to Know

Phonograph In addition to the light bulb, Thomas Edison invented the original phonograph (or "record player") and the motion picture camera.

Primary Source

"Anything that won't sell, I don't want to invent. Its sale is proof of utility, and utility is success."
–Thomas A. Edison

Skills Focus: Making Generalizations

Level Tag

Reading Skill
Advances in Transportation

1. Have each student choose the one form of transportation discussed in this chapter—railroads, automobiles, or airplanes—that they think had the most far-reaching effects. Have students write an editorial telling why their chosen the form of transportation is so revolutionary. Have students predict the changes that will be brought about as a result of the new mode of transportation.
2. Poll the class to see how many students chose to write about each of the three modes of transportation. Which received the most votes? Which received the fewest?
3. Have volunteers read their editorials to the class.
4. Guide the class in a discussion of student editorials. **LS Verbal-Linguistic**

Alternative Assessment Handbook, Rubric 43: Writing to Persuade

Answers

Interpreting Maps **1.** *in the northeast and Midwest;* **2.** *possible answer—spurred growth, made it easier for people to move west*

Direct Teach

Reading Focus

Advances in Transportation

Summarize How did expansion of the railroad benefit trade? *Markets for goods increased, travel time decreased, and new products became available.*

Predict How will Henry Ford's "motor car for the great multitude" change life in the United States? *Affordable cars will give Americans freedom to travel anywhere at any time.*

Activity Modern Transportation Have students sketch modern-day versions of each mode of transportation shown in the transportation feature. How are they similar? How are they different? LS **Visual-Spatial**

CRF: Biography: Granville Woods

Info to Know

Assembly Lines Ransom Eli Olds founded the first automobile factory in 1897. The Olds Motor Vehicle Company was also the first to use an assembly line. In 1913, Henry Ford became the first manufacturer to use a conveyor belt on an assembly line, more than tripling production. Assembly lines with conveyor belts soon became the norm.

The rapid expansion of the railroad helped both travel and trade. As a result, markets for goods increased. Because trains could move huge loads efficiently, transportation costs declined, bringing a wide range of low-cost products to market. In addition, new products became available. Shoppers had more food choices. Perishable foods could get to market before they spoiled. For example, merchants in the United States shipped frozen beef by rail from the west to the east.

THE IMPACT TODAY

The auto industry continues its technological innovations. For example, in 2002 the Ford Motor Company began production of a car that runs on fuel cells powered by hydrogen. Water is the only emission.

Steamships Just as trains revolutionized land transportation, steamships changed ocean travel. Sailing ships depended on wind for power, but steamships could travel through any kind of weather.

In 1849 regular U.S. steamship service began, traveling from the west coast, around South America, to the east coast. Within a few years, engineers had made mechanical improvements to steamships. By 1870, long-distance movement of goods by steamship was economically viable. People also came on board. A long ocean voyage became an option for people looking for jobs or for fun.

The Automobile As early as 1769, several Europeans had tried to build a form of personal transportation. For more than a century only small advances were made. Finally, German engineers Carl Benz and Gottlieb Daimler both developed practical automobiles. In 1885 Benz built a three-wheeled vehicle. A year later, Daimler put an internal combustion engine on a horse carriage. Daimler also developed the carburetor, which mixed fuel with air for proper combustion in the engine.

At about the same time, several Americans developed their own automobile models. These early cars were too expensive for most buyers, but **Henry Ford** wanted to change that. In 1908 he announced, "I will build a motor car for the great multitude." He did it. Using mass-production methods in modern factories, Ford built a line of affordable cars called the Model T.

By 1920 the Model T made up 40 to 50 percent of U.S. automobile production. With cars, Americans gained a new freedom that allowed them to travel anywhere at any time. Road builders had to keep up. By 1915 American roads spanned more miles than rail lines.

New Ways to Travel

New modes of transportation revolutionized travel in the 1800s and early 1900s. One of the new ways to travel was introduced by Orville and Wilbur Wright, pictured below, when they flew their airplane at Kitty Hawk, North Carolina, in 1903.

A train arriving in a New Mexico station

The Train at Glorieta Summit, by Roy Anderson, 1800s

The Wright Brothers at Kitty Hawk, N. Carolina, artist unknown, 1900s

Model T Fords in a St. Louis park in the 1920s

The Granger Collection, N

Skills Focus: Comparing and Contrasting

Above Level

Research Required

Reading Skill

Powering Transportation

1. Organize students into small groups. Have the groups conduct outside research using reliable Internet or print sources to find out how steam engines and internal combustion engines work. Students should investigate the kinds of fuels that can be used to power steam engines and internal combustion engines.
2. Have each group make a before-and-after chart describing why internal combustion engines quickly replaced steam engines.
3. Have volunteers share the information from their charts with the entire class. Guide students in a discussion of the changes that were made possible as a result of the internal combustion engine. What, if any, alternatives are there to using internal combustion engines powered by fossil fuels? LS **Interpersonal, Visual-Spatial**

Alternative Assessment Handbook, Rubrics 7: Charts; and 30: Research

Linking TO Today

Telephone Technology

Although Alexander Graham Bell and Thomas Watson made the first telephone in 1876, improvements were gradual. Rural areas and small towns, especially, were often behind the cities in technological progress.

For example, only 50 years ago many calls still required the help of a live operator. To place a call, a person picked up the receiver, and an operator said "Number, please." The caller replied with a series of numbers. The operator made the connection, the other phone rang, and the call was completed.

The first telephone operators were boys who had experience as telegraph operators. But customers complained that the boys were rude to them. In 1878 the telephone companies began hiring women operators. Emma Nutt, a Boston woman, was the first one hired.

Today, of course, we can talk, send instant messages, surf the Internet, and take photos on our phones—without any help.

Analyze How would your daily life be different if you did not have access to advanced telephone technology?

A modern cell phone ▶

An operator connects two callers on a switchboard in about 1900.

The Airplane Advances in transportation were not limited to land and sea. People also wanted to fly. Hot air balloons made their debut in 1783 and became useful for wartime spying and aerial photography. However, balloons were at the mercy of the wind.

A big step forward in controlled flight happened at Kitty Hawk, North Carolina, on December 17, 1903. On that date, American brothers **Wilbur and Orville Wright** succeeded in flying a powered airplane in sustained flight.

Drawing from the work of earlier aviation engineers, the Wrights had spent four years developing their lightweight airplane. They used principles of aerodynamics, which is the study of how forces act on solid surfaces moving through the air. The Wrights designed a glider with specially shaped wings. To power their plane, they attached a version of the internal combustion engine. The first powered flight went only 120 feet, but the plane's performance improved rapidly. This first flight paved the way for the use of airplanes to travel the globe, transport goods, and fight wars.

READING CHECK **Identifying Cause and Effect** What effect did advances in transportation have on daily life?

Advances in Communication

Today, news and messages travel around the world in mere seconds by e-mail and telephone. In the early 1800s, though, news traveled much more slowly, by boat or by messenger on foot, horseback, or carriage. As a result, entrepreneurs and inventors started to look for better and faster ways to communicate.

The Telegraph Putting electricity to use made possible the invention of the **telegraph**, a machine that sent messages instantly over wires. American **Samuel Morse** is credited with inventing the telegraph in 1837. Morse also developed a "language," which became known as Morse code, for sending telegraph messages. Morse code is a series of long and short signals that represent letters and numbers. These telegraph messages were transmitted as electrical pulses of different lengths.

In 1844 Morse received funding from the United States government to lay 35 miles of telegraph wires between Washington, D.C., and Baltimore., Maryland The first telegraph message Morse tapped out was, "What hath God wrought?" With this message, a new era in communication technology began.

Direct Teach

Reading Focus

3 What were the advances in communication, and how were they achieved? *telegraph, telephone, radio; made possible by the invention of electricity; telephone and telegraph sent messages over wires, radio provided wireless communication*

Advances in Communication

Recall Where did funding for the first telegraph wires come from? *the United States government*

Make Inferences Why could the telegraph not have been invented earlier? *It relied on electricity.*

Linking to Today

Telephone Technology

Predict Remind students that cellular telephone technology is relatively new, and currently changing. Have students predict what the next generation of cell phones will look like—and what they will do.

Skills Focus: Identifying Cause and Effect

At Level

Advances in Communication

Standard English Mastery

1. Guide students in a discussion of the advances in communication that were made during the 1800s.
2. Tell students that it is 1850 and they are writing a magazine article about the effects of the telegraph. Have students use the following questions to guide them: How have changes in the speed of communication changed life? Would these changes constitute a revolution in communication? Why or why not? What other changes might occur as the country is linked by telegraph wires? What might happen if telegraph wires someday link the United States with Europe and England with India? What future developments might further revolutionize communication?
3. Have students check their articles for correct spelling and grammar. Ask volunteers to read their articles to the class. **LS Verbal-Linguistic**

Alternative Assessment Handbook, Rubrics 11: Discussions; and 40: Writing to Describe

Answers

Linking to Today *possible answers—much more complicated, harder to communicate quickly, more in-person contact*

Reading Check *better and faster means of transportation; made it possible to get more goods to market at lower costs, increasing consumers' choices*

Direct Teach

Reading Focus

Advances in Communication

Sequence In what order were the major developments in communication made? *telegraph, telephone, radio*

Make Judgments Which of the three advances in communication had the biggest impact? Why? *possible answer—telegraph, first to make communication instantaneous*

Review & Assess

Close

Have students summarize the technological breakthroughs that took place during the Industrial Age.

Review

Online Quiz, Section 1

Assess

SE Section 1 Assessment

Progress Assessment: Section 1 Quiz

Alternative Assessment Handbook

Reteach/Intervene

Interactive Reader and Study Guide, Section 1

Interactive Skills Tutor CD-ROM

As the United States grew, the importance of the telegraph increased. By 1851 more than 50 telegraph companies were in operation in the United States. About 10 years later, telegraph wires strung on poles along established railroad tracks linked much of the country. At railroad stations, passengers could send messages, or telegrams, to friends and family.

Communication between the United States and Europe also improved with the laying of a telegraph cable on the floor of the Atlantic Ocean in 1866. By 1870 telegraph wires stretched from England to India.

The telegraph revolutionized more than personal communication. In many countries, businesses could keep in close contact with suppliers and markets. News traveled around the world in hours instead of weeks. Newspapers sent correspondents to the front lines of wars, from where they telegraphed back vivid reports of victories and defeats. The reading public was very impressed by these timely reports. The reports were one way in which the telegraph globalized communication.

The Telephone As use of the telegraph spread around the world, inventors tried to improve on it. American **Alexander Graham Bell**, a teacher of hearing-impaired students, was one of the scientists working in sound technology. Bell tried to create a way to send multiple telegraph messages at the same time.

While working on that device, Bell made a remarkable discovery. One day in 1876 he was in one room and his assistant Thomas Watson was in another. Bell said, "Mr. Watson, come here, I want to see you!" Watson could hear Bell's voice not just through the air but also through the device's receiver. The telephone was born.

During the 1880s demand for telephones increased. Telephone companies laid thousands of miles of phone lines across the United States. By 1900 almost 1.5 million telephones were installed in American homes and offices.

The Radio and Phonograph Although the telephone revolutionized communication, the technology was limited. Wires could only stretch so far. A new wireless technology was based on theories about electromagnetic waves. In 1895 Italian physicist **Guglielmo Marconi** used the discoveries to build a wireless telegraph, or radio. First used as a communication method for ships, the radio was later used for entertainment and news. Entertainment options increased when Thomas Edison recorded sound with one of his many inventions. It was the phonograph, which became the record player. With these inventions, music was available to everyone.

READING CHECK **Contrast** How did the telegraph differ from the telephone?

SECTION 1 ASSESSMENT

go.hrw.com
Online Quiz
Keyword: SHL LIF HP

Reviewing Ideas, Terms, and People

1. **a. Recall** What did **Michael Faraday** invent?
   b. Draw Conclusions What impact did electricity have on industry?
   c. Evaluate Assess the validity of this statement: **Thomas Edison** contributed to all aspects of electrical technology.
2. **a. Define** What is the **Bessemer process**?
   b. Explain What advantages did rail travel have over canal and river travel?
   c. Develop What advantages did the automobile provide?
3. **a. Define** What is the **telegraph**?
   b. Analyze How did advances in communication technology change the way people lived in the late 1800s?
   c. Evaluate Do you think the telegraph, telephone, radio, and phonograph could have had both positive and negative effects on daily life in the late 1800s? Explain your answer.

Critical Thinking

4. **Identify Supporting Details** Use your notes and a graphic organizer like this one to record details that support the main idea about one type of technological advance. Write the subsection's main idea in the center circle.

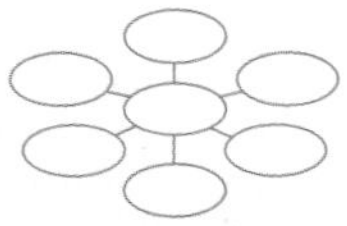

FOCUS ON WRITING

5. **Narrative** Write a paragraph that tells the story of one of the advances in technology during the 1800s. Include details from this section.

Section 1 Assessment Answers

1. **a.** the dynamo,
   b. Factories no longer relied on steam engines or water sources; production increased as workday lengthened.
   c. possible answer—valid, he created many different electrical inventions
2. **a.** a steel-making process that made steel stronger
   b. faster, not tied to waterways
   c. gave Americans the freedom to travel
3. **a.** a machine that sends messages instantly over wires with electricity
   b. revolutionized communication, allowing news to travel quickly
   c. possible answer—revolutionized communication, made life complicated
4. electric power—transformed industry and daily life; transportation—increased availability of products; people free to travel; communication—allowed news to travel quickly
5. Paragraphs should discuss the innovation's development and impact.

Answers

Reading Check *telegraph transmitted coded messages; telephone transmitted voice*

Focus on Themes

Science and Technology

Humanity's fascination with electricity has a long history. The first people were probably awed by lightning. In the 600s BC a Greek scholar noticed that rubbing a piece of amber produced a spark. More than 2,000 years later a German physicist made a device that generated static electricity. Then in 1831 Michael Faraday saw the connection between magnetism and electricity, and a new technology was born. Since then, electricity has changed practically all aspects of daily life in industrialized countries.

▲ **NOW This NASA image shows where artificial lights shine from the earth at night. The composite of satellite images took a year to complete.**

BEFORE ELECTRICITY Before the development of electricity, people depended on several sources of power for their daily needs. They burned candles and oil lamps for light. To drive machines, they used the power of muscle, water, coal, and steam. For other activities, people depended on themselves and each other. For entertainment, audiences attended live performances. To communicate long distances, they wrote letters. Today, it is hard for us to imagine what life was like before the widespread use of electricity.

The Granger Collection, New York

◀ **THEN This lightbulb is a replica of the one invented by Thomas Edison in 1879.**

AFTER ELECTRICITY What aspect of daily life has not been transformed by electricity? Think about how electricity makes your daily routine possible, starting with the alarm clock that wakes you in the morning. Drying your hair, cooking breakfast, checking the weather on the Internet before you decide what to wear—electricity makes it all possible. Throughout your whole day, from lighted classrooms and the computer lab to instant messages on your cell phone and late-night TV talk shows, electricity powers your modern lifestyle.

There is a price to pay for all this convenience. Much of the world's electricity is generated by burning fossil fuels, which pollute air around the world. As a result, even people who live where electricity is not available are affected by its use. Another type of pollution is the result of so much light. In big cities, people cannot see the stars because the lights are so bright. To avoid this light pollution, astronomers must build their telescopes in remote locations or send them into space. Still, there are probably few among us who would want to go back to the "dark" ages.

Skills Focus UNDERSTANDING THEMES

1. **Contrast** How would your daily life be different if you did not have electricity?
2. **Support a Position** Would you give up some conveniences to reduce the burning of fossil fuels? Explain your answer.

Focus on Themes

Science and Technology

Info to Know

Life Before Electricity Before electricity, artificial light was dim, sooty, and smelly. Even regular cleaning could not get rid of the grime and odor left throughout the house by candles, kerosene lamps, and gas lights. Because of their flames, these light sources could cause fires. In addition, gas lights released dangerous fumes if the flame went out.

Houses were designed to be functional, with doors to shut off individual rooms for airing and to minimize draft. Rooms were decorated in dark colors to hide soot.

Skills Focus: Identifying Problem and Solution

At Level

Research Required

Reading Skill

The Impact of Electricity

Background: In addition to polluting the air, fossil fuels are becoming increasingly expensive, driving up the cost of generating electricity.

1. Organize students into six groups. Have each group research one of the following alternatives to fossil fuels for creating electricity: nuclear energy, solar energy, geothermal energy, wind power, water power, burning wood or other biomass such as garbage. Have students make a list of the pros and cons of using each.
2. Have volunteers from each group share their lists with the class. Ask members of the class to name any additional benefits or disadvantages they can think of for each energy source.
3. Guide students in a discussion of the best ways to reduce dependency on fossil fuels. **LS Interpersonal**

Alternative Assessment Handbook, Rubrics 14: Group Activity; and 30: Research

Answers

Understanding Themes 1. *Answers will vary. Students should recognize that almost every device in their homes is powered by electricity.* **2.** *possible answers—Yes, giving up some conveniences would be worth it if pollution decreased; no, it would be difficult to give up the conveniences to which we are accustomed.*

Preteach

Getting Started

Use the **Interactive Reader and Study Guide** to familiarize students with the section content.

Interactive Reader and Study Guide, Section 2

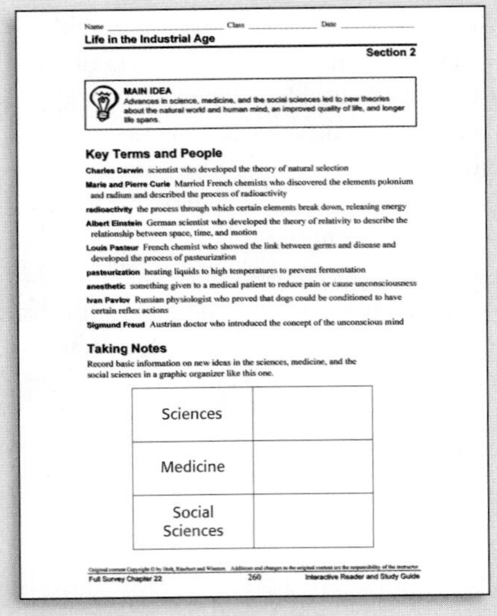

Name ____________ Class ________ Date ________

Life in the Industrial Age

Section 2

MAIN IDEA
Advances in science, medicine, and the social sciences led to new theories about the natural world and human mind, an improved quality of life, and longer life spans.

Key Terms and People

Charles Darwin scientist who developed the theory of natural selection

Marie and Pierre Curie Married French chemists who discovered the elements polonium and radium and described the process of radioactivity

radioactivity the process through which certain elements break down, releasing energy

Albert Einstein German scientist who developed the theory of relativity to describe the relationship between space, time, and motion

Louis Pasteur French chemist who showed the link between germs and disease and developed the process of pasteurization

pasteurization heating liquids to high temperatures to prevent fermentation

anesthetic something given to a medical patient to reduce pain or cause unconsciousness

Ivan Pavlov Russian physiologist who proved that dogs could be conditioned to have certain reflex actions

Sigmund Freud Austrian doctor who introduced the concept of the unconscious mind

Taking Notes

Record basic information on new ideas in the sciences, medicine, and the social sciences in a graphic organizer like this one.

Sciences	
Medicine	
Social Sciences	

Full Survey Chapter 22 260 Interactive Reader and Study Guide

Academic Vocabulary

Review with students the high-use academic term in this section.

theories plausible general principles offered to explain what has been observed (p. 269)

CRF: Vocabulary Builder: Section 2

Taking Notes

Sciences—theory of evolution; modern atomic theory; periodic table; radioactivity; relativity; Medicine—pasteurization, new vaccinations; anesthetics; more modern hospitals; decline in infant mortality; Social Sciences—new fields of study including psychology, archaeology, anthropology, sociology

go.hrw.com
Online Resources

KEYWORD: SHL LIF
ACTIVITY: Introduction to Anesthesia to Surgery

SECTION 2

Scientific and Medical Achievements

Before You Read

Main Idea

Advances in science, medicine, and the social sciences led to new theories about the natural world and human mind, an improved quality of life, and longer life spans.

Reading Focus

1. What were some of the new ideas in the sciences?
2. What medical breakthroughs affected the quality of life?
3. What new ideas developed within the social sciences?

Key Terms and People

Charles Darwin
Marie and Pierre Curie
radioactivity
Albert Einstein
Louis Pasteur
pasteurization
anesthetic
Ivan Pavlov
Sigmund Freud

TAKING NOTES Use a graphic organizer like this one to record new ideas in the sciences, medicine, and the social sciences.

Sciences	
Medicine	
Social Sciences	

Tracking a Killer

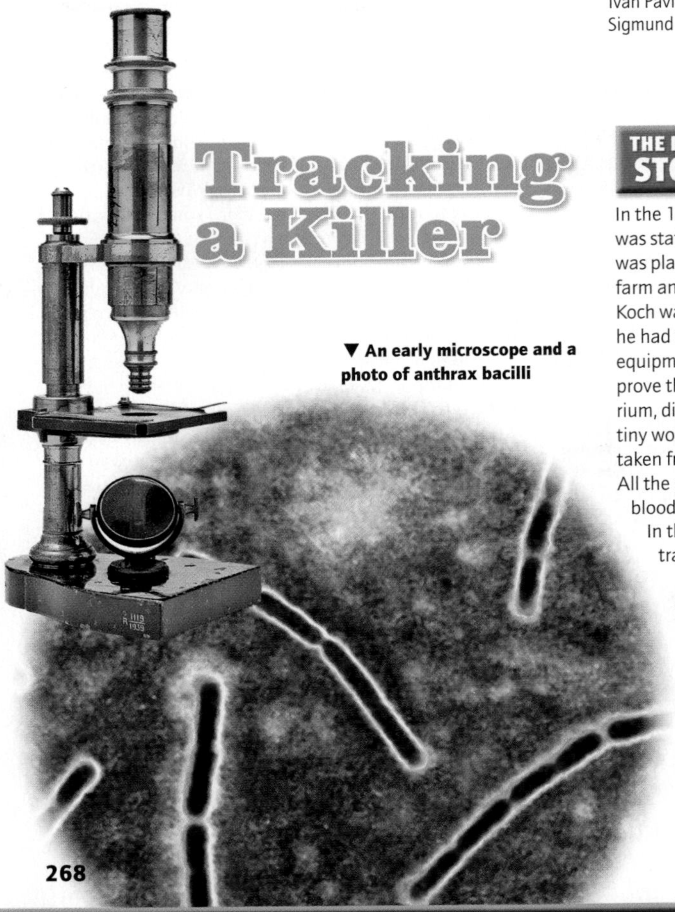

▼ **An early microscope and a photo of anthrax bacilli**

THE INSIDE STORY ***How did a poorly equipped country doctor make major discoveries about disease?***

In the 1870s a military doctor named Robert Koch was stationed in the German countryside. The region was plagued by anthrax, a disease that killed many farm animals and could be transmitted to people. Koch wanted to learn more about the disease. But he had no library, no assistants, and practically no equipment besides a microscope. He first hoped to prove that a previously discovered bacillus, or bacterium, did indeed cause anthrax. To do so, Koch carved tiny wood slivers to inject mice with anthrax bacillus taken from the blood of animals killed by the disease. All the mice died. Then he injected other mice with blood from healthy animals, and they all survived. In this way, Koch proved that anthrax could be transmitted by the blood of infected animals.

Koch went on to discover that the anthrax bacillus produced seedlike bodies called spores that could spread the disease. Later, Koch made additional discoveries that led to treatments for malaria, tuberculosis, and other diseases. Koch's discoveries are among countless scientific advances made during the 1800s. ■

268

Teach the Main Idea

At Level

Scientific and Medical Achievements

1. **Teach** Ask students the Reading Focus questions to teach this section.
2. **Apply** Have students create an outline of the section using the red headings as main points. Have students identify at least two main ideas under each of the blue subheadings.
3. **Review** Review student outlines as a class. Have students identify the points in their outlines that they feel are most important or most interesting. Guide students in a discussion of the similarities and the differences between science and social science.
4. **Practice/Homework** Have students write letters to the editor of a scientific journal about an important scientific or medical achievement described in this section. Letters should persuade readers that the achievement is of utmost importance.

LS Verbal-Linguistic

Alternative Assessment Handbook, Rubrics 11: Discussion; and 17: Letters to Editors

Reading like a Historian

A Scientist's Report on Island Animals

Analyzing Primary Sources During his long voyage on the HMS *Beagle*, Charles Darwin recorded his observations on practically everything he saw and experienced. In the passage given here, he describes the iguanas and birds of the Galapagos Islands, which lie in the Pacific Ocean about 600 miles west of South America.

As you read, think about how a report from 1835 might differ from a present-day scientific report from the same islands. Consider:

- the author's background
- scientific knowledge at the time
- details of scientific observation

These islands appear paradises for the whole family of Reptiles . . . The black Lava rocks on the beach are frequented by large (2–3 ft) most disgusting, clumsy Lizards. They are as black as the porous rocks over which they crawl & seek their prey from the Sea. Somebody calls them "imps of darkness." They assuredly well become the land they inhabit . . . The birds are Strangers to Man & think him as innocent as their countrymen the huge Tortoises. Little birds within 3 & four feet, quietly hopped about the Bushes & were not frightened.

—Charles Darwin's *Beagle Diary*, 1835

Darwin's comments about the birds' behavior indicate that few if any people had ever visited the islands.

Skills Focus READING LIKE A HISTORIAN

1. **Author** What does the passage reveal about Darwin's previous experiences? about knowledge at the time?
2. **Details** What details demonstrate Darwin's skills of scientific observation?

See **Skills Handbook**, p. H25

New Ideas in Science

Among the many new ideas of the 1800s were those developed by a young geologist named **Charles Darwin**. He had taken a long voyage during which he studied variations among plants and animals. Many years later, Darwin published his theories in a book titled *On the Origin of Species*.

Darwin's Theories Through careful observation of what he saw on his journey, Darwin developed the concept of natural selection. According to this theory, creatures that are well adapted to their environments have a better chance of surviving to produce offspring. The offspring will inherit the physical features that help the creatures survive. Over time, Darwin argued, the species will evolve, or change to improve its survival chances. This idea became known as the theory of evolution.

Darwin's theory was controversial, however. The theory indicated that human beings were descended from other animals. Many people thought this possibility was simply ridiculous. Others opposed Darwin because his theory differed from the creation story in the Bible.

Advances in Chemistry and Physics In the early 1800s chemists and physicists also made landmark discoveries. For centuries, scientists had proposed that tiny particles, or atoms, made up chemical elements. Moreover, most scientists thought that all elements were made of the same kinds of atoms. But in 1803 English chemist John Dalton developed modern atomic theory. An essential part of this theory is the idea that atoms of different elements are themselves of different size and mass.

In 1871 Russian chemist Dmitri Mendeleyev arranged all the chemical elements into a chart called the periodic table. The table revealed previously unknown patterns among the elements. Mendeleyev left gaps in the periodic table, knowing that some elements were yet to be discovered. He even described what those elements would be like.

As Mendeleyev had predicted, scientists that came after him discovered more elements that fit into the periodic table. For example, in France in 1898 chemists **Marie and Pierre Curie** discovered polonium and radium. The Curies also concluded that certain elements release energy when they break down. Marie Curie called this process **radioactivity**.

ACADEMIC VOCABULARY
theories plausible general principles offered to explain what has been observed

Direct Teach

Reading Focus

1 What were some of the new ideas in the sciences? *ideas that provided a much better understanding of the way the universe works, including the origins of species, atomic structure, and the relationships between space, time, and motion*

New Ideas in Science

Identify What is the periodic table? *a chart in which all the chemical elements are arranged*

Explain Why was Darwin's theory of evolution controversial? *Some people thought the idea that humans descended from animals was ridiculous. The theory differed from the creation story in the Bible.*

Evaluate How important were Einstein's ideas to science? *revolutionary—overturned what Newton and many others had said about how the universe worked*

Info to Know

Birds in the Galapagos Darwin collected a large number of animal specimens on the Galapagos Islands. After analyzing the specimens, he realized that several Galapagos birds, which he had first thought to be totally different kinds of birds, were actually closely related to a species of finches. The beaks of the different birds varied greatly in size and shape. Darwin realized the beaks were specialized according to what the birds ate.

Differentiating Instruction

Above Level

Advanced Learners/Gifted and Talented

Research Required

Background: Tell students that in the early 1800s French biologist Jean-Baptist Lamarck set forth a theory of evolution, which stated that living things changed their form in response to their environments. For example, giraffes developed long necks because they always had to stretch high up in trees. He believed that such acquired changes were then passed on by inheritance to offspring. Many of Lamarck's ideas were later proven wrong, but he did influence Charles Darwin.

1. Have students construct a Venn diagram showing the major ideas of Lamarck and Darwin and what points the two scientists had in common.
2. Have volunteers share their Venn diagrams.
3. Guide students in a discussion of the theories of Lamarck and Darwin. On what points did they agree? On what points did they disagree? **LS Visual-Spatial**

Alternative Assessment Handbook, Rubrics 13: Graphic Organizers; and 30: Research

Answers

Reading Like a Historian

1. *suggests he and many others had not seen birds and animals like this before;* **2.** *the many descriptive details about the size, appearance, and behavior of the animals and birds; shows that he feels superior to the people he is describing, and pities them for their "miserable" life*

Direct Teach

Reading Focus

New Ideas in Science

Describe According to Ernest Rutherford, what is the nucleus of an atom like? *a heavy core at the center of an atom, made up of positively charged particles called protons*

Analyze Where does the relativity in Einstein's theory of relativity come into play? *the idea that motion can only be measured relative to a particular observer*

Reading Focus

2 What medical breakthroughs affected the quality of life? *Pasteur discovered methods of preventing disease through pasteurization and vaccines. Other scientists developed anesthetics and antiseptics.*

Medical Breakthroughs

Recall What was the concept of spontaneous generation? *the idea that bacteria, flies, or other tiny animals could spring to life out of nonliving matter*

Evaluate In addition to being useful in combating diseases, how could an understanding of bacteria have negative effects? *Bacteria can be used in biological warfare.*

Primary Source

"I am one of those who think like Nobel, that humanity will draw more good than evil from new discoveries."
–Marie Curie

Answers

Faces of History *because she helped stockpile radioactive materials for use in health care and research; because she won the Nobel Prize*

Reading Check *evolution, radioactivity, relativity*

Other scientists developed theories based on the Curies' work. In 1911 British chemist Ernest Rutherford realized that in the center of an atom lay a core called a nucleus. In addition, he found that the nucleus is made up of positively charged particles, which he called protons. These findings disproved the long-held belief that an atom is a solid piece of matter.

Einstein's Genius In 1905 German-Jewish scientist **Albert Einstein** revolutionized physics. In an early work, Einstein used mathematics to show that light can act not only as a wave, but also like tiny particles of energy. In another paper, Einstein developed the special theory of relativity, based on two crucial ideas. One was that no particle of matter can move faster than the speed of light. The other is that motion can be measured only from the viewpoint of a particular observer. Therefore, scientists cannot speak of absolute motion, space, or time.

Among Einstein's ideas was a now-famous formula: $E = mc^2$. The formula means that a small amount of mass can be converted into a huge amount of energy. Einstein also proposed that space itself is curved and that one must include time in the study of space. These theories overturned what Sir Isaac Newton and many scientists who came after Newton had said about how the universe worked.

READING CHECK **Summarize** What new theories revolutionized science?

THE IMPACT TODAY

Pasteurization technology is still improving. With ultra-high-temperature (UHT) pasteurization, milk is heated to above the boiling point for one or two seconds. If in a sterile container, UHT milk can be stored without refrigeration for months.

FACES OF HISTORY

Marie CURIE
1867–1934

Marie Curie's accomplishments went beyond her discoveries related to radioactivity. At a girls' school, she introduced the idea of teaching science through experiments. Curie was the first woman to teach at the Sorbonne, the oldest university in Paris. She also helped stockpile rare and valuable radioactive minerals for use in health care and further research.

Curie shared the Nobel Prize for Physics in 1903 with her husband and another physicist. Then in 1911, she received the Nobel Prize for chemistry on her own. Although Curie's work was brilliant, it was ultimately fatal. She died from leukemia caused by exposure to radiation.

Draw Conclusions Why do you think Marie Curie is respected and revered by workers in many health care professions?

Medical Breakthroughs

During the late 1800s breakthroughs in medicine occurred as a result of the scientific advances made earlier in the century. Fundamental concepts of disease, medical care, and sanitation were revealed.

Preventing Disease For thousands of years, people had been mystified by what caused disease. Part of the mystery was solved in 1870 when French chemist **Louis Pasteur** showed the link between microbes and disease. He also disproved a concept called spontaneous generation—the idea that bacteria, flies, or other tiny animals could spring to life out of nonliving matter. Instead, Pasteur showed that bacteria are always present in the air, although we cannot see them, and reproduce like other living things.

Pasteur also discovered that bacteria present in the air cause fermentation, the process that makes grape juice turn into wine and milk turn sour. By heating liquids and foods to high temperatures, Pasteur killed the bacteria and prevented fermentation. His process became known as **pasteurization**. The process also destroys bacteria that cause disease. Today, most milk, cheese, and juice on our grocery shelves has been sterilized, or made germ-free, through pasteurization.

Pasteur next targeted a deadly disease that was a constant threat to people and their livestock—anthrax. To prevent anthrax, Pasteur injected animals with a vaccine containing weakened anthrax germs, which prevented the animals from getting sick. His vaccine worked because the body builds up substances called antibodies to fight weakened germs when they enter the body.

Preventing rabies was Pasteur's next goal. He developed a vaccine in 1885 and saved the life of a young boy who had been bitten by a rabid dog. Pasteur's fame was secured.

Improving Medical Care Other medical practices improved also. One was the treatment of pain. Surgery patients suffered terribly. American surgeon Crawford W. Long discovered a solution. Long had his patients breathe in a gas called ether. It was an **anesthetic**, a drug that reduces pain and in large doses makes the patient unconscious.

Collaborative Learning

At Level

Emergency Room in the 1800s

1. Organize the class into small groups. Have each group write a skit illustrating the state of medicine in the early 1800s, before the development of anesthetics and antiseptics. Each of the students in the group should have a role in the skit. (Students may wish to conduct additional research to find out more about medical practices of the early 1800s.)
2. Have each group present its skit to the rest of the class.
3. Guide students in a discussion of advances in medical science between the early 1800s and today. What further developments can students envision? **LS Interpersonal, Kinesthetic**

Alternative Assessment Handbook, Rubrics 14: Group Activity; and 33: Skits and Reader's Theater

FORENSICS in History

Do the Prints Match?

Forensics advanced in the 1800s along with the other sciences. The use of fingerprints in solving crimes was a major development.

Who solved the crimes? Around the world today, fingerprints are the most commonly used forensic evidence. Scientists and law enforcement officers in many countries contributed to their use.

In the 1820s a Czech scientist classified fingerprints into categories but did not note that fingerprints were unique. Decades later, a British official in India required fingerprints on contracts. Over time, he noticed that a person's prints did not change with age. A Scottish doctor working in Japan is probably the first person to prove a suspect's innocence by showing that fingerprints left at the crime scene did not match those of the suspect. In Argentina in 1892, a police officer matched a bloody fingerprint to a woman who had killed her sons but cut her own throat to avoid arrest. By the end of the 1800s, police around the world were using fingerprints to solve crimes.

Analyze Why do you think the value of fingerprints was not recognized more quickly?

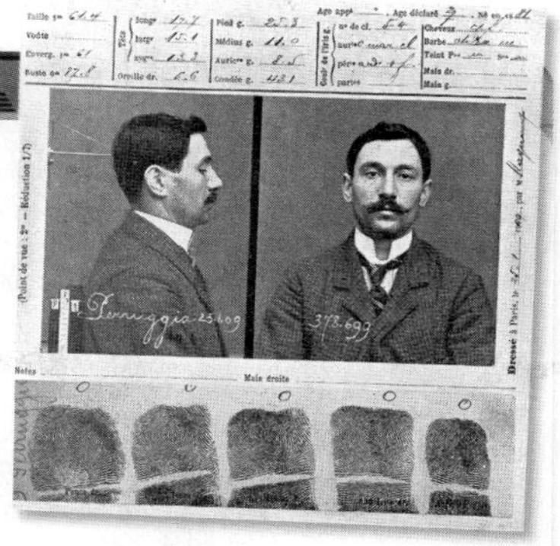

▲ The police record of the thief who stole the *Mona Lisa* in 1911 includes his fingerprints.

In 1842 Long performed the first painless operation by administering ether. Other types of anesthetics were soon developed.

Still, many surgical patients later died from infections. In the 1860s English surgeon Joseph Lister began cleaning wounds and equipment with an antiseptic—a germ-killing agent containing carbolic acid. By using the antiseptic, Lister reduced post-surgery deaths in one hospital ward from 45 to 15 percent.

Another improvement in public health was the building of more modern hospitals. More physicians, nurses, and other medical professionals were trained. Nursing schools trained large numbers of women as nurses or physicians' assistants. Some women even enrolled in medical school to become doctors. By 1900, 5 percent of American physicians were women.

A major result of these developments in medical care and public health was a dramatic decline in infant mortality, or deaths in infancy. Statistics from Sweden provide a clear example. In 1800 Sweden reported 240 deaths of infants under one year old per 1,000 live births. By 1898 that figure had dropped to 91 deaths.

READING CHECK **Identify Cause and Effect** What medical advances allowed people to live longer?

New Ideas in Social Sciences

In the late 1800s scientists expanded their focus to include the study of the mind and human societies. These new fields became known as the social sciences and include psychology, archaeology, anthropology, and sociology.

Psychology In the 1890s the study of the mind and human behavior emerged as a separate field known as psychology. Observation and experiments helped psychologists explore their subject.

To better understand human behavior some scientists studied animal behavior. Russian physiologist **Ivan Pavlov** used dogs as research subjects to prove that animals could be conditioned, or taught, to have certain reflex actions. In his study, Pavlov rang a bell each time he fed the dogs. Over time Pavlov discovered that instead of only salivating at the sight or smell of food, the dogs salivated when they heard the bell. Pavlov called this reaction the conditioned reflex. By studying the dogs' behavior, Pavlov concluded that human behaviors are also a series of connected conditioned reflexes.

Direct Teach

Reading Focus

3 What new ideas developed within the social sciences? *new ideas about human behavior; new ideas about communities and culture*

New Ideas in Social Sciences

Identify What are the social sciences? *fields that study the mind and human societies, including psychology, archaeology, anthropology, and sociology*

Draw Conclusions Why might some people object to the idea that human behaviors are a series of conditioned reflexes? *possible answer—might feel that it reduces them to the same level as animals*

CRF: Biography: Elizabeth Blackwell

Info to Know

Louis Pasteur In the 1990s historians revealed that they had learned from Pasteur's notebooks that the scientist had committed several misdeeds. He "borrowed" a technique from a competitor who was also working on an anthrax vaccine; he lied in his published paper about the kind of vaccine he used in his anthrax experiment; and he used his newly developed rabies vaccine on a human subject when it had not yet been tested on animals. Historians believe that Pasteur and other great scientists of his day, such as Michael Faraday, regularly violated scientific ethics.

Skills Focus: Identifying Main Idea and Details

At Level

Reading Skill

Charting the Social Sciences

1. Guide the class in a discussion of the social sciences using the following questions as a guide: What are the social sciences? In addition to the social sciences discussed in this section, what other branches of study could be considered social sciences? How do the social sciences differ from the natural sciences? How did science influence the study of the social sciences?
2. Have students make charts showing the various social sciences and explaining what is studied in each field.
3. Have volunteers share their charts with the class. **LS Verbal-Linguistic, Visual-Spatial**

Alternative Assessment Handbook, Rubrics 7: Charts; and 11: Discussions

Answers

Forensics in History *possible answer—It may not have occurred to anyone that each person's fingerprints would be unique, just that there were different general patterns.*

Reading Check *pasteurization, antiseptics, and anesthetics*

Direct Teach

Reading Focus

New Ideas in Social Sciences

Identify Why was Freud interested in dreams? *He believed dreams revealed repressed thoughts, thoughts that might cause mental illness.*

Contrast How did archaeology change in the 1800s? *Early excavations were little more than treasure hunts; modern archaeology takes a scientific approach, recording and carefully preserving all the work.*

CRF: Literature: *Frankenstein*

Quick Facts Transparency: New Ideas in the Sciences

Review & Assess

Close

Guide students in a discussion of 19th-century achievements in science, medicine, and the social sciences.

Review

Online Quiz, Section 2

Assess

SE Section 2 Assessment

Progress Assessment: Section 2 Quiz

Alternative Assessment Handbook

Reteach/Intervene

Interactive Reader and Study Guide, Section 2

Interactive Skills Tutor CD-ROM

QUICK FACTS: New Ideas, Advancements and Developments in the Sciences

New Ideas in Science	Natural selection and evolution Modern atomic theory Mendeleyev's periodic table Radioactivity Atomic nucleus Theory of relativity
Advancements in Medicine	Pasteurization and vaccination Anesthetics Antiseptics Modern hospitals More training for nurses and doctors
Developments in the Social Sciences	Pavlov's theories of conditioned response Freud's theories of the unconscious Scientific approach to archaeology Anthropology Sociology

READING SKILLS

Identifying Stated Main Ideas Which sentence states the main idea of this paragraph? How do details contribute to the main idea?

Studies of human behavior continued with the work of Austrian-Jewish physician **Sigmund Freud** (FROYD). Freud argued that an unconscious part of the mind contains thoughts of which one is unaware. Hypnotism was one of the techniques Freud used to explore the unconscious with his patients. He wrote his first paper on hypnotism in 1893. Freud also encouraged patients to tell him about their dreams. He felt that repressed thoughts revealed in dreams could cause mental illness. Freud called his method of therapy psychoanalysis.

Other Social Sciences Just as Freud studied individuals, other scientists studied people as members of groups. These scholars were interested in societies, or communities of people who share a common culture.

One field that received much attention was archaeology, the study of the past based on artifacts. Archaeology was not an entirely new field of study. Many early archaeological expeditions, however, had been little more than treasure hunts. Then, starting in the mid-1800s, archaeologists started to take a more scientific approach to their investigations. They carefully recorded all stages of their work and preserved their finds for education, not just for riches.

As more evidence of the human past was unearthed, anthropology became an organized discipline. Anthropology is the study of humanity and human ancestors. Physical anthropologists are interested in how *Homo sapiens* developed as a species over time. In the 1920s cultural anthropology, which deals more with the structures of societies, became a separate field. In general, cultural anthropologists study cultures other than their own.

Closely related to anthropology is sociology, which emerged as a social science in the late 1800s. Sociologists also study people in groups. More often, though, the groups are in their own societies. As part of their work, sociologists examine societies' institutions and sub-groups, such as those organized around racial or ethnic identity, gender, or age.

READING CHECK **Draw Conclusions** How did new ideas contribute to the social sciences?

Section 2 Assessment

go.hrw.com Online Quiz Keyword: SHL LIF HP

Reviewing Ideas, Terms, and People

1. **a. Define** What are theories?
   b. Explain What did **Albert Einstein** say about the connection between space and time?
   c. Evaluate Why would later discoveries in physics and chemistry depend on Dalton's conclusion?
2. **a. Describe** How does **pasteurization** affect bacteria?
   b. Draw Conclusions How do you think people's opinion of surgery changed after the development of **anesthetics**?
3. **a. Describe** How did **Sigmund Freud** contribute to the field of psychology?
   b. Identify Cause and Effect What effect did **Ivan Pavlov**'s study of dog behavior have on the study of human behavior?

Critical Thinking

4. **Infer** Using your notes and a chart like this one, record the effects of key scientific advances.

Advance	Effects

Focus on Writing

5. **Persuasive** Imagine you are a scientist in the late 1800s working on cures for diseases. Write a letter to a U.S. senator asking for help with funding for your research. Explain how you think your research will benefit society.

Section 2 Assessment Answers

1. **a.** plausible general principles offered to explain what has been observed
   b. that one must include time in the study of space
   c. because it showed that atoms of different elements have different size and mass
2. **a.** destroys bacteria
   b. probably feared it much less
3. **a.** introduced the idea of the unconscious mind and therapy through psychoanalysis
   b. It suggested that human behaviors are a series of connected conditioned reflexes.
4. evolution—contributed to field of physical anthropology; atoms—led to periodic table, discovery of radioactivity, knowledge of structure of atoms; germs—pasteurization and vaccines; advances in medical care—saved lives, led to more modern hospitals, more physicians and nurses; psychology—led to knowledge of the way human minds work, allowing mental illness to be treated
5. Letters will vary but should include logical reasons for funding research.

Answers

Reading Skills *the first sentence; supporting sentences detail the contributions Freud made to the study of human behavior*

Reading Check *Ideas of human behavior and societies led to new fields of study, including psychology, archaeology, anthropology, and sociology.*

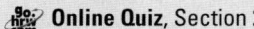

SECTION 3

Daily Life in the Late 1800s

Before You Read

Main Idea

During the late 1800s, cities grew and changed, while education, leisure time activities, and the arts reflected those changing times.

Reading Focus

1. How did cities grow and change in the late 1800s?
2. What developments affected education, leisure, and the arts?

Key Terms and People

urbanization
romanticism
William Wordsworth
Ludwig van Beethoven
realism
Charles Dickens
Leo Tolstoy
Henrik Ibsen
impressionism

TAKING NOTES Take notes on the ways in which cities and daily life changed. Add more boxes as needed.

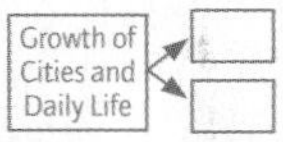

THE INSIDE STORY ***How did a new garment and a new sport give women more freedom?*** In 1850 American social reformer Amelia Jenks Bloomer wore a startling new outfit in public. Instead of the floor-length skirt that most women wore, Bloomer had on long, baggy pants that showed beneath her short skirt. Although she did not invent this new costume, called bloomers, she helped popularize it.

By the 1890s the term "bloomers" referred to a different version of the outfit—short, baggy pants worn with knee-high stockings. Women often wore bloomers for a new sport—bicycling. With clothing that allowed freedom of movement and with the availability of bicycles that were light and safe, thousands of women in Europe and the United States began cycling through city streets and parks. Cycling gave women the freedom to leave their homes alone and travel long distances. Although some people claimed that bike riding might be harmful to women's health because of "the organic weakness of women," riding bikes was fun and provided women with a new form of exercise. Women did give up floor-length skirts, but they did not give up their bikes. ■

In this illustration, women and men enjoy bicycling along the seashore in Belgium.

Preteach

Getting Started

Use the **Interactive Reader and Study Guide** to familiarize students with the section content.

Interactive Reader and Study Guide, Section 3

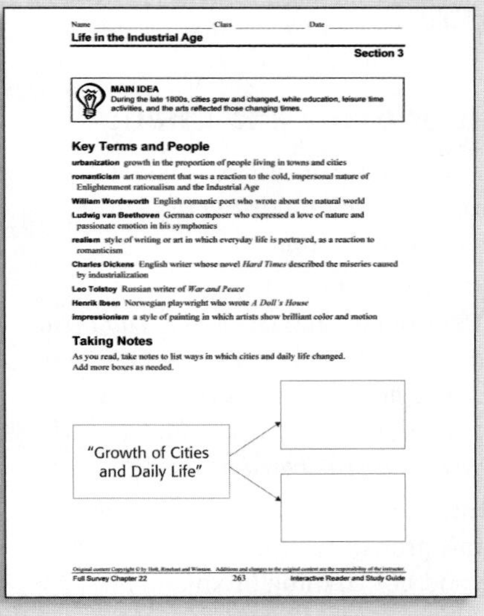
Name ____________ Class ________ Date ________

Life in the Industrial Age

Section 3

MAIN IDEA
During the late 1800s, cities grew and changed, while education, leisure time activities, and the arts reflected those changing times.

Key Terms and People

urbanization growth in the proportion of people living in towns and cities
romanticism art movement that was a reaction to the cold, impersonal nature of Enlightenment rationalism and the Industrial Age
William Wordsworth English romantic poet who wrote about the natural world
Ludwig van Beethoven German composer who expressed a love of nature and passionate emotion in his symphonies
realism style of writing or art in which everyday life is portrayed, as a reaction to romanticism
Charles Dickens English writer whose novel *Hard Times* described the miseries caused by industrialization
Leo Tolstoy Russian writer of *War and Peace*
Henrik Ibsen Norwegian playwright who wrote *A Doll's House*
impressionism a style of painting in which artists show brilliant color and motion

Taking Notes

As you read, take notes to list ways in which cities and daily life changed. Add more boxes as needed.

"Growth of Cities and Daily Life"

Original content Copyright © by Holt, Rinehart and Winston. Additions and changes to the original content are the responsibility of the instructor.
Full Survey Chapter 22 263 Interactive Reader and Study Guide

Academic Vocabulary

Review with students the high-use academic term in this section.

immigrate move to another country to live (p. 275)

CRF: Vocabulary Builder: Section 3

Taking Notes

growth of industrial factories; migration of workers; cities became crowded; unhealthy conditions; increase in education, leisure and arts; improvements in city life; suburbs less crowded, cleaner

Teach the Main Idea

At Level

Daily Life in the Late 1800s

1. **Teach** Ask students the Reading Focus questions to teach this section.
2. **Apply** Have students write a brief summary of the section. Student summaries should include at least two main ideas from under each of the red subheadings.
3. **Review** Review student summaries as a class. Have students identify the points in their summaries that they feel are most important or most interesting. Guide students in a discussion of the ways in which life changed as a result of urbanization.
4. **Practice/Homework** Have students write a journal entry from the point of view of a teenager in the 1800s. The entry should describe some recent changes in the teenager's daily life. **LS Verbal-Linguistic**

Alternative Assessment Handbook, Rubric 37: Writing Assignments

Direct Teach

Reading Focus

1 How did cities grow and change in the late 1800s? *Industrial cities grew rapidly. They required a large workforce to gather raw materials, produce manufactured goods, and distribute those goods, and attracted many people to fill those jobs.*

Cities Grow and Change

Define What is urbanization? *the growth in the proportion of people living in towns and cities*

Contrast How did industrial cities differ from traditional cities? *Traditional cities served political, military, religious, or trade functions. Industrial cities gathered raw materials, manufactured goods, and distributed them.*

Make Judgments Was the enormous growth of cities in the late 1800s a good or bad thing? Explain. *possible answer—a bad thing; cities became overcrowded, and living conditions were not healthy*

History Close-up

New York City in the Late 1800s

Transportation In 1883 the Brooklyn Bridge was completed, linking New York City with Brooklyn across the East River. It was the longest suspension bridge in the world. Urban mass transit improved steadily in the second half of the 19th century. Horse-drawn streetcars were introduced by the 1850s, elevated trains by the 1870s, and electric trolleys by the 1890s. The first subway was opened in 1904.

About the Illustration

This illustration is an artist's conception based on available sources. Historians, however, are uncertain exactly what this scene looked like.

Interactive HISTORY CLOSE-UP

New York City in the Late 1800s

Like many cities of the late 1800s New York was a busy, crowded place. To make city life more pleasant and convenient, the age's new technologies were put to use.

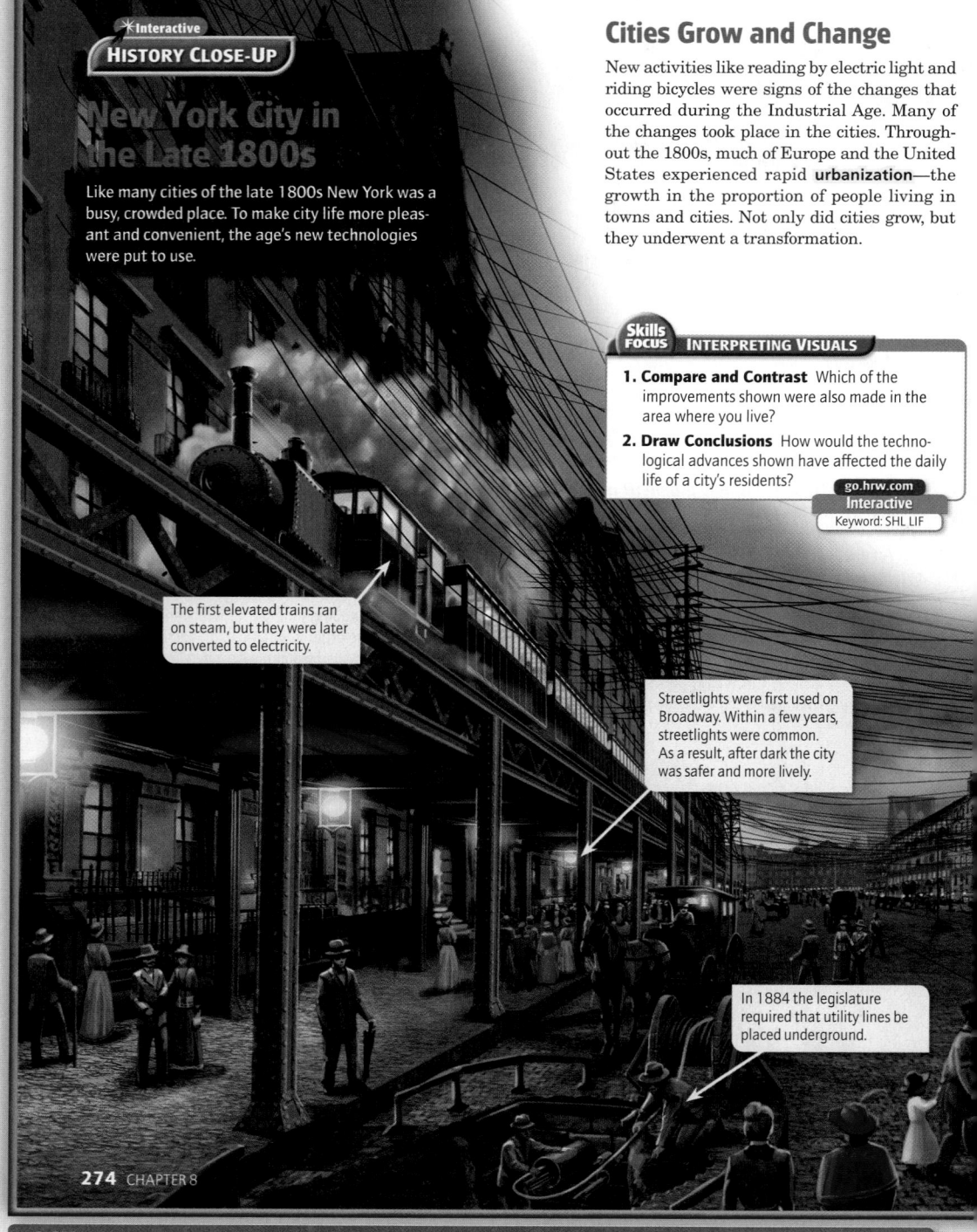

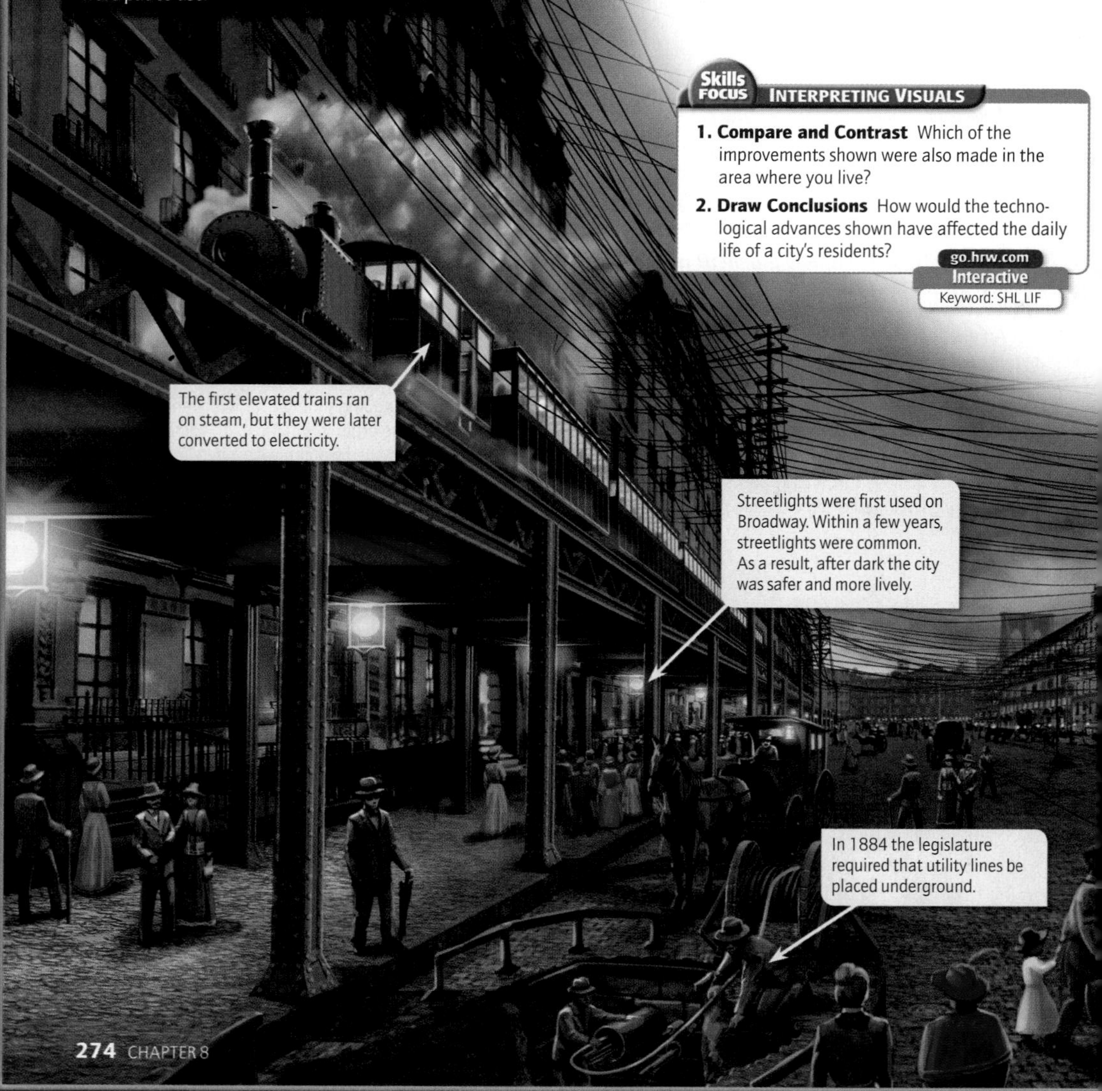

The first elevated trains ran on steam, but they were later converted to electricity.
Streetlights were first used on Broadway. Within a few years, streetlights were common. As a result, after dark the city was safer and more lively.
In 1884 the legislature required that utility lines be placed underground.
274 CHAPTER 8

Cities Grow and Change

New activities like reading by electric light and riding bicycles were signs of the changes that occurred during the Industrial Age. Many of the changes took place in the cities. Throughout the 1800s, much of Europe and the United States experienced rapid **urbanization**—the growth in the proportion of people living in towns and cities. Not only did cities grow, but they underwent a transformation.

Skills Focus INTERPRETING VISUALS

1. **Compare and Contrast** Which of the improvements shown were also made in the area where you live?
2. **Draw Conclusions** How would the technological advances shown have affected the daily life of a city's residents?

go.hrw.com Interactive Keyword: SHL LIF

Skills Focus: Analyzing Costs and Benefits

Above Level

Social Studies Skill

The Growth of Cities

1. Organize students into small groups. Tell them that it is 1825 and they are industrialists planning a new factory town. Have each group develop a plan for the city, including a map showing the location of the factory, housing, public buildings, and recreational opportunities. Remind students that in 1825 industrialists needed to take into consideration the power needs of factories as well as transportation, recreation, and services that would be available. At the same time, they needed to try to keep factories profitable and cities affordable.
2. Have volunteers from each group share their plans with the rest of the class.
3. Guide the class in comparing and contrasting the "ideal" cities designed by students with the actual cities that developed during the Industrial Age. **LS Kinesthetic, Visual-Spatial**

Alternative Assessment Handbook, Rubrics 14: Group Activity; and 20: Map Creation

The Industrial City Before the Industrial Age, most cities existed to serve trade, political, military, or religious functions. The industrial city, in contrast, did more. In the industrial city raw materials had to be sent to factories, new products manufactured in the factories, and the products distributed to buyers. To meet these functions, industrial cities needed factories, a large workforce, a reliable transportation network, warehouses, stores, and offices.

One of the first cities to have all these supports for industry was Lowell, Massachusetts. At the heart of Lowell's growth was its textile factories, which employed young women from the surrounding countryside and newcomers from Europe.

Other industries besides textiles fueled the growth of cities. Meat-packing was one of several industries that lured workers to Chicago. As a result, Chicago's population grew from 30,000 in 1850 to 1.7 million in 1900. Another example is Pittsburgh, Pennsylvania, where jobs in the steel industry attracted workers.

Industrial cities were lively, fast-paced places. For example, in growing cities a constant stream of pedestrians competed with electric streetcars and horse-drawn carriages for space on the streets. Merchants advertised their wares by shouting out prices from their doorways. Construction crews produced a constant sound of hammering as they built new banks, office buildings, and homes for the growing population.

With high population density, the health of many city residents suffered. One of the hazards was smoky air from the coal that was burned to run steam engines and to warm homes. London had a special problem with smoke that combined with the fog that is common in damp climates. The word *smog* was coined to describe the thick, choking, lung-burning result. In 1873 a smog episode caused 268 deaths. An 1879 episode lasted for four long months.

By the 1880s the city's sky was criss-crossed with telephone wires.

Trolley car lines spurred the development of suburbs. Trolleys also took passengers to holiday spots like Coney Island.

Migration to Cities Despite the cities' unhealthy conditions, people kept arriving during the late 1800s. They wanted not just jobs, but also to escape hunger, political oppression, or discrimination.

Just as the goals of the new city residents differed, so did their origins. Some people came to the cities from the countryside. Boatloads of people, though, left their own countries behind and went to cities in a different country. Many Europeans sailed to Latin America, Australia, and other places. But the United States drew the most people.

Between 1870 and 1900, about 12 million people immigrated to the United States. Many came from Ireland, England, Germany, Italy, Russia, and China. In 1890, 42 percent of New Yorkers were foreign-born. Immigrants poured into other major U.S. cities, including Boston, Chicago, and San Francisco, where the newcomers gradually created their own unique communities.

ACADEMIC VOCABULARY

immigrate to move to another country to live

When they first arrived, though, most of the immigrants lived in miserable, crowded conditions. Journalist and photographer Jacob Riis described what he saw in New York's dismal apartment buildings, or tenements.

HISTORY'S VOICES

"Bedrooms in tenements were dark closets, utterly without ventilation. There couldn't be any. The houses were built like huge square boxes, covering nearly the whole of the lot. Some light came in at the ends, but the middle was always black."

—Jacob Riis, *The Battle with the Slum*, 1902

Direct Teach

Info to Know

Lowell Girls Lowell, Massachusetts, is named for Francis Cabot Lowell, a pioneer in the American cotton industry. One of his innovations was to hire young farm girls to work in his cotton mill. Although he paid them less than he paid men, he provided clean company boarding houses. Religious and educational activities were also available for the "Lowell girls."

Smog The term smog is a combination of the words *smoke* and *fog*. It was coined in 1905 by Dr. H. A. des Voeux in a paper called "Fog and Smoke." He was describing one of the "products" of city life, the smoky fog of London. Today the term is used for the air pollution that plagues urban areas, primarily as a result of automobile emissions. Photochemical smog is formed when radiation from the sun causes nitrogen oxides to react with hydrocarbons. It irritates the membranes of the eyes and respiratory tract, as well as harming plants.

CRF: History and Geography: The Growth of Cities

CRF: Biography: Sarah Winnemucca

Collaborative Learning

At Level

Research Required

Immigration

1. Organize students into small groups. Have each group conduct research about immigration in your area using the following questions as a guide: When did the first non-native settlers arrive? Where did they come from, elsewhere in the United States, other countries, or both? What attracted them to the area? What major ethnic groups settled in your area, and when did each first arrive? How has the area changed since the first non-native settlers began to arrive?
2. Each member of the group should take responsibility for investigating one topic. Then, have each group put its findings into a report. Reports should include maps, graphs, or other visual materials to help track immigration.
3. Have volunteers from each group present the reports to the class.

LS **Interpersonal, Verbal-Linguistic**

Alternative Assessment Handbook, Rubrics 30: Research; and 42: Writing to Inform

Answers

Interpreting Visuals 1. *Answers will vary. Students should identify at least one improvement made where they live.* **2.** *telephone wires—aided communication; streetlights—made city safer; trains and trolleys—made transportation easier, allowed workers to live outside the city*

Direct Teach

Reading Focus

Cities Grow and Change

Explain Why did suburbs develop? *Public transportation made it possible to move outside a city, where it was less crowded, quieter, and cleaner.*

Summarize How did reforms make cities more livable? *improved sanitation, clean water made cities healthier and cleaner; transportation improved, parks were built*

CRF: Primary Source: The Public Park Movement

Info to Know

Leisure Time In the Industrial Age, shorter workdays and higher wages gave people more free time. Team sports became favorite pastimes. As these sports became more popular, increasing numbers of people came to cheer for their team. Families played games together or went bicycling. Trips to the beach, parks, and museums were also popular activities.

Football The teams of the earliest football games usually consisted of whole villages, and the field could cover more than a dozen square miles. The ball was advanced by kicking, punching, and carrying. The game was very violent and could lead to injury and even death. In the 1600s a less violent form of football was played in England in schools, although many authorities thought it too rowdy.

The Livable City Eventually, reforms eased the squalid conditions. Improvements were made in cities' infrastructure. For example, cities modernized their water and sewer systems. These improvements also extended to the home. Better plumbing allowed more families to have clean drinking water, toilets, and bathtubs. Sanitation and overall health improved as a result.

Electricity also made homemaking more convenient. In the early 1900s appliances such as vacuum cleaners, refrigerators, and electric stoves became available.

With more people moving to the cities, working and living space became scarce. Constructing taller buildings was one solution. In 1883 architect William Le Baron Jenney designed the first multistory steel-framed building, or skyscraper, in Chicago. It was 10 stories tall. Four years later, the high-speed elevator was perfected. Skyscrapers could get taller still.

Growing populations caused congestion on city streets. Underground railway systems, or subways, helped relieve the crowding. In 1863 London opened the world's first subway line. Other cities followed. For example, the city of Budapest, Hungary, opened its subway in 1896. The original purpose of this subway was so residents could get to a city park easily.

As cities spread out, city planners made an effort to preserve green spaces within the city. In the 1860s Napoleon III created parks in Paris to give working people places for healthy recreation. In the United States, Frederick Law Olmsted designed city parks that were equally accessible to all residents.

The Suburbs As cities in Europe and the United States became more congested, their boundaries expanded to include surrounding areas. As a result, people moved out of the cities to new areas called suburbs.

People moved to the suburbs because they were less crowded, quieter, and cleaner than the central city. Public transportation helped suburbs grow. In the early 1800s streetcar and ferry transportation linked cities to the suburbs. Later, suburbs developed along railroad and bus lines.

READING CHECK **Identify Cause and Effect** Why did people migrate to cities?

Education, Leisure, and Arts

With the growth of cities in the 1800s, new educational opportunities developed. In addition, new sports, other leisure activities, and changes in the arts world affected society.

A Day at the Beach

Blackpool, in northwestern England, offered working families a holiday. In the background, the photo shows an observation tower modeled on the Eiffel Tower in Paris and a gigantic Ferris wheel. In the foreground, couples enjoy rides along the beach in horse-drawn carts.

Differentiating Instruction

Level Tag

Learners Having Difficulty

Standard English Mastery

1. Ask students what types of activities they enjoy doing in their spare time. As students mention activities, write them for the class to see.
2. Tell students that people in the 1800s did some of these same activities for fun. After students have read the text titled Education, Leisure, and Arts, ask how people in the 1800s spent their leisure time. As students mention activities, make a new list for students to see.
3. Guide the class in a discussion of the ways in which leisure activities of the 1800s differed from those of today.
4. Have students write a paragraph summarizing the class discussion. Tell students to check their paragraphs for correct grammar, spelling, and punctuation to align them with standard English usage. **LS Verbal-Linguistic**

Alternative Assessment Handbook, Rubrics 9: Comparing and Contrasting; and 11: Discussions

Answers

Reading Check *to work in factories*

Education and Information During the 1800s increased industrialization created a need for a more educated workforce. Factories wanted managers who could read and write and engineers with technical skills. Armed forces grew larger, and military leaders wanted officers who knew about the wider world. Because people became more involved in politics they supported public education as a way to develop informed, patriotic citizens.

After 1870 governments in western Europe and the United States passed laws requiring education for all children. Many countries required only elementary education. Eventually, some governments funded education through high school.

Not all social classes were educated equally, however. Most children of the lower classes stayed in school only as long as the law required. Then, many of them quit school to go to work. However, the establishment of vocational and technical training schools gave some members of the working class more opportunities. For instance, in Tuskegee, Alabama, in 1881, Booker T. Washington founded a private school to train African Americans to be teachers.

Just as education for lower classes lagged behind, so did education for girls. Although more industrialized countries guaranteed free public education, some countries did not require that girls go beyond elementary school. Even in countries that provided basic education for girls, few girls in high schools took the science and math classes that could lead directly to careers in the industrialized world. Because few colleges allowed women to enroll as students, educators who thought women should have more opportunities began founding colleges just for women.

With a more educated populace, more cities began printing newspapers. The new papers expanded their coverage from current events to the arts and sciences. Lively stories published in weekly installments kept readers coming back to follow the adventures of favorite fictional characters. Political cartoons often poked fun at public figures. Because newspapers usually held specific viewpoints, one could choose a newspaper that agreed with a certain political or religious stance. For example, some French papers supported the king, while others supported a republican form of government.

QUICK FACTS

Increase in Leisure Activities

CAUSES

- Higher incomes, more free time
- Public transportation to recreational areas
- Public funding of cultural activities

EFFECTS

- Time for sports: soccer, rugby, football, baseball
- More people enjoying vacation spots and resorts
- More opportunities to hear music, enjoy art

New technology, including the linotype machine and the electric press, improved newspaper printing processes. Reporting of foreign affairs improved when the telegraph made up-to-date coverage possible. Foreign correspondence was just one area within a growing profession—journalism.

Leisure Time As leisure time increased, people had more time to play and watch sports. In Britain, football—known as soccer in the United States—became more popular. Rugby and American football were also developed. Baseball became a popular pastime for troops during the American Civil War and grew quickly as an amateur and professional sport. With the growth of railroads, sports fans could travel to see their favorite teams play.

In fact, railroads allowed more families to enjoy a range of activities. For example, in Britain in the mid-1800s, working-class families could take the train to vacation spots. Seaside resorts such as Blackpool provided entertainment, relaxation, and fresh air.

Cultural activities, too, became available to more people. Before the 1800s musicians usually performed in private homes or at religious services. During the 1800s, though, city governments began building new concert halls and theaters and supporting more orchestras, bands, and choral groups. With public funding, ticket prices were within the budget of more audience members.

READING SKILLS

Identifying Stated Main Ideas In the first paragraph about leisure time, what indicates that the first sentence contains the main idea?

Direct Teach

Reading Focus

2 What developments affected education, leisure, and the arts? *factory workers could afford leisure activities; with railroad, people could travel; the arts idealized nature, then turned to realistic works and impressionism; educated workforce developed, which led to an increase in number of newspapers and magazines*

Education, Leisure, and Arts

Compare How are the novels of Dickens similar to photographs? *They are both examples of the realist movement.*

Analyze How did railroads contribute to leisure activity? *They led to the development of tourist resorts and professional sports, as people could travel to watch their favorite teams play.*

Predict What industries besides newspapers might have been affected as the population became increasingly educated? *possible answer—the publishing industry; more people would read books, and books are necessary for schools*

Quick Facts Transparency: Increase in Leisure Activities

Biography

Émile Zola (1840–1902) Émile Zola was the chief proponent of French naturalism. He applied scientific techniques to his novels, observing characters and their surroundings objectively. He tried to show how heredity and the environment affected his characters and shaped their behavior.

Skills Focus: Identifying Cause and Effect

At Level

Reading Skill

The Importance of Education

1. Remind students that education was not always compulsory, and was once the luxury of those who could afford it. Then guide the class in a discussion of the ways in which education affects their daily lives.
2. Point out to students that life is much more complex today than it was in the 1800s. What skills do they think are needed in today's society and workplaces? How can they best learn those skills?
3. Have students write an essay describing what life would be like today for someone who could not read or write. How would the inability to read and write affect their own lives? Conversely, what kinds of changes could learning to read and write make in their lives?
4. Have volunteers read their essays to the class. **LS Verbal-Linguistic**

Alternative Assessment Handbook, Rubric 40: Writing to Describe

Answers

Reading Skills *possible answer—It is a general statement; other sentences give details.*

Direct Teach

Reading Focus

Education, Leisure, and Arts

Recall What was realism? *a movement in the arts that revealed the details in everyday life, no matter how unpleasant*

Interpret What characteristics did the romantic movement value, and why? *love of nature, deep emotions, the individual, the past, and imagination; a response to Enlightenment rationalism and problems of the Industrial Revolution*

Review & Assess

Close

Have students explain how industrialization contributed to urbanization.

Review

Online Quiz, Section 3

Assess

SE Section 3 Assessment

Progress Assessment: Section 3 Quiz

Alternative Assessment Handbook

Reteach/Intervene

Interactive Reader and Study Guide, Section 3

Interactive Skills Tutor CD-ROM

Just as performances moved from private homes to new spaces, so did art. Museums such as the Louvre (LOOV) in Paris made great works of art available to all. Public libraries also opened their doors. For example, the reading room of London's British Museum opened, making its huge collection of books accessible to scholars.

Changes in the Arts With all the discoveries, inventions, and new ideas of the 1800s, it is no wonder that the world of the arts underwent change as well. Artists, writers, and musicians developed new styles in response to what was going on around them.

A literary and artistic development of the early 1800s was called **romanticism**. With an emphasis on intuition and feeling, the romantic movement was a reaction to Enlightenment rationalism and the early abuses of the Industrial Revolution. Major characteristics of the movement were love of nature, deep emotions, value of the individual, affection for the past, and the importance of the imagination. Political revolutions that swept through Europe in the 1800s released a spirit of liberty and equality that were also common in works of the romantic era.

THE IMPACT TODAY

Original impressionist paintings are still immensely popular—and expensive. For example, in 1990 a painting by Auguste Renoir sold for more than $78 million.

Poet **William Wordsworth** expressed the romantic spirit in his definition of poetry as "the spontaneous overflow of powerful feelings from emotions recollected in tranquility." In music, nature inspired composers such as German **Ludwig van Beethoven**, who also celebrated human freedom in his work. Among many great romantic painters was Frenchman Theodore Gericault (zhay-REE-KOH), whose scenes of suffering heroes caught the public's attention. William Blake, an English artist and writer, painted scenes of mystical beauty.

In the mid-1800s, a movement known as **realism** developed in reaction to romanticism. The realist movement revealed the details of everyday life, no matter how unpleasant. For example, in his novel *Hard Times* Englishman **Charles Dickens** wrote about the struggles of London's poor. That novel also described pollution, exploitation, and miseries caused by industrialization. In the novel *War and Peace,* Russian writer **Leo Tolstoy** showed that war is chaotic and horrible. Norwegian playwright **Henrik Ibsen** broke new ground in *A Doll's House*. The play revealed the unfair treatment of women within families.

Painters also turned to realism as a reaction against romanticism. Instead of painting imaginary or emotional scenes, they painted ordinary working people as they really lived. Many realist paintings show people of the lower classes as possessing quiet dignity.

Later in the century, beginning in the 1860s, a group of French painters introduced a new way of looking at the world. They started a movement that came to be called **impressionism**. These artists wanted to capture an impression of a scene using light, vivid color, and motion, rather than just showing its realistic details.

READING CHECK **Find the Main Idea** How did the arts reflect how people viewed the world in the 1800s?

SECTION 3 ASSESSMENT

go.hrw.com Online Quiz Keyword: SHL LIF HP

Reviewing Ideas, Terms, and People

1. **a. Describe** What were industrialized cities of the 1800s like?
   b. Explain How did technological innovations help make cities more livable?
   c. Evaluate Do you think the industrialized cities were better places to live than the countryside in the late 1800s? Why or why not?
2. **a. Identify** What literary style did **William Wordsworth** follow? What style did **Charles Dickens** follow?
   b. Contrast How did **realism** differ from **romanticism**?
   c. Elaborate How might increased educational opportunities have benefited society in general in the 1800s?

Critical Thinking

3. **Identifying Cause and Effect** Copy the chart below. Use it and your notes to describe causes and effects of urbanization.

Causes of Urbanization	Effects of Urbanization

FOCUS ON WRITING

4. **Persuasive** Imagine that you live in a big city in the 1880s. Write a letter to the editor of your local newspaper arguing for or against the development of suburbs.

Section 3 Assessment Answers

1. **a.** contained factories, transportation network, stores and offices; attracted large workforce; lively and fast-paced; high population density; unhealthy living conditions
   b. water and waste systems improved, improving sanitation and health; electricity led to invention of home appliances; taller buildings created more living space; public transportation improved travel; parks enabled recreation
   c. possible answer—yes, work was available and life was fast-paced
2. **a.** Wordsworth—romanticism; Dickens—realism
   b. realism—details of everyday life, romanticism —life idealized
   c. educated society, stronger workforce
3. causes—growth of industrial factories, migration of workers; effects—crowded cities, unhealthy conditions, increase in education, leisure and arts, improvements in city life
4. Student letters should include details from the section to support their arguments.

Answers

Reading Check *The arts reflected the struggle between the ways of the past and the new inventions of the Industrial Age.*

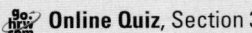

THE ARTS AROUND THE WORLD

Painting

Impressionism

Young Girl Lying in the Grass, by Auguste Renoir

What is it? Several painters caused a sensation in the French art world in the 1860s. They were rebelling against the definition of art promoted by France's official art school, the Academy of Fine Arts. The Academy wanted the subject matter to be clear and the painting method to be realistic. The rebel painters, who shared a style of painting called impressionism, were more concerned about the effects of shadows and light, the use of color, and the suggestion of movement. They tried to capture these effects by painting outdoors, rather than in a studio. They wanted to show an "impression" of the scene rather than an exact record of it, and they experimented with different kinds of brushstrokes to achieve that effect. Although impressionism was controversial when it first developed, it has become one of the best-loved artistic styles of all time.

The scene in this painting by Auguste Renoir is dappled with light and shade, and the outline of the figure is blurry. The combination of these techniques gives the impression of a warm, hazy, summer day.

Why is it important?

- Impressionism helped artists and the general public see the world in new ways.
- The new style freed artists to paint as they wished, not as they were told.

Key characteristics:

Impressionist painters focused on

- everyday life and ordinary people
- outdoor settings
- light, weather, and atmosphere
- visible brushstrokes

Banks of the Loing River, by Alfred Sisley, 1885

Claude Monet painted many views of water lilies. The play of light on water was a favorite subject of the impressionist painters.

Skills FOCUS INTERPRETING VISUALS

1. **Summarize** How did the impressionists' style vary from the style that the Academy approved?
2. **Predict** How do you think the impressionists' rebellion affected other artists over time?

The Arts Around the World

Impressionism

Info to Know

Impressionism The term *impressionist* was first used in 1874 by a French art critic, Louis Leroy, in a review of an exhibit of paintings by "The Anonymous Society of Painters, Sculptors, Engravers, etc." The name was suggested by one of the paintings in the show, *Impression, Sunrise,* by Claude Monet. In his satirical review, Leroy argued that the artists were satisfied with the impression given by a few quick brushstrokes and had left their paintings unfinished. In spite of its original negative connotations, the term impressionism stuck. The term was also used to describe a style of classical music that emerged in the late 1800s. It is most strongly identified with the music of French composer Claude Debussy. The dreamlike qualities of Debussy's music reminded critics of impressionist paintings. Other composers, including Maurice Ravel, Paul Dukas, and Albert Roussel, adopted the impressionist style.

Skills Focus: Analyzing Visuals

At Level

Reading Like a Historian Skill

Impressionism

1. Guide students in a discussion of the two paintings shown on this page using the following questions: What similarities do you notice? What differences do you notice? Which key characteristics does each display? What makes both of these pictures examples of impressionism?
2. Have each student choose one of the two paintings and write a poem or song lyrics based on it.
3. Have volunteers share their poems or lyrics with the class. **LS Auditory-Musical**

Alternative Assessment Handbook, Rubrics 9: Comparing and Contrasting; and 26: Poems and Songs

Answers

Interpreting Visuals 1. *The French Academy wanted subject matter to be clear and the painting method to be realistic. Impressionists were more interested in capturing an "impression" of a scene rather than an exact record of it.* **2.** *possible answer—It probably freed other artists from the constraints of painting in an officially accepted style, allowing them to give free rein to their imaginations.*

Document-Based Investigation

Artistic Responses to the Industrial Age

Word Help

list a field or arena designed for jousting
recoil jump back
visor front piece of a helmet

Info to Know

Caspar David Friedrich Friedrich is considered to be one the greatest German Romantic artists. His landscapes and seascapes usually depict a sense of the helplessness of man in the face of nature. He is known for capturing quiet, isolated landscapes, and his scenes of nature usually show some element of mystery or awe, as in the painting on this page.

Activity **Analyzing Visuals** Have students write a short description of the view shown in Friedrich's painting Wanderer Above the Sea of Fog.

Teaching Tip

Before reading the excerpt from *Ivanhoe*, you might wish to review the chapter, Early Middle Ages, so that students can refresh their memories about kings, knights, and jousting.

CHAPTER 8

Document-Based Investigation

Artistic Responses to the Industrial Age

Historical Context These four documents show examples of two major artistic movements of the Industrial Age—romanticism and realism.

Task Study the selections and answer the questions that follow. After you have studied the documents, you will be asked to write an essay analyzing why writers and artists responded to the Industrial Age in various ways.

DOCUMENT 1

A German Painter's View

Caspar David Friedrich was one of Germany's foremost artists in the early 1800s. The painting shown is one of his most famous. But Friedrich did not just paint. He also wrote about painting. On the issue of subject matter, Friedrich had this to say:

> The artist should paint not only what he sees before him, but also what he sees within him. If, however, he sees nothing within him, then he should also refrain from painting that which he sees before him.

Wanderer Above the Sea of Fog, by Caspar David Friedrich, 1818

DOCUMENT 2

A Medieval Tale

Sir Walter Scott wrote several novels set during the Middle Ages. One of the most famous, *Ivanhoe*, was published in 1819. It relates the adventures of bold knights, fair ladies, and wicked nobles. In the passage here, the author describes the scene as a tournament, or contest between knights, begins.

> The trumpets had no sooner given the signal, than the champions vanished from their posts with the speed of lightning, and closed in the centre of the lists with the shock of a thunderbolt. The lances burst into shivers up to the very grasp, and it seemed at the moment that both knights had fallen, for the shock had made each horse recoil backward upon its haunches. The address of the riders recovered their steeds by use of the bridle and spur; and having glared on each other for an instant with eyes which seemed to flash fire through the bars of their visors, each . . . received a fresh lance from the attendants.

Recognizing Bias in Primary Sources

Above Level

Prep Required

Reading Like a Historian Skill
Realism and Romanticism

1. Prepare copies of a short excerpt or scene from a novel written in the style of realism for students. Works by Charles Dickens, such as *Hard Times,* work well for this activity.
2. Have students read the excerpts, and then rewrite the scene in a romantic style. Rewrites can take the form of poems, scenes for a play, or prose.
3. Have volunteers share their writings with the class. Then guide students in a discussion of the differences between the two styles. Which style do they prefer? Which style do they feel has less bias?
4. Have students reread the excerpt from Scott and explain if they believe it is a biased or factual account of a joust. **LS Verbal-Linguistic**

Alternative Assessment Handbook, Rubrics 9: Comparing and Contrasting; and 41: Writing to Express

DOCUMENT 3

A French Painter's View

Gustave Courbet (koor-BAY) painted common people he saw in the French countryside. The painting here is titled *Girls Sifting Corn*. Like Friedrich, Courbet had something to say about an artist's subject matter:

"An *abstract* object, invisible or nonexistent, does not belong to the domain of painting."

"Show me an angel and I'll paint one."

Girls Sifting Corn, by Gustave Courbet, 1855

DOCUMENT 4

A Norwegian Playwright's View

Henrik Ibsen's 1883 play *An Enemy of the People* focuses on Dr. Stockman, a man who has found that his town's public baths are badly polluted. He feels that people should be alerted to the danger. However, because the baths are a major source of income, the townspeople agree that Dr. Stockman must be silenced. In fact, they insist that he be declared "an enemy of the people." In this excerpt, Stockman defends himself at a public meeting and attacks the townspeople's way of thinking.

No, it's ignorance and poverty and ugliness in life that do the devil's work! In a house that isn't aired and swept every day—my wife Katherine maintains that the floors ought to be scrubbed as well, but that's debatable—anyway—I say in a house like that, within two or three years, people lose all power for moral thought and action. Lack of oxygen dulls the conscience. And there must be a woeful dearth of oxygen in the houses of this town, it seems, if the entire solid majority can numb their consciences enough to want to build this town's prosperity on a quagmire [swamp] of duplicity and lies.

Skills FOCUS READING LIKE A HISTORIAN

DOCUMENT 1

a. **Explain** To which movement did Friedrich belong? What elements in the painting provide clues?
b. **Infer** What connections can you make between the quote from Friedrich and the scene in the painting?

DOCUMENT 2

a. **Categorize** How does Scott's choice of words show that he wrote within the romantic movement?
b. **Develop** How might a realist writer have described the scene? Provide examples to illustrate your answer.

DOCUMENT 3

a. **Explain** How does Courbet's choice of subject matter indicate the movement he helped found? How does the style of painting indicate the movement?
b. **Compare and Contrast** How do Courbet's statements about subject matter compare to Friedrich's statements?

DOCUMENT 4

a. **Identify** According to Dr. Stockman, what does "the devil's work"?
b. **Support a Position** Defend or dispute this statement: "Ibsen probably thought that the new middle class was too pleased with its own success." Support your argument.

DOCUMENT-BASED ESSAY QUESTION

The Industrial Revolution and the Industrial Age affected both individuals and societies. Recall what you have learned about the many positive and negative effects. Write an essay in which you discuss the results of industrialization and later changes and how writers and authors responded to those results. Discuss what drove or inspired them to respond as they did.

See **Skills Handbook**, pp. H25–H26

Differentiating Instruction

Special Education Students

Below Level

Have students copy the painting of the girl sifting corn and label the various parts of the drawing including the sifter, the sacks of corn, and the oven. Then have students explain the relationship between the people and the objects shown in the painting. **LS Visual-Spatial**

Advanced Learners/ Gifted and Talented

Above Level

Have students conduct outside research on Gustave Courbet, his life and his paintings. Have students use their research to prepare a collage showing Courbet's development as an artist. **LS Visual-Spatial**

Alternative Assessment Handbook, Rubric 8: Collages

Document-Based Investigation

Info to Know

Gustave Courbet Courbet was the leader of the Realist movement in France. He was one of the first to rebel against Romanticism and chose to paint common, everyday events. In his paintings, Courbet gives dignity to people going about their everyday chores.

Answers

Reading Like a Historian

Document 1. a. *romantic; it depicts a view of man and nature;* **b.** *possible answer— the painting shows emotion; man is alone, facing the power of the sea; scene reflects the struggle between man and nature;* **Document 2. a.** *Verbs and adjectives romanticize the nature of the battle; phrases such as "speed of lightning; lances burst into shivers; seemed to flash fire" reflect romanticism.* **b.** *would write a literal description of the scene; students should describe two knights, armed with lances, mounted on horses;* **Document 3. a.** *He shows women at work, doing everyday jobs; realistic view of the job;* **b.** *Friedrich says artist should paint more than what he sees; Courbet paints only what he sees, not abstract objects;* **Document 4. a.** *ignorance, poverty, ugliness in life;* **b.** *possible answer—Defend: reference of building prosperity on "duplicity and lies";* **Essay** *Student essays should discuss the many problems that arose in cities because of rapid population growth, as well as the steps that were taken to improve city life and help city residents. Essays should address romanticism and realism, and how and why these artistic movements grew out of industrialization.*

Answers

Visual Summary

Review and Inquiry Organize students into groups of three. Have each group prepare a visual and written summary of the New Ideas of the Industrial Age, including technology, science and medicine, and daily life. Have volunteers share their work with the class.

Quick Facts Transparency: Visual Study Guide: Life in the Industrial Age

Review Key Terms and People

1. Samuel Morse
2. Ludwig van Beethoven
3. anesthetic
4. Guglielmo Marconi
5. Louis Pasteur
6. Marie Curie
7. Albert Einstein
8. impressionism
9. immigrate

Comprehension and Critical Thinking

10. a. light bulb, electric motors, generators, light sockets, first permanent electric power plant
b. markets for goods increased, travel time decreased, transportation costs declined, low-cost products became available, new products became available
c. possible answer—Communication improved dramatically so that diplomats could talk to each other, resolve conflicts and problems quickly, rather than waiting for weeks for mail to arrive.

11. a. heating liquids and foods to high temperatures to kill bacteria and prevent fermentation; destroys bacteria that cause disease
b. first systematic arrangement of chemical elements; revealed unknown patters among elements, and gaps showed that some elements had yet to be discovered
c. that human behavior may be a series of connected conditioned reflexes

CHAPTER 8

Chapter Review

QUICK FACTS

VISUAL STUDY GUIDE

New Ideas of the Industrial Age

Technology
- Faraday and electrical power
- Swan, Edison, and the lightbulb
- Bessemer process
- Expansion of railroads
- Steamships
- Benz, Daimler, Ford, and cars
- Wright Brothers and the airplane
- Morse and the telegraph
- Bell and the telephone
- Marconi and the radio
- Edison and the phonograph

Science and Medicine
- Darwin and evolution
- Dalton and atomic theory
- Mendeleyev and periodic table
- Curies and radioactivity
- Einstein's theories
- Pasteur's fight against disease
- Anesthetics and antiseptics
- Pavlov, Freud, and the mind
- Advances in archaeology
- Anthropology and sociology

Daily Life
- Growth of industrial cities
- Migration to cities
- Improvements in utilities
- Skyscrapers, subways, parks
- Growth of suburbs
- More education and newspapers
- Sports, other uses of leisure time
- Public museums and libraries
- Romanticism
- Realism
- Impressionism

Key Events of the Industrial Age

1803 ▪ John Dalton develops modern atomic theory.
1830 ▪ Railroad links Manchester and Liverpool.
1831 ▪ Michael Faraday discovers connection between magnetism and electricity.
1835 ▪ Charles Darwin's *Beagle* diary describes discoveries made about animals on voyage.
1842 ▪ Crawford W. Long performs surgery using ether as anesthetic.
1844 ▪ Samuel Morse sends telegram.
1871 ▪ Dmitri Mendeleyev's periodic table reveals patterns among elements.
1873 ▪ London smog kills 268 people.
1876 ▪ Bell and Watson invent the telephone.
1881 ▪ Booker T. Washington opens school.
1883 ▪ First skyscraper is built in Chicago.
1885 ▪ Carl Benz builds three-wheeled vehicle.
▪ Pasteur develops vaccine against rabies.
1891 ▪ Trans-Siberian Railroad construction starts.
1893 ▪ Sigmund Freud publishes first paper on use of hypnotism.
1898 ▪ Curies discover polonium and radium.
1900 ▪ Paris Exhibition displays power of electricity.
1903 ▪ Wright Brothers fly at Kitty Hawk.
1908 ▪ Henry Ford announces the Model T.

Review Key Terms and People

Identify the correct term or person from the chapter that best fits each of the following descriptions.

1. invented the telegraph and a code for sending messages by telegraph
2. great German composer of the romantic movement
3. a drug that dulls pain
4. Italian who invented the radio
5. French scientist who used his knowledge of germs to develop vaccines against anthrax and rabies
6. scientist who died because of her research with radioactivity
7. scientist whose new theories about the universe disagreed with those of Sir Isaac Newton
8. artistic style that used light, movement, outdoor settings, and ordinary people as subject matter
9. to take up residence in a new country

12. a. the growth in the proportion of people living in towns and cities; new factories in cities attracted millions of workers, who left the countryside to work in the factories
b. Romanticism is an idealized view of life, as writers and painters imagined life might or could be; artists of the realism movement showed realistic, often harsh details from everyday life.
c. possible answer—Not all social classes were educated equally. Education for lower classes and girls lagged behind.

Reading Skills

13. the first sentence, especially the phrase, "...scientists that came after him discovered additional elements that fit into the periodic table."

History's Impact video program
Review the video to answer the closing question: What are the impacts of new technologies on the world today?

Comprehension and Critical Thinking

SECTION 1 *(pp. 260–267)*

10. a. Summarize What were Thomas Edison's contributions to advances in technology?

b. Explain How did the expansion of railroads affect commerce?

c. Predict How might the invention of the telegraph have affected global diplomacy?

SECTION 2 *(pp. 268–272)*

11. a. Identify What is pasteurization?

b. Explain Why was Mendeleyev's chart of elements important?

c. Draw Conclusions What did Pavlov's experiment with dogs seem to indicate about people?

SECTION 3 *(pp. 273–279)*

12. a. Recall What is urbanization, and why did it increase during the 1800s?

b. Analyze Why did some artists and writers turn to romanticism?

c. Make Judgments What is one way that advances of the 1800s did not apply equally to all people?

Reading Skills

Identifying Stated Main Ideas *Read the passage below from this chapter. Then answer the question that follows.*

"As Mendeleyev had predicted, scientists that came after him discovered additional elements that fit into the periodic table. For example, in France in 1898 chemists Marie and Pierre Curie discovered polonium and radium. The Curies also concluded that certain elements release energy when they break down. Marie Curie called this process radioactivity."

13. Which statement in this passage expresses the main idea of the paragraph?

Using the Internet

go.hrw.com
Practice Online
Keyword: SHL LIF

14. The chapter discusses just a few of the advances of the Industrial Age. Use the keyword to explore the Internet for other inventions and discoveries. Choose one and research it fully. Then create a report that includes information on the person(s) responsible for the discovery, the process he or she went through to make the discovery, and graphics that help explain it to a nonexpert audience.

Analyzing Primary Sources

Reading Like a Historian *The excerpt below is from the records of a doctor who treated the poor people of Manchester, England, during an outbreak of cholera, a devastating intestinal disease.*

"I had requested the younger members of the staff, charged with the visitation of the outpatients of the infirmary, to give me the earliest information of the occurrence of any cases indicating the approach of cholera. I had a scientific wish to trace the mode of its propagation [origin], and to ascertain if possible by what means it would be introduced into the town. My purpose also was to discover whether there was any, and if so what, link or connection between the physical and social evils, to which my attention had been so long directed."

—Sir James Kay-Shuttleworth,
The Moral and Physical Condition of the Working Classes Employed in the Cotton Manufacture in Manchester, 1832

15. Draw Conclusions What was an important piece of information about cholera that doctors did not yet know in 1832?

16. Elaborate Think about what you learned in this chapter and the previous one about the effects of the Industrial Age. What do you think Sir Kay-Shuttleworth meant by "physical and social evils"?

WRITING FOR THE SAT

Think about the following issue.

The development of railroads, steamship lines, automobiles, and air travel during the late 1800s and early 1900s has been called the Transportation Revolution.

17. Assignment: Think about the events and trends throughout your study of world history that have been characterized as revolutions. Some were quick and violent, while others happened over many years and were relatively peaceful. What qualities do these two types of revolutions have in common? Do the changes in transportation qualify as a revolution? Why or why not? Write an essay in which you develop your position on this issue. Support your point of view with reasoning and examples from your reading and studies.

Answers

Using the Internet

14. Go to the HRW Web site and enter the keyword shown to access a rubric for this activity.

KEYWORD: SHL LIF

Analyzing Primary Sources

15. Doctors wanted to know how cholera was introduced into towns.

16. possible answer—He was probably referring to problems that were caused by rapid expansion of towns and cities, including child labor, illiteracy, and unhealthy living and working conditions.

Writing for the SAT

17. Students should discuss the meaning of the term revolution, and how changes in transportation dramatically changed commerce, trade, and travel. A rubric for the activity is provided in **CRF:** Writing for the SAT.

HOLT
History's Impact
► **Video Program: Life in the Industrial Age**
See the Video Program Teacher's Guide for the answer to the closing question.

Review and Assessment Resources

Review and Reinforce

- **CRF:** Chapter Review
- **Quick Facts Transparency**: Visual Study Guide: Life in the Industrial Age
- **Spanish Chapter Summaries Audio CD Program**
- OSP **Holt PuzzlePro**: Quiz Show for ExamView
- **Quiz Game CD-ROM**

Assess

- **PASS**: Chapter Test, Forms A and B
- **Alternative Assessment Handbook**
- OSP **ExamView Test Generator**, Chapter Test
- **Differentiated Instruction Modified Worksheets and Tests CD-ROM**: Chapter Test
- HOAP **Holt Online Assessment Program** (in the Premier Online Edition)

Reteach/Intervene

- **Interactive Reader and Study Guide**
- **Differentiated Instruction Teacher Management System**: Lesson Plans for Differentiated Instruction
- **Differentiated Instruction Modified Worksheets and Tests CD-ROM**: Chapter Test
- **Interactive Skills Tutor CD-ROM**

go.hrw.com
Online Resources
KEYWORD: SHL TEACHER

Chapter 9 Planning Guide

Reforms, Revolutions, and War

Chapter Overview	Reproducible Resources	Technology Resources
CHAPTER 9 **pp. 284–709** **Overview: In this chapter, students will learn about the reforms that took place in Europe and the Americas during the 1800s. They will also study the causes and effects of the Civil War.**	**Differentiated Instruction Teacher Management System:** • Pacing Guide • Lesson Plans for Differentiated Instruction **Interactive Reader and Study Guide:** Chapter Summary* **Chapter Resource File*** • Writing About History • Social Studies Skill • Chapter Review **World History Outline Maps**	**Live Ink© Online Reading Help** **Student Edition on Audio CD Program** **Differentiated Instruction Modified Worksheets and Tests CD-ROM** **World History Primary Source Library CD-ROM** **Power Presentations with Video CD-ROM** **History's Impact: World History Video Program (VHS/DVD):** Reforms, Revolutions, and War
Section 1: **Reforms in the British Empire** **The Main Idea:** During the 1800s Great Britain passed many democratic reforms that changed the way people lived and worked.	**Differentiated Instruction Teacher Management System:** Section 1 Lesson Plan* **Interactive Reader and Study Guide:** Section 1 Summary* **Chapter Resource File*** • Vocabulary Builder: Section 1 • Biography: Sir Apirana Tupura Ngata • Literature: *A Vindication of the Rights of Woman*	**Daily Test Practice Transparency:** Section 1* **Map Transparency:** European Possessions, 1800* **Quick Facts Transparency:** British Reforms*
Section 2: **Revolution and Change in France** **The Main Idea:** During the 1800s opposing groups in France struggled to determine what kind of government France would have—a republic, a constitutional monarchy, or an absolute monarchy.	**Differentiated Instruction Teacher Management System:** Section 2 Lesson Plan* **Interactive Reader and Study Guide:** Section 2 Summary* **Chapter Resource File*** • Vocabulary Builder: Section 2 • Biography: Gustave Eiffel	**Daily Test Practice Transparency:** Section 2*
Section 3: **Independence in Latin America** **The Main Idea:** Revolutionary ideas took hold in Latin America as colonies fought for independence from Europe.	**Differentiated Instruction Teacher Management System:** Section 3 Lesson Plan* **Interactive Reader and Study Guide:** Section 3 Summary* **Chapter Resource File*** • Vocabulary Builder: Section 3 • Biography: José Martí	**Daily Test Practice Transparency:** Section 3* **Map Transparency:** Independence in Latin America* **Quick Facts Transparency:** Causes and Effects of Revolution in Latin America*
Section 4: **Expansion and War in the United States** **The Main Idea:** As the United States began to expand west, conflicts erupted over territory and slavery.	**Differentiated Instruction Teacher Management System:** Section 4 Lesson Plan* **Interactive Reader and Study Guide:** Section 4 Summary* **Chapter Resource File*** • Vocabulary Builder: Section 4 • Biography: Harriet Tubman • Primary Source: The Secession of South Carolina • History and Geography: Issue of Slavery Divides States	**Daily Test Practice Transparency:** Section 4* **Map Transparency:** Westward Expansion of the United States* **Quick Facts Transparency:** Causes and Effects of Westward Expansion*

go.hrw.com | Print Resource | Transparency
LS Learning Styles | Audio CD | CD-ROM
Video | SE Student Edition | TE Teacher's Edition
OSP One-Stop Planner CD-ROM
*also on One-Stop Planner CD-ROM

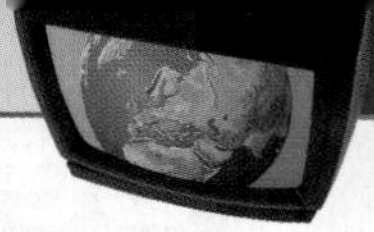

HOLT
History's Impact
World History Video Program (VHS/DVD)
Reforms, Revolutions, and War

Review, Assessment, Intervention

- **Quick Facts Transparency:** Reforms, Revolutions, and War*
- **Spanish Chapter Summaries Audio CD Program**
- **Progress Assessment Support System (PASS):** Chapter Test*
- **Differentiated Instruction Modified Worksheets and Tests CD-ROM:** Modified Chapter Test
- OSP **One-Stop Planner CD-ROM:** ExamView Test Generator (English/Spanish)
- HOAP **Holt Online Assessment Program (HOAP),** in the Holt Premier Online Student Edition

- **PASS:** Section 1 Quiz*
- **Online Quiz:** Section 1
- **Alternative Assessment Handbook**

- **PASS:** Section 2 Quiz*
- **Online Quiz:** Section 2
- **Alternative Assessment Handbook**

- **PASS:** Section 3 Quiz*
- **Online Quiz:** Section 3
- **Alternative Assessment Handbook**

- **PASS:** Section 4 Quiz*
- **Online Quiz:** Section 4
- **Alternative Assessment Handbook**

Power Presentation with Video CD-ROM

Power Presentations with Video are visual presentations of each chapter's main ideas. Presentations can be customized by including Quick Facts charts, images and maps from the textbook, and video clips.

Holt Online Learning

go.hrw.com
Teacher Resources
KEYWORD: SHL TEACHER

go.hrw.com
Student Resources
KEYWORD: SHL REF

- Document-Based Questions
- Interactive Multimedia Activities
- Current Events
- Chapter-Based Internet Activities
- and more!

Holt Premier
Online Student Edition

Complete online support for interactivity, assessment, and reporting
- Interactive Maps and Notebook
- Homework Practice and Research Activities Online

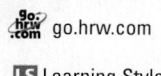

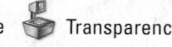

Before You Teach

The Big Picture

Peter N. Stearns

Currents of Reform The aftermath of the French and American revolutions spawned a number of movements to broaden social and political reform. New ideas about human improvability and equality, social tensions generated by expanding industrialization, and efforts by newly vigorous conservatives to forestall further change created the context for a variety of new efforts on both sides of the Atlantic. Four key cases, each with roots early in the 19th century, important in their own right, illustrate the larger processes involved.

Britain and France The British adopted the reform route, beginning with the gradual expansion of voting rights from 1832 through the rise of feminism toward the century's end. British politics also contended with demands from Ireland, Canada and Australia. Patterns of revolution resumed in France in 1830, with the uprising of 1848 and then the establishment of the Third Republic after 1871. Changes in education and some social reform followed from political change, along with new efforts to resolve old tensions between church and state. Britain and France can be usefully compared: why reform in one, revolutions in another, and did the long-term results point essentially in the same directions?

Latin America While Haiti ventured a genuine and important revolution, much of Latin America produced wars for independence. The causes of these wars can be compared with the causes of reform and revolution in Europe, as can the goals. But independence movements must be seen as somewhat different from revolution. Political independence ushered in a new era in Latin American history, even though the dreams of many leaders foundered on ensuing territorial divisions and frequent political instability.

The United States Reform impulses in the United States showed in the advent of Jacksonian democracy, dramatic expansion of education, and some social reform. Great energy also went into territorial expansion, with results that did not always mesh easily with the reform impulses. Slavery focused the most important set of political and social issues, and ultimately the Civil War responded to the bitter divisions involved.

Recent Scholarship

The abolition of slavery was one of the key developments in 19th-century world history. Seymour Drescher's *From Slavery to Freedom: Comparative Studies in the Rise and Fall of Atlantic Slavery* (1999) focuses both on the extended geography and chronology of emancipation, and at basic causes. His essays chart the beginning of the process, through attacks on West Indian slavery and the slave trade—attacks closely associated with the age of revolution and reform. He also treats later emancipations, which became such a central part of United States and Latin American history. Drescher considers many factors in the emancipation process, but highlights the rise of a new kind of humanitarian ideology, also closely linked to the revolutionary era but capable of spreading more widely in place and time. Several sections also treat what happened to workers after slavery ended.

Differentiating Instruction

Differentiated Instruction Teacher Management System
- Pacing Guide
- Lesson Plans for Differentiated Instruction

Interactive Reader and Study Guide

Spanish Chapter Summaries Audio CD Program

Student Edition on Audio CD Program

Differentiated Instruction Modified Worksheets and Tests CD-ROM
- Vocabulary Flash Cards
- Modified Vocabulary Builder Activities
- Modified Chapter Review Activity
- Modified Chapter Test

OSP **One-Stop Planner CD-ROM**
- ExamView Test Generator (English/Spanish)
- PuzzlePro
- Quiz Show for ExamView
- Transparencies and Videos

TE **Differentiated Activities in the Teacher's Edition**
- Arts and Culture of the Victorian Era, p. 289
- France's Road to Democracy, p. 294
- Brazil's Steps to Independence, p. 301
- Charting the Expansion of U.S. Territory, p. 304

Reading Like a Historian

Sam Wineburg

Haitian Independence Drawing inspiration from the American Revolution, in 1797 the former slave Toussaint L'Ouverture and his force of black and mulatto soldiers set out to cast off French rule on the island of Saint Domingue, present-day Haiti.

Despite his capture by the 20,000-strong force sent by Napoleon to quell the rebellion, and his imprisonment in France's Jura Mountains, L'Ouverture predicted that his brethren in bondage would soon be free. Some 7,000 French and an estimated 200,000 to 300,000 Haitian deaths later, L'Ouverture was proven right. On January 1, 1804, the Republic of Haiti was born.

One might assume that the two western hemisphere countries that had overthrown European rule—one against the British, the other against the French—would have much in common. But from the start, Haiti's neighbor to the north cast a suspicious eye on this nation of former slaves. The young American government—still under the Washington administration—provided aid ($726,000 for the purchase of guns and ammunition) to French planters to suppress the revolt.

The author of the Declaration of Independence, Thomas Jefferson, believed that it would be against American interests for former slaves to achieve self-government, fearing that if they did they would send "black crews, & supercargoes & missionaries" to the southern states to foment rebellion. Jefferson wrote, "If this combustion can be introduced among us under any veil whatever, we have to fear it."

American Policy As president, Jefferson did more than fear. He sought to isolate the black nation. American policy toward the newly independent Haiti was summarized by Jefferson's Secretary of the Treasury Albert Gallatin: "San Domingo is a French colony, recognized as such by the United States and by every European nation, a colony in a state of rebellion against the mother–country." Continuing to trade with Haiti would be "altogether illegal."

With the help of Congress, Gallatin's stance became law. On February 28, 1806, President Jefferson signed a trade ban, putting an embargo on commerce with Haiti. In so doing, Jefferson supported his son-in-law, John W. Eppes, congressman from Virginia, who argued that American businessmen should have little to do with a race that Americans needed "to depress and keep down."

Congress hoped that an isolated Haiti might become so desperate that it would seek the protection of its former French rulers. This didn't happened. The only lasting effect of the trade ban (which disintegrated four years later—Haitian sugar was too valuable) was that it "firmly established American hostility toward the black republic," in the words of historian Donald R. Hinkey.

Americans wanted Haitian sugar but southern lawmakers could not tolerate establishing relations with a nation of slaves that rose up and killed many of their masters. It wasn't until after the outbreak of the Civil War—when it was no longer necessary to placate the south—that Congress finally recognized Haiti and the hypocrisy of denying it the very rights that Americans claimed in 1776.

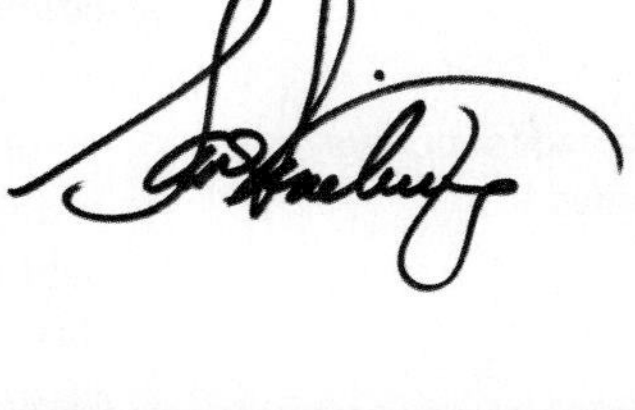

• Chapter Preview •

Chapter Main Ideas

Section 1 During the 1800s Great Britain passed many democratic reforms that changed the way people lived and worked.

Section 2 During the 1800s opposing groups in France struggled to determine what kind of government France would have—a republic, a constitutional monarchy, or an absolute monarchy.

Section 3 Revolutionary ideas took hold in Latin America as colonies fought for independence from Europe.

Section 4 As the United States began to expand west, conflicts erupted over territory and slavery.

CHAPTER 9

1800–1900

Reforms, Revolutions, and War

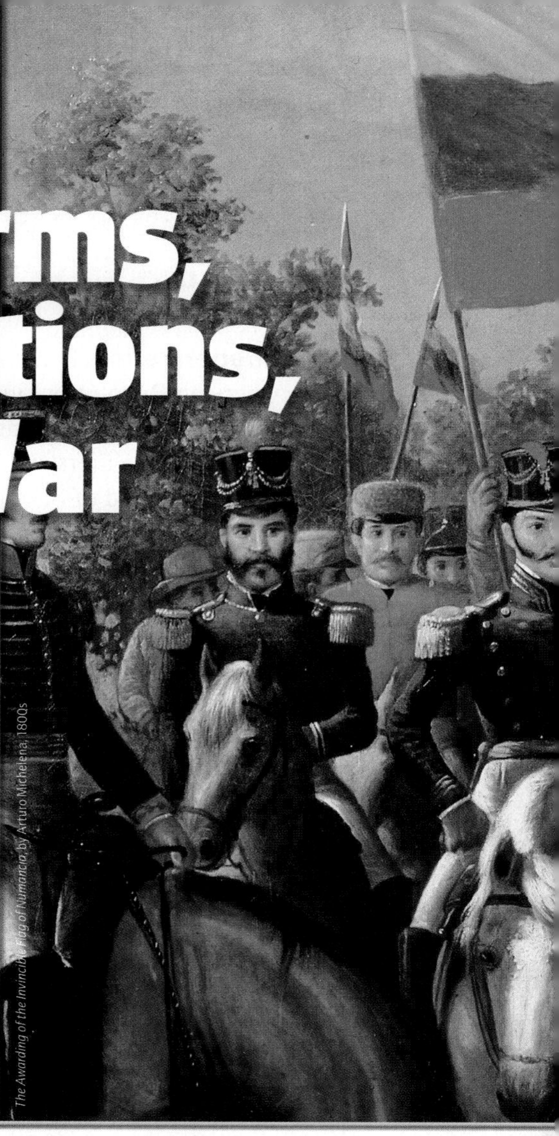

The Awarding of the Invincible Flag of Numancia, by Arturo Michelena, 1800s

THE BIG PICTURE Major reforms took place in Europe and the Americas during the 1800s. Both Great Britain and France made democratic reforms. In Latin America, colonies won independence from Europe. The United States abolished slavery after a bloody Civil War.

Theme GOVERNMENT AND CITIZENSHIP

In the 1800s reforms, revolutions, and war transformed government and citizenship in many places around the world. In this chapter you will learn how changes in government affected citizens in Great Britain, France, Latin America, and the United States.

TIME LINE

CHAPTER EVENTS

- **1803** U.S. president Thomas Jefferson purchases the Louisiana Territory from France, doubling the size of the United States.
- **1821** Mexico declares independence from Spain.
- **1832** The Reform Act doubles the number of voters in Great Britain.

1800 — 1820 — 1840

WORLD EVENTS

- **1804** Napoleon is crowned emperor of France.
- **1812** Egyptian forces capture Mecca and Medina.
- **1829** The Ottoman Empire recognizes Greece's independence.
- **1852** The Republic of South Africa is formed.

Key to Differentiating Instruction

Below Level

Basic-level activities designed for all students encountering new material

At Level

Intermediate-level activities designed for average students

Above Level

Challenging activities designed for honors and gifted and talented students

Standard English Mastery

Activities designed to improve standard English usage

Introduce the Chapter

At Level

Reforms, Revolutions, and War

1. Remind students that the Industrial Revolution changed life profoundly. Not only was it accompanied by rapid urbanization, but it also brought about revolutions in science, medicine, transportation, and communication.
2. Organize students into small groups. Have each group prepare a list of possible changes or reforms—both political and social—that they would expect to come about as a result of the Industrial Revolution. Have volunteers from each group share their lists with the class.
3. Guide the class in a discussion of the ideas presented.
4. Tell students that in this chapter they will learn about the wars, revolutions, and reforms that helped shape the modern world. **LS Interpersonal**

Alternative Assessment Handbook, Rubrics 11: Discussions; and 14: Group Activity

History's Impact video program
Watch the video to understand the impact of the women's suffrage movement.

1861 The Civil War begins in the United States.

1863 U.S. president Abraham Lincoln signs the Emancipation Proclamation, freeing slaves in the Confederate states.

1860 — 1880

1864 The Taiping Rebellion in China leaves 20 million Chinese dead.

Reading like a Historian This painting shows Simón Bolívar and members of the Venezuelan army after they defeated Spanish troops at the Battle of Carabobo on June 24, 1821. Bolívar is shown congratulating one of his generals by presenting him with a flag of liberation.

Analyzing Visuals How did the artist make Simón Bolívar the focal point of this painting? Explain your answer.

See **Skills Handbook**, p. H26

• Chapter Preview •

HOLT
History's Impact
► **Video Program: Reforms, Revolutions, and War**
See the Video Teacher's Guide for strategies for using the video segment.

Reading Like a Historian

Simón Bolívar Simón Bolívar was born into an aristocratic Venezuelan family of Spanish descent. Raised in wealth and privilege, Bolívar received an excellent education, in the course of which he was influenced by the thinking of John Locke, Thomas Hobbes, and the French writers of the Enlightenment. He led popular revolutions against Spanish rule in what is now Bolivia, Colombia, Ecuador, Peru, and Venezuela. Today Bolívar is known throughout Latin America as El Libertador—"The Liberator."

Explore the Time Line

1. What did the Reform Act accomplish? *doubled the number of voters in Britain*
2. When was Napoleon crowned emperor of France? *1804*
3. How did the United States double in size? *Thomas Jefferson bought the Louisiana Territory from France.*
4. What did the Emancipation Proclamation do? *freed the slaves in the Confederate states*

Info to Know

An Early Revolutionary Among the first serious rebellions against Spain's rule was an Indian uprising in the Viceroyalty of Peru in 1780. Led by Tupac Amarú, who claimed descent from an Inca emperor of the same name, a poorly armed force of more than 10,000 Indians attacked the city of Cuzco. Although Tupac was captured the revolt continued and spread to Bolivia.

Make Judgments Why do you think claiming descent from an Inca emperor would have helped Amarú's cause? *possible answer —It would have made others more likely to follow him.*

go.hrw.com
Online Resources
Chapter Resources:
KEYWORD: SHL REF
Teacher Resources:
KEYWORD: SHL TEACHER

Answers

Reading Like a Historian *possible answer—The artist depicted Bolívar on a white horse to make him the focal point of the painting. Bolívar is also shown in brighter light than the other figures in the painting.*

Preteach

Geography Starting Points

The British Empire In 1897 Queen Victoria celebrated her Diamond Jubilee—60 years on the throne of Great Britain. Her empire comprised one-fourth of the earth and over 400 million people. British influence was evident in virtually every country on Earth. Today little remains of the British Empire, but Britain's legacy is still apparent. Capitalism was a British invention, and English has become the international language for business and culture. Britain's successor on the world stage, the United States, continues to export the message of democracy that was first learned from the British.

Primary Source

"If France were to establish itself permanently in North Africa, to penetrate to central Africa, to make its influence felt in the entire Sahara and to win the [Western] Sudan; if in these immense regions where only fanaticism and brigandage [plundering by roving bands] reign today, it were to bring—even at the price of spilled blood—peace, commerce, tolerance, who could say this was a poor use of force? ... Having taught millions of men civilization and freedom would fill it with the pride that makes great peoples."

—Gabriel Charmes

Map Transparency: European Possessions, 1800

World History Outline Maps

Interactive Map: European Possessions, 1800

Answers

Geography Starting Points

1. *possible answers—may have signed treaties with other European nations; may have used force to defend colonies in Latin America;* **2.** *possible answer—They probably resented being controlled by a country so far away.*

GEOGRAPHY Starting Points

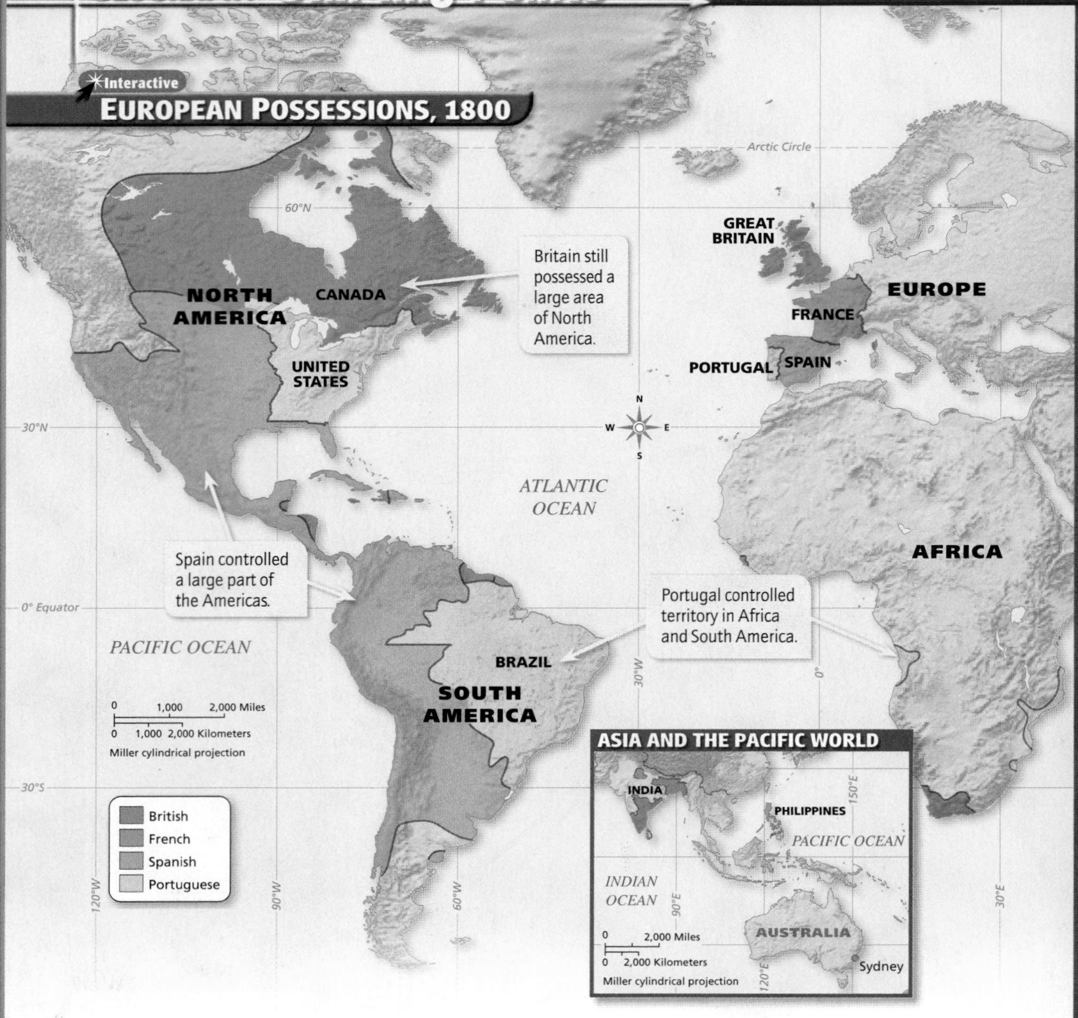

Starting Points In 1800 Great Britain, France, Spain, and Portugal controlled territories around the world. Most of the Americas was colonial territory that provided valuable natural resources to European nations.

1. **Analyze** How do you think Spain was able to control much of Latin America?
2. **Predict** How might the people in faraway colonies like India react to being ruled by a European country?

Listen to History

Go online to listen to an explanation of the starting points for this chapter.

go.hrw.com

Keyword: SHL REF

Skills Focus: Analyzing Maps

At Level

Social Studies Skill
European Possessions in 1800

1. Have students compare the map on this page with a map of the world in 1900. Guide the class in a discussion of the differences using the following questions as a guide: What happened to the great colonial empires? Which empires virtually disappeared? Which empires expanded greatly? How would having an empire affect the ruling nation? How would being part of an empire affect a colony?
2. Have each student write an essay describing how history might have been different if Spain, Portugal, France, Great Britain, and other European nations had *not* built empires.
3. Have volunteers read their essays to the class.

LS Visual-Spatial, Verbal-Linguistic

Alternative Assessment Handbook, Rubrics 21: Map Reading; and 40: Writing to Describe

SECTION 1

Reforms in the British Empire

BEFORE YOU READ

MAIN IDEA

During the 1800s Great Britain passed many democratic reforms that changed the way people lived and worked.

READING FOCUS

1. How did social and political reforms change life in Britain during the early 1800s?
2. What reforms helped to shape the Victorian Era?
3. What changes transformed the British empire?

KEY TERMS AND PEOPLE

Queen Victoria
Victorian Era
Benjamin Disraeli
suffrage
Emmeline Pankhurst

TAKING NOTES Take notes on the three types of reforms discussed in this section.

Reforms	
Social	
Political	
Voting	

STARVING FOR THE VOTE

THE INSIDE STORY ***What did British women have to endure to gain the right to vote?*** Some British women took extreme measures in the their fight for voting rights. In the late 1800s and early 1900s, hundreds of British women protested Parliament's refusal to grant women voting rights through criminal acts. They broke windows, set fires, and assaulted police officers. As a result, British police arrested the women and brought them to the Holloway prison in London. In prison, some of the women went on hunger strikes and refused to eat. They thought they would have to be released from prison if they starved themselves. But to their surprise, instead of releasing them, prison officials force fed them, holding the women down and sticking feeding tubes up their noses.

Some British citizens protested this harsh treatment. As a result, Parliament passed an act that allowed women who were sick from hunger to leave prison to recover. Once they were well, the police would then take them back to the prison. Still, this act ensured that the women could not use hunger strikes to shorten their prison times. ■

A group of British women celebrate their release from Holloway prison in 1908. ▶

Teach the Main Idea

At Level

Reforms in the British Empire

1. **Teach** Ask students the Reading Focus questions to teach this section.
2. **Apply** Guide students in a discussion of the ways in which democracy changed in the British Empire during the 1800s. Why is it significant that a British possession, New Zealand, was the first nation in which women gained the right to vote? Have students make a time line of the major voting reforms that led to universal adult suffrage in 1928.
3. **Review** Review student lists as a class, writing each reform for students to see.
4. **Practice/Homework** Britain has been called the "mother of democracies" and the "mother of nations." Have students write a brief essay based on material in this section explaining why they think those nicknames either fit or do not fit. **LS Visual-Spatial, Verbal-Linguistic**

Alternative Assessment Handbook, Rubrics 11: Discussions; and 43: Writing to Persuade

Preteach

Getting Started

Use the **Interactive Reader and Study Guide** to familiarize students with the section content.

Interactive Reader and Study Guide, Section 1

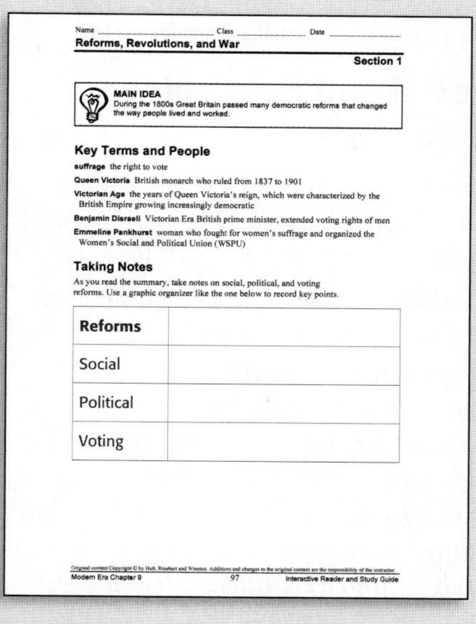

Name Class Date

Reforms, Revolutions, and War

Section 1

MAIN IDEA
During the 1800s Great Britain passed many democratic reforms that changed the way people lived and worked.

Key Terms and People

suffrage the right to vote
Queen Victoria British monarch who ruled from 1837 to 1901
Victorian Age the years of Queen Victoria's reign, which were characterized by the British Empire growing increasingly democratic
Benjamin Disraeli Victorian Era British prime minister, extended voting rights of men
Emmeline Pankhurst woman who fought for women's suffrage and organized the Women's Social and Political Union (WSPU)

Taking Notes
As you read the summary, take notes on social, political, and voting reforms. Use a graphic organizer like the one below to record key points.

Reforms	
Social	
Political	
Voting	

Modern Era Chapter 9 97 Interactive Reader and Study Guide

Academic Vocabulary

Review with students the high-use academic term in this section.

liberal supporter of political and social reform (p. 288)

CRF: Vocabulary Builder: Section 1

Taking Notes

Social—Factory Acts of 1833 and 1839, abolition of slavery; Political—Reform Act of 1832, some self-government granted to British possessions; Voting—voting reforms of 1867–1885 give more men of all classes the right to vote, New Zealand becomes the first country in which women gain the right to vote, British women gain right to vote on the same basis as men in 1928

go.hrw.com Online Resources

KEYWORD: SHL REF
ACTIVITY: The Settling of Australia

Direct Teach

Reading Focus

1 How did social and political reforms change life in Britain during the early 1800s? *reformed parliamentary representation, expanded voting rights; abolished slavery, improved conditions of workers, legalized trade unions*

Social and Political Reforms

Recall Why were some British prevented from voting? *They were poor, did not meet property requirements.*

Evaluate What was the significance of the People's Charter? *It was a petition sent to Parliament in 1839 demanding a number of additional reforms, such as voting rights for all men and a secret ballot. Although it was rejected by Parliament, Chartists gained wide support, and by the end of the century Parliament had passed many of its reforms.*

Teaching Tip

Suggest that students create their own time lines of the various social and political reforms. Students can use their time lines as a study guide when reviewing the chapter.

Social and Political Reforms

Before the 1800s Britain was dominated by the interests of wealthy landowners and aristocrats. During the 1830s, however, industrialization led to rapid changes in society. The growth of factories created a new class of workers, but these new industrial workers were not well represented in government. Recognizing the changing times, some British citizens began to call for social and political reform.

Reform Act of 1832 The growing prosperity of the working and middle classes produced by the Industrial Revolution in Britain led to greater demands for political reform. In 1800 landowning aristocrats made up most of Parliament. Some industrial cities, such as Birmingham and Manchester, had no representatives at all. Throughout Britain, only wealthy male property owners could vote. Catholics, Jews, and other minority groups could hold few political offices. In addition, members of Parliament's House of Commons were not paid for their services, so public office was largely restricted to men of great wealth.

ACADEMIC VOCABULARY
liberal supporter of political and social reform

By the 1830s, however, demands for reform became too strong to ignore. In Britain, as in the rest of Europe, liberals were challenging the old aristocratic and conservative order. Unrest increased throughout the country as ordinary people demanded greater political participation. Finally, Parliament agreed to change the electoral laws.

The Reform Act of 1832 gave industrial cities representation in Parliament for the first time. The bill also gave the vote to middle-class men, which increased the number of eligible voters by about 50 percent and significantly reduced the power of the aristocracy. However, political leaders continued to assume that only men with property and education would be responsible voters. Consequently, the bill stated that only men with a certain amount of property could vote. This requirement effectively prevented many working-class men from voting. Furthermore, British law continued to exclude women from voting.

Sadler and the Factory Act At the same time Parliament was debating the Reform Act of 1832, one of its members set out to investigate the treatment of children in Britain's textile factories. This member of Parliament, Michael Sadler, showed the harmful conditions endured by child workers—including physical mistreatment, long hours, and low wages.

In Sadler's report, one former child worker, who had worked in a mill in the early 1830s, remembered what it was like to work 13-hour days as a young boy.

Themes Through Time

Women's Suffrage

SOCIETY It was not until the late 1800s and early 1900s that women began to receive the right to vote. Before that, women fought to gain equal voting rights with men. Today, women exercise the freedom to vote in democratic countries around the world.

1792 Mary Wollstonecraft publishes a book advocating women's rights in Britain.

1848 Elizabeth Cady Stanton and Lucretia Mott organize the first women's rights convention in Seneca Falls, New York.

1800 — 1900

1888 Supporters of women's voting rights from Europe and the United States meet in Washington, D.C.

1893 New Zealand becomes the first country to grant women voting rights.

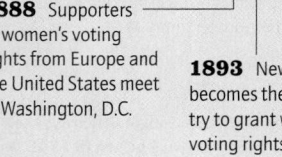

Skills Focus: Analyzing Alternative Points of View

At Level

Reading Like a Historian Skill

Chartists

1. Guide the class in a discussion of the demands made by the People's Charter using the following questions as a guide: What demands did the Chartists make? Do any of their demands seem radical or unreasonable? Why do you think the Chartists did not request voting rights for women as well as for men?
2. Tell students that they are newspaper editors in 1839 who oppose the People's Charter. Have each student write an editorial giving reasons why the provisions of the People's Charter should not be passed by Parliament.
3. Have volunteers read their editorials to the class. **LS Verbal-Linguistic**

Alternative Assessment Handbook, Rubrics 11: Discussions; and 43: Writing to Persuade

HISTORY'S VOICES

"My school life came to an end when I was about eight years old . . . I now went to work at John Sharpe's mill at the bottom of the town and close to the school I had left . . . We could count whole families of children who worked with us who had gone to an early grave."

—Thomas Wood, child mill worker, quoted in *Useful Toil*

Because of Sadler's report, Parliament passed the Factory Act in 1833. This act limited the working hours of children in textile factories. The act made it illegal for teenagers to work more than 12 hours a day. In addition, children between the ages of 9 and 13 had to receive two hours of schooling a day.

Other Reforms As workers gained more rights, the British Parliament also passed other social reforms. In 1833 Parliament abolished slavery in Great Britain and all of the British Empire. However, the Slavery Abolition Act did not immediately free slaves. For another four years, slaves over the age of six remained only partly free. In addition, the act stated that the British government would compensate slave owners depending on how many slaves they freed. Parliament also passed new public health and crime laws to improve living conditions in industrial cities.

Chartism By 1839 many people still could not vote. To remedy this problem, a group called the Chartists worked for universal manhood suffrage: voting rights for all men.

The Chartists got their name from the People's Charter, a petition sent to Parliament in 1839. The People's Charter demanded voting rights for all men, vote by secret ballot, annual elections, and pay for representatives in Parliament. The secret ballot was important because it meant people could not be intimidated to vote in a certain way. Pay for representatives in Parliament meant that working people could become members.

Parliament rejected the People's Charter. In response, the Chartists gained wide popular support and staged uprisings, including one large revolt in 1848. Based on the number of signatures on the 1848 petition, there may have been several million Chartist supporters.

READING SKILLS
Identifying Implied Main Ideas What is the main idea of this paragraph?

Although the Chartists did not see immediate results of the petition they sent to Parliament, they did draw attention to their cause. By the end of the 1800s, many reforms in the original People's Charter had been passed in Parliament.

READING CHECK **Compare** How did the demands of Chartism compare to the voting reforms passed in 1832?

1914 Activist Emmeline Pankhurst is arrested in London for speaking out on women's rights.

2006 Kuwaiti women vote for the first time in their country's national election.

2000

1920 American women gain the right to vote with the passage of the Nineteenth Amendment.

Skills FOCUS **UNDERSTANDING THEMES**

Identify Cause and Effect What early events in the history of the women's suffrage movement affected voting rights for women around the world?

Direct Teach

Reading Focus

Social and Political Reforms

Recall In what year did the British Parliament abolish slavery? What was the result? *1833; slaves over age six remained only partly free.*

Summarize What was the Sadler Report? *a report on an investigation by Michael Sadler on the treatment of children in the textile factories; led to the Factory Act in 1833*

Info to Know

Abolition of Slavery The Abolition of the Slave Trade Act was passed by Parliament in 1807. Although it made the slave trade illegal throughout the British Empire, slave trade continued between the Caribbean colonies until 1811. Most plantation owners lived in Britain, although their plantations were in the Caribbean. They often brought their household slaves back with them when they returned to Britain.

Differentiating Instruction

Above Level

Advanced Learners/Gifted and Talented

Research Required

Background: Tell students that Queen Victoria's reign was not only marked by political and social reforms and economic progress, but also by the development of a distinct culture.

1. Have students use reliable primary and secondary sources to search for information on the arts and culture of the Victorian Era.
2. Have students make a collage or multimedia presentation based on their findings. Presentations may either focus on a particular aspect of Victorian culture, such as architecture, furniture, fashions, art, literature, religion, or morality, or they may take a more general approach.
3. Have volunteers share their presentations with the class.
4. Guide students in a discussion of Victorian culture based on the presentations.
LS Visual-Spatial

Alternative Assessment Handbook, Rubrics 22: Multimedia Presentations; and 30: Research

Answers

Reading Skills *possible answer—Despite Parliament's rejection of the People's Charter, chartists gained popularity.*

Themes Through Time *1792: Mary Wollstonecraft publishes a book advocating women's rights; 1848: first women's rights convention held in Seneca Falls, New York; 1888: supporters of women's voting rights meet in Washington, D.C.*

Reading Check *1832 voting reforms redrew borough lines, extended vote to many middle-class property owners, gave parliamentary representation to many industrial towns, but not to industrial workers; Chartists called for additional reforms, extending the vote to all men, vote by secret ballot, annual elections, payment of representatives in Parliament*

Direct Teach

Reading Focus

2 What reforms helped to shape the Victorian Era? *voting rights expanded for men, secret ballot created*

Victorian Era Voting Reforms

Recall What was Queen Victoria's attitude toward women's suffrage? *She was opposed to it.*

Summarize What reasons did Disraeli give for believing that women should have the right to vote? *Women were considered capable of other responsibilities connected with both church and state.*

Predict Do you think that the Women's Social and Political Union's use of destructive means will help or hurt the cause of women's suffrage? Explain. *possible answers—may hurt the cause by making women appear to be irrational and their opponents justified; may help the cause by gaining recognition*

Quick Facts Transparency: British Reforms

CRF: Literature: *A Vindication of the Rights of Woman*

Info to Know

British Labor Movement Only about 10 to 15 percent of British laborers enjoyed high pay, regular employment, and membership in trade unions during the late 1800s. This so-called "labour aristocracy"—consisting of skilled artisans such as engineers, cotton spinners, printers, and cabinet-makers—provided the leadership of the working class. Although its members generally adopted a lower-middle-class lifestyle, the leadership of radical reform movements frequently came from this "aristocracy."

British Reforms

QUICK FACTS

During the 1800s and early 1900s, the British Parliament passed a series of reforms that gave more rights and freedoms to its citizens.

Reform Act of 1832	Redrew political boundaries to give more equal representation in Parliament
Abolition of Slavery, 1833	Abolished slavery in both Britain and its colonies
Factory Acts of 1833 and 1839	Limited the working hours of women and children in factories
People's Charter, 1839	Charter sent to Parliament that called for voting rights for all men and for voting by secret ballot
Voting Reforms, 1867–1885	Several different acts that gave more men of all classes voting rights
Women's Suffrage, 1918 and 1928	Granted women over 30 the right to vote (1918) and all British women the right to vote (1928)

Victorian Era Voting Reforms

In 1837 **Queen Victoria** became the ruler of Great Britain. Her reign, the longest in British history, lasted until 1901 and is known as the **Victorian Era**. It was a time of great change in Britain, including voting reforms that made the country more democratic. Britain had long been a constitutional monarchy, but the voting reforms of the Victorian Era made it increasingly democratic.

Disraeli and Gladstone During the years 1868–1885, two influential prime ministers, **Benjamin Disraeli** and William Gladstone, were elected prime minister several times. Disraeli was a member of the Conservative party, which wanted to preserve the best traditions of the past. The Conservatives were slow in accepting modern reforms. Gladstone was a member of the Liberal party, which adopted a more progressive approach to solving society's problems.

Voting Rights for Men Disraeli put forth a new reform bill that would extend voting rights to more working men. Passed in 1867, the bill meant about one out of every three men could now vote. Another law created the secret ballot, to ensure voters would not be bribed or intimidated. In 1885 Gladstone pushed through a reform bill that extended voting rights still further.

Women's Suffrage While Gladstone and Disraeli were trying to extend voting rights for men, some members of Parliament were also pushing for women's **suffrage**, or the right to vote. The question of women's rights had first been raised during the Enlightenment. But during most of the 1800s, women were still not seen as equals. They could not own property and they were not even considered the legal guardians of their children.

Many women thought the right to vote could increase their power in society. In contrast, Queen Victoria was against women's suffrage, calling it "mad, wicked folly."

In spite of the Queen's opposition, Disraeli argued in favor of women's voting rights in a speech before the House of Commons in 1866. He argued that if a woman could be queen or own land, she should to be able to vote:

HISTORY'S VOICES

> **"I say that in a country governed by a woman . . . [and] where a woman by law may be a churchwarden and overseer of the poor—I do not see, when she has so much to do with the state and the Church, on what reasons . . . she has not a right to vote."**
>
> —Benjamin Disraeli, speech before House of Commons, 1866

Disraeli and other members of Parliament tried to add women's suffrage to the 1867 reform bill. But they did not succeed.

For nearly 40 years, suffragists—people who work to achieve voting rights for women—made little progress, but not from lack of trying. One group of suffragists, led by Millicent Garrett Fawcett, used a gradual approach to winning the vote. They lobbied members of Parliament, signed petitions, and worked on educating the public. But the government largely ignored their efforts.

By the early 1900s, some women grew frustrated with the slow pace of the suffrage movement. **Emmeline Pankhurst**, founder of the Women's Social and Political Union (WSPU),

Skills Focus: Analyzing Alternative Points of View

At Level

Reading Like a Historian Skill
Women's Suffrage

1. Review the information in the text about women's suffrage with students. Organize students into two groups. Have one group represent the point of view of British citizens who supported women's suffrage. Have the other group represent British citizens who opposed women's suffrage. Have each group prepare arguments to support its position.
2. Conduct a classroom debate on women's suffrage.
3. Guide the class in a discussion of the results of the debate. What reasons were students able to give for denying the vote to women? Why do they think that Queen Victoria—a woman—would want to deny equal rights to other women? **LS Interpersonal, Verbal-Linguistic**

Alternative Assessment Handbook, Rubrics 10: Debates; and 11: Discussions said that in order to achieve reform, "You have to make more noise than anybody else." As the government continued to ignore the issue of women's suffrage, the WSPU adopted more destructive tactics, such as breaking windows and arson. For these acts, many suffragists went to prison.

Finally, in 1918, Parliament granted the vote to women over the age of 30. Not until 1928, however, did British women gain the right to vote on the same basis as men.

READING CHECK **Summarize** What reforms were passed during the late 1800s?

Changes in the British Empire

Beyond Britain, people living in other parts of the British Empire were also moved by the spirit of reform. In the mid-1800s people in Ireland, Canada, Australia, and New Zealand took steps to rule themselves.

Ireland Since 1801 Ireland had been part of the United Kingdom after the Act of Union joined it with England, Scotland, and Wales. Some Irish hated their British rulers, especially British landlords. These landlords owned much of Ireland's land and had the power to evict Irish farmers. In addition, policies created to help British industry hurt Irish agriculture.

Several times in the mid-1800s, the potato crop failed. Because many Irish peasants depended on potatoes as their main food source, famine swept Ireland. The failure of the potato crop left many with no food and no income. Without the money to pay rent, many peasants were evicted from their homes.

HISTORY'S VOICES

"In many places the wretched people were seated on the fences of their decaying gardens, wringing their hands and wailing bitterly the destruction that had left them foodless."

—Father Matthew, Irish priest, in a letter to Prime Minister Trevelyan

Ireland's Potato Famine

In the early 1800s, about half of Ireland's population depended on potatoes as their main food source. Beginning in 1845, a disease, or blight, struck Ireland's potato crop. As a result, about 1 million people died from starvation or famine-related diseases. To make matters worse, the British government did little to help the starving Irish. ***Based on the graph below, when did the Irish population finally stop declining after the famine?***

POPULATION OF IRELAND, 1780–1920

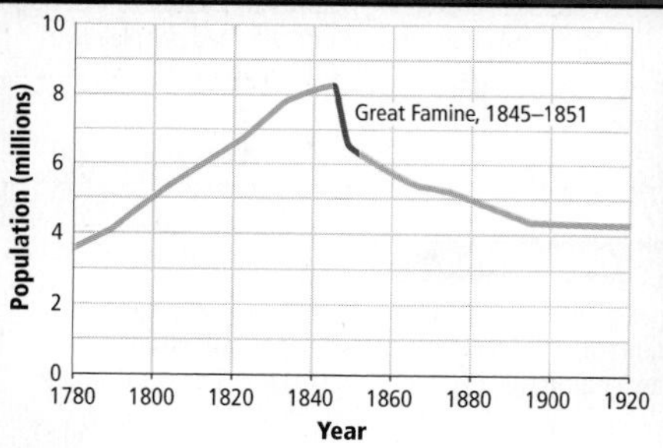

Source: Hearth Tax Returns, Irish Census

This British cartoon from 1846 shows a wealthy British landowner offering potatoes to a poor Irish family. ▼

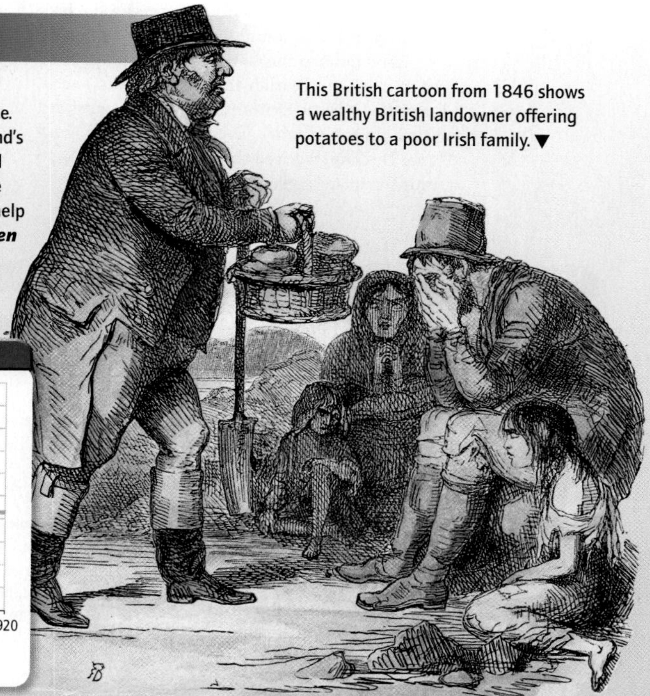

"Union is Strength," *Punch*, 1846

Collaborative Learning

At Level

Canadian Unity

1. Organize students into small groups. Tell groups that they are members of the Canadian governor-general's staff working to get the support of the colonists for a dominion. Have each group either create posters and flyers or put together a multimedia presentation designed to convince colonists that forming a dominion is in their best interest. Remind students that their presentations should be historically accurate, even though they are using modern public relations methods.
2. Have each group share its presentation with the class.
3. Guide the class in a discussion of the advantages and disadvantages of combining several colonies to make a larger dominion, from the point of view of the colonies and from that of the ruling nation.

LS Interpersonal, Visual-Spatial

Alternative Assessment Handbook, Rubrics 14: Group Activity; and 24: Multimedia Presentations

Direct Teach

Reading Focus

3 What changes transformed the British empire? *Canada, Australia, and New Zealand all gained some level of self-government.*

Changes in the British Empire

Recall Why did the Irish resent the British? *British landowners owned much of Ireland's land; British policies hurt Irish agriculture.*

Make Judgments Do you think the British should be held responsible for the high death rate in Ireland during the potato famine? Explain. *possible answer—Yes, Britain probably had the resources to feed the starving people of Ireland but chose not to do so.*

Info to Know

Irish Immigration to the U.S. The Irish Potato Famine of 1845 is considered to be the primary reason for the enormous wave of Irish immigration to the United States that occurred during the 1840s. Between 1820 and 1860, over one third of all U.S. immigrants were Irish, and in the 1840s, the Irish made up almost half of all U.S. immigrants.

Quebec Separatists The differences between French and British Canadians remain strong today. A separatist movement exists in Quebec, where more than 80 percent of the population is French-speaking. In recent years, Quebec voters have narrowly defeated referendums calling for the province's independence from the rest of Canada.

Answers

Ireland's Potato Famine *It stopped declining in about 1900.*

Reading Check *voting rights expanded for men, secret ballot created*

Direct Teach

Reading Focus

Changes in the British Empire

Recall In what year were women in New Zealand allowed to vote? *1893*

Infer What kind of society do you think resulted from Britain sending criminals to Australia? *possible answer—probably chaotic and dangerous*

CRF: Biography: Sir Apirana Tupura Ngata

Review & Assess

Close

Have the class summarize the growth of democracy in Great Britain.

Review

Online Quiz, Section 1

Assess

SE Section 1 Assessment

Progress Assessment: Section 1 Quiz

Alternative Assessment Handbook

Reteach/Intervene

Interactive Reader and Study Guide, Section 1

Interactive Skills Tutor CD-ROM

Answers

Reading Check *potato famine left Irish resentful, 1920: limited self-rule; 1867: British granted some Canadian colonies self-rule; Australia granted self-rule; Maoris in New Zealand exchanged land for self-rule*

During the years of the famine, about 1 million people starved, and about 1.5 million others emigrated—many to the United States.

Tragically, Ireland continued to export food throughout the famine years. Food shipments left Irish ports for England under heavy guard by British soldiers. British officials encouraged this trade because they believed that interfering with this trade would harm the British economy.

The famine left many Irish people more resentful of British rule than ever. By the 1860s, many Irish began to fight for change. Some wanted independence and staged violent protests. Others struggled for home rule, in which Ireland would govern itself within the United Kingdom. Parliament debated several bills to grant home rule to Ireland in the 1800s, but they did not pass. Ireland did not receive limited self-government until 1920.

Canada Like Ireland, Canada was also controlled by Britain. Britain's colonies in Canada were very different, however. Some were mainly French-speaking, and others were mainly English-speaking. This diversity created a lack of unity in Canada and led to calls for reform.

Rebellions in the Canadian colonies in 1837 convinced the British that reform was necessary. In 1838 the British government sent Lord Durham to serve as governor-general to Canada. Durham wanted the Canadian colonies to unite to form "a great and powerful people."

By 1867 the British Parliament united several Canadian colonies and granted them the power to govern themselves. With this act, Canada became a dominion, or a self-governing colony. For Canada, this was the first step toward independence from Britain.

The new dominion continued to expand westward until it eventually reached the Pacific coast. Although Canada was developing its own identity, it remained closely tied to Britain.

Australia and New Zealand Canada became a model for self-government in other British colonies on the other side of the globe—Australia and New Zealand. Since the late 1700s, Britain had used Australia as a place to send its criminals. In the mid-1800s, however, other British colonists, attracted by the discovery of rich copper and gold deposits, began to settle in Australia. In 1901 Britain granted self rule to the Commonwealth of Australia, which established its own parliament but still remained part of the British empire.

In New Zealand, the British government made an agreement with the local Maori people for land in exchange for self rule. In this way, New Zealand became a dominion of Great Britain. In 1893 New Zealand became the first country to give women the vote.

READING CHECK **Compare and Contrast** How did self-rule come about in Ireland, Canada, Australia, and New Zealand?

Section 1 Assessment

go.hrw.com Online Quiz Keyword: SHL REF HP

Reviewing Ideas, Terms, and People

1. **a. Recall** What was Chartism?
   b. Analyze Why did the Chartists fail to gain universal manhood suffrage in 1848?
   c. Evaluate Why do you think the first labor reforms dealt with child labor?
2. **a. Identify** Name two reforms of the late 1800s.
   b. Explain What reforms did **Benjamin Disraeli** argue for?
   c. Evaluate Do you think **Emmeline Pankhurst** was right when she said reformers had to "make more noise than anybody else" in order to be successful? Why or why not?
3. **a. Recall** What was the purpose of the Act of Union?
   b. Compare and Contrast How were New Zealand and Australia similar and how were they different?

Critical Thinking

4. **Categorize** Copy the graphic organizer below and use it to list social, political, and voting reforms in Great Britain during the 1800s. Identify how each reform affected people's lives.

Social	Political	Voting

Focus on Writing

5. **Exposition** Choose a reform discussed in the section and decide whether you think it was a beneficial reform or not. Write a paragraph explaining the reasons for your decision.

Section 1 Assessment Answers

1. **a.** a movement that got its name from the People's Charter, a voting rights petition sent to Parliament in 1839
   b. Parliament rejected the People's Charter.
   c. possible answer— It was a cause that might appeal to all people.
2. **a.** extension of voting rights to all men; creation of the secret ballot
   b. extending voting rights to more working men; women's suffrage
   c. possible answer—no, destructive and violent acts may have convinced some people to oppose women's suffrage
3. **a.** to create a United Kingdom joining England, Scotland, and Wales to Ireland
   b. similar: far from Britain; Australia—place to send criminals, immigrants attracted by minerals, granted self-rule in 1901; New Zealand—Maoris exchange land for self rule
4. Reform Act of 1832—eliminated unequal representation in Parliament; extended vote to middle class; abolition of slavery—freed many slaves; public health and crime laws—improved conditions in cities; Factory Act of 1833—limited women and children's hours in textile factories; made working all night illegal; voting reforms—extended vote to men of all classes; created secret ballot
5. Paragraphs should focus on one reform and its benefits or drawbacks.

SECTION 2

Revolution and Change in France

BEFORE YOU READ

MAIN IDEA

During the 1800s opposing groups in France struggled to determine what kind of government France would have—a republic, a constitutional monarchy, or an absolute monarchy.

READING FOCUS

1. What happened during the Revolution of 1830?
2. What were the results of the birth of the French republic?
3. How did the Dreyfus affair reveal divisions within French society?

KEY TERMS AND PEOPLE

Louis Philippe
Louis Napoleon
Dreyfus affair
anti-Semitism
Theodor Herzl
Zionism

TAKING NOTES Take notes on the different eras in French history during the 1800s.

Years	
Leader	
Key events and policies	

During the Revolution of 1830, Parisians built barricades in the streets. ▲

THE INSIDE STORY ***What led France to revolution again?*** The year was 1830. Fifteen years had passed since the Congress of Vienna. Charles X—the last of the French Bourbon monarchs—was now king of France.

Liberals had just won a majority of seats in the French legislature, but Charles was a conservative. To prevent the liberals from exercising power, he passed laws that broke up the legislature and called for new elections. The new laws also limited the freedom of the press.

The king's actions reminded some people of the absolute monarchs who had ruled before the French Revolution. In 1830 the people revolted, and protesters took over the center of Paris. They built large barricades and waved the tricolor flag, shouting "Down with the Bourbons!" Another revolution was underway. ■

Teach the Main Idea

At Level

Revolution and Change in France

1. **Teach** Ask students the Reading Focus questions to teach this section.
2. **Apply** Have students create an outline of the section using the heads as main points. Have students identify at least two main ideas under each of the blue subheadings.
3. **Review** Review student outlines as a class. Have students identify the points in their outlines that they feel are most important or most interesting. Have students explain why anti-Semitism would emerge so forcefully during the Third Republic.
4. **Practice/Homework** Write the following statement for students to see: It is acceptable for the government to limit civil liberties if more jobs and a stronger France are the result. Have each student write an editorial either supporting or opposing the statement. Student editorials should support opinions with facts and examples from this section. **LS Visual-Spatial, Verbal-Linguistic**

Alternative Assessment Handbook, Rubrics 11: Discussions; and 17: Letters to Editors

Preteach

Getting Started

Use the **Interactive Reader and Study Guide** to familiarize students with the section content.

Interactive Reader and Study Guide, Section 2

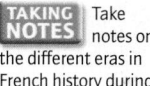

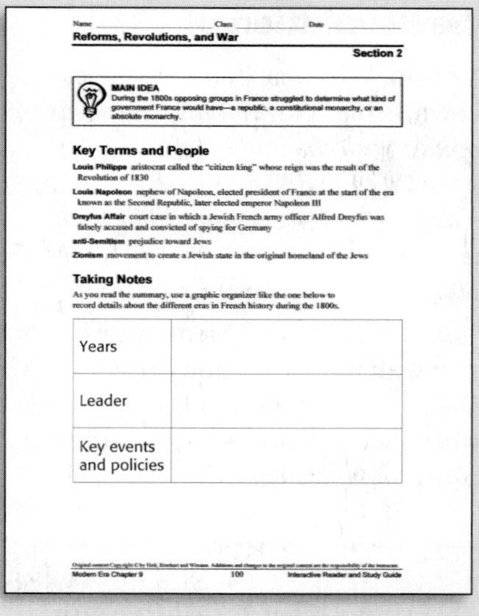

Name ______ Class ______ Date ______

Reforms, Revolutions, and War

Section 2

MAIN IDEA
During the 1800s opposing groups in France struggled to determine what kind of government France would have—a republic, a constitutional monarchy, or an absolute monarchy.

Key Terms and People

Louis Philippe aristocrat called the "citizen king" whose reign was the result of the Revolution of 1830
Louis Napoleon nephew of Napoleon, elected president of France at the start of the era known as the Second Republic, later elected emperor Napoleon III
Dreyfus Affair court case in which a Jewish French army officer Alfred Dreyfus was falsely accused and convicted of spying for Germany
anti-Semitism prejudice toward Jews
Zionism movement to create a Jewish state in the original homeland of the Jews

Taking Notes

As you read the summary, use a graphic organizer like the one below to record details about the different eras in French history during the 1800s.

Years	
Leader	
Key events and policies	

Original content Copyright © by Holt, Rinehart and Winston. Additions and changes to the original content are the responsibility of the instructor.
Modern Era Chapter 9 100 Interactive Reader and Study Guide

CRF: Vocabulary Builder: Section 2

Taking Notes

1815–1830—Charles X: broke up legislature, limited freedom of press and number of voters; 1830–1848—Louis Philippe: number of voters expanded, some freedoms limited, economic troubles by mid-1840s; 1848–1852—Second Republic—Louis Napoleon: created support for idea of French republic, fueled women's rights movement, revolution inspired revolutions across Europe, arrested members of National Assembly who opposed him; 1852–1870—Second Empireaa—Louis Napoleon (now Napoleon III): increased voting rights, economic prosperity, new railroads increased trade and development, 1870—Third Republic—trade unions become legal, working hours reduced, Dreyfus affair, new constitution, public education laws, universal male suffrage

The Revolution of 1830

At the end of the Napoleonic era, the Congress of Vienna restored Louis XVIII to the French throne. The French had a constitution and a legislature, but most power remained with the king. The French people would not remain content with their government for long.

A King Abdicates After Louis XVIII died, his brother Charles X inherited the throne. Charles tried to rule as an absolute monarch. But when he suspended the power of the legislature, angry citizens revolted in an uprising known as the Revolution of 1830. Within days they controlled Paris. Charles abdicated, or gave up the throne, and fled to England.

News of the revolution in France quickly reached Klemens von Metternich in Austria. "My life's work is destroyed!" he exclaimed. The reactionary ideals and absolute monarchies he had supported at the Congress of Vienna were beginning to crumble. Metternich feared that revolution threatened to spread throughout the continent. His fears would soon come true.

The Reign of Louis Philippe Having rid the country of King Charles, moderate liberal leaders formed a constitutional monarchy and chose **Louis Philippe** to be the new king. Louis Philippe was an aristocrat who was popular with the middle class. He dressed like them, wearing long pants rather than the knee-length breeches worn by the nobility. Because he appeared to live simply, like ordinary citizens, many French people referred to him as the "citizen king."

Over time, however, Louis Philippe seemed less like a citizen and more like a king. He increased the number of voters—but only by extending the vote to more wealthy citizens. To protect the power of the government, he limited the freedom of the press. His rule became increasingly repressive, and he silenced most people who opposed him.

During Louis Philippe's reign, working people grew poorer, while the middle class and aristocracy became more prosperous. The popularity of the king deteriorated rapidly in 1846 when an economic depression made life even more difficult for all but the wealthiest French people. Discontent would lead France to revolution once more.

READING CHECK **Identify Cause and Effect** What were the effects of the Revolution of 1830?

Birth of a Republic

The economic troubles and general unhappiness simmered in France until 1848. Then revolution exploded again, and another republic was born.

The Revolution of 1848 The Revolution of 1848 was sparked when the French government banned a banquet planned by reformers. Angry protesters, both middle and working class, took to the streets.

Louis Philippe quickly abdicated and the monarchy came to an end. The French citizens formed a new government, a republic headed by a president. Voters elected Napoleon's nephew, **Louis Napoleon** as president.

TIME LINE

Changes in France's Government

1830 King Charles X flees France during the Revolution of 1830. Louis Philippe is crowned king.

1848 In the Revolution of 1848, Louis Philippe abdicates and the Second Republic is formed with Louis Napoleon as president.

1852 Louis Napoleon dissolves the National Assembly and is elected emperor by the people.

1870 After the Franco-Prussian War, a democratic government is restored during the Third Republic.

Second Republic — Second Empire — Third Republic

Skills Focus **INTERPRETING TIME LINES**

In which year did the French government replace a king with a president?

Direct Teach

Reading Focus

1 What happened during the Revolution of 1830? *King Charles X abdicated and was replaced by King Louis Philippe, the "citizen king"*

The Revolution of 1830

Explain Why was Louis Philippe known as the "citizen king"? *He was popular with the middle class; he appeared to live like ordinary people; he dressed in long pants rather than the knee-length breeches worn by the nobility.*

Evaluate Why was Metternich so upset with the Revolution of 1830? *A revolution—especially one to overthrow an absolute monarch—went against his reactionary ideals.*

Reading Focus

2 What were the results of the birth of the French republic? *King Louis Philippe abdicated. A new republican government formed, with Louis Napoleon as president.*

Birth of a Republic

Recall What positive effects did the Revolution of 1848 have in France? *gave French men the right to vote; created support for republican government; fueled a new women's movement in France*

Explain What was unusual in the way that Napoleon III became emperor? *He was elected by the voters.*

CRF: Biography: Gustave Eiffel

Differentiating Instruction

Below Level

Learners Having Difficulty

1. Organize students into mixed-ability pairs. Have students use the information in their texts to create a chart comparing and contrasting the rise to power, rule, and fall from power of Louis XVI, Napoleon, Louis Philippe, and Louis Napoleon (Emperor Napoleon III).
2. Review student charts as a class. Create a master chart for students to see and fill it in as students call out the points of comparison. Ask students what parallels existed among the rule of these four men.
3. Guide the class in a discussion of France's rocky road to democracy during the 1800s. What do the repeated returns to monarchy indicate about the nation? **LS Visual-Spatial**

Alternative Assessment Handbook, Rubrics 7: Charts; and 9: Comparing and Contrasting

Answers

Time Line *1848*

Reading Check *King Charles X abdicated and was replaced by King Louis Philippe, the "citizen king"*

Reading like a Historian

The Dreyfus Affair

Interpreting Political Cartoons In 1894 the French government put Alfred Dreyfus, a captain in the French army, on trial for spying for Germany, even though he was innocent. At the time, many French were anti-Semitic, or prejudiced toward Jews. Because Dreyfus was Jewish, he suffered from this anti-Semitism.

To interpret what this cartoon suggests about anti-Semitism, think about

- the details of the cartoon
- the message or point of the cartoon
- the message versus known facts

Alfred Dreyfus is shown as a mythical dragon in this anti-Semitic cartoon.

The French government called Dreyfus *le traitre,* the traitor.

Skills Focus READING LIKE A HISTORIAN

1. **Details** What details do you see in the cartoon? How do the details dehumanize Dreyfus?
2. **Message** What is the message of the cartoon? How is that message contradicted by facts?

See **Skills Handbook**, p. H28

The era that followed was known as the Second Republic; the First Republic had existed during the years between the French Revolution and the reign of Napoleon.

The Revolution of 1848 had far-reaching effects. From that point on, all adult French men had the right to vote and never lost it again. The Revolution of 1848 also created support for republican government, fueled a new women's rights movement, and inspired other revolutions across Europe.

Napoleon III and the Second Empire

The French constitution allowed the president to serve only four years, but Louis Napoleon wanted to remain in office. In 1851 he sent his troops to Paris and arrested members of the National Assembly who opposed him. Then he called for a national vote to decide whether he should be given the power to draft a new constitution. Voters approved the measure.

In another vote the following year, the French people elected him emperor Napoleon III. Thus began the period known as the Second Empire. During the Second Empire Napoleon III made some reforms, such as increasing voting rights, but he always kept absolute power as emperor. He ruled during a time of economic prosperity and built many miles of railroads, which helped increase trade and improve communications in France.

The Third Republic In 1870 Napoleon III drew France into a war with Prussia. In the Franco-Prussian War, Napoleon III was captured in battle and surrendered to the Prussians. This shameful defeat led the French Assembly to depose Napoleon and proclaim the Third Republic. The new republic immediately faced a crisis as the Prussians invaded France and began a siege of Paris.

Despite this troubled beginning, the Third Republic made some important reforms. In 1882 the government made primary education available for children between the ages of 6 and 13. In 1884 trade unions were legalized, and by 1900 working hours had been reduced. In addition, in 1906 a new act required employers to give their workers one day off per week.

READING CHECK **Draw Conclusions** Why did the French elect Louis Napoleon as their president?

Direct Teach

Recent Scholarship

The Dreyfus Affair by Leslie Derfler contains primary sources, reference material and background information that put the affair into context. Derfler examines the tension that developed in France over the incident and addresses the history of anti-Semitism in France.

The Dreyfus Affair by Leslie Derfler. Greenwood Press, 2002.

Info to Know

Louis Napoleon A liberal who was influenced by his uncle Napoleon I's ideas, Louis Napoleon was deeply involved in revolutionary activities. In 1836, he attempted a military coup against King Louis Philippe and was exiled to the United States. Returning to France in 1840 he launched another uprising against the king, for which he was sentenced to life in prison.

Skills Focus: Making Inferences

At Level

Reading Skill

The Dreyfus Affair

1. Review the information in the text and the political cartoon about the Dreyfus affair. Tell students that they are foreign correspondents in the 1890s covering the Dreyfus affair for an American newspaper. Have each student write an article about the affair from the perspective of an American reporter of the time.
2. Have volunteers read their articles to the class.
3. Guide the class in a discussion of the Dreyfus affair using the following questions as a guide: Could something like the Dreyfus affair have happened in the United States in the 1890s? Could something like that happen today? What other groups have been singled out for similar treatment in the United States? What other instances of scapegoating—fixing the blame on someone other than the perpetrator—can students name? **LS Verbal-Linguistic**

Alternative Assessment Handbook, Rubrics 11: Discussions; and 42: Writing to Inform

Answers

Reading Like a Historian **1.** *the words "le traitre" (traitor) attached to the dragon's body, the snakes around Dreyfus's head depict him as a monster;* **2.** *The message depicts Dreyfus as a traitor, but he was innocent.*

Reading Check *possible answer—because of his famous name and family legacy*

Direct Teach

Reading Focus

3 How did the Dreyfus affair reveal divisions within French society? *It was at the bottom of the Dreyfus affair. The controversy split the French into those who sided with Dreyfus, a Jewish army officer, and those who were against him.*

The Dreyfus Affair

Recall What effect did Zola think the Dreyfus affair would have on France? *Anti-Semitism would destroy the liberal France of the Rights of Man.*

Identify Cause and Effect What were some effects of the Dreyfus affair, both inside and outside of France? *in France—set off anti-Semitic riots; united many political groups into just two—supporters and opponents of Dreyfus; outside France—Zionist movement began and gained strength*

Review & Assess

Close

Guide the class in a discussion about democracy in 19th-century France.

Review

Online Quiz, Section 2

Assess

SE Section 2 Assessment

Progress Assessment: Section 2 Quiz

Alternative Assessment Handbook

Reteach/Intervene

Interactive Reader and Study Guide, Section 2

Interactive Skills Tutor CD-ROM

Answers

Reading Check *polarized the French into two groups; inspired Theodor Herzl to begin the movement called Zionism, with the objective of creating a Jewish state in Palestine*

The Dreyfus Affair

These reforms did not solve all of France's problems. Divisions continued to split French society. In 1894 these divisions came to a head over the controversial court case known as the **Dreyfus affair**. The Dreyfus affair revealed the extent of **anti-Semitism**, or prejudice toward Jews, in France.

In 1894 Alfred Dreyfus (DRAY-fuhs), a captain in the French army who was Jewish, was falsely accused and convicted of betraying French military secrets to Germany. Even though they knew he was not guilty, anti-Semitic military officers let Dreyfus take the blame rather than admit their error.

A month after Dreyfus was found guilty a public military ceremony was held to humiliate him. The stripes on his uniform were removed, and his sword was broken. A crowd that had gathered to watch shouted, "Kill him! Kill him!" Later evidence suggested that another officer may actually have done the spying. But the second officer, who was not Jewish, was found not guilty in court. A few years later army officers came forward with the real story, but Dreyfus was not cleared until 1906.

The Dreyfus affair divided people in France. One famous French writer, Émile Zola came to Dreyfus's defense. Zola published a letter in 1898 called "J'accuse" (I accuse). This letter accused the French government of anti-Semitism and led the French courts to reopen Dreyfus's case.

HISTORY'S VOICES

> **"It is a crime to poison the minds of the lowly and the humble, to exasperate the passions of reaction and intolerance, while seeking shelter behind odious [horrible] anti-Semitism, which, if not suppressed, will destroy the great liberal France of the Rights of Man."**
>
> —Émile Zola, "J'accuse"

Zola's letter set off anti-Semitic riots in more than 50 towns. Zola eventually went to trial himself and was found guilty of libel, or publishing false information.

The Dreyfus affair had an important effect on the growth of Jewish nationalism. **Theodor Herzl** was a Hungarian-born Jewish journalist who covered the trial. He was shocked by the anti-Semitism he saw in France and in other parts of Europe. Herzl came to believe that the root of the problem was that Jews in Europe did not have a nation of their own. In 1896 Herzl published *The Jewish State*, which outlined plans for an independent Jewish country developed with the support of the international community. Herzl's work helped spark **Zionism**, a Jewish nationalist movement to re-create a Jewish state in its original homeland.

By the early 1900s, a growing number of Jews were returning to their ancient homeland in the eastern Mediterranean. These settlements encouraged other Jews to follow, and the Zionist movement gained strength.

READING CHECK **Identify Cause and Effect** What were two major effects of the Dreyfus affair?

SECTION 2 ASSESSMENT

go.hrw.com
Online Quiz
Keyword: SHL REF HP

Reviewing Ideas, Terms, and People

1. **a. Identify** Who was **Louis Philippe**?
   b. Analyze Why was it significant that Louis Philippe wore long pants and lived more simply than other aristocrats?
   c. Develop Why do you think it was important to some people that the new king be a "citizen king"?
2. **a. Recall** What reforms were made during the Second and Third republics?
   b. Identify Cause and Effect What effect did the Revolution of 1848 have on the rest of Europe?
   c. Evaluate In your opinion, was Napoleon III a good leader for France? Why or why not?
3. **a. Describe** Describe the events of the Dreyfus affair.
   b. Analyze What is **Zionism** and how was it related to **anti-Semitism** in Europe?

Critical Thinking

4. **Compare and Contrast** Use your notes and the graphic organizer below to compare achievements of each era of French government. How do they compare with one another?

Government	Achievement

FOCUS ON SPEAKING

5. **Narration** Using information in the section, write a short speech that tells the story of the creation of the Third Republic and its goals.

Section 2 Assessment Answers

1. **a.** king of France who replaced Charles X
   b. It made him popular with the middle class.
   c. possible answer—reassured them that he didn't wasn't an absolute monarch.
2. **a.** all French men gained right to vote, primary education established, trade unions legalized, working hours reduced
   b. It inspired similar revolutions across Europe.
   c. possible answer—yes, had support of people, reign marked by economic prosperity
3. **a.** French army officer accused of spying for Germany because he was Jewish; charges polarized France, led to Zionism movement
   b. Theodor Herzl believed anti-Semitism arose because Jews in Europe did not have their own nation.
4. Second Republic—all French men gained right to vote; Second Empire—increased voting rights, built railroads; Third Republic—primary education established; trade unions legalized; working hours reduced
5. Speeches should include details about the Third Republic.

SECTION 3

Independence in Latin America

BEFORE YOU READ

MAIN IDEA

Revolutionary ideas took hold in Latin America as colonies fought for independence from Europe.

READING FOCUS

1. How did early struggles in Latin America affect Haiti and other colonies?
2. What events led to independence in Mexico?
3. Who were the key revolutionary leaders in South America, and what did they achieve?

KEY TERMS AND PEOPLE

Toussaint L'Ouverture
creoles
peninsulares
Miguel Hidalgo
José María Morelos
Simón Bolívar
José de San Martín
Pedro I

TAKING NOTES Take notes on independence movements and revolutionary leaders in Latin America during the 1800s.

Independence Movements	
Revolutionary Leaders	

FROM SLAVE TO SOLDIER

THE INSIDE STORY ***How did a former slave become a military hero?*** Toussaint L'Ouverture (TOO-san loo-vehr-TOOR) was born into slavery in a French colony on the Caribbean island of Hispaniola. As a young man, Toussaint was chosen to be a house servant. He learned to read and write in the slaveholder's home. Toussaint read about Enlightenment philosophers and their ideas of liberty and equality, as well as about military heroes such as Julius Caesar and Alexander the Great.

In 1771 Toussaint was legally freed. His life changed dramatically in 1791 when a major slave revolt broke out on the island. Toussaint helped his former slaveholder escape, then joined the rebellion. Soon afterward, he became a soldier in the Spanish army. During that time Toussaint took the last name L'Ouverture, which means "an opening" in French. Toussaint went on to become a military leader. Well respected for his leadership, he soon commanded a force of more than 4,000 men. ■

◀ **Toussaint L'Ouverture presents a document to French army officers.**

Preteach

Getting Started

Use the **Interactive Reader and Study Guide** to familiarize students with the section content.

Interactive Reader and Study Guide, Section 3

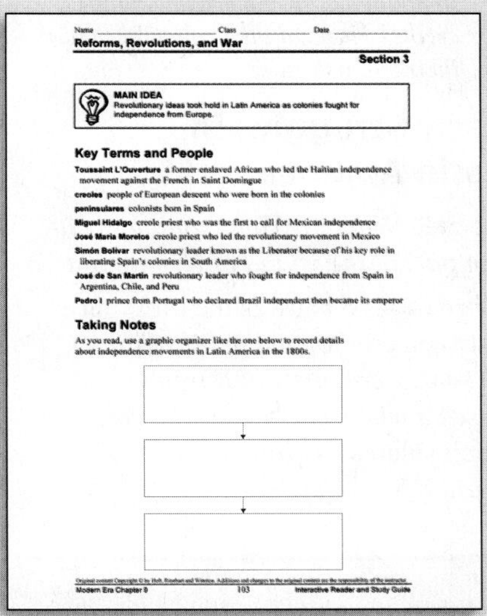

Name ______ Class ______ Date ______

Reforms, Revolutions, and War

Section 3

MAIN IDEA
Revolutionary ideas took hold in Latin America as colonies fought for independence from Europe.

Key Terms and People

Toussaint L'Ouverture a former enslaved African who led the Haitian independence movement against the French in Saint Domingue
creoles people of European descent who were born in the colonies
peninsulares colonists born in Spain
Miguel Hidalgo creole priest who was the first to call for Mexican independence
José Maria Morelos creole priest who led the revolutionary movement in Mexico
Simón Bolívar revolutionary leader known as the Liberator because of his key role in liberating Spain's colonies in South America
José de San Martín revolutionary leader who fought for independence from Spain in Argentina, Chile, and Peru
Pedro I prince from Portugal who declared Brazil independent then became its emperor

Taking Notes
As you read, use a graphic organizer like the one below to record details about independence movements in Latin America in the 1800s.

Academic Vocabulary

Review with students the high-use academic term in this section.

export item sent to other regions for trade (p. 298)

CRF: Vocabulary Builder: Section 3

Taking Notes

Independence Movements—Haiti gains independence in 1804; conflict between creoles and peninsulares in Latin America; Napoleon invades Spain and Portugal in 1807; several Latin American countries gain independence in 1831; Revolutionary Leaders—Miguel Hidalgo, José Maria Morelos, and Agustín de Iturbide, Mexico; Simón Bolívar and José de San Martín, South America; Pedro I, Brazil

Teach the Main Idea

At Level

Independence in Latin America

1. **Teach** Ask students the Reading Focus questions to teach this section.
2. **Apply** Have students make a time line showing the major events from this section, beginning with the slave revolt in Haiti (1791) and ending with San Martín's death (1850).
3. **Review** Review student time lines as a class. Guide the class in a discussion of the events on their time lines. How do the time lines clarify what was happening concurrently in different parts of Latin America?
4. **Practice/Homework** Tell students that Latin American independence movements were inspired by the ideas of Enlightenment philosophers but used the political turmoil in Europe to their advantage. Have students write a short essay explaining what they think was the primary reason that Latin American colonies sought independence when they did, and why. **LS Visual-Spatial, Verbal-Linguistic**

Alternative Assessment Handbook, Rubrics 36: Time Lines; and 43: Writing to Express

Direct Teach

Reading Focus

1 How did early struggles in Latin America affect Haiti and other colonies? *Haiti declared independence in 1804 after a war against France. In Spain's Latin American colonies, creoles resented the* peninsulares *and their Spanish rulers.*

Early Struggles in Latin America

Recall Where is Haiti? *on the western part of the island of Hispaniola*

Contrast What was the difference between creoles and *peninsulares*? *Creoles—colonists of European descent who were born in the colonies;* Peninsulares*—colonists who had been born in Spain*

Info to Know

Toussaint L'Ouverture Although there are many sketches and engravings of Toussaint L'Ouverture, there are no existing portraits that were done from life. Many engravings were based on oral descriptions of the man, and some of these drawings reflect the artists' biases.

Teaching Tip

Explain to students that in Spanish America, creoles were people of pure European descent. People of mixed European and native heritage were referred to as mestizos.

Early Struggles in Latin America

By the early 1800s growing tensions among the different ethnic and social groups of Latin American society, as well as reforms imposed by colonial authorities in Europe, were leading to demands for change. The Enlightenment and the American and French Revolutions also inspired some in Latin America to seek greater freedom. Soon new nations began to emerge from colonial domination throughout Latin America.

Haiti Becomes Independent The first Latin American territory to break its ties with Europe was Saint Domingue, located on the western half of the Caribbean island of Hispaniola. Sugar exports had made Saint Domingue one of France's richest possessions. But this prosperity was built on slave labor.

ACADEMIC VOCABULARY
export item sent to other regions for trade

The French Revolution had had a dramatic effect on Saint Domingue. The Declaration of the Rights of Man and of the Citizen gave the right to vote to all free men, including mulattoes, people of mixed African and European ancestry. French settlers on Saint Domingue, however, resisted the new law. As tensions rose, **Toussaint L'Ouverture**, a former enslaved African, led a group of mulattoes and slaves in a bloody revolt against the French settlers.

Toussaint's military and political actions made him a hero in Hispaniola. Back in France, the emperor Napoleon was worried. Napoleon sent a French general to Hispaniola to take control of the colony away from Toussaint. The island forces struggled for months, but in 1802 Toussaint agreed to an armistice. The French broke the agreement and sent him to prison in France, where he died in 1803.

Still the fight for independence continued. In 1804 the revolutionaries of Saint Domingue declared their independence from France and named their new nation Haiti.

Colonies of Spain and Portugal At the same time, another kind of independence movement was beginning to form in the colonies of Spain and Portugal. In the 1800s, Spain controlled most of Latin America, including what is today Mexico and a large portion of Central and South America. Portugal governed the huge colony of Brazil.

In the 1700s Spanish kings had made improvements in their colonies, building roads and regulating trade. As a result, the colonies grew in wealth and prosperity. This wealth gave some in Latin America greater access to education and new ideas. As a result, educated colonists read the works of Enlightenment philosophers and learned about revolutions in France and America. One scholar named Antonio Nariño translated the Declaration of the Rights of Man and of the Citizen into Spanish.

At the same time, tensions were growing between two groups in Latin America: **creoles** (KREE-ohlz), people of European descent who were born in the colonies, and ***peninsulares*** (peh-neen-soo-LAHR-ayz), colonists who were born in Spain. A similar distinction was made between Brazilian-born and Portuguese-born colonists. Creoles were excluded from the highest-level government or church positions, which were reserved for *peninsulares*. Together, creoles and *peninsulares* made up the highest social class; lower on the social scale were people of mixed race, Africans, and Indians.

As their prosperity grew, creoles began to resent the *peninsulares*. Creoles also resented their faraway Spanish rulers. One bishop said that if the Creoles "could empty their veins of the Spanish part of their blood, they would gladly do so."

In 1807 the French emperor Napoleon invaded Spain and Portugal. The king of Spain went to prison and the king of Portugal fled to Brazil. This invasion seriously weakened the power of Spain and Portugal in Latin America. Some creole revolutionaries decided the time was right to fight for independence.

READING CHECK **Sequence** How did Haiti win independence from France?

Independence in Mexico

Napoleon's conquest of Spain was the spark for independence in the colony of New Spain, as Mexico was known at the time. Mexico was a Spanish colony with a mixture of creoles, *peninsulares*, Indians, and people of mixed race.

Father Hidalgo In 1810 in a small town in southern Mexico, a creole priest named Father **Miguel Hidalgo** (mee-GEHL ee-DAHL-goh) made the first public call for Mexican independence.

Skills Focus: Identifying Problem and Solution

At Level

Reading Skill

Colonial Reforms

1. Have students write letters to the king of Spain urging him to make reforms in his American colonies. Tell students to choose a point of view from one of the following classes: creoles, *peninsulares*, or one of the other social classes who made up the population of Spain's American colonies. Student letters should discuss specific problems and propose solutions.
2. Have volunteers read their letters to the class. How well does each letter fit the point of view of the selected social class?
3. Discuss with students how history might have been different if Spain had made changes in the way its colonies were run. **LS Verbal-Linguistic**

Alternative Assessment Handbook, Rubric 43: Writing to Persuade

Answers

Reading Check *A rebellion of slaves and mulattoes became a revolution against France after Napoleon tried to take power from the revolutionary leader Toussaint L'Ouverture.*

INDEPENDENCE IN LATIN AMERICA

During the early 1800s, revolutionary leaders Simón Bolívar and José de San Martín led independence movements across South America. Inspired by their efforts, other revolutions flared up across the region, and neither Spain or Portugal could hold onto their empires in the Americas. By 1831 a dozen nations had declared their independence.

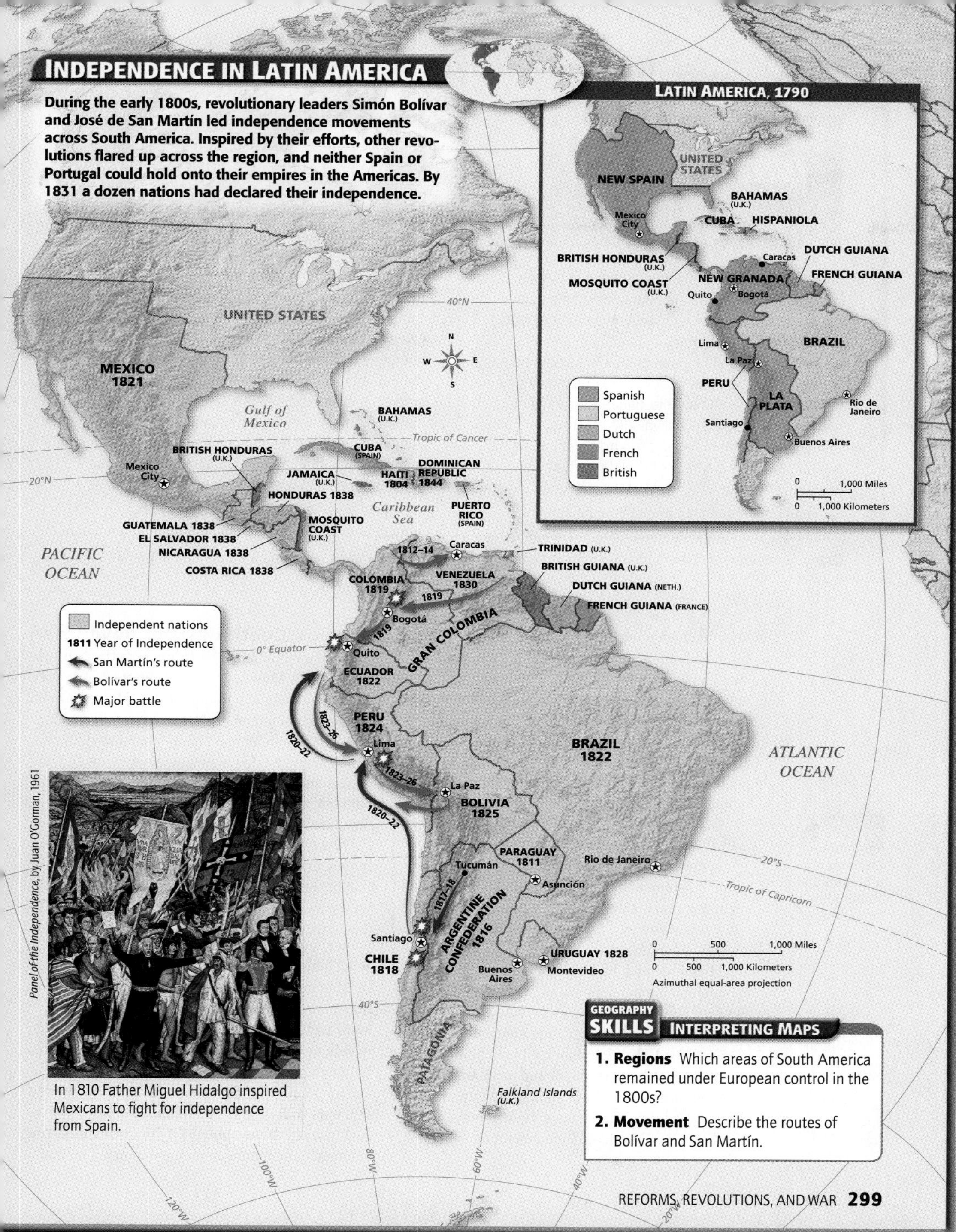

In 1810 Father Miguel Hidalgo inspired Mexicans to fight for independence from Spain.

GEOGRAPHY SKILLS INTERPRETING MAPS

1. **Regions** Which areas of South America remained under European control in the 1800s?
2. **Movement** Describe the routes of Bolívar and San Martín.

Direct Teach

Reading Focus

❷ What events led to independence in Mexico? *Father Hidalgo called for the peasants to revolt against the* peninsulares, *beginning a revolution in 1810. In 1821, Mexico finally won independence after a revolutionary war when the leader of the royalists, Agustín de Iturbide, switched sides.*

Independence in Mexico

Recall How did Mexico's fight for independence begin? *with a speech by Father Miguel Hidalgo calling the peasants to fight for their independence from the* peninsulares

Evaluate Why do you think the Spanish authorities in Mexico investigated Father Hidalgo for leading discussions of literature and art in his home? *They may have thought the discussions were about Enlightenment ideas, or that they served as a cover for subversive plans.*

Map Transparency: Independence in Latin America

CRF: Biography: José Martí

Info to Know

Fanny Calderón de la Barca (1804–1882) Frances ("Fanny") Erskine Inglis was born in Edinburgh, Scotland, but grew up in the United States. In 1838 she married the Spanish-born Don Angel Calderón de la Barca, who was appointed Minister to Mexico. The historian William H. Prescott assembled her letters from Mexico into a book, which was published in 1843. *Life in Mexico* was so accurate American officers used it as a guide four years later during the Mexican-American War.

Skills Focus: Analyzing Maps

At Level

Social Studies Skill

Latin America Then and Now

1. Have students study the maps on this page. Point out that the smaller map shows Latin America under colonial rule, while the larger map shows Latin America after independence. Ask students to theorize why larger colonies broke up into smaller nations.
2. Have students use the atlas in their text to compare the larger map with a current map of Latin America. Guide students in a discussion of the differences between the map of Latin America shortly after independence and the modern map. What can they infer from the differences in the old and modern maps? Why might Latin America's internal situation have encouraged European intervention? **LS Visual-Spatial**

Alternative Assessment Handbook, Rubrics 11: Discussions; and 21: Map Reading

Answers

Interpreting Maps 1. *Trinidad, British Guiana, Dutch Guiana, French Guiana;* **2.** *Bolívar began in the north and moved southward; San Martín began in the south and moved northward; the two leaders met in Lima, Peru.*

Direct Teach

Reading Focus

Independence in Mexico

Compare Describe the similarities between Hidalgo and Morelos. *Both were priests; both included people of all races and backgrounds in their plans; both were captured and executed by the Spanish.*

Identify Cause and Effect Why did Iturbide change sides in the Mexican war for independence? *There was a liberal revolution in Spain that he thought might reduce his power.*

Evaluate Why do you think Mexico lost so much of its territory so soon after becoming independent? *possible answer—It was too large to be easily governed, especially by inexperienced leaders.*

Info to Know

Agustín de Iturbide An officer in the colonial forces in Mexico, Iturbide supported the Spanish government after his hacienda was sacked by Hidalgo's Indian army. However, he was denied a promotion because he was a creole. Iturbide rethought his loyalties and switched to the rebel side, where he quickly rose to a leadership position. After he was overthrown in 1823, he was bribed to accept exile in Europe. When the payments were not made, he disguised himself and slipped back into Mexico, ignoring the advice of fellow exile José de San Martín to not return. Despite Iturbide's disguise, a soldier recognized him by his style of mounting a house. He was arrested, tried, and shot.

FACES OF HISTORY Two Revolutionary Leaders

Simón BOLÍVAR

1783–1830

Known as the "George Washington of South America," Simón Bolívar was a revolutionary general. In the early 1800s he liberated several South American colonies from Spanish rule.

Beginning in 1811 Bolívar helped free his native Venezuela. He was president of Gran Colombia (present-day Venezuela, Colombia, Panama, and Ecuador) and then Peru. Because Bolívar also helped free Bolivia, the country was named in his honor. Today Bolívar's birthday is a national holiday in both Venezuela and Bolivia.

Summarize What were Bolívar's accomplishments?

José de SAN MARTÍN

1778–1850

José de San Martín was the son of a royal official in the colony of La Plata, which later became Argentina. San Martín was the main leader against Spanish rule in southern South America. By 1821 he had liberated not only La Plata but also Chile and much of Peru. As Spanish resistance continued, San Martín helped fellow revolutionaries such as Simón Bolívar.

San Martín is perhaps best known for skillfully leading his troops into Chile through the difficult terrain of the Andes Mountains. There, he defeated royalist troops and liberated Chile.

Analyze How did San Martín liberate Chile?

Draw Conclusions What impact did the accomplishments of Bolívar and San Martín have on Latin America?

Hidalgo had a history of challenging authority. He had been investigated by Spanish authorities for leading discussions of literature and art in his home. Hidalgo invited many people to these discussions, including creoles, *peninsulares*, Indians and people of mixed race. Eventually he met creoles who wanted to take power from the *peninsulares*. Hidalgo became a leader and helped to plan a rebellion.

On September 16, 1810, Hidalgo rang a bell in his home town, calling the members of his church to the churchyard. There he delivered a famous speech calling on peasants to fight for their independence against the Spanish *peninsulares* in Mexico. He shouted, "Death to bad government and death to Spaniards!"

THE IMPACT TODAY Mexicans celebrate Mexican Independence Day on September 16.

Hidalgo was calling for the peasants to revolt against the *peninsulares*, not against Spain. In fact, in his speech he said he was loyal to the Spanish king. But the Spanish authorities realized Hidalgo was behind the growing revolution. He was captured and executed, but the Mexican independence movement had begun. Hidalgo would later become known as the Father of Mexican Independence.

Morelos Continues the Revolution

After the death of Hidalgo, another creole priest, **José María Morelos**, became the leader of the revolutionary movement. He organized a Mexican congress with representatives from many places in Mexico. Morelos wanted all people born in Mexico, whether they were Indian, mixed race, or creole, to be called Americans. He also wanted Mexico to be an independent republic with guaranteed freedoms.

Morelos was a strong military leader. He led troops and took control of parts of Mexico for the independence movement. But eventually he too was captured. The Spanish authorities found him guilty of treason and executed him.

A Creole King for Mexico Not all creoles in Mexico wanted independence from Spain. Some remained royalists, people who were loyal to the Spanish king. One of these creole royalists was a military officer named Agustín de Iturbide (ah-goos-TEEN day ee-toor-BEE-day).

In 1820 the Spanish authorities asked Iturbide to lead a final battle against the revolutionaries. They believed he could end the Mexican independence movement for good.

Skills Focus: Comparing and Contrasting

Below Level

Reading Skill

Wars of Independence

1. Have students make a chart comparing and contrasting the wars of independence in Mexico and in South America.
2. Have volunteers use the information from their charts to make a master chart for all students to see. Have students correct their own work as needed.
3. Guide the class in a discussion about the Latin American wars of independence. Ask students why they think the leaders of the independence movements were creoles and not peasants. Which form of government—a monarchy or a republic—would have been the more common choice in those days?

LS Visual-Spatial

Alternative Assessment Handbook, Rubrics 7: Charts; and 9: Comparing and Contrasting

Answers

Faces of History (left) *Bolívar freed Venezuela, helped free Bolivia, and served as president of Gran Colombia.* **(right)** *San Martín liberated Chile by crossing the Andes Mountains and defeating royalist forces.* **(bottom)** *Together, the two leaders helped liberate much of South America from colonial rule.*

However, that same year a liberal revolution was underway in Spain. Iturbide believed this revolution might take away some of his power, so he decided to switch sides and fight for the Mexican revolutionaries.

Iturbide made a three-part proposal to the leader of the revolution. First, Mexico would gain its independence but would be ruled by a monarch. Second, creoles and *peninsulares* would have equal rights. Third, the Roman Catholic Church would be the official church of Mexico. This independence proposal was very different from the ideas of Hidalgo and Morelos. But after 10 years of fighting, the compromise brought together many different groups, including the creoles and the *peninsulares* and the revolutionaries and the royalists. Both royalist and rebel troops joined Iturbide to win independence from Spain.

In 1821 Mexico declared its independence from Spain. That same year Mexico named as its emperor the creole military leader who had made independence happen. Iturbide became Emperor Agustín I of Mexico.

READING CHECK **Compare and Contrast** How were the goals of Hidalgo, Morelos, and Iturbide different, and how were they similar?

Revolutionary Leaders in South America

The revolutions in Haiti and Mexico, as well earlier revolutions in the United States and France, inspired leaders in South America. Soon, independence movements began to form in these colonies, and several capable revolutionary leaders emerged.

Simón Bolívar The most influential leader in the South American independence movement was **Simón Bolívar** (see-MOHN boh-LEE-vahr) He is known as simply "the Liberator" because of his key role in liberating Spain's colonies in South America.

Bolívar was born into a wealthy creole family in what is now Venezuela. He often traveled to Europe and was an admirer of Napoleon's leadership. Once, while in Rome, he made a famous pledge to liberate South America.

In 1811 Venezuela declared independence from Spain. For the next 10 years, Bolívar led a series of military campaigns against Spanish forces. Finally, in 1821, Bolívar's troops had defeated the Spanish in most of northern South America.

Bolívar had a dream for the newly independent South America. He wanted to form one large, united country called the Federation of the Andes. That dream, however, never became reality. Bolívar did set up the state of Gran Colombia, which included what are now Venezuela, Colombia, Panama, and Ecuador. But other leaders set up separate countries in Peru, Bolivia, and other places. "America is ungovernable," Bolívar complained.

READING SKILLS
Identifying Implied Main Ideas What is the main idea of this paragraph?

José de San Martín While Simón Bolívar was fighting for independence in the north, **José de San Martín** was fighting for independence from Spain in the south. San Martín was a soldier who had fought against Napoleon in Spain. Born in Argentina, he returned home when he learned that his country was rising up against Spanish rule. Eventually, San Martín would lead the independence movement not only in Argentina, but in most of southern South America.

PRIMARY SOURCES

Bolívar's Message to the Congress of Angostura

In 1819 Simón Bolívar wrote to members of Congress in the city of Angostura asking for the abolition of slavery.

> "Americans by birth and Europeans by law, we find ourselves engaged in a dual conflict: we are disputing with the natives for title of ownership, and at the same time we are struggling to maintain ourselves in the country that gave us birth against the opposition of the invaders . . . As our role has always been strictly passive and political existence nil, we find our quest for liberty is now even more difficult to achieve; for we, having been placed in a state lower than slavery, had been robbed not only of our freedom but also of the right to exercise an active domestic tyranny."

Skills FOCUS **READING LIKE A HISTORIAN**

Draw Conclusions Who is Bolívar referring to when he mentions the "invaders"?

See **Skills Handbook**, p. H25

Direct Teach

Reading Focus

3 Who were the key revolutionary leaders in South America, and what did they achieve? *Bolívar and San Martín, Pedro I; Venezuela declared independence in 1811, took 10 years before independence became reality; Argentina won independence in 1816; Bolívar and San Martín led fight for independence in northern and western South America; Pedro I declares Brazil independent in 1822.*

Revolutionary Leaders in South America

Identify What was the Federation of the Andes? *the nation that Bolívar hoped to establish in western South America; would have included Venezuela, Colombia, Ecuador, Peru, and Bolivia*

Contrast How did Bolívar and San Martín's opinions of Napoleon differ? *Bolívar admired Napoleon's leadership, but San Martín had fought against Napoleon's armies in Spain.*

Differentiating Instruction

Below Level

Learners Having Difficulty

1. Copy the sequence chart for students to see. Omit the italicized answers. Have students work individually or in pairs to fill in the steps by which Brazil gained its independence.
2. Guide the class in a discussion of the similarities and differences between the way Brazil and the Spanish colonies gained independence. **LS Visual-Spatial**

Alternative Assessment Handbook, Rubrics 7: Charts; and 9: Comparing and Contrasting

1807: Napoleon invades Portugal.
↓
Portuguese royal family flees to Brazil.
↓
Prince João changes status of the colony.
↓
Napoleon falls from power.
↓
King João returns to Portugal, leaving Prince Pedro to rule Brazil
↓
1822: Prince Pedro declares Brazil independent
↓
Prince Pedro crowned Emperor Pedro I of Brazil.

Answers

Primary Sources peninsulares

Reading Skills *Despite his establishment of the state of Gran Colombia, Bolívar's dream for an independent South America never became a reality.*

Reading Check *Hidalgo wanted the peasants to revolt against the* peninsulares, *not against Spain; Morelos wanted independence from Spain and an "American" identity to unify all people born in Mexico; Iturbide wanted to create an independent monarchy, give creoles and* peninsulares *equal rights, make the Roman Catholic Church the official church of Mexico*

Direct Teach

Reading Focus

Revolutionary Leaders in South America

Recall What changes came about in Brazil as a result of the king's residence there? *Rio de Janeiro was named capital of the Portuguese empire; Brazil was allowed to trade directly with the rest of the world.*

Identify Cause and Effect What effect did the independence movements in Spain's colonies have on Brazil? *Brazilian colonists wanted their independence, too.*

Quick Facts Transparency: Causes and Effects of Revolution in Latin America

Review & Assess

Close

Have students summarize the paths to freedom that were taken by the nations of Latin America.

Review

Online Quiz, Section 3

Assess

SE Section 3 Assessment

Progress Assessment: Section 3 Quiz

Alternative Assessment Handbook

Reteach/Intervene

Interactive Reader and Study Guide, Section 3

Interactive Skills Tutor CD-ROM

After declaring independence for Argentina in 1816, San Martín moved on to Chile. There he helped lead troops over a 15,000-foot summit in the Andes Mountains. The feat helped his forces surprise the Spanish troops and win independence for Chile.

Next San Martín moved on to Gran Colombia. There he met the northern revolutionary leader Simón Bolívar. Historians do not agree on what the two men discussed when they met. What is known is that San Martín resigned his position after the meeting. This left Bolívar in power. San Martín returned to Europe, where he lived until his death in 1850.

Pedro I The story of independence was a bit different in the Portuguese colony of Brazil. When Napoleon invaded Portugal in 1807, the reigning Portuguese monarch John VI and his family fled. They took a long journey to their colony in Brazil, where they lived for more than 10 years. Having the Portuguese monarch in Brazil raised the status of the colony. John VI named the Brazilian city of Rio de Janeiro as the capital of the entire Portuguese empire. He also allowed Brazil to trade directly with the rest of the world, rather than through Portugal.

After a revolution in Portugal in 1820, John VI returned to Portugal. He left his son Pedro to rule Brazil. Then, at about the time that Bolívar and San Martín were liberating the rest of South America, Brazilian-born colonists began to protest their colonial status. Brazil wanted independence too. But the transition to independence happened more smoothly in Brazil than anywhere else in Latin America. In September 1822, Prince Pedro simply declared Brazil independent. Soon afterward, he was crowned Emperor **Pedro I** of Brazil. Brazil had achieved independence with very little violence.

READING CHECK Contrast In what ways was the independence movement in Brazil different from independence movements elsewhere in South America?

QUICK FACTS

Causes and Effects of Revolution in Latin America

CAUSES

- Tensions between ethnic and social groups
- The French Revolution and American Revolution
- Limited freedoms under Spanish rule

EFFECTS

- Independence from Spain
- New nations and governments formed
- Ethnic and social groups work together

Section 3 Assessment

go.hrw.com
Online Quiz
Keyword: SHL REF HP

Reviewing Ideas, Terms, and People

1. **a. Identify** Who was **Toussaint L'Ouverture**?
   b. Identify Cause and Effect What effect did Napoleon's invasion of Spain and Portugal have on independence movements in Latin America?
2. **a. Identify** Whose speech launched the Mexican independence movement?
   b. Interpret Why was the congress organized by **José María Morelos** important?
   c. Evaluate Why do you think Agustín de Iturbide's plan for Mexican independence worked?
3. **a. Identify** Which two generals led independence movements in much of South America ?
   b. Infer What do you think happened in the meeting between **Simón Bolívar** and **José de San Martín**?

Critical Thinking

4. **Sequence** Use the graphic organizer below to show the sequence of events that led to Latin American nations gaining independence.

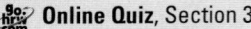

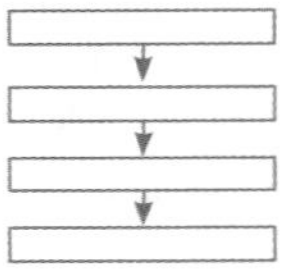

FOCUS ON WRITING

5. **Description** Choose a revolutionary leader from this section and write a paragraph on his life, his achievements, and his goals for revolution.

Section 3 Assessment Answers

1. **a.** former slave, military leader, appointed governor of Hispaniola for life
   b. It led some creole revolutionaries to decide to fight for independence.
2. **a.** Father Miguel Hidalgo
   b. It included representatives from many places in Mexico.
   c. it was a compromise; brought together many different groups, including creoles and *peninsulares*, revolutionaries, and royalists
3. **a.** Simón Bolívar and José de San Martín
   b. possible answer—probably argued about South America's future, since San Martín resigned after the meeting
4. Students should list key events, in order of their occurrence, that led to Latin American countries' independence.
5. Paragraphs should contain details about Toussaint L'Ouverture, Father Miguel Hidalgo, José María Morelos, Agustín de Iturbide, Simón Bolívar, or José de San Martín.

Answers

Reading Check *Brazil won independence more smoothly and without violence.*

302

SECTION 4

Expansion and War in the United States

BEFORE YOU READ

MAIN IDEA

As the United States began to expand west, conflicts erupted over territory and slavery.

READING FOCUS

1. How did the United States expand during the first half of the 1800s?
2. What issues led to civil war in the United States?

KEY TERMS AND PEOPLE

Louisiana Purchase
Monroe Doctrine
manifest destiny
Trail of Tears
abolition
Abraham Lincoln
secession
Emancipation Proclamation

TAKING NOTES Take notes on the causes and effects of westward expansion and civil war in the United States.

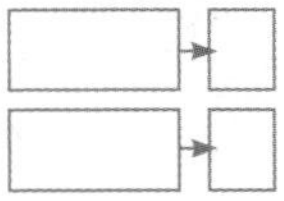

THE INSIDE STORY ***Did the president of the United States have the power to purchase foreign territory?*** That was the question on Thomas Jefferson's mind in 1803. The French emperor, Napoleon, had offered to sell the enormous Louisiana Territory to the United States for about $15 million. Napoleon no longer wanted to build a French empire in North America, and the United States wanted to expand westward. It seemed like the perfect deal. But did the U.S. Constitution give the president the power to buy it?

Jefferson, who believed in a strict interpretation of the Constitution, thought that buying territory was "an act beyond the Constitution." He wanted to amend the Constitution to include such a purchase. Others in the government, however, believed there was no need for an amendment. Eventually, American diplomats in Paris signed the Louisiana Purchase treaty on April 30, 1803. The treaty gave more than 800,000 square miles of land to the United States and doubled the size of the young country. ■

A PRESIDENT'S PURCHASE

▲ The Louisiana Purchase included this stretch of land near the edge of the Great Plains.

Teach the Main Idea

At Level

Expansion and War in the United States

1. **Teach** Ask students the Reading Focus questions to teach this section.
2. **Apply** Have students create a sequence chart showing how westward expansion led to increased tensions in the United States during the 19th century.
3. **Review** Review student charts as a class. Have students describe how the following groups were affected by manifest destiny: white settlers, African Americans, Native Americans.
4. **Practice/Homework** Have students write scenarios describing what they think would have happened if the South had been allowed to secede and the Civil War had never taken place. **LS Visual-Spatial, Verbal-Linguistic**

Alternative Assessment Handbook, Rubrics 7: Charts; and 40: Writing to Describe

Preteach

Getting Started

Use the **Interactive Reader and Study Guide** to familiarize students with the section content.

Interactive Reader and Study Guide, Section 4

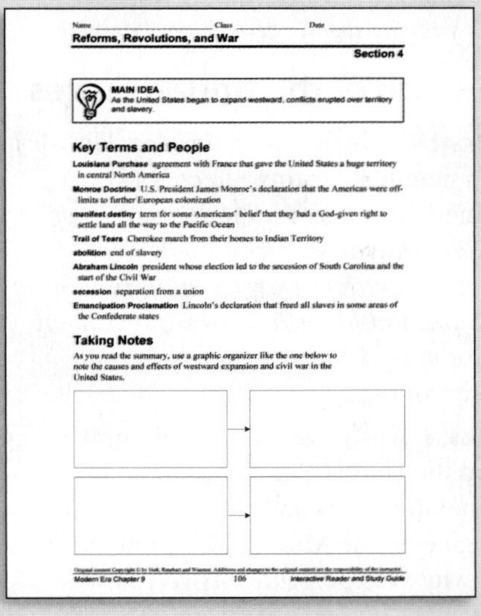

Name ____________ Class ____________ Date ____________

Reforms, Revolutions, and War

Section 4

MAIN IDEA
As the United States began to expand westward, conflicts erupted over territory and slavery.

Key Terms and People

Louisiana Purchase agreement with France that gave the United States a huge territory in central North America

Monroe Doctrine U.S. President James Monroe's declaration that the Americas were off-limits to further European colonization

manifest destiny term for some Americans' belief that they had a God-given right to settle land all the way to the Pacific Ocean

Trail of Tears Cherokee march from their homes to Indian Territory

abolition end of slavery

Abraham Lincoln president whose election led to the secession of South Carolina and the start of the Civil War

secession separation from a union

Emancipation Proclamation Lincoln's declaration that freed all slaves in some areas of the Confederate states

Taking Notes

As you read the summary, use a graphic organizer like the one below to note the causes and effects of westward expansion and civil war in the United States.

Modern Era Chapter 9 106 Interactive Reader and Study Guide

Academic Vocabulary

Review with students the high-use academic term in this section.

amendment a written change to a legal document (p. 307)

CRF: Vocabulary Builder: Section 4

Taking Notes

Westward Expansion—causes: Louisiana Purchase, manifest destiny, discovery of gold; effects: millions move, Native Americans forced to relocate, Trail of Tears; Civil War—causes: nation expands, debate over slavery and states' rights, Lincoln elected, secession of southern states, Confederate states draft their own constitution, attack on Fort Sumter; effects: over 500,000 killed, slavery ends, much of South left in ruins, nation reunites

Direct Teach

Reading Focus

1 How did the United States expand during the first half of the 19th century? *bought Louisiana from France in 1803, annexed Texas in 1845, then annexed the Mexican Cession after winning the Mexican-American War*

Growth of the United States

Identify Cause and Effect How did manifest destiny affect Native Americans? *The Indian Removal Act made Native American lands available to white settlers by relocating Indian nations to Indian Territory. Subsequent laws moved Native Americans onto reservations.*

Make Judgments Do you think that the United States was justified in annexing Texas and forcing Mexico to give up the Mexican Cession? Why or why not? *possible answers—No, Americans essentially stole the land from Mexico; yes, the Texas settlers wanted to be part of the United States.*

Map Transparency: Westward Expansion of the United States

Info to Know

Florida The Adams-Onís Treaty formalized the United States' acquisition of Florida in 1819. It also settled a 16-year-old dispute between the United States and Spain over the western boundary of the Louisiana Purchase.

Growth of the United States

In 1803 the United States completed the **Louisiana Purchase** with France, an agreement that gave the United States a huge territory in central North America. During the rest of the 1800s, the United States would continue to grow and expand westward.

A Young Nation At the beginning of the 1800s the United States was still a young nation. It had only recently won independence from Great Britain. Yet Britain was still harassing its former colony, seizing American sailors to use in its naval war against Napoleon. This angered Americans. In addition, Britain was helping Native Americans fight American settlers in the Northwest. As a result, Great Britain and the United States went to war in 1812. When the fighting ended, no territory had changed hands, but some Americans felt they had proved their country to be an independent nation.

By the 1820s the young nation was growing in national pride and beginning to build a world reputation. President James Monroe went so far as to declare the Americas off limits to further European colonization. This policy became known as the **Monroe Doctrine**.

Texas and Mexico In 1820 an American named Moses Austin got permission from Spain to found small settlements in Texas. Texas was a part of Mexico at this time. But when Mexico gained its independence from Spain, strict laws were imposed on the settlers in Texas. Eventually these settlers fought for and achieved independence for the Republic of Texas.

In 1845 the United States admitted Texas as a state. The Mexican government, however, claimed Texas was still part of Mexico. This dispute and others led to the Mexican-American War from 1846 to 1848, which the United States won. The result of the war was that the United States gained a large territory that is now the southwestern United States.

Westward Expansion of the United States

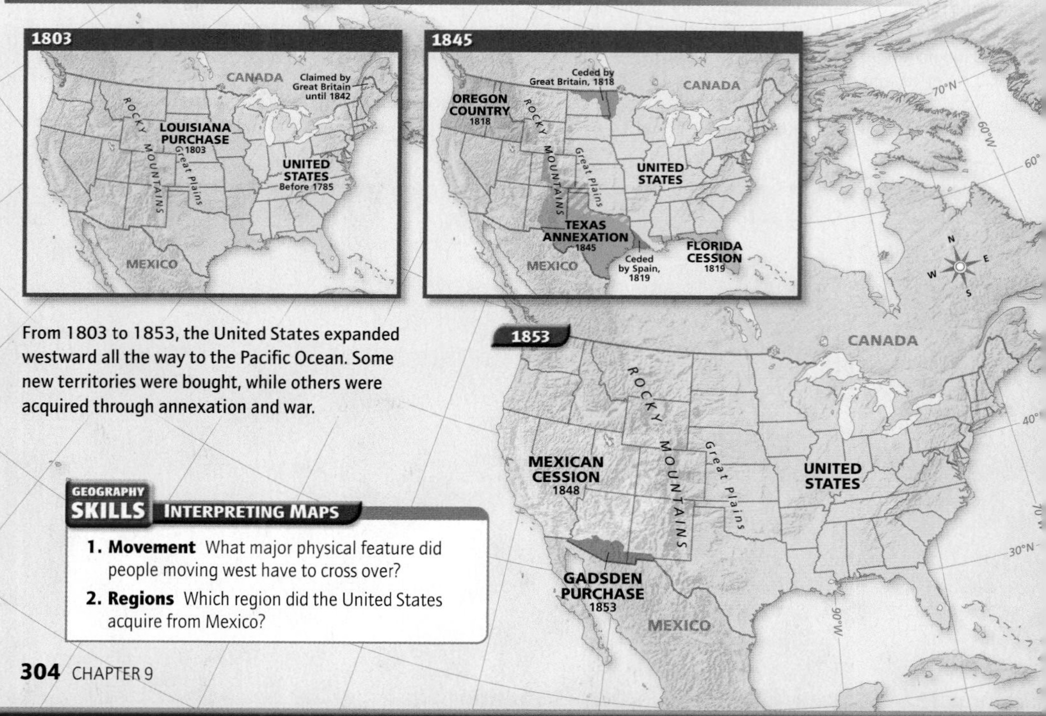

From 1803 to 1853, the United States expanded westward all the way to the Pacific Ocean. Some new territories were bought, while others were acquired through annexation and war.

GEOGRAPHY SKILLS INTERPRETING MAPS

1. **Movement** What major physical feature did people moving west have to cross over?
2. **Regions** Which region did the United States acquire from Mexico?

Differentiating Instruction

At Level

English-Language Learners

1. Copy the chart for students to see. Omit the italicized information. Have students copy and fill in the chart. Have students use the maps on this page to identify the states formed either completely or partly from each land acquisition. Students may need to consult another U.S. map to identify the states.
2. Fill in the master chart and have students correct their charts as needed. **LS Visual-Spatial**

Alternative Assessment Handbook, Rubrics 7: Charts; and 21: Map Reading

Territory	How Obtained	States
Louisiana	*bought from France*	*Minnesota, Iowa, Missouri, Arkansas, Louisiana, Oklahoma, Kansas, Nebraska, South Dakota, North Dakota, Montana, Wyoming, Colorado*
Texas	*annexed by United States*	*Texas, Oklahoma, Kansas, Colorado, Wyoming, New Mexico*
Mexican Cession	*war with Mexico*	*New Mexico, Colorado, Wyoming, Utah, Arizona, Nevada, California*

Answers

Interpreting Maps 1. *the Rocky Mountains;* **2.** *Refer to map.*

The Move West By 1850 the westward expansion of the United States had been ongoing for more than half a century. The United States had claimed territory all the way to the Pacific Ocean, including the Louisiana Territory, Florida, Texas, the Mexican Cession, and the Oregon Territory.

This rapid expansion led some Americans to believe that they had a God-given right to settle land all the way to the Pacific Ocean. One journalist arguing for Texas annexation came up with the term **manifest destiny** to describe this belief:

HISTORY'S VOICES

> "Other nations have tried to check . . . the fulfillment of our manifest destiny to overspread the continent allotted by Providence [God] for the free development of our yearly multiplying millions."
>
> —John O'Sullivan, editorial, 1845

Settlers headed west for many reasons. In 1848 gold was discovered in California, which led to massive immigration. In addition, a national law promised 160 acres of free land to anyone who made the trip west. Thousands of Americans packed all of their belongings into covered wagons and traveled west.

Effects on Native Americans By moving west, American settlers were often moving onto land that had been inhabited for thousands of years by Native Americans. Conflict between Native Americans and settlers was frequent. Some people believed the solution was to push Native Americans further west.

In 1830 the Indian Removal Act called for the relocation of five Indian nations to Indian Territory, part of the Louisiana Territory in the Great Plains. Under the control of the United States army, Indians from the Cherokee, Choctaw, Chickasaw, Seminole, and Creek nations were forced from their homes and moved into Indian Territory.

The Cherokee march to the Indian Territory was so deadly that it became known as the **Trail of Tears**. It is estimated that a quarter of the Cherokees who made the trip died. As Americans moved further west, subsequent laws moved Native Americans into designated areas, called reservations.

READING CHECK **Summarize** What territories did the United States acquire between 1803 and 1850?

Causes and Effects of Westward Expansion (QUICK FACTS)

CAUSES

- United States acquires new territories
- Desire for land and opportunity
- Discovery of gold in California

EFFECTS

- Millions of people move to new territories
- Native Americans are forcibly relocated
- Population of California explodes

The Civil War

As the United States expanded west, the issue of slavery became a national problem. Since colonial times Americans had used enslaved Africans and African Americans as unpaid workers. Slave labor helped support the American economy, especially in the South. Yet many Americans believed denying freedom to enslaved people was wrong. Some fought for **abolition**, or the end of slavery.

The Road to War As new territories and states were added to the country, Americans had to decide whether the new states would allow slavery or not. Some Southerners worried that new states where slavery was not allowed might cause a shift of power in congress, which could end slavery in all states. For the first half of the 1800s, however, a series of compromises preserved the balance between slave states and free states.

In 1854 the Kansas-Nebraska Act created two new territories in the west, Kansas and Nebraska. The decision of whether to allow slavery or not in each state was left to the residents. This act set off a bitter debate. Tensions were so great between antislavery and proslavery Americans that after the election of **Abraham Lincoln** as president, South Carolina decided to secede, or separate from the Union. This separation is called **secession**.

Direct Teach

Reading Focus

2 What issues led to civil war in the United States? *conflict over slavery and states' rights; Lincoln's election as president; secession of southern states; attack on Fort Sumter*

The Civil War

Recall Why were people in the South concerned that new free states might be admitted to the Union? *thought that new free states would cause Congress to outlaw slavery in the entire country*

Make Judgments Do you think that the issue of slavery should have been left to the states or decided by the federal government? Explain. *possible answer—decided by the federal government; leaving it to the states resulted in violence between antislavery and pro-slavery groups*

Quick Facts Transparency: Causes and Effects of Westward Expansion

CRF: Biography: Harriet Tubman

CRF: Primary Source: The Secession of South Carolina

Teaching Tip

Explain to students that a civil war is a war in which citizens of the same country fight against one another. The American Civil War, in which one part of the nation fought for independence from the other, illustrates one kind of civil war. More common is the kind that occurs when factions within a country struggle for control of the entire nation. For example, in the English Civil War, fought in the 1640s and 1650s, Parliament established supremacy over the monarchy.

Collaborative Learning

At Level

Territorial Rights

1. Organize students into two groups to debate whether people already living in territories taken over by the United States in the 1800s—for example, the Louisiana Purchase and the Mexican Cession—should have had the same rights and legal status as people in the existing states. Have one group support equal rights for residents of territories and one group oppose them. Give students time to develop their arguments.
2. Conduct a classroom debate on the rights and status of residents of territories.
3. Ask students what their opinions on this question would be if it pertained to people today who live in American territories such as Puerto Rico and Guam. **LS Interpersonal, Verbal-Linguistic**

Alternative Assessment Handbook, Rubric 10: Debates

Answers

Reading Check *Louisiana, Texas, Mexican Cession*

Direct Teach

Reading Focus

The Civil War

Analyze Why was the Battle of Gettysburg important? *The victory made Union troops think that they could win the war.*

Evaluate How many slaves were immediately freed by the Emancipation Proclamation? *none, actually, since it applied only to Confederate states, which were not under Lincoln's control at the time it was issued*

CRF: History and Geography: Issue of Slavery Divides States

Biography

Mathew Brady (c. 1823-1896) While Mathew Brady began as a portrait photographer in New York, he is perhaps best known today for his groundbreaking photographs of the Civil War. In 1862 Brady shocked New Yorkers with his photographs of the bloody aftermath of the Battle of Antietam, showing northerners the war's gruesome results. Though he never gained financial success, his work showed that photography could be used for more than just portraits: it could document real-life events.

Info to Know

Legalized Segregation After the Civil War, most southern states passed "Jim Crow" laws to enforce racial segregation in businesses, buses and trains, and public institutions such as schools. Under these laws, it was also illegal to marry someone of a different race.

A Nation Divided

From 1861 to 1865 the Civil War war between the North, or Union states, and the South, or Confederate states, tore the country apart. ***What were some main causes and results of the Civil War?***

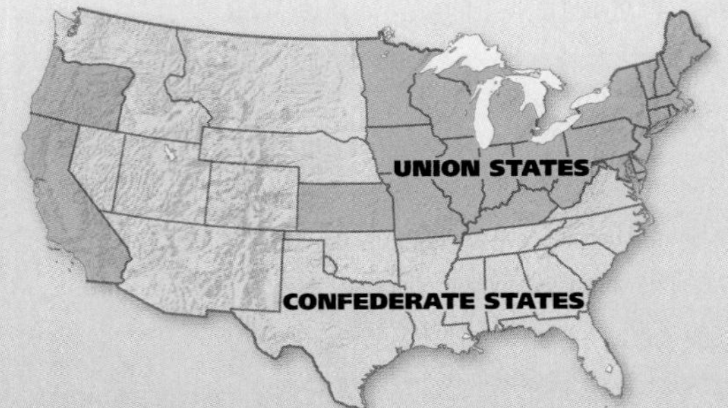

Causes of the Civil War
- Conflicts over slavery and states' rights
- Lincoln's election as president
- The secession of southern states
- The attack on Fort Sumter

Battle of Lookout Mountain, by Kurz and Allison, 1889

The Civil War In November 1863 the Union army defeated the Confederate army in battles near Chattanooga, Tennessee.

Results of the Civil War
- The end of slavery
- More than 500,000 dead
- The South left in ruins
- A reunited nation

Other states soon followed. The states that seceded from the Union adopted the name the Confederate States of America and elected Jefferson Davis as their president. Soon after, the leaders of the Confederate states drafted a constitution.

War Begins President Lincoln did not believe that the Constitution gave states the right to secede. In April 1861 he gave orders to bring supplies to an American fort in South Carolina. There, at Fort Sumter, the first shots of the Civil War were fired.

The Civil War continued for four years. During the war more than 500,000 soldiers died from battle or disease—more soldiers than in any other American war before or since. As the deadly conflict grew and spread, the future of the country was in the balance.

The Emancipation Proclamation In January 1863 Lincoln took a historic step. With the **Emancipation Proclamation**, Lincoln declared all slaves free in some areas of the Confederate states. The proclamation did not apply to areas that had already been conquered by Union armies.

The Emancipation Proclamation helped the North in several ways. First, many Southern slaves fled to the North, which hurt the Southern economy. The proclamation also gave renewed purpose to Union soldiers, who now saw their cause as abolition as well as the preservation of the Union. In addition, the Emancipation Proclamation caused European powers to withdraw support for the Confederacy.

The Union Prevails Later in 1863, the Battle of Gettysburg in Pennsylvania represented a turning point in the war. In this battle, Union soldiers defeated Confederate troops and began to believe they could actually win the war. Later that year Lincoln delivered a famous speech at a cemetery dedication ceremony for the soldiers killed in the Battle of the Gettysburg.

HISTORY'S VOICES

> **"We here highly resolved that these dead shall not have died in vain—that this nation, under God, shall have a new birth of freedom—and that government of the people, by the people, for the people, shall not perish from the earth."**
>
> —Abraham Lincoln, Gettysburg Address, 1863

Skills Focus: Making Inferences

At Level

Reading Skill

Social Changes Following the Civil War

1. Have students identify three major social changes that resulted from the Civil War. Have students explain which of these changes affected women, and how they affected women.
2. Have each student write a short essay predicting how the Fifteenth Amendment will affect women. Tell students to explain their predictions in the body of their essays.
3. Have volunteers read their essays to the class.
4. Guide the class in a discussion of student essays. **LS Verbal-Linguistic**

Alternative Assessment Handbook, Rubrics 11: Discussions; and 40: Writing to Describe

Answers

A Nation Divided *Causes—conflicts over slavery and states' rights, Lincoln's election, secession, attack on Fort Sumter; Results—end of slavery, 500,000 deaths, South left in ruins, a reunited nation*

The war continued for about one and half more years with the Union forces gradually gaining an advantage. Finally, after several significant Union victories in the South, Confederate general Robert E. Lee surrendered to Union general Ulysses S. Grant at Appomattox, Virginia, in 1865. The Civil War was over, but the issues that caused it still plagued the United States.

Effects of the Civil War After the Civil War much of the South lay in ruins. Large areas were destroyed, and economies were ruined. The final battles of the war had also damaged railroads, roads, and bridges. Many Americans wondered how the federal government would treat the former Confederate states.

How would the slavery issue be resolved? How would the South rebuild? In an era known as Reconstruction—the period of rebuilding in the South—congress and the president sought to answer these questions.

Reconstruction was a difficult time for the United States because people had different ideas on how to solve the problems caused by the war. Despite these disagreements, however, the government passed several important laws and constitutional amendments.

The Civil Rights Act protected some rights of formerly enslaved people. The Fourteenth Amendment granted citizenship to all freed African Americans and "equal benefit of all laws and proceedings for the security of person and property, as is enjoyed by white citizens." The Fifteenth Amendment stated that voting rights could not be denied based on race.

Reconstruction did not fully achieve the goal of equal rights for former slaves, however. Some Southern states continued to pass discriminatory laws. In reality many freed African Americans were still prevented from making a decent living after the war. Nevertheless, the constitutional amendments passed during Reconstruction did provide a foundation for later civil rights movement in the United States during the 1900s.

READING CHECK **Contrast** In what ways did Reconstruction succeed and in what ways did it fail?

ACADEMIC VOCABULARY
amendment a written change to a legal document

FACES OF HISTORY

Abraham LINCOLN
1809–1865

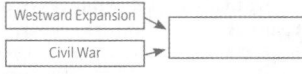

Abraham Lincoln is considered one of the best presidents in U.S. history. He kept the Union together during the war and ended slavery.

Before his presidency, Lincoln ran against Senator Stephen Douglas for a senate seat in Illinois. In a series of debates with Douglas, Lincoln expressed his views on slavery and defended democracy and the Union. As president, Lincoln opposed extending slavery into the territories. In addition, in the Emancipation Proclamation, he proclaimed the freedom of slaves in the Confederate states. As a result, about 180,000 African-American men volunteered to fight in the Union army during the Civil War.

Find the Main Idea How did Lincoln's efforts help end slavery?

SECTION 4 ASSESSMENT

go.hrw.com
Online Quiz
Keyword: SHL REF HP

Reviewing Ideas, Terms, and People

1. **a. Define** What is **manifest destiny**?
   b. Analyze Why did President James Monroe issue the Monroe Doctrine?
   c. Elaborate How do you think the idea of manifest destiny influenced the settlement of the west?
2. **a. Recall** What did the Kansas-Nebraska Act say about expansion and slavery?
   b. Analyze What were the main causes of the Civil War, and what were the war's effects?
   c. Evaluate How successful was Reconstruction? Provide reasons for your answer.

Critical Thinking

3. **Analyze** Use the graphic organizer below and your notes to analyze ways in which westward expansion and the Civil War were related.

Westward Expansion → [ ]
Civil War → [ ]

FOCUS ON WRITING

4. **Persuasion** Using information from the section, write a paragraph persuading others how the expansion of the United States will be good for the country.

Review & Assess

Close
Have students summarize the causes and effects of the American Civil War. To what extent was the war caused by the nation's expansion?

Review
Online Quiz, Section 4

Assess
SE Section 4 Assessment
Progress Assessment: Section 4 Quiz
Alternative Assessment Handbook

Reteach/Intervene
Interactive Reader and Study Guide, Section 4
Interactive Skills Tutor CD-ROM

Answers

Faces of History *He opposed extending slavery into the territories and called for the freedom of slaves in the Confederate states.*

Reading Check *It succeeded by passing the Civil Rights Act and the Fourteenth and Fifteenth Amendments, protecting and extending rights of African Americans. It failed because southern states continued to pass discriminatory laws and prevented many African Americans from making a decent living.*

Section 4 Assessment Answers

1. **a.** belief of Americans' "God-given right" to settle land all the way to the Pacific Ocean
   b. to make the Americas off limits to further European colonization
   c. possible answers—probably encouraged Americans to push Native Americans further west; the idea of manifest destiny also led to war against Mexico
2. **a.** It left the decision on whether to allow slavery to the residents of each of the territories.
   b. Major causes—disagreement over slavery and states' rights; secession of the southern states; Major effects—ended slavery, reunited the nation
   c. possible answer—Reconstruction was successful in passing the Civil Rights Act and the Fourteenth and Fifteenth Amendments. It was unsuccessful in preventing southern states from passing discriminatory laws. However, the laws passed during Reconstruction provided a foundation for America's civil rights movement in the 1900s.
3. Westward expansion led to more territory. Addition of new states fueled th e debate over slavery. The Civil War resulted.
4. Student paragraphs should point out that expansion west will strengthen the worldwide reputation of the United States; bring natural resources, including gold, to the nation; and bring new opportunities and prosperity to individual Americans.

Document-Based Investigation

Independence in Latin America

Info to Know

Diego Rivera Diego Rivera is considered to be the greatest Mexican painter of the 20th century. Rivera studied art in Mexico City and then in Paris where he became acquainted w ith the work of the impressionists, post-modernists, and Cubists. He also studied the Italian Renaissance frescoes, and using frescoes, brought art to everyday people.

Activity **Analyzing Visuals** Have students work together in pairs to name the various groups of people shown in the mural on this page.

Primary Source

"The painter can and must abstract from many details in creating his painting. Every good composition is above all a work of abstraction. All good painters know this. But the painter cannot dispense with subjects altogether without his work suffering impoverishment."
—Diego Rivera

CHAPTER 9 **Document-Based Investigation**

Independence in Latin America

Historical Context These four documents are accounts of several Latin American revolutions by people involved in or affected by these revolutions.

Task Study the documents and answer the questions that follow. After you have studied all the documents, you will be asked to write an essay outlining similarities and differences between several Latin American revolutions.

From the Conquest to 1930, by Diego Rivera, 1900s

DOCUMENT 1

Mexico's History Reflected in Art

In the 1900s Mexican artist Diego Rivera painted enormous murals throughout Mexico City. This section of Rivera's mural in the city's National Palace shows the history of Mexico. Rivera depicts Father Hidalgo and other prominent figures in Mexico's struggle for independence standing above the eagle in the center of the mural.

DOCUMENT 2

Freedom in Haiti

Several months after he seized power in France in 1799, Napoleon issued a proclamation to the people of Haiti promising to respect the rights of the colony's free black citizens. He decreed that the words "Remember, brave blacks, that the French people alone recognize your freedom and equality of rights" should be written on the flags of the colony. But Toussaint L'Ouverture refused to follow the order and responded with the following words.

It is not a circumstantial freedom conceded to ourselves alone that we want. It is the absolute adoption of the principle that any man born red, black or white cannot be the property of his like. We are free today because we are the stronger party. The Consul maintains slavery in Martinique and Bourbon; we will thus be slaves when he will be stronger.

308 CHAPTER 9

Collaborative Learning

At Level

Independence Mural

Materials: poster paper, colored markers

1. Organize students into small groups. Assign each group one of the countries that fought for independence discussed in this chapter.
2. Have students reexamine the Diego Rivera mural shown on this page. Guide students in a discussion of the style, the groups of people shown, and the emblem in the foreground. Then have students review the information in the text about their assigned country.
3. Have students work together to design and then sketch that country's fight for independence in the same style as the Rivera mural.
4. Have students use the art supplies to create their own mural. Have volunteers from each group share the finished mural with the class.
LS **Visual-Spatial**

Alternative Assessment Handbook, Rubric 3: Artwork

DOCUMENT 3

A Bolivian Supports Independence

In 1885 Bolivian writer and statesman Nataniel Aguirre published *The Memoirs of Juan de la Rosa,* a novel about a fictional soldier in the Bolivian revolution. In the excerpt below, de la Rosa's teacher tells him about some of the motivations behind the revolution.

> The country where we were born, as well as many other countries in this part of the world, obey a king who is two thousand leagues away, on the other side of the ocean. It takes one year for our complaints to reach his feet, and we never know when—if at all—the resolutions that his Council dictates, or even his sovereign dispositions, will arrive here. His agents believe that they are demigods, high above us. His subjects who come from there consider themselves nothing more and nothing less than our masters and lords. Those of us who are their very children —the criollos [Bolivian-born people with only Spanish blood]—are looked upon with disdain; they think that we should never aspire to the honors and public positions that are reserved just for them. The mestizos [people with mixed Spanish and Indian blood], whose blood is half like theirs, are scorned and condemned to suffer innumerable humiliations.

DOCUMENT 4

A Cuban's View of San Martín

José Martí, a supporter of the Cuban revolution, published an article in 1891 describing José de San Martín. In the article Martí describes the life of the liberator of Argentina, Chile, and Peru through the eyes of a Cuban revolutionary.

> His veins flowed with the blood of a soldier from León and a granddaughter of conquistadors; his father was governor of Yapeyú on the banks of one of America's great rivers. He learned to read on the mountain slopes and grew up in the town as a gentleman's son in the shade of the palms and the urundays [kinds of trees]. He was taken to Spain to learn dancing and Latin in a school for the sons of noblemen. At the age of 12 the child "who seldom laughed" became a cadet. When as a Spanish lieutenant-colonel of 34 he returned to fight against Spain, he was no longer the man forged by the wind and rain of the pampas [grasslands] deep in his America, but the soldier who, in the glow of his native memories, had nurtured in the shadows of the Masonic Lodge of Lautaro, among young patricians and noblemen from Madrid, the will to work systematically and according to plan for American independence.

Skills Focus READING LIKE A HISTORIAN

DOCUMENT 1

a. Describe How does Rivera represent the leaders of the Mexican Revolution?

b. Analyze How does Rivera represent the people of Mexico in this mural?

DOCUMENT 2

a. Interpret Why did Toussaint L'Ouverture refuse to follow Napoleon's order?

b. Analyze How do Toussaint L'Ouverture's words indicate that a rebellion in Haiti might occur in the future?

DOCUMENT 3

a. Interpret How does Aguirre characterize the Spanish?

b. Identify Main Ideas Why should Bolivians support the revolution, according to Aguirre?

DOCUMENT 4

a. Interpret Do you think Martí respects San Martín? Why or why not?

b. Compare and Contrast What are some similarities and differences between San Martín and other revolutionaries you have read about?

DOCUMENT-BASED ESSAY QUESTION

People supported independence in the Americas for many reasons. What were some of these reasons, and how did they affect Latin American independence? Using the documents above and information from this chapter, form a thesis that expresses your opinion. Then write a short essay to support your opinion.

See **Skills Handbook**, pp. H25, H28

Document-Based Investigation

Word Help

demigod person with more power than a mortal, but with less power than a god

innumerable countless

patrician person of noble birth

Activity. Drawing José de San Martín Have students create drawings of José de San Martín based on the description provided in Document 4 and details in the chapter. When the drawings are complete, have volunteers share their drawings, noting what features the drawings share. **LS Visual-Spatial**

Alternative Assessment Handbook, Rubric 3: Artwork

Skills Focus: Interpreting Literature as Historical Evidence

Reading Like a Historian Skill

The Memoirs of Juan de la Rosa

At Level

1. Remind students that Document 3 is an excerpt from a novel written during the period of the Latin American independence movements. Then, have them reread Document 3. Ask the following questions: What makes the excerpt seem like a novel? Can this novel be considered historical evidence as well?
2. Have students review the material in this chapter about creoles and peninsulares. Then, copy this chart for all to see. Have students complete the chart with facts from the textbook and facts from Document 3. What do the two columns of the chart suggest about Document 3? After comparing the two columns, ask students if they would consider *The Memoirs of Juan de la Rosa* to be a good source of historical evidence. Why or why not? **LS Visual-Spatial, Interpersonal**

Alternative Assessment Handbook, Rubrics 7: Charts, and 9: Comparing and Contrasting

Answers

Reading Like a Historian

Document 1. a. *The mural represents the leaders of the Mexican Revolution as just one part of Mexico's long history from empire, to conquest, to independence.* **b.** *The people of Mexico are looking up to the revolutionary leaders and looking back on their history.* **Document 2. a.** *because slavery still existed in other areas of the French empire;* **b.** *L'Ouverture lists several demands for change.* **Document 3. a.** *The Spanish believe they are almost gods, and that they should be the masters of the Bolivians.* **b.** *because they have suffered scorn and humiliation under Spanish rule;* **Document 4. a.** *possible answer—yes, seems to respect San Martin; traces his educational background and development as a leader;* **b.** *possible answer—came from a background of prosperity and was well-educated;* **Essay** *possible thesis—Latin American independence movements brought together people with many different goals, including independence from colonial rulers, change in Latin America's social structure, and an end to slavery.*

Answers

Visual Summary

Review and Inquiry Remind students that the title of the chapter is Reforms, Revolutions, and War. Have students classify the events in Great Britain, France, Latin America, and the United States as reforms, revolutions, or wars. Some events may fit in more than one category. As a class, discuss the reasons that change sometimes happens peacefully, and sometimes through revolution and war.

Quick Facts Transparency: Visual Study Guide: Reforms, Revolutions, and War

Review Key Terms and People

1. Simón Bolívar
2. Emancipation Proclamation
3. potato famine
4. creole
5. manifest destiny
6. liberal
7. suffrage
8. Victoria
9. anti-Semitism
10. abolition

Comprehension and Critical Thinking

11. **a.** limited working hours of children and teenagers, children aged 9 to 13 had to receive two hours of schooling per day
b. broke windows, set fires, assaulted police officers, went on hunger strikes
c. possible answer—might not have established different cultures

12. **a.** reactionary leader in Austria
b. extended vote to wealthy citizens; limited freedom of the press, silenced opposition caused economic depression and discontent
c. possible answer—Dreyfus was a scapegoat because he was Jewish.

13. **a.** He led a slave revolt that became an independence movement.
b. liberated several South American colonies, served as president of Gran Colombia
c. possible answer—It was unfair that colonists born in Spain had more rights and opportunities.

14. **a.** encouraged westward expansion as a "God-given" right
b. forced Native Americans from their homes; many died on march west, the Trail of Tears
c. ended slavery; killed more than 500,000 Americans; left South in ruins; reunited the nation

Reading Skills

15. that the Factory Act of 1833 improved working conditions for children and teenagers
16. details about limited working hours and mandatory schooling

CHAPTER 9

Chapter Review

QUICK FACTS

VISUAL STUDY GUIDE

Reforms, Revolutions, and War

Great Britain

- The British Parliament passes many social reforms.
- British women gain the right to vote.
- About 1 million Irish die from starvation in the potato famine, and more than 1 million emigrate.

France

- Louis Philippe is crowned king in 1830.
- The Second Republic is established in 1848.
- Louis Napoleon becomes emperor in 1852.
- The Third Republic passes reforms in the late 1800s.
- Alfred Dreyfus is falsely accused of spying in 1894.

Latin America

- Haiti gains independence from France in 1804.
- Tensions grow between creoles and *peninsulares*.
- Mexico gains independence from Spain in 1821.
- Other nations gain independence.

United States

- The United States expands in the 1800s.
- Americans move westward.
- The North defeats the South in the Civil War.

Key People

Queen Victoria
- Ruled Great Britain from 1837 to 1901 during an era of reform

Benjamin Disraeli
- Influential British prime minister who argued for women's suffrage

Emmeline Pankhurst
- Led the British women's suffrage movement

Louis Philippe
- French monarch who expanded voting rights

Louis Napoleon
- Ruled France during the Second Republic

Toussaint L'Ouverture
- Liberated Haiti from the French

Miguel Hidalgo
- Mexican priest who made the first public call for independence from Spain

José María Morelos
- Mexican military leader who led the fight for independence

Simón Bolívar
- Leader of several independence movements in South America

José de San Martín
- Leader of independence movements in southern South America

Pedro I
- Declared Brazil independent in 1822

Review Key Terms and People

Identify the correct term or person from the chapter that best matches each of the following descriptions.

1. Venezuelan leader who was called "the Liberator"
2. American Civil War document that freed slaves in states that were in rebellion
3. disaster that killed nearly 1 million Irish
4. term for a colonist of European descent who was born in the Americas
5. the belief that Americans had a God-given right to settle the North American continent all the way to the Pacific Ocean
6. supporter of political and social reform
7. the right to vote
8. the British monarch who had the longest reign
9. prejudice towards Jews
10. the movement to end slavery

History's Impact video program
Watch the video to answer the closing question: How have voting rights for women affected politics around the world today?

Comprehension and Critical Thinking

SECTION 1 *(pp. 287–292)*

11. a. Recall How did the Factory Act of 1833 change working conditions?

b. Explain What extreme measures did women take to gain the right to vote in Britain?

c. Predict How might British colonies be different today if they had not become independent?

SECTION 2 *(pp. 293–296)*

12. a. Identify Who was Klemens von Metternich?

b. Explain In what ways did Louis Philippe change France?

c. Evaluate What do you think about how the French government treated Alfred Dreyfus?

SECTION 3 *(pp. 297–302)*

13. a. Describe How did Toussaint L'Ouverture free Haiti from French rule?

b. Identify Cause and Effect How did Simón Bolívar gain independence for South America?

c. Evaluate What do you think of the peninsulares' role in Latin American society during the 1800s?

SECTION 4 *(pp. 303–307)*

14. a. Recall What effect did manifest destiny have on the westward expansion of the United States?

b. Cause and Effect How did the Indian Removal Act change the way Native Americans lived?

c. Elaborate In what ways did the Civil War affect the United States?

Reading Skills

Identifying Implied Main Ideas *Read the passage below and use what you know about identifying implied main ideas to answer the questions that follow.*

> "Because of Sadler's report, Parliament passed the Factory Act in 1833. This act limited the working hours of children in textile factories. The act made it illegal for teenagers to work more than 12 hours a day. In addition, children between the ages of 9 and 13 had to receive two hours of schooling a day."

15. What is the implied main idea of this paragraph?

16. What details help you find the implied main idea?

Interpreting Political Cartoons

Reading Like a Historian *The 1863 cartoon below shows Lady Liberty representing the Union by defending herself against members of Congress who are represented by snakes.*

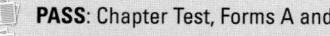

The Granger Collection, New York

17. Draw Conclusions Why do you think the cartoonist chose to use Lady Liberty to represent the Union?

18. Explain Why are the members of congress attacking the Union?

Using the Internet

go.hrw.com
Practice Online
Keyword: SHL REF

19. Beginning in the early 1800s, Mexicans fought for their independence from Spain. Several leaders led the fight, including Father Miguel Hidalgo, José María Morelos, and Agustín de Iturbide. Using the Internet, research more about one of these revolutionary leaders. Then write a report about how the leader helped Mexico gain its independence from Spain.

WRITING ABOUT HISTORY

Exposition: Analyzing Causes and Effects *In Great Britain during the 1800s political and social reforms changed people's lives for the better.*

20. Assignment: In an essay, analyze the causes and effects of British reforms during the 1800s. To provide support for your essay, use specific examples from the chapter and from other research sources if needed.

Answers

Interpreting Political Cartoons

17. possible answer—to represent the Union's fight for freedom and emancipation

18. possible answer—were against Lincoln's anti-secession belief's

Using the Internet

19. Go to the HRW Web site and enter the keyword shown to access a rubric for this activity.

KEYWORD: SHL REF

Writing About History

20. possible answer—Student essays should discuss how industrialization created a new class of workers and new problems in Great Britain. This led to calls for increased representation and certain factory reforms. In turn, those early reforms led to further social and political reforms. A rubric for the activity is provided in **CRF:** Writing About History.

HOLT
History's Impact
▶ **Video Program: Reforms, Revolutions, and War**
See the Video Program Teacher's Guide for the answer to the closing question.

Review and Assessment Resources

Review and Reinforce

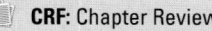

- **CRF:** Chapter Review
- **Quick Facts Transparency:** Visual Study Guide: Reforms, Revolutions, and War
- **Spanish Chapter Summaries Audio CD Program**
- OSP **Holt PuzzlePro:** Quiz Show for ExamView
- **Quiz Game CD-ROM**

Assess

- **PASS:** Chapter Test, Forms A and B
- **Alternative Assessment Handbook**
- OSP **ExamView Test Generator,** Chapter Test
- **Differentiated Instruction Modified Worksheets and Tests CD-ROM:** Chapter Test
- HOAP **Holt Online Assessment Program** (in the Premier Online Edition)

Reteach/Intervene

- **Interactive Reader and Study Guide**
- **Differentiated Instruction Teacher Management System:** Lesson Plans for Differentiated Instruction
- **Differentiated Instruction Modified Worksheets and Tests CD-ROM:** Chapter Test
- **Interactive Skills Tutor CD-ROM**

go.hrw.com
Online Resources
KEYWORD: SHL TEACHER

Chapter 10 Planning Guide

Nationalism in Europe

Chapter Overview	Reproducible Resources	Technology Resources
CHAPTER 10 **pp. 312–339** **Overview: In this chapter, students will learn how nationalism led to revolutions across Europe, causing monarchies to fall and dramatically changing the map of Europe.**	**Differentiated Instruction Teacher Management System:*** • Pacing Guide • Lesson Plans for Differentiated Instruction **Interactive Reader and Study Guide:** Chapter Summary* **Chapter Resource File*** • Writing for the SAT • Social Studies Skill • Economics and History • Chapter Review	**Live Ink© Online Reading Help** **Student Edition on Audio CD Program** **Differentiated Instruction Modified Worksheets and Tests CD-ROM** **Interactive Skills Tutor CD-ROM** **World History Primary Source Library CD-ROM** **History's Impact: World History Video Program (VHS/DVD):** Nationalism in Europe
Section 1: **Italian Unification** **The Main Idea:** In the 1800s, Italian states rebelled against Austria and unified as the Kingdom of Italy.	**Differentiated Instruction Teacher Management System:** Section 1 Lesson Plan* **Interactive Reader and Study Guide:** Section 1 Summary* **Chapter Resource File*** • Vocabulary Builder: Section 1 • Biography: Giuseppe Verdi	**Daily Test Practice Transparency:** Section 1* **Map Transparency:** The Unification of Italy, 1858–1870* **Quick Facts Transparency:** Elements of Nationalism* **Internet Activity:** The Making of a Hero: Giuseppe Garibaldi
Section 2: **German Unification** **The Main Idea:** In the late 1800s, Otto von Bismark transformed Germany from a loose confederation of separate states into a powerful empire.	**Differentiated Instruction Teacher Management System:** Section 2 Lesson Plan* **Interactive Reader and Study Guide:** Section 2 Summary* **Chapter Resource File*** • Vocabulary Builder: Section 2 • Biography: Johann Gottlieb Fichte	**Daily Test Practice Transparency:** Section 2* **Map Transparency:** The Unification of Germany, 1865–1871* **Quick Facts Transparencies:** Steps to Unification in Germany; Germany's Economic Growth, 1890–1913*
Section 3: **Austria-Hungary and the Ottoman Empire** **The Main Idea:** Nationalism broke down two old European empires—the Austrian Hapsburg Empire and the Ottoman Empire.	**Differentiated Instruction Teacher Management System:** Section 3 Lesson Plan* **Interactive Reader and Study Guide:** Section 3 Summary* **Chapter Resource File*** • Vocabulary Builder: Section 3 • Biography: Mustafa Kemal • Primary Source: Hungary's National Song, 1848	**Daily Test Practice Transparency:** Section 3* **Map Transparencies:** Ethnic Groups in Austria-Hungary, 1867; The Ottoman Empire*
Section 4: **Unrest in Russia** **The Main Idea:** In the 1800s and early 1900s, Russians rebelled against the absolute power of the czar and demanded social reforms.	**Differentiated Instruction Teacher Management System:** Section 4 Lesson Plan* **Interactive Reader and Study Guide:** Section 4 Summary* **Chapter Resource File*** • Vocabulary Builder: Section 4 • Biography: Karl Marx • Literature: *Dead Souls* • History and Geography: Russian Expansion	**Daily Test Practice Transparency:** Section 4* **Quick Facts Transparencies:** Last Czars of Russia; Russian Revolution of 1905* **Internet Activity:** Russian Revolution

go.hrw.com | Print Resource | Transparency
LS Learning Styles | Audio CD | CD-ROM
Video | SE Student Edition | TE Teacher's Edition
OSP One-Stop Planner CD-ROM
*also on One-Stop Planner CD-ROM

Review, Assessment, Intervention

- **Quick Facts Transparency:** Nationalism in Europe*
- **Spanish Chapter Summaries Audio CD Program**
- **Progress Assessment Support System (PASS):** Chapter Test*
- **Differentiated Instruction Modified Worksheets and Tests CD-ROM:** Modified Chapter Test
- OSP **One-Stop Planner CD-ROM:** ExamView Test Generator (English/Spanish)
- HOAP **Holt Online Assessment Program (HOAP),** in the Premier Online Edition

- **PASS:** Section 1 Quiz*
- **Online Quiz:** Section 1
- **Alternative Assessment Handbook**

- **PASS:** Section 2 Quiz*
- **Online Quiz:** Section 2
- **Alternative Assessment Handbook**

- **PASS:** Section 3 Quiz*
- **Online Quiz:** Section 3
- **Alternative Assessment Handbook**

- **PASS:** Section 4 Quiz*
- **Online Quiz:** Section 4
- **Alternative Assessment Handbook**

HOLT
History's Impact
World History Video Program (VHS/DVD)
Nationalism in Europe

Power Presentation with Video CD-ROM

Power Presentations with Video are visual presentations of each chapter's main ideas. Presentations can be customized by including Quick Facts charts, images and maps from the textbook, and video clips.

Holt Online Learning

go.hrw.com
Teacher Resources
KEYWORD: SHL TEACHER

go.hrw.com
Student Resources
KEYWORD: SHL NAT

- Document-Based Questions
- Interactive Multimedia Activities
- Current Events
- Chapter-Based Internet Activities
- and more!

Holt Premier
Online Student Edition

Complete online support for interactivity, assessment, and reporting

- Interactive Maps and Notebook
- Homework Practice and Research Activities Online

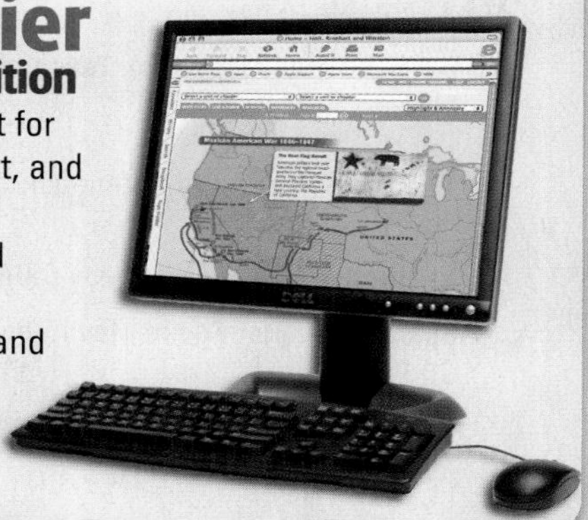

The Big Picture

Peter N. Stearns

The Nature of Nationalism Nationalism became such a powerful force around the world that it is hard to remember how new it is. While hints of nationalism can be found earlier, the force was only fully defined in the late 18th century. Intellectuals, especially in Germany, helped define the importance of national cultures. Social changes spurred many groups to seek new loyalties, as opposed to more traditional regional and religious identities. The French Revolution aided nationalism by breaking down barriers between citizens and the state and by causing nationalist resistance in places like Spain, Italy and Germany. By the early 19th century, nationalism was a powerful force in European politics, despite conservative efforts to keep it under control. Nationalist revolts occurred in Greece, Poland, and Belgium.

Unification Nationalism caused major intellectual and political movements in Italy and Germany. The revolutions of 1848 in these countries highlighted demands for national unification and though they failed, the efforts continued. Leaders like Cavour and Bismarck took advantage of nationalist sentiments to increase their power and to use force to cement loyalty to moderate-liberal and conservative governments. Such unions provided the leading diplomatic developments of the third quarter of the 19th century. After unifications, nationalism helped maintain domestic stability, amid some new foreign adventurism, though it could not prevent a growing challenge from socialism.

Disruption In the Hapsburg, Ottoman, and, to an extent, Russian empires nationalism proved to be a disruptive force. It became increasingly difficult to maintain multinational empires against demands by smaller groups for cultural and political independence. Austria tried to compromise with Hungarian nationalism, but faced growing agitation from Slavic groups. The Ottomans could not prevent independence movements in the Balkans; around 1900 a Turkish nationalist group arose as the Ottoman Empire visibly declined. Russia faced some nationalist pressure, but social issues loomed larger. Peasant reforms did not suffice, and Marxist and other movements gained ground against a tsarist regime that refused fundamental political change. The revolution of 1905 foreshadowed larger upheaval.

Recent Scholarship

Benedict Anderson's *Imagined Communities: Reflections on the Origin and Spread of Nationalism* (1991) is not brand new, but it remains the most widely cited recent work on nationalism. Using various European and Southeast Asian examples, Anderson discusses how nations came to be defined, despite no really objective prior existence. This leads in turn to a discussion of what other interests nationalism served. The emphasis is on nationalism as a historic product, not some inevitable force of nature. An important companion piece, heavily focused on nationalist traditions in various parts of the world, is *The Invention of Tradition* (1983) edited by Eric Hobsbawm and Terence Ranger.

Differentiating Instruction

Differentiated Instruction Teacher Management System
- Pacing Guide
- Lesson Plans for Differentiated Instruction

Interactive Reader and Study Guide

Spanish Chapter Summaries Audio CD Program

Student Edition on Audio CD Program

Differentiated Instruction Modified Worksheets and Tests CD-ROM
- Vocabulary Flash Cards
- Modified Vocabulary Builder Activities
- Modified Chapter Review Activity
- Modified Chapter Test

OSP **One-Stop Planner CD-ROM**
- ExamView Test Generator (English/Spanish)
- PuzzlePro
- Quiz Show for ExamView
- Transparencies and Videos

TE **Differentiated Activities in the Teacher's Edition**
- German Unification Chart, p. 321
- Serfdom in Europe Chart, p. 331
- Causes and Effects of the Revolution of 1905, p. 333
- Analyzing Prince Andrew's Attitudes, p. 335

Reading Like a Historian

Sam Wineburg

Siege of Paris By New Year's Eve, 1870, Bismarck's siege of Paris was coming onto three months. With food deliveries halted from the countryside, Parisians took to drastic measures. Today, a plaque at the Paris zoo commemorates one of them. "Famine required the sacrifice of any animal which would be a contribution, however small, to the public food supply; it was necessary . . . to slaughter the two elephants, Castor and Pollux."

In the first weeks of 1871, rich Parisians wolfed down elephant. The poor, however, took to a more gruesome sort of protein seeking—the most desperate form short of cannibalism. They hunted and roasted flea-infested rats—or "rat pâté" as it was known.

On January 28, the siege ended. Old, beaten, suffering from gallstones that gave him little respite, a haggard Napoleon III capitulated to Bismarck. Paris was in shambles and France shamed. On the other hand, intoxicated by his stunning victory, Bismarck seized the French provinces of Alsace and Lorraine. But the Prussian victory had greater internal ramifications than this territorial conquest. Victory cemented German unification, providing the glue that would bind Europe's German-speaking states into the continent's most formidable fighting machine. A French defeat paved the way to German unification.

The Franco-Prussian war was a historical oil spill, the consequences of which were not felt for decades. Forty years later, France would again go to war to regain its pride—and Alsace-Lorraine—in World War I. This war was the prelude to World War II, the Holocaust, and the carving up of Europe into new spheres of superpower influence. Nearing the midpoint of the 20th century, blood stained the European continent.

Counterfactual History What if this whole chain of events had been stopped at its source? Let's go back to that decisive moment in 1870 before the siege. The French attaché pays a visit to the Prussian king seeking assurance that he will not try to place a minor German prince, one of several possible candidates, on Spain's throne. The king pays the attaché no heed and snubs him by refusing to speak further about the issue. An account of the meeting, a telegram actually, is released. French newspapers have a field-day playing up this diplomatic slight. Their passions enflamed by lurid headlines, crowds gather in Paris feverously chanting "À Berlin."

Instead of yielding to this warmongering, suppose that Napoleon proceeds with caution. Who knows what will happen to Spain? Instead of fanning flames, Napoleon chooses to turn the other cheek.

This thought experiment is what historians call a "counterfactual," a "what if" that lays out an alternative history that might have occurred had a different path been pursued. This particular scenario is the brainchild of historian Alistair Horne, the author (with Richard Cobb) of *The Fall of Paris: The Siege and the Commune 1870-71.*

Had Napoleon ignored Bismarck's slight, the ramifications would have been greater than saving Castor and Pollux. Bismarck would have been deprived of his crowning victory, and German unification would have been stalled. Catholic Bavaria, imagines Horne, may have joined with Catholic Austria, counterbalancing Prussian might and the military titan known as Germany would be stillborn. No World War I, no World War II, and that little boy Adolf, born in Braunau am Inn, would have died a second-rate artist and small-town rabble-rouser.

The counterfactual teaches us that the past could have been different. In so doing, it reminds us that the future is ours to make.

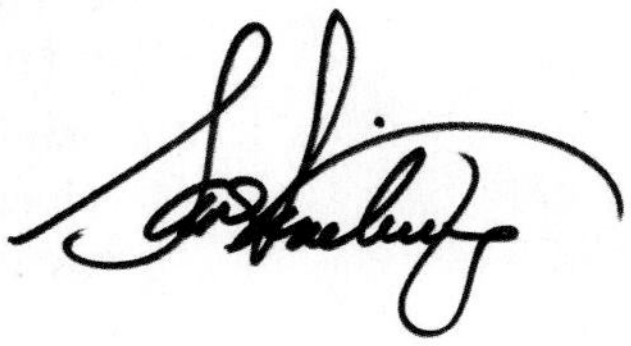

• Chapter Preview •

Chapter Main Ideas

Section 1 In the 1800s, Italian states rebelled against Austria and unified as the Kingdom of Italy.

Section 2 In the late 1800s, Otto von Bismarck transformed Germany from a loose confederation of separate states into a powerful empire.

Section 3 Nationalism broke down two old European empires—the Austrian Hapsburg Empire and the Ottoman Empire.

Section 4 In the 1800s and early 1900s, Russians rebelled against the absolute power of the czar and demanded social reforms.

CHAPTER 10

1800–1920

Nationalism in Europe

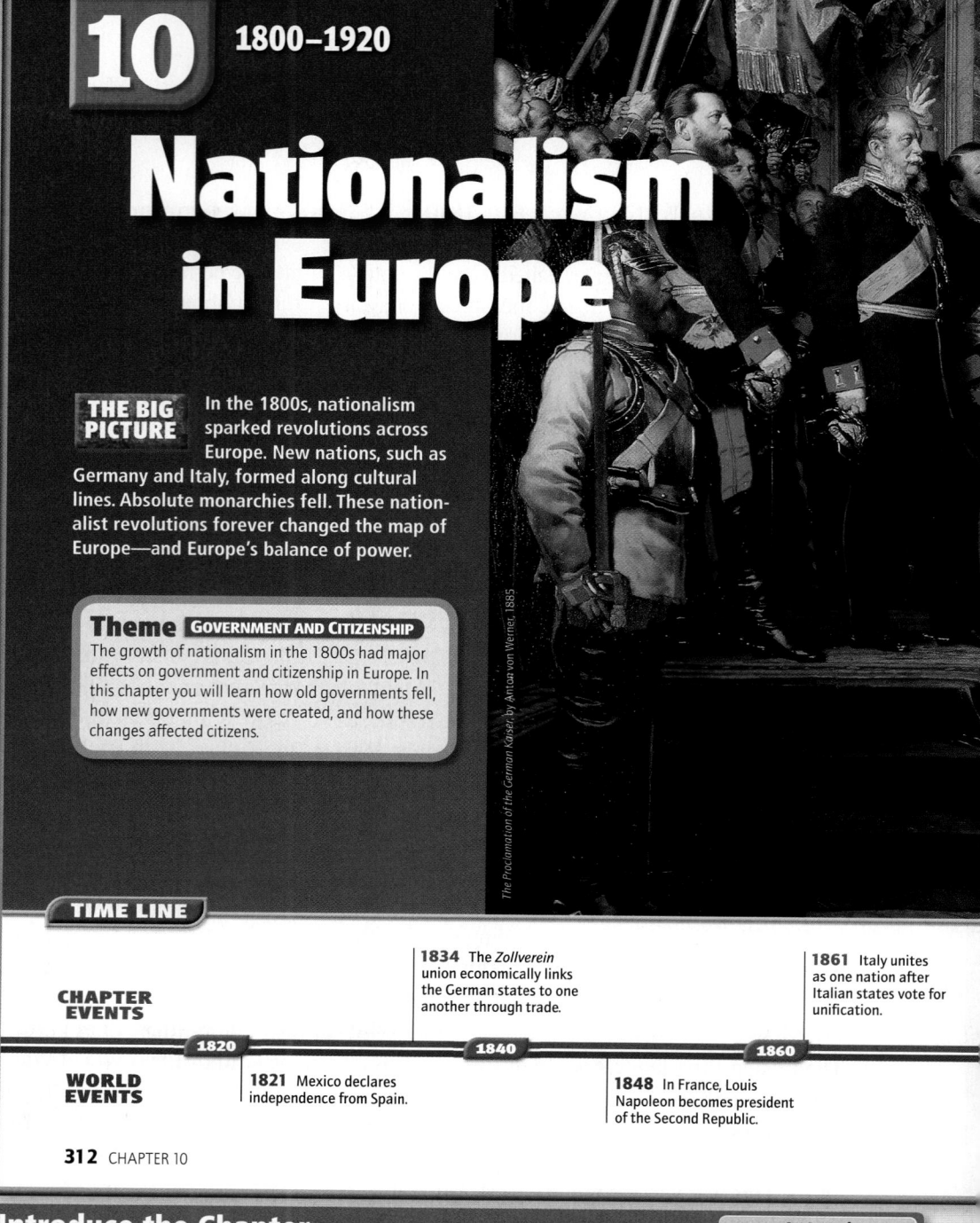

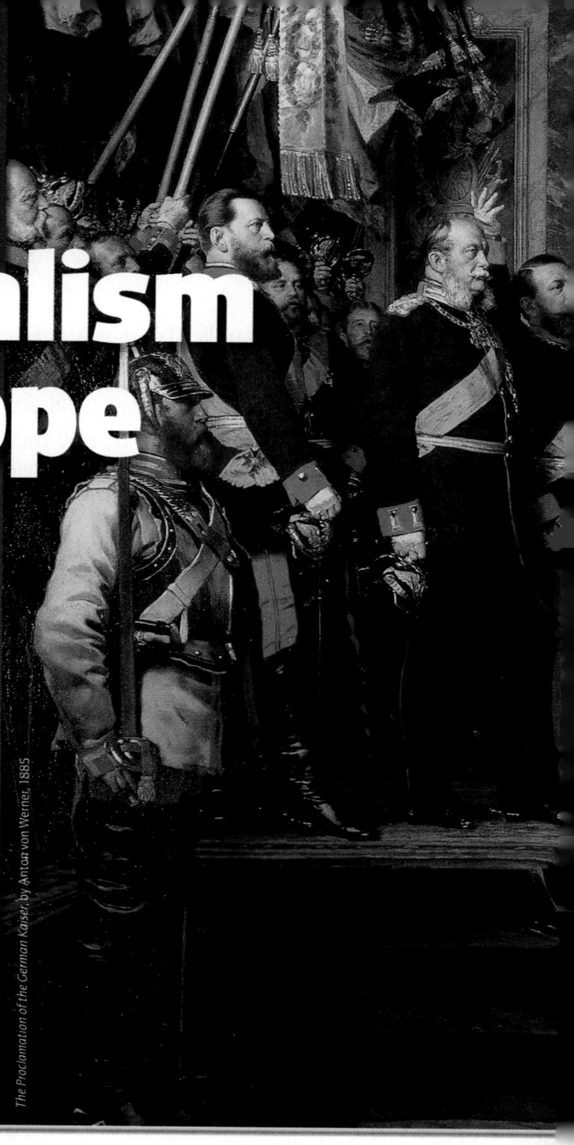

The Proclamation of the German Kaiser, by Anton von Werner, 1885

THE BIG PICTURE In the 1800s, nationalism sparked revolutions across Europe. New nations, such as Germany and Italy, formed along cultural lines. Absolute monarchies fell. These nationalist revolutions forever changed the map of Europe—and Europe's balance of power.

Theme GOVERNMENT AND CITIZENSHIP

The growth of nationalism in the 1800s had major effects on government and citizenship in Europe. In this chapter you will learn how old governments fell, how new governments were created, and how these changes affected citizens.

TIME LINE

	1820	1840	1860
CHAPTER EVENTS		**1834** The *Zollverein* union economically links the German states to one another through trade.	**1861** Italy unites as one nation after Italian states vote for unification.
WORLD EVENTS	**1821** Mexico declares independence from Spain.	**1848** In France, Louis Napoleon becomes president of the Second Republic.	

Key to Differentiating Instruction

Below Level

Basic-level activities designed for all students encountering new material

At Level

Intermediate-level activities designed for average students

Above Level

Challenging activities designed for honors and gifted and talented students

Standard English Mastery

Activities designed to improve standard English usage

Introduce the Chapter

At Level

Nationalism in Europe

1. Remind students that in 1815 Europe was recovering from the Napoleonic wars. The Congress of Vienna had tried to restore the old order, but the seeds of nationalism had been planted.
2. Organize students into small groups. Have each group try to define nationalism and write predictions of the ways in which nationalism would change the map of Europe.
3. Review student predictions as a class. Then guide students in a discussion of nationalism and its probable outcomes.
4. Tell students that in this chapter they will learn what effects nationalism had and how it changed the map of Europe. **LS Interpersonal**

Alternative Assessment Handbook, Rubrics 14: Group Activity; and 38: Writing to Classify

History's Impact video program
Watch the video to understand the impact of nationalism.

HOLT
History's Impact
► **Video Program: Nationalism in Europe**
See the Video Teacher's Guide for strategies for using the video segment.

Reading Like a Historian
Analyzing Visuals During the Franco-Prussian War, the Prussian army captured the French emperor, Napoleon III. The French formed a Government of National Defense to carry on the war until it ended in January 1871. Prussian statesman Otto von Bismarck rubbed in his victory by annexing the provinces of Alsace and Lorraine, demanding an indemnity of 5 billion francs, and organizing a victory march through Paris. He also proclaimed Wilhelm I of Prussia the new German emperor in the Hall of Mirrors at Versailles, just outside of Paris.

Reading like a Historian
In this painting, Prussian prime minister Otto von Bismarck (in white) proclaims the Prussian king Wilhelm I (on podium) to be Emperor of Germany on January 18, 1871. This ceremony marked the creation of the German Empire following Prussia's defeat of France in the Franco-Prussian War.

Analyzing Visuals How can you tell that this painting commemorates an important event?
See **Skills Handbook**, p. H26

1867 Austria and Hungary become two separate, equal states under the Dual Monarchy.

1905 Revolution breaks out in Russia after troops kill some protesters on Bloody Sunday.

1880 ———— **1910**

1869 Suez Canal opens in Egypt.

1901 Theodore Roosevelt becomes president of the United States.

NATIONALISM IN EUROPE **313**

Explore the Time Line
1. What was the purpose of the *Zollverein*? *to link the German states through trade*
2. When did Italy unite as one nation? *1861*
3. When did the Dual Monarchy begin? *1867*
4. Who became president of the United States in 1901? *Theodore Roosevelt*

Info to Know
German Nationalism During the early 1800s, many Germans associated nationalism with liberalism. They believed that representative government and individual freedoms would advance along with nationalistic principles. However, Otto von Bismarck used nationalism mainly as a tool to help Prussia gain control over the rest of Germany.
Analyze How did different people view the connection between nationalism and government rule in Germany? *Some believed nationalism would advance representative government; Bismarck believed it would advance the power of the kaiser.*

go.hrw.com
Online Resources
Chapter Resources:
KEYWORD: SHL NAT
Teacher Resources:
KEYWORD: SHL TEACHER

Answers
Reading Like a Historian *The men are wearing dress uniforms and raising their swords to the new emperor. Their facial expressions reflect their intense interest in the event.*

Geography Starting Points

Switzerland Switzerland is a confederation of cantons that has traditionally been neutral in times of war. The country was occupied by France under Napoleon, who forced upon the Swiss a constitution and a strong central government. After Napoleon's downfall, Switzerland once more became a confederation of states. A new constitution expanded federal power in 1848. In 1874 the constitution was revised to change Switzerland into a unified nation.

Info to Know

Confederations Frederick K. Lister served for 34 years in the secretariat of the United Nations. He recently studied three confederations—the early United States, the Swiss Confederation, and the German Confederation. None of those confederations succeeded in the long run, but he blames their failure on the lack of modern means of communication, which forced them to create more centralized federal governments. Today, he believes that they could serve as a model for such international organizations as the European Union, NAFTA, and the United Nations.

Map Transparency: Europe, 1815

World History Outline Maps

Interactive Map: Europe, 1815

GEOGRAPHY Starting Points

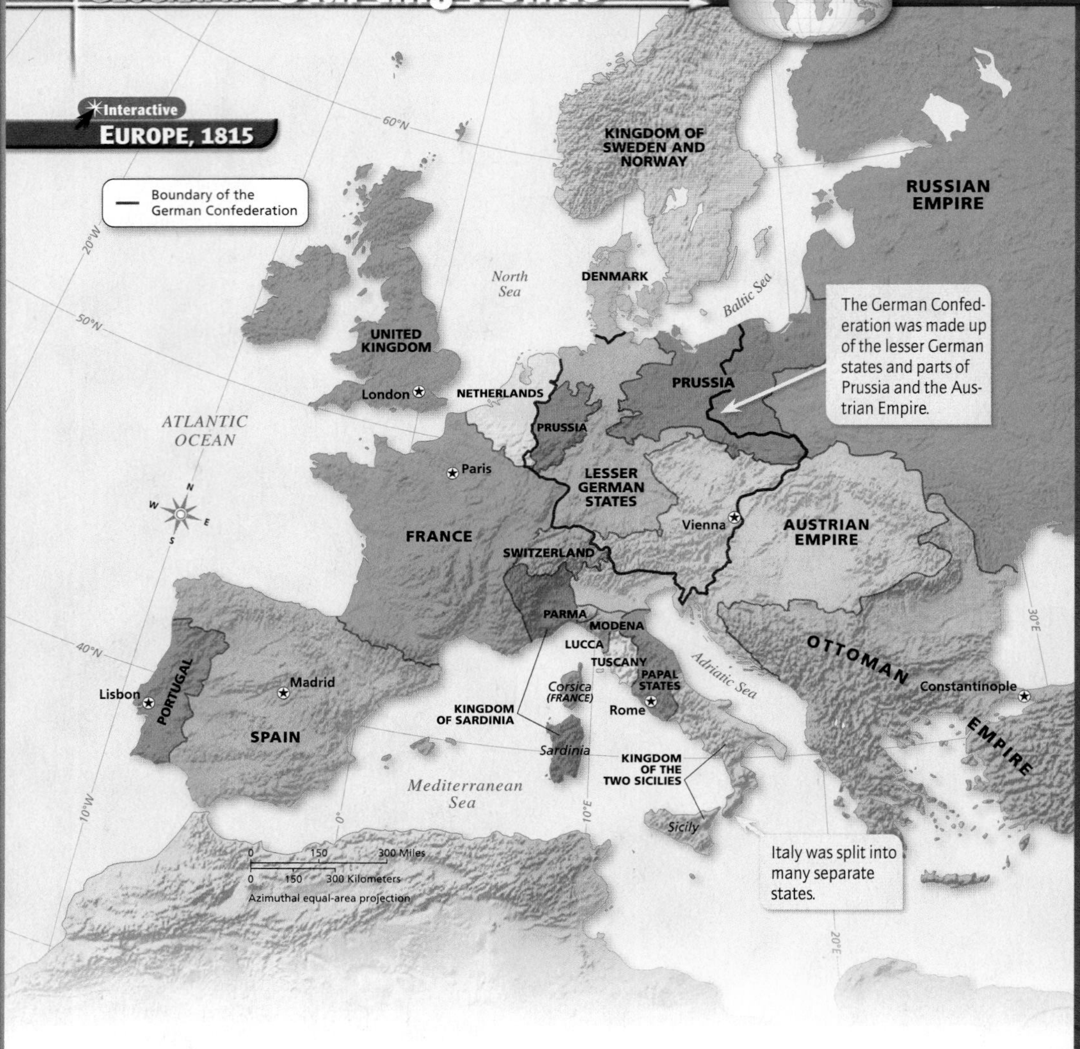

Starting Points In 1815 the Congress of Vienna divided Europe with little regard for the nationalities of the people who lived there. By the mid-1800s, nationalist movements arose which would lead to the breakup of empires and the creation of new nations. In Russia, a revolution threatened the power of the czar.

1. **Analyze** How would you describe the political geography of Germany and Italy at this time?
2. **Predict** Based on the map, what challenges do you think Italy would face as it unified?

Listen to History

Go online to listen to an explanation of the starting points for this chapter.

go.hrw.com
Keyword: SHL NAT

314 CHAPTER 10

Skills Focus: Analyzing Maps

At Level

Social Studies Skill
Europe, 1815

1. Have students compare the map on this page with a map of Europe after World War I. Guide students in a discussion of the following questions: What nations disappeared between 1815 and 1918? What new nations emerged between 1815 and 1918? Which nations lost the most land?
2. To help students see the continuing effects of nationalism, have them compare the 1918 map of Europe with a present-day map of Europe. Discuss the differences using the following questions: What new nations have emerged since 1918? What nations have lost land since 1918? What nations have gained land since 1918?
3. Finally, ask students how nationalism continues to play a part in world affairs today. **LS Verbal-Linguistic**

Alternative Assessment Handbook, Rubrics 9: Comparing and Contrasting; and 21: Map Reading

Answers

Geography Starting Points

1. *Each consisted of many separate states.* 2. *possible answer—many of the separate Italian states did not border one another, so it might prove difficult to govern them as one nation.*

SECTION 1

Italian Unification

BEFORE YOU READ

MAIN IDEA

In the 1800s, Italian states rebelled against Austria and unified as the Kingdom of Italy.

READING FOCUS

1. How did nationalism stir in Italy after the Congress of Vienna?
2. What role did Cavour and Sardinia play in the path toward Italian unification?
3. How did Garibaldi and the Red Shirts help unite Italy?
4. What challenges did Italy face after unification?

KEY TERMS AND PEOPLE

Giuseppe Mazzini
Camillo di Cavour
Giuseppe Garibaldi
Red Shirts
Victor Emmanuel

TAKING NOTES Take notes on how nationalism in Italy led to unification and, later, challenges.

Nationalism → Unification → Challenges

THE INSIDE STORY ***How did the lyrics of an opera help unite all Italians?*** During the 1800s most Italians were unhappy being part of the Austrian Empire. They were beginning to yearn to have their own nation, an Italian nation.

Someone had to put these yearnings into words, however, and that someone was Giuseppe Verdi, an Italian composer. In the lyrics to some of his operas, Verdi called for the Italian people to unite. Italians especially identified with his opera, *Nabucco.* It featured singers praising their homeland with the lyrics, "Go, settle on the cliffs and hills, where the sweet breezes bring the warm, soft fragrances of your native land. . . Oh my fatherland so beautiful and lost!" These words reminded Italians of the beauty of their own land and the fact that it was under Austria's control.

Verdi's music became a kind of national anthem for Italians seeking unification, inspiring them and urging them to act. The popularity of his music not only made Verdi an international star, but also helped spread the message of Italian nationalism. ■

A COMPOSER INSPIRES A NATION

Giuseppe Verdi conducts an orchestra in Paris in 1880. ▶

Illustration of Giuseppe Verdi conducting in Paris, by Stefano Bianchetti, 1800s

Teach the Main Idea

At Level

Italian Unification

1. **Teach** Ask students the Reading Focus questions to teach this section.
2. **Apply** Have students work in pairs to make visual representations of the events that led to Italian unification. Encourage students to use visual symbolism such as two rivers flowing toward unification.
3. **Review** Review student visual representations as a class. Guide students in a discussion of Italian unification. Ask students to name what they consider to be the most important event on the road to unification.
4. **Practice/Homework** Have students write an essay that describes what might have happened in Italy if Garibaldi and Cavour had not been able to reach an agreement to unite Italy under the king of Sardinia.

LS Visual-Spatial, Verbal-Linguistic

Alternative Assessment Handbook, Rubrics 14: Group Activity; and 40: Writing to Describe

Preteach

Getting Started

Use the **Interactive Reader and Study Guide** to familiarize students with the section content.

Interactive Reader and Study Guide, Section 1

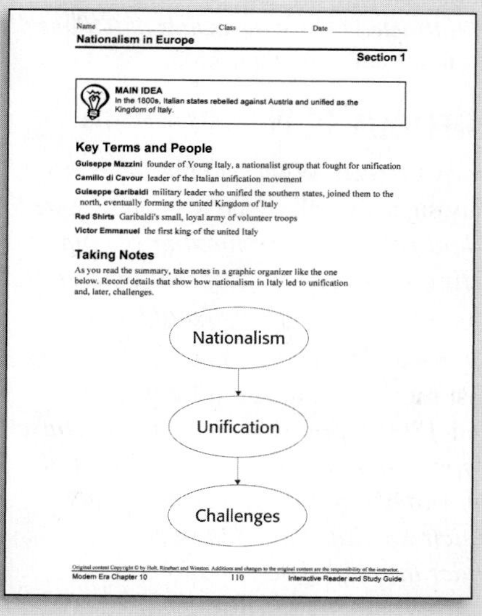

Name ________ Class ________ Date ________

Nationalism in Europe

Section 1

MAIN IDEA
In the 1800s, Italian states rebelled against Austria and unified as the Kingdom of Italy.

Key Terms and People

Guiseppe Mazzini founder of Young Italy, a nationalist group that fought for unification
Camillo di Cavour leader of the Italian unification movement
Guiseppe Garibaldi military leader who unified the southern states, joined them to the north, eventually forming the united Kingdom of Italy
Red Shirts Garibaldi's small, loyal army of volunteer troops
Victor Emmanuel the first king of the united Italy

Taking Notes

As you read the summary, take notes in a graphic organizer like the one below. Record details that show how nationalism in Italy led to unification and, later, challenges.

Nationalism → Unification → Challenges

Modern Era Chapter 10 110 Interactive Reader and Study Guide

Academic Vocabulary

Review with students the high-use academic term in this section.

ethnic common background or culture (p. 714)

CRF: Vocabulary Builder: Section 1

Taking Notes

Nationalism—It inspired uprisings in 1848; some states rebelled against Austrian rule; by 1860 northern Italy had freed itself from the control of the Austrian Empire.
Unification—Cavour and Garibaldi united Italy with the Two Sicilies; most of Papal States joined soon after.
Challenges—Regional differences kept nation from being truly united; Pope forbade Catholics from voting; social tensions were building; widespread poverty caused many Italians to emigrate; only wealthy males could vote; working class was beginning to campaign for change.

go.hrw.com
Online Resources
KEYWORD: SHL NAT
ACTIVITY: The Making of a Hero: Giuseppe Garibaldi

Direct Teach

Reading Focus

1 How did nationalism stir in Italy after the Congress of Vienna? *Some Europeans believed that people of the same background should form separate nation-states. Mazzini's Young Italy attracted tens of thousands of Italians to the cause of unification.*

Stirrings of Nationalism

Summarize What had happened to Italy since the fall of the Roman Empire? *It had consisted of a number of competing states for most of that time until it was united briefly by Napoleon.*

Evaluate Why do you think a nationalist movement arose in Italy in the mid-1800s? *possible answer —because Napoleon had united many of the Italian states into the Kingdom of Italy, which was later divided once again under the rule of other nations*

Quick Facts Transparency: Elements of Nationalism

Teaching Tip

Explain to students that nationalism can take many forms. In one form, national groups broke away from larger nations or empires that included people of many different back grounds. Greece, which broke away from the Ottoman Empire, is an example of this type of nationalism. In another form, smaller states that shared a language and culture united to form larger states. Italy and Germany are examples of this type of nationalism.

Answers

Elements of Nationalism *possible answer—A shared past connects people.*

QUICK FACTS

Elements of Nationalism

In Europe in the 1800s, devotion to one's national group, or nationalism, swept through the continent. The elements of nationalism listed below help bond a nation together.
How is history an element of nationalism?

Culture	Shared beliefs and a way of life create a common bond.
History	A shared past connects people as a group.
Religion	A common religion helps unite people.
Language	A common language is a key element of nationalism.
Territory	A shared land gives people a sense of unity.

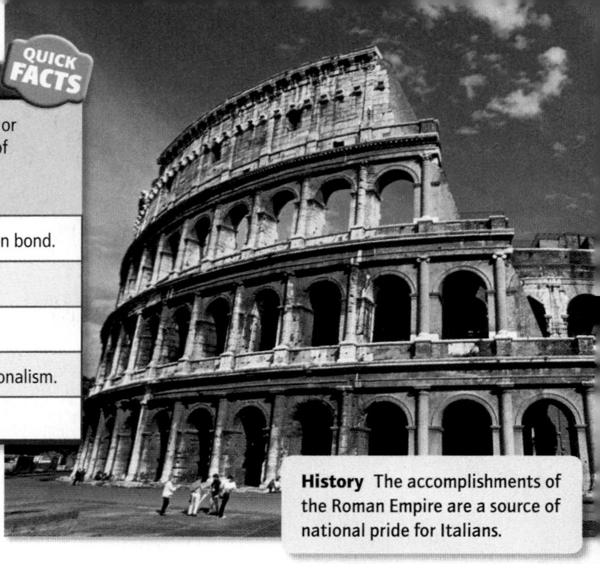

History The accomplishments of the Roman Empire are a source of national pride for Italians.

Stirrings of Nationalism

The Italian Peninsula had not been unified since the fall of the Roman Empire. Although most people spoke the same language, the peninsula was divided into several competing states, each with its own government. When Napoleon invaded Italy, he united many of these states under one government, but that unification did not last.

After Napoleon was defeated, the Congress of Vienna split the Italian states apart once more. This time, however, a spirit of nationalism, or a devotion to one's national group, was on the rise throughout Europe.

After the Congress of Vienna Prince Metternich of Austria had wanted the Congress of Vienna to maintain the old Europe with its old relationships. But just 15 years after the Congress met, a tired Metternich admitted that "the old Europe is nearing its end." Despite his efforts to halt change, the old order had been destroyed beyond repair.

Nationalism was a growing force in Europe during the 1800s, fostered in part by some of the decisions made at the Congress of Vienna. The Congress had created political boundaries that ignored national groups, instead placing these groups under the control of large empires.

ACADEMIC VOCABULARY
ethnic common background or culture

Some of Europe's empires included people of different ethnic groups. For example, the Austrian Empire was home to Croats, Czechs, Germans, Hungarians, Italians, Poles, Serbs, Slovaks, and Slovenes. The Italians were split into three groups. The Congress of Vienna had placed much of northern Italy under Austrian rule, other Italian states under control of the Hapsburgs, and still others under control of a French ruler. Italian nationalism grew in opposition to these conditions.

Mazzini and Young Italy As Italian artists, writers, and thinkers became interested in celebrating Italy's cultural traditions, other Italians in Austria formed secret societies to work for political change. They began plotting to overthrow the Austrian government in Italy.

In 1831 a popular writer launched a nationalist group called Young Italy to fight for unification of the separate Italian states. This writer, **Giuseppe Mazzini**, had been exiled because of his outspoken nationalism, but he smuggled his patriotic pamphlets into Italy. Mazzini believed that Europe needed to redraw the lines set by the Congress of Vienna in 1815.

HISTORY'S VOICES

> **"Europe no longer possesses unity of faith, of mission, or of aim . . . The question of nationality can only be resolved by destroying the treaties of 1815 and changing the map of Europe and its public law."**
>
> —Giuseppe Mazzini, "On Nationality," 1852

Skills Focus: Making Oral Presentations

At Level

Research Required

Reading Like a Historian Skill
Italian Nationalists

1. Organize students into four groups. Have each group research one of the following leaders in the Italian independence movement: Giuseppe Mazzini, Camillo di Cavour, Giuseppe Garibaldi, or King Victor Emmanuel. Each student within the group should find a different source, and each group's sources should include both print and online sources. Sources should include visuals such as pictures of the leaders and maps. Have students look for reliable sources of information and get approval before continuing.
2. Have each group prepare a multimedia presentation on its assigned leader.
3. Have each group give its presentation to the class. **LS Interpersonal, Verbal-Linguistic**

Alternative Assessment Handbook, Rubrics 22: Multimedia Presentations; and 30: Research

Mazzini's Young Italy attracted tens of thousands of Italians to the cause of unification. Italians were ready to unite behind a strong nationalist leader.

READING CHECK **Define** What is nationalism?

The Path Toward Unity

As Italian nationalism grew, some Italians led unsuccessful rebellions. Then two men, Camillo di Cavour and Giuseppe Garibaldi, rose to lead a successful movement to unify Italy.

Uprisings and Revolutions Nationalist-inspired revolutions spread throughout Europe in 1848, and Italian nationalists led rebellions of their own. In some of the Italian states, citizens rebelled against Austrian rule. For example, the state of Piedmont declared war against Austria. That war lasted only a year and ended in Piedmont's defeat.

In 1849 other revolutionaries seized Rome and set up a republic that Mazzini and two others leaders governed. French troops, however, helped the pope gain control of Rome again.

The only successful revolt was in Sardinia. The rebellion there forced the rulers of Sardinia to grant a new constitution, and Sardinia remained independent.

Cavour and Sardinia The failures of the rebellions of 1848 and 1849 did not seriously weaken the nationalist movement. One of the most important leaders of the Italian unification movement, **Camillo di Cavour**, emerged at this time.

Before the rebellions Cavour had expressed his belief that the Italian nationalist movement was strong enough to unite Italy, despite differences among the many Italian states.

HISTORY'S VOICES

"Nationalism has become general; it grows daily; and it has already grown strong enough to keep all parts of Italy united despite the differences that distinguish them."

—Camillo di Cavour, 1846

Cavour founded a nationalist newspaper called *Il Risorgimento*, which means "resurgence" or "rebirth." The movement for Italian unification and freedom from Austrian control also became known as *Il Risorgimento*.

In 1852 Cavour became prime minister of the independent Kingdom of Sardinia. He believed that a thriving economy was important in order for the nation of Italy to be reborn. Therefore, he worked to build the Sardinian economy. He also believed that Italy should be reborn as a monarchy.

By this time, Cavour was in a position to cultivate a powerful ally. He supported France in a war with Russia and gave France the provinces of Savoy and Nice. France, in turn, agreed to support Sardinia in its planned war against Austria. The plan worked. By 1860 the northern Italian states were liberated from the control of the Austrian Empire.

READING CHECK **Identify Cause and Effect** How did Cavour help Sardinia break free from the Austrian Empire?

PRIMARY SOURCES

Mazzini's Young Italy

In 1831 the Italian writer Giuseppe Mazzini founded a nationalist movement called Young Italy. In just a few years, Young Italy had about 60,000 members. This excerpt is from Mazzini's instructions to new members of the movement:

> "Young Italy is a brotherhood of Italians who believe in Progress and Duty, and are convinced that Italy is destined to become one nation—convinced also that she possesses sufficient strength within herself to become one, and that the ill success of her former efforts is to be attributed not to the weakness, but to the misdirection of the revolutionary elements within her—that the secret of force lies in constancy and unity of effort. They join this association in the firm intent of consecrating both thought and action to the great aim of reconstituting Italy as one independent sovereign nation of free men and equals."

Skills Focus **READING LIKE A HISTORIAN**

1. **Interpret** Why do you think Mazzini links a united Italy with "Progress and Duty"?
2. **Analyze Primary Sources** From reading this excerpt, what can you learn about Mazzini's goal to unite Italy?

See **Skills Handbook**, p. H25

Direct Teach

Reading Focus

2 What role did Cavour and Sardinia play in the path toward Italian unification? *Cavour supported France in a war in return for France's support of Sardinia in its planned war against Austria.*

The Path Toward Unity

Identify What was *Il Risorgimento*? *a nationalist newspaper founded by Cavour as well as the name for the Italian movement for unification*

Identify Cause and Effect How did the revolutions of 1848 indirectly help Cavour? *Cavour was able to get support in Italy's fight against Austria; support for nationalism grew.*

Make Judgments If a nation is trying to unite, does it make sense to give some of its territory to another nation in exchange for support? Explain. *possible answer—No, it would be better to have the other nation's support without resorting to bribery, since a nation that would take a bribe of land from one group might also accept bribes from the opposition.*

Skills Focus: Comparing and Contrasting

At Level

Reading Skill
Cavour and Garibaldi

1. Have each student make a chart comparing and contrasting Camillo di Cavour and Giuseppe Garibaldi.
2. Review student charts as a class. Guide students in a discussion of the similarities and differences between the two leaders.
3. Have students explain how Italy's history might have been different if Cavour and Garibaldi had not been willing to cooperate. Have each student write a paragraph describing the possible outcome.
4. Have volunteers read their paragraphs to the class. **LS Visual-Spatial, Verbal-Linguistic**

Alternative Assessment Handbook, Rubrics 9: Comparing and Contrasting; and 40: Writing to Describe

Answers

Primary Sources 1. *possible answer—to inspire people to follow him;* **2.** *He hopes that people will dedicate themselves wholeheartedly to that goal.*

Reading Check (left) *devotion to one's national group*

Reading Check (right) *He cultivated an alliance with the French.*

Direct Teach

Reading Focus

3 How did Garibaldi and the Red Shirts help unite Italy? *Garibaldi led the Red Shirts to victory in Sicily and Naples; gained control of the southern Italian states, led to a united Italy*

Garibaldi and the Red Shirts

Identify Who was Giuseppe Garibaldi? *military commander, rose to lead a successful unification movement in Italy*

Contrast How did Garibaldi's approach to Italian unification differ from Cavour's approach? *Cavour worked through the political system in the north; Garibaldi led a military revolt in the south.*

Predict What do you think would have happened if Garibaldi had invaded the Papal States? *possible answer—It would have set the pope more firmly against unification, and might have alienated Catholics in other parts of Italy.*

Map Transparency: The Unification of Italy, 1858–1870

Garibaldi and the Red Shirts

Many Italians consider Cavour the "brain" of Italian unification and Mazzini its "heart." Equally important was **Giuseppe Garibaldi** (GAR-uh-BAWL-dee), whom many have called the "sword" of Italy.

Garibaldi joined Mazzini's Young Italy movement in 1833. Because of his nationalist activities, however, he was forced to flee from Italy twice. While living in exile in South America, he learned the techniques of guerrilla warfare. He then returned to Italy several times to continue the fight to free Italy from Austrian domination.

Garibaldi returned to Italy for good in 1854. Five years later, Cavour asked him to lead part of the Sardinian army in the war against Austria. Garibaldi accepted. After a few months of bitter fighting, the Austrians agreed to give up Lombardy, while keeping Venetia.

The Red Shirts Garibaldi and his followers, known as the **Red Shirts** because of their colorful uniforms, next turned their attentions to the Kingdom of the Two Sicilies. Using tactics of guerrilla warfare, Garibaldi and the Red Shirts gained control of the island of Sicily by July 1860. Then they crossed to the mainland. Meanwhile, Cavour had annexed territory in central Italy. In September, Sardinian troops helped Garibaldi conquer Naples. The Red Shirts now controlled the southern part of the Italian peninsula.

Unification Though he favored a republic, Garibaldi offered the Kingdom of the Two Sicilies to King **Victor Emmanuel** of Sardinia. The territories throughout Italy held elections in 1861, and all agreed to unification. The only holdouts were Venetia, which still belonged to Austria, and the Papal States, where French troops supported the pope.

GEOGRAPHY SKILLS INTERPRETING MAPS

1. **Movement** In what city did Garibaldi end his military campaign through Italy?
2. **Regions** Which territory did Italy gain from Austria in 1866?

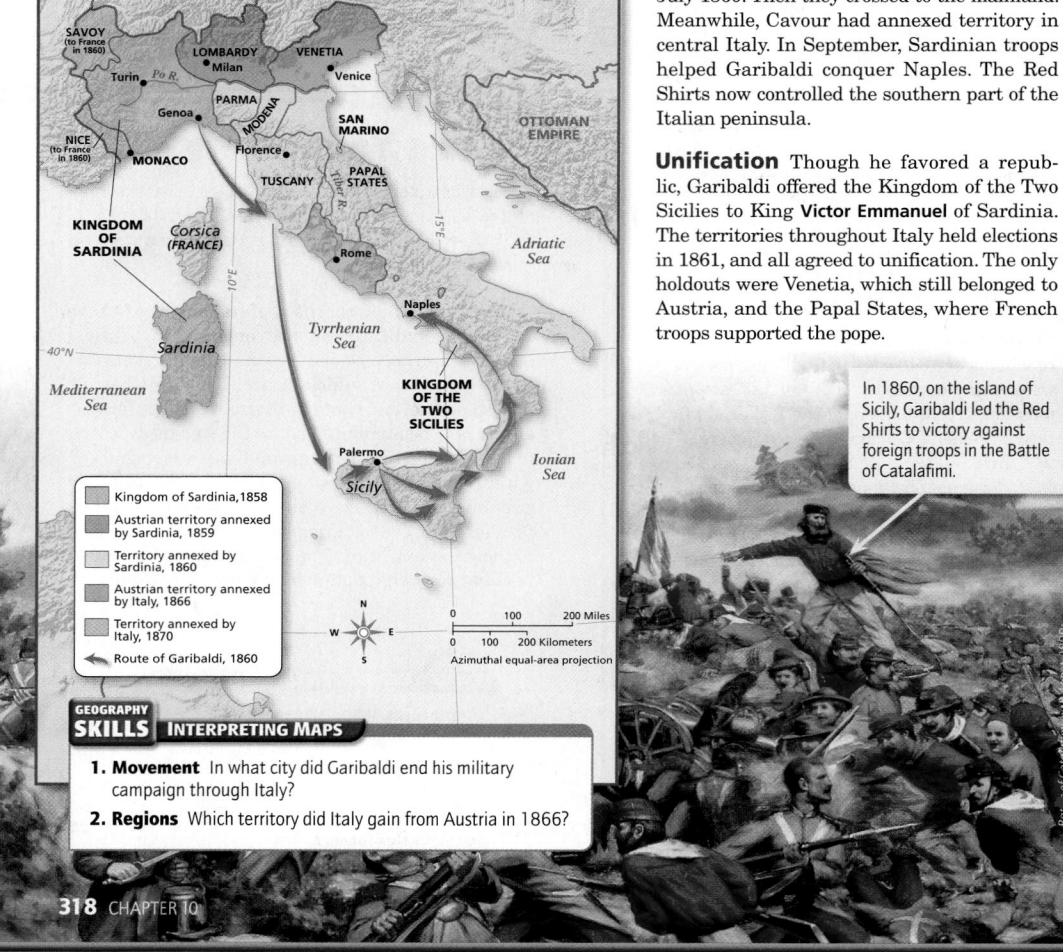

In 1860, on the island of Sicily, Garibaldi led the Red Shirts to victory against foreign troops in the Battle of Catalafimi.

Collaborative Learning

At Level

Unifying Italy

Background: With Camillo Cavour as prime minister, the Kingdom of Sardinia led the movement to unify Italy. Giuseppe Garibaldi united the Kingdom of the Two Sicilies with the Kingdom of Sardinia.

1. Organize students into two groups. Have one group represent people of the Kingdom of Sardinia supporting the unification. Have the other group represent people of the Kingdom of the Two Sicilies opposing unification. Give each side time to do research and prepare arguments in support of its position.
2. Conduct a classroom debate on Italian unification.
3. Guide students in a discussion of the debate. Which group was able to make the most convincing arguments for its position? What reasons did supporters of unification present? What reasons were opponents able to present?

LS Interpersonal, Verbal-Linguistic

Alternative Assessment Handbook, Rubrics 10: Debates; and 14: Group Activity

Answers

Interpreting Maps 1. *Naples;* **2.** *Venetia*

Those territories, however, did not hold out for long. In 1866 war broke out between Austria and Prussia. The Italians sided with the Prussians, and after Austria's defeat, Prussia gave Venetia to Italy. In 1870 war between France and Prussia forced the French to withdraw their troops from Rome. Italian troops entered Rome later that year, thus completing the unification of Italy under King Victor Emmanuel.

READING CHECK **Find the Main Idea** What actions led Garibaldi to be called the "sword" of Italian unification?

Challenges After Unification

In the years after unification, Italy faced many new challenges. Although politically unified, Italy had to deal with a number of social and economic problems. During the late 1800s, the new nation would take steps to catch up with the rest of Europe in industrialization, foreign policy, and social reform.

Social and Economic Problems

Although Italy was now politically united, strong regional differences still led to a lack of unity among many Italians. For example, some southern Italians resented being governed by Rome, which became the new capital of Italy in 1871. Meanwhile, the Catholic Church did not recognize Italy as a legitimate nation, and the pope prohibited Catholics from voting.

Widespread poverty was a serious problem. Unemployment and rising taxes often led to rioting in the towns, and violence was common. Poverty also led many Italians to emigrate. In the 1880s, large numbers of Italians began to leave Italy, many headed for the Americas. By 1920, some 4.5 million Italians had emigrated.

Reforms The Italian government soon began to address some of the problems facing the new nation. Voting reform was a major priority. At the time of unification, only the wealthiest Italian men could vote. By the late 1800s, most adult male taxpayers could vote.

As Italy industrialized, particularly in the north, the government passed reforms, including laws limiting working hours and prohibiting child labor. The government also encouraged the building of transportation and water systems to improve cities and encourage industry.

A New Foreign Policy In 1882 Italy formed a military alliance with Austria-Hungary and Germany. The three nations agreed to defend each other against any possible attack. This mutual arrangement was known as the Triple Alliance. As you will read in the next chapters, this alliance and others combined with political developments brought most of Europe to war in 1914.

Italy also tried to build an empire. It tried to gain control over Ethiopia, but failed after being defeated by a larger Ethiopian army in 1896. Then, in 1911, Italy declared war on the Ottoman empire. As a result, Italy gained territory in Africa.

READING CHECK **Summarize** What problems did Italy face after unification?

SECTION 1 ASSESSMENT

go.hrw.com
Online Quiz
Keyword: SHL NAT HP

Reviewing Ideas, Terms, and People

1. **a. Describe** What was Young Italy?
   b. Analyze Why did **Mazzini** think the territory lines set by the Congress of Vienna needed to be changed?
   c. Elaborate What effect did the Congress of Vienna have on the development of nationalism in Italy?
2. **a. Recall** Who was **Camillo di Cavour**?
   b. Interpret Why did Cavour form an alliance with France?
   c. Develop What role could a newspaper like *Il Risorgimento* play in the Italian unification movement?
3. **a. Identify** Who were the **Red Shirts**?
   b. Interpret Given that he favored a republic, why do you think Garibaldi handed over the southern states to **Victor Emmanuel**?
4. **a. Recall** Name two problems Italy faced after unification.
   b. Contrast How did social reform in Italy compare to reforms in Great Britain and France during the same period?

Critical Thinking

5. **Identify Cause and Effect** Use your notes from the section and a graphic organizer like this one to list causes and effects of Italian unification. Which effects were positive? Which were negative?

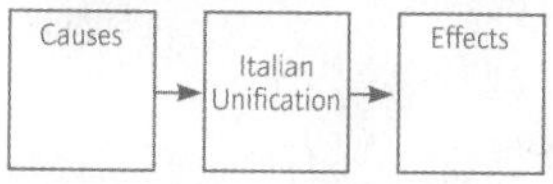

FOCUS ON WRITING

6. **Persuasion** Suppose you are Giuseppe Garibaldi. Write a letter to Camillo di Cavour, explaining why you believe a unified Italy would be better off as a republic than a monarchy.

Direct Teach

Reading Focus

4 What challenges did Italy face after unification? *regional differences; pope forbade Catholics from voting; social tensions; widespread poverty; only wealthy males could vote*

Challenges After Unification

Explain Why did 4.5 million Italians emigrate in the decades after unification? *to escape widespread poverty*

Analyze What can you tell about Italy from its foreign policy? *that it must have made peace with its old enemy, Austria-Hungary, by the time they joined in an alliance; was ready to try to acquire an overseas empire*

Review & Assess

Close

Guide students in a discussion of the causes and effects of Italy's unification movement.

Review

Online Quiz, Section 1

Assess

SE Section 1 Assessment

Progress Assessment: Section 1 Quiz

Alternative Assessment Handbook

Reteach/Intervene

Interactive Reader and Study Guide, Section 1

Interactive Skills Tutor CD-ROM

Section 1 Assessment Answers

1. **a.** a nationalist group
   b. He believed that people of the same background needed to form separate nation-states.
   c. possible answer—encouraged the development of nationalism by drawing political boundaries that ignored national groups
2. **a.** a leader of the Italian unification movement
   b. He wanted France's support in Italy's fight against Austria.
   c. might spread the message of nationalism
3. **a.** volunteer troops led by Garibaldi
   b. possible answer—for the sake of Italian unity
4. **a.** regional differences, poverty
   b. possible answers—There was still a lack of unity in Italy; Italy needed strong allies.
5. Causes—dissatisfaction with Congress of Vienna, nationalism, international politics; Effects—regional political differences (negative), industrialization (positive), voting reforms (positive), widespread poverty and mass emigration (negative)
6. Student letters should show an understanding of the characteristics of republics and monarchies.

Answers

Reading Check (left) *He used guerilla tactics to gain control of the southern Italian states.* **(right)** *Regional differences kept the nation from being truly united; pope did not recognize Italy as a legitimate nation; widespread poverty caused many Italians to emigrate.*

Preteach

Getting Started

Use the **Interactive Reader and Study Guide** to familiarize students with the section content.

Interactive Reader and Study Guide, Section 2

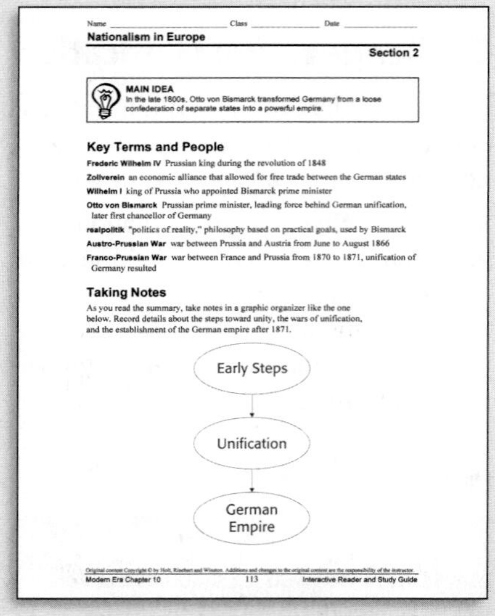
Name ______________ Class __________ Date __________

Nationalism in Europe

Section 2

MAIN IDEA
In the late 1800s, Otto von Bismarck transformed Germany from a loose confederation of separate states into a powerful empire.

Key Terms and People

Frederic Wilhelm IV Prussian king during the revolution of 1848

Zollverein an economic alliance that allowed for free trade between the German states

Wilhelm I king of Prussia who appointed Bismarck prime minister

Otto von Bismarck Prussian prime minister, leading force behind German unification, later first chancellor of Germany

realpolitik "politics of reality," philosophy based on practical goals, used by Bismarck

Austro-Prussian War war between Prussia and Austria from June to August 1866

Franco-Prussian War war between France and Prussia from 1870 to 1871, unification of Germany resulted

Taking Notes

As you read the summary, take notes in a graphic organizer like the one below. Record details about the steps toward unity, the wars of unification, and the establishment of the German empire after 1871.

Early Steps → Unification → German Empire

Original content Copyright © by Holt, Rinehart and Winston. Additions and changes to the original content are the responsibility of the instructor.

Modern Era Chapter 10 113 Interactive Reader and Study Guide

CRF: Vocabulary Builder: Section 2

Taking Notes

Early Steps—German Confederation; revolutions of 1848; creation of Zollverein; Bismarck's wars with Denmark and Austria;

Unification—Austro-Prussian War joined together north German states; Franco-Prussian War united southern German states with the north;

German Empire—created a federalist government of 25 separate states with Wilhelm I as head of the government; Bismarck worked to limit the power of the Catholic Church in Germany; joined in alliances with Austria-Hungary, Italy, and Russia

SECTION 2

German Unification

Before You Read

MAIN IDEA

In the late 1800s, Otto von Bismarck transformed Germany from a loose confederation of separate states into a powerful empire.

READING FOCUS

1. What steps did Germany take toward unification?
2. What was Bismarck's plan for Germany and how did he hope to achieve it?
3. How did wars lead to the unification of a German Empire?
4. In what ways did Germany grow and change after unification?

KEY TERMS AND PEOPLE

Frederick Wilhelm IV
Zollverein
Otto von Bismarck
Wilhelm I
realpolitik
Austro-Prussian War
Franco-Prussian War

TAKING NOTES Take notes on the steps toward unity, the wars of unification, and the establishment of the German Empire after 1871.

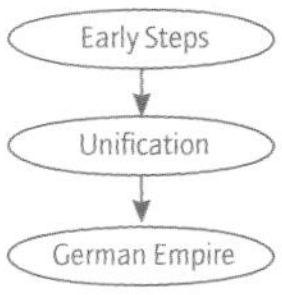

THE INSIDE STORY ***How did a revolution help lead to the unification of Germany?*** In 1848 revolution spread through Europe. At this time, German liberals also revolted. When the people of Berlin heard that Metternich had been ousted in Vienna, they encircled the royal palace to hear the response of the Prussian king, Frederick Wilhelm IV. The crowd erupted when edgy soldiers accidently fired two shots. They felt tricked that a peaceful celebration had turned into a confrontation. To fight the royal soldiers, the Berliners set up wooden barricades, which forced the soldiers to retreat. Hundreds died in the two days of fighting.

Soon after the revolt, the king gave in to nationalist demands and proclaimed, "From now on Prussia merges with Germany!" However, the king quickly reasserted his power. Even though the revolution failed, German unification would eventually be accomplished with new policies enacted by a king and his powerful chancellor. ■

BARRICADES IN BERLIN

In 1848 Berliners fight Prussian troops in the city's streets.

Lithograph of the barricades at Alexanderplatz, Berlin during the night of March 18-19, 1848, c. 1848

Teach the Main Idea

At Level

German Unification

1. **Teach** Ask students the Reading Focus questions to teach this section.
2. **Apply** Tell students that in the mid-1800s Germany was divided into numerous independent states. Have students work in pairs to make lists of reasons for and against unification.
3. **Review** Review student lists as a class. Guide students in a discussion of the ways in which both liberal nationalists and conservative rulers seemed to get what they wanted.
4. **Practice/Homework** Have students write a paragraph predicting how German unification will unfold, using what they have read about Italian unification to form their predictions. Remind students that the two nations might not necessarily have unified in the same manner. **LS Interpersonal, Verbal-Linguistic**

Alternative Assessment Handbook, Rubrics 11: Discussions; and 43: Writing to Persuade

Steps Toward Unification

Like Italy, Germany was not a unified nation in 1848. However, the patchwork of independent German states did have a common language and culture. In addition, Napoleon had nurtured nationalism when he united the German states into a confederation. Following Napoleon's defeat in 1815, the leaders at the Congress of Vienna retained that organization but renamed it the German Confederation. Thus, a group of 39 separate states with a common language and culture was poised for the movement to unite.

Revolution in Prussia As revolution swept through Europe in 1848, German liberals in the state of Prussia also took the opportunity to revolt. Though liberals differed over whether to support a republic or a constitutional monarchy, they agreed that German unity would promote individual rights and liberal reforms.

Facing calls for increased democracy, Prussian king **Frederick Wilhelm IV** quickly promised a constitution and other reforms. These changes did not become reality, however. By the end of 1848, the king went back on many of his promises. "Now I can be honest again," he told one of his ambassadors. He banned publications and organizations that supported democracy, and the constitution was never written.

Economic and Cultural Unity Another early step toward creating a unified Germany was an economic alliance between some of the German states. Created in 1834, the **Zollverein**, (TSOHL-fer-yn) or customs union, allowed for the removal of tariffs, or taxes, on products traded between the German states. The Zollverein inspired businesspeople to support unification and encouraged the growth of railroads connecting the German states. It also helped join Germans economically, if not yet politically, to each other. By 1844 the Zollverein included almost all of the German states.

As the German economy was growing, the sense of a distinctly German culture was growing. For example, German composers such as Richard Wagner wrote music glorifying German myths and traditions.

READING CHECK **Identify** What was the outcome of the revolution of 1848 in Prussia?

Steps to Unification in Germany (QUICK FACTS)

In the mid-1800s many Germans were driven by nationalistic feelings to support a unified Germany.

The Revolution of 1848
- Inspired by revolution in France and a desire for a united Germany, Germans revolt against the Prussian king.

The Promise of Reforms
- At first, the Prussian king Frederick Wilhelm IV agrees to bring about democratic reforms, but later breaks his promises.

The Zollverein
- Germans create an economic alliance between the German states, the Zollverein, which promotes trade and a strong economy.

German Unification
- Otto von Bismarck leads Germany towards unification using his political philosophy of realpolitik, or "the politics of reality."

Bismarck's Plan for Germany

Otto von Bismarck, a conservative and a politician, was the leading force behind German unification. He became prominent in Prussian politics in 1847 when he gave a strongly conservative speech at the National Assembly. In 1862 **Wilhelm I**, the new Prussian king, chose Bismarck as Prussia's prime minister.

Bismarck's Philosophy Bismarck was not a liberal like the people involved in the revolution. Instead, he was a conservative who supported the king of Prussia and believed that it was Prussia's destiny to lead the German people to unification. Bismarck's philosophy about government was practical rather than idealistic. Practicing what would later be known as **realpolitik** (ray-AHL-poh-luh-TEEK), he developed policies based on the interests of Prussia.

"Blood and Iron" Bismarck's politics of reality were soon made evident in his push to increase the power of the Prussian military. In a speech to the Prussian parliament, he argued that German unity would not be won by speeches and majority vote but by "blood and iron." When the liberal parliament would not approve funds to expand the military, he dismissed the assembly and collected the taxes anyway. He then built the Prussian army into a great war machine, one that could use force to unite Germany.

Direct Teach

Reading Focus

1 What steps did Germany take toward unification? *German Confederation formed by Congress of Vienna; German revolt, Prussian king promises reform, but breaks promises, Zollverein allowed for free trade among German states*

Steps Toward Unification

Identify What was the German Confederation? *a group of 39 separate states, including Austria and Prussia, set up by the Congress of Vienna*

Analyze What did Frederick Wilhelm IV mean when he said "Now I can be honest again"? *that he did not have to pretend to support a republic*

Elaborate How would free trade help in the development of railroads? *would encourage trade, which would increase the need for transporting goods*

Quick Facts Transparency: Steps to Unification in Germany

Reading Focus

2 What was Bismarck's plan for Germany and how did he hope to achieve it? *to lead the German people to unification by increasing the power of the Prussian military.*

Bismarck's Plan for Germany

Define What was realpolitik? *Bismarck's "politics of reality," a belief in practical goals instead of theory*

Contrast How did Bismarck's beliefs differ from those of the German revolutionaries? *did not believe in liberal democracy; was a conservative who supported the king*

Differentiating Instruction

At Level

English-Language Learners

1. Copy the chart for students to see. Omit the italicized answers. Have students work in pairs to complete the chart.
2. Review student charts as a class, filling in the master chart as you go. Guide students in a discussion of German unification.

LS Interpersonal, Visual-Spatial

Alternative Assessment Handbook, Rubrics 7: Charts; and 11: Discussions

State that led unification	Prussia
Land acquired in unification process	*Schleswig, Holstein, north German states, south German states, Alsace, Lorraine*
Major factors leading to unification	*German nationalism* *Zollverein* *Realpolitik* *Military alliances* *Bismarck's Prussian army*

Answers

Reading Check *failed to bring democratic reform to Prussia*

Direct Teach

Reading Focus

3 How did wars lead to the unification of a German Empire? *Austro-Prussian War joined northern German states; Franco-Prussian War declared unification of all German states*

Unification and Empire

Recall What were the results of the Austro-Prussian War? *dissolved German Confederation; forced Austria to give territory to Prussia; joined together the north German states*

Identify Cause and Effect What caused the south German states to join together with the north German states in the Franco-Prussian War? *feelings of nationalism over Alsace and Lorraine*

Make a Judgment Why do you think that Wilhelm I chose to be proclaimed emperor of Germany at Versailles? *possible answer—to get revenge against France; Versailles associated with French kings*

Bismarck's First War A disagreement over two border states, called Schleswig and Holstein, eventually gave Bismarck a way to start a war with Denmark. In 1864 Bismarck formed a military alliance with Austria against Denmark, believing both Schleswig and Holstein should be controlled by the German Confederation. After a brief fight, Denmark gave the territory to Austria and Prussia. Prussia would control Schleswig, and Austria would control Holstein. However, this meant that Austria now held a small bit of territory inside Prussia's borders. Bismarck knew that if he were to unite Germany, war with Austria was inevitable.

READING SKILLS
Understanding Word Origins If you know that the term *confederate* comes from the Latin word *confoederare* meaning "to unite by a league," how would you define confederation?

READING CHECK **Describe** What was the plan of Bismarck to unite Germany?

Unification and Empire

Bismarck could not increase Prussia's power as long as Austria was in the way. Austria was a leader in the German Confederation and it had influence over some of the German states that opposed Prussia's leadership. With two short wars, Bismarck moved Austria out of the way and established a unified German Empire.

The Austro-Prussian War To prepare for the war with Austria that he knew he had to wage and win, Bismarck worked behind the scenes. He met with the Italian prime minister and promised that, in exchange for support against Austria, Italy could have the territory of Venetia. He also persuaded Napoleon III to keep France neutral if war broke out between the German states. Then, to provoke Austria, Bismarck sent Prussian troops into the Austrian state of Holstein. In response, Austria declared war against Prussia.

The skirmish in Holstein was just what the Prussian leaders needed to gain support for the war with Austria. In an address to the Prussian people, king Wilhelm I blamed Austria for starting the war. His address clearly appealed to the people's sense of nationalism.

The war between Prussia and Austria unfolded just as the king and Bismarck planned. The highly skilled and well-equipped Prussian army defeated the Austrians in only seven weeks. The treaty ending the **Austro-Prussian War** dissolved the German Confederation and forced Austria to surrender the state of Holstein. When several other states in the North united with Prussia, only three states in the South remained outside Prussian control.

Together, Bismarck and Wilhelm used the victory to rally other German states around Prussia. The German Confederation, which had joined Austria to Prussia, had been destroyed by the war. By joining together the North German states, the Austro-Prussian War was the first step toward German unification.

The Franco-Prussian War Despite the victory in the Austro-Prussian War, it would take another war to create a unified Germany. The southern German states were still not included in the North German Confederation.

In 1870 a conflict was brewing with France over the disputed territory of Alsace and Lorraine. These provinces had been a part of the Holy Roman Empire, which included Prussia. The issue over Alsace and Lorraine sparked feelings of nationalism in the south German states. As a result, these states supported Prussia and the north German states in a war against France. In 1871 with the southern German states' help, Bismarck secured a Prussian victory in the **Franco-Prussian War**. Prussia won the war, and the peace treaty declared the unification of Germany.

Creating the German Empire The peace treaty following the Franco-Prussian War had far-reaching consequences. For example, the victory established a unified German empire.

FACES OF HISTORY

Otto von BISMARCK
1815–1898

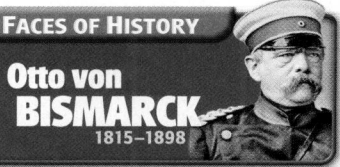

The revolutions of the mid-1800s gave Otto von Bismarck his first taste of power. In 1847, Bismarck gave a strongly conservative speech to the German National Assembly. He soon became the leader of the conservative politicians who supported the king and opposed the liberal revolution of 1848.

In 1862 Wilhelm I, the new Prussian king, appointed Bismarck as head of the Prussian cabinet. Bismarck believed it was Prussia's destiny to lead the German people to unification. Bismarck is perhaps best known for his build up of the Prussian army into a great war machine. With this army, Bismarck forcibly united the German states.

Draw Conclusions How did Bismarck's beliefs affect Germany?

Skills Focus: Comparing and Contrasting

At Level

Reading Skill

Roads to Unification

1. Have students work in pairs to create charts that compare and contrast unification in Germany and Italy. Student charts should show the causes of unification in each nation, which state led the unification process, leaders of the unification processes, the methods they used to bring unification about, who ruled the unified nations, and the after-effects of unification.
2. Review student charts as a class. Guide students in a discussion of the similarities and differences between unification in Germany and Italy. **LS Interpersonal, Visual-Spatial**

Alternative Assessment Handbook, Rubrics 7: Charts; and 9: Comparing and Contrasting

Answers

Faces of History *believed government policies should be based on realistic interest, not idealism; led to unification*

Reading Skills *a league of united states*

Reading Check *increase the Prussian military, go to war with Austria*

GEOGRAPHY SKILLS INTERPRETING MAPS

1. **Movement** From which German states did the Prussian armies begin their march during the Austro-Prussian War?
2. **Regions** When did the region of southern Germany join the German Empire?

Representatives of the allied German states met at Versailles, near Paris. The representatives proclaimed Wilhelm I the first kaiser, or emperor, of the German Empire. Wilhelm then appointed Bismarck as his first chancellor. The German victory also significantly changed the balance of power in Europe. With Napoleon III gone, France was no longer as powerful. As Germany grew economically, a new empire rose in power.

READING CHECK **Sequence** How did the Austro-Prussian and the Franco-Prussian War lead to German unification?

The Empire's Growth and Change

In the years after 1871, Germany prospered. Under the leadership of Wilhelm I and Bismarck, Germany developed into a strong empire. This period was known as the Second Reich, or empire, because Germans considered the Holy Roman Empire to be the First Reich.

A New Government Germany's 25 separate states wanted to retain some power. As a result, the government of the new German empire took a federalist form. Similar to the United States government, power was shared between state and national governments. Wilhelm I led the government. According to the law, all men in Germany over the age of 25 could vote. But in reality the government placed many restrictions on voters. Political parties also developed.

The Government and the Church Bismarck also believed that the Roman Catholic Church posed a threat to his government. He believed the government and not the church should control aspects of culture such as education. Bismarck worked to pass laws limiting the influence of the Catholic Church in Germany. This struggle between the government and the church was known as Kulturkampf, which in German means "the struggle for culture."

Economic Growth After unification Germany experienced a time of economic growth.

Direct Teach

Reading Focus

4 In what ways did Germany grow and change after unification? *vote was given to all men over 25; political parties developed; economic growth as Germany caught up with other European industrial economies; new alliances with other nations; Kulturkampf limited influence of Catholic Church*

The Empire's Growth and Change

Define What are reparations? *money paid for damages*

Make Inferences Why do you think that the new German Empire took a federalist form and allowed all men over the age of 25 to vote? *possible answer—It was probably a concession to the states that had voluntarily banded together with Prussia to form the empire.*

Evaluate Why do you think that Bismarck did not want Austria to be part of the German Empire? *possible answer—Austria already had an empire of its own, and he probably feared that Prussia would be in constant conflict with Austria if the two nations were joined.*

Map Transparency: The Unification of Germany, 1865–1871

Skills Focus: Making Inferences

At Level

Reading Skill

Bismarck and the King

Background: Tell students that the term *Machiavellian* is an adjective that can be summarized by the statement, "The end justifies the means."

1. Have students look for images of Otto von Bismarck and Wilhelm I. You might wish to refer students to the chapter opener. Have students use information from this chapter to draw political cartoons either supporting or opposing the policies of Bismarck and Wilhelm I.
2. Display student cartoons for the class to see.
3. After students have had a chance to view all the cartoons, guide the class in a discussion of Bismarck's and Wilhelm's policies and the contributions they made to uniting Germany. Which of their policies were Machiavellian?
LS Visual-Spatial

Alternative Assessment Handbook, Rubrics 11: Discussions; and 27: Political Cartoons

Answers

Interpreting Maps 1. *Saxony and Silesia;* **2.** *1871*

Reading Check *The Austro-Prussian War joined together the north German states. After Prussia won the Franco-Prussian War, the peace treaty declared the unification of Germany.*

Review & Assess

Close

Guide students in a discussion of the causes of Germany's unification movement.

Review

go.hrw.com **Online Quiz**, Section 2

Assess

SE Section 2 Assessment

Progress Assessment: Section 2 Quiz

Alternative Assessment Handbook

Reteach/Intervene

Interactive Reader and Study Guide, Section 2

Interactive Skills Tutor CD-ROM

Answers

Interpreting Graphs *created economic growth and general prosperity; improved infrastructure; caused Germany to experience some of the same problems of other industrialized European nations*

Reading Check *vote was given to all men over 25, political parties developed, economic growth as Germany caught up with other European industrial economies, new alliances with other nations, Kulturkampf limited influence of Catholic Church*

QUICK FACTS

GERMANY'S ECONOMIC GROWTH, 1890–1913

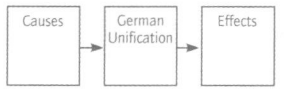

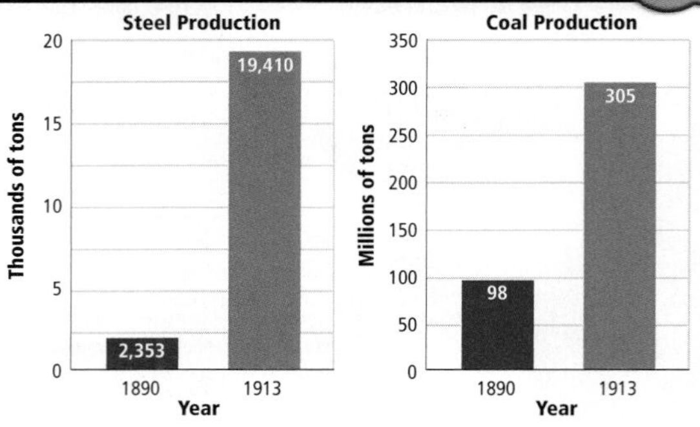

Source: *Oxford Atlas of World History*

Skills FOCUS INTERPRETING GRAPHS

Infer How do you think the growth in steel and coal production between 1890 and 1913 affected life in Germany?

France had paid reparations, or money for damages, to Germany after the Franco-Prussian War. German leaders used some of the money to build railroads to link the German states. Other funds helped build German businesses. Over the next half century, the new empire quickly caught up with the other industrial countries of Europe. Coal mines and steel factories flourished in Germany's major cities.

The Path to Social Reforms As in other nations, industrialization had its critics in Germany. German socialists protested against harsh factory conditions and called for state control of all industries. In the late 1870s Bismarck blamed socialists for two assassination attempts made on the emperor.

Even as Bismarck tried to destroy socialism, he also sought to reduce its appeal among the German people by enacting his own reforms. Beginning in the early 1880s, Bismarck pushed through legislation that provided benefits for health, accidents, old age, and disability.

Bismarck and the Wilhelm II After unification, Bismarck did not want to expand Germany's borders any further. He did, however, believe that France remained a threat. To counteract that threat, he entered a number of alliances with other European nations, including Austria-Hungary, Italy, and Russia. These nations agreed to help protect one another from a possible attack.

In 1888 Wilhelm I's grandson became kaiser of Germany. After a disagreement, the new kaiser, Wilhelm II, fired Bismarck as prime minister. In the early 1900s, the Wilhelm II continued to make alliances with other European nations and build up the most powerful military forces in Europe.

READING CHECK **Describe** How did Germany change both economically and politically in the years following unification?

SECTION 2 ASSESSMENT

go.hrw.com **Online Quiz** Keyword: SHL NAT HP

Reviewing Ideas, Terms, and People

1. **a. Define** What was the **Zollverein**?
   b. Explain What did German liberals in Prussia want?
2. **a. Identify** Who was **Otto von Bismarck**?
   b. Explain Why were the states of Schleswig and Holstein significant?
   c. Evaluate In your opinion, what are the pros and cons of the policy of **realpolitik**? List two pros and two cons.
3. **a. Identify** What was the North German Confederation?
   b. Explain How did the **Franco-Prussian War** affect German unification?
4. **a. Identify** What was the structure of government in the new German Empire?
   b. Summarize How did Bismarck struggle with the church?
   c. Elaborate Why do you think Germany's economy grew so quickly in the years after unification?

Critical Thinking

5. **Identify Cause and Effect** Use your notes from this section and a graphic organizer like the one below to list causes and effects of German unification.

Causes	→	German Unification	→	Effects

FOCUS ON SPEAKING

6. **Exposition** Imagine you are a reporter and are about to interview Otto von Bismarck. Write three short questions you will ask him about German unification.

Section 2 Assessment Answers

1. **a.** an economic alliance between the German states
   b. individual rights and liberal reforms
2. **a.** prime minister of Prussia; largely responsible for uniting Germany
   b. border states between the German Confederation and Denmark; disagreement over these states gave Bismarck an excuse to start a war with Denmark
   c. possible answer—Pros: a realistic approach, would result in a unified German nation; Cons: involved using force to get what Prussia wanted; students may infer that it was not a democratic policy
3. **a.** northern German states that fought for German unification
   b. joined south German states to the north German states, treaty ending the war unified Germany
4. **a.** a federation of 25 separate states
   b. He believed the Catholic Church posed a threat to his government; he passed laws limiting the Church's influence.
   c. France had paid reparations, putting money into the German economy; Germany industrialized
5. Causes—revolutions of 1848; promise of reforms; Zollverein; Bismarck's policies of realpolitik; wars; Effects—federalist government of 25 separate states with Wilhelm I as head of government; economic growth and industrialization; certain reforms
6. Student questions might focus on Bismarck's policies of realpolitik, his reasons for war, and his vision for the German Empire.

SECTION 3

Austria-Hungary and the Ottoman Empire

Before You Read

Main Idea

Nationalism broke down two old European empires—the Austrian Hapsburg Empire and the Ottoman Empire.

Reading Focus

1. In what ways did the Austrian Empire struggle with nationalism in 1848 and beyond?
2. What was the dual monarchy of Austria-Hungary, and why was it created?
3. How did nationalism create conflict in the Ottoman Empire?

Key Terms and People

Franz Joseph I
Magyars
Dual Monarchy
Crimean War
Balkan Wars
Young Turks

TAKING NOTES Take notes about nationalism in Austria, Hungary, and the Ottoman Empire.

Nationalism	
Austria	
Hungary	
Ottoman Empire	

THE INSIDE STORY ***How did a British woman revolutionize the field of nursing?*** The Crimean War, fought in the 1850s between Russia on one side and Great Britain, France, the Ottoman Empire, and Sardinia on the other, has been called "the most unnecessary war in history." Fierce battles took a heavy toll on soldiers. In addition, conditions in the crowded and filthy field hospitals caused diseases to spread. Florence Nightingale, a British nurse, described one hospital by stating, "Civilians have little idea, from reading the newspapers, of the horror and misery in a military hospital of operating upon these dying exhausted men . . . We have now 4 miles of beds and not 18 inches apart."

When she arrived at the war hospitals in 1854, Nightingale immediately took charge. She had the hospital wards cleaned to control the spread of disease. She obtained food, eating utensils, clothes, and bedding for wounded soldiers. These supplies, and the care given by the nurses, helped improve morale and reduce the mortality rate.

After the war, Nightingale helped set up training programs for nurses and worked to reform British military hospitals. She received the British Order of Merit for her dedication to nursing. ■

A Nurse's Care Saves Lives

▲ Florence Nightingale and other nurses tend to patients during the Crimean War.

Florence Nightingale at Scutari, Crimean War

Teach the Main Idea

At Level

Austria-Hungary and the Ottoman Empire

1. **Teach** Ask students the Reading Focus questions to teach this section.
2. **Apply** Have students create an outline of the section using the heads as main points. Have students identify at least two main ideas under each of the red subheadings.
3. **Review** Review student outlines as a class. Have students identify the points in their outlines that they feel are most important or most interesting. Guide students in a discussion comparing the problems of the Austrian and Ottoman empires.
4. **Practice/Homework** Tell students that it is 1867 and Franz Josef has asked them to write a speech for him to explain how the Dual Monarchy will work and how it will benefit the people of Austria, Hungary, and the Austro-Hungarian Empire. Have students present their speeches. LS **Visual-Spatial, Verbal-Linguistic**

Alternative Assessment Handbook, Rubrics 13: Graphic Organizers; and 43: Writing to Persuade

Preteach

Getting Started

Use the **Interactive Reader and Study Guide** to familiarize students with the section content.

Interactive Reader and Study Guide, Section 3

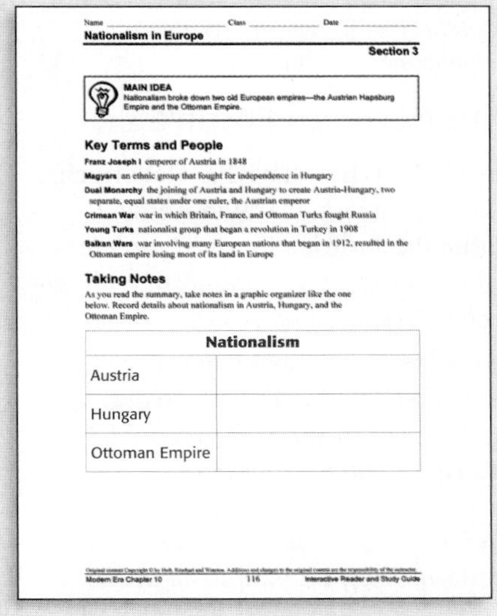

Name ________ Class ________ Date ________

Nationalism in Europe

Section 3

MAIN IDEA
Nationalism broke down two old European empires—the Austrian Hapsburg Empire and the Ottoman Empire.

Key Terms and People

Franz Joseph I emperor of Austria in 1848
Magyars an ethnic group that fought for independence in Hungary
Dual Monarchy the joining of Austria and Hungary to create Austria-Hungary, two separate, equal states under one ruler, the Austrian emperor
Crimean War war in which Britain, France, and Ottoman Turks fought Russia
Young Turks nationalist group that began a revolution in Turkey in 1908
Balkan Wars war involving many European nations that began in 1912, resulted in the Ottoman empire losing most of its land in Europe

Taking Notes

As you read the summary, take notes in a graphic organizer like the one below. Record details about nationalism in Austria, Hungary, and the Ottoman Empire.

Nationalism	
Austria	
Hungary	
Ottoman Empire	

Modern Era Chapter 10 116 Interactive Reader and Study Guide

CRF: Vocabulary Builder: Section 3

Taking Notes

Austria—against nationalist activities; Congress of Troppau attempted to unite European nations against nationalist revolutions; resignation of Metternich and the Austrian emperor;

Hungary—1848 revolution stopped by Austria; Dual Monarchy created in 1867, making Austria and Hungary two separate and equal states under one ruler; ethnic groups remained divided

Ottoman Empire—nationalist groups began revolutions in the Balkans, war cost Ottoman Empire most of its land in Europe; Young Turks began revolution in 1908, leading to more representative and liberal government

Direct Teach

Reading Focus

1 In what ways did the Austrian Empire struggle with nationalism in 1848 and beyond? *rebellions in Vienna led to resignations by Metternich and Ferdinand, empire unstable, continued rebellion; despite efforts, naturalist movement continued to grow*

The Austrian Empire

Identify What steps did Metternich take to confront liberal movements within the Austrian Empire? *prohibited reforms conflicting with absolute monarchy; formed alliances*

Analyze How was Metternich able to maintain control over Europe during the first half of the 19th century? *The Austrian Empire was one of the strongest and largest in Europe, and as leader of the German Confederation Metternich kept nationalism in check.*

Reading Focus

2 What was the Dual Monarchy of Austria-Hungary, and why was it created? *agreement that made Austria and Hungary two separate, equal states under one ruler, Austrian emperor and Hungarian nationalist leaders created Dual Monarchy as compromise*

The Dual Monarchy

Recall What were the economic advantages of the Dual Monarchy? *Hungary could provide raw materials to Austria; Austria could provide industrial products to Hungary.*

Evaluate Was the Dual Monarchy successful? Explain. *possible answer—yes: there were economic and political advantages.*

The Austrian Empire

The Hapsburg family, rulers of the Austrian Empire at the beginning of the 1800s, had controlled much of the region for nearly four centuries. When the Congress of Vienna met after the fall of Napoleon, Prince Metternich of Austria was a powerful voice in determining how to restore the balance of power in Europe. Nevertheless, this powerful empire would not remain intact through the remainder of the 1800s.

Resistance to Change After the Congress of Vienna, the Austrian emperor, Franz I, and his foreign minister, Prince Metternich, worked together to maintain the power of the Austrian Empire and the Hapsburg monarchy. They were determined to hold onto the empire and resist liberal ideas and movements that might endanger it.

As revolts spread through other parts of Europe, Metternich clamped down on the universities, accusing them of creating "a whole generation of revolutionaries." As leader of the German Confederation, he called a meeting at Carlsbad and helped pass the Carlsbad Decrees. These decrees, or laws, prohibited any reforms that conflicted with absolute monarchy. In addition, the decrees established censorship of newspapers and created a secret police force that spied on students who were suspected of liberal or nationalist revolutionary activities.

In addition to creating these restrictive laws for the empire, Metternich formed alliances with other European powers that were trying to prevent nationalist revolutions. In 1820 he and the leaders of these powers convened a meeting called the Congress of Troppau. At that Congress, the leaders agreed to provide military intervention to support governments against internal revolution.

Turmoil in Europe and Austria Metternich was able to protect the power of the Austrian Empire for a few years. But events in Europe and changes within the empire itself eventually caught up with him.

Revolutions in France, Italy, and the German states set off revolts in the Austrian Empire. People of many different nationalities living within the Austrian Empire wanted independence. In Vienna, demonstrators and the army clashed in the streets. A frightened emperor Ferdinand ordered Metternich to resign, and Metternich fled Austria. Later in 1848 Ferdinand abdicated, and the throne went to his young nephew, **Franz Joseph I**.

Response to Revolution During his long reign, Franz Joseph I ruled over an unstable empire. In 1848 the Hungarian **Magyars** rebelled against Austrian rule, and for a long time it looked as though they would win their independence. However, czar Nicholas I of Russia sent Russian troops to help Austria crush the revolt. Franz Joseph I then abolished the liberal reforms enacted in 1848, but he could not stamp out nationalism in his multiethnic empire. Franz Joseph I revoked the new constitution. The revolutions had been stopped, at least for a while.

READING CHECK **Find the Main Idea** What was the purpose of the Congress of Troppau?

The Dual Monarchy

Although Franz Joseph I abolished the liberal reforms of 1848 and restored the power of the monarchy, he could not stop the nationalist movement. Change had to come to the Austrian Empire. It came in the form of the **Dual Monarchy**, also known as Austria-Hungary.

Forming a New Government As the nationalist movement continued in Europe, Austria lost the province of Lombardy to Italy in 1859. In 1866 Austria's defeat in the war with Prussia brought new demands from the Hungarians. Finally, Franz Josef I and leaders of the Hungarian nationalist movement reached an agreement. Known as the Compromise of 1867, this agreement created the dual monarchy of Austria-Hungary.

Under the dual monarchy, Austria and Hungary became two separate, equal states. They would have one ruler, Franz Joseph I, whose title would be emperor of Austria and king of Hungary. Austria and Hungary shared the ministries of war, finance, and foreign affairs, but each had its own parliament.

An Uneven Solution The Dual Monarchy lasted for about 50 years, until 1918. In addition to easing some of the pressure for nationalism, the Dual Monarchy had other benefits.

Collaborative Learning

At Above

The Congress of Troppau

Research Required

Background: The Congress of Troppau was convened to decide what action to take in response to liberal uprisings across Europe.

1. Organize students into five groups. Assign each group one of the nations that met at the Congress of Troppau: Austria, Prussia, Russia, Great Britain, and France. Tell each group that it is the delegation from its country to the Congress of Troppau. Have each group research its country's position toward repressing nationalist revolutions.
2. Tell students that the Congress of Troppau is called to order. Act as moderator as each group presents its case either for or against suppressing revolutions.
3. Guide students in a discussion of the results of the Congress of Troppau. Why did Austria, Prussia, and Russia vote to suppress nationalist revolutions? Why did France and Great Britain refuse to go along with them? **LS Interpersonal**

Alternative Assessment Handbook, Rubrics 11: Discussions; and 14: Group Activity

Answers

Reading Check *to unite European powers in trying to prevent nationalist revolutions*

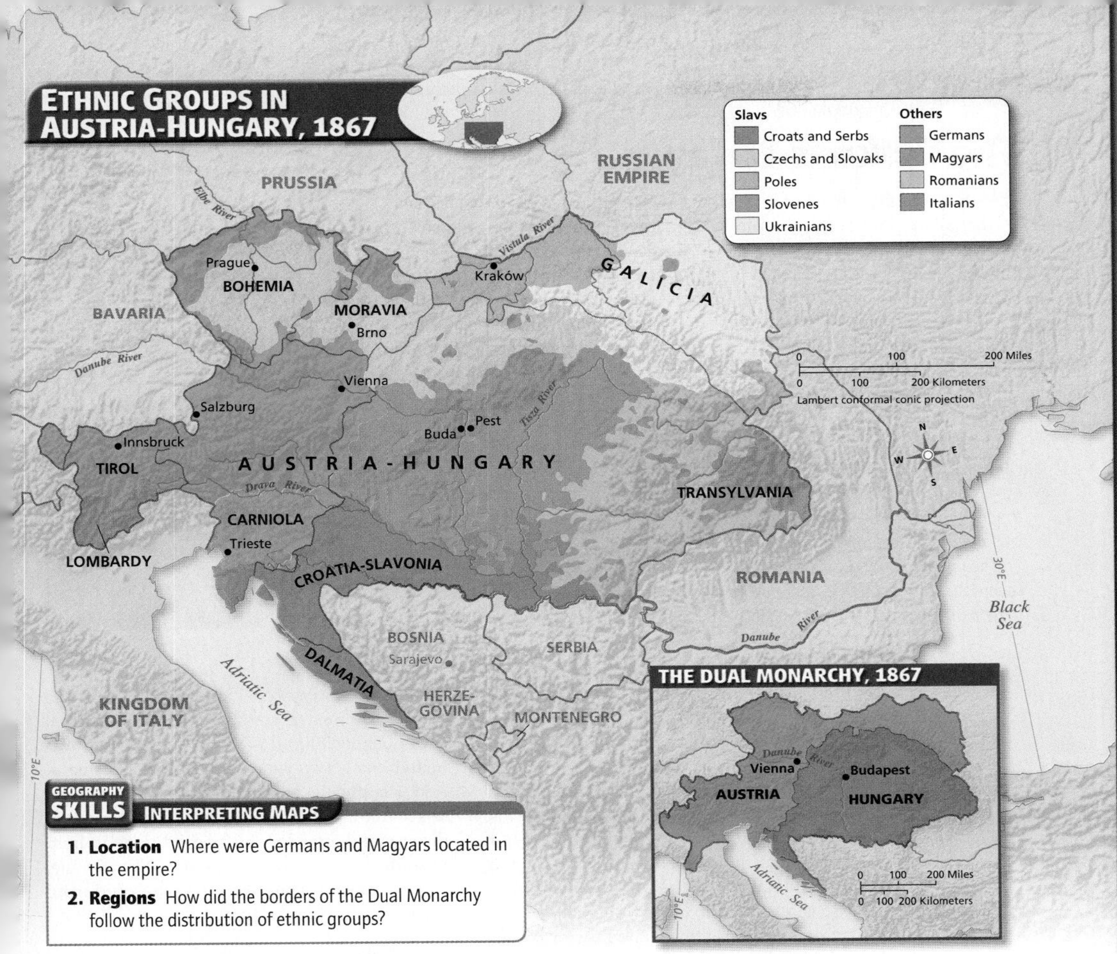

GEOGRAPHY SKILLS INTERPRETING MAPS

1. **Location** Where were Germans and Magyars located in the empire?
2. **Regions** How did the borders of the Dual Monarchy follow the distribution of ethnic groups?

For example, there were some economic advantages to the arrangement. Hungary, mostly rural and agricultural, could provide raw materials and food to Austria. Austria, which was more industrialized, could in turn provide industrial products to Hungary.

The unrest in the empire did not go away, however. Divisions remained among the various nationalities. Austrian Germans and Hungarian Magyars did not speak the same language. Also, ethnic minorities received little benefit from the Dual Monarchy and continued to seek self-government.

READING CHECK **Describe** What was the basic structure of the government in Austria-Hungary?

The Ottoman Empire

Like the Austrian Empire, the Ottoman Empire had existed for centuries and controlled a vast multiethnic territory. Within its borders were many different religious and ethnic groups, including Greeks, Bulgarians, Turks, Kurds, Arabs, and Jews. This empire had been in decline since the late 1600s, and it could not survive the winds of change blowing across Europe in the 1800s.

The Eastern Question In the early 1800s, it became clear that the Ottoman Empire could no longer defend itself against independence movements or against external threats.

Direct Teach

Reading Focus

3 How did nationalism create conflict in the Ottoman Empire? *Crimean War erupted over access to the Holy Land; diverse ethnic groups fought for independence in the Balkan Wars; Young Turks fought against absolute rule of the sultan.*

The Ottoman Empire

Recall What was the Eastern Question? *concern over what would happen to the European balance of power if the Ottoman Empire collasped*

Predict What do you think happened between the various religious and ethnic groups in the Balkans in the 1800s? *possible answer—fought for independence and separate states*

Map Transparency: Ethnic Groups in Austria-Hungary, 1867

Skills Focus: Comparing and Contrasting

At Level

Research Required

Two Examples of Nationalism

1. Copy the chart for students to see. Have students fill in the chart, using their textbooks and other sources, if necessary.
2. Guide students in a comparison of Austria-Hungary and the Ottoman Empire. How was nationalism similar and different in each empire? **LS Visual-Spatial**

Alternative Assessment Handbook, Rubrics 7: Charts; and 30: Research

	Austria-Hungary	The Ottoman Empire
Government (leader, legislature, voting rights)		
Economy		
Ethnic groups		
Response to nationalism		

Answers

Interpreting Maps 1. *in the central part of the empire;* **2.** *divided Croats and Serbs, Magyars, and Romanians from the rest of the empire (some Germans remained in Hungary, however)*

Reading Check *two separate, equal states under one ruler, with separate parliaments but some shared government ministries, as well as a joint government*

Direct Teach

Reading Focus

The Ottoman Empire

Identify Cause and Effect What were the results of the Crimean War? *ended in a stalemate; resulted in approximately half a million deaths*

Analyze Why were the Balkans important to Russia? *The area would provide access to the Mediterranean.*

Info to Know

The Balkans The Balkan region has often been at the center of conflict over the centuries because it is strategically located at the southern crossroads of Europe and Asia, just across the Adriatic Sea east of Italy. From the 300s BC until modern times, the Balkans have been invaded and conquered or contested by the Roman, Byzantine, Slav, Bulgar, Venetian, Ottoman, and Austro-Hungarian empires.

Linking TO Today

The Balkans Today

The ethnic diversity in the Balkans that led to the Balkan Wars has also led to ethnic conflicts in more recent times. This incredibly diverse region, which includes Croats, Serbs, Montenegrins, Bosnians, Macedonians, and many other ethnic groups, has unfortunately had a long history of conflict.

After World War I, European leaders created the country of Yugoslavia. It included many formerly independent countries and ethnic groups under one government. Yugoslavia did not last. In the early 1990s, it broke up amidst civil war and ethnic and religious violence.

The violence in Yugoslavia was so severe that other countries stepped in to help put an end to the conflict. In 1995 countries around the world sent troops to one of the hardest hit regions, Bosnia and Herzegovina, to help bring an end to the fighting. A peace accord was later signed which resulted in the end of the former Yugoslavia and the creation of five new countries that had been Yugoslav republics.

In 2006 another country was born. Montenegro, which was part of the former Yugoslav republic of Serbia and Montenegro, narrowly voted to declare its independence. It became the world's newest nation without conflict.

Draw Conclusions How has ethnic diversity affected the political history of the Balkans?

Montenegrins rally for independence in 2006.

By 1830, for example, Greece had gained independence. Russian had forced the Ottomans to accept Russian control of territory in the Caucasus and self-rule for Serbia.

This situation greatly worried European powers and created what they called "The Eastern Question." What would happen if the Ottoman Empire collapsed? In particular, what would happen to the city of Constantinople? Russia wanted to control that city so that it would have access to the Mediterranean. To keep Russia from gaining control of Constantinople, the French and British propped up the Ottoman Empire.

The Crimea The situation between the Ottomans and Europeans grew worse in the 1850s with a dispute over the Holy Land. The Ottomans, who controlled the region, gave Roman Catholics the control of the holy places in Palestine. When the Ottomans denied Orthodox Christians these same rights, the Russians invaded Ottoman territories. In addition, Great Britain saw Russia's move as a potential threat against its interests in India and joined in an alliance with France. Great Britain and France then joined with the Ottoman Empire in a war against Russia.

This war, most of which was fought in the Russian Crimea on the shores of the Black Sea, accomplished almost nothing. The **Crimean War** lasted about two years, ended in a stalemate, and resulted in approximately half a million deaths. Many of those deaths were the result of disease and crowded, filthy conditions in field hospitals. British nurse, Florence Nightingale, is well-known for her work to save lives during the Crimean War.

The Balkans The Balkans were another hot spot in the Ottoman Empire. The rise of nationalism in Europe had created discontent among the diverse ethnic groups in the region. Serbs, Romanians, Bulgarians, Albanians, and Greeks all wanted independence and their own nation state. These conditions, along with the competing interests of several European countries, let to a series of conflicts and wars in the 1800s and early 1900s.

Russia was involved in several of these conflicts in the Balkans. The Russians saw the Balkans as a route to the Mediterranean, which they wanted to gain. Great Britain and France were looking after their own interests in the region, so they sometimes sided with the Russians and sometimes sided with the Ottomans.

Skills Focus: Analyzing Alternative Points of View — At Level

Reading Like a Historian Skill

Balkan Nationalism

1. Organize students into five groups. Assign each group one of the following: the Ottoman Empire, the Austrian Empire, Russia, Prussia, France. Tell students that it is 1865 and they are newspaper editors in the country they represent. Have each student write an editorial discussing the situation in the Balkans. Students should consider the balance of power and attitudes of their nation toward nationalism in general and toward Balkan nationalism in particular.
2. Have volunteers read their editorials to the class. How well did students grasp the probable attitudes of their nation toward the Balkan nationalist revolutions?
3. Guide students in a discussion of the causes and effects of the Balkan nationalist movements. **LS Verbal-Linguistic**

Alternative Assessment Handbook, Rubric 23: Newspapers

Answers

Linking to Today *Civil war and ethnic and religious violence have plagued this region for hundreds of years. Yugoslavia broke up in the early 1900s; violence in Bosnia and Herzegovina, new countries created in peace accord*

Germany and Austria wanted to secure Austrian control over the various ethnic groups. When all was said and done, the **Balkan Wars** had cost the Ottoman Empire most of its land in Europe and the Balkan issues were far from settled.

With Russian troops almost at the gates of Constantinople, however, the other European powers became alarmed. In 1878 Prussian chancellor Bismarck hosted the Congress of Berlin to discuss the situation. In fact, the real purpose of the Congress was to overturn the gains Russia had made against the Ottomans.

The Congress of Berlin also gave Austria-Hungary land in the Balkans with no consideration of ethnic or national ties. As a result, conflicts between ethnic groups would erupt in the region for many years to come.

Political Reform One conflict occurred in 1908 when a nationalist group called the **Young Turks** began a revolution. The Young Turks were fighting against the absolute power of the sultan, the ruler of the Ottoman Empire. Mainly educated men, the Young Turks were devoted to restoring the constitution. Their revolution helped ensure a more representative, liberal government. Education improved, and the government took steps to provide some individual liberties.

READING CHECK **Recall** How were European nations involved in the affairs of the Ottoman Empire?

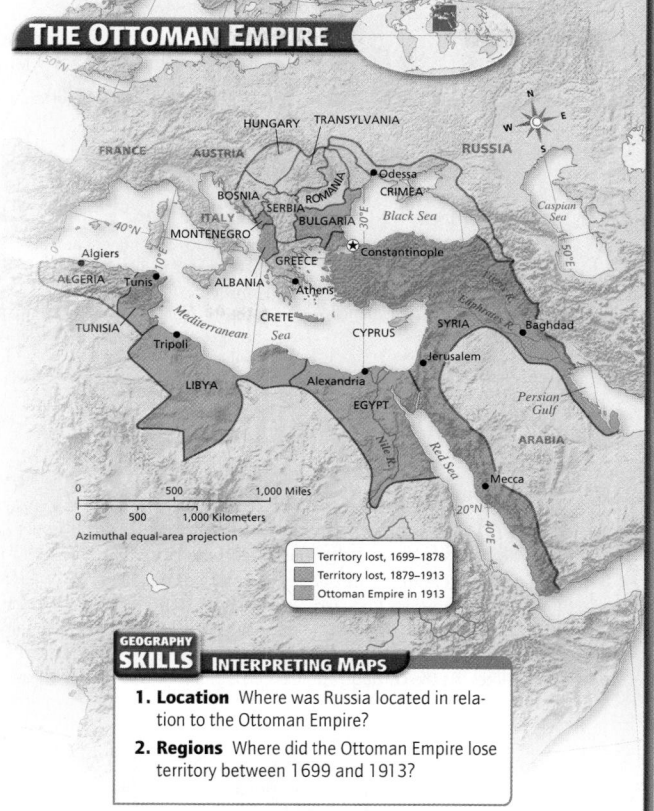

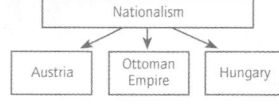

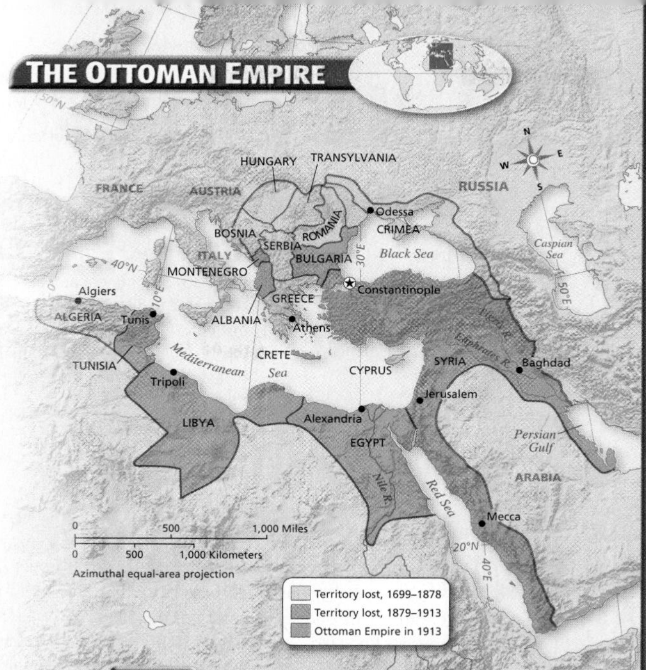

GEOGRAPHY SKILLS INTERPRETING MAPS

1. **Location** Where was Russia located in relation to the Ottoman Empire?
2. **Regions** Where did the Ottoman Empire lose territory between 1699 and 1913?

SECTION 3 ASSESSMENT

go.hrw.com
Online Quiz
Keyword: SHL NAT HP

Reviewing Ideas, Terms, and People

1. **a. Recall** What were the Carlsbad Decrees?
   b. Analyze Why was Metternich's resignation significant?
   c. Evaluate Why do you think the revolution of 1848 failed in Austria?
2. **a. Define** What was the **Dual Monarchy**?
   b. Interpret How did Hungary benefit from Austria-Hungary's economy?
   c. Evaluate Do you think the dual monarchy of Austria-Hungary would have been formed if Austria had won the Austro-Prussian War? Explain your answer.
3. **a. Identify** What was the Eastern Question?
   b. Identify Cause and Effect What was the major effect of the **Balkan Wars**?

Critical Thinking

4. **Identify Cause and Effect** Copy the graphic organizer below and use it and your notes on the section to identify the effects of nationalism in Austria, Hungary, and the Ottoman Empire.

Nationalism → Austria | Ottoman Empire | Hungary

FOCUS ON WRITING

5. **Persuasion** You belong to a minority ethnic group in Austria-Hungary. Write a letter to Emperor Franz Joseph I outlining why your group should have independence. Use details from the chapter in your notes.

Direct Teach

Info to Know

The Ottoman Empire The Ottoman Empire was once feared as the conqueror of Europe. However, beginning with the unsuccessful Siege of Vienna in 1683, its domination of eastern Europe declined. Failure to centralize power led local officials to take control of many provinces.

Map Transparency: The Ottoman Empire

Review & Assess

Close

Have students summarize the ways in which the Austrian and Ottoman empires dealt with nationalist movements.

Review

Online Quiz, Section 3

Assess

SE Section 3 Assessment

Progress Assessment: Section 3 Quiz

Alternative Assessment Handbook

Reteach/Intervene

Interactive Reader and Study Guide, Section 3

Interactive Skills Tutor CD-ROM

Section 3 Assessment Answers

1. **a.** a series of restrictive laws to censor and investigate liberal and nationalist groups
   b. possible answer—Ferdinand might have hoped it would end the revolution; instead it led to further demands.
   c. possible answer—because the revolutionaries could not win against military action
2. **a.** the two nations of Austria and Hungary, with a government led by Franz Joseph I
   b. Austria provided industrial products.
   c. possible answer—No, Austria probably would have remained an independant nation.
3. **a.** concern over how the fate of the Ottoman Empire would affect the rest of Europe
   b. The Ottoman Empire lost most of its land in Europe.
4. Austria and Hungary—creation of Dual Monarchy; Ottoman Empire—loss of territory
5. Student letters should discuss the benefits of independence for separate ethnic groups.

Answers

Interpreting Maps 1. *to the east and northeast;* **2.** *in north Africa and the Balkans*

Reading Check *became involved in wars to protect their own territorial interests and the overall balance of power*

Preteach

Getting Started

Use the **Interactive Reader and Study Guide** to familiarize students with the section content.

Interactive Reader and Study Guide, Section 4

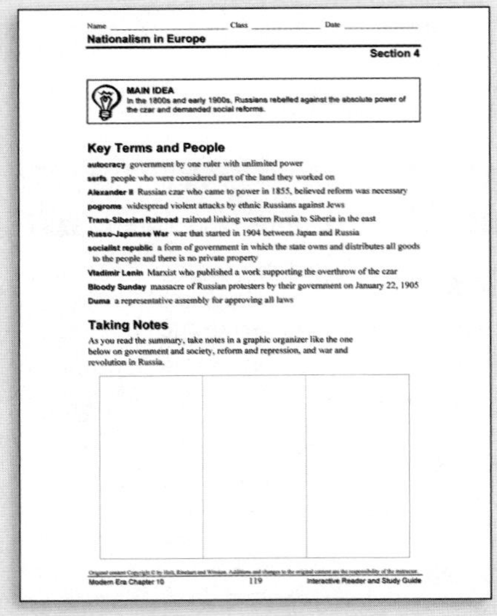

Name ______________ Class ______________ Date ______________

Nationalism in Europe

Section 4

MAIN IDEA
In the 1800s and early 1900s, Russians rebelled against the absolute power of the czar and demanded social reforms.

Key Terms and People

autocracy government by one ruler with unlimited power
serfs people who were considered part of the land they worked on
Alexander II Russian czar who came to power in 1855, believed reform was necessary
pogroms widespread violent attacks by ethnic Russians against Jews
Trans-Siberian Railroad railroad linking western Russia to Siberia in the east
Russo-Japanese War war that started in 1904 between Japan and Russia
socialist republic a form of government in which the state owns and distributes all goods to the people and there is no private property
Vladimir Lenin Marxist who published a work supporting the overthrow of the czar
Bloody Sunday massacre of Russian protesters by their government on January 22, 1905
Duma a representative assembly for approving all laws

Taking Notes

As you read the summary, take notes in a graphic organizer like the one below on government and society, reform and repression, and war and revolution in Russia.

Academic Vocabulary

Review with students the high-use academic term in this section.

sector a subdivision of society (p. 334)

CRF: Vocabulary Builder: Section 4

Taking Notes

Government and Society—czars were autocrats, serfdom was a problem in Russian society; Reform and Repression—Decembrist Revolt fought against czar's rule, Alexander II freed the serfs, pogroms were violent attacks against Jews, industry developed rapidly under Nicholas II, Trans-Siberian Railroad built; War and Revolution—Russo-Japanese War; Marxist ideas spread; Bloody Sunday killings inspired Revolution of 1905 against the czar; October Manifesto promised reform and democratic government after revolution, but czar still maintained significant power

go.hrw.com
Online Resources

KEYWORD: SHL NAT
ACTIVITY: Russian Revolution

SECTION 4

Unrest in Russia

Before You Read

Main Idea

In the 1800s and early 1900s, Russians rebelled against the absolute power of the czar and demanded social reforms.

Reading Focus

1. What was government and society like in Russia in the first half of the 1800s?
2. What were some examples of reform and repression in Russia?
3. How did war and revolution affect Russia in the early 1900s?

Key Terms and People

autocracy
serfs
Alexander II
pogroms
Trans-Siberian Railroad
Russo-Japanese War
socialist republic
Vladimir Lenin
Bloody Sunday
Duma

TAKING NOTES Take notes on government and society, reform and repression, and war and revolution in Russia.

THE INSIDE STORY ***Why did terrorists kill Russia's leader?*** It was the same day that Czar Alexander II signed a document granting major political reforms to the people. The czar was traveling through the snow in his iron-clad carriage to the Winter Palace in St. Petersburg. His guards kept close by him on open sleighs. Terrorists had already tried to assassinate the czar several times. As the carriage approached a street corner, a bomb exploded, and some of the guards were wounded. Alexander II stepped out of the carriage to check on the wounded guards' condition. After he got out, a terrorist threw another bomb—fatally injuring the czar.

The terrorist who assassinated Alexander II belonged to a radical group called The People's Will. Members of The People's Will believed that Russian society needed radical reforms, and the only way to make that happen was to overthrow the government and start over. Alexander II had made many reforms during his rule, but it was not enough. ■

Surprise Attack

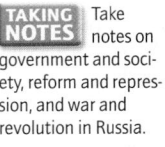

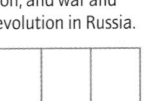

▲ A terrorist explodes a bomb as Czar Alexander II and his guards travel outside the Winter Palace.

Contemporary drawing of the assassination of Alexander II at St. Petersburg, 1881

Teach the Main Idea

At Level

Unrest in Russia

1. **Teach** Ask students the Reading Focus questions to teach this section.
2. **Apply** Have students make a time line showing the major events from this section. Student time lines should begin with the death of Czar Alexander I in 1825 and end with the October Manifesto of 1905.
3. **Review** Review student time lines as a class. Guide students in a discussion of the events on their time lines. Call students' attention to the swing back and forth from repression to reform, to repression under different czars.
4. **Practice/Homework** Tell students that they are advisers to the czar of Russia. Have students make a list of proposed reforms to improve the economic and social conditions of the country. **LS Visual-Spatial, Verbal-Linguistic**

Alternative Assessment Handbook, Rubrics 36: Time Lines; and 42: Writing to Inform

LAST CZARS OF RUSSIA

QUICK FACTS

The last czars of Russia passed some reforms but still ruled with nearly unlimited power.

Nicholas I (ruled 1825–1855) put down the Decembrist Revolt and led Russia during the Crimean War.

Alexander II (ruled 1855–1881) enacted social and economic reforms and freed Russia's serfs.

Alexander III (ruled 1881–1894) used the secret police and censorship to quell unrest.

Nicholas II (ruled 1894–1917) led Russia during the Russo-Japanese War and issued the October Manifesto promising reforms.

▲ Nicholas II and his wife, Alexandra, are crowned in 1896.

Government and Society

In the first half of the 1800s, Russia was one of the great powers of Europe. Russian troops helped defeat Napoleon, and Russia's leaders helped reorganize Europe after his fall. Yet Russia was very different from Europe's other powers. The Russian Empire was huge. It stretched eastward far into Asia and included many different ethnic groups.

To govern this large and diverse empire, Russian monarchs ruled with absolute power. They were called czars and they had control over most aspects of Russian life. The czars believed in **autocracy**, or government by one ruler with unlimited power.

Russian society under the czars was mainly agricultural. Unlike many other countries in Europe, Russia had not industrialized very much. Much of the country's population consisted of peasants. Many of these Russian peasants were **serfs**—agricultural workers who were considered part of the land on which they worked.

Serfs were controlled by lords, the wealthy nobles who owned the land. Technically, serfs were not slaves because they were not legally considered property. However, their poor living conditions and lack of freedom resembled slavery. For example, serfs were not allowed to leave the property on which they were born and they did not own the land on which they worked. In addition, serfs had to make regular payments of both goods and labor to their lords.

Some government leaders wanted to improve conditions for the serfs, but they were unable to make reforms. Russian serfdom remained a way of life for many people and was a major problem in Russian society.

READING CHECK **Summarize** What was Russian government and society like in the first half of the 1800s?

Reform and Repression

As in other European countries at this time, revolutionary ideas began to grow in Russia. Russians wanted more freedoms and more democracy. But Russia's conservative czars were resistant to reform, which led to revolts, unrest, and repression.

The Decembrist Revolt Some revolutionaries formed secret societies to fight against the czar's rule. When Czar Alexander I died in 1825, they saw it as an opportunity for change.

A group of revolutionaries later referred to as the Decembrists rebelled against the government. The Decembrists included many military officers. They led a group of some 3,000 soldiers that assembled near the Winter Palace, publicly refusing to declare their allegiance to the new czar, Nicholas I.

READING SKILLS

Understanding Word Origins If you know that the term *serf* comes from a Latin word meaning "slave," what might that tell you about their status in society?

Direct Teach

Reading Focus

1 What was government and society like in Russia in the first half of the 1800s? *It was ruled by czars with absolute power. Most of the population consisted of peasants, and most of them were serfs, who were ruled by the wealthy nobles who owned the land.*

Government and Society

Draw Conclusions Why did Russia have a role in reorganizing Europe after Napoleon's fall? *because it was on the winning side*

Elaborate Why might an absolute monarchy seem to be well suited to a nation of large geographic size? *possible answer—An absolute monarchy could keep nationalism in check and prevent movements from gaining power.*

Quick Facts Transparency: Last Czars of Russia

Reading Focus

2 What were some examples of reform and repression in Russia? *Reform—serfs freed, judicial system and some local self-government, industrialization, Trans-Siberian Railroad, Repression—Decembrist Revolt crushed; pogroms*

Reform and Repression

Identify Who were the Decembrists? *Russian revolutionary group that rose up against Nicholas I*

Identify Cause and Effect What short-term and long-term effects did the Decembrist Revolt have? *short-term—the revolt was crushed; long-term—inspired other revolutionaries*

Differentiating Instruction

Above Level

Advanced Learners/Gifted and Talented

Research Required

1. Tell students that Russia was not the only country in Europe where serfdom survived into modern times. Have students research serfdom in Europe after the Middle Ages until serfdom ended. Have students make a chart with the following information: Where else did serfdom continue to exist? What similarities or differences were there between serf systems in different countries? When did serfdom end in each country? How did serfdom end? Who ended it?
2. Review student charts as a class.
3. Guide students in a discussion of serfdom, and of the similarities and differences between the European serf system and the American slave system. LS **Visual-Spatial**

Alternative Assessment Handbook, Rubrics 9: Comparing and Contrasting; and 30: Research

Answers

Reading Skills *possible answer—that even though serfs were not techically considered property, they were much like slaves*

Reading Check *autocratic government led by czar, country's population mainly peasants, many peasants were serfs.*

Direct Teach

Reading Focus

3 How did war and revolution affect Russia in the early 1900's? *Russia's defeat in the war with Japan amplified social unrest and led to protests against the czar's strict rules. In response, some reforms were made but the czar still held absolute power.*

War and Revolution

Recall Why did Japan attack Russia in what became known as the Russo-Japanese War? *Japan viewed Russia as a threat to its growing empire.*

Make Inferences Why do you think Marx's ideas gained popularity in the late 1800's? *possible answer—his ideas probably appealed to the large working class*

Identify Cause and Effect Why did Czar Nicholas issue the October Manifesto? *in response to Bloody Sunday and other protests, in hopes of quelling future rebellions and strikes*

Info to Know

Emperor Nicholas When news of Czar Alexander's death reached his family, his brother Nicholas declared loyalty to their other brother Konstantin, as the new emperor. However, Alexander had named Nicholas heir apparent in a manifesto. Konstantin had married a Polish woman not of royal blood and had renounced his rights to the throne. Nevertheless, Nicholas swore allegiance to Konstantin but eventually took the throne anyway because the threat of revolt was spreading.

Answers

Reading Check *freeing of serfs; system whereby peasants could buy the land they worked; reformed judicial system and some local self-government*

Nicholas responded by crushing the rebellion. Many of the Decembrists were captured and sent to Siberia, an isolated region in far eastern Russia. Five were executed. The Decembrist revolt had failed, but it began a revolutionary movement in Russia that would only grow in the years ahead.

Reforms of Alexander II The next czar, **Alexander II**, came to power in 1855 near the end of the Crimean War, which Russia lost to Great Britain, France, the Ottoman Empire, and Sardinia. The loss showed how far behind Russia was from the rest of Europe. Russia did not have the modern technology and industry necessary to build a military that could compete with Europe's powers. To solve these problems, Alexander II began a program of reforms.

In 1861 Alexander II took the historic step of freeing Russia's serfs and giving them the right to own land as part of a commune. He believed that if the terrible living conditions continued for the serfs, a rebellion was likely. In addition, he hoped that giving serfs their own land would help build a market economy in Russia. The government set up a system in which peasants would buy the land they worked on from the landowner, usually with government help.

Alexander II made other reforms to modernize Russia. He set up a new judicial system and allowed some local self-government. In addition, he reorganized the army and navy.

Despite these reforms, revolutionary movements continued to gain strength and call for more radical changes. In 1881 a radical group called the People's Will assassinated Czar Alexander II.

Unrest Under Alexander III Alexander's son, Alexander III, became the next czar. He was a reactionary, or a person who wants to go back to the way things were in the past. Alexander III ended the reforms of his father. He responded to revolutionary threats by going after individuals and groups suspected of plotting against the government.

THE IMPACT TODAY
About 2 million Jews fled the Russian Empire between 1880 and 1914 because of the pogroms, many to the United States and Great Britain.

Meanwhile, a different sort of unrest was building. Mobs of people started attacking Jews, killing them and destroying their property. These widespread violent attacks were known as **pogroms**, and there were several waves of them in Russia.

The first wave of pogroms began after Alexander II was assassinated. Some people in the government and in society wrongly blamed Jews for the assassination. As a result, groups of anti-Semitic rioters attacked and killed innocent Jews, and the authorities did nothing to stop them.

Industrialization under Nicholas II Nicholas II was crowned czar in 1894. Like his father, he ruled as an autocrat. Early in his reign, industry developed rapidly in Russia. During the 1890s Russia began building the **Trans-Siberian Railroad** to link western Russia with Siberia. But Russian expansion in the east would soon led to a conflict and war.

READING CHECK **Identify** What were some key reforms in Russia during the 1800s?

War and Revolution

As Russia expanded in the east, it came into conflict with another imperial power—Japan. At the same time, revolutionary ideas were growing again, and revolution was brewing.

War with Japan In the early 1900s, Japan was building an empire in the east and viewed Russia as a threat to its plans. As a result, in 1904 Japanese forces attacked and eventually defeated Russia in the **Russo-Japanese War**. The defeat shocked many Russians and added to growing unrest and calls for change.

Marxist Ideas One group calling for change in Russia was the Marxists, Russians who followed the communist theories of Karl Marx. In the late 1800s, Marx's ideas gained popularity in Russia. Marx's followers wanted to create a **socialist republic**, a society in which there would be no private property and the state would collectively own and distribute goods.

In 1902 a Marxist named **Vladimir Lenin** published a work supporting the overthrow of the czar. He called for revolutionaries to rise up against "the shame and the curse of Russia."

The Revolution of 1905 By 1905 many Russians were ready to rebel against the czar. On January 22, 1905, an Orthodox priest named Father Gapon planned to bring a petition to the czar at the Winter Palace. The petition listed a number of demands.

Skills Focus: Identifying Main Idea and Details — At Level

Reading Skill

Repression and Reform

1. Write the names of the following Russian czars for students to see: Nicholas I, Alexander II, and Alexander III. Have students copy each of the three names. Under each name, have students make a list of the acts of repression or reform that marked that czar's rule. Have students identify the reason for that czar's policies of repression or reform.
2. Review student lists as a class.
3. Guide students in a discussion of the alternating patterns of repression and reforms. **LS Verbal-Linguistic**

Alternative Assessment Handbook, Rubrics 11: Discussions; and 38: Writing to Classify

Reading like a Historian

Bloody Sunday in St. Petersburg

Analyzing Visuals One source that historians study to learn about the past is art. The painting below, *Death in Snow,* is by Russian artist Vladimir Makovsky. It shows protesters in St. Petersburg, Russia, on January 22, 1905—an event known as Bloody Sunday.

To analyze what this painting suggests about this event and about the Russian Revolution of 1905, think about

- the subject of the painting
- the details in the painting
- the title of the work

On Bloody Sunday, Russian troops killed and wounded hundreds of peaceful protesters, igniting the Russian Revolution of 1905.

Father Gapon, a Russian priest, led the march.

The protesters included poor workers, women, and children. They had marched to the czar's Winter Palace to ask for better working conditions.

Skills Focus READING LIKE A HISTORIAN

1. **Subject** Why do you think Makovsky chose to paint this event? What might his decision indicate about the importance of Bloody Sunday?
2. **Details** How would you describe the expressions and body language of the people shown?
3. **Title** What statement did Makovsky make by titling the painting *Death in Snow*?

See **Skills Handbook**, p. H26

Direct Teach

Reading Like a Historian

Bloody Sunday in St. Petersburg

Analyzing Visuals Does this painting present a point of view about Bloody Sunday? How can you tell? *Yes, it emphasizes the suffering of poor workers, women, and children; it seems to be sympathetic to their cause.*

Activity Artistic Interpretation Have students draw a scene from Bloody Sunday from the perspective of the czar and the Russian troops. **LS Visual-Spatial**

Alternative Assessment Handbook, Rubrics 3: Artwork

Recent Scholarship

Historian Sheila Fitzpatrick presents the Russian Revolution as a series of stages, not just a single event that occurred in 1905. In her work *The Russian Revolution,* Fitzpatrick examines the changes that occurred in Russia from the time of the Bolsheviks through the purges of the 1930.

The Russian Revolution by Sheila Fitzpatrick. Oxford University Press, 2001.

Differentiating Instruction

Below Level

Learners Having Difficulty

Materials: construction paper, colored markers

1. Guide the class in a discussion of the Revolution of 1905 to make sure that students understand its causes and effects. Use the following questions as a guide: What were the causes of the revolution? What part did Bloody Sunday play in the revolution? What did the revolutionaries hope to accomplish? What was the outcome of the revolution? What were the long-term effects of the revolution? Was the revolution a success or a failure? Why?
2. Have each student make a poster designed to inspire people to join the Revolution of 1905.
3. Place student posters on display for the class to see. **LS Visual-Spatial**

Alternative Assessment Handbook, Rubrics 11: Discussions; Rubric 28: Posters

Answers

Reading Like a Historian 1. *to depict the fear and suffering of the protesters; to show that the protesters were not zealous revolutionaries, but ordinary people, including poor workers, women, and children; shows that Bloody Sunday inspired more discontent with the czar;* **2.** *possible answer—desperate, fearful;* **3.** *possible answer—that the killings were even more brutal because they happened in winter*

Direct Teach

Biography

Nikolay Rimsky-Korsakov (1844–1908) Nikolay Rimsky-Korsakov was educated at the Russian naval academy in St. Petersburg but began to compose a symphony in 1861. After his graduation in 1862, he sailed on a clipper ship to the United States at the height of the American Civil War. He finished his first symphony after returning to St. Petersburg, and it was premiered in 1865. In the 1860s Rimsky-Korsakov joined four other composers to create a truly national school of Russian music known as "The Five." By 1871 he was hired to teach composition at the St. Petersburg Conservatory. One of his biggest services to Russian music was as editor of many of his colleagues' musical scores for publication; his work guaranteed the survival of those works.

Quick Facts Transparency: Russian Revolution of 1905

Review & Assess

Close

Have students summarize the periods of repression and reform in Russia between 1825 and 1905.

Review

Online Quiz, Section 4

Assess

SE Section 4 Assessment

Progress Assessment: Section 4 Quiz

Alternative Assessment Handbook

Reteach/Intervene

Interactive Reader and Study Guide, Section 4

Interactive Skills Tutor CD-ROM

ACADEMIC VOCABULARY
sector a subdivision of society

When Gapon and the protesters neared the Winter Palace, troops fired at the group, and hundreds died. The day became known in Russian history as **Bloody Sunday**.

Bloody Sunday inspired many sectors of society to rise up against the czar. In the cities and across the countryside, rebellions broke out. Workers went on strike, and university students protested in the streets. Peasants rebelled against their landlords. People everywhere began to disobey the czar's strict rules. The Russian Revolution of 1905 had begun.

At first the czar firmly supported the autocracy. Then he promised reform but did not follow through with his promises. Finally, in October, a massive worker's strike seemed to be the final straw. Some 2 million workers protested in the streets of Russia. Railroads stopped because of lack of workers. Czar Nicholas II had to do something.

QUICK FACTS

RUSSIAN REVOLUTION OF 1905

CAUSES
- The slow pace of reforms by Russia's czars
- Desire for better living conditions and freedoms
- The growth of revolutionary groups

EFFECTS
- Nicholas II issues October Manifesto promising some reforms, Duma as representative body
- Political parties and voting rights are allowed, but czar maintains absolute power

The October Manifesto In response to the rebellions and strikes, Nicholas II issued the October Manifesto, an official promise for reform and a more democratic government. The October Manifesto promised a Russian constitution. It guaranteed individual liberties to all Russians, including freedom of speech and freedom of assembly. Many Russians also gained the right to vote.

The October Manifesto stated that voters would elect representatives to the **Duma** (doo-muh), an assembly that would approve all laws. Although the czar would continue to rule Russia, he promised not to pass any laws without the approval of the elected Duma.

Nicholas II hoped that the October Manifesto would end the revolution. But he still did not want to give up the absolute power he had always known. In 1906 when the first Duma met, the czar ended the meeting when the Duma made too many demands.

Nicholas II and his advisers did make more reforms in the years after the Russian Revolution of 1905. However, it was clear that the czar had not achieved a balance between his own power and the growing support for democracy. People still wanted reform and change. Eventually they would get it.

READING CHECK **Cause and Effect** What were some causes of the Russian Revolution of 1905?

SECTION 4 ASSESSMENT

go.hrw.com
Online Quiz
Keyword: SHL NAT HP

Reviewing Ideas, Terms, and People

1. **a. Define** What is an **autocracy**?
   b. Explain What was life like for Russia's **serfs**?
   c. Evaluate Why do you Russia's czars failed to improve living conditions for serfs?
2. **a. Recall** What historic action did **Alexander II** take in 1861?
   b. Contrast In what ways did Alexander II differ from Russia's other czars?
   c. Evaluate Why do you think the Decembrist Revolt failed?
3. **a. Identify** What was the **Duma**?
   b. Interpret Why was **Bloody Sunday** a significant event?
   c. Predict How do you think the refusal of Russia's czars to make lasting reforms would affect Russia?

Critical Thinking

4. **Rank** Use your notes from the section and a graphic organizer like this one to rank three major problems facing Russian society in the late 1800s and early 1900s.

1 2 3

FOCUS ON WRITING

5. **Narration** Write a short paragraph from the point of view of a newspaper reporter describing the events of Bloody Sunday.

Section 4 Assessment Answers

1. **a.** government by one ruler with unlimited power;
   b. poor living conditions; lack of freedom
   c. possible answer—There were so many serfs that it was difficult to make a change.
2. **a.** freed the serfs
   b. Nicholas I's rule was marked by repression, whereas Alexander II's rule was marked by liberal reforms.
   c. possible answer—did not have widespread support
3. **a.** the Russian legislative assembly set up after the Revolution of 1905
   b. It led to the October Manifesto promising reforms and more democratic government.
   c. possible answer—might result in another revolution
4. Possible answer—serfdom; military defeats; growth of revolutionary groups
5. Student paragraphs should include details from the section about the protest and the response.

Answers

Reading Check *growing unrest, pogroms, crack down on revolutionary movements, defeat in Russo-Japanese War led to discontent, Bloody Sunday inspired rebellions against czar*

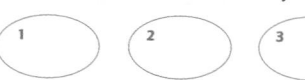

World Literature

Leo Tolstoy (1828–1910)

About the Reading Leo Tolstoy's novel *War and Peace*, published from 1865 to 1869, is considered one of the greatest novels of all time. It follows the lives of five Russian families in the early 1800s and presents a picture of Russian society during this time. In the passage below, two of the novel's characters, Pierre Bezukhov and Prince Andrew Bolkonsky, argue about whether or not people should live their lives to help others or to help themselves.

AS YOU READ **Think about how Prince Andrew views Russia's serfs.**

Excerpt from

War and Peace

by Leo Tolstoy

"Come on let's argue then," said Prince Andrew. "You talk of schools," he went on, crooking a finger, "education and so forth; that is you want to raise him" (pointing to a peasant who passed by them taking off his cap) "from his animal condition and awaken in him spiritual needs, while it seems to me that animal happiness is the only happiness possible, and that is just what you want to deprive him of. I envy him, but you want to make him what I am, without giving him my means. Then you say, 'lighten his toil.' But as I see it, physical labor is as essential to him, as much a condition of his existence, as mental activity is it to you or me. You can't help thinking. I go to bed after two in the morning, thoughts come and I can't sleep but toss about till dawn, because I think and can't help thinking, just as he can't help plowing and mowing; if he didn't, he would go to the drink shop or fall ill. Just as I could not stand his terrible physical labor but should die of it in a week, so he could not stand my physical idleness, but would grow fat and die. The third thing—what else was it you talked about?" and Prince Andrew crooked a third finger. "Ah, yes, hospitals, medicine. He has a fit, he is dying, and you come and bleed him and patch him up. He will drag about as a cripple, a burden to everybody, for another ten years. It would be far easier and simpler for him to die. Others are being born and there are plenty of them as it is. It would be different if you grudged losing a laborer—that's how I regard him—but you want to cure him from love of him. And he does not want that. And besides, what a notion that medicine ever cured anyone! Killed them, yes!" said he, frowning angrily and turning away from Pierre.

Dinner at the Zemstvo, by Grigori Mjasoedov, 1872

This painting shows Russian serfs in the 1800s.

Skills FOCUS **READING LIKE A HISTORIAN**

go.hrw.com
World Literature
Keyword: SHL WRLIT

1. **Describe** How would you describe Prince Andrew's attitude toward Russia's serfs?
2. **Interpret Literature as a Source** Do you think this novel accurately portrays the views of some upper-class Russians toward serfs? Why or why not?

See **Skills Handbook**, p. H28

World Literature

War and Peace

Word Help

condition state of being
toil work

Meet the Writer

Leo Tolstoy (1828–1910) Tolstoy was born into a noble family. In about 1876 he experienced a religious conversion, after which he preached nonviolence and advocated a simple life. He considered any organizations that ruled by force—including both the government and the church—to be wrong. A Tolstoy cult developed, attracting pilgrims to his estate. The Russian Church excommunicated Tolstoy in 1901. Because of his prestige, however, the government left him alone. Tolstoy's belief in practicing what he preached led him to abandon all earthly goods, including his home. In 1910, with no destination, he left home with his youngest daughter, caught a chill, and died.

Info to Know

War and Peace Many people consider *War and Peace* to be the one of the greatest novels ever written. It combines three kinds of material—an actual history of the Napoleonic wars, biographies of fictional characters, and essays in which Tolstoy attempts to formulate laws of history. In his view, history is not a result of major decisions by great men, but is the sum total of all the little decisions made by ordinary people.

Differentiating Instruction

English-Language Learners — Below Level

Review through this passage with students to make sure that they understand its meaning. Have each student write a paragraph responding to Prince Andrew. Have volunteers read their paragraphs to the class. Then guide students in a discussion of Prince Andrew's attitudes toward the peasants and their responses. **LS Verbal-Linguistic**

Alternative Assessment Handbook, Rubrics 11: Discussions; and 37: Writing Assignments

Advanced Learners/Gifted and Talented — Above Level

Have students write a brief essay analyzing Prince Andrew's attitudes toward peasants. Which of the two men would probably be considered a conservative? Which would probably be a liberal nationalist? Have volunteers read their essays to the class. Then guide students in a discussion of the condition of peasants in Russia at the time.
LS Verbal-Linguistic

Alternative Assessment Handbook, Rubrics 11: Discussions and 37: Writing Assignments

Answers

Reading Like a Historian **1.** *He is not sympathetic about their living conditions; believes serfs are meant to live the way they do.* **2.** *possible answer—probably accurate, the upper-class Russians probably looked for a justification to the way the serfs were treated.*

Document-Based Investigation

Revolution and Unification

Word Help

prolongation a lengthening in time
intolerable unbearable

Primary Source

"The passions of the mob broke loose like a bursting dam. The people, seeing the dead and dying carried away in all directions, the snow on the streets and pavements soaked with blood, cried aloud for vengeance . . . Men, women, and children fell at each volley, and were carried away in ambulances, sledges, and carts. The indignation and fury of every class were aroused. Students, merchants, all classes of the population alike were inflamed. At the moment of writing, firing is going on in every quarter of the city."
—*Eyewitness account of Bloody Sunday, published in London Weekly Times, January 1905*

CHAPTER 10

Document-Based Investigation

Revolutions and Unification

Historical Context The four documents below provide different views and accounts of revolutions and unification in Europe during the late 1800s and early 1900s.

Task Study the documents and answer the questions that follow. After you have studied the documents, you will be asked to write an essay about the causes of revolutions and unification in Europe. You will need to use evidence from these selections and from the chapter to support the position you take in your essay.

DOCUMENT 1

Petition to the Czar

In St. Petersburg, Russia, in 1905, Father Gapon wrote a petition to Russian Czar Nicolas II expressing the desires of the Russian people for more equal rights under the law.

> Oh Sire, we working men and inhabitants of St. Petersburg, our wives, our children and our parents, helpless and aged women and men, have come to you our ruler, in search of justice and protection. We are beggars, we are oppressed and overburdened with work, we are insulted, as slaves. The moment has come for us when death would be better than the prolongation of our intolerable sufferings. We are seeking here our last salvation. Do not refuse to help your people. Destroy the wall between yourself and your people.

DOCUMENT 2

Germany's Military Might

In the early 1900s, as kaiser of a united Germany, Wilhelm II built up a powerful military as a show of strength and national pride. This 1914 Russian cartoon shows Wilhelm II surprised by an invasion of Germany by the Russian army.

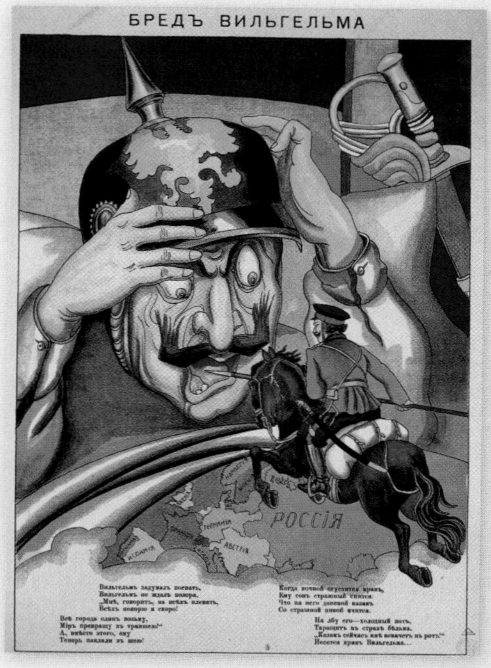

Russian engraving, by Machistov, 1914

Skills Focus: Analyzing Alternative Points of View

At Level

Reading Like a Historian Skill

Petition to the Czar

1. Remind students that Father Gapon led the Bloody Sunday protest of 1905.
2. Ask students what words Gapon uses to describe the Russian working people. How does he get his message across? Which words show his point of view? How might the Russian czar describe the situation from his point of view?
3. Have students compare Document 1 with the artwork *Death in Snow* in Section 4 of this chapter. Do Vladimir Makovsky and Father Gapon share the same point of view? How can you tell?
4. Have students write a brief essay comparing the points of view expressed in "Petition to the Czar" and *Death in Snow*, focusing on the portrayal of the protesters. **LS Verbal-Linguistic**

Alternative Assessment Handbook, Rubrics 9: Comparing and Contrasting, and 38: Writing to Classify

DOCUMENT 3

Bismarck's "Blood and Iron" speech

In this speech to the Prussian parliament in 1862, Otto von Bismarck argues for a buildup of the Prussian military. Bismarck went on to build the Prussian army into a great war machine that would use "blood and iron" to forcibly unite the German states under Prussia.

> Public opinion changes, the press is not [the same as] public opinion; one knows how the press is written; members of parliament have a higher duty, to lead opinion, to stand above it. We are too hot-blooded, we have a preference for putting on armor that is too big for our small body; and now we're actually supposed to utilize it. Germany is not looking to Prussia's liberalism, but to its power; Bavaria, Württemberg, Baden may indulge liberalism, and for that reason no one will assign them Prussia's role; Prussia has to coalesce and concentrate its power for the opportune moment, which has already been missed several times; Prussia's borders according to the Vienna Treaties [of 1814–1815] are not favorable for a healthy, vital state; it is not by speeches and majority resolutions that the great questions of the time are decided—that was the big mistake of 1848 and 1849—but by iron and blood.

DOCUMENT 4

Revolution Spreads to the German States

In his memoir, Carl Schurz describes the excitement he witnessed on the streets of Berlin during the German Revolution of 1848.

> Great news came from Vienna! There the students of the university were the first to assail the Emperor of Austria with the cry for liberty and citizens' rights . . . In the Prussian capital the masses surged upon the streets, and everybody looked for events of great import.
>
> On the 18th of March we too had our mass demonstration. A great multitude gathered for a solemn procession through the streets of the town [Berlin] . . . At the head of the procession Professor Kunkel bore the tricolor—black, red, and gold—which so long had been prohibited as the revolutionary flag. He spoke with wonderful eloquence, his voice ringing out in its most powerful tones as he depicted a resurrection of German unity and greatness and new liberties and rights of the German people, which now must be conceded by the princes or won by force by the people. And when at last he waved the black-red-gold banner, and predicted to a free German nation a magnificent future, enthusiasm without bounds broke forth. People clapped their hands; they shouted; they embraced one another; they shed tears.

Skills FOCUS READING LIKE A HISTORIAN

DOCUMENT 1

a. Describe How does Father Gapon describe the people of St. Petersburg?

b. Explain What is Father Gapon asking the czar to destroy?

DOCUMENT 2

a. Identify How does the artist reveal his views about Russia in this cartoon?

b. Infer Why do you think the artist chose to show the German kaiser so surprised?

DOCUMENT 3

a. Describe What does Bismarck want most from Prussia?

b. Interpret What kind of mistake do you think Bismarck is referring to that occurred in 1848 and 1849?

DOCUMENT 4

a. Explain What event in Vienna inspired people to march in Berlin?

b. Evaluate What symbol was the professor using to show the crowd his national pride?

DOCUMENT-BASED ESSAY QUESTION

What were some reasons that people in Prussia and Russia wanted change? Using the documents above and information from the chapter, form a thesis to explain the desires and causes of revolution and unification. Then write a short essay to support your position.

See **Skills Handbook**, pp. H25, H27, H29

Document-Based Investigation

Info to Know

Carl Schurz After participating in the unsuccessful revolutions of 1848 in Berlin, Carl Schurz emigrated to the United States, where he became an American citizen. He was involved in the antislavery movement in the United States and served as a brigadier general in the Union army during the American Civil War. Schurz was also elected as a United States senator and, later, named secretary of the interior. As secretary of the interior, Schurz fought for the rights of Native Americans as the United States expanded westward.

Teaching Tip

Remind students that revolution broke out in Vienna in March 1848. That year, protesters called for a constitution and the resignation of Austria's foreign minister, Prince Metternich. As a result Metternich fled Austria. Have students connect these events in Austria to the events described in Document 4.

Differentiating Instruction

Above Level

Advanced Learners/Gifted and Talented

Research Required

1. Draw a time line for all to see, beginning in 1850 and ending in 1920, with marks at 10-year increments. Have students add Documents 1, 2, 3, and 4 to the class time line and copy the time line onto their own papers.
2. Have students conduct research to add several important events to the time line, including Bloody Sunday, the Franco-Prussian War, German unification, the revolutions of 1848, and the beginning of World War I.
3. Using the time lines as a starting point, ask students what new observations they can make about the documents. Ask students the following questions: What was Bismarck trying to accomplish with the blood and iron speech? Did Russia and Germany go to war? What happened after Gapon's petition? How are Documents 3 and 4 related? **LS Visual-Spatial**

Alternative Assessment Handbook, Rubrics 12: Drawing Conclusions, and 36: Time Lines

Answers

Reading Like a Historian

Document 1 a. *as suffering beggars, slaves;* **b.** *the division between the czar and the people;* **Document 2 a.** *shows Russia as a strong force to be feared by Germany;* **b.** *possible answer—because Germany did not expect to be invaded by Russia; kaiser thought German military was unbeatable, thought fighting would take place in the west;* **Document 3 a.** *power, a unified Germany;* **b.** *the resignation of Metternich, the revolutions of 1848 and calls for liberal reform;* **Document 4 a.** *protests calling for liberty and citizens' rights;* **b.** *a black, red, and gold flag;* **Essay** *Student essays should explain that revolutions of the 1800s were caused both by nationalism and the call for liberal reforms. Using examples from the documents and the chapter, students might choose to argue that the forces of nationalism and liberal reform were often in conflict in Prussia and Russia during this period.*

Answers

Visual Summary

Review and Inquiry Organize students into five groups. Have each group review the history of nationalism in one of the countries shown in the Visual Study Guide. Have groups create and perform a skit summarizing the key events in their country.

Quick Facts Transparency: Visual Study Guide: Nationalism in Europe

Review Key Terms and People

1. Guiseppe Mazzini
2. Red Shirts
3. Zollverein
4. Otto von Bismarck
5. Balkan Wars
6. autocracy
7. Duma
8. ethnic

Comprehension and Critical Thinking

9. a. growing nationalism; opposition to Austrian rule; Cavour unified Kingdom of Sardinia; Garibaldi unified Kingdom of Two Sicilies
b. regional differences; widespread poverty; emigration; industrialization and reform; new foreign policy
c. led Italians to support their actions

10. a. first kaiser, or emperor, of the German Empire
b. similarity—both examples of realpolitik; difference—Austro-Prussian war fought only by Prussia; Franco-Prussian war also involved the southern German states
c. encouraged trade between them

11. a. Austria and Hungary were two separate, equal states, with one ruler as both emperor of Austria and king of Hungary
b. set off revolts in the Austrian empire
c. possible answer—disagree; ultimately led to conflict between ethnic groups

CHAPTER 10

Chapter Review

QUICK FACTS

VISUAL STUDY GUIDE

Nationalism in Europe, 1800–1920

Italy

- In 1815 the Congress of Vienna split the Italian states apart.
- In 1831 Giuseppe Mazzini formed a nationalist group called Young Italy to fight for the unification of Italy.
- In 1852 Camillo di Cavour united states in northern Italy.
- In the 1860s Giuseppe Garibaldi continued the fight for unification of the rest of the Italian states.
- In 1861 under Victor Emmanuel's reign, Italians voted for unification.

Germany

- In 1834 the German states formed the Zollverein, or customs union, that made trade easier between the states.
- In 1848 German liberals revolted in the state of Prussia.
- In the mid-1800s Otto von Bismarck built up the Prussian military and pushed for the unification of Germany.
- In 1866 Prussia defeated Austria in the Austro-Prussian War.
- In 1871 Prussia defeated France in the Franco-Prussian War, and Germany was unified.

Austria-Hungary

- After the Congress of Vienna in 1815, Austrian foreign minister Metternich passed laws limiting reforms and formed alliances with other European powers to deter uprisings.
- In 1848 Hungarian Magyars made an unsuccessful attempt at a revolution.
- In 1867 the Dual Monarchy was set up, and Austria and Hungary became two separate, equal states.

Ottoman Empire

- The power of the Ottoman Empire declined during the 1800s.
- In the 1850s the Ottomans fought with Great Britain, France, and Sardinia against Russia in the Crimean War.
- The Ottoman Empire lost much territory in Europe after the Balkan Wars.
- In 1908 a nationalistic movement called the Young Turks began a revolution against the Ottoman sultan.

Russia

- In the first half of the 1800s, many Russian peasants were serfs—agricultural workers who were considered part of the land on which they worked.
- In 1825 Russian revolutionaries rebelled against the Czar Nicholas I but were defeated.
- From the 1860s to the 1880s Czar Alexander II freed the serfs and made other reforms.
- The Russian Revolution of 1905 began after Bloody Sunday because people were upset with the slow pace of reform.

Review Key Terms and People

Identify the correct term or person from the chapter that best matches each of the following descriptions.

1. Founded the Italian nationalist movement called Young Italy
2. Followers of Giuseppe Garibaldi
3. German customs union that allowed for the removal of tariffs between the German states
4. Prussian leader who helped unify Germany by "blood and iron"
5. wars that cost the Ottoman Empire most of its land in Europe
6. government by one ruler with unlimited power
7. an assembly in Russia that approved all laws
8. common background and culture

338 CHAPTER 10

12. a. guaranteed individual liberties to all Russians, including freedom of speech and freedom of assembly; some Russians gained the right to vote
b. regular payments of goods and labor
c. by staging rebellions across Russia

Reading Skills

13. nation: from roots meaning "birth" or "race;" examples of nationalism in the chapter involve people of common background

14. empire: from roots meaning "absolute authority" or "to command;" empires in the chapter had absolute rulers

15. autocrat: from roots meaning "one" and "rule;" autocracy means rule by one person with absolute power

Analyzing Visuals

16. They are pulling it by a rope and appear to be tied together.

17. that the serfs lived under extremely poor conditions

History's Impact video program
Review the video to answer the closing question: What impact did nationalism have on Europe during the 1800s?

Comprehension and Critical Thinking

SECTION 1 *(pp. 315–319)*

9. a. Describe What led to the unification of Italy?

b. Analyze What new challenges did Italians face after unification ?

c. Evaluate How did feelings of nationalism affect the actions of Italian leaders such as Giuseppe Mazzini and Camillo di Cavour?

SECTION 2 *(pp. 320–324)*

10. a. Identify Who was Wilhelm I?

b. Compare and Contrast What was one similarity and one difference between the Austro-Prussian War and the Franco-Prussian War?

c. Elaborate How did the Zollverein strengthen ties between the German states?

SECTION 3 *(pp. 325–329)*

11. a. Describe What was the government of Austria-Hungary like under the Dual Monarchy?

b. Identify Cause and Effect How did revolutions elsewhere in Europe affect uprisings in the Austrian Empire?

c. Make Judgments Do you agree or disagree on how the Congress of Berlin ignored ethnic groups when they gave land to Austria-Hungary?

SECTION 4 *(pp. 330–334)*

12. a. Recall How did the October Manifesto benefit Russians?

b. Explain What did serfs owe to the lords who owned the land they worked on?

c. Elaborate How did Russians react to the news of violence on Bloody Sunday?

Reading Skills

Understanding Word Origins *Using a dictionary, find the origins of the following words. Then explain how the origin of each word relates to the use of the word in this chapter.*

13. nation

14. empire

15. autocrat

Analyzing Visuals

Reading Like a Historian *The painting below shows Russian serfs on the banks of the Volga River.*

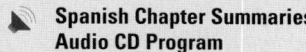

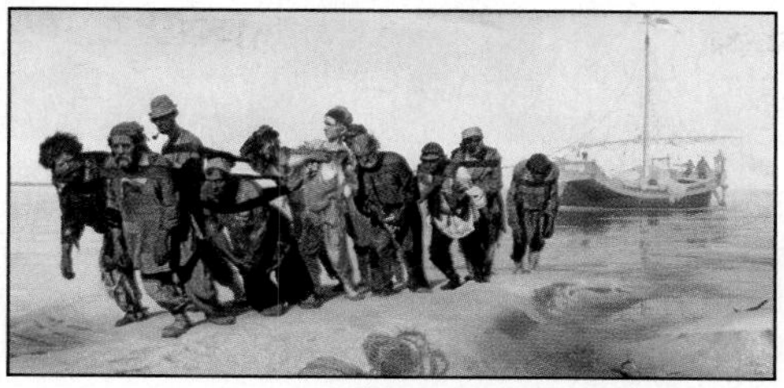

The Bargemen on the Volga, by Ilya Repin, 1870s

16. Identify How are the serfs pulling this ship down the river?

17. Draw Conclusions Many of the serfs in the painting have ragged clothing, no shoes, and look exhausted. What do you think the artist was trying to say by showing the serfs in this condition?

Using the Internet

go.hrw.com
Practice Online
Keyword: SHL NAT

18. During the 1800s in Italy and Germany, several key people led nationalist movements that resulted in their country's unification. Enter the activity keyword and choose one Italian or German leader to learn more about. Then write a short newspaper article that describes this person's life and achievements.

WRITING FOR THE SAT

Think about the following issue:

Nationalism was a major force in Europe during the 1800s as people began to feel an allegiance to others who shared a common language, religion, and history. As a result, the nations of Italy and Germany achieved unification, and old multinational empires started to crumble. In some places, representative government began to replace the absolute power of monarchs.

19. Assignment: In your opinion, what was the most important effect of European nationalism in the 1800s? Write an essay in which you develop your position on this issue. Support your point of view with reasoning and examples from the chapter.

Answers

Using the Internet

18. Go to the HRW Web site and enter the keyword shown to access a rubric for this activity.

KEYWORD: SHL NAT

Writing for the SAT

19 Student essays might address liberal reforms, the formation of new nations, the new balance of power in Europe, or some other effect of nationalism. Essays should be supported by logic and specific examples from the chapter.
A rubric for this activity is provided in **CRF:** Writing for the SAT

HOLT History's Impact

► **Video Program: Nationalism in Europe**
Refer to the Video Program Teacher's Guide for the answer to the closing question.

Review and Assessment Resources

Review and Reinforce

- **CRF:** Chapter Review
- **Quick Facts Transparency**: Visual Study Guide: Nationalism in Europe
- **Spanish Chapter Summaries Audio CD Program**
- OSP **Holt PuzzlePro**: Quiz Show for ExamView
- **Quiz Game CD-ROM**

Assess

- **PASS**: Chapter Test, Forms A and B
- **Alternative Assessment Handbook**
- OSP **ExamView Test Generator**, Chapter Test
- **Differentiated Instruction Modified Worksheets and Tests CD-ROM**: Chapter Test
- HOAP **Holt Online Assessment Program** (in the Premier Online Edition)

Reteach/Intervene

- **Interactive Reader and Study Guide**
- **Differentiated Instruction Teacher Management System**: Lesson Plans for Differentiated Instruction
- **Differentiated Instruction Modified Worksheets and Tests CD-ROM**: Chapter Test
- **Interactive Skills Tutor CD-ROM**

go.hrw.com
Online Resources
KEYWORD: SHL TEACHER

Chapter 11 Planning Guide

The Age of Imperialism

Chapter Overview	Reproducible Resources	Technology Resources
CHAPTER 11 **pp. 340–371** **Overview:** **In this chapter, students will learn about the age of imperialism from 1800 to 1920, when European powers ruled over much of Africa and Asia, and the United States influenced its neighbors.**	**Differentiated Instruction Teacher Management System:** • Pacing Guide • Lesson Plans for Differentiated Instruction **Interactive Reader and Study Guide:** Chapter Summary* **Chapter Resource File*** • Writing About History • Social Studies Skill • Chapter Review **World History Outline Maps**	**Live Ink© Online Reading Help** **Student Edition on Audio CD Program** **Differentiated Instruction Modified Worksheets and Tests CD-ROM** **World History Primary Source Library CD-ROM** **Power Presentations with Video CD-ROM**
Section 1: **The British in India** **The Main Idea:** One of the first examples of European imperialism in Asia, the British rule over India changed Indian politics, economics, and society and led to the rise of Indian nationalism.	**Differentiated Instruction Teacher Management System:** Section 1 Lesson Plan* **Interactive Reader and Study Guide:** Section 1 Summary* **Chapter Resource File*** • Vocabulary Builder: Section 1 • Biography: Ramanujan	**Daily Test Practice Transparency:** Section 1* **Map Transparencies:** European Imperialism*; The British in India, 1767–1858* **Quick Facts Transparency:** Forms of Imperialism*
Section 2: **East Asia and the West** **The Main Idea:** While Western nations focused their imperial ambitions on East Asia, the reactions and results differed in China, Japan, and Southeast Asia.	**Differentiated Instruction Teacher Management System:** Section 2 Lesson Plan* **Interactive Reader and Study Guide:** Section 2 Summary* **Chapter Resource File*** • Vocabulary Builder: Section 2 • Biography: Hokusai • History and Geography: Japan Opens Trade Routes	**Daily Test Practice Transparency:** Section 2* **Map Transparencies:** Imperialism in China, 1842–1900*; Southeast Asia, 1895*; Imperialism and a Global Economy* **Quick Facts Transparency:** The Meiji Reforms*
Section 3: **The Scramble for Africa** **The Main Idea:** In the late 1800s and early 1900s, European powers claimed land in much of Africa.	**Differentiated Instruction Teacher Management System:** Section 3 Lesson Plan* **Interactive Reader and Study Guide:** Section 3 Summary* **Chapter Resource File*** • Vocabulary Builder: Section 3 • Biography: Samuel Ajayi Crowther • Literature: *Heart of Darkness*	**Daily Test Practice Transparency:** Section 3* **Map Transparency:** Imperialism in Africa* **Quick Facts Transparency:** The New Imperialism in Africa* **Internet Activity:** Democratic Republic of the Congo Today
Section 4: **Imperialism in Latin America** **The Main Idea:** Imperialism in Latin America involved the United States and European nations seeking to strengthen their political and economic influence over the region.	**Differentiated Instruction Teacher Management System:** Section 4 Lesson Plan* **Interactive Reader and Study Guide:** Section 4 Summary* **Chapter Resource File*** • Vocabulary Builder: Section 4 • Biography: José Guadalupe Posada • Primary Source: U.S. Imperialism	**Daily Test Practice Transparency:** Section 4* **Map Transparency:** United States Intervention in the Caribbean* **Internet Activity:** Report on Imperialism

go.hrw.com | Print Resource | Transparency
Learning Styles | Audio CD | CD-ROM
Video | **SE** Student Edition | **TE** Teacher's Edition
OSP One-Stop Planner CD-ROM
*also on One-Stop Planner CD-ROM

Review, Assessment, Intervention

- **Quick Facts Transparency**: The Age of Imperialism*
- **Progress Assessment Support System (PASS)**: Chapter Test*
- **Differentiated Instruction Modified Worksheets and Tests CD-ROM**: Modified Chapter Test
- OSP **One-Stop Planner CD-ROM**: ExamView Test Generator (English/Spanish)
- HOAP **Holt Online Assessment Program (HOAP)**, in the Holt Premier Online Student Edition

- **PASS**: Section 1 Quiz*
- **Online Quiz**: Section 1
- **Alternative Assessment Handbook**

- **PASS**: Section 2 Quiz*
- **Online Quiz**: Section 2
- **Alternative Assessment Handbook**

- **PASS**: Section 3 Quiz*
- **Online Quiz**: Section 3
- **Alternative Assessment Handbook**

- **PASS**: Section 4 Quiz*
- **Online Quiz**: Section 4
- **Alternative Assessment Handbook**

HOLT
History's Impact
World History Video Program (VHS/DVD)
The Age of Imperialism

Power Presentation with Video CD-ROM

Power Presentations with Video are visual presentations of each chapter's main ideas. Presentations can be customized by including Quick Facts charts, images and maps from the textbook, and video clips.

Holt Online Learning

go.hrw.com
Teacher Resources
KEYWORD: SHL TEACHER

go.hrw.com
Student Resources
KEYWORD: SHL IMP

- Document-Based Questions
- Interactive Multimedia Activities
- Current Events
- Chapter-Based Internet Activities
- and more!

Holt Premier
Online Student Edition

Complete online support for interactivity, assessment, and reporting

- Interactive Maps and Notebook
- Homework Practice and Research Activities Online

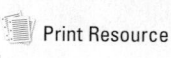

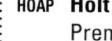

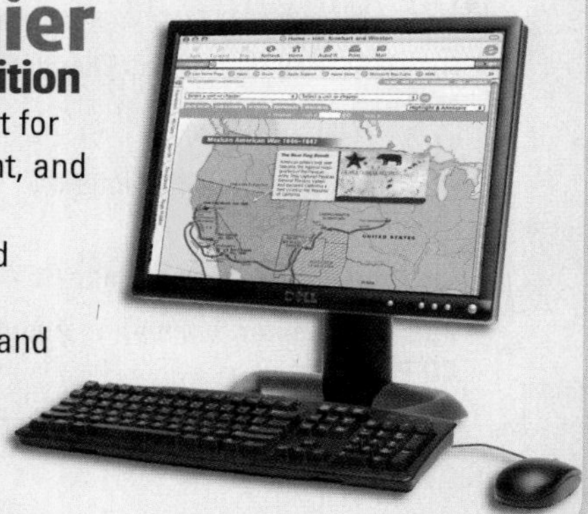

Before You Teach

The Big Picture

Susan Ramírez

Forms of Imperialism In contrast to the conquest and annexation style of imperialism common in the Americas earlier in history, this era saw new forms of international control. Protectorates and spheres of influence were important types involving not only Europeans and the nations of Africa and Asia, but also Japan in Korea and China.

The Benefits of Imperialism Foreigners benefited disproportionately from imperialism. Foreign governments collected taxes. Foreign traders sold manufactured goods in distant markets and entrepreneurs exported gold, diamonds, silk, tea, cotton, indigo, spices, sugar, coffee, and jute to supply industry and consumption at home. The peoples of India, Asia, and Africa benefited from the extent that they found employment in the export-import sector or worked on the railroads, canals, and roads constructed in their countries. Too many, however, especially in the rural areas, lost land or were saddled with paying the high taxes that paid for the infrastructure built to service world trade.

Resistance to Foreign Domination The inequality that developed in colonized states was not accepted by all. The control of a country by foreigners generated local protests, rebellion, and more subtle forms of resistance. Eventually, these movements coalesced into a rising tide of nationalism.

Recent Scholarship

The necessary brevity and synthesis of a textbook sometimes sacrifices the impact of great events or trends on ordinary people. "Everyday Forms of Resistance" by James C. Scott (a chapter in *Everyday Forms of Peasant Resistance* (1989), edited by Forrest D. Colburn restores the popular perspective to history. He analyzes the sometimes disguised opposition to domination by persons with little formal power. Individual and small group resistance include poaching, squatting [on land], desertion, evasion [of taxes], and foot dragging. Revenge, smuggling, folk religion, social banditry, and class heroes are other forms.

Differentiating Instruction

Differentiated Instruction Teacher Management System
- Pacing Guide
- Lesson Plans for Differentiated Instruction

Interactive Reader and Study Guide

Spanish Chapter Summaries Audio CD Program

Student Edition on Audio CD Program

Differentiated Instruction Modified Worksheets and Tests CD-ROM
- Vocabulary Flash Cards
- Modified Vocabulary Builder Activities
- Modified Chapter Review Activity
- Modified Chapter Test

OSP **One-Stop Planner CD-ROM**
- ExamView Test Generator (English/Spanish)
- PuzzlePro
- Quiz Show for ExamView
- Transparencies and Videos

TE **Differentiated Activities in the Teacher's Edition**
- African Colonies, p. 342
- The East India Company and the Raj, p. 345
- Downfall of the Qing Dynasty, p. 352
- Effects of Rubber in a Global Economy, p. 357
- U.S. Actions, p. 386
- Chinese Nationalist Editorials, p. 368

Reading Like a Historian

Sam Wineburg

Our students have come of age when wars are fought with infrared night goggles, and terrorist groups, using cell phones to detonate road-side explosives, send live video feed via satellite back to their mountain hideouts.Technology so defines modern warfare that it will be difficult for today's students to imagine anything different. Few will be able to grasp the true import of our chapter's statement that "repeating rifles, machine guns and exploding shells made European armies more lethal." What exactly did "more lethal" mean?

Outgunned! Technology and Power So lopsided were the contests between Africans and European imperialists that these encounters "resembled hunting more than war" in the words of Daniel R. Headrick, author of the *Tools of Empire: Technology and European Imperialism in the Nineteenth Century*. Fatality rates provide a rough sense of this mismatch. In the 1898 Battle of Omdurman, a force of 50,000 Sudanese soldiers, armed with spears and the previous decade's collection of European arms, faced a combined British and Egyptian force half that size. The British possessed the Maxim machine gun. The first automatic machine gun in history, the Maxim could fire up to 600 rounds of ammunition a minute. At the end of five hours of battle, 11,000 Sudanese lay dead, versus 20 British soldiers and 20 Egyptian allies.

Still, such numbers fail to convey the full horror of this bloodbath. Winston Churchill, a 24-year-old officer with the British forces, documented this battle by sending accounts back to London's *Morning Post* (he got around the prohibition forbidding dispatches from the front by writing letters to his mother, who then forwarded them to the newspaper). Churchill wrote: "At the critical moment the gunboat arrived on the scene and began suddenly to blaze and flame from Maxim guns, quick-firing guns and rifles. The range was short; the effect tremendous . . . The charging Dervishes sank down in tangled heaps."

These Maxim-equipped soldiers held such an upper hand that the adrenaline of warfare eventually dissipated into boredom: "The infantry fired steadily and stolidly, without hurry or excitement . . . Besides, the soldiers were interested in the work and took great pains. But presently the mere physical act became tedious."

To the Sudanese, British tedium spelled hellish fury: "Bullets were shearing though flesh, smashing and splintering bone; blood spouted from terrible wounds; valiant men were struggling on through a hell of whistling metal, exploding shells, and spurting dust—suffering, despairing, dying." With more than a hint of bravado, Churchill summarized the tally sheet at the end of day: "The strongest and best-armed savage army yet arrayed against a European power had been destroyed and dispersed, with hardly any difficulty, comparatively small risk, and insignificant losses to the victors."

Similar scenes with only slight variations in detail would be repeated many times. To give just one example, in 1899 in Chad, a French force of 320 vanquished the armies of Rabah, 12,000 strong and armed with 2,500 antiquated firearms.

A Moral Compass Gone Awry The irony of these bloodbaths was that the victors explained their ease of conquest not as the consequence of Hiram Maxim figuring out how to cool the exploding chamber of his weapon with a constant stream of water so that it would continue to fire unabated. Rather, the Europeans interpreted technological prowess as proof of their inherent moral and cultural superiority.

As our chapter notes, the encounters between Europeans and Africans were fatal in terms of human cost. But the first fatality was the moral compass of the European invaders.

Chapter Preview

Chapter Main Ideas

Section 1 One of the first examples of European imperialism in Asia, the British rule over India changed Indian politics, economics, and society and led to the rise of Indian nationalism.

Section 2 While Western nations focused their imperial ambitions on East Asia, the reactions and results differed in China, Japan, and Southeast Asia.

Section 3 In the late 1800s and early 1900s, European powers claimed land in much of Africa.

Section 4 Imperialism in Latin America involved the United States and European nations seeking to strengthen their political and economic influence over the region.

CHAPTER 11

1800–1920

The Age of Imperialism

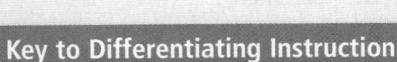

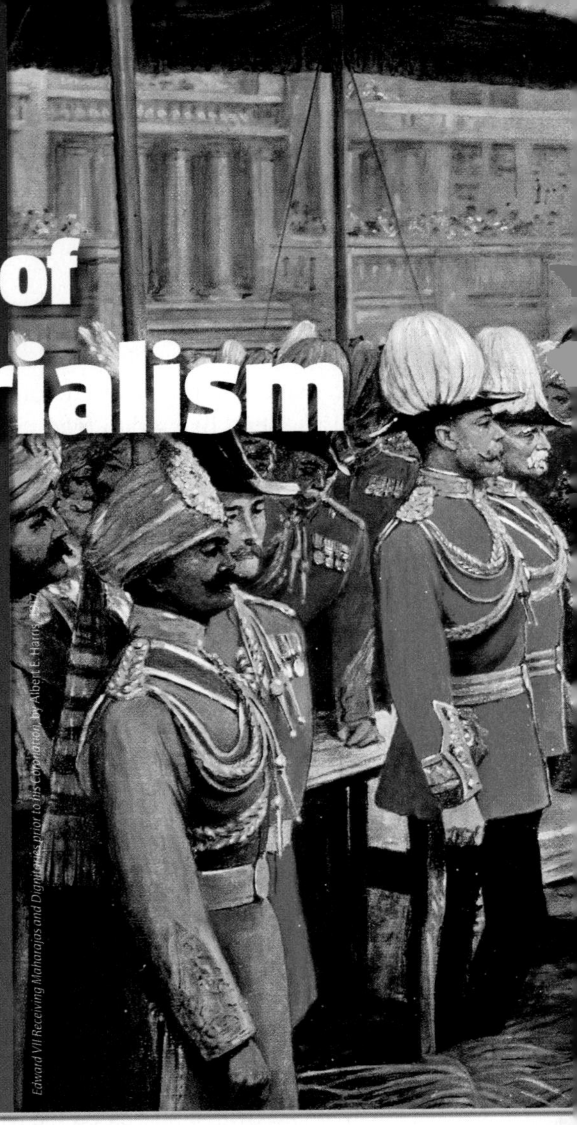

Edward VII Receiving Maharajas and Dignitaries prior to his Coronation by Albert E. Harris, 1907

THE BIG PICTURE European powers came to rule a large portion of Africa and Asia between 1800 and 1920. Only Japan emerged as an independent power capable of challenging the West. In the Americas, the United States exercised greater influence over the affairs of its neighbors.

Theme ECONOMIC SYSTEMS

In the 1800s industrialized nations looked beyond their own borders for ways to build their economic and political strength. In this chapter you will examine how this economic drive contributed to an intense competition for global empire.

TIME LINE

CHAPTER EVENTS

- **1842** The first Opium War ends in China.
- **1862** France gains control of Vietnam.
- **1884–1885** The Berlin Conference sets the rules for dividing Africa.
- **1885** The Indian National Congress is founded.

1840 — 1860 — 1880

WORLD EVENTS

- **1845** The Irish Potato Famine begins.
- **1861** The American Civil War begins.
- **1871** German unification is complete.

Key to Differentiating Instruction

Below Level

Basic-level activities designed for all students encountering new material

At Level

Intermediate-level activities designed for average students

Above Level

Challenging activities designed for honors and gifted and talented students

Standard English Mastery

Activities designed to improve standard English usage

Introduce the Chapter

At Level

The Age of Imperialism

1. Tell students that imperialism involves nations gaining power by gaining territory. Have students name some reasons why European nations might have wanted to build empires in the years between 1880 and 1920. Tell students about the economic, political, and cultural reasons for the rise of imperialism.
2. Organize students into small groups. Assign one group economic reasons, one group political reasons, and one group cultural reasons.
3. Have each group scan the chapter to find reasons for imperialism that relate to its category. Have a volunteer from each group explain some of their reasons to the rest of the class. **LS Interpersonal**

Alternative Assessment Handbook, Rubric 1: Acquiring Information

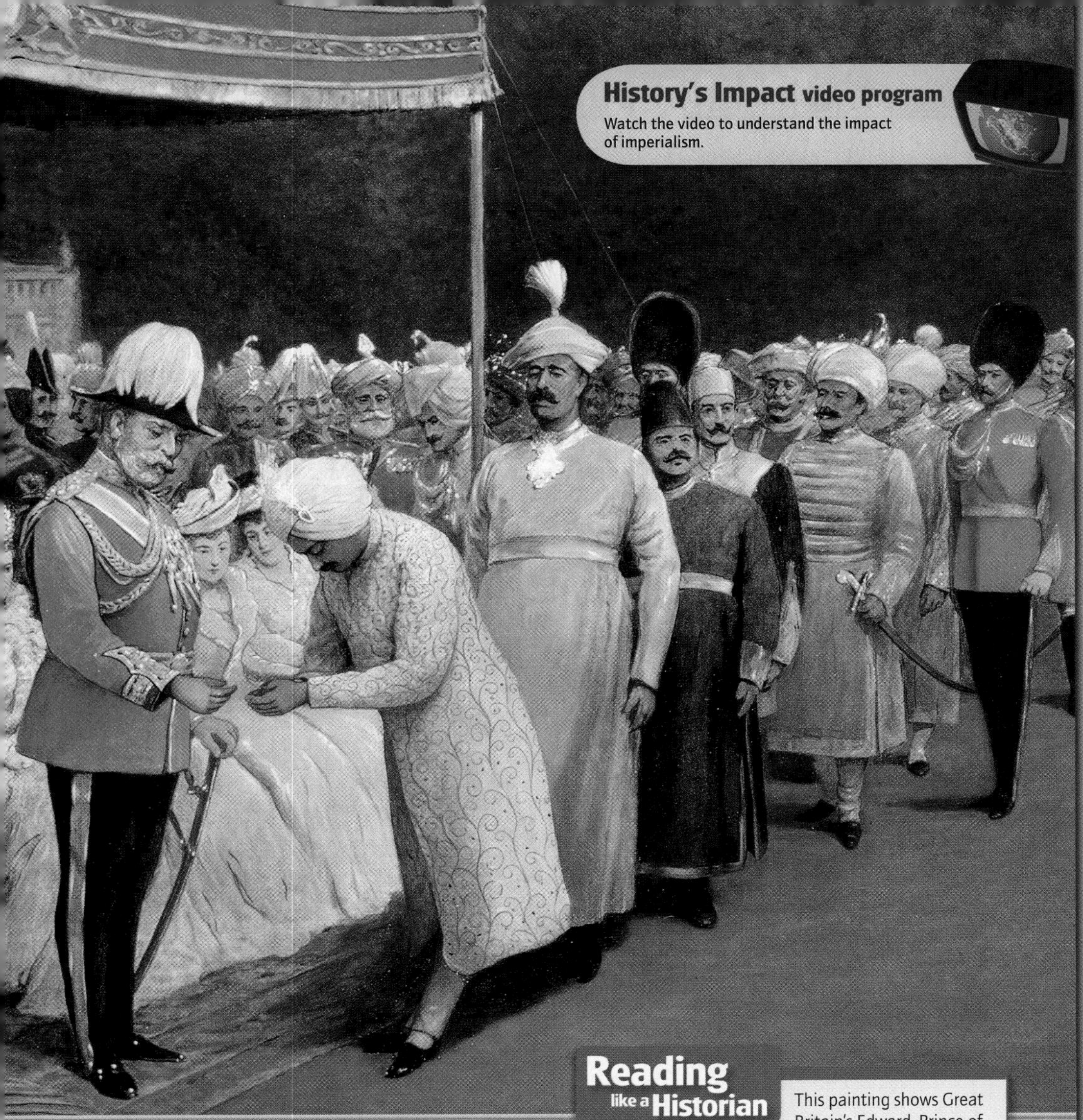

History's Impact video program
Watch the video to understand the impact of imperialism.

Reading like a Historian This painting shows Great Britain's Edward, Prince of Wales, being greeted by Indian princes during an official visit to India in 1875.

Analyzing Visuals The artist painted this scene in 1917, when Britain's position as a major world power was being threatened by the events of World War I. Why do you think the artist chose to look back at this particular moment?

See **Skills Handbook**, p. H26

1895 Japan wins the Sino-Japanese War.

1898 The United States gains control of Cuba and the Philippines.

1900

1901 Edward VII becomes king of the United Kingdom.

1914 World War I begins.

1920

Chapter Preview

HOLT

History's Impact

► **Video Program: The Age of Imperialism**
See the Video Teacher's Guide for strategies for using the video segment.

Reading Like a Historian

Analyzing Visuals Indian nationalism was rising in the late 1800s. Prince Edward's visit to India in 1875-1876, as shown in this painting, was intended to improve the relationship between Britain and India.

Explore the Time Line

1. How many years passed between the end of the Sino-Japanese War and the beginning of World War I? *19 years*
2. In what year was the Indian National Congress founded? *1885*
3. When did the United States gain control of Cuba and the Philippines? *1898*
4. What was the purpose of the Berlin Conference? *to set the rules for dividing Africa*

Info to Know

Economics and Imperialism Britain experienced a slight economic depression from 1873 to 1896. Feeling the effects of this decline, the country's leaders intensified the policies of imperialism. They hoped to claim an empire before other nations did.

Make Inferences Why might an economic depression have intensified policies of imperialism? *Colonies could provide resources and new markets.*

go.hrw.com

Online Resources

Chapter Resources:
KEYWORD: SHL IMP
Teacher Resources:
KEYWORD: SHL TEACHER

Answers

Reading Like a Historian *possible answer—This painting probably was created to remind people of Britain's glory, because it depicts a scene at the height of the British empire's power and wealth.*

Direct Teach

Geography Starting Points

Different Kinds of Imperialism Imperialists from Britain and France held vastly different views about the future of their African colonies. Britain expected them to mature into independent nations. Some French imperialists, on the other hand, wanted to merge the colonies with their home country. Colonized peoples were later represented in France's legislature.

The Economics of Imperialism Whether their colonial holdings were of substantial economic value to the imperialist powers remains unclear. A look at three Western countries provides an interesting counterargument. Before the height of imperialism in the 1890s, Britain had reached its economic peak. Despite continued imperial expansion throughout the early twentieth century, Britain continued to lose its economic lead. Germany, which held barely any important colonies, was ready to surpass Britain and become Europe's richest power. Meanwhile, the United States, with fewer overseas colonial possessions, was richer still than Germany.

GEOGRAPHY Starting Points

Interactive

EUROPEAN IMPERIALISM

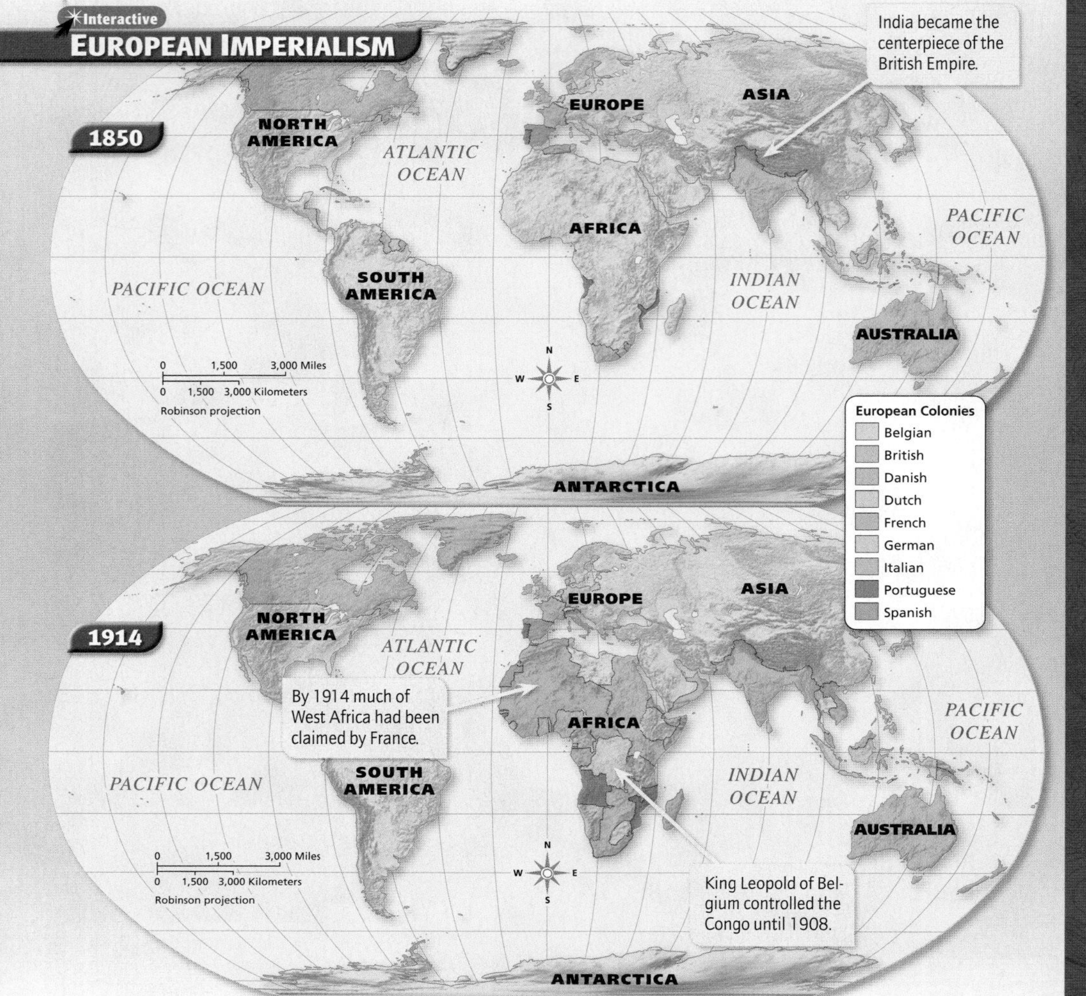

Starting Points Starting in the late 1700s, European nations began a renewed campaign of competitive empire building that would eventually span the globe. By the early 1900s, European nations controlled territory on nearly every continent. The legacy of imperialism would affect the world for decades to come.

1. **Analyze** Why do you think there were more European colonies in 1914 than in 1850?
2. **Predict** How do you think the change in political control in Africa between 1850 and 1914 affected Africa's people?

Listen to History

Go online to listen to an explanation of the starting points for this chapter.

go.hrw.com
Keyword: SHL IMP

Differentiating Instruction

Above Level

Advanced Learners/Gifted and Talented

Research Required

1. Remind students that most of Africa was colonized by European nations between the years 1850 and 1914. Have students predict how they think colonization affected Africa, and how Africans reacted to it.
2. Organize students into small groups. Have each group pick an African colony and research its history from colonization to independence, if applicable. Student research should help answer the following questions: which country controlled this part of Africa from 1850-1914? Did the Africans eventually gain independence? How?
3. Have groups create a multimedia presentation showing how imperialism affected the part of Africa they researched.

LS **Interpersonal, Visual-Spatial**

Alternative Assessment Handbook, Rubric 22: Multimedia Presentations

Answers

Geography Starting Points 1. *The nations of Europe were competing for colonies during those years, and each probably wanted to claim as much territory as possible.* **2.** *possible answer—probably influenced by European culture; may also have resisted colonization*

SECTION 1

The British in India

BEFORE YOU READ

MAIN IDEA
One of the first examples of European imperialism in Asia, the British rule over India changed Indian politics, economics, and society and led to the rise of Indian nationalism.

READING FOCUS
1. What changes set the stage for European imperialism in Asia and Africa?
2. What role did the British East India Company play in British imperialism in India?
3. What was life like in India when it became a British colony?

KEY TERMS
British East India Company
Sepoy Mutiny
Raj
Indian National Congress
Muslim League

TAKING NOTES As you read, take notes on the development and effects of British rule in India.

Development
↓
British Rule in India
↓
Effects

Robert Clive and Mir Jaffar after the Battle of Plassey, by Francis Hayman, 1857

◀ **British general Robert Clive made a secret deal to gain territory for Britain.**

THE INSIDE STORY ***When does a secret work better than an army?*** The year was 1756, and British power in India was rising. To secure their position in India, the British began fortifying their position in the rich trading city of Calcutta. This effort angered the ruler of Bengal, the region in which Calcutta lay, and he sent his army to attack the British fortifications at Fort William. The fort fell quickly, and more than 140 British defenders were imprisoned in a small, poorly ventilated jail cell for the night. All but 23 of the prisoners died of dehydration and suffocation.

Outraged, the British sent general Robert Clive to recapture Calcutta. Clive secretly met with a commander of the Bengal army. Later, when the British met the Bengal army, the commander refused to join in the battle. Why did the commander not fight? He and Clive had made a secret deal. The deal helped the British recapture Calcutta, and the commander became the ruler of Bengal.

By taking control of Calcutta, the British had essentially become the rulers of the richest province in the Mughal Empire. Remarkably, the conquest of Bengal had been won not through military might, but through deceit. ■

Teach the Main Idea

At Level

The British in India

1. **Teach** Ask students the Reading Focus questions to teach this section.
2. **Apply** Organize the class into small groups. Have each group discuss the meaning of the word *imperialism* and then write its definition. Then have each group make a list of the different ways in which modern European empires used imperialism to extend their power.
3. **Review** Review student definitions and lists as a class. Guide students in a discussion of the reasons the British Crown took direct control of India from the East India Company.
4. **Practice/Homework** Tell students they are Indian nationalists. Have each student write a speech explaining why the British should withdraw from India and leave the country to its rightful owners and citizens, the Indians. **LS Interpersonal, Verbal-Linguistic**

Alternative Assessment Handbook, Rubrics 14: Group Activity; and 43: Writing to Persuade

Preteach

Getting Started

Use the **Interactive Reader and Study Guide** to familiarize students with the section content.

Interactive Reader and Study Guide, Section 1

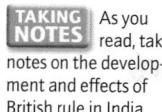

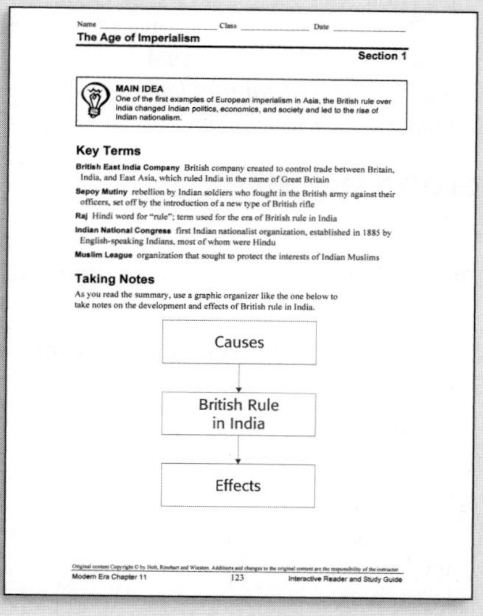

Name ________ Class ________ Date ________

The Age of Imperialism

Section 1

MAIN IDEA
One of the first examples of European imperialism in Asia, the British rule over India changed Indian politics, economics, and society and led to the rise of Indian nationalism.

Key Terms

British East India Company British company created to control trade between Britain, India, and East Asia, which ruled India in the name of Great Britain

Sepoy Mutiny rebellion by Indian soldiers who fought in the British army against their officers, set off by the introduction of a new type of British rifle

Raj Hindi word for "rule"; term used for the era of British rule in India

Indian National Congress first Indian nationalist organization, established in 1885 by English-speaking Indians, most of whom were Hindu

Muslim League organization that sought to protect the interests of Indian Muslims

Taking Notes

As you read the summary, use a graphic organizer like the one below to take notes on the development and effects of British rule in India.

Causes
↓
British Rule in India
↓
Effects

Modern Era Chapter 11 123 Interactive Reader and Study Guide

Academic Vocabulary

Review with students the high-use academic term in this section.

prejudiced biased against a racial, religious, or national group (p. 345)

CRF: Vocabulary Builder: Section 1

Taking Notes

Development—new technology; weakening of great empires of Asia and North Africa; Effects—Sepoy Mutiny in 1857; devastation of India's pre-existing industry; rise of Indian nationalism; founding of Indian National Congress; swadeshi (boycott) movement; founding of Muslim League

Direct Teach

Reading Focus

1. What changes set the stage for European imperialism in Asia and Africa? *The Industrial Revolution introduced new technologies that increased the European military advantage over the rest of the world, and the great empires of Asia and North Africa all had severe internal problems at the time when European power was rising.*

Setting the Stage

Define What is imperialism? *the process of one people ruling or controlling another*

Make Inferences Why do you think Europeans did not try to control Africa and Asia earlier? *possible answer—lacked technology to compete with empires of Asia and North Africa*

Quick Facts Transparency: Forms of Imperialism

Reading Focus

2. What role did the British East India Company play in British imperialism in India? *controlled trade between Britain, India, and East Asia; ruled India in Britain's name*

British East India Company

Identify Who were the Sepoys? *Indian soldiers who had fought in the British armyn*

Summarize How was the British Empire in India built? *British East India Company established trading posts; after decline of Mughal Empire placed allies on the thrones of Indian states and waged wars against the most powerful kingdoms of India; after Sepoy Mutiny British Crown took direct control*

Setting the Stage

The arrival of the British in India was an example of European imperialism, the process of one people ruling or controlling another. By 1700, Spain, Great Britain, France, and Portugal ruled vast territories in the Americas. Europeans had less success, however, in ruling territory in Asia and Africa. While Europeans had built trading posts along those continents' coasts, they held little territory farther inland.

By the late 1700s, however, European states began expanding their power in Asia and Africa. Two factors that made this possible were new technologies and the weakening of the great empires of Asia and North Africa.

New Technologies Advances in technology gave Europeans a huge military advantage over Africans and Asians. Steam-powered gunboats could attack even inland targets, while repeating rifles, machine guns, and exploding shells made European armies more lethal than ever. Asian and African weapon makers simply could not match these new technologies.

Weakening Empires Meanwhile, the great empires of Asia and North Africa were weakening, and Europeans took advantage. The Mughal Empire in India entered a deep decline after 1707. The Ottoman Empire lost strength throughout the 1700s and had a weak grasp on its North African provinces. The Qing dynasty in China faced several major rebellions. By the late 1700s, European armies faced limited resistance as they claimed new territories.

THE IMPACT TODAY
English is still widely spoken in India today and serves as a major language of government and business.

READING CHECK **Summarize** Why did European power begin to expand in the late 1700s?

QUICK FACTS

FORMS OF IMPERIALISM

Imperial nations developed several different ways of organizing and governing the many territories in their empires.

- **Colony** a territory governed by a foreign power
- **Protectorate** a territory that has its own government but is controlled by a foreign power
- **Sphere of influence** a territory in which a country claims exclusive political or economic rights.

British East India Company

Early British imperialism in India was not carried out by the government but by a trading company, the **British East India Company**. Created to control trade between Britain, India, and East Asia, the company soon became embroiled in Indian politics. By 1800 it had come to rule much of India in the name of Great Britain.

The British Take Control As long as the Mughal Empire remained strong in India, the East India Company's activity was limited to coastal trading cities. When the empire began to break apart into small states in the mid-1700s, though, leaders of the East India Company sensed a chance to take over Indian lands. They manipulated the rulers of these new states, suggesting to each ruler that he needed British support to keep his throne. By playing rulers against each other and keeping them from cooperating, the British kept India in chaos. The company then swept in with its own armies and took over much of India, claiming to have done so just to restore order.

Changes in India Once in control, the East India Company made changes to Indian society. They introduced a new education system and the English language. They also introduced British laws that banned certain customs, such as sati, the practice of Hindu widows throwing themselves on their husbands' funeral fires. The British also invited Christian missionaries to spread their beliefs through India.

Eventually, some Indians began to believe the British were trying to destroy their society. They thought the British wanted to eliminate Indian customs and Hinduism completely. As a result, relations between Indians and British became increasingly strained.

The Sepoy Mutiny In 1857 these strained relations exploded into a rebellion, the **Sepoy Mutiny**. Sepoys were Indian soldiers who fought in the British army. The spark that set off their rebellion was the introduction of a new type of British rifle. Before inserting a cartridge into the rifle, a soldier had to bite off the end of an ammunition cartridge, which was greased with pork and beef fat. This offended both Muslim sepoys, who did not eat pork, and Hindu sepoys, who did not eat beef.

Skills Focus: Identifying Main Idea and Details

At Level

Prep Required

Reading Skill

European Imperialism

1. Organize the class into small groups. Have each group create a chart showing the causes of European imperialism between 1800 and 1920. Tell students to group the causes under the following headings: Technology and Weakening Empires.
2. Review student charts as a class, creating a master chart for students to see.
3. Guide students in a discussion of the causes of the new wave of European colonization.

LS Interpersonal, Visual-Spatial

Alternative Assessment Handbook, Rubrics 7: Charts; and 11: Discussions

Answers

Reading Check *Europeans had an advantage in the quality of their weapons and military training, and took advantage of the decline of the great empires in Asia and Africa.*

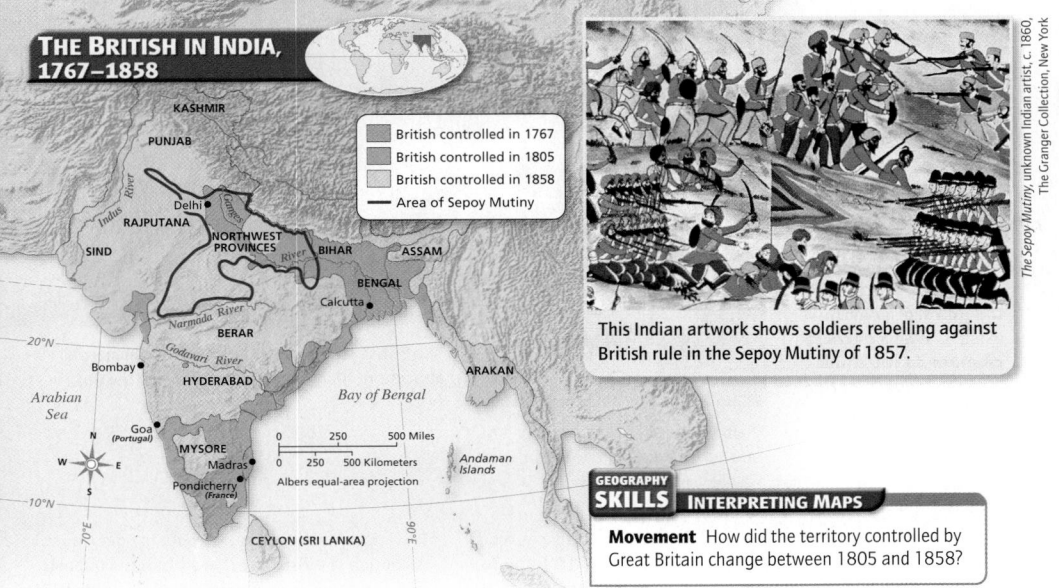

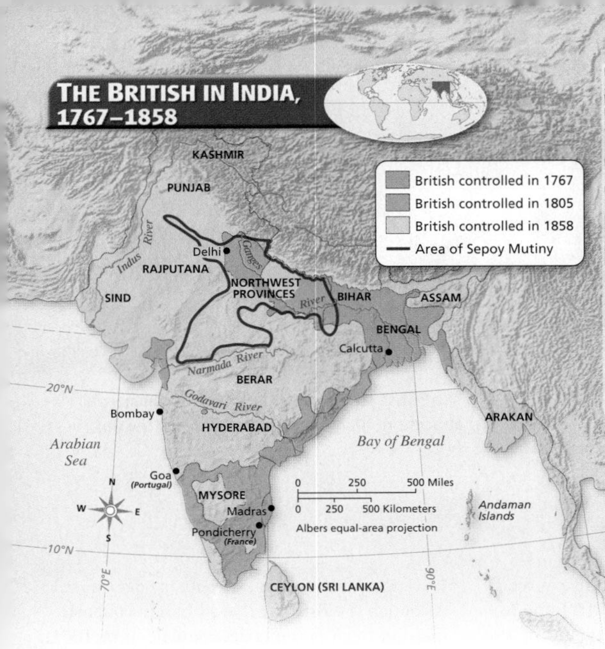

The Sepoy Mutiny, unknown Indian artist, c. 1860, The Granger Collection, New York

This Indian artwork shows soldiers rebelling against British rule in the Sepoy Mutiny of 1857.

GEOGRAPHY SKILLS INTERPRETING MAPS

Movement How did the territory controlled by Great Britain change between 1805 and 1858?

Already resentful of the British efforts to westernize India, many sepoys balked. Thinking that the new cartridges were a plot to make them abandon Hinduism and Islam, sepoys in the town of Meerut refused to use them. For their protest, these sepoys were punished. In response, sepoys all over northern India rose up against British officers. Before long the rebellious sepoys had gained control of Delhi.

The violence of this rebellion was ferocious, with both sides committing atrocities. Sepoys killed not only their officers but also British women and children. The British responded with extreme brutality. Captured mutineers were strapped to cannons and shot. Villages suspected of supporting rebels were burned. The fighting continued for two years.

As a result of the mutiny, the British ended the rule of the East India Company in 1858. From then on, the British government would rule India directly. Although the British moved away from some of the social regulations that had angered many Indians, distrust continued between the British and the Indians.

READING CHECK **Identify Cause and Effect** How did the decline of the Mughal Empire contribute to the rise of British power in India?

India as a British Colony

India was Britain's most important colony—the "jewel in the crown" of the British Empire. Ruling India gave the British great political and financial rewards, as well as national pride. But for many Indians, British rule was a source of frustration and humiliation. This frustration gave rise to powerful feelings of nationalism.

The Raj The era of British rule in India is often called the British **Raj** (RAHZH), a Hindi word meaning "rule." The administration of India was carried out by a government agency called the Indian Civil Service (ICS). Though they were ruling India, most officials of the ICS were British. The ICS employed very few Indians, leaving many educated Indians frustrated at having no say in their own government.

Many British officials in India believed themselves superior to the people they governed. As a result, they lived in segregated neighborhoods and belonged to exclusive clubs. Most of these officials believed that they were improving the lives of the Indian people through westernization. Yet many prejudiced British officials believed that Indians were utterly incapable of governing themselves.

ACADEMIC VOCABULARY
prejudiced biased against a racial, religious, or national group

Direct Teach

Reading Focus

3 What was life like in India when it became a British colony? *administration of India mainly carried out by British officials; British lived in segregated neighborhoods; few opportunities for Indians to participate in government; Indian nationalism grew; boycotts started*

India as a British Colony

Recall What is the term for the British rule of India? *the British Raj*

Interpret In what ways did ruling India profit Great Britain? *India became a market for British manufactured goods, and also a source of raw materials such as cotton, tea, indigo, and jute.*

Map Transparency: The British in India, 1767–1858

Info to Know

The East India Connection In 1775 the American colonies adopted the Grand Union flag. At that time, members of Congress still hoped that the colonies could be reconciled to England. The Grand Union flag was virtually identical to the flag of the East India Company, which had been adopted following the Act of Union in 1707. Colonists would have been familiar with that flag because the tea they drank was transported on the company's ships. The current U.S. flag, with 13 alternating red and white stripes, is a mere modification of that design.

Differentiating Instruction

At Level

English-Language Learners

Standard English Mastery

1. Have students work in pairs or small groups to make a chart comparing the British East India Company's role in India with that of the British Raj.
2. Review student charts as a class, creating a master chart for students to see. Have students correct their own work as needed.
3. Guide students in a discussion of British involvement in India. Have students take notes during the discussion.
4. Have students use the information from their charts and class notes to write a paragraph addressing this question: What lessons might the British have learned from the experiences of the East India Company? Have students work in pairs to review their first drafts, correcting spelling and grammar. **LS Visual-Spatial, Verbal-Linguistic**

Alternative Assessment Handbook, Rubrics 7: Charts; and 37: Writing Assignments

Answers

Interpreting Maps *By 1858, Great Britain controlled most of India.*

Reading Check *As the Mughal Empire weakened, the British were able to take control of more land in India.*

Direct Teach

Reading Focus

India as a British Colony

Identify Who was Ram Mohun Roy and what was his message? *an Indian nationalist; believed that Indians should have the same rights as Europeans*

Identify Cause and Effect What were the effects of the swadeshi boycott movement? *convinced the British to make concessions to the Indian people; formation of Muslim League*

Evaluate In what ways did British rule help India? In what ways did it harm India? *possible answer—helped: built railroads, roads, and canals; harmed: devastated India's pre-existing industry, kept Indians from participating in government*

CRF: Biography: Ramanujan

Info to Know

British Rule Under the Raj, the British ruled India through a network of Indian politicians and civil servants. While it appeared to be stable, the Raj was constantly under threat from within as Indians aspired to self-rule, as well as from the plotting of other imperialist nations. Russia also had designs on the subcontinent. The competition between Britain and Russia for control came to be called "the great game."

Impact of the Raj on India

The era of British control in India brought many changes. The British introduced their own governmental, legal, and educational systems, the English language, and new forms of technology and industry. These changes to India's economy and society, combined with unhappiness over foreign control, led to the growth of nationalism in India. ***Which of these changes do you think had the longest lasting effects in India? Why?***

The British encouraged the growth of commercial agriculture, India's main industry during the Raj.

Ram Mohun Roy, an Indian nationalist, argued for India's right to govern itself.

During the Raj the British built railroads, roads, and canals in India. By 1910 India had the fourth-largest railroad network in the world. Britain invested in transportation for two reasons: to move troops to trouble spots more easily and to help sell British products throughout India.

India was an important market for British manufactured goods, but that was not its only economic significance. It was a source of raw materials, such as cotton, tea, indigo, and jute. In fact, India became one of the most significant sources of raw cotton for British textile factories in the 1860s, after cotton from the United States became unavailable during the American Civil War. In addition, taxes collected from Indian landowners paid for the administration of India and the Indian army.

Though it was profitable for Britain, the introduction of British manufactured goods, especially textiles, devastated India's pre-existing industry. Although India had been a major exporter of textiles to Asia until the early 1800s, the British closed Indian textile factories to prevent competition with British companies. By the mid-1800s, India primarily exported raw materials rather than manufactured goods.

The Rise of Indian Nationalism Many groups in India found the changes that came with British rule deeply disturbing. Indian elites and middle classes resented having so few opportunities to participate in government. Although the British allowed Indians to participate in town and district councils after 1861, Indians had little power to influence decisions at higher levels of government.

Still, it took more than resentment to build a nationalist movement. That movement did not take off until Indians began to see themselves as having the same rights as Europeans. This idea was first expressed by the reformer Ram Mohun Roy in the 1820s. Roy, an activist who wanted to abolish several aspects of traditional Indian society, felt that the British were violating the Indian people's rights, including the rights of free speech and religion. Roy wrote texts and opened schools to spread his nationalist ideas throughout India.

Despite Roy's efforts, it took several decades for the nationalist movement to become active. The first Indian nationalist organization, the **Indian National Congress**, was not founded until 1885. A popular organization, the Indian National Congress was established by English-speaking Indians, most of whom were Hindu. In the early years, the requests of the Congress to the British were modest, such as more positions for Indians in the ICS and better representation on government councils.

Indian nationalism became more radical, though, when the British announced plans to partition Bengal. Officials claimed that breaking Bengal into two provinces would make it

Collaborative Learning

At Level

Research Required

The British in India

1. Organize students into two groups. Have each group prepare for a classroom debate about the positive and negative effects of British rule on India. Have students use reliable print and online sources to gather information for the debate. Each group should be prepared to either defend or attack the overall effects of British rule.
2. After each group has had time to conduct its research and prepare its arguments, hold a classroom debate. Which side was able to present the more convincing arguments?
3. Guide students in a discussion of the overall effects of British rule on India. How did researching both sides of the issue help them understand the ongoing controversy over it?

LS Interpersonal, Kinesthetic

Alternative Assessment Handbook, Rubrics 10: Debates; 11: Discussions; and 30: Research

Answers

Impact of the Raj on India *possible answer—new technology and industry; because those things helped modernize India, a lasting effect even after independence*

Under British rule, thousands of miles of railroads were built across India. Here, workers build the East Bengal Railway around 1870.

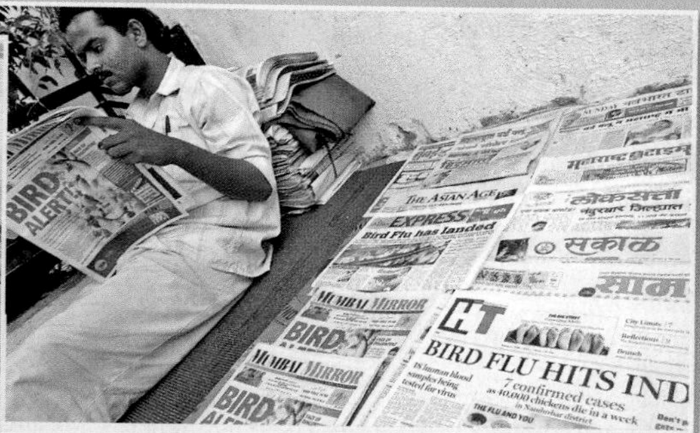

A lingering effect of the Raj is the prevalence of the English language in India today. One of the country's most widely spoken languages, English is often used in politics and business.

easier to govern, but some nationalists thought the partition was an attempt to break up Bengal's Hindu population. In response, radicals in the Congress called for a boycott of British goods. This boycott, or *swadeshi* ("own country"), movement lasted from 1905 to 1908.

Participants in the *swadeshi* boycotts vowed to wear only Indian-made garments. As part of their protest, some publicly burned piles of British cloth. A few militant nationalists, not thinking the boycott to be a strong enough statement of their feelings, attacked British officials. The militants were punished, but the *swadeshi* movement convinced the British to make concessions to the Indian people.

In addition to political concessions, the *swadeshi* movement had some unintended consequences. One was the formation of the **Muslim League** in 1906. Many Muslim leaders feared that Hindus had opposed the partition of Bengal for political reasons—to preserve the power of Hindus at the expense of Muslims. As a result, the Muslim League sought to protect the interests of Indian Muslims. The Indian National Congress and the Muslim League later became the main organizations in the struggle for Indian independence.

READING CHECK **Infer** Why did Indian nationalists respond to the plan to partition Bengal with a boycott of British goods?

SECTION 1 ASSESSMENT

go.hrw.com
Online Quiz
Keyword: SHL IMP HP

Reviewing Ideas, Terms, and People

1. **a. Recall** What military technologies did the Industrial Revolution provide to Europeans?
   b. Identify Cause and Effect How did internal problems in Asian empires contribute to the success of European imperialism?
2. **a. Identify** What was the **Sepoy Mutiny**?
   b. Explain How did Britain gain control over most of India by 1858?
3. **a. Define** What was the **Raj**?
   b. Explain How did the *swadeshi* movement lead to the creation of the **Muslim League**?

Critical Thinking

4. **Categorize** Using the chart below and your notes from this section, summarize the effects of British rule on India in each category listed. Which effect was most significant?

Category	Effects
Politics	
Economics	
Society	

FOCUS ON SPEAKING

5. **Persuasion** Write a short speech arguing that British rule helped India or harmed India. Use details from the section.

Direct Teach

Info to Know

Gandhi's Spinning Wheel Mohandas Gandhi, the great leader of the Indian independence movement, was often photographed at his spinning wheel. His spinning wheel represented resistance to the forced importation of British textiles that had undermined the Indian weaving industry. It also represented resistance to the British rulers and the way of life they had tried to impose on India.

Review & Assess

Close

Guide students in a discussion of the overall effects of British rule on India's economy, society, and government.

Review

Online Quiz, Section 1

Assess

SE Section 1 Assessment

Progress Assessment: Section 1 Quiz

Alternative Assessment Handbook

Reteach/Intervene

Interactive Reader and Study Guide, Section 1

Interactive Skills Tutor CD-ROM

Section 1 Assessment Answers

1. **a.** steam-powered boats, repeating rifles, machine guns, and exploding shells
   b. by weakening them so that they could only offer limited resistance to European armies
2. **a.** Muslim and Hindu soldiers refused to use a rifle that had a cartridge greased with animal fat. They were punished, leading to mutiny.
   b. by placing allies on the thrones of Indian states, and through a series of wars against the most powerful kingdoms of India
3. **a.** the age of British rule in India
   b. because the boycotts seemed to protect the rights of Hindus at the expense of Muslims
4. Politics—introduced British system of government; Economics—hurt India's existing industry, made India an exporter of raw materials rather than manufactured goods; Society—introduced English language, led to growth of Indian nationalism
5. Students should support their arguments with information from the text.

Answers

Reading Check *They thought the partition was intended to weaken the Hindu population.*

Preteach

Getting Started

Use the **Interactive Reader and Study Guide** to familiarize students with the section content.

Interactive Reader and Study Guide, Section 2

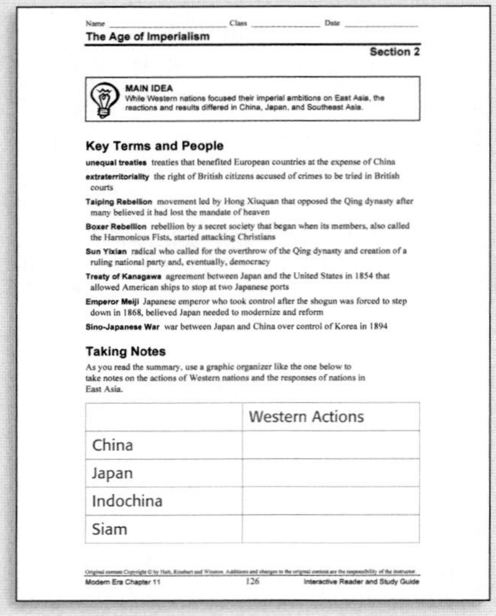

Name ______ Class ______ Date ______

The Age of Imperialism

Section 2

MAIN IDEA
While Western nations focused their imperial ambitions on East Asia, the reactions and results differed in China, Japan, and Southeast Asia.

Key Terms and People

unequal treaties treaties that benefited European countries at the expense of China

extraterritoriality the right of British citizens accused of crimes to be tried in British courts

Taiping Rebellion movement led by Hong Xiuquan that opposed the Qing dynasty after many believed it had lost the mandate of heaven

Boxer Rebellion rebellion by a secret society that began when its members, also called the Harmonious Fists, started attacking Christians

Sun Yixian radical who called for the overthrow of the Qing dynasty and creation of a ruling national party and, eventually, democracy

Treaty of Kanagawa agreement between Japan and the United States in 1854 that allowed American ships to stop at two Japanese ports

Emperor Meiji Japanese emperor who took control after the shogun was forced to step down in 1868, believed Japan needed to modernize and reform

Sino-Japanese War war between Japan and China over control of Korea in 1894

Taking Notes

As you read the summary, use a graphic organizer like the one below to take notes on the actions of Western nations and the responses of nations in East Asia.

	Western Actions
China	
Japan	
Indochina	
Siam	

CRF: Vocabulary Builder: Section 2

Taking Notes

China—Treaty of Nanjing; Taiping Rebellion; Boxer Rebellion; 1911 Revolution; Japan—Treaty of Kanagawa; Meiji Restoration and reforms; modernization and industrialization; Dutch East Indies—established large plantations in Southeast Asia; British took control parts of the Malay Peninsula; Indochina—French conquered Indochina; Vietnam—French controlled most of the South; Siam—retained independence; served as buffer between British Burma and French Indochina

SECTION 2

East Asia and the West

Before You Read

Main Idea

While Western nations focused their imperial ambitions on East Asia, the reactions and results differed in China, Japan, and Southeast Asia.

Reading Focus

1. How did Western nations gain power and influence in China in the 1800s?
2. What led to the rise of Japan as a major power?
3. How did European power and influence increase in Southeast Asia?

Key Terms and People

unequal treaties
extraterritoriality
Taiping Rebellion
Boxer Rebellion
Sun Yixian
Treaty of Kanagawa
Emperor Meiji
Sino-Japanese War

Taking Notes Take notes about the actions of Western nations and the responses of nations in East Asia.

Western Actions	Response of East Asian Nations

The Inside Story

Why did Great Britain go to war over the sale of illegal drugs? During the 1700s tea became a popular drink among the British. China was the sole source of tea. Despite Britain's position as the world's greatest industrial power, China had little interest in buying anything Britain produced. So, to pay for its tea habit, Britain sent vast quantities of silver to China. Year after year, silver was leaving Britain for China, and little money was coming back.

To correct the imbalance, Britain needed to find a product that the Chinese would buy, and it found one—opium. Opium had been grown in Asia for centuries, but the Chinese emperor had outlawed the opium trade in 1729. Even so, British traders had been smuggling in small quantities of opium from Britain's territories in India for years. Because of the desire to send silver back to Britain, the British East India Company increasingly ignored opium smuggling in the territory it controlled.

Opium had a devastating effect on China. Workers and peasants fell victim to the drug. It is impossible to know exact figures, but some historians estimate that as many as 1 out of every 10 Chinese were addicted to opium.

The drug's destructive effects on Chinese society led the emperor to stand firm against the British smuggling. Commissioner Lin Zixu wrote a letter to Queen Victoria, stating the Chinese case.

"Let us ask, where is your conscience? I have heard that the smoking of opium is very strictly forbidden by your country; that is because the harm caused by opium is clearly understood. Since it is not permitted to do harm to your own country, then even less should you let it be passed on to the harm of other countries—how much less to China!"

The British never responded to Lin's letter. When Lin ordered the destruction of British opium stored in the city of Guangzhou, the British struck back by sending warships to China. The Opium War had begun.

British ships attacking Chinese warships during the Opium War ▶

Iron Steam Ship Nemesis *Destroying the Chinese War Junks,* by Edward Duncan, 1841

Teach the Main Idea

At Level

East Asia and the West

1. **Teach** Ask students the Reading Focus questions to teach this section.
2. **Apply** Have students create an outline of the section using the headings as main points. Have students identify two main ideas under each of the blue subheadings.
3. **Review** Review student outlines as a class. Have students identify the points in their outlines that they feel are most important to the section entitled East Asia and the West. Then guide students in a discussion of the ways in which China, Japan, and Southeast Asia were affected by Western imperialism.
4. **Practice/Homework** Have students write a paragraph explaining why a government might try to limit its people's trade and contact with other nations. **LS Visual-Spatial, Verbal-Linguistic**

Alternative Assessment Handbook, Rubric 42: Writing to Inform

Western Nations Gain Power

In 1800 trade with European merchants was profitable for the Chinese, but the Chinese did not view the Europeans as particularly important. They were just another set of foreigners who might pay tribute to the emperor.

All of that changed in the 1800s. Little by little, the Qing dynasty lost its power, its prestige, and its sovereignty over China.

The Opium War Chinese rulers had long believed that all nations outside China were barbaric, and they wanted little contact with the outside world. When Europeans pushed for trading rights in China, the Chinese restricted their trade to a single city, Guangzhou.

The Chinese did not want European goods, but they did want silver. They were pleased when tea became popular in Britain and British silver flowed into China. But the British were distressed by the imbalance of trade.

In the late 1700s the British discovered a solution to the trade imbalance—opium. In China there was a great demand for the drug, and opium addiction became such a problem that the Chinese government banned the import of opium in 1796. But foreign merchants continued to smuggle the drug into China.

In 1839 Chinese officials ordered the destruction of British opium in Guangzhou. The British responded by sending a naval force to launch an attack. After capturing Shanghai in 1842, the British forced the Chinese to sign a peace treaty, the Treaty of Nanjing.

The Treaty of Nanjing was the first of the **unequal treaties**—so called because they benefited European countries at the expense of China. The treaty opened five more ports to Western trade. It also gave **extraterritoriality** to the British, meaning that British citizens accused of crimes had the right to be tried in British courts rather than in Chinese courts.

In the next two decades, China was forced to sign more treaties with Britain, France, the United States, and Russia. Slowly but surely, the Qing dynasty was losing control over China to Western intruders.

The Taiping Rebellion The failure of the Qing dynasty to resist the Western powers led some Chinese to believe that the dynasty had lost the mandate of heaven. That belief led to a series of rebellions starting in 1850.

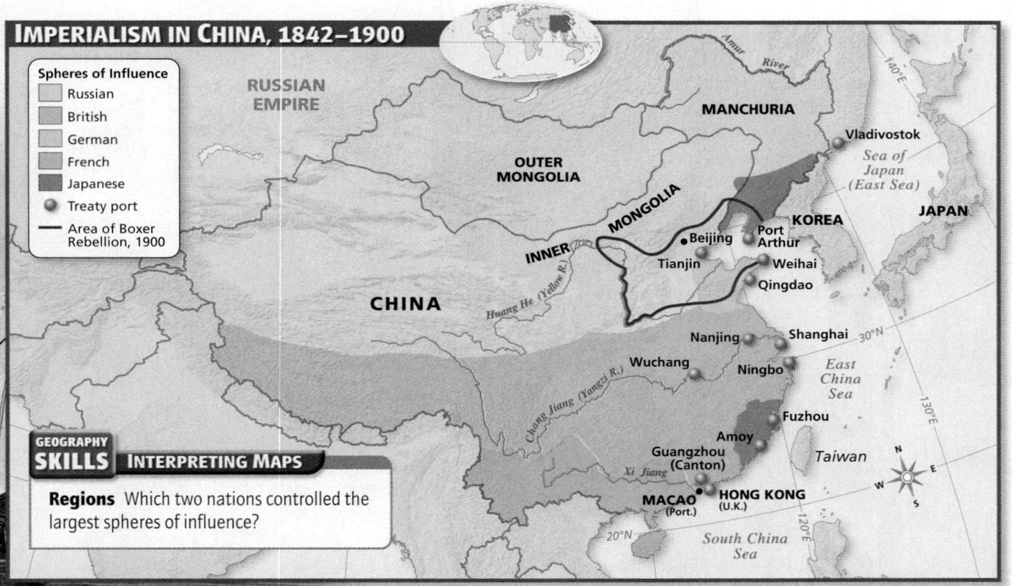

GEOGRAPHY SKILLS INTERPRETING MAPS

Regions Which two nations controlled the largest spheres of influence?

Direct Teach

Reading Focus

1 How did Western nations gain power and influence in China in the 1800s? *Britain smuggled opium to China; forced Chinese to sign unequal treaties benefiting Europeans at China's expense*

Western Nations Gain Power

Describe How did the Chinese view Europeans in the 1800s? *as just another set of foreigners who might pay tribute to the emperor*

Make Inferences Why did the Chinese restrict trade with Europe? *believed all nations outside China were barbaric*

Make Judgments Were Chinese fears about Western intentions warranted? Explain. *possible answer—Yes; by the end of the 19th century, China had lost much of its sovereignty to Western powers, and the Chinese empire was overthrown in 1911.*

Activity **Asia Past and Present** Have students compare this map of Asia with a current map in the atlas of their text. Have students identify what has changed between 1900 and the present. **LS Visual-Spatial**

Map Transparency: Imperialism in China, 1842–1900

Collaborative Learning — At Level

Opening Doors to Trade

1. Organize the class into three groups. One group represents a Western government that wants to open China to Western trade. The second group represents the Qing government's attitudes toward Western trade. The third group represents the point of view of Chinese merchants. Have each group conduct research if necessary and prepare arguments to support the views of the group it represents.
2. Conduct a classroom debate on the desirability of opening China to Western trade, and whether or not this should have been a Chinese or Western decision. When the debate has ended, have students decide which group or groups made the most convincing arguments and explain why.
3. Have each student write a brief essay discussing the long-term effects on China of trade with the West. **LS Interpersonal, Verbal-Linguistic**

Alternative Assessment Handbook, Rubrics 10: Debates; and 42: Writing to Inform

Answers

Interpreting Maps *Great Britain*

Direct Teach

Reading Focus

Western Nations Gain Power

Identify Cause and Effect What were the effects of the Taiping Rebellion? *more than 20 million Chinese died; Qing dynasty ended the rebellion*

Explain How did the Boxer Rebellion start and end? *In 1899, the Boxers started attacking Christians in China; 20,000 foreign troops captured Beijing and suppressed the uprising*

Info to Know

Hong Kong The Chinese island of Hong Kong was ceded to Great Britain after the first Opium War in 1842. Hong Kong and the peninsula of Kowloon were leased to Great Britain for 99 years. The lease expired in 1997, and the area reverted to Chinese control.

In the 1850s the most serious rebellion was led by Hong Xiuquan (shee-oo-CHOO-ahn), who believed that he was the brother of Jesus. He wanted to create a "Heavenly Kingdom of Great Peace," (*Taiping Tianguo*) where no one would be poor. His followers formed a movement called the **Taiping Rebellion**.

Hong and his followers captured large territories in southeastern China and by 1853 controlled the city of Nanjing. Qing soldiers, as well as British and French armies, attacked the Taiping army and finally defeated it in 1864. Although the Qing dynasty emerged victorious, the cost was great—more than 20 million Chinese died in the Taiping Rebellion.

READING SKILLS
Identifying Supporting Details What kind of reforms did Qing officials make?

Foreign Influence Takes Hold After the Taiping Rebellion, reform-minded officials of the Qing dynasty tried to make changes. For example, they pushed to build coal mines, factories, and railroads. They encouraged the government to make modern weapons and ships. They tried to introduce Western knowledge and languages to China. This movement, called the self-strengthening movement, ultimately failed because of strong resistance from traditional Confucian scholars and powerful officials.

While China struggled to reform, Japan was emerging as a major military power. China went to war with Japan over Korea in 1894, but the Japanese soundly defeated China.

Noting the weakness of the Chinese military, Western powers rushed to claim more territory in China. Germany, Russia, Great Britain, and France all carved out spheres of influence there.

By the late 1890s the United States got involved. Americans feared that European nations would divide China among themselves and the United States would lose its profitable trade in China. To prevent such a loss, U.S. secretary of state John Hay proposed the Open Door Policy, which would allow free trade in the Chinese ports under European control. This policy would allow the United States to continue its trade in China. Although the European nations never formally agreed to the Open Door Policy, they did allow free trade in their ports.

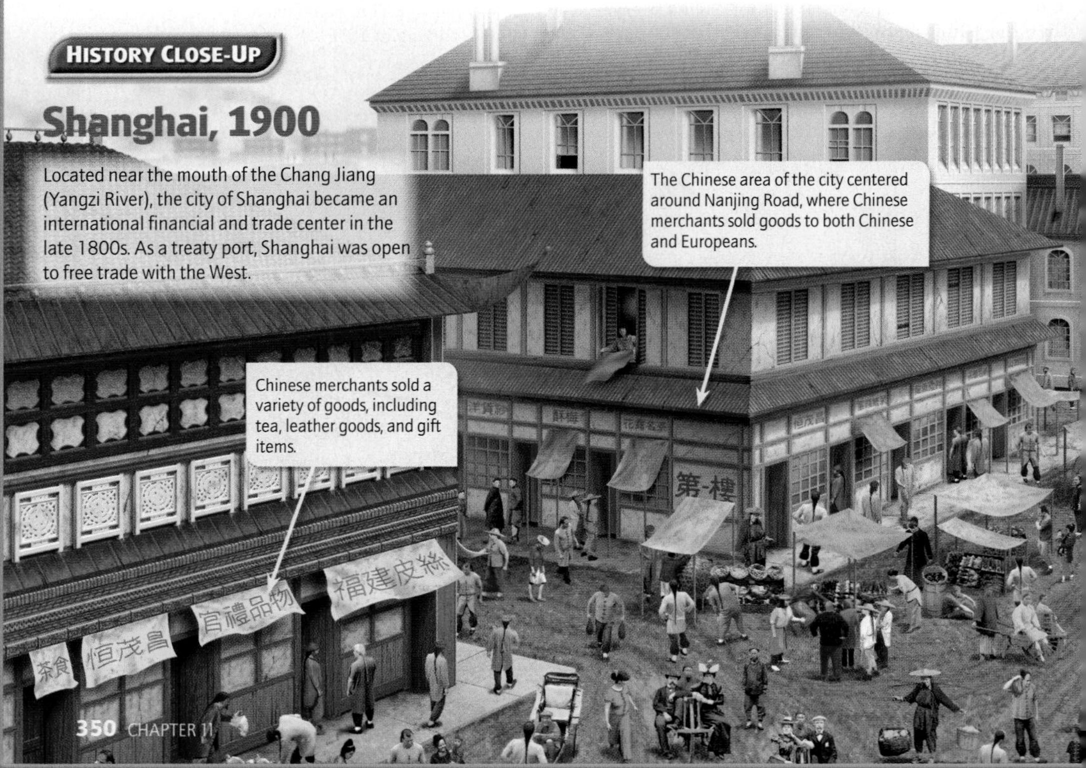

HISTORY CLOSE-UP
Shanghai, 1900
Located near the mouth of the Chang Jiang (Yangzi River), the city of Shanghai became an international financial and trade center in the late 1800s. As a treaty port, Shanghai was open to free trade with the West.
The Chinese area of the city centered around Nanjing Road, where Chinese merchants sold goods to both Chinese and Europeans.
Chinese merchants sold a variety of goods, including tea, leather goods, and gift items.
350 CHAPTER 11

Skills Focus: Summarizing

At Level

Reading Skill
Chinese Isolationism

1. Have students create charts summarizing the ways in which contact with Europeans affected China. Have students list advantages and disadvantages of contact with the West.
2. Review student charts as a class, creating a master chart for students to see. Have students correct their own charts as needed.
3. Tell students they are editors of an early Western-style Chinese newspaper. Have each student write an editorial discussing whether China should have remained isolated from Westerners. Student editorials should take a stand either for or against isolationism, and should include valid arguments.

LS Visual-Spatial, Verbal-Linguistic

Alternative Assessment Handbook, Rubrics 7: Charts; and 17: Letters to Editors

Answers

Reading Skills *pushed to build coal mines, factories, and railroads; encouraged government to make modern weapons and ships; tried to introduce Western knowledge and languages to China*

By the end of the 1800s, China was in a desperate position. The war with Japan had exposed China's military weakness, and Europeans now controlled large portions of Chinese territory. Something had to be done if China were to remain independent.

In 1898 the Chinese emperor decided to enact a series of reforms, including changing the civil service examinations and building a modern army. But Empress Dowager Cixi, the most powerful person in China, stopped the reforms because she believed they threatened the rule of the Qing dynasty. People who believed the reforms were necessary now began to call for an end to the Qing dynasty.

The Boxer Rebellion The humiliation of China by the West produced several nationalist movements intent on restoring China's glory. The most important was the Harmonious Fists, or Boxers. This secret society combined martial arts training, hatred of foreigners, and a belief that they were invulnerable to Western weapons. The **Boxer Rebellion** began in 1899 when the Boxers started attacking missionaries and Chinese converts to Christianity.

In June 1900 the Boxers laid siege to the foreign compounds in Beijing and held the foreigners hostage for 55 days. A few weeks later, an army of 20,000 foreign troops captured Beijing and suppressed the uprising. The foreign powers imposed a heavy fine on the Chinese government for secretly supporting the Boxers. The result was more humiliation for the Chinese government at the hands of foreigners.

The 1911 Revolution With the defeat of the Boxers, Qing officials finally began to enact reforms. They eliminated the system of examinations for officials and tried to establish primary and secondary schools. Qing officials took steps to create a new national army. They even created elected provincial assemblies, which began to meet in 1909.

Still, these reforms were too little, too late. Radicals living in Japan and the United States called for the overthrow of the Qing dynasty and the creation of a new Chinese republic.

Skills Focus INTERPRETING VISUALS

Draw Conclusions Why do you think Europeans considered Shanghai an important trading port?

Europeans controlled the area of the city along the river. This stretch of land included European banks, hotels, clubs, and restaurants.

Chinese merchants sold raw materials such as cotton and silk to European traders, who shipped the goods to Europe by steamship.

Direct Teach

Info to Know

Shanghai Today Today Shanghai is a bustling, modern city with a population well over 16 million. It is China's leading scientific and technological research center, and one of China's largest industrial centers.

The Taiping Rebellion The Taiping rebel force at its greatest consisted of about one million people. After they captured the city of Nanjing in 1853, they made it the capital of their kingdom. They were not driven out of Nanjing until 1864.

The Rise of the Chinese Press Toward the end of the 1800s, many Chinese scholars shifted from traditional to modern ideas and practices. Western religious texts were translated, along with a variety of other written works. The 1870s brought newspapers and magazines that circulated information about current events—a distinct break from the Confucian focus of the past. Large numbers of people were able to read the same periodicals at the same time. The press included satirical and critical pieces aimed at the government and foreign nations, which provoked reactions from the mass populace.

About the Illustration

This illustration is an artist's conception based on available sources. Historians, however, are uncertain exactly what this scene looked like.

Skills Focus: Identifying Main Idea and Details

At Level

Reading Skill

Western Influence and the Qing Dynasty

1. Have students make two lists, one describing Western influence on China and the other identifying problems with Qing rule.
2. Review student lists as a class, creating a master list for students to see. Have students identify examples of each type of Western influence or each problem with Qing rule.
3. Have each student write an analysis of the economic, political, and social problems of Qing rule. Which of the problems were directly attributable to Western influence? How might history have been different if China had been able to successfully resist foreign influence? **LS Verbal-Linguistic**

Alternative Assessment Handbook, Rubric 38: Writing to Classify

Answers

History Close-Up *was open to free trade with the West; traded tea, leather goods, and gift items, as well as raw materials such as cotton and silk*

Direct Teach

Reading Focus

Western Nations Gain Power

Recall What were the three principals of Sun Yixian's ideology? *nationalism, democracy, and "people's livelihood"*

Analyze How did Sun Yixian's philosophy incorporate both democracy and socialism? *possible answer—belief in independence, elected rulers, and individual freedoms, but also in equality in land ownership to remedy problems of the past in China*

Primary Sources

"An individual should not have too much freedom. A nation should have absolute freedom."
—Sun Yat-Sen

FACES OF HISTORY

SUN Yixian
1866–1925

Known as the Father of Modern China, Sun Yixian first became interested in pursuing a political career after China's disastrous defeat in the Sino-Japanese War. By 1905 he began developing a plan to restore economic and political strength to China. His ideas centered around the concept of political tutelage—that a strong government would teach the Chinese people the principles of representative government until a true democracy could emerge. Sun Yixian was practical and formed many alliances—even with Russian Communists—in an effort to unite the Chinese people.

Draw Conclusions What was Sun Yixian's main goal throughout his career?

Sun Yixian, known in the West as Sun Yat-sen, was the most prominent of these radicals. Sun based his revolutionary ideology on three basic principles—nationalism, democracy, and "people's livelihood." The last of these principles involved equality in landownership and was often translated as socialism.

Sun believed that China should eventually become a democracy, but that the Chinese people were not ready yet. First, he called for the overthrow of the Qing dynasty and its replacement by a ruling nationalist party. He wanted this party to act as a guardian of the Chinese people until they were ready for democracy.

Other people in China also began to call for the overthrow of the Qing dynasty. Revolutionary ideas took root among intellectuals and junior officers in military academies. In October 1911 a group of young officers led a revolt in the city of Wuchang. Support for the revolt grew rapidly. In January 1912 the revolutionaries declared a republic.

The Qing wanted a general named Yuan Shikai to quash the rebellion. Instead of crushing the rebels, though, Yuan negotiated peace with them. At the peace talks, Yuan convinced the Chinese emperor to abdicate. This event brought an end to the 268-year rule of the Qing dynasty. After the abdication, Yuan Shikai agreed to become the first president of the new Republic of China.

READING CHECK **Find the Main Idea** How did European intervention in China contribute to the downfall of the Qing dynasty?

The Rise of Modern Japan

Japan learned from the Chinese example about how *not* to respond to the West. Like China, Japan resisted contact at first. But once that contact was made in the mid-1800s, Japan reacted differently. Instead of descending into turmoil and revolution, Japan emerged as a great military and imperial power.

The U.S. Renews Contact The Tokugawa regime ruled Japan from 1603 to 1867 and tried to limit contact with the outside world. Yet American and European merchants wanted to trade with Japan. To open up trade, in 1852 U.S. president Millard Fillmore sent Commodore Matthew Perry on a mission to Japan. Perry appeared in Edo (Tokyo) Bay in 1853 with four warships and again in 1854 with nine ships.

The threat of the U.S. navy convinced Japanese officials to sign the **Treaty of Kanagawa** in 1854. This treaty allowed American ships to stop at two Japanese ports. Another treaty in 1858 opened five more Japanese ports to Western merchants. This treaty also established extraterritoriality for Westerners in Japan.

Many Japanese found these treaties deeply humiliating. They were especially angry that Westerners committing crimes in Japan received extremely mild punishments or no punishment at all. These treaties contributed to the rise of Japanese nationalism.

The Meiji Restoration Throughout the Tokugawa period, the emperor had been little more than a symbolic figure. The shogun, or supreme military ruler, was the real power in Tokugawa Japan. But many Japanese people, resenting the way that the shogun had given in to Western demands, forced the shogun to step down. This ended the military control of the Japanese government.

The young emperor, Mutsuhito, took back the power of the government in 1868, taking the name **Emperor Meiji**, which means "enlightened rule." The period of his reign from 1868 to 1912 is called the Meiji period, and the emperor's return to power is called the Meiji Restoration.

From China's example, the Meiji emperor learned about the risk of resisting Western demands. China had clung to its traditional ways and had been unsuccessful in keeping

Differentiating Instruction

Below Level

Learners Having Difficulty

1. Have students work in mixed-ability pairs to review the information in the text about the Qing dynasty. Then have students work in pairs to create a sequence diagram showing the steps that led to the dynasty's downfall.
2. Review student sequence charts as a class, creating a master chart for students to see. Have volunteers explain steps on the chart. Have students correct their work as needed.
3. Guide students in a discussion of the downfall of the Qing dynasty. Have volunteers suggest measures that could have been taken at each step to help strengthen the dynasty.

LS Visual-Spatial

Alternative Assessment Handbook, Rubric 7: Charts

Answers

Faces of History *to restore economic and political strength to China*

Reading Check *Western actions in China led to nationalist movements and rebellions. In 1911 Chinese revolutionaries ended the 268-year Qing dynasty and declared the Republic of China.*

its sovereignty, or independent control of its government. The Meiji emperor believed that the best way to preserve and build Japan's strength was to modernize and reform.

Meiji Reforms The reforms undertaken during the Meiji era were far-reaching. A group of Japanese officials made a two-year journey called the Iwakura Mission, in which they traveled to the United States and Europe to learn about Western society, military practices, and economics. The officials were to determine which aspects of Western life would help Japan modernize efficiently.

Japan soon required all children to attend school and allowed some students to study abroad. Japanese military officials adapted practices of the U.S. and European armed forces to strengthen their own military.

Most significantly, the emperor supported rapid industrialization. The government financed the construction of the infrastructure necessary for a modern industrial economy. It built telegraph lines, set up a postal service, established a national currency, and helped build a railroad system. By the 1890s, the Japanese economy was booming. In fact, between 1895 and 1915, manufacturing grew more rapidly in Japan than in the United States. Japan was quickly becoming one of the world's great industrial powers.

Becoming an Imperial Power Now that Japan had modernized, it was ready to take its place on the world stage. It began by strengthening its influence over Korea. In the 1870s Japan forced Korea to open three ports to Japanese merchants—even though Korea had traditionally pledged its allegiance to China. When a rebellion broke out in Korea in 1894, Japan and China both sent troops to Korea. This action led to the **Sino-Japanese War**, which lasted only a few months and ended in a humiliating defeat for China.

Japan Reacts to U.S. Military Might

Commodore Matthew Perry Arrives in Japan, by Yoshitoshi Taiso

Skills Focus READING LIKE A HISTORIAN

In this print, artist Yoshitoshi Taiso depicts the arrival of Commodore Perry in Edo Bay in 1853. Perry's hulking black warships sent the Japanese a strong message about U.S. military power.

Analyzing Visuals How did the artist show the difference between Japanese and American power?

See **Skills Handbook**, p. H26

Direct Teach

Reading Focus

2 What led to the rise of Japan as a major power? *During the Meiji period, Japan made reforms and modernized.*

The Rise of Modern Japan

Identify What was the main point of the Treaty of Kanagawa? *allowed American ships to stop at two Japanese ports*

Interpret Why did Japan agree to the Treaty of Kanagawa? *The threat of the U.S. navy convinced Japan to sign the treaty, even though many Japanese found the treaty humiliating.*

Contrast How did Japan's response to the West differ from China's response? *Instead of rebelling against Western influences, Japan made reforms and modernized.*

CRF: Biography: Hokusai

CRF: History and Geography: Japan Opens Trade Routes

Info to Know

Modernizing the Silk Industry In the late 1800s Japan acquired Western techniques and machinery to mechanize its silk industry. Using steam or water power instead of turning the reel by hand produced silk filaments of uniform size and greater strength at faster speed. A large labor force was still required to prepare silkworm cocoons and tend the machines. Most of the employees were women. Under Meiji rule, the silk industry progressed due to the use of more advanced methods of production and numerous mills.

Skills Focus: Identifying Problem and Solution

At Level

Reading Skill

Japan Responds to Perry

1. Tell the class that they are daimyo, and the Japanese shogun has asked for their advice on how to respond to Commodore Perry's demands for U.S. trading privileges in Japan.
2. Organize the class into small groups, and have the daimyo discuss among themselves whether opening trade with the United States is in Japan's best interests.
3. Then have the daimyo propose courses of action that might satisfy the United States but still preserve Japan's culture and desire for isolation.
4. Have each daimyo write a draft of a letter of response for Perry to take back to the American president. Each letter should include the reasoning behind that daimyo's decision. **LS Interpersonal, Verbal-Linguistic**

Alternative Assessment Handbook, Rubrics 14: Group Activity; and 41: Writing to Express

Answers

Reading Like a Historian *possible answer—Perry's ship appears large and intimidating in comparison to the small Japanese boats in the foreground.*

Direct Teach

Reading Focus

3 How did European power and influence increase in Southeast Asia? *Dutch, British, and French claimed colonies in Southeast Asia.*

Europeans in Southeast Asia

Recall Where did Great Britain and France claim colonies in Southeast Asia? *Great Britain—Malaysia; France—Indochina*

Contrast How was Siam different from other parts of Southeast Asia? *It was the only Southeast Asian country to retain its independence in the 1800s.*

Quick Facts Transparency: The Meiji Reforms

Map Transparency: Southeast Asia, 1895

Info to Know

Government Reforms The new Japanese government abolished feudalism. Most of the feudal lords willingly gave up their privileges, but those who resisted were ruthlessly crushed. As compensation for their losses, former lords were awarded European titles and public offices. Thus counts, barons, and marquises began to appear as key figures in the Japanese government.

The Meiji Reforms

QUICK FACTS

During the Meiji era, a number of significant reforms quickly transformed Japan into a modern industrialized nation.

Governmental Reforms
- Ended feudalism; local government based on prefectures (districts)
- Enacted European-style constitution

Rapid Industrialization
- Government invested in transportation and communication
- Government directly supported businesses and industries

Military Reforms
- Modeled army and navy after those of Prussia and Britain
- Required three years' military service from all men

▲ Factory workers during the Meiji era

The Japanese victory established Japan as the most powerful state in Asia. As a result of the war, China recognized Korea's independence. Japan gained control of Taiwan, which became its colony, and won the right to build factories in China. Western powers treated Japan with a newfound respect, giving in to Japan's request to end extraterritoriality.

Japan's status as a great power was confirmed by its victory in the Russo-Japanese War of 1904–1905. This war was caused by Russian competition with Japan over influence in Manchuria and Korea. Although the Japanese won a series of battles, they could not get the Russians to surrender. Instead, the two sides asked U.S. president Theodore Roosevelt to help negotiate a peace treaty, called the Treaty of Portsmouth.

The treaty gave Japan control over Russian railway lines in southern Manchuria and transferred Russian leases on two Manchurian ports to Japan. The treaty also recognized Korea as under Japanese influence.

Japan's victory over Russia was celebrated all over Asia. It showed that an Asian power could defeat a European power. But growing Japanese power also presented a threat to its Asian neighbors. In 1910 Japan annexed Korea as a Japanese colony, demonstrating that its power in Asia was growing.

READING CHECK **Draw Conclusions** How did Japan gain the strength to become an imperial power?

Europeans in Southeast Asia

Southeast Asia had long been a source of spices, such as cloves and pepper, that Europeans valued highly. To get these spices, Europeans established colonies there in the 1500s.

In the 1600s and 1700s, the Dutch controlled the spice trade by holding key Southeast Asian ports and fortifications. The Dutch began to grow sugar and coffee on large plantations in their Southeast Asian colonies. This shift to plantation agriculture set the pattern for future colonies in Southeast Asia.

In the 1800s the British began to compete with the Dutch in Malaysia. The British attained control of Malacca (part of modern-day Malaysia) from the Dutch in 1824. Britain already controlled the port cities of Singapore and Penang on the Malay Peninsula. In the late 1800s, the British moved into the interior of the peninsula. There, they established rubber plantations to provide raw material for bicycle-tire factories in Britain.

While the British increased their control over Malaysia, the French conquered part of Indochina. French missionaries and traders were active in Vietnam in the early 1800s. The ruling Nguyen (NGWEEN) dynasty saw the French as a threat and tried to expel French missionaries from the country. They also tried to crack down on Vietnamese converts to Christianity. In response, French emperor Napoleon III sent a fleet to Vietnam. The French defeated the Vietnamese forces in the Mekong

Skills Focus: Identifying Problem and Solution

At Level

Reading Skill

The Meiji Reforms

1. Tell students they will act as advisers to Emperor Meiji. Direct students' attention to the Quick Facts chart on this page.
2. Organize students into small groups and have them come up with several good reasons behind each of the reforms listed on the chart. Remind students to think about the reforms as a response to Western influence and to consider the long-term effects of each reform for Japan.
3. Have students write drafts of a letter to Emperor Meiji. Letters should propose that he enact several of the reforms and explain why each one will be beneficial to Japan.

LS **Interpersonal, Verbal-Linguistic**

Alternative Assessment Handbook, Rubrics 14: Group Activity; and 41: Writing to Express

Answers

Reading Check *Japan modernized and industrialized, which gave it the power to begin expanding.*

Delta and forced the Vietnamese ruler to sign the Treaty of Saigon in 1862. This treaty gave the French control of most of the territory in southern Vietnam.

France took control of the rest of Vietnam in 1884 and annexed neighboring Laos and Cambodia, creating a territory known as French Indochina. Like the British in India, the French built roads, railroads, and irrigation systems in Indochina. They also introduced some reforms in education and medical care.

French colonialism in Indochina largely benefited the French, however. Many French citizens became rich from their large tea and rubber plantations. Meanwhile, many Vietnamese farmers fell into debt when they were unable to pay high taxes. Due to these factors, Vietnamese peasants often lost their farms and were forced to become wage laborers. Vietnamese resentment against the French rulers grew throughout the 1800s and early 1900s.

Siam (called Thailand today) was the only Southeast Asian country to retain its independence in the 1800s. Siam served as a buffer between British-controlled Burma and French Indochina. By skillful exploitation of European rivalries and by careful modernization, the monarchs of Siam preserved the nation's freedom.

READING CHECK **Summarize** Why were Europeans interested in colonizing Southeast Asia?

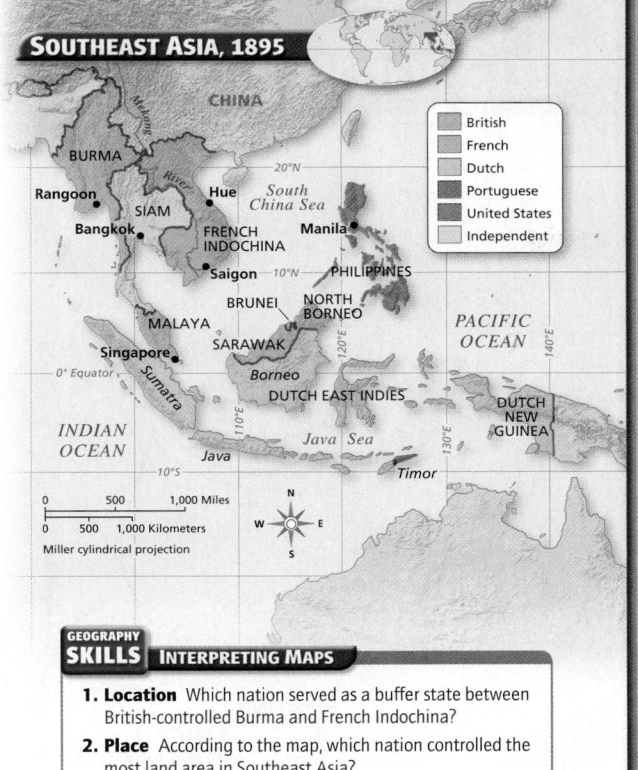

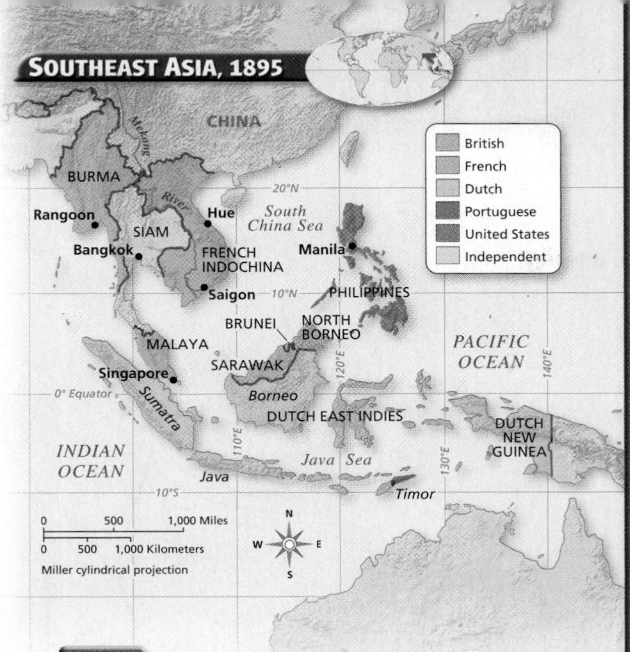

GEOGRAPHY SKILLS **INTERPRETING MAPS**

1. **Location** Which nation served as a buffer state between British-controlled Burma and French Indochina?
2. **Place** According to the map, which nation controlled the most land area in Southeast Asia?

SECTION 2 ASSESSMENT

go.hrw.com
Online Quiz
Keyword: SHL IMP HP

Reviewing Ideas, Terms, and People

1. **a. Recall** What were the **unequal treaties**?
   b. Draw Conclusions How did European imperialism lead to problems for the Qing dynasty?
   c. Elaborate How did the Chinese people react to the growing influence of Westerners in China?
2. **a. Identify** Who was **Emperor Meiji**?
   b. Contrast How did Japan's reaction to Western imperialism differ from China's?
   c. Evaluate Why was Japan more successful than China in maintaining its independence?
3. **a. Recall** What was the Treaty of Saigon?
   b. Make Generalizations How did Siam retain its independence?

Critical Thinking

4. **Compare and Contrast** Using your notes from the section and the chart below, compare and contrast European imperialism's effects on China and Japan.

	Effects on Japan	Effects on China
Political		
Economic		
Cultural		
Military		

FOCUS ON SPEAKING

5. **Persuasion** Suppose you are an official at the court of the Chinese emperor, just after China's defeat in the Sino-Japanese War. Prepare a short presentation to the emperor explaining the types of reforms China needs to make to become a great power again.

• Review & Assess •

Close

Have students summarize the ways in which China, Japan, and Southeast Asia responded to Western influences.

Review

Online Quiz, Section 2

Assess

SE Section 2 Assessment

Progress Assessment: Section 2 Quiz

Alternative Assessment Handbook

Reteach/Intervene

Interactive Reader and Study Guide, Section 2

Interactive Skills Tutor CD-ROM

Answers

Interpreting Maps **1.** *Siam;* **2.** *The Netherlands*

Reading Check *to obtain valuable spices such as cloves and pepper*

Section 2 Assessment Answers

1. **a.** treaties that benefited Europeans at the expense of the Chinese
   b. Humiliating defeats at the hands of European imperialists weakened the Qing dynasty, causing rebellions.
   c. They rebelled against their leaders.
2. **a.** the young emperor who returned to power in Japan in 1868
   b. Japan made reforms; Chinese resisted change.
   c. possible answer—Japan's modernization and industrialization allowed it to protect itself and expand its borders.
3. **a.** treaty that gave France control of most of the territory in southern Vietnam
   b. by exploiting European rivalries; modernizing
4. Political—Japan: rise in nationalism led to Meiji Restoration; China: rise in nationalist movements led to rebellions that weakened government; Economic—Japan: modernized industry, economy; China: British introduced opium, weakening China's economy Cultural—Japan: Meiji emperor made all children attend school, allowed some study abroad—China: Christian missionaries indirectly influenced rebellions; Military—Japan: modernized military; China: weak military led to loss of Sino-Japanese War and carving out of spheres of influence by Western nations
5. Student presentations might recommend reforms similar to the Meiji Reforms, which helped Japan emerge as a world power.

History and Geography

Imperialism and a Global Economy

Info to Know

Before Imperialism Western trade with China from 1760 to 1842 was considered by the Chinese to be a gracious grant by the Son of Heaven to foreigners. However, the Chinese government would not directly involve itself in dealings with Western traders. Instead, this task was assigned to special Chinese merchants known as the Cohong. Foreigners were allowed to live in specific areas in the port of Guangzhou only while engaged in trade, were not allowed the company of their wives, and were discouraged from learning Chinese. Foreign merchants could only communicate with government officials through Cohong intermediaries. Western traders endured these cumbersome regulations and restrictions. The end of the Cohong system was a major British goal in negotiating the Treaty of Nanjing.

HISTORY & Geography

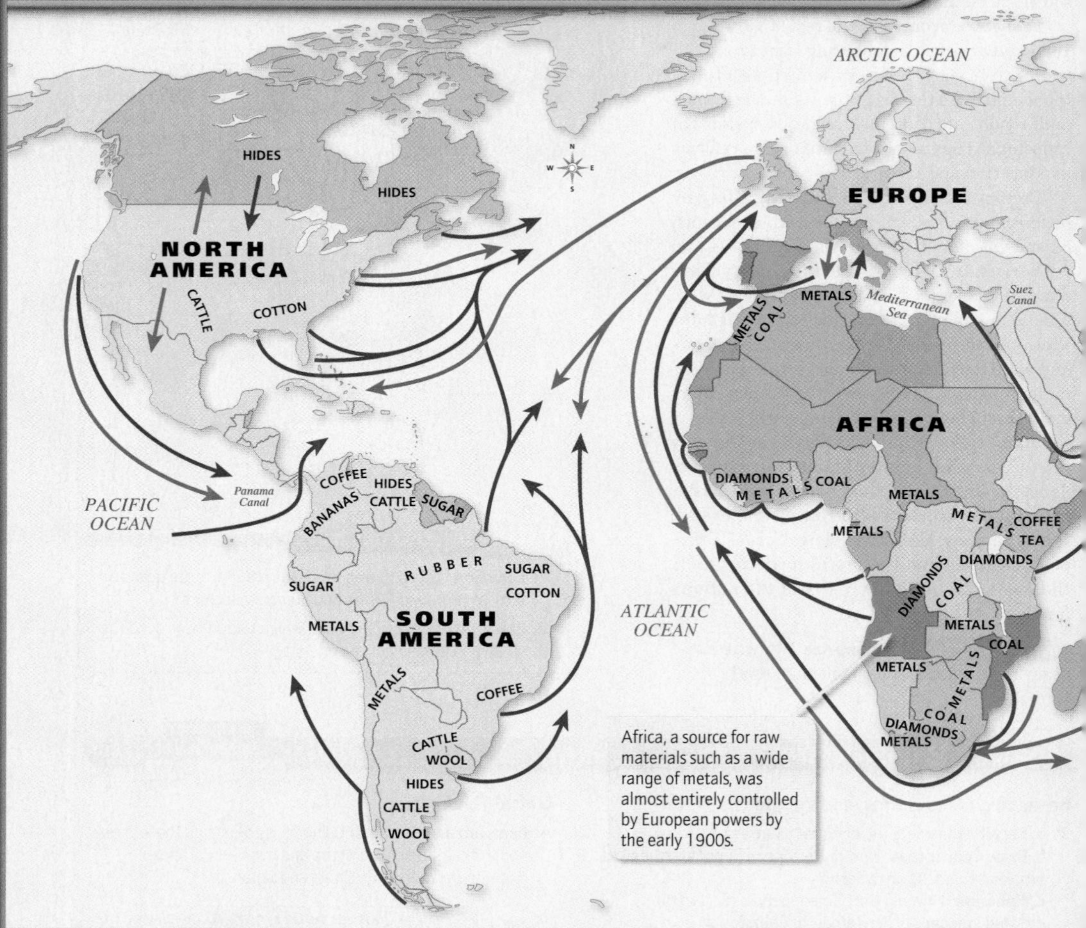

Africa, a source for raw materials such as a wide range of metals, was almost entirely controlled by European powers by the early 1900s.

Imperialism and a Global Economy

One result of the growth of imperialism was the creation of a global economy. As European nations competed for power and influence, they set up colonies around the world, especially in Africa and Asia. The colonies provided Europe's powers with the raw materials they needed for their rapidly industrializing economies. At the same time, the colonies provided new markets for European exports of manufactured goods. As a result, global trade grew dramatically, and a two-way traffic of goods developed—raw materials went to Europe, and manufactured goods went to the colonies.

356 CHAPTER 11

Skills Focus: Identifying Cause and Effect

At Level

Research Required

Reading Skill

The Effect of the Suez Canal

1. Review with students the information about the Suez Canal. Remind them that control of the Suez Canal was an important goal of imperialists, and that the canal was strategically located for shipping between Asia and Europe.
2. Have students conduct independent research on the impact to shipping of the 1867 opening of the Suez Canal.
3. Organize students into groups of four to six. Each group will prepare a multimedia presentation that explains the importance of the Suez Canal. Students may use photographs, graphs and charts, and/or time lines in their presentations.
4. Have groups give their presentations to the rest of the class. LS **Interpersonal, Visual-Spatial**

Alternative Assessment Handbook, Rubrics 14: Group Activity; 22: Multimedia Presentations; and 30: Research

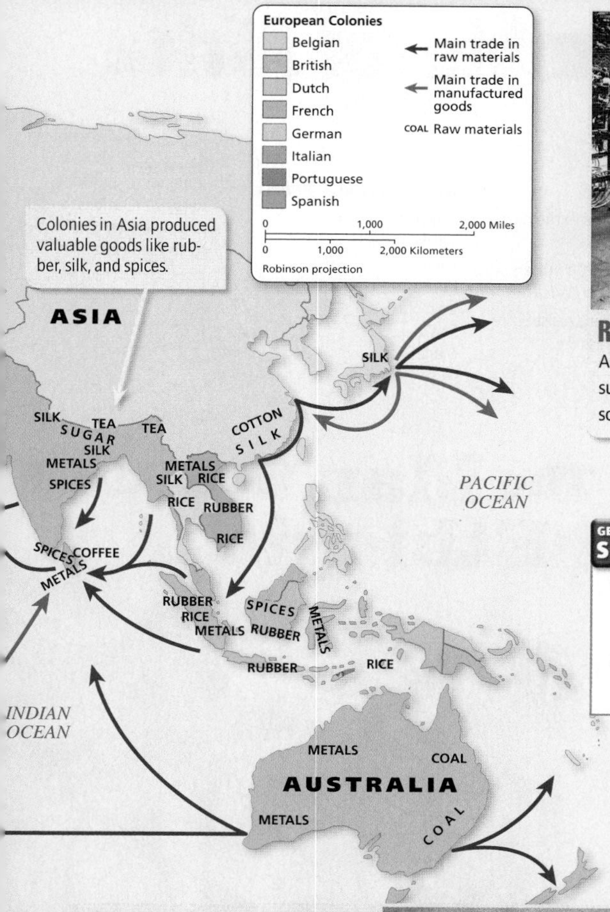

Raw Materials and Industry

As industry in Europe grew, so did the need for raw materials, such as rubber to make bicycle tires. Rubber is a tropical crop, so Europeans had to import it from their colonies.

GEOGRAPHY SKILLS INTERPRETING MAPS

1. **Place** Which European countries controlled colonies in Africa? What kinds of resources did Africa have?
2. **Regions** Based on the map, where were the major manufacturing regions at this time?

Transportation Technology

Improvements in transportation technology were key to the growth of the global economy. Giant new steamships could carry more goods more quickly than ever before. These ships sailed along major shipping routes and relied on coaling stations and strategic waterways such as the Suez Canal, shown here. The canal, opened in 1869, dramatically cut the time and cost of shipping goods from Asia to Europe, further increasing global trade.

History and Geography

Interpreting Maps

Imperialism and a Global Economy

Location Name three raw materials listed on the map, and where they were found. *Asia: rubber, silk, spices; Africa: metals*

Movement What effect did steamships have upon global trade? *steamships could carry more goods, more quickly than ever before*

Activity **Canal Routes** Have students locate the Panama Canal and the Suez Canal on the map. Ask students what routes must have been used before these canals existed. Then, have students write a short paragraph about the importance of key canals to the global economy. **LS Visual-Spatial, Verbal-Linguistic**

Differentiating Instruction

Below Level

Learners Having Difficulty

Standard English Mastery

Materials: Outline map showing Asia and Europe

1. Review with students where rubber came from, where it went, and its many uses. Explain to students that rubber is just one example of a raw material found in European colonies that could be used in manufactured goods.
2. On outline maps, have students draw the journey of a rubber plant from Asia to Europe. On their maps, students should label the line, and the continents of Asia and Europe.
3. Have students write a short paragraph describing rubber as an example of imperialism and the global economy. **LS Visual-Spatial, Verbal-Linguistic**

Alternative Assessment Handbook, Rubrics 20: Map Creation; and 40: Writing to Describe

Answers

Interpreting Maps 1. *Belgium, Great Britain, France, Germany, Italy, Portugal, Spain; metals;* **2.** *U.S., Europe, Japan*

Preteach

Getting Started

Use the **Interactive Reader and Study Guide** to familiarize students with the section content.

Interactive Reader and Study Guide, Section 3

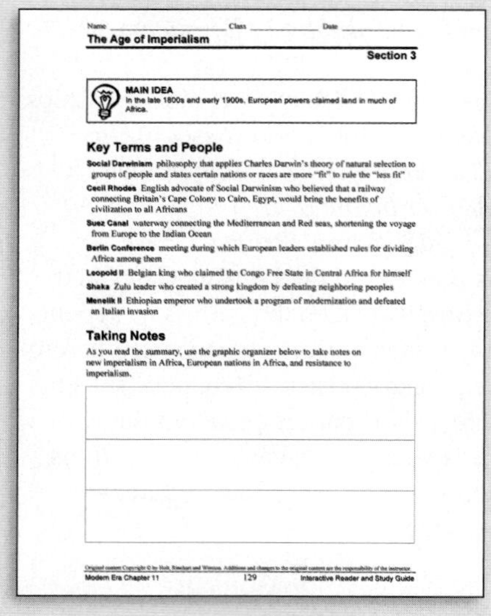

Name ______________ Class ________ Date ________

The Age of Imperialism

Section 3

MAIN IDEA
In the late 1800s and early 1900s, European powers claimed land in much of Africa.

Key Terms and People

Social Darwinism philosophy that applies Charles Darwin's theory of natural selection to groups of people and states certain nations or races are more "fit" to rule the "less fit"

Cecil Rhodes English advocate of Social Darwinism who believed that a railway connecting Britain's Cape Colony to Cairo, Egypt, would bring the benefits of civilization to all Africans

Suez Canal waterway connecting the Mediterranean and Red seas, shortening the voyage from Europe to the Indian Ocean

Berlin Conference meeting during which European leaders established rules for dividing Africa among them

Leopold II Belgian king who claimed the Congo Free State in Central Africa for himself

Shaka Zulu leader who created a strong kingdom by defeating neighboring peoples

Menelik II Ethiopian emperor who undertook a program of modernization and defeated an Italian invasion

Taking Notes

As you read the summary, use the graphic organizer below to take notes on new imperialism in Africa, European nations in Africa, and resistance to imperialism.

Modern Era Chapter 11 129 Interactive Reader and Study Guide

Academic Vocabulary

Review with students the high-use academic term in this section.

discrimination the act of treating a person differently because of race, gender, or national origin (p. 359)

CRF: Vocabulary Builder: Section 3

Taking Notes

New Imperialism in Africa—rapid division of Africa by European powers to obtain manufacturing materials during Industrial Revolution; competition among European nations contributed to imperialism, as did discrimination and Social Darwinism

European Nations in Africa—aided by advanced in medicine, weapons, communication, and transportation; Suez Canal influenced Britain's interest in Egypt; Berlin Conference mediated European disputes; Boer War fought over southern Africa; Belgian king controlled Congo with brutal methods

Resistance to Imperialism—Zulu fought the British; Ethiopians defeated Italians; Malinke people fought against French rule in West Africa; Maji Maji Rebellion was put down by Germans in East Africa

go.hrw.com
Online Resources
KEYWORD: SHL IMP
ACTIVITY: Democratic Republic of the Congo Today

SECTION 3 The Scramble for Africa

BEFORE YOU READ

MAIN IDEA

In the late 1800s and early 1900s, European powers claimed land in much of Africa.

READING FOCUS

1. What factors led to the new imperialism?
2. How did European powers claim territory in Africa?
3. How did Africans resist European imperialism?

KEY TERMS AND PEOPLE

Social Darwinism
Cecil Rhodes
Suez Canal
Berlin Conference
Leopold II
Shaka
Menelik II

TAKING NOTES Take notes on new imperialism in Africa, European nations in Africa, and resistance to imperialism.

The Man Who Saved Ethiopia

THE INSIDE STORY ***How did Ethiopia remain independent?*** In 1889 the emperor of Ethiopia, Menelik II, signed a treaty with Italy. This treaty gave control over what is now Eritrea to the Italians in exchange for weapons and a sum of money. An error in the translation of the treaty, however, led both sides to war.

The Italian translation of the treaty led Italy to believe that it not only controlled Eritrea but that it also had a protectorate over Ethiopia. The version of the treaty in Amharic—the official language of Ethiopia—led Menelik to believe he was only giving up Eritrea. Menelik rejected the claim over Ethiopia and denounced the entire treaty, knowing it would lead to war.

Menelik initiated the war, amassing some 100,000 Ethiopian soldiers and advancing upon the Italian forces at Adwa. The Italian force was disorganized, and the Ethiopians quickly defeated it on March 1, 1896, in the Battle of Adwa. About 70 percent of the Italian forces perished in the battle. The Italians retreated through unfamiliar terrain while local peoples harassed them.

The Battle of Adwa marked a high point of African resistance to European imperialism. An African army had crushed a European army in battle and in doing so had ensured the continued independence of Ethiopia. ■

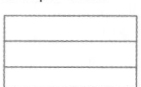

The Negus Menelik II at Battle of Aduwa, 1896

▲ **Menelik II at the Battle of Adwa**

Teach the Main Idea

At Level

The Scramble for Africa

1. **Teach** Ask students the Reading Focus questions to teach this section.
2. **Apply** Have students work in pairs to make graphic organizers showing which European countries controlled which African colonies, along with the date they established their control.
3. **Review** Review student graphic organizers as a class. Guide students in a discussion of the reasons European nations felt entitled to take control of Africa.
4. **Practice/Homework** Have each student write a letter to the editor about the results of the Berlin Conference from the point of view of an American living at that time. **LS Visual-Spatial, Verbal-Linguistic**

Alternative Assessment Handbook, Rubrics 13: Graphic Organizers; and 17: Letters to Editors

The New Imperialism

European countries controlled only a small part of Africa in 1880, but by 1914, only Ethiopia and Liberia remained independent. During the period known as the "Scramble for Africa" European powers rapidly divided Africa.

Historians view the scramble as the most visible example of the new imperialism. Unlike the imperialism of the 1500s and 1600s, the new imperialism was not based on settlement of colonies. Instead, European powers worked to directly govern large areas occupied by non-European peoples. Europeans were driven by economic interests, political competition, and cultural motives.

Economic Interests Before the early 1800s, several European nations profited from the slave trade in Africa. However, after some nations passed laws abolishing the slave trade, Europeans looked to Africa instead as a source for raw materials. During the Industrial Revolution, Europeans needed materials such as coal and metals to manufacture goods. These needs fueled Europeans' desire for land with plentiful natural resources—resources that were available in Africa.

To gather and export these natural resources, European entrepreneurs, or independent businesspeople, developed their own mines, plantations, and trading routes. Sometimes the entrepreneurs would call on their home countries to protect their economic interests from European competitors. In this way, the drive for colonization sometimes came from ambitious individuals, rather than from European governments.

Political Competition Imperialism in Africa reflected struggles for power in Europe, such as the long-term rivalry between France and Britain. As France expanded its control over West and Central Africa, Britain began to expand its colonial empire to block the French. The rise of Germany and Italy as European powers also contributed to the new imperialism. Both nations jumped into the race for colonies to assert their status as great powers.

Nationalism also contributed to the rise of the new imperialism. European leaders believed that controlling colonies would gain them more respect from other leaders.

Cultural Motives In addition to practical matters of economics and politics, the new imperialism was motivated by cultural attitudes. In particular, European imperialists felt they were superior to non-European peoples. These Europeans argued that humanity was divided into distinct peoples, or races, and there were significant biological differences between the races. Most Europeans who held these views believed that people of European descent were biologically superior to people of African or Asian descent.

As a result, some Europeans believed their rule in Africa was justified because they were teaching Africans good government, European customs, and Christian values. Some imperialists even believed their actions in Africa were noble. They saw it as their duty to educate those people they considered inferior. They referred to their influence in Africa as "the white man's burden," after a poem by the English writer Rudyard Kipling.

Defenders of imperialism also often applied Charles Darwin's theory of natural selection to the struggle between nations and races. Darwin argued that species that are more fit for their environment will survive and reproduce. The notion of **Social Darwinism** stated that certain nations or races are more fit than others. Social Darwinists believed these "fit" nations came to rule over the nations that are "less fit," and often showed discrimination against citizens of the ruled nations.

ACADEMIC VOCABULARY
discrimination the act of treating a person differently because of race, gender, or national origin

One outspoken advocate of Social Darwinism was Englishman **Cecil Rhodes**. A wealthy businessman, Rhodes once explained how he felt about British influence in Africa:

HISTORY'S VOICES

> **"I contend that we are the finest race in the world and that the more of the world we inhabit the better it is for the human race . . . What an alteration there would be if they [Africans] were brought under Anglo-Saxon influence."**
>
> —Cecil Rhodes, *Confessions of Faith*, 1877

Rhodes believed that a railway linking Britain's Cape Colony in southern Africa to Cairo, Egypt, in the north would bring what he saw as the benefits of civilization to all Africans.

READING CHECK **Find the Main Idea** What were some reasons that European powers scrambled to claim colonies in Africa?

Direct Teach

Reading Focus

1 What factors led to the new imperialism? *desire for markets for their manufactured goods and investment; desire for raw materials; desire to protect European entrepreneurs; rivalry between European powers*

The New Imperialism

Describe How did the map of Africa change between 1880 and 1914? *In 1880 European countries controlled only a small part of Africa. By 1914, only two nations—Ethiopia and Liberia—remained independent.*

Summarize Why did European nations establish colonies? *to provide a market for manufactured goods and investment; source of raw materials*

CRF: Biography: Samuel Ajayi Crowther

Recent Scholarship

The Troubled Heart of Africa: The History of the Congo explores why one of the richest countries in Africa has become one of its most troubled. Roger Edgerton examines the devastation that occurred to the country and its people from 1908, when it became a Belgian colony, until 1960, when it became independent. Edgerton discusses the ongoing problems of the Congo under corrupt leadership.

—*The Troubled Heart of Africa: The History of the Congo* by Roger Edgerton. St Martin's Press, 2002.

Collaborative Learning — Below Level

The New Imperialism

1. Organize students into mixed-ability pairs
2. Copy this chart omitting the italicized entries. Have pairs complete the chart by categorizing information from "The New Imperialism" subhead in the text. Have students retain charts as a study guide. **LS Visual-Spatial, Verbal-Linguistic**

Alternative Assessment Handbook, Rubrics 7: Charts; and 16: Judging Information

Motives for the New Imperialism	
Economic	*need for raw materials to manufacture goods*
Political	*Rivalry between European nations created competition over establishing African colonies.*
Cultural	*racist beliefs that Europepeans were superior and that Africans needed to be taught good government, European customs, Christian values*
Scientific	*Darwin's theory of natural selection applied to struggle between nations and races (Social Darwinism)*

Answers

Reading Check *for their own economic interests; to compete with one another, and to teah the Africans good government, European customs, and Christian values*

Direct Teach

Reading Focus

2 How did European powers claim territory in Africa? *Britain took control of Egypt, began to compete with France over trade in West Coast of Africa; Belgium began to develop commercial interests; Germany declared protectorates over four African territories*

European Claims in Africa

Recall What was the extent of European control of Africa prior to the 1880s? *They controlled only some parts of the African coast.*

Summarize What developments spurred European expansion in Africa after 1880? *British takeover of Egypt to ensure security of the Suez Canal; British and French competition over trade to the interior of West Coast colonies; development of Belgian commercial interests in the Congo; rise of new powers that sought colonial empires*

CRF: Literature: *Heart of Darkness*

READING SKILLS
Identifying Supporting Details What details are given that explain European claims in Africa?

European Claims in Africa

Prior to the 1880s, Europeans controlled some parts of the African coast. In the 1880s, driven by their new economic, political, and cultural motives, Europeans began to compete for additional territory in Africa.

Scientific Advances and Imperialism

In Africa Europeans faced a huge continent with rugged terrain that could make travel and control difficult. In the 1880s, however, several European scientific advances came together to make traveling in and controlling Africa easier. With the discovery of the drug quinine, Europeans protected themselves against one of the biggest threats, malaria. With the development of the first automatic machine gun, they created a strong military advantage, one that enabled them to defeat and subdue African peoples who had no modern weapons. Finally, with the development of telegraphs, railroads, and steamships, Europeans overcame many of the problems of communication and travel.

Suez Canal In 1869 another technological advancement, the **Suez Canal**, influenced Britain's interest in Egypt. The canal linked the Mediterranean with the Red Sea, drastically shortening the trip from Europe to the Indian Ocean by eliminating the need for ships to sail around the southern tip of Africa.

When the Egyptian government appeared unstable in 1882, the British occupied Egypt to protect British interests in the Suez Canal. Britain later established partial control over Egypt as a protectorate to ensure British access to the canal.

Division of Africa Meanwhile, European nations continued to compete aggressively for other territories in Africa. To create order and prevent conflict between European nations, European leaders met in Berlin, Germany, in 1884–1885 to divide African territory. Leaders at the **Berlin Conference** agreed that when a European nation claimed a new African territory, it had to notify other European nations and prove that it could control the territory. As they divided Africa, European leaders paid no attention to Africans' traditional ethnic boundaries. This disregard for the African peoples land would later cause conflict.

The Boer War In southern Africa, the British met opposition to land claims. Dutch settlers, known as Boers, had lived in the region since the 1600s. After gold was discovered there in the late 1800s, the Boers refused to grant political rights to foreigners, including the British. Tensions between the two groups heightened as Britain tried to make Boer territory a part of the British Empire. In 1899 war broke out.

During the Boer War, British forces vastly outnumbered Boer forces. Nevertheless, using guerrilla tactics, the Boers quickly gained an advantage over British troops. The British responded by destroying Boer farms and imprisoning women and children in concentration camps. More than 20,000 Boer women and children died of disease in the camps. In the end the British defeated the Boers, and in 1902, Boer territory became the self-governing Union of South Africa under British control.

Belgian Congo Unlike most of Africa, the Congo Free State in Central Africa was not ruled by a European country. Instead, the king of Belgium, **Leopold II**, claimed the territory for himself. Leopold created a personal fortune by exploiting the Congo's natural resources.

In the 1890s and early 1900s in Europe and the United States, the demand for rubber increased as the need for bicycle and automobile tires increased. To meet this demand, Leopold forced his Congolese subjects to extract rubber from the region's rubber trees. Millions of workers died from overwork and disease. Eventually an international outcry over Leopold's brutal tactics caused the Belgian government to take control of the Congo in 1908.

READING CHECK **Infer** How did the Berlin Conference contribute to the Scramble for Africa?

African Resistance

Africans did not passively accept European claims to rule over them. As European troops advanced on African territory, they often met stiff resistance from local rulers and peoples.

The Zulu The Zulu people resisted colonialism for more than 50 years. In the early 1800s the Zulu leader **Shaka** built a strong Zulu kingdom by subduing several neighboring peoples.

Skills Focus: Identifying Problem and Solution

At Level

Reading Skill
The Scramble for Africa

1. Tell students they are delegates to the Berlin Conference. Students may choose to represent any of the nations that actually sent delegations to the conference. Have students write a list of their country's goals for the conference and ways in which they hope that their goals will be accomplished.
2. Have volunteers identify the nation they represent and read their goals and solutions.
3. Guide students in a discussion of the Berlin Conference.
4. As an extension, have students prepare scripts and re-enact the Berlin Conference for the class. **LS Verbal-Linguistic, Kinesthetic**

Alternative Assessment Handbook, Rubrics 33: Skits and Reader's Theater; and 38: Writing to Classify

Answers

Reading Skills *scientific advances—quanine, machine gun, telegraphs, railroads, steamships; Suez Canal—shortened trip from Europe to Indian Ocean; Berlin Conference—agreement to create order and prevent conflict among Europeans; Boer War—Dutch vs. British in southern Africa; Belgian Congo—King Leopold II overworked subjects to extract rubber to sell*

Reading Check *set rules for the division of Africa among the European nations*

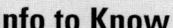

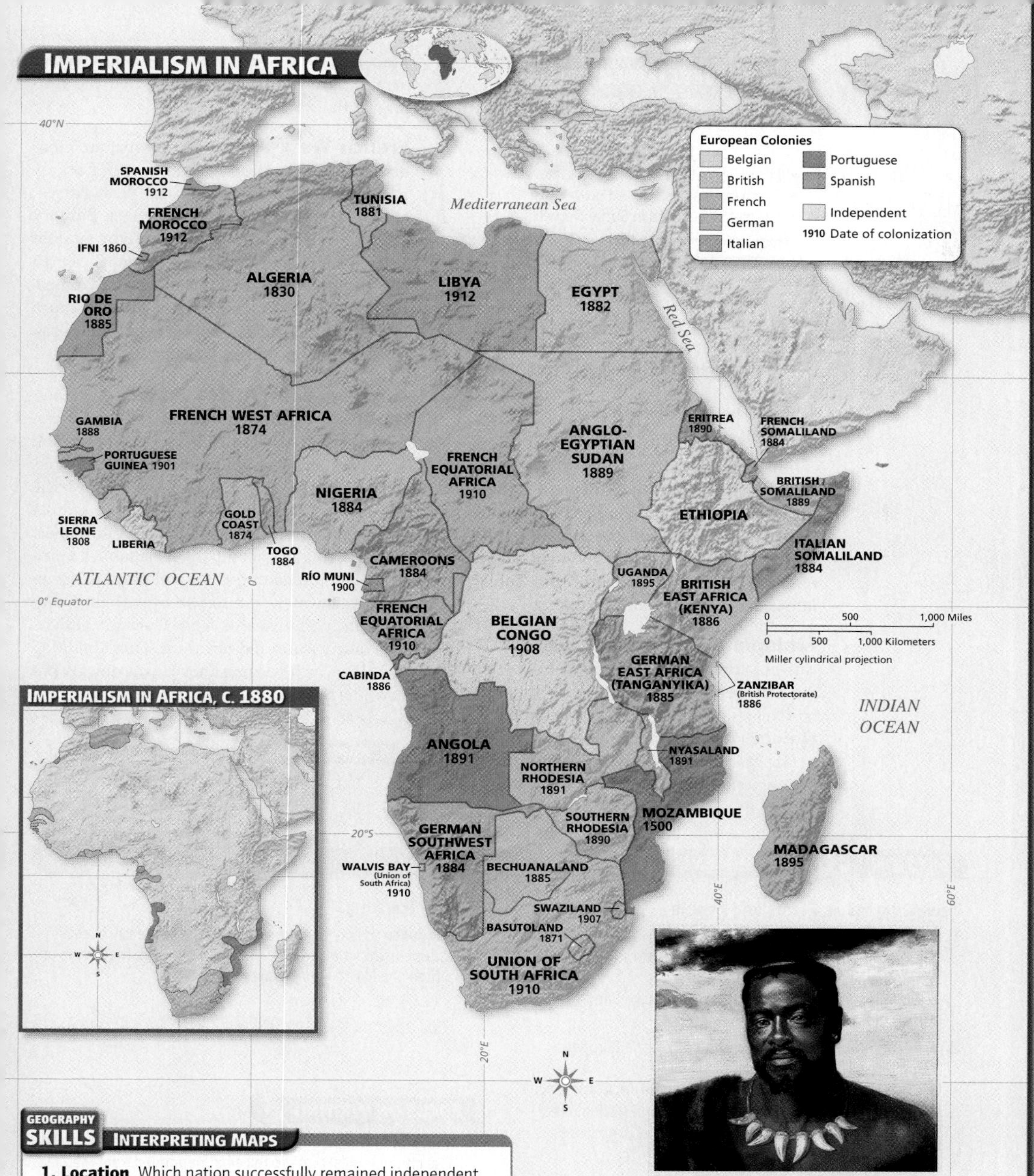

GEOGRAPHY SKILLS INTERPRETING MAPS

1. **Location** Which nation successfully remained independent during the Scramble for Africa?
2. **Regions** During which decade did European nations seize the greatest amount of land in Africa?

Cetshwayo, king of the Zulu nation, led his army to resist imperial control. Though Zulu resistance was fierce, the British defeated them in 1879.

Direct Teach

Info to Know

The Berlin Conference In 1884 European leaders met in Germany to resolve potential conflicts over African colonies. With no regard for the boundaries the Africans already had in place (which were often based on the location of ethnic groups), the Europeans carved up Africa among themselves. The decisions made at the Berlin Conference continue to hamper the continent's development.

Activity **Africa Today** Have students compare the map of Africa on this page with a map of Africa today. Have them list the countries that now exist that were once European colonies. **LS Visual-Spatial**

Map Transparency: Imperialism in Africa

Skills Focus: Analyzing Secondary Sources

At Level

Reading Like a Historian Skill

African Resistance

Research Required

1. Organize students into four groups and assign one of the following nationalities to each group: The Zulu, Ethiopia, French West Africa, and German East Africa
2. Have students use the information about African resistance in the text and from reliable print and online sources to create posters that illustrate the key people and events of the New Imperialism.
3. Have students include several of the following on their posters: pictures, photographs, first-person accounts, contemporary newspaper stories, maps, charts, graphs, and time lines.
4. Have groups present their posters to the class. Display posters in the classroom for students to see. **LS Verbal-Spatial, Kinesthetic**

Alternative Assessment Handbook, Rubrics 1: Acquiring Information; 24: Oral Presentations; and 28: Posters

Answers

Interpreting Maps *1. Ethiopia; 2. the 1880s*

Direct Teach

Reading Focus

3 How did Africans resist European imperialism? *in battle, sometimes with modern weapons and sometimes without them*

African Resistance

Recall What was the only nation in Africa that was able to retain its independence? *Ethiopia*

Summarize What happened in German East Africa? *In the Maji Maji Rebellion, Africans rebelled, using so-called magic water to protect themselves. Tens of thousands of them died.*

Quick Facts Transparency: The New Imperialism in Africa

Review & Assess

Close

Have students summarize the events that occurred in the European scramble for Africa.

Review

Online Quiz, Section 3

Assess

SE Section 3 Assessment

Progress Assessment: Section 3 Quiz

Alternative Assessment Handbook

Reteach/Intervene

Interactive Reader and Study Guide, Section 3

Interactive Skills Tutor CD-ROM

THE NEW IMPERIALISM IN AFRICA — QUICK FACTS

CAUSES

- European nations needed raw materials.
- European leaders wanted power and land.
- Europeans believed in Social Darwinism.

EFFECTS

- Africans lost their land and independence.
- Many Africans died resisting the Europeans.

In 1879 the British invaded Zulu territory. The Zulus, led by Shaka's nephew Cetshwayo (kech-WAH-yoh), won a major victory, but the Zulus could not resist the superior military might of the British for long. In about six months, the British defeated the Zulus and annexed their kingdom as a colony.

Ethiopia Only the African nation of Ethiopia was able to retain its independence by matching European firepower. In 1889 the emperor of Ethiopia, **Menelik II**, undertook a program of modernization that included a modern army.

In 1895 Italian forces invaded Ethiopia over a treaty dispute. Within a year, however, Menelik's forces—more numerous and better armed than the Italians— defeated the Italians at the Battle of Adwa.

French West Africa Even without modern weapons, other Africans still fiercely resisted European powers. In West Africa, the leader of the Malinke peoples, Samory Touré, formed his own army to fight against French rule. Touré fought the French for 15 years and proclaimed himself king of Guinea. However, in 1898 the French captured Touré and defeated his army. This act ended all resistance to French rule in West Africa.

German East Africa Religious symbolism often played a significant role in African resistance as Africans called on their gods and ancestors for spiritual guidance. For example, in 1905 in the colony of German East Africa, several African peoples united to rebel against the Germans' order to grow cotton for export to Germany. To combat the Germans, a spiritual leader encouraged his followers to sprinkle magic water, or *maji*, all over their bodies to protect themselves from German bullets. The magic water did not work. This Maji Maji Rebellion, as it became known, was quickly put down by the Germans, who killed tens of thousands of Africans.

READING CHECK **Draw Conclusions** How did Ethiopia resist imperialism?

SECTION 3 ASSESSMENT

go.hrw.com
Online Quiz
Keyword: SHL IMP HP

Reviewing Ideas, Terms and People

1. **a. Define** What is **Social Darwinism**?
   b. Explain Why did European nations want raw materials from Africa?
   c. Evaluate What drove European leaders to claim African territory?
2. **a. Recall** What advances in technology made European domination of Africa possible?
   b. Explain What was the purpose of the **Berlin Conference**?
   c. Support a Position Do you think **Leopold II** should have claimed the Belgian Congo for himself? Why or why not?
3. **a. Identify** Who were the Zulu?
   b. Draw Conclusions How did Ethiopians under **Menelik II** defeat the Italians?

Critical Thinking

4. **Sequence** Using your notes, make a list of the key events in European imperialism in Africa. Then organize the events on a time line like the one below.

FOCUS ON WRITING

5. **Narration** Write a brief news report on the Battle of Adowa. Use chronological order to tell what happened from the beginning to the end of the battle.

Section 3 Assessment Answers

1. **a.** the notion that certain nations or races are more fit than others and that those nations should rule over the "less fit" nations
   b. in order to manufacture goods.
   c. for political reasons, as evidence of power, and economic reasons, as a source of raw materials for factories and a potential market for finished products
2. **a.** quinine, the machine gun, telegraphs, railroads, and steamships
   b. to divide African territory among the European nations
   c. possible answer—no, because he was a brutal leader
3. **a.** an African group who resisted colonialism for more than 50 years
   b. Ethiopia had a modern army that was larger and better armed than the Italian army.
4. 1869, Suez Canal opens; 1879, British vs. Zulu; 1882, British occupy Egypt; 1884, Berlin Conference; 1895, Ethiopia defeats Italy; 1902, Boer territory becomes British
5. Students should explain how the Ethiopians won the battle.

Answers

Reading Check *by building a modern army, matching European firepower, and defeating the Italians at the Battle of Adowa*

SECTION 4

Imperialism in Latin America

BEFORE YOU READ

MAIN IDEA

Imperialism in Latin America involved the United States and European nations seeking to strengthen their political and economic influence over the region.

READING FOCUS

1. How did various groups struggle for power in Mexico before and during the Mexican Revolution?
2. How did growing U.S. influence in Latin America change the region?

KEY TERMS AND PEOPLE

Antonio López de Santa Anna
Porfirio Díaz
Emiliano Zapata
Francisco "Pancho" Villa
Venustiano Carranza
José Martí
Spanish-American War
Emilio Aguinaldo
Roosevelt Corollary

TAKING NOTES Take notes on the sequence of events in Latin America from 1820 to 1920.

1820 1920

◀ Pancho Villa leads other Mexican rebels on horseback.

THE INSIDE STORY ***How did a revolutionary win by running?*** Of all of the leaders of the Mexican Revolution, Francisco "Pancho" Villa fascinated Americans the most. Villa's successes in battle and his colorful personality made him a darling of the American media in 1913 and 1914. He gave interviews to U.S. journalists and allowed a Hollywood film crew to make a movie about his life. Because of Villa's revolutionary battles against wealth and privilege, journalists called him a "Mexican Robin Hood."

But the media adoration began to change in 1916. Villa became angry that the United States had recognized the government of Venustiano Carranza, his rival for power. He launched an attack on Columbus, New Mexico, in which 19 U.S. citizens were killed, and then retreated to Mexico. Villa's goal was to provoke the United States into invading Mexico, an act Villa thought would destroy relations between the United States and Carranza governments.

U.S. president Woodrow Wilson sent General John J. Pershing on an expedition across the Mexican border to capture Villa—dead or alive. For 11 months Pershing pursued Villa through northern Mexico, but he never caught him. The pursuit accomplished Villa's goal, however. It soured relations between Mexico and the United States. ■

Preteach

Getting Started

Use the **Interactive Reader and Study Guide** to familiarize students with the section content.

Interactive Reader and Study Guide, Section 4

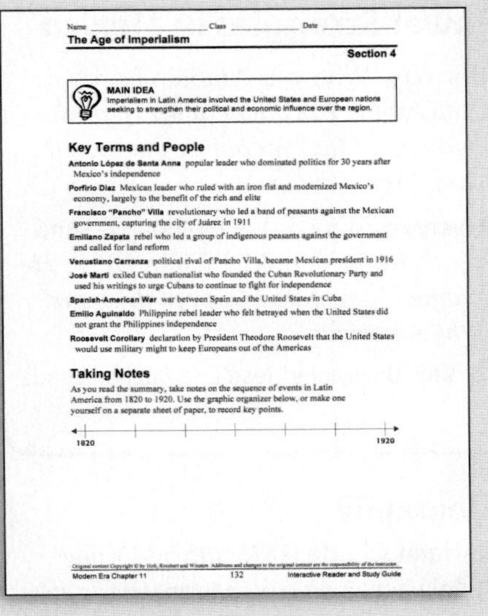
Name ________ Class ________ Date ________

The Age of Imperialism

Section 4

MAIN IDEA
Imperialism in Latin America involved the United States and European nations seeking to strengthen their political and economic influence over the region.

Key Terms and People

Antonio López de Santa Anna popular leader who dominated politics for 30 years after Mexico's independence

Porfirio Díaz Mexican leader who ruled with an iron fist and modernized Mexico's economy, largely to the benefit of the rich and elite

Francisco "Pancho" Villa revolutionary who led a band of peasants against the Mexican government, capturing the city of Juárez in 1911

Emiliano Zapata rebel who led a group of indigenous peasants against the government and called for land reform

Venustiano Carranza political rival of Pancho Villa, became Mexican president in 1916

José Martí exiled Cuban nationalist who founded the Cuban Revolutionary Party and used his writings to urge Cubans to continue to fight for independence

Spanish-American War war between Spain and the United States in Cuba

Emilio Aguinaldo Philippine rebel leader who felt betrayed when the United States did not grant the Philippines independence

Roosevelt Corollary declaration by President Theodore Roosevelt that the United States would use military might to keep Europeans out of the Americas

Taking Notes

As you read the summary, take notes on the sequence of events in Latin America from 1820 to 1920. Use the graphic organizer below, or make one yourself on a separate sheet of paper, to record key points.

1820 1920

Original content Copyright © by Holt, Rinehart and Winston. Additions and changes to the original content are the responsibility of the instructor.

Modern Era Chapter 11 132 Interactive Reader and Study Guide

CRF: Vocabulary Builder: Section 4

Taking Notes

1821: Mexico declares independence from Spain; 1855: Mexican president Santa Anna is overthrown; 1861: French emperor Napolean III overthrows Mexican goverment, installs archduke Maximilian as emperor; 1895: José Marti returned to Cuba to join uprising against the Spanish; 1898: Spanish American War begins; 1904-1914: Panama Canal is built; 1911: Rebels led by Pancho Villa capture Juárez in the Mexican Revolution; 1917: new Mexican constitution goes into effect

Teach the Main Idea

At Level

Imperialism in Latin America

1. **Teach** Ask students the Reading Focus questions to teach this section.
2. **Apply** Have students make a time line showing the major events from this section. Student time lines should begin with Mexican independence in 1821 and end with the Mexican Constitution of 1917.
3. **Review** Review student time lines as a class. Discuss the ways in which European and U.S. imperialism has affected Latin America in the early 19th century.
4. **Practice/Homework** Tell students they are newspaper editors in Mexico City in 1861. Have students write an editorial about the installation of the Austrian archduke Maximilian as emperor of Mexico by the French. Students may take either the liberal or conservative view, but should maintain their selected editorial perspective.

LS Visual-Spatial, Verbal-Linguistic

Alternative Assessment Handbook, Rubrics 36: Time Lines; and 43: Writing to Persuade

go.hrw.com
Online Resources

KEYWORD: SHL IMP
ACTIVITY: Report on Imperialism

Direct Teach

Reading Focus

1 How did various groups struggle for power in Mexico before and during the Mexican Revolution? *civil war, jailing opposition, peasant revolt*

Power Struggles in Mexico

Identify Who was Antonio López de Santa Anna? *President of Mexico who dominated Mexican politics in the 30 years after independence*

Analyze Why did Napoleon III send French troops into Mexico in 1861? *He dreamed of restoring a French empire in the Americas.*

CRF: Biography: José Guadalupe Posada

Biography

Mariano Azuela (1873-1952) Mariano Azuela began writing newspaper articles against the regime of Porfirio Díaz in 1896, while working on a degree in medicine. He wrote his most famous novel, *Los de abajo* (The Underdogs), while serving as an army doctor for Pancho Villa's revolutionary forces. After Villa's defeat in 1915, Azuela fled to El Paso, Texas, where he finished the novel. *Los de abajo* follows the career of an imaginary revolutionary leader, Demetrio Macías, as he rises from the leadership of a group of Native Americans to the position of general under Pancho Villa.

Teaching Tip

The sequence of events in Mexico may be confusing for some students. If so, have students create a sequencing chart of the leaders and retain it as a study tool.

FACES OF HISTORY

Emiliano ZAPATA
1879–1919

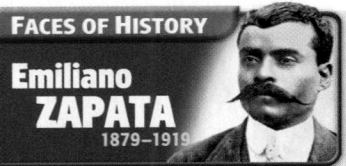

Emiliano Zapata was a Mexican revolutionary who fought for the rights of the rural poor. Orphaned at age 17, Zapata led his neighbors in taking back land that had been seized from them. Later, he helped Francisco Madero overthrow Díaz as president of Mexico but quickly grew dissatisfied with the pace of land reform. He led a campaign that seized land and returned it to peasants. He later helped defeat Victoriano Huerta, occupied Mexico City with Pancho Villa, and implemented land reform. His campaign came to a swift end after he was ambushed and killed by the forces of Venustiano Carranza.

Infer Why do you think the cause of land reform was so important to Emiliano Zapata?

Power Struggles in Mexico

Although Mexico won its independence from Spain in 1821 and became a republic in 1823, political factions struggled for control of the government. Conflict among political groups caused violence well into the next century.

Early Conflicts In the 30 years after independence, Mexican politics was dominated by **Antonio López de Santa Anna**. His popularity relied on numerous military victories, and he served as president five times between 1833 and 1855. He began his career aligned with liberal reformers, but as his power increased his rule became more conservative. He was exiled from the country several times, only to return to power as his enemies were defeated. Finally, in 1855 a group of reformers overthrew and exiled Santa Anna, and he did not return.

The leader of these reformers, Benito Juárez, put forth a series of major reforms that reduced the power of the Catholic Church and the military. Conservatives were outraged by these efforts. Soon, a civil war erupted. With support from the U.S. government, Juárez and his liberal allies triumphed.

The Second Mexican Empire The conservatives found a powerful ally in Europe. French emperor Napoleon III dreamed of restoring a French empire in the Americas. In 1861 he sent French troops into Mexico, overthrew the Mexican government, and installed Austrian archduke Maximilian as emperor of Mexico.

Mexican conservatives supported Maximilian at first because they believed he would restore the power of the church. But Maximilian ended up alienating both conservatives and liberals. When the French withdrew their troops, Maximilian did not have enough support to stay in power. Forced to surrender, Maximilian was executed by Republican troops.

The Mexican Republic was restored, and Juárez was reelected as president. Because of Juárez's courageous resistance to Maximilian and the French, he became one of Mexico's greatest national heroes.

The Mexican Revolution After the death of Juárez, **Porfirio Díaz** came to power. Ruling with an iron fist, he maintained law and order in Mexico. Díaz imprisoned his opponents and used the army to keep the peace at any cost.

Díaz helped modernize Mexico by encouraging foreign investment. Mexican exports boomed, and railroads expanded quickly. Yet most Mexicans remained extremely poor. Wealth was concentrated in the hands of foreign investors and a small Mexican elite. Half of the population was bound to debt-slavery, and discontent began to grow.

In the election of 1910, Díaz controlled the outcome. He jailed his opponent, the reform-minded Francisco Madero. After being released from jail, however, Madero fled to Texas and declared himself president of Mexico. He called for a revolution against the Díaz government.

When Madero returned to Mexico later that year, he found rebellion spreading across the nation. Two men gathered support from the lowest classes and began attacking government forces. **Francisco "Pancho" Villa** led a band of rebels who supported Madero's ideas. They disgraced Díaz's government by capturing the city of Juárez in 1911. At the same time, a group of indigenous peasants led by **Emiliano Zapata** arose and called for land reforms. Díaz was soon forced to resign.

More Violence Madero was elected president later that year, but turmoil in Mexico continued. Within months, army chief Victoriano Huerta seized power and imprisoned Madero. Former supporters of Madero opposed Huerta. In the north, Pancho Villa's army of small ranchers, unemployed workers, and cowboys also rose up against Huerta. Zapata's peasant

Collaborative Learning

At Level

Power Struggles in Mexico

1. Organize students into small groups. Tell half of the groups they represent Mexican conservatives who oppose Benito Juárez. Tell the other groups they represent Mexican liberals led by Benito Juárez. Have each group prepare arguments in support of its position, either for or against Juárez's series of reforms. You might wish to have students conduct additional research to help them prepare their arguments.
2. Hold a classroom debate on reforms in Mexico. At the end of the debate, ask students to identify which side presented the most convincing arguments and to explain why.
3. Guide students in a discussion of the causes and effects of Juárez's series of reforms. Ask students why they think conservatives would prefer to be ruled by a foreign emperor rather than a popularly elected native president.

LS Interpersonal, Verbal-Linguistic

Alternative Assessment Handbook, Rubric 10: Debates

Answers

Faces of History *possible answer—because he grew up among people whose land was taken from them*

Mexican Revolution

This mural by David Siquieros depicts the solidarity of Mexican peasants, led by Emiliano Zapata, in their struggle to regain the land once taken from them.

army revolted against Huerta in the south. Even the United States opposed him after Madero was executed in 1914.

The United States intervened by sending Marines to occupy the city of Veracruz, bringing Mexico and the United States close to war. Huerta struggled to stay in power but resigned in July and fled to Spain.

Carranza as President With Huerta gone, Carranza declared himself president. Zapata and Villa, however, refused to support Carranza, and the nation was plunged into another civil war. But by the end of 1915, Carranza had defeated his rivals.

Villa continued to lead attacks against the Carranza government. Upset that the United States recognized Carranza as president, Villa launched an attack across the U.S. border. U.S. forces pursued Villa back across the Mexican border, but were unable to capture him. In 1920 he finally agreed to halt his attacks.

With his political position now secure, Carranza took on the task of nation building. A new constitution went into effect in 1917. allowing the government to redistribute land, limited the power of the church, and protected the rights of citizens. Despite these improvements, Mexico still struggled with the problem of widespread poverty made worse by the damage done by years of revolution.

READING CHECK **Sequence** What were the major events of the Mexican Revolution?

Growing U.S. Influence

The United States had become a growing economic force in Latin America by the late 1800s. Economic power and political power grew together, and the United States exerted its influence and control in many ways.

Uprising in Cuba One of Spain's colonies in the Americas was the island of Cuba. In the 1860s Cuban nationalists began fighting for independence. Spain's response was to exile the leaders of the nationalist revolts.

One exiled leader managed to continue the struggle for independence from New York City. A poet and journalist, **José Martí**, communicated to Cubans through his writing, urging them to continue to fight for independence. While exiled, he founded the Cuban Revolutionary Party and in 1895 he returned to Cuba to join an uprising against the Spanish.

The Spanish responded brutally to the uprising. Martí was killed, and thousands of Cubans were forced into camps controlled by the Spanish army. The conditions were terrible, and many died from disease or starvation.

THE IMPACT TODAY

A statue of José Martí stands in New York City's Central Park. The statue was a gift of the Cuban government in 1965.

Direct Teach

Reading Focus

2 How did growing U.S. influence in Latin America change the region? *Cuba gained independence from Spain; Panama Canal was built; Roosevelt Corollary threatened miliary force to keep Europe out of the Americas*

Growing U.S. Influence

Identify Who was José Martí? *poet and journalist who founded the Cuban Revolutionary Party*

Summarize How did people in the United States respond to the Cuban Revolution? *They sympathized with the Cuban rebels, seeing their struggle as similar to the American Revolution.*

Activity **Yellow Journalism** Explain to students that yellow journalism uses sensationalism to put forth a message. Have students write yellow journalism headlines about the Spanish American War. Display the headlines for all to see. As an extension, have students write a brief article using yellow journalism. **LS Verbal-Linguistic**

Alternative Assessment Handbook, Rubric 23: Newspapers

Primary Source

"... therefore I come to ask your approval that I should use the armed forces of the United States in such ways and to such an extent as may be necessary to obtain from General Huerta...the fullest rights and dignity of the United States..."
–Woodrow Wilson, Address to Congress, April 20, 1914

Skills Focus: Recognizing Bias in Primary Sources

At Level

Research Required

Reading Like a Historian Skill

Mexican Leaders of the 1800s

1. Organize the class into small groups. Have each group conduct outside research to find pictures of Antonio López de Santa Anna, Benito Juárez, and Emperor Maximilian. Pictures may include paintings, drawings, and cartoons.
2. Have each student choose a picture of one of the three men and write a brief essay analyzing it. Students should answer these questions: How is the leader portrayed, favorably or unfavorably? What can you tell about the leader from his picture? What is the point of view of the artist or creator of the drawing? How can you tell?
3. Have volunteers share the pictures and their analyses with the rest of the class.
4. Guide the class in a discussion of the three Mexican leaders. How does each man represent his type—the caudillo, the reformer, and the European imperialist? **LS Visual-Spatial**

Alternative Assessment Handbook, Rubrics 3: Artwork; and 38: Writing to Classify

Answers

Reading Check *President Porforío Diaz jailed his opponent, Francisco Madero; Madero called for a revolution; Francisco "Pancho" Villa led a band of rebels who captured city of Juárez; Emiliano Zapata called for land reforms; Diaz resigned*

Direct Teach

Reading Focus

Growing U.S. Influence

Recall What territory did the United States acquire at the end of the Spanish-American War? *Puerto Rico, Guam, the Philippines*

Sequence List the events that led to the Spanish-American War. *The U.S. battleship* Maine *exploded in Havana's harbor; Americans assumed Spain was responsible; Congress declared war*

CRF: Primary Source: U.S. Imperialism

Map Transparency: United States Intervention in the Caribbean

The Spanish-American War In the United States, many people already felt sympathy for the Cuban rebels. They viewed the Cuban struggle for freedom as similar to their own American Revolution. U.S. newspapers printed scandalous stories and large, shocking illustrations about events in Cuba. Newspapers using this sensationalist style of reporting, known as yellow journalism, urged the United States to enter the war.

In February 1898 the U.S. battleship *Maine* mysteriously exploded in Havana's harbor, and many Americans immediately assumed that Spain was responsible. Congress declared war, and the **Spanish-American War** began.

The war was a disaster for Spain. The Spanish army was defeated in Cuba, and Spanish navy fleets were destroyed in the Philippines and Cuba. Within three months, the United States had won the war. In the treaty ending the war, the United States received Puerto Rico and Guam, and agreed to purchase the Philippines for $20 million.

Even though Spain agreed to give up Cuba, some Americans did not want Cuba to have full independence. Instead the United States made Cuba a protectorate by forcing it to include the Platt Amendment as part of its new constitution. The Platt Amendment allowed the United States to intervene in Cuba, to approve foreign treaties, and to lease land at Guantánamo Bay for a naval base.

Revolt in the Philippines In the Philippines, another Spanish colony, nationalists believed that the Spanish-American War would bring them independence. But rather than grant the Philippines independence, the United States made it an American colony. Rebel leader **Emilio Aguinaldo**, who had cooperated with U.S. forces against the Spanish, felt betrayed.

Filipino rebels revolted against the U.S. occupation. In three years of fighting, more than 200,000 Filipinos died from combat or disease. They did not win independence. The United States ruled the Philippines through a governor appointed by the U.S. president until 1935. The Philippines were not granted full independence until 1946.

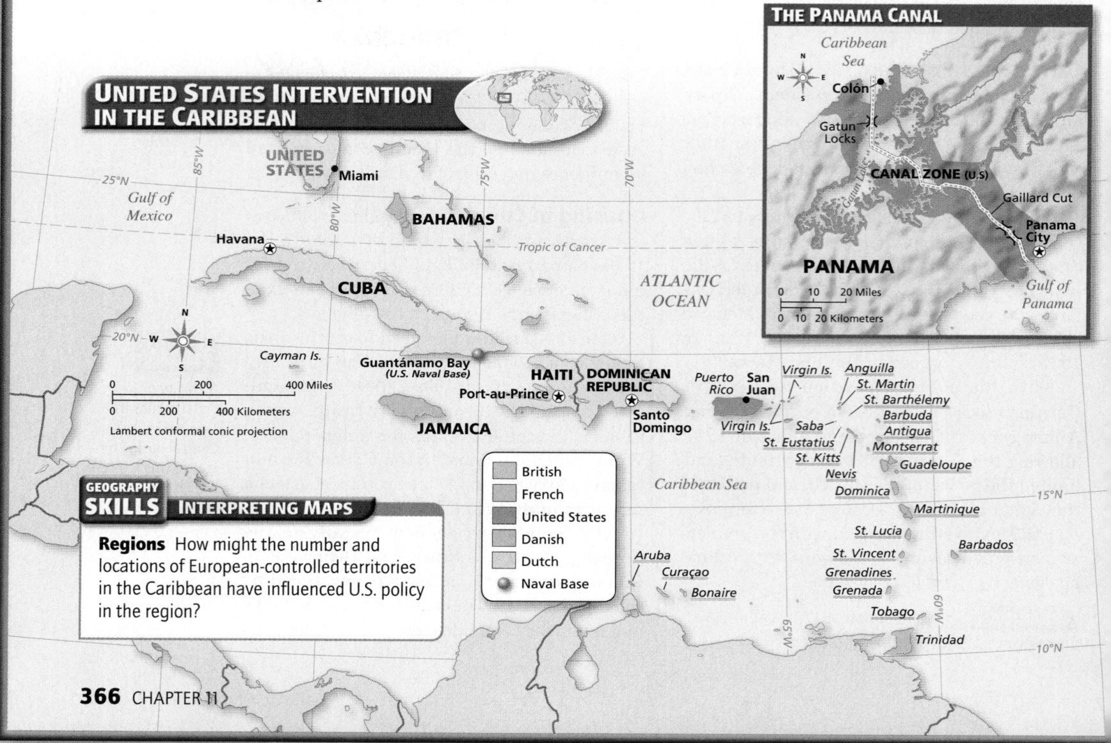

GEOGRAPHY SKILLS INTERPRETING MAPS

Regions How might the number and locations of European-controlled territories in the Caribbean have influenced U.S. policy in the region?

Differentiating Instruction

Below Level

Special Education Students

1. Draw the chart as shown, omitting the italicized answers. Have students copy the charts onto their own paper.
2. Have students use the information in the section to complete the chart, showing the actions of the United States in each area. When students have finished, create a chart for all to see. Have students correct their work and retain the charts as a study tool. **LS Visual-Spatial**

Area	Actions
Cuba	*entered Spanish-American War; made Cuba a protectorate*
Philippines	*made Philippines an American colony; granted independence in 1946*
Colombia	*supported uprising against Colombia; ruled Panama Canal Zone*

Alternative Assessment Handbook, Rubric 7: Charts

Answers

Interpreting Maps *possible answer—The United States may have attempted to limit future European colonization.*

The Panama Canal With the building of the Panama Canal, the United States gained control over more territory. A French company had tried unsuccessfully to build a canal across the Isthmus of Panama, then part of Colombia, in the 1880s. In 1903 the United States bought the French property and equipment, but Colombia refused to allow the United States to build the canal.

Determined to build the canal, U.S. president Theodore Roosevelt sent U.S. warships to support an uprising against Colombia. After Panama was declared independent, the new nation quickly signed a treaty granting the United States a strip of land to build the canal. This became the Panama Canal Zone, which was ruled directly by the United States.

The Panama Canal was built between 1904 and 1914. Its construction was a marvel of modern engineering but major medical advances were required to control the effects of yellow fever and malaria upon canal workers. When the Panama Canal opened, it shortened the sea voyage from San Francisco to New York City by about 8,000 miles.

A Warning to Europeans In 1823, with the proclamation of the Monroe Doctrine, the United States declared the Americas off-limits to European imperialism except for colonies that already existed. Until the end of the Spanish-American War, however, the Monroe Doctrine was seen by European powers as no more than an idle threat.

By the late 1800s, Europe and the United States had considerable financial interests in Latin America. Many Latin American nations had become deeply indebted to foreign creditors. In 1904 European creditors threatened to use military force to collect their debts in the Dominican Republic.

To protect U.S. interests and maintain stability in the region, President Roosevelt announced the **Roosevelt Corollary** to the Monroe Doctrine.

HISTORY'S VOICES

> **"Chronic wrongdoing . . . in the Western Hemisphere . . . may force the United States, however reluctantly, . . . to the exercise of an international police power."**
>
> —Theodore Roosevelt, Roosevelt Corollary, 1904

The United States vowed to use its military might to keep Europeans out of the Americas.

Increasing U.S. Power The United States sent troops to several nations in the early 1900s. U.S. forces entered Haiti, the Dominican Republic, Nicaragua, and Cuba with the stated goal of restoring civil order. The United States took control of the finances of these countries, claiming a need to prevent financial chaos. In reality, the United States used the Roosevelt Corollary to become even more involved in the political affairs of Latin American countries.

READING CHECK **Find the Main Idea** How did the United States gain control over more territory in the late 1800s and early 1900s?

SECTION 4 ASSESSMENT

go.hrw.com
Online Quiz
Keyword: SHL IMP HP

Reviewing Ideas, Terms, and People

1. **a. Identify** Who was **Porfirio Díaz**?
   b. Identify Cause and Effect What was the effect of Victoriano Huerta's seizing power and imprisoning Madero?
   c. Elaborate How successful was **Venustiano Carranza** in quelling the turmoil of the Mexican Revolution?
2. **a. Recall** What event pushed the United States into war with Spain?
   b. Draw Conclusions Why did President Roosevelt develop the **Roosevelt Corollary** to the Monroe Doctrine?
   c. Predict What do you think was the Latin American reaction to increasing U.S. power in the early 1900s?

Critical Thinking

3. **Identify Cause and Effect** Copy this chart and use your notes from the section to explain the causes of the Mexican Revolution.

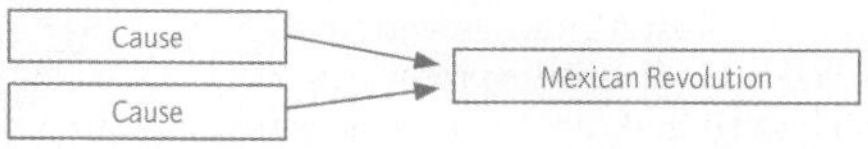

FOCUS ON WRITING

4. **Persuasion** Using details from the section, write an editorial on the growing influence of the United States in Latin America. Take the point of view of a Latin American.

Direct Teach

Info to Know

U.S. Intervention At different times, the United States created military governments in Nicaragua, Haiti, the Dominican Republic, and Cuba. The United States intervened in these countries for several reasons. During the early 1900s, the economies of several nations in the area almost collapsed. The United States feared that governments would refuse to pay debts owed to foreign banks. European nations might have used a refusal to pay debts as a pretext for large-scale intervention in the region.

Review & Assess

Close

Have students summarize the effects of imperialism in Latin America, particularly the role played by the United States.

Review

go.hrw.com **Online Quiz**, Section 4

Assess

SE Section 4 Assessment
Progress Assessment: Section 4 Quiz
Alternative Assessment Handbook

Reteach/Intervene

Interactive Reader and Study Guide, Section 4
Interactive Skills Tutor CD-ROM

Section 4 Assessment Answers

1. **a.** ruler of Mexico who came to power after the death of Juárez; overthrown in Mexican Revolution
   b. the United States sent Marines to occupy the city of Veracruz
   c. possible answer—he was somewhat successful, but civil war and widespread poverty persisted
2. **a.** the sinking of the U.S. battleship *Maine*
   b. in order to protect U.S. interests and maintain stability in Latin America
   c. possible answer—Latin American nations may have resented the foreign influence.
3. Most Mexicans were poor; wealth was in the hands of foreign investors and the elite; Díaz jailed his opponent Francisco Madero
4. Student editorials should describe the actions of the United States in Latin America, including in Mexico, Cuba, and Colombia, from the point of view of a Latin American.

Answers

Reading Check *gained Guam, Puerto Rico, and the Philippines after the Spanish-American War; ruled the Panama Canal Zone after supporting an uprising against Colombia; added the Roosevelt Corollary to the Monroe Doctrine; sent troops to Haiti, the Dominican Republic, Nicaragua, and Cuba*

Document-Based Investigation

Imperialism

Word Help

coerced forced

assimilate to make part of a culture or group

yoke bondage; something that is oppressive and restrictive

Info to Know

Dollar Diplomacy Dollar diplomacy was started in 1909 by President William H. Taft to help Americans make money in other countries. It was used mainly in Central America and the Caribbean. American companies started businesses there. Then the United States used its economic strength to protect the businesses. In this way, the business continued to make money and the United States maintained power in these nations. Over time, many people resisted U.S. efforts to control them through dollar diplomacy. By 1912 President Taft had given up on dollar diplomacy. Today the phrase is used to describe efforts by one country to control another through money.

CHAPTER 11 **Document-Based Investigation**

Imperialism

Historical Context The documents that follow reveal a number of different attitudes concerning the effects of imperialism.

Task Examine the selections and answer the questions that follow. After you have studied the documents, you will be asked to write an essay contrasting the views of people on both sides of the imperialism debate. You will need to use evidence from the selections and from the chapter to support the position you take in your essay.

DOCUMENT 1

A Chinese View of Democracy

Sun Yixian, the spokesman of Chinese nationalism, fiercely opposed imperialism. He did not believe that China needed any help from other countries to thrive. In fact, in his *History of the Chinese Revolution*, Sun argued that China was at its best when it remained free from any outside influence.

> Revelations of Chinese history prove that the Chinese as a people are independent in spirit and in conduct. Coerced into touch with other people, they could at times live in peace with them by maintaining friendly relations and at others assimilate them. . . During the periods when their political and military prowess declined, they could not escape for the time from the fate of a conquered nation, but they could eventually vigorously reassert themselves. Thus the Mongol rule of China, lasting nearly a hundred years was finally overthrown by Tai Tse of the Ming dynasty and his loyal follower. So in our own time was the Manchu yoke thrown off by the Chinese. Nationalistic ideas in China did not come from a foreign source; they were inherited from our remote forefathers.

DOCUMENT 2

Roosevelt in the Caribbean

Under President Theodore Roosevelt, the United States expanded its influence over nations in the Caribbean and the rest of Latin America after the Spanish-American War. In this cartoon, Roosevelt marches through the Caribbean while carrying a club, a reference to a West African proverb that was one of his favorite expressions: "Speak softly and carry a big stick; you will go far."

Differentiating Instruction

Below Level

Learners Having Difficulty

1. Review with students the material in the text about Sun Yixian, Chinese nationalism, and the end of the Qing dynasty.
2. Organize students into mixed-ability groups, and have groups review Document 1. Have each student write answers to the following questions: How does Sun Yixian describe China in the past? What does he say the past indicates about China's future?
3. Have students write newspaper editorials from the point of view of a Chinese nationalist who opposes Western influence. Editorials should use the same logic used by Sun Yixian in Document 1, but students should use their own words. **LS Interpersonal, Verbal-Linguistic**

Alternative Assessment Handbook, Rubric 17: Letters to Editors

DOCUMENT 3

Kipling's "The White Man's Burden"

British poet Rudyard Kipling was born in India—at the time a British colony—and was a great supporter of imperialism. He believed that the countries of Europe and the United States had a duty to help the people of Africa, Asia, and Latin America, a duty he referred to as the "White Man's Burden" in the 1899 poem of that name, part of which is printed below.

Take up the White Man's burden—
Ye dare not stoop to less—
Nor call too loud on Freedom
To cloke your weariness;
By all ye cry or whisper,
By all ye leave or do,
The silent, sullen peoples
Shall weigh your gods and you.

Take up the White Man's burden—
Have done with childish days—
The lightly proferred laurel,
The easy, ungrudged praise.
Comes now, to search your manhood
Through all the thankless years
Cold, edged with dear-bought wisdom,
The judgments of your peers!

DOCUMENT 4

Letter to the Emperor of Japan

In 1853 U.S. president Millard Fillmore sent Commodore Matthew Perry and four large warships to Japan. His purpose was the request the opening of Japan to trade with the United States. An excerpt from Fillmore's letter to the emperor of Japan appears below.

GREAT AND GOOD FRIEND: I send you this public letter by Commodore Matthew C. Perry, an officer of the highest rank in the navy of the United States, and commander of the squadron now visiting Your imperial majesty's dominions.

I have directed Commodore Perry to assure your imperial majesty that I entertain the kindest feelings toward your majesty's person and government, and that I have no other object in sending him to Japan but to propose to your imperial majesty that the United States and Japan should live in friendship . . . with each other.

These are the only objects for which I have sent Commodore Perry, with a powerful squadron, to pay a visit to your imperial majesty's renowned city of Yedo: friendship, commerce, a supply of coal and provisions, and protection for our shipwrecked people.

Skills Focus: READING LIKE A HISTORIAN

DOCUMENT 1

a. Recall What does Sun Yixian say are two characteristics of the Chinese people?

b. Draw Conclusions Do you think Sun would have welcomed Europeans to China? Why or why not?

DOCUMENT 2

a. Explain What does the "big stick" symbolize?

b. Infer Do you think this cartoonist approved of American imperialism? Why or why not?

DOCUMENT 3

a. Describe What does the "White Man's Burden" mean?

b. Analyze Why does Kipling urge European nations to become involved in other societies?

DOCUMENT 4

a. Identify Why does President Fillmore say he has sent Perry and his squadron to Japan?

b. Infer Why do you think President Fillmore mention that Perry has arrived "with a powerful squadron"?

DOCUMENT-BASED ESSAY QUESTION

How did attitudes toward imperialism differ between the people who were founding colonies and those whose countries were colonized? Using the documents above and information from the chapter, form a thesis that explains your position. Then write a short essay to support it.

See **Skills Handbook**, p. H25

Document-Based Investigation

Word Help

sullen gloomy, repressed

proferred given

Biography

Rudyard Kipling (1865–1936) Rudyard Kipling was a British writer of poems, novels, and short stories. His best known works include the children's books *Just So Stories* and *The Jungle Book* and the novel *Kim*, whose main character is an Irish orphan in India who adopts Indian customs. Like Kim, Kipling was born in India, where he learned the Hindi language at a young age. Unlike his character, however, Kipling began attending school in England at the age of five.

Skills Focus: Analyzing Primary Sources

At Level

Reading Like a Historian Skill
Reasons for Imperialism

1. Have students review Documents 3 and 4 and identify the reasons given for imperialism. Remind students that these documents are written from an imperialist point of view; people in the colonized countries probably had a different perspective.
2. Organize students into mixed ability groups. Have each group identify the reasons each document presents for Western influence in other parts of the world.
3. Guide a class discussion about Documents 3 and 4. Ask the following questions: In what ways do these documents represent an imperialist point of view? What would people in the colonized countries think of the concept of the "White Man's Burden"? How might the emperor of Japan have responded to Fillmore's letter? **LS Interpersonal**

Alternative Assessment Handbook, Rubric 11: Discussions

Answers

Reading Like a Historian

Document 1 a. *They are independent both in their thoughts and in their actions.* **b.** *possible answer—No, Sun Yixian believes the Chinese people are meant to be independent and will eventually rebel against outside influence.* **Document 2 a.** *The big stick represents the use of force against enemies.* **b.** *possible answer—No, because it looks as if Roosevelt is using too much influence in too small an area;* **Document 3 a.** *the idea that it is a white person's duty to help the people of Africa, Asia, and Latin America;* **b.** *because they have wisdom; because it is their responsibility;* **Document 4 a.** *to become friends with Japan, to open trade with Japan, to provide coal, provisions, and protection for shipwrecked Americans in Japan;* **b.** *possible answer—because he wished to intimidate Japan.* **Essay** *Student essays should contrast the attitudes of colonized countries with the attitudes of imperialists, using details and examples from the documents and the chapter.*

Answers

Visual Summary

Review and Inquiry Review the cause-and-effect chart with students. Then, have students work individually or in groups to find an example of each concept. Have volunteers share their examples with the class.

Quick Facts Transparency: Visual Study Guide: The Age of Imperialism

Review Key Terms and People

1. Roosevelt Corollary
2. Raj
3. Menelik II
4. Boxer Rebellion
5. Venustiano Carranza
6. Emperor Meiji
7. Social Darwinism

Comprehension and Critical Thinking

8. **a.** ruled India in the name of Great Britain
b. British rule led to the rise of Indian nationalism.
c. possible answer—more benefits, because the British modernized the country, and India eventually gained its independence

9. **a.** the idea that people living in other countries have the right to be tried in the courts of their own home country
b. Chinese nationalists rose up against their Qing leaders because of Western influence.
c. Japan's reforms involved modernization and industrialization, which better prepared it for becoming a world power, rather than simply isolating the nation.

10. **a.** It set rules for how European nations should divide Africa.
b. to gain new markets and new raw materials; did not want other nations to gain territory in Africa first
c. possible answer—The lines Europeans drew to divide African territory did not take into account Africa's traditional borders, which might lead to ethnic conflict later.

CHAPTER 11

Chapter Review

VISUAL STUDY GUIDE

QUICK FACTS

Imperialism in the 1800s

CAUSES

Desire for Resources and Markets
- Western industrializing countries needed raw materials and consumers for manufactured goods.

Political Competition Among Western Nations
- Long-standing rivalries and the rise of nationalism led countries to compete for power.

Western Belief in Cultural Superiority
- Westerners believed it was their duty and their right to rule over and "civilize" other peoples.

Imperialism

EFFECTS

Colonization
- European nations, and to a lesser degree the United States and Japan, exerted their power and influence over much of the globe.

Rise of Nationalism
- The experience of colonial rule, as well as exposure to Western ideas, led to the development of nationalism in parts of Asia and Africa.

Exploitation of Peoples Under Colonial Rule
- Through exploitation of resources and the labor of peoples under colonial rule, imperial nations benefited at the expense of those they ruled.

Key Events of Imperialism

1842	Opium War and Treaty of Nanjing
1853	Commodore Perry opens Japan
1857	Sepoy Mutiny results in British government taking direct control over India
1861	France installs Austrian archduke Maximilian as the emperor of Mexico
1862	Treaty of Saigon gives France control over most of Vietnam
1868	Meiji era begins in Japan
1884	Berlin Conference sets the rules for European control over Africa
1885	Indian National Congress founded
1894	Japan wins the Sino-Japanese War
1898	U.S. wins the Spanish-American War
1900	Boxer Rebellion in China
1906	The Muslim League founded
1911	Chinese and Mexican revolutions begin
1914	Panama Canal opens

Review Key Terms and People

Fill in each blank with the name or term that correctly completes the sentence.

1. The _______ declared that the United States would use its military power to prevent Europeans from gaining control in the Americas.
2. The period of British rule in India is often referred to as the _______.
3. _______ successfully resisted Western attempts to conquer Ethiopia.
4. During the _______, Chinese nationalists laid siege to foreign compounds in Beijing for 55 days.
5. _______ declared himself president of Mexico after Huerta was forced to flee in 1914.
6. _______ began an era of modernization in Japan.
7. The notion that certain nations or races are more fit than others is called_______ .

11. **a.** a leader of the Mexican Revolution; president of Mexico
b. Madero called for a revolution; rebel groups led by Pancho Villa and Emiliano Zapata staged attacks
c. Napoleon III made Archduke Maximilian of Austria the emperor of Mexico, leading to conflict between Mexicans who supported Maximilian and those who opposed him. The United States supported Benito Juárez in his rebellion against Santa Anna and later, Maximilian.

Reading Skills

12. The Indian National Congress, which was mainly Hindu, led boycotts of British goods to protest a partition. The Muslim League was founded because Muslims believed the Indian National Congress might be preserving the interests of Hindus at the expense of Muslims.

13. information about Western society, military practices, and economics

History's Impact video program
Review the video to answer the closing question: What impact did imperialism have on India during the 1800s and early 1900s?

Comprehension and Critical Thinking

SECTION 1 *(pp. 343–347)*

8. a. Recall What role did the British East India Company have in India until 1857?

b. Identify What effect did British rule have on the development of Indian nationalism?

c. Evaluate Did the British bring more benefits or more harm to India? Explain your answer.

SECTION 2 *(pp. 348–355)*

9. a. Define What was extraterritoriality?

b. Identify Cause In what ways did European imperialism contribute to the downfall of the Qing dynasty in China?

c. Elaborate Why were Japan's reforms more effective at resisting Western imperialism than China's reforms were?

SECTION 3 *(pp. 358–362)*

10. a. Identify What did the Berlin Conference achieve?

b. Draw Conclusions Why were Europeans so eager to gain control over Africa?

c. Predict Given how Europeans gained control over Africa, what might be the long-term effects?

SECTION 4 *(pp. 363–367)*

11. a. Recall Who was Francisco Madero?

b. Sequence What were the major events of the Mexican Revolution?

c. Evaluate How did interference from outside nations contribute to unrest in Mexico in the 1800s and early 1900s?

Reading Skills

Identifying Supporting Details *Use what you know about identifying supporting details to answer the questions below.*

12. As Indian nationalism began to develop in the late 1800s and early 1900s, why were two different organizations created to fight for the rights of Indians?

13. What information did the Iwakura Mission seek on its two-year journey through the United States and Europe?

Analyzing Primary Sources

Reading Like a Historian *This political cartoon below was drawn by American cartoonist Thomas Nast in 1885.*

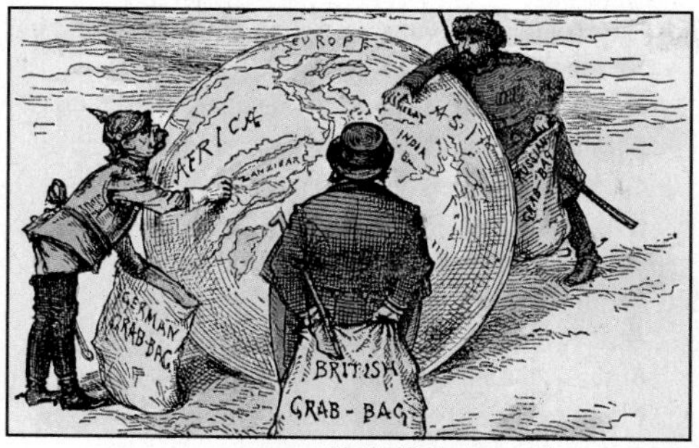

The World's Plunderers, by Thomas Nast, 1885
The Granger Collection, New York

14. Explain What do the "grab bags" symbolize?

15. Draw Conclusions What do you think the artist thought about European imperialism?

Using the Internet

go.hrw.com
Practice Online
Keyword: SHL IMP

16. The Berlin Conference set the ground rules for the European nations that wanted to divide Africa amongst themselves. Using the Internet, research the decisions made at the Berlin Conference. Then make a list of all provisions contained in the General Act of the Berlin Conference, including a map that shows the territorial decisions.

Writing About History

Exposition: Writing a News Article *In 1853 Commodore Perry and his warships ended two centuries of Japan's isolation from the West.*

17. Assignment: Write a news article in which you explain what happened as a result of Commodore Perry's missions to Japan in 1853 and 1854. Be sure to include the reactions of the Japanese and the Americans to this contact. To provide depth to your story, use specific details from the chapter and from other research.

Answers

Analyzing Primary Sources

14. African territories

14. possible answer—he probably disliked it; the title of the cartoon "The World's Plunderers" gives a negative connotation.

Using the Internet

16. Go to the HRW Web site and enter the keyword shown to access a rubric for this activity.

KEYWORD: SHL IMP

Writing About History

17. Student articles should describe the reasons behind Commodore Perry's visit to Japan, and Japanese reactions to the visit. Articles should use details and examples from the chapter to analyze the effects of the visit upon both Americans and Japanese. A rubric for the activity is provided in **CRF**: Writing for the SAT.

HOLT
History's Impact
► **Video Program: The Age of Imperialism**
Refer to the Video Program Teacher's Guide for the answer to the closing question.

Review and Assessment Resources

Review and Reinforce

- **CRF**: Chapter Review
- **Quick Facts Transparency**: Visual Study Guide: The Age of Imperialism
- **Spanish Chapter Summaries Audio CD Program**
- OSP **Holt PuzzlePro**: Quiz Show for ExamView
- **Quiz Game CD-ROM**

Assess

- **PASS**: Chapter Test, Forms A and B
- **Alternative Assessment Handbook**
- OSP **ExamView Test Generator**, Chapter Test
- **Differentiated Instruction Modified Worksheets and Tests CD-ROM**: Chapter Test
- HOAP **Holt Online Assessment Program** (in the Premier Online Edition)

Reteach/Intervene

- **Interactive Reader and Study Guide**
- **Differentiated Instruction Teacher Management System**: Lesson Plans for Differentiated Instruction
- **Differentiated Instruction Modified Worksheets and Tests CD-ROM**: Chapter Test
- **Interactive Skills Tutor CD-ROM**

go.hrw.com
Online Resources
KEYWORD: SHL TEACHER

Unit Review

You can use these pages to have students simultaneously review the unit and practice taking standardized tests.

Answers

1. D
The Industrial Revolution, Section 1
2. C
The Industrial Revolution, Section 2
3. A
The Industrial Revolution, Section 2
4. D
The Industrial Revolution, Section 3
5. A
Life in the Industrial Age, Section 1
6. B
Life in the Industrial Age, Section 2
7. C
Life in the Industrial Age, Section 3
8. D
Reforms, Revolutions, and War Section 1
9. D
Reforms, Revolutions, and War Section 2
10. D
Reforms, Revolutions, and War Section 3

UNIT 3

Standardized Test Practice

Directions Write your answer for each statement or question on a separate answer sheet. Choose the letter of the word or expression that best completes the statement or answers the question.

1 The Industrial Revolution began in Great Britain in part because

A Britain imported technology from the United States.
B Britain had laws against the enclosure movement.
C Britain had a large number of immigrant workers.
D Britain had key resources like iron and coal.

2 As factories in Great Britain grew,

A mass production decreased.
B the textile industry became less important.
C cottage industries declined.
D workers moved away from cities.

3 Why did some factory owners prefer to hire women and children to work in their factories?

A because women and children would work for lower wages
B because women and children were less likely to get sick
C because it was illegal for men to work in factories
D because men preferred to work outdoors

4 Which thinker called for workers around the world to unite and overthrow the capitalist system?

A Adam Smith
B Thomas Malthus
C Thomas Edison
D Karl Marx

5 Industrialization led to

A technological advances like railroads and electricity.
B the decline of the middle class.
C less leisure time for ordinary people.
D the decline of capitalist economies.

6 How did medical advances of the 1800s change industrial societies?

A They enabled governments to provide free health care.
B They helped to lower infant mortality rates.
C They caused a decrease in the amount of pollution.
D They ended the need for vaccinations.

7 Many industrial cities in the 1800s

A severely restricted the growth of suburbs.
B had traffic problems as cars became common.
C started to become more livable as infrastructure improved.
D lost population as workers moved back to rural areas.

8 How did government reforms in Britain affect women's suffrage?

A Women lost the right to vote.
B Women could vote only if they were over 50.
C Women could only vote in local elections.
D Women could vote in all elections.

9 Which letter on the map below indicates the country where the Dreyfus affair occurred?

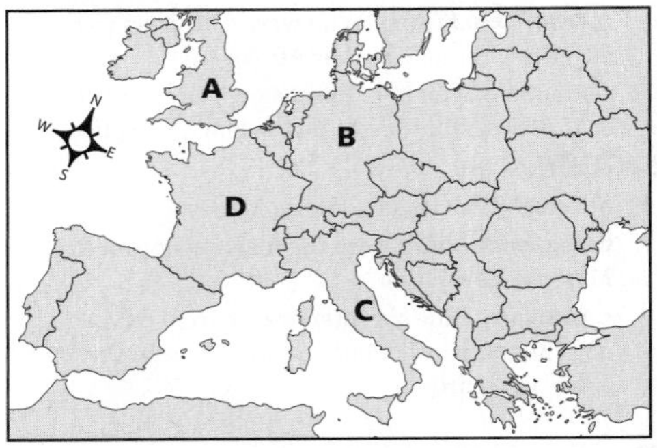

A A
B B
C C
D D

10 Both Toussaint L'Ouverture and Simón Bolívar

A served as colonial governors for Spain in the Americas.
B were priests who argued for better treatment of native peoples.
C fought against the spread of Enlightenment ideas.
D led independence movements in the Americas.

11 **When was slavery abolished in the United States?**
- **A** at the beginning of the Revolutionary War
- **B** during the Civil War
- **C** before the Louisiana Purchase
- **D** at the end of the French and Indian War

12 **Two of the first countries in Europe to unify under nationalist movements were**
- **A** Austria and Poland.
- **B** Norway and Greece.
- **C** Spain and Austria.
- **D** Italy and Germany.

13 **Giuseppe Garibaldi is associated with Italian**
- **A** exploration.
- **B** monarchy.
- **C** isolationism.
- **D** nationalism.

14 **The quote below by France's minister of foreign affairs in 1883 is an attempt to justify what policy?**

> *"The policy of colonial expansion is a political and economic system . . . One can relate this system to three orders of ideas: economic ideas, ideas of civilization in its highest sense, and ideas of politics and patriotism."*

- **A** industrialization
- **B** imperialism
- **C** nationalism
- **D** reform

15 **One reason the British wanted to control India was**
- **A** to encourage Indian nationalism.
- **B** to buy manufactured goods from India.
- **C** to get access to India's raw materials.
- **D** to set up a democracy in India.

16 **What caused the Boxer Rebellion in China?**
- **A** military duties that were forced on the Chinese
- **B** resentment against foreigners
- **C** resistance to the introduction of modern technology
- **D** the fear of a Japanese invasion

17 **How did the Meiji Restoration affect Japan?**
- **A** Japan's economy became modern and industrialized.
- **B** Japan became more isolated.
- **C** China invaded and occupied Japan.
- **D** Japan moved away from Western ideas

18 **What happened at the Berlin Conference?**
- **A** Germany and France signed an agreement to end the Franco-Prussian War.
- **B** European leaders met to decide how to divide Africa.
- **C** Great Britain and Germany met to discuss how to prevent the spread of industrial technologies.
- **D** Austria demanded that Germany renounce claims to its territory.

Reviewing the Unit

Constructed Response Industrialization, nationalism, and imperialism are all related. Recall what you have learned about each topic. Then write a brief essay in which you summarize how industrialization influenced the rise of nationalism in Europe and how nationalism and the growth of industrial economies contributed to the growth of imperialism.

Connecting to the Previous Unit

Constructed Response Basic ideas about science, knowledge, and progress that developed during the Scientific Revolution contributed to the development of the Industrial Revolution. Recall the major changes that occurred during the Scientific Revolution. Then write a brief essay on how those changes set the stage for the beginnings of the Industrial Revolution.

Unit Review

Answers

11. B
Reform, Revolutions, and War Section 4

12. D
Nationalism in Europe, Sections 1 & 2

13. D
Nationalism in Europe, Section 1

14. B
The Age of Imperialism, Section 3

15. C
The Age of Imperialism, Section 1

16. B
The Age of Imperialism, Section 2

17. A
The Age of Imperialism, Section 2

18. B
The Age of Imperialism, Section 3

Reviewing the Unit

Student essays should mention that industrialized nations sought colonies as a source of raw materials and to provide a market for their manufactured goods.

Connecting to the Previous Unit

Student essays should indicate that the scientific method, which evolved during the Scientific Revolution, helped set the stage for the Industrial Revolution. Observation and experimentation led to many of the developments that made the Industrial Revolution possible. For example, British inventors learned to harness the power of steam. The result was the steam engine that revolutionized both manufacturing and transportation.

Unit Review

Science and Technology

Interchangeable Parts The idea of using of interchangeable parts dates back to Gutenberg's printing press, which depended on type that was completely interchangeable. Early attempts at interchangeability in manufacturing met with only limited success. As early as 1828, however, interchangeable parts were used in clocks. By the time of the Civil War, rifles and muskets were made with interchangeable parts. After the war, first sewing machines and then typewriters used them. But it took Henry Ford to revolutionize manufacturing by using assembly lines along with interchangeable parts.

Economic Systems

"Gentlemanly Capitalism" In 1995 a pair of books on British imperialism presented the idea of "gentlemanly capitalism" as the driving force in the economic development of Britain and its empire. According to this theory, it was the British upper classes, not the industrialists, that invested around the world and shaped British imperialism; they had the political power to shape imperial policies to fit their investments.

Themes & Global Connections

THEME

Science and Technology

What new advances in science and technology occurred during the Industrial Revolution?

During the Industrial Revolution, scientists and engineers made major advances in the science and technology of industry. They invented new machines, learned how to harness new sources of power, created a system of factory production, and developed ways to mass produce goods.

Technological Advances During the Industrial Revolution

New Inventions
New inventions, such as the spinning jenny and steam engine, changed the way people produced goods. Large and complex machines of iron and steel became the main tools of industry.

New Sources of Power
To power their new inventions, people burned fossil fuels like coal. Fossil fuels provided abundant energy to move steam-powered machines and generate electricity.

Creation of Factories
With new machines and new sources of power, the very nature of how work was organized changed. The huge new industrial machines required people to come together in large factories to produce goods like cotton and wool textiles, railroad cars, and iron and steel.

Mass Production of Goods
The scale of industrial production was so enormous that mass production became common, and factories produced more goods than ever before.

THEME

Economic Systems

How did the Industrial Revolution change the world's economic systems?

The technological advances made during the Industrial Revolution had far-reaching effects on the world economy. In industrializing countries, production increased and economies boomed as a new urban middle class developed. At the same time, a global economy began to emerge that was dominated by the world's industrial countries.

Effects of the Industrial Revolution on Economic Systems

- The amount of manufactured goods in industrializing countries increased dramatically, causing prices to fall and standards of living to rise.
- A new middle class of workers developed.
- Cities grew rapidly into industrial centers as people flocked to factories to work.
- Industrial countries worked to secure access to raw materials for their factories and to export their manufactured goods.
- A global economic system dominated by industrial countries began to develop.

Skills Focus: Identifying Cause and Effect

At Level

Reading Skill

The Effects of Nationalism

1. Have students come up with examples of nationalism from the last 20 years. As they mention examples, make a list for the class to see. *Examples might include the former Soviet Union, the former Yugoslavia, Rwanda, the Kurds in Iraq and Turkey, etc.*
2. Have each student choose one of the places from the list and conduct research about what the effects of nationalism were in that instance. Students should try to find essays on nationalism from a variety of different places. Have students write a paragraph explaining their research findings.
3. Have volunteers read their paragraphs to the class.
4. Guide the class in a discussion of the effects nationalism continues to have in the modern world. **LS Verbal-Linguistic**

Alternative Assessment Handbook, Rubrics 6: Cause and Effect and 11: Discussions

THEME

GOVERNMENT AND CITIZENSHIP

How did nationalism affect government and citizenship?

In the 1800s, the rise of nationalism, or devotion to one's national group, had major impacts on government and citizenship around the world. Nationalism led to revolutions and the rise of the nation-state as the main form of government.

EFFECTS OF NATIONALISM ON GOVERNMENT AND CITIZENSHIP

- Revolutions in Europe and Latin America led to the creation of new governments based on national groups—people that share a common identity and features such as language, religion, or culture.
- Citizens felt a connection to their government through a shared identity, common history, and national symbols.
- Nonnational states that were imposed by rulers from the top down were challenged, overthrown, and replaced by new governments.
- The nation-state became the dominant form of government.

Skills FOCUS

UNDERSTANDING THEMES

How have industrialization and nationalism shaped the world today? Use your textbook and other resources to gather information about what the world was like before the Industrial Revolution and the rise of modern nationalist movements and what it is like now. Then create a chart like the one below and use it to compare how the world has changed.

	Then	Now
Science and Technology		
Economic Systems		
Government and Citizenship		

Global Connections

Making Connections This chart shows basic economic data for three different countries today. What does this data indicate about the different levels of industrialization in each country? How do you think the Industrial Revolution affected these countries differently? Write a short essay explaining how this data relates to the Industrial Revolution and its uneven effects around the world.

	Major Industries	Labor Force	Urban	Per Capita GDP
United Kingdom	Machine tools, electric power equipment, automation equipment, railroad equipment, shipbuilding, aircraft	Agriculture 1.5%, industry 19.1%, services 79.5%	89.1%	$29,600
Nigeria	Crude oil, mining, palm oil, peanuts, cotton, rubber	Agriculture 70%, industry 10%, services 20%	46.7%	$1,000
Thailand	Tourism, textiles and garments, agricultural processing, beverages, tobacco, cement	Agriculture 49%, industry 14%, services 37%	31.9%	$8,100

Source: *The World Almanac and Book of Facts, 2006*

Differentiating Instruction

Above Level

Advanced Learners/Gifted and Talented

Research Required

1. Draw a table like the one at the bottom of this page for students to see, but label the first row with the name of your community and the second with the name of your state. The third row should be labeled United States. Leave the cells under the headings empty.
2. Organize students into small groups. Have each group copy the table and conduct research about the local, state, and national economies to fill it in. Students should use reliable and current sources, such as census records, economic development Web sites, etc.
3. Have volunteers provide information to fill in the master chart.
4. Guide the class in a discussion of the economy in your community compared with the state as a whole and the national economy. Then compare those economies with the ones listed in the table on this page. **LS Interpersonal, Visual-Spatial**

Alternative Assessment Handbook, Rubrics 7: Charts; 9: Comparing and Contrasting; and 14: Group Activity

Unit Review

Government and Citizenship

The Changing Face of Nationalism

Nationalism was originally a liberal cause. Liberals believed that every people had the right to a state of their own. They believed that governments owed their existence to the consent of the governed. After the failure of the revolutions in 1848, conservative monarchs with notions of cultural or racial unity took the lead in nation-building. They used war and diplomacy rather than reforms to build nation-states in Germany and Italy.

Activity Analyzing Primary Sources Write the following quotation from French President Charles De Gaulle for students to see: "Patriotism is when love of your own people comes first; nationalism, when hate for people other than your own comes first." Have students write a paragraph explaining what this means in the context of this unit.

Understanding Themes

Answers will vary. Charts should include details from the unit that depend on which examples students choose. Under "Government and Citizenship" students should indicate that most Western nations were monarchies in which common people had few rights, whereas today most Western nations have democratic governments with universal adult suffrage.

Global Connections

Answers will vary, but student essays should note that the United Kingdom is the most industrialized nation, as well as the most urban. Agricultural workers account for very little of the labor force, compared with Nigeria, where 70% of the labor force is engaged in agriculture, and Thailand, where nearly half the labor force is engaged in agriculture. Major British industries tend to involve more sophisticated technology than those in Thailand, and most of Nigeria's industries are "low tech." These differences probably reflect the fact that Britain was an industrial and colonial power, and Nigeria is a former colony, where there was no incentive to industrialize until after it achieved independence.

Unit Review

Summarizing the Unit

During the period covered in this unit, the world went through many changes. Write the following terms for students to see: *technology, industrialization, urbanization, nationalism,* and *imperialism.* Ask students what effects these things had on the world during this period. *New technology fueled industrialization, which in turn led to urbanization, improvements in education, and growing democracy. Nationalism changed the map of Europe, while imperialism changed the map of the world as European nations scrambled for colonies.*

UNIT 3 IN BRIEF

Below is a chapter-by-chapter summary of the main ideas in this unit, followed by a summary activity for the unit.

CHAPTER 7 The Industrial Revolution 1700–1900

MAIN IDEA The Industrial Revolution and the factory system changed how goods were made as industry moved from the home and into factories.

SECTION 1 The Industrial Revolution began in Great Britain, which had the necessary factors of production, and later spread to other countries.

SECTION 2 The factory system changed life for workers and created new labor conditions.

SECTION 3 New economic ideas such as Marxism arose in response to industrialization.

CHAPTER 8 Life in the Industrial Age 1800–1900

MAIN IDEA During the Industrial Age, cities grew and changed, new inventions and advances changed life, and people enjoyed new cultural pursuits.

SECTION 1 The telegraph, telephone, and railroad led to a transportation and communication revolution.

SECTION 2 New ideas in the sciences included discoveries in biology, physics, chemistry, and medicine.

SECTION 3 As cities grew larger and became more livable, a growing middle class enjoyed new leisure activities and new movements in the arts.

CHAPTER 9 Reforms, Revolutions, and War 1800–1900

MAIN IDEA In the 1800s, industrialization in Britain led to reform, a new government formed in France, much of Latin America achieved independence, and a costly civil war struck the United States.

SECTION 1 Reforms in Britain increased voting rights, abolished slavery, and improved working conditions.

SECTION 2 After a revolution against the monarchy, France worked to create a democratic government.

SECTION 3 In the Americas, new countries formed after gaining independence from European rule.

SECTION 4 The United States expanded westward in the 1800s and suffered through a bloody civil war.

CHAPTER 10 Nationalism in Europe 1800–1920

MAIN IDEA During the 1800s, nationalist movements spread throughout Europe, and people united to form their own nation-states.

SECTION 1 After years of rebellion against Austrian control, several Italian states unified to form Italy.

SECTION 2 Otto von Bismarck successfully led the German people in two wars against Austria and France, which finally unified German states into one nation.

SECTION 3 In central and eastern Europe, ethnic groups struggled for independence against two powerful empires—the Austrian Empire and the Ottoman Empire.

SECTION 4 In the 1800s and early 1900s, Russians revolted against the absolute power of the czars.

CHAPTER 11 The Age of Imperialism 1800–1920

MAIN IDEA In the 1800s, European nations colonized large areas of Africa, Asia, and Latin America.

SECTION 1 British rule over India supplied British factories with raw materials like cotton and tea.

SECTION 2 While China was controlled by European traders, Japan had limited contact with the West.

SECTION 3 Europe's imperial powers divided up and colonized most of Africa despite African resistance.

SECTION 4 While nations in Latin America gained independence from Spain and Portugal, the United States exerted its influence in the Caribbean.

Thinking like a Historian — Summary and Extension Activity

The Industrial Revolution had dramatic effects on Europe and the rest of the world. Write one paragraph on each of the following topics to describes how industrialization influenced each:

A. Economies and societies

B. Nationalism

C. The rise of imperialism

Answers

Thinking Like a Historian

*possible answers—***A.** *Industrialization led to capitalism and urbanization.* **B.** *Industrialization let to increased nationalism because nations were competing for natural resources to fuel the demands of their growing industries.* **C.** *As nations became industrialized, they sought colonial empires to provide raw materials as well as markets for their manufactured goods.*

Unit Resources

Review and Reinforce

- **CRF:** Chapter Review
- **Spanish Chapter Summaries Audio CD Program**
- OSP **Holt PuzzlePro**: Quiz Show for ExamView
- **Quiz Game CD-ROM**

Assess

- **PASS**: Unit Test, Forms A and B
- **Alternative Assessment Handbook**
- OSP **ExamView Test Generator**
- **Differentiated Instruction Modified Worksheets and Tests CD-ROM**: Chapter Test
- HOAP **Holt Online Assessment Program** (in the Premier Online Edition)

Reteach/Intervene

- **Interactive Reader and Study Guide**
- **Differentiated Instruction Teacher Management System**: Lesson Plans for Differentiated Instruction
- **Differentiated Instruction Modified Worksheets and Tests CD-ROM**: Chapter Test
- **Interactive Skills Tutor CD-ROM**

go.hrw.com Online Resources

KEYWORDS: SHL IND, SHL LIF, SHL REF, SHL NAT, SHL IMP

The World at War
1914–1945

UNIT 4

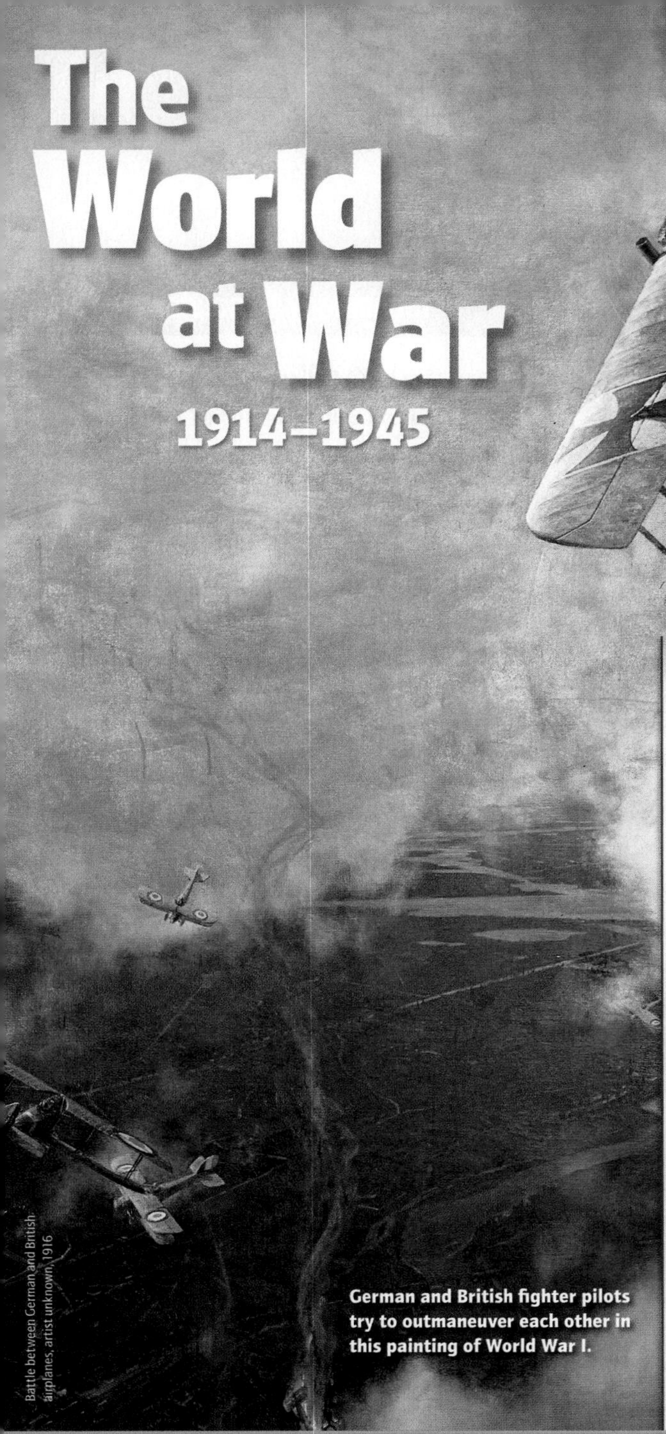

German and British fighter pilots try to outmaneuver each other in this painting of World War I.

Battle between German and British airplanes, artist unknown, 1916

Themes

GOVERNMENT AND CITIZENSHIP
Nationalism in Europe caused government rivalries and alliances that led to devastating world wars and inspired citizens to fight for their countries.

SCIENCE AND TECHNOLOGY
New inventions changed the science and technology of modern warfare, which became more deadly and destructive than ever before.

SOCIETY
Entire countries were mobilized for war, and the global conflicts left millions of soldiers and civilians dead and societies in ruins.

377

Unit Preview

Introducing the Unit

In this unit, students will read about two world wars that shaped relations between nations for the years that followed. Discuss with students the overall causes of war. Have students compare and contrast the causes of World War I and II with the war in Iraq and the war on terrorism.

Connecting to Themes

Activity **New Weaponry** Explain to students that trench warfare gave way to advancements in science and technology as new weaponry was developed. Have students explain how poison gas, tanks, and aircraft gave the Allies and the Axis Powers new advantages in combat. Guide students in a discussion about how the resulting death tolls affected societies across the globe.

Reading Like a Historian

Interpreting Visuals

Fighter Planes At the beginning of World War I, planes were generally unarmed. Aerial combat consisted of pilots shooting at each other with rifles and pistols. Air warfare was revolutionized in May 1915, however, with Germany's introduction of an "interrupter gear" that allowed a machine gun mounted near the front of a plane to fire forward without hitting its own propeller. This invention was quickly copied by the Allies and led directly to the development of specialized "fighter" planes.

Unit Resources

Planning

- **Differentiated Instruction Teacher Management System:** Unit Pacing Guide
- OSP **One-Stop Planner CD-ROM:** Teacher Management System
- **Power Presentations with Video CD-ROM**

Differentiating Instruction

- **Differentiated Instruction Teacher Management System:** Lesson Plans for Differentiated Instruction
- **Differentiated Instruction Modified Worksheets and Tests CD-ROM**

Enrichment

- **A World History Teacher's Guide to Analyzing Movies**
- **Document-Based Activities for World History**
- **World History Outline Maps**
- **Reading Like a Historian: World History Toolkit**
- **World History Primary Source Library CD-ROM**

Assessment

- **PASS:** Unit Test, Forms A and B
- **Alternative Assessment Handbook**
- OSP **ExamView Test Generator**
- HOAP **Holt Online Assessment Program** (in the Premier Online Edition)

Chapter 12 Planning Guide

World War I

Chapter Overview	Reproducible Resources	Technology Resources
CHAPTER 12 **pp. 378–405** **Overview: In this chapter, students will learn about the causes, battles, and effects of World War I.**	**Differentiated Instruction Teacher Management System:*** • Pacing Guide • Lesson Plans for Differentiated Instruction **Interactive Reader and Study Guide:** Chapter Summary* **Chapter Resource File*** • Writing for the SAT • Social Studies Skill • Chapter Review **World History Outline Maps**	**Live Ink© Online Reading Help** **Student Edition on Audio CD Program** **Differentiated Instruction Modified Worksheets and Tests CD-ROM** **World History Primary Source Library CD-ROM** **Power Presentations with Video CD-ROM** **History's Impact: World History Video Program (VHS/DVD):** World War I
Section 1: **The Great War Begins** **The Main Idea:** Europe in 1914 was on the brink of war. After an assassination, the nations of Europe were drawn one by one into what would be called the Great War, or World War I.	**Differentiated Instruction Teacher Management System:** Section 1 Lesson Plan* **Interactive Reader and Study Guide:** Section 1 Summary* **Chapter Resource File*** • Vocabulary Builder: Section 1 • Biography: Sophie, Duchess von Hohenberg • History and Geography: World War I: Early Fighting	**Daily Test Practice Transparency:** Section 1* **Map Transparency:** European Alliances and Military Forces, 1914* **Map Transparency:** World War I Battles, 1914* **Quick Facts Transparency:** Causes of World War I*
Section 2: **A New Kind of War** **The Main Idea:** With the introduction of new types of warfare and new technologies, World War I resulted in destruction on a scale never before imagined.	**Differentiated Instruction Teacher Management System:** Section 2 Lesson Plan* **Interactive Reader and Study Guide:** Section 2 Summary* **Chapter Resource File*** • Vocabulary Builder: Section 2 • Biography: Edith Wharton	**Daily Test Practice Transparency:** Section 2* **Map Transparency:** World War I Battles, 1915–1917* **Internet Activity:** Propaganda Poster
Section 3: **Revolution in Russia** **The Main Idea:** The war and social unrest combined to push Russia to the edge of a revolution. The events that followed led to Russia's exit from the war and became a major turning point in world history.	**Differentiated Instruction Teacher Management System:** Section 3 Lesson Plan* **Interactive Reader and Study Guide:** Section 3 Summary* **Chapter Resource File*** • Vocabulary Builder: Section 3 • Biography: Leon Trotsky	**Daily Test Practice Transparency:** Section 3* **Internet Activity:** Treaty of Versailles
Section 4: **The War Ends** **The Main Idea:** After several years of bloody stalemate—and the entry of the United States into the conflict—the Allied Powers finally prevailed. The peace, however, proved difficult to establish.	**Differentiated Instruction Teacher Management System:** Section 4 Lesson Plan* **Interactive Reader and Study Guide:** Section 4 Summary* **Chapter Resource File*** • Vocabulary Builder: Section 4 • Biography: Arhtur Zimmerman • Literature: *The Sun Also Rises* • Primary Source: The Fourteen Points	**Daily Test Practice Transparency:** Section 4* **Map Transparency:** Europe and the Middle East* **Quick Facts Transparency:** Effects of World War I*

go.hrw.com | Print Resource | Transparency
LS Learning Styles | Audio CD | CD-ROM
Video | SE Student Edition | TE Teachers Edition
OSP One-Stop Planner CD-ROM
*also on One-Stop Planner CD-ROM

Review, Assessment, Intervention

- **Quick Facts Transparency:** World War I*
- **Spanish Chapter Summaries Audio CD Program**
- **Progress Assessment Support System (PASS): Chapter Test**
- **Differentiated Instruction Modified Worksheets and Tests CD-ROM:** Modified Chapter Test
- OSP **One-Stop Planner CD-ROM:** ExamView Test Generator (English/Spanish)
- HOAP **Holt Online Assessment Program (HOAP),** in the Holt Premier Online Student Edition

- **PASS:** Section 1 Quiz*
- **Online Quiz:** Section 1
- **Alternative Assessment Handbook**

- **PASS:** Section 2 Quiz*
- **Online Quiz:** Section 2
- **Alternative Assessment Handbook**

- **PASS:** Section 3 Quiz*
- **Online Quiz:** Section 3
- **Alternative Assessment Handbook**

- **PASS:** Section 4 Quiz*
- **Online Quiz:** Section 4
- **Alternative Assessment Handbook**

HOLT
History's Impact
World History Video Program (VHS/DVD)
World War I

Power Presentation with Video CD-ROM

Power Presentations with Video are visual presentations of each chapter's main ideas. Presentations can be customized by including Quick Facts charts, images and maps from the textbook, and video clips.

Holt Online Learning

go.hrw.com
Teacher Resources
KEYWORD: SHL TEACHER

go.hrw.com
Student Resources
KEYWORD: SHL WWI

- Document-Based Questions
- Interactive Multimedia Activities
- Current Events
- Chapter-Based Internet Activities
- and more!

Holt Premier
Online Student Edition

Complete online support for interactivity, assessment, and reporting

- Interactive Maps and Notebook
- Homework Practice and Research Activities Online

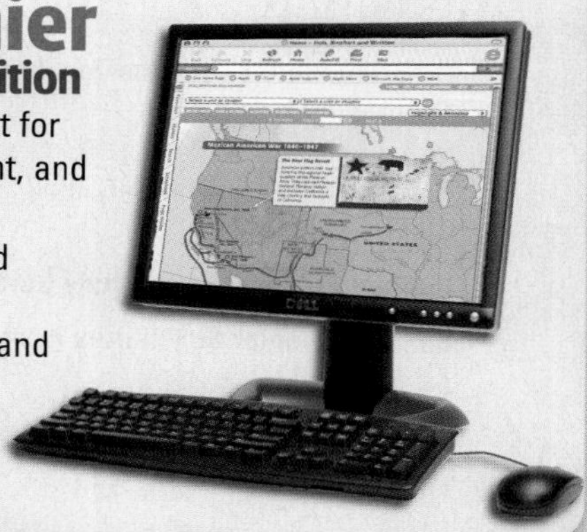

The Big Picture

Peter N. Stearns

Perspective Almost any history of anything, that reaches 1914, sees World War I as a watershed. Obviously the war introduced massive changes into European history. It profoundly affected the United States, the emerging British Commonwealth, and the Middle East—putting a final touch to the collapse of the Ottoman Empire. Participation in the war stimulated significant changes in South Asia and Africa, spurring new levels of nationalist frustration, while shifting the balance in East Asia as well, particularly in creating new opportunities but also new concerns for Japan. The war must be evaluated in another sense as well, as the first clearly modern war in terms of the impact of industrial weaponry and forms of organization. Not only new weapons and unprecedented death rates, but also new government controls and propaganda introduced novel, often troubling, innovations into world history. Comparing this war to earlier types of warfare, and looking to the war as cause of major subsequent developments in world history, provides vital analytical opportunities.

Origins Causes of World War I were once hotly debated, as many people sought to place particular blame on one country or another. At this point, historians more commonly agree that the alliance system and rising levels of armament constrained choice, and when a particular crisis emerged—the assassination of the Austrian archduke—the system was too inflexible to avoid major conflict. To what extent the war reflected larger tensions in the industrial economy and society can still be debated: a number of participants may initially have been inclined to see war as an escape hatch from pressing domestic tensions.

The Peace Settlement Fairly obviously, the peace settlement did not work well. It may usefully be compared with other settlements such as Vienna in 1815. Punitive measures toward Germany and the creation of weak states in east-central Europe were at least part of the problem. Efforts to innovate through the League of Nations were well intentioned but inadequate against ongoing tensions. Several major empires were permanently destroyed, and the map both of Europe and the Middle East was redrawn. Victorious European powers hoped to resume attention to empire, though new de facto colonies were now held as League mandates; but the war had created forces—new weaknesses in Europe, new demands outside—that would increasingly jeopardize imperialism.

Recent Scholarship

With *Sites of Memory, Sites of Mourning: The Great War in European Cultural History* (1995), Jay Winter expresses a leading theme in recent history: the way modern wars, and World War I in particular, inspire new kinds of historical memories which in turn mark major disruptions in popular culture. Winter captures the impact of unprecedented bloodshed and the hardships of the domestic front, as they would help form later memories and monuments. He is adept at portraying similarities and distinctions in the major national experiences. The war itself is well treated in John Keegan's *The First World War* (1999).

Differentiating Instruction

Differentiated Instruction Teacher Management System
- Pacing Guide
- Lesson Plans for Differentiated Instruction

Interactive Reader and Study Guide

Spanish Chapter Summaries Audio CD Program

Student Edition on Audio CD Program

Differentiated Instruction Modified Worksheets and Tests CD-ROM
- Vocabulary Flash Cards
- Modified Vocabulary Builder Activities
- Modified Chapter Review Activity
- Modified Chapter Test

OSP **One-Stop Planner CD-ROM**
- ExamView Test Generator (English/Spanish)
- PuzzlePro
- Quiz Show for ExamView
- Transparencies and Videos

TE **Differentiated Activities in the Teacher's Edition**
- Geography's Effects on the Course of War, p. 382
- Tanks and Aircraft of World War I, p. 386
- Lenin's Decree, p. 394
- Propaganda Pamphlet, p. 400
- World War I Speeches, p. 403

Reading Like a Historian
Sam Wineburg

The U.S. in Haiti Woodrow Wilson campaigned for re-election on the slogan "He Kept us Out of War," and our chapter describes the former president as reluctant to embroil the United States in "the affairs of other nations." This is true if these "other nations" happened to be located in Europe. When it came to our own hemisphere, Wilson and American forces meddled in the affairs of Cuba, Mexico, Panama, and Nicaragua. Indeed, it was under Wilson's watch that the longest American military intervention—an occupation that lasted 19 years and cost thousands of lives—began in Haiti.

With Haiti experiencing social turmoil and political instability, Wilson feared that Germany might invade the island nation and threaten free access to the Panama Canal. On July 28, 1915, he ordered the U.S. Marines to occupy the island, ostensibly to restore order and protect American financial interests. Before long, the Marines introduced a system of "corveé labor," a kind of indentured servitude in which Haitian peasants were forced to work on public works projects at subsistence wages under conditions resembling a chain gang. In his memoirs, Lieutenant General Lewis B. Puller compared these projects to the "building of the pyramids." Watching peasants collapse from heavy labor under the Haitian heat, Puller's conscience wore thin. "I may go to hell for this," he later disclosed to a confidant.

Revolts In the period between 1915 and 1920, some 2,000 to 3,000 Haitians perished in revolts against American rule, many of them followers of Charlemagne Péralte, the rebel leader who waged a guerrilla war against the American forces. Under the pretense of spreading democracy, Americans "helped" Haitians write a constitution. But the document was a sham. Wilson's Assistant Secretary of the Navy, Franklin Delano Roosevelt, indiscreetly boasted in his 1920 campaign for vice president that he was qualified to run a nation: "You know I have had something to do with the running of a couple of little republics. The facts are that I wrote Haiti's Constitution myself, and, if I do say it, I think it a pretty good Constitution." Haiti's "new" constitution allowed Americans, among other things, the "right" to buy Haitian land.

Indeed, the "agreements" signed with Haiti under Wilson virtually turned the nation into a vassal state in which American banks held controlling interests in the Haitian treasury, and granted concessions to American companies to build railroads and run agricultural plantations. These developments did not go unnoticed—particularly among black Americans. Writing in the magazine *The Crisis*, the official publication of the NAACP, W.E.B. Dubois conceded that Haiti had suffered from poor government but noted that the Wilson Administration should "help Haiti rid herself of thieves and not try to fasten American thieves on her." Pressure by the NAACP helped lead to two 1920 fact-finding missions, one by the Navy and the other by the Marines. Both commissions admitted individual acts of wrongdoing, but unsurprisingly concluded that these were isolated incidents and not part of general policy. This did not stop the Haiti-Santo Domingo Independence Society from publishing an advertisement in *The Nation* on November 9, 1921, under the banner "Why Should YOU Worry About Haiti?" which told readers that "Your Government killed two or three thousand harmless Haitians—as against thirteen Marines killed; Your Government is still maintaining martial law in Haiti and continuing an 'American' rule which is in effect 'government of, for, and by, the National City Bank'; and Because You, as an American, are responsible."

Wilson's re-election slogan "he kept us out of war" was true only on one condition: that America turn a blind eye to events in its own backyard.

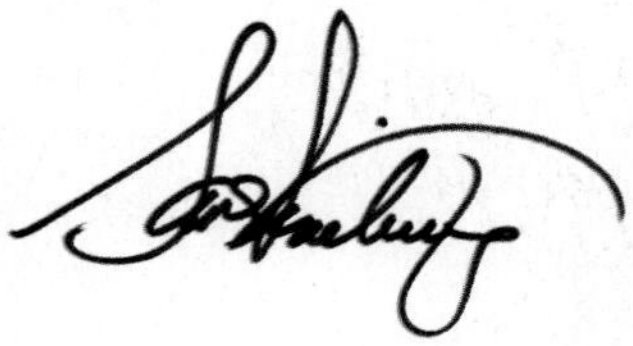

• Chapter Preview •

Chapter Main Ideas

Section 1 Europe in 1914 was on the brink of war. After an assassination, the nations of Europe were drawn one by one into what would be called the Great War, or World War I.

Section 2 With the introduction of new types of warfare and new technologies, World War I resulted in destruction on a scale never before imagined.

Section 3 The war and social unrest combined to push Russia to the edge of a revolution. The events that followed led to Russia's exit from the war and became a major turning point in world history.

Section 4 After several years of bloody stalemate—and the entry of the United States into the conflict—the Allied Powers finally prevailed. The peace, however, proved difficult to establish.

CHAPTER 12 1914–1918

World War I

THE BIG PICTURE A variety of powerful forces—including growing nationalism, a tangle of alliances, and decades of rivalry and competition—created conditions that transformed a single assassination into a worldwide war. After years of unprecedented bloodshed and political upheaval, the warring nations finally reached an uneasy peace.

Theme GOVERNMENT AND CITIZENSHIP
The role of governments and citizens in wartime has varied greatly throughout history. In this chapter you will examine how citizens contributed to the war effort during World War I.

TIME LINE

CHAPTER EVENTS

June 28, 1914 Archduke Franz Ferdinand is assassinated in Sarajevo.

July 28, 1914 Austria-Hungary declares war on Serbia, and World War I begins.

May 1915 Germany attacks and sinks the *Lusitania.*

December 1915 The Gallipoli Campaign ends.

February 1916 The Battle of Verdun begins.

1914 — 1916

WORLD EVENTS

August 1914 The Panama Canal opens.

November 1916 Germany and Austria-Hungary establish the Kingdom of Poland.

Key to Differentiating Instruction

Below Level
Basic-level activities designed for all students encountering new material

At Level
Intermediate-level activities designed for average students

Above Level
Challenging activities designed for honors and gifted and talented students

Standard English Mastery
Activities designed to improve standard English usage

Introduce the Chapter

At Level

World War I, 1914–1918

1. Review with students the definition of *alliance.*
2. Organize students into small groups and have each group make a list of reasons alliances are formed between nations. *trade, shared resources, mutual economic aid, defense*
3. Have students picture what happens when a pebble is thrown into a pond. *Ripples fan out far beyond where the pebble landed.* Explain that World War I began with just one man assassinating another, but this seemingly small event affected the lives of millions of people. Tell students that because of political alliances, many nations became involved in World War I.
4. Have students list the countries that became involved in World War I. Have them decide which countries were allied to one another. Have students work in pencil so they can revise their lists as needed. **LS Interpersonal**

Alternative Assessment Handbook, Rubric 14: Group Activity

Reading like a Historian This photograph shows a British tank and British soldiers during a battle in 1917. World War I marked the first time that tanks were used in combat.

Analyzing Visuals How do you think the use of tanks during World War I would change the nature of warfare? Explain your answer, referring to details from the photograph.

See **Skills Handbook**, p. H26

November 1917 Communists take control of Russia in the Bolshevik Revolution.

November 11, 1918 An armistice ends the war.

1918

June 1917 The first Pulitzer Prizes are awarded.

• Chapter Preview •

HOLT

History's Impact

► **Video Program: World War I**
See the Video Teacher's Guide for strategies for using the video segment.

Reading Like a Historian

Analyzing Primary Sources Have students examine the photograph on these pages. Have them observe where the soldiers are, how they are standing, and where they are looking. Have students determine whether or not they think the photographer was in danger.

Explore the Time Line

1. Where was Archduke Ferdinand assassinated? *Sarajevo*
2. What action did Germany take in May of 1915? *attacked and sank the* Lusitania
3. When was the Kingdom of Poland established? *November 1916*
4. When did an armistice end the war? *November 11, 1918*

Info to Know

Inventing the Tank In 1914, Col. E.D. Swinton of Britain suggested mounting armor and firepower on an American Caterpillar Tractor. When the vehicles were sent to France, the shipping label read "water tanks," to disguise the shipment from the Germans. Such vehicles are still called "tanks" today.

Make Inferences Why would armor help a tank in trench warfare? *would protect it from barbed wire and enemy fire*

go.hrw.com
Online Resources

Chapter Resources:
KEYWORD: SHL WW1
Teacher Resources:
KEYWORD: SHL TEACHER

Answers

Reading Like a Historian *help armies cross wide, trenches; better protect soldiers; larger gun more deadly*

Preteach

Geography Starting Points

The Schlieffen Plan Before the war broke out, Count Alfred von Schlieffen, the chief of the German general staff, developed a planned invasion of France in 1905. From several points along the border, German troops would sweep through Belgium into northeastern France and destroy the French armies at Paris. Schlieffen emphasized the need for a strong right wing of the German army, advancing as far west as possible. The plan was abandoned, however, by the circumstances of the war.

- **Map Transparency:** European Alliances and Military Forces, 1914
- **World History Outline Maps**
- **Interactive Map:** European Alliances and Military Forces, 1914

Answers

Geography Starting Points

1. *Allied Powers—France, Montenegro, Russia, Serbia, United Kingdom; Central Powers—Austria, Hungary, Germany;*
2. *possible answer—The Allied Powers have more troops and would likely win, but would face a difficult challenge defeating Germany.*

GEOGRAPHY Starting Points

Interactive

EUROPEAN ALLIANCES AND MILITARY FORCES, 1914

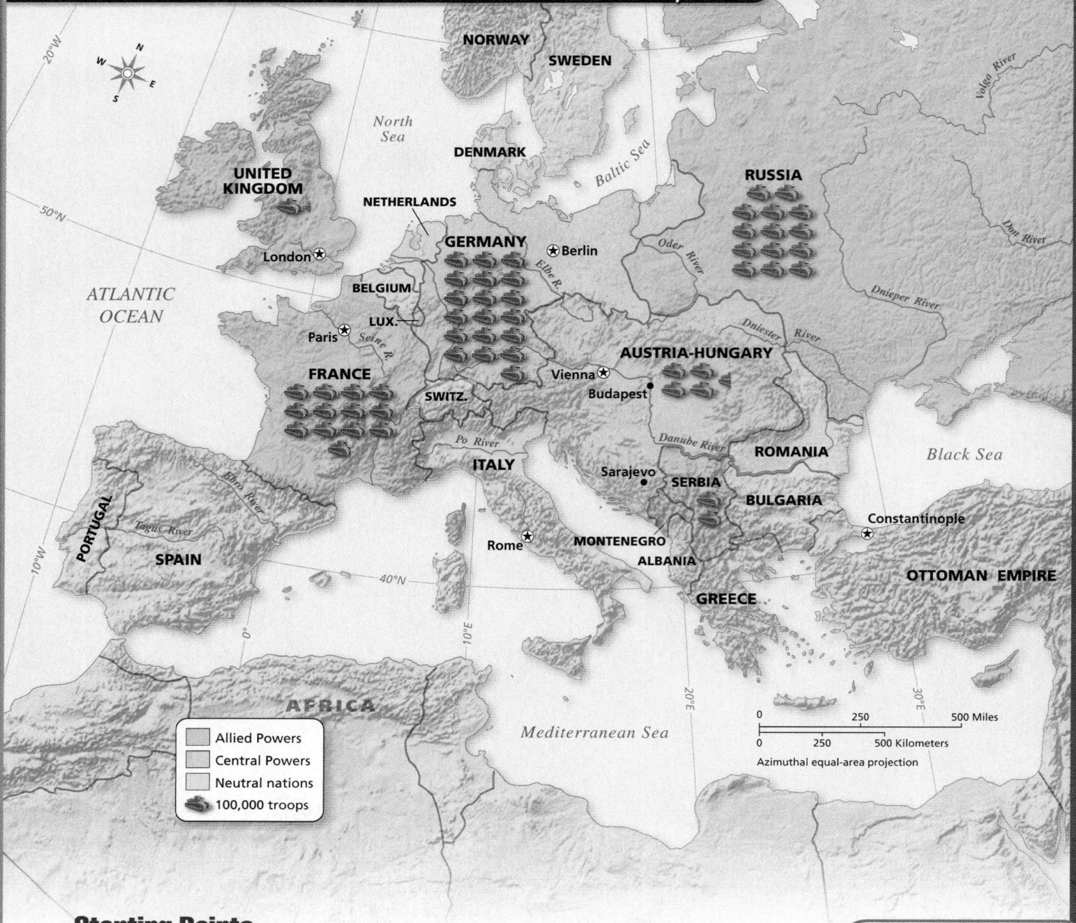

Starting Points In the late 1800s and early 1900s, European nations began a massive military buildup, in part to protect their overseas colonies from rival powers. At the same time, these nations formed a complicated network of alliances to protect themselves from opposing armed forces. By 1914 the uneasy peace was about to end.

1. **Identify** Which nations were members of the Allied Powers in 1914? Which nations made up the Central Powers?
2. **Predict** Given the alliances and the size of the armed forces in Europe in 1914, what might happen if conflict broke out?

Listen to History

Go online to listen to an explanation of the starting points for this chapter.

go.hrw.com
Keyword: SHL WW1

Skills Focus: Analyzing Maps

At Level

Social Studies Skill
Comparing Troop Strengths

1. Draw the chart for students to see. Omit the italicized answers. Have students work in pairs to copy and fill in their charts. Students should list the names of all the Central Powers first, and list all the Allied Powers below them.
2. Have students determine the correct number of troops and have them record the numbers next to each country. **LS Visual-Spatial**

Alternative Assessment Handbook, Rubrics 13: Graphic Organizers; and 21: Map Reading

Comparative Troop Strengths	
Countries	**Troops**
Germany	***1,900,000***
Austria-Hungary	***450,000***
United Kingdom	***100,000***
France	***1,300,000***
Serbia	***200,000***
Russia	***1,400,000***

SECTION 1

The Great War Begins

Before You Read

Main Idea

Europe in 1914 was on the brink of war. After an assassination, the nations of Europe were drawn one by one into what would be called the Great War, or World War I.

Reading Focus

1. Why was Europe on the brink of war in 1914?
2. Why did war break out?
3. What were the results of the fighting in 1914?

Key Terms and People

Triple Alliance
Triple Entente
Franz Ferdinand
Gavrilo Princip
neutral
Central Powers
Allied Powers
Western Front

TAKING NOTES Take notes on the events leading up to the outbreak of war.

[ ] → [ ] → World War I Begins

THE INSIDE STORY ***How did an archduke's trip lead to war?*** It seemed like a bad idea for Austrian archduke Franz Ferdinand to make a trip to the Bosnian city of Sarajevo (SAR-uh-YAY-voh). After all, Austria had taken over Bosnia and Herzegovina just six years earlier, and many Bosnians were still bitterly opposed to Austrian rule.

Bosnia was also the home of many Serbs and ethnic Slavs who were equally outraged by Austria's actions. Serbian leaders hoped to expand Serbia by uniting the ethnic Slavs in Bosnia, but Austria-Hungary stood in the way. Now the future ruler of the Austro-Hungarian Empire was coming to pay a visit.

Franz Ferdinand's visit to Sarajevo fell on June 28, which was also St. Vitus Day, a holiday that symbolized Serbian unity. Members of a Serbian terrorist group known as the Black Hand plotted to kill Franz Ferdinand.

On the day that the archduke visited Sarajevo, seven members of the Black Hand positioned themselves around the city to watch for him. One would-be assassin, 19-year-old Gavrilo Princip, had just stepped out of a sandwich shop when Franz Ferdinand's car pulled up in front of him. Unable to believe his luck, Princip grabbed his pistol and fired, killing both the archduke and the archduke's wife, Sophie. This assassination started a chain of events that, within weeks, would pull most of Europe into the largest war the world had ever seen. ■

▼ Soldiers arrest Gavrilo Princip after he shoots Archduke Franz Ferdinand.

A MURDER IN BOSNIA

Teach the Main Idea

At Level

Events of World War I

Materials: chart paper

1. **Teach** Ask students the Reading Focus questions to teach this section.
2. **Apply** Organize students into small groups. Have each group create a two-column chart listing several causes and effects they identify in each section of this chapter.
3. **Review** Using chart paper, create a large causes-and-effects chart for students to see. For each section, have volunteers from each group record causes and effects they discovered.
4. **Practice/Homework** Have each student write a one-paragraph summary of the major events of the Great War. **LS Verbal-Linguistic, Visual-Spatial**

Alternative Assessment Handbook, Rubric 6: Cause and Effect

Preteach

Getting Started

Use the **Interactive Reader and Study Guide** to familiarize students with the section content.

Interactive Reader and Study Guide, Section 1

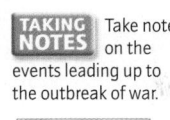

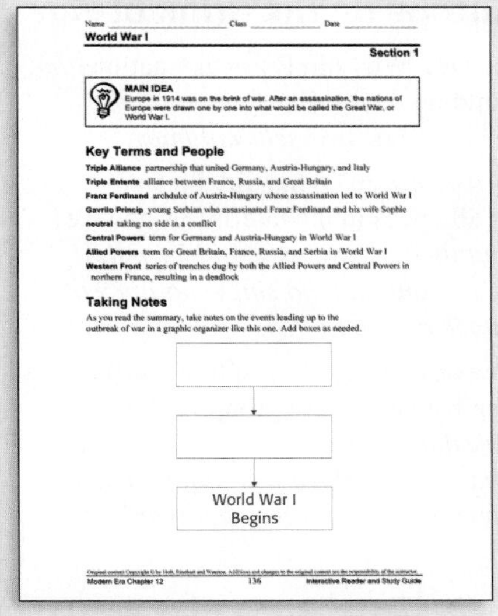

Name ______ Class ______ Date ______

World War I

Section 1

MAIN IDEA
Europe in 1914 was on the brink of war. After an assassination, the nations of Europe were drawn one by one into what would be called the Great War, or World War I.

Key Terms and People

Triple Alliance partnership that united Germany, Austria-Hungary, and Italy
Triple Entente alliance between France, Russia, and Great Britain
Franz Ferdinand archduke of Austria-Hungary whose assassination led to World War I
Gavrilo Princip young Serbian who assassinated Franz Ferdinand and his wife Sophie
neutral taking no side in a conflict
Central Powers term for Germany and Austria-Hungary in World War I
Allied Powers term for Great Britain, France, Russia, and Serbia in World War I
Western Front series of trenches dug by both the Allied Powers and Central Powers in northern France, resulting in a deadlock

Taking Notes

As you read the summary, take notes on the events leading up to the outbreak of war in a graphic organizer like this one. Add boxes as needed.

[ ] → [ ] → World War I Begins

Modern Era Chapter 12 136 Interactive Reader and Study Guide

CRF: Vocabulary Builder: Section 1

Taking Notes

assassination of Archduke Ferdinand starts a chain of events; militarism, alliances, imperialism, and nationalism cause tensions in Europe

Direct Teach

Reading Focus

1 Why was Europe on the brink of war in 1914? *rising tensions resulting from militarism, alliances, imperialism, and nationalism*

Europe on the Brink of War

Recall Why did European nations build up their military forces? *to protect their overseas colonies*

Summarize What did the leaders of alliances in the late 1800s believe? *that their alliances would keep the peace, and that no single nation would attack another*

Predict What do you think will happen between these groups of allies? *possible answer—When one nation is attacked, its allies will join to defend them, resulting in a larger war.*

Info to Know

Heart Surgery Cardiac surgery was first performed during World War I. In 1896 author Stephen Paget wrote the opinion that heart surgery was impossible and should not be attempted by surgeons. In 1917, however, British surgeon George Grey Turner removed a bullet from a soldier's heart. Even though there was no blood bank, no antibiotics, only primitive anesthesia, and poor lighting at the time, the soldier lived through the surgery and was still living in 1940 when the case was finally reported. Nearly half a century after Paget's statement, heart surgery at last became accepted and techniques advanced rapidly.

QUICK FACTS Causes of World War I

Analyze Which factor listed in the chart most influenced ethnic Serbs to rebel against Austria-Hungary? *nationalism*

Quick Facts Transparency: Causes of World War I

Answers

Reading Check *rising tensions as result of militarism, alliances, imperialism, and nationalism*

Europe on the Brink of War

In 1914, rising tensions in Europe had the continent on the brink of war. These tensions were the result of four factors: militarism, alliances, imperialism, and nationalism.

Militarism Throughout the late 1800s and early 1900s, European countries had undertaken a massive military buildup. This militarism was caused mostly by the desire to protect overseas colonies from other nations. Across Europe, the size of armed forces and navies had risen sharply, particularly in Germany.

The growing power of Europe's armed forces left all sides anxious and ready to act at the first sign of trouble. In this nervous environment, even a minor disagreement had the potential to turn quickly into armed conflict.

Alliances Seeking to protect themselves from opposing armed forces, the nations of Europe formed a series of alliances, or partnerships. For example, in the late 1800s, the so-called **Triple Alliance** united Germany, Austria-Hungary, and Italy. France and Russia feared Germany's growing power and formed their own alliance. Soon Great Britain joined with France and Russia in a less formal promise to cooperate—an entente (ahn-TAHNT). France, Russia, and Great Britain thus became known as the **Triple Entente**. Leaders hoped that these alliances would help keep the peace. They believed that no single nation would attack another, since that action would prompt the attacked nation's allies to join the fight.

Imperialism The quest to build empires in the late 1800s and early 1900s had created much rivalry and ill will among the nations of Europe. Germany, France, Russia, and Great Britain each saw themselves as great imperial nations. They believed they could not afford to stand by while a rival empire gained power.

Nationalism An important part of the rising tensions in Europe was an increase in nationalism beginning in the late 1800s. Nationalism is a strong devotion to one's national group or culture. In Europe, nationalism led to the formation of new countries, including Germany and Italy, and struggles for power.

The most visible of these power struggles was in the Balkan Peninsula, a region of southeastern Europe that was home to many ethnic groups. In the early 1900s, some of these ethnic groups were trying to break free from the Ottoman Empire, which had ruled the Balkans for hundreds of years but was now nearing collapse.

Some of the strongest nationalist tensions in the Balkans were in Serbia. At the time, Serbia was an independent nation. Many ethnic Serbs, however, lived outside Serbia in other areas of the Balkans. Serbian leaders wanted to expand the nation's borders and unite all their people in a "greater Serbia." But Austria-Hungary, the powerful empire to the north of Serbia, opposed any Serbian expansion, fearing that such growth might encourage ethnic groups within Austria-Hungary to rebel. Tensions between Austria-Hungary and Serbs would continue to rise in the early 1900s.

READING CHECK **Summarize** Why was Europe on the brink of war in 1914?

QUICK FACTS: Causes of World War I

MILITARISM
- European nations engage in a massive military buildup.

ALLIANCES
- European countries form partnerships to protect themselves.

IMPERIALISM
- Rival empires seek to keep power.

NATIONALISM
- People feel loyalty and devotion to their country or culture.

War Breaks Out

In the midst of the tensions and resentment the Serbs felt toward Austria-Hungary, the archduke of Austria-Hungary, **Franz Ferdinand**, decided to visit the Bosnian city of Sarajevo (SAR-uh-YAY-voh). On June 28, 1914, as Franz Ferdinand's car drove through the Sarajevo

Differentiating Instruction

At Level

Research Required

Special Education Students

Materials: chart paper

1. Review with students the locations of countries that became involved in World War I.
2. Organize students into groups of four or five. Assign each group one border area between two non-allied nations.
3. Have each group find and trace a detailed map of its assigned area, including landform details and routes across the borders. Ask each group to select a member to find and print out detailed aerial photos of the border area. It may take several prints to cover the full border. Have students attach the printouts to the outside of the drawn maps, using arrows to indicate which sections they represent.
4. Based on their observations, have group members write their predictions about how the landforms might affect the course of war at that location. Allow time for groups to share their work. **LS Interpersonal, Visual-Spatial**

Alternative Assessment Handbook, Rubrics 20: Map Creation; and 30: Research

World War I Battles, 1914

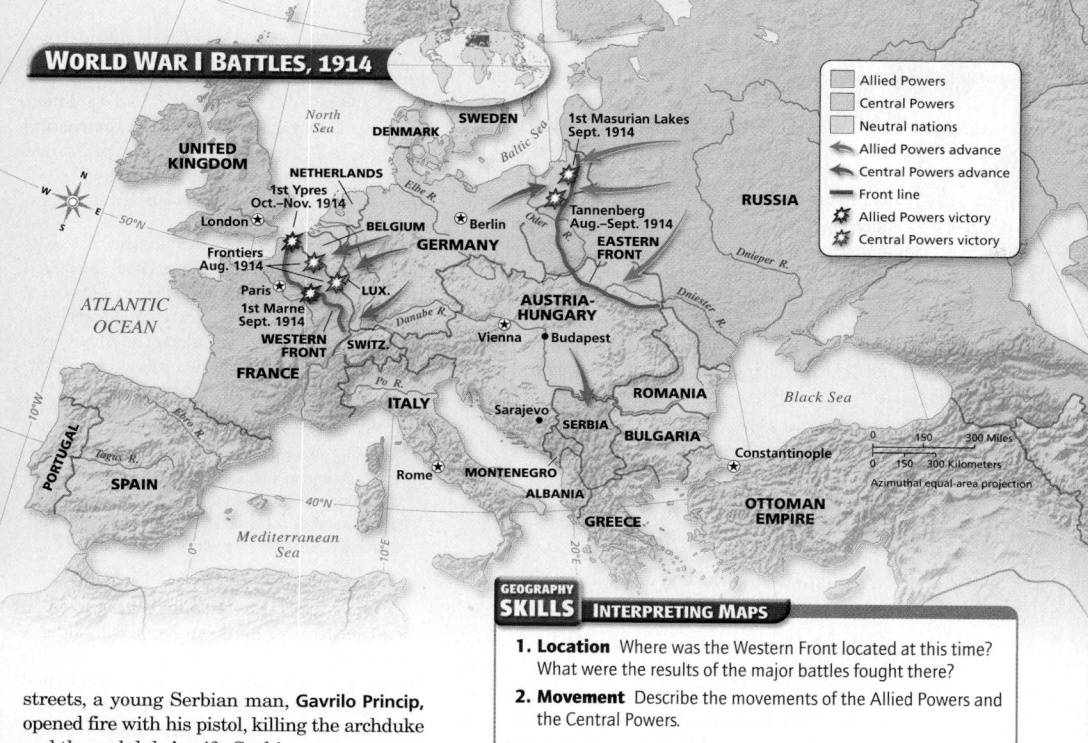

GEOGRAPHY SKILLS INTERPRETING MAPS

1. **Location** Where was the Western Front located at this time? What were the results of the major battles fought there?
2. **Movement** Describe the movements of the Allied Powers and the Central Powers.

streets, a young Serbian man, **Gavrilo Princip,** opened fire with his pistol, killing the archduke and the archduke's wife, Sophie.

The Impact Princip was arrested after the assassination. When he was identified as a Serb, Austria-Hungary decided to use the murder as an excuse to punish Serbia. Austria-Hungary made a series of humiliating demands of Serbia and then declared war on July 28, 1914.

Russia, a country with many people of Slavic ethnicity, had previously promised to support the Serbs if Austria-Hungary attacked. When Russia prepared to fulfill its promise to the Serbs, Austria-Hungary's ally Germany saw the Russian action as a threat. Germany declared war on Russia and then on Russia's ally, France. Thus, Europe's alliances and rivalries turned the action of a single assassin into a major conflict.

Fighting Begins Located in central Europe, Germany faced a war on two fronts—against Russia to the east and France to the west. Years earlier, German military planners had developed the Schlieffen Plan, which called for German troops to quickly defeat France in the west and then head east to fight Russia. German leaders believed this strategy would be effective because Russia's vast size meant that the Russian military would need some time to move toward the German border.

Germany began with a quick strike into Belgium, which was located between Germany and France. Belgium was a **neutral** country, or a country that takes no side in a conflict. Still, Germany planned to sweep through that country and then move on to France. Germany's attack on a neutral country led Great Britain to declare war on Germany.

The main players of what came to be called World War I, or the Great War, were now in place. Germany and Austria-Hungary made up one side, known as the **Central Powers**. Great Britain, France, Russia, and Serbia were known as the **Allied Powers.**

READING CHECK **Sequence** What events led to the outbreak of World War I?

READING SKILLS

Understanding Sequencing In what order did the Allied Powers become involved in the war?

Direct Teach

Reading Focus

2 Why did war break out? *Austria-Hungary blamed Serbia for the assassination of Archduke Ferdinand, leading to war between both countries' allies.*

War Breaks Out

Recall Which country did Germany attack on its way to invade France? *Belgium*

Explain Why did Germany declare war on Russia? *Germany, an ally of Austria-Hungary, saw Russia's plan to support the Serbs as a threat.*

Activity **Russian Advancement** Have students refer to the map and propose an alternate position for the advance of Russia. Use sticky notes on a wall map, if available, to indicate proposed Russian positions. Have students discuss and explain their ideas. **LS Visual-Spatial**

Alternative Assessment Handbook, Rubric 6: Cause and Effect

Map Transparency: World War I Battles, 1914

CRF: Biography: Sophie, Duchess von Hohenberg

Skills Focus: Interpreting Movement Maps

At Level

Prep Required

Social Studies Skill

Troop Strength

Materials: one black outline map per student, glue, punched holes from two colors of paper

1. Distribute black outline maps of Europe to each student. Review the numbers of troops shown on the Geography Starting Points map, European Alliances and Military Forces, 1914.
2. Have students lightly pencil in the front lines and the arrows representing advances from the map on this page. Distribute piles of two colors of paper punch-outs to each row of students.
3. Using the punch-outs to represent each group of 100,000 troops, have students distribute the appropriate number of troops as they were likely to have been placed by the Allied Powers and the Central Powers. Use different colors to represent each allied group. Display student work. **LS Visual-Spatial**

Alternative Assessment Handbook, Rubric 20: Map Creation

Answers

Reading Skills *Germans attack Belgium, Great Britain declares war on Germany, French and British fight in Battle of the Frontiers, Russia attacks Germany from east*

Interpreting Maps **1.** *along the border of Germany and France; refer to map;* **2.** *The Central Powers advanced toward Russia to the east, France to the west, and Serbia to the south; the Allied Powers advanced along the Eastern Front.*

Reading Check *Serbian Gavrilo Princip killed Austrian Archduke Ferdinand and his wife; Germany (an ally of Austria-Hungary) declared war on Russia (an ally of Serbia); Germany attacked Belgium; Great Britain declared war on Germany*

Direct Teach

Reading Focus

3 What were the results of the fighting in 1914? *Both sides suffered heavy losses; Russia attacked East Prussia; trench warfare began; the war became a bloody stalemate.*

Fighting in 1914

Identify What was the name of the disastrous Russian battle? *The Battle of Tannenberg*

Identify Cause and Effect What effect did the Russian attack on East German territory have on the Western Front? *It distracted the Germans and removed pressure on France.*

CRF: History and Geography: World War I: Early Fighting

Review & Assess

Close

Have students explain how alliances caused World War I to expand quickly.

Review

Online Quiz, Section 1

Assess

SE Section 1 Assessment

Progress Assessment: Section 1 Quiz

Alternative Assessment Handbook

Reteach/Intervene

Interactive Reader and Study Guide, Section 1

Interactive Skills Tutor CD-ROM

FACES OF HISTORY

Kaiser WILHELM II
1859–1941

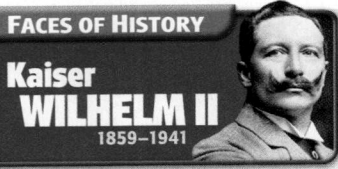

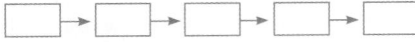

Friedrich Wilhelm Viktor Albert became emperor of Germany when he was only 29 years old. Wilhelm believed the ideal ruler was someone who would make a nation powerful and respected. He was determined to make Germany a world power.

Under Wilhelm's rule, the German armed forces underwent a massive expansion. Wilhelm believed that his personal relationships with the leaders of Great Britain and Russia would help prevent war, but he was mistaken. His aggressive, tactless actions, combined with his desire to build a powerful German military, helped lead the world into a devastating war.

Find the Main Idea How did Wilhelm help cause World War I?

Fighting in 1914

Germany's plans for a swift victory in France soon failed. By the end of 1914, the Great War had become a bloody stalemate.

Early Battles Beginning in August 1914, German troops fought French and British forces in a series of clashes known as the Battle of the Frontiers. Both sides suffered heavy losses, but the result was a German victory.

While France was struggling to fight off Germany during the Battles of the Frontiers, Russia attacked German territory from the east. The results for the Russians were disastrous. In the Battle of Tannenberg, German forces crushed the Russian invasion.

The Russian attack had failed to defeat the Germans, but it succeeded in distracting German forces from their advance on France. This distraction allowed Allied forces to collect themselves and turn on the German invaders.

Trench Warfare Begins In the Battle of the Marne in early September 1914, the Allied troops succeeded in driving the Germans back. After retreating, German forces dug a series of trenches, or deep ditches, along the Aisne (AYN) River and awaited the Allied attack. One British soldier described the German trenches:

HISTORY'S VOICES

> **"[German] infantry are holding strong lines of trenches among and along the edge of the numerous woods which crown the slopes. These trenches are elaborately constructed and cleverly concealed. In many places there are wire entanglements."**
>
> —British colonel Ernest Swinton, September 18, 1914

From their strongly defended trenches on the Aisne, the Germans were able to fight back the Allied forces. But the Allied forces soon dug trenches of their own. As a result, German and Allied positions would change little in the coming months, despite a series of major battles. The deadlocked region in northern France became known as the **Western Front**.

READING CHECK **Summarize** What were the major events of the fighting in 1914?

SECTION 1 ASSESSMENT

go.hrw.com
Online Quiz
Keyword: SHL WW1 HP

Reviewing Ideas, Terms, and People

1. **a. Identify** What were the **Triple Alliance** and the **Triple Entente**?
   b. Explain Why do you think European governments expanded the size of their armed forces?
   c. Draw Conclusions How did the increased size and power of military forces make fighting more likely?
2. **a. Describe** What was the crime that led to the start of World War I?
   b. Make Inferences After **Franz Ferdinand** was killed, why do you think that Austria-Hungary chose to take the actions it did?
   c. Develop How might Germany have worked to stop the war from beginning?
3. **a. Recall** What forces fought in the war's first major battle?
   b. Analyze How did the construction of trenches affect the war in 1914?

Critical Thinking

4. **Identify Cause and Effect** Using your notes on the section and a graphic organizer like the one below, explain how the events of the late 1800s and early 1900s led up to the outbreak of World War I.

→	→	→	→	

FOCUS ON SPEAKING

5. **Persuasion** Write notes for a speech that a European leader trying to prevent the outbreak of war might have given in July 1914. Use details from the chapter in your notes.

Section 1 Assessment Answers

1. **a.** The Triple Alliance united Germany, Austria-Hungary, and Italy. The Triple Entente included France, Russia, and Great Britain.
   b. possible answer—to protect overseas colonies from other nations
   c. The growing power of Europe's armed forces left all sides ready for war.
2. **a.** the assassination of Archduke Franz Ferdinand and his wife by Gavrilo Princip
   b. possible answer—Austria-Hungary opposed Serbian expansion, so they used the assassination as an excuse to punish Serbia.
   c. possible answer—Germany could have avoided attacking Serbia's allies.
3. **a.** German troops fought French and British
   b. Trench warfare would cause higher casualties.
4. buildup of armed forces in Europe; alliances formed; assassination of Archduke Franz Ferdinand; Germany invaded Belgium and France; Great Britain and Russia join the war
5. possible speech topics—alliances will not prevent war; militarism should be avoided; nationalism and imperialism may lead to war

Answers

Faces of History *was aggressive and tactless, determined to make Germany a world power*

Reading Check *Germany advanced though Belgium to attack France; Russia attacked East Prussia; Russians crushed in Battle of Tannenberg; British and French forces regrouped; millions died or were wounded; trench warfare resulted in a stalemate*

SECTION 2

A New Kind of War

Before You Read

Main Idea

With the introduction of new types of warfare and new technologies, World War I resulted in destruction on a scale never before imagined.

Reading Focus

1. How was the World War I battlefield different than those of earlier wars?
2. How did the war affect the home front?
3. What happened on the Western Front?
4. How did the war spread around the world?

Key Terms

trench warfare
total war
propaganda
Battle of Verdun
Gallipoli Campaign
genocide

TAKING NOTES Take notes on the weapons and technology of the battlefield and the events of the war.

POISON FROM THE SKY

THE INSIDE STORY ***Can you protect yourself against the air?*** The exhausted British soldiers were taking a break from the bitter fighting with German forces. In the distance, they could see the other end of their own line of trenches. This section was occupied by British allies, including soldiers from France and from the French colony of Algeria.

The resting British soldiers noticed a curious thing. Floating through the air from the German lines toward the Allied trenches was a slow-moving cloud of yellowish smoke. Soon, from the direction of the strange cloud came a steady stream of running men, throwing away clothing, equipment, and anything else that might slow them down.

The British were at first horrified at what they thought was the cowardly retreat of the French and Algerians. They soon learned, however, that the terrified men had good reason to run. The yellow cloud that had floated into their trenches was chlorine gas, a deadly poison. When inhaled, this gas damages lung tissue and causes victims to cough violently and choke. In some cases, the gas kills.

The poison gas used against the Allied troops was one of many new weapons that first appeared in World War I. Together these weapons produced a horrifying level of death and destruction. ■

▲ **Gas masks were vital equipment for soldiers in the World War I trenches.**

The World War I Battlefield

Poison gas and the other new weapons developed during World War I were a response to a massive deadlock. By the end of 1914, two systems of trenches stretched for hundreds of miles over western Europe. Across the Western Front, millions of Allied and Central Powers soldiers lived in these trenches, surrounded by flying bullets, bombs, and grenades.

Teach the Main Idea

At Level

A New Kind of War

1. **Teach** Ask students the Reading Focus questions to teach this section.
2. **Apply** Organize students into small groups. Write these topics for all to see: On the Battlefield, At Home, Around the Globe. Have groups write newspaper articles about the changes war brought to these three areas. Group members should write articles about each topic.
3. **Review** Have groups share their newspaper articles with the class. As you review the section, have students revise their articles as needed.
4. **Practice/Homework** Have each student write a list of changes for each of the three locations covered. LS **Interpersonal, Visual-Spatial**

Alternative Assessment Handbook, Rubrics 14: Group Activity; and 23: Newspapers

Preteach

Getting Started

Use the **Interactive Reader and Study Guide** to familiarize students with the section content.

Interactive Reader and Study Guide, Section 2

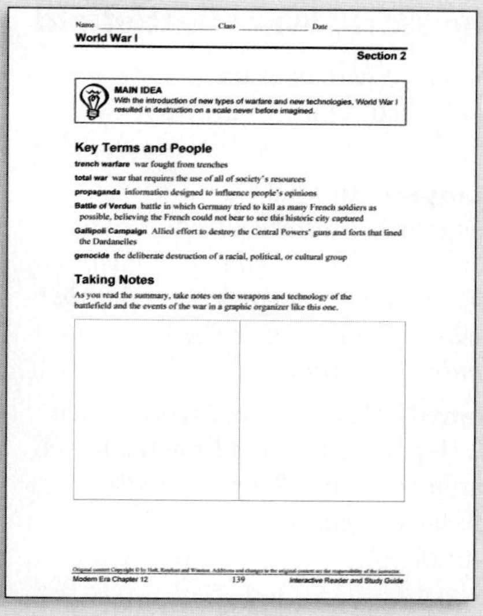

Name ________ Class ________ Date ________

World War I

Section 2

MAIN IDEA
With the introduction of new types of warfare and new technologies, World War I resulted in destruction on a scale never before imagined.

Key Terms and People

trench warfare war fought from trenches
total war war that requires the use of all of society's resources
propaganda information designed to influence people's opinions
Battle of Verdun battle in which Germany tried to kill as many French soldiers as possible, believing the French could not bear to see this historic city captured
Gallipoli Campaign Allied effort to destroy the Central Powers' guns and forts that lined the Dardanelles
genocide the deliberate destruction of a racial, political, or cultural group

Taking Notes

As you read the summary, take notes on the weapons and technology of the battlefield and the events of the war in a graphic organizer like this one.

Modern Era Chapter 12 139 Interactive Reader and Study Guide

CRF: Vocabulary Builder: Section 2

Taking Notes

soldiers on the battlefields face miserable life in the trenches; new weapons such as poison gas, machine guns, tanks, and faster aircraft used; Ottoman Empire joins Central Powers; Italy joins Allied Powers; war spreads to Asia and Africa

go.hrw.com
Online Resources
KEYWORD: SHL WW1
ACTIVITY: Propaganda Poster

Direct Teach

Reading Focus

1 How was the World War I battlefield different than those of earlier wars? *poison gas, new weapons, trench warfare*

The World War I Battlefield

Recall Where does the term "no-man's-land" come from? *from the dangerous open area between trenches*

Compare In what way were the new trenches different from earlier warfare? *Soldiers had long hidden behind mounds of earth for safety, but now systems of trenches stretched for hundreds of miles.*

Identify Cause and Effect What developments resulted from the trench warfare stalemate? *new technology such as gas warfare, tanks, and aircraft*

Recent Scholarship

Historian Hew Strachan takes a less traditional stance in his book *The First World War,* which describes the war as less about soldiers' courage and more about a race for the latest warfare technology. According to Strachan, World War I generals focused mainly on new weapons and tactics rather than on troop strength and bravery. *The First World War* also outlines the far-reaching effects of the war and discusses how it affected soldiers.

The First World War by Hew Strachan. Viking, 2004.

THE IMPACT TODAY

The use of chemical weapons like poison gas was outlawed in 1997 by the Chemical Weapons Convention.

Trench Warfare The idea of **trench warfare**, or fighting from trenches, was not new. Soldiers had long hidden behind mounds of earth for safety. But no one had ever experienced trench warfare on the scale seen in Europe in 1914.

Life in the trenches was often miserable. Rainstorms produced deep puddles and thick mud, and sanitation was a constant problem. Sometimes removing dead bodies from trenches or the surrounding area was impossible. Lice, rats, and other unpleasant creatures were always present.

Occasionally soldiers would be ordered "over the top" of their trench to attack the enemy. They would jump out of their trench and sprint across the area between opposing trenches, called no-man's-land. As they ran, many were cut down by enemy guns. Thousands of soldiers on both sides died in no-man's-land, their bodies left where they fell.

New Weapons Neither the Allies nor the Central Powers were able to make significant advances past the enemy's trenches. As a result, each side turned to new weapons and technology to win the war.

Poison gas was one of the new weapons used in the war. Different types of gas could blind, choke, or burn the victims. Gas killed or injured thousands of people, but its value was limited. A change in wind direction, for example, could blow the gas back toward the troops who had launched it. Also, both sides developed gas masks, which provided some protection.

Other new weapons were far more effective. For example, rapid-fire machine guns came into wide use during the war. Modern industry also produced artillery and high-explosive shells with enormous destructive power.

Tanks and Aircraft Both tanks and aircraft were first used in World War I. Tanks, armored vehicles that could cross rough battlefield terrain, were pioneered by the British. Because reliability was a problem, however, they would not make a contribution until late in the war.

Aircraft, on the other hand, were useful from the beginning. At the start of the war, few

Interactive HISTORY CLOSE-UP

Trench Warfare

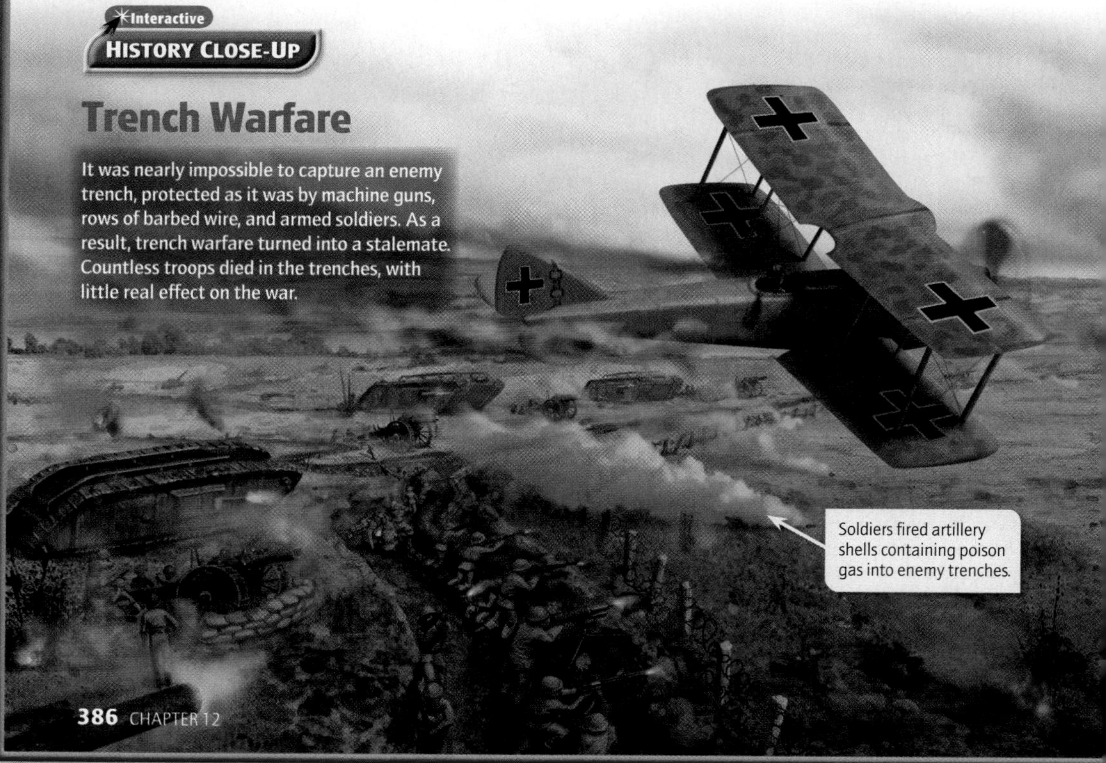
Soldiers fired artillery shells containing poison gas into enemy trenches.

It was nearly impossible to capture an enemy trench, protected as it was by machine guns, rows of barbed wire, and armed soldiers. As a result, trench warfare turned into a stalemate. Countless troops died in the trenches, with little real effect on the war.

Differentiating Instruction

Above Level

Advanced Learners/Gifted and Talented

Research Required

1. Remind students that tanks and aircraft were developed for battlefield use in World War I.
2. Organize students into groups of four or five. Groups should designate an illustrator, a researcher, and two or more capabilities analysts. Have each group choose either tanks or aircraft of World War I as their subject.
3. Have groups conduct research about the development of their vehicle type. Tell students to focus on new developments and capabilities as well as the appearance of their vehicle type.
4. Ask each group to create a detailed poster illustrating and explaining the capabilities of the vehicles they are researching and their value in the battlefield. Allow time for groups to present their posters. **LS Interpersonal, Visual-Spatial**

Alternative Assessment Handbook, Rubrics 28: Posters; and 30: Research aircraft existed, and they were used mainly to observe enemy positions. Soon, mechanics began to attach machine guns to airplanes, and pilots began to drop bombs from the air. As the war dragged on, new, faster airplanes proved useful in attacking battlefields and cities.

Despite the new technologies, however, neither side was able to gain an advantage on the battlefield. Trench warfare, with all its miseries, dragged on.

READING CHECK **Summarize** How did new technology affect the World War I battlefield?

War on the Home Front

The nations fighting in World War I soon realized that winning this new type of war would require the use of all of society's resources. This tactic is called **total war**. Governments began to take stronger control of their citizens' lives.

Government Actions In some countries, new controls resulted in changes to the nation's industries and economy. Factories began to produce military equipment. Civilians conserved food and other goods for military use.

Governments also sought to control public opinion. They censored newspaper reports about the fighting, worried that truthful descriptions of casualties might discourage the public. Governments also created **propaganda**, information designed to influence people's opinions, in order to encourage support of the war effort. Posters, pamphlets, and articles urged people to volunteer or told stories of the enemy's brutal actions.

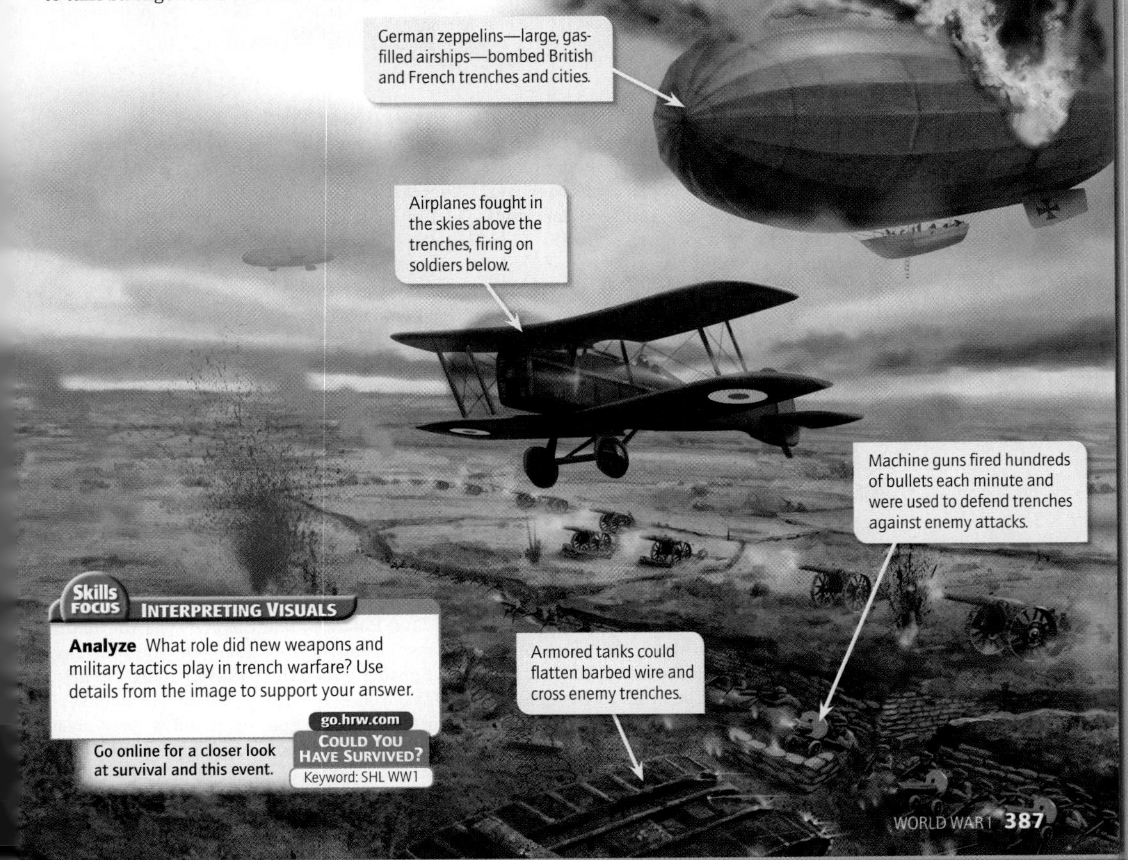

German zeppelins—large, gas-filled airships—bombed British and French trenches and cities.
Airplanes fought in the skies above the trenches, firing on soldiers below.
Machine guns fired hundreds of bullets each minute and were used to defend trenches against enemy attacks.
Armored tanks could flatten barbed wire and cross enemy trenches.

Skills FOCUS **INTERPRETING VISUALS**

Analyze What role did new weapons and military tactics play in trench warfare? Use details from the image to support your answer.

go.hrw.com
Go online for a closer look at survival and this event.
COULD YOU HAVE SURVIVED?
Keyword: SHL WW1

Direct Teach

Reading Focus

❷ How did the war affect the home front? *Involved nations' governments took control of the lives of their people and women entered the workforce.*

War on the Home Front

Describe What is total war? *the tactic of using all of society's resources to fight a war*

Rate What is your opinion of the use of propaganda and censorship? *possible answer—It would unify people to support the war effort, but it is wrong to keep people from knowing about what is happening.*

Teaching Tip

Some wartime music reflected propaganda's positive spin on the war. Locate some recordings and share them with your class.

About the Illustration

This illustration is an artist's conception based on available sources. Historians, however, are uncertain exactly what this scene looked like.

Skills Focus: Recognizing Bias in Primary Sources — At Level

Reading Like a Historian Skill
Influencing Public Opinion

1. Tell students that governments of nations involved in World War I felt a need to influence public opinion. Tell students that catchy tunes often painted a rosy picture of the war.
2. Organize students into small groups. Have each group conduct research using reliable online or print sources to locate World War I propaganda.
3. Using the propaganda material found in their research as a model, have groups create propaganda by writing new lyrics to a well-known melody such as "Happy Birthday" or "Clementine." Tell students that their lyrics should represent the positive attitude that the government would have wanted to use in propaganda.
4. Encourage volunteers to sing or recite their songs to the class. **LS Interpersonal, Auditory-Musical**

Alternative Assessment Handbook, Rubrics 14: Group Activity; and 26: Poems and Songs

Answers

History Close-Up *New weapons and tactics made fighting deadlier—zeppelins and airplanes fired from the skies; machine guns fired hundreds of bullets per minute; tanks crossed enemy trenches.*

Reading Check *New technologies such as poison gas and rapid-firing machine guns made the battlefield more dangerous; faster airplanes proved useful in attacking battlefield positions, factories, and cities; neither side was able to gain an advantage.*

Direct Teach

Reading Focus

3 What happened on the Western Front? *France and Germany both suffered enormous casualties in the Battle of Verdun; the Battle of the Somme resulted in enormous casualties for the British and Germans; Germans defeated British in the Third Battle of Ypres; front lines remained unchanged.*

Battles on the Western Front

Recall What made the Verdun location special to the French? *It had been an important fortress since Roman times.*

Explain What did the Germans mean by saying they would "bleed France white"? *Germany intended to kill as many French soldiers as possible.*

Evaluate Was Britain successful in reaching their goal for the Battle of the Somme? *possible answer—Only partly: many Germans were killed, but there was no major breakthrough.*

CRF: Biography: Edith Wharton

Info to Know

Women's Roles In addition to working at critical jobs and serving in Europe, American women contributed to the Allies' war effort in another important way by conserving food. Some 20 million homemakers signed pledge cards distributed by the government, promising not to serve meat on Mondays, to conserve other foodstuffs, and to grow their own vegetables in "Victory Gardens." In return, they received stickers to display in the windows of their homes, indicating that they were cooperating with the war effort.

Linking TO Today

Women in War

In World War I, only a few hundred women fought as soldiers, nearly all in the Russian army. These soldiers were the exceptions.

Most women who wanted to help the war effort had only two options: assist on the home front or work as nurses for the armed forces. Thousands of women chose to serve as nurses. Many worked in hospitals or medical-aid stations near the war's front lines, where they faced terrible conditions while helping wounded soldiers.

The role of women in the armed forces began to change slowly after the war. In World War II, most women were still limited to non-combat roles, but some fought as soldiers or as part of organized resistance movements. Today, women serve in many of the world's armed forces, filling roles ranging from soldiers on the front lines to support staff on the home front.

Summarize How has the role of women in war changed since World War I?

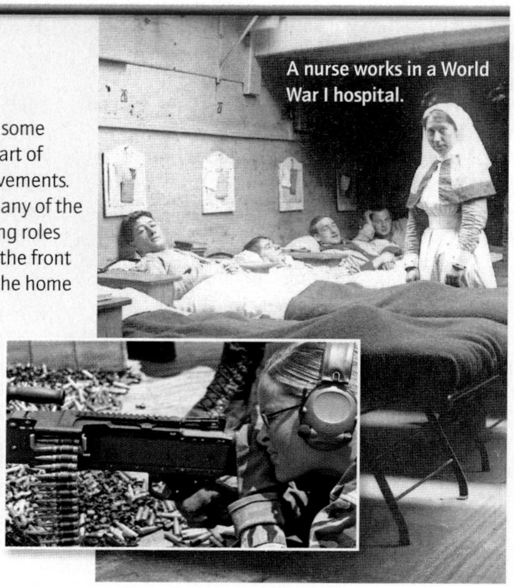

A nurse works in a World War I hospital.

An American soldier fires a machine gun. ▶

Women and the War With millions of men at battle, much of the work on the home front was done by women. Some worked in factories producing weapons and other war supplies. These women helped send important shipments of food and weapons to the front lines. Others served as nurses to wounded soldiers. The contributions women made during the war helped transform public views of what women could do. In some countries, this change helped women finally win the right to vote.

READING CHECK **Find the Main Idea** In what ways did the war affect the home front?

Battles on the Western Front

While people on the home front supported their troops, the war in Western Europe was going badly for the Allied Powers. In 1915, a series of battles had resulted in many Allied casualties.

The Italian Front In May 1915, Italy entered World War I by joining the Allied Powers. Italy's first move was to send its forces against Austria-Hungary on the Italy-Austria border. In a long series of back-and-forth battles, Italy made little progress.

The Battle of Verdun Meanwhile, the Germans were making plans for an assault on the French fortress of Verdun. Verdun had been an important French fortress since Roman times. German leaders believed that the French, unable to bear seeing the city captured, would defend it at all costs. The **Battle of Verdun** was meant solely to kill or injure as many French soldiers as possible—to "bleed France white," said the German commander.

From the start of the battle in February 1916 to its end that December, France suffered some 400,000 casualties. Germany, however, endured nearly as many. The battle left both sides weakened, and the stalemate continued.

The Battle of the Somme The British launched their own attack, intended partly to pull German troops away from Verdun, in June 1916. This British attack took place in the Somme River area of France.

The Battle of the Somme was the main Allied assault during 1916. On the first day of fighting alone, the British suffered nearly 60,000 casualties. Just as in the Battle of Verdun, by the time fighting ended in December 1916 there had been no major breakthroughs. Both sides lost an enormous number of troops.

Collaborative Learning

At Level

Women of the New Century

Research Required

1. Remind students that prior to World War I, most women worked in their homes. Tell students that there were rare exceptions in which women made history and furthered the cause of women's rights.
2. Organize students into small groups. Have students conduct research about women who made an impact on the early twentieth century, such as Marie Curie, or Amelia Earhart. Each group should select a different person.
3. Have students assign specific tasks to each group member: note taking, compiling research, etc. Presentations should include an illustration or photograph of the person and her most important accomplishments.
4. Have each group prepare a short presentation to share with the class. **LS Verbal-Linguistic**

Alternative Assessment Handbook, Rubrics 14: Group Activity; 24: Oral Presentations; and 30: Research

Answers

Linking to Today *Today, women fill many roles in the armed forces, ranging from soldiers on the front lines to support staff on the home front, whereas in World War I women were mostly nurses.*

Reading Check *The government took over factories; civilians conserved food and materials; propaganda was produced; women joined the work force.*

The Third Battle of Ypres The year 1917 went badly for the Allies. That spring, a failed French offensive caused rebellion among some French soldiers. In July, the British began an offensive near Ypres (ee-pruh), Belgium, where two earlier German attacks had taken place. The Third Battle of Ypres was a disaster for the British, who ended the attack in November. After three years of battle in western Europe, the front lines were virtually unchanged.

READING CHECK **Summarize** What was the result of the battles on the Western Front?

War around the World

Much of the early fighting took place in Europe, but the conflict quickly became a true world war as fighting spread around the globe. Over 30 nations officially took sides in the war, and other countries became involved in less formal ways.

The Gallipoli Campaign A new power had entered the battle on the Eastern Front in late 1914, when the Ottoman Empire joined the Central Powers. The vast empire was weakening, but it still had a vital location. The Ottomans controlled an important sea passage called the Dardanelles (dahr-den-ELZ), which was part of the water route between the Black Sea and the Mediterranean. The Allies used the Dardanelles to ship supplies to Russia.

To destroy the guns and forts that lined the Dardanelles, the Allies landed a force on the Gallipoli Peninsula in the spring of 1915. After months of fighting and nearly 200,000 casualties, the Allies gave up. The **Gallipoli Campaign** was a failure.

The Ottoman Empire did suffer a major loss later in the war when its subjects in the Arabian Peninsula rebelled. To take advantage of this revolt, the British sent officer T. E. Lawrence to support the Arabs. With Lawrence's help, the Arabs overthrew Ottoman rule.

WORLD WAR I BATTLES, 1915–1917

GEOGRAPHY SKILLS **INTERPRETING MAPS**

Location What were the results of the major battles fought on the Western Front during this time?

Skills Focus: Evaluating Information on the Internet

Above Level

Research Required

Social Studies Skill
The Armenian Massacre

1. Remind students that during World War I, many people accused the Turks of Armenian genocide. Tell students that since the Turks had a different view of this, research on such a subject will reflect different viewpoints. Materials on the Internet have been written by people with varying amounts of expertise on the subject.
2. Organize students into small groups. Have students conduct research to locate and print out several documents about the Armenian Massacre. Students should record the URLs, publishers, copyrights, and authors of each site they use in their research.
3. Have students in each group rate the expertise and credibility of the source for each article, giving reasons for their opinions. **LS Verbal-Linguistic, Interpersonal**

Alternative Assessment Handbook, Rubrics 14: Group Activity; 16: Judging Information; and 30: Research

Direct Teach

Reading Focus

4 How did the war spread around the world? *over 30 nations officially took sides; Ottoman Empire joined Central Powers; war fought in Asia, in the Pacific, and in Africa; Allied colonists contributed to the war*

War around the World

Recall How did the stalemate influence warring nations? *They had to look elsewhere for ways to win the war.*

Identify Where was the special defensive position controlled by the Ottoman Empire? *the Dardanelles, which connected the Black Sea and the Mediterranean*

Analyze How did the Ottoman Empire affect the war? *helped Central Powers win Battle of Gallipoli*

Map Transparency: World War I Battles, 1915–1917

Interpreting Maps

World War I Battles, 1915–1917

Location Which nations in the Central Powers guarded the entrance to the Black Sea? *Bulgaria and the Ottoman Empire*

Human/Environment Interaction What factors would have made delivery of goods to Russia more difficult via the Baltic Sea? *The Central Powers had control of much of the Baltic Sea and extreme winter cold would cause transportation problems in northwestern Russia.*

Answers

Interpreting Maps *The Western Front stayed about the same; Russia lost a large area to the Central Powers; the Allies failed at Gallipoli.*

Reading Check *Both sides suffered extreme casualties, but the front lines remained virtually unchanged.*

Direct Teach

Reading Focus

War around the World

Recall What did Turkish leaders claim about the Armenians? *that they were aiding the Russians*

Make Generalizations Why do you think some colonists were reluctant to help colonial rulers? *possible answer—They may have felt that their contribution would make no difference.*

Review & Assess

Close

Review with students the new kinds of technology developed for use in World War I and how war spread quickly around the world.

Review

go.hrw.com **Online Quiz**, Section 2

Assess

SE Section 2 Assessment

Progress Assessment: Section 2 Quiz

Alternative Assessment Handbook

Reteach/Intervene

Interactive Reader and Study Guide, Section 2

Interactive Skills Tutor CD-ROM

The Armenian Massacre As the Gallipoli Campaign went on, a different conflict occurred elsewhere in the Ottoman Empire. In late 1914, Russia had launched an attack in the Caucasus (KAW-kuh-suhs), a mountain region that lies between the Black and Caspian seas and borders northeastern Turkey. The area was home to ethnic Armenians. Because most were Christians, Armenians formed a minority group in the largely Muslim Ottoman Empire.

THE IMPACT TODAY

The Turkish government officially denies that the Armenian deaths should be considered genocide, although most historians disagree.

Ottoman leaders claimed that the Armenians were aiding the Russians. In the spring of 1915, Ottoman leaders began forcibly removing Armenians from the Caucasus. Some 600,000 Armenians died from violence and starvation. Ottoman leaders were accused by many of **genocide**—the deliberate destruction of a racial, political, or cultural group.

Other Fighting Battles were also fought elsewhere in Asia and in Africa. Japan, for example, had declared war on Germany in 1914 as part of a military agreement with Great Britain. Far from the battlefields of Europe, Japanese forces captured German colonies in China and the Pacific. British and French troops attacked German colonies in Africa.

Allied colonies scattered around the world made many contributions to the war. For example, soldiers from all parts of the British Empire—India, Australia, Canada, New Zealand—took part in the war. Some of these people worked as laborers to keep the armies supplied. Many others fought and died in battle, such as the Algerians who fought for France.

THE ARMENIAN MASSACRE

Nearly 2 million ethnic Armenians were deported to Mesopotamia and what is now Syria during World War I. During this forced relocation, hundreds of thousands starved to death or were killed by Ottoman soldiers and police.

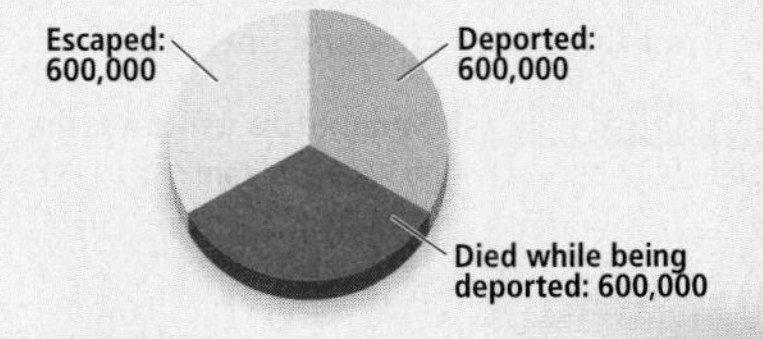

Source: Encyclopedia Britannica

▲ Armenians who escaped during the relocation arrive in a refugee camp.

Although some colonial peoples were reluctant to help their rulers, others volunteered to fight in the hopes that their service would help win independence. They would soon discover that these hopes were in vain.

READING CHECK **Summarize** In what areas of the world did the war take place?

SECTION 2 ASSESSMENT

go.hrw.com Online Quiz Keyword: SHL WW1 HP

Reviewing Ideas, Terms, and People

1. **a. Describe** How did World War I differ from previous wars?
   b. Identify Cause and Effect How did the technological developments of World War I affect **trench warfare**?
2. **a. Recall** How did civilians help support the war effort?
   b. Infer How do you think **total war** affected life on the home front?
3. **a. Recall** What were the results of the **Battle of Verdun** and the Battle of the Somme?
   b. Explain Why did the Western Front change very little between 1915 and 1917?
4. **a. Recall** What happened in the **Gallipoli Campaign**?
   b. Summarize List the war's events outside of Europe.

Critical Thinking

5. **Compare** Using your notes on the section and a graphic organizer like the one below, explain how the war on the Western Front was different from the war elsewhere in the world.

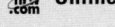

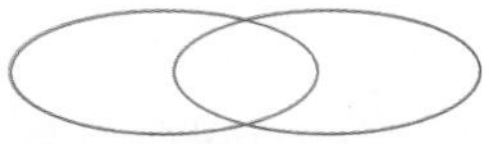

FOCUS ON WRITING

6. **Description** From the perspective of a World War I soldier, write a letter describing life in the trenches. Use details from the section in your letter.

Section 2 Assessment Answers

1. **a.** new technologies and types of warfare; involved many nations
   b. Tanks, aircraft, and poison gas killed millions.
2. **a.** Civilians conserved food and materials; women joined the work force.
   b. Women joined the work force for the first time; citizens united to help their countries.
3. **a.** Both battles resulted in enormous casualties but the front lines were virtually unchanged.
   b. Both sides were evenly matched, developing technology at the same pace.
4. **a.** Allies suffered nearly 200,000 losses.
   b. The Japanese captured German colonies in China and the Pacific; British and French troops attacked German colonies in Africa.
5. West—German forces attacked first, front lines did not move, trench warfare and new technology used; Both—suffered massive casualties; East—Russian forces attacked first, front lines moved east
6. Answers will vary but should include details about trench warfare.

Answers

Reading Check *Europe, Asia, Africa, and the Pacific*

SECTION 3

Revolution in Russia

BEFORE YOU READ

MAIN IDEA
The war and social unrest combined to push Russia to the edge of a revolution. The events that followed led to Russia's exit from the war and became a major turning point in world history.

READING FOCUS
1. What was Russia's experience in World War I?
2. What were the main events of the Russian Revolution?
3. What major events took place after the Russian Revolution?

KEY TERMS AND PEOPLE
Bolsheviks
Grigory Rasputin
Marxism-Leninism
Leon Trotsky
New Economic Policy

TAKING NOTES Take notes on Russia during the war, during the Revolution, and after the Revolution.

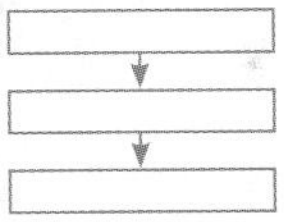

THE INSIDE STORY ***How could an illiterate peasant control the Russian Empire?*** Grigory Rasputin was filthy, illiterate, and believed by some people to be insane. But he was also a self-proclaimed holy man and healer as well as a trusted adviser to Russia's Czarina Alexandra.

Rasputin's influence on the Russian royal family began in the early 1900s, when he first met Czar Nicholas II and Czarina Alexandra. Their son, Alexis, suffered from hemophilia, a disease in which injuries can result in uncontrolled bleeding. Rasputin had a reputation as a man who could heal the sick, and the royal family was eager to see if he could help their son. Indeed, Rasputin seemed to relieve the boy's suffering. Rasputin soon became a common sight at the royal palace.

In the presence of the royal family, Rasputin was careful to appear as a humble, holy peasant. But his actions were very different outside the palace, where his immoral behavior soon created a scandal. When outraged Russians protested, the czar refused to believe their stories.

After Nicholas went off to lead Russia's armies in World War I, Rasputin became Alexandra's personal adviser. He helped her make decisions on a variety of issues, including political appointments and military actions. Nearly all of the decisions proved disastrous for Russia.

In December 1916, a group of Russian nobles formed a plan to murder Rasputin and save Russia from his influence. The nobles poisoned and shot Rasputin, but he did not die. Finally, they drowned him in an icy Russian river. While Rasputin could do no more harm to Russia, the nation was anything but saved. ■

◀ **Known as the Mad Monk, Rasputin had great power over Russia.**

Teach the Main Idea

Revolution in Russia

1. **Teach** Ask students the Reading Focus questions to teach this section.
2. **Apply** Organize students into small groups. Have each group identify and list the major events in this section. Caution students not to rely solely on the time line in the chapter, as many other details are important.
3. **Review** Ask volunteers to share events they identified and write them for students to see. Have students help number the events in order while they write their own lists.
4. **Practice/Homework** Have each student create a flow chart of the major events of the Russian Revolution. **LS Verbal-Linguistic, Visual-Spatial**

Alternative Assessment Handbook, Rubric 13: Graphic Organizers

Preteach

Getting Started

Use the **Interactive Reader and Study Guide** to familiarize students with the section content.

Interactive Reader and Study Guide, Section 3

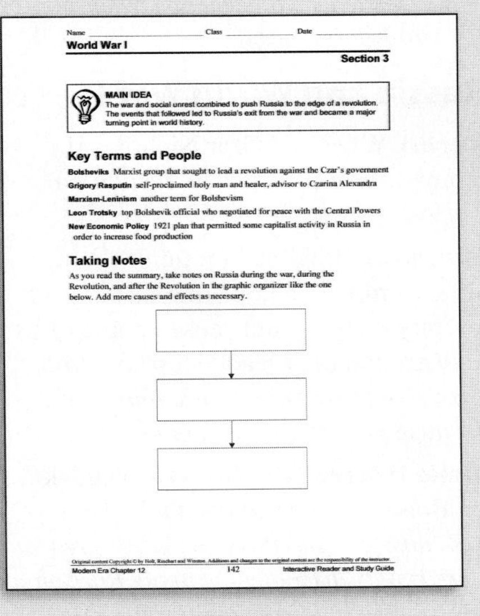
Name Class Date
World War I
Section 3

MAIN IDEA
The war and social unrest combined to push Russia to the edge of a revolution. The events that followed led to Russia's exit from the war and became a major turning point in world history.

Key Terms and People
Bolsheviks Marxist group that sought to lead a revolution against the Czar's government
Grigory Rasputin self-proclaimed holy man and healer, advisor to Czarina Alexandra
Marxism-Leninism another term for Bolshevism
Leon Trotsky top Bolshevik official who negotiated for peace with the Central Powers
New Economic Policy 1921 plan that permitted some capitalist activity in Russia in order to increase food production

Taking Notes
As you read the summary, take notes on Russia during the war, during the Revolution, and after the Revolution in the graphic organizer like the one below. Add more causes and effects as necessary.

Modern Era Chapter 12 142 Interactive Reader and Study Guide

Academic Vocabulary

Review with students the high-use academic term in this section.

fundamental important or vital (p. 394)

CRF: Vocabulary Builder: Section 3

Taking Notes

Russia entered the war unprepared to meet its army's needs; Russia was crushed; Bolsheviks revolted against Czar Nicholas II; Trotsky accepted the Treaty of Brest-Litovsk; ussia had a civil war; the economy improved; the USSR was formed.

go.hrw.com
Online Resources
KEYWORD: SHL WW1
ACTIVITY: Treaty of Versailles

Direct Teach

Reading Focus

1 What was Russia's experience in World War I? *After the revolution in 1905, there were economic problems, worker strikes, and a Marxist group sought to lead a revolution against the czar's government.*

Russia and World War I

Recall When did Czar Nicholas II promise reform? *after the revolution in 1905*

Evaluate What do you think about the government's hope that the military crisis would cause people to rally around their leadership? *possible answer—Their hopes were unrealistic because people wanted change.*

Make Inferences Why do you think the Bolsheviks gained popularity? *possible answer—the Russian people grew increasingly discontent with the Russian government and wanted reform.*

Info to Know

Russian Weather Notice the Russian soldiers' clothing in the photograph on this page. Most of Russia's extreme climate is best compared to that of Alaska, Antarctica, and Northern Canada. The huge Russian landmass is inland, away from the warming influence of coastal waters. It is also located at high latitudes, where it is cold year-round. The weather is so severe that, even today, water, rail, and road transport are interrupted or stopped entirely during winter.

Russia and World War I

On the eve of World War I, Russia was a troubled nation. Czar Nicholas II had promised reform after the revolution of 1905, but he delivered little real change. Economic conditions grew worse, and another revolution seemed near.

The Years Before the War A small Marxist group known as the **Bolsheviks** (BOHL-shuh-viks) sought to change life in Russia through revolution. Led by Vladimir Lenin, the Bolsheviks wanted to overthrow the czar so that the proletariat—the industrial workers—could gain the power to rule Russia as a socialist country. This plan was an adaptation of Marxist ideas. Marx had predicted a spontaneous uprising of the proletariat to overthrow capitalism, but Bolsheviks had other plans. They wanted an elite group—themselves—to lead a revolution and keep much of the power over Russia. Although the Bolsheviks had little influence in the early 1900s, they gained followers as Russia's problems grew more serious.

By 1914, economic conditions in Russia were so bad that the arrival of World War I provided some relief for Nicholas and his top government officials. They hoped that the military crisis would help unite the country and cause the people to rally around their leadership.

Russia in World War I At the start of the war, Russia had an enormous army of some 6 million soldiers. As the czar had hoped, the outbreak of fighting did help provide a burst of patriotism. People from across the country rushed to join the military.

In many other ways, however, Russia was ill-prepared for war. Russian factories were not able to produce ammunition and other military supplies quickly enough to meet the army's needs. In addition, the nation's transportation system was weak. As a result, moving troops and equipment to the right places at the right times proved very difficult.

To make matters worse, the Russian military was not prepared to fight a major war. Its equipment was outdated, and many of its leaders were of poor quality. Russian officers commonly advanced on the basis of personal connections rather than actual ability.

Initially, the Russians enjoyed success on the battlefield, but the losses soon outnumbered the victories. In both victory and defeat, however, Russia's costs in human life were great. Millions of Russian soldiers were wounded or killed during the war's early battles.

Conditions Grow Worse In 1915, Czar Nicholas II decided to take personal command of the Russian forces. The move made little sense. As one of Russia's top commanders said, the czar "understood literally nothing about military matters." Nevertheless, it was now clear that the czar's fate was linked with the fate of Russia's armed forces. If they failed, so would he.

TIME LINE

Russia in Turmoil

August 1914 Russia enters World War I on the side of the Allied Powers.

March 1917 Russian citizens revolt and force Czar Nicholas II to give up power. A provisional government is established.

November 1917 In the Bolshevik Revolution, Communists led by Vladimir Lenin take over the Russian government.

392 CHAPTER 12

Skills Focus: Comparing and Contrasting

At Level

Reading Skill

Battle Preparations

1. Have students review sections two and three to recall information about German and Russian preparedness for war. Discuss with students each side's strengths and weaknesses as they went into battle.
2. Have volunteers call out their ideas about these topics as you raise them: ammunition, weapons, leadership, troops, and supplies.
3. Have each student write a paragraph contrasting the two nations' preparedness for war. **LS Verbal-Linguistic**

Alternative Assessment Handbook, Rubrics 9: Comparing and Contrasting; and 37: Writing Assignments

The war had been going badly for Russia, but once the czar took command, the situation for Russia grew even worse. A few months later the Central Powers were able to stop a major Russian offensive. That defeat destroyed the Russian soldiers' faith in their leaders. With little strength and even less confidence, the Russian army seemed doomed.

Conditions in Russia itself were even worse than they were on the battlefield. Food and other goods were growing scarce in Russian cities, and impoverished Russian peasants were growing desperate. The czar had left his wife, the unpopular Czarina Alexandra, in control of the country when he went off with the troops. She relied on the advice of **Grigory Rasputin**, a self-proclaimed holy man and healer whom many Russians viewed as corrupt and immoral. With the government under his influence, the already shaky Russian support for the monarchy dipped even lower.

READING CHECK **Find the Main Idea** How did World War I affect Russia?

The Russian Revolution

By the end of 1916, Russia was once again on the edge of a revolution. As the new year began and conditions in Russia continued to worsen, the Russian people clearly wanted change.

Revolution Begins On March 8, 1917, unhappy citizens took to the streets of Petrograd, the Russian capital, to protest the lack of food and fuel. Sympathetic police and soldiers in Petrograd refused to follow orders to shoot the rioters. The government was helpless.

While protests raged in the streets, Czar Nicholas II ordered the Duma, Russia's legislature, to disband. The Duma defied this order. With Russia's citizens, soldiers, and government all refusing to obey Nicholas, it was clear that he had lost control of the nation. On March 15, Nicholas was forced to abdicate, or step down, as czar. The Russian monarchy had come to an end.

The March revolution that forced Nicholas to step down is known as the February Revolution in Russia. At the time of the revolution, Russia used an old type of calendar that was 13 days behind the one used in the rest of Europe and the United States. Russia adopted the new calendar in 1918.

The Provisional Government After the fall of the czar, the Duma established a provisional, or temporary, government. This government was led by Aleksandr Kerensky.

READING SKILLS

Understanding Sequencing What events took place in Russia in 1917 before the czar stepped down?

◀ A Bolshevik poster seeks to recruit soldiers during the Russian Civil War.

March 1918 The Bolshevik government signs the Treaty of Brest-Litovsk, which ends Russian involvement in World War I.

November 1920 After three years of fighting, the Russian Civil War ends with a Bolshevik victory.

December 1922 The Soviet Union is formed.

Skills Focus **INTERPRETING TIME LINES**

Summarize What actions did the Bolsheviks take in Russia between 1914 and 1922?

Direct Teach

Reading Focus

2 What were the main events of the Russian Revolution? *With the Russian citizens, the army, and the Duma against him, Czar Nicholas abdicated; the Duma formed a provisional government; the Russian army collapsed; the Bolsheviks took over*

The Russian Revolution

Identify What were the Russian citizens protesting? *the lack of food and fuel*

Define What was the Duma? *Russia's legislature*

Contrast Explain the difference between Kerensky's leadership and that of Vladimir Lenin. *Kerensky's provisional government called for continued fighting in World War I, an unpopular stance with the Russians, who were tired of the war. Lenin was popular with Russians because he attacked Kerensky's government and represented change.*

Skills Focus: Interpreting Time Lines

At Level

Research Required

Social Studies Skill

A More Detailed Time Line

Materials: tape, lined paper

1. Have students tape three sheets of lined paper together end-to-end.
2. Have students use information from their text and reliable online sources to find other events that occurred in Russia during this period and add them to their time lines. Students should leave the same amount of space for each year and may attach more paper as needed. *Time lines should include some of the following events: late 1915: Czar Nicholas II takes command of Russian forces; late 1916: Russia on verge of a revolution; December 1916: Rasputin murdered by Russian nobles; late 1918: Russia adopts calendar used by Europe and the U.S.*
3. Have students share their time lines with the class and use them as a study guide.

LS Visual-Spatial

Alternative Assessment Handbook, Rubric 36: Time Lines

Answers

Reading Skills *Citizens protested in Petrograd, Czar Nicholas ordered Duma to be disbanded, Duma refused.*

Time Line *took over Russian government; ended Russia's involvement in World War I; claimed victory in Russian Civil War*

Reading Check *poor economic conditions, worker strikes, unpopular czar*

Direct Teach

Reading Focus

The Russian Revolution

Describe What was Marxism-Leninism? *a political philosophy that called for the abolition of private property and the enforcement of social equality*

Analyze How did events in the war help the Bolsheviks? *Russia's failed military offensive in 1917 collapsed the Russian army and led to support for the Bolsheviks.*

Reading Focus

3 What major events took place after the Russian Revolution? *Russia signed peace treaty and lost a huge territory; civil war between Bolsheviks and the White Army; Lenin's New Economic Policy*

After the Revolution

Identify What was the White Army? *a group opposing the Bolsheviks, including army leaders, political opponents, and wealthy Russians who opposed communism*

Make Inferences Why were many Russians upset by the treaty ending the war? *Russia was forced to give up huge chunks of its empire.*

CRF: Biography: Leon Trotsky

FACES OF HISTORY

Vladimir LENIN
1870–1924

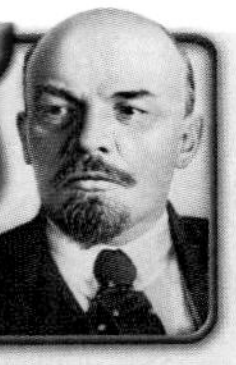

The son of a teacher, Vladimir Lenin graduated first in his class from high school and seemed destined to be a scholar. Instead, he soon became a Marxist and fought for revolution in Russia.

When Lenin was 17 years old, his older brother was hanged for plotting to kill the Russian czar. Lenin himself soon turned against the Russian government. He founded the Bolshevik Party and sought to establish a Communist social system, in which there would be no economic classes and no private property. Today he is considered the father of the Russian Revolution.

Infer Why is Lenin considered the father of the Russian Revolution?

ACADEMIC VOCABULARY
fundamental basic

Many Russians were unhappy with their new leadership. The government planned to continue fighting in World War I, even though most Russians were thoroughly tired of war. Russian peasants, who simply wanted land and food, felt that Kerensky's government was doing too little to help.

Leading the opposition to Kerensky's provisional government were the Bolsheviks, who wanted a fundamental change in Russian government and society—an immediate Marxist revolution. They planned to abolish private property and enforce social equality, and believed that this revolution would soon sweep the world.

Bolshevism later became known as **Marxism-Leninism**, after Bolshevik leader Vladimir Lenin. Lenin had been forced to live outside Russia because of his revolutionary ideas, but he returned to Russia in April 1917. This return was arranged by Germany, which hoped Lenin would stir unrest in Russia and weaken the Russian effort in World War I.

The Bolshevik Revolution In mid-1917, Kerensky's government ordered a final military offensive against the Central Powers along the Eastern Front. The drive failed. Even worse, it led to widespread rebellion in the Russian army. "I have received word," wrote one officer, "that in some units the officers are being slaughtered by their own men." The weakened Russian army had collapsed.

The conditions were ideal for Lenin to lead a Bolshevik takeover. In November 1917, armed Bolshevik factory workers known as the Red Guard attacked the provisional government. The October Revolution—its name came from the old Russian calendar—was brief. After a nearly bloodless struggle, Kerensky's government collapsed. Russia was now in Bolshevik hands, and Lenin became the nation's leader.

Lenin wasted no time in establishing a radical Communist program. He soon made private ownership of land illegal.

HISTORY'S VOICES

> **"All private ownership of land is abolished immediately without compensation [payment to the owners]. All landowners' estates and all land belonging to the Crown, to monasteries, church lands with all their livestock and . . . property . . . are transferred to the disposition [control] of the township Land Committees."**
>
> —Vladimir Lenin, *Decree on Land*, October 26, 1917

The Bolsheviks gave this land to peasants. Similarly, the Bolsheviks seized Russia's factories and gave control of the factories to workers. With these actions, millions of Russians gained new power over their daily lives, but this power did not ensure that good times lay ahead.

READING CHECK **Summarize** What were the main events of the Russian Revolution?

After the Revolution

After the Bolshevik Revolution, Lenin set about ending Russia's involvement in World War I. He sent **Leon Trotsky**, a top Bolshevik official, to negotiate for peace with the Central Powers. Because Russia's army was virtually powerless, Trotsky had to accept an agreement that was harsh on Russia. Russia had finally gained peace, but was forced to give up huge chunks of its empire.

Civil War The Bolsheviks' acceptance of the treaty upset many Russians deeply. As a result, some of the Bolsheviks' opponents organized into what came to be called the White Army. The Whites included some army leaders, political opponents of the Bolsheviks, and wealthy Russians who opposed Lenin's Communist system. The only thing that united them was their opposition to the Bolsheviks. The Whites received some military help from countries that opposed the Bolsheviks, such as France and the United States.

Differentiating Instruction

Below Level

Struggling Readers

Standard English Mastery

1. Have students read Lenin's decree in the text labeled History's Voices above. Read it aloud to students to facilitate understanding.
2. Have students paraphrase each of the two sentences of Lenin's decree in their own words.
3. Have students add several more sentences to the decree, in which Lenin explains to the people the reason he is taking these drastic steps.
4. Allow time for students to exchange papers and read each other's work. Students should make any necessary revisions to align their work with standard English usage. LS **Verbal-Linguistic**

Alternative Assessment Handbook, Rubric 43: Writing to Persuade

Answers

Faces of History *Lenin founded the Bolshevik Party and sought to establish a Communist social system.*

Reading Check *the February Revolution and the Bolshevik Revolution*

For three years, civil war raged between Lenin's Bolshevik Red Army and the White Army. Millions of Russians died in the fighting and famines that swept across Russia, until the Bolsheviks triumphed in late 1920.

New Economic Policy The civil war pushed Russia's collapsing economy to the edge of total ruin. Especially hard hit were poor peasants and workers, who had been forced to endure terrible sacrifices in order to win the war.

Lenin responded to this crisis in 1921. He introduced the **New Economic Policy**, a plan that permitted some capitalist activity. Peasants, for example, could sell their food at a profit. The plan was meant to encourage more food production, which Russia badly needed.

The Soviet Union By 1922 the Russian economy was beginning to improve. That same year, Russia reunited with several neighboring lands that had been part of the Russian Empire before 1917. The new country was called the Union of Soviet Socialist Republics—also known as the Soviet Union. Russia's Communist leadership dominated the new country.

While the Soviet Union's economy gained strength, Lenin's own health was failing. After a series of strokes, he died in 1924. Lenin had no clear successor, and his death soon led to a struggle for control of the Soviet Union.

READING CHECK **Sequence** What events took place after the Russian Revolution?

PRIMARY SOURCES

Lenin's Call to Power

Lenin issued his "Call to Power" on October 24, 1917—according to the old Russian calendar—urging Russians to rise up and seize power from the provisional government.

"I am writing these lines on the evening of the 24th. The situation is critical in the extreme. In fact it is now absolutely clear that to delay the uprising would be fatal.

"With all my might I urge comrades to realize that everything now hangs by a thread; that we are confronted by problems which are not to be solved by conferences or congresses (even congresses of Soviets), but exclusively by peoples, by the masses, by the struggle of the armed people.

". . . We must not wait. We must at all costs, this very evening, this very night, arrest the government, having first disarmed the officer cadets, and so on.

"We must not wait! We may lose everything! . . .

"All districts, all regiments, all forces must be mobilized at once . . .

"The government is tottering. It must be given the death-blow at all costs."

Skills FOCUS **READING LIKE A HISTORIAN**

1. **Explain** What did Lenin want Russians to do? Why?
2. **Analyzing Primary Sources** What words does Lenin use to try to convince readers to follow his instructions?

See **Skills Handbook**, p. H25

SECTION 3 ASSESSMENT

go.hrw.com
Online Quiz
Keyword: SHL WW1 HP

Reviewing Ideas, Terms, and People

1. **a. Recall** What was the condition of the Russian military at the beginning of World War I?
   b. Summarize How did the **Bolsheviks** plan to change Russian society?
   c. Make Judgments Do you think that Czar Nicholas II's decision to take over as commander in chief of the Russian army was wise? Why or why not?
2. **a. Identify** What role did Vladimir Lenin have in Russia in 1917?
   b. Elaborate Why do you think many Russians were anxious for radical change in 1917?
3. **a. Recall** When did the Russian Civil War begin?
   b. Identify Cause and Effect Why did the Russian economy begin to improve after the civil war?

Critical Thinking

4. **Sequence** Using your notes on the section and a graphic organizer like the one below, identify the causes and effects of the Russian Revolution.

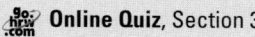

FOCUS ON WRITING

5. **Exposition** In a paragraph, explain why Lenin and the Bolsheviks took the actions they did between 1917 and 1924. Use details from the section to support your explanation. Be sure to include information about Bolshevik political and economic goals.

Section 3 Assessment Answers

1. a. big army, but not modernized
   b. by abolishing private property and establishing social equality
   c. possible answer—No, because he understood little about military matters.
2. a. Lenin was the Bolshevik leader when conditions were ideal for a takeover of the government.
   b. Most Russians were tired of war, and the peasants wanted land and food.
3. a. when the White Army rose up against the Bolsheviks
   b. Allowing the peasants to sell their food for a profit encouraged more food production and improved the economy.
4. Causes—Russia signs peace treaty and loses huge part of its empire; opponents of Bolshevism organize into the White Army; Effects—millions die in fighting and famine; Russia's economy collapses
5. possible details—poor economic conditions; unpopular czar; Bolsheviks believed that Marxism-Leninism would solve Russia's problems

Direct Teach

Reading Focus

After the Revolution

Recall What was the Union of Soviet Socialist Republics, and how was it formed? *a new country formed in 1917, made up of Russia and neighboring lands that had previously been part of the Russian Empire*

Analyze How did Lenin's New Economic Policy address problems in Russia's economy? *permitted some capitalist activity in order to encourage more food production*

Predict How do you think Lenin's death affected Russian's citizens? *possible answer—They may have lost faith in Russia's leadership because he had been a popular leader*

Review & Assess

Close

Review with students the time line in this section. Emphasize how difficult it was for the Russians to endure so many leadership changes.

Review

Online Quiz, Section 3

Assess

SE Section 3 Assessment

Progress Assessment: Section 3 Quiz

Alternative Assessment Handbook

Reteach/Intervene

Interactive Reader and Study Guide, Section 3

Interactive Skills Tutor CD-ROM

Answers

Primary Sources **1.** *seize power from the government;* **2.** *urgent words and phrases such as "extreme, fatal, hangs by a thread, at all costs;"*

Reading Check *The Bolsheviks formed the Red Army which fought against the White Army. The White Army was made up of army leaders, political opponents of the Bolsheviks, and wealthy Russians*

Preteach

Getting Started

Use the **Interactive Reader and Study Guide** to familiarize students with the section content.

Interactive Reader and Study Guide, Section 4

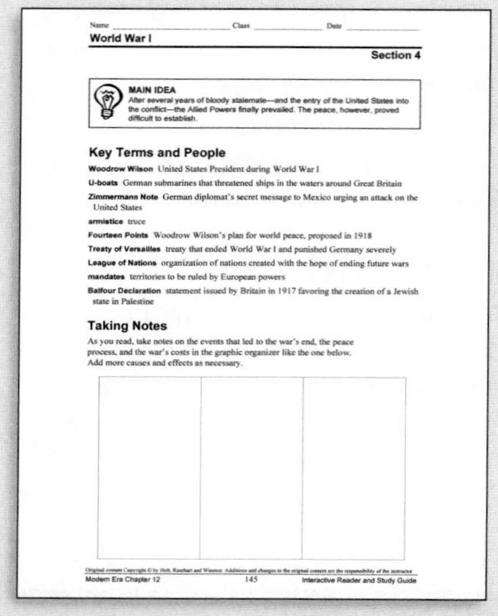
Name ______ Class ______ Date ______

World War I

Section 4

MAIN IDEA
After several years of bloody stalemate—and the entry of the United States into the conflict—the Allied Powers finally prevailed. The peace, however, proved difficult to establish.

Key Terms and People

Woodrow Wilson United States President during World War I
U-boats German submarines that threatened ships in the waters around Great Britain
Zimmermann Note German diplomat's secret message to Mexico urging an attack on the United States
armistice truce
Fourteen Points Woodrow Wilson's plan for world peace, proposed in 1918
Treaty of Versailles treaty that ended World War I and punished Germany severely
League of Nations organization of nations created with the hope of ending future wars
mandates territories to be ruled by European powers
Balfour Declaration statement issued by Britain in 1917 favoring the creation of a Jewish state in Palestine

Taking Notes

As you read, take notes on the events that led to the war's end, the peace process, and the war's costs in the graphic organizer like the one below. Add more causes and effects as necessary.

Modern Era Chapter 12 145 Interactive Reader and Study Guide

Academic Vocabulary

Review with students the high-use academic terms in this section.

assessed evaluated or determined (p. 399)

generation group of people born and living about the same time (p. 400)

CRF: Vocabulary Builder: Section 4

Taking Notes

The United States entered the war; Germany advanced into France; Allied forces combined tank and aircraft use; Central Powers were defeated; peace treaties were negotiated; economies were devastated; many countries experienced political unrest.

SECTION 4 The War Ends

Before You Read

Main Idea

After several years of bloody stalemate—and the entry of the United States into the conflict—the Allied Powers finally prevailed. The peace, however, proved difficult to establish.

Reading Focus

1. Why did the United States enter the war?
2. What events led to the end of the fighting?
3. What issues made the peace process difficult?
4. What were the costs of the war?

Key Terms and People

Woodrow Wilson
U-boats
Zimmermann Note
armistice
Fourteen Points
Treaty of Versailles
League of Nations
mandates
Balfour Declaration

TAKING NOTES Take notes on the events that led to the war's end, the peace process, and the war's costs.

THE INSIDE STORY

Why would Germany attack a passenger liner? For passengers packing their bags for the ocean voyage from New York to Great Britain, the advertisement in the newspaper must have been alarming. The notice was from the German government, and it warned that any ship approaching Great Britain was subject to attack.

Still, the *Lusitania* was a passenger liner. It carried nearly 2,000 innocent civilians. Surely German submarines would not attack a helpless, harmless vessel like the *Lusitania*.

The Germans, however, felt that they could not trust passenger ships. The British routinely hid war supplies on civilian ships, using them to transport guns and ammunition across the ocean. Germany couldn't afford to simply ignore passenger ships. Sinking anything that sailed into or out of Great Britain was a safer policy.

In early May 1915, when a German submarine spotted the *Lusitania* off the coast of Ireland in the Atlantic Ocean, the submarine's commander did not hesitate. The submarine fired a single torpedo, which struck the ship squarely. This blast set off another, larger explosion inside the ship. Badly damaged, the *Lusitania* sank in a mere 18 minutes. Nearly 1,200 people lost their lives, including more than 120 U.S. citizens. ■

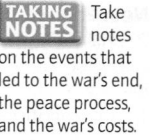

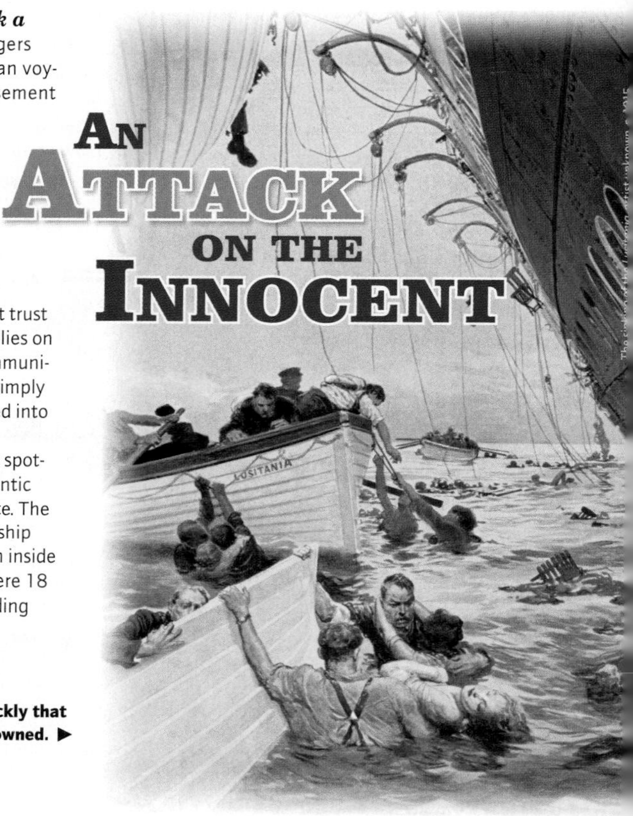

The *Lusitania* sank so quickly that many passengers were drowned. ▶

Teach the Main Idea

At Level

The War Ends

1. **Teach** Ask students the Reading Focus questions to teach this section.
2. **Apply** Have students create a cause-and-effect flow chart listing the main events they identify in each section of this chapter.
3. **Review** For each section, ask volunteers to share the events they discovered. Write the events on a class flow chart for students to see and have them revise the flow charts as necessary. Encourage students to add to their flow charts as they review the section and to use them as a study guides.
4. **Practice/Homework** Have each student write a one-paragraph summary of the major events of the war's end. **LS Verbal-Linguistic, Visual-Spatial**

Alternative Assessment Handbook, Rubric 13: Graphic Organizers

The United States Enters the War

German attacks on ships carrying American passengers angered the American people and their leaders. Those attacks, as well as information about a German plan to have Mexico attack the United States, pushed the United States into World War I.

American Neutrality In the early years of the war the United States was neutral, although the American public generally supported the Allies. Still, most Americans agreed with President **Woodrow Wilson**, who did not want to become involved in the huge conflict on the other side of the Atlantic Ocean. He believed that the United States should stay out of the affairs of other nations. In 1916, in fact, Wilson used the slogan "He kept us out of war" to help win reelection.

Trouble on the Seas Remaining neutral was not easy when Germany attacked civilian ships. These attacks were part of a policy called unrestricted submarine warfare. Under this policy, any ship traveling in the waters around Great Britain was subject to attack by German submarines, or **U-boats**. Germany initially used its U-boats to attack British naval vessels, but then began targeting merchant ships delivering goods to Great Britain. Targeting merchant ships was an effective tactic, since the island of Great Britain depended heavily on supplies shipped on the seas.

The passenger ship *Lusitania* was sunk under the German policy of unrestricted warfare, killing some 1,200 people, including over 120 Americans. The sinking of the *Lusitania* was followed in August and September 1915 by two more sinkings in which more American citizens died.

The U.S. government complained bitterly to Germany about the loss of American lives. Fearing U.S. entry into the war, Germany finally agreed to stop attacking passenger ships.

By 1917, though, German leaders realized that, to defeat the powerful British navy, they would need to return to unrestricted submarine warfare. This act might bring the United States into the war. The German leaders hoped, however, that they could defeat the Allied Powers before U.S. forces could have an impact.

FACES OF HISTORY

Woodrow WILSON
1856–1924

U.S. president Woodrow Wilson is often remembered for his efforts for world peace. During the early years of World War I, Wilson worked tirelessly for peace, winning reelection in 1916 in part by promising to keep the United States out of the war.

By the following year, however, Wilson felt that the war was becoming a serious threat to the world's future. He hoped that a victory by the Allied Powers could help bring about a lasting peace and urged Congress to declare war. His Fourteen Points speech proposed the League of Nations, which would help prevent future wars. For his peacemaking efforts, Wilson earned the Nobel Peace Prize in 1919.

Summarize How did Wilson work for world peace?

The Zimmermann Note The repeated attacks on shipping moved the United States closer to declaring war against Germany. In February of 1917, the discovery of the so-called Zimmermann Note provided the final push. The **Zimmermann Note** was a secret message from German diplomat Arthur Zimmermann to officials in Mexico in which Germany proposed that Mexico attack the United States. In return, Germany promised, Mexico would gain the U.S. states of Texas, Arizona, and New Mexico, all of which had once belonged to Mexico. German leaders hoped that an American war with Mexico would keep the United States out of the war in Europe.

The Zimmermann Note greatly angered the American public, which now began to call for war against Germany. After all, Americans had much in common with the Allied Powers. Many Americans traced their ancestry to Great Britain, for example, and the two nations shared the same language and many cultural traditions. The United States also had strong financial ties to the Allied Powers and was selling millions of dollars' worth of war goods to Britain each week.

By early 1917, the various forces pushing the United States toward war were too strong to resist. In April 1917, the United States entered the war on the side of the Allied Powers.

READING CHECK **Identify Cause and Effect** How did unrestricted submarine warfare affect U.S. entry into the war?

Skills Focus: Analyzing Alternative Points of View — At Level

Reading Like a Historian Skill

War Planners Skits

1. Tell students they are participants in a war-planning meeting. Have students think about what the room might look like, the tension of the planners, and the marks on the wall map.
2. Organize students into groups of six to eight. Assign half of the groups to represent British planners, and half to represent German planners.
3. Ask students to create a realistic skit in which planners discuss German submarine attacks on ships near Britain.
4. When groups have had adequate time to prepare, have them perform their skits for the rest of the class. **LS Kinesthetic, Verbal-Linguistic**

Alternative Assessment Handbook, Rubrics 14: Group Activity; and 33: Skits and Reader's Theater

Direct Teach

Reading Focus

1 Why did the United States enter the war? *Germany attacked the* Lusitania *and other ships, killing many Americans. German leaders tried to push Mexico into attacking the United States. Many Americans felt strong ties to Great Britain.*

The United States Enters the War

Explain How did President Wilson feel about American involvement in the war in 1916? *He felt that the United States should stay out of the affairs of other nations.*

Summarize How did Germany's policy on submarine warfare change? *They began with unrestricted attacks, but fearing U.S. entry into war, agreed to stop attacking passenger ships. Finally, they returned to unrestricted submarine warfare.*

CRF: Biography: Arthur Zimmerman

Info to Know

The Arts and War Strong feelings inspired by war are often expressed in the arts. Dadaism, an artistic movement that developed during World War I, is known for its witty, shocking images. Dada pieces ridicule aesthetic standards and society, exhibiting everyday objects in shocking contexts. One well-known piece is Marcel Duchamp's *Fountain*, which is actually a urinal. Another is George Grosz's *A Victim of Society*, which portrays the first president of the Weimar Republic grotesquely decorated with a button sewn to his skull, a mechanical device for a nose, and perhaps most meaningfully, a straight razor at his throat.

Answers

Faces of History *tried to keep United States out of war; proposed League of Nations after the war*

Reading Check *Germany broke its promise to the United States to stop attacking passenger ships.*

Direct Teach

Reading Focus

❷ What events led to the end of the fighting? *As Germany advanced toward Paris, they lost 900,000 troops. American troops arrived, and the Alllies combined the use of tanks and aircraft.*

The End of the Fighting

Explain Even though the Americans had just declared war, what reasons for hope did the Germans have? *It would be months before American troops would arrive, and Russia was out of the war.*

Identify What did the Russian collapse allow Germany to do? *transfer troops from the Eastern Front back to France*

Evaluate In what ways were the Germans likely unprepared for the Allies' use of tanks and aircraft at the Second Battle of the Marne? *possible answer—They had suffered heavy losses, had young recruits and a poor food supply, and could not compete with the new technology.*

Teaching Tip

Suggest that students read the novel *All Quiet on the Western Front,* which was first published in 1928. Set late in World War I, the book gives a clear picture of the war's impact on both sides.

Reading like a Historian

U.S. Neutrality

Interpreting Political Cartoons Many Americans initially thought of World War I as a far-off European conflict that had little effect on the United States. They did not want to become involved in the fighting. However, as the war continued and as Germany attacked neutral ships with American passengers, American feelings slowly changed. This cartoon took a stand on the American position of neutrality.

To interpret what this cartoon says about American involvement in the war, think about

- the text and symbols used in the cartoon
- the artist's message

PATIENCE WITH GERMANY
The figure of Uncle Sam represents the United States.
This block of ice labeled "Patience with Germany" is melting.

Melting, by Lute Pease, c. 1917

Skills Focus READING LIKE A HISTORIAN

1. **Symbols** Why did the artist use a fan and a block of ice in this cartoon?
2. **Message** Was this cartoon created by a supporter or an opponent of U.S. entry into the war? How can you tell?

See **Skills Handbook**, p. H27

The End of the Fighting

German leaders knew that the U.S. decision to enter the war would dramatically increase the strength of the Allied Powers. To win the war, Germany and the other Central Powers would have to deal a decisive blow before the United States had time to raise an army, train soldiers, and ship troops and supplies to the front lines.

A New German Offensive Germany's opportunity to win the war before the U.S. military could mobilize came with Russia's withdrawal from the war. Russia had endured revolution and civil war, and by the end of 1917 was out of the war entirely. With German troops no longer needed to fight Russia on the Eastern Front, Germany could launch a new offensive in the west.

Germany transferred troops back to France, and in March 1918, launched a major assault on the Western Front. For a while, German forces made great progress against Allied defenders, advancing to within 40 miles of the French capital of Paris.

The offensive came at a high cost to Germany, however. By the end of June, they had lost 800,000 troops. Also by that time, hundreds of thousands of Americans had arrived in Europe. These soldiers helped on the battlefield, but they also gave the Allies hope—and discouraged the Germans.

German Collapse Slowly, the balance of power shifted. In the Second Battle of the Marne, Allied forces stopped the German assault—just as they had stopped the

Skills Focus: Making Oral Presentations

At Level

Reading Like a Historian Skill

A BBC News Report

1. Organize students into groups of six or seven. Tell students they are reporters preparing a radio newscast for the British Broadcasting Corporation (BBC) about the collapse of Germany in 1918.
2. Tell students to organize their groups as follows: one member is the anchor at the news desk who introduces each reporter, another is a reporter describing the retreat of Allied troops; another reporter interviews people on the streets of London; the remaining students are the people being interviewed.
3. Have groups perform their broadcasts for the class. Encourage students to speak with appropriate accents and use expressions of the period. **LS Verbal-Linguistic, Kinesthetic**

Alternative Assessment Handbook, Rubrics 24: Oral Presentations; 33: Skits and Reader's Theater

Answers

Reading Like a Historian 1. *fan—shows it was hot; block of ice—shows that American patience was lessening;* **2.** *a supporter, because it appears that the ice will certainly melt; Uncle Sam appears angry or frustrated*

Germans at the Marne in 1914. Now the Allies went on the offensive. Combining effective use of tanks and aircraft, Allied forces gained huge amounts of territory. Many Germans simply gave up without a fight, knowing that Germany was a defeated force.

HISTORY'S VOICES

"[German] officers in particular inform us of the weakness of their forces, the youth of their recruits, and the influence of the American entry. They are depressed by their heavy losses, by the poor quality of their food . . . They are worried and begin to doubt German power."

—French report on German morale, September 1918

In October Allied forces broke through the heavily fortified Hindenburg Line. Germany's end was near. Soon German leaders approached the Allies seeking an **armistice**, or truce. Peace terms were agreed to on November 11, 1918. By this time, the other Central Powers had admitted defeat. World War I was over.

READING CHECK **Summarize** How did fighting come to an end?

A Difficult Peace

Although peace had come to the battlefield, the leaders of the war's major countries still had to work out a formal peace agreement. This task would prove to be difficult.

Differing Allied Goals In early 1918, while fighting was still going on, Woodrow Wilson had announced his vision of world peace. This plan for peace was called the **Fourteen Points**. These points included the reduction of weapons and the right of all people to choose their own governments. He also proposed forming an organization in which the world's nations would join to protect one another from aggression.

Not everyone shared Wilson's goals. In fact, the leaders of the four major Allies—Great Britain, France, the United States, and Italy—had very different ideas about a peace treaty. The French, led by Georges Clemenceau, wanted to punish Germany. Clemenceau also wanted Germany to pay for the costs of the war.

Great Britain's David Lloyd George stood somewhere between Clemenceau and Wilson. He also wanted to punish Germany, yet he did not want to see Germany weakened. He was anxious, for example, that Germany be able to stop the spread of communism from Russia.

Italy's leader Vittorio Orlando hoped to gain territory for his nation. He was disappointed to find himself largely ignored by other leaders during the peace talks.

The Treaty of Versailles After difficult negotiations, the Allies finally compromised on the **Treaty of Versailles**. The treaty was named after the French Palace of Versailles, where the treaty signing took place.

The treaty came much closer to Clemenceau's vision than to Wilson's. Germany was forced to pay an enormous amount of money to the war's victims. The treaty also assessed responsibility for the war. Germany was forced to take full responsibility for the conflict.

ACADEMIC VOCABULARY
assessed evaluated or determined

Other parts of the Treaty of Versailles were designed to weaken Germany. The treaty forced Germany to limit the size of its military. Germany also had to return conquered lands to France and to Russia. Other German lands were taken to form the newly independent nation of Poland, and German colonies around the globe were given to various world powers.

Germans were furious about the humiliating terms of the treaty, but they had no choice but to accept them. Germany signed the treaty on June 28, 1919. The reparations crippled the German economy and the bitterness caused by the Treaty of Versailles would have an effect on German politics in the years to come.

Yet the treaty did contain one victory for Wilson. It established the organization of world governments he had envisioned in his Fourteen Points. This organization was called the **League of Nations**. The League's main goals were to encourage international cooperation and to keep peace between nations. But the League did not represent all the world's nations. Germany, for example, was excluded from the League. In addition, Wilson was unable to convince the U.S. government to ratify the Treaty of Versailles, as some Americans worried that the League of Nations would drag them into another far-off war. The U.S. absence greatly weakened the League.

Other Treaties Allied leaders also created separate agreements with all of the defeated Central Powers. These treaties made important changes to Europe.

Direct Teach

Reading Focus

3 What issues made the peace process difficult? *Each of the four major Allies had different goals, which made it difficult for them to come to an agreement.*

A Difficult Peace

Explain What did France want to do to Germany? Why? *to severely punish Germany and have them pay for the costs of the war; because France had been severely damaged in the war*

Contrast In what way was the goal of Italy's leader different from those of the other negotiators? *He wanted to gain territory for his nation.*

Evaluate What are some possible reasons Allied leaders created separate agreements with all the defeated Central Powers? *possible answer—Many of the nations caused little of the war's destruction and would not likely pose a threat to the Allies in the future.*

CRF: Primary Source: The Fourteen Points

Biography

Joan Miró (1893–1983) Spanish oil painter Joan Miró is known for his Surrealist works characterized by bright colors and fanciful shapes. Miró was born in Barcelona, Spain, where he studied art. Many of his works depict a light-hearted fantasy world, and others are somewhat disturbing. Both types were typical of Surrealist work. In 1919 Miró traveled to Paris, where his work was influenced by Dada and Cubism. Though he worked in other media such as ceramics and tapestry, he is known today for his delightful, amusing paintings.

Skills Focus: Analyzing Alternative Points of View

At Level

Research Required

Reading Like a Historian Skill
Each Country's Wish

1. Have students list the five Allied Powers. *France, Russia, Great Britain, Italy, the United States*
2. Organize the class into four groups. Assign one group to each of the following: France, Russia, Great Britain, and Italy.
3. Have each group conduct research about its assigned country in World War I and write goals, as Woodrow Wilson did for the peace negotiations, representing their country.
4. Have volunteers share their ideas while their classmates take notes. Ask students to select one idea and write a paragraph supporting it.
LS Interpersonal, Verbal-Linguistic

Alternative Assessment Handbook, Rubrics 14: Group Activity; and 43: Writing to Persuade

Answers

Reading Check *The Allies used tanks and aircraft at the Marne, then broke through the Hindenburg Line, and Germans sought an armistice.*

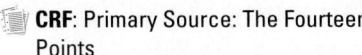

Direct Teach

Reading Focus

4 What were the costs of the war? *Nearly nine million soldiers died and millions more were wounded or taken prisoner; many national economies were destroyed; some nations and English colonies experienced political unrest.*

The Costs of the War

Explain How did influenza spread worldwide? *The disease spread rapidly in crowded military conditions and soldiers carried it home at war's end.*

Contrast How were the economies of the United States and Japan different from those of France and Russia? *The United States and Japan prospered during the war; France and Russia's economies were destroyed.*

Map Transparency: Europe and the Middle East

Interpreting Maps

Europe and the Middle East

Location Name the seven new nations that were formed from formerly Russian land after the war. *Finland, Estonia, Latvia, Lithuania, East Prussia, Poland*

Human/Environment Interaction What are some reasons that Luxembourg became an occupied zone? *It shared a long border with the newly-reduced Germany and needed protection from invasion.*

EUROPE AND THE MIDDLE EAST

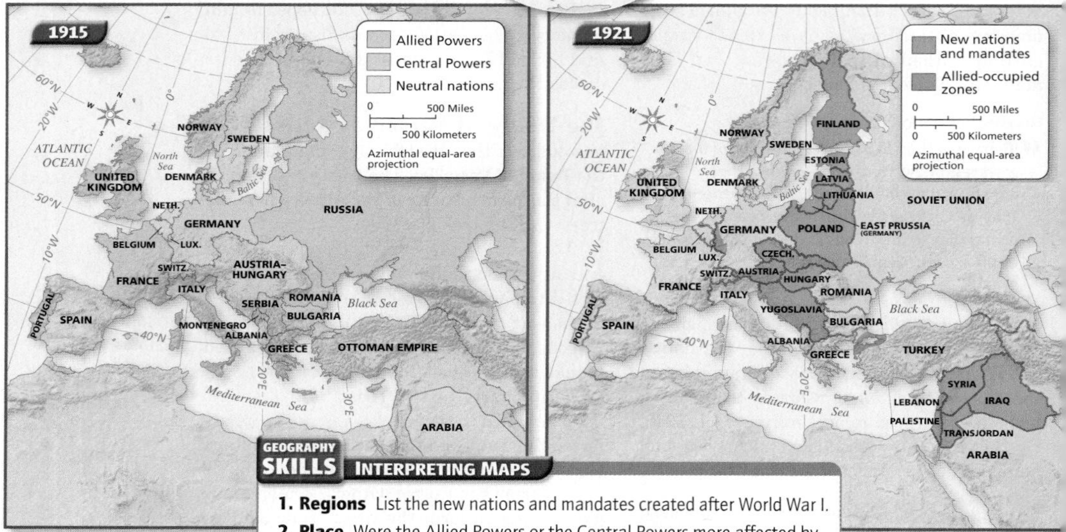

GEOGRAPHY SKILLS INTERPRETING MAPS

1. **Regions** List the new nations and mandates created after World War I.
2. **Place** Were the Allied Powers or the Central Powers more affected by the changes in national boundaries?

The vast lands of Austria-Hungary and the Ottoman Empire were broken apart, forming the independent nations of Austria, Hungary, Yugoslavia, Czechoslovakia, and Turkey. German territories in Africa and the Pacific Ocean were also given to other countries to control.

In the Middle East, former Ottoman lands were turned into **mandates**, or territories to be ruled by European powers. Syria and Lebanon became French mandates, and Palestine and Iraq became British mandates. Meanwhile in Europe, the Zionist movement to create a Jewish state in the Middle East was growing. In 1917, Britain issued the **Balfour Declaration**, which favored establishing a Jewish state in Palestine, the ancient Jewish homeland. Later, Britain created Transjordan from the Palestine Mandate and named Abdullah as Transjordan's first ruler. European nations were supposed to control the mandates only until those territories were able to govern themselves. In reality, mandates became colonies.

ACADEMIC VOCABULARY
generation group of people born and living about the same time

THE IMPACT TODAY
Scientists today are worried that a type of influenza known as avian flu, or bird flu, might turn into another worldwide flu epidemic.

READING CHECK **Summarize** Why was it so difficult to work out a peace agreement?

The Costs of the War

World War I was the most devastating conflict the world had ever seen. It would take years for the nations involved to recover.

Human Costs Nearly 9 million soldiers were killed in battle. Millions more were wounded or taken prisoner. In nations such as Germany, Russia, and France, almost an entire generation of young men died or were wounded in the war.

In the spring of 1918, the suffering became worse when a deadly outbreak of influenza swept across the globe. The disease spread rapidly in crowded military conditions and as soldiers made their way home at the war's end. Worldwide, perhaps 50 million people or more died in the epidemic.

Economic Costs The war also destroyed national economies. In places such as France, Belgium, and Russia, where much fighting took place, farmland and cities alike were devastated. Economic chaos soon spread misery throughout many parts of Europe.

Answers

Interpreting Maps 1. *Finland, Estonia, Latvia, Lithuania, East Prussia, Poland, Austria, Hungary, Czechoslovakia, Yugoslavia, Iraq, Palestine, Lebanon, Syria;* **2.** *Refer to map*

Reading Check *because each of the four major Allies had different goals*

Differentiating Instruction

Below Level

English-Language Learners

Materials: 8 ½ x 11" unlined paper, colored markers

1. Have students picture how farms in eastern France would have looked after battles were fought. Remind students that most men had been killed or wounded.
2. Tell students they will create uplifting propaganda to inspire people rebuilding their lives after the war. Suggest songs and poems, recipes appropriate for those with limited resources, workshop ideas for repairing homes, instructions for how to reclaim battle-scarred farmland, and so on.
3. Have each student develop one concept to contribute to a class pamphlet. Instruct students to leave a 1" margin on the left side blank for binding
4. Compile the pamphlet ideas into a simple binder and display in the classroom.

LS Intrapersonal, Visual-Spatial

Alternative Assessment Handbook, Rubrics 3: Artwork; and 40: Writing Assignments

The war also cost Europe its role as the dominant economic region of the world. Countries such as the United States and Japan prospered during the war. In addition, countries that had formerly relied on European imports turned to new sources or developed their own products.

Political Changes World War I caused widespread political unrest, including the Communist revolution in Russia. After the war, the monarchies in Austria-Hungary, Germany, and the Ottoman Empire were all overthrown, and many other countries also experienced political upheaval. This widespread political and social turmoil would help shape the world in the years to come.

Unrest in Colonies The growing unrest affected European colonies as well. Many colonists who had fought in the war had heard the Allied leaders speak noble words about the importance of democracy and freedom. After they shed blood for these ideals on behalf of their colonial rulers, the colonists came to expect these rights for themselves.

Instead, the colonists soon found that their wartime sacrifices had not won them any new freedoms. The powers of Europe simply split up the lands controlled by the German, Austro-Hungarian, and Ottoman empires and distributed them to other colonial powers. Independence would have to wait.

READING CHECK **Find the Main Idea** What were the costs of the war?

Effects of World War I

QUICK FACTS

HUMAN COSTS	ECONOMIC COSTS
• 8.5 million soldiers died. • 13 million civilians died. • 21.2 million soldiers were wounded.	• The war cost the world's nations an estimated $332 billion.

POLITICAL CHANGES

- Austria-Hungary and the Ottoman Empire were broken apart.
- Germany was greatly weakened.
- The Russian monarchy was overthrown.
- New countries and colonies formed in Europe and the Middle East.
- European colonies in Africa and Asia changed hands.

▲ The war destroyed large areas of Europe.

Section 4 Assessment

go.hrw.com
Online Quiz
Keyword: SHL WW1 HP

Reviewing Ideas, Terms, and People

1. **a. Describe** What role did **U-boats** have in World War I?
   b. Identify Cause and Effect Why did the United States enter the war in 1917?
2. **a. Recall** What was the outcome of Germany's last offensive?
   b. Explain What effect did U.S. troops have on the war?
3. **a. Describe** How did the **Treaty of Versailles** affect Germany?
   b. Compare and Contrast How did the various Allied goals for peace differ?
4. **a. Recall** What event that began in 1918 added to the suffering caused by the fighting in World War I?
   b. Predict How do you think the political unrest after World War I will affect the world in the years that follow?

Critical Thinking

5. **Identify Cause and Effect** Using your notes on the section and a graphic organizer like the one below, explain what you believe was the most significant effect of World War I.

World War I → [ ]

Focus on Writing

6. **Description** Choose one of the three types of costs of World War I—human, economic, or political. Write a newspaper article explaining those costs.

Section 4 Assessment Answers

1. **a.** used by Germans to attack ships near Britain, causing U.S. to enter war.
   b. Germany broke its promise to stop attacking passenger ships and attempted to push Mexico to attack the United States.
2. **a.** They lost 800,000 troops.
   b. helped shift the balance of power
3. **a.** Reparations required by the Treaty of Versailles hurt the German economy.
   b. France wanted to punish Germany; Italy wanted territory; U.S. wanted peace; Great Britain wanted to punish Germany without weakening it
4. **a.** a deadly outbreak of influenza
   b. possible answer—Monarchies would be overthrown and new governments formed.
5. possible answer—World War I resulted in the overthrowing of many monarchies and the growth of communism, which would shape the world for many years to come.
6. possible answers—human: millions of lives lost; economic: some nations' economies badly hurt; political: redrawn boundaries

Direct Teach

Reading Focus

The Costs of the War

Identify Cause and Effect What effect did the war have on the monarchies of the Central Powers? *Political unrest after the war caused the monarchies to be overthrown.*

Elaborate Defend the postwar expectations of the colonists. *possible answer—Countries whose citizens fought for democracy and freedom deserve to enjoy these rights themselves, and not be held under the rule of another nation.*

Quick Facts Transparency: Effects of World War I

CRF: Literature: *The Sun Also Rises*

Review & Assess

Close

Guide students in a discussion about the close of the war and review the economic costs and political unrest caused by the war.

Review

Online Quiz, Section 4

Assess

SE Section 4 Assessment

Progress Assessment: Section 4 Quiz

Alternative Assessment Handbook

Reteach/Intervene

Interactive Reader and Study Guide, Section 4

Interactive Skills Tutor CD-ROM

Answers

Reading Check *Millions of people died or were wounded. Some nations' economies were devastated while others prospered. Some people enjoyed the benefits of freedom and democracy after the war, but others remained under the control of colonial rulers.*

Document-Based Investigation

Causes of World War I

Word Help

sheathe place into a case or covering

commend to entrust for care or preservation

implore to call or pray for earnestly

premeditated deliberately planned; calculated

conciliatory that which will gain goodwill or favor

Info to Know

Wilhelm II When his grandfather died and his father passed soon after, Wilhelm became Kaiser of Germany at age 29. During his thirty-year reign, the indecisive leader lost control of the military and failed to negotiate peace when it was within his grasp. When Germany at last surrendered, Wilhelm gave up the throne and exiled himself in the Netherlands. This ended the monarchy in Germany and soon after, Hitler rose to power.

Activity Analyzing Primary Sources Have students volunteer what they know about sound technology of the World War I era. *Examples include victrolas, microphones, the telegraph, and early radios.* Tell students they are news reporters in 1918. Ask them the following questions: How would you make sure the news you report is accurate? What tools are used today that help to ensure accurate reporting?

CHAPTER 12

Document-Based Investigation

Causes of World War I

Historical Context The documents below provide information about the causes of World War I.

Task Examine the documents and answer the questions that follow. After you have studied all the documents, you will be asked to write an essay about the causes of World War I. You will need to use evidence from these selections and from the chapter to support the position you take in your essay.

DOCUMENT 1

The German Perspective

Wilhelm II, the ruler of Germany, gave this speech from the balcony of the royal palace in Berlin on July 31, 1914.

> A momentous hour has struck for Germany. Envious rivals everywhere force us to legitimate defense. The sword has been forced into our hands. I hope that in the event that my efforts to the very last moment do not succeed in bringing our opponents to reason and in preserving peace, we may use the sword, with the help of God, so that we may sheathe it again with honor. War will demand enormous sacrifices by the German people, but we shall show the enemy what it means to attack Germany. And so I commend you to God. Go forth into the churches, kneel down before God, and implore his help for our brave army.

DOCUMENT 2

The British Perspective

On January 5, 1918, British prime minister David Lloyd George made this statement about Great Britain's war goals.

> We are not fighting a war of aggression against the German people. Their leaders have persuaded them that they are fighting a war of self-defence against a league of rival nations bent on the destruction of Germany. That is not so. The destruction or disruption of Germany or the German people has never been a war aim with us from the first day of this war to this day. Most reluctantly, and indeed quite unprepared for the dreadful ordeal, we were forced to join in this war in self-defence . . . we had to join in the struggle or stand aside and see Europe go under and brute force triumph over public right and international justice. It was only the realization of that dreadful alternative that forced the British people into war.

DOCUMENT 3

The Allied Powers Perspective

After the war's end, the victorious Allied Powers formed a commission to determine responsibility for the war. Below are the conclusions of the commission, which were issued on May 6, 1919.

> 1. The War was premeditated by the Central Powers together with their Allies, Turkey and Bulgaria, and was the result of acts deliberately committed in order to make it unavoidable.
>
> 2. Germany, in agreement with Austria-Hungary, deliberately worked to defeat all the many conciliatory proposals made by the Entente Powers and their repeated efforts to avoid war.

Skills Focus: Recognizing Bias in Primary Sources

At Level

Reading Like a Historian Skill

Kaiser Wilhelm II

1. Read Wilhelm II's speech above aloud to the students. Explain that this indecisive leader encouraged his military leaders to make their own decisions. Thus, he lost control of them even when he might have been able to negotiate peace.
2. Have groups identify key words or phrases in Document 1 above that support Kaiser Wilhelm's view of Germany as a peaceful nation that is under attack.
3. Guide students in a discussion of the persuasiveness of Kaiser Wilhelm's speech. If they were Germans living in 1914, would they have believed the speech? Why or why not? **LS Interpersonal, Verbal-Linguistic**

Alternative Assessment Handbook, Rubrics 16: Judging Information; and 40: Writing to Describe

DOCUMENT 4

The American Perspective

The cartoon at right was created by American artist Orson Lowell. Published in March 1918, it shows Germany's Kaiser Wilhelm II hanging by a noose attached to a plank of wood marked "Greedy Ambition." Other figures in the cartoon represent Great Britain, the United States, France, and other countries that fought the Central Powers during World War I.

Now Then, All Together!, by Orson Lowell, 1918

Skills FOCUS READING LIKE A HISTORIAN

DOCUMENT 1

a. Interpret Who does Wilhelm blame for the war?

b. Make Judgments The day after Wilhelm gave this speech, Germany declared war on Russia. Do you think that action supports or contradicts what he said in his speech?

DOCUMENT 2

a. Explain What words does Lloyd George use to suggest that Great Britain did not want war?

b. Evaluate Would Lloyd George agree or disagree with Document 1?

DOCUMENT 3

a. Identify What nation or nations does this document blame for causing the war?

b. Evaluate Do you think the authors of this document were biased about the causes of the war? Why or why not?

DOCUMENT 4

a. Draw Conclusions What are the figures attempting to do to the globe? Why?

b. Interpret Who does the artist blame for the war? Does he believe that others feel the same way?

DOCUMENT-BASED ESSAY QUESTION

Why might the different sides in the war view the causes of the war differently? Using the documents above and information from the chapter, form a thesis that explains your position. Then write a short essay to support your position.

See **Skills Handbook**, pp. H25, H27, H29

Document-Based Investigation

Info to Know

The Allied Powers Commission The Allied Powers Commission was a group formed in January 1919 made up of twenty-five people, two from each main Allied power (the United States, Britain, France, Italy, and Japan), and one each from Belgium, Greece, Poland, Romania, and Serbia. The group's full title was The Commission on the Responsibility of the Authors of the War and on Enforcement of Penalties.

Differentiating Instruction

Above Level

Advanced Learners/Gifted and Talented

Research Required

Background: Tell students that leaders of free nations often present formal addresses to their countrymen and their allies like the one given by David Lloyd George in Document 2. Sometimes such speeches are written by professionals known as ghost writers.

1. Have a volunteer read George's address aloud dramatically.
2. Organize students into small groups and have each group choose a country that was involved in World War I, and is not represented among the documents. Have students conduct research to identify the country's leader and the reasons that nation became involved in the war.
3. Have groups write a speech as if the leader they chose were addressing his nation about its involvement in World War I.
4. Allow time for presentations of the speeches.

LS Interpersonal, Verbal-Linguistic

Alternative Assessment Handbook, Rubrics 24: Oral Presentations; and 30: Research

Answers

Reading Like a Historian

Document 1. a. *the nations he claims has attacked Germany;* **b.** *possible answer—contradicts, because he claims that he is trying to preserve peace and that Germany is the victim;* **Document 2. a.** *possible answers—"reluctantly, quite unprepared, dreadful ordeal, forced to join this war in self-defence";* **b.** *He would disagree.* **Document 3. a.** *The Central Powers and their allies;* **b.** *Yes, because they had recently been fighting the Central Powers in a costly, deadly war.* **Document 4. a.** *push it from under Kaiser Wilhelm II; would cause him to be hanged;* **b.** *blames the ambition and greed of Kaiser Wilhelm II; believes all those who fought the Central Powers agree.*

Essay *Student essays will vary but should discuss the different viewpoints on the causes of the war.*

CHAPTER 12

Chapter Review

QUICK FACTS

VISUAL STUDY GUIDE

Causes and Effects of World War I

CAUSES

- Military buildup in Europe
- European countries form alliances
- Rival European empires try to keep and expand their power
- Growing nationalism
- Assassination of Archduke Franz Ferdinand

World War I

EFFECTS

- Tens of millions of people killed or wounded
- Much of Europe destroyed
- Widespread political unrest and economic problems
- New countries formed in Europe
- Mandates established in the Middle East
- League of Nations established

Key Events of World War I

1881	▪ Triple Alliance formed
1907	▪ Triple Entente formed
1914	▪ Archduke Franz Ferdinand murdered ▪ Austria-Hungary declares war on Serbia ▪ Germany declares war on Russia and France and invades Belgium ▪ Trench warfare begins
1915	▪ German U-boat sinks *Lusitania* ▪ Czar Nicholas II takes command of Russian forces ▪ Armenian Massacre takes place
1916	▪ Tanks first used in the war ▪ Battle of Verdun becomes longest battle of the war
1917	▪ Russian Revolution takes place ▪ United States enters the war
1918	▪ Armistice ends the fighting
1919	▪ Treaty of Versailles signed

Review Key Terms and People

Match each numbered definition with the letter of the correct item from the list below.

Column I

a. Grigory Rasputin
b. Central Powers
c. armistice
d. League of Nations
e. Bolshevik
f. total war
g. fundamental
h. U-boat

Column II

1. Germany, Austria-Hungary, Ottoman Empire
2. War using all of society's resources
3. Important or vital
4. German submarine
5. Truce that ended the fighting in World War I
6. Controversial adviser to the czar during World War I
7. Radical Communist group that took over Russia in 1917
8. Organization of countries proposed in Wilson's Fourteen Points

Answers

Visual Summary

Review and Inquiry Organize students into small groups. Assign each group one cause or effect from the Visual Study Guide. Have groups write a paragraph to present orally, explaining their item and its importance.

Quick Facts Transparency: Visual Study Guide: World War I

Review Key Terms and People

1. b.
2. f.
3. g.
4. h.
5. c.
6. a.
7. e.
8. d.

Comprehension and Critical Thinking

9. a. the Triple Alliance and the Triple Entente
b. The Austrians blamed Serbia for the assassination, which led to the involvement of both sides' allies.
c. The growing power of European armed forces added to the tension, and the alliances led many more nations to join the war.

10. a. Soldiers lived in and fought from a massive system of trenches that stretched for hundreds of miles.
b. possible answer—It involved new weapons such as gas and machine guns, and technology such as tanks and aircraft, which caused millions of casualties.
c. Without propaganda, fewer people would have supported the war and volunteered to fight.

11. a. Czar Nicholas II became increasingly unpopular and many wanted to overthrow the government.
b. The defeat of Russian troops led to the abdication of the czar and the Bolshevik Revolution.
c. possible answer—It would cause a struggle for control of the Soviet Union.

12. a. It proposed the League of Nations, which intended to keep peace between nations. Some countries were excluded from the League, however, which weakened it.
b. The United States helped on the battlefield, helped shift the balance of power, and influenced peace negotiations.
c. War reparations would cripple Germany's economy.

Reading Skills

13. before the United States
14. after the war
15. citizens protested lack of food and fuel; police shot rioters; czar ordered Duma to disband; Duma defied the order

History's Impact video program
Review the video to answer the closing question: What impact has modern warfare had on the world today?

Comprehension and Critical Thinking

SECTION 1 *(pp. 380–384)*

9. a. Recall What were the two major alliances in Europe in the years leading up to World War I?

b. Explain How did the assassination of Franz Ferdinand contribute to the start of World War I?

c. Elaborate How did militarism and alliances help cause World War I?

SECTION 2 *(pp. 385–390)*

10. a. Describe What was trench warfare?

b. Make Generalizations What general statement could you make to describe the fighting in World War I?

c. Evaluate How important was the role of propaganda in World War I? Explain your answer.

SECTION 3 *(pp. 391–395)*

11. a. Describe What was the general attitude of the Russian people toward their government in the early 1900s?

b. Identify Cause and Effect How did World War I affect the Russian people and their relationship with their government?

c. Predict How do you think Lenin's death would affect the Soviet Union?

SECTION 4 *(pp. 396–401)*

12. a. Identify How did the Fourteen Points affect the peace agreement at the end of the war?

b. Identify Cause and Effect What was the result of the U.S. entry into the war?

c. Support a Position Which effect of World War I do you think will have the greatest impact on the world? Why?

Reading Skills

Understanding Sequencing *Use what you know about understanding sequencing to answer the questions below.*

13. Did Austria-Hungary enter the war before or after the United States did?

14. Did the creation of mandates in the Middle East take place before or after the war?

15. What events led up to Czar Nicholas II stepping down as leader of Russia?

Interpreting Political Cartoons

Reading Like a Historian *The cartoon below shows a hand carving up a map of the southwestern United States.*

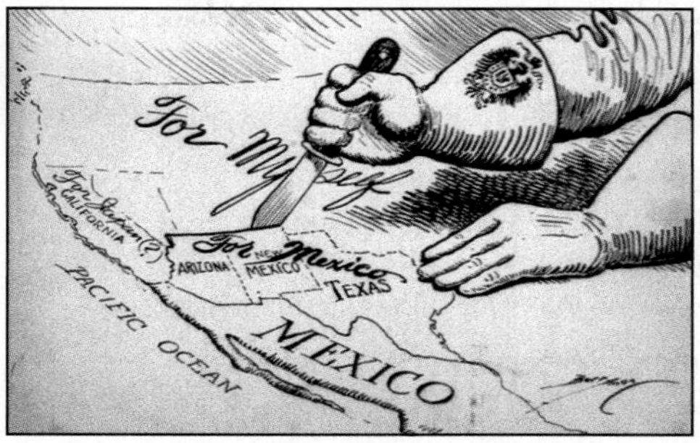

Carving up the United States, by Clifford Berryman, 1917

16. Draw Conclusions The eagle on the glove symbolizes Germany. Whose hands are in the cartoon?

17. Analyze To what event was the cartoonist referring? What do you think the cartoonist thought about this event?

Using the Internet

go.hrw.com
Practice Online
Keyword: SHL WW1

18. The Treaty of Versailles had an enormous effect on Germany and the rest of Europe following World War I. Using the Internet, research the Treaty of Versailles. Then write a detailed report about the treaty, its terms, and its effects on Germany. Be sure to include an evaluation of the treaty's strengths and weaknesses.

WRITING FOR THE SAT

Think about the following issue:

The forces of nationalism and imperialism played a major role in causing World War I. The war was the largest conflict the world had ever seen, and years of battles took place before the armistice and the Treaty of Versailles finally brought an end to the fighting.

19. Assignment: Did World War I resolve the disagreements that had caused the war? Write a short essay in which you develop your position on this issue. Support your point of view with reasoning and examples from your reading and studies.

Answers

Interpreting Political Cartoons

16. German Foreign Secretary Arthur Zimmerman

17. the Zimmerman Note; probably blamed Zimmerman for German aggression

Using the Internet

18. Go to the HRW Web site and enter the keyword shown to access a rubric for this activity.

KEYWORD: SHL WWI

Writing for the SAT

19. Student essays might include one of the following ideas—did resolve, by punishing Germany for the invasions; did not resolve, because the Treaty of Versailles did not provide for a lasting peace.
A rubric for this activity is provided in **CRF:** Writing for the SAT.

HOLT

History's Impact

► **Video Program: World War I**
See the Video Program Teacher's Guide for the answer to the closing question.

Review and Assessment Resources

Review and Reinforce

- **CRF:** Chapter Review
- **Quick Facts Transparency**: Visual Study Guide: World War I
- **Spanish Chapter Summaries Audio CD Program**
- OSP **Holt PuzzlePro**: Quiz Show for ExamView
- **Quiz Game CD-ROM**

Assess

- **PASS**: Chapter Test, Forms A and B
- **Alternative Assessment Handbook**
- OSP **ExamView Test Generator**, Chapter Test
- **Differentiated Instruction Modified Worksheets and Tests CD-ROM**: Chapter Test
- HOAP **Holt Online Assessment Program** (in the Premier Online Edition)

Reteach/Intervene

- **Interactive Reader and Study Guide**
- **Differentiated Instruction Teacher Management System**: Lesson Plans for Differentiated Instruction
- **Differentiated Instruction Modified Worksheets and Tests CD-ROM**: Chapter Test
- **Interactive Skills Tutor CD-ROM**

go.hrw.com
Online Resources
KEYWORD: SHL TEACHER

Chapter 13 Planning Guide

The Interwar Years

Chapter Overview	Reproducible Resources	Technology Resources
CHAPTER 13 **pp. 406–433** **Overview: In this chapter, students will learn how different nations' leaders dealt with social, political, and economic chaos during the period between World War I and II.**	**Differentiated Instruction Teacher Management System:** • Pacing Guide • Lesson Plans for Differentiated Instruction **Interactive Reader and Study Guide:** Chapter Summary* **Chapter Resource File*** • Writing for the SAT • Social Studies Skill • Interdisciplinary Project • Economics and History • Chapter Review **World History Outline Maps**	**Live Ink© Online Reading Help** **Student Edition on Audio CD Program** **Differentiated Instruction Modified Worksheets and Tests CD-ROM** **Interactive Skills Tutor CD-ROM** **World History Primary Source Library CD-ROM** **Power Presentations with Video CD-ROM** **History's Impact: World History Video Program (VHS/DVD):** The Interwar Years
Section 1: **Unrest in Asia and Africa** **The Main Idea:** During the chaotic years following World War I, nationalist feeling increased in Asia and Africa. The resulting unrest continued into the 1930s.	**Differentiated Instruction Teacher Management System:** Section 1 Lesson Plan* **Interactive Reader and Study Guide:** Section 1 Summary* **Chapter Resource File*** • Vocabulary Builder: Section 1 • Biography: Reza Shah Pahlavi • Primary Source: British White Paper of June 1922 • Literature: *A Passage to India*	**Daily Test Practice Transparency:** Section 1* **Map Transparency:** Postwar Colonies and Nationalism, 1920s* **Map Transparency:** The Long March, 1934–1935* **Internet Activity:** Mustafa Kemal Atatürk
Section 2: **The Great Depression** **The Main Idea:** In the late 1920s an economic depression started in the United States and quickly spread around the globe, causing great hardship and creating ideal conditions for political unrest.	**Differentiated Instruction Teacher Management System:** Section 2 Lesson Plan* **Interactive Reader and Study Guide:** Section 2 Summary* **Chapter Resource File*** • Vocabulary Builder: Section 2 • Biography: Bessie Smith • History and Geography: The Great Depression	**Daily Test Practice Transparency:** Section 2* **Quick Facts Transparency:** Causes of the 1929 Stock Market Crash* **Quick Facts Transparency:** Major U.S. Social Reforms* **Internet Activity:** U.S. Economy
Section 3: **Japanese Imperialism** **The Main Idea:** A modernized Japan emerged from World War I as one of the world's leading powers. Dreams of empire, however, led the country in a dangerous direction.	**Differentiated Instruction Teacher Management System:** Section 3 Lesson Plan* **Interactive Reader and Study Guide:** Section 3 Summary* **Chapter Resource File*** • Vocabulary Builder: Section 3 • Biography: Sadao Araki	**Daily Test Practice Transparency:** Section 3* **Map Transparency:** Japanese Aggression, 1931–1937* **Quick Facts Transparency:** Major Japanese Events 1920 to 1940*
Section 4: **Dictators in Europe** **The Main Idea:** The political and social unrest that followed World War I helped totalitarian dictators rise to power in Europe.	**Differentiated Instruction Teacher Management System:** Section 4 Lesson Plan* **Interactive Reader and Study Guide:** Section 4 Summary* **Chapter Resource File*** • Vocabulary Builder: Section 4 • Biography: Haile Selassie I	**Daily Bellringer Transparency:** Section 4* **Quick Facts Transparency:** Common Features of Totalitarian Governments*

go.hrw.com | Print Resource | Transparency
Learning Styles | Audio CD | CD-ROM
Video | **SE** Student Edition | **TE** Teachers Edition
OSP One-Stop Planner CD-ROM
*also on One-Stop Planner CD-ROM

Review, Assessment, Intervention

- **Quick Facts Transparency:** The Interwar Years*
- **Spanish Chapter Summaries Audio CD Program**
- **Progress Assessment Support System (PASS):** Chapter Test*
- **Differentiated Instruction Modified Worksheets and Tests CD-ROM:** Modified Chapter Test
- OSP **One-Stop Planner CD-ROM:** ExamView Test Generator (English/Spanish)
- HOAP **Holt Online Assessment Program (HOAP),** in the Holt Premier Online Student Edition

---

- **PASS:** Section 1 Quiz*
- **Online Quiz:** Section 1
- **Alternative Assessment Handbook**

- **PASS:** Section 2 Quiz*
- **Online Quiz:** Section 2
- **Alternative Assessment Handbook**

- **PASS:** Section 3 Quiz*
- **Online Quiz:** Section 3
- **Alternative Assessment Handbook**

- **PASS:** Section 4 Quiz*
- **Online Quiz:** Section 4
- **Alternative Assessment Handbook**

HOLT
History's Impact
World History Video Program (VHS/DVD)
The Interwar Years

Power Presentation with Video CD-ROM

Power Presentations with Video are visual presentations of each chapter's main ideas. Presentations can be customized by including Quick Facts charts, images and maps from the textbook, and video clips.

Holt Online Learning

go.hrw.com
Teacher Resources
KEYWORD: SHL TEACHER

go.hrw.com
Student Resources
KEYWORD: SHL IWY

- Document-Based Questions
- Interactive Multimedia Activities
- Current Events
- Chapter-Based Internet Activities
- and more!

Holt Premier Online Student Edition

Complete online support for interactivity, assessment, and reporting

- Interactive Maps and Notebook
- Homework Practice and Research Activities Online

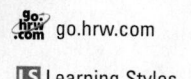

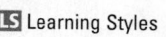

Before You Teach

The Big Picture

Peter N. Stearns

A Balance Sheet World War I substantially weakened the major European powers, but not, initially, their ambitions. There was every interest in maintaining and even expanding empire, with a slight bow to new commitments to the League of Nations. But the war had accelerated new currents in Africa and Asia. This involved new nationalist agitation, including the emergence of an independent Turkey. It also involved the enhancement of power centers in Asia, in China to an extent, and even more in Japan. Despite these larger developments, European struggles held pride of place, and key nationalist tensions were not resolved during the aftermath of the war. Then, when new economic woes hit Europe through the great Depression, forces of totalitarianism, particularly in Nazi Germany, made European stabilization virtually impossible.

The 1920s and the Depression Various initiatives occurred during the 1920s, including dramatic changes in popular culture; some efforts to resolve diplomatic tensions with Germany; and some signs of renewed economic vitality in the Western world. But basic issues were not resolved, including a number of clear economic weaknesses. This set a context for the dramatic reverberations of the Depression literally around the world. Unemployment increased widely and social tensions grew rapidly. While some societies responded to the Depression successfully, global economic recovery remained incomplete even in 1939.

Collapse of Globalization Developments in the interwar decades called into serious question the network of global economic, political and cultural relationships built up, under Western sponsorship, in the later 19th century. The Soviet Union pulled away, into substantial economic isolation. Japan tried to build its own empire as an alternative to full global involvement, and of course the United States turned away from global alliances as well while still participating in international economic activity. Full globalization would resume only some decades later, after another devastating war.

Recent Scholarship

The Ebbing of European Ascendancy: An International History of the World, 1914-1945 (2002), by Sally Marks, has become the standard treatment of international relations in a busy and troubled period. Marks covers the essential landmarks—including world wars, the frenzied diplomacy of the 1920s, and the failed response to the rise of fascism—but she keeps in mind the bigger picture. European developments are carefully linked to emerging global power centers and challenges. In these three decades, European powers fatally weakened their capacity to retain global dominance by two brutal and wasting internal struggles, while other societies and movements began to see new opportunities for self-assertion. This is a masterful study of a watershed period in contemporary world history.

Differentiating Instruction

Differentiated Instruction Teacher Management System
- Pacing Guide
- Lesson Plans for Differentiated Instruction

Interactive Reader and Study Guide

Spanish Chapter Summaries Audio CD Program

Student Edition on Audio CD Program

Differentiated Instruction Modified Worksheets and Tests CD-ROM
- Vocabulary Flash Cards
- Modified Vocabulary Builder Activities
- Modified Chapter Review Activity
- Modified Chapter Test

OSP **One-Stop Planner CD-ROM**
- ExamView Test Generator (English/Spanish)
- PuzzlePro
- Quiz Show for ExamView
- Transparencies and Videos

TE **Differentiated Activities in the Teacher's Edition**
- Comparing Gandhi and Atatürk, p. 411
- Failing Economy Posters, p. 415
- Japan's Economic Problems, p. 421
- Hirohito and the Nanjing Massacre, p. 423

BEFORE YOU TEACH

Reading Like a Historian

Sam Wineburg

Maps as Historical Texts Many students regard maps as neutral representations of three-dimensional spaces. But for historians, maps are like any other historical text. They reflect a point of view, are rooted in a particular context, and shed light on one facet of a multi-faceted historical reality.

Consider the map on page 820, whose title heralds its purpose: to convey information about Japan's aggressive seizure of territory in the years before World War II. The map's colored legend paints "Japan and her colonies" in red and the "area invaded by Japan" in orange. Aside from providing the name of the Soviet Union to the north, the countries that do not fall under Japan's sphere go unmarked. We might surmise that the map's purpose is to focus our attention on the issue before us—"Japanese Aggression"—and to show that by seizing Korea and conquering broad swaths of China, Japan's voracious expansionism succeeded in more than doubling its territory.

What would happen if we tinkered with this map and started to label the unmarked countries? We might begin underneath Taiwan by labeling the Philippines and adding to the map's legend "area colonized by the United States" (or, if we were writing from a Philippine perspective, "territory invaded by the United States"). Moving west, we would then label the territory that constitutes present-day Vietnam, Laos, and Cambodia as French Indochina—part of the French colonial venture that was justified by Prime Minister Jules Ferry, who proclaimed "We must say openly that indeed the high races have a right over the lower races."

Examining Scope If we zoomed out to enlarge the map's scope, we would label Indonesia as the Dutch West Indies, except for East Timor, which was Portugal's. And the biggest colonial overlord in this enlarged picture would be Great Britain, whose prizes would include Malaya, Hong Kong, Burma, and the glimmering jewel in the crown, India. Our new map would show a Far East ringed by the expansionist outposts of European countries and the Johnny-come-lately colonialist, the United States. As the Pulitzer-prize winning historian John Dower observed in *Embracing Defeat: Japan in the Wake of World War II:* "Colonialism and imperialism more generally, defined the twentieth century Asia in which Japan was accused of having conspired to wage an aggressive war. Japan's colonial and neo-colonial domain (Formosa, Korea, and Manchuria) existed alongside the Asian overseas possessions of . . . Britain, France, the Netherlands, and the United States. China itself, nominally sovereign, had been a congeries of Japanese, European, and American 'special rights and interests'."

None of this is to excuse Japanese aggression, which was unqualifiedly brutal. It does, however, put into perspective Japan's behavior prior to World War II, which employed many of the same tactics Western nations used in ravenously gobbling up huge chunks of Africa and Asia. This double standard did not go unnoticed during the 1946 Tokyo war trials. The Indian jurist Radhabinod Pal trenchantly pointed out the hypocrisy of Western nations who, on one hand, condemned Japan's brutal acquisition of Manchuria while, on the other, knew full well that the colonial map of Asia was "acquired by such aggressive measures." Indeed, observed Pal, the "Amau Doctrine" under which Japan claimed "special rights" over China found "obvious precedent in the conduct of the United States in pursuance of the Monroe Doctrine."

Maps, like all historical documents, capture one slice of geographic reality. Every map discloses some facts while remaining mute about others. Our map is no exception.

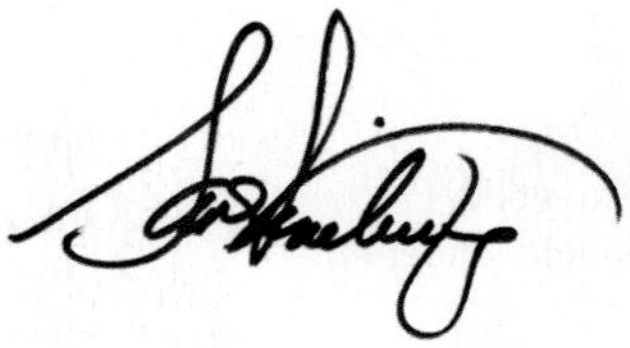

• Chapter Preview •

Chapter Main Ideas

Section 1 During the chaotic years following World War I, nationalist feeling increased in Asia and Africa. The resulting unrest continued into the 1930s.

Section 2 In the late 1920s, an economic depression started in the United States and quickly spread around the globe, causing great hardship and creating ideal conditions for political unrest.

Section 3 A modernized Japan emerged from World War I as one of the world's leading powers. Dreams of empire, however, led the country in a dangerous direction.

Section 4 The political and social unrest that followed World War I helped totalitarian dictators rise to power in Europe.

CHAPTER 13

1919–1939

The Interwar Years

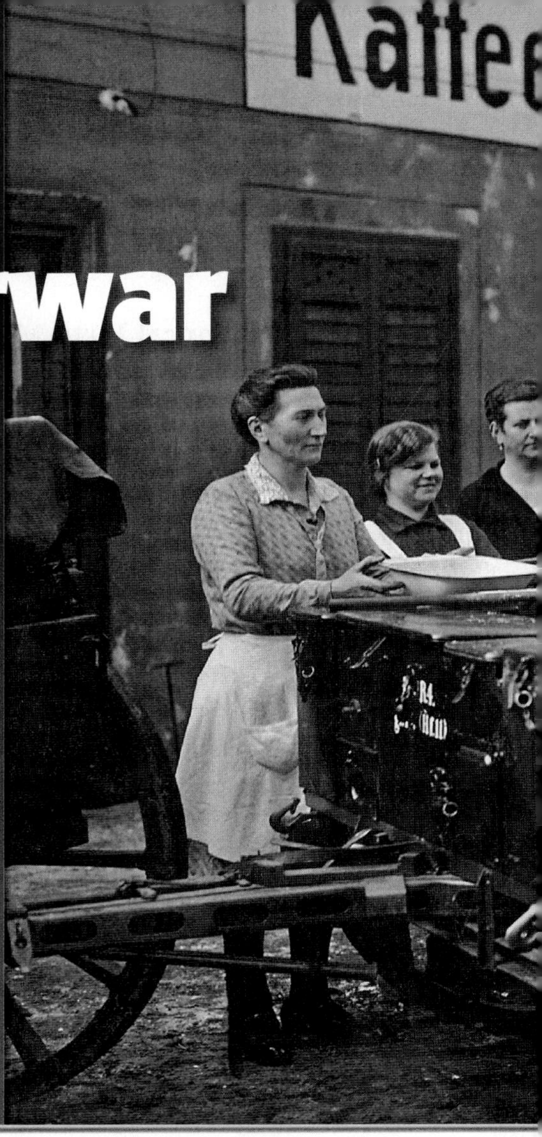

THE BIG PICTURE World War I left millions of people dead and the map of Europe transformed. With Europe in chaos, nationalism spread to parts of the world that had long been under imperialist control, and a new generation of strong leaders promised power and glory. By the end of the 1930s, these leaders' aggressive actions had the world on the brink of another devastating global war.

Theme SOCIETY

Economic problems and political unrest can result in major changes in society. In this chapter you will learn how the troubled times after World War I affected societies across the world.

TIME LINE

CHAPTER EVENTS

- **April 1919** British troops kill hundreds of Indian protestors in Amritsar.
- **April 1921** The kingdom of Transjordan is created.
- **February 1922** Egypt wins independence from Great Britain.
- **October 1929** The U.S. stock market crashes.

1920 — 1925 — 1930

WORLD EVENTS

- **1921** Ireland achieves independence.
- **1928** A scientist in Scotland discovers penicillin, an antibacterial agent.

406 CHAPTER 13

Key to Differentiating Instruction

Below Level

Basic-level activities designed for all students encountering new material

At Level

Intermediate-level activities designed for average students

Above Level

Challenging activities designed for honors and gifted and talented students

Standard English Mastery

Activities designed to improve standard English usage

Introduce the Chapter

At Level

The Interwar Years

Materials: construction paper

1. Tell students that during the period they will be studying, the world had become more interconnected. Students will make posters to represent the content of each section of the chapter.
2. Organize students into four groups (or eight if the class is large). Assign one section of the chapter to each group. Have groups scan the sections they were assigned, listing important facts and events.
3. Distribute paper. Have each group prepare a poster representing the content of its assigned section.
4. Allow time for groups to display and present their finished posters. **LS Interpersonal, Visual-Spatial**

Alternative Assessment Handbook, Rubrics 14: Group Activity; and 28: Posters

History's Impact video program
Watch the video to understand the impact of the 1929 stock market crash.

Reading like a Historian This photograph shows a soldier distributing food to hungry Germans in 1931 during a severe economic depression. Germany's economic problems soon helped lead to the rise of a powerful dictator.

Analyzing Visuals How do you think these German women felt about the food provided by the army? How might Germany's economic problems have contributed to the rise of a dictator?

See **Skills Handbook**, p. H26

September 1931 Japan invades Manchuria.

January 1933 Adolf Hitler becomes chancellor of Germany.

October 1935 Italian forces invade Ethiopia.

November 1938 Anti-Jewish riots sweep Germany.

1935 — 1939

1933 Prohibition ends in United States.

1935 An earthquake kills 20,000 people in Pakistan.

1939 The Spanish Civil War ends with a Fascist victory.

• Chapter Preview •

HOLT
History's Impact
► **Video Program: The Interwar Years**
See the Video Teacher's Guide for strategies for using the video segment.

Reading Like a Historian
Analyzing a Photograph Have students examine the photograph on these pages and then explain what is happening. Guide students in a discussion of what this photograph tells us about the people and their living conditions.

Explore the Time Line
1. In what year did Ireland achieve independence? *1921*
2. When did the U.S. stock market crash? *October 1929*
3. Name the two countries that invaded other countries during the 1930s. *Japan and Italy*
4. When did anti-Jewish riots sweep Germany? *November 1938*

Info to Know
Globalization of the Depression The Great Depression in the United States spread through Europe and beyond. Though most economies usually recover at the end of a decade-long cycle of business, the worldwide aspect of this depression made it far worse. Germany, already paying reparations after World War I, suffered hyperinflation, making its currency worthless.
Draw Conclusions Why was Germany's economy suffering even before the Great Depression began? *Germany was paying reparations for World War I damages.*

go.hrw.com
Online Resources
Chapter Resources:
KEYWORD: SHL IWY
Teacher Resources:
KEYWORD: SHL TEACHER

Answers
Reading Like a Historian *possible answer—The women appear pleased and grateful; because of Germany's economic problems, Germans may have been likely to accept a dictator who promised aid.*

Preteach

Geography Starting Points

Activity Analyzing Proverbs Read the African proverbs below to students, and write them for all to see. Have students explain how the proverbs might have related to African struggles with colonial rule. *possible answers—In British colonies, the British took over the justice systems; African colonies were controlled by Europeans, and conflicts fairly frequent.* As an extension, have students write their own proverbs reflecting the images shown on this page.

Map Transparency: Postwar Colonies and Nationalism, 1920s

World History Outline Maps

Interactive Map: Postwar Colonies and Nationalism, 1920s

Primary Source

African Proverbs

"Show me your friend and I will show you your character."
—Kwaku Boateng

"Where the leopard is made the judge the goat will never get a fair judgment."
—Makanze Emeka

"Great towns grow with peace but not killing and intimidation."
—Prince Arusi Obi

GEOGRAPHY Starting Points

Interactive

POSTWAR COLONIES AND NATIONALISM, 1920s

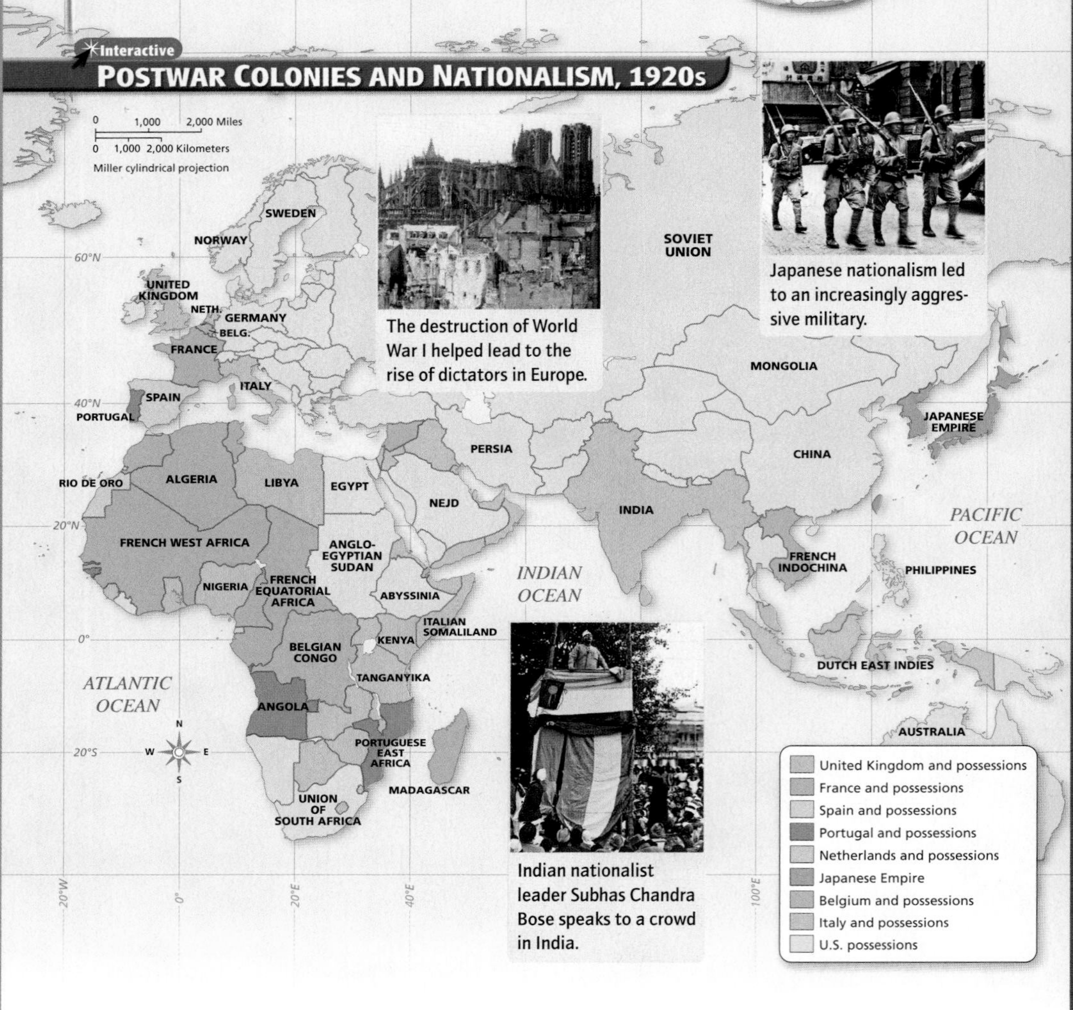

The destruction of World War I helped lead to the rise of dictators in Europe.

Japanese nationalism led to an increasingly aggressive military.

Indian nationalist leader Subhas Chandra Bose speaks to a crowd in India.

Starting Points During the years of political and economic instability that followed World War I, nationalism grew in areas that had long been under the power of other nations. In some places this nationalism led to struggles for independence, while in others it led to the rise of powerful leaders who promised to build new empires—by force.

1. **Analyze** During the 1920s, where were most colonial possessions located?
2. **Predict** How do you think the growth of nationalism might affect the area of the world shown in this map? How might the map be different in the 1940s? In the 1960s?

Listen to History

Go online to listen to an explanation of the starting points for this chapter.

go.hrw.com
Keyword: SHL IWY

Skills Focus: Analyzing Maps

At Level

Social Studies Skill

Nationalism's Impact

1. Draw the chart for students to see. Omit the italicized answers. Have students copy the chart, and fill the Impact column with a sentence about each of the areas listed.
2. Have students refer to the map on this page and create a statement explaining its title. Have volunteers share their answers.

LS Visual-Spatial, Verbal-Linguistic

Alternative Assessment Handbook, Rubrics 13: Graphic Organizers; and 21: Map Reading

Nationalism's Impact	
Area	*Impact*
Western Europe	***People struggle to rebuild after World War I.***
British Colonies	***Nationalism in Asia and Africa causes unrest in the colonies.***
Japan	***Japan modernizes its military, hoping to enlarge its empire.***

Answers

Geography Starting Points

1. *Africa;* 2. *possible answer—might cause colonies to rebel; later maps might show fewer colonial possessions*

SECTION 1

Unrest in Asia and Africa

BEFORE YOU READ

MAIN IDEA

During the chaotic years following World War I, nationalist feeling increased in Asia and Africa. The resulting unrest continued into the 1930s.

READING FOCUS

1. What happened in China after World War I?
2. What changes took place in India?
3. How did nationalism affect the Middle East?
4. How did nationalism affect Africa?

KEY TERMS AND PEOPLE

Jiang Jieshi
Mao Zedong
Long March
Amritsar Massacre
Mohandas Gandhi
Kemal Atatürk

TAKING NOTES Take notes about the rise of nationalism in China, India, the Middle East, and Africa.

◀ **Mao Zedong led the Chinese Communist troops during the Long March.**

THE INSIDE STORY ***Would you march 6,000 miles for your beliefs?*** In 1934 the civil war in China was going poorly for the Chinese Communist army. The Communists were trapped near their base in southeastern China, with some 700,000 nationalist troops, known as Guomindang, waiting to attack. Communist leaders knew they needed to escape to continue their struggle for a Communist China.

That October, the remaining 100,000 Communist troops and supporters broke through Guomindang lines and fled toward northern China. Led by Mao Zedong, they struggled to cross rivers and swamps and to climb over high, snow-covered mountains in their search for safety. During the first three months of their journey, the Communists faced near-constant attacks from the Guomindang air force and ground troops. Many marchers died as a result.

Finally, after traveling thousands of miles across some of the harshest terrain in China, the Communists arrived at a safe haven. Only 8,000 of the marchers had survived. In the years to come, however, their vision of a Communist China would get closer to reality. ■

China after World War I

World War I had devastated large parts of Europe, and postwar treaties and political unrest had reshaped many nations. Although China's role in the war had been small, it faced unrest during the postwar period.

Preteach

Getting Started

Use the **Interactive Reader and Study Guide** to familiarize students with the section content.

Interactive Reader and Study Guide, Section 1

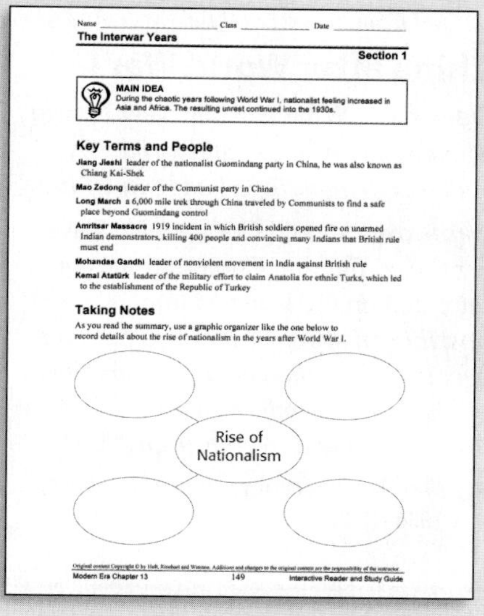
Name ______ Class ______ Date ______

The Interwar Years

Section 1

MAIN IDEA
During the chaotic years following World War I, nationalist feeling increased in Asia and Africa. The resulting unrest continued into the 1930s.

Key Terms and People

Jiang Jieshi leader of the nationalist Guomindang party in China, he was also known as Chiang Kai-Shek

Mao Zedong leader of the Communist party in China

Long March a 6,000 mile trek through China traveled by Communists to find a safe place beyond Guomindang control

Amritsar Massacre 1919 incident in which British soldiers opened fire on unarmed Indian demonstrators, killing 400 people and convincing many Indians that British rule must end

Mohandas Gandhi leader of nonviolent movement in India against British rule

Kemal Atatürk leader of the military effort to claim Anatolia for ethnic Turks, which led to the establishment of the Republic of Turkey

Taking Notes

As you read the summary, use a graphic organizer like the one below to record details about the rise of nationalism in the years after World War I.

Rise of Nationalism

Original content Copyright © by Holt, Rinehart and Winston. Additions and changes to the original content are the responsibility of the instructor.

Modern Era Chapter 13 149 Interactive Reader and Study Guide

CRF: Vocabulary Builder: Section 1

Taking Notes

Chinese student protests gave rise to the nationalist Guomindang, whose members attacked rival Communists. Mao Zedong led Communist supporters to northern China. Nationalist feelings in British-controlled India sparked protests, one of which resulted in the Amritsar Massacre. Mohandas Gandhi inspired nonviolent civil disobedience. Ethnic Turks, under the leadership of Kemal Atatürk, turned Turkey into a modern nation. Reza Kahn overthrew the Persian shah, becoming emperor, and sought to make the new nation of Iran independent. Arab nationalists hoped for an independent Arab state. Zionism, the Jewish national movement, grew stronger. France and Great Britain set up mandates in the Middle East, and both Arabs and Jews were unhappy with the decision. Nationalism in Africa led to desire for independence. Egypt gained its independence.

go.hrw.com
Online Resources
KEYWORD: SHL IWY
ACTIVITY: Mustafa Kemal Atatürk

Teach the Main Idea

At Level

Unrest in Asia and Africa

1. **Teach** Ask students the Reading Focus questions to teach this section.
2. **Apply** Organize students into four groups. Tell students they will create a news briefing, to inform western world leaders about developing events in the world regions discussed in the section—China, India, the Middle East, and Africa. Assign each group a different area. Briefings should be supported with maps of the region.
3. **Review** Have groups present their news briefings to the class. Guide students in a discussion of the information presented in the briefings.
4. **Practice/Homework** Have each student write a one-paragraph summary of the major events in Asia and Africa during this time.
LS Interpersonal, Kinesthetic

Alternative Assessment Handbook, Rubrics 24: Oral Presentations; and 42: Writing to Inform

Direct Teach

Reading Focus

1 What happened in China after World War I? *Chinese student protests led to rise in nationalism; Communist Party formed; nationalist Guomindang Party attacked rival Communists; Mao Zedong led Communists on Long March*

China after World War I

Describe What was the May Fourth Movement? *protests and strikes by students demanding change in China*

Evaluate Should Communists have continued fighting Chinese forces or retreated on the Long March? *possible answers—continued fighting, because many thousands of them died on the Long March; retreated, because they were able to regain strength*

Map Transparency: The Long March, 1934–1935

Recent Scholarship

In *The Great Wall: China Against the World, 1000 BC—2000 AD,* author Julia Lovell reveals the many faces of the Great Wall, its reality, image, and how it has shaped its nation with new understanding. Lovell views it in a modern perspective, as she equates it to a "Great Fire-wall" of the Internet, protecting China from international attack.

The Great Wall: China Against the World, 1000 BC—2000 AD by Julia Lovell. Grove Press, 2006

The May Fourth Movement In 1917 China had declared war on Germany, hoping that after the war the grateful Allied Powers would return German-controlled Chinese territories to China. The Treaty of Versailles, however, gave Germany's Chinese territories to Japan, which had captured this land during the war. To the Chinese, the Versailles treaty was a sign that the world still saw China as a weak nation.

On May 4, 1919, thousands of angry students in Beijing demanded change. Strikes and protests swept the country in what came to be called the May Fourth Movement.

An Uneasy Partnership The Guomindang nationalists still had the support of some Chinese, but many others believed that communism was the best way to strengthen and modernize China. In 1921 the Communist Party of China was formed. The Communists and the Guomindang formed an uneasy partnership, working together to fight the warlords who controlled many areas of China.

This partnership made many gains in the early 1920s. Under the leadership of **Jiang Jieshi** (jee-AHNG jee-ay-SHEE), also known as Chiang Kai-Shek (jee-AHNG ky-SHEK), continued to fight the warlords and foreign imperialism. Soon, the Guomindang controlled much of China.

Jiang eventually turned against his Communist allies. Because the success of the Communist-Guomindang partnership had expanded Communist influence in China, some Guomindang nationalists were upset. They urged Jiang to take action. In 1927 Jiang had his forces attack Communists in several cities, killing thousands of people. This action marked the beginning of the Chinese Civil War.

The Long March A number of Communists survived Jiang's attack, among them a leader named **Mao Zedong**. Mao and his fellow survivors tried to rebuild their organization. By 1934, however, the Guomindang had the Communists under serious military pressure. To escape, Mao led 100,000 Communist supporters on a 6,000-mile trek through China. The purpose of this **Long March** was to find a safe place for the Chinese Communists in a part of China beyond Guomindang control.

Only 8,000 of Mao's followers survived the terrible conditions of the Long March. Eventually, however, they would regain their strength and begin another battle against Jiang.

READING CHECK **Sequence** What happened in China after World War I?

Changes in India

The early 1900s also saw the rise of nationalist feeling in India. This soon led to increasing tension between Indians and their British rulers.

THE LONG MARCH, 1934–1935

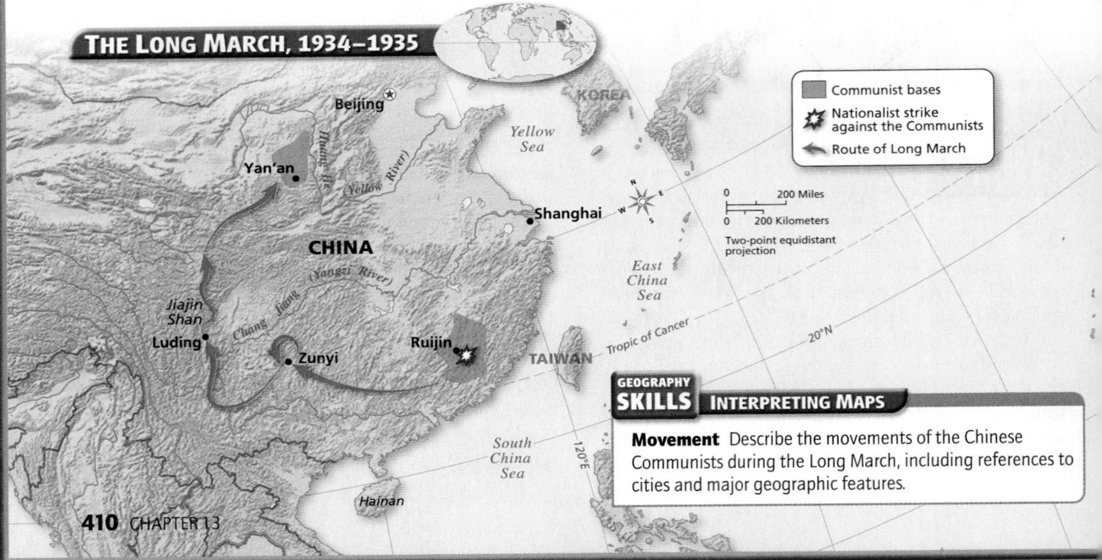

GEOGRAPHY SKILLS **INTERPRETING MAPS**

Movement Describe the movements of the Chinese Communists during the Long March, including references to cities and major geographic features.

Skills Focus: Interpreting Movement Maps

At Level

Research Required

Social Studies Skill

The Long March

Materials: poster paper

1. Review the route followed by Mao Zedong and his Communist followers to Yan'an. Have students create their own outline maps of China, based on the map on this page.
2. Have students work in pairs or small groups to determine the landforms that would have presented barriers on the Long March and those that would have made the route easier. Have students add these landforms to their maps.
3. Ask students what factors other than landforms might have influenced Mao's route.
4. Have students write a short essay about the challenges posed by the Long March route, and how this rigorous journey might have influenced the determination of Mao's Chinese Communists to preserve their beliefs.

LS Visual-Spatial, Verbal-Linguistic

Alternative Assessment Handbook, Rubrics 12: Drawing Conclusions; and 20: Map Creation

Answers

Interpreting Maps *They traveled around the city of Zunyi, across the Chang Jiang (Yangzi River), to the city of Luding, then crossed the Jiang Shan mountains, and finally arrived in the northern city of Yan'an.*

Reading Check *1919: strikes and protests; 1921: Communist Party of China formed; 1927: nationalists attack Communists; 1934: Long March*

India and World War I Some 800,000 Indians had served with the British in World War I, fighting on the Western Front and in the Middle East. After the war's end, the surviving Indian soldiers returned home to find that their wartime sacrifices had not won them any new freedoms. It was clear that Britain planned to keep firm control over India. Anger and unrest among the Indian population grew.

In 1919 the British passed the Rowlatt Acts, which allowed the British to deal harshly with the growing opposition in India. Indians were outraged. At an April 1919 protest in the Indian city of Amritsar (uhm-RIT-suhr), British soldiers opened fire on a large crowd of peaceful, unarmed demonstrators. Nearly 400 people were killed. The **Amritsar Massacre** helped convince many Indians that they must rid themselves of their British rulers.

Gandhi's Protests After the Amritsar Massacre, Indian lawyer **Mohandas Gandhi** started to organize protests against Britain. Gandhi believed in two important concepts. One was ahimsa, or nonviolence toward living things, which was an important value in Gandhi's Hindu religion. The second was civil disobedience, or a refusal to obey unjust laws.

In 1920 Gandhi began his first nonviolent action against British rule. He encouraged Indians to boycott all British products. For example, Gandhi stopped wearing clothes made from British cloth. Many Indians began to make their own thread and cloth, and the spinning wheel became a symbol of Gandhi's peaceful movement for change.

In 1930 Gandhi launched a protest against the British monopoly on salt. The issue seemed minor, but it captured the interest of the public. Soon, thousands of Indians were producing their own salt—and defying British law.

Gandhi's Progress Gandhi inspired millions of Indians to resist British rule. He and his followers were arrested often, but this increased public sympathy for their cause.

Gandhi's efforts did lead to some changes. In 1935 the British Parliament gave Indians a limited degree of self-rule. Still, this was far from the full independence that Gandhi sought, and India's struggle did not end.

READING CHECK **Identify the Main Idea** How did Gandhi work for change in India?

FACES OF HISTORY

Mohandas GANDHI
1869–1948

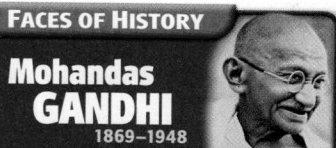

Mohandas Gandhi believed that nonviolent resistance is the best way to achieve change in a society where others hold all the power. This strategy was greatly influenced by his religious beliefs.

Gandhi grew up in a deeply religious home. His mother practiced a form of Hinduism that emphasized nonviolence and held that everything in the universe is eternal. As a result, Gandhi came to believe in the importance of causing no harm to other living beings. This emphasis on nonviolence became an important element of India's struggle for independence from Great Britain, which Gandhi led.

Summarize How did Gandhi's religious beliefs affect the Indian independence movement?

The Middle East

The years after World War I saw nationalist hopes and dreams flourish throughout much of the Middle East too. Some of these nationalist movements achieved their goals—but others did not.

Turkey and Atatürk Under the Treaty of Sèvres after World War I, the Ottoman Empire agreed to give up control of much of its territory, including the homeland of the ethnic Turkish population. The Allied Powers planned to give these lands to Greece and other nations.

But the Turks, led by a World War I hero named Kemal Mustafa, fought these plans. They defeated Greek forces sent to claim Turkish territory, and in October 1923 Kemal Mustafa announced the establishment of the Republic of Turkey. He later came to be known as **Kemal Atatürk**, or "Father of the Turks."

As the first president of Turkey, Atatürk sought to turn it into a modern nation. He believed this modernization required ending the influence of the Muslim religion on government and personal life. Thus, he made Turkey's government completely secular, or nonreligious. Until his death in 1938, Atatürk's leadership in Turkey led to advances in industry, education, and many other fields.

Persia Similar reforms took place in Persia. In 1921 Reza Khan led an overthrow of Persia's shah, or emperor. Khan himself became shah in 1925.

READING SKILLS
Understanding Comparison and Contrast How were reforms in Turkey and Persia alike?

Direct Teach

Reading Focus

2 What changes took place in India? *protests and boycotts led to limited self-rule*

Changes in India

Identify What were Gandhi's two most two important concepts? *nonviolence, civil disobedience*

Analyze What was the result of the Amritsar Massacre? *convinced many Indians that British rule should end*

CRF: Biography: Reza Shah Pahlavi

CRF: Literature: *A Passage to India*

Reading Focus

3 How did nationalism affect the Middle East? *Republic of Turkey established; new Persian shah worked to make Iran modern, independent; French and British mandates formed; Zionist movement grew; Arab nationalism grew*

The Middle East

Identify Why did Turkey fight Greek forces? *to gain full control of Anatolia, the Turkish homeland*

Analyze What changes did Atatürk bring to Turkey? *made government completely secular, improved industry, education*

Primary Source

"Nonviolence is the first article of my faith. It is also the last article of my creed."
—Mohandas Gandhi, 1922

Differentiating Instruction

Below Level

Learners Having Difficulty

1. Guide students in a discussion comparing and contrasting the leadership of Gandhi in India and Atatürk in Turkey. Have students take notes during the discussion.
2. Have students use the information from the discussion and their notes to create a two-column chart in which they list the leadership characteristics of each man.
3. Have volunteers create a class chart for all to see. Have students compare, add to, and correct the class chart and their own work.
4. As an extension, have each student write a short paragraph about the leader who most appeals to them. Students should explain their choice and justify their answer with information from the text and class discussion. **LS Verbal-Linguistic, Visual-Spatial**

Alternative Assessment Handbook, Rubrics 7: Charts; and 9: Comparing and Contrasting

Answers

Faces of History *caused him to believe in nonviolence*

Reading Skills *both involved advances in industry and education*

Reading Check *organized protests, promoted independence in industries within India, resisted British authority*

Direct Teach

Reading Focus

The Middle East

Recall What did Arab nationalists want at the end of World War I? *an independent Arab state*

Describe What was one result of the Balfour Declaration? *thousands of Jews immigrated to Palestine*

CRF, Primary Source: British White Paper of June 1922

Reading Focus

4 How did nationalism affect Africa? *African colonies wanted independence from Europe; pan-African movement*

Nationalism in Africa

Identify Why did African nationalism grow after World War I? *Many Africans had served in European armies during the war.*

Explain How was the African economy affected by the war? *suffered, trade dried up, European spending almost stopped*

Teaching Tip

Some students may have very strong feelings about issues in the Middle East. If so, review events from the history of the area, presenting a balance of opinions.

Linking TO Today

Roots of the Arab-Israeli Conflict

The modern Arab-Israeli conflict over the control of land in the Middle East has long resisted attempts at resolution. The roots of this conflict can be traced back many years.

In the late 1800s Jews from Europe began to establish small colonies in Palestine, their ancient homeland, as part of an effort to rebuild a Jewish state. By the early 1900s, a growing Arab nationalist movement had also developed, which wanted to form an independent Arab state in the Middle East.

When World War I ended, France and Great Britain set up mandates in the Middle East. Both Arabs and Jews were unhappy with this decision. Still, after the war, thousands of foreign-born Arabs and Jews moved to Palestine. Tensions increased, and violence between the two groups broke out.

In an attempt at compromise, the United Nations issued a plan to divide Palestine between Jews and Arabs in 1947. Although the Jews accepted this plan, Arabs felt it was unfair and rejected it. In 1948 Britain pulled out of Palestine and the state of Israel was created. Five Arab states immediately attacked Israel. Although Israel won this war, it was the first of many Arab-Israeli wars that followed. Today, the Arab-Israeli conflict continues.

Summarize What are the origins of the conflict between Arabs and Jews?

▲ Jewish settlers arrive in the newly formed state of Israel.

Khan, who ruled as Reza Shah Pahlavi (ri-ZAH SHAH PA-luh-vee), wanted to make Iran into a modern and fully independent nation. Reza Shah sought to advance industry and to improve education. In 1935 he changed Persia's name to Iran.

French and British Mandates Arab nationalists, supported by the British, had rebelled against the Ottoman Empire in 1916. Led by Husayn bin Ali (hoo-SAYN bin ah-LEE), they wanted to create an independent Arab state stretching from Syria to Yemen.

Meanwhile, another national movement was growing stronger. The Jewish national movement, called Zionism, hoped to rebuild a Jewish state in the ancient Jewish homeland. In the 1917 Balfour Declaration, the British government declared its support for a Jewish homeland in Palestine, while respecting the "rights of existing non-Jewish communities."

Instead of fulfilling these Arab and Jewish nationalist hopes, the postwar peace agreements established French and British mandates in the Middle East. France gained control of Syria and Lebanon, and Britain gained control of Iraq and what was called the Palestine Mandate. Both Arabs and Jews were unhappy, believing wartime promises had been broken.

In 1921 the British gave the eastern part of the Palestine Mandate to Husayn's son Abdullah as the kingdom of Transjordan (now Jordan). That same year the British installed Husayn's son Faisal as the king of Iraq, the British mandate on Transjordan's northeastern border. Palestine's population soon expanded greatly as tens of thousands of Jews and Arabs immigrated to the land. Palestinian Arab anger over this Jewish immigration led to conflict in the mid-1930s. Indeed, the conflict in this region continues today.

READING CHECK **Compare** What issues did nations in the Middle East face after World War I?

Nationalism in Africa

During World War I, Africa had been almost entirely under the rule of European colonial powers. Hundreds of thousands of Africans served in European armies during the war, and tens of thousands of them lost their lives. This wartime experience did much to increase nationalist feeling in Africa.

Skills Focus: Analyzing Alternative Points of View

At Level

Reading Like a Historian Skill

African Freedom and Colonialism

1. Have students review the information about Africa in the text, and guide them in a discussion about African colonies after World War I.
2. Organize students into small groups. Remind students that many African songs, poems, and even speeches are written with a refrain throughout the work. Have each group write two songs or poems using this technique. One poem or song should reflect the desire for freedom in African colonies. The other should reflect the viewpoint of Europeans who stand to lose valuable resources in Africa.
3. Guide students in a discussion of the viewpoints presented. Who lost and gained the most in Africa's quest for independence?

LS Auditory-Musical

Alternative Assessment Handbook, Rubric 26: Poems and Songs

Answers

Linking to Today *both wanted states in Palestine; after World War I, France and Great Britain set up mandates in the Middle East; many Arabs and Jews moved to Palestine; a plan to divide Palestine between them failed; state of Israel was created, war broke out*

Reading Check *reforms and independence in Turkey and Persia;*

Nationalist Feeling Grows Many Africans believed they had earned independence from European control through their wartime sacrifices. Further, the war had caused great economic hardship in many parts of Africa. Trade with Europe, on which many African colonies depended, dried up, and European spending in African colonies slowed to a trickle. In short, Africans felt that they had suffered a great deal for Europe and had little to show for it.

African anger further increased because of the Treaty of Versailles. No Africans were involved in the negotiations, and the European powers simply gave Germany's African colonies to other countries as mandates rather than granting them independence.

Africans United

Speakers gather at the Second Pan-African Congress, held in Belgium in 1921. American W.E.B. Du Bois, one of the organizers of the congress, is second from the right.

Working for Independence In the years after World War I, Africans' frustrations at the actions of the European powers led them to seek greater independence. For example, a series of meetings known as Pan-African Congresses began in 1919. Organized by people of African heritage living around the world, these conferences led to a series of demands for African independence.

North African Arabs also took action to win independence in British-controlled Egypt. After the war, in which hundreds of thousands of Egyptians had served, a group of Egyptians tried to bring a demand for independence to the British government. When some members of the group were arrested, protests swept the country. Many Egyptians were killed.

The British eventually recognized that they could not maintain full control of Egypt. In February 1922 they formally declared that Egypt was an independent nation.

Egypt's independence was a victory for nationalism in Africa, but it was not the start of a trend in the postwar years. Indeed, the continent remained almost entirely under European control in the 1920s and 1930s. During this time, African desire for reform and independence continued to grow. Yet it would take time—and another world war—before nationalism in Africa would lead to major change on the continent.

READING CHECK **Summarize** How did World War I help inspire feelings of nationalism in Africa?

SECTION 1 ASSESSMENT

go.hrw.com **Online Quiz** Keyword: SHL IWY HP

Reviewing Ideas, Terms, and People

1. **a. Identify** Who were **Jiang Jieshi** and **Mao Zedong**?
   b. Draw Conclusions Why do you think the Guomindang and the Communists worked together in China in the early 1920s?
2. **a. Describe** What two key concepts did **Mohandas Gandhi** use in his protests?
   b. Evaluate Why do you think Gandhi's repeated arrests helped build sympathy for his cause?
3. **a. Recall** Why did many Arabs feel mistreated at the end of World War I?
   b. Elaborate Explain how the Balfour Declaration influenced events in the Middle East following World War I.
4. **a. Describe** How did World War I affect Africa?
   b. Summarize What happened in Egypt after World War I?

Critical Thinking

5. **Sequence** Use your notes on the section to summarize how the growth of nationalism was similar in each region.

CHINA	
INDIA	
MIDDLE EAST	
AFRICA	

FOCUS ON SPEAKING

6. **Exposition** Write a brief speech that might have been given at the First Pan-African Congress in 1919. In a few sentences, summarize the arguments in favor of independence for African colonies.

Direct Teach

Reading Focus

Nationalism in Africa

Identify Cause and Effect Why did Britain grant independence to Egypt? *They realized they could not maintain full control of the country.*

Rate Was the Versailles Treaty fair to Africans? Why or why not? *possible answer—No, African colonies were not included in the negotiations and were not given independence.*

Review & Assess

Close

Have students explain events and conflicts in the regions discussed in the section.

Review

Online Quiz, Section 1

Assess

SE Section 1 Assessment

Progress Assessment: Section 1 Quiz

Alternative Assessment Handbook

Reteach/Intervene

Interactive Reader and Study Guide, Section 1

Interactive Skills Tutor CD-ROM

Section 1 Assessment Answers

1. **a.** Jiang Jieshi—led Guomindang; Mao Zedong—Chinese Communist leader
   b. shared similar goals
2. **a.** nonviolence and civil disobedience
   b. possible answer—He hurt no one.
3. **a.** expected an independent Arab state
   b. Britain supported the Zionist movement
4. **a.** Africans died fighting; war caused great economic hardship
   b. Egyptians killed in independence protests; Egypt eventually won independence
5. China—May Fourth Movement: Communist Party formed: the Long March; India—Amritsar Massacre: Ghandi's nonviolent protests: India gains partial independence; Middle East—Turks defeat Greek forces and establish Republic of Turkey: Reza Khan overthrows Persia's shah and founds Iran; Africa—Pan-African Congresses: Egyptian independence
6. Speeches might argue that Africans earned their independence by serving in World War I.

Answers

Reading Check *Many Africans believed they had earned independence through wartime service.*

Preteach

Getting Started

Use the **Interactive Reader and Study Guide** to familiarize students with the section content.

Interactive Reader and Study Guide, Section 2

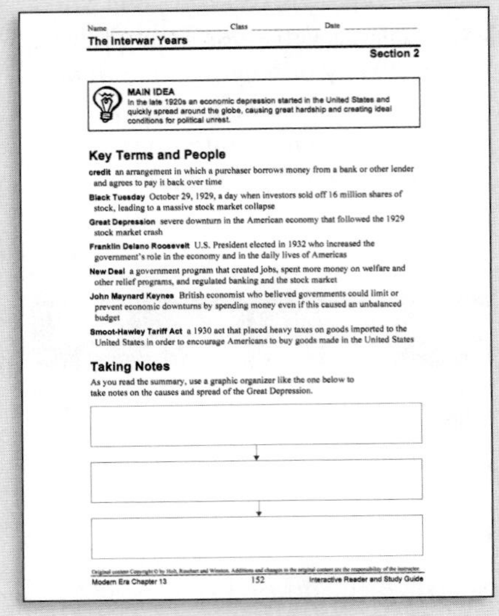

Name ________ Class ________ Date ________

The Interwar Years

Section 2

MAIN IDEA
In the late 1920s an economic depression started in the United States and quickly spread around the globe, causing great hardship and creating ideal conditions for political unrest.

Key Terms and People

credit an arrangement in which a purchaser borrows money from a bank or other lender and agrees to pay it back over time

Black Tuesday October 29, 1929, a day when investors sold off 16 million shares of stock, leading to a massive stock market collapse

Great Depression severe downturn in the American economy that followed the 1929 stock market crash

Franklin Delano Roosevelt U.S. President elected in 1932 who increased the government's role in the economy and in the daily lives of Americas

New Deal a government program that created jobs, spent more money on welfare and other relief programs, and regulated banking and the stock market

John Maynard Keynes British economist who believed governments could limit or prevent economic downturns by spending money even if this caused an unbalanced budget

Smoot-Hawley Tariff Act a 1930 act that placed heavy taxes on goods imported to the United States in order to encourage Americans to buy goods made in the United States

Taking Notes

As you read the summary, use a graphic organizer like the one below to take notes on the causes and spread of the Great Depression.

Original content Copyright © by Holt, Rinehart and Winston. Additions and changes to the original content are the responsibility of the instructor.

Modern Era Chapter 13 152 Interactive Reader and Study Guide

Academic Vocabulary

Review with students the high-use academic term in this section.

prosperity wealth or success (p. 415)

CRF: Vocabulary Builder: Section 2

Taking Notes

The U.S. economy was booming during the 1920s, so many Americans bought stock. Poor consumers could no longer buy products. In 1929, a huge sell-off led to the stock market crash. The Great Depression was caused by many factors. Hoover's minimal governmental response didn't work. Roosevelt fought the crisis with the New Deal, employing people and regulating banking and the stock market. The Depression had a worldwide impact. The Smoot-Hawley Tariff Act slowed world trade, ruining some foreign economies. War recovery and economic problems in Europe led to political unrest, and changes in government.

go.hrw.com
Online Resources
KEYWORD: SHL IWY
ACTIVITY: U.S. Economy

SECTION 2

The Great Depression

Before You Read

Main Idea

In the late 1920s an economic depression started in the United States and quickly spread around the globe, causing great hardship and creating ideal conditions for political unrest.

Reading Focus

1. What happened to the U.S. economy during the 1920s?
2. How did the Depression spread throughout the United States?
3. How did the Depression affect the world?

Key Terms and People

credit
Black Tuesday
Great Depression
Franklin Delano Roosevelt
New Deal
John Maynard Keynes
Smoot-Hawley Tariff Act

TAKING NOTES Take notes on the causes and spread of the Great Depression.

Causes	Spread

THE INSIDE STORY ***Could the good times last forever?*** During the decade known as the Roaring Twenties, times were good for many Americans. The economy was booming, unemployment was low, and the stock market was climbing steadily. It was an exciting time for American popular culture as well. Movies and radio exploded in popularity and artists and writers throughout the country documented the great economic and social changes taking place. It seemed the good times would never end.

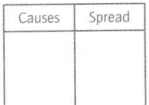

▲ **This 1929 magazine cover shows a woman enjoying the good times.**

The growing stock market was one thing that seemed likely to last forever. In fact, many Americans in 1929 believed that the price of stocks would always rise. Who could blame them? In the two years before 1929, the stock market had doubled in value. Investing in stocks seemed like an easy way to wealth.

In the summer of 1929, businessman John J. Raskob wrote a magazine article about investing in the stock market. The article's title sums up what he and many other people felt about buying stocks in the 1920s: "Everybody Ought to Be Rich." In the article, Raskob said that investing in the stock market was a simple matter, and that the average American could—and should—do so. But just two months after "Everybody Ought to Be Rich" was published, many stock investors were not even close to being rich. They were flat broke. ■

The U.S. Economy in the 1920s

At the end of World War I, the United States was the world's leading economic power. That position grew stronger during the boom times of the 1920s, but by the end of the decade the U.S. economy was crashing.

Economic Growth During World War I, American farms and factories supplied much of the world with the food and supplies needed to fight the war. Although the American economy slowed down briefly when the war ended, it was booming again by 1921. Growth was steady throughout most of the 1920s.

Most of this economic growth occurred in industry, with automobile manufacturing a huge part of the boom. In addition, American factories also busily turned out a wide range of consumer goods—from radios to vacuum cleaners to washing machines.

Teach the Main Idea

At Level

The Great Depression

Materials: construction paper

1. **Teach** Ask students the Reading Focus questions to teach this section.
2. **Apply** Organize students into small groups. Have groups scan the section and list the factors that caused the Great Depression, and the reasons it had a worldwide impact. Distribute construction paper. Have groups use the atlas in their texts to sketch a simple outline map of the world and write their facts in boxes with arrows pointing to the areas affected.
3. **Review** Display students' labeled maps for all to see.
4. **Practice/Homework** Have each student write a summary paragraph about the causes of the Great Depression and its worldwide impact. **LS Verbal-Linguistic, Visual-Spatial**

Alternative Assessment Handbook, Rubrics 1: Acquiring Information; and 20: Map Creation

The success of American industry was reflected in the stock market. During the 1920s the overall value of the stocks traded at the nation's stock markets rose an astounding 400 percent. Many Americans rushed to buy stocks, afraid they would miss out on the prosperity. Some borrowed money from stockbrokers in order to buy stocks, in what is known as buying on margin. This increasing investment in the stock market drove stock prices even higher.

Hidden Problems The stock market was booming, but there were hidden problems affecting the American economy. For example, the new wealth being created was not distributed evenly. The richest 1 percent of the population earned 19 percent of the nation's income.

Also, for much of the 1920s, the easy availability of credit allowed Americans to increase their spending on consumer goods. **Credit** is an arrangement in which a purchaser borrows money from a bank or other lender and agrees to pay it back over time. By the end of the decade, many consumers were reaching the limit of their credit and could no longer afford to buy the products that had kept the U.S. economy expanding.

The Stock Market Crash By the fall of 1929, consumer spending had slowed, and sales of some products had suffered badly. Fears began to grow that stock prices might soon drop. Then, at the end of October, some nervous investors began to sell off their stocks. Others joined in, and a huge sell-off began.

The worst day was October 29, known as **Black Tuesday**. On that single day, investors sold off 16 million shares. With few people wanting to buy the stocks that flooded the market, stock prices collapsed completely. Many investors who had borrowed money to buy stocks were forced to sell at a loss to repay their loans.

ACADEMIC VOCABULARY

prosperity wealth or success

The massive stock market crash ruined many investors, but they were not the only ones affected. Banks that had lent money to these investors were in deep financial trouble as well. Furthermore, the crash delivered a devastating blow to American industry, which had already been struggling. Indeed, the effects of the great crash would soon be felt throughout the country—and beyond.

READING CHECK **Sequence** What happened to the U.S. economy during the 1920s?

The Depression Spreads

Following the stock market crash, the American economy took a severe downward dive. This economic downturn became known as the **Great Depression**. The Depression was the result of a number of complex factors.

Causes of the 1929 Stock Market Crash

QUICK FACTS

- Increasing speculation in stock market
- Stock prices at unrealistic levels
- Increasing consumer reliance on credit
- Declining consumer spending
- Struggling businesses

↓

Stock Market Crash

During the Depression, many businesses failed and millions of people were unemployed.

Direct Teach

Reading Focus

1. What happened in the U.S. economy during the 1920s? *Until 1929, it boomed; Americans bought products and stock on credit.*

The U.S. Economy in the 1920s

Explain What happened on Black Tuesday? *Investors sold about 16 million shares of stock, prices collapsed, and the stock market crashed.*

Identify Cause and Effect What two problems led to the crash? *consumer spending slowed; some feared stock prices might soon drop*

Quick Facts Transparency: Causes of the 1929 Stock Market Crash

Info to Know

Soup Kitchens During the Great Depression, soup kitchens fed the 12 million Americans who were out of work. The first were run by churches and private charities. Notorious gangster Al Capone ran one in order to improve his image. The need for soup kitchens became so great that the states and the federal government began to run them. Why soup? Water could be added to serve more people.

Teaching Tip

Some students have little idea of the cost of living. Create a sample budget for an average family in the 1920s and a family today to share with students.

Differentiating Instruction

Below Level

English-Language Learners

Materials: fake money, certificates representing manufactured goods and groceries

1. Have three volunteers represent a Manufacturer, Grocer, and Worker. As the Employer, you will distribute pay to the Worker every round, which represents a month. Have the Worker buy goods from the Manufacturer and the Grocer each month. Increase the cost of the goods until the Worker cannot buy from one of them.
2. When this occurs, stop the simulation and guide students in a discussion about where the money goes after it is paid to the Manufacturer. What will happen when people cannot buy their products?
3. Have each student create a poster illustrating the route of money through a failing economic system. LS **Kinesthetic, Visual-Spatial**

Alternative Assessment Handbook, Rubrics 11 Discussions; and 28: Posters

Answers

Reading Check *The economy boomed; Americans bought goods and stock on credit; when consumer spending slowed, a stock sell-off began, resulting in the 1929 stock market crash.*

Direct Teach

Reading Focus

2 How did the Depression spread throughout the United States? *Industry slowed, people lost jobs, and government response did not work.*

The Depression Spreads

Explain What caused some banks to go out of business? *Businesses and investors failed to pay off loans; anxious depositors withdrew their savings.*

Identify Cause and Effect What effect did joblessness have on Americans? *They could not buy needed goods or food, hurting industry further.*

Make Inferences How do you think Americans felt about Herbert Hoover? *possible answer—frustrated that the president would not take action to help those who lost jobs*

CRF: Biography: Bessie Smith

Biography

Langston Hughes (1902–1967) The Harlem Renaissance fueled creative genius, as can be seen in the poetry and novels of Langston Hughes. Hughes was born in Missouri. He was raised by his grandmother in Kansas, and in his teens moved to Illinois and then to Ohio with his mother. He very nearly followed the path of a developing musical sensation, the blues. In his work, Hughes honored the American poor as they struggled through the Depression with determination and strength. Hughes gave some of his poems to the famous critic Vachel Lindsay, whose praise helped him gain recognition.

Industry Slows One cause of the Depression was a slowdown in industry. This slowdown had begun before the crash but worsened quickly after it. As industry slowed, workers lost their jobs. By 1933 one out of every four workers was unemployed. Joblessness and poverty reduced Americans' ability to buy food and goods, which hurt industry even further.

As businesses and investors failed to pay off loans, banks also suffered. At the time, a bank's failure meant that people who had savings in the bank could lose their money. As a result, the rumor that a bank was struggling could cause anxious depositors to withdraw all their savings, driving the bank out of business.

Government Response U.S. president Herbert Hoover believed that the federal government should have a limited role in business affairs. As a result, he favored a minimal government response to the crisis. In fact, some of his advisers believed the Great Depression was a normal, healthy adjustment to an overheated economy. Hoover eventually took some actions to fight the Depression, but many Americans felt that he was doing too little.

Roosevelt Elected In 1932 U.S. voters elected **Franklin Delano Roosevelt** as president. Under Roosevelt, the federal government's role in the lives of Americans greatly increased. Roosevelt pushed forward a program known

THE ARTS AROUND THE WORLD

Music
The Blues

What is it? The blues is a simple yet expressive form of music that developed in the American South in the late 1800s. Blues songs evolved in African American communities, combining aspects of spirituals, work songs, and traditional African music. Most blues songs express feelings of sadness, often about problems in love. When southern African Americans moved to northern cities in search of work during World War I and the Great Depression, they took the blues with them. As a result, the music spread throughout the north.

Why is it important?
- Blues is an important African American contribution to modern culture.
- Blues has been a major influence on later forms of music, including jazz, rock, and hip-hop.

Blues musician Robert Johnson is sometimes called the grandfather of rock and roll.

Bessie Smith was one of the most popular blues singers of the 1920s and 1930s.

The deep poverty in the Mississippi Delta influenced the early blues. ▶

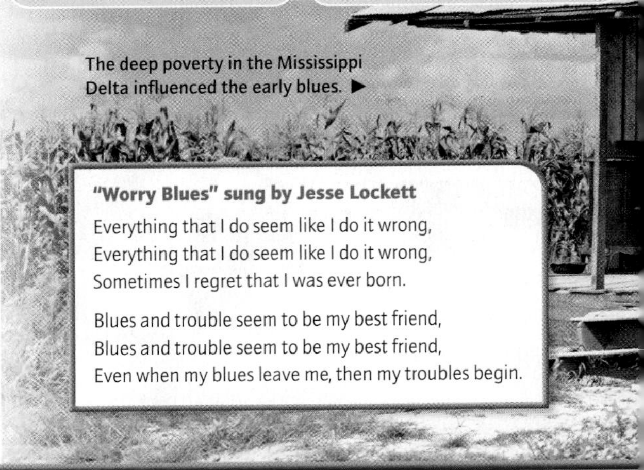

"Worry Blues" sung by Jesse Lockett

Everything that I do seem like I do it wrong,
Everything that I do seem like I do it wrong,
Sometimes I regret that I was ever born.

Blues and trouble seem to be my best friend,
Blues and trouble seem to be my best friend,
Even when my blues leave me, then my troubles begin.

Skills Focus INTERPRETING VISUALS

1. **Summarize** How did blues music spread?
2. **Infer** How did the Great Depression affect blues music?

416 CHAPTER 13

Skills Focus: Analyzing Secondary Sources

At Level

Research Required

Reading Like a Historian Skill
Opinions of Hoover's Response

1. Remind students that President Hoover did very little to boost the economy when the stock market crashed because he believed that government should take a limited role in business affairs.
2. Organize students into small groups. Have each group conduct research to find information about Hoover's responses to the stock market crash. Have students examine sources for possible bias.
3. Have groups prepare a display of the articles they found, accompanied by their conclusions about potential bias in each source.
4. Have students form a generalization about President Hoover's response to the crash.
   LS Verbal-Linguistic, Interpersonal

Alternative Assessment Handbook, Rubrics 12: Drawing Conclusions; and 30: Research as the **New Deal**, aimed at fighting the Great Depression. Roosevelt and his advisers believed that government spending could help start an economic recovery. The New Deal established public works programs that gave jobs to the unemployed and it provided government money for welfare and other relief programs. The New Deal also created new regulations to reform and protect the stock market and the banking system.

New Economic Theories The increased government spending was supported by the theories of **John Maynard Keynes**, a British economist. Keynes believed that governments could limit or even prevent economic downturns. He argued that governments could do this by spending money—even if it meant having an unbalanced budget. In an economic depression, Keynes said, government spending would help increase economic output. Factories would have to hire workers to meet the new demand, providing workers with income. Eventually, the workers would begin spending—and the depression would end.

Indeed, increased government spending seemed to help the U.S. economy, at least initially. But the Great Depression lingered on throughout the 1930s.

READING CHECK **Identify Cause and Effect** Explain the factors that led to the Great Depression.

THE SPREAD OF THE BLUES

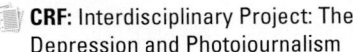

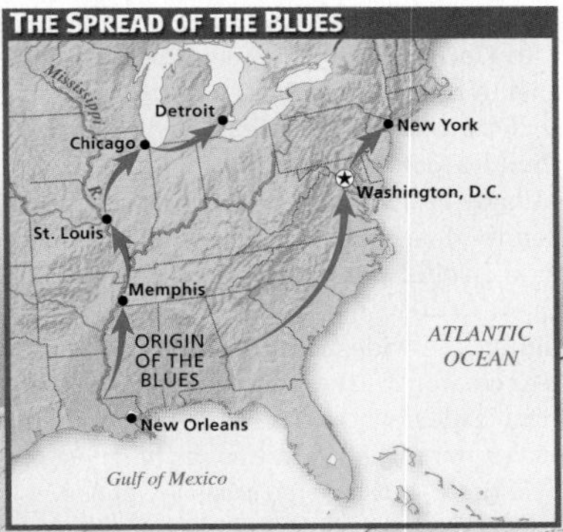

The Worldwide Depression

In 1929 American businesses were responsible for much of the world's industrial output. America was also one of the world's leading importers and lenders of money. Thus, events affecting the American economy were sure to have an impact on other countries. The Great Depression that began in the United States soon spread around the world.

Before the Crash Some areas of the world were having economic difficulties even before the American stock market crash. In Europe, most countries were still struggling to recover from the devastating effects of World War I. Many of the former Allied Powers were deeply in debt to the United States. In Great Britain, high interest rates in the late 1920s led to decreased spending and high unemployment. In Germany, the steep reparations the nation had been forced to pay after the war led to severe inflation, making German money virtually worthless and crippling the German economy. In Japan, a severe economic depression in 1927 had forced many banks to close. For these and other countries, the Great Depression was just the latest in a long series of economic crises. The effects of this latest collapse, however, were far worse.

A Slowdown in Trade In 1930 President Hoover signed the **Smoot-Hawley Tariff Act**. This act placed heavy taxes on imported goods in an attempt to encourage Americans to buy goods and products made in the United States.

Direct Teach

Reading Focus

The Depression Spreads

Identify What was the New Deal? *government program aimed at fighting the Depression through jobs, welfare, and other relief programs*

Summarize What did John Maynard Keynes believe would limit or prevent economic downturns? *increased government spending*

Reading Focus

3 How did the Depression affect the world? *ruined foreign economies, led to political instability*

The Worldwide Depression

Explain Why was the Depression deeper in many European countries than elsewhere? *European countries were still recovering from World War I.*

Contrast How did the purpose of the Smoot-Hawley Tariff Act differ from its result? *It was designed to encourage Americans to buy U.S. goods; resulted in slowing world trade, crippling foreign economies.*

CRF: History and Geography: The Great Depression

CRF: Interdisciplinary Project: The Depression and Photojournalism

Skills Focus: Summarizing

At Level

Research Required

Reading Skill
Foreign Concerns in the 1930s

1. Remind students that foreign countries suffered greatly because of the American economic collapse.
2. Organize students into small groups. Assign each group a European, Asian, or Latin American country. Have each group conduct research on its assigned country's economic struggles after 1930.
3. Students should investigate and record the most important problems related to the Great Depression in their assigned country. Then have students create a slogan for a banner representing peoples' concerns at the time.
4. When students have finished, have volunteers from each group share their banners with the class. **LS Verbal-Linguistic, Interpersonal**

Alternative Assessment Handbook, Rubrics 30: Research; and 34: Slogans and Banners

Answers

The Arts Around the World
1. *When African Americans moved north in search of work, they took blues music with them.* **2.** *caused it to spread throughout the northern United States*

Reading Check *unequal distribution of wealth; buying stock and products on credit; spending slowed; stock market crashed; a slowdown in industry followed*

Direct Teach

Reading Focus

The Worldwide Depression

Recall Name two countries in which extremists gained strength as economies worsened. *Germany, Italy*

Make Inferences How did the Great Depression contribute to the rise of totalitarian leaders? *Widespread misery led people to trust powerful leaders who promised to fix problems.*

Review & Assess

Close

Review the factors that led to the worldwide Great Depression and its political consequences.

Review

go.hrw.com **Online Quiz**, Section 2

Assess

SE Section 2 Assessment

Progress Assessment: Section 2 Quiz

Alternative Assessment Handbook

Reteach/Intervene

Interactive Reader and Study Guide, Section 2

Interactive Skills Tutor CD-ROM

UNEMPLOYMENT, 1929–1933

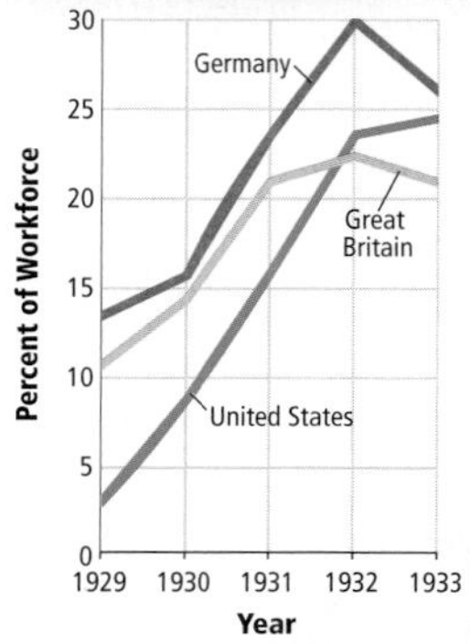

Source: *Historical Statistics of the United States; European Historical Statistics*

DECLINE OF WORLD TRADE, 1929–1933

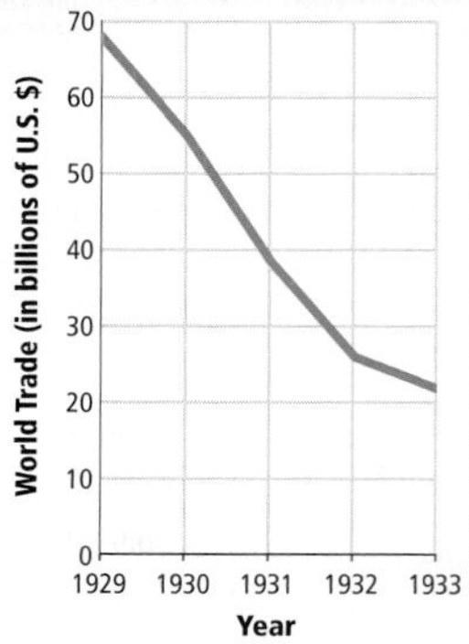

Source: *Economic Discrimination and Political Exchange*

Skills Focus INTERPRETING GRAPHS

Summarize How did the Great Depression affect unemployment and world trade?

These American goods would be cheaper than the imported goods which were taxed. The act backfired. The new tariff led countries around the world to increase their own tariffs on American goods. As a result, world trade slowed to a standstill. For many nations, the loss of foreign trade crippled their economies.

As trade slowed, the prices for trade goods collapsed. In Japan, for example, the price of silk dropped sharply. This product was a major export and responsible for nearly 20 percent of Japanese farm income. The decline of Japan's silk industry is just one example of the collapsing markets and economic hardship found all over the world.

Political Impact The postwar era had been challenging for many European governments. The difficult peace process and the formation of new nations out of the ruins of empires had left many countries politically unstable.

As the Depression continued, unrest grew worse. Political instability in Great Britain and France led to the formation of several new governments during the Depression, as desperate citizens looked for leaders who could help them.

In other countries, extremist political groups gained strength as economies worsened. In Germany, for example, the National Socialist (Nazi) Party unfairly blamed Jews for many of the country's problems and promised to rebuild a powerful German empire. Italy had already fallen under the rule of the dictator Benito Mussolini. During the Depression years, Mussolini tightened his control on the nation.

Indeed, the widespread misery and hopelessness created ideal conditions for the rise of powerful leaders who promised to restore their nations to glory. The world was in the midst of troubled times, but a worse crisis lay ahead.

READING CHECK **Summarize** How did the Depression spread to the rest of the world?

SECTION 2 ASSESSMENT

go.hrw.com **Online Quiz** Keyword: SHL IWY HP

Reviewing Ideas, Terms, and People

1. **a. Describe** What role did **credit** play in the success of the U.S. economy in the 1920s?
   b. Identify Cause and Effect How did the success of the stock market in the 1920s contribute to its collapse?
2. **a. Identify** How did the slowdown in American industry affect the economy?
   b. Compare and Contrast Compare and contrast the policies of Herbert Hoover and **Franklin Delano Roosevelt**.
3. **a. Recall** Why and how did the **Great Depression** spread from the United States to other countries?
   b. Elaborate Why do you think economic and political turmoil in Europe may have made some people more willing to accept a dictator?

Critical Thinking

4. **Compare and Contrast** Use your notes on the section to compare and contrast the Great Depression in the United States and in the rest of the world.

United States | World

FOCUS ON WRITING

5. **Exposition** Write a letter that someone who lost his or her job in the Great Depression might have written to a friend.

Section 2 Assessment Answers

1. **a.** People bought goods and stocks on credit, creating jobs and fueling the economy.
   b. Investors who borrowed money to buy stocks were forced to sell at a loss.
2. **a.** workers lost their jobs, could not buy goods, hurting industry even more
   b. Hoover—limited government role in business affairs; Roosevelt—increased government spending for jobs program, welfare, relief
3. **a.** United States was a world leader in lending, importing, and manufacturing; Smoot-Hawley Tariff Act backfired
   b. People were desperate for strong leadership to solve the economic crisis.
4. U.S.—stock market crash, eventually New Deal started; both—farmers hit hard, Smoot-Hawley Tariff Act slowed trade, widespread misery and hopelessness; World—still recovering from war, owed U.S. and other nations money, political instability, rise of dictatorships
5. Student letters should include details from the section about life during the Great Depression.

Answers

Interpreting Graphs *Unemployment rose in the United States, Great Britain, and Germany, and world trade declined.*

Reading Check *World trade slowed, ruining some foreign economies. War recovery and economic problems in Europe led to political unrest and changes in government.*

Focus on Themes

Society

During the Great Depression, many people around the world depended on government-administered social welfare programs to provide food and jobs. In the United States, social welfare programs to help poor and unemployed Americans were first established during this time period. Today, many nations have similar programs to aid their citizens.

SOCIAL WELFARE PROGRAMS THEN The first modern social programs were established in Germany in the late 1800s and included health insurance, workers' compensation, and pensions for the elderly and the disabled. By the 1920s similar social welfare programs had become common in Europe and in much of the Western Hemisphere.

In the United States, however, social services were the responsibility of state and local governments, churches, and voluntary organizations. The crippling effects of the Great Depression changed that. Beginning with Franklin Roosevelt's New Deal, the federal government established a variety of national social welfare programs to aid poor, unemployed, and elderly Americans in need of help.

▲ THEN Workers at a Chicago soup kitchen serve food to unemployed men during the Great Depression.

SOCIAL PROGRAMS IN SELECTED COUNTRIES (QUICK FACTS)

DENMARK
- Government-funded benefits for health, education, disability, unemployment, and old age are available for all Danes.

UNITED STATES
- The federal government provides retirement and unemployment benefits, health-care programs for elderly and low-income Americans, and housing and welfare benefits for low-income citizens.

SOUTH KOREA
- Government welfare programs are relatively new and limited but provide benefits for disabled war veterans; housing facilities for elderly, homeless, and orphaned citizens; and job training for women.

NIGERIA
- There is no national health insurance or social welfare system; instead, family members serve as an unofficial social welfare network for elderly and low-income Nigerians.

SOCIAL WELFARE PROGRAMS NOW Social programs are widespread today but are most common in Western Europe. In many countries, social welfare programs to help those in need are seen as an important government responsibility.

While most countries offer some form of social welfare, there is much disagreement about the services that should be offered as well as the amount of money that should be spent on them. Most programs are funded by a combination of contributions from employers, persons covered by insurance programs, and general government revenue. Some people worry that offering generous welfare programs can cause governments to spend too much money and may discourage the unemployed from finding jobs.

Skills Focus: UNDERSTANDING THEMES

1. **Summarize** How did the Great Depression affect social welfare programs in the United States?
2. **Infer** Why do some people object to welfare programs?
3. **Draw Conclusions** Why do you think national social welfare programs were established later in the United States than in many European countries?

Focus on Themes

Society

Info to Know

Daily Life To help students understand how the Great Depression affected people's daily lives and changed the very fabric of society, mention the following true events and statistics from the United States during the 1930s: a group of 50 desperate men were seen behind a Chicago restaurant fighting violently over a garbage can; some Americans emigrated to Russia to seek jobs; the suicide rate reached its peak; jurors acquitted two families who shot their landlords to prevent being evicted.

Quick Facts Transparency: Major U.S. Social Reforms

Skills Focus: Making Oral Presentations

At Level

Research Required

Reading Like a Historian Skill
Town Hall Forum Speaker

1. Discuss the Understanding Themes questions with students. Have students explain why the U.S. government agreed to implement the New Deal.
2. Organize students into seven groups. Assign one Social Reform from the Quick Facts list to each group. Have each group discuss and list the benefits and problems associated with its assigned program. Students should conduct outside research on their assigned project to determine its effects.
3. Have each group prepare two short speeches, one supporting the program, and one opposing the program.
4. Next, have volunteers present their speeches while the rest of the class listens and takes notes. **LS Interpersonal, Verbal-Linguistic**

Alternative Assessment Handbook, Rubrics 18: Listening; and 24: Oral Presentations

Answers

Understanding Themes 1. *shifted responsibility for social services to federal government (away from state and local governments, churches, and voluntary organizations);* **2.** *Some people worry that programs are too costly and may discourage the unemployed from finding jobs.* **3.** *possible answer—Economic conditions in the United States were generally prosperous before the Great Depression.*

Preteach

Getting Started

Use the **Interactive Reader and Study Guide** to familiarize students with the section content.

Interactive Reader and Study Guide, Section 3

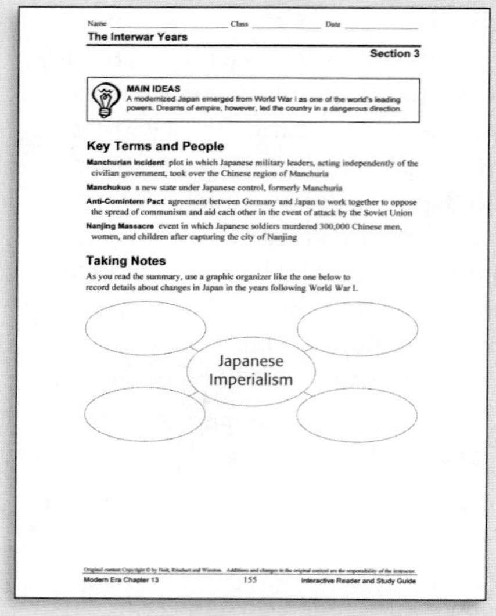

Name ______________ Class ____________ Date ____________

The Interwar Years

Section 3

MAIN IDEAS
A modernized Japan emerged from World War I as one of the world's leading powers. Dreams of empire, however, led the country in a dangerous direction.

Key Terms and People

Manchurian Incident plot in which Japanese military leaders, acting independently of the civilian government, took over the Chinese region of Manchuria

Manchukuo a new state under Japanese control, formerly Manchuria

Anti-Comintern Pact agreement between Germany and Japan to work together to oppose the spread of communism and aid each other in the event of attack by the Soviet Union

Nanjing Massacre event in which Japanese soldiers murdered 300,000 Chinese men, women, and children after capturing the city of Nanjing

Taking Notes

As you read the summary, use a graphic organizer like the one below to record details about changes in Japan in the years following World War I.

Japanese Imperialism

Modern Era Chapter 13 155 Interactive Reader and Study Guide

Academic Vocabulary

Review with students the high-use academic term in this section.

subsequent later; following in time (p. 424)

CRF: Vocabulary Builder: Section 3

Taking Notes

Japan needed natural resources and raw materials to support its growing industry and population. Japan was quickly becoming an urban, industrialized nation. The military sought and was gaining more power in government. The 1924 American law barring Japanese immigration offended the Japanese, who were becoming increasingly nationalistic.

SECTION 3

Japanese Imperialism

Before You Read

Main Idea

A modernized Japan emerged from World War I as one of the world's leading powers. Dreams of empire, however, led the country in a dangerous direction.

Reading Focus

1. How did Japan change in the 1920s?
2. Why did the Japanese military's influence grow?
3. What were the reasons for Japanese aggression in the 1930s?

Key Terms

Manchurian Incident
Manchukuo
Anti-Comintern Pact
Nanjing Massacre

TAKING NOTES Take notes on Japanese imperialism in the years following World War I.

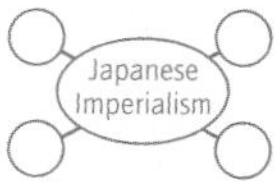

THE INSIDE STORY ***Why would an army bomb its own railway?*** In 1931, a bomb exploded in the Chinese region of Manchuria, damaging a Japanese-controlled railway line. Japanese soldiers stationed in Manchuria immediately blamed the blast on Chinese sabotage. Given Chinese unhappiness with the Japanese presence in China, it was easy to believe that China was responsible for the attack.

However, China had nothing to do with the explosion. The bomb had been planted by Japanese soldiers who wanted to use the excuse of this alleged Chinese attack to quickly take over Manchuria. Japan would then have access to the region's rich natural resources, which were badly needed by Japanese industry.

The Japanese plot worked perfectly, except for one thing: Japan's government did not support the military action. Indeed, Japan's civilian leaders had known nothing about the plot. But when Japanese troops began to move into northern Manchuria three days after the explosion, military leaders refused to obey the government's orders to stop the invasion. The Japanese public supported the army's actions, and the government had little choice but to go along. Soon, the Japanese military dominated Manchuria—and was growing ever more aggressive. ■

A SECRET PLOT

A Chinese city burns after a devastating Japanese attack. ▼

420 CHAPTER 13

Teach the Main Idea

At Level

Japanese Imperialism

1. **Teach** Ask students the Reading Focus questions to teach this section.
2. **Apply** Have students work individually or in mixed-ability pairs to create their own two-column charts showing the problems within Japan and the problems Japan was having with other nations during this time period. For problems within Japan, students should include the economy, strikes, and lack of natural resources.
3. **Review** Have students share the information on their charts, and create a class chart for all to see. Have students retain their charts to use as a study tool.
4. **Practice/Homework** Have students use their charts to write an "in-depth" magazine article about the rise of Japanese imperialism.
   LS Verbal-Linguistic, Visual-Spatial

Alternative Assessment Handbook, Rubrics 7: Charts; and 19: Magazines

Japan in the 1920s

At the end of World War I, Japan stood as one of the world's foremost powers. It was a remarkable accomplishment for a country that just a half-century before had been a relatively weak agricultural nation. Even so, Japan's postwar years were not easy ones.

Economic Challenges Japan's economy had undergone many changes during the Meiji restoration, when the nation's economy first began to industrialize. By the early 1920s this rapid industrialization had begun to create problems. Peasants and rural workers had not shared in the nation's new prosperity, and once World War I ended many industries experienced slowdowns. As a result, businesses began to lay workers off, and unrest grew. Strikes and labor disputes increased sharply in the 1920s.

Japan faced other economic challenges during the 1920s as well. The small island country did not have the natural resources needed to supply modern industry and was forced to import these materials. To pay for them, Japan sold its manufactured goods abroad. But because other countries passed tariffs to protect their own products against foreign competition, Japan had difficulty exporting enough goods to survive economically. To get the natural resources needed to support its growing population, Japanese leaders decided their nation needed to expand.

Social Changes Japan's rapid shift from a feudal agricultural nation to a more urban industrial country affected more than just its economy. The shift, combined with universal education and new ideas from the West, led to changes in Japanese society. Democracy began to flourish, and a vibrant system of political parties emerged. Some young people adopted Western fashions and beliefs and began to question traditional Japanese values, such as obedience and respect for authority. More conservative Japanese, including military leaders, resented these changes and believed that straying from traditional Japanese beliefs and interests had corrupted the country.

READING CHECK **Summarize** What changes took place in Japan during the 1920s?

Events in Japan, 1929–1940

QUICK FACTS

1929	The Great Depression hits Japan.
1931	Japan takes control of Manchuria, China.
1933	Japan withdraws from the League of Nations.
1934	Japan announces it will no longer submit to limits on its navy.
1936	Japan signs agreement with Germany.
1937	Japanese troops kill hundreds of thousands of civilians in Nanjing, China.
1940	Japan attempts to expand its power in Asia by proposing an economic alliance of Asian nations.

▼ Japanese troops invade China.

Growing Military Influence

A serious economic crisis struck Japan in 1927, followed shortly thereafter by the Great Depression. Many Japanese lost faith in their government, which seemed unable to help them, and began to look to the Japanese military for leadership during this time of crisis.

The Military's Vision Military officers envisioned a united Japan—a society devoted to the emperor and to the glory of the nation ruled by the military leadership. Thus, they began to seek more power over Japan's civilian government.

Direct Teach

Reading Focus

1 How did Japan change in the 1920s? *rapid urbanization, democracy began to flourish, universal education and ideas from the west led to changes in values and politics*

Japan in the 1920s

Describe What occurred within the Japanese labor force after the war? *layoffs, strikes, labor disputes*

Analyze What two factors caused a slowdown in Japanese industry? *lack of natural resources, reduction in exports*

Reading Focus

2 Why did the Japanese military's influence grow? *economic crisis; people lost confidence in government, put faith in the military whose leaders opposed the government's foreign policy*

Growing Military Influence

Recall How would Japanese military officers describe a united Japan? *a society devoted to its emperor and to the glory of the nation, under the rule of military leadership*

Interpret Why did some Japanese lose faith in their government? *possible answer—The government seemed unable to help them but the military leaders seemed strong enough to do so.*

Quick Facts Transparency: Major Japanese Events, 1929 to 1940

Differentiating Instruction

Below Level

Standard English Mastery

Learners Having Difficulty

1. Remind students that the Great Depression affected economies worldwide. Review the information in the text about the particular economic problems that faced Japan.
2. Have students make a table showing how Japan's economy changed in the years after World War I. Students should list specific problems and how Japan began to address each problem.
3. Have students use the information in their tables to write a paragraph contrasting Japan before and after industrialization. Have students review their paragraphs to check for correct spelling, grammar, and standard English usage. LS **Verbal-Linguistic, Visual-Spatial**

Alternative Assessment Handbook, Rubrics 9: Comparing and Contrasting; and 42: Writing to Inform

Answers

Reading Check *rapid industrialization, economic problems, universal education, democracy began to flourish, tension between traditional values and new ideas*

Direct Teach

Reading Focus

3 What were the reasons for Japanese aggression in the 1930s? *Military leaders realized they could not compete with industrialized nations.*

Japanese Aggression

Explain How did Japan's military leaders make up for industrial limitations? *by building a fighting spirit in the Japanese troops and members of the public*

Contrast How was the Japanese military different from that of industrialized nations? *Japan had not yet developed technology and industrial power.*

Map Transparency: Japanese Aggression, 1931–1937

Info to Know

The Great Kanto Earthquake Just as Japan was undergoing significant changes and facing serious economic challenges, a natural disaster hit. In September 1923, a strong earthquake devastated a large area around Yokohama and Tokyo. It destroyed buildings and took the lives of approximately 145,000 people.

Foreign Relations The military's influence in Japan grew in part because of public opposition to the Japanese government's foreign policy. After World War I, the civilian leaders of Japan's government had made several treaties with the West to limit the size of the Japanese navy. Military officials were furious over these agreements, which seemed to put an end to Japan's overseas expansion.

In 1924 the United States passed a law barring Japanese immigration. This action by one of Japan's supposed allies deeply offended Japanese pride, and some Japanese began to question their government's policy of cooperation with the West. Increasingly, the Japanese public began to put its faith in the military, drawn to its nationalist vision of a strong Japan that would defer to no other country.

READING CHECK **Analyze** Why did the Japanese military's influence increase in the 1920s?

Japanese Aggression

As the 1920s came to an end, Japan's military gained power, widening the gap between the military and the civilian government. Without civilian controls, Japan's military became more aggressive toward other nations.

Building a Fighting Spirit World War I had shown that modern war would rely on technology and industrial power. Japan's military leaders realized that Japan would have difficulty contending directly with the large industrial nations of the world. First, they did not have the industrial capacity; and, second, they had been forced to limit the size of their navy after the war.

To make up for their nation's industrial limitations, Japan's military leaders focused on a different kind of weapon: the Japanese soldiers. They began to promote the fighting spirit of the Japanese troops. This bravery, many officers claimed, could make up for a lack of modern weaponry. "If against tanks you have no anti-tank guns," said one officer, "it becomes a matter of using human bullets." In the Japanese military's instruction manual, the words *surrender*, *retreat*, and *defense* were removed to encourage the idea that these were no longer possibilities.

Japan's military leaders also tried to inspire a fighting spirit among members of the public. One way they did so was by placing military personnel in the public schools to shape the thinking of Japanese children. One Japanese leader described the military's goals:

HISTORY'S VOICES

"To impart the belief in ultimate victory to the people and the army . . . I applied education and training to the schools and to the youths, and I planned for soundness of heart and mind among the people. At the same time, by encouraging unity . . . between the people and the army, I worked to secure the position of the army as the pillar of the nation."

—Ugaki Kazushige, army minister, 1928

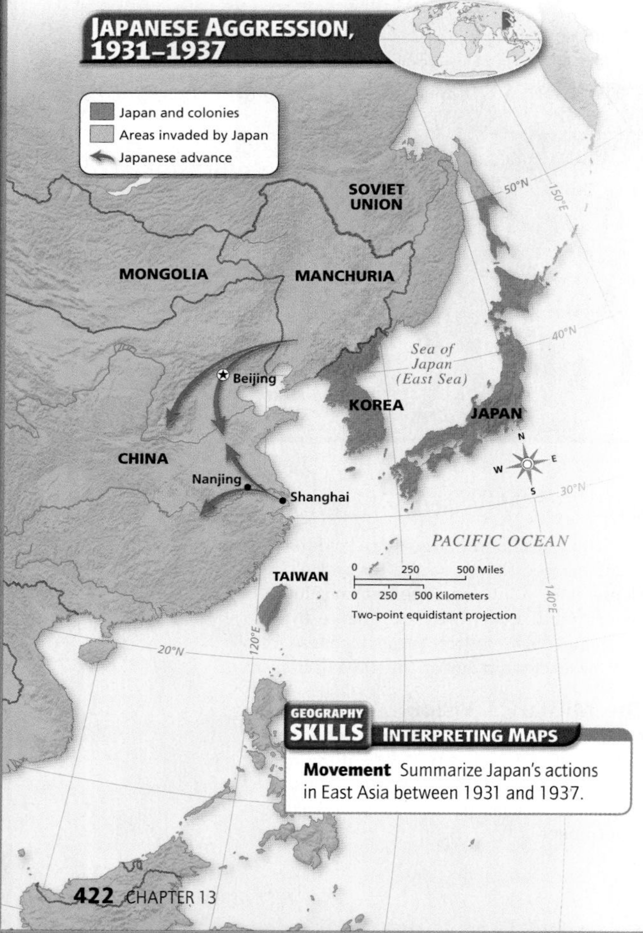

GEOGRAPHY SKILLS **INTERPRETING MAPS**

Movement Summarize Japan's actions in East Asia between 1931 and 1937.

Skills Focus: Analyzing Primary Sources

Below Level

Standard English Mastery

Reading Like a Historian Skill
Ugaki Kazushige's Goals

1. Remind students that the Japanese military was determined to increase its political power, as well as its military might.
2. Read the quote from Ugaki Kazushige in History's Voices to students. Then have students copy the quote onto their own papers, leaving space between lines. Have students underline their copy of the quote to separate each of Kazushige's thoughts. Have students rewrite each goal as a sentence.
3. Write this goal of Japanese officers for students to see, "…a united Japan—a society devoted to its emperor and to the glory of the nation, under the rule of military leadership." Have students write a paragraph explaining how Kazushige's statement supports this goal. **LS Verbal-Linguistic**

Alternative Assessment Handbook, Rubric 37: Writing Assignments

Answers

Interpreting Maps *Refer to map.*

Reading Check *People lost faith in their government's leadership and began to look to military leadership to help overcome economic problems.*

Reading like a Historian

The Nanjing Massacre

Recognizing Bias in Secondary Sources

In 1937 the Japanese army killed many Chinese civilians and soldiers in Nanjing, China. Historians generally agree that the total number of deaths was at least 100,000, but the events at Nanjing remain controversial. In China, the story of Nanjing is told very differently from in Japan.

Even accounts of historical events that are meant to be neutral can show bias. As you read these excerpts from Chinese and Japanese textbooks, consider these factors:

- the country the textbook came from
- the textbook's point of view
- the words used to describe the Japanese soldiers' actions

What word does this selection use to describe the Japanese soldiers? What does this suggest?

Wherever they went, the Japanese aggressors burned, killed, raped, looted, and committed the most heinous crimes imaginable. After the Japanese army occupied Nanjing, they unleashed the bloodiest massacre of the city's residents, and committed monstrous crimes. Some peaceful residents were shot as practice targets, others were butchered as bayonet practice targets, and still others were buried alive.

—From a Chinese middle school history textbook

How does this selection describe the ways that Chinese civilians were killed?

What does this selection imply with the wording "It is said to have killed"?

The Japanese army encountered fierce resistance everywhere. It is said to have killed 200,000 people after occupying Nanking (Nanjing), and it was censured by various foreign governments. But the Japanese people were not informed of these facts.

—From a Japanese middle school history textbook

Look at the last sentence of this selection. Why do you think the textbook included this sentence?

Skills Focus READING LIKE A HISTORIAN

1. **Language** Compare and contrast the words used to describe the Japanese soldiers' actions in Nanjing.
2. **Point of View** How are the two versions of this event similar and different? How can you explain these similarities and differences?

See **Skills Handbook**, p. H31

Taking Over the Government A group of Japanese military leaders plotted to replace the nation's government with a military dictatorship, believing that aggressive nationalist leadership was vital to Japan's future. They wanted to build a Japanese empire. During the 1930s, Japanese soldiers, military leaders, and members of nationalist organizations carried out a series of assassinations of government officials, including prime ministers and cabinet members. Some of these crimes were punished, but Japan's civilian government gradually gave in to the military's demands for power. Slowly, Japan's government grew more dominated by the military.

Conquering Manchuria The Japanese military's aggression soon became clear. In the **Manchurian Incident** in 1931, Japanese military leaders decided to conquer the Manchuria region of northeastern China, which was rich in natural resources such as coal and iron. Many in the army believed that Manchuria's resources would help free Japan from economic reliance on trade with the West and would thus allow Japan to compete with large industrial nations.

Japanese forces moved quickly to gain control of Manchuria. The Japanese public supported this action, and the civilian government was virtually powerless to stop it.

Direct Teach

Reading Focus

Japanese Aggression

Identify List two ways Japan isolated itself from the western powers. *withdrew from the League of Nation; announced it would no longer agree to any limits on its naval forces*

Analyze Why did Japan invade Manchuria? *Manchuria had rich natural resources, which Japan needed.*

Activity **Nanjing Massacre** Have students conduct research to find more sources on the Nanjing Massacre, examining each for possible bias. Have each student write an essay comparing the accounts and giving a possible explanation of what happened in Nanjing in 1937. **LS Verbal-Linguistic**

Alternative Assessment Handbook, Rubrics 30: Research; and 37: Writing Assignments

CRF: Biography: Sadao Araki

Differentiating Instruction

Above Level

Advanced Learners/ Gifted and Talented

1. Review the information in the text about the growing strength of the Japanese military. Tell students that Hirohito became emperor of Japan in 1926. The emperor had supreme authority over Japan, but some historians believe that Hirohito simply accepted the advice of the Japanese ministers and military advisers.
2. Have students conduct outside research on the role of Hirohito in Japanese political and military affairs prior to World War II. Students should focus their research on the role Hirohito played, or did not play, in formulating Japan's expansionist policies and in the Nanjing Massacre.
3. Have students prepare a multimedia presentation showing the results of their research. **LS Verbal-Linguistic**

Alternative Assessment Handbook, Rubric 22: Multimedia Presentations

Answers

Reading Like a Historian **1.** *Chinese textbook uses emotionally charged words like "heinous," "monstrous;" Japanese textbook describes event more neutrally, states that Japanese people were not informed of the massacre;* **2.** *Chinese version shows strong opinion, because so many Chinese people died in the massacre; Japanese version describes the event in terms of the supposed facts, probably because the Japanese government did not share the facts of the massacre with the people at the time.*

• Review & Assess •

Reading Focus

Japanese Aggression

Recall Approximately how many Chinese men, women, and children do historians believe were killed in the Nanjing Massacre? *as many as 300,000*

Develop What do you think the Anti-Comintern Pact nations had in common? *possible answers—anti-Communist, strong military influence in government*

Elaborate What might Southeast Asians have thought of the Japanese proposal to create the Greater East Asia Co-Prosperity Sphere? *possible answer—Many would not have trusted the aggressive Japanese.*

• Review & Assess •

Close

Have students describe the modernization and subsequent militarization of Japan.

Review

go.hrw.com **Online Quiz**, Section 3

Assess

SE Section 3 Assessment

Progress Assessment: Section 3 Quiz

Alternative Assessment Handbook

Reteach/Intervene

Interactive Reader and Study Guide, Section 3

Interactive Skills Tutor CD-ROM

Answers

Reading Check *military dominated the Japanese government; Japan needed more natural resources, wanted to increase the size of its empire*

THE IMPACT TODAY

In April 2005, some 20,000 Chinese demonstrators attacked the Japanese embassy in Beijing, China, furious about a new Japanese high school textbook that referred to the Nanjing Massacre only as an "incident."

ACADEMIC VOCABULARY

subsequent later; following in time

Eventually, Japanese troops set up a government in the region. They announced that Manchuria was a new state under Japanese control called **Manchukuo** (man-CHOO-kwoh).

Forming New Alliances The League of Nations strongly condemned Japan's aggressive actions in Manchuria. In response, Japan simply withdrew from the league in 1933. The following year, Japan further isolated itself from the Western powers by announcing that it would no longer agree to limits on the size of its navy.

While Japan was making its break with much of the West, it was growing closer to Germany. In 1936 the two nations signed an agreement known as the Anti-Comintern Pact. In the **Anti-Comintern Pact**, Japan and Germany agreed to work together to oppose the spread of communism. Each nation promised to come to the aid of the other if that country was attacked by the Soviet Union. The following year, Italy joined the pact.

War in China Conflict between Japan and China had continued ever since the Manchurian Incident, but grew worse as Japan became increasingly aggressive and seized more territory in eastern China. Some in Japan began to worry that the Chinese Communists and Guomindang nationalists might again join forces and turn on Japan, perhaps with the support of Japan's old enemy, the Soviet Union. With tensions rising, a series of violent incidents in the summer of 1937 between Chinese troops and Japanese forces stationed in China led to open warfare between the two nations. This conflict became known as the Second Sino-Japanese War.

One of the war's early battles occurred in Nanjing, also known as Nanking. After capturing the city, Japanese troops went on a murderous rampage, killing Chinese soldiers and civilians alike. At least 100,000 Chinese men, women, and children were killed in the **Nanjing Massacre**. The world reacted in horror to the bloody incident.

A Move toward Wider War Japan had some early victories in China, but subsequent battles did not go Japan's way. China was simply too large for Japan to conquer easily, and the war turned into a long, costly struggle.

In search of natural resources to supply its military needs, Japan looked to Southeast Asia. This region was rich in rubber, oil, and other key resources. In 1940 Japan's foreign minister proposed the creation of what he called the Greater East Asia Co-Prosperity Sphere. This was to be a group of nations whose combined resources would allow independence from Western control. The proposal was presented as an economic benefit for the region, but it was little more than another attempt to build a Japanese empire.

Japan's aggression in Asia was viewed with alarm by other nations. They did not welcome the expansion of a Japanese empire.

READING CHECK **Analyze** Why did Japanese aggression increase in the 1930s?

SECTION 3 ASSESSMENT

go.hrw.com **Online Quiz** Keyword: SHL IWY HP

Reviewing Ideas, Terms, and People

1. **a. Describe** What were some of the challenges facing the Japanese in the 1920s?
   b. Explain How did Japanese society change after World War I?
2. **a. Recall** What did Japanese military leaders believe their nation should be like?
   b. Summarize Why did the Japanese people begin to put their faith in the military?
3. **a. Identify** Identify the following event and its significance to Japan in the 1930s: **Manchurian Incident**
   b. Evaluate Why do you think the people of Japan supported their military's aggressive actions?

Critical Thinking

4. **Sequence** Copy the time line below and use your notes from the section to identify key events and changes in Japan in the years after World War I.

1920 ——————————————— 1940

FOCUS ON SPEAKING

5. **Persuasion** Were the Japanese army's actions in Manchuria good or bad for Japan? Write a short conversation from the 1930s in which two Japanese people debate this question.

Section 3 Assessment Answers

1. **a.** poverty, industrial slowdown, unemployment, labor disputes, and reduced exports
   b. economic changes, urbanization, universal education, and other social changes
2. **a.** a society devoted to its emperor and to the glory of the nation, under military rule
   b. lost faith in their government
3. **a.** 1931 invasion to gain Manchuria's natural resources, resulted in condemnation by the League of Nations
   b. possible answer—felt they needed strong, military leadership to end the economic crisis
4. 1922—agrees to limit the size of its navy; 1927—serious economic crisis; 1931—takes control of Manchuria; 1933—withdraws from the League of Nations; 1934—announces it will no longer limit its navy's size; 1936—Anti-Comintern Pact; 1937—Nanjing Massacre, Anti-Comintern Pact with Italy; 1940—Greater East Asia Co-Prosperity Sphere proposed
5. possible conversation topics—good, increased natural resources; bad, resulted in split with League of Nations

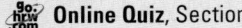

SECTION 4

Dictators in Europe

BEFORE YOU READ

MAIN IDEA

The political and social unrest that followed World War I helped totalitarian dictators rise to power in Europe.

READING FOCUS

1. How did Benito Mussolini rule Italy?
2. How did Joseph Stalin rule the Soviet Union?
3. How did Adolf Hitler rule Germany?

KEY TERMS AND PEOPLE

Benito Mussolini
fascism
totalitarianism
Joseph Stalin
Gulag
Adolf Hitler
Nazi Party
anti-Semitism
Nuremberg Laws
Kristallnacht

TAKING NOTES Take notes on the rise of totalitarian dictators in Italy, the Soviet Union, and Germany in the 1920s and 1930s.

Italy	Soviet Union	Germany

THE INSIDE STORY

How could someone take over a nation without a fight? Dreaming of greatness for his beloved Italy, Benito Mussolini plotted to take over the Italian government. His plan called for his followers to capture key buildings in the Italian capital of Rome, while some 30,000 more supporters waited outside the city, ready to march in for support. This show of force was impressive, but it might not be enough to defeat the Italian armed forces.

Mussolini's plan, however, was a triumph. Italy's king was worried that the Italian armed forces would not remain loyal to him and was unwilling to risk a battle with Mussolini's protestors. Mussolini realized this and rushed by train to Rome. After entering the city he met with the king, who asked Mussolini to form a new Italian government. Only then did Mussolini order his followers into the city for a triumphant "March on Rome." ■

A POWER GRAB IN ITALY

▲ **Mussolini (center) and his followers enter Rome in 1922.**

Mussolini's Italy

After the end of World War I, new ideas about government power arose in Italy. Those ideas, promoted by **Benito Mussolini**, led to drastic change in the Italian government and its view of Italy's role in the world.

Fascist Ideology Mussolini, who became known as *Il Duce* (il DOO-chay), or "the leader," wanted to build a great and glorious Italian empire. In 1919 he founded the National Fascist Party. The party took its name from the Latin word *fasces*, which referred to an ancient Roman symbol for the unity and strength of the state.

Fascism is an authoritarian form of government that places the good of the nation above all else, including individual needs and rights. Fascists envision an aggressive state ruled by a dictator, an all-powerful leader who makes all major decisions.

Mussolini in Power By 1922 the Fascists had become a significant force in Italian politics. But that wasn't enough for Mussolini. He wanted to rule Italy. In October he led the so-called March on Rome. This show of force convinced Italy's king to put Mussolini at the head of Italy's government.

Teach the Main Idea

At Level

Dictators in Europe

1. **Teach** Ask students the Reading Focus questions to teach this section.
2. **Apply** Have students create a Venn diagram in which they show the similarities and differences among the three leaders discussed in this section: Mussolini, Stalin, and Hitler. Have students include a simple sketch of each leader, based on images in the section.
3. **Review** Have volunteers share and discuss their diagrams. Have students compare and correct their own work.
4. **Practice/Homework** Have each student write a one-paragraph summary of the similarities between these three leaders.
   LS Verbal-Linguistic, Visual-Spatial

Alternative Assessment Handbook, Rubric 9: Comparing and Contrasting

Preteach

Getting Started

Use the **Interactive Reader and Study Guide** to familiarize students with the section content.

Interactive Reader and Study Guide, Section 4

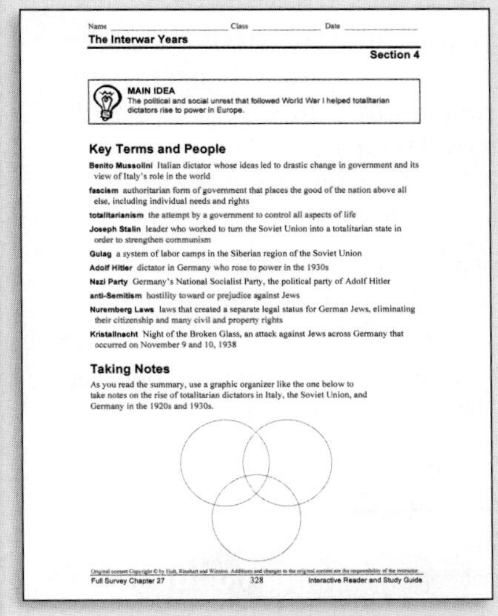

Name ______ Class ______ Date ______

The Interwar Years

Section 4

MAIN IDEA
The political and social unrest that followed World War I helped totalitarian dictators rise to power in Europe.

Key Terms and People

Benito Mussolini Italian dictator whose ideas led to drastic change in government and its view of Italy's role in the world

fascism authoritarian form of government that places the good of the nation above all else, including individual needs and rights

totalitarianism the attempt by a government to control all aspects of life

Joseph Stalin leader who worked to turn the Soviet Union into a totalitarian state in order to strengthen communism

Gulag a system of labor camps in the Siberian region of the Soviet Union

Adolf Hitler dictator in Germany who rose to power in the 1930s

Nazi Party Germany's National Socialist Party, the political party of Adolf Hitler

anti-Semitism hostility toward or prejudice against Jews

Nuremberg Laws laws that created a separate legal status for German Jews, eliminating their citizenship and many civil and property rights

Kristallnacht Night of the Broken Glass, an attack against Jews across Germany that occurred on November 9 and 10, 1938

Taking Notes

As you read the summary, use a graphic organizer like the one below to take notes on the rise of totalitarian dictators in Italy, the Soviet Union, and Germany in the 1920s and 1930s.

Original content Copyright © by Holt, Rinehart and Winston. Additions and changes to the original content are the responsibility of the instructor.

Full Survey Chapter 27 328 Interactive Reader and Study Guide

CRF: Vocabulary Builder: Section 4

Taking Notes

Italy—1919: Mussolini founds the National Fascist Party, develops totalitarian government; 1935: Italy overtakes Ethiopia; Soviet Union—1924: Stalin leads the Soviet Union; 1927: Stalin introduces first Five Year Plan, Stalin orders collectivization and responds to resistance with violence, 1932: Ukranians starve, Stalin begins the Great Purge, totalitarian rule indoctrinates children, discourages religion, and idealizes Stalin; Germany—Nation suffers postwar turmoil; 1923: Hitler's first attempt to overthrow the government, writes Mein Kampf in jail, supports anti-Semitism; 1933: Hitler becomes Chancellor, 1935: Nuremburg laws established; 1938: Kristallnacht occurs

Direct Teach

Reading Focus

1 How did Benito Mussolini rule Italy? *as the all-powerful leader of a totalitarian government*

Mussolini's Italy

Explain Describe the type of government fascists envision. *Under fascism, an authoritarian from of government that places the good of the nation above all else, fascists envision an aggressive state ruled by a dictator.*

Analyze Why did Italy invade Ethiopia? *to show military strength, expand Italy's territories*

CRF: Economics and History: Defense Spending in the 1930s

Reading Focus

2 How did Joseph Stalin rule the Soviet Union? *totalitarian rule, with violence, fear, propaganda*

Stalin's Soviet Union

Recall What were the goals of Stalin's Five-Year Plans? *modernize Soviet economy, increase Soviet industrial output*

Contrast How do capitalism and central planning differ? *capitalism: market forces influence production; central planning: government controls production of goods*

Quick Facts Transparency: Common Features of Totalitarian Governments

CRF: Biography: Haile Selassie

Common Features of Totalitarian Governments

QUICK FACTS

Examples of totalitarian governments include Italy under Mussolini, the Soviet Union under Stalin, and Germany under Hitler. These governments shared many common features.

Political
- The state is more important than individuals.
- The government is controlled by a single political party.
- A powerful dictator unites the people and symbolizes the government.

Social
- The government controls all aspects of daily life.
- Secret police use terror and violence to enforce government policies.
- Citizens are denied basic rights and liberties.

Economic
- The government controls businesses and directs the national economy.
- Labor and business are used to fulfill the objectives of the state.

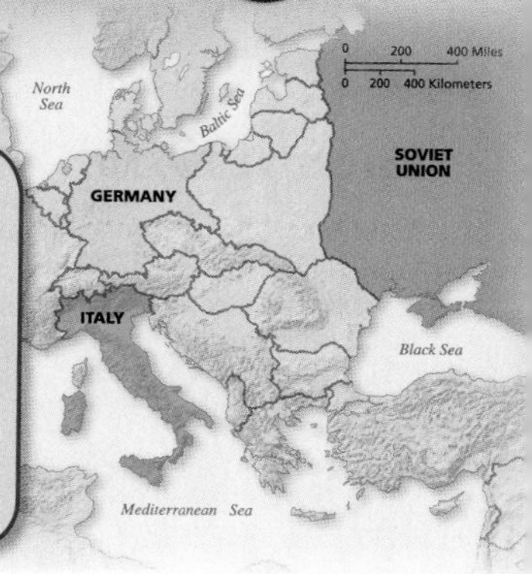

Once in power, Mussolini moved to establish a dictatorship. Using threats, violence, and his political skill, he had soon outlawed all opposition and taken unlimited power.

Fascist Italy Mussolini was not satisfied merely with political control. He tried to influence Italians' thoughts, feelings, and behaviors. The attempt by a government to control all aspects of life is called **totalitarianism**.

Mussolini's totalitarian program had many parts. Two of the most effective parts of this program were his use of propaganda to promote Italy's greatness and his establishment of festivals and holidays that reminded modern Italians of their proud Roman heritage.

The Invasion of Ethiopia Mussolini set out to make Italy a strong military power. To that end, he looked around for an easy target and spotted Ethiopia. Ethiopia had two serious disadvantages. It was located between two Italian colonies and its military was ill-equipped. Italian forces crushed the Ethiopians in 1935.

Ethiopian leader Haile Selassie (HY-lee suh-LA-see) appealed to the League of Nations to take action against Italy's aggression. Although much of the world condemned Italy's attack, no nation was willing to get involved and risk another world war. The League placed some economic sanctions on Italy but took no real action.

READING CHECK **Identify the Main Idea** How did Mussolini rule Italy?

READING SKILLS
Understanding Comparison and Contrast How did Stalin's approach differ from Marx's prediction?

Stalin's Soviet Union

Soviet leader Vladimir Lenin had died in 1924, shortly after the Communist Soviet Union was formed. After a struggle for power, **Joseph Stalin** became the new Soviet leader.

Communism Under Stalin Although Karl Marx had predicted that the state would gradually wither away under communism, Stalin took a very <u>different</u> approach. Instead of reducing the government's power, he worked to turn the Soviet Union into a totalitarian state, intent on controlling every aspect of Soviet life. Stalin believed this was necessary in order to strengthen communism in the Soviet Union.

The Five-Year Plans A major part of Stalin's plan to strengthen Soviet communism was the modernization of the Soviet economy. In 1928 he began the first Five-Year Plan. Other such plans would follow later. Under the Five-Year Plans, each factory and mine had production goals set by the state.

These plans reflected the Soviet system of central planning, in which the government makes major decisions about the production of goods. Central planning differs from a capitalist economic system, such as that of the United States. In capitalism, market forces are the major influence on production.

The Five-Year Plans did, as Stalin had hoped, lead to increases in Soviet industrial output. During the first two Five-Year Plans, for example, Soviet production of oil more

Skills Focus: Comparing and Contrasting

At Level

Reading Skill
Comparing Empire Builders

1. Remind students about the empire builders and dictators of other nations and time periods they have studied. Have students create a class list for all to see. Students may wish to refer to their texts to create the list.
2. Organize students into small groups. Have each group pick one leader from this section and one from the past. Have students use their texts to review the ways in which each leader built his empire.
3. Have groups make a list of factual comparisons between the two leaders. Then have each group form a closing generalization statement about the similarities and differences between the two.
4. Have volunteers from each group present their comparisons to the rest of the class.

LS Interpersonal, Verbal-Linguistic

Alternative Assessment Handbook, Rubrics 9: Comparing and Contrasting; and 24: Oral Presentations

Answers

Reading Check *with unlimited power; totalitarianism*

Reading Skills *Marx predicted the state would wither away, but Stalin increased government control.*

than doubled, while coal and steel production quadrupled. The demands placed on Soviet workers, however, were high.

Collectivization and Famine Stalin also wanted to increase Soviet farm input. He believed that the millions of small, individually owned Soviet farms would be more productive if they were combined to form larger, mechanized farms. This combining of small farms was called collectivization.

After the Russian Revolution, one of Lenin's first acts had been to give land to Russian peasants. Now Stalin tried to take that land back. When peasants resisted, Stalin responded violently. Stalin's forces executed thousands and sent many more to a remote and frigid region of the Soviet Union called Siberia. In Siberia these Soviets worked—and often died—in a system of labor camps called the **Gulag**.

Still, resistance to collectivization continued. One center of this resistance was the republic of Ukraine (yoo-KRAYN). To punish the Ukrainians, Stalin refused to send food to aid them when a famine struck the region in 1932. Millions of Ukrainians starved to death.

Political Purges By the mid-1930s Stalin had absolute power, but he still feared that people were plotting against him. In response, he began a campaign known as the Great Purge, or the Great Terror. To purge is to get rid of people or things considered undesirable. In a series of purges, Stalin attacked real and imagined opponents of his rule. Thousands of Communist leaders, military officers, and ordinary citizens were executed or sent to the Gulag.

Totalitarian Rule Stalin's regime dominated Soviet life. Children were encouraged to join youth organizations where they were taught the attitudes and beliefs that Soviet leaders wanted them to have. Religion was discouraged, and many churches were closed.

All across Russia, portraits of Stalin decorated public places, creating a heroic and idealized image of the Soviet leader. Streets and towns were renamed in his honor. By promoting this cult of personality and ruthlessly removing any opposition, Stalin gained a stranglehold over Soviet society.

READING CHECK **Summarize** How did Stalin use fear and violence to rule the Soviet Union?

Soviet leader Joseph Stalin delivers a speech at a rally. ▶

PRIMARY SOURCES

Stalin's Five-Year Plan

In January 1933, Joseph Stalin delivered this report on the results of the first Five-Year Plan.

"What is the five-year plan? . . .

"The fundamental task of the five-year plan was to transfer our country, with its backward . . . technology, on to the lines of new, modern technology.

"The fundamental task of the five-year plan was to convert the U.S.S.R. [Soviet Union] from an agrarian and weak country . . . into an industrial and powerful country.

"The fundamental task of the five-year plan was . . . to ensure the economic basis of socialism in the countryside and thus to eliminate the possibility of the restoration of capitalism in the U.S.S.R.

"Finally, the task of the five-year plan was to create all the necessary technical and economic prerequisites for increasing to the utmost the defensive capacity of the country, enabling it to organize determined resistance to any attempt at military intervention from abroad, to any attempt at military attack from abroad."

Skills Focus READING LIKE A HISTORIAN

1. **Summarize** What was the Five-Year Plan?
2. **Analyze Primary Sources** In the last paragraph, what does Stalin seem to be worried about? Why might this be?

See **Skills Handbook**, p. H25

Direct Teach

Reading Focus

Stalin's Soviet Union

Explain What led to the starvation of Ukranian peasants in 1932? *They resisted collectivization, so Stalin refused to send food when famine struck the region.*

Contrast How did the farm ownership actions of Lenin and Stalin differ? *Lenin gave land to peasants; Stalin took the land back and placed it under government control.*

Make Inferences Why was Stalin determined to influence the attitudes and behavior of the Russian people? *possible answers—He was obsessed with power. He feared opposition.*

Info to Know

Joseph Stalin When Stalin was only ten years old, his father died, leaving his illiterate mother to raise him alone. He was awarded a scholarship and attended the Orthodox theological seminary from his early teen years until he was expelled five years later, about the time he became involved with a group that spread nationalistic and socialistic ideas in Georgia. Though Stalin eventually turned against his church, his religious background influenced his speeches.

Skills Focus: Analyzing Primary Sources

At Level

Research Required

Reading Like a Historian Skill

Five-Year Plans

1. Have students review the Primary Sources feature, Stalin's Five-Year Plan. Guide students in a discussion of the excerpt to help ensure that all students understand it.
2. Have students conduct outside research using reliable print and Internet sources on the effectiveness of Stalin's Five-Year Plans and their effect on the Soviet economy. Students should try to find one article that defends the plans and one article that criticizes their effects on the Soviet economy and people.
3. Have students write an essay summarizing the two documents and explaining any bias they believe the authors might have.

Alternative Assessment Handbook, Rubrics 30: Research; and 42: Writing to Inform

Answers

Primary Sources 1. *a plan to modernize the Soviet Union in terms of its economy and its military;* **2.** *military attack from abroad; because the country had recently faced attack in World War I*

Reading Check *executed those who resisted him; sent opponents to Siberia to work in labor camps*

Direct Teach

Reading Focus

3 How did Adolf Hitler rule Germany? *used fear, violence, and propaganda to maintain power*

Hitler's Germany

Explain What does *Mein Kampf* reveal about Hitler? *describes his major political ideas and his belief in racial superiority of the German people*

Identify Cause and Effect What led to the growth of the Nazi Party? *The message of restoring German greatness appealed to Germans who wanted a strong leader to help solve Germany's problems.*

Biography

René Magritte (1898–1967) Belgian surrealist painter René Magritte served in the military at the close of World War I. The images left in his mind were likely things he would rather have forgotten, so it isn't surprising to see idealized or otherworldly objects appear in his paintings. Clever compositions, such as one with an eye served on a plate, compel viewers to closely examine his unusual work.

Info to Know

The Weimar Republic The failure of Germany's democratic postwar government was brought on by many complex issues. The average German was unaware of the enormous spending during the war and tended to blame the country's economic condition on its leadership. The Weimar Republic had to triple the taxes it imposed on citizens in order to pay off war debts, to help pay for social services, and to pay the reparations agreed to in the Versailles Treaty.

Answers

Faces of History *possible answer—Germany had suffered a humiliating defeat in World War I, followed by years of economic trouble. Hitler's message of German greatness probably appealed to Germans who were suffering.*

Hitler's Germany

Germany underwent great changes after World War I. Like Mussolini and Stalin, Germany's **Adolf Hitler** rose to power during a time of conflict and political instability.

Postwar Germany After World War I, Germany formed a new republican government known as the Weimar (VY-mahr) Republic. This government was extremely unpopular among Germans, who blamed it for the humiliating Versailles treaty and for the economic problems that overwhelmed Germany after the war. Inflation soared in Germany in the early 1920s, and the German mark became virtually worthless. Many Germans saw their savings wiped out. Although an economic recovery began in the late 1920s, the Great Depression soon brought even more political and economic chaos to Germany.

Hitler's Early Career Adolf Hitler, born in Austria in 1889, served in the German army during World War I. In the chaos of postwar Germany, he became involved with a group of right-wing extremists and soon joined the Nationalist Socialist Party, or **Nazi Party**.

THE IMPACT TODAY
The Nazi Party has been outlawed in Germany since the end of World War II. Still, extremist Neo-Nazi groups that hold racist or anti-Semitic beliefs exist today in Germany, the United States, and other nations.

With the Nazis, Hitler discovered that he had a talent for public speaking and leadership. He soon became a key figure in the party, but he wanted greater power. In October 1923 he led an attempt to overthrow Germany's government. The effort failed, and Hitler received a short prison term. While in prison, he wrote a book titled *Mein Kampf*—German for "My Struggle." The book described Hitler's major political ideas, including nationalism and the racial superiority of the German people, whom he called Aryans.

Hitler Gains Power After Hitler was released from prison, he continued to work to gain power. The economic effects of the Great Depression helped his cause, as the German people were desperate for a strong leader who would improve their lives. Hitler promised to rebuild Germany's military. He spoke of a mighty German empire and said that Germans were the "master race." His claims about German greatness won the Nazi Party many new supporters who wanted to believe that his words were true.

Through Hitler's efforts the Nazis continued to gain strength in the early 1930s. They became the most popular of Germany's many political parties. As a result, in 1933 Hitler was appointed to the position of chancellor, the most powerful post in the German government.

Hitler Controls Germany Once in power, Hitler began to crush his opposition. Many of his opponents were arrested; others were intimidated by Nazi thugs. By these means, Hitler bullied the German legislature into giving him dictatorial powers.

Increasingly, Hitler's rule took the form of a totalitarian regime. Nazi propaganda built up a cult of personality glorifying Hitler as the Führer (FYOOR-uhr), or "leader." Nazi youth organizations shaped the minds of young Germans, who pledged complete loyalty to Hitler and Germany.

Hitler began to rebuild the German military and improve the German economy. Strict wage controls and massive government spending on public works programs helped reduce unemployment. Much of the spending was for the rearmament of the German military, although it also included the construction of new public buildings and roads.

Nazi Anti-Semitism A key component of the Nazi system was strong anti-Semitic beliefs. **Anti-Semitism** is hostility toward or prejudice against Jews. Hitler blamed Jews for many of Germany's problems, including its defeat in World War I.

FACES OF HISTORY
Adolf HITLER
1889–1945

After Germany's humiliating defeat in World War I, a soldier named Adolf Hitler vowed to rebuild a German empire. After the war ended he became active in a small German political party.

A master of propaganda and a stirring public speaker, Hitler soon became known for his attacks on the Treaty of Versailles, Communists, Jews, and anyone or anything else he believed to be a threat to German greatness. Twisting facts to suit his purposes, Hitler used German anger over World War I and the economic effects of the Great Depression to convince Germans that he would restore their nation to glory.

Infer Why do you think so many Germans found Hitler's ideas appealing in the years after World War I?

Skills Focus: Making Generalizations

At Level

Prep Required

Reading Skill

The Nuremberg Laws

1. Obtain copies of one or more of the Nuremberg Laws and read the laws to the class. Then review the information in the text about the Nuremberg Laws. Guide students in a discussion of its effects on Jewish citizens of Germany.
2. Have students write letters to the editor of a newspaper protesting the new laws. In their letters students should explain why these laws are unjust and discriminatory.
3. Have students share their letters with the class. **LS Verbal-Linguistic**

Alternative Assessment Handbook, Rubric 17: Letters to Editors

Anti-Semitism had a long history in largely Christian Europe. In fact, Christian hostility toward Jews had existed since the Middle Ages. Nazi anti-Semitism combined this religious hostility with modern—and false—beliefs that Jews were a separate race. Under the Nazis, anti-Semitism combined prejudice based on religion with hatred based on ancestry.

During the 1930s Hitler's Nazi government passed many laws aimed at excluding Jews from mainstream German life. They prohibited Jews from marrying Germans. In 1935 the **Nuremberg Laws** created a separate legal status for German Jews, eliminating their citizenship and many civil and property rights, such as the right to vote. Jews' right to work in certain jobs was limited. The Nuremberg Laws defined a person as Jewish based on the ancestry of grandparents—not religious beliefs.

The Nazis also mounted more direct attacks. On the nights of November 9 and 10, 1938, they encouraged anti-Jewish riots across Germany and Austria. This attack came to be known as **Kristallnacht** (KRIS-tahl-nahkt), or the Night of Broken Glass. During the riots, nearly 100 Jews were killed, and thousands of Jewish businesses and places of worship were damaged and destroyed. Yet as terrifying as this anti-Jewish violence and destruction were, greater horrors were yet to come. Indeed, Hitler's Germany was about to lead the world into history's bloodiest war.

READING CHECK **Analyze** How did Hitler's anti-Semitism affect the way he ruled Germany?

The Nuremberg Rallies

Under Adolf Hitler, the Nazi Party staged enormous public rallies in Nuremberg, Germany, during the 1930s. At the rallies, hundreds of thousands of Germans listened to pro-Nazi speeches and took part in parades and demonstrations.

SECTION 4 ASSESSMENT

go.hrw.com
Online Quiz
Keyword: SHL IWY HP

Reviewing Key Terms and People

1. **a. Describe** How did **Benito Mussolini** use **fascism** and **totalitarianism** to rule Italy?
   b. Sequence Trace the major steps in Mussolini's rise to power in Italy.
2. **a. Recall** What steps did **Joseph Stalin** take to try to modernize the Soviet economy?
   b. Make Generalizations How did Stalin respond to public or internal opposition?
3. **a. Identify** Identify the following: **Nazi Party**, **Nuremberg Laws**, and **Kristallnacht**.
   b. Develop How did economic and political conditions in postwar Germany contribute to **Adolf Hitler's** rise to power?

Critical Thinking

4. **Make Generalizations** Using your notes on the section, compare and contrast the ways that Mussolini, Stalin, and Hitler rose to power and kept power.

	Mussolini	Stalin	Hitler
Rise to power			
Methods used to keep power			

FOCUS ON WRITING

5. **Description** Write a journal entry that a Soviet citizen might have written in the 1930s describing daily life in the Soviet Union under Stalin.

Direct Teach

Reading Focus

Hitler's Germany

Recall What is anti-Semitism? *hostility toward or prejudice against Jews*

Analyze Why is Kristallnacht remembered as a significant event? *signifies the beginning of Nazi violence against Jews*

Review & Assess

Close

Have students compare and contrast the totalitarian dictatorships of Mussolini, Stalin, and Hitler.

Review

go.hrw.com **Online Quiz**, Section 4

Assess

SE Section 4 Assessment

Progress Assessment: Section 4 Quiz

Alternative Assessment Handbook

Reteach/Intervene

Interactive Reader and Study Guide, Section 4

Interactive Skills Tutor CD-ROM

Answers

Reading Check *Anti-Semitism led to the Nuremberg Laws, riots, and direct attacks on Jews.*

Section 4 Assessment Answers

1. **a.** tried to control Italians' thoughts, feelings, and behaviors; used threats and violence
   b. March on Rome; king placed Mussolini at head of Italy's parliamentary government; used violence, political skills to establish a dictatorship
2. **a.** set up Five-Year Plans; set production goals; collectivized farms
   b. with violence; people were exiled to labor camps in Siberia, starved, executed, and imprisoned
3. **a.** Nazi Party—the National Socialist Party that gave Hitler his start; Nuremberg Laws—anti-Semitic laws passed in 1935; Kristallnacht—anti-Jewish riots resulting in the death of nearly 100 Jews and damage to thousands of Jewish businesses and places of worship
   b. possible answer— German people wanted change, end to economic problems, hoped for a strong empire
4. Mussolini—1922; used political skill, threats, violence, and propaganda; outlawed all opposition; Stalin—1924; used fear, violence, propaganda, purged opponents; Hitler—1933; used political skill, fear, violence, crushed his opposition, used propaganda; passed anti-Semitic laws; all came to power in post-war economic depression
5. Student letters should include details from the section about daily life under Stalin.

Document-Based Investigation

Nationalism in India and Germany

Word Help

perpetuate to cause to last indefinitely

diplomacy negotiations between nations

Activity Analyzing Primary Sources Have students volunteer information they can infer from the photograph of the Salt March. Ask students what questions they might ask to determine what this photograph represents.

Info to Know

Mohandas Gandhi Gandhi lived in South Africa for a number of years, where he led protests against government discrimination toward Indians, a struggle that lasted for more than seven years. After his return to India, Gandhi began to lead protests there; some critics charged that he was moving too quickly; others said he moved too slowly. Today, most agree that Gandhi was a great mediator who was able to reconcile the interests and beliefs of many different groups.

CHAPTER 13 Document-Based Investigation

Nationalism in India and Germany

Historical Context The documents below provide information about the rise of different forms of nationalism in India and Germany during the early 1900s.

Task Examine the documents and answer the questions that follow. After you have studied all the documents, you will be asked to write an essay about different responses to the rise of nationalism during the early 1900s. You will need to use evidence from these selections and from the chapter to support the position you take in your essay.

DOCUMENT 1

The Salt March

In 1930 Indian nationalist leader Mohandas Gandhi led the so-called Salt March as a peaceful protest against the British rule of India. The British arrested some 60,000 Indians during the protest, which drew worldwide attention and helped advance Indian efforts for independence. In this photograph, Gandhi is the fourth person from the left.

DOCUMENT 2

Gandhi's Philosophy

During a visit to Great Britain in 1931 as part of his efforts to win independence for India, Gandhi gave this speech on an American radio station. The following passage describes the Indian independence movement.

> India is by itself almost a continent. It contains one-fifth of the human race. It represents one of the most ancient civilizations. It has traditions handed down from tens of thousands of years, some of which, to the astonishment of the world, remain intact. If India is to perpetuate the glory of her ancient past, it can do so only when it attains freedom. The reason for the struggle having drawn the attention of the world, I know does not lie in the fact that we Indians are fighting for our liberty, but in the fact that the means adopted by us for attaining that liberty are unique and, as far as history shows us, have not been adopted by any other people of whom we have any record. The means adopted are not violence, not bloodshed, not diplomacy as one understands it nowadays, but they are purely and simply truth and non-violence. No wonder that the attention of the world is directed towards this attempt to lead a successful, bloodless revolution.

Skills Focus: Recognizing Bias in Primary Sources

At Level

Reading Like a Historian Skill

The Other View

1. Remind students that historical documents often show clear bias when they are analyzed today. Have students carefully review Documents 2, 3, and 4.
2. Have students identify statements that exhibit bias. Have students write these statements onto their own papers, and then write down their reactions to these statements.
3. Organize students into mixed-ability pairs. Have pairs write an unbiased statement that corresponds to each biased statement on their lists. Have each pair share its biased and unbiased statements, as well as its reaction to the biased statements with the class.

LS **Interpersonal, Verbal-Linguistic**

Alternative Assessment Handbook, Rubric 16: Judging Information

DOCUMENT 3

The Nazi Party's Goals

In a speech in 1920, Germany's Adolf Hitler outlined the Twenty Five Points of the Nazi Party, which summarized Nazi goals. Selected points are listed below.

1. We demand the union of all Germans in a Great Germany on the basis of the principle of self-determination of all peoples . . .

3. We demand land and territory (colonies) for the maintenance of our people and the settlement of our surplus population.

4. Only those who are our fellow countrymen can become citizens. Only those who have German blood, regardless of creed, can be our countrymen. Hence no Jew can be a countryman . . .

7. We demand that the State shall above all undertake to ensure that every citizen shall have the possibility of living decently and earning a livelihood. If it should not be possible to feed the whole population, then aliens (non-citizens) must be expelled from the Reich.

8. Any further immigration of non-Germans must be prevented. We demand that all non-Germans who have entered Germany since August 2, 1914, shall be compelled to leave the Reich immediately.

DOCUMENT 4

Nationalism in Germany

Hitler gave this speech at a Nazi rally in Nuremberg, Germany, in 1927.

Our fellow party member . . . began his speech by saying that it is critical for a nation that its territory correspond to its population. As he put it so well: 'The nation needs space' . . . The question confronts us today as insistently as ever: No government, of whatever kind, can long escape dealing with it. Feeding a nation of 62 million means not only maintaining our agricultural productivity, but enlarging it to meet the needs of a growing population . . .

The first way to satisfy this need, the adjustment of territory to population, is the most natural, healthy and long-lasting . . .

If a nation today proclaims the theory that it will find happiness in lasting peace, and attempts to live according to that theory, it will one day inevitably succumb to this most basic form of cowardice. Pacifism is the clearest form of cowardice, possessing no willingness to fight for anything at all . . .

62 million people have an impossible amount of land. There are 20 million 'too many.' This nation cannot survive in the long term. It must find a way out.

Skills FOCUS READING LIKE A HISTORIAN

DOCUMENT 1

a. Describe According to this photograph, was the Salt March a peaceful protest or a violent one?

b. Analyze What does this photograph tell you about the type of people on the Salt March and their behavior?

DOCUMENT 2

a. Identify What means does Gandhi say are being used by Indians in their struggle for independence?

b. Contrast How are these means different from those used in other struggles for independence?

DOCUMENT 3

a. Make Generalizations How does this document suggest that non-Germans be treated?

b. Summarize How does this document express an aggressive form of nationalism?

DOCUMENT 4

a. Identify What does Hitler believe that Germany must do in order to survive?

b. Compare and Contrast How does Hitler's opinion about peace differ from the belief that Gandhi expresses in Document 2?

DOCUMENT-BASED ESSAY QUESTION

How and why did expressions of nationalism differ in Gandhi's India and Hitler's Germany? Using the documents above and information from the chapter, form a thesis that supports your position. Then write a short essay to support your position.

See **Skills Handbook**, pp. H25, H26

Skills Focus: Identifying Problem and Solution — At Level

Reading Like a Historian Skill
Overpopulation Solutions

1. Tell students that in recent years many people have come to believe that the world is becoming crowded and overpopulated, the same problem that brought about the impassioned speeches presented in Documents 3 and 4.
2. Organize students into small groups. Have each group devise a logical plan to address the problem of crowding and then prepare a speech discussing its solution and persuading others that this is the best course of action. Allow time for students to rehearse their speeches.
3. When students are ready, have the presenters deliver speeches.
4. As an extension, have students write a paragraph expressing support for the solution they feel would work best. **LS Interpersonal, Verbal-Linguistic**

Alternative Assessment Handbook, Rubrics 11: Discussions; and 24: Oral Presentations

Document-Based Investigation

Word Help

creed set of beliefs or guiding principles

pacifism nonresistance or nonviolence in settling disputes

succumb give in, yield to an overpowering appeal or desire

Info to Know

The Nuremberg Trials The city of Nuremberg, Germany was the site of many Nazi rallies during the 1930s. After World War II, it also became the site of the historic Nuremberg Trials, in which Allied Powers put Nazi war criminals on trial for killing more than 6 million Jews and 5 million other Europeans during the war. The Nuremberg Trials sentenced many Nazi leaders to death for their actions, showing that military orders from superiors are not a valid reason for committing war crimes. This marked the first war crimes trial in modern history.

Answers

Reading Like a Historian

Document 1. a. *a peaceful protest;* **b.** *they appear patient and nonviolent;* **Document 2. a.** *truth and nonviolence;* **b.** *Other struggles use violence, bloodshed, and diplomacy.* **Document 3. a.** *The document suggests that non-Germans should be denied citizenship, and expelled from the country if there is ever not enough food. Furthermore, it states that non-Germans should not be allowed to enter Germany, and that any non-German who entered after a certain date should be expelled.* **b.** *It bases nationalism on heritage and discriminates against anyone without "German blood."* **Document 4. a.** *fight for more territory;* **b.** *Hitler—believed peace is a form of cowardice, which shows lack of purpose; Gandhi—believed non-violence is the best form of revolution;* **Essay** *Student essays should show an understanding of different views of nationalism and should include information from each of the four documents.*

Answers

Visual Summary

Review and Inquiry Organize students into three groups. Have each group create a poster depicting information about one of the following topics: Causes and Effects of the Great Depression, Japanese Imperialism, and Growing Nationalism and Aggression.

Quick Facts Transparency: Visual Study Guide: The Interwar Years

Review Key Terms and People

1. Kemal Atatürk, or Kemal Mustafa
2. Smoot-Hawley Tariff Act
3. Gulag
4. Manchurian Incident
5. Mohandas Gandhi
6. Joseph Stalin
7. Anti-Comintern Pact
8. Mao Zedong
9. National Socialist Party, also known as the Nazi Party
10. New Deal
11. prosperity

Comprehension and Critical Thinking

12. a. Jiang Jieshi—leader of the Chinese nationalist Guomindang party; Mao Zedong—Chinese Communist party leader who led Communists on the Long March
b. In each area, nationalism led to desire for independence.
c. possible answer—Gandhi's nonviolent actions and acts of civil disobedience required patience, but they increased sympathy for the cause and harmed no one.

13. a. The economy was booming, unemployment was low, and the stock market was climbing steadily.
b. It caused other nations to increase tariffs on American goods, which brought world trade to a standstill.
c. possible answer—Yes, people wanted quick changes, and the democratically elected leaders who were in office often could not make quick, drastic changes so they turned to dictators for help.

CHAPTER 13

Chapter Review

QUICK FACTS

VISUAL STUDY GUIDE

Causes

- U.S. economic growth in the 1920s hides serious problems in the economy.
- Speculation in the U.S. stock market drives up prices
- U.S. stock market crashes in October 1929.
- Crash devastates U.S. businesses, investors, and banks.
- Economic crisis begins to spread around the world.

Great Depression

Effects

- In Europe, countries still struggling to recover from World War I are hit hard by the Depression.
- World trade slows and national economies are crippled.
- Political unrest grows.
- In some countries, extremist political groups and totalitarian leaders take power.

Growing Japanese Aggression

- Social and economic changes in Japan lead many Japanese people to lose faith in their government.
- Nationalist military leaders gradually take control of Japan's government.
- Japan begins to pursue aggressive, expansionist policies.
- Japan invades Manchuria in 1931.
- War with China begins in 1937, leading to the Nanjing Massacre. Japan looks elsewhere for the natural resources needed to supply its war machine.

Growing Nationalism and Aggression

1917 ▪ In the Balfour Declaration, Britain announces its support for a Jewish state

1919 ▪ China's nationalist May Fourth Movement begins

1920 ▪ Mohandas Gandhi begins boycott of British products

1921 ▪ Reza Khan overthrows Persia's shah
▪ China's Communist Party formed

1922 ▪ Benito Mussolini takes power in Italy
▪ Egypt gains independence

1923 ▪ Republic of Turkey formed
▪ Adolf Hitler tries to overthrow German government

1924 ▪ Joseph Stalin begins to take power in the Soviet Union

1927 ▪ Stalin announces first Five-Year Plan

1931 ▪ Japan takes control of Manchuria

1933 ▪ Hitler becomes chancellor of Germany

1935 ▪ Italy invades Ethiopia
▪ Germany's Nazi government passes anti-Semitic Nuremberg Laws
▪ Chinese Communist Party finishes the Long March

1937 ▪ Japan begins war with China

Review Key Terms and People

Identify the correct person or term from the chapter that best fits each of the following descriptions.

1. Founder of modern Turkey
2. Action by U.S. government during the Great Depression that led to a drop in world trade
3. Soviet system of prison camps
4. Japanese plot to take over part of China
5. Leader who used nonviolence and civil disobedience in struggle for Indian independence
6. Totalitarian leader of the Soviet Union
7. 1930s agreement between Japan and Germany
8. Leader of Chinese Communists
9. Adolf Hitler's political party
10. Franklin Roosevelt's response to the Depression
11. Wealth or success

432 CHAPTER 13

14. a. Japan stood as one of the world's foremost powers, but began to have economic problems.
b. The military grew dissatisfied with the civilian government because of its foreign policy, especially treaties with the west that limited the size of Japan's navy.
c. possible answer—Japan effectively compensated for its lack of industrial power by encouraging a fighting spirit.

15. a. a leader who has complete political control, and also seeks to influence the thoughts, feelings, and behaviors of the people
b. similar—totalitarian dictators who used threats, violence and propaganda to control and influence their people; different—Hitler and Stalin encouraged the cult of personality; Hitler won the appointment of German chancellor; Mussolini used show of force to convince king to place him at head of government
c. possible answer—Citizens are somewhat responsible for the rise of dictators, especially when dictators replace democratic leaders. They might believe a change in leadership, no matter how aggressive, can fix a country's problems.

History's Impact video program

Review the video to answer the closing question: How do changes made after the 1929 stock market crash help protect the American economy today?

Comprehension and Critical Thinking

SECTION 1 *(pp. 409–413)*

12. a. Identify Who were Jiang Jieshi and Mao Zedong?

b. Compare How were China, India, Middle Eastern countries, and African countries similar in their reaction to the aftermath of World War I?

c. Evaluate What were the strengths and weaknesses in Gandhi's methods for seeking independence in India?

SECTION 2 *(pp. 414–418)*

13. a. Describe What was the state of the American economy throughout most of the 1920s?

b. Explain Why did the Smoot-Hawley Tariff Act have such a dramatic effect on trade?

c. Evaluate Do you think the effects of the Great Depression were the main cause of the rise of dictators? Why or why not?

SECTION 3 *(pp. 420–424)*

14. a. Recall What was Japan's position in the world after World War I?

b. Summarize Why was the Japanese military growing increasingly dissatisfied with Japan's civilian government in the 1920s?

c. Make Judgments What do you think of the Japanese military's commitment to the notion of fighting spirit as a key weapon? Why?

SECTION 4 *(pp. 425–429)*

15. a. Describe What is a totalitarian dictator?

b. Compare and Contrast In what ways were Mussolini, Stalin, and Hitler similar and different?

c. Evaluate To what extent were the citizens of Italy, the Soviet Union, and Germany responsible for the rise of Mussolini, Stalin, and Hitler?

Reading Skills

Understanding Comparison and Contrast *Use what you know about understanding comparison and contrast to answer the questions below.*

16. How were Arab and Jewish responses to postwar mandates similar and different?

17. Did the Great Depression affect the United States and Europe in similar ways? Explain your answer.

Recognizing Bias in Secondary Sources

Reading Like a Historian

"The two lines of Chinese soldiers defended either side of the railroad bridge. Facing hundreds of Japanese attackers, they were not cowed in the least, and they engaged in intense hand-to-hand fights with [the] enemies. Nearly all of them died at the end of the battle of the bridge. Seeing their comrades fall in the battle, other soldiers, without showing too much sorrow, clenched their teeth. They fought forward. Even the wounded who were ordered to retreat were still charging ahead."

—From a Chinese history textbook

18. Explain How does this excerpt demonstrate bias? What words or phrases show bias?

19. Infer How might a Japanese textbook describe this battle differently?

Using the Internet

go.hrw.com
Practice Online
Keyword: SHL IWY

20. Although Adolf Hitler and Joseph Stalin shared some characteristics in the way they ruled their nations, there are also important differences between the two. Using the Internet, research how Hitler and Stalin led their countries. Then write a detailed report that compares and contrasts the two leaders. Be sure to include information about how each person rose to power, as well as how each used that power to control his country. You may wish to discuss each leader's goals for his nation, as well as his use of propaganda, threats, and secret police to maintain power.

WRITING FOR THE SAT

Think about the following issue:

In the 1920s and 1930s the Japanese military gradually took control of Japan's civilian government. The military's aggressive nationalism became increasingly popular with the Japanese public, but expansion in Asia in the early 1930s led to a costly war with China.

21. Assignment: Why did the Japanese people support their military's aggressive actions? Write a short essay in which you develop your position on this issue. Support your point of view with reasoning and examples from your reading and studies.

Answers

Reading Skills

16. both disliked mandates; Jews accepted UN plan, Arabs rejected it

17. No, for Europe, the Great Depression was just the latest in a series of economic crises.

Recognizing Bias in Secondary Sources

18. depicts Chinese soldiers as brave; "not cowed in the least;" "without showing too much sorrow"

19. possible answer—might emphasize bravery of Japanese soldiers

Using the Internet

20. Go to the HRW Web site and enter the keyword shown to access a rubric for this activity.

KEYWORD: SHL IWY

Writing for the SAT

21. Student essays might discuss the need for an improved farming economy, as the United States might become dependent upon other nations for its food supply.
A rubric for the activity is provided in **CRF:** Writing for the SAT..

HOLT
History's Impact
► **Video Program: The Interwar Years**
See to the Video Program Teacher's Guide for the answer to the closing question.

Review and Assessment Resources

Review and Reinforce

- **CRF:** Chapter Review
- **Quick Facts Transparency:** Visual Study Guide: The Interwar Years
- **Spanish Chapter Summaries Audio CD Program**
- OSP **Holt PuzzlePro:** Quiz Show for ExamView
- **Quiz Game CD-ROM**

Assess

- **PASS:** Chapter Test, Forms A and B
- **Alternative Assessment Handbook**
- OSP **ExamView Test Generator**, Chapter Test
- **Differentiated Instruction Modified Worksheets and Tests CD-ROM:** Chapter Test
- HOAP **Holt Online Assessment Program** (in the Premier Online Edition)

Reteach/Intervene

- **Interactive Reader and Study Guide**
- **Differentiated Instruction Teacher Management System:** Lesson Plans for Differentiated Instruction
- **Differentiated Instruction Modified Worksheets and Tests CD-ROM:** Chapter Test
- **Interactive Skills Tutor CD-ROM**

go.hrw.com
Online Resources
KEYWORD: SHL TEACHER

Chapter 14 Planning Guide

World War II

Chapter Overview	Reproducible Resources	Technology Resources
CHAPTER 14 **pp. 434–469** **Overview: In this chapter, students will learn about events that led up to World War II, the battles involving the Allies and Axis Powers, and the war's effects.**	**Differentiated Instruction Teacher Management System:*** • Pacing Guide • Lesson Plans for Differentiated Instruction **Interactive Reader and Study Guide:** Chapter Summary* **Chapter Resource File*** • Writing for the SAT • Social Studies Skill • Chapter Review **World History Outline Maps**	**Live Ink© Online Reading Help** **Student Edition on Audio CD Program** **Differentiated Instruction Modified Worksheets and Tests CD-ROM** **World History Primary Source Library CD-ROM** **Power Presentations with Video CD-ROM** **History's Impact: World History Video Program (VHS/DVD):** World War II
Section 1: **Axis Aggression** **The Main Idea:** While Hitler became increasingly aggressive in the late 1930s, other leaders sought to appease him. The effort backfired and led to the outbreak of World War II.	**Differentiated Instruction Teacher Management System:** Section 1 Lesson Plan* **Interactive Reader and Study Guide:** Section 1 Summary* **Chapter Resource File*** • Vocabulary Builder: Section 1 • Biography: Queen Elizabeth • Primary Source: The Atlantic Charter	**Daily Test Practice Transparency:** Section 1* **Map Transparency:** Axis Advances, 1939–1941* **Map Transparency:** The London Blitz, 1940*
Section 2: **The Allied Response** **The Main Idea:** The early years of World War II went poorly for the Allies. But after the United States joined the war, the Allies soon recovered and began making gains against the Axis.	**Differentiated Instruction Teacher Management System:** Section 2 Lesson Plan* **Interactive Reader and Study Guide:** Section 2 Summary* **Chapter Resource File*** • Vocabulary Builder: Section 2 • Biography: Rosie the Riveter • History and Geography: Japanese Internment Camps	**Daily Test Practice Transparency:** Section 2* **Map Transparency:** World War II in Europe and North Africa, 1941–1943* **Map Transparency:** War in the Pacific, 1942–1944*
Section 3: **The Holocaust** **The Main Idea:** During World War II, Germany's Nazi government murdered some 6 million Jews and 5 million others in Europe. These actions became known as the Holocaust.	**Differentiated Instruction Teacher Management System:** Section 3 Lesson Plan* **Interactive Reader and Study Guide:** Section 3 Summary* **Chapter Resource File*** • Vocabulary Builder: Section 3 • Biography: Raoul Wallenberg	**Daily Test Practice Transparency:** Section 3* **Internet Activity:** Report on Anne Frank
Section 4: **The End of the War** **The Main Idea:** In 1945 the Allies finally triumphed over the Axis Powers in Europe and Asia but the war left many nations in ruins.	**Differentiated Instruction Teacher Management System:** Section 4 Lesson Plan* **Interactive Reader and Study Guide:** Section 4 Summary* **Chapter Resource File*** • Vocabulary Builder: Section 4 • Biography: Harry S Truman	**Daily Test Practice Transparency:** Section 4* **Quick Facts Transparency:** Causes and Effects of World War II* **Map Transparency:** The End of the War, 1944–1945* **Internet Activity:** D-Day

go.hrw.com | Print Resource | Transparency
Learning Styles | Audio CD | CD-ROM
Video | **SE** Student Edition | **TE** Teachers Edition
OSP One-Stop Planner CD-ROM
*also on One-Stop Planner CD-ROM

Review, Assessment, Intervention

- **Quick Facts Transparency:** World War II*
- **Spanish Chapter Summaries Audio CD Program**
- **Program Assessment Support System (PASS):** Chapter Test*
- **Differentiated Instruction Modified Worksheets and Tests CD-ROM:** Modified Chapter Test
- **OSP One-Stop Planner CD-ROM:** ExamView Test Generator (English/Spanish)
- **HOAP Holt Online Assessment Program (HOAP),** in the Holt Premier Online Student Edition

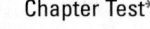

- **PASS:** Section 1 Quiz*
- **Online Quiz:** Section 1
- **Alternative Assessment Handbook**

- **PASS:** Section 2 Quiz*
- **Online Quiz:** Section 2
- **Alternative Assessment Handbook**

- **PASS:** Section 3 Quiz*
- **Online Quiz:** Section 3
- **Alternative Assessment Handbook**

- **PASS:** Section 4 Quiz*
- **Online Quiz:** Section 4
- **Alternative Assessment Handbook**

HOLT
History's Impact
World History Video Program (VHS/DVD)
World War II

Power Presentation with Video CD-ROM

Power Presentations with Video are visual presentations of each chapter's main ideas. Presentations can be customized by including Quick Facts charts, images and maps from the textbook, and video clips.

Holt Online Learning

go.hrw.com
Teacher Resources
KEYWORD: SHL TEACHER

go.hrw.com
Student Resources
KEYWORD: SHL WW2

- Document-Based Questions
- Interactive Multimedia Activities
- Current Events
- Chapter-Based Internet Activities
- and more!

Holt Premier
Online Student Edition

Complete online support for interactivity, assessment, and reporting

- Interactive Maps and Notebook
- Homework Practice and Research Activities Online

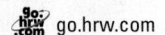

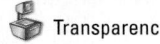

The Big Picture

Peter N. Stearns

The Course of the War Both in Europe and in Asia, the 1930s saw sequences of events that prepared for World War II, provoking inadequate and divided responses from the Western democracies and the Soviet Union. Not surprisingly, the early years of outright war saw key gains by Germany and Japan and their allies—"their finest hour," as Churchill might have put it. In both cases, however, turning points occurred that reversed the tide and brought steady, if gradual, Allied advances until ultimate victory.

Beneath the Surface World War II continued trends visible in World War I—governments' mobilization of labor, materials, and propaganda along with military developments themselves. This was a pattern that has been called total war. More than the previous world war, however, World War II further blurred the distinction between military and civilians with the massive bombardments of civilian populations by all major participants. The first use of nuclear weapons added further innovation to this category. The Holocaust deserves major attention as a particularly horrible offshoot of the war.

Global Patterns The war's settlement was conclusive in some respects, confirming the defeat of the Axis powers, but inconclusive in others given the emerging disputes between the Soviet Union and the United States-led West. The war also should be reviewed in patterns of impact levels. The war and its immediate consequences recast relationships in East and Southeast Asia, and to an extent India as well, setting conditions for further upheaval in China and for rapid decolonization. The same applies to North Africa. Europe was redefined not only by the new Soviet-Western division but also by the realization that a continent of warring nation-states was a recipe for failure. The war was also decisive in Jewish history and in the growth of the government in the United States as well as in United States global power. Ripple effects also apply to Africa, the Middle East and Latin America, though with descending urgency.

Recent Scholarship

Civilians and the War World War II had devastating effects on civilians. A.C. Grayling's *Among the Dead Cities: The History and Moral Legacy of the WWII Bombing of Civilians in Germany and Japan* (2006) deals with crucial aspects of this feature of the war. The treatment is even-handed: Grayling gives careful attention to the arguments of those who pushed for the bombing of cities, including the precedents set by German and Japanese actions. He ultimately contends, however, that the policies were both misguided and unnecessary. This is a challenging global vantage point that can promote constructive debate.

Differentiating Instruction

Differentiated Instruction Teacher Management System
- Pacing Guide
- Lesson Plans for Differentiated Instruction

Interactive Reader and Study Guide

Spanish Chapter Summaries Audio CD Program

Student Edition on Audio CD Program

Differentiated Instruction Modified Worksheets and Tests CD-ROM
- Vocabulary Flash Cards
- Modified Vocabulary Builder Activities
- Modified Chapter Review Activity
- Modified Chapter Test

OSP **One-Stop Planner CD-ROM**
- ExamView Test Generator (English /Spanish)
- PuzzlePro
- Quiz Show for ExamView
- Transparencies and Videos

TE **Differentiated Activities in the Teacher's Edition**
- The Munich Conference, p. 439
- Attack Pearl Harbor, p. 443
- Battles in North Africa, p. 448
- German Invasion of the Soviet Union, p. 450
- The Allied Advance in the Pacific, p. 451
- Illustrating Poetic Images, p. 453
- "Hatred" Essays, p. 453
- Battle of the Bulge, p. 462

Reading Like a Historian

Sam Wineburg

Exhibition Controversy During Fall, 1994, opinion pages of major newspapers raged with arguments for and against a proposed exhibition at the Smithsonian Institution commemorating the fiftieth anniversary of the dropping of the atomic bomb and the end of World War II. The fury unleashed by the proposed exhibit made one thing absolutely clear: while the war might have ended fifty years before, the battle over its meaning continued to rage.

Veterans' groups took offense at the thought that there might be other reasons for dropping the bomb besides bringing the Japanese to a speedy surrender. The mere suggestion, they claimed, disrespected the memory of their fallen comrades. After the museum made some changes in response, a group of professional historians and authors accused the museum of "intellectual corruption" and "historical cleansing," with one author claiming that the Smithsonian had traded historical integrity for "feel-good national myths."

By January 1995, the exhibit was pronounced dead on arrival, gasping its last breath before a single person passed through the turnstiles. Smithsonian secretary I. Michael Heyman, a man who months before spoke about the museum's need to "explore and present the complexities of our subjects," wondered whether the very idea was conceived in error. It had been a mistake, he concluded, to have tried "to couple an historical treatment of the use of atomic weapons with the 50th anniversary commemoration of the end of the war."

Rethinking the Past Can celebration of history be reconciled with its critical evaluation? In his post-mortem on the Smithsonian affair, Pulitzer-prize winning MIT historian John Dower was pessimistic. We celebrate the past in order to cultivate pride in the rightness of "our side" and to deepen the attachment we feel to our cause. On the other hand, according to Dower, to examine the past historically means that we must "use the perspective of time, together with access to previously unavailable materials, to rethink the past." This "rethinking" yields questions and ambiguity. For example, thinking historically pits the commonly accepted belief that the US used the bomb to defeat Japan quickly against interpretations that draw on little-known documents. A government report, first released in 1946, estimated that even without dropping the bomb Japan was ready to capitulate to Allied forces by the end of 1945. Other documents reveal that before the bomb was dropped, military brass already anticipated a post-war power struggle with the USSR. They saw the bomb as a powerful way to warn the Soviets about what awaited them should they fall out of line.

Adding to these factors were domestic pressures on the Truman administration, which had inherited a top-secret and pricey Manhattan Project and needed something to show for it.

Other declassified government documents reveal that the president and his advisors drew on reports drafted by America's top scientists. In a 1945 report, Arthur Compton sounded an argument for using the bomb in order to teach the world a lesson. "If the bomb were not used in the present war the world would have no adequate warning as to what was to be expected if war should break out again."

None of these factors—flexing our muscles before the Soviets, justifying the expenses of the Manhattan Project, or acting as a deterrent for the nations of the world—were immediately tied to bringing the Japanese to a hasty surrender. Neither do they cancel out that reason. All told, we must contend with the thorny fact that complex decisions often have sets of complex causes.

Thinking historically means embracing this complexity, not shrinking from it.

• Chapter Preview •

Chapter Main Ideas

Section 1 While Hitler became increasingly aggressive in the late 1930s, other leaders sought to appease him. The effort backfired and led to the outbreak of World War II.

Section 2 The early years of World War II went poorly for the Allies. But after the United States joined the war, the Allies soon recovered and began making gains against the Axis.

Section 3 During World War II, Germany's Nazi government deliberately murdered some 6 million Jews and 5 million others in Europe. These actions became known as the Holocaust.

Section 4 In 1945 the Allies finally triumphed over the Axis Powers in Europe and Asia, but the war left many nations in ruins.

CHAPTER 14

1930–1945

World War II

Invasion of Italy, by William G. Lawrence, 1943

THE BIG PICTURE The aggression of tyrants in Europe and Asia exploded in another world war in 1939. At first, the Axis armies of Germany, Japan, and Italy gained territory and inflicted great suffering. But after years of conflict, the Allies, led by Great Britain, the United States, and the Soviet Union, prevailed.

Theme SCIENCE AND TECHNOLOGY

The needs of wartime have often resulted in the creation of new weapons, with sometimes terrifying consequences. In this chapter you will learn how the Allies and the Axis Powers used science and technology in their efforts to win World War II.

TIME LINE

CHAPTER EVENTS

- **September 1939** German forces invade Poland, beginning World War II.
- **May 1940** Germany invades France.
- **December 7, 1941** Japan attacks Pearl Harbor, drawing the United States into World War II.
- **The Battle of Stalingrad August 1942–February 1943**
- **June 6, 1944** The Allies storm ashore at Normandy, France, on D-Day.

1939 — 1941 — 1943

WORLD EVENTS

- **August 1940** Former Soviet revolutionary Leon Trotsky is killed in Mexico.
- **August 1942** Gandhi is arrested after calling for Britain to leave India.
- **1943** Penicillin comes into wide use as an antibiotic.

Key to Differentiating Instruction

Below Level

Basic-level activities designed for all students encountering new material

At Level

Intermediate-level activities designed for average students

Above Level

Challenging activities designed for honors and gifted and talented students

Standard English Mastery

Activities designed to improve standard English usage

Introduce the Chapter

At Level

World War II

1. Write the following scenario for students to see: You are an American living in Europe in 1939, at the outbreak of war in Poland. Should you stay and fight, or return home as soon as possible? If you decide to return home, would you try to encourage the United States to enter the war?
2. Give students time to consider the question and lead a class discussion of the scenario and questions. List students' answers for the class to see. Encourage students to explain their reasoning and opinions.
3. Tell students that in this chapter they will learn how the aggression of dictators in Europe and Asia after World War I led to a second world war starting in 1939. LS **Verbal-Linguistic**

Alternative Assessment Handbook, Rubric 11: Discussions

History's Impact video program
Watch the video to understand the impact of World War II.

Reading like a Historian This painting shows the Allied invasion of Italy in 1943—the first major Allied advance into Europe since the beginning of the war.

Analyzing Visuals The man who created this painting was an artist with the United States Coast Guard. What do you think he tried to show in this painting? Explain your answer.

See **Skills Handbook**, p. H26

July 1944 Soviet troops discover an abandoned Nazi death camp.

May 7, 1945 Germany formally surrenders.

August 15, 1945 Japan surrenders after atomic bombs are dropped on Hiroshima and Nagasaki.

1945

1944 The first large automatic computer is developed.

• Chapter Preview •

HOLT
History's Impact
▶ **Video Program: World War II**
See the Video Teacher's Guide for strategies for using the video segment.

Reading Like a Historian

Analyzing Visuals Have students look closely at the image on these pages. Explain to students that there were many bloody battles in World War II, both in Europe and in the Pacific. Ask students what type of warfare this painting captures. *attacks from the air with bombers, by sea with naval warfare, and ground warfare with tanks*

Explore the Time Line

1. What event caused the United States to enter World War II? *Japan attacked Pearl Harbor.*
2. How long did World War II last? *nearly six years*
3. What event occurred on June 6, 1944? *D-Day—Allies stormed ashore at Normandy, France*

Info to Know

Admiral Chester W. Nimitz Late in 1941, U.S. Admiral Chester W. Nimitz was appointed to command the U.S. Pacific fleet. Nimitz was the mastermind behind the complex strategy used in the Pacific known as island hopping, in which U.S. naval and land forces seized one Pacific island after another, advancing closer to Japan.

Make Inferences Why do you think Nimitz planned to seize islands closer and closer to Japan? *possible answer—He wanted islands near Japan as bases for bombing and ultimately invading Japan.*

go.hrw.com
Online Resources
Chapter Resources:
KEYWORD: SHL WW2
Teacher Resources:
KEYWORD: SHL TEACHER

Answers

Reading Like a Historian *possible answer—people storming the beaches, the role of amphibious landing craft and airplanes, the dangerous landing conditions*

Preteach

Geography Starting Points

Roots of Facism The word facism comes from the Italian word *fascio,* which refers to peasant organizations and labor unions. The word is derived from the Latin word *fasces,* which are bundles of wooden rods tightly bound together and used to hold an axe blade. Fasces were used by ancient Roman bodyguards and became a symbol of strength and unity, which is one reason Italian dictator Benito Mussolini chose it as a symbol for the Fascist Party. The fasces symbol has even appeared on some American coins.

Map Transparency: Europe, 1930s

World History Outline Maps

Teaching Tip

If a world map is not available in your classroom, have students refer to an atlas and find a current map of Europe and Asia. Discuss any differences between the map shown on this page and a current map.

GEOGRAPHY Starting Points

*Interactive

EUROPE, 1930s

Adolf Hitler dreamed of a mighty German empire. He began to secretly build up the German military.

Communist dictator Joseph Stalin crushed his political opponents and dominated all aspects of Soviet life.

Fascist dictator Francisco Franco held power in Spain after the Spanish Civil War ended in the 1930s.

Fascist Benito Mussolini promised to restore Italy's greatness. He had a vision of a strong, powerful Italian military.

Starting Points As Europe struggled to recover and rebuild following World War I, many citizens looked for strong leaders. By the mid-1930s, some countries had fallen under the rule of dictators who promised power and glory for their nations. As the decade continued, their aggressive actions would lead the world closer to another devastating war.

1. **Analyze** What do you think happened in Europe as dictators tried to make their nations more powerful?
2. **Predict** How do you think other countries in Europe reacted to the rise of aggressive dictators?

Listen to History

Go online to listen to an explanation of the starting points for this chapter.

go.hrw.com
Keyword: SHL WW2

Skills Focus: Analyzing Maps

At Level

Research Required

Social Studies Skill

World Leaders, 1930s

1. Draw the chart as shown for students to see. Omit the italicized answers. Have students copy the chart onto their own papers.
2. Have students scan the chapter and use information from the map on this page to fill in the chart. Suggest to students that they add a Notes column to add information about each leader as they study the chapter and use their charts as a study guide. **LS Visual-Spatial, Logical-Mathematical**

Alternative Assessment Handbook, Rubric 7: Charts

Country	Leader in 1930s
Spain	*Fransisco Franco*
France	*Edouard Daladier*
England	*Neville Chamberlain*
Germany	*Adolf Hitler*
Italy	*Benito Mussolini*
U.S.S.R.	*Joseph Stalin*

Answers

Geography Starting Points

1. *possible answer—Nations might attack other nations or form an alliance.*
2. *possible answer—They might try to wage war or make deals with other dictators.*

SECTION 1

Axis Aggression

BEFORE YOU READ

MAIN IDEA

In the late 1930s Germany and Japan used military force to build empires. Their aggressive actions led to the outbreak of World War II.

READING FOCUS

1. In what ways did Germany expand in the late 1930s?
2. What alliances did Axis nations make in the 1930s?
3. How did the war begin?
4. What were the causes and effects of Japan's attack on the United States?

KEY TERMS AND PEOPLE

appeasement
Winston Churchill
Axis Powers
nonaggression pact
blitzkrieg
Allies
Battle of Britain
Hideki Tojo
isolationism

TAKING NOTES Take notes on the events leading up to the start of World War II.

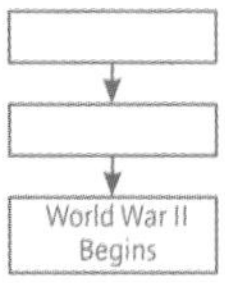

Adolf Hitler meets with German military leaders.

THE INSIDE STORY ***How did a secret meeting outline Hitler's plan for world war?*** A secret meeting took place deep in the heart of Nazi Germany on November 5, 1937. Present were German leader Adolf Hitler and a few of his top military and government advisers. One of those advisers, Colonel Friedrich Hossbach, took notes. These notes give a chilling description of Hitler's vision for the future of Germany.

Earlier in the day, Hitler had assured the Polish ambassador that Germany would respect Poland's territory on its eastern border. He also had stated that Germany had no intention of taking any Polish land. But at this secret meeting, Hitler said something very different.

Hitler began by swearing those present to secrecy. The subject that he was about to discuss was of vital importance. Germany, he said, faced a bleak future unless it could solve the problem of its limited territory. Simply put, Germany in its present form was too small to be self-sufficient.

According to Hossbach's notes, Hitler believed there was just one possible answer. "Germany's problem," Hossbach wrote, "could only be solved by means of force." Germany needed to act quickly. Within a few years, the powerful German military, newly rebuilt after its post–World War I destruction, would become outdated while other nations grew stronger. Hitler argued that Germany must soon seize Eastern Europe and prepare for conflict with Great Britain and France. The time to strike was coming soon.

Hossbach compiled his report several days after hearing Hitler's words. They provide a clear picture of the threat growing in Europe in the late 1930s as Germany headed down the road to war. ■

Preteach

Getting Started

Use the **Interactive Reader and Study Guide** to familiarize students with the section content.

Interactive Reader and Study Guide, Section 1

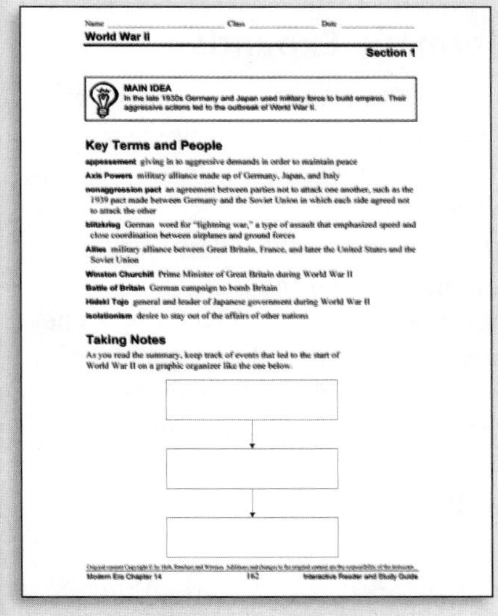
Name ________ Class ________ Date ________

World War II

Section 1

MAIN IDEA
In the late 1930s Germany and Japan used military force to build empires. Their aggressive actions led to the outbreak of World War II.

Key Terms and People

appeasement giving in to aggressive demands in order to maintain peace
Axis Powers military alliance made up of Germany, Japan, and Italy
nonaggression pact an agreement between parties not to attack one another, such as the 1939 pact made between Germany and the Soviet Union in which each side agreed not to attack the other
blitzkrieg German word for "lightning war," a type of assault that emphasized speed and close coordination between airplanes and ground forces
Allies military alliance between Great Britain, France, and later the United States and the Soviet Union
Winston Churchill Prime Minister of Great Britain during World War II
Battle of Britain German campaign to bomb Britain
Hideki Tojo general and leader of Japanese government during World War II
isolationism desire to stay out of the affairs of other nations

Taking Notes
As you read the summary, keep track of events that led to the start of World War II on a graphic organizer like the one below.

Academic Vocabulary

Review with students the high-use academic terms in this section.

violate break or ignore (p. 438)

hypothesis assumption or theory (p. 439)

CRF: Vocabulary Builder: Section 1

Taking Notes

Germany rebuilds military, militarizes the Rhineland, annexes Austria and the Sudetenland, and invades Poland.

Teach the Main Idea

At Level

Axis Aggression

1. **Teach** Ask students the Reading Focus questions to teach this section.
2. **Apply** Draw a blank time line for students to see with the years 1938 through 1942. Have students copy the time line onto their own papers and work in pairs to place events and dates discussed in this section in the proper order. *Anschluss (March, 1938); Annexation of Sudetenland (Sept. 1938); Attack on Poland (Sept. 1939); Attack on France (May 1940); Battle of Britain (Aug.–Oct. 1940); Invasion of the Soviet Union (June 1941); Attack on Pearl Harbor (Dec. 7, 1941); U.S. enters the war (Dec. 8, 1941)*
3. **Review** Review student time lines as a class. Add events as students name them.
4. **Practice/Homework** Have each student write a newspaper article describing the attack on Pearl Harbor. **LS Visual-Spatial, Verbal-Linguistic**

Alternative Assessment Handbook, Rubrics 36: Time Lines; and 40: Writing to Describe

Direct Teach

Reading Focus

1 In what ways did Germany expand in the late 1930s? *It took over German-speaking Austria and the Czech Sudetenland, which had large German-speaking populations.*

Germany Expands

Recall What was the reason Hitler gave for building submarines and warships? *to resist the spread of communism*

Predict What do you think would have happened if the British and French had stood up to Hitler when he threatened to annex the Sudetenland? *possible answer—Hitler might have stopped annexing land and been satisfied with Austria.*

CRF: Writing for the SAT

Info to Know

English Roots of Nazi Geopolitics Hitler's plans for German expansion owed much to theories of geopolitics, or the relationship between land and foreign policy. In the early 1900s English geopolitician Sir Halford Mackinder argued that a nation's power depended on its control of large areas of land. Mackinder believed the most important area was Eurasia and Africa, a vast connected landmass that he called the World Island. Whoever controlled the central regions of Eurasia that included Germany and Russia could control the rest of the World Island as well. His ideas received little attention in Great Britain before World War II, but they were used in Germany to support the Nazis' geopolitical ideas.

Answers

Reading Skills *He wanted Germany to have more territory.*

Reading Check *followed a policy of appeasement, giving in to Hitler's demands to maintain peace*

READING SKILLS
Understanding Causes and Effects Why did Hitler want Germany to expand?

Germany Expands

The Treaty of Versailles, which ended World War I, had seriously damaged the German economy. The terms of the treaty left Germans feeling humiliated. Adolf Hitler came to power in 1933 with a promise to restore German greatness. He wanted the nation to have lebensraum (LAY-buhnz-rowm), or "living space," in which the German people could grow and prosper. In other words, Hitler wanted Germany to have more territory. Germany's neighbors were well aware of the threat of German expansion. But with memories of the devastation of World War I still fresh, no one was willing to fight over Hitler's words.

Rebuilding the German Military Hitler soon realized that European leaders were no more willing to fight over his actions than over his words. After gaining control of the government when he became chancellor in 1933, Hitler secretly began to rebuild the German military, which had been greatly weakened after World War I. Before long, however, he was openly stating his plan to rearm Germany. Even though this action would violate the Treaty of Versailles, it went virtually unchallenged. In 1935, for example, Britain agreed to a new treaty allowing Germany to build submarines and other warships—again, in violation of the Treaty of Versailles. Hitler claimed that he was building German military strength to resist the spread of communism. Hitler's claim was a diversion, though. He was actually planning to make war to build a mighty German empire.

ACADEMIC VOCABULARY
violate break or ignore

Militarizing the Rhineland By 1936 Hitler was ready to take more direct action. In March he sent a small armed force into the Rhineland. This was German territory that bordered France. Hitler claimed to be reacting to a recent French-Soviet military agreement, which he said threatened Germany. The militarization of the Rhineland was another violation of the Treaty of Versailles, which required that German troops stay out of the region.

The French, along with the British, complained about Germany's treaty violations. They took no direct action, however. German troops remained in the Rhineland, and Hitler grew bolder.

Annexing Austria Hitler knew that his opponents in Europe hoped to avoid war. Therefore, he began to plot more aggressive moves.

His next target was Austria, a German-speaking country that bordered Germany and was Hitler's birthplace. He had long dreamed of uniting all the German-speaking people in Europe. In fact, Hitler's Nazi party already had many supporters in Austria.

In early 1938 Hitler began to demand that Austrian officials accept annexation by Germany. Annexation is the formal joining of one country to another. The German term for this annexation with Austria was *Anschluss* (AHN-shloos). When it became clear that Hitler would conquer Austria by force and that many of the Austrian people supported unification with Germany, the Austrian government gave in. In March 1938 German forces marched into Austria without opposition. The independent country of Austria was no more.

A Growing Crisis After the takeover of Austria, Hitler was convinced that no one dared to stop him. Next he turned to Czechoslovakia. It had a large German-speaking population, many of whom lived in a region known as the Sudetenland (soo-DAY-tuhn-land). These people were eager to join Germany. Hitler began to threaten the Czech government. The Czechs, in turn, prepared for war. The Czechs believed that if fighting began they could count on the support of France.

Though the growing crisis alarmed the French and British, they were still more interested in avoiding conflict than in confronting Hitler. At a meeting in September 1938 in Munich, Germany, British prime minister Neville Chamberlain and French leader Edouard Daladier agreed not to block Hitler's way. Czechoslovakia was told that if it fought Germany, it would do so alone.

Chamberlain returned to Great Britain believing that his policy of **appeasement**, or giving in to aggressive demands in order to maintain peace, had prevented an unnecessary war. However, others were convinced that this was wrong, and that Hitler would not stop after annexing the Sudetenland. In Britain's Parliament, **Winston Churchill** had spoken out against Chamberlain's plans. "Why not make a stand [against Hitler] while there is still a good company of united, very

Skills Focus: Making Inferences

At Level

Reading Skill
Czechoslovakia's Fate

Background: Remind students that Czechoslovakia was one of the new nations formed from the former Austro-Hungarian Empire in 1918 after World War I.

1. Guide the class in a discussion of Hitler's early actions that violated the terms of the Treaty of Versailles, including rebuilding the German military, moving troops into the Rhineland and the Anschluss with Austria.
2. Tell students that it is September 1938 and they are students in Czechoslovakia. Have them write a letter to a relative in the United States explaining how they feel about having the rest of Europe stand by as the Sudetenland—a part of Czechoslovakia—is taken over by Germany.
3. Ask volunteers to read their letters to the class. **LS Verbal-Linguistic, Intrapersonal**

Alternative Assessment Handbook, Rubric 25: Personal Letters

Interactive
AXIS ADVANCES, 1939–1941

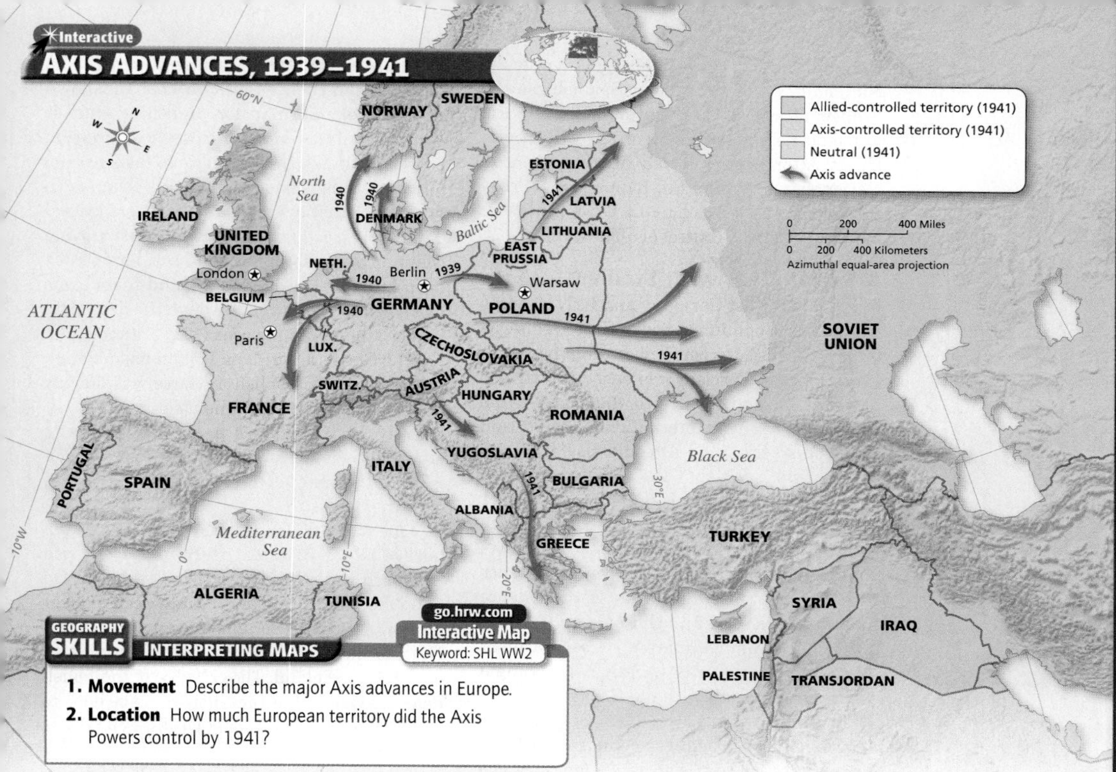

go.hrw.com
Interactive Map
Keyword: SHL WW2

GEOGRAPHY SKILLS INTERPRETING MAPS

1. **Movement** Describe the major Axis advances in Europe.
2. **Location** How much European territory did the Axis Powers control by 1941?

powerful countries?" Churchill asked. Few listened to his hypothesis. In Great Britain, Chamberlain was greeted as a hero. "I believe it is peace for our time," he told an audience. "Go home and get a nice quiet sleep."

READING CHECK **Make Generalizations** How did the British and French respond to Germany's expansion and aggression?

Alliances and Civil War

While Hitler was threatening Europe in the 1930s, he was also busy building alliances with other totalitarian governments. These alliances put him in league with some of the world's other major aggressors.

The Axis Forms Aggressive and totalitarian regimes had also emerged in Italy and Japan in the years after World War I. These countries demonstrated a willingness to use military force to achieve their goals. They also showed a disregard for the opinions of other nations.

Not surprisingly, perhaps, the similarities between Germany, Italy, and Japan led to a series of agreements that joined them together in a military alliance. These countries later came to be known as the **Axis Powers**.

One important agreement came in 1936, when Germany and Japan agreed to the Anti-Comintern Pact. This agreement united the two countries in an effort to prevent the spread of communism and to oppose the Soviet Union. The next year, Italy joined in the agreement. Later, in 1939, Italy and Germany signed a military alliance in which each side pledged to aid the other in the event of war.

The Spanish Civil War Italy and Germany also worked for an alliance with Spain. In 1936 fierce political conflict there had led to the outbreak of the Spanish Civil War. On one side were the Nationalists, a Fascist group.

ACADEMIC VOCABULARY
hypothesis assumption or theory

Direct Teach

Reading Focus

2 What alliances did Axis nations make in the 1930s? *Germany and Japan agreed to the Anti-Comintern Pact, and were joined by Italy a year later. Italy and Germany signed a military alliance.*

Alliances and Civil War

Recall What did Italy and Japan have in common with Germany in the years following World War I? *willingness to use military force to achieve goals; disregard for opinions of other nations*

Identify What was the Anti-Comintern Pact? *a 1936 agreement between Germany and Japan to prevent the spread of communism*

Activity **Analyzing Maps** Have students make a three-column chart. Have them label the first column Axis, the second column Allied, and the third column Neutral. Then have them use the map on this page to categorize each of the European countries under the appropriate heading. **LS Visual-Spatial**

Alternative Assessment Handbook, Rubric 7: Charts

Map Transparency: Axis Advances, 1939–1941

Interactive Map: Axis Advances, 1931-1941

Differentiating Instruction

Above Level

Advanced Learners/Gifted and Talented

1. Guide the class in a discussion of the meeting in Munich, Germany, at which leaders of Great Britain and France agreed not to block Hitler's attempt to annex the Sudetenland.
2. Tell students that they are newspaper editors. Have each student decide what position to take on appeasement. Do they think it will guarantee "peace in our time"? Is it just a tactic to delay an armed confrontation? Do they think that Chamberlain and Daladier should have stood up to Hitler, calling his bluff? What, if any, other options were available to them? Have students write an editorial expressing their opinion on what took place at the Munich Conference and taking a position for or against appeasement.
3. Take a poll to determine how many students supported appeasement and how many opposed it. Did they suggest any other options? If so, what were they?
4. Ask volunteers to read their editorials to the class. **LS Verbal-Linguistic**

Alternative Assessment Handbook, Rubric 43: Writing to Persuade

Answers

Interpreting Maps **1.** *Axis troops moved in every direction from Germany to France, Norway, Russia, and Greece.* **2.** *Axis Powers controlled most of continental Europe.*

Direct Teach

Reading Focus

Alliances and Civil War

Analyze What was the international impact of the Spanish Civil War? *Italy and Germany supported the Nationalists. The Soviet Union supported the Republicans. The victory of the Nationalists further strengthened the positions of Italy and Germany.*

Make Inferences What might be an effect of Hitler's alliances and the rise of dictatorships after the Spanish Civil War? *possible answer—Hitler would have little to stop his expansion in Europe.*

Biography

Pablo Picasso (1881–1973) Pablo Picasso is regarded as one of the most important artists of the 20th century. He was born in Málaga, Spain, where his father taught art. After 1900 Picasso spent most of his time in France, where he became one of the pioneers in the modern art movement known as cubism.

Picasso was a strong supporter of the Republican cause during the Spanish Civil War. In 1937 Picasso created a mural for Spain's pavilion at an international exposition in Paris. Soon afterward he heard that the Spanish town of Guernica had been bombed by the Nazis in support of General Francisco Franco's attempt to overthrow the Spanish republic. His painting "Guernica" expresses his outrage over the bombing. Picasso created the painting in black and white to reflect the seriousness of the subject. Picasso asked that "Guernica" be kept in the United States until democracy returned to Spain. In 1981, after Franco's death, the painting was placed in a museum in Madrid.

Answers

Reading Check *Japan and Italy; he also signed a nonaggression pact with the Soviet Union*

Italy and Germany gave military support to the Nationalists, who were led by Spanish general Francisco Franco. On the other side were the Republicans, who were supported by the Soviet Union. After years of bloody fighting, Franco's Nationalists defeated the Republicans. Franco's victory added Spain to the list of European nations under the control of a Fascist dictator.

A Secret Deal with Stalin During the late 1930s Fascist Germany and Italy strongly opposed the Communist Soviet Union. This was in part because fascism and communism were very different. Fascism was based in extreme nationalism and loyalty to the state, while communism sought international change and a classless society. As a result, Soviet leader Joseph Stalin felt that the German military expansion threatened his nation.

In the summer of 1939 British and French officials, concerned about Hitler's aggressive actions, were discussing a possible alliance with the Soviets. But Stalin had lost confidence that the British and French would help protect his country from Germany's growing armies. As a result, Stalin was secretly negotiating a separate agreement with the Germans.

That agreement, the Nazi-Soviet Non-Aggression Pact, was revealed in August 1939. A **nonaggression pact** is an agreement in which each side promises not to attack the other. This pact was designed to allow further German aggression in Europe. A secret section of the pact also recognized each side's right to take territory in Eastern Europe, including dividing Poland into Soviet and German areas.

News of the pact shocked the British and French, who had hoped that the Soviets would support them in the event of a German attack. But it was now clear that Hitler was on the march. Only force would stop him.

READING CHECK **Identify Supporting Details** With whom did Hitler seek alliances in the late 1930s?

The War Begins

Just days after reaching his agreement with the Soviets, Hitler was ready for all-out war. On September 1, 1939, Germany launched an attack on Poland. This assault marked the start of World War II.

Lightning Attacks German forces used a new tactic in their assault on Poland. Known as **blitzkrieg**, German for "lightning war," it emphasized speed and close coordination between planes in the air and fast-moving forces on the ground. A blitzkrieg began with air attacks that damaged defenses and caused panic among civilians. Meanwhile, fast-moving columns of tanks and mobile artillery struck deep into the countryside. Behind them came foot soldiers, who swept through the area looking for any remaining areas of resistance.

The German attack on Poland had a devastating effect. The Polish air force was quickly destroyed. On land, Polish soldiers fought bravely, but they were nearly powerless to stop the German forces. In addition, the Polish countryside offered few natural barriers to slow the blitzkrieg.

One thing Poland did have was the support of Great Britain and France. Both had promised to help if Poland was attacked. On September 3, Britain and France declared war on Germany. They became known as the **Allies**. Neither country, however, gave any significant help to Poland. The collapse of the Polish defenses was so fast that little could be done to stop Poland's defeat. In just weeks, Poland was in German hands.

Even before the conquest of Poland was complete, German troops began to move into position on Germany's western border. Hitler wanted to destroy his major enemies in Europe, and he was eager to begin an assault on France. Throughout the winter of 1939–1940, German leaders made their plans for an invasion.

The Attack on France The German assault began in the spring of 1940. First came a quick, well-planned invasion of lightly defended Denmark and Norway. Capturing these countries helped improve Germany's access to the Atlantic Ocean. Then, on May 10, the long-expected attack on France began.

The German assault slammed first into the Netherlands and Belgium, countries that lay between Germany and France. Allied forces rushed to meet the invasion, but they were no match for the German attack.

At the same time, another German force was attacking farther to the south, in the Ardennes (ahr-DEN); a dense forest region along the border between France and Belgium.

Collaborative Learning

At Level

Social Studies Skill

The Soviet Factor

1. Organize the class into four groups to represent the military high commands of Germany, Great Britain, France, and Poland. Have each group discuss what course a war in Europe might take and how the Soviet Union might be a factor.
2. Have each group draft a memorandum detailing a recommended plan of action for its national leaders. Each plan should include two alternatives—one that assumes the Soviet Union will continue to cooperate with Germany and another that assumes that the Soviet Union will enter the war on the side of the Allies.
3. Have volunteers from each group present their plans of action to the class.
4. Guide the class in a discussion of each group's plans of action. **LS Interpersonal, Verbal-Linguistic**

Alternative Assessment Handbook, Rubrics 14: Group Activity; and 24: Oral Presentations

The London Blitz

The London Blitz began in September 1940, when Germany bombed London, the British capital. The German goal was to terrorize the British people so that they would lose the will to fight. For 57 straight nights, German bombs pounded London. They destroyed huge areas of the city and killed tens of thousands of people. Despite the destruction, the British people refused to surrender.

Some 200 German bombers attacked London each night. British fighters shot them down faster than German factories could replace them.

Searchlights targeted German aircraft for British anti-aircraft guns.

Fires raged throughout London, and many of the city's buildings lay in ruins.

Many Londoners found shelter from German bombs in the city's subway system—the Underground.

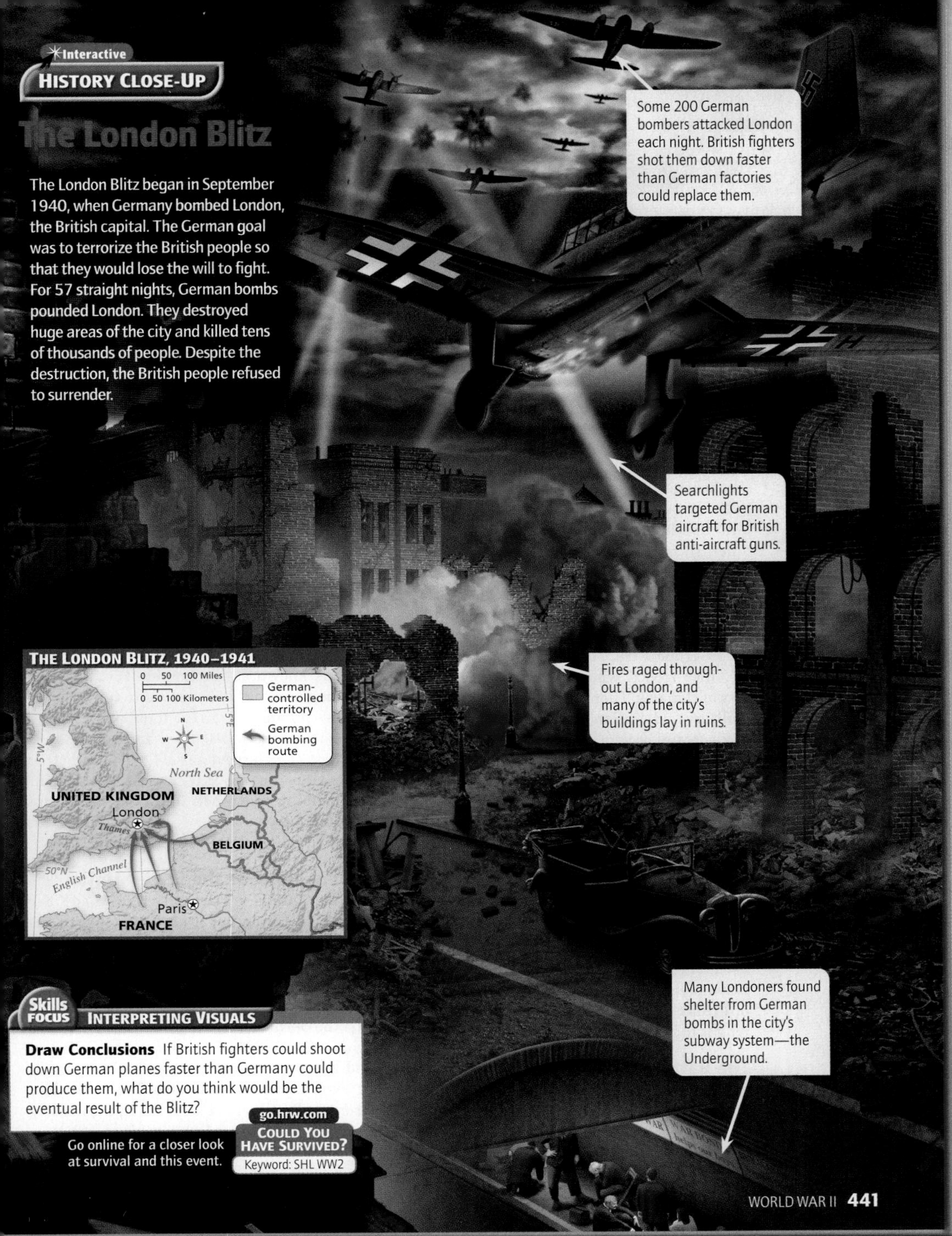

THE LONDON BLITZ, 1940–1941

0 50 100 Miles
0 50 100 Kilometers

German-controlled territory

→ German bombing route

North Sea

UNITED KINGDOM NETHERLANDS
London
Thames
BELGIUM
English Channel
Paris ★
FRANCE

Skills FOCUS INTERPRETING VISUALS

Draw Conclusions If British fighters could shoot down German planes faster than Germany could produce them, what do you think would be the eventual result of the Blitz?

go.hrw.com
COULD YOU HAVE SURVIVED?
Go online for a closer look at survival and this event.
Keyword: SHL WW2

WORLD WAR II **441**

Collaborative Learning

At Level

The Blitz

Research Required

1. Organize students into small groups. Have each group conduct outside research on the London Blitz, including at least one eyewitness account of the Blitz.

2. Have each group write a short scene from a play or film about the London Blitz using research and information on this page. Scripts should provide roles for each of the group's members. Students can focus on the Blitz from the point of view of the Royal Air

Force pilots who defended Britain, London civilians, or German pilots.

3. Have groups present their scenes for the class as reader's theater.

4. Guide the class in a discussion of the scenes. What did they all have in common? What aspects were unique? What do students think it would have been like to live in London during the Blitz? **LS** Interpersonal, Kinesthetic

Alternative Assessment Handbook, Rubrics 30: Research; and 33: Skits and Reader's Theater

Reading Focus

③ How did the war begin? *the invasion of Poland, followed by the massing of German troops on its western border*

The War Begins

Explain How did the blitzkrieg get its name? *from the German words for "lightning war"*

Contrast How did the reaction of Great Britain and France to the invasion of Poland differ from reaction to previous German expansion? *When Germany invaded Poland, Great Briain and France declared war on Germany. Previously, they stood by, allowing Hitler to have his way.*

History Close-Up

Blackouts During the Blitz, Londoners were subject to blackout restrictions and had to cover their windows at night with black material. Streetlights were not lit, and drivers were not permitted to turn on their headlights. These precautions were taken to make it harder for German bombers to find their target, but all the bombers had to do was follow the River Thames to the docks on London's East End.

Map Transparency: The London Blitz, 1940

Info to Know

Saving Children As early as September 1939, fearing potential air attacks, British authorities prepared to evacuate children from London. Thousands of children relocated from the city to temporary homes in the countryside beyond the reach of German bombers. Although relocating children separated families, it saved many lives as Germans persistently bombed London during the Blitz.

Answers

Interpreting Visuals *possible answer— Germany would stop the attacks; they would run out of airplanes.*

Direct Teach

Reading Focus

The War Begins

Recall Why was the Soviet Red Army, with millions of soldiers, unable to withstand the German blitzkrieg? *because its troops were poorly trained and equipped, and Germany's attack was unexpected*

Contrast How did Hitler's attack on Great Britain differ from his attack on France? *He used armies with tanks to invade France, but he used aircraft to attack Britain.*

Predict How do you think the rescue of the Allied troops from Dunkirk affected the outcome of the war? *possible answer—If it hadn't taken place, the Allies would have been weakened and the Germans might have won the war.*

CRF: Biography: Queen Elizabeth

CRF: Primary Source: The Atlantic Charter

Info to Know

The Maginot Line After World War I, the French spent millions of francs building a defensive structure known as the Maginot Line. It consisted of a vast series of underground bunkers and fortresses, which were connected by underground tunnels and underground railways. This system could be used to defend the entire border with Germany against attack. What the builders did not anticipate, however, was that the Germans would overrun the Netherlands and Belgium and invade France through them. The Maginot Line proved virtually useless against the German attack in 1940.

FACES OF HISTORY

Winston CHURCHILL
1874–1965

One of the great leaders of World War II was Winston Churchill. The prime minister of Great Britain, Churchill used his gift for words to rally the British people to victory during the early years of the war, when all hope seemed lost.

Churchill had been active in British politics since 1900, but it was the growing danger posed by Germany in the 1930s that brought out his finest qualities as a leader and speaker. He became prime minister after war broke out. In that role, he led the British people throughout the war, urging them to remain strong in their opposition to Nazi Germany. His refusal to consider surrendering helped preserve Britain as a base from which the Allies could eventually attack Hitler's armies.

Find the Main Idea What qualities of leadership did Churchill display?

French leaders believed that the thick forest was impossible for an army to pass through and had left it virtually undefended. Consequently, when German tanks emerged from the Ardennes, they quickly overwhelmed the light resistance they met there.

From the Ardennes the German tanks rumbled northwest toward the French coast. The Germans trapped hundreds of thousands of Allied troops, who retreated to the coastal city of Dunkirk. There, in a heroic rescue, Allied military and civilian ships saved over 300,000 soldiers and brought them to Great Britain.

Although disaster had been avoided at Dunkirk, France was doomed. The remaining Allied forces were unable to slow the Germans' steady march toward Paris. On June 22, 1940, France surrendered to Germany.

Germany occupied much of France, but placed part of the country under the control of French officials who cooperated with Hitler. This area was known as Vichy (VEE-shee) France. Some French leaders, including Charles de Gaulle, escaped to Britain. There they organized resistance to German and Vichy control of France. Within France, resistance fighters fought to liberate their country.

The Battle for Britain Despite the French resistance effort, Great Britain now stood alone against what appeared to be an unstoppable German war machine. But conquering Britain would prove to be far more difficult for Hitler than taking the rest of Europe had been. Britain was now led by Winston Churchill, who had replaced Neville Chamberlain as prime minister in May 1940. Churchill's fighting spirit inspired confidence among the British people.

HISTORY'S VOICES

> **"We shall fight on the beaches, we shall fight on the landing grounds, we shall fight in the fields and in the streets, we shall fight in the hills. We shall never surrender."**
>
> —Winston Churchill, June 4, 1940

Between August and October of 1940 Germany sent thousands of aircraft over the English Channel to attack British targets in what became known as the **Battle of Britain**. Hitler's plan was to destroy the British Royal Air Force and thus make it possible to invade Britain. For the first time in the war, the Germans failed. The British were aided by a new technology called radar. Radar uses radio signals to locate and create an image of distant objects. In the Battle of Britain, radar allowed the British to detect incoming German air attacks before the German planes were visible. This made British air defenses much more effective.

As the battle continued into the fall of 1940, German planes began to bomb British ports and cities, including London. This assault became known as the London Blitz. Hitler's goal in attacking civilians was to terrorize the British public and break their will to fight. German bombs killed thousands of civilians and destroyed large areas of London and other major cities, but the British refused to give in.

Bombing continued into early 1941, but German losses increased. Finally, Hitler was forced to call off his plans to invade Britain.

The Invasion of the Soviet Union The German failure in Great Britain may have frustrated Hitler, but it did not stop him. He quickly shifted his attention back to the east. In June 1941 Hitler broke his nonaggression pact with Stalin and sent some 3 million German troops pouring into the Soviet Union. At first the German blitzkrieg was highly effective against the Soviets. Just as they had in Poland and France, German tanks and soldiers raced across the Soviet countryside. The Soviet Red Army had millions of soldiers, but its poorly trained and equipped troops were no match for the overwhelming German forces.

Skills Focus: Making Inferences

At Level

Reading Skill

The Battle of Britain

1. Guide the class in a discussion of the Battle of Britain using the following questions as a guide: What factors helped Britain resist German attacks? *it is an island; Churchill's inspiration; radar* What was Great Britain's strategic importance to the Germans? *could help them protect rest of Western Europe if U.S. entered war* What was Great Britain's strategic importance to the Allies? *could provide a base to stage an Allied attack on Europe's mainland*
2. Have each student write a journal entry describing life in Great Britain if the Germans had won the Battle of Britain.
3. Have volunteers read their entries to the class.

LS Verbal-Linguistic, Intrapersonal

Alternative Assessment Handbook, Rubrics 11: Discussions; and 15: Journals

Answers

Faces of History *gift for words to rally British people; faced danger posed by Germany*

Reading Check *invasion of Poland, followed by the massing of German troops on its western border*

Despite the steep losses suffered by the Soviet army, the Soviet Union did not collapse. By autumn the Germans had pushed deep into Soviet territory, but they had not managed to reach their major goals of Leningrad and Moscow, the Soviet capital. Further, they had not prepared for the extremely harsh temperatures of the Soviet winter. German troops lacked warm clothing, and their vehicles and equipment worked poorly in the frigid conditions. As winter set in, their progress slowed, then stopped.

At the same time, the Soviets were beginning to recover from the huge number of casualties they had suffered in the early fighting. The vast population of the Soviet Union allowed the Soviet armies to rebuild quickly. The Soviets had survived the mighty German onslaught, and for the first time they were beginning to fight back.

READING CHECK **Sequence** With what events did the war begin?

Japan Attacks

While war spread across Europe, another threat to peace was taking shape halfway around the world. Recall that Japan's military expansion and aggression in Asia during the 1930s had concerned many observers, including American leaders. Most Americans, however, wanted to stay out of the growing conflict overseas.

In 1941 Japan moved its forces into French Indochina, a French colony in Southeast Asia. This region was rich in oil, rubber, and other natural resources that Japan would need to supply its military. In response, nervous American leaders banned the sale of oil to Japan, a move that was designed to slow the Japanese war machine. This was a serious threat to Japan's future plans.

The Japanese government continued to hold peace talks with the United States. Meanwhile, Japan secretly planned for war.

Pearl Harbor For months, Japanese military leaders under General **Hideki Tojo** had been developing plans for a surprise attack on the American naval base at Pearl Harbor, Hawaii. This base was home to the U.S. Navy's Pacific Fleet. As the sun rose on Sunday morning, December 7, 1941, the Japanese attack began.

PRIMARY SOURCES

The Attack on Pearl Harbor

The day after the attack on Pearl Harbor, President Franklin D. Roosevelt asked Congress to declare war on Japan.

"Yesterday, December 7th, 1941—a date which will live in infamy—the United States of America was suddenly and deliberately attacked by naval and air forces of the Empire of Japan . . .

"As commander in chief of the Army and Navy, I have directed that all measures be taken for our defense. But always will our whole nation remember the character of the onslaught against us.

"No matter how long it may take us to overcome this premeditated invasion, the American people in their righteous might will win through to absolute victory . . .

"Hostilities exist . . . our people, our territory, and our interests are in grave danger.

"With confidence in our armed forces, with the unbounding determination of our people, we will gain the inevitable triumph—so help us God."

Skills FOCUS **READING LIKE A HISTORIAN**

1. Analyze Primary Sources How does President Roosevelt describe Japan's actions?

2. Infer In what way do you think the American public would have responded to Roosevelt's speech?

See **Skills Handbook**, p. H25

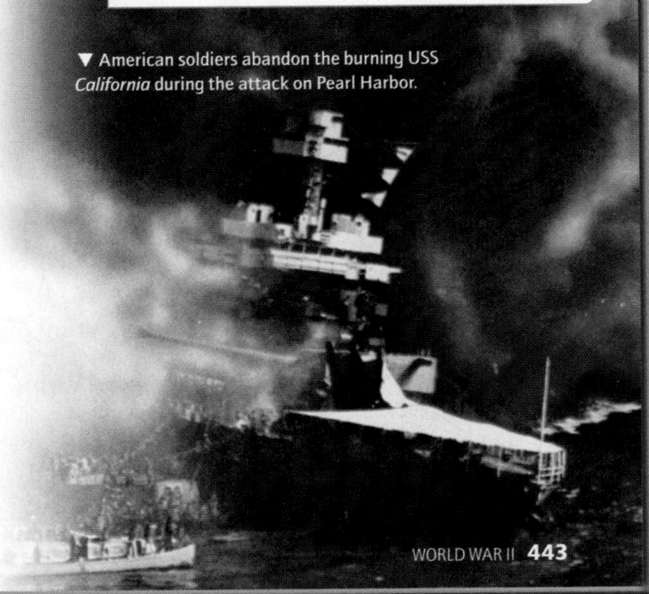

▼ American soldiers abandon the burning USS *California* during the attack on Pearl Harbor.

Direct Teach

Reading Focus

4 What were the causes and effects of Japan's attack on the United States? *Causes—Japan's military expansion and aggression; alliance with Germany and Italy; response to America's ban on the sale of oil; Effects—U.S. declared war on Japan.*

Japan Attacks

Identify Who was General Hideki Tojo? *the head of the Japanese government*

Cause and Effect Why did American leaders ban oil sales to Japan? *in response to the Japanese invasion of French Indochina*

Primary Source

In an excerpt from his book *At Dawn We Slept,* historian Gordon Prange relates an eyewitness account of the attack on Pearl Harbor:

"When the attack began, … the explosion of bombs, the whine of bullets, the roar of planes, the belching guns of aroused defenders, the acrid smell of fire and smoke—all blended into a nerve-racking cacophony [sound] of chaos. … Bombardiers still dropped their torpedoes, while dive bombers pounced like hawks. … Far above, high-level bombers rained their deadly missiles as fighters shuttled in and out, weaving together the fearful tapestry of destruction."

Differentiating Instruction

Below Level

Learners Having Difficulty

Materials: butcher paper, paints or colored markers

1. Guide the class in a discussion of the attack on Pearl Harbor using the following questions:
   - Describe the attack. *Hundreds of Japanese fighters and bombers dropped bombs on the American base.*
   - What was the result of the attack? *2,400 Americans dead, nearly 200 aircraft destroyed, eight battleships sunk or damaged*
   - What good news was there? *Three aircraft carriers were out to sea and therefore spared.*
   - How did the attack affect Americans? *Isolationism disappeared as news of attack spread. Congress declared war on Japan.*
2. Organize the class into small groups. Have groups create murals of the Pearl Harbor attack.
3. Display students' murals in a classroom exhibit. **LS Interpersonal, Visual-Spatial**

Alternative Assessment Handbook, Rubrics 3: Artwork; 11: Discussions; and 14: Group Activity

Answers

Reading Like a Historian

1. *shameful, sudden, deliberate;*
2. *possible answer—They would feel encouraged, determined, and patriotic.*

Review & Assess

Close

Have students summarize the Axis aggression that led up to the entry of the United States into the war.

Review

Online Quiz, Section 1

Assess

SE Section 1 Assessment

Progress Assessment: Section 1 Quiz

Alternative Assessment Handbook

Reteach/ Intervene

Interactive Reader and Study Guide, Section 1

Interactive Skills Tutor CD-ROM

Answers

Reading Check *American leaders banned the sale of oil to Japan, which threatened Japan's future plans in French Indochina.*

For nearly two weeks Japanese aircraft carriers had been approaching Pearl Harbor from the north, undetected by the American military. When the attack started, hundreds of Japanese fighters and bombers launched from the carriers and sped over Pearl Harbor, dropping bombs and torpedos on the American base below. The raid was a complete surprise.

American Eddie Jones was onboard the USS *California* in Pearl Harbor when the attack began.

HISTORY'S VOICES

"You couldn't believe it was happening. You could see it in front of your eyes, but you couldn't believe it. Here it was, a beautiful morning—a beautiful Sunday morning—and you see everything blowing up and ships sinking and men in the water. And you think, we're at peace with the world. This can't be happening."

—Seaman Second Class Eddie Jones, in *War Stories: Remembering World War II*

Although American military planners had long believed that an attack on Pearl Harbor was a possibility, the base was lightly defended. Most American planes never had the chance to leave the ground.

The attack lasted less than two hours, but the destruction was enormous. Some 2,400 Americans were dead. Nearly 200 aircraft were destroyed, and all eight battleships in the harbor were sunk or damaged. Perhaps the only good news for the Americans was that the three aircraft carriers normally stationed at Pearl Harbor were out to sea during the attack and were unharmed.

The American Response The attack on Pearl Harbor had a profound effect on the American public. Until then, many Americans had believed that the United States should stay out of Europe's war and protect its own interests. This desire to avoid involvement in the affairs of other nations is known as **isolationism**. Isolationism was common in the United States after World War I, when many Americans questioned what the costly Allied victory in that war had actually accomplished. But as news of the attack on Pearl Harbor spread, most isolationism quickly disappeared. On December 8 the U.S. Congress declared war on Japan. Three days later, Germany and Italy declared war on the United States. With these actions, the United States joined the Allies in the global fight against the Axis Powers.

READING CHECK **Find the Main Idea** Why did Japan attack the United States?

SECTION 1 ASSESSMENT

go.hrw.com
Online Quiz
Keyword: SHL WW2 HP

Reviewing Ideas, Terms, and People

1. **a. Identify** What are some examples of Hitler's growing military aggression in the late 1930s?
   b. Compare and Contrast Compare and contrast Germany's actions in the Rhineland, Austria, and Czechoslovakia.
   c. Evaluate How would you describe Neville Chamberlain's policy toward Hitler in the late 1930s?
2. **a. Recall** Who were the **Axis Powers**?
   b. Make Inferences Why do you think Hitler sought allies in the late 1930s?
   c. Evaluate What do you think about Stalin's decision to make a deal with Hitler rather than trust the British and French to help stop the Germans? Explain.
3. **a. Recall** What event marked the start of World War II?
   b. Compare and Contrast Describe Germany's successes and failures in France, Great Britain, and the Soviet Union.
4. **a. Recall** What events led up to the Japanese attack on Pearl Harbor?
   b. Identify Cause and Effect What was the significance of the attack on Pearl Harbor in terms of American public opinion?

Critical Thinking

5. **Sequence** Use your notes and a graphic organizer like this one to explain how events of the 1930s led to the outbreak of World War II. How did the world react to each event.

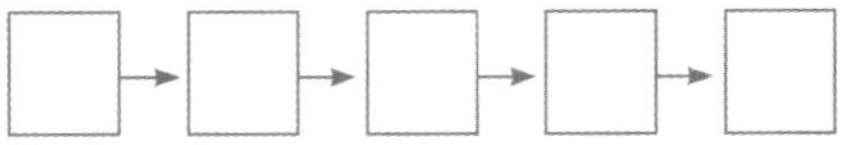

FOCUS ON SPEAKING

6. **Persuasion** Write a brief conversation between Neville Chamberlain and Winston Churchill. In your conversation, have the speakers discuss what Great Britain should do about Germany's increasingly aggressive actions.

Section 1 Assessment Answers

1. **a.** rebuilding the German military, militarizing the Rhineland, annexing Austria
   b. possible answer—hoped to avoid or delay war by giving Hitler what he wanted
   c. possible answer—He believed that appeasement would prevent war.
2. **a.** Germany, Italy, and Japan
   b. possible answer—He knew he needed allies to get what he wanted.
   c. possible answer—Stalin should have known that Hitler would act aggressively because Germans had been untrustworthy.
3. **a.** Germany's invasion of Poland
   b. Success—forced French surrender in 1940; destroyed much of London in Blitz; blitzkrieg effective against Soviets; Failures—French resistance in Vichy; British refuse to surrender, German troops ill-equipped for winter, Soviet army rebuilds.
4. **a.** Japan had moved into French Indochina. In response, American leaders banned the sale of oil to Japan. Japan held peace talks with the U.S. while secretly planning for war.
   b. Many Americans no longer felt U.S. should stay out of the war.
5. Germany rebuilds military, militarizes the Rhineland, annexes Austria and the Sudetenland, invades Poland.
6. Student conversations should show an understanding of the viewpoints of both Chamberlain and Churchill.

SECTION 2

The Allied Response

BEFORE YOU READ

MAIN IDEA

The early years of World War II went poorly for the Allies. But after the United States joined the war, the Allies soon recovered and began making gains against the Axis.

READING FOCUS

1. In what ways were Americans involved in the early years of the war?
2. How did the war in North Africa and Italy progress?
3. What was the turning point in the Soviet Union?
4. What was the turning point in the Pacific?

KEY TERMS AND PEOPLE

Erwin Rommel
Battle of El Alamein
Dwight D. Eisenhower
Siege of Leningrad
Battle of Stalingrad
Douglas MacArthur
Bataan Death March
Battle of Midway
Battle of Guadalcanal
kamikazes

TAKING NOTES List the main instances of Allied success in the war in 1942 and 1943.

THE INSIDE STORY ***Could old newspapers help win a war?*** Defeating the Axis armies required a huge effort from the Allies. In the Allied nations, millions of people volunteered to fight. Others found different ways to help.

The war effort required enormous amounts of raw materials to make the supplies needed to win the war, from airplanes to ammunition to food. In Great Britain and the United States, civilians took part in efforts to save these precious resources for the soldiers fighting overseas.

Rationing and recycling were two ways the average British or American civilian helped the war effort. The federal government rationed, or limited, many products during the war, including certain foods, clothing, and gasoline. Rationing meant sacrifices for all. Civilians received a certain number of ration stamps, which could be used to buy rationed products such as meats, butter, and canned vegetables. Many people planted "victory gardens" to grow extra food.

Recycling was another way people on the home front contributed to the war effort. They collected metal, rubber, newspapers, even kitchen fat, all of which could be used in the war effort. For example, metal cans could be turned into ammunition or guns, while kitchen fat was used to make glycerin, an ingredient in explosives and medicines.

These scrap drives provided scarce materials for the war effort and they also brought civilians together to support the Allied struggle. They helped people at home stay strong during the uncertain days of the bloodiest war the world had ever seen. ■

RECYCLING FOR VICTORY

▶ **American children collect old paper for the Allied war effort.**

Preteach

Getting Started

Use the **Interactive Reader and Study Guide** to give students a quick preview of the section.

Interactive Reader and Study Guide, Section 2

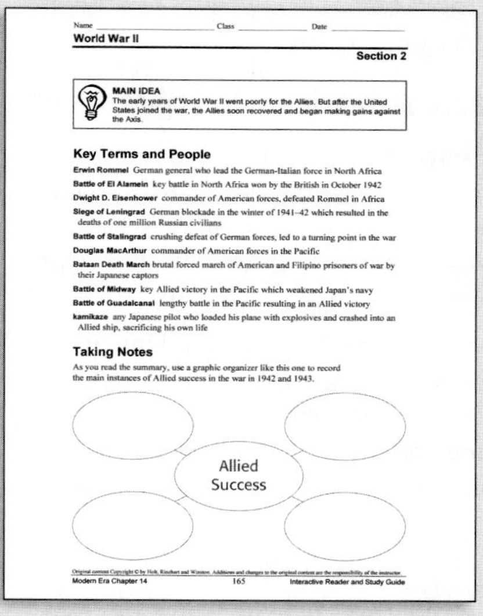
Name ______ Class ______ Date ______

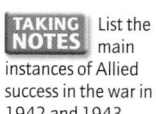

World War II

Section 2

MAIN IDEA
The early years of World War II went poorly for the Allies. But after the United States joined the war, the Allies soon recovered and began making gains against the Axis.

Key Terms and People

Erwin Rommel German general who lead the German-Italian force in North Africa
Battle of El Alamein key battle in North Africa won by the British in October 1942
Dwight D. Eisenhower commander of American forces, defeated Rommel in Africa
Siege of Leningrad German blockade in the winter of 1941–42 which resulted in the deaths of one million Russian civilians
Battle of Stalingrad crushing defeat of German forces, led to a turning point in the war
Douglas MacArthur commander of American forces in the Pacific
Bataan Death March brutal forced march of American and Filipino prisoners of war by their Japanese captors
Battle of Midway key Allied victory in the Pacific which weakened Japan's navy
Battle of Guadalcanal lengthy battle in the Pacific resulting in an Allied victory
kamikaze any Japanese pilot who loaded his plane with explosives and crashed into an Allied ship, sacrificing his own life

Taking Notes

As you read the summary, use a graphic organizer like this one to record the main instances of Allied success in the war in 1942 and 1943.

Allied Success

Modern Era Chapter 14 165 Interactive Reader and Study Guide

CRF: Vocabulary Builder: Section 2

Taking Notes

better equipment and breaking of a key German code help Allies gain control of the Atlantic; Allies win control of North Africa, move north through Italy; German forces defeated at Stalingrad; Japan's navy suffers terrible blow in Battle of Midway

Teach the Main Idea

At Level

The Allied Response

1. **Teach** Ask students the Reading Focus questions to teach this section.
2. **Apply** Have students create four-column charts about the information in this chapter. Each chart should have the following headings: Atlantic, North Africa/Italy, Europe, and Pacific. Students should list significant battles and events under each heading.
3. **Review** Review students' charts as a class. Ask students which event covered in this chapter is the most important. Write their responses for the class to see.
4. **Practice/Homework** Ask students to write a short essay comparing the treatment of the Japanese during World War II with the treatment of people of Middle Eastern or Islamic background following the terrorist attacks of September 11, 2001. **LS Visual-Spatial, Verbal-Linguistic**

Alternative Assessment Handbook, Rubrics 7: Charts; and 37: Writing Assignments

Direct Teach

Reading Focus

1 In what ways were Americans involved in the early years of the war? *The U.S. gave military aid to Great Britain, which led to shooting between American vessels and German craft and the sinking of an American escort ship by a German U-boat.*

Early American Involvement

Recall Before declaring war on Japan, how did the United States help the Allies? *by offering military aid to Great Britain in the form of ships and military escorts for convoys*

Summarize How did the United States mobilize for war? *Men volunteered to fight or were drafted, women filled non-combat roles, factories converted to producing weapons and supplies.*

CRF: Biography: Rosie the Riveter

Info to Know

U.S. Neutrality In 1940 the United States was officially neutral. Congress had passed Neutrality Acts in 1937 and 1939 to keep the United States from being drawn into European wars. Nevertheless, President Roosevelt believed that the United States should serve as a "great arsenal of democracy." After his reelection that year, he presented a military aid bill to Congress. His proposal would "lend-lease" or otherwise provide supplies needed by any country whose security was considered vital to the defense of the United States. Congress passed the Lend-Lease Act, providing much-needed assistance to Great Britain while buying time for the United States to prepare for war.

Early American Involvement

The Japanese attack on Pearl Harbor ended most American resistance to entering the war. But even before the United States declared war on Japan, the country had been helping the Allies by shipping supplies across the Atlantic Ocean.

The Battle of the Atlantic Control of the Atlantic Ocean was a critical factor in World War II. Great Britain and the Soviet Union depended heavily on supplies shipped by sea to their ports. If Germany gained control of the seas and cut off Allied access to food and equipment, the war would soon be lost.

Germany's navy was powerful, but it did not have enough ships to match the battleships of Great Britain. As a result, the Germans came to rely on the same weapon they had used in World War I—the U-boat, or submarine. U-boats inflicted enormous damage on the Allies, sinking hundreds of merchant supply ships in the early years of the war.

THE IMPACT TODAY

The Manzanar internment camp in California is now a national historic site operated by the National Park Service.

Before entering the war, the United States offered military aid to Great Britain in the form of ships and military escorts for convoys. Convoys were groups of many ships that offered safety in numbers. This aid led to shooting between American and German vessels. In October 1941 a U-boat sank the American escort ship USS *Reuben James*, killing most of its crew. It was the first U.S. Navy ship sunk by Germany during the war.

The American Home Front Less than two months after the *Reuben James* went down, Japan attacked Pearl Harbor. After the United States entered the war, the nation had to mobilize, or bring its military forces into readiness. This was an enormous task. To defeat the powerful Axis armies, the United States would need soldiers, sailors, and pilots, as well as a great deal of military equipment and supplies.

Millions of American men volunteered to fight for their country, and still more were drafted, or required to serve. While women were not permitted to take part in combat, they filled other roles in the military, working as pilots, clerks, and in other positions. The nation also responded quickly to the need for war supplies. For example, many factories that made consumer goods were converted to produce weapons and supplies. The enormous demand for workers gave new employment opportunities to many women and African Americans.

Americans at home found other ways to help their country. They made do with less food, fuel, and other items, all of which were needed by the armed forces. They participated in scrap drives to collect materials such as iron and rubber, which could be recycled for military purposes.

But wartime patriotism had negative effects too. Some government officials worried that Americans of German, Italian, and Japanese descent would help the enemy. German Americans and Italian Americans faced certain restrictions during the war, but Japanese Americans were treated most harshly.

More than 100,000 Japanese Americans on the West Coast were forced to leave their homes and businesses and travel to internment camps. Most were American citizens, but the government was concerned only with their racial background. Life in the camps was hard. Many were located in desert areas with a harsh climate and were surrounded by guards and barbed wire fences. Families lived in small facilities, and the quality of education and health care was poor. It was not until later in the war that they were released.

Winning the Atlantic After the United States was officially at war, Germany sent its U-boats into American waters. They hoped to destroy American merchant ships. Indeed, hundreds of American ships went down.

By 1943, however, the Allies had made a number of adjustments in the war for the Atlantic. For one thing, Allied factories finally began producing ships and planes in large numbers. This meant better equipped convoys, which had more firepower to find and destroy U-boats. The Allies had also broken a key German code system used to transmit information about German plans. This helped the Allies learn the locations of German U-boats.

Thanks to these improvements, losses to U-boats dropped sharply. The vital supply line to Great Britain and the Soviet Union was kept open, and the Atlantic belonged to the Allies.

READING CHECK **Find the Main Idea** How were Americans on the home front involved in the war?

Skills Focus: Analyzing Alternative Points of View

At Level

Reading Like a Historian Skill

America's Role in World War II

1. Organize students into five groups. Tell them that they are members of Congress in 1939, planning U.S. response to events in Europe including the German invasion of Poland.
2. Have each group split into two teams. One student in each group should serve as moderator. One team should support entering the war on the side of the Allies to prevent further German aggression. The other team should favor isolationism.
3. Have each group conduct a debate. Students may use information from their textbooks and may conduct additional research to support their arguments.
4. Have moderators announce the winners based on the most convincing argument.

LS Interpersonal, Verbal-Linguistic

Alternative Assessment Handbook, Rubrics 10: Debates; and 14: Group Activity

Answers

Reading Check *Many factories converted to produce weapons and supplies; Americans made do with less food, fuel, and other items; people planted "victory gardens."*

Interactive
WORLD WAR II IN EUROPE AND NORTH AFRICA, 1941–1943

Legend:
- Allied-controlled territory (1942)
- Allied advance
- Axis-controlled territory (1942)
- Axis advance
- Neutral (1942)
- ✹ Major battle

0 300 600 Miles
0 300 600 Kilometers
Azimuthal equal-area projection

GEOGRAPHY SKILLS — **INTERPRETING MAPS**

go.hrw.com
Interactive Map
Keyword: SHL WW2

1. **Movement** Describe the major Allied advances in North Africa and Italy.
2. **Location** What areas of Europe and North Africa did the Allies control in 1942?

War in North Africa and Italy

While the fighting for the Atlantic was still raging, Italian and British forces began a battle for the control of North Africa. This territory was vital for the Allies. If the British could control North Africa, they would be able to protect the Suez Canal, the shipping route that linked the Mediterranean Sea with the oil fields of the Middle East. Keeping this oil supply flowing was essential to the British war effort.

In the fall of 1940, Italian forces based in Libya attacked British-controlled Egypt. This attack was a failure. British forces not only eliminated the Italian threat to Egypt, they soon drove into Libya and threatened to gain control of all of North Africa. Hitler was forced to send German forces to support the Italians.

Back-and-Forth Fighting The new German and Italian force in Africa—called the Afrika Korps—was led by German general **Erwin Rommel**. He quickly earned his nickname, the Desert Fox, by skillfully pushing the British out of Libya and back into Egypt.

The Afrika Korps, however, had trouble supplying its forces, and this limited its effectiveness. Throughout 1941 and into 1942, the British and the Afrika Korps traded blows.

A key battle took place in October 1942, at El Alamein (el a-luh-MAYN) in Egypt. British troops under General Bernard Montgomery took advantage of Rommel's supply problems.

WORLD WAR II **447**

Collaborative Learning

Japanese Internment

At Level

Research Required

Materials: maps of the United States

1. Organize students into groups of four or five. Have each group conduct research on Japanese internment facilities in the United States during World War II.

2. Have students list each of the centers, along with its location and the number of people who were held there during the war. Give each group a map of the United States. Have them locate each of the internment facilities on the map.

3. Review students' lists and maps as a class.

4. Tell students that they are Japanese teenagers who have been sent with their families to an internment camp. Have them write letters describing their feelings on being sent to a strange place and separated from their friends and everything that is familiar to them.

LS Intrapersonal, Verbal-Linguistic

Alternative Assessment Handbook, Rubrics 14: Group Activity; 25: Personal Letters; and 30: Research

● **Direct Teach** ●

Reading Focus

❷ How did the war in North Africa and Italy progress? *Allies drove Axis out of North Africa; used as base for launching invasion of Europe through Italy*

War in North Africa and Italy

Explain Why was control of North Africa important to the British? *to protect the Suez Canal to keep supply of Middle Eastern oil flowing to support the British war effort*

Identify Cause and Effect How did the Germans get drawn into the war in North Africa? *After Italian forces based in Libya attacked Egypt, British forces drove into Libya and threatened to control North Africa.*

🗺 **Map Transparency:** World War II in Europe and North Africa, 1941–1943

✱ **Interactive Map:** World War II in Europe and North Africa, 1941–1943

Info to Know

Breaking the Code During World War II, the German military used a device called Enigma to encode their strategic messages. (The word enigma means "riddle.") The Poles first broke the code in the early 1930s. When they faced invasion in 1939, the Poles gave the information to the Allies. By then, the Germans had made changes in Enigma's operating procedures and had supplied the Japanese with a version of the Enigma machine. The British secret service set up a project north of London to intercept and decode Enigma's messages. The British used the first electronic computers to break Germany's secret military codes. This project, known as Ultra, remained an official British secret until 1974.

Answers

Interpreting Maps 1. *The Allies moved from the west by sea through Morocco and Algeria, into Tunisia, then north into Italy through Sicily.* **2.** *most of Egypt, the United Kingdom, parts of the Soviet Union*

Direct Teach

Reading Focus

War in North Africa and Italy

Recall Recall How did German general Erwin Rommel earn his nickname, the Desert Fox? *by skillfully pushing the British out of Libya and back into Egypt*

Summarize How did the Germans respond to the Allied invasion of Italy? *The Germans fought to keep the Allies from moving north.*

Recent Scholarship

The women of Leningrad share their perspective in *Writing the Siege of Leningrad: Women's Diaries, Memoirs and Documentary Prose,* by Cynthia Simmons and Nina Perlina. Because the men were at the front, women were forced to run the city and defend their homes. Industry continued to operate and schools were open, even though the city was being constantly bombed, supplies were cut off, and people were dying of starvation. Stories of Leningrad's inhabitants have more in common with those of concentration camp prisoners than with typical war stories. Recently scholars have begun to focus on the writings of the women of Leningrad, which often differ from official Soviet depictions of the siege.

Writing the Siege of Leningrad: Women's Diaries, Memoirs and Documentary Prose by Cynthia Simmons and Nina Perlina. Greta Bucher, 2004.

Answers

Faces of History *He was patient, diplomatic, and a skilled military planner.*

Reading Check *They drove the Axis out of North Africa and used it as a base for launching an invasion of Europe through Italy.*

Using information gained from secret German codes, the British won a smashing victory. As a result of the **Battle of El Alamein**, Axis power in North Africa was severely weakened.

The Americans Join the Battle As the British and the Afrika Korps fought in Libya and Egypt, Allied leaders were planning to bring American troops to the European battlefield. The Soviets wanted the Allies to invade Europe, creating a second front that would force Hitler to pull troops away from Soviet territory. British and American leaders insisted that planning for such a huge action would take time. They decided to invade the western part of North Africa first, in the French colonies of Morocco, Algeria, and Tunisia.

In November 1942 a combined American and British force landed in North Africa. It was led by American general **Dwight D. Eisenhower**. The Allies faced little resistance after landing, and French forces soon joined them.

The landing put Rommel in a difficult spot, with strong Allied forces both to the east and west. His supply problems also continued to worsen. After several battles, during which the Americans first experienced combat in the war, the Germans and Italians were finally trapped. In May 1943, they surrendered. Nearly 250,000 Axis soldiers were taken prisoner. All of North Africa was now in Allied hands.

Fighting in Italy The next goal for the Allies was Italy itself. In July 1943 Allied soldiers moved north from Africa and landed on the Italian island of Sicily. Italian resistance was weakening, and by the end of the month the Italian government had forced dictator Benito Mussolini from power. The Allies captured the island a few weeks later and made plans to invade mainland Italy.

But Hitler was not going to allow the Allies to simply march through Italy into the center of Europe. After the Allies moved into southern Italy in September 1943, the invasion was slowed by German resistance as troops moved north. Bloody fighting there would continue for months to come.

READING CHECK **Summarize** What did Allied troops accomplish in the war in North Africa and Italy?

FACES OF HISTORY

Dwight D. EISENHOWER

1890–1969

Dwight D. Eisenhower was known for being patient, diplomatic, and a skilled planner. With these character traits, he proved to be the ideal person to lead the Allied armies in World War II.

Born in Texas and raised in the small farm town of Abilene, Kansas, Eisenhower attended the U.S. Military Academy and rose steadily through the ranks of the Army. During World War II, he was named supreme commander of the Allied forces in Europe. In this role Eisenhower planned and commanded D-Day, the invasion of France. After the war, Eisenhower served two terms as president.

Draw Conclusions In what ways did Eisenhower's character traits help make him a good leader?

A Turning Point in the Soviet Union

The 1941 German invasion of the Soviet Union had sputtered to a halt when the Soviet winter set in. German equipment failed in the brutally cold conditions, and Hitler's poorly equipped troops suffered greatly.

Their suffering, however, was mild compared to that of the citizens of Leningrad. After German troops failed to capture the city in 1941, Hitler ordered a siege, or a military blockade designed to force the city to surrender. "In this war for existence," he said, "we have no interest in keeping even part of this great city's population." In the winter of 1941–1942, Soviet civilians starved to death at a rate of 3,000–4,000 a day. Eventually, as many as 1 million civilians would perish in the **Siege of Leningrad**.

The Battle of Stalingrad As the weather warmed in the spring of 1942, Hitler ordered renewed assaults on the Soviet Union. To aid in the attack, he assembled a large force, including troops drawn from Italy, Romania, and Hungary.

At first, Axis forces fought well, though shortages of fuel slowed their advance. By the end of the summer, a large Axis force was poised to take the industrial city of Stalingrad on the Volga River. Stalingrad was one of the largest cities in the Soviet Union. Its factories produced tanks, guns, and other military equipment for the Soviet armies. Stalingrad's ports on the Volga shipped grain, oil, and other products throughout the Soviet Union.

Differentiating Instruction

At Level

Struggling Readers

Research Required

Materials: outline maps of North Africa and the Mediterranean

1. Organize students into groups of four or five. Have each group conduct research to follow the progress of the battles in North Africa from 1941 to 1943. Have each group make a chart listing the battles, their locations, the major participants, and their outcomes.
2. Give each group an outline map of North Africa and the Mediterranean. Have each group work together to map the battles in North Africa, labeling them with their names and dates.
3. Conduct a discussion of the war in North Africa. Point out that much of North Africa is desert, and ask students to explain North Africa's strategic importance. *controlled the Suez Canal; provided a launching pad for the invasion of Italy* **LS Visual-Spatial, Interpersonal**

Alternative Assessment Handbook, Rubrics 14: Group Activity; 20: Map Creation; and 30: Research

Reading like a Historian

Propaganda Posters

Analyzing Visuals Many countries used propaganda during World War II to try to influence the way people thought. Propaganda is information and ideas designed to promote a certain cause. In World War II, governments would create propaganda posters to encourage citizens to support the war effort. Some posters urged people to join the armed forces or to conserve food and gasoline for soldiers. Others warned about the evil intentions of the enemy.

To analyze what these posters suggest about World War II, think about

- the words in the poster
- the similarities and differences in the two posters

This German poster was created in 1942. It shows a German soldier on the battlefield.

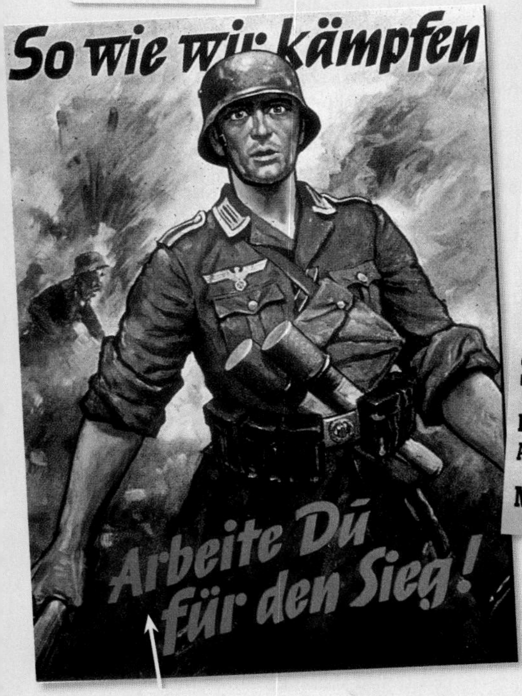

So wie wir kämpfen
Arbeite Du für den Sieg!

The German text means "This is how we fight. You, too, must work for victory."

This American poster was created in 1942. It shows a German airplane in flames.

YOUR SCRAP
...brought it down
KEEP SCRAPPING
IRON AND STEEL—RUBBER
ALL OTHER METALS—RAGS
MOVE ALL SCRAP NOW!

"Scrap" refers to the products Americans recycled to help the war effort. "Scrapping" also means "fighting."

Skills Focus READING LIKE A HISTORIAN

1. **Words** What does the German poster mean by "You, too, must work for victory"?
2. **Message** Are the messages of the two posters similar or different? Why do you think that is?

See **Skills Handbook**, p. H26

Direct Teach

Reading Focus

❸ What was the turning point in the Soviet Union? *the Battle of Stalingrad*

A Turning Point in the Soviet Union

Recall What were the results of the Siege of Leningrad? *During the winter of 1941–1942, 3,000 to 4,000 civilians starved to death each day. In all, as many as one million civilians perished.*

Summarize Why did Axis forces want to take Stalingrad? *It was one of the largest cities in the Soviet Union, a major industrial center, and a center for shipping.*

CRF: Social Studies Skills: Interpreting Infographics

Reading Like a Historian

Propaganda Posters

Compare and Contrast Compare and contrast the two posters shown on this page. How are they similar? How are they different? *possible answer—Similar: both motivate intended audience to action to help a nation; Different: German poster promotes helping Germany, American poster promotes fighting Germany.*

Skills Focus: Analyzing Visuals

At Level

Reading Like a Historian Skill

Propaganda Posters

Materials: poster board, colored pencils, markers

1. Guide the class in a discussion of the propaganda posters on this page. Remind students that propaganda is information about an organization to promote a policy or idea. Ask students what these posters have in common. Point out that propaganda can take many forms, such as articles, books, and movies.
2. Have students use reliable online or print sources to find other examples of propaganda posters. Students may find posters from other periods, such as World War I and World War II.
3. Display posters for the class to see. Guide the class in a discussion about why each poster classifies as propaganda.
4. Have students create their own propaganda posters. Display student posters in a classroom exhibit. **LS Visual-Spatial**

Alternative Assessment Handbook, Rubrics 11: Discussions; and 28: Posters

Answers

Reading Like a Historian 1. *It is encouraging German citizens to help their country.* **2.** *possible answer—The posters' messages are similar because they are both encouraging citizens to support the war effort.*

Direct Teach

Reading Focus

A Turning Point in the Soviet Union

Explain Why was Stalin so determined to hold Stalingrad? *The city was named for him.*

Summarize What was the outcome of the Battle of Stalingrad? *Over a million Soviet soldiers died, but Hitler suffered a crushing defeat; German army was forced to retreat to the west, — a turning point in the war.*

Make Judgements Why do you think Hitler stated "Surrender is forbidden"? *possible answer—He was probably blinded by his own ambition and refused to admit defeat.*

Info to Know

MacArthur and the Philippines Ten hours after attacking Pearl Harbor, the Japanese attacked Clark Air Force Base in the Philippines, which at that time was a U.S. possession. American General Douglas MacArthur had been put in charge of building a Philippine army. After the Japanese attack, MacArthur took his forces to the island fortress of Corregidor in Manila Bay and to the nearby Bataan Peninsula. The United States was concentrating its forces in Europe, and ordered MacArthur to evacuate members of the Philippine government and lead the war against Japan from Australia. Although it went against his belief in an officer's duty, MacArthur left his men, promising them, "I shall return." He fulfilled his promise in October 1944, when he waded ashore at Leyte Gulf and drove the Japanese out of the Philippines.

Answers

Reading Skills *It showed the Allies that the German army was no longer invincible.*

Reading Check *The German army had seemed invincible, but after failing to take Stalingrad, it was now retreating to the west.*

The **Battle of Stalingrad** was one of the most brutal of the war. After having bombed the city into rubble with air and artillery attacks, German troops moved into the ruins to wipe out the surviving Soviets. The Soviet defenders, pinned between the Germans and the Volga River, fought furiously for each bombed-out building and cellar hole. Soviet leader Joseph Stalin wanted to save the city that was named after him and insisted on holding it at all costs. Those costs were high. Estimates vary, but many tens of thousands of soldiers on each side died in this phase of the battle alone.

While somehow managing to hold off the German attack through the fall of 1942, Soviet marshal Georgy Zhukov (ZOO-kov) gathered his remaining forces for a counterattack. By November, the Soviets were ready to strike. A strong force broke through the Axis defenses, quickly surrounding some 250,000 men.

There was still a chance for the trapped Axis soldiers to retreat to the west and try to break through the trap, but Hitler refused to allow it. Instead, he insisted that they stand and fight, promising to supply the force by air. This effort fell far short. Hunger, cold, and Soviet attacks soon took a dreadful toll. One German soldier recorded the scene in the overflowing field hospital.

HISTORY'S VOICES

> **"Here was the greatest misery that I have seen in my whole life. An endless wailing of wounded and dying men . . . most of them had received nothing to eat for days."**
>
> —Alois Dorner, German soldier, January 1943

In late January, the German commander told Hitler that his troops had no ammunition, food, or medicine. "Surrender is forbidden," was Hitler's reply. Within days, 90,000 half-dead Axis survivors were finally captured. Many of them would soon die in Soviet prison camps.

Over 1 million Soviet soldiers had died in the defense of Stalingrad, but the result was a crushing defeat for Hitler. The seemingly invincible German army was now retreating to the west. This, along with the Allied victories in North Africa and Italy, marked a turning point in the war.

READING SKILLS
Understanding Causes and Effects What was the effect of Germany's loss at Stalingrad?

READING CHECK **Summarize** Why was the Battle of Stalingrad a turning point?

A Turning Point in the Pacific

Meanwhile in the Pacific, the attack on Pearl Harbor had been an enormous success for Japan. The damage to the U.S. Navy's Pacific Fleet took time to overcome and limited the American ability to strike back at Japan. In addition, in the early years of the war the Allies chose to focus on the fighting in Europe.

The Allies Fight Back Fortunately for the Allies, the Pacific Fleet's three aircraft carriers were not damaged in the attack on Pearl Harbor. Without the air power that aircraft carriers provided, Allied ground and naval forces would have been at the mercy of Japanese bombers. Still, following the devastation of Pearl Harbor, the Japanese navy ruled the seas.

The early months in the Pacific were difficult for the Allies. The Japanese forces were better equipped and fighting closer to home. They moved almost at will, conquering vital territory—Singapore, Hong Kong, Burma, and many strategic islands in the Pacific.

Another target was the American-held Philippines. There General **Douglas MacArthur** led a small number of American soldiers and poorly equipped Filipino troops in a doomed defense. Following the American surrender of the Philippines in April 1942, the Japanese forced 70,000 prisoners to march up the Bataan Peninsula to a distant prison camp. During this **Bataan Death March**, tropical heat, lack of food and water, and brutal violence from their captors killed 600 American and up to 10,000 Filipino prisoners. Thousands more of the survivors later perished in the inhumane prison camp.

The Battle of Coral Sea Japan was at the height of its power in May 1942 when Japanese and American aircraft carriers first came together in battle. The location was the Coral Sea, a body of water off the northeast coast of Australia. The battle took place as Japanese forces were preparing to invade the British-controlled Port Moresby on the island of New Guinea. A group of Allied vessels tried to block the attack. Both sides lost an aircraft carrier in the Battle of Coral Sea. This hurt the Americans more than it hurt the Japanese. Yet the battle marked the first time that the relentless Japanese advance had been stopped.

Differentiating Instruction

Below Level

Learners Having Difficulty

1. Have students create a short story, journal entry, or political cartoon about the German invasion of the Soviet Union.
   - A short story might tell of an invasion-related event through the eyes of a German or Soviet soldier, a guerilla fighter, or a Russian civilian.
   - A journal entry might express the feelings of a German soldier, a Soviet soldier defending his homeland, a woman left behind during the Siege of Leningrad, or a teenage survivor of the Battle of Stalingrad.
   - A cartoon might portray the changing relationship between Hitler and Stalin.
2. Have volunteers share their creations with the rest of the class.
3. Guide the class in a discussion of students' creations. How accurate or believable is each student's work? How well do students reflect their chosen point of view? **LS Verbal-Linguistic, Intrapersonal**

Alternative Assessment Handbook, Rubrics 27: Political Cartoons; and 37: Writing Assignments

The Battle of Midway A month later, in June 1942, Japanese and American carriers again fought on the high seas in the **Battle of Midway**. The Japanese had planned to capture the strategic island of Midway in the middle of the Pacific Ocean, home to a key American military base. Japanese leaders wanted the island, but they also wanted to lure the American fleet into a naval battle in which the Americans would be outnumbered and destroyed.

The Japanese had the advantage in the number of ships and aircraft carriers they could bring to Midway. But the Americans had a more important advantage: they had broken the secret Japanese code used to transmit messages. As a result, the Americans knew the date and location of the planned Japanese attack. American admiral Chester Nimitz was therefore able to plan an effective defense that overcame the Japanese superiority in firepower. Nimitz's plan worked perfectly. In the battle that followed, the Americans destroyed four Japanese carriers with a loss of only one of their own. The Allies had won a great victory, and Japan's navy had suffered a terrible blow.

The aircraft carrier USS *Yorktown* burns after being hit by Japanese torpedoes during the Battle of Midway.

Interactive

WAR IN THE PACIFIC, 1942–1944

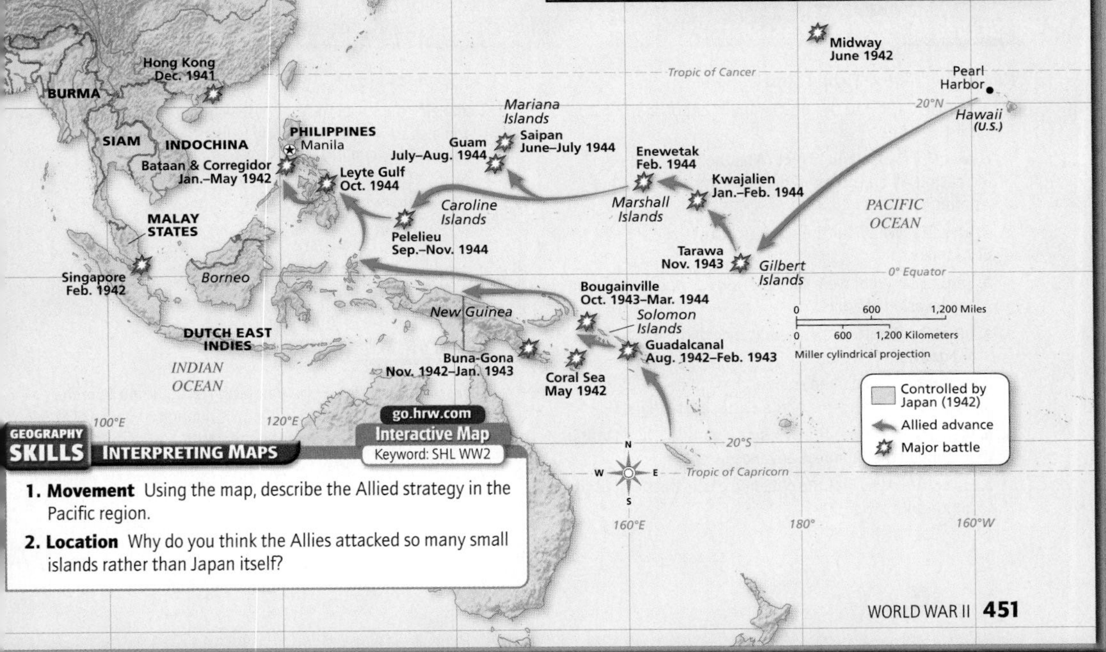

GEOGRAPHY **SKILLS** INTERPRETING MAPS

1. **Movement** Using the map, describe the Allied strategy in the Pacific region.
2. **Location** Why do you think the Allies attacked so many small islands rather than Japan itself?

Direct Teach

Reading Focus

4 What was the turning point in the Pacific? *the Battle of Midway*

A Turning Point in the Pacific

Recall What part of the U.S. Pacific fleet had not been damaged in the attack on Pearl Harbor? *aircraft carriers*

Summarize What advantage did the U.S. military have that helped overcome the Japanese forces in the Battle of Midway? *Americans had broken the secret Japanese code used to transmit messages and knew the date and location of the planned attack.*

Evaluate Why do you think that there was only a small force of Americans in the Philippines when the Japanese attacked in December 1941? *possible answer—The U.S. had just entered the war, and hadn't had a chance to station more troops there.*

Map Transparency: War in the Pacific, 1942–1944

Interactive Map: War in the Pacific

Answers

Interpreting Maps **1.** *The Allies moved from one island to another, making their way to the Philippines.* **2.** *possible answer—The Allies skipped Japanese strongholds, capturing weaker targets to use as bases to move closer to Japan.*

Differentiating Instruction

Above Level

English-Language Learners

1. Have students look at the map on this page. Ask them what is significant about the Allied advance in the Pacific. *There are two lines of Allied advance.* Draw the graphic organizer for students to see, leaving space for several boxes and arrows on each side. Omit the sample italicized answers.
2. Have students copy the graphic onto their own papers and tell them to add boxes as needed to show the principle Allied lines of advance in the Pacific and the dates and locations of individual battles. Have students work in pairs to fill in the graphic organizer showing how the two lines of advance come together. Add boxes to the class graphic organizer as volunteers call out the correct answers. **LS Interpersonal, Visual-Spatial**

Alternative Assessment Handbook, Rubric 13: Graphic Organizers

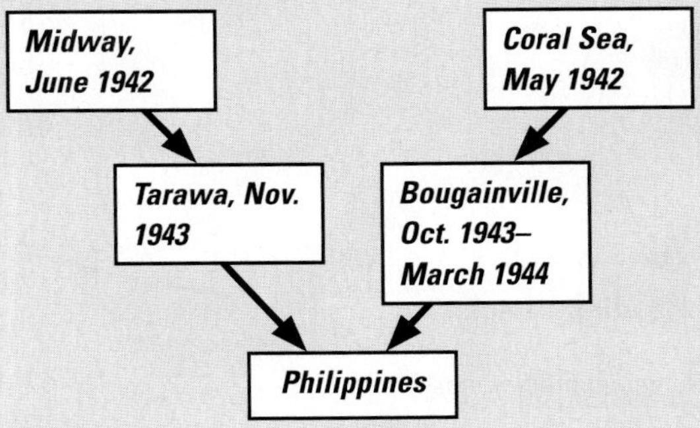

Direct Teach

Reading Focus

A Turning Point in the Pacific

Describe Describe the Allied island-hopping strategy. *The Allies skipped over Japanese strongholds and captured weaker targets, which were then used as bases for the next attacks, moving ever closer to Japan. This cut Japanese strongholds off from outside supplies, eventually weakening them.*

Evaluate What effect did Japanese kamikaze attacks have? *They didn't change the outcome of the Battle of Leyte Gulf, although they did sink dozens of Allied ships during the closing years of the war.*

CRF: History and Geography: Japanese Internment Camps

Review & Assess

Close

Guide the class in a discussion of this question: What difference do you think U.S entry into World War II made?

Review

Online Quiz, Section 2

Assess

SE Section 2 Assessment

Progress Assessment: Section 2 Quiz

Alternative Assessment Handbook

Reteach/Intervene

Interactive Reader and Study Guide, Section 2

Interactive Skills Tutor CD-ROM

Island Hopping The Battle of Midway had changed the balance of power in the Pacific. The once great Japanese advantage on the seas no longer existed, and the Allies could finally go on the offensive.

In the Pacific, the Allies pursued a strategy that became known as island hopping. This involved skipping over Japanese strongholds and capturing weaker targets. These captured islands were then used as bases for the next attacks, which moved ever closer to Japan. The bypassed Japanese strongholds, meanwhile, were cut off from outside supplies and would eventually weaken.

This was not always an easy task. For example, the Allied invasion of the island of Guadalcanal, near Australia, led to a series of brutal battles in late 1942 and early 1943. For six months, American forces fought Japanese troops on the swamp- and jungle-covered island in the **Battle of Guadalcanal**. Each side won small victories until the Japanese troops finally fled the island in February 1943.

Many other bloody battles followed. During the fighting, the Japanese demonstrated a willingness to fight to the death that amazed and terrified the Allied soldiers. Still, the Allies made steady progress in the South Pacific. From 1942 through 1944, the Allies captured locations in the Solomon, Gilbert, Marshall, Caroline, and Mariana islands. By the middle of 1944, Allied forces had fought to within striking distance of the Philippines. General MacArthur, who had surrendered the Philippines in 1942, led the Allied troops.

The first major battle in the Philippines was the Battle of Leyte (LAY-tee) Gulf, which took place in October 1944. It was the largest naval battle ever fought. Leyte Gulf saw the first major use of a new Japanese weapon—the kamikaze attack. The **kamikazes** were Japanese pilots who loaded their planes with explosives and deliberately crashed into Allied ships, sacrificing their own lives in the process. Kamikaze attacks did not change the outcome of Leyte Gulf, but they did sink dozens of Allied ships during the closing years of the war.

The Battle of Leyte Gulf ended in an Allied victory. It would take months more of fighting for the Allies to take control of the Philippines, but Japan's once-mighty naval power was virtually destroyed.

READING CHECK **Find the Main Idea** How was the Battle of Midway a turning point in the war in the Pacific?

SECTION 2 ASSESSMENT

go.hrw.com
Online Quiz
Keyword: SHL WW2 HP

Reviewing Ideas, Terms, and People

1. **a. Recall** What was the key German weapon in the battle for the Atlantic?
   b. Identify Cause and Effect What helped lead to the increasing Allied success in the battle for control of the Atlantic?
2. **a. Identify** What was the significance of the **Battle of El Alamein**?
   b. Sequence What were the main events leading up to the Allied invasion of Italy?
3. **a. Identify** What was the significance of the **Battle of Stalingrad**?
   b. Evaluate How did the stubbornness of both Hitler and Stalin affect the outcome of the Battle of Stalingrad?
4. **a. Identify** What was the first major battle in World War II that stopped the Japanese advance?
   b. Elaborate Why was the outcome of the **Battle of Midway** so important to the Allies?

Critical Thinking

5. **Identify Cause and Effect** Use your notes for this section and a chart like the one below to identify the main turning points of the war in 1942–1943.

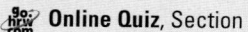

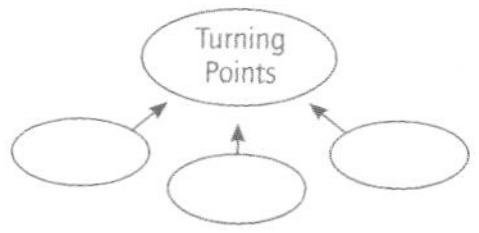

FOCUS ON WRITING

6. **Description** Write a one-paragraph letter home from the viewpoint of a civilian in Stalingrad during the Battle of Stalingrad. In your letter, describe the battle and its outcome.

Section 2 Assessment Answers

1 **a.** U-boats
b. better equipped Allied convoys and the breaking of a key German code system

2. **a.** It was a smashing victory for the British, and severely weakened Axis power in North Africa.
b. the defeat of Axis forces in North Africa; the move of Allied soldiers from Africa to Sicily; weakened resistance among the Italians; Mussolini's fall from power

3. **a.** It was one of the turning points of the war, as Soviet forces broke through Axis defenses and forced them to retreat to the west.
b. Stalin held the city at all costs; Hitler refused to allow his troops to retreat; over a million Soviet soldiers died; Hitler suffered a crushing defeat.

4. **a.** Battle of Coral Sea
b. changed balance of power in Pacific

5. Answers should include three of the following: Battle of El Alamein; Battle of Stalingrad; Battle of Coral Sea; Battle of Midway

6. Student letters will vary but should show an understanding of the Battle of Stalingrad.

Answers

Reading Check *It changed the balance of power in the Pacific, eliminating the once great Japanese advantage on the seas, and allowing the Allies to go on the offensive.*

World Literature

Wislawa Szymborska (1923–)

About the Reading Poet Wislawa Szymborska was born in western Poland in 1923. She studied Polish literature and sociology in college and published her first poem in 1945. Many of her poems are less than a page in length, but they are powerful reflections on subjects such as war, love, and human suffering. Szymborska was awarded the Nobel Prize for Literature in 1996.

AS YOU READ **Think about what this poem might have to do with World War II.**

Nazi soldiers round up Polish Jews in Warsaw in 1942.

Excerpt from

Hatred

by Wislawa Szymborska

See how efficient it still is,
how it keeps itself in shape—
our century's hatred.
How easily it vaults the tallest obstacles.
How rapidly it pounces, tracks us down.

It's not like other feelings.
At once both older and younger.
It gives birth itself to the reasons
that give it life.
When it sleeps, it's never eternal rest.
And sleeplessness won't sap its strength; it feeds it.

One religion or another—
whatever gets it ready, in position.
One fatherland or another—
whatever helps it get a running start.
Justice also works well at the outset
until hate gets its own momentum going.
Hatred. Hatred.
Its face twisted in a grimace
of erotic ecstasy . . .

Hatred is a master of contrast—
between explosions and dead quiet,
red blood and white snow.
Above all, it never tires
of its leitmotif—the impeccable executioner
towering over its soiled victim.

It's always ready for new challenges.
If it has to wait awhile, it will.
They say it's blind. Blind?
It has a sniper's keen sight
and gazes unflinchingly at the future
as only it can.

Skills FOCUS **READING LIKE A HISTORIAN**

go.hrw.com
World Literature
Keyword: SHL WRLIT

1. **Analyze** What words does Szymborska use to suggest that hatred is a living thing?
2. **Interpret Literature as a Source** How do you think Szymborska's Polish background may have affected this poem?

See **Skills Handbook**, p. H28

World Literature

"Hatred"

Word Help

vault to jump or leap over
outset begining
momentum the force a moving object has as a result of its motion
grimace twisted or distorted facial expression
impeccable flawless; incapable of wrong-doing

Meet the Writer

Wislawa Szymborska (1923-) Wislawa Szymborska did not have to look far for the subject of her poem "Hatred." The twentieth century was a very difficult one for her native country. Poland was one of the new nations on the map of Europe in 1918, following World War I. Just 21 years later it was overrun by Germany and the Soviet Union and became a Soviet satellite after World War II.

Szymborska's first collection of poems was published in 1952, when Poland was under Communist control. In that book and her next, she tried to conform to Socialist Realism, the Communist government's officially approved literary style. She now disowns these, saying that Socialist Realism did not represent her poetic intentions.

When Szymborska won the Nobel Prize in 1996 she had published 16 volumes of poetry. In Poland, many people memorize and recite her poems. Instead of seeking publicity, however, she does her best to stay out of the spotlight.

Differentiating Instruction

Learners Having Difficulty — Below Level

Tell students that poetry often presents very powerful images. In her poem "Hatred," Witislawa Szymborska has used words to paint a vivid image of that emotion. Have students work in pairs to create pictures that illustrate Szymborska's images. Display students' pictures for the class to see. Guide the class in a discussion of the pictures. **LS Interpersonal, Visual-Spatial**

Alternative Assessment Handbook, Rubric 3: Artwork

Advanced Learners/Gifted and Talented — Above Level

Have students write an essay about an event of the past century that could have been inspired by hatred. Students' essays should answer the following questions: What violent act(s) did it inspire? What, if anything, could be done to change that hatred to acceptance? Ask volunteers to read their essays to the rest of the class. **LS Verbal-Linguistic**

Alternative Assessment Handbook, Rubrics 35: Solving Problems; and 41: Writing to Express

Answers

Reading Like a Historian **1.** *vaults, pounces, sleeps;* **2.** *possible answer—Szymborska's poem may describe the "hatred" with which German forces devastated Poland in the blitzkrieg.*

History and Geography

The Battle of Stalingrad

Activity **Victory and Defeat** Have students write two short newspaper articles and headlines—one announcing the victory at Stalingrad for an American newspaper, the other announcing the defeat for a German newspaper.

Info to Know

What's in a Name? Some historians have argued that Hitler was determined to take Stalingrad because of his deep-seated hatred for Russian leader, Joseph Stalin. It has also been argued that the Russians put up an incredible defense because the city was named for their Russian leader. In 1961, Stalingrad was renamed Volgograd, "the town on the Volga."

Primary Source

"Surrender is forbidden. 6 Army will hold their positions to the last man and last round and by their heroic endurance will make an unforgettable contribution towards the establishment of a defensive front and the salvation of the Western world."

—Supreme Commander (Hitler) to 6 Army, January 24, 1943

Info to Know

General Friedrich von Paulus Friedrich von Paulus served as commander of the German Sixth Army and was ordered by Hitler to take Stalingrad. When it became clear that the German Army might become trapped, he requested that the army be allowed to withdraw his troops from Stalingrad. Hitler refused. The surrender of the German Army in February 1943 infuriated Hitler, who ordered a day of national mourning for the men who had been killed and to recognize the shame of the defeat. Von Paulus was imprisoned by the Russians and then later testified at the Nuremberg Trials.

HISTORY & Geography

The Battle of Stalingrad

Battles and wars are fought to control territory. For Germany, capturing the city of Stalingrad was a key goal—it would help the Germans take the rich oil fields and industrial areas of the southern Soviet Union.

But geography helped the Soviets win the Battle of Stalingrad. First, Stalingrad was located far from Germany, which made it hard for the Germans to supply and reinforce their troops. Second, the Soviets used the city's environment to their advantage, fighting a deadly urban war. Finally, the Soviet winter killed German soldiers and ruined equipment. In the end, Germany suffered a major defeat.

The Factory District
Some of the most intense fighting took place in the ruins of the factories in northern Stalingrad. Soviet defenders hid in the wreckage to ambush German attackers.

THE INVASION OF THE SOVIET UNION, 1941–1943

▲ German tanks and equipment lay in ruins after a Soviet attack outside Stalingrad.

Differentiating Instruction

Below Level

Learners Having Difficulty

Materials: colored markers, drawing paper, map of Europe showing the Soviet Union

1. Organize the class into mixed-ability pairs. Have each pair create its own map of the Soviet Union. Maps should show the city of Stalingrad.
2. Have each pair draw the German advance across the Soviet Union on their maps. Maps should also include a key showing the dates of the German siege of Stalingrad.
3. Have students include the length of the siege on their map keys.
4. Have volunteers share their maps with the class. Have students keep the maps as a study tool. **LS Interpersonal, Logical-Mathematical**

Alternative Assessment Handbook, Rubric 20: Map Creation

▲ Soviet troops engaged in house-to-house fighting during the battle.

The Volga River
The wide river helped protect the Soviets from a German attack from the rear, but it also meant that getting supplies and reinforcements was difficult.

GEOGRAPHY SKILLS INTERPRETING MAPS

1. **Location** How did Stalingrad's location on the Volga River both help and hurt the Soviet defenders?
2. **Human-Environment Interaction** How was the Battle of Stalingrad affected by geography?

History and Geography

Info to Know

Combat in Stalingrad Over one million soldiers were killed in the fighting in Stalingrad. It has been reported that the average life-expectancy of Soviet soldiers during the fighting was about one day, 24 hours. German troops, who had experienced easier victories during the Blitzkrieg, were suddenly involved in hand-to-hand, door-to-door combat. They suffered from lack of fuel, ammunition, and clothing. Many died from exposure to the cold winter weather, disease, and hunger.

Primary Source

"The Red Army and Navy and the whole of the Soviet people must fight for every inch of Soviet soil, fight to the last drop of blood for our towns and villages…onward to victory!"

—Joseph Stalin, July 1941

Primary Source

"The disaster of Stalingrad profoundly shocked the German people and armed forces alike…Never before in Germany's history had so large a body of troops come to so dreadful an end."

—General Siegfried von Westphal, 1943

Skills Focus: Identifying Main Idea and Details

At Level

Reading Skill
Military Decisions

1. Review the information in the feature and in the text about the Battle of Stalingrad. Remind students that the German army was ordered to stay in the city and continue the battle despite the difficult conditions.
2. Have students write a petition to Hitler and military leaders in Berlin asking permission to withdraw the German troops from the city. Students should focus on the bitter cold, lack of supplies, and hopeless fighting conditions faced by the army.
3. Have volunteers share their letters with the class. **LS Verbal-Linguistic**

Alternative Assessment Handbook, Rubric 43: Writing to Persuade

Answers

Interpreting Maps 1. *The Volga was used to transport goods and soldiers into Stalingrad, for either Russia or Germany.* **2.** *Stalingrad was far from Germany, which made it difficult for Germans to supply and reinforce their troops; Soviets used the urban environment to their advantage; harsh Soviet winter killed many ill-equipped German troops.*

Preteach

Getting Started

Use the **Interactive Reader and Study Guide** to give students a quick preview of the section.

Interactive Reader and Study Guide, Section 3

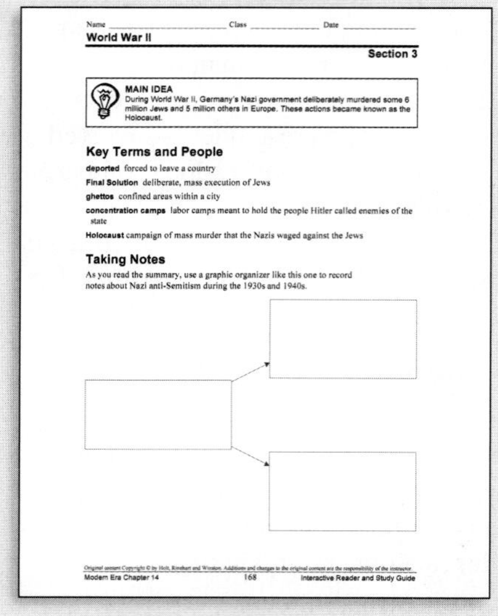
Name ______ Class ______ Date ______

World War II

Section 3

MAIN IDEA
During World War II, Germany's Nazi government deliberately murdered some 6 million Jews and 5 million others in Europe. These actions became known as the Holocaust.

Key Terms and People

deported forced to leave a country

Final Solution deliberate, mass execution of Jews

ghettos confined areas within a city

concentration camps labor camps meant to hold the people Hitler called enemies of the state

Holocaust campaign of mass murder that the Nazis waged against the Jews

Taking Notes

As you read the summary, use a graphic organizer like this one to record notes about Nazi anti-Semitism during the 1930s and 1940s.

Modern Era Chapter 14 168 Interactive Reader and Study Guide

CRF: Vocabulary Builder: Section 3

Taking Notes

Nazi Anti-Semitism—Nazi government passes a variety of restrictive laws targeting German Jews; thousands of Jews are deported or flee Germany; Nazi leaders implement the "Final Solution;" Jews are forced into ghettos and sent to concentration camps; six million Jews are killed.

go.hrw.com
Online Resources
KEYWORD: SHL WW2
ACTIVITY: Report on Anne Frank

Section 3 The Holocaust

Before You Read

Main Idea

During World War II, Germany's Nazi government deliberately murdered some 6 million Jews and 5 million others in Europe. These actions became known as the Holocaust.

Reading Focus

1. What was the history of Nazi anti-Semitism during the 1930s?
2. What was the Nazi government's "Final Solution"?
3. How did the world react to Hitler's efforts to destroy European Jews?

Key Terms and People

deported
Final Solution
ghetto
concentration camps
Holocaust

Taking Notes Take notes about Nazi anti-Semitism during the 1930s and 1940s.

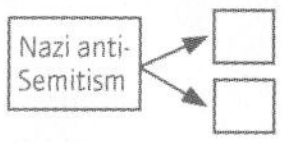

The Inside Story

Can music keep you alive? As a young musician played Chopin's Nocturne in C-sharp Minor for a radio broadcast, a German attack knocked the radio station off the air. That was the last broadcast of Polish Radio until the end of World War II. The year was 1939, and the young musician was Wladyslaw Szpilman (SPEEL-man), a Jewish pianist.

After German forces stormed through Poland, Szpilman—with his family and thousands of other Jews—was forced into a small, confined area of the city of Warsaw. When other Warsaw Jews were shipped off to Nazi labor camps, Szpilman managed to escape. He survived by hiding in the ruins of Warsaw, living in the rubble of bombed out buildings. Somehow, he managed to find enough food to stay alive. He kept his sanity by playing musical pieces in his head, mentally performing everything he had ever played or composed.

Near the end of the war, Szpilman was discovered by a German soldier, Wilm Hosenfeld. When Hosenfeld found out that Szpilman was a pianist, he demanded that Szpilman prove this by playing an abandoned piano. Szpilman had not touched a piano in over two years, but his fingers slowly remembered what to do. Soon, the sounds of Chopin echoed through the ruined building. Hosenfeld had grown to hate his government's murderous policies toward Jews and decided to protect the pianist. In the closing days of the war, Hosenfeld helped Szpilman survive by bringing him food and keeping his hiding place a secret.

When Polish radio returned to the air after the end of the war in 1945, its first broadcast was performed by Wladyslaw Szpilman—playing the same Chopin piece that had been interrupted by Nazi bombs six years earlier. ■

◄ Wladyslaw Szpilman at his piano

Nazi Anti-Semitism

At the time of Hitler's rise to power in Germany, there were about 9 million Jews in Europe. Most lived outside Germany, but Hitler still blamed Jews for many of Germany's problems. He also promoted a belief in the racial superiority of the German people. There was no factual basis for Hitler's anti-Semitism or for his claims about the German "master race." However, for many Germans who had suffered through World War I, the humiliation of the Treaty of Versailles, and the economic crises of the 1920s and 1930s, there was something appealing in Hitler's twisted vision. Jews were a convenient scapegoat—a group to blame for Germany's problems.

Teach the Main Idea

At Level

The Holocaust

1. **Teach** Ask students the Reading Focus questions to teach this section.
2. **Apply** Organize students into small groups. Have groups discuss the Holocaust and then list factors that allowed it to happen. *The Holocaust was Hitler's genocidal campaign against the Jews. Factors: anti-Semitism; Hitler's ideas of a "master race;" countries' limited immigration; many of the countries Hitler's armies conquered had large Jewish populations*
3. **Review** Ask volunteers from each group to read their definitions and lists to the class. Guide the class in a discussion of the Holocaust.
4. **Practice/Homework** Have each student write a one-page essay about whether the Holocaust, or something similar to it, could happen today. **LS Interpersonal, Verbal-Linguistic**

Alternative Assessment Handbook, Rubrics 11: Discussions; and 14: Group Activity

Hitler's anti-Semitism was not new. As you read in the previous chapter, there was a long history of anti-Semitism in Europe. But in Nazi Germany this hostility based on religion changed into hatred based on race. During the 1930s, Hitler's Nazi government passed the Nuremberg Laws, creating a separate legal status for German Jews. Thousands of Jews were deported from Germany. To be **deported** is to be forced to leave a country. Many thousands of others left Germany on their own.

Emigration, however, was not an option for all German Jews. Nazi laws had left many without money or property, and countries were often unwilling to take in poor immigrants. The United States and many European nations were still recovering from the Great Depression and would not accept newcomers who would compete for scarce jobs. Furthermore, some countries, including the United States, had strict limits on the number of Germans who could enter the country.

As a result, at the start of World War II, about 250,000 Jews still lived in Germany and Austria. With the outbreak of war, emigration became even more difficult, and Germany finally outlawed it in late 1941. The remaining Jews under German rule were trapped.

READING CHECK **Summarize** Describe Nazi anti-Semitism in the 1930s.

The "Final Solution"

As Hitler's powerful armies conquered large areas of Europe during the early years of World War II, millions of Jews came under Nazi control. As a result, Nazi leaders eventually adopted a plan they called the **Final Solution**: the deliberate mass execution of Jews.

The Killing Begins The Nazis used several brutal methods to deal with the Jewish civilians who came under German control. At first, some Jews were forced into a **ghetto**, or a confined area within a city. Often, walls or barbed wire fences prevented the Jews from leaving, and armed guards shot those trying to escape. The most notorious ghetto was in the Polish city of Warsaw, which housed 400,000 people. Most of these people eventually died of starvation or were murdered by the Nazis.

Other Jews were sent to labor camps called **concentration camps**, which were meant to hold the people Hitler called enemies of the state. At the camps, Jews and other prisoners were forced to work as slave laborers. Some were subjected to cruel medical experiments. All endured severe hunger, which killed many.

Hitler's forces also carried out large-scale executions of Jews and other civilians in villages across Poland. German soldiers gunned down men, women, and children without mercy.

During Germany's invasion of the Soviet Union in 1941, the Nazis established mobile killing units to destroy the Jews who lived in Soviet territory. These mobile killing units carried out executions on a massive scale, often aided by local people and police, known as collaborators. For example, in one two-day period in September 1941, nearly 35,000 Jews were murdered at a place called Babi Yar, near the Soviet city of Kiev.

Yet as bloody as this work was, Nazi leaders were not satisfied. The killing was simply leaving behind too much evidence of Nazi crimes. Therefore, the Germans established a number of special concentration camps in Poland for the main purpose of killing large numbers of Jews and destroying their bodies. These death camps, such as Auschwitz, had specially designed gas chambers in which thousands of people were killed every day. The camps also had furnaces for the disposal of bodies.

READING SKILLS
Understanding Causes and Effects Why did the Nazis establish death camps?

FACES OF HISTORY

Anne FRANK
1929–1945

Anne Frank was a young Jewish girl who lived in Germany when Hitler came to power. Anne and her family soon fled to the Netherlands. After war erupted, German troops began rounding up Jews in the Netherlands, and the Franks were forced to hide above Anne's father's office. Anne kept a diary of her family's two years in hiding.

In 1944 the Nazi secret police discovered the Franks and sent them to a concentration camp. Anne was eventually transferred to the Bergen-Belsen camp, where she died of disease in March 1945. Just a few weeks later, the camp was liberated by Allied troops.

Anne's diary was published following the war. It has since been translated into more than 50 languages.

Make Inferences Why do you think Anne Frank's diary has been translated into so many languages?

Direct Teach

Reading Focus

1 What was the history of Nazi anti-Semitism during the 1930s? *Nazis passed laws creating separate legal status for Jews, denying citizenship, right to government jobs, and limiting right to work and own property; thousands of Jews deported*

Nazi Anti-Semitism

Identify How did many Germans view Hitler's anti-Semitic vision for a master race? *Jews were a scapegoat.*

Evaluate Why do you think the German government changed its position from encouraging Jews to emigrate to outlawing emigration in late 1941? *possible answer—may have known that Jews with the means to do so would go, leaving all their money and property behind*

Reading Focus

2 What was the Nazi government's "Final Solution"? *deliberate, mass execution of Jewish prisoners in German control*

The "Final Solution"

Recall What happened at Babi Yar? *Germans used mobile killing units to massacre nearly 35,000 people in two days.*

Summarize How did the Nazis carry out their "Final Solution"? *forced Jews into ghettos and concentration camps in Soviet Union; executed many Jews*

Skills Focus: Analyzing Primary Sources

At Level

Reading Like a Historian Skill
The "Final Solution"

1. Remind students that Hitler's belief in a "master race" led him to kill Jews and others he considered inferior. Guide the class in a discussion of Hitler's anti-Semitism. How did he go about blaming his victims? Why would they have felt a sense of helplessness?
2. Have students find primary sources written by concentration camp survivor. Primary sources may include letters, diary entries, memoirs, or book excerpts.
3. Tell students that they are historians assembling a book of readings by concentration camp survivors. Have students write a short essay introducing the selection. Student essays should provide background material on the writer.
4. Have volunteers read their essays to the class. Guide the class in a discussion of the essays. **LS Verbal-Linguistic**

Alternative Assessment Handbook, Rubrics 11: Discussions; and 37: Writing Assignments

Answers

Faces of History *possible answer—It is a true account that people from different cultures can appreciate.*

Reading Skills *to eliminate evidence of Nazi crimes by destroying bodies of Jews*

Reading Check *Jews had separate legal status, no citizenship and no right to hold government jobs, limited right to work and own property; thousands of Jews deported*

Direct Teach

Reading Focus

3 How did the world react to Hitler's efforts to destroy European Jews? *with disbelief; when reports were confirmed, U.S. and Great Britian officials met to discuss possible responses*

The World Reacts

Recall What evidence of German atrocities did the Allies find at Bergen-Belsen? *35,000 bodies and 60,000 survivors, many too starved or ill to be saved*

Make Inferences Why do you think it took so long to respond to the reports of Germany's widespread killing of Jews in Europe? *possible answer—The reports seemed too horrific to believe, so there was little incentive to come up with a response.*

CRF: Biography: Raoul Wallenburg

Info to Know

Efficient Murder Soon after invading the Soviet Union, the Nazis began to experiment on Russian Jews and other Soviet prisoners to determine the most efficient way to kill large numbers of people. The first method tried—machine-gunning massed groups of prisoners—was rejected as labor-intensive, inefficient, and hard to keep secret. The first experiment with gas—confining prisoners in trucks with altered exhaust systems until they were overcome by carbon monoxide fumes—was also rejected as too slow. In September 1941, some 600 Soviet POWs were placed in a sealed area with crystals of Zyklon B, a commercial pesticide. The victims quickly died of asphyxiation. The Germans later used this method to kill millions of Jews.

Answers

Forensics in History *possible answer—to prove that he was dead so that attempts to find him and bring him to justice could end*

Reading Check *Nazi leaders adopted a plan they called the "Final Solution"—the deliberate, mass execution of Jewish prisoners.*

FORENSICS in History

Was It the Angel of Death?

The body of Wolfgang Gerhard, dug up in Embu, Brazil, in 1985 was little more than rotting bones. But Nazi hunters believed Gerhard was actually the Nazi war criminal Josef Mengele—known as the Angel of Death for his cruel medical experiments on concentration camp prisoners. Could modern science find out once and for all?

How could he be identified? All the cells in the human body contain DNA. DNA directs the formation, growth, and reproduction of cells. Sections of DNA called genes can be used to tell one human being apart from another through a process called genetic fingerprinting. Genes can also be used to establish whether people are related.

In 1985, documents were discovered that connected Mengele to Gerhard, and a team of forensics scientists set out to determine whether the bones in Brazil were those of the Angel of Death.

The scientists used genetic fingerprinting to find the answer. They took DNA samples from the remains of Gerhard's body and compared them to DNA from Mengele's son, who still lived in Germany. The results? The odds were 1,800 to 1 that the remains were from anyone other than Mengele. Later, dental records and other DNA tests found the same results. In other words, the man who had been calling himself Wolfgang Gerhard was indeed Josef Mengele, the Angel of Death.

▲ Josef Mengele in 1945

Draw Conclusions Why do you think it was important to determine the identity of Josef Mengele?

The Victims Jews were not the only victims of Nazi concentration and death camps. The Nazis also imprisoned other groups they viewed as inferior, including Poles, Slavs, homosexuals, people with disabilities, and the Romany, an ethnic group also known as Gypsies. By the end of the war, some 5 million people from these groups had died in Nazi camps.

It was Jews, however, who suffered the most under the Nazis. During the war, 6 million Jews—two of every three in Europe—died at Nazi hands. Entire families were killed. Today we refer to this mass murder of Jews as the **Holocaust**.

THE IMPACT TODAY

January 27—the anniversary of the Soviet liberation of the Auschwitz death camp—is marked in many countries as Holocaust Memorial Day.

READING CHECK **Find the Main Idea** What was the Final Solution, and how did the Nazis attempt to carry out this plan?

The World Reacts

Other countries were aware of the Nazi government's anti-Semitism in the 1930s. After the outbreak of war, however, the full extent of Hitler's brutality was shielded from the outside world.

In 1942 people in the United States and Europe began to hear disturbing reports of widespread killing of Jews in Europe. At first, these reports seemed too horrific to believe. But as the reports were investigated and confirmed, officials in the United States and Great Britain met to discuss possible responses. No concrete action was taken, however.

Finally, in January 1944, after millions of Jews had already died, the United States established the War Refugee Board to help rescue European Jews. The board helped save some 200,000 Jews. But Allied leaders were unwilling to take actions such as bombing the railroad lines that led to the death camps. This government inaction was in part because Allied leaders did not want to do anything that might interfere with the war effort. Apathy and anti-Semitism also contributed to this inaction.

As Allied forces in Europe started to push back the Germans, they came upon Nazi camps. In the summer of 1944, Soviet troops made one of the first discoveries, an abandoned death camp in Poland. The Germans had tried to cover up evidence of their crimes before leaving—including removing or killing the prisoners.

Collaborative Learning

At Level

Saving the Jews

1. Organize students into groups of four or five. Tell them that it is 1942 and they have just heard about Hitler's widespread killing of Jews in Europe.
2. Have each group develop a campaign to convince the U.S. government to take action to save European Jews. Campaigns may include letters to editors or elected officials, speeches, posters, or other materials they think would help convince people to stop Hitler's widespread killing of Jews.
3. Have each group present its campaign to the rest of the class.
4. Lead the class in a discussion of student campaign materials. **LS Interpersonal**

Alternative Assessment Handbook, Rubric 14: Group Activity

Eventually, though, the Germans were unable to hide their actions. When the Soviets liberated the Auschwitz death camp in January of 1945, they found about 7,000 starving survivors. They also found hundreds of thousand of pieces of clothing—a strong indication that many more people had been held there.

In April 1945, American forces reached the Buchenwald camp. There they found thousands of corpses as well as many inmates who were nearly dead. Around the same time, the British reached the Bergen-Belsen camp, where tens of thousands had been murdered.

The soldiers who discovered the death camps were shocked at what they found. American soldier Reid Draffen visited the Dachau camp after it had been liberated by the Allies, and remembered the horrible scene:

HISTORY'S VOICES

> **"I thought I had seen everything. I was a hardened soldier. I had been in combat since October 1944, and I had seen death and destruction that was unparalleled in modern times. But this—there are no words to describe this."**
>
> —Captain Reid Draffen, in *War Stories: Remembering World War II*

The scenes of horror at the death camps gave the world a clear picture of what a world controlled by Adolf Hitler might have been like. But Nazi hopes of world domination were about to come to an end.

READING CHECK **Summarize** How did the world react to Nazi killing of Jews and other prisoners?

▲ **Prisoners at the Buchenwald concentration camp after their liberation by Allied troops**

EUROPE'S JEWISH POPULATION

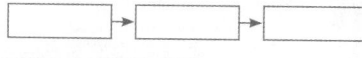

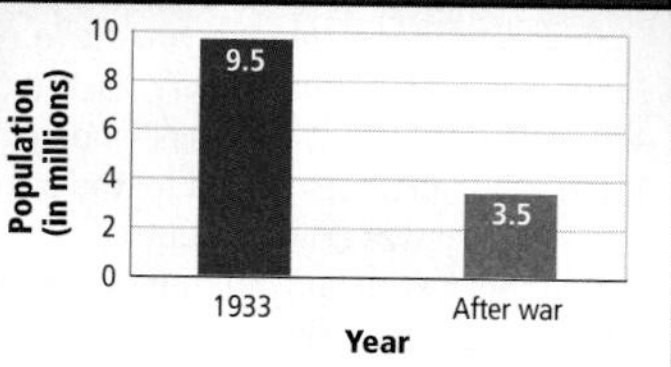

Source: United States Holocaust Memorial Museum

Skills Focus INTERPRETING GRAPHS

Analyze How many fewer Jews lived in Europe in 1950 than had lived there in 1933, before World War II began?

SECTION 3 ASSESSMENT

go.hrw.com
Online Quiz
Keyword: SHL WW2 HP

Reviewing Ideas, Terms, and People

1. **a. Describe** What was the official Nazi policy toward Jews prior to World War II?
   b. Identify Cause and Effect What were the effects of Nazi anti-Jewish policies on Germany's Jewish population?
2. **a. Identify** What was the Nazi government's **Final Solution**?
   b. Contrast Contrast Nazi policies toward Jews before and after the start of the war.
   c. Elaborate Why did the Germans build death camps?
3. **a. Identify** What was the significance of the War Refugee Board?
   b. Analyze Why did the Allies fail to take more actions to stop the Nazi killing of Jews?
   c. Predict What might have happened if the Allies had made liberating the Jews a priority early in the war?

Critical Thinking

4. **Sequence** Copy the chart below and use your notes from the section to describe the main events of the Holocaust.

→	→	

FOCUS ON WRITING

5. **Persuasion** Could the Allies have done more to lessen the loss of life during the Holocaust? If so, what actions should the Allies have taken? Using information from the section, write a newspaper editorial that presents your views.

Review & Assess

Close

Guide students in a discussion about the atrocities of the Holocaust and how comparable events continue to occur today, such as in Rwanda, Bosnia, and Darfur.

Review

Online Quiz, Section 3

Assess

SE Section 3 Assessment

Progress Assessment: Section 3 Quiz

Alternative Assessment Handbook

Reteach/Intervene

Interactive Reader and Study Guide, Section 3

Interactive Skills Tutor CD-ROM

Answers

Interpreting Graphs *about six million*

Reading Check *At first they didn't believe them, but as the reports were confirmed, they met to discuss possible responses. In January 1944, the United States established the War Refugee Board to help rescue Jews in Europe.*

Section 3 Assessment Answers

1. **a.** Germany passed a variety of restrictive laws creating a separate legal status for Jews, denying them citizenship and the right to hold government jobs, and severely limiting their right to work and own property. Thousands of Jews were deported.
   b. Many fled Germany, but Nazi laws left many German Jews without money or property. Also, some countries were unwilling to take in poor immigrants.
2. **a.** deliberate, mass execution of Jewish prisoners
   b. Before the war, the Nazis just stripped the Jews of their rights and property. After the start of the war, they decided to kill them all.
   c. to efficiently kill large numbers of Jews and dispose of their bodies
3. **a.** It helped save some 200,000 Jews.
   b. They were focused on defeating the Axis Powers.
   c. possible answer—It probably would have been difficult, since the concentration camps were behind enemy lines. It could have shifted the focus of the war and allowed Hitler to concentrate on defending the German homeland, prolonging the war.
4. German Jews stripped of rights and property; Jews forced into ghettos, sent to concentration camps; Einsatzgruppen carry out mass executions; Germans set up death camps; Allies free concentration camps
5. Editorials will vary but should present convincing ideas about lessening the loss of life during the Holocaust.

Preteach

Getting Started

Use the **Interactive Reader and Study Guide** to give students a quick preview of the section.

Interactive Reader and Study Guide, Section 4

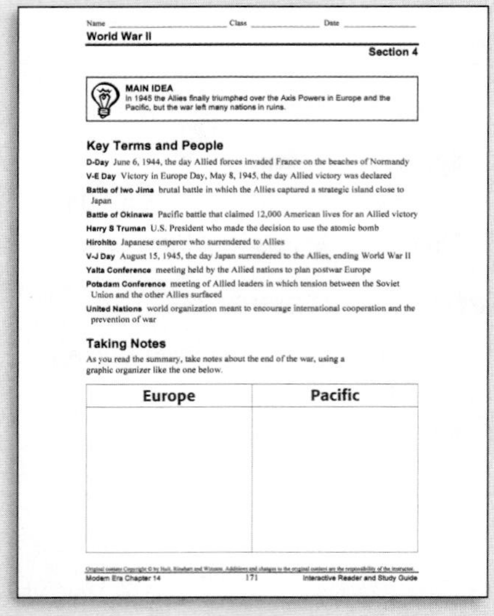
Name ______ Class ______ Date ______

World War II

Section 4

MAIN IDEA
In 1945 the Allies finally triumphed over the Axis Powers in Europe and the Pacific, but the war left many nations in ruins.

Key Terms and People

D-Day June 6, 1944, the day Allied forces invaded France on the beaches of Normandy

V-E Day Victory in Europe Day, May 8, 1945, the day Allied victory was declared

Battle of Iwo Jima brutal battle in which the Allies captured a strategic island close to Japan

Battle of Okinawa Pacific battle that claimed 12,000 American lives for an Allied victory

Harry S Truman U.S. President who made the decision to use the atomic bomb

Hirohito Japanese emperor who surrendered to Allies

V-J Day August 15, 1945, the day Japan surrendered to the Allies, ending World War II

Yalta Conference meeting held by the Allied nations to plan postwar Europe

Potsdam Conference meeting of Allied leaders in which tension between the Soviet Union and the other Allies surfaced

United Nations world organization meant to encourage international cooperation and the prevention of war

Taking Notes

As you read the summary, take notes about the end of the war, using a graphic organizer like the one below.

Europe	Pacific

Modern Era Chapter 14 171 Interactive Reader and Study Guide

Academic Vocabulary

Review with students the high-use academic term in this section.

sufficient enough of what is needed (p. 859)

CRF: Vocabulary Builder: Section 4

Taking Notes

Europe—Allies fight strong German defenses on D-Day, quickly recover most of France; Germany defeated at Battle of the Bulge; Hitler commits suicide; Germany surrenders; Pacific—Battle of Iwo Jima and Battle of Okinawa claim thousands of lives; atomic bombs dropped on Hiroshima and Nagasaki; Japanese emperor Hirohito surrenders

go.hrw.com
Online Resources
KEYWORD: SHL WW2
ACTIVITY: D-Day

Section 4 The End of the War

Before You Read

Main Idea

In 1945 the Allies finally triumphed over the Axis Powers in Europe and the Pacific, but the war left many nations in ruins.

Reading Focus

1. How did the war end in Europe?
2. How did the war end in the Pacific?
3. What were the Allied plans for the postwar world?

Key Terms and People

D-Day
V-E Day
Battle of Iwo Jima
Battle of Okinawa
Harry S Truman
Hirohito
V-J Day
Yalta Conference
United Nations
Potsdam Conference

Taking Notes

As you read, compare the end of the war in Europe and in the Pacific.

Europe	Pacific

The Inside Story

How do you take back an entire continent? Packed tightly onto thousands of landing craft, more than 150,000 Allied troops set out for the beaches of German-held France. It was D-Day—June 6, 1944. When the ships neared shore, each landing craft's gate went down, and the soldiers had to plow through waist-deep water directly into German gunfire. Some were killed before they reached land. Those who made it to shore had to race past mines, ruined equipment, and their dead and wounded friends to find temporary shelter from the deadly fire.

Still, the invaders pushed on. As thousands of soldiers fell, thousands more fought their way up the bluffs that overlooked the beaches. One by one, they captured the German positions. By the end of the day, the Allies had taken all five beaches they had attacked. With over 10,000 Allied casualties, the price was high.

The first battle in the invasion of Europe was successful. The Allies had taken more than a year to plan the massive invasion, but it was worth the time it took. Germany now had to contend with a major Allied force in Western Europe and with the Soviets in the east. It was the beginning of the end for Germany.

◀ Allied troops land at Normandy on D-Day.

Teach the Main Idea

At Level

The End of the War

1. **Teach** Ask students the Reading Focus questions to teach this section.
2. **Apply** Have students create an outline of the section using the heads as main points. Have them identify at least two main ideas under each of the subheadings.
3. **Review** Review students' outlines as a class. Have students identify the points in their outlines that they feel are most important or most interesting. Guide students in a discussion of the Tehran, Yalta, and Potsdam conferences, at which the Allies made plans for the future.
4. **Practice/Homework** Tell students that they are newspaper reporters covering the Yalta Conference. Have each student write a news story explaining what took place and the results of the conference. **LS Logical-Mathematical, Verbal-Linguistic**

Alternative Assessment Handbook, Rubrics 36: Time Lines; and 37: Writing Assignments

War Ends in Europe

While American and British military leaders were planning the invasion of France, German soldiers were busy fighting the Soviet armies in the east. After the Soviet triumph at Stalingrad in early 1943, the Soviets eventually pushed the Germans backward. By the end of the year, Axis forces had suffered 2 million casualties. Outnumbered, they were unable to stop the relentless Soviet advance.

Soviet Victories In early 1944 the Soviets finally ended the Siege of Leningrad. A major offensive in the summer achieved great success for the Soviets, leading to another 800,000 German casualties. Other important victories followed, driving Axis forces out of the Soviet Union and back into central Europe. By the end of January 1945 Soviet forces were within 40 miles of the German capital of Berlin.

D-Day As the Soviets forced the Axis armies back toward Germany, the other Allies were finalizing their plans for a massive invasion of Western Europe.

An effective invasion of Europe would be difficult. For one thing, the assault would have to come by sea. It would also have to be made directly against strong German positions.

The Allied preparations were led by American generals George Marshall and Dwight Eisenhower. In addition to assembling and training sufficient troops, the Allies needed to develop specialized equipment for transporting tanks and troops across open water. They also staged a complex plan to mislead Hitler about where the invasion would take place.

On June 6, 1944—**D-Day**—Allied forces invaded France. Over 150,000 troops landed on the beaches of Normandy that first day, forcing through the strong German defenses. Casualties were high, but D-Day was a huge victory for the Allies. With the beaches secured, more Allied forces poured into France. By July nearly 1 million soldiers had come ashore.

After some bloody fighting in the first few weeks following the landing, the Allied forces broke through German defenses in July. The Allies quickly reconquered much of France. By the end of August, the Germans had surrendered Paris. Eisenhower reported that "the enemy is routed [defeated] and running."

The Battle of the Bulge But Hitler was not yet finished. In December 1944 he ordered one last, massive counterattack in Belgium. At first the Germans made solid advances, producing a bulge in the Allied battle lines. Thus, the battle became known as the Battle of the Bulge.

ACADEMIC VOCABULARY

sufficient enough of what is needed

The End of the War, 1944–1945

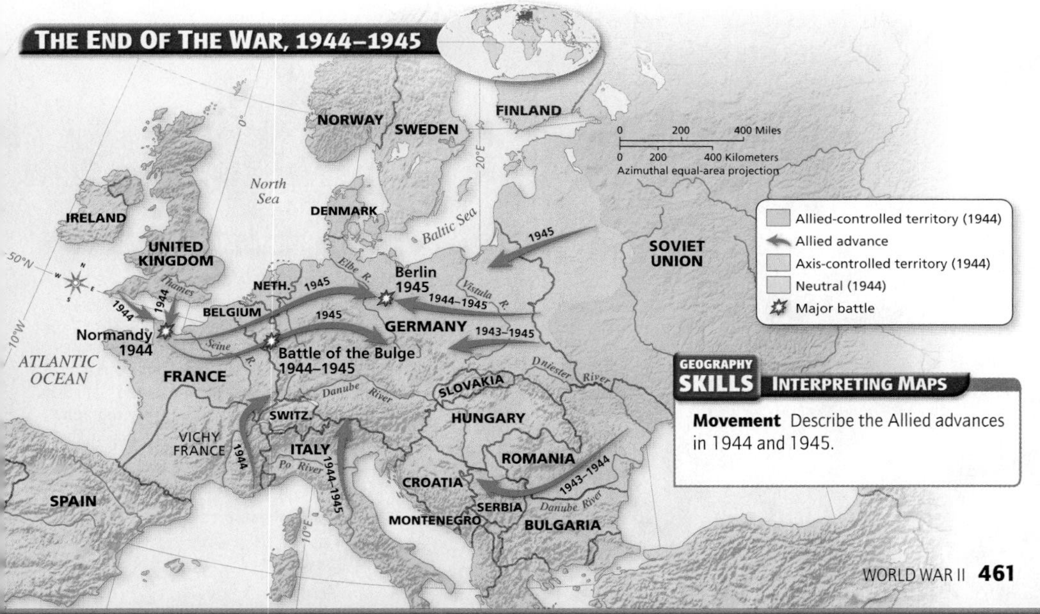

GEOGRAPHY SKILLS INTERPRETING MAPS

Movement Describe the Allied advances in 1944 and 1945.

Direct Teach

Reading Focus

1 How did the war end in Europe? *Soviets pushed Hitler's troops backward in the east and Allies launched D-Day invasion of France in the west, pushing toward Germany.*

War Ends in Europe

Recall When did the Siege of Leningrad end? *early 1944*

Analyze Why was it so difficult to open a second front in the war in Europe? *It had to come by sea, and had to be made against strong German positions.*

Evaluate Why do you think Hitler ordered the massive counterattack that led to the Battle of the Bulge? *possible answer—He wanted to make one last-ditch effort to turn back the Allies.*

Map Transparency: The End of the War, 1944–1945

Misconception Alert

You won't find it in many encyclopedias, but the largest Allied offensive operation of World War II took place in the Soviet Union, not on the shores of Normandy. In the summer of 1944, a Soviet offensive called Operation Bagration inflicted far more damage to the Germans than the D-Day landings. Stalin's campaign wiped out three Axis armies to support the Allied invasion of France, free Soviet territory from the Germans, and break the German war machine.

Skill Focus: Making Inferences

At Level

Reading Skill

What If D-Day Had Failed?

Background: Remind students that Allied casualties were high during the D-Day invasion because the attack came by sea and the Germans had strong coastal defenses.

1. Guide a discussion with students about what might have happened if the Allies' D-Day invasion of France had failed. How might it have affected the outcome of the war?
2. Have students write a scenario about what could have happened if the Germans had been expecting the attack to come from where it did and had been able to turn back the invasion.
3. Have volunteers read their scenarios to the class.
4. Guide the class in a discussion of students' scenarios. **LS Verbal-Linguistic**

Alternative Assessment Handbook, Rubric 37: Writing Assignments

Answers

Interpreting Maps *Allies advanced west from Soviet Union through Eastern Europe toward Germany; moved from United Kingdom to Normandy, France, and then to Germany; advanced north from Italy and southern France*

Direct Teach

Reading Focus

2 How did the war end in the Pacific? *The Allies continued their island-hopping strategy and attacked the major islands of Japan from the air; then the U.S. dropped two atomic bombs on Japanese cities.*

War Ends in the Pacific

Explain Why did the Allies dread the idea of invading the major islands of Japan? *Japanese defenders' willingness to fight to the death led Allied military leaders to believe that an invasion could cost up to one million Allied killed and wounded.*

Elaborate Do you think that the United States was justified in dropping atomic bombs on civilian targets in Japan? Why or why not? *possible answer—No, civilized nations don't kill civilians.*

Info to Know

Iwo Jima The famous photograph on this page shows U.S. servicemen raising the American flag on Iwo Jima after winning one of the bloodiest battles of the war. The tiny island was honeycombed with caves and tunnels, protecting many guns. After attacking the island for more than two months with shells and bombs, some 30,000 U.S. marines stormed ashore in February of 1945. Japanese resistance was so fierce that after three days of combat, the marines had advanced only about 700 yards inland.

By January 1945, the Allies had crushed the German offensive at the Battle of the Bulge. Germany's defeat marked the end of major German resistance. Within two months, Allied forces had crossed the Rhine River into Germany and were racing toward Berlin. At the same time, Soviet troops were advancing through Germany from the east.

The Germans Surrender The Soviets were the first to reach Berlin, surrounding the city in late April 1945. On May 2 they found the body of Adolf Hitler near his Berlin bunker. He had taken his own life. Berlin surrendered that same day.

With Hitler dead and Berlin in Allied hands, the war in Europe was all but over. Germany surrendered on May 7. The next day was proclaimed **V-E Day**—Victory in Europe Day. After nearly six years of bloody battle, the war in Europe was over.

READING CHECK **Draw Conclusions** What effect did D-Day have on the war in Europe?

War Ends in the Pacific

Although the Allies had achieved victory in Europe, war was still raging in the Pacific. The Allied island-hopping strategy continued to push back the Japanese, but there were several battles yet to come.

Final Battles By mid-1944 American bombers had begun making regular bombing raids on Japanese cities, including the capital, Tokyo. The attacks did severe damage, but the great distance American pilots had to travel from their bases to Japan made the raids risky.

To reduce these risks, the Americans needed bases closer to Japan. In February 1945 Allied troops landed on the Japanese island of Iwo Jima (EE-woh JEE-muh), some 750 miles south of Tokyo. During the month-long **Battle of Iwo Jima**, nearly 7,000 Americans died to capture the tiny island. More than 20,000 Japanese defenders had been on the island when the Americans attacked. All but a thousand of them fought to the death.

Iwo Jima

The Marine Corps War Memorial is located at Arlington National Cemetery in Virginia.

Skills Focus READING LIKE A HISTORIAN

The photograph at left was taken on the top of Iwo Jima's Mount Suribachi on February 23, 1945, during the Battle of Iwo Jima. The image was immediately popular in the United States and was used by the U.S. government as part of a campaign to help raise money for the war effort. It later won the Pulitzer Prize for photography.

Analyzing Visuals Why do you think the Marine Corps memorial statue was modeled on the photo of the flag raising at Iwo Jima?

See **Skills Handbook**, p. H26

Differentiating Instruction

Above Level

Research Required

Advanced Learners/Gifted and Talented

1. Have students conduct research on the Battle of the Bulge, making a list of facts about the battle, including the following:
   - When and where it took place
   - How long it lasted
   - Who was involved in it
   - Why it was important
   - Number of casualties
2. Have students find and read at least one eyewitness account of the Battle of the Bulge.
3. Have students write a brief essay explaining which material made the battle more interesting—the "cold facts" or the personal account. Students should reinforce their opinions with examples.
4. Have volunteers read their essays to the class.

LS Verbal-Linguistic

Alternative Assessment Handbook, Rubrics 30: Research; and 37: Writing Assignments

Answers

Reading Like a Historian *possible answer—It is a powerful image that portrays U.S. Marines' determination and strength against a persistent enemy.*

Reading Check *The Allies quickly reconquered much of France and started to push into Germany from the west.*

After Iwo Jima, the Americans invaded Okinawa (OH-kee-NAH-wah), an island barely 350 miles from Japan. The **Battle of Okinawa**, which lasted nearly three months, claimed 12,000 American lives. The Japanese lost the battle along with nearly all of the more than 100,000 defenders.

The Atomic Bomb After Okinawa, the next step for the Allies was to take Japan itself. But the experiences of Iwo Jima and Okinawa made the Allies dread the idea of invading the major islands of Japan. The Japanese defenders' willingness to fight to the death led American military leaders to conclude that an invasion of Japan would be too costly. They calculated that an invasion could cost up to 1 million killed or wounded Allied soldiers.

As a result, American leaders considered another option: the atomic bomb. This weapon used the energy released by the splitting of atoms and was far more powerful than ordinary bombs. A program to develop the bomb had begun in 1939, and a bomb had been successfully tested in July 1945.

Harry S Truman, who had become president when Franklin Roosevelt died in May 1945, was forced to make a difficult decision. Should the United States use the atomic bomb? Many of Truman's advisers believed that using the atomic bomb would help bring the war to a quick end and save American lives. Others believed that such a powerful weapon should be used only as a last resort. In the end, Truman decided to drop the bomb on a Japanese city in the hopes that the mighty new weapon would cause Japan to surrender.

On July 26, 1945, the Allies issued a demand for Japan's surrender. When the Japanese did not respond, plans to use the bomb went forward. On August 6, an American plane dropped an atomic bomb on the Japanese city of Hiroshima. The devastation was extreme. More than 70,000 people were killed instantly, and thousands of buildings were destroyed. Yet even this horror was not enough to bring a quick Japanese surrender. On August 9, the Americans dropped a second bomb, this time over the city of Nagasaki. Another 75,000 people died. Tens of thousands of residents of both cities would later die from radiation poisoning, an effect of their exposure to the bombs' radioactive materials.

A mushroom cloud rises over Nagasaki after the explosion of the atomic bomb.

PRIMARY SOURCES

Hiroshima

Father John A. Siemes, a German priest, was in Hiroshima when the atomic bomb was dropped on August 6, 1945. He later described the explosion:

> "Suddenly . . . the whole valley is filled by a garish light which resembles the magnesium light used in photography, and I am conscious of a wave of heat. I jump to the window to find out the cause of this remarkable phenomenon, but I see nothing more than that brilliant yellow light . . . I realize now that a bomb has burst . . .
>
> "The bright day now reveals the frightful picture ... Where the city stood everything, as far as the eye could reach, is a waste of ashes and ruin. Only several skeletons of buildings completely burned out in the interior remain. The banks of the river are covered with dead and wounded, and the rising waters have here and there covered some of the corpses . . .
>
> "As a result of the explosion of the bomb ... almost the entire city was destroyed at a single blow."

Skills Focus READING LIKE A HISTORIAN

1. **Make Generalizations** What does this source tell you about the power of the atomic bomb?
2. **Analyze Primary Sources** How would you expect the Japanese government to respond to the bombing of Hiroshima?

See **Skills Handbook**, p. H25

Direct Teach

Primary Sources

Hiroshima

Analyze Was it really necessary to use atomic weapons against Japan? Many of the top U.S. military leaders did not think so. Dwight D. Eisenhower, supreme commander of the Allies in Europe during World War II and later President of the United States, was one of them. In his 1963 book *Mandate for Change, 1953–1956,* Eisenhower wrote of being told by Secretary of War Henry L. Stimson that an atomic bomb was about to be dropped on a Japanese city:

"During his recitation of the relevant facts, I had been conscious of a feeling of depression and so I voiced to him my grave misgivings, first on the basis of my belief that Japan was already defeated and that dropping the bomb was completely unnecessary, and secondly because I thought that our country should avoid shocking world opinion by the use of a weapon whose employment was, I thought, no longer mandatory as a measure to save American lives."

Other World War II military leaders who felt that the bombing was unnecessary included President Truman's chief of staff, Admiral William D. Leahy; General Douglas MacArthur, who served as supreme commander in the Pacific during the war; and Admiral Chester W. Nimitz, commander in chief of the Pacific Fleet.

CRF: Biography: Harry S Truman

Skills Focus: Identifying Problem and Solution

At Level

Reading Skill

Defeating Japan

1. Tell students that it is 1945 and they are advisers to President Truman. The Allies have captured Okinawa, and they plan to invade the major islands of Japan. Have each student write a memorandum recommending an action to bring the war to an end. Students should weigh the feasibility of using traditional methods, such as strategic air strikes backed up by marines on shore, as opposed to more radical options, such as dropping an atomic bomb. Students should also look at the ethical and long-term consequences of their recommendations. Have them list the pros and cons of each in their memorandums and make a recommendation based on their lists.
2. Have volunteers read their memorandums to the class. Guide the class in a discussion of students' memorandums. **LS Verbal-Linguistic**

Alternative Assessment Handbook, Rubric 43: Writing to Persuade

Answers

Reading Like a Historian **1.** *It is extremely powerful and devastating.* **2.** *possible answer—Japan would immediately surrender.*

Reading Check *the dropping of atomic bombs on the Japanese cities of Hiroshima and Nagasaki*

Direct Teach

Reading Focus

3 What were the Allied plans for the postwar world? *Roosevelt and Churchill wanted no territorial gain and wanted a peaceful world in which nations chose their own governments and worked together for mutual prosperity. Stalin joined the two leaders at a conference, and agreed to work toward peace, but wanted former Polish territory.*

The Postwar World

Identify What was the Atlantic Charter? *a joint declaration by Franklin Roosevelt and Winston Churchill outlining what the two men saw as the purpose of the war*

Summarize What were some of the challenges that faced the postwar world? *Much of Europe and Asia lay in ruins, national economies were near collapse, millions of displaced people had to rebuild their lives, and concerns increased about the spread of communism and Soviet influence.*

Quick Facts Transparency: World War II Casualties

Primary Source

The eighth point of the Atlantic Charter stated that "all of the nations of the world, for realistic as well as spiritual reasons, must come to the abandonment of the use of force. Since no future peace can be maintained if land, sea or air armaments continue to be employed by nations which threaten, or may threaten, aggression outside of their frontiers, they believe… that the disarmament of such nations is essential. They will likewise aid and encourage all other practicable measures which will lighten for peace-loving peoples the crushing burden of armaments."

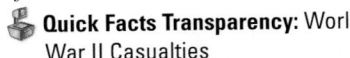

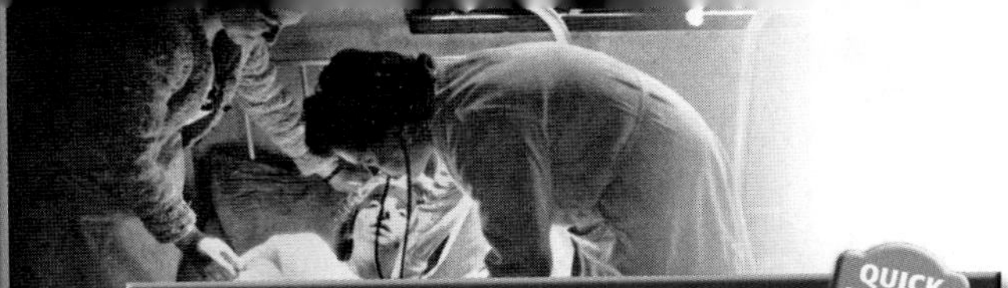

World War II Casualties

QUICK FACTS

		MILITARY DEAD	MILITARY WOUNDED	CIVILIAN DEAD
ALLIES	**China**	1,310,000	1,753,000	1,000,000+
	France	213,000	4,000,000	350,000
	Great Britain	264,000	277,000	93,000
	Soviet Union	11,000,000	unknown	7,000,000+
	United States	292,000	672,000	6,000
AXIS	**Germany**	3,500,000	5,000,000	780,000
	Italy	242,000	66,000	153,000
	Japan	1,300,000	4,000,000	672,000

Source: Encyclopedia Britannica

Finally acknowledging Japan's utter defeat, Japanese emperor **Hirohito** surrendered on August 15, 1945, the date now known as **V-J Day**. World War II was finally over.

READING CHECK **Find the Main Idea** What brought an end to the war in the Pacific?

The Postwar World

At the end of the war, much of Europe and Asia lay in ruins. Tens of millions of people had died in the war, many of them civilians. The heaviest losses were in the nations of Eastern Europe, including Poland, Yugoslavia, and the Soviet Union, but Germany, Japan, and China had also suffered greatly. In these areas the physical devastation was nearly complete. Entire cities, villages, and farms had been destroyed or damaged heavily, and national economies were near collapse. Food, shelter, and medicine were scarce.

The war also uprooted millions of people in Europe and Asia. These displaced persons included former prisoners of war, survivors of Nazi concentration camps, people who had fled their homes when fighting grew near, and even people who had been forced out when national borders changed after the war. These millions of people had to begin to rebuild their lives. Tragically, this was made even more difficult for some Polish Jews, who returned to their homes to find that their property had been taken. Dozens of these Holocaust survivors were murdered by hostile neighbors.

Planning for the Future For years, Allied leaders had been planning for the day the war would finally end. For example, in July 1941, even before the United States entered the war, President Franklin Roosevelt met with Winston Churchill. They issued a joint declaration called the Atlantic Charter. The charter outlined what the two leaders saw as the purpose of the war. Together they proclaimed that they sought no territorial gain, and they looked forward to a peaceful world in which all nations chose their own governments and worked together for mutual prosperity.

In late November 1943 Roosevelt and Churchill were joined by Joseph Stalin at a conference in Tehran, Iran. There the three leaders agreed on a schedule for the D-Day invasion. They also agreed to work together in the peace that would follow the war.

HISTORY'S VOICES

> **"We shall seek the cooperation and active participation of all nations, large and small, whose peoples in heart and mind are dedicated . . . to the elimination of tyranny and slavery, oppression and intolerance. We will welcome them . . . into a world family of Democratic Nations."**
>
> —Declaration of the Three Powers, December 1, 1943, Tehran

Yalta and Potsdam In early 1945, when the Allies were on the brink of victory, they were having difficulties agreeing on the plans for peace. These difficulties came to the surface at the **Yalta Conference**, held in Soviet territory.

The primary goal of the conference was to reach agreement on what to do with postwar Europe. Roosevelt, Stalin, and Churchill agreed on plans for governing the soon-to-be conquered

Skills Focus: Analyzing Visuals

At Level

Research Required

Reading Like a Historian Skill

After the War

1. Have students conduct research to find photographs depicting war damage. If possible, students should find photographs that show the same locations before and after the war. *Possible locations—Hiroshima and Nagasaki, Japan; Dresden, Germany; London, England; Berlin, Germany; Warsaw, Poland; Manila, the Philippines; and Stalingrad, USSR.*
2. Have students make copies of their photographs and conduct research on the location using the following questions as guidelines: How extensive was the damage? What happened to the people who lived in the vicinity where damage occurred? How long did it take to rebuild afterward?
3. Have students present their photos and describe the war's damage. LS **Interpersonal, Visual-Spatial**

Alternative Assessment Handbook, Rubrics 24: Oral Presentations; and 30: Research

Germany. Stalin, however, was able to get his way on other key points, such as keeping territory that had formerly been part of Poland. In return, he promised to respect democratic ideals in the Eastern European countries his armies now occupied. President Roosevelt also managed to win some points. For example, he persuaded Stalin to join the fight against Japan soon after the war in Europe ended.

Roosevelt also convinced Stalin to agree to join a new world organization proposed by the Allies—the **United Nations**. Like the earlier League of Nations, the United Nations (UN) was designed to encourage international cooperation and prevent war. In June 1945 representatives of many of the world's nations signed the UN charter. The United States, Great Britain, France, the Soviet Union, and China formed the UN Security Council and had more power than other member nations.

In July 1945, Allied leaders met again, this time in the German city of Potsdam. The **Potsdam Conference** took place amid growing ill will between the Soviet Union and the other Allies. The Allies discussed many issues concerning postwar Europe, but often had difficulty reaching agreement.

Soviet Plans In the closing months of the war, American and British leaders were concerned about Stalin's intentions in Eastern Europe. They worried that communism and Soviet influence would spread in the postwar world. As you will learn, they were correct: Stalin would soon break his promises about respecting democracy in Eastern Europe. World War II had ended, but another struggle was about to begin.

READING CHECK **Summarize** What major decisions did Allied leaders make at Yalta and Potsdam?

CAUSES AND EFFECTS OF WORLD WAR II

QUICK FACTS

CAUSES

- Economic hardship and political unrest following World War I
- Aggressive leaders in Germany, Italy, and Japan wanted to expand their nations.
- Germany invaded Poland, and Japan attacked the United States.

EFFECTS

- Millions of people were killed, and large areas of Europe and Asia were damaged or destroyed.
- The Allies occupied Japan and parts of Europe.
- The United Nations was created to help prevent future wars.
- Conflict began between the Soviet Union and the other Allies over the fate of Eastern Europe.
- The United States and the Soviet Union emerged as the world's two major powers.

SECTION 4 ASSESSMENT

go.hrw.com
Online Quiz
Keyword: SHL WW2 HP

Reviewing Ideas, Terms, and People

1. **a. Identify** What was the significance of **D-Day** in the war in Europe?
   b. Identify Cause and Effect How did the Allies' careful planning pay off in the D-Day invasion?
   c. Predict If the D-Day invasion had failed, how might the outcome of the war have been different?
2. **a. Describe** What enabled the Americans to go on the offensive in the Pacific?
   b. Make Inferences How did the experiences of Iwo Jima and Okinawa affect the Allied decision to drop the atomic bomb?
   c. Predict How do you think the American development of the atomic bomb would affect the world in the years after the war?
3. **a. Identify** Identify one of the conferences attended by the leaders of the Allied nations.
   b. Evaluate How do you think the coordination of military efforts may have helped the Allies in World War II?

Critical Thinking

4. **Explain** Copy the chart below and use your notes from the section to explain what led to the end of the war.

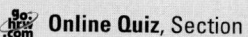

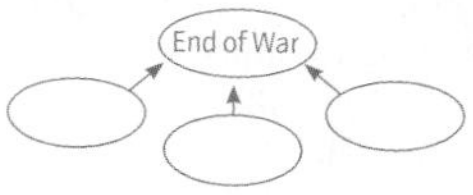

FOCUS ON SPEAKING

5. **Narration** Using details from the section, write a speech that an Allied leader might have given about the Allied plans for the postwar world.

Section 4 Assessment Answers

1. **a.** gave Allies a foothold in the west; opened a second front, hastening the war's end
   b. They broke through German defenses and quickly reconquered much of France.
   c. possible answer—It could have delayed the end of the war.
2. **a.** The island-hopping strategy continued to push the Japanese back.
   b. Americans knew Japan fought fiercely to defend the islands and feared that would continue.
   c. possible answer—Other nations will try to develop atomic weapons, which will lead to increased tension.
3. **a.** Yalta or Potsdam
   b. possible answer—By pooling their resources and coordinating military attacks, Allies were able to defeat the enemy.
4. Soviets invade Germany from the east; Allies invade Germany from the west; island hopping and bombing of Hiroshima and Nagasaki lead Japan to surrender
5. Student speeches should show an understanding of postwar Allied plans.

Direct Teach

QUICK FACTS Causes and Effects of World War II

Make Inferences How do you think the effects of World War II affected relations between nations? *possible answer—While the United Nations worked together toward peaceful resolutions, some nations' resentments may have lingered due to damage caused during the war, such the bombings in Japan.*

Quick Facts Transparency: Causes and Effects of World War II

Review & Assess

Close

Guide students in a discussion of the final days of the war and how hopes for the postwar world soon faded.

Review

Online Quiz, Section 4

Assess

SE Section 4 Assessment

Progress Assessment: Section 4 Quiz

Alternative Assessment Handbook

Reteach/Intervene

Interactive Reader and Study Guide, Section 4

Interactive Skills Tutor CD-ROM

Answers

Reading Check *At Yalta, Allied leaders agreed on what to do with postwar Europe. Roosevelt persuaded Stalin to join the fight against Japan and to join the United Nations. At Potsdam, the three sides discussed many issues concerning postwar Europe, but often had difficulty reaching agreement.*

Document-Based Investigation

The Holocaust

Word Help

crematorium a building containing an oven for cremating, or burning, dead bodies

cordwood wood stacked in cords, or piles

Recent Scholarship

In 1994, a book titled *"The Good Old Days": The Holocaust as Seen by Its Perpetrators and Bystanders* gave a chilling picture of what really happened during the Holocaust. It shows that thousands of people in Germany and eastern Europe went along with the "Final Solution." Maximilian Grabner tried to excuse his participation by saying that he did it out of consideration for his family. Grabner was investigated by the Nazis for killing 2,000 prisoners and was sentenced to death.

"The Good Old Days": The Holocaust as Seen by Its Prepetrators and Bystandars edited by Ernst Klee, Willi Dressen, and Volker Reiss. Free Press, 1994.

Info to Know

The Shanghai Ghetto When many countries, including the United States, were turning back Jewish refugees, China welcomed them. About 30,000 mostly German Jews managed to make their way to the Chinese port of Shanghai. During World War II, Shanghai was occupied by Japan. As a German ally, Japan imprisoned Jews and set up a ghetto. After Shanghai was liberated at the end of the war, most of the Jewish refugees left to try to rebuild their lives in elsewhere.

CHAPTER 14

Document-Based Investigation

The Holocaust

Historical Context The documents below provide information about the Holocaust.

Task Examine the selections and answer the questions that follow. After you have studied the documents, you will be asked to write an essay about how an event like the Holocaust could have taken place. You will need to use evidence from these selections and from the chapter to support the position you take in your essay.

DOCUMENT 1

An American Soldier's Reaction

Leon Bass was an African American soldier who visited the Buchenwald camp in April 1945, shortly after it had been liberated by the Allies.

> Then we saw the crematorium where the dead bodies were outside, stacked up like cordwood, and we went into the crematorium and you could see the residue in the ovens—the rib cages, the skulls. And it was so hard to believe—to understand why. What did these people do that merited this kind of treatment? And it boggles the mind when you think that it had gone on for almost ten years before we got into the war! Why wasn't it dealt with? Why did nobody scream and shout, 'Stop!' They never did.

DOCUMENT 2

A Gestapo Officer's Justification

Maximilian Grabner was the head of the Gestapo, or secret police, at the Auschwitz-Birkenau death camp. After the war's end, he tried to explain his actions.

> To kill three million people is in my view the greatest crime of all. I only took part in this crime because there was nothing I could do to change anything. The blame for this crime lay with National Socialism [the Nazi Party]. I myself was never a National Socialist. Nevertheless, I still had to join the Party.
>
> . . . I only took part in the murder of some three million people out of consideration for my family.

DOCUMENT 3

Nazi Camp Locations

Nazi prison camps spread throughout Europe as military victories brought more Jews under German control. Death camps were designed mainly to kill large numbers of Jews, while mobile killing units were Nazi police forces that traveled throughout Europe to execute Jews. Many of the Nazi camps were located near towns or cities in areas that had large Jewish populations.

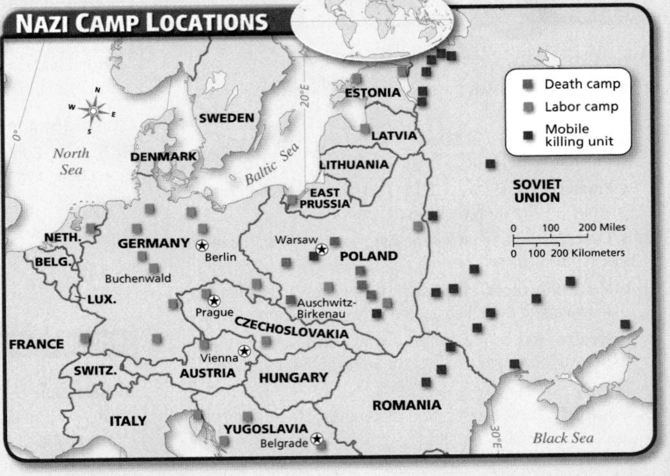

Skills Focus: Making Oral Presentations

At Level

Reading Like a Historian Skill

Genocide

Background: Remind students that *genocide* means the systematic killing of a group of people. Tell the class that, although the word was first used in connection with Hitler's "Final Solution," genocide has taken place throughout history.

1. Guide the class in a discussion of genocide. What other examples of genocide can they think of in the last century? *Cambodia, Rwanda, Iraq, Bosnia, Sri Lanka, Guatemala, East Timor, etc.*
2. Organize students into small groups. Have each group research one of the other examples of genocide and write a report about its causes and how (or if) it was stopped.
3. Ask each group to present its report to the class.
4. Guide the class in a discussion of genocide based on student reports. **LS Interpersonal, Verbal-Linguistic**

Alternative Assessment Handbook, Rubrics 14: Group Activity; and 30: Research

DOCUMENT 4

A German Witness

Herman Graebe was a German engineer working in the Ukraine. On October 5, 1942, he accidentally discovered a Nazi mobile killing unit executing Ukrainian Jews. He later described what he saw.

> I heard rifle shots in quick succession from behind one of the earth mounds . . . I walked around the mound and found myself confronted by a tremendous grave. People were closely wedged together and lying on top of each other so that only their heads were visible. Nearly all had blood running over their shoulders from their heads. Some of the people shot were still moving. Some were lifting their arms and turning their heads to show that they were still alive. The pit was nearly two-thirds full. I estimated that it already contained about a thousand people. I looked for the man who did the shooting. He was an SS [Nazi military police] man, who sat at the edge of the narrow end of the pit, his feet dangling into the pit. He had a tommy-gun on his knees and was smoking a cigarette.

DOCUMENT 5

An American Learns about Hitler's Plan

Howard Elting, Jr., was an American official stationed in Switzerland. The document below is from a letter he wrote to the U.S. secretary of state on August 10, 1942.

> This morning Mr. Gerhart M. RIEGNER, Secretary of the World Jewish Congress in Geneva, called in great agitation. He stated that he had just received a report from a German business man of considerable prominence, who is said to have excellent political and military connections in Germany and from whom reliable and important political information has been obtained on two previous occasions, to the effect that there has been and is being considered in Hitler's headquarters a plan to exterminate all Jews from Germany and German controlled areas in Europe after they have been concentrated in the east (presumably Poland). The number involved is said to be between three-and-a-half and four millions and the object is to permanently settle the Jewish question in Europe. The mass execution if decided upon would allegedly take place this fall.

Skills FOCUS READING LIKE A HISTORIAN

DOCUMENT 1

a. **Recall** What did Bass see at the camp?

b. **Infer** Do you think Bass believed that the Allies should have done more to stop the Holocaust? Why or why not?

DOCUMENT 2

a. **Explain** How does Grabner try to justify his actions?

b. **Analyze** What does Grabner mean by saying he took part in the murder "out of consideration for my family"?

DOCUMENT 3

a. **Identify** Which large cities were Nazi camps near?

b. **Draw Conclusions** Where were most Nazi camps and killing units located? Why?

DOCUMENT 4

a. **Recall** How many bodies does Graebe say were in the mass grave?

b. **Infer** What was the executioner's attitude toward the mass murder? How can you tell?

DOCUMENT 5

a. **Identify** What did Gerhart Riegner believe was going to happen to European Jews?

b. **Infer** Compare the date of Elting's letter to the date of the War Refugee Board's establishment. What do these dates suggest about the U.S. response to the Holocaust?

DOCUMENT-BASED ESSAY QUESTION

How could an event as large and as terrible as the Holocaust have taken place? Using the documents above and information from the chapter, form a thesis that explains your position. Then write a short essay to support it.

See **Skills Handbook**, p. H25

Skills Focus: Analyzing Primary Sources

Below Level

Reading Like a Historian Skill
Speaking Out

Materials: poster paper, colored markers

1. Guide the class in a discussion of Documents 1, 4, and 5. Ask students to think about the graphic atrocities described in Documents 1 and 4 and contrast them with the information in Document 5.
2. Have students work in pairs to create posters against the persecution of European Jews.
3. Ask volunteers to share their posters with the class, explaining them as they show them.
4. Guide the class in a discussion of students' posters. **LS Interpersonal, Visual-Spatial**

Alternative Assessment Handbook, Rubrics 11: Discussions; and 28: Posters

Document-Based Investigation

Info to Know

Stopping Racism Leon Bass was only 19 years old when he witnessed the liberation of Buchenwald in 1945. As an African American, he was a member of a segregated army unit. After Buchenwald, he realized that human suffering is universal, and that the Nazis had practiced the ultimate racism in their death camps. In the 1960s Bass became involved in the American civil rights movement. He continued to work in the field of Holocaust education and to promote understanding between African Americans and Jews.

Answers

Reading Like a Historian

Document 1. a. *describes horrific conditions at Buchenwald, such as seeing bodies "stacked up like cordwood;"* **b.** *possible answer— Yes, because no one did anything to stop it.* **Document 2. a.** *He says there was nothing he could do to change anything, and that he only did it out of consideration for his family.* **b.** *possible answer—that his family might have come to some harm if he had refused.* **Document 3. a.** *Poland, Warsaw;* **b.** *in areas with a large Jewish population; eliminated transportation issues for Germans;* **Document 4. a.** *about a thousand;* **b.** *indifference; casually smoking, dangling his feet;* **Document 5. a.** *they would be exterminated;* **b.** *Elting's letter is dated about a year and a half before the War Refugee Board was established, which shows that U.S. response was slow;* **Document 6.** *Students' essays should show an understanding of the fact that Germans did little to stop the crimes. If the people of Germany had refused to allow Hitler to carry out his "Final Solution," they could have stopped it.*

Answers

Visual Summary

Review and Inquiry Organize students into four groups, and assign each group one of the topics in the quick facts chart: German aggression leads to war, Axis Powers make early gains, The Allies fight back, and The War ends. Have each group write a short summary of its assigned topic.

Quick Facts Transparency: Visual Study Guide: World War II: 1939–1945

Review Key Terms and People

1. appeasement
2. Axis
3. radar
4. Holocaust
5. violate
6. Battle of Stalingrad
7. ghettos
8. Final Solution
9. D-Day
10. Battle of Okinawa

Comprehension and Critical Thinking

11. a. They took no direct action, hoping to avoid war.
b. Britain's use of radar in the Battle of Britain made their air defences more effective when German planes flew over the English Channel, whereas the German assualt on France was quick and well planned.
c. possible answer—The attack on Pearl Harbor caused many Americans to rethink isolationism; as a result, American forces became a determined enemy of Japan.

12. a. the Allies
b. It changed the balance of power in the Pacific, allowing Allies to go on the offensive.
c. He failed to plan for the harsh Soviet winter. By refusing to allow his troops to retreat, many of them ran out of ammunition, food, and medicine.

CHAPTER 14

Chapter Review

QUICK FACTS

VISUAL STUDY GUIDE

World War II: 1939–1945

German aggression leads to war	Axis Powers make early gains	The Allies fight back	The war ends
• Rhineland militarized • Austria and parts of Czechoslovakia annexed • Poland invaded	• Germany conquers Denmark, Norway, France, invades Soviet Union • Nazis adopt the Final Solution and establish death camps • Japan attacks Pearl Harbor, rules the Pacific	• British and Americans win in North Africa, Italy • Soviets win at Stalingrad • Americans win at Midway, begin island hopping	• Soviets push back Germans from the east • After D-Day, other Allies push toward Germany from the west • Americans win in Pacific; atomic bomb ends war

Major Events of World War II

1939
- Nazi-Soviet nonaggression pact
- German troops invade Poland and the war begins

1940
- Germany conquers France
- Battle of Britain begins

1941
- Germany invades the Soviet Union
- Japan attacks Pearl Harbor
- United States enters the war

1942
- Allies win the Battle of Midway
- Allied victory at El Alamein
- Allies begin to hear reports of widespread killings of Jews in Europe

1943
- Soviets win the Battle of Stalingrad
- Allies invade Italy

1944
- Allies invade France in D-Day
- Allies begin to discover death camps

1945
- Allies meet at Yalta and Potsdam
- Germany surrenders
- Allies win battles of Iwo Jima and Okinawa
- Allies drop atomic bombs on Hiroshima and Nagasaki
- Japan surrenders and the war ends

Review Key Terms and People

Complete each sentence by filling the blank with the correct term or person.

1. Neville Chamberlain pursued a policy known as ________ in dealing with the Germans.
2. Germany, Italy, and Japan formed an alliance known as the ________.
3. The British used the technology of ________ to help them win the Battle of Britain.
4. In 1941, Hitler's forces began the widespread, systematic killing that marked the start of the __________.
5. Hitler's plan to rearm Germany was an action that would __________ the Treaty of Versailles.
6. The Germans lost the ___________ after being surrounded by Soviet troops.
7. In some cities the Nazis forced Jews to live in a ________, or confined area.
8. The _________ was the Nazi plan for the deliberate, mass execution of Jews.
9. On _________ , the Allies launched a major, long-planned invasion of Europe.
10. The _________ was formed after the war to encourage international cooperation and prevent war.

13. a. They tried to get rid of German Jews by deporting them or forcing them to leave by stripping them of their citizenship and property rights.
b. As the Germans moved into new areas of Europe, millions of Jews came under their power. Nazi leaders came up with the "Final Solution"—the deliberate, mass execution of Jewish prisoners.
c. possible answer—Only after the Allies had forced the Germans to retreat were they able to liberate the prisoners.

14. a. Hitler ordered one last, massive counterattack in Belgium in December 1944, but the D-Day attack let to Germany's surrender on May 7, 1945.
b. President Truman's decision to drop two atomic bombs in Japan—one on Hiroshima, and one on Nagasaki
c. millions killed; much of Europe and Asia destroyed; Allies occupied Japan and parts of Europe; United Nations created; U.S. and Soviet Union become world's two major powers

History's Impact video program
Review the video to answer the closing question: How did events after World War II lead to the beginning of the Cold War?

Comprehension and Critical Thinking

SECTION 1 *(pp. 437–444)*

11. a. Recall How did Great Britain and France respond to Hitler's aggression in the late 1930s?

b. Explain Why were the results of German attacks on France and Britain so different?

c. Predict How might the Japanese success at Pearl Harbor have later hurt their cause?

SECTION 2 *(pp. 445–452)*

12. a. Identify Who won the battle to control the Atlantic?

b. Explain In what ways did the Allied victory at Midway affect the war in the Pacific?

c. Make Judgments How did the Battle of Stalingrad demonstrate Hitler's poor judgment?

SECTION 3 *(pp. 456–459)*

13. a. Describe How did the Nazi government treat German Jews before World War II began?

b. Identify Cause and Effect How did German military victories lead to the Nazi's Final Solution?

c. Evaluate What do you think of the Allies' decision to focus on winning the war rather than immediately trying to save the people in Nazi death camps?

SECTION 4 *(pp. 460–465)*

14. a. Recall What effect did D-Day have on the war in Europe?

b. Cause and Effect What events helped bring about an end to the war in the Pacific?

c. Elaborate In what ways did World War II affect the world?

Reading Skills

Understanding Causes and Effects *Use what you know about understanding causes and effects to answer the questions below.*

15. Why did Germany begin to threaten much of Europe in the 1930s?

16. What effects did Japan's attack on Pearl Harbor have on the war?

17. List the causes and effects of Nazi anti-Semitism during the 1930s and 1940s.

Analyzing Visuals

Reading Like a Historian *The American propaganda poster below shows a man being urged to be quiet by Uncle Sam, a symbol of the United States.*

Quiet! Loose Talk Can Cost Lives, Dal Holcomb, 1942

18. Explain Why is the man—and the viewer—being told to be quiet? How can talk "cost lives"?

19. Draw Conclusions Why do you think the artist used the symbol of Uncle Sam?

Using the Internet

go.hrw.com
Practice Online
Keyword: SHL WW2

20. The Allied invasion of France, or D-Day, began on June 6, 1944, when 150,000 soldiers landed on the beaches of Normandy. Using the Internet, research what happened in Normandy on D-Day. Then write a report about the first 24 hours after the landing, using eyewitness accounts and other documents to support your work.

WRITING ABOUT HISTORY

Persuasion: Writing an Evaluation *In the late 1930s, many Americans did not want to become involved in conflict in Europe, believing that the United States should stay out of troubles overseas. Others thought it was dangerous to ignore the aggressive actions of dictators in Europe and Asia.*

21. Assignment: In an essay, evaluate the wisdom of American isolationism. To provide support for your evaluation, use specific reasons and examples from the chapter and from other research.

Answers

Reading Skills

15. Hitler sought to rebuild Germany, build up the military, and plan for war.

16. caused isolationism to disappear; United States joined Allies

17. Causes—Hitler's belief in a "superior race," Germans accept Hitler's view of Jews as scapegoat; separate status for Ger man Jews; Effects—thousands of Jews deported; Nazi leaders adopt "Final Solution;" 6 million Jews murdered

Analyzing Visuals

18. possible answer—If he speaks out, it might jeopardize the U.S. government.

19. possible answer—to show that the U.S. government suppressed its citizens.

Using the Internet

20. Go to the HRW Web site and enter the keyword shown to access a rubric for this activity.

KEYWORD: SHL WW2

Writing for the SAT

Student essays should show an understanding of isolationism.

A rubric for this activity is provided in **CRF:** Writing for the SAT

HOLT
History's Impact
► **Video Program**
Refer to the Video Program Teacher's Guide for a discussion of the closing question.

Review and Assessment Resources

Review and Reinforce

- **CRF:** Chapter Review
- **Quick Facts Transparency:** Visual Study Guide: World War II
- **Spanish Chapter Summaries Audio CD Program**
- OSP **Holt PuzzlePro:** Quiz Show for ExamView
- **Quiz Game CD-ROM**

Assess

- **PASS:** Chapter Test, Forms A and B
- **Alternative Assessment Handbook**
- OSP **ExamView Test Generator**, Chapter Test
- **Differentiated Instruction Modified Worksheets and Tests CD-ROM:** Chapter Test
- HOAP **Holt Online Assessment Program** (in the Premier Online Edition)

Reteach/Intervene

- **Interactive Reader and Study Guide**
- **Differentiated Instruction Teacher Management System:** Lesson Plans for Differentiated Instruction
- **Differentiated Instruction Modified Worksheets and Tests CD-ROM:** Chapter Test
- **Interactive Skills Tutor CD-ROM**

go.hrw.com
Online Resources
KEYWORD: SHL TEACHER

Unit Review

You can use these pages to have students simultaneously review the unit and practice taking standardized tests.

Answers

1. D
   World War I, Section 1
2. D
   World War I, Section 1
3. A
   World War I, Section 1
4. C
   World War I, Section 3
5. D
   World War I, Section 2
6. D
   World War II, Section 1
7. C
   World War I, Section 4
8. D
   The Interwar Years, Section 2
9. A
   The Interwar Years, Sections 3 and 4
10. B
    The Interwar Years, Section 3
11. A
    The Interwar Years, Section 4

UNIT 4

Standardized Test Practice

Directions Write your answer for each statement or question on a separate answer sheet. Choose the letter of the word or expression that best completes the statement or answers the question.

1 In 1914 many European leaders believed that alliances would

A improve world trade.
B support the League of Nations.
C lead to war.
D help prevent war.

2 What event triggered the outbreak of World War I?

A the Russian Revolution
B Germany's invasion of Poland
C the assassination of Archduke Franz Ferdinand
D French aggression toward Italy

3 During World War I trench warfare led to

A a military stalemate.
B very few casualties.
C a quick end to the war.
D war in the Pacific.

4 Who led the Bolsheviks during their October Revolution against the Russian czar?

A Joseph Stalin
B Karl Marx
C Vladimir Lenin
D Alexander Kerensky

5 During World War I, more than 1 million Armenians were deported or killed in

A Germany.
B Russia.
C France.
D the Ottoman Empire.

6 The terms of the Treaty of Versailles are often blamed for contributing to

A the Russian Revolution.
B the rise of Nazism in Germany.
C Japanese aggression in China.
D U.S. isolationism.

7 Which of the following was one political outcome of World War I?

A The Bolsheviks in Russia were overthrown.
B Tensions in European colonies decreased.
C The Ottoman Empire broke apart.
D The United Nations was formed.

8 The Great Depression helped lead to

A World War I.
B a rise in world trade.
C the growth of free trade associations.
D the rise of dictators in Europe.

9 In the 1930s, Germany, Italy, and Japan

A worked to build empires around the globe.
B became more democratic.
C reduced the size of their militaries.
D pursued isolationist policies.

10 Why did Japan invade Manchuria?

A in response to a Manchurian attack on Japan
B to gain control of Manchuria's natural resources
C the people of Manchuria wanted to join Japan
D Japan had an alliance with China

11 What was a common feature of the totalitarian dictators who rose to power after World War I?

A They used violence and fear to maintain power.
B They were elected democratically.
C They were Communist.
D They were Fascist.

12 **The quotation below by British prime minister Neville Chamberlain in 1938 is an example of what policy? Base your answer on the passage and on your knowledge of history.**

> *"We should seek by all means in our power to avoid war, by analysing possible causes, by trying to remove them, by discussion in a spirit of collaboration and good will. I cannot believe that such a programme would be rejected by the people of this country, even if it does mean the establishment of personal contact with the dictators."*

A isolationism
B appeasement
C aggression
D containment

13 **France and Great Britain declared war on Germany in 1939 as a direct result of**

A Germany's annexation of Austria.
B Germany's attack on France.
C Germany's invasion of Poland.
D Germany's militarization of the Rhineland.

14 **Which of the following was a key turning point in Germany's invasion of the Soviet Union?**

A the Blitz
B the Battle of the Bulge
C the Battle of Midway
D the Battle of Stalingrad

15 **Why did Japan attack Pearl Harbor?**

A Japan saw the United States as a threat to Japanese expansion in Asia.
B Japan's leaders had promised Germany they would attack the United States.
C Japan wanted Pearl Harbor's natural resources.
D Japan wanted to oust the U.S. military from China.

16 **What was the goal of the Nazis' Final Solution?**

A to take control of the Soviet Union
B to murder all European Jews
C to drop atomic bombs on Great Britain
D to invade the United States

17 **What best explains the data on the chart below? Base your answer on the data and on your knowledge of history.**

World War II Casualties

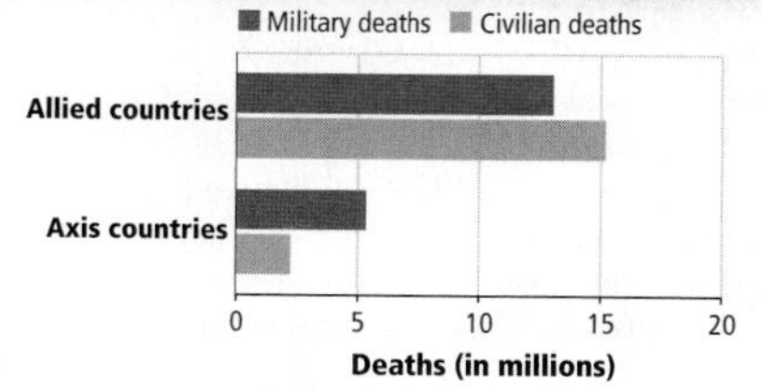

Source: Encyclopedia Britannica

A new military technologies and total war
B trench warfare and poison gas
C atomic weapons
D U-boats and torpedoes

18 **The main purpose of the Yalta Conference was to decide**

A how to destroy Nazi concentration camps.
B what to do with postwar Europe.
C how to stop the spread of communism.
D when to invade Germany.

Reviewing the Unit

Constructed Response World leaders played key roles in the events of World Wars I and II. These leaders included Kaiser Wilhelm II, Woodrow Wilson, Winston Churchill, Franklin Roosevelt, Adolf Hitler, Joseph Stalin, Emperor Hirohito, and Dwight Eisenhower. Recall the roles that two world leaders played in these world wars. Then write a brief essay in which you summarize how each was involved in and influenced the course of these wars and history.

Connecting to the Previous Unit

Constructed Response Industrialization, nationalism, and imperialism all helped to set the stage for World Wars I and II. Choose one of these topics to explore. Write a brief essay in which you explain how your topic affected key countries in Europe and was one of the causes of the world wars.

Unit Review

12. B
World War II, Section 1

13. C
World War II, Section 1

14. D
World War II, Section 2

15. A
World War II, Section 1

16. B
World War II, Section 3

17. A
World War II, Section 4

18. B
World War II, Section 4

Reviewing the Unit

Essays should discuss two world leaders who were involved in World War I or World War II and should summarize the involvement and influence of the leaders in the war and in history.
possible brief essay—
Dwight Eisenhower and Emperor Hirohito both played important roles in history and in World War II. Eisenhower was supreme commander of the Allies in Europe and the commander on D-Day. An integral part of the Allies' success, Eisenhower became president of the United States after the war, continuing his leadership. Japanese Emperor Hirohito also played an important, if less valiant, role. Following the dropping of the atomic bomb, Hirohito surrendered, ending World War II.

Connecting to the Previous Unit

Student essays should explain how industrialization, nationalism, or imperialism affected key European countries and helped cause the world wars.
possible essay topic—
Industrialism and its inception and impact on Great Britain's economy and society

Unit Review

Government and Citizenship

Rise of Fascism Following World War I, many Europeans were looking for new leadership to restore pride in their countries. As a result, ambitious militant leaders had the opportunity to take control of a vulnerable public. In Italy, Benito Mussolini led the Fascist Party, which was formed in 1919. The Fascists gained the nickname the Blackshirts for the black shirts they wore as part of their uniform. They fought against trade unionists, Communists, farm organizations, and Socialists, which was ironic, as Mussolini was a former Socialist.

Science and Technology

Gases in World War I Gas warfare was first used by German troops in 1915. Chlorine gas, a lung irritant, was released by soldiers from a cylinder. The wind spread the gas to enemy trenches. Other gases used during this time caused tearing, sneezing, vomiting, and skin irritation and burning. At the time, soldiers had little or no protection from such attacks.

Recent Scholarship

According to British Scholar Martin Pugh, fascism may not have gained popularity in other parts of Europe, but its ideas were widely adopted in Great Britain during the interwar years. In his book *Hurrah for the Blackshirts: Fascists and Fascism in Britain Between the Wars,* Pugh states that England's leadership during this time reflected fascism's influence.

Hurrah for the Blackshirts: Fascists and Fascism in Britain Between the Wars by Martin Pugh. Pimlico, 2006.

Themes & Global Connections

THEME
Government and Citizenship

How did nationalism affect government and citizenship in World Wars I and II?

Nationalism, which was a driving force behind the world wars of the 1900s, had many significant effects on government and citizenship in Europe. Nationalism led to government rivalries and alliances, opened the door to new forms of government, and inspired citizens to fight for and defend their countries.

Effects of Nationalism on Government and Citizenship in Europe, 1914–1945

Government Rivalries and Alliances
- Europe's countries competed for power, resources, and influence.
- National rivalries led governments to build strong militaries and form alliances for security and protection.
- When conflict broke out, government leaders were committed to supporting their allies, which led to world wars.

New Forms of Government
- After World War I, some citizens wanted new leaders to rebuild their countries and restore national pride.
- As a result, fascist leaders rose to power and formed new governments in Germany and Italy.

Citizens Defend Their Government
- In warring countries, feelings of national pride and duty led many citizens to volunteer for military service.
- These citizens responded to their governments' calls to defend and protect their homeland from enemy armies.

THEME
Science and Technology

How did industrialization change the science and technology of warfare?

The advances made during the Industrial Revolution enabled scientists and engineers to invent many new military technologies. As new weapons and equipment became a key part of battles, the nature of warfare changed. Industrial facilities became key components of a country's ability to wage war—and key targets for its enemies.

Causes and Effects of Modern Warfare Technologies

CAUSES
- Military engineers developed new technologies like machine guns, tanks, submarines, artillery, poison gas, and atomic weapons.
- Existing technologies, like airplanes and steamships, were modified for war.

EFFECTS
- Battle zones became scenes of enormous death and destruction.
- War became an industrial competition as countries produced huge amounts of weapons and supplies to keep up with their enemies.
- Factories and industries became military targets and were attacked to weaken an opponent's ability to wage war.

Differentiating Instruction

Below Level

Learners Having Difficulty

Standard English Mastery

1. Review with students the technological advancements that contributed to new weapons used in the world wars.
2. Tell students they are soldiers fighting in Europe during World War I or World War II. Have each student write a letter home to a friend or family member. The letter should describe what war is like with the new technology. For example, a soldier might be stationed on a submarine or be living in a World War I trench.
3. Tell students to use descriptive words and active verbs in their letters so the recipient will get a vivid picture of what the fighting was like.
4. Have volunteers read their letters to the class. Discuss what life must have been like for soldiers who served in one of the world wars.

LS **Verbal-Linguistic**

Alternative Assessment Handbook, Rubric 25: Personal Letters

THEME
SOCIETY

In what ways did the world wars affect society in Europe?

World Wars I and II affected society like never before. As entire countries mobilized for war, governments placed new controls on society to help achieve victory. But in the end, the massive scale of the wars left societies devastated.

World Wars

Mobilizing Society
Countries mobilized for total war and devoted all resources to it. Soldiers went off to fight, and men and women worked in factories to produce weapons, vehicles, and other war-related goods.

Controlling Society
Governments controlled information to shape public opinion and keep morale high. They also set up rationing systems and restricted the rights of groups they mistrusted.

Societies in Ruins
The wars caused millions of military and civilian casualties. Huge areas were reduced to rubble, leaving towns, farms, and economies ruined.

Skills FOCUS **UNDERSTANDING THEMES**

How did World Wars I and II affect government and citizenship, science and technology, and society in one country? Choose a country in Europe that fought in both World War I and II. Use your textbook and other resources to gather information about how each war affected that country. Then create a chart like the one below that compares and contrasts the effects of the two wars.

	World War I	World War II
Effects on Government and Citizenship		
Effects on Science and Technology		
Effects on Society		

Global Connections

World Wars I and II affected the entire world. Even places far away from the battle zones were affected as fighting interrupted trade routes, used valuable resources, and forced countries to choose sides.

Making Connections This map shows German U-boat attacks during World War II. How do you think these attacks affected places far away from the fighting? Which areas were affected? Use the map to write a short paragraph explaining how U-boat attacks are one example of the worldwide effects of World War II.

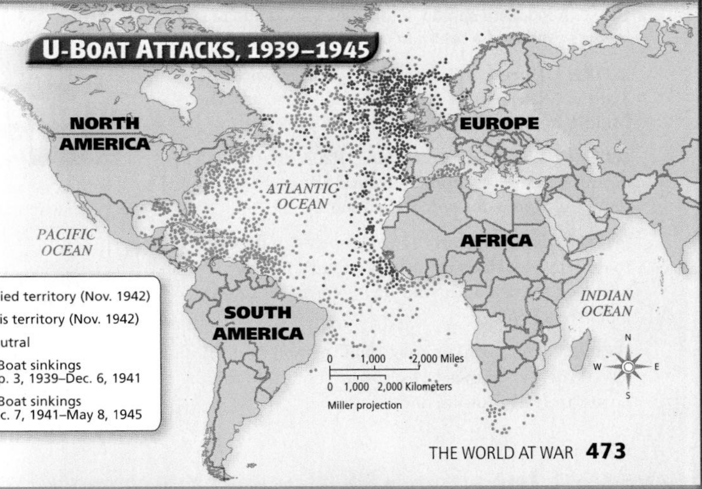

Unit Review

Society

Women's War Efforts Many women in Europe had suspended their efforts for women's rights and suffrage to help with the war effort. After World War I women demanded recognition for their wartime contributions. They gained voting rights in many countries, including Germany, Sweden, Spain, Austria, Poland, and Canada. Women gained a stronger legal position in Great Britain. Although many women stopped working outside the home after the war, they were presented with a greater variety of job opportunities.

Understanding Themes

Student charts should compare how the world wars affected the country's government and citizenship, science and technology, and society.

Global Connections

Student paragraphs should explain how U-boat attacks during World War II affected countries throughout the world. possible short paragraph—
As the map shows, most countries chose sides in the war, while only a few were neutral. Even countries far away from the most devastating fighting chose sides. The map also shows that there were U-Boat sinkings far from the main battles—in the Caribbean, around South America, and as far south as the tip of Africa.

Collaborative Learning

At Level

Research Required

War Effort Slogans

Materials: poster board, colored markers

1. Organize students into small groups. Have each group conduct research using reliable online sources to locate information about the U.S. war effort at home during World War I or World War II.
2. Have students choose one particular program associated with the war effort, such as liberty bonds or victory gardens. Have students use the information found in their research to brainstorm a slogan for their chosen program.
3. Have each group create a poster that illustrates its chosen slogan.
4. Have volunteers present their posters to the class. **LS Visual-Spatial, Verbal-Linguistic**

Alternative Assessment Handbook, Rubrics 14: Group Activity; and 34: Slogans and Banners

Unit Review

Summarizing the Unit

In this unit, students learned that Europe endured drastic changes—geographically, economically, and politically. For example, Austria and Poland were new nations created by treaty. While established nations such as France had to rebuild, the new nations of eastern Europe had to start from scratch. Have students name some of the challenges these new countries faced. *New nations lacked democratic traditions and had to establish new governments, choose new leaders, and deal with unfamiliar political conflicts.*

Answers

Thinking Like a Historian

Student charts, graphs, or graphic organizers should show how the world wars affected the economy and government of either Germany or Japan. possible responses—

A. *Reparations crippled the German economy; after World War II, the economy was again devastated; many cities, villages, and farms were destroyed or damaged.*

B. *Germany forced to pay reparations and limit the size of its military; German land was lost; Weimar Republic was founded; political unrest; Hitler gained power; after World War II, Germany lost lands and eventually developed a democratic government*

C. *Much of Europe and Asia were left in ruins; United States and Soviet Union emerge as world's two major powers.*

UNIT 4 IN BRIEF

Below is a chapter-by-chapter summary of the main ideas in this unit, followed by a summary activity for the unit.

CHAPTER 12 World War I 1914–1918

MAIN IDEA A host of powerful factors, including growing nationalism, military alliances, and European rivalries, created conditions that quickly transformed a single assassination into a bloody worldwide war.

SECTION 1 Europe in 1914 was on the brink of war. The assassination of Archduke Franz Ferdinand quickly led to the outbreak of what came to be called the Great War, or World War I.

SECTION 2 The development of new technologies and new types of warfare during World War I caused destruction on a scale never before imagined.

SECTION 3 Russia's losses in the war and widespread social unrest led to the Russian Revolution, which was led by Vladimir Lenin and the Bolsheviks.

SECTION 4 After several years of stalemate—and the U.S. entry into the war—the Allied Powers finally prevailed. The war was over, but the peace proved difficult to establish.

CHAPTER 13 The Interwar Years 1919–1939

MAIN IDEA Following the destruction and chaos of World War I, the postwar world suffered from instability and serious economic and social problems. Under these conditions, nationalism spread, and a new generation of strong leaders promised a return to power and glory.

SECTION 1 During the chaotic years after World War I nationalist feelings grew in Asia, Africa, and the Middle East, leading to widespread unrest.

SECTION 2 Beginning in the late 1920s, an economic depression quickly spread around the globe, creating ideal conditions for political change.

SECTION 3 Economic and social changes in Japan led to growing tensions in society. Japan's military gradually took control of the nation's government and attacked China.

SECTION 4 The social and political turmoil that followed the war allowed totalitarian dictators to take power in Italy, Russia, and Germany.

CHAPTER 14 World War II 1930–1945

MAIN IDEA The aggressive actions of Germany, Italy, and Japan led to the outbreak of World War II in 1939. At first the Axis armies won many battles, but after years of conflict the Allies triumphed.

SECTION 1 In the late 1930s, Germany, Italy, and Japan used military force to build growing empires. Their aggressive actions led to the start of World War II.

SECTION 2 The early years of World War II went poorly for the Allies. After the United States joined the war, however, the Allies recovered and began making gains against the Axis armies.

SECTION 3 During World War II Germany's Nazi government deliberately murdered some 6 million Jews and 5 million others in Europe. These actions became known as the Holocaust.

SECTION 4 In 1945 the Allies finally defeated the Axis Powers. But the war had disastrous consequences for many countries around the world. It left millions of people dead, millions uprooted, and many lives destroyed. Some entire nations were in ruins.

Thinking like a Historian — Summary and Extension Activity

The two world wars of the 1900s had dramatic effects on many countries' economies, governments, and relations with other nations. Perhaps no two countries were affected more than Germany and Japan. Choose one of these countries and create a chart, graph, or graphic organizer to show how world wars affected its:

A. Economy

B. Government

C. International Relations

Unit Resources

Review and Reinforce

- **CRF:** Chapter Review
- **Spanish Chapter Summaries Audio CD Program**
- OSP **Holt PuzzlePro**: Quiz Show for ExamView
- **Quiz Game CD-ROM**

Assess

- **PASS**: Unit Test, Forms A and B
- **Alternative Assessment Handbook**
- OSP **ExamView Test Generator**
- **Differentiated Instruction Modified Worksheets and Tests CD-ROM**: Chapter Tests
- HOAP **Holt Online Assessment Program** (in the Premier Online Edition)

Reteach/Intervene

- **Interactive Reader and Study Guide**
- **Differentiated Instruction Teacher Management System**: Lesson Plans for Differentiated Instruction
- **Differentiated Instruction Modified Worksheets and Tests CD-ROM**: Chapter Tests
- **Interactive Skills Tutor CD-ROM**

go.hrw.com
Online Resources
KEYWORDS: SHL WW1, SHL IWY, SHL WW2

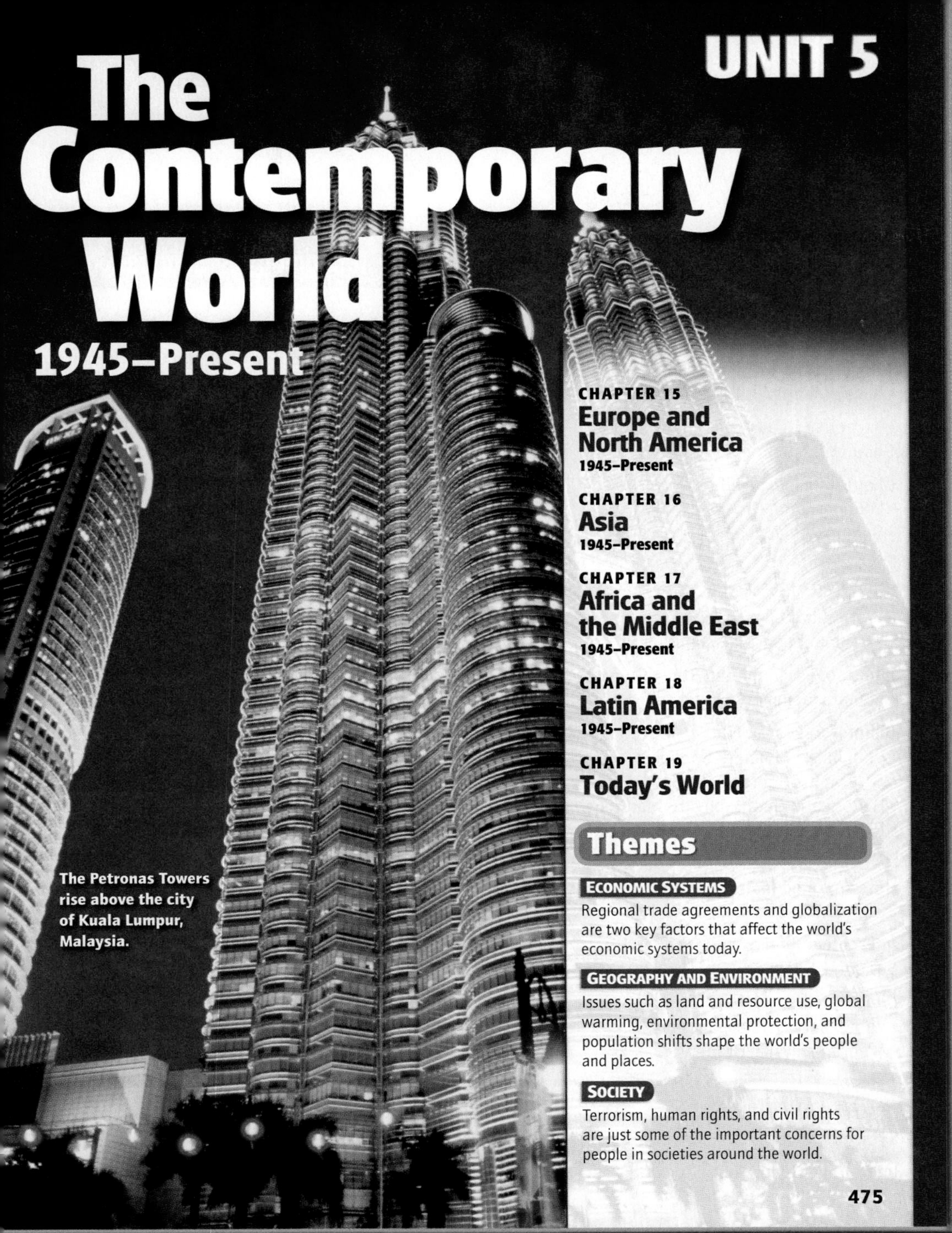

UNIT 5

The Contemporary World
1945–Present

The Petronas Towers rise above the city of Kuala Lumpur, Malaysia.

Themes

ECONOMIC SYSTEMS
Regional trade agreements and globalization are two key factors that affect the world's economic systems today.

GEOGRAPHY AND ENVIRONMENT
Issues such as land and resource use, global warming, environmental protection, and population shifts shape the world's people and places.

SOCIETY
Terrorism, human rights, and civil rights are just some of the important concerns for people in societies around the world.

475

Unit Preview

Introducing the Unit

Have students name the most significant historical events since the end of World War II. As they name them, make a list of the events for the class to see. Then have students to help rank the events in order of importance, from most important to least important. Which event did students choose as the most significant? Why?

Connecting to Themes

Activity **Globalization** Tell students that globalization is the process in which trade and culture link together countries around the world. Guide students in a discussion of the ways in which globalization affects them and their community.
LS Verbal-Linguistic

Reading Like a Historian

Interpreting Visuals

The Petronas Towers At 1,483 feet (452 meters), the Petronas Towers are the tallest buildings in the world. The buildings' developers wanted to create a monument that would commemorate Kuala Lumpur's position as a commercial and cultural capital. The basic design is meant to evoke Malaysia's Islamic heritage while embracing the nation's future.

Unit Resources

Planning

- **Differentiated Instruction Teacher Management System:** Unit Pacing Guide
- OSP **One-Stop Planner CD-ROM:** Teacher Management System
- **Power Presentations with Video CD-ROM**

Differentiating Instruction

- **Differentiated Instruction Teacher Management System:** Lesson Plans for Differentiated Instruction
- **Differentiated Instruction Modified Worksheets and Tests CD-ROM**

Enrichment

- **A World History Teacher's Guide to Analyzing Movies**
- **Document-Based Activities for World History**
- **World History Outline Maps**
- **Reading Like a Historian: World History Toolkit**
- **World History Primary Source Library CD-ROM**

Assessment

- **PASS:** Unit Test, Forms A and B
- **Alternative Assessment Handbook**
- OSP **ExamView Test Generator**
- HOAP **Holt Online Assessment Program** (in the Premier Online Edition)

Chapter 15 Planning Guide

Europe and North America

Chapter Overview	Reproducible Resources	Technology Resources
CHAPTER 15 **pp. 476–507** **Overview: In this chapter, students will learn how World War gave way to new alliances, but also to a new war, resulting in a rivalry between two superpowers: the United States and the Soviet Union.**	**Differentiated Instruction Teacher Management System:** • Pacing Guide • Lesson Plans for Differentiated Instruction **Interactive Reader and Study Guide:** Chapter Summary* **Chapter Resource File*** • Writing About History • Social Studies Skill • Chapter Review	**Live Ink© Online Reading Help** **Student Edition on Audio CD Program** **Differentiated Instruction Modified Worksheets and Tests CD-ROM** **World History Primary Source Library CD-ROM** **History's Impact: World History Video Program (VHS/DVD):** Europe and North America
Section 1: **Beginnings of the Cold War** **The Main Idea:** Once partners in war, the Soviet Union and the other former Allies found it much more difficult to cooperate in peace. The result was an era of conflict and confrontation called the Cold War.	**Differentiated Instruction Teacher Management System:** Section 1 Lesson Plan* **Interactive Reader and Study Guide:** Section 1 Summary* **Chapter Resource File*** • Vocabulary Builder: Section 1 • Biography: George Marshall • History and Geography: Berlin Crisis • Primary Source: The North Atlantic Treaty	**Daily Test Practice Transparency:** Section 1* **Map Transparencies:** Communist and NATO Countries, 1949; The Iron Curtain, 1949; The Korean War, 1950–1951* **Quick Facts Transparency:** Causes and Effects of the Cold War*
Section 2: **Superpower Rivalries** **The Main Idea:** As the Cold War continued, the world's two superpowers—the Soviet Union and the United States—competed for power and influence around the world.	**Differentiated Instruction Teacher Management System:** Section 2 Lesson Plan* **Interactive Reader and Study Guide:** Section 2 Summary* **Chapter Resource File*** • Vocabulary Builder: Section 2 • Biography: Willy Brandt	**Daily Test Practice Transparency:** Section 2* **Map Transparencies:** The Cuban Missle Crisis; Cold War Hot Spots* **Internet Activity:** The Cold War
Section 3: **Changing Societies** **The Main Idea:** The Cold War brought tremendous economic and social change to North America, Western Europe, and Eastern Europe and the Soviet Union.	**Differentiated Instruction Teacher Management System:** Section 3 Lesson Plan* **Interactive Reader and Study Guide:** Section 3 Summary* **Chapter Resource File*** • Vocabulary Builder: Section 3 • Biography: Rosa Parks • Literature: *Invisible Man*	**Daily Test Practice Transparency:** Section 3* **Quick Facts Transparency:** Contrasting Economic Systems* **Internet Activity:** Report on Europe and North America in the Postwar Years
Section 4: **After the Cold War** **The Main Idea:** The Soviet Union collapsed in 1991 and the Cold War came to an end, bringing changes to Europe and leaving the United States as the world's only superpower.	**Differentiated Instruction Teacher Management System:** Section 4 Lesson Plan* **Interactive Reader and Study Guide:** Section 4 Summary* **Chapter Resource File*** • Vocabulary Builder: Section 4 • Biography: Condoleezza Rice	**Daily Test Practice Transparency:** Section 4* **Map Transparencies:** The Breakup of the Soviet Union, 1991; The European Union, 2006* **Quick Facts Transparency:** Recent U.S. Military Involvement, 2001–Present*

go.hrw.com | Print Resource | Transparency
LS Learning Styles | Audio CD | CD-ROM
Video | SE Student Edition | TE Teacher's Edition
OSP One-Stop Planner CD-ROM
*also on One-Stop Planner CD-ROM

Review, Assessment, Intervention

- **Quick Facts Transparency:** Europe and North America*
- **Progress Assessment Support System (PASS):** Chapter Test*
- **Differentiated Instruction Modified Worksheets and Tests CD-ROM:** Modified Chapter Test
- OSP **One-Stop Planner CD-ROM:** ExamView Test Generator (English/Spanish)
- HOAP **Holt Online Assessment Program (HOAP),** in the Holt Premier Online Student Edition

---

- **PASS:** Section 1 Quiz*
- **Online Quiz:** Section 1
- **Alternative Assessment Handbook**

- **PASS:** Section 2 Quiz*
- **Online Quiz:** Section 2
- **Alternative Assessment Handbook**

- **PASS:** Section 3 Quiz*
- **Online Quiz:** Section 3
- **Alternative Assessment Handbook**

- **PASS:** Section 4 Quiz*
- **Online Quiz:** Section 4
- **Alternative Assessment Handbook**

HOLT
History's Impact
World History Video Program (VHS/DVD)
Europe and North America

Power Presentation with Video CD-ROM

Power Presentations with Video are visual presentations of each chapter's main ideas. Presentations can be customized by including Quick Facts charts, images and maps from the textbook, and video clips.

Holt Online Learning

go.hrw.com
Teacher Resources
KEYWORD: SHL TEACHER

go.hrw.com
Student Resources
KEYWORD: SHL ENA

- Document-Based Questions
- Interactive Multimedia Activities
- Current Events
- Chapter-Based Internet Activities
- and more!

Holt Premier
Online Student Edition

Complete online support for interactivity, assessment, and reporting

- Interactive Maps and Notebook
- Homework Practice and Research Activities Online

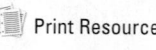

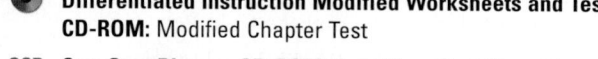

The Big Picture

Peter N. Stearns

Postwar Trends After World War II, in Europe and North America, a Cold War and an arms race led to dramatic social and economic change and, in the case of Western Europe, dramatic political innovation as well. The United States replaced Western Europe as the dominant global power, taking the lead in many of the conflicts that developed during and after the Cold War.

The Cold War Tensions between the United States and the Soviet Union emerged quickly after World War II. Soviet desire for a protective belt against Germany combined with the opportunity to force-feed communist states in Eastern Europe. The West responded with rapid rearmament and an anti-Soviet alliance system. Specific crises in Germany, Korea, Vietnam, Cuba, and elsewhere dotted the Cold War. Equally ominous was the steady buildup of nuclear weapons. Negotiations led to arms control measures from the 1960s onward. The Cold War finally ended with the collapse of the Soviet Union, amid severe economic pressure, between 1985 and 1991.

Social and Political Change Economic growth after World War II created many social changes. Consumerism advanced. Class differentiation receded. Racial tensions led to new civil rights movements, but new patterns of immigration created further divisions. The women's movement and dramatic new work patterns ushered in major changes in gender relations and family life. Some of these currents touched Eastern Europe, but economic and social developments there lagged despite rapid economic recovery from World War II. Democracy spread widely, first in Western Europe and then after 1989 in most of Eastern Europe. The most dramatic international relations initiative in the region was Europe's Common Market, now the European Union. This reduced centuries-old national tensions, spreading after 2000 to much of East-Central Europe. The end of the Cold War was disrupted by new conflicts, particularly with terrorist movements, and growing United States involvement in the Middle East.

Recent Scholarship

In *Europe Recast: A History of the European Union* (2004), Desmond Dinan offers a balanced study of one of the most striking developments in contemporary world history. Dinan discusses the factors that led to this dramatic innovation and probes the tensions and issues that have plagued the experiment since its founding. The gains and strains of recurrent expansion are given careful attention. Overall, the book makes it clear how much Europe has changed, while allowing discussion of continuing issues and constraints. Europe has both declined as a world player and has addressed some key problems with imaginative vigor. This study encourages discussion about what the future holds, as new power centers arise in other parts of the world.

Differentiating Instruction

Differentiated Instruction Teacher Management System
- Pacing Guide
- Lesson Plans for Differentiated Instruction

Interactive Reader and Study Guide

Spanish Chapter Summaries Audio CD Program

Student Edition on Audio CD Program

Differentiated Instruction Modified Worksheets and Tests CD-ROM
- Vocabulary Flash Cards
- Modified Vocabulary Builder Activities
- Modified Chapter Review Activity
- Modified Chapter Test

OSP **One-Stop Planner CD-ROM**
- ExamView Test Generator (English/Spanish)
- PuzzlePro
- Quiz Show for ExamView
- Transparencies and Videos

TE **Differentiated Activities in the Teacher's Edition**
- The Bay of Pigs, p. 486
- The European Union, p. 492
- Conflicts in Yugoslavia's Republics, p. 498
- Creating a Political Cartoon, p. 504

Reading Like a Historian

Sam Wineburg

On October 4, 1957, the USSR successfully launched an R-7 intercontinental ballistic missile that carried a 58-centimeter steel globe dubbed "Sputnik." This metal ball, weighing 184 pounds, orbited the earth and punctured American pride.

The Space Race As our chapter describes, American reaction was swift, bordering on panic. A new government agency, the National Aeronautics and Space Administration (NASA) was hastily formed, signaling a major new commitment in government support for research and development in science. Americans read commentaries like those in the Chicago Daily News, which warned that if the Russians could hurl a metal ball around the earth it wouldn't be long before a larger object, carrying a nuclear payload, had our address on it. Private citizens rushed to construct backyard bomb shelters and schools conducted air raid drills in which schoolchildren were taught to cover their eyes to protect them from the flash of a nuclear explosion.

Predictable reactions, we might say. But ask your students if they can imagine other reactions. Students may be able to come up with other ideas, but I doubt that they will chance on this one: Americans interpreted Sputnik as a crushing indictment of their schools.

The Birth of a Crisis The March 24, 1958 cover of Life Magazine declared that there was a "Crisis in Education." Life offered a damning comparison of the rigors of the Soviet system versus the Mickey Mouse, happy-go-lucky atmosphere of American schooling. The magazine profiled two students, Chicago's Stephen Lapekas and Moscow's Alexei Kutzhov. Stephen boasted that he was reading Robert Louis Stevenson's *Kidnapped*, while Alexei had already mastered English as a second language, the complete works of Shakespeare, and George Bernard Shaw.

Accompanying the main article was an essay by Sloan Wilson, author of *The Man in the Grey Flannel Suit,* itself a critique of American conformism. Wilson's piece, entitled "It's Time to Close our Carnival," pulled no punches: "The facts of the school crisis are out and in plain sight ...A surprisingly small percentage of high school students is studying what used to be considered basic subjects...It is hard to deny that America's schools, which were supposed to reflect one of history's noblest dreams and to cultivate the nation's youthful minds, have degenerated into a system for coddling and entertaining the mediocre."

On the heals of this "crisis" Congress passed the one billion "National Defense Education Act" (NDEA) making education an issue of national security. Pouring money into math, science, and language instruction—recall the "New Math"—the NDEA represented a major shift in Federal education policy, which to that point had largely been an issue at the local and state level. At the initiative of President Eisenhower, the nation's top scientists, such as Glenn T. Seaborg, the 1951 Nobel laureate in chemistry and the discoverer of plutonium, occupied their time writing high school curriculum—this was after all an issue of national security. Overnight American schools went from being hunky-dory to being "in crisis."

Continuity and change is a major theme running throughout all of history. Much has changed since the Soviets launched Sputnik and the fallout landed on American schools. But the notion that the "schools are to blame," that they are "in crisis," perpetual crisis, remains a fixture in American rhetoric and culture—displaying a wondrous staying power that seemingly knows no time.

• Chapter Preview •

Chapter Main Ideas

Section 1 Once partners in war, the Soviet Union and the other former Allies found it much more difficult to cooperate in peace. The result was an era of conflict and confrontation called the Cold War.

Section 2 As the Cold War continued, the world's two superpowers—the Soviet Union and the United States—competed for power and influence around the world.

Section 3 The Cold War brought tremendous economic and social change to North America, Western Europe, and Eastern Europe and the Soviet Union.

Section 4 The Soviet Union collapsed in 1991 and the Cold War came to an end, bringing changes to Europe and leaving the United States as the world's only superpower.

CHAPTER 15

1945–Present

Europe and North America

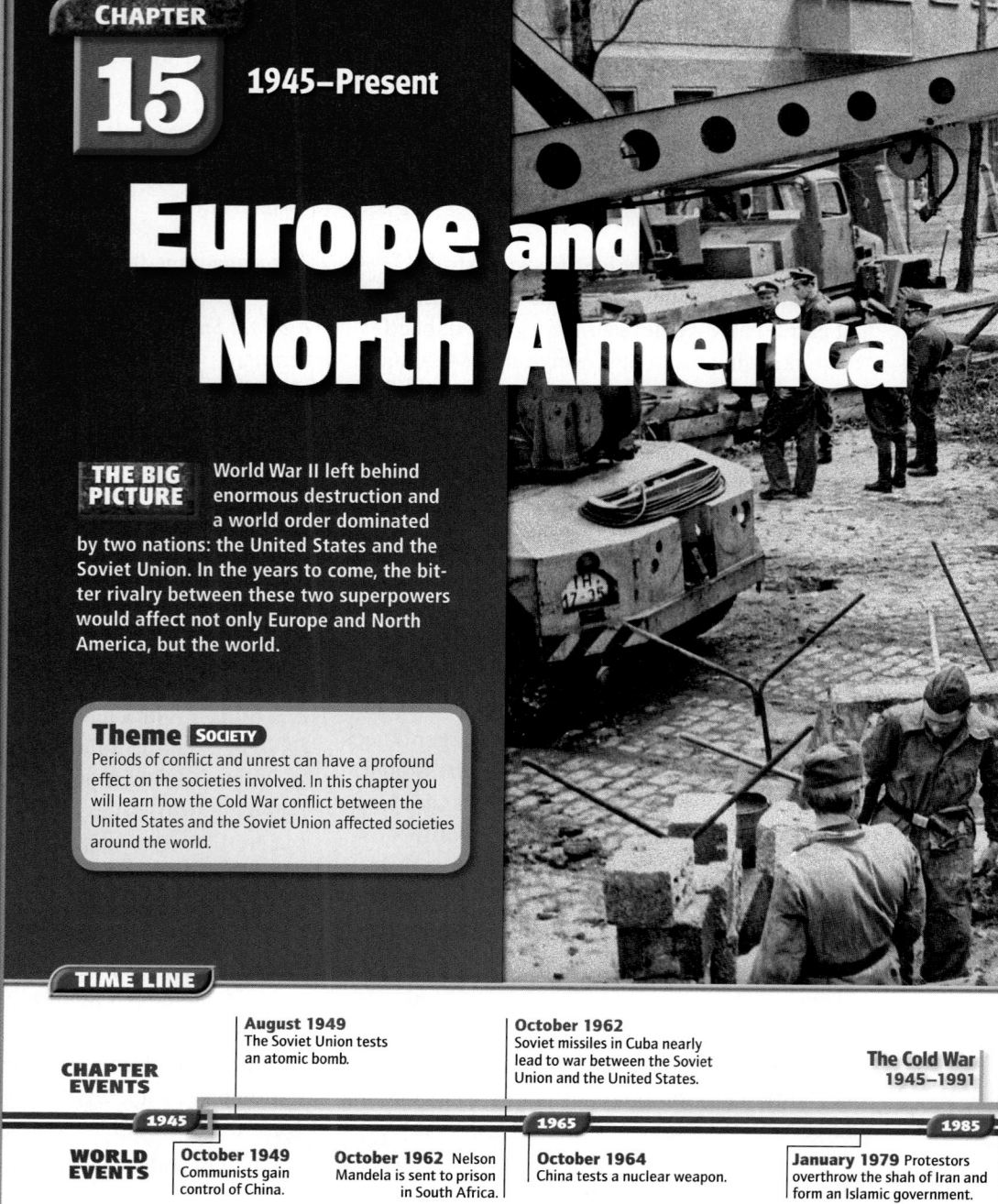

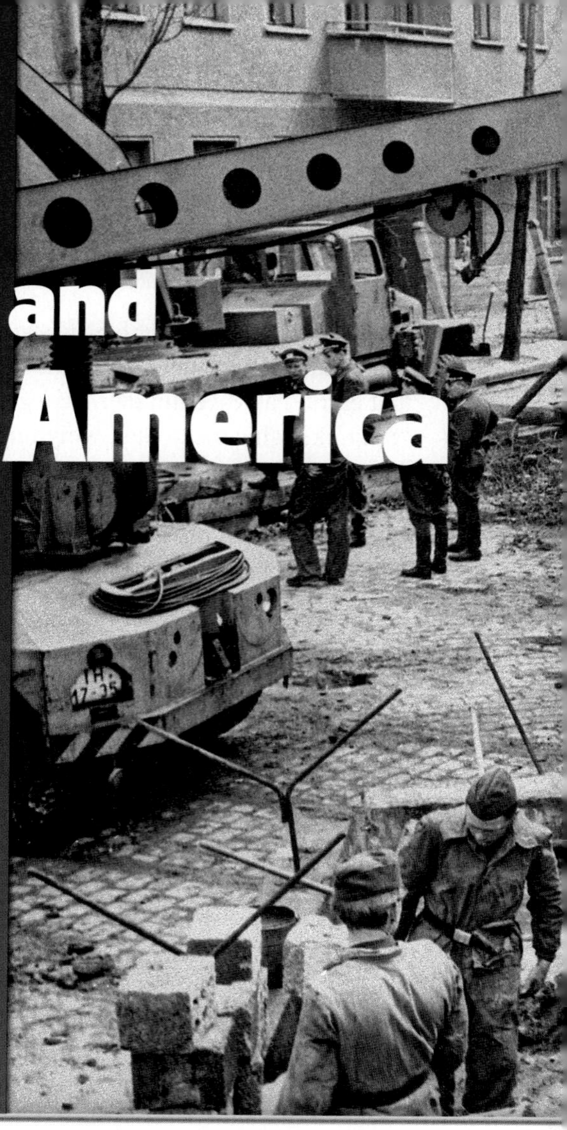

THE BIG PICTURE World War II left behind enormous destruction and a world order dominated by two nations: the United States and the Soviet Union. In the years to come, the bitter rivalry between these two superpowers would affect not only Europe and North America, but the world.

Theme SOCIETY
Periods of conflict and unrest can have a profound effect on the societies involved. In this chapter you will learn how the Cold War conflict between the United States and the Soviet Union affected societies around the world.

TIME LINE

CHAPTER EVENTS

August 1949 The Soviet Union tests an atomic bomb.

October 1962 Soviet missiles in Cuba nearly lead to war between the Soviet Union and the United States.

The Cold War 1945–1991

1945 — 1965 — 1985

WORLD EVENTS

October 1949 Communists gain control of China.

October 1962 Nelson Mandela is sent to prison in South Africa.

October 1964 China tests a nuclear weapon.

January 1979 Protestors overthrow the shah of Iran and form an Islamic government.

Key to Differentiating Instruction

Below Level

Basic-level activities designed for all students encountering new material

At Level

Intermediate-level activities designed for average students

Above Level

Challenging activities designed for honors and gifted and talented students

Standard English Mastery

Activities designed to improve standard English usage

Introduce the Chapter

At Level

Europe and North America

1. Explain the following scenario to students: World War II, a long, devastating conflict that involved almost every country in the world, has ended. New conflicts over government, land, and control of people, have begun to emerge between two large, dominant countries. Have students answer the following questions: How would you reduce the conflict and solve the dispute between the nations? What steps would you take to prevent another war?
2. List student answers for the class to see. Review with students what they learned in the last chapter about World War II and the "Big Three," the United States, Great Britain, and the Soviet Union.
3. Tell students that in this chapter they will learn about a period of hostility and tension between the Soviet Union and the United States called the Cold War. **LS Verbal-Linguistic**

Alternative Assessment Handbook, Rubric 11: Discussions

History's Impact video program
Watch the video to understand the impact of the European Union.

Reading like a Historian This 1963 photograph shows the Berlin Wall, which divided Communist East Berlin from democratic West Berlin. In the photo, East Berlin police rebuild a section of the wall that was damaged when an East German teenager rammed a truck through it and escaped to the West.

Analyzing Visuals What does this image suggest about the way some Communist leaders treated citizens?

See **Skills Handbook**, p. H26

November 1989 The Berlin Wall falls.

December 1991 The Soviet Union collapses.

March 2003 The U.S.-led invasion of Iraq begins.

1985 — 2005

November 1995 Israeli leader Yitzhak Rabin is assassinated.

• Chapter Preview •

HOLT
History's Impact
► **Video Program:**
Europe and North America
See the Video Teacher's Guide for strategies for using the video segment.

Reading Like a Historian

The Berlin Wall Approximately 2.5 million people from East Germany fled to the west between 1949 and 1961. Many of those who left were skilled and well educated. To prevent further loss of its skilled workforce, East Germany decided to erect a wall, and on the night of August 12-13, 1961, the first Berlin Wall, which was built with cinder blocks and barbed wire, went up.

Explore the Time Line

1. When did the Communists take control of China? *October 1949*
2. What events occurred in 1962? *Cuban Missile Crisis, Nelson Mandela imprisoned in South Africa*
3. How many years after the Soviet Union test of an atomic bomb did China test a nuclear bomb? *15 years*
4. How long did the Cold War last? *46 years*

Info to Know

The Wall Comes Down The following is an eyewitness account of the night the Berlin Wall was torn down in 1989: "…people cheered and clapped. East Germans drove through the applause, grinning, dazed, as thousands of flashbulbs went off. …streams of people were walking, talking together. Despite the brilliantly cold night, car windows were open and everyone talked to each other."

Make Inferences What do you think the fall of the Berlin Wall symbolized? *possible answer—hope, unity among Germans, freedom*

go.hrw.com
Online Resources
Chapter Resources: KEYWORD: SHL ENA
Teacher Resources: KEYWORD: SHL TEACHER

Answers

Reading Like a Historian *lack of trust, felt a wall was needed to keep citizens inside East Germany*

Preteach

Geography Starting Points

NATO NATO was formed in April 1949 and had 12 members; by 2006, there were 26 member nations from North America and Europe. The goal and role of NATO is to protect the freedom and security of member nations through political and military means. Russia is not a member, but is considered a partner country, and in May 2002, a NATO-Russia Council was established, strengthening the partnership between NATO and Russia.

Primary Source

"It was, frankly, very gratifying to sit at this table with the members of this NATO alliance to remember its extraordinary past, which, . . . managed to, through common values and resoluteness, face down imperial communism on this continent and to see the emergence of a Europe whole, free and at peace with itself."

—Remarks by Secretary of State Condoleezza Rice at NATO Headquarters, Brussels, February 9, 2005

- **Map Transparency:** Communist and NATO Countries, 1949
- **World History Outline Maps**
- **Interactive Map:** Communist and NATO Countries, 1949

GEOGRAPHY Starting Points

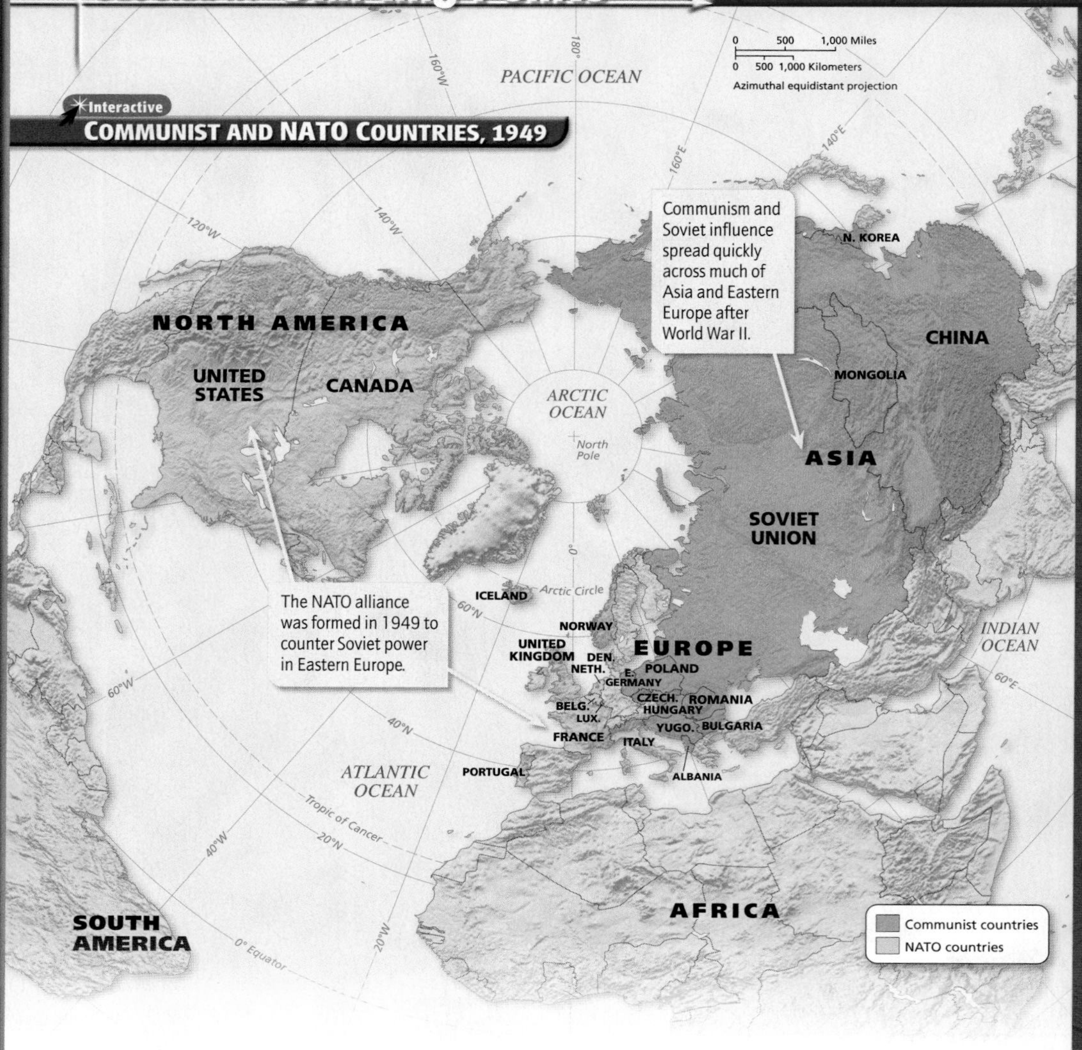

Starting Points While communism spread across Asia and Eastern Europe after World War II, the United States and other democratic nations worried about the possibility of another world war. As conflict between the two sides grew, a new era of competition for power and influence began.

1. **Identify** Which nations were members of NATO in 1949? Which countries were Communist?
2. **Predict** How might the increasing competition between NATO countries and Communist countries affect the world?

Listen to History

Go online to listen to an explanation of the starting points for this chapter.

go.hrw.com
Keyword: SHL ENA

Skills Focus: Drawing Conclusions

At Level

Reading Skill
NATO Countries

1. Have students use the map on this page to locate the 12 founding members of NATO: Belgium, Canada, Denmark, France, Iceland, Italy, Luxembourg, Netherlands, Norway, Portugal, the United Kingdom, and the United States.
2. Have students write a list of reasons why they think Germany and Spain were not among the original members.
3. Have volunteers read their lists to the class.
4. Guide students in a class discussion about the founding of NATO. Do they think a military alliance such as NATO is an effective way to counter Communist powers? **LS Verbal-Linguistic**

Alternative Assessment Handbook, Rubrics 11: Discussions; and 21: Map Reading

Answers

Geography Starting Points

1. *NATO—U.S., Canada, Iceland, Norway, U.K., Denmark, Netherlands, Belgium, Luxembourg, France, Portugal, Italy; Communist—N. Korea, China, Soviet Union, Poland, E. Germany, Czechoslovakia, Romania, Hungary, Yugoslavia, Bulgaria, Albania* **2.** *possible answer—increased tension, desire for power and control*

SECTION 1

Beginnings of the Cold War

BEFORE YOU READ

MAIN IDEA

Once partners in war, the Soviet Union and the other former Allies found it much more difficult to cooperate in peace. The result was an era of conflict and confrontation called the Cold War.

READING FOCUS

1. How did peace create problems for the Allies?
2. How did the Cold War conflict worsen in the late 1940s?
3. What were some of the early Cold War confrontations?

KEY TERMS

Nuremberg trials
Cold War
iron curtain
Truman Doctrine
Marshall Plan
containment
Berlin airlift
NATO
Warsaw Pact

TAKING NOTES Take notes on the problems, containment effects, and confrontations of the beginning of the Cold War.

Problems
Containment
Confrontations

TROUBLE AT POTSDAM

Joseph Stalin and Harry Truman pose for the camera at the Potsdam Conference.

THE INSIDE STORY ***How did a hot war turn cold?*** On the final day of the Potsdam Conference in 1945, U.S. president Harry S Truman was worried. He thought that Soviet leader Joseph Stalin had been stubborn and difficult to deal with and was concerned about Soviet plans for postwar Eastern Europe.

Truman made an appeal to Stalin on a minor issue, hoping that Stalin would demonstrate his goodwill and agree to compromise. Before Truman could even complete his request, Stalin interrupted him. "No!" shouted the Soviet leader.

It was an awkward moment, and Truman felt insulted by Stalin's manner. Little did he know that this difficult exchange was just a taste of what was to come in the increasingly tense U.S.-Soviet relationship. ■

The Problems of Peace

In World War II the Allies had worked together to defeat the Axis armies. With the war over, the Allies had to decide what to do with the shattered nations of Europe. This task placed a great strain on the alliance.

Occupying Germany When the war in Europe ended in May 1945, much of Germany was in ruins and it had no functioning government. The victorious Allies needed to establish a system to govern Germany and rebuild the nation. The Allies had thought ahead to the end of the war and had begun to plan for Germany's future even before fighting ceased. At the Potsdam Conference, they agreed on several major issues.

Teach the Main Idea

At Level

Beginnings of the Cold War

1. **Teach** Ask students the Reading Focus questions to teach this section.
2. **Apply** Have students work in mixed-ability pairs to make a list of the maps and other visuals in the chapter. Then have students scan the section and write a brief explanation about the significance of each visual and how it relates to the section title, Beginnings of the Cold War.
3. **Review** Have volunteers share their explanations with the class. Then guide students in a discussion about the significance of the iron curtain and the Korean War in the Cold War.
4. **Practice/Homework** Have students write a short essay explaining the reasons for the Cold War and whether or not they think it could have been prevented. **LS Visual-Spatial, Verbal-Linguistic**

Alternative Assessment Handbook, Rubric 37: Writing Assignments

Preteach

Getting Started

Use the **Interactive Reader and Study Guide** to familiarize students with the section content.

Interactive Reader and Study Guide, Section 1

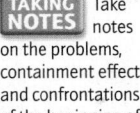

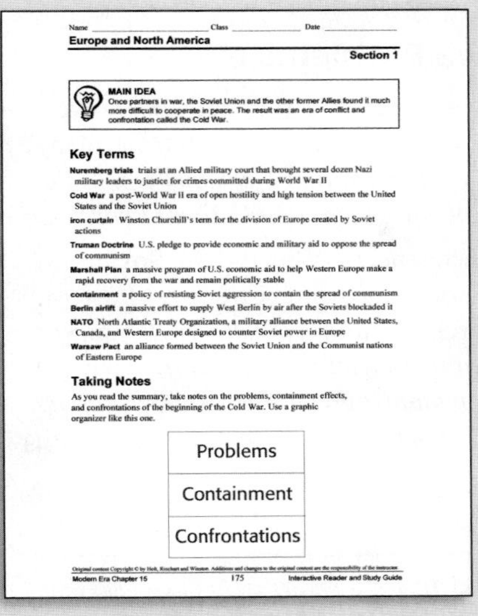

Name ______________ Class ______________ Date ______________

Europe and North America

Section 1

MAIN IDEA
Once partners in war, the Soviet Union and the other former Allies found it much more difficult to cooperate in peace. The result was an era of conflict and confrontation called the Cold War.

Key Terms

Nuremberg trials trials at an Allied military court that brought several dozen Nazi military leaders to justice for crimes committed during World War II

Cold War a post-World War II era of open hostility and high tension between the United States and the Soviet Union

iron curtain Winston Churchill's term for the division of Europe created by Soviet actions

Truman Doctrine U.S. pledge to provide economic and military aid to oppose the spread of communism

Marshall Plan a massive program of U.S. economic aid to help Western Europe make a rapid recovery from the war and remain politically stable

containment a policy of resisting Soviet aggression to contain the spread of communism

Berlin airlift a massive effort to supply West Berlin by air after the Soviets blockaded it

NATO North Atlantic Treaty Organization, a military alliance between the United States, Canada, and Western Europe designed to counter Soviet power in Europe

Warsaw Pact an alliance formed between the Soviet Union and the Communist nations of Eastern Europe

Taking Notes

As you read the summary, take notes on the problems, containment effects, and confrontations of the beginning of the Cold War. Use a graphic organizer like this one.

Problems
Containment
Confrontations

Modern Era Chapter 15 175 Interactive Reader and Study Guide

Academic Vocabulary

Review with students the high-use academic terms in this section.

currency money (p. 878)

import bring goods into a place (p. 880)

CRF: Vocabulary Builder: Section 1

Taking Notes

Problems—fight over Eastern Europe; the Soviets refuse to move out of Iran; Soviets spread communism to Eastern Europe; Soviet blockade of West Berlin; Containment—Truman Doctrine, Marshall Plan; Confrontations—Berlin airlift, NATO, Warsaw Pact, Korean War

Direct Teach

Reading Focus

1 How did peace create problems for the Allies? *Allies disagreed on what to do with Eastern Europe and how governments of these countries should be organized.*

The Problems of Peace

Describe How did the Allies solve the issue of reparations with Germany? *They decided that Germany would pay with equipment in addition to currency.*

Summarize Why did the Soviet Union want more power over Eastern Europe? *Stalin wanted to make sure that the Soviet Union had friendly, Communist governments as neighbors.*

Map Transparency: The Iron Curtain, 1949

Primary Source

"A shadow has fallen upon the scenes so lately lighted by the Allied victory. Nobody knows what Soviet Russia and its Communist international organization intends to do in the immediate future, or what are the limits, if any, to their expansive... tendencies... It is my duty to place before you certain facts about the present position of Europe. From Stettin in the Baltic to Trieste in the Adriatic an iron curtain has descended across the Continent."

—Winston Churchill, speech at Westminster College, March 5, 1946

Interactive Map: The Iron Curtain, 1949

Interactive

THE IRON CURTAIN, 1949

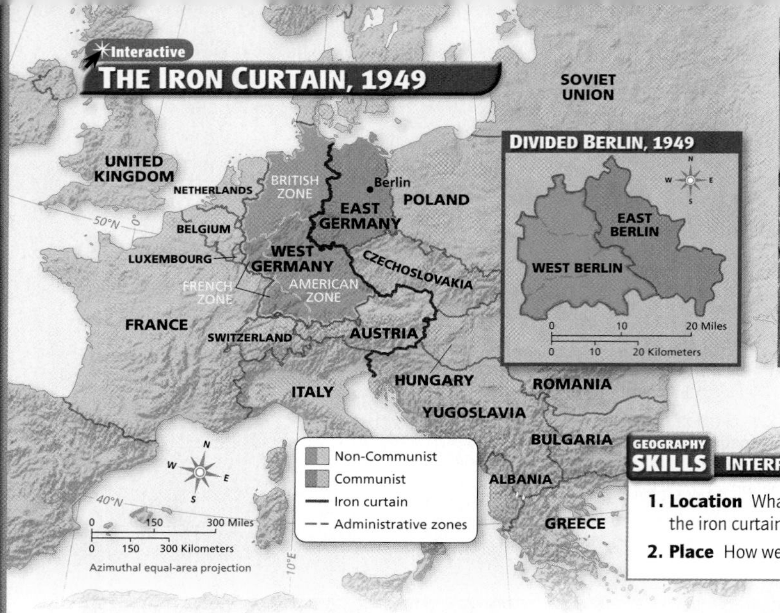

▲ In a famous speech, Winston Churchill described a Communist "iron curtain" descending on Europe.

go.hrw.com
Interactive Map
Keyword: SHL ENA

GEOGRAPHY SKILLS INTERPRETING MAPS

1. **Location** What countries were on the eastern side of the iron curtain?
2. **Place** How were Germany and Berlin divided?

First, the Allies agreed to temporarily divide Germany into four zones of occupation. The Soviet Union would control about one-third of the country. The remaining two-thirds would be divided into three zones, to be controlled by the United States, France, and Great Britain.

Second, the Allies also divided the German capital, Berlin. Though this city lay deep within the Soviet-controlled region of Germany, it was divided into four zones of occupation.

Third, the Allies worked together to establish a plan to rid Germany of any remnants of the Nazi Party and Nazi beliefs, in part by bringing former Nazi and military leaders to justice for crimes committed during the war. At the **Nuremberg trials**, which were held in Nuremberg, Germany, between 1945 and 1949, Allied military courts tried more than two hundred Nazi and military officials. Several dozen were sentenced to death for their roles in the Holocaust and in other war crimes.

Finally, the Allies agreed on a plan for Germany to pay reparations for the destruction caused by the war. These reparations were in the form of German currency and German industrial equipment. The Soviet Union received the largest share, since that country had suffered the greatest destruction.

ACADEMIC VOCABULARY
currency money

Eastern Europe While the Allies were able to agree on postwar Germany, deciding what to do with the rest of Europe proved more difficult. Even before the war ended, the major Allied powers were in conflict. American and British leaders argued with each other, and the Soviets often disagreed with both.

At the Potsdam Conference in the summer of 1945, the two sides argued over Eastern Europe, which bordered the Soviet Union and was occupied by Soviet forces. The Soviet Union had been invaded by Germany during both world wars, and Soviet leaders believed that they needed a buffer zone of friendly governments in Eastern Europe to guard against another such attack.

Soviet dictator Joseph Stalin promised to respect the rights of people in Eastern Europe to choose their own governments. American and British leaders, however, believed that Stalin planned to establish pro-Soviet Communist governments throughout Eastern Europe and beyond. Although the war in Europe had ended, growing tensions between the Allies were about to lead to another conflict.

READING CHECK **Identify Supporting Details** What problems did peace bring for the Allies?

Skills Focus: Analyzing Maps

At Level

Prep Required

Social Studies Skill
Potsdam Conference

1. Display political maps of Europe before and after World War I, after World War II, and Europe as it is today.
2. Distribute blank outline maps of Europe. Have students show and compare the national boundaries of individual countries after the two wars. Point out that after World War II, Poland, Czechoslovakia, Hungary, Romania, Bulgaria, Albania, and East Germany came under Soviet control. Estonia, Latvia, and Lithuania became part of the USSR. Yugoslavia also had a Communist government.
3. Have students compare the map of Europe after World War II with the map of the iron curtain on this page. Then have volunteers explain why the iron curtain appeared where it did. **LS Visual-Spatial**

Alternative Assessment Handbook, Rubrics 20: Map Creation; and 21: Map Reading

Answers

Interpreting Maps 1. *Soviet Union, East Germany, Poland, Czechoslovakia, Romania, Hungary, Yugoslavia, Bulgaria, Albania, Greece* **2.** *Both were divided into east and west sections.*

Reading Check *how to treat defeated countries, disagreements on what to do with Eastern Europe*

The Conflict Worsens

The relationship between the Soviet Union and the Western nations continued to worsen after the war. Soon the United States and the Soviet Union entered an era of tension and hostility, which became known as the **Cold War**.

The Struggle Begins The Cold War was more than a military rivalry. It was a struggle for power and control between two nations with very different forms of government, economic systems, and ways of life. In short, the Cold War was a conflict between communism and capitalist democracy.

With the backing of Soviet troops, pro-Soviet Communist governments were soon established throughout Eastern Europe. Only Yugoslavia avoided Soviet domination, although that nation was also led by a Communist dictator. As communism spread throughout Eastern Europe, tension between the Soviet Union and the western democracies continued to grow. This tension was worsened by the Soviet failure to remove troops from northern Iran, which the Soviet Union had occupied during the war. In January 1946, President Truman warned his secretary of state, "Another war is in the making."

In February 1946 Stalin stated publicly that he believed war between the East and West was bound to happen in the future. The next month, former British leader Winston Churchill gave a speech in the United States. Churchill used the image of an **iron curtain** to describe the sharp division of Europe that was the result of Soviet actions. This division, he said, was a serious threat to peace.

HISTORY'S VOICES

> "Our difficulties and dangers will not be removed by closing our eyes to them. They will not be removed by mere waiting to see what happens; nor will they be removed by a policy of appeasement."
>
> —Winston Churchill, speech, March 5, 1946

The West Resists The democratic nations of the West soon faced a test of their resolve to contain the Communist East. In early 1947 Soviet-backed Communists were threatening the governments of Greece and Turkey. President Truman used the opportunity to announce what became known as the Truman Doctrine. The **Truman Doctrine** was a pledge to provide economic and military aid to oppose the spread of communism. The United States was committed, Truman said, to helping free peoples resist takeover by "armed minorities or outside pressures." The U.S. Congress agreed to send hundreds of millions of dollars in aid to Greece and Turkey.

Similar war-related economic problems existed throughout much of Europe. Truman believed that if conditions grew worse, more Europeans might turn to communism. So in mid-1947, the U.S. government launched a massive program of economic aid. The **Marshall Plan**, named after U.S. secretary of state George Marshall, provided $13 billion for rebuilding Europe. The plan helped Western Europe make a rapid recovery from the war, and it also helped preserve political stability.

READING CHECK **Summarize** How did conflict between East and West worsen after World War II?

PRIMARY SOURCES

The Marshall Plan

In a speech at Harvard University on June 15, 1947, U.S. secretary of state George C. Marshall outlined his plan to help rebuild the postwar European economy.

> "The truth of the matter is that Europe's requirements for the next three or four years of foreign food and other essential products—principally from America—are so much greater than her present ability to pay that she must have substantial additional help or face economic, social, and political deterioration of a very grave character . . .
>
> "It is logical that the United States should do whatever it is able to do to assist in the return of normal economic health in the world, without which there can be no political stability and no assured peace. Our policy is directed not against any country or doctrine but against hunger, poverty, desperation, and chaos."

Skills Focus **READING LIKE A HISTORIAN**

1. **Summarize** Why does Marshall say that the United States needs to help Europe?
2. **Analyze Primary Sources** Is Marshall worried about the spread of communism? Explain your answer.

See **Skills Handbook**, p. H25

Direct Teach

Reading Focus

2 How did the Cold War conflict worsen in the late 1940s? *establishment of Communist governments in Europe, Soviet Union did not remove troops from Iran, U.S. commitment to provide economic and military aid to countries threatened by spread of communism*

The Conflict Worsens

Explain Why did President Truman issue the Truman Doctrine? *to show of force against Communist aggression and to prevent spread of communism; to help countries struggling to fight communism*

Evaluate Do you think the Marshall Plan was a success in establishing peace in Europe? *possible answers—yes, made rebuilding possible, increased support for democracy; no, may have increased tensions between Eastern Europe and the West*

CRF: Biography: George Marshall

Primary Source

"I believe that our help should be primarily through economic and financial aid which is essential to economic stability and orderly political processes."
—Harry S Truman, speech to joint session of Congress, March 12, 1947

Skills Focus: Analyzing Costs and Benefits

Above Level

Research Required

Social Studies Skill
The Marshall Plan

1. Have students conduct outside research using both print and Internet sources to learn more about the Marshall Plan, what it entailed, and its consequences in Europe and within the United States.
2. Have students write an economic and political analysis about the ways in which the Marshall Plan helped make the United States a superpower. Students should include charts and graphs with economic data to support the arguments in their analyses.
3. Have volunteers present their research papers to the class. Then guide students in a discussion of the importance and effectiveness of the Marshall Plan.

LS Logical-Mathematical, Verbal-Linguistic

Alternative Assessment Handbook, Rubrics 1: Acquiring Information; and 42: Writing to Inform

Answers

Primary Sources 1. *believed that if Europe didn't receive U.S. aid, it would face "economic, social, and political deterioration;"* **2.** *possible answers—no, because he says his policy isn't directed at "any country or doctrine;" yes, because he wanted to preserve political stability*

Reading Check *communism spread to most of Eastern Europe, the Soviet Union would not withdraw troops from Iran, the West resists with Truman Doctrine, aid to Turkey and Greece*

Direct Teach

Reading Focus

3 What were some of the early Cold War confrontations? *Berlin blockade and Airlift, Korean War*

Cold War Confrontations

Explain Were the UN efforts in Korea effective? How can you tell? *possible answer—The UN did not achieve all its military goals, but neither did North Korean forces; the border remained where it was before the conflict.*

Make Predictions What might have happened if the Berlin airlift had been unsuccessful? *possible answer—Soviet Union would have taken control of Berlin; might have led to Soviet control of Germany, possibly war*

Map Transparency: The Korean War, 1950–1951

CRF: History and Geography: Berlin Crisis Forges New Alliances

CRF: Primary Source: The North Atlantic Treaty

Interactive Map: The Korean War, 1950–1951

Recent Scholarship

John Lewis Gaddis provides a comprehensive history of the Cold War from beginnings to aftermath in *The Cold War: A New History*. While Gaddis provides a complete analysis of the beginnings of the Cold War, he focuses on the failed ideologies, class struggles, and economic woes that led to the downfall of the Soviet Union.

The Cold War: A New History by John Lewis Gaddis. Penguin Press, 2005.

Answers

Interpreting Maps *invades the south, June 1950; pushed back by UN forces, Sept.–Oct. 1950; China helps North Korea advance south again, November 1950–January 1951*

Interactive

THE KOREAN WAR, 1950–1951

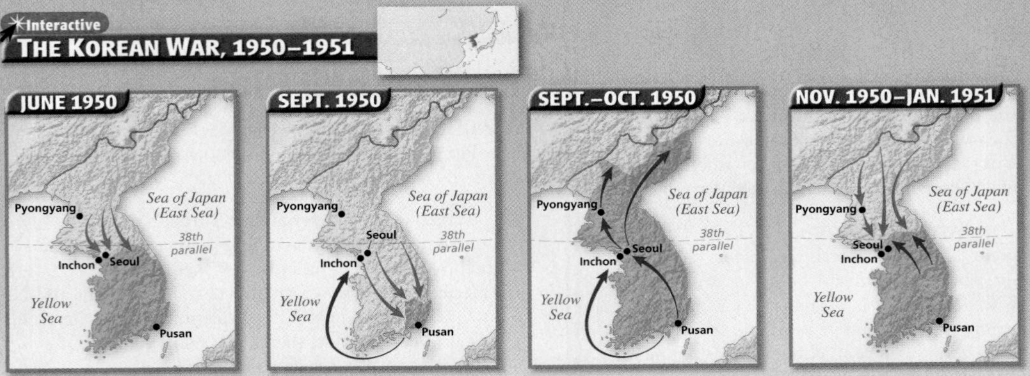

1 In a surprise attack, North Korean troops invade the South.

2 UN forces land at Inchon, attacking behind North Korean lines.

3 UN forces quickly push north from Pusan and Inchon.

4 China enters the war on the side of North Korea.

Controlled by North Korea
Controlled by South Korea
North Korean forces
UN forces
0 150 300 Miles
0 150 300 Kilometers
Lambert conformal conic projection

GEOGRAPHY SKILLS INTERPRETING MAPS

go.hrw.com Interactive Map Keyword: SHL ENA

Territory changed hands frequently during the Korean War as troops moved over an area smaller than the state of California.

Movement Describe North Korean movements during the war.

Cold War Confrontations

The Truman Doctrine and the Marshall Plan demonstrated the West's Cold War policy of **containment**, which involved resisting Soviet aggression in order to contain the spread of communism. The confrontations between East and West soon became increasingly severe.

Crisis in Berlin The division of Germany and of Berlin was originally meant to be temporary. In 1947, however, Western leaders began planning for the creation of an independent democratic German nation, to be formed from the three western zones of occupation. They also planned to establish a democratic government in West Berlin, deep inside the Soviet zone. The Soviets opposed this plan.

In June 1948, the Soviets blocked off all land, rail, and water routes into West Berlin. As a result, Berlin's 2 million residents were no longer able to import food, coal, and other vital supplies. The Soviets hoped these measures would force the West to leave Berlin.

ACADEMIC VOCABULARY
import bring goods into a place

Western leaders refused to give in. They organized the **Berlin airlift**, a massive effort to supply West Berlin by air. At one point, a cargo plane was taking off from or landing in Berlin every 30 seconds. The Berlin airlift was a success, and the Soviets called off the blockade of Berlin in May 1949.

New Nations and Alliances Within days of the end of this crisis, the western zones of Germany formed the Federal Republic of Germany, or West Germany. A few months later, the Soviet zone became the German Democratic Republic, or East Germany.

Also in the aftermath of the airlift, the United States, Canada, and most Western European countries joined together in a military alliance. The alliance, called the North Atlantic Treaty Organization, or **NATO**, was designed to counter Soviet power in Europe. In 1955, the Soviet Union and the Communist nations of Eastern Europe formed their own alliance, known as the **Warsaw Pact**.

War in Korea After Japan's surrender in World War II, the Allies had gained control of the Korean Peninsula. The Soviet Union and the United States agreed to temporarily divide the country in half. The Soviets quickly established a Communist government in the northern half of Korea. In the South, the United States supported a non-Communist regime.

Skills Focus: Sequencing

Below Level

Reading Skill
The Korean War

1. Draw the chart for students to see. Omit the italicized answers.
2. Have students work in mixed-ability pairs to copy and complete the chart with the events that led up to UN involvement in the Korean War. **LS Visual-Spatial**

Alternative Assessment Handbook, Rubric 13 Graphic Organizers

- **Allies agree at Yalta that Korea should be free, but temporarily divided, following the war.**
- **Japan surrenders.**
- ***Soviet Union establishes Communist government in North Korea, United States promotes democratic system in South Korea.***
- ***North Korea builds up forces along the 38th parallel.***
- ***United States and Soviet Union withdraw troops from South and North Korea, respectively.***
- ***North Korea invades South Korea, captures Seoul***
- **Truman commits U.S. troops and asks the UN to approve use of force to stop North Korean invasion.**

In June 1950 the North Koreans attacked South Korea. Their goal was to unite the country under a Communist government. Believing that a failure to defend South Korea might lead to other attempts at Communist expansion, the United States asked the United Nations to approve the use of force to stop the invasion. U.S. Army general Dwight Eisenhower warned, "We'll have a dozen Koreas soon if we don't take a firm stand." The United Nations soon formed a military force with troops from 17 nations and sent these soldiers to Korea. Most of the soldiers were Americans.

In spite of the UN involvement, the North Koreans nearly conquered the South within a matter of months. Then, UN forces led by American general Douglas MacArthur carried out a daring invasion at Inchon, behind enemy lines. The Inchon landing tipped the balance back in favor of the UN forces. Soon, they had pushed the North Koreans out of South Korea and driven deep into North Korea, near the Chinese border.

The war shifted once more when Communist Chinese forces poured into Korea to aid the North Koreans. With overwhelming numbers, they drove the UN forces back out of North Korea.

During 1951, the war settled into a stalemate. The battle lines lay just about where they had been before North Korea's initial invasion. In 1953 both sides agreed to an armistice.

Causes and Effects of the Cold War

QUICK FACTS

CAUSES

- Disagreements between the Allies during World War II
- Differing U.S. and Soviet political and economic systems
- Differing goals for postwar Germany and Eastern Europe
- Soviet expansion of communism in Eastern Europe
- Resistance to Soviet aggression by United States

EFFECTS

- Political and military struggles around the world
- Increased military spending, leading to an arms race
- The ever-present danger of nuclear war

After three years of fighting and some 4 million casualties, the Korean War was over. But little had changed since the war began. North Korea remained a Communist state, and South Korea was an ally of the West.

READING CHECK **Summarize** What were some Cold War confrontations of the 1940s and 1950s?

THE IMPACT TODAY

The tension between North and South Korea is still a major regional and international problem.

Section 1 Assessment

go.hrw.com
Online Quiz
Keyword: SHL ENA HP

Reviewing Ideas, Terms, and People

1. **a. Describe** What questions about postwar Europe did the Allies face?
   b. Infer Why do you think the Allies decided to divide Germany into four zones of occupation?
   c. Evaluate How did Soviet plans for Eastern Europe differ from those of the other Allies?
2. **a. Identify** Identify the following: **iron curtain**, **Truman Doctrine**, **Marshall Plan**
   b. Make Inferences Why do you think President Truman believed that poverty and suffering created conditions in which communism might spread?
3. **a. Recall** What were two major conflicts between the East and the West in the late 1940s and early 1950s?
   b. Evaluate Was the Korean War a success for the United States? Explain your answer.

Critical Thinking

4. **Identify Supporting Details** Using your notes on the section, identify the causes of the Cold War and its effects during these early years.

Causes	→	Effects

Focus on Writing

5. **Exposition** Write a paragraph that summarizes Soviet actions in Europe after World War II. Be sure to include details from the section.

Direct Teach

Causes and Effects of the Cold War

QUICK FACTS

Interpret How did the Cold War differ in size, length, and location from other wars? *Size—included millions from both sides, most wars did not include so many people; length—lasted 46 years, most wars not so lengthy; location—fought around the world, most wars between enemies geographically closer together*

Quick Facts Transparency: Causes and Effects of the Cold War

Review & Assess

Close

Have students review events of the Cold War discussed in the section.

Review

Online Quiz, Section 1

Assess

SE Section 1 Assessment

Progress Assessment: Section 1 Quiz

Alternative Assessment Handbook

Reteach/Intervene

Interactive Reader and Study Guide, Section 1

Interactive Skills Tutor CD-ROM

Answers

Reading Check *Soviet blockade of West Berlin, Berlin airlift, Korean War,*

Section 1 Assessment Answers

1. **a.** what to do with Germany; how to handle reparations; Eastern Europe
   b. possible answer—to give control of Germany to the Allied nations
   c. The Soviet Union insisted on having Communist governments as neighbors, but had promised to respect rights of people living in these countries; other Allies wanted people in Eastern Europe to choose their own form of government.
2. **a.** iron curtain—division of Europe into East and West; Truman Doctrine—promise to provide economic aid to countries opposing spread of communism; Marshall Plan—U.S. provided $13 billion to rebuild Europe
   b. possible answer—communism caters to poor by promising same opportunities and social status to all
3. **a.** Soviet blockade of West Berlin and Korean War
   b. possible answers—yes; showed that world would not tolerate forceful Communist-inspired invasions; no, war ended in stalemate, with same boundaries after the war
4. Causes—fight over Eastern Europe; Soviet refusal to remove troops from Iran; Communist governments in Eastern Europe; Effects—Soviet blockade of West Berlin; Korean War; iron curtain; Truman Doctrine
5. Student paragraphs should include details from the section about Soviet actions in Europe after World War II.

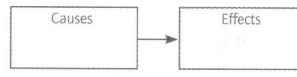

Preteach

Getting Started

Use the **Interactive Reader and Study Guide** to familiarize students with the section content.

Interactive Reader and Study Guide, Section 2

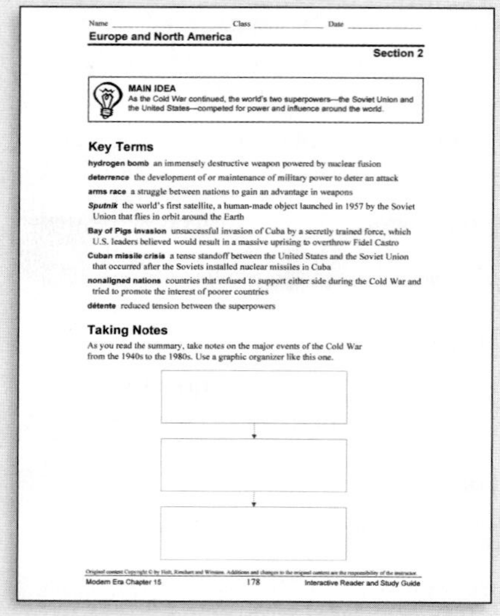

Name ______________ Class __________ Date __________

Europe and North America

Section 2

MAIN IDEA
As the Cold War continued, the world's two superpowers—the Soviet Union and the United States—competed for power and influence around the world.

Key Terms

hydrogen bomb an immensely destructive weapon powered by nuclear fusion
deterrence the development of or maintenance of military power to deter an attack
arms race a struggle between nations to gain an advantage in weapons
Sputnik the world's first satellite, a human-made object launched in 1957 by the Soviet Union that flies in orbit around the Earth
Bay of Pigs invasion unsuccessful invasion of Cuba by a secretly trained force, which U.S. leaders believed would result in a massive uprising to overthrow Fidel Castro
Cuban missile crisis a tense standoff between the United States and the Soviet Union that occurred after the Soviets installed nuclear missiles in Cuba
nonaligned nations countries that refused to support either side during the Cold War and tried to promote the interest of poorer countries
détente reduced tension between the superpowers

Taking Notes

As you read the summary, take notes on the major events of the Cold War from the 1940s to the 1980s. Use a graphic organizer like this one.

Original content Copyright © by Holt, Rinehart and Winston. Additions and changes to the original content are the responsibility of the instructor.

Modern Era Chapter 15 178 Interactive Reader and Study Guide

CRF: Vocabulary Builder: Section 2

Taking Notes

Cuban Missile Crisis, arms race, Sputnik, Vietnam War, Berlin Wall, Bay of Pigs invasion, battle over the Suez Canal, battle over Angola, SALT I and II, ABM Treaty

go.hrw.com
Online Resources
KEYWORD: SHL ENA
ACTIVITY: The Cold War

SECTION 2

Superpower Rivalries

Before You Read

Main Idea

As the Cold War continued, the world's two superpowers—the Soviet Union and the United States—competed for power and influence around the world.

Reading Focus

1. How did the arms race begin in the 1950s and early 1960s?
2. How did the Cold War contribute to conflict around the world?
3. How did the superpowers attempt to achieve arms control during the Cold War?

Key Terms

hydrogen bomb
deterrence
arms race
Sputnik
Bay of Pigs invasion
Cuban missile crisis
nonaligned nations
détente

TAKING NOTES Take notes on the major events of the Cold War from the 1940s through the 1980s.

THE INSIDE STORY

Was nuclear war at hand? President John F. Kennedy was in his White House bedroom eating breakfast when he heard about a startling discovery—an American spy plane had photographed several Soviet nuclear missiles on a launching pad on the island of Cuba, just 90 miles from American territory. A missile fired from Cuba could potentially hit targets in the eastern United States within a few minutes. Was nuclear war at hand?

During the first frantic days after this discovery, U.S. officials tried to decide what actions to take. Should the United States invade Cuba? Bomb the missile sites? Attack the Soviet Union?

The Soviets claimed that the missiles were only intended to protect Cuba from an American attack, not to attack the United States. Still, President Kennedy demanded that the Soviets remove the missiles. He also considered military options—options he knew might trigger a nuclear war.

The tense standoff lasted for nearly two weeks. Finally, after much negotiation, the Soviets removed the missiles. In exchange, the United States agreed to remove U.S. missiles from Turkey and promised not to attack Cuba. Nuclear disaster had been avoided—at least for a while. ■

The Arms Race Begins

During the 1950s and early 1960s nuclear war seemed to draw ever closer as the Soviet Union and the United States raced to develop powerful new weapons. This rivalry between the world's two superpowers became increasingly tense—and dangerous.

The Nuclear Arms Race In 1949 the West was deeply shaken by news of a successful Soviet test of an atomic bomb. Suddenly, the great military advantage the United States had enjoyed over the Soviet Union was gone.

Immediately, the United States sought to develop even more powerful weapons. Atomic bombs used energy created by splitting apart atoms; but using nuclear fusion, or the fusing together of atoms, could produce a much larger explosion. Fusion is the process that creates the enormous energy of the sun and stars.

Crisis in CUBA

A U.S. surveillance photograph shows eight missiles carried by a Soviet cargo ship. ▶

Teach the Main Idea

At Level

Superpower Rivalries

1. **Teach** Ask students the Reading Focus questions to teach this section.
2. **Apply** Organize students into groups of three. Assign one Reading Focus question to each student in the group and have students scan the section to answer the question. Have each member of the group teach the others in the group the answer to the question.
3. **Review** Make a class list of all the regions mentioned in the section and guide students in a discussion of their significance to the Cold War and the rivalries between the superpowers.
4. **Practice/Homework** Have students identify one conflict involving the United States and the Soviet Union. Have students write letters to the editor describing the conflict and expressing their opinions about whether the conflict was justified or not. **LS Verbal-Linguistic**

Alternative Assessment Handbook, Rubric 17: Letters to Editors

In the fall of 1952 the United States tested the first fusion-powered **hydrogen bomb** with spectacular results, completely vaporizing the island on which the bomb was tested. As with the atomic bomb, the U.S. technological advantage was short-lived. Less than one year later the Soviets tested their own hydrogen bomb.

This development of nuclear weapons forced both sides to change their military tactics. Instead of relying upon conventional forces, such as troops and tanks, U.S. and Soviet leaders increased their stockpiles of nuclear weapons. These weapons soon became central to each side's defense strategy, a strategy based on the principle of deterrence. **Deterrence** is the development of or maintenance of military power to deter, or prevent, an attack.

The two superpowers were locked in an **arms race**, a struggle between nations to gain an advantage in weapons. The United States soon had far more nuclear weapons than the Soviet Union, and it was clear that a nuclear attack by either side would lead to terrible destruction.

HISTORY CLOSE-UP

The Cuban Missile Crisis

During October 1962, the U.S.-Soviet confrontation over Soviet missiles in Cuba brought the world close to a nuclear war. This map—which is based on a map created for President John F. Kennedy by a U.S. intelligence agency—shows major U.S. cities within the 1,200-mile range of Soviet medium-range missiles fired from Cuba. Long-range missiles could hit targets as far as 4,000 miles away.

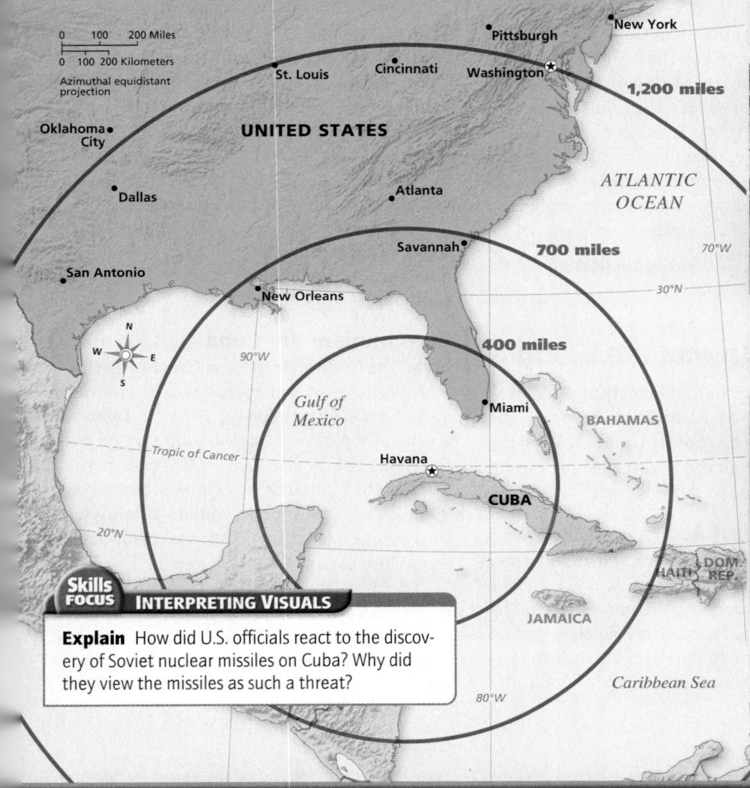

Skills Focus INTERPRETING VISUALS

Explain How did U.S. officials react to the discovery of Soviet nuclear missiles on Cuba? Why did they view the missiles as such a threat?

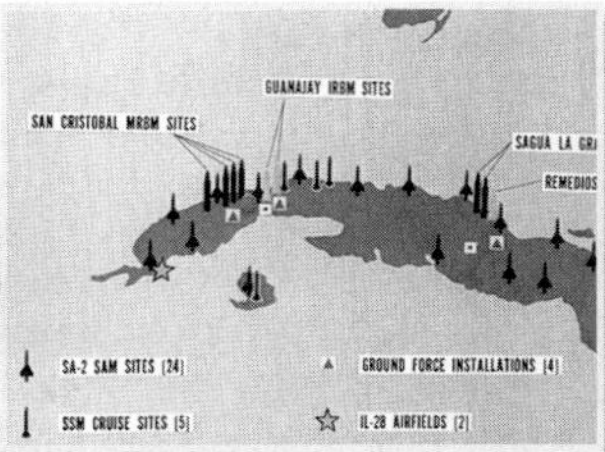

October 14, 1962 A U.S. spy plane first photographs a missile on a launching site. Other sites are soon identified.

October 23, 1962 A Soviet nuclear warhead bunker is under construction at San Cristobal, Cuba.

October 25, 1962 The U.S. ambassador to the United Nations confronts the Soviet ambassador, displaying photos of the Soviet missiles.

Direct Teach

Reading Focus

❶ How did the arms race begin in the 1950s and early 1960s? *Soviets developed and tested atomic bomb; U.S. followed and countered with hydrogen bomb; both countries developed ICBMs*

The Arms Race Begins

Identify What did the United States test in 1952? *the first fusion-powered hydrogen bomb*

Make Judgments Do you agree with the U.S. response to the Soviet testing of an atomic bomb? Why or why not? *possible answer—No, it intensified already strained relations.*

History Close-up

The Cuban Missile Crisis

Kennedy's Reaction President Kennedy's reaction to the Cuban Missile crisis was not one of diplomatic negotiation. His plan was to isolate Cuba in order to prevent any more military shipments from the Soviet Union. His next move was to address the Soviets in a televised statement on the evening of October 22, 1962; a few days later the Soviets agreed to remove the missiles.

Map Transparency: The Cuban Missile Crisis

Primary Source

"I call upon Chairman Khrushchev to halt and eliminate this clandestine, reckless, and provocative threat to world peace and to stable relations between our two nations. I call upon him further to abandon this course of world domination and to join in an historic effort to end the perilous arms race and transform the history of man.

—John F. Kennedy, Address on the Cuban Crisis, October 22, 1962

Skills Focus: Comparing and Contrasting

At Level

Reading Skill

The Cuban Missile Crisis

1. Review with students the information about the Cuban Missile Crisis. Then have students create two political cartoons. One cartoon should show the Soviets removing their missiles from Cuba. The other cartoon should show Kennedy winning a fight against Khrushchev in the crisis.
2. Have volunteers share their cartoons with the class.
3. Guide students in a discussion of the cartoons and the role that the Cuban Missile Crisis may have played in the Strategic Arms Limitations Talks. LS **Visual-Spatial**

Alternative Assessment Handbook, Rubric 27: Political Cartoons

Answers

History Close-Up *wanted immediate removal of the missiles; could have destroyed a number of U.S. citites*

Direct Teach

Reading Focus

2 How did the Cold War contribute to conflict around the world? *Directly and indirectly, the United States and the Soviet Union entered into military battles in an effort to stop or assist in the spread of communism.*

Cold War Around the World

Explain What were the causes of the Vietnam War? *Vietnam had been partitioned into Communist-controlled North and anti-Communist South. When the North began fighting to unify the country, the United States intervened.*

Analyze Do you think the United States should have prevented Castro's forces from taking over Cuba's government? Explian your answer. *possible answer—yes, would have prevented installation of Communist government; no, was not clear that Castro would create a Communist dictatorship and Cuba's previous government was corrupt*

CRF: Biography: Willy Brandt

Soviet Union Launches *Sputnik* In October 1957 the arms race took another leap forward with the Soviet Union's successful launch of *Sputnik*. ***Sputnik*** was history's first artificial satellite—an object that orbits the earth.

Americans had always believed they had a technological advantage over the Soviets. With the launch of *Sputnik*, Americans feared that Soviet military technology had leaped ahead of their own. In response, the U.S. government established the National Aeronautics and Space Administration, or NASA, in 1958. This agency would eventually return the United States to the forefront of space research.

Public Fears The growing threat of nuclear war had a significant impact on people in the United States and other nations. Many people built bomb shelters in hopes that these structures would help protect them from a nuclear explosion. American schools led air-raid drills to prepare students for a possible Soviet attack; and a number of movies, books, and comic books had plots centered on the dangers of radiation and nuclear war.

READING SKILLS

Making Inferences Why do you think that so many Americans feared Communists in the United States?

Most significantly, the Cold War led to a so-called Red Scare in the United States as many Americans feared possible Communist influence in the U.S. government. In the late 1940s and early 1950s Senator Joseph McCarthy and a congressional committee led the effort to expose Communists in the American film industry and government, accusing many innocent people of Communist activities.

READING CHECK **Identify Supporting Details** How did the arms race begin?

Cold War Around the World

THE IMPACT TODAY

The United States enforces a trade embargo against Cuba that was first enacted in 1962, after Fidel Castro's government confiscated hundreds of millions of dollars worth of U.S. property and businesses.

The Korean War had shown that Cold War rivalry could lead to conflict far from the United States or the Soviet Union. During the Cold War, this rivalry led to struggles for influence in countries around the world.

War in Southeast Asia At the end of World War II, France sought to reestablish its former colonial control over Southeast Asia. In one Southeast Asian country, Vietnam, Communist rebels fought back, forcing the French to give up control of Vietnam. In the resulting peace agreement, Vietnam was temporarily divided into northern and southern halves. Communists controlled the North and an anti-Communist regime ruled the South.

American officials were concerned about the spread of communism in Vietnam. They had supported the French struggle against the Communists; and after Vietnam's division, they supported the non-Communist government of the South. When a revolution began in the South, the United States sent military aid to fight the rebels. Eventually, the North Vietnamese began to fight alongside the rebels in an effort to reunite Vietnam.

Although the American military commitment grew, the Vietnam War dragged on until the mid-1970s. You will read more about this war in the next chapter.

Another Crisis in Berlin After Communist East Germany and democratic West Germany formed in 1949, tens of thousands of East Germans left their country by crossing from East Berlin into West Berlin. Some wanted to live in a free, democratic nation, while others simply crossed the border in search of work. By 1961 as many as 1,000 people a day were making the daily trip between their homes in East Germany and jobs in West Berlin. To stop this exodus, East Germany began erecting a tall barrier between the two halves of the city. This barrier, known as the Berlin Wall, was heavily guarded. Anyone attempting to cross it risked being shot by East German guards.

The Berlin Wall succeeded in slowing the flight of East Germans to West Germany. It also came to symbolize the brutality of the Communist system.

Communism in Cuba In 1959 rebels under the leadership of Fidel Castro overthrew Cuba's dictator and installed a Communist government. Once in power, Castro established a centrally planned economy and forged close ties with the Soviet Union. Castro's actions worried the United States. Cuba is located only 90 miles south of Florida, and its alliance with the Soviet Union brought the Cold War alarmingly close to American territory.

The U.S. government, seeking to overthrow Castro, secretly trained an invasion force of approximately 1,500 Cubans who had fled Castro's regime. In April 1961 this force came ashore at Cuba's Bay of Pigs. American

Differentiating Instruction

Below Level

Learners Having Difficulty

1. Write the following questions for students to see: What was the Bay of Pigs? Why did the administration support the invasion? What were some consequences of the failed invasion?
2. Have students work in mixed-ability pairs to copy and answer the questions. Then have students develop five questions that President Kennedy might have asked about the plans for the invasion. Have students exchange papers and answer each other's questions.
3. Have volunteers share their questions and answers.
4. Guide students in a discussion of the Bay of Pigs. **LS Verbal-Linguistic**

Alternative Assessment Handbook, Rubrics 11: Discussions; and 12: Drawing Conclusions

Answers

Reading Skills *possible answer—Heightened tensions in U.S.-Soviet relations coupled with the threat of nuclear war caused many American to fear Communists in the United States.*

Reading Check *development of atomic and hydrogen bombs*

Cold War Hot Spots

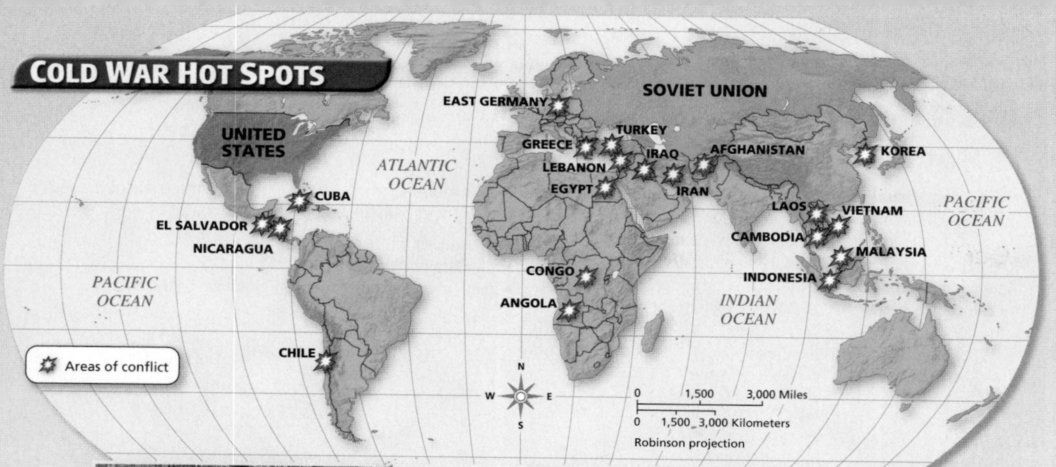

Built by Communist East Germany, the Berlin Wall divides Berlin.

Refugees search for safety during the Angolan civil war.

U.S. troops fight Communist rebels in Vietnam.

officials had believed the **Bay of Pigs invasion** would start a massive Cuban uprising against Castro. Instead, the invaders were quickly defeated.

In 1962 came the **Cuban missile crisis**, a confrontation between the United States and the Soviet Union over the installation of Soviet nuclear missiles in Cuba. After a two-week standoff, Soviet leaders removed the missiles when the United States agreed to remove U.S. missiles from Turkey and promised not to attack Cuba.

Other Cold War Conflicts The Cold War rivalry also played out in the Middle East, Africa, and Central and South America.

In 1956 Egypt angered the West by taking over the Suez Canal, which had been controlled primarily by Great Britain and France. After Britain, France, and Israel attacked Egypt, the Soviet Union threatened to fight on Egypt's side. Afraid of a larger war, the United States quickly demanded that its Western allies halt their attack; and the conflict came to an end.

GEOGRAPHY SKILLS **INTERPRETING MAPS**

1. **Regions** Where did Cold War conflicts take place?
2. **Location** Why do you think there were no conflicts in the United States or the Soviet Union?

In Africa, the final years of European colonial rule created numerous power struggles, as well as much involvement by the superpowers. In 1960, for example, Belgium ended its colonial control of the Congo (now the Democratic Republic of the Congo). After the Belgians left the Congo, military leader Joseph Mobutu gradually took control. The United States and other Western countries supported his dictatorship because they believed he would be a good ally against the Soviet Union.

The African country of Angola won independence from Portugal in 1975, but years of civil war followed. The United States and the Soviet Union supported opposing sides in this conflict, which lasted until 1991.

Direct Teach

Reading Focus

Cold War Around the World

Describe What led to the end of the Suez Canal crisis? *The United States insisted that its Western allies end the conflict with Egypt.*

Make Judgments Do you think the United States was justified in supporting Joseph Mobutu? Explain your answer. *possible answer—Yes, he was an ally against communism; no, the United States should not support brutal dictatorships; the goal is democracy and freedom.*

Interpreting Maps

Cold War Hot Spots

Region Why were these countries considered Cold War hotspots? *possible answer—They were turning or had turned to communism, and the United States was trying to prevent the spread of communism.*

Map Transparency: Cold War Hot Spots

Teaching Tip

Tell students that the Spanish name for the Bay of Pigs is Bahía de los Cochinos. The bay is located on Cuba's southern coast, not too far from the town of Cienfuegos. Havana is on the other side of the island.

Skills Focus: Analyzing Visuals

Below Level

Reading Like a Historian Skill

Cold War Hot Spots

1. Have students examine the map on this page. Copy the chart for students to see. Have students use information from the text to complete the chart.
2. As an extension, have students explain why so many of the Cold War hot spots were located in the Middle East. **LS Visual-Spatial, Verbal-Linguistic**

Alternative Assessment Handbook, Rubric 13: Graphic Organizers

Country/Conflict	Results
Cuba	
Angola	
Congo	

Answers

Interpreting Maps 1. *Refer to map.* **2.** *possible answer—Each country wanted to avoid conflict on its home turf.*

Direct Teach

Reading Focus

Cold War Around the World

Identify Cause and Effect What caused Chile's military to overthrow Allende and what was the result? *The United States had secretly supported opposition to Allende; the Communist regime was ousted.*

Make Inferences Why do you think non-aligned countries refused to take sides? *possible answer—They wanted to avoid conflict and keep peace in their own countries.*

Reading Focus

3 How did the superpowers attempt to achieve arms control during the Cold War? *United States tried open skies treaty, signed Test Ban Treaty, SALT I, ABM Treaty, SALT II, Intermediate-Range Nuclear Forces Treaty*

Attempts at Arms Control

Identify What was the ABM Treaty? *Anti-Ballistic-Missle Treaty; prevented development of weapon that would shoot down nuclear missiles*

Contrast What were the differences between SALT I and SALT II? *SALT I led to signed ABM Treaty; SALT II produced treaty that was never ratified.*

Reading like a Historian

A Soviet Military Parade

Analyzing Visuals The Cold War strategy of deterrence relied upon the threat of nuclear war. As a result, the enemy's perception of a nation's military power could be nearly as important as the military power itself. In this 1986 photograph, a Soviet military parade travels through Moscow's Red Square in celebration of the anniversary of the 1917 Bolshevik Revolution.

To interpret what this photograph suggests about the use of military force in the Cold War, think about

- the subject of the photo
- the details of the photo
- the reasons why this parade might have been held

This banner shows Vladimir Lenin, the leader of the Bolshevik Revolution, and the socialists Friedrich Engels and Karl Marx.
Thousands of Soviet citizens watch the parade.
These Soviet military vehicles are SCUD nuclear missile launchers.

Skills Focus READING LIKE A HISTORIAN

1. **Subject** Why do you think banners showing Soviet slogans and figures were displayed?
2. **Details** Why might there be so many people watching the parade?
3. **Reasons** Why might this parade of military equipment have taken place?

See **Skills Handbook**, p. H26

Superpower rivalries also affected Central and South America, where the United States supported efforts to overthrow regimes allied with the Soviet Union. In the early 1970s the United States secretly supported opposition to Chile's democratically elected leader, Salvador Allende, a socialist. As a result, Chile's military overthrew Allende in 1973. In 1983 U.S. forces ousted a Communist regime that had seized power on the island of Grenada.

Many countries sought to avoid being caught up in this worldwide rivalry between superpowers. Starting in the 1950s a number of nations refused to support either side. Instead, these so-called **nonaligned nations** sought to use their combined strength to promote the interests of poorer countries.

READING CHECK **Find the Main Idea** How did the Cold War play out around the world?

Skills Focus: Drawing Conclusions

Below Level

Standard English Mastery

Reading Skill
Arms Control Treaties

1. Review with students the information in the text about SALT I and II. Have students work in mixed-ability pairs to write brief summaries of the information in the text about the talks.
2. Guide students in a discussion of the importance, effectiveness, and limitations of treaties that prevent or limit development of weapons and missiles. Have students take notes during the discussion.
3. Have students use the information in their written summaries and class discussion notes to write a paragraph supporting or opposing arms control treaties. Have students work in pairs to review their first-draft paragraphs. Have students incorporate corrections into their final drafts. **LS Verbal-Linguistic**

Alternative Assessment Handbook, Rubrics 11: Discussions; and 37: Writing Assignments

Answers

Reading Like a Historian 1. *possible answer—to show its enemies that it was strong and united;* **2.** *possible answers—They wanted to show pride in their country; they were curious about the actions of their leader.* **3.** *possible answer—It was a show of military force to both citizens and enemies.*

Reading Check *Communism was spreading to many other countries, and the United States became involved in an attempt to stop its spread around the world.*

Attempts at Arms Control

While relations between East and West were largely hostile throughout the Cold War, some attempts at cooperation were made. Both sides worked to limit the spread of nuclear weapons and avoid the threat of nuclear war.

Early Arms Control In 1955 President Eisenhower proposed a so-called open skies treaty with the Soviet Union. This agreement would allow each side to fly over the other's territory and gather accurate information about its weapons. With accurate information, Eisenhower argued, neither side would have to imagine the worst about their enemy. Soviet leaders rejected this idea but proposed arms control measures of their own, periodically suggesting total nuclear disarmament. The United States rejected the Soviet proposals.

Eisenhower was followed in office by President John F. Kennedy. Kennedy favored limiting nuclear weapons tests as a means of slowing the development of new and more deadly technologies. The Cuban missile crisis helped convince both sides that it was important to make some progress on arms control; and in 1963 the United States and the Soviet Union agreed on a Test Ban Treaty. This treaty outlawed nuclear testing in the atmosphere, in outer space, and underwater.

SALT I and II In 1968 Richard Nixon was elected U.S. president. He sought what he called **détente** (day-TAHNT), or reduced tension between the superpowers. One result of his efforts was the start of negotiations known as the Strategic Arms Limitations Talks, or SALT I. The talks led to agreements limiting the number of nuclear weapons held by each side. SALT I also led to the Anti-Ballistic Missile (ABM) Treaty, which prevented the development of weapons designed to shoot down nuclear missiles. The ABM Treaty was meant to ensure that each side remained vulnerable to the other's nuclear weapons. This vulnerability was an important element of the principle of deterrence, which many people felt had been a key factor in the prevention of nuclear war.

The two sides then began a new round of talks, called SALT II. These talks resulted in an arms control treaty in 1979, although it was never ratified by the U.S. Senate.

The 1980s Ronald Reagan was elected U.S. president in 1980. He took an aggressive position against the Soviet Union and spoke of developing a missile defense system, an idea that seemed to violate the spirit of the ABM Treaty. But President Reagan also began arms reduction talks with Soviet leader Mikhail Gorbachev. In 1988 the two countries ratified the Intermediate-Range Nuclear Forces (INF) Treaty, which called for the elimination of certain types of missiles. After many years of conflict, the relationship between the Soviet Union and the United States was finally beginning to improve.

READING CHECK **Sequence** What were the major arms control agreements negotiated by the Soviet Union and the United States?

SECTION 2 ASSESSMENT

go.hrw.com
Online Quiz
Keyword: SHL ENA HP

Reviewing Ideas, Terms, and People

1. **a. Recall** What were some of the key technological developments affecting the Cold War in the 1950s?
   b. Explain How did an **arms race** develop between the Soviet Union and the United States?
   c. Evaluate Do you believe that **deterrence** was the best strategy to prevent nuclear war?
2. **a. Identify** What was the significance of the **Cuban missile crisis**?
   b. Explain Why did the Cold War spread around the world?
   c. Make Judgments Do you think the United States was justified in supporting the overthrow of Communist governments during the Cold War?
3. **a. Recall** What were some of the arms control agreements reached during the Cold War?
   b. Evaluate What do you think of the reasoning behind the Anti-Ballistic Missile Treaty?

Critical Thinking

4. **Evaluate** Using your notes on the section and a graphic organizer like the one below, identify the five most important events of the Cold War and rank them in their order of importance.

FOCUS ON SPEAKING

5. **Exposition** Write a brief conversation that two U.S. officials might have had during the Cuban missile crisis. The topic of the conversation should be possible ways to resolve the crisis.

Review & Assess

Close

Have students name and describe significant Cold War disputes.

Review

Online Quiz, Section 2

Assess

SE Section 2 Assessment

Progress Assessment: Section 2 Quiz

Alternative Assessment Handbook

Reteach/Intervene

Interactive Reader and Study Guide, Section 2

Interactive Skills Tutor CD-ROM

Answers

Reading Check *Test Ban Treaty, SALT I, reducing the number of nuclear weapons each side held, ABM Treaty that prevented the development of weapons that shoot down nuclear missiles*

Section 2 Assessment Answers

1. **a.** hydrogen bombs, ICBMs, satellites
   b. Each side was trying to develop more advanced weaponry than the other.
   c. possible answers—Yes, it showed other nations that nuclear war was not an acceptable option; no, it provoked the enemy.
2. **a.** It showed the world that both the United States and the Soviet Union could decrease their nuclear weaponry, and ultimately led to a reduction of weaponry in the arms race.
   b. The U.S.-Soviet rivalry for control led to conflicts in other parts of the world.
   c. possible answer—No, ultimately these efforts were not successful in establishing democracies and respecting human rights.
3. **a.** Test Ban Treaty, SALT I agreements, ABM Treaty
   b. possible answer—did not stop the development or production of nuclear missiles; was an attempt to end the arms race
4. Answers should include five of the following: arms race, *Sputnik*, Cuban Missile Crisis, Vietnam War, Berlin Wall, Bay of Pigs invasion, battle over the Suez Canal, battle over Angola, SALT I and II, ABM Treaty
5. Conversations should demonstrate an understanding of the Cuban Missile Crisis and its ramifications.

Preteach

Getting Started

Use the **Interactive Reader and Study Guide** to familiarize students with the section content.

Interactive Reader and Study Guide, Section 3

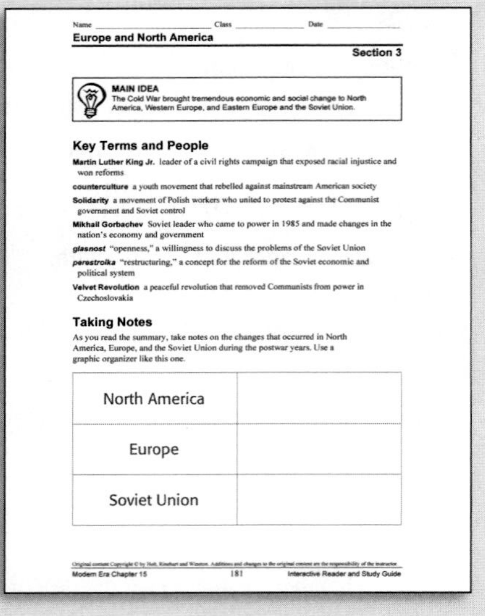
Name ______ Class ______ Date ______

Europe and North America

Section 3

MAIN IDEA
The Cold War brought tremendous economic and social change to North America, Western Europe, and Eastern Europe and the Soviet Union.

Key Terms and People

Martin Luther King Jr. leader of a civil rights campaign that exposed racial injustice and won reforms

counterculture a youth movement that rebelled against mainstream American society

Solidarity a movement of Polish workers who united to protest against the Communist government and Soviet control

Mikhail Gorbachev Soviet leader who came to power in 1985 and made changes in the nation's economy and government

glasnost "openness," a willingness to discuss the problems of the Soviet Union

perestroika "restructuring," a concept for the reform of the Soviet economic and political system

Velvet Revolution a peaceful revolution that removed Communists from power in Czechoslovakia

Taking Notes

As you read the summary, take notes on the changes that occurred in North America, Europe, and the Soviet Union during the postwar years. Use a graphic organizer like this one.

North America	
Europe	
Soviet Union	

Modern Era Chapter 15 181 Interactive Reader and Study Guide

CRF: Vocabulary Builder: Section 3

Taking Notes

North America—boom immediately followed war, social movements; Europe—economic unity, overall prosperity, many immigrants look for jobs, Common Market; Soviet Union—recovery, de-Stalinization, communism continues, anti-Communist revolts in Eastern Europe, Gorbachev implements glasnost and perestroika

go.hrw.com
Online Resources

KEYWORD: SHL ENA
ACTIVITY: Report on Europe and North America in the Postwar Years

SECTION 3 Changing Societies

Before You Read

Main Idea

The Cold War brought tremendous economic and social change to North America, Western Europe, and Eastern Europe and the Soviet Union.

Reading Focus

1. What were the major social changes taking place in North America after World War II?
2. How did Western Europe recover economically in the postwar era?
3. How did Eastern Europe and the Soviet Union change after World War II?

Key Terms and People

Martin Luther King Jr.
counterculture
Solidarity
Mikhail Gorbachev
glasnost
perestroika
Velvet Revolution

TAKING NOTES Take notes on the changes that occurred in North America, Europe, and the Soviet Union during the postwar years.

North America	
Europe	
Soviet Union	

THE INSIDE STORY

Were kids and cars everywhere in postwar America? It seemed that children were everywhere in 1950s America. Millions of American veterans started families when they returned home after World War II, and the number of babies born each year soared. At the same time the nation entered this so-called baby boom, it also entered an economic boom.

In the 1950s the American economy was red hot. Jobs were plentiful, wages were increasing, and Americans were eagerly spending their paychecks on cars, homes, and other consumer goods. Car manufacturers spurred demand with exciting new features, such as aircraft-inspired tailfins, and designs that changed each year. Meanwhile, American builders were putting up countless houses and suburban developments throughout the country. These new homes were filled with a variety of shiny new products: refrigerators, stoves, radios, television sets. While the 1950s was a time of peace and prosperity for many Americans, great social changes lay ahead. ■

THE POSTWAR BOOM

Enjoying their new car, an American family poses for a photograph. ▼

Teach the Main Idea

At Level

Changing Societies

1. **Teach** Ask students the Reading Focus questions to teach this section.
2. **Apply** Have students create an outline of the section using the heads as main points. Have students list at least two main ideas under each of the blue subheadings.
3. **Review** Review student outlines as a class. Have students identify the points in their outlines that they feel best reflect the section title, Changing Societies.
4. **Practice/Homework** Have students create a "Before and After" poster showing how society in Eastern Europe changed during the postwar era. **LS Verbal-Linguistic, Visual-Spatial**

Alternative Assessment Handbook, Rubrics 28: Posters; and 42: Writing to Inform

490 CHAPTER 15

North America

The postwar United States was a land of tremendous prosperity. At the same time, the country was undergoing rapid social change.

The U.S. Economy Overall, the U.S. economy—already the most powerful in the world—enjoyed great success in the years after World War II. By 1960 the total value of all U.S. goods and services was two-and-a-half times greater than it had been in 1940. Much of this economic growth was driven by consumer spending. After years of economic depression and war, Americans were ready to buy consumer goods.

By the early 1970s, however, rapid inflation and high unemployment had slowed the U.S. economy dramatically. At the same time, events in the Middle East disrupted the distribution of the world's oil supply. This disruption led to a steep spike in the cost of energy, which drove the prices of other goods higher. The nation's economic problems lasted into the early 1980s before unemployment dropped and the economy began another period of sustained growth. At the same time, however, the nation's debts grew sharply as the federal government increasingly spent more money than it received in taxes.

The postwar decades also brought major structural changes to the economy. The nation's heavy industry suffered during the 1970s and 1980s, as American shipbuilders, automakers, and steel companies found it more difficult to compete with companies in other countries. Many Americans lost their jobs when U.S. companies closed their factories. American companies in other industries still proved successful, creating many new jobs in advanced technology and in service industries such as banking, health care, and sales.

Social Changes During the 1950s, the booming U.S. economy helped raise the living standard of millions of Americans. So, too, did the so-called G.I. Bill of Rights, a law that helped millions of American veterans attend college—a choice that used to be available mainly to the wealthy. Also during this time, many World War II veterans married and started families. Birthrates rose, and the nation entered a so-called baby boom.

FACES OF HISTORY

Martin Luther KING Jr.
1929–1968

A Baptist minister and social activist, Martin Luther King Jr. was a leader of the African American civil rights movement. King was known for his powerful speaking ability as well as his reliance on nonviolence and civil disobedience in his protests against racial injustice.

King first came to national attention in 1955, when he led a boycott of the segregated bus system in Montgomery, Alabama. He and other leaders soon organized marches and protests throughout the United States, which eventually led to sweeping civil rights reform. King received the Nobel Peace Prize in 1964, but four years later, he was assassinated by an opponent of civil rights.

Summarize How did King work for civil rights for African Americans?

African Americans made major advances in the postwar era. During the war they had served bravely—but in units segregated from whites. Recognizing this injustice, in 1948 President Truman issued an executive order ending segregation in the armed forces.

The desegregation of the military was just the first in a series of victories for African Americans. In 1954 the U.S. Supreme Court ruled in *Brown* v. *Board of Education* that the segregation of public schools had to end. This decision was followed by a civil rights campaign led by **Martin Luther King Jr.**, James Farmer, Malcolm X, and many other activists and organizations. After years of struggle against racial injustice, the civil rights movement achieved some major reforms. In 1964 the U.S. Congress passed the Civil Rights Act, and the following year the Voting Rights Act. These laws knocked down longstanding barriers to equality for African Americans. The laws did not end racism, but they laid the groundwork for future progress.

The civil rights movement helped inspire a renewed women's rights movement in the 1960s and 1970s. The core belief of this movement was that women and men should be socially, politically, and economically equal. Some women also wanted to change traditional ideas about women's roles, including the idea that women would be happiest as wives, mothers, and homemakers. This effort met with opposition from others—including some women—who believed in the importance of maintaining traditional family roles.

Skills Focus: Analyzing Primary Sources

At Level

Research Required

Reading Like a Historian Skill

Martin Luther King, Jr. and Mohandas Gandhi

Materials: construction paper, colored markers

1. Have students use reliable print and online sources to conduct research about the lives of Martin Luther King, Jr. and Mohandas Gandhi, focusing on the nonviolent protests they both organized. In their research, students should find three quotes from each leader about his quest for freedom and civil rights.
2. Have students create posters about their quotes. Students should choose one quote from each leader and create a visual to illustrate the chosen quotes.
3. Have students share their posters with the class and explain why they selected the quotes shown on the poster.

Alternative Assessment Handbook, Rubrics 28: Posters; and 30: Research

Direct Teach

Reading Focus

1. What were the major social changes taking place in North America after World War II? *civil rights movement, feminism, counterculture movement, returning soldiers buying homes and attending college, baby boom*

North America

Recall What was the main driving factor for economic growth in the United States after the war? *consumer spending*

Analyze What were the long-term results of *Brown* v. *Board of Education*? *ended segregation in public schools, paved the way for broader civil rights reforms for minorities and for women*

CRF: Biography: Rosa Parks

CRF: Literature: *Invisible Man*

Biography

Betty Friedan (1921–2006) Betty Friedan graduated from Smith College in 1942, settled in New York, became a journalist, married, and continued to work as a freelance writer for a variety of magazines. In 1957, in response to a college questionnaire, Friedan discovered that many of her friends were unhappy with their traditional roles as housewives. She began to conduct extensive research, which she published in her book *The Feminine Mystique*. This bestseller challenged the established, restricted role of women as mothers and wives. In 1966 Friedan help found the National Organization for Women and throughout her life, she helped shape society's attitudes toward women and women's views of themselves.

Answers

Faces of History *powerful speaker, promoted nonviolence, protested racial injustice, organized marches to fight for civil rights reform*

Direct Teach

Reading Focus

North America

Identify Cause and Effect What caused the counterculture in the 1960s? *civil rights movement inspired many teenagers and young adults to rebel against social norms*

Explain How did Canadian military veterans receive help? *Government programs helped them attend college, establish businesses, and buy homes.*

CRF: Interdisciplinary Project: The Youth Market Emerges

Reading Focus

2 How did Western Europe recover economically in the postwar era? *slowly at first, but with the help of the Marshall Plan, most of Western Europe recovered better than before the war*

Western Europe

Recall Why were immigrants attracted to Europe following World War II? *availability of jobs*

Draw Conclusions Why do you think European farms produced more after the war than before? *possible answer—With help from the Marshall Plan, farmers bought more advanced machinery, and farms became more mechanized, leading to higher yields.*

Summarize What were the goals of the Common Market? *to eliminate trade barriers in Europe and create unified economic policies and a market that would rival the U.S*

Women were not alone in questioning social norms. In the 1960s the **counterculture**—a rebellion of teenagers and young adults against mainstream American society—spread across the country. Many young people adopted unconventional values, clothing, and behavior, which shocked some mainstream Americans. Some young Americans questioned the government's actions in the Vietnam War.

READING SKILLS

Making Inferences Why do you think Canada underwent many of the same changes as the United States?

Changes in Canada Canada underwent many of the same economic and social changes. Government programs helped military veterans go to college, establish a business, or buy a home. The economy provided many jobs, and birthrates rose. Canada also had an active civil rights movement, women's movement, and counterculture. During the Vietnam War, Canada sheltered many American men who fled the military draft in the United States.

During the 1960s the province of Quebec experienced what was called the Quiet Revolution. This movement featured a growing nationalism among French-speaking residents of Quebec as well as a call for the separation of Quebec from the rest of Canada. It remains a significant force in Canadian politics today.

READING CHECK **Summarize** What postwar changes took place in North America?

Western Europe

Western Europe faced a challenging future after World War II. But, in spite of the devastation left by the war, the region made a remarkable recovery.

Postwar Recovery At the end of World War II, much of Western Europe lay in ruins. Vast amounts of property and farmland had been destroyed, national economies had collapsed, and millions of people had been displaced from their homes.

Western Europe seemed to be on the brink of chaos. Nevertheless, chaos did not come, thanks in large part to the Marshall Plan. With American aid, Western Europe's factories and farms were producing more by the early 1950s than they had before the war. West Germany grew into a major economic power, and growth was strong in most other countries.

Prosperity did not eliminate poverty, however. Certain countries enjoyed more success than others, and the region endured some difficult economic times. When the availability of jobs attracted many immigrants from European nations' former colonies, the influx of people from different cultures caused strain in some places as Europeans struggled to adapt to the newcomers. The overall story of postwar

▲ Allied troops move toward the Reichstag after Germany's surrender in May 1945.

Rebuilding Europe

Much of Europe lay in ruins after World War II, but the region was quickly rebuilt. In Berlin, the Reichstag—home to Germany's parliament—was reconstructed in the early 1960s.

Differentiating Instruction

Above Level

Research Required

Advanced Learners/Gifted and Talented

1. Have students read the information under the heading Alliances and Economic Unity about the European Economic Community and the European Free Trade Association. Then have students conduct outside research to learn more about these organizations, how they function, and what problems they encountered. In their research students should investigate how the European Union came into being, what its functions are, and how successful it has been in meeting its economic and political goals. Students should support their findings with appropriate analytical data showing the growth of the European Union.
2. Have students prepare multimedia presentations of their research findings and present them to the class. **LS Visual-Spatial, Logical-Mathematical**

Alternative Assessment Handbook, Rubrics 22: Multimedia Presentations; and 30: Research

Answers

Reading Skills *possible answer—Canada had similar economic and social issues as the United States, such as civil rights and women's movements.*

Reading Check *economic boom; veterans bought homes and consumer goods, went to college; the civil rights, feminist, and counterculture movements*

Western Europe, however, is one of remarkable success.

Alliances and Economic Unity World War II had changed Europe's place in the world. The continent was no longer the center of world power; instead, the United States and the Soviet Union were the centers of power. During the postwar years, European nations began to end longstanding rivalries with one another and work together for their common good. The formation of NATO in 1949 helped unify many European nations in a strong military alliance with the United States and Canada. Through NATO, countries that had warred for centuries now relied on each other for security. Despite ongoing tension with the Soviet Union and Eastern Europe, Western Europe remained at peace during the Cold War.

Many nations in Western Europe also moved toward economic unity. Early efforts led to cooperation in the coal and steel industries and in the development of atomic energy. Over time, Western European countries undertook broader efforts to develop a single regional market free of trade barriers and with unified economic policies. The goal was to create a single market that might rival that of the United States.

In 1957 six European nations founded the European Economic Community, also known as the Common Market. In 1960, seven other European countries formed the rival European Free Trade Association. True economic unity in Europe, however, was still years in the future.

READING CHECK **Find the Main Idea** Describe the economic recovery in Western Europe after World War II.

CONTRASTING ECONOMIC SYSTEMS

QUICK FACTS

COMMAND ECONOMIES (such as the Soviet Union)	**MARKET ECONOMIES** (such as the United States)
The government makes all economic decisions.	The government has minimal involvement in the economy.
The government decides what goods and products to make and how much to produce.	Market forces such as supply and demand determine the type and quantity of goods and products.
The government decides what wages to pay and what prices to charge for goods.	Wages and prices are set largely by market forces.
The government owns most property.	Private citizens and businesses own most property.

Eastern Europe and the Soviet Union

The challenges facing the Soviet Union and the Eastern European nations under its control were even more overwhelming than those facing Western Europe. Like Western Europe, however, the region soon began to recover.

The Postwar Soviet Union Tens of millions of Soviet citizens had been killed in World War II, and the nation's cities, farms, and industries had suffered heavy damage. Soviet dictator Joseph Stalin was determined to rebuild quickly. Remember that the Soviet Union had a centrally planned economy, or a command economy. In a command economy the government controls all economic decisions. Under strict government controls, the country was producing goods at prewar levels by 1953.

Nikita Khrushchev eventually became the leader of the Soviet Union and undertook an effort to "de-Stalinize" the Soviet Union, tearing down statues of Stalin and renaming streets and towns named after Stalin. Khrushchev also loosened some of the more drastic Stalin-era economic and political restrictions.

Despite these changes, Khrushchev and his successors remained committed Communists. They continued to limit the individual freedoms of Soviet citizens, and they maintained a generally hostile stance against the West.

Revolts in Eastern Europe The changes in the Soviet Union after Stalin's death led some in Eastern Europe to hope that the Soviets might end their domination of the region. Soviet leaders, however, made it clear that the reforms were limited. The Soviets used—or threatened—force to crush public protests in many countries and to assert their control. Soviet troops put down revolts in East Germany (1953), Poland (1956), Hungary (1956), and Czechoslovakia (1968).

Direct Teach

Reading Focus

3 How did Eastern Europe and the Soviet Union change after World War II? *The Soviet Union had complete control over Eastern Europe and crushed revolts in 1950s and 1960s; in 1989, countries began to throw off Soviet-backed regimes, ending Soviet domination of Eastern Europe.*

Eastern Europe and the Soviet Union

Recall How did World War II affect Europe's place in the world? *It was no longer the center of world power; the United States and the Soviet Union became the centers of power.*

Describe How does a command economy work? *government controls all economic decisions, what to produce, how much to produce, sets wages and prices, owns most property*

Primary Source

"About the capitalist states, it doesn't depend on you whether or not we exist. If you don't like us, don't accept our invitations, and don't invite us to come and see you. Whether you like it or not, history is on our side. We will bury you."
—Nikita Khrushchev, November 18, 1956

QUICK FACTS Contrasting Economic Systems

Activity **Analyzing Charts** Have students provide examples of each item on the Quick Facts chart, and then list benefits and disadvantages of each point. Remind students that most economies are mixed, neither completely command nor completely market. **LS Verbal-Linguistic**

Quick Facts Transparency: Contrasting Economic Systems

Skills Focus: Recognizing Bias

At Level

Research Required

Reading Like a Historian Skill

Glasnost and Perestroika

1. Have students conduct outside research on the changes that occurred within the Soviet Union and Eastern European countries in the late 1980s. Have students focus on how glasnost and perestroika affected ordinary citizens. Tell students to look for primary and secondary sources published in Europe, the Soviet Union, and the United States.
2. Have students use their research findings to write an essay explaining the changes brought about by glasnost and perestroika, and their consequences. Students should compare and contrast the various points of view presented in their research documents.
3. In the conclusions to their essays, students should address the issue of bias, how it was used, and why it was apparent.

Alternative Assessment Handbook, Rubrics 30: Research; and 37: Writing Assignments

Answers

Reading Check *uneven, some countries recovered quickly with the Marshall Plan; others lagged; generally high standard of living*

Direct Teach

Reading Focus

Eastern Europe and the Soviet Union

Recall How did glasnost affect the people of the Soviet Union? *was a beginning of free speech; people were able to discuss national problems*

Explain Why did Gorbachev want to reduce spending on weapons? *needed to reform the economy, spend more on consumer products*

Analyze Were the uprisings in Poland, Hungary, and Czechoslovakia successful? Explain your answer. *in the short-term, no; in the long-term, yes, because they paved the way for further protest and end of Soviet control*

Info to Know

Velvet Revolution The Velvet Revolution was a six-week long student demonstration that led to the end of the Czechoslovakian Communist regime without any violence. It began on November 17, 1989, exactly 50 years to the day after a famous student protest against the Nazi occupation. It was a peaceful transition that split the country in two, the Czech Republic and Slovakia.

Uprisings in Eastern Europe

Revolutions swept across Eastern Europe in 1989 after Mikhail Gorbachev loosened Soviet controls on the region. ***How did Eastern Europeans react to Gorbachev's reforms?***

1 Polish demonstrators march in support of the democratic Solidarity movement.

The Soviet crackdowns did not end the protests in Eastern Europe. For example, in 1980 Polish electrician Lech Walesa led hundreds of thousands of workers in an anti-government protest movement known as **Solidarity**. Poland's Communist government used martial law to suppress this anti-Communist movement but could not destroy it.

Glasnost and Perestroika The Soviet economy that had performed so well after the war began to falter in the 1960s. By the 1980s the Soviet Union faced a crisis. The command economy system had worked when the country was establishing its basic industries; but as these industries expanded, central planning proved inefficient. Government planners set production goals with little regard for the wants and needs of the marketplace. These goals stressed heavy industry, neglecting the goods that consumers needed. As a result, most sectors of the Soviet economy ceased to grow.

When **Mikhail Gorbachev** came to power in the Soviet Union in 1985, he saw the need for change. Gorbachev proposed two radical concepts: **glasnost** and **perestroika**. Glasnost means "openness," and it meant a willingness to discuss openly the Soviet Union's problems. Perestroika means "restructuring" and referred to the reform of the Soviet economic and political system.

FACES OF HISTORY

Mikhail GORBACHEV
1931–

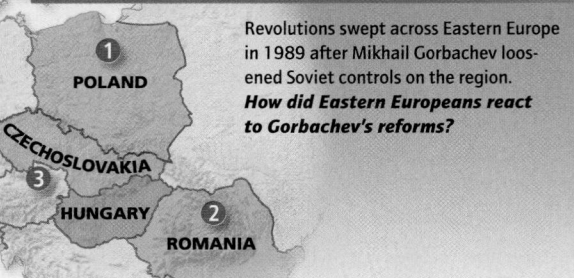

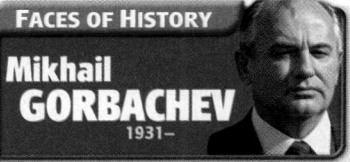

Mikhail Gorbachev was the leader of the Soviet Union from 1985 to 1991. The son of Russian peasants, he joined the Soviet Communist Party in the 1950s and rose steadily through the party's ranks.

As Soviet leader, Gorbachev's primary goal was to rebuild the nation's stagnant economy. He called for major reforms of the Soviet economic and political system. Under his leadership the Soviet Union began to end its domination of Eastern Europe. Gorbachev also worked to build better relations with the United States and the West and is credited with helping bring an end to the Cold War. For his efforts to improve international relations, Gorbachev received the Nobel Peace Prize in 1990.

Summarize How did Gorbachev work to change the Soviet Union, and how did Soviet relations with the West change under his leadership?

HISTORY'S VOICES

> **"*Perestroika* is an urgent necessity . . . This society is ripe for change. It has long been yearning for it. Any delay in beginning perestroika could [lead] to . . . serious social, economic and political crises."**
>
> —Mikhail Gorbachev, *Perestroika: New Thinking for Our Country and the World*, 1987

Gorbachev pushed through a number of major reforms. Hoping to reduce Soviet spending on weapons programs, he aggressively pursued arms control agreements with the United States. Gorbachev also reduced central planning of the Soviet economy and introduced some free-market mechanisms.

Knowing that the Soviet Union could no longer afford to prop up the Communist governments of Eastern Europe, Gorbachev began to pull Soviet troops out of the region, urging local leaders to adopt reforms. His actions reversed decades of Soviet policy in Eastern Europe.

Skills Focus: Comparing and Contrasting

At Level

Reading Skill

Uprisings in Eastern Europe

1. Have students examine the images in the feature Uprising in Eastern Europe, and review the captions for each image.
2. Have students select one of the three locations and write a newspaper article about the uprising in their chosen location. Students should create first-hand observations of the scene portrayed in the image, provide a historical background, and context for their articles. Articles should also include a map, based on the map in the feature.
3. Have volunteers share their newspaper articles with the class. **LS Verbal-Linguistic, Visual-Spatial**

Alternative Assessment Handbook, Rubric 23: Newspapers

Answers

Uprisings in Eastern Europe *led protests before waiting for Gorbachev's reforms were in place*

Faces of History *installed major reforms to Soviet's economic and political systems, fostered improved relations with the United States and the West, introduced glasnost and perestroika*

② The struggle for democracy turns violent in Romania, where tanks operated by pro-democracy troops fire on government supporters.

③ Thousands of Czechoslovakians protest against the nation's Communist regime.

Revolutions in Eastern Europe The citizens of Eastern Europe, longing for freedom, did not wait for reform. In 1989 revolution quickly spread across the region as citizens rose up and overthrew their Soviet-backed leaders. Gorbachev, no longer willing to keep Eastern Europe under control, did nothing to interfere.

In most cases, the revolutions were peaceful. In Czechoslovakia the **Velvet Revolution**—so called because it was peaceful—pushed the Communists out of power. In Poland the Solidarity movement forced free elections, and in 1990 Lech Walesa was elected president. Only in Romania, where some military forces remained loyal to the Communist dictator, was there significant bloodshed.

Perhaps the most dramatic changes took place in East Germany. The changes began when Hungary opened its border with Austria in August 1989. By the thousands, East Germans traveled to Hungary to cross this now-open border to the West. Powerless to stop the flood of its citizens streaming into West Germany, the East German government opened the gates of the Berlin Wall in November 1989. Overjoyed Berliners spontaneously began tearing down the wall. The strongest symbol of Soviet repression—and of the Cold War itself—had finally fallen. Less than one year later, East Germany and West Germany were reunified as a single nation.

READING CHECK **Summarize** What changes took place in the Soviet Union and Eastern Europe after World War II?

SECTION 3 ASSESSMENT

go.hrw.com
Online Quiz
Keyword: SHL ENA HP

Reviewing Ideas, Terms, and People

1. **a. Describe** How has the U.S. economy changed since World War II?
   b. Identify Cause and Effect What social changes did the United States experience in the postwar years?
2. **a. Describe** What were the major problems facing Western Europe after the war?
   b. Explain What was the significance of NATO and of the formation of organizations such as the European Economic Community?
   c. Elaborate How might economic unity have contributed to peace in Western Europe in the postwar years?
3. **a. Recall** What were **glasnost** and **perestroika**?
   b. Compare How did Stalin's death affect both the Soviet Union and Eastern Europe?
   c. Evaluate What effect did glasnost and perestroika have on Eastern Europe?

Critical Thinking

4. **Identify Supporting Details** Using your notes on the section and a graphic organizer like the one below, identify 10 important events that took place during the postwar years in North America, Western Europe, and Eastern Europe and the Soviet Union, and put the events in chronological order.

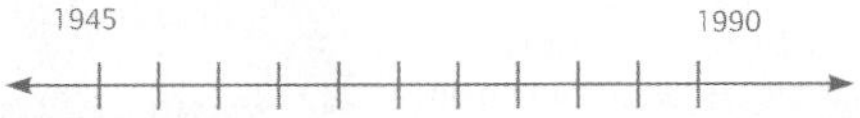

FOCUS ON SPEAKING

5. **Persuasion** Write an outline for a speech that Mikhail Gorbachev might have given to persuade the Soviet people to support his policies of glasnost and perestroika. Support your outline with details from the section.

Review & Assess

Close
Have students explain how the actions of Mikhail Gorbachev helped bring about the end of the Soviet Union.

Review
Online Quiz, Section 3

Assess
SE Section 3 Assessment
Progress Assessment: Section 3 Quiz
Alternative Assessment Handbook

Reteach/Intervene
Interactive Reader and Study Guide, Section 3
Interactive Skills Tutor CD-ROM

Answers
Reading Check *Krushchev tried to "de-Stalinize" and loosen political restrictions, revolts after Stalin's death, Solidarity, Gorbachev introduced reforms, glasnost and perestroika*

Section 3 Assessment Answers

1. **a.** enjoyed great success overall, consumer spending increased, heavy industry suffered, but new jobs still created
   b. consumer spending, homeownership, more people attending college, baby boom, increased government spending
2. **a.** rebuilding infrastructures and economies, increased immigration, loss of global prestige and power
   b. helped to unify Western Europe, end long-standing rivalries among countries, created a single European bloc that could compete with superpowers
   c. Countries were connected, worked together, and were dependent upon each other for success.
3. **a.** glasnost—openness, ability to discuss problems; perestroika—reform of Soviet economy and political system
   b. reign of Soviet terror ended, Soviet Union maintained tight control over Eastern Europe, some restrictions relaxed
   c. opened a window of opportunity, used to gain independence
4. Student time lines should list 10 significant events from the section, listed in chronological order. Events might include the postwar boom and U.S. economic recovery, civil rights and women's movements, European economic unity, founding of EEC and EFTA, Gorbachev's reforms, and Eastern Europe's revolts.
5. Student outlines should demonstrate an understanding of Gorbachev's reforms and the effects of glasnost and perestroika on Soviet citizens.

Preteach

Getting Started

Use the **Interactive Reader and Study Guide** to familiarize students with the section content.

Interactive Reader and Study Guide, Section 4

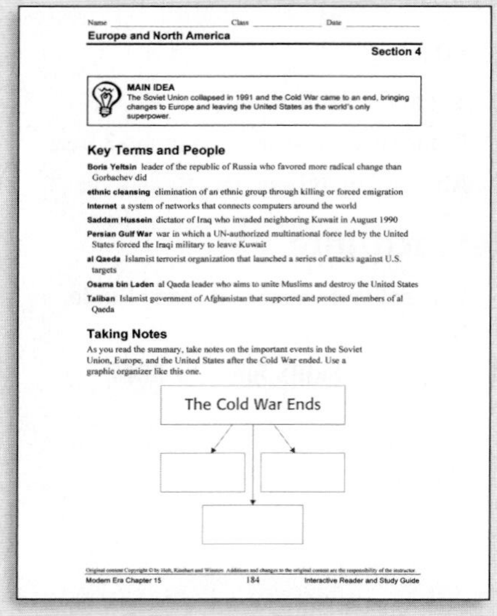

Name ____________ Class ________ Date ________

Europe and North America

Section 4

MAIN IDEA
The Soviet Union collapsed in 1991 and the Cold War came to an end, bringing changes to Europe and leaving the United States as the world's only superpower.

Key Terms and People

Boris Yeltsin leader of the republic of Russia who favored more radical change than Gorbachev did

ethnic cleansing elimination of an ethnic group through killing or forced emigration

Internet a system of networks that connects computers around the world

Saddam Hussein dictator of Iraq who invaded neighboring Kuwait in August 1990

Persian Gulf War war in which a UN-authorized multinational force led by the United States forced the Iraqi military to leave Kuwait

al Qaeda Islamist terrorist organization that launched a series of attacks against U.S. targets

Osama bin Laden al Qaeda leader who aims to unite Muslims and destroy the United States

Taliban Islamist government of Afghanistan that supported and protected members of al Qaeda

Taking Notes

As you read the summary, take notes on the important events in the Soviet Union, Europe, and the United States after the Cold War ended. Use a graphic organizer like this one.

The Cold War Ends

Modern Era Chapter 15 184 Interactive Reader and Study Guide

CRF: Vocabulary Builder: Section 4

Taking Notes

development of the European Union in Europe, former Soviet Union is still trying to recover and transition from command economy to market economy and different government systems; United States had economic growth, low unemployment, but involved in new conflicts

SECTION 4

After the Cold War

Before You Read

Main Idea

The Soviet Union collapsed in 1991 and the Cold War came to an end, bringing changes to Europe and leaving the United States as the world's only superpower.

Reading Focus

1. How did the Soviet Union break up?
2. What changes occurred in Europe after communism ended?
3. What challenges does the United States face today?

Key Terms and People

Boris Yeltsin
ethnic cleansing
Internet
Saddam Hussein
Persian Gulf War
al Qaeda
Osama bin Laden
Taliban

TAKING NOTES Take notes on the important events in the Soviet Union, Europe, and the United States after the Cold War ended.

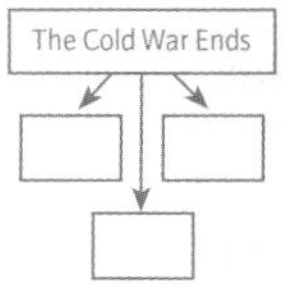

THE INSIDE STORY ***How long can the desire for freedom be held down?*** The crackdown began one cold Friday in January 1991, as Soviet Red Army tanks rumbled into Vilnius, the capital of Lithuania. Lithuania was a Soviet republic that had declared independence the previous spring. Soviet leaders had rejected this claim of independence but had taken little action to punish Lithuania—until this moment.

The Soviets quickly seized government buildings in Vilnius. But as Soviet tanks pushed toward the Vilnius radio and television broadcasting facilities, a crowd of 1,000 Lithuanian protestors met them. The protestors aimed to stop the Soviets from taking over the broadcast stations. In a violent response the Soviets opened fire on the unarmed protestors, driving the tanks through the crowd. Fourteen Lithuanians died during the brief, one-sided attack, and dozens more were injured.

Even as they faced the Soviet assault, the protestors did not give up. Inside the radio station one last defiant message was sent over the airwaves before the Soviets broke into the building: "It is possible that [the army] can break us with force," the broadcast declared, "but no one will make us renounce freedom and independence." Indeed, although the Soviets soon gained control of Vilnius, tens of thousands of protestors gathered in the city's center to march for independence. Lithuanians had died in the Soviet crackdown, but the desire for freedom could not be put down. ■

A Struggle for FREEDOM

Lithuanian demonstrators face down a Soviet tank during protests in Vilnius.

The Breakup of the Soviet Union

The 1989 fall of the Berlin Wall and the collapse of Soviet-backed regimes in Eastern Europe showed the dramatic crumbling of Soviet power. Soon the Soviet Union itself was falling apart.

The Soviet Union Collapses The Soviet Union consisted of 15 separate republics. Some, such as the Baltic republics of Lithuania, Latvia, and Estonia, which had been independent nations before World War II, had

Teach the Main Idea

At Level

After the Cold War

1. **Teach** Ask students the Reading Focus questions to teach this section.
2. **Apply** Have students scan the section and make a time line of the events discussed. You might wish to have students work in small groups or mixed-ability pairs for this activity.
3. **Review** Review student time lines as a class, and create a class time line for all to see. Have students correct their work as needed as you fill in the class time line. Have students identify the events on the class time line they believe contributed most to the end of the Soviet Union.
4. **Practice/Homework** Have students write a paragraph or one-page essay in which they answer this question: Is the world is safer now that the Cold War is over? Why or why not? **LS Verbal-Linguistic, Visual-Spatial**

Alternative Assessment Handbook, Rubrics 36: Time Lines; and 43: Writing to Persuade long wanted their freedom. When Lithuania declared independence in 1990, it appeared that other republics planned to do the same. Soviet troops occupied Lithuania, but it was far from certain that the Soviet government had the will—or the power—to stop the independence movement.

In fact, the Soviet government was in crisis. In August 1991 hard-line Communist Party leaders sought to end Mikhail Gorbachev's reforms and preserve the Soviet Union by taking over the Soviet government in a coup d'état. The effort failed, largely because of the opposition of **Boris Yeltsin**, the leader of the republic of Russia. Yeltsin favored even more radical changes for the Soviet Union than Gorbachev had proposed and did not want to see hard-liners take over the Soviet Union.

Although the coup had failed, Gorbachev's power was largely gone. Republic after republic declared independence; and by the end of 1991, the Soviet government had ceased to function. Twelve of the republics eventually united in a loose confederation known as the Commonwealth of Independent States; but the mighty Soviet Union, once one of the two most powerful countries on the globe, no longer existed. After more than 40 years of tension and conflict, the Cold War was finally over.

Economic Change With the fall of the Soviet Union came the end of communism in the former Soviet republics. In Russia, the largest republic, Boris Yeltsin began a massive campaign to alter the economy's basic structure. His goal was to make the economy function more like a capitalist system.

Under the new market reforms, Yeltsin began to allow private ownership of businesses and land. Business owners and workers received more freedom to take advantage of economic opportunity. In return, however, they lost the guarantee of a government-backed job and other government supports.

Early results of Russia's reforms were mixed. A few entrepreneurs prospered, but most ordinary Russians did not. Meanwhile, prices rose sharply, and many Russians could not afford to buy goods in stores. Some began to question the benefits of market reform.

By the early 2000s Russia had rebounded somewhat from the economic crises that came with market reform. Still, the path from communism to capitalism was not an easy one.

Other Issues After the Soviet Union fell, underlying issues in the region bubbled to the top. Two of these issues were ethnic unrest and the need for new governments.

THE BREAKUP OF THE SOVIET UNION, 1991

GEOGRAPHY SKILLS **INTERPRETING MAPS**

1. **Place** What are the 15 republics that made up the Soviet Union? Which republic is the largest?
2. **Regions** How might the large number of Soviet republics have contributed to the breakup of the Soviet Union?

Direct Teach

Reading Focus

1 How did the Soviet Union break up? *Gorbachev's power reduced, republics within the Soviet Union declared independence, Soviets unable to quell the unrest*

The Breakup of the Soviet Union

Explain Why did the coup d'état in the Soviet Union fail? *Boris Yeltsin, leader of the Russian republic, opposed the coup.*

Analyze Why did Russia's first attempt at market reform result in an economic crisis? *people had never lived in a market economy, difficult adjustment for all*

CRF: Biography: Condoleezza Rice

Info to Know

Boris Yeltsin In 1985 Boris Yeltsin was chosen by Gorbachev to investigate and reform the Moscow Party organization, which was at the time very corrupt. In 1986 Yeltsin was made a nonvoting member of the Politburo, but he had to resign in 1988. In 1990 he quit the Communist Party, and in 1991 he became the first popularly elected leader in Russia's history.

Collaborative Learning

At Level

Impact of Soviet Union's Breakup

Research Required

1. Organize students into small groups.
2. Assign each group a country that emerged after the fall of the Soviet Union.
3. Have groups research their countries focusing on how the country gained independence, conflicts that may have developed, and the current status of the country today.
4. Have each group create a multimedia presentation, and present a culmination of its research to the class. **LS Verbal-Linguistic, Visual-Spatial**

Alternative Assessment Handbook, Rubrics 14: Group Activity; and 22: Multimedia Presentations

Answers

Interpreting Maps 1. *Lativa, Kaliningrad, Estonia, Lithuania, Belarus, Moldova, Ukraine, Georgia, Armenia, Azerbaijan, Turkmenistan, Uzbekistan, Kyrgyzstan, Tejikistan, Kazakhstan, Russia.* **2.** *possible answer—As each declared its independence, the republics united, limiting Soviet's power.*

Direct Teach

Reading Focus

2 What changes occured in Europe after communism ended? *conflict in Yugoslavia, unemployment, migration from east to west, European Union*

Europe after Communism

Identify In which of Yugoslavia's republics did the most violent conflict occur? *Bosnia and Herzegovina*

Summarize What happened in Yugoslavia after communism ended? *conflict between ethnic and religious groups, violence in Serbia and Bosnia and Herzegovina, bloodshed between ethnic Serbs and Muslims in Bosnia, fighting in Serbia, NATO peacekeepers help maintain order*

Activity **Compare** Review with students the information about genocide in the World War II chapter of the text, and have students compare the two situations.

Forensics in History

Identifying the Dead

Genocide Bosnia is a very diverse country with three main populations Serbs—make up about 37 percent, Muslims (Bosniaks) 48 percent, and Croatians 14 percent. Because of this diversity, conflicts between the ethnic groups occurred, resulting in the mass murder of thousandsof people.

One example of ethnic unrest took place in Chechnya (CHECH-nya), an area in the Caucasus region of southwestern Russia. Unlike the republics that had broken away from the Soviet Union, Chechnya was considered part of Russia. When the Chechens tried to gain their independence from Russia, the dispute eventually led to bloody fighting and to an insurgency that still affects the region today. Another example of ethnic conflict occurred in a former Soviet republic in the early 1990s when the ethnic Armenian minority sought to break away from the country of Azerbaijan. Tens of thousands died in the fighting that followed.

For some of the former republics, the transition from communism to a new government has been challenging. For example, Ukraine held an election in 2004. Among widespread charges of fraud, the election had to be repeated. Still controversial, the results of the elections left Ukraine deeply divided. Such transitions continue to trouble the region.

READING CHECK **Summarize** How and why did the Soviet Union break up?

Europe after Communism

The collapse of the iron curtain brought new opportunities and new challenges to Europe. The end of communism brought much economic change as well as new threats to peace.

Conflict in Yugoslavia In Eastern Europe, Communist governments had maintained strict control over their people. In Yugoslavia this control had helped suppress tensions between the many different ethnic and religious groups that lived in that country's six republics. But as communism slowly collapsed, those tensions began to come to the surface.

Feelings of nationalism in Yugoslavia's republics grew as ethnic and religious tensions increased. Some republics declared independence. Serbia—and ethnic Serbs living in other republics—tried to prevent the breakup of Yugoslavia, and conflict soon broke out in several republics.

The most violent of these wars took place in the republic of Bosnia and Herzegovina, which

FORENSICS in History

Identifying the Dead

Thousands of Bosnian Muslims were executed by Serb forces during the war in Bosnia, their bodies buried in mass graves. As a result, the human remains have become mixed together. Can such remains be identified?

What facts do we have? Scientists and human rights groups have created databases with data about the victims. One database collects information from close relatives of missing persons, including a description of the person's height, hair color, and other identifying features. This database also collects information about the clothing and personal items the person might have had on him or her at the time of death, such as eyeglasses, jewelry, or personal documents. This data is then compared to the corpses in the mass graves, while photographs of jewelry or clothing found on exhumed bodies are shown to relatives. One woman, for example, identified her husband by the socks found on his body.

▲ Scientists gather remains from a mass grave in Bosnia.

Another database is a DNA database. The International Commission for Missing Persons has collected DNA samples from the bodies and from the relatives of missing people. Scientists then compare these DNA samples in order to match family members. By 2006 nearly 10,500 bodies had been identified through DNA testing.

Draw Conclusions Why do you think it is important for people to identify the remains of their loved ones?

Differentiating Instruction

Below Level

Learners Having Difficulty

1. Have students read the Forensics in History feature and review the information in the text about the division of Yugoslavia and the conflicts that followed.
2. Have students work in mixed-ability pairs to develop a written summary and a sequencing chart of the information.
3. Have volunteers share their summaries and charts with the class. Have students review and correct their work as needed.
4. As an extension for more advanced learners, have students write an essay suggesting ways that the bloodshed in Bosnia could have been prevented. **LS Visual-Spatial, Verbal-Linguistic**

Alternative Assessment Handbook, Rubrics 7: Charts; and 37: Writing Assignments

Answers

Forensics in History *possible answer—to provide closure and solace to families*

Reading Check *Republics fought for freedom and independence, Communist Party leaders tried to overthrow the government and end Gorbachev's reforms, and republics gained independence.*

THE EUROPEAN UNION, 2006

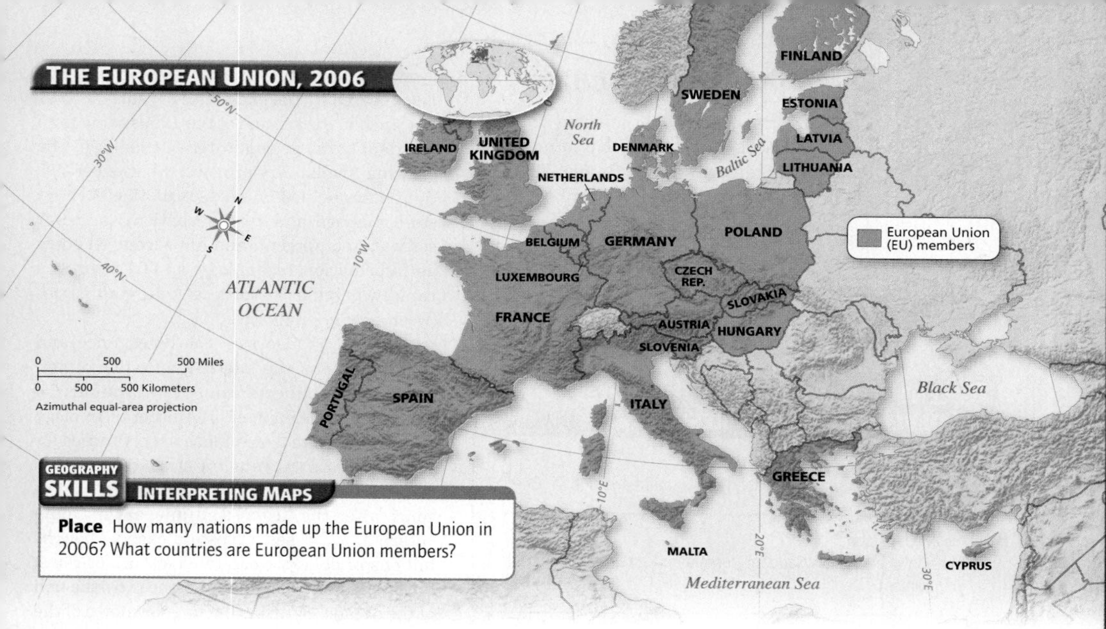

GEOGRAPHY SKILLS INTERPRETING MAPS

Place How many nations made up the European Union in 2006? What countries are European Union members?

declared its independence from Yugoslavia in 1992. Many Bosnian Serbs wanted to remain part of Yugoslavia, and they began a war to prevent Bosnian independence. During this war, Serbs used a policy of ethnic cleansing against Bosnian Muslims. **Ethnic cleansing** is the elimination of an ethnic group from society through killing or forced emigration. After much bloodshed a U.S.-led diplomatic effort finally ended the violence in Bosnia in 1995.

Soon after, another conflict began in the region. This time, fighting was located in the Serbian province of Kosovo, where Serbs and ethnic Albanians fought over control of the area. In the spring of 1999, after peace negotiations had failed, NATO airplanes bombed Serbian targets in an attempt to stop the conflict. NATO peacekeepers eventually took up positions in the region to help maintain order, although Kosovo remains a Serbian province today.

Economic Change The end of communism brought mixed results for the economies of Eastern Europe. The introduction of market reforms created new opportunities for many people. Some started new businesses. The highly skilled got well-paying management or technical jobs in newly private enterprises.

Others in Eastern Europe have fared less well. Earnings have not risen for all workers, and many state-supported factories have closed, leading to high unemployment in some areas. These economic problems have led many Eastern Europeans to move to Western Europe, hoping to take advantage of opportunities there. This has led to strain in some parts of Western Europe, as newcomers compete with longtime residents for jobs and other resources.

The European Union Ongoing efforts to build an economic and political union among the nations of Europe resulted in the establishment of the European Union (EU) in 1992. In recent years a number of Eastern European nations and former Soviet republics have joined the EU, and others are scheduled to join in 2007. These steps have created a single economic unit that is large enough to compete with the United States. Many of the newer members, however, are far poorer than the older Western Europe members. As a result, some people in the wealthier nations worry that their own economies will suffer.

THE IMPACT TODAY

A proposed European Constitution would further unify the members of the EU. All member states need to ratify the treaty for it to take effect; by mid-2006, 15 of the 25 members had ratified it.

READING CHECK **Summarize** How has Europe changed since the end of communism?

Direct Teach

Reading Focus

Europe after Communism

Explain How successful were the economic reforms in Eastern Europe? Explain your answer. *possible answers—very successful, created new opportunities; unsuccessful, led to high unemployment, wage discrepancies between those with high paying jobs and those in low-paying jobs*

Predict How might the European Union help ensure peace within Europe? *Nations depend on each other for economic development, which creates unity and a means for resolving conflicts.*

Map Transparency: The European Union, 2006

Info to Know

The European Union The European Union consists of 25 members and almost half a billion people, and its accomplishments are notable. For example, there have been no wars between member countries in the past 60 years. In order for a country to join the European Union it must apply and meet certain criteria. Countries must have a stable democratic government with a competitive market economy.

Skills Focus: Analyzing Visuals

Below Level

Prep Required

Reading Like a Historian Skill

The European Union

1. Before class, visit the Web site for the European Union and prepare a list of member nations and candidate countries. Distribute the list to students or create a class list for all students to see.
2. Have students use the map on this page to create their own maps of Europe showing the countries that belong to the European Union and those that do not.
3. Guide students in a discussion of the goals of the European Union and how effective it has been in achieving those goals and in unifying Europe. **LS Visual-Spatial**

Alternative Assessment Handbook, Rubrics 11: Discussions; and 20: Map Creation

Answers

Interpreting Maps *Refer to map.*

Reading Check *High unemployment has led many Eastern Europeans to move to Western Europe for jobs and opportunites.*

Direct Teach

Reading Focus

3 What challenges does the United States face today? *The U.S. economy did well in the 1990s with the beginning of the information age, but conflicts continue in the Middle East, as does war on terror*

The United States Today

Recall What fueled the U.S. economy during the 1990s? *developments in computer technology, jobs in information technology, Internet-related companies*

Identify Cause and Effect What led to the Persian Gulf War and how did it end? *Iraq attacked and invaded Kuwait; UN forces moved in, liberated Kuwait, and pushed Iraq back into its own borders.*

Quick Facts Transparency: Recent U.S. Military Involvement, 2001–Present

Teaching Tip

Explain and emphasize the differences among the Taliban, Afghanistan, Osama bin Laden, Iraq, and Saddam Hussein.

The United States Today

The end of the Cold War affected the economic, political, and military situation facing the United States. In the 1990s and 2000s the nation adjusted to this new reality.

The Economy For the United States the 1990s was a time of economic success. Economic growth was strong and unemployment was low. Even the budget deficits that had grown so alarmingly in the 1980s shrank and disappeared by the end of the decade.

Much of the success of the 1990s came from developments in computer technology. The growing availability of powerful, inexpensive computers helped businesses more efficiently store, manage, and use information. Computer software, equipment, and knowledge—known as information technology, or IT—improved rapidly, helping workers in many industries become more productive.

The 1990s also saw the emergence and rapid growth of the **Internet**, a system of networks that connects computers around the world. The development of Internet technology seemed to create tremendous opportunities for commerce. Entrepreneurs started hundreds of Internet-related companies known as dot-coms, after the ".com" that appears in many Internet addresses. Investors eagerly bought billions of dollars worth of stock in dot-coms, but many had gone out of business by the end of the decade, contributing to a slowdown of the U.S. economy.

Although the economy began to improve in the early 2000s, high energy costs, increased government spending, and a rising national debt remained areas of economic concern. At the same time, the gap between the incomes of the richest and poorest Americans continued to widen. The U.S. poverty rate also increased during the early 2000s, leading to a higher rate than in most other industrialized nations.

New Conflicts Even as the Cold War was coming to an end, the United States faced a new conflict in the Middle East. Iraq, led by dictator **Saddam Hussein**, attacked neighboring Kuwait in August 1990. The invasion troubled the United States in part because Iraq seemed to threaten the oil supplies produced by Kuwait and nearby Saudi Arabia.

After negotiations failed to convince Iraq to leave Kuwait, the United States led a multinational force into battle in the **Persian Gulf War**. The coalition troops quickly freed Kuwait, and Saddam agreed to obey firm new limits on his military forces and weapons.

U.S. forces also took part in peacekeeping missions around the globe, including the NATO operations in Kosovo. In the early 1990s, 43 American soldiers died in the African country of Somalia when the UN famine relief program

Recent U.S. Military Involvement, 2001–Present

QUICK FACTS

Afghanistan, 2001–present
- Invasion to overthrow the Taliban government and fight al Qaeda

Iraq, 2003–present
- Invasion to overthrow Saddam Hussein and establish democratic government

Haiti, 2004
- Peacekeeping efforts after Haiti's leader was overthrown

South Asia, 2004–2005
- Humanitarian aid following a devastating tsunami

Pakistan, 2005–2006
- Relief and rebuilding efforts following a major earthquake

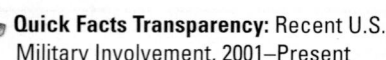

In Sri Lanka U.S. soldiers and aid workers deliver food supplies to the victims of a 2004 tsunami.

Skills Focus: Recognizing Bias in Primary Sources

At Level

Research Required

Reading Like a Historian Skill

Current Events

Materials: construction paper

1. Review the information in the Quick Facts chart with students. Have students select one event that they wish to know more about.
2. Have students find at least three newspaper, magazine, or Internet features on their chosen event. Have students read the articles carefully and write a summary of each. Have students post their summaries on a single sheet of construction paper. At the end of each summary, have students write a few sentences describing the bias in each article that they found and reasons why they believe that the authors may have taken the position they did.
3. Have volunteers share and explain their posters. Create a class display of student work. LS **Verbal-Linguistic, Visual-Spatial**

Alternative Assessment Handbook, Rubrics 16: Judging Information; and 30: Research they were assisting became involved in conflict. In 1994 U.S. forces helped restore Haiti's elected government after a coup.

U.S. leaders also continued to work toward a solution to the conflict between Israel and the Palestinians. There were some bright spots, including the 1993 Oslo Accords, in which the Palestine Liberation Organization (PLO) recognized Israel's right to exist and Israel recognized the PLO as the representative of the Palestinian people. Overall, however, the conflict continued to defy a peaceful resolution.

The War on Terror The 1990s also saw the beginning of a series of terrorist attacks on American targets within the United States and overseas, including bombings of the World Trade Center, in New York City, in 1993 and the U.S. embassies in Kenya and Tanzania in 1998. Over time, U.S. officials began to see that these and other attacks were planned and carried out by the Islamist terrorist organization **al Qaeda**, which was led by **Osama bin Laden**. Bin Laden saw the United States as an enemy of Islam and claimed that his goal of a worldwide Islamic revolution required the destruction of the United States.

Al Qaeda launched its deadliest attack on September 11, 2001. On that day, terrorists hijacked four passenger airplanes and crashed them into the World Trade Center and the Pentagon, outside Washington, D.C. One plane crashed in rural Pennsylvania. Nearly 3,000 people died in the attacks.

In what soon became known as the war on terror or the war on terrorism, U.S. officials responded quickly to the attacks, targeting al Qaeda and the Taliban. The **Taliban** was a group that was then governing Afghanistan according to a strict interpretation of Islamic law. The Taliban supported and protected members of al Qaeda. In the fall of 2001, a U.S.-led military campaign invaded Afghanistan and forced out the Taliban.

President George W. Bush then focused on Iraq. Saddam Hussein had used chemical weapons against Iran in the 1980s, and some U.S. officials claimed that he still possessed such weapons and that he supported anti-American terrorist organizations.

A U.S.-led invasion attacked Iraq in March 2003 and quickly toppled the Iraqi government. American weapons inspectors, however, failed to find stockpiles of biological or chemical weapons or any evidence proving Saddam had a role in the September 11 attacks.

After the invasion U.S. and coalition forces occupied Iraq and began a massive rebuilding program. Iraqis elected a new government and approved a new constitution, but the nation faced ongoing violence as religious extremists and former Saddam loyalists attacked non-Iraqis as well as Iraqis who cooperated with foreign troops. As U.S. and Iraqi casualties increased, it became clear that rebuilding a stable Iraq would take years.

READING CHECK **Summarize** What threats does the United States face today?

SECTION 4 ASSESSMENT

go.hrw.com
Online Quiz
Keyword: SHL ENA HP

Reviewing Ideas, Terms, and People

1. **a. Recall** What events led to the breakup of the Soviet Union?
   b. Identify Cause and Effect How did the breakup of the Soviet Union affect Russia and the other former Soviet republics?
   c. Make Judgments Was the end of communism in the Soviet Union positive or negative for the former Soviet republics? Explain your answer.
2. **a. Recall** Which country experienced widespread ethnic conflict following the collapse of its Communist regime?
   b. Make Generalizations What effect did the fall of communism have on European economies?
3. **a. Identify** How have **al Qaeda** and **Osama bin Laden** affected U.S. policy in the post–Cold War era?
   b. Summarize How has the U.S. economy changed in the years following the end of the Cold War?
   c. Evaluate Do you think the United States has become safer and more secure since the end of the Cold War, or less so? Explain.

Critical Thinking

4. **Identify Supporting Details** Use your notes on the section and a graphic organizer like this one to describe the similarities and differences among the former Soviet Union, other parts of Europe, and the United States during the years after the Cold War.

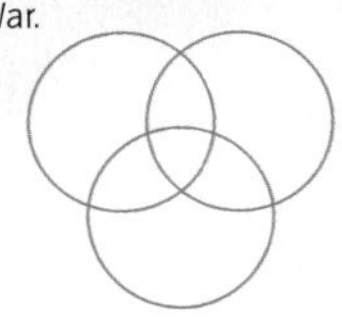

FOCUS ON SPEAKING

5. **Description** Write an outline for a three-minute story for a radio report describing life in Eastern Europe and the former Soviet Union after the collapse of the Soviet Union. Be sure to use details from the section in your news story.

Direct Teach

Reading Focus

The United States Today

Identify What is al Qaeda? *an Islamic terrorist organization led by Osama bin Laden*

Explain What is the relationship among the Taliban, Afghanistan, and Osama bin Laden? *The Taliban ruled Afghanistan and supported and protected members of al Qaeda, including Osama bin Laden.*

Review & Assess

Close

Guide students in a discussion of the events around the world that followed the Cold War.

Review

Online Quiz, Section 4

Assess

SE Section 4 Assessment

Progress Assessment: Section 4 Quiz

Alternative Assessment Handbook

Reteach/Intervene

Interactive Reader and Study Guide, Section 4

Interactive Skills Tutor CD-ROM

Section 4 Assessment Answers

1. **a.** Communist leaders tried to overthrow the government; Gorbachev lost power, and republics gained independence.
   b. some prospered, others failed, bloody fighting in Chechnya, ethnic conflicts
   c. possible answers—positive: it allowed republics to become independent; negative: ethnic unrest still exists
2. **a.** Yugoslavia
   b. mixed results: market reforms created businesses, but low earnings, high unemployment, competitive job market
3. **a.** resulted in war on terror, U.S. military responses in Afghanistan and Iraq
   b. Internet, technology created economic success
   c. possible answer—safer, threat of large-scale attacks by Soviet Union gone
4. **a.** Charts should show the economic, political, and social similarities and differences in countries following the Cold War.
5. Outlines should demonstrate an understanding of the conditions in Eastern Europe following the Soviet Union collapse.

Answers

Reading Check *conflicts in the Middle East and the war on terror*

History and Geography

The Nuclear Age

Info to Know

Anti-Ballistic Missile Treaty In 2001 the United States withdrew themselves from the Anti-Ballistic Treaty with Russia. President George W. Bush declared that the ABM Treaty hindered the United States from properly defending the country from terrorism. President Bush also declared that the Cold War was "long gone" and that Russia and the world have no need to worry about the U.S. withdrawal from the treaty.

Nuclear Power There are just over 100 licensed, commercial nuclear reactors in the United States, which generate about 20 percent of the electricity produced in the country. About 400 commercial nuclear reactors exist in the world today.

Info to Know

Star Wars The Strategic Defense Initiative (SDI) was referred to as Star Wars. President Ronald Reagan believed that the nation needed to develop new ways to defend itself against nuclear weapons. In response to critics of SDI, the U.S. Department of Defense argued that in pursuing strategic defenses, the U.S. goal was not to eliminate or replace the policy of deterrence, but to enhance it.

HISTORY & Geography

The Nuclear Age

Today nuclear weapons and other nuclear materials are found around the world. Although nuclear materials can be used for peaceful purposes, the spread of nuclear weapons poses a serious threat to the world's safety. Mounted on long-range missiles, these weapons can travel thousands of miles in minutes and in the hands of terrorists or aggressive governments could cause widespread devastation.

As fears of nuclear war grew during the Cold War, so did international efforts to limit nuclear weapons. By 2006 nearly all the world's nations had signed an agreement pledging to prevent the further spread of nuclear weapons. Still, at least nine nations possess nuclear weapons today and others are believed to be secretly developing such weapons.

United States
Despite the end of the Cold War and the collapse of the Soviet Union, the United States still has more nuclear weapons than any other nation.

Global Nuclear Weapons, 1945–2005

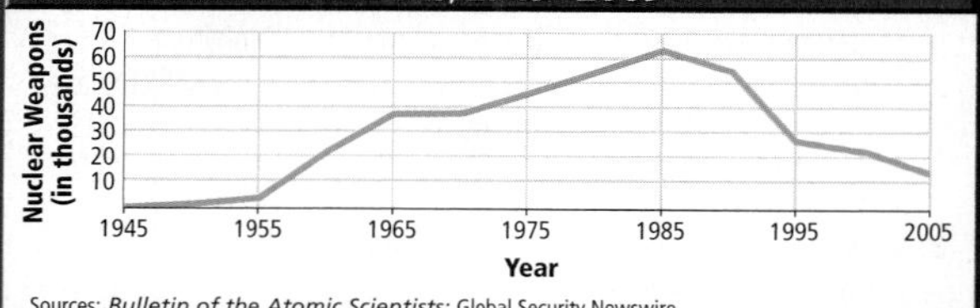

Sources: *Bulletin of the Atomic Scientists;* Global Security Newswire

TIME LINE

Nuclear Weapons

July 16, 1945 In New Mexico, the United States tests the world's first atomic bomb.

EXTRA
TRUMAN GETS EVIDENCE RUSSIANS HAVE A-BOMB
"Explosion Occurred in U.S.S.R. Within Recent Weeks," President Tells Cabinet—Stresses Need for Control
Globe
FINAL SCORE

August 29,1949 The Soviet Union tests its first atomic bomb, years earlier than most U.S. experts had predicted.

1972 Soviet leader Leonid Brezhnev and U.S. president Richard Nixon sign the Anti-Ballistic Missile Treaty.

Skills Focus: Making Oral Presentations

At Level

Reading Like a Historian Skill

Strategic Defense Initiative

1. Remind students that President Ronald Reagan was known as the "Great Communicator" partly because of his clear, simple way of explaining policy. Remind students, too, that the Strategic Defense Initiative was not without its critics.
2. Have students prepare a persuasive speech that President Reagan could have delivered to the American people explaining why he believes that the United States must invest in the SDI. Students should include reasons why Reagan believes that the program will successfully defend the United States and ensure that the nation is not attacked by nuclear weapons.
3. Have students practice their speeches. Choose volunteers to deliver their speeches to the class. **LS Verbal-Linguistic, Auditory-Musical**

Alternative Assessment Handbook, Rubric 24: Oral Presentations

200 Number of nuclear warheads

Selected nuclear facility (production, research, or weapons-related material)

Nuclear weapons nation

UNITED KINGDOM
200

RUSSIA
7,300

FRANCE
350

NORTH KOREA
6-8 ?

CHINA
400

ISRAEL
100-200

PAKISTAN
30-50

INDIA
40-90

Pakistan
In 2004, Pakistani engineer A.Q. Khan confessed to selling nuclear weapons technology to Libya, Iran, and North Korea.

Israel
The Israeli government has never officially confirmed Israel's possession of nuclear weapons, but most experts believe that Israel had become a nuclear power by the early 1970s.

History and Geography

Info to Know

Nuclear Technology in Asia In 2006, the United States signed an agreement with India to allow the transfer of U.S. nuclear technology, for civilian and military purposes. India agreed to accept the conditions of the Non-Proliferation Treaty, and to continue its moratorium on the testing of nuclear weapons.

North Korea In early October 2006, North Korean officials announced that the country had successfully tested a nuclear weapon in the capital city of Pyongyang. The announcement received immediate condemnation from the United States, China, and other nations.

Primary Source

"The transfer of nuclear weapons... would be considered a grave threat to the United States. And we would hold North Korea fully accountable for the consequences of such action."
—President George W. Bush, October 10, 2006

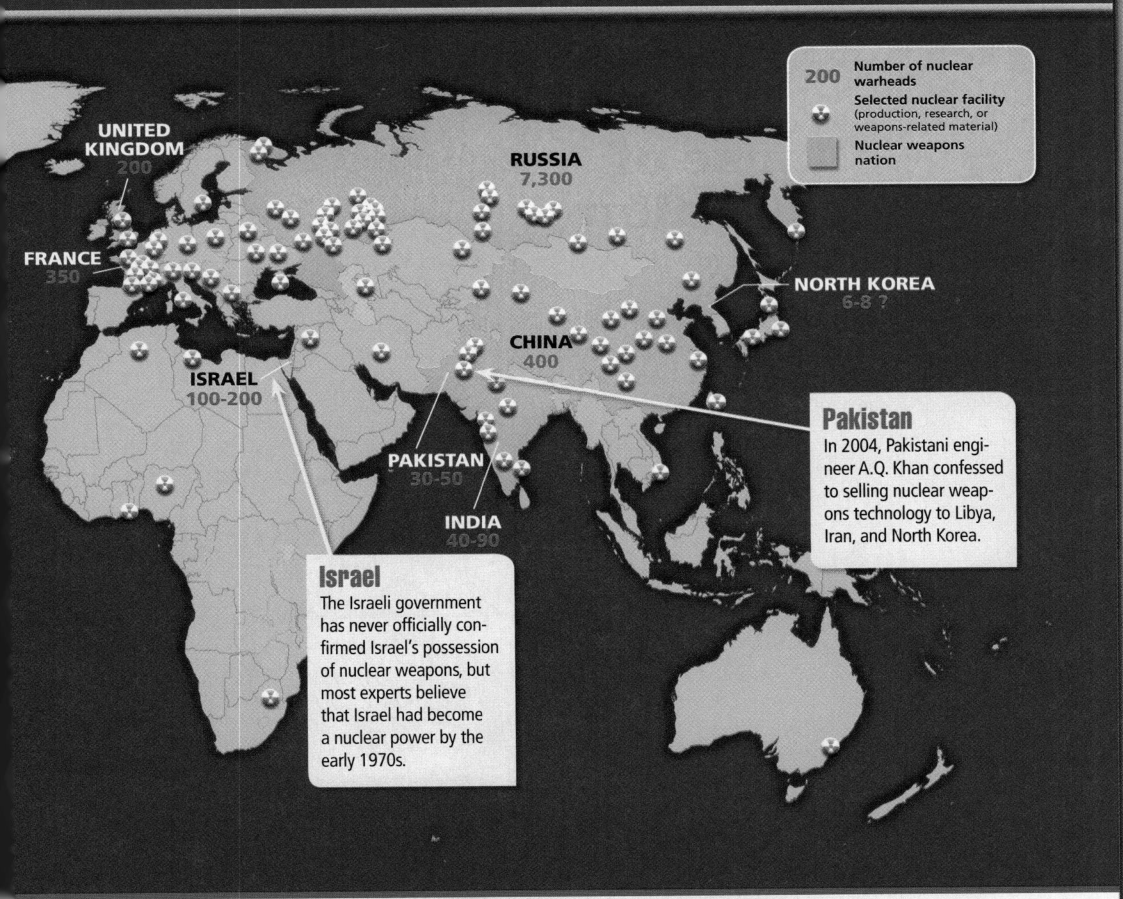

1983 U.S. president Ronald Reagan proposes the Strategic Defense Initiative (SDI), a missile defense system in space.

2006 North Korea continues to develop nuclear weapons at its Yongbyon nuclear facility.

GEOGRAPHY SKILLS INTERPRETING MAPS

1. **Place** Which countries have nuclear weapons?

2. **Regions** Which areas of the world have the greatest number of nuclear facilities? Do all countries with nuclear facilities have nuclear weapons?

EUROPE AND NORTH AMERICA **503**

Skills Focus: Drawing Conclusions

At Level

Reading Skill
Nuclear Power Debate

1. Organize students into small groups.

2. Have groups conduct research using reliable Internet sources to locate current information about the status of using nuclear energy for power, and nuclear materials in the world's nations.

3. Have groups take notes on their findings. Each group should come to a consensus about the benefits and potential negative impact of the use of nuclear energy.

4. When groups have had enough time to prepare their arguments, conduct a class debate about the pros and cons of nuclear power. **LS** **Verbal-Linguistic**

Alternative Assessment Handbook, Rubrics 10: Debates; and 30: Research

Answers

Interpreting Maps **1.** *United States, U.K., France, Israel, Russia, China, Pakistan, India, North Korea;* **2.** *Europe and Russia, no*

Document-Based Investigation

The Collapse of the Soviet Union

Word Help

accelerating faster
anew for an additional time

Info to Know

Russian Economy Between 1998 and 2005, the Russian economy grew on average 6.4 percent each year. Poverty continues to decline today, and the middle class continues to grow. Russia's foreign debt has also been decreasing in recent years.

Teaching Tip

Make sure that students understand what the phrase "Mayday" means." The term is the voice radio signal for ships and people in serious trouble at sea. It is officially recognized around the world. Mayday comes from the French term *m'aidez*, or "help me."

CHAPTER 15 Document-Based Investigation

The Collapse of the Soviet Union

Historical Context The documents below provide information about the final years of the Soviet Union.

Task Study the selections and answer the questions that follow. After you have studied all the documents, you will be asked to write an essay about the collapse of the Soviet Union. You will need to use evidence from these selections and from the chapter to support the position you take in your essay.

DOCUMENT 1

A Cartoonist's View

The cartoon at right, created by the American artist Dick Adair, shows a crowd of angry Soviet citizens protesting conditions in their country. The men looking down at the crowd represent Soviet government officials and military leaders.

DOCUMENT 2

A U.S. Intelligence Report

The following document is an excerpt from a June 1991 Central Intelligence Agency report to the U.S. Congress.

> Six years after Mikhail Gorbachev launched the policies and reforms that have come to be known as *perestroyka*, the Soviet economy is in crisis. Output is declining at an accelerating rate, inflation threatens to rage out of control, interregional trade has broken down, and the center and the republics are engaged in a fierce political struggle over the future of the multinational state . . . Even if reform proceeds anew, tough economic times are in store for the Soviets.

DOCUMENT 3

The Soviet Premier's Complaint

At a government meeting in October 1990, the premier of the Soviet Union, Nikolai Ryzhkov, complained about the country's deteriorating situation.

> How long can we take this?! The government has turned into whipping boys! No one listens to us! You summon someone and they don't even show up! No one follows directions! The country is out of control! We're in the midst of a complete collapse! All the media are against us . . . We have to get back the support of [Soviet newspapers] . . . And get rid of, fire, half of those in television.

Differentiating Instruction

At Level

English-Language Learners

1. Have students examine the political cartoon on this page. Then read Document 2 aloud, explaining what each sentence means.
2. Have students create their own political cartoon reflecting the same idea as shown in Document 1. Student cartoons should have a caption and carry a clear message.
3. Have volunteers share their cartoons with the class. Then guide students in a discussion of the problems facing the Soviet Union just before its collapse. **LS Visual-Spatial**

Alternative Assessment Handbook, Rubric 27: Political Cartoons

Document 4

Mikhail Gorbachev's Opinion

Former Soviet leader Mikhail Gorbachev wrote about the causes of the nation's collapse in his 2000 book, *On My Country and the World*.

> Were there problems in the Soviet Union, including ethnic problems? Yes, there were political, economic, and social problems—and problems between nationalities . . .
>
> [Under Stalin's rule the Soviet Union's] borders were carved out arbitrarily, the rights of one or another nationality were flagrantly violated, and during and immediately after World War II many nationalities were subjected to wholesale repression. They were deported from their ancient homelands and resettled in remote parts of the country. Tens of thousands of people perished in the process. Even under these conditions, however, closer ties and joint efforts among the various nationalities in the Soviet Union allowed all of them to accelerate their development sharply . . . The different nations and nationalities grew stronger, and each acquired an increasingly profound sense of its own identity.
>
> In other words, contradictory processes were at work . . . Severe problems accumulated and were not resolved. Why did this happen? The official conception was that relations among the nationalities . . . were in sufficiently good shape, that in general there were no serious problems.

Document 5

Ronald Reagan's View

During a January 1989 speech, U.S. president Ronald Reagan remembered a visit to the Soviet Union.

> Once, during the heady days of the Moscow summit, Nancy [Reagan] and I decided to . . . visit the shops on Arbat Street—that's a little street just off Moscow's main shopping area. Even though our visit was a surprise, every Russian there immediately recognized us and called out our names and reached for our hands. We were just about swept away by the warmth. You could almost feel the possibilities in all that joy. But within seconds, [Soviet secret police] pushed their way toward us and began pushing and shoving the people in the crowd. It was an interesting moment. It reminded me that while the man on the street in the Soviet Union yearns for peace, the government is Communist. And those who run it are Communists, and that means we and they view such issues as freedom and human rights very differently.
>
> We must keep up our guard, but we must also continue to work together to lessen and eliminate tension and mistrust. My view is that President Gorbachev is different from previous Soviet leaders. I think he knows some of the things wrong with his society and is trying to fix them. We wish him well.

Skills Focus: Reading Like a Historian

Document 1
- **a. Describe** What are Soviet citizens complaining about?
- **b. Analyze** According to the cartoonist, how are Soviet officials reacting to these problems?

Document 2
- **a. Recall** What does the report say about the Soviet Union?
- **b. Evaluate** Would the authors of this document agree or disagree with Document 1?

Document 3
- **a. Identify** What is Ryzhkov complaining about?
- **b. Interpret** Does he believe the government is responsible for the country's problems? Explain your answer.

Document 4
- **a. Summarize** What problems does Gorbachev say the Soviet Union had?
- **b. Interpret** Does he blame Soviet officials for contributing to this problem?

Document 5
- **a. Recall** What does Reagan believe his experience showed about the nature of the Communist Soviet Union?
- **b. Interpret** Do you think he was biased about the Soviet system? Why or why not?

Document-Based Essay Question

What events or causes helped bring about the collapse of the Soviet Union? Using the documents above and information from the chapter, form a thesis that explains your position. Then write a short essay to support your position.

See **Skills Handbook**, pp. H25, H27, H33

Skills Focus: Analyzing Primary Sources

At Level

The Collapse of the Soviet Union

1. Have students review Documents 3 and 4 carefully, focusing on the tone and visual elements in each.
2. Have students choose one of the documents and then use the information in the documents to create a "live" television report of the incident reported.
3. If possible, have students record their report and present the videotape to the class, or have students present their "live" reports to the class.
4. When all reports have been delivered, guide students in a discussion of the causes that resulted in the collapse of the Soviet Union. **LS Kinesthetic, Verbal-Linguistic**

Alternative Assessment Handbook, Rubric 24: Oral Presentations

Document-Based Investigation

Word Help

summon call, ask to appear

Izvestia daily newspaper in the Soviet Union, expressed official views of the Soviet government

Pravda daily newspaper in the Soviet Union; expressed views of Communist Party, was closed in 1991

entourage escorts, staff members

Info to Know

Lithuania Lithuania was the first Soviet republic to declare its independence. It was not until 1993 that Russian military removed itself from the country. Immediately, Lithuania strived to form a government and economy that would fit into the Western countries. It joined the European Union and NATO in 2004 and has also gained access to the World Trade Organization.

Answers

Reading Like a Historian

Document 1. a. *poor conditions in their country;* **b.** *shouting "Mayday," which is a call for help during a crisis;* **Document 2. a.** *that it is in crisis due to inflation and political struggles;* **b.** *agree; both call attention to problems in Soviet Union;* **Document 3. a.** *the country's deteriorating situation and lack of support from the media;* **b.** *possible answer—yes, calls the government "whipping boys;"* **Document 4. a.** *political, economic, social, ethnic, and international problems, which included arbitrarily drawn borders, repression, and human rights violations;* **b.** *yes, says they believed relations were "in sufficiently good shape;"* **Document 5. a.** *People yearned for peace, but were repressed by Communist government.* **b.** *possible answer—Yes, he runs a capitalist, democratic country, so he is biased about other forms of government; no, he simply sees the Soviet system as flawed and unfair.* **Essay** *Student essays should illustrate causes of the Soviet Union's collapse and should include supporting details from the chapter.*

Answers

Visual Summary

Review and Inquiry Have students list one detail from the text that explains or supports each date on the time line in the Visual Study Guide.

Quick Facts Transparency: Visual Study Guide: Europe and North America

Review Key Terms and People

1. Containment was a policy that involved resisting Soviet aggression to contain the spread of communism.
2. Perestroika was a reform of the Soviet economic and political system.
3. Saddam Hussein was an Iraqi dictator who began the Persian Gulf War after invading Kuwait.
4. The world's first successfully launched satellite was *Sputnik*, created by the Soviet.
5. The iron curtain refers to the division betwwn Communist Eastern Europe and democratic Western Europe.
6. Détente is the reduction of U.S.-Soviet tensions.
7. The development of the hydrogen bomb fueled the arms race.
8. The Marshall Plan provided $13 billion in U.S. aid to rebuild Europe.
9. Al Qaeda is an Islamic terrorist group, responsible for the September 11, 2001 terrorists attacks.
10. The effects of the Cold War included ongoing military struggles and increased military spending.

Comprehension and Critical Thinking

11. **a.** during the 1945 Potsdam Conference; conflict over the establishment of governments in Eastern Europe
b. The Soviet Union wanted control over Eastern Europe; Allies wanted them to establish their own governments.
c. possible answer—No, it increased East/West conflicts.

12. **a.** arms race, space race, Korean War, Cuba, Vietnam War
b. causes—Soviet missiles in Cuba, close to the U.S. mainland; effects—missiles removed, Soviet Union and U.S. remained enemies
c. possible answer—Soviet Union wanted to spread communism; U.S. opposed communism; these regions have significant natural resources and economic opportunities

13. **a.** postwar economic boom, unemployment dropped but national debt grew, civil rights and women's movement inspired fight for individual freedom, counterculture
b. to reform poor economy
c. possible answer—very effective until the late 1980s; when people could voice dissent, countries began declaring independence

14. **a.** collapse of Soviet-back regimes in Eastern Europe, fall of Berlin Wall
b. conflict in Middle East, terrorist attacks
c. possible answer—yes, because the Soviet economy was failing, consumers not provided for, economic structure had to change completely for improvements to occur

CHAPTER 15

Chapter Review

QUICK FACTS

VISUAL STUDY GUIDE

Causes and Effects of the Cold War

CAUSES

Systems of Government
- Soviet Union was a Communist dictatorship.
- United States is a democratic republic.

Postwar Conflict
- Both sides disagreed over Eastern Europe.
- Soviet Union established Communist governments throughout Eastern Europe.
- United States resisted Soviet expansion and aided countries seeking to resist communism.

↓

Cold War

↓

EFFECTS

Military
- Arms race between Soviet Union and United States led to the threat of nuclear war.
- Confrontations took place around the world, including Germany, Cuba, Korea, and many other locations.

Political
- Both sides formed a variety of alliances.
- Soviet Union eventually collapsed, and United States became the world's sole superpower.

Major Events in Europe and North America since 1945

1948	Berlin airlift begins
1949	NATO forms
1950	Korean War starts
1952	United States tests hydrogen bomb
1955	Warsaw Pact forms
1957	Soviets launch *Sputnik*
1961	Construction begins on Berlin Wall
1962	Cuban missile crisis takes place
1972	SALT I agreement is signed
1985	Mikhail Gorbachev comes to power
1988	Major arms control agreement is reached
1989	Iron curtain begins to crumble in Eastern Europe
1991	Soviet Union collapses
1992	European Union established
2001	Al Qaeda attacks the United States
2003	United States invades Iraq

Review Key Terms and People

For each term or name below, write a sentence explaining its significance to Europe or North America between 1945 and the present.

1. containment
2. perestroika
3. Saddam Hussein
4. *Sputnik*
5. iron curtain
6. détente
7. hydrogen bomb
8. Marshall Plan
9. al Qaeda
10. Cold War

History's Impact video program
Review the video to answer the closing question: How has the European Union changed the way Europeans live today?

Comprehension and Critical Thinking

SECTION 1 *(pp. 479–483)*

11. a. Recall When and why did Cold War tensions begin to appear?

b. Contrast How did Allied plans for Eastern Europe differ?

c. Make Judgments Was the U.S. policy of containment effective at preventing the spread of communism? Why or why not?

SECTION 2 *(pp. 484–489)*

12. a. Describe How did the United States and Soviet Union compete during the Cold War?

b. Identify Cause and Effect What were the causes and effects of the Cuban missile crisis?

c. Elaborate Why do you think the United States and the Soviet Union cared about having influence in countries around the world?

SECTION 3 *(pp. 490–495)*

13. a. Identify How did cultural changes affect the United States in the years after World War II?

b. Identify Cause and Effect Why did Mikhail Gorbachev propose glasnost and perestroika?

c. Make Judgments How effective do you think the Soviet system was at controlling public dissent? Explain your answer.

SECTION 4 *(pp. 496–501)*

14. a. Describe What events brought about the breakup of the Soviet Union?

b. Summarize What threats has the United States faced since the end of the Cold War?

c. Evaluate Was the end of communism in Eastern Europe completely positive for those nations? Why or why not?

Reading Skills

Making Inferences *Use what you know about making inferences to answer the questions below.*

15. Given what you know about the Cold War, how do you think Americans reacted to the Soviet test of a hydrogen bomb in 1955?

16. How do you think Soviet citizens responded to Mikhail Gorbachev's policies of *glasnost* and *perestroika*?

Analyzing Primary Sources

Reading Like a Historian *This photograph shows demonstrators in the Soviet republic of Lithuania in 1991, protesting the Soviet military crackdown after Lithuania declared its independence.*

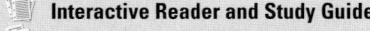

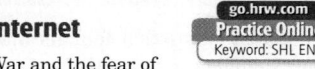

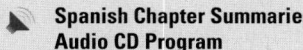

17. Describe How would you describe the people taking part in this protest?

18. Infer Why do you think the protest march was a peaceful march instead of a violent uprising?

Using the Internet

go.hrw.com
Practice Online
Keyword: SHL ENA

19. The Cold War and the fear of nuclear war had a profound effect on people in the United States, the Soviet Union, and around the world. Using the Internet, research the effects of Cold War anxieties on movies, books, and other aspects of popular culture. Then write an illustrated report about your findings.

WRITING ABOUT HISTORY

Persuasion: Writing an Evaluation *During the Cold War, each side developed weapons that were capable of completely destroying the enemy. Defense strategies centered on the idea that the threat of massive nuclear retaliation would deter the enemy from starting a conflict.*

20. Assignment: In an essay, evaluate the wisdom of a war strategy that involved the assured destruction of both sides. To provide support for your evaluation, use information from this chapter and from other research as needed.

Answers

Reading Skills

15. possible answer—people probably feared Soviet attacks

16. possible answer—probably embraced them because of frustration with the old system

Analyzing Primary Sources

17. possible answer—calm, but determined

18. possible answer—because people had faith that their government would address their concerns

Using the Internet

19. Go to the HRW Web site and enter the keyword shown to access a rubric for this activity.

KEYWORD: SHL ENA

Writing About History

20. Students should recognize the benefits and disadvantages of deterrents, and the power of the weapons developed during the Cold War. A rubric for this activity is provided in **CRF**: Writing for the SAT.

HOLT
History's Impact
► **Video Program: Europe and North America**
Refer to the Video Program Teacher's Guide for the answer to the closing question.

Review and Assessment Resources

Review and Reinforce

- **CRF**: Chapter Review
- **Quick Facts Transparency**: Visual Study Guide: Europe and North America
- **Spanish Chapter Summaries Audio CD Program**
- OSP **Holt PuzzlePro**: Quiz Show for ExamView
- **Quiz Game CD-ROM**

Assess

- **PASS**: Chapter Test, Forms A and B
- **Alternative Assessment Handbook**
- OSP **ExamView Test Generator**, Chapter Test
- **Differentiated Instruction Modified Worksheets and Tests CD-ROM**: Chapter Test
- HOAP **Holt Online Assessment Program** (in the Premier Online Edition)

Reteach/Intervene

- **Interactive Reader and Study Guide**
- **Differentiated Instruction Teacher Management System**: Lesson Plans for Differentiated Instruction
- **Differentiated Instruction Modified Worksheets and Tests CD-ROM**: Chapter Test
- **Interactive Skills Tutor CD-ROM**

go.hrw.com
Online Resources
KEYWORD: SHL TEACHER

Chapter 16 Planning Guide

Asia

Chapter Overview	Reproducible Resources	Technology Resources
CHAPTER 16 **pp. 508–535** **Overview: In this chapter, students will learn about challenges and economic growth in India, Southeast Asia, China and the Pacific Rim following World War II.**	**Differentiated Instruction Teacher Management System:** • Pacing Guide • Lesson Plans for Universal Access **Interactive Reader and Study Guide:** Chapter Summary* **Chapter Resource File*** • Writing for the SAT • Social Studies Skill • Economics and History • Chapter Review **World History Outline Maps**	**Live Ink© Online Reading Help** **Student Edition on Audio CD Program** **Differentiated Instruction Modified Worksheets and Tests CD-ROM** **Interactive Skills Tutor CD-ROM** **World History Primary Source Library CD-ROM** **Power Presentations with Video CD-ROM** **History's Impact: World History Video Program (VHS/DVD):** Asia
Section 1: **South Asia after Empire** **The Main Idea:** India, long a part of the British empire, finally gained its independence, but entered an era of conflict.	**Differentiated Instruction Teacher Management System:** Section 1 Lesson Plan* **Interactive Reader and Study Guide:** Section 1 Summary* **Chapter Resource File*** • Vocabulary Builder: Section 1 • Biography: Mohandas Gandhi • History and Geography: The Partition of India	**Daily Test Practice Transarency:** Section 1* **Map Transparency:** Asia, 1945* **Map Transparency:** Religious Groups in India and Pakistan, 1947*
Section 2: **Independence Struggles in Southeast Asia** **The Main Idea:** A region long under colonial domination, Southeast Asia saw many of its countries achieve independence in the postwar years. The transition, however, was not always a smooth one.	**Differentiated Instruction Teacher Management System:** Section 2 Lesson Plan* **Interactive Reader and Study Guide:** Section 2 Summary* **Chapter Resource File*** • Vocabulary Builder: Section 2 • Biography: Loung Ung	**Daily Test Practice Transarency:** Section 2* **Map Transparency:** Southeast Asia, 1965* **Map Transparency:** The Vietnam War, 1964–1975*
Section 3: **Communist China** **The Main Idea:** In 1949, Communist forces led by Mao Zedong had gained control of mainland China. This introduced decades of turmoil, which has just recently given way to reform.	**Differentiated Instruction Teacher Management System:** Section 3 Lesson Plan* **Interactive Reader and Study Guide:** Section 3 Summary* **Chapter Resource File*** • Vocabulary Builder: Section 3 • Biography: Zhang Yimou • Primary Source: A Red Guard Describes the Cultural Revolution	**Daily Test Practice Transarency:** Section 3* **Internet Activity:** Biography of an Asian Leader
Section 4: **The Rise of Pacific Rim Economies** **The Main Idea:** The postwar era in East Asia is in many cases a story of remarkable economic growth. In spite of this success, however, significant challenges remain.	**Differentiated Instruction Teacher Management System:** Section 4 Lesson Plan* **Interactive Reader and Study Guide:** Section 4 Summary* **Chapter Resource File*** • Vocabulary Builder: Section 4 • Biography: Soichiro Honda • Literature: *Hiroshima Notes*	**Daily Test Practice Transparency:** Section 4*

go.hrw.com | Print Resource | Transparency
LS Learning Styles | Audio CD | CD-ROM
Video | SE Student Edition | TE Teacher's Edition
OSP One-Stop Planner CD-ROM
*also on One-Stop Planner CD-ROM

Review, Assessment, Intervention

- **Quick Facts Transparency:** Asia*
- **Progress Assessment Support System (PASS):** Chapter Test*
- **Differentiated Instruction Modified Worksheets and Tests CD-ROM:** Modified Chapter Test
- OSP **One-Stop Planner CD-ROM:** ExamView Test Generator (English/Spanish)
- HOAP **Holt Online Assessment Program (HOAP),** in the Holt Premier Online Student Edition

---

- **PASS:** Section 1 Quiz*
- **Online Quiz:** Section 1
- **Alternative Assessment Handbook**

- **PASS:** Section 2 Quiz*
- **Online Quiz:** Section 2
- **Alternative Assessment Handbook**

- **PASS:** Section 3 Quiz*
- **Online Quiz:** Section 3
- **Alternative Assessment Handbook**

- **PASS:** Section 4 Quiz*
- **Online Quiz:** Section 4
- **Alternative Assessment Handbook**

HOLT
History's Impact
World History Video Program (VHS/DVD)
Asia

Power Presentation with Video CD-ROM

Power Presentations with Video are visual presentations of each chapter's main ideas. Presentations can be customized by including Quick Facts charts, images and maps from the textbook, and video clips.

Holt Online Learning

go.hrw.com
Teacher Resources
KEYWORD: SHL TEACHER

go.hrw.com
Student Resources
KEYWORD: SHL ASA

- Document-Based Questions
- Interactive Multimedia Activities
- Current Events
- Chapter-Based Internet Activities
- and more!

Holt Premier
Online Student Edition

Complete online support for interactivity, assessment, and reporting

- Interactive Maps and Notebook
- Homework Practice and Research Activities Online

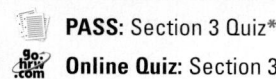

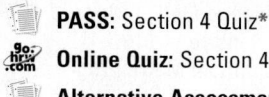

Before You Teach

The Big Picture

Peter N. Stearns

South Asia Asia is a huge continent, with many separate cultures and traditions. This makes comparison a vital analytical tool. In India, decolonization began in the 1940s. National unity could not be retained in the face of religious disputes, some of which had been encouraged by the British. Three separate nations resulted amid diplomatic and military tensions. India itself developed a vigorous and durable democracy. The new nation struggled with economic change, population growth, and rural conservatism. Still agricultural productivity was strong and, from the 1990s, industrial growth surged forward as well.

Southeast Asia Decolonization in Vietnam, Laos, and Cambodia involved massive conflict, first with the French and later against American military intervention. A communist revolutionary effort accompanied the struggle. Vietnamese independence and unification introduced greater flexibility into the communist system, allowing for some market-based economic development. Indonesia, the largest nation in the region, gained independence more peacefully, but then faced a long period of authoritarian rule that later yielded to democratic political forms and new regional strife.

China The big news here was the communist triumph by 1949, and the successive Maoist experiments in economic and political control. Systematic changes involved educational reforms and new public health measures that dramatically reduced infant mortality. In 1978 the regime shifted gears, allowing more market capitalism that generated intense industrial growth and a new global economic role. Still, China continued its authoritarian political controls against democratic movements.

Japan and the Pacific Rim This region featured dramatic economic growth, after a brief post-World War II recovery period. Japan led the way, developing new political institutions and a new level of economic development. Other Pacific Rim nations, notably South Korea and Taiwan, also produced latter day industrial revolutions.

Recent Scholarship

Alan T. Wood's *Asian Democracy in World History* (2004) takes up one of the more interesting and complex trends in South and East Asia. Wood carefully defines democracy and notes European precedents. He explores early post-World War II democracies in India, Japan, and the Philippines, noting reasons for their emergence amidst a regional climate of communist and authoritarian rule. Later democratic developments include South Korea, Taiwan, and the abortive surge in China. A third major section treats the flowering of democracy in Southeast Asia, including Indonesia. Overall, this is a carefully comparative book, combining clear description with lucid, explanatory analysis.

Differentiating Instruction

Differentiated Instruction Teacher Management System
- Pacing Guide
- Lesson Plans for Differentiated Instruction

Interactive Reader and Study Guide

Spanish Chapter Summaries Audio CD Program

Student Edition on Audio CD Program

Differentiated Instruction Modified Worksheets and Tests CD-ROM
- Vocabulary Flash Cards
- Modified Vocabulary Builder Activities
- Modified Chapter Review Activity
- Modified Chapter Test

OSP **One-Stop Planner CD-ROM**
- ExamView Test Generator (English/Spanish)
- PuzzlePro
- Quiz Show for ExamView
- Transparencies and Videos

TE **Differentiated Activities in the Teacher's Edition**
- Religions in India Poster, p. 512
- Colonial Independence Maps, p. 517
- The Tet Offensive, p. 519
- Political Cartoon: Mao's Programs, p. 524
- Japanese Postwar Recovery, p. 529
- Asian Imports and Exports, p. 530
- Cultural Revolution Posters, p. 533

Reading Like a Historian

Sam Wineburg

"Once upon a time ..." begins our children's stories, but how should we begin a historical story? This is not a trick question. A narrative's opening reflects a historian's choices and assumptions. A different historian coming to the same event may locate its beginning in another place entirely.

In narrating the struggles for independence in Southeast Asia, our chapter first notes American involvement with its participation at the 1954 Geneva Peace Conference on the future status of Vietnam. Until then, our chapter seems to suggest, Vietnamese independence was a French affair, with the "Viet Minh fighting France to win independence." The United States, we are told, only becomes actively involved in 1956, when President Eisenhower becomes convinced that Vietnam would be the next domino to fall in the communist struggle for world domination.

Once Upon a Time in Vietnam How else might we begin the story of America's tangled involvement in Vietnam? Consider these different possibilities:

Scenario One: Our story would begin in the waning days of World War II with President Roosevelt's antipathy for European colonial policy, particularly the venality of the French. In a note to Secretary of State Cordell Hall, Roosevelt wrote, "Indochina should not go back to France but [should] be administered by an international trusteeship ... France has milked it for one hundred years. The people of Indochina are entitled to something better than that." In this beginning, the US opposes the return of corrupt French rule and supports the aspirations of the Vietnamese for self-determination.

Scenario Two: This story begins with Ho Chi Minh, the leader of the Viet Minh, long before he became the archenemy of the US. We find Ho in the foggy days of 1945-46, before American policy has crystallized, a period in which Ho wrote eight different letters to President Truman, including one in which he requested that "the United States as guardians and champions of World Justice ... take a decisive step in support of our independence ... Like the Philippines, our goal is full independence and full cooperation with the United States. We will do our best to make this independence profitable to the whole world." We might try to explain why, on the record at least, Ho's appeals to President Truman went unanswered. (This letter was dated February 16, 1945, but not declassified until 1972).

Scenario Three: This story begins with a seven-hour meeting between President Truman and Charles de Gaulle on August 21, 1945, on the fate of French Indochina. It then moves to the collapse of the Chinese Nationalists and Mao's declaration in 1949 of a "People's Republic of China." Viewing all of Southeast Asia as a battleground against communism, President Truman on July 26, 1950, authorized 15 million dollars of military aid to the French, still holding, albeit precariously, onto power in Vietnam. If we started here, we would have to rewrite the French collapse at Dien Bien Phu in 1954 as the defeat of a regime propped up by American military aid and American military advisers in a nation that had already become a Cold War chessboard.

The beginnings of stories do not innocently present themselves to the storyteller. They are matters of choice and judgment—as well as political leaning. Often the key to discerning historical interpretation is by engaging in an intellectual experiment in alternative beginnings.

Indeed, the more we learn about the tangled web of Vietnam—and the role the United States played in it—the more alternative beginnings start to multiply.

• Chapter Preview •

Chapter Main Ideas

Section 1 India gained its independence from Great Britain, but the region entered an era of conflict and challenges.

Section 2 Long under colonial domination, many Southeast Asian nations achieved independence in the postwar years. The transition, however, was not always a smooth one.

Section 3 China has undergone many changes since becoming a Communist nation in 1949. Today, after making many market reforms, China has a rapidly growing economy.

Section 4 The nations of the Asian Pacific Rim underwent remarkable economic growth in the years after World War II, but significant challenges remain.

CHAPTER

16 1945–Present

Asia

THE BIG PICTURE Following World War II, the nations of Asia worked to win political and economic independence. Their efforts were complicated by Cold War tensions, religious and ethnic conflicts, and struggles for political power. Despite these obstacles, some nations achieved great success in building strong, vibrant economies, and improved the lives of people throughout the region.

Theme ECONOMIC SYSTEMS

In the years after World War II, many Asian nations looked for ways to build their economic and political strength. In this chapter you will examine how these nations worked toward economic development and how some achieved economic success.

TIME LINE

CHAPTER EVENTS

- **August 1947** India is partitioned.
- **May 1954** Vietminh defeat French at Dien Bien Phu.
- **Mao Zedong leads China 1949–1976**
- **April 1975** North Vietnam wins the Vietnam War.

1945 — 1965 — 1985

WORLD EVENTS

- **May 14, 1948** Israel declares its statehood.
- **1954** Gamal Abdel Nasser seizes power in Egypt.
- **1961** The Soviet Union sends the first human into outer space.
- **1979** Sandinista rebels win control of Nicaragua.

Key to Differentiating Instruction

Below Level

Basic-level activities designed for all students encountering new material

At Level

Intermediate-level activities designed for average students

Above Level

Challenging activities designed for honors and gifted and talented students

Standard English Mastery

Activities designed to improve standard English usage

Introduce the Chapter

At Level

Asia

Materials: 12" x 18" construction paper

1. Organize students into four groups. Assign a section to each group and give each group a sheet of construction paper.
2. Have groups copy their section number and Main Idea paragraph in the center of their papers. Have groups work together to write subheads and important details beneath each subhead. Have students add appropriate illustrations to their posters.
3. When groups have finished, have them display their work and present it to the class.
4. As homework, ask students to write a short paragraph about why the information in this chapter might be important. **LS Interpersonal, Visual-Spatial**

Alternative Assessment Handbook, Rubrics 14: Group Activity; and 28: Posters

History's Impact video program
Watch the video to understand the impact of Vietnam's location.

Reading like a Historian This photograph was taken during China's Cultural Revolution of the late 1960s, an effort by Chinese leaders to rid the nation of its old ways. The Chinese characters on the large signs translate as "Long live the proletariat's [workers'] great cultural revolution."

Analyzing Visuals How do you think a large public rally like this might have helped the Chinese government maintain power and minimize dissent?

See **Skills Handbook**, p. H26

1993 Apartheid officially ends in South Africa.

June 1989 Chinese troops attack pro-democracy demonstrators in Tiananmen Square.

1997 A financial crisis slows growth in the Pacific Rim.

March 2003 A U.S.-led force invades Iraq.

2005

• Chapter Preview •

HOLT
History's Impact
► **Video Program: Asia**
See the Video Teacher's Guide for strategies for using the video segment.

Reading Like a Historian

Analyzing Visuals Have students examine the photograph on these pages. Tell them that the portrait hanging on the wall depicts Mao Zedong, leader of the Chinese Communist Party. Ask students what they think might happen to a person who did not attend the rally, or who questioned its message.

Explore the Time Line

1. What major world event occurred in 1961? *The Soviet Union sent the first human being into outer space.*
2. How long did Mao Zedong lead China? *27 years*
3. When was Iraq invaded by U.S.-led forces? *2003*
4. When did a financial crisis slow growth in the Pacific Rim? *1997*

Info to Know

The Red Guard The Red Guard was formed to carry out Mao's goals for the Cultural Revolution. They were mostly urban youths, mobilized as their schools were shut down. They were told to attack all traditional values and "bourgeois things" and to publicly criticize party officials.

Predict How might people respond to the Red Guard? *possible answer—Some people might begin to question communism; others might avoid dissent for fear of being harmed.*

go.hrw.com
Online Resources
Chapter Resources:
KEYWORD: SHL ASA
Teacher Resources:
KEYWORD: SHL TEACHER

Answers

Reading Like a Historian *possible answer—People would be less likely to dissent when they saw how many others supported the government.*

Preteach

Geography Starting Points

Himalayan Ascents Nepalese sherpa Tenzing Norgay climbed Mt. Everest over 50 years ago with Britain's Sir Edmund Hillary. It was the first time that the daunting 29,035 foot high summit had been touched by man. Hillary has since made it his mission to help with another ascent, the rise of the sherpa standard of living. Hillary's Himalayan Trust has built twenty-seven schools, a dozen medical clinics, two hospitals, two airfields, and several bridges under "Sir Ed's" watchful care.

Interpreting Maps

Asia, 1945

Location Which four countries were under British rule in 1945? *India, Burma, Malaysia, Brunei*

Human/Environment Interaction What geographic feature may have served to protect Nepal and Bhutan from British control? *The Himalayas*

What are some possible advantages to controlling western Malaysia? *possible answer—Malaysia lies along the logical shipping routes between the Far East and India and Africa, so Singapore could be a major trade center and shipping port.*

Map Transparency: Asia, 1945

World History Outline Maps

Interactive Map: Asia, 1945

GEOGRAPHY Starting Points

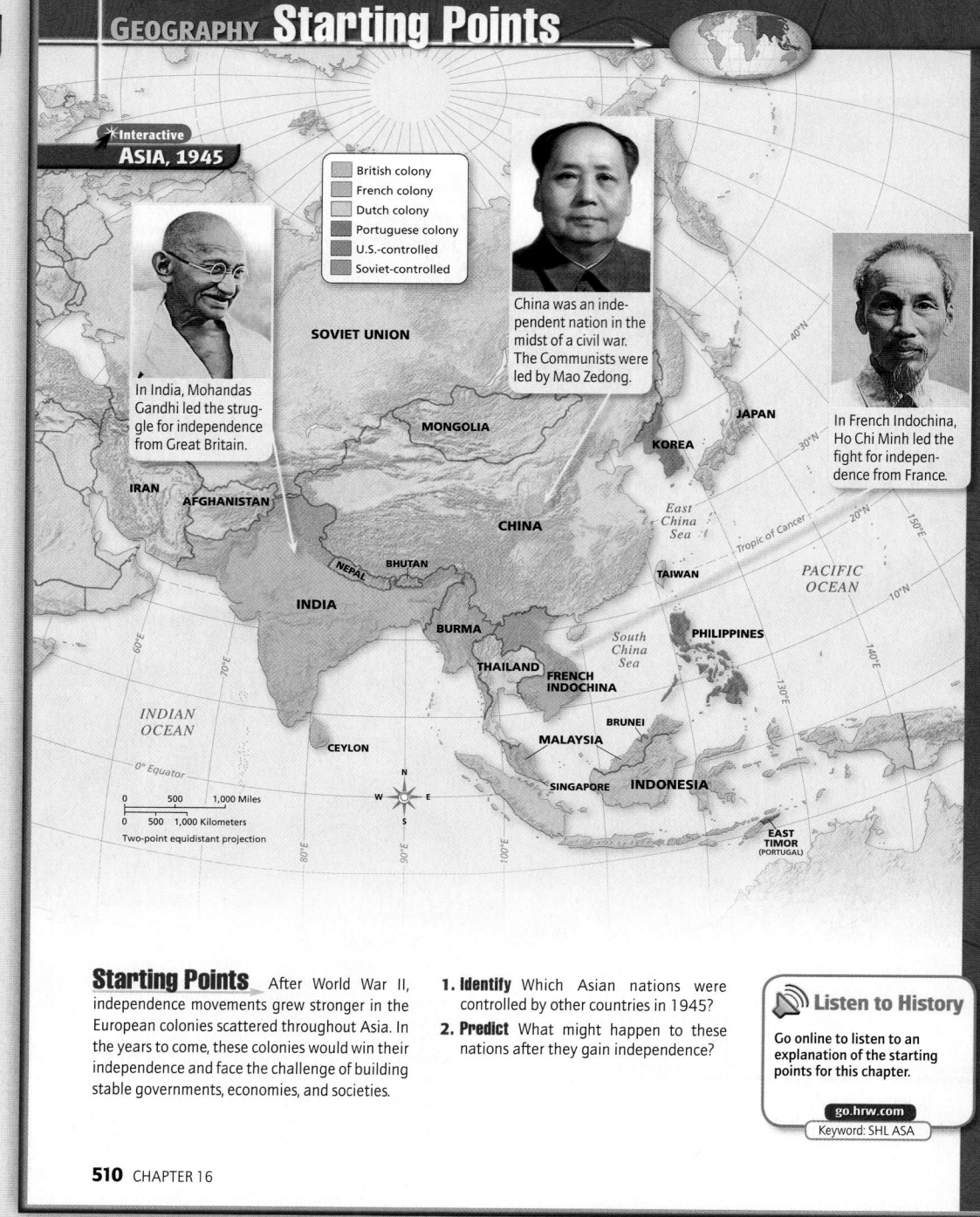

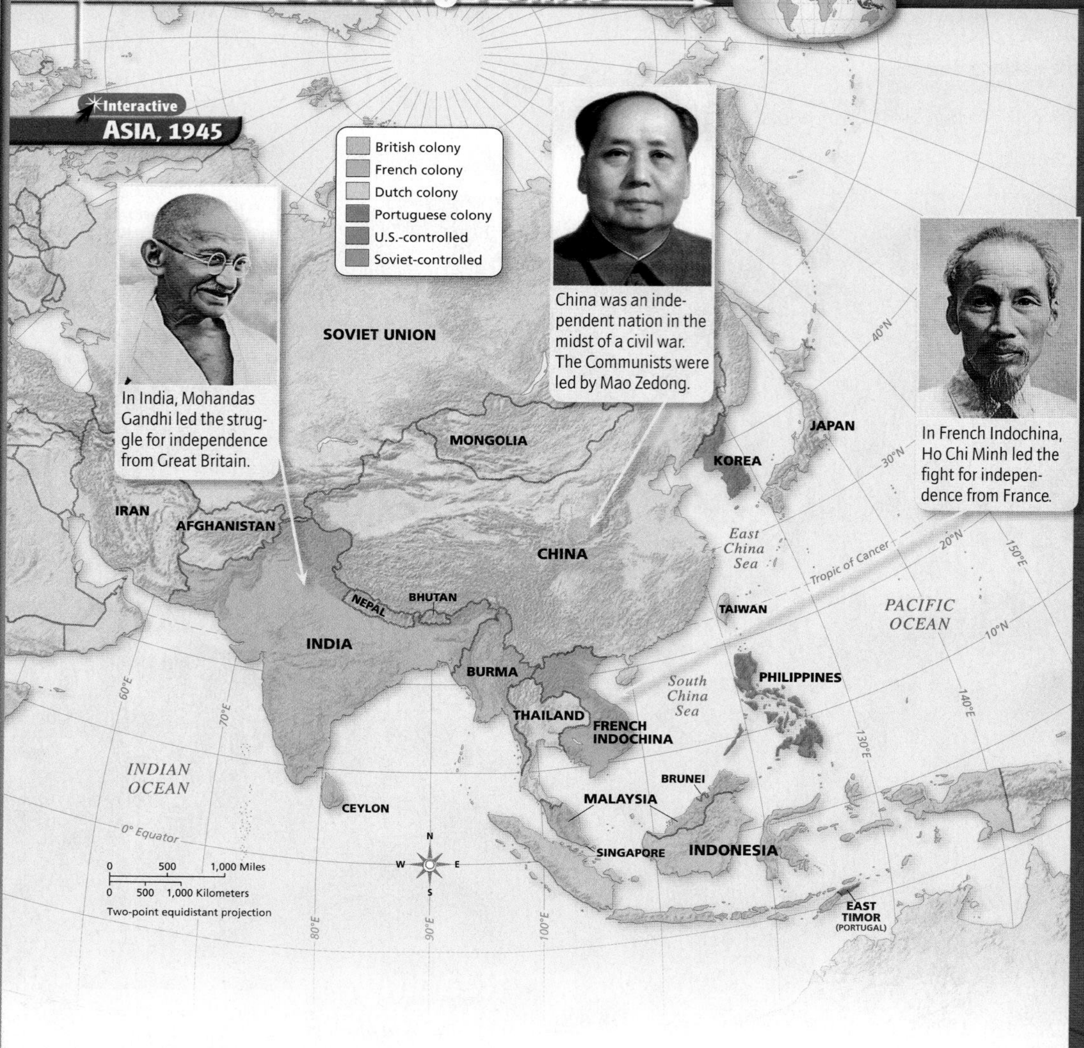

Starting Points After World War II, independence movements grew stronger in the European colonies scattered throughout Asia. In the years to come, these colonies would win their independence and face the challenge of building stable governments, economies, and societies.

1. **Identify** Which Asian nations were controlled by other countries in 1945?
2. **Predict** What might happen to these nations after they gain independence?

Listen to History

Go online to listen to an explanation of the starting points for this chapter.

go.hrw.com
Keyword: SHL ASA

Skills Focus: Analyzing Maps

At Level

Social Studies Skill

Factors Influencing Economic Independence

1. Remind students that various factors influenced whether nations' economies could survive on their own. Tell students they will determine the economic advantages of different areas of Asia in 1945.
2. Organize students into small groups. Assign each group one country from the map on this page. Write the following headings for students to see: Location, Climate, Products, and Political Climate for Trade. Have groups conduct research and record observations about their assigned country. Have groups make a prediction about the country's potential economic success. Have groups share their observations and prediction with the class.
3. As homework, have students list factors that might indicate potential economic success of a country. **LS Interpersonal, Verbal-Linguistic**

Alternative Assessment Handbook, Rubrics 12: Drawing Conclusions; and 21: Map Reading

Answers

Geography Starting Points

1. *India, Burma, Ceylon, French Indochina, Malaysia, Brunei, Phillippines, East Timor, Korea;* **2.** *possible answer—They would have to form their own governments and maintain stability.*

SECTION 1

South Asia after Empire

BEFORE YOU READ

MAIN IDEA

India gained its independence from Great Britain, but the region entered an era of conflict and challenges.

READING FOCUS

1. What events led to independence and conflict in India?
2. What happened to India after the nation won its independence?
3. What challenges face the countries of South Asia?

KEY TERMS AND PEOPLE

Muhammad Ali Jinnah
partition
Jawaharlal Nehru
Indira Gandhi
Pervez Musharraf

TAKING NOTES Take notes about the events in India and Pakistan that followed partition.

Partition → [ ]

THE INSIDE STORY

What is the price of independence? It is the summer of 1947, and more than 10 million Indians are on the move across the British colony of India. The British Parliament has just passed an act dividing India into two independent nations—Hindu India and Islamic Pakistan. People have one month to decide which country to live in and to travel to their new home.

People are scrambling for trains or trying to find other forms of transportation. They're deciding what personal belongings they can take to their new country and what they must leave behind. Most Hindus and Sikhs opt for India, while most Muslims choose Pakistan. As their paths cross, violence erupts—hundreds of thousands of people are dying.

Indians have finally won their independence from Great Britain. But peace will have to wait.

A Nation Torn Apart

▼ **Millions traveled across the Indian subcontinent on overcrowded trains.**

Teach the Main Idea

At Level

South Asia after Empire

1. **Teach** Ask students the Reading Focus questions to teach this section.
2. **Apply** Organize students into small groups. Assign one part of this section to each group: Independence and Conflict, India after Independence, and Challenges in South Asia. Have groups create news headlines about their topic that might appear in various Asian newspapers.
3. **Review** Have groups share their headlines with the class. Guide the class in a discussion about the accuracy of the headlines.
4. **Practice/Homework** Have each student write a newspaper article about the main topics in this section. **LS Interpersonal, Verbal-Linguistic**

Alternative Assessment Handbook, Rubrics 14: Group Activity; and 23: Newspapers

Preteach

Getting Started

Use the **Interactive Reader and Study Guide** to familiarize students with the section content.

Interactive Reader and Study Guide, Section 1

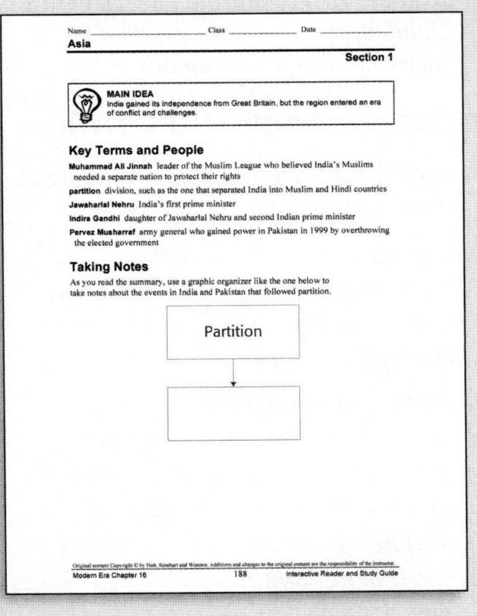

Name ______ Class ______ Date ______

Asia

Section 1

MAIN IDEA
India gained its independence from Great Britain, but the region entered an era of conflict and challenges.

Key Terms and People

Muhammad Ali Jinnah leader of the Muslim League who believed India's Muslims needed a separate nation to protect their rights
partition division, such as the one that separated India into Muslim and Hindi countries
Jawaharlal Nehru India's first prime minister
Indira Gandhi daughter of Jawaharlal Nehru and second Indian prime minister
Pervez Musharraf army general who gained power in Pakistan in 1999 by overthrowing the elected government

Taking Notes
As you read the summary, use a graphic organizer like the one below to take notes about the events in India and Pakistan that followed partition.

Partition → [ ]

Modern Era Chapter 16 188 Interactive Reader and Study Guide

Academic Vocabulary

Review with students the high-use academic term in this section.

utilize to make use of (p. 513)

CRF: Vocabulary Builder: Section 1

Taking Notes

Indian National Congress win some self rule by the mid-1930s; Gandhi imprisoned; British leave India; separate Muslim and Hindu countries created; Nehru India's first prime minister; partition heightened tensions between Muslims, Hindus, and Sikhs; Gandhi killed in riots; control of Kashmir divided between Pakistan and India; East Pakistan becomes Bangladesh; Sikhs occupy India's Golden Temple; Indira Gandhi orders them out, hundreds killed, Sikh bodyguards assassinate her; anti-Sikh violence leaves thousands dead; India and Pakistan test nuclear weapons; religious and ethnic tensions cause conflicts; Ceylon, now Sri Lanka, wins independence from Britain; Gen. Musharraf overthrows Pakistan's government

Direct Teach

Reading Focus

1 What events led to independence and conflict in India? *"Quit India" campaign; Gandhi's imprisonment, and riots; Muslims call for partition; Britain believed partition would ensure stability; they ended rule of India, formed two separate nations*

Independence and Conflict

Recall Who led the Muslim League at this time? *Muhammad Ali Jinnah*

Sequence Place the following in order: a. India becomes independent, b. World War II begins, c. Gandhi is imprisoned. *b, c, a*

Evaluate Do you think partition helps people of different faiths get along? *possible answer—No, they will still fight over the borders. Learning about other faiths and practicing tolerance is a better solution.*

CRF: Biography: Mohandas Gandhi

CRF: History and Geography: The Partition of India

Interpreting Maps

Religious Groups in India and Pakistan, 1947

Human/Environment Interaction How might Kashmir and Ceylon have become Buddhist? *possible answer—Chinese Buddhists must have traveled over the mountains to reach Kashmir, and Chinese ships probably brought sailors to Ceylon.*

Movement Why do you suppose partition created two distant lands for Pakistan? *possible answer—Large populations of Muslims must have been in both areas and it would have been a great hardship for those in the east to move to the far western half.*

Map Transparency: Religious Groups in India and Pakistan, 1947

Answers

Interpreting Maps **1.** *Muslim;* **2.** *India*

Religious Groups in India and Pakistan, 1947

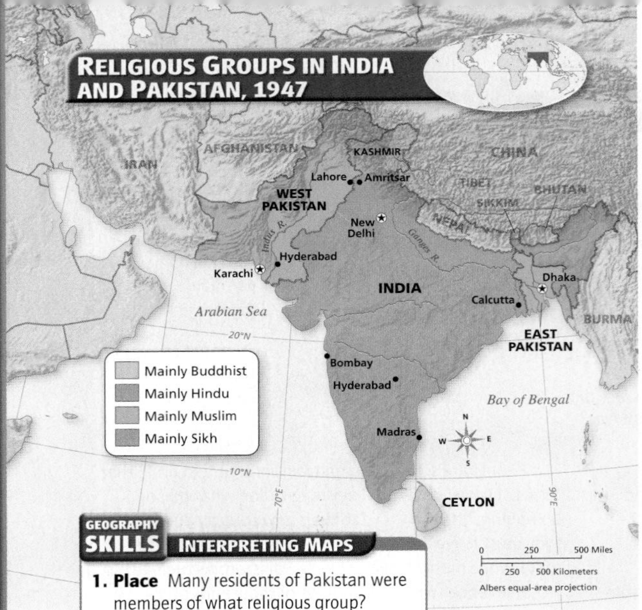

GEOGRAPHY SKILLS INTERPRETING MAPS

1. **Place** Many residents of Pakistan were members of what religious group?
2. **Location** Where did many Hindus live?

Independence and Conflict

Great Britain had controlled India for nearly two hundred years, but by the early 1900s the British control of the region was starting to weaken. At the same time, religious tensions were pulling India apart.

Indian Nationalism Grows A movement for independence in India gained strength throughout the early 1900s. By the mid-1930s the Indian National Congress and Mohandas Gandhi had won some self-rule for Indians.

When World War II began, the British informed India that Indians would have to fight for the Allies. Furious at being forced to participate in a war for democracy while being denied their own independence, the Indian National Congress refused to support the war effort. Instead, Gandhi began the so-called "Quit India" campaign. This effort was a nonviolent protest that aimed to drive the British from India.

The British immediately imprisoned Gandhi and thousands of Congress officials. These actions increased anti-British feelings, and riots erupted throughout India. The violence and increasing Indian nationalism helped convince the British that maintaining control of India was too costly. When the war ended, the British began making plans to leave India.

Religious Conflict and Partition India had long had two main religious groups: Hindus and Muslims. In 1940 India was home to about 255 million Hindus and 92 million Muslims. Smaller numbers of Indians were Sikhs (SEEKS), Christians, or Buddhists. As hopes for Indian independence rose, so did religious tensions. Some Muslims, fearing that an independent democratic India would be dominated by India's large Hindu population, believed that Indian Muslims needed a separate nation in order to protect their rights.

Muhammad Ali Jinnah led the Muslim League, an organization that worked for the interests of India's Muslims. In 1940 the Muslim League formally called for a **partition**, or division, of India and the creation of separate Muslim and Hindu countries. Gandhi strongly opposed the division of India, but there was little he could do to prevent it.

As violence between Muslims and Hindus increased during the early 1940s, British leaders came to believe that partition was the best way to ensure a safe and stable region. They decided to divide India into separate Hindu and Muslim nations.

Great Britain formally ended its colonial rule of India in August 1947 and two new nations were created: Muslim East and West Pakistan and Hindu India. **Jawaharlal Nehru** (juh-WAH-huhr-lahl NAY-roo), who would be India's first prime minister, spoke on the eve of independence.

HISTORY'S VOICES

> **"It is a fateful moment for us in India, for all Asia and for the world. A new star rises, the star of freedom in the East, a new hope comes into being, a vision long cherished materializes."**
>
> —Jawaharlal Nehru, speech, August 14, 1947

Violence after Partition The division of India into two nations also divided the religious groups that lived in India. Most of the residents of Pakistan were Muslims and many in India were Hindu, but followers of other religions lived in each new country as well. As a result, millions of people on each side of the bor-

Differentiating Instruction

Advanced Learners/ Gifted and Talented

Research Required

Materials: 12" x 18" construction paper

1. Point out to students that religious differences contributed to much conflict in mid-20th century India. Tell students they will create posters representing basic facts about the four main faiths of 1947 India.
2. Organize students into four groups. Assign one of the following to each group: Buddhism, Hinduism, Islam, and Sikhism.
3. Have groups research the development of their assigned religion, and create a Basic Facts poster for display. Encourage students to investigate customs, holy cities, famous people, and nations with large populations of each religion's followers.
4. When groups have finished their posters, have groups share them with the class.

LS Interpersonal, Visual-Spatial

Alternative Assessment Handbook, Rubrics 14: Group Activity; 28: Posters; and 30: Research der decided to move. Muslims in India moved to Pakistan. Hindus and Sikhs in Pakistan left for India. As millions of people crossed the subcontinent, violence between different religious groups flared. Over a million people died.

Gandhi himself was a victim of the bloodshed. In January 1948 he was shot and killed by a fellow Hindu who blamed Gandhi for the partition of India and believed that Gandhi had sacrificed Hindu interests to protect Muslims.

War over Kashmir Complicating relations between India and Pakistan was the fact that not all border issues had been settled at partition. One major point of conflict was the region of Kashmir, near the northern border of India and Pakistan. Soon after partition, India and Pakistan began to fight over control of Kashmir. This continued until a cease-fire in 1949 divided the region into two parts, one controlled by India and the other by Pakistan. Later, China claimed control of part of Kashmir as well. Kashmir was the site of frequent conflicts between India and Pakistan in the years after partition.

READING CHECK **Identify Cause and Effect** How did India's independence lead to conflict?

India after Independence

India became the world's largest democracy when the nation won its independence in 1947. In the years after independence, India faced many challenges.

India under Nehru Prime Minister Jawaharlal Nehru led India through the difficult early years of independence. Nehru emphasized the need for unity and economic and social reforms, as well as a respect for democratic ideals. He worked to increase the legal rights of women, to improve the lives of the poor, and to prevent discrimination based on caste, or inherited status. Under Nehru's leadership, India utilized modern science and technology to improve its industry and agriculture. During the Cold War, India played an important role in the formation of the nonaligned movement when it chose to focus on economic development instead of taking sides in the conflict.

ACADEMIC VOCABULARY
utilize to make use of

After Nehru Nehru died in 1964. Two years later his daughter, **Indira Gandhi**, was elected prime minister. Her rise to power showed that the role of women in Indian society had improved in the years after independence.

Linking TO Today

The Conflict in Kashmir

On top of the frigid Siachen Glacier, some 20,000 feet above sea level, Indian and Pakistani troops struggle to control the region of Kashmir. This conflict on the world's highest battlefield has its roots in India's 1947 partition.

When Great Britain partitioned India, the Hindu ruler of Kashmir agreed to join India. This decision left Kashmir's largely Muslim population furious. Pakistan soon sent forces into the region to take control of Kashmir, which it considered a part of its territory, and India immediately followed suit. War broke out.

The war in Kashmir lasted until a UN-brokered cease-fire took effect at the start of 1949 and temporarily divided Kashmir at the battle line. In the cease-fire, both sides agreed to hold a vote to determine the preference of the people of Kashmir. That vote was never held.

Today, Kashmir is still disputed territory. Much of the region's Muslim population lives in the Indian-controlled area, and militants there fight this Indian control. India claims that these fighters are terrorists supported by Pakistan, but Pakistan claims that the fighters are Kashmir residents rising up in an independence movement. Thousands of people have died in the fighting in Kashmir.

Summarize Why is Kashmir disputed territory?

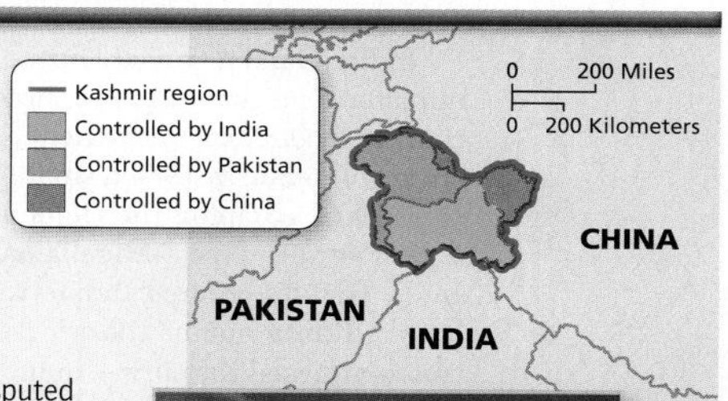

A Pakistani soldier guards the Pakistan-controlled section of Kashmir.

Direct Teach

Reading Focus

2 What happened to India after the nation won its independence? *Jawaharial Nehru and Indira Gandhi each served as prime minister, reforms, Sikh independence movement, Indira Gandhi assassinated*

India after Independence

Recall What were some reforms Nehru made? *increased legal rights of women, improved life for poor, prevented discrimination based on caste, emphasized need for unity and economic development*

Describe What happened in 1984 in the Indian state of Punjab? *small group of militant Sikhs occupied the Golden Temple; Indira Gandhi orders them driven out; hundreds killed at the temple and sacred items destroyed; Gandhi assassinated, touching off a wave of anti-Sikh violence in India*

Info to Know

Mahatma In references to Mohandas Gandhi, the names Mohandas and Mahatma seem to be used interchangeably. However, his given name was Mohandas, but Mahatma is a term bestowed upon him by the people of India to honor him. This title is given only to people of exceptional merit. It comes from maha-atman, which means great self. In Gandhi's case, "great soul" might be the best translation.

MISCONCEPTION ALERT

Indira Gandhi is no relation to Mohandas Gandhi. She is the daughter of Jawaharlal Nehru.

Skills Focus: Comparing and Contrasting

At Level

Reading Skill
Disputes Involving New Nations

1. Remind students that the formation of new nations often involves violent conflict.
2. Draw the chart for students to see, omitting the italicized answers. Have students copy the chart and fill in the answers. When students have completed their charts, have them write a short essay comparing the two disputes. **LS Visual-Spatial, Verbal-Linguistic**

Alternative Assessment Handbook, Rubrics 6: Cause and Effect; and 13: Graphic Organizers

	Kashmir	East Pakistan
Date	*1949; 1964*	*1971*
Cause	*unresolved border dispute*	*distance from West Pakistan, ethnic differences, government policies*
Goal	*to gain territory*	*independence*
Action	*wars*	*civil war*
Result	*division of Kashmir; still unresolved*	*formation of independent Bangladesh*

Answers

Linking to Today *because both India and Pakistan claim the territory*

Reading Check *When India gained independence, new nations were formed along religious lines, leading to conflicts between the groups.*

Direct Teach

Reading Focus

India after Independence

Describe What problem does India continue to face today? *Millions of Indians live in poverty in crowded cities such as Mumbai and Kolkata.*

Identify Cause and Effect What actions did India take in the 1990s, leading to significant economic gains? *loosened control of many industries, reduced trade barriers*

Info to Know

Henotheism It is difficult and confusing to assign an "-ism" to the Hindu faith. It has been called Trinitarian, because Brahman is viewed as three persons: Brahma the Creator, Vishnu the Preserver, and Shiva the Destroyer. However, Hinduism is more accurately described as henotheism. While Hindus believe in one supreme God, they also worship multiple deities, though each is considered a form or facet of the supreme God. Especially important to an area where religious tension has often led to violence is Hinduism's accepting attitude toward other faiths, expressed by this saying: "The truth is One, but different Sages call it by Different Names."

World Religions

Hinduism

Hinduism is one of the world's oldest religions. It is the largest religion in India today and the third largest in the world.

Origins of Hinduism Unlike other religions, Hinduism has no single founder. Instead, it evolved gradually over thousands of years and was influenced by the cultures and traditions of many peoples.

Hinduism teaches that everything in the world is a reflection of Brahman, a single universal spirit. Most Hindus believe that various aspects of Brahman, called *devas*, are active in the world and help keep order in nature.

Hindus believe that the universe and everyone in it are part of a continual pattern of birth, death, and rebirth. After death, they believe that the *atman*, or soul, will be released from the body and later reborn in another body through a process called reincarnation. The nature of the person's new life will be shaped by his or her karma, the sum effect of his or her deeds and actions during the past life. For Hindus, the ultimate goal of existence is *moksha*, or escape from the cycle of death and rebirth and a reunion with Brahman.

Hinduism Today Hinduism is practiced primarily in India, where it originated. Based on many sacred texts and practices, Hinduism often combines new ideas with existing practices. In part because of the religion's many influences, the practice of Hinduism varies widely, with certain beliefs and customs more common in some regions than others. Hinduism is composed of countless sects, with no governing organization.

Summarize What are the major beliefs of Hinduism?

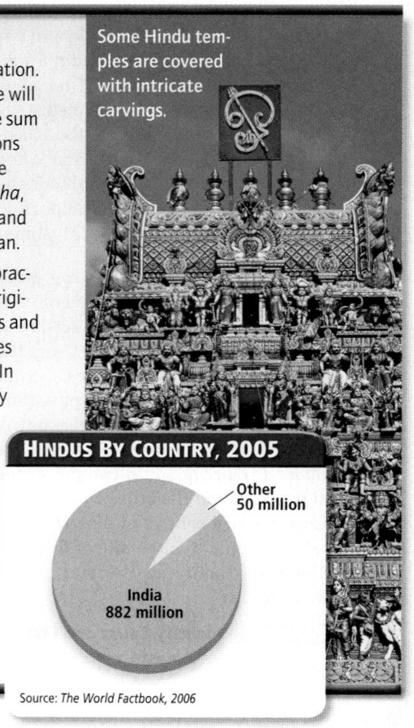

Some Hindu temples are covered with intricate carvings.

HINDUS BY COUNTRY, 2005

Source: *The World Factbook, 2006*

Indira Gandhi served four terms as prime minister. One challenge she faced was from a Sikh independence movement in the Indian state of Punjab. In 1984 a small group of militant Sikhs occupied the Golden Temple, the holiest shrine of the Sikh religion, in Amritsar, India. Gandhi ordered Indian troops to drive the militants out of the temple. When the troops attacked the shrine, hundreds of people were killed, including many who had nothing to do with the temple's occupation. The attack damaged the temple and Sikh holy scriptures.

The violent attack on the temple outraged many Sikhs—including Sikhs who had not supported the militants. In October 1984 Indira Gandhi's Sikh bodyguards assassinated her. This killing touched off a wave of anti-Sikh violence in India that left thousands dead.

The events of 1984 remain a bitter subject today. The incidents greatly harmed relations between India's Sikh minority and the Indian government.

Modern India In the 1990s India undertook some reforms that have led to significant economic gains. For example, the government loosened its controls on many industries and reduced its trade barriers, which helped encourage the growth of new businesses. Although most Indians still work in agriculture, service industries, particularly information technology and the customer-service industry, have expanded rapidly. In recent years, the Indian economy has grown at a remarkable rate.

The strong economy has brought prosperity to only a minority of the country's 1.1 billion people. Millions of Indians live in poverty in crowded cities such as Mumbai and Kolkata. A variety of charity groups work to provide food, clothing, and medical aid to India's poor. One of the best-known groups is the Missionaries of Charity, founded in Kolkata by Roman Catholic nun Mother Teresa.

READING CHECK **Summarize** How did India change after winning its independence?

Skills Focus: Analyzing Primary Sources

At Level

Reading Like a Historian Skill

The Functions of the Vedas

Materials: copies of several Yajur Vedas, printed out from the Internet or other sources

1. Remind students that the Vedas are rituals, hymns, incantations, and sacrifices meant to aid people in the practice of Hinduism.
2. Organize students into small groups. Distribute one veda per group. Have groups read their assigned veda and discuss how its words would relate to the lives of poor, agrarian Hindus. Groups should explain the purpose of the veda. Was it written to teach a lesson, guide a worship ritual, or offer praise to a deity? Have groups share their findings with the class.
3. As homework, have students write a short essay on the function of the veda in the lives of Hindus. Essays should draw parallels to other religious practices. **LS Interpersonal, Verbal-Linguistic**

Alternative Assessment Handbook, Rubrics 12: Drawing Conclusions; and 14: Group Activity

Answers

World Religions *that everything in the world is a reflection of Brahman, the universal spirit; that there is a continual pattern of birth, death, and rebirth*

Reading Check *focused on economic development; increased rights for women and the poor; became the world's largest democracy*

Challenges in South Asia

The history of other nations in South Asia has been as turbulent as that of India. Today, those nations face a range of challenges.

Civil War in Pakistan When Pakistan was created in 1947 it had two parts—West Pakistan and East Pakistan. The areas were separated by over 1,000 miles and by deep differences in language, religion, and culture. In addition, the west, though smaller in population, controlled the country's government. Government policies and spending favored the west while the east remained desperately poor.

In 1971 East Pakistan decided to seek independence. The Pakistani government responded with armed force, and in the civil war that followed, many thousands of people died. After India sent troops to support East Pakistan, Pakistan was forced to accept the independence of the East—now called Bangladesh.

Troubles in Bangladesh Bangladesh faced very difficult times after the civil war. The nation is one of the poorest and most densely populated countries in the world. Much of Bangladesh is just a few feet above sea level, and devastating floods and storms have often swept across the country, killing many people and leading to widespread famine. The nation has seen a series of governments since independence, but in recent years Bangladesh has attempted to build a stable democracy.

Instability in Pakistan Pakistan has also faced instability in the years since the civil war. Ethnic and religious conflicts have been common, including disagreements about the role of Islam in government. A series of leaders have taken power, some through election and some through military coups, as when General **Pervez Musharraf** took power in 1999 by overthrowing the elected government. Musharraf's government has worked with the United States to fight al Qaeda and the Taliban in neighboring Afghanistan.

Nuclear Weapons Even in the best of times, relations between India and Pakistan have been tense, with war a near-constant threat. This tension is one reason that India's testing of a nuclear weapon in 1974 caused alarm around the world. In 1998, after another Indian test, Pakistan tested its own nuclear bomb. The threat of nuclear war has kept tensions high.

Ethnic and Religious Tensions The region continues to experience powerful divisions and conflict based on religious and ethnic differences. Much of this stems from the long-standing hostility between Hindus and Muslims, which continues to cause conflict between India and Pakistan.

Ethnic fighting also plagues India's neighbor, Sri Lanka. This island nation, formerly known as Ceylon, was a British colony until winning independence in the late 1940s. Since the 1980s, fighting between the Buddhist Sinhalese majority, which holds most political power, and the Hindu Tamil minority has killed tens of thousands. Religious tension has intensified this struggle between ethnic groups.

READING SKILLS
Identifying Problems and Solutions What problem does Sri Lanka face?

READING CHECK **Identify Supporting Details** What challenges do the nations of South Asia face today?

SECTION 1 ASSESSMENT

go.hrw.com
Online Quiz
Keyword: SHL ASA HP

Reviewing Key Terms and People

1. **a. Recall** Why did the Muslim League propose the **partition** of India?
   b. Explain How has the dispute over Kashmir affected the relationship between India and Pakistan?
   c. Make Judgments Do you believe that the partition was the best way to ensure a safe and stable region, given the events that followed?
2. **a. Recall** What important events took place in India in 1984?
   b. Summarize What political, economic, and social changes took place in India after independence?
3. **a. Describe** Why did East Pakistan seek independence in 1971?
   b. Explain How have ethnic and religious tensions affected South Asia?

Critical Thinking

4. **Identify Supporting Details** Use your notes on the section and a graphic organizer like the one below to compare and contrast the events that followed partition in India and Pakistan.

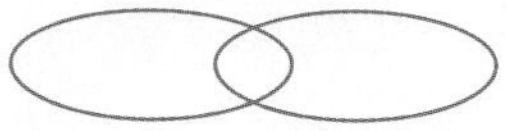

FOCUS ON SPEAKING

5. **Exposition** Write an outline for a brief television news report on the history of India and Pakistan since the partition in 1947. Be sure to include details from the section in your outline.

Section 1 Assessment Answers

1. **a.** partition to separate India by faiths
   b. increased tensions
   c. possible answer—No, the partition probably increased religious tensions.
2. **a.** Sikh independence movement in Punjab, assassination of Indira Gandhi
   b. economic development, reforms increasing rights of women and the poor, limiting discrimination based on caste, nonaligned in the Cold War
3. **a.** because of differences in religion, poverty in the east
   b. resulted in civil war in Bangladesh, tension between India and Pakistan, ethnic fighting in Sri Lanka
4. India—economic and social reforms, democracy, Sikh independence movement, assassination of Indira Gandhi; Pakistan—Bangladesh independence movement, civil war, instability, Musharraf overthrows elected government in 1999; Both—independence movements, nuclear weapons
5. Student outlines should include events from the graphic organizer in question 4.

Direct Teach

Reading Focus

3 What challenges face the countries of South Asia? *nuclear weapons, religious and ethnic tensions, extreme poverty, political upheaval*

Challenges in South Asia

Recall Which two groups continue fighting in Sri Lanka? *the Sinhalese and the Tamils*

Sequence What events led to the independence of Bangladesh? *East Pakistan decided to seek independence in 1971; government responded with force; thousands died in civil war; India sent troops to support East Pakistan, which became Bangladesh*

Review & Assess

Close

Review with students the independence and partition of India, the major challenges facing the new nation, and the ongoing challenges facing South Asia.

Review

Online Quiz, Section 1

Assess

SE Section 1 Assessment

Progress Assessment: Section 1 Quiz

Alternative Assessment Handbook

Reteach/Intervene

Interactive Reader and Study Guide, Section 1

Interactive Skills Tutor CD-ROM

Answers

Reading Skills *ethnic fighting between Buddhist Sinhalese majority and Hindi Tamil minority*

Reading Check *poverty, religious and ethnic tensions, nuclear weapons, famine, political upheaval*

Preteach

Getting Started

Use the **Interactive Reader and Study Guide** to familiarize students with the section content.

Interactive Reader and Study Guide, Section 2

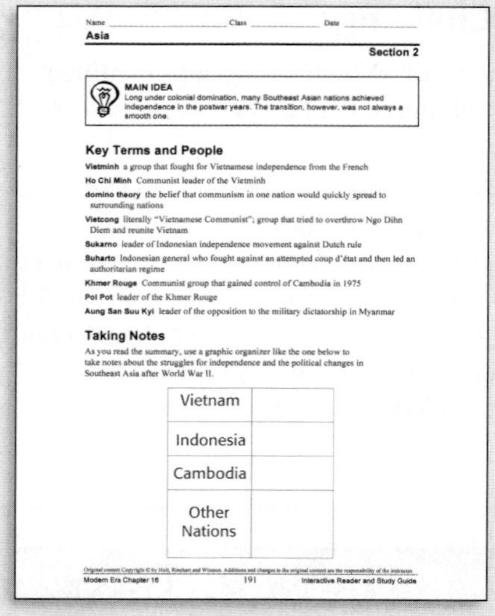

Name ______________ Class ______________ Date ______________

Asia

Section 2

MAIN IDEA
Long under colonial domination, many Southeast Asian nations achieved independence in the postwar years. The transition, however, was not always a smooth one.

Key Terms and People

Vietminh a group that fought for Vietnamese independence from the French

Ho Chi Minh Communist leader of the Vietminh

domino theory the belief that communism in one nation would quickly spread to surrounding nations

Vietcong literally "Vietnamese Communist"; group that tried to overthrow Ngo Dihn Diem and reunite Vietnam

Sukarno leader of Indonesian independence movement against Dutch rule

Suharto Indonesian general who fought against an attempted coup d'état and then led an authoritarian regime

Khmer Rouge Communist group that gained control of Cambodia in 1975

Pol Pot leader of the Khmer Rouge

Aung San Suu Kyi leader of the opposition to the military dictatorship in Myanmar

Taking Notes

As you read the summary, use a graphic organizer like the one below to take notes about the struggles for independence and the political changes in Southeast Asia after World War II.

Vietnam	
Indonesia	
Cambodia	
Other Nations	

Modern Era Chapter 16 191 Interactive Reader and Study Guide

CRF: Vocabulary Builder: Section 2

Taking Notes

Vietnam—Vietminh fight French for Vietnamese independence; Ho Chi Minh leads resistance; French surrender; country divided; U.S. leaders want South Vietnam independent; Gulf of Tonkin Resolution increases American presence; North's Tet Offensive atrocities weaken U.S. public support; U.S. fighting spreads north; U.S. and North Vietnam peace agreement reached in 1973; Vietnam unified in 1976; Indonesia—a military dictatorship, but has returned to democracy; Cambodia— Pol Pot leads Khmer Rouge to gain control of Cambodia in 1975; brutal Khmer Rouge regime fights Vietnam; Pol Pot forced from power; UN helps Cambodia become democratic; Myanmar— a military dictatorship since 1960s, has resisted democracy;

SECTION 2

Independence Struggles in Southeast Asia

Before You Read

Main Idea

Long under colonial domination, many Southeast Asian nations achieved independence in the postwar years. The transition, however, was not always a smooth one.

Reading Focus

1. How did independence come to Southeast Asia?
2. What were the main causes of the Vietnam War?
3. How has Southeast Asia changed in recent decades?

Key Terms and People

Vietminh
Ho Chi Minh
domino theory
Vietcong
Sukarno
Suharto
Khmer Rouge
Pol Pot
Aung San Suu Kyi

TAKING NOTES Take notes about the struggles for independence and the political changes in Southeast Asia after World War II.

Vietnam	
Indonesia	
Cambodia	
Other Nations	

A TERRIBLE DECISION

THE INSIDE STORY ***How did the French lose a war with one bad decision?*** After World War II the French struggled to regain control of their colonies in Southeast Asia. In Vietnam, French troops fought a guerrilla group, known as the Vietminh, that sought to win Vietnam's independence. French leaders decided to build a new military base at Dien Bien Phu (DYEN BYEN FOO) to help defeat the Vietminh. It was a terrible decision.

The French base was located at the bottom of a bowl-shaped valley. When the Vietminh cut off all the roads leading to the area, the fort could be supplied only from the air. Still, French leaders were unconcerned, believing the Vietminh were too weak to defeat them.

When the Vietminh attacked Dien Bien Phu in March 1954, they quickly overwhelmed the French defenses above the valley. Then the Vietminh began to pound the French base below with powerful artillery fire. Under constant bombardment, the French were unable to fly supply aircraft in or out of Dien Bien Phu. Heavy monsoon rains added to their misery. By early May, the French were completely defeated and were forced to surrender to the Vietminh. French control of Southeast Asia had come to an end. ■

◀ **French troops parachute into Dien Bien Phu.**

Teach the Main Idea

At Level

Independence Struggles in Southeast Asia

1. **Teach** Ask students the Reading Focus questions to teach this section.
2. **Apply** Organize students into three groups. Assign one part of this section to each group. Have groups create a list of important events from their assigned part of this section.
3. **Review** When groups have completed their lists, have them present their work. Have students use sticky notes to indicate the location of important events.
4. **Practice/Homework** Have each student write a one paragraph summary about the struggles for independence in Southeast Asia. **LS Interpersonal, Visual-Spatial**

Alternative Assessment Handbook, Rubrics 1: Acquiring Information; and 14: Group Activity

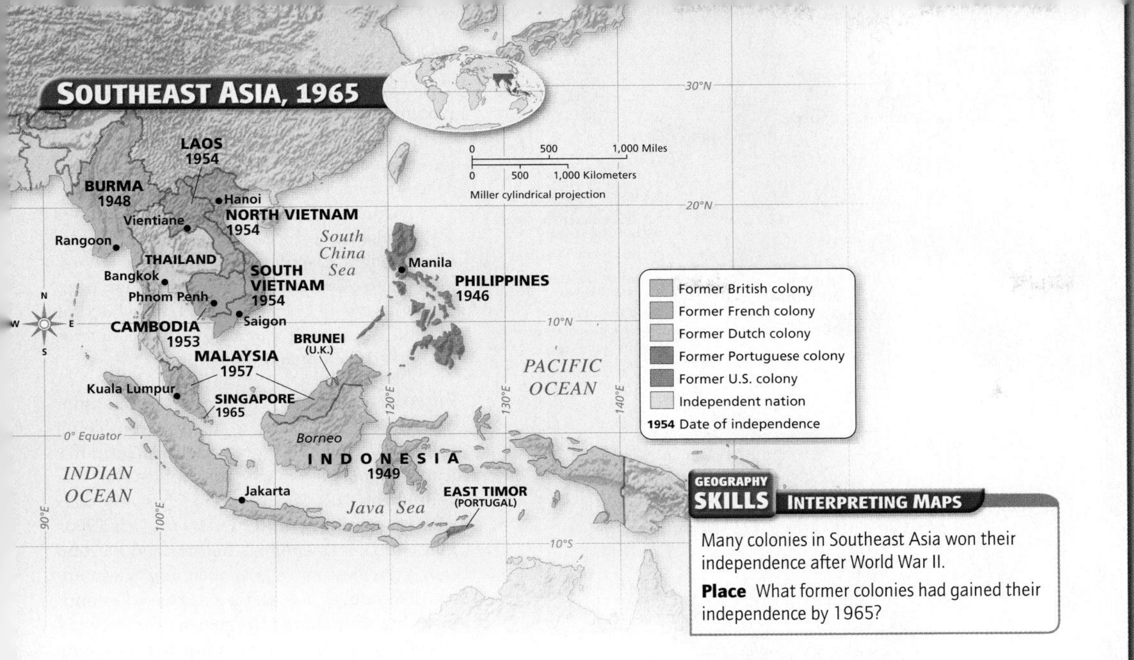

GEOGRAPHY SKILLS INTERPRETING MAPS

Many colonies in Southeast Asia won their independence after World War II.

Place What former colonies had gained their independence by 1965?

Independence in Southeast Asia

Before World War II much of Southeast Asia was controlled by major colonial powers. For example, Burma (now known as Myanmar) and Malaya (now Malaysia) were controlled by the British. The Philippines was under the control of the United States, while the country now known as Indonesia was a Dutch colony. The modern-day countries of Vietnam, Laos, and Cambodia were part of a French colony known as French Indochina.

During the war, the Japanese occupied these Southeast Asian colonies. This occupation helped weaken the grip of the European and American powers. When World War II ended, some nations decided to end their colonial presence in the region. The United States, for example, granted independence to the Philippines in 1946, while the British gave up control of Burma in 1948.

In other cases, however, independence came only with struggle. Communist rebels in Malaya, for example, fought the British before they achieved independence. In Indochina, a group known as the **Vietminh** fought French troops to win Vietnamese independence. The leader of the Vietminh, **Ho Chi Minh**, was a Communist. He received assistance in his effort from China and the Soviet Union. His major goal, however, was independence for Vietnam, not the expansion of communism. After years of fighting, the Vietminh finally defeated France, and French control of Indochina came to an end.

READING CHECK **Make Generalizations** How did Southeast Asian nations achieve independence?

The Vietnam War

The fighting with France had ended, but the conflict in Vietnam was far from over. Ho Chi Minh's dream of a united, independent Vietnam would only be achieved after years of war.

Planning Vietnam's Future In 1954 representatives from France, Vietnam, the United States, the Soviet Union, and other nations met in Switzerland to establish a peace agreement for Vietnam. The talks reflected the Cold War tensions of the mid-1950s. Worried about the spread of communism, the Western powers did not want to give Ho Chi Minh and the Communists complete control of Vietnam.

Direct Teach

Reading Focus

1 How did independence come to Southeast Asia? *many struggles for independence from foreign colonial rule*

Independence in Southeast Asia

Identify Before World War II, which parts of Southeast Asia were controlled by Great Britain? *Burma (now known as Myanmar) and Malaya (now Malaysia)*

Predict Given that the French had western allies from past world wars, what do you think might happen in the conflict with the Vietminh? *possible answer— Allies of the French might come to their aid.*

Map Transparency: Southeast Asia, 1965

Reading Focus

2 What were the main causes of the Vietnam War? *Vietnam divided after defeat of French; U.S fears spread of communism; Vietcong joined by North Vietnamese to defeat South Vietnamese fighters.*

The Vietnam War

Recall What worried Western leaders at the conference in Switzerland? *the spread of communism*

Explain What was the domino theory? *the belief that if Vietnam fell to communism, other Southeast Asian countries would quickly follow*

Differentiating Instruction

Below Level

Learners Having Difficulty

Materials: black outline masters of Southeast Asia, colored pencils

1. Remind students that between the end of World War II and 1975, many colonies in Southeast Asia gained independence. Tell students they will create maps to show which colonies did so peacefully, and which ones had to fight for independence.
2. Distribute maps and have students copy the country names and dates of independence from the map on this page.
3. Have students refer to this page to find how some former colonies achieved independence. If war was involved, students should color the country red. If the transition was peaceful, they should color it blue.
4. As homework, ask students to write a short paragraph, reviewing how these countries achieved independence. **LS Visual-Spatial, Verbal-Linguistic**

Alternative Assessment Handbook, Rubrics 1: Acquiring Information; and 20: Map Creation

Answers

Interpreting Maps *Burma, Laos, Cambodia, North Vietnam, South Vietnam, Malaysia, Singapore, Indonesia, Philippines*

Reading Check *In some areas, Japanese occupation during World War II helped weaken the grip of the European and American powers in the region. In others, independence came with struggle.*

Direct Teach

Reading Focus

The Vietnam War

Identify What resolution served to escalate the United States' involvement? *the Gulf of Tonkin Resolution*

Explain Why did the United States support South Vietnam? *to keep it from being taken over by the North, and therefore becoming Communist*

Analyze In what way did the U.S. involvement cause North Vietnam and the Vietcong to change their strategy? *Instead of pressing for a quick victory, the Vietcong focused on outlasting their enemies.*

Map Transparency: The Vietnam War, 1964–1975

Interactive Map: The Vietnam War, 1964–1975

Info to Know

Diem's Values When the Viet Minh first took over in 1945, Ngo Dinh Diem was offered a job in the Ho Chi Minh government. Diem, who felt that Communists posed a threat to his Catholic values and to Vietnamese independence, turned down the job. A few years later, Diem exiled himself and came to live in the United States. It was then that the Eisenhower administration chose him to serve as first prime minister of South Vietnam. Diem's "values" did not include religious tolerance, however. His nepotism, corruption, and cruelty moved several Buddhist monks to set fire to themselves in public protest. News and photos of this shocked the American people and led to the end of U.S. support for Diem.

Answers

Interpreting Maps *The Vietcong controlled most of South Vietnam, excluding some small areas.*

Faces of History *inspired him to demand independence for Vietnam*

Interactive

THE VIETNAM WAR, 1964–1975

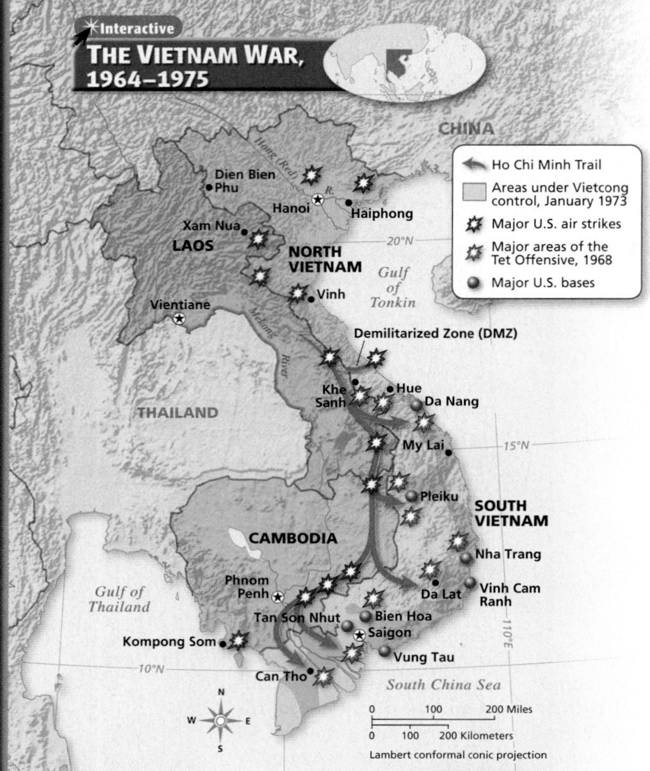

go.hrw.com
Interactive Map
Keyword: SHL ASA

GEOGRAPHY SKILLS INTERPRETING MAPS

Place How much of South Vietnam did the Vietcong control by January 1973?

FACES OF HISTORY

HO Chi Minh
1890–1969

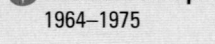

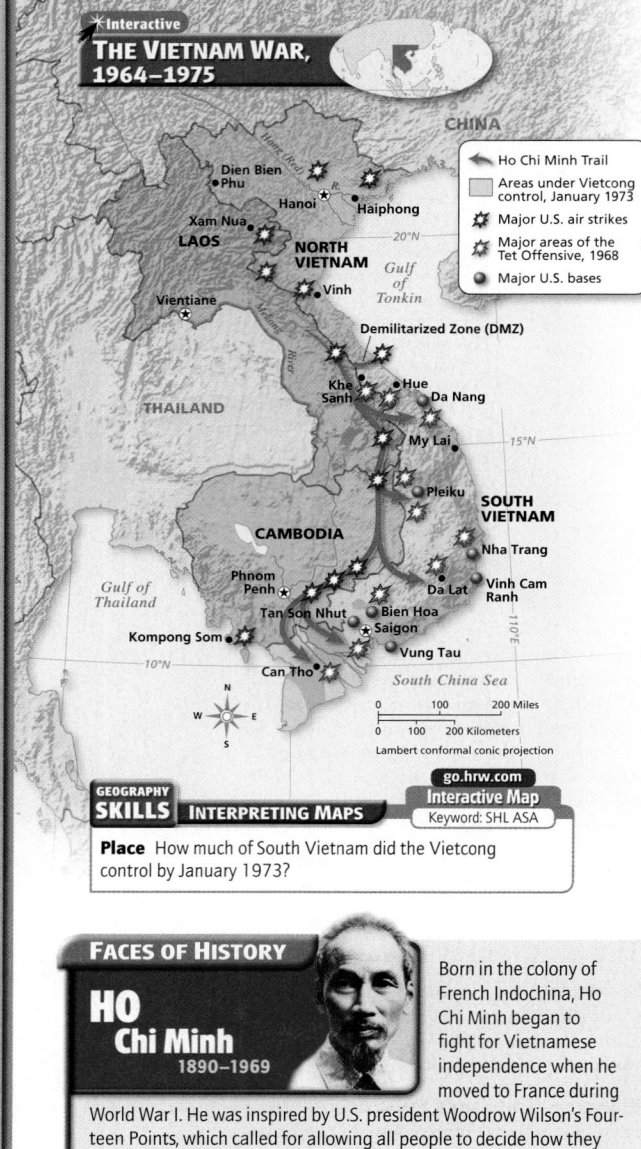

Born in the colony of French Indochina, Ho Chi Minh began to fight for Vietnamese independence when he moved to France during World War I. He was inspired by U.S. president Woodrow Wilson's Fourteen Points, which called for allowing all people to decide how they want to be governed.

When world leaders met in Paris to negotiate the post-World War I peace treaty, Ho Chi Minh sent them a petition demanding Vietnam's independence, but received no response. He soon began to use Communist ideas in his struggle for independence, believing that peasants would play a key role in the fight for an independent Vietnam.

Find the Main Idea How did the Fourteen Points affect Ho Chi Minh?

Thus, Vietnam was divided temporarily into northern and southern halves. The Communists would control the north. According to the agreement, in 1956 Vietnamese voters would choose a government for a reunited Vietnam.

The United States feared that Communists would take control of South Vietnam. U.S. president Dwight Eisenhower warned that if Vietnam fell to communism, other Southeast Asian countries would quickly follow. This belief that communism would spread to other countries was called the **domino theory**.

Fighting Begins The United States supported South Vietnam to keep it from being taken over by the North. South Vietnam's leader, Ngo Dinh Diem (NGOH DIN dee-EM), prevented the 1956 election and made enemies with his corrupt, brutal rule. By the late 1950s many of Diem's enemies had formed a group called the **Vietcong**, a term meaning "Vietnamese Communist." Not all Vietcong were Communists, but they shared the goal of overthrowing Diem's government and reuniting Vietnam. Soon, North Vietnamese forces entered South Vietnam to fight alongside the Vietcong.

Fighting Escalates As Vietcong influence spread, the United States increased its aid to South Vietnam. The United States also sent thousands of military advisers to help South Vietnamese forces.

In August 1964 U.S. president Lyndon B. Johnson informed Congress that two U.S. Navy ships sailing off North Vietnam's coast had been the victims of an unprovoked attack by North Vietnamese gunboats. It was true that one U.S. ship had been fired upon by North Vietnamese who believed the ship had attacked them the previous day, but the second attack seems to have been a misunderstanding. Johnson did not mention the full facts, and Congress passed the Gulf of Tonkin Resolution. This resolution gave Johnson the power to expand U.S. involvement without a formal declaration of war. As a result, the American military presence in Vietnam grew quickly, with hundreds of thousands of combat troops sent to the region.

The increased U.S. involvement forced North Vietnam and the Vietcong to change their military strategy in South Vietnam. Rather than pressing for a quick victory, they focused on outlasting their enemies.

Skill Focus: Analyzing Primary Sources

At Level

Research Required

Reading Like a Historian Skill
Letters From Vietnam

1. Remind students that when people were sent to war in Vietnam, the letters they sent home often revealed the reality of war that was not reported in the news.
2. Organize students into small groups. Have students conduct online research to locate letters written by soldiers and medical personnel who served in Vietnam. Have students print out one or more letters to analyze.
3. Have groups discuss the letters and highlight areas that might be of particular interest to historians, and explain their highlighted choices.
4. As homework, have students write a short paragraph explaining the value of letters as primary sources. **LS Interpersonal, Verbal-Linguistic**

Alternative Assessment Handbook, Rubrics 16: Judging Information; and 30: Research

COUNTERPOINTS

Two Views on The Domino Theory

President Dwight Eisenhower and many other U.S. leaders believed that if one nation fell to communism, others might quickly follow.

"You have a row of dominoes set up, you knock over the first one, and what will happen to the last one is the certainty that it will go over very quickly. So you could have the beginning of a disintegration that would have the most profound influences . . . Asia, after all, has already lost some 450 millions of her peoples to the Communist dictatorship, and we simply can't afford greater losses."

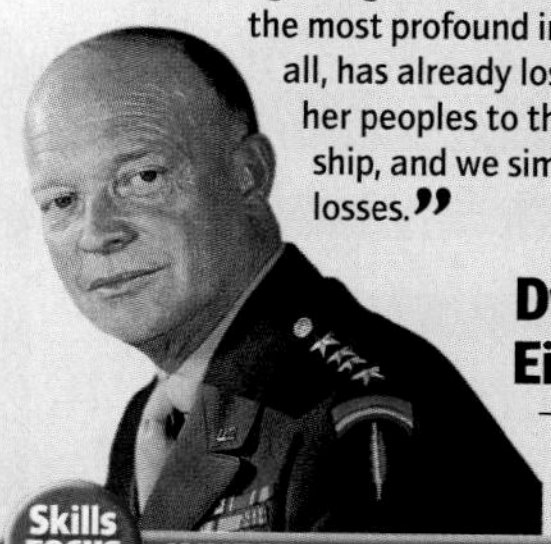

Dwight Eisenhower
—April 7, 1954

Robert McNamara was the U.S. secretary of defense during the first part of the Vietnam War. At the time, he believed in the domino theory, but he later came to regret the U.S. actions in Southeast Asia.

"I am certain we exaggerated the threat. Had we never intervened, I now doubt that the dominoes would have fallen; I doubt that all of Asia would have fallen under Communist control. I doubt that the security of the West would have been materially and adversely affected had we not intervened . . . That was our major error."

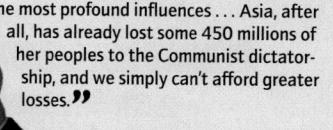

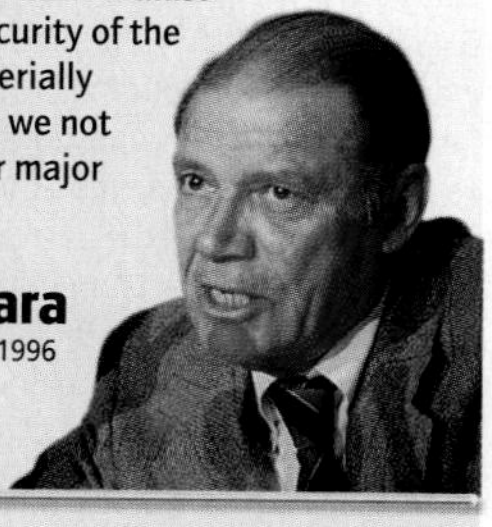

Robert McNamara
—April 16, 1996

Skills FOCUS **INVESTIGATING HISTORY**

Infer Do you think world events that took place after Eisenhower spoke had any effect on McNamara's opinion? Why or why not?

Tet: A Turning Point In 1968 the North Vietnamese army and the Vietcong carried out a daring strike against cities and other targets across South Vietnam. Because the attack began on the Vietnamese New Year, called *Tet*, it came to be called the Tet Offensive.

The offensive was a military setback for the Vietcong, but it still delivered a heavy political blow to the U.S. and South Vietnamese effort. American leaders had claimed that victory in Vietnam was close at hand, but the Tet Offensive dramatically showed this was not the case. Thus, the attacks greatly weakened American public support for the war.

After the Tet Offensive, the war expanded into Laos and Cambodia, Vietnam's neighbors, where the North Vietnamese had built a supply network known as the Ho Chi Minh Trail. U.S. efforts to destroy the trail largely failed.

As more American soldiers were killed or wounded in the conflict, the American public's opposition to the war grew. After long negotiations, the United States reached a peace agreement with North Vietnam in 1973 and withdrew its military support. Without that support, the South quickly lost ground. In April 1975 North Vietnamese tanks rolled into Saigon, South Vietnam's capital, ending the war.

After the War Vietnam was reunited officially in 1976, but the nation faced major problems. Millions of Vietnamese had died or been made homeless during the war, and the Vietnamese economy was severely crippled.

Vietnam abandoned its Soviet-style planned economy in the mid-1980s and adopted economic reforms, which resulted in slow but largely steady economic growth. In 1995 the United States formally recognized the united Vietnam, and soon after, the two nations agreed to improve their trade relationship. Although Vietnam has undergone many economic reforms since the war ended, political reforms have been slower to arrive. Today, Vietnam remains a Communist nation.

READING CHECK **Summarize** Summarize the course of the Vietnam War.

THE IMPACT **TODAY**

In the fall of 2006 Vietnam was working to join the World Trade Organization, an act that would open up the country to more foreign trade and investment.

Direct Teach

Reading Focus

The Vietnam War

Recall Why was the 1968 offensive known as the Tet Offensive? *because it took place on the Vietnamese New Year, called Tet*

Evaluate Which side benefited most from the Tet Offensive? *possible answer—The Vietcong showed they were capable of effective attacks against American forces; they also benefited from the secondary effect of weakened American public support.*

Describe Describe the political situation in Vietnam today. *It is a Communist nation. The united Vietnam is formally recognized by the United States.*

Info to Know

Lunar New Year The celebration of the Tet is significant to the Vietnamese, providing three days of celebration that emphasize their cultural identity. The Tet festival dates back to the Bronze Age and emphasizes the cultural identity of the Vietnamese. Though there are several Tet festivals per year, the most significant one marks the lunar new year. Entire villages celebrate together, expressing the unities of man and nature, of people with their ancestors, of families with faraway members, and of people with their neighbors.

Differentiating Instruction

Below Level

Learners Having Difficulty

1. Remind students that the Tet Offensive resulted in a major decline in the American public's support for the war.
2. Have students read each view presented in the Counterpoints feature on this page. When students have a clear understanding of each quote, have them paraphrase each point of view in their own words.
3. Have volunteers read their paraphrases aloud to the class.
4. Guide students in a class discussion about each point of view, and the tense atmosphere in the United States during this time.

LS Intrapersonal, Verbal-Linguistic

Alternative Assessment Handbook, Rubrics 11: Discussions; and 37: Writing Assignments

Answers

Counterpoints *Since all of Asia did not fall to the communists, it is likely McNamara based his conclusion on world events.*

Reading Check *United States feared Communists would take control of South Vietnam; war began and U.S. involvement increased American public opposition to the war grew; United States removed troops; North Vietnamese took control of South Vietnam.*

Direct Teach

Reading Focus

3 How has Southeast Asia changed in recent decades? *Many nations have gained independence from colonial rule and have struggled to build stable, independent countries.*

Changes in Southeast Asia

Identify When did Indonesia win its independence? *1949*

Describe How did the Cold War affect Indonesia? *Sukarno, Indonesia's first president, adopted policies that supported communism.*

Evaluate What was positive and what was negative about Suharto's rule? *positive—Indonesian economy revived temporarily; negative—authoritarian regime was corrupt*

CRF: Biography: Loung Ung

World Religions

Buddhism

Describe What are Buddhists to do while they seek enlightenment? *lead virtuous, moral lives, and attempt to purify their minds in order to reach nirvana*

Analyze Rounding to the nearest hundred years, how long has it been since the death of Siddhartha Gautama, the Buddha? *2,500 years*

Info to Know

Buddhism's Growth The American Buddhist population has increased dramatically in the last decade. Buddhism is now listed among the top ten organized religions in the United States.

World Religions

Buddhism

Buddhism is one of the most common religions in Southeast Asia. Many of the people of Vietnam, Cambodia, and Laos are Buddhists.

Origins of Buddhism The religion and philosophy of Buddhism developed from the teachings of a man named Siddhartha Gautama, a Hindu who was born in India around 563 BC. As a young man, Siddhartha spent years wandering throughout India, searching for answers to his questions about the meaning of human life. After much meditation he found the answers he had been looking for. From that point on, he was known as the Buddha, or the "Enlightened One." The Buddha spent the rest of his life traveling across northern India, teaching people his ideas. By the time of his death around 483 BC, the Buddha's teachings were spreading rapidly.

Buddhism is based on the teachings of the Buddha. A key aspect of Buddhism is the search for enlightenment, or the understanding of the true nature of reality. Buddhists seek to lead virtuous, moral lives, and attempt to purify their minds in order to reach nirvana, or a state of perfect peace.

Buddhism Today Some 350–400 million people in the world are Buddhists. Buddhists live on every continent, but the majority of the religion's followers are in Asia. Buddhism is a powerful religious, political, and cultural force in many parts of the world today.

Today, two major branches of Buddhism exist: Theraveda and Mahayana. Mahayana is the larger branch.

Summarize How did Buddhism develop?

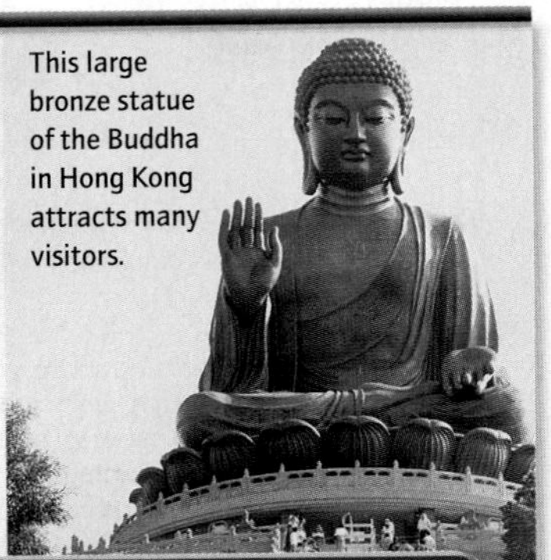

This large bronze statue of the Buddha in Hong Kong attracts many visitors.

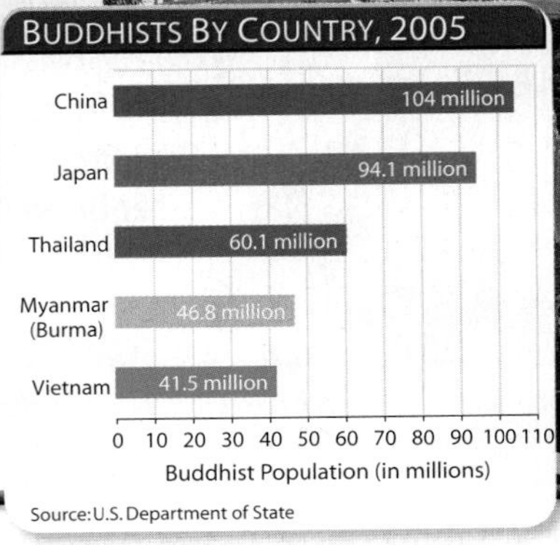

Changes in Southeast Asia

Some of the political and social forces that tore apart Vietnam were also at work elsewhere in the region. During the years after World War II, other nations in Southeast Asia struggled to build stable, independent countries.

Indonesia The nation now known as Indonesia consists of over 13,000 islands spread across the Indian and Pacific oceans. Before being taken over by Japan in World War II, Indonesia had been a Dutch colony known as the Dutch East Indies. When the Dutch tried to regain control after the war, they faced an independence movement led by **Sukarno**. After several years of fighting, Indonesia won its independence in 1949.

Sukarno became Indonesia's first president and eventually moved to take greater control of the government, replacing the elected parliament with his supporters. Although Sukarno initially tried to stay out of the Cold War, he later adopted policies that allied Indonesia with the Soviet Union and supported the growth of Indonesia's Communist party. At the same time, Sukarno's economic policies pushed the nation close to bankruptcy.

In 1965 a group of army officers and Communists tried to seize power in a coup d'état. The head of the army, General **Suharto**, fought back. In the struggle for power that followed the attempted coup, hundreds of thousands of Communists and alleged Communists were murdered. When the struggle ended, Suharto took control of the country.

Suharto ruled Indonesia for many years. His authoritarian regime was corrupt, but under his rule the Indonesian economy revived. By the 1980s, however, some Indonesians had started to turn against him, resenting his corruption and his use of power. When the Indonesian economy collapsed in 1997, protests and riots broke out; and Suharto stepped down the

---

Skills Focus: Making Written Presentations

At Level

Research Required

Reading Like a Historian Skill

Sukarno and Suharto

1. Explain to students that Sukarno and Suharto were two early leaders in Indonesia.
2. Refer students to the Faces of History biography of Ho Chi Minh in this section. Have students conduct independent research to create their own Faces of History biography of either Sukarno or Suharto. Biographies should include years lived, interesting facts about the person, and a question at the end.
3. Collect the biographies and redistribute them. Each student should have a biography written by another student. Tell students to read the biographies and answer the questions.

LS Verbal-Linguistic

Alternative Assessment Handbook, Rubrics 4: Biographies; 30: Research; and 42: Writing to Inform

Answers

World Religions *Siddharta Gautama became known as the Buddha and traveled across India teaching his ideas.*

following year. In subsequent years, a series of democratic governments worked to rebuild the nation's economy.

Today, Indonesia has the fourth-largest population in the world and is home to over 300 ethnic groups. Most Indonesians are Muslims, but a large Christian minority exists, as well as Hindus and Buddhists. At times, this diversity has led to conflict. On the island of Sulawesi, for example, thousands of Indonesians died in fighting between Christians and Muslims. In the early 2000s, Muslim radicals were linked to several terrorist attacks in Indonesia.

The nation was faced with a new challenge in 2004 when a devastating tsunami struck Indonesia and other parts of Southeast Asia, killing over 225,000 people and causing widespread destruction.

East Timor In 1975 Indonesia seized control of East Timor, a former Portuguese colony that had declared its independence just days before. For nearly three decades, East Timorese fought against the Indonesian invasion. Over 100,000 people died. In 2002 East Timor finally won its independence.

Cambodia Cambodia endured years of struggle after it won independence from France in 1953. In 1975 a Communist group called the **Khmer Rouge** (kuh-MER roozh) gained control of the country. Led by **Pol Pot**, the Khmer Rouge established a Communist government and renamed the country Democratic Kampuchea (cam-pooh-CHEE-uh).

The Khmer Rouge also began a radical program to rebuild Cambodian society. The goal was to create a country in which nearly everyone would work as a simple peasant. The Khmer Rouge believed that in order to achieve this goal, all the influences of urban life and modern civilization had to be destroyed.

The Khmer Rouge set about their task with tremendous brutality. All opposition—real or imagined—was destroyed. Anyone who showed any sign of having been educated was killed, and many others were worked or starved to death. At least 1.5 million Cambodians died—out of a population of 7 million.

Growing conflict between the Khmer Rouge and Vietnam soon turned into war. Vietnam invaded Cambodia, forcing Pol Pot from power in 1979. Peace did not come quickly, however, as Pol Pot led Khmer Rouge guerrillas in a civil war that raged in Cambodia throughout the 1980s. In 1993 the United Nations helped organize an election, and today Cambodia is a constitutional monarchy with a democratically elected parliament. The nation is slowly rebuilding itself after many years of war.

THE IMPACT TODAY

In 2006 Cambodia approved the selection of 30 judges to preside over genocide trials for surviving Khmer Rouge leaders.

Myanmar Burma, which is now known as Myanmar, won independence from Great Britain in 1948. The new nation faced many difficulties, including a weak central government and severe ethnic tensions. A military dictatorship seized power in the 1960s, and the military still controls Myanmar today. An opponent of the government, **Aung San Suu Kyi** (AWNG SAHN SOO CHEE), won the Nobel Peace Prize in 1991 for her efforts to promote democracy in Myanmar. Yet the government has held her in prison or under house arrest for much of the time since the late 1980s.

READING CHECK **Make Generalizations** How have nations in Southeast Asia changed?

SECTION 2 ASSESSMENT

go.hrw.com
Online Quiz
Keyword: SHL ASA HP

Reviewing Key Terms and People

1. **a. Identify** Who were the **Vietminh** and **Ho Chi Minh**?
   b. Contrast How did colonies in Southeast Asia achieve independence in different ways?
2. **a. Define** Define the following terms: **domino theory**, **Vietcong**
   b. Analyze How did the Tet Offensive affect the Vietnam War?
   c. Evaluate How do you think U.S. belief in the domino theory affected American involvement in the Vietnam War?
3. **a. Recall** What did the **Khmer Rouge** do in Cambodia?
   b. Summarize Summarize the events in Indonesia after World War II.

Critical Thinking

4. **Compare and Contrast** Use your notes and a graphic organizer like the one below to answer the following questions: In what ways were postwar events in Vietnam similar to events in other nations in Southeast Asia? How were they different?

Similarities	Differences

FOCUS ON WRITING

5. **Narration** Write a one-paragraph encyclopedia entry on the life of Ho Chi Minh. Include the main events of his life in chronological order.

Review & Assess

Close

Review with students the changes in Southeast Asia in the postwar years, the effects of the Vietnam War, and the recent changes in Southeast Asia.

Review

go.hrw.com **Online Quiz**, Section 2

Assess

SE **Section 2 Assessment**

Progress Assessment: Section 2 Quiz

Alternative Assessment Handbook

Reteach/Intervene

Interactive Reader and Study Guide, Section 2

Interactive Skills Tutor CD-ROM

Answers

Reading Check *Many of its natioons have gained independence from colonial rule, but have struggled to build stable, independent governments.*

Section 2 Assessment Answers

1. a. Vietminh—guerrilla group that fought for Vietnamese independence; Ho Chi Minh—Communist leader of the Vietminh
   b. Some granted independence; others struggled for independence.
2. a. domino theory: the belief that if Vietnam fell to communism, other Southeast Asian countries would quickly follow; Vietcong: Vietnamese Communists
   b. heavy blow to American forces proved victory was not close at hand, and weakened public's support for the war.
   c. possible answer—Without this belief, the United States might never have become involved in the Vietnam War.
3. a. began radical program to rebuild Cambodian society; killed 1.5 million people suspected of opposition
   b. won independence; Sukarno adopted Communist policies; General Suharto fought back against coup; Suharto took control of government, stepped down in 1997; democratic governments worked to rebuild economy
4. all endured years of struggle; Vietminh fought for independence; North became Communist; South backed by United States; after Vietnam War North takes control of Vietnam; Other Countries—Khmer Rouge begins radical program, kills 1.5 million in Cambodia; Indonesia seizes East Timor in 1975, and East Timor finally wins independence in 2002; military dicatorship in Myanmar
5. Student entries should include details and events from the life of Ho Chi Minh.

Preteach

Getting Started

Use the **Interactive Reader and Study Guide** to familiarize students with the section content.

Interactive Reader and Study Guide, Section 3

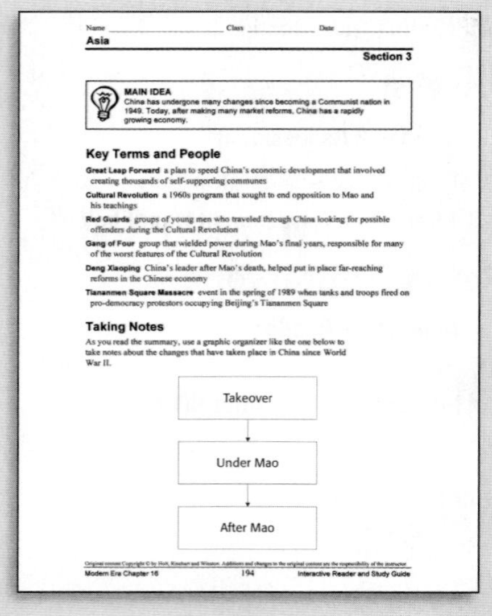

Name ______ Class ______ Date ______

Asia

Section 3

MAIN IDEA
China has undergone many changes since becoming a Communist nation in 1949. Today, after making many market reforms, China has a rapidly growing economy.

Key Terms and People

Great Leap Forward a plan to speed China's economic development that involved creating thousands of self-supporting communes

Cultural Revolution a 1960s program that sought to end opposition to Mao and his teachings

Red Guards groups of young men who traveled through China looking for possible offenders during the Cultural Revolution

Gang of Four group that wielded power during Mao's final years, responsible for many of the worst features of the Cultural Revolution

Deng Xiaoping China's leader after Mao's death, helped put in place far-reaching reforms in the Chinese economy

Tiananmen Square Massacre event in the spring of 1989 when tanks and troops fired on pro-democracy protestors occupying Beijing's Tiananmen Square

Taking Notes

As you read the summary, use a graphic organizer like the one below to take notes about the changes that have taken place in China since World War II.

Takeover → Under Mao → After Mao

Modern Era Chapter 16 194 Interactive Reader and Study Guide

Academic Vocabulary

Review with students the high-use academic terms in this section.

ideology a system of ideas, often political (p. 523)

initiate to begin (p. 524)

CRF: Vocabulary Builder: Section 3

Taking Notes

Takeover—civil war resumed between nationalist Guomindang and Chinese Communists; China became Communist in 1949; Under Mao—many so-called opponents killed or sent to labor camps; Great Leap Forward; Cultural Revolution; After Mao—reforms began, Gang of Four imprisoned, Deng Xiaoping made market reforms known as the Four Modernizations; protests lead to Tiananmen Square Massacre in 1989; today China's economy is second largest in the world

go.hrw.com
Online Resources
KEYWORD: SHL ASA
ACTIVITY: Biography of an Asian Leader

SECTION 3 Communist China

Before You Read

Main Idea

China has undergone many changes since becoming a Communist nation in 1949. Today, after making many market reforms, China has a rapidly growing economy.

Reading Focus

1. How did the Communists take over China?
2. What were the main events that took place in China under Mao's leadership?
3. How did China change in the years after Mao's death?

Key Terms and People

Great Leap Forward
Cultural Revolution
Red Guards
Gang of Four
Deng Xiaoping
Tiananmen Square Massacre

TAKING NOTES Take notes about the changes that have taken place in China since World War II.

Takeover → Under Mao → After Mao

A LITTLE RED BOOK

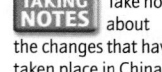

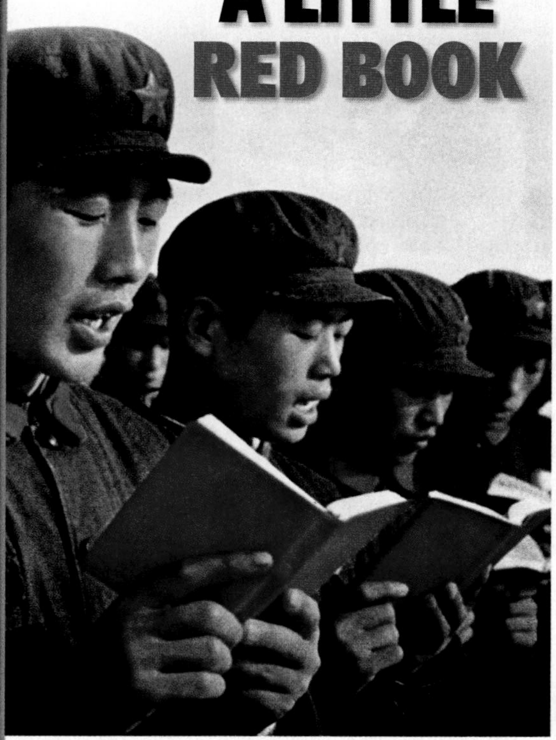

▲ **Chinese soldiers recite passages from Mao's writings.**

THE INSIDE STORY ***Did everyone in China have a little red book?*** In 1960s-era Communist China, the color red symbolized the Communist revolution that had swept over the nation two decades earlier. Red was everywhere in China—on posters, banners, and flags—but it may have been most visible on the pocket-sized red books that nearly all Chinese people carried with them. This so-called "Little Red Book," or *Quotations From Chairman Mao*, was a collection of Mao Zedong's writings and political ideas. Originally published to shape Chinese soldiers' political beliefs, by the late 1960s the book was enormously popular among the public.

The adoration of Mao's words extended to Mao himself. In newspapers, photographs, and propaganda posters, the Chinese government actively encouraged virtual worship of Mao, showing him as a larger-than-life, godlike figure. It was expected that a Chinese home would have an official portrait or bust of Mao displayed in a prominent location. In fact, the failure to possess a book of Mao's writings or a portrait of the leader was often interpreted as a sign that a person was anti-Mao or anti-Communist and could lead to punishment. In one case, a man was jailed for seven years for accidentally breaking a bust of Mao. Having a "Little Red Book," then, was a way to demonstrate loyalty to the Communist leader—and to provide protection against being accused of disloyalty. ■

Communists Take Over China

During World War II the Chinese Communists and the nationalist Guomindang had agreed to put aside their differences in order to fight the Japanese invaders. Once the war ended with Japan's defeat, however, the civil war resumed.

Teach the Main Idea

At Level

Communist China

Materials: 3 sheets of chart paper

1. **Teach** Ask students the Reading Focus questions to teach this section.
2. **Apply** Organize students into three groups. Assign one of the following topics to each group: Communists Take Over China, China under Mao, and China After Mao. Distribute chart paper and have groups design and assemble collages made up of notes and drawings representing the information presented in their assigned part of this section.
3. **Review** Allow time for groups to share their work with the class.
4. **Practice/Homework** Have each student write a short paragraph about China from 1934 to the present. **LS Visual-Spatial, Verbal-Linguistic**

Alternative Assessment Handbook, Rubrics 1: Acquiring Information; 14: Group Activity; and 8: Collages

Although the Guomindang forces outnumbered Mao's Communists, the Communists had wide support among China's peasants, who made up the vast majority of the nation's population. Rural Chinese peasants had long been oppressed by brutal landlords and high taxes, as well as by the policies of Jiang Jieshi's corrupt government. Because the Communists promised to take land from the landlords and distribute it to the peasants, public support for the Communists was widespread.

By 1949 the Communists had driven the Guomindang almost entirely from China, with Guomindang control limited to a few small areas on the mainland and several islands, including Taiwan. On October 1 Mao Zedong stood before a huge crowd in Beijing and announced the formation of the People's Republic of China.

China faced many difficulties, including a crippled economy and the lack of a functional government. Some countries that opposed communism, such as the United States, refused to recognize Mao, claiming that Jiang's government on Taiwan was China's true government. But Mao was in power to stay.

READING CHECK **Summarize** Why did peasants support the Communist takeover of China?

FACES OF HISTORY

MAO Zedong
1893–1976

As a teenager, Mao Zedong was forced to work full-time on his family's farm. Rebelling against his parents, Mao left home to continue his education and by 1918 was working as a librarian's assistant at Beijing University, where he was first introduced to Marxist theory.

Mao joined the Chinese Communist Party in 1921 and soon after realized the potential power of China's rural peasants. Mao believed that, unlike the Bolshevik revolution in Russia, which depended on urban workers, China's hundreds of millions of peasants would be the revolutionaries. It was Mao's strategy of guerrilla warfare in rural China that would eventually lead to Communist victory.

Summarize How did Mao believe that China differed from Russia?

China under Mao

Having defeated the Guomindang, Mao set about building a Communist China. His first concern was rebuilding a country that had been torn apart by years of civil war.

Rebuilding China Communist ideology shaped the new government's efforts to change China's political and economic systems. The government discouraged the practice of religion and, as Communist leaders had promised peasants during the civil war, seized the property of rural landowners and redistributed it among the peasants. China soon put in place Soviet-style five-year plans for industrial development. The first plan, completed in 1957, succeeded in doubling China's small industrial output. Indeed, the early efforts to build the Chinese economy were remarkably successful at improving the economy and reducing rural poverty, and they had much public support. Mao's policies led to improvements in literacy rates and public health, and Chinese life expectancy increased sharply over the next few decades.

These improvements came at a cost, however. To consolidate Communist control over China, the government soon began to eliminate the so-called "enemies of the state" who had spoken out against the government's policies. Many thousands of Chinese—including public officials, business leaders, artists, and writers—were killed or sent to labor camps in the early years of Communist rule.

The Great Leap Forward The Soviet Union provided much financial support and other aid to China in its first years as a Communist nation. China modeled many of its new political, economic, and military policies on the Soviet system. During the 1950s, however, territorial disputes and differences in ideology slowly pushed China away from its Soviet ally. In a break from Soviet-style economic planning, in 1958 Mao announced a program, the **Great Leap Forward**, designed to increase China's industrial and agricultural output. The plan created thousands of communes, or collectively owned farms, of about 20,000 people each. Each commune was to produce food and to have its own small-scale industry.

The plan was a disaster. The small commune factories failed to produce the quantity or quality of goods that China needed, and a combination of poor weather and farmers' neglect led to sharp drops in agricultural production.

ACADEMIC VOCABULARY
ideology a system of ideas, often political

Direct Teach

Reading Focus

1 How did the Communists take over China? *The Guomindang and the Communists fought the Japanese invasion. Afterwards, with wide support from peasants, the Communists drove the Guomindang out of China.*

Communists Take Over China

Recall How did the United States feel about the People's Republic of China? *They refused to recognize it and claimed that Jiang's government was the true Chinese government.*

Rate What is your opinion of a leader who can raise an army of one million within a few years? *possible answer—He must have had great charisma and persuasive powers to do so.*

Reading Focus

2 What were the main events that took place in China under Mao's leadership? *the Great Leap Forward, the Cultural Revolution*

China under Mao

Explain Why did Mao institute the Great Leap Forward? *to increase China's agricultural and industrial output*

Make Inferences From your knowledge of Mao's ordered executions of hundreds of thousands, what sort of person do you think he was? *possible answer—He feared opposition, and may have been paranoid.*

Skills Focus: Recognizing Bias in Primary Sources

At Level

Prep Required

Reading Like a Historian Skill
Mao's Little Red Book

Materials: copies of various pages from *Quotations from Chairman Mao,* available in English on the Internet.

Background: Tell students that many Chinese citizens had a copy of *Quotations from Chairman Mao* during his rule. The "Little Red Book" was a guide to life as a loyal Communist.

1. Organize students into small groups. Distribute copies of several quotations to each group. Ask groups to discuss their assigned quotations, marking wording that reflects any sort of bias. Have students record the observations and opinions expressed by group members about each quotation.
2. Have groups share their results with the class.
3. As homework, have students write a paragraph summarizing Mao Zedong's ideas.

LS Interpersonal, Verbal-Linguistic

Alternative Assessment Handbook, Rubrics 14: Group Activity; and 16: Judging Information

Answers

Faces of History *Mao believed that, the peasants would be the revolutionaries.*

Reading Check *because the Communists promised them land*

Direct Teach

Reading Focus

China under Mao

Describe What were the early results of the Great Leap Forward? *Factories and farms failed to produce well and there was widespread famine.*

Explain What was the purpose of the Cultural Revolution? *Mao tried to regain some of the power and prestige he had lost under the Great Leap Forward.*

Identify Cause and Effect What caused China's complete isolation? *Mao's harsh treatment of his citizens and the failure of the Great Leap Forward led other nations, including the Soviet Union, to criticize him. Relations between the two countries broke down completely by the 1960s.*

CRF: A Red Guard Describes the Cultural Revolution

Biography

Qi Shu Fang (c.1943—) Qi Shu Fang is a significant contributor in the history of Chinese opera. She began her studies of opera in 1947 when she was only 4 years old. By the 1960s, she was performing nationally, but the Cultural Revolution (1966-1976) limited performances to only a few patriotic plays. At 22, she was among those selected to perform in one of them. Millions saw her play the part of a courageous peasant girl, Chang Bao, or "Constant Treasure." Later, political change reopened the traditional repertory, and she performed in other countries as well. In 1987 Qi Shu Fang immigrated to the United States, where she established her own Chinese opera troupe.

As a result, famine spread throughout rural China. Tens of millions of Chinese starved to death between 1959 and 1961.

The failure of the Great Leap Forward led to criticism of Mao by many people, including Soviet leaders. The Soviet criticism, and the withdrawal of Soviet industrial aid in 1960, helped widen the rift between the two Communist nations. By the early 1960s relations between the two countries had broken down completely. Communist China found itself virtually isolated in the world community.

ACADEMIC VOCABULARY
initiate to begin

The Cultural Revolution In the mid-1960s Mao tried to regain some of the power and prestige he had lost after the Great Leap Forward. He initiated a new movement called the **Cultural Revolution**, which sought to rid China of its old ways and create a society in which peasants and physical labor were the ideal. This campaign of social change meant eliminating intellectuals such as teachers, skilled workers, and artists, who Mao feared wanted to end communism and bring back China's old ways.

Mao shut down China's schools and encouraged militant high school and college students known as **Red Guards** to carry out the work of the Cultural Revolution by criticizing intellectuals and traditional values. But Mao soon lost control of the movement. The Red Guards traveled through China's cities and villages, looking for possible offenders and torturing or killing people they believed to be politically corrupt. They murdered hundreds of thousands of people. By the late 1960s China was on the verge of civil war before Mao managed to regain control and break up the Red Guards.

Although the Cultural Revolution reestablished Mao's dominance in China, it caused terrible destruction in Chinese society. In many areas, civil authority collapsed, while economic activity fell off sharply.

READING CHECK **Analyze** How did life in China change under Mao?

HISTORY CLOSE-UP

Tiananmen Square, 1989

More than 1 million pro-democracy protestors occupied Beijing's Tiananmen Square in the spring of 1989. At first, Chinese leaders tolerated the demonstration, but as the protest grew larger they decided to crack down. In the evening hours of June 3, the government sent tanks and troops into the square to crush the protestors, killing hundreds.

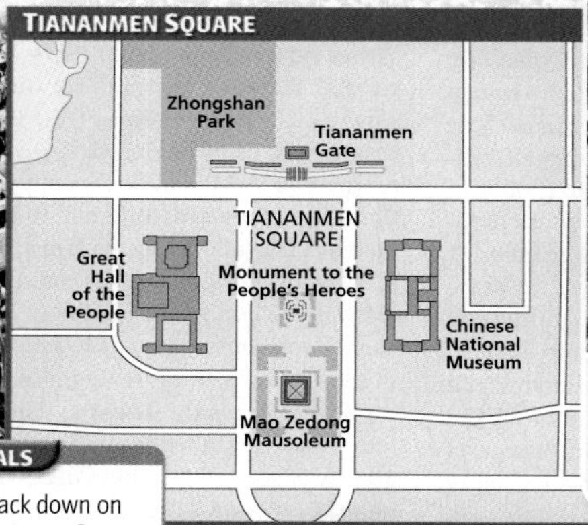

DAY 1

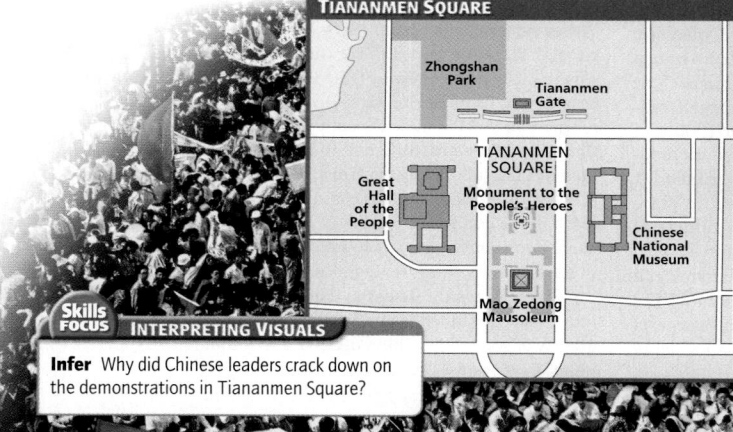

April 15 After the death of a reformist Chinese political leader, students gather in Tiananmen Square to call for democratic reform.

Skills Focus INTERPRETING VISUALS

Infer Why did Chinese leaders crack down on the demonstrations in Tiananmen Square?

Differentiating Instruction

Below Level

Struggling Readers; Learners Having Difficulty

1. Copy the chart for students to see, omitting the italicized words. Have students copy and fill in the chart alone, or in pairs.
2. When students have had adequate time to fill in their charts, allow them to compare and complete their work. Have students draw a political cartoon that relates to one of Mao's programs. **LS Verbal-Linguistic, Visual-Spatial**

Alternative Assessment Handbook, Rubrics 7: Charts; and 27: Political Cartoons

	Great Leap Forward	Cultural Revolution
Date	*1958*	*mid-1960s*
Goal	*to speed China's development*	*create a society where peasants and physical labor were the ideal*
Actions	*formed communes, set production goals*	*Red Guard tortured or killed suspected offenders*
Result	*famine, China's isolation*	*destruction in Chinese society*

Answers

History Close-Up *possible answer—The protest grew larger, and the Chinese government did not agree with its pro-democracy message.*

Reading Check *The failure of the Great Leap Forward and the isolation of China triggered the Cultural Revolution.*

China After Mao

Mao Zedong died in 1976. Though Mao was a revered figure in China, his death was followed by a retreat from many of his policies.

Reforms Begin China began to end its isolation from the rest of the world in the early 1970s. U.S. president Richard Nixon ended decades of U.S. hostility toward the nation by visiting China in 1972 and meeting with Mao, who by that time was in poor health.

During the last years of Mao's life, much of the power in China was wielded by a group of four people known as the **Gang of Four**. This group, which included Mao's wife, Jiang Qing (jee-AHNG ching), was responsible for many of the worst features of the Cultural Revolution. After Mao's death, more moderate leaders imprisoned the Gang of Four.

Deng Xiaoping (DUHNG SHOW-ping) eventually became China's leader and helped put in place far-reaching market reforms in the Chinese economy. Deng's reform plan was called the Four Modernizations after the four economic areas it sought to modernize: agriculture, industry, science and technology, and national defense. The plan gave businesses new freedom to make economic decisions.

Tiananmen Square Inspired by the movement toward economic freedom, many Chinese demanded more political freedom. In the spring of 1989, as democratic reforms were sweeping through Eastern Europe, more than 1 million pro-democracy protestors occupied Beijing's Tiananmen (tee-AN-uhn-men) Square.

China's leaders became increasingly impatient with the protests. After repeatedly asking the protestors to leave the square, they finally responded with force. Tanks and troops moved into the square in June 1989, killing many protestors in the **Tiananmen Square Massacre**. True freedom had not yet arrived in China.

China Today China's economy has grown rapidly as market reforms have continued.

READING SKILLS
Identifying Problems and Solutions How did Deng try to solve China's economic problems?

DAY 16

May 30 Near the official portrait of Mao Zedong, students build a large statue that comes to be known as the "Goddess of Democracy."

DAY 19

June 3 Chinese soldiers move into Tiananmen Square to force out the protestors. Hundreds of protestors are killed.

DAY 21

June 5 In this famous image from the events at Tiananmen Square, an unarmed man faces down a line of Chinese tanks.

Direct Teach

Reading Focus

3 How did China change in the years since Mao's death? *New reforms have dramatically improved the economy and the standard of living for the Chinese, and increased China's participation in the world economy.*

China After Mao

Recall When did Mao Zedong die? *1976*

Explain What happened to the Gang of Four after Mao's death? *They were arrested and imprisoned.*

Develop What are some possible reasons so many people were killed in Tiananmen Square? *possible answer—Frustration caused leaders to call for force, and the military did not issue a warning, or fire a few shots, but they responded with the full force of tanks and troops.*

CRF: Biography: Zhang Yimon

Teaching Tip

Remind students that Mao Zedong led a popular revolution to save his people from what many people felt was a corrupt regime. Guide a discussion about the positive and negative effects of his leadership.

Skills Focus: Comparing and Contrasting

At Level

Reading Skill

Mao Zedong and Deng Xiaoping

1. Copy the chart for all to see. Omit the italicized answers. Have students copy and complete the chart.
2. Guide a class discussion comparing and contrasting Mao's Great Leap Forward and Deng's Four Modernizations. Which plan succeeded and which plan failed? Why? **LS Verbal-Linguistic**

Alternative Assessment Handbook, Rubrics 7; Charts; and 9: Comparing and Contrasting

Great Leap Forward (Mao Zedong)	Four Modernizations (Deng Xiaoping)
20,000 communes, or collectively owned farms	*economic reforms in four areas: agriculture, industry, science and technology, and national defense*
resulted in famine, starvation of millions of Chinese people	*businesses had freedom to make economic decisions*
Soviet Union criticized Mao	*Chinese economy grew rapidly*

Answers

Reading Skills *made market reforms to modernize the economy*

Review & Assess

Close

Review with students how the Communists took control, Mao's leadership, and the changes in China since Mao's death.

Review

Online Quiz, Section 3

Assess

SE Section 3 Assessment

Progress Assessment: Section 3 Quiz

Alternative Assessment Handbook

Reteach/Intervene

Interactive Reader and Study Guide, Section 3

Interactive Skills Tutor CD-ROM

Answers

Primary Sources 1. *combining elements of a planned economy with elements of a market economy;* **2.** *"no alternative," "only road to prosperity"*

Reading Check *isolation lessened, more moderate leaders took power, new economic freedom led to call for political freedom, improved standard of living*

PRIMARY SOURCES

Economic Reforms in China

In 1985 Chinese leader Deng Xiaoping spoke about the economic reforms that China was undergoing.

> "There is no fundamental contradiction between socialism and a market economy . . . If we combine a planned economy with a market economy, we shall be in a better position to liberate the productive forces and speed up economic growth . . .
>
> "It is clear now that the right approach is to open to the outside world, combine a planned economy with a market economy and introduce structural reforms . . .
>
> "In short, the overriding task in China today is to throw ourselves heart and soul into the modernization drive. While giving play to the advantages inherent in socialism, we are also employing some capitalist methods—but only as methods of accelerating the growth of the productive forces . . . China has no alternative but to follow this road. It is the only road to prosperity."

Skills Focus READING LIKE A HISTORIAN

1. **Summarize** What economic changes was Deng advocating?
2. **Analyze Primary Sources** What words does Deng use to justify the economic reforms?

See **Skills Handbook**, p. H25

Today, China's economy is the second largest in the world, behind only the United States. As the economy has improved, so has the standard of living for many Chinese. Still, economic growth has not reached all of China's 1.3 billion people. To prevent further population growth from harming economic development, the Chinese government encourages families to have only one child.

China faces other challenges as its large population and rapidly expanding industries place high demands on the nation's resources and environment. The country has been forced to import enormous quantities of coal, iron ore, oil, and natural gas to meet its energy and resource needs, leading to shortages—and higher costs—of these resources on the global market. Furthermore, the rapid industrial expansion has led to widespread air and water pollution within China.

Human rights abuses are another concern for many critics of China. The Chinese government continues to limit free speech and religious freedoms, and it exercises strict control over the media. Political protestors can be jailed, and the nation's courts are accused of failing to provide fair trials. Critics increased their calls for reforms after Beijing was chosen to host the 2008 Olympic Games.

READING CHECK **Make Generalizations** How did China change in the years after Mao's death?

SECTION 3 ASSESSMENT

go.hrw.com
Online Quiz
Keyword: SHL ASA HP

Reviewing Key Terms and People

1. **a. Describe** What happened in China after the end of World War II?
   b. Explain Why did most Chinese peasants support the Communists?
2. **a. Identify** Summarize the following events: **Great Leap Forward, Cultural Revolution**
   b. Explain Why did the Cultural Revolution lead to such chaos and disorder in China?
   c. Evaluate Evaluate the successes and failures of Communist China under Mao Zedong.
3. **a. Recall** Summarize the challenges that China faces today.
   b. Contrast Contrast Chinese leaders' willingness to make economic reforms with their willingness to make democratic reforms.

Critical Thinking

4. **Identify Cause and Effect** Use your notes on the section and a graphic organizer like the one below to describe the effects of the events listed.

Mao Takes Power →	
Great Leap Forward →	
Cultural Revolution →	
Mao Dies →	

FOCUS ON SPEAKING

5. **Persuasion** Write a brief speech that a protestor might have given in Tiananmen Square in May 1989 about the need for democratic reform in China.

Section 3 Assessment Answers

1. **a.** Mao Communists drove the Guomindong out of China; people's Republic of China is formed; Mao is in power
   b. because the Communists promised to take land from landlords and give it to the peasants
2. **a.** Great Leap Forward—an economic plan that created thousands of communes and assigned food and industrial production quotas but resulted in famine; Cultural Revolution—a plan for Mao to regain some of his former power and prestige
   b. Civil authority collapsed, economic activity fell off sharply.
   c. possible answer—Mao had some early successes, but his later plans and brutality were a disaster for China.
3. **a.** economic growth has not reached all people; pollution; human rights abuses
   b. possible answer—Deng Xiaoping was willing to introduce some capitalist elements into the economy, but today, Chinese people still lack basic rights.
4. Mao Takes Power—a campaign to strengthen his control and transform the Chinese economy and culture; Great Leap Forward—factory and farm failures and famine led to the isolation of China from the rest of the world; Cultural Revolution—the killing of thousands, collapse of civil authority, fall off of economic activity; Mao Dies—retreat from many of his policies
5. Student speeches should point out that political freedoms should accompany economic freedoms.

SECTION 4

The Rise of Pacific Rim Economies

Before You Read

Main Idea

The nations of the Asian Pacific Rim underwent remarkable economic growth in the years after World War II, but significant challenges remain.

Reading Focus

1. How did Japan change during the postwar years?
2. How did the nations of the Pacific Rim change after World War II?
3. How did the Asian Tigers develop?

Key Terms and People

Ferdinand Marcos
Corazon Aquino
Kim Il Sung
Kim Jong Il
Asian Tigers

TAKING NOTES Take notes on the causes and effects of Asian economic growth.

Causes → Growth → Effects

AN EMPEROR SURRENDERS

◀ **Three weeping Japanese girls react to Emperor Hirohito's announcement that Japan had surrendered to end World War II.**

THE INSIDE STORY ***What happens after an emperor surrenders?*** To the Japanese people, Emperor Hirohito was more than an emperor. To them, he was a living god and the latest in a line of divine rulers that stretched back hundreds of years.

Japanese citizens had never heard Hirohito's voice—until August 14, 1945. Speaking over the radio following the devastating atomic bomb attacks on Hiroshima and Nagasaki, Hirohito informed his stunned subjects that World War II was over. "The hardships and sufferings to which our nation is to be subjected hereafter will be certainly great," he warned.

Indeed, much would change in Japan in the years after the war. Emperor Hirohito would remain on his throne, but he would lose his authority and his divine status as a living god. Japan's economy, government, and many of its basic institutions would be rebuilt under U.S. occupation and control, and Japanese society would undergo many changes.

Yet while the changes ahead, as Hirohito had predicted, would be difficult and painful, Japan's rapid recovery from the war would become one of history's great success stories. The nation had lost the war, but in the space of a few short years, Japan would become one of the world's leading economic powers. ■

Teach the Main Idea

At Level

The Rise of Pacific Rim Economies

Materials: 4 ½" x 12" construction paper in a variety of colors, tape

1. **Teach** Ask students the Reading Focus questions to teach this section.
2. **Apply** Organize students into three groups. Assign a heading from this section to each group: Postwar Japan, The Pacific Rim, and The Asian Tigers. Have groups record causes and effects for their assigned heading, neatly copy each pair onto a strip of construction paper, and tape each pair together.
3. **Review** Display and discuss the cause-and-effect chains.
4. **Practice/Homework** Have each student write a short paragraph about the economies of the Pacific Rim countries. **LS Verbal-Linguistic, Visual-Spatial**

Alternative Assessment Handbook, Rubrics 6: Cause and Effect; and 13: Graphic Organizers

Preteach

Getting Started

Use the **Interactive Reader and Study Guide** to familiarize students with the section content.

Interactive Reader and Study Guide, Section 4

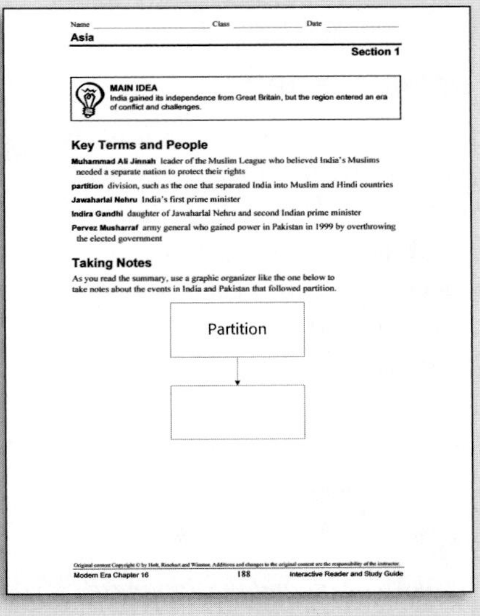

Name ______ Class ______ Date ______

Asia

Section 1

MAIN IDEA
India gained its independence from Great Britain, but the region entered an era of conflict and challenges.

Key Terms and People

Muhammad Ali Jinnah leader of the Muslim League who believed India's Muslims needed a separate nation to protect their rights
partition division, such as the one that separated India into Muslim and Hindi countries
Jawaharlal Nehru India's first prime minister
Indira Gandhi daughter of Jawaharlal Nehru and second Indian prime minister
Pervez Musharraf army general who gained power in Pakistan in 1999 by overthrowing the elected government

Taking Notes

As you read the summary, use a graphic organizer like the one below to take notes about the events in India and Pakistan that followed partition.

Partition → [ ]

Original content Copyright © by Holt, Rinehart and Winston. Additions and changes to the original content are the responsibility of the instructor.
Modern Era Chapter 16 188 Interactive Reader and Study Guide

CRF: Vocabulary Builder: Section 4

Taking Notes

Causes—economic and military aid, Japan provided supplies to U.S. and U.N. forces during Korean War; work ethic, skilled workforce, increased exports; Effects—population growth; Japan has become a major economic power, improved standard of living

Direct Teach

Reading Focus

1 How did Japan change during the postwar years? *Japan's citizens gained new civil rights, a democratic government was established, new political parties formed, the economy grew, the standard of living improved*

Postwar Japan

Identify Which American was given control of occupied Japan? *General Douglas MacArthur*

Recall How did the building of a democratic government begin? *a new constitution went into effect in 1947.*

CRF: Literature: *Hiroshima Notes*

Recent Scholarship

In *America and the Japanese Miracle: The Cold War Context of Japan's Postwar Economic Revival, 1950-1960*, Aaron Forsberg describes how the Cold War fears of the United States and its allies governed many aspects of foreign relations in Asia. The American government became deeply involved in the recovery of Japan after that country's surrender at the end of World War II. This unusually deep involvement influenced America's international relations for many years, which is outlined in Forsberg's book.

America and the Japanese Miracle: The Cold War Context of Japan's Postwar Economic Revival, 1950-1960 by Aaron Forsberg. The University of North Carolina Press, 2000.

Postwar Japan

Japan suffered terrible destruction during World War II. After the war, the nation needed to rebuild its government and economy.

American Occupation After World War II, U.S. troops occupied Japan, and American general Douglas MacArthur took control of the Allied efforts to rebuild the nation. The rebuilding process had three basic steps: demilitarizing Japan, building a democratic government, and establishing an economy that could support a peaceful and democratic Japan.

MacArthur's first job was to demilitarize Japan. He removed all wartime political, military, and business leaders from power. Many were tried as war criminals. MacArthur also dismantled the armed forces and shut down Japan's military industries.

The second step, building a democratic government, began with a new constitution for Japan, which went into effect in 1947. The new constitution gave far more power to the Japanese people than the previous constitution had, establishing a parliamentary democracy and giving all Japanese adults the right to vote for Japan's Diet, or parliament. The emperor was no longer a sacred being but was now simply a symbol of the state. The constitution placed great emphasis on the importance of human rights and greatly expanded Japanese citizens' civil rights, including the rights of freedom of speech, assembly, and religion. The constitution forbade Japan from building a military capable of attacking other countries.

THE IMPACT TODAY

Nationalist Japanese leaders have expressed a desire to revise the constitution to give the military more power.

The new constitution also guaranteed the right to organize political parties, which led to the formation of countless new parties, both small and large. The most important new party was the Liberal Democratic Party (LDP), a generally conservative party with a pro-U.S. foreign policy that dominated Japanese politics after the party's formation in 1955.

Reading like a Historian

Occupation of Japan

Analyzing Primary Sources After World War II, American troops occupied Japan under the command of General Douglas MacArthur. MacArthur's main tasks were to demilitarize Japan, to establish a new, democratic national government, and to create a successful economy. This document is an excerpt from the official orders given to MacArthur concerning the occupation of Japan.

As you read the selection, consider these factors:

- the point of view of the authors
- the words used to describe Japan, and what the choice of words suggests about Allied views of Japan

The ultimate objective of the United Nations [in] Japan is to foster conditions which will give the greatest possible assurance that Japan will not again become a menace to the peace and security of the world and will permit her eventual admission as a responsible and peaceful member of the family of nations . . .

By appropriate means you will make clear to all levels of the Japanese population the fact of their defeat. They must be made to realize that their suffering and defeat have been brought upon them by the lawless and irresponsible aggression of Japan, and that only when militarism has been eliminated . . . will Japan be admitted to the family of nations.

—Joint Chiefs of Staff Instructions to General Douglas MacArthur, 1945

Skills Focus READING LIKE A HISTORIAN

1. **Point of View** Who or what do the authors blame for the war?
2. **Words** What does the "family of nations" metaphor suggest about how the authors viewed Japan's role in the world? In this "family," who is the child and who is the parent?

See **Skills Handbook**, p. H25

Skill Focus: Analyzing Alternative Points of View

At Level

Reading Like a Historian Skill
Two Views of Occupation

1. Tell students that films of American life were shown to people in occupied Japan. Some had never seen a color movie or used electricity.
2. Have students choose the viewpoint of one of the following Japanese people: a peasant farmer, an industrial worker, an urban survivor of the Allied bombing, or a suburban housewife.
3. Have each student write a letter to the American head of the Occupation Forces Educational Services. Letters should be written from the assigned viewpoints, expressing their reaction to the educational films they have seen, and their needs during their nation's recovery.
4. Have volunteers read their letters to the class.

LS Verbal-Linguistic, Intrapersonal

Alternative Assessment Handbook, Rubrics 25: Personal Letters; 41: Writing to Express

Answers

Reading Like a Historian 1. *Japan;* 2. *as a threat; Japan is the child and the United Nations is the parent*

The third step, rebuilding the Japanese economy, led MacArthur to make many economic changes. For example, he sought to break up the large organizations known as zaibatsu that had dominated Japanese industry. He also established a land reform program that gave farmland to farmers who had previously rented their land.

Economic Recovery U.S. economic aid flowed freely, but perhaps the biggest boost to the Japanese economy came with the outbreak of the Korean War in 1950. During the conflict, Japan served as a key source of supplies for the U.S. and UN forces fighting in nearby Korea.

After the Korean War, Japan built its economy around foreign trade and the production of consumer goods. Japan constructed modern factories and quickly rebuilt its heavy industry, including steel and automobile manufacturing. The strong Japanese work ethic and good relations between management and labor contributed to the industrial growth, and exports rose quickly. In the 1970s Japan began to focus on electronics and computer technology and soon became a world leader in those areas.

Even compared to the postwar growth of most western democracies, Japan's success was stunning. The U.S. occupation of Japan ended in 1952; by 1968, Japan had the world's second-largest economy. Despite some problems in recent years, including a recession in the 1980s, Japan is still a major economic power.

Social Changes The postwar economic growth led to an improved standard of living for Japanese workers and brought many other social changes to Japan. The new urban industries attracted workers from agriculture and small businesses, and the population of Japan's cities grew rapidly. In the late 1800s only 15 percent of all Japanese lived in urban areas; by 1970, more than 80 percent did so.

Japanese culture and family life changed as well. In the postwar years, many Japanese young people adopted American customs, music, movies, and food. Gender roles changed as more women began attending high school and college and won new social and legal freedoms. At the same time, the importance of the extended family began to decline.

READING CHECK **Summarize** How did Japan change in the postwar years?

After World War II, the Japanese economy came to rely heavily on automobile production and electronics and computer technology.

The Pacific Rim

The Pacific Rim refers to the countries that border or are located in the Pacific Ocean. Like Japan, other nations in the Asian Pacific Rim worked to build their economies and support the growth of democracy after World War II.

The Philippines The Philippines, a group of islands in Southeast Asia, won independence from U.S. control in 1946. The nation established a democratic government and kept close ties to the United States. By the early 1970s, however, President **Ferdinand Marcos** had become an authoritarian dictator. Marcos imposed martial law, arrested his opponents, and stole millions of dollars from the nation.

As public opposition to Marcos increased in the early 1980s, one of his chief rivals, Benigno Aquino, was assassinated. This killing, which many thought Marcos had ordered, led to antigovernment riots across the Philippines. Facing international pressure, Marcos allowed elections in 1986. Voters elected **Corazon Aquino**, Aquino's widow, as the nation's new president.

Under Corazon Aquino and later leaders, the Philippines struggled to return to democracy, as well as to build the nation's economy. Although the economy began to improve in the 1990s, many Filipinos still live in poverty. Other challenges include groups of separatist Communist and Muslim rebels who have used guerrilla warfare and terrorist attacks in their fights to establish independent states.

Direct Teach

Reading Focus

Postwar Japan

Explain How did the attitude of Japanese people contribute to their own recovery? *Their work ethic contributed to strong economic performance.*

Contrast How did Japanese industry change from prewar to postwar? *The prewar economy had more light industry, but postwar efforts focused on rebuilding heavy industries.*

CRF: Biography: Soichiro Honda

CRF: Economics and History: Exports of East Asian Nations Since 1950

Reading Focus

2 How did the nations of the Pacific Rim change after World War II? *worked to build their economies and support the growth of democracy*

The Pacific Rim

Recall When did the Philippines gain independence from the United States? *1946*

Contrast How did the presidencies of Ferdinand Marcos and Corazon Aquino differ? *Marco was an authoritarian dictator, and Aquino struggled to return to democracy.*

Differentiating Instruction

Below Level

Special Education Students

Materials: 12" x 4" construction paper strips

1. Remind students that after the war, Americans and the Japanese worked to help Japan recover from the war's effects.
2. Review with students the information that follows the heading, Postwar Japan, starting on the previous page. Read aloud one paragraph at a time, asking volunteers to name specific aids to recovery. When volunteers call one out, give them paper strips on which to record their ideas in bold letters.
3. When you have reviewed all of Postwar Japan, ask students to arrange the "aids to recovery" strips for display.
4. As homework, have students write about what one example most helped the recovery of Japan. **LS Verbal-Linguistic, Visual-Spatial**

Alternative Assessment Handbook, Rubric 1: Acquiring Information

Answers

Reading Check *standard of living improved; economy grew; culture adopted some American elements; gender roles changed*

Direct Teach

Reading Focus

The Pacific Rim

Identify Who is Kim Jong Il and how is he related to Kim Il Sung? *the ruler of North Korea; Kim Jong Il is the son of Kim Il Sung*

Contrast How has the economy of North Korea differed from the economy of South Korea? *The Communist North Korean economy has deteriorated; the South Korean economy has improved, with U.S. economic aid.*

Info to Know

World's Tallest Buildings As of 2006, 47 of the 100 tallest buildings in the world are located in Asia. Eight of the top ten are in Asian countries. Though the Sears Tower and the Empire State Building each have more stories, (110 and 102 respectively), the Taipei 101 rises 1,667 feet from ground level. Its base is topped by eight tiers of eight pagoda-like structures.

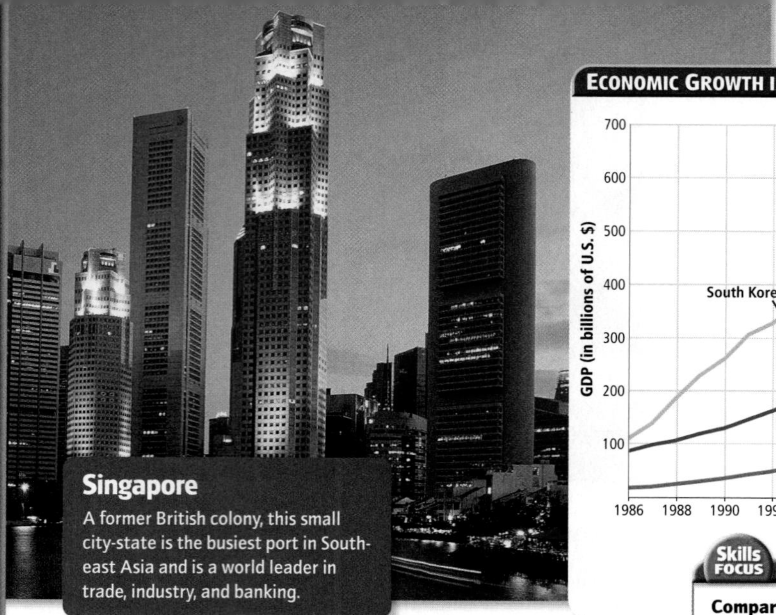

Singapore
A former British colony, this small city-state is the busiest port in Southeast Asia and is a world leader in trade, industry, and banking.

Economic Growth in Asia, 1986–2004

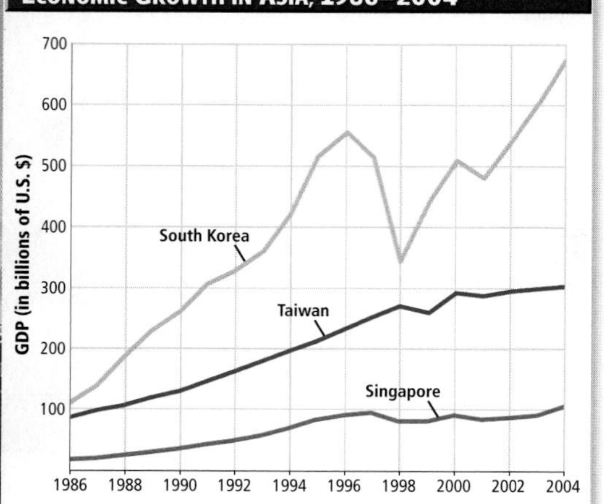

Skills Focus INTERPRETING GRAPHS

Compare and Contrast How did the economies of South Korea, Taiwan, and Singapore change between 1986 and 2004? Was this a time of constant economic growth for all three countries?

North Korea and South Korea Korea, on China's northeastern border, remained a divided nation after the end of the Korean War in 1953. In North Korea, Communist dictator **Kim Il Sung** formed a government based on the Soviet model, with the state controlling much of the economy and most spending devoted to heavy industry and the military. With Soviet and Chinese aid, North Korea made significant gains; but poverty and food shortages spread across the nation as foreign aid decreased.

When Kim Il Sung died in 1994, his son, **Kim Jong Il**, took power. Under Kim Jong Il's rule, the North Korean economy has continued to deteriorate. Despite its economic problems, the North has funded an expansion of its military programs. In 2006 North Korea tested a nuclear weapon for the first time.

South Korea followed a different path. With the help of heavy U.S. economic aid, Syngman Rhee and other leaders built up the nation's industries, emphasizing foreign trade and the production of consumer goods. Despite much economic success, South Koreans had little freedom or political stability, and repeated uprisings and military coups replaced one authoritarian government with another. Reform finally began in the late 1980s with the adoption of a more democratic constitution. South Korea has tried to improve its relationship with the North in recent years, but North Korea's possession and testing of nuclear weapons has led to more tension in the region.

Taiwan The Guomindang nationalists settled on the island of Taiwan after they were driven from mainland China by the Communists in 1949. With economic and military aid from the United States, Taiwan was able to build a successful economy based on international trade and the production of consumer goods. The Guomindang ruled Taiwan under martial law until the 1980s, when they ended martial law and allowed other political parties to form. This movement toward democracy continued in later years. Today, China views Taiwan as an integral part of China and insists that the two areas will eventually be reunited. Taiwan, however, resists this pressure from China.

READING CHECK **Summarize** How did most of the Pacific Rim nations move toward democracy?

Differentiating Instruction

Above Level

Advanced Learners/Gifted and Talented

Research Required

1. Organize students into small groups. Tell students that the U.S. Census bureau keeps extensive records about trade.
2. Have each group conduct online research to determine which Asian nations have been top trading partners with the United States over the last year. Remind students to record information for imports as well as exports.
3. Next, have groups discuss their data, whether or not is it is complete, what precisely it represents, and what they can conclude from it. Have each group record its conclusions.
4. Allow class time for groups to share their discoveries with the class. LS **Interpersonal, Logical-Mathematical**

Alternative Assessment Handbook, Rubrics 12: Drawing Conclusions; 14: Group Activity; and 30: Research

Answers

Interpreting Graphs *GDP increased; No, South Korea saw a sharp decline in GDP in 1998, but continued to grow after that.*

Reading Check *with U.S. economic aid*

The Asian Tigers

While Japan was building one of the world's strongest economies in the years after World War II, other Asian nations were also making great economic gains. Because of their economic success, South Korea, Hong Kong, Taiwan, and Singapore became known as the **Asian Tigers**.

Spectacular Growth The Asian Pacific Rim entered the 1960s as a largely poor and underdeveloped region. Over the next few decades, however, the Asian Tiger economies performed spectacularly, with average growth far higher than that of similar economies in Latin America or Africa.

To achieve these results, these countries followed a pattern similar to the one used by postwar Japan. For example, they generally provided ample education and training for their citizens, which helped produce the skilled workforce necessary for industrial expansion. The nations also received large amounts of economic aid from the United States during the early stages of the Cold War and further benefited from their access to the major shipping routes of the Pacific Ocean.

As in Japan, the Asian Tigers focused on growth through exports of consumer goods, primarily to the United States. Low costs for labor and production, as well as a loyal, dedicated workforce, allowed them to make low-cost products that could sell in the United States.

An Economic Crisis The economies of Japan and the Asian Tigers suffered a shock when a severe financial crisis hit the region in 1997. The crisis was in many ways a result of the region's great success. The decades of superior performance had led many foreign companies to invest heavily in the region's economies, and a lack of government regulation allowed Asian Tiger banks to borrow far more money than they needed.

The crisis began when banks began to fail in Thailand. The financial panic quickly spread through the region: foreign investors sold their holdings, stock and real estate prices collapsed, currencies lost value, and the region was overwhelmed by debts that it could not pay. The collapse undid years of progress.

An Asian Century Over the following decade, the region began to recover from the economic disaster, and nations like Indonesia, Malaysia, Thailand, and the Philippines began to emerge as economic powers. The great success of many Asian economies had many observers celebrating a so-called Asian miracle. Some predicted that the 2000s would be an "Asian century" in which Asia would surpass Europe and North America as the dominant economic region in the world.

READING CHECK **Find the Main Idea** How did the Asian Tigers follow Japan's model of economic growth?

READING SKILLS

Identifying Problems and Solutions What problem did the Asian Tigers face in 1997?

SECTION 4 ASSESSMENT

go.hrw.com
Online Quiz
Keyword: SHL ASA HP

Reviewing Key Terms and People

1. **a. Recall** What role did the United States play in postwar Japan?
   b. Summarize Why did Japan make such an impressive economic recovery after World War II?
   c. Make Judgments In your opinion, did Japan's government, economy, or society change the most in the years after World War II? Why do you think so?
2. **a. Recall** Summarize the political changes in the Philippines after the nation won its independence.
   b. Compare and Contrast Compare and contrast the development of North Korea and South Korea after the Korean War.
3. **a. Identify** What are the **Asian Tigers**?
   b. Make Generalizations Describe the basic features of the Asian Tigers and their approach to economic growth.

Critical Thinking

4. **Compare** Use your notes on the section and a graphic organizer like the one below to compare economic changes in Japan and the Asian Tigers.

Japan → Asian Tigers

FOCUS ON WRITING

5. **Exposition** Write a brief paragraph that explains how and why Japan changed in the years after World War II. Be sure to mention changes in Japan's government, economy, and society. Use details from the section to support your conclusions.

Direct Teach

Reading Focus

3. How did the Asian Tigers develop? *They provided their citizens with education and training, took advantage of economic aid from the United States, and focused on producing goods for export.*

The Asian Tigers

Identify Which Asian countries are known as Asian Tigers? Why? *South Korea, Hong Kong, Taiwan, and Singapore; because they made great economic gains in the years after World War II*

Identify Cause and Effect What led to the financial crisis of 1997? *Foreign companies invested heavily in Asian Tiger economies, and lack of government regulations led to problems, so banks began to fail.*

Review & Assess

Close

Review the effects of changes made in Japan following World War II, and the reasons behind economic growth in the Pacific Rim.

Review

Online Quiz, Section 4

Assess

SE Section 4 Assessment

Progress Assessment: Section 4 Quiz

Alternative Assessment Handbook

Reteach/Intervene

Interactive Reader and Study Guide, Section 4

Interactive Skills Tutor CD-ROM

Section 4 Assessment Answers

1. **a.** occupied Japan; provided economic aid
   b. Japan focused rebuilding efforts on heavy industry and exports rose. The people's work ethic also contributed.
   c. possible answer—society, because it adopted parts of American culture
2. **a.** first was an authoritarian dictatorship, then became more democratic
   b. North Korea's economy declined, while South Korea's improved dramatically.
3. **a.** Pacific Rim nations who experienced great economic gains after World War II
   b. provided education and training to create a skilled workforce; received U.S. economic aid; focused on growth through exports
4. Changes—economic aid, work ethic, education and training to create skilled workforce, increased exports
5. Student paragraphs should describe the American occupation, as well as Japan's economic recovery and social changes, using details from the section.

Answers

Reading Skills *severe financial crisis*

Reading Check *provided education and training for workers; focused on exports*

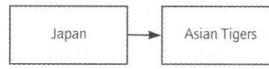

Document-Based Investigation

The Cultural Revolution

Info to Know

Four Goals In his last decade of leadership, Chairman Mao worried that his country would develop problems similar to those in the Soviet Union. He also wanted to renew the revolutionary spirit of his people. He set four goals for the Cultural Revolution: to replace his designated successors with leaders more faithful to his current thinking; to rectify the Chinese Communist Party; to provide China's youths with a revolutionary experience; and to achieve some specific policy changes to make the educational, health care, and cultural systems less elitist.

CHAPTER 16

Document-Based Investigation

The Cultural Revolution

Historical Context The documents below provide information about China's Cultural Revolution, the movement during the 1960s that sought to rid China of its old ways and create a society in which peasants and physical labor were the ideal.

Task Examine the selections and answer the questions that follow. After you have studied the documents, you will be asked to write an essay about the Cultural Revolution. You will need to use evidence from these selections and from the chapter to support the position you take in your essay.

DOCUMENT 1

Mao and the Army

The poster at right was created during 1969, at the height of the Cultural Revolution. It shows Mao watching over a group of Chinese soldiers, most of whom are holding a copy of the so-called "Little Red Book"—a collection of Mao's writings and political ideas. The Chinese characters at the bottom of the poster translate as "The Chinese People's Liberation Army is the great school of Mao Zedong thought."

中国人民解放军是毛泽东思想大学校

The Chinese People's Liberation Army is the Great School of Mao Zedong Thought

DOCUMENT 2

The Song of Ox-Ghosts and Snake-Demons

This song was composed by a Chinese student and quickly spread throughout the country during the Cultural Revolution. The Red Guards punished certain teachers in part by forcing the teachers to sing this song several times a day. If the singing was unsatisfactory, the teachers would be beaten or otherwise punished.

I am an ox-ghost and snake-demon.
I am an ox-ghost and snake-demon.
I am guilty. I am guilty.
I committed crimes against the people,
So the people take me as the object of the dictatorship.
I have to lower my head and admit to my guilt.
I must be obedient. I am not allowed to speak or act incorrectly.
If I speak or act incorrectly,
May you beat me and smash me,
Beat me and smash me.

Skills Focus: Analyzing Visuals

At Level

Reading Like a Historian Skill
Analyzing Posters

1. Remind students that posters have long communicated ideas to the masses. In China, they were particularly effective in reaching uneducated peasants who could not read. Tell students they will conduct research and analyze a specific poster from the Cultural Revolution.
2. Organize students into small groups. Have each group conduct online research to locate Chinese propaganda posters online. Have students select one poster and print it out.
3. Write the following questions for students to see and have students answer them on their own papers: Do any objects shown symbolize something? What message do you think the poster is trying to convey?
4. Have students write a short paragraph about the objectives of propaganda posters.
   LS Verbal-Linguistic, Interpersonal

Alternative Assessment Handbook, Rubrics 14: Group Activity; and 30: Research

DOCUMENT 3

Violence Against Teachers

This excerpt from a 1996 paper written by historian Youqin Wang describes the violence against teachers that was common during the Cultural Revolution.

> In the afternoon of August 5, 1966, some tenth grade students at the Girls Middle School attached to Beijing Teachers University started [beating] . . . a group comprised of three vice principals and two deans . . . Many students came to join them. The students . . . forced them to kneel on the ground, hit them with nail-spiked clubs, scalded them with boiling water, and so on. After three hours of torture, the first vice principal, Bian Zhongyun, lost consciousness and was put into a garbage cart. Two hours later she was sent to the hospital across the street. There, she was later found to have been dead for some time . . .
>
> In most cases, beatings were a collective activity, conducted not by single students but by a group of Red Guards. A group of Red Guards acted together, inciting each other and encouraging hostilities. Sometimes, a beating happened in front of hundreds of people . . . Bian Zhongyun, the first victim of the violence of 1966, died after being beaten by many students. During the several hours of torture, no one at this school of more than 1,600 students tried to dissuade the beaters from these inhuman actions . . . There was no sense of guilt, but rather an excited, giddy atmosphere.

DOCUMENT 4

The Cultural Revolution's Goals

The document below is from a June 7, 1966, editorial in the *People's Liberation Army Daily*, the official newspaper of the Chinese military.

> The current great socialist cultural revolution is a great revolution to sweep away all monsters and a great revolution that remoulds the ideology of people and touches their souls. What weapon should be used to sweep away all monsters? What ideology should be applied to arm people's minds and remould their souls? The most powerful ideological weapon, the only one, is the great Mao Tse-tung's thought . . .
>
> In this great, stormy cultural revolution, the masses of workers, peasants and soldiers are playing the role of the main force—this is the result of their efforts in creatively studying and applying Mao Tse-tung's thought and arming their ideology with it . . .
>
> Chairman Mao is the radiant sun lighting our minds. Mao Tse-tung's thought is our lifeline. Those who oppose Mao Tse-tung's thought, no matter when they do so and what kind of "authorities" they are, will be denounced by the entire Party and the whole nation.

Skills Focus: READING LIKE A HISTORIAN

DOCUMENT 1

a. Describe How is Mao depicted in this poster?

b. Infer According to this poster, what is the military's role during the Cultural Revolution?

DOCUMENT 2

a. Recall What are singers of this song allegedly guilty of?

b. Explain Why did Red Guards believe that the singers were guilty of these actions?

DOCUMENT 3

a. Identify Main Ideas What does the author of this document say that Red Guards did to teachers?

b. Compare and Contrast How does this description of the Cultural Revolution differ from that shown in Document 1?

DOCUMENT 4

a. Identify What are the goals of the Cultural Revolution?

b. Interpret How will the "weapon" described here help win the Revolution?

DOCUMENT-BASED ESSAY QUESTION

How did the reality of the Cultural Revolution differ from the government's claims about the Revolution? Using the documents above and information from the chapter, form a thesis that explains your position. Then write a short essay to support your position.

See **Skills Handbook**, pp. H25, H26, H33

Differentiating Instruction

At Level

Learners Having Difficulty

Materials: 12" x 18" construction paper, colored markers

1. Tell students they are members of the Red Guards who want to spread Mao's ideology. Remind students that at the outset, these young people were enthusiastic, not destructive.
2. Have students refer to information in this chapter to choose an idea to express in their poster. Student work should show Chinese people participating in an activity that reflects the ideals of the Cultural Revolution. A brief slogan should also be added.
3. Allow adequate time for students to plan their posters. They may need homework time to complete their work.
4. Display the posters and guide a class discussion about the ideals of Mao Zedong's followers. **LS Visual-Spatial**

Alternative Assessment Handbook, Rubrics 28: Posters; and 34: Slogans and Banners

Document-Based Investigation

Info to Know

Four Rights Mao's ideological "Little Red Book" *(Quotations from Chairman Mao)* included four ideas that were so important that they eventually became part of the state constitution. These rights were: "speaking out freely, airing views fully, holding great debates, and writing big-character posters." Many Chinese youths enthusiastically followed Mao's guidelines. As the army and party authorities were told not to suppress the Red Guards, their actions finally led to widespread disorder in the nation.

Answers

Reading Like a Historian

Document 1 a. *he is depicted as large, watchful, content;* **b.** *to further Mao's ideas;* **Document 2 a.** *speaking and acting incorrectly, which is considered a crime against the people;* **b.** *possible answer—They assumed the words were an admission of guilt.* **Document 3 a.** *The Red Guards beat groups of teachers.* **b.** *This description claims that the Red Guards were ruthless and lacked guilt, whereas in Document 1 the Red Guards simply look happy;* **Document 4 a.** *to "sweep away" thoughts of the past and old ideologies;* **b.** *possible answer—Mao Zedong's teachings will help rid China of past ways of thinking.* **Essay** *Student essays should point out that although the Chinese government claimed that the Cultural Revolution was a glorious thing, in reality, the revolution was often brutally violent. Essays should support this position with details from the documents and from Section 3 of this chapter.*

CHAPTER 16

Chapter Review

QUICK FACTS

VISUAL STUDY GUIDE

Independence in Asia

- The postwar years saw many struggles for independence in Asia. Some were peaceful, but others were violent conflicts.
- The Philippines gains independence from the United States in 1946.
- India and Pakistan gain independence from Great Britain after the 1947 partition of India.
- Burma (Myanmar) gains independence from Great Britain in 1948.
- Indonesia wins independence from the Netherlands in 1949 after years of fighting.
- France is forced out of Indochina in the early 1950s, leading to independence for Cambodia, Laos, and Vietnam.
- Bangladesh wins independence after a civil war with Pakistan in 1971.
- East Timor wins independence from Indonesia in 2002.

Pacific Rim Economies

- Japan builds its postwar economy around foreign trade and the production of consumer goods, becoming one of the world's leading economies.
- Other Pacific Rim nations follow Japan's model to achieve great economic growth.
- An economic crisis in 1997 sets the region back, but economic growth continues today.
- Some predict that the 2000s will be a century dominated by Asian nations.

The Rise of Modern China

- Communists led by Mao Zedong defeat the nationalist Guomindang and take power in China in 1949.
- China's government puts in place Soviet-style five year plans for industrial development, successfully improving the economy and reducing rural poverty.
- Mao announces the Great Leap Forward, a plan designed to increase China's agricultural and industrial output. The plan fails, and tens of millions starve.
- Mao launches the Cultural Revolution to rid China of its old ways, eliminating intellectuals. Red Guards attack people they believe to be politically corrupt.
- After Mao's death, Deng Xiaoping puts in place market reforms in the Chinese economy. Troops attack pro-democracy protestors at Tiananmen Square.
- China's economy grows rapidly in recent years, but population growth, environmental problems, and human rights abuses remain areas of concern.

Review Key Terms and People

Identify the correct term or person from the chapter that best fits each of the following descriptions.

1. leader of the Vietminh in the Vietnam War
2. disastrous plan to increase China's industrial and agricultural output
3. authoritarian general who ruled Indonesia for many years
4. first prime minister of India
5. Chinese leader who put in place market reforms
6. group that used violence to destroy the influences of modern civilization in Cambodia
7. authoritarian dictator of the Philippines
8. division of India into two independent nations
9. Pacific Rim nations with great economic success
10. a system of ideas, often political
11. belief that communism would quickly spread to other countries

Answers

Visual Summary

Review and Inquiry Organize students into three groups. Assign each group one section from the Visual Study Guide. Have groups plan a set of political cartoons to express the main concepts taught in their assigned section. Distribute 8 ½" x 11" unlined paper and have students draw their ideas. Display cartoons grouped by the subjects South Asia, Southeast Asia, China, and Pacific Rim Economies.

Quick Facts Transparency: Visual Study Guide: Asia

Review Key Terms and People

1. Ho Chi Minh
2. Great Leap Forward
3. Suharto
4. Jawaharlal Nehru
5. Deng Xiaoping
6. Khmer Rouge
7. Ferdinand Marcos
8. partition
9. Asian Tigers
10. ideology
11. domino theory

Comprehension and Critical Thinking

12. **a.** After Gandhi was imprisoned, riots erupted throughout India, convincing the British that maintaining control of India was too costly.
b. Following independence from Great Britain, the main basis for partition was border issues.
c. possible answer—No, because the violence after partition created even more tension.

13. **a.** American leaders wanted to prevent the spread of communism.
b. Indonesia—ruled by military leader; Suharto stepped down in 1997 and subsequent democratic governments worked to rebuild economy; Cambodia—Khmer Rouge instituted brutal program to root out opposition, killing at least 1.5 million people; war with Vietnam; Both—were Communist, now are democratic
c. because they have struggled with political tensions and war; have not received aid

14. **a.** Great Leap Forward—Mao's 1958 plan to speed economic development; was a horrible disaster, resulting in famine, and the isolation of China; Cultural Revolution—Mao's plan to regain power and prestige
b. China saw a retreat from many of Mao's policies.
c. possible answer—Mao made some achievements in his early years. However, in carrying out his plans during his last years, he lost control and there was terrible destruction in China. The negative aspects of his rule outweigh the positive ones.

15. **a.** After Japan's defeat, U.S. forces occupied the country and MacArthur took control of the country. Japan's economy grew.
b. began as an authoritarian dictatorship but slowly became more democratic
c. Some nations of the Pacific Rim, known as Asian Tigers, have achieved great economic gains since World War II. Others have struggled with political problems that have harmed their economies.

History's Impact video program
Review the video to answer the closing question: What role did North and South Vietnam's location have on the domino theory?

Comprehension and Critical Thinking

SECTION 1 *(pp. 511–515)*

12. a. Recall How did India and Pakistan gain their independence?

b. Summarize Summarize the changes in India and Pakistan after partition.

c. Make Judgments Given the events that followed, do you believe Great Britain's decision to partition India was wise? Why or why not?

SECTION 2 *(pp. 516–521)*

13. a. Recall Why did the United States become involved in the Vietnam War?

b. Compare and Contrast Compare and contrast the political changes in Indonesia and Cambodia in the years after World War II.

c. Make Judgments Why do you think some countries in Southeast Asia had difficulty building stable, independent nations?

SECTION 3 *(pp. 522–526)*

14. a. Identify What were the Great Leap Forward and the Cultural Revolution?

b. Make Generalizations In what ways did China change after Mao Zedong's death?

c. Evaluate Do Mao's positive contributions to China's development outweigh the negative aspects of his years in power? Why or why not?

SECTION 4 *(pp. 527–531)*

15. a. Describe How did Japan's government and economy change after World War II?

b. Summarize Summarize the history of the Philippines after the nation gained its independence.

c. Evaluate Evaluate the economic successes and failures of Pacific Rim nations.

Reading Skills

Identifying Problems and Solutions *Read the passage below, which comes from Section 1 of this chapter. Then answer the question that follows.*

"The violence and increasing Indian nationalism helped convince the British that maintaining control of India was too costly. When the war ended, the British began making plans to leave India."

16. What problem did British leaders face in India? What was their solution to this problem?

Analyzing Primary Sources

Reading Like a Historian *The passage below is an excerpt from an editorial in a Chinese newspaper written during the Cultural Revolution.*

"Every sentence by Chairman Mao is the truth, and carries more weight than ten thousand ordinary sentences. As the Chinese people master Mao Tse-Tung's thought, China will be prosperous and ever-victorious."

–*People's Liberation Army Daily* Editorial, June 7, 1966

17. Explain How does the writer feel about Mao Zedong?

18. Draw Conclusions How did beliefs like that expressed in this document lead to violence during the Cultural Revolution?

Using the Internet

go.hrw.com
Practice Online
Keyword: SHL ASA

19. China and India are the world's two most populous countries, and both have an enormous—and growing—influence on the world economy. Using the keyword above, research how the Chinese and Indian economies have developed over the past several decades. Then write a report about these economies and their influence on the world. Include details about how the economies have developed and how government leaders are trying to shape the economies in the future.

WRITING FOR THE SAT

Think about the following issue:

The years after World War II saw independence movements spread across Asia. Many former colonies gained their independence—some peacefully, but others through armed conflict. After independence, some nations turned toward democracy, but others were led by authoritarian regimes or Communist governments.

20. Assignment: Why did some Asian nations become democratic while others were led by dictators or Communist governments? Write a short essay in which you develop a position on this issue. Support your point of view with reasoning and examples from your reading.

Answers

Reading Skills

16. violence and nationalism; left India

Analyzing Primary Sources

17. The writer greatly admires Mao.

18. possible answer—Such admiration for Mao Zedong led to violence against those who opposed him or were suspected of opposing him.

Using the Internet

19. Go to the HRW Web site and enter the keyword shown to access a rubric for this activity.

KEYWORD: SHL ASA

Writing for the SAT

20. Student responses should include a clear position statement and supporting details. Examples of former Asian colonies might include Cambodia and Indonesia, which eventually became democratic, and Vietnam, which became Communist.
A rubric for the activity is provided in **CRF:** Writing for the SAT.

HOLT
History's Impact
► **Video Program: Asia**
Refer to the Video Program Teacher's Guide for the answer to the closing question.

Review and Assessment Resources

Review and Reinforce

- **CRF:** Chapter Review
- **Quick Facts Transparency**: Visual Study Guide: Asia
- **Spanish Chapter Summaries Audio CD Program**
- OSP **Holt PuzzlePro**: Quiz Show for ExamView
- **Quiz Game CD-ROM**

Assess

- **PASS**: Chapter Test, Forms A and B
- **Alternative Assessment Handbook**
- OSP **ExamView Test Generator**, Chapter Test
- **Differentiated Instruction Modified Worksheets and Tests CD-ROM**: Chapter Test
- HOAP **Holt Online Assessment Program** (in the Premier Online Edition)

Reteach/Intervene

- **Interactive Reader and Study Guide**
- **Differentiated Instruction Teacher Management System**: Lesson Plans for Differentiated Instruction
- **Differentiated Instruction Modified Worksheets and Tests CD-ROM**: Chapter Test
- **Interactive Skills Tutor CD-ROM**

go.hrw.com
Online Resources
KEYWORD: SHL TEACHER

Chapter 17 Planning Guide

Africa and the Middle East

Chapter Overview	Reproducible Resources	Technology Resources
CHAPTER 17 **pp. 536–565** **Overview:** In this chapter, students will learn how many countries in Africa and the Middle East struggled to gain their independence after World War II, and the political, religious, and economic issues that followed.	**Differentiated Instruction Teacher Management System:*** • Pacing Guide • Lesson Plans for Differentiated Instruction **Interactive Reader and Study Guide:** Chapter Summary* **Chapter Resource File*** • Writing About History • Social Studies Skill • Chapter Review **World History Outline Maps**	**Live Ink© Online Reading Help** **Student Edition on Audio CD Program** **Differentiated Instruction Modified Worksheets and Tests CD-ROM** **World History Primary Source Library CD-ROM** **Power Presentations with Video CD-ROM** **History's Impact: World History Video Program (VHS/DVD):** Africa and the Middle East
Section 1: **African Nations Gain Independence** **The Main Idea:** After World War II, almost all countries in Africa gained independence from ruling European powers.	**Differentiated Instruction Teacher Management System:** Section 1 Lesson Plan* **Interactive Reader and Study Guide:** Section 1 Summary* **Chapter Resource File*** • Vocabulary Builder: Section 1 • Biography: Léopold Senghor • Primary Source: Independence in Kenya	**Daily Test Practice Transparency:** Section 1* **Map Transparency:** Africa and the Middle East, 1950* **Map Transparency:** Independence in Africa*
Section 2: **Post-Colonial Africa** **The Main Idea:** Newly independent African nations struggled with poverty, conflict, and ineffective governments. In recent years some countries sought better government by holding democratic elections.	**Differentiated Instruction Teacher Management System:** Section 2 Lesson Plan* **Interactive Reader and Study Guide:** Section 2 Summary* **Chapter Resource File*** • Vocabulary Builder: Section 2 • Biography: Nelson Mandela • Literature: *Things Fall Apart*	**Daily Test Practice Transparency:** Section 2* **Quick Facts Transparency:** Political Trends in Post-Colonial Africa* **Internet Activity:** Desmond Tutu
Section 3: **Nationalism in North Africa and the Middle East** **The Main Idea:** The rise of nationalism in North Africa and the Middle East led to independence for some countries and to conflicts with the West.	**Differentiated Instruction Teacher Management System:** Section 3 Lesson Plan* **Interactive Reader and Study Guide:** Section 3 Summary* **Chapter Resource File*** • Vocabulary Builder: Section 3 • Biography: Danièle Djamila Amrane-Minne	**Daily Test Practice Transparency:** Section 3* **Quick Facts Transparency:** Causes and Effects of the Suez Canal Crisis*
Section 4: **Conflicts in the Middle East** **The Main Idea:** Regional issues in the Middle East have led to conflicts between Israel and its neighbors and to conflicts in and between Iran and Iraq.	**Differentiated Instruction Teacher Management System:** Section 4 Lesson Plan* **Interactive Reader and Study Guide:** Section 4 Summary **Chapter Resource File*** • Vocabulary Builder: Section 4 • Biography: Hanan Ashrawi • History and Geography: Conflicts in the Persian Gulf	**Daily Test Practice Transparency:** Section 4* **Map Transparency:** Creation of Israel, 1947–2006*

go.hrw.com | Print Resource | Transparency
LS Learning Styles | Audio CD | CD-ROM
Video | SE Student Edition | TE Teacher's Edition
OSP One-Stop Planner CD-ROM
*also on One-Stop Planner CD-ROM

Review, Assessment, Intervention

- **Quick Facts Transparency:** Africa and the Middle East*
- **Progress Assessment Support System (PASS):** Chapter Test*
- **Differentiated Instruction Modified Worksheets and Tests CD-ROM:** Modified Chapter Test
- OSP **One-Stop Planner CD-ROM:** Exam View Test Generator (English/Spanish)
- HOAP **Holt Online Assessment Program (HOAP),** in the Holt Premier Online Student Edition

- **PASS:** Section 1 Quiz*
- **Online Quiz:** Section 1
- **Alternative Assessment Handbook**

- **PASS:** Section 2 Quiz*
- **Online Quiz:** Section 2
- **Alternative Assessment Handbook**

- **PASS:** Section 3 Quiz*
- **Online Quiz:** Section 3
- **Alternative Assessment Handbook**

- **PASS:** Section 4 Quiz*
- **Online Quiz:** Section 4
- **Alternative Assessment Handbook**

HOLT
History's Impact
World History Video Program (VHS/DVD)
Africa and the Middle East

Power Presentation with Video CD-ROM

Power Presentations with Video are visual presentations of each chapter's main ideas. Presentations can be customized by including Quick Facts charts, images from the text, and video clips.

Holt Online Learning

go.hrw.com Teacher Resources KEYWORD: SHL TEACHER

go.hrw.com Student Resources KEYWORD: SHL AFR

- Document-Based Questions
- Interactive Multimedia Activities
- Current Events
- Chapter-Based Internet Activities
- and more!

Holt Premier
Online Student Edition

Complete online support for interactivity, assessment, and reporting

- Interactive Maps and Notebook
- Homework Practice and Research Activities Online

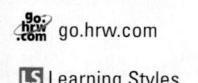

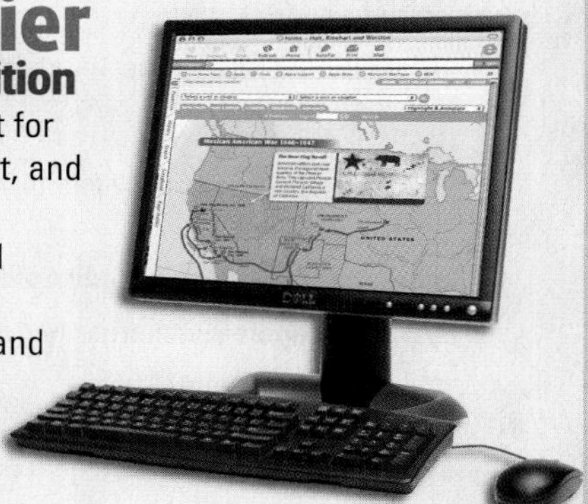

The Big Picture

Peter N. Stearns

Patterns in Africa Decolonization in sub-Saharan Africa began in the 1950s. In many cases it was relatively peaceful, but there were sharp conflicts in a few regions. The South African struggle against the apartheid system was both distinctive and significant. Most new nations in Africa began with democratic intentions, but quickly turned to authoritarian rule. Various internal ethnic conflicts occurred, and some trouble spots expanded in the 1990s and 2000s. Massive bloodshed resulted in several tragic cases. Many African regions also suffered from low levels of economic development and continued exploitation by industrial nations eager to acquire resources. In some regions environmental degradation, famine, and disease produced even greater hardship. By the 1990s a new democratic current gained strength, producing new regimes in several African countries. Cultural developments included a strong focus on adapting traditional arts, adjusting to the growing importance of Islam and Christianity, and the expansion of urban consumerism.

Patterns in North Africa and the Middle East Violent independence struggles were acute in Algeria, but new nations emerged more peacefully in most of North Africa and the Middle East. A brief dispute accompanied Egypt's takeover of the Suez Canal. The establishment of the state of Israel and ensuing conflicts, both with neighboring Arab states and with the large Palestinian minority, created ongoing tensions in much of the region. Monarchies or one-party rule were common. Secular interests predominated in many states, despite the ongoing importance of Islam. Along with independence, several Middle Eastern states gained greater control over oil reserves and generated considerable wealth. At the same time, poverty in cities, resentment against widespread Western diplomatic influence, and reactions to authoritarian states helped generate a growing fundamentalist movement within Islam, which would exert important political strength in the region from the late 1970s onward. While dramatic conflicts punctuated much of contemporary Middle Eastern history, other important developments involved significant new opportunities for many women, expansion of education, and the emergence of industrial sectors in several regions.

Recent Scholarship

Analyzing the rise of religious fundamentalism is one of the most important and most challenging tasks for world historians. *In Understanding Fundamentalism: Christian, Islamic, and Jewish Movements* (2001), Richard Antoun offers a useful comparative framework for dealing with all three of the "religions of Abraham." He looks at the scriptural arguments and bases for fundamentalism, in terms of their shared impulses and different interpretations. He sees three different strategies emerging, one per religion, for seeking new levels of purity. He also deals with fundamentalism as a common experience in terms of total involvement and high levels of activism.

Differentiating Instruction

Differentiated Instruction Teacher Management System
- Pacing Guide
- Lesson Plans for Differentiated Instruction

Interactive Reader and Study Guide

Spanish Chapter Summaries Audio CD Program

Student Edition on Audio CD Program

Differentiated Instruction Modified Worksheets and Tests CD-ROM
- Vocabulary Flash Cards
- Modified Vocabulary Builder Activities
- Modified Chapter Review Activity
- Modified Chapter Test

OSP **One-Stop Planner CD-ROM**
- ExamView Test Generator (English /Spanish)
- PuzzlePro
- Quiz Show for ExamView
- Transparencies and Videos

TE **Differentiated Activities in the Teacher's Edition**
- Comparing Independence in Ghana and Kenya, p. 541
- African Sculpture, p. 544
- History of the Congo, p. 547
- "After the Deluge" Poetry, p. 550
- David Ben-Gurion Obituary, p. 554

Reading Like a Historian

Sam Wineburg

Let's imagine that a reader comes to our chapter knowing little about Ghana—indeed, nothing more than what's on page 938: that Kwame Nkrumah was a leader in Ghana's nationalist movement, that he organized demonstrations against the British and became Ghana's first prime minister. Armed with this scanty information, the reader, who in this case also happens to be a historian—but not a specialist on Africa—turns to the "Reading Like a Historian" feature at the page's bottom. How might a historian with only the barest knowledge of Africa—a specialist in, say, Medieval France, approach this document?

Facing a new document, the first thing a historian does is to scan its attribution—a process known as sourcing. What is the document: a letter? A book? A speech? What do we know about its author? When was it written and what else was going on at the same time? What clues about the author are revealed in the document's title? In other words, before examining a text's substance, its attribution is carefully interrogated. The clues it yields generate questions the historian then brings to the reading of the actual text.

Our document's title seems straightforward with one exception: the charged word "ideology." Ideology emits negative connotations, tainted by foiled grand plans and failed social visions. But these are today's associations, formed in history's hindsight: we've seen with our own eyes the dissolution of Soviet ideologies and witnessed the disintegration of the Iron Curtain. Back in 1961, however, "ideology" still carried high hopes. Used as a title as it is here—"A Statement of African Ideology"—the word typically signaled a socialist project influenced by the Marxist-Leninist tradition.

A historian would also note the document's date, 1961, and situate it as two years after the Cuban revolution, when socialism was on the rise among developing nations. With these hunches, the historian would move to the text itself, noting that Nkrumah champions "economic development" that "must be planned and pursued as a whole." Knowing little about Nkrumah, our historian would develop a strong hunch that the document's author was, himself, a socialist.

A little digging on the Web shows this to be correct. Nkrumah was heavily influenced by the Pan-Africanist ideas of Marcus Garvey and the classic communist writings of Vladimir Lenin. At Ghana's helm in the early sixties, he embraced socialist ideas of a planned, state-directed economy that, in Ghana's case, took a lucrative cacao industry and by fixing state prices (often set below the world market, which led to widespread smuggling) brought it to ruin.

In 1961, Nkrumah visited the Soviet Union and returned home entranced by mammoth public works projects and multi-year development plans. In short order, he unveiled his own Seven-Year plan—that because of inflexible economic assumptions and widespread corruption—failed to realize even a fraction of its inflated hopes.

Clearly this information fills in the initial hunches of our historian. But the general contours of this direction were evident—in skeletal form—just from the document's attribution. By the time students reach Chapter 31, they will have encountered many of these ideas—communism, capitalism, ideology, the Cold War, the Five Year Plans of the USSR and state-sponsored central planning. Some students will in fact possess the background knowledge they need to form similar hunches, but will not know how to draw on this knowledge to move beyond the document's literal meaning.

It is our job to model for them how to do just that.

Chapter Preview

Chapter Main Ideas

Section 1 After World War II, almost all countries in Africa gained independence from ruling European powers.

Section 2 Newly independent African nations struggled with poverty, conflict, and ineffective governments. In recent years some countries sought better government by holding democratic elections.

Section 3 The rise of nationalism in North Africa and the Middle East led to independence for some countries and to conflicts with the West.

Section 4 Regional issues in the Middle East have led to conflicts between Israel and its neighbors and to conflicts in and between Iran and Iraq.

CHAPTER 17

1945–Present

Africa and the Middle East

THE BIG PICTURE After World War II, many countries in Africa and the Middle East struggled for independence from European rule. After they gained that independence, they faced other challenges created by political, religious, and economic issues.

Theme GEOGRAPHY AND ENVIRONMENT

Throughout history the political geography of many of the world's regions has changed because of conflicts and imperialism. In this chapter you will learn how the political geography of Africa and the Middle East has changed since World War II.

TIME LINE

CHAPTER EVENTS

- **1948** The State of Israel is established.
- **1963** Kenya achieves independence from Great Britain.
- **1978** Egypt and Israel sign a peace agreement known as the Camp David Accords.

1945 — 1965

WORLD EVENTS

- **1945** Following World War II the United Nations is established.
- **1968** Martin Luther King Jr. is assassinated.
- **1975** The North Vietnamese take Saigon, reuniting Vietnam.

Key to Differentiating Instruction

Below Level

Basic-level activities designed for all students encountering new material

At Level

Intermediate-level activities designed for average students

Above Level

Challenging activities designed for honors and gifted and talented students

Standard English Mastery

Activities designed to improve standard English usage

Introduce the Chapter

At Level

Africa and the Middle East

1. Have students create a list of what they already know about Africa and the Middle East. Have volunteers share their statements with the class.
2. Write down student statements for all to see.
3. Guide students in a discussion of these statements about Africa and the Middle East. As a class, sort out assumptions, stereotypes, and statements that are factual.
4. Guide students in a discussion of present-day economic, political, and social conditions in Africa and the Middle East. Remind students that Africa is a vast continent, and that conditions vary from country to country. Also remind students that the Middle East consists of a number of countries, cultures, religions, and government styles. LS **Verbal-Linguistic**

Alternative Assessment Handbook, Rubric 11: Discussions

History's Impact video program
Watch the video to understand the impact of oil.

Reading like a Historian After spending 27 years in prison for his activities against South Africa's apartheid government, Nelson Mandela was released in 1990 and became South Africa's president four years later. In this photo, Mandela visits a school in Johannesburg.

Analyzing Visuals How does this photograph show Nelson Mandela's importance as a leader to black South Africans?

See **Skills Handbook**, p. H26

1985

1982 Great Britain and Argentina go to war over the Falkland Islands.

1994 Nelson Mandela is elected president of South Africa.

1997 Hong Kong reverts to Chinese control.

1999 The United States and NATO stop "ethnic cleansing" in Kosovo.

2005 Iraq holds democratic elections.

2005

Chapter Preview

HOLT
History's Impact
▶ **Video Program: Africa and the Middle East**
See the Video Teacher's Guide for strategies for using the video segment.

Reading Like a Historian

Analyzing Visuals Nelson Mandela was chosen to be president by South Africa's National Assembly, after the first election in which black people were allowed to vote. The election represented a turning point in the history of South Africa.

Explore the Time Line

1. In what year was the state of Israel established? *1948*
2. What were the Camp David Accords? *a peace agreement between Israel and Egypt, signed in 1978*
3. What nation declared independence from Great Britain in 1963? *Kenya*
4. Who worked together to stop "ethnic cleansing" in Kosovo in 1999? *NATO and the United States*

Info to Know

South Africa and Russia South Africa and Russia have pledged to become closer partners. As the world's mineral and diamond superpowers, an alliance might give them a monopoly over the world's mineral and diamond market. Between diamond firms in South Africa and Russia, the two nations hold 75 percent of the world's diamond mining.
Predict How might this alliance affect both the South African and Russian economy? *possible answer—The price of diamonds would probably increase, which might help both countries in producing revenue and jobs.*

go.hrw.com
Online Resources

Chapter Resources:
KEYWORD: SHL AFR
Teacher Resources:
KEYWORD: SHL TEACHER

Answers

Reading Like a Historian *possible answer—The crowd seems to be cheering for Mandela, suggesting that he is a popular leader in South Africa.*

Preteach

Geography Starting Points

1948 Election in South Africa The 1948 elections in South Africa marked a turning point for the nation. The two political parties, the United Party and the HNP, or Reunited National Party, had very different ideas about segregation. The United Party argued that segregation was impossible especially because many Africans and people of African descent had moved into the cities. The United Party also had members of mixed ancestry. The HNP argued for complete segregation and for no representation for Africans in South Africa's parliament. The HNP proposed that African laborers in the cities should be considered a temporary solution to labor problems, and that these laborers should be moved back into countryside whenever needed to meet the country's agricultural needs. The HNP also called on a ban of interracial marriages, the creation of black trade unions, and stricter enforcement of job reservation. The HNP won the 1948 election, began apartheid, and ruled South Africa until 1994.

Map Transparency: Africa and the Middle East, 1950

World History Outline Maps

Interactive Map: Africa and the Middle East, 1950

Teaching Tip

Show students a large map of Africa and the Middle East to make sure that they have an overall understanding of the geography of the areas they will be studying this chapter.

GEOGRAPHY Starting Points

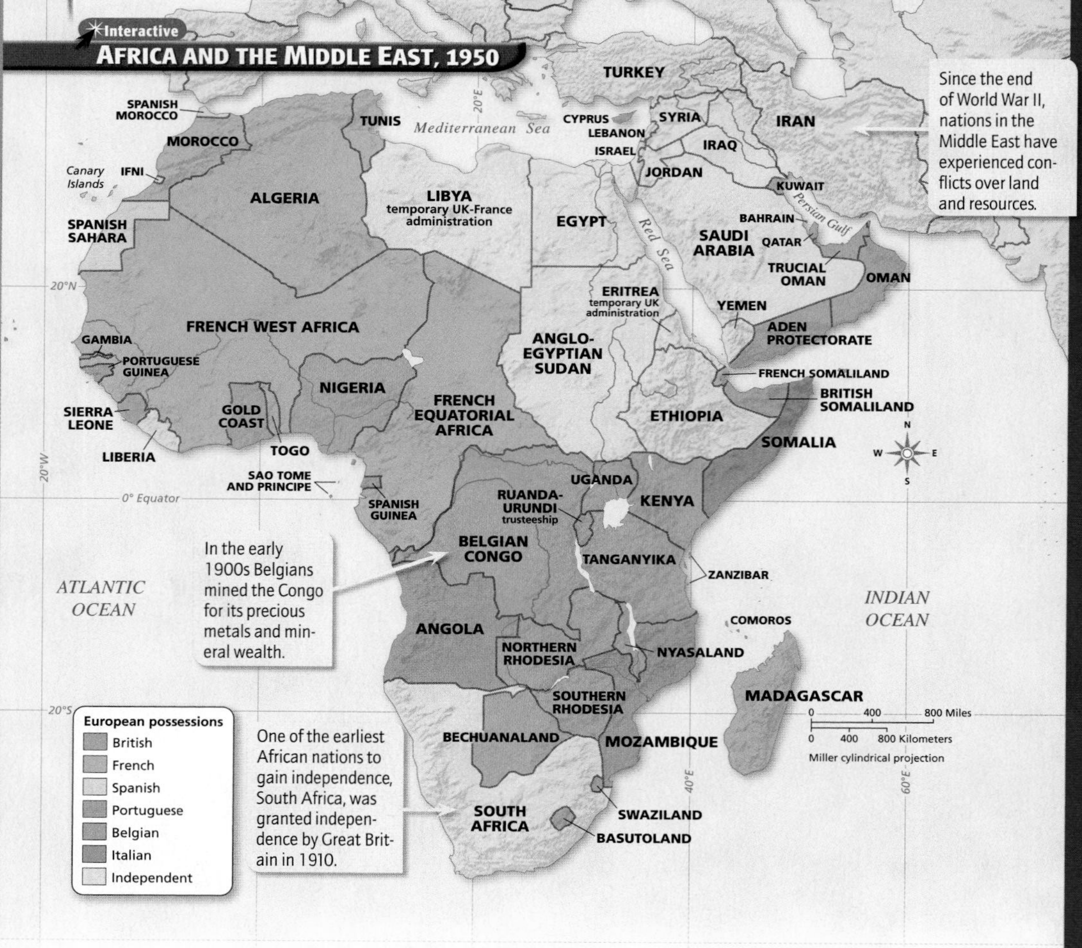

Starting Points At the end of World War II European powers still controlled much of Africa. Great Britain, France, Spain, Portugal, Belgium, and Italy all had African colonies. Forces of change were brewing, however, and most African colonies would become independent nations in the coming years.

1. **Analyze** What challenges do you think Africans faced living under European colonial rule?
2. **Predict** How do you think African countries gained independence from European colonial governments?

Listen to History

Go online to listen to an explanation of the starting points for this chapter.

go.hrw.com
Keyword: SHL AFR

Skills Focus: Analyzing Maps

At Level

Social Studies Skills
Africa and the Middle East, 1950

1. Have students study the map on this page, paying close attention to the different regions of Africa and the Middle East and the countries that colonized them.
2. Have students identify regions where colonization might have created the most difficulties. For example, French West Africa was a gigantic area; its size could have presented many difficulties in governing, transportation, building infrastructures, etc.
3. Have students compare this map with a current map of Africa. Have students identify and list the countries that emerged from the colonial holdings shown on this map.
4. Guide students in a discussion about the colonization of Africa and how it continues to affect the continent today. **LS Verbal-Linguistic, Visual-Spatial**

Alternative Assessment Handbook, Rubrics 12: Drawing Conclusions; and 21: Map Reading

Answers

Geography Starting Points

1. *possible answer—Africans did not have equal rights, were not treated with dignity or respect by their colonial rulers and had no say in their own county's affairs;* **2.** *possible answer—through protest and rebellion*

SECTION 1

African Nations Gain Independence

Before You Read

Main Idea

After World War II, almost all countries in Africa gained independence from ruling European powers.

Reading Focus

1. What ideas and actions led to independence for British and French colonies?
2. Why did Portuguese and Belgian colonies have difficulty achieving independence?
3. What effect did apartheid have on the lives of black South Africans?

Key Terms and People

Kwame Nkrumah
Jomo Kenyatta
Mau Mau
apartheid

TAKING NOTES Take notes on African independence movements.

British and French	
Portuguese and Belgian	
South Africa	

From PRISONER to PRIME MINISTER

◀ Kwame Nkrumah speaks to a crowd of supporters.

THE INSIDE STORY ***How did a jailed radical become leader of an African nation?*** In 1951 Kwame Nkrumah sat in jail in the Gold Coast, a British colony, serving a three-year jail sentence for subversive activities. Nkrumah was the head of the Convention People's Party (CPP), and the British saw him as a dangerous radical.

At the same time, the British were holding elections in the Gold Coast. Assuming that these elections would be the first step toward self-government in the colony, the British hoped moderates would win the elections. The moderates did not win. Instead, the Convention People's Party won a majority of the seats.

The British governor of the Gold Coast now faced a dilemma. He could ignore the election results and keep Nkrumah in jail, or he could release Nkrumah and ask him to form a government. On November 12, 1951, the governor released Nkrumah from prison and asked him to form a government, which he did. In 1952 Nkrumah became the prime minister of the Gold Coast, and when the country achieved independence from Britain in 1957, he became the prime minister of the new nation—Ghana. ■

Teach the Main Idea

At Level

African Nations Gain Independence

1. **Teach** Ask students the Reading Focus questions to teach this section.
2. **Apply** Organize students into groups of three, and assign each student one of the three topics in the section. Have each student create a time line for the assigned topic. Then have students share and copy each time line. Have students explain the significance of the information in their time lines to their group members.
3. **Review** Have volunteers share their time lines with the class, and create a class time line for all to see. Have students add to and correct their own work as needed.
4. **Practice/Homework** Have students illustrate their time lines, choosing images that show the events recorded. **LS Visual-Spatial**

Alternative Assessment Handbook, Rubrics 14: Group Activity, and 36: Time Lines

Preteach

Getting Started

Use the **Interactive Reader and Study Guide** to familiarize students with the section content.

Interactive Reader and Study Guide, Section 1

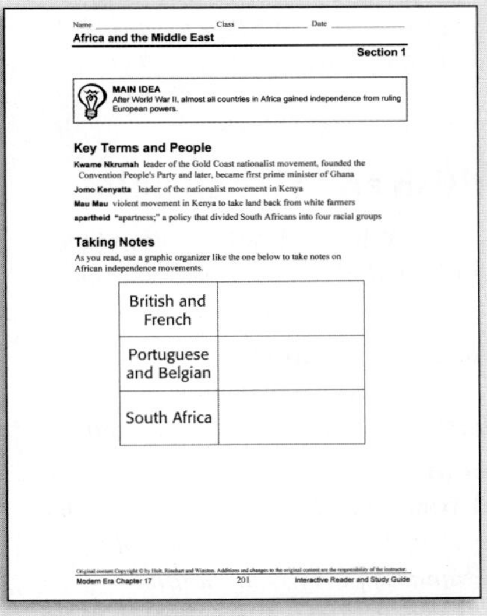
Name ______ Class ______ Date ______
Africa and the Middle East
Section 1

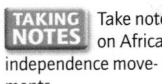

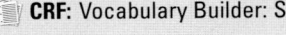

MAIN IDEA
After World War II, almost all countries in Africa gained independence from ruling European powers.

Key Terms and People
Kwame Nkrumah leader of the Gold Coast nationalist movement, founded the Convention People's Party and later, became first prime minister of Ghana
Jomo Kenyatta leader of the nationalist movement in Kenya
Mau Mau violent movement in Kenya to take land back from white farmers
apartheid "apartness;" a policy that divided South Africans into four racial groups

Taking Notes
As you read, use a graphic organizer like the one below to take notes on African independence movements.

British and French	
Portuguese and Belgian	
South Africa	

Modern Era Chapter 17 201 Interactive Reader and Study Guide

Academic Vocabulary

Review with students the high-use academic term(s) in this section.

institute to originate and establish (p. 543)

CRF: Vocabulary Builder: Section 1

Taking Notes

British and French—Ghana: Convention People's Party; Kenya: Mau Mau; French Africa: French Community; Portuguese and Belgian—Congo: African nationalists; Angola, Portuguese Guinea, and Mozambique: various African leaders who went to war with Portugal; South Africa—limited by National Party's policy of apartheid

Direct Teach

Reading Focus

1 What ideas and actions led to independence for British and French colonies? *desire for self-government, nationalism; Ghana—Britain tried experiment of self-government, elected leader pushed for full independence; Kenya—rebel insurgency against white settlers; French colonies—given choices, granted independence*

British and French Colonies

Define What is decolonization? *the withdrawal of colonial powers from their colonies and areas of influence*

Recall What was the first British colony to achieve independence? *the Gold Coast, which was renamed Ghana*

Summarize How did Ghana achieve independence? *Britain decided to hold elections for a national assembly; Nkrumah's party won majority, embarked on a campaign for self-government and independence; Britain granted colony full independence*

CRF: Biography: Léopold Senghor

CRF: Primary Source: The Independence Movement in Kenya

Reading Like a Historian

Kwame Nkrumah's *I Speak of Freedom*

Activity **Powerful Words** Have students identify words and phrases in the speech that show pride and invite action. **LS Verbal-Linguistic**

Primary Source

"It is far better to be free to govern or misgovern yourself than to be governed by anybody else."
—Kwame Nkrumah

Answers

Reading Like a Historian **1.** *that he believes African nations should unite* **2.** *He thinks economic development is within Africa's grasp.*

British and French Colonies

After 1945 European colonial powers began a process of decolonization—the withdrawal of colonial powers from their colonies and areas of influence. Great Britain and France led the way by gradually leaving their colonies and granting them independence.

Ghana After World War II the British colony of the Gold Coast in West Africa was the first British colony to achieve independence. To gain independence, some African leaders in the Gold Coast established a convention to demand greater participation in government. The goal of the convention was to cooperate with the British and gain influence as peacefully as possible.

However, a less cooperative nationalist movement was brewing in the Gold Coast. In 1947 **Kwame Nkrumah** became the leader of the Gold Coast nationalist movement and established the Convention People's Party (CPP). As leader of the CPP, Nkrumah led strikes and demonstrations. The British responded by jailing him. Yet, even while in jail, Nkrumah transformed the CPP into a major political party with considerable popular support. Faced with this kind of pressure, the British eventually agreed to allow national elections in the Gold Coast in 1951. The CPP swept the national elections.

In part because Nkrumah continued to press for independence, Britain granted the Gold Coast full self-government in 1957. Nkrumah became the first prime minister of the new nation, which he named Ghana.

Kenya In Kenya in the 1950s, the path to independence did not go as smoothly as it did in Ghana. The ownership of land and the possibility of independence led to conflict between white Kenyan farmers and the native Kikuyu people. The farmers feared independence would cause them to lose large tracts of valuable cash crops, such as coffee, which they grew in the Kenyan highlands. The Kikuyu considered the highlands their ancestral homeland, and they wanted the land back.

A leader of Kenya's nationalist movement, **Jomo Kenyatta**, argued for the Kikuyu's right to the land and its importance.

Reading like a Historian

Kwame Nkrumah's *I Speak of Freedom*

Analyzing Primary Sources One way we can learn about the past is by carefully analyzing primary sources. Primary sources are valuable to historians because these sources provide critical information about an event or time period.

In this excerpt, Kwame Nkrumah writes about the need for African nations to unite. He describes the value of Africa's natural resources and the need for African nations to come together to profit from these resources. When analyzing this primary source, think about

- the author of the source
- the point of view of the author

> Never before have a people had within their grasp so great an opportunity for developing a continent endowed with so much wealth. Individually, the independent states of Africa, some of them potentially rich, others poor, can do little for their people. Together, by mutual help, they can achieve much. But the economic development of the continent must be planned and pursued as a whole . . . Only a strong political union can bring about full and effective development of our natural resources for the benefit of our people.
>
> —Kwame Nkrumah, *I Speak of Freedom: A Statement of African Ideology*, 1961

Skills Focus READING LIKE A HISTORIAN

1. **Author** What can you learn about Kwame Nkrumah by reading this excerpt?
2. **Point of View** How does Nkrumah view Africa's future?

See **Skills Handbook**, p. H25

Skills Focus: Analyzing Primary Sources

Above Level

Reading Like a Historian Skill

I Speak of Freedom

1. Have students review the excerpt from Nkrumah's speech on this page. Guide students in a discussion of the points Nkrumah makes, and ensure that students understand the vocabulary, tone, message, and the audience for whom this speech was intended. Have students take notes during the discussion.
2. Then have students write another speech with the same tone that Nkrumah might have written to make the same point he makes in this speech.
3. Have students practice their speeches. Choose volunteers to deliver their speeches to the class. **LS Verbal-Linguistic, Auditory-Musical**

Alternative Assessment Handbook, Rubric 24: Oral Presentations

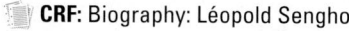

HISTORY'S VOICES

> "It is the key to the people's life; it secures them that peaceful tillage [cultivation] of the soil which supplies their material needs and enables them to perform their magic and traditional ceremonies in undisturbed serenity."
>
> —Jomo Kenyatta, *Facing Mount Kenya*

To rid Kenya of the white farmers and gain their land back, many Kikuyu farmers formed a violent movement called the **Mau Mau**. For several years the group terrorized the highlands of Kenya. They murdered anyone who opposed them, including other Africans who cooperated with the white settlers.

The British eventually regained control of the colony by murdering and torturing some members of the Mau Mau movement. Nevertheless, by the late 1950s the British were convinced that they must accept decolonization. A few years later, in 1963, Kenya became an independent nation with Jomo Kenyatta as the nation's first prime minister.

French Africa Whereas the British colonies followed one path toward independence, France's African colonies followed another path. Unlike the British, the French had always insisted that their goal was to incorporate their African colonies into France itself. After World War II, France's prime minister, Charles de Gaulle, tried to pursue that goal. At the same time, he tried to respond to calls for greater African participation in France's colonial government.

Some African leaders in France's colonies believed they should have greater opportunities for self-rule, but rejected a final break with France. These leaders believed Africans could attain economic and cultural benefits from a continuing relationship with France. In 1958, de Gaulle called for a referendum on the continuing union between France and its African colonies. He gave African leaders the choice between remaining tied to France through a new organization of colonies known as the French Community and becoming completely independent. Most colonies voted to become part of the French Community. A few years later France granted most of the colonies of the French Community independence.

READING CHECK **Find the Main Idea** How did Britain grant independence to its African colonies?

FACES OF HISTORY

Jomo KENYATTA
1894–1978

As a young man in the 1920s, Kenyatta joined a group that protested against Kenya's white-minority government. As a member of the Kikuyu tribe of Kenya, Jomo Kenyatta spent most of his life fighting to gain more rights for the Kikuyu.

In 1952 the Kenyan government arrested and jailed Kenyatta for leading a movement—called the Mau Mau—against European settlers in Kenya. Although, Kenyatta denied he had any involvement in the movement, he remained in jail for seven years. In 1963, several years after Kenyatta's release from prison, Kenyans celebrated their independence and elected Kenyatta as their prime minister.

Infer Why do you think Kenyans elected Kenyatta as prime minister?

Portuguese and Belgian Colonies

For the Belgian and Portuguese colonies in Africa, the transition to independence was more difficult than for the British and French colonies. The Belgians and the Portuguese held on to their African colonies longer than any other European nations until violence forced them to decolonize.

After World War II, the Belgian government agreed that it should prepare the people of the Belgian Congo for self-government. In the 1950s, African nationalists in the Congo demanded immediate self-government. In 1960 the Belgians suddenly announced that they would withdraw completely from the Congo. Soon violence toward Belgian settlers and a civil war in the Congo erupted.

As Portugal continued to hold on to its colonies, African leaders emerged in the colonies of Angola, Portuguese Guinea, and Mozambique. These leaders organized their own armies to fight for independence. As a result, long years of bloody warfare between the Africans and the Portuguese marked the last decades of Portuguese rule. Years of war and a military coup in Portugal drained Portugal's economy, making it impossible for the Portuguese to support their colonies. In 1974 Portugal withdrew completely from Africa.

READING CHECK **Summarize** How did Africans in the Portuguese colonies achieve independence?

Direct Teach

Reading Focus

2 Why did Portuguese and Belgian colonies have difficulty achieving independence? *Portugal and Belgium hung on to their colonies until violence forced them to decolonize.*

Portuguese and Belgian Colonies

Recall Where did Portugal have colonies in Africa? Where did Belgium have a colony? *Portugal—Angola, Portuguese Guinea, and Mozambique; Belgium—Belgian Congo*

Analyze Why did Portugal ultimately withdraw from Africa? *War and a military coup drained Portugal's economy.*

Info to Know

Early History of Kenya Before the Europeans came to Kenya, the economy was simple. Wealth was determined by land and livestock. The British introduced money and taxation, and they claimed land for themselves. In order to provide for themselves and their families, African men had to serve the British. The Kenyans received one-fifth the amount whites received for doing the same work, so it's not surprising that revolt and rebellion occurred.

Differentiating Instruction

Above Level

Advanced Learners/Gifted and Talented

1. Have students read the information in the text on the quest for independence in both Ghana and Kenya.
2. Then read this quote from Kwame Nkrumah to students: "Freedom is not something that one people can bestow on another as a gift. They claim it as their own and none can keep it from them."
3. Have students write an essay in which they discuss how this quotation can be applied to both Ghana and Kenya as they fought to achieve independence from the British.

LS Verbal-Linguistic

Alternative Assessment Handbook, Rubric 37: Writing Assignments

Answers

Faces of History *possible answer—Kenyatta was a hero to Kenyans because of his involvement in the independence movement.*

Reading Check (left) *Britain granted independence to its colonies after they began nationalist movements.* **(right)** *African leaders organized armies to fight for independence; years of bloody warfare ended Portuguese rule.*

Direct Teach

Interpreting Maps

Independence in Africa

Activity Sequence Have students list the countries shown on the map in order of when each achieved its independence. **LS Logical-Mathematical**

Map Transparency: Independence in Africa

Info to Know

Sub-Saharan Africa While conditions vary from country to country, poverty and lack of education are widespread in sub-Saharan Africa. About 700 million people live in 47 countries, and 34 of the world's poorest countries are in Africa. The country's gross national income ranges from under $100 per person in Burundi to over $7,000 in the Seychelles. In 2001, the number of Africans living in poverty was about 314 million—just under half of the population.

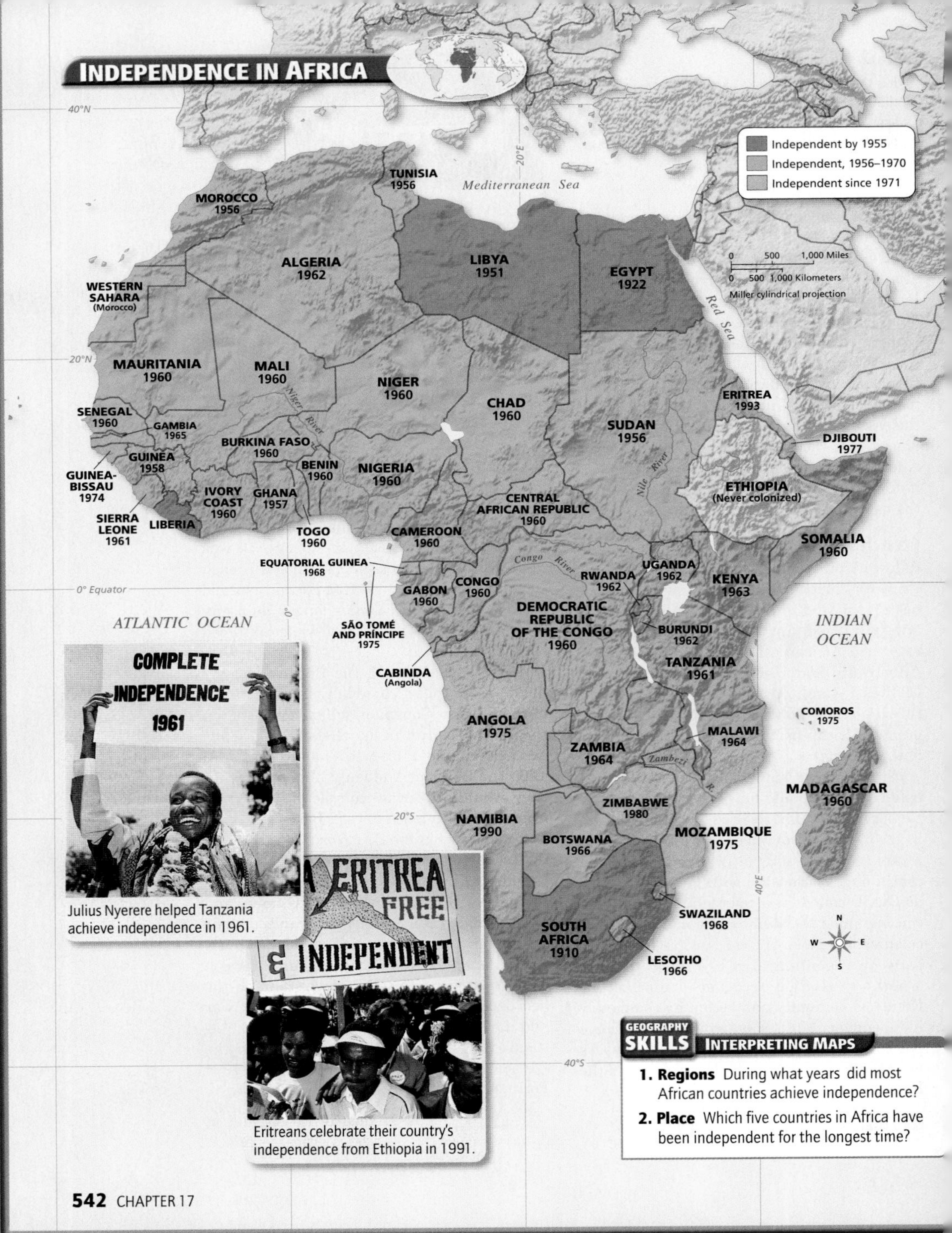

Julius Nyerere helped Tanzania achieve independence in 1961.

Eritreans celebrate their country's independence from Ethiopia in 1991.

GEOGRAPHY SKILLS INTERPRETING MAPS

1. **Regions** During what years did most African countries achieve independence?
2. **Place** Which five countries in Africa have been independent for the longest time?

Collaborative Learning

At Level

Research Required

Independence in Africa

1. Organize students into small groups, and have each group list three or four African countries that students want to learn more about.
2. Have each group vote to select one country. Create a class list of each group's country. Try to avoid duplication of countries on the list. Some groups may have to vote again to choose another country.
3. Have groups conduct outside research about their chosen country. Research should focus on current events, problems, challenges, advantages, and resources the country possesses. Remind students to use reliable sources.
4. Have groups prepare multimedia presentations for the class about their chosen countries. Reports should include maps, charts, and graphs as a means of telling the country's story. **LS Verbal-Linguistic, Visual-Spatial**

Alternative Assessment Handbook, Rubrics 14: Group Activity; and 22: Multimedia Presentations

Answers

Interpreting Maps 1. *1950s and 1960s;* **2.** *Ethiopia, Liberia, Libya, Egypt, South Africa*

South Africa

In the early 1900s South Africa was run by white Afrikaners—descendants of the original Dutch settlers. Even though South Africa had received its official independence from Great Britain in 1910, nonwhites in South Africa were not free under the Afrikaner government of South Africa. The government passed restrictive laws meant to limit the freedom of nonwhites in South Africa.

Apartheid In 1948 racial discrimination heightened when the Afrikaner-dominated National Party came to run the South African government. The National Party instituted a policy of **apartheid**, which means "apartness" in the Afrikaans language. This policy divided people into four racial groups: White, Black, Colored (mixed ancestry), and Asian.

Apartheid attempted to create a greater separation between nonwhites and whites and impose harsh controls over nonwhites. Apartheid laws banned interracial marriages, and placed further restrictions on African ownership of land and businesses.

Apartheid laws were especially harsh on blacks in South Africa. They were required to carry passes or identity books, which indicated where they lived and worked. Further restrictions blacks faced included imprisonment if the police found them in an area for more than 72 hours without a pass.

Under apartheid, only white South Africans could vote or hold political office. Blacks, who made up nearly 75 percent of the population, were denied South African citizenship and were restricted to certain occupations with very little pay.

Homelands Apartheid laws also placed strict limits on where blacks could live. In cities, blacks were required to live in impoverished areas called townships. Government laws restricted the types of businesses allowed in townships, ensuring that the people would stay poor. Starting in the 1950s, the government created rural "homelands" for different African tribes or groups. Most of these areas did not include good farmland or resources.

The South African government used these homelands as an excuse for depriving millions of black South Africans of citizenship. In addition, millions of black men were forced to migrate miles from the homelands to work in mines, factories, and farms. These men were not permitted to bring their families with them. As a result, the homeland policy made millions of black South Africans resident aliens in their own country.

READING CHECK **Find the Main Idea** What was apartheid, and how did it function?

ACADEMIC VOCABULARY

institute to originate and establish

READING SKILLS

Drawing Conclusions What can you conclude about the effects of South Africa's independence?

SECTION 1 ASSESSMENT

go.hrw.com
Online Quiz
Keyword: SHL AFR HP

Reviewing Ideas, Terms, and People

1. **a. Identify** Who was Kwame Nkrumah?
   b. Compare and Contrast How did the process of gaining independence differ for British and French colonies in Africa?
   c. Evaluate Do you think the Kikuyu people had a right to the land the white farmers owned? Why or why not?
2. **a. Recall** What happened in the Belgian Congo after independence?
   b. Identify Cause and Effect What caused Portugal to finally withdraw from its African colonies?
3. **a. Define** What was apartheid?
   b. Explain How were the lives of blacks in South Africa restricted by apartheid laws?
   c. Elaborate How did homelands deny citizenship to blacks in South Africa?

Critical Thinking

4. **Identify Cause and Effect** Copy the graphic organizer here and use it and your notes from this section to list the causes of African independence movements and their effects.

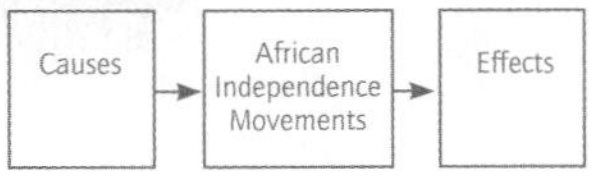

FOCUS ON WRITING

5. **Exposition** In a brief paragraph, compare and contrast the nationalist movements in Ghana and Kenya. Be sure to use supporting details from the section.

Direct Teach

Reading Focus

3 What effect did apartheid have on the lives of black South Africans? *had to carry passes or identity books; could not vote, hold political office, or work in certain jobs; were not considered citizens; were required to live in impoverished areas*

South Africa

Identify Who were the Afrikaners? *white descendants of the original Dutch settlers of South Africa*

Interpret How does the meaning of the word apartheid relate to its policies? *means "apartness;" apartheid separated nonwhites and whites, discriminating against nonwhites*

Review & Assess

Close

Have students compare and contrast the African countries that struggled the most to gain independence with countries struggled the least.

Review

go.hrw.com **Online Quiz**, Section 1

Assess

SE Section 1 Assessment

Progress Assessment: Section 1 Quiz

Alternative Assessment Handbook

Reteach/Intervene

Interactive Reader and Study Guide, Section 1

Interactive Skills Tutor CD-ROM

Section 1 Assessment Answers

1. **a.** leader of the Convention People's Party; first prime minister and president of Ghana
   b. British colonies rebelled; French colonies granted independence without fighting
   c. possible answer—Yes, it was their ancestral homeland.
2. **a.** Civil war erupted.
   b. War and a military coup drained Portugal's economy.
3. **a.** a policy in South Africa that divided whites and nonwhites into four groups, separating them and placing harsh controls on nonwhites
   b. interracial marriages banned, land and business ownership restricted, blacks had to carry identification, could not vote, hold political office or certain jobs, had to live in certain places
   c. made millions of black South Africans resident aliens in their own country
4. Causes—nationalism, desire for self-government; Effects—civil wars, violence, independence, formation of new nations
5. Students should cite the desire for self-government, and the unfair colonial system.

Answers

Reading Skills *possible answer—Even after independence, nonwhites in South Africa did not have freedom.*

Reading Check *policy of separating whites and nonwhites and placing restrictions upon nonwhites; enforced by police, laws*

The Arts Around the World

African Sculpture

Info to Know

African Sculpture African sculpture was not created for beauty or to be sold but to recall important events or feelings. The most common types of African sculpture are of the human form, and wood is the most commonly used material. African art is designed to show laws and history, and to teach these to young people. Another purpose of African art is to serve as a transmitter between human and supernatural happenings; it also shows the wealth and status of those who possess it.

THE ARTS AROUND THE WORLD

Sculpture

African Sculpture

What is it? African sculpture includes many different forms such as masks, statues, and carvings. In Africa, peoples of different regions and cultures create styles of sculpture that reflect their unique cultures. Many of these styles use the human form as a subject. One of the highest compliments an African artist can receive is someone praising their work by saying it "looks like a human being."

Key characteristics:

- Highly skilled artists learn to sculpt at an early age from a master sculptor.
- Sculptures usually represent royalty, ancestors, animals, or spirits.
- Traditional materials used to create sculptures include wood, metals, and clay.

Why is it important?

- Sculpture shows us the rich diversity of cultures throughout Africa.
- African sculpture is a significant art form that is passed on from generation to generation to keep African history and cultures alive.

This Yoruba artist is from Nigeria. Over the past 700 years the Yoruba have been known for their skilled craftsmanship and the bronze sculptures they produce like the one pictured above.

These masks from South Africa represent the diversity of styles among African artists who created them.

Skills FOCUS INTERPRETING VISUALS

Compare What characteristics do these three forms of African sculpture have in common?

Differentiating Instruction

Below Level

Special Education Students

Materials: modeling clay, paper, colored markers

1. Read the information in the feature to students and explain any words that might be unfamiliar to them. Help students understand the information, and have them examine the artwork on the page.
2. Have students draw a sculpture that they would like to make. Student sculptures should reflect the information in the text.
3. Have students use the clay to create their own African sculpture. Display the sculptures in a classroom exhibit. You might wish to hold an exhibit "opening" by inviting other classes to view the artwork. Encourage students to create invitations to the classroom exhibit.

LS Visual-Spatial, Kinesthetic

Alternative Assessment Handbook, Rubric 3: Artwork

Answers

Interpreting Visuals *All of the sculptures depict human faces, appear to be made of wood*

SECTION 2

Post-Colonial Africa

BEFORE YOU READ

MAIN IDEA

Newly independent African nations struggled with poverty, conflict, and ineffective governments. In recent years some countries sought better government by holding democratic elections.

READING FOCUS

1. What political challenges did Africans face after independence?
2. What economic and environmental challenges did Africans face after independence?
3. How did Africans revive their culture after independence?

KEY TERMS AND PEOPLE

African National Congress
Nelson Mandela
Sharpeville Massacre
Soweto Uprising
F. W. de Klerk
one-party system
patronage
Mobutu Sese Seko
desertification
negritude movement

TAKING NOTES Take notes on the challenges Africa faced after independence and the challenges it faces today.

Political Challenges
Economic Challenges
Environmental Challenges

THE INSIDE STORY

Dawn of a New Day

How did black South Africans end 300 years of white rule in only four days? First the elderly and the ill came to vote. Some came in wheelchairs and some with canes to cast their ballots in South Africa's first democratic election. On the following day, April 27, 1994, South Africa's general population began to vote. In some black areas voters waited in line for more than 10 hours. In rural areas, some voters had to cast their ballots by candlelight.

In some cases, black voters went to cast ballots in white areas where the lines were shorter. The racial hostility that had dominated South Africa for so long seemed to have disappeared. Black and white voters shared a sense of elation as they participated in the rebirth of their nation—the new, democratic South Africa.

For older black voters, the chance to vote was empowering. Many thought that it would never be possible for them to choose their own government. "My parents never saw this day. My husband never saw this day," said Mildred Motsuenane. "I can tell you dawn is breaking and the dark light is gone." For voters like Mildred, this was not merely an election, but was a chance for people to get their dignity back. ■

South Africans line up to cast their votes in the country's democratic elections. ▶

Teach the Main Idea

At Level

Post-Colonial Africa

1. **Teach** Ask students the Reading Focus questions to teach this section.
2. **Apply** Have students create an outline of the section using the heads as main points. Have students identify at least two main ideas under each of the red subheadings.
3. **Review** Review student outlines as a class. Have students identify the points in their outlines that they feel are most important in the development of post-colonial Africa.
4. **Practice/Homework** Have students make generalizations to answer this question: Why did African countries turn to dictatorships and one-party governments instead of pursuing democracy and free elections? Have students write a brief essay explaining their answers. **LS Verbal-Linguistic, Visual-Spatial**

Alternative Assessment Handbook, Rubric 37: Writing Assignments

Preteach

Getting Started

Use the **Interactive Reader and Study Guide** to familiarize students with the section content.

Interactive Reader and Study Guide, Section 2

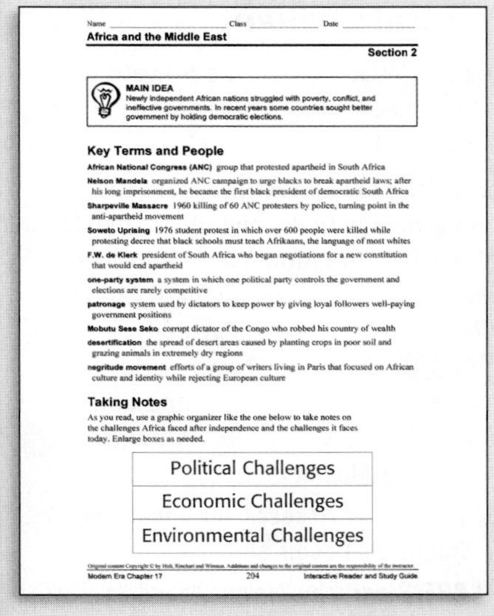

Name ____________ Class ________ Date ________

Africa and the Middle East

Section 2

MAIN IDEA
Newly independent African nations struggled with poverty, conflict, and ineffective governments. In recent years some countries sought better government by holding democratic elections.

Key Terms and People

African National Congress (ANC) group that protested apartheid in South Africa

Nelson Mandela organized ANC campaign to urge blacks to break apartheid laws; after his long imprisonment, he became the first black president of democratic South Africa

Sharpeville Massacre 1960 killing of 60 ANC protesters by police, turning point in the anti-apartheid movement

Soweto Uprising 1976 student protest in which over 600 people were killed while protesting decree that black schools must teach Afrikaans, the language of most whites

F.W. de Klerk president of South Africa who began negotiations for a new constitution that would end apartheid

one-party system a system in which one political party controls the government and elections are rarely competitive

patronage system used by dictators to keep power by giving loyal followers well-paying government positions

Mobutu Sese Seko corrupt dictator of the Congo who robbed his country of wealth

desertification the spread of desert areas caused by planting crops in poor soil and grazing animals in extremely dry regions

negritude movement efforts of a group of writers living in Paris that focused on African culture and identity while rejecting European culture

Taking Notes

As you read, use a graphic organizer like the one below to take notes on the challenges Africa faced after independence and the challenges it faces today. Enlarge boxes as needed.

Political Challenges
Economic Challenges
Environmental Challenges

Original content Copyright © by Holt, Rinehart and Winston. Additions and changes to the original content are the responsibility of the instructor.

Modern Era Chapter 17 204 Interactive Reader and Study Guide

Academic Vocabulary

Review with students the high-use academic term in this section.

infrastructure public works, such as buildings and roads, that are needed to support a population (p. 548)

CRF: Vocabulary Builder: Section 2

Taking Notes

Political—apartheid, Sharpeville Massacre, Soweto Uprising; military dictatorships, ethnic conflicts, civil war

Economic—many nations not industrialized at time of independence, turned to international organizations like the World Bank for loans

Environmental—diseases like malaria and AIDS, desertification

go.hrw.com
Online Resources
KEYWORD: SHL AFR
ACTIVITY: Apartheid in South Africa

Direct Teach

Reading Focus

1 What political challenges did Africans face after independence? *dictatorships; ethnic conflict and civil war; protests against apartheid*

Political Challenges

Recall What caused the Soweto Uprising? *a new policy that black students be taught Afrikaans*

Explain How did F.W. de Klerk's actions help with the end of apartheid? *released Nelson Mandela from prison, reinstated the African National Congress, allowed the first non-racial elections*

Activity **Soweto Poems** Have students write a poem or song commemorating the Soweto Uprising.
LS Auditory-Musical

Alternative Assessment Handbook, Rubric 26: Poems and Songs

CRF: Biography: Nelson Mandela

Recent Scholarship

In His Own Words, by Nelson Mandela, is a collection of the prolific leader's speeches covering a wide variety of topics. Whether discussing politics, education, or culture, Mandela offers compelling thoughts about his experiences as a leader dedicated to preserving freedom.

In His Own Words by Nelson Mandela. Little Brown & Co., 2004.

Political Challenges

In the 1950s and 1960s many former European colonies in Africa were ruled by dictators and some nations fell into civil war. However, the 1990s brought renewed hope with the return of democracy in many African countries and the end of the apartheid system in South Africa.

Protesting South Africa's Apartheid In the early 1900s a group of blacks in South African had formed the **African National Congress (ANC)**. The ANC petitioned the government and held peaceful protests against apartheid. In the 1940s, however, younger and more radical members joined the organization, including a young lawyer named **Nelson Mandela**. In 1952 Mandela helped organize a campaign that urged blacks in South Africa to break apartheid laws. The ANC gained a mass following from this campaign.

In 1960 the ANC drastically changed its peaceful philosophy after police fired on demonstrators in the township of Sharpeville, killing more than 60 people. The **Sharpeville Massacre** was a turning point in the anti-apartheid movement. Some ANC leaders, including Mandela, decided that they would have to meet violence with violence. In response to this decision, the government banned the ANC and jailed Mandela.

In 1976, a major student protest movement took place in the township of Soweto. The **Soweto Uprising** was set off by a government decree that black schools teach their students Afrikaans—the language spoken by the majority of white South Africans. When police killed a protesting student, the peaceful march developed into a revolt. The police crushed the uprising, but more than 600 people were killed and 4,000 wounded.

After the uprising, violence erupted in many black townships, while the ANC fought to end apartheid. At the same time, much of the international community imposed trade sanctions, or restrictions, on South Africa in an attempt to force the nation to abandon apartheid.

Democracy in South Africa In 1990 under President **F.W. de Klerk**, South Africa legalized the ANC and began negotiations to enact a new constitution that would end apartheid. De Klerk released Mandela from prison and lifted the long-standing ban on the African National Congress. De Klerk also abolished the homelands and held South Africa's first democratic elections. The ANC swept the elections, and

PRIMARY SOURCES

Mandela's Trial Speech

In 1964 Nelson Mandela gave a speech at the Rivona Trial, in which 10 ANC leaders were accused of promoting acts of sabotage and violent revolution. In the speech, Mandela explained why ANC leaders felt they had no choice but to use violence to resist the government. He also eloquently expressed his commitment to his principles.

> "During my lifetime I have dedicated myself to this struggle of the African people. I have fought against white domination, and I have fought against black domination. I have cherished the ideal of a democratic and free society in which all persons live together in harmony and with equal opportunities. It is an ideal which I hope to live for and to achieve. But if needs be, it is an ideal for which I am prepared to die."
>
> —Nelson Mandela, April 20, 1964

Skills Focus READING LIKE A HISTORIAN

1. **Explain** To what cause does Mandela say he is committed?
2. **Analyze Primary Sources** What impact do you think Mandela's speech had on his cause?

See **Skills Handbook**, p. H25

Nelson Mandela in Johannesburg in the early 1960s.

Skills Focus: Making Generalizations

Below Level

Standard English Mastery

Reading Skill
Apartheid

1. Review the information in the text about apartheid, the Soweto Uprising, and the imprisonment of Nelson Mandela. Have students work in mixed-ability pairs to create a graphic organizer that summarizes the information.
2. Guide students in a discussion of the anti-apartheid movement, and have students take notes during the class discussion. Focus student attention on the embargoes and divestments in businesses that occurred.
3. Have students use their notes and graphic organizers to write a letter to the editor of a South African newspaper encouraging an end to apartheid. Have students review their drafts in mixed-ability pairs, correct their work, and turn in the final letter. **LS Verbal-Linguistic**

Alternative Assessment Handbook, Rubrics 11: Discussions; and 17: Letters to Editors

Answers

Primary Sources **1.** *a democratic and free society in which people of all races have equal oppor-tunities;* **2.** *possible answer—He probably inspired followers with his dedication.*

Nelson Mandela became the first black president of a democratic South Africa.

Military Dictatorships By the end of the 1960s almost all of the newly independent African nations had adopted a **one-party system**. In this system, a single political party controls the government and elections are rarely competitive. In many countries opposition parties were outlawed.

Dictators ruled many of these African nations by maintaining their power through **patronage**, giving their loyal followers well-paying positions in the government. Some corrupt officials required bribes for government contracts or licenses. These officials also ran government enterprises for their own personal profit, and sometimes stole money from the public treasury.

This new generation of African dictators robbed their countries of their wealth. For example, **Mobutu Sese Seko**, dictator of the Congo, amassed a personal fortune of about $5 billion and built a $100 million palace. While Mobutu enriched himself, his nation's people fell into poverty. Other dictators committed similar offenses.

Ethnic Conflicts and Civil War When the European powers divided Africa into colonies, preexisting political units were not maintained. After independence, rival ethnic groups competed for control.

Some of these conflicts led to destructive civil wars. In 1967 in Nigeria people of the Igbo-speaking ethnic group of eastern Nigeria proclaimed their own independent state of Biafra. As a result, a bloody civil war erupted. About 2 million Nigerians died from fighting, and just as many died of starvation. After Biafra collapsed, the territory rejoined Nigeria.

Similarly, a civil war and a severe drought led to enormous suffering in Somalia in 1992. Hundreds of thousands of Somalis died when warring militias stole food sent to Somalia from international relief agencies. The United States and the United Nations tried to help but were unsuccessful.

In the 1990s tensions between two ethnic groups, the Hutu and the Tutsi, in Rwanda erupted in widespread violence. In 1994 the Hutu-led government encouraged a genocide of Tutsi and moderate Hutu civilians, which resulted in the massacre of about 1 million Tutsi and moderate Hutus. Many more civilians fled to refugee camps in the neighboring countries of Burundi, Uganda, and the Democratic Republic of the Congo.

Democracy for Some Despite conflicts and war throughout the late 1900s, many African countries were still dictatorships. During the Cold War, the United States and the Soviet Union had each provided large amounts of money to dictators who were friendly to their side. But when the Cold War ended in 1989, most of that money dried up. The lack of funding began to weaken some of the dictators' governments. Many Africans saw this weakness as an opportunity to create democratic governments and they demanded elections.

By 2005, more than 30 African countries had abandoned one-party systems and held elections. Results of these elections were mixed, however. Some former dictators resorted to fraud and intimidation to win elections. Others were elected because the people preferred them to other alternatives.

READING CHECK **Draw Conclusions** Why did most African states adopt a one-party system?

Political Trends in Post-Colonial Africa

QUICK FACTS

Since gaining independence, many African countries have struggled to build stable governments.

ONE-PARTY RULE AND MILITARY DICTATORSHIPS

After many African countries gained independence following World War II, strong leaders seized power and set up one-party rule or military dictatorships. Although some of these regimes lasted for many years, others were toppled and replaced in military coups, which were common.

ETHNIC CONFLICTS AND CIVIL WAR

Africa's ethnic diversity and rivalries, combined with country borders that were drawn without consideration of ethnic homelands, led to conflicts and civil wars in many countries.

STRUGGLES WITH DEMOCRACY

Beginning in the early 1990s many African countries began to make progress toward democracy and overcome their history of dictatorship and conflict. However, most countries still struggled to hold free and fair elections and maintain stability.

Differentiating Instruction

Above Level

Advanced Learners/Gifted and Talented

Research Required

1. Have students review the information about Mobutu Sese Seko and the Congo. Tell students that the history of the Congo, a country rich in natural resources, is one of tragedy, bloodshed, and wasted wealth.
2. Have students research the history of the Congo from the time of Patrice Lumumba to the current day. Students should follow the events that occurred when Mobutu was dictator. Student research should include Mobutu's replacement by both Laurent Kabila and his son Joseph Kabila, and the presidential elections held since that time.
3. Have students prepare a multimedia presentation of their research with maps, charts, and statistics supporting their findings. In their conclusions students should predict what lies ahead for the Congo. LS **Verbal-Linguistic, Visual-Spatial**

Alternative Assessment Handbook, Rubrics 22: Mulitimedia Presentations; and 30: Research

Direct Teach

Reading Focus

Political Challenges

Identify What led to the genocide in Rwanda? *Hutu-led government encouraged a genocide of Tutsi and moderate Hutus*

Explain What caused a weakening of dictatorships following the Cold War? *lack of funding from United States and Soviet Union, countries that previously had given money to dictators who were on their side*

Quick Facts Transparency: Political Trends in Post-Colonial Africa

go.hrw.com
Online Resources
KEYWORD: SHL AFR
ACTIVITY: Desmond Tutu

Biography

Alexander Skunder Boghossian (1937–2003) Alexander Skunder Boghossian is one of Africa's most renowned artists. He was born to an Ethiopian mother and an Armenian father. In 1955, he went to London to study art, and in 1957, he moved to Paris where he taught and studied art. In 1966, he returned to Ethiopia and taught at the Fine Arts School in Addis Ababa, his birth place. Boghossian's work are colorful, vibrant, and feature symbols, motifs, forms, and shapes from his Ethiopian background. He was the first Ethiopian artist to have pieces bought by the Museum of Modern Art in New York City and the Musée d'Art Moderne in Paris. Several of his works have also been purchased by the Smithsonian Museum of African Art.

Answers

Reading Check *U.S. and Soviet Union each provided large amounts of money to dictators friendly to their side*

Direct Teach

Reading Focus

Economic and Environmental Challenges

Define What is desertification? *the spread of desertlike conditions, contributing to drought and famine*

Make Inferences Why do you think such a small percentage of Africans with AIDS are receiving treatment? *possible answers—lack of education, lack of infrastructure to deliver treatment, lack of money to pay for expensive treatments*

Interpreting Graphs

Challenges in Post-Colonial Africa

Make Generalizations Why has the number of people with HIV risen so rapidly since 1992? *possible answer—Resources to help the people with HIV are lacking; people are not being educated about the disease.*

Info to Know

Facts about AIDS in Sub-Saharan Africa AIDS is the leading cause of death in Africa; 70 percent of all people infected with HIV live in sub-Saharan Africa. In 2004, 3.1 million people in sub-Saharan Africa were newly infected with HIV. Because of HIV and AIDS, schools are being closed due to the deaths of teachers.

Challenges in Post-Colonial Africa

Poverty and health issues like HIV are two of the main challenges in Africa today. Many poor Africans live in makeshift housing in shantytowns like this one in Soweto, South Africa.

HIV in Sub-Saharan Africa

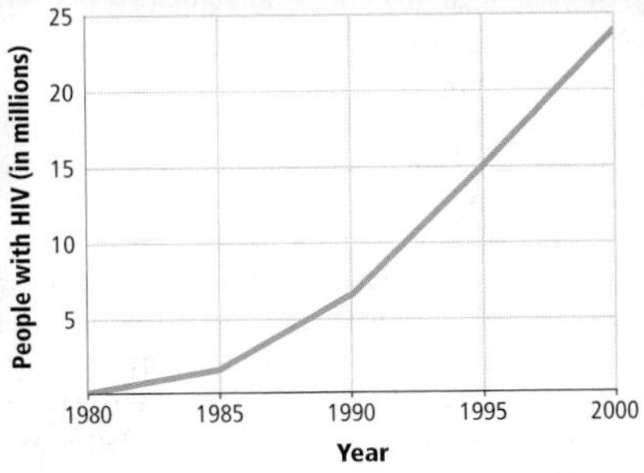

Source: World Health Organization

Skills Focus INTERPRETING GRAPHS

Analyze In what ways do you think the growth of HIV in sub-Saharan Africa affects society?

Economic and Environmental Challenges

After achieving independence, many African nations faced economic challenges that came with their new status. In addition, Africans had to combat the spread of disease and environmental problems.

Struggling Economies After independence, the economies of most African nations were fragile because they depended on only one or two exports for their support. African nations were not yet industrialized and depended on farming or the mining of raw materials. For example, Ghana depended on cocoa, and Nigeria, on oil.

To support themselves, many African nations turned to international organizations, such as the World Bank, for development loans. However, even with economic help, bad planning and corrupt leaders left these nations with huge debts and no infrastructure.

ACADEMIC VOCABULARY
infrastructure public works, such as buildings and roads, that are needed to support a population

Disease African nations have also been challenged by the management of deadly diseases. Malaria, a disease that is spread by mosquitoes, continues to be one of the most common causes of death in much of Africa today.

In the 1980s a new disease, acquired immune deficiency syndrome (AIDS), spread rapidly through Africa. The HIV virus that causes AIDS weakens the body's immune system and results in death. The social costs of HIV/AIDS in sub-Saharan Africa are staggering. Millions of children are orphans because their parents died from AIDS. A small percentage of infected Africans are receiving AIDS treatment, but prevention programs continue to be somewhat effective in several countries.

Desertification The scarcity of fertile farmland and pastures for livestock is a challenge for many Africans today. Farmers must plant crops in poor soil, and herders have to graze their animals in extremely dry regions. As a result, the soil in these areas dries out, and the natural grasses cannot grow. The Sahara and the Sahel in North Africa are expanding today due to **desertification**, the spread of desertlike conditions. Desertification threatens the future of Africa by contributing to the cycles of drought and famine that plague many African countries today.

READING CHECK **Identify Cause and Effect** What causes desertification in Africa?

Skills Focus: Identify Problem and Solution

Above Level

Reading Skill

Fighting AIDS in Africa

1. Have students review the information in the text about HIV/AIDS in sub-Saharan Africa.
2. Have students conduct independent research using reliable online resources to learn about organizations working to reduce the spread of AIDS in Africa, and to treat those who already have the disease.
3. Have students choose one organization about which to write a report. Have students write a few paragraphs describing the organization's goals, and evaluating how successful the organization has been to date. Students might wish to include graphs or charts in their reports. Each report should include a bibliography of sources. **LS Verbal-Linguistic**

Alternative Assessment Handbook, Rubrics 30: Research; and 37: Writing Assignments

Answers

HIV in Sub-Saharan Africa *possible answers—results in many deaths, leaves many children orphans, makes people fearful*

Reading Check *planting crops in poor soil and grazing animals in dry areas, causing soil to dry out even more*

Revival of African Culture

In spite of the challenges African countries have faced since independence, Africans have experienced a cultural revival. Many Africans lost faith in their own culture during the colonial era, but a new generation of African writers, artists, and musicians has emerged to establish a powerful African identity.

Language and Literature During colonial rule Africans preserved their culture and used it as a means of expressing dissatisfaction with colonial rule. For example, many Africans in East Africa continued to study Swahili, an African language. After independence in the early 1960s, Swahili became the national language in both Kenya and Tanzania. Swahili writers maintained a strong tradition of poetry, plays, and novels.

A new type of African literature developed in the French-speaking colonies of West Africa. A group of African and Caribbean students living in Paris in the 1930s founded the **negritude movement**. Their writings rejected European culture and focused on African culture and identity.

In the years after independence, African writers shifted their focus from a criticism of European colonialism to a criticism of African leaders. However, many of these writers faced censorship and harassment by the African governments they ridiculed. Writers such as Wole Soyinka spent time in prison for opposing the Nigerian government through his writings. Other African writers fled Africa to escape possible imprisonment.

Art, Music, and Dance Just as literature became a new means of expressing African identity, so did the traditional arts such as sculpture, music, and dance. African artists began to produce traditional pieces, such as ceremonial masks, African musical instruments, and sculptures carved from wood or cast in bronze. These African artists incorporated new ideas and materials into their work, giving the revival of African art a new vitality and creativity. As a result, African art is highly valued on the world market today.

Music and dance are also an important art form in many African societies. African musicians have traditionally played music to honor their history and mark special occasions. Traditional dances are also performed in many African cultures to celebrate specific events or special ceremonies.

In the 1960s African musicians began to blend traditional African styles with Western musical styles. To create this new music, African musicians used common Western instruments in addition to traditional African instruments. Later, in the 1980s, African popular music, or Afro-Pop, became popular in Europe and throughout the world. As a result, many African musicians are internationally known today.

READING CHECK **Find the Main Idea** What subject did many African writers focus on after independence?

SECTION 2 ASSESSMENT

go.hrw.com
Online Quiz
Keyword: SHL AFR HP

Reviewing Ideas, Terms, and People

1. **a. Define** What are **one-party systems**?
   b. Draw Conclusions Why were civil wars common in post-colonial Africa?
   c. Elaborate How important was the end of apartheid?
2. **a. Recall** What caused African economies to struggle and depend on outside aid?
   b. Explain Why has economic development been so difficult in Africa?
   c. Develop What do you think African leaders should do to improve economic conditions in their countries?
3. **a. Define** What was the **negritude movement?**
   b. Analyze In what ways have Africans preserved their traditional culture?

Critical Thinking

4. **Summarize** Copy the graphic organizer below and use it to list the key people or events that are related to Africa's challenges.

	Key People or Event
Apartheid	
Dictatorship and War	
Struggling economies	
Disease	
Desertification	

FOCUS ON WRITING

5. **Narration** Write a brief radio report that might have been broadcast after Nelson Mandela was elected president of South Africa in 1994. In your report, relate the sequence of events that ended apartheid in South Africa.

Direct Teach

Reading Focus

3 How did Africans revive their culture after independence? *through literature, art, music, and dance*

Revival of African Culture

Identify Who is Wole Soyinka? *a writer who spent time in prison for criticizing the Nigerian government*

Explain How was the Swahili language significant in post-colonial Africa? *possible answer—represented African culture, became national language in some places, used in African literature*

CRF: Literature: *Things Fall Apart*

Review & Assess

Close

Guide students in a discussion about post-colonial Africa and why some countries continue to struggle.

Review

Online Quiz, Section 2

Assess

SE Section 2 Assessment

Progress Assessment: Section 2 Quiz

Alternative Assessment Handbook

Reteach/Intervene

Interactive Reader and Study Guide, Section 2

Interactive Skills Tutor CD-ROM

Section 2 Assessment Answers

1. **a.** single political party controls the government
   b. Colonies had been divided without regard to cultures or ethnic groups.
   c. very important; ended white domination, led to democracy and increased liberties
2. **a.** Few exports supported their economies.
   b. bad planning, corrupt leaders resulted in debt, lack of infrastructure
   c. possible answers—work to prevent desertification, end spread of disease, and place good leaders in power
3. **a.** a literary movement rejecting European culture and focusing on African identity
   b. through language and the arts
4. Apartheid—ANC, Mandela, de Klerk, Sharpeville Massacre, Soweto Uprising, Mandela's election; Dictatorship and War—Mobutu Sese Seko, civil war, genocide; Struggling economies: many depend on loans; Disease: malaria, AIDS; Desertification: creates drought, famine
5. Reports should discuss apartheid and the actions of President F.W. de Klerk.

Answers

Reading Check *criticism of African leaders*

World Literature

"After the Deluge"

Word Help

denomination value (as of money)
bullion uncoined gold or silver in bars

Meet the Writer

Wole Soyinka (1934–) Wole Soyinka was born in 1934 in western Nigeria. In 1960 he formed a theater group called "The 1960 Masks" and then in 1964, he formed the "Orison Theatre Company" that served as a way for him to produce and act in his own plays. During the civil war in Nigeria, he asked for a cease fire in a 1967 article. In response, he was arrested and accused of conspiring with the Biafra rebels. He was detained for 22 months. In 1986 Soyinka became the first African to win the Nobel Prize for Literature.

World Literature

Wole Soyinka (1934–)

About the Reading In 1967 the Nigerian government arrested Wole Soyinka for his outspoken criticism of the military dictator who had forcibly seized power of the government. The subject of this poem is a nameless dictator who, like many corrupt African leaders, took money from his nation's fortune while people in his country were suffering from poverty.

AS YOU READ **Think about how the dictator's lifestyle led to his demise.**

In 1997 the Central African Republic crowned an emperor.

"After the Deluge"

by Wole Soyinka

Once, for a dare,
He filled his heart-shaped swimming pool
With bank notes, high denomination
And fed a pound of caviar to his dog.
The dog was sick; a chartered plane
Flew in replacement for the Persian rug.

He made a billion yen
Leap from Tokyo to Buenos Aires,
Turn somersaults through Brussels,
New York, Sofia and Johannesburg.
It cracked the bullion market open wide.
Governments fell, coalitions cracked
Insurrection raised its bloody flag
From north to south.

He knew his native land through iron gates,
His sight was radar bowls, his hearing
Electronic beams. For flesh and blood,
Kept company with a brace of Dobermans.
But—yes—the worthy causes never lacked
His widow's mite, discreetly publicized.

He escaped the lynch days. He survives.
I dreamt I saw him on a village
Water line, a parched land where
Water is a god
That doles its favors by the drop,
And waiting is a way of life.
Rebellion gleamed yet faintly in his eye
Traversing chrome-and-platinum retreats. There,
Hubs of commerce smoothly turn without
His bidding, and cities where he lately roosted
Have forgotten him, the preying bird
Of passage.

They let him live, but not from pity
Or human sufferance. He scratches life
From earth, no worse a mortal man than the rest.
Far, far away in dreamland splendor,
Creepers twine his gates of bronze relief.
The jade-lined pool is home
To snakes and lizards; they hunt and mate
On crusted algae.

Skills FOCUS **READING LIKE A HISTORIAN**

go.hrw.com
World Literature
Keyword: SHL WRLIT

1. **Explain** How did the dictator live?
2. **Interpret Literature as a Source** What bias does Soyinka show in this poem? How do you think Soyinka's experiences shaped his point of view?

See **Skills Handbook**, p. H28

Differentiating Instruction

English-Language Learners; Special Education Students

Below Level

Read the excerpt from the poem "After the Deluge" to students. Have students visualize what Soyinka is referring to in the poem as you read it. Have students draw their visualizations. **LS Visual-Spatial**

Alternative Assessment Handbook, Rubric 3: Artwork

Advanced Learners/Gifted and Talented

Above Level

Have students read the excerpt of the poem "After the Deluge." Then, have students write their own poems using similar language, tone, and ideas. **LS Auditory-Musical**

Alternative Assessment Handbook, Rubric 26: Poems and Songs

Answers

Reading Like a Historian **1.** *He lived in extreme luxury, protecting himself from rebellion behind iron gates.* **2.** *writes from the people's point of view; biased against the dictator*

SECTION 3

Nationalism in North Africa and the Middle East

BEFORE YOU READ

MAIN IDEA

The rise of nationalism in North Africa and the Middle East led to independence for some countries and to conflicts with the West.

READING FOCUS

1. How did independence come to French North Africa?
2. What events led to the creation of Israel?
3. How did nationalism cause changes in Egypt and Iran?

KEY TERMS AND PEOPLE

David Ben-Gurion
Gamal Abdel Nasser
Suez Crisis
Baghdad Pact
Pan-Arabism
Mohammad Reza Pahlavi

TAKING NOTES Take notes on key events and dates in the history of North Africa and the Middle East.

French North Africa	
Israel	
Egypt	
Iran	

BATTLE of ALGIERS

▲ French troops patrol the streets of Algiers.

THE INSIDE STORY ***How did Algerians win their independence?*** Bombs explode in crowded cafes, restaurants, and markets in the French section of Algiers. In response, government troops close off the Casbah, the old section of the city. They search houses and arrest thousands of people. Many of those arrested are tortured.

This was the scene in Algiers in 1956 when an Algerian nationalist group, the National Liberation Front (FLN), decided to take its war for independence against Algeria's French rulers to the cities. The FLN launched a campaign of bombings and assassinations aimed at both police and civilians. The French responded with a harsh crackdown on Arab residents.

Through tough interrogations of the people they had arrested, the French were able to track down most of the leadership of the FLN. The leaders were killed or thrown into prison, effectively shutting down the FLN's terror campaign.

Even though the French won the Battle of Algiers, they lost Algeria. The harsh tactics the French used increased popular support for the FLN, and six years later Algeria won its independence. ■

Teach the Main Idea

At Level

Nationalism in North Africa and the Middle East

1. **Teach** Ask students the Reading Focus questions to teach this section.
2. **Apply** Have each student draw a map of North Africa and the Middle East. Then organize students into groups of three, and assign each student one of the topics discussed in the section. Have students use their maps to locate the countries discussed in their assigned section and record one pertinent fact about the country on the map.
3. **Review** Create or show a large class map for all to see. Have volunteers identify the countries and facts about each. Have students add to or correct their own work as needed.
4. **Practice/Homework** Have students select one country in the section and write a summary of its independence movement. **LS Visual-Spatial, Verbal-Linguistic**

Alternative Assessment Handbook, Rubrics 20: Map Creation; and 37: Writing Assignments

Preteach

Getting Started

Use the **Interactive Reader and Study Guide** to familiarize students with the section content.

Interactive Reader and Study Guide, Section 3

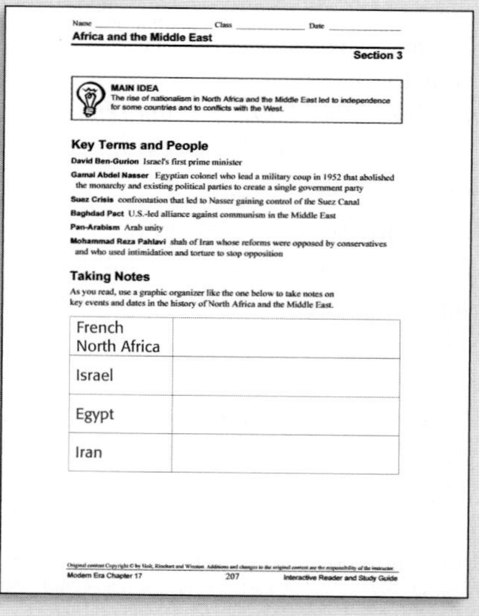

Name ____ Class ____ Date ____

Africa and the Middle East

Section 3

MAIN IDEA
The rise of nationalism in North Africa and the Middle East led to independence for some countries and to conflicts with the West.

Key Terms and People

David Ben-Gurion Israel's first prime minister
Gamal Abdel Nasser Egyptian colonel who lead a military coup in 1952 that abolished the monarchy and existing political parties to create a single government party
Suez Crisis confrontation that led to Nasser gaining control of the Suez Canal
Baghdad Pact U.S.-led alliance against communism in the Middle East
Pan-Arabism Arab unity
Mohammad Reza Pahlavi shah of Iran whose reforms were opposed by conservatives and who used intimidation and torture to stop opposition

Taking Notes

As you read, use a graphic organizer like the one below to take notes on key events and dates in the history of North Africa and the Middle East.

French North Africa	
Israel	
Egypt	
Iran	

Modern Era Chapter 17 207 Interactive Reader and Study Guide

Academic Vocabulary

Review with students the high-use academic term(s) in this section.

valid correct or justified (p. 953)

CRF: Vocabulary Builder: Section 3

Taking Notes

French North Africa—Morocco and Tunisia granted independence in 1956; Charles de Gaulle appointed prime minister of France in 1958; Algeria granted independence in 1962; Israel—Britain gives up control of mandate in 1947; Israel formed on May 14, 1948; first Arab-Israeli war in May-December 1948; Egypt—gained formal independence from Britain in 1922; coup led by Gamal Abdel Nasser in 1952; Suez Crisis; Baghdad Pact; Iran—Mohammad Reza Pahlavi became shah in 1941; Iranian parliament named Mohammad Mosaddeq prime minister in 1951

Direct Teach

Reading Focus

1 How did independence come to French North Africa? *North Africans resisted colonialism by force.*

French North Africa

Recall Why did France give up its protectorates in Morocco and Tunisia? *decided it could not fight guerrilla wars in Morocco, Tunisia, and Algeria at the same time*

Make Inferences Why did France launch such a violent counterattack in Algeria? *possible answer—believed that if they reacted with force the FLN would stop its attacks*

Draw Conclusions Why did France decide that Algeria was more important to fight for than Morocco and Tunisia? *possible answer—Algeria had more resources, wealth, and a large European population.*

CRF: Biography: Danièle Djamila Amrane-Minne

Info to Know

Pied Noir The French words *pied noir* mean "black foot" and refer to the French settlers in Algeria prior to 1962. In 1962 roughly 900,000 pied noirs fled Algeria. They took the motto, "suitcase or coffin" on justifying their mass exodus.

French North Africa

After World War II, France faced growing nationalist movements in its North African protectorates of Morocco, Tunisia, and Algeria. In all three places, resistance to colonialism had a strong influence on national identity.

Morocco and Tunisia In both Morocco and Tunisia, nationalist campaigns for independence began to grow in the early and mid-1900s. Attempts by France to crack down on these growing movements eventually led to increasing unrest, demonstrations, and guerrilla wars.

Meanwhile, Algeria was also struggling for independence. Algeria was far more important to the French because it was home to a large French settler population. Eventually, the French government concluded that it could not fight guerrilla wars in Algeria, Morocco, and Tunisia at the same time. As a result, France decided to negotiate with nationalist leaders in Morocco and Tunisia. Both countries were granted independence in 1956.

Algeria France had been involved in Algeria since 1830, when it first took control of some areas there. Later, France began to encourage large-scale European settlement in Algeria. By the 1950s there were more than 1 million European settlers in the area. These settlers owned the best land, dominated the economy, and had a grip on political power.

In 1954 a group of Algerian nationalist leaders formed the National Liberation Front (FLN). When the FLN began a campaign of armed attacks against French targets in November 1954, the French responded with mass arrests and raids on Muslim towns.

The next year the FLN decided to directly target French settlers. In one city, attacks killed more than 100 people. French forces and groups of settlers responded by attacking Muslims. Between 1,200 and 12,000 Muslims were killed in these reprisal attacks. These attacks set the pattern for the deadly war in Algeria—the FLN targeted French civilians, and the French responded by attacking the Muslim population.

In Algiers, the Algerian capital, the FLN launched a campaign of bombings and assassinations directed at both civilians and the military. The French responded with a harsh counterterrorism campaign that included torture of suspected FLN members. By the summer of 1957, the FLN had been largely defeated in Algiers. But the war was far from over.

French settlers in Algeria became increasingly angry over a perceived lack of support from the French government. In May 1958 French troops and a mob of settlers seized power in Algiers, demanding a change in government in Paris. Their demands were met when Charles de Gaulle was appointed prime minister in June 1958. De Gaulle was seen as a strong supporter of the settler population of Algeria.

De Gaulle hoped to satisfy both the French settlers and the Algerian nationalists by giving Algeria a limited degree of self-government. But he faced a violent reaction from the French settlers, who did not want France to give up any degree of control over Algeria, and the nationalists, who wanted full independence for Algeria.

De Gaulle finally decided that French rule in Algeria could not be maintained. He opened peace talks with the FLN in February 1961 and signed an agreement granting Algeria independence in 1962.

READING CHECK **Contrast** How was the struggle for independence in Algeria different from the struggle in Morocco and Tunisia?

The Creation of Israel

Nationalism also led to the creation of Israel. Since the late 1800s the Jewish nationalist movement known as Zionism had been growing, and Jews had been calling for an independent state in their ancient homeland. After World War II, Jewish dreams of an independent Jewish state were finally realized.

End of the British Mandate After World War I, the League of Nations gave Britain control over the mandate of Palestine and required Britain to make preparations for a Jewish homeland there. Following World War II, Jewish leaders in Palestine pressed the British to create a Jewish state. With the horrors of the Holocaust revealed to the world, the international community was sympathetic to the Zionist cause.

Skills Focus: Comparing and Contrasting

At Level

Reading Skill

Middle East Conflicts

1. Organize students into small, mixed-ability groups. Have each group copy and complete the chart as shown.
2. When groups have finished, create a large class chart for all to see, and post it in the classroom. Have students copy the chart and retain it as a study tool. **LS Visual-Spatial**

Alternative Assessment Handbook, Rubrics 6: Cause and Effect, and 7: Charts

Conflicts in the Middle East

Location	Causes	Effects

Answers

Reading Check *The French government negotiated with nationalist leaders in Morocco and Tunisia and allowed them independence, but fought the FLN to keep control of Algeria.*

World Religions

Judaism

The country of Israel sits in the heart of the Middle East. Israel is also the heart of Judaism, serving as a homeland and spiritual center for followers of one of the world's most ancient religions.

Origins of Judaism Before 1200 BC, nomadic Hebrew tribes settled in Canaan, a region on the eastern Mediterranean Sea. Over time, their beliefs developed into Judaism, the earliest monotheistic religion still in existence.

Jews believe that their religion was revealed by God to Moses, an early prophet who according to Jewish belief led the Israelites out of slavery from Egypt. These events are outlined in the Torah, the most sacred text of Judaism. The Torah is the first part of the Hebrew Bible, or Tanach.

By about 930 BC, kings had united the different tribes of the Israelites, and the Temple in Jerusalem became the Israelites' major religious center. By the 500s BC, invaders from outside conquered the region. As a result, many Jews were forced out. They later returned and established the Kingdom of Judea.

Judaism Today Today about 15 million Jews live around the world. The majority live in Israel and the United States, but many other countries have Jewish minorities.

Jews are a very diverse group. They have different beliefs and follow many different customs. They are united by common beliefs, a shared history, and a shared language—Hebrew. It is the language of the Hebrew Bible, of prayer, and is the everyday language of the State of Israel.

Infer How do you think common beliefs and history unite the Jewish people?

WORLD JEWISH POPULATION BY COUNTRY, 2005

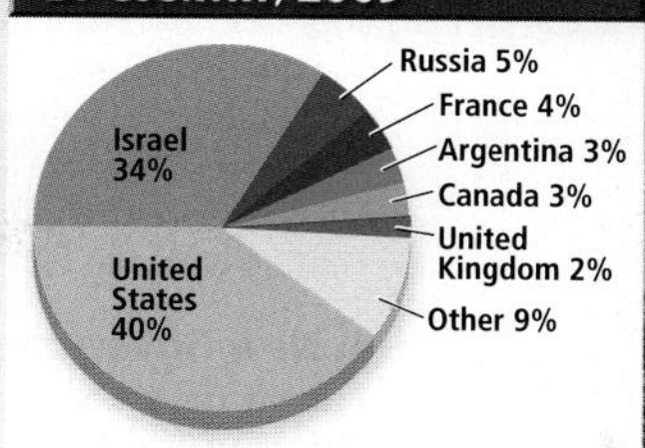

Source: Jewish Virtual Library

Jews pray at the Western Wall in Jerusalem.

In 1947 Britain announced that it was giving up control of the mandate and turning the matter over to the United Nations. The UN proposed to partition, or divide, Palestine into a Jewish state and an Arab state with Jerusalem under international control. Jewish leaders accepted the proposal, but Arab leaders rejected it. Despite Arab objections, the UN General Assembly passed a resolution supporting the partition as valid.

Independence and War As the British left Palestine, **David Ben-Gurion** and other Jewish leaders declared the birth of the democratic State of Israel on May 14, 1948. Ben-Gurion later became Israel's first prime minister.

The day after Israel declared its independence, armies from the Arab countries of Egypt, Syria, Lebanon, Transjordan, and Iraq invaded Israel, launching the first Arab-Israeli war. The war lasted from May to December 1948. In the end, the Arab armies were soundly defeated. Arab states negotiated cease-fire agreements with Israel, but they would not sign permanent peace treaties.

One result of this first Arab-Israeli war was that the Arab state proposed by the UN did not come into existence. Instead, during the fighting both Israel and neighboring Arab countries seized and held the land that had been planned for the new state. At the end of the war, Egypt controlled the Gaza Strip, and Transjordan controlled the territory west of the Jordan River known as the West Bank.

The war also caused massive refugee problems. By the end of the fighting, around 700,000 Palestinian Arabs had become refugees. They fled or were expelled from areas that Israel took control of as well as from the general war and chaos. Meanwhile, many Jewish refugees fled or were expelled from Arab countries and resettled in Israel.

READING CHECK **Summarize** What events led to the creation of Israel as an independent state?

ACADEMIC VOCABULARY
valid correct or justified

Direct Teach

Reading Focus

2 What events led to the creation of Israel? *1947: Britain announced it was giving up control of the mandate; UN proposed to partition Palestine into a Jewish state and an Arab state; 1948: Jewish leaders declared birth of the State of Israel*

The Creation of Israel

Describe What was the UN's plan for Palestine? *to divide Palestine into Jewish and Arab states*

Make Inferences What role did World War II play in the establishment of Israel? *The Holocaust created great sympathy for Jews who survived and created support for a separate Jewish state.*

Identify Cause and Effect What were some effects of the first Arab-Israeli war? *proposed Arab state did not come into existence; 700,000 Palestinian Arabs became refugees*

World Religions

Judaism

Analyzing Graphs Which country has the largest population of Jewish people? *the United States*

Skills Focus: Analyzing Alternative Points of View — Above Level

Reading Like a Historian Skill
Palestine and Israel

1. Review the information about the creation of Israel with students, and remind students that both Palestine and Israel have legitimate claims to land in the Middle East. Have students conduct outside research to find several articles about the creation of Israel from both the Arab and Israeli points of view. Tell students to look for scholarly, historical articles that are sensitive to the needs and claims of both.
2. Have students answer the questions who, what, why, when and how about each of their articles. Then have students analyze the articles for language that shows bias.
3. Have students present their research findings to the class. **LS Verbal-Linguistic**

Alternative Assessment Handbook, Rubrics 24: Oral Presentations; and 30: Research

Answers

World Religions *possible answer—by providing them with a shared history*

Reading Check *1947: Britain announced it was giving up control of the mandate; UN proposed to partition Palestine into a Jewish state and and Arab state; 1948: Jewish leaders declared birth of the State of Israel*

Direct Teach

Reading Focus

3 How did nationalism cause changes in Egypt and Iran? *The two countries began to reclaim land, and nationalize industries and resources.*

Changes in Egypt and Iran

Explain Why were Egyptians dissatisfied with King Farouk? *corruption, loss in First Arab-Israeli War, growing gap between rich and poor*

Sequence What led to the Suez Canal crisis? *Egypt signed arms deal with Czechoslovakia; U.S. refused to lend Egypt money to build Aswan Dam; Nasser nationalized Suez Canal; Britain, France, Israel attacked Egypt*

Quick Facts Transparency: Causes and Effects of the Suez Canal Crisis

Changes in Egypt and Iran

Israel's victory in the first Arab-Israeli war had effects throughout the Arab world. The victory discredited many of the region's leaders. As the pro-Western leaders lost popular support, a group of young nationalist leaders came to power in places such as Egypt and Iran. These new nationalist leaders soon came into conflict with the West.

A New Government in Egypt Egypt had gained its formal independence from Great Britain in 1922. But in many ways Egypt was not a fully independent country. British troops occupied the Suez Canal Zone, and a 1936 treaty allowed Britain to defend Egypt if it was attacked. The Egyptian monarch, King Farouk I, was strongly pro-British and seen as dependent on the British for his power.

Egypt's loss in the first Arab-Israeli war discredited King Farouk I and the leaders of Egypt's parliament. Many Egyptians believed that corruption in the palace, the parliament, and the army contributed to the defeat. The growing gap between rich and poor under the post-independence government also angered many Egyptians.

Out of this dissatisfaction came a 1952 military coup led by a 34-year-old colonel named **Gamal Abdel Nasser**. A group of young nationalist army officers staged the coup. Nasser and his co-conspirators moved quickly to consolidate power. They forced King Farouk out of power, abolished the monarchy, banned existing political parties, and created a single government party. Nasser also undertook an ambitious program of land reform to gain support among the poor.

The Suez Crisis Nasser became the most important figure in the Arab world after his confrontation with Britain, France, and Israel over the Suez Canal. This confrontation, known as the **Suez Crisis**, had its roots in the politics of the Cold War.

After Nasser came to power, he refused to join the **Baghdad Pact**, the U.S.-led alliance against communism in the Middle East. Then, when Nasser requested that western countries sell him arms, they refused. As a result, Nasser turned to Czechoslovakia, which was controlled by the Soviet Union, and signed an arms deal. The United States and Britain responded by refusing to loan Egypt money to build a dam on the Nile River at Aswan.

Nationalism in Egypt
Gamal Abdel Nasser led Egypt from the mid-1950s until 1970. A popular leader, he promoted nationalism in Egypt and the Arab world.

Causes and Effects of the Suez Canal Crisis (Quick Facts)

Causes

- Egypt signs an arms deal with Czechoslovakia.
- The United States and Great Britain decide not to help Egypt fund the Aswan High Dam.
- Egypt blocks Israeli shipping and supports raids against Israel.
- Egypt takes over control of the Suez Canal.
- Great Britain, France, and Israel secretly agree to attack Egypt and take the canal back.

Effects

- Egypt is defeated militarily, but Nasser emerges as a hero for standing up to the West.
- A desire for Arab unity, or Pan-Arabism, increases.
- Hostility between Egypt and Israel increases.

Differentiating Instruction

Below Level

Learners Having Difficulty

Materials: blank outline maps of the Middle East, colored pencils or markers

1. Review the information in the text about the Suez Canal crisis. Have students locate the Suez Canal in the atlas of their textbooks. Tell students that the Suez was an important waterway because it shortened the sea voyage to Asia.
2. Distribute outline maps to students. Have students label Egypt, the Mediterranean Sea, the Red Sea, and the Suez Canal.
3. Have students draw a sea route from the Mediterranean to the Red Sea, using one color. Then, in another color, have students draw the sea route that European ships would have to take if Egypt closed the Suez Canal. **LS Visual-Spatial**

Alternative Assessment Handbook, Rubric 20: Map Creation

Nasser was enraged that the United States and Britain denied him the funding necessary to build the dam. In response, he decided to nationalize, or take control of, the Suez Canal, which was owned by an international company controlled by Britain and France.

For many people in the Arab world, Nasser's action was celebrated as an act of defiance against European imperialism. But the British and French were outraged by this seizure of property. Hostility between Egypt and Israel was also growing.

In October 1956 Britain, France, and Israel launched a coordinated attack on Egypt. Israel invaded the Sinai Peninsula, and British and French troops occupied the Suez Canal Zone. Militarily, they defeated the Egyptian forces.

The United States did not support these actions, which created tensions with the Soviet Union. The U.S. government pressured Britain, France, and Israel to withdraw, which they did. When these countries withdrew and Egypt was left in control of the Suez Canal, the Suez Crisis became a great victory for Nasser. He became a hero in the Arab world.

Nasser promoted **Pan-Arabism**, or Arab unity, hoping to unite the Arab world. He brought Egypt and Syria together in 1958 as the United Arab Republic, but Syria withdrew two years later. Despite this failure, Nasser remained very popular in the Arab world.

Conflict in Iran When **Mohammad Reza Pahlavi** became shah of Iran in 1941, British and Russian troops occupied parts of the country. A British-run company also controlled Iran's highly profitable oil industry and kept most of the profits.

Iranian nationalists were determined to take control of the country's oil resources, reduce the power of the shah, and establish a constitutional monarchy. These nationalists were led by Mohammad Mosaddeq, an opponent of foreign influence in Iran.

In 1951 the Iranian parliament named Mosaddeq prime minister and voted to nationalize the Iranian oil industry. In response, Britain and the United States called for a boycott of Iranian oil, preventing Iran from selling much of its oil on the world market.

Meanwhile, Mosaddeq worked to reduce the power of the monarchy. He placed army forces under the control of the government, not the shah. He reduced the size of the army and forced officers loyal to the shah to leave.

Many military officers were upset with these reforms, and some joined a coup to replace Mosaddeq that was supported by the United States and Britain. When the coup was successful. Mosaddeq was overthrown and the shah returned to power.

After returning to power, the shah began an ambitious program of reforms, including land reform and a campaign to increase literacy. Iran's industry, education, and health care improved. Education and employment opportunities for women also improved.

The shah continued to rule with an iron hand, however. He used his secret police to spy on, intimidate, and torture the opposition. The shah's reforms were also opposed by conservatives who viewed them as moving Iran away from traditional Islamic values.

READING CHECK **Find the Main Idea** What changes occurred in Egypt and Iran, and how were they related to nationalism?

SECTION 3 ASSESSMENT

go.hrw.com
Online Quiz
Keyword: SHL AFR HP

Reviewing Ideas, Terms, and People

1. **a. Recall** How did the large population of French settlers in Algeria affect Algeria's history?
   b. Compare and Contrast What tactics were used by the FLN and by the French in the struggle in Algeria?
2. **a. Describe** What was the UN plan for the partition of Palestine?
   b. Sequence What happened after **David Ben-Gurion** and other Jewish leaders announced the creation of the State of Israel in 1948?
   c. Predict How might the events of 1947 and 1948 have set the stage for more conflicts between Israel and Arab states in the Middle East?
3. **a. Describe** Who was **Gamal Abdel Nasser**, and how did he promote Pan-Arabism?
   b. Summarize What events led to the **Suez Crisis**?
   c. Develop How did the policies of **Mohammad Reza Pahlavi** both help and hurt Iran?

Critical Thinking

4. **Sequence** Use your notes from this section and a graphic organizer like this one to create a time line of the key events in North Africa and the Middle East.

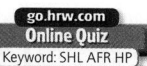

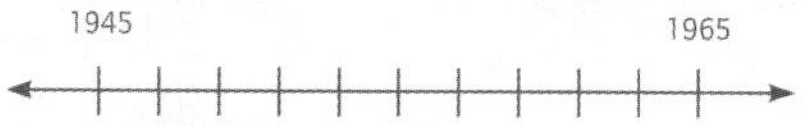

FOCUS ON WRITING

5. **Exposition** Write a brief newspaper article that describes the crisis over the Suez Canal.

Direct Teach

Reading Focus

Changes in Egypt and Iran

Recall What was Pan-Arabism? *unity of Arab nations*

Contrast What were some positive and negative aspects of the shah's rule in Iran? *positive—made reforms; negative—spied on and tortured the opposition*

Review & Assess

Close

Have students name the countries discussed in the section and how each gained independence.

Review

Online Quiz, Section 3

Assess

SE Section 3 Assessment

Progress Assessment: Section 3 Quiz

Alternative Assessment Handbook

Reteach/Intervene

Interactive Reader and Study Guide, Section 3

Interactive Skills Tutor CD-ROM

Section 3 Assessment Answers

1. **a.** French settlers owned the best land and had political power, leading to Algerian opposition.
   b. bombings, assassinations, torture
2. **a.** to divide it into two states, one Jewish and one Arab
   b. The first Arab-Israeli war began.
   c. no permanent peace treaty signed; many Palestinians from Israel left homeless
3. **a.** led military coup, forced King Farouk to abdicate, eliminated opposition
   b. Egypt signed arms deal with Czechoslovakia; U.S. refused to lend Egypt money for Aswan Dam; Suez Canal nationalized; Britain, France, Israel attacked Egypt
   c. help—improved industry, education, health care; hurt—used torture, conservatives disliked reforms
4. 1941: Pahlavi becomes shah of Iran; 1948: Israel formed, first Arab-Israeli war; 1951: Mosaddeq becomes Iran prime minister; 1952: Nasser leads coup in Egypt; 1956 and 1962: Morocco, Tunisia, Algeria granted independence
5. Students should argue logically and use information from the text to support their position.

Answers

Reading Check *Egypt—Nassir overthrew King Farouk, who was seen as too pro-British; promoted Pan-Arabism; Iran—nationalized oil industry; U.S. and Britain supported overthrow of Shah Mosaddeq, who had opposed foreign influence*

Preteach

Getting Started

Use the **Interactive Reader and Study Guide** to familiarize students with the section content.

Interactive Reader and Study Guide, Section 4

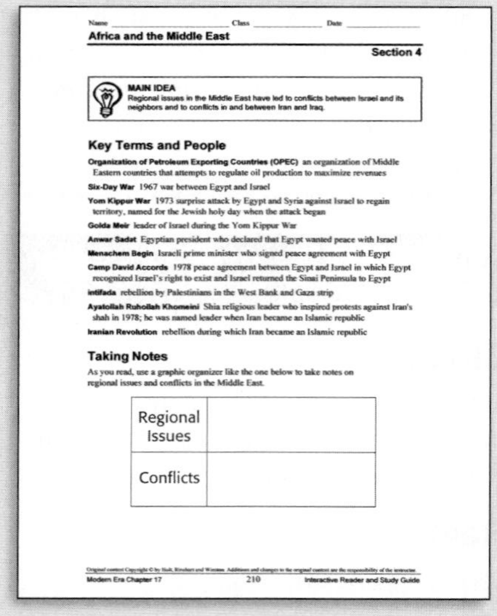
Name ______ Class ______ Date ______

Africa and the Middle East

Section 4

MAIN IDEA
Regional issues in the Middle East have led to conflicts between Israel and its neighbors and to conflicts in and between Iran and Iraq.

Key Terms and People

Organization of Petroleum Exporting Countries (OPEC) an organization of Middle Eastern countries that attempts to regulate oil production to maximize revenues

Six-Day War 1967 war between Egypt and Israel

Yom Kippur War 1973 surprise attack by Egypt and Syria against Israel to regain territory, named for the Jewish holy day when the attack began

Golda Meir leader of Israel during the Yom Kippur War

Anwar Sadat Egyptian president who declared that Egypt wanted peace with Israel

Menachem Begin Israeli prime minister who signed peace agreement with Egypt

Camp David Accords 1978 peace agreement between Egypt and Israel in which Egypt recognized Israel's right to exist and Israel returned the Sinai Peninsula to Egypt

intifada rebellion by Palestinians in the West Bank and Gaza strip

Ayatollah Ruhollah Khomeini Shia religious leader who inspired protests against Iran's shah in 1978; he was named leader when Iran became an Islamic republic

Iranian Revolution rebellion during which Iran became an Islamic republic

Taking Notes

As you read, use a graphic organizer like the one below to take notes on regional issues and conflicts in the Middle East.

Regional Issues	
Conflicts	

Modern Era Chapter 17 210 Interactive Reader and Study Guide

CRF: Vocabulary Builder: Section 4

Taking Notes

Regional Issues—oil production, growth of Islamism, conflicts with Israel

Conflicts—Six-Day War, Yom Kippur War, intifada, Iranian Revolution, Iran-Iraq War, Persian Gulf War, Iraq War

SECTION 4

Conflicts in the Middle East

Before You Read

Main Idea

Regional issues in the Middle East have led to conflicts between Israel and its neighbors and to conflicts in and between Iran and Iraq.

Reading Focus

1. How have regional issues contributed to conflicts in the Middle East?
2. What were some key events in the Arab-Israeli conflict?
3. What caused a revolution in Iran?
4. How have conflicts in Iraq affected that country?

Key Terms and People

Organization of Petroleum Exporting Countries (OPEC)
Six-Day War
Yom Kippur War
Golda Meir
Anwar Sadat
Menachem Begin
Camp David Accords
intifada
Ayatollah Ruhollah Khomeini
Iranian Revolution

TAKING NOTES Take notes on regional issues and conflicts in the Middle East.

Regional Issues	
Conflicts	

A Difficult Peace

THE INSIDE STORY ***How did a meeting in Maryland lead to peace between Egypt and Israel?*** In the summer of 1978 Egypt and Israel were holding peace talks after decades of conflict. U.S. president Jimmy Carter decided to bring together Egyptian and Israeli leaders for face-to-face negotiations. Carter invited Egyptian president Anwar Sadat and Israeli prime minister Menachem Begin to a meeting at Camp David, the U.S. presidential retreat in northern Maryland.

At first, the meetings went poorly. Israeli and Egyptian delegates sat in different sections of the dining room. On the third day of talks, discussions between Begin and Sadat broke down into heated arguments. One of Begin's advisers suggested that Begin and Sadat be kept apart for the remainder of the negotiations.

President Carter and his staff kept working for an agreement. The U.S. team went back and forth between the Egyptians and the Israelis, gathering comments and suggested changes to a proposed peace agreement. U.S negotiators wrote 23 drafts of an agreement before coming up with a version that both sides would accept. After 13 days of intense negotiations, Begin and Sadat finally signed the agreement—the first peace treaty between Israel and one of its Arab neighbors. ■

▲ **Anwar Sadat (left), Jimmy Carter (middle), and Menachem Begin (right) in 1978**

Regional Issues

Over the last few decades, major conflicts have erupted in the Middle East. Although the circumstances surrounding each of these conflicts were unique, some general regional issues have contributed to the conflicts. These regional issues include the presence of huge oil reserves, the growth of Islamism, and the conflict between Israel and its neighbors.

Oil in the Middle East About two-thirds of the world's known oil reserves are located in the Middle East. These vast oil reserves have been a great source of wealth for Saudi Arabia, Iran, Iraq, Kuwait, and other countries. Most of the region's oil-rich countries

Teach the Main Idea

At Level

Conflicts in the Middle East

1. **Teach** Ask students the Reading Focus questions to teach this section.
2. **Apply** Organize students into groups of three, and assign each student one of the three topics in the section. Have students scan their assigned topic and create a graphic organizer showing the main points of their assigned topic. Have students share and copy their graphic organizers, so that students have organizers for the entire section. Have students retain their work as a study tool.
3. **Review** Have volunteers share their graphic organizers with the class. Guide students in a discussion about conflicts in the Middle East and their affect on the rest of the world.
4. **Practice/Homework** Have students select one conflict in the Middle East and write a short summary describing it and the outcome. **LS Visual-Spatial, Interpersonal**

Alternative Assessment Handbook, Rubrics 17: Graphic Organizers; and 37: Writing Assignments are members of the **Organization of Petroleum Exporting Countries (OPEC)**, which attempts to regulate the production of oil exports to maximize revenues.

Oil revenues have allowed governments in the Middle East to modernize their countries and promote industrialization, economic development, and social programs. However, oil has also been a source of conflict. Some governments have used oil revenues to build up their military, maintain power, and even threaten their neighbors. Oil wealth has also caused internal clashes within countries and societies. In addition, the region's strategic importance as a source of oil has led outside nations to become involved in Middle Eastern affairs and politics.

Growth of Islamism Another regional issue that has led to conflict is the growth of Islamism, or Islamic fundamentalism, a movement to reorder government and society according to Islamic laws. Islamists believe that Muslim countries have strayed from the path of true Islam by following Western models of political and economic development. Over the last decades, countries such as Egypt, Iran, and Iraq have seen a growth in Islamism, which has led to conflicts within society and government. Furthermore, some Islamic extremists have used violence to try to bring about the changes they want. These radical extremists have attacked regional governments, their allies, and innocent civilians.

Conflicts with Israel A third regional issue that has been a source of conflict in the Middle East involves Israel. Since Israel was established in 1948, most Middle Eastern countries have refused to recognize its right to exist. Some countries have repeatedly attacked Israel and funded militant groups that conduct raids and terrorist attacks against Israelis. A series of wars between Israel and its neighbors has led to the expansion of Israel, which controls more land now than it did in 1948. As a result, many Palestinian Arabs live under Israeli control, another source of tension and conflict in the region.

READING CHECK **Summarize** What regional issues have led to conflicts in the Middle East?

CREATION OF ISRAEL, 1947–2006

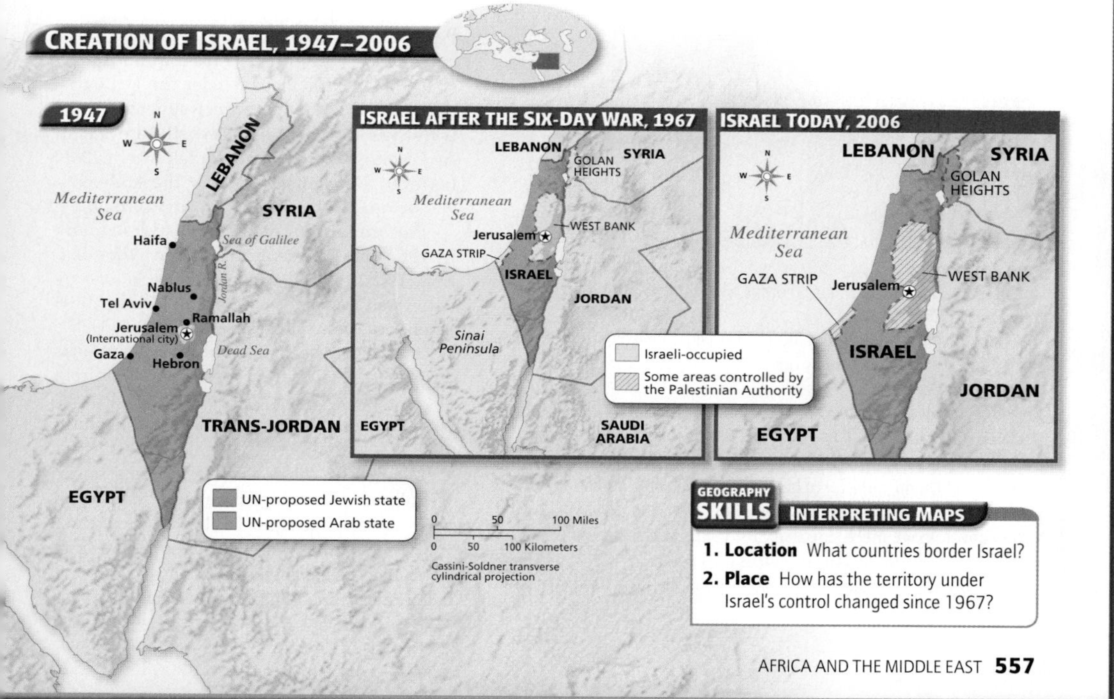

GEOGRAPHY SKILLS **INTERPRETING MAPS**

1. **Location** What countries border Israel?
2. **Place** How has the territory under Israel's control changed since 1967?

Direct Teach

Reading Focus

1 How have regional issues contributed to conflicts in the Middle East? *Oil revenues have been used to build up military power, growth of Islamism has led to conflict, and most Middle Eastern countries do not recognize Israel's right to exist.*

Regional Issues

Recall How have Middle Eastern nations used their profits from oil? *industrialization, health care, education, military*

Make Generalizations How has political Islam hindered the relationship between the Middle East and the Western world? *Radical extremists have used violence to try to bring about the changes they want.*

Interpreting Maps

Creation of Israel, 1947–2006

Activity **Summarizing Events**

Have students examine each of the maps and summarize what happened in Israel between the two time periods.

LS Visual-Spatial

Map Transparency: Creation of Israel, 1947–2006

Skills Focus: Sequencing

Below Level

Reading Skill

Creation of Israel

1. Organize students into mixed-ability pairs or small groups. Have students review the maps on this page showing Israel in 1947, 1967, and 2006. Then have students create a time line of events discussed in the section. Students should include the consequences or results of each event.
2. Have volunteers share their time lines and create a class time line for all to see. Have students add to or correct their work as needed.
3. As an extension, have students create a visual to illustrate each event on their time lines. Visuals could include charts, graphs, or small maps. **LS Visual-Spatial, Interpersonal**

Alternative Assessment Handbook, Rubric 36: Time Lines

Answers

Interpreting Maps **1.** *Egypt, Jordan, Syria, Lebanon;* **2.** *in 2006, Sinai Peninsula under Egypt's control, some areas of Jerusalem controlled by Palestinian Authority, Golan Heights no longer just occupied by Israel*

Reading Check *use of oil revenues; growth of Islamism; conflicts with Israel*

Direct Teach

Reading Focus

2 What were some key events in the Arab-Israeli conflict? *Six-Day War, Yom-Kippur War, Camp David Accords, intifada, Oslo Accords, second intifada, Israel withdraws from Gaza*

The Arab-Israeli Conflict

Sequence How did the Six-Day War lead to the Yom Kippur War? *At the end of the Six-Day War in 1967, Israel controlled territory in the West Bank and Gaza; Egypt and Syria launched the Yom Kippur War in 1973 in an attempt to win the territory back.*

Explain Why did Israel invade Lebanon in 1978 and 1982? *to stop PLO guerrilla attacks against Israel*

Info to Know

Golda Meir Golda Meir moved from Ukraine to Milwaukee, Wisconsin in 1906. Meir joined the Labor Zionist Party in 1915 and in 1939, Meir attended the Zionist Congress in Geneva to ensure the safety of European Jews. She became part of the People's Council that signed the proclamation starting the State of Israel in 1948. From 1969 to 1974 she served as the Prime Minister of Israel.

Primary Source

"The Egyptians could run to Egypt, the Syrians into Syria. The only place we could run was into the sea, and before we did that we might as well fight."
—Golda Meir

The Arab-Israeli Conflict

The Arab-Israeli conflict that began in 1948 has continued through the years. In 1967 and again in 1973, war erupted. Six years after the 1973 war, Egypt and Israel signed a peace agreement, but unrest among Palestinian Arabs in Israel remained a major problem.

War in 1967 and 1973 In 1967 Egypt demanded that the UN remove its troops from Gaza and the Sinai Peninsula. Egyptian troops then moved into the Sinai, and Egypt began to close off the Gulf of Aqaba, Israel's route to the Red Sea. Expecting a large-scale Arab attack, Israel decided to strike first.

Israel launched air strikes against Egypt, Syria, and Jordan, destroying most of their airplanes on the ground. Israeli ground troops then moved in and rapidly defeated Arab forces. In this war, called the **Six-Day War**, Israel took control of the Golan Heights, Sinai Peninsula, Gaza Strip, West Bank, and East Jerusalem. Israel gained control of land in the West Bank and Gaza with a large Palestinian population.

Determined to win their territory back Egypt and Syria launched the **Yom Kippur War**, a surprise attack against Israel in 1973. The war takes its name from the Jewish holy day when the attack began. At first, Arab troops made gains in the war. Israel's government, led by **Golda Meir**, was not fully prepared for the attack and needed military support from the United States. With U.S. support, Israeli forces regrouped and pushed back the Egyptian and Syrian armies. After weeks of fighting, both sides agreed to a cease-fire.

During the war, Arab members of OPEC declared an oil embargo, or a refusal to sell oil, to countries supporting Israel, including the United States. The price of oil around the world rose dramatically as a result.

A Peace Agreement Until the late 1970s no Arab nation had recognized Israel's right to exist. Then, in 1977, Egyptian president **Anwar Sadat** made a momentous declaration: Egypt wanted peace with Israel. To help facilitate this historic peace, U.S. president Jimmy Carter invited Sadat and Israeli prime minister **Menachem Begin** to Camp David, the presidential retreat in Maryland. There, in 1978, Sadat and Begin reached an agreement known as the **Camp David Accords**. Egypt recognized Israel, and Israel returned the Sinai Peninsula to Egypt. The treaty ended 30 years of hostility between Egypt and Israel.

Palestinian Unrest As Egypt and Israel made peace, Palestinian Arabs continued their struggle for nationhood. Under the UN partition plan of 1947, there were supposed to be two states in Palestine—a Jewish state and an Arab state. After the Arab-Israeli war of 1948, however, the land set aside for the Arab state was occupied by Israel, Egypt, and Jordan.

Palestinian nationalism was strong, and in 1964 the Palestine Liberation Organization (PLO) formed with a pledge to destroy Israel and replace it with a Palestinian state. After Yasser Arafat became leader in 1969, the PLO launched a campaign of guerrilla attacks against Israel, first from Jordan and later from Lebanon. In an effort to stop the PLO attacks, Israel invaded Lebanon in 1978 and again in 1982.

Meanwhile, tensions were building in the West Bank and Gaza, where Israel had begun building settlements. In 1987 Palestinian resentment of Israeli occupation boiled over into a rebellion called the **intifada**. During the intifada, Palestinian youths battled Israeli troops

FACES OF HISTORY

Golda MEIR
1898–1978

Golda Meir was one of the founders of the State of Israel and one of the first women to lead a national government in the modern era. She spent much of her life working toward the creation of Israel and helping build the foundation of the new country after it achieved independence in 1948.

Golda Meir was born in Ukraine. In 1906 her family immigrated to the United States, where Meir went to school and became active in the Zionist movement. In 1921 she moved to the British Mandate of Palestine and eventually became very influential there. When Israel declared its establishment in 1948, she was one of 24 people to sign the document. She later served in Israel's government as ambassador to the Soviet Union, minister of labor, foreign minister, and finally prime minister. In all of these positions, Golda Meir worked to build a strong government, make sure that the country was secure, and see to it that Israel's citizens had the resources they needed.

Summarize How did Golda Meir help establish the State of Israel?

Skills Focus: Analyzing Maps

At Level

Israel and Its Neighbors

Materials: construction paper, colored pencils

1. Have students examine the maps in this section and then create their own maps of Israel and neighboring countries. Have students use the atlas in their text to add capitals, major cities, and physical features.
2. Have students trace the events in the section about Arab-Israel conflicts on their maps. Students should show land lost and gained, areas of disputes, and where wars took place.
3. When students have finished their maps, guide students in a discussion of the role of geography in Middle East conflicts, and remind them of the size of the region.
LS Visual-Spatial

Alternative Assessment Handbook, Rubrics 11: Discussions; and 20: Map Creation

Answers

Faces of History *was active in Zionist movement, signed document declaring the establishment of Israel*

World Religions

Islam

Islam, one of the world's largest religions, has its roots in the Middle East. For more than 1,300 years, Islam has provided the rhythm for daily life in much of the region.

Origins of Islam The center of Islam is in Mecca, Saudi Arabia. Muslims believe that Muhammad received his first message from God in Mecca in about 610. Soon, Muhammad began to tell others about these messages, which form the basis of Islamic beliefs.

The sacred text of Islam is the Qur'an, which contains the messages Muhammad is said to have received from God. Muslims believe that the words in the Qur'an are the direct word of God. Believers around the world memorize the Qur'an and recite its teachings. As a result, the Qur'an is one of the most widely read texts in the world.

After Muhammad died in 632, his followers spread Islam rapidly across much of the Middle East and North Africa. In the following centuries, Islam continued to spread even more, eventually reaching farther into Africa, Asia, and Europe.

Islam Today About 1.3 billion Muslims live in the world today. The majority live in the Middle East, Africa, and Asia. Millions of Muslims also live in major cities throughout the world. Every year, as many as 3 million Muslims make a religious pilgrimage, or hajj, to Mecca.

Summarize How is Islam rooted in the Middle East?

The Blue Mosque in Istanbul, Turkey

Muslim Population by Country, 2006

COUNTRY	TOTAL NUMBER OF MUSLIMS (Percentage of total population)
Indonesia	212,937,000 (88%)
Pakistan	157,547,000 (97%)
India	140,434,000 (13%)
Bangladesh	119,785,000 (83%)
Egypt	72,855,000 (94%)
Turkey	69,660,000 (99.8%)
Iran	67,338,000 (99%)
Nigeria	64,383,000 (50%)
Ethiopia	34,700,000 (47.5%)
Algeria	32,207,000 (99%)

Source: *The World Almanac and Book of Facts, 2006*

in widespread street violence. Israel responded with strong military and police resistance, but the fighting continued until the early 1990s.

In 1993 PLO leader Yasser Arafat and Israeli prime minister Yitzhak Rabin negotiated the Oslo Accords to end the violence. The agreement called for the Palestinians to gradually gain control over the governing of the West Bank and Gaza. Israel and the PLO were supposed to sign a permanent agreement by 1998.

Extremists on both sides worked hard to undermine the peace process. The militant group Hamas launched suicide bombings in Israel. An Israeli religious fanatic assassinated Rabin in 1995. Eventually, relations between the Israeli and Palestinian leadership soured.

In 2000 a second intifada began. This time, Palestinian youths were joined by Palestinian security forces with guns. Hamas sent suicide bombers into Israel to attack civilians. The Israelis countered by sending troops backed by tanks, fighter jets, and helicopter gunships into cities in the West Bank and Gaza.

In 2004 Yasser Arafat died and was succeeded by Mahmoud Abbas. That same year, Israeli prime minister Ariel Sharon decided that Israel would withdraw from Gaza and parts of the West Bank. Israeli troops compelled Israeli settlers to leave Gaza and turned it over to the Palestinians in 2005. But tensions grew once more when Hamas, which many countries consider a terrorist organization, won control of the Palestinian parliament in 2006.

Also in 2006, armed conflict erupted after militants kidnapped several Israeli soldiers along the borders with Gaza and Lebanon. Israel launched massive air strikes and ground offensives in Gaza and southern Lebanon to root out extremists and secure its borders.

READING CHECK **Sequence** Describe the sequence of events in the Arab-Israeli conflict.

Direct Teach

Reading Focus

The Arab-Israeli Conflict

Identify Name the two leaders who participated in the Oslo Accords. *PLO leader Yasser Arafat and Israeli Prime Minister Yitzhak Rabin*

Sequence What are some developments of the Arab-Israeli conflict in the 2000s? *2000: second intifada began; 2005: Israeli settlers leave Gaza and turn it over to Palestinians; 2006: Hamas won control of Palestinian parliament; 2006: militants kidnapped several Israeli soldiers along the border of Gaza and Lebanon, Israel launched air strikes*

CRF: Biography: Hanan Ashrawi

Primary Source

"Peace for us means the destruction of Israel. We are preparing for an all-out war, a war which will last for generations."

"I come bearing an olive branch in one hand, and the freedom fighter's gun in the other. Do not let the olive branch fall from my hand."

—Yasser Arafat

Activity Analyzing Primary Sources Have students contrast these two quotes by Yasser Arafat and suggest reasons Arafat changed his position so dramatically. Remind students that Arafat won the Nobel Peace Prize in 1994.

LS Verbal-Linguistic

Skills Focus: Comparing and Contrasting

At Level

Research Required

Reading Skill

Islam and Judaism

1. Have students review the features on Islam and Judaism in this chapter. Then have students conduct outside research using reliable print and online sources to learn more about the two religions.
2. Have student show the results of their research in a chart in which they compare and contrast the two religions. Students should show similarities as well as the differences between the two.
3. Have volunteers share their charts with the class. **LS Verbal-Linguistic, Visual-Spatial**

Alternative Assessment Handbook, Rubrics 7: Charts; 9: Comparing and Contrasting; and 30: Research

Answers

Reading Check *1967: Six-Day War; 1973: Yom Kippur War; 1978: Camp David Accords; 1987: intifada; 1993: Oslo Accords; 2000: second intifada; 2005: Israel withdraws from Gaza*

Direct Teach

Reading Focus

3 What caused a revolution in Iran? *protests against the rule of the shah*

Revolution in Iran

Identify Who is Ayatollah Ruhollah Khomeini? *Shia religious leader, coordinated rebellion against shah, became Iran's leader in 1979*

Make Inferences Why were Khomeini's policies so strongly anti-Western? *The shah had been ousted because of his ties to Western governments and oil companies; Islamists opposed such ties to the west.*

Reading Focus

4 How have conflicts in Iraq affected that country? *Wars, economic sanctions, and insurgency have created the potential for civil war; ongoing violence has devestated much of the country.*

Conflict in Iraq

Identify Cause and Effect What was the cause of the Iran-Iraq War? *border disputes, Iran called for revolution among Iraq's Shiite population*

Evaluate Do you think Iraq could have been successful in taking control of Kuwait if the UN had not intervened? *possible answer—Yes, Iraq had the largest army in Arab world, Kuwait is much smaller*

CRF: History and Geography: Conflicts in the Persian Gulf

TIME LINE

Conflict in Iraq

1958 Army officers overthrow Iraq's monarchy and kill King Faisal II.

1968 The nationalist Baath Party takes power in Iraq.

1979 Saddam Hussein, a leader of the Baath Party, becomes president of Iraq.

1980 Iraq invades Iran, sparking the deadly Iran-Iraq War (1980–1988).

Revolution in Iran

A different kind of conflict erupted in Iran, where a revolution ousted the shah, Mohammad Reza Pahlavi. The shah had close ties to Western governments and oil companies. With their support, Iran westernized, and foreign influence grew. By the 1970s, Iran had changed from a traditional rural society to a more industrialized and urban one. Many Iranians felt threatened by this rapid change, while others felt betrayed by a government they viewed as corrupt. Islamists, in particular, opposed the shah because of his ties to the West.

In 1978 Iranians began to protest against the shah's rule. These protests were inspired by **Ayatollah Ruhollah Khomeini** (koh-MAY-nee), a Shia religious leader. Unable to calm the unrest, the shah fled Iran in 1979. During the **Iranian Revolution** Iran became an Islamic republic with Khomeini as its leader.

Under Khomeini's regime, the government suppressed political opposition and enforced strict social and religious values. Iran's foreign policy became strongly anti-Western, especially after the shah went to the United States for medical treatment.

In 1979 Iranian revolutionaries seized the U.S. embassy in Tehran and took 66 Americans hostage. The Iranians demanded that the shah be returned to Iran to stand trial. Although the shah left the United States shortly thereafter, the Iranians continued to hold the hostages until January 1981.

THE IMPACT TODAY

Since the hostage crisis, the United States Government has not reestablished an embassy in Tehran or any diplomatic relations with the Iranian government.

READING CHECK **Sequence** What was the sequence of events that led to the Iranian Revolution?

Conflict in Iraq

As Iran's new government was dealing with the hostage crisis, it soon found itself at war with its neighbor, Iraq. Later, Iraq fought two wars against U.S.-led coalitions before the government of Saddam Hussein was overthrown.

The Iran-Iraq War In 1980 Iraq attacked Iran because of border disputes and because Iran's new government called for revolution among Iraq's Shiite population. The war was long and costly, with as many as 500,000 dead on both sides. During the war, Iraq used chemical weapons against Iranian troops as well as Kurdish Iraqis who supported Iran. In 1988, after years of stalemate, Iran and Iraq agreed to a cease-fire.

The Persian Gulf War After the cease-fire, Saddam Hussein continued to build up Iraq's military, even though Iraq already had the largest army in the Arab world. In 1990 Iraq accused neighboring Kuwait of drilling into an Iraqi oil field and stealing oil. Hussein used this excuse to invade Kuwait.

In an effort to end the Iraqi occupation of Kuwait, the UN passed economic sanctions against Iraq. Those sanctions failed. As a result, a U.S.-led coalition launched the Persian Gulf War, attacking the Iraqi forces in Kuwait. In weeks, Kuwait was freed.

After the war, the UN continued its economic sanctions, insisted that Iraq destroy its chemical and biological weapons and agree not to develop nuclear weapons. But Iraq failed to fully cooperate with UN weapons inspectors

Skills Focus: Identifying Main Ideas and Details

At Level

Research Required

Reading Skill

Reporting on Iraq

1. Organize students into nine groups. Assign one of the events from the Conflict in Iraq time line to each group.
2. Tell students they are newspaper reporters covering their assigned event. Have students conduct research on the event, using reliable online sources.
3. When students have had enough time to gather research, have them create the front page of a newspaper about the event, including a headline, at least two articles, and a map or graphic. Articles should convey details about the event using the five Ws and one H of journalism (who, what, where, when, why, and how.)
4. Have each group present its newspaper page to the class **LS Verbal-Linguistic, Visual-Spatial**

Alternative Assessment Handbook, Rubrics 14: Group Activity; 23: Newspapers; and 30: Research

Answers

Reading Check *Protests began against the shah; the shah fled Iran in 1979; Iran became an Islamic republic with Khomeini as its leader.*

1991 A U.S.-led coalition forces Iraq out of Kuwait in the Persian Gulf War.

2005 Millions of Iraqis vote for a transitional national assembly.

1988 Iraq uses poison gas against its Kurdish minority for supporting Iran in the war.

1990 Iraq invades Kuwait.

2003 In the Iraq War, a U.S.-led coalition overthrows Hussein's government and occupies Iraq.

Skills Focus INTERPRETING TIME LINES

Identify What major wars did Iraq fight under Saddam Hussein?

who had been sent to verify that Iraq's weapons had been destroyed.

The Iraq War Following the attacks of September 11, 2001, some U.S. leaders believed that Saddam Hussein posed a greater threat to the United States than before. They worried that Hussein might have deadly weapons that he could give to terrorists. A new round of UN weapons inspections did not find any stockpiles of chemical, biological, or nuclear weapons; but again, Iraq did not fully cooperate with the inspections. Some U.S. officials were convinced that Hussein was hiding weapons. As a result, in 2003 another U.S.-led coalition invaded Iraq, quickly forcing Hussein out of power.

The coalition then moved to bring order to the nation, but efforts to restore peace were thwarted. A growing insurgency, or armed rebellion, by different groups from both inside and outside Iraq targeted coalition forces, their Iraqi allies, and innocent civilians. Insurgent attacks grew more and more deadly.

Meanwhile, the coalition worked to create a new, democratic government in Iraq. In 2004 political power was transferred to the Iraqis. In 2005 Iraqis voted in the country's first multiparty election in 50 years and later approved a new constitution that would make Iraq an Islamic federal democracy. But even as Iraq made progress toward a new government, continuing violence and the potential for civil war made the country's future highly uncertain.

READING CHECK **Infer** What are the main problems Iraq has faced in recent years?

SECTION 4 ASSESSMENT

go.hrw.com
Online Quiz
Keyword: SHL AFR HP

Reviewing Ideas, Terms, and People

1. **a. Recall** How has oil affected conflicts in the Middle East?
   b. Summarize What is Islamism?
2. **a. Describe** Describe the wars of 1967 and 1973.
   b. Support a Position What key steps do you think must be taken to begin to resolve the Arab-Israeli conflict?
3. **a. Describe** What was **Ayatollah Ruhollah Khomeini's** role in the **Iranian Revolution**?
   b. Analyze How do you think Iran's seizure of the U.S. embassy affected its relations with the West?
4. **a. Recall** Why did Iraq invade Kuwait, and what resulted from this action?
   b. Predict What challenges do you think Iraq will face in the coming years?

Critical Thinking

5. **Identify Cause and Effect** Using your notes, fill in a graphic organizer like the one below to identify causes and effects of the Arab-Israeli conflict, Iranian Revolution, and wars in Iraq.

Causes	Effects

FOCUS ON WRITING

6. **Description** For a library display on the Camp David Accords, write a paragraph describing the scene at Camp David when the agreement was reached.

• Review & Assess •

Close

Guide students in a discussion of recent conflicts in the Middle East and how they have been or might be resolved.

Review

go.hrw.com Online Quiz, Section 4

Assess

SE Section 4 Assessment

Progress Assessment: Section 4 Quiz

Alternative Assessment Handbook

Reteach/Intervene

Interactive Reader and Study Guide, Section 4

Interactive Skills Tutor CD-ROM

Answers

Time Lines *Iran-Iraq War, Persian Gulf War, Iraq War*

Reading Check *wars, economic sanctions, insurgency, potential for civil war*

Section 4 Assessment Answers

1. **a.** Oil revenues have been used for military buildup.
   b. a movement to reorder government and society according to Islamic laws
2. **a.** 1967: Israel takes control of territory, including land in the West Bank and Gaza, in Six-Day War; 1973: Egypt and Syria launch Yom Kippur War to regain territory
   b. possible answer—A peace agreement needs to be created that will be acceptable to both Arabs and Israelis.
3. **a.** inspired protests against shah, became Iran's leader after the shah fled Iran
   b. possible answer—probably made the West distrust Iran even more
4. **a.** accused Kuwait of drilling into an Iraqi oil field and stealing oil; UN passed economic sanctions; U.S.-led coalition launched the Persian Gulf War
   b. possible answer—to continue to hold elections and develop its new, democratic government; to stop violence and the insurgency
5. Arab-Israeli Conflict—Causes: dispute beween Arabs and Israelis over territory; Effects: wars, continuing violence; Iranian Revolution—Causes: protests against shah; shah's ties to West; Effects: new Islamic republic formed; Wars in Iraq—Causes: disputes over oil; Iraq's occupation of Kuwait; Iraq's failure to fully cooperate with UN inspections; Effects—growing insurgency; new, democratic government in Iraq
6. Students should draw upon information in this section to create detailed descriptions.

Document-Based Investigation

The Iranian Revolution

Info to Know

Khomeini and Technology Despite his rejection of Western values and his call for a return to strict Shia customs, Khomeini did not oppose the use of modern Western technology. After being exiled from Iran, he eventually settled in Paris where he coordinated the opposition movement against the shah of Iran through telecommunications. He used tape-recorded messages to express his revolutionary ideas. With the help of supporters in Paris, the messages were relayed to the people of Iran by telephone. Protests and demonstrations in Iran became more radical, and in 1979 Khomeini replaced the shah as the new ruler.

CHAPTER 17 Document-Based Investigation

The Iranian Revolution

Historical Context The four documents below present opinions from both sides of the Iranian Revolution of 1979.

Task Study the selections and answer the questions that follow. After you have studied all the documents, you will be asked to write an essay explaining why the Iranian Revolution occurred. You will need to use evidence from these selections and from the chapter to support the position you take in your essay.

DOCUMENT 1

Iran before the Revolution

Before the Revolution of 1979, Iran was ruled by Mohammad Reza Pahlavi, who worked to modernize and Westernize the country. As part of his effort to change Iran—a goal not shared by all Iranians—the shah wanted closer ties with the United States, a desire he expressed in a toast delivered to U. S. president Richard Nixon at a state dinner in 1972.

> Depending upon 25 centuries of national heritage and sovereignty, we today have started a new period of renewing our past glories, based on the eternal values of our culture and civilization, and hope that the pages of our future history will also be thumbed through with the same national pride based on honor, righteousness, peace, and justice.
>
> We have based our independent national policy on international understanding in the path of national reconstruction and the strengthening of world peace, coexistence, and, above all, cooperation. It is to be noted that we shall not tolerate any inequality from any quarter in our relations with other countries. Certainly under no circumstances will we allow any violation of our land or of our rights.

DOCUMENT 2

Leader of the Revolution

The Iranian Revolution was led by Ayatollah Ruhollah Khomeini, a Muslim leader who had been exiled from Iran for making derogatory comments against both the shah and the United States. Though the ayatollah died in 1989, images of him, such as this mural in a busy Tehran street, can still be seen all over Iran.

Skills Focus: Analyzing Visuals

At Level

Standard English Mastery

Reading Like a Historian Skill

A Tehran Mural

1. Have students review Document 2. Tell students that the image is a photograph of a mural in Tehran that depicts Ayatollah Khomeini.
2. Guide a class discussion about the mural. What might its purpose have been? Does the ayatollah look like someone to be feared, or someone to be loved? Why was the mural painted in this style? Why might it still exist in Tehran today, even though the ayatollah died in 1989, and Iran is now led by different people?
3. Have students write a paragraph explaining why they think the mural showing the ayatollah is significant, and why similar murals can still be seen all over Iran today. **LS Verbal-Linguistic,**

Alternative Assessment Handbook, Rubric 37: Writing Assignments

Document 3

The Ayatollah Speaks

Shortly after the overthrow of the shah, Ayatollah Khomeini addressed the people of Iran about the events that inspired the revolution.

> Your opponents, oppressed people, have never suffered. In the time of the *taghut* [impurity], they never suffered because either they were in agreement with the regime and loyal to it, or they kept silent. Now you have spread the banquet of freedom in from of them and they have sat down to eat. Xenomaniacs, people infatuated with the West, empty people, people with no content! Come to your senses; do not try to westernize everything you have! Look at the West, and see who the people are in the West that present themselves as champions of human rights and what their aims are. Is it human rights they really care about, or the rights of the superpowers? What they really want to secure are the rights of the superpowers. Our jurists should not follow or imitate them. You should implement human rights as the working classes of our society understand them. Yes, they are the real Society for the Defense of Human Rights. They are the ones who secure the well-being of humanity; they work while you talk; for they are Muslims and Islam cares about humanity.

Document 4

An American View of the Revolution

The revolution in Iran drew attention around the world. Scholars tried to explain its causes. One such scholar was Lewis Ware, who published this passage in the *Air University Review* in 1980. In his article, Ware points out that many Iranians did not consider the shah to be their legitimate ruler. He had already been overthrown once before, in 1953, and only regained his position through the intervention of the CIA. As a result, many Iranians considered him a puppet of the U. S. government.

> The Shah was the great modernizer of Iran. To further his goals he chose an autocratic model of nation-building bequeathed to him by his father, Reza Shah. During his reign a need for independence informed Muhammad Reza Pahlavi's vision of Iranian grandeur from which he never wavered and to which he applied the limitless resources of absolute monarchy. He failed to unite Iran under his person and destroyed in the process any possibility for Iran to act in an unrestrained environment . . . The Shah's debacle came about because there had never been, nor could there ever be under the circumstances, a general agreement on the meaning of progress. As a consequence, the Shah was denied the very security and legitimacy his regime needed to exist.

Skills Focus: Reading Like a Historian

Document 1

a. Identify What values does the shah say he wants Iran to be known for?

b. Elaborate How do you think the shahs' opinions would have been received by those who did not share his goals?

Document 2

a. Explain Why do you think the ayatollah's image can still be seen throughout Iran?

b. Develop What does the popularity of the ayatollah's image suggest about people's views of his ideas?

Document 3

a. Describe What does the ayatollah say is Westerners' real motivation for their involvement in Iran?

b. Contrast How did the ayatollah's views differ from the shah's? Which do you think were shared by more Iranians?

Document 4

a. Analyze How does Ware characterize the shah's reign?

b. Interpret Why does Ware think the shah's government was overthrown?

Document-Based Essay Question

The Iranian Revolution of 1979 was led by Ayatollah Khomeini, but he did not fight alone. Khomeini was supported by a huge segment of Iran's population. Could the revolution have been successful without the people's support? Using the documents above and information from the chapter, form a thesis about the role of the Iranian people in the revolution. Then write a short essay to support your position.

See **Skills Handbook**, pp. H25–H26, H30

Skills Focus: Analyzing Alternative Points of View — At Level

Reading Like a Historian Skill

Two Speeches

1. Tell students that Document 1 was a toast delivered to the U.S. president several years before the Iranian Revolution. Have a volunteer read it aloud. Which words in the speech emphasize the ties between Iran and the United States?
2. Tell students that Document 3 was a speech meant to support the new leadership of Ayatollah Khomeini. Have a volunteer read the speech aloud. Have students identify the words and phrases that emphasize the ayatollah's message.
3. Guide a class discussion about the two speeches. How is Iran's relationship with the West different after the Iranian Revolution?
4. Have students write a brief description of how Iran's relationship to the West changed after the Iranian Revolution. **LS Verbal-Linguistic**

Alternative Assessment Handbook, Rubric 40: Writing to Describe

Document-Based Investigation

Word Help

bequeathed handed down

debacle violent disruption

Teaching Tip

Explain to students that the word *ayatollah* is not a first name. It is a term meaning a Shia religious teacher of the highest rank, used most often in Iran.

Answers

Reading Like a Historian

Document 1. a. *honor, righteousness, peace, and justice;* **b.** *possible answer—The shah's opponents might have argued that he was too concerned with Western interests and not concerned enough with the interests of Iran.* **Document 2. a.** *possible answer—He is seen as a great leader who brought Iran its current form of government;* **b.** *that they continue to agree with his views;* **Document 3. a.** *He says Westerners are only motivated by their own interests, not by interests in human rights.* **b.** *The ayatollah did not want Western influence in Iran, while the shah wanted closer ties with the United States.* **Document 4. a.** *shah's goals for Iran were imposed with force on the country, resulting in the failure of the shah to maintain changes and his position;* **b.** *because there was no agreement on the shah's goals, nor did the people see him as a legitimate ruler;* **Essay** *Student essays should point out that the people of Iran played an important role in the Iranian Revolution of 1979. Essays should use details from Documents 1–4 and the chapter to support their position.*

Answers

Visual Summary

Review and Inquiry Have students write a summary of the key events in Africa and the Middle East listed on this page.

Quick Facts Transparency: Visual Study Guide: Africa and the Middle East

Review Key Terms and People

1. Jomo Kenyatta
2. apartheid
3. one-party system
4. negritude movement
5. Gamal Abdel Nasser
6. David Ben-Gurion
7. Pan-Arabism
8. Camp David Accords
9. intifada
10. Ayatollah Ruhollah Khomeini
11. Organization of Petroleum Exporting Countries (OPEC)
12. institute

Comprehension and Critical Thinking

13. a. a leader of Kenya's nationalist movement
b. by establishing the Convention People's Party (CPP) and leading strikes and demonstrations
c. possible answer—The establishment of homelands implied that black people were not citizens of South Africa.

14. a. helped organize a campaign that encouraged blacks in South Africa to break apartheid laws
b. about 1 million Tutsi and moderate Hutus massacred; many more became refugees
c. possible answer—by removing corrupt leaders from power

CHAPTER 17

Chapter Review

QUICK FACTS

VISUAL STUDY GUIDE

Conflicts in the Middle East

- The region's oil wealth has led to the build up of military forces, internal clashes within countries and societies, and outside influence by the world powers.
- The growth of Islamism in countries such as Egypt, Iran, and Iraq has led to conflicts within societies and governments.
- Since the State of Israel was established in 1948, a conflict between Arabs and Israelis has existed.
- During the Iranian Revolution in 1979, Islamists ousted the shah and Iran became an Islamic republic.
- In the late 1900s and early 2000s, Iraq was involved in three wars: the Iran-Iraq War, the Persian Gulf War, and the Iraq War.

Challenges in Africa

- Decades of protest against apartheid led to its end, and South Africans elected the country's first black president—Nelson Mandela.
- Dictators led governments with one-party systems in many newly independent countries.
- After independence, ethnic conflicts and civil war broke out in some African countries.
- Many countries struggled to establish democratic governments, while some countries were ruled by corrupt leaders.
- Today Africa faces many economic and environmental challenges, such as struggling economies, disease, and desertification.

Key Events in Africa and the Middle East, 1945–Present

- **1948** The State of Israel is established, and the first Arab-Israeli war begins.
- **1956** Morocco and Tunisia gain independence from France.
- **1956** Egypt seizes the Suez Canal, sparking the Suez Crisis.
- **1957** Ghana gains independence.
- **1960** Belgium withdraws from the Belgian Congo.
- **1963** Britain grants independence to Kenya, and Jomo Kenyatta becomes prime minister.
- **1967** Israel fights Egypt, Syria, and Jordan in the Six-Day War.
- **1973** Egypt and Syria attack Israel in the Yom Kippur War.
- **1974** Portugal withdraws from its African colonies after years of war.
- **1978** Egypt and Israel sign the Camp David Accords.
- **1991** A U.S.-led coalition forces Iraq out of Kuwait in the Persian Gulf War.
- **1994** South Africans elect Nelson Mandela as president.
- **2003** A U.S.-led coalition invades Iraq and forces Saddam Hussein from power.

Review Key Terms and People

Identify the term or person from the chapter that best fits each of the following descriptions.

1. leader of Kenya's independence movement
2. policy of racial segregation in South Africa
3. system in which a single political party controls the government
4. a literature movement focused on African identity
5. Egyptian nationalist leader
6. first Israeli prime minister
7. Arab unity
8. peace agreement between Egypt and Israel
9. Palestinian rebellion
10. leader of the Iranian Revolution
11. organization of oil-rich countries
12. to originate and establish

15. a. A nationalist movement known as Zionism called for an independent Jewish state.
b. In Egypt, the rise of a nationalist leader led to the Suez crisis; in Iran, nationalism led to opposition to foreign influence.
c. possible answer—a stronger claim, because the prime minister felt obligated to support the French settlers in Algeria

16. a. oil and the growth of Islamism
b. the Six-Day War, the Yom Kippur War, the Camp David Accords, intifada, the Oslo Accords
c. possible answer—There has been continuing violence and a growing insurgency.

History's Impact video program

Watch the video to answer the closing question: How has oil impacted the Arabian Peninsula and the rest of the world?

Comprehension and Critical Thinking

SECTION 1 *(pp. 539–543)*

13. a. Recall Who was Jomo Kenyatta?

b. Explain How did Kwame Nkrumah help gain independence for the Gold Coast?

c. Evaluate How do you think the establishment of homelands prevented black South Africans from gaining equal rights in South Africa?

SECTION 2 *(pp. 545–549)*

14. a. Describe What role did Nelson Mandela play in the ANC in the 1950s and 1960s?

b. Summarize How did ethnic conflict affect the peoples of Rwanda in the 1990s?

c. Predict How do you think Africans should work to overcome economic and environmental challenges such as disease and desertification?

SECTION 3 *(pp. 551–555)*

15. a. Recall How did nationalism lead to the creation of the State of Israel?

b. Contrast How did the rise of nationalist leaders in both Egypt and Iran affect those countries differently?

c. Support a Position Do you think the French settler population in Algeria gave France a stronger or weaker claim to Algeria? Explain.

SECTION 4 *(pp. 556–561)*

16. a. Describe Describe two regional issues that have contributed to conflicts in the Middle East.

b. Summarize What were the key events of the Arab-Israeli conflict since the 1960s?

c. Elaborate How have events in Iraq made it difficult for Iraqis to establish a stable democracy?

Reading Skills

Drawing Conclusions *Use what you know about drawing conclusions to answer the questions below.*

17. If you know that South Africa's apartheid system was abolished, what can you conclude about how life for black South Africans changed?

18. If you know that most of world's countries depend on oil and the Middle East has most of the world's oil, what can you conclude about the future of the Middle East?

Analyzing Primary Sources

Reading Like a Historian *The excerpt below is from a speech that Nelson Mandela gave in 1994 after he was inaugurated as the president of South Africa.*

> "We have triumphed in the effort to implant hope in . . . our people. We enter into a covenant that we shall build the society in which all South Africans, both black and white, will be able to walk tall, without any fear in their hearts, assured of their inalienable right to human dignity—a rainbow nation at peace with itself and the world."
>
> —Nelson Mandela, Inaugural Address, May 10,1994

19. Infer What former South African policy might have affected what Mandela says in his speech?

20. Interpret What do you think Mandela means by the phrase "a rainbow nation at peace with itself and the world"?

Using the Internet

go.hrw.com
Practice Online
Keyword: SHL AFR

21. In 1947 the United Nations proposed a plan to divide Palestine into separate Jewish and Arab states. Using the Internet, research the proposal and the reaction it received. Then write a report about the UN plan, using maps and other documents to support your work. Be sure to include information about how people living in Palestine reacted to the proposal.

WRITING ABOUT HISTORY

Exposition: Comparing and Contrasting *After World War II, nationalist movements grew in many areas European powers controlled in Africa and the Middle East. In some countries, the transition to independence took very different forms.*

22. Assignment: In an essay, compare and contrast nationalist movements in two nations discussed in this chapter. To provide support for your essay, use information from this chapter and from other research as needed. Be sure to collect facts and examples to clearly illustrate the points you are making about how the struggles for independence in these nations were similar and different.

Answers

Reading Skills

17. that black South Africans gained more rights and freedoms

18. that the future of the Middle East will vcontinue to be important to the world

Analyzing Primary Sources

19. apartheid

20. possible answer—a nation in which people of all races live in harmony with each other and the rest of the world

Using the Internet

21. Go to the HRW Web site and enter the keyword shown to access a rubric for this activity.

KEYWORD: SHL AFR

Writing About History

22. Student essays should compare and contrast two nationalist movements covered in this chapter, using details and examples to strengthen the comparison.
A rubric for the activity is provided in **CRF:** Writing for the SAT.

HOLT
History's Impact
▶ **Video Program: Africa and the Middle East**
Refer to the Video Teacher's Guide for the answer to the closing question.

Review and Assessment Resources

Review and Reinforce

- **CRF:** Chapter Review
- **Quick Facts Transparency:** Visual Study Guide: Africa and the Middle East
- **Spanish Chapter Summaries Audio CD Program**
- OSP **Holt PuzzlePro:** Quiz Show for ExamView
- **Quiz Game CD-ROM**

Assess

- **PASS:** Chapter Test, Forms A and B
- **Alternative Assessment Handbook**
- OSP **ExamView Test Generator,** Chapter Test
- **Differentiated Instruction Modified Worksheets and Tests CD-ROM:** Chapter Test
- HOAP **Holt Online Assessment Program** (in the Premier Online Edition)

Reteach/Intervene

- **Interactive Reader and Study Guide**
- **Differentiated Instruction Teacher Management System:** Lesson Plans for Differentiated Instruction
- **Differentiated Instruction Modified Worksheets and Tests CD-ROM:** Chapter Test
- **Interactive Skills Tutor CD-ROM**

go.hrw.com
Online Resources
KEYWORD: SHL TEACHER

Chapter 18 Planning Guide

Latin America

Chapter Overview	Reproducible Resources	Technology Resources
CHAPTER 18 **pp. 566–589** **Overview: In this chapter, students will learn about the political and economic problems in Latin America from 1945 to the present.**	**Differentiated Instruction Teacher Management System:*** • Pacing Guide • Lesson Plans for Differentiated Instruction **Interactive Reader and Study Guide:** Chapter Summary* **Chapter Resource File*** • Writing for the SAT • Social Studies Skill • Chapter Review **World History Outline Maps**	**Live Ink© Online Reading Help** **Student Edition on Audio CD Program** **Differentiated Instruction Modified Worksheets and Tests CD-ROM** **Interactive Skills Tutor CD-ROM** **World History Primary Source Library CD-ROM** **Power Presentations with Video CD-ROM** **History's Impact: World History Video Program (VHS/DVD):** Latin America
Section 1: **Revolution and Intervention** **The Main Idea:** In reaction to economic and social conditions in Latin America after World War II, many Central American countries experienced revolutions that involved intervention by the United States.	**Differentiated Instruction Teacher Management System:** Section 1 Lesson Plan* **Interactive Reader and Study Guide:** Section 1 Summary* **Chapter Resource File*** • Vocabulary Builder: Section 1 • Biography: Juan José Arévalo • Primary Source: Nicaraguans Protest U.S. Support of the Contras • History and Geography: Superpower Showdown	**Daily Test Practice Transparency:** Section 1* **Map Transparency:** Turmoil in Latin America, 1945–Present* **Internet Activity:** Latin America
Section 2: **The Rise of Dictatorships** **The Main Idea:** Spiraling economic and social problems and political turmoil in Latin America led military leaders to seize power and install repressive regimes.	**Differentiated Instruction Teacher Management System:** Section 2 Lesson Plan* **Interactive Reader and Study Guide:** Section 2 Summary* **Chapter Resource File*** • Vocabulary Builder: Section 2 • Biography: Enriqueta Barnes de Carlotto • Literature: *My Invented Country*	**Daily Test Practice Transparency:** Section 2*
Section 3: **Democratic and Economic Reforms** **The Main Idea:** In the 1980s, repressive regimes in Latin America fell, and more moderate elected leaders brought some measure of political and economic progress.	**Differentiated Instruction Teacher Management System:** Section 3 Lesson Plan* **Interactive Reader and Study Guide:** Section 3 Summary* **Chapter Resource File*** • Vocabulary Builder: Section 3 • Biography: Luiz Inácio Lula da Silva	**Daily Test Practice Transparency:** Section 3* **Map Transparency:** Poverty in Latin America, 2006* **Quick Facts Transparency:** Mexico Then; Mexico Now* **Internet Activity:** Current Events in Latin America

go.hrw.com | Print Resource | Transparency
LS Learning Styles | Audio CD | CD-ROM
Video | SE Student Edition | TE Teachers Edition
OSP One-Stop Planner CD-ROM
*also on One-Stop Planner CD-ROM

Review, Assessment, Intervention

- **Quick Facts Transparency:** Latin America*
- **Spanish Chapter Summaries Audio CD Program**
- **Progress Assessment Support System (PASS):** Chapter Test*
- **Differentiated Instruction Modified Worksheets and Tests CD-ROM:** Modified Chapter Test
- OSP **One-Stop Planner CD-ROM:** ExamView Test Generator (English/Spanish)
- HOAP **Holt Online Assessment Program (HOAP),** in the Holt Premier Online Student Edition

---

- **PASS:** Section 1 Quiz*
- **Online Quiz:** Section 1
- **Alternative Assessment Handbook**

- **PASS:** Section 2 Quiz*
- **Online Quiz:** Section 2
- **Alternative Assessment Handbook**

- **PASS:** Section 3 Quiz*
- **Online Quiz:** Section 3
- **Alternative Assessment Handbook**

HOLT
History's Impact
World History Video Program (VHS/DVD)
Latin America

Power Presentation with Video CD-ROM

Power Presentations with Video are visual presentations of each chapter's main ideas. Presentations can be customized by including Quick Facts charts, images and maps from the textbook, and video clips.

Holt Online Learning

go.hrw.com
Teacher Resources
KEYWORD: SHL TEACHER

go.hrw.com
Student Resources
KEYWORD: SHL LAT

- Document-Based Questions
- Interactive Multimedia Activities
- Current Events
- Chapter-Based Internet Activities
- and more!

Holt Premier
Online Student Edition

Complete online support for interactivity, assessment, and reporting

- Interactive Maps and Notebook
- Homework Practice and Research Activities Online

The Big Picture

Peter N. Stearns

Inequality The division between rich and poor is a long-standing problem in Latin America. The elite's control of natural resources, such as land, coupled with their control over economic and political institutions has severely limited the opportunities open to less powerful members of society. Extreme poverty and inadequate political representation have led to social and political instability. These circumstances have also led to a crisis of confidence among investors that has undermined economic growth in many nations.

Dictatorship The long-term rule of one man or one party (like the PRI of Mexico) characterized the governments of many Latin American countries in the second half of the twentieth century. The populace supported or endured heavy-handed leaders who promised to maintain order. But, continued and increasingly violent repression, sometimes exacerbated by corruption, brought resistance by ordinary folk into the open. In time, such protests precipitated the downfall of oppressive and corrupt regimes in Latin America.

Open Societies Recently, many governments in Latin America have returned to democratic rule. More responsive political and economic institutions have not solved new problems, such as those associated with the North American Free Trade Association (NAFTA). More open political structures do, however, give voice to the masses. In recent years, voters in many Latin American countires have excercised their right to vote by electing populist political leaders who promise to improve their standard of living.

Recent Scholarship

One of the best and most readable accounts of the modern era in Latin America is a text entitled *Born in Blood and Fire: A Concise History of Latin America* (2001), by John C. Chasteen. In addition to providing an excellent overview of this region's complicated history, the author analyzes political cartoons, paintings and murals, as well as movies that portray historical events. Special attention should be paid to the author's short essays called "Countercurrents." These essays highlight special dimensions of the broader themes covered in the chapters.

Differentiating Instruction

Differentiated Instruction Teacher Management System
- Pacing Guide
- Lesson Plans for Differentiated Instruction

Interactive Reader and Study Guide

Spanish Chapter Summaries Audio CD Program

Student Edition on Audio CD Program

Differentiated Instruction Modified Worksheets and Tests CD-ROM
- Vocabulary Flash Cards
- Modified Vocabulary Builder Activities
- Modified Chapter Review Activity
- Modified Chapter Test

OSP **One-Stop Planner CD-ROM**
- ExamView Test Generator (English/Spanish)
- PuzzlePro
- Quiz Show for ExamView
- Transparencies and Videos

TE **Differentiated Activities in the Teacher's Edition**
- Brazilian Lifestyles, p. 968
- Castro's Agrarian Reform Law, p. 969
- Victims of the "Dirty War", p. 974
- Economic Conditions and Changes, p. 981
- Analyzing Primary Sources, p. 985
- Higher Trade and Lower Employment, p 985

Reading Like a Historian

Sam Wineburg

Exploring Context How might historians approach the photo essay on Cuba that appears on page 972? Even before viewing this essay, they would note the context in which these photos appear: a textbook produced in the United States. Why would it matter that it was an American textbook rather than, say, a Canadian one? Because the United States has imposed a travel and trade embargo on Cuba for the last 45 years and maintains no diplomatic relations with this island nation. Canada, on the other hand, is Cuba's largest trading partner and more Canadians visit Cuba per year than tourists from any other nation. Just knowing where our book was published leads to certain expectations over others.

Have your students examine the five images and captions under the title "Communism in Cuba." The caption at the top of the essay announces that "Castro's policies have had mixed results." From this, we might indeed expect something mixed, a balance of good and bad attributes. But three of the four titles—"Stalled Economy," "Lack of Political Freedom," and "Scarcity of Food"—are decidedly in one direction.

Point of View The image that accompanies the Cuba's "stalled economy" is a close up of a vintage American car. "Because Cuba's communist policies have led to trade embargos . . . most cars in Cuba are from the 1950s." Have your students think about agency in this caption. Ask them how they might rewrite it if they wanted the reader to form a different impression. Compare the book's caption to this rewritten one: "Because the American government does not allow Ford, GE, and Chrysler to sell new cars to Cuba, many people, especially the poor, are forced to drive American automobiles dating back to the 1950s." How does each caption make us feel about the image before us?

We could use the same picture and, by writing a different caption, give it a different spin. We could turn the image/caption pairing into something positive, accentuating the ingenuity of the Cuban people, who have created cottage industries to make parts that keep classic cars running.

Farfetched? This is exactly what National Geographic photographer David Allen Harvey did in a 2006 photo essay. Accompanying an image of a vintage American car driving by a boxy Russian Lada on the sandy roadway alongside Havana's Malecón seaside avenue, Harvey wrote: "I think that the steel they made cars from in the 1950s must be tougher than today's materials. People drive those old cars in salt air and even drive them in flooded areas where the ocean comes over the [seawall]. But they don't seem to rust out and those guys keep them up somehow, they're able to just keep them going."

If we were to go to Cuba we might certainly see many cars like the one depicted in our textbook. But camera in hand, we could choose to shoot pictures of different scenes. In a six-part investigative report published in the *Bangor Daily News* in 2000, Gordon Bonin also observed fleets of vintage autos cruising Havana's streets. But he also noted "the roads swarm with new Hyundais, Daewoos, Citroens, Peugeots and Toyotas. Fewer in number, but more prominent by their rarity, are the black Mercedes and Audis." A photo of 'swarming' Asian imports would give a different impression of Cuba still.

The process of connecting a photograph to its caption is so spontaneous that many students don't even realize that their eye has been directed. To the question students are asked at the bottom of 972—"What can you say about life in Cuba based on these photographs?"—historians would ask, "What do the caption writers of this essay want us to say about life Cuba based on these photographs and captions?"

• Chapter Preview •

Chapter Main Ideas

Section 1 In reaction to economic and social conditions in Latin America after World War II, many Central American countries experienced revolutions that involved intervention by the United States.

Section 2 Spiraling economic and social problems and political turmoil in Latin America led military leaders to seize power and install repressive regimes.

Section 3 In the 1980s, repressive regimes in Latin America fell, and more moderate elected leaders brought some measure of political and economic progress.

CHAPTER 18

1945–Present

Latin America

THE BIG PICTURE Latin America has experienced many political and economic shifts since 1945. Revolutions and repressive governments have coincided with shifts toward government-controlled economies or more open market economies. In recent years, Latin America has made great strides toward democracy but still faces many economic and political challenges.

Theme ECONOMIC SYSTEMS

A common theme in Latin American history has been how to develop strong, diverse economies that meet the needs of the people. In this chapter you will learn about Latin America's struggles to create modern and productive economic systems.

TIME LINE

CHAPTER EVENTS

- **1959** The Cuban Revolution brings Fidel Castro to power.
- **1973** Augusto Pinochet takes power in Chile in a military coup.
- **Argentina's "dirty war" 1976–1983**

1945 — 1965

WORLD EVENTS

- **1949** The Chinese Communist Party takes full control of China.
- **1967** The Six-Day War takes place between Israel and Arab nations.
- **1980** Zimbabwe wins independence from Great Britain.

Key to Differentiating Instruction

Below Level
Basic-level activities designed for all students encountering new material

At Level
Intermediate-level activities designed for average students

Above Level
Challenging activities designed for honors and gifted and talented students

Standard English Mastery
Activities designed to improve standard English usage

Introduce the Chapter

At Level

Latin America

1. Have students make a list of all the material things people need in order to survive. Then have students make a list of basic rights and freedoms that people need in order to live in a just and fair society.
2. Have volunteers share their ideas and create a class list for all to see. You may wish to add several amendments from the Bill of Rights to the class list if students do not include them.
3. Have students name common traits of dictatorships, such as lack of security, little freedom, poor economy, and poor standard of living.
4. Guide students in a discussion of conditions in countries run by dictators. Why do people in these countries often lack material necessities and basic human rights?
LS Verbal-Linguistic

Alternative Assessment Handbook, Rubrics 11: Discussions; and 12: Drawing Conclusions

History's Impact video program
Watch the video to understand the impact of NAFTA.

Reading like a Historian Thousands of supporters attend a political rally for a presidential candidate in Uruguay. Rallies like this one are common in Latin America, as people express their support for or opposition to their government.

Analyzing Visuals What does this scene tell you about politics in modern Latin America?

See **Skills Handbook**, p. H26

1985 — **2005**

1992 Mexico, the United States, and Canada sign the North American Free Trade Agreement (NAFTA).

1992 A treaty to establish the European Union is signed.

2001 Terrorists attack the World Trade Center and the Pentagon in the United States.

2006 In reaction to failed economic reforms, Bolivians elect a leftist president.

• Chapter Preview •

HOLT
History's Impact
► **Video Program: Latin America**
See the Video Teacher's Guide for strategies for using the video segment.

Reading Like a Historian

Analyzing Visuals Uruguay is a small coastal country in southeast South America. Like many countries in South America, it faced political problems starting in the 1950s and 1960s, including a period of military rule. Since 1985, however, Uruguay has been ruled by democratically elected presidents. Have students take a moment to examine the photograph on this page. Ask students why a presidential rally might be so popular in Uruguay, considering the country's recent history.

Explore the Time Line

1. When did Castro come to power in Cuba? *1959*
2. How long was the "dirty war" in Argentina? *about 7 years*
3. What two significant events occurred in 1992? *NAFTA was signed; treaty to establish European Union was signed*

Info to Know

NAFTA and Mexico The North American Free Trade Agreement has not yet achieved all of its goals. Mexico has experienced some economic success and growth, but not as much as the United States and Canada. Mexico's northern states are seeing more benefits from NAFTA, while the southern states continue to lag behind. Overall, Mexico is benefiting, but not as much as proponents of NAFTA had hoped.

Draw Conclusions Why do you think Mexico has not benefited as much from NAFTA as the United States and Canada? *possible answer—lack of infrastructure found in U.S. and Canada*

go.hrw.com
Online Resources
Chapter Resources:
KEYWORD: SHL LAT
Teacher Resources:
KEYWORD: SHL TEACHER

Answers

Reading Like a Historian *People in some Latin American countries have the right to gather and demonstrate their political beliefs.*

Preteach

Geography Starting Points

Response to Argentina's "dirty war" In 1983 Argentina's new democratic government began to prosecute members of its former military government. Hundreds of military personnel and five members of the military junta were prosecuted and convicted of human rights violations.

Biography

Tomás Eloy Martínez (1934–) Tomás Eloy Martínez was born in Argentina in 1934 and wrote for a number of newspapers and publications. From 1972 to 1975 he wrote opinion columns that were staples in the dissent against Argentina's military dictatorship. In response, the government forced Martínez into exile. He moved to Venezuela, where he began to work for a newspaper called *El Nacional*. In 1979 he founded his own daily publication, *El Diario,* which is still in circulation today. In addition to his work as a newspaper journalist, Martínez as written several screenplays and books and is the recipient of seven honorary doctorates. Referring to the journalism profession, Martínez once stated, "To query, to learn, and to doubt a hundred times over before reporting about something: these are the most important verbs in the most risky, passionate profession of the world."

Map Transparency: Turmoil in Latin America, 1945–Present

World History Outline Maps

Interactive Map: Turmoil in Latin America, 1945–Present

GEOGRAPHY Starting Points

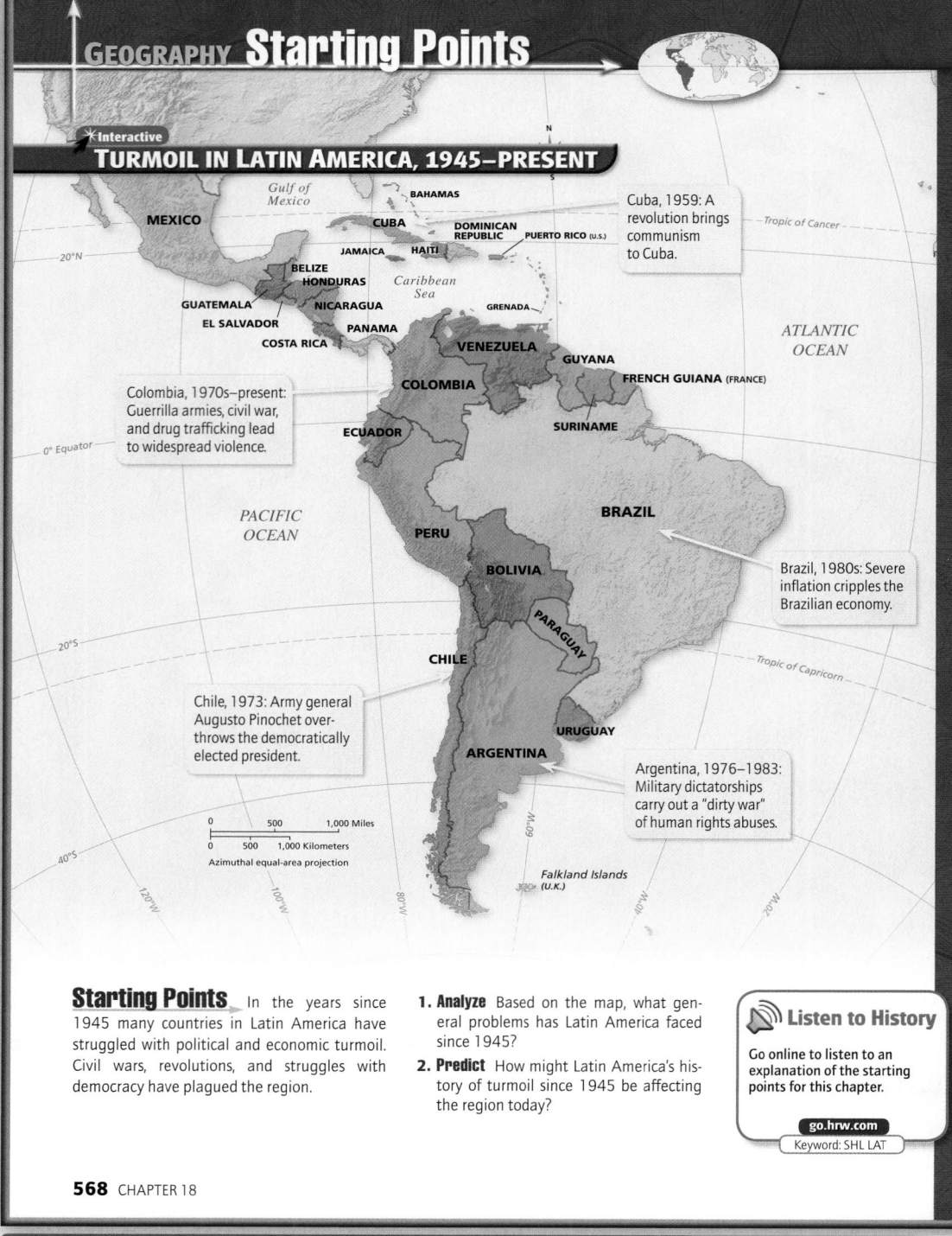

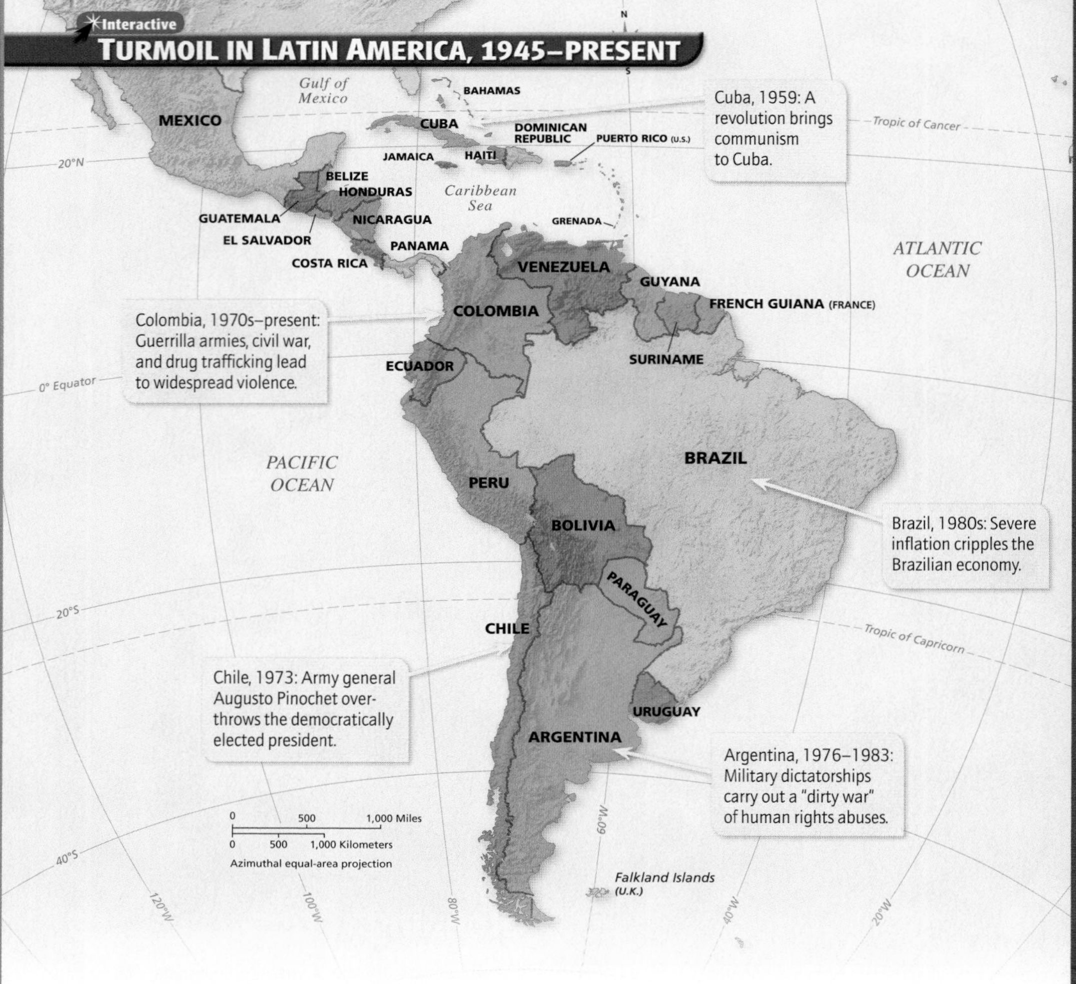

Starting Points In the years since 1945 many countries in Latin America have struggled with political and economic turmoil. Civil wars, revolutions, and struggles with democracy have plagued the region.

1. **Analyze** Based on the map, what general problems has Latin America faced since 1945?
2. **Predict** How might Latin America's history of turmoil since 1945 be affecting the region today?

Listen to History

Go online to listen to an explanation of the starting points for this chapter.

go.hrw.com
Keyword: SHL LAT

Skills Focus: Analyzing Maps

At Level

Social Studies Skill
Latin America Time Lines

1. To help students understand the information on the map, have them create their own time lines of Latin American events, using the information in the text boxes.
2. Organize students into small groups, and assign each group one of the five countries discussed: Argentina, Brazil, Chile, Columbia, and Cuba.
3. Have students use information from their texts to add information to their time lines about their assigned country and its political and economic problems.
4. Have volunteers from each group present their time lines to the class. **LS Visual-Spatial, Verbal-Linguistic**

Alternative Assessment Handbook, Rubrics 14: Group Activity; and 36: Time Lines

Answers

Geography Starting Points

1. *revolutions, economic hardships, social changes, dictatorships, wars*
2. *possible answer—Countries are still recovering from economic hardships and trying to establish stable, democratic governments.*

SECTION 1

Revolution and Intervention

BEFORE YOU READ

MAIN IDEA

In reaction to economic and social conditions in Latin America after World War II, many Central American countries experienced conflicts that involved intervention by the United States.

READING FOCUS

1. What were some key economic and social trends in postwar Latin America?
2. How did the Cuban Revolution come about and what changes did it bring?
3. What other conflicts arose in Central America?

KEY TERMS AND PEOPLE

import-substitution led industrialization
Liberation Theology
Fidel Castro
Che Guevara
Sandinistas
junta
Contras

TAKING NOTES Take notes on trends in Latin America and on the conflicts in this section.

Trends	Conflicts

LAND FOR THE LANDLESS

◀ **Members of Brazil's Landless Workers' Movement march to the capital.**

THE INSIDE STORY ***Who has a right to a country's land?*** In Brazil, less than 3 percent of the population owns about two-thirds of the country's farmland. As a result, more than 1.5 million landless workers have joined together to try to get land for Brazil's poor citizens.

Brazil's huge Landless Workers' Movement, known as the MST for its initials in Portuguese, was founded in 1984. The MST organizes groups of landless farmers to invade and build camps on large, unused private lands. One MST leader explained the reasons for these land invasions: "You have a right to land. There are unused properties in the region. There is only one way to force the government to expropriate [take] them. You think they'll do it if we write them a letter? Asking the mayor is a waste of time, especially if he's a landowner. You could talk to the priest, but if he's not interested, what's the point? We have to organize and take over that land ourselves."

Over the years, the MST has gained legal rights to much land. About 350,000 families have acquired land through land invasions and takeovers. However, these invasions naturally anger Brazil's large landowners. As a result, the MST is regularly in conflict with the police and other government officials. ■

Teach the Main Idea

At Level

Revolution and Intervention

1. **Teach** Ask students the Reading Focus questions to teach this section.
2. **Apply** Have students use the atlas in their textbooks to create their own maps of Latin America. Have students scan the section and take notes on each country discussed, using the maps as their note paper.
3. **Review** Organize students into pairs. Have one student read one of the notes, and have the other student identify the country where the event took place.
4. **Practice/Homework** Have students use reliable outside sources, such as newspapers, online news articles, or news magazines to locate an article about current events in Latin America. Have students share their articles, and then create a classroom "Current Events" display with the articles. LS **Verbal-Linguistic**

Alternative Assessment Handbook, Rubrics 1: Acquiring Information; and 24: Oral Presentations

Preteach

Getting Started

Use the **Interactive Reader and Study Guide** to familiarize students with the section content.

Interactive Reader and Study Guide, Section 1

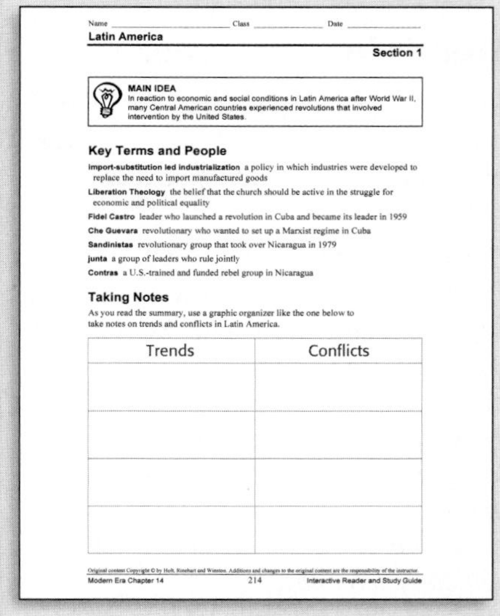

Name Class Date

Latin America

Section 1

MAIN IDEA
In reaction to economic and social conditions in Latin America after World War II, many Central American countries experienced revolutions that involved intervention by the United States.

Key Terms and People

Import-substitution led industrialization a policy in which industries were developed to replace the need to import manufactured goods
Liberation Theology the belief that the church should be active in the struggle for economic and political equality
Fidel Castro leader who launched a revolution in Cuba and became its leader in 1959
Che Guevara revolutionary who wanted to set up a Marxist regime in Cuba
Sandinistas revolutionary group that took over Nicaragua in 1979
junta a group of leaders who rule jointly
Contras a U.S.-trained and funded rebel group in Nicaragua

Taking Notes

As you read the summary, use a graphic organizer like the one below to take notes on trends and conflicts in Latin America.

Trends	Conflicts

Modern Era Chapter 14 214 Interactive Reader and Study Guide

Academic Vocabulary

Review with students the high-use academic term in this section.

intervene to enter into an event to affect its outcome (p. 573)

CRF: Vocabulary Builder: Section 1

Taking Notes

Trends—import-substitution led industrialization; land redistribution; urbanization; Conflicts—Cuban Revolution; civil wars in Guatemala and El Salvador; war between Sandinistas and Contras in Nicaragua

go.hrw.com
Online Resources

Chapter Resources:
KEYWORD: SHL LAT
ACTIVITY: Latin America

Direct Teach

Reading Focus

1 What were some key economic and social trends in postwar Latin America? *economic—land reform, industrialization; social—gap between rich and poor, urbanization*

Trends in Latin America

Recall What is Liberation Theology? *belief that the church should be active in the struggle for economic and political equality*

Elaborate Why do you think some Latin American countries were still dependent upon the United States even after the import-substitution led industrialization? *possible answers—They still needed money to develop to manufacturing plants; they were still developing their countries; it takes time to develop an independent and self-sufficient economy.*

Info to Know

Liberation Theology Liberation Theology first became popular in the 1960s and 1970s, but lost its popularity during the 1980s when it came under intense criticism from Cardinal Joseph Ratzinger, now Pope Benedict XVI. In Brazil, however, the movement is still very strong. Today, however, priests who have been drawn to Liberation Theology now tackle social issues such as women's rights, environmental conservation, homelessness, and AIDS.

Trends in Latin America

Latin America includes the countries south of the United States, from Mexico and the Caribbean to South America. After World War II, many countries in the region struggled to address problems of poverty and inequality. The roots of these problems go back to Latin America's long history of colonialism. Under colonialism, most land and wealth were concentrated in the hands of the elite, and economies were based mainly on agricultural exports.

Economic Trends One main economic trend in Latin America was industrialization. Economies in the region had long been based on the export of cash crops and raw materials and the import of manufactured goods. To decrease dependence on foreign countries, many countries adopted a policy of **import-substitution led industrialization**. Under this policy, local industries are developed to replace the need to import manufactured goods. However, even as industry grew, Latin America still depended on foreign countries for investment, technology, loans, and military aid.

As Latin America's countries industrialized, rural land use remained a major issue. A small group of elites, many tied to U.S. business interests, owned much of the land in Latin America, while many peasants struggled to find land to farm. Some countries tried to address this issue by taking land from large landholders and giving it to landless peasants. Although this policy had mixed results, it became another major economic trend in the region.

Social Trends The large gap between rich and poor in Latin America was also a major social issue. Some groups, including the church, tried to address this issue. Many priests began to promote **Liberation Theology**, the belief that the church should be active in the struggle for economic and social equality. Although it was criticized by the Catholic Church, the Liberation Theology movement became popular in heavily Catholic Latin America.

While some people looked to the church for help with their problems, others looked to the cities. Unable to make a living in rural areas, people flocked to the region's cities. This movement caused rapid urbanization. But many people found that life was no easier in the cities. Shortages of food, housing, and safe drinking water continued to present challenges for many in Latin America.

READING CHECK **Summarize** How did people in Latin America try to deal with some of the region's economic and social problems?

Urbanization in Latin America

Huge, rapidly growing cities are a common feature in Latin America. In many cities, such as Fortaleza, Brazil, upscale apartment buildings and offices are concentrated downtown and are surrounded by massive slums on the city's outskirts. ***How might the gap between rich and poor people affect life in the cities?***

Differentiating Instruction

At Level

English-Language Learners

Standard English Mastery

1. Have students examine the image of Fortaleza, Brazil on this page.
2. Have students work in pairs to create a list contrasting the lifestyle of someone who lives in a luxury, high-rise apartment in Brazil with someone who lives in a slum like the one in the image. Have volunteers share their lists and create a class list for all to see.
3. Have students use the information from the class list to write four journal entries; two should describe life in a high-rise, and the other two should describe life in the slum.
4. Have volunteers share their journal entries, either in small groups or with the entire class.
LS Verbal-Linguistic

Alternative Assessment Handbook, Rubric 15: Journals

Answers

Urbanization in Latin America *tension among the rich and poor, class struggles, increased crime*

Reading Check *industrialization, land reform, migration to cities, Liberation Theology movement*

The Cuban Revolution

In Cuba, social and economic trends led to a revolution. There, social inequality and heavy U.S. influence led to a revolt that brought communism to this large Caribbean island.

Reasons for Revolt Like much of Latin America, Cuba was very dependent on the United States. By the 1950s Cuba's modern hotels and gambling casinos were owned by wealthy Americans and Cuba's elite. U.S. businesses also owned huge sugar and tobacco plantations. These plantations produced valuable exports, but little land was left for average people to grow food. Cuba was one of the richest, most developed countries in Latin America. Yet most Cubans struggled to get by and earn a decent living.

Business interests encouraged the U.S. government to support a string of corrupt dictators in Cuba. The last of these dictators was Fulgencio Batista, an anticommunist who seized power in a 1952 military coup. Batista's Cuba was "a rich country with too many poor people," critics charged. Batista's coup stirred a wave of discontent and nationalism among the poor.

In 1953 a young lawyer named **Fidel Castro** led an unsuccessful attack on a Cuban army barracks. Castro was arrested and imprisoned. But two years later, he returned with a group of revolutionaries and launched a guerrilla war that became a full-scale revolution. When Batista fled the country on January 1, 1959, Cuba was left in the control of Castro, a brash leader who would outlast at least 10 U.S. presidents and the rest of the Cold War.

Goals of the Revolution Although there was broad public support for the revolution to remove Batista, most people did not know exactly what kind of revolution Castro would lead. Many middle-class Cubans supported moderate democratic reforms. But many of Castro's revolutionaries, including his brother Raul and the fiery leader **Che Guevara**, wanted to set up a Marxist regime. Castro was mainly focused on ending U.S. dominance, redistributing wealth, and reforming society.

To achieve these goals, Castro threw his energies into restructuring Cuba's economy, society, government, and foreign policy. In 1961 he launched a program that virtually ended illiteracy within one year. He also created a system of free, nationwide medical care that helped raise life expectancy to near-U.S. levels. To reduce economic inequality, Castro limited the size of landholdings and nationalized all private property and businesses in Cuba.

To ensure that he had the power to make such radical changes, Castro took full control over the government. Then he took away freedom of the press. These radical actions led Cuba more and more toward communism and a confrontation with the United States, which saw communism anywhere in the Americas as a threat to U.S. security.

PRIMARY SOURCES

Fidel Castro Speech

In the early years of the Cuban Revolution, Fidel Castro felt he needed to defend the policies of Cuba's new government. He did so in this speech to the UN General Assembly on September 26, 1960.

"Then followed the next law, an essential and inevitable law for our country, and a law which sooner or later will have to be adopted by all countries of the world, at least by those which have not yet adopted it: the Agrarian Reform Law. Of course, in theory everybody agrees with the Agrarian Reform Law. Nobody will deny the need for it unless he is a fool. No one can deny that agrarian reform is one of the essential conditions for the economic development of the country . . . In my country it was absolutely necessary: more than 200,000 peasant families lived in the countryside without land on which to grow essential food crops.

". . . Was it a radical agrarian reform? We think not. It was a reform adjusted to the needs of our development, and in keeping with our own possibilities of agricultural development. In other words, [it] was an agrarian reform which was to solve the problems of the landless peasants, the problem of supplying basic foodstuffs, the problem of rural unemployment, and which was to end, once and for all, the ghastly poverty which existed in the countryside of our native land."

Skills Focus — READING LIKE A HISTORIAN

1. **Explain** Why did Castro think it was necessary to pass the Agrarian Reform Law?
2. **Analyze Primary Sources** Against what criticisms do you think Castro felt he needed to defend his policies?

See **Skills Handbook**, p. H25

Direct Teach

Reading Focus

❷ How did the Cuban Revolution come about and what changes did it bring? *discrepancy between rich and poor, corrupt dictator, Fidel Castro led revolt; virtually ended illiteracy, provided free healthcare, nationalized properties and businesses, communism, loss of civil liberties*

The Cuban Revolution

Describe What changes did Castro and Che Guevara want for Cuba? *a Marxist regime; end to U.S. dominance, wealth redistribution, reformed society*

Summarize What were Castro's first actions after seizing power? *virtually ended illiteracy, established free medical care, limited size of landholdings, nationalized private properties and businesses*

Activity **Cuba Time Line** Have students make a time line focusing on important events and dates in Cuban history from the 1950s to the present day. **LS Visual-Spatial**

Alternative Assessment Handbook, Rubric 36: Time Lines

Primary Source

Fidel Castro Speech

Analyze Why did Castro defend his actions before the United Nations? *possible answer—concerned about international reaction to seizing land from its owners and giving it to the poor*

Differentiating Instruction

Above Level

Advanced Learners/ Gifted and Talented

Research Required

1. Have students read the excerpt on this page from the speech Fidel Castro gave to the United Nations on his Agrarian Reform Law.
2. Then have students conduct outside research on Castro's Agrarian Reform Law and its effects. Have students focus their research on both the negative and positive outcomes of the law.
3. Have students use their research to write a two-page petition to the United Nations persuading it to support Cuba's Agrarian Reform Law and to insist that other countries adopt this land reform measure. **LS Verbal-Linguistic**

Alternative Assessment Handbook, Rubrics 5: Business Letters; and 43: Writing to Persuade

Answers

Primary Sources **1.** *to improve the economy, supply basic food for peasants, help end rural unemployment and poverty;* **2.** *possible answer—that it was unfair, radical*

Direct Teach

History Close-Up

Info to Know

Communism in Cuba Fidel Castro took power of Cuba in 1959. In 1962, 78,000 Cubans fled Cuba and migrated to the United States. Castro then restricted travel between the United States and Cuba until 1965 when the government decided to permit air travel to Miami. During the next eight years, approximately 50,000 Cubans left their country and moved to the United States. Then in 1980, in what is known as the Mariel immigration, about 125,000 people fled Cuba in boats. In 1994 and 1995, the United States and Cuba signed agreements that allowed 20,000 Cubans to immigrate each year.

Fidel Castro Fidel Castro graduated from the School of Law at the University of Havana in 1950 and became involved in politics. He was imprisoned in Cuba after leading a rebel attack against Batista. Both he and his brother Raul were granted political amnesty in 1955 and moved to Mexico. They returned to Buba in 1956, and in 1959, Castro and his group of 800 guerrillas had forced Batista to flee, winning against the Cuban army of 30,000. One U.S. diplomat, Wayne Smith, has said that Fidel Castro will be remembered because "he stood up to the United States and survived." In August 2006, Fidel Castro was hospitalized and turned power over, at least temporarily, to his brother, Raul.

Teaching Tip

Remind students that Fidel Castro has ruled Cuba since 1959. Many Cubans have only known one leader for their entire lifetime.

HISTORY CLOSE-UP

Communism in Cuba

The Cuban Revolution affected many aspects of life in Cuba. Today the government controls the press, the economy, and social services. But Castro's communist policies have had mixed effects on the island and its people.

Lack of Political Freedoms While many Cubans support Castro and his policies, those who oppose the government are not free to express their opinions openly.

A Stalled Economy
A U.S. embargo on trade with Cuba has been in place since the 1960s. As a result, most cars in Cuba date from the 1950s, and many old buildings are in disrepair.

Scarcity of Food and Goods The Cuban government regulates the distribution of food and other goods, and scarcity is a major problem.

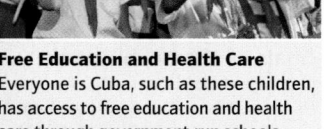

Free Education and Health Care Everyone is Cuba, such as these children, has access to free education and health care through government-run schools and clinics.

Skills Focus INTERPRETING VISUALS

Infer What can you say about life in Cuba based on these photographs?

Skills Focus: Comparing and Contrasting

Above Level

Reading Skill

Revolutions in History

1. Have students read the information about the revolution that took place in Cuba and the effects it had on the country.
2. Have students use the information in their texts to compare and contrast the revolution in Cuba that led to communism with other revolutions they have studied including the U.S. fight for freedom from Great Britain, the French Revolution, the revolutions of 1848, and the rise of communism in China and Russia.
3. Have students write an essay or create a multimedia presentation in which they explain why some revolutions have led to democracy, freedom, and civil rights, and others have led to dictatorships and communism. LS **Verbal-Linguistic, Visual-Spatial**

Alternative Assessment Handbook, Rubric 42: Writing to Inform

Answers

Interpreting Visuals *possible answers—Cubans have access to free education and health care; they must support the government; scarcity of food and goods continues; U.S. embargo has affected available products*

U.S. Involvement Cuba's move toward communism during the Cold War troubled U.S. leaders. They viewed Latin America as part of a U.S. sphere of influence and wanted to keep communism out of the region. Shortly after World War II, the United States helped set up the Organization of American States (OAS), an organization of countries in the Americas that promotes economic and military cooperation. The OAS was strongly anticommunist.

Repeated U.S. attempts to oust Cuba's communist leaders failed. In 1961 a U.S.-trained invasion force of Cuban exiles landed in the Bay of Pigs, along Cuba's southern coast. Their mission was designed to spark a nationwide uprising against Castro. But it was a disaster. Cuban troops easily defeated the invaders.

Still stinging from this defeat, U.S. president John F. Kennedy soon found himself in a far more serious crisis with Cuba and the Soviet Union. In 1962 the CIA learned that the Soviet Union was building nuclear missile sites in Cuba. Missiles from these sites would be able to easily hit targets in America. Kennedy ordered a naval blockade to intercept Soviet ships loaded with missiles for Cuba. This tense confrontation, known as the Cuban missile crisis, brought the world as close to nuclear war as it had ever been. In the end, however, a compromise was reached, and the Soviet Union removed the missile sites.

Results of the Revolution In the years since these Cold War conflicts, the Cuban Revolution has had mixed results. For example, Cubans have good access to health care and education. However, people's civil liberties are restricted under a one-party system. The government jails opponents and watches citizens through a network of neighborhood spies.

Economic effects have also been mixed. Castro's policies led many Cubans to leave the country. Most went to the United States, and Cuba's economy struggled as a result. Castro relied on the Soviet Union for economic support. But when the Soviet Union collapsed in 1991, Cuba's economy suffered. Cuba has also suffered for decades because of a U.S. economic embargo.

READING CHECK **Identify Cause and Effect** What were some of the causes and effects of the Cuban Revolution?

Other Conflicts

As in Cuba, economic inequality was a serious problem in other Central American countries. Yet economic conditions were not the only cause of conflicts. Political corruption and repression affected many places as well. In addition, U.S. support for anticommunist but corrupt governments stirred nationalist passions in Guatemala, El Salvador, and Nicaragua.

READING SKILLS
Understanding Causes and Effects What caused conflicts in Central America?

Guatemala In 1952 Guatemala's president, Jacobo Arbenz, used land reform to take over large landholdings and distribute the land to peasants. This policy hurt the United Fruit Company, an American company that owned huge amounts of mostly uncultivated land in Guatemala.

Pressure from the United Fruit Company, along with concerns that Arbenz was a leftist, or radical, persuaded the U.S. government that Guatemala's president must be removed from power. The CIA intervened in a coup that toppled Arbenz in 1954 and replaced him with a military dictator. The coup was the start of nearly a half century of repressive dictatorships in Guatemala.

ACADEMIC VOCABULARY
intervene to enter into an event to affect its outcome

The harshness of the government and the end of social reforms upset many peasants. Some joined rural guerrilla forces, and civil war raged from the 1970s to the 1990s between the guerrillas and government troops. Finally, in 1996, a peace accord brought an end to the fighting.

El Salvador Civil war also struck El Salvador, where military dictatorships kept power through unfair elections and repression. In 1980 government assassins gunned down Archbishop Oscar Romero, an outspoken government critic, as he was leading mass. Romero was one of many priests in Latin America who supported Liberation Theology.

Romero's murder sparked a bloody civil war between Communist-supported guerrilla groups and the army. Peasant villagers were often caught in the middle as government-sponsored "death squads" roamed the countryside killing civilians suspected of aiding the opposition. The Reagan administration supported the Salvadoran government and the army by providing money and military aid. Violence continued into the 1990s.

Direct Teach

Reading Focus

3 What other revolutions arose in Central America? *Guatemala—civil war between guerilla fighters and military; El Salvador—civil war between Communist-supported guerrillas and the army; Nicaragua—Sandinistas came to power, Contras, a rebel group, continued violent attacks on the country*

Other Revolutions

Explain What event sparked the civil war in El Salvador? *murder of Archbishop Oscar Romero, who supported Liberation Theology*

Analyze Why did the United States support the Somoza family and the Contras in Nicaragua? *Somozas opposed communism and the Contras opposed socialism.*

CRF: Biography: Juan José Arévalo

CRF: Primary Source: Nicaraguans Protest U.S. Support of the Contras

CRF: History and Geography: Superpower Showdown

Skills Focus: Drawing Conclusions

At Level

Reading Skill
Castro in Cuba

1. Have students review the information on this page about Cuba's relationship with the United States, focusing on the Cuban economy.
2. Have students use the information to create a political cartoon showing the problems in Cuba that resulted from the U.S. trade embargo and from Castro's economic policies. Students should create a cartoon and an appropriate caption.
3. Have students share their cartoons in small groups and then post the cartoons for all to see. **LS Visual-Spatial**

Alternative Assessment Handbook, Rubric 27: Political Cartoons

Answers

Reading Skills *economic inequality, political corruption, repression, and U.S. support for anticommunist but corrupt governments stirred nationalist passions in Central American countries*

Reading Check *Causes—social inequality, U.S. influence, revolts; Effects—access to health care and education, but restricted freedom, economy still suffers*

Review & Assess

Close

Have students name the countries discussed in the section, and discuss the economic and political problems facing each country.

Review

go.hrw.com **Online Quiz**, Section 1

Assess

SE Section 1 Assessment

Progress Assessment: Section 1 Quiz

Alternative Assessment Handbook

Reteach/Intervene

Interactive Reader and Study Guide, Section 1

Interactive Skills Tutor CD-ROM

Answers

Reading Check *civil war, violence, some corrupt leaders overthrown, economic problems, some financial and military aid*

Civil War

In 1979 leftist guerrillas in El Salvador launched a civil war against the country's military government. Here, a guerrilla fighter guards a roadblock in the country's rural interior, where much of the fighting took place.

Nicaragua Nicaragua also struggled with instability. Nicaragua had been ruled for four decades by members of the Somoza family. This wealthy family controlled about a quarter of the country's farmland. The Somozas' anticommunist views kept them in favor with the United States, but their corruption and violent repressive tactics alarmed many Nicaraguans. An anti-Somoza movement gained strength. In 1979 Somoza was forced to flee after a revolutionary group known as the **Sandinistas** took over the capital.

The Sandinistas ruled as a **junta** (HOON-tuh), a group of leaders who rule jointly. To deal with the country's many problems, they launched a program of economic and social reform. They set up some state-owned collective farms but also allowed private ownership of land. The Sandinistas also passed laws to protect workers' rights and began a Castro-style campaign to increase literacy. Unlike Castro, however, they allowed political opposition, both in the media and in elections.

Eventually, several factors pushed the Sandinistas to become more radical. The Reagan administration cut off financial aid to Nicaragua, leaving the Sandinistas to look to socialist countries for financial aid. In addition, a U.S.-trained and funded rebel group, the **Contras**, carried out a campaign of violence in Nicaragua that made it harder and harder for the junta to govern.

Eager to prove their government was still democratic in spite of its socialist leanings, the Sandinistas held an election in 1984. They were easily reelected. However, increasing economic troubles and violence continued throughout the 1980s.

READING CHECK **Make Generalizations** How did U.S. influence affect conflicts in Guatemala, El Salvador, and Nicaragua?

SECTION 1 ASSESSMENT

go.hrw.com **Online Quiz** Keyword: SHL LAT HP

Reviewing Ideas, Terms, and People

1. **a. Describe** What conditions in postwar Latin America made many countries politically unstable?
   b. Infer Why did **Liberation Theology** become popular in Latin America?
   c. Evaluate What was one benefit and one drawback of **import-substitution led industrialization**?
2. **a. Identify** Who is **Fidel Castro**? How did he come to power?
   b. Summarize How has the Cuban Revolution affected life for people in Cuba?
   c. Predict What challenges might Cuba's government face after Castro's rule has ended? Explain your answer.
3. **a. Recall** Why did the United States get involved in Guatemalan politics in the 1950s?
   b. Analyze What factors led to the failure of the **Sandinista** government?
   c. Support a Position Do you think the United States should have become involved in civil wars in Central America? Why or why not?

Critical Thinking

4. **Identify Cause and Effect** Using your notes, identify major causes and effects of revolutions and civil wars in Central America. How were these causes and effects similar and different from country to country?

	Cause	Effect
Cuba		
Guatemala		
El Salvador		
Nicaragua		

FOCUS ON WRITING

5. **Exposition** Imagine you are a citizen of Cuba, El Salvador, or Nicaragua. Write a short letter to a friend explaining the conflict in your country, identifying who is fighting, and analyzing what people are fighting for.

Section 1 Assessment Answers

1. **a.** poverty and inequality
   b. People hoped the Church would help solve economic and political problems.
   c. helped countries become more self-sufficient; countries relied on U.S. and other countries for investments, led to high debt
2. **a.** Cuba's leader; led revolt that forced Batista to flee, seized control of government
   b. virtually ended illiteracy, provided free health care; became Communist; restricted civil liberties; caused economic problems
   c. possible answers—a democratic revolt; U.S. aid; end to trade embargo
3. **a.** A U.S. company risked losing land in a land reform movement.
   b. The U.S. cut off financial aid to Nicaragua, funded the Contras
   c. possible answers—Yes, the United States should support democracy and its own interests in Latin America; no, many Latin American leaders are elected and are trying to solve various problems.
4. Cuba—inequality, heavy U.S. influence; Communist dictator; Guatemala—U.S. helped overthrow president; military dictator, civil war; El Salvador—murder of archbishop; civil war; Nicaragua— Sandinistas seized power, war between the Sandinistas and Contras
5. Student letters should address the issues that faced Nicaragua, Cuba, or El Salvador.

SECTION 2

The Rise of Dictatorships

Before You Read

Main Idea

Spiraling economic and social problems and political turmoil in Latin America led military leaders to seize power and install repressive regimes.

Reading Focus

1. How did life change under dictatorships in Argentina?
2. What changes occurred during the dictatorship in Brazil?
3. What was life like in Chile during Pinochet's dictatorship?
4. How did dictatorships affect life in other countries?

Key Terms and People

Juan Perón
populist
hyperinflation
Augusto Pinochet
Manuel Noriega
Shining Path

TAKING NOTES As you read, take notes on life during the dictatorships in these countries.

Argentina	
Brazil	
Chile	
Other countries	

VOICE OF THE PEOPLE

▲ Evita waves to her admirers.

THE INSIDE STORY ***Why was a dictator's wife so loved by her people?*** To her admirers, Eva Perón was the voice of Argentina's poor working class. As her husband, Argentine president Juan Perón, became more and more powerful, Evita ("little Eva") never let him forget the workers—the people whose support had helped him rise to power.

Although she never held any official posts during her husband's presidency, Evita essentially ran the government's health and labor departments. Focusing on charity work, she created the Eva Perón foundation to help the poor. This foundation built hospitals, schools, orphanages, and other institutions to help Argentina's poor and needy citizens. In addition, Evita championed the rights of women.

In 1952 Evita died tragically from cancer at the age of 33. The nation was devastated. Massive crowds of mourners lined up for miles to attend her funeral. Even today Evita's popularity lives on in books, films, and a Broadway musical. ■

Argentina

After World War II, when many countries around the world got rid of dictators, Argentina and other Latin American countries saw a rise of dictatorships. Many of these rulers did not come to power with the intent to rule as dictators. But social and economic conditions allowed them to take tremendous power at the expense of people's personal freedoms.

Teach the Main Idea

At Level

The Rise of Dictatorships

1. **Teach** Ask students the Reading Focus questions to teach this section.
2. **Apply** Organize the students into groups of four. Have each student scan one of the topics covered in the section and write down the main points. Have students share their notes and add the information about each topic covered in the section.
3. **Review** Have volunteers share the information and create a class outline of the section. Have students correct their own work and retain the notes and the outline as a study tool.
4. **Practice/Homework** Have students create an illustrated time line chronicling the important events discussed in the section.
LS Verbal-Linguistic, Visual-Spatial

Alternative Assessment Handbook, Rubrics 14: Group Activity; and 36: Time Lines

Preteach

Getting Started

Use the **Interactive Reader and Study Guide** to familiarize students with the section content.

Interactive Reader and Study Guide, Section 2

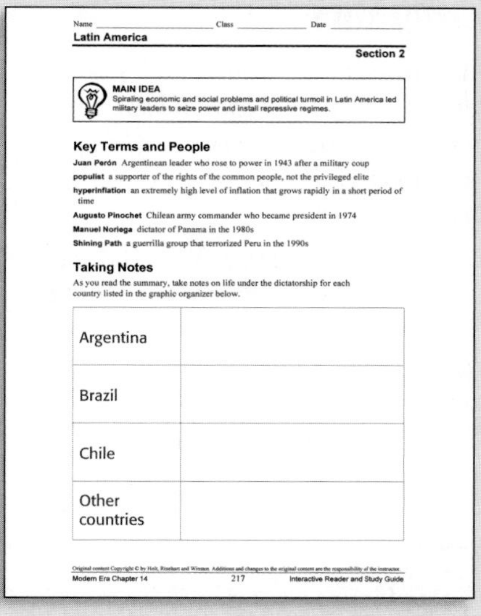

Name ____ Class ____ Date ____
Latin America
Section 2

MAIN IDEA
Spiraling economic and social problems and political turmoil in Latin America led military leaders to seize power and install repressive regimes.

Key Terms and People
Juan Perón Argentinean leader who rose to power in 1943 after a military coup
populist a supporter of the rights of the common people, not the privileged elite
hyperinflation an extremely high level of inflation that grows rapidly in a short period of time
Augusto Pinochet Chilean army commander who became president in 1974
Manuel Noriega dictator of Panama in the 1980s
Shining Path a guerrilla group that terrorized Peru in the 1990s

Taking Notes
As you read the summary, take notes on life under the dictatorship for each country listed in the graphic organizer below.

Argentina	
Brazil	
Chile	
Other countries	

Modern Era Chapter 14 217 Interactive Reader and Study Guide

CRF: Vocabulary Builder: Section 2

Taking Notes

Argentina—"dirty war", fear and violence, unemployment, inflation, foreign debt; Brazil—dictatorship froze wages, living standards dropped, death squads, economy crashed, hyperinflation; Chile—poor economy, disappearance of people; Other countries—turmoil, poor economy, loss of rights

Direct Teach

Reading Focus

1 How did life change under dictatorships in Argentina? *the economy took a downturn, personal freedoms were denied, "dirty war" of violence and fear*

Argentina

Summarize How did the Peróns reform Argentina? *established minimum wage, eight-hour workday, paid vacations; built schools, hospitals, homeless shelters*

Draw Conclusions Why did the Argentinean government carry out the "dirty war"? *to eliminate opposition, maintain complete control over Argentina through fear and repression.*

CRF: Biography: Enriqueta Barnes de Carlotto

Reading Like a Historian

Mothers of Plaza de Mayo The Mothers of Plaza de Mayo are still protesting. They are still on a mission to bring justice for their disappeared loved ones and they are tackling current events as well. This group of politically minded women continues to be a source of active resistance, whose movement is based on respect for human dignity and human life.

Answers

Reading Like a Historian 1. *less biased; written by outsider; perhaps favoring the point of view of those she interviewed;* **2.** *benefits—fresh in memory; disadvantages—can be emotionally charged, not placed within historical context;* **3.** *possible answer—might be a little biased in support of mothers who were hoping to find their children*

Perónism Beginning in 1943, **Juan Perón** rose to power following a military coup. With the help of his wife, Eva, Perón quickly proved himself to be a **populist**, a supporter of the rights of the common people as opposed to the privileged elite. With Eva in charge of labor and social programs, Perón made radical changes. He created a minimum wage, an eight-hour workday, and paid vacations. He built schools, hospitals, and homeless shelters. A booming postwar economy helped pay for these benefits.

However, there was a downside to Perón's rule. He tried to boost industrialization, but the effort failed because of a lack of resources. He also placed the cattle and wheat industries under government control. Farm production plunged as a result, damaging the nation's economy. In addition, Perón ruled with an iron fist. He turned Argentina into a one-party state and suppressed opposition and freedom of speech. Perón had become a dictator.

Military Dictatorships Perón's eventual downfall in 1955 was followed by decades of economic and political turmoil. For many years, right-wing military dictatorships ruled Argentina. They struggled with declining industry and rising unemployment, inflation, and foreign debt. Meanwhile, they cracked down on dissent by severely limiting people's personal freedoms.

Argentina entered a particularly ugly period in history from 1976 to 1983. During those years, the government carried out a "dirty war," as it was known, against suspected dissidents. It was a secret war carried out in the middle of the night. Soldiers seized people from their homes and took them to detention centers, where they were tortured and often killed. Some 10,000 to 30,000 people vanished during this time. The victims included both critics of the government and those falsely accused of being critics.

Reading like a Historian

Mothers of Plaza de Mayo

Evaluating Historical Interpretation When historians interpret the past, they build on and add to the knowledge, information, and sources of other scholars who have come before them. Through this process, historians arrive at their own interpretation of events based on their sources and their personal background and experiences.

The selection here is one historian's interpretation of the role of the Mothers of Plaza de Mayo. To evaluate this historical interpretation, think about

- the author of the source
- the date the source was created
- the author's background or perspective

The decision to install a permanent weekly presence in Plaza de Mayo was an act of desperation rather than one of calculated political resistance. It was a sense of desperation which the women believed only other mothers who had lost their children would share. . . . The Mothers, however, who had no legal or political expertise, recognized that their only weapon was direct action. They were committed to their illegal meetings in the square. Only by demonstrating their collective strength would they have any chance of breaking through the wall of silence erected by the authorities . . .

—Jo Fisher, from *Mothers of the Disappeared,* 1989

This book was published in 1989, soon after the events it describes had taken place.

Skills Focus READING LIKE A HISTORIAN

1. **Author** Jo Fisher based her book on interviews with more than 40 mothers and grandmothers in Argentina. How does that affect the author's credibility?
2. **Date** What benefits and drawbacks are there for historical interpretation when it occurs soon after an event takes place?
3. **Background** The author developed a close connection with the mothers and their cause. How might that affect her interpretation?

See **Skills Handbook**, p. H32

Differentiating Instruction

Below Level

Special Education Students

Materials: plain paper, pencils

1. Review the information in the text about the "dirty war" and the efforts of the Mothers of Plaza de Mayo.
2. Have students create a "Child Missing" poster for a young Argentine man or woman who became a victim of the "dirty war."
3. As an extension or for more advanced students, have students write an obituary for the person they have drawn in the poster.
4. Have students share their posters and obituaries with the class. **LS Visual-Spatial**

Alternative Assessment Handbook, Rubrics 3: Artwork; and 28: Posters

Desperate relatives tried to find out what happened to their loved ones. A group of mothers of the disappeared marched every week in the Plaza de Mayo, a square outside government buildings in Buenos Aires. Although they did not get the answers they wanted from the government, they did manage to bring national and international attention to the tactics of Argentina's military dictatorship.

READING CHECK **Find the Main Idea** How did dictatorships affect society in Argentina?

Brazil

Brazil followed a path similar to Argentina's. For a while, however, it seemed like Brazil would take a more stable and democratic route. With the death of a dictator in 1954, Juscelino Kubitschek (zhoo-se-LEE-noh KOO-bih-shek) came to power in a free election. Kubitschek promised "fifty years of progress in five." Foreign investment flowed into Brazil and helped the president achieve his goal. The results of this economic progress can be seen in the capital city of Brasília. The city, built in just three years at a cost of about $2 billion, became a symbol of pride and modernity.

The modernization effort, however, bankrupted Brazil's economy. As a result, military rulers seized control in 1964. For a time, they achieved success, creating the "Brazilian miracle" of 1968 to 1973. Industrial exports, farming, and mining grew. In fact, during this time Brazil's economy grew faster than any other in the world.

To achieve such rapid growth, Brazil's military dictatorship froze wages. Living standards declined sharply as a result. If people complained about the government, they risked becoming victims of government death squads that kidnapped, tortured, and killed.

As opposition to the military dictatorship grew, the economy crashed again. When oil prices rose in the 1970s, the economy spiraled into debt and **hyperinflation**, an extremely high level of inflation that grows rapidly in a short period of time. By 1990 the inflation rate was more than 2,500 percent.

READING CHECK **Identify Cause and Effect** What caused Brazil's economic problems?

HISTORY and Economics

Budgeting Money and Preventing Debt

Money is a limited resource, and using it wisely requires a plan for spending called a budget. A budget that is carefully planned and followed can help ensure that needs and wants are provided for appropriately. Responsible budgeting can also help prevent debt.

Budgeting and Debt in History In the 1960s and 1970s Brazil's leaders decided to borrow money to pay for the development of the nation's industries. They believed accumulating this debt was justified because future economic growth would create trade surpluses that the country could use to repay its loans. But that did not happen. Instead, the cost of oil skyrocketed in 1973 and 1979. Higher oil prices made industrialization dramatically more expensive than Brazil's leader had planned on when making the country's budget. As a result, Brazil's national and foreign debt spiraled out of control.

BRAZIL'S FOREIGN DEBT, 1965–1985

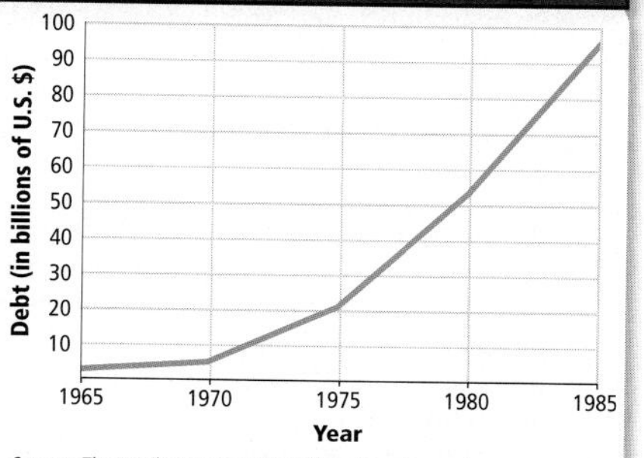

Sources: *The Brazilian Economy: Growth and Development; A Divida Externa Brasileira 1964–1982: Evolução e Crise*

Budgeting and Debt in Your Life In your life, you will also need to budget to pay the bills and stay out of debt. For example, will you take out loans to pay for college? How much debt should you take on to buy a car or a house? Answering questions like these will require you to carefully budget your earnings and expenses. Of course, you will not be able to anticipate all the factors that may affect your personal finances in the future. As a result, you may decide that the best approach will be to keep your budget balanced, take on as little debt as possible, and have enough savings to cover any emergencies.

Draw Conclusions Why is it important for people to budget their money?

Direct Teach

Reading Focus

❷ What changes occurred during the dictatorship in Brazil? *incurred great debt, living standards declined; death squads; economy crashed, inflation skyrocketed*

Brazil

Explain Why did military leaders seize control of the government? *Modernization had crippled the economy; military leaders thought they could fix the problem.*

Evaluate Do you think Brazil's phenomenal economic growth hurt or helped the country? *possible answers—helped: exports, farming, mining expanded; hurt: with wage freezes, living standards declined*

History and Economics

Budgeting Money and Preventing Debt

The Cruzado Plan In 1982, Brazil could no longer borrow money internationally and so it started to borrow domestically. By 1986 Brazil's domestic and international debt had risen to the same level. To help reduce inflation and to solve its economic woes, Brazil began the Cruzado Plan and froze prices and wages. The results were that inflation was brought down dramatically, but Brazil's currency was overvalued, which led to new economic problems.

Skills Focus: Identifying Main Idea and Details

Below Level

Standard English Mastery

Reading Skill
Current Events in Brazil

Materials: newspapers, magazines, scissors

1. Have the students review the information about Brazil's economy.
2. Have students find an article about Brazil in magazines, newspapers, or from reliable online sources.
3. Have students answer the following questions about their articles on a separate piece of paper: Who was involved? What happened? Where did it happen? When did it happen? Why is it important?
4. Have students use the information from their answers to these questions to write a summary of their articles.
5. Have volunteers share their summaries and discuss as a class. **LS Verbal-Linguistic**

Alternative Assessment Handbook, Rubric 42: Writing to Inform

Answers

History and Economics *possible answer—so they can keep debt at a minimum and become less dependent upon others*

Reading Check (top) *people lived in fear; economy suffered;* **(bottom)** *foreign investment, excessive domestic spending, dependence on imported petroleum products*

Direct Teach

Reading Focus

3 What was life like in Chile during Pinochet's dictatorship? *civil rights restricted, no free speech, no opposition tolerated*

Chile

Describe What changes did Allende make in Chile? *improvements in housing, education, health care, land reform*

Compare How was repression in Chile similar to repression in Argentina and Brazil? *government used violence as a tool to keep power; thousands of people were arrested and disappeared*

CRF: Literature: *My Invented Country*

Reading Focus

4 How did dictatorships affect life in other countries? *caused turmoil, economic disasters, and instability, raised international concern*

Other Dictatorships

Explain Why was President Aristide unsuccessful? *was unable to solve Haiti's economic problems*

Summarize Why did the United States intervene in Panama? *believed that Manuel Noreiga, a drug smuggler, would abuse his power over the Panama Canal*

The Pinochet Regime

Augusto Pinochet led a military coup in Chile in 1973.

During Pinochet's regime, thousands of people disappeared. Their relatives continue to protest against the government, demanding to know what happened. ***What tactics are the protesters using?***

Chile

As in Argentina and Brazil, economic problems led to drastic changes in Chile's government. Like so many other Latin American countries, Chile spent a period of time under the rule of a dictator.

Allende's Presidency In 1970 Chileans elected the leftist Salvador Allende president. Allende tried to improve the lives of the working class and stimulate the economy. He spent huge amounts of money on housing, education, and health care. The government broke up large estates and distributed the land to peasants. It also nationalized foreign-owned companies. For a time, Allende's measures were successful and widely popular.

However, Allende soon ran into trouble. Industrial and farm production fell, prices rose, and food shortages spread. In addition, Allende's leftist policies alienated business owners and worried the U.S. government. The CIA began providing secret funding and military training to opposition groups in hopes of triggering a coup.

As the economy failed and more people turned against Allende, the military rebelled. On September 11, 1973, fighter planes bombed the presidential palace. Allende and more than 3,000 others died in the coup.

READING SKILLS

Understanding Causes and Effects What was one cause and one effect of the 1973 coup?

The Pinochet Regime Several weeks before the coup, Allende had appointed a new commander in chief of the army, **Augusto Pinochet** (peen-oh-SHAY). General Pinochet was closely involved in the coup. He took command of the new military junta and became president in 1974.

Pinochet moved quickly to destroy the opposition. He disbanded congress, suspended the constitution, and banned opposition parties. He also censored the media. Within three years, an estimated 130,000 people were arrested for opposing the government. As in Argentina and Brazil, the government used violence as a tool to keep power. Thousands of people disappeared, were tortured, or fled into exile.

Despite the political crackdown, during this period the economy experienced several periods of rapid growth. Pinochet's government promoted capitalism, and exports grew.

READING CHECK **Summarize** How did events in Chile lead to a dictatorship?

Other Dictatorships

Military coups and elections brought other dictators to power throughout Latin America from the 1960s to the 1980s. These dictators had negative effects on their countries and caused serious international concern.

Skills Focus: Making Generalizations

Below Level

Reading Skill

Art as Protest

Materials: construction paper, art supplies, photographs of *arpilleras*, (a type of Latin American tapestry)

1. Display the sample arpilleras for all to see. Tell students that arpilleras are tapestries created to show daily life, and that they were first used as a form of protest in Chile.
2. Have students make their own arpillera depicting the daily life of a person living in Chile during the military dictatorship.
3. Have students share their work in small groups or with the entire class. **LS Visual-Spatial**

Alternative Assessment Handbook, Rubric 3: Artwork

Answers

The Pinochet Regime *displaying images of loved ones*

Reading Skills *cause—socialist-style policies; effect—Pinochet became dictator*

Reading Check *economic problems, socialist-style policies, CIA provided funding and training to opposition, a coup took place*

Haiti In Haiti, one family headed a dictatorship for 28 years. In 1957 François Duvalier was elected president, but he quickly began to repress any opposition. When he died, his son carried on the dictatorship.

The corruption of the Duvaliers made Haiti's bad economy even worse. In 1986 riots broke out in protest, and Duvalier was forced to flee. After several years of turmoil, Haitians elected Jean-Bertrand Aristide president in 1990. He had a plan to improve living standards for the poor. However, his presidency lasted just seven months before he was pushed from power by a military coup.

Aristide returned to power in 1994 when, faced with an invasion by U.S. troops, the Haitian military stepped down. But although he was popular with the poor, he was unable to solve the country's economic problems and was eventually pushed from power again.

Panama During the 1980s Panama came under the control of a dictator, **Manuel Noriega**. Noriega brutally crushed his enemies and used the country as a base for drug smuggling.

Noriega caused international concern. The Panama Canal, which had been under the control of the United States since its construction, was scheduled to be handed over to Panama in 1999. Because of the economic importance of the canal to worldwide shipping, Noriega's misrule posed a threat to worldwide economic interests.

In 1989 the United States sent troops to Panama City to arrest Noriega. Noriega surrendered and was sent to a prison in Florida on charges of drug trafficking. Democratic elections in Panama followed in 1994, and transfer of the canal occurred smoothly in 1999.

Peru In 1990 Peru faced the challenges of a poor economy and a guerrilla group known as the **Shining Path** that was terrorizing the countryside. In these conditions, Alberto Fujimori won the presidential election. Fujimori took drastic measures to improve the economy and stop the Shining Path. When congress complained that he had abused his power as president, Fujimori disbanded congress and suspended the constitution.

Although Fujimori had essentially become a dictator, Peru held elections in 1995. With the economy booming and significant progress being made against guerrilla activity, Fujimori won again. However, scandals and fraud eventually forced him to resign after the election of 2000.

READING CHECK **Compare** What did the dictators in Haiti, Panama, and Peru have in common?

SECTION 2 ASSESSMENT

go.hrw.com
Online Quiz
Keyword: SHL LAT HP

Reviewing Ideas, Terms, and People

1. **a. Define** What is a **populist**?
   b. Infer Why do you think Argentina's military dictatorships cracked down on dissent?
   c. Make Judgments Do you think the results achieved by the mothers of the disappeared were worth the risk of protesting against the government? Explain your answer.
2. **a. Describe** What was life like in Brazil during the military dictatorships?
   b. Analyze What led to **hyperinflation** in Brazil?
   c. Elaborate How might Brazil have avoided its economic troubles?
3. **a. Identify** Who became dictator of Chile after the coup that ended Allende's rule?
   b. Sequence What events led to a military coup in Chile?
   c. Support a Position What is your reaction to the argument that strong, repressive leadership was needed to achieve economic progress in Chile?
4. **a. Identify** Who was **Manuel Noriega**?
   b. Infer What role did the **Shining Path** play in allowing Fujimori to essentially become a dictator?
   c. Elaborate How might the situation in Panama have been different if the Panama Canal were not at stake?

Critical Thinking

5. **Compare and Contrast** Choose two countries from this section. Using your notes and a graphic organizer like this one, describe similarities and differences between those countries.

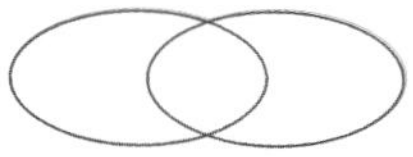

FOCUS ON WRITING

6. **Description** Imagine you live in Chile in 1974. Write a short journal entry describing the recent changes in your government and how those changes might affect Chile's future.

Direct Teach

Reading Focus

Other Dictatorships

Explain Why was the Panama Canal important to the United States and the rest of the world? *Closing it would threaten worldwide economic interests.*

Sequence How did Fujimori become a dictator in Peru? *won election; disbanded congress, suspended constitution*

Review & Assess

Close

Have students explain the connections between the economic problems and political turmoil in Latin America.

Review

Online Quiz, Section 2

Assess

SE Section 2 Assessment

Progress Assessment: Section 2 Quiz

Alternative Assessment Handbook

Reteach/Intervene

Interactive Reader and Study Guide, Section 2

Interactive Skills Tutor CD-ROM

Answers

Reading Check *abuse of power, economic problems, repression of opposition*

Section 2 Assessment Answers

1. **a.** a supporter of common people's rights
   b. did not want authority questioned, wanted to maintain complete control and power
   c. possible answer— Yes, the protests attracted the world's attention.
2. **a.** very difficult, inflation, no wage increases, no opposition tolerated
   b. high foreign debt, skyrocketing fuel prices, need to import oil
   c. possible answer—developed alternative fuel sources
3. **a.** Augusto Pinochet
   b. food shortages, economic problems, socialist-style policies, CIA's secret funding
   c. possible answer—Murdering opposition and curtailing human rights does not help solve economic problems.
4. **a.** drug smuggler, dictator of Panama
   b. Fujimori took drastic measures to stop the group; was told he had overstepped his powers, disbanded congress
   c. Noriega might have retained power
5. Students should describe similarities and differences of two countries discussed in this section.
6. Journal entries should discuss improvements and problems that occurred during Allende's rule and Pinochet's oppressive regime.

Preteach

Getting Started

Use the **Interactive Reader and Study Guide** to familiarize students with the section content.

Interactive Reader and Study Guide, Section 3

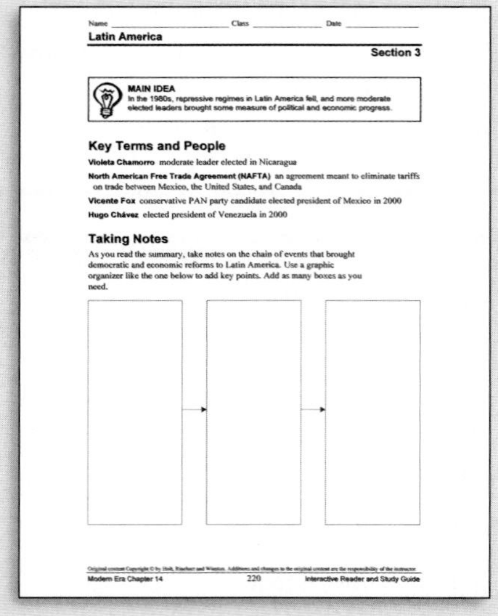
Name ______ Class ______ Date ______

Latin America

Section 3

MAIN IDEA
In the 1980s, repressive regimes in Latin America fell, and more moderate elected leaders brought some measure of political and economic progress.

Key Terms and People

Violeta Chamorro moderate leader elected in Nicaragua

North American Free Trade Agreement (NAFTA) an agreement meant to eliminate tariffs on trade between Mexico, the United States, and Canada

Vicente Fox conservative PAN party candidate elected president of Mexico in 2000

Hugo Chávez elected president of Venezuela in 2000

Taking Notes

As you read the summary, take notes on the chain of events that brought democratic and economic reforms to Latin America. Use a graphic organizer like the one below to add key points. Add as many boxes as you need.

Modern Era Chapter 14 220 Interactive Reader and Study Guide

Academic Vocabulary

Review with students the high-use academic terms in this section.

integrate to blend or join together (p. 581)

security freedom from danger or fear (p. 583)

CRF: Vocabulary Builder: Section 3

Taking Notes

new conditions in order to receive loans; outside groups pushing for voting rights; NAFTA; more exports

go.hrw.com
Online Resources

Chapter Resources:
KEYWORD: SHL LAT
ACTIVITY: Current Events in Latin America

SECTION 3

Democratic and Economic Reforms

Before You Read

Main Idea

In the 1980s, repressive regimes in Latin America fell, and more moderate elected leaders brought some measure of political and economic progress.

Reading Focus

1. How did democracy return to Latin America?
2. How has democracy in Mexico changed in recent years?
3. What have been the results of market reforms in Latin America?

Key Terms and People

Violeta Chamorro
North American Free Trade Agreement (NAFTA)
Vicente Fox
Hugo Chávez

TAKING NOTES Take notes on the chain of events that brought democratic and economic reforms to Latin America.

THE INSIDE STORY

How did a dictator's attempt to distract his people lead to war? In early 1982 Argentina's military government was faced with a weakening economy and public outcry over the mysterious disappearances of government critics. Argentina's government, led by General Leopoldo Galtieri, wanted to distract the country from its problems. So Galtieri started a war. On April 2, about 9,000 Argentine troops invaded the British-controlled Falkland Islands in the South Atlantic, about 300 miles off Argentina's coast.

The Falklands—known as the Malvinas in Argentina—consist of two main islands and hundreds of tiny ones. The 2,000 or so Falklands residents were mainly sheep-farming British citizens. Great Britain and Argentina had both claimed these small islands for about 150 years. But Galtieri wanted to take them from the British once and for all.

Galtieri's political gamble failed. First, Galtieri did not expect the British to fight back, but they did. Second, he did not count on the role the United States would play in the conflict. Argentina and the United States had recently enjoyed good relations, and Galtieri thought the United States would remain neutral. Instead, the United States supported Great Britain.

In addition to these political miscalculations, Argentina's armed forces suffered a major defeat. The country's poorly trained troops were no match for the British army. The situation quickly got so bad that some Argentine commanders abandoned their soldiers. The British easily recaptured the islands and took many Argentine soldiers prisoner. About 700 Argentines and some 250 British troops lost their lives in the fighting.

To make things worse, military leaders lied to the public about the war by giving them false reports of victory. When the truth was discovered, the ruling military was humiliated and discredited. Although the war lasted just 74 days, it helped bring down the dictatorship.

A WAR OF DISTRACTION

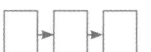

Teach the Main Idea

At Level

Democratic and Economic Reforms

1. **Teach** Ask students the Reading Focus questions to teach this section.
2. **Apply** Have students work in pairs to create their own "Quick Facts" chart for the section.
3. **Review** Have volunteers share their charts with the class, explaining the information they chose to include. Then guide students in a discussion of the democratic and economic reforms that occurred and are still occurring in Latin America.
4. **Practice/Homework** Have students write a letter to the editor of a Latin American newspaper explaining why economic reforms will help pave the way to democratic reform, peace, and stability in Latin America. **LS Verbal-Linguistic**

Alternative Assessment Handbook, Rubric 17: Letters to Editors

Return of Democracy

After decades of struggling through civil wars and conflicts, dictatorships across Latin America started falling in the 1980s and 1990s. Voters were finally able to elect leaders who put an end to military rule, and moderate civilian politicians began a series of political and economic reforms.

The Failures of Dictatorships Latin America's military governments fell for a number of reasons. One major reason was that many had failed to achieve social and economic reforms. Poverty, malnutrition, and infant mortality remained high throughout most of the region. As a result, poor, landless peasants continued to stream into cities and settled in giant shantytowns in search of work. Even the "Brazilian miracle" had gone sour. It turned out to be a miracle for the few—the military, large landowners, and wealthy businesspeople.

In addition to failing to improve people's economic lives, the dictatorships did not manage to bring about stability and security. In Central America, death squads roamed cities and the countryside while civil wars raged. In South America, civil rights were severely repressed. Governments in Argentina, Brazil, and Chile dealt with opposition through mysterious disappearances, torture, and killings carried out by the military dictatorships. Some people began to demand a change.

British soldiers fight Argentine forces in the Falkland Islands. ▼

FACES OF HISTORY

Violeta CHAMORRO

1929–

Violeta Chamorro began her political career as a member of Nicaragua's Sandinista government. However, she soon became an outspoken critic of the Marxist policies of the Sandinistas.

In 1990 the Sandinistas allowed a presidential election, and Chamorro defeated the Sandinista candidate, Daniel Ortega, to become the first female president in Central America. During her presidency, she worked to unify the country, which had been deeply divided by civil war. She brought the war to an end and reversed many Sandinista policies, such as Sandinista control of the military and restrictions on freedom of the press.

Summarize How did Violeta Chamorro change politics in Nicaragua?

A Peaceful Transition Despite this history of violence and repression, the return of democracy in Latin America was actually fairly peaceful. The change came when a combination of internal and external forces began to apply pressure for reform. International lenders, including the International Monetary Fund (IMF), the World Bank, and large corporate banks, began to demand changes in the way countries were governed as a condition for receiving loans. Also, pro-democracy groups inside and outside the region, such as the Organization of American States, began calling for countries to restore voting rights and allow political opposition. Military leaders began to realize that they needed to relax some of the restrictions on society and integrate some limited freedoms into their policies.

ACADEMIC VOCABULARY
integrate to blend or join together

Given a chance to vote, people did. Countries across the region voted out the military and voted in new civilian governments.

Democracy in Brazil returned in the early 1970s. Argentina followed after the Falklands War in 1982. Central American countries returned to relative calm in the 1980s and 1990s with the election of moderate governments, such as that of **Violeta Chamorro** in Nicaragua. In Chile, which enjoyed more economic success than most of the region, the Pinochet regime fell in 1990.

READING CHECK **Identify Cause and Effect** What factors brought about the return of democracy in Latin America?

Direct Teach

Reading Focus

1 How did democracy return to Latin America? *military governments forced to relax restrictions in order to obtain loans, severe social and economic problems, pro-democracy groups encouraged political opposition military dictatorships voted out*

Return of Democracy

Explain What were the major problems facing military governments? *poverty, death squads, ongoing economic and social problems*

Summarize Why was the transition to democracy relatively peaceful? *totalitarian governments forced to make changes, relaxed restrictions, pro-democracy groups formed, people able to vote, voted military governments out*

CRF: Biography: Luiz Inácio Lula da Silva

Primary Source

"In my homeland, the advent of democracy did not occur through violence or force. It took place solely through free elections. For the first time in the history of the twentieth century, the result of a vote ended a totalitarian dictatorship and the two civil war opponents agreed on peace—not because of the victory of one group, but because of the conviction of both."
—Violeta Chamorro, 1991 speech to the National Endowment for Democracy

Collaborative Learning

At Level

Return of Democracy

1. Organize students into small groups.
2. Have each group write and rehearse a skit that describes how Latin American citizens feel about their country becoming democratic. As an alternative, students might wish to create a formal ceremony announcing sweeping democratic reforms to the public.
3. Have students present their skits to the class. **LS Kinesthetic**

Alternative Assessment Handbook, Rubric 33: Skits and Reader's Theater

Answers

Faces of History *won presidency, reversed Sandinista socialist policies*

Reading Check *severe social and economic problems; new requirements for reform from IMF and other lenders in order to obtain loans; pro-democracy groups*

Direct Teach

Reading Focus

❷ How has democracy in Mexico changed in recent years? *A non-PRI president in office; signing of NAFTA*

Democracy in Mexico

Describe What is the purpose of NAFTA? *improve economies of Canada, U.S., and Mexico by eliminating tariffs among the three nations*

Analyze How did PRI retain its control over the Mexican government? *fraudulent elections, use of force, bought votes*

Recent Scholarship

Two timely issues are examined in *Free Trade and the Environment: Mexico, NAFTA, and Beyond.* Author Kevin Gallagher argues that Mexico's free trade policies have had environmental benefits and have not resulted in lax environmental standards nor in incentives for polluting industries, as others have suggested would happen.

Free Trade and the Environment: Mexico, NAFTA, and Beyond by Kevin Gallagher. Stanford University Press, 2004.

Democracy in Mexico

Mexico's path to democracy was different from other countries in the region. Unlike most other Latin American countries, Mexico experienced relative political stability in the second half of the 1900s. Although Mexico was never really a dictatorship, it was not very democratic either.

One-Party Rule For more than 70 years, the Institutional Revolutionary Party, or PRI, ruled Mexico with almost no opposition. It controlled congress, and PRI candidates won every presidential election. Often these political victories were achieved through fraud and force. At election time, candidates gave gifts of food and other goods to poor people to win their votes.

In spite of the political situation, Mexico's economy remained quite strong. Boosted by Mexico's rich oil reserves, industry grew for many years. However, because of the PRI economic policies, Mexican industry became increasingly dominated by foreign companies. As these companies' profits increased, more money went to foreign countries. Mexico's foreign debt grew tremendously, and poverty and inequality remained.

Demands for Reform Worsening economic conditions and growing frustration with political corruption left the ruling party open to take all the blame. In addition, a number of crises struck Mexico that caused more dissatisfaction with the PRI.

The first crisis occurred in 1968 when police and military forces opened fire on a group of peaceful student protesters. The event left hundreds dead and wounded. To make matters worse, the government tried to cover up the extent of the tragedy. A Mexican teacher explained how the massacre affected people's views of the government:

HISTORY'S VOICES

> **"The . . . incident led those who sincerely believed that great improvements had been made in our democratic institutions, and that the political and social system of our country was basically sound except for certain minor failings and mistakes, to re-examine all their most cherished beliefs."**
>
> —Elena Quijano de Rendón, quoted in *Massacre in Mexico*, by Elena Poniatowska

Another crisis occurred in the 1980s when world oil prices fell. Mexico's economy relied heavily on oil production and exports, and the fall in prices caused oil revenues to be cut in half. The country fell into a severe economic decline. High inflation and unemployment meant that many people struggled to support themselves. When a major earthquake destroyed large parts of Mexico City in 1985, the huge cost of rebuilding created more problems for the government and the economy. Public dissatisfaction with the PRI increased.

Events of the 1990s brought even more concern to Mexicans. In 1992 Mexico, the United States, and Canada signed the **North American Free Trade Agreement (NAFTA)**, a free-trade agreement that eliminated tariffs on trade between the three countries. NAFTA was designed to improve the countries' economies, but many Mexicans feared the economic effects of increased competition from foreign imports.

In 1994 a peasant uprising in the Mexican state of Chiapas and the government's decision to devalue the Mexican currency again shook the public's confidence. As more Mexicans faced new hardships in their daily lives, something had to change.

Changes in Mexico

Mexico has made much progress toward a fairer and more inclusive political system in recent years. No longer dominated by one party, Mexico's government is more democratic today and is working to improve the country's economy.

▲ Mexican riot police arrest student protesters in 1968 following violent clashes that killed as many as 300 people.

Skills Focus: Analyzing Primary Sources

At Level

Research Required

Reading Like a Historian Skill
Mexico's Elections, 2006

Materials: plain paper, colored markers

1. Have students conduct outside research using reliable print and online sources to learn more about the 2006 presidential candidates in Mexico, their parties, and their platforms.
2. Have students use the information from their research to prepare a campaign slogan for one of the principal candidates.
3. Organize students into small groups, based on the candidate they selected, and have groups create a campaign poster for each candidate using their slogans.
4. Have volunteers share their posters, and put them on display in the classroom.

LS Visual-Spatial

Alternative Assessment Handbook, Rubrics 28: Posters; and 34: Slogans and Banners

QUICK FACTS

Mexico Then	Mexico Now
One political party, the PRI, controlled congress.	The PRI is just one of many political parties to have representation in congress.
The PRI candidate won every presidential election.	Mexicans have elected presidents from opposition parties.
Elections were characterized by corruption and fraud.	Elections are much more open and are closely monitored for fraud.
The government crushed dissent, sometimes violently.	People can openly criticize the government.
Mexico had tremendous foreign debt, inflation, and unemployment.	Economic problems remain, but foreign debt, inflation, and unemployment are down.
Many industries were nationalized, and imports and exports were limited.	Imports and exports are up, and Mexicans have access to more goods.

Felipe Calderón won Mexico's closely contested presidential election in 2006. ▶

A New Era Change began in 1997 when opposition parties won a number of seats in congress. In 2000, voters ended 71 years of PRI rule when they elected as president **Vicente Fox**, a member of the conservative PAN party.

Fox faced the challenge of creating a functioning government and stable economy. In addition, he worked to end the uprising in Chiapas, end corruption, and improve relations with the United States. Fox made progress on most of his goals. However, relations between the two countries were strained in 2006 when political leaders in the United States worked to reform immigration laws and improve border security. Fox argued that both countries needed to address the economic disparities that encouraged illegal immigration and to recognize the status of immigrant workers in the United States.

Mexico maintained its commitment to democracy with elections in 2006. Felipe Calderón, of the conservative PAN party, won an extremely close race. He faced the recurring challenge of improving Mexico's economy.

READING CHECK **Find the Main Idea** In what way was Mexico not very democratic until 2000?

Market Reforms

The shift to democracy that swept through countries from Mexico to Argentina brought economic changes as well. Under pressure from Western banks, deeply indebted Latin American countries began a series of reform measures in the 1990s. These measures were difficult, but they held out the promise of economic progress and stability. The reforms included

- drastically cutting government spending, including funding for social programs
- ending some government subsidies of businesses
- selling government services to private enterprise
- returning inefficient, government-controlled businesses to private ownership
- strengthening regional trade agreements and establishing new ones.

These cost-cutting, free-market measures were intended to stabilize shaky economies by reducing inflation and expanding exports. They were also expected to enable countries to pay their debts.

ACADEMIC VOCABULARY
security freedom from danger or fear

Direct Teach

Reading Focus

❸ What have been the results of market reforms in Latin America? *mixed results, some economic growth; poverty continues; election of leftist-leaning governments*

Market Reforms

Recall What were the goals of free-market reforms? *stabilize economy by reducing inflation and expanding exports*

Identify What were three major market reforms? *cut government spending, privatize enterprises, establish and strengthen trade agreements*

Predict How well do you think the market reforms will work in the future? *possible answer—In some countries, results will be positive; in other countries, reforms may not work as hoped.*

Quick Facts Transparency: Mexico Then; Mexico Now

Info to Know

Presidential Election 2006 Democracy is still a challenge for Mexico. In July 2006, Mexico held its presidential election. It first seemed that Manuel Lopez Obrador, the favorite of the poor, won. After further calculations and recounts, the PAN candidate, Felipe Calderon, was declared winner by about ½ percent, about 240,000 votes. Controversy erupted over the voting and the accuracy of the counting of ballots. Supporters of Obrador participated in many protests demanding a recount of the votes.

Differentiating Instruction

Above Level

Advanced Learners/Gifted and Talented

Research Required

1. Have students review the chapter, focusing on the economic problems in each of the countries discussed.
2. Have students select one of the following countries: Cuba, Guatemala, El Salvador, Nicaragua, Brazil, Argentina, Chile, Haiti, Panama, Peru, Mexico, or Venezuela.
3. Have students research the current economic conditions in the country and chart the changes over the past ten years.
4. Have students prepare reports summarizing the results of their research, supporting their work with charts and graphs that show the economic changes. **LS Logical-Mathematical**

Alternative Assessment Handbook, Rubrics 1: Acquiring Information; and 7: Charts

Answers

Reading Check *One party ruled the government for over 70 years.*

Direct Teach

Reading Focus

Market Reforms

Recall How has the gap between rich and poor changed? *It has gotten worse.*

Draw Conclusions What led to the elections of leftist-leaning leaders in the early 2000s? *inability of existing governments to solve economic problems*

Info to Know

Latin American Poverty Though poverty levels are still high, Latin America is making progress. In 2003 the total number of people living in poverty was about 44 percent, but by 2005 it had dropped to about 40 percent. Latin American economies have been growing; in 2004, economies grew 5.6 percent, the largest increase in 25 years. The infant mortality rate has dropped from 43 deaths per 1000 in 1990 to 25 death per 1000 in 2003.

Map Transparency: Poverty in Latin America

Primary Source

"Brazil has rediscovered itself, and this coming together is visible in the enthusiasm felt throughout society and in the mobilization of the country to deal with the enormous problems ahead."
—Luis Inácio Lula da Silva, in a speech at the World Economic Forum, Davos, Switzerland, 2003

"We have to reinvent socialism. It can't be the kind of socialism that we saw in the Soviet Union, but it will emerge as we develop new systems that are built on cooperation, not competition."
—Hugo Chávez, in a speech at the World Social Forum, Porto Alegre, Brazil, 2005

Answers

Interpreting Maps *Lowest—Brazil; Chile; Dominican Republic; Highest—Bolivia, Guatemala, Suriname*

Reading Check *by electing leftist-leaning governments or those who are sympathetic to the plight of the poor*

THE IMPACT TODAY

Many people from Latin America migrate to the United States hoping for economic opportunities they do not have at home.

Results of Market Reforms The free-market reforms of the 1990s had mixed results. Many countries experienced economic growth and stability as private enterprise became stronger, but others suffered.

Some successes occurred in Brazil and Chile. Brazil's inflation fell from quadruple digits in 1994 to less than 7 percent in 2006. In Chile, reforms cut the poverty rate in half between 1990 and 2003. In addition, fruit exports soared as new markets opened. Business owners celebrated the economic changes. Reassured bankers, as well as international lenders such as the International Monetary Fund and the World Bank, loaned billions of dollars for increased economic development in Latin America.

Struggles continued in other parts of Latin America. Overall, exports from the region generally remained sluggish, as many countries were dependent on single commodities. In addition, the many reform measures caused hardships in some countries.

One country that suffered from these reform measures was Argentina. Once viewed as a model for economic growth and stability, Argentina experienced a deep recession in 2001 and 2002. When the country could not pay its multi-billion-dollar debt, the president responded by devaluing Argentina's currency. Therefore, people's money was suddenly worth less than it was before. As a result, banks failed, and the unemployment rate reached more than 20 percent. Many middle-class people who had held good jobs suddenly found themselves struggling to buy basic necessities. By the end of 2003, however, the economy had mostly stabilized once more.

Even where market reforms have benefited national economies, many people have not felt the positive effects. For example, poverty is still widespread in Latin America. Nearly one-third of the population lives on less than two dollars a day. In addition, the gap between rich and poor has widened. In 2003 about 10 percent of the region's population earned nearly half of all income.

Still, supporters of market reforms insist that the reforms simply have not gone far enough or had enough time to make an impact. They argue that key elements of reform, such as laws to protect property rights and business contracts, have not been made. Also, political corruption cripples businesses in much of Latin America.

Reactions to Market Reforms Latin Americans' dissatisfaction with economic problems and with their governments' seeming inability to solve them has led to more political and economic shifts in the region. Starting in the late 1990s elections brought populist, left-leaning leaders to power in some countries.

In 1998 Venezuelans elected **Hugo Chávez** president. Popular among the poor, Chávez set out to eliminate poverty. To do so, however, he rejected certain aspects of capitalism. Chávez's policies appear to have had limited success, but problems remain. Also, critics both within and outside Venezuela are concerned that he has turned the country away from democracy and toward dictatorship.

Another dramatic shift occurred in Bolivia. There, indigenous leader Evo Morales defeated

POVERTY IN LATIN AMERICA, 2006

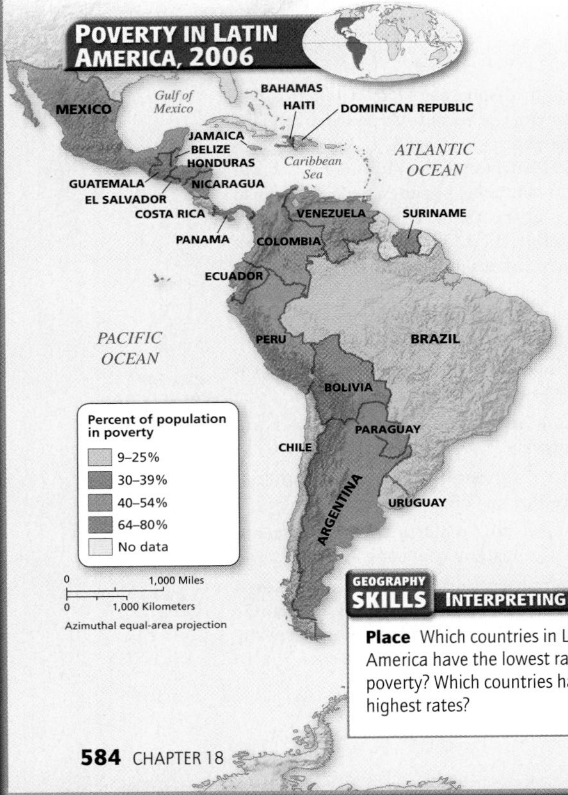

GEOGRAPHY SKILLS INTERPRETING MAPS

Place Which countries in Latin America have the lowest rates of poverty? Which countries have the highest rates?

Skills Focus: Analyzing Maps

Below Level

Social Studies Skill
Poverty in Latin America

1. To help students understand the map on this page, ask: Which country or countries have the highest percentage of poverty? Which country or countries have the lowest percentage?
2. Have students create a chart like the one shown to record poverty levels in each country. **LS Visual-Spatial**

Country	% of population living in poverty
Argentina	*30–39%*
Brazil	*5-25%*
Chile	*5-25%*

Alternative Assessment Handbook, Rubrics 7: Charts; and 21: Map Reading

Latin American Economies Today

Economies are growing in most Latin American countries today. As industries become more competitive and exports and imports grow, the middle class is expanding and people are gaining more access to consumer goods. Still, not everyone benefits from these changes. ***Why do you think an improved national economy might not benefit everyone?***

An autoworker assembles trucks in Mexico. ▶

Skills FOCUS INTERPRETING GRAPHS

Analyze How would you describe Latin America's growth in GDP per capita based on the information in this graph?

GDP PER CAPITA IN LATIN AMERICA

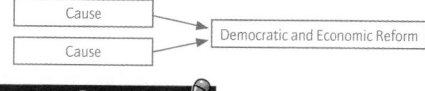

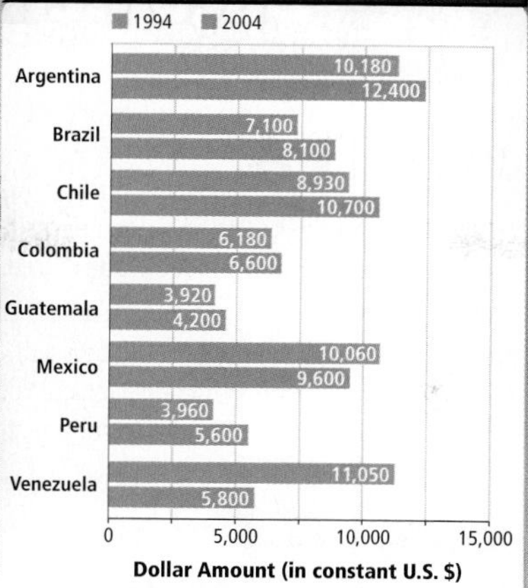

Sources: *The World Almanac and Book of Facts, 1997; The World Almanac and Book of Facts, 2006*

a former IMF official in a 2005 election. Morales nationalized the natural gas industry in an effort to enable all Bolivians to benefit from their resources. He also supported farmers who grew coca leaves, which have traditional uses but can also be used to make cocaine.

In Brazil voters turned to a leftist president when they elected Luiz Inácio Lula da Silva in 2002. They hoped that Lula, a former union leader, would be sympathetic to the problems of the poor. Although people were concerned that Lula's former ties to the Communist Party would lead Brazil in the wrong direction, Lula managed to balance the interests of social reformers and businesses.

READING CHECK Make Generalizations How have people in Latin America reacted to market reforms in recent years?

SECTION 3 ASSESSMENT

go.hrw.com **Online Quiz** Keyword: SHL LAT HP

Reviewing Ideas, Terms, and People

1. **a. Describe** What failures caused the fall of dictators in Latin America?
   b. Analyze What factors made possible a peaceful transition to democracy?
   c. Make Judgments Did foreign countries have a right to push for political changes in Latin America? Explain your answer.
2. **a. Describe** Why was the election of **Vicente Fox** significant for Mexico?
   b. Sequence What were the major crises facing Mexico, in chronological order, that led to the end of one-party rule?
   c. Make Judgments Several crises helped bring about the end of PRI rule. Were Mexicans right to blame their government for the situation in their country? Explain your answer.
3. **a. Describe** Describe two market reforms that took place in Latin America.
   b. Analyze What were the positive and negative effects of the economic reforms of the 1990s?
   c. Predict How do you think the move toward leftist leaders might affect Latin America in the future?

Critical Thinking

4. **Identify Cause and Effect** Using your notes, fill in a graphic organizer like the one below with at least two main causes of democratic and economic reform in Latin America.

Cause → Democratic and Economic Reform
Cause → Democratic and Economic Reform

FOCUS ON SPEAKING

5. **Persuasion** Imagine you are a citizen of a Latin American country in the 1970s or 1980s. Write a short speech explaining why there is a need for political or economic reform in your country.

Direct Teach

Teaching Tip

Remind students that GDP stands for gross domestic product, the total value of the goods and services produced by a nation during a defined period of time.

Review & Assess

Close

Have students name the expected and unexpected consequences of economic reforms measures in Latin America.

Review

Online Quiz, Section 3

Assess

SE Section 3 Assessment

Progress Assessment: Section 3 Quiz

Alternative Assessment Handbook

Reteach/Intervene

Interactive Reader and Study Guide, Section 3

Interactive Skills Tutor CD-ROM

Answers

Latin American Economies Today *possible answers—jobs might not be available to most workers; social services still lacking*

Interpreting Graphs *GDP per capita has increased in all countries except Mexico and Venezuela.*

Section 3 Assessment Answers

1. **a.** did not solve economic and social problems, death squads, repression of civil rights
   b. internal and external pressure; new requirements for loans; pro-democracy groups
   c. possible answer—Yes, they forced governments to institute basic human rights and civil liberties.
2. **a.** he was the first non-PRI president in 71 years; fair election
   b. 1968, police attack student protesters; 1980s, oil prices fell, severe economic decline; 1985, devastating earthquake in Mexico City; 1992, NAFTA; 1994, peasant uprising in Chiapas, devaluation of currency
   c. possible answer—Not entirely, the drop in oil prices and the earthquake created severe economic hardships.
3. **a.** cost-cutting, free-market measures; turning government enterprises to private ownership; ending some government subsidies of businesses
   b. positive—inflation slowed; money flowed in from outside sources; negative—widespread poverty; gap between rich and poor widened
   c. possible answers—curtailment of human rights, political instability
4. pressure from IMF and World Bank; pro-democracy groups; military leaders began to relax restrictions
5. Speeches should include government-sponsored violence, repression of civil rights, and growing poverty.

Document-Based Investigation

Info to Know

NAFTA NAFTA has not been a complete success in all of Mexico. Guillermo Perry, World Bank Chief Economist for Latin America and the Caribbean has said the following: "NAFTA definitely further plugged Mexico into the most dynamic economy in the world, but the country's development across the 1990s, including the NAFTA period, was unequal … The most developed and competitive regions and sectors have clearly benefited from the trade liberalization, while those lagging behind have not. Extending the benefits of greater integration [to] all society remains the challenge."

CHAPTER 18

Document-Based Investigation

NAFTA

Historical Context The four documents below represent different views of the effect the North American Free Trade Agreement (NAFTA) has had on Mexico.

Task Study the selections and answer the questions that follow. After you have studied all the documents, you will be asked to write an essay explaining whether NAFTA has been good or bad for Mexico. You will need to use evidence from these selections and from the chapter to support the position you take.

DOCUMENT 1

Mexico's Balance of Trade

This table shows Mexico's trade balance with the United States and Canada from 1993 to 2003. Negative numbers mean that Mexico imported more than it exported. Positive numbers mean that Mexico exported more than it imported.

MEXICO'S TRADE BALANCE, 1993–2003

YEAR	WITH THE UNITED STATES	WITH CANADA
1993	–1,164*	1,723*
1994	–1,350	1,713
1995	15,393	2,527
1996	17,506	2,677
1997	14,549	3,081
1998	15,857	2,863
1999	22,812	3,474
2000	24,577	4,109
2001	30,3041	3,587
2002	37,146	3,609
2003	40,648	4,588

*in millions of U.S. dollars

Sources: *The World Almanac and Book of Facts, 2006*; The Canadian Trade Commissioner Service

DOCUMENT 2

A Political Cartoon

This cartoon ran in a Mexico City newspaper in 2004. It shows one artist's opinion of NAFTA's effects.

Mr. Dumping, published in *El Universal*, October 13, 2004

Skills Focus: Interpreting

At Level

Reading Like a Historian Skill

NAFTA Cartoons

1. Have students examine the political cartoon shown in Document 2.
2. Have students work in mixed-ability pairs to write a few sentences describing what the cartoon represents and the cartoonist's point of view. Have volunteers share their work.
3. Have students create two political cartoons, one supporting NAFTA and the other opposing it.
4. Have students share their cartoons with the class. **LS Visual-Spatial**

Alternative Assessment Handbook, Rubric 27: Political Cartoons

DOCUMENT 3

Report of the World Bank

Economists studied NAFTA's effects on Mexico for a report published by the World Bank in 2003. The excerpt below contains some of their findings.

> The report's main conclusion regarding NAFTA is that the treaty has helped Mexico get closer to the levels of development of its NAFTA partners. The research suggests, for example, that Mexico's global exports would have been about 25% lower without NAFTA, and foreign direct investment (FDI) would have been about 40% less without NAFTA. Also, the amount of time required for Mexican manufacturers to adopt U.S. technological innovations was cut in half. Trade can probably take some credit for moderate declines in poverty, and has likely had positive impacts on the number and quality of jobs. However, NAFTA is not enough to ensure economic convergence among North American countries and regions. This reflects both limitations of NAFTA's design and, more importantly, pending domestic reforms.

DOCUMENT 4

An Economic Report

Researchers Timothy A. Wise and Kevin P. Gallagher published their analysis of NAFTA's effects on the Mexican economy in 2002 through an organization called Foreign Policy in Focus.

> Official figures from both the World Bank and the Mexican government show that trade liberalization has succeeded in stimulating both trade and investment, and it has brought inflation under control. Mexico's exports have grown at a rapid annual rate of 10.6% in real terms since 1985, and foreign direct investment (FDI) has nearly tripled, posting a real 21% annual growth rate. Inflation has been significantly tamed.
>
> Unfortunately, these figures have not translated into benefits for the Mexican population as a whole. The same official sources show that:
>
> • . . . There has been little job creation, falling far short of the demand in Mexico from new entrants into the labor force. Even the manufacturing sector, one of the few sectors to show significant economic growth, has seen a net loss in jobs since NAFTA took effect.
>
> • Wages have declined nationally, with real wages down significantly. The real minimum wage is down 60% since 1982, 23% under NAFTA.

Skills Focus: READING LIKE A HISTORIAN

DOCUMENT 1

a. Describe What has happened to Mexico's balance of trade with the United States since NAFTA took effect?

b. Analyze How do you think the change in balance of trade has affected Mexico's economy?

DOCUMENT 2

a. Describe What is happening in the political cartoon?

b. Infer What does the artist think about NAFTA's effects on Mexico?

DOCUMENT 3

a. Identify Main Ideas What is the main idea of the World Bank's report?

b. Analyze How can you tell that the writers are confident about some of their conclusions and less confident about others? Which conclusions are they less confident about? Which words indicate they are more or less confident?

DOCUMENT 4

a. Identify Main Ideas What is the main idea of the researchers' report?

b. Interpret Does the report give a mostly positive or mostly negative evaluation of NAFTA? Explain your answer.

DOCUMENT-BASED ESSAY QUESTION

Opinions about NAFTA's effect on Mexico range from very positive to very negative. How has NAFTA affected the different segments of Mexican society in different ways? Using the documents above and information from the chapter, form a thesis that expresses your opinion. Then write a short essay to support your opinion.

See **Skills Handbook**, pp. H25, H27

Differentiating Instruction

Learners Having Difficulty — Below Level

Have students work in mixed-ability pairs and reread Documents 3 and 4. Then have students work individually to write a paraphrase of the two documents. Have pairs share their paraphrases. **LS Verbal-Linguistic**

Alternative Assessment Handbook, Rubric 37: Writing Assignments

Advanced Learners/Gifted and Talented — Above Level

Have students examine Documents 3 and 4. Then have students explain or theorize why the balance of trade has increased so dramatically, while real wages have declined and job creation has stalled. **LS Verbal-Linguistic**

Alternative Assessment Handbook, Rubric 37: Writing Assignments

Document-Based Investigation

Word Help

exports goods shipped to another country

innovation modernization, new ways of doing something

convergence merging into a unified whole

MISCONCEPTION ALERT

NAFTA has not led to an increase in U.S. agricultural imports. Instead, it has led to an increase in exports. Between 1994 and 2005, U.S. agricultural exports increased to Mexico and Canada jumped from $9.5 billion to about $19 billion. Mexico accounted for $4.5 billion of that increase.

Answers

Reading Like a Historian

Document 1. a. *It increased dramatically; exports exceeded imports.* **b.** *strengthened it;* **Document 2. a.** *The supply of American-made goods in Mexico is hurting Mexican industry.* **b.** *The artist thinks NAFTA has negatively impacted Mexico.* **Document 3. a.** *that NAFTA is helping Mexico's economy; Mexico's exports have increased;* **b.** *Confidence is shown by the use of specific numbers and statistics; words such as "probably" and "likely" indicate areas where the authors are less confident.* **Document 4. a.** *Most Mexicans are not benefiting from NAFTA.* **b.** *negative, focuses more on the problems.* **Essay** *Student essays should recognize that NAFTA had mixed results in Mexico. Exports and productivity have increased, but not everyone has benefited.*

Answers

Visual Summary

Review and Inquiry Have students match the political trends on the left with the events on the time line.

Quick Facts Transparency: Visual Study Guide: Latin America

Review Key Terms and People

1. junta
2. Fidel Castro
3. NAFTA
4. Augusto Pinochet
5. Juan Perón
6. Contras
7. intervene

Comprehension and Critical Thinking

8. **a.** Church became active in social and economic struggles.
   b. similarities—the U.S. intervened, between guerilla and military armies; differences—led to dictatorship in Guatemala; Sandinistas instituted some reforms
   c. positive—established free health care, virtually ended illiteracy; reduced economic inequality; negative—civil liberties are restricted; there is a one-party system
9. **a.** supported the poor and working class; established minimum wage, eight-hour working day; built schools, hospitals, and homeless shelters
   b. similar—absolute dictatorships, controlled people with violence; economies suffered; different—mothers protested in Argentina; Brazil, opposition grew, Chile, not everyone suffered
   c. possible answer—Yes, the U.S. helped establish less corrupt governments and institute democratic reforms.
10. **a.** It was a one party rule; won victories through corruption and fraud.
   b. mixed results; rate of inflation has decreased, poverty rate has decreased, increase in some exports; poverty gap has widened

CHAPTER 18

Chapter Review

QUICK FACTS

VISUAL STUDY GUIDE

Political Trends in Latin America

Dictatorships
- Argentina under Perón and the military
- Brazil under the military
- Chile under Pinochet
- Haiti under the Duvaliers
- Panama under Noriega

↓

Moderate Reforms
- Argentina after the Falklands War
- Brazil with the end of the military dictatorship
- Chile after Pinochet
- Nicaragua under Chamorro
- Mexico with the election of Fox

↓

Leftist Movements
- Cuban Revolution under Castro
- Sandinistas in Nicaragua
- Shining Path in Peru
- Chávez in Venezuela
- Morales in Bolivia
- Lula in Brazil

Key Events in Latin America

- **1954** ■ Jacobo Arbenz, an elected leftist, is overthrown in Guatemala.
- **1959** ■ The Cuban Revolution brings Fidel Castro to power.
- **1968** ■ The Mexican army kills hundreds of unarmed student protesters.
- **Early 1970s** ■ Oil prices surge, which benefits Mexico and Venezuela but hurts Brazil.
- **1973** ■ President Salvador Allende is killed in a coup in Chile, and Augusto Pinochet takes power the next year.
- **1976** ■ Argentina's "dirty war" begins.
- **1979** ■ Nicaraguan revolution brings leftist Sandinistas to power.
- **1980** ■ Archbishop Oscar Romero is assassinated in El Salvador, which worsens that country's civil war.
- **1980s** ■ Debt and hyperinflation bring Latin American countries to the brink of economic collapse.
- **1982** ■ The Falklands War helps bring down Argentina's dictatorship.
- **2000** ■ One-party rule ends in Mexico with the election of Vicente Fox.

Review Key Terms and People

Identify the term or person from the chapter that best fits each of the following descriptions.

1. a group of leaders who rule jointly
2. dictator who brought a communist revolution to Cuba
3. agreement to eliminate tariffs on trade between Mexico, the United States, and Canada
4. dictator in Chile who improved the economy but severely repressed personal freedoms
5. leader who supports the rights of the common people as opposed to the privileged elite
6. U.S.-trained and funded rebel group in the Nicaraguan civil war
7. to enter into an event to affect its outcome

c. possible answer—They hope for solutions to their economic problems and want a better standard of living.

Reading Skills

11. pressure from pro-democracy groups; new requirements from the IMF and World Bank
12. positive—drop in the rate of inflation, some stability; negative—unemployment high, high poverty rates, gap between rich and poor grew, not equal benefits to all countries
13. economy was failing; dictator took power, limited civil rights
14. discredited and brought down the military dictatorship
15. too much debt, excessive dependence on imported oil

Evaluating Historical Interpretation

16. leftist, holy crusade, campaign of public misinformation, covert terrorist operations
17. He does not agree with U.S. involvement.

History's Impact video program
Review the video to answer the closing question:
What impact does NAFTA have on Mexico?

Comprehension and Critical Thinking

SECTION 1 *(pp. 569–574)*

8. a. Recall What influence did Liberation Theology have on Latin American politics?

b. Compare and Contrast What were two similarities and two differences between the civil wars in Guatemala and Nicaragua?

c. Evaluate How did Fidel Castro's policies change Cuba in both positive and negative ways?

SECTION 2 *(pp. 575–579)*

9. a. Describe What aspects of Juan Perón's rule show that he was a populist?

b. Compare and Contrast How were the military dictatorships in Argentina, Brazil, and Chile both similar and different?

c. Make Judgments The United States played a role in the politics of Chile, Haiti, and Panama. Was intervention by the United States justified in each of these cases? Explain your answer.

SECTION 3 *(pp. 580–585)*

10. a. Describe In what ways was the PRI like a dictatorship?

b. Make Generalizations How have market reforms changed Latin American economies in recent years?

c. Elaborate Why do you think people in many Latin American countries have been looking to populist, left-leaning leaders in recent years?

Reading Skills

Understanding Causes and Effects *Use what you know about understanding causes and effects to answer the questions below.*

11. What were two causes of the end of dictatorships in Latin America?

12. What have been the positive and negative effects of market reforms in Latin America?

13. What was one cause and one effect of the 1973 coup in Chile?

14. What major effect did the Falklands War have on Argentina?

15. What were two causes of economic trouble in Brazil during the military dictatorship?

Evaluating Historical Interpretation

Reading Like a Historian *The selection below is one historian's interpretation of U.S. influence in Central American civil wars.*

> "Ronald Reagan's campaigns against the leftist Sandinista regime in Nicaragua and the leftist . . . guerrillas in El Salvador took on all the characteristics of a holy crusade against communist forces in Central America. From the beginning of his first term, President Reagan sought to overthrow the Sandinistas, employing tactics that included economic sanctions, a campaign of public misinformation, support of rightist counterrevolutionary armies (the contras), and covert terrorist operations aided by the CIA."
>
> —Benjamin Keen, *A History of Latin America*, 1996

16. Analyze Which words or phrases suggest the writer might have a bias one way or another?

17. Infer What do you think the writer thinks of U.S. involvement in Nicaragua and El Salvador?

Using the Internet

go.hrw.com
Practice Online
Keyword: SHL LAT

18. Latin America faces many political and economic challenges today. Using the keyword above, research current events in Latin America that relate to some of these challenges. Then write a one-paragraph summary of two of the articles that you find.

WRITING FOR THE SAT

Think about the following issue:

Countries in Latin America have experimented with different types of governments. Leftist leaders believed that the way to achieve economic progress in societies where few people held most of the wealth was for the common people to take over the government. Rightist leaders believed that only a leader who ruled with an iron fist could force a country to take the painful steps required to reform an inefficient economy.

19. Assignment: Is either of these theories valid in Latin America? Is neither valid? Is either partly valid? Write a short essay in which you develop your position on this issue. Support your point of view with reasoning and examples from your reading and studies.

Answers

Using the Internet

18. Go to the HRW Web site and enter the keyword shown to access a rubric for this activity.

KEYWORD: SHL LAT

Writing for the SAT

19. Student essays should mention that rebellions can have unexpected consequences, as their study of this chapter shows. Essays should also discuss that while dictatorships can solve problems in the short-run, human rights usually suffer.
A rubric for this activity is provided in **CRF:** Writing for the SAT.

HOLT
History's Impact
► **Video Program**
See the Video Program Teacher's Guide for the answer to the closing question.

Review and Assessment Resources

Review and Reinforce

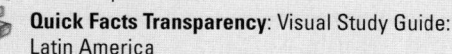

- **CRF:** Chapter Review
- **Quick Facts Transparency**: Visual Study Guide: Latin America
- **Spanish Chapter Summaries Audio CD Program**
- OSP **Holt PuzzlePro**: Quiz Show for ExamView
- **Quiz Game CD-ROM**

Assess

- **PASS**: Chapter Test, Forms A and B
- **Alternative Assessment Handbook**
- OSP **ExamView Test Generator**, Chapter Test
- **Differentiated Instruction Modified Worksheets and Tests CD-ROM**: Chapter Test
- HOAP **Holt Online Assessment Program** (in the Premier Online Edition)

Reteach/Intervene

- **Interactive Reader and Study Guide**
- **Differentiated Instruction Teacher Management System**: Lesson Plans for Differentiated Instruction
- **Differentiated Instruction Modified Worksheets and Tests CD-ROM**: Chapter Test
- **Interactive Skills Tutor CD-ROM**

go.hrw.com
Online Resources
KEYWORD: SHL TEACHER

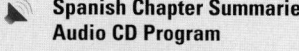

Chapter 19 Planning Guide

Today's World

Chapter Overview	Reproducible Resources	Technology Resources
CHAPTER 19 **pp. 590–615** **Overview: In this chapter, students will learn about the economic, environmental, and technological changes and challenges in the world today.**	**Differentiated Instruction Teacher Management System:** • Pacing Guide • Lesson Plans for Universal Access **Interactive Reader and Study Guide:** Chapter Summary* **Chapter Resource File*** • Writing About History • Social Studies Skill • Chapter Review	**Live Ink© Online Reading Help** **Student Edition on Audio CD Program** **Differentiated Instruction Modified Worksheets and Tests CD-ROM** **World History Primary Source Library CD-ROM** **History's Impact: World History Video Program (VHS/DVD):** Today's World
Section 1: **Trade and Globalization** **The Main Idea:** Trade and culture link economies and lives around the world.	**Differentiated Instruction Teacher Management System:** Section 1 Lesson Plan* **Interactive Reader and Study Guide:** Section 1 Summary* **Chapter Resource File*** • Vocabulary Builder: Section 1 • Biography: Amadou and Mariam • History and Geography: Economic Interdependence • Primary Source: The Impact of Globalization on World Cultures	**Daily Test Practice Transparency:** Section 1* **Map Transparency:** World per Capita GDP, 2006* **Quick Facts Transparency:** Major Trade Organizations and Agreements* **Internet Activity:** Television: Its History and Impact
Section 2: **Social Challenges** **The Main Idea:** People and countries are working together to protect human rights, help solve problems such as poverty and disease and adjust to new patterns of migration.	**Differentiated Instruction Teacher Management System:** Section 2 Lesson Plan* **Interactive Reader and Study Guide:** Section 2 Summary* **Chapter Resource File*** • Vocabulary Builder: Section 2 • Biography: Louise Arbour • Literature: *Cry, the Beloved Country*	**Daily Test Practice Transparency:** Section 2* **Map Transparency:** World Average Life Expectancy, 2002*
Section 3: **Threats to World Security** **The Main Idea:** Terrorism, the potential use of weapons of mass destruction, and ethnic and religious tensions threaten security around the world.	**Differentiated Instruction Teacher Management System:** Section 3 Lesson Plan* **Interactive Reader and Study Guide:** Section 3 Summary* **Chapter Resource File*** • Vocabulary Builder: Section 3 • Biography: Rose Riso	**Daily Test Practice Transparency:** Section 3* **Map Transparency:** World Terrorism Incidents, 1995–2005*
Section 4: **Environment and Technology** **The Main Idea:** People are working together to protect the environment and using science and technology to improve living conditions around the world.	**Differentiated Instruction Teacher Management System:** Section 4 Lesson Plan* **Interactive Reader and Study Guide:** Section 4 Summary* **Chapter Resource File*** • Vocabulary Builder: Section 4 • Biography: Yuet Wai Kan	**Daily Test Practice Transparency:** Section 4* **Quick Facts Transparency:** World Internet Access, 2006* **Internet Activity:** Investigate Global Warming

go.hrw.com | Print Resource | Transparency
LS Learning Styles | Audio CD | CD-ROM
Video | SE Student Edition | TE Teachers Edition
OSP One-Stop Planner CD-ROM
*also on One-Stop Planner CD-ROM

Review, Assessment, Intervention

- **Quick Facts Transparency:** Today's World*
- **Spanish Chapter Summaries Audio CD Program**
- **Differentiated Instruction Modified Worksheets and Tests CD-ROM:** Modified Chapter Test
- OSP **One-Stop Planner CD-ROM:** ExamView Test Generator (English/Spanish)
- HOAP **Holt Online Assessment Program (HOAP),** in the Holt Premier Online Student Edition

- **PASS:** Section 1 Quiz*
- **Online Quiz:** Section 1
- **Alternative Assessment Handbook**

- **PASS:** Section 2 Quiz*
- **Online Quiz:** Section 2
- **Alternative Assessment Handbook**

- **PASS:** Section 3 Quiz*
- **Online Quiz:** Section 3
- **Alternative Assessment Handbook**

- **PASS:** Section 4 Quiz*
- **Online Quiz:** Section 4
- **Alternative Assessment Handbook**

HOLT
History's Impact
World History Video Program (VHS/DVD)
Today's World

Power Presentation with Video CD-ROM

Power Presentations with Video are visual presentations of each chapter's main ideas. Presentations can be customized by including Quick Facts charts, images and maps from the textbook, and video clips.

Holt Online Learning

go.hrw.com
Teacher Resources
KEYWORD: SHL/TEACHER

go.hrw.com
Student Resources
KEYWORD: SHL TOD

- Document-Based Questions
- Interactive Multimedia Activities
- Current Events
- Chapter-Based Internet Activities
- and more!

Holt Premier
Online Student Edition

Complete online support for interactivity, assessment, and reporting

- Interactive Maps and Notebook
- Homework Practice and Research Activities Online

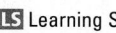

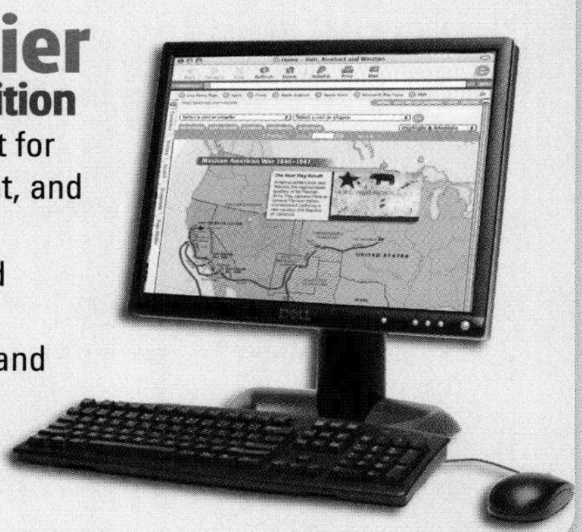

The Big Picture

Peter N. Stearns

Globalization The big news, after the end of the cold war, was the process of globalization and resistance to it. Globalization involves an intensification of international contacts and the consequences of those contacts, in areas of human endeavor from economics through politics to culture. Today, economic globalization involves multinationals and movements toward free trade, but also debate and resistance. Globalization has differential economic results for advanced industrial countries and those countries that are still largely agricultural. Still, a key development of the early 21st century has been the rapid economic growth of countries like China and India.

Cultural and Political Aspects Cultural influences have spread widely thanks to the activities of multinational organizations and information technologies. The consumer styles of the United States, Western Europe, and Japan have had a global impact that has sparked resistance in the name of traditional and regional identities. Organizations, including international NGOs, have worked for adherence to human rights standards with mixed results. Global contacts have increased the potential for the rapid dissemination of disease. Today. new patterns of migration involve longer distances and lead to greater cultural diversity. Resistance to migration has developed as well.

Terrorism and Conflict Terrorism has a long human history. Over the past few decades terrorist methods and effects have become more sophisticated. Contemporary terrorism reflects many problems and tensions, particularly in the Middle East. Some observers point to government-sponsored attacks on civilians as another component of today's terrorism. Many societies have taken increasing measures against terrorism, and terrorists rarely win significant political results. Other international tensions have involved concern about the spread of new types of weapons, particularly nuclear weaponry.

Environmental Change Increased pollution levels caused growing concern around 2000. Environmental globalization involves all the human activities that cause global environmental deterioration. Population growth and advancing consumerism has underwritten environmental change, with particular involvement from the United States. Global technologies and the rapid spread of scientific research rounded out the world's agenda by the early 21st century.

Recent Scholarship

Historians have fruitfully explored globalization around two themes: first, the different patterns of regional adjustment and resistance to globalization in historical perspective, and second the more fundamental issue of how new globalization is compared to previous surges in global contacts. *The New Global History* (2006) by Bruce Mazlish takes the lead in arguing for dramatic novelty, as against earlier passages in world history. His new book makes the case strongly, while also illustrating different facets of globalization and regional-global interactions. His approach should stimulate serious discussion, as its contentions are central to the challenge of relating contemporary changes to past patterns.

Differentiating Instruction

Differentiated Instruction Teacher Management System
- Pacing Guide
- Lesson Plans for Differentiated Instruction

Interactive Reader and Study Guide

Spanish Chapter Summaries Audio CD Program

Student Edition on Audio CD Program

Differentiated Instruction Modified Worksheets and Tests CD-ROM
- Vocabulary Flash Cards
- Modified Vocabulary Builder Activities
- Modified Chapter Review Activity
- Modified Chapter Test

OSP **One-Stop Planner CD-ROM**
- ExamView Test Generator (English/Spanish)
- PuzzlePro
- Quiz Show for ExamView
- Transparencies and Videos

TE **Differentiated Activities in the Teacher's Edition**
- Global Automobile Production, p. 595
- Terrorist Attacks, p. 603
- Terrorism in Recent Years, p. 604
- Global Warming, p. 611

Reading Like a Historian

Sam Wineburg

"Fair Trade" It has been called "the book that killed colonialism" but few Americans know its name. Published in 1860 by Eduard Douwes Dekker, the semi-autobiographical *Max Havelaar* chronicles the exploits of a colonial official in the Dutch East Indies. *Max Havelaar* leaves no doubt as to the brutality of a regime that ordered the Javanese to cultivate coffee and tea under a system ("cultuurstelsel") that required them to turn over a proportion of their crop to the government. When crops failed or a drought hit, farmers were left with nothing to fall back on. Starvation and malnutrition raged in the Indonesian countryside.

On publication, *Max Havelaar* caused only a minor stir. But after a few years, its message sparked reformist efforts all over Europe. The book led to changes in Dutch colonial policy—especially the repeal of cultuurstelsel—and helped initiate a program of building schools and hospitals.

We can assess the influence of *Max Havelaar* because we have the distance and perspective from which to view it. However, if we were trying to write about the book's impact in 1862, we would have little idea of its ultimate fate. Such is the problem of writing contemporary history.

The Impact Today A similar problem confronts us in trying to assess the impact of the contemporary movement known as "fair trade," which our chapter describes as a counterbalance to "free trade." After petroleum, coffee is the largest commodity on the world market, and the US is world's largest consumer—accounting for 40 percent of international consumption.

When Americans go to their specialty roaster and spend $10.00/lb for their fragrant "Breakfast Blend," the farmer who grew these beans gets as little as twenty cents—a measly 2 percent—of this sum. Those who benefit most in this web of financial excess are the middlemen who stand between us and the grower: throngs of buyers, exporters, importers, wholesalers, roasters, and retailers, each inflating the price before they pass on the beans to the next link in the chain.

In 1992 the inequities built into this system led a group of European reformers to create the first "fair trade" coffee organization, appropriately named "Max Havelaar" (http://www.maxhavelaar.ch/en/) and headquartered in Basel, Switzerland. Its goal was to eliminate the middlemen from this system—or at least some of them—so that the growers could earn a decent wage for their beans. Today, the going price paid to farmers is stabilized at $1.26, far higher than the open market but one that is ultimately passed on to consumers in higher prices.

Will coffee aficionados put their money where their conscience is? In Western Europe at least, the answer seems to be yes. Fair trade coffee now accounts for 3 percent of all sales in countries like the Netherlands, Switzerland, and Luxembourg. In contrast, as of 2001, fair trade accounted for a minuscule fraction of the American coffee market—a mere 0.2 percent.

A 2003 study by political scientists Margaret Levi and April Linton and published in the journal *Politics & Society*, found that in Seattle, America's coffee capital, when the choice came down to caffeine scruples or a tasty brew, consumers leaned decidedly toward the latter: "Store buyers report that their decisions to stock Fair Trade coffees and customers' decisions to buy them are based as much on good taste in the cup as on a desire to help coffee farmers."

It is impossible know whether Fair Trade will become more than a flash in the cup, or whether it will alter how we think not only about coffee—but about the ethics of all kinds of foodstuffs.

Trying to answer this question remains little more than a guess. This is why historians stick to writing about the past.

• Chapter Preview •

Chapter Main Ideas

Section 1 Trade and culture link economies and lives around the world.

Section 2 People and countries are working together to protect human rights, help solve problems such as poverty and disease, and adjust to new patterns of migration.

Section 3 Terrorism, the potential use of weapons of mass destruction, and ethnic and religious tensions threaten security around the world.

Section 4 People are working together to protect the environment and using science and technology to improve living conditions around the world.

CHAPTER 19

Today's World

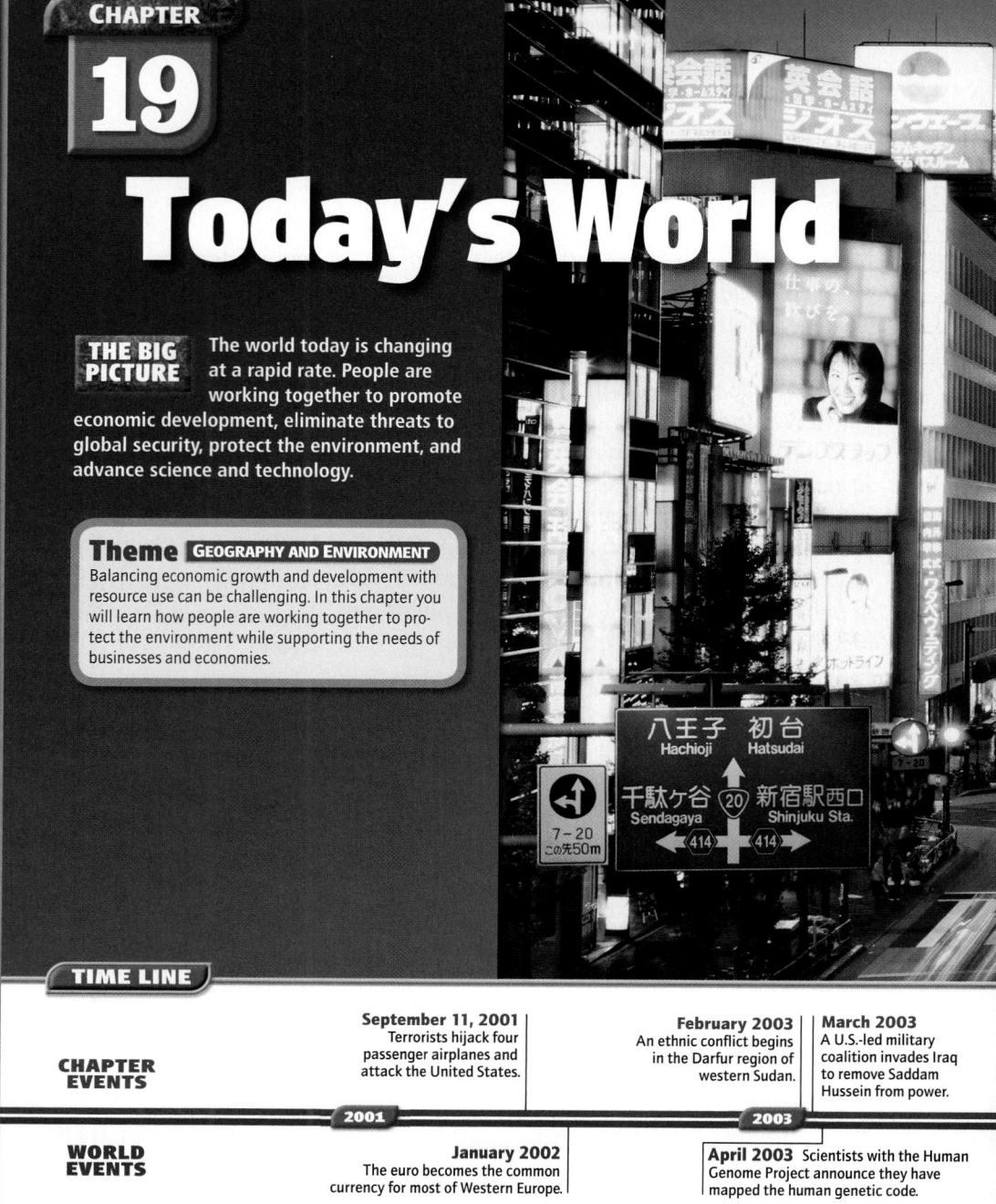

THE BIG PICTURE The world today is changing at a rapid rate. People are working together to promote economic development, eliminate threats to global security, protect the environment, and advance science and technology.

Theme GEOGRAPHY AND ENVIRONMENT

Balancing economic growth and development with resource use can be challenging. In this chapter you will learn how people are working together to protect the environment while supporting the needs of businesses and economies.

TIME LINE

CHAPTER EVENTS

September 11, 2001 Terrorists hijack four passenger airplanes and attack the United States.

February 2003 An ethnic conflict begins in the Darfur region of western Sudan.

March 2003 A U.S.-led military coalition invades Iraq to remove Saddam Hussein from power.

2001 — **2003**

WORLD EVENTS

January 2002 The euro becomes the common currency for most of Western Europe.

April 2003 Scientists with the Human Genome Project announce they have mapped the human genetic code.

Introduce the Chapter

At Level

Today's World

1. Have students name important events in the United States and the world that have happened during their lifetimes. Remind students not to focus solely on wars or conflicts, but to name positive changes that have occurred in the world as well.
2. Create a class list for all to see and broadly categorize them, using such heads as medicine, science and technology, global conflicts, etc.
3. Review the list of events with students, and have volunteers explain the importance and possible consequences of each event.
4. Tell students that in this chapter they will learn about the important issues facing today's world, including terrorism, security, the environment, technology, human rights, trade, and globalization.
LS Verbal-Linguistic

Alternative Assessment Handbook, Rubric 11: Discussions

Key to Differentiating Instruction

Below Level

Basic-level activities designed for all students encountering new material

At Level

Intermediate-level activities designed for average students

Above Level

Challenging activities designed for honors and gifted and talented students

Standard English Mastery

Activities designed to improve standard English usage

History's Impact video program
Watch the video to understand the impact of September 11, 2001.

Reading like a Historian This photograph shows a busy nighttime scene in the Shinjuku area of Tokyo, Japan. Shinjuku is a major commercial center and is home to the world's busiest train station as well as to a large number of successful stores, restaurants, and night clubs.

Analyzing Visuals What does this photograph tell you about life in Japan? What does it indicate about Japan's level of technology and resource use?

See **Skills Handbook**, p. H26

December 2004 A tsunami strikes Southeast Asia, killing more than 225,000 people.

August 2005 Hurricane Katrina hits New Orleans and the Gulf Coast of the United States.

2005 — 2007

August 2005 South Korean scientists announce the first successful cloning of a dog.

March 2006 CAFTA, a free trade agreement between the United States and several Caribbean countries, goes into effect.

• Chapter Preview •

HOLT
History's Impact
▶ **Video Program: Today's World**
See the Video Teacher's Guide for strategies for using the video segment.

Reading Like a Historian

Shinjuku, Japan Shinjuku makes up one of the 23 wards, or districts, of Tokyo, but is a thriving metropolis in its own right. Its train station, for example, accommodates more than two million passengers each day. The Shinjuku business district contains some of Tokyo's tallest skyscrapers.

go.hrw.com
Online Resources
Chapter Resources:
KEYWORD: SHL TOD
Teacher Resources:
KEYWORD: SHL TEACHER

Explore the Time Line

1. What two natural disasters occurred within a year of each other? *tsunami in Southeast Asia; Hurricane Katrina in the United States*
2. When did two major scientific achievements involving DNA occur, and what were they? *April 2003, scientists announce they have mapped the human genetic code; August 2005, South Korean scientists announce the successful cloning of a dog*
3. How long after September 11, 2001, did the U.S. invade Iraq? *18 months*

Info to Know

Human Genome Project Scientists have discovered that genetics may play an important role in health. It is thought that a person's DNA can determine how susceptible or resistant a person is to certain diseases. Some scientists believe that in the future, doctors will be able to look at a newborn's DNA to determine the diseases and illnesses to which the child might be susceptible. **Predict** How would this new research help? *possible answer—Doctors could use the information to treat children before they become seriously ill, perhaps reducing infant mortality rates.*

Answers

Reading Like a Historian *possible answer—Japan's economy has thrived, as shown by its modern cities with bustling business districts.*

Preteach

Geography Starting Points

Per capita Income in the United States Per capita income in the United States has risen dramatically in the last half century. In 1935, per capita income was $474; in 1945, $1,235. In 1965, it was approximately $2,800, in 1985, $14,758, and in 2005, it was $34,586.

Activity **Per capita Income** Have students calculate the percentage increase in the United States' per capita income from 1985 to 2006. **LS Logical-Mathematical**

- **Map Transparency:** World Per Capita GDP, 2006
- **World History Outline Maps**
- **Interactive Map:** World Per Capita GDP, 2006

Teaching Tip

Remind students that two very reliable sources of current economic data on foreign countries are available online through the World Bank and the CIA World Factbook. Have students explain why the World Bank tracks GDP and per capita income of individual countries.

GEOGRAPHY Starting Points

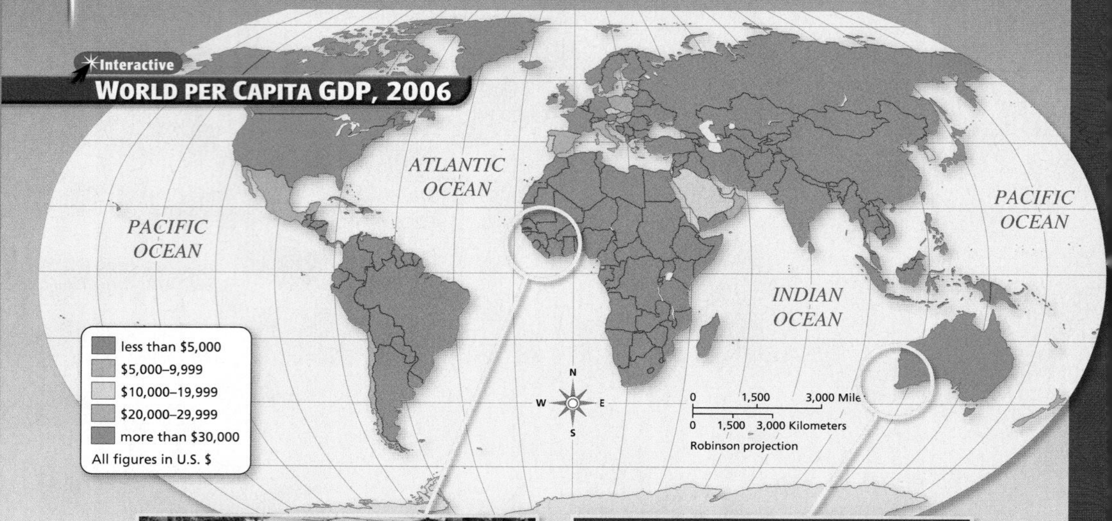

Senegal Developing countries like Senegal have low per capita GDPs, slow economic growth, and a low standard of living.

Australia Developed countries like Australia have high per capita GDPs, modern and industrial economies, and a high standard of living.

Starting Points In recent years, the world has changed rapidly as a global economy develops. New methods of transportation and communication continue to bring nations and cultures closer together. Despite economic growth in some areas, however, many countries are still working hard to build strong economies and provide opportunities for their citizens.

1. **Analyze** Which parts of the world have the lowest and highest per capita GDPs? What might explain this regional difference?
2. **Predict** How do you think the continued growth of global trade might affect this map? Do you think the map will look the same in 2020? in 2040?

Listen to History

Go online to listen to an explanation of the starting points for this chapter.

go.hrw.com
Keyword: SHL TOD

Skills Focus: Interpreting Cartograms

At Level

Social Studies Skill
World Economy

1. Review with students what cartograms are, how they differ from normal maps, and the types of information they show. Have students explain why economic data is often showed in cartogram form. You might wish to show students examples of cartograms.
2. Have students work in pairs to create a cartogram showing the data represented on the world map in the feature.
3. Have volunteers share their cartograms with the class and explain how they converted the data into this format. **LS Logical-Mathematical, Visual-Spatial**

Alternative Assessment Handbook, Rubric 20: Map Creation

Answers

Geography Starting Points

1. *Lowest—South America and parts of Central America, much of Asia, Eastern Europe, Africa; Highest—Western Europe, United States, Canada, Australia; areas with lower GDPs are poorer, many are not yet industrialized;* **2.** *possible answer—As global trade increases, the map might show less difference in GDP between countries.*

SECTION 1

Trade and Globalization

BEFORE YOU READ

MAIN IDEA

Trade and culture link economies and lives around the world.

READING FOCUS

1. How does economic interdependence affect countries around the world?
2. What are some patterns and effects of global trade?
3. How does globalization lead to cultural exchange?

KEY TERMS

globalization
interdependence
multinational corporations
outsourcing
free trade
popular culture
cultural diffusion

TAKING NOTES Take notes on the causes and effects of globalization.

Causes → Globalization → Effects

CHOPPING DOWN THE FUTURE

◀ **A pile of logs in Naren awaits the construction of more new homes.**

THE INSIDE STORY ***Does prosperity have its own risks?*** People living in the small Chinese village of Naren were once among the poorest people in the world. Now, however, they are relatively rich—and all because of a wild mushroom.

The mushrooms that grow beneath the oak and pine trees of Naren can bring high prices in Japan, where they are considered a rare delicacy. Beginning in the 1980s, Naren villagers began to gather these mushrooms to sell to Japanese consumers. It is possible for a villager to earn more than one thousand dollars in a single summer by harvesting mushrooms—an enormous amount of money in Naren.

The money from mushrooms has changed life in Naren. People who used to live in small shacks have been able to build huge wooden houses and fill them with modern luxuries, including TVs, CD players, and satellite dishes.

However, this increased prosperity has brought problems as well. As villagers chop down trees to build their new wooden houses, the forests of Naren are slowly shrinking. Without forests to absorb rainfall, disastrous floods are becoming more common. Some villagers worry that even more tree cutting could mean the end of the valuable mushrooms that grow under those trees—and of their new modern lifestyle. ■

Preteach

Getting Started

Use the **Interactive Reader and Study Guide** to familiarize students with the section content.

Interactive Reader and Study Guide, Section 1

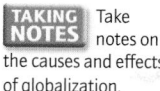

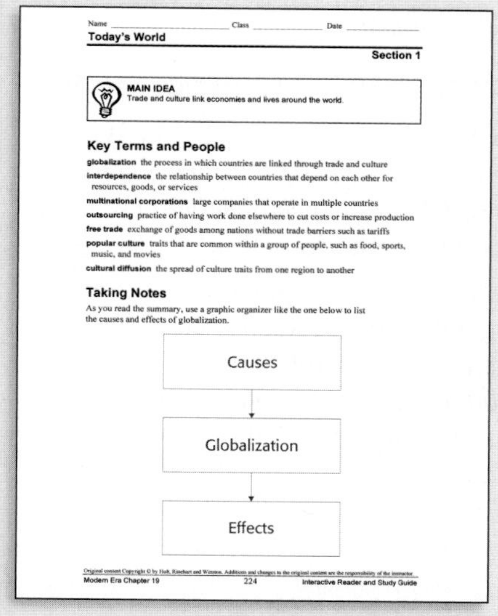

Name ______ Class ______ Date ______

Today's World

Section 1

MAIN IDEA
Trade and culture link economies and lives around the world.

Key Terms and People

globalization the process in which countries are linked through trade and culture
interdependence the relationship between countries that depend on each other for resources, goods, or services
multinational corporations large companies that operate in multiple countries
outsourcing practice of having work done elsewhere to cut costs or increase production
free trade exchange of goods among nations without trade barriers such as tariffs
popular culture traits that are common within a group of people, such as food, sports, music, and movies
cultural diffusion the spread of culture traits from one region to another

Taking Notes

As you read the summary, use a graphic organizer like the one below to list the causes and effects of globalization.

Causes → Globalization → Effects

Modern Era Chapter 19 224 Interactive Reader and Study Guide

CRF: Vocabulary Builder: Section 1

Taking Notes

Causes—the need to have closer relationships between the world's nations; easier, faster global trade; Effects—economic interdependence; links between developed and developing countries; outsourcing with multinational countries; free trade; cultural exchange; changes in popular culture

go.hrw.com
Online Resources

KEYWORD: SHL TOD
ACTIVITY: Television: Its History and Impact

Teach the Main Idea

At Level

Trade and Globalization

1. **Teach** Ask students the Reading Focus questions to teach this section.
2. **Apply** Have students create an outline of the section using the heads as main points. Have students identify at least two main ideas under each of the blue subheadings.
3. **Review** Review student outlines as a class. Have students identify the points in their outlines that they feel are most important or most interesting and have them explain their reasoning to the class. Guide students in a discussion about the ways their everyday lives are affected by international trade and globalization.
4. **Practice/Homework** Have students think about what they wear, what they do for fun, where they work, and what transportation their families use. Have students write a short essay explaining how globalization affects them personally. **LS Verbal-Linguistic**

Alternative Assessment Handbook, Rubrics 11: Discussions; and 42: Writing to Inform

Direct Teach

Reading Focus

1 How does economic interdependence affect countries around the world? *Countries are linked through trade and culture; developing and developed countries depend upon one another for goods and services.*

Economic Interdependence

Define What is economic interdependence? *relationship between countries in which they depend one another for a variety of resources, goods, or services*

Predict How do you think outsourcing will affect developed countries in the future? *possible answer—It could lead to higher unemployment in the developed countries, help lower the cost of goods, and increase prosperity and employment rates around the world.*

CRF: History and Geography: Economic Interdependence

Info to Know

Outsourcing to India In the early 2000s, India was the leader in outsourcing. India was receiving about 80 to 90 percent of the outsourcing jobs in the world. This is helping to raise the standard of living in India and is providing much needed jobs in the country. India has equipped itself with the technology and resources to manage international contracts and to provide services to other developed countries.

Economic Interdependence

At the beginning of the twenty-first century, the world was divided over a number of political, cultural, and economic issues. At the same time, however, countries around the world found themselves tied together like never before.

Globalization The force behind the new, closer relationships among the world's nations is globalization. **Globalization** is the process in which trade and culture link together countries around the world. Trade between nations is not new, but improvements in transportation and communication in recent years have made global trade much easier.

One major effect of global trade is increased economic interdependence among the world's countries. **Interdependence** is a relationship among countries in which they depend on one another for resources, goods, and services. Economic interdependence occurs because countries vary greatly in the types of goods and services they need and can provide.

Developed and Developing Countries

The goods and services a nation can provide, and those it needs, depend on the level of economic development in that country. The world's countries are often grouped into two basic categories—developed and developing countries—based on their level of economic development.

Developed countries are industrialized nations with strong economies and a high standard of living. The world's wealthiest and most powerful nations, such as the United States and Japan, are developed countries. People in developed countries generally have access to good health care, education, and technology.

READING SKILLS
Making Generalizations Combine what you already know about Japan with the information in this paragraph. Form a generalization about Japan's economy.

About 20 percent of the world's nations are considered to be developed, while the remainder are known as developing countries. Developing countries are those with less productive economies and a lower standard of living, such as Guatemala and the Philippines. Many people in these countries lack adequate education and health care.

Not all developing countries are in similar economic situations. The world's poorest nations making the least economic progress are known as least-developed countries. Most of the least-developed countries are located in Africa and southern Asia. These nations suffer from great poverty, a lack of political and social stability, and ongoing war or other conflict.

Multinational Corporations The increasing interdependence of the world's countries has been accompanied by the dramatic growth of multinational corporations. **Multinational corporations** are large companies that operate in multiple countries.

One benefit to multinational corporations from their international operations comes from **outsourcing**, the practice of having work done elsewhere to cut costs or increase production. For example, multinational corporations often build manufacturing facilities in developing countries, where materials and labor are relatively inexpensive.

Advocates of multinational corporations believe they create jobs and wealth in the developing countries they operate in. Critics say that they fail to improve the standard of living in developing countries and that outsourcing causes job loss in the company's home country.

Global Economic Ties One effect of economic interdependence is that certain events or actions can affect the economies of many nations. This global interdependence is particularly evident in times of uncertainty.

In the early 2000s, for example, the price of crude oil rose dramatically, nearly tripling in just two years. One factor in this increase was the rising world demand for oil, especially in rapidly industrializing countries like China and India. Another factor was growing concern about the available supply of oil in the world, both because of fears about dwindling oil reserves and because of unrest in some of the oil-producing regions of the Middle East.

Since all countries depend on oil for energy in some way, the rise in oil prices was felt around the world. Developed countries such as the United States that rely heavily on oil for shipping, transportation, and energy were faced with dramatically higher costs. Some poor nations in Africa could not afford to import oil at the higher prices and faced shortages. The rise in oil prices led to increased demand for alternative energy sources as well as attempts to reduce oil consumption.

READING CHECK **Summarize** How does economic interdependence affect the world?

Collaborative Learning

At Level

Outsourcing

Research Required

1. Review the information in the text about multinational corporations and outsourcing. Then organize the students into two groups. Have one group represent members of a multinational corporation that believes that outsourcing has a positive worldwide effect; the other group should represent those who oppose outsourcing to foreign countries.
2. Have students use reliable Internet or current print sources to acquire information about both sides of this issue.
3. Have each group prepare its arguments and then debate the effects and consequences of outsourcing. Have all students take notes during the debate.
4. Have students use the information from their notes to write a letter to the editor stating and supporting their own position on this topic. **LS Verbal-Linguistic**

Alternative Assessment Handbook, Rubrics 10: Debates; and 17: Letters to Editors

Answers

Reading Skills *possible answer—Japan is an industrialized nation with advanced technology and a strong economy.*

Reading Check *helps to provide jobs in developing countries, increases production and decreases cost for multinational companies*

Global Trade

Globalization often leads to or promotes free trade. **Free trade** is the exchange of goods among nations without trade barriers such as tariffs. Supporters of free trade believe that it gives producers more markets in which to sell goods and allows consumers to purchase higher-quality goods at lower prices.

International Trade Organizations A variety of international trade organizations exist today, many of which work to promote and regulate free trade. The first major international agreement on free trade came in 1948, when the General Agreement on Tariffs and Trade (GATT) was signed. Member countries worked to limit trade barriers and settle trade disputes. In 1995, GATT was replaced by the World Trade Organization (WTO). Some 150 countries are members of the WTO, which monitors national trade policies and helps resolve trade disputes.

Another group that has a major effect on international trade today is the Organization of Petroleum Exporting Countries, or OPEC. A group of oil-rich nations, OPEC works to control the production and price of oil.

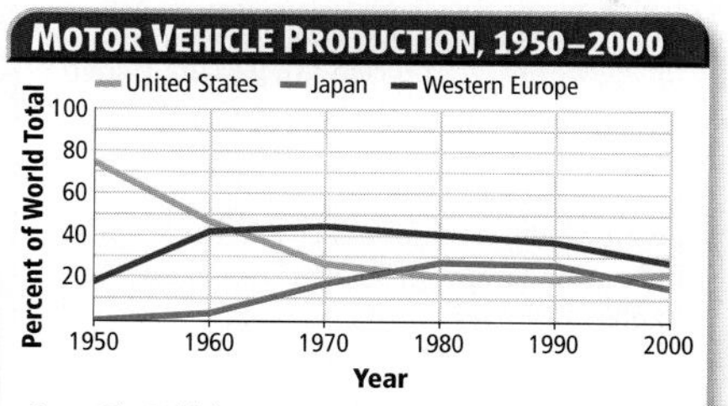

Source: *The World Almanac and Book of Facts, 2006*

Skills Focus INTERPRETING GRAPHS

Analyze How has the global production of motor vehicles changed between 1950 and 2000?

HISTORY CLOSE-UP

A Global Economy

It takes about 15,000 parts to make a typical modern automobile. The growth of the global economy means that automakers can buy these parts from countries all over the world, depending on where they can get the best prices and the highest-quality parts.

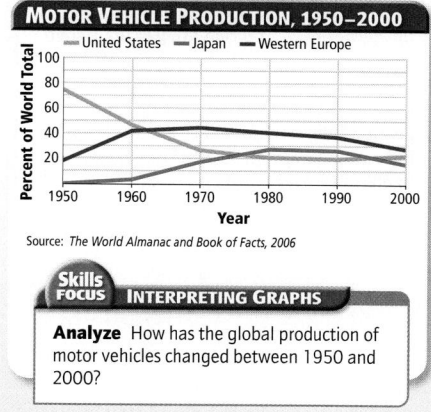

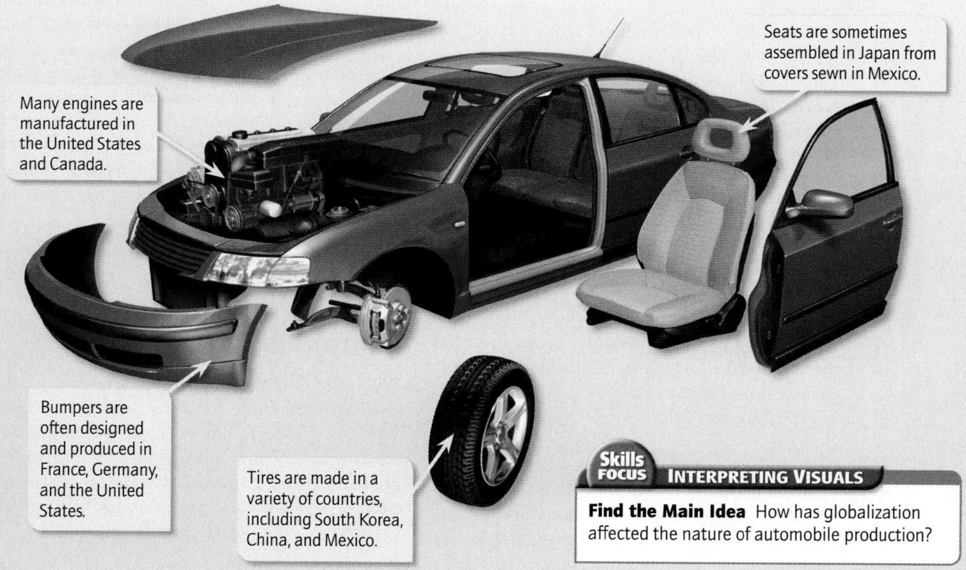

Many engines are manufactured in the United States and Canada.
Seats are sometimes assembled in Japan from covers sewn in Mexico.
Bumpers are often designed and produced in France, Germany, and the United States.
Tires are made in a variety of countries, including South Korea, China, and Mexico.

Skills Focus INTERPRETING VISUALS

Find the Main Idea How has globalization affected the nature of automobile production?

Direct Teach

Reading Focus

2 What are some patterns and effects of global trade? *free trade, international trade organizations, developing countries provide new markets for goods and services, developed countries provide technology and money to raise standard of living in the developing countries*

Global Trade

Explain What do supporters of free trade believe? *that free trade gives producers more markets to sell their goods and allows for high-quality, low cost goods*

Summarize What was the purpose of GATT, and what was its successor? *General Agreement on Tariffs and Trade worked to limit trade barriers, settle trade disputes; replaced in 1995 by the World Trade Organization*

CRF: Primary Source: The Impact of Globalization on World Cultures

Info to Know

Car Manufacturing Remind students that many cars, including luxury cars, are the result of outsourcing. For example, in 2005, about 80 percent of Porsche production was outsourced. According to an October 2005 article in *Business Week*, "Buyers of the highly successful Porsche Cayenne sport-utility vehicle, which starts at $41,000, are probably unaware that VW workers produce more than 85 percent of the wholesale value of every Cayenne, and that the Cayenne shares 65 percent of its parts and modules with VW's Touareg."

Differentiating Instruction

Below Level

Special Education Students

1. Remind students that cars are not made in just one factory in a single country. Have students work in mixed-ability pairs to list the countries mentioned in the History Close-Up feature. Make a class list for all to see.
2. Use a large world map to show students where these countries are located. Then have students create their own world maps highlighting the countries mentioned in the feature.
3. As a class, calculate the distances between the countries discussed in the feature. LS **Visual-Spatial, Logical-Mathematical**

Alternative Assessment Handbook, Rubric 20: Map Creation

Answers

Interpreting Graphs *In 1950, the United States produced the most cars; in 2000, Western Europe, Japan, and the United States each produced roughly the same percentage of cars.*

Interpreting Visuals *allows one car to be manufactured with parts made in many different countries*

Direct Teach

Reading Focus

3 How does globalization lead to cultural exchange? *cultural diffusion, increased travel to other countries for work or vacation, goods from other countries available*

Cultural Exchange

Analyze What benefits of globalization do you see in your life? *possible answers—video games, different foods, electronics, books, new cultures*

Evaluate What steps can countries take to ensure that their own cultural heritage is not lost? *possible answers—celebrate national holidays, emphasize cultural pride, patriotism, and family values*

CRF: Biography: Amadou and Mariam

Quick Facts Transparency: Major Trade Organizations and Agreements

Info to Know

Globalization Developing countries have increased their trade overall, from 19 percent in 1971 to 29 percent in 1999. Some developing countries have benefited more than others. For example, countries in Asia are profiting, while African nations struggle. Successfully increasing trade and raising the standard of living in developing countries means that the need for international aid is decreasing.

Reading like a Historian

Globalization

Analyzing Points of View There are a variety of opinions about the effects of globalization on the world. In these excerpts from a discussion about globalization, two experts debate the subject. To analyze these views on globalization, consider:

- the main points in each argument
- the emotional or factual language used

> And you see it in the streets of every city in the world . . . The rich are getting richer . . . and then the poor, the people at the bottom of the barrel . . . seem to be getting poorer . . . I suggest we get realistic and we acknowledge the undoubted fact that globalization is very good for the rich and very bad for the poor.
>
> —Leslie Sklair, sociologist, 2001

> Inequality is growing, but poverty is going down . . . The whole level [of wealth] moves such that people who used to be classified as poor are no longer poor . . . The last 20 years of growth has made more people get out of poverty than at any time in history. Today . . . the maximum amount of people in poverty is about 20 percent. . . . In 1800, it would be 80 percent.
>
> —Meghnad Desai, economist, 2001

Skills Focus READING LIKE A HISTORIAN

1. Point of View How do these opinions on globalization vary?

2. Language How do the authors use emotional and factual language in support of their points of view?

See **Skills Handbook**, p. H33

Regional Trade Many countries belong to at least one regional trade bloc, or group, which they form to promote free trade and to deal with economic issues with neighboring nations. The largest regional trade bloc is the European Union (EU), with 25 member countries. Other regional trade blocs include the North American Free Trade Agreement (NAFTA), the Association of Southeast Asian Nations (ASEAN), and the Southern African Development Community (SADC).

Effects of Global Trade Global trade has some clear benefits. Developing countries can provide new and valuable markets for goods and services produced by developed countries. In return, the technology, services, and money provided by developed countries can improve public services and raise the standard of living in developing countries.

On the other hand, opponents of globalization argue that the process benefits wealthy developed nations at the expense of developing nations. For example, they say that free trade encourages practices that exploit workers and destroy the environment in developing countries. Anti-globalization activists sometimes take part in protests against the World Trade Organization, the International Monetary Fund, the World Bank, and other organizations that seek to regulate the global economy.

Other people who oppose free trade work to promote what they call fair trade. One example is the fair trade coffee movement, which guarantees that fair prices are paid to the farmers who grow coffee beans in an effort to improve farmers' standard of living. Companies involved in fair trade see it as a way of promoting social responsibility.

READING CHECK **Find the Main Idea** How does global trade affect the world?

Cultural Exchange

With globalization, countries are linked not only through trade but also through culture. While people have had cultural exchanges for thousands of years, modern methods of transportation and communication allow these exchanges of ideas and customs to happen faster than ever before.

Collaborative Learning

At Level

Cultural Diffusion

1. Organize students into small groups. Have students in each group develop a list of their favorite foods, communication and music items, sports, and entertainment.
2. Have students use the information in their texts or outside sources to research the origin of their favorite items.
3. Have students present their findings to the class and explain how these items came to be a part of American culture and daily life. Then guide students in a discussion about cultural diffusion and globalization.

LS **Verbal-Linguistic**

Alternative Assessment Handbook, Rubrics 11: Discussions; and 14: Group Activity

Answers

Reading Like a Historian **1.** *Sklair believes globalization hurts the poor; Desai believes globalization has caused poverty to go down.* **2.** *Sklair uses repetition for emotional effect; Desai cites factual information, such as the percentage of people living in poverty.*

Reading Check *can provide opportunities for developing countries; opponents believe global trade exploits developing nations, supporters believe it provides for the production and sale of high-quality, low cost goods*

Culture Traits Spread Globalization leads to changes in popular culture. **Popular culture** refers to culture traits such as food, sports, and music, that are common within a group of people. Although popular cultures vary from one country to another, globalization is causing **cultural diffusion**, or the spread of culture traits from one region to another. Rapid modern transportation systems permit many people to travel to different countries for work or vacation. When people travel, they see new styles of clothing, try other foods, and hear different types of music. Other people move permanently from one country to another, bringing with them elements of their own culture to their new homes.

Television, movies, music, and other forms of mass media are the most powerful methods of cultural diffusion. For example, people around the world can readily watch satellite news channels and movies from the United States and Europe, while people in Western nations can listen to traditional African or Asian music on the radio. The Internet is another means for the exchange of images and ideas. In this way, mass media plays a huge role in cultural changes.

Effects of Cultural Changes Some people believe that these changes are largely negative. They argue that mass media and advertising encourage the growth of consumerism, or a preoccupation with the buying of consumer goods. For example, as people in developing countries become wealthier, many begin to spend their new money on consumer goods from toothpaste to clothing to automobiles. This market for consumer goods, opponents say, is shaped by the media and advertising rather than by actual needs. Thus, they worry that globalization is beginning to create a common world culture and is encouraging traditional cultures to lose some of their uniqueness.

Globalization is creating a world community where people are linked together through economics and culture. One of the biggest challenges of globalization may be to preserve valuable traditional cultures and at the same time provide enrichment from other places around the world.

READING CHECK **Summarize** How is cultural exchange a part of globalization?

Major Trade Organizations and Agreements

QUICK FACTS

ORGANIZATION (date formed)	Current Members and Goals
General Agreement on Tariffs and Trade (GATT) (1948)	125 members (in 1995); worked to reduce tariffs and other international trade barriers; replaced by WTO
World Trade Organization (WTO) (1995)	Nearly 150 members; promotes lower trade barriers
Group of Eight (G-8) (1975, as G-6)	8 major industrial democracies; discuss international economic, environmental, and other issues
Organization of Petroleum Exporting Countries (OPEC) (1960)	11 major oil-exporting countries, most in Middle East; coordinate oil policies of members
European Union (EU) (1993)	25 European nations; work for European economic and political integration

Section 1 Assessment

go.hrw.com
Online Quiz
Keyword: SHL TOD HP

Reviewing Ideas, Terms, and People

1. **a. Define** What is **globalization**?
   b. Explain How are **multinational corporations** an example of economic **interdependence** between developed and developing countries?
   c. Evaluate What are some benefits and drawbacks of **outsourcing**?
2. **a. Identify** What is the World Trade Organization?
   b. Compare and Contrast How do supporters and opponents of global **free trade** differ in their views of it?
   c. Elaborate Why do you think countries may want to join multiple regional trade blocs?
3. **a. Recall** What types of culture traits make up **popular culture**?
   b. Explain How do mass media affect **cultural diffusion**?
   c. Evaluate What recent change do you think has been the biggest cause of global diffusion?

Critical Thinking

4. **Make Judgments** Do you think globalization has had a greater effect on developed countries or developing countries? Use your notes on the section to explain your answer.

Globalization → Greater Effects

FOCUS ON SPEAKING

5. **Persuasion** Prepare a list of points that a government official in a developing country might use in a speech to convince other government and business leaders that the country should sign a free trade agreement.

Direct Teach

Recent Scholarship

Though many people believed the world was flat before explorations in the 1400s proved them wrong, author Thomas L. Friedman says the world today actually is flat, at least in a metaphorical sense. In his book *The World Is Flat*, Friedman analyzes patterns of globalization in recent years and how electronic communication has enabled the world to become interconnected. Providing an example of just how progressive technology has become, Friedman issued an update of his book a year after the hardcover was published, adding revised content.

The World Is Flat by Thomas Friedman. Farrar, Straus and Giroux, 2005. (Updated edition, 2006)

Review & Assess

Close

Have students explain what globalization is and summarize its possible positive and negative effects.

Review

Online Quiz, Section 1

Assess

SE Section 1 Assessment

Progress Assessment: Section 1 Quiz

Alternative Assessment Handbook

Reteach/Intervene

Interactive Reader and Study Guide, Section 1

Interactive Skills Tutor CD-ROM

Section 1 Assessment Answers

1. **a.** process in which countries are linked to each other through trade and culture
   b. Multinational companies sometimes outsource work to developing countries.
   c. benefits—goods and services at lower cost, jobs in developing countries; drawbacks—developed countries lose some jobs, become more dependent on corporations
2. **a.** international organization that monitors trade policies and helps solve disputes
   b. supporters—both developing and developed countries benefit; opponents—helps developed nations more, exploits developing nations
   c. possible answer—for resources and labor
3. **a.** food, sports, music, and movies
   b. allows sharing and exchange of cultures
   c. possible answers—ease of transportation and communication, the Internet
4. possible answer—developing countries; they are provided with jobs and resources
5. Lists should include free tariffs, more resources, and an increase in jobs.

Answers

Reading Check *leads to cultural diffusion, more travel to other countries for work or vacation, exotic goods from other countries available*

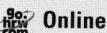

Preteach

Getting Started

Use the **Interactive Reader and Study Guide** to familiarize students with the section content.

Interactive Reader and Study Guide, Section 2

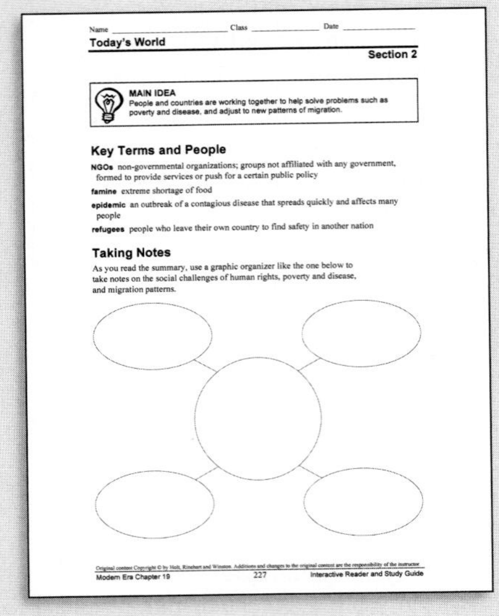

Name ______ Class ______ Date ______

Today's World

Section 2

MAIN IDEA
People and countries are working together to help solve problems such as poverty and disease, and adjust to new patterns of migration.

Key Terms and People

NGOs non-governmental organizations; groups not affiliated with any government, formed to provide services or push for a certain public policy

famine extreme shortage of food

epidemic an outbreak of a contagious disease that spreads quickly and affects many people

refugees people who leave their own country to find safety in another nation

Taking Notes

As you read the summary, use a graphic organizer like the one below to take notes on the social challenges of human rights, poverty and disease, and migration patterns.

Modern Era Chapter 19 227 Interactive Reader and Study Guide

Academic Vocabulary

Review with students the high-use academic terms in this section.

welfare displace to force to leave home or homeland (p. 599)

displace to force to leave home or homeland (p. 600)

CRF: Vocabulary Builder: Section 2

Taking Notes

Human Rights—problems include torture, slavery, killing; United Nations and NGOs work to improve and protect human rights; human rights usually better protected in democratic countries; Poverty and Disease—more than 20 percent of people in the world live on less than $1 per day; poverty more common in developing countries; international health organizations seek to control diseases; Population Movement—movement has increased dramatically in recent years; globalization makes movement easier; wealthy developed nations in North America and Europe are traditional destinations for migrants; fastest growing cities are in developing countries

SECTION 2

Social Challenges

Before You Read

Main Idea

People and countries are working together to protect human rights, help solve problems such as poverty and disease, and adjust to new patterns of migration.

Reading Focus

1. How are individuals, groups, and nations working to protect human rights?
2. What global challenges do people around the world face?
3. What are the causes and effects of population movement?

Key Terms

NGO
famine
epidemic
refugees

TAKING NOTES Take notes on the social challenges of human rights, poverty and disease, and population movement.

Social Challenges
1.
2.
3.

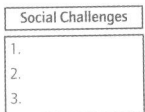

RUNNING FOR FREEDOM

THE INSIDE STORY ***Can running keep you alive?*** During his final year of high school in the Central African nation of Burundi, champion runner Gilbert Tuhabonye dreamed of attending college in the United States. Instead, an outbreak of ethnic violence nearly killed him.

Tuhabonye is a Tutsi, one of the two main ethnic groups in Burundi. The other group is the Hutu. In October 1993, a mob of Hutus attacked Tuhabonye's village and forced the Tutsis into the school building, which they set on fire. For hours, Tuhabonye lay trapped in the flames, protected only by the bodies of his dead classmates.

Finally, he gathered the strength to break free. With his back on fire, he broke through a window and escaped into the nearby woods. His legs were so badly burned that they barely functioned, but he refused to give up. Tuhabonye made his way to a hospital for treatment, where he had to learn again how to walk and, eventually, to run.

Less than three years after Tuhabonye nearly died, he was a member of Burundi's Olympic team. Soon after, he enrolled in college in the United States—where he was given a running scholarship. Today, Gilbert Tuhabonye lives in the United States, where he trains runners and tells his story of how running helped him survive. ■

◀ **Runner Gilbert Tuhabonye trains in Texas.**

Teach the Main Idea

At Level

Social Challenges

1. **Teach** Ask students the Reading Focus questions to teach this section.
2. **Apply** Organize students into groups of three. Assign one of the three topics in the section, Human Rights, Global Challenges, and Population Movement, to each student in a group. Have students write a summary of the information about their topic, and read them to the rest of the group. Have students ask and answer questions about the summaries.
3. **Review** Guide students in a discussion of the importance of human rights, and develop a class list of the rights students believe to be most important in a democratic society.
4. **Practice/Homework** Have students select one of the global challenges discussed in the section and write a proposal containing workable solutions to their chosen problem.
LS Interpersonal, Verbal-Linguistic

Alternative Assessment Handbook, Rubrics 14: Group Activity; and 37: Writing Assignments

Human Rights

Violence and human rights abuses are not new, but globalization has made the world more aware of such events. In recent years, many nations have pledged to respect human rights.

Statements on Human Rights In 1948 the United Nations issued the Universal Declaration of Human Rights. It states that all people deserve basic rights "without distinction of any kind, such as race, color, sex, language, religion, political or other opinion, national or social origin, property, birth or other status." Countries that signed the Helsinki Accords in 1975 agreed to respect human rights.

Human Rights Abuses In spite of these agreements, torture, slavery, killing, and other human rights abuses are daily occurrences in some countries. These abuses are most common in countries that are not democracies or are in the process of establishing democracy.

Some groups of people are at a greater risk of human rights abuses than others. People who disagree with their government or people who are members of a religious or ethnic minority are more likely to be victims of human rights abuses. Women and children are also at increased risk for violence and abuse.

Working for Rights Many individuals and groups are working to improve and protect human rights around the world. The United Nations investigates human rights abuses and works with national governments to protect rights. In addition, some groups called NGOs work to protect the rights of particularly threatened groups. An **NGO** is a nongovernmental organization that is formed to provide services or to promote certain public policies. NGOs such as the International Red Cross work to improve the welfare of groups such as women, children, and indigenous peoples and have played key roles in the fights against slavery, violence against women, and apartheid.

Other changes in the world have also led to improved human rights. Human rights are usually better protected in democratic countries, and the spread of democracy has led to the spread of human rights.

READING CHECK **Make Generalizations** How are human rights threatened and protected?

FACES OF HISTORY

Aung San SUU KYI
1945–

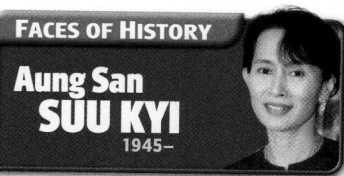

An activist for democracy in her native Myanmar (Burma), Aung San Suu Kyi has long been an opponent of her country's harsh military government. In 1990 her political party won a large majority of the seats in Myanmar's parliament, but the military rulers refused to give up power. Instead, they placed Aung San and other democratic leaders under house arrest.

Despite her imprisonment, she continued to fight for democratic reform and free elections in Myanmar. For her nonviolent struggle for democracy, Aung San was awarded the Nobel Peace Prize in 1991. As of 2006 she remained under house arrest.

Summarize What does Aung San hope to achieve in Myanmar?

Global Challenges

Although globalization is improving the lives of some people, many still face major challenges, including poverty, disease, and natural disasters. These challenges greatly affect worldwide life expectancy.

Poverty Poverty is a major problem in many countries. More than 20 percent of the world's people live on less than $1 per day and do not have access to basic services such as education and health care. Poverty can have many causes, including a lack of natural resources, wars, poor government planning, and rapid population growth. One result of poverty can be a **famine**, or an extreme shortage of food.

Although poverty is found in even the world's wealthiest countries, it is more common in developing countries. In an attempt to reduce poverty, developed countries give or loan billions of dollars every year to poor countries. When used carefully, this foreign aid can make a vital contribution to reducing poverty.

ACADEMIC VOCABULARY
welfare well-being

Disease Although many diseases have their largest impact on a local or regional level, globalization has made controlling disease a challenge for the entire world. International air travel allows diseases to spread rapidly as infected people move from place to place. For example, in November 2002 a type of pneumonia known as SARS appeared in China. Over the next few months, SARS spread to other countries in Asia, Europe, and the Americas.

Direct Teach

Reading Focus

1 How are individuals, groups, and nations working to protect human rights? *United Nations investigates abuses, works with governments; NGOs form; democracy has spread*

Human Rights

Recall What is the Universal Declaration of Human Rights? *a document issued by the U.N. in 1948, stating that all people deserve basic rights*

Describe Which groups are more likely to suffer from human rights abuses? *those who disagree with their government, members of a religious or ethnic minority, women and children*

CRF: Biography: Louise Arbour

CRF: Literature: *Cry, the Beloved Country*

Reading Focus

2 What global challenges do people around the world face? *poverty, disease, natural disasters*

Global Challenges

Recall How many people in the world live on less than $1 a day? *more than 20 percent*

Summarize What are the some causes of poverty? *lack of natural resources, wars, poor government planning, rapid population growth*

Skills Focus: Summarizing

Above Level

Research Required

Reading Skill

Non-Governmental Organizations

1. Have students conduct outside research to find an NGO that interests them. Then have students find the goals of the organization, where it is based, how many people are involved in the group, and where it operates, its annual budget, funding sources, and other pertinent information.
2. Have students compile their research into a multimedia or video presentation, and have students present their finished work to the class. **LS Verbal-Linguistic, Visual-Spatial**

Alternative Assessment Handbook, Rubrics 22: Multimedia Presentations; and 30: Research

Primary Source

"The only real prison is fear, and the only real freedom is freedom from fear."
—Aung San Suu Kyi

Answers

Faces of History *democratic reform and free elections*

Reading Check *threatened—torture, slavery, and killing; protected—actions of United Nations, NGOs; increased democracy, globalization*

Direct Teach

Reading Focus

Global Challenges

Explain Why do diseases spread more quickly today? *air travel and the number of people traveling*

Make Generalizations How does disease affect population and life expectancy? *possible answer—many diseases that plague the world are deadly, and others can be deadly if left untreated; reduce population*

Map Transparency: World Average Life Expectancy, 2002

Reading Focus

3 What are the causes and effects of population movement? *causes—war, persecution, poverty, jobs, education; effects—urbanization, crowded cities, lack of jobs for newcomers*

Population Movement

Explain What are migration push-pull factors? *reasons people leave their home country, such as war, persecution, or poverty; reasons people move to a new country, for jobs and better life*

Make Inferences What makes people in developing countries move from the rural to urban areas? *possible answer—search for a better life, higher-paying jobs*

World Average Life Expectancy, 2002

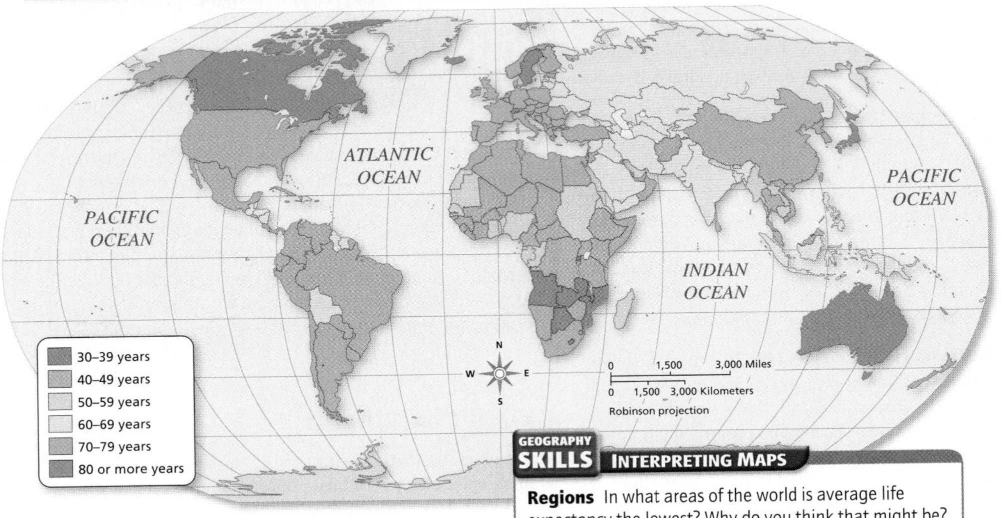

Geography SKILLS **INTERPRETING MAPS**

Regions In what areas of the world is average life expectancy the lowest? Why do you think that might be?

Hundreds of people were killed in the epidemic. An **epidemic** is an outbreak of contagious disease that spreads quickly and affects many people. HIV/AIDS is another recent epidemic. Over 25 million people have died from AIDS since 1981, and millions more are infected by the disease.

International health organizations and local governments have had some success controlling the spread of certain diseases. Much of the success has come from educating people about the prevention of disease, as well as making medicines cheaper and more available.

ACADEMIC VOCABULARY
displace to force to leave home or homeland

READING SKILLS
Making Generalizations Combine what you already know with what you have learned in this paragraph. Form a generalization about natural disasters.

Natural Disasters Natural disasters such as hurricanes, earthquakes, and floods also affect many areas of the world, often causing deaths and destroying homes and businesses. In December 2004, for example, a tsunami devastated large areas of Southeast Asia, killing over 225,000 people. Fortunately, many individuals, governments, and humanitarian organizations provide aid to regions suffering from natural disasters.

READING CHECK **Summarize** What are some of the challenges facing people around the world?

Population Movement

The movement of people around the world has increased dramatically in recent years. Some people choose to move in search of better opportunities in new places, while others are **refugees**, people who flee violence in their home country to seek safety in another nation.

Migration Many factors can cause people to leave their homes and migrate to a new place. Some of these factors "push" people to leave their homeland, while others "pull" people to a new place. Typical push factors that displace people include war, persecution, and poverty. Pull factors include opportunities in a particular country for jobs and a better life.

Migration has been changed significantly by globalization. With modern air transportation, migrants today can quickly travel far from their home countries. As a result, they can settle in places that are very different from their former homes, and the mixing of cultures can be dramatic. Furthermore, migrants are often able to return to their native countries to visit, which makes it easier to retain their own cultures, languages, and habits.

Skills Focus: Making Generalizations

At Level

Reading Skill
Natural Disasters

1. Review with students some of the natural disasters that have occurred recently. Students might mention Hurricane Katrina, recent tsunamis, earthquakes, etc. Make a class list for all to see. Then review the ways in which the national and international community responded to each disaster on the list.
2. Have students write a song or poem commemorating one of the events on the class list. Student work should be sensitive to the loss of life, property, and way of life that occurs during a severe natural disaster.

LS Auditory-Musical

Alternative Assessment Handbook, Rubric 26: Poems and Songs

Answers

Interpreting Maps *much of Africa and parts of Asia; more poverty and exposure to deadly diseases, inadequate health care*

Reading Skills *possible answer—Natural disasters can have devastating effects on a community's economy and on people's lives.*

Reading Check *poverty, disease, natural disasters*

The countries that have traditionally been the destinations of most migrants are wealthy developed nations in North America and Europe. Often, migrants do manage to find work and provide a better life for themselves and their families. Sometimes, however, they fail to find jobs or they face discrimination in their new countries. Some people want to limit the number of migrants allowed into their countries because they think the newcomers take away jobs and services from native citizens. Others worry that the traditions and languages of the migrants will change the culture of the country.

Urbanization Another type of migration happens within countries. In many parts of the world, people in search of jobs or better opportunities are moving in large numbers to urban areas from rural areas. This increase in the percentage of people who live in cities is called urbanization.

The world's fastest-growing cities are located in developing countries. As the populations of these countries grow, more of their people move to the cities looking for work. The vast urban areas of Mumbai, India, and São Paulo, Brazil, are examples of rapidly growing cities. Urban growth in developed countries is much slower, but rapid urbanization is a main factor in worldwide population movement.

READING CHECK **Find the Main Idea** What are some main reasons for population movement?

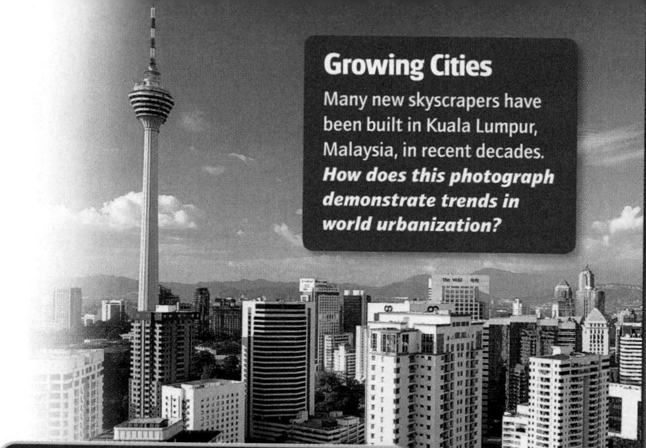

Growing Cities
Many new skyscrapers have been built in Kuala Lumpur, Malaysia, in recent decades.
How does this photograph demonstrate trends in world urbanization?

WORLD URBANIZATION, 1950–2030

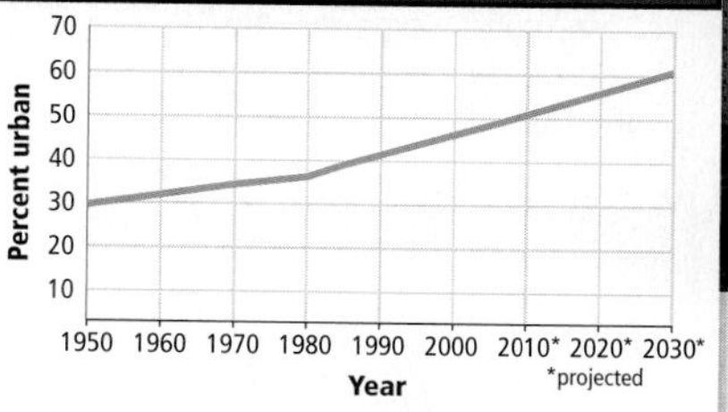

Source: United Nations Population Fund

Skills FOCUS **INTERPRETING GRAPHS**

Summarize How has world urbanization changed since 1950? How is it projected to change in the future?

SECTION 2 ASSESSMENT

go.hrw.com
Online Quiz
Keyword: SHL TOD HP

Reviewing Ideas, Terms, and People

1. a. **Identify** What is the purpose of the Universal Declaration of Human Rights?
   b. **Explain** What role do **NGOs** play in protecting human rights?
   c. **Predict** How do you think the spread of democracy might affect human rights around the world? Explain your answer.
2. a. **Identify** What are some of the main challenges facing certain people and countries around the world today?
   b. **Explain** How can an **epidemic** of a disease affect a country's economy?
   c. **Elaborate** Why is it so difficult to reduce poverty?
3. a. **Identify** What are some push and pull factors of migration?
   b. **Make Inferences** Why are the world's fastest-growing cities found in developing countries?

Critical Thinking

4. **Elaborate** Use your notes on the section and a graphic organizer like the one below to explain how social challenges affect the world today.

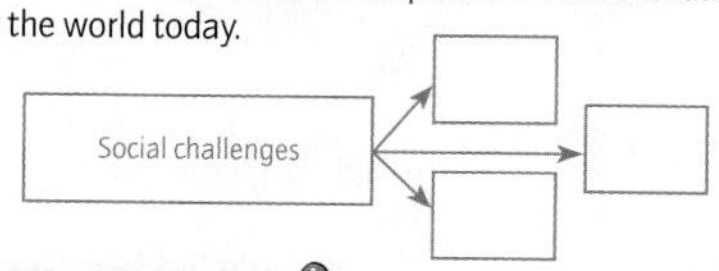

FOCUS ON WRITING

5. **Exposition** Write a letter from a person who has migrated to a new country to a friend back home. Tell the friend what you like and do not like about the new country.

Section 2 Assessment Answers

1. **a.** to assert the basic rights of all people
   b. provide services or promote public policies
   c. possible answer—will probably improve human rights, because democratically elected leaders are held accountable for their actions by the voters
2. **a.** poverty, disease, natural disasters
   b. possible answer—can hurt economy by decreasing workers and consumers
   c. possible answer—it is widespread; some causes are difficult to prevent
3. **a.** war, persecution, poverty; jobs, education, opportunities
   b. Rapid population growth leads people to move to cities looking for work.
4. Social challenges—poverty, disease, human rights abuses; Effects—increased urbanization, migration, globalization
5. Student letters should demonstrate an understanding of the causes and effects of migration.

Review & Assess

Close

Have students list human rights violations, problems associated with worldwide poverty and disease, and the effects of population movement.

Review

go.hrw.com **Online Quiz**, Section 2

Assess

SE Section 2 Assessment

Progress Assessment: Section 2 Quiz

Alternative Assessment Handbook

Reteach/Intervene

Interactive Reader and Study Guide, Section 2

Interactive Skills Tutor CD-ROM

Answers

Growing Cities *shows increase in urbanization because large, modern skyscrapers indicate population growth in the city*

Interpreting Graphs *The percentage of people living in urban areas has increased, and it is projected to continue increasing.*

Reading Check *to escape war, persecution, poverty; search for better jobs, education, better life*

Preteach

Getting Started

Use the **Interactive Reader and Study Guide** to familiarize students with the section content.

Interactive Reader and Study Guide, Section 3

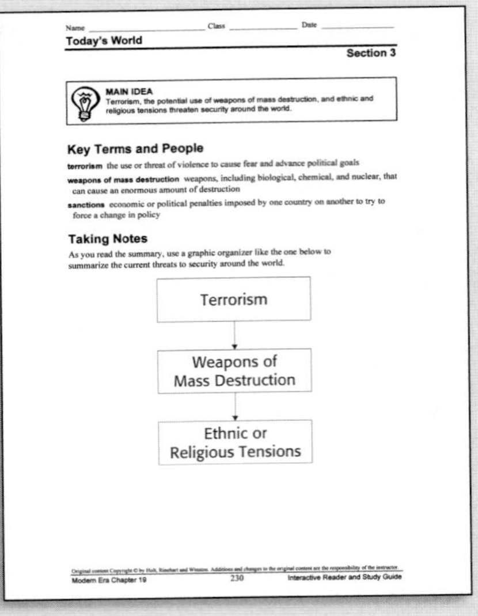

Name ____________ Class ________ Date ________

Today's World

Section 3

MAIN IDEA
Terrorism, the potential use of weapons of mass destruction, and ethnic and religious tensions threaten security around the world.

Key Terms and People

terrorism the use or threat of violence to cause fear and advance political goals

weapons of mass destruction weapons, including biological, chemical, and nuclear, that can cause an enormous amount of destruction

sanctions economic or political penalties imposed by one country on another to try to force a change in policy

Taking Notes

As you read the summary, use a graphic organizer like the one below to summarize the current threats to security around the world.

Terrorism

Weapons of Mass Destruction

Ethnic or Religious Tensions

Original content Copyright © by Holt, Rinehart and Winston. Additions and changes to the original content are the responsibility of the instructor.
Modern Era Chapter 19 230 Interactive Reader and Study Guide

Academic Vocabulary

Review with students the high-use academic term in this section.

legislation laws or rules passed by a governing body (p. 604)

CRF: Vocabulary Builder: Section 3

Taking Notes

Terrorism—unlawful use or threat of violence to cause fear and to advance political, religious, or ideological goals; Weapons of Mass Destruction—weapons that can cause enormous destruction; Ethnic or Religious Tensions—create willingness to destroy or kill; can cause civil war within countries or regions, genocide

SECTION 3 Threats to World Security

BEFORE YOU READ

MAIN IDEA
Terrorism, the potential use of weapons of mass destruction, and ethnic and religious tensions threaten security around the world.

READING FOCUS
1. How does the threat of terrorism affect today's world?
2. What other threats to world security exist today?

KEY TERMS
terrorism
weapons of mass destruction (WMD)
sanctions

TAKING NOTES Use this graphic organizer to take notes on the threats to world security.

Terrorism

Weapons of Mass Destruction

Ethnic or Religious Tensions

PREPARING FOR AN ATTACK

During a terrorism preparedness drill, emergency response workers aid a "victim" of a simulated attack.

THE INSIDE STORY ***How do you prepare for the worst?*** One November day, three people dressed as maintenance workers walked into a crowded Oklahoma mall. They calmly went about their business tending the mall's plants and then left. But the plant sprayers they used actually contained a deadly contagious disease—smallpox. Soon, dozens of people in Oklahoma had come down with smallpox, and the disease continued to spread.

Fortunately, this incident was only a test. The "smallpox" outbreak was a simulated crisis planned by the federal government and carried out at an Air Force base near Washington, D.C. The goal was to see how prepared the nation was to deal with a possible terrorist attack and to learn how the government's response to an attack could be improved. Indeed, the government learned valuable lessons from the exercise. Exercises like this have become increasingly common in the world today as governments work to protect their citizens from the threat of terrorist attacks. ■

The Threat of Terrorism

A major threat to global security today is terrorism. **Terrorism** is the unlawful use or threat of violence to cause fear and to advance political, religious, or ideological goals. Terrorists often intentionally target unarmed and unsuspecting civilians during their attacks.

Teach the Main Idea

At Level

Threats to World Security

1. **Teach** Ask students the Reading Focus questions to teach this section.
2. **Apply** Have students review the terrorism time line that appears in this section. Then have students draw a world map using the atlas in their text book as a reference. Have students locate and show the site of each event on the time line on their maps. Student maps should also contain a key to the events.
3. **Review** Review student maps as a class. Have volunteers explain what happened in each country that was targeted by terrorist groups.
4. **Practice/Homework** Have students write a one-page memo describing how life in the United States, and in other countries, changed following the September 11, 2001, attacks on the World Trade Center.

LS Visual-Spatial, Verbal-Linguistic

Alternative Assessment Handbook, Rubrics 20: Map Creation; and 40: Writing to Describe

WORLD TERRORISM INCIDENTS, 1995–2005

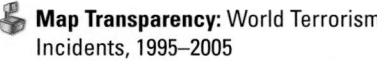

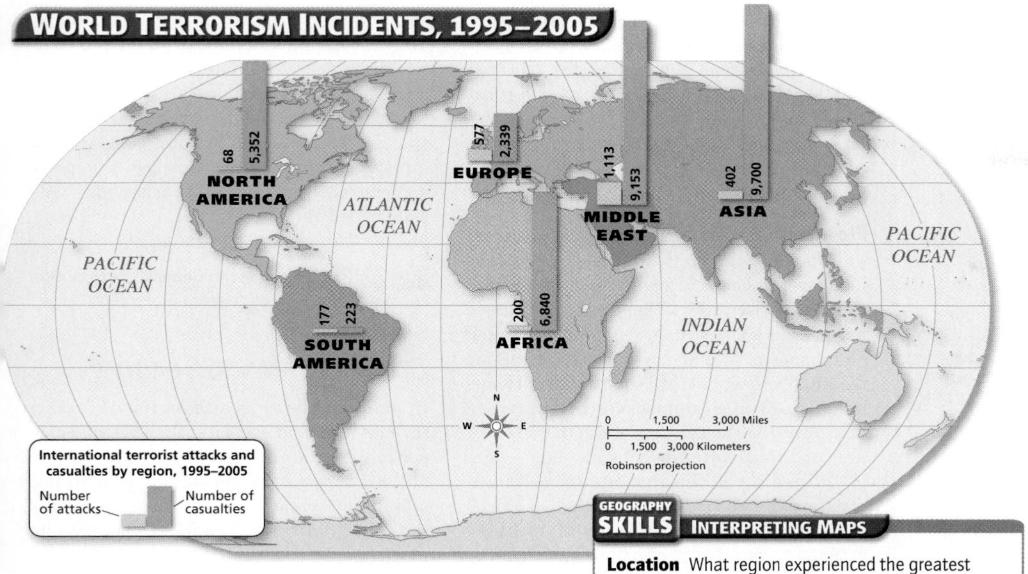

GEOGRAPHY SKILLS INTERPRETING MAPS

Location What region experienced the greatest number of terrorist attacks between 1995 and 2005?

Terrorism in History Terrorism is not a modern phenomenon, but over the last 200 years acts of terrorism have become far more common. Traditionally, terrorist groups have used terrorism to overthrow governments, fight for independence, or change society. In the late 1800s and early 1900s, for example, different terrorist groups around the world killed a number of kings, presidents, and other political leaders.Other terrorists attacked ordinary citizens in order to further their goals.

Terrorist Attacks Over the past few decades, the number of worldwide terrorist attacks has increased, as has the violence of these attacks. Few regions of the world have been spared from terrorism. In Latin America, terrorism connected to the illegal drug trade is a major problem in Colombia and Peru. In Great Britain, the Irish Republican Army (IRA) for many years engaged in terrorist attacks on British targets in an attempt to end British control of Northern Ireland. In South Asia, the Tamil Tigers in Sri Lanka have used suicide bombings and other terrorist tactics in their fight for an independent state.

Terrorism in the Middle East Increasingly, the Middle East has become a focus of efforts against international terrorist groups. In part this is because of the ongoing Arab-Israeli conflict as well as the region's history of Western colonial domination, which have led to resentment of the West among some Arabs. The region is home to some radical Muslim organizations that claim that Islam justifies terrorist attacks against innocent civilians. These terrorist actions, however, are contrary to Islamic law, and are condemned by most Muslims.

In the 1980s, Islamist groups such as Hamas, Hezbollah, and al Qaeda increasingly used terrorist tactics against Israel and some Western nations. Some of these groups, such as Hamas, seek to destroy Israel and create an independent Palestinian state, while others want to rid the Middle East of Western influences. In some cases, these groups are funded or otherwise aided by certain governments in what is known as state-sponsored terrorism.

The Lebanese group Hezbollah, for example, is supported by Iran. Hezbollah formed after the 1982 Israeli invasion of Lebanon and has the primary goal of the destruction of Israel.

Direct Teach

Reading Focus

1 How does the threat of terrorism affect today's world? *increased security and intelligence gathering, military actions to fight terrorism*

The Threat of Terrorism

Describe What have been historical reasons for terrorism? *to fight for independence, overthrow governments, change society*

Make Inferences Why might terrorists choose to target civilians? *possible answer—creates more fear than attacks on military would create*

Map Transparency: World Terrorism Incidents, 1995–2005

CRF: Biography: Rose Riso

Interpreting Maps

World Terrorism Incidents, 1995–2005

Region Which region had the most casualties from terrorist attacks? *Asia* Which region has the highest average casualty rate per attack? *North America*

MISCONCEPTION ALERT

Be sure to remind students that not all terrorist attacks originate in the Middle East region or from members of a single religious group. If students question this, remind them of the Oklahoma City bombing, which resulted in 168 deaths.

Differentiating Instruction

Below Level

English-Language Learners

Standard English Mastery

Materials: newspapers, news magazines, scissors, glue

1. Have students work in mixed-ability pairs to find current articles on terrorism and responses to terrorist attacks and organizations.
2. Have each student select two articles. In their pairs, have students review the articles to ensure that they understand the article completely.
3. Have students write a short essay answering the following questions about each of their articles: Who does it involve and affect? What happened? Where did it happen? When did it happen? Why is it important to know about this event? Encourage students to use dictionaries as needed, and to write clearly, focusing on the main ideas. **LS Verbal-Linguistic**

Alternative Assessment Handbook, Rubric 40: Writing to Describe

Answers

Interpreting Maps *the Middle East*

Direct Teach

Reading Focus

2 What other threats to world security exist today? *weapons of mass destruction, ethnic and religious conflicts*

Other Threats to Security

Identify What is a biological weapon? *weapon made from organisms or toxins found in nature that are deadly to humans, also diseases and poisons*

Recall How many nations signed a treaty prohibiting biological weapons, and in what year was the treaty signed? *more than 70 nations; 1972*

Themes Through Time

Terrorism

Identify How many people were killed in the Pan Am Flight 103 attack? *270*

Sequence What two events happened in 1995, and how long was the period between the events? *attack on Tokyo subway system, Oklahoma City bombing; about 1 month*

Although Israel, the United States, and several other nations consider Hezbollah to be a terrorist organization, in some nations it is seen as a legitimate resistance movement against Israel. In July 2006 Hezbollah kidnapped two Israeli soldiers and fired rockets into Israeli, triggering a month-long conflict between Israel and Lebanon.

Fighting Terrorism After al Qaeda attacked the United States on September 11, 2001, the U.S. government took many actions to prevent future terrorist attacks. The government passed new legislation to strengthen its international and domestic intelligence services, including the establishment of the Department of Homeland Security. Government leaders increased their focus on the security of the nation's borders and transportation networks and sought to find and cut off the funding sources for terrorist networks.

ACADEMIC VOCABULARY
legislation laws or rules passed by a governing body

The government also used military action—or the threat of action—to pressure countries it suspected of supporting terrorists. In 2001, for example, a U.S.-led military campaign invaded Afghanistan and forced out the Taliban government, which had supported and protected members of al Qaeda. In 2003, another U.S.-led invasion targeted Iraq and its dictator Saddam Hussein. Some American officials claimed that Saddam possessed dangerous biological and chemical weapons and supported anti-American terrorist groups. This was later found not to be the case.

Other countries faced similar security issues. Bomb attacks on trains and buses in Madrid, London, and Jerusalem, for example, spurred Spain, Great Britain, and Israel to investigate ways to use technology to improve security for their transportation systems. Officials hoped that these measures would help prevent future terrorist attacks.

READING CHECK **Make Generalizations** How are countries working to prevent terrorism?

Other Threats to Security

In addition to terrorist attacks, there are other threats to global security. Dangerous weapons in the hands of terrorist groups or certain nations threaten public safety. In addition, ethnic and religious tensions in some areas of the world contribute to a lack of security for many people.

Dangerous Weapons Countries around the world possess weapons of mass destruction. **Weapons of mass destruction (WMD)** are weapons, including biological, chemical, and nuclear weapons, that can cause an enormous amount of destruction. Terrorist groups or governments may seek to use these weapons for their own purposes.

Themes Through Time

TERRORISM

SOCIETY Acts of terrorism go back thousands of year—at least as far as the times of ancient Greece and Rome. Over the last four decades, however, terrorism has grown far more common—and more violent. Today, terrorism is a major threat to the world's security.

September 1972 Palestinian terrorists take hostage and kill 11 Israeli athletes at the 1972 Olympic Games in Munich, Germany.

December 1988 Pan Am Flight 103 explodes over Scotland, killing 270 people. A Libyan man is later convicted for his role in the bombing.

1975

1985

April 1983 A suicide bomber attacks the U.S. embassy in Beirut, Lebanon, killing 63 people. The group Hezbollah is believed to be responsible.

Differentiating Instruction

Above Level

Advanced Learners/Gifted and Talented

Research Required

1. Have students study the terrorism time line.
2. Have students select one event on the time line that they would like to research.
3. Have students conduct research about the terrorist event they have chosen. Students should investigate the causes, the event itself, and the consequences, both international and within the country where the attack took place.
4. Have students develop a multimedia presentation describing the attack, what might have led to the attack, the implications of the attack, and the effect that it had on its country. **LS Verbal-Linguistic, Visual-Spatial**

Alternative Assessment Handbook, Rubrics 6: Cause and Effect; and 22: Multimedia Presentations

Answers

Reading Check *strengthened intelligence services, increased security, military actions*

Biological weapons are made with organisms or toxins found in nature, including diseases and poisons such as anthrax, plague, and smallpox. In 1972 more than 70 nations signed a treaty prohibiting the production or possession of biological weapons. Nevertheless, officials have begun to worry about biological attacks by terrorist groups, in part because biological weapons are relatively easy and inexpensive to develop. In 2001, for example, anthrax sent through the mail killed five Americans.

Chemical weapons such as mustard gas and nerve gas use chemical toxins to kill or injure. Like biological weapons, chemical weapons can do much damage. Chemical weapons were used during both world wars, and in the 1980s Saddam Hussein used them in the Iran-Iraq War and against Iraqi Kurds. In 1995 a Japanese religious group used the nerve gas sarin in an attack on the Tokyo subway system.

Nuclear weapons are the biggest threat to the world in the twenty-first century. Experts fear that such weapons will fall into the hands of terrorists. During the Cold War, the United States, the Soviet Union, and 60 other nations signed the Nuclear Non-proliferation Treaty, an arms control agreement meant to stop the spread of nuclear weapons.Today, nearly every nation in the world has agreed to this treaty. Still, at least nine countries are known to possess nuclear weapons, while others are believed to be trying to develop them.

One difficulty in controlling nuclear weapons is that nuclear technology can be used for legitimate purposes, such as generating energy. Because of the international concern over the development of nuclear weapons, many countries and international organizations are making efforts to ensure that nuclear technology is used safely. For example, the International Atomic Energy Agency (IAEA) routinely monitors countries suspected of developing nuclear weapons. In addition, countries have also placed sanctions on other nations they consider nuclear threats. **Sanctions** are economic or political penalties imposed by one country on another to try to force a change in policy.

Ethnic and Religious Conflicts High-tech weapons are a threat to world security because of their power to destroy and kill. Ethnic and religious conflicts are a threat because they create a willingness to destroy or kill. These conflicts have led to suicide bombings, mass killings, and other abuses.

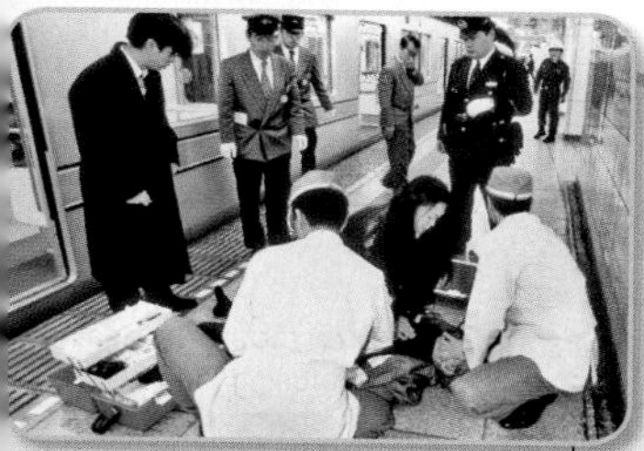

1995

2005

March 1995 A Japanese religious group releases poisonous sarin gas in the Tokyo subway system, killing 12 and injuring hundreds.

April 1995 American anti-government radicals bomb a government building in Oklahoma City, Oklahoma, killing 168 people.

September 2001 Al Qaeda terrorists use four hijacked airplanes to attack U.S. targets, killing some 3,000 people.

September 2004 Some 330 people taken hostage by Chechen terrorists are killed in a battle between the terrorists and Russian soldiers.

Skills Focus UNDERSTANDING THEMES

Summarize How have acts of terrorism affected the world since the early 1970s?

Direct Teach

Reading Focus

Other Threats to Security

Identify What are chemical weapons, and what are some examples? *weapons that use chemical toxins to kill or injure; nerve gas, mustard gas*

Analyze Why are nuclear weapons such a big threat? *may fall into hands of terrorists, would cause mass destruction if used, hard to control development of nuclear weapons*

Biography

Khaled Hosseini (1965–) Khaled Hosseini is a physician who was born in Afghanistan. His family moved to the United States in 1980 where he received his bachelor's degree in Biology and then his medical degree. The novel *The Kite Runner* was his first attempt at writing a novel, and the work was met with critical success. The novel tells the story of an Afghan whose family immigrates to the United States when the Taliban comes to power, and it recounts life for those who were left to deal with the changes in the country.

Info to Know

Rwanda In 2004 Rwandans marked the 10th anniversary of the 100-day genocide during which about 1 million Tutsi and Hutu were murdered.

Skills Focus: Identifying Main Idea and Details

At Level

Reading Skill

Ethnic and Religious Conflicts

1. Have students review the information in the text about the conflicts in Rwanda and the Darfur region of Sudan. Have students locate these two countries on a world map. Then guide students in a discussion of the destruction caused by these two conflicts to the population and to each country.
2. Have students select one of the two conflicts and write a petition to the United Nations asking for immediate international assistance to help enforce peace within the selected country. Students should discuss the number of people being killed, the reason for the internal conflict, and why immediate assistance is needed. **LS Verbal-Linguistic**

Alternative Assessment Handbook, Rubrics 35: Solving Problems; and 42: Writing to Inform

Answers

Themes Through Time *have killed many people and threatened world security, heightened awareness about security threats*

Direct Teach

Primary Sources

Ethnic Conflict in Darfur

Activity Interpreting Maps Have students locate the Darfur region, Sudan, and Chad on a map of Africa.
LS Visual-Spatial

Review & Assess

Close

Have students review threats to world security and identify what actions governments have taken to confront those threats.

Review

Online Quiz, Section 3

Assess

SE Section 3 Assessment

Progress Assessment: Section 3 Quiz

Alternative Assessment Handbook

Reteach/Intervene

Interactive Reader and Study Guide, Section 3

Interactive Skills Tutor CD-ROM

PRIMARY SOURCES

Ethnic Conflict in Darfur

The conflict in the Darfur region of Sudan between rebel forces and government-supported Janjaweed fighters had spread to the Sudan-Chad border by 2006. In this interview, a 48-year-old man from Djawara, Chad, describes a Janjaweed attack on his village. The Janjaweed killed some 75 villagers within a few hours.

Hijab generally refers to a headscarf worn by some Muslim women, but here means an amulet that is filled with printed verses from the Qur'an.

"I ran away but I was caught with others by a group of Janjaweed at 500 meters from the village. They took off my hijab. We were surrounded by Janjaweed, more than fifty I would say, maybe one hundred. They tried to kill us with machetes and knives. I was hit on the head. At some point, the Janjaweed decided to finish us off and asked someone in the group to shoot us. The guy took his Kalashnikov and shot. Everybody collapsed. I felt that I had been shot in the arm, and I fell down."

A Kalashnikov is an assault rifle.

Skills Focus READING LIKE A HISTORIAN

1. **Describe** What is the speaker describing?
2. **Analyze Primary Sources** According to the speaker, how did his fellow villagers die?

See **Skills Handbook**, p. H25

For example, in 1994 in the African nation of Rwanda, tensions between Tutsi and Hutu ethnic groups led to massacres in which some 1 million people were killed. Most of the victims were Tutsis, killed by Hutu militias. Another 2 million Tutsi and Hutu refugees fled to neighboring countries, where food shortages and disease killed thousands, despite international humanitarian aid. French and UN troops worked to maintain a ceasefire in Rwanda until a new government could establish order and end the violence. In 1998, some of the people involved in the genocide were convicted and executed for their crimes.

A similar situation occurred in the early 2000s in the Darfur region of Sudan. There, Arab militias, supported by the government, attacked African villagers and looted and destroyed their homes. The African Union sent a peacekeeping force to Sudan to try to end the conflict, but the violence continues. By 2006 some 400,000 people had been killed in Darfur, and more than 2 million others had fled to refugee camps.

Violence caused by ethnic and religious hatred is a significant threat to people in many places around the world. As nations face the risk of terrorist attacks, the use of weapons of mass destruction, and ethnic and religious conflict, people around the world are working hard to protect public safety.

READING CHECK Identify Problem and Solution How are countries and international groups dealing with threats to world security?

SECTION 3 ASSESSMENT

go.hrw.com
Online Quiz
Keyword: SHL TOD HP

Reviewing Ideas, Terms, and People

1. **a. Define** What is **terrorism**?
   b. Explain How did the United States seek to prevent future terrorist attacks after September 11, 2001?
   c. Evaluate Do you think the measures being taken in Europe, Israel, and the United States to prevent future terrorist attacks will be successful? Why or why not?
2. **a. Recall** What are three main types of **weapons of mass destruction (WMD)**?
   b. Make Inferences How have ethnic and religious tensions affected the world?
   c. Predict How do you think countries involved in threatening activities might respond to **sanctions**?

Critical Thinking

3. **Evaluate** Identify three threats to national security and rank them from least threatening to most threatening. Use your notes from the section and a graphic organizer like the one below to support your answer.

Most
Least

FOCUS ON WRITING

4. **Persuasion** Write a letter to the editor. Propose one way to eliminate or reduce a threat to society. Identify two reasons why your proposal would work.

Section 3 Assessment Answers

1. **a.** the unlawful use or threat of violence to cause fear and advance political, religious, or ideological goals
   b. strengthened domestic and international intelligence, increased security, military action in Afghanistan to remove Taliban government
   c. possible answer—Yes, nations will work together to eradicate terrorism, but there is always new technology, new ways to attack, and terrorist groups determined to cause havoc and fear.
2. **a.** biological, chemical, nuclear
   b. have caused a significant threat of violence in many parts of the world
   c. possible answer—They might choose to change their policies.
3. possible answer—from least to most: WMDs, terrorism, ethnic and religious conflict
4. Student letters should identify a realistic threat, a reasonable solution, and two reasons supporting the solution.

Answers

Primary Sources 1. *an ethnic attack;* **2.** *They were attacked with machetes, knives, and guns.*

Reading Check *peacekeeping missions, imposing sanctions*

SECTION 4

Environment and Technology

Before You Read

Main Idea

People are working together to protect the environment and using science and technology to improve living conditions around the world.

Reading Focus

1. What are people doing to protect the environment?
2. What changes are recent advances in science and technology bringing to the world?

Key Terms and People

sustainable development
deforestation
global warming
biotechnology
genetic engineering
green revolution
cloning

TAKING NOTES Take notes on the effects of recent advances in science and technology.

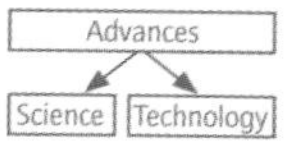

Thinking Globally, Acting Locally

THE INSIDE STORY ***Can planting a tree improve people's lives?*** Wangari Maathai was born in Kenya in 1940. It was rare in those days for girls in Kenya to receive an education, but Maathai studied biology and eventually earned a doctoral degree. She was the first woman in all of East and Central Africa to do so.

Maathai saw that environmental problems were harming Kenya. Soil erosion meant that grazing lands for livestock were disappearing. Also, Kenyans had to travel farther and farther from home to find wood for their cooking fires. These problems were leading to poverty. In 1977, Maathai decided to take action and founded the Green Belt Movement to restore Africa's forests.

Since then, the Green Belt Movement has planted 30 million trees across Africa. It has also worked to fight poverty, hunger, and political corruption. In 2004, Maathai was awarded the Nobel Peace Prize for her work. ■

Teach the Main Idea

Environment and Technology

1. **Teach** Ask students the Reading Focus questions to teach this section.
2. **Apply** Have students scan the section and make a list of the visuals, including charts. Then organize the class into small groups and have each group explain how the image relates to the section title. Have volunteers share their explanations with the class.
3. **Review** Guide students in a discussion of the growing importance of technology and of protecting the environment.
4. **Practice/Homework** Have students select one scientific or technological breakthrough discussed in the section and write a paragraph explaining how that breakthrough has affected their own lives. **LS Verbal-Linguistic**

Alternative Assessment Handbook, Rubrics 11: Discussions; and 37: Writing Assignments

Preteach

Getting Started

Use the **Interactive Reader and Study Guide** to familiarize students with the section content.

Interactive Reader and Study Guide, Section 4

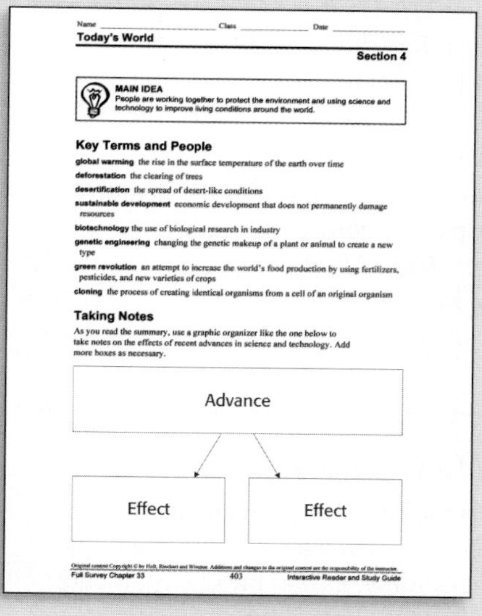
Name ______ Class ______ Date ______

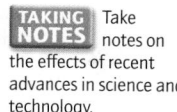

Today's World

Section 4

MAIN IDEA
People are working together to protect the environment and using science and technology to improve living conditions around the world.

Key Terms and People

global warming the rise in the surface temperature of the earth over time
deforestation the clearing of trees
desertification the spread of desert-like conditions
sustainable development economic development that does not permanently damage resources
biotechnology the use of biological research in industry
genetic engineering changing the genetic makeup of a plant or animal to create a new type
green revolution an attempt to increase the world's food production by using fertilizers, pesticides, and new varieties of crops
cloning the process of creating identical organisms from a cell of an original organism

Taking Notes

As you read the summary, use a graphic organizer like the one below to take notes on the effects of recent advances in science and technology. Add more boxes as necessary.

Advance
Effect
Effect

Original content Copyright © by Holt, Rinehart and Winston. Additions and changes to the original content are the responsibility of the instructor.
Full Survey Chapter 33 403 Interactive Reader and Study Guide

CRF: Vocabulary Builder: Section 4

Taking Notes

use of satellites for cell phones and televisions, Internet, sharing of information, genetic engineering, more productive crops, cloning, medical advances

go.hrw.com
Online Resources

KEYWORD: SHL TOD
ACTIVITY: Investigate Global Warming

Direct Teach

Reading Focus

1 What are people doing to protect the environment? *improving resource use, reducing pollution*

Protecting the Environment

Recall What has caused the world's population to increase over the past 200 years? *improved nutrition and medical treatment*

Summarize Explain the negative impact of deforestation. *After trees are cleared from forest areas, animals and plants that lived there can become extinct.*

Info to Know

Green Buildings Green buildings are designed to reduce the negative impact the building has on the environment. These buildings use less energy and water, and are usually built near public transportation to reduce the need to drive cars. To promote land recycling, the green buildings are built on already developed land.

Desertification The desertification in the Sahel region of West Africa began in about 1968. It has led to the deaths of over 100,000 people, and desertification and overgrazing has led to the deaths of over 12 million cattle.

Protecting the Environment

As globalization increases and the world's population continues to grow, so do our demands on the environment. The challenge we face today is how to balance growth and development with practices that will help protect the resources and environments we all count on.

Resource Use Over the past 200 years, improved nutrition and medical treatment have led to a dramatic increase in the world's population. Since 1800 the earth's population has grown from 1 billion to well over 6 billion. As the population has increased, industrialization and development have placed great strain on the world's resources and environment.

Development can improve lives and strengthen a nation's economy, but achieving sustainable development is a major challenge. **Sustainable development** is economic development that does not permanently damage resources. With sustainable development, people try to balance the need for development with protection of the environment. In some parts of the world, for example, people seek to protect resources by limiting their use or by setting aside areas where no development is allowed. In other parts of the world, however, the environment receives little protection.

In areas of Africa, Asia, and Latin America, particularly in the Amazon region of Brazil, **deforestation**, or the clearing of trees, is taking place at a rapid rate. In these places, trees are burned or cut down in order to dig mines or to clear land for farming or cattle ranching. As a result, some species of animals and plants that live in these forests have become extinct because of deforestation.

In the Sahel region of West Africa, people are struggling with desertification, or the spread of desert-like land conditions. Desertification is caused partly by drought and partly by human activity. People cut trees for firewood and allow livestock to overgraze the land. Without plants to anchor the soil, wind blows rich soil away, and the land becomes useless.

Pollution The global environment has been seriously affected by pollution. Human beings have always polluted their environments, but pollution did not become a serious issue until the Industrial Revolution. That revolution brought new industrial processes, which created waste products that harmed the air, water, and land. By the 1960s, pollution had increased so much that some scientists had begun to see it as a growing threat to human survival.

Green Buildings

So-called green buildings are designed to reduce the building's use of resources and its impact on the environment.

The roof of Chicago's City Hall is largely covered with plants, which reduces energy use and filters rainwater.

Insulation and construction techniques, such as solar panels, help reduce this home's energy consumption.

Skills Focus: Making Oral Presentations

At Level

Reading Like a Historian Skill

Public Service Announcement

1. Have students review the information on environmental issues in this section.
2. Have students pick one environmental issue and conduct research about it using reliable online sources.
3. Have students prepare a public service announcement about their chosen issue. The announcement should inform people about the environmental problem, its consequences, and ways to help solve the problem. Students might wish to make a multimedia presentation with both video and audio components.

LS Kinesthetic

Alternative Assessment Handbook, Rubric 24: Oral Presentations

Countries around the world find it hard to agree on how best to fight pollution. One debate surrounds the issue of **global warming**, or the rise in the surface temperature of the earth over time. This rise could bring about disastrous changes in the earth's climate. Scientists agree that the earth's temperature has increased slightly over the past 100 years, and many believe that air pollution caused by human activity has brought about this rise.

Although some governments have taken action against pollution and global warming by passing laws to protect the world's air and water, many nations do not have strict pollution controls in place. The United States, for example, has passed many environmental laws but is one of the world's largest polluters. Some nations fear that placing strict limits on the emissions of carbon dioxide and other gases that contribute to global warming might harm economic development. Preventing and reducing pollution while protecting businesses and economies is a major international challenge.

Even when environmental laws are in place, pollution and toxic waste can be released because of accidents at industrial facilities. In 1984, for example, a leak of toxic gas from an Indian factory killed over 15,000 people and injured a half-million more. Two years later, the meltdown of the Soviet Union's Chernobyl nuclear plant sent deadly radiation into the air over parts of Europe.

READING CHECK **Find the Main Idea** What environmental issues face the world today?

Science and Technology

Advances in science and technology have greatly changed the world in recent years. While new discoveries have brought great benefits, they have also raised new questions and challenges.

Space Exploration Some of the greatest discoveries and scientific advances in recent years have come from space exploration. Data collected from satellites and during space shuttle missions have given scientists new information about the origins and development of stars, galaxies, and planets. Other data is helping scientists understand climate change on the earth.

QUICK FACTS

World Internet Access, 2006

REGION	POPULATION	INTERNET ACCESS
North America	331 million	68.6%
Oceania	34 million	54.1%
Europe	807 million	38.2%
South and Central America	554 million	15.1%
Middle East	190 million	10.0%
Asia	3,668 million	9.9%
Africa	915 million	3.6%

Source: Internet World Stats

Space exploration has also led to the development of technologies that are widely used today. Consumer products ranging from scratch-resistant eyeglass lenses to farther-flying golf balls are the results of experiments performed by scientists for the world's space programs.

The Information Age Other advances in science and technology have led to great changes in the way we transmit and receive information. In fact, the exchange of information is such an important part of modern life that some people say we are living in the Information Age.

Today, space satellites transmit the signals for cell phones and satellite television, both of which have become increasingly common around the world. Personal computers and the Internet link people, educational institutions, businesses, and governments around the world, allowing instant communication. More and more people are working, shopping, and maintaining friendships online.

Not all areas of the world have joined the Information Age, however. This difference in access to the Internet and other information and communications technologies is called the digital divide. Given the importance of information technology in aiding economic development, the digital divide is an obstacle that many people are trying to overcome.

Direct Teach

Reading Focus

2 What changes are recent advances in science and technology bringing to the world? *new products, increased knowledge, better and faster access to information, better medical care, larger crops*

Science and Technology

Recall What advances in consumer products have come from space exploration? *scratch-resistant eyeglass lenses, farther-flying golf balls*

Describe What is the digital divide? *difference in access to the Internet and other information and communications technologies*

Predict How will genetic engineering affect the world in ten years? *possible answer—new crops, larger crop production, less hunger*

Quick Facts Transparency: World Internet Access, 2006

CRF: Biography: Yuet Wai Kan

Skills Focus: Comparing and Contrasting

At Level

Reading Skill

Genetically Engineered Crops

Materials: construction paper, colored markers

1. Have students review the information about the green revolution and genetically engineered crops. Discuss the advantages of and concerns about genetic engineering, and have students take notes during the discussion.
2. Have students create a print advertisement to promote or discredit genetically engineered crops. Ads should carry a distinct message, a slogan, and a brief argument or comment supporting the position stated in the ad.
3. Have students present their advertisements to the class.

LS Verbal-Linguistic

Alternative Assessment Handbook, Rubric 2: Advertisements

Answers

Reading Check *pollution, global warming, deforestation, desertification*

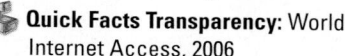

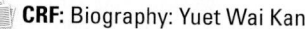

Direct Teach

Faces of History

James D. Watson

Identify Who is James Watson, and what did he do? *an American scientist; one of the discoverers of the structure of DNA; later led the Human Genome Project*

Analyze What are some possible benefits and risks of genetically modified crops? *Benefits—better crops, more food production; Risks—potential harm to humans and the environment*

Review & Assess

Close

Have students explain the impact of technology on the environment.

Review

Online Quiz, Section 4

Assess

SE Section 4 Assessment

Progress Assessment: Section 4 Quiz

Alternative Assessment Handbook

Reteach/Intervene

Interactive Reader and Study Guide, Section 4

Interactive Skills Tutor CD-ROM

FACES OF HISTORY

James D. WATSON

1928–

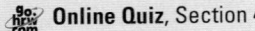

An American scientist, James D. Watson was one of the discoverers of the structure of DNA, the material that carries genetic information in all forms of life. This discovery in the 1950s played a crucial role in the later study of genetics and in genetic engineering.

In later years, Watson continued to research human biology and genetics and led the Human Genome Project, a scientific project to determine the chemical structure of every human gene. Watson is a strong supporter of genetically modified crops and other genetic engineering, believing that the benefits outweigh any possible risks.

Infer Given Watson's scientific background, why might he support genetic engineering?

Medicine and Genetic Engineering The world has greatly benefited from the medical advances that took place in the years after World War II. Scientists and doctors developed many medicines and vaccines that prevent the spread of contagious diseases and treat physical and mental illnesses, as well as techniques that allow surgeons to transplant human organs. Advances in medical technology, including ultrasound, laser, and computer technology, have allowed doctors to more easily treat the human body.

Developments in genetics—the study of genes and heredity—have led to the rapid growth of the field of **biotechnology**, or the use of biological research in industry. Some biotechnology companies manufacture vaccines to treat diseases, while other companies have genetically modified types of food plants—grains, fruits, and vegetables. Altering the genetic makeup of a plant or animal is called **genetic engineering**. Genetically modified plants can be hardier and more productive than conventional ones and are often grown in areas of the world where other crops struggle.

Genetically modified plants are one part of the green revolution. The **green revolution** is an ongoing attempt by agricultural scientists to increase the world's food production by developing new types of wheat, rice, and other food crops. With enough water, fertilizer, and pesticides, the genetically modified crops can produce much more food than unmodified crops. Advocates believe that genetically modified crops can reduce pesticide use and bring higher profits for farmers. Others, however, are concerned about the crops' unknown effects on humans and the environment as well as a possible reduction of genetic diversity.

Another use of genetic engineering that has brought debate is cloning. **Cloning** is the process of creating identical organisms from a cell of an original organism. Although cloning offers possibilities for improving livestock and for medical research, it also presents serious moral, ethical, and legal questions. As we go forward into the twenty-first century, we will continue to use science and technology to solve problems and improve lives, while dealing with the important ethical questions these new technologies may raise.

READING CHECK **Make Generalizations** How have recent advances in science and technology brought both great benefits and new challenges?

SECTION 4 ASSESSMENT

go.hrw.com
Online Quiz
Keyword: SHL TOD HP

Reviewing Ideas, Terms, and People

1. **a. Define** What is **deforestation**?
   b. Make Inferences Why might some people not want to limit pollution?
   c. Elaborate How might politics and economics interfere with achieving **sustainable development**?
2. **a. Describe** How have improvements in information and communication technologies affected the world?
   b. Identify Cause and Effect What have been some results of the **green revolution**?
   c. Elaborate What moral, ethical, and legal questions do you think **cloning** presents?

Critical Thinking

3. **Make Judgments** Using your notes, explain what recent scientific or technological achievement you believe has had the biggest impact on the world today.

Achievement → Impact

FOCUS ON WRITING

4. **Exposition** Write a short paragraph in which you explain the benefits and drawbacks of genetic engineering.

Section 4 Assessment Answers

1. **a.** the clearing of trees
   b. possible answer—Limiting pollution might harm economic development.
   c. possible answer—takes more time to achieve, requires ongoing dedication, is not a quick fix
2. **a.** satellites; new information on stars, galaxies, and planets; improvements in communications technology; scratch-resistant lenses; farther-flying golf balls
   b. new types of wheat, rice, other crops
   c. Student answers should focus on the moral, ethical, and legal problems involved in cloning a human or animal.
3. possible answer—Internet, because it improves access to information information
4. Student paragraphs should present the benefits and drawbacks of genetic engineering, and should be supported by logic and information from the text.

Answers

Faces of History *may support practical application of his original discovery*

Reading Check *possible answer—hardier crops, larger yields; debate on the ethics of DNA research and work such as cloning*

Focus on Themes

Geography and Environment

Many factors shape the earth's climate. Some are natural, such as volcanic eruptions, ocean circulation, and changes in the earth's orbit. In recent years, however, scientists have begun to understand that human activities have also contributed to climate change. Climate change can take many forms, including higher ocean levels, decreased precipitation, and increased surface temperatures. These changes are commonly known as global warming.

▲ **NOW The frozen Arctic region has gradually melted as the earth's temperature has increased.**

CLIMATE CHANGE THEN The global climate is constantly changing. By the end of the 1800s, most scientists had come to understand that global temperatures have warmed and cooled repeatedly over millions of years, leading to ice ages and periods of tropical weather.

In 1896 a Swedish chemist proposed that increases in carbon dioxide and other so-called greenhouse gases—those produced by burning fossil fuels such as coal and oil—might lead to an increase in the earth's temperature by trapping heat from the sun's rays. At first, few scientists took the idea seriously, but by the 1970s, some scientists had begun to explore the possibility that human actions can contribute to climate change.

▲ **THEN Glaciers began to melt and retreat around 1850 as the world's climate warmed.**

CLIMATE CHANGE NOW The rise of the environmentalist movement in the 1960s and 1970s brought new public attention to the idea that human activity could affect the planet, and scientific research on climate change increased. Studies have shown that carbon dioxide can indeed build up in the atmosphere and has done so steadily since the mid-1800s, when fossil fuels began to be burned in large amounts during the Second Industrial Revolution.

Decades of scientific research have made it clear that the world's climate is changing. The human effect on that change, however, is less clear. Some scientists and government officials argue that the recent global warming is due to natural changes in the earth's climate rather than to human actions. By the late 1980s, however, many countries were attempting to limit their production of greenhouse gases. There is disagreement about the appropriate actions to take, but climate change is an issue that will continue to affect the world in coming years.

Skills Focus UNDERSTANDING THEMES

1. **Summarize** How has the world's climate changed over time?
2. **Find the Main Idea** Why do many scientists believe that humans have contributed to climate change?
3. **Infer** Why might people have different opinions about the causes of climate change?

Focus on Themes

Geography and Environment

Info to Know

Facts about Global Warming Spring ice thaw and fall freezing happens 9 days earlier and 10 days later, respectively, than it did 150 years ago. Alaska, western Canada, and eastern Russia's average temperature has risen 5 to 7 degrees over what it was 50 years ago. In 1910, there were approximately 150 glaciers in Montana's Glacier Park; now only 30 glaciers are left. Average global sea level has risen 4 to 8 inches, and since the 1860s, the atmosphere's carbon dioxide level has risen almost 100 parts per million.

Differentiating Instruction

At Level

Standard English Mastery

English-Language Learners

1. Have students review the information in the text about global warming. Guide students in a discussion about the ways in which scientists believe the problem could be alleviated or perhaps solved. Have students take notes during the discussion and then review their notes in small groups.
2. Have volunteers propose solutions that might work in their own community to solve the problems of global warming. Create a class list for all to see and have students copy the list.
3. Have students use their notes from the class discussion and the class list of solutions to write a letter to the editor describing a solution and steps the community could take to implement it.
4. Have students use proper grammar, style, and a dictionary to help them as they write their letters. **LS Verbal-Linguistic**

Alternative Assessment Handbook, Rubric 17: Letters to Editors

Answers

Understanding Themes 1. *warmed and cooled repeatedly;* 2. *because studies have shown that carbon dioxide can build up in the atmosphere, and has done so steadily since humans began to burn fossil fuels in large amounts;* 3. *because many factors shape the earth's climate*

Document-Based Investigation

Genetically Modified Crops

Word Help

biotechnology biological sciences applied to genetic engineering and some DNA techniques

erosion gradually worn away

biodiversity variety of organisms found within a specified geographic region

Info to Know

Norman Borlaug Norman Borlaug spent 27 years of his career working with Mexican scientists to improve their wheat production. He also began working with scientists all around the world helping them with their production of wheat. He won the Nobel Peace Prize in 1970 for his work with the green revolution and genetically engineered crops.

Teaching Tip

Make sure that students understand the abbreviations used in the cartoon. B.G.H. is Bovine Growth Hormone, which increases milk production in cows. D.D.T., dichloro-diphenyl-trichloroethane, is a toxic pesticide, once widely used, no longer legal in the United States. P.C.Bs, Polychlorinated Biphenyls, are mixtures of man-made chemicals that were widely used in plastics, rubber products, and numerous other industrial ways, are toxic. Their manufacture, processing and distribution are now prohibited under the 1976 Toxic Substances Control Act.

CHAPTER 19

Document-Based Investigation

Genetically Modified Crops

Historical Context The documents below provide information about the debate over genetically modified crops.

Task Examine the documents and answer the questions that follow. After you have studied all the documents, you will be asked to write an essay about genetically modified crops. You will need to use evidence from these selections and from the chapter to support the position you take in your essay.

DOCUMENT 1

A Cartoonist's View

The cartoon at right was created by American cartoonist Andy Singer. Published in 2002, it shows a farmer singing about farm life while spraying crops, using the children's song "Old MacDonald Had a Farm" as a basis for the song's lyrics.

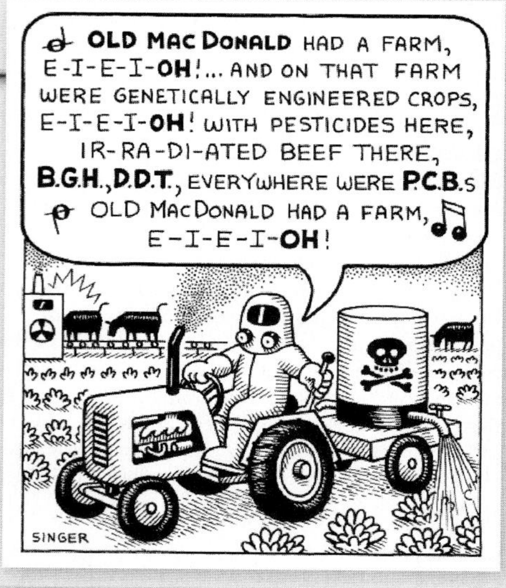

Old MacDonald's Agribusiness Farm, by Andy Singer, 2002

DOCUMENT 2

Norman Borlaug's Opinion

A scientist and crop researcher, American Norman Borlaug received the Nobel Peace Prize in 1970 for his work to end world hunger. In this 2002 interview, he speaks about the use of biotechnology and the development of genetically modified crops.

> Biotechnology will help these [developing] countries accomplish things that they could never do with conventional plant breeding. The technology is more precise and farming becomes less time consuming. The public needs to be better informed about the importance of biotechnology in food production so it won't be so critical . . .
>
> You can philosophize about this but I've been in the field for a long time and I believe genetically modified food crops will stop world hunger . . .
>
> If we had continued practicing conventional farming, we would have cut down millions of acres of forest, thereby destroying wildlife habitat, in order to increase cropland to produce enough food for an escalating population. And we would have to use more herbicides in more fields, which would damage the environment even more. Technology allows us to have less impact on soil erosion, biodiversity, wildlife, forests, and grasslands.

Skills Focus: Analyzing Alternative Points of View — Below Level

Reading Like a Historian Skill

Debating Genetically Modified Crops

1. Have students review the information in the chapter regarding genetically modified crops. Then have students write a paraphrase of each of the documents, using simpler vocabulary. Students should be sure to note whether each document is in favor of genetic modification, or against it.
2. Organize students into two groups for a class debate on genetic engineering. Students should use arguments presented in the documents during the debate.
3. After the debate, have students make their own political cartoons reflecting one viewpoint or the other. **LS Interpersonal, Visual-Spatial**

Alternative Assessment Handbook, Rubrics 10: Debates; and 27: Political Cartoons

DOCUMENT 3

A Concern about Food Safety

The excerpt below is from *Fatal Harvest: The Tragedy of Industrial Agriculture*, a 2002 collection of essays edited by Andrew Kimbrell, the director of the Center for Food Safety. The Center opposes genetically modified crops.

> The myths of industrial agriculture share one underlying and interwoven concept—they demand that we accept that technology always equals progress. This blind belief has often shielded us from the consequences of many farming technologies. Now, however, many are asking the logical questions of technology: A given technology may be progress, but progress toward what? What future will that technology bring us? . . . As a growing portion of society realizes that pesticides, fertilizers, monoculturing, and factory farming are little more than a fatal harvest, even the major agribusiness corporations are starting to admit that some problems exist. Their solution to the damage caused by the previous generation of agricultural technologies is—you guessed it—more technology. "Better" technology, biotechnology, a technology that will fix the problems caused by chemically intensive agriculture. In short, the mythmakers are back at work.

DOCUMENT 4

The History of Genetic Modification

In this October 2000 essay in the plant biology journal *Plant Physiology*, Norman Borlaug writes about genetically modified crops.

> The fact is that genetic modification started long before humankind starting altering crops by artificial selection. Mother Nature did it, and often in a big way. For example, the wheat groups we rely on for much of our food supply are the result of unusual (but natural) crosses between different species of grasses . . . Neolithic humans domesticated virtually all of our food and livestock species over a relatively short period 10,000 to 15,000 years ago. Several hundred generations of farmer descendants were subsequently responsible for making enormous genetic modifications in all of our major crop and animal species . . . Thanks to the development of science over the past 150 years, we now have the insights into plant genetics and breeding to do purposefully what Mother Nature did herself in the past by chance.
>
> Genetic modification of crops is not some kind of witchcraft; rather, it is the progressive harnessing of the forces of nature to the benefit of feeding the human race.

Skills FOCUS READING LIKE A HISTORIAN

DOCUMENT 1

a. Identify What is the cartoonist's opinion about genetically modified crops?

b. Make Judgments Do you think the cartoonist's use of humor to support his opinion is effective? Why or why not?

DOCUMENT 2

a. Identify What is Borlaug's opinion about genetically modified crops? What words or phrases support your answer?

b. Explain What arguments does Borlaug use to support his opinion?

DOCUMENT 3

a. Identify What is the author's opinion about genetically modified crops?

b. Analyze How does the author use factual and emotional language to support this view?

DOCUMENT 4

a. Compare and Contrast Does the author agree or disagree with the writer of Document 3? What words or phrases support your answer?

b. Make Judgments How does the author support his position? Do you think his arguments are valid?

DOCUMENT-BASED ESSAY QUESTION

Why might people view genetically modified crops differently? Using the documents above and information from the chapter, form a thesis that explains your position. Then write a short essay to support your position.

See **Skills Handbook**, pp. H25, H27, H29

Collaborative Learning

At Level

Choosing the Best Argument

1. Organize students into groups of four. Assign each student in each group one document, and have the students write a paraphrase or summary of the assigned document. Have students share the information within their groups, so that all four documents are reviewed by the groups.
2. Have groups decide which document they think makes the best argument. Tell groups they should consider the following questions when making their choice: Does the document use facts or emotional language? Is the argument persuasive? Why or why not?
3. Have groups list specific reasons to support their choice.
4. Have volunteers present their group's chosen document and cite specific examples and information that support their choice.

LS Verbal-Linguistic

Alternative Assessment Handbook, Rubrics 14: Group Activity; and 24: Oral Presentations

Document-Based Investigation

Word Help

monoculture cultivation of a single crop on a farm or in a region or country

agribusiness farm industry

Info to Know

Green Revolution and the World

The green revolution set out to eliminate hunger and famine by developing heartier or productive varieties of crops. By the 1990s, 75 percent of Asian rice had new varieties, and almost 50 percent of the wheat in Africa also had new varieties.

Answers

Reading Like a Historian

Document 1. a. *that they are harmful;* **b.** *possible answers—no, because if the plants hurt people it would be a serious matter; yes, humor gets his message across;* **Document 2. a.** *that they will end world hunger and help the environment; "genetically modified food crops will stop world hunger;" "would have cut down millions of acres of forest;"* **b.** *argues that his opinion is more valid because he has been in the field for a long time, and that others are merely philosophizing;* **Document 3. a.** *that these crops may have unintended negative consequences; that technology does not necessarily mean progress;* **b.** *asks rhetorical questions, labels supporters of genetic modification as "blind" and "mythmakers;"* **Document 4. a.** *disagrees; "not some kind of witchcraft," "progressive;"* **b.** *states that nature and many earlier farmers also genetically modified crops; possible answers—no, because the outcome of the earlier modifications has no bearing on the outcome of today's genetic engineering; yes, his argument gives good examples for why people should not fear the new technology;* **Essay** *Student essays should explore both sides of the debate over genetically modified crops, using details from the documents and the chapter to explain the differing opinions.*

CHAPTER 19

Chapter Review

QUICK FACTS

VISUAL STUDY GUIDE

Globalization

Effects of Globalization

Economic Effects

- Increased economic interdependence among the world's nations
- Growth of the free trade movement
- Establishment of international trade organizations and agreements
- Rise of multinational corporations

Social Effects

- Population movement around the world through migration and urbanization
- Spread of culture traits from one region to another
- International efforts to fight poverty and disease and provide aid to regions suffering from national disasters
- Efforts to protect human rights by NGOs and other groups

Environmental Issues

- Population growth strains the world's resources and the environment
- Achieving sustainable development is a major challenge
- Limiting pollution and fighting global warming while protecting businesses and economies is an important international issue

Threats to World Security

- Acts of terrorism
- Terrorist groups or dangerous nations using biological, chemical, or nuclear weapons
- Ethnic and religious hatred and violence

Review Key Terms

Identify the correct term or person from the chapter that best fits each of the following descriptions.

1. laws or rules passed by a governing body
2. the rise in the surface temperature of the earth over time
3. biological, chemical, and nuclear weapons
4. changing the genetic makeup of a plant or animal to create a new type
5. a relationship between countries in which they rely on one another for resources, goods, and services
6. economic development that does not permanently damage resources
7. the process in which countries are linked to each other through trade and culture

Answers

Visual Summary

Review and Inquiry Have students name one specific example of each of the issues found in the Visual Study Guide. Then, create a class list of examples of Globalization, Environmental Issues, and Threats to World Security. Display the list for all to see.

Quick Facts Transparency: Visual Study Guide: Today's World

Review Key Terms and People

1. legislation
2. global warming
3. weapons of mass destruction
4. genetic engineering
5. economic interdependence
6. sustainable development
7. globalization

Comprehension and Critical Thinking

8. **a.** developed—strong economies with a high standard of living, technologically advanced, industrialized; developing—weak economies, lower standard of living, lack of adequate education and health care
b. They are able to outsource jobs to cut costs and increase profits.
c. possible answer—positive, it provides a global community, people around the world able to connect

9. **a.** lack of natural resources, war, poor government planning, rapid population growth
b. possible answer—could be due to a fight for power; abuse of human rights is used as a means to instill fear, stop opposition
c. possible answer—Cities would grow; globalization and cultural diffusion might increase.

10. **a.** possible answer—bombing of Pan Am Flight 103 over Scotland; gas attack in Tokyo subway; bombing in Oklahoma City; destruction of World Trade Center in New York City and Pentagon in Washington, D.C.
b. Terrorism threatens civilians; weapons of mass destruction, if used, could result in enormous loss of life.
c. nuclear technology has legitimate uses, can generate energy; little proof that countries are using it to create weapons; difficult to determine purpose of research

11. **a.** genetically engineered crops; stable, hardier, larger yields create adequate food supplies
b. causes—drought, overgrazed land, trees cut; effects—erosion occurs, land becomes useless
c. possible answer—protecting environment: must be able to grow food, have clean air and water

Reading Skills

12. possible answer—The growth of the global economy allows for increased economic interdependence.
13. possible answer—Due to advances in technology, in addition to globalization, people are able to travel quickly, and communicate easily around the world.
14. possible answer—Migration effects globalization, because people move into new areas, bringing their cultures with them.

History's Impact video program
Review the video to answer the closing question: How have the events of September 11th changed the world?

Comprehension and Critical Thinking

SECTION 1 *(pp. 593–597)*

8. a. Describe What are some main differences between developed and developing countries?

b. Explain How do multinational corporations benefit from global economic interdependence?

c. Make Judgments Do you think cultural diffusion has mostly positive or negative effects? Explain your answer.

SECTION 2 *(pp. 598–601)*

9. a. Recall What are some factors that can contribute to poverty?

b. Make Inferences Why do you think threats to human rights have occurred particularly in countries that are not democracies or are just trying to establish democracy?

c. Predict How might increasing migration and urbanization affect the world?

SECTION 3 *(pp. 602–606)*

10. a. Describe Name four examples of recent terrorism and list where they occurred.

b. Summarize Summarize the threats posed to the world's security by terrorism and weapons of mass destruction.

c. Elaborate What issues are involved in trying to stop the spread of nuclear weapons?

SECTION 4 *(pp. 607–610)*

11. a. Recall What kinds of improvements in living conditions have recent advances in biology brought about?

b. Identify Cause and Effect What are some causes and effects of desertification?

c. Evaluate Do you think protecting the environment or encouraging development is more important? Explain your answer.

Reading Skills

Making Generalizations *Use what you have learned in this chapter to make a generalization about each topic below.*

12. the global economy

13. technology and globalization

14. migration and globalization

Analyzing Points of View

Reading Like a Historian *The two selections below show alternative points of view on the use of genetic engineering in corn production.*

"There are a number of Oaxacans, especially campesinos [farmers], who consider the presence of any transgenes in maize [corn] as an unacceptable risk to their traditional farming practices, and the cultural, symbolic, and spiritual value of maize. That sense of harm is independent of its scientifically studied potential or actual impact upon human health, genetic diversity, and the environment."

—Report of the Commission for Environmental Cooperation, a division of NAFTA, 2004

"The report also fails to consider the potential benefits of biotechnology . . . Biotechnology offers the world . . . opportunities to combat hunger and protect the environment."

—Joint statement of the Environmental Protection Agency and the U.S. Trade Representative on the NAFTA report, 2004

15. Explain On what basis does the NAFTA report claim that genetically modified corn is bad for Mexico?

16. Interpret What differences are at the root of the disagreement between the two sources?

Using the Internet

go.hrw.com
Practice Online
Keyword: SHL TOD

17. Global warming is an important—and controversial—issue. Using the Internet, research the ongoing debate about the causes and impact of global warming. Then write a report that summarizes and evaluates the major positions and arguments about climate change.

WRITING ABOUT HISTORY

Exposition: Writing and Explanation *Advances in science and technology have encouraged economic growth and population growth. These results have, in turn, threatened the environment in many places around the world.*

18. Assignment: In an essay, explain how societies balance their need for economic development with the pressures development places on the environment. To support your explanation, use information from this chapter and from other research as needed. Be sure to collect facts and examples that clearly illustrate the points you are making.

Answers

Analyzing Points of View

15. that it hurts traditional farming practices, as well as the cultural, symbolic, spiritual value of corn

16. impact of biotechnology in solving world hunger

Using the Internet

17. Go to the HRW Web site and enter the keyword shown to access a rubric for this activity.

KEYWORD: SHL TOD

Writing About History

18. Students should mention that economic development and environmental protection are not mutually exclusive, that societies can find ways to support both environments and economies.

A rubric for this activity is provided in **CRF:** Writing About History.

HOLT
History's Impact
▶ **Video Program: Today's World**
Refer to the Video Program Teacher's Guide for an answer of the closing question.

Review and Assessment Resources

Review and Reinforce

- **CRF:** Chapter Review
- **Quick Facts Transparency**: Visual Study Guide: Today's World
- **Spanish Chapter Summaries Audio CD Program**
- OSP **Holt PuzzlePro**: Quiz Show for ExamView
- **Quiz Game CD-ROM**

Assess

- **PASS**: Chapter Test, Forms A and B
- **Alternative Assessment Handbook**
- OSP **ExamView Test Generator**, Chapter Test
- **Differentiated Instruction Modified Worksheets and Tests CD-ROM**: Chapter Test
- HOAP **Holt Online Assessment Program** (in the Premier Online Edition)

Reteach/Intervene

- **Interactive Reader and Study Guide**
- **Differentiated Instruction Teacher Management System**: Lesson Plans for Differentiated Instruction
- **Differentiated Instruction Modified Worksheets and Tests CD-ROM**: Chapter Test
- **Interactive Skills Tutor CD-ROM**

go.hrw.com
Online Resources
KEYWORD: SHL TEACHER

Unit Review

You can use these pages to have students simultaneously review the unit and practice taking standardized tests.

Answers

1. D
   Europe and North America, Section 1
2. B
   Europe and North America, Section 1
3. A
   Europe and North America, Section 2
4. C
   Europe and North America, Section 2
5. D
   Europe and North America, Section 4
6. B
   Asia, Section 1
7. C
   Asia, Section 2
8. B
   Asia, Section 3

UNIT 5

Standardized Test Practice

Directions Write your answer for each statement or question on a separate answer sheet. Choose the letter of the word or expression that best completes the statement or answers the question.

1 The U.S. effort to rebuild Europe after World War II was known as

A the Truman Doctrine.
B the Monroe Doctrine.
C the domino theory.
D the Marshall Plan.

2 The quote below from Winston Churchill in 1946 came at the beginning of what conflict?

"From Stettin in the Baltic to Trieste in the Adriatic, an iron curtain has descended across the Continent . . . All these famous cities and the populations around them lie in the Soviet sphere and are subject, in one form or another, not only to Soviet influence, but to a very high degree and increasing measure of control from Moscow."

A World War II
B the Cold War
C the Korean War
D the Vietnam War

3 What caused the Cuban missile crisis?

A The Soviet Union began transporting nuclear missiles to Cuba.
B The Cuban government sold nuclear missiles to Venezuela.
C The United States aimed nuclear missiles at Cuba.
D The Soviet Union agreed to buy nuclear missiles from Cuba.

4 In what ways did the Cold War conflict between the Soviet Union and the United States affect the rest of the world?

A The United States set up satellite states in Eastern Europe.
B The Soviet Union formed NATO to guard against a possible attack by Western powers.
C The United States and the Soviet Union competed to gain influence and control around the world.
D Soviet and U.S. troops fought each other directly in many countries.

5 Which event led to the end of the Cold War?

A The United States and the Soviet Union signed a truce to end the war after the Cuban missile crisis.
B The United States and the Soviet Union both decided to reduce military spending.
C The United States developed a missile defense system that neutralized the threat of nuclear weapons.
D The Soviet Union suffered from serious economic problems and collapsed.

6 India was partitioned in 1947 largely because

A India's neighbors feared a unified India would dominate the region.
B differences between Hindus and Muslims created religious conflict.
C the Soviet Union was trying to set up a Communist government in eastern India.
D Great Britain and the United States feared that India had nuclear weapons.

7 How was the Vietnam War related to the domino theory?

A Vietnam had built up its military and planned to invade Cambodia and Thailand.
B The Soviet Union invaded China to prevent it from attacking Vietnam.
C The United States did not want a Communist government to take control of Vietnam.
D France agreed to allow Vietnam to set up a democracy to stop the spread of communism.

8 Under Deng Xiaoping, China

A became a Communist country.
B began economic reforms.
C launched the Cultural Revolution.
D battled the nationalist Guomindang forces.

9 **What event in China's history does this photo represent?**

A the Communist takeover of China
B China's long conflict with Taiwan
C the Cultural Revolution
D the protests at Tiananmen Square

10 **The term Asian Tigers refers to**

A countries in Asia that experienced tremendous economic growth in the 1980s.
B countries in Asia that have used their strong militaries to threaten their neighbors.
C the Communist countries of Asia.
D countries in Asia that have nuclear weapons.

11 **Both Kwame Nkrumah and Jomo Kenyatta**

A were imprisoned in South Africa during apartheid.
B were Arab nationalists.
C led independence movements in Africa.
D were African dictators in the 1980s.

12 **What was a key result of the Camp David Accords?**

A Israel agreed to return to its 1948 boundaries.
B Syria and Lebanon agreed to a common border.
C Iran and Iraq ended their long war.
D Egypt and Israel settled their conflict peacefully.

13 **How did the Iranian Revolution change Iran?**

A A conservative religious government came to power.
B Iran established better relations with the West.
C Iran became a Communist country.
D Freedom of religion and speech were allowed.

14 **How has the United States been involved in Central America in the postwar era?**

A The United States invaded Nicaragua and El Salvador in the 1980s.
B The United States has repeatedly blockaded the Panama Canal.
C The United States has supported anticommunist governments and insurgent groups.
D The United States has worked to end free trade agreements in the region.

15 **One thing that Juan Perón and Augusto Pinochet have in common is that both**

A led military dictatorships in Latin America.
B served as president of Argentina.
C led Communist uprisings in Central America.
D refused to join NAFTA.

16 **How is globalization changing the world?**

A It is eliminating poverty in many countries.
B It is linking countries through trade and culture.
C It is reducing economic interdependence.
D It is eliminating free trade.

17 **Which international agency works to resolve international conflicts and humanitarian crises?**

A GATT
B NAFTA
C UN
D G-8

REVIEWING THE UNIT

Constructed Response The superpower rivalry between the United States and the Soviet Union affected the whole world. Pick two world regions from this unit and write a brief essay on how superpower conflicts affected their history since 1945. What conflicts occurred, and how were superpowers involved?

CONNECTING TO THE PREVIOUS UNIT

Constructed Response The roots of the Cold War can be traced back to events at the end of World War II. What were some of these events, and how did they set the stage for postwar conflict? Write a brief essay outlining how two events at the end of World War II laid the foundation for Cold War conflicts.

Unit Review

Answers

9. D
Asia, Section 3

10. A
Asia, Section 4

11. C
Africa and the Middle East, Section 1

12. D
Africa and the Middle East, Section 4

13. A
Africa and the Middle East, Section 4

14. C
Latin America, Section 1

15. A
Latin America, Section 2

16. B
Today's World, Section 1

17. C
Africa and the Middle East, Sections 2–4; Today's World, Sections 2–3

Reviewing the Unit

Student essays will vary, but might mention the Soviet blockade of Berlin and the Cuban missile crisis. In the first case, the Soviet Union hoped to force the Western nations to abandon Berlin. The Soviets were forced to lift their blockade after the Western allies used an airlift to deliver food and other supplies to West Berlin. In the second instance, after the failed Bay of Pigs invasion, the Soviet Union installed missiles in Cuba, 90 miles from the United States. After the United States threatened to take military action—which could have resulted in a nuclear war—the Soviets removed the missiles.

Connecting to the Previous Unit

Student essays should discuss two critical events that occurred at the end of World War II and their connection to later Cold War conflicts.

Unit Review

Economic Systems

Cultural Protection In 2005 the UN Educational, Scientific and Cultural Organization (UNESCO) approved the first international treaty designed to protect cultures from foreign competition. The measure was a response to increasing globalization, which threatens to diminish local cultures. U.S. officials objected to the measure, saying that it could be used to block the flow of ideas, goods, and services. The measure was supported by Canada and Britain, normally among America's closest allies. Only Israel joined the United States in voting against the measure.

Society

Globalization and Terrorism
A connection can be made between globalization and terrorism. Computers, jets, and other technology have sped up globalization and broken down traditional ideas of sovereign nation-states. At the same time, tools of globalization can be used to spread terror.

Primary Source

"Analyzing terrorism as something separate from globalization is misleading and potentially dangerous. Indeed globalization and terrorism are intricately intertwined forces characterizing international security in the twenty-first century."
—Audrey Kurth Cronin, Specialist in International Terrorism at the Congressional Research Service at the Library of Congress

Activity **Analyzing Primary Sources** Write the quote by Audrey Kurth Cronin above for students to see. Have students write two or three paragraphs explaining what the quote means, whether they agree or not, and why. **LS Verbal-Linguistic**

Themes & Global Connections

THEME
ECONOMIC SYSTEMS

How is globalization changing the world's economic systems?

Globalization is the process by which countries are linked through trade and culture. Improvements in mass communication and modern transportation technologies have allowed people, goods, and information to spread around the globe faster than ever before. As a result, global and regional trade are growing, and countries are increasingly linked economically and culturally.

Effects of Globalization

- **Free Trade** Regional trade organizations that seek to lower trade barriers and increase trade among countries are growing.
- **Global Culture** A global culture is developing as people have more access to the same information and products.
- **Growth of Trade** Global and regional trade are growing as the world economy expands.
- **Outsourcing** Companies are sending more work overseas, creating jobs in some places but eliminating them in others.
- **Interdependence** Countries are relying on each other more than ever for goods and services.
- **Multinational Corporations** Large companies that operate around the world are growing in size and influence.

THEME
SOCIETY

What challenges do societies around the world face today?

In both developed and developing countries, people face many difficult issues that affect their societies. These include safeguarding human rights, fighting poverty and health problems, providing services and economic opportunities to migrants and immigrants, and protecting societies from the threats of terrorism and conflict.

Challenges Facing Societies Today

Human Rights Despite government commitments to protect human rights, people around the world are still victims of human rights abuses.

Poverty Poverty is a major problem in both developed and developing countries, despite global efforts to reduce it.

Health Fighting disease and hunger, making quality health care available, and educating people about health issues are worldwide challenges.

Migration and Urbanization As cities grow and people migrate to new places, providing them with jobs and services is a challenge.

Terrorism and Security Societies around the world face increasing threats from terrorism and regional conflicts.

Differentiating Instruction

Below Level

English-Language Learners

Materials: poster paper, colored pencils or markers

1. Organize students into mixed-ability pairs. Ask students what they think is the biggest challenge facing societies today. Have each pair decide on a challenge and write it on a sheet of paper. (Students may choose one of those listed in the chart at the bottom of this page, or another challenge, such as an aging population.)
2. Have pairs create a poster to build awareness of the challenge they identified.
3. Display student posters for the class to see.
4. Guide students in a discussion of the challenges they illustrated. What are some possible ways of dealing with these challenges? **LS Visual-Spatial**

Alternative Assessment Handbook, Rubrics 11: Discussions; 28: Posters; and 35: Solving Problems

ENVIRONMENTAL CHALLENGES TODAY

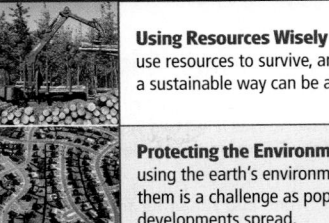

	**Using Resources Wisely** People need to use resources to survive, and using them in a sustainable way can be a major challenge.
	**Protecting the Environment** Living in and using the earth's environments while protecting them is a challenge as populations grow and developments spread.
	**Reducing Pollution** Preventing and cleaning up pollution of the land, water, and air is a challenge in many places.
	**Fighting Global Warming** Reducing greenhouse gases without disrupting economies is an international challenge.

THEME

GEOGRAPHY AND ENVIRONMENT

What environmental challenges are affecting the world's people and places?

As populations and economies grow, so too does the need for resources and the demands on the environment. The challenge that people face around the globe is how to balance growth and development with practices that will help preserve and protect the natural resources and environments that we depend on.

Skills FOCUS UNDERSTANDING THEMES

How have globalization, challenges facing society, and environmental issues affected the community you live in? Read a local newspaper to gather information about current events in your community. Then create a chart like this one and use it to describe how these global themes are affecting the area where you live.

	Effects on My Community
Globalization	
Societal Challenges	
Environmental Challenges	

Global Connections

With globalization, places around the world are connected more than ever before. The people, culture, and businesses in one place can affect those of other places far away.

Making Connections This map shows the store locations and major resource locations of a multinational coffee company. How does the information on this map show some of the effects of globalization around the world? Write a short essay identifying three effects of globalization based on this map.

STARBUCKS™ AROUND THE WORLD

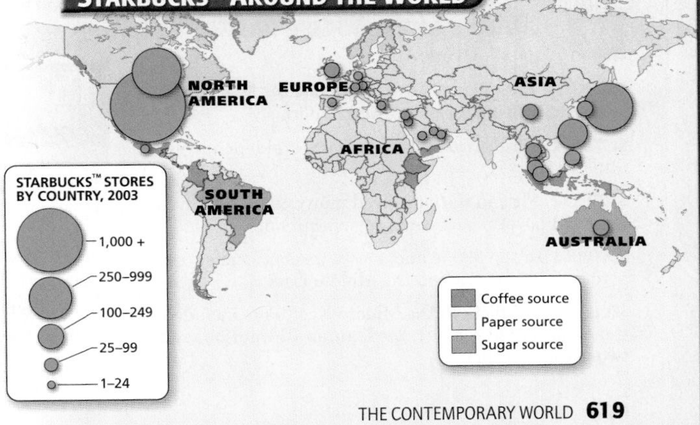

Sources: starbucks.com; U.S. Department of Agriculture; *Fortune Magazine*
Starbucks is a registered trademark of Starbucks U.S. Brands, LLC Ltd.

Unit Review

Geography and Environment

The Kyoto Accord In February 2005 the Kyoto Accord went into effect. This is an international agreement to reduce emissions of carbon dioxide and other greenhouse gasses that have been blamed for global warming. The treaty became legally binding after Russia ratified it in November 2004. However, the world's top polluter, the United States, has not ratified the treaty, saying the changes would be too costly. In one of his first acts upon taking office in 2001, President George W. Bush took the United States out of the Kyoto negotiations. He objected to the fact that large developing countries such as China and India are exempted from its requirements.

Understanding Themes

Answers will vary but might include the loss of jobs due to outsourcing, coping with an aging population, and challenges such as pollution or urban sprawl.

Global Connections

One effect of globalization is that Starbucks depends on raw materials from nations around the world for coffee beans, sugar, and paper. A second effect is that Starbucks is an American-based company that has stores in many nations. A third effect is the spreading of American culture to places like Japan and China. Still another effect is that around the world, Starbucks stores may drive locally owned cafés out of business.

Collaborative Learning

At Level

Reducing Pollution to Fight Global Warming

1. Tell students about the Kyoto Accord (see "Geography and Environment: The Kyoto Accord" in the side margin on this page).
2. Organize students into two groups for a class debate. Tell one group that it will argue in favor of U.S. participation in the Kyoto Accord. Tell the other group that it will argue against U.S. participation in the Kyoto Accord. Give students time to prepare arguments and conduct additional research, if necessary.
3. Moderate a class debate on the desirability of U.S. participation in the Kyoto Accord to reduce pollution and slow global warming.
4. Guide students in a discussion of the Kyoto Accord. What alternatives are there to such an international agreement? **LS Interpersonal**

Alternative Assessment Handbook, Rubrics 10: Debates; 11: Discussions; and 14: Group Activity

Unit Review

Summarizing the Unit

The decades following World War II have been marked by dramatic technological and social changes. At the beginning of the period, there was an ideological Cold War between two superpowers—the United States and the Soviet Union. At the beginning of the new millennium, only one superpower remained, and American culture was spreading throughout the world. Have students create a class chart showing the current state of each of the areas covered in this unit: Europe and North America, Asia, Africa and the Middle East, and Latin America.

UNIT 5 IN BRIEF

Below is a chapter-by-chapter summary of the main ideas in this unit, followed by a summary activity for the unit.

CHAPTER 15 Europe and North America
1945–Present

MAIN IDEA The end of World War II left two superpowers: the United States and the Soviet Union. For decades, their rivalry shaped world politics.

SECTION 1 The Soviet Union and the other former Allies found it difficult to cooperate during peacetime.

SECTION 2 During the Cold War, the Soviet Union and the United States competed for power and influence.

SECTION 3 The postwar boom and the Cold War caused social changes in Europe and North America.

SECTION 4 The Soviet Union collapsed in 1991, leaving the United States as the world's only superpower.

CHAPTER 16 Asia
1945–Present

MAIN IDEA After World War II, the nations of Asia continued their quest for political and economic independence.

SECTION 1 India, a former British colony, achieved independence but also suffered from conflicts.

SECTION 2 Many countries in Southeast Asia achieved independence in the postwar years.

SECTION 3 Communist forces led by Mao Zedong took control of China in 1949 and reshaped the country.

SECTION 4 In East Asia, the postwar era has been a time of great economic growth in countries like Japan, South Korea, and Singapore.

CHAPTER 17 Africa and the Middle East
1945–Present

MAIN IDEA After World War II, Africa and the Middle East struggled with independence and conflict.

SECTION 1 Most African nations gained independence after 1950.

SECTION 2 African nations faced many challenges that included poverty and corrupt governments.

SECTION 3 In the 1950s and 1960s, nationalism spread` across North Africa and the Middle East.

SECTION 4 Conflicts in the Middle East have included the Arab-Israeli conflict, the Iranian Revolution, and two wars in Iraq.

CHAPTER 18 Latin America
1945–Present

MAIN IDEA Latin America has experienced a transition from repressive military dictatorships to more open democratic societies. The region's economies have suffered from many problems but have been improving.

SECTION 1 After World War II, revolutions, civil war, and U.S. intervention affected many countries in Central America.

SECTION 2 Economic and social problems allowed dictators to seize control in Argentina, Brazil, Chile, and other countries.

SECTION 3 In the 1980s, dictatorships fell, and moderate governments began political and economic reforms.

CHAPTER 19 Today's World

MAIN IDEA The world is changing rapidly today as people face issues like globalization, human rights, terrorism and conflict, and changes in science and technology.

SECTION 1 Global trade and cultural exchange are affecting people around the world.

SECTION 2 Fighting poverty, protecting human rights, and preventing disease are major societal challenges.

SECTION 3 Terrorism and ethnic and religious tensions threaten regional and global security.

SECTION 4 People are working together to protect the environment and use resources wisely. At the same time, new developments in science and technology are improving living conditions around the world.

Thinking like a Historian — Summary and Extension Activity

People around the world face many difficult challenges today. What are some of these challenges, and how do they affect the world's major regions? Draw a simple map of the world that includes Europe, North America, Asia, Africa, and Latin America. On each continent, identify key challenges that affect:

A. Government and politics
B. Economies
C. Societies

Answers

Thinking Like a Historian *Student maps and challenges will vary. possible answers—***A.** *the precarious democracies of the former Soviet Union, the rise of fundamental Islamic republics in the Middle East;* **B.** *the effects of globalization, the effects of regional trade blocs;* **C.** *aging populations, epidemics such as avian flu.*

Unit Resources

Review and Reinforce
- **CRF:** Chapter Review
- **Spanish Chapter Summaries Audio CD Program**
- OSP **Holt PuzzlePro**: Quiz Show for ExamView
- **Quiz Game CD-ROM**

Assess
- **PASS**: Unit Test, Forms A and B
- **Alternative Assessment Handbook**
- OSP **ExamView Test Generator**
- **Differentiated Instruction Modified Worksheets and Tests CD-ROM**: Chapter Test
- HOAP **Holt Online Assessment Program** (in the Premier Online Edition)

Reteach/Intervene
- **Interactive Reader and Study Guide**
- **Differentiated Instruction Teacher Management System**: Lesson Plans for Differentiated Instruction
- **Differentiated Instruction Modified Worksheets and Tests CD-ROM**: Chapter Test
- **Interactive Skills Tutor CD-ROM**

go.hrw.com
Online Resources

KEYWORDS: SHL ENA, SHL ASA, SHL AFR, SHL LAT, SHL TOD

UNIT 6

CASE STUDIES: Issues in the Contemporary World

Document-Based Investigation

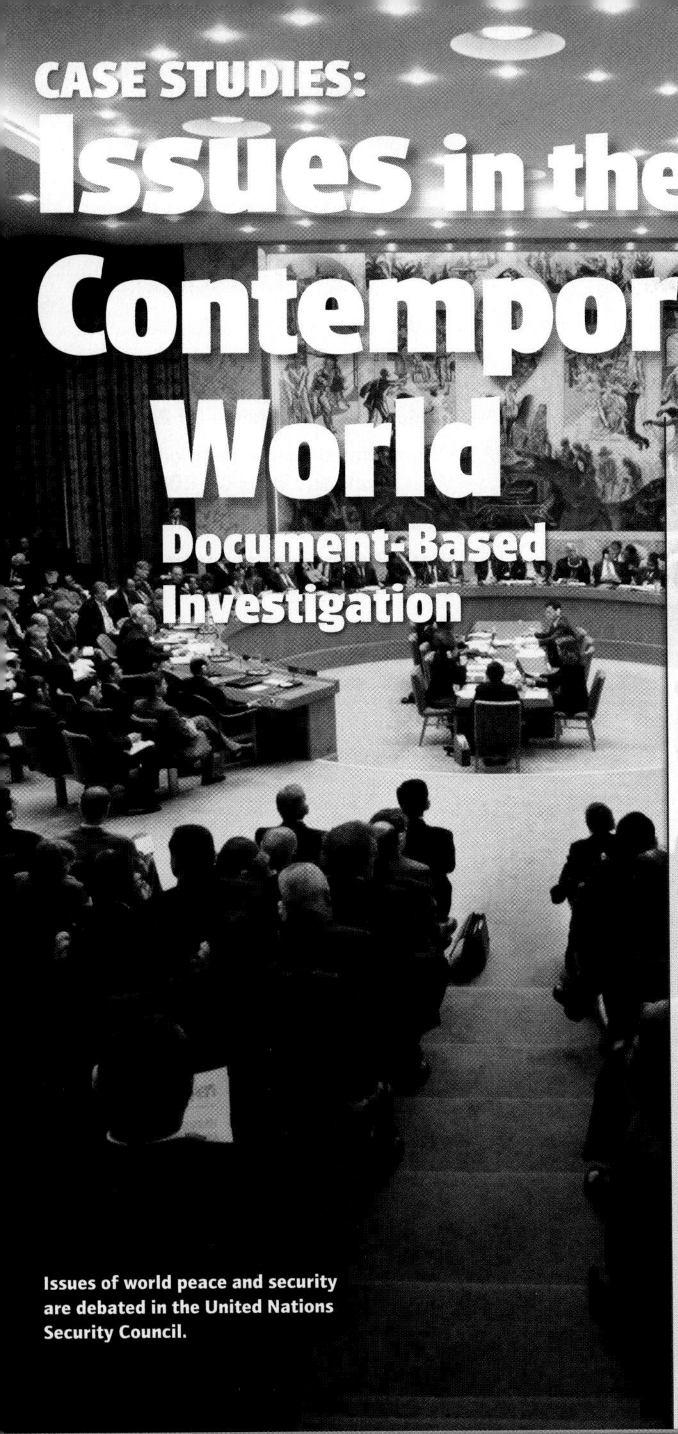

Issues of world peace and security are debated in the United Nations Security Council.

CASE STUDY 1
Civic Participation
The United Kingdom and South Africa

CASE STUDY 2
Developing Societies
Brazil and Mexico

CASE STUDY 3
Building Economic Powerhouses
China and India

CASE STUDY 4
Women in Society
Ireland and Turkey

CASE STUDY 5
The Role of the United Nations

Themes

ECONOMIC SYSTEMS
Globalization is transforming the world's economic landscape.

GOVERNMENT AND CITIZENSHIP
Democracies are struggling to increase citizen participation. Meanwhile, nations are trying to define the role of the United Nations.

SOCIETY
Changes in political structures, economic systems, and belief systems are fundamentally reshaping societies.

621

Unit Preview

Introducing the Unit

Have students list what they believe are the major global issues of today. Write several of their ideas on the board. Have students review the issues discussed in this unit. For each issue, have students write a sentence explaining how they think the issue could affect them personally. Have students read their sentences to the class.

Connecting to Themes

Activity **A Global Economy** Have students consider the issue of globalization. Have students write a definition of the term in their own words. Then have students list ways that globalization has impacted their lives. Explain that events and trends in nations such as China and India can have a major effect on the economies of nations around the world. Guide a class discussion about the positives and negatives of globalization.

Reading Like a Historian

Analyzing Visuals

The United Nations Have students take a moment to examine the photograph on this page. Ask students how the arrangement of participants might affect debates of the United Nations Security Council. *possible answer—People are seated in a circular shape, so it is a non-confrontational setting that might foster peaceful debate.*

Unit Resources

Planning

- **Differentiated Instruction Teacher Management System:** Pacing Guide
- OSP **One-Stop Planner CD-ROM:** Teacher Management System

Differentiating Instruction

- **Differentiated Instruction Teacher Management System:** Lesson Plans for Differentiated Instruction
- **Differentiated Instruction Modified Worksheets and Tests CD-ROM**

Enrichment

- **Civic Participation Activities Guide**
- **World History Primary Source Library CD-ROM**

Assessment

- **PASS:** Unit Test A and B
- **Alternative Assessment Handbook**

Unit 6 Planning Guide

Issues in the Contemporary World

Chapter Overview	Reproducible Resources	Technology Resources
UNIT 6 **pp. 621–646** **Overview: Issues in the Contemporary World:** **In this unit, students will learn about some important issues facing the world today. Students will analyze these contemporary issues and how they affect the United States and its relations with other countries.**	**Differentiated Instruction Teacher Management System:** • Pacing Guide • Lesson Plans for Differentiated Instruction **Interactive Reader and Study Guide:** Unit Summary* **World History Outline Maps**	**Live Ink© Online Reading Help** **Student Edition on Audio CD Program** **Differentiated Instruction Modified Worksheets and Tests CD-ROM** **Interactive Skills Tutor CD-ROM** **World History Primary Source Library CD-ROM** **Power Presentations with Video CD-ROM** **History's Impact: World History Video Program (VHS/DVD):** Issues in the Contemporary World
Issue 1: **Civic Participation** **The Main Idea:** The United Kingdom, an old democracy, and South Africa, a new democracy, are both experiencing significant declines in voter turnout.	**Differentiated Instruction Teacher Management System:** Issue 1 Lesson Plan* **Interactive Reader and Study Guide:** Issue 1 Summary*	**Differentiated Instruction Modified Worksheets and Tests CD-ROM**
Issue 2: **Developing Societies** **The Main Idea:** To build national prosperity, the countries of Latin America seek to establish political, economic, and social stability.	**Differentiated Instruction Teacher Management System:** Issue 2 Lesson Plan* **Interactive Reader and Study Guide:** Issue 2 Summary*	**Differentiated Instruction Modified Worksheets and Tests CD-ROM**

go.hrw.com | Print Resource | Transparency
Learning Styles | Audio CD | CD-ROM
Video | SE Student Edition | TE Teacher's Edition
OSP One-Stop Planner CD-ROM
*also on One-Stop Planner CD-ROM

Review, Assessment, Intervention

- **Spanish Chapter Summaries Audio CD Program**
- **Progress Assessment Support System (PASS):** Unit Test A and B*
- **Differentiated Instruction Modified Worksheets and Tests CD-ROM:** Modified Chapter Test
- OSP **One-Stop Planner CD-ROM:** ExamView Test Generator (English/Spanish)
- HOAP **Holt Online Assessment Program (HOAP),** in the Holt Premier Online Student Edition

- **Alternative Assessment Handbook**

- **Alternative Assessment Handbook**

HOLT
History's Impact
World History Video Program (VHS/DVD)
Issues in the Contemporary World

Power Presentation with Video CD-ROM

Power Presentations with Video are visual presentations of each chapter's main ideas. Presentations can be customized by including Quick Facts charts, images and maps from the textbook, and video clips.

Holt Online Learning

go.hrw.com
Teacher Resources
KEYWORD: SHL TEACHER

go.hrw.com
Student Resources
KEYWORD: SHL ISSUES

- Document-Based Questions
- Interactive Multimedia Activities
- Current Events
- Chapter-Based Internet Activities
- and more!

Holt Premier
Online Student Edition

Complete online support for interactivity, assessment, and reporting

- Interactive Maps and Notebook
- Homework Practice and Research Activities Online

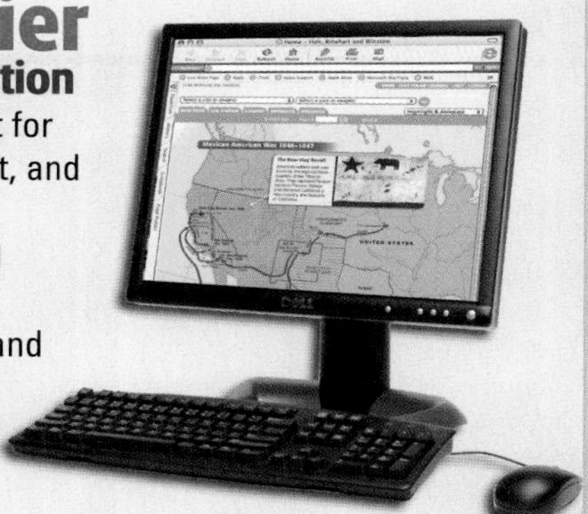

Unit 6 Planning Guide

Issues in the Contemporary World

Chapter Overview	Reproducible Resources	Technology Resources
Issue 3: **Building Economic Power Houses** **The Main Idea:** China and India have produced massive economic growth in recent decades.	**Differentiated Instruction Teacher Management System:** Issue 3 Lesson Plan* **Interactive Reader and Study Guide:** Issue 3 Summary*	**Differentiated Instruction Modified Worksheets and Tests CD-ROM**
Issue 4: **The Status of Women** **The Main Idea:** Though world governments have recently pledged to promote gender equality, women in many countries still face discrimination and limited opportunities.	**Differentiated Instruction Teacher Management System:** Issue 4 Lesson Plan* **Interactive Reader and Study Guide:** Issue 4 Summary*	**Differentiated Instruction Modified Worksheets and Tests CD-ROM**
Issue 5: **The Role of the United Nations** **The Main Idea:** The United Nations' mission and size have grown in the six decades since it was founded, but so too have the problems the organization faces.	**Differentiated Instruction Teacher Management System:** Issue 5 Lesson Plan* **Interactive Reader and Study Guide:** Issue 5 Summary*	**Differentiated Instruction Modified Worksheets and Tests CD-ROM**

go.hrw.com | Print Resource | Transparency
LS Learning Styles | Audio CD | CD-ROM
Video | SE Student Edition | TE Teacher's Edition
OSP One-Stop Planner CD-ROM
*also on One-Stop Planner CD-ROM

HOLT
History's Impact
World History Video Program (VHS/DVD)
Issues in the Contemporary World

Review, Assessment, Intervention

Alternative Assessment Handbook

Alternative Assessment Handbook

Alternative Assessment Handbook

Differentiating Instruction

Differentiated Instruction Teacher Management System
- Lesson Plans for Differentiated Instruction
- Pacing Guide
- Interactive Reader and Study Guide

Spanish Chapter Summaries Audio CD Program

Student Edition on Audio CD Program

Differentiated Instruction Modified Worksheets and Tests CD-ROM
- Vocabulary Flash Cards
- Modified Vocabulary Builder Activities
- Modified Chapter Review Activity
- Modified Chapter Test

OSP **One-Stop Planner CD-ROM**
- ExamView Test Generator (English/Spanish)
- PuzzlePro
- Quiz Show for ExamView
- Transparencies and Videos

TE **Differentiated Activities in the Teacher's Edition**
- Poster: Civic Participation in the UK and South Africa, p. 627
- Collage: Successes and Challenges in Daily Life, p. 629
- Multimedia Presentation: China's Economic Growth, p. 633
- Political Cartoon: India's/China's Economic Growth, p. 636
- Poem/Song: Women's Issues in Turkey and Ireland, p. 641
- Diorama: The UN'S Activities, p. 643

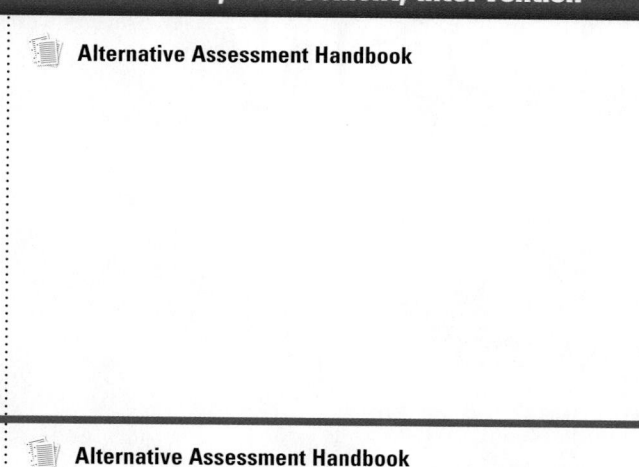

Unit Preview

Issues in the Contemporary World

By now you've read about many issues in world history. What issues do people around the world continue to face today? In the following five sections you will read about some important contemporary issues in today's world.

Issue 1

Civic Participation (pp. 624–627)

The United Kingdom, an old democracy, and South Africa, a new democracy, are both experiencing significant declines in voter turnout. What challenges do old and new democracies face in promoting civic participation?

Issue 2

Developing Societies (pp. 628–631)

To build national prosperity, the countries of Latin America seek to establish political, economic, and social stability. How are developing countries such as Brazil and Mexico trying to meet the needs of their peoples?

Issue 3

Building Economic Powerhouses (pp. 632–637)

China and India have produced massive economic growth in recent decades. How are the giant emerging economies of India and China affecting the world?

CASE STUDIES: Issues in the Contemporary World

THE BIG PICTURE The world today is a rapidly changing place. New technologies are reshaping the way economies operate and people interact. But how people and nations react to change is often rooted in the past. That's why studying the past can give you the tools you need to understand the present. The following case studies look at some key issues facing the world today. Use what you have learned to form opinions about these key issues.

Voters in Cape Town line up in the early morning hours to vote in a South Africa election ▶

622 CASE STUDIES: CONTEMPORARY ISSUES

History's Impact video program
Watch the video to learn more about the role of the United Nations.
Case Study 1 Civic Participation
What challenges do old and new democracies face in promoting civic participation?
Case Study 2 Developing Societies
How are developing nations such as Brazil and Mexico trying to meet the needs of their peoples?
Case Study 3 Building Economic Powerhouses
How are the giant emerging economies of India and China affecting the world?
Case Study 4 Women in Society
How do political and social trends affect the roles of women?
Case Study 5 The Role of the United Nations
What should the role of the United Nations be in international affairs?
623

Unit Preview

HOLT

History's Impact

► **Video Program: Issues in the Contemporary World**
See the Video Teacher's Guide for strategies for using the video segment.

Issue 4

Women in Society (pp. 638–641)

Though world governments have recently pledged to promote gender equality, women in many countries still face discrimination and limited opportunities. How do historical and cultural trends affect women's status?

Issue 5

The Role of the United Nations (pp. 642–646)

The mission and size of the United Nations have grown in the six decades since it was founded, but so too have the problems the organization faces. What should the role of the United Nations be in international affairs?

Preteach

Focusing on the Issue

What challenges do old and new democracies face in promoting civic participation? *possible answer—a declining voter turnout and little civic participation in democratic processes*

Key Terms

Preteach the following term:

devolution the redistribution of power from the central government to local governments (p. 625)

Case Study 1

Document-Based Investigation

Civic Participation The United Kingdom and South Africa

Focusing on the Issue

What challenges do old and new democracies face in promoting civic participation?

Key Terms
devolution

In a 2005 survey, "Voice of the People," about two-thirds of the respondents in 68 countries said they were generally satisfied with democracy. Yet only one-third said that their own countries were ruled by the will of the people. Citizens may respect the idea of rule by the people, but many do not see it as a reality in their countries.

When people feel they have little voice in their government or that their votes do not count, they may become discouraged about participating in their democratic institutions. In recent years, voter turnout has declined in many countries. Some observers fear that this decline suggests a more general disinterest in civic participation.

Civic participation involves more than voting, of course. There is a range of political activities aimed at influencing government policies, structures, laws, and the use of public resources. Contacting elected representatives, staging protests, and building coalitions to have a louder voice on issues—these are just some of the ways people participate. In addition, factors such as fair elections, honest government, a lively opposition, and free speech help keep citizens engaged.

Participation in a democracy extends beyond politics as well. Nongovernmental organizations (NGOs) have a strong role in many countries, tackling issues from hunger to election monitoring. Local charities and other volunteer organizations also provide crucial support for communities.

The United Kingdom has over a century of democratic tradition. South Africa began its great experiment in rule by the people in 1994, with its first-ever multiethnic elections. Yet both countries are undergoing political changes that will affect the future of their democracies.

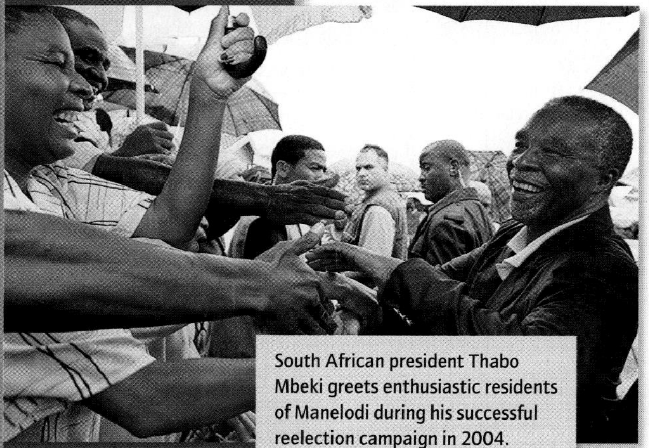

South African president Thabo Mbeki greets enthusiastic residents of Manelodi during his successful reelection campaign in 2004.

Teach the Main Idea

At Level

Civic Participation

1. **Teach** Ask students the Focusing on the Issue question to teach this section.
2. **Apply** Have students work in groups of three to compile a list of five problems they believe are common in contemporary democracies. Have groups rank their lists in order of most serious to least serious.
3. **Review** Have groups share their lists with the class. Using a point system (each group's top-ranked problem = 5 pts; 2nd problem = 4 pts; 3rd problem = 3 pts; 4th problem = 4 pts; 5th problem = 1 pt) tally the different problems each group listed. Using the overall point totals, compile a list of the top five problems the class believes face democracies today.
4. **Practice/Homework** For each item on the class top five list, have students write a paragraph suggesting ways that democracies should try to overcome the problem.
LS Interpersonal, Verbal-Linguistic

Alternative Assessment Handbook, Rubrics 35: Solving Problems; and 37: Writing Assignments

Exploring the Issue

Old and new democracies each have their own advantages and problems. The United Kingdom has a stable society, respect for long-established laws and democratic institutions, and a healthy culture of civic volunteerism. In recent years, however, it has been troubled by a declining level of voter turnout in elections. South Africa's young democracy has seen its initially high level of voter turnout drop rapidly. It is struggling to create trustworthy institutions amid social and political unrest. Increasingly, South Africans are participating in civic life through informal organizations.

UK Conservative Party leader David Cameron faces a group of reporters at his party's conference in April 2006.

Democracy in the UK The United Kingdom's parliamentary traditions stretch back at least 700 years. Over the centuries, political change has come slowly. It was not until the twentieth century that the country became fully democratic, extending voting rights to all adult citizens.

Since it was elected in 1997, Britain's Labor government has sought to reform the country's democratic institutions. In part, these efforts are a response to declining voter participation, especially among poor and young voters. "The turnout freefall has triggered a national debate about the public's loss of interest in politics and what to do about it," one university study noted.

One of the Labor government's key reforms has been **devolution**. Devolution is the redistribution of power from the central government to local governments. Devolution of authority to the UK countries of Wales and Scotland took place in the late 1990s. At the time, devolution was hailed as a victory for democratic reform. However, it has not fulfilled the hopes of some of its proponents. They are disappointed because major areas of power remain in the hands of the central government.

Democracy in South Africa In the 2005 "Voice of the People" survey, South Africa topped the charts for optimism. Nearly two-thirds of South Africans said their country was governed by the will of the people—the highest ranking of any country.

In the first few years of independence, South Africans demonstrated their support for democracy by going to the polls in impressive numbers. High voter turnout in 1994 brought President Nelson Mandela to power. Since then, however, election turnout among the voting-age population has begun to drop sharply.

The main beneficiary of voter participation in South Africa has been the ruling African National Congress (ANC). The ANC has seen its majorities rise in each of the three national elections since the end of apartheid. Voters continue to reward the party for its role in the anti-apartheid struggle. But without an opposition party to challenge and monitor it, the ANC has been troubled by corruption and inefficiency.

Despite a lack of reliable institutions of governance, South Africans' commitment to civic participation remains strong. Membership in informal institutions, such as anti-crime organizations, women's organizations, and trade unions, has soared. Social scientists believe that societies that have a dense network of informal institutions are healthier ones.

Informal institutions strengthen a society. They offer flexible, creative options for solving a society's problems. Albert Oupamoloto is a resident of Soweto, one of South Africa's poorest cities yet one known for its vibrant political life. He describes the optimism that drives much civic participation in South Africa; "Many people think their lives are better because they are free citizens," Oupamoloto says, "and I agree with them."

Direct Teach

Reading Focus

Exploring the Issue

Identify Who was elected president of South Africa in 1994? *Nelson Mandela*

Explain Why was the United Kingdom not considered a fully democratic nation until the twentieth century? *All adult citizens in the nation did not have voting rights until the twentieth century.*

Compare and Contrast How are the democracies of the United Kingdom and South Africa similar and different? *possible answer—similarities: Both nations hold elections for governmental offices; civic participation in both countries has declined in recent years; differences: Britain has a long democratic tradition, while South Africa is a new democracy; the United Kingdom has faced challenges relating to the power balance between central and local governments, while South Africa is still experiencing the impact of its long anti-apartheid struggle.*

Biography

Desmond Tutu (1931–) Desmond Tutu has long been one of South Africa's leading champions for democracy and human rights. A high school teacher as a young adult, Tutu studied religion and became an Anglican priest in 1960. Soon after, he emerged as a major spiritual leader and a vocal critic of apartheid. Questioning the morals of his nation's white-dominated government, Tutu supported economic sanctions against South Africa. In 1984 Tutu won the Nobel Peace Prize for his anti-apartheid work. After his country ended apartheid and became a true democracy, Tutu headed a commission investigating the human rights abuses of the previous regime.

Skills Focus: Making Generalizations

At Level

Reading Skill

The United Kingdom and South Africa Today

1. Have students examine recent newspapers and magazines to find an article about democracy in the United Kingdom or South Africa.
2. Have students write a report about the article they selected. In their reports students should generalize about the status of democracy in the country described in the article.
3. Have students present their reports to the class. Guide students in a discussion about the current political situation in the United Kingdom and South Africa today. LS **Verbal-Linguistic**

Alternative Assessment Handbook, Rubrics 23: Newspapers; and 37: Writing Assignments

Direct Teach

Word Help

persistent continuing (p. 627)
profoundly completely (p. 627)
apathy lack of interest (p. 627)

Reading Focus

Investigating the Issue

Recall What percentage of voting-age South Africans voted in the 1999 elections? *71.8%*

Make Inferences What does the information in Document 1 and Document 2 suggest about how the number of people who voted for the African National Congress changed between 1994 and 2004? *possible answer—fewer South Africans voted in 2004, though the ANC won more provinces that year; thus, the number of people who voted for the ANC might have stayed about the same in actual number.*

Info to Know

Capitals of South Africa Unlike most other nations, South Africa has three capital cities. Each capital is home to a branch of government. Cape Town, the legislative capital, is the site of the South African Parliament. Pretoria (or Tshwane), the administrative capital, is where South Africa's president and cabinet members meet. Bloemfontein, the judicial capital, is home to South Africa's Supreme Court of Appeal, the nation's highest court.

Answers

Analyzing the Document (left) *possible answers—Both countries experienced a drop in voter turnout; the decline was sharper in South Africa; the decline in the UK may be related to long-term voter apathy while the decline in South Africa may be related to the problems of building a new democracy.* **(right)** *The ANC gained political strength, dominating the 2004 elections; possible consequences include decline of voter interest in uncontested elections.*

Investigating the Issue

Democracy in the United Kingdom and in South Africa presents strong comparisons and contrasts. The documents that follow explore these issues by presenting different points of view and arguments. Examine the documents, keeping in mind what you have read about these democracies, and answer the questions that follow.

Document 1

The United Kingdom and South Africa—an old democracy and a new one—both have experienced declines in voter turnout in recent years. Both are trying to identify possible causes for the decline and to inspire citizens to participate in the democratic process. This graph shows the election trends in the two countries.

Election Turnout, United Kingdom

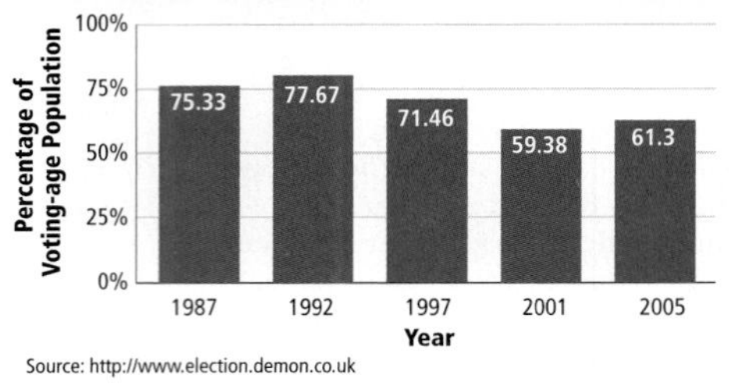

Source: http://www.election.demon.co.uk

Election Turnout, South Africa

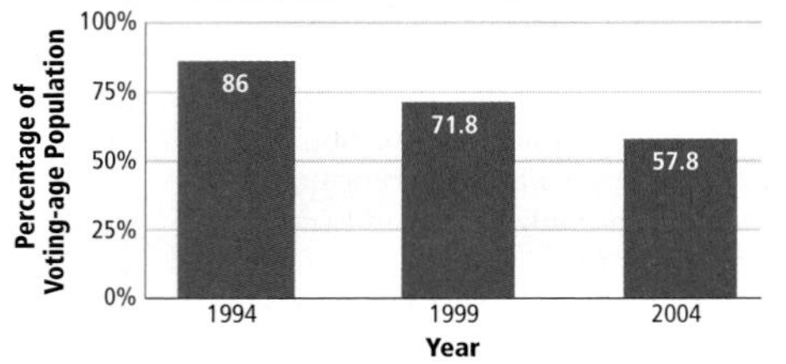

Source: http://www.ccc.nps.navy.mil/si/2004/may/piomboMay04.asp

Analyzing the Document
Describe the changes in voter turnout in the two countries during the time period shown here. Compare and contrast the two countries' turnout results. Which country experienced the sharpest decline?

Document 2

This series of maps shows the results of South African national elections from 1994, when apartheid ended and the country held its first multiethnic vote.

African National Elections, 1994–2004

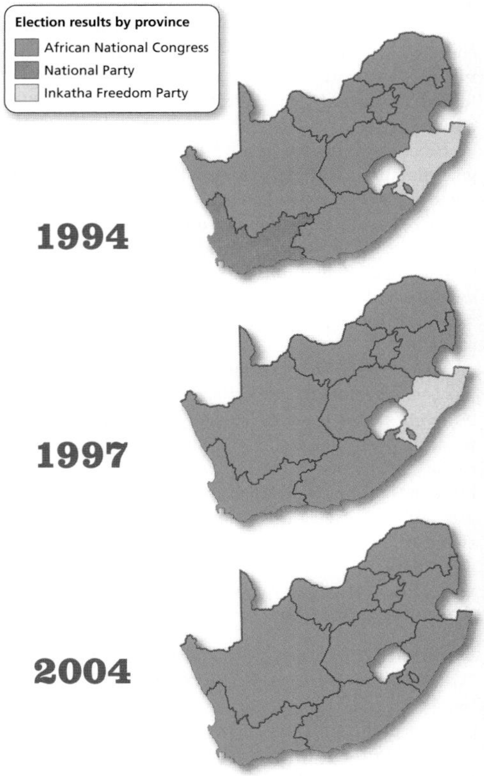

Analyzing the Document
What political change does this series of maps show? What are some possible consequences of this change?

Skills Focus: Interpreting Pie and Bar Graphs — Above Level

Social Studies Skill
Voter Turnout

1. Have students examine the bar graphs on this page. Guide students in a discussion about recent voting trends in the United Kingdom and South Africa.
2. Have students conduct research to find comparable voter turnout percentages in elections in the United States since 1990.
3. Using the data from their research, have students prepare a bar graph of U.S. voter turnout.
4. Have students compare the bar graph they created with the ones on this page. Discuss with the class how American voter participation trends compare with those of the United Kingdom and South Africa. **LS Visual-Spatial, Logical-Mathematical**

Alternative Assessment Handbook, Rubrics 7: Charts; and 30: Research

DOCUMENT 3

In 2006 the British government released a study of declining voter turnout. A British magazine examined the report.

> "The real problem . . . lies not with the political system at all, but with changes in society itself. As [the report] observes, two contrasting groups have emerged to whom conventional politics has little appeal.
>
> On one hand there are the relatively well-educated, relatively well-informed, relatively young who expect to make their own decisions, find self-expression in buying what they want when they want it, and see themselves as individuals free of geographic, institutional or social bonds.
>
> On the other are the casualties of de-industrialisation who suffer from persistent poverty and social exclusion. The former are cynical about political leaders and irritated that voting is not more like shopping, while the latter feel bullied and let down by the institutions they rely on for their survival.
>
> Constitutional reform . . . is well worth doing for its own sake. But whether it will make much difference to people who are already profoundly detached from the habits and modes of representative democracy is another matter."
>
> —*The Economist*, March 4, 2006

Analyzing the Document
What two groups does the report describe?

DOCUMENT 4

Analyzing the factors underlying the decline in voter turnout has been a source of heated debate in South Africa. This writer remains hopeful that the trend signals a "normalizing" of politics in South Africa.

> "[T]he fact that the major worries of political leaders and analysts was about potential apathy, rather than electoral violence, signifies the politics are becoming increasingly routine, a sign of the institutionalization of democracy in South Africa. . . .
>
> The election process and results demonstrated that politics are normalizing in South Africa, while at the same time pointing to areas that need to be monitored. For now, democracy is stable, institutionalizing itself and performing well. If the country can avoid the pitfalls of permanent party dominance and the slow erosion of democratic freedoms (as occurred in neighboring Zimbabwe after 1980), the second ten years of democracy will be worth celebrating."
>
> —Jessica Piombo, "Politics in a Stabilizing Democracy: South Africa's 2004 Elections," *Strategic Insights*, May 2004

Analyzing the Document
Why does this writer think dropping voter turnout signals a "normalizing" of South African politics? What does she believe needs to be monitored if democracy in South Africa is to grow stronger?

ANALYZING THE ISSUE

go.hrw.com
Research Online
SD7 Case Study

1. Review the documents presented on this issue. What similarities and what differences do they reveal about the challenges to democratic participation in the United Kingdom and in South Africa? What effect, if any, does the age of these democracies have on citizen participation?
2. Review the graph showing South African voter turnout and the map showing election results. What possible connection is there between declining voter turnout and the increased election success of the ANC?
3. Do library or online research to learn more about another democratic reform proposed in the United Kingdom—the elimination of hereditary lordships in Parliament's House of Lords. What effect might the change have on democracy and representation in the United Kingdom?
4. What sort of informal organizations are there in your community? in the United States? Do research to learn about one such organization. Write a one-page paper describing the organization, including its purpose, goals, and membership.

Direct Teach

Reading Focus

Investigating the Issue

Describe What does Jessica Piombo not want to see happen in South Africa? *permanent dominance of one political party; loss of democratic freedoms*

Make Inferences What do you think are the goals of the British government commission that issued the report in Document 3? *possible answer—to increase civic participation and democracy in the United Kingdom*

Predict What seems likely to happen in Great Britain if the government adopts the proposed constitutional reforms? *possible answer—little will change; the two major social groups that are currently removed from politics will continue to refrain from participating in democratic processes*

Differentiating Instruction

Below Level

English-Language Learners

1. Organize the class into mixed-ability pairs. Have students review each of the documents included in this case study so they understand the main issues.
2. Have each pair of students create a poster promoting civic participation in government in either the United Kingdom or South Africa.
3. Encourage students to include photographs, charts, newspaper headlines, and cartoons, as well as their own original drawings in their posters.
4. Display the posters for students to see. Allow class time for each pair to explain the concepts included in their posters. LS **Visual-Spatial, Verbal-Linguistic**

Alternative Assessment Handbook, Rubric 28: Posters

Answers

Analyzing the Document (left) *"well-educated, well-informed, relatively young" and the poor, socially excluded* **(right)** *possible answer—believes the decline is due to apathy and the institutionalizing of politics in South Africa; party dominance and democratic freedoms of citizens*

Analyzing the Issue 1. *possible answers—both nations face challenges in inspiring citizens to vote and participate in politics; differences: voter turnout declined more sharply in South Africa; effect—the newness of democracy in South Africa may account for the sharp drop in voter turnout there since people likely lost interest as one party gained dominance.* **2.** *possible answer—The growing political strength of the ANC has caused citizens to lose interest in voting since the party's candidates face little competition in many districts.* **3.** *Answers should reflect knowledge of British public opinion about hereditary lordships in the House of Lords.* **4.** *Answers should accurately describe an informal organization in your community.*

Direct Teach

Focusing on the Issue

How are developing countries such as Brazil and Mexico trying to meet the needs of their peoples? *possible answer—expanding sources of trade; attracting more foreign investment; improving management of government finances*

Key Terms

Preteach the following terms:

indigenous native (p. 628)

megacity city with a population of 10 million or more (p. 629)

maquiladora large industrial assembly plant in a Mexican border town that produces finished goods for export to the United States (p. 629)

Case Study 2

Document-Based Investigation

Developing Societies Brazil and Mexico

Focusing on the Issue

How are developing nations such as Brazil and Mexico trying to meet the needs of their peoples?

Key Terms
megacity, maquiladora

In order to become more prosperous, developing countries strive to create political, economic, and social stability. The three elements are interconnected. Political stability is one factor that helps businesses take root and thrive. It attracts much-needed foreign investment that strengthens the economy. A strong economy creates jobs, wealth, and consumer markets, helping to build a middle class—the backbone of a stable society. Finally, a contented, stable society promotes political order and helps democracy take root.

Like many developing regions, Latin America has had its share of instability in all three categories. For more than a century, political revolutions have stemmed in part from severe economic gaps between rich and poor. Economically, a reliance on exporting cash crops has kept the region trapped in boom-and-bust cycles; a drop in world prices for commodities can send developing economies into a tailspin. Socially, large migrations have unsettled societies in recent decades, as poor and landless peoples move to urban areas seeking work. Further upheaval has come from the efforts of indigenous peoples in Mexico and elsewhere to gain recognition and equality.

In recent years, however, the region's two most populous countries, Brazil and Mexico, have undergone remarkable political transformations. Brazil emerged from a string of repressive military dictatorships in the 1960s and 1970s to form a modern democracy. In 2000 Mexico set aside more than seven decades of one-party rule and held its first true two-party election.

Economic security, however, has proved more difficult to achieve. Globalization is pitting the two countries against new economic competitors such as India and China. Still, leaders in the both countries are seeking dynamic solutions to produce long-term stability and make use of one of their greatest assets: the enormous human resources they possess in their large populations.

Maquiladora factories, like the one shown above, have fueled much of Mexico's growth but are vulnerable to swings in the world economy.

Teach the Main Idea

At Level

Developing Societies

1. **Teach** Ask students the Focusing on the Issue question to teach this section.
2. **Apply** Organize students into two groups. One group will represent Brazil, the other will represent Mexico. Have each group brainstorm strategies for improving political, economic, and social conditions in its country. Have each group present its top five strategies.
3. **Review** Discuss the lists as a class. Have each group evaluate the potential effectiveness of the strategies listed by the other group.
4. **Practice/Homework** Have students write a paragraph explaining how "their country" will be different in 10 years after implementing the proposed strategies.

LS Verbal-Linguistic, Interpersonal

Alternative Assessment Handbook, Rubric 37: Writing Assignments

EXPLORING THE ISSUE

Economically and socially, Brazil and Mexico face many of the same challenges. Both are attempting to broaden their economic bases by expanding their sources of trade and foreign investment. Both are also seeking new solutions to the chronic problem of poverty and inequity in society.

Progress and Problems in Brazil Latin America's largest country, Brazil also has the region's largest economy. The nation made considerable economic progress starting in the mid-1990s despite some severe downturns. It expanded its presence in global markets for agricultural, mining, and manufactured goods. Exports surged, the economy grew, infant mortality dropped, and school enrollment increased. Laws requiring better management of government finances have been praised.

Yet Brazil also has some of the world's most desperate poverty, especially in the **megacities** of São Paulo and Rio de Janeiro. Megacities are those with populations of 10 million or more. Most of Brazil's urban poor live on the fringes of its two megacities. In Rio the *favelas*, or shantytowns, that climb the hillsides are so dangerous the police won't go there. São Paulo is one of the world's most murderous cities, wracked by gang violence. The streets are so dangerous that many wealthy people travel by helicopter, hopping among the city's 240 heliports.

To ease the population pressure on the cities, since the 1970s Brazil has turned to one of its most valuable resources: space. Brazil opened up its vast interior for resettlement and large-scale development. The resulting destruction of rain forests, however, has produced an international outcry and spurred calls for Brazil to limit rural overdevelopment.

Mexico Seeks Solutions Mexico has the second-largest economy in Latin America, now exceeding a trillion dollars. It has large petroleum reserves and a thriving tourism industry. Its location next to the United States has made it possible to expand trade under the North American Free Trade Agreement (NAFTA). Mexico benefits from its **maquiladoras**, the large industrial assembly plants throughout its border towns that produce finished goods for export to the United States.

In its drive to develop, Brazil has become a leader in the production of alternate fuels such as ethanol, refined here in São Tome.

Mexicans enjoy the highest per-capita income in Latin America. But such averages mask the huge gaps between rich and poor. In 2005 the richest 10 percent of Mexicans earned 25 times what the poorest 10 percent earned—just as they had two decades before. The government estimated extreme poverty at 17.3 percent in 2004.

Efforts to address rural poverty are limited by the fact that only 15 percent of Mexico's large, dry land mass is arable. The lack of land continues to draw peasants from the countryside to the nation's megacity, Mexico City, where nearly one-fifth of the nation's population lives. Not surprisingly, Mexican government policies now focus on urban poverty, because of the massive spinoff problems it creates: violence, political instability, and environmental destruction.

Despite protests from some U.S. leaders, the Mexican government encourages migration to the United States. Migrants, legal and illegal, send much-needed dollars back home to support their families.

Meanwhile, Mexico is focusing on creating a more highly educated work force, a priority the era of globalization. The government pays parents to keep their children in school instead of pulling them out to work in the fields and family businesses.

Direct Teach

Reading Focus

Exploring the Issue

Explain Why do wealthy residents of Sao Paulo travel by helicopter? *to avoid the city's violent streets*

Analyze What economic advantages does Mexico possess? *location next to the United States; large petroleum reserves; attractive to tourists; maquiladoras*

Compare What challenges do both Mexico and Brazil face? *poverty; huge gaps between rich and poor; crime*

MISCONCEPTION ALERT

Many Americans believe that the largest suppliers of oil to the United States are Arab nations in the Middle East. Since 2003, however, Mexico has been America's top supplier of crude oil. In 2005 the United States imported 1,568 thousand barrels of oil *each day* from its neighbor to the south.

Differentiating Instruction

Below Level

Learners Having Difficulty

1. Have students choose one of the two nations described in this case study. Have students create a collage depicting political, economic, and social life in the country they selected.
2. Students may use photographs from newspapers, magazines, or printouts of pictures they find on the Internet for their collages. Instruct students to find images reflecting both successes and challenges in their chosen country.
3. Display collages in a classroom exhibit. Have volunteers share their collages with the class. Volunteers should explain what the images they selected represent. **LS Visual-Spatial, Intrapersonal**

Alternative Assessment Handbook, Rubric 8: Collages

Direct Teach

Word Help

infrastructure transportation, communication, and public works systems of a country (p. 630)

Reading Focus

Investigating the Issue

Identify According to Luiz Ignácio Lula da Silva, what is the combined total of Brazil's exports to Latin America, the European Union, and the United States? *$78 billion*

Predict How do you think auto production in Brazil will change in the coming years? *possible answer—Production of alternate fuel vehicles will continue to rise sharply.*

Info to Know

Brazilian Trade In 2004 Brazil's total exports were $95 billion. The nation's imports for that year totaled $61 billion, creating a trade surplus of $34 billion. The United States accounts for more than one-fifth of Brazil's total exports and imports.

Investigating the Issue

Over the years Brazil and Mexico have adopted a number of strategies to boost economic development—and to lessen its potential negative effects. The documents that follow explore the issue of development in Brazil and Mexico. Examine the documents, keeping in mind what you have just read about economic development efforts in the two countries.

Document 1

Brazil has taken a lead in forming regional trade agreements in Latin America and trade ties outside the region, as a way of broadening and stabilizing its economy. President Luiz Ignácio Lula da Silva explained the philosophy behind this course of action.

> "I think Latin America is going through an important moment in its history. . . . [O]ur way forward is to consolidate the process of integration, . . . physical integration, with infrastructure, with roads, with railways, with communications, with energy. Based on this Brazil has decided to make some investments in other countries. Brazil today has some $3bn of investments in other South American countries, so that we can give South America more infrastructure.
>
> We believe that it is necessary to do much more, because only infrastructure is going to make more circulation possible. Not just goods but people as well. And we have had some results in the period in which we have been in government. Today, Latin America is Brazil's biggest market. We export almost $28bn to the rest of Latin America. . . . With the European Union we have $27bn and with the US $23bn. This is an extremely important thing. We are showing that it is possible through partnership and with seriousness, that we can help each other, we can help ourselves to grow. . . .
>
> —Brazilian President Luiz Ignácio Lula da Silva, interview, *Financial Times*, July 2006

Analyzing the Document

Why, according to Lula da Silva, does it make sense for a Brazil to invest money in other countries in the region?

Document 2

In 1979 Brazil launched a national program to develop alternate fuels. Ethanol, a type of alcohol produced from refined sugar cane, is the leading alternate fuel. Today, 34,000 gas stations in Brazil have at least one pump dedicated to alternate fuel. The program has drastically reduced Brazil's need for oil and has cut down on auto pollution. But the vast acreage devoted to sugar cane production is causing worry among environmentalists, who fear a loss of biodiversity.

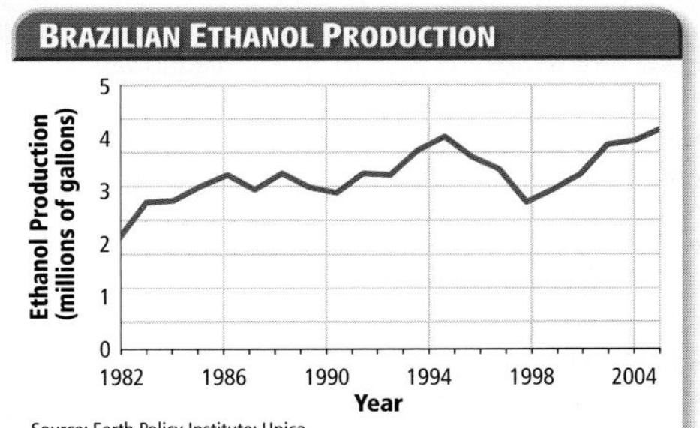

Source: Earth Policy Institute; Unica

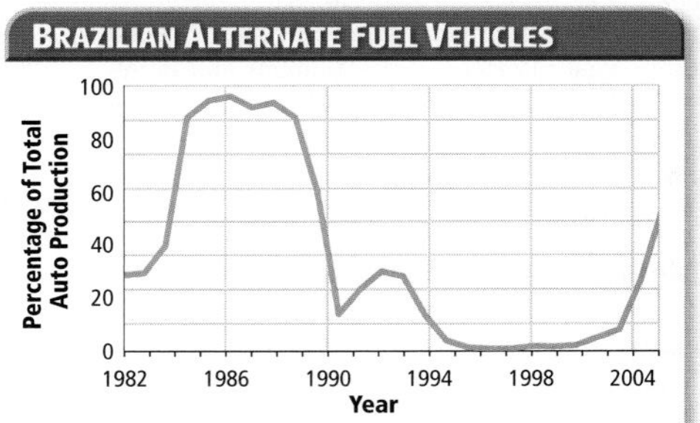

Source: Unica

Analyzing the Document

What is the trend in ethanol production? How does the trend correspond to trends in auto manufacturing?

Skills Focus: Interpreting Line Graphs

Social Studies Skill

Population Growth

1. Have students study the graphs titled Brazilian Ethanol Production and Brazilian Alternate Fuel Vehicles on th,is page.
2. Have students conduct research about ethanol production and alternate fuel vehicle production in the United States between the years 1982 and 2004.
3. Have students prepare a graph, similar to the ones on this page, based on the information they found.
4. Have students compare the graphs they created with the Brazil graphs. Discuss with the class how ethanol and alternate fuel vehicle production in the United States and Brazil are similar and different. **LS Visual-Spatial, Logical-Mathematical**

Alternative Assessment Handbook, Rubrics 9: Comparing and Contrasting; and 11: Discussions

Answers

Analyzing the Document (left) *By investing in other Latin American countries, Brazil is strengthening the infrastructure and economies of its major trading partners—this in turn will help increase Brazil's trade income;* **(right)** *Ethanol production has mostly increased since 1982; after a decline in the late 1980s and early 1990s, production of alternative fuel vehicles has increased sharply since 1998.*

DOCUMENT 3

About a third of the people in the Mexican state of Chiapas are descended from the Maya, or "people of the corn," as they call themselves. Since 1994 the indigenous people of Chiapas have waged a battle to end political and cultural repression by the government and bring decent living conditions to the extremely impoverished region. The woman in this photograph participated in a protest by the Zapatista rebels of Chiapas that was held in Mexico City. Such demonstrations drew worldwide support to their cause.

Analyzing the Document

What does this photograph suggest about the cultural identity of the people of Chiapas?

DOCUMENT 4

There were 14 megacities worldwide in 1995. By 2015 there will be 21. Mexico and Brazil have some of the world's largest megacities. These statistics provide a snapshot of population growth in some of the world's megacities.

MEGACITIES

City/Metropolitan Areas (rank)	Population* (2000)	Percentage of Population (2000)	Projected Population Growth (2000–2015)
Tokyo, Japan (1)	34,450	27.1%	5.1%
Mexico City, Mexico (2)	18,066	18.3%	14.3%
New York City, USA (3)	17,846	6.3%	10.5%
São Paolo, Brazil (4)	17,099	10.0%	16.7%
Mumbai, India (5)	16,086	1.6%	40.8%
Rio de Janeiro, Brazil (14)	10,803	6.3%	14.4%

*All population figures in thousands.

Source: *World Almanac Book of Facts*, 2005

Analyzing the Document

Compare and contrast the statistics for the Mexican and Brazilian cities listed in the table. Which city has a higher percentage of its country's population? Which city is projected to grow the fastest?

ANALYZING THE ISSUE

go.hrw.com
Research Online
SD7 Case Study

1. Review the documents presented on this issue. What evidence do they present to suggest that development in Brazil and Mexico is a complex challenge?
2. What goals do Brazil and Mexico share in terms of economic development? What are some problems unique to each country?
3. Do online research to learn more about life in the Chiapas region of Mexico. How has life there changed, or not changed, since the Zapatista rebellion in 1994? Why did the rebellion evoke sympathy throughout Mexico and the world? Do you think economic development in Mexico would benefit Chiapas? Why or why not?
4. Research Brazil's policy of alternative fuel development. Compare the positive and negative effects. Do you think the government is justified in pursuing this policy? Explain your reasoning.

Collaborative Learning

At Level

The Chiapas Conflict

1. Organize students into small groups. Have each group use reliable Internet or print sources to conduct research about the major issues of Mexican government's conflict with the indigenous peoples of Chiapas.
2. Have each group write a skit about the Chiapas conflict. In their skits, students should cover the origins of the controversy, the lives of the Maya people in Chiapas, the role of Zapatista rebels, and the responses of the government.
3. Have students rehearse and perform their skits for the class. LS **Kinesthetic, Interpersonal**

Alternative Assessment Handbook, Rubrics 30: Research; and 33: Skits and Reader's Theater

Direct Teach

Reading Focus

Investigating the Issue

Identify Which megacity is projected to grow at the fastest rate between 2000 and 2015? *Mumbai, India*

Predict How would Mexico benefit from resolving the grievances of the people of Chiapas? *possible answer—internal stability; fewer protests at home and abroad; greater economic production from Chiapas*

Answers

Analyzing the Document (top) *possible answer—The woman wears traditional clothing and carries a basket of corn; this suggests that the people of Chiapas are proud of their Mayan heritage, which is a major part of their identity.* **(bottom)** *highest: Mexico City, Mexico; fastest; Sao Paulo, Brazil*

Analyzing the Issue 1. *possible answer—Latin American economies are interdependent; cultural issues have created unrest in Mexico; megacities are growing even larger adding to urban poverty challenges; Brazil's increased use of alternative fuel reduces dependency on oil, but creates environmental problems.* **2.** *possible answers—Both nations seek to increase trade, attract more foreign investment, improve their infrastructures, and reduce poverty. Brazil's megacities are wracked by violent crime and it faces international opposition to its rural migration program; Mexico faces unrest in Chiapas and has little arable land.* **3.** *Answers should demonstrate an understanding of the reasons for the rebellion in Chiapas, including the major economic issues in the state since 1994.* **4.** *possible answers— positive effects: less pollution and reduced dependency on foreign oil; negative effects: destruction of rain forests harms the environment, increasing international opposition to Brazil; responses about the government's justification should be supported by an assessment of the policy's effects*

Preteach

Focusing on the Issue

How are the giant emerging economies of India and China affecting the world? *possible answers—Export goods have flooded global markets, lowering prices; enterprises in other nations have made profits investing in China and India; enterprises in other nations have moved their factories to China; Indian employees provide a host of services at low wages, taking some jobs away from people in other nations.*

Key Terms

Preteach the following terms:

offshoring moving an entire factory or other business enterprise abroad (p. 633)

privatization the private ownership of industries as opposed to government control (p. 634)

joint venture business partnerships and co-ownership (p. 634)

Case Study 3

Document-Based Investigation

Building Economic Powerhouses China and India

Focusing on the Issue

How are the giant emerging economies of India and China affecting the world?

Key Terms
offshoring, privatization, joint ventures

To many observers the question is not whether India and China will bump the United States from its position as the world's largest economy. The question is when, and which country will get there first.

The world's two most populous nations have embarked on ambitious programs to move from failed planned or semi-planned economies to vibrant market economies. Their pathways to success have differed, and each faces challenges that could derail them. China is still a one-party Communist dictatorship, and India's thriving democracy struggles to contain explosive religious conflict. Yet few experts dispute that the changes underway in these two countries are shaking up the world's economies.

The economic successes of India and China are no accident. China began limited economic reforms in the late 1970s and then threw open its doors to private enterprise 20 years later, determined to become the manufacturing capital of the world. India opened its economy later, in the 1990s, but quickly and seized the opportunities of the telecommunications revolution. High-speed Internet connections opened up sudden opportunities for these countries to connect their large labor pools with potential employers and customers around the globe.

The vigorous moves of India and China onto the world stage are affecting economic planning, markets, and wages in other countries. No one is quite sure how this scenario will play out either for India and China—potential competitors who also happen to share a disputed border—or for the Western and Asian industrial giants of the twentieth century. One thing we is for certain: the twenty-first century is truly a new era of global economic interdependence.

China's heavy industry manufacturers, like this tractor factory in the city of Luoyang, have grown increasingly competitive in world markets.

Teach the Main Idea

At Level

Emerging Economic Giants

1. **Teach** Ask students the Focusing on the Issue question to teach this section.
2. **Apply** Have students list the different ways that India and China have changed in recent decades. Have students write a sentence assessing how each change affected the home country (India or China) and how it affected the other nations of the world.
3. **Review** Have students meet in small groups to discuss their lists. Guide a class discussion about whether India and China should continue on their current paths in the coming years.
4. **Practice/Homework** Have students write a brief essay about how they think China and India will be impacting the global economy in 10 years. **LS Verbal-Linguistic, Interpersonal**

Alternative Assessment Handbook, Rubrics 11: Discussions; and 37: Writing Assignments

EXPLORING THE ISSUE

The rise of Asian economies began in the 1960s, when Japan, South Korea, and the other so-called "Asian tigers" began to industrialize at a breathtaking rate. These countries developed efficient, streamlined manufacturing processes that flooded the global market with inexpensive export goods.

Today's "Asian tigers," India and China, may not yet match Japan's GDP, but their rapid economic growth makes for a promising future. Up until now, China has emphasized traditional manufacturing industries. India has focused on new service industries provided via the Internet, from tax preparation to computer technical support.

Factories, like this textile plant in Hubei province, have sprouted up in China's interior.

China's Communist Economy Under Maoist Communism, China's government tightly controlled all aspects of the nation's economy. Communist leaders tried to move the ancient agricultural society into the modern age. But massive industrialization efforts eventually stalled. The government allowed virtually no private enterprise. The lack of free-market incentives produced low productivity and inefficiency. While Japan and other "Asian tigers" were roaring, China's living standards remained relatively low.

Chinese Capitalism Takes Hold With the rise to power of Deng Xiaoping in 1978, China cautiously started down a new economic path. Since then, agricultural, industrial, and market reforms have come slowly but steadily.

In the agricultural sector, the government began to allow farmers to sell some of their crops on the free market. Centralized economic planning was relaxed. That allowed regional officials to make free-market decisions on some issues, including trade.

The government also began to encourage foreign investment, although not on the scale that India later embraced. Initially, economic liberalization was confined to the creation of a few "special economic zones," such as the city of Shenzen. These areas served as testing grounds for China's limited capitalism.

The results were impressive. Farm output doubled during the 1980s. Industrial growth and investment in the special economic zones blossomed. Another round of market reforms was launched in the 1990s, creating what the government called "a socialist market economy." At the same time, China placed strict curbs on its population growth, holding it to a rate of about 13 per 1,000 people. This helped to ease poverty, but it created controversy at home and abroad.

Economic growth surged. By 2005 China had become the second-largest economy in the world, although still far behind the United States in terms of production. Since 1980 China has doubled its share of world trade every five years. It now supplies one-fifth of the world's clothing and one-third of all mobile phones.

In 2001 China's entered the World Trade Organization (WTO). In joining the WTO, China agreed to follow its laws and standards of competitive business and trade practices. The move made China an even more attractive place for foreign investment and for **offshoring**. Unlike outsourcing, which involves moving a part of a business operation, like computer tech support, to another country, the offshoring involves moving an entire factory or other business enterprise abroad.

Direct Teach

Reading Focus

Exploring the Issue

Recall How did the economies of Japan, Korea, and the other "Asian tigers" change in the late twentieth century? *They rapidly industrialized and dramatically increased their manufacturing output.*

Explain Why did China depart from strict Communist economic policies to adopt market reforms? *Under communism, China's economy stagnated in low production and inefficiency.*

Evaluate How has the shift to limited capitalism affected China's economy? *possible answer—massive economic growth, greater industrial and agricultural output; increased world trade; large amounts of foreign investment; rise in economic crimes and pollution, widespread inequality*

Primary Source

Lester R. Brown, the founder and president of the Earth Policy Institute made the following comments about China's economic power in a 2005 article:

"The United States, the world's largest debtor nation, is not heavily dependent on Chinese capital to underwrite its fast-growing debt. If China ever decides to divert this capital surplus elsewhere, either to internal development or to the development of oil, gas, and mineral resources elsewhere in the world, the U.S. economy will be in trouble. China is no longer just a developing country. It is an emerging economic superpower, one that is writing economic history. If this last century was the American century, this one looks to be the Chinese century."

Differentiating Instruction

Above Level

Advanced Learners/Gifted and Talented

1. Organize students into small groups.
2. Have students conduct research on China's recent economic growth using reliable print or online sources. Students should focus their research on foreign investment, trade, and/or other aspects of China's economic interactions with other nations.
3. Have students prepare a multimedia presentation based on their research findings. Allow enough time for groups to gather research, organize their notes, and prepare their presentations.
4. Have groups make their presentations to the class. **LS Visual-Spatial, Verbal-Linguistic**

Alternative Assessment Handbook, Rubrics 22: Multimedia Presentations; and 30: Research

Direct Teach

Reading Focus

Exploring the Issue

Identify Which American company announced in 2006 that it would invest $6 billion in India over the following three years? *IBM*

Explain How does the legacy of British colonial rule continue to affect India's economy? *As English speakers, Indians can provide services to other English-speaking nations, including the United States*

Predict Which nation do you believe will have the stronger economy in 20 years, China or India? Explain your answer. *possible answers—India, because of its ties to the West and its capacity to provide services to the English-speaking world; China, because its socialist-capitalist economy combines the strengths of both systems to create massive production.*

Teaching Tip

The World Trade Organization website includes a wealth of information about the trading activities of the nations of the world. Have students access the WTO website and then navigate to find trade statistics relating to India and China. *Trade statistics can be accessed by clicking the Resources link at the top of the WTO homepage (www.wto.org).*

High-tech business parks (left) are sprouting up around Bangalore and other Indian cities. The Internet allows Indian software engineers (right) to serve world customers.

China has struggled to decide how far and how fast to implement reforms. Corruption and slow government decision-making hamper progress. The easing of restrictions on business has produced a rise in economic crimes, widespread inequality, and worrisome levels of pollution. Nevertheless, China is clearly on a path from which it does not intend to turn back.

India's Closed Economy Since it achieved independence from Great Britain in 1948, India has struggled to overcome desperate, grinding poverty. Inspired by the philosophy of independence leader Mohandas K. Gandhi, India adopted a socialist economy. It strove for economic self-sufficiency, with limits on imports and foreign investment. For more than four decades, India's economy was largely closed.

The government embarked on large-scale industrialization in order to meet its own needs and to limit dependence on foreign investment and imports. However, heavy government regulation resulted in decades of inefficiency, overregulation, poor output, and quality goods.

India Opens Its Doors In the 1990s a democratic India embraced capitalism and began to move to a market economy. The government allowed increasing **privatization**, the private ownership of industries as opposed to government control. It opened the door to limited private investment in some industries. Over time, more and more foreign companies were allowed to operate in India. At first they formed **joint ventures**—business partnerships and co-ownership—with Indian companies.

In the early 2000s, direct foreign investment in India, particularly in telecommunications, took hold. In 2006 the American computer giant IBM announced that it would triple its investment in India over the following three years, to $6 billion.

Government efforts to revamp India's ways of doing business have helped the economy grow at an impressive rate of 7 percent a year since 1991. In addition to a more open business climate, two factors have contributed to making India a world leader in providing high-tech services to businesses worldwide. An emphasis on higher education over the last fifteen years has given India a large pool of highly skilled workers. There are also a large number of English speakers—the legacy of British colonial rule. Looking to the future, many observers believe India's democratic government will give it the flexibility it needs to meet the challenges ahead.

Barriers to Success India still faces formidable obstacles to economic success. High import tariffs and restrictions on direct foreign investment have remained, sparking a national debate on how far to liberalize, or open up, the economy. India's huge population, most of whom still work on farms and in small, traditional businesses, can be an economic asset. Already home to one-sixth of the world's people, the country is expected to become the most populous nation within the 50 years. But the rapid creation of vast wealth has further highlighted the "two Indias": one largely rural and poor; the other urban and prosperous.

Skills Focus: Comparing and Contrasting

At Level

Reading Skill

The Two Indias

1. Review with students the information in the text about the "two Indias."
2. Have students conduct research about India to learn more about the dual nature of its economy.
3. Based on their research, have students write two paragraphs: one describing a rural Indian, the other describing an urban Indian.
4. Have volunteers share their paragraphs with the class. Guide a class discussion about how the daily life of people in rural India is similar to and different from the daily lives of urban Indians. LS **Verbal-Linguistic**

Alternative Assessment Handbook, Rubrics 30: Research; and 38: Writing to Classify

Investigating the Issue

Today, university graduates in cities like Bangalore, India, are preparing the tax returns of millions of Americans—overnight, half a world away, via the Internet—for far lower wages than tax preparers get in the United States. China is promoting a balance of high-technology "knowledge jobs" as well, while also boosting manufacturing to become a giant exporter. The opening of these economies poses both challenges and opportunities for the rest of the world.

Document 1

In his influential book *The World Is Flat*, Thomas Friedman argued that India and China are leveling, or flattening, the economic playing field. Western industrialized countries are losing their advantages, and other developing countries risk falling farther behind.

> "Because China can amass so many low-wage workers at the unskilled, semiskilled, and skilled levels, because it has such a voracious [huge] appetite for factory, equipment, and knowledge jobs to keep its people employed, and because it has such a massive and burgeoning [growing] consumer market, it has become an unparalleled zone for offshoring. . . .
>
> The more attractive China makes itself as a base for offshoring, the more attractive other developed and developing countries competing with it, like Malaysia, Thailand, Ireland, Mexico, Brazil, and Vietnam, have to make themselves. . . . This has created a process . . . in which countries scramble to see who can give companies the best tax breaks, education incentives, and subsidies, on top of their cheap labor, to encourage offshoring to their shores. . . .
>
> In Cairo, the skyline seems forever the same. In China, if you miss visiting a city for a year, it's like you haven't been there in forever. And in Mexico City, just when Mexicans thought they had turned the corner forever, they ran smack into China, coming the other way and running much faster. . . .
>
> —Thomas Friedman, *The World Is Flat*, 2005

Analyzing the Document

Why, according to Friedman, does China pose a problem for developing countries like Mexico and Brazil?

Document 2

As China industrializes and modernizes, its demand for energy is soaring, as shown in this graph. The increasing need causes concern about the possible effect on global energy prices and supplies.

China's Oil Consumption, 1980–2005

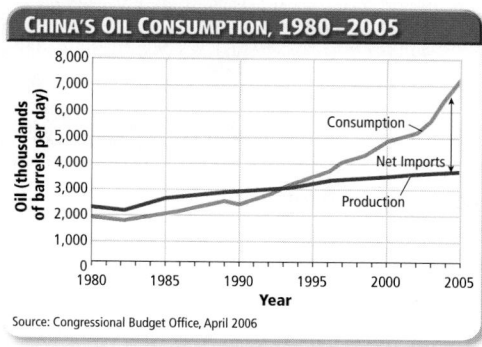

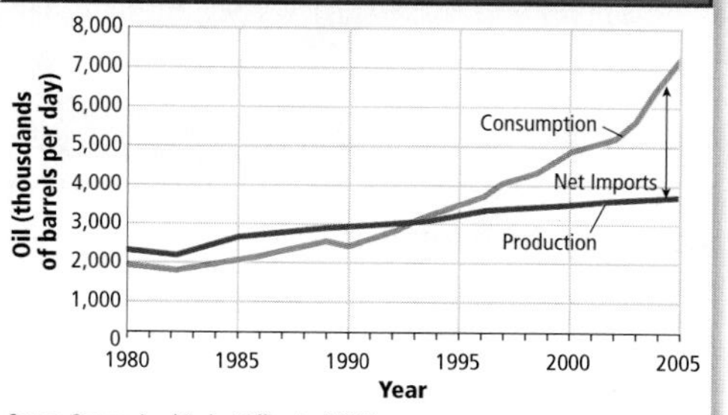

Source: Congressional Budget Office, April 2006

Analyzing the Document

By roughly how much did China's energy consumption increase between 1980 and 2005? Explain the gap between the two lines since about 1995. What effect could that have on the rest of the world?

Direct Teach

Word Help

lucrative profitable (p. 636)

geopolitical relating to the political and geographic factors that influence a nation's foreign policy (p. 637)

adage traditional saying that expresses a common observation (p. 637)

Reading Focus

Investigating the Issue

Identify What was China's oil production rate in 1990? *3,000,000 barrels per day*

Explain According to Friedman, how is China affecting the developing nations of the world? *possible answer—To compete with China economically, developing countries are scrambling to offer better incentives to attract offshoring.*

Info to Know

World Energy As of 2003, the United States, Russia, and China were the top three producers of energy, accounting for 39% of the world's total production. The three nations were also the top consumers of energy, accounting for 41% of the world's total consumption. The United States was the leader in both categories by wide margins. The United States alone accounted for nearly one quarter of the planet's energy consumption. Americans consumed 40% more energy than they produced.

Skills Focus: Interpreting Line Graphs

Social Studies Skill

U.S. Oil Consumption and Production

1. Have students review the line graph on this page and write down the trend(s) it reveals.
2. Have students create a similar line graph based on United States oil production and consumption between 1980 and 2005. This information is available at the Energy Information Administration's Web site.
3. Have students compare the line graph they create with the one on this page.
4. Have students write a paragraph describing the possible conclusions they could draw from their comparisons of the line graphs. Have students discuss their conclusions with the class. **LS Visual-Spatial, Logical-Mathematical**

Alternative Assessment Handbook, Rubrics 7: Charts; and 9: Comparing and Contrasting

Answers

Analyzing the Document (left) *possible answer—China, with its large workforce, strong industrial base, and huge consumer market, is able to draw foreign business enterprises away from developing nations.* **(right)** *approximately 5,000,000 barrels a day; possible answers—China's consumption of oil has increased at a much faster rate than its production of oil since 1995; because of this gap, China will have to import more oil, increasing demand, which may cause oil prices to rise for all nations.*

Direct Teach

Reading Focus

Investigating the Issue

Draw Conclusions What does Aravind Adiga suggest about the impact of remittances on the economy of India? *possible answer—Remittances have had a major impact; the flow of money has transformed cities and towns and helped many Indians rise in economic class.*

Draw Conclusions Do you think India should continue to promote outsourcing and the sending of its young people to work abroad? *possible answer—Yes, outsourcing and remittances have stimulated economic growth and brought new wealth to many Indians; no, India is too dependent upon foreign countries—the nation's economy could crash if trends change overseas.*

Info to Know

Outsourcing in India In 2006 exports of computer software and outsourced services such as call centers and back office operations generated over $23 billion in annual income for India. These sources of revenue continue to grow rapidly each year. By 2010 the country's software and services sector are projected to generate $60 billion in annual revenue.

DOCUMENT 3

For decades, the United States has promoted free trade and capitalism around the world. It continues to do so today. In the early years of the twenty-first century, however, the United States ran up large budget and trade deficits.

MORIN/The Miami Herald

Analyzing the Document

Who are the characters in this cartoon? What are they concerned about? How does the cartoonist depict China, and why?

DOCUMENT 4

Economic change is transforming India and China. In this article, the writer, who lives in the United States, talks about the cultural changes he observed when returned to visit his hometown of Mangalore, India.

"Back in 1991, when I left, about 300,000 people lived there. Since then its population has doubled But that doesn't begin to describe its transformation. . . .

[The] past decade has seen extraordinary change—and extraordinary excess—in Mangalore. The fastest-growing industry is education. During the 1980s, higher education became the only way out of a broken system for many frustrated young Indians. The best doctors and computer engineers had a fighting chance of nabbing a lucrative job offer from Silicon Valley [California] or Manhattan. So boys and girls throughout India streamed into colleges and institutes, where they studied calculus and organic chemistry with a passion that was probably unrivaled anywhere in the world. In recent years, the trend has accelerated. Mangalore had one medical college when I left; it now has five as well as at least four dental schools and 14 physiotherapy colleges. Some 350 schools, colleges and polytechnics are listed in its yellow pages.

. . . A flood of new money has arrived, thanks to outsourcing jobs, surging real estate prices and expatriate remittances [money that Indians who leave send back to support their families at home]. As a result, many locals have become middle-class, upper-middle-class or even rich. . . .

For better or worse, Mangalore's fate is in the hands of outsiders."

—Aravind Adiga, "My Lost World", *Time*, June 26, 2006

Analyzing the Document

What kinds of changes does the writer identify in his booming hometown? How do you think he feels about the changes?

Differentiating Instruction

Below Level

Learners Having Difficulty

1. Have students review the cartoon on this page. Discuss with the class the issues addressed in the cartoon.
2. Organize students into mixed-ability pairs.
3. Have each pair create a political cartoon that addresses an issue or issues relating to India's or China's economic growth. Cartoons may address the economic relationship of one or both of those nations to the United States.
4. Have students present their cartoons to the class. **LS Visual-Spatial**

Alternative Assessment Handbook, Rubric 27: Political Cartoons

Answers

Analyzing the Document (left) *Lady Liberty, Uncle Sam, the country of China; how free trade and capitalism will affect budgets; China depicted as wealthy because it benefited from free trade;* **(right)** *greater emphasis on education, more schools and colleges, more wealth in the city; possible answer—The writer is, for the most part, pleased with the changes though he is concerned that his hometown is so dependent upon foreign countries.*

DOCUMENT 5

Today, a relatively small segment of India's labor force generates the largest share of its income, as measured in gross domestic product (GDP). These pie graphs illustrate that fact.

INDIA'S GDP BY SECTOR, 2005

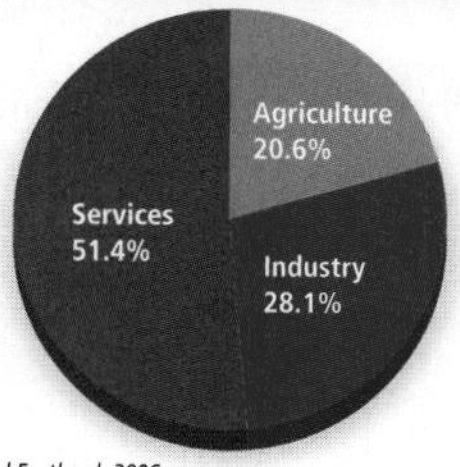

Source: *CIA World Factbook 2006*

INDIA'S LABOR FORCE BY SECTOR, 1999

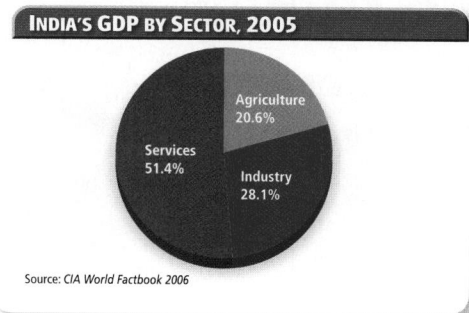

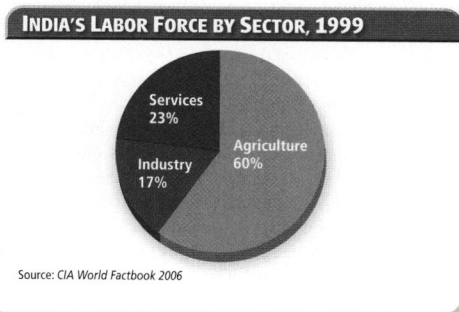

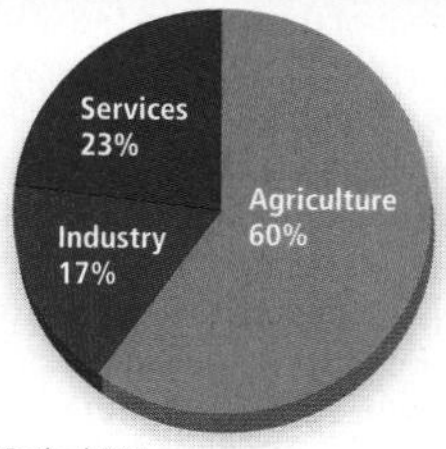

Source: *CIA World Factbook 2006*

Analyzing the Document

What proportion of India's labor force produces the largest share of its wealth, as measured in GDP? What do you think accounts for this fact?

DOCUMENT 6

The writer is a former governor of Hong Kong and former European Commissioner for External Relations. He notes the high stakes in the India-China competition.

> "India now trains a million engineering graduates a year (against 100,000 each in America and Europe) and stands third in technical and scientific capacity—behind America and Japan but ahead of China. Now when we play the geopolitical game of who will dominate the century to come, we add India to the stand-off between America and China.
>
> . . . I recognise the growing interest in whether we should—businessmen and politicians—place our bets on China's authoritarian model of development or India's democratic approach. The question is given more edge if you accept (which I don't) the old Chinese adage, "No mountain can accommodate two tigers."
>
> —Chris Patten, "Mystery Candidate," *Financial Times*, August 4, 2006

Analyzing the Document

According to Patten, in what way is the competition more than an economic one? Rewrite the last sentence in your own words. What is Patten's view of the issue?

ANALYZING THE ISSUE

go.hrw.com
Research Online
SD7 Case Study

1. Review the documents presented on this issue. What are some ways the economic rise of India and China are affecting the world?
2. What do the documents suggest about the advantages and disadvantages India and China each possess in their effort to become the world's biggest economic power?
3. Read excerpts and reviews of Thomas Friedman's book, *The World is Flat*. What does the title of his book mean? What effect does he think India and China are having on the world economy?
4. What steps do you think the United States could take to meet the challenge of global competition? Consider possibilities relating to education and business growth.

Direct Teach

Reading Focus

Investigating the Issue

Recall Most Indians work in which sector? *agricultural*

Identify How many more engineering graduates a year does India train than America and Europe combined? *800,000*

Collaborative Learning

At Level

World Economy

1. Organize students into three groups.
2. Have one group conduct research and prepare arguments to defend the position: "China will be the dominant economic power in the world by 2030." Have the second group conduct research and prepare arguments to defend the position: "India will be the dominant economic power in the world by 2030." Have the third group conduct research about both positions and prepare questions to ask the other two groups.
3. Hold a debate in which the first two groups present their arguments. The third group should ask each side relevant questions during the debate.
4. Have the third group decide which side won the debate. Students should explain why they thought the winning group's arguments were strongest. LS **Verbal-Linguistic, Interpersonal**

Alternative Assessment Handbook, Rubrics 10: Debates; and 30: Research

Answers

Analyzing the Document (left) *services; possible answer—These services include high tech businesses that generate large revenues from foreign sources.* **(right)** *possible answer—The competition between India and China is also a battle between rival political ideologies. "There can be only one dominant nation in Asia."; Patten does not believe that is true—he believes the both India and China can prosper.*

Analyzing the Issue 1. *possible answer—Their labor force continues to take some jobs away from people in other countries.* **2.** *possible answers—Advantages include large educated workforces, cheap labor and other incentives to attract foreign business enterprises, and growing high tech industries; disadvantages include competition with each other and other nations, and reliance upon foreign businesses for prosperity.* **3.** *possible answers—Technological and political forces have created a global marketplace in which competition and exchanges now occur on a level playing field; China and India have become competitive in economic sectors around the world, and are vying to become the dominant powers in the global economy.* **4.** *Answers will vary, but should consider the U.S.'s economic strengths in knowledge-based resources, science, and technology.*

Preteach

Focusing on the Issue

How do historical and cultural trends affect the status of women? *possible answers—Longstanding traditions have denied equality to women in many developing nations; religious beliefs have limited the rights and opportunities of women in certain countries; recent cultural and political trends have increased equality and opportunities for women in many nations.*

Key Terms

Preteach the following term:

secular non-religious (p. 639)

Case Study 4

Document-Based Investigation
Women in Society Ireland and Turkey

FOCUSING ON THE ISSUE

How do historical and cultural trends affect the status of women?

KEY TERMS
secular

Global studies of women in recent years have painted a bleak picture of the status of women around the world. For example, a 1999 survey revealed that women did about 66 percent of the work, earned 10 percent of the income, and owned 1 percent of the land. Moreover, women held only about 16 percent of the seats in the world's parliaments. A United Nations report noted in 2005, "Gender is one of the world's strongest markers for disadvantage."

The world's governments have pledged themselves to improve conditions for women. The United Nations Millennium Development Goals set a timetable of 2015 for increasing standards for women. It calls for improvements in the areas of educational opportunities, literacy, employment in non-farm jobs, and participation in national parliaments.

Globalization has helped produce a gradual shift in attitudes in some societies. Globalization emphasizes that countries need to value women as a human resource in order to become economically competitive. Studies show that countries that hold women back from participating in society consistently lag behind in development. In addition, as globalization helps women throughout the world gain greater access to new role models, information, and opportunities, their expectations grow.

Yet as governments try to improve the lives of women, they often must struggle to balance competing demands. Empowerment for women can clash with traditional cultural and religious beliefs. Even some women wonder if too much is lost in the rush for change. Ireland and Turkey are two nations that have faced and continue to face these challenges. The paths they have followed have taken some surprising twists.

Tansu Ciller (left) of Turkey and Mary McAleese (right) of Ireland have risen to the top ranks of government in their respective countries in recent years.

638

Teach the Main Idea

At Level

The Status of Women

1. **Teach** Ask students the Focusing on the Issue question to teach this section.
2. **Apply** Organize students into two large groups. Have one group list examples of the progress Irish women have made and give examples of inequality Irish women still face. Have the second group do the same for Turkish women.
3. **Review** Have the two groups share their lists. Discuss as a class how the status of women in Ireland and Turkey is similar and different.
4. **Practice/Homework** Have students write an essay describing opportunities and challenges for a woman living in either Ireland or Turkey today. **LS Verbal-Linguistic, Interpersonal**

Alternative Assessment Handbook, Rubrics 14: Group Activity; and 40: Writing to Describe

Exploring the Issue

Ireland is a predominantly Roman Catholic country, and Turkey is a predominantly Muslim country. In each, religious tradition and, in some cases, religious doctrine, have played a role in shaping the roles of women in society.

Ireland in Transition As recently as the 1970s, an Irish woman who got married could be forced to quit her job. In a largely Roman Catholic country opposed to abortion and birth control, the majority of women stayed home and raised families.

Starting in the 1970s, however, and gathering force in the 1990s, a number of changes began to reshape Irish society. In 1973, Ireland joined the European Economic Community, forerunner to the European Union (EU). As a member of the EU, Ireland has gradually conformed to EU standards on the treatment of women. Also, EU membership has opened Ireland to the world, helping to change attitudes on a number of social issues.

While EU influence has grown, the influence of the Roman Catholic Church has begun to diminish. In 1972 a clause recognizing the "special position" of the Catholic Church in Irish society was removed from the constitution. Since then, the Church has continued to play a large role in politics, but not always successfully. So far, it has convinced Irish voters to uphold restrictions on abortion, but it failed in its efforts to keep divorce illegal.

Social, political, economic, and cultural changes have combined to open up opportunities for women. After a long struggle, the right of married women to work outside the home was guaranteed. The employment of women has risen steadily, from roughly 36 percent of the workforce in 1994 to about 47 percent in 2004. Much of that increase came during the 1990s, when an Irish economic boom produced a need for more workers.

Yet women in Ireland still face inequities. Men earn more than women do, and they have greater access both to living-wage jobs and to high-paying management jobs. Despite success at the top of the political ranks, overall participation of women in public office is low. Ireland ranks 77th out of 188 nations in terms of the proportion of women members of Parliament.

Modern Turkish women express themselves in different ways. Some adopt Western dress and others wear traditional headscarves.

Diverging Trends in Turkey When the modern nation of Turkey was founded in 1923, its leaders built a **secular**, or nonreligious, state in which government and religion are strictly separated by law. Women's rights were written into laws regarding property ownership, inheritance, and suffrage.

Turkey is trying to join the European Union. To further that effort, it has taken numerous steps to bring its laws closer in line with EU requirements and to promote women's rights generally. Yet the reality of equal opportunity has been more difficult to achieve. Women have trouble rising to managerial levels in the workplace. Although Turkish law mandates equal pay, estimates of inequities between women and men range from 10 percent to 40 percent. (In the United States, pay inequities range from 8 to 25 percent.)

In 2002 Turkey took what many saw as a turn away from secular politics. That year, they elected a party with Islamic ties. Commentators were quick to point out, however, that the shift was partly a reaction to corruption in the secular governments of the 1990s.

Recently, a generational divide has opened up among some Turkish women. To older generations, being a "modern" women meant being secular—seeing yourself as a Turkish citizen first and as a Muslim second. Among the new generation, however, some women seek to redefine women's rights and feminism in accordance with their religious beliefs.

Direct Teach

Reading Focus

Exploring the Issue

Explain In Ireland, how has the influence of the European Union and the influence of the Roman Catholic Church changed in recent years? *the influence of the European Union has grown; the influence of the Roman Catholic Church has declined*

Make Judgments In which nation, Ireland or Turkey, do you think women will make greater progress in achieving equality in the coming years? *possible answers—Ireland: religious restrictions against equality are weakening; as a member of the EU, Ireland's economy will produce more opportunities for women; women in high-ranking offices will inspire more women to participate in politics; Turkey: because it has a long legal tradition mandating equal pay, it seeks to gain EU membership and is motivated to demonstrate the gender equality in its nation to the rest of Europe; women's rights and feminism are becoming more compatible with the nation's Islamic religious beliefs*

Primary Source

"New opportunities in education, employment, business, politics and religion have been seized with enthusiasm by women, transforming their expectations and self-confidence as individuals but also, and crucially, radically transforming the potential of family, of community and of country. Their genius, their energy has flowed much more freely than ever before into the human energy grid and we in Ireland have seen first-hand the manifest resulting uplift in economic, social and political fortunes."

—Mary McAleese, president of Ireland, in a speech at the Cornerstone Conference of the International Women's Forum, May 22, 2003

Skills Focus: Making Oral Presentations

At Level

Reading Like a Historian Skill

Women Leaders

1. Have students compile a list of interview questions to ask a woman who is in a leadership position. Questions should focus on the challenges and professional experiences of this person.
2. Have students select a woman to interview. This person could be in politics, the business world, organized religion, academia, etc.
3. Have students conduct the interviews and then prepare an oral report based on the interviewees' answers.
4. Have students present their reports to the class. LS **Interpersonal, Verbal-Linguistic**

Alternative Assessment Handbook, Rubrics 18: Listening; and 24: Oral Presentations

Direct Teach

Word Help

fundamentally radically (p. 640)

particularistic unique to oneself or one's own group (p. 641)

Reading Focus

Investigating the Issue

Compare A higher percentage of which country's citizens can read and write: Ireland or Turkey? *Ireland*

Interpret What do you think is Mary Robinson's primary goal for giving the speech in Document 2? *possible answer—to encourage the citizens of her country to use new strategies to address women's issues and help bring about gender equality*

Make Inferences How do you think Document 1 influenced Document 2? *possible answer—Ireland's low rank in women's legislative office-holding likely helped inspire Robinson's call for a fundamental reappraisal of women's issues in her country.*

Info to Know

The Supreme Court of Ireland The highest court in Ireland is the Supreme Court. It consists of a Chief Justice and seven regular judges. As of 2006, three of the eight judges on the Supreme Court were women: Susan Denham, Catherine McGuinness, and Fidelma Macken.

Investigating the Issue

The changing role of women in societies around the world raises many questions. The documents that follow present data and opinions about how two countries—Ireland and Turkey—are addressing some of these questions. Examine the documents, keeping in mind what you have read about how women's roles are changing in each country. Then answer the questions that follow.

Document 1

This chart compares key facts about the populations of Ireland and Turkey. Note that while both countries have had female heads of state, neither is a leader when it comes to electing women to the national legislature.

Ireland and Turkey Comparison, 2005

	IRELAND	TURKEY
Population	4.1 million	70.5 million
Religion	88.4% Roman Catholic	99.8% Muslim
Adult Literacy Rate	Men 99%, Women 99%	Men 94.3%, Women 78.7%
Women in Parliament, world ranking*	Ranked 77 out of 188	Ranked 126 out of 188

*USA Ranking = 66 out of 188

Source: CIA; International Parliamentary Union

Analyzing the Document

In what way are Ireland and Turkey fairly similar, according to this data? How are they different?

Document 2

The election of Ireland's first woman president, Mary Robertson, focused more attention on women's issues. In this speech, Robertson called for new thinking about roles for women in Irish society.

"If the imbalances of the past came, and I believe they did, not simply from legislative and economic inequality but from profound resistances and failures of perception, then it follows that to right that balance we must do more than review our legislation and re-state our economic structures. We must also fundamentally re-appraise our view of who and what is valuable in our society. We must look with fresh and unprejudiced eyes at the work of women, the views of women, their way of organising and their interpretation of social priorities. To achieve this, we must, I believe, begin at the beginning and alter our way of thinking."

—Speech by Mary Robinson, president of Ireland, 1992

Analyzing the Document

According to Robinson, what combination of factors produced inequalities in Irish society?

Collaborative Learning

At Level

Female Heads of State

1. Organize students into five groups. Assign one of the following continents to each group: North America, South America, Europe, Asia, and Africa.
2. Have each group compile a list of all past and current female heads of state in the countries on their continent since 1900.
3. Have groups share their lists with the class. Note the differences in the total number of names on the lists.
4. Guide students in a discussion about possible reasons for the different total numbers on the lists. **LS Visual-Spatial, Logical-Mathematical**

Alternative Assessment Handbook, Rubrics 11: Discussions; and 14: Group Activity

Answers

Analyzing the Document (top) *similarities: men have a high literacy rate, religion is important, low rank in terms of the proportion of women MPs; differences: Ireland is primarily Catholic, Turkey is primarily Muslim, Turkey has a much larger population than Ireland, Irish women have a much higher literacy rate than Turkish women;* **(bottom)** *legislative and economic inequalities, lack of understanding of women's issues, prejudices against women*

DOCUMENT 3

Like many countries, Turkey is struggling to live up to its promises of gender equality. This table shows the education gender gap.

EDUCATION RATES IN TURKEY, 2004

	GIRLS	BOYS	GENDER GAP
Primary school	93	100	7.8
Secondary school	57.2	74.3	17.1
College	18.7	24.3	8.3
Adult literacy	78.5	94.4	15.9
Adult literacy, rural	69.2	91	21.8
Adult literacy, urban	83.4	96.1	12.7

Analyzing the Document

Where is the gender gap greatest? Where is it lowest? What do you think accounts for the differences in urban and rural literacy rates?

DOCUMENT 4

The controversy over the Muslim head scarf symbolizes the current tensions in Turkey over the role of women. This writer, a Turkish professor of sociology, has studied the attitudes of young Turkish women who are rebelling against secularism and wearing the head scarf.

"What really distinguishes the contemporary Islamic movement [in Turkey] is this presence of women in these movements, so they are the motor of change. . . .

But what happens is that each time these Muslim girls—or women, now—go to public life, pursue their professional career, for instance, they go from home to outside, from private to public life. Each time there is a tension within the [Islamic] movement and, therefore, there is a kind of debate among Islamic women who want to go even more public and Islamic men who remind them that, first of all, they have to be wives and mothers—their sacred roles. . . .

. . . [A]lthough we are in a country where the majority of the population is Muslim, nevertheless we define the republic as a secular republic. And secularism meant this neutral space where you are not allowed to bring your religious, ethnic, particularistic [individual] identities. So there is this debate now ongoing to what extent we are going to enlarge democratic rights to include this kind of new demands of difference.

—Nilufer Gole, online interview, *Frontline,* PBS, June 2001

Analyzing the Document

How are attitudes toward women's participation in Turkish society changing?

ANALYZING THE ISSUE

go.hrw.com
Research Online
SD7 Case Study

1. How has religious tradition played a role in the shaping women's roles in Ireland and in Turkey? What similarities and differences exist between the two countries on this issue?
2. In what ways is there a gap between the laws and the realities of life for women in both countries? Provide specific examples.
3. Research the role of the president in Ireland. Do you think the function of that position made it easier for women to reach that post? Why or why not?
4. Do research to create a time line of major events in history of women's rights in Ireland, Turkey, and the United States from the 1900s to the present.

Direct Teach

Reading Focus

Investigating the Issue

Recall What portion of Turkish boys is college educated? *about one fourth, or 24.3%*

Make Inferences Why does Gole believe that young Turkish women are "motors of change"? *possible answer—Young Turkish women are participating in a public movement that creates tension among much of the Muslim population. This tension sparks debates that can lead to social change.*

Differentiating Instruction

Above Level

Advanced Learners/Gifted and Talented

1. Have students select a topic relating to women's issues in either Ireland or Turkey. Possible topics include individuals (e.g. Tansu Ciller), groups (e.g. textile workers), or conditions (e.g. unequal wages).
2. Have students write a poem or song about the issue they selected. Students having difficulty writing lyrics may choose a popular song and write new words for their topic.
3. Have student present their songs or poems to the class. Students who wrote songs may wish to include music as part of their presentation.
4. Discuss with the class how music and poetry can inspire social change. **LS Auditory-Musical, Verbal-Linguistic**

Alternative Assessment Handbook, Rubrics 11: Discussions; and 26: Poems and Songs

Answers

Analyzing the Document (left) *greatest: adult literacy in rural areas; lowest: primary school education; possible answer—Modern secular values are likely stronger in urban areas, resulting in more educational opportunities for girls; in rural areas, where traditional religious beliefs are stronger, education for girls is less emphasized.* **(right)** *women want increased role in public life, debate about increasing democratic rights*

Analyzing the Issue 1. *Religious tradition has generally limited women's rights in Ireland and Turkey; similar—young women in both countries are seeking greater equality and professional opportunities while still honoring the values of their religion. differences—Turkish women seem more at odds with Muslim faith, which emphasizes "sacred" roles of wives and mothers.* **2.** *possible answers—Though Ireland and Turkey legislate equality, women in both nations still face inequalities. In both Ireland and Turkey women are not paid as much as men and have less access to management-level jobs.* **3.** *Answers will vary, but students should support their arguments with specific examples from their research about the Irish president.* **4.** *Answers will vary, but should include relevant events such as gaining the right to vote, passage of laws guaranteeing women's rights and dates woman attained high offices.*

Preteach

Focusing on the Issue

What should the role of the United Nations be in international affairs? *possible answer—to debate and settle disputes among nations, to preserve human rights, and to foster peaceful relations among nations*

Key Terms

Preteach the following terms:

charter the document that created the United Nations (p. 642)

General Assembly entity of the United Nations consisting of all member nations (p. 643)

Security Council entity of the United Nations consisting of 15 member nations that serve as peacekeepers (p. 643)

Secretariat entity of the United Nations that carries out the organization's administrative tasks (p. 643)

peacekeeping sending multinational forces into countries to enforce ceasefires or truces among warring countries or warring groups within a single country (p. 643)

Case Study 5

Document-Based Investigation

The Role of the United Nations

Focusing on the Issue

What should the role of the United Nations be in international affairs?

Key Terms

charter, General Assembly, Security Council, Secretariat, peacekeeping

It was an ambitious idea: Create an organization to settle disputes among nations and solve tough global problems. Since its founding in 1945—the outcome of efforts by the United States and its World War II allies—the United Nations has struggled to live up to those high ideals.

The United Nations **charter**, the document that created the organization, lays out four major goals. It aims "to maintain international peace and security; to develop friendly relations among nations; to cooperate in solving international problems and in promoting respect for human rights; and to be a centre for harmonizing the actions of nations." Security, human rights, economic development, healthcare, disaster relief, and refugee aid are among its top concerns today.

From the start, the UN's mission was a delicate balancing act. The charter establishes the principle of equality among nations; yet it assigns an unequal role to the world's powerful nations in maintaining global security—often to the frustration of smaller countries. The United Nations consists of a diversity of shifting alliances, values, voices, interests, and goals. Even within the host country itself, the United States, debate over the very existence of the UN has raged for years.

Since 1945 UN membership has grown from 51 to 191 nations. As the organization has grown, so has its mission. Indeed, the modern-day rise of globalization, terrorism, and nuclear proliferation has challenged the UN in ways its founders never could have imagined. With expansion have come problems: waste, corruption, scandals. Failures to prevent or resolve wars and genocides in various parts of the world during the 1990s and beyond further damaged the UN's image and credibility.

Starting around 2005, the UN launched reforms aimed at dealing with these acknowledged problems. Leaders vowed to retool the organization to effectively meet twenty-first century needs. Critics remained skeptical about whether the UN could succeed in reforming itself.

United Nations Secretary-General Kofi Annan addressing the General Assembly at the opening ceremonies of the sixtieth session of the UN in 2005.

642

Teach the Main Idea

At Level

The Role of the United Nations

1. **Teach** Ask students the Focusing on the Issue question to teach this section.
2. **Apply** Organize students into two groups. Have one group compile a list of general functions and goals of the United Nations. Have the second group make a list of specific operations or policies the United Nations is currently pursuing.
3. **Review** Have volunteers write each list on the board. Have students match the general function or goal to each specific operation or policy with which it corresponds. Guide a discussion about how the United Nations is currently working to achieve its goals.
4. **Practice/Homework** Have each student write an essay evaluating the success of the United Nations, suggesting future directions the organization should take. **LS Verbal-Linguistic, Intrapersonal**

Alternative Assessment Handbook, Rubrics 14: Group Activity; and 37: Writing Assignments

Exploring the Issue

The UN consists of six main entities: the General Assembly, the Security Council, the Secretariat, the Economic and Social Council, the Trusteeship Council, and the International Court of Justice. The court is held at The Hague, in the Netherlands, while the rest of the operations are based at the UN's global headquarters in New York City.

The **General Assembly** includes all the member nations, and each nation gets one vote on matters before the assembly. The votes are not binding, but they carry weight as a statement of world opinion.

The role of the **Security Council** is to be the guardian of peace. It sends armies to trouble spots to keep the peace, arranges cease-fires, and brokers peace agreements. If countries violate agreements, the Council may impose sanctions. It can even order military action against the offenders. Of the 15 Security Council members, five are permanent—China, France, Russia, the United Kingdom, and the United States. The others serve two-year terms. Each of the permanent members has veto power over Security Council decisions. This arrangement guarantees that the interests of the powerful nations are protected. Recently, there have been discussions about expanding the Security Council to include other powerful nations, such as Japan and Germany.

The **Secretariat** carries out the administrative tasks of the UN, from conducting studies to providing services around the globe. The head of the UN, the secretary-general, is elected for up to two five-year terms.

An Expanding Role Since the end of the Cold War, the UN's mission has expanded. UN workers are now dispersed throughout the world. More than half of the UN's 30,000 nonmilitary employees serve in the field. Civilian field operations include humanitarian relief operations, human rights monitoring, election monitoring, and efforts to combat the drug trade and other global criminal activity.

The major field operation of the UN is **peacekeeping**, or the sending multinational forces into countries to enforce ceasefires or truces among warring countries or warring groups within a single country. In 2006, approximately 80,000 troops from member nations served in UN peacekeeping forces around the globe. In 2006 roughly 70 percent of the UN's budget was dedicated to field operations, up from 50 percent 10 years earlier.

UN peacekeeping troops on patrol in Sudan in 2006. In 1998, the UN received the Nobel Peace Prize for its peacekeeping operations.

Criticism and Scandal Critics of the UN fault it for reacting slowly to the ethnic genocides in Rwanda and Bosnia in the 1990s. They say the UN is ineffective in combating terrorism and in preventing the spread of nuclear technology to countries such as Iran and North Korea. Some fault the UN for not taking stronger action against the dictatorship of Saddam Hussein in Iraq prior to the U.S. invasion of the country in 2003.

The worst blow to the UN's image in recent times was the Oil-for-Food scandal that broke in 2004. The UN Oil for Food program allowed Iraq to sell its oil to buy humanitarian supplies for its people. Instead of using the oil money to buy food and medicine for suffering Iraqis, Saddam Hussein skimmed billions from the program. UN officials were implicated in profiting from the theft as well.

Direct Teach

Reading Focus

Exploring the Issues

Identify Which nations are permanent members of the UN Security Council? *China, France, Russia, the United Kingdom, and the United States*

Explain How has the UN changed since the end of the Cold War? *expanded mission, greater emphasis on field operations*

Evaluate What, if anything, do you think the UN should have done differently in the past 15 years? *possible answers—quicker and more forceful response to stop the genocides in Rwanda and Bosnia; stronger action in preventing Iran and North Korea from acquiring nuclear technology; stricter regulation of its Oil for Food program with Iraq*

Recent Scholarship

Noted scholar Paul Kennedy is known for his work describing the histories of the world's great powers. In his recent book *The Parliament of Man: The Past, Present, and Future of the United Nations,* Johnson examines the UN. The author, in this thorough history, describes the organization's precursors, its founding, and its evolution over the past 60 years. Though Johnson covers the UN's many shortcomings, he presents convincing arguments that the organization has played an important role in the modern world.

The Parliament of Man: The Past, Present, and Future of the United Nations by Paul Kennedy. Random House, 2006.

Differentiating Instruction

Below Level

Struggling Readers

1. Organize students into mixed-ability pairs. Have each pair select a major activity (or activities) of the United Nations for further study.
2. Have each pair create a diorama depicting one or more of the UN's activities in the world today.
3. Have students display their dioramas throughout the classroom.
4. Have pairs describe their diorama to the class. Hold a summary discussion about how students' work illustrates the current activities of the UN. LS **Visual-Spatial**

Alternative Assessment Handbook, Rubrics 11: Discussions; and 3: Artwork

Direct Teach

Word Help

eradicate eliminate completely (p. 644)

ad-hoc concerned with a specific purpose (p. 645)

Reading Focus

Investigating the Issue

Recall What are the three primary categories of UN expenses? *extra-budgetary, peacekeeping, regular*

Describe How does the UN pursue its health care agenda? *through the World Health Organization, a UN branch that coordinates disease-prevention efforts; by including health care issues among its Millennium Development Goals*

Make Generalizations Summarize the information in the three documents on this page in a single statement. *possible answer—The UN has recently achieved notable successes as its vast agenda has continued to expand.*

Investigating the Issue

Controversy continues to rage around the United Nations. The documents that follow explore these issues by presenting different points of view and arguments. Examine the documents, keeping in mind what you have read about the organization's history, mission, and challenges.

Document 1

Reflecting the scope of the UN's mission, in 2005 all 191 UN member countries pledged to achieve the following list of ambitious goals, called the Millennium Development Goals, by 2015.

UN Millennium Development Goals

1. Eradicate extreme poverty and hunger
2. Achieve universal primary education
3. Promote gender equality and empower women
4. Reduce child mortality
5. Improve maternal health
6. Combat HIV/AIDS, malaria and other diseases
7. Ensure environmental sustainability
8. Develop a global partnership for development

Analyzing the Document

How would you characterize the type of goals listed here? Do you think the goals are realistic in the time frame established? Why or why not?

Document 2

The World Health Organization, a branch of the UN, has spearheaded efforts to combat disease worldwide. With funding from member states and private groups, the WTO coordinates disease-prevention efforts, such as the drive to eliminate smallpox, which achieved success in 1977. Currently, the WTO is conducting a drive to wipe out polio. The graph below shows the progress of the effort.

World Cases of Polio, 1980–2005

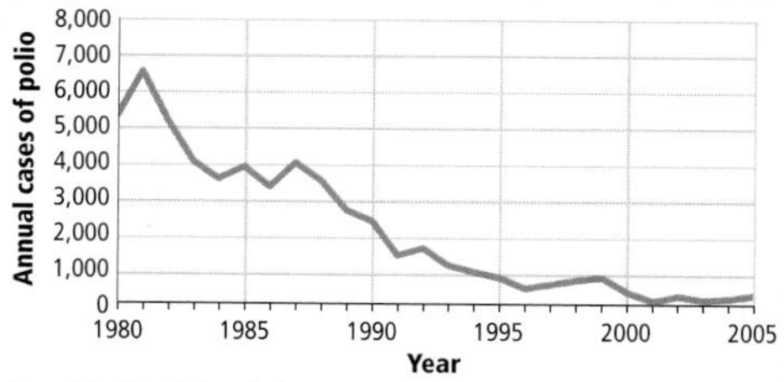

Source: World Health Organization

Analyzing the Document

What is the trend in world cases of polio? What happened between 2000 and 2005?

Document 3

The UN's expenses have grown as its mission has expanded. The budget for peacekeeping alone in 2004-2005 was greater than the UN's entire budget in 1996-1997.

Analyzing the Document

During the decade shown here, what portion of UN expenses grew the most? What do you think accounts for that dramatic increase?

UN Budgets, 1996–2005

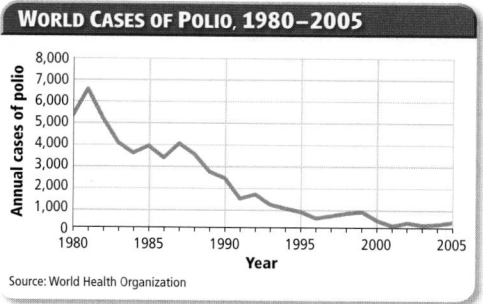

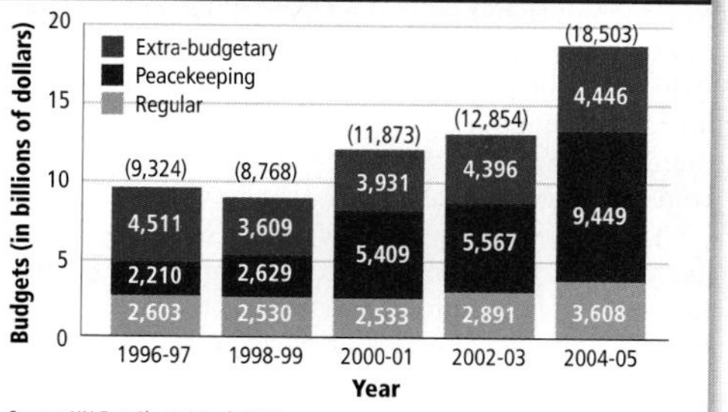

Source: UN Fact Sheet, March 2006

Skills Focus: Analyzing

At Level

Social Studies Skill

United Nations Peacekeeping Missions

1. Have students visit the UN cartography webpage (http://www.un.org/Depts/Cartographic/english/htmain.htm). Have students select one of the peacekeeping maps listed.
2. Have students research the operation(s) depicted on their chosen map.
3. Have students prepare an informational essay describing the operations shown on their map. For example, students could explain why various troop units are deployed in certain locations.
4. Have students print out their maps and present their essays to the class. LS **Visual-Spatial, Verbal-Linguistic**

Alternative Assessment Handbook, Rubrics 21: Map Reading; and 42: Writing to Inform

Answers

Analyzing the Document (top left) *possible answers—ambitious, optimistic; no, too much opposition and conflict in the world; yes, with an increasing budget and resources, UN can match success it had with polio with these goals;* **(top right)** *rise in polio cases in early 1980s, then decline in cases; polio almost completely eliminated;* **(bottom)** *peacekeeping; possible answer—The UN has committed more resources to field operations in recent years.*

DOCUMENT 4

American conservatives have been particularly critical of the United Nations over the years. At times they have called for the United States to withdraw from the UN, and they have successfully worked to withhold US funding from the UN.

In this piece from *Commentary* magazine, one of the leading conservative journals in the United States, the writer finds fault with the very structure of the UN. As UN responsibilities grow, the writer argues, so do opportunities for inefficiencies and corruption.

Analyzing the Document

From what you read, do you believe that Rosett believes the United Nations can ever be reformed?

"Since its founding, the institution has added untold numbers of agencies, funds, commissions, programs, "ad-hoc bodies," and "other entities," to the point where most of the UN's own personnel do not know who reports to whom, or how. . . .

There is almost no way to hold the UN accountable for most of what goes on in this growing empire. . . . In fact, there is no procedure at the UN for impeaching or firing the Secretary-General. . . .

The founding purpose of the UN was to bring peace and prosperity to the globe. As to the former, the UN in the age of terror has been in most ways useless and in some ways positively dangerous. The lesson that Saddam Hussein quickly grasped was that the UN lends itself to money-laundering [illegally hiding the transfer of funds]. . . .

Like the Soviet Union of old, the UN is unwieldy, gross, inefficient, and incompetent. . . ."

—"How Corrupt Is the United Nations?"
Claudia Rosett, *Commentary* magazine, April 2006

DOCUMENT 5

As of late 2006, the United Nations had sponsored 59 peacekeeping operations since its founding. Sixteen were ongoing. UN peacekeeping has had some notable successes, such as El Salvador and Mozambique in the early 1990s and East Timor in the early 2000s.

In the case of the Arab-Israeli conflict, success has been more elusive. Indeed, over the years there have been seven separate UN peacekeeping missions triggered by the Arab-Israeli conflict. UN peacekeepers have successfully monitored truces or agreements between Israel and its neighbors Syria and Egypt. But a lasting regional peace has remained out of reach. A UN monitoring force in Lebanon since 1978 has been powerless to stop repeated attacks against Israel or two full-scale invasions of Lebanon by Israel. The cartoonist, a supporter of Israel, reflects the frustration that many felt during the Israel-Lebanon War of 2006.

Michael Ramirez, *Investor's Business Daily*, July 24, 2006

Analyzing the Document

How does the cartoonist characterize the UN's response to Middle East conflict?

Direct Teach

Reading Focus

Exploring the Issue

Recall To what does Claudia Rosett compare the United Nations? *the Soviet Union*

Make Connections What connections can you identify between the two documents on this page? *possible answer—The lack of success of the UN in dealing with the Israel-Lebanon War of 2006 likely caused people to criticize the organization using arguments similar to those of Claudia Rosett.*

Info to Know

UN Relief Efforts Relief to nations across the globe is one of the United Nations' primary missions: the UN carries out this work primarily through four organizations: the World Food Program (provides food to victims of disaster, long-term refugees, and displaced persons), the Office of the UN High Commissioner for Refugees (helps and protects refugees), the UN Children's Fund (addresses the needs of children in developing countries), and the UN Relief and Works Agency for Palestinian Refugees in the Near East (provides health, education, and social services to Palestinian refugees).

Collaborative Learning

At Level

Opinions about the UN

1. Organize students into groups of five. Have groups prepare a set of three survey questions to ask people they know about their opinions of the UN. Examples of possible questions include: "Do you approve of the UN's current policies?" and "Should the United States continue to support the UN financially?"
2. Have students in each group interview four people of different ages about the UN. When finished with the interviews, each group should have a sample of 20 responses.
3. Have groups prepare a report summarizing the results of their interviews.
4. Compare each of the group's reports. Have the class identify trends in American public opinion about the United Nations.

LS Interpersonal, Verbal-Linguistic

Alternative Assessment Handbook, Rubrics 1: Acquiring Information; and 14: Group Activity

Answers

Analyzing the Document (top) *possible answer—No, Rosett believes the problems with the UN are deep-seated and structural—she believes that the UN, like the Soviet Union, is inefficient dissolved.* **(bottom)** *unreliable; asleep at the wheel, inferring that the UN could do more to keep peace in the region*

Direct Teach

Reading Focus

Investigating the Issue

Recall According to Florini, how many nations are equally represented in the General Assembly? *191*

Explain How does Florini believe that the United States has hindered reform in the UN? *inconsistent diplomatic efforts to build consensus for meaningful change, withholding dues*

Make Inferences Why do you think the nations listed by Florini as opponents of reform are actively working against the UN? *possible answers—Those nations do not want outsiders interfering in their domestic business; their governments pursue policies that conflict with the UN's mission.*

Answers

Analyzing the Document *yes; structural flaws ("a fundamentally unsound institutional base"), inefficiency ("mess of largely pointless debates"), overt opposition from several nations ("actively subvert attempts to make the UN function efficiently"), and inconsistent U.S. policies ("only fitfully invested in the long-term, patient diplomacy needed to build consensus for meaningful change")*

Analyzing the Issue 1. *possible answers—The UN has ambitious goals that will present many challenges; the UN needs a lot of money to carry out its agenda; the UN has many opponents.* **2.** *possible answer—A conservative author is more likely to oppose the UN for not supporting recent U.S. foreign policy; a liberal author is more likely to support the UN's humanitarian and peacekeeping missions.* **3.** *possible answers—Several countries on the commission were criticized for human rights abuses; Americans criticized the commission's lack of discussion about human rights issues; the U.S. criticized the addition of Sudan to the commission.* **4.** *Letters will vary, but should discuss specific UN policies, and possible reform strategies.*

DOCUMENT 6

Ann Florini is an analyst for the Brookings Institution, a nonpartisan think tank that often takes positions perceived as liberal. Like Claudia Rosett, she believes that the UN as currently organized is fundamentally flawed. Still, she believes the UN can be reformed.

"But all this [UN] activity depends on a fundamentally unsound institutional base. The UN's fifteen-country Security Council, the only UN body with teeth, gives lopsided power to the victors of World War II. The General Assembly, where all 191 nations theoretically have equal voice, has degenerated [fallen] into a . . . mess of largely pointless debates on a mind-numbing agenda covering every conceivable issue. The fifty-three-member Economic and Social Council is essentially worthless. The Secretariat suffers from a deadwood-ridden staff, extreme micro-management by member states, and an inadequate oversight system that allows plenty of waste, fraud, and abuse . . .

Step one [in reform] is to assign responsibility where it belongs: overwhelmingly with the member countries. . . .

The member countries have never invested the financial and human resources needed to make the UN work well. . . . A few hard-core opponents of reform—insiders point to Syria, Pakistan, Venezuela, Cuba, Egypt, and Iran—actively subvert [undermine] attempts to make the UN function efficiently and effectively. The U.S., where Congress goes into periodic fits of rage over revelations of misdeeds such as the oil-for-food scandal, has only fitfully invested in the long-term, patient diplomacy needed to build consensus [agreement] for meaningful change, and has sometimes shot itself in the foot with bullying tactics like withholding of dues. . . .

The small reforms agreed upon to date may still prove the spark for a real UN renaissance—if a whole lot of people act quickly. . . .

[The United States] must engage effectively but, given the realities of anti-Americanism, quietly with pro-reform forces in New York. . . . And the member states need to regain control of their own delegations in New York, who too often serve personal interests at the expense of national ones.

If all this is done, the UN may be reborn.

—Ann Florini, "The UN at 60: Senescence or Renaissance?"
The Brookings Institution, 2005

Analyzing the Document

Does the writer support the existence of the United Nations? What does she see as the key challenges to its success? Use passages from the excerpt to support your answers.

ANALYZING THE ISSUE

go.hrw.com
Research Online
SD7 Case Study

1. Review the documents presented on this issue. What do they tell you about the difficulties of carrying out the UN's mission?
2. Review the descriptions of the authors of the passages excerpted here. How might their backgrounds affect their point of view about the UN?
3. Research viewpoints about the UN Human Rights Commission. What controversies have surrounded its membership? Why has the United States objected to some of its activities?
4. Considering all the challenges involved in getting UN members to agree on actions and respond quickly to crises, do you think the UN has outlived its usefulness? Do you think it should be strengthened? Do you have another viewpoint? Write a letter to the editor explaining your position and offering reasons to support it.

Skills Focus: Analyzing Alternative Points of View — At Level

Reading Like a Historian Skill
Opinions About the United Nations

1. Have students examine recent newspapers, magazines, or online sources to find two opinion pieces about the United Nations. One article should be pro-UN, and the other should be critical of the UN.
2. Have students write an essay assessing the two articles they selected. Students should recognize if the authors supported their arguments with facts or if their writing is excessively biased to advance an agenda.
3. Have students present their conclusions about the articles they selected to the class.
LS Verbal-Linguistic

Alternative Assessment Handbook, Rubric 16: Judging Information

Reference Section

THE WORLD ALMANAC®

go.hrw.com
Research Online
Keyword: SS World Almanac

Key Events in World History

The World Almanac Key Events in World History is a brief summary of important turning points in world history. It provides capsule descriptions of events or movements along with brief accounts of their significance. Use this section to review the content in *Human Legacy.*

Millions of years ago First Hominids

About 5–7 million years ago several species of "hominids," or upright walking, human-like primates, were roaming the African continent. By about 2–3 million years ago, early hominids lived in groups, made tools, and gathered food.

Significance These first hominids are the most distant ancestors of modern humans. Fossil records are gradually filling in a still murky picture of these early hominid ancestors.

200,000–100,000 years ago First Modern Humans

Homo sapiens, the species to which all modern humans belong, first lived in East Africa about 200,000 years ago. By 100,000 years ago humans had reached Southwest Asia, and by 35,000 years ago they had reached Europe.

Significance *H. sapiens* spread and thrived. They soon became the sole hominid species, supplanting Neanderthals among others.

14,000 years ago End of the Last Ice Age

Approximately 2 million years ago Earth's atmosphere cooled. Large sheets of ice formed and eventually covered vast portions of the planet's surface. This period, which lasted until about 12,000 BC, is called the Pleistocene epoch, or the last Ice Age. The end of the Pleistocene was marked by a gradual increase in Earth's temperatures. Land that had been covered by ice for millennia gradually became exposed to the sun once again.

Significance As the ice sheets receded, Earth became a more hospitable place. New plant and animal species developed. The Bering Land Bridge, which had connected Asia and the Americas, receded under the ocean, isolating the Americas and their inhabitants.

12,000–10,000 years ago Invention of Agriculture

For thousands of years humans had survived by hunting wild animals and gathering wild plants. Around 10,000 BC, with the climate warmer and drier, some humans discovered that animals and plants could be domesticated, or made to serve their needs directly. Domestication is one of the signs of the transition to the Neolithic Era, or New Stone Age. This happened around the same time in many parts of the world.

Significance Agriculture freed humans from the need to migrate in search of animals and plants for food. This allowed for permanent settlements, labor specialization and, eventually, civilization.

c. 4000 BC Rise of Mesopotamian Cultures

The Sumerians, a people who lived in the area between the Tigris and Euphrates rivers in what is now Iraq, developed what many consider the world's first civilization. Sumerian society was centered on large cities that were supported by irrigated farms in the countryside. Sumerians made use of the first known system of writing, which developed into the wedge-shaped script called cuneiform.

Significance As the world's first civilization, with the first developed system of writing, the Sumerians stand at the beginning of recorded history.

c. 4000–3500 BC Invention of the Wheel

Evidence suggests that people in the Mesopotamian cultures of the Near East had invented wheeled vehicles by as early as the fourth millennium BC. The concept spread rapidly to other civilizations. Remains of an early wooden disk wheel dating to around 3500 BC have been found at a site in what is now the Netherlands.

Significance The wheel was a milestone technological achievement. It made many tasks, from transporting people and goods to making pottery, far easier to accomplish.

c. 3100 BC Upper and Lower Egypt Unite

In ancient times the abundance of the Nile River valley gave rise to the two kingdoms of Upper and Lower Egypt. Around 3100 BC, according to tradition, Menes, an Upper Egyptian king, marched his army north to invade Lower Egypt. His efforts resulted in unification of the civilizations along the Nile into one Egypt. Menes established Egypt's first dynasty, and is considered to be Egypt's first pharaoh.

Significance The unification of Egypt by Menes represents the beginning of a great ancient civilization that lasted nearly 3,000 years.

3000–1500 BC Indus Valley Civilization

Around 3000 BC the Indus Valley civilization developed along the Indus River, in the northwest of the Indian subcontinent. Ruins from the cities of Harappa and Mohenjo Daro show that the Indus Valley civilization possessed strong governments and an economy based on agriculture. The Indus Valley civilization also developed a written language.

Significance The story of civilization in one of the world's most historically rich regions, the Indian subcontinent, began with this first Indus River valley culture.

c. 2700–2300 BC Egyptian Pyramids Built

Egyptians began constructing pyramids to serve as tombs for their pharaohs during the Old Kingdom, in the 2700s BC. The largest of the pyramids, the Great Pyramid of Khufu near Giza, was built during this time. The pyramids are evidence of the Egyptian belief in an afterlife and in the godly stature of their pharaohs.

Significance With nearly 80 pyramids still standing along the west bank of the Nile, the pyramids of Egypt serve as a testament to the strength, material wealth, and ability to mobilize vast resources characteristic of ancient Egypt under the pharaohs.

c. 1750 BC Code of Hammurabi

The Babylonian king Hammurabi rose to power around 1792 BC. By the end of his reign the Babylonian Empire extended through much of the Tigris-Euphrates Valley—a testament to his prowess as a military leader. But Hammurabi is best known for the code of written laws that survives from his reign. The laws, which were written down for all to see, dealt with matters ranging from trade and business to crimes and personal injuries.

Significance The Code of Hammurabi is the earliest known collection of written laws. Combining Sumerian and Semitic traditions, the code represented an advance beyond tribal codes.

c. 1700 BC Hyksos Invasion of Egypt

As the Middle Kingdom in Egypt weakened, a people known as the Hyksos migrated into Egypt from the east. With superior military technology, such as the horse-drawn chariot and the compound bow, the Hyksos were eventually able to establish their power. They ruled Egypt for more than a century, extending the kingdom's boundaries as far as Syria and Palestine, and maintaining peace and prosperity throughout their lands.

Significance The Hyksos kings ushered in a new phase in ancient Egyptian history. They introduced the horse-drawn chariot, which pharaohs of the New Kingdom period would use to build strong armies and expand their territory.

c. 1540–1075 BC New Kingdom in Egypt

Around 1540 BC an Egyptian named Ahmose declared himself pharaoh and drove the Hyksos from Egypt. This was the beginning of the New Kingdom, the period that would see Egypt rise to the peak of its power and glory. Fearful of invasion, future Egyptian pharaohs succeeded in establishing control over possible invasion routes. In the process, they overtook foreign lands and established an empire. Military conquests also expanded Egyptian trade and made the kingdom wealthy. The most famous New Kingdom pharaoh is Ramses II (died c. 1235 BC), who left behind numerous monuments.

Significance The New Kingdom period was the last great flourish of Egyptian power and culture before the empire's long, slow decline.

c. 1500 BC India's Vedic Period Begins

By around 1500 BC a new element became apparent in the Indus Valley region. Many scholars believe that a nomadic people known as the Aryans, originating from the area near the Black Sea, entered the Indus Valley in search of pastureland for their livestock. The synthesis between these new peoples and the indigenous population produced a rich culture, which we can glimpse today through the *Vedas*, one of the great religious texts of Hinduism.

Significance The languages of classical Sanskrit, in which the *Vedas* are written, and modern Bengali and Hindi derive from the Indo-Aryan language.

c. 1766–1100 BC Shang Dynasty in China

The Shang dynasty, the first Chinese dynasty for which solid historical evidence exists, created the first strong state in China, in the Huang River valley. Far-flung irrigation and flood-control systems spurred the Shang to develop a complex bureaucracy. Over time, the Shang expanded their lands. They are known for their outstanding bronzework.

Significance The Shang bureaucracy became a model for later Chinese dynasties. The earliest Chinese system of writing dates from the Shang period.

1200 BC Olmec Civilization in Mexico

Settlements dating from around 1500 BC along the southern Gulf of Mexico coast developed into the Olmec civilization by around 1200 BC. Remains of ceremonial cities that included temples and large stone statues date from this time. Olmec society was supported primarily by agriculture. The Olmec developed a calendar and a writing system. They worshipped a jaguar-like god.

Significance The Olmec developed the first historically known civilization in the Americas. Elements of Olmec civilization can be seen in many later Mesoamerican cultures.

c. 1200 BC Phoenicians Dominate Trade in the Mediterranean Sea

Having settled along the eastern Mediterranean coast by around 2800 BC, the Phoenicians developed a loose union of city-states supported by sea trade with the other Mediterranean cultures of Egypt and Greece. By 1200 BC the Phoenicians were the leading Mediterranean trading power. They established colonies throughout the Mediterranean, including Carthage in North Africa.

Significance As a trading people, the Phoenicians mingled the cultures of Egypt, Mesopotamia, and Greece. Their alphabet was adopted, with some modifications, by the Greeks and later the Romans, becoming the basis of our own.

960 BC Solomon Builds the Temple

King Solomon built the Temple to God in Jerusalem, the center of Israelite worship, in which the Ark of the Covenant containing the Ten Commandments was kept. Religion was the foundation upon which the Israelites, and later the Jews, based their society. Belief in one God and a strong code of ethics are central beliefs of Judaism. The standards of fairness, justice, and righteousness central to Judaism have sustained the Jewish people and their religion for more than 3,000 years. Even though the Temple was destroyed in 586 BC, rebuilt, and destroyed again in AD 70, the Jewish religion and people still thrive.

Significance One of the earliest monotheistic faiths, Judaism has had a major influence on Western society and is one of the world's major religions. The Jewish ethical tradition was later carried forward into Christianity and became known as Judeo-Christian ethics.

c. 700 BC Kushite Dynasty Rules Egypt

As neighbors in the Nile River valley, Kush and Egypt had a long history of relations, including a 500-year period of Egyptian rule of Kush. Following the decline of the New Kingdom in Egypt, Kushite kings launched military attacks against Egypt. Around 716 BC a Kushite king named Piankhi rose to power and declared himself pharaoh. This marked the beginning of the Kushite dynasty in Egypt.

Significance Kushite rulers of Egypt sought to restore Egyptian cultural traditions. They built new temples and pyramids and made efforts to preserve Egyptian writings.

509 BC Founding of the Roman Republic

According to tradition, Rome was founded in 753 BC and ruled by a succession of kings. The last of these was overthrown by nobles in 509 BC, and the Roman Republic was born. Over the next 500 years the Republic greatly expanded in size and power and evolved politically to include democratic elements.

Significance As the Republic expanded, it proved unable to reconcile rule of vast territories with the traditions of self-governance conceived for a city-state. Its example—good, bad, and idealized—nonetheless inspired the efforts of later ages to found republican governments.

500 BC Confucius in China

A Chinese philosopher who lived from 551 to 479 BC during the Zhou dynasty, Confucius urged a system of morality that stressed the importance of family, respect for elders, reverence for ancestors, and honest and just government. His teachings were compiled by his followers in the *Analects*.

Significance The body of thought derived from Confucius's teachings, Confucianism, exerted a profound influence on China and other East Asian culture.

500 BC Buddhism Develops in India

Siddhartha Gautama of India lived from around 563 to 483 BC. Revered for having found true wisdom, he came to be called the Buddha, or Enlightened One. For the remainder of his life the Buddha taught others the way to achieve an enlightened state.

Significance From the Buddha's life and experience arose one of the world's great religions, Buddhism. In the centuries following the Buddha's death, his teachings gained wide acceptance in Asia, shaping the cultural life of the region. In recent times Buddhism's influence has spread to non-Asian cultures.

500 BC Persian Empire under Darius

The largest empire to date at that time, stretching from Asia Minor and Egypt to India, the Persian Empire reached its peak under the emperor Darius, who ruled from 522 to 486 BC. Darius reorganized the administration of the empire and recognized a diversity of religions. His efforts to extend Persian rule to Greece, however, met with defeat.

Significance Darius's reforms helped solidify the power of his dynasty, the Achaemenids. Despite defeat in Greece, the Persian Empire remained the dominant power in the Near East for more than a century.

c. 500–479 BC Persian Wars

When Athens aided Greek city-states in Asia Minor in rebelling against the Persian Empire, a conflict began that became known as the Persian Wars. The Persian leader Darius, and later his son Xerxes, sought to punish Athens by launching invasions of Greece. The Persians captured and burned Athens, but in the end the Greek forces, though fewer in number, defeated the Persians in a great sea battle at Salamis and saved their homeland.

Significance Victory in the Persian Wars led to an expansion of Greek power in the eastern Mediterranean and a flowering of ancient Greek culture and artistic achievement.

c. 480–404 BC Golden Age of Athens

Athens reached the peak of its cultural development during the time of the statesman Pericles (around 460–429 BC) and after. Thanks to the reforms of Pericles, Athenian democracy was at its strongest. Greek art, architecture, poetry, drama, and philosophy flourished at this time.

Significance The cultural legacy of Athens is one of the great sources of Western civilization, serving to influence later art, governments, and philosophy.

431–404 BC Peloponnesian War

Following the Persian Wars, Athens transformed a mutual defense league into an empire, earning enemies and starting it on a collision course with Sparta, its rival for dominance in the Greek world. In 31 BC the rivalry between Athens and Sparta erupted into war, which lasted for 27 years. Ultimately Sparta, with assistance from Persia, was able to cut off food supplies to Athens. This forced Athens to surrender to Sparta in 404 BC.

Significance The Peloponnesian War was the watershed moment in the struggle for power in ancient Greece. Weakened, the Greek city-states declined and were eventually conquered by Philip II of Macedon.

330 BC Alexander the Great's Conquests

After inheriting a united Greece following the assassination in 336 BC of his father, Philip II of Macedon, Alexander set out to conquer the known world. By 331 BC Alexander and his armies had conquered Asia Minor, Syria, Egypt, Mesopotamia, and all of the lands of the Persian Empire east to the Indus River. For his political and military successes he was called Alexander the Great. He ruled over his vast empire until his death in 323 BC.

Significance Alexander's conquests spread Greek culture from the Mediterranean Sea to India. This Hellenistic, or Greek-like, culture thrived between the time of Alexander's death and the Roman conquest of Greece in 146 BC.

218–201 BC Second Punic War

Rome's expanding borders and increased influence in the western Mediterranean brought the Republic into conflict with Carthage, a powerful commercial city in North Africa. In 218 BC the second of three major wars between the two powers began when the Carthaginian general Hannibal invaded Roman territory. Rome countered by invading North Africa and forcing Hannibal to return to his city. In 202 BC the Romans, led by Scipio, defeated Hannibal and his army at Zama, near Carthage.

Significance The Second Punic War established Rome as the most powerful force in the western Mediterranean. Within 100 years Rome brought the rest of the Mediterranean region under its control.

27 BC Augustus Becomes Rome's Emperor

When the Roman leader Julius Caesar was assassinated in 44 BC, Octavian, his grandnephew and chosen heir, struggled initially to consolidate his own rule. By 31 BC Octavian had quelled unrest in the Roman territories and defeated both his rivals for power. In 27 BC the Roman Senate officially conferred on him the title Augustus, which means "the revered one." Under Augustus the Roman Republic became the Roman Empire.

Significance The roughly 200-year period of political stability in the Roman Empire known as the Pax Romana began with the reign of Augustus.

c. AD 30 Jesus of Nazareth Preaches

Around AD 30, in the Roman province of Judea, Jesus of Nazareth, a Jewish teacher and prophet, began attracting followers. According to the Gospels of the New Testament, he preached a message of repentance and love of God and neighbor. A few years after he began teaching, Jesus was put to death by the Romans.

Significance The story of Jesus and his teachings are the basis for one of the world's great religions. Today over 2 billion people are Christians.

c. AD 47–62 Paul Spreads Christianity

Saul, a Jewish religious official from Tarsus in Asia Minor, at first opposed the spread of Christian beliefs. Better known by his Greek name Paul, he converted to Christianity and devoted his life to preaching and helped establish Christian churches throughout the eastern Mediterranean. Paul also wrote many of the letters that are part of the New Testament. He was imprisoned, and likely executed, by the Romans around 62.

Significance Through his journeys and writings, Paul played a key role in the development of Christian thought and the spread of Christianity in parts of the Roman empire.

250–900 Maya Classic Age

Early Maya villages on the Yucatán Peninsula of Mesoamerica gave rise, though increased trade, to larger towns and cities. During the Maya Classic Age, which lasted from 250 to 900, there were as many as 40 Maya cities with 5,000 to 50,000 inhabitants each. The cities had stone pyramids, temples, palaces, and plazas for public gatherings. Canals controlled the flow of water. Mayans developed systems of astronomy and mathematics to aid in their religious practices. By 900, for uncertain reasons, the Maya civilization rapidly declined.

Significance The Maya were one of the great ancient civilizations of the Western Hemisphere. Today their descendants in Mexico, Belize, and Guatemala still speak variants of the Maya language.

312 Constantine Converts to Christianity

In 284 the Roman Empire was divided in two. Following the death of his father in 306, Constantine became emperor of the Western Roman Empire. The eastern emperor, however, refused to recognize his status and he was forced to contend with a series of rivals. Constantine met one such rival in battle in 312. Before the battle he is said to have had a vision that would later lead him to convert to Christianity. He triumphed and the following year issued the Edict of Milan declaring Christianity to be a legal religion within the empire.

Significance With legal status and support in Rome, the Christian religion, once persecuted and suppressed, was able to grow and flourish. By the end of the fourth century it was the official religion of the Roman Empire.

476 Fall of the Western Roman Empire

Nearly a century of invasions by peoples expanding their territory left the Western Roman Empire in a severely weakened state. In 410 a Germanic people known as the Visigoths captured the city of Rome. The Western Empire continued to be plagued by invaders through 476. In that year a Germanic commander overthrew Romulus Augustulus, the last Roman emperor in the West.

Significance The fall of the Western Roman Empire fractured the unity of the Roman world and marked the beginning of a period in Europe when there were no strong central governments.

529–535 Justinian Preserves Roman Laws

The Eastern Roman Empire, called the Byzantine Empire, carried on after the fall of the Western Roman Empire. Its leaders sought to preserve the power and glory of Rome in the east. In about 529 the emperor Justinian had his scholars begin compiling the laws of the Roman Empire. The result was Justinian's Code. The collection of older laws was issued in Latin; newer ones were issued in Greek, the language of the Byzantines. Central to the code was the idea that established laws prevent people from being subject to the whims of their leaders.

Significance By establishing a clear reference for judicial decisions, Justinian's Code enhanced the stability of the Byzantine Empire. It later influenced legal systems throughout Europe.

622 Muhammad Leaves Mecca

According to Islamic tradition, around 610 an Arab merchant named Muhammad received a calling from God. He began preaching a monotheistic faith to the people of his home city of Mecca, on the Arabian Peninsula. The pagan rulers of Mecca were not receptive to his teachings and harassed Muhammad and his followers, who were called Muslims. In 622 Muhammad left Mecca for the town of Medina, where Islam gained a larger following.

Significance The journey of Muhammad from Mecca to Medina is known as the hegira. Later, Muslims marked the year in which the hegira took place as the first year of the Islamic calendar.

634–711 Spread of Islam

Following Muhammad's death, his successors, known as caliphs, led Arab armies in a rapid conquest of much of the Byzantine Empire, including North Africa, and the Persian Empire. The new Muslim empire stretched as far east as India and as far west as the Atlantic Ocean. In 711 Muslim forces conquered Spain, leading to the development of Muslim civilization in southern Europe.

Significance As Arabic language and Muslim patterns of life became prominent, the conquered peoples slowly converted to Islam. In many of those lands, Islam remains the majority religion today and provides a basis for shared cultural identity.

c. 661–680 Sunni-Shia Split

Disputes over the succession as caliph eventually led to the division of Muslims into several groups. Sunni Muslims accepted the legitimacy of the first four caliphs; Shia Muslims, who considered only Ali a rightful leader, did not. The deaths of Ali (661) and his son Husayn (680) widened the rift. Differing opinions among early Muslims regarding proper theological and religious ideas solidified the differences between Sunni and Shia groups.

Significance Today Sunnis and Shias continue to be the main groups of Muslims, with Sunni Muslims accounting for about 90 percent of Muslims. Shia Muslims live mainly in Iran, Iraq, Lebanon, the Arabian Peninsula, India, and Pakistan.

750–1258 Abbasid Caliphate

The first dynasty of caliphs, the Umayyads, oversaw the initial expansion of the caliphate. In 747 a competing family, the Abbasids, with the support of the Shia, began a rebellion against the Umayyads. By 750 the head of the Abbasid family had become caliph over the Muslim empire, with the Umayyads surviving only in Spain. The Abbasids moved the capital of the caliphate from Damascus to the new city of Baghdad. The Abbasids remained in power, which progressively diminished, until 1258, when Baghdad was overrun by Mongol invaders.

Significance The Abbasid Caliphate ushered in a golden age for the Muslim Empire. Art, literature, music, and scholarship thrived in the caliphate.

800 Charlemagne Crowned Emperor

Charlemagne inherited the Frankish throne from his father in 768. After gaining greater power upon his brother's death, he sought to carry out his vision of building a new Rome. He conquered the Lombards, Saxons, and Avars before finally being repelled by the Moors in Spain. In 799 a new pope, Leo III, asked Charlemagne for help in fighting off opposition to his papacy. Charlemagne obliged, the next year the pope crowned him Emperor of the Romans.

Significance Charlemagne's coronation by the pope granted legitimacy to his conquests and solidified his rule. Charlemagne's realm was the basis of what became known as the Holy Roman Empire, which lasted in various guises until 1806.

c. 800–1591 West African Trading States

In West Africa, along the gold-rich banks of the Niger River, a succession of three powerful kingdoms arose: Ghana, Mali, and Songhai. Control of trans-Saharan trade gave all three their power. Ghana reached its peak under Tunka Manin in about 1067. Early in the 13th century Ghana was overtaken by Mali's empire; its greatest ruler was Mansa Musa, who made a notable pilgrimage to Mecca. In 1468 Mali gave way to Songhai after Sonni Ali captured the important commercial city of Timbuktu. Songhai controlled the trade routes of West Africa until 1591, when a Moroccan force defeated the empire.

Significance Links between West African and Arab traders helped bring Islam into sub-Saharan Africa. The West African trading states developed a rich oral history.

850–1150 Viking Invasions

The Vikings were Scandinavian warriors who, beginning about 850, began a series of invasions of Europe. Many Viking raids were hit-and-run attacks, but sometimes Vikings settled where they raided, as in England and Normandy, France. A Viking leader named Rurik and his clan, the Rus, took control of a town in Eastern Europe. The Rus remained and expanded their domain. From these invasions, the history of Russia began.

Significance The Viking raids destabilized Europe for 200 years. Where the Vikings settled, however, they melded with the local population, contributing customs and language.

850–1250 Manorial and Feudal Systems in Europe

Two related systems governed social relations in medieval Europe. The feudal system, or feudalism, began as a means of mutual defense in the chaos of invasions by Vikings, Magyars, and Muslims. Lords enlisted trained warriors known as knights to defend their lands in return for a fief, a portion of those lands. Lords and vassals, those who accepted fiefs, owed each other service and protection. The manorial system was an economic arrangement that tied serfs, or peasants, to a lord's land. The serfs farmed the lord's land in return for a plot of the lord's land to farm for themselves, the lord's protection, and other services.

Significance The feudal and manorial systems provided the social, economic, and political structures for European society for about 400 years.

c. 1000 Toltecs Dominate Central Mexico

A semi-nomadic people, the Toltec settled in the region around present-day Mexico City around 900. By about 1000 they dominated the region and had spread southward, into the lands of the Maya.

Fierce warriors, the Toltec established three military orders—the Coyote, the Jaguar, and the Eagle—and incorporated military imagery into their art and architecture. They were the dominant power in the region until the mid-1200s.

Significance The Toltec's militaristic culture influenced the late Maya and the emergent Aztec, who eventually established themselves as the dominant power in Mesoamerica in the early 1400s.

1066 Norman Conquest of England

When Edward the Confessor, the king of England, died in 1066 without leaving an heir, Duke William of Normandy, France, a distant relative of Edward's, claimed the English throne. The English selected another man to be their king and William launched an invasion of the island. Backed by a powerful force of Norman knights, he was victorious in the Battle of Hastings in 1066. Shortly thereafter he was crowned King William I of England.

Significance The Norman Conquest ended Anglo-Saxon rule in England. William introduced military feudalism. Over time, a blending of Anglo-Saxon and Norman laws, customs, and language occurred.

1071 Seljuk Turks Conquer Asia Minor

Around 1000 the Seljuk Turks, a Muslim people from Central Asia, began conquering territory in the Middle East. In 1055 they conquered Baghdad, and from there, under the nominal authority of the Abbasid caliph, they ruled Iran, Iraq, and Syria. In 1071 the Seljuk Turks conquered most of the Byzantine territory in Asia Minor. When their power receded elsewhere, Asia Minor, today called Turkey, became the last Seljuk stronghold.

Significance The Seljuks established a system of Islamic schools (called the madrasa) throughout their domain. In Persia their rule led to a revival of Persian as a literary language. Their defeat of the Byzantines was one factor that led to the Crusades.

1095–1291 Crusades

A series of military expeditions from Europe to the Holy Land between 1095 and 1291, the Crusades began when the hard-pressed Byzantine emperor turned to his fellow Christians in Western Europe for help in fending off the Muslim Seljuks. In 1095 Pope Urban II called on Europe's feudal lords to supply soldiers for a war to defend the Byzantine Empire and to take Jerusalem and the area around it, known as the Holy Land, from the Muslims. The First Crusade (1096–1099) succeeded in taking Antioch and Jerusalem. Over the next 200 years at least ten expeditions were undertaken, with varied leadership and diverse purposes. The Crusades ended in 1291, when Muslims captured the city of Acre, the last Christian stronghold in the Holy Land.

Significance The Crusades led to increased trade between Europe and the East. They also spurred political change in Europe, as nobles gained power at the expense of kings.

c. 1200–1294 Mongol Invasions

The Mongol invasions began in the early 1200s, when Genghis Khan and his army began taking territory in China. From there they conquered Central Asia and most of Persia. Other Mongol armies, led by relatives of Genghis Khan, continued the conquests. Kublai Khan finished conquering China, and also captured Tibet and parts of Southeast Asia. Meanwhile Batu, another relative, invaded Europe. He succeeded in bringing Kievan Russia and parts of Poland and Hungary into the Mongol Empire.

Significance By 1294 the Mongols controlled the largest land empire in history. In China, Kublai Khan founded the Yuan dynasty. Kievan Russia remained under Mongol control for nearly 200 years.

c. 1200 Rise of European Trading Cities

Trade in Europe, which had declined following the collapse of the Roman Empire, began to revive following the Crusades. Merchants in Italian city-states like Venice and Genoa controlled the transfer of goods from ships to overland routes; as a result they grew wealthy from trade. In northern Europe, German cities along the Baltic and North Seas created the Hanseatic League to regulate and profit from trade in their region. At its peak the Hanseatic League had 100 member cities.

Significance The revival of trade increased European wealth and power, and brought Europeans into closer contact with the world.

1215 Magna Carta

Frustrated by the demands of King John II, English nobles forced him in 1215 to consent to the provisions in the document known as Magna Carta. The original charter contained 63 clauses, many of which were intended to ensure the feudal rights of nobles. Other clauses, though, sought to protect the rights of all the king's subjects.

Significance In time Magna Carta came to be seen as the foundation of constitutional government in England. The document established that everyone, including monarchs, was subject to the rule of law.

1347–1351 Black Death

Increased trade between Europe and Asia had unintended consequences. One such consequence was the ease with which diseases could spread. The Black Death probably traveled to Europe from China along sea and overland trade routes. The outbreak of this epidemic in the mid-1300s decimated the populations of both continents.

Significance The Black Death severed some of the bonds that held the manorial system together. The shortage of labor gave peasants more bargaining power. Europe's population did not completely rebound until the 1500s.

1350–1600 Renaissance

Literally "rebirth," the Renaissance was a period of cultural renewal starting first in Italy and spreading to all of Europe. Based on the rediscovery of Greek and Roman writings and new appreciation for secular culture and individual achievement, or humanism, the Renaissance inspired advances in the arts and sciences.

Significance The Renaissance profoundly changed how Europeans viewed themselves and their world. The movement's onset represents the close of the Middle Ages, a term invented during the Renaissance to mark its separation from the earlier time.

1400–1500 Inca Empire Flourishes

Having begun as an isolated tribe near Cuzco, in what is now Peru, the Inca, through conquest of neighboring tribes, rose to become a mighty empire. By the mid-1400s the Inca presided over a territory that stretched nearly 2,000 miles along the Andes Mountains from present-day Ecuador to Chile. The Inca are known in history for the strength of their central government, the complexity of their system of roads, and their building skills, shown most dramatically at Machu Picchu.

Significance The Inca Empire ruled 12 million people at its peak, which occurred at the brink of European contact. Ironically, their sophisticated road system sped the Spaniards along on their conquest.

c. 1415–1650 Age of Exploration

Seeking new ways to trade with the civilizations of the Far East, Europeans at the beginning of the 1400s began exploring possible sea routes to Asia. On his 1486–1487 voyage Bartolomeu Dias rounded Africa's southern tip. Later missions led Europeans to America, and ultimately, with Ferdinand Magellan's 1519–1522 voyage, around the world. The Age of Exploration continued through the 1600s with the search for a Northwest Passage that led to the opening of the interior of North America.

Significance The Age of Exploration expanded knowledge of the world and made possible the European colonization of Asia, Africa, and the Americas.

1453 Ottoman Turks Take Constantinople

Toward the end of the 1200s, a new power, the Ottoman Turks, arose in Asia Minor. In the 1300s the Ottomans began to threaten the remaining territory of the Byzantine Empire. They conquered the Balkans and took Adrianople, a Byzantine city, in 1361. In 1453 the Ottomans succeeded in capturing Constantinople, which they renamed Istanbul and made the capital of their empire.

Significance The fall of Constantinople marked the end of the Byzantine Empire. The Ottoman Turks would build a vast empire embracing Egypt, Syria, and much of North Africa that lasted until 1922.

1455 Gutenberg's Printing Press

Though the Chinese developed a printing process in the 100s, printing in Europe exploded after Johannes Gutenberg pioneered the use of movable type in the mid-1400s. Using metal block letters individually laid onto a plate that was then rolled with ink and pressed over paper, Gutenberg began printing copies of the Bible around 1455. The new technology spread quickly. By 1475 printing presses were operating in nations throughout Europe.

Significance The printing press helped make literacy common, spread the ideas of the Renaissance, and introduced a new method of mass communication.

1492 Spanish Unification and Expansion

Ferdinand of Aragon and Isabella of Castile married in 1469 and joined their kingdoms in 1479 to form a united Spain. They used the Inquisition, an investigative body of the Roman Catholic Church, to enforce religious conformity. In 1492 they conquered Granada, the last remaining Muslim kingdom on the Iberian Peninsula. In that year they ordered all Jews and Muslims (whom they called Moors) to become Christians or leave Spain and sponsored Christopher Columbus's voyage across the Atlantic.

Significance United Spain became Europe's dominant power for 100 years. Columbus's voyage led to a Spanish empire in the Americas. The expulsion of non-Christians, however, robbed Spain of much of its commercial and intellectual talent.

1494 Treaty of Tordesillas

Voyages of exploration created conflict as Spain and Portugal staked competing claims over newly discovered lands. In 1493 Pope Alexander VI sought to resolve the disputes by drawing an imaginary line through the Atlantic Ocean. Spain was given rights to all non-Christian lands claimed west of the line, while Portugal was given rights to new claims in the east. The following year, Spain and Portugal agreed to the Treaty of Tordesillas, which moved the demarcation line farther west.

Significance Other European powers largely ignored the line. However, because of the agreement, Portugal was able to establish a colony in Brazil, which is why today Brazilians speak Portuguese, while the rest of Latin America speaks Spanish.

c. 1500–1865 Atlantic Slave Trade

The economies of the European colonies in the Americas were based on plantation agriculture and the extraction of raw materials. Such labor-intensive enterprises required large numbers of workers. To meet these labor needs the colonial powers began transporting Africans across the Atlantic to serve as slaves. In time the slave trade solidified into a system of triangular trade. The journey of Africans from their homelands to the Americas was called the Middle Passage. Conditions for Africans on the journey were brutal, and many died along the way. By the time the slave trade ended in the mid-1800s, some 10 million Africans had been transported to slavery in the Americas.

Significance The slave trade devastated the lives of those who were enslaved and ravaged the countries from which they were taken. In the Americas, slavery contributed to economic development but left lingering social scars.

1502–1722 Persia's Safavid Dynasty

As the 1500s began, a Muslim religious leader named Ismail rose to power over the Safavids, a Shia Muslim clan that had lived in Persia for generations. By 1512 Ismail had succeeded in establishing a Safavid dynasty in Persia. Most Persians were Sunni Muslims, but Ismail proclaimed Shi'ism the empire's official religion. Under Abbas the Great, who reigned from 1578 to 1629, the Safavid Empire reached its peak, with successful wars against the Ottoman Turks. Following Abbas's death in 1629 the empire began a slow decline.

Significance Safavid culture represented a blending of Arab, Persian, and Chinese styles. Safavid adherence to Shia Islam made Persia distinct among Muslim states.

1517 Luther's Ninety-Five Theses

In 1517 Martin Luther, then a 34-year-old Catholic clergyman, posted a list of 95 theses, or statements, critical of the Roman Catholic Church's practice of selling letters of forgiveness, called indulgences. Luther's intent in posting these statements was to spark reform within the church. By 1521, however, Luther's ideas had led to his expulsion from the Roman Catholic Church and sparked the Protestant Reformation. With the break from Rome official, Luther went on to establish a religious movement that became known as the Lutheran Church. Other Protestant movements quickly developed.

Significance With its emphasis on a personal interpretation of scripture, the Protestant Reformation contributed to the growth of individualism. The passions it aroused, however, sparked religious wars that roiled Europe for the next century and a half.

1519–1533 Spanish Conquests in the Americas

In less than fifteen years, Spain overthrew the two most powerful empires in the Americas, the Aztec and the Inca, and established an empire of their own. In 1519 Hernán Cortés landed in Mexico with 600 men. Within two years Cortés succeeded in capturing and destroying the Aztec capital of Tenochtitlán. In 1530 Francisco Pizarro led an expedition to conquer the Inca of South America. By 1533 Pizarro had won the Inca territories from present-day Ecuador to Chile for Spain. Superior weapons, Native American allies, and European diseases that weakened the Indians contributed to Spanish victory.

Significance Wealth from Spain's empire in the Americas fueled Spain's military and political efforts in Europe for 100 years. Disease and exploitation decimated native populations. Over time, a new culture, mixing Spanish and native elements, developed in Central and much of South America.

1526 Mughal Empires of India

Muslim armies entered the Indus River valley as early as the 700s. By the early 1200s the Delhi sultanate extended Muslim rule into the Ganges River valley. In 1526 a Muslim chieftain named Babur led a combined Turk and Mongol army into India from the north. Babur defeated the Delhi sultanate and established the Mughal Empire. Babur's grandson Akbar, greatest of the Mughal rulers, expanded the empire, sponsored inter-religious discussions, and encouraged a blending of Hindu and Muslim cultures. By the early 1700s the Mughals controlled most of the Indian subcontinent, but England's increasing economic and military power was already undermining their rule.

Significance At its height the Mughal Empire ruled as many as 100 million people, making it one of the world's most powerful states. Art, architecture, and literature flourished under the Mughals.

c. 1540–1725 Scientific Revolution

A movement in Europe during the 1500s and 1600s, the Scientific Revolution rejected medieval scholasticism in favor of direct observation of nature and a program of hypothesis tested by experiment (i.e., the scientific method). In 1543 Nicolaus Copernicus (1473–1543) published *On the Revolution of Celestial Spheres,* in which he argued that the sun rather than the Earth was the center of the universe, marks the symbolic birth of the Scientific Revolution. Other notable contributors included Galileo Galilei (1564–1642), who developed the telescope and used experiments to test theories; and Sir Isaac Newton (1642–1727), who invented calculus and codified the laws of motion and gravity.

Significance The Scientific Revolution transformed Europeans' view of the universe, weakened the authority of religion, and, by establishing the scientific method, started an ongoing expansion of human knowledge and technological innovation.

1545–1563 Council of Trent

The Roman Catholic Church responded to the Protestant Reformation with its own reforms. The Catholic, or Counter-, Reformation began under Pope Paul III, who convened the Council of Trent in 1545. The Council acted to correct some of the abuses most criticized by Protestants, such as the sale of indulgences. At the same time, the Council reaffirmed other church doctrines and traditions.

Significance The Council of Trent largely satisfied Catholics' demand for reform. A newly reinvigorated church began to reassert its power.

1588 Defeat of the Spanish Armada

King Phillip II of Spain saw himself as Roman Catholicism's defender. Hoping to depose Queen Elizabeth I, a Protestant, from the English throne, Phillip assembled a fleet of 130 ships known as the Spanish Armada. In August 1588 the English fleet attacked the Armada, causing severe damage. Less than half the Armada returned home to Spain.

Significance The Armada's defeat spared England from invasion, aided its ally, the Netherlands, which was at war with Spain, and began to shift the balance of power in the Atlantic from Spain to England.

1600–1800 Absolute Monarchs in Europe

In the 1600s, as the feudal structure broke down, European monarchs began to assert their right to rule absolutely, without consulting nobles, common people, or their representative bodies. The archetype of an absolute monarch was Louis XIV of France who once famously uttered, "I am the state." Other notable absolute monarchs included Peter the Great (1672–1725) and Catherine the Great (1729–1796), who "westernized" Russia.

Significance By consolidating fiefs into larger kingdoms, breaking down the feudal system, and centralizing authority, absolute monarchs hastened the development of European nation-states.

1603–1868 Japan's Tokugawa Shogunate

In the Japanese feudal system, the shogun was the emperor's military commander and the actual ruler of the country. From the late 1400s, however, no shogun was able to assert authority over rival, warring factions. In 1603 Tokugawa Ieyasu won a struggle for supremacy and declared himself shogun. He introduced changes to the feudal system that tied peasants to the land, outlawed social mobility, and centralized power in his hands.

Significance The Tokugawa shoguns brought Japan about 200 years of relative calm. However, in the 1630s, fearing destabilization that Christian missionaries might cause, they also closed the country to the outside world.

1618–1648 Thirty Years' War

Tensions between Roman Catholics and Protestants frequently erupted into warfare. When Ferdinand II, King of Bohemia and later Holy Roman Emperor, attempted to impose Catholicism on his subjects, Protestants rebelled. Religion was used to further territorial ambitions, as other European nations, including Denmark, Sweden, and France, involved themselves in the fighting. In the ensuing years a series of devastating wars were fought, mainly on German territory. The fighting came to end with the signing of the Treaty of Westphalia in 1648.

Significance The Thirty Years' War devastated the German territories. The power of the Holy Roman Empire was greatly reduced. Its territories were granted sovereignty, forming the foundation for the modern system of European nation-states.

1688 England's Glorious Revolution

During the 1600s the Stuart monarchs of England tried to assert absolute authority over Parliament. The efforts of Charles I triggered the English Civil War (1641–1649), which resulted in his execution. Oliver Cromwell ruled England as a Commonwealth for eleven years, until the Stuarts were restored in 1660. Conflict between king and Parliament erupted anew in 1685 when James II became king of England. Though most English were Protestant, James was Roman Catholic. Fearing a line of Catholic kings, Parliament asked James to surrender the throne and invited his daughter Mary and her husband William to serve as joint rulers. James fled to exile in France, and William and Mary were crowned after signing the English Bill of Rights.

Significance The bloodless transfer of power, known as the Glorious Revolution, ratified Parliament's power over the monarch.

1700–1800 Age of Enlightenment

A period in European history in which belief in rationalism, natural law and natural rights, secularism, and progress held sway, the Enlightenment is also known as the Age of Reason. Enlightenment thinkers, known in France as *philosophes*, included John Locke, Baron de Montesquieu, and Voltaire.

Significance Enlightenment thinkers advocated reforms in government. The influence of these ideas can be seen in the American and French revolutions and in the governments they produced.

c. 1750–1850 Industrial Revolution

An era in Europe and the United States that saw a rapid expansion of industry and machine-driven production of goods at the expense of farming and handicraft production, the Industrial Revolution began first in Great Britain. New technologies such as the steam engine and iron smelting led to advances in textile manufacturing and transportation (railroads and steamboats).

Significance The Industrial Revolution transformed nations like few events before it. Cities grew quickly, and became crowded and unhealthy, as workers relocated in search of factory jobs. Goods became cheaper for a swelling middle class, but workers suffered terrible exploitation.

1754–1763 Seven Years' War and French and Indian War

The rivalry between Great Britain and France for status as colonial powers and the struggle between Austria and Prussia for dominance over the German states erupted into nine years of warfare. In the French and Indian War, which lasted from 1754 to 1763, France and Great Britain fought for control of North America. In Europe the two nations were also involved in the Seven Years' War. Between 1756 and 1763 a British-Prussian alliance fought a French-Austrian alliance for control of the German states of Saxony and Silesia.

Significance In Europe, no clear victor emerged from the Seven Years' War. Prussia held onto the region of Silesia, but Austria made gains elsewhere. However, Great Britain's victory in the French and Indian War brought it control of France's North American territory.

1775–1781 American Revolution

The American Revolution began in April 1775 with the battles of Lexington and Concord. Initially the Americans' undermanned and poorly equipped Continental Army faced numerous setbacks and almost certain defeat. The first official call for American independence came in 1775, leading to the adoption of the Declaration of Independence on July 4, 1776. An American military victory at Saratoga in 1777 proved a turning point, as it convinced the French to enter the war on the American side. Britain's decision to challenge the Americans in the South ultimately proved fatal. It led to the defeat of the British army at Yorktown, Virginia, in 1781.

Significance The American Revolution was the first successful struggle of a colony for independence from its ruler. The United States of America was established as a democratic republic.

1789 United States Constitution Adopted

Seeking to address some of the problems it faced under the Articles of Confederation, the United States drafted a new Constitution in 1787. Ratified in 1788 and officially adopted in 1789, the United States Constitution established a federal system of shared power between the national and state governments. It created a system of three branches of federal government, with the power of each countered by checks and balances. The Bill of Rights, added in 1791, guaranteed key rights.

Significance The United States Constitution ushered in a new era of constitutional democracy. However, this democracy was incomplete. Most white males and all white females could not vote, and slavery was still legal.

1789 French Revolution Begins

French society evolved through the 1700s, but its political institutions remained static. By 1789 the situation proved unsustainable. At the meeting called by King Louis XVI of the Estates General, France's parliament, representatives of the Third Estate rebelled, declaring themselves to be the National Assembly. In July the citizens of Paris looted and destroyed the Bastille prison. In August, the National Assembly adopted The Declaration of the Rights of Man and of the Citizen, which expressed the revolutionary principles of liberty, equality, and fraternity. A series of constitutions transformed

France into a republic. In 1793 the King was executed, and a Reign of Terror against internal opponents of the revolution began.

Significance The French Revolution completely transformed French government and society. Its successes served as a beacon and its excesses as a caution for later revolutionary movements.

1791–1824 Independence Movements in the Americas

From the atmosphere of liberty inspired by the American and French revolutions arose the Latin American independence movements. The first blow came on the island of Santo Domingo, where Toussaint L'Ouverture led a revolt of African slaves that eventually established an independent Haiti. Mexico achieved independence from Spain in 1821, following a ten-year struggle. In South America, charismatic leaders Simón Bolívar and José de San Martín helped push the Spanish entirely off the continent by 1824. Brazil declared its independence from Portugal in 1822.

Significance Latin American independence brought to an end 300 years of colonial rule in the region.

1796–1815 Napoleonic Wars

Out of the chaos of the French Revolution arose the dramatic personality of General Napoleon Bonaparte. Napoleon used his popularity as a military leader to establish political authority in France in 1799. As emperor, Napoleon reorganized the French state and launched a series of wars to gain control of Europe. Great Britain remained his implacable foe, checking his ambitions at sea and supporting a shifting coalition of allies in Europe. The failure of Napoleon's invasion of Russia in 1812 assured his fall. He made one last bid for power in 1815 but met defeat in the Battle of Waterloo.

Significance The Napoleonic Wars hastened the growth of nationalism and of mass armies, as well as the spread of democratic ideals. The Congress of Vienna, a meeting of European Powers in 1815 to establish a balance of power, ushered in a period of peace and political reaction.

1828–1832 Growth of Democracy in the United States and Great Britain

In the United States the elimination of property ownership requirements for voting increased political participation and ushered in the era of Jacksonian Democracy. The period is named after Andrew Jackson, whose election to the presidency in 1828 symbolized the shift in political power in the United States from the elite to the common citizen. In Great Britain, years of agitation led to the passage of the Reform Bill of 1832, which redistributed seats in the House of Commons to provide more balanced representation for the country's urban districts. Expansion of the right to vote in Great Britain came later, in stages, starting in 1867.

Significance While full democracy in Great Britain and the United States would have to wait until the 20th century, the period from 1828 to 1832 represented a shift to more representative governments.

1845–1849 Irish Potato Famine

From 1845 to 1849 a fungus devastated Ireland's potato crop. With much of the Irish population living in poverty and dependent on potatoes as a main food source, a severe famine resulted. Great Britain, of which Ireland was a part at that time, did little to provide assistance to the Irish people. Other food products grown in Ireland were not affected by the fungus but were exported because the Irish people could not afford them.

Significance Of the 8.4 million Irish before the famine, 1.1 million are believed to have died of starvation and malnutrition, while another 1.5 million emigrated to the United States or Great Britain.

1848 Revolutions Sweep Europe

In 1848 the monarchies restored by the Congress of Vienna in 1815 began to unravel. Beginning with the February Revolution in France, a series of republican revolutions swept through Europe. One by one, governments fell and monarchs fled. In Paris, Berlin, and Vienna, the urban poor turned radical. Moderates drew back from social revolution. By August of 1849 most of the old governments had been restored. Austria defeated nationalist uprisings in Italy and Hungary, though it was forced to grant Hungary autonomy and abolish serfdom.

Significance Following the failure of the revolutions, many liberals felt disillusioned. Tens of thousands of people from German lands emigrated to the United States to escape political repression at home. Karl Marx's *Communist Manifesto*, published in February of 1848, foretold a new round of more radical revolutions to come.

1859–1871 German and Italian Unification

In the German states and the Italian states—38 and 9 of them respectively—the revolutions of 1848 had been as much about national unification as democratic change. Through warfare, an uprising led by Giuseppe Garibaldi in the south, and by direct vote, a unified Italian kingdom with its capital in

Rome was established by 1870. German unification was accomplished largely through warfare. Led by Otto von Bismarck, Prussia fought the Danish War (1863–64), the Austro-Prussian War (1866), and the Franco-Prussian War (1870–71). Out of these wars arose a united German Empire in 1871 with its capital in Berlin.

Significance Italian and German unification showed the power of nationalism in the late 1900s. A united Germany became the most powerful country in Europe, triggering rivalries that ultimately led to the outbreak of World War I in the 20th century.

1850–1864 Taiping Rebellion in China

By the 1840s China's Qing dynasty, which began in 1644, had grown weak and corrupt. European powers were able to extract valuable trade concessions, which only made the Qing's weakness more apparent. A large increase in population and poverty produced social unrest. In 1850 a Christian convert who believed himself the brother of Jesus of Nazareth started a rebellion that soon gathered wide-spread support. Fearing the loss of trade that the collapse of the Qing dynasty might bring, Western powers eventually stepped in and helped put down the rebellion in 1864.

Significance The Taiping Rebellion lasted for 14 years, caused terrible destruction, and cost millions of lives. The Qing dynasty never recovered control of the country. Western influence grew. Some of the ideas of the Taiping rebels—for instance, common ownership of property—inspired the Chinese Communists in the 20th century.

1854 End of Japanese Isolation

In 1853 United States president Millard Fillmore dispatched Commodore Matthew Perry to Japan with the intention of opening the country to foreign trade. Fearing the use of force, the Japanese reluctantly agreed to the Treaty of Kanagawa in 1854, which opened two Japanese ports to American vessels for obtaining fuel, shelter, and supplies.

Significance The opening of the two ports allowed trade between Japan and the United States. Within two years Japan signed similar treaties with Great Britain, the Netherlands, and Russia. Japan's isolationism was effectively ended.

1861–1865 American Civil War

The election of Abraham Lincoln as United States president in 1860 led to secession of the slaveholding southern states and the formation of the Confederacy. The Civil War began in April 1861 with the Confederate attack on Fort Sumter. The Confederacy won key early battles, thanks largely to the superior military skill of its general. Northern victories at Vicksburg and Gettysburg in 1863 helped turn the tide of the war. Fighting ended in April 1865, with the surrender of Confederate commander Robert E. Lee to Union commander Ulysses S. Grant at Appomattox Court House in Virginia.

Significance More than 600,000 Americans died in the Civil War, making it the nation's costliest war. Northern victory ensured the preservation of the United States and led to the end of slavery.

1868 Meiji Restoration in Japan

Believing the shogun had failed to stand up to the Western powers, a group of samurai forced the shogun to step down and restore authority to the emperor in 1868. The leaders of the Meiji Restoration wanted to make Japan powerful enough to rival the West. They encouraged the Meiji emperor to implement policies that would enrich the country and strengthen the military.

Significance The Meiji Restoration triggered a rapid transformation of Japanese society. The feudal system ended, educational opportunities improved, and the country industrialized. By the turn of the 20th century Japan had become a world power.

1880–1920 Age of Imperialism

Heightened nationalism, a desire for raw materials and new markets, and a paternalistic missionary zeal all contributed to the rise of Western imperialism. By 1914 the major European powers had divided nearly all of Africa among themselves. Parts of Asia were similarly divided, though many countries, including China, managed to maintain their independence. The United States also became involved in the imperial age by acquiring territories in the Pacific and the Caribbean.

Significance Imperialism drew Africa and Asia into a world economic system whose hubs were Europe and the United States. The relationship between colonizer and colonized, however, was often exploitative and dehumanizing.

1903 Wright Brothers Flight

Orville and Wilbur Wright, two bicycle mechanics from Dayton, Ohio, built the first successful powered airplane. On December 17, 1903, at Kitty Hawk, North Carolina, the Wright brothers made four successful tests of their design.

Significance The Wright brothers and others soon began manufacturing airplanes. Improved designs revolutionized transportation, increased demand for oil, and affected the conduct of warfare.

1914–1918 World War I

Increasingly intense rivalries in Europe, along with heightened feelings of nationalism and a system of military alliances, led to the start of World War I in 1914. The primary opponents were the Central Powers (Germany, Austria-Hungary, and Turkey) and the Allied Powers (Great Britain, France, and Russia). New technologies such as machine guns and four years of stalemated trench warfare made World War I the deadliest war—14 million killed—the world had seen to that point. The U.S. entry into the war in 1917 helped the Allies win.

Significance World War I led to the end of monarchies in Russia, Austria-Hungary, Germany, and Turkey. The horrific number of casualties produced widespread disillusionment. The Treaty of Versailles imposed harsh penalties on Germany, contributing to the outbreak of World War II.

1917 Russian Revolution

Defeats and high casualties in World War I led to revolution in Russia. In the February Revolution of 1917 Czar Nicholas II was forced from power. An interim government was established, but it was ineffectual. In the October Revolution of 1917 the Bolsheviks, a Communist revolutionary group led by Vladimir Lenin, overthrew the interim government and established power. In 1918 a civil war broke out, in which the Bolsheviks prevailed. Collectively the two 1917 revolutions and the years of civil war that followed are known as the Russian Revolution.

Significance The Russian Revolution led to the establishment of the Soviet Union in 1922. The Soviets eventually succeeded in creating a world power, but at a steep cost for some Soviet citizens.

1914–1939 Women Win Voting Rights

As early as 1792, British writer Mary Wollstonecraft called for women's voting rights in *A Vindication of the Rights of Women*. In the United States, the Seneca Falls Convention of 1848 issued a similar call for United States women. However, the first country to grant women voting rights was New Zealand, then still a British colony, in 1893. Between 1914 and 1939, however, 28 nations, including the United States (1920), granted women voting rights.

Significance The extension of voting rights to women placed many societies on a firmer democratic footing. In 1952 the United Nations adopted a resolution calling on all member states to grant women the right to vote on an equal basis with men. Not every nation has complied.

1929–1939 Great Depression

A variety of factors, including reckless investments in stocks, an overreliance by consumers on credit, and a radically uneven distribution of wealth, contributed to the collapse of the United States economy in 1929. The U.S. downturn soon affected other countries, and protectionist trade policies made the situation worse. Countries experienced crushing unemployment and sharply reduced economic output. World trade fell by more than two thirds. For its unprecedented duration and severity, the event came to be called the Great Depression.

Significance In addition to its economic effects, the Great Depression caused political instability in Europe. In Germany, it was one factor in the rise of Nazism and Adolph Hitler. In the United States, the New Deal of President Franklin Roosevelt helped the country avoid serious unrest.

1933–1945 Holocaust

Soon after gaining power in Germany in 1933, Adolf Hitler and his Nazi Party began using the power of the government to persecute German Jews. German conquests early in World War II brought nearly all of Europe's 9 million Jews under Nazi control. In the largest genocide in world history the Nazis attempted to exterminate the entire Jewish population of Europe. This became known as the Holocaust.

Significance The Nazis murdered 6 million Jews in the Holocaust, decimating the Jewish population of Europe. Nazis also killed about 5 million other people from groups they considered undesirable. After the war, many Nazi leaders were convicted of war crimes by an international court.

1939–1945 World War II

Aggressive, militaristic regimes in Italy, Germany, and Japan threatened the uneasy peace that followed World War I. With the German invasion of Poland on September 1, 1939, World War II began. The main participants in the war were the Axis Powers (Germany, Italy and Japan), and the Allied Powers (Great Britain, France, and the Soviet Union). After the Japanese bombed Pearl Harbor on December 7, 1941, the United States entered the war on the Allied side. Initial Axis gains began to erode by 1943. The Allied invasion of France on D-Day (June 6, 1944) and the simultaneous push from the Soviet Union in the east led to victory in Europe in May of 1945. The United States dropped atomic bombs on Hiroshima and Nagasaki, Japan, in August 1945, bringing an end to the Pacific war in September.

Significance With the deaths of 40 to 50 million soldiers and civilians, World War II was by far the most destructive conflict in world history. The United States and the Soviet Union emerged as the world's two superpowers, but competing political systems soon made enemies of the former allies.

1939–1945 Manhattan Project

The Manhattan Project was a top-secret U.S. government program to develop an atomic bomb during World War II. It was motivated by the danger that Germany might be the first to develop atomic weapons. Manhattan Project scientists worked in Los Alamos, New Mexico. They successfully tested the first atomic bomb near Alamogordo, New Mexico, on July 16, 1945.

Significance The creation of the atomic bomb began the age of nuclear weapons. During the Cold War that followed World War II, the United States and the Soviet Union competed in a nuclear-arms race.

1945 United Nations Founded

The failure of the League of Nations to prevent World War II led to calls for a new, stronger international organization. All countries that had declared war on the Axis Powers by March 1, 1945, were invited to the founding conference of the new organization, which was held in San Francisco from April to June of 1945. Conference members drafted a charter declaring the new organization's goals: to maintain international peace and security, promote cordial relations among countries, and develop systems of cooperation for solving a wide range of international problems. The charter was ratified on October 24, 1945, marking the official founding of the United Nations (UN).

Significance The development of Cold War tensions between the United States and Soviet Union meant that the UN never quite functioned as it was intended to. Despite this, the organization has played, and continues to play, a major role in international affairs.

1947–1975 Asia and Africa Decolonized

Following World War II, the economically strained and war-weary European countries had little ability to resist independence movements in their colonies. A wave of decolonization began. British India was one of the first to be decolonized, with its partition into the independent countries of India and Pakistan in 1947. Independence for other Asian nations soon followed. The French were slower to withdraw, fighting losing battles in Vietnam, Algeria, and elsewhere. Decolonization also occurred throughout Africa. By the mid-1960s, most of the continent had achieved independence.

Significance The large number of newly independent countries changed the face of international organizations like the UN. The legacy of colonialism, however, often left the newly formed nations economically dependent and politically ill-prepared for self-government. Violent ethnic disputes and dictatorships were the result.

1947–1989 Cold War

Efforts by the Soviet Union to extend its influence in Eastern Europe and elsewhere led U.S. president Harry Truman to declare the spread of communism a threat to democracy that the United States would resist (the Truman Doctrine, 1947). He also endorsed the Marshall Plan for rebuilding the economies of Europe. The ensuing Cold War was a decades-long rivalry of the United States and its democratic allies against the Soviet Union and its Communist allies. The Cold War led to the formation of new political and military alliances. In April 1949, Western nations formed the North Atlantic Treaty Organization (NATO). The Soviet Union and its allies formed the Warsaw Pact in May 1955.

Significance The Cold War shaped international affairs for decades. The creation of NATO checked Soviet expansion in Europe. The main antagonists avoided a direct confrontation elsewhere, but numerous wars were fought in developing countries as a direct result of the Cold War rivalry.

1948–Present Arab-Israeli Conflicts

Faced with mounting opposition and unrest in Palestine, Great Britain gave up its mandate over the region in 1947. Later that year, the UN voted to partition Palestine into separate Jewish and Arab states. In May 1948 Israel declared itself an independent country. Arab states refused to recognize the new nation. In a series of wars, Israel prevailed over neighboring Arab countries and gained more territory. Large numbers of Palestinian Arabs and Jewish refugees from Arab countries were displaced by the wars. Alternating periods of open warfare and tense quiet have continued to the present day.

Significance Despite peace treaties between Israel and two of its neighbors, Egypt and Jordan, as well as various peace proposals, the region remains unstable. The unsettled matter of Palestinian statehood, the Israeli presence in the West Bank, Palestinian attacks, and hostility from many of Israel's neighbors contribute to the situation's volatility.

1949 Communists Seize Control of China

During World War II, Chinese Nationalists and Chinese Communists ceased their civil war in order to combat Japanese aggression. With the defeat of Japan in 1945, the civil war resumed. In 1949 the Communists under the leadership of Mao Zedong finally succeeded in driving the Nationalists from power. Nationalist leaders and their supporters fled to Taiwan. On the Chinese mainland Mao Zedong's Communists formed the People's Republic of China on October 1, 1949.

Significance Nearly 1 million people died in the Communist takeover of China. Communist efforts to modernize China caused millions more deaths through famine and political persecution. Taiwan grew a vibrant economy but only slowly embraced democracy. The emergence of another Communist state further heightened Cold War tensions.

1950–1953 Korean War

The conflict between the Democratic People's Republic of Korea (North Korea) and the Republic of Korea (South Korea) began when North Korean forces invaded the South. A UN force, made up mostly of U.S. troops, entered the war to block the North Korean invasion. Chinese troops fought alongside the North Koreans. The war ended with North and South Korea divided along almost the same border as before the war. At least 2.5 million people lost their lives in the war.

Significance The Korean War was the first "shooting war" in the Cold War between Communists and U.S. forces. The United States defended South Korea to show that it would protect nations from Communist attack. Following the war, South Korea built a strong economy and a democratic political structure. North Korea remains a Communist dictatorship whose people are impoverished.

1954–1975 Vietnam War

When French colonial rule ended in Vietnam in 1954, the country was divided into North and South Vietnam. The North's government was Communist, while the South's government allied with the West. When South Vietnam's president cancelled elections in 1956 that would have benefited Communists allied with the North, a civil war began. South Vietnam sought and was granted assistance from the United States. U.S. troops began arriving in 1961. By 1968, some 500,000 U.S. troops were on the ground. With victory nowhere in sight and public opinion turning against the war, the United States began withdrawing troops. The last U.S. soldiers left in 1973. Vietnam unified as a Communist state in 1975.

Significance More than 3 million Vietnamese and 58,000 Americans died in the Vietnam War, which also spilled into the neighboring countries of Laos and Cambodia, resulting in the deaths of at least 1 million more people. Vietnam remains a Communist country, but in the late 1980s it began to introduce free market elements into its economy.

1957 European Economic Community Founded

In 1957 Belgium, France, Italy, Luxembourg, the Netherlands, and West Germany established the European Economic Community (EEC). The six members sought economic growth through common policies on tariffs and production quotas. The organization has expanded in scope and ambition over the years. In 1993 it became the European Union (EU), a block of 25 nations with a common currency and common citizenship rights.

Significance The formation of the EEC signaled the beginning of a new era of cooperation among the nations of Europe. As the predecessor to the EU of today, the EEC was important to the formation of modern Europe.

1978–Present Capitalist Reforms in China

Under leader Deng Xiaoping, China began to move toward a market economy by implementing a reform plan called the Four Modernizations. The goal of the plan was to improve agriculture, industry, science and technology, and national defense. Pursuit of these goals led Deng Xiaoping to seek closer ties with the West, including the United States.

Significance China's embrace of market reforms has powered an impressive economic rise, increasing its stature on the world stage. A parallel movement for political reform, however, was cut short by a government crackdown (the Tiananmen Square Massacre) in 1989.

1989–1991 Fall of Communism in Europe

In the 1980s Soviet leader Mikhail Gorbachev attempted to reform the Soviet economy and political system (perestroika and glasnost). The move led to calls for greater freedom in the Soviet Union and Eastern Europe. Under pressure from their people, Communist governments in Eastern Europe began collapsing in 1989. Gorbachev refused to prop them up. The Berlin Wall, one of the most potent symbols of Communist oppression, was dismantled in late 1989. In 1991 the Soviet Union collapsed, as former Soviet republics declared their independence.

Significance The fall of the Soviet Union marked the end of the Cold War. Millions of people in Eastern Europe and the former Soviet Union gained freedom from Communist dictatorships. The United States was left as the world's only superpower.

1994 Genocide in Rwanda

One legacy of European colonial rule in Africa was the establishment of national borders that did not reflect the divisions of African ethnic groups. As a result, ethnically based warfare has been common in postcolonial Africa. The worst case occurred in 1994, when long-simmering hostilities between Hutus and Tutsis in Rwanda erupted. Between 500,000 and 1 million people, mostly Tutsis and moderate Hutus, were killed before the violence ended. Another 2 million people fled the country as refugees.

Significance Civil strife continues to plague Rwanda and its neighbors. The lack of an effective international response to the Rwandan genocide led many to criticize the UN and the major world powers.

1994 Apartheid Ends in South Africa

Apartheid, or legalized racial segregation, became official South African government policy in 1948. A series of laws culminating in the Bantu Homelands Citizenship Act (1970), which stripped black South Africans of voting rights, extended the reach of apartheid into virtually every area of South African life. Opponents of apartheid were treated harshly. Nelson Mandela, leader of the African National Congress, spent 28 years in prison. From 1990 to 1991, South African president F. W. de Klerk's government repealed most apartheid laws. In 1994 Nelson Mandela became president after South Africa's first multiracial election.

Significance The end of apartheid removed the last vestige of white European rule in Africa. The relatively nonviolent transition provided a hopeful sign that other long-standing disputes might one day be resolved peacefully.

1995 World Trade Organization Created

Globalization—the process by which trade and culture link the nations of the world—has been an increasingly prominent part of the post–World War II world. In 1947, efforts to promote free trade and to regulate international trade resulted in the General Agreement on Tariffs and Trade (GATT). The GATT was replaced in 1995 by the World Trade Organization (WTO). The WTO's mandate includes monitoring national trading policies, mediating trade disputes, and enforcing the GATT's provisions.

Significance Globalization is transforming the world, making nations more interdependent and standardizing cultures, and the WTO is a powerful contributor to the process. Critics, however, charge that the WTO provides inadequate protections for labor and the environment and that globalization erodes national sovereignty.

1999 World Population Exceeds 6 Billion

World population has been growing at a startling rate in modern times. It took over 120 years to grow from 1 to 2 billion, but only 33 years to add another billion. In 40 years, from 1959 to 1999, world population doubled to 6 billion—and it continues to grow.

Significance The rate at which world population is increasing has raised concerns about our ability to feed such a large population and the negative effects humans are having on the earth's environment.

2001 Terrorist Attacks of 9/11

On September 11, 2001, terrorists hijacked four American commercial passenger planes. Two planes were crashed into the towers of the World Trade Center in New York City. Another plane was crashed into the Pentagon, near Washington, D.C. The fourth plane went down in a field in Pennsylvania after passengers attempted to take back the aircraft from the terrorists. Approximately 3,000 people, mostly from the United States but from numerous other countries as well, were killed in the attacks.

Significance After the attacks, U.S. president George W. Bush declared a "war on terror." The hijackers were identified as members of al Qaeda, an Islamist terrorist group led by Osama bin Laden and based at the time in Afghanistan. In October 2001, U.S. forces invaded Afghanistan after its government refused to turn over bin Laden and other al Qaeda figures. The invasion toppled the government but failed to capture bin Laden.

2003–Present Iraq War

In 1991 the United States had led an international military coalition that ousted an Iraqi occupying force from Kuwait. A decade later, with Iraq still under UN sanctions for failing to comply with demands to disarm, U.S. president George W. Bush accused Iraqi leader Saddam Hussein of building weapons of mass destruction that could be used against the United States or its allies. Saddam insisted that Iraq had no such weapons but failed to cooperate fully with UN weapons inspectors. Although many nations argued against going to war, the United States insisted that the Iraqi threat be countered. With the support of Great Britain and other allies, U.S. forces invaded Iraq in 2003 and quickly toppled Saddam's government. No weapons of mass destruction were found.

Significance In June 2004, the United States handed control over to an Iraqi government. Over 130,000 U.S. troops remained in Iraq, though, as violence continued. Insurgents carried out frequent attacks against U.S. troops and Iraqi civilians. By 2006, the threat loomed of a prolonged Iraqi civil war.

Using Maps to Understand History

by Dr. Peter Stearns

History is most obviously about time—about when things happen and how change occurs over time. But history makes no sense without place as well as time, since events happen in place as well as in time. This is where maps come in. Maps make place—geographic locations—visible and visual.

Maps are essential in the study of history. They can be used to show specific events, such as battles or wars. They can trace routes of trade, migration, or the diffusion of culture or diseases. They can show change in political alignments, territories, and boundaries. Maps show spatial relationships—where things are in relation to other things. If you want to know if one society is likely to be influenced by another, like Mexico by the United States, look at a map. Much of world history revolves around patterns of connection among regions, and maps help both to illustrate and explain these patterns.

A study of maps can also suggest the possibilities for development that a society might have. Is a region well supplied with easily navigable rivers? Its history will surely be different from a region with fewer or less open rivers. Some geographers argue, in fact, that much of the character of a given society is determined by its geography—whether it will be rich or poor, populous or sparse, centralized or localized. Figuring how far geography defines a region, and for how long in its history, is a key analytical challenge for the historian, and it starts with maps.

Indeed, take a risk, particularly early in your study of world history: try to predict what a society will be like from looking at its features on a map. See how well your effort at geographic determinism works, as you learn about the region's actual history. When you study more recent periods, see if major regions have been able to break through their geographic limits by new forms of technology and organization—or whether, in fact, their patterns can still be pretty well read from their maps.

In the following pages, you will find a refresher on some map and geography basics. Review these concepts. They will help you understand maps—and understand history.

Comparing maps of Europe at two different times can reveal how boundaries shift over time, in this case as a result of World War I.

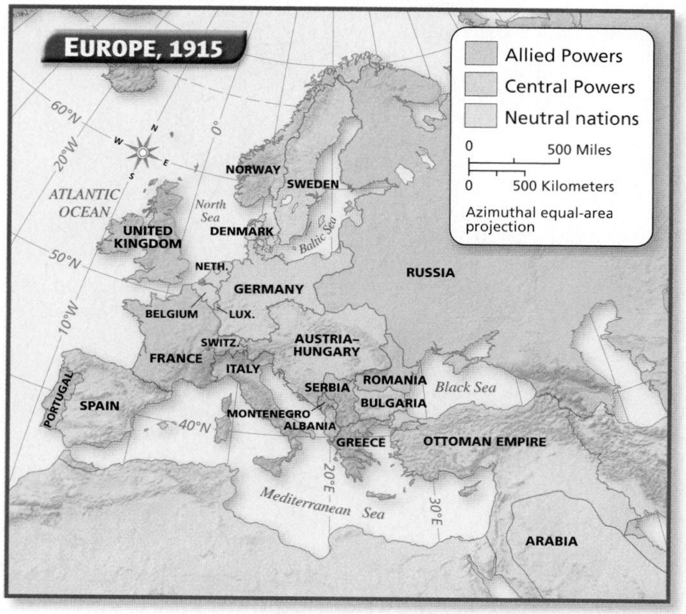

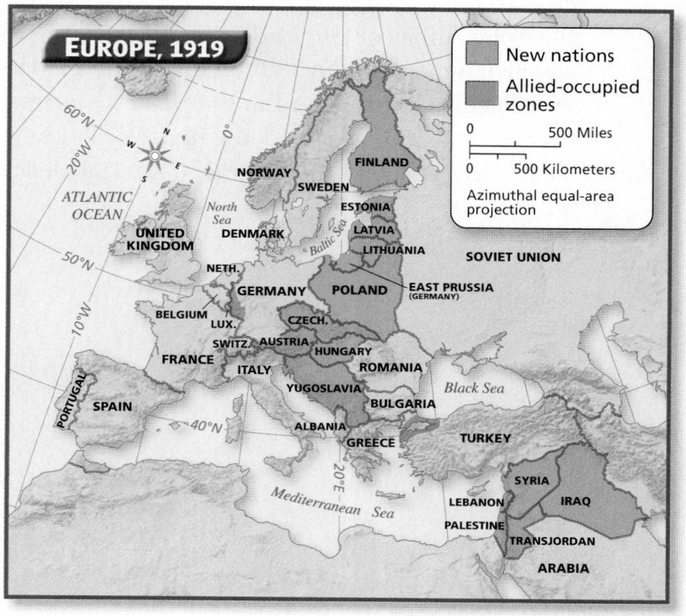

Mapping the Earth
Using Latitude and Longitude

A **globe** is a scale model of the earth. It is useful for showing the entire earth or studying large areas of the earth's surface.

A pattern of lines circles the globe in east-west and north-south directions. It is called a **grid.** The intersection of these imaginary lines helps us find places on the earth.

The east-west lines in the grid are lines of **latitude.** Lines of latitude are called **parallels** because they are always parallel to each other. These imaginary lines measure distance north and south of the **equator**. The equator is an imaginary line that circles the globe halfway between the North and South Poles. Parallels measure distance from the equator in **degrees**. The symbol for degrees is °. Degrees are further divided into **minutes**. The symbol for minutes is ´. There are 60 minutes in a degree. Parallels north of the equator are labeled with an N. Those south of the equator are labeled with an S.

The north-south lines are lines of **longitude**. Lines of longitude are called **meridians**. These imaginary lines pass through the Poles. They measure distance east and west of the **prime meridian**. The prime meridian is an imaginary line that runs through Greenwich, England. It represents 0° longitude.

Lines of latitude range from 0°, for locations on the equator, to 90°N or 90°S, for locations at the Poles. Lines of longitude range from 0° on the prime meridian to 180° on a meridian in the mid-Pacific Ocean. Meridians west of the prime meridian to 180° are labeled with a W. Those east of the prime meridian to 180° are labeled with an E.

Lines of Latitude

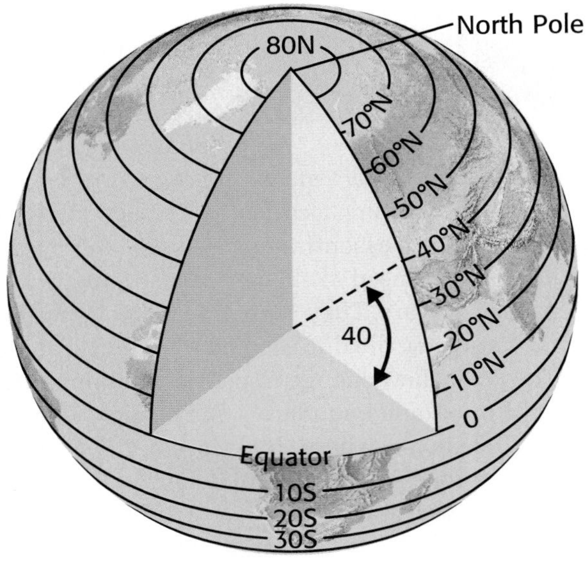

Lines of Longitude

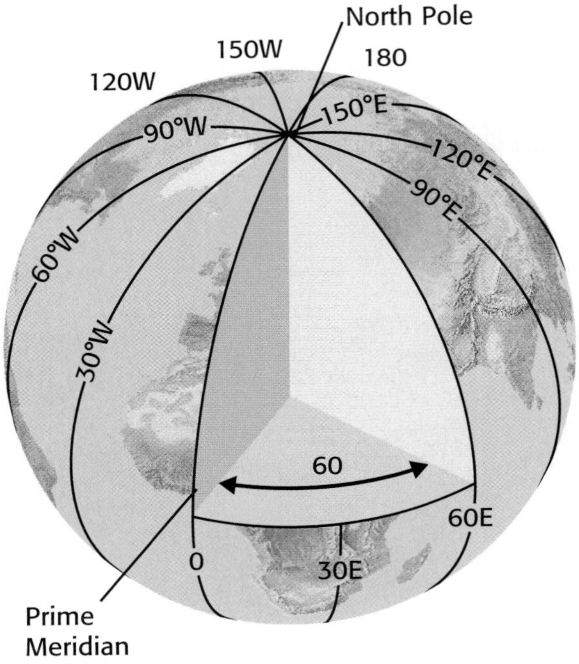

The equator divides the globe into two halves, called **hemispheres**. The half north of the equator is the Northern Hemisphere. The southern half is the Southern Hemisphere. The prime meridian and the 180° meridian divide the world into the Eastern Hemisphere and the Western Hemisphere. However, the prime meridian runs right through Europe and Africa. To avoid dividing these continents between two hemispheres, some mapmakers divide the Eastern and Western hemispheres at 20°W. This places all of Europe and Africa in the Eastern Hemisphere.

Our planet's land surface is divided into seven large landmasses, called **continents**. They are identified in the maps on this page. Landmasses smaller than continents and completely surrounded by water are called **islands**.

Geographers also organize Earth's water surface into parts. The largest is the world ocean. Geographers divide the world ocean into the Pacific Ocean, the Atlantic Ocean, the Indian Ocean, and the Arctic Ocean. Lakes and seas are smaller bodies of water.

Northern Hemisphere

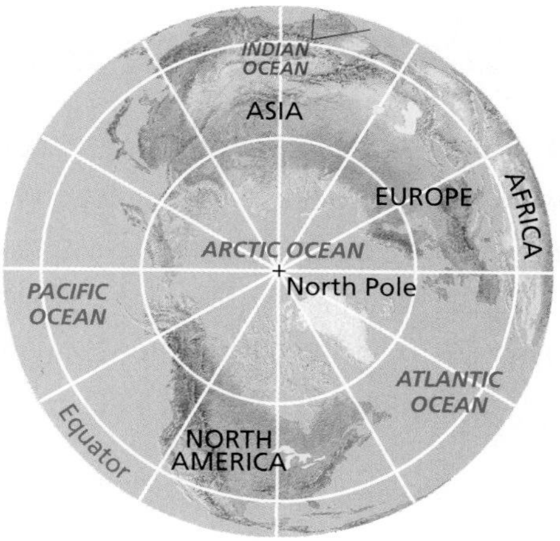

Southern Hemisphere

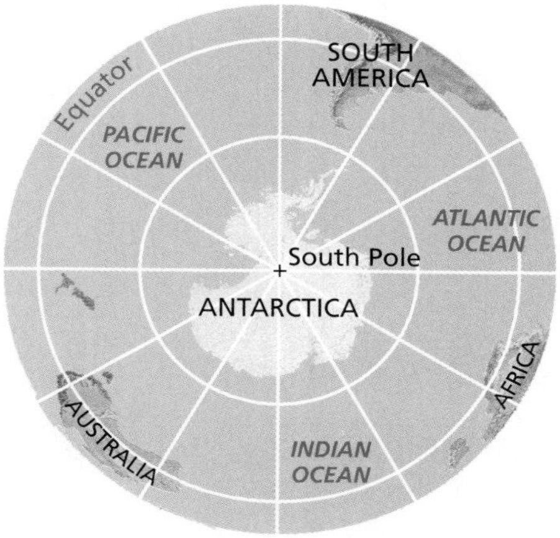

Western Hemisphere

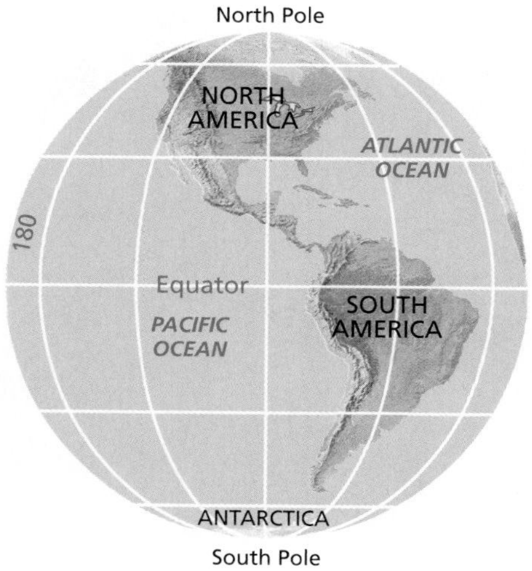

Eastern Hemisphere

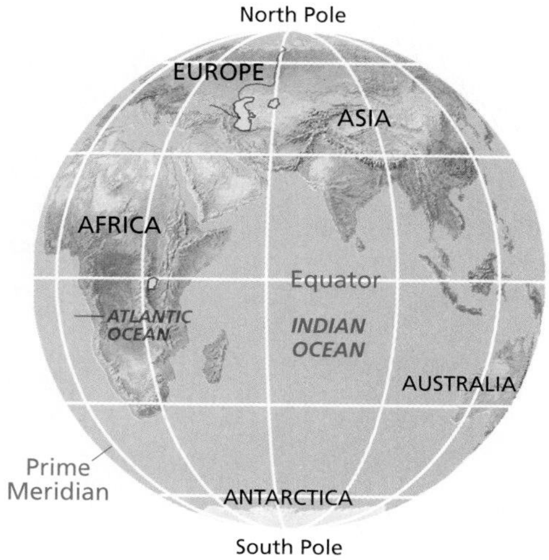

Mapmaking
Understanding Map Projections

A **map** is a flat diagram of all or part of the earth's surface. Mapmakers have created different ways of showing our round planet on flat maps. These different ways are called **map projections**. Because the earth is round, there is no way to show it accurately in a flat map. All flat maps are distorted in some way. Mapmakers must choose the type of map projection that is best for their purposes. Many map projections are one of three kinds: cylindrical, conic, or flat-plane.

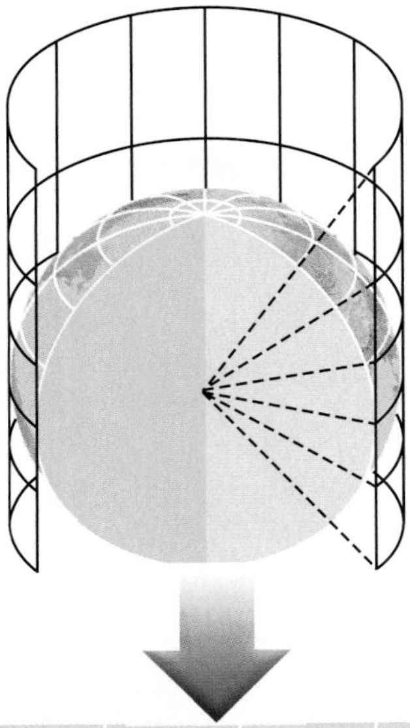

Paper cylinder

Cylindrical Projections

Cylindrical projections are based on a cylinder wrapped around the globe. The cylinder touches the globe only at the equator. The meridians are pulled apart and run parallel to each other instead of meeting at the Poles. This causes landmasses near the Poles to appear larger than they really are. The map below is a Mercator projection, one type of cylindrical projection. Navigators use the Mercator projection because it shows true direction and shape. However, it distorts the size of land areas near the Poles.

Mercator projection

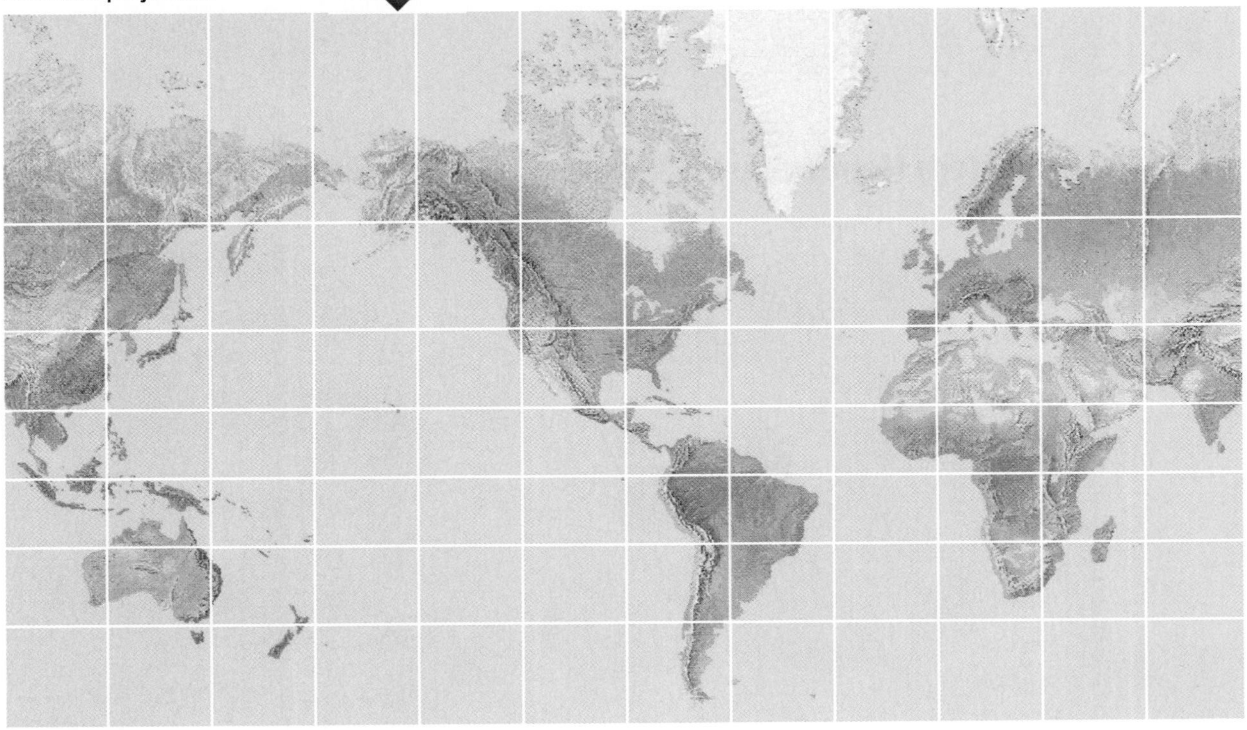

Conic Projections

Conic projections are based on a cone placed over the globe. A conic projection is most accurate along the lines of latitude where it touches the globe. It retains almost true shape and size. Conic projections are most useful for showing areas that have long east-west dimensions, such as the United States.

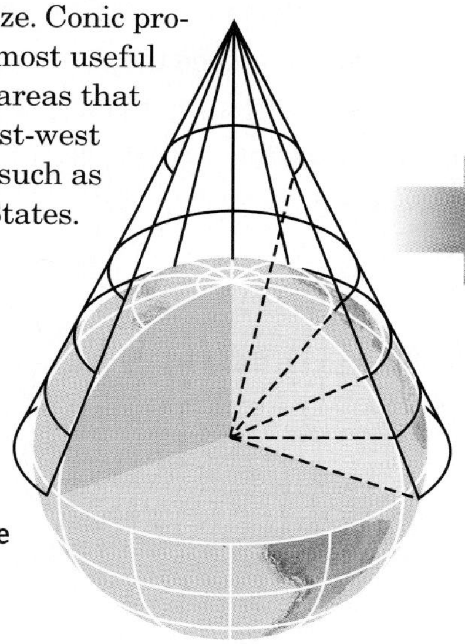

Paper cone

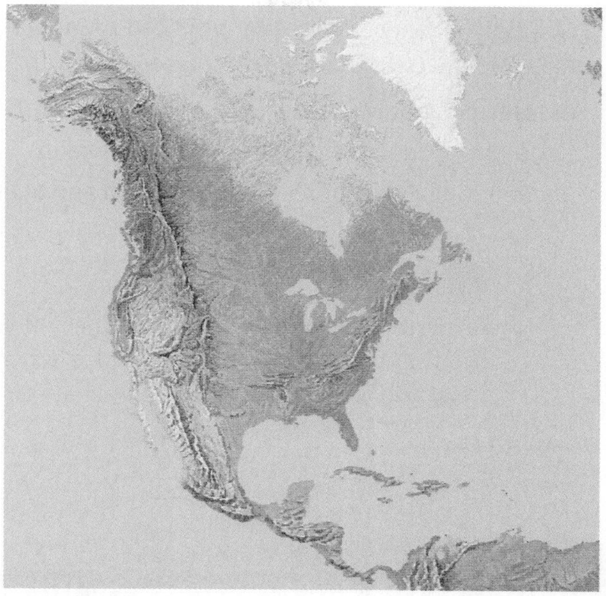

Conic projection

Flat-plane Projections

Flat-plane projections are based on a plane touching the globe at one point, such as at the North Pole or South Pole. A flat-plane projection is useful for showing true direction for airplane pilots and ship navigators. It also shows true area. However, it distorts the true shapes of land masses.

Flat plane

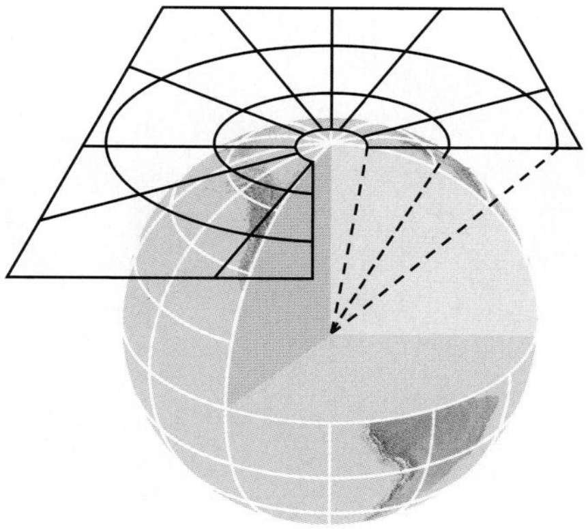

Flat-plane projection

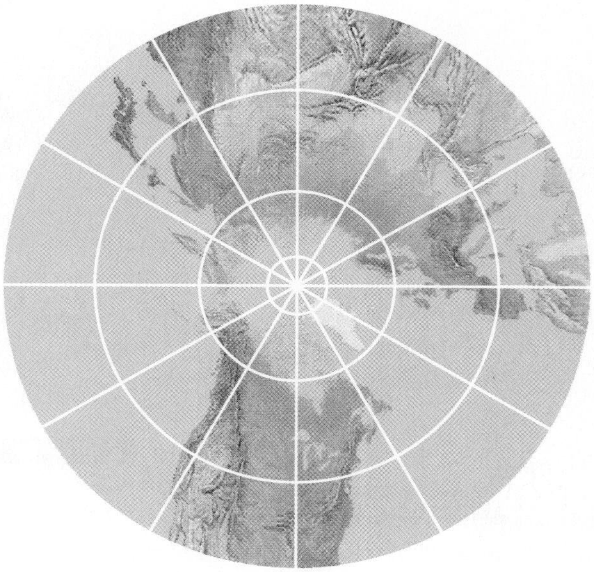

Map Essentials

How to Read a Map

Maps are like messages sent out in code. Mapmakers provide certain elements that help us translate these codes. These elements help us understand the message they are presenting about a particular part of the world. Of these elements, almost all maps have titles, directional indicators, scales, and legends. The map below has all four of these elements, plus two more—a locator map and an interactive keyword.

1 Title

A map's **title** shows what the subject of the map is. The map title is usually the first thing you should look at when studying a map, because it tells you what the map is trying to show.

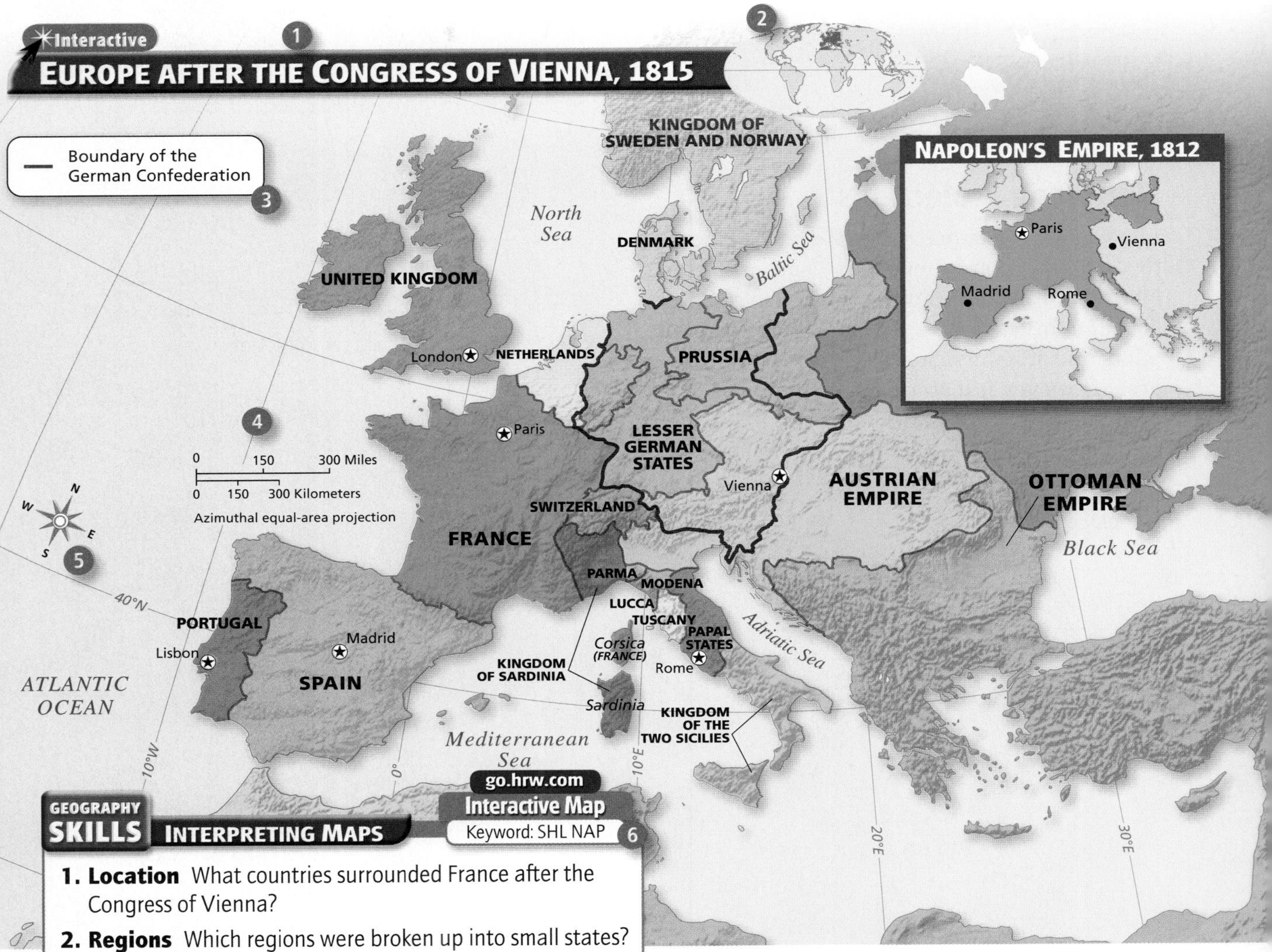

GEOGRAPHY SKILLS INTERPRETING MAPS

1. **Location** What countries surrounded France after the Congress of Vienna?
2. **Regions** Which regions were broken up into small states?

2 Locator Map

A **locator** map shows where in the world the area on the map is located. The area shown on the main map is shown in red on the locator map. The locator map also shows surrounding areas so the map reader can see how the information on the map relates to neighboring lands.

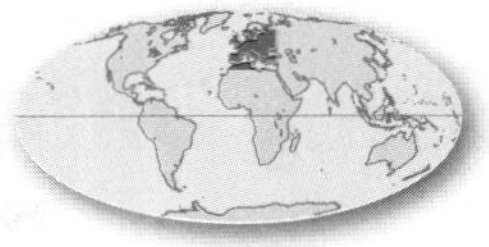

3 Legend

The **legend**, or key, explains what the symbols on the map represent. Point symbols are used to specify the location of things, such as cities, that do not take up much space on the map. Some legends show colors that represent elevations. Other maps might have legends with symbols or colors that represent things such as roads, the movement of military forces and battles. Legends can also show political divisions, economic resources, land use, population density, and climate.

— Boundary of the German Confederation

4 Scale

Mapmakers use scales to represent show the distances between points on a map. Scales may appear on maps in several different forms. The maps in this textbook provide a bar **scale**. Scales give distances in miles and kilometers. The scale is often found in the legend. In this textbook, the type of projection used to make the map is shown below the scale bar.

To find the distance between two points on the map, place a piece of paper so that the edge connects the two points. Mark the location of each point on the paper with a line or dot. Then compare the distance between the two dots with the map's bar scale. Because distances on a scale are given in large intervals, you may have to approximate the actual distance.

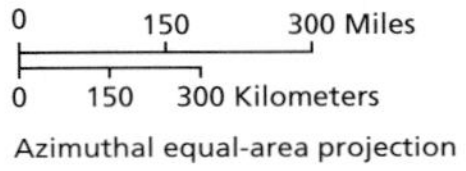

5 Compass Rose

A directional indicator shows which way north, south, east, and west lie on the map. Some mapmakers use a "north arrow," which points toward the North Pole. Remember, "north" is not always at the top of a map. The way a map is drawn and the location of directions on that map depend on the perspective of the mapmaker. Most maps in this textbook indicate direction by using a compass rose. A **compass rose** has arrows that point to all four principal directions, as shown.

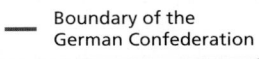

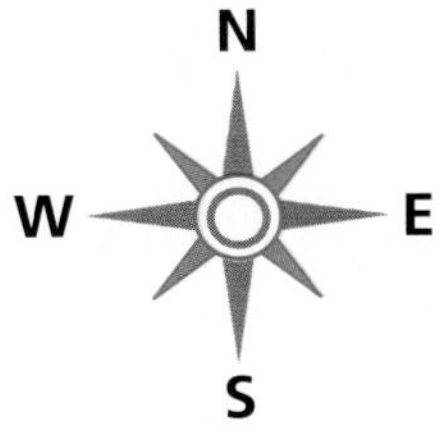

6 Interactive Keyword

Some maps in this textbook are interactive. If you go online to the Holt website and type in the map's keyword, you can learn more about the places and events shown on the map.

go.hrw.com
Interactive Map
Keyword: SHL NAP

Working with Maps
Using Different Kinds of Maps

The Atlas in this textbook includes both physical and political maps. **Physical maps** show the major physical features in a region. These features include things like mountain ranges, rivers, oceans, islands, deserts, and plains. **Political maps** show the major political features of a region, such as countries and their borders, capitals, and other important cities.

Historical Map

In this textbook most of the maps you will study are historical maps. Historical maps, such as the one below, show information about the past. This information might include which lands a country controlled, where a certain group of people lived, what large cities were located in a region, or how a place changed over time. Often colors are used to indicate the different things on the map. Be sure to look at the map title and map legend first to see what the map is showing. What does this map show?

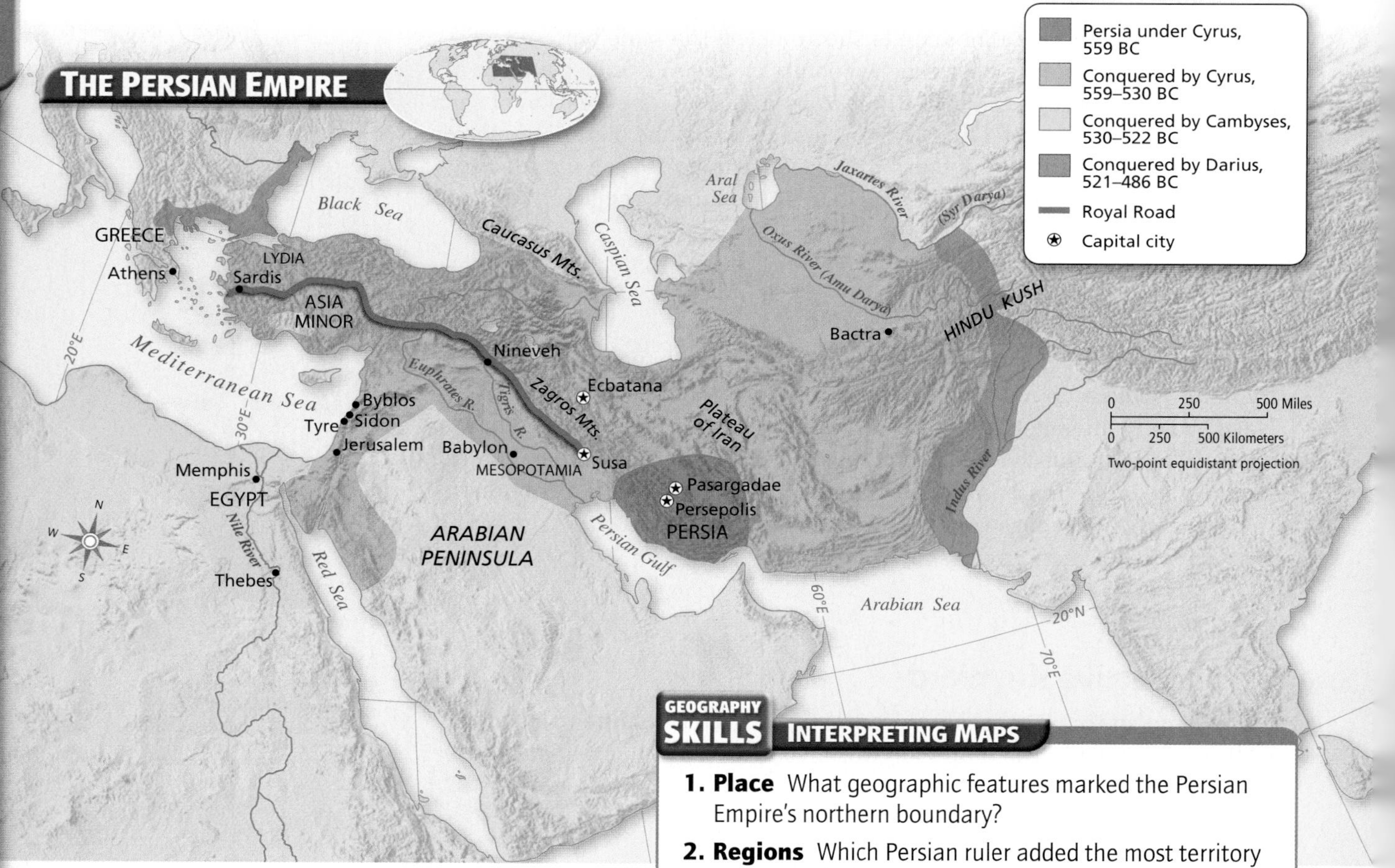

GEOGRAPHY SKILLS **INTERPRETING MAPS**

1. **Place** What geographic features marked the Persian Empire's northern boundary?
2. **Regions** Which Persian ruler added the most territory to the empire?

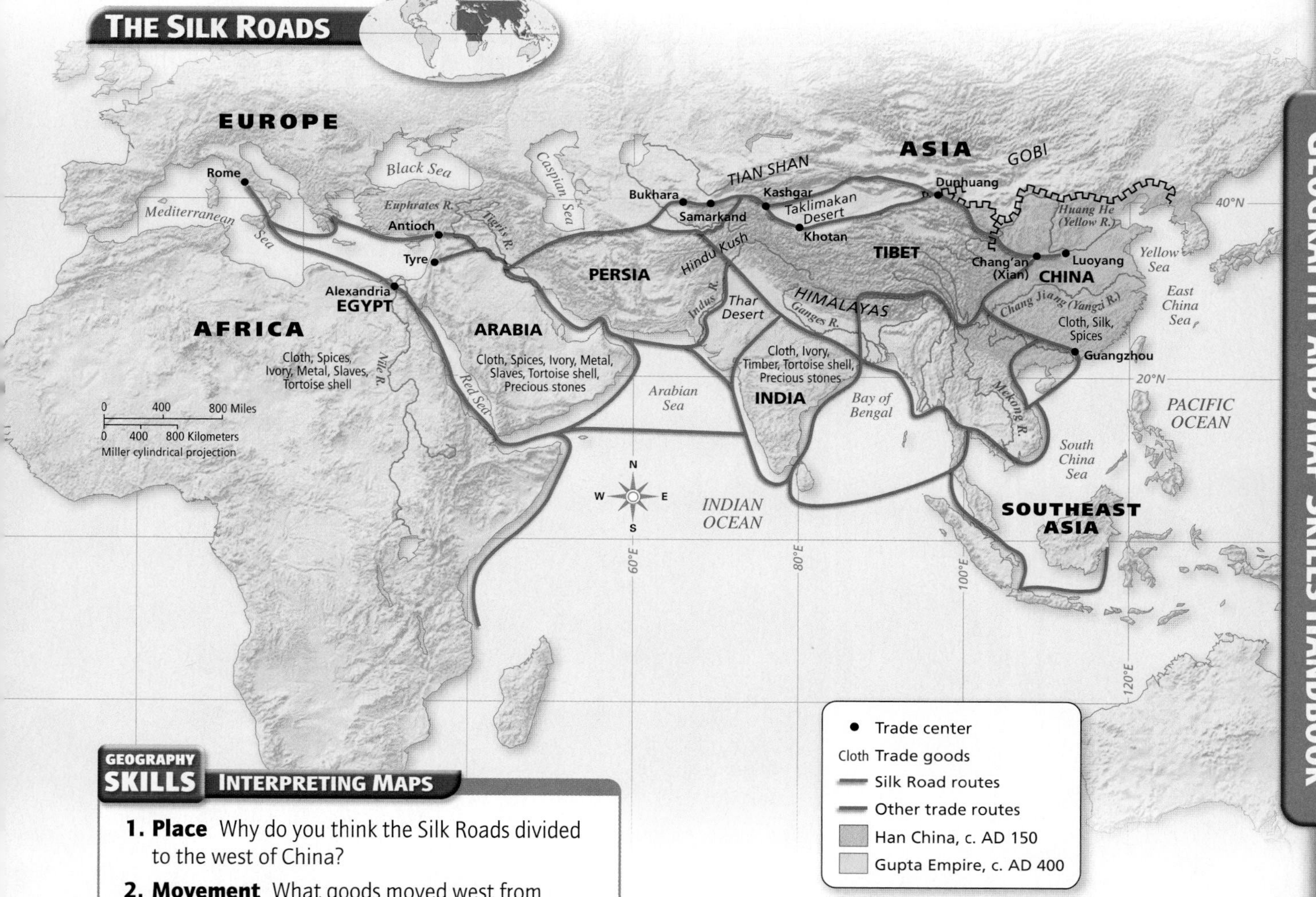

GEOGRAPHY SKILLS **INTERPRETING MAPS**

1. **Place** Why do you think the Silk Roads divided to the west of China?
2. **Movement** What goods moved west from China over the Silk Roads?

Route Map

One special type of historical map is called a route map. A route map, like the one above, shows the route, or path, that someone or something followed. Route maps can show things like trade routes, invasion routes, or the journeys and travels of people. The routes on the map are usually shown with an arrow. If more than one route is shown, several arrows of different colors may be used. What does this route map show?

The maps in this textbook will help you study and understand history. By working with these maps, you will see where important events happened, where empires rose and fell, and where people moved. In studying these maps, you will learn how geography has influenced history.

Geographic Dictionary

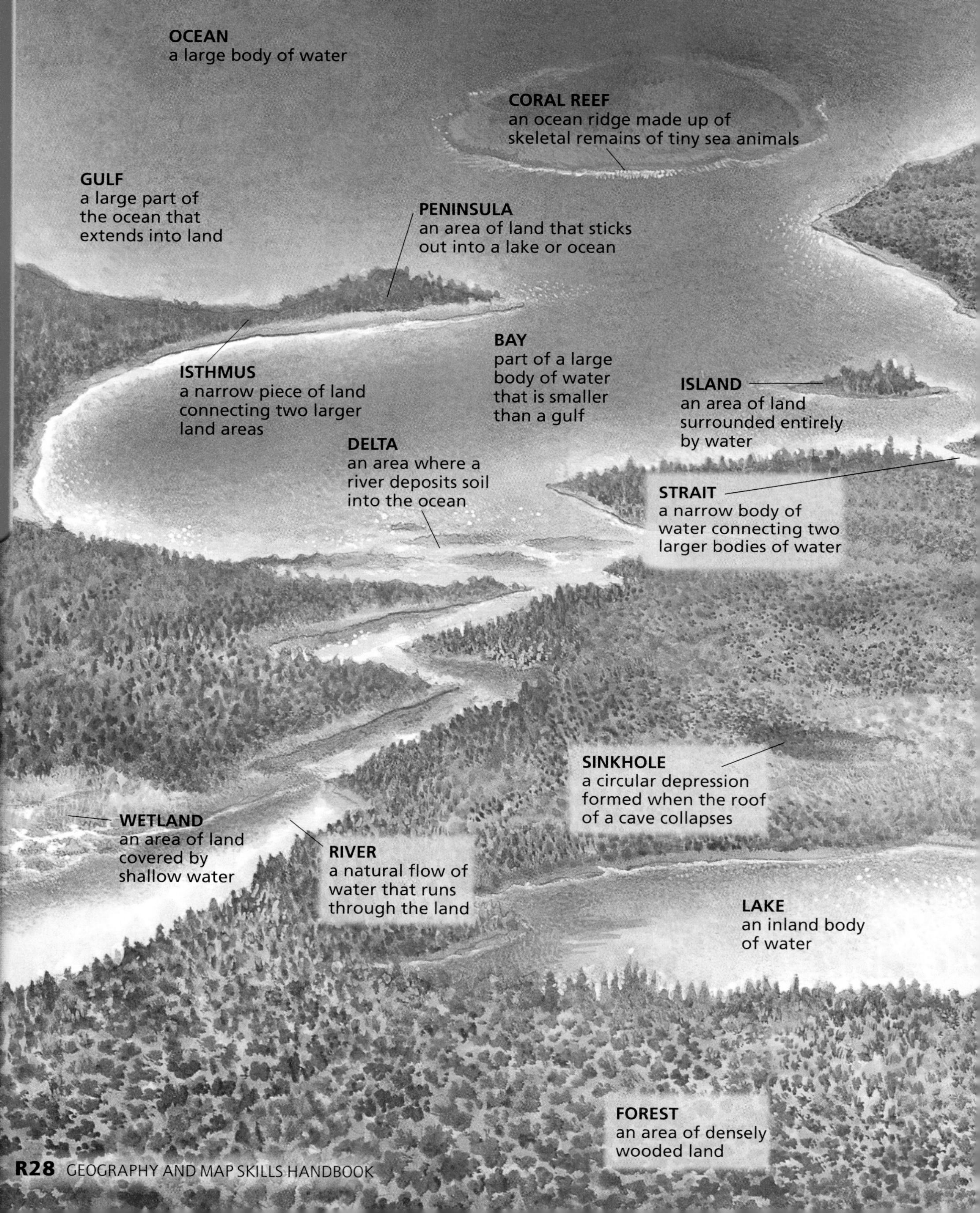

OCEAN
a large body of water
CORAL REEF
an ocean ridge made up of skeletal remains of tiny sea animals
GULF
a large part of the ocean that extends into land
PENINSULA
an area of land that sticks out into a lake or ocean
BAY
part of a large body of water that is smaller than a gulf
ISTHMUS
a narrow piece of land connecting two larger land areas
ISLAND
an area of land surrounded entirely by water
DELTA
an area where a river deposits soil into the ocean
STRAIT
a narrow body of water connecting two larger bodies of water
SINKHOLE
a circular depression formed when the roof of a cave collapses
WETLAND
an area of land covered by shallow water
RIVER
a natural flow of water that runs through the land
LAKE
an inland body of water
FOREST
an area of densely wooded land

COAST
an area of land near the ocean
MOUNTAIN
an area of rugged land that generally rises higher than 2,000 feet
VALLEY
an area of low land between hills or mountains
GLACIER
a large area of slow-moving ice
VOLCANO
an opening in Earth's crust where lava, ash, and gases erupt
CANYON
a deep, narrow valley with steep walls
HILL
a rounded, elevated area of land smaller than a mountain
PLAIN
a nearly flat area
DUNE
a hill of sand shaped by wind
OASIS
an area in the desert with a water source
DESERT
an extremely dry area with little water and few plants
PLATEAU
a large, flat, elevated area of land

Themes and Essential Elements of Geography

by Dr. Christopher L. Salter

To study the world, geographers have identified 5 key themes, 6 essential elements, and 18 geography standards.

"How should we teach and learn about geography?" Professional geographers have worked hard over the years to answer this important question.

In 1984 a group of geographers identified the 5 Themes of Geography. These themes did a wonderful job of laying the groundwork for good classroom geography instruction. Teachers used the 5 Themes in classrooms, and geographers taught workshops on how to apply the 5 themes in everyday life.

By the early 1990s, however, some geographers felt the 5 Themes were too broad. They created the 18 Geography Standards and the 6 Essential Elements. The 18 Geography Standards include more detailed information about what geography is, and the 6 Essential Elements are like a bridge between the 5 Themes and 18 Standards.

Look at the chart to the right. It shows how each of the 5 Themes connects to the 6 Essential Elements and 18 Geography Standards. For example, the theme of Location is related to The World in Spatial Terms and, through it, to the first three Standards. Study the chart carefully to see how the other Themes, Elements, and Standards are related.

The last Essential Element and the last two Standards cover The Uses of Geography. These key parts of geography were not covered by the 5 Themes. They emphasize how geographical knowledge can be applied to the study of history and current events and also be used to plan for the future.

5 Themes of Geography

Location The theme of location describes where something is.

Place Place describes the features that make a site unique.

Regions Regions are areas that share common characteristics.

Movement This theme looks at how and why people and things move.

Human-Environment Interaction People interact with their environment in many ways.

6 Essential Elements

18 Geography Standards

I. The World in Spatial Terms

1. How to use maps and other tools
2. How to use mental maps to organize information
3. How to analyze the spatial organization of people, places, and environments

II. Places and Regions

4. The physical and human characteristics of places
5. How people create regions to interpret Earth
6. How culture and experience influence people's perceptions of places and regions

III. Physical Systems

7. The physical processes that shape Earth's surface
8. The distribution of ecosystems on Earth

IV. Human Systems

9. The characteristics, distribution, and migration of human populations
10. The complexity of Earth's cultural mosaics
11. The patterns and networks of economic interdependence on Earth
12. The patterns of human settlement
13. The forces of cooperation and conflict

V. Environment and Society

14. How human actions modify the physical environment
15. How physical systems affect human systems
16. The distribution and meaning of resources

VI. The Uses of Geography

17. How to apply geography to interpret the past
18. How to apply geography to interpret the present and plan for the future

World: Political

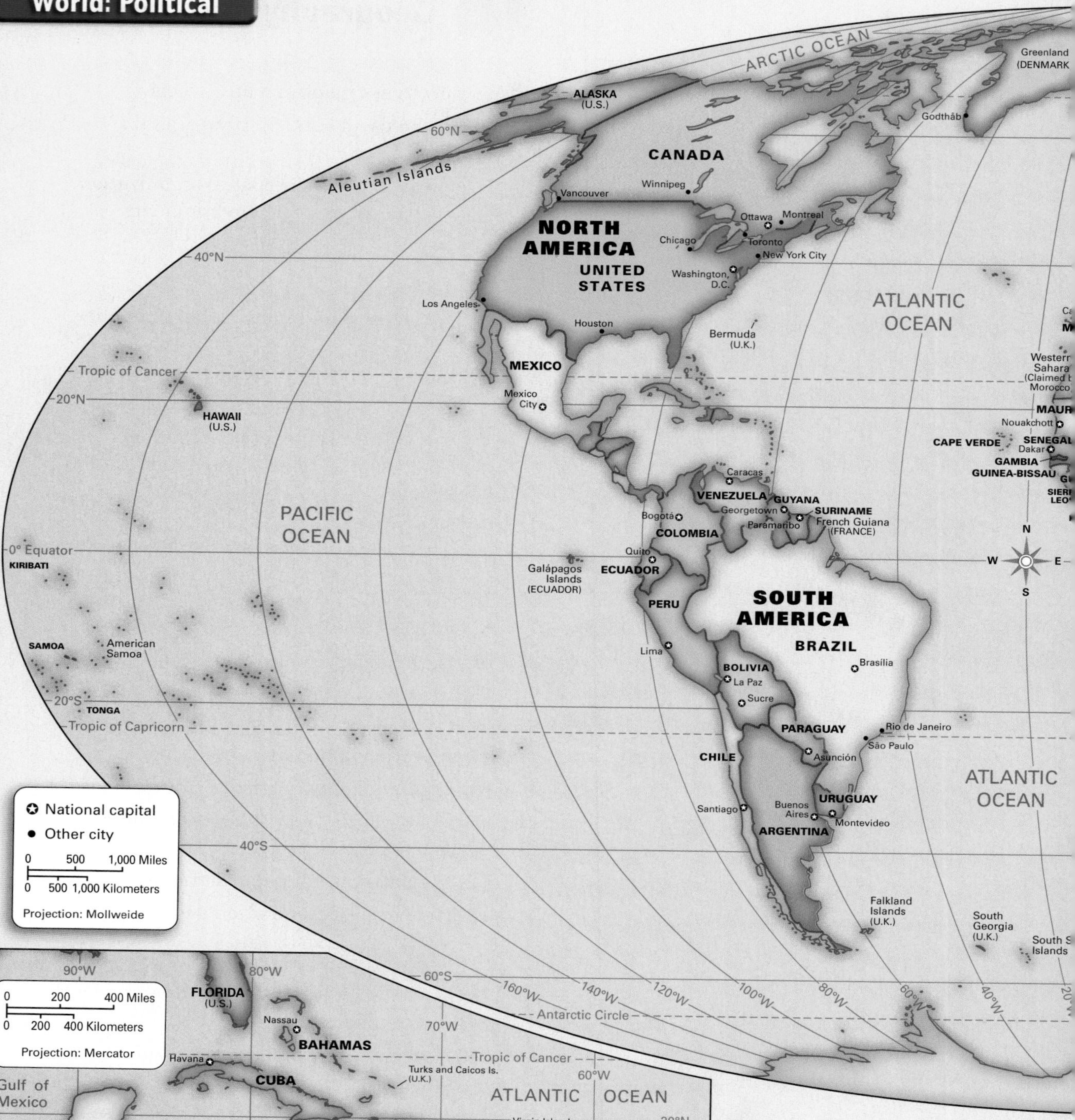

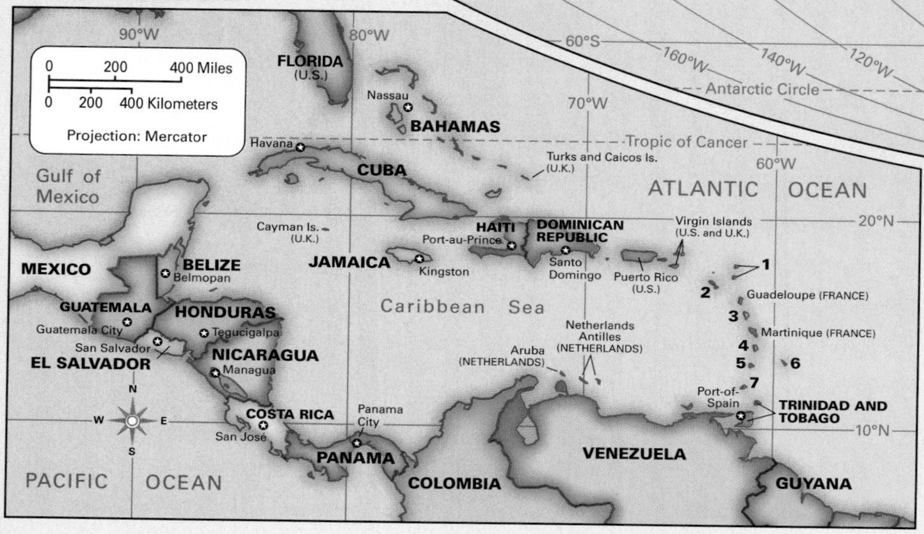

	COUNTRY	CAPITAL
1	Antigua and Barbuda	St. Johns
2	St. Kitts and Nevis	Basseterre
3	Dominica	Roseau
4	St. Lucia	Castries
5	St. Vincent and the Grenadines	Kingstown
6	Barbados	Bridgetown
7	Grenada	St. George's

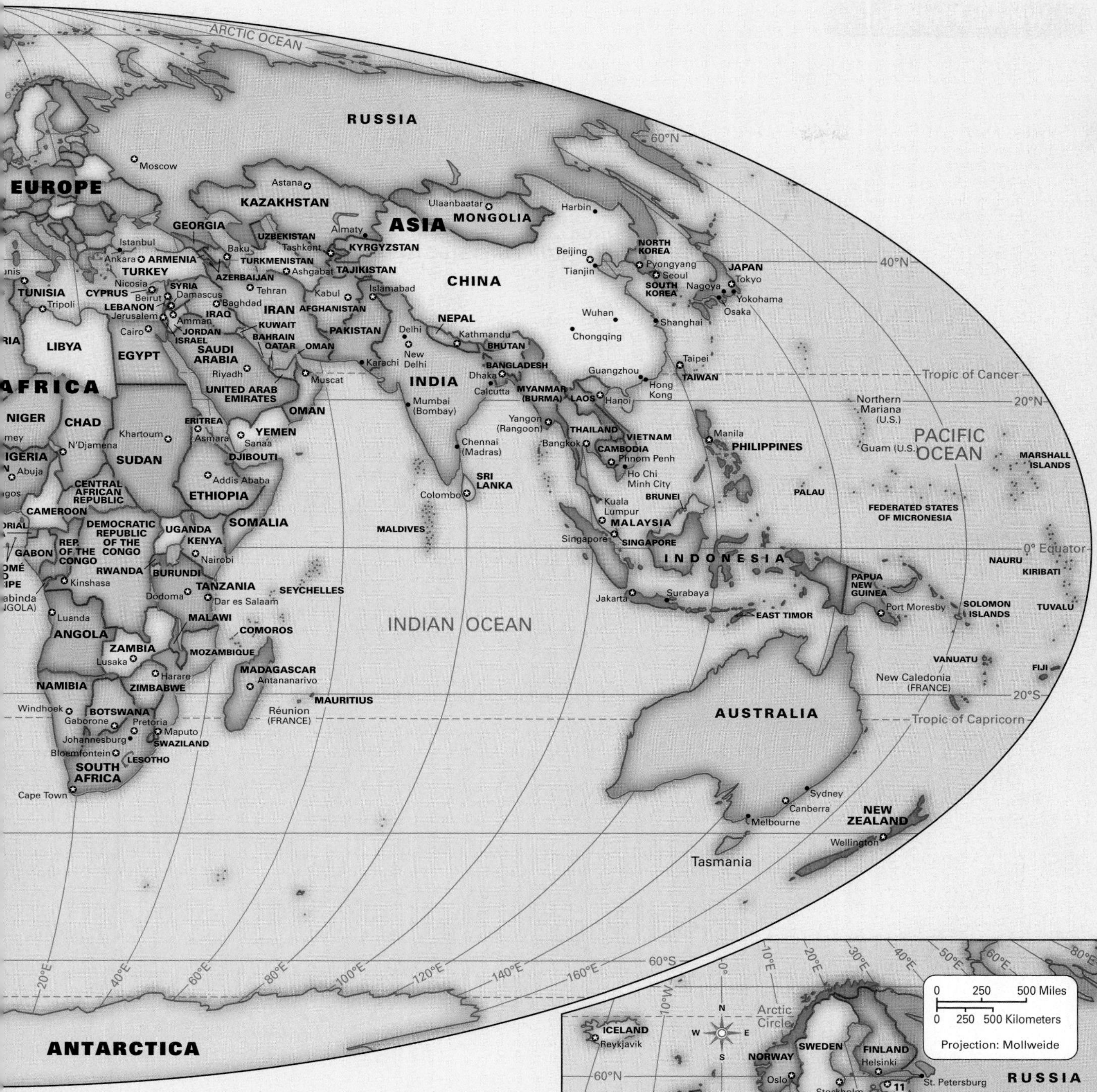

	COUNTRY	CAPITAL
1	Czech Republic	Prague
2	Slovakia	Bratislava
3	Slovenia	Ljubljana
4	Croatia	Zagreb
5	Bosnia and Herzegovina	Sarajevo
6	Macedonia	Skopje
7	Serbia	Belgrade
8	Montenegro	Podgorica
9	Lithuania	Vilnius
10	Latvia	Riga
11	Estonia	Tallinn

World: Physical

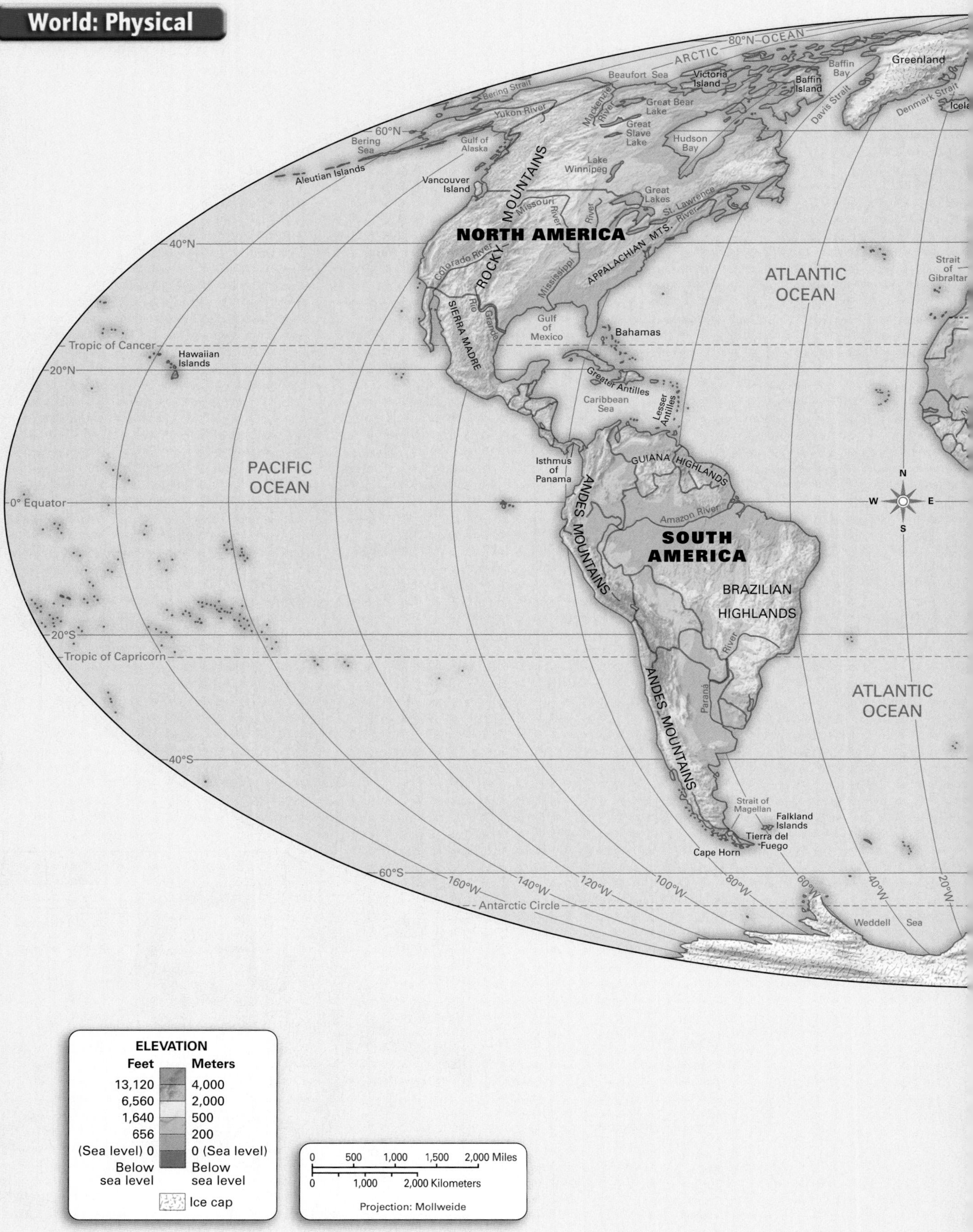
ARCTIC
80°N
OCEAN
Beaufort Sea
Victoria Island
Baffin Bay
Baffin Island
Greenland
Bering Strait
Yukon River
Mackenzie River
Great Bear Lake
Great Slave Lake
Davis Strait
Denmark Strait
60°N
Bering Sea
Gulf of Alaska
Hudson Bay
Lake Winnipeg
Aleutian Islands
Vancouver Island
ROCKY MOUNTAINS
Missouri River
River
Great Lakes
St. Lawrence River
NORTH AMERICA
APPALACHIAN MTS.
40°N
Colorado River
Mississippi
ATLANTIC OCEAN
Strait of Gibraltar
SIERRA MADRE
Rio Grande
Gulf of Mexico
Bahamas
Tropic of Cancer
Hawaiian Islands
20°N
Greater Antilles
Lesser Antilles
Caribbean Sea
Isthmus of Panama
GUIANA HIGHLANDS
PACIFIC OCEAN
N
W
E
S
0° Equator
ANDES MOUNTAINS
Amazon River
SOUTH AMERICA
BRAZILIAN HIGHLANDS
20°S
Tropic of Capricorn
River
Paraná
ATLANTIC OCEAN
40°S
Strait of Magellan
Falkland Islands
Tierra del Fuego
Cape Horn
60°S
160°W
140°W
120°W
100°W
80°W
60°W
40°W
20°W
Antarctic Circle
Weddell Sea
ELEVATION
Feet
Meters
13,120
4,000
6,560
2,000
1,640
500
656
200
(Sea level) 0
0 (Sea level)
Below sea level
Below sea level
Ice cap
0
500
1,000
1,500
2,000 Miles
0
1,000
2,000 Kilometers
Projection: Mollweide

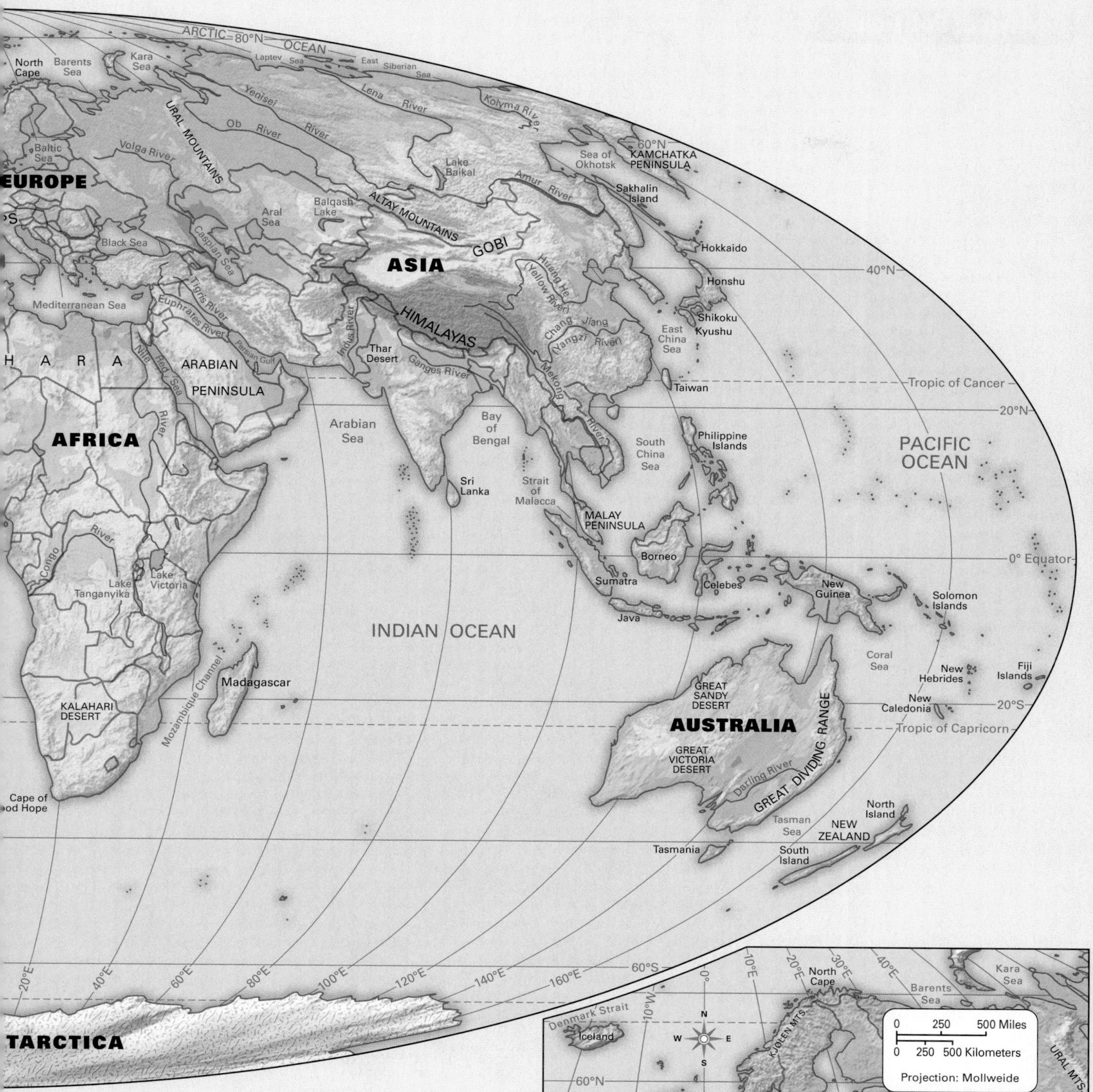
ARCTIC OCEAN
80°N
North Cape
Barents Sea
Kara Sea
Laptev Sea
East Siberian Sea
Lena River
Kolyma River
Yenisei River
URAL MOUNTAINS
Ob River
Baltic Sea
Volga River
EUROPE
Lake Baikal
Amur River
60°N
Sea of Okhotsk
KAMCHATKA PENINSULA
Sakhalin Island
Aral Sea
Balqash Lake
ALTAY MOUNTAINS
GOBI
Black Sea
Caspian Sea
ASIA
Hokkaido
Huang He (Yellow River)
Honshu
40°N
Mediterranean Sea
Tigris River
Euphrates River
Indus River
HIMALAYAS
Chang Jiang (Yangzi River)
East China Sea
Shikoku
Kyushu
Persian Gulf
Thar Desert
Ganges River
Mekong River
Taiwan
Tropic of Cancer
ARABIAN PENINSULA
Nile River
Red Sea
20°N
AFRICA
Arabian Sea
Bay of Bengal
South China Sea
Philippine Islands
PACIFIC OCEAN
Sri Lanka
Strait of Malacca
MALAY PENINSULA
Congo River
Borneo
0° Equator
Lake Tanganyika
Lake Victoria
Sumatra
Celebes
New Guinea
Solomon Islands
Java
INDIAN OCEAN
Coral Sea
New Hebrides
Fiji Islands
Madagascar
Mozambique Channel
GREAT SANDY DESERT
New Caledonia
20°S
KALAHARI DESERT
AUSTRALIA
GREAT DIVIDING RANGE
Tropic of Capricorn
GREAT VICTORIA DESERT
Darling River
Cape of Good Hope
North Island
Tasman Sea
NEW ZEALAND
Tasmania
South Island
20°E
40°E
60°E
80°E
100°E
120°E
140°E
160°E
60°S
ANTARCTICA

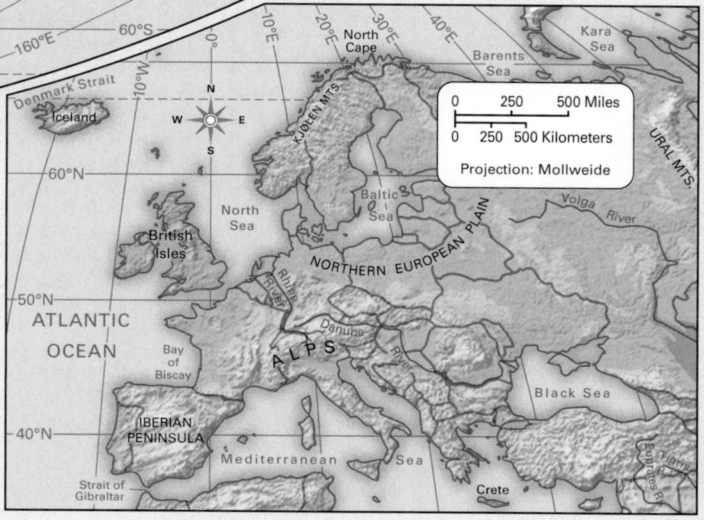
0°
10°E
20°E
30°E
40°E
North Cape
Barents Sea
Kara Sea
Denmark Strait
10°W
N
W
E
S
Iceland
KJØLEN MTS.
0 250 500 Miles
0 250 500 Kilometers
Projection: Mollweide
URAL MTS.
60°N
North Sea
Baltic Sea
Volga River
British Isles
NORTHERN EUROPEAN PLAIN
Rhine River
50°N
ATLANTIC OCEAN
Danube River
ALPS
Bay of Biscay
Black Sea
40°N
IBERIAN PENINSULA
Mediterranean Sea
Strait of Gibraltar
Crete
Euphrates River
Tigris River

Africa: Political

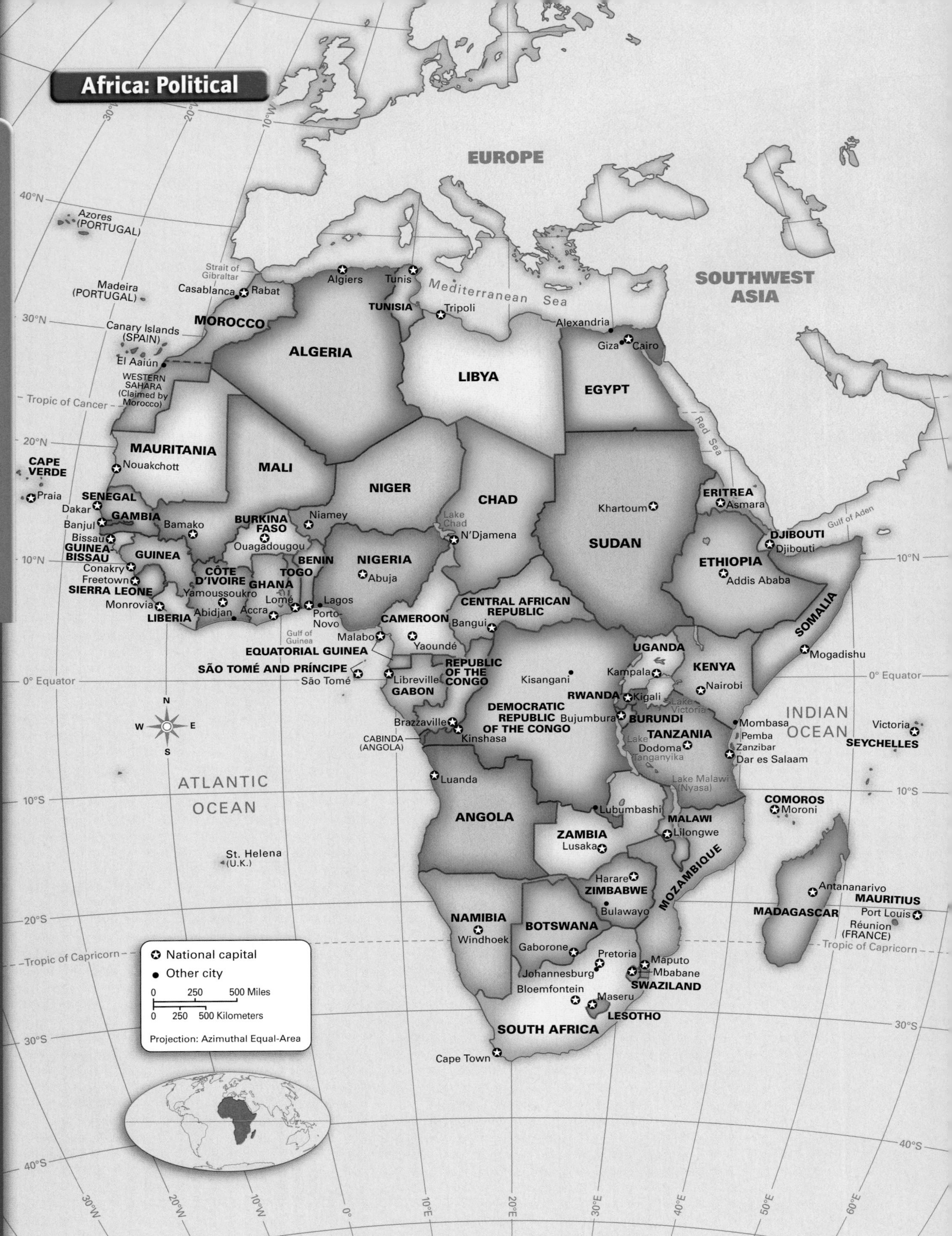

ATLAS

Africa: Physical

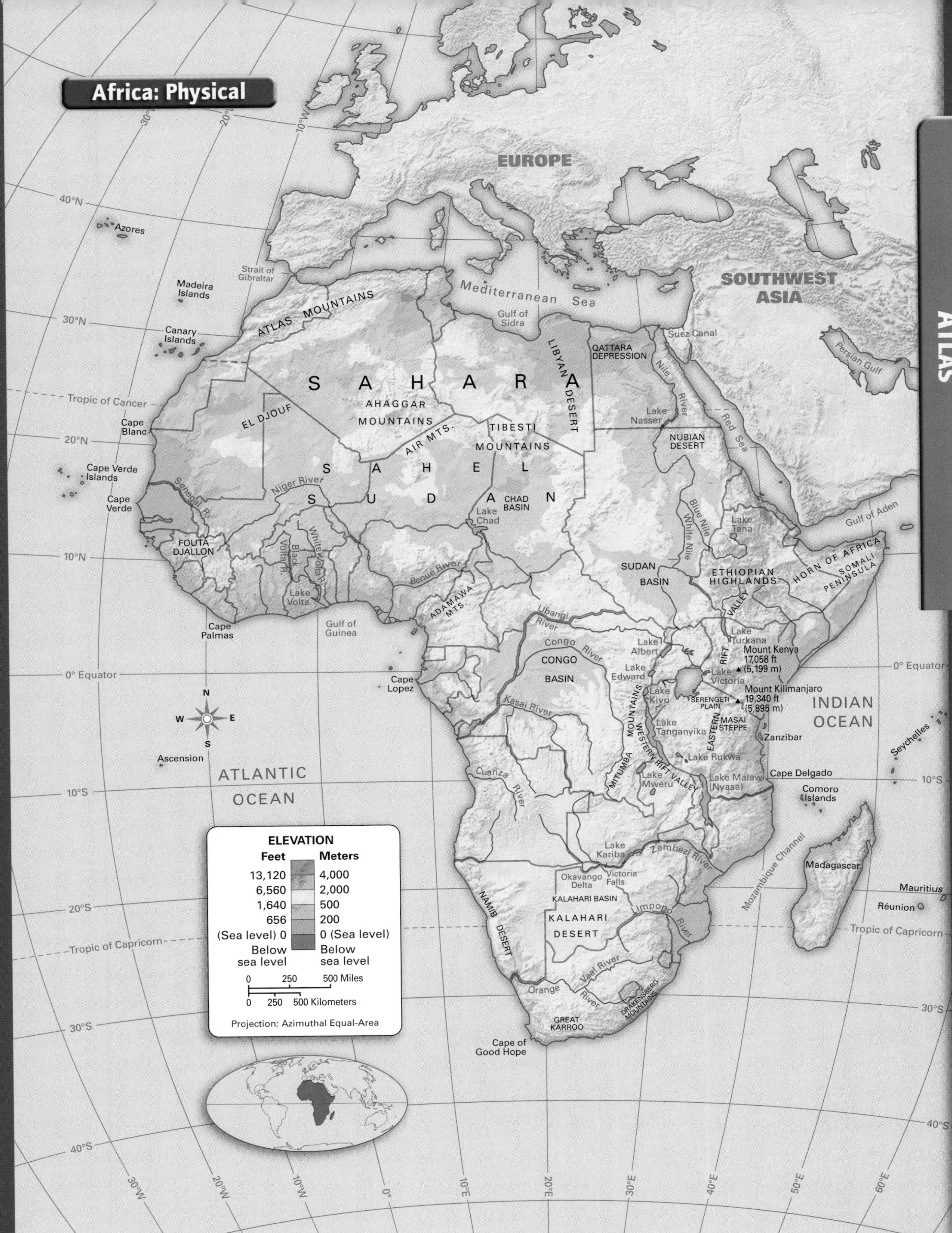
EUROPE
SOUTHWEST ASIA
Azores
Madeira Islands
Canary Islands
Strait of Gibraltar
Mediterranean Sea
Gulf of Sidra
Suez Canal
Persian Gulf
ATLAS MOUNTAINS
QATTARA DEPRESSION
LIBYAN DESERT
Nile River
S A H A R A
AHAGGAR MOUNTAINS
EL DJOUF
AIR MTS.
TIBESTI MOUNTAINS
Lake Nasser
NUBIAN DESERT
Red Sea
Tropic of Cancer
Cape Blanc
Cape Verde Islands
Cape Verde
S A H E L
S U D A N
Niger River
Senegal R.
CHAD BASIN
Lake Chad
Blue Nile
White Nile
Lake Tana
Gulf of Aden
HORN OF AFRICA
SOMALI PENINSULA
ETHIOPIAN HIGHLANDS
SUDAN BASIN
FOUTA DJALLON
Black Volta R.
White Volta R.
Volta R.
Lake Volta
Benue River
ADAMAWA MTS.
Cape Palmas
Gulf of Guinea
Ubangi River
Congo River
CONGO BASIN
Lake Albert
Lake Edward
Lake Turkana
EASTERN RIFT VALLEY
Mount Kenya 17,058 ft (5,199 m)
Lake Victoria
Mount Kilimanjaro 19,340 ft (5,895 m)
SERENGETI PLAIN
MASAI STEPPE
Lake Kivu
MITUMBA MOUNTAINS
WESTERN RIFT VALLEY
Lake Tanganyika
Lake Rukwa
Lake Mweru
Lake Malawi (Nyasa)
Zanzibar
Cape Delgado
Comoro Islands
Seychelles
INDIAN OCEAN
Cape Lopez
Kasai River
Cuanza River
ATLANTIC OCEAN
Ascension
0° Equator
Lake Kariba
Zambezi River
Mozambique Channel
Madagascar
Mauritius
Réunion
Okavango Delta
Victoria Falls
KALAHARI BASIN
KALAHARI DESERT
NAMIB DESERT
Limpopo River
Tropic of Capricorn
Vaal River
Orange River
DRAKENSBERG MOUNTAINS
GREAT KARROO
Cape of Good Hope
N
S
E
W
ELEVATION
Feet
Meters
13,120
6,560
1,640
656
(Sea level) 0
Below sea level
4,000
2,000
500
200
0 (Sea level)
Below sea level
0 250 500 Miles
0 250 500 Kilometers
Projection: Azimuthal Equal-Area
40°N
30°N
20°N
10°N
10°S
20°S
30°S
40°S
30°W
20°W
10°W
0°
10°E
20°E
30°E
40°E
50°E
60°E

ATLAS

Asia: Political

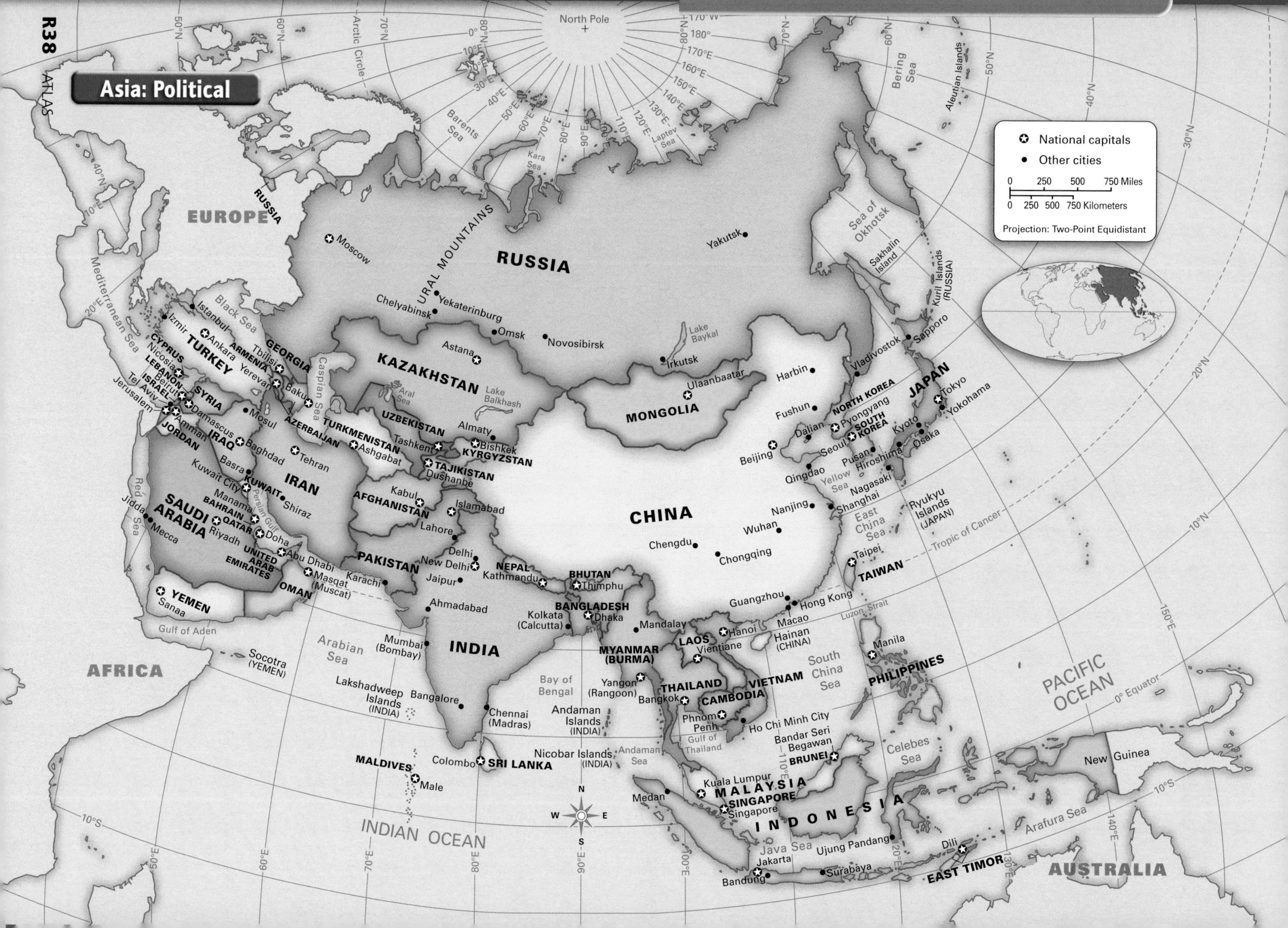

Asia: Physical

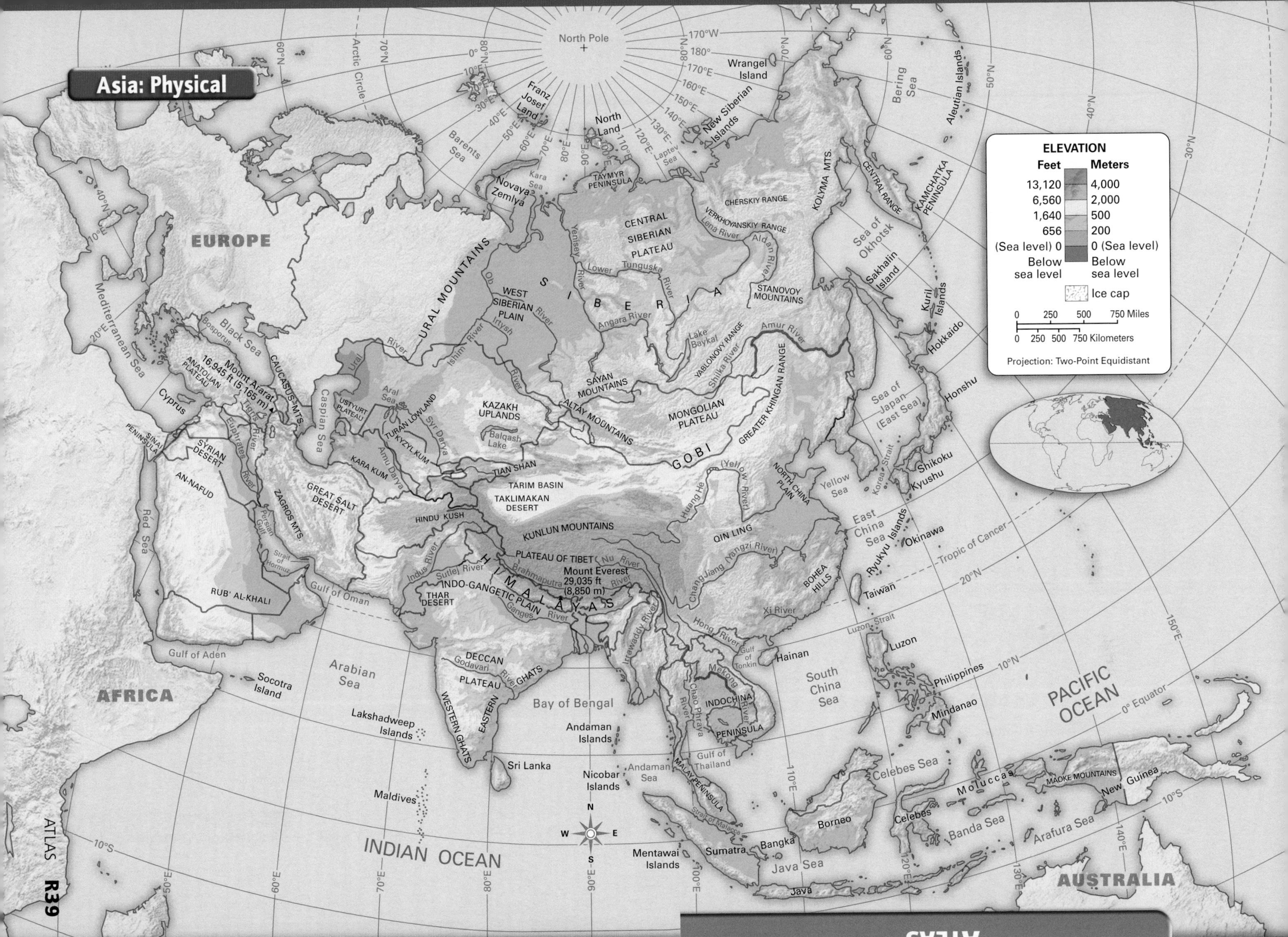
ELEVATION
Feet
Meters
13,120
6,560
1,640
656
(Sea level) 0
Below sea level
4,000
2,000
500
200
0 (Sea level)
Below sea level
Ice cap
0 250 500 750 Miles
0 250 500 750 Kilometers
Projection: Two-Point Equidistant
North Pole
Arctic Circle
Tropic of Cancer
0° Equator
EUROPE
AFRICA
AUSTRALIA
URAL MOUNTAINS
S I B E R I A
WEST SIBERIAN PLAIN
CENTRAL SIBERIAN PLATEAU
TAYMYR PENINSULA
CHERSKIY RANGE
VERKHOYANSKIY RANGE
KOLYMA MTS.
CENTRAL RANGE
KAMCHATKA PENINSULA
STANOVOY MOUNTAINS
YABLONOVY RANGE
SAYAN MOUNTAINS
ALTAY MOUNTAINS
MONGOLIAN PLATEAU
GREATER KHINGAN RANGE
GOBI
KAZAKH UPLANDS
TURAN LOWLAND
USTYURT PLATEAU
KYZYL KUM
KARA KUM
TIAN SHAN
TARIM BASIN
TAKLIMAKAN DESERT
HINDU KUSH
KUNLUN MOUNTAINS
PLATEAU OF TIBET
H I M A L A Y A S
Mount Everest 29,035 ft (8,850 m)
INDO-GANGETIC PLAIN
THAR DESERT
DECCAN PLATEAU
EASTERN GHATS
WESTERN GHATS
QIN LING
NORTH CHINA PLAIN
BOHEA HILLS
INDOCHINA PENINSULA
MALAY PENINSULA
MAOKE MOUNTAINS
CAUCASUS MTS.
Mount Ararat 16,945 ft (5,165 m)
ANATOLIAN PLATEAU
SINAI PENINSULA
SYRIAN DESERT
AN-NAFUD
RUB' AL-KHALI
ZAGROS MTS.
GREAT SALT DESERT
Mediterranean Sea
Black Sea
Bosporus
Caspian Sea
Aral Sea
Balqash Lake
Lake Baykal
Red Sea
Persian Gulf
Strait of Hormuz
Gulf of Oman
Gulf of Aden
Arabian Sea
Bay of Bengal
INDIAN OCEAN
Andaman Sea
Gulf of Thailand
Strait of Malacca
South China Sea
Gulf of Tonkin
Luzon Strait
East China Sea
Yellow Sea
Korea Strait
Sea of Japan (East Sea)
Sea of Okhotsk
Bering Sea
Barents Sea
Kara Sea
Laptev Sea
PACIFIC OCEAN
Celebes Sea
Banda Sea
Arafura Sea
Java Sea
Ural River
Ob River
Irtysh
Ishim River
Yenisey River
Lower Tunguska River
Angara River
Lena River
Aldan River
Amur River
Shilka River
Syr Darya
Amu Darya
Tigris River
Euphrates River
Indus River
Sutlej River
Ganges River
Brahmaputra River
Nu River
Irrawaddy River
Mekong River
Chao Phraya River
Hong River
Xi River
Chang Jiang (Yangzi River)
Huang He (Yellow River)
Franz Josef Land
Novaya Zemlya
North Land
New Siberian Islands
Wrangel Island
Aleutian Islands
Kuril Islands
Sakhalin Island
Hokkaido
Honshu
Shikoku
Kyushu
Ryukyu Islands
Okinawa
Taiwan
Hainan
Luzon
Philippines
Mindanao
Borneo
Celebes
Moluccas
New Guinea
Sumatra
Bangka
Java
Mentawai Islands
Nicobar Islands
Andaman Islands
Sri Lanka
Maldives
Lakshadweep Islands
Socotra Island
Cyprus
N
S
E
W

Europe: Political

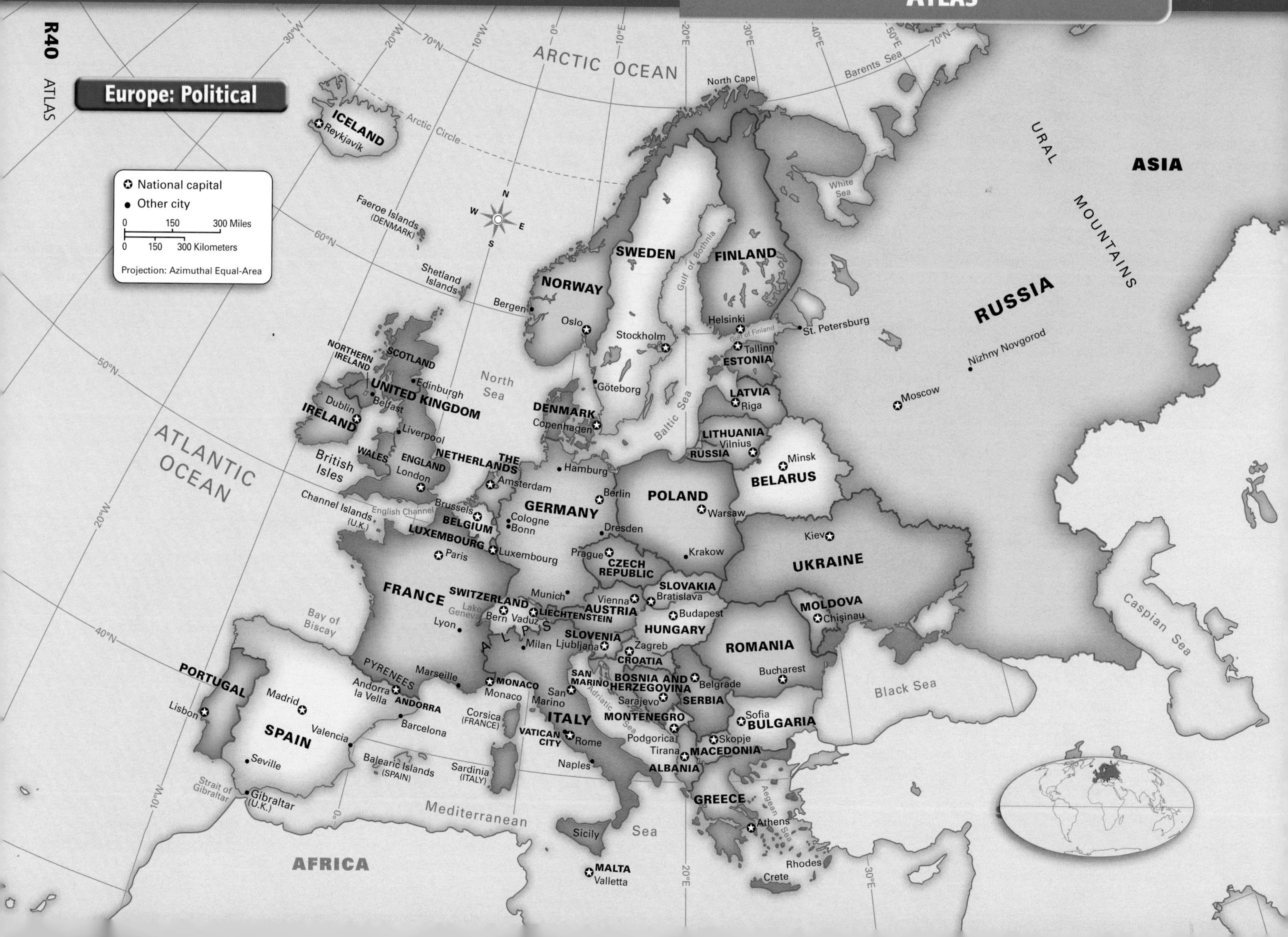

Europe: Physical
ELEVATION
Feet
Meters
13,120
4,000
6,560
2,000
1,640
500
656
200
(Sea level) 0
0 (Sea level)
Below sea level
Below sea level
Ice cap
0
150
300 Miles
0
150
300 Kilometers
Projection: Azimuthal Equal Area
ARCTIC OCEAN
Norwegian Sea
North Sea
ATLANTIC OCEAN
Barents Sea
North Cape
Arctic Circle
Iceland
Faeroe Islands
Shetland Islands
Orkney Islands
Hebrides
British Isles
Irish Sea
PENNINES
Thames River
English Channel
KJOLEN MOUNTAINS
Gulf of Bothnia
Gulf of Finland
Lake Vänern
Lake Vättern
Skagerrak
Kattegat
Baltic Sea
KOLA PENINSULA
White Sea
North Dvina River
Lake Onega
Lake Ladoga
Rybinsk Reservoir
Pechora River
URAL MOUNTAINS
Kama River
Ural River
Volga River
Don River
Dnipro River
Daugava R.
Dzvina River
BALTIC PLAINS
NORTHERN EUROPEAN PLAIN
Elbe River
Oder River
Vistula River
Rhine River
Seine River
Loire River
Garonne River
Rhone River
Danube River
Dnestr River
Nistru River
CARPATHIAN MTS.
TRANSYLVANIAN ALPS
Lake Geneva
Mont Blanc 15,781 ft (4,810 m)
ALPS
Po River
Bay of Biscay
Cape Finisterre
PYRENEES
Douro River
Ebro River
Tagus River
Guadiana River
Guadalquivir River
IBERIAN PENINSULA
Strait of Gibraltar
Balearic Islands
Corsica
Sardinia
Tyrrhenian Sea
APENNINES
Tiber River
Adriatic Sea
DINARIC ALPS
BALKAN PENINSULA
Sea of Marmara
Aegean Sea
Rhodes
Crete
Sicily
Malta
Mediterranean Sea
AFRICA
Sea of Azov
CRIMEAN PENINSULA
Black Sea
Mt. Elbrus 18,510 ft (5,642 m)
CAUCASUS MTS.
Caspian Sea
ASIA
N
E
S
W
70°N
60°N
40°N
30°N
40°W
30°W
20°W
10°W
0°
10°E
20°E
30°E
40°E
50°E

ATLAS

North America: Political

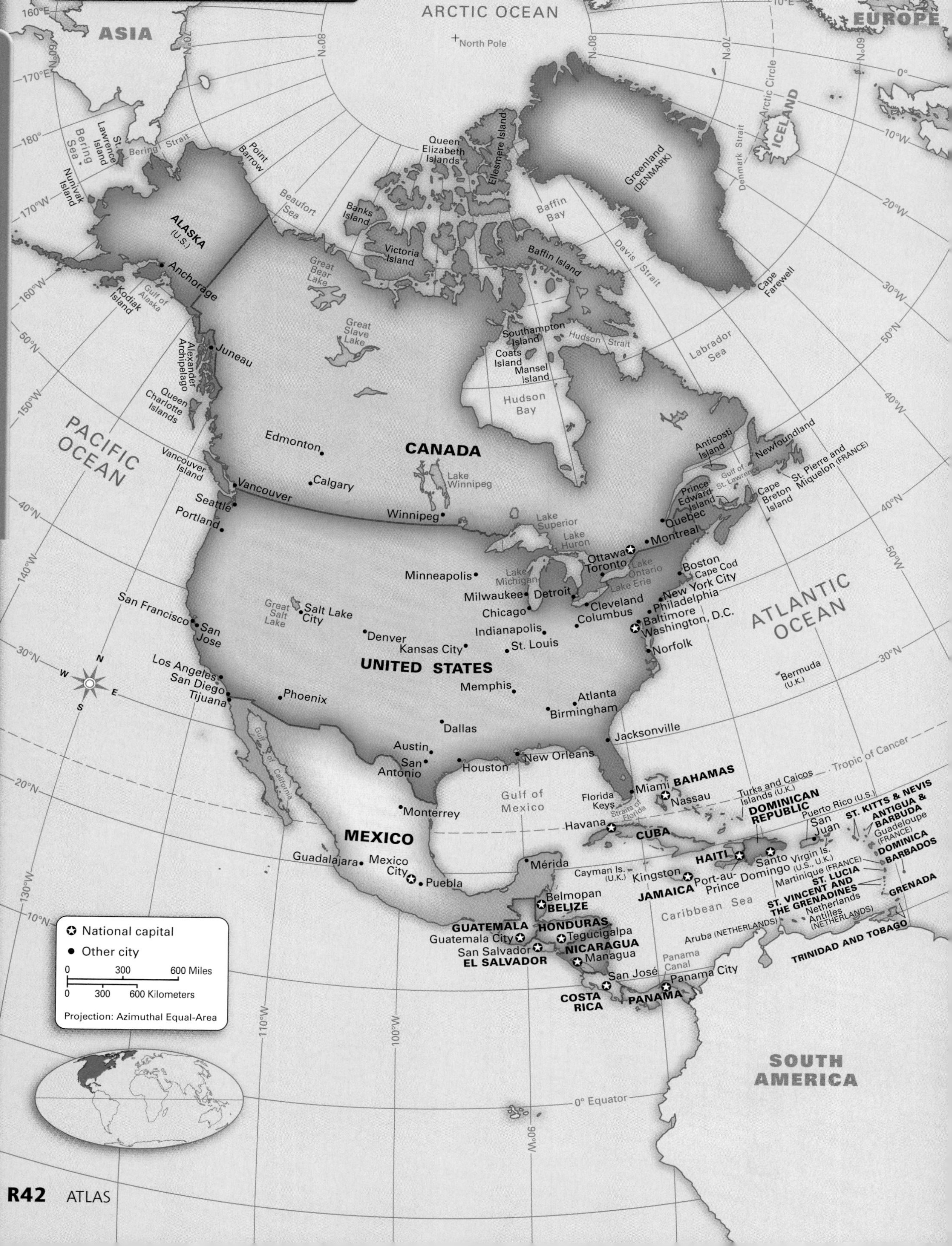
ARCTIC OCEAN
North Pole
ASIA
EUROPE
160°E
170°E
180°
170°W
160°W
150°W
140°W
130°W
10°E
0°
10°W
20°W
30°W
40°W
50°W
60°N
70°N
80°N
50°N
40°N
30°N
20°N
10°N
110°W
100°W
90°W
Arctic Circle
ICELAND
Denmark Strait
Greenland (DENMARK)
Cape Farewell
Bering Sea
Bering Strait
St. Lawrence Island
Nunivak Island
Point Barrow
Beaufort Sea
ALASKA (U.S.)
Anchorage
Gulf of Alaska
Kodiak Island
Juneau
Alexander Archipelago
Queen Charlotte Islands
Vancouver Island
Queen Elizabeth Islands
Ellesmere Island
Banks Island
Victoria Island
Baffin Bay
Baffin Island
Davis Strait
Great Bear Lake
Great Slave Lake
Southampton Island
Coats Island
Mansel Island
Hudson Strait
Labrador Sea
Hudson Bay
Anticosti Island
Newfoundland
Gulf of St. Lawrence
St. Pierre and Miquelon (FRANCE)
Prince Edward Island
Cape Breton Island
PACIFIC OCEAN
Edmonton
CANADA
Lake Winnipeg
Calgary
Vancouver
Seattle
Portland
Winnipeg
Lake Superior
Lake Huron
Quebec
Montreal
Ottawa
Toronto
Lake Ontario
Lake Michigan
Lake Erie
Boston
Cape Cod
New York City
Philadelphia
Baltimore
Washington, D.C.
Norfolk
Minneapolis
Milwaukee
Detroit
Cleveland
Chicago
Columbus
Indianapolis
St. Louis
ATLANTIC OCEAN
San Francisco
San Jose
Great Salt Lake
Salt Lake City
Denver
Kansas City
UNITED STATES
Los Angeles
San Diego
Tijuana
Phoenix
Memphis
Atlanta
Birmingham
Bermuda (U.K.)
Dallas
Jacksonville
Austin
San Antonio
Houston
New Orleans
Gulf of California
Tropic of Cancer
Gulf of Mexico
Miami
BAHAMAS
Nassau
Florida Keys
Straits of Florida
Turks and Caicos Islands (U.K.)
DOMINICAN REPUBLIC
Puerto Rico (U.S.)
San Juan
ST. KITTS & NEVIS
ANTIGUA & BARBUDA
Guadeloupe (FRANCE)
DOMINICA
BARBADOS
Monterrey
MEXICO
Havana
CUBA
HAITI
Santo Domingo
Port-au-Prince
Virgin Is. (U.S., U.K.)
Martinique (FRANCE)
ST. LUCIA
ST. VINCENT AND THE GRENADINES
GRENADA
Guadalajara
Mexico City
Puebla
Mérida
Cayman Is. (U.K.)
Kingston
JAMAICA
Belmopan
BELIZE
Caribbean Sea
Netherlands Antilles (NETHERLANDS)
Aruba (NETHERLANDS)
TRINIDAD AND TOBAGO
GUATEMALA
Guatemala City
HONDURAS
Tegucigalpa
San Salvador
EL SALVADOR
NICARAGUA
Managua
Panama Canal
San José
Panama City
COSTA RICA
PANAMA
SOUTH AMERICA
0° Equator
N
S
E
W
National capital
Other city
0 300 600 Miles
0 300 600 Kilometers
Projection: Azimuthal Equal-Area

North America: Physical

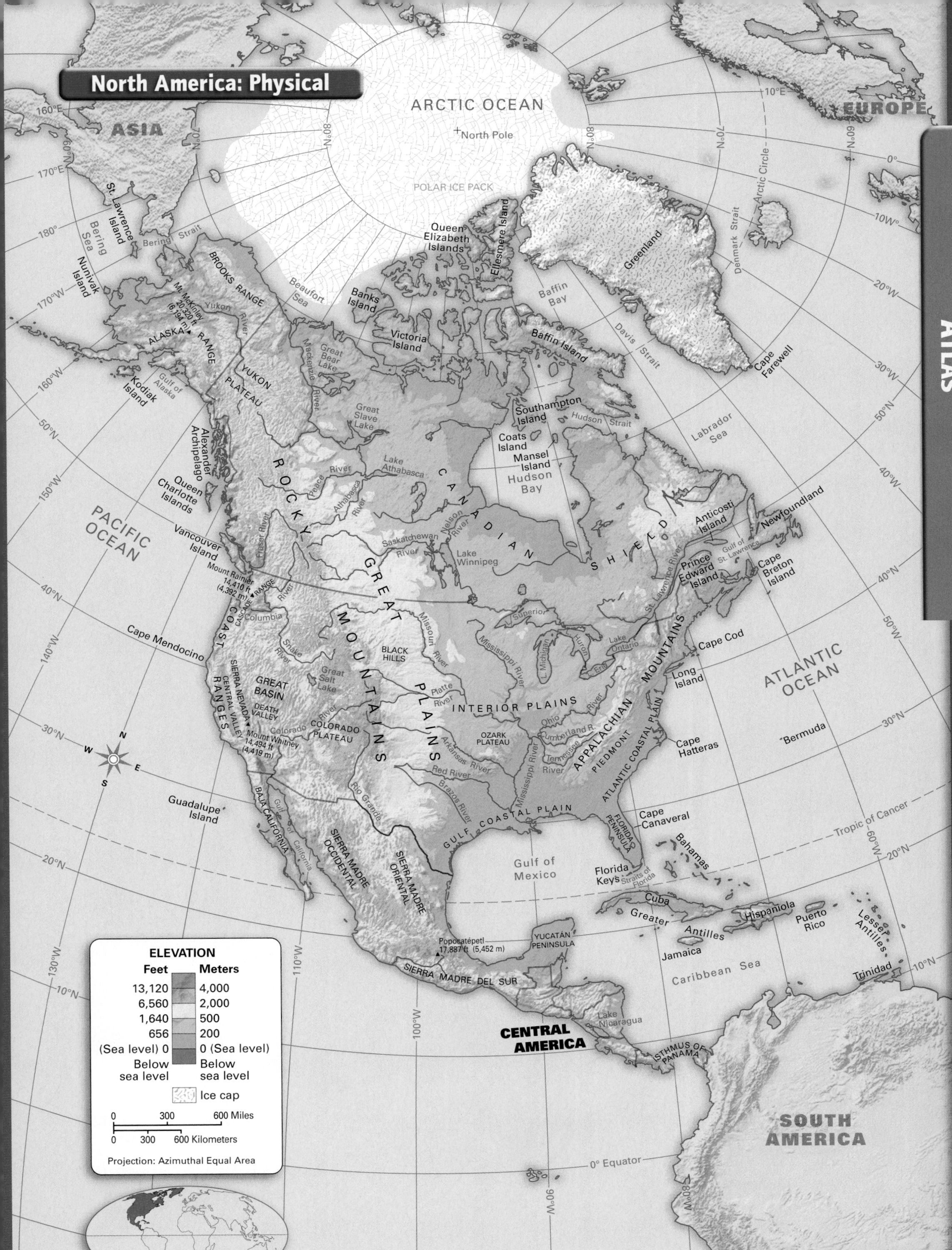
ARCTIC OCEAN
North Pole
POLAR ICE PACK
ASIA
EUROPE
St. Lawrence Island
Bering Sea
Bering Strait
Nunivak Island
BROOKS RANGE
Mt. McKinley 20,320 ft (6,194 m)
ALASKA RANGE
Yukon River
Beaufort Sea
Banks Island
Queen Elizabeth Islands
Ellesmere Island
Greenland
Denmark Strait
Arctic Circle
Baffin Bay
Victoria Island
Baffin Island
Davis Strait
Cape Farewell
Gulf of Alaska
Kodiak Island
YUKON PLATEAU
Mackenzie River
Great Bear Lake
Great Slave Lake
Southampton Island
Hudson Strait
Coats Island
Mansel Island
Hudson Bay
Labrador Sea
Alexander Archipelago
Queen Charlotte Islands
ROCKY
Peace River
Lake Athabasca
Athabasca River
CANADIAN SHIELD
Anticosti Island
Newfoundland
Gulf of St. Lawrence
Prince Edward Island
Cape Breton Island
PACIFIC OCEAN
Vancouver Island
Fraser River
Nelson River
Saskatchewan River
Lake Winnipeg
St. Lawrence River
Mount Rainier 14,410 ft (4,392 m)
CASCADE RANGE
COAST RANGES
Columbia River
GREAT PLAINS
MOUNTAINS
Superior
Cape Mendocino
Snake River
Missouri River
BLACK HILLS
Mississippi River
L. Michigan
Huron
Lake Ontario
Erie
Cape Cod
MOUNTAINS
Great Salt Lake
GREAT BASIN
SIERRA NEVADA
CENTRAL VALLEY
DEATH VALLEY
Mount Whitney 14,494 ft (4,419 m)
Colorado River
COLORADO PLATEAU
Platte River
INTERIOR PLAINS
Ohio River
Cumberland R.
OZARK PLATEAU
Tennessee River
APPALACHIAN
PIEDMONT
ATLANTIC COASTAL PLAIN
Long Island
ATLANTIC OCEAN
Cape Hatteras
Bermuda
Arkansas River
Red River
Brazos River
Rio Grande
GULF COASTAL PLAIN
Guadalupe Island
BAJA CALIFORNIA
Gulf of California
SIERRA MADRE OCCIDENTAL
SIERRA MADRE ORIENTAL
Cape Canaveral
FLORIDA PENINSULA
Bahamas
Tropic of Cancer
Gulf of Mexico
Florida Keys
Straits of Florida
Cuba
Greater Antilles
Hispaniola
Puerto Rico
Lesser Antilles
Jamaica
Popocatépetl 17,887 ft (5,452 m)
YUCATÁN PENINSULA
SIERRA MADRE DEL SUR
Caribbean Sea
Trinidad
Lake Nicaragua
CENTRAL AMERICA
ISTHMUS OF PANAMA
SOUTH AMERICA
0° Equator
ELEVATION
Feet
Meters
13,120
4,000
6,560
2,000
1,640
500
656
200
(Sea level) 0
0 (Sea level)
Below sea level
Below sea level
Ice cap
0 300 600 Miles
0 300 600 Kilometers
Projection: Azimuthal Equal Area

ATLAS

South America: Political

Caribbean Sea
CENTRAL AMERICA
Barranquilla
Cartagena
Caracas
Lake Maracaibo
VENEZUELA
Medellín
Bogotá
COLOMBIA
Cali
Malpelo Island (COLOMBIA)
Georgetown
Paramaribo
Cayenne
GUYANA
SURINAME
French Guiana (FRANCE)
ATLANTIC OCEAN
Quito
ECUADOR
Guayaquil
Galápagos Islands (ECUADOR)
0° Equator
Belém
PERU
BRAZIL
Recife
Trujillo
Callao
Lima
Lake Titicaca
La Paz
Lake Poopó
BOLIVIA
Sucre
Arequipa
PACIFIC OCEAN
Brasília
Salvador
Belo Horizonte
Campinas
São Paulo
Rio de Janeiro
Curitiba
PARAGUAY
Asunción
Tropic of Capricorn
San Félix Island (CHILE)
San Ambrosio Island (CHILE)
CHILE
Pôrto Alegre
Córdoba
Rosario
URUGUAY
Juan Fernández Islands (CHILE)
Valparaíso
Santiago
Buenos Aires
Montevideo
ATLANTIC OCEAN
ARGENTINA
National capital
Other city
0 250 500 Miles
0 250 500 Kilometers
Projection: Azimuthal Equal-Area
Strait of Magellan
Falkland Islands (U.K.)
Tierra del Fuego
South Georgia Island (U.K.)
N
S
E
W
20°N
10°N
10°S
20°S
30°S
40°S
50°S
100°W
90°W
80°W
70°W
60°W
50°W
40°W
30°W
20°W

South America: Physical

CENTRAL AMERICA

Caribbean Sea

Panama Canal

Gulf of Panama

Malpelo Island

Margarita Island
Tobago
Trinidad
Orinoco River Delta

Lake Maracaibo

LLANOS

Meta River
Orinoco River
Cauca River
Magdalena River

Mount Tolima 18,425 ft (5,616 m)

GUIANA
Angel Falls

HIGHLANDS

Devil's Island
Cape Orange

ATLANTIC OCEAN

Amazon River Delta

Galápagos Islands

0° Equator

Gulf of Guayaquil

Mount Chimborazo 20,561 ft (6,267 m)

Caqueta River

Japurá River

Orinoco River

Rio Negro

AMAZON

BASIN

Amazon River

Amazon River

Marañón River

Juruá River
Purus River
Ucayali River

Madeira River

Tapajós River

Xingu River

Araguaia River

Tocantins River

Parnaiba River

São Francisco River

BRAZILIAN

HIGHLANDS

Mount Huascarán 22,205 ft (6,768 m)

ANDES

MATO GROSSO PLATEAU

Beni River

Mamoré River

Ancohuma Peak 20,958 ft (6,388 m)

PACIFIC OCEAN

Lake Titicaca

Lake Poopo

ATACAMA DESERT

San Félix Island
San Ambrosio Island

CHACO

Pilcomayo

Paraguay River

BRAZILIAN PLATEAU

Salado River
Paraná River
Uruguay River

Juan Fernández Islands

Mount Aconcagua 22,834 ft (6,960 m)

ANDES

Salado River

PAMPAS

Rio de la Plata

ATLANTIC OCEAN

Colorado River

Gulf of San Matías

Chiloé Island

Chonos Archipelago

PATAGONIA

Gulf of San Jorge

Cape Tres Puntas

Bahía Grande

Strait of Magellan

Tierra del Fuego

Cape Horn

Falkland Islands

South Georgia Islands

ELEVATION

Feet		Meters
13,120		4,000
6,560		2,000
1,640		500
656		200
(Sea level) 0		0 (Sea level)
Below sea level		Below sea level

0 250 500 Miles

0 250 500 Kilometers

Projection: Azimuthal Equal Area

20°N
10°N
0° Equator
10°S
Tropic of Capricorn
20°S
30°S
40°S
50°S

90°W 80°W 70°W 60°W 50°W 40°W 30°W 20°W

100°W

Oceania: Political

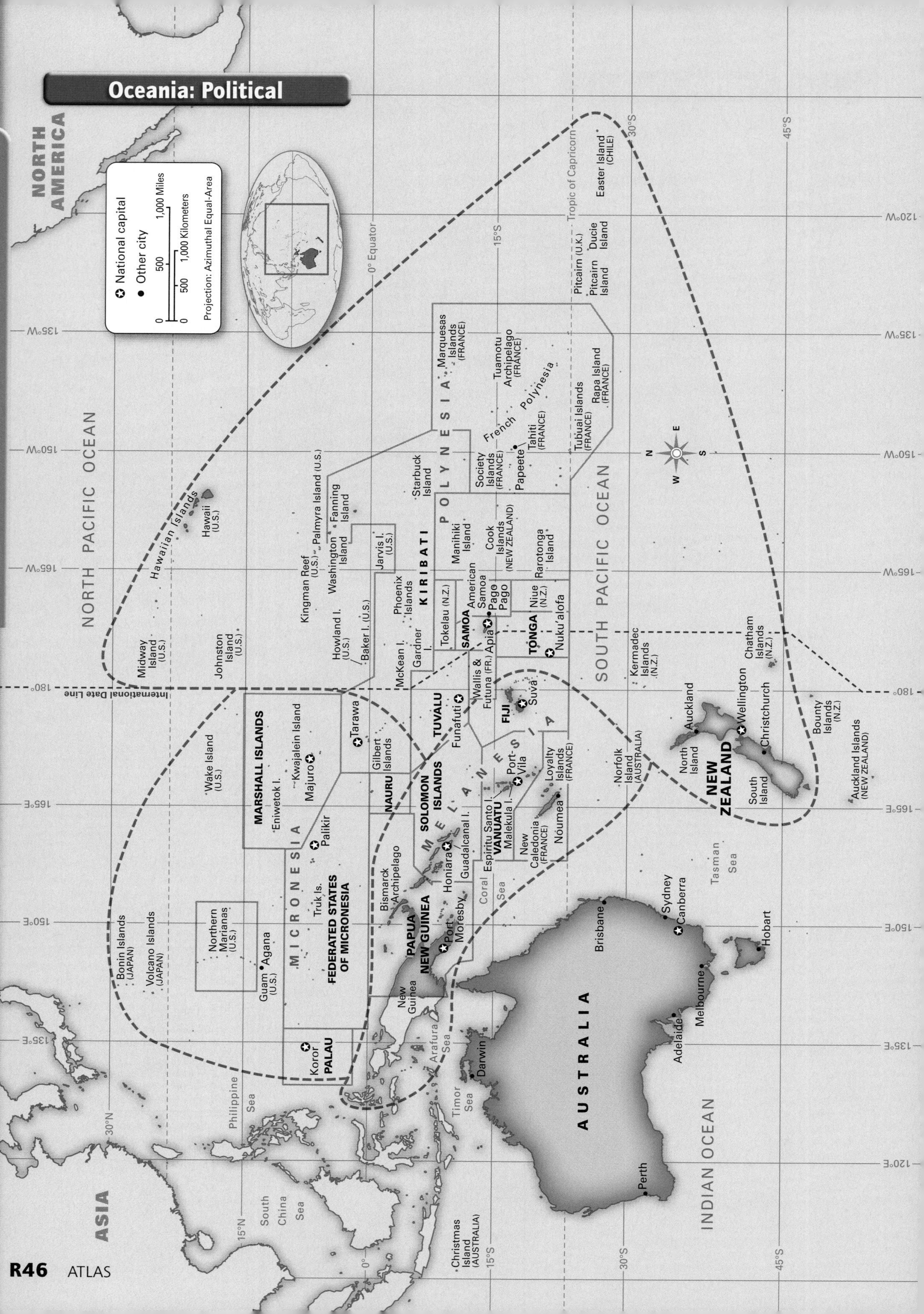
National capital
Other city
0 500 1,000 Miles
0 500 1,000 Kilometers
Projection: Azimuthal Equal-Area
NORTH AMERICA
ASIA
NORTH PACIFIC OCEAN
SOUTH PACIFIC OCEAN
INDIAN OCEAN
Philippine Sea
South China Sea
Timor Sea
Arafura Sea
Coral Sea
Tasman Sea
0° Equator
Tropic of Capricorn
International Date Line
MICRONESIA
MELANESIA
POLYNESIA
AUSTRALIA
NEW ZEALAND
North Island
South Island
PAPUA NEW GUINEA
New Guinea
PALAU
Koror
FEDERATED STATES OF MICRONESIA
Palikir
Truk Is.
MARSHALL ISLANDS
Majuro
Eniwetok I.
Kwajalein Island
NAURU
KIRIBATI
Tarawa
Gilbert Islands
Phoenix Islands
TUVALU
Funafuti
SOLOMON ISLANDS
Honiara
Guadalcanal I.
VANUATU
Port-Vila
Espiritu Santo I.
Malekula I.
FIJI
Suva
SAMOA
Apia
TONGA
Nuku'alofa
New Caledonia (FRANCE)
Nouméa
Loyalty Islands (FRANCE)
Norfolk Island (AUSTRALIA)
Bismarck Archipelago
Port Moresby
Guam (U.S.)
Agana
Northern Marianas (U.S.)
Bonin Islands (JAPAN)
Volcano Islands (JAPAN)
Wake Island (U.S.)
Midway Island (U.S.)
Johnston Island (U.S.)
Hawaiian Islands
Hawaii (U.S.)
Kingman Reef (U.S.)
Palmyra Island (U.S.)
Washington Island
Fanning Island
Howland I. (U.S.)
Baker I. (U.S.)
Jarvis I. (U.S.)
McKean I.
Gardner I.
Starbuck Island
Tokelau (N.Z.)
Wallis & Futuna (FR.)
American Samoa
Pago Pago
Niue (N.Z.)
Manihiki Island
Cook Islands (NEW ZEALAND)
Rarotonga Island
Society Islands (FRANCE)
Papeete
Tahiti (FRANCE)
French Polynesia
Marquesas Islands (FRANCE)
Tuamotu Archipelago (FRANCE)
Tubuai Islands (FRANCE)
Rapa Island (FRANCE)
Pitcairn (U.K.)
Pitcairn Island
Ducie Island
Easter Island (CHILE)
Kermadec Islands (N.Z.)
Chatham Islands (N.Z.)
Bounty Islands (N.Z.)
Auckland Islands (NEW ZEALAND)
Auckland
Wellington
Christchurch
Darwin
Brisbane
Sydney
Canberra
Melbourne
Adelaide
Perth
Hobart
Christmas Island (AUSTRALIA)
N
S
E
W
0°
15°N
30°N
15°S
30°S
45°S
120°E
135°E
150°E
165°E
180°
165°W
150°W
135°W
120°W

Polar Regions

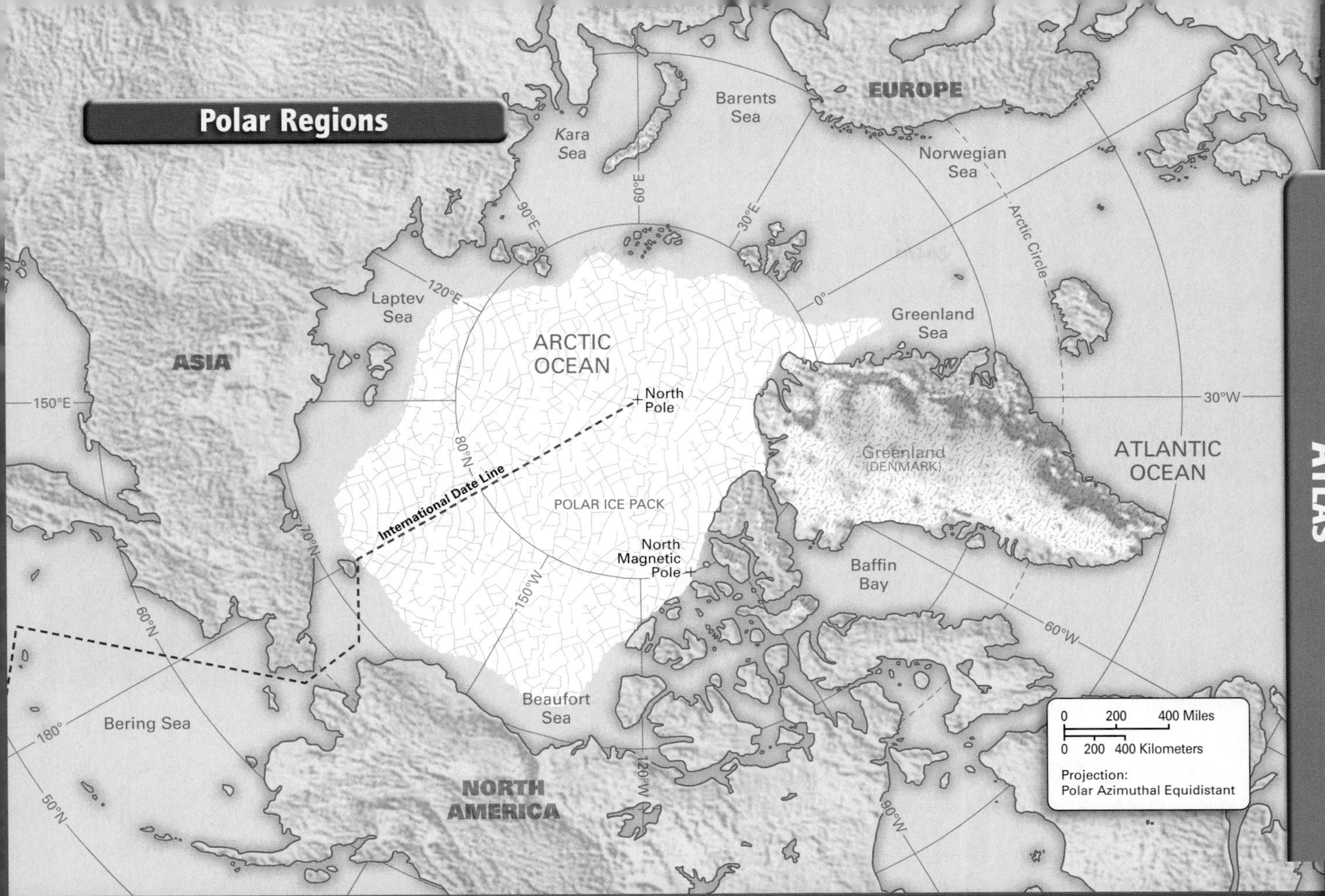

Kara Sea
Barents Sea
EUROPE
Norwegian Sea
Laptev Sea
ARCTIC OCEAN
Greenland Sea
ASIA
North Pole
Greenland (DENMARK)
ATLANTIC OCEAN
International Date Line
POLAR ICE PACK
North Magnetic Pole
Baffin Bay
Bering Sea
Beaufort Sea
NORTH AMERICA
0 200 400 Miles
0 200 400 Kilometers
Projection: Polar Azimuthal Equidistant
90°E
60°E
30°E
120°E
0°
150°E
30°W
80°N
70°N
60°N
50°N
180°
150°W
120°W
90°W
60°W
Arctic Circle

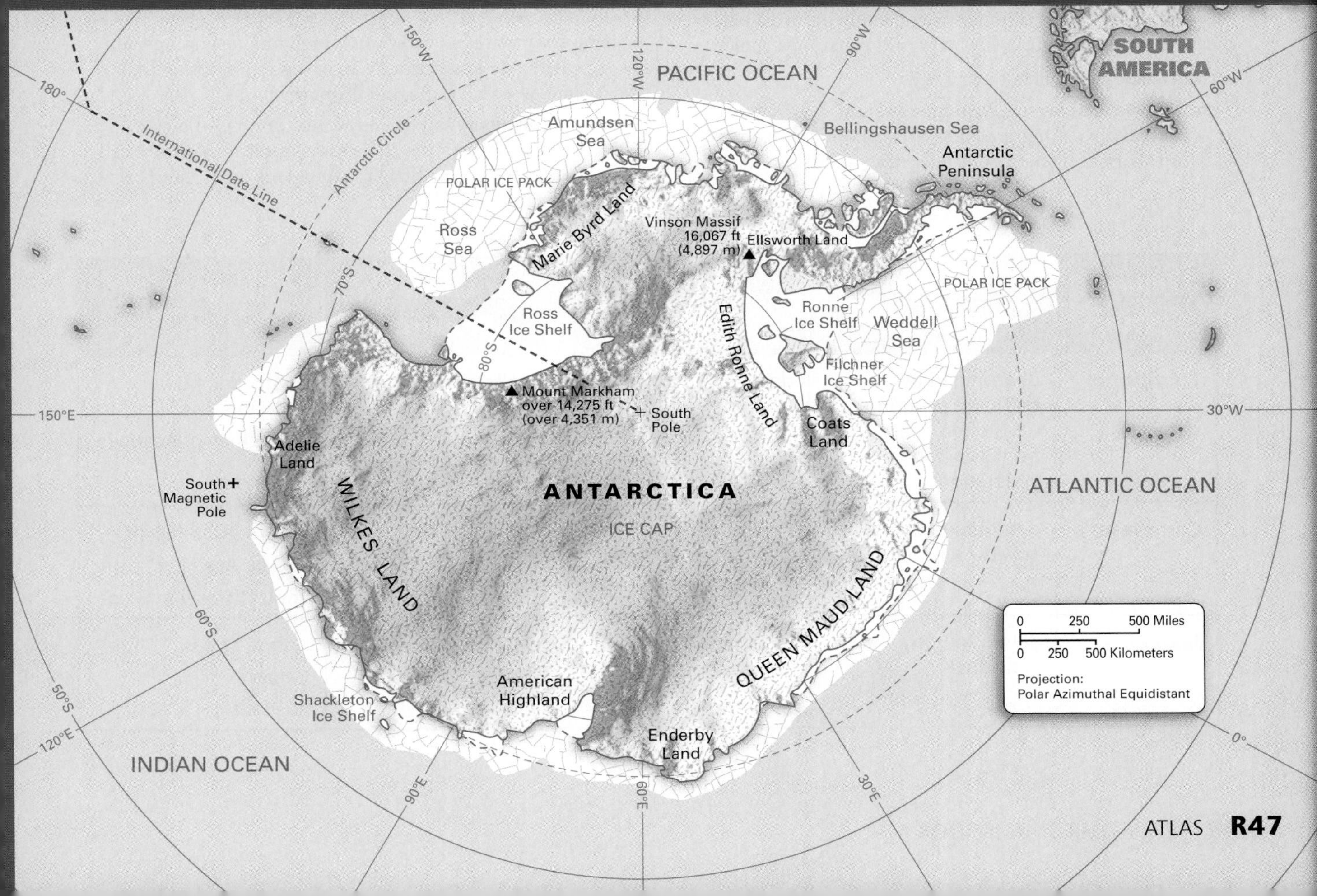

SOUTH AMERICA
PACIFIC OCEAN
Amundsen Sea
Bellingshausen Sea
Antarctic Peninsula
International Date Line
Antarctic Circle
POLAR ICE PACK
Ross Sea
Marie Byrd Land
Vinson Massif 16,067 ft (4,897 m)
Ellsworth Land
POLAR ICE PACK
Ross Ice Shelf
Ronne Ice Shelf
Weddell Sea
Edith Ronne Land
Filchner Ice Shelf
Mount Markham over 14,275 ft (over 4,351 m)
South Pole
Coats Land
Adelie Land
South Magnetic Pole
ANTARCTICA
ICE CAP
ATLANTIC OCEAN
WILKES LAND
QUEEN MAUD LAND
0 250 500 Miles
0 250 500 Kilometers
Projection: Polar Azimuthal Equidistant
American Highland
Shackleton Ice Shelf
Enderby Land
INDIAN OCEAN
150°W
120°W
90°W
60°W
180°
150°E
120°E
30°W
0°
90°E
60°E
30°E
80°S
70°S
60°S
50°S

ATLAS

Economics Handbook

ECONOMICS HANDBOOK

What Is Economics?

We can think of economics as a study of the choices people make to satisfy their needs or their wants. Which pair of shoes do you buy—the ones on sale or the ones you really like? Economics may sound dull, but it touches almost every part of your life.

Economics is also one of the major forces in world history. Societies with healthy economies tend to perform better than those with weaker economies. When a civilization decays, a weakened economy is often a leading factor. Learning a little about economics can help in your study of world history.

Glossary of Economic Terms

Here are some of the terms we use to talk about economics:

ECONOMIC SYSTEMS

Countries have developed different economic systems to help them make choices, such as what goods and services to produce, how to produce them, and for whom to produce them. The most common economic systems in the world today are market economies and mixed economies. Market economies generally perform better in terms of worker productivity and consumer choice.

capitalism See market economy.

command economy an economic system in which the central government makes all economic decisions; in theory, the means of production—industrial and agricultural—are "owned" by the people, but since the government makes all economic decisions, it is the true owner; also known as "centrally planned"; the countries of Cuba and North Korea are examples of command economies

communism a political system in which the government owns all property and runs a command economy

free enterprise a system in which businesses operate with little government involvement, such as in a country with a market economy

market economy an economic system based on private ownership, free trade, and competition; the government has little to say about what, how, or

Economic Systems	What to Produce	How to Produce	For Whom to Produce	Examples
Traditional	determined by tradition; economic roles often passed from generation to generation	determined by custom	usually centered around traditional family and social units such as a tribe	Prehistoric hunter-gatherers Aborigines of Australia
Command	determined by government officials	determined by government officials	determined by government officials	Old Kingdom Egypt Middle Ages in Europe Zhou Dynasty in China
Market	determined by individuals	determined by individuals	determined by individuals	United States Canada Australia

for whom goods and services are produced; these decisions are made by individual buyers and sellers in the marketplace; examples include Germany and the United States

mixed economy an economy that is a combination of command, market, and traditional economies; private ownership is allowed

scarcity a condition of limited resources and unlimited wants by people; a fundamental concept in economics

traditional economy an economy in which production is based on customs and tradition, and in which people often grow their own food, make their own goods, and use barter to trade

THE ECONOMY AND MONEY

People, businesses, and countries obtain the items they need and want through economic activities such as producing, selling, and buying goods or services. Countries differ in the amount of economic activity that they have and in the strength of their economies.

balance of payments the accounting record of what a nation owes to and is owed by foreign countries and international organizations

boom and bust a period of rapid economic growth followed by rapid economic contraction; see business cycle

business any commercial enterprise or establishment

business cycle the periodic fluctuation in economic activity, usually reflected in levels of employment, prices, and production or gross domestic product (GDP); there are four phases: expansion, peak, contraction, trough

THE BUSINESS CYCLE

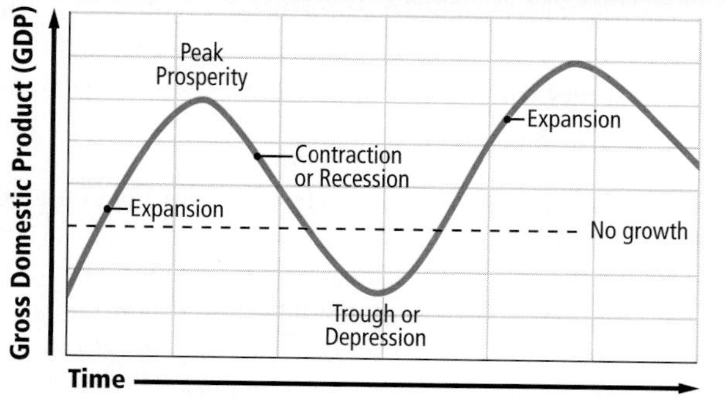

consumer a person who buys goods or services for personal use

consumer good a finished product sold to consumers for personal or home use

corporation a business in which a group of owners share in the profits and losses; as a legal entity separate from its owners, a corporation provides some protection to its owners, who are liable for the corporation's debts and losses only to the extent of their ownership investment in that corporation

currency paper or coins that a country uses for its money supply

demand the amount of goods and services that consumers are willing and able to buy at a given time; see supply and demand

devaluation a reduction in the value of a nation's currency

depression a severe drop, or contraction, in overall business activity over a long period of time; the most severe depression in modern history occurred between 1929–1939, affected nearly every country on Earth, and is known as the Great Depression

developed countries nations with strong economies and a high quality of life; often have high per capita GDPs and high levels of industrialization and technology

developing countries nations with less productive economies and a lower quality of life; often have less industrialization and technology

economic development the level of a country's economic activity, growth, and quality of life

economy the structure of economic life in a country; the total of all economic activity in a given country

entrepreneur someone who undertakes and develops a new business or develops a new product, risking failure or loss for the possibility of financial gain

foreign exchange rate the rate at which one nation's currency can get exchanged for another's

goods objects or materials that humans can purchase to satisfy their wants and needs

gross domestic product (GDP) total market value of all goods and services produced in a country in a given year; *per capita GDP* is the average value of goods and services produced per person in a country in a given year

industrialization the process of using machinery for all major forms of production

inflation an increase in overall prices

investment the purchase of something with the expectation that it will gain in value; usually property, stocks, etc.

leading indicators a set of economic factors, such as GDP and new housing construction starts, that economists use to predict a new phase of the business cycle

money any item, usually coins or paper currency, that is used in payment for goods or services

private property property that is owned by individuals and businesses, rather than the government

producer a person or group that makes goods or provides services to satisfy consumers' wants and needs

productivity the amount of goods or services that a worker or workers can produce within a given amount of time

profit the gain or excess made by selling goods or services over their costs

profit motive the desire to make profits

purchasing power the amount of income that people have available to spend on goods and services

ECONOMICS HANDBOOK

recession a period in which economic activity drops a moderate amount; technically defined as two consecutive quarters of negative growth in GDP

scarcity a condition of limited resources and unlimited wants by people; a fundamental concept in economics

services any activities that are performed for a fee

specie coined money

standard of living how well people are living; determined by the amount of goods and services they can afford

stock a share of ownership in a corporation

stock market an organized market for the sale, purchase, or exchange of shares or stocks in corporations; also known as a "stock exchange;" the origins of stock exchanges date to the Middle Ages

supply the amount of goods and services that are available at a given time; see supply and demand

supply and demand a theory describing how prices vary according to the supply of an item available and the demand for that item: when supply exceeds demand, prices drop; when demand exceeds supply, prices rise.

SUPPLY AND DEMAND

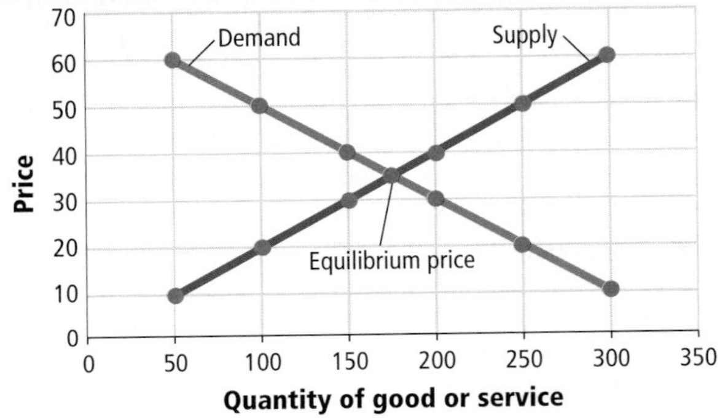

INTERNATIONAL TRADE

Countries trade with each other to obtain resources, goods, and services. Networks of trade in the ancient world, for instance, linked the Roman Empire and China. Beginning in the Age of Exploration, growing global trade led to the development of a global economy.

absolute advantage the ability of a nation, region, or company to produce a certain good or service more efficiently and cheaply than any other nation, region, or company

balance of payments the difference between the value of a country's exports and imports

balance of trade the difference between the value of a country's exports and imports

barter the exchange of one good or service for another

black market the illegal buying and selling of goods, often at high prices

commodity a product that is the same no matter who produces it

comparative advantage the ability of a company or country to produce something at a lower cost than other companies or countries

competition rivalry between businesses selling similar goods or services; a condition that often leads to lower prices or improved products

e-commerce the electronic trading of goods and services, such as over the Internet

exports goods or services that a country sells and sends to other countries

fair trade trade between a company in a developed nation and producers in less-developed nations that aims to make sure that producers receive fair prices for their goods

free trade trade among nations that is not affected by financial or legal barriers; trade without barriers

globalization the process of rapid economic integration among countries, characterized by the free flow of capital, goods, services, and labor

imports goods or services that a country brings in or purchases from another country

interdependence a relationship between countries in which they rely on one another for resources, goods, or services

market the free exchange of goods and services; also called the market place

market clearing price the price of a good or service at which supply equals demand

mercantilism an economic theory that defined a nation's power in terms of specie; used to direct most European economies from 1500 to 1800

multinational corporation a business that is based in one nation but operates divisions or subsidiaries in other nations

one-crop economy an economy that is dominated by the production of a single product

opportunity cost the value of the next-best alternative that is sacrificed when choosing to consume or produce another good or service

outsourcing the practice of using workers from outside of a company

protectionism the use of trade barriers to protect a nation's industries against foreign competition

specialization a focus on only one or two aspects of production in order to produce a product more quickly and cheaply; for example, one worker washes the wheels of the car, another cleans the interior, and another washes the body

tariff a tax charged by a government on imported goods, usually designed to make the imported goods more expensive relative to domestic goods

trade barriers financial or legal limitations to trade; prevention of free trade; see also tariff

trade deficit a condition in international trade in which the value of a nation's imports from another country exceeds the value of its exports to that country

trade-offs the goods or services sacrificed in order to consume or produce another good or service

trade surplus a condition in international trade in which the value of a nation's exports to a particular country exceeds the value of its imports from that country

underground economy illegal economic activities and unreported legal economic activities

PERSONAL ECONOMICS

Individuals make personal choices in how they manage and use their money to satisfy their needs and desires. Individuals have the choice to spend, save, or invest their money.

asset anything of value that is owned by an individual

budget a plan listing the expenses and income of an individual or organization

bankruptcy a legal process in which an individual or business whose debts exceed the value of their assets is forgiven those debts in excess of their assets

credit a system that allows consumers to pay for goods and services over time

credit bureau a company that collects and reports to its clients information about a person's financial condition and past record in meeting his or her financial obligations

credit rating an evaluation of a person's or a company's financial condition and reliability, especially concerning its record of meeting financial obligations

debt an amount of money that is owed

disposable income money that remains after all taxes have been paid

financial institutions businesses that keep and invest people's money and loan money to people; include banks or credit unions

income a gain of money that comes typically from labor or capital

interest the money that a borrower pays to a lender in return for a loan

investment the purchase of something of value with the expectation that over time it will increase in value and produce a profit

loan money given on the condition that it will be paid back, often with interest

need an economic good or service that is basic to survival, such as food, clothing, and shelter

purchasing power the amount of income that people have available to spend on goods and services

savings money or income that is not used to purchase goods or services

stock a share of ownership in a corporation

tax a required payment to a local, state, or national government; different kinds of taxes include sales taxes, income taxes, and property taxes

wage the payment a worker receives for his or her labor

want a desire for goods and services, not necessarily accompanied by the power to satisfy them

value the worth of a good or service for the purposes of exchange, usually expressed as the amount of money a consumer is willing to pay for that good or service

RESOURCES

People and businesses need resources—such as land, labor, and money—to produce goods and services.

capital generally refers to wealth, in particular wealth that can be used to finance the production of goods or services

human capital sometimes used to refer to human skills and education that affect the production of goods and services in a company or country

labor force all people who are legally old enough to work and are either working or looking for work

natural resource any material in nature that people use and value

nonrenewable resource a resource that cannot be replaced naturally, such as coal or petroleum

raw material a natural resource used to make a product or good

renewable resource a resource that Earth replaces naturally, such as water, soil, and trees

INTERNATIONAL ORGANIZATIONS AND TRADE AGREEMENTS

Countries have formed many organizations to promote economic cooperation, growth, and trade. These organizations are important in today's global economy.

European Union (EU) an organization that promotes political and economic cooperation in Europe

International Monetary Fund (IMF) a UN agency that promotes cooperation in international trade and that works to maintain stability in the exchange of countries' currencies

North American Free Trade Agreement (NAFTA) a 1993 agreement in which Canada, Mexico, and the United became one large free-trade zone, meaning that most products could be sold across borders without any sort of tariffs or trade barriers.

Organization of Petroleum Exporting Countries (OPEC) an organization that coordinates the petroleum policies of major oil producing countries

Organization of Economic Cooperation and Development (OECD) an organization of countries that promotes democracy and market economies

United Nations (UN) an organization of countries that promotes peace and security around the globe

World Bank a UN agency that provides loans to countries for development and recovery

World Trade Organization (WTO) an international organization dealing with trade between nations

Economics Handbook

Answers

Economic Systems

1. A. *free enterprise*
B. *command economy*
C. *Communism*
D. *mixed economies*
E. *Capitalism*

The Economy and Money

2. A. *Goods*
B. *service*
C. *consumer; producer*
D. *demand*
E. *gross domestic product (GDP)*

International Trade

3. A. *scarcity*
B. *outsourcing*
C. *globalization*
D. *comparative advantage*
E. *free trade*

Personal Economics

4. A. *tax*
B. *savings*
C. *credit*
D. *wage*
E. *purchasing power*

Resources

5. A. *natural resources*
B. *labor force*
C. *capital*
D. *nonrenewable resource*
E. *renewable resources*

Organizations

6. A. *European Union (EU)*
B. *United Nations (UN)*
C. *World Bank*
D. *International Monetary Fund (IMF)*
E. *Organization of Economic Cooperation and Development (OECD)*

Economic Handbook Review

REVIEWING VOCABULARY AND TERMS

On a separate sheet of paper, fill in the blanks in the following sentences:

ECONOMIC SYSTEMS

1. A. Businesses are able to operate with little government involvement in a _______ system.
B. In a _______, a central government makes all economic decisions.
C. _______ is a political system in which the government owns all property and runs a command economy.
D. Economies that combine parts of command, market, or traditional economies are called _______.
E. _______ is another name for a market economy, which is based on private ownership, free trade, and competition.

THE ECONOMY AND MONEY

2. A. _______ are objects or materials that people can buy to satisfy their needs and wants.
B. A _______ is any activity that is performed for a fee.
C. A person who buys goods or services is a _______, and a person or group that makes goods or provides services is a _______.
D. The amount of goods and services that consumers are willing and able to buy at any given time is known as _______.
E. The total value of all the goods and services produced in the United States in one year is its _______.

INTERNATIONAL TRADE

3. A. If we have an unlimited demand for a natural resource, such as oil, and there is only so much oil in the ground, we have a condition called _______.
B. The practice of using workers from outside of a company is called _______.
C. The process of rapid economic integration among countries is called _______.
D. If a country is able to produce a good or service at a lower cost than other countries, it is said to have a _______.
E. Trade among nations that is not limited by legal or economic barriers is called _______.

PERSONAL ECONOMICS

4. A. A _______ is a required payment to a local, state, or national government that is used to support public services such as education, road construction, and government aid.
B. The money we do not spend on goods or services is our _______.
C. You can use _______ to pay for goods and services over time.
D. The payment that a worker receives for his or her labor is called a _______.
E. The amount of income that people have available to spend on goods and services is known as their _______.

RESOURCES

5. A. Diamonds and gold are examples of _______, which are any materials in nature that people use and value.
B. The _______ consists of all people who are legally able to work and are working or looking for work.
C. Wealth that can be used to finance the production of goods and services is called _______.
D. Oil is an example of a _______, which is a resource that cannot be replaced naturally.
E. Water and trees are examples of _______, resources that Earth replaces naturally.

ORGANIZATIONS

6. A. Many European countries have joined the _______ to help promote political and economic cooperation across Europe.
B. The _______ consists of many agencies that promote peace and security around the world.
C. The _______ is a UN agency that provides loans to countries to help them develop their economies.
D. The _______ is a UN agency that helps protect the stability of countries' currencies.
E. Many democratic countries promote market economies through the _______.

Activities

1. With a partner, compare prices in two grocery stores. Create a chart showing the price of five items in the two stores. Also, figure the average price of the items in each store. How do you think the fact that the stores are near each other affects prices? How might prices be different if one store went out of business? How might the prices be different or similar if the United States had a command economy?

2. With a group, choose four countries from the last unit of your textbook to research. Use your library or the Internet to find out what kind of economic system each country currently has—traditional, command, or market. Do library or Internet research to find the per capita GDP, life expectancy rate, literacy rate, and the number of TVs per 1,000 people for each country. Organize this information in a five-column table. Study the information to see if you can find any patterns. Do countries with higher per capita GDPs have higher life expectancy rates, for example?

3. Work with a partner to identify some of the many types of currency used in either Latin America, Africa, Europe, or Asia. Then imagine that you are the owners of a business in the United States. You have created a new product that you want to sell in the region you selected, but people there do not use the same currency as you do. To sell your product, you will need to be able to exchange one type of currency for another. Search the Internet or look in a newspaper to find a list of currency exchange rates. For example, if your product sells for 1,000 dollars, what should the cost be in euros? In South African rand? In Japanese yen?

4. With three or four partners, create a skit that illustrates one of the following basic economic concepts: scarcity and limited resources, supply and demand, or opportunity costs and trade-offs. For example, a skit might illustrate supply and demand by showing how the high demand for the best seats at a concert increases the prices for those seats. Perform your skit for the class.

5. You can increase your purchasing power by saving money. One effective way to do this is to deposit savings in a bank account that earns you interest. Suppose you want to save $3,000 for a new computer. You decide to put $300 each month in a savings account that earns three percent interest compounded each month. If the interest is compounded, that means you earn interest on the money you deposit plus on the interest itself. Copy the chart below. Then complete it to show the value of savings at the end of six months.

Month	Monthly Deposit	Compounded Interest Earned (at 3%)	Value of Savings
1	$300	$9	$309.00
2	$300	$18.27	$627.27
3	$300		
4	$300		
5	$300		
6	$300		

Answers

1. *Students should recognize that competition keeps prices in the two stores close. If one store went out of business, the closing store might lower prices to sell remaining stock; with no competition, the other store might raise its prices. Student answers will vary but should be logical.*

2. *While answers will vary depending upon countries and factors chosen for comparison, higher GDP is usually correlated to higher life expectancies.*

3. *Answers will vary depending upon chosen currency and exchange rates.*

4. *See Alternative Assessment Handbook, Rubric 33: Skits and Reader's Theater.*

5. *Month 3: Interest: $27.82, Value of Savings: $955.09; Month 4: Interest: $37.65, Value of Savings: $1,292.74; Month 5: Interest: $47.78, Value of Savings: $1,640.52; Month 6: Interest: $58.21, Value of Savings: $1,998.73*

Excerpt from

The Dao De Jing

by Laozi

道

▲The Chinese character for Dao

About the Reading *The* Dao De Jing *was written about 2,500 years ago. It forms the basis of Daoism, an ancient Chinese belief system that influenced many Asian cultures. Daoism holds that all things in nature are part of a unified whole. Light balances dark, hot balances cold, yin balances yang, to produce a harmony. The word "Dao" is usually translated as "the path" or "the way." The Daoist way counsels retreat from the everyday world. By accepting and living in harmony with the laws of nature, a person can find peace.*

Chapter Two

All under heaven see beauty as beauty only because they also see ugliness.
All announce that good is good only because they also denounce what is bad.
Therefore, something and nothing give birth to one another
Difficult and easy complete one another.
Long and short fashion one another.
High and low arise from one another.
Notes and tones harmonize with one another.
Front and back follow one another.
Thus, the True Person acts without striving and teaches without words.
Deny nothing to the ten thousand things.
Nourish them without claiming authority,
Benefit them without demanding gratitude,
Do the work, then move on.
And, the fruits of your labor will last forever.

Chapter Fifteen

The ancient followers of the Dao were subtle, mysterious, and penetrating.
They were too deep to be fathomed.
All we can do is describe their appearance.
Hesitant, as if crossing a winter stream.
Watchful, as if aware of neighbors on all sides.
Respectful, like a visiting guest.
Yielding, like ice beginning to melt.
Simple, like an uncarved block.
Open, like a valley.
Obscure, like muddy water.
Who else can be still and let the muddy water slowly become clear?
Who else can remain at rest and slowly come to life?
Those who hold fast to the Dao do not try to fill themselves to the brim.
Because they do not try to be full they can be worn out and yet ever new.

fathomed understood
obscure unclear, hidden from view

Skills Focus READING LIKE A HISTORIAN

1. **Identify** In your own words, state the main idea of Chapter Two.
2. **Elaborate** Daoism arose at a time of political instability in China. How would the ideas expressed in Daoism be appealing in a time of unrest?

Answers

Reading Like a Historian

1. *Students should recognize that the chapter discusses the balance in nature. Students should also recognize the significance of the last sentence, "…the fruits of your labor will last forever."*

2. *Students should discuss the Dao idea of retreating from everyday conflicts and strife. In their responses, students should mention the significant passages and words supporting this idea, including watchful, respectful, yielding.*

Excerpt from

The Apology

from the *Dialogues* of Plato

About the Reading *The Greek philosopher Plato (c. 429–c. 347 BC) was a student of Socrates. Socrates was known for his relentless pursuit of truth and his questioning of authority. In 399 BC, in a time of unrest following Athens' defeat in the Peloponnesian War, Socrates was brought to trial on charges of corrupting the minds of his young students. He was sentenced to death. "The Apology" is Plato's version of Socrates' defense at his trial. As used here, "apology" means a formal defense of one's beliefs or actions.*

A bust of Plato ▲

Let us reflect in another way, and we shall see that there is great reason to hope that death is a good, for one of two things: either death is a state of nothingness and utter unconsciousness, or, as men say, there is a change and migration of the soul from this world to another.

Now if you suppose that there is no consciousness, but a sleep like the sleep of him who is undisturbed even by the sight of dreams, death will be an unspeakable gain. For if a person were to select the night in which his sleep was undisturbed even by dreams, and were to compare with this the other days and nights of his life, and then were to tell us how many days and nights he had passed in the course of his life better and more pleasantly than this one, I think that any man, . . . will not find many such days or nights, when compared with the others. Now if death is like this, I say that to die is gain; for eternity is then only a single night.

But if death is the journey to another place, and there, as men say, all the dead are, what good, O my friends and judges, can be greater than this? If indeed when the pilgrim arrives in the world below, he is delivered from the professors of justice in this world, and finds the true judges who are said to give judgment there, . . . that pilgrimage will be worth making. . . . Nay, if this be true, let me die again and again. . . . Above all, I shall be able to continue my search into true and false knowledge; as in this world, so also in that; I shall find out who is wise, and who pretends to be wise, and is not. What would not a man give, O judges, to be able to examine the leader of the great Trojan expedition;. . . What infinite delight would there be in conversing with them and asking them questions! For in that world they do not put a man to death for this; certainly not. For besides being happier in that world than in this, they will be immortal, if what is said is true.

Wherefore, O judges, be of good cheer about death, and know this of a truth—that no evil can happen to a good man, either in life or after death. . . .

The hour of departure has arrived, and we go our ways—I to die, and you to live. Which is better God only knows.

Skills Focus READING LIKE A HISTORIAN

1. **Describe** Describe how Socrates feels about death. Does he believe in an afterlife?
2. **Analyze** What does Socrates mean when he says that "in that world they do not put a man to death for this"?
3. **Elaborate** Why might Athenians turn against their tradition of free speech in a time of uncertainty?

Answers

Reading Like a Historian

1. *Socrates does not fear death; he states that no evil can happen to a good man, in life or after death. He does not know if the afterlife exists or not.*

2. *In the afterlife, Socrates would be able to ask questions freely; he could continue his pursuit of knowledge and not be put to death for these actions.*

3. *Free speech means that people have the right to question policies, practices, and their leaders. During times of unrest, government leaders may feel this right adds to unrest.*

Primary Source Library

Excerpt from

Politics

by Aristotle

A bust of Aristotle ▲

About the Reading *One of the most influential ancient Greek philosophers, Aristotle (384–322 BC) wrote about many subjects, including biology, government, physics, and poetry. Aristotle's* Politics *is one of the most important works of political philosophy. After more than 2,000 years, it is still discussed by political scholars. In this excerpt, Aristotle describes the characteristics of a democracy.*

The basis of a democratic state is liberty; which, according to the common opinion of men, can only be enjoyed in such a state; this they affirm to be the great end of every democracy. One principle of liberty is for all to rule and be ruled in turn, . . . whence it follows that the majority must be supreme, and that whatever the majority approve must be the end and the just. Every citizen, it is said, must have equality, and therefore in a democracy the poor have more power than the rich, because there are more of them, and the will of the majority is supreme. This, then, is one note of liberty, which all democrats affirm to be the principle of their state. Another is that a man should live as he likes. This, they say, is the privilege of a freeman, since, on the other hand, not to live as a man likes is the mark of a slave. This is the second characteristic of democracy, whence has arisen the claim of men to be ruled by none, if possible, or, if this is impossible, to rule and be ruled in turns; and so it contributes to the freedom based upon equality.

. . . [T]he characteristics of democracy are as follows: the election of officers by all out of all; and that all should rule over each, and each in his turn over all; that the appointment to all offices, or to all but those which require experience and skill, should be made by lot; that no property qualification should be required for offices, or only a very low one; that a man should not hold the same office twice, or not often, or in the case of few except military offices: that the tenure of all offices, or of as many as possible, should be brief, that all men should sit in judgment, or that judges selected out of all should judge, in all matters, or in most and in the greatest and most important . . . ; that the assembly should be supreme over all causes, or at any rate over the most important, and the magistrates over none or only over a very few. . . .

These are the points common to all democracies; but democracy and demos in their truest form are based upon the recognized principle of democratic justice, that all should count equally; for equality implies that the poor should have no more share in the government than the rich, and should not be the only rulers, but that all should rule equally according to their numbers.

magistrates government officials
demos democratic populace or citizenry

Skills Focus READING LIKE A HISTORIAN

1. **Identify** According to Aristotle, what are two principles of liberty? How are they related?
2. **Evaluate** Aristotle asserts that "the majority must be supreme." Do you agree or disagree? Explain your answer.

Answers

Reading Like a Historian

1. *for all to rule and be ruled in turn; man should live as he likes, freedom is based upon equality*

2. *Student answers will vary, but students should discuss the importance of "one person, one vote" in a democracy.*

Excerpt from

The Gallic Wars

by Julius Caesar

About the Reading *Soldier and statesman, Julius Caesar helped transform ancient Rome from a republic to an empire. From 58 to 50 BC, he led a Roman army that conquered Gaul, a land that included modern-day France, Belgium, and parts of Switzerland. He published an account of his campaign in* The Gallic Wars *(50 BC). In this excerpt, Caesar describes the role of the Druids, or priests, in the lives of the Gauls.*

A statue of Julius Caesar ▲

Throughout all Gaul there are two orders of those men who are of any rank and dignity. . . . But of these two orders, one is that of the Druids, the other that of the knights. The former are engaged in things sacred, conduct the public and the private sacrifices, and interpret all matters of religion. To these a large number of the young men resort for the purpose of instruction, and they [the Druids] are in great honor among them. For they determine [judge] respecting almost all controversies, public and private; and if any crime has been perpetrated, if murder has been committed, if there be any dispute about an inheritance, if any about boundaries, these same persons decide it; they decree rewards and punishments; if any one, either in a private or public capacity, has not submitted to their decision, they interdict him from the sacrifices. This among them is the most heavy punishment. Those who have been thus interdicted are esteemed in the number of the impious and the criminal: all shun them, and avoid their society and conversation, lest they receive some evil from their contact; nor is justice administered to them when seeking it, nor is any dignity bestowed on them. Over all these Druids one presides, who possesses supreme authority among them. Upon his death, if any individual among the rest is pre-eminent in dignity, he succeeds; but, if there are many equal, the election is made by the suffrages [votes] of the Druids; sometimes they even contend for the presidency with arms. These assemble at a fixed period of the year in a consecrated [holy] place in the territories of the Carnutes, which is reckoned the central region of the whole of Gaul. Hither all, who have disputes, assemble from every part, and submit to their decrees and determinations. This institution is supposed to have been devised in Britain, and to have been brought over from it into Gaul; and now those who desire to gain a more accurate knowledge of that system generally proceed thither [Britain] for the purpose of studying it.

resort turn to, make use of
interdict prohibit, forbid, ban

Skills Focus READING LIKE A HISTORIAN

1. **Describe** Are Druids religious leaders or political leaders? Explain your answer. What does this say about the Gauls?
2. **Draw Conclusions** Why might Julius Caesar want to give an account of his military triumphs in Gaul on the eve of his own war with Pompey?

Answers

Reading Like a Historian

1. *Druids were religious leaders, but since they also served as judges and their leaders were elected, they were also political leaders.*

2. *to make people aware of his triumphs and to call attention to the importance of knights; remind everyone that he is a strong, victorious military leader*

Excerpt from

Beowulf

by Anonymous (translated by Burton Raffel)

About the Reading *The epic poem* Beowulf *is the first great work of English literature. It tells of Beowulf, a warrior from Sweden who sails to Denmark to rid King Hrothgar's people from the monster Grendel. Much of the story is based on early Celtic and Scandinavian folk legends. In this excerpt, Beowulf and Grendel are fighting. Beowulf has seized Grendel's arm. Shrieking with pain and defeat, Grendel tries to flee. But he cannot break Beowulf's powerful grip.*

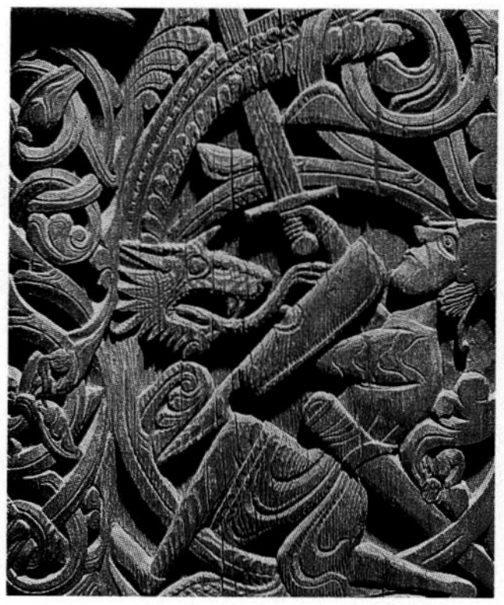

Viking carving, c. 1100s ▲

That mighty protector of men
Meant to hold the monster till its life
Leaped out, knowing the fiend was no use
To anyone in Denmark. All of Beowulf's
Band had jumped from their beds, ancestral
Swords raised and ready, determined
To protect their prince if they could. Their
courage
Was great but all wasted: they could hack at
Grendel
From every side, trying to open
A path for his evil soul, but their points
Could not hurt him, the sharpest and hardest
iron
Could not scratch at his skin, for that sin-
stained demon
Had bewitched all men's weapons, laid spells
That blunted every mortal man's blade.
And yet his time had come, his days
Were over, his death near; down
To hell he would go, swept groaning and
helpless
To the waiting hands of still worse
fiends.
Now he discovered—once the afflictor
Of men, tormentor of their days—what it
meant
To feud with Almighty God: Grendel
Saw that his strength was deserting him, his
claws
Bound fast, Higlac's brave follower tearing at
His hands. The monster's hatred rose higher,
But his power had gone. He twisted in pain,
And the bleeding sinews deep in his shoulder
Snapped, muscle and bone split
And broke. The battle was over, Beowulf
Had been granted new glory; Grendel escaped,
But wounded as he was could flee to his den,
His miserable hole at the bottom of the marsh,
Only to die, to wait for the end
Of all his days.

Higlac's brave follower meaning Beowulf; Higlac is Beowulf's uncle and feudal lord

Skills Focus READING LIKE A HISTORIAN

1. **Recall** According to this excerpt, why can Beowulf's men not harm Grendel?
2. **Draw Conclusions** In what way is the poem's blending of Christian belief with ancient mythology characteristic of the Middle Ages?

Answers

Reading Like a Historian

1. *Grendel had bewitched the weapons of Beowulf's men, and his spells had blunted their sword blades.*
2. *Student answers will vary. Students should recognize that Grendel is a mythical being with mythical powers; now he is fighting against Christian forces who will overcome him. Like other stories from the Middle Ages, it is a tale of good and evil.*

Excerpt from

Magna Carta

About the Reading Magna Carta, *or Great Charter, is an agreement between King John of England and a group of English nobles. The nobles forced the king to sign the agreement in 1215. It required the king to give up certain rights, follow certain basic legal procedures, and accept that his power was subject to law.* Magna Carta *is one of the earliest documents limiting the powers of a ruler and listing the rights of the ruled. The "we" and "us" in* Magna Carta *refer to the king.*

Presenting Magna Carta to King John ▲

[1] In the first place we have granted to God, and by this our present charter confirmed for us and our heirs forever that the English Church shall be free, and shall have her rights entire, and her liberties inviolate; . . . We have also granted to all freemen of our kingdom, for us and our heirs forever, all the underwritten liberties, to be had and held by them and their heirs, of us and our heirs forever.

[7] A widow, after the death of her husband, shall forthwith and without difficulty have her marriage portion and inheritance; nor shall she give anything for her dower, or for her marriage portion, or for the inheritance which her husband and she held on the day of the death of that husband; and she may remain in the house of her husband for forty days after his death, within which time her dower shall be assigned to her.

[8] No widow shall be compelled to marry, so long as she prefers to live without a husband; provided always that she gives security not to marry without our consent, if she holds of us, or without the consent of the lord of whom she holds, if she holds of another.

[38] No bailiff for the future shall, upon his own unsupported complaint, put anyone to his "law," without credible witnesses brought for this purposes.

[39] No freemen shall be taken or imprisoned or disseised or exiled or in any way destroyed, nor will we go upon him nor send upon him, except by the lawful judgment of his peers or by the law of the land.

[40] To no one will we sell, to no one will we refuse or delay right or justice.

[45] We will appoint as justices, constables, sheriffs, or bailiffs only such as know the law of the realm and mean to observe it well.

bailiff official employed by an English sheriff to make arrests and executions

disseised deprived of legal possession of property

Skills Focus READING LIKE A HISTORIAN

1. **Identify Main Ideas** What are the main ideas in the first paragraph?
2. **Analyze** Paragraphs 38–40 and 45 discuss how justice should be carried out. What do they suggest about justice under King John?
3. **Make Judgments** What does *Magna Carta* tell you about the relationship between kings and nobles under the feudal system?

Answers

Reading Like a Historian

1. *Paragraph 1: The Church shall be free, not subject to control by the king, and that the rights and liberties granted in the charter would be granted to English citizens forever.*

2. *King John may not have carried out laws fairly or justly. People may have been imprisoned capriciously, without a fair trial, or without any trial. Judges may have served the king, not the law, and they may not have understood the law.*

3. *Students should recognize that under the feudal system, kings had the power to accuse people of crimes, imprison and execute people, and that people had no recourse against a king.*

Primary Source Library

Excerpt from

Summa Theologica

by Thomas Aquinas

About the Reading *Thomas Aquinas (c.1225–1274) was a Roman Catholic philosopher and theologian. Many Catholics consider Aquinas to be the church's greatest theologian. The excerpt below is from Aquinas's most famous work, the* Summa Theologica, *a systematic description of Roman Catholic theology. Aquinas's method is to pose questions and then answer them. In this excerpt, he discusses who may make laws, the purpose of laws, and the limits of laws.*

Thomas Aquinas, from a 1442 book ▲

PRIMARY SOURCE LIBRARY

Whether the reason of any man is competent to make laws?

. . . A law, properly speaking, regards first and foremost the order to the common good. Now to order anything to the common good, belongs either to the whole people, or to someone who is the viceregent of the whole people. And therefore the making of a law belongs either to the whole people or to a public personage who has care of the whole people: since in all other matters the directing of anything to the end concerns him to whom the end belongs. . . .

Whether it belongs to the human law to repress all vices?

. . . Human law is framed for a number of human beings, the majority of whom are not perfect in virtue. Wherefore human laws do not forbid all vices, from which the virtuous abstain, but only the more grievous vices, from which it is possible for the majority to abstain; and chiefly those that are to the hurt of others, without the prohibition of which human society could not be maintained: thus human law prohibits murder, theft and such like.

. . . The purpose of human law is to lead men to virtue, not suddenly, but gradually. Wherefore it does not lay upon the multitude of imperfect men the burdens of those who are already virtuous, viz. that they should abstain from all evil. Otherwise these imperfect ones, being unable to bear such precepts, would break out into yet greater evils: thus it is written . . . (Mt. 9:17) that if "new wine," i.e. precepts of a perfect life, "is put into old bottles," i.e. into imperfect men, "the bottles break, and the wine runneth out."

viceregent assistant to a regent or ruler
repress to check, put down, or prevent
abstain refrain, keep from doing
grievous serious, grave
Mt. 9:17 A passage from the Gospel of Matthew in the Christian Bible. Aquinas frequently cites the Bible.

Skills Focus READING LIKE A HISTORIAN

1. **Identify** According to Aquinas, who can make laws?
2. **Make Inferences** What is the purpose of human law? Does Aquinas believe that governments should exercise unlimited powers when it comes to making laws?

Answers

Reading Like a Historian

1. *The people or the ruler who takes care of all the people should make laws.*

2. *to promote the common good, to take care of people; to prevent horrible deeds; to lead men to virtue*

Excerpt from

Travels in Asia and Africa, 1325–1345

by Ibn Battutah

About the Reading *Ibn Battutah (1304–1369?) was one of the greatest travelers of all time. A scholar, judge, and explorer, Battutah traveled throughout the Muslim world for nearly 30 years, covering some 75,000 miles. He visited Turkey, Iran, China, Sri Lanka, Southeast Asia, India, East Africa, and North Africa. Battutah dictated the stories of his journeys to a scholar named Ibn Juzay al-Kalbi. This record of his travels was published as his book* Travels in Asia and Africa, 1325–1345. *This excerpt describes Battutah's visit to Baghdad in 1327, when it was ruled by the Mongols.*

Baghdad garden, 1396 ▲

Thence we travelled to Baghdad, the Abode of Peace and Capital of Islam. Here there are two bridges . . . on which the people promenade night and day, both men and women. The town has eleven cathedral mosques, eight on the right bank and three on the left, together with very many other mosques and madrasas, only the latter are all in ruins.

The baths at Baghdad are numerous and excellently constructed, most of them being painted with pitch, which has the appearance of black marble. This pitch is brought from a spring between Kufa and Basra, from which it flows continually. It gathers at the sides of the spring like clay and is shovelled up and brought to Baghdad. Each establishment has a large number of private bathrooms, every one of which has also a wash-basin in the corner, with two taps supplying hot and cold water. Every bather is given three towels, one to wear round his waist when he goes in, another to wear round his waist when he comes out, and the third to dry himself with. In no town other than Baghdad have I seen all this elaborate arrangement, though some other towns approach it in this respect.

The western part of Baghdad was the earliest to be built, but it is now for the most part in ruins. In spite of that there remain in it still thirteen quarters, each like a city in itself and possessing two or three baths. The hospital [*maristan*] is a vast ruined edifice, of which only vestiges remain.

The eastern part has an abundance of bazaars, the largest of which is called the Tuesday bazaar. On this side there are no fruit trees, but all the fruit is brought from the western side, where there are orchards and gardens.

Abode home
madrasa (Arabic) school, often associated with a mosque
pitch sticky, oil-based substance used for waterproofing

Skills Focus READING LIKE A HISTORIAN

1. **Interpret** Why do you think Battutah found the baths in Baghdad worth highlighting in his account? Explain your answer.
2. **Draw Conclusions** What did it say about Muslim civilization at the time that someone like Ibn Battutah could travel so widely in many different lands?

PRIMARY SOURCE LIBRARY

Primary Source Library

Answers

Reading Like a Historian

1. *Students should recognize that Battutah was surprised by the extensive number and the careful construction of the baths, at a time when many people did not bathe regularly.*
2. *Students should note that foreigners were welcome; although the logistics were probably difficult, it was possible to travel from country to country.*

Excerpt from

The Chronicle

by Jean de Venette

About the Reading *Jean de Venette (c. 1307–c. 1370) was a Roman Catholic monk in Paris. His* Chronicle *covers 1340 to 1368, the years when the Black Death appeared in Europe. De Venette's eyewitness account of the plague and other events provides valuable information about social, religious, and political life of the fourteenth century.*

Burying plague victims in France, 1349 ▲

In the month of August, 1348, after Vespers when the sun was beginning to set, a big and very bright star appeared above Paris, toward the west. . . . It is . . . possible that it was a presage of the amazing pestilence to come, which, in fact, followed very shortly. . . .

This plague, it is said, began among the unbelievers, came to Italy, and then crossing the Alps reached Avignon, where it attacked several cardinals and took from them their whole household. Then it spread, unforeseen, to France, through Gascony and Spain, little by little, from town to town, from village to village, from house to house, and finally from person to person. It even crossed over to Germany, though it was not so bad there as with us. . . .

Some said that this pestilence was caused by infection of the air and waters, since there was at this time no famine nor lack of food supplies, but on the contrary great abundance. As a result of this theory of infected water and air as the source of the plague the Jews were suddenly and violently charged with infecting wells and water and corrupting the air. The whole world rose up against them cruelly on this account. In Germany and other parts of the world where Jews lived, they were massacred and slaughtered by Christians, and many thousands were burned everywhere, indiscriminately. The unshaken, if fatuous, constancy of the men and their wives was remarkable. For mothers hurled their children first into the fire that they might not be baptized and then leaped in after them to burn with their husbands and children. It is said that many bad Christians were found who in like manner put poison into wells. But in truth, such poisonings, granted that they actually were perpetrated, could not have caused so great a plague nor have infected so many people. There were other causes; for example, the will of God and the corrupt humors and evil inherent in air and earth. Perhaps the poisonings, if they actually took place in some localities, reinforced these causes. The plague lasted in France for the greater part of the years 1348 and 1349 and then ceased. Many country villages and many houses in good towns remained empty and deserted. Many houses, including some splendid dwellings, very soon fell into ruins. Even in Paris several houses were thus ruined, though fewer here than elsewhere.

presage sign
fatuous silly and pointless
constancy faithfulness
humors bodily fluids whose balance was thought to be essential to well-being

Skills Focus **READING LIKE A HISTORIAN**

1. **Describe** What does Venette think about some of the explanations for the causes of the plague?
2. **Analyze** What do the words "fatuous" and "constancy" used to describe those Jews who chose death rather than abandon their religious faith indicate about the author's point of view?

Answers

Reading Like a Historian

1. *He does not believe that some explanations could be true, for example, poisoning could not have caused so many deaths. Venette does state that the plague could have been the will of God or problems in the air or earth.*

2. *Although Venette's words imply that he believes Jews should have chosen to convert to Christianity and live rather than die, he is impressed with the commitment of the Jewish people to their religion.*

Excerpt from

The Canterbury Tales

by Geoffrey Chaucer

About the Reading *The* Canterbury Tales *are a collection of stories that give us a picture of life in the Middle Ages. By placing travelers together on a pilgrimage, or religious journey, Chaucer (1343–1400) was able to include the entire range of English medieval society in his story. The excerpt, from the Prologue to the poem, introduces a handful of Chaucer's large cast of characters.*

Pilgrims leaving Canterbury, early 1500s ▲

It happened in that season that one day
In Southwark, at The Tabard, as I lay
Ready to go on pilgrimage and start
For Canterbury, most devout at heart,
At night there came into that hostelry
Some nine and twenty in a company
Of sundry folk happening then to fall
In fellowship, and they were pilgrims all
That towards Canterbury meant to ride. . .
There was a *Knight*, a most distinguished man,
Who from the day on which he first began
To ride abroad had followed chivalry,
Truth, honor, generousness, and courtesy.
He had done nobly in his sovereign's war
And ridden into battle, no man more,
As well in Christian as in heathen places,
And ever honored for his noble graces. . .
A *Monk* there was, one of the finest sort
Who rode the country; hunting was his sport.
A manly man, to be an Abbot able;
Many a dainty horse he had in stable. . .
He did not rate that text at a plucked hen
Which says that hunters are not holy men. . .
There was a *Merchant* with a forking beard
And motley dress; high on his horse he sat,
Upon his head a Flemish beaver hat
And on his feet daintily buckled boots. . .
This estimable Merchant so had set
His wits to work, none knew he was in debt. . .
An *Oxford Cleric,* still a student though,
One who had taken logic long ago
Was there; his horse was thinner than a rake,
And he was not too fat, I undertake,
But had a hollow look, a sober stare;
The thread upon his overcoat was bare. . .
A worthy *woman* from beside *Bath* city
Was with us, somewhat deaf, which was a pity.
In making cloth she showed so great a bent
She bettered those of Ypres and of Ghent. . . .
A worthy woman all her life, what's more
She'd had five husbands, all at the church door,
Apart from other company in youth;
No need just now to speak of that, forsooth. . .
There was a *Plowman* with him there. . .
Many a load of dung one time or other
He must have carted through the morning dew.
He was an honest worker, good and true.

hostelry inn; The Tabard is a lodging place
heathen pagan; for Chaucer, a non-Christian
motley multi-colored
cleric clergyman; Oxford University trained clergymen

Skills Focus — Reading Like a Historian

1. **Identify** Who are some of the people on the pilgrimage?
2. **Analyze** How does Chaucer's cast of characters represent the changes that were taking place during the High Middle Ages?

PRIMARY SOURCE LIBRARY

Answers

Reading Like a Historian

1. *a variety of people, including a knight, a monk, a merchant, a student from Oxford, a clothmaker from Bath, and a plowman*

2. *People from different backgrounds and classes mixed and traveled together. They were all making a religious pilgrimage.*

Primary Source Library

PRIMARY SOURCE LIBRARY

Excerpt from

Refusal at the Diet of Worms

by Martin Luther

About the Reading *After being excommunicated by Pope Leo X, Martin Luther (1483–1546) was summoned by Emperor Charles V to appear before the Diet of Worms in 1521. He was given an opportunity to renounce his writings. Luther asked for a day to consider his response. His speech the following day became a ringing defense of individual conscience.*

Martin Luther, c. 1521 ▶

"Your Imperial Majesty and Your Lordships: I ask you to observe that my books are not all of the same kind.

"There are some in which I have dealt with piety in faith and morals with such simplicity and so agreeably with the Gospels that my adversaries themselves are compelled to admit them useful, harmless, and clearly worth reading by a Christian . . .

"The second kind consists in those writings leveled against the papacy and the doctrine of the papists, as against those who by their wicked doctrines and precedents have laid waste Christendom by doing harm to the souls and the bodies of men . . . Through the Pope's laws and through man-made teachings the consciences of the faithful . . . have been devoured . . . by unbelievable tyranny, . . . If then I recant these, the only effect will be to add strength to such tyranny, to open not the windows but the main doors to such blasphemy . . .

"The third kind consists of those books which I have written against private individuals, . . . who have exerted themselves in defense of the Roman tyranny and to the overthrow of that piety which I have taught. I confess that I have been more harsh against them than befits my religious vows and my profession . . . But it is not in my power to recant them, because that recantation would give that tyranny and blasphemy an occasion to lord it over those whom I defend and to rage against God's people more violently than ever . . .

"And so, through the mercy of God, I ask Your Imperial Majesty, and Your Illustrious Lordships, or anyone of any degree, to defeat them [Luther's books] by the writings of the Prophets or by the Gospels; for I shall be most ready, if I be better instructed, to recant any error, and I shall be the first in casting my writings in the fire . . ."

Thereupon the Orator of the Empire, in a tone of upbraiding . . . asked for a plain reply . . . Was he prepared to recant, or no?

Luther then replied: . . . "Unless I am convicted [convinced] of error by the testimony of Scripture, . . . I cannot and will not recant anything, for to act against our conscience is neither safe for us, nor open to us. On this I take my stand. I can do no other. God help me. Amen."

recant withdraw and renounce
upbraiding disapproval

Skills Focus **READING LIKE A HISTORIAN**

1. **Identify** What are the three categories into which Luther places his books? Why does he say that he cannot recant the second kind?
2. **Explain** Why would Luther's position have posed a threat to the authority both of the pope and of the emperor?

Answers

Reading Like a Historian

1. *One group deals with piety in faith and morals; the second group consists of writings critical of the papacy and the ways in which Church doctrines have been interpreted and applied; the third group consists of criticisms of various individuals.*

2. *Students should recognize that Luther's refusal to recant opened the door to strong challenges to the pope and emperor.*

Excerpt from

Don Quixote

by Miguel de Cervantes

About the Reading *Miguel de Cervantes (1547–1616) lived during the peak and decline of Spain's Golden Age. His masterpiece* Don Quixote *(1606; 1615) is a parody of medieval stories of knights and chivalry, which were extremely popular in Cervantes's time. It reflects the disillusionment that began to affect Spanish society as the country declined in power.*

Picasso's drawing of Don Quixote and the windmill ▲

At this point they caught sight of thirty or forty windmills which were standing on the plain there, and no sooner had Don Quixote laid eyes upon them than he turned to his squire and said, "Fortune is guiding our affairs better than we could have wished; for you see there before you, friend Sancho Panza, some thirty or more lawless giants with whom I mean to do battle. I shall deprive them of their lives, and with the spoils from this encounter we shall begin to enrich ourselves; for this is righteous warfare, and it is a great service to God to remove so accursed a breed from the face of the earth."

"What giants?" said Sancho Panza.

"Those that you see there," replied his master, "those with the long arms, some of which are as much as two leagues in length."

"But look, your Grace, those are not giants but windmills, and what appear to be arms are their wings which, when whirled in the breeze, cause the millstone to go."

"It is plain to be seen," said Don Quixote, "that you have had little experience in this matter of adventures. If you are afraid, go off to one side and say your prayers while I am engaging them in fierce, unequal combat."

Saying this, he gave spurs to his steed Rocinante, without paying any heed to Sancho's warning that these were truly windmills and not giants that he was riding forth to attack. Nor even when he was close upon them did he perceive what they really were, but shouted at the top of his lungs, "Do not seek to flee, cowards and vile creatures that you are, for it is but a single knight with whom you have to deal!"

At that moment a little wind came up and the big wings began turning.

He thereupon commended himself with all his heart to his lady Dulcinea, beseeching her to succor him in this peril; and, being well covered with his shield and with his lance at rest, he bore down upon them at a full gallop and fell upon the first mill that stood in his way, giving a thrust at the wing, which was whirling at such a speed that his lance was broken into bits and both horse and horseman went rolling over the plain, very much battered indeed.

squire a young nobleman who attends a knight
millstone large stone used for grinding
succor help

Skills Focus READING LIKE A HISTORIAN

1. **Describe** Use examples from this excerpt to show how Cervantes portrays Don Quixote as both noble and foolish.
2. **Analyze** In your opinion, is Don Quixote a crazy person who refuses to see things as they really are, or is he more like a person who refuses to compromise his ideals so he can achieve a greater good?

Answers

Reading Like a Historian

1. *noble—fighting for the lady Dulcinea, unafraid, courageous; foolish—fights windmills, does not listen to his friend, gets hurt*

2. *Answers will vary, but based on the excerpt, most students will probably conclude that Don Quixote was a bit crazy.*

Excerpt from

Leviathan

by Thomas Hobbes

About the Reading *Thomas Hobbes (1588–1679) wrote* Leviathan *in 1651, while in exile in France. At the time England was ruled by Parliament, making it unsafe for Royalists like Hobbes. In* Leviathan, *Hobbes argues that in their natural state people are selfish and constantly at war. The only way society can be established is if people surrender some rights to an authority that offers safety. In this excerpt, Hobbes discusses the possible forms of sovereign governments.*

Cover page of *Leviathan* ▲

The difference of Commonwealths consisteth in the difference of the sovereign, or the person representative of all and every one of the multitude. And because the sovereignty is either in one man, or in an assembly of more than one; and into that assembly either every man hath right to enter, or not every one, but certain men distinguished from the rest; it is manifest there can be but three kinds of Commonwealth. For the representative must needs be one man, or more; and if more, then it is the assembly of all, or but of a part. When the representative is one man, then is the Commonwealth a monarchy; when an assembly of all that will come together, then it is a democracy, or popular Commonwealth; when an assembly of a part only, then it is called an aristocracy. Other kind of Commonwealth there can be none: for either one, or more, or all, must have the sovereign power (which I have shown to be indivisible) entire.

There be other names of government in the histories and books of policy; as tyranny and oligarchy; but they are not the names of other forms of government, but of the same forms misliked [misnamed]. For they that are discontented under monarchy call it tyranny; and they that are displeased with aristocracy call it oligarchy: so also, they which find themselves grieved under a democracy call it anarchy, which signifies want of government; and yet I think no man believes that want of government is any new kind of government: nor by the same reason ought they to believe that the government is of one kind when they like it, and another when they mislike it or are oppressed by the governors.

commonwealth an independent state or community
manifest clear, plain, apparent
want lack, absence

Skills Focus READING LIKE A HISTORIAN

1. **Describe** In your own words, describe Hobbes's three basic forms of commonwealth. What do they have in common?
2. **Draw a Conclusion** What does Hobbes mean when he says that "sovereign power" is "indivisible"? Does that leave any room for compromise in the struggle between king and Parliament?

Answers

Reading Like a Historian

1. *monarchy, one man; democracy, when all come together; aristocracy, assembly of one part; each is a recognized form of government with an accepted sovereign*

2. *Only one person or group can serve as a government; students should support their answers with reason and logic.*

Excerpt from

The Spirit of Laws

by Charles de Secondat, Baron de Montesquieu

About the Reading *Charles de Secondat, Baron de Montesquieu (1689–1755), was a French jurist and influential political thinker during the Enlightenment. He drew on the classical past of ancient Greece and Rome and the contemporary government of Great Britain for some of his ideas. His best-known work,* The Spirit of Laws *(1748), contains his theories of separation of governing powers and checks and balances, two ideas that strongly influenced the United States Constitution.*

Baron de Montesquieu ▲

In every government there are three sorts of power: the legislative; the executive, in respect to things dependent on the law of nations; and the executive, in regard to things that depend on the civil law.

By virtue of the first, the prince or magistrate enacts temporary or perpetual laws, and amends or abrogates those that have been already enacted. By the second, he makes peace or war, sends or receives embassies; establishes the public security, and provides against invasions. By the third, he punishes criminals, or determines the disputes that arise between individuals. The latter we shall call the judiciary power, and the other simply the executive power of the state.

The political liberty of the subject is a tranquility of mind, arising from the opinion each person has of his safety. In order to have this liberty, it is requisite the government be so constituted as one man need not be afraid of another.

When the legislative and executive powers are united in the same person, or in the same body of magistrates, there can be no liberty; because apprehensions may arise, lest the same monarch or senate should enact tyrannical laws, to execute them in a tyrannical manner.

Again, there is no liberty, if the power of judging be not separated from the legislative and executive powers. Were it joined with the legislative, the life and liberty of the subject would be exposed to arbitrary control, for the judge would then be the legislator. Were it joined to the executive power, the judge might behave with all the violence of an oppressor.

There would be an end of every thing were the same man, or the same body, whether of the nobles or of the people to exercise those three powers that of enacting laws, that of executing the public resolutions, and that of judging the crimes or differences of individuals.

What a situation must the poor subject be in, under those republics! The same body of magistrates are possessed, as executors of the laws, of the whole power they have given themselves in quality of legislators. They may plunder the state by their general determinations; and as they have likewise the judiciary power in their hands, every private citizen may be ruined by their particular decisions.

---

abrogates abolishes

arbitrary unrestrained; based on individual whim

Skills Focus READING LIKE A HISTORIAN

1. **Analyze** Why does Montesquieu say it is a bad idea to combine legislative and executive powers in one person?
2. **Make Judgments** Review the excerpt from Hobbes on R66. How do his ideas and Montesquieu's differ?

Answers

Reading Like a Historian

1. *If legislative and executive functions are carried out by the same person, the laws may be tyrannical and carried out in a tyrannical manner, creating fear among the people; if judges are also legislators, then judges might behave as oppressors.*

2. *Hobbes discusses three forms of government, monarchy, democracy, and aristocracy. Montesquieu discusses the importance of separating legislative, executive, and judicial functions within a government or governing body.*

Excerpt from

The Declaration of Independence

by Thomas Jefferson

Thomas Jefferson ▲

About the Reading *In April 1775, American colonists fought English soldiers at Lexington and Concord. By the summer of 1776, events had advanced far enough that the Continental Congress voted for independence. The job of writing a formal declaration of that independence fell to Thomas Jefferson. Only 33 years old at the time, Jefferson was respected by his colleagues for his writing ability. Still, Congress revised about one-fifth of his draft. The passage that begins "We hold these truths to be self-evident," however, they left untouched. It has become a lasting statement of America's founding ideals.*

In Congress, July 4, 1776

The unanimous Declaration of the thirteen united States of America,

When in the Course of human events it becomes necessary for one people to dissolve the political bands which have connected them with another and to assume among the powers of the earth, the separate and equal station to which the Laws of Nature and of Nature's God entitle them, a decent respect to the opinions of mankind requires that they should declare the causes which impel them to the separation.

We hold these truths to be self-evident, that all men are created equal, that they are endowed by their Creator with certain unalienable Rights, that among these are Life, Liberty and the pursuit of Happiness. — That to secure these rights, Governments are instituted among Men, deriving their just powers from the consent of the governed, — That whenever any Form of Government becomes destructive of these ends, it is the Right of the People to alter or to abolish it, and to institute new Government, laying its foundation on such principles and organizing its powers in such form, as to them shall seem most likely to effect their Safety and Happiness.

impel force

endowed provided, given

unalienable cannot be taken away, given away, or transferred

Skills Focus READING LIKE A HISTORIAN

1. **Identify Main Ideas** What is the main idea in the first paragraph of this excerpt?
2. **Interpret** How are Jefferson's words consistent with the Enlightenment's ideas of John Locke and Jean-Jacques Rousseau?
3. **Support a Position** Is it the right of the people to alter or abolish a government if they wish to? Give reasons that support your position.

Answers

Reading Like a Historian

1. *When a political relationship between peoples is dissolved, the reasons or causes should be publicly stated.*

2. *Each individual has rights that cannot be denied; these are basic human rights to which each of us is entitled. This is one of the Enlightenment ideals.*

3. *Students should recognize that throughout history, oppressed people have sought and won independence, the right to self-govern. Students should support their answers with concrete examples and logic.*

Excerpt from

The Wealth of Nations

by Adam Smith

About the Reading *Adam Smith (1723–1790) was a Scottish philosopher and economist. In his best-known work,* The Wealth of Nations *(1776), Smith asserted the value of free trade and few, if any, governmental regulations or restraints on trade. Smith's arguments exerted a tremendous force in shaping an era of free trade in the 1800s. In this excerpt, Smith describes how a person's self-interest guides him or her to buy and sell things in order to have the "necessaries of life."*

Adam Smith ▲

In civilized society he [man] stands at all times in need of the cooperation and assistance of great multitudes, while his whole life is scarce sufficient to gain the friendship of a few persons. In almost every other race of animals each individual, when it is grown up to maturity, is entirely independent, and in its natural state has occasion for the assistance of no other living creature. . . But man has almost constant occasion for the help of his brethren, and it is in vain for him to expect it from their benevolence only. He will be more likely to prevail if he can interest their self-love in his favour, and show them that it is for their own advantage to do for him what he requires of them. Whoever offers to another a bargain of any kind, proposes to do this. Give me that which I want, and you shall have this which you want, is the meaning of every such offer; and it is in this manner that we obtain from one another the far greater part of those good offices which we stand in need of. It is not from the benevolence of the butcher, the brewer, or the baker, that we expect our dinner, but from their regard to their own interest. We address ourselves, not to their humanity but to their self-love, and never talk to them of our own necessities but of their advantages. Nobody but a beggar chuses [chooses] to depend chiefly upon the benevolence of his fellow-citizens. Even a beggar does not depend upon it entirely. The charity of well-disposed people, indeed, supplies him with the whole fund of his subsistence. But though this principle ultimately provides him with all the necessaries of life which he has occasion for, it neither does nor can provide him with them as he has occasion for them. The greater part of his occasional wants are supplied in the same manner as those of other people, by treaty, by barter, and by purchase. With the money which one man gives him he purchases food. The old cloaths [clothes] which another bestows upon him he exchanges for other old cloaths which suit him better, or for lodging, or for food, or for money, with which he can buy either food, cloaths, or lodging, as he has occasion.

brethren literally brothers; here, fellow men
benevolence kindness
good offices goods and services

Skills Focus READING LIKE A HISTORIAN

1. **Recall** According to Smith, how does man in civilized society differ from "almost every other race of animals"?
2. **Analyze** Why is it necessary for a person to obtain goods by treaty, barter, or purchase?
3. **Predict** Based on this excerpt, why do you think that Smith was an advocate of liberal free trade among nations?

Answers

Reading Like a Historian

1. *We need to cooperate and work together to satisfy our needs, we cannot survive alone.*
2. *By appealing to the needs and wants of another person, we can satisfy our own needs; people do not respond or give out of kindness, but want to get something in return.*
3. *Students should recognize that Smith is advocating trading what you have for what you want with no barriers to the trade.*

Excerpt from the Introduction to

A Vindication of the Rights of Woman

by Mary Wollstonecraft

Mary Wollstonecraft ▲

About the Reading *In 1789 the French Revolution erupted and, with its stirring slogan of "liberty, equality, fraternity," shook European society. Inspired by the ideas of the revolution in France, in 1792 Wollstonecraft wrote* A Vindication of the Rights of Woman. *It is a strong and passionate criticism of the social and economic institutions that lead to inequality for women.*

I have sighed when obliged to confess, that either nature has made a great difference between man and man, or that civilization . . . has been very partial. I have . . . a profound conviction, that the neglected education of my fellow creatures is the grand source of the misery I deplore; and that women in particular, are rendered weak and wretched by a variety of concurring causes. . . . The conduct and manners of women, in fact, evidently prove, that their minds are not in a healthy state; for, like the flowers that are planted in too rich a soil, strength and usefulness are sacrificed to beauty; and the flaunting leaves, after having pleased a fastidious eye, fade, disregarded on the stalk, long before the season when they ought to have arrived at maturity. One cause of this barren blooming I attribute to a false system of education, gathered from the books written on this subject by men, who, considering females rather as women than human creatures, have been more anxious to make them alluring mistresses than rational wives; and the understanding of the sex has been so bubbled by this specious homage, that the civilized women of the present century, with a few exceptions, are only anxious to inspire love, when they ought to cherish a nobler ambition, and by their abilities and virtues exact respect. . . .

Yet, because I am a woman, I would not lead my readers to suppose, that I mean violently to agitate the contested question respecting the equality and inferiority of the sex; but . . . I shall stop a moment to deliver, in a few words, my opinion. In the government of the physical world, it is observable that the female, in general, is inferior to the male. The male pursues, the female yields—this is the law of nature; and it does not appear to be suspended or abrogated in favor of woman. This physical superiority cannot be denied—and it is a noble prerogative! But not content with this natural pre-eminence, men endeavor to sink us still lower, merely to render us alluring objects for a moment; and women, intoxicated by the adoration which men, under the influence of their senses, pay them, do not seek to obtain a durable interest in their hearts, or to become the friends of the fellow creatures who find amusement in their society. . . .

partial biased
fastidious overly fussy; picky
specious showy but false; lacking genuineness
abrogated abolished; repealed

Skills Focus READING LIKE A HISTORIAN

1. **Identify Main Ideas** What is the main idea of this excerpt?
2. **Explain** In your own words, explain how Wollstonecraft responds to the issue of the equality of the sexes.
3. **Elaborate** How did Wollstonecraft's ideas differ from those of other Enlightenment thinkers? Explain.

Answers

Reading Like a Historian

1. *that men consider and treat women as inferior; women are denied education, which makes them inferior; that women should not consider themselves objects of adoration, but aspire to a larger role*
2. *She argues that women should not accept their roles as inferior beings.*
3. *Students should support their positions with logic and refer to specific arguments from the excerpt.*

Excerpt from

The Communist Manifesto

by Karl Marx and Friedrich Engels

About the Reading *In the 1840s, a new philosophy of history and the nature of human beings—communism—appeared. Communism views humans as historical beings whose lives and work are determined by the material conditions of the society in which they live. Communism also envisions a society in which there is no private property and in which workers will not be exploited and forced to live in poverty and misery. Marx and Engels wrote* The Communist Manifesto *(1848) as an explanation of the doctrines and theories of communism.*

Karl Marx ▲

The history of all hitherto existing society is the history of class struggles. . . .

Freeman and slave, patrician and plebian, lord and serf, guild-master and journeyman, in a word, oppressor and oppressed, stood in constant opposition to one another, carried on an uninterrupted, now hidden, now open fight, a fight that each time ended, either in a revolutionary reconstitution of society at large, or in the common ruin of the contending classes. . . .

We have seen above that the first step in the revolution by the working class is to raise the proletariat to the position of ruling class to win the battle of democracy.

The proletariat will use its political supremacy to wrest, by degree, all capital from the bourgeoisie, to centralize all instruments of production in the hands of the state, i.e., of the proletariat organized as the ruling class; and to increase the total productive forces as rapidly as possible. . . .

When, in the course of development, class distinctions have disappeared, and all production has been concentrated in the hands of a vast association of the whole nation, the public power will lose its political character. Political power, properly so called, is merely the organized power of one class for oppressing another. If the proletariat during its contest with the bourgeoisie is compelled, by the force of circumstances, to organize itself as a class; if, by means of a revolution, it makes itself the ruling class, and, as such, sweeps away by force the old conditions of production, then it will, along with these conditions, have swept away the conditions for the existence of class antagonisms and of classes generally, and will thereby have abolished its own supremacy as a class.

In place of the old bourgeois society, with its classes and class antagonisms, we shall have an association in which the free development of each is the condition for the free development of all.

The Communists disdain to conceal their views and aims. They openly declare that their ends can be attained only by the forcible overthrow of all existing social conditions. Let the ruling classes tremble at a communist revolution. The proletarians have nothing to lose but their chains. They have a world to win.

Proletarians of all countries, unite!

proletariat workers or working-class people
bourgeoisie the wealthy middle class; capitalists

Skills Focus READING LIKE A HISTORIAN

1. **Recall** How have all previous "class struggles" ended?
2. **Analyze** According to Marx, how and why will a communist revolution take place? Is his prediction realistic?

Answers

Reading Like a Historian

1. *either in a revolutionary change in society or in the ruin of the classes (rulers and subjects, oppressors and oppressed) that were fighting each other*
2. *A Communist revolution will occur as an open fight; it will occur because oppressed and oppressors are in constant opposition. Students should show an understanding of the failure of communism in Russia and the Soviet Union.*

Excerpt from

All Quiet on the Western Front

by Erich Maria Remarque

Trench in World War I ▲

About the Reading *Erich Maria Remarque (1898–1970) was born in Germany and served in the German army during World War I. His novel* All Quiet on the Western Front *(1929) describes the routine horrors of war that soldiers faced in the trenches that spread across Western Europe.*

There are so many airmen here, and they are so sure of themselves that they give chase to single individuals, just as though they were hares. For every one German plane there come at least five English and American. For one hungry, wretched German soldier come five of the enemy, fresh and fit. For one German army loaf there are fifty tins of canned beef over there. We are not beaten, for as soldiers we are better and more experienced; we are simply crushed and driven back by overwhelming superior forces.

Behind us lay rainy weeks—grey sky, grey fluid earth, grey dying. If we got out, the rain at once soaks through our overcoat and clothing;—and we remain wet all the time we are in the line. We never get dry. Those who will wear high boots tie sand bags round the tops so that the mud does not pour in so fast. The rifles are caked, the uniforms caked, everything is fluid and dissolved, the earth one dripping, soaked, oily mass in which lie yellow pools with red spiral streams of blood and into which the dead, wounded, and survivors slowly sink down.

The storm lashes us, out of the confusion of grey and yellow the hail of splinters whips forth the child-like cries of the wounded, and in the night shattered life groans painfully into silence.

Our hands are earth, our bodies clay and our eyes pools of rain. We do not know whether we still live.

Then the heat sinks heavily into our shell-holes like a jelly fish, moist and oppressive and on one of those late summer days, while bringing food, Kat falls. We two are alone. I bind up his wound; his shin seems to be smashed. It has got the bone, and Kat groans desperately: "At last—just at the last—"

I comfort him. "Who knows how long this mess will go on yet! Now you are saved—"

The wound begins to bleed fast. Kat cannot be left by himself while I try to find a stretcher. Anyway, I don't know of a stretcher-bearer's post in the neighborhood.

Kat is not very heavy; so I take him up on my back and start off to the dressing station with him.

Twice we rest. He suffers acutely on the way. We do not speak much. I have opened the collar of my tunic and breathe heavily, I sweat and my face is swollen with the strain of carrying. All the same I urge him to let us go on, for the place is dangerous.

Skills Focus READING LIKE A HISTORIAN

1. **Describe** How does the narrator describe the conditions on the battlefield?
2. **Infer** After Kat is wounded, why do you think the narrator tells him "Now you are saved"?

Answers

Reading Like a Historian

1. *The narrator paints a grim picture of the battlefield, wet, grey, muddy, lack of food and supplies, wounded and dying soldiers.*

2. *Students should recognize that Kat will be removed from the battlefield.*

Excerpt from

On Nonviolent Resistance

by Mohandas K. Gandhi

About the Reading *Mohandas K. Gandhi (1869–1948) was the leader of India's fight for independence from British rule. Though Gandhi was often arrested and imprisoned for his actions, he urged his followers to adhere to the principles of nonviolence. The following excerpt is from a 1916 speech made to Gandhi's Hindu supporters at Kochrab Ashram in India. It was collected with other of Gandhi's writings and published in 1922.*

Mohandas K. Gandhi ►

There are two ways of countering injustice. One way is to smash the head of the man who perpetrates injustice and to get your own head smashed in the process. All strong people in the world adopt this course. Everywhere wars are fought and millions of people are killed. . . . Pride makes a victorious nation bad-tempered. It falls into luxurious ways of living. Then for a time, it may be conceded, peace prevails. But after a short while, it comes more and more to be realised that the seeds of war have not been destroyed but have become a thousand times more nourished and mighty. No country has ever become, or will ever become, happy through victory in war. A nation does not rise that way, it only falls further. In fact, what comes to it is defeat, not victory. And if, perchance, either our act or our purpose was ill-conceived, it brings disaster to both belligerents.

But through the other method of combating injustice, we alone suffer the consequences of our mistakes, and the other side is wholly spared. This other method is satyagraha. One who resorts to it does not have to break another's head; he may merely have his own head broken. He has to be prepared to die himself suffering all the pain. . . . [N]o State is possible without two entities (the rulers and the ruled). You are our sovereign, our Government, only so long as we consider ourselves your subjects. When we are not subjects, you are not the sovereign either. So long as it is your endeavour to control us with justice and love, we will let you do so. But if you wish to strike at us from behind, we cannot permit it. Whatever you do in other matters, you will have to ask our opinion about the laws that concern us. If you make laws to keep us suppressed in a wrongful manner and without taking us into confidence, these laws will merely adorn the statute-books. We will never obey them. Award us for it what punishment you like, we will put up with it. Send us to prison and we will live there as in a paradise. Ask us to mount the scaffold and we will do so laughing. Shower what sufferings you like upon us, we will calmly endure all and not hurt a hair of your body. We will gladly die and will not so much as touch you. But so long as there is yet life in these our bones, we will never comply with your arbitrary laws.

satyagraha power of truth without force or violence to change political and other circumstances; insistence on truth

scaffold raised wooden platform used for public executions

Skills Focus **READING LIKE A HISTORIAN**

1. **Identify Main Ideas** What are the two ways to counter injustice to which Gandhi refers?
2. **Explain** How did Gandhi use nonviolent resistance in the struggle for Indian independence?

Answers

Reading Like a Historian

1. *react violently and then be treated with violence;* satyagraha, *nonviolent protest and response*

2. *refusal to obey laws that suppress the people; accept prison sentences; endure suffering, punishment, and if necessary, death*

Guernica

by Pablo Picasso

About the Artist *Pablo Picasso (1881–1973) was one of the most famous artists of the twentieth century, restlessly pioneering bold, new styles. Born in Barcelona, Spain, Picasso spent much of his career in Paris, then the art capital of the world. Picasso mostly avoided politics, but during the Spanish Civil War (1936–1939), he sided with the Republican government, which commissioned a painting to commemorate the bombing of the small town of Guernica by Fascist forces in 1937.*

About the Painting Mondays were market days in Guernica, a town of about 5,000 people with no military significance. On Monday, April 27th, 1937, Nazi bombers dumped 100,000 pounds of bombs on the town, reducing it to rubble. The Nazis, who were allies of the Spanish Nationalists, later admitted that the purpose of this unprecedented attack was to test a new military tactic—carpet-bombing civilians to kill them and break their morale.

Guernica is a large oil-on-canvas painting measuring 11.5 feet high by 25.5 feet wide. It is done in Cubist style, which uses interlocking geometric shapes to portray the world in a nonrealistic fashion. Picasso restricted his palette of colors to back, white, and shades of gray. He set the scene inside a room open at the left. A bull stands over a woman grieving over a dead child in her arms. Other images in the painting include a horse, wounded by a spear or lance; a dead soldier; a female figure floating into the room (above and to the right of the horse), carrying a lamp; and another female figure (at the far right) falling through a burning building. Interpretations of the painting and the individual images in it vary widely. Picasso said, "If you give a meaning to certain things in my paintings it may be very true, but it is not my idea to give this meaning. . . . I make the painting for the painting. I paint the objects for what they are."

Skills Focus READING LIKE A HISTORIAN

1. **Describe** How does Picasso show the bombing of Guernica in his painting?
2. **Interpret** Why do you think Picasso chose to create such a large painting in the Cubist style and in such stark colors? Select one part of the painting and interpret its meaning.
3. **Evaluate** Would you say that Picasso's painting is as effective a statement about the horror and destruction of war today as it was in 1937? Why or why not? Refer to images in the painting to support your answer.

Answers

Reading Like a Historian

1. *Students should recognize that people and animals have been killed, dismembered, and that this is a scene of total destruction.*
2. *Students should recognize that Picasso was a Cubist and that in the fragmentation, he was able to capture the destructive forces of the bombs. Student answers will vary depending upon the image chosen.*
3. *Student answers will vary but should show an understanding of the painting.*

Never Shall I Forget

by Elie Wiesel

About the Reading *Elie Wiesel (1928–) was fifteen years old when he and all the other Jews in his Romanian village were shipped to Nazi concentration camps in Poland and Germany during World War II. In 1955 Wiesel wrote a nine-hundred-page memoir, which was later condensed and republished under the title* Night. *The following excerpt originally appeared as a prose passage in* Night.

Elie Wiesel ▲

Never Shall I Forget

Never shall I forget that night, the first night in camp, that turned my life into one long night seven times sealed.

Never shall I forget that smoke.

Never shall I forget the small faces of the children whose bodies I saw transformed into smoke under a silent sky.

Never shall I forget those flames that consumed my faith for ever.

Never shall I forget the nocturnal silence that deprived me for all eternity of the desire to live.

Never shall I forget those moments that murdered my God and my soul and turned my dreams to ashes.

Never shall I forget those things, even were I condemned to live as long as God Himself.

Never.

Skills Focus READING LIKE A HISTORIAN

1. **Describe** What is the effect on the reader of Wiesel's repeated use of the word "never"?
2. **Interpret** What does Wiesel mean by "bodies . . . transformed into smoke"?
3. **Elaborate** How did Wiesel's time in the concentration camp affect him?

Answers

Reading Like a Historian

1. *Students should recognize the force of the repetition of the word "never;" these are memories that Wiesel will never forget.*

2. *Students should remember that during the Holocaust, Jewish people were murdered in a variety of ways, including in crematoriums.*

3. *It deprived him of the desire to live, filled him with horrific memories that he will never forget.*

Primary Source Library

PRIMARY SOURCE LIBRARY

Excerpt from

Address to the United Nations

by Eleanor Roosevelt

Eleanor Roosevelt ▲

About the Reading *As the world learned of the atrocities committed by Nazi Germany, members of the United Nations saw the need to clarify fundamental human rights. A UN commission drafted the Universal Declaration of Human Rights. Former First Lady Eleanor Roosevelt (1884–1962) represented the United States when the UN General Assembly adopted the document on December 10, 1948. The excerpt below is taken from her speech to the General Assembly.*

In giving our approval to the Declaration today it is of primary importance that we keep clearly in mind the basic character of the document . . . It is a Declaration of basic principles of human rights and freedoms . . . to serve as a common standard of achievement for all peoples of all nations.

We stand today at the threshold of a great event both in the life of the United Nations and in the life of mankind. This Universal Declaration of Human Rights may well become the international Magna Carta of all men everywhere[,] . . . an event comparable to the proclamation of the Declaration of the Rights of Man by the French people in 1789, the adoption of the Bill of Rights by the people of the United States, and the adoption of comparable declarations at different times in other countries.

. . . This must be taken as testimony of our common aspiration first voiced in the Charter of the United Nations to lift men everywhere to a higher standard of life and to a greater enjoyment of freedom. Man's desire for peace lies behind this Declaration. The realization that the flagrant violation of human rights by Nazi and Fascist countries sowed the seeds of the last world war has supplied the impetus for the work which brings us to the moment of achievement here today.

In a recent speech in Canada, Gladstone Murray said:

> The central fact is that man is fundamentally a moral being. That the light we have is imperfect does not matter so long as we are always trying to improve it. . . . We are equal in sharing the moral freedom that distinguishes us as free men. Man's status makes each individual an end in himself. No man is by nature simply the servant of the state, or of another man . . . the ideal and fact of freedom—and not technology—are the true distinguishing marks of our civilization.

This Declaration is based upon the spiritual fact that man must have freedom in which to develop his full stature and through common effort to raise the level of human dignity. We have much to do to fully achieve and to assure the rights set forth in this Declaration.

Skills Focus READING LIKE A HISTORIAN

1. **Recall** To what other documents does Roosevelt compare this Declaration?
2. **Explain** How were the events of World War II important in spurring the adoption of the Universal Declaration of Human Rights?

Answers

Reading Like a Historian

1. *Magna Carta, 1789 French Declaration of the Rights of Man, U.S. Constitutional Bill of Rights*
2. *The loss of life during battles, the genocide that occurred in the Holocaust, and the loss of freedom that occurred in Nazi and Fascist countries all helped spur this declaration.*

Excerpt from

Inaugural Address

by Nelson Mandela

About the Reading *After years of imprisonment for opposing white rule in South Africa, Nelson Mandela (1918–) was freed in 1990. He led his party, the African National Congress, in negotiations with the government of President F. W. de Klerk. The two leaders agreed to a timetable for the end of apartheid and a date for South Africa's first democratic elections. In that election, held in 1994, Mandela was elected president.*

Nelson Mandela ▲

Today, all of us do, by our presence here, and by our celebrations in other parts of our country and the world, confer glory and hope to newborn liberty . . .

Our daily deeds as ordinary South Africans must produce an actual South African reality that will reinforce humanity's belief in justice, strengthen its confidence in the nobility of the human soul and sustain all our hopes for a glorious life for all . . .

To my compatriots, I have no hesitation in saying that each one of us is as intimately attached to the soil of this beautiful country as are the famous jacaranda trees of Pretoria and the mimosa trees of the bushveld . . . .
That spiritual and physical oneness we all share with this common homeland explains the depth of the pain we all carried in our hearts as we saw our country tear itself apart in a terrible conflict, and as we saw it spurned, outlawed and isolated by the peoples of the world. . . .

The time for the healing of the wounds has come.

The moment to bridge the chasms that divide us has come.

The time to build is upon us.

We have, at last, achieved our political emancipation. We pledge ourselves to liberate all our people from the continuing bondage of poverty, deprivation, suffering, gender and other discrimination. . . .

We have triumphed in the effort to implant hope in the breasts of the millions of our people. We enter into a covenant that we shall build the society in which all South Africans, both black and white, will be able to walk tall, without any fear in their hearts, assured of their inalienable right to human dignity—a rainbow nation at peace with itself and the world. . . .

We understand it still that there is no easy road to freedom.

We know it well that none of us acting alone can achieve success.

We must therefore act together as a united people, for national reconciliation, for nation building, for the birth of a new world. . . .

Never, never and never again shall it be that this beautiful land will again experience the oppression of one by another and suffer the indignity of being the skunk of the world.

Let freedom reign.

Skills Focus **READING LIKE A HISTORIAN**

1. **Identify** What does Mandela want South Africans to do—for themselves and for the people of the world?
2. **Explain** What goals does Mandela set out for South Africa's future?

Answers

Reading Like a Historian

1. *liberate people from poverty, deprivation, suffering, all types of discrimination; build a society where all people are respected*

2. *national reconciliation, nation building, end oppression*

Excerpt from

Nobel Peace Prize Acceptance Speech

by Aung San Suu Kyi

About the Reading *Aung San Suu Kyi (1945–), a pro-democracy activist in Myanmar (Burma), has repeatedly been arrested by Myanmar's military dictatorship. In 1991 she was awarded the Nobel Peace Prize. Her son delivered her acceptance speech, as she was under house arrest.*

Aung San Suu Kyi ▲

I stand before you here today to accept on behalf of my mother, Aung San Suu Kyi, this greatest of prizes, the Nobel Prize for Peace. Because circumstances do not permit my mother to be here in person, I will do my best to convey the sentiments I believe she would express.

Firstly, I know that she would begin by saying that she accepts the Nobel Prize for Peace not in her own name but in the name of all the people of Burma. She would say that this prize belongs not to her but to all those men, women and children who, even as I speak, continue to sacrifice their wellbeing, their freedom and their lives in pursuit of a democratic Burma. . . .

I know that if she were free today my mother would, in thanking you, also ask you to pray that the oppressors and the oppressed should throw down their weapons and join together to build a nation founded on humanity in the spirit of peace.

Although my mother is often described as a political dissident who strives by peaceful means for democratic change, we should remember that her quest is basically spiritual. As she has said, "The quintessential revolution is that of the spirit," and she has written of the "essential spiritual aims" of the struggle. The realization of this depends solely on human responsibility. At the root of that responsibility lies, and I quote, "the concept of perfection, the urge to achieve it, the intelligence to find a path towards it, and the will to follow that path if not to the end, at least the distance needed to rise above individual limitation . . . To live the full life," she says, "one must have the courage to bear the responsibility of the needs of others. . . ." And she links this firmly to her faith when she writes, ". . . Buddhism . . . places the greatest value on man, who alone of all beings can achieve the supreme state of Buddhahood. Each man has in him the potential to realize the truth through his own will and endeavor and to help others to realize it." Finally she says, "The quest for democracy in Burma is the struggle of a people to live whole, meaningful lives as free and equal members of the world community. It is part of the unceasing human endeavor to prove that the spirit of man can transcend the flaws of his nature."

Buddhahood in Buddhism, a peaceful and gentle state

Skills Focus READING LIKE A HISTORIAN

1. **Identify** To whom would Aung San Suu Kyi say that the Nobel Peace Prize belongs?
2. **Analyze** For Suu Kyi, what is the nature of the struggle for democratic change, and how will success in that struggle be realized?

Answers

Reading Like a Historian

1. *all of the people of Burma, especially those who are working for democracy*
2. *struggle—for people to "join together to build a nation founded on humanity in the spirit of peace," for people to be able "to live whole, meaningful lives as free and equal members of the world community"; success—when Burma has a democratic government and people accept their human responsibilities*

Biographical Dictionary

A

'Abbas (1571–1629) Shah of the Safavid Empire in Persia (1588–1629); his military victories against the Ottomans and skilled administration brought about a golden age in Safavid history. (p. (p. 105)

Akbar the Great (1542–1605) Mughal emperor of India; he ruled from 1556 until 1605 and continued the policy of conquest put in place under regent Bairim Khan, enlarging his empire to include nearly all of the Indian peninsula north of the Godavari River. (p. 107)

Akhenaton (died c. 1362 BC) King of Egypt; he practiced monotheism and attempted to change the religious beliefs of his people. (p. 12)

Aguinaldo, Emiliano (1869–1964) Self-proclaimed President of the new Philippine Republic in 1899; he fought for Filipino independence from the United States. (p. 366)

Alexander the Great (356–323 BC) King of Macedon and conqueror of much of Asia; he is considered one of the greatest generals of all time. (p. 16)

Alexander I (1777–1825) Czar of Russia from 1801 to 1825; after the defeat of the Napoleon's army in 1812, he became one of Europe's most powerful leaders, supporting the suppression of revolutionary movements in Russia and Europe. (p. 217)

Alexander II (1818–1881) Czar of Russia from 1855 to 1851; he freed the Russian serfs and passed other liberal reforms in Russia. (p. 322)

Aquino, Corazon (1933–) Philippine politician and president of the Philippines from 1986 until 1992; she struggled to overcome political instability, return to democracy, and rebuild the nation's economy. (p. 529)

Arkwright, Richard (1732–1792) English inventor; in 1769 he patented the spinning frame, which spun stronger, thinner, thread. (p. 238)

Ashoka (died c. 232 BC) Mauryan emperor from c. 273–c. 232 BC; he was one of the greatest rulers of ancient India and brought nearly all of India under one authority for the first time in history. He also promoted the spread of Buddhism. (p. 14)

Atahualpa (c. 1502–1533) Last Inca king of Peru; he was taken prisoner by Pizarro and his army after refusing to accept Christianity and hand over his empire to the Spanish. He was killed by the Spanish and his empire was taken over. (p. 80)

Atatürk, Kemal (1881–1938) Turkish leader and founder of modern Turkey; he sought to transform Turkey into a modern, secular state with separation between religion (Islam) and government. (p. 411)

Augustus (63 BC–AD 14) First emperor of Rome; he established the Second Triumvirate with Mark Antony and Lepidus. He created the imperial system of administration, established new coinages, and encouraged trade. (p. 17)

Aung San Suu Kyi (1945–) Burmese political leader; she won the Nobel Peace Prize in 1991 for her efforts to promote democracy in the country of Myanmar (Burma). (p. 521)

Aurangzeb (1618–1707) Mughal emperor of India (1658-1707); he expanded Mughal power to its greatest extant, but his efforts to impose his strict religious views weakened Mughal rule. (p. 109)

B

Babur (1483–1530) Founder of the Mughal empire of India; he invaded Afghanistan and India and established an empire there. (p. 107)

Begin, Menachem (1913–1992) Israeli politician and prime minister; he signed a peace treaty with Anwar Sadat that ended thirty years of conflict between Israel and Egypt. (p. 558)

Beethoven, Ludwig van (1770–1827) German composer who spanned the Classical and Romantic periods; often considered the greatest composer; wrote symphonies, quartets, and sonatas. (p. 278)

Bell, Alexander Graham (1847–1922) American inventor and educator; his interest in electrical and mechanical devices to aid people with hearing impairments led to the development and patent of the telephone. (p. 266)

Ben-Gurion, David (1886–1973) Israeli statesman; he founded the Histadrut labor organization and was head of the Mapai Labor Party from 1930 to 1965. (p. 553)

bin Laden, Osama (1957–) Founder of al Qaeda, the terrorist network responsible for the attacks of September 11, 2001, and other attacks. (p. 501)

Bismarck, Otto von (1815–1898) German statesman; he became the leading force behind German unification. His main political goal was for Prussia to gain power over Austria. (p. 321)

Bolívar, Simón (1783–1830) South American revolutionary who led independence wars in the present nations of Venezuela, Colombia, Panama, Ecuador, Peru, and Bolivia. (p. 301)

Bonaparte, Napoleon (1769–1821) general; Emperor of France; he seized power in a coup d'état in 1799; he led French armies in conquering much of Europe, placing his relatives in positions of power. Defeated at the Battle of Waterloo, he was exiled on the island of Elba. (p. 211)

Borromeo, Charles (1538–1584) Archbishop of Milan from 1560 to 1584; he took steps to implement the reforms ordered by the Council of Trent. (p. 59)

Buonarroti, Michelangelo (1475–1564) Italian Renaissance sculptor, architect, painter, and poet; he sculpted the *Pieta* and the *David* and he painted the ceiling of the Sistine Chapel. (p. 45)

C

Caesar, Julius (100–47 BC) Roman general and one of the greatest military leaders in history; he conquered most of Gaul and was named dictator for life, but was later murdered by a group of senators. (p. 17)

Calvin, John (1509–1564) French Protestant theologian of the Reformation; he founded Calvinism, which was associated with the doctrine of predestination. (p. 54)

Carnegie, Andrew (1835–1919) American industrialist and humanitarian; he led the expansion of the American steel industry. (p. 249)

Carranza, Venustiano (1859–1920) Mexican revolutionist and politician: he led forces against Victoriano Huerta during the Mexican Revolution. (p. 365)

Castiglione, Baldassare (1479–1529) Italian diplomat and writer; he wrote *The Courtier*, one of the most important books of the Renaissance, in which he explained the correct behavior for a courtier to adopt to win favor from a ruler. (p. 42)

Castro, Fidel (1926–) Communist political leader of Cuba; he helped overthrow the Cuban government in 1959 and seized control of the country, exercising total control of the government and economy. (p. 571)

Catherine the Great (1729–1796) Czarina of Russia from 1762 to 1796; ruling with absolute power, she introduced a number of reforms that extended Peter the Great's policy of "westernization." (p. 157)

Cavour, Camillo di (1810–1861) Italian statesman and premier of the kingdom of Sardinia; architect of the Italian unification movement in the late 1800s. (p. 317)

Cervantes, Miguel de (1547–1616) Spanish novelist, dramatist, and poet; he wrote *Don Quixote de la Mancha.* (p. 139)

Chamorro, Violetta (1929–) President of Nicaragua from 1990 to 1997; she was the first woman to govern a Central American nation. (p. 581)

Chandragupta Maurya (c. 321–c. 298 BC) Founder of the Mauryan Empire in India; he conquered much of northern India and ruled over parts of Pakistan. (p. 14)

Charlemagne (c. 742–814) King of the Franks from 768 to 814; he united much of France, Germany and northern Italy in on Frankish empire; crowned Emperor of the e Roman people in 800. (p. 30)

Charles I (1600–1649) King of England, Scotland, and Ireland from 1625 to 1649; his conflict with Parliament started the English Civil War. He was beheaded in 1649. (p. 149)

Charles II (1630–1685) King of England, Scotland, and Ireland from 1660 to 1685 and eldest son of King Charles I; he was asked by Parliament to rule England after the death of Oliver Cromwell. (p. 151)

Charles V (1500–1558) King of Spain (as Charles I); Holy Roman Emperor (as Charles V) from 1519 to 1558; his opposition to the Protestant Reformation embroiled Spain in a series of wars throughout his reign. (p. 138)

Chávez, Hugo (1954–) Venezuelan political leader and president; he set out to eliminate poverty in his country, but his methods of doing so tended to turn his country away from democracy and toward a dictatorship. (p. 584)

Churchill, Winston (1874–1965) British prime minister; he opposed the policy of appeasement and led Great Britain through World War II. (p. 438)

Columbus, Christopher (1451–1506) Italian explorer, sailing for Spain, who reached the Americas in 1492 while searching for a western sea route from Europe to Asia. (p. 75)

Confucius (551–479 BC) Chinese philosopher; he was the most influential teacher in Chinese history. His teachings, Confucianism, focused on morality, family, society, and government. (p. 15)

Constantine (died 337) Emperor of Rome from 306 to 377; he ordered the building of Constantinople, which became a gateway between Asia and Europe. (p. 28)

Copernicus, Nicolaus (1473–1543) Polish astronomer; he proposed the heliocentric, or sun-centered, theory of the universe. (p. 171)

Cortés, Hernan (1485–1547) Spanish conquistador; from 1519 to 1521, he defeated the Aztec Empire, conquering Mexico for Spain. (p. 79)

Cromwell, Oliver (1599–1658) Lord Protector of England; in 1642 he led Parliament's forces in deposing King Charles I. (p. 149)

Cruz, Sister Juana Ines de la (1651–1695) Mexican nun and poet; she wrote poetry, prose, and plays. (p. 139)

Curie, Marie (1867–1934) and **Pierre** (1859–1906) European chemists and physicists; they discovered radium and polonium in 1898. (p. 269)

D

Darwin, Charles (1809–1882) English scientist; he proposed the theory of evolution through natural selection. (p. 269)

Deng Xiaoping (1904–1997) Chinese revolutionary and government leader; after a struggle for power following Mao's death, Deng took power in 1981; he made far-reaching market reforms in the Chinese economy. (p. 525)

Descartes, René (1596–1650) French philosopher, mathematician, and scientist; his belief that all things should be doubted until they could be proved by reason became one of the underpinnings of the scientific method. (p. 171)

Díaz, Porfirio (1830–1915) Mexican general and politician; he was president and dictator of Mexico for a total of 30 years. He encouraged foreign investment but ruled the people of Mexico harshly. (p. 364)

Dickens, Charles (1812–1870) English author during the Victorian era; he wrote *Great Expectations, A Christmas Carol, Oliver Twist,* and *A Tale of Two Cities,* among many other works. (p. 278)

Disraeli, Benjamin (1804–1881) British statesman; as prime minister, he passed key reforms, including an extension of male suffrage. (p. 290)

Drake, Sir Francis (c. 1540–1596) English admiral; he rounded the tip of South America and explored the west coast. He ended up heading west to return to England, thus becoming the second man to circumnavigate the globe. (p. 76)

Dürer, Albrecht (1471–1528) German painter, engraver, and theoretician; he combined Italian Renaissance techniques of realism and perspective with elements unique to the northern Renaissance, such as the use of oils in his painting. (p. 49)

E

Edison, Thomas (1847–1931) American inventor of over 1,000 patents; he invented the light bulb and established a power plant that supplied electricity to parts of New York City. (p. 262)

BIOGRAPHICAL DICTIONARY

BIOGRAPHICAL DICTIONARY

Einstein, Albert (1879–1955) American theoretical physicist; he developed the theory of relativity among his many scientific theories and was awarded the Nobel Prize for physics in 1921. (p. 270)

Eisenhower, Dwight D. (1890–1969) General; thirty-fourth president of the United States; as Supreme Allied Commander in Europe during World War II, he led the Allied invasions of North Africa and of France (D-Day). (p. 448)

El Greco (c. 1541–1614) Greek painter in Spain; chiefly religious in nature, his works express the spirit of the Counter, or Catholic, Reformation. (p. 139)

Elizabeth I (1533–1603) Queen of England from 1558 to 1603; a skillful politician and diplomat, she reasserted Protestant supremacy in England. (p. 56)

Equiano, Olaudah (c.1750–1797) African American abolitionist; he was an enslaved African who was eventually freed, became a leader of the abolitionist movement, and wrote *The Interesting Narrative of the Life of Olaudah Equiano.* (p. 91)

Erasmus, Desiderius (1466–1536) Dutch priest and humanist; he wrote on the need for a pure and simple Christian life. To his regret, his writings fanned the flames of discontent with the Roman Catholic Church. (p. 47)

Eyck, Jan van (c. 1390–1441) Flemish painter; his paintings focused on landscapes and domestic life and fused the everyday with the religious. (p. 49)

Ezana (c. AD 300s) Aksumite ruler; he destroyed the Kush capital of Meroë and took over the kingdom of Kush around AD 320. (p. 25)

F

Faraday, Michael (1791–1867) English scientist; he invented the dynamo—a machine that generated electricity. His invention eventually led to today's electrical generators. (p. 262)

Ford, Henry (1863–1947) American business leader; he revolutionized factory production through use of the assembly line and popularized the affordable automobile (Model T). (p. 264)

Fox, Vicente (1942–) Mexican political leader and president of Mexico; he was the first democratically elected opposition candidate in Mexico's history. (p. 583)

Francis of Sales (1567–1622) French Roman Catholic leader and preacher; he worked to win back the district of Savoy from Calvinism. (p. 59)

Franklin, Benjamin (1706–1790) American statesman; he was a philosopher, scientist, inventor, writer, publisher, first U.S. postmaster, and member of the committee to draft the Declaration of Independence. (p. 184)

Franz Ferdinand (1863–1914) Heir to the throne of Austria-Hungary whose assassination by a Serb nationalist started World War I. (p. 382)

Franz Josef I (1830–1916) Emperor of Austria-Hungary from 1848 to 1916; during his long reign he took small steps to address the democratic and nationalist aspirations of his people. (p. 326)

Frederick the Great (1712–1786) King of Prussia from 1740 to 1786; through victories in a series of wars with Austria, Prussia's main rival for dominance among the German states, Frederick made Prussia a major European power in the late 1700s. (p. 159)

Frederick Wilhelm IV (1795–1861) King of Prussia from 1840 to 1861; when revolution broke out in Prussia in 1848, Frederick Wilhelm promised a constitution and other reforms, which he later disavowed. (p. 321)

Freud, Sigmund (1856–1939) Austrian psychiatrist and founder of psychoanalysis; he treated hysteria using hypnosis and believed that complexes of repressed and forgotten impressions underlies all abnormal mental states. (p. 272)

Fulton, Robert (1765–1815) American engineer and inventor; he built the first commercially successful, full-sized steamboat, the *Clermont,* which led to the development of commercial steamboat ferry services for goods and people. (p. 239)

G

Galilei, Galileo (1564–1642) Italian astronomer, mathematician, and physicist; he discoveries, including the law of motion of falling objects, put him into conflict with the Roman Catholic Church. (p. 172)

Gama, Vasco da (c. 1469–1524) Portuguese navigator; he was the first European to sail around Africa and reach India by sea. (p. 74)

Gandhi, Indira (1917–1984) Indian politician; daughter and mother of Indian prime ministers, she was India's first female prime minister; her term was marred by sectarian violence involving India's Sikh minority (p. 513)

Gandhi, Mohandas (1869–1948) Leader of India's struggle for independence from Great Britain; he organized the population for protest through the methods of nonviolent resistance and civil disobedience. (p. 411)

Garibaldi, Guiseppe (1807–1882) Italian military and nationalist leader; he unified the southern states of Italy and joined them to the north to form the united Kingdom of Italy. (p. 318)

Genghis Khan (c. 1162–1227) Mongol warrior and ruler; he forged the Mongol tribes into a fighting force that conquered much of Asia, including parts of China. (p. 27)

Gorbachev, Mikhail (1931–) Russian politician; he was the last president of the Soviet Union before the country's collapse in 1991. (p. 494)

Guevara, Che (1928–1967) Argentinean revolutionary leader; he was an aide to Fidel Castro during the Cuban revolution. (p. 571)

Gutenberg, Johannes (c. 1397–1468) German inventor and printer; he invented movable type. His first printed publication was a 1,282-page Bible. (p. 47)

H

Henry IV (1553–1610) King of France (1589–1610); he issued the Edict of Nantes, which allowed Protestant worship, in order to restore peace to France. (p. 143)

Henry VIII (1491–1547) King of England from 1509 to 1547; his desire to annul his marriage led to a conflict with the pope, England's break with the Roman Catholic Church, and its embrace of Protestantism. Henry established the Church of England in 1532. (p. 55)

Henry the Navigator (1394–1460) Prince of Portugal and patron of exploration; he made no voyages himself but spent his life directing voyages of discovery along the African coast. (p. 73)

Herzl, Theodor (1860–1904) Hungarian Zionist leader; in 1896 he wrote *The Jewish State*, which outlines plans for an independent Jewish country. (p. 296)

Hidalgo, Miguel (1753–1811) Mexican priest and revolutionary; he made the first public call for Mexican independence. In 1810 he rang a bell in his hometown calling the peasants to fight for their independence from Spain. He was captured and executed. (p. 298)

Hirohito (1901–1989) Emperor of Japan from 1926 to 1989; he led Japan during World War II and was forced into unconditional surrender following the atomic-bomb attacks on Hiroshima and Nagasaki. (p. 463)

Hitler, Adolf (1889–1945) Totalitarian dictator of Germany; his invasion of European countries led to World War II. He espoused notions of racial superiority and was responsible for the mass murder of millions of Jews and others in the Holocaust. (p. 428)

Ho Chi Minh (1890–1969) Vietnamese nationalist and revolutionary leader; president of the Democratic Republic of Vietnam (North Vietnam) from 1945 to 1969; he wanted to bring communism to South Vietnam. (p. 517)

BIOGRAPHICAL DICTIONARY

Hongwu (1328–1398) First emperor of the Ming dynasty in China; he drove the Mongols out of China, Korea, and Manchuria. He concentrated all power in his own hands. (p. 112)

Hudson, Henry (died 1611) English navigator; he sailed for the Dutch East India Company and discovered the Hudson River in present-day New York. (p. 76)

Hussein, Saddam (1937–) President of Iraq from 1979 to 2003; he established a brutal dictatorship and led Iraq into wars with Iran (1980–1990) and Kuwait (1991). He was removed from power in 2003 by U.S.-led forces. (p. 500)

I

Ibsen, Henrik (1828–1906) Norwegian poet and dramatist; he wrote *A Doll's House,* which revealed the unfair treatment of women in the home. (p. 278)

Ignatius of Loyola (1491–1556) Spanish churchman and founder of the Jesuits (1534), a Roman Catholic order of priests that helped revive Catholicism during the Catholic Reformation. (p. 58)

Ivan IV (1530–1584) Grand duke of Russia and the first Russian ruler to assume to title of czar; also known as Ivan the Terrible. He instituted a campaign of terror against disfavored boyars. He killed his son, leaving no heir to the throne. (p. 155)

J

Jefferson, Thomas (1743–1826) American statesman; he was a member of two Continental Congresses, chairman of the committee to draft the Declaration of Independence, the Declaration's main author and one of its signers, and the third president of the United States. (p. 184)

Jesus of Nazareth (AD 1–30) First-century Jewish teacher and prophet; he founded Christianity and taught about kindness and love of God. His teachings spread through the Roman Empire and, eventually, the rest of the world. (p. 17)

Jiang Jieshi (1887–1975) Chinese general and politician; he succeeded Sun Yixian as leader of the Nationalist Party in China and led attacks against Communists in China in the 1920s. (p. 410)

Jinnah, Muhammad Ali (1876–1948) Indian politician and founder of Pakistan; as leader of the Muslim League, he believed that Indian Muslims needed a separate nation and called for a partition in 1940 (p. 512)

Justinian (483–565) Byzantine emperor from 527 to 565; he reunited parts of the Roman Empire, simplified Roman laws with Justinian's Code, and ordered Hagia Sophia built. (p. 28)

K

Kangxi (1654–1722) Chinese emperor of the Qing dynasty from 1661 to 1722; his reign was one of relative internal peace. He constructed many public works and was a patron of the arts. (p. 114)

Kenyatta, Jomo (c. 1893–1978) African political leader and first president of Kenya from 1964 to 1978; he was a leader of the African nationalist movement. (p. 540)

Keynes, John Maynard (1883–1946) British economist; his revolutionary economic theory, which stated that governments could prevent economic downturns by deficit spending, provided the basis for some of Franklin D. Roosevelt's New Deal policies. (p. 417)

Khomeini, Ayatollah Ruhollah (c. 1900–1946) Iranian political and religious leader; he led a revolution to overthrow Iran's government in 1979; he ruled the country for the next ten years. (p. 560)

Kim Il Sung (1912–1994) North Korean political leader and chief of state of the Democratic People's Republic of Korea from 1948 until 1994; he established a governmental party based on the Soviet model, with the state controlling much of the economy, financing heavy industry and the military. (p. 530)

Kim Jong Il (1941–) Dictatorial leader of North Korea; under his rule the North Korean economy has continued to deteriorate. (p. 530)

King, Martin Luther Jr. (1929–1968) American civil rights leader; he was a celebrated and charismatic advocate of civil rights for African Americans in the 1950s and 1960s. He was assassinated in 1968. (p. 491)

Klerk, F. W. de (1936–) South African statesman and president of South Africa from 1989 to 1994; he began the process of ending apartheid in South Africa by lifting the ban on antiapartheid parties and releasing Nelson Mandela from prison. (p. 944)

Kublai Khan (1215–1294) Mongol emperor and founder of the Yüan Dynasty, grandson of Ghengis Khan; he continued his grandfather's wars of conquest in China. He moved the Mongol capital to China and expanded his empire beyond China. (p. 27)

L

Las Casas, Bartholomé de (1474–1566) Spanish missionary and historian; he sought to protect Native Americans against Spanish mistreatment by replacing them as laborers with imported African slaves. (p. 81)

Lenin, Vladimir (1870–1924) Russian revolutionary and founder of Bolshevism; he rose to power in Russia following the Russian Revolution in 1917. (p. 332)

Leonardo da Vinci (1452–1519) Italian painter, sculptor, architect, musician, engineer, and scientist; his interests and talents spanned numerous disciplines. He painted the *Mona Lisa.* (p. 45)

Leopold II (1835–1909) King of Belgium from 1865 to 1909; he financed an expedition to the Congo and assumed the title of sovereign of the Congo Free State. His armies treated the Congolese brutally and exploited them as workers. (p. 360)

Lincoln, Abraham (1809–1865) Sixteenth president of the United States; his election led to the secession of the Southern states and the Civil War; Lincoln successfully preserved the Union and issued the Emancipation Proclamation. (p. 305)

Locke, John (1632–1704) English philosopher and founder of British empiricism; he developed political and economic theories during the Enlightenment. He wrote *Two Treatises on Government* in which he declared that people have a right to rebel against governments that do not protect their rights. (p. 177)

Louis XIII (1601–1643) King of France from 1610 to 1643; a relatively weak ruler, he let Cardinal Richelieu, his chief minister, hold great sway during his reign. (p. 143)

Louis XIV (1638–1715) King of France from 1643 to 1715; known as the Sun King, he built the palace at Versailles as a means to consolidate absolute power; a series of wars at the end of his long reign drained France's wealth. (p. 144)

Louis XVI (1754–1793) King of France from 1774 to 1792; his unpopular policies, including harsh taxes, helped trigger the French Revolution. Deposed by the National Convention, he was executed by guillotine. (p. 196)

Louis Philippe (1773–1850) King of France from 1830 to 1848; he came to power after the July Revolution and was known as the "citizen king" for showing an interest in the working class and having much in common with the middle class. (p. 294)

Louis Napoleon (1808–1873) Emperor of France from 1852 to 1870; after winning the presidential election in 1848, he staged a coup d'état and took absolute power. He ruled during a time of economic prosperity in France. (p. 294)

Luther, Martin (1483–1546) German monk whose protests against the Catholic Church in 1517 (the Ninety-Five Theses) led to calls for reform and to the movement known as the Reformation. (p. 52)

BIOGRAPHICAL DICTIONARY

M

Macartney, Lord George (1737–1806) British diplomat; he visited China in 1793 to discuss expanding trade. He was sent away after his goods were found to be inferior and he refused to kowtow to the emperor. (p. 115)

MacArthur, Douglas (1880–1964) American general, he commanded U.S. troops in the southwest Pacific during World War II and administered Japan after the war ended. He later commanded UN forces at the beginning of the Korean War, until he was removed by President Truman. (p. 450)

Machiavelli, Niccolo (1469–1527) Italian political philosopher and statesman; he wrote *The Prince,* which advised rulers to separate morals from politics. He insisted that a ruler do whatever is necessary to succeed and that the ends would justify the means. (p. 42)

Madison, James (1751–1836) American statesman; he was a delegate to the Constitutional Convention and the fourth president of the United States. He is known as the "father of the Constitution." (p. 186)

Magellan, Ferdinand (c. 1480–1521) Portuguese navigator; his ships were the first to circumnavigate the globe, though he died on the journey. (p. 76)

Malthus, Thomas (1766–1834) English economist and sociologist; his theory that population growth would exceed the growth of food production and that poverty would always exist was used to justify low wages and laws restricting charity to the poor. (p. 249)

Mandela, Nelson (1918–) Former guerrilla fighter; statesman; he helped end apartheid and became the first black president of South Africa. (p. 546)

Mansa Musa (died 1332) Leader of Mali who held power from 1307 to 1332; he conquered the Kingdom of Songhai. He expanded trade, supported the arts, and promoted Islam. (p. 24)

Mao Zedong (1893–1976) Leader of the Chinese Communists; he led a successful revolution and established a Communist government in China in 1949. (p. 410)

Marconi, Guglielmo (1874–1937) Italian physicist; he experimented with wireless telegraphy and established communication across the English Channel between France and England. (p. 266)

Marcos, Ferdinand (1917–1989) Philippine politician; he was elected president of the Philippines in 1965; but soon became an authoritarian dictator. He imposed martial law, arrested his political opponents, and stole millions from his country's treasury. (p. 529)

Maria Theresa (1717–1780) Austrian archduchess, queen of Bohemia and Hungary from 1740 to 1780; she took the throne after the War of the Austrian Succession. She was on of the most beloved monarchs in the history of Austria. (p. 158)

Marie-Antoinette (1755–1793) Queen of France, wife of King Louis XVI; she was queen during the French Revolution and was disliked by many French citizens. She was found guilty of treason and guillotined. (p. 196)

Martí, José (1853–1895) Cuban writer and independence fighter; he was killed in battle but became a symbol of Cuba's fight for freedom. (p. 365)

Marx, Karl (1818–1883) German social philosopher and chief theorist of modern socialism and communism; he declared that as capitalism grew, more and more workers would become impoverished and miserable. He advocated for a state in which the workers own the means of production and govern themselves. Along with Friedrich Engels, he wrote the *Communist Manifesto* in 1848, explaining their philosophy. (p. 251)

Mazzini, Guiseppe (1805–1872) Italian patriot; he formed the nationalist group called Young Italy to fight for the unification of the separate Italian states into one nation. (p. 316)

Medici, Lorenzo de (1449–1492) Florentine ruler; he supported some of the most talented Renaissance artists. He was known for his patronage and liberal mind. (p. 44)

Mehmed II (1432–1481) Sultan of the Ottoman Empire from 1444 to 1446 and again from 1451 to 1481; he was a strong military leader who conquered the Byzantine capital of Constantinople. (p. 103)

Meiji, Emperor (1852–1912) Emperor of Japan from 1867 to 1912; he restored imperial rule to Japan and with the help of samurais pushed for many reforms in Japan. (p. 352)

Meir, Golda (1898–1978) Israeli politician; she was prime minister of Israel during the Yom Kippur War and sought assistance and supplies from the United States. (p. 558)

Menelik II (1844–1913) Emperor of Ethiopia after 1889; he gained Ethiopian independence from Italy in 1896. (p. 362)

Menes (fl. 3100 BC) First pharaoh of Egypt; he is credited with uniting Upper and Lower Egypt and is said to have founded the city of Memphis, the capital of unified Egypt. (p. 12)

Metternich, Prince Klemens von (1773–1859; Austrian statesman and diplomat; he was the Austrian representative at the Congress of Vienna. (p. 219)

Mobutu Sese Seko (1930–1997) President of Zaire; he made himself dictator and, over the course of his rule, amassed great wealth for himself at the expense of his people, who remained poor. (p. 547)

Moctezuma II (1466–1520) Aztec ruler from 1502 to 1520; he was the emperor of the Aztecs when Cortés and his army conquered the empire. He was taken prisoner and killed during battle with the Spanish army. (p. 79)

Montesquieu, Baron de (1689–1755) French jurist and political philosopher; he explored democratic theories of government. He proposed a government divided into three branches and greatly influenced the United States Constitution. (p. 178)

More, Sir Thomas (1478–1535) English statesman and author; he wrote *Utopia,* which describes an ideal society. (p. 48)

Morelos, José María (1765–1815) Creole priest; he became the leader of the revolutionary movement in Mexico after Hidalgo's death. (p. 300)

Morse, Samuel (1791–1872) American artist and inventor; he applied scientists' discoveries of electricity and magnetism to develop the telegraph. (p. 265)

Muhammad (c. 570–632) Prophet of Islam whom Muslim recognize as Allah's messenger to all humankind. His teachings form the basis of Islam. (p. 22)

Muhammad, Askia (died 1538) Ruler of the West African kingdom of Songhai from 1493 to 1598; he was known for encouraging a revival of Muslim learning during his rule. (p. 24)

Musharaf, Pervez (1943–) Pakistani general; he overthrew the elected government of Pakistan in 1999 and became president. (p. 515)

Mussolini, Benito (1883–1945) Italian Fascist leader; he ruled as Italy's dictator for more than 20 years beginning in 1922. His alliance with Hitler brought Italy into World War II. (p. 425)

N

Nasser, Gamal Abdal (1918–1970) Egyptian army officer, political leader, and first president of the republic of Egypt; he helped lead a military coup that forced King Faruq to abdicate. He banned existing political parties and undertook an ambitious land reform program to gain support for his regime among the poor. (p. 554)

Nehru, Jawaharlal (1889–1964) Indian statesman; he was the first prime minister of independent India at the end of British colonial rule. (p. 512)

Nelson, Admiral Horatio (1758–1805) British admiral; he defeated Napoleon's navy in Egypt and again at the Battle of Trafalgar (1805). (p. 211)

Newton, Isaac (1642–1727) English mathematician and natural philosopher; he discovered the law of gravity as well as laws on the physics of objects. (p. 172)

Nkrumah, Kwame (1909–1972) Ghanaian nationalist leader and statesman; he pushed for Ghanaian independence from Great Britain and was elected Ghana's first president in 1957. (p. 540)

Noriega, Manuel (1938–) Panamanian general and dictator; he brutally crushed his enemies and used the country as a base for drug smuggling. (p. 579)

P

Pahlavi, Mohammad Reza (1919–1980) Shah of Iran from 1941 to 1979; during his reign, Iran's oil industry was controlled by foreign interests. He was overthrown in a revolution led by the Ayatollah Khomeini. (p. 555)

Pankhurst, Emmeline (1858–1928) British woman suffragist; she founded the Women's Social and Political Union in 1903. In support of women's suffrage, she led hunger strikes and was arrested often for her actions. (p. 290)

Pasteur, Louis (1822–1895) French chemist; his experiments with bacteria disproved the theory of spontaneous generation and led to the germ theory of infection. He also developed vaccines for anthrax and rabies. (p. 270)

Pavlov, Ivan (1849–1936) Russian physiologist and experimental psychologist; he researched the physiology of the heart, the digestive system, the brain, and the higher nervous system. He conducted a famous experiment with dogs demonstrating conditioned reflex. (p. 271)

Pedro I (1798–1834) First emperor of Brazil (1822–1831); he declared Brazil's independence from Portugal, where Pedro's father was king. (p. 302)

Perón, Juan (1895–1974) President of Argentina from 1946 to 1955 and again from 1973 to 1974; he rose to power following a military coup d'état and was a supporter of the rights of the people. (p. 576)

Peter the Great (1672–1725) Czar of Russia from 1682 to 1725; he transformed Russia into a modern state. He was an absolute monarch who brought the ways of Western Europe to Russia and made various reforms. (p. 155)

Philip II (1527–1598) King of Spain (1556–1598), Naples from (554–1598), and Portugal (1580–1598); he led Roman Catholic efforts to recover parts of Europe from Protestantism. He was defeated by England and the Netherlands. (p. 138)

Pinochet, Augusto (1915–) President and dictator of Chile from 1973 to 1990; he planned and carried out a coup of Salvador Allende's government in Chile. (p. 578)

Pisan, Christine de (1364–c. 1430) French poet and author; her *The City of Women* discusses the role of women in society. She championed the causes of equality and education for women. (p. 48)

Pizarro, Francisco (c. 1476–1541) Spanish conquistador; founder of Lima, Peru. From 1530 to 1533, he conquered the Inca Empire. (p. 80)

Pol Pot (1925–1998) Cambodian political leader; he led the Khmer Rouge guerillas in establishing a Communist government in Cambodia. Once in power, the Communists' brutal efforts to restructure Cambodian society left 1.5 million people dead. (p. 521)

Princip, Gavrilo (1894–1918) Serbian nationalist; he assassinated Archduke Franz Ferdinand of Austria-Hungary, which started World War I. (p. 383)

Q

Qianlong (1711–1799) Emperor of the Qing dynasty from 1735 to 1796; he was the grandson of Kangxi. During his reign, China expanded to its greatest size. He limited foreign contacts and ordered traders to conduct business with the Chinese government, not with private merchants. (p. 114)

R

Ramses II (died c. 1237 BC) Pharaoh of Egypt; he led an army against Hittite invaders in Egypt. He ruled Egypt with extravagance and built more temples and monuments than any other Egyptian pharaoh. (p. 12)

Raphael (1483–1520) Italian Renaissance painter; he painted frescos, his most famous being *The School of Athens.* (p. 45)

Rasputin, Grigory (1872–1916) A self-proclaimed Russian holy man and prominent figure at the court of Czar Nicholas II. He was viewed as corrupt, and support for czarist Russia deteriorated because of him. (p. 393)

Rhodes, Cecil (1853–1902) British imperialist and business magnate; he was one of the foremost advocates of expanding the British Empire and was a strong believer in the superiority of the "Anglo-Saxon" race. (p. 359)

Ricci, Matteo (1552–1610) Italian missionary; he traveled to China in 1583. He learned the language and adopted many Chinese customs, which gained him entry to the Ming court. He introduced China to European learning in mathematics, science, and technology. (p. 113)

Richelieu, Cardinal (1585–1642) French minister and chief minister of King Louis XIII; he wanted to strengthen the monarchy and fought against Huguenot resistance to the Catholic monarchy. (p. 143)

Robespierre, Maximilien (1758–1794) Leading figure of the French Revolution; he was known for his intense dedication to the Revolution. He became increasingly radical and led the National Convention during its most bloodthirsty time. (p. 204)

Rommel, Erwin (1891–1944) German general during World War II; he commanded the Afrika Korps and was nicknamed the Desert Fox for his leadership. (p. 447)

Roosevelt, Franklin Delano (1882–1945) Thirty-second president of the United States; he was elected president four times. He led the United States during the major crises of the Great Depression and World War II. (p. 416)

Rousseau, Jean-Jacques (1712–1778) Swiss-French political philosopher; he valued the social contract and addressed the nature of man in his work, *On the Origin of Inequality.* (p. 177)

S

Sadat, Anwar (1918–1981) Egyptian soldier and statesman; he launched the Yom Kippur War against Israel. (p. 558)

San Martín, José de (1778–1850) South American revolutionary; he led troops in Argentina, Chile, and Peru and gained independence for these nations. (p. 301)

Santa Anna, Antonio López de (1794–1876) Mexican general, president, and dictator; he fought in the Texas Revolution and seized the Alamo but was defeated and captured by Sam Houston at San Jacinto. (p. 364)

Shah Jahan (1592–1666) Mughal emperor of India from 1628 to 1658; under his rule, Mughal power reached its height and his age was the golden period of Muslim art and architecture. (p. 109)

Shaka (died 1828) Founder of the Zulu Empire; he reorganized the army and introduced new fighting tactics. He exterminated many clans and conquered most of southern Africa. (p. 360)

Shakespeare, William (1564–1616) English dramatist and poet; he is considered one of the greatest dramatists of all time and wrote such works as *Romeo and Juliet, Hamlet,* and *A Midsummer Night's Dream.* (p. 48)

Smith, Adam (1723–1790) Scottish economist; he became the leading advocate of laissez faire economics and is considered by some to be the "father of modern economics." He wrote the first true text on economics *The Wealth of Nations,* in 1776. (p. 249)

Solomon (1000s BC) King of Israel; he led Israel during the height of its wealth and power. (p. 13)

Stalin, Joseph (1879–1953) Totalitarian dictator of the Soviet Union; he led the Soviet Union through World War II and created a powerful Soviet sphere of influence in Eastern Europe after the war. (p. 426)

Suharto (1921–) President of Indonesia from 1967 to 1998; he seized power in Indonesia from Sukarno in a coup d'état. His authoritarian and corrupt rule eventually led to his ouster. (p. 520)

Sukarno (1901–1970) Indonesian politician; he became Indonesia's first president after leading an independence movement. A strong anti-communist, whose policies resulted in the deaths of hundreds, he was deposed in a coup led by Suharto. (p. 520)

BIOGRAPHICAL DICTIONARY

Suleyman I (1495–1566) Sultan of the Ottoman Empire from 1520 to 1566; he expanded the empire and took on a large economic and political role in the affairs of Europe and the Mediterranean. (p. 103)

Sunni Ali (died 1492) First great leader of Africa's Songhai Empire; he organized an uprising against Malian rule and established a new empire in Songhai. (24)

Sun Yixian (1866–1925) Chinese statesman and revolutionary leader; he believed that China should be a democracy but that it first needed to replace the Qing dynasty with a ruling nationalist party. He founded the Revolutionary Alliance in 1905. (p. 352)

T

Talleyrand, Charles Maurice de (1754–1838) French statesman and diplomat; he was one of the negotiators at the Congress of Vienna. He represented France on behalf of Louis XVIII. (p. 219)

Teresa of Avila (1515–1582) Spanish Carmelite nun of the Roman Catholic Church; she reformed the Carmelite order. Her fervor for the Catholic Church proved inspiring for many people during the Reformation period. (p. 60)

Thomas Aquinas (1225–1274) Italian philosopher and theologian; he argued that rational thought could be used to support Christian belief. (p. 33)

Tokugawa, Ieyasu (1542–1616) Japanese warrior and dictator; he was appointed shogun by the emperor, thus assuming complete control of the government and establishing the Tokugawa shogunate. (p. 121)

Tojo, Hideki (1884–1948) Japanese nationalist and general; he took control of Japan during World War II. He was later tried and executed for war crimes. (p. 443)

Tolstoy, Leo (1828–1910) Russian novelist; his novel *War and Peace* portrayed war as confusing and horrible. (p. 278)

Toussaint L'Ouverture (c. 1744–1803) Haitian patriot and martyr; he took control of Hispaniola for the French and was a hero of the people. Napoleon felt threatened by his growing popularity and had him captured and killed in 1803. (p. 298)

Trotsky, Leon (1879–1940) Russian Communist revolutionary; he negotiated the peace between Russia and the Central Powers to end Russian involvement in World War I. (p. 394)

Truman, Harry S (1884–1972) Thirty-third president of the United States; he became president upon the death of Franklin D. Roosevelt. He led the United States through the end of World War II and the beginning of the Cold War. (p. 463)

Tull, Jethro (1674–1741) British inventor; he invented the seed drill. (p. 236)

V

Velázquez, Diego (1465–1524) Spanish painter; he painted in a realistic style but also worked in impressionism towards the end of his career. (p. 139)

Victor Emmanuel (1820–1878) King of Sardinia-Piedmont from 1849 to 1861 and king of Italy from 1861 to 1878; he was the first king of a united Italy. (p. 318)

Victoria, Queen (1819–1901) Queen of Great Britain and Ireland from 1837 to 1901 and empress of India from 1876 to 1901; she had the longest reign in all of British history and allowed Parliament to become more involved in running the government. (p. 290)

Villa, Francisco "Pancho" (1878–1923) Mexican bandit and revolutionary leader; he led revolts against Victoriano Huerta. He was pursued by the United States but evaded General Pershing. (p. 364)

Vladimir I (c. 965–1015) Grand prince of Kiev; he converted to Orthodox Christianity in the 980s and made it the state religion. (p. 29)

Voltaire (1694–1778) French philosopher and author; he was a supporter of Deism, the idea that God was no longer involved with the universe after creating it. He also advocated a tolerant approach to religion. (p. 178)

W

Washington, George (1732–1799) First president of the United States; he commanded the Continental Army during the Revolutionary War and served as a representative to the Continental Congress. (p. 185)

Watt, James (1736–1819) Scottish inventor; he developed crucial innovations to make the steam engine efficient, fast, and better able to power machinery. (p. 239)

Wellington, Duke of (1769–1852) British soldier and statesman; he led the British troops against Napoleon at the Battle of Waterloo. (p. 218)

Wilhelm I (1797–1888) King of Prussia from 1861 to 1888 and emperor of Germany from 1871 to 1888; he chose Otto von Bismarck as Prussia's prime minister, and together they unified Germany. (p. 321)

William and Mary King William III (1650–1702) and Queen Mary II (1662–1694), rulers of Great Britain who replaced King James II as a result of the Glorious Revolution. (p. 152)

William the Conqueror (c. 1027–1087) King of England from 1060 to 1087; he was a powerful French noble who conquered England and brought feudalism to Britain. (p. 32)

Wilson, Woodrow (1856–1924) Twenty-eighth president of the United States; he proposed the League of Nations after World War I as a part of his Fourteen Points. (p. 397)

Wordsworth, William (1770–1850) English poet; his works included *The Evening Walk, Descriptive Sketches, The Prelude,* and *The Excursion*. (p. 278)

Wright, Orville (1871–1948) and **Wilbur** (1867–1912) American pioneers of aviation; they went from experiments with kites and gliders to piloting the first successful gas-powered airplane flight. (p. 265)

Y

Yaroslav the Wise (978–1054) Grand duke of Kiev from 1019 to 1054; he promoted Christianity and civilization in Russia and began a codification of the law. (p. 29)

Yeltsin, Boris (1931–) Russian politician and president of Russia in the 1990s; he was the first popularly elected leader of the country. (p. 497)

Yi Song-gye (1335–1408) Founder of the Korean Choson dynasty; his dynasty became one of the longest continuous dynasties in history. (p. 123)

Yonglo (1360–1424) Third emperor of the Ming dynasty in China; he ordered the reconstruction of Beijing and made it the new capital of China. He also commissioned an encyclopedia that covered history, philosophy, literature, astronomy, medicine, and numerous other topics. (p. 112)

Z

Zapata, Emiliano (1879–1919) Mexican revolutionary; he led the revolt against Porfirio Díaz in the south of Mexico during the Mexican Revolution. (p. 364)

Zheng He (1371–c. 1433) Admiral, diplomat, and explorer during China's Ming dynasty; his Chinese fleet visited more than 30 countries. (p. 112)

BIOGRAPHICAL DICTIONARY

English and Spanish Glossary

MARK	AS IN	RESPELLING	EXAMPLE
a	alphabet	a	*AL-fuh-bet
ā	Asia	ay	AY-zhuh
ä	cart, top	ah	KAHRT, TAHP
e	let, ten	e	LET, TEN
ē	even, leaf	ee	EE-vuhn, LEEF
i	it, tip, British	i	IT, TIP, BRIT-ish
ī	site, buy, Ohio	y	SYT, BY, oh-HY-oh
	iris	eye	EYE-ris
k	card	k	KAHRD
ō	over, rainbow	oh	OH-vuhr, RAYN-boh
ù	book, wood	ooh	BOOHK, WOOHD
ȯ	all, orchid	aw	AWL, AWR-kid
ȯi	foil, coin	oy	FOYL, KOYN
àu	out	ow	OWT
	cup, butter	uh	KUHP, BUHT-uhr
ü	rule, food	oo	ROOL, FOOD
yü	few	yoo	FYOO
zh	vision	zh	VIZH-uhn

* A syllable printed in small capital letters receives heavier emphasis than the other syllable(s) in a word.

Phonetic Respelling and Pronunciation Guide

Many of the key terms in this textbook have been respelled to help you pronounce them. The letter combinations used in the respelling throughout the narrative are explained in the following phonetic respelling and pronunciation guide. The guide is adapted from **Webster's Tenth New College Dictionary, Merriam-Webster's New Geographical Dictionary, and Merriam-Webster's New Biographical Dictionary.**

A

Abbasid dynasty that overthrew the Umayyad dynasty to rule the Muslim caliphate from 750 to 1258; for 150 years the Abbasids maintained the unity of the caliphate and Islamic culture and civilization flourished (p. 22)
Abasida gobernantes del Imperio musulmán que derrocaron a la familia Umayyad y establecieron un régimen que contribuyó a fortalecer el imperio, lo cual brindó gran prosperidad y crecimiento cultural a la cultura islámica (pág. 22)

abolition abolishment of slavery (p. 305)
abolición eliminación de la esclavitud (pág. 305)

absolute monarch a ruler that has unlimited power and authority over his or her people (p. 137)
monarca absoluto gobernante con poder y autoridad ilimitados sobre su pueblo (pág. 137)

African Diaspora the dispersal of people of African descent throughout the Americas and Western Europe due to the slave trade (p. 93)
diáspora africana resultado del comercio de esclavos, cuando muchos africanos y sus descendientes fueron llevados a la Américas y a Europa Occidental (pág. 93)

African National Congress political organization in South Africa; founded in 1912, it developed into the main opposition force to apartheid (p. 546)
Congreso Nacional Africano organización política de Sudáfrica; fundada en 1912, comenzó como una agrupación pacífica que luchaba por los derechos civiles y se oponía al apartheid (pág. 546)

al Qaeda "the base"; Islamist terrorist organization responsible for the September 11 attacks (p. 501)
al Qaeda literalmente significa "la base"; grupo fundamentalista islámico (pág. 501)

Allied Powers the alliance formed between Britain, France, and Russia during World War I (p. 383)
Potencias Aliadas alianza que formaron Gran Bretaña, Francia y Rusia durante la Primera Guerra Mundial (pág. 383)

Allies the alliance of Britain, France, and Russia in World War II; joined by the United States after the Japanese bombing of Pearl Harbor in 1941 (p. 440)
Aliados alianza de Gran Bretaña, Francia y Rusia durante la Segunda Guerra Mundial; Estados Unidos se unió tras el bombardeo de Pearl Harbor en 1941 (pág. 440)

Amritsar Massacre (1919) an event in which British troops fired on a large crowd of peaceful, unarmed Indian protestors, killing some 400 people; it led to a campaign of protest led by Gandhi (p. 411)
masacre de Amritsar (1919) suceso ocurrido en la India en el cual los soldados británicos dispararon contra una multitud de manifestantes pacíficos que no llevaban armas; murieron aproximadamente 400 personas (pág. 411)

anesthetic a drug that inhibits pain during surgery (p. 270)
anestesia droga que inhibe el dolor durante una cirugía (pág. 270)

Anti-Comintern Pact (1936) agreement signed between Germany and Japan in which they established their opposition to the Comintern, a Soviet-sponsored international organization aimed at spreading communism (p. 424)
Pacto Anti-Comintern (1936) acuerdo firmado entre Alemania y Japón para establecer su oposición al Comintern, una organización internacional promovida por la Unión Soviética que se dedicaba a difundir el comunismo (pág. 424)

anti-Semitism hostility or prejudice towards Jews (pp. 296, 428)
antisemitismo creencias en contra de los judíos (pág. 296, 428)

annulled declared invalid based on church laws (p. 55)
anular declarar inválido según las leyes de la Iglesia (pág. 55)

apartheid the South African government's official policy of legalized racial segregation throughout the society (p. 543)
apartheid política oficial del gobierno sudafricano que consiste en la segregación racial legalizada en toda la sociedad (pág. 543)

appeasement giving in to aggressive demands in order to avoid war (p. 438)
pacificación ceder a las demandas de potencias intransigentes para evitar una guerra (pág. 438)

armistice an agreement to cease fighting, usually in a war (p. 399)
armisticio acuerdo para cesar una lucha, generalmente en una guerra (pág. 399)

arms race competition between nations to gain an advantage in weapons (p. 485)
carrera armamentística competencia entre naciones para tener ventaja en cuanto a la cantidad de armas (pág. 485)

artifacts any object made by early humans such as a tool, a piece of pottery, or a weapon (p. 10)
artefactos todo objeto hecho por los primeros humanos, como una herramienta, una pieza de cerámica o un arma (pág. 10)

artisans skilled craftspeople who make goods, such as pottery or baskets, by hand (p. 11)
artesanos trabajadores que hacen productos a mano, como piezas de cerámica o canastas (pág. 11)

Aryans members of a warrior civilization that came to power in India following the Harappas (p. 14)
arios civilización guerrera que tomó el poder en la India después de los harappa (pág. 14)

Asian Tigers term referring to South Korea, Hong Kong, Taiwan, and Singapore, which built strong export-driven economies in the late 1900s (p. 531)
tigres asiáticos países de Asia que siguen un modelo de desarrollo económico similar al japonés (pág. 531)

assembly a group of persons gathered for a particular purpose; in Ancient Greece, they gathered for political purposes (p. 3)
asamblea grupo de personas reunidas con un determinado propósito; en la antigua Grecia, se reunían con fines políticos (pág. 3)

assembly line a mass-production process in which a product is moved forward through many work stations, where workers perform specific tasks (p. 247)
línea de montaje proceso de producción en masa en el que un producto pasa por varias etapas en las que los trabajadores hacen tareas específicas (pág. 247)

Austro-Prussian War (1866) war fought between Prussia and Austria lasting seven weeks; Prussian victory dissolved the German Confederation and led to the exclusion of Austria from German affairs (p. 322)
Guerra austro-prusiana (1866) guerra entre Prusia y Austria; la victoria prusiana provocó la exclusión de Austria de Alemania (pág. 322)

autocracy a government in which the ruler holds absolute power (p. 331)
autocracia forma de gobierno en la que el gobernante tiene poder absoluto (pág. 331)

Axis Powers the alliance of Germany, Italy, and Japan in World War II (p. 439)
Potencias del Eje alianza de Alemania, Italia y Japón durante la Segunda Guerra Mundial (pág. 439)

B

Baghdad Pact during the Cold War, a U.S.-led alliance against communism in the Middle East (p. 554)
Pacto de Bagdad alianza dirigida por Estados Unidos contra el comunismo en Medio Oriente (pág. 554)

balance of trade the difference in value between what a nation imports and exports over a period of time (p. 86)
balance comercial la diferencia en valor entre lo que una nación importa y lo que exporta a lo largo de un período de tiempo (pág. 86)

Balfour Declaration a statement issued by the British foreign secretary in favor of establishing a Jewish homeland in Palestine (p. 400)
Declaración de Balfour declaración escrita por el Ministro de Asuntos Exteriores británico a un líder sionista de Palestina (pág. 400)

Balkan Wars (1912–1913) two wars that cost the Ottomon Empire all of its European territories except the area around Constantinople (Istanbul) (p. 329)
Guerras de los Balcanes (1912–1913) dos guerras que se libraron por el último de los territorios europeos del Imperio otomano; a causa de ellas, el área que rodea a Constantinopla (Estambul) quedó como el único territorio otomano en Europa (pág. 329)

Bataan Death March (1942) a forced march of American and Filipino prisoners of war captured by the Japanese in the Philippines in World War II (p. 450)
marcha de la muerte de Bataan (1942) marcha forzada de los prisioneros de guerra estadounidenses y filipinos capturados por los japoneses en Filipinas durante la Segunda Guerra Mundial (pág. 450)

Battle of Britain (1940) three month air battle between Germany and Great Britain fought over Great Britain during World War II; Britain's victory forestalled a German invasion (p. 442)
batalla de Inglaterra (1940) serie de batallas aéreas entre Alemania y Gran Bretaña que se libraron en Gran Bretaña durante la Segunda Guerra Mundial (pág. 442)

Battle of El Alamein (1942) World War II battle in which the Britain won a decisive victory over Germany in Egypt, securing the Suez Canal (p. 448)
batalla de El Alamein (1942) batalla clave de la Segunda Guerra Mundial donde los británicos obtuvieron una victoria aplastante sobre los alemanes en Egipto (pág. 448)

Battle of Guadalcanal (1942–1943) World War II battle in the Pacific; it represented the first Allied counterattack against Japanese forces; Allied victory forced Japanese forces to abandon the island (p. 452)
batalla de Guadalcanal (1942–1943) batalla de la Segunda Guerra Mundial que se libró en el Pacífico por tierra, mar y aire; la victoria aliada obligó a las fuerzas japonesas a abandonar la isla (pág. 452)

Battle of Iwo Jima (1945) World War II battle between Japanese forces and invading U.S. troops (p. 462)
batalla de Iwo Jima (1945) batalla de la Segunda Guerra Mundial entre las fuerzas japonesas y el ejército invasor estadounidense (pág. 462)

Battle of Midway (1942) World War II naval battle fought in the Pacific; the Americans broke the Japanese code and knew the date and location of the attack, setting the stage for a major American victory (p. 451)
batalla de Midway (1942) batalla de la Segunda Guerra Mundial librada en el Pacífico; los estadounidenses descifraron el código japonés y averiguaron dónde y cuándo atacarían los japoneses, lo que les permitió obtener una victoria importante (pág. 451)

Battle of Okinawa (1945) World War II victory for the Allied troops that resulted in the deaths of almost all of the 10,000 Japanese defenders; the battle claimed 12,000 American lives (p. 462)
batalla de Okinawa (1945) victoria de los Aliados en la Segunda Guerra Mundial que tuvo como consecuencia la muerte de los casi 10,000 defensores japoneses; los estadounidenses perdieron 12,000 soldados en la batalla (pág. 462)

Battle of Stalingrad (1942) World War II battle between invading German forces and Soviet defenders for control of Stalingrad, a city on the Volga River; each side sustained hundreds of thousands casualties; Germany's defeat marked turning point in the war (p. 450)
batalla de Stalingrado (1942) una de las batallas más sangrientas de la Segunda Guerra Mundial, en la que los soviéticos defendieron la ciudad, a costa de decenas de miles de vidas, y lograron echar a los alemanes de la ciudad (pág. 450)

Battle of Verdun (1916) the longest battle of World War I; it ended in stalemate, with both sides suffering hundreds of thousands of casualties (p. 388)
batalla de Verdún (1916) la batalla más larga de la Primera Guerra Mundial; ambos bandos quedaron muy debilitados tras perder decenas de miles de vidas (pág. 388)

Bay of Pigs invasion (1961) the failed attempt of Cuban exiles backed by the U.S. to overthrow the Cuban socialist government of Fidel Castro (p. 487)
invasión de la Bahía de Cochinos (1961) intento frustrado de los exiliados cubanos, apoyados por Estados Unidos, de derrocar al gobierno socialista de Fidel Castro (pág. 487)

Berlin airlift (1948–1949) a program in which the United States and Britain shipped supplies by air to West Berlin during the Soviet blockade of all routes to the city (p. 482)
puente aéreo de Berlín (1948–1949) programa de envío de suministros a Berlín occidental por parte de Estados Unidos y Gran Bretaña durante el bloqueo soviético de todas las vías de acceso a la ciudad (pág. 482)

Berlin Conference (1884–1885) a meeting at which representatives from European nations agreed upon rules for the European colonization of Africa (p. 360)
Conferencia de Berlín (1884–1885) encuentro en el que representantes de países europeos acordaron reglas para la colonización europea de África (pág. 360)

Bessemer process a process developed in the 1850s that led to faster, cheaper steel production (p. 263)
proceso de Bessemer proceso desarrollado en la década de 1850 que permitió producir acero de forma más rápida y económica (pág. 263)

Bill of Rights the first 10 amendments to the United States Constitution (p. 7)
Declaración de Derechos primeras 10 enmiendas hechas a la Constitución de Estados Unidos (pág. 7)

biotechnology the use of biological research in industry (p. 610)
biotecnología usa de la investigación biológica en la tecnología (pág. 610)

Black Death a terrible outbreak of bubonic plague that swept through Europe, beginning in 1347; (p. 33)
Peste Negra terrible plaga de peste bubónica, propagada por las pulgas que tenían las ratas, que comenzó en 1347 y arrasó Europa (pág. 33)

Black Tuesday October 29, 1929, the day that the United States stock market crashed (p. 415)
martes negro 29 de octubre de 1929, día en que el mercado de valores de Estados Unidos colapsó (pág. 415)

blitzkrieg a German word meaning "lightning war"; a fast, forceful style of fighting used by Germans in World War II (p. 440)
blitzkrieg palabra alemana que significa "guerra relámpago"; estilo de combate rápido y contundente que usaron los alemanes en la Segunda Guerra Mundial (pág. 440)

Bloody Sunday January 22, 1905, the day that czarist troops fired on protestors at the Winter Palace, igniting the Russian Revolution of 1905 (p. 334)
Domingo sangriento 22 de enero de 1905 acontecimiento inspirador de la Revolución rusa de 1905, cuando el ejército disparó contra unos manifestantes frente al Palacio de Invierno (pág. 334)

Bolsheviks Marxists whose goal was to seize state power and establish a dictatorship of the proletariat; Soviet Communists (p. 392)
bolcheviques seguidores de Marx cuyo objetivo era apropiarse del poder estatal y establecer una dictadura del proletariado; comunistas soviéticos (pág. 392)

bourgeoisie the urban middle class; merchants, professionals, and manufacturers (p. 197)
burguesía la clase media urbana; mercaderes, profesionales y fabricantes (pág. 197)

Boxer Rebellion (1900) a siege of a foreign settlement in Beijing by Chinese nationalists who were angry at foreign involvement in China (p. 351)
rebelión de los boxers (1900) asedio a un asentamiento extranjero en Beijing por parte de nacionalistas chinos que estaban en desacuerdo con la intervención extranjera en China (pág. 351)

boyars wealthy Russian landowners (p. 154)
boyars ricos terratenientes ruso (pág. 154)

British East India Company a joint-stock company granted a royal charter by Elizabeth I in 1600 for the purpose of controlling trade in India (p. 344)
British East India Company sociedad por acciones a la que Isabel I otorgó un cédula real en 1600 para controlar el comercio en la India (pág. 344)

Buddhism the religion founded by Siddhartha Gautama, which teaches the Four Noble Truths and following the Eightfold Path (p. 14)
budismo religión fundada por Siddhartha Gautama que enseña las Cuatro Nobles Verdades y a seguir el sendero óctuple (pág. 14)

Bushido "way of the warrior;" code of behavior of Japanese samurai warriors, stressing bravery, loyalty, and honor (p. 119)
bushido "vía del guerrero"; código de conducta de los guerreros samuráis japoneses que destacaba la valentía, la lealtad y el honor (pág. 119)

C

caliph "successor to the Prophet"; title given to the political and religious leader of Muslims(p. 22)
califa "sucesor del Profeta"; título dado al líder político y religioso de los musulmanes (pág. 22)

Camp David Accords (1978) a peace agreement mediated by U.S. President Carter between Egyptian President Anwar Sadat and Israeli Prime Minister Menachem Begin (p. 558)
Acuerdos de Camp David (1978) acuerdos de paz entre el presidente egipcio Anwar Sadat y el primer ministro israelí Menachem Begin en los que el presidente Carter actuó como mediador (pág. 558)

canon law the code of laws that govern a Christian church (p. 31)
derecho canónico código de leyes que gobiernan una iglesia cristiana (pág. 31)

capitalism economic system in which most businesses are privately owned (p. 89)
capitalismo sistema económico donde la mayoría de las empresas son de propiedad privada (pág. 89)

caravel a sailing vessel that uses square and triangular sails to help it sail against the wind (p. 73)
carabela barco de velas triangulares y cuadradas que permiten navegar con el viento en contra (pág. 73)

Central Powers the alliance between Germany, Austria-Hungary, and the Ottoman Empire during World War I (p. 383)
Potencias Centrales alianza entre Alemania, el Imperio austrohúngaro y el Imperio otomano durante la Primera Guerra Mundial (pág. 383)

charter a founding document or agreement, such as the one that created the United Nations (p. 642)
carta de constitución documento que crea organizaciones, como Naciones Unidas (pág. 642)

checks and balances a system in which the powers of government are balanced among different branches so that each branch can check, or limit, the power of the other branches (p. 4)
equilibrio de poderes sistema mediante el cual el poder de un gobierno está distribuido entre las distintas ramas, de manera que cada rama pueda limitar el poder de las demás (pág. 4)

circumnavigate to proceed completely around (p. 76)
circunnavegar dar una vuelta completa alrededor de algo (pág. 76)

civilization a complex, organized society that has advanced cities, a government, religion, record keeping and writing, job specialization, social classes, and arts and architecture (p. 11)
civilización sociedad compleja y organizada que tiene ciudades desarrolladas, un gobierno, una religión, registros escritos, especialización laboral, clases sociales y arte y arquitectura (pág. 11)

cloning the process of making a genetically identical copy of an animal's cell (p. 610)
clonación proceso de hacer una copia genéticamente idéntica de la célula de un animal (pág. 610)

Cold War an era of high tension and bitter rivalry between the United States and the Soviet Union in the decades following World War II (p. 481)
Guerra Fría época de mucha tensión y rivalidad implacable entre Estados Unidos y la Unión Soviética tras el fin de la Segunda Guerra Mundial (pág. 481)

Columbian Exchange the transfer of plants, animals, and disease between the Americas and Europe, Asia, and Africa (p. 85)
intercambio colombino intercambio de plantas, animales y enfermedades entre las Américas, Europa, Asia y África (pág. 85)

commonwealth a republican government based on the common good of all the people (p. 150)
commonwealth gobierno democrático basado en el bien común de todos los ciudadanos (pág. 150)

communism economic and political system in which government owns the means of production and controls economic planning; a socialist economic system without social classes (p. 251)
comunismo sistema político y económico en que el gobierno posee los medios de producción y controla la planificación económica; sistema económico socialista sin clases sociales (pág. 251)

concentration camps detention sites created for military or political purposes to confine, terrorize, and, in some cases, kill civilians (p. 457)
campos de concentración lugares de detención creados con fines militares o políticos para confinar, intimidar y, en algunos casos, matar a civiles (pág. 457)

conquistador a Spanish soldier and explorer who led military expeditions in the Americas and captured land for Spain (p. 79)
conquistador soldado y exploradore español que encabezó expediciones militares en América y capturó territorios en nombre de España (pág. 79)

constitutional monarchy a monarchy limited by certain laws (p. 152)
monarquía constitucional monarquía limitada por ciertas leyes (pág. 152)

containment the United States policy adopted in the 1940s to stop the spread of communism by providing economic and military aid to countries opposing the Soviets (p. 482)
contención política estadounidense adoptada en la década de 1940 para detener la difusión del comunismo; se proporcionó ayuda económica y militar a los países que se oponían a los soviéticos (pág. 482)

Continental System the system of commercial blockades of Britain and continental Europe, set in place by Napoleon with the intent of destroying Britain's economy (p. 212)
Sistema Continental sistema de bloqueos comerciales a Gran Bretaña y Europa continental impuestos por Napoleón para intentar destruir la economía británica (pág. 212)

Contras rebels seeking to overthrow Nicaragua's Sandinista government in the 1980s; financed by the United States (p. 574)
contras rebeldes que intentaban derrocar el gobierno sandinista de Nicaragua; financiados por Estados Unidos (pág. 574)

cottage industry a usually small-scale industry carried on at home by family members using their own equipment (p. 237)
industria casera industria que los miembros de una familia desarrollan en el hogar, generalmente a pequeña escala y con sus propias herramientas (pág. 237)

Council of Trent a meeting of church leaders in the 1500s whose purpose was to clearly define Catholic doctrines for the Catholic Reformation (p. 58)
Concilio de Trento encuentro de los líderes de la Iglesia en el siglo XVI con el fin de definir claramente las doctrinas católicas para la Reforma católica (pág. 58)

counterculture a rebellion of teens and young adults against mainstream American culture in the 1960s (p. 492)
contracultura rebelión de adolescentes y adultos jóvenes contra la cultura masiva estadounidense en la década de 1960 (pág. 492)

Counter-Reformation the Catholic Church's series of reforms in response to the spread of Protestantism (p. 58)
Contrarreforma serie de reformas que emprendió la Iglesia católica como respuesta a la difusión de las iglesias protestantes (pág. 58)

counterrevolution a revolution against a government established by a revolution (p. 206)
contrarrevolución revolución contra un gobierno establecido por una revolución (pág. 206)

coup d'état "stroke of state"; the sudden overthrow of a government by force (p. 211)
golpe de estado derrocamiento súbito de un gobierno por la fuerza (pág. 211)

credit an arrangement by which a purchaser borrows money from a bank or other lender and agrees to pay it back over time (p. 415)
crédito acuerdo por el cual un comprador pide dinero a un banco o a otro prestamista para hacer una compra y se compromete a devolverlo en determinado tiempo (pág. 415)

creoles people of Spanish or Portuguese descent born in the Americas (p. 298)
criollos nativos de las Américas descendientes de españoles o portugueses (pág. 298)

Crimean War (1853–1856) war between the Ottoman Empire and Russia, ostensibly over access for Eastern Orthodox Christians to the Holy Land, controlled by the Ottomans; Britain and France allied with the Ottomans to check Russian expansion (p. 328)
Guerra de Crimea (1853–1856) guerra entre Gran Bretaña, Francia y los turcos otomanos por un lado y Rusia por el otro, causada por disputas religiosas entre los cristianos católicos y los cristianos ortodoxos en Palestina (pág. 328)

Crusades (1096–1204) a series of wars carried out by European Christians to gain control of the Holy Land from their Muslim rulers (p. 33)
Cruzadas (1096–1204) serie de guerras santas encabezadas por los católicos para recuperar partes de Medio Oriente, en posesión de los musulmanes (pág. 33)

Cuban Missile Crisis (1962) confrontation between the United States and the Soviet Union over Soviet missiles in Cuba (p. 487)
crisis de los misiles en Cuba (1962) confrontación entre Estados Unidos y la Unión Soviética acerca de los misiles soviéticos en Cuba (pág. 487)

cultural diffusion the spreading of culture from one society to another (pp. 11, 597)
difusión cultural transmisión cultural de una sociedad a otra (pág. 11, 597)

Cultural Revolution the violent attempt at social change in China, launched by Mao Zedong in 1966 (p. 524)
Revolución cultural intento violento de cambiar la sociedad china, ideado por Mao Tsé-Tung en 1966 (pág. 524)

cuneiform Sumerian writing (p. 13)
cuneiforme tipo de escritura que usaban los sumerios (pág. 13)

czar "caesar"; title taken by the ruler of Russia (p. 154)
zar "césar"; título que llevaba el gobernante del ruso (pág. 154)

D

daimyo a warrior lord in feudal Japan who controlled vast amounts of land and commanded a private army of samurai (pp. 27, 121)
daimyo señor guerrero del Japón feudal que controlaba grandes extensiones de tierra y lideraba un ejército privado de samuráis (pág. 27, 121)

Daoism a system of ideas and beliefs based on the teachings of Chinese thinker Laozi, who believed that people should live a simple, honest life and not interfere with the course of natural events (p. 15)
taoísmo sistema de ideas y creencias basadas en las enseñanzas del pensador chino Laozi, quien creía que se debe vivir una vida sencilla y honesta sin interferir con el desarrollo natural de los acontecimientos (pág. 15)

D-Day June 6, 1944; the first day of the Allied invasion of Normandy in World War II (p. 461)
Día D 6 de junio de 1944; el primer día de la invasión de los Aliados a Normandía durante la Segunda Guerra Mundial (pág. 461)

Declaration of the Rights of Man and of the Citizen a document that laid out the basic principles of the French Revolution—liberty, equality, and fraternity (pp. 7, 200)
Declaración de los Derechos del Hombre y del Ciudadano documento que estableció los principios básicos de la Revolución francesa: libertad, igualdad y fraternidad (pág. 7, 200)

Declaration of Independence statement of the Second Continental Congress that formally announced the American colonies break with Britain (p. 7)
Declaración de Independecia pronunciamiento del Segunda Congreso Continental que anunció formalmente la separación de las colonias de Gran Bretaña (pág. 7)

deforestation the clearing of forests (p. 608)
deforestación tala de árboles (pág. 608)

democracy a government run by the people (p. 16)
democracia gobierno del pueblo (pág. 16)

deported forced to leave a country (p. 457)
deportado obligado a dejar un país (pág. 457)

desertification the transformation of habitable land to desert through a change in climate or destructive land use (p. 548)
desertificación transformación de una región habitable en un desierto, a través de un cambio en el clima o el uso destructivo de la tierra (pág. 548)

détente efforts taken by President Nixon in the late 1960s and early 1970s to lower Cold War tensions (p. 489)
détente intento que hizo el presidente Nixon a finales de la década de 1960 y comienzos de la década de 1970 para reducir la tensión de la Guerra Fría (pág. 489)

deterrence the development of or maintenance of military power to deter, or prevent, an attack (p. 485)
disuasión desarrollo o mantenimiento de un poder militar para disuadir, o impedir, un ataque (pág. 485)

devolution the redistribution of power from the central government to local governments (p. 625)
devolución redistribución del poder del gobierno central a los gobiernos locales (pág. 625)

Diaspora the dispersal of the Jews from their homeland in Palestine during the 2,600 years that followed the destruction of the Solomon's Temple in Jerusalem in 586 BC by the Chaldeans (p. 13)
diáspora dispersión de los judíos desde su tierra natal en Palestina durante los 1,800 años que siguieron a la destrucción del Templo de Jerusalén, en el año 70 d.C., por parte de los romanos (pág. 13)

direct democracy the type of governing system where all people vote directly on an issue (p. 3)
democracia directa sistema de gobierno donde todos los ciudadanos votan directamente sobre una cuestión (pág. 3)

divine right the belief that a ruler's authority comes directly from God (p. 137)
derecho divino creencia de que la autoridad de un gobernante viene directamente de Dios (pág. 137)

division of labor when certain people do a specific task or type of work (p. 11)
división del trabajo cuando ciertas personas hacen una tarea o trabajo específicos (pág. 11)

domino theory the belief during the Cold War that the fall of one non-communist country to communism would cause neighboring non-communist countries also to fall to communists (p. 518)
teoría del dominó creencia de que el comunismo se difundiría a otros países (pág. 518)

Dreyfus affair a political scandal that divided France in the 1890s, involving the wrongful conviction of Jewish army officer Alfred Dreyfus for treason (p. 296)
caso Dreyfus escándalo político que dividió a Francia en la década de 1890 y que se inició cuando el militar judío Alfred Dreyfus fue condenado erróneamente por traición (pág. 296)

Dual Monarchy Austria-Hungary (1867–1918), two separate, equal states ruled by one monarch (p. 326)
monarquía dual sistema de gobierno donde un mismo rey gobierna a dos estados (pág. 326)

Duma the Russian assembly formed after the Revolution of 1905 in charge of approving all laws (p. 334)
Duma asamblea rusa formada después de la Revolución de 1905 que aprobaba todas las leyes (pág. 334)

E

Edict of Nantes (1598) a declaration of French king Henry IV in which he promised that Protestants could live peacefully in France and were free to establish houses of worship in selected French cities (p. 143)
Edicto de Nantes (1598) declaración del rey francés Enrique IV, donde prometía que los protestantes podrían vivir en paz en Francia y eran libres de establecer sus lugares de culto en ciertas ciudades francesas (pág. 143)

Emancipation Proclamation (1862) an order issued by President Abraham Lincoln freeing the enslaved people in areas rebelling against the Union (p. 306)
Proclamación de Emancipación (1862) decreto emitido por el presidente Abraham Lincoln para liberar a los esclavos en las áreas que se rebelaban contra la Unión (pág. 306)

enclosure movement a process in Europe from 1700s to the mid-1800s where landowners fenced small fields to create large farms, allowing for more efficient farming methods and increased the food supply (p. 237)
movimiento de cercamiento proceso por el cual los terratenientes cercaban pequeños campos para crear grandes granjas; esto permitía aplicar métodos agrícolas más rentables y aumentó el suministro de alimentos (pág. 237)

encomienda Spanish colonial system in which a colonist was given a certain amount of land and a number of Native Americans to work the land in exchange for teaching the Native Americans Christianity (p. 79)
encomienda sistema por el cual un colono recibía una porción de tierra y un grupo de indígenas norteamericanos lo cultivaban a cambio de recibir enseñanzas cristianas (pág. 79)

English Bill of Rights document drafted by Parliament that set limits on the monarch's power (p. 6)
Declaración de Derechos inglesa documento redactado por el Parliamento que limitaba el poder del monarca (pág. 6)

enlightened despots the absolute monarchs in 18th- century Europe who ruled according to the principles of the Enlightenment (p. 180)
déspotas ilustrados los monarcas absolutos europeos del siglo XVIII, que gobernaban según los principios de la Ilustración (pág. 180)

Enlightenment a time of optimism and possibility from the late 1600s to the late 1700s; also called the Age of Reason (pp. 6, 176)
Ilustración época de optimismo y nuevas posibilidades que comenzó en Europa en el siglo XVII; tambien llamada Edad de la Razón (pág. 6, 176)

entrepreneur a risk taker who starts a new business within the economic system of capitalism (p. 249)
empresario persona que corre un riesgo para emprender un negocio dentro del sistema económico capitalista (pág. 249)

epidemic an outbreak of a contagious disease that spreads rapidly and affects many people (p. 600)
epidemia algo que afecta a muchas personas y se propaga o extiende rápidamente (pág. 600)

ethnic cleansing the elimination of an ethnic group from society through killing or forced migration (p. 499)
limpieza éthnica eliminación de un grupo éthnico de una sociedad, ya sea asesinando o expulsando del área a los miembros de dicho grupo (pág. 499)

extraterritoriality the right of citizens to be tried in the courts of their native country rather than in the courts of the country that they are living in (p. 349)
extraterritorialidad derecho de un ciudadano a ser juzgado por una corte de su país natal y no del país donde vive (pág. 349)

F

factors of production the basic resources for industrialization, such as necessary land, labor, and capital (p. 237)
factores de producción recursos básicos para la industrialización, como la tierra necesaria, la mano de obra y el capital (pág. 237)

factory a place where goods are manufactured in mass quantity (p. 238)
fábrica lugar de producción masiva de bienes (pág. 238)

famine an extreme shortage of food (p. 599)
hambruna escasez extrema de alimentos (pág. 599)

fascism a totalitarian system of government that focuses on the good of the state rather than on the good of the individual citizens (p. 425)
fascismo sistema totalitario de gobierno que se centra en el bien del estado y no en el bienestar de los ciudadanos individuales (pág. 425)

federal system a system of government in which power is divided between a central, or a federal, government and individual states (p. 7)
sistema federal sistema de gobierno donde el poder se divide entre un gobierno central o federal, y estados individuales (pág. 7)

feudal system a political and social system based on the granting of land in exchange for loyalty, military assistance, and other services (p. 31)
sistema feudal sistema político y social basado en la cesión de tierras a cambio de lealtad, protección militar y otros servicios (pág. 31)

fief a grant of land from a lord to a vassal (p. 31)
feudo cesión de tierras por parte de un señor a un vasallo (pág. 31)

Final Solution the Nazi Party's plan to murder the entire Jewish population of Europe and the Soviet Union (p. 457)
Solución Final plan del Partido Nazi para asesinar a toda la población judía de Europa y la Unión Soviética (pág. 457)

First Estate in pre-Revolution France, the clergy (p. 196)
primer estado en la Francia prerrevolucionaria, el clero (pág. 196)

Fourteen Points President Woodrow Wilson's plan for organizing post-World War I Europe and for avoiding future wars (p. 399)
Catorce Puntos plan del presidente Woodrow Wilson para organizar Europa después de la Primera Guerra Mundial y evitar futuras guerras (pág. 399)

Franco-Prussian War (1870–1871) a war fought between France and Prussia that ended in the defeat of France and the unification of Germany (p. 322)
Guerra franco-prusiana (1870–1871) guerra entre Francia y Prusia que terminó con la derrota de Francia y la fundación de Alemania (pág. 322)

free trade the exchange of goods among nations without barriers such as tariffs, or taxes (p. 595)
libre comercio intercambio de bienes entre naciones sin barreras como aranceles o impuestos (pág. 595)

G

Gallipoli Campaign (1915) failed attempt by the Allies in World War I to take control of the Dardanelles (p. 389)
campaña de Gallipoli (1915) intento de los Aliados en la Primera Guerra Mundial de tomar el control de los Dardanelos; terminó en un fracaso para los Aliados (pág. 389)

Gang of Four powerful group of radicals, including Madame Mao, responsible for many of the excesses of China's Cultural Revolution in the 1960s and 1970s; they lost power after Mao's death in the 1976 (p. 525)
Banda de los Cuatro grupo comunista radical de la señora Mao, que quería continuar la Revolución cultural en China (pág. 525)

General Assembly a United Nations body consisting of all the member nations (p. 643)
Asamblea General de Naciones Unidas; está formada por todas las naciones miembro (pág. 643)

genetic engineering changing the genetic makeup of a plant or animal to create a new type (p. 610)
ingeniería genética cambio de la estructura genética de una planta o un animal para crear un nuevo tipo (pág. 610)

genocide the killing of an entire people (p. 390)
genocidio asesinato de todo un pueblo (pág. 390)

geocentric theory scientific theory that has the earth as the center of the universe with the sun and stars revolving around it (p. 170)
teoría geocéntrica teoría científica que afirma que la Tierra es el centro del universo y el Sol y las estrellas giran a su alrededor (pág. 170)

ghazis warriors for the Islamic faith (p. 102)
gazis guerreros de la fe islámica (pág. 102)

ghetto an area where minority groups live (p. 457)
gueto área donde vive un grupo de personas de un determinado origen étnico (pág. 457)

glasnost "openness"; refers to a new era of media freedom in the Soviet Union under Mikhail Gorbachev in the 1980s (p. 494)
glasnost "apertura": se refiere a una nueva era de libertad de los medios de comunicación en la Unión Soviética bajo el gobierno de Mikhail Gorbachev (pág. 494)

global warming an increase in the average temperature of the earth's atmosphere (p. 609)
calentamiento global aumento de la temperatura promedio de la atmósfera terrestre (pág. 609)

globalization the process in which trade and culture link together countries around the world (p. 594)
globalización hacer global o universal el alcance o la aplicación de algo (pág. 594)

Glorious Revolution (1688) a nonviolent revolution in which leaders of Britain's Parliament invited Mary, daughter of King James II, and her husband, the Dutch ruler William of Orange, to replace King James II (p. 152)
Revolución gloriosa (1688) revolución pacífica en que los líderes del Parlamento británico invitaron a María, hija del rey Jacobo II, y a su marido, el gobernante holandés Guillermo de Orange, a sustituir al rey Jacobo II (pág. 152)

Gothic a style of church architecture characterized by tall spires and flying buttresses developed during the 1100s (p. 33)
gótica estilo de arquitectura religiosa caracterizado por chapiteles altos y arbotantes que se desarrolló en el siglo XII (pág. 33)

Great Depression (1929–1930s) a severe worldwide depression that followed the collapse of the United States stock market; prices and wages fell, business activity slowed, and unemployment rose (p. 415)
Gran Depresión (1929–década de 1930) grave crisis económica mundial que siguió al colapso del mercado de valores de Estados Unidos; los precios y los salarios bajaron, la actividad comercial disminuyó y aumentó el desempleo (pág. 415)

Great Leap Forward (1958) Mao Zedong's second Five-Year Plan for China; its goal was to speed progress (p. 523)
Gran Salto Adelante (1958) segundo plan de cinco años para China de Mao Tsé-Tung, cuyo fin era acelerar el progreso (pág. 523)

green revolution a significant increase in agricultural productivity resulting from the introduction of high-yield varieties of grains, the use of pesticides, and improved management techniques (p. 610)
revolución verde aumento significativo de la productividad agrícola debido a la introducción de variedades de cereales de alto rendimiento, el uso de pesticidas y la mejora de las técnicas de administración (pág. 610)

guillotine a device used during the French Revolution for beheading people (p. 204)
guillotina aparato usado durante la Revolución francesa para decapitar a las personas (pág. 204)

Gulag a Soviet forced labor camp or prison, used especially for political dissidents (p. 427)
gulag campo de trabajos forzados de la Unión Soviética, destinado especialmente para los prisioneros políticos (pág. 427)

H

haiku a Japanese poem that consists of 17 syllables set in three lines (p. 123)
haiku poema japonés que consiste en 17 sílabas dispuestas en tres versos (pág. 123)

heliocentric theory scientific theory that has the sun as the center of the universe with the earth rotating around the sun (p. 171)
teoría heliocéntrica teoría científica que afirma que el Sol es el centro del universo y la Tierra gira a su alrededor (pág. 171)

Hellenistic the blending of Greek cultures with those of Persia, Egypt, and Central Asia following the conquests of Alexander the Great (p. 16)
helenístico mezcla de las culturas griegas con las culturas de Persia, Egipto y Asia Central (pág. 16)

Hinduism the largest religion in India; Hindus believe in reincarnation and strive to break free from the cycle of rebirth (p. 14)
hinduismo la religión más importante de la India; los hindúes creen en la reencarnación y se esfuerzan por liberarse del ciclo de renacimiento (pág. 577)

Holocaust the killing of millions of Jews and others by the Nazis during World War II (p. 458)
Holocausto asesinato de millones de judíos y otras personas por los nazis durante la Segunda Guerra Mundial (pág. 458)

Huguenot a French Protestant (p. 143)
hugonote protestante francés (pág. 143)

human equality the belief that all people are equal (p. 4)
igualdad humana creencia de que todas las personas son creadas iguales (pág. 4)

humanism an intellectual movement during the Renaissance that focused on the study of worldly subjects, such as poetry and philosophy, and on human potential and achievements (p. 41)
humanismo movimiento intelectual del Renacimiento que se centró en el estudio de temas terrenales como la poesía y la filosofía, y en el potencial humano y sus logros (pág. 41)

Hundred Days (1815) period that marks the time between Napoleon's return to Paris from Elba (March 20), his final defeat at Waterloo (June 18), and the restoration of King Louis XVIII (June 28) p. 218)
Cien Días (1815) también llamados campaña de Waterloo; período que marca la época entre el regreso de Napoleón a París desde Elba (20 de marzo) y la restauración del rey Luis XVIII (28 de junio) (pág. 218)

hydrogen bomb a nuclear weapon that gets its power from the fusing together of hydrogen atoms (p. 485)
bomba de hidrógeno arma nuclear que debe su potencia a la fusión de átomos de hidrógeno (pág. 485)

hyperinflation an extremely high level of inflation that grows rapidly in a short period of time (p. 577)
hiperinflación nivel de inflación extremadamente alto que aumenta con rapidez en un corto período de tiempo (pág. 577)

I

icon a painting or carving of Jesus, the Virgin Mary, or a saint (p. 29)
icono pintura o grabado de Jesús, la Virgen María o un santo (pág. 29)

import-substitution led industrialization an economic policy of replacing certain imported goods with a country's own manufactured goods (p. 570)
industrialización de sustitución de importaciones política económica que consiste en reemplazar ciertos bienes importados por bienes producidos en el país (pág. 570)

impressionism a new style of painting that began in France in the 1860s in which artists used light, vivid color, and seeming motion to capture an impression of a scene (p. 278)
impresionismo novedoso estilo de pintura que comenzó en Francia en la década de 1860 en la que los artistas usaban juegos con la luz, el moviemento y el uso de colores vivos (pág. 278)

indemnity compensation that is paid to a nation for the damage inflicted upon it (p. 220)
indemnización compensación que se paga a una nación por los daños causados a dicha nación (pág. 220)

independent judiciary a branch of the government that includes the court system and remains separate from the other branches of government (p. 6)
poder judicial rama del gobierno que incluye el sistema de cortes y permanece separada de los otros poderes del gobierno (pág. 6)

Indian National Congress a major political party in India; founded in 1885 to press for greater rights for Indians under British rule, it later became one of the main forces calling for Indian independence (p. 346)
Congreso Nacional de la India importante partido político de la India, fundado en 1885 con el fin de organizar a los ciudadanos en la lucha contra el Imperio británico (pág. 346)

indulgences pardons issued by the pope of the Roman Catholic Church that could reduce a soul's time in purgatory; from the 1100s to the 1500s, indulgences could be purchased, which led to corruption (p. 52)
indulgencias perdones comprados a la Iglesia católica con el fin de evitar un castigo por un pecado (pág. 52)

Industrial Revolution a period of rapid growth in the use of machines in manufacturing and production that began in the mid-1700s (p. 235)
revolución industrial período de rápido crecimiento del uso de las máquinas para la producción; comenzó a mediados del siglo XVIII (pág. 235)

industrialization developing industries for the production of goods (p. 237)
industrialización desarrollo de las industrias que producen bienes (pág. 237)

interchangeable parts identical parts that can replace each other (p. 247)
piezas intercambiables partes idénticas que se pueden reemplazar entre sí (pág. 247)

interdependence a relationship between countries in which they rely on one another for resources, goods, or services (p. 594)
interdependencia relación entre países que se produce cuando dependen mutuamente para poder obtener recursos, bienes o servicios (pág. 594)

Internet an electronic system that allows the linking of millions of individual computers around the world (p. 500)
Internet sistema electrónico que conecta a millones de computadoras individuales de todo el mundo (pág. 500)

intifada a violent uprising by Palestinians against the Israeli occupation of the West Bank and Gaza Strip in the late 1980s (p. 558)
intifada levantamiento violento de los palestinos contra la ocupación israelí de Cisjordania y la franja de Gaza a finales de la década de 1980 (pág. 558)

Iranian Revolution (1978–1979) a revolution against the shah of Iran led by the Ayatollah Ruhollah Khomeini, which resulted in Iran becoming an Islamic republic with Khomeini as its leader (p. 560)
Revolución iraní (1978–1979) revolución contra el sha de Irán dirigida por el ayatolá Ruhollah Khomeini, cuyo resultado fue que Íran se transformó en una república islámica dirigida por Khomeini (pág. 560)

iron curtain term coined by Winston Churchill in 1946 to describe an imaginary line dividing Communist countries in the Soviet bloc from countries in Western Europe during the Cold War (p. 481)
cortina de hierro término creado por Winston Churchill en 1946 para describir una línea imaginaria que separaba a los países comunistas del bloque soviético de los países de Europa occidental durante la Guerra Fría (pág. 481)

Islam a monotheistic religion whose prophet is Muhammad and whose holy book is the Qur'an; the term means "achieving peace through surrender to God" (p. 22)
Islam religión enseñada por Mahoma; el término significa literalmente "entregarse" o "someterse" (pág. 22)

isolationism staying out of the affairs and wars of other nations; the position initially held by the United States at the beginning of World War II (p. 444)
aislacionismo permanecer al margen de los asuntos y los conflictos bélicos de otras naciones; postura que mantenía Estados Unidos al comienzo de la Segunda Guerra Mundial (pág. 444)

J

Janissaries highly trained soldiers in the elite guard of the Ottoman Empire (p. 102)
Jenízaros soldados sumamente entrenados de la guardia de élite del Imperio otomano (pág. 102)

Jesuits members of a Catholic religious order, the Society of Jesus, founded by Ignatius Loyola in 1534 (p. 58)
jesuitas miembros de la orden católica de la Compañía de Jesús, fundada por Ignacio de Loyola en 1534 (pág. 58)

joint-stock companies businesses formed by groups of people who jointly make an investment and share in the profits and losses (p. 89)
sociedad por acciones empresas formada por personas que realizan una inversión conjunta y comparten las ganancias y las pérdidas (pág. 89)

joint ventures business partnerships and co-ownership (p. 634)
empresa conjunta asociación comercial y copropiedad (pág. 634)

junta a group of leaders who rule jointly (p. 574)
junta grupo de líderes que gobiernan juntos (pág. 574)

K

kabuki a form of Japanese theater dating from the 1600s, featuring a highly stylized blend of singing and dancing; performances can last all day (p. 123)
kabuki forma de teatro japonés que podía durar todo un día y en la cual los actores cantaban, bailaban e interactuaban con el público (pág. 123)

kamikazes in World War II, Japanese pilots who loaded their aircraft with bombs and crashed them into enemy ships (p. 452)
kamikazes en la Segunda Guerra Mundial, pilotos que se estrellaban con su avión cargado de explosivos contra un barco enemigo (pág. 452)

Khmer Rouge Communists trained by the Vietcong who came to power in Cambodia in 1975 (p. 521)
Khmer Rouge comunistas entrenados por el Vietcong que se hicieron con el poder en Camboya en 1975 (pág. 521)

kivas underground chambers in a Pueblo village, used by the men for religious ceremonies or councils (p. 19)
kivas cámaras subterráneas de los indios Pueblo, usadas por los hombres para celebrar ceremonias religiosas o consejos (pág. 19)

Kristallnacht (1938) "night of broken glass"; an event that occurred on the nights of November 9 and 10 in which Hitler's Nazis encouraged Germans to riot against Jews; nearly 100 Jews died (p. 428)
Kristallnacht (1938) "noche de cristales rotos"; suceso que tuvo lugar en las noches del 9 y 10 de noviembre, en el que ciudadanos alemanes, alentados por los nazis de Hitler, atacaron a los judíos; murieron casi 100 judíos (pág. 429)

L

labor union an organization representing workers' interests (p. 246)
sindicato organización que representa los intereses de los trabajadores (pág. 246)

laissez-faire a business system where companies are allowed to conduct business without interference by the government (p. 248)
laissez-faire sistema comercial donde las empresas pueden llevar a cabo actividades comerciales sin interferencia del gobierno (pág. 248)

League of Nations an international body of nations formed after World War I to prevent future wars (p. 399)
Liga de las Naciones cuerpo internacional de naciones formado después de la Primera Guerra Mundial para evitar futuras guerras (pág. 399)

Legalism a Chinese political philosophy that holds that the most effective government is that which rules the people by a harsh set of laws (p. 15)
legalismo filosofía política china que sostiene que el gobierno más eficaz es el que gobierna mediante un conjunto de leyes severas (pág. 15)

Liberation Theology the belief, common in Latin America in the late 1900s, that the Roman Catholic Church should be active in the struggle for economic and political equality (p. 570)
teología de la liberación creencia de que la iglesia cristiana debe participar activamente en la lucha por la igualdad política y económica (pág. 570)

limits on executive power the restriction of a particular ruler's power (p. 5)
límites del poder ejecutivo restricciones al poder de un gobernante en particular (pág. 5)

Long March (1934) the 6,000-mile journey made by Communist Chinese to escape Nationalist troops (p. 410)
Larga Marcha (1934) viaje de 6,000 millas hecho por los comunistas chinos para escapar de las tropas nacionalistas (pág. 410)

Louisiana Purchase (1803) the purchase of land between the Mississippi River and the Rocky Mountains that nearly doubled the size of the United States (p. 304)
Compra de Luisiana (1803) compra de tierra entre el río Mississippi y las montañas Rocallosas que casi duplicó el tamaño de Estados Unidos (pág. 304)

M

Magna Carta (1215) a charter agreed to by King John of England that granted nobles certain rights and restricted the king's powers (pp. 5, 32)
Carta Magna (1215) carta de libertades aceptadas por el rey Juan de Inglaterra, que obligaban al rey a obedecer las mismas leyes que los ciudadanos (pág. 5, 32)

Magyars a Hungarian ethnic group (p. 326)
magiares grupo étnico de Hungría (pág. 326)

maize corn (p. 18)
maíz grano (pág. 18)

ENGLISH AND SPANISH GLOSSARY

Manchukuo Japanese puppet state (1932–1945) formed in Manchuria and eastern Inner Mongolia (p. 424)
Manchukuo antiguo estado del este de Asia en Manchuria y el este de Mongolia Interior; fue establecido como estado títere en 1932 después de que los japoneses invadieran Manchuria en 1931 (pág. 424)

Manchurian Incident (1931) using an explosion on a Japanese-controlled Southern Manchurian railroad as an excuse, Japanese military forces conquered Manchuria and set up a puppet government (p. 423)
incidente de Manchuria (1931) plan de los japoneses para incriminar a los chinos en la explosión de una bomba en un ferrocarril controlado por los japoneses en la región china de Manchuria; el gobierno japonés se negó a apoyar la acción con sus tropas, lo que produjo una importante crisis diplomática en Japón (pág. 423)

Mandate of Heaven the Chinese belief that royal authority is the result of divine approval (p. 15)
Mandato del Cielo creencia china de que la autoridad del rey es el efecto de la aprobación divina (pág. 15)

mandates territories once part of the Ottoman Empire that the League of Nations gave to other European powers to rule after World War I (p. 400)
mandatos después de la Primera Guerra Mundial, los territorios del Imperio otomano que serían gobernados por potencias europeas (pág. 400)

manifest destiny a belief shared by many Americans in the mid-1800s that the United States should expand from Atlantic to Pacific oceans (p. 305)
destino manifiesto creencia compartida por muchos estadounidenses a mediados del siglo XIX de que Estados Unidos debía expandirse desde el océano Atlántico hasta el Pacífico (pág. 305)

manorial system an economic system in the Middle Ages that was built around large estates called manors (p. 31)
sistema de feudos sistema económico de la Edad Media cuya base eran grandes propiedades llamadas feudos (pág. 31)

maquiladora a large industrial assembly plant located in the border towns of Mexico that produces finished goods for export to the United States (p. 629)
maquiladora gran planta de montaje industrial ubicada en las ciudades fronterizas de México en la que se fabrican productos elaborados para exportar a Estados Unidos (pág. 629)

Marshall Plan (1947) plan for the economic reconstruction of Europe after World War II (p. 481)
Plan Marshall (1947) plan para la reconstrucción económica de Europa tras la Segunda Guerra Mundial (pág. 481)

Marxism-Leninism the political and economic philosophy of the Bolsheviks, expounded by Vladimir Lenin, which looked to an uprising of the proletariat that would abolish private property and enforce social equality (p. 394)
marxismo-leninismo filosofía política y económica de los bolcheviques; se concentraba en el levantamiento contra los burgueses; refutaba el capitalismo y tenía como objetivo final la creación de una sociedad sin clases (pág. 394)

mass production the system of manufacturing large numbers of identical items (p. 247)
producción en masa sistema de fabricación que consiste en producir gran cantidad de artículos idénticos (pág. 247)

Mau Mau a violent movement in Kenya during the 1960s, led by Kikuyu farmers, to rid the country of white settlers(p. 541)
Mau Mau movimiento emprendido por los agricultores kikuyu con el fin de expulsar de Kenia por medios violentes a los agricultores blancos (pág. 541)

megacity an urban area with a population or 10 million of more (p. 629)
megalópolis ciudad con una población de 10 o más millones de habitantes (pág. 629)

mercantilism an economic system used from about the 1500s to the 1700s, which held that a nation's power was directly related to its wealth (p. 86)
mercantilismo sistema económico usado desde el siglo XVI hasta el siglo XVIII aproximadamente, que afirmaba que el poder de una nación estaba directamente asociado a su riqueza (pág. 86)

Middle Passage name for voyages that brought enslaved Africans across the Atlantic Ocean to North America and the West Indies (p. 91)
Paso Central viaje en el que los esclavos africanos atravesaban el océano Atlántico hasta llegar a América del Norte y las Antillas (pág. 91)

monotheism the belief in one god (p. 12)
monoteísmo creencia en un solo dios (pág. 12)

Monroe Doctrine (1823) U.S. President James Monroe's statement forbidding further colonization in the Americas and declaring that any attempt by a foreign country to colonize would be considered an act of hostility by the United States (p. 304)
Doctrina Monroe (1823) declaración del presidente Estados Unidos James Monroe en la que se prohibía la colonización del continente americano y se advertía que todo intento de colonización por parte de cualquier país extranjero sería considerado un acto hostil (pág. 304)

Mughal Empire a Muslim empire in India (1526–1761) founded by Babur (p. 107)
Imperio mughal imperio musulmán en la India (1526–1761) fundado por Babur (pág. 107)

multinational corporations large companies that operate in several different countries and sell their products around the world (p. 594)
corporaciones multinacionales grandes empresas que operan en varios países diferentes y venden sus productos en todo el mundo (pág. 594)

Muslim League political group founded in 1906 to protect the rights of Indian Muslims; it later became one of the main forces calling for India independence and a separate nation for Indian Muslims (p. 347)
Liga musulmana grupo político de musulmanes de la India que buscaban proteger sus derechos (pág. 347)

Muslims followers of Islam (p. 22)
musulmanes seguidores del Islam (pág. 22)

N

Nanjing Massacre (1937) the murder of as many as 300,000 Chinese men, women, and children by Japanese troops (p. 424)
masacre de Nanjing (1937) asesinato de nada menos que 300 mil hombres, mujeres y niños chinos por parte de las tropas japonesas (pág. 424)

nationalism sense of pride and devotion to one's nation (p. 215)
nacionalismo sentido de orgullo y lealtad por la propia nación (pág. 215)

NATO North Atlantic Treaty Organization; a defensive military alliance of twelve Western nations formed in 1949 (p. 482)
OTAN Organización del Tratado del Atlántico Norte; alianza militar defensiva de doce naciones occidentales formada en 1949 (pág. 482)

natural rights rights that every person is granted, such as life, liberty, and the pursuit of happiness (p. 4)
derechos naturales derechos que tienan todas las personas, como el derecho a la vida, a la libertad y a el búsqueda de la felicidad (pág. 4)

Nazi Party National Socialist Party; fascist political party of Adolf Hitler governed on totalitarian lines and advocating German racial superiority (p. 428)
Partido Nazi Partido Nacional Socialista de los Trabajadores Alemanes; partido político fascista liderado por Adolf Hitler que se basaba en el totalitarismo, la superioridad racial y el control gubernamental de la industria (pág. 428)

negritude movement African and Afro-Caribbean literary movement founded in Paris in the 1930s that rejected European models and promoted pride in African cultural identity (p. 549)
movimiento de la negritud movimiento literario fundado por un grupo de estudiantes africanos y afrocaribeños que vivían en París en la década de 1930 (pág. 549)

neutral in a war, not aiding either side (p. 383)
neutral en una guerra, que no apoya a ningún bando (pág. 383)

New Deal U.S. President Franklin D. Roosevelt's plan of economic relief, recovery, and reforms for the country during the Great Depression (p. 417)
Nuevo Trato plan del presidente Franklin D. Roosevelt destinado a proporcionar ayuda económica, y a recuperar y reformar económicamente al país después de la Gran Depresión (pág. 417)

New Economic Policy Lenin's plan, started in 1921, to allow limited capitalism, especially among farmers, in order to restore the Soviet economy (p. 395)
Nueva Política Económica Respuesta de Lenin a los campesinos y trabajadores que sufrían después de la Revolución Rusa; autorizó un poco de capitalismo para que estas personas pudieran recuperarse (pág. 395)

NGO a non-governmental organization, or a group not affiliated with any government, that is formed to provide services or to push for a certain public policy (p. 599)
ONG organización no gubernamental, o grupo no afiliado a ningún gobierno, que se forma para brindar servicios o promover cierta política pública (pág. 599)

nomads people who move from place to place in search of food and water (p. 11)
nómadas personas que se trasladan de un lugar a otro en busca de comida y agua (pág. 11)

nonaggression pact an agreement between nations to not attack one another (p. 440)
pacto de no agresión acuerdo entre naciones de no atacarse entre sí (pág. 440)

nonaligned nations nations who refused to ally with either side in the Cold War between the United States and the Soviet Union (p. 488)
naciones no alineadas naciones que se niegan a aliarse con uno de los bandos en un conflicto (pág. 488)

North American Free Trade Agreement (NAFTA) a free trade agreement that eliminated tariffs on trade between Mexico, the United States, and Canada (p. 582)
Tratado de Libre Comercio de América del Norte (TLCAN o NAFTA) organización que une México, Estados Unidos y Canadá en una gran zona de libre comercio (pág. 582)

Nuremberg Laws Nazi laws that eliminated citizenship and many civil and property rights for Jews (p. 429)
Leyes de Nuremberg leyes de los nazis que negaban la ciudadanía y muchos derechos civiles y de propiedad a los judíos (pág. 429)

Nuremberg trials (1945–1949) trials in which an Allied military tribunal tried several dozen top Nazi and military officials; many were executed for war crimes (p. 878)
juicios de Nuremberg (1945–1949) juicios en los que un tribunal militar de los Aliados juzgó a varias decenas de autoridades militares y nazis de alto rango; muchos fueron ejecutados por crímenes de guerra (pág. 878)

O

Old Order the political and social system in place in France before the Revolution (p. 195)
Viejo Orden sistema político y social que funcionaba en Francia antes de la Revolución (pág. 195)

offshoring the movement of an entire factory or other business enterprise abroad (p. 633)
externalización acto de trasladar al extranjero una fábrica o negocio al completo (pág. 633)

one-party system political system in which a single political party controls the government and elections are rarely competitive (p. 547)
sistema de partido único sistema político donde un único partido controla el gobierno y las elecciones no suelen ser competitivas (pág. 547)

Organization of Petroleum Exporting Countries (OPEC) an organization that coordinates petroleum policies of major producing countries (p. 557)
Organización de Países Exportadores de Petróleo (OPEP) organización que coordina las políticas sobre el petróleo de las empresas productoras más importantes (pág. 557)

Orthodox Church the church that followed the Eastern traditions of Christianity as opposed to the Western traditions (p. 29)
iglesia ortodoxo iglesia que siguió las tradiciones cristianas orientales, en lugar de las tradiciones occidentales (pág. 29)

Ottomans ruling dynasty of the Ottoman Empire (1293–1922), named for Osman I, the founder; at the Empire's height, the Ottomans ruled a vast area that encompassed southwest Asia, northeast Africa, and southeast Europe (p. 102)
otomanos descendientes de Osmán I, que gobernó el vasto sultanato turco del suroeste de Asia, el noreste de África y el sureste de Europa hasta su disolución tras la Primera Guerra Mundial (pág. 102)

outsourcing the practice of using workers from outside a company to cut costs or increase production (p. 594)
tercerización práctica de las empresas de usar trabajadores externos para reducir los costos o aumentar la producción (pág. 594)

P

Pan-Arabism political movement in the 1950s and 1960s promoting Arab unity (p. 555)
panarabismo la unidad de los pueblos de ascendencia árabe (pág. 555)

Parliament the governing body of England (p. 5)
Parlamento el cuerpo que gobierna Inglaterra (pág. 5)

partition division (p. 512)
partición división (pág. 512)

pasteurization the process of heating liquids to kill bacteria and prevent fermentation (p. 270)
pasteurización proceso de calentar los líquidos para matar las bacterias y evitar la fermentación (pág. 270)

patronage the practice of rewarding political loyalty with well-paying government positions (p. 547)
tráfico de influencias dar puestos bien pagados en el gabinete gubernamental a los seguidores leales de un funcionario del gobierno (pág. 547)

Pax Romana a period of peace in Roman Empire lasting from the beginning of Augustus's reign until the death of Marcus Aurelius (27 BC–AD 180) (p. 17)
Pax Romana período de paz en Roma que duró desde el comienzo del gobierno de Augusto hasta la muerte de Marco Aurelio (pág. 17)

Peace of Augsburg (1555) an agreement between states in the Holy Roman Empire that gave each German prince the right to decide whether his state would be Catholic or Protestant (p. 138)
Paz de Augsburgo (1555) acuerdo por el cual la religión de cada estado alemán sería decidida por su gobernante (pág. 138)

peacekeeping sending multinational forces into countries to enforce ceasefires or truces among warring countries or warring groups within a single country (p. 643)
mantenimiento de la paz envío de fuerzas internacionales a otros países para que se respete un cese del fuego o una tregua entre países en guerra o entre grupos en guerra dentro de un mismo país (pág. 643)

Peloponnesian War (431 BC) war fought between Athens and Sparta; the war effectively ended the Classical Age in Greece (p. 16)
Guerra del Peloponeso (431 a.C.) guerra entre Atenas y Esparta; significó el fin de la época clásica griega (pág. 16)

peninsulares colonists in Latin American who were born on the Iberian Peninsula, in Spain or Portugal (p. 298)
peninsulares europeos que nacieron en la península ibérica, es decir, en España o Portugal (pág. 298)

perestroika "restructuring"; restructuring of the corrupt government bureaucracy in the Soviet Union begun by Mikhail Gorbachev (p. 494)
perestroika "reestructuración"; la reestructuración de la burocracia corrupta del gobierno soviético que se realizó bajo la presidencia de Mikhail Gorbachev (pág. 494)

Persian Gulf War (1990–1991) war in which U.S.-led forces liberated Kuwait from Iraq (p. 500)
Guerra del Golfo (1990–1991) guerra en que las fuerzas lideradas por Estados Unidos liberaron Kuwait de Irak (pág. 500)

pharaoh ruler of ancient Egypt (p. 12)
faraón gobernador de Egipto antigua (pág. 12)

philosophes philosophers of the Enlightenment (p. 178)
philosophes filósofos de la Ilustración (pág. 178)

plantations large farms that usually specialized in the growing of one type of crop for a profit (p. 90)
plantación establecimientos agrícolas grande, generalmente especializado en un tipo de cultivo con el fin de obtener una ganancia (pág. 90)

plebiscite the procedure used to submit the constitution of a new government to the people for a yes-or-no vote (p. 212)
plebiscito procedimiento para someter a votación la aprobación de una nueva constitución o gobierno; los ciudadanos votan a favor o en contra (pág. 212)

pogroms the organized persecutions and massacres of Jews in Russia in the 1880s (p. 332)
pogroms persecucións organizadas y masacres de los judíos en Rusia en la década de 1880 (pág. 332)

polis a city-state of ancient Greece (p. 16)
polis ciudad estado de la antigua Grecia (pág. 16)

polytheism the belief in many gods (p. 12)
politeísmo creencia en muchos dioses (pág. 12)

popular culture cultural traits such as food, sports, and music, that are common within a group of people (p. 597)
cultura popular rasgos culturales que son bien conocidos y aceptados (pág. 597)

popular sovereignty the idea that political authority belongs to the people (p. 6)
soberanía popular idea de que la autoridad política pertenece al pueblo (pág. 6)

populist a supporter of the rights of the common people as opposed to the privileged elite (p. 576)
populista defensor de los derechos y el poder del pueblo (pág. 576)

Potsdam Conference (1945) a meeting of Allied leaders in the German city of Potsdam to address issues about the post-World War II Europe (p. 465)
Conferencia de Potsdam (1945) encuentro de los líderes Aliados hacia el final de la Segunda Guerra Mundial (pág. 465)

predestination the belief that at the beginning of time God decided who would gain salvation (p. 54)
predestinación creencia de que al comienzo de los tiempos Dios decidió quién alcanzaría la salvación (pág. 54)

privatization the process of converting businesses or industries from public to private ownership (p. 634)
privatización el control privado de las industrias, en contraposición al control del gobierno (pág. 634)

propaganda information such as posters and pamphlets created by governments in order to influence public opinion (p. 387)
propaganda información difundida con la intención de influir en la opinión pública (pág. 387)

Protestant Reformation a religious movement in the 1500s that split the Christian church in western Europe and led to the establishment of a number of new churches (p. 51)
Reforma protestante revolución religiosa del siglo XVI que dividió la iglesia de Europa occidental y llevó al establecimiento de una serie de iglesias nuevas (pág. 51)

Puritans English Protestants of the late 1500s and most of the 1600s who wanted to "purify" the Church of England through reforms (p. 149)
puritanos protestantes inglés que quería "purificar" la Iglesia de Inglaterra a través de reformas (pág. 149)

Q

Qur'an the sacred text of Islam (p. 22)
Corán texto sagrado del Islam (pág. 22)

R

radical a person with extreme views (p. 201)
radical persona con opiniones extremas (pág. 201)

radioactivity a process in which atoms of certain elements constantly break down and release energy (p. 269)
radioactividad proceso por el cual los átomos de ciertos elementos se desintegran constantemente y liberan energía (pág. 269)

Raj the British rule of India from 1757 until 1947 (p. 345)
Raj gobierno británico en la India desde 1757 hasta 1947 (pág. 345)

reactionary an extremist who not only opposes change but also wants to undo certain changes (p. 220)
reaccionario extremista que no solamente se opone al cambio, sino que también quiere revertir algunos cambios (pág. 220)

realism a mid-1800s movement in art and literature that rejected romanticism and sought to depict the details of everyday life, no matter how unpleasant (p. 278)
realismo movimiento artístico y literario de mediados del siglo XIX que rechazaba el romanticismo y prefería representar el mundo tal cual es (pág. 278)

realpolitik "the politics of reality"; the belief in practical goals instead of theory in political philosophy (p. 321)
realpolitik "la política de la realidad"; la creencia en los objetivos prácticos en lugar de en la teoría de la filosofía política (pág. 321)

Red Guards a group of young men who carried out the work of the Cultural Revolution; they roamed the cities and villages, identifying possible opposition to Mao Zedong's leadership (p. 524)
Guardias Rojos grupo de jóvenes que llevaron a cabo el trabajo de la Revolución cultural; recorrían las ciudades y los pueblos en busca de posibles opositores al liderazgo de Mao Tsé-Tung (pág. 524)

Red Shirts army of volunteer troops led by Guiseppe Garibaldi; in 1860 they attacked the island of Sicily and won it for the Italians (p. 318)
Camisas Rojas ejército de tropas voluntarias dirigidas por Guiseppe Garibaldi; en 1860 atacaron la isla de Sicilia y la conquistaron para los italianos (pág. 318)

refugees people who leave their country to escape danger or persecution (p. 600)
refugiados personas que dejan su país para escapar de un peligro o una persecución (pág. 600)

Reign of Terror a period during the French Revolution in which the Robespierre-led government executed thousands of political figures and ordinary citizens (p. 206)
Reino del Terror período de la Revolución francesa en que el gobierno dirigido por Robespierre ejecutó a miles de figuras políticas y ciudadanos comunes (pág. 206)

Renaissance "rebirth"; following the Middle Ages, a movement that centered on the revival of interest in the classical learning of Greece and Rome (p. 41)
Renacimiento movimiento posterior a la Edad Media que se centró en revivir el interés por el legado clásico de Grecia y Roma (pág. 41)

representative government a government in which citizens elect officials to represent them (p. 4)
gobierno representativo gobierno en el cual los ciudadanos eligen a los funcionarios que los representan (pág. 4)

republic a political system in which the citizens of a region elect representatives to run the government (pp. 3, 17)
república sistema político en el que los ciudadanos de una región eligen representantes para dirigir el gobierno (pág. 3, 17)

Restoration the period of the reign of Charles II in England when the monarchy was restored after the collapse of Oliver Cromwell's government; there was also a rebirth of English culture during this time (p. 151)
Restauración período de la historia de Inglaterra durante el reinado de Carlos II en el que se restauró la monarquía tras la caída del gobierno de Oliver Cromwell; durante este período, también hubo un renacimiento de la cultura inglesa (pág. 151)

romanticism an artistic and literary movement at the beginning of the 1800s which rejected the rationalism of the Enlightenment in favor of emotion, intuition, and imagination (p. 278)
romanticismo movimiento intelectual de comienzos del siglo XIX que se concentró en el sentimiento y la imaginación, y se ocupó del tema del romance de la vida en contraposición a la razón (pág. 278)

Roosevelt Corollary a policy proposed by U.S. president Theodore Roosevelt as an addition, or corollary, to the Monroe Doctrine; it pledged to use U.S. military force to prevent European interference in the internal affairs of Latin American nations while reserving for the United States the right to intervene (p. 367)
Corolario de Roosevelt cambio en la Doctrina Monroe en la que se declaraba que Estados Unidos podía intervenir en los asuntos internos de los países latinoamericanos (pág. 367)

Royalists supporters of government by a monarch; used as a name for supporters of England's King Charles I (p. 149)
monárquicos defensors de un gobierno monárquico (pág. 149)

rule of law a system in which government leaders must act according to a set of laws (p. 4)
gobierno de la ley sistema en el que los líderes de un gobierno deben actuar de acuerdo a una serie de leyes establecidas (pág. 4)

Russo-Japanese War (1904–1905) an imperialistic conflict that stemmed from the rival designs of Russia and Japan on Manchuria and Korea, resulting in the defeat of Russia (p. 332)
Guerra ruso-japonesa (1904–1905) conflicto entre imperios que surgió debido a las intenciones rivales de Rusia y Japón respecto a Manchuria y Corea; terminó con la derrota de Rusia (pág. 332)

S

Saint Bartholomew's Day Massacre August 24, 1572; a massacre of 6,000 to 8,000 Huguenots in Paris authorized by King Charles IX and his mother Catherine de Médici (p. 143)
masacre del día de San Bartolomé 24 de agosto de 1572; sangriento episodio que ocurrió durante las guerras religiosas en Francia después del intento de asesinato de un líder militar hugonote, planeado por Catalina de Médici; el resultado fue un extenso combate donde murieron entre 6,000 y 8,000 hugonotes (pág. 143)

salons gatherings in which intellectual and political ideas were exchanged during the Enlightenment (p. 177)
salóns reunión donde se intercambiaban ideas intelectuales y políticas durante la Ilustración (pág. 177)

samurai a professional Japanese warrior hired by wealthy landowners for protection in feudal Japan (pp. 27, 119)
samurai guerrero profesional japonés contratado por los terratenientes ricos del Japón feudal para obtener protección (pág. 27, 119)

sanctions economic or political penalties imposed by one country on another to try and force a change in policy (p. 605)
sanciones penalidades económicas o políticas impuestas por un país a otro para obligarlo a cambiar su política (pág. 605)

Sandinistas Marxist group who led the revolution against the dictator of Nicaragua and then ruled the country from 1979 to 1990 (p. 574)
sandinistas grupo marxista que dirigió la revolución contra el dictador de Nicaragua (pág. 574)

sansculottes "without breeches"; a radical group of shopkeepers and wage earners during the French Revolution who wanted a larger voice in government and an end to food shortages (p. 197)
sansculottes "sin pantalones"; grupo radical de comerciantes y trabajadores a sueldo que, durante la Revolución francesa, querían tener más participación en el gobierno y poner fin a la escasez de comida (pág. 197)

scholasticism in the Middle Ages, the theological and philosophical school of thought that attempted to reconcile faith and reason (p. 33)
escolasticismo escuela de pensamiento teológico y filosófico de la Edad Media que intentaba reconciliar la fe y la razón (pág. 33)

scientific method a method of inquiry that promotes observing, measuring, explaining, and verifying as a way to gain scientific knowledge (p. 170)
método científico método de investigación basado en la observación, medición, explicación y verificación como la verdadera manera de adquirir el conocimiento científico (pág. 170)

Scientific Revolution a transformation in European thought in the 1500s and 1600s that called for scientific observation, experimentation, and the questioning of traditional opinions (p. 170)
revolución científica transformación del pensamiento que ocurrió durante los siglos XVI y XVII debida a la observación, experimentación y cuestionamiento científico de las opiniones tradicionales (pág. 170)

secession the act of separating from (p. 305)
secesión acto de separarse de algo (pág. 305)

Second Estate in pre-Revolution France, the nobles (p. 196)
Segundo Estado en la Francia anterior a la Revolución, los nobles (pág. 196)

Secretariat body of the United Nations responsible for carrying out the administrative tasks (p. 643)
Secretaría de Naciones Unidas; grupo se encarga de las tareas administrativas de NU (pág. 643)

secular having to do with worldly, as opposed to religious, matters (pp. 41, 639)
secular relacionado con cuestiones terrenales, en contraposición a las cuestiones religiosas (pág. 41, 639)

Security Council body of the United Nations, consisting of 15 members, five of them permanent, charged with being the guardians of world peace (p. 643)
Consejo de Seguridad de Naciones Unidas; su función es mantener la paz (pág. 643)

separation of powers the distribution of political power among the branches of government, giving each branch a particular set of responsibilities (p. 4)
separación de poderes distribución del poder político que da a cada poder del gobierno un conjunto particular responsabilidades (pág. 4)

Sepoy Mutiny (1857) a rebellion of Hindu and Muslim soldiers against the British in India (p. 344)
Motín de Sepoy (1857) rebelión de los soldados hindúes y musulmanes contra los británicos que estaban en la India (pág. 344)

serfs peasants who were legally bound to their lord's land (p. 331)
siervos campesinos que estaban legalmente obligados a quedarse en las tierras de su señor (pág. 331)

shah name given to a king of the Safavid Empire (p. 104)
shah nombre dado al rey del Imperio safavida (pág. 104)

Sharpeville massacre (1960) an incident in which South African police fired on a crowd of apartheid protestors, killing 67 people (p. 546)
masacre de Sharpeville (1960) incidente en el cual una organización nacionalista africana convocó a una manifestación frente a la estación de policía del municipio de Sharpeville; la policía abrió fuego contra los manifestantes y mató a 67 (pág. 546)

Shining Path guerrilla group in Peru that terrorized the countryside in the 1980s and 1990s (p. 579)
Sendero Luminoso grupo guerrillero de Perú que sembró el terror en las áreas rurales en la década de 1990 (pág. 579)

shogun the hereditary chief of Japan's warrior class who held the real power, while the emperor ruled in name only (pp. 27, 121)
shogun jefe hereditario de la clase guerrera japonesa que poseía el verdadero poder, mientras que el emperador sólo gobernaba nominalmente (pág. 27, 121)

Siege of Leningrad (1941–1942) Nazi army's unsuccessful attempt to capture the city of Leningrad in the Soviet Union during World War II; as many as 1 million civilians perished during the siege (p. 448)
sitio de Leningrado (1941–1942) toma de Leningrado por parte de Hitler en Rusia; durante este sitio, murieron nada menos que un millón de civiles (pág. 448)

Sikhism an Indian religion founded in the late 1400s whose beliefs blend elements of Hinduism and Islam (p. 108)
sikhismo religión no violenta cuyas creencias unen las religiones hinduista y musulmana (pág. 108)

Sino-Japanese War (1894) war fought between China and Japan for influence over Korea; Japan's victory symbolized its successful modernization (p. 353)
Guerra sinojaponesa (1894) guerra entre China y Japón a causa de una rebelión en Corea; ambas naciones enviaron tropas para someter a los rebeldes coreanos (pág. 353)

Six-Day War (June, 1967) war between Israel and Egypt, Syria, and Jordan; Israel's victory gave it control of areas with large Palestinian populations, including the West Bank and Gaza (p. 558)
Guerra de los Seis Días (junio de 1967) guerra entre Israel y Egipto a causa del deseo de Egipto de ser la figura dominante del mundo árabe; terminó con una victoria aplastante para Israel (pág. 558)

Smoot-Hawley Tariff Act (1930) a U.S. law that set extremely high tariffs on imports in an effort to protect American farmers and manufacturers; the result was a worsening of the Great Depression (p. 417)
Ley arancel Smoot-Hawley (1930) arancel extremadamente alto sobre los productos agrícolas y manufacturados (pág. 417)

social contract an agreement between a people and their government, stating that people would give up some of their freedom and in return, their government would provide them with peace, security, and order (pp. 6, 177)
contrato social acuerdo entre un pueblo y su gobierno que establece que el pueblo cederá parte de su libertad a cambio de que el gobierno brinde paz, seguridad y orden (pág. 6, 177)

Social Darwinism an application of Charles Darwin's scientific theories of natural selection and the survival of the fittest to the struggle between nations and races; used in the late 1800s to justify imperialism and racism (p. 359)
darwinismo social visión de la sociedad basada en la teoría científica de la selección natural de Charles Darwin (pág. 359)

socialism a political and economic system in which society, usually in the form of the government, owns the means of production (p. 250)
socialismo sistema económico y político en el cual la sociedad, generalmente en la forma del gobierno, posee los medios de producción (pág. 250)

socialist republic a type of republic in which there is no private property and the state owns and distributes all goods to people (p. 332)
república socialista tipo de república en la cual no hay propiedad privada y el estado posee todos los bienes y los distribuye entre los ciudadanos (pág. 332)

Solidarity an independent labor union founded in Soviet-controlled Poland in 1980 (p. 494)
Solidaridad sindicato independiente fundado en 1980 en la Polonia controlada por los soviéticos (pág. 494)

Soweto Uprising (1976) a major student protest against apartheid that took place in the township of Soweto; the peaceful march turned violent, killing more than 600 people and wounding 4,000 (p. 546)
rebelión de Soweto (1976) importante protesta estudiantil contra el apartheid que ocurrió en el municipio de Soweto; la marcha pacífica se tornó violenta, con más de 600 muertos y 4,000 heridos (pág. 546)

Spanish-American War (1898) war fought between Spain and the United States that began after the sinking of the battleship USS *Maine*; the United States won the war in four months, gaining control of Puerto Rico, Guam, and the Philippines (p. 366)
Guerra hispano-estadounidense (1898) guerra entre España y Estados Unidos que comenzó tras el hundimiento de *Maine*; fue un desastre para España y Estados Unidos ganó la guerra en cuatro meses, tomando el poder de Puerto Rico, Guam y las Filipinas (pág. 366)

Spanish Armada a great fleet (130 ships and 20,000 men) assembled by Spain in 1588 for an invasion of England (p. 140)
Armada española gran flota de barcos; incluía aproximadamente 130 barcos y 20,000 marineros y soldados (pág. 140)

Sputnik (1957) the first artificial satellite; launched by the Soviet Union (p. 486)
Sputnik (1957) primer satélite artificial; lanzado por la Unión soviética (pág. 486)

Stamp Act (1765) a law passed by the British Parliament that raised tax money by requiring the American colonists to pay for an official stamp whenever they bought paper items (p. 183)
Ley del Sello (1765) ley aprobada por el Parlamento británico que aumentaba los impuestos para los colonos estadounidenses, obligándoles a pagar un sello oficial cada vez que compraran artículos de papel (pág. 183)

standard of living a measure of the quality of life (p. 253)
nivel de vida medida de la calidad de vida (pág. 253)

strike a work stoppage (p. 246)
huelga detención del trabajo (pág. 246)

subsidies grants of money (p. 87)
subsidios dinero que se otorga (pág. 87)

Suez Canal Egyptian waterway connecting the Mediterranean and Red seas; built in 1869 by Franco-Egyptian company; in 1875 Britain bought Egypt's share in the canal (p. 360)
canal de Suez canal de agua egipcio del que se apoderaron los ingleses en 1882 (pág. 360)

Suez Crisis (1956) Egypt's confrontation with Britain, France, and Israel over control of the Suez Canal (p. 554)
crisis de Suez confrontación entre Egipto por un lado y Gran Bretaña, Francia e Israel por el otro, sobre el control del Canal de Suez (pág. 554)

suffrage the right to vote (p. 290)
sufragio derecho a votar (pág. 290)

sultan title for the ruler of the Ottoman Empire (p. 102)
sultán título del gobernador del Imperio otomano (pág. 102)

surplus excess (p. 11)
excedente lo que sobra (pág. 11)

sustainable development economic development that is maintained over a period of time but does not harm the environment (p. 608)
desarrollo sostenible desarrollo económico que se mantiene durante cierto tiempo, pero que no daña el medio ambiente (pág. 608)

T

Taiping Rebellion (1850–1864) revolt against the Qing dynasty in China led by Hong Xiuquan, a convert to Christianity; over 20 million Chinese died; eventually suppressed with British and French aid (p. 350)
rebelión de Taiping (1850–1864) rebelión en China encabezada por Hong Xiuquan, quien declaró que se establecería una nueva dinastía (pág. 350)

Taj Mahal a mausoleum built from 1632–1643 by India's Mughal emperor Shah Jahan to honor his wife (p. 109)
Taj Mahal maravilla arquitectónica creada por el Shah Jahan (pág. 109)

Taliban Islamist group that took control over much of Afghanistan in the late 1990s; were ousted by the United States invasion of 2001 (p. 501)
talibanes grupo que tomó el control de gran parte de Afganistán después de la ocupación soviética en 1979 (pág. 501)

telegraph a machine perfected by Samuel F. B. Morse in 1832; it uses pulses of electric current to send messages across long distances through wires (p. 265)
telégrafo máquina perfeccionada por Samuel F.B. Morse en 1832 que usa pulsaciones de corriente eléctrica para enviar mensajes a larga distancia mediante cables (pág. 265)

terrorism the use of violence by individuals and groups to advance political goals (p. 602)
terrorismo uso de la violencia, por parte de individuos o grupos, para conseguir objetivos políticos (pág. 602)

theocracy a government ruled by religious leaders who claim God's authority (p. 54)
teocracia gobierno de líderes religiosos que afirman tener la autoridad de Dios (pág. 54)

Third Estate in pre-Revolution France, the bourgeoisie, artisans, workers, and peasants (p. 197)
Tercer Estado en la Francia antes de la Revolución, la burguesía, los artesanos, los trabajadores y los campesinos (pág. 197)

Thirty Years' War (1618–1648) a conflict in Europe that began in Prague as a Protestant rebellion against the Holy Roman Empire; fought over religion and power among ruling dynasties (p. 158)
Guerra de los Treinta Años (1618–1648) conflicto europeo que comenzó en Praga como una rebelión protestante contra el Santo Imperio Romano; fue una guerra por motivos religiosos y de poder entre familias dominantes (pág. 158)

Tiananmen Square Massacre violent suppression by the Chinese communist government of a large pro-democracy protest in Beijing's central square in 1989 (p. 525)
masacre de la plaza de Tiananmen gran protesta en favor de la democracia realizada en China en 1989 y que el gobierno reprimió con fuerzas militares; en consecuencia, murieron cientos de personas (pág. 525)

totalitarianism form of government in which the person or party in charge has absolute control over all aspects of life (p. 426)
totalitarismo forma de gobierno en la cual la persona o partido que está en el poder tiene un control absoluto de todos los aspectos de la vida (pág. 426)

total war a war that requires the use of all society's resources (p. 387)
guerra total guerra que requería el uso de todos los recursos de una sociedad (pág. 387)

Trail of Tears (1838—39) an 800-mile march made by the Cherokee from their homeland in Georgia to Indian Territory; resulted in the deaths of almost one-fourth of the Cherokee people (p. 305)
Ruta de las Lágrimas (1838–39) marcha de 800 millas que hizo la tribu cherokee desde su territorio natal en Georgia hasta el Territorio Indígena; tuvo como consecuencia la muerte de casi la cuarta parte del pueblo cherokee (pág. 305)

Trans-Siberian Railroad railroad, begun in 1891, linking western Russia to Siberia in the east (p. 332)
ferrocarril transiberiano ferrocarril que unió Rusia occidental y el este de Siberia (pág. 332)

Treaty of Kanagawa (1854) trade treaty between Japan and the United States opening up two Japanese ports to U.S. trade; signed in response to a show of force by U.S. admiral Matthew Perry (p. 352)
Tratado de Kanagawa (1854) tratado que permitió a los barcos estadounidenses detenerse en dos puertos japoneses (pág. 352)

Treaty of Paris (1783) the agreement that officially ended the American Revolution and established British recognition of the independence of the United States (p. 186)
Tratado de París (1783) acuerdo que puso fin oficialmente a la Guerra de Independencia estadounidense y esta- bleció el reconocimiento británico de la independencia de Estados Unidos (pág. 186)

Treaty of Tordesillas (1494) the agreement between Spain and Portugal that created an imaginary north-south line dividing their territory in the Americas (p. 81)
Tratado de Tordesillas (1494) acuerdo entre España y Portugal que creaba una línea imaginaria de norte a sur que dividía el territorio de las Américas (pág. 81)

Treaty of Utrecht (1713) treaty that ended the War of the Spanish Succession; it gave the throne to Louis XIV's grandson but also stated that France and Spain would never be ruled by the same monarch (p. 146)
Tratado de Utrecht (1713) tratado que supuso el fin de la Guerra de Sucesión Española y dio el trono al nieto de Luis XIV, pero también impuso la condición de que Francia y España nunca serían gobernadas por el mismo rey (pág. 146)

Treaty of Versailles (1919) treaty ending World War I; required Germany to pay huge war reparations and established the League of Nations (p. 797)
Tratado de Versalles (1919) tratado que puso fin a la Primera Guerra Mundial; exigía a Alemania que pagara enormes indemnizaciones de guerra y estableció la Liga de las Naciones (pág. 797)

Treaty of Westphalia (1648) treaty ending the Thirty Years' War; it reduced the power of the Holy Roman Emperor; it extended religious toleration to Protestants and Catholics within most of the empire (p. 158)
Tratado de Westfalia (1648) tratado que puso fin a la Guerra de los Treinta Años; en un sentido general, fue una victoria protestante y extendió la tolerancia religiosa (pág. 158)

trench warfare a form of combat in which soldiers dug trenches, or deep ditches, to seek protection from enemy fire and to defend their positions (p. 386)
guerra de trincheras forma de combate en que los soldados cavaban trincheras, o pozos profundos, para protegerse del fuego enemigo y defender sus posiciones (pág. 386)

triangular trade trading network lasting from the 1600s to the 1800s that carried goods and enslaved people between Europe, the Americas, and Africa (p. 91)
comercio triangular redes de intercambio de bienes y esclavos entre Inglaterra, las colonias norteamericanas y África (pág. 91)

Triple Alliance an alliance between Germany, Austria-Hungary, and Italy (p. 382)
Triple Alianza alianza entre Alemania, el Imperio austrohúngaro e Italia (pág. 382)

Triple Entente an alliance between France, Russia, and Great Britain (p. 382)
Triple Entente alianza entre Francia, Rusia y Gran Bretaña (pág. 382)

Truman Doctrine (1947) U.S. President Truman's pledge to provide economic and military aid to countries threatened by communism (p. 481)
Doctrina Truman (1947) compromiso del presidente dos Estados Unidos Truman para prestar ayuda económica y militar a los países amenazados por el comunismo (pág. 481)

U

U-boats submarines used by Germans in World Wars I and II (p. 397)
U-boats nombre que recibieron los pequeños submarinos que usaron los alemanes en la Primera y la Segunda Guerra Mundial (pág. 397)

Umayyad (661–750) first ruling dynasty over the Muslim Caliphate (p. 22)
Umayyad califato de Mu'awiya que marcó un período de enorme crecimiento y cambio para el imperio musulmán (pág. 22)

unequal treaties trade treaties that China signed under pressure of invasion; gave Western powers trade benefits (p. 349)
tratados desiguales tratados comerciales que China firmó bajo amenaza de invasión y que dieron beneficios comerciales a las potencias occidentales (pág. 349)

United Nations international organization formed in 1945 to maintain world peace and encourage cooperation among nations (p. 465)
Naciones Unidas organización internacional que promueve la cooperación entre las naciones (pág. 465)

United States Constitution the governmental structure of the United States (p. 7)
Constitución de Estados Unidos estructura da gobierno de Estados Unidos (pág. 7)

urbanization the migration of people from rural areas to cities (p. 274)
urbanización migración de las áreas rurales a las ciudades (pág. 274)

V

vassal in medieval Europe, a person granted land from a lord in return for services (p. 31)
vasallo en la Europa medieval, persona que recibía tierras de un señor a cambio de ciertos servicios (pág. 31)

V-E Day (1945) May 8, 1945; a term used by the Allies, it stands for "victory in Europe" during World War II (p. 462)
Día V-E (1945) 8 de mayo de 1945; fecha en que los Aliados celebraron su victoria en Europa en la Segunda Guerra Mundial (pág. 462)

Vedas sacred writings of the Indo-Aryans (p. 14)
Vedas escrituras sagradas de los indoarios (pág. 14)

Velvet Revolution (1989) a quick, peaceful revolution that swept the Communists from power in Czechoslovakia (p. 495)
revolución de terciopelo (1989) revolución rápida y pacífica que expulsó a los comunistas del poder en Checoslovaquia (pág. 495)

viceroys officials who ruled Spain's American empire (p. 81)
virreyes funcionarios que gobernaban en el imperio español en las Américas (pág. 81)

Victorian Era the era spanning the reign of Queen Victoria of England (1837–1901) (p. 290)
época victoriana reinado de la reina Victoria entre los años 1837 y 1901; el reinado más largo de la historia de los monarcas británicos (pág. 290)

Vietcong communist guerilla force allied with North Vietnam which fought to overthrow the government of South Vietnam from the 1950s to 1975 (p. 518)
Vietcong fuerzas militares del Frente Nacional de Liberación, grupo que quería derrocar al gobierno de Vietnam (pág. 518)

Vietminh nationalist organization led by Ho Chi Minh that fought for Vietnamese independence from French rule in the 1940s and 1950s (p. 517)
Vietminh fuerza dirigida por Ho Chi Minh que desafió la autoridad de los franceses en Indochina (pág. 517)

V-J Day (1945) August 15, 1945; a term used by the Allies, it stands for "victory over Japan" during World War II (p. 464)
Día V-J (1945) 15 de agosto de 1945; fecha en que los Aliados declararon la victoria sobre Japón en la Segunda Guerra Mundial (pág. 464)

W

War of the Spanish Succession (1701–1713) war fought over the Spanish throne; Louis XIV wanted it for his son and fought a war against the Dutch, English, and the Holy Roman Empire to gain the throne for France (p. 146)
Guerra de Sucesión Española (1701–1713) guerra por la sucesión al trono de España; Luis XIV lo quería para su hijo y luchó contra los holandes, los españoles y el Santo Imperio Romano para que el trono quedra en manos francesas (pág. 146)

Warsaw Pact a military alliance of the Soviet-dominated countries of Eastern Europe, established in 1955 (p. 482)
Pacto de Varsovia alianza militar entre los países controlados por los soviéticos de Europa oriental, establecida en 1955 (pág. 482)

weapons of mass destruction (WMD) weapons that kill or injure civilian as well as military personnel, usually nuclear, chemical, and biological weapons (p. 604)
armas de destrucción masiva (WMD, por sus siglas en inglés) armas que matan o hieren a los civiles así como a los militares; generalmente, armas nucleares, químicas y biológicas (pág. 604)

Western Front during World War I, the deadlocked region in northern France where German and Allied armies faced off (p. 384)
frente occidental durante la Primera Guerra Mundial, área del norte de Francia donde los combates habían llegado a un punto en que ninguno de los bandos podía avanzar (pág. 384)

westernization the adoption of the culture and ideas of Western society, namely Europe and America (p. 155)
occidentalización adopción de la cultura e ideas de la sociedad occidental, es decir, de Europa y Estados Unidos (pág. 155)

Y

Yalta Conference (February, 1945) a meeting between Franklin Roosevelt, Winston Churchill, and Joseph Stalin to reach an agreement on what to do with Germany after World War II (p. 464)
Conferencia de Yalta (1945) encuentro entre Franklin Roosevelt, Winston Churchill y Joseph Stalin para llegar a un acuerdo sobre qué hacer con Alemania después de la Segunda Guerra Mundial (pág. 464)

Yom Kippur War (1973) war launched by Egypt and Syria against Israel on the Jewish holy day of Yom Kippur; the Israeli counterattack, supported by the United States repulsed the Syrians and Egyptians (p. 558)
Guerra de Yom Kippur (1973) ataque a Israel por parte de Egipto y Siria el día de Yom Kippur; tuvo como consecuencia un contraataque de los israelíes, que expulsaron a los sirios y pasaron a Egipto cruzando el canal de Suez (pág. 558)

Young Turks Turkish reformist and nationalist political party active in the early 20th century (p. 329)
Jóvenes Turcos partido político reformista y nacionalista turco, activo a comienzos del siglo XX (pág. 329)

Z

Zen Buddhism sect of Buddhism that stresses meditation as a means of achieving enlightenment; became popular among Japanese aristocrats and was a part of the samurai's code (p. 119)
budismo zen secta del budismo que enfatiza el valor de la meditación como medio para alcanzar la iluminación; se hizo popular entre los aristócratas japoneses y era parte del código samurai (pág. 119)

ziggurat a Sumerian temple made of sun-dried brick that was dedicated to the chief god or goddess of a particular city-state (p. 13)
zigurat templo sumerio hecho de ladrillos secados al sol, dedicado al dios o diosa principal de una determinada ciudad estado (pág. 13)

Zimmermann Note a telegram sent to a German official in Mexico prior to U.S. entrance into World War I; proposed an alliance between Germany and Mexico (p. 397)
Telegrama Zimmermann telegrama enviado a un funcionario alemán que estaba en México antes de que Estados Unidos entrara en la Primera Guerra Mundial, con la propuesta de una alianza entre Alemania y México (pág. 397)

Zionism a nationalist movement, begun in the 1890s, to establish a Jewish state in Palestine (p. 296)
sionismo movimiento nacionalista para establecer un estado judío en Palestina (pág. 296)

Zollverein an economic alliance of most German states in 1834; allowed for free trade among themselves and common tariffs on imports, exports, and transit (p. 321)
Zollverein alianza económica entre la mayor parte de los estados alemanes en 1834, que autorizaba el libre comercio y establecía aranceles comunes para las importaciones, las exportaciones y el tránsito (pág. 321)

Index

KEY TO INDEX

c = chart g = graph m = map
q = quotation p = picture

A

INDEX

INDEX

B

C

E

INDEX

F

G

I

J

K

L

INDEX

M

INDEX

O

P

Q

R

INDEX

S

INDEX

INDEX

T

U

V

W

Y

Z

Credits and Acknowledgments

Photo Credits

Front Cover, (t), Panoramic Images/Getty Images; (c-frame), © Jean-Yves Bruel/Masterfile; (c), © Robert Maass/CORBIS; (bl), © CORBIS; (bkgd), Art Resource, NY.

Forensics in History feature: (tl), ©Stockbyte/Getty Images; (tr), ©Comstock Images/Getty Images.

All History of Economics features: (tl-border) FreeStockPhotos.com; (tc-border), (tr-border).

Table of Contents: Page vi, Jon Arnold/ DanitaDelimont.com; Vii (t), Scala/Art Resource, NY; vii (b), The Art Archive/Musée de la Marine Paris/ Dagli Orti ; viii (t), akg-images, London/National Palace Museum, Taipei; viii (b), Dinodia Picture Agency; ix (b), akg-images, London/Bibliotheque Nationale, France; ix (t), Scala/Art Resource, NY ; x (b), ©Christie's Images/CORBIS; xi (t), The Art Archive; xi (b), ©Superstock/SuperStock; xii (t), AKG-Images, London; xii (b), akg-images, London/ Bismarck-Museum, Friedrichsruh ; xiii, © National Maritime Museum, London; xiv (b), © Austrian Archives/CORBIS; xv (t), © CORBIS; xvi (t), VincentThian/AP/Wide World Photos; xvi (b), akg-images, London; xvii (t), Andrew Parsons/AP/Wide World Photos; xvii (b), © Viviane Moos/CORBIS; xviii (t), © Santo Visalli/TIPS Images; xviii (b), © William Campbell/Sygma/Corbis; xix (l), Fredrik Renander/ Redux; xix (r), Jiro Ose/Redux; xx (l), Library of Congress #LC-USZ62-75334; xx (r), REUTERS/Zohra Bensemra; xxi, Erich Lessing/Art Resource, NY; xxiii, PPP/Popperfoto.com; xxvi (t), Popperfoto.com; xxvi (b), Popperfoto.com; xxvii (l), Copyright The New York Public Library; xxvii (r), ©Stone/Getty Images; xxix, Library of Congress, General Collections; xxx (t), NASA; xxx (b), ©Caroline Penn/CORBIS; xxxiv (t), Image Club Graphics; xxxiv (c), ©Brand X Pictures; xxxiv (bkgd), Image Club Graphics; xxxiv (b), Library of Congress. **Handbook:** Page H1, Usher Gallery, Lincoln, Lincolnshire County Council; H17, popper-foto.com/ Robertstock; H22, HRW Photo/Gary Benson Photography; H26, Imagno/Austrian Archives/Getty Images; H27, Best of Latin America / Cagle Cartoons H39, © Charles Gupton /CORBIS; H42, Erich Lessing/Art Resource, NY; H49, Library of Congress LC-USZ62-42464, cartoon by Lute Pease; CT9, Scala/Art Resoure, NY; CT11, akg-images, London. **Connect Unit:** Page 01, Jon Arnold/ DanitaDelimont. com; 03 (l), © Gianni Dagli Orti/CORBIS; 03 (r), ©SIME s.a.s. /eStock Photo; 04, © Adam Woolfitt/ CORBIS; 05 (l), ©Bettmann/CORBIS; 05 (c), Private Collection/© Philip Mould, Historical Portraits Ltd, London, UK/ Bridgeman Art Library; 05 (r), © Stefano Blancketti/CORBIS; 06 (l), ©Bettmann/CORBIS; 06 (r), © Bettmann/CORBIS; 08, (detail) Courtesy, Musee du Quai Branly ; 10 (t), ©Pascal Goetgheluck/Photo Researchers, Inc.; 11 (t), Erich Lessing/Art Resource, NY; 11 (b), Natural History Museum, British Museum; 12, ©Archivo Iconografico, S.A./CORBIS; 13 (l), The Art Archive / Musée du Louvre Paris/ Dagli Orti (A); 13 (c), Ankara National Museum, Turkey; 13 (r), © Michael Holford; 14, ©The Art Archive/CORBIS; 15 (tl), Bildarchiv Preussischer Kulturbesitz /Art Resource, NY; 15 (tr), The Art Archive/Musé Guimet Paris / Dagli Orti; 15 (br), Snark/Art Resource, NY; 16 (tl), Ronald Sheridan/Ancient Art & Architecture Collection; 16 (c), Ancient Art and Architecture Collection Ltd.; 16 (b), akg-images, London/ Peter Connolly; 18 (t), © age fotostock/SuperStock; 18 (b), ©Robert Frerck/Odyssey/Chicago; 19 (tl), The British Museum/HIP/The Image Works; 19 (c), The Art Archive/Museum of Mankind London/Eileen Tweedy; 19 (br), ©Tony Linck/SuperStock; 20, The Art Archive/ Bibliothéque Universitaire de Médecine, Montpellier/ Dagli Orti; 22 (t), Peter Sanders Photography; 22 (b), Getty Images; 24, The Art Archive / Musée des Arts Africains et Océaniens / Dagli Orti; 25, Ariadne Van Zandbergen /Alamy; 26, Réunion des Musées Nationaux/Art Resource, NY; 27, Courtesy Dr. Yushin Yoo; 28 (l), SuperStock; 28 (r), ©AAAC/Topham/The Image Works; 29, SIME s.a.s/eStock Photo; 30, © Gianni Dagli Orti/CORBIS; 31, ©The British Library/ HIP/The Image Works; 32, Bibliotheque National, Paris, France/ Bridgeman Art Library; 33, ©age fotos-tock/SuperStock.

Unit One: Page 35, The Art Archive /Musée de la Marine Paris / Dagli Orti. **Chapter 1:** Pages 36-37, Alinari/Art Resource, NY; 39, Scala/Art Resource, NY; 40, 42, 43 (all), Scala/Art Resource, NY; 44 (l), Private Collection, Italy/Dagli Orti/The Art Archive; 44 (r), Scala/Art Resource, NY; 46, Alte Pinakothek, Munich, Germany/The Bridgeman Art Library International; 47 (t), ©Stock Montage/SuperStock; 47 (b), Huntington Library/SuperStock; 48 (l), Erich Lessing/ Art Resource, NY; 48 (r), The Art Archive/Bibliothèque des Arts Décoratifs Paris / Dagli Orti ; 49, Bildarchiv Preussischer Kulturbesitz/Art Resource, NY; 50 (l), ©National Trust Photographic Library/Horst Kolo/The Image Works; 50 (r), British Library, London/ Bridgeman Art Library; 51, AKG-Images, London/Wartburg Collection, Eisenach; 53 (both), AKG-Images, London; 54, The Reformed Church of France, Paris, France, Lauros / Giraudon/ Bridgeman Art Library International; 55 (t), Palazzo Barberini, Rome, Italy/Bridgeman Art Library International; 55, © Corporation of London/Topham- HIP/The Image Works; 55 (b), Victoria & Albert Museum, London/ Art Resource, NY; 57, The Art Archive/ College of St. Michel Fribourg Switzerland / Dagli Orti; 58, Phillips, The International Fine Art Auctioneers, UK, ©Bonhams, London, UK/Bridgeman Art Library International; 61, ©Tim Hursley/SuperStock; 63 (b), Erich Lessing/Art Resource, NY; 63 (t), Martin Harvey/Gallo Images/Getty Images; 64, National Gallery, London, UK/ Bridgeman Art Library; 67, Scala/Art Resource, NY. **Chapter 2:** Pages 68-69, The Art Archive; 70, Bridgeman Art Library/Getty Images; 71, ©Farrell Grehan/CORBIS; 72 (t), Bibliotheque nationale de France; 72 (b), ©Bridgeman Art Library/SuperStock; 73 (l), ©Bridgeman Art Library/Getty Images; 73 (r), ©NASA/Time-Life Pictures/Getty Images; 73 (b), ©ICONE/Martel/The Image Works; 74 (l), Erich Lessing/Art Resource, NY; 74 (r), The Art Archive/Museo de Arte Antiga Lisbon/Dagli Orti; 75 (l), Victoria & Albert Museum, London/The Bridgeman Art Library; 75 (r), The Art Archive/Marine Museum Lisbon/Dagli Orti; 77, The Granger Collection, New York; 78, Biblioteca Nacional, Madrid/Giraudon/Bridgeman Art Library; 81, Library and Archives Canada #C-002774; 82, The Granger Collection, New York; 84, Institut Amatller d'Art Hispanic; 87 (l), ©Bettmann/CORBIS; 87 (r), Bibloteca Nacional de Madrid; 88, Visual Connection Archive; 90, Sam Dudgeon/HRW; 92, Bebeto Matthews/AP/ Wide World Photos; 93, Visual Connection Archive; 94 (t), C. Chesek/J.Becket/Negatives/Transparencies #4051, Courtesy Department of Library Services, American Museum of Natural History; 94 (b), North Wind Picture Archives; 97, The Granger Collection, New York. **Chapter 3:** Pages 98-99, Dinodia Picture Agency; 100, ©Bruno Barbey/Magnum Photos; 101, Bibliotheque nationale de France, MS. Fr. 9087, fol. 207/Visual Connection Archive; 103, The Art Archive/ Museo Correr Venice/Dagli Orti; 105, ©Madrasa-yi Madar-i Shah, Isfahan, Iran/Bridgeman Art Library; 106, Borromeo /Art Resource, NY; 107 (t), Victoria & Albert Museum, London, UK/The Stapleton Collection/The Bridgeman Art Library; 107 (b), Willem Proos/ World 2C Pictures Gallery; 109, ©Reuters/ CORBIS; 111, ©Free Agents Limited/CORBIS; 112-13, ©Dennis Cox/ChinaStock; 114 (l), ©The Palace Museum, Beijing; 114 (r), The Art Archive/ British Museum/Eileen Tweedy; 115, akg-images, London/ National Palace Museum, Taipei; 116, ©Philadelphia Museum of Art/CORBIS; 117, Image courtesy of Mr. Chung Chee Kit and National Library Board, Singapore, 2006; 118, Ira Bloch/National Geographic Image Collection ; 122, ©Arena Pal/Topham/The Image Works; 124 (l), ©Jon Arnold/Danita Delimont. com; 124 (r), ©Michael Holford; 127, The Art Archive/ The Bodleian Library Oxford/The Bodleian Library Ouseley Add 166 folio 8r; 128, The Granger Collection, New York; 131 (t), ©Jon Arnold/Danita Delimont.com; 131 (b), ©Michael Holford.

Unit Two: Page 133, Chateau de Versailles, France, Lauros / Giraudon/The Bridgeman Art Library. **Chapter 4:** Pages 134-35, HIP /Art Resource, NY; 136 (tl), The Art Archive; 136 (tr), Museum of Art, Serpukhov, Russia, Giraudon/ Bridgeman Art Library International; 136 (l), The Art Archive / Galleria degli Uffizi Florence / Dagli Orti (A); 136 (bl), The Art Archive / Museo del Prado Madrid; 136 (br), ©Lviv State Picture Gallery, Ukraine/ Bridgeman Art Library International; 137, The Art Archive / Farnese Palace Caprarola / Dagli Orti (A) ; 138 (l), Erich Lessing / Art Resource, NY ; 138 (r), The Art Archive / Metropolitan Museum of Art New York; 139 (l), Prado, Madrid, Spain, Giraudon /The Bridgeman Art Library International; 139 (c), Erich Lessing / Art Resource, NY; 139 (r), The Granger Collection, New York; 142, ©Krause, Johansen/Archivo Iconografico, SA/Corbis; 143, Art Resource, NY; 144 (r), The Art Archive / Musée du Château de Versailles / Dagli Orti (A); 147, Scala / Art Resource, NY ; 148, ©Pool/Tim Graham Photo Library/Corbis; 153 (t), ©Reuters/ CORBIS; 153 (b), ©The Art Archive/CORBIS; 153 (bkgd), British Library, London, UK/ Bridgeman Art Library International; 154, Tretyakov Gallery, Moscow, Russia/ Bridgeman Art Library International; 156 (l), Bildarchiv Preussischer Kulturbesitz / Art Resource, NY; 156 (r), HIP / Art Resource, NY ; 158, Bildarchiv Preussischer Kulturbesitz/ Art Resource, NY; 160 (b), ©Gianni Dagli Orti/CORBIS; 161 (both), ©age fotostock/ SuperStock ; 160-161, akg-images, London; 162 (b), Réunion des Musées Nationaux/ Art Resource, NY; 165, ©Bettmann/CORBIS. **Chapter 5:** Pages 166-67, The Derby Museum; 168 (tl), Erich Lessing/Art Resource, NY; 168 (tr), ©Paul Almasy/ CORBIS; 168 (bl), Giraudon/Art Resource, NY; 168 (br), Erich Lessing/Art Resource, NY; 169, National Museum in Cracow, Poland/ Bridgeman Art Library; 170, ©Micheline Pelletier/CORBIS SYGMA; 172, Jorge Perez de Lara; 173 (tc), ©Bettmann/CORBIS; 173 (tr), NASA, ESA, HEIC, and The Hubble Heritage Team (STScI/AURA); 173 (bl), Bildarchiv Preussischer Kulturbesitz /Art Resource, NY; 174 (l), Louvre, Paris, France/Peter Willi/ Bridgeman Art Library; 174 (r), Erich Lessing/Art Resource, NY; 176, Private Collection/ Bridgeman Art Library; 178 (l), The Granger Collection, New York; 178 (r), Private Collection/©Philip Mould, Historical Portraits Ltd, London, UK/ Bridgeman Art Library; 180 (t, inset), Erich Lessing/ Art Resource, NY; 182, akg-images, London/Bibliotheque Nationale, France; 183, (art reference) Phoenix Museum of Art, Arizona/ Bridgeman Art Library; 187, Hall of Representatives, Washington DC/ Bridgeman Art Library. **Chapter 6:** Pages 192-93, Musee Carnavalet Paris/Dagli Orti/The Art Archive; 195, Marc Charmet/The Art Archive; 196, Erich Lessing/Art Resource, NY; 197, Musee de la Ville de Paris, Musee Carnavalet, Paris, France/ Bridgeman Art Library; 199, ©Gianni Dagli Orti/CORBIS; 202 (t), ©Chris Heller/CORBIS; 202 (b), The Bridgeman Art Library/Getty Images; 203, Imagno/ Austrian Archives/Getty Images; 204, ©Bettmann/CORBIS; 205 (t), Private Collection, Archives Charmet/Bridgeman Art Library; 205 (c), Private Collection/Bridgeman Art Library; 205 (c) (frame), ©1999 Image Farm Inc.; 205 (b), Musee de la Revolution Francaise; 206 (l), Dagli Orti/Musee Carnavalet Paris/The Art Archive; 206 (r), Giraudon/ Art Resource, NY; 207 (t), Musee de la Revolution Francaise, Vizille, France/ Visual Arts Library, London, UK/ Bridgeman Art Library; 207 (b), Hulton Archive/Getty Images; 209 (b), North Wind Picture Archives; 209 (t), Pascal Le Segretain/Getty Images; 210, ©Historical Picture Archive/CORBIS; 211, Erich Lessing/Art Resource, NY; 213 (l), ©Francis G. Mayer/ CORBIS; 213 (r), Musée de l'Armée/AKG-Images; 214 (tl), Réunion des Musées Nationaux/Art Resource, NY; 214 (tc), Palazzo Pitti (Galleria d'Arte Moderna), Florence, Italy/Bridgeman Art Library; 214 (tr), Dagli Orti /Musée du Château de Versailles/The Art Archive; 214 (br), Erich Lessing/Art Resource, NY; 214 (bc), Dagli Orti /Musée du Château de Versailles/The Art Archive; 214 (bl), Musée Nat. du Château/AKG-Images, London; 216-17, ©Christie's Images /CORBIS; 219, Dr. David E. J. Jones; 221, Dagli Orti/Museo Glauco Lombardi Parma/The Art Archive; 222, Erich Lessing/Art Resource, NY; 225, Private Collection, Archives Charmet/The Bridgeman Art Library.

CREDITS AND ACKNOWLEDGMENTS

Unit Three: Page 231, Conservatoire des Arts et Métiers Paris /Marc Charmet /The Art Archive. **Chapter 7:** Pages 232-33, The Art Archive; 234 (t), Ironbridge Gorge Museum, Telford, Shropshire, UK/ The Bridgeman Art Library; 234 (b), ©Towneley Hall Art Gallery and Museum, Burnley, Lancashire/ The Bridgeman Art Library; 235, Usher Gallery, Lincoln, Lincolnshire County Council; 236 (r), AFP PHOTO/Jimin Lai/NewsCom ; 237, 239, The Granger Collection, New York; 240, ©SSPL/The Image Works; 242, Private Collection/ Bridgeman Art Library; 246, The Art Archive/Ecomusée de la Communauté Le Creusot/Dagli Orti; 248, Victoria and Albert Museum London/Eileen Tweedy/The Art Archive; 249, Library of Congress, General Collections; 251 (t), Fine Art Photographic Library, London / Art Resource, NY ; 251 (b), Scala /Art Resource, NY ; 254, ©Bettmann/ CORBIS; 255, HIP /Art Resource, NY. **Chapter 8:** Pages 258-59, Royal Holloway and Bedford New College, Surrey, UK/ Bridgeman Art Library; 261, Courtesy, Civiche Raccolte d'Art Applicata ed Incisioni (Raccolte Bertarelli) Photo: Foto Saporetti; 262, The Art Archive/Culver Pictures; 264 (tr), Artist: Roy Anderson. Image in the public domain, Courtesy of Pecos National Historical Park; 264 (bl), Private Collection/ Bridgeman Art Library; 264 (br), The Granger Collection, New York; 265 (l), ©Royalty-Free/ CORBIS; 265 (r), ©Topham Picturepoint/The Image Works; 267 (t), NASA; 267 (b), The Granger Collection, New York; 268 (t), ©SSPL/The Image Works; 268 (b), ©James Cavallini/Photo Researchers, Inc.; 270, Image Select/Art Resource, NY; 271, ©Roger-Viollet/The Image Works; 273, ©Superstock/SuperStock; 277, HIP/Art Resource, NY; 279 (t), Giraudon/Art Resource, NY; 279 (b), Erich Lessing/Art Resource, NY; 279, ©The Philadelphia Museum of Art/Art Resource, NY; 280, ©Archivo Iconografico, S.A./CORBIS; 281, ©The Art Archive/CORBIS. **Chapter 9:** Pages 284-84: The Art Archive/Museo Bolivar Caracas/Dagli Orti; 287, ©Museum of London/HIP/The Image Works; 288 (tl), SWEM Library/The College of William & Mary; 288 (tr), Tate Gallery, London/Art Resource, NY; 288 (bl), The Art Archive/Culver Pictures; 289 (tl), The Granger Collection, New York; 289 (tr), REUTERS /Zohra Bensemra/ Newscom; 289 (b), Library of Congress #LC-USZ62-75334; 291, The Granger Collection, New York; 293, Réunion de Musées Nationaux/Art Resource, NY; 295, AKG-Images, London; 297, ©CORBIS; 299, ©Juan O'Gorman Estate, courtesy Landucci Editorial, Mexico City/ Schalkwijk/Art Resource, NY; 300 (both), The Granger Collection, New York; 303, ©Jonathan Blair/CORBIS; 306, The Art Archive/Culver Pictures; 307, Library of Congress LC-USZ62-13016; 308, ©2008 Banco de México Diego Rivera & Frida Kahlo Museums Trust. Av. Cinco de Mayo No. 2, Col Centro, Del. Cuauhtémoc 06059, México, D.F. Reproduction authorized por el Instituto Nacional de Bellas Artes y Literature/Schalkwijk/Art Resource, NY; 311, The Granger Collection, New York. **Chapter 10:** Pages 312-13, akg-images, London/ Bismarck-Museum, Friedrichsruh; 315, ©Stefano Blanchetti/CORBIS; 316 (l), ©Alessandra Benedetti/ CORBIS; 316 (r), ©Bill Bachmann/Photo Researchers, Inc.; 318, Scala/Art Resource, NY; 321, Bildarchiv Preussischer Kulturbesitz /Art Resource, NY; 322, akg-images, London; 325, Image Select/Art Resource, NY; 328, Risto Bozovic/AP/Wide World Photos; 330, The Granger Collection, New York; 331, Bibliotheque des Arts Decoratifs, Paris/Bridgeman Art Library; 333, Museum of the Revolution, Moscow /RIA Novosti/ The Bridgeman Art Library; 335 (t), The Granger Collection, New York; 335 (b), Tretyakov Gallery, Moscow, Russia/The Bridgeman Art Library; 336, The Art Archive/Musee des 2 Guerres Mondiales Paris/ Dagli Orti; 339, ©Sovfoto/Eastfoto; **Chapter 11:** Pages 340-41, Roy Miles Fine Paintings/ Bridgeman Art Library; 343, National Portrait Gallery, London; 345, The Granger Collection, New York; 346 (l) © Bristol City Museum and Art Gallery, UK/The Bridgeman Art Library; 346 (r), ©Mary Evans Picture Library/The Image Works; 347 (l), ©Topham/The Image Works; 347 (r) INDRAMIL MUKHERJEE/AFP/Getty Images;; 347 (r), ©Bristol City Museum and Art Gallery, UK/ Bridgeman Art Library; 348, ©National Maritime Museum, London; 352, ©Private Collection/The Bridgeman Art Library; 353, The Art Archive/British Museum; 354 (from 347) The Art Archive/ Private Collection/Laurie Platt Winfrey; 356, ©Hulton-Deutsch Collection/CORBIS; 357,358, The Granger Collection, New York; 358, ©Mary Evans Picture Library/The Image Works; 361, The Royal Collection, Windsor, ON; 363, ©Topham/The Image Works; 364, ©The Image Works Archives; 365, ©Estate of David Siqueiros/Artists Rights Society (ARS), NY. Photo by Schalkwijk/Art Resource, NY. ; 368, The Granger Collection, New York.

Unit Four: Page 377, Erich Lessing /Art Resource, NY. **Chapter 12:** Pages 378-79, ©Hulton-Deutsch/ CORBIS; 381, ©CORBIS; 384, ©Bettmann/CORBIS; 385, Everett Collection ; 388 (t), IWM/Popperfoto/ Robertstock; 388 (b), U.S. Air Force photo/Senior Airman Jason P. Robertson; 390, ©Bettmann/CORBIS; 391, ©Hulton-Deutsch Collection /CORBIS; 392 (both), Popperfoto.com; 393 (l), Copyright The New York Public Library; 393 (r), ©Stone/Getty Images; 394, ©Bettmann/CORBIS; 396, ©Mansell/Time Life Pictures/Getty Images; 397, ©CORBIS; 398, 400, Library of Congress; 401, ©Mansell/Time & Life Pictures/Getty Images; 402, 405, Library of Congress. **Chapter 13:** Pages 406-07, ©Austrian Archives/ CORBIS; 408 (tl), Bibliohèque Nationale de France, Paris; 408 (tr, b), popperfoto.com; 409, Collection J.A. Fox/Magnum Photos; 411, ©Bettmann/CORBIS; 412, PPP/Popperfoto.com; 413, Special Collections Department, W.E.B. Du Bois Library, University of Massachusetts Amherst; 414, ©Condé Nast Archive/ CORBIS; 415, ©The Image Bank/Getty Images; 416 (tl), ©1989 Delta Haze Corporation. All Rights Reserved. Used by Permission; 416 (tr), ©Frank Driggs Collection/Getty Images; 416-17 (bkgd), Library of Congress; 419, ©Underwood & Underwood/ CORBIS; 420, 421, popperfoto.com; 425, ©Hulton Deutsch Collection/CORBIS; 427, ©Hulton Archive/ CORBIS; 428, Hulton Archive/Getty Images; 429, ©Photo by Hugo Jaeger/Timepix/ Time Life Pictures/ Getty Images; 430, ©Time Life Pictures/Getty Images. **Chapter 14:** Pages 434-35, United States Coast Guard Museum; 436 (tl), ©Hulton/Getty Images; 436 (tr), ©Hulton Archive/CORBIS; 436 (bl), ©Bettmann/ CORBIS; 436 (br), AP/Wide World Photos; 437, Walter-Frentz- Collection, Berlin; 442, ©Bettmann/CORBIS; 443, ©Getty Images; 445, ©Minnesota Historical Society/CORBIS; 448, ©Bettmann/CORBIS; 449 (l), Courtesy of the German Propaganda Archive; 449 (r), ©Swim Ink 2, LLC/CORBIS; 451, The Granger Collection, New York; 453 (t), Maria Soderberg/ Ordfront; 453 (b), ©Bettmann/CORBIS; 454, akg-images; 455, ©Soviet Group/Magnum Photos; 456, Leo Spellman Collection/United States Holocaust Memorial Museum; 457, ©Handout/Reuters/CORBIS; 458, ©Hulton Archive/Getty Images; 459, Time & Life Pictures/Getty Images; 462 (l), ©CORBIS; 462 (r), ©SuperStock; 463, ©Nagasaki Atomic Bomb Museum/ epa/Corbis; 464, 467, ACQ/Popperfoto/Classicstock; 469, ©Swim Ink 2, LLC/CORBIS.

Unit Five: Page 475, ©Tibor Bognar/CORBIS. **Chapter 15:** Pages 476-77, ©Bettmann/CORBIS; 479, Courtesy Harry S. Truman Library; 480, 484, 485 (l, br), ©Bettmann/CORBIS; 485 (tr,cr), ©CORBIS; 487 (l), ©Bettmann /CORBIS; 487 (c), ©Louise Gubb/CORBIS SABA; 487 (r), ©Bettmann/CORBIS; 488, TASS/Sovfoto; 490, Robertstock.com; 491, ©Flip Schulke/Corbis; 492 (t), ©Yevgeny Khaldei/CORBIS; 492 (b), ©Peter Horree/Alamy; 494 (t), ©Francis Lochon/ Time Life Pictures/Getty Images; 494 (bl), ©Peter Turnley/CORBIS; 494 (br), ©Reuters/CORBIS; 495, ©David Turnley/CORBIS; 496, ©Pascal Le Segretain/CORBIS SYGMA; 498, AP/Wide World Photos; 500, Vincent Thian/AP/Wide World Photos; 502 (l,r), ©Bettmann/CORBIS; 502 (c), Republished with permission of Globe Newspaper Company, Inc. Photo by AP/Wide World Photos; 503 (l), AP/Wide World Photos; 503 (r), ©Digital Globe/Handout/epa/ Corbis; 504, Dick Adair/Honolulu Advertiser/Rothco Cartoons ; 507, Mindaugas Kulbis/AP/Wide World Photos; **Chapter 16:** Pages 508-09, ©Bettmann/ CORBIS; 510 (tl), ©Roman Sourmar /CORBIS; 510 (r), ©Hulton Archive/Getty Images; 510 (bl), ©Bettmann/ CORBIS; 511, AP/Wide World Photos; 513, Photo by Robert Nickelsberg//Time Life Pictures/Getty Images; 514, ©age fotostock/ SuperStock ; 516, ©Photo by RDA Getty Images; 518, ©Hulton Archive/Getty Images; 519 (both), ©Bettmann/CORBIS; 520, ©So Hing-Keung/CORBIS; 522, AFP/Getty Images; 523, ©Roman Sourmar/CORBIS; 524, Mark Avery/AP/Wide World Photos; 525 (l,r), AP /Wide World Photos/Jeff Widener; 525 (c), ©Koichi Imaeda / Magnum Photos; 524-25 (bkgd), ©Peter Turnley/CORBIS; 527, AP/ Wide World Photos; 529, ©TWPhoto/CORBOS; 530, ©Steve Vidler/SuperStock. **Chapter 17:** Pages 536-37, ©Louise Gubb/CORBIS SABA; 539, ©Bettmann/ CORBIS; 541, ©Keystone/Getty Images; 542 (t), ©Bettmann/CORBIS; 542 (b), ©Patrick Durand/ CORBIS SYGMA; 544 (tr), ©Christie's Images/ CORBIS; 544 (l), Bruno Barbey/Magnum Photos; 544 (b), Timothy O' Keefe/Index Stock Imagery, Inc.; 545, Naashon Zalk/AP/Wide World Photos ; 546, ©Reuters/CORBIS; 548, ©Jon Hrusqa/epa/CORBIS ; 550, Alan Mothner/AP/Wide World Photos; 551, ©Marc Garanger/ CORBIS ; 553, ©Eitan Simanor/Alamy; 554, ©Popperfoto.com; 556, 558, ©Bettmann/CORBIS; 559, ©Richard T. Nowitz/CORBIS; 560 (l), ©Bettmann/ CORBIS; 560 (r), AP/Wide World Photos; 561 (l), ©Allen Tannenbaum/Time Life Pictures/Getty Images; 561 (r), Andrew Parsons/AP/Wide World Photos; 562, ©Kaveh Kazemi/CORBIS. **Chapter 18:** Pages 566-67, Eduardo de Baia/AP/Wide World Photos; 569, Eraldo Peres /AP/Wide World Photos; 570 (both), ©Viviane Moos/CORBIS; 572 (l), Keith Levit Photography/ NewsCom; 572 (tr), Claudia Daut/REUTERS; 572 (cr), AFP Photo Archive/NewsCom; 572 (br), REUTERS/Claudia Daut; 574, ©Reuters/CORBIS; 575, ©Bettmann/CORBIS; 578 (l), ©Horacio Villalobos/ CORBIS; 578 (r), ©Reuters/CORBIS; 580-581, ©Fox Photos/Getty Images; 581, ©Photo by Cindy Karp/ Time Life Pictures/Getty Images; 582, AP/Wide World Photos; 583, Dario Lopez-Mills/AP/Wide World Photos; 585, ©Danny Lehman/CORBIS; 586, Best of Latin America / Politicalcartoons.com. **Chapter 19:** Pages 590-91, ©Jose Fuste Raga/CORBIS; 592 (l), Sam Dudgeon/HRW; 592 (r), ©David Lawrence/CORBIS; 593, ©Bob Sacha/Corbis; 599, ©Reuters/CORBIS; 601, ©Robert Harding/Getty Images; 602, Debra Reid/AP/ Wide World Photos; 604 (t), Kurt Strumpf/AP/Wide World Photos; 604 (b), AP/Wide World Photos; 605 (l), ©TOKYO SHIMBUN/CORBIS SYGMA; 605 (r), ©Hubert Boesl/dpa/CORBIS; 607, ©William Campbell/ Sygma/Corbis; 608 (l), ©Santo Visalli/TIPS Images;; 610, ©GRAHAM DONALD/CORBIS SYGMA; 611 (t), NASA; 611 (b), ©age fotostock/SuperStock; 612, Andy Singer/Darryl Cagle Political Cartoons; 614 (t), ©age fotostock/SuperStock; 614 (b), Kurt Strumpf/AP/ Wide World Photos; 617, AP /Wide World Photos/Jeff Widener; 619 (t), ©Royalty Free/CORBIS; 619 (tc), ©Charles O'Rear/CORBIS; 619 (bc), ©Michael St. Maur Shell/CORBIS; 619 (b), ©Lester Lefkowicz/ CORBIS.

Unit Six: Page 621, Photo by Michael Nagle/Getty Images. **Case Studies:** Pages 622-23, REUTERS/Mike Hutchings; 624, RAJESH JANTILAL/AFP/Getty Images; 625, Christopher Furlong/Getty Images; 628, ©Annie Griffiths Belt/CORBIS; 629, REUTERS/Paulo Whitaker; 631, Images & Stories; 632, REUTERS/ Claro Cortes IV; 633, CHINA OUT REUTERS/ Stringer; 634 (l), Fredrik Renander/Redux; 634 (r), Jiro Ose/Redux; 636, Cartoon © Jim Morin in THE MIAMI HERALD. Courtesy CWS/CARTOONARTS INTERNATIONAL; 638 (r), AP Photo/John Coghill; 638 (l), ©Reuters Photographer/ Reuters; 639, REUTERS/Euan Denholm; 642, Daniel Berehulak/ Getty Images; 643, REUTERS/Euan Denholm; 645, Michael Ramirez/Copley News Service/Newscom.

End Matter.

Reference: R1, Art Resource, NY; R54, Formosa-Translation .com; R55, © The Art Archive/CORBIS; R56, Kunsthistorisches Museum/ Bridgeman Art Library; R57, Art Resource, NY; R58, Werner Forman/ Art Resource, NY; R59, Royal Exchange/ Bridgeman Art Library; R60, British Library/ Bridgeman Art Library; R61, The Art Archive/British Library; R62, Snark/Art Resource, NY; R63, British Library/The Art Archive; R64, Scala/Art Resource, NY; R65, © Mary Evans Picture Library/The Image Works; R66, British Library/The Art Archive; R67, Erich Lessing/Art Resource, NY; R68, © Burstein Collection/ CORBIS; R69, Scottish National Portrait Gallery/ Bridgeman Art Library; R70, Private Collection/ Bridgeman Art Library; R71, The Art Archive/Karl Marx Museum Trier/Dagli Orti; R72, Bibliotheque-Musee Forney/Bridgeman Art Library; R73, Archives Larousse/ Bridgeman Art Library; R74 , © Succession Picasso/Archivo Iconografico, S.A./CORBIS, Picasso, Pablo (1881-1973) © ARS, NY; R75, © JEFF CHRISTENSEN/ Reuters/CORBIS; R76, ©Bettmann/ CORBIS; R77, ©Peter Turnley/CORBIS; R78, Richard Vogel/AP/Wide World Photos.

For permission to reproduce copyrighted material, grateful acknowledgment is made to the following sources:

From *The Settlement of the Americas* by Thomas D. Dillehay. Copyright © 2000 by Thomas D. Dillehay. Reproduced by permission of **Basic Books, a member of the Perseus Book Group.**

From *Naser-e Khosraw's Book of Travels (Safarnama)* by Narir-i Khusraw, translated by W. M. Thackston Jr. Copyright © 1986 by **Bibliotheca Persica Press, a division of Persian Heritage Foundation.** Reproduced by permission of the publisher.

From "Biotechnology and the Green Revolution," an interview with Norman Borlaug from *ActionBioscience* web site, accessed at http://www.actionbioscience.org/biotech/borlllaug.html. Copyright © 2002 by Norman Borlaug. Reproduced by permission of Norman Borlaug and electronic format by permission of ActionBioscience.org.

From "Ending World Hunger. The Promise of Biotechnology and the Threat of Antiscience Zealotry" by Norman Borlaug from *Plant Physiology* web site, accessed at http://www.plantphysiol.org/misc/about shtml. Copyright © 2000 by Norman Borlaug. Reproduced by permission of **Norman Borlaug and electronic format by permission of PlantPhysiolorg.**

From *Hanfeitzu*, translated by Lydia Gerber, from *Reading About the World*, Vol. 1, edited by Paul Brians, Mary Gallwey, Douglas Hughes, Azfar Hussain, Richard Law, Michael Myers, Michael Neville, Roger Schlesinger, Alice Spitzer, and Susan Swan. Copyright © 1999 by **Paul Brians.** Originally published by Harcourt Custom Publishing. Reproduced by permission of the copyright holder.

From *History and Description of Africa* by Leo Africanus from *Reading About the World*, Vol., 2, edited by Paul Brians, Mary Gallwey, Douglas Hughes, Azfar Hussain, Richard Law, Michael Myers, Michael Neville, Roger Schlesinger, Alice Spitzer, and Susan Swan. Copyright © 1999 by **Paul Brians**. Originally published by Harcourt Custom Publishing. Reproduced by permission of the copyright holder.

From *The Cambridge Illustrated History of China* by Patricia Buckley Ebrey. Copyright © 1996 by **Cambridge University Press.** Reproduced by permission of the publisher.

From *Prehistory of the Americas* by Stuart J. Fiedel. Copyright © 1987 by **Cambridge University Press.** Reproduced by permission of the publisher.

From *The World of Rome* by Peter Jones and Keith Sidwell. Copyright © 1997 by **Cambridge University Press.** Reproduced by permission of the publisher.

From "Julius Caesar" from *The Twelve Caesars* by Suetonius, translated by Robert Graves, revised with an introduction by Michael Grant. Copyright © 1957 by Robert Graves; copyright © 1979 by Michael Grant Publication Limited. Reproduced by permission of **Carcanet Press Limited and electronic format by permission of A. P. Watt, Ltd. on behalf of the Trustees of the Robert Graves Copyright Trust.** Users must not reproduce, download, store in any medium, distribute, transmit or retransmit, or manipulate any text reproduced on web site www.apwatt.co.uk.

From "Kilwa in 1331" by Ibn Battatah from *African Civilization Revisited*, translated by G. S. P. Freeman-Grenville. Copyright © 1962 by G. S. P. Freeman-Grenville. Reproduced by permission of **Clarendon Press, a division of Oxford University Press.**

From *The Analects by Confucius from Sources of Chinese Tradition*, compiled by Wm. Theodore de Bary, Wing-tsit Chan, Burton Watson, with contribution by Yi-pao Mei, Leon Hurvitz, T'ung-tsu Ch'u, Chester Tan, and John Meskill. Copyright © 1960 by **Columbia University Press, New York.** Reproduced by permission of the publisher.

From *On My Country and the World* by Mikhail Gorbachev, translated from Russian by George Shriver. Copyright © 2000 by **Columbia University Press.** Reproduced by permission of the publisher.

From *The Pillow Book of Sei Shonagon*, translated by Ivan Morris. Copyright © 1967 by Ivan Morris. Reproduced by permission of **Columbia University Press.**

From *Arda Wiraz Namag: The Iranian 'Divina Commedia,'* translated by Fereydun Vahman. Copyright © 1986 by Fereydun Vahman. Reproduced by permission of **Curzon Press Ltd.**

From *Medieval Russia's Epics, Chronicles, and Tales*, edited and translated by Serge A. Zenkovsky. Copyright © 1963, 1974 by Serge A. Zenkovsky. All rights reserved. Reproduced by permission of **Dutton, a division of Penguin Group (USA) Inc.**

From "The Fall of Troy" from *The Aeneid* by Virgil, translated by Robert Fitzgerald. Translation copyright © 1980, 1982, 1983 by Robert Fitzgerald. Reproduced by permission of **Penelope Fitzgerald for the Estate of Robert Fitzgerald.**

From "NAFTA: A Cautionary Tale" by Timothy A. Wise and Kevin P. Gallagher from *Foreign Policy in Focus*, October 24, 2002. Copyright © 2002 by **Foreign Policy in Focus.** Reproduced by permission of the publisher.

From "History" by Herodotus from *Classics of Western Thought: The Ancient World*, edited by Stebelton H. Nulle. Copyright © 1964 by Harcourt, Brace & World, Inc. Reproduced by permission of Harcourt, Inc.

From quote by Pericles from "History of the Peloponnesian War" by Thucydides from Classics of Western Thought: The Ancient World, edited by Stebelton H. Nulle. Copyright © 1964 by Harcourt, Brace & World, Inc. Reproduced by permission of **Harcourt, Inc.**

From "Oration on the Dignity of Man" by Giovanni Pico della Mirandola from *Classics of Western Thought: Middle Ages, Renaissance, and Reformation*, Vol. II, edited by Karl F. Thompson. Copyright © 1964, 1973, 1980 by Harcourt Brace Jovanovich, Inc. Reproduced by permission of **Harcourt, Inc.**

From "Hatred" from *Poems: New and Collected, 1957-1997* by Wislawa Szymborska, translated from the Polish by Stanislaw Baranczak and Clare Cavanagh. English translation copyright © 1998 by Harcourt Brace & Company. Reproduced by permission of **Harcourt, Inc.** and electronic format by permission of **Stanislaw Baranczak** and **Clare Cavanagh.**

Adapted from *History of the Indies* (retitled "Bartolomé de las Casas Condemns Spanish Treatment of the Indians") by Bartolomé de las Casas, translated and edited by Andrée Collard. Copyright © 1971 by Andrée Collard. Reproduced by permission of **HarperCollins Publishers, Inc.**

From *China: A New History* by John King Fairbank. Copyright © 1992 by the **President and Fellows of Harvard College, Cambridge, MA.** Reproduced by permission of the publisher.

From *I Speak of Freedom: A Statement of African Ideology* by Kwame Nkrumah. Copyright © 1961 by Kwame Nkrumah. Reproduced by permission of **William Heinemann, Ltd., London.**

From *Travels in Asia and Africa 1325-1354* by Ibn Battuta, translated by H.A.R. Gibb. Copyright 1929 by Broadway House, London. Reproduced by permission of **David Higham Associates Limited.**

From *East Asia: The Great Tradition* by Edwin O. Reischauer and John K. Fairbank. Copyright © 1958, 1960 by Edwin O. Reischauer and John K. Fairbank. All rights reserved.Reproduced by permission of **Houghton Mifflin Company.**

Letter from King Ferdinand and Queen Isabella, adapted from *Readings in Latin American Civilization: 1492 to the Present*, edited by Benjamin Keen. Copyright © 1955 by Benjamin Keen. All rights reserved. Reproduced by permission of **Houghton Mifflin Company.**

Exodus 3:7–14 from *The Holy Scriptures according to the Masoretic Text, A New Translation with The Aid of Previous Versions and with Constant Consultation of Jewish Authorities.* Copyright 1917, © 1955 by **The Jewish Publication Society of America.** Reproduced by permission the publisher.

Exodus 20:2–14 from *The Holy Scriptures according to the Masoretic Text, A New Translation with The Aid of Previous Versions and with Constant Consultation of Jewish Authorities.* Copyright 1917, © 1955 by **The Jewish Publication Society of America.** Reproduced by permission the publisher.

From *The Tale of Genji* by Lady Muraskai Shikibu, translated by Edward G. Seidensticker. Copyright © 1976 by Edward G. Seidensticker. Reproduced by permission of **Alfred A. Knopf, a division of Random House, Inc., www.randomhouse.com.**

From *Ibn Jubayr Voyages*, translated and annotated by Maurice Gaudefroy-Demonbynes. Copyright 1949-1951 by Paul Geuthner, Paris. Reproduced by permission of **Librairie Orientaliste Paul Geuthner.**

From "The Importance of the Hajj" from *The Koran Interpreted*, translated by A. J. Arberry. Copyright © 1955 by A. J. Arberry. Reproduced by permission of **Macmillan Publishing Company.**

From "The Garland of Madurai" from *The Wonder that Was India: A Survey of the Culture of the Indian Sub-continent before the Coming of the Muslims* by A. L. Basham. Copyright © 1954 by **Macmillan Company.** Reproduced by permission of the publisher.

From "Prehistory: The Harappa Culture and the Aryans" from *The Wonder that Was India: A Survey of the Culture of the Indian Sub-continent before the Coming of the Muslims* by A. L. Basham. Copyright © 1954 by **Macmillan Company.** Reproduced by permission of the publisher.

From "Great Zimbabwe (11th-15th Century)" from *Timeline of Art History.* Copyright © 2000 by **The Metropolitan Museum of Art, New York.** Reproduced by permission of the copyright holder.

From "Swahili Coast" by Robert Caputo from *National Geographic* Magazine, vol. 200, no. 4, October 2001. Copyright © 2001 by **National Geographic Society.** Reproduced by permission of the publisher.

"Quiet Night Thoughts" by *Li Po from Li Po and Tu Fu: Poems,* translated by Arthur Cooper. Copyright © 1973 by Arthur Cooper. Reproduced by permission of **Penguin Books, Ltd.**

From "The Merciful" from *The Koran,* translated with notes by N. J. Dawood (Penguin Classics 1956, Fifth revised edition 1990). Copyright © 1956, 1959, 1966, 1968, 1974, 1990, 1993, 1997, 1999, 2003 by N. J. Dawood. Reproduced by permission of **Penguin Books, Ltd.**

From *The Epic of Gilgamesh*, translated by N. K. Sandars (Penguin Classics 1960, Third Edition, 1972). Copyright © 1960, 1964, 1972 by N. K. Sandars. Reproduced by permission of **Penguin Books Ltd.**

From *The Travels of Ibn Jubayr: Being the Chronicle of a Mediaeval Spanish Moor concerning His Journey to the Egypt of Saladin, the Holy Cities of Arabia, Baghdad the City of the Caliphs, the Latin Kingdom of Jerusalem, and the Norman Kingdom of Sicily*, translated by R.J.C. Broadhurst. Copyright 1952 by Jonathan Cape, Ltd., London. Reproduced by permission of **The Random House Archive & Library.**

From "After the Deluge" from *Mandela's Earth and Other Poems* by Wole Soyinka. Copyright © 1988 by Wole Soyinka. Reproduced by permission of **Random House, Inc., www.randomhouse.com.**

From "Description of the World" from *The Travels of Marco Polo*, a modern translation by Teresa Waugh, from the Italian by Maria Bellonci. Copyright © 1984 by **Sidgwick and Jackson Limited.** Reproduced by permission of the publisher.

From *Kokinshu from An Introduction to Japanese Court Poetry* by Earl Miner, with translations by the author and Robert H. Brower. Copyright © 1968 by the Board of Trustees of the Leland Stanford Junior University. Reproduced by permission of **Stanford University Press.**

From "This Old House" from *The Leopard's Tale: Revealing the Mysteries of Çatalhöyük* by Ian Hodder. Copyright © 2006 by Ian Hodder. Reproduced by permission of **Thames & Hudson.**

From "Unmarked Boxes" from *Open Secret: Versions of Rumi,* translated by John Moyne and Coleman Barks. Copyright © 1984 by **Threshold Books.** Reproduced by permission of the publisher.

From *African Kingdoms* by Basil Davidson. Copyright © 1966 by **Time-Life Books.** Reproduced by permission of the publisher.

"From "Canto I" from *Inferno* from *The Divine Comedy of Dante Alighieri*, translated by Allen Mandelbaum. Copyright © 1980 by Allen Mandelbaum. Reproduced by permission of **University of California Press.**

From "Student Attacks Against Teachers: The Revolution of 1966" by Youqin Wang, a paper presented at the conference "The Cultural Revolution in Retrospect,"at the Hong Kong University of Science and Technology, July 4-6, 1996. Copyright © 1996 by **Youqin Wang.** Reproduced by permission of the author.

"An old silent pond" by Matsuo Bashō, translated by Harry Behn from *One Hundred Frogs: From Renga to Haiku to English* by Hiroaki Sato. Copyright © 1983 by John Weatherhill, Inc. Reproduced by permission of **Weatherhill, an imprint of Shambhala Publications, Inc.**

SOURCES CITED

From *Al-Masalik wa 'l-Mamalik* by Abdullah Abu-Ubayd al Bekri, translated from the French by MacGuckin de Slane, and translated into English by Basil Davidson. Published by Adrien-Maisonneuve, Paris, 1965.

From "Song of Ox-Ghosts and Snake-Demons" by a student of Beijing Fourth Middle School.

From *The Indus Civilization*, 3rd edition by Sir M. Wheeler. Published by Cambridge University Press, London, 1968.

From "Abuses by Sudanese 'Janjaweed' and Chadian militiamen" from *Human Rights Watch* web site. Published by Human Rights Watch, New York, 2006.

From "The Decline and Fall of Meroe" from Kush, translated by L. P. Kirwan. Published in London, 1960.

From *Sundiata: an epic of old Mali* by D. T. Niane, translated by G. D. Pickett. Published by Longmans, London, 1965.

From *Sight-Seeing Journeys* by Ibn Fadl Allah al Omari.

From *The Country of Zanj* by Abdul Hassan ibn Ali Al-Masudi, translated by C. Pellat. Published in Paris, 1962.

from "Preface" from *Facing Mount Kenya: The Tribal Life of the Gilkuyu* by Jomo Kenyatta. Published by Warburg Ltd., 1938.

From the *Records of the Grand Historian* (Shi Ji 122) by Sima Qian, translated by Burton Watson.

From *The Literature of Ancient Egypt: an anthology of stories, instructions, and poetry,* edited with an introduction by William Kelly Simpson and translations by R. O. Faulkner, Edward F. Wente, Jr., and Kelly Simpson. Published by Yale University Press, New Haven, 1973.

Staff Credits:

Bruce Albrecht, Lissa Anderson, Charlie Becker, Julie Beckman-Key, Paul Blankman, Gillian Brody, Erin Cornett, Christine Devall, Mescal Evler, Kristin Franckiewicz, Susan Franques, Bob Fullilove, Betsy Harris, Leora Harris, Wendy Hodge, Cathy Jenevein, Stephanie Jones, Shannon Johnston, David Knowles, Laura Lasley, Betty Mayo, Bob McClellan, Joe Melomo, Ivonne Mercado, Andrew Miles, Michael Neibergall, Janice Noske, Nathan O'Neal, Karl Pallmeyer, Jarred Prejean, Shelly Ramos, Allison Rudmann, Gene Rumann, Michelle Rumpf-Dike, Paul Selfa, Kay Selke, Ken Shepardson, Jeannie Taylor, Lisa Vecchione, Joni Wackwitz, Diana Walker, Tracy Wilson, Sherri Whitmarsh, Nadyne Wood

KEEP CURRENT WITH HOLT!
HOLT
History doesn't stop when you reach the end of the book. History continues to happen every day.
KEEP CURRENT WITH HOLT!
GO.HRW.COM
http://go.hrw.com/gopages/ss.html
News
HOLT, RINEHART AND WINSTON
go.hrw.com
Social Studies Home Page
Holt Online Learning
Online Textbooks
<< Select your subject
American History
Geography
World History
Government & Civics
Psychology & Sociology
Economics
State Resources
Holt Researcher
HRW World Atlas
CURRENT EVENTS
Holt's Current Events weblink gives students and teachers the tools they need to understand history as it unfolds.
When events happen around the world, turn to Holt for:
• background
• perspective
• Links to recommended web resources
Click here to keep current with Holt.
Log on to www.go.hrw.com to access Holt's online resources